CASES AND MATERIALS

REMEDIES

SIXTH EDITION

by

EDWARD D. RE
Chief Judge Emeritus, United States Court
of International Trade
Distinguished Professor of Law Emeritus
St. John's University

JOSEPH R. RE
of the California and New York Bars

FOUNDATION PRESS

NEW YORK, NEW YORK

2005

© 1975, 1982, 1987, 1992, 1996, 2000 FOUNDATION PRESS
© 2005 By FOUNDATION PRESS
        395 Hudson Street
        New York, NY 10014
        Phone Toll Free 1–877–888–1330
        Fax (212) 367–6799
        fdpress.com
Printed in the United States of America

ISBN 1–58778–901–9

TEXT IS PRINTED ON 10% POST CONSUMER RECYCLED PAPER

TO

The Memory of

JAMES BARR AMES

ROSCOE POUND

ZECHARIAH CHAFEE, JR.

SIDNEY POST SIMPSON

and

JOHN PHILIP MALONEY

GIFTED TEACHERS and SCHOLARS

whose contributions have greatly benefited
generations of law students, and
profoundly influenced the progressive
development of the law

*

PREFACE

As with all prior editions, the tradition is continued of making the book a guide to the authoritative statutes, cases and other materials in this important area of the law. All of the materials are valuable not only to law students and law teachers, but also to practicing lawyers who seek practical solutions to the countless legal problems presented.

The unexpected privilege of returning to law school teaching has afforded Judge Edward D. Re, the senior editor, the opportunity to return to the calling of teaching law, including the subject of Remedies as presently offered in most American law schools. The return to the teaching of Remedies has greatly facilitated the most recent 5th and 6th Editions of Re and Re on Remedies. The junior editor, Joseph R. Re, beyond updating materials, has contributed the viewpoint and experience of the practicing lawyer who, daily, is faced with the task of seeking the most appropriate available remedy to solve the legal problems presented by clients.

In this preface, it is most appropriate to record one's gratitude and to acknowledge one's indebtedness to others who have contributed to the present work. The greatest debt is owed to Dean James Barr Ames and to Professors Pound and Chafee, Jr., the original editors of this work. A debt is also owed to those teachers, colleagues, and former students who have urged that the book be kept current to enhance its continued use as a course book in the course on remedies in the modern law school curriculum, and in the practice of law.

Commencing with the introductory materials, the goal has been to present cases, statutes and other materials to teach a modern course on Remedies. The abundance of cases, some classic and others very recent, underscore not only the origins and continuing significance of equitable remedies, but also illustrate the timeliness and critical importance of equitable concepts for the contemporary practicing lawyer. All of the cases should facilitate a lively class discussion highlighting the availability of an appropriate judicial remedy, whether formerly denominated legal or equitable, to vindicate a legally enforceable right.

This book traces its origins to Dean James Barr Ames' seminal casebook entitled Cases in Equity Jurisdiction.[1] Successor editors include Dean Roscoe Pound, Professor Zechariah Chafee, Jr., Professor Sidney Post Simpson and Professor John Philip Maloney. In the preface to the 1934 edition of Chafee and Simpson on Equity, Professors Chafee and Simpson gratefully acknowledged that "[t]his book builds on the pioneer work of Dean Ames

---

1. JAMES BARR AMES, CASES IN EQUITY JURISDICTION (1902).

and on Dean Pound's long experience in teaching equity." Judge Re's contribution commenced with Chafee and Re's Cases and Materials on Equity, the 4th edition (1958) of Chafee and Simpson, Cases on Equity.

As in the more recent editions, this sixth edition contains six parts. Commencing with an introductory Part I, the various parts contain the following subject matter: Part II, Equity; Part III, Restitution and Unjust Enrichment; Part IV, Damages; Part V, Remedies in Context; and Part VI, Completing the Remedy.

The cases and materials are cross-referenced and each part, although a self-contained unit, complements and completes the powers of the courts to grant a party the appropriate judicial relief requested and desired. The book, therefore, presents a most useful and important survey of judicial remedies whether formerly denominated legal or equitable.

It may be added that the American Law Institute has announced that a Restatement Third on Restitution and Unjust Enrichment will supplant the original Restatement of Restitution. The editors are confident that, under the leadership of Professor Lance Liebman, director, and Professor Andrew Kull, reporter, of the Restatement of the Law Third, Restitution and Unjust Enrichment, the new venture will prove a worthy successor to the initial effort of the distinguished scholars, Professors Warren A. Seavey and Austin W. Scott, who were the Reporters of the original Restatement on Restitution.[2]

Judge Re's association with Professor Zechariah Chafee, Jr. commenced more than forty years ago when he was asked by Professor Chafee to revise his widely used casebook on Equity.[3] That unique privilege offered the extraordinary opportunity of meeting one of the great law teachers of our country. To have taught a variety of law school courses, in addition to the subject of Equity for many years has afforded Judge Re the invaluable experience to observe not only the development of American law through the years, but also changes in the law school curriculum.

There are law teachers who recall the unique contribution of the former course in Equity and regret the loss of the separate course on Equity.[4] Some feel that the stressing of moral principles as the underlying foundation of law, and the attainment of justice and equity in the particular case, by and large, may have been lost by the removal of Equity as a separate course in the law school curriculum. It was in the teaching of Equity that the teacher was best able to stress the giving of legal effect to moral norms. Much of this blending of law and ethics may have been lost except to the brightest students who are able to discern the continuing role of equity in cases that stress the application of equitable principles and doctrines.

---

2. *See* Professor Liebman's Foreword to the "Discussion Draft" to Restatement of the Law Third, The American Law Institute, Restatement of the Law, Restitution and Unjust Enrichment, Discussion Draft (Mar. 31, 2000).

3. *See* EDWARD D. RE, FREEDOM'S PROPHET 349 (1981).

4. For a statement of the cultural, professional and practical benefits of a course in equity, see STEVENS, *A Brief on Behalf of a Course in Equity*, 8 J. LEGAL ED. 422 (1956).

The procedural merger of law and equity is usually given as a main reason for the elimination of Equity from the curriculum of most law schools. Remedies is now a well established course in the American law school curriculum. The important role of Remedies in the curriculum is appreciated since it is clear that the value of a "right" depends upon the ability to obtain a legally enforceable remedy. Hence, the role of the teacher of Remedies is not only to teach the equitable and other judicial remedies, but also to instill in the student a yearning to achieve the true purpose of law, namely, the attainment of a just and fair result or solution in each case brought for adjudication. Hence, the present task is to teach judicial remedies, whether formerly denominated legal or equitable, in an environment or context that inculcates the animating spirit of equity.

As a result of the suggestions of judges, practicing lawyers and law teachers, many of the historical and textual notes included in prior recent editions of this book have been updated and included in this sixth edition. The present edition is a modern coursebook on the law of Remedies as may be gleaned not only from the many recent cases, but also from the many federal and state statutes and rules that have been included.

It is probably accurate to state that, although we find ourselves in an almost completely statutory environment, in both the federal and state courts, many students believe that America is still a common law country as it was in the days of Lord Elden or Justice Cardozo. Indeed, Cardozo, more than seventy–five years ago, stated that "[t]he truth is that many of us, bred in common law traditions, view statutes with a distrust which we may deplore, but not deny."[5] Statutes today are often the starting point for most legal or judicial analysis. In 1975, the senior editor referred to the importance of legislation at a Seminar for United States Appellate Judges by stating that "[t]oday legislation so extensively covers practically every branch of law, both public and private, that the principle or point of beginning can no longer be presumed to be a judicial precedent. Often the point of beginning must be the legislative policy set forth in a relevant statute."[6] Hence, since, with the exception of only a few states, there are no longer any courts of Chancery or Equity, in view of the importance of statutes one may lose sight of the *equitable factors or "equities"* that should be considered in deciding cases justly and according to equity and good conscience.

Professor Zechariah Chafee, Jr., appropriately dubbed "the Last of the Harvard Chancellors,"[7] with characteristic simplicity of expression, made the following observations about the nature and scope of equity:

> Equity is a way of looking at the administration of justice; it is a set of effective and flexible remedies admirably adapted to the needs of a complex society; it is a body of substantive rules.[8]

A major objective of this book is to present to the reader those important aspects of the law embraced in Professor Chafee's previously quoted

5. BENJAMIN N. CARDOZO, THE PARADOXES OF LEGAL SCIENCE 8, (1928).

6. EDWARD D. RE, *Stare Decisis*, 79 Fed. R. Dec. 509, 515 (1979).

7. Professor John M. Maguire, *in* 24 HARV. L. REC. 4 (Feb. 14, 1957).

8. Professor Chafee in *Foreword*, Edward D. Re, SELECTED ESSAYS ON EQUITY iii (1955).

description of equity as well as other judicial remedies whether formerly denominated legal or equitable.

Beyond the inclusion of textual notes and references to recent cases and statutes, the book adheres essentially to the plan and sequence followed in prior recent editions of Re and Re on Remedies. A careful examination of the presentation of materials, as may be noted from the table of contents, will indicate that it is justified by both custom and logic. Furthermore, it facilitates the use of the new 6th edition by those teachers who have been using the prior editions.

Commencing with the initial volume of Chafee and Re, the book has contained a chapter on Jury Trials. The jury trial requirement of the Constitution is the one remaining consideration or factor that prevents a total or complete merger of law and equity. In the event of a demand for a jury trial, the question still persists, "Is the cause of action, by virtue of its nature and relief requested, a common law or equitable cause of action, that is, one that would formerly have been tried in equity without a jury?" Hence, the chapter on Jury Trial has been retained and updated. The notes that present and explain the merger of law and equity, both in the federal and state courts, have been updated and indicate that only a few states still retain separate courts of law and equity. To facilitate comprehension of all textual material throughout the book, Latin words and phrases, as well as unfamliar words, are followed by a bracket which contains a translation or definition.

The editors have resisted the temptation of including important civil rights cases brought under Title 42, Section 1983 of the United States Code, or under *Bivens v. Six Unknown Named Agents of Federal Bureau of Narcotics,* 403 U.S. 388, 91 S. Ct. 1999, 29 L. Ed. 2d (1971), pursuant to which persons are granted a remedy against local and federal officials who have violated their constitutionally protected rights. The leading cases that have been retained are included since they teach important remedies available to litigants.

This edition contains recent decisions of the Supreme Court of the United States that are important in the area of Remedies, including *Pounders v. Watson,* 521 U.S. 982 (1997) (reviewing summary contempt procedures); *International Union, United Mine Workers of America v. Bagwell,* 512 U.S. 821 (1994) (reviewing civil and criminal contempt; *Grupo Mexicano de Desarrollo, S.A. v. Alliance Bond Fund, Inc.,* 119 S. Ct 1961 (1999) (reviewing the equitable jurisdiction of federal district courts); *Missouri v. Jenkins,* 495 U.S. 33 (1990) (reviewing the scope and breadth of structural injunctions); *BMW v. Gore,* 517 U.S. 559 (1996) (reviewing the constitutionality of a punitive damage award); *Correctional Services Corp. v. Malesko,* 534 U.S. 61, (2001) (reviewing an implied right of action for damages against a private entity operating under contract from the Bureau of Prisons); *Great-West Life & Annuity Insurance Co. v. Knudson,* 534 U.S. 708 (2001) (reviewing whether ERISA authorizes an action for specific performance of the plan's reimbursement provision); *Buckhannon Board and Care Home, Inc. v. West Virginia Department of Health and Human Resources,* 532 U.S. 598 (2001) (reviewing a party must either obtain a judgment on the merits or a court-ordered consent decree in order to qualify as a prevailing party entitled to attorney's fees under the FHAA and ADA); and *Cooper Industries v. Leatherman Tool Group, Inc.*, 532 U.S. 424 (2001) (reviewing whether a de novo standard should be used by the circuit courts when reviewing district court determinations of the constitutionality of punitive damages awards).

Numerous other cases and text notes which summarize cases and subject matter have been added. Included in Chapter 6 on the Specific Enforcement of Contracts are two cases in which courts enforced restrictive covenants in employment contracts: *Ticor Title Insurance Co. v. Cohen,* 173 F.3d 63 (2d Cir. 1999) (enforcing a non-competition clause) and *BDO Seidman v. Hirshberg,* 93 N.Y.2d 382, 712 N.E. 2d 1220 (1999) (enforcing a non-solicitation clause). Cognizant of the ever expanding demands on students to absorb greater amounts of information in each of their law school courses, the editors have endeavored to select cases with readily understandable fact patterns that contain a clear statement of the applicable law, as well as an explanation of minority and majority views. A good example is *Austin Hill Country Realty, Inc. v. Palisades Plaza, Inc.,* 948 S.W. 2d 293 (Texas 1997), in which the Supreme Court of Texas held that a landlord has a duty to make reasonable efforts to mitigate damages when a tenant defaults on a lease. In *Austin Hill,* the court digests the applicable rule in all 50 states, distinguishing between residential and commercial leases. Other cases include *Kaepa v. Achilles Corp.,* 76 F.3d 624 (5th Cir. 1996) (reviewing whether the defendant-appellant could be enjoined from prosecuting an action in Japan that mirrored one previously filed in state court and then prosecuted in federal district court); and *In re Covert,* 761 N.E.2d 571 (N.Y. 2001) (reviewing whether a wongdoer's heirs are disallowed from sharing in his victim's estate).

Judge Re assumes full responsibility for all changes, omissions and innovations in the book. A special debt of gratitude is owed to Professor William H. Manz of St. John's University School of Law and member of the New York Bar. His scholarly interest and diligence were indispensable in the completion of this 6th edition.

It is probably true that most law books, designed to be used as teaching tools, are too big. This book is no exception. The editors, nevertheless, find comfort in the statement in the preface to the 1934 edition that "this book errs on the side of abundance rather than paucity of materials." It is hoped that it will serve the purposes intended by the editors in the training of law students for the profession of the law as a "calling in the spirit of public service."[9]

EDWARD D. RE
JOSEPH R. RE

*

---

9. ROSCOE POUND, THE LAWYER FROM ANTIQUITY TO MODERN TIMES 5 (1953).

SUMMARY OF CONTENTS

*

TABLE OF CONTENTS

PART   V.   REMEDIES IN CONTEXT

PART VI. COMPLETING THE REMEDY

CHAPTER 19. Attorneys' Fees, Costs, Prejudgment Interest, & Foreign Currency Judgments

TABLE OF CASES

Principal cases are in bold type. Non-principal cases are in roman type. References are to Pages.

CASES AND MATERIALS

REMEDIES

*

PART I

INTRODUCTION TO REMEDIES

CHAPTER 1   Introduction

CHAPTER 1

INTRODUCTION

The Study of Judicial Remedies: Rights and Remedies

The importance of the study of *Remedies* ought to be obvious. The *remedy* is the goal of litigation. An aggrieved person who resorts to the courts for judicial relief must consider the availability of the remedy sought. *Ubi jus ibi remedium* is a classic maxim of the law which means that where there is a right there is a remedy. Is this maxim a statement of law, or is it merely an ideal? The course on Remedies will teach the judicial remedies that are legally available for an aggrieved party who resorts to the courts for justice. Another relevant Latin maxim is *"Judex aequitatem semper spectare debit,"* meaning "A judge should always consider equity."

A discussion of the *remedies* granted or afforded by the courts is of immense practical importance. To say that a plaintiff may be able to sue, or may have a valid "cause of action," may have little significance unless it is known precisely what the plaintiff may recover after resorting "to the law." To state that a plaintiff has been wronged in a way cognizable by the law of the land does not mean, necessarily, that the plaintiff will recover the particular relief that is desired. Indeed, a plaintiff may conclude that it is not worthwhile to resort to the courts if the particular relief requested is not obtainable.

Knowledge of the subject of remedies is essential to the lawyer who must advise clients who deem themselves wronged or aggrieved, and who wish to have their rights vindicated in the courts. A course in remedies is designed to teach the judicial remedies that may be available to a plaintiff who resorts to the courts for a vindication of a right allegedly violated by a defendant.

To understand the available judicial remedies will require a knowledge of substantive law, procedure, and, often, legal history. The goal, however, is to appreciate and acquire the knowledge of the available remedies provided by the courts. In all cases, the student or lawyer should be "remedies conscious," and should ascertain the availability of the particular relief or remedy desired by the aggrieved party. If the particular remedy requested is not available, is there another remedy that may be suitable and satisfactory? The answers to these questions are a major purpose of a study of remedies.

The study of remedies is rewarding since it concentrates upon the specific or tangible results of the lawsuit, and adds a dimension of reality to the study of law. Over and beyond its cultural benefits, the subject will yield enormous practical benefits for the lawyer and counselor.

Practicing lawyers must advise and remind clients that legal rights are not self-executing. Resorting to the courts for judicial relief highlights the importance of both substantive law and the law of remedies. The lawyer must know the rules that prescribe access to the courts, as well as the guiding principles and rules that determine the judicial remedies available for the vindication of legal rights. The client will also wish to know the effectiveness of the remedy that may be granted. As a practical matter, can and will the remedy be enforced, and, if damages will be awarded, are there enforcement procedures to compel the losing party to pay?

Courts and the adjudicatory process provide the vehicle or means for the resolution of disputes. The goal of both substantive law and procedure is to achieve a fair and just resolution of the litigation. Courts, however, do more than merely determine who is right and who is wrong. The courts must also provide a *remedy* for the party that has been wronged. Principles of substantive law are important because they determine the rights of the parties, i.e., who is right and who is wrong. Merely to be found to be right by a court or to have been deemed wronged by a defendant is usually not a rewarding outcome for the successful litigant. The reward or satisfaction of the successful party to the litigation is *the remedy* that the court has granted. The courts, therefore, do more than merely decide who is right, but must also grant a remedy that is sought and deemed satisfactory to the successful party. The practical goal and benefit of the litigation is *the remedy* granted by the court.

Assuming that a plaintiff has established that a substantive right has been violated, what remedy may be pursued for its vindication? Hence the importance of knowing both substantive rights and the available remedies. The inquiry may well lead to a revival of the jurisprudential discussion whether *rights* can exist without *remedies* for their enforcement. Enlightened societies have attempted to give vitality to the maxim "ubi jus ibi remedium," that is, where there is a right, there is a remedy. Even assuming that this is true, it is still necessary to know not only whether the law recognizes the existence of a right, but also whether it will grant a remedy for its violation. Hence the necessity of reading all cases keeping in mind both aspects of the inquiry: whether the interest or right sought to be vindicated is a legally protected interest, and if it is, in the event of its violation or infringement, what remedies are available for its vindication or enforcement?

Our subject, however, is not limited to private wrongs, i.e., a wrong inflicted upon a plaintiff by another individual. The defendant may be the government itself, a public official or a government employee. Hence, it also includes what may be termed public litigation.

In this area as well we can see the relevance and applicability of the notion that "where there is a right, there is a remedy." A splendid example is the case of *Bivens v. Six Unknown Agents of the Federal Bureau of Narcotics*, found infra in Chapter 17 "Remedies and Public law" under the heading of "Implied Causes of Action." In that case Justice Brennan's opinion quotes and invokes the concept expressed by Chief Justice John Marshall in *Marbury v. Madison* that "the very essence of civil liberty certainly consists in the right of every individual to claim the protection of the laws whenever he receives an injury. One of the first duties of government is to afford that protection." Justice Marshall, in that seminal decision, also wrote, "... where a specific duty is assigned by law, and individual rights depend upon the performance of that duty, it seems equally clear, that the individual who considers himself injured has a right to resort to the laws of his country for a [remedy]." *Marbury v. Madison*, 1 Cranch (5 U.S.) 137, 163, 2 L.Ed. 60 (1803). In effect, in *Bivens* since the plaintiff asserted a right found in the Fourth Amendment to the Constitution, the court concluded that the plaintiff had a right which gave rise to a cause of action. In the words of Justice Brennan: "petitioner's complaint states a cause of action under the Fourth Amendment," and the court concluded "that petitioner [was] entitled to recover money damages for any injuries he had suffered as a result of the agents' violation of the Amendment." The Bivens case, under the American constitutional system, adds a new element to the ancient debate whether it is true that where there is a right there is a remedy. This new American contribution to the debate is highlighted by the dissenting opinions in the *Bivens* case. Note, for example, the dissent of Chief Justice Burger who wrote: "I dissent from today's holding which judicially creates a damage remedy not provided for by the Constitution and not enacted by Congress."

Other notes and cases in that section illustrate when the court will imply a remedy for a violation of a right found in the Constitution or a statute. These cases and others throughout this coursebook will show the present vitality of the questions that flow from the classic maxim that "where there is a right there is a remedy."

————

Remedies: Substitutional and Specific

With the exceptions of *ejectment*, for the recovery of the possession of land, *replevin*, for the recovery of the possession of chattels, and the recovery of a *debt*, the ordinary common law remedy consisted of *damages*. A judgment for *damages* denotes the monetary award designed to compensate a plaintiff for harm sustained that is reasonably attributable to the defendant. The remedy or redress of damages is *substitutional* since, at best, it is an equivalent of the harm sustained.

Specific redress or relief required a resort to equity for an *equitable remedy.* Hence, the phraseology that the specific relief or remedy in equity was *extraordinary*. By this specific relief the court would order defendants specifically to do what they had wrongfully omitted to do e.g., to convey land they contracted to convey, or to undo what they had wrongfully done, e.g., the removal of a nuisance. Of course, the equitable *preventive remedy* is the *preventive injunction*, whereby a defendant is ordered to refrain from doing or continuing a particular injurious act.

An understanding of the process whereby a court may order a defendant to do or refrain from doing something requires a study and understanding of the origin and development of this judicial power. An exercise of this power and our common-law system requires a study and knowledge of courts that came to be called Courts of Chancery or Courts of Equity; Chancery, because the presiding officer was a Chancellor and Equity because equity denoted a "correction of the law where it was defective owing to its universality." The court would do justice *ex aequo et bono*, i.e., according to equity and good conscience. A study of the vast array of judicial remedies, both legal and equitable, will prove to be intellectually rewarding as well as of invaluable practical use in the practice of law

———

Equitable Remedies

In the English legal system as it existed over a century ago, if a particular remedy was not available in the common law courts, the plaintiff may have had to resort to equity. Those remedies available in equity, that reflect the enduring contribution of the English Chancellor[1], continue to be called *equitable remedies*. The Chancellor's remedies were innovative, ingenious and effective. Not only did the Chancellor fashion a remedy where none was available by resort to common law actions, but the Chancellor also granted a more perfect remedy specifically designed to do justice in the particular case.

As compared with the system of the royal writs, chancery was not only flexible but remarkably effective. The Chancellor, acting in personam, would summon a defendant by subpoena, and could order the defendant to do right and justice—*ex aequo et bono*. The Chancellor could order the defendant to perform a contract specifically according to its terms, or enjoin the defendant to cease and desist in conduct harmful or prejudicial to the plaintiff. Not only was chancery not limited to any particular remedy, but once having acquired jurisdiction, it would do "complete justice." Furthermore, in the event of the disobedience of its orders or decrees, it could order the arrest of the defendant, and imprison for contempt.

Equitable Remedies: To the well–known equitable remedies such as the *injunction, specific performance, reformation, rescission, declaratory judgment, foreclosure, partition,* and the appointment of a *receiver,* one may add such titles as *account, contribution, subrogation,* the *marshalling of assets, ne exeat, discovery, perpetration of testimony, creditor's bills, interpleader, bills of peace, bills quia timet, equitable mortgage, equitable lien, equitable assignment and constructive trust.*

———

"Equitable Relief" and "Equitable Discretion"

As a result of historical development, remedies are still classified as either legal or equitable. Questions pertaining to the availability of a jury trial continue to give the dichotomy life and vigor. Additionally, it is still

---

1. As stated by Professor Carlton: "The lord chancellor originally had been the king's chaplain and confessor, who through his role as keeper of the royal conscience had come to administer equity, a form of justice based on fairness and common sense. In the sixteenth century Chancery greatly expanded the scope of equity to compensate for the growing inadequacies of the common law." *Changing Jurisdictions in 16th and 17th Century England: The Relationship Between the Courts of Orphans and Chancery,* 18 AMERICAN JOURNAL OF LEGAL HISTORY 124, 130 (1974).

important to know which remedies are deemed to be "purely equitable" and therefore "discretionary." In those cases, where the remedy sought is "equitable," the court may examine or inquire into the *equities of the parties*. These may indeed refer to ethical considerations pertaining to the conduct of the parties and their moral culpability. Hence, it is fundamental to say that plaintiff must come into equity with clean hands, and that one who seeks equity must do equity. Furthermore, a plaintiff who has improperly delayed in the bringing of the suit may be barred by laches. Many of the maxims of equity pertain to the conduct of the parties in the granting or withholding of equitable relief.

For cases in which "equitable relief" is sought, the court, in the exercise of its "equitable discretion," may "balance the hardship" of the parties to determine how it will exercise its discretion. Hence in such a case a court may write:

> A court of equity can never be justified in making an inequitable decree. If the protection of a legal right even would do a plaintiff but comparatively little good and would produce great public or private hardship, equity will withhold its discreet and beneficent hand and remit the plaintiff to his legal rights and remedies.

McCann v. Chasm Power Company, 211 N.Y. 301, 305, 105 N.E. 416 (1914).

Many of the cases set forth in this book are designed to show the attitudes of the courts in the *exercise of discretion*, in the granting or withholding of "equitable relief." Also, they indicate the standards that have been established by the courts for the control or review of the exercise of judicial discretion.

The cases offer countless examples. Most of them teach not only the nature of the substantive right sought to be protected, but also the availability of an appropriate remedy.

Discretion: Judicial and "Equitable"

The heart of equity may be said to be the exercise of a wise and just discretion in the granting or withholding of equitable relief. Equitable relief is traditionally regarded as "extraordinary," and, therefore, "discretionary." It is important to know what is meant by "discretion." The specific performance cases are good examples of the considerable measure of latitude in the granting or withholding of relief. The same elements of discretion apply to the defenses that are considered in the granting or denial of relief. Thus whether a plaintiff will be denied an equitable remedy due to laches, "unclean hands," or balance of hardship, is a consideration entrusted to the discretion of the court. Discretion also includes matters such as inadequacy of consideration, plaintiff's default, the adequacy of the remedy at law, and the practicality of the remedy sought in equity. In a sense, therefore, all of these defenses or considerations introduced to defeat the granting of the equitable relief sought may be said to be "discretionary."

The materials that discuss equitable discretion also serve to introduce the reader to the exercise of *judicial discretion* found in all areas of the law. Notwithstanding a few early statements to the contrary, the granting of equitable relief "in the discretion of the chancellor" was always understood to mean a *judicial discretion* to be exercised by the application of established principles and precedents. To imply whim or caprice does violence to the wisdom and integrity of the chancellors who strove to give vitality to Justinian's three main principles of justice: "[t]o live honestly, to hurt no one, and give everyone his due."[2]

Judicial discretion implies a prudence and correctness of judgment that is just and fair under all of the circumstances. It does not mean a decision or conclusion based upon unknown or questionable assumptions and idiosyncratic factors. Rather, judicial discretion implies the exercise of a judicial value judgment based upon pertinent and relevant factual data. This value judgment has also taken into consideration the existing precedents in like cases. Hence, the importance of recognizing and presenting the factors or *equities* that affect that judgment—i.e., the exercise of judicial discretion. An appeal to "equity," therefore, requires a knowledge of these factors or equities, and not a tugging at the heartstrings and an appeal to emotions. What the courts have said, in the cases that follow, and more important, what they have done—in the granting or withholding of the relief sought—offer helpful and valuable guides.

In equity cases, a point of beginning for the exercise of judicial discretion is often found in the various equitable maxims.[3]

The Relief Sought by Plaintiff

What relief does plaintiff seek? Does plaintiff seek an award of damages? *Damages* consist of compensation in money for the loss or harm that the plaintiff has sustained. The next question pertains to the measure and quantum of damages recoverable.

Does the plaintiff wish to be restored to the position he would have held, had the defendant not committed the wrong? *Restitution* may also involve a money judgment, but the goal is to prevent the defendant's unjust enrichment. Hence, the measure of recovery will be the defendant's gain rather than plaintiff's loss. An example is the fiduciary who wrongfully invests plaintiff's money, and earns a substantial profit. Several restitutionary remedies are available to the plaintiff who may claim from the fiduciary the increased fund.

May the plaintiff compel a defendant to do specifically what the defendant promised to do? If the plaintiff seeks *specific relief*, under what circumstances is it available? An example is the defendant who breached the contract, and plaintiff seeks specific performance—not damages for its

---

2. INSTITUTES 1.1.3. *See* EDWARD D. RE, *The Roman Contribution to the Common Law*, 29 FORDHAM L. REV. 447, 455, n.36 (1961).

3. See materials at pp. 33–35, infra.

breach. When will a court compel the defendant specifically to do or refrain from doing something? The study here pertains to the entire area of specific relief, and the availability of a mandatory or prohibitory injunction. The injunction is, of course, a *coercive remedy*, enforceable by the contempt power of the court.

Often a plaintiff does not seek damages, nor does plaintiff wish that the defendant do or refrain from doing something. The relief that plaintiff seeks is a declaration of rights, i.e., *declaratory relief*. The cases offer many examples where the relief sought is a declaratory judgment. Illustrative are cases where a plaintiff may wish to have the court construe a contract to declare the rights of the parties. Likewise, a plaintiff may wish a declaration that a statute, under which the plaintiff is about to be tried, is unconstitutional. The request for the declaration of the unconstitutionality of the statute is often coupled with a request to *enjoin* the district or state attorney from prosecuting the plaintiff.

The specific performance, and other cases in this book, offer many examples of decrees which command a defendant to do or not to do something, i.e., perform the contract, not chop down shade trees, stop polluting a river, etc. They have been included, not only because they teach the nature of the substantive right sought to be protected, but also the availability of an appropriate remedy.

Frequently, the individual who has been wronged will be able to choose from among several different remedies. Depending upon which remedy or remedies is chosen, a different interest may be protected. In an appropriate case, an individual may obtain an injunction to restrain another from committing a tort. If the tort has already been committed, damages may be awarded. In contract cases, a recovery in both restitution and in damages may be available.

Equity

The Problem of Individualized Justice

DEVLIN, THE JUDGE 84 (1979).

Judgment according to law is *not* invariably the same thing as judgment according to the merits of the particular case from which the judgment flows. The hallmark of judgment according to law is conformity with a set of rules. The rules should be designed so as to ensure justice in the normal case and also in any foreseeable exceptions, at least to the extent that provision for the exceptions does not make the rule intolerably cumbersome. But to frame a set of rules that would do justice in every case which could be brought within them would be, if not theoretically impossible, at any rate practically unattainable. So lawyers perforce accept the distinction between justice according to law and justice on the merits, or *ex aequo et bono* [in equity and good conscience] as they call it.

Aristotle defined equity similarly, as "a correction of law where it is defective owing to its universality."[4] Aristotle explains what is "equity" or "equitable" in his discussion of "epieikeia," a necessary element because of the imperfect generalization of legal rules. How, then, does equity differ from statutory interpretation or common law rulemaking? How can this exercise of equity powers by judges be reconciled with the idea of the rule of law that is so central to our notion of law and government and our commitment to democracy?

Riggs v. Palmer

Court of Appeals of New York, 1889.
115 N.Y. 506, 22 N.E. 188.

■ EARL, J. On the 13th day of August 1880, Francis B. Palmer made his last will and testament, in which he gave small legacies to his two daughters, ... the plaintiffs in this action, and the remainder of his estate to his grandson, the defendant, Elmer E. Palmer.... The testator at the date of his will owned a farm and considerable personal property.... At the date of the will, and, subsequently, to the death of the testator, Elmer lived with him as a member of his family, and at his death was sixteen years old. He knew of the provisions made in his favor in the will, and, that he might prevent his grandfather from revoking such provisions, which he had manifested some intention to do, and to obtain the speedy enjoyment and immediate possession of his property, he willfully murdered him by poisoning him. [When this suit was filed, Elmer had already been convicted of murdering Francis, and he was serving time in a reformatory.] He now claims the property, and the sole question for our determination is, can he have it? The defendants say that the testator is dead; that his will was made in due form and has been admitted to probate, and that, therefore, it must have effect according to the letter of the law.

It is quite true that statutes regulating the making, proof and effect of wills, and the devolution of property, if literally construed, and if their force and effect can in no way and under no circumstances be controlled or modified, give this property to the murderer.

. . . .

Such a construction ought to be put upon a statute as will best answer the intention which the makers had in view, for [one who considers merely the letter of an instrument goes but skin deep into its meaning].... In some cases the letter of a legislative act is restrained by an equitable construction; in others it is enlarged; in others the construction is contrary

---

4. "Our next subject is equity ... When the law speaks universally, then and a case arises on it which is not covered by the universal statement, then it is right when the legislator fails us and has erred by oversimplicity, to correct the omission—to say what the legislator himself would have said had he been present, and would have put into his law if he had known. Hence the equitable is just, and better than one kind of justice—not better than absolute justice but better than the error that arises from the absoluteness of the statement. And this is the nature of the equitable, a correction of law where it is defective owing to its universality...." the Nicomachean Ethics of Aristotle *quoted in* EDWARD D. RE, SELECTED ESSAYS ON EQUITY xi (1955).

to the letter. The equitable construction which restrains the letter of a statute is defined by Aristotle, as frequently quoted, in this manner: [Equity is a correction of the law where it is defective owing to its universality.] If the law-makers could, as to this case, be consulted, would they say that they intended by their general language that the property of a testator or of an ancestor should pass to one who had taken his life for the express purpose of getting his property? In 1 Blackstone's Commentaries (91) the learned author, speaking of the construction of statutes, says: "If there arise out of them any absurd consequences manifestly contradictory to common reason, they are, with regard to those collateral consequences, void.... When some collateral matter arises out of the general words, and happen to be unreasonable, then the judges are in decency to conclude that the consequence was not foreseen by the parliament, and, therefore, they are at liberty to expound the statute by equity and only [as to this] disregard it;" and he gives as an illustration, if an act of parliament gives a man power to try all causes that arise within his manor of Dale, yet, if a cause should arise in which he himself is party, the act is construed not to extend to that because it is unreasonable that any man should determine his own quarrel.

. . . .

What could be more unreasonable than to suppose that it was the legislative intention in the general laws passed for the orderly, peaceable and just devolution of property, that they should have operation in favor of one who murdered his ancestor that he might speedily come into the possession of his estate? Such an intention is inconceivable....

Besides, all laws as well as all contracts may be controlled in their operation and effect by general, fundamental maxims of the common law. No one shall be permitted to profit by his own fraud, or to take advantage of his own wrong, or to found any claim upon his own iniquity, or to acquire property by his own crime. These maxims are dictated by public policy, have their foundation in universal law administered in all civilized countries, and have nowhere been superseded by statutes....

These maxims, without any statute giving them force or operation, frequently control the effect and nullify the language of wills. A will procured by fraud and deception, like any other instrument, may be decreed void and set aside, and so a particular portion of a will may be excluded from probate or held inoperative if induced by the fraud or undue influence of the person in whose favor it is. So a will may contain provisions which are immoral, irreligious or against public policy, and they will be held void.

Here there was no certainty that this murderer would survive the testator, or that the testator would not change his will, and there was no certainty that he would get this property if nature was allowed to take its course. He, therefore, murdered the testator expressly to vest himself with an estate. Under such circumstances, what law, human or divine, will allow him to take the estate and enjoy the fruits of his crime? The will spoke and became operative at the death of the testator. He caused that death, and thus by his crime made it speak and have operation. Shall it speak and operate in his favor? If he had met the testator and taken his property by force, he would have had no title to it. Shall he acquire title by murdering him? If he had gone to the testator's house and by force compelled him, or by fraud or undue influence had induced him to will him his property, the law would not allow him to hold it. But can he give effect and operation to a will by murder, and yet take the property? To answer these questions in the affirmative, it seems to me, would be a reproach to the jurisprudence of our state, and an offense against public policy.

Under the civil law evolved from the general principles of natural law and justice by many generations of jurisconsults, philosophers and statesmen, one cannot take property by inheritance or will from an ancestor or benefactor whom he has murdered. In the Civil Code of Lower Canada the provisions on the subject in the Code Napoleon have been substantially copied. But, so far as I can find, in no country where the common law prevails has it been deemed important to enact a law to provide for such a case. Our revisers and law-makers were familiar with the civil law, and they did not deem it important to incorporate into our statutes its provisions upon this subject. This is not a *casus omissus* [a case or event for which no provision has been made]. It was evidently supposed that the maxims of the common law were sufficient to regulate such a case and that a specific enactment for that purpose was not needed.

For the same reasons the defendant Palmer cannot take any of this property as heir. Just before the murder he was not an heir, and it was not certain that he ever would be. He might have died before his grandfather, or might have been disinherited by him. He made himself an heir by the murder, and he seeks to take property as the fruit of his crime. What has before been said as to him as legatee applies to him with equal force as an heir. He cannot vest himself with title by crime.

My view of this case does not inflict upon Elmer any greater or other punishment for his crime than the law specifies. It takes from him no property, but simply holds that he shall not acquire property by his crime, and thus be rewarded for its commission.

. . . .

The judgment of the General Term and that entered upon the report of the referee should, therefore, be reversed and judgment should be entered as follows: That Elmer E. Palmer and the administrator be enjoined from using any of the personalty or real estate left by the testator for Elmer's benefit; that the devise and bequest in the will to Elmer be declared ineffective to pass the title to him; that by reason of the crime of murder committed upon the grandfather he is deprived of any interest in the estate left by him; that the plaintiffs are the true owners of the real and personal estate left by the testator, subject to the charge in favor of Elmer's mother and the widow of the testator, under the ante-nuptial agreement, and that the plaintiffs have costs in all the courts against Elmer.

■ GRAY, J. (dissenting) . . . .

To sustain their position the appellants' counsel has submitted an able and elaborate brief, and, if I believed that the decision of the question could be affected by considerations of an equitable nature, I should not hesitate to assent to views which commend themselves to the conscience. But the matter does not lie within the domain of conscience. We are bound by the rigid rules of law, which have been established by the legislature, and within the limits of which the determination of this question is confined. The question we are dealing with is, whether a testamentary disposition can be altered, or a will revoked, after the testator's death, through an appeal to the courts, when the legislature has, by its enactments, prescribed exactly when and how wills may be made, altered and revoked, and, apparently, as it seems to me, when they have been fully complied with, has left no room for the exercise of an equitable jurisdiction by courts over such matters. Modern jurisprudence, in recognizing the right of the individual, under more or less restrictions, to dispose of his property after his death, subjects it to legislative control, both as to extent and as to mode of exercise. Complete freedom of testamentary disposition of one's property has not been and is not the universal rule; as we see from the provisions of the Napoleonic Code, from those systems of jurisprudence in other countries which are modeled upon the Roman law, and from the statutes of many of our states. To the statutory restraints, which are imposed upon the disposition of one's property by will, are added strict and systematic statutory rules for the execution, alteration and revocation of the will; which must be, at least, substantially, if not exactly, followed to insure validity and performance. The reason for the establishment of such rules, we may naturally assume, consists in the purpose to create those safeguards about these grave and important acts, which experience has demonstrated to be the wisest and surest. That freedom, which is permitted to be exercised in the testamentary disposition of one's estate by the laws of the state, is subject to its being exercised in conformity with the regulations of the statutes. The capacity and the power of the individual to dispose of his property after death, and the mode by which that power can be exercised, are matters of which the legislature has assumed the entire control, and has undertaken to regulate with comprehensive particularity.

The appellants' argument is not helped by reference to those rules of the civil law, or to those laws of other governments, by which the heir or legatee is excluded from benefit under the testament, if he has been convicted of killing, or attempting to kill, the testator. In the absence of such legislation here, the courts are not empowered to institute such a system of remedial justice. The deprivation of the heir of his testamentary succession by the Roman law, when guilty of such a crime, plainly, was intended to be in the nature of a punishment imposed upon him. The succession, in such a case of guilt, escheated to the exchequer.

. . . .

The judgment should be affirmed, with costs.

■ All concur with EARL, J., except GRAY, J., who reads dissenting opinion, and DANFORTH, J., concurring.

Judgment in accordance with the prevailing opinion.

In re Covert

Court of Appeals of New York, 2001.
97 N.Y.2d 68, 761 N.E.2d 571, 735 N.Y.S.2d 879.

■ CIPARICK, J.

The issue on this appeal is whether the doctrine of *Riggs v. Palmer*, 115 N.Y. 506, 22 N.E. 188, which disallows a wrongdoer from profiting by his or her crime at the expense of the victim's estate, mandates the disinheritance of the wrongdoer's heirs and distributees, thereby negating their entitlement to an express testamentary bequest made in the victim's will. We conclude, under the circumstances of this case, that where a victim's will makes bequests to the wrongdoer's family—innocent distributees—their status as legatees under the victim's will is not vitiated, and they are not disinherited by virtue of their familial relationship to the wrongdoer.

I

This case involves a dispute between two families over the estates of a deceased couple, Edward M. and Kathleen Covert. Tragically, on April 3, 1998, Edward shot and killed Kathleen, then turned the gun on himself and took his own life. Edward was survived by his parents, Edward F. Covert and Joan Covert, and his siblings, Theresa Guinan, Gayle Diffendorf and Phyllis Thompson (the Coverts). Excluding Edward, Kathleen was survived by her parents, Robert L. Millard and Carol A. Millard, and her siblings, Robert L. Millard, II and Kelly Hawley (the Millards).

Prior to this incident, on December 14, 1995, Edward and Kathleen executed a joint will providing for the final disposition of their property. The will designated Kelly Hawley as executrix. The second paragraph of the will provided,

> "[u]pon the death of one of us leaving the other of us surviving, all the property and estate of every kind and nature and wheresoever situate, of the one so dying first of which he or she has the power of disposal, is hereby given, devised and bequeathed to the survivor absolutely and without any limitation or restriction whatsoever."

Upon the death of the surviving spouse, the fifth paragraph of the will bequeathed the couple's jointly owned time share and jewelry to Kelly Hawley or to named alternative legatees. Also upon the death of the survivor, the residuary estate was to be distributed into three equal shares—one third each to Edward's parents, Kathleen's parents and decedents' siblings.

At the time of her death, Kathleen's combined probate and nonprobate assets were valued at $225,000. Edward's assets—including two life insurance policies and a union retirement fund payable to Kathleen as primary beneficiary and to his parents as contingent beneficiaries—were worth approximately $71,000. The couple further held assets valued at $121,000 as joint tenants.

On May 21, 1998, the court admitted the will to probate and issued letters testamentary to Hawley as executor. In March 1999, Hawley petitioned Surrogate's Court requesting direction in the distribution of the estates. The Coverts filed an answer to the petition in June 1999, demanding strict compliance with the express terms of the will, and requesting division of the estates in equal shares among Kathleen's parents, Edward's parents and the surviving siblings. In response, the Millards requested that the court preclude the Coverts from taking under the will due to Edward's role in Kathleen's death. Thereafter, the Coverts moved for summary judgment to dismiss the Millards' answer and to compel distribution according to the terms of the will.

Surrogate's Court denied the Coverts' motion and granted summary judgment to the Millards, opining that "the *Riggs* precedent must sweep away all other arguments and require a forfeiture of the Covert family's interest in Kathleen's property including her insurance and the couple's joint property." The court precluded the Coverts from taking any of Kathleen's property, yet allowed them to receive a share of Edward's individual property. The Appellate Division unanimously modified the order, treating Edward as having fictionally predeceased Kathleen and directing that all property pass through Kathleen's estate, ultimately to be distributed in equal thirds. Additionally, the Court ordered that Edward's two life insurance policies and retirement fund proceeds pass to the respective contingent beneficiaries (279 A.D.2d 48, 717 N.Y.S.2d 392). We granted the Millards leave to appeal (96 N.Y.2d 711, 727 N.Y.S.2d 697, 751 N.E.2d 945) and now affirm, for different reasons.

II

Our analysis begins with a restatement of settled principles regarding will construction and testamentary distribution. A validly executed joint will is a proper and legally tenable means of effecting a testamentary disposition of property . . . This Court has long recognized that testamentary instruments are strictly construed so as to give full effect to the testator's clear intent. . . .

Notwithstanding the exceptional degree of deference afforded testator intent, this Court has consistently reaffirmed the equitable principle that "[no] one shall be permitted to profit by his [or her] own fraud, or to take advantage of [their] own wrong, or to found any claim upon [their] own iniquity, or to acquire property by [their] own crime" . . . In *Riggs*, this Court fashioned an equitable rule that prevented a grandson legatee who murdered his grandfather from profiting from his crime. This Court voided the gift to the grandson, Elmer Palmer, and allowed the estate to pass to the testator's daughters and to Elmer's mother, in accord with the provisions of the will. The Court did not force the estate into intestacy, nor did the Court prevent the wrongdoer's mother from taking under the will.

The *Riggs* rule prevents wrongdoers from acquiring a property interest, or otherwise profiting from their own wrongdoing. However, we have never applied the doctrine to cause a wrongdoer's forfeiture of a vested property interest. Indeed, public policy, as embodied in Civil Rights Law § 79–b, militates against application of *Riggs* as a means of effecting a proprietary forfeiture. Section 79–b provides, in pertinent part, that "[a] conviction of a person for any crime, does not work a forfeiture of any property, real or personal, or any right or interest therein" (Civil Rights Law § 79–b).

Because Kathleen died at Edward's hand, the *Riggs* doctrine nullifies any and all bequests by Kathleen to him. There is no need to employ the Appellate Division's fiction that Edward "predeceased" Kathleen. Since

Riggs voids the gift to Edward, any testamentary bequests to which he would have been entitled pass directly into the residuary.

The Millards would apply *Riggs* to void the gift to the Coverts, as well. Absent a showing that the Coverts are anything other than innocent distributees, *Riggs* is inapplicable. The Millards would further have us disregard settled principles in favor of invalidation of the residuary clause and an intestate distribution, arguing that the will's residuary clause applied only if Kathleen survived Edward and received his property. Contrary to the Millards' assertions, however, failure of the preceding gift does not destroy, but accelerates, the residuary. ... Furthermore, the mere existence of a testamentary instrument gives rise to a presumption against intestacy ... Application of the presumption against intestacy further supports validation of the residuary clause by preventing a portion of the estate from falling into intestacy. We conclude that neither the will, nor any clause thereof, is invalid, and accordingly, no portion of either estate falls into intestacy.

III

This appeal centers on three main types of property to be distributed—individual property owned outright and independently by Edward and Kathleen respectively, joint property with a right of survivorship and individual assets with named beneficiaries. Each type of property is subject to its own analysis.

The individual assets owned outright, other than the specific bequest to Hawley (which is uncontested), must pass through decedents' respective wills, and into the residuary. Similarly, Edward's individual property owned outright passes through his will. In that Kathleen predeceased him, his property passes into the residuary, also to be distributed into equal thirds to the Covert parents, the Millard parents and the siblings.

In contrast to individual property, a joint tenant is entitled to an immediate one-half interest in the joint property.... This interest is immediately vested, entitling either tenant to a half portion, even though only one tenant may have established and contributed to the asset.... Thus, before their deaths, Edward and Kathleen each owned an undivided one-half interest, with a right of survivorship, in their joint property. Allowing Edward the one-half interest in that property would not afford him any benefit from his wrongdoing. Consistent with the public policy articulated in Civil Rights Law § 79–b, his one-half interest is not forfeited.

Riggs, however, prevents Edward from profiting from his own wrongdoing. Because Edward killed Kathleen, he cannot succeed to the survivorship interest that would ordinarily arise on the death of his joint tenant. Therefore, the joint property should be divided evenly, half passing through Edward's estate and half through Kathleen's.

Finally, the insurance and pension plan proceeds must pass to their alternative beneficiaries. Insurance policies are, in essence, creatures of contract, and accordingly, subject to principles of contract interpretation ... "It is unquestionably the rule that '[c]ontracts of insurance, like other contracts, are to be construed according to the sense and meaning of the terms which the parties have used, and if they are clear and unambiguous the terms are to be taken and understood in their plain, ordinary and proper sense' " . . . Pension plans are also contracts subject to construction under similar principles . . .

Neither party claims that the terms of the relevant instruments are deficient or ambiguous. Edward's insurance policies name Kathleen as primary beneficiary, and his father as contingent beneficiary. His retirement plan is payable primarily to Kathleen and in the alternative to his parents. The Millards claim that our decision in *Petrie v. Chase Manhattan Bank*, 33 N.Y.2d 846, 352 N.Y.S.2d 194, 307 N.E.2d 253 precludes payment to the contingent beneficiaries. Their reliance on *Petrie* is misplaced.

In *Petrie*, the murderer was a beneficiary of his victim's trust and first in line to benefit. He would have directly profited by his wrongful act and acquired property to which he was not otherwise entitled. Applying *Riggs* prevented him from benefitting from his criminal act. Likewise, we further concluded that *Riggs* equally applied to prevent the contingent beneficiaries, chosen by the murderer, not by the settlor of the trust, from recovering trust proceeds.

Unlike *Petrie*, here we are concerned with the disposition of the slayer's property. The insurance and pension funds were Edward's own property both before and after Kathleen's death. Because the alternative beneficiaries are innocent distributees of his property, they are entitled to take pursuant to the provisions of the respective instruments.

Accordingly, the order of the Appellate Division should be affirmed, with costs to all parties appearing separately and filing separate briefs payable out of the estates.

CHIEF JUDGE KAYE and JUDGES SMITH, LEVINE, WESLEY, ROSENBLATT and GRAFFEO concur.

Order affirmed, etc.

Graf v. Hope Building Corp.

Court of Appeals of New York, 1930.
254 N.Y. 1, 171 N.E. 884.

■ O'BRIEN, J. Plaintiffs, as executors of Joseph L. Graf, are the holders of two consolidated mortgages forming a single lien on real property the title to which is vested in defendant Hope Building Corporation. According to the terms of the agreement consolidating the mortgages the principal sum is made payable January 1, 1935. Nevertheless, a clause provides that the whole shall become due after default for twenty days in the payment of any installment of interest. David Herstein is the controlling stockholder and also president and treasurer of defendant. He alone was authorized to sign checks in its behalf. Early in June, 1927, he went to Europe. Before his departure a clerical assistant who was also the nominal secretary of the corporation computed the interest due July 1, and through an error in arithmetic incorrectly calculated it. Mr. Herstein signed the check for the erroneous amount but before the date upon which the interest became due, the secretary discovered the error, notified the mortgagee of the shortage of

$401.87, stated that on the president's return from Europe the balance would be paid and on June 30 forwarded to the mortgagee the check as drawn. It was deposited by the mortgagee and paid by defendant. On July 5 Mr. Herstein returned, but, through an omission in his office, he was not informed of the default in the payment of interest. At the expiration of twenty-one days this action of foreclosure was begun. Defendant made tender of the deficiency but the mortgagee, strictly insisting on his contract rights, refused the tender and elected to assert the power created by the acceleration clause in the consolidation agreement.

On the undisputed facts as found, we are unable to perceive any defense to the action and are, therefore, constrained to reverse the judgment dismissing the complaint. Plaintiffs may be ungenerous, but generosity is a voluntary attribute and cannot be enforced even by a chancellor. Forbearance is a quality which under the circumstances of this case is likewise free from coercion. Here there is no penalty, no forfeiture, nothing except a covenant fair on its face to which both parties willingly consented. It is neither oppressive nor unconscionable. In the absence of some act by the mortgagee which a court of equity would be justified in considering unconscionable, he is entitled to the benefit of the covenant. The contract is definite and no reason appears for its reformation by the courts. We are not at liberty to revise while professing to construe. Defendant's mishap, caused by a succession of its errors and negligent omissions, is not of the nature requiring relief from its default. Rejection of plaintiffs' legal right could rest only on compassion for defendant's negligence. Such a tender emotion must be exerted, if at all, by the parties rather than by the court....

. . . .

The judgment of the Appellate Division and that of the Special Term should be reversed and judgment ordered in favor of plaintiff for the relief demanded in the complaint, with costs in all courts.

■ CARDOZO, C.J. (dissenting)....

There is no undeviating principle that equity shall enforce the covenants of a mortgage, unmoved by an appeal *ad misericordiam* [to mercy], however urgent or affecting. The development of the jurisdiction of the chancery is lined with historic monuments that point another course. Equity declines to treat a mortgage upon realty as a conveyance subject to a condition, but views it as a lien irrespective of its form. Equity declines to give effect to a covenant, however formal, whereby in the making of a mortgage, the mortgagor abjures and surrenders the privilege of redemption. Equity declines, in the same spirit, to give effect to a covenant, improvident in its terms, for the sale of an inheritance, but compels the buyer to exhibit an involuntary charity if he is found to have taken advantage of the necessities of the seller. Equity declines to give effect to a covenant for liquidated damages if it is so unconscionable in amount as to be equivalent in its substance to a provision for a penalty. One could give many illustrations of the traditional and unchallenged exercise of a like dispensing power. It runs through the whole rubric of accident and mistake. Equity follows the law, but not slavishly nor always. If it did, there could never be occasion for the enforcement of equitable doctrine.

To all this, acceleration clauses in mortgages do not constitute an exception.... In general, it is true, they will be enforced as they are written. In particular this has been held of a covenant in a mortgage accelerating the maturity of the principal in default of punctual payment of an installment of the interest. If the quality of a penalty inheres in such a covenant at all, it is not there to such a degree as to call, in ordinary circumstances, for mitigation or repression. Less favor has been shown to a provision for acceleration of a mortgage in default of punctual payment of taxes or assessments. We have held that such a provision, though not a penalty in a strict or proper sense, is yet so closely akin thereto in view of the forfeiture of credit that equity will relieve against it if default has been due to mere venial inattention and if relief can be granted without damage to the lender....

There is neither purpose nor desire to impair the stability of the rule, which is still to be enforced as one of general application, that non-payment of interest will accelerate the debt if the mortgage so provides. The rule is well understood, and is fair to borrower and lender in its normal operation. Especially is it fair if there is a period of grace (in this case twenty days) whereby a reasonable leeway is afforded to inadvertence and improvidence. In such circumstances, with one period of grace established by the covenant, only the most appealing equity will justify a court in transcending the allotted period and substituting another. There is a difference, however, between a denial of power, without heed to the hardship calling for its use, and a definition of hardship that will limit the occasions upon which power shall be exercised.... However fixed the general rule and the policy of preserving it, there may be extraordinary conditions in which the enforcement of such a clause according to the letter of the covenant will be disloyalty to the basic principles for which equity exists.... The exercise of a dispensing power was deemed to be a branch of the jurisdiction of equity to relieve against the consequences of accident or mistake. "This does not mean that such provisions for accelerating payments are provisions for forfeitures. Fairly made and fairly enforced they are not." Even so, "a court of equity may intervene to prevent the creditor from taking an unconscionable advantage of the letter of his bargain."

When an advantage is unconscionable depends upon the circumstances. It is not unconscionable generally to insist that payment shall be made according to the letter of a contract. It may be unconscionable to insist upon adherence to the letter where the default is limited to a trifling balance, where the failure to pay the balance is the product of mistake, and where the mortgagee indicates by his conduct that he appreciates the mistake and has attempted by silence and inaction to turn it to his own advantage. The holder of this mortgage must have understood that he could have his money for the asking. His silence, followed, as it was, by immediate suit at the first available opportunity, brings conviction to the mind that he was avoiding any act that would spur the mortgagor to payment. What he did was almost as suggestive of that purpose as if he had kept out of the way in order to avoid a tender. Demand was, indeed, unnecessary to bring the debt to maturity at law. There is not a technical estoppel. The consequence does not follow that, in conditions so peculiar, the omission to make demand is without significance in equity. Significant it may then be in helping the court to a determination whether the conduct of a suitor in taking advantage of a default, so easily averted and so plainly unintentional, is consistent with good conscience. True, indeed, it is that accident and mistake will often be inadequate to supply a basis for the granting or withholding of equitable remedies where the consequences to be corrected might have been avoided if the victim of the misfortune had ordered his affairs with reasonable diligence. The restriction, however, is not obdurate, for always the gravity of the fault must be compared with the gravity of the hardship. Let the hardship be strong enough, and equity will find a way, though many a formula of inaction may seem to bar the path.

Cases such as Klein v. New York Life Ins. Co., 104 U.S. 88, 26 L.Ed. 662; Wheeler v. Connecticut Mut. Life Ins. Co., 82 N.Y. 543, and Whiteside v. North American Acc. Ins. Co., 200 N.Y. 320, 93 N.E. 948, do not derogate from the doctrine that a postulant in equity for affirmative relief may be dismissed without a remedy where he is attempting as an actor in the lawsuit to make himself the beneficiary of accident or error. In those cases and in others like them there was an attempt to charge a defendant with a contractual liability in disregard of the conditions limiting its creation. The party insisting on the condition was before the court as a defendant resisting a liability which could only arise if the condition was a nullity. Here, on the other hand, there is no endeavor by the owner of the property to charge the mortgagee with an obligation to do anything affirmative. The operation of the decree will be negative altogether. There is nothing more than a refusal to give active aid and countenance to one who seeks the aid of equity and is unwilling as a price to do equity himself. In equity as in mechanics action and reaction are equal and opposite. The equity that one asks one must be ready to concede. The maxim applies "whatever be the nature of the controversy between two definite parties, and whatever be the nature of the remedy" (Pomeroy, Equity Jurisprudence, vol. 1, § 385). The court will stand aside when by intervening it will make itself an instrument of injustice. . . .

In this case, the hardship is so flagrant, the misadventure so undoubted, the oppression so apparent, as to justify a holding that only through an acceptance of the tender will equity be done. The omission to pay in full had its origin in a clerical or arithmetical error that accompanied the act of payment, the very act to be performed. The error was not known to the debtor except in a constructive sense, for the secretary, a subordinate clerk, omitted to do her duty and report it to her principal. The deficiency, though not so small as to be negligible within the doctrine of *de minimis,* was still slight and unimportant when compared with the payment duly made. The possibility of bad faith is overcome by many circumstances, of which not the least is the one that instantly upon the discovery of the error, the deficiency was paid, and this only a single day after the term of grace was at an end. Finally, there is no pretense of damage or even inconvenience ensuing to the lender. On the contrary, and this is the vital point, the inference is inevitable that the lender appreciated the blunder and was unwilling to avert it. From his conduct on the day immediately succeeding the default, we can infer his state of mind as it existed the day before. When all these circumstances are viewed in their cumulative significance, the enforcement of the covenant according to its letter is seen to approach in hardship the oppression of a penalty, just as truly as in Noyes v. Anderson there was unconscionable hardship in an insistence upon a default in the discharge of an assessment. Ninety-one per cent of the interest had been paid when it matured. The other nine per cent was paid as soon as the underpayment became known to an agent competent to act, and only a day too late. Equity declines to intervene at the instance of a suitor who after fostering the default would make the court his ally in an endeavor to turn it to his benefit.

The judgment should be affirmed with costs.

■ Pound, Crane and Hubbs, JJ., concur with O'Brien, J.; Cardozo, C.J., dissents in opinion in which Lehman and Kellogg, JJ., concur.

Judgment accordingly.

————

NOTE

DeMare sold Plaintiff a parcel of land. Plaintiff recorded the deed. DeMare then sold the same land to Selden Land Corp., which recorded its deed. Fifteen years later, Selden built homes on the land and sold them to Defendants. Defendants, who bought in good faith, lived on the land for six years. Like Plaintiff, Defendants paid real estate taxes on the property during those years. Finally, when Plaintiff learned that the land she thought was vacant was occupied by Defendants, she brought an action for ejectment. In Miceli v. Riley, 79 A.D.2d 165, 436 N.Y.S.2d 72 (1981), the court held that, inasmuch as this was an action at law, the trial judge erred by considering the parties' relative hardships when deciding whether Plaintiff (who had legal title and the right to possess the land) was entitled to Defendants' unconditional ejectment. (However, the court also ruled that, in light of Defendants' good faith and the value of the improvements on the land, Plaintiff could not collect any damages.). See Peters v. Archambault, *infra* p. 482, Somerville v. Jacobs, *infra* p. 705, and Cal. Civ. Proc., Section 871.3(b) *infra* p. 712.

————

Weinberger v. Romero–Barcelo

Supreme Court of the United States, 1982.
456 U.S. 305, 102 S.Ct. 1798, 72 L.Ed.2d 91.

[The Navy, in the course of using an island off the Puerto Rico coast for air-to-ground weapons training, discharged ordnance into the waters surrounding the island. Romero–Barcelo brought an action in United States district court to enjoin the Navy's operation, alleging a violation of the Federal Water Pollution Control Act (FWPCA). Although the district court found that the discharges did not harm the quality of the water, it held that the Navy had violated the FWPCA by discharging ordnance into the water without first obtaining a permit from the Environmental Protection Agency. It ordered the Navy to apply for a permit but refused to enjoin the operation pending consideration of the permit application.

On appeal, the United States Court of Appeals for the First Circuit vacated the district court's order and remanded with instructions that the district court order the Navy to cease the violations until a permit was obtained. Relying on TVA v. Hill, 437 U.S. 153, 98 S.Ct. 2279, 57 L.Ed.2d 117 (1978), a case in which the Supreme Court held that an imminent violation of the Endangered Species Act required injunctive relief, the court of appeals concluded that the district court erred in undertaking a traditional balancing of the parties' competing interest.]

■ JUSTICE WHITE delivered the opinion of the Court.

. . . .

II

It goes without saying that an injunction is an equitable remedy. It "is not a remedy which issues as of course," or "to restrain an act the injurious consequences of which are merely trifling." An injunction should issue only where the intervention of a court of equity "is essential in order effectually to protect property rights against injuries otherwise irremediable." The Court has repeatedly held that the basis for injunctive relief in the federal courts has always been irreparable injury and the inadequacy of legal remedies.

Where plaintiff and defendant present competing claims of injury, the traditional function of equity has been to arrive at a "nice adjustment and reconciliation" between the competing claims. In such cases, the court "balances the conveniences of the parties and possible injuries to them according as they may be affected by the granting or withholding of the injunction." "The essence of equity has been the power of the chancellor to do equity and to mold each decree to the necessities of the particular case. Flexibility rather than rigidity has distinguished it."

In exercising their sound discretion, courts of equity should pay particular regard for the public consequences in employing the extraordinary remedy of injunction. Thus, the Court has noted that "the award of an interlocutory injunction by courts of equity has never been regarded as strictly a matter of right, even though irreparable injury may otherwise result to the plaintiff," and that "where an injunction is asked which will adversely affect a public interest for whose impairment, even temporarily, an injunction bond cannot compensate, the court may in the public interest withhold relief until a final determination of the rights of the parties, though postponement may be burdensome to the plaintiff." The grant of jurisdiction to insure compliance with a statute hardly suggests an absolute duty to do so under any and all circumstances, and a federal judge sitting as chancellor is not mechanically obligated to grant an injunction for every violation of law.

These commonplace considerations applicable to cases in which injunctions are sought in the federal courts reflect a "practice with a background of several hundred years of history," a practice of which Congress is assuredly well aware. Of course, Congress may intervene and guide or control the exercise of the courts' discretion, but we do not lightly assume that Congress has intended to depart from established principles. As the

Court said in Porter v. Warner Holding Co., 328 U.S. 395, 398, 66 S.Ct. 1086, 1089, 90 L.Ed. 1332 (1946):

"Moreover, the comprehensiveness of this equitable jurisdiction is not to be denied or limited in the absence of a clear and valid legislative command. Unless a statute in so many words, or by a necessary and inescapable inference, restricts the court's jurisdiction in equity, the full scope of that jurisdiction is to be recognized and applied. 'The great principles of equity, securing complete justice, should not be yielded to light inferences, or doubtful construction.' . . ."

In TVA v. Hill, we held that Congress had foreclosed the exercise of the usual discretion possessed by a court of equity. There, we thought that "one would be hard pressed to find a statutory provision whose terms were any plainer" than that before us. The statute involved, the Endangered Species Act, 87 Stat. 884, 16 U.S.C. § 1531 et seq., required the district court to enjoin completion of the Tellico Dam in order to preserve the snail darter, a species of perch. The purpose and language of the statute under consideration in *Hill,* not the bare fact of a statutory violation, compelled that conclusion. Section 1536 of the Act requires federal agencies to "insure that actions authorized, funded, or carried out by them do not jeopardize the continued existence of [any] endangered species . . . or result in the destruction or habitat of such species which is determined . . . to be critical." The statute thus contains a flat ban on the destruction of critical habitats.

It was conceded in *Hill* that completion of the dam would eliminate an endangered species by destroying its critical habitat. Refusal to enjoin the action would have ignored the "explicit provisions of the Endangered Species Act." Congress, it appeared to us, had chosen the snail darter over the dam. The purpose and language of the statute limited the remedies available to the district court; only an injunction could vindicate the objectives of the Act.

That is not the case here. An injunction is not the only means of ensuring compliance. The FWPCA itself, for example, provides for fines and criminal penalties. 33 U.S.C. § 1319(c) and (d). Respondents suggest that failure to enjoin the Navy will undermine the integrity of the permit process by allowing the statutory violation to continue. The integrity of the nation's waters, however, not the permit process, is the purpose of the FWPCA. As Congress explained, the objective of the FWPCA is to "restore and maintain the chemical, physical and biological integrity of the Nation's waters." 33 U.S.C. § 1251(a).

This purpose is to be achieved by compliance with the Act, including compliance with the permit requirements. Here, however, the discharge of ordnance had not polluted the waters, and, although the District Court declined to enjoin the discharges, it neither ignored the statutory violation nor undercut the purpose and function of the permit system. The court ordered the Navy to apply for a permit. It temporarily, not permanently, allowed the Navy to continue its activities without a permit.

In *Hill,* we also noted that none of the limited "hardship exemptions" of the Endangered Species Act would "even remotely apply to the Tellico

Project." The prohibition of the FWPCA against discharge of pollutants, in contrast, can be overcome by the very permit the Navy was ordered to seek. The Senate Report to the 1972 Amendments explains that it was enacting the permit program because "the Committee recognizes the impracticality of any effort to halt all pollution immediately." S.Rep. 92–414, 92d Cong., 1st Sess. 43 (1971), U.S.Code Cong. & Admin.News 1972, p. 3709. That the scheme as a whole contemplates the exercise of discretion and balancing of equities militates against the conclusion that Congress intended to deny courts their traditional equitable discretion in enforcing the statute.

Other aspects of the statutory scheme also suggest that Congress did not intend to deny courts the discretion to rely on remedies other than an immediate prohibitory injunction. Although the ultimate objective of the FWPCA is to eliminate all discharges of pollutants into the navigable waters by 1985, the statute sets forth a scheme of phased compliance. As enacted, it called for the achievement of the "best practicable control technology currently available" by July 1, 1977 and the "best available technology economically achievable" by July 1, 1983. 33 U.S.C. § 1311(b) (Supp. IV 1970). This scheme of phased compliance further suggests that this is a statute in which Congress envisioned, rather than curtailed, the exercise of discretion.

. . . .

Because Congress, in enacting the FWPCA, has not foreclosed the exercise of equitable discretion, the proper standard for appellate review is whether the district court abused its discretion in denying an immediate cessation order while the Navy applied for a permit. We reverse and remand to Court of Appeals for proceedings consistent with this opinion.

It is so ordered.

■ [The concurring opinion of POWELL, J., and the dissenting opinion of STEVENS, J., are omitted.]

*

PART II

EQUITY

CHAPTER 2

THE HISTORY OF EQUITY

A. THE ORIGINS OF EQUITY[1]

Suppose that we ask the question—What is Equity? We can only answer it by giving some short account of certain courts of justice which were abolished over thirty years ago. In the year 1875 we might have said "equity is that body of rules which is administered only by those Courts which are known as Courts of Equity." The definition of course would not have been very satisfactory, but nowadays we are cut off even from this unsatisfactory definition. We have no longer any courts which are merely courts of equity. Thus we are driven to say that Equity now is that body of rules administered by our English courts of justice which, were it not for the operation of the Judicature Acts, would be administered only by those courts which would be known as Courts of Equity.

This, you may well say, is but a poor thing to call a definition. Equity is a certain portion of our existing substantive law, and yet in order that we may describe this portion and mark it off from other portions we have to make reference to courts that are no longer in existence. Still I fear that nothing better than this is possible. The only alternative would be to make a list of the equitable rules and say that Equity consists of those rules. This, I say, would be the only alternative, for if we were to inquire what it is that all these rules have in common and what it is that marks them off from all other rules administered by our courts, we should by way of answer find nothing but this, that these rules were until lately administered, and administered only, by our courts of equity.

Therefore for the mere purpose of understanding the present state of our law, some history becomes necessary. . . .

In Edward I's day [(r. 1272–1307)], at the end of the thirteenth century, three great courts have come into existence, the King's Bench, the Common Bench or Court of Common Pleas and the Exchequer. Each of these has its own proper sphere, but as time goes on each of them attempts to extend its sphere and before the middle ages are over a plaintiff has often a choice between these three courts and each of them will deal with his case in the same way and by the same rules. The law which these courts administer is in part traditional law, in part statute law. Already in Edward I's day the phrase "common law" is current. It is a phrase that has been borrowed from the canonists—who used *"jus commune"* to denote the general law of the Catholic Church; it describes that part of the law that is unenacted, nonstatutory, that is common to the whole land and to all Englishmen. It is contrasted with statute, with local custom, with royal

1. Reprinted from MAITLAND, EQUITY 1–11 (1909).

prerogative. It is not as yet contrasted with equity, for as yet there is no body of rules which bears this name.

One of the three courts, namely, the Exchequer, is more than a court of law. From our modern point of view it is not only a court of law but a "government office," an administrative or executive bureau; our modern Treasury is an offshoot from the old Exchequer. What we should call the "civil service" of the country is transacted by two great offices or "departments"; there is the Exchequer which is the fiscal department, there is the Chancery which is the secretarial department, while above these there rises the king's permanent Council. At the head of the Chancery stands the Chancellor, usually a bishop; he is we may say the king's secretary of state for all departments, he keeps the king's great seal and all the already great mass of writing that has to be done in the king's name has to be done under his supervision.

He is not as yet a judge, but already he by himself or his subordinates has a great deal of work to do which brings him into a close connection with the administration of justice. One of the duties of that great staff of clerks over which he presides is to draw up and issue those writs whereby actions are begun in the courts of law—such writs are sealed with the king's seal. A man who wishes to begin an action must go to the Chancery and obtain a writ. Many writs there are which have been formulated long ago; such writs are writs of course (*brevia de cursu*), one obtains them by asking for them of the clerks—called Cursitors—and paying the proper fees. But the Chancery has a certain limited power of inventing new writs to meet new cases as they arise. That power is consecrated by a famous clause of the Second Statute of Westminster authorizing writs *in consimili casu*. Thus the Chancellor may often have to consider whether the case is one in which some new and some specially worded writ should be framed. This however is not judicial business. The Chancellor does not hear both sides of the story, he only hears the plaintiff's application, and if he grants a writ the courts of law may afterwards quash that writ as being contrary to the law of the land.

But by another route the Chancellor is brought into still closer contact with the administration of justice. Though these great courts of law have been established there is still a reserve of justice in the king. Those who can not get relief elsewhere present their petitions to the king and his council praying for some remedy. Already by the end of the thirteenth century the number of such petitions presented in every year is very large, and the work of reading them and considering them is very laborious. In practice a great share of this labour falls on the Chancellor. He is the king's prime minister, he is a member of the council, and the specially learned member of the council. It is in dealing with these petitions that the Chancellor begins to develop his judicial powers.

In course of time his judicial powers are classified as being of two kinds. It begins to be said that the Court of Chancery, "Curia Cancellariae"—for the phrase is used in the fourteenth century—has two sides, a common law side and an equity side, or a Latin side and an English side. Let us look for a moment at the origin of these two kinds of powers, and first at that which concerns us least.

(1) Many of these petitions of which I have spoken seek for justice not merely from the king but against the king. If anybody is to be called the wrongdoer, it is the king himself. For example, he is in possession of land which has been seized by his officers as an escheat while really the late tenant has left an heir. Now the king can not be sued by action—no writ will go against him; the heir if he wants justice must petition for it humbly. Such matters as these are referred to the Chancellor. Proceedings are taken before him; the heir, it may be, proves his case and gets his land. The number of such cases, cases in which the king is concerned, is very large— kings are always seizing land on very slight pretexts—and forcing other people to prove their titles. Gradually a quite regular and ordinary procedure is established for such cases—a procedure very like that of the three courts of law. The proceedings are enrolled in Latin—just as the proceedings of the three courts of law are enrolled in Latin (hence the name "Latin side" of the Court of Chancery)—and if a question of fact be raised, it is tried by jury. The Chancellor himself does not summon the jury or preside at the trial, he sends the question for trial to the King's Bench. All this is by no means unimportant, but it does not concern us very much at the present time.

(2) Very often the petitioner requires some relief at the expense of some other person. He complains that for some reason or another he can not get a remedy in the ordinary course of justice and yet he is entitled to a remedy. He is poor, he is old, he is sick, his adversary is rich and powerful, will bribe or will intimidate jurors, or has by some trick or some accident acquired an advantage of which the ordinary courts with their formal procedure will not deprive him. The petition is often couched in piteous terms, the king is asked to find a remedy for the love of God and in the way of charity. Such petitions are referred by the king to the Chancellor. Gradually in the course of the fourteenth century petitioners, instead of going to the king, will go straight to the Chancellor, will address their complaints to him and adjure him to do what is right for the love of God and in the way of charity. Now one thing that the Chancellor may do in such a case is to invent a new writ and so provide the complainant with a means of bringing an action in a court of law. But in the fourteenth century the courts of law have become very conservative and are given to quashing writs which differ in material points from those already in use. But another thing that the Chancellor can do is to send for the complainant's adversary and examine him concerning the charge that has been made against him. Gradually a procedure is established. The Chancellor having considered the petition, or "bill" as it is called, orders the adversary to come before him and answer the complaint. The writ whereby he does this is called a subpoena—because it orders the man to appear upon pain of forfeiting a sum of money, e.g. *subpoena centum librarum*. It is very different from the old writs whereby actions are begun in the courts of law. They tell the defendant what is the cause of action against him—he is to answer why he assaulted and beat the plaintiff, why he trespassed on the plaintiff's land, why he detains a chattel which belongs to the plaintiff. The subpoena, on the other hand, will tell him merely that he has got to come before the Chancellor and answer complaints made against him by A.B. Then when he comes before the Chancellor he will have to answer on oath,

and sentence by sentence, the bill of the plaintiff. This procedure is rather like that of the ecclesiastical courts and the canon law than like that of our old English courts of law. It was in fact borrowed from the ecclesiastical courts, not from their ordinary procedure but from the summary procedure of those courts introduced for the suppression of heresy. The defendant will be examined upon oath and the Chancellor will decide questions of fact as well as questions of law.

I do not think that in the fourteenth century the Chancellors considered that they had to administer any body of substantive rules that differed from the ordinary law of the land. They were administering the law but they were administering it in cases which escaped the meshes of the ordinary courts. The complaints that come before them are in general complaints of indubitable legal wrongs, assaults, batteries, imprisonments, disseisins and so forth—wrongs of which the ordinary courts take cognizance, wrongs which they ought to redress. But then owing to one thing and another such wrongs are not always redressed by courts of law. In this period one of the commonest of all the reasons that complainants will give for coming to the Chancery is that they are poor while their adversaries are rich and influential—too rich, too influential to be left to the clumsy processes of the old courts and the verdicts of juries. However this sort of thing can not well be permitted. The law courts will not have it and parliament will not have it. Complaints against this extraordinary justice grow loud in the fourteenth century. In history and in principle it is closely connected with another kind of extraordinary justice which is yet more objectionable, the extraordinary justice that is done in criminal cases by the king's council. Parliament at one time would gladly be rid of both—of both the Council's interference in criminal matters, and the Chancellor's interference with civil matters. And so the Chancellor is warned off the field of common law—he is not to hear cases which might go to the ordinary courts, he is not to make himself a judge of torts and contracts, of property in lands and goods.

But then just at this time it is becoming plain that the Chancellor is doing some convenient and useful works that could not be done, or could not easily be done by the courts of common law. He has taken to enforcing uses or trusts. Of the origin of uses or trusts you will have read and I shall have something to say about it on another occasion. I don't myself believe that the use came to us as a foreign thing. I don't believe that there is anything Roman about it. I believe that it was a natural outcome of ancient English elements. But at any rate I must ask you not to believe that either the mass of the nation or the common lawyers of the fourteenth and fifteenth centuries looked with disfavour upon uses. No doubt they were troublesome things, things that might be used for fraudulent purposes, and statutes were passed against those who employed them for the purpose of cheating their creditors or evading the law of mortmain. But I have not a doubt that they were very popular, and I think we may say that had there been no Chancery, the old courts would have discovered some method of enforcing these fiduciary obligations. That method however must have been a clumsy one. A system of law which will never compel, which will never even allow, the defendant to give evidence, a system which sends every question of fact to a jury, is not competent to deal adequately with fiduciary relationships. On the other hand the Chancellor had a procedure which was very well adapted to this end. To this we may add that very possibly the ecclesiastical courts (and the Chancellor you will remember was almost always an ecclesiastic) had for a long time past been punishing breaches of trust by spiritual censures, by penance and excommunication. And so by general consent, we may say, the Chancellor was allowed to enforce uses, trusts or confidences.

Thus one great field of substantive law fell into his hand—a fruitful field, for in the course of the fifteenth century uses became extremely popular. Then, as we all know, Henry VIII [(r. 1509–47)]—for it was rather the king than his subservient parliament—struck a heavy blow at uses. The king was the one man in the kingdom who had everything to gain and nothing to lose by abolishing uses, and as we all know he merely succeeded in complicating the law, for under the name of "trusts" the Chancellors still reigned over their old province. And then there were some other matters that were considered to be fairly within his jurisdiction. An old rhyme[2] allows him "fraud, accident, and breach of confidence"—there were many frauds which the stiff old procedure of the courts of law could not adequately meet, and "accident," in particular the accidental loss of a document, was a proper occasion for the Chancellor's interference. No one could set any very strict limits to his power, but the best hint as to its extent that could be given in the sixteenth century was given by the words "fraud, accident and breach of confidence." On the other hand he was not to interfere where a court of common law offered an adequate remedy. A bill was "demurrable for want of equity" on that ground.

In the course of the sixteenth century we begin to learn a little about the rules that the Chancellors are administering in the field that is thus assigned to them. They are known as "the rules of equity and good conscience." As to what they have done in remoter times we have to draw inferences from very sparse evidence. One thing seems pretty plain. They had not considered themselves strictly bound by precedent.[3] Remember

---

2. "These three give place in court of conscience, Fraud, accident, and breach of confidence."

3. One seventeenth century critic put it this way:

Equity in Law is the same that the spirit is in Religion, what ever one pleases to make it. Sometimes they Goe according to conscience sometime according to Law some time according to the Rule [i.e., practice] of the Court. Equity is A Roguish thing, for Law wee have a measure know what to trust too. Equity is according to the conscience of him that is Chancellor, and as that is larger or narrower soe is equity. Tis all one as if they should make the Standard for the measure wee call A foot, to be the Chancellors Foot; what an uncertain measure would this be; One Chancellor ha's a long foot another A short foot a third an indifferent foot; this the same thing in the Chancellors Conscience.

SELDEN, TABLE TALK 43 (Pollock ed. 1927).

Compare Lord Eldon, L.C., in Gee v. Pritchard, 2 Swanst. 402, 414 (1818):

[The doctrines of this Court ought to be as well settled, and made as uniform almost as those of the common law, laying down fixed principles, but taking care that they are applied according to the circumstances of each case. I cannot agree that the doctrines of this Court are to be changed with every succeeding judge. Nothing would inflict on me greater pain, in quitting this place, than the recollection that I had done any thing to justify the reproach that the equity of this Court varies like the Chancellor's foot.]

this, our reports of cases in courts of law go back to Edward I's day—the middle ages are represented to us by the long series of Year Books. On the other hand our reports of cases in the Court of Chancery go back no further than 1557; and the mass of reports which come to us from between that date and the Restoration in 1660 is a light matter. This by itself is enough to show us that the Chancellors have not held themselves very strictly bound by case law, for men have not cared to collect cases. Nor do I believe that to any very large extent the Chancellors had borrowed from the Roman Law—this is a disputed matter, Mr. Spence has argued for their Romanism, Mr. Justice Holmes against it. No doubt through the medium of the canon law these great ecclesiastics were familiar with some of the great maxims which occur in the *Institutes* or the *Digest*. One of the parts of the *Corpus Juris Canonici,* the Liber Sextus, ends with a bouquet of these high-sounding maxims—*Qui prior est tempore potior est jure,* and so forth, maxims familiar to all readers of equity reports. No doubt the early Chancellors knew these and valued them—but I do not believe that we ought to attribute to them much knowledge of Roman law or any intention to Romanise the law of England. For example, to my mind the comparison sometimes drawn between the so-called double ownership of England, and the so-called double ownership of Roman law can not be carried below the surface. In their treatment of uses or trusts the Chancellors stick close, marvelously close, to the rules of the common law—they often consulted the judges, and the lawyers who pleaded before them were common lawyers, for there was as yet no "Chancery Bar." On the whole my notion is that with the idea of a law of nature in their minds they decided cases without much reference to any written authority, now making use of some analogy drawn from the common law, and now of some great maxim of jurisprudence which they have borrowed from the canonists or the civilians.

In the second half of the sixteenth century the jurisprudence of the court is becoming settled. The day for ecclesiastical Chancellors is passing away. Wolsey is the last of the great ecclesiastical Chancellors, though in Charles I's day [(r. 1625–49)] we have one more divine in the person of Dr. Williams. Ellesmere, Bacon, Coventry, begin to administer an established set of rules which is becoming known to the public in the shape of reports and they begin to publish rules of procedure. In James I's day [(r. 1603–25)] occurred the great quarrel between Lord Chancellor Ellesmere and Chief Justice Coke which finally decided that the Court of Chancery was to have the upper hand over the courts of law. If the Chancery was to carry out its maxims about trust and fraud it was essential that it should have a power to prevent men from going into the courts of law and to prevent men from putting in execution the judgments that they had obtained in courts of law. In fraud or in breach of trust you obtain a judgment against me in a court of law; I complain to the Chancellor, and he after hearing what you have to say enjoins you not to put in force your judgment, says in effect that if you do put your judgment in force you will be sent to prison. Understand well that the Court of Chancery never asserted that it was superior to the courts of law; it never presumed to send to them such mandates as the Court of King's Bench habitually sent to the inferior courts, telling them that they must do this or must not do that or quashing their proceedings—the Chancellor's injunction was in theory a very different thing from a mandamus, a prohibition, a certiorari, or the like. It was addressed not to the judges, but to the party. You in breach of trust have obtained a judgment—the Chancellor does not say that this judgment was wrongly granted, he does not annul it, he tells you that for reasons personal to yourself it will be inequitable for you to enforce that judgment, and that you are not to enforce it. For all this, however, it was natural that the judges should take umbrage at this treatment of their judgments. Coke declared that the man who obtained such an injunction was guilty of the offence denounced by the Statutes of Praemunire, that of calling in question the judgments of the king's courts in other courts (these statutes had been aimed at the Papal curia). King James had now a wished-for opportunity of appearing as supreme over all his judges, and all his courts, and acting on the advice of Bacon and other great lawyers he issued a decree in favour of the Chancery. From this time forward the Chancery had the upper hand. It did not claim to be superior to the courts of law, but it could prevent men from going to those courts, whereas those courts could not prevent men from going to it.

Its independence being thus secured, the court became an extremely busy court. Bacon said that he had made 2000 orders in a year, and we are told that as many as 16,000 causes were pending before it at one time: indeed it was hopelessly in arrear of its work. Under the Commonwealth [(1649–60)] some vigorous attempts were made to reform its procedure. Some were for abolishing it altogether. It was not easily forgotten that the Court of Chancery was the twin sister of the Court of Star Chamber. The projects for reform came to an end with the Restoration. Still it is from the Restoration or thereabouts—of course a precise date can not be fixed—that we may regard the equity administered in the Chancery as a recognised part of the law of the land. Usually, though not always, the great seal is in the keeping of a great lawyer—in 1667 Sir Orlando Bridgman, the great conveyancer, has it; in 1673 Sir Heneage Finch, afterwards Lord Nottingham, who has been called the father of equity; in 1682 Sir Francis North, afterwards Lord Guilford; in 1693 Sir John Somers, afterwards Lord Somers, a great common lawyer. I think that Anthony Ashley, Earl of Shaftesbury, the famous Ashley of the Cabal, was the last non-lawyer who held it, and he held it for but one year, from 1672 to 1673. Then during the eighteenth century there comes a series of great Chancellors. In 1705 Cowper, in 1713 Harcourt, in 1725 King, in 1733 Talbot, in 1737 Hardwicke, in 1757 Northington, in 1766 Camden, in 1778 Thurlow, in 1793 Loughborough, in 1801 Eldon. In the course of the century the Chancery reports improve; the same care is spent upon reporting the decrees of the Chancellors that has long been spent on reporting the judgments of the judges in the courts of common law. Gradually, too, a Chancery bar forms itself, that is to say, some barristers begin to devote themselves altogether to practising before the Chancellor, and do not seek for work elsewhere. Lastly, equity makes its way into the textbooks as a part, and an important part, of the law of the land.

Origin of Separate Equity Courts[4]

In the Anglo–American system of jurisprudence, ... [equity] has reference to the substantive principles (those defining rights and duties) and remedial devices formerly administered in England by the High Court of Chancery in the exercise of its extraordinary jurisdiction, and in the U.S. by courts of chancery or equity in the exercise of similar powers.

The following gives, in its barest outline, the origin of the separate Court of Equity in English jurisprudence. The office of chancellor first appeared during the reign of Edward the Confessor. He was keeper of the royal seal and the secretary of the King. Partly because of the literary qualifications of the office, the chancellor was always an ecclesiastic, schooled in the Canon and moral law of the Church. Up to the time of St. Thomas More, the first layman to be lord chancellor, practically all of the chancellors had been "churchmen" or ecclesiastics, many of them of high rank in the Church such as bishops and cardinals. To the end of Cardinal Wolsey's chancellorship in 1530, the office had been held by no less than 160 "ecclesiastics." The contribution of these early chancellors is deemed to have been an exceedingly beneficial one, for it may well be doubted whether judges trained in the practice of the common law would have possessed the courage to interfere with its rules, in the face of the professional opinion of their brethren, or indeed have been sufficiently detached in mind to discover that the rules stood in need of correction. Sir Henry Maine states that the early ecclesiastical chancellors contributed to the Court of Chancery, from the Canon Law, many of the principles which lie deepest in its structure.

The power of the chancellor continued to grow until he became the principal legal officer and most powerful member of the King's Council. Under the circumstances it seemed natural to refer to him those petitions addressed to the King or the Council seeking justice in cases where the King's regularly established tribunals were deficient and ineffective. The referral of these petitions to the chancellor became so commonplace that by the middle of the 14th century the Chancery had attained the status of a separate judicial tribunal or court. Since one of the titles of the chancellor was that of Keeper of the King's Conscience, the court he administered also came to be called a Court of Conscience.

Maxims of Equity

Some equitable principles and notions have come to be expressed in the form of maxims. An English authority speaking of the maxims has noted: "The maxims do not cover the whole of the ground, and moreover, they overlap, one maxim containing by implication what belongs to another. Indeed, it would not be difficult to reduce them all under [two] 'Equity will

4. Reprinted from EDWARD D. RE, *Anglo–American Law of Equity*, 5 NEW CATHOLIC ENCYCLOPEDIA 503 (1967).

not suffer a wrong to be without a remedy', and 'Equity acts on the person.'[5] The maxims influenced the creative period of the development of equity. Although they do not always show the particular path to be followed, they invariably indicate the right direction. Courts have also used them to justify the application of principles of obvious fairness.

The maxims are occasionally classified as "enabling" or "restrictive." The enabling maxims, of which "equity will not suffer a wrong to be without a remedy" is an example, pertain to the exercise of equitable jurisdiction, and the granting of equitable relief. The restrictive maxims impel or constrain the court to deny equitable relief. A few examples are "one who seeks equity must do equity," "one who comes into equity must come with clean hands," and "equity aids the vigilant, not those who slumber on their rights."

There is no agreement on the exact number and source of these maxims. Nevertheless, they are frequently referred to and relied upon by the courts.

1. *One Who Seeks Equity Must Do Equity.*

2. *One Who Comes Into Equity Must Come with Clean Hands.* The maxim is an application of the broader doctrine *ex turpi causa non oritur actio*: no action arises out of an illegal consideration (transaction). Perhaps the earliest application of the underlying principle is found in the famous case of the *Highwayman*:

> It is stated the Lord Kenyon once said, by way of illustration, that he would not sit to take account between two robbers on Hounslow Heath, and it was questioned whether the legend in regard to the highwayman did not arise from the saying. It seems, however, that the case was a real one. He did file a bill in equity for an accounting against a partner, although it was no sooner filed and its real nature discovered than it was dismissed with costs, and the solicitors for the plaintiff were summarily dealt with by the court as for a contempt in bringing such a case.[6]

3. *Equity Aids the Vigilant, Not Those Who Slumber on Their Rights* (unconscionable delay).

4. *Equity Acts in Personam* (aequitas agit in personam).

5. *Equity Follows the Law* (aequitas sequitur legem).

6. *Equity Delights to Do Justice and Not by Halves.*

7. *Equity Will Not Suffer a Wrong to Be Without a Remedy* (see also ubi jus ibi remedium–where there is a right, there is a remedy, and lex semper dabit remedium–the law always gives a remedy).

8. *Equity Regards as Done That which Ought to Be Done.*

9. *Equity Regards Substance Rather than Form.*

---

5. SNELL, PRINCIPLES OF EQUITY 24 (27th ed. 1973).

6. McMullen v. Hoffman, 174 U.S. 639, 654, 19 S.Ct. 839, 845, 43 L.Ed. 1117 (1899)(citation omitted). *See also*, RIDDELL, *A Legal Scandal Two Hundred Years Ago*, 16 A.B.A.J. 422 (1930).

10. *Equity Imputes an Intent to Fulfill an Obligation.*

11. *Equality is Equity.*

12. *Between Equal Equities the Law Will Prevail.*

13. *Between Equal Equities the First in Order of Time Shall Prevail.*

14. *Equity Abhors a Forfeiture.*

15. *Equity Will Not Aid a Volunteer.*

#16. First in time, first in right.

these are different

Equity in the United States[7]

The American colonies were settled before English equity had been reduced to a system under Lord Eldon. Under the pioneer conditions in America, there was little need for the elaborate machinery of the English Court of Chancery, which was in large part concerned with family settlements and the transactions of wealthy landowners. Whether there was any substantial hostility in the colonies to equity as such has been disputed. Pound takes the position that the very notion of equity and of discretion in the application of law went counter to Puritan ideas, and that this was an important reason for the hostility to equity in England during the Commonwealth and in the New England colonies. Chafee has suggested that there was no real hostility to equity as such in the colony of Massachusetts Bay, and explains the failure of some of the colonies to set up separate courts of chancery on the ground that this would have been unnecessary and expensive. Whether this was the primary reason for the reluctance of the New England colonies to set up separate equity courts, or whether the reason lay rather in Puritan hostility to equity and to a feeling that the Court of Chancery in England was sister to the hated Courts of Star Chamber and High Commission, are questions which cannot be answered with confidence in the present state of the colonial records. It seems clear that the fact that in some colonies chancery powers were vested in the royal governors or persons appointed by them did not increase the popularity of equity, and it is also clear that the colonists generally became much attached to the institution of trial by jury in civil cases. For whatever combination of reasons, while "courts of chancery had existed in some shape or other in every one of the thirteen colonies"[8] prior to the Revolution, in many instances those courts were legislative bodies, while in other instances equity powers were exercised by the ordinary courts of law. In Massachusetts, for example, the General Court or colonial legislature exercised the powers of an equity court for many years, and the regular courts of law exercised a considerable amount of equity jurisdiction. There were, however, regularly constituted courts of chancery in some of the colonies.

7. Reprinted from SCOTT & SIMPSON, CASES AND OTHER MATERIALS ON CIVIL PROCEDURE 161–64 (1951).

8. WILSON, *Courts of Chancery in the American Colonies*, 18 AM.L.REV. 226 (1884), *reprinted in* 2 SELECT ESSAYS IN ANGLO-AMERICAN LEGAL HISTORY 779 (1908).

After the Revolution, most of the newly constituted states established courts of chancery, but at first these for the most part administered only a rough layman's equity. There was no American equity jurisprudence; the English precedents were inaccessible and not well settled, and there was in any event a hostility to all things English; many of the judges were laymen. The history of equity in the United States as a system of law as distinguished from a system of lay magisterial discretion in hard cases dates from the second decade of the last century. Joseph Story became a Justice of the Supreme Court of the United States and began to sit in equity cases in the Circuit Court for Massachusetts in 1811; James Kent became Chancellor of New York in 1814. At that time the equity of the English Court of Chancery was becoming settled under Lord Eldon, and the time was ripe for the building of an American equity jurisprudence. The judicial labors of Kent and Story did much to domesticate equity in the United States; their writings, perhaps, did even more. Most of the original states developed courts with full equity powers comparatively early in the last century, and the newer states created such courts.

But history has left its mark. The New England states were slow in developing full equity jurisdiction—indeed, Massachusetts did not have it until 1877—so that early New England equity cases are apt to turn upon the meaning of particular statutes granting partial jurisdiction. Pennsylvania equity, also, has had a checkered history; prior to 1836 there were no equity courts at all, with the result that the common-law courts absorbed a considerable amount of equity into the law, sometimes in a rather awkward fashion, and that there was a considerable amount of equitable relief by special acts of the legislature. In Georgia, there were jury trials in all equity cases as late as 1830; and in North Carolina, there is jury trial of right in some equity cases today. Moreover, the civil law origin of the law of Louisiana and the Spanish influences on the law of Texas have had their effect on equity in those states.

By Article III, Section 2 of the Constitution of the United States "The judicial Power shall extend to all Cases, in Law and Equity" of certain classes. By the second clause of the same section the Supreme Court is given original jurisdiction of certain cases, chiefly "those in which a State shall be a Party." Since this clause makes no distinction between law and equity, it is apparent that the original jurisdiction of the Supreme Court extends to both. When the first Congress created the inferior federal courts by the Judiciary Act of 1789, it followed the same plan. No separate equity courts were created; the same courts, circuit and district, were to administer law and equity, but on different sides of the court and by a different procedure. Some of the states followed this lead; others retained the system of separate courts. Then, beginning with 1848, when the Code of Procedure proposed and drafted by David Dudley Field was adopted in New York, there came a vigorous movement to merge or fuse law and equity. This movement spent its original force by about 1887, when some twenty-two states and territories had adopted codes of procedure purporting to abolish the distinction between actions at law and suits in equity, but was revived, as evidenced by the Illinois Civil Practice Act of 1933 and the Federal Rules of Civil Procedure of 1938....

Equity Acts in Personam

J.R. v. M.P.

Court of Common Pleas, 1459.
Yearbook, 37 Henry 6, 13, pl. 3.[9]

Debt upon an obligation [(a sealed bond)] by J.R. of London against M.P. and J.B., citizens and aldermen of London.

Choke, for the defendants. The action lies not; for formerly, on such a day in the feast of the Holy Trinity, in the year last past, the said defendants made a bill to the Chancellor of England containing the matter following: that the defendants had purchased of J.R. certain debts due to him, giving their obligation therefor; that these debts being only choses in action could not vest in the defendants so as to give them any action for the recovery of the debts, but the duty remained all the time in J.R., so that the defendants had no *quid pro quo;* that their obligation was, on this account, void and worthless, but that the common law gave them no relief against their obligation; wherefore they prayed for a writ against J.R. to appear, under a certain penalty, before the king in Chancery to answer to this matter. A *subpoena* issued. The parties appeared, and because the matter was doubtful in law, the Chancellor [Waynflete] adjourned them to the Exchequer Chamber. There the matter was rehearsed and well debated before him and the justices of both benches [(i.e., King's Bench and Common Pleas)]. And it was the opinion of all the justices that, as no duty was vested in the defendants by the bargain, the obligation ought in conscience to be surrendered to them, or the plaintiff ought to release the defendants. The Chancellor ordered him to give up the obligation to be cancelled in the Chancery or to make an acquittance or release. The plaintiff refusing to do either, was committed for contempt to the Fleet prison until he should obey, and still remains there. And we do not think an action lies upon the obligation.

Demurrer. And now a *supersedeas* is issued out of Chancery, relating all these matters and commanding that they shall not proceed.[10]

Billing, for the plaintiff. The decree is not that the obligation is null and void in the law, but that the plaintiff shall bring it in to be cancelled. This proves clearly that the obligation is in force until cancelled. The decree is not a bar here.

Littleton, for the defendants. I think otherwise, that it is a bar. What was done in Chancery was by the advice of all the justices, and by the order

---

9. [Translation by Dean Ames.]

10. [A *supersedeas* commands a lower court to stay proceedings before it. This *supersedeas* aimed to stay the proceedings at law. Counsel for the plaintiff argued successfully that it should not be obeyed by the Common Bench in this instance. However, he recognized that the situation would be differ- ent if the *supersedeas* concerned a matter of privilege. "If an officer of the Chancery be impleaded here, in that case if he wishes to buy a *supersedeas* because he is minister of that court, you would stop proceedings because of their privilege, for otherwise all the clerks and ministers of Chancery might be impleaded here."]

to bring in the obligation to be cancelled, the obligation loses its force. For as soon as he brings it in, the court will cancel it or redeliver it to the defendants, and so in effect it is null and void in law.

Laicon, contra. Sir, the decree is merely that he bring in the obligation to be cancelled, so it is clear that it is still in force. For if the obligation by this decree had lost its force, the plaintiff would not be ordered to prison.

Boef. It is proved that the obligation is not yet surrendered, but remains with the plaintiff. Therefore it is still in force, and that is why he is still in prison.

Needham, J. The matter is [not] a bar, because the obligation is still in force....

Danby, J., contra. By the decree the obligation loses its force as fully as if it had been cancelled.

Moyle, J., to the same effect.

Danvers, J. This is not like an obligation made by an infant, or under duress. In those cases the obligation is void; not so here. The plea is bad.

Ashton, J., contra. The decree is the same in effect as if it had ordered that the obligation should be null and void.

Prisot, C.J. In the use of writs of *subpoena* the Chancery is not a court of record,[11] for it is only to examine the conscience. We here are bound to the law, and cannot go beyond. It belongs to them to examine the conscience. For when the deed is good and always has been so, their examination will not make it bad, nor will their examination make it good and legal in our law. And since the defendants cannot have any remedy by our law, they shall sue there to be restored to their obligation; and the effect of their power and decree is to restore the party to his obligation, or to compel the plaintiff to make an acquittance or release. But to execute this, the Chancery can do nothing but order him to prison, there to remain until he will obey. And this is all that court can do. And if the party will lie in prison rather than give up the obligation, the other is without remedy, and so the Chancellor has no power to nullify the obligation.

NOTES

1. "If judgment be given in an action at common law, the Chancellor cannot alter or meddle with the judgment, but he may proceed against the person for corrupt conscience, because he will take advantage of the law against conscience." Anonymous, Litt. 37, 124 Eng.Rep. 124 (C.P.1626).

2. The grounds for equitable relief against judgments invariably involve fraud, accident, mistake, surprise and duress. Injunctions against domestic judgments have lost much of their former importance for two reasons: *First,* substantive equitable objections to the law plaintiff's cause of action can usually be raised as equitable defenses in the action at law, under codes and practice acts. Thus there is no longer much need for the

---

11. [At the time of this decision, this meant that the Chancery did not follow the common law.]

law defendant to go into equity and try to enjoin the law plaintiff's inequitable action after judgment or before. If the equitable defense is good, the defendant obtains judgment in his own favor in the law court. Rule 8(e) of the Federal Rules of Civil Procedure likewise provides that a party may state all claims or defenses "regardless of consistency and whether based on legal, equitable, or maritime grounds."

Second, most procedural injustices in legal proceedings are now corrected by the law courts themselves, through the exercise of wide powers to vacate their own judgments, or grant new trials. Law courts can control their own proceedings, and give a remedy against judgments resulting from fraud, accident and mistake.

3.   C, a judgment creditor of D, sued D and got a temporary injunction in July against any transfer of D's land until the hearing. On August 11, before any hearing, D paid C, and with his consent sold the land to X. The injunction remained pending until November when C obtained an order dissolving it and dismissing the bill. Meanwhile, on August 17, P, another judgment creditor of D, filed a bill against D and X to set aside the sale as in violation of the injunction. The sale was held valid. Herman v. Sartor, 107 Tenn. 235, 63 S.W. 1120 (1901).

4.   B has a right with respect to A's land which is enforceable only in equity. A conveys the land to X with a covenant against incumbrances. X is subject to B's equitable right. X can recover damages from A in an action at law for breach of the covenant. Roberts v. Levy, 3 Abb.Pr., N.S., 311 (N.Y.1867); New York v. New York & South Brooklyn Ferry & Steam Transp. Co., 231 N.Y. 18, 131 N.E. 554 (1921).

Summary of Equity Pleading[12]

Indeed, as a rule, the chancellor, like the ecclesiastical courts, had no jurisdiction *in rem,* and hence could only enforce his orders and decrees by process *in personam;* though whether this was a cause or a consequence of his adopting the ecclesiastical procedure may be doubtful. To some extent, however, the chancellor has asserted and maintained the right to proceed *in rem.* Thus, when all process against the person has been exhausted without effect, he will issue a writ of sequestration against the property of the delinquent. So when a defendant has been decreed to deliver possession of land to the plaintiff, as a last resort a writ of assistance will be issued to the sheriff to put the plaintiff in possession. But, with these exceptions, chancery exercises all its powers by process of contempt against the person.

After all, these are scarcely exceptions to the rule that the chancellor has no jurisdiction *in rem.* When he issues and enforces a writ of sequestration, or a writ of assistance, he merely exerts physical power over the possession of property, and this he can do, though he have no jurisdiction whatever *in rem.* A court which possesses that jurisdiction can by its judgment or decree take the title to property out of one person and put it in another. Thus, courts of admiralty are in the constant habit of ordering the sale of property against which proceedings *in rem* are taken, and when property is thus sold all existing titles to it are extinguished, and the entire

12. Reprinted from LANGDELL, SUMMARY OF EQUITY PLEADING 35, n.4 (2d ed. 1883).

ownership of it becomes vested in the purchaser. So when the property of a judgment debtor is seized and sold to satisfy the judgment, the title of the judgment debtor is as effectively transferred to the purchaser as if the sale had been made by the judgment debtor himself. So when common-law courts were in the habit of entertaining suits for the partition of land, the partition was made by the court itself without any act of the owners of the property whatever. The court first rendered judgment that partition be made (*quod partitio fiat*); whereupon a writ was issued to the sheriff, directing him to make a partition of the land pursuant to the judgment, and report the same to the court. When this had been done, the court rendered another and final judgment that the partition so made remain firm and stable forever (*firma et stabilis in perpetuum teneatur*); and by force of this latter judgment each party acquired the exclusive title to the share allotted to himself, and ceased to have any title to the shares allotted to the others. This power of creating and extinguishing titles the chancellor never had nor claimed to have, except when it was given him by statute. It is true that he frequently directed the sale of property, but it was by his control over the person of the owner that he made the sale effective, i.e., when the sale had been made he compelled the owner to execute a deed pursuant to the sale; and hence, when the owner was out of the jurisdiction, or labored under any incapacity, e.g., that of infancy, the chancellor was powerless. He could not even make the appointment of a new trustee effective, except by compelling the old trustee or his heir, or whoever held the legal title, to convey to the new trustee. When it became the practice to resort to chancery for the partition of land, what the chancellor really did was, first, to inquire and ascertain *how* the property should be divided, and then to compel the parties to divide accordingly by the execution of mutual conveyances. So when the chancellor undertook the settlement of a disputed boundary, he first ascertained what the true boundary line was, and then compelled the parties by mutual conveyances to establish that as the boundary line. When the chancellor placed property in the hands of a receiver, the latter acquired no title to the property, but possession merely. If he had occasion to assert a title to the property in a court of law, he had to do it in the name of the owner; and if the owner brought an action against him to recover the property, he had no defence to the action, and his only security was in the power of the chancellor to punish for contempt any one who interfered with the possession of his receiver. It is often said to have been one of the functions of the chancellor to set aside, for fraud or other sufficient cause, judgments, awards, accounts stated, conveyances and contracts; but this is an incorrect use of language. If a judgment had been obtained by fraud, he would enjoin the judgment creditor from enforcing it; if an award or an account stated was infected with fraud, he would not permit it to be used against the defrauded party, either as a cause of action or as a defence to the original cause of action; if a conveyance of property was obtained by fraud, he would compel a reconveyance of it; if a written instrument purporting to constitute a contract was infected with fraud, he would, in a proper case, require it to be delivered up and cancelled; but he never did nor could set anything aside by his decree. Indeed, it may be stated broadly that a decree in chancery has not in itself (i.e., independently of what may be done under it) any legal operation whatever. If a debt, whether by simple contract or by specialty, be sued for in a court of law, and judgment recovered, the original debt is merged in the judgment, and extinguished by it, and the judgment creates a new debt of a higher nature, and of which the judgment itself is conclusive evidence. But if the same debt be sued for in the court of chancery (as it frequently may be) and a decree obtained for its payment, not one of the effects before stated is produced by the decree. Undoubtedly it has often been said by chancellors that their decrees are equal to judgments at law, but that only means that they will, to the extent of their power, secure for their decrees the same advantages that judgments have by law; it does not mean that a decree is by law equal to a judgment. Again, if a claim be made the subject of an action at law, and judgment be rendered for the defendant upon the merits, the judgment is conclusive evidence that the claim was not well founded, and it will therefore furnish a perfect defence to any future action upon the same claim; but a decree in equity against the validity of a claim is never a defence to an action at law upon the same claim. Here again, however, the chancellor will make his decrees equal to judgments so far as it is in his power to do so; and therefore a decree in chancery against a claim upon its merits will always be a defence to any future suit in chancery upon the same claim, not as destroying the claim or as proving conclusively its invalidity, but as furnishing a sufficient reason why chancery should not again take cognizance of it. Such a decree will also be (what is sometimes called) an equitable defence to any action at law upon the same claim, i.e., the chancellor will enjoin the prosecution of any such action, upon the ground that the plaintiff having elected to make his claim the subject of a suit in equity, and that suit having been defended successfully upon the merits, it is not right that the defendant should be vexed again by the same claim. Accordingly, when A and B demand the same thing of C, and for that reason C, the demand being a legal one, files a bill of interpleader against A and B, and the chancellor decides that the thing demanded belongs to A, and awards it to him, he also directs a perpetual injunction to issue against B to restrain him from suing C at law for the same thing, and that is C's only protection.

Upon the whole, therefore, the weakness of the chancellor's jurisdiction is as conspicuous as its strength; its strength being that it can always command the obedience of suitors; its weakness being that it has substantially no resource beyond commanding such obedience. It should be observed, however, that, while its element of strength is necessary to the existence of the jurisdiction, its element of weakness is not. The chancellor might in the beginning, like the court of admiralty, have been clothed with the same jurisdiction *in rem* as *in personam;* but if he had been, equity would now be a very different thing from what it is, and its machinery would be very different from what it is. If the system were to be constructed anew, probably its element of weakness would be eliminated from it, and if it could be reconstructed in an enlightened manner (a thing which is not at all likely to happen), it would probably be improved. However that may be, any one who wishes to understand the English system of equity as it is, and as it has been from the beginning, must study its weakness as well as its strength.

B.   The Merger of Law and Equity

Steps Toward Merger[13]

The movement for the procedural merger of law and equity had its chronological beginning in the United States with the activities of the New York Commissioners on Practice and Pleading. Their report of 1848 proposed that the distinction between law and equity be abolished, and this proposal was embodied in the Code of Procedure adopted by the legislature of New York in that year and widely copied in many other states within a relatively brief period. A little later, as a result of the investigations of two Royal Commissions, substantial legislative changes were made in the English practice which brought about some degree of fusion but of a less complete character. The English legislation, unlike that of New York and the states which copied the New York code, did not purport to combine law and equity, but did permit equitable defenses and some degree of equitable relief in actions at law and extended the jurisdiction of the Court of Chancery to decide questions of law. Later English legislation (1858) gave the courts of law a limited jurisdiction to grant equitable relief in some cases. Legislation of somewhat similar character has been enacted in many of the non-code states. In 1875, England made effective a completely unified procedure. In 1915, Congress for the first time permitted equitable defenses in actions at law in the federal courts, and allowed the transfer of causes from law to equity or from equity to law. In the provision as to transfer of causes, Congress followed the lead of a number of non-code states. In recent years the movement for more complete unification of civil procedure has made considerable headway, the most noteworthy events being the adoption of a new system of practice by the state of Illinois in 1933 and the promulgation by the Supreme Court of the United States in 1938 of unified rules of civil procedure for the federal district courts, pursuant to the statutory authorization of 1934, and the thoroughgoing merger in New Jersey in 1948.

In studying the procedural merger of law and equity, four main types of legislation come into consideration.

1. *Equitable Defenses and Counterclaims at Law.* The English legislation of 1854, the federal legislation of 1915, and the statutes of most non-code states permit the defendant in an action at law to set up what are commonly denominated "equitable defenses." The main purpose of the earlier legislation of this character seems to have been to deal with cases where the defendant in an action at law could secure in equity a perpetual and unconditional injunction against the prosecution of the action, as for example where the plaintiff sued in covenant on a sealed instrument

---

13. Reprinted from Scott & Simpson,   232–46 (1951).
Cases and Other Material on Civil Procedure

obtained by fraud in the inducement, in a jurisdiction where such fraud was not a legal defense. Later these statutes were extended in many jurisdictions to allow equitable counterclaims or sometimes equitable relief at law in some cases.

By the Common Law Procedure Act, 1854, 17 & 18 Vict. c. 125, §§ 83–86, it was provided that where in an action at law the defendant would be entitled on equitable grounds to relief against the judgment, he might plead the facts which entitle him to such relief as a defense in the action at law; but that if the court is of the opinion that any such equitable plea cannot be dealt with by a court of law so as to do justice between the parties, it may order the plea to be struck out on such terms as to costs and otherwise as to it may seem reasonable.

By the United States Judicial Code, § 274b, as inserted in 1915, it was provided that "in all actions at law equitable defenses may be interposed by answer, plea, or replication without the necessity of filing a bill on the equity side of the court." This provision which was formerly 28 U.S.C.A. § 398 has been repealed, since the distinction between actions at law and suits in equity has been done away with in the federal courts. . . .

Under the code system of unified procedure it would appear that no special statutory authorization of equitable defenses or counterclaims was necessary, but doubts which arose under the pioneer New York Code of Procedure led to its amendment to include the following provision:

> The defendant may set forth by answer, as many defences and counterclaims as he may have, whether they be such as have been heretofore denominated legal or equitable, or both.

Similar sections are contained in most of the codes of civil procedure in the states which have adopted code practice.

2. *Expansion of the Power of Equity.* Under the classical English practice, the powers of the Court of Chancery were limited by three self-imposed restrictions: (1) The Court was reluctant to decide questions of legal right or title in suits to enjoin torts; (2) it was sometimes reluctant to decide questions of law and was in the habit of stating cases for the opinion of one of the courts of common law on such questions; (3) it would not give damages in lieu of specific performance or damages in cases where equitable relief turned out to be impracticable or was refused for some other reason not affecting the merits. The first two of these limitations were removed by statute in 1852, the third by statute in 1858.

By the Chancery Amendment Act, 1852, 15 & 16 Vict. c. 86, §§ 61, 62, it was provided that the Court of Chancery should not direct a case to be stated for the opinion of any court of common law, but it should have full power to determine any questions of fact which in its judgment should be necessary to be decided previously to the decision of the equitable question at issue between the parties; and that the Court of Chancery might itself determine the legal title or right of the parties without requiring them to proceed at law.

By Lord Cairns' Act, 21 & 22 Vict. c. 27 (1858), *see infra* pp. 1018–1019, it was provided that where the Court of Chancery has jurisdiction to enjoin a breach of contract or any wrongful act or to grant specific performance of a contract, it may, if it should think fit, award damages, either in addition to or in substitution for such injunction or specific performance, and that such damages may be assessed in such manner as the court should direct.

The difficulties met by this English legislation have not been so serious in the United States, and there is little legislation of similar character in this country.

3. *Transfer of Causes From Law to Equity or From Equity to Law.* Under the old practice a plaintiff who failed in a suit in equity because he was found to have an adequate remedy at law or for some other reason not affecting the merits such as impracticability of the remedy in equity, had to begin a new action at law. Similarly, a plaintiff who sought relief at law which could be given only in equity had to bring a new suit in equity. According to the better view he was not precluded from so doing by any election of remedies. This resulted in substantial and unnecessary expense in every such case, and in some cases the Statute of Limitations had run on the plaintiff's cause of action before he found out that he had sued in the wrong court. Where law and equity are administered in the same court but by different procedures, as in a considerable number of the United States, these difficulties could readily be met by providing that an action or suit brought on the wrong side of the court might be transferred to the other side of the court, with appropriate amendment of the pleadings. Such statutes have been enacted in a number of the non-code states.

By the United States Judicial Code, § 274a, as inserted in 1915, it was provided that "in case any of said courts shall find that a suit at law should have been brought in equity or a suit in equity should have been brought at law, the court shall order any amendments to the pleadings which may be necessary to conform them to the proper practice," and that "The cause shall proceed and be determined upon such amended pleadings." This section is now repealed.

In those states which still have separate courts at law and equity, this procedure of transfer seems unavailable, although there would seem to be no reason why some statutory provision for removal from one court to the other of actions or suits brought in the wrong court might not be provided for.

4. *Unification of Legal and Equitable Procedure.* None of the methods heretofore discussed eliminates all the difficulties resulting from separate law and equity procedure. In consequence, the most usual form of legislative change to meet these difficulties has been some kind of unification of legal and equitable procedure.

5. *Equitable Remedies and Defenses and "The Extraordinary Writs."* On occasion equitable remedies and defenses granted or allowed by a court having equitable jurisdiction are referred to as *extraordinary remedies.* They are extraordinary in the sense that they were not originally granted or available in a common law court but only in courts of Chancery or Equity, i.e., courts having equitable jurisdiction. These equitable causes of action or defenses are not to be confused with the *extraordinary rememdies* traditionally granted by the common law courts. Prof. Chester J. Antieau in

his book entitled *The Practice of Extraordinary Remedies Habeas Corpus and the Other Common Law Writs* covers these common law extraordinary writs.

The extraordinary writs covered are the writs of mandamus, habeas corpus, prohibition, quo warranto and certiorari. In the Preface he states: "Throughout the common law world, freedom of the individual person has been principally protected against the temporary trustees of political power by what were once called 'the prerogative writs' and are now generally known as the extraordinary writs' of habeas corpus, mandamus, prohibition, quo warranto and certiorari. They are in the words of the United States Supreme Court both 'the symbols and guardians of individual liberty.'" [Peyton v. Rowe, 391 U.S. 54, 58, 88 S.Ct. 1549, 20 L.Ed.2d 426 (1968)]. Professor Antieau adds that "The extraordinary writs give protection and meaning to the constitutional rights of free people" and makes the cogent observation that "Substantive constitutional rights have been readily expressed in the organic laws of nation, but they remain virtually meaningless without the procedural remedies to vindicate them." This observation by Prof. Antieau is followed by a quotation of Justice Frankfurter: "The history of liberty has largely been the history of observance of procedural safeguards." [McNabb v. United States, 318 U.S. 332, 347, 63 S.Ct. 608, 87 L.Ed. 819 (1943) and cf. Malinkski v. New York, 324 U.S. 401, 414, 65 S.Ct. 781, 89 L.Ed. 1029 (1945)].

———

Grupo Mexicano de Desarrollo, S.A. v. Alliance Bond Fund, Inc., et al.

Supreme Court of the United States, 1999.
527 U.S. 308, 119 S.Ct. 1961, 144 L.Ed.2d 319.

■ JUSTICE SCALIA delivered the opinion of the Court.

This case presents the question whether, in an action for money damages, a United States District Court has the power to issue a preliminary injunction preventing the defendant from transferring assets in which no lien or equitable interest is claimed.

I

Petitioner Grupo Mexicano de Desarrollo, S.A. (GMD), is a Mexican holding company. In February 1994, GMD issued $250 million of 8.25% unsecured, guaranteed notes due in 2001 (Notes), which ranked *pari passu* in priority of payment with all of GMD's other unsecured and unsubordinated debt. Interest payments were due in February and August of every year. Four subsidiaries of GMD (which are the remaining petitioners) guaranteed the Notes. Respondents are investment funds which purchased approximately $75 million of the Notes.

Between 1990 and 1994, GMD was involved in a toll road construction program sponsored by the Government of Mexico. In order to elicit private financing, the Mexican Government granted concessions to companies that would build and operate the system of toll roads. GMD was both an investor in the concessionaries and among the construction companies hired by the concessionaries to build the toll roads. Problems in the Mexican economy resulted in severe losses for the concessionaries, who were therefore unable to pay contractors like GMD. In response to these problems, in 1997, the Mexican Government announced the Toll Road Rescue Program, under which it would issue guaranteed notes (Toll Road Notes) to the concessionaries, in exchange for their ceding to the Government ownership of the toll roads. The Toll Road Notes were to be used to pay the bank debt of the concessionaries, and also to pay outstanding receivables held by GMD and other contractors for services rendered to the concessionaries (Toll Road Receivables). In the fall of 1997, GMD announced that it expected to receive approximately $309 million of Toll Road Notes under the program.

Because of the downturn in the Mexican economy and the related difficulties in the toll road program, by mid–1997 GMD was in serious financial trouble. In addition to the Notes, GMD owed other debts of about $450 million. GMD's 1997 Form 20–F, which was filed with the Securities and Exchange Commission on June 30, 1997, stated that GMD's current liabilities exceeded its current assets and that there was "substantial doubt" whether it could continue as a going concern. As a result of these financial problems, neither GMD nor its subsidiaries (who had guaranteed payment) made the August 1997 interest payment on the Notes.

Between August and December 1997, GMD attempted to negotiate a restructuring of its debt with its creditors. On August 26, Reuters reported that GMD was negotiating with the Mexican banks to reduce its $256 million bank debt, and that it planned to deal with this liability before negotiating with the investors owning the Notes. On October 28, GMD publicly announced that it would place in trust its right to receive $17 million of Toll Road Notes, to cover employee compensation payments, and that it had transferred its right to receive $100 million of Toll Road Notes to the Mexican Government (apparently to pay back taxes). GMD also negotiated with the holders of the Notes (including respondents) to restructure that debt, but by December these negotiations had failed.

On December 11, respondents accelerated the principal amount of their Notes, and, on December 12, filed suit for the amount due in the United States District Court for the Southern District of New York (petitioners had consented to personal jurisdiction in that forum). The complaint alleged that "GMD is at risk of insolvency, if not insolvent already"; that GMD was dissipating its most significant asset, the Toll Road Notes, and was preferring its Mexican creditors by its planned allocation of Toll Road Notes to the payment of their claims, and by its transfer to them of Toll Road Receivables; and that these actions would "frustrate any judgement" respondents could obtain. App. 29–30. Respondents sought breach-of-contract damages of $80.9 million, and requested a preliminary injunction restraining petitioners from transferring the Toll Road Notes or Receivables. On that same day, the District Court entered a temporary restraining order preventing petitioners from transferring their right to receive the Toll Road Notes.

On December 23, the District Court entered an order in which it found that "GMD is at risk of insolvency if not already insolvent"; that the Toll Road Notes were GMD's "only substantial asset"; that GMD planned to use the Toll Road Notes "to satisfy its Mexican creditors to the exclusion of [respondents] and other holders of the Notes"; that "[i]n light of [petitioners'] financial condition and dissipation of assets, any judgment [respondents] obtain in this action will be frustrated"; that respondents had demonstrated irreparable injury; and that it was "almost certain" that respondents would succeed on the merits of their claim. App. to Pet. for Cert. 25a–26a. It preliminarily enjoined petitioners "from dissipating, disbursing, transferring, conveying, encumbering or otherwise distributing or affecting any [petitioner's] right to, interest in, title to or right to receive or retain, any of the [Toll Road Notes]." *Id.*, at 26a. The court ordered respondents to post a $50,000 bond.

The Second Circuit affirmed. 143 F.3d 688 (1998). We granted certiorari, 525 U.S. 1015, 119 S.Ct. 537, 142 L.Ed.2d 447 (1998).

III

We turn, then, to the merits question whether the District Court had authority to issue the preliminary injunction in this case pursuant to Federal Rule of Civil Procedure 65.[3] The Judiciary Act of 1789 conferred on the federal courts jurisdiction over "all suits ... in equity." § 11, 1 Stat. 78. We have long held that "[t]he 'jurisdiction' thus conferred ... is an authority to administer in equity suits the principles of the system of judicial remedies which had been devised and was being administered by the English Court of Chancery at the time of the separation of the two countries." *Atlas Life Ins. Co. v. W.I. Southern, Inc.*, 306 U.S. 563, 568, 59 S.Ct. 657, 83 L.Ed. 987 (1939). ... "Substantially, then, the equity jurisdiction of the federal courts is the jurisdiction in equity exercised by the High Court of Chancery in England at the time of the adoption of the Constitution and the enactment of the original Judiciary Act, 1789 (1 Stat. 73)." A. Dobie, Handbook of Federal Jurisdiction and Procedure 660 (1928). "[T]he substantive prerequisites for obtaining an equitable remedy as well as the general availability of injunctive relief are not altered by [Rule 65] and depend on traditional principles of equity jurisdiction." 11A Charles Alan Wright, Arthur R. Miller, & Mary Kay Kane, Federal Practice and Procedure § 2941, p. 31 (2d ed.1995). We must ask, therefore, whether the relief respondents requested here was traditionally accorded by courts of equity.

A

Respondents do not even argue this point. The United States as *amicus curiae*, however, contends that the preliminary injunction issued in this case is analogous to the relief obtained in the equitable action known as a

---

3. Although this is a diversity case, respondents' complaint sought the injunction pursuant to Rule 65, and the Second Circuit's decision was based on that rule and on federal equity principles. Petitioners argue for the first time before this Court that under *Erie R. Co. v. Tompkins*, 304 U.S. 64, 58 S.Ct. 817, 82 L.Ed. 1188 (1938), the availability of this injunction under Rule 65 should be determined by the law of the forum State (in this case New York). Because this argument was neither raised nor considered below, we decline to consider it.

"creditor's bill." This remedy was used (among other purposes) to permit a judgment creditor to discover the debtor's assets, to reach equitable interests not subject to execution at law, and to set aside fraudulent conveyances. See 1 D. Dobbs, Law of Remedies § 2.8(1), pp. 191–192 (2d ed.1993); 4 S. Symons, Pomeroy's Equity Jurisprudence § 1415, pp. 1065–1066 (5th ed.1941); 1 G. Glenn, Fraudulent Conveyances and Preferences § 26, p. 51 (rev. ed.1940). It was well established, however, that, as a general rule, a creditor's bill could be brought only by a creditor who had already obtained a judgment establishing the debt. ... The rule requiring a judgment was a product, not just of the procedural requirement that remedies at law had to be exhausted before equitable remedies could be pursued, but also of the substantive rule that a general creditor (one without a judgment) had no cognizable interest, either at law or in equity, in the property of his debtor, and therefore could not interfere with the debtor's use of that property. As stated by Chancellor Kent: "The reason of the rule seems to be, that until the creditor has established his title, he has no right to interfere, and it would lead to an unnecessary, and, perhaps, a fruitless and oppressive interruption of the exercise of the debtor's rights." ...

The United States asserts that there were exceptions to the general rule requiring a judgment. The existence and scope of these exceptions is by no means clear. Cf. G. Glenn, The Rights and Remedies of Creditors Respecting Their Debtor's Property §§ 21–24, pp. 18–21 (1915). Although the United States says that some of them "might have been relevant in a case like this one," Brief for United States as *Amicus Curiae* 11, it chooses not to resolve (or argue definitively) whether any particular one would have been, *id.*, at 12. For their part, as noted above, respondents do not discuss creditor's bills at all. Particularly in the absence of any discussion of this point by the lower courts, we are not inclined to speculate upon the existence or applicability to this case of any exceptions, and follow the well-established general rule that a judgment establishing the debt was necessary before a court of equity would interfere with the debtor's use of his property.

JUSTICE GINSBURG concedes that federal equity courts have traditionally rejected the type of provisional relief granted in this case. She invokes, however, "the grand aims of equity," and asserts a general power to grant relief whenever legal remedies are not "practical and efficient," unless there is a statute to the contrary. *Post*, at 1979 (internal quotation marks omitted). This expansive view of equity must be rejected. Joseph Story's famous treatise reflects what we consider the proper rule, both with regard to the general role of equity in our "government of laws, not of men," and with regard to its application in the very case before us: ...

We do not question the proposition that equity is flexible; but in the federal system, at least, that flexibility is confined within the broad boundaries of traditional equitable relief. To accord a type of relief that has never been available before—and especially (as here) a type of relief that has been specifically disclaimed by longstanding judicial precedent—is to invoke a "default rule," *post*, at 1979, not of flexibility but of omnipotence. When there are indeed new conditions that might call for a wrenching departure from past practice, Congress is in a much better position than we both to perceive them and to design the appropriate remedy. Despite JUSTICE GINSBURG'S allusion to the "increasing complexities of modern business relations," *post*, at 1977 (internal quotation marks omitted), and to the bygone "age of slow-moving capital and comparatively immobile wealth," *ibid.*, we suspect there is absolutely nothing new about debtors' trying to avoid paying their debts, or seeking to favor some creditors over others—or even about their seeking to achieve these ends through "sophisticated ... strategies," *ibid.* The law of fraudulent conveyances and bankruptcy was developed to prevent such conduct; an equitable power to restrict a debtor's use of his unencumbered property before judgment was not.

Respondents argue (supported by the United States) that the merger of law and equity changed the rule that a general creditor could not interfere with the debtor's use of his property. But the merger did not alter substantive rights. "Notwithstanding the fusion of law and equity by the Rules of Civil Procedure, the substantive principles of Courts of Chancery remain unaffected." *Stainback*, 336 U.S., at 382, n. 26, 69 S.Ct. 606. Even in the absence of historical support, we would not be inclined to believe that it is merely a question of procedure whether a person's unencumbered assets can be frozen by general-creditor claimants before their claims have been vindicated by judgment. It seems to us that question goes to the substantive rights of all property owners. In any event it appears, as we have observed, that the rule requiring a judgment was historically regarded as serving, not merely the procedural end of assuring exhaustion of legal remedies (which the merger of law and equity could render irrelevant), but also the substantive end of giving the creditor an interest in the property which equity could then act upon. See *supra*, at 1968–1969.

B

Respondents contend that two of our postmerger cases support the District Court's order "in principle." Brief for Respondents 22. We find both of these cases entirely consistent with the view that the preliminary injunction in this case was beyond the equitable authority of the District Court.

In *Deckert v. Independence Shares Corp.*, 311 U.S. 282, 61 S.Ct. 229, 85 L.Ed. 189 (1940), purchasers of certificates that entitled the holders to invest in a trust of common stocks sued the company that sold the certificates and the company administering the trust, and related officers and affiliates, under the Securities Act of 1933, alleging that the sale was fraudulent. They further alleged that the company that sold the certificates was insolvent, that it was likely to make preferential payments to certain creditors, and that its assets were in danger of dissipation. They sought the appointment of a receiver and an injunction restraining the company administering the trust from transferring any assets of the corporations or of the trust. The District Court preliminarily enjoined the company from transferring a fixed sum. *Id.*, at 285–286, 61 S.Ct. 229. After deciding that the Securities Act permitted equitable relief, we concluded that the bill stated a cause of action for the equitable remedies of rescission of the contracts and restitution of the consideration paid, *id.*, at 287–288, 61 S.Ct.

229, and that the preliminary injunction "was a reasonable measure to preserve the status quo pending final determination of the questions raised by the bill," *id.*, at 290, 61 S.Ct. 229. *Deckert* is not on point here because, as the Court took pains to explain, "the bill state[d] a cause [of action] for equitable relief." *Id.*, at 288, 61 S.Ct. 229.

"The principal objects of the suit are rescission of the Savings Plan contracts and restitution of the consideration paid. . . . That a suit to rescind a contract induced by fraud and to recover the consideration paid may be maintained in equity, at least where there are circumstances making the legal remedy inadequate, is well established." *Id.*, at 289, 61 S.Ct. 229.

The preliminary relief available in a suit seeking equitable relief has nothing to do with the preliminary relief available in a creditor's bill seeking equitable assistance in the collection of a legal debt.

In the second case relied on by respondents, *United States v. First Nat. City Bank*, 379 U.S. 378, 85 S.Ct. 528, 13 L.Ed.2d 365 (1965), the United States, in its suit to enforce a tax assessment and tax lien, requested a preliminary injunction preventing a third-party bank from transferring any of the taxpayer's assets which were held in a foreign branch office of the bank. *Id.*, at 379–380, 85 S.Ct. 528. Relying on a statute giving district courts the power to grant injunctions " 'necessary or appropriate for the enforcement of the internal revenue laws,' " id., at 380, 85 S.Ct. 528 (quoting former 26 U.S.C. § 7402(a) (1964 ed.)), we concluded that the temporary injunction was "appropriate to prevent further dissipation of assets," 379 U.S., at 385, 85 S.Ct. 528. We stated that if a district court could not issue such an injunction, foreign taxpayers could avoid their tax obligations.

First National is distinguishable from the present case on a number of grounds. First, of course, it involved not the Court's general equitable powers under the Judiciary Act of 1789, but its powers under the statute authorizing issuance of tax injunctions. Second, *First National* relied in part on the doctrine that courts of equity will " 'go much farther both to give and withhold relief in furtherance of the public interest than they are accustomed to go when only private interests are involved,' " *id.*, at 383, 85 S.Ct. 528 (quoting *Virginian R. Co. v. Railway Employees*, 300 U.S. 515, 552, 57 S.Ct. 592, 81 L.Ed. 789 (1937)). And finally, although the Court did not rely on this fact, the creditor (the Government) asserted an equitable lien on the property, see 379 U.S., at 379–380, 85 S.Ct. 528, which presents a different case from that of the unsecured general creditor.

That *Deckert* and *First National* should not be read as establishing the principle relied on by respondents is strongly suggested by *De Beers Consol. Mines, Ltd. v. United States*, 325 U.S. 212, 65 S.Ct. 1130, 89 L.Ed. 1566 (1945).

The requirement that the creditor obtain a prior judgment is a fundamental protection in debtor-creditor law—rendered all the more important in our federal system by the debtor's right to a jury trial on the legal claim. There are other factors which likewise give us pause: The remedy sought here could render Federal Rule of Civil Procedure 64, which authorizes use of state prejudgment remedies, a virtual irrelevance. Why go through the trouble of complying with local attachment and garnishment statutes when this all-purpose prejudgment injunction is available? More importantly, by adding, through judicial fiat, a new and powerful weapon to the creditor's arsenal, the new rule could radically alter the balance between debtor's and creditor's rights which has been developed over centuries through many laws—including those relating to bankruptcy, fraudulent conveyances, and preferences. Because any rational creditor would want to protect his investment, such a remedy might induce creditors to engage in a "race to the courthouse" in cases involving insolvent or near-insolvent debtors, which might prove financially fatal to the struggling debtor.

We do not decide which side has the better of these arguments. We set them forth only to demonstrate that resolving them in this forum is incompatible with the democratic and self-deprecating judgment we have long since made: that the equitable powers conferred by the Judiciary Act of 1789 did not include the power to create remedies previously unknown to equity jurisprudence. Even when sitting as a court in equity, we have no authority to craft a "nuclear weapon" of the law like the one advocated here. Joseph Story made the point many years ago:

> "If, indeed, a Court of Equity in England did possess the unbounded jurisdiction, which has been thus generally ascribed to it, of correcting, controlling, moderating, and even superceding the law, and of enforcing all the rights, as well as charities, arising from natural law and justice, and of freeing itself from all regard to former rules and precedents, it would be the most gigantic in its sway, and the most formidable instrument of arbitrary power, that could well be devised. It would literally place the whole rights and property of the community under the arbitrary will of the Judge, acting, if you please, *arbitrio boni judicis*, and it may be, *ex aequo et bono*, according to his own notions and conscience; but still acting with a despotic and sovereign authority. A Court of Chancery might then well deserve the spirited rebuke of Seldon; 'For law we have a measure, and know what to trust to— Equity is according to the conscience of him, that is Chancellor; and as that is larger, or narrower, so is Equity. T is all one, as if they should make the standard for the measure the Chancellor's foot. What an uncertain measure would this be? One Chancellor has a long foot; another a short foot; a third an indifferent foot. It is the same thing with the Chancellor's conscience.' " 1 Commentaries on Equity Jurisprudence § 19, at 21.

The debate concerning this formidable power over debtors should be conducted and resolved where such issues belong in our democracy: in the Congress.

* * *

Because such a remedy was historically unavailable from a court of equity, we hold that the District Court had no authority to issue a preliminary injunction preventing petitioners from disposing of their assets pending adjudication of respondents' contract claim for money damages.

We reverse the judgment of the Second Circuit and remand the case for further proceedings consistent with this opinion.

It is so ordered.

■ JUSTICE GINSBURG, with whom JUSTICE STEVENS, JUSTICE SOUTER, and JUSTICE BREYER join, concurring in part and dissenting in part.

I

Uncontested evidence presented to the District Court at the preliminary injunction hearing showed that petitioner Grupo Mexicano de Desarrollo, S.A. (GMD), had defaulted on its contractual obligations to respondents, a group of GMD noteholders (Alliance), see App. to Pet. for Cert. 24a, 31a, that Alliance had satisfied all conditions precedent to its breach of contract claim, see *id.*, at 25a, and that GMD had no plausible defense on the merits, see *id.*, at 25a, 36a. Alliance also demonstrated that GMD had undertaken to treat Alliance's claims on the same footing as all other unsecured, unsubordinated debt, see *id.*, at 24a, but that GMD was in fact satisfying Mexican creditors to the exclusion of Alliance, *id.*, at 26a. Furthermore, unchallenged evidence indicated that GMD was so rapidly disbursing its sole remaining asset that, absent provisional action by the District Court, Alliance would have been unable to collect on the money judgment for which it qualified. See *id.*, at 26a, 32a.

Had it been possible for the District Judge to set up "a pie-powder court ... on the instant and on the spot," *Parks v. Boston*, 32 Mass. 198, 208 (1834) (Shaw, C. J.), the judge could have moved without pause from evidence taking to entry of final judgment for Alliance, including an order prohibiting GMD from transferring assets necessary to satisfy the judgment. Lacking any such device for instant adjudication, the judge employed a preliminary injunction "to preserve the relative positions of the parties until a trial on the merits [could] be held." *University of Texas v. Camenisch*, 451 U.S. 390, 395, 101 S.Ct. 1830, 68 L.Ed.2d 175 (1981). The order enjoined GMD from distributing assets likely to be necessary to satisfy the judgment in the instant case, but gave Alliance no security interest in GMD's assets, nor any preference relative to GMD's other creditors. Moreover, the injunction expressly reserved to GMD the option of commencing proceedings under the bankruptcy laws of Mexico or the United States. App. to Pet. for Cert. 27a. In addition, the District Judge recorded his readiness to modify the interim order if necessary to keep GMD in business. See id., at 53a. The preliminary injunction thus constrained GMD only to the extent essential to the subsequent entry of an effective judgment.

The Court nevertheless disapproves the provisional relief ordered by the District Court, holding that a preliminary injunction freezing assets is beyond the equitable authority of the federal courts. I would not so disarm the district courts. As I comprehend the courts' authority, injunctions of this kind, entered in the circumstances presented here, are within federal equity jurisdiction. Satisfied that the injunction issued in this case meets the exacting standards for preliminary equitable relief, I would affirm the judgment of the Second Circuit.

II

The Judiciary Act of 1789 gave the lower federal courts jurisdiction over "all suits ... in equity." § 11, 1 Stat. 78. We have consistently interpreted this jurisdictional grant to confer on the district courts "authority to administer ... the principles of the system of judicial remedies which had been devised and was being administered" by the English High Court of Chancery at the time of the founding. *Atlas Life Ins. Co. v. W.I. Southern, Inc.*, 306 U.S. 563, 568, 59 S.Ct. 657, 83 L.Ed. 987 (1939).

As I see it, the preliminary injunction ordered by the District Court was consistent with these principles. We long ago recognized that district courts properly exercise their equitable jurisdiction where "the remedy in equity could alone furnish relief, and ... the ends of justice requir[e] the injunction to be issued." *Watson v. Sutherland*, 5 Wall. 74, 79, 18 L.Ed. 580 (1867). Particularly, district courts enjoy the "historic federal judicial discretion to preserve the situation [through provisional relief] pending the outcome of a case lodged in court." 11A Charles Alan Wright, Arthur R. Miller, & Mary Kay Kane, Federal Practice and Procedure § 2943, p. 79 (2d ed. 1995). The District Court acted in this case in careful accord with these prescriptions, issuing the preliminary injunction only upon well-supported findings that Alliance had "[no] adequate remedy at law," would be "frustrated" in its ability to recover a judgment absent interim injunctive relief, and was "almost certain" to prevail on the merits. App. to Pet. for Cert. 26a.

The Court holds the District Court's preliminary freeze order impermissible principally because injunctions of this kind were not "traditionally accorded by courts of equity" at the time the Constitution was adopted. Ante, at 1968; see ante, at 1975. In my view, the Court relies on an unjustifiably static conception of equity jurisdiction. From the beginning, we have defined the scope of federal equity in relation to the principles of equity existing at the separation of this country from England, see, e.g., Payne v. Hook, 7 Wall. 425, 430, 19 L.Ed. 260 (1869); Gordon v. Washington, 295 U.S. 30, 36, 55 S.Ct. 584, 79 L.Ed. 1282 (1935); we have never limited federal equity jurisdiction to the specific practices and remedies of the pre-Revolutionary Chancellor.

Since our earliest cases, we have valued the adaptable character of federal equitable power. See *Seymour v. Freer*, 8 Wall. 202, 218, 19 L.Ed. 306 (1869) ("[A] court of equity ha[s] unquestionable authority to apply its flexible and comprehensive jurisdiction in such manner as might be necessary to the right administration of justice between the parties."); *Hecht Co. v. Bowles*, 321 U.S. 321, 329, 64 S.Ct. 587, 88 L.Ed. 754 (1944) ("Flexibility rather than rigidity has distinguished [federal equity jurisdiction]."). We have also recognized that equity must evolve over time, "in order to meet the requirements of every case, and to satisfy the needs of a progressive social condition in which new primary rights and duties are constantly arising and new kinds of wrongs are constantly committed." *Union Pacific R. Co. v. Chicago, R.I. & P.R. Co.*, 163 U.S. 564, 601, 16 S.Ct. 1173, 41 L.Ed. 265 (1896) (internal quotation marks omitted); see also 1 S. Symons, Pomeroy's Equity Jurisprudence § 67, p. 89 (5th ed. 1941) (the "American system of equity is preserved and maintained ... to render the national jurisprudence as a whole adequate to the social needs.... [I]t possesses an inherent capacity of expansion, so as to keep abreast of each succeeding generation and age."). A dynamic equity jurisprudence is of special importance in the commercial law context. As we observed more than a century ago: "It must not be forgotten that in the increasing complexities of modern business relations equitable remedies have necessarily and steadily been expanded, and no inflexible rule has been permitted to circumscribe them." *Union Pacific R. Co.*, 163 U.S., at 600–601, 16 S.Ct. 1173. On this understanding of equity's character, we have upheld diverse injunctions that would have been beyond the contemplation of the 18th-century Chancellor.

I do not question that equity courts traditionally have not issued preliminary injunctions stopping a party sued for an unsecured debt from disposing of assets pending adjudication. (As the Court recognizes, however, see *ante*, at 1968–1969, the historical availability of prejudgment freeze injunctions in the context of creditors' bills remains cloudy.) But it is one thing to recognize that equity courts typically did not provide this relief, quite another to conclude that, therefore, the remedy was beyond equity's capacity. I would not draw such a conclusion.

Chancery may have refused to issue injunctions of this sort simply because they were not needed to secure a just result in an age of slow-moving capital and comparatively immobile wealth. By turning away cases that the law courts could deal with adequately, the Chancellor acted to reduce the tension inevitable when justice was divided between two discrete systems. See Wasserman, *supra*, at 319. But as the facts of this case so plainly show, for creditors situated as Alliance is, the remedy at law is worthless absent the provisional relief in equity's arsenal. Moreover, increasingly sophisticated foreign-haven judgment proofing strategies, coupled with technology that permits the nearly instantaneous transfer of assets abroad, suggests that defendants may succeed in avoiding meritorious claims in ways unimaginable before the merger of law and equity. See LoPucki, The Death of Liability, 106 Yale L.J. 1, 32–38 (1996). I am not ready to say a responsible Chancellor today would deny Alliance relief on the ground that prior case law is unsupportive.

III

A

The Court worries that permitting preliminary injunctions to freeze assets would allow creditors, " 'on a mere statement of belief that the defendant can easily make away with or transport his money or goods, [to] impose an injunction on him, indefinite in duration, disabling him to use so much of his funds or property as the court deems necessary for security or compliance with its possible decree.' " *Ante*, at 1972 (quoting *De Beers Consol. Mines, Ltd. v. United States*, 325 U.S. 212, 222, 65 S.Ct. 1130, 89 L.Ed. 1566 (1945)). Given the strong showings a creditor would be required to make to gain the provisional remedy, and the safeguards on which the debtor could insist, I agree with the Second Circuit "that this 'parade of horribles' [would] not come to pass." 143 F.3d 688, 696 (1998).

Under standards governing preliminary injunctive relief generally, a plaintiff must show a likelihood of success on the merits and irreparable injury in the absence of an injunction. See *Doran v. Salem Inn, Inc.*, 422 U.S. 922, 931, 95 S.Ct. 2561, 45 L.Ed.2d 648 (1975). Plaintiffs with questionable claims would not meet the likelihood of success criterion. See 11A Charles Alan Wright, Arthur R. Miller, & Mary Kay Kane, Federal Practice and Procedure § 2948.3, at 184–188 (as a general rule, plaintiff seeking preliminary injunction must demonstrate a reasonable probability of success). The irreparable injury requirement would not be met by unsubstantiated allegations that a defendant may dissipate assets. See *id.*, § 2948.1, at 153 ("Speculative injury is not sufficient."); see also Wasserman, 67 Wash.L.Rev., at 286–305 (discussing application of traditional preliminary injunction requirements to provisional asset-freeze requests). As the Court of Appeals recognized, provisional freeze orders would be appropriate in damages actions only upon a finding that, without the freeze, "the movant would be unable to collect [a money] judgment." 143 F.3d, at 697. The preliminary asset-freeze order, in short, would rank and operate as an extraordinary remedy.

Federal Rule of Civil Procedure 65(c), moreover, requires a preliminary injunction applicant to post a bond "in such sum as the court deems proper, for the payment of such costs and damages as may be incurred or suffered by any party who is found to have been wrongfully enjoined." As an essential condition for a preliminary freeze order, a district court could demand sufficient security to ensure a remedy for wrongly enjoined defendants. Furthermore, it would be incumbent on a district court to "match the scope of its injunction to the most probable size of the likely judgment," thereby sparing the defendant from undue hardship. See *Hoxworth v. Blinder, Robinson & Co.*, 903 F.2d 186, 199 (C.A.3 1990); cf. App. to Pet. for Cert. 53a (District Court expressed readiness to modify the preliminary injunction if necessary to GMD's continuance in business).

The protections in place guard against any routine or arbitrary imposition of a preliminary freeze order designed to stop the dissipation of assets that would render a court's judgment worthless.

B

Contrary to the Court's suggestion, see *ante*, at 1974, this case involves no judicial usurpation of Congress' authority. Congress, of course, can instruct the federal courts to issue preliminary injunctions freezing assets pending final judgment, or instruct them not to, and the courts must heed Congress' command. See *Guaranty Trust Co. v. York*, 326 U.S. 99, 105, 65 S.Ct. 1464, 89 L.Ed. 2079 (1945) ("Congressional curtailment of equity powers must be respected."). Indeed, Congress has restricted the equity jurisdiction of federal courts in a variety of contexts. See *Yakus v. United States*, 321 U.S. 414, 442, n. 8, 64 S.Ct. 660, 88 L.Ed. 834 (1944) (cataloging statutes regulating federal equity power).

The Legislature, however, has said nothing about preliminary freeze orders. The relevant question, therefore, is whether, absent congressional direction, the general equitable powers of the federal courts permit relief of the kind fashioned by the District Court. I would find the default rule in the grand aims of equity. Where, as here, legal remedies are not "practical and efficient," *Payne*, 7 Wall. at 431, 19 L.Ed. 260, the federal courts must rely on their "flexible jurisdiction in equity . . . to protect all rights and do justice to all concerned," *Rubber Co. v. Goodyear*, 9 Wall. 805, 807, 19 L.Ed. 828 (1870). No countervailing precedent or principle holds the federal courts powerless to prevent a defendant from dissipating assets, to the destruction of a plaintiff's claim, during the course of judicial proceedings. Accordingly, I would affirm the judgment of the Court of Appeals and uphold the District Court's preliminary injunction.

Methods of Effectuating the Merger

Two somewhat different techniques have been used to bring about the procedural unification of law and equity, which may be described for the sake of brevity as the New York method and the English method.

(1) The New York method involves the formal abolition of the distinction between actions at law and suits in equity. The New York Code of Procedure of 1848 provided in § 62 that: "The distinctions between actions at law and suits in equity, and the forms of all such actions and suits, heretofore existing, are abolished; and, there shall be in this state, hereafter, but one form of action, for the enforcement or protection of private rights and the redress of private wrongs, which shall be denominated a civil action."

The present provision in New York is to be found in section 103(a) of the New York Civil Practice Law and Rules, which became effective September 1, 1963. It provides, as did Section 8 of the Civil Practice Act before September 1, 1963, that: "There is only one form of civil action. The distinctions between actions at law and suits in equity, and the forms of those actions and suits, have been abolished."

The New York Code and most of the other codes distinguish between a civil action and a special proceeding. Special proceedings include such judicial proceedings as habeas corpus, quo warranto, mandamus, prohibition, enforcement of mechanics' liens, applications to punish for criminal contempt in a civil action, and a considerable number of other proceedings of a rather miscellaneous character. . . .

(2) The characteristics of the English method of unified procedure have been well stated by Millar:[14]

> "The English statute proceeded differently. It explicitly faced the fact that, owing to the manner of the law's growth, the distinction between legal and equitable rules, though purely artificial, had so embedded itself in the fabric of the law as to be insusceptible of any outright abolition, and that what really was being aimed at in speaking of fusion was the concurrent administration of the two kinds of rules in

14. MILLAR, *The Old Regime and the New in Civil Procedure*, in 1 LAW: A CENTURY OF PROGRESS 207, 224 (1937).

the same suit when the circumstances so required. Resultingly, it enacted that 'in every civil cause or matter . . . law and equity shall be administered' according to a series of detailed provisions which followed, covering the various contingencies calling for that concurrent administration. To this was added a section regulating certain special situations involved in the change, which concluded with the significant declaration that 'generally in all matters not hereinbefore particularly mentioned, in which there is any conflict or variance between the rules of equity and the rules of the common law, with reference to the same matter, the rules of equity shall prevail.' Thus equity, as before, was to have the last word, but now that word was to be spoken in time to foreclose the adverse word of the common law. This difference between the two statutes in the manner of approach accounts in some measure, at least, for the smoother working of the English system in the present regard."

Equity in the U.S. Today

In addition to the merger in the federal courts, under the Federal Rules of Civil Procedure, the state systems are administered as follows:

(1) Equity may be administered in the same court and by the same procedure as law. This is now the system in Alabama, Alaska, Arizona, California, Colorado, Connecticut, the District of Columbia, Florida, Georgia, Hawaii, Idaho, Illinois, Indiana, Kansas, Kentucky, Louisiana, Maine, Maryland, Massachusetts, Michigan, Minnesota, Missouri, Montana, Nebraska, Nevada, New Hampshire, New Mexico, New York, North Carolina, North Dakota, Ohio, Oklahoma, Oregon, Rhode Island, South Carolina, South Dakota, Texas, Utah, Vermont, Washington, West Virginia, Wisconsin, and Wyoming. This is also true of the federal courts.

(2) Equity may be administered in the same court as law, but on a different side of the court. This was the federal system prior to September 16, 1938, and is the system in Iowa, New Jersey, Pennsylvania and Virginia. Where this system prevails, statutes usually provide for the easy transfer of cases from law to equity and the reverse.

(3) Equity may be administered in a separate court from law and by a different procedure. This was the English system prior to 1875, and is still the system followed in Arkansas, Delaware, Mississippi, and Tennessee.

NOTE

Powers of Courts of Equity: "Traditional" Remedies and New Applications of "Equitable Relief"

For a discussion of the powers of courts of equity, see Grupo Mexicano de Desarrollo S.A. v. Alliance Bond Fund, Inc., 527 U.S. 308, 119 S.Ct. 1961, 144 L.Ed.2d 319 (1999). This case ought to be read in its entirety. In Desarrollo, respondents, investment funds, purchased unsecured notes (Notes) from petitioner Grupo Mexicano de Desarrollo, S.A. (GMD), a

Mexican holding company. Four GMD subsidiaries (also petitioners) guaranteed the Notes. After GMD fell into financial trouble and missed an interest payment on the Notes, respondents accelerated the Notes' principal amount and filed suit for the amount due in a U.S. District Court. Respondents alleged that GMD was at risk of insolvency, or was already insolvent, that it was preferring its Mexican creditors by its planned allocation to them of its most valuable assets, and that these actions would frustrate any judgment respondents would obtain, respondents requested a preliminary injunction restraining petitioners from transferring the assets. The U.S. District Court issued the preliminary injunction and ordered respondents to post a $50,000 bond. The Court of Appeals for the Second Circuit affirmed.

In this 5 to 4 decision the U.S. Supreme Court held that the District Court lacked the authority to issue a preliminary injunction preventing petitioners from disposing of their assets pending adjudication of respondents' contract claim for money damages because such a remedy was historically unavailable from a court of equity.

Writing for the majority, Justice Scalia stated that the federal courts have the equity jurisdiction that was exercised by the English Court of Chancery at the time the Constitution was adopted and the Judiciary Act of 1789 was enacted, and that the well established general rule was that a judgment fixing the debt was necessary before a court of equity would interfere with the debtor's use of its property.

In the dissenting opinion, Justice Ginsburg stated that: "the uncontested evidence presented to the District Court at the preliminary injunction hearing showed that petitioner ... (GMD) had defaulted on its contractual obligations to respondents, a group of GMD noteholders (Alliance), ... that Alliance had satisfied all conditions precedent to its breach of contract claim, ..., and that GMD had no plausible defense on the merits.... Alliance also demonstrated that GMD had undertaken to treat Alliance's claims on the same footing as all other unsecured, unsubordinated debt, ... but that GMD was in fact satisfying Mexican creditors to the exclusion of Alliance.... Furthermore, the unchallenged evidence indicated that GMD was so rapidly disbursing its sole remaining asset that, absent provisional action by the District Court, Alliance would have been unable to collect on the money judgment for which it qualified."

"From the beginning, we have defined the scope of federal equity in relation to the principles of equity existing at the separation of this country from England, see e.g., Payne v. Hook, 74 U.S. 425, 430, 19 L.Ed. 260 (1868); Gordon v. Washington, 295 U.S. 30, 36, 55 S.Ct. 584, 79 L.Ed. 1282 (1935); we have never limited federal equity jurisdiction to the specific practices and remedies of the pre-Revolutionary Chancellor.... [W]e have valued the adaptable character of federal equitable power."

The dissent quoted from Hecht Co. v. Bowles, 321 U.S. 321, 329, 64 S.Ct. 587, 88 L.Ed. 754 (1944) "('Flexibility rather than rigidity has distinguished [federal equity jurisdiction].')." It also quoted from Pomeroy on Equity Jurisdiction (5th ed. 1941) that equity "possesses an inherent capacity of expansion, so as to keep abreast of each succeeding generation and age.", and concluded: "On this understanding of equity's character, we have upheld diverse injunctions that would have been beyond the contemplation of the eighteenth century Chancellor." Justice Ginsburg added that "it is one thing to recognize that equity courts typically did not provide this relief, quite another to conclude that, therefore, the remedy was beyond equity's capacity. I would not draw such a conclusion."

Was the question in Grupo Mexicano whether the District Court had jurisdiction or whether the facts were such that it should have been exercised in the particular case by enjoining or restraining petitioners from transferring their assets? See discussion in Yuba Consolidated Gold Fields v. Kilkeary, *infra* p. 347.

Countless cases illustrate the "flexibility" of equity and its ability to "fashion" an appropriate remedy in cases where the remedy at law is inadequate and an equitable remedy is necessary to do justice in the particular case. Strank v. Mercy Hospital of Johnstown is a good example.

NOTES

1. The leading case of Erie R. Co. v. Tompkins, 304 U.S. 64, 58 S.Ct. 817, 82 L.Ed. 1188 (1938) which overruled Swift v. Tyson, 41 U.S. (16 Pet.) 1 (1842), held that in diversity cases, except for cases governed by the U.S. Constitution and Acts of Congress, the substantive law to be applied is that of the state in which the federal court is located. For a thorough discussion of the applicability of the Erie doctrine to this case, see John T. Cross, "The Erie Doctrine in Equity," 60 La. L. Rev. 173–232 (1999).

For the impact of the Grupo Mexicano case on bankruptcy law, see "Grupo Mexicana. and the Death of Substantive Consolidation," 8 Am. Bankr. Inst. L. Rev. 427 (2000).

2. In Quackenbush, California Insurance Commissioner v. Allstate Insurance Co., 517 U.S. 706, 116 S.Ct. 1712, 135 L.Ed.2d 1 (1996), the U.S. Supreme Court considered "whether an abstention-based remand order is appealable as a final order under 28 U.S.C. § 1291, and whether the abstention doctrine first recognized in Burford v. Sun Oil Co., 319 U.S. 315, 63 S.Ct. 1098, 87 L.Ed. 1424 (1943), can be applied in a common-law suit for damages." Although the court held that the remand order was appealable, the court stated that "the federal interests in this case are pronounced, as Allstate's motion to compel arbitration under the Federal Arbitration Act [FAA] implicates a substantial concern for the enforcement of arbitration agreements," and that the Burford abstention applied only to cases where equitable relief was sought and not to a case where the plaintiff sought solely legal relief, such as common law damages.

Strank v. Mercy Hospital of Johnstown

Supreme Court of Pennsylvania, 1955.
383 Pa. 54, 117 A.2d 697.

■ STERN, C.J. . . . .

The facts are set forth in the opinion of this court on a former appeal. Briefly stated, they are that the defendant institution conducts a school of nursing in conjunction with its hospital, that plaintiff, then a minor, enrolled in the school as a student nurse and paid the expenses incidental thereto, that she successfully completed the work prescribed for the first two years of the course but was dismissed in her third and final year of training because she had broken a rule of the school in remaining away overnight without permission; (she explained the circumstances of this infraction). She does not seek reinstatement as a student in the school but only that defendant give her transfer credits for the work she has completed in order that she may secure advanced standing in some other nursing school; this the defendant has refused to do. Plaintiff brought an action in mandamus to compel defendant to give her the credits; to her complaint defendant filed a preliminary objection raising the question of jurisdiction. We held that a writ of mandamus could not issue to enforce a right or duty which was not imposed by law but rested solely on contract, and therefore that the complaint in mandamus must be dismissed.

Following this decision plaintiff instituted the present proceedings in equity. She filed a complaint, and, after defendant filed preliminary objections thereto, an amended complaint, in which she set forth her oral arrangements with the school at the time she entered, later confirmed in part by writing and carried out by both parties for a period of two years. She alleged that these arrangements and understandings imposed upon defendant the legal duty to give her proper credits for work completed, and that, because of defendant's refusal to do so, she has suffered great damage by loss of time for which she has no adequate remedy at law. Defendant again filed preliminary objections, among them that the court did not have jurisdiction to entertain such an action in equity. The court below entered a decree dismissing the objections and ordering defendant to file an answer to the complaint. Thereupon defendant took the present appeal . . . , thereby again raising the sole question of jurisdiction.

There is not the slightest merit in defendant's contention that the court in equity was without jurisdiction to enter upon these proceedings; indeed the case is one peculiarly for determination by such a court. Under the Acts of June 16, 1836, P.L. 784, § 13, 12 P.S. § 1221, and February 14, 1857, P.L. 39, 17 P.S. § 283, the courts of common pleas have the jurisdiction and powers of a court of chancery in all cases such as those in which they had theretofore possessed jurisdiction and powers under the Constitution and laws of the Commonwealth, and also so far as relates to the affording of specific relief when a recovery in damages would be an inadequate remedy. They have jurisdiction not only for the prevention of acts contrary to law and prejudicial to the rights of individuals, but also for the enforcement of obligations whether arising under express contracts, written or oral, or implied contracts, including those in which a duty may have resulted from long recognized and established customs and usages, as in this case, perhaps, between an educational institution and its students. Moreover, it is the peculiar province of equity to afford relief where the measurement of damages in such cases cannot be formulated and applied in a suit at law because of their being necessarily speculative and indeterminate, and therefore the legal remedy is not adequate and complete. Indeed it might be said that it would be a reproach to our system of jurisprudence if plaintiff should be found entitled to the transfer credits which she seeks, but nevertheless neither law nor equity can furnish her any adequate means of redress.

The decree of the court below is affirmed, costs to abide the event.

————

Unified Civil Procedure

Contributions of the Federal Rules of Civil Procedure

In any discussion of the effort to unify and simplify the law of procedure, reference must be made to the contribution of the Federal Rules of Civil Procedure. In addition to the merger of law and equity in Rule 2 which states that "[t]here shall be one form of action to be known as 'civil action,'" in Rule 1 it is stated that the purpose of the Rules is "to secure the just, speedy, and inexpensive determination of every action." Rule 104 of the Civil Practice Act and Rules of the State of New York also states that "the civil practice law and rules shall be liberally construed to secure the just, speedy and inexpensive determination of every civil judicial proceeding."

In addition to preserving, in Rule 38, the right to a jury trial as declared by the Seventh Amendment to the United States Constitution, the Federal Rules also incorporate procedural devices formerly available only in equity courts. Hence, under these modern procedural Rules a court may grant a successful litigant the relief or remedy to which that litigant is entitled whether the relief was formerly denominated legal or equitable. Furthermore, the defendant may also raise any defense whether formerly denominated legal or equitable.

Problems resulting from legislative attempts partly or completely to unify legal and equitable procedure may arise from several sources.

(1) The substantive law which has developed at law and in equity is sometimes different. Where both systems are administered in one procedure, one must yield to the other where conflict occurs. The one to yield is always the law, either by reason of an express statutory provision as in England, or simply as a necessary consequence of unifying two systems where one already had the upper hand. This aspect of unification thus has caused little difficulty.

(2) Equitable relief is often specific; legal relief is ordinarily substitutional. But even classical equity often gave money decrees which were sometimes by way of substitutional relief, and the courts of law gave specific relief in replevin and ejectment and by the extraordinary legal remedies of mandamus and habeas corpus. Procedural fusion thus merely gave to a single court powers to give specific and substitutional relief which each of two separate courts had given to some degree.

(3) Legal relief is usually as of course; equitable relief is frequently discretionary. But the courts of law had a discretion in administering the extraordinary legal remedies, and the equity courts in many cases gave their relief as of course. Here again there was no very serious problem to arise from procedural fusion.

(4) The theory of the pleadings has tended to prevent complete disappearance of the forms of action at common law and the effect of the theory of the bill in suits in equity. The same sort of difficulty has arisen under unified procedure, particularly with regard to the manner of pleading causes of action or defenses formerly at law and those formerly equitable. We have seen how far Illinois has carried over into its reformed procedure the notion that complaints must be characterized as legal or equitable. Perhaps more significant is the fact that the New York courts, a hundred years after the "distinction between actions at law and suits in equity [has] been abolished," still constantly refer to "actions in equity" and "equitable relief." This is to a considerable degree inevitable so long as there is no complete fusion of the legal and equitable elements of the substantive law. This distinction has been perpetuated unnecessarily by the courts in deciding procedural questions.

(5) The most important obstacle to complete procedural unification in the United States is the presence in the federal constitution and in most state constitutions of guarantees of trial by jury in civil cases at law. As it has been graphically put, this guarantee of jury trial "is the sword in the bed that prevents the complete union of law and equity."[15] Where trial by jury may constitutionally be abolished, as in England, this difficulty may be met. Or it might be met by requiring jury trial as of right in cases of equitable cognizance, as in a few states; although it may be suggested that this cure would be worse than the disease. But as matters stand in the federal courts and most of the states, the problem of preserving the right to trial by jury in cases formerly at law raises serious problems for a unified procedure, ... Problems of the theory of the pleadings may be evanescent; but problems as to jury trial are perennial in any unified civil procedure in the United States today.

Great–West Life & Annuity Insurance Company v. Janette Knudson and Eric Knudson.

Supreme Court of the United States, 2002.
534 U.S. 204, 122 S.Ct. 708, 151 L.Ed.2d 635.

SCALIA, J., delivered the opinion of the Court, in which REHNQUIST, C.J., and O'CONNOR, KENNEDY, and THOMAS, JJ., joined. STEVENS, J., filed a dissenting opinion, *post*, p. 719. GINSBURG, J., filed a dissenting opinion, in which STEVENS, SOUTER, and BREYER, JJ., joined, *post*, p. 720.

■ JUSTICE SCALIA delivered the opinion of the Court.

The question presented is whether § 502(a)(3) of the Employee Retirement Income Security Act of 1974 (ERISA), 88 Stat. 891, 29 U.S.C. § 1132(a)(3) (1994 ed.), authorizes this action by petitioners to enforce a reimbursement provision of an ERISA plan.

I

Respondent Janette Knudson was rendered quadriplegic by a car accident in June 1992. Because her then-husband, respondent Eric Knud-

15. Professor Zechariah Chafee, Jr., in an unpublished lecture.

son, was employed by petitioner Earth Systems, Inc., Janette was covered by the Health and Welfare Plan for Employees and Dependents of Earth Systems, Inc. (Plan). The Plan covered $411,157.11 of Janette's medical expenses, of which all except $75,000 was paid by petitioner Great–West Life & Annuity Insurance Co. pursuant to a "stop-loss" insurance agreement with the Plan.

The Plan includes a reimbursement provision that is the basis for the present lawsuit. This provides that the Plan shall have "the right to recover from the [beneficiary] any payment for benefits" paid by the Plan that the beneficiary is entitled to recover from a third party. App. 58. Specifically, the Plan has "a first lien upon any recovery, whether by settlement, judgment or otherwise," that the beneficiary receives from the third party, not to exceed "the amount of benefits paid [by the Plan] ... [or] the amount received by the [beneficiary] for such medical treatment...." If the beneficiary recovers from a third party and fails to reimburse the Plan, "then he will be personally liable to [the Plan] ... up to the amount of the first lien." *Id.*, at 59. Pursuant to an agreement between the Plan and Great–West, the Plan "assign[ed] to Great–West all of its rights to make, litigate, negotiate, settle, compromise, release or waive" any claim under the reimbursement provision. ...

In late 1993, the Knudsons filed a tort action in California state court seeking to recover from Hyundai Motor Company, the manufacturer of the car they were riding in at the time of the accident, and other alleged tortfeasors. The parties to that action negotiated a $650,000 settlement, a notice of which was mailed to Great–West. This allocated $256,745.30 to a Special Needs Trust under Cal. Prob. Code Ann. § 3611 (West 1991 and Supp.1993) to provide for Janette's medical care; $373,426 to attorney's fees and costs; $5,000 to reimburse the California Medicaid program (Medi–Cal); and $13,828.70 (the portion of the settlement attributable to past medical expenses) to satisfy Great–West's claim under the reimbursement provision of the Plan.

The day before the hearing scheduled for judicial approval of the settlement, Great–West, calling itself a defendant and asserting that the state-court action involved federal claims related to ERISA, filed in the United States District Court for the Central District of California a notice of removal pursuant to 28 U.S.C. § 1441 (1994 ed.). That court concluded that Great–West was not a defendant and could not remove the case, and therefore remanded to the state court, which approved the settlement. The state court's order provided that the defendants would pay the settlement amount allocated to the Special Needs Trust directly to the trust, and the remaining amounts to respondents' attorney, who, in turn, would tender checks to Medi–Cal and Great–West.

Great–West, however, never cashed the check it received from respondents' attorney. Instead, at the same time that Great–West sought to remove the state-law tort action, it filed this action in the same federal court (the United States District Court for the Central District of California), seeking injunctive and declaratory relief under § 502(a)(3) to enforce the reimbursement provision of the Plan by requiring the Knudsons to pay the Plan $411,157.11 of any proceeds recovered from third parties. Great–

West subsequently filed an amended complaint adding Earth Systems and the Plan as plaintiffs and seeking a temporary restraining order against continuation of the state-court proceedings for approval of the settlement. The District Court denied the temporary restraining order, a ruling that petitioners did not appeal. After the state court approved the settlement and the money was disbursed, the District Court granted summary judgment to the Knudsons. It held that the language of the Plan limited its right of reimbursement to the amount received by respondents from third parties for past medical treatment, an amount that the state court determined was $13,828.70. The United States Court of Appeals for the Ninth Circuit affirmed on different grounds. Judgt. order reported at 208 F.3d 221 (C.A.9 2000). Citing *FMC Medical Plan v. Owens*, 122 F.3d 1258 (C.A.9 1997), it held that judicially decreed reimbursement for payments made to a beneficiary of an insurance plan by a third party is not equitable relief and is therefore not authorized by § 502(a)(3). We granted certiorari. ...

II

We have observed repeatedly that ERISA is a " 'comprehensive and reticulated statute,' the product of a decade of congressional study of the Nation's private employee benefit system." Mertens v. Hewitt Associates, 508 U.S. 248, 251, 113 S.Ct. 2063, 124 L.Ed.2d 161 (1993) (quoting Nachman Corp. v. Pension Benefit Guaranty Corporation, 446 U.S. 359, 361, 100 S.Ct. 1723, 64 L.Ed.2d 354 (1980)). We have therefore been especially "reluctant to tamper with [the] enforcement scheme" embodied in the statute by extending remedies not specifically authorized by its text. Massachusetts Mut. Life Ins. Co. v. Russell, 473 U.S. 134, 147, 105 S.Ct. 3085, 87 L.Ed.2d 96 (1985). Indeed, we have noted that ERISA's "carefully crafted and detailed enforcement scheme provides 'strong evidence that Congress did not intend to authorize other remedies that it simply forgot to incorporate expressly.' " Mertens, supra, at 254, 113 S.Ct. 2063 (quoting Russell, supra, at 146–147, 105 S.Ct. 3085).

Section 502(a)(3) authorizes a civil action:

"by a participant, beneficiary, or fiduciary (A) to enjoin any act or practice which violates ... the terms of the plan, or (B) to obtain other appropriate equitable relief (i) to redress such violations or (ii) to enforce any provisions of ... the terms of the plan." 29 U.S.C. § 1132(a)(3) (1994 ed.).

As we explained in Mertens, " '[e]quitable' relief must mean something less than all relief." 508 U.S., at 258, n. 8, 113 S.Ct. 2063. Thus, in Mertens we rejected a reading of the statute that would extend the relief obtainable under § 502(a)(3) to whatever relief a court of equity is empowered to provide in the particular case at issue (which could include legal remedies that would otherwise be beyond the scope of the equity court's authority). Such a reading, we said, would "limit the relief not at all" and "render the modifier ['equitable'] superfluous." Id., at 257–258, 113 S.Ct. 2063. Instead, we held that the term "equitable relief" in § 502(a)(3) must refer to "those categories of relief that were typically available in equity.... " Id., at 256, 113 S.Ct. 2063.

Here, petitioners seek, in essence, to impose personal liability on respondents for a contractual obligation to pay money—relief that was not typically available in equity. "A claim for money due and owing under a contract is 'quintessentially an action at law.' " Wal–Mart Stores, Inc. v. Wells, 213 F.3d 398, 401 (C.A.7 2000) (Posner, J.). "Almost invariably . . . suits seeking (whether by judgment, injunction, or declaration) to compel the defendant to pay a sum of money to the plaintiff are suits for 'money damages,' as that phrase has traditionally been applied, since they seek no more than compensation for loss resulting from the defendant's breach of legal duty." Bowen v. Massachusetts, 487 U.S. 879, 918–919, 108 S.Ct. 2722, 101 L.Ed.2d 749 (1988) (SCALIA, J., dissenting). And "[m]oney damages are, of course, the classic form of legal relief." *Mertens, supra,* at 255, 113 S.Ct. 2063.

Nevertheless, petitioners, along with their *amicus* the United States, struggle to characterize the relief sought as "equitable" under the standard set by Mertens. We are not persuaded.

A

First, petitioners argue that they are entitled to relief under § 502(a)(3)(A) because they seek "to enjoin a[n] act or practice"—respondents' failure to reimburse the Plan—"which violates . . . the terms of the plan." But an injunction to compel the payment of money past due under a contract, or specific performance of a past due monetary obligation, was not typically available in equity. See, e.g., 3 Restatement (Second) of Contracts § 359 (1979); 3 Dobbs § 12.8(2), at 199; 5A A. Corbin, Contracts § 1142, p. 119 (1964) (hereinafter Corbin). Those rare cases in which a court of equity would decree specific performance of a contract to transfer funds were suits that, unlike the present case, sought to prevent future losses that either were incalculable or would be greater than the sum awarded. For example, specific performance might be available to enforce an agreement to lend money "when the unavailability of alternative financing would leave the plaintiff with injuries that are difficult to value; or to enforce an obligor's duty to make future monthly payments, after the obligor had consistently refused to make past payments concededly due, and thus threatened the obligee with the burden of bringing multiple damages actions." Bowen, supra, at 918, 108 S.Ct. 2722 (SCALIA, J., dissenting). See also 3 Dobbs § 12.8(2), at 200; 5A Corbin § 1142, at 117–118. Typically, however, specific performance of a contract to pay money was not available in equity. . . .

Thus, the suit was not merely for past due sums, but for an injunction to correct the method of calculating payments going forward. Bowen, supra, at 889, 108 S.Ct. 2722. Bowen has no bearing on the unavailability of an injunction to enforce a contractual obligation to pay money past due.

B

Second, petitioners argue that their suit is authorized by § 502(a)(3)(B) because they seek restitution, which they characterize as a form of equitable relief. However, not all relief falling under the rubric of restitution is available in equity. . . . Thus, "restitution is a legal remedy when ordered in a case at law and an equitable remedy ... when ordered in an equity case," and whether it is legal or equitable depends on "the basis for [the plaintiff's] claim" and the nature of the underlying remedies sought. *Reich v. Continental Casualty Co.*, 33 F.3d 754, 756 (C.A.7 1994) (Posner, J.).

restitution can be both at law and equity

→ In cases in which the plaintiff "could *not* assert title or right to possession of particular property, but in which nevertheless he might be able to show just grounds for recovering money to pay for some benefit the defendant had received from him," the plaintiff had a right to restitution *at law* through an action derived from the common-law writ of assumpsit. 1 Dobbs § 4.2(1), at 571. See also Muir, *supra*, at 37. In such cases, the plaintiff's claim was considered legal because he sought "to obtain a judgment imposing a merely personal liability upon the defendant to pay a sum of money." Restatement of Restitution § 160, Comment *a*, pp. 641–642 (1936). Such claims were viewed essentially as actions at law for breach of contract (whether the contract was actual or implied).

In contrast, a plaintiff could seek restitution *in equity*, ordinarily in the form of a constructive trust or an equitable lien, where money or property identified as belonging in good conscience to the plaintiff could clearly be traced to particular funds or property in the defendant's possession. See 1 Dobbs § 4.3(1), at 587–588; Restatement of Restitution, *supra*, § 160, Comment a, at 641–642; 1 G. Palmer, Law of Restitution § 1.4, p. 17; § 3.7, p. 262 (1978). A court of equity could then order a defendant to transfer title (in the case of the constructive trust) or to give a security interest (in the case of the equitable lien) to a plaintiff who was, in the eyes of equity, the true owner. But where "the property [sought to be recovered] or its proceeds have been dissipated so that no product remains, [the plaintiff's] claim is only that of a general creditor," and the plaintiff "cannot enforce a constructive trust of or an equitable lien upon other property of the [defendant]." Restatement of Restitution, *supra*, § 215, Comment *a*, at 867. Thus, for restitution to lie in equity, the action generally must seek not to impose personal liability on the defendant, but to restore to the plaintiff particular funds or property in the defendant's possession. ...

We need not decide these issues because, as we explained in *Mertens*, "[e]ven assuming ... that petitioners are correct about the pre-emption of previously available state-court actions" or the lack of other means to obtain relief, "vague notions of a statute's 'basic purpose' are nonetheless inadequate to overcome the words of its text regarding the *specific* issue under consideration." 508 U.S., at 261, 113 S.Ct. 2063. In the very same section of ERISA as § 502(a)(3), Congress authorized "a participant or beneficiary" to bring a civil action "to enforce his rights under the terms of the plan," without reference to whether the relief sought is legal or equitable. 29 U.S.C. § 1132(a)(1)(B) (1994 ed.). But Congress did not extend the same authorization to fiduciaries. Rather, § 502(a)(3), by its terms, only allows for *equitable* relief. We will not attempt to adjust the "carefully crafted and detailed enforcement scheme" embodied in the text that Congress has adopted. *Mertens, supra*, at 254, 113 S.Ct. 2063. Because petitioners are seeking legal relief—the imposition of personal liability on respondents for a contractual obligation to pay money—§ 502(a)(3) does not authorize this action. Accordingly, we affirm the judgment of the Court of Appeals.

It is so ordered.

■ JUSTICE STEVENS, dissenting.

In her lucid dissent, which I join, JUSTICE GINSBURG has explained why it is fanciful to assume that in 1974 Congress intended to revive the obsolete distinctions between law and equity as a basis for defining the remedies available in federal court for violations of the terms of a plan under the Employee Retirement Income Security Act of 1974 (ERISA). She has also convincingly argued that the relief sought in the present case is permissible even under the Court's favored test for determining what qualifies as "equitable relief" under § 502(a)(3)(B) of ERISA. I add this postscript because I am persuaded that Congress intended the word "enjoin," as used in § 502(a)(3)(A), to authorize any appropriate order that prohibits or terminates a violation of an ERISA plan, regardless of whether a precedent for such an order can be found in English Chancery cases.

I read the word "other" in § 502(a)(3)(B) as having been intended to enlarge, not contract, a federal judge's remedial authority. Consequently, and contrary to the Court's view in *Mertens v. Hewitt Associates*, 508 U.S. 248, 256, 113 S.Ct. 2063, 124 L.Ed.2d 161 (1993), I would neither read § 502(a)(3)(B) as placing a *limitation* on a judge's authority under § 502(a)(3)(A), nor shackle an analysis of what constitutes "equitable relief" under § 502(a)(3)(B) to the sort of historical analysis that the Court has chosen. . . .

I respectfully dissent. . . .

■ JUSTICE GINSBURG, with whom JUSTICE STEVENS, JUSTICE SOUTER, and JUSTICE BREYER join, dissenting.

Today's holding, the majority declares, is compelled by "Congress's choice to limit the relief available under § 502(a)(3)." Ante, at 717. In the Court's view, Congress' placement of the word "equitable" in that provision signaled an intent to exhume the "fine distinction[s]" borne of the "days of the divided bench," ante, at 714, 715; to treat as dispositive an ancient classification unrelated to the substance of the relief sought; and to obstruct the general goals of ERISA by relegating to state court (or to no court at all) an array of suits involving the interpretation of employee health plan provisions. Because it is plain that Congress made no such "choice," I dissent. . . .

———

Recognition of Equity Decrees at Law (And Judgments in Equity)

———

Mutual Life Insurance Co. v. Newton

Supreme Court of New Jersey, 1888.
50 N.J.L. 571, 14 A. 756.

On motion to strike out plea.

The declaration is upon a bond for $8000, made by the defendant to the plaintiffs. It states that this bond was accompanied by a mortgage, made by the defendant upon certain lands of his, to the plaintiffs, to secure the sum mentioned in said bond. That upon the foreclosure of this mortgage a sum was realized, which was applied to the payment of the said $8000, leaving a balance of $3877.53 still due.

The defendant filed a plea, setting up that the sum of $3877.53 is the amount of a deficiency declared and decreed by the Court of Chancery as still due and owing upon the proceeding in foreclosure set forth in the declaration. That the bond sued on is the bond which accompanied the mortgage, and was set forth in the bill of complaint to foreclose the said mortgage. That after such decree of foreclosure was made and entered in the Court of Chancery, and after the sale of the lands, there remained the said deficiency of $3877.53, which was decreed by the Court of Chancery to be still due. That on the 15th day of August, 1881, a statement or abstract of such decree was filed in the office of the clerk of the Supreme Court, whereby the said sum became a judgment of this court, and is still a judgment.

The opinion of the court was delivered by

■ REED, J. The motion to strike out the plea raises the question, whether a party who has taken a personal decree in equity for a deficiency in the amount raised on the foreclosure of a mortgage, can afterwards bring an action at law upon the accompanying bond.

The view of the pleader was that the recovery, by way of a decree under the statute, was a bar against any other action upon the original cause of action. The notion of the plaintiffs' counsel is, that a decree is not a judgment in a sense that implies a merger of the original cause of action, and that, therefore, the bond is still suable.

The point made is, that no action will lie on a decree as it will upon a judgment, and therefore a decree has not the qualities of a judgment, in respect to its effect in extinguishing the original ground of the suit. . . .

The law in England may be regarded as settled, that upon foreign decrees an action at law will lie. . . .

The right to bring actions upon domestic decrees the English courts had denied, but this denial was put upon the ground that such actions were unnecessary, because the court which made the decree could, within its own jurisdiction, enforce it, and so an action was unnecessary.

The Chief Justice, in Van Buskirk v. Mulock [3 Har. 184], relied upon the case of Hugh v. Higgs, 21 U.S. 697, 5 L.Ed. 719, 8 Wheat. 697, as establishing the law in the federal courts against an action at law on a decree. Whatever force this case may have once had, is now entirely dissipated by the case of Pennington v. Gibson, 57 U.S. 65, 14 L.Ed. 847, 16 How. 65, in his opinion in which case, Mr. Justice Daniels remarked: "We lay it down as the general rule that in every instance in which an action of debt can be maintained upon a judgment at law for a sum of money awarded by such judgment, the like action can be maintained upon a decree in equity for an ascertained and specific amount, and nothing more."

... In treating the question as an open one, I have no doubt that an action will lie upon a domestic decree for the payment of money only, in the same degree as it will lie upon a judgment.... I think it might be admitted that the right of an action at law upon a domestic decree could be denied, upon the ground that such an action is unnecessary and vexatious, because of the fact that the court which made the decree can enforce it in all respects. It was upon this ground that the English courts and one or two of the American courts early denied the right of bringing such an action at law.

The denial of a right of action upon such ground would not, in my judgment, render such a decree less conclusive in bar of another suit for the same cause of action, for the question is, whether the decree amounts to a determination of the rights of the parties in respect to the identical matter involved in the present action. If so it is a bar. The doctrine of *res adjudicata* is plain and intelligible, and amounts simply to this, that a cause of action once finally determined without appeal, between the parties, on the merits, by a competent tribunal, cannot afterwards be litigated by a new proceeding, either by the same or any other tribunal....

And this is true, whether the first adjudication is in a court of law or equity.

A decree in chancery may be given in evidence between the same parties, or those claiming under them, for their judgments must be of authority in those cases where the law gives them jurisdiction, for it were very absurd that the law should give them jurisdiction and yet not suffer what is done by force of that jurisdiction to be full proof.

Hence, it is settled that a verdict and judgment of a court of record or a decree in chancery puts an end to all further controversy concerning the points thus decided between the parties to the suit....

If the decree is final, then its result is to merge the original cause of action. As was remarked in the case of Barnes v. Gibbons, 7 Vr. 319, in regard to a judgment, the doctrine of merger arises out of the quality which renders the judgment conclusive upon the parties as to the question which is involved. If the plaintiff be permitted to sue on the original cause of action, it is treating it, although judicially settled, as open to controversy.

I am of the opinion that when the plaintiff invoked the Court of Chancery to give him the statutory decree for deficiency, and he obtained it, his right to bring a new suit on the bond was gone. Nor is it easy to perceive the occasion for such an action.

The power to file the decree of the court in the supreme [court] clerk's office, the power to have execution in any county in the state, the right to sue upon the decree in foreign jurisdictions, all tend to make the decree an efficient instrument for the collection of the debt.

The motion to strike out is refused, with costs.

———

NOTES ON THE RES JUDICATA EFFECT OF EQUITY DECREES

1. A town, after issuing bonds, sued a bondholder to cancel the bonds as invalid for non-compliance with various statutory requisites. The bonds were held valid and the complaint dismissed. The bondholder then brought an action to recover upon unpaid interest coupons attached to the bonds. The defense raised was that the bonds were invalid. A directed verdict for plaintiff was held proper in Williamsburgh Savings Bank v. Solon, 136 N.Y. 465, 32 N.E. 1058 (1893). The court's explanation for this ruling was as follows:

> [The bank in the first suit] might have defended upon other grounds, those peculiar to equity, and independent of the main and central issue, but it did not. One such ground might have been that there was an adequate remedy at law, but that was waived because not raised by demurrer on the one hand, or by pleading the defense on the other. There was no such issue in the case, for if not pleaded, it cannot be made available.... The defendant submitted itself to the jurisdiction of equity by abandoning its claim to meet its enemy only in a court of law. Another such defense might possibly have been laches, but that was not interposed, and was explicitly shut out from the decision.... On the trial, no merely equitable question was raised, save and except that if the bonds were invalid on their face, the remedy was at law, which the court correctly overruled. The defendant's final motion at the close of the case for a dismissal of the complaint rested upon no such ground, but wholly and entirely on the contention that the bonds were valid and the lawful obligations of the town. That therefore was the sole issue involved, and the sole issue ultimately decided. The plaintiff municipality deliberately chose the forum of equity, saying that it was afraid of the courts of law and of the multitude of suits which might follow and especially of some in the Federal courts; and before the tribunal which it voluntarily selected was bound to show, and could only succeed by showing, that the identical bonds here in controversy were void.... The town has had its day in court, a full opportunity to assail and test the bonds, a patient hearing and direct decision upon all the questions now raised. It would be hard to find a case to which the doctrine of *res judicata* could more justly and clearly apply than this.

2. The Restatement (Second) of Judgments § 25 comment i makes these observations about the effect of the merger of law and equity on the doctrines of merger and bar:

> *"Legal" and "equitable" phases of a claim.* When "law" and "equity" with their distinctive remedies were separately administered, a plaintiff had to choose between the two "sides" when he brought his action, and the choice could be difficult, as the dividing line was not exact. Also, it was sometimes impossible to dispose completely in a single action of an entire transaction or controversy, since it might require a

combination of legal and equitable remedies. The difficult remedial situation created by the law-equity division naturally had important restrictive effects on the operation of the doctrines of merger and bar. These are overcome when law and equity are "merged" or unified into the "one form of action" so that a pleader may and is expected to demand in a single action any and all remedies suited to the case. The point is emphasized by the customary provision in modern rules or codes of procedure that, except where judgment is by default, "every final judgment shall grant the relief to which the party in whose favor it is rendered is entitled, even if the party has not demanded such relief in his pleadings." See Rule 54(c) of the Federal Rules of Civil Procedure.

(1) Remission from "law" to "equity" or "equity" to "law" unnecessary and improper. Formerly, if the plaintiff brought an action at law in which judgment was given for the defendant because the plaintiff's remedy was solely by a suit in equity, the plaintiff was not precluded from maintaining a suit in equity. Conversely, if the plaintiff brought a suit in equity which was dismissed because his remedy was solely by an action at law, the plaintiff was not precluded from maintaining an action at law; this was true, for example, where the suit in equity was dismissed because the plaintiff had an adequate remedy at law, or on the ground of such delay or hardship or impropriety of the plaintiff's conduct as barred a suit in equity but not an action at law.

In a unified system of procedure, the plaintiff in the situations mentioned would ordinarily be entitled to be awarded in the first action any remedy called for by the facts, whether the remedy would formerly have been denominated legal or equitable; hence, one action should suffice. . . .

(2) "Legal" and "equitable" relief possible in single action. Formerly, a plaintiff who brought a suit in equity to enjoin the continuance of wrongful conduct might not be permitted to demand in the same suit the prior damages resulting from the wrong, or, where the system was somewhat less strict, might be permitted, but would not be obligated to make the demand in the same suit (a demand for "cleanup" damages). Accordingly, judgment in the equity suit either would not preclude an action by the plaintiff at law to recover the damages, or in the laxer systems, would preclude the action only if the plaintiff had in fact sought the damage remedy in the equity suit. Today, after unification, the damage remedy would be considered part of the unitary claim for purposes of merger and bar. . . . So also a judgment granting or denying specific performance of a contract should preclude an action for money damages for breach.

(3) Alternative relief in a single action on a contract as written or as reformed. Formerly, when the plaintiff brought an action at law for breach of a written contract and failed to prove a breach, and judgment was accordingly given for the defendant, the plaintiff was not precluded from a suit in equity to reform the contract on the ground of mistake or fraud or some other ground, and to enforce the contract as reformed. Today, in a unified system, he would ordinarily be precluded

from a second action, assuming, as would very likely be the case, that the facts basing the proposed second action were part of the same transaction as those grounding the first.

C.   THE RIGHT TO TRIAL BY JURY

The United States Constitution Seventh Amendment provides:

> In suits at common law, where the value in controversy shall exceed twenty dollars, the right of trial by jury shall be preserved, and no fact tried by jury, shall be otherwise re–examined in any Court of the United States, than according to the rules of the Common Law.

Hence, in the courts of the United States the right to trial by jury is preserved by the Seventh Amendment "[i]n suits at common law, where the value in controversy shall exceed twenty dollars." Also, when Congress authorized the Supreme Court of the United States to prescribe rules of procedure for the district courts, the Act provided:

> The court may at any time unite the general rules prescribed by it for cases in equity with those in actions at law so as to secure one form of action and procedure for both: *Provided, however,* That in such union of rules the right of trial by jury as at common law and declared by the seventh amendment to the Constitution shall be preserved to the parties inviolate.[16]

Although the Seventh Amendment does not guarantee a trial by jury in state courts, the right is generally preserved by state constitutional provisions.

In brief, the right exists in actions at law, i.e. common law causes of action, but not in actions in equity.

For purposes of ascertaining whether a litigant is entitled to a jury trial, a reading of even the most recent cases will reveal that, for jury trial purposes, a complete merger of law and equity has not been achieved. In this area the distinction between "legal" and "equitable" causes still perseveres.

Some basic rules may be stated with certainty. For example, a case involving only a *legal* claim, and an answer thereto, is within the constitutional guarantee of a jury trial. Likewise, a case involving only an *equitable* claim, and an answer thereto, does not come within the constitutional guarantee. Quite apart from the traditional role of equity in granting "incidental" or "complete" relief once equity jurisdiction has attached, the problems today are further complicated by the assertion of new causes of action, the joinder of causes of action and by counterclaims. Even assuming

16.   48 Stat. 1064.

that there will be no question as to whether a cause of action is "legal" or "equitable," a variety of problems have had to be dealt with by the courts. Illustratively, what is the effect, upon the parties' right to a jury trial, of the plaintiff's request for both legal and equitable relief? What is the effect of the defendant's raising of equitable defenses and counterclaims? The *Chauffeurs* case reflects the approach of the Supreme Court.

Chauffeurs, Teamsters and Helpers, Local No. 391 v. Terry

Supreme Court of the United States, 1990.
494 U.S. 558, 110 S.Ct. 1339, 108 L.Ed.2d 519.

[Plaintiff truck drivers brought action against their employer for breach of a collective bargaining agreement and their union for breach of the duty of fair representation. Plaintiff voluntarily dismissed action against employer (after employer filed for Bankruptcy), leaving the claim for compensatory damages against the union. The issue before the Court was whether plaintiff had a right to a jury trial in a duty of fair representation suit. The district court decided in favor of the plaintiffs and the court of appeals affirmed.

The underlying controversy concerned the interpretation of seniority rights under the collective bargaining agreement. Plaintiffs had been transferred to a new location where other truckers were inactive, having already been laid off. A subsequent round of layoffs and recalls created tension in the Union between the two groups of truckers. Further layoffs and recalls prompted grievance hearings in which a union representative presented the arguments of both factions to the Grievance Committee. Ultimately, the union decided against the plaintiffs, favoring an interpretation of seniority rights that benefitted the inactive drivers. Plaintiffs then commenced suit against their employer and the union.]

■ JUSTICE MARSHALL delivered the opinion of the Court, except as to Part III–A.

This case presents the question whether an employee who seeks relief in the form of backpay for a union's alleged breach of its duty of fair representation has a right to trial by jury. We hold that the Seventh Amendment entitles such a plaintiff to a jury trial.

II

The duty of fair representation is inferred from unions' exclusive authority under the National Labor Relations Act (NLRA), . . . to represent all employees in a bargaining unit. The duty requires a union "to serve the interests of all members without hostility or discrimination toward any, to exercise its discretion with complete good faith and honesty, and to avoid arbitrary conduct." Vaca v. Sipes, 386 U.S. 171, 177, 87 S.Ct. 903, 909–910, 17 L.Ed.2d 842 (1967). A union must discharge its duty both in bargaining with the employer and in its enforcement of the resulting collective-bargaining agreement. Thus, the Union here was required to pursue respondents' grievances in a manner consistent with the principles of fair representation.

Because most collective-bargaining agreements accord finality to grievance or arbitration procedures established by the collective-bargaining agreement, an employee normally cannot bring a § 301 action against an employer unless he can show that the union breached its duty of fair representation in its handling of his grievance. Whether the employee sues both the labor union and the employer, or only one of those entities, he must prove the same two facts to recover money damages: that the employer's action violated the terms of the collective-bargaining agreement and that the union breached its duty of fair representation.

III

We turn now to the constitutional issue presented in this case—whether respondents are entitled to a jury trial. The Seventh Amendment provides that "[i]n Suits at common law, where the value in controversy shall exceed twenty dollars, the right of trial by jury shall be preserved." The right to a jury trial includes more than the common-law forms of action recognized in 1791; the phrase "Suits at common law" refers to "suits in which legal rights [are] to be ascertained and determined, in contradistinction to those where equitable rights alone [are] recognized, and equitable remedies [are] administered." Parsons v. Bedford, 3 Pet. 433, 447, 7 L.Ed. 732 (1830). . . . The right extends to causes of action created by Congress. Since the merger of the systems of law and equity, this Court has carefully preserved the right to trial by jury where legal rights are at stake. . . .

To determine whether a particular action will resolve legal rights, we examine both the nature of the issues involved and the remedy sought. "First, we compare the statutory action to 18th-century actions brought in the courts of England prior to the merger of the courts of law and equity. Second, we examine the remedy sought and determine whether it is legal or equitable in nature." Tull, supra, 481 U.S. 412, 417–418 (1987). The second inquiry is the more important in our analysis.[4]

A

An action for breach of a union's duty of fair representation was unknown in 18th-century England; in fact, collective bargaining was unlawful. We must therefore look for an analogous cause of action that existed in the 18th century to determine whether the nature of this duty of fair representation suit is legal or equitable.

---

4. Justice Stevens' analysis emphasizes a third consideration, namely whether "the issues [presented by the claim] are typical grist for the jury's judgment." This Court, however, has never relied on this consideration "as an independent bases for extending the right to a jury trial under the Seventh Amendment." Tull v. United States, 481 U.S. at 418 n.4 (1987). We recently noted that this consideration is relevant only to the determination "whether Congress has permissibly entrusted the resolution of certain disputes to an administrative agency or specialized courts of equity, and whether jury trials would impair the functioning of the legislative scheme." Granfinanciera, S.A. v. Nordberg, 492 U.S. 33, 42 n. 4.

The Union contends that this duty of fair representation action resembles a suit brought to vacate an arbitration award because respondents seek to set aside the result of the grievance process. In the 18th century, an action to set aside an arbitration award was considered equitable....

The arbitration analogy is inapposite, however, to the Seventh Amendment question posed in this case. No grievance committee has considered respondents' claim that the Union violated its duty of fair representation; the grievance process was concerned only with the employer's alleged breach of the collective-bargaining agreement....

The Union next argues that respondents' duty of fair representation action is comparable to an action by a trust beneficiary against a trustee for breach of fiduciary duty. Such actions were within the exclusive jurisdiction of courts of equity. This analogy is far more persuasive than the arbitration analogy. Just as a trustee must act in the best interests of the beneficiaries, a union, as the exclusive representative of the workers, must exercise its power to act on behalf of the employees in good faith, Vaca v. Sipes, 386 U.S. 171, 177 (1967). Moreover, just as a beneficiary does not directly control the actions of a trustee, an individual employee lacks direct control over a union's actions taken on his behalf, see Cox, The Legal Nature of Collective Bargaining Agreements.

The trust analogy extends to a union's handling of grievances. In most cases, a trustee has the exclusive authority to sue third parties who injure the beneficiaries' interest in the trust, including any legal claim the trustee holds in trust for the beneficiaries. The trustee then has the sole responsibility for determining whether to settle, arbitrate, or otherwise dispose of the claim. Similarly, the union typically has broad discretion in its decision whether and how to pursue an employee's grievance against an employer. Just as a trust beneficiary can sue to enforce a contract entered into on his behalf by the trustee only if the trustee "improperly refuses or neglects to bring an action against the third person," Restatement (Second) of Trusts, § 282(2)(1959), so an employee can sue his employer for a breach of the collective-bargaining agreement only if he shows that the union breached its duty of fair representation in its handling of the grievance.

Respondents contend that their duty of fair representation suit is less like a trust action than an attorney malpractice action, which was historically an action at law....

The attorney malpractice analogy is inadequate in several respects. Although an attorney malpractice suit is in some ways similar to a suit alleging a union's breach of its fiduciary duty, the two actions are fundamentally different. The nature of an action is in large part controlled by the nature of the underlying relationship between the parties. Unlike employees represented by a union, a client controls the significant decisions concerning his representation. Moreover, a client can fire his attorney if he is dissatisfied with his attorney's performance. This option is not available to an individual employee who is unhappy with a union's representation, unless a majority of the members of the bargaining unit share his dissatisfaction. Thus, we find the malpractice analogy less convincing than the trust analogy.

Nevertheless, the trust analogy does not persuade us to characterize respondents' claim as wholly equitable. The Union's argument mischaracterizes the nature of our comparison of the action before us to 18th-century forms of action. As we observed in Ross v. Bernhard, 396 U.S. 531 (1970), "The Seventh Amendment question depends on the nature of the *issue* to be tried rather than the character of the overall action." Id. at 538 (emphasis added). As discussed above, to recover from the Union here, respondents must prove both that McLean violated § 301 by breaching the collective-bargaining agreement and that the Union breached its duty of fair representation.[6] When viewed in isolation, the duty of fair representation issue is analogous to a claim against a trustee for breach of fiduciary duty. The § 301 issue, however, is comparable to a breach of contract claim—a legal issue.

Respondents' action against the Union thus encompasses both equitable and legal issues. The first part of our Seventh Amendment inquiry, then, leaves us in equipoise as to whether respondents are entitled to a jury trial.

B

Our determination under the first part of the Seventh Amendment analysis is only preliminary. In this case, the only remedy sought is a request for compensatory damages representing backpay and benefits. Generally, an action for money damages was "the traditional form of relief offered in the courts of law." Curtis v. Loether, 415 U.S. 189, 196 (1974). This Court has not, however, held that "any award of monetary relief must *necessarily* be 'legal' relief." Id. (emphasis added). Nonetheless, because we conclude that the remedy respondents seek has none of the attributes that must be present before we will find an exception to the general rule and characterize damages as equitable, we find that the remedy sought by respondents is legal.

First, we have characterized damages as equitable where they are restitutionary, such as in "action[s] for disgorgement of improper profits," *Tull*, 481 U.S. at 424. The backpay sought by respondents is not money wrongfully held by the Union, but wages and benefits they would have received from McLean had the Union processed the employees' grievances properly. Such relief is not restitutionary.

Second, a monetary award "incidental to or intertwined with injunctive relief" may be equitable. *Tull*, 481 U.S. at 424. See, e.g., Mitchell v. Robert DeMario Jewelry, Inc., 361 U.S. 288, 291–292, 80 S.Ct. 332, 334–

---

6. The dissent characterizes this opinion as "pars[ing] legal elements out of equitable claims." The question whether the Seventh Amendment analysis requires an examination of the nature of each element of a typical claim is not presented by this case. The claim we confront here is not typical; instead, it is a claim consisting of discrete issues that would normally be brought as two claims, one against the employer and one against the union. Had the employer re-

mained a defendant in this action, the dissent would surely agree that the § 301 claim against the employer was a separate claim. The Seventh Amendment analysis should not turn on the ability of the plaintiff to maintain his suit against both defendants, when the issues in the suit remain the same even when he can sue only the union. Consideration of the nature of the two issues in this hybrid action is therefore warranted.

335, 4 L.Ed.2d 323 (1960)(District Court had power, incident to its injunctive powers, to award backpay under the Fair Labor Standards Act; also backpay in that case was restitutionary). Because respondents seek only money damages, this characteristic is clearly absent from the case.[8]

The Union argues that the backpay relief sought here must nonetheless be considered equitable because this Court has labeled backpay awarded under Title VII, of the Civil Rights Act of 1964, 42 U.S.C. § 2000e et seq. (1982), as equitable. It contends that the Title VII analogy is compelling in the context of the duty of fair representation because the Title VII backpay provision was based on the NLRA provision governing backpay awards for unfair labor practices, 29 U.S.C. § 160(c)(1982). We are not convinced.

The Court has never held that a plaintiff seeking backpay under Title VII has a right to a jury trial. Assuming, without deciding, that such a Title VII plaintiff has no right to a jury trial, the Union's argument does not persuade us that respondents are not entitled to a jury trial here. Congress specifically characterized backpay under Title VII as a form of "equitable relief." 42 U.S.C. § 2000e–5(g)(1982). Congress made no similar pronouncement regarding the duty of fair representation. Furthermore, the Court has noted that backpay sought from an employer under Title VII would generally be restitutionary in nature, in contrast to the damages sought here from the Union. Thus, the remedy sought in this duty of fair representation case is clearly different from backpay sought for violations of Title VII.

Moreover, the fact that Title VII's backpay provision may have been modeled on a provision in the NLRA concerning remedies for unfair labor practices does not require that the backpay remedy available here be considered equitable. The Union apparently reasons that if Title VII is comparable to one labor law remedy it is comparable to all remedies available in the NLRA context. Although both the duty of fair representation and the unfair labor practice provisions of the NLRA are components of national labor policy, their purposes are not identical.... Thus, the remedies appropriate for unfair labor practices may differ from the remedies for a breach of the duty of fair representation, given the need to vindicate different goals. Certainly, the connection between backpay under Title VII and damages under the unfair labor practice provision of the

---

8. Both the Union and the dissent argue that the backpay award sought here is equitable because it is closely analogous to damages awarded to beneficiaries for a trustee's breach of trust. Such damages were available only in courts of equity because those courts had exclusive jurisdiction over actions involving a trustee's breach of his fiduciary duties. The Union's argument, however, conflates the two parts of our Seventh Amendment inquiry. Under the dissent's approach, if the action at issue were analogous to an 18th-century action within the exclusive jurisdiction of the courts of equity, we would necessarily conclude that the remedy sought was also equitable because it would have been unavailable in a court of law. This view would, in effect, make the first part of our inquiry dispositive. We have clearly held, however, that the second part of the inquiry—the nature of the relief—is more important to the Seventh Amendment determination. The second part of the analysis, therefore, should not replicate the "abstruse historical" inquiry of the first part, Ross v. Bernhard, 396 U.S. 531, 538 n. 10 (1970), but requires consideration of the general types of relief provided by courts of law and equity.

NLRA does not require us to find a parallel connection between Title VII backpay and money damages for breach of the duty of fair representation.

We hold, then, that the remedy of backpay sought in this duty of fair representation action is legal in nature. Considering both parts of the Seventh Amendment inquiry, we find that respondents are entitled to a jury trial on all issues presented in their suit.

IV

On balance, our analysis of the nature of respondents' duty of fair representation action and the remedy they seek convinces us that this action is a legal one. Although the search for an adequate 18th-century analog revealed that the claim includes both legal and equitable issues, the money damages respondents seek are the type of relief traditionally awarded by courts of law. Thus, the Seventh Amendment entitles respondents to a jury trial, and we therefore affirm the judgment of the Court of Appeals.

■ JUSTICE BRENNAN, concurring,

I agree with the Court that respondents seek a remedy that is legal in nature and that the Seventh Amendment entitles respondents to a jury trial on their duty of fair representation claims. I therefore join Parts I, II, III–B, and IV of the Court's opinion. I do not join that part of the opinion which reprises the particular historical analysis this Court has employed to determine whether a claim is a "Sui[t] at common law" under the Seventh Amendment, because I believe the historical test can and should be simplified.

The current test, first expounded in Curtis v. Loether, 415 U.S. 189, 194 (1974), requires a court to compare the right at issue to 18th-century English forms of action to determine whether the historically analogous right was vindicated in an action at law or in equity, and to examine whether the remedy sought is legal or equitable in nature. However, this Court, in expounding the test, has repeatedly discounted the significance of the analogous form of action for deciding where the Seventh Amendment applies. I think it is time we dispense with it altogether. I would decide Seventh Amendment questions on the basis of the relief sought. If the relief is legal in nature, i.e., if it is the kind of relief that historically was available from courts of law, I would hold that the parties have a constitutional right to a trial by jury—unless Congress has permissibly delegated the particular dispute to a non-Article III decisionmaker and jury trials would frustrate Congress' purposes in enacting a particular statutory scheme.

I believe that our insistence that the jury trial right hinges in part on a comparison of the substantive right at issue to forms of action used in English courts 200 years ago needlessly convolutes our Seventh Amendment jurisprudence. For the past decade and a half, this Court has explained that the two parts of the historical test are not equal in weight, that the nature of the remedy is more important than the nature of the right. Since the existence of a right to jury trial therefore turns on the nature of the remedy, absent congressional delegation to a specialized decisionmaker, there remains little purpose to our rattling through dusty attics of ancient writs. The time has come to borrow William of Occam's razor and sever this portion of our analysis.

We have long acknowledged that, of the factors relevant to the jury trial right, comparison of the claim to ancient forms of action, "requiring extensive and possibly abstruse historical inquiry, is obviously the most difficult to apply." Ross v. Bernhard, 396 U.S. 531, 538 n. 10 (1970). Requiring judges, with neither the training nor time necessary for reputable historical scholarship, to root through the tangle of primary and secondary sources to determine which of a hundred or so writs is analogous to the right at issue has embroiled courts in recondite controversies better left to legal historians. . . .

To be sure, it is neither unusual nor embarrassing for members of a court to disagree and disagree vehemently. But it better behooves judges to disagree within the province of judicial expertise. Furthermore, inquiries into the appropriate historical analogs for the rights at issue are not necessarily susceptible of sound resolution under the best of circumstances. . . .

In addition, modern statutory rights did not exist in the 18th century, and even the most exacting historical research may not elicit a clear historical analog. The right at issue here, for example, is a creature of modern labor law quite foreign to Georgian England. . . . I have grappled with this kind of inquiry for three decades on this Court and have come to the realization that engaging in such inquiries is impracticable and unilluminating.

To rest the historical test required by the Seventh Amendment solely on the nature of the relief sought would not, of course, offer the federal courts a rule that is in all cases self-executing. Courts will still be required to ask which remedies were traditionally available at law and which only in equity. But this inquiry involves fewer variables and simpler choices, on the whole, and is far more manageable than the scholasticist debates in which we have been engaged. . . .

This is not to say that the resulting division between claims entitled to jury trials and claims not so entitled would exactly mirror the division between law and equity in England in 1791. But it is too late in the day for this Court to profess that the Seventh Amendment preserves the right to jury trial only in cases that would have been heard in the British law courts of the 18th century.

Indeed, given this Court's repeated insistence that the nature of the remedy is always to be given more weight than the nature of the historically analogous right, it is unlikely that the simplified Seventh Amendment analysis I propose will result in different decisions than the analysis in current use. In the unusual circumstance that the nature of the remedy could be characterized equally as legal or equitable, I submit that the comparison of a contemporary statutory action unheard of in the 18th century to some ill-fitting ancient writ is too shaky a basis for the resolution of an issue as significant as the availability of a trial by jury. If, in the rare case, a tie breaker is needed, let us break the tie in favor of jury trial. . . .

■ JUSTICE STEVENS, concurring.

Because I believe the Court has made this case unnecessarily difficult by exaggerating the importance of finding a precise common-law analogue to the duty of fair representation, I do not join Part III–A of its opinion. Ironically, by stressing the importance of identifying an exact analogue, the Court has diminished the utility of looking for any analogue.

As I have suggested in the past, I believe the duty of fair representation action resembles a common-law action against an attorney for malpractice more closely than it does any other form of action. Of course, this action is not an exact counterpart to a malpractice suit. Indeed, by definition, no recently recognized form of action—whether the product of express congressional enactment or of judicial interpretation—can have a precise analogue in 17th-or 18th-century English law. Were it otherwise the form of action would not in fact be "recently recognized."

But the Court surely overstates this action's similarity to an action against a trustee. Collective bargaining involves no settlor, no trust corpus, and no trust instrument executed to convey property to beneficiaries chosen at the settlor's pleasure.... Beneficiaries are protected from their own judgment. The attorney-client relationship, by contrast, advances the client's interests in dealings with adverse parties. Clients are saved from their lack of skill, but their judgment is honored. Union members, as a group, accordingly have the power to hire, fire, and direct the actions of their representatives—prerogatives anathema to the paternalistic forms of the equitable trust....

In most duty of fair representation cases, the issues, which require an understanding of the realities of employment relationships, are typical grist for the jury's judgment. Indeed, the law defining the union's duty of fair representation has developed in cases tried to juries....

Duty of fair representation suits are for the most part ordinary civil actions involving the stuff of contract and malpractice disputes. There is accordingly no ground for excluding these actions from the jury right....

I therefore join [in the] opinion except for Part III–A.

■ JUSTICE KENNEDY, with whom JUSTICE O'CONNOR and JUSTICE SCALIA join, dissenting.

This case asks whether the Seventh Amendment guarantees the respondent union members a jury trial in a duty of fair representation action against their labor union. The Court is quite correct, in my view, in its formulation of the initial premises that must govern the case. Under Curtis v. Loether, 415 U.S. 189, 194 (1974), the right to a jury trial in a statutory action depends on the presence of "legal rights and remedies." To determine whether rights and remedies in a duty of fair representation action are legal in character, we must compare the action to the 18th-century cases permitted in the law courts of England, and we must examine the nature of the relief sought. I agree also with those Members of the Court who find that the duty of fair representation action resembles an equitable trust action more than a suit for malpractice.

I disagree with the analytic innovation of the Court that identification of the trust action as a model for modern duty of fair representation actions is insufficient to decide the case. The Seventh Amendment requires us to determine whether the duty of fair representation action "is more similar to cases that were tried in courts of law than to suits tried in courts of equity." Tull v. United States, 481 U.S. 412, 417 (1987). Having made this decision in favor of an equitable action, our inquiry should end. Because the Court disagrees with this proposition, I dissent.

I

Both the Union and the respondents identify historical actions to which they find the duty of fair representation action most analogous. The Union contends that the action resembles a traditional equitable suit by a beneficiary against a trustee for failing to pursue a claim that he holds in trust. In other words, the Union compares itself to a trustee that, in its discretion, has decided not to press certain claims. The respondents argue that the duty of fair representation action resembles a traditional legal malpractice suit by a client against his lawyer for mishandling a claim. They contend that the Union, when acting as their legal representative, had a duty to press their grievances.

JUSTICE MARSHALL, speaking for four Members of the Court, states an important and correct reason for finding the trust model better than the malpractice analogy. He observes that the client of an attorney, unlike a union member or beneficiary, controls the significant decisions concerning his litigation and can fire the attorney if not satisfied. Put another way, although a lawyer acts as an agent of his client, unions and trustees do not serve as agents of their members and beneficiaries in the conventional sense of being subject to their direction and control in pursuing claims. An individual union member cannot require his union to pursue a claim and cannot choose a different representative. A trustee, likewise, may exercise proper discretion in deciding whether to press claims held in trust.

Further considerations fortify the conclusion that the trust analogy is the controlling one here. A union's duty of fair representation accords with a trustee's duty of impartiality. The duty of fair representation requires a union "to make an honest effort to serve the interests of all of [its] members, without hostility to any." Ford Motor Co. v. Huffman, 345 U.S. 330, 337 (1953). This standard may require a union to act for the benefit of employees who, as in this case, have antithetical interests.

A lawyer's duty of loyalty is cast in different terms. Although the union is charged with the responsibility of reconciling the positions of its members, the lawyer's duty of loyalty long has precluded the representation of conflicting interests. A lawyer, at least absent knowing waiver by the parties, could not represent both the respondents and the senior laid off workers as the Union has done in this case.

The relief available in a duty of fair representation action also makes the trust action the better model. To remedy a breach of the duty of fair representation, a court must issue an award "fashioned to make the injured employee whole." Electrical Workers v. Foust, 442 U.S. 42, 49 (1979). The court may order an injunction compelling the union, if it is still able, to pursue the employee's claim, and may require monetary compensation, but it cannot award exemplary or punitive damages. This relief parallels the remedies prevailing in the courts of equity in actions against trustees for failing to pursue claims.

These remedies differ somewhat from those available in attorney malpractice actions. . . .

For all these reasons, the suit here resembles a trust action, not a legal malpractice action. By this I do not imply that a union acts as a trustee in all instances or that trust law, as a general matter, should inform any particular aspects of federal labor law. Obvious differences between a union and a trustee will exist in other contexts. I would conclude only that, under the analysis directed by our precedents, the respondents may not insist on a jury trial. When all rights and remedies are considered, their action resembles a suit heard by the courts of equity more than a case heard by the courts of law. From this alone it follows that the respondents have no jury trial right on their duty of fair representation claims against the Union.

II

The Court relies on two lines of precedents to overcome the conclusion that the trust action should serve as the controlling model. The first consists of cases in which the Court has considered simplifications in litigation resulting from modern procedural reforms in the federal courts. Justice Marshall asserts that these cases show that the Court must look at the character of individual issues rather than claims as a whole. The second line addresses the significance of the remedy in determining the equitable or legal nature of an action for the purpose of choosing the most appropriate analogy. Under these cases, the Court decides that the respondents have a right to a jury because they seek money damages. These authorities do not support the Court's holding.

A

In three cases we have found a right to trial by jury where there are legal claims that, for procedural reasons, a plaintiff could have or must have raised in the courts of equity before the systems merged. In Beacon Theatres, Inc. v. Westover, 359 U.S. 500 (1959), Fox, a potential defendant threatened with legal antitrust claims, brought an action for declaratory and injunctive relief against Beacon, the likely plaintiff. Because only the courts of equity had offered such relief prior to the merger of the two court systems, Fox had thought that it could deprive Beacon of a jury trial. Beacon, however, raised the antitrust issues as counterclaims and sought a jury. We ruled that, because Beacon would have had a right to a jury trial on its antitrust claims, Fox could not deprive it of a jury merely by taking advantage of modern declaratory procedures to sue first. The result was consistent with the spirit of the Federal Rules of Civil Procedure, which allow liberal joinder of legal and equitable actions, and the Declaratory Judgment Act, 28 U.S.C. §§ 2201, 2202 (1982), which preserves the right to jury trial to both parties.

In Dairy Queen, Inc. v. Wood, 369 U.S. 469 (1962), we held, in a similar manner, that a plaintiff, by asking in his complaint for an equitable accounting for trademark infringement, could not deprive the defendant of a jury trial on contract claims subsumed within the accounting. Although a court of equity would have heard the contract claims as part of the accounting suit, we found them severable under modern procedure.

In Ross v. Bernhard, 396 U.S. 531 (1970), a shareholder-plaintiff demanded a jury trial in a derivative action asserting a legal claim on behalf of his corporation. The defendant opposed a jury trial. In deciding the case, we recognized that only the courts of equity had procedural devices allowing shareholders to raise a corporation's claims. We nonetheless again ruled that modern procedure allowed trial of the legal claim to a jury.

These three cases responded to the difficulties created by a merged court system. They stand for the proposition that, because distinct courts of equity no longer exist, the possibility or necessity of using former equitable procedures to press a legal claim no longer will determine the right to a jury. Justice Marshall reads these cases to require a jury trial whenever a cause of action contains legal issues and would require a jury trial in this case because the respondents must prove a breach of the collective-bargaining agreement as one element of their claim.

I disagree. The respondents, as shown above, are asserting an equitable claim. Having reached this conclusion, the Beacon, Dairy Queen, and Ross cases are inapplicable. Although we have divided self-standing legal claims from equitable declaratory, accounting, and derivative procedures, we have never parsed legal elements out of equitable claims absent specific procedural justifications. Actions which, beyond all question, are equitable in nature may involve some predicate inquiry that would be submitted to a jury in other contexts. For example, just as the plaintiff in a duty of fair representation action against his union must show breach of the collective-bargaining agreement as an initial matter, in an action against a trustee for failing to pursue a claim the beneficiary must show that the claim had some merit. But the question of the claim's validity, even if the claim raises contract issues, would not bring the jury right into play in a suit against a trustee. . . .

We have not deemed the elements of a duty of fair representation action to be independent of each other. Proving breach of the collective-bargaining agreement is but a preliminary and indispensable step to obtaining relief in a duty of fair representation action. . . . The absence of distinct equitable courts provides no procedural reason for wresting one of these elements from the other.

B

The Court also rules that, despite the appropriateness of the trust analogy as a whole, the respondents have a right to a jury trial because they seek money damages. The nature of the remedy remains a factor of considerable importance in determining whether a statutory action had a legal or equitable analog in 1791, but we have not adopted a rule that a statutory action permitting damages is by definition more analogous to a legal action than to any equitable suit. In each case, we look to the remedy to determine whether, taken with other factors, it places an action within the definition of "Suits at common law."

In *Curtis*, 415 U.S. at 195–196, for example, we ruled that the availability of actual and punitive damages made a statutory antidiscrimination action resemble a legal tort action more than any equitable action. We made explicit that we did not "go so far as to say that any award of monetary relief must necessarily be 'legal' relief." Id. at 196. Although monetary damages might cause some statutory actions to resemble tort suits, the presence of monetary damages in this duty of fair representation action does not make it more analogous to a legal action than to an equitable action. Indeed, as shown above, the injunctive and monetary remedies available make the duty of fair representation suit less analogous to a malpractice action than to a suit against a trustee.

In *Tull*, 481 U.S. at 422, the availability of damages again played a critical role in determining the right to a jury trial. In an environmental suit by the Government for injunctive relief and a civil penalty, both an equitable public nuisance action and a legal action in debt seemed appropriate historical models. We decided between them by noting that only the courts of law could award civil penalties. In the present case, however, one cannot characterize both the trust analogy and the legal malpractice comparisons as appropriate; the considerations discussed above, including the remedy available, all make the trust model superior. As we stated in Tull, "[o]ur search is for a single historical analog, taking into consideration the nature of the cause of action and the remedy as two important factors." Id. at 421 n. 6. The trust action alone satisfies this standard.

In Granfinanciera, S.A. v. Nordberg, 492 U.S. 33 (1989), we again found the presence of monetary relief critical in determining the nature of a statutory action as a whole. We held that, despite some evidence that both the courts of law and equity had jurisdiction over fraudulent conveyances, only a court of law could entertain an action to recover an alleged fraudulent transfer of a determinate sum of money. As in *Curtis* and *Tull*, however, the particular importance of monetary damages in *Granfinanciera* does not carry forward into this case. The courts of equity could and did award the kind of damages sought by the respondents here. The respondents' mere request for backpay in no way entitles them to a jury under the Seventh Amendment.

III

The Court must adhere to the historical test in determining the right to a jury because the language of the Constitution requires it. The Seventh Amendment "preserves" the right to jury trial in civil cases. We cannot preserve a right existing in 1791 unless we look to history to identify it. Our precedents are in full agreement with this reasoning and insist on adherence to the historical test. No alternatives short of rewriting the Constitution exist. If we abandon the plain language of the Constitution to expand the jury right, we may expect Courts with opposing views to curtail it in the future.

It is true that a historical inquiry into the distinction between law and equity may require us to enter into a domain becoming less familiar with time. Two centuries have passed since the Seventh Amendment's ratification, and the incompleteness of our historical records makes it difficult to know the nature of certain actions in 1791. The historical test, nonetheless, has received more criticism than it deserves. Although our application of the analysis in some cases may seem biased in favor of jury trials, the test has not become a nullity. We do not require juries in all statutory actions. The historical test, in fact, resolves most cases without difficulty.

I would hesitate to abandon or curtail the historical test out of concern for the competence of the Court to understand legal history. We do look to history for the answers to constitutional questions. Although opinions will differ on what this history shows, the approach has no less validity in the Seventh Amendment context than elsewhere.

IV

Because of the employer's bankruptcy, the respondents are proceeding only against the Union in the suit before us. In a typical duty of fair representation action, however, union members may sue both their union and their employer. The Union argues that a duty of fair representation action against an employer also would have an equitable character because it resembles another trust action entertained in the courts of equity. It contends that, if a trustee fails to pursue a claim according to his duty, the beneficiary may join the trustee and the third party in one action and assert in his own name both the claim of breach of fiduciary duty and the claim against the third party. In this case, we do not have to determine the correctness of this analogy, nor must we decide whether Beacon, Dairy Queen, or Ross would require a jury trial in a suit against an employer. I would deny a jury trial to the respondents here, but would leave these other questions for a later time. Because the Court has reached a different result, I dissent.

NOTES ON THE RIGHT TO TRIAL BY JURY

1. Under the Federal Rules of Civil Procedure a right to a jury trial is preserved and may be waived:

Rule 38. Jury Trial of Right

(a) Right Preserved. The right of trial by jury as declared by the Seventh Amendment to the Constitution or as given by a statute of the United States shall be preserved to the parties inviolate.

(b) Demand. Any party may demand a trial by jury of any issue triable of right by a jury by (1) serving upon the other parties a demand therefor in writing at any time after the commencement of the action and not later than 10 days after the service of the last pleading directed to such issue, and (2) filing the demand as required by Rule 5(d). Such demand may be indorsed upon a pleading of the party

(c) Same: Specification of Issues. In the demand a party may specify the issues which the party wishes so tried; otherwise the party shall be deemed to have demanded trial by jury for all the issues so triable. If the party has demanded trial by jury for only some of the issues, any other party within 10 days after service of the demand or such lesser time as the court may order, may serve a demand for trial by jury of any other or all of the issues of fact in the action.

(d) Waiver. The failure of a party to serve and file a demand as required by this rule constitutes a waiver by the party of trial by jury. A demand for trial by jury made as herein provided may not be withdrawn without the consent of the parties.

(e) Admiralty and Maritime Claims. These rules shall not be construed to create a right to trial by jury of the issues in an admiralty or maritime claim within the meaning of Rule 9(h).

If there is no right to a jury trial or that right has been waived, a jury may nonetheless be used to help decide the case:

Rule 39.   Trial by Jury or by the Court

(a) By Jury. When trial by jury has been demanded as provided in Rule 38, the action shall be designated upon the docket as a jury action. The trial of all issues so demanded shall be by jury, unless (1) the parties or their attorneys of record, by written stipulation filed with the court or by an oral stipulation made in open court and entered in the record, consent to trial by the court sitting without a jury or (2) the court upon motion or of its own initiative finds that a right of trial by jury of some or all of those issues does not exist under the Constitution or statutes of the United States.

(b) By the Court. Issues not demanded for trial by jury as provided in Rule 38 shall be tried by the court; but, notwithstanding the failure of a party to demand a jury in an action in which such a demand might have been made of right, the court in its discretion upon motion may order a trial by a jury of any or all issues.

(c) Advisory Jury and Trial by Consent. In all actions not triable of right by a jury the court upon motion or of its own initiative may try any issue with an advisory jury or, except in actions against the United States when a statute of the United States provides for trial without a jury, the court, with the consent of both parties, may order a trial with a jury whose verdict has the same effect as if trial by jury had been a matter of right.

2.   A plaintiff asserting a substantive legal claim may demand a jury trial even though the procedure for commencing the action is deemed equitable. Ross v. Bernhard, 396 U.S. 531, 90 S.Ct. 733, 24 L.Ed.2d 729 (1970)(plaintiff asserting legal claim in a shareholder's derivative action entitled to jury trial notwithstanding equitable procedure for commencing suit). Similarly, a defendant will not be denied a jury trial simply because the plaintiff has commenced an equitable action. Beacon Theatres, Inc. v. Westover, 359 U.S. 500, 79 S.Ct. 948, 3 L.Ed.2d 988 (1959) (plaintiff used equitable procedural device of declaratory judgment action to deprive

adversary of a jury trial on antitrust claims), or because the plaintiff has cloaked legal claims within an equitable proceeding. Dairy Queen, Inc. v. Wood, 369 U.S. 469, 82 S.Ct. 894, 8 L.Ed.2d 44 (1962)(plaintiff's request for an equitable accounting for trademark infringement could not deprive the defendant of a jury trial on contract claims subsumed within the accounting). Prior to *Beacon Theatres* and *Dairy Queen* federal courts hearing equitable actions exercised "clean up" or incidental jurisdiction to decide related legal claims. For example, the clean up doctrine permitted a court granting an injunction against further patent infringement to simultaneously award damages for the defendant's misconduct. The *Beacon* and *Dairy Queen* decisions curbed this practice at the federal level by forcing a closer examination of cases with both equitable and legal claims to insure that the clean up doctrine did not deprive litigants of their constitutional right to a trial by jury.

3.   An equitable action may typically precede a legal action in which the triable issues are identical. In such a circumstance the judge's decision as to the equitable action will have a preclusive effect on the latter without offending the seventh amendment. Parklane Hosiery Company, Inc. v. Shore, 439 U.S. 322, 99 S.Ct. 645, 58 L.Ed.2d 552 (1979). In *Parklane* plaintiffs sued defendant corporation after the Securities and Exchange Commission had obtained a declaratory judgment against the same defendant. In the second action, the defendant did not have the right to relitigate the same issues before a jury.

When a plaintiff presses both legal and equitable claims, and nothing requires the equitable claim to precede the legal claim, the claims should be severed and the legal claim tried to a jury first. In Lytle v. Household Manufacturing, Inc., 494 U.S. 545, 110 S.Ct. 1331, 108 L.Ed.2d 504 (1990), the plaintiff was entitled to sever her § 1981 (legal) claims and present them to a jury before her Title VII (equitable) claims were heard by the Judge. In *Lytle* the trial judge had erroneously dismissed plaintiffs § 1981 claims without submitting them to a jury.

4.   "[T]he seventh amendment is generally inapplicable in administrative proceedings, where jury trials would be incompatible with the whole concept of administrative adjudication." Curtis v. Loether, 415 U.S. 189, 194, 94 S.Ct. 1005, 1008, 39 L.Ed.2d 260 (1974). In *Curtis*, however, the Court unanimously held that the defendant had a right to a jury trial because the enforcement of statutory rights (the fair housing provisions of the Civil Rights Act of 1968) had been committed to a *court*, not an *agency*. In Atlas Roofing Co. v. Occupational Safety and Health Review Commission, 430 U.S. 442, 97 S.Ct. 1261, 51 L.Ed.2d 464 (1977), enforcement of statutory penalties was committed to an agency, and therefore, the defendant had no right to a jury trial. In answer to the argument that Congress could "utterly destroy the right to a jury trial by always providing for administrative rather than judicial resolution of a vast range of cases," *Id.* at 457, 97 S.Ct. at 1270, the Court distinguished between public and private rights: the seventh amendment would be inapplicable only when Congress assigned public rights to an agency, but the amendment would retain its full force for "[w]holly private tort, contract, and property cases . . ." *Id.* at 458, 97 S.Ct. at 1271.

5.   Parties that are within the equitable jurisdiction of a bankruptcy court generally do not have a right to a jury trial. Langenkamp v. Culp, 498 U.S. 42, 111 S.Ct. 330, 112 L.Ed.2d 343 (1990); Katchen v. Landy, 382 U.S. 323, 86 S.Ct. 467, 15 L.Ed.2d 391 (1966). In Granfinanciera, S.A. v. Nordberg, 492 U.S. 33, 109 S.Ct. 2782, 106 L.Ed.2d 26 (1989) the Court held that a nonparty to a Bankruptcy action, (i.e., neither a debtor, creditor or trustee of the estate), pursued by a party to recover fraudulent transfers or unlawful preferences, is nonetheless entitled to a jury trial.

6.   Tull v. United States, 481 U.S. 412, 107 S.Ct. 1831, 95 L.Ed.2d 365 (1987), held that the seventh amendment applies to an action seeking civil penalties under the federal Clean Water Act. The Court stated that the relief sought "was a type of remedy at common law that could only be enforced in courts of law." The court in dictum, in a portion of the decision that has been criticized by scholars, intimated that the defendant did not have a right to have a jury determine the amount of damages. This dictum appears to have been cast aside by the Court's decision in Feltner v. Columbia Pictures Television, 523 U.S. 340, 118 S.Ct. 1279, 140 L.Ed.2d 438 (1998), described in the following note, in which the Court explained that damages have always been for the jury.

7.   Section 504(c) of the Copyright Act permits a copyright owner "to recover, instead of actual damages and profits, an award of statutory damages, in a sum of not less than $500 or more than $20,000 as the court considers just." In 1998 the Supreme Court considered whether Section 504(c) or the Seventh Amendment grants a right to a jury trial when a copyright owner elects to recover statutory damages. The court held that although the statute is silent on the point, the Seventh Amendment provides a right to a jury trial, which includes a right to a jury determination of the amount of statutory damages.

Justice Thomas writing for the Court stated:

The Seventh Amendment provides that "[i]n Suits at common law where the value in controversy shall exceed twenty dollars, the right of trial by jury shall be preserved * * *." Since Justice Story's time, the Court has understood "Suits at common law" to refer "not merely [to] suits, which the common law recognized among its old and settled proceedings, but [to] suits in which legal rights were to be ascertained and determined, in contradistinction to those where equitable rights alone were recognized, and equitable remedies were administered." Parsons v. Bedford, 3 Pet. 433, 447 (1830). The Seventh Amendment thus applies not only to common-law causes of action, but also to "actions brought to enforce statutory rights that are analogous to common-law causes of action ordinarily decided in English law courts in the late 18th century, as opposed to those customarily heard by courts of equity or admiralty." Granfinanciera, S.A. v. Nordberg, 492 U.S. 33, 42 (1989). To determine whether a statutory action is more analogous to cases tried in courts of law than to suits tried in courts of equity or admiralty, we examine both the nature of the statutory action and the remedy sought.

Feltner v. Columbia Pictures Television, 523 U.S. 370, 118 S.Ct. 1279, 140 L.Ed.2d 438 (1998).

8.   The issues in an action commenced under 42 U.S.C. § 1983 seeking legal relief in the form of money damages for an unconstitutional denial of just compensation are for the jury. City of Monterey v. Del Monte Dunes, Ltd., 526 U.S. 687, 119 S.Ct. 1624, 143 L.Ed.2d 882 (1999) (plurality opinion). In *Del Monte*, a property owner brought a § 1983 action alleging that a municipality's repeated rejection of proposals for development violated the property owner's equal protection and due process rights, and effected a regulatory taking. In a concurring opinion, Justice Scalia stated, "In my view, all § 1983 actions must be treated alike insofar as the Seventh Amendment right to jury trial is concerned; that right exists when monetary damages are sought; and the issues submitted to the jury in the present case were properly sent there." 119 S.Ct. at 1645.

CHAPTER 3

POWERS OF COURTS OF EQUITY

A. ENFORCEMENT OF EQUITABLE DECREES

1. NOTICE

The Cape May and Schellinger's Landing Railroad Co. v. Johnson

Court of Chancery of New Jersey, 1882.
35 N.J.Eq. 422.

■ VAN FLEET, V.C. The defendants are before the court on a charge of contempt. On the 20th day of June, 1881, an order was made directing the city council of the city of Cape May to desist and refrain from passing a certain ordinance, and also to show cause, at a subsequent day, why an injunction should not issue restraining the same act. The order was granted at Newark about midday on the day of its date. The council, it was understood, were to meet on the evening of the same day for the purpose of doing the act which the order was intended to restrain. The distance between the point where the order was made and the point where the defendants were to meet, rendered an actual service of the order impossible before the next day. Notice of the fact that an order had been made prohibiting the passage of the ordinance was sent to the president of the council by telegraph, which he received before the council convened on the evening of the 20th, and afterwards read to the council in open meeting. A special messenger, sent by the complainants, gave the council the same notice while they were in session on the evening of the 20th. The council the next day (June 21st) passed the ordinance.

The facts just stated are undisputed. They show that the defendants are guilty. The regularity, validity or correctness of the order contemned cannot be examined on this proceeding. While an order of a court remains in force it must be obeyed. Even if it was improvidently granted or irregularly obtained, it must nevertheless be respected until it is annulled by the proper authority. The rule upon this subject has been laid down with great clearness and force by Lord Truro. He says: "It is an established rule of this court that it is not open to any party to question the orders of this court, or any process issued under the authority of this court, by disobedience. I know of no act which this court may do which may not be questioned in a proper form and on a proper application; but I am of opinion that it is not competent for any one . . . to disobey an injunction, or any other order of the court, on the ground that such orders were made improvidently. Parties must take a proper course to question their validity, but while they exist they must be obeyed. I consider the rule to be of such

90

importance to the interests and safety of the public, and to the due administration of justice, that it ought on all occasions to be inflexibly maintained.".....

The notice that the defendants had of the order, at the time they violated the command, was, according to the authorities, entirely sufficient. Where the charge is that the defendant has willfully contemned the authority of the court, all that need be shown is that he knew of the existence of the order at the time he violated it.... Lord Eldon held that if a defendant is in court when an injunction is granted, he has sufficient notice of it to make it his duty to respect it. He also held that if the defendant is not in court when an order for an injunction is made, but is informed that such an order has been made, by a person who was in court when the order was made, he has sufficient notice of the injunction to render him liable to punishment for its breach....

Notice given by telegraph has recently been adjudged in England to be sufficient. The solicitor of the party obtaining the injunction, immediately after it was granted, notified the defendant, by telegram, that an injunction had been granted. The defendant disregarded the notice, and proceeded to do what the notice informed him he had been commanded not to do. The defendant was brought before the court on a charge of contempt, and Bacon, V.C., held that the telegram constituted sufficient notice, and adjudged the defendant guilty of contempt.

Notice, to be sufficient, need possess but two requisites—first, it must proceed from a source entitled to credit; and second, it must inform the defendant clearly and plainly from what act he must abstain. The notice in the case under consideration possessed both requisites. It was sent by the counsel who obtained the order, and it not only informed the defendants what act the order prohibited, but warned them, if they disregarded the order, their disobedience would be a contempt of the authority of the court. There is nothing in the conduct of the defendants indicating that they had the least doubt concerning the authenticity of the notice or the truth of its contents. They made no inquiry respecting its authenticity or its truth, but say that they consulted counsel whether or not they could safely disregard it, and were advised that they could. This advice, to say the least of it, was both injudicious and dangerous. It affords the defendants neither justification nor palliation. They must be adjudged guilty of contempt.

The complainants, since the proceeding for contempt was instituted, have voluntarily brought the order to show cause why an injunction should not issue to hearing, and it has been decided against them. While the fact that the order contemned was improvidently or erroneously made, neither justifies nor excuses the defendants, it is a matter which it is proper the court should consider in awarding punishment.

Each of the six defendants must pay to the clerk, for the use of the state, a fine of $10, and they must also jointly pay the taxed costs of this proceeding.

2. PERSONS BOUND BY THE DECREE

Lord Wellesley v. Earl of Mornington

Chancery, 1848.
11 Beavan 180, 50 Eng.Rep. 786.

The plaintiff, having failed in his motion to commit [(i.e., imprison)] Mr. Batley for a breach of the injunction, which applied to the Earl only, and not to his agents, now moved to commit him for the contempt, in being party and privy to, and in aiding and assisting the breach of the injunction, which restrained the defendant, the Earl of Mornington, from cutting timber, & c., Batley at the time knowing that these acts were forbidden.

It was proved that Batley, who was the agent and manager of the Earl, from the time of granting the injunction in 1846, had cut trees and underwood, and appropriated the produce to the purposes of the Earl, and that he had interfered in letting the property and taking fines [(payments from tenants to lords)]. All these acts were in breach of the injunction, and some of them had been done after Batley had been served with clear and distinct notice of the terms of the injunction.

Mr. Roupell and *Mr. Heathfield,* in support of the motion. The former motion failed in consequence of this technical objection:—that it was to commit for a breach of an injunction which accidentally omitted the words "servants and agents." The present motion is in a different form, and seeks to commit for the contempt, in knowingly assisting in a breach of the injunction.

The court will interfere, where a person, though not enjoined, willfully assists in the act forbidden by the court, as in Lewes v. Morgan, 5 Price, 42, where after an injunction granted against Morgan from receiving rents, Lewes, the solicitor of Morgan, with knowledge of the order, received them, an order was made for his committal for the contempt.

So, where a party assaults an officer of the court in the discharge of his duty; or displaces a receiver; or interferes with the execution of its process; or obstructs or interferes with the due course of justice; the court interferes and punishes for the contempt. . . .

THE MASTER OF THE ROLLS [LANGDALE]. Does the plaintiff press for a committal?

Mr. Roupell stated that it was not his desire to press for the committal.

THE MASTER OF THE ROLLS. By the forbearance of the plaintiff, I am spared the painful necessity of making an order. If the matter had been pressed, I should have found it my duty to commit Mr. Batley for his contempt in intermeddling with these matters; some of his acts in contravention of the injunction are distinctly proved, though with respect to others there may be some shadow of doubt.

Batley in the position in which he was, and knowing the duty of the Earl of Mornington, ought to have taken care not to do any acts, in violation of the order of the court. I am glad to be relieved from the necessity of ordering a committal, but Batley must pay the costs of the motion.

NOTE

In Iveson v. Harris, 7 Ves.Jun. 251, 32 Eng.Rep. 102 (1802), Lord Eldon, L.C., made the following remarks:

> I have no conception that it is competent to this court to hold a man bound by an injunction, who is not a party in the cause for the purpose of the cause. The old practice was that he must be brought into court, so as according to the ancient laws and usages of the country [to] be made a subject of the writ.... I find the court has adhered very closely to the principle, that you cannot have an injunction except against a party to the suit.... The court has no right to grant an injunction against a person whom they have not brought or attempted to bring before the court by subpoena.

contradicts the Mornington case.

Rigas v. Livingston

NY

Court of Appeals of New York, 1904.
178 N.Y. 20, 70 N.E. 107.

P = fruit stand owner

Appellant = Tenant of store front.
— appellant wants stone front removed
facts

■ CULLEN, J. The plaintiff was the occupant of a fruit stand on the sidewalk in front of No. 89 Park Row, in the city of New York. The appellant, Levy, was the tenant and occupant of the store in front of which the plaintiff's stand was located. Levy was anxious that the stand should be removed, and applied to the city authorities to have such removal effected. Thereupon the plaintiff brought an action in the Supreme Court against the commissioner of public works of the borough of Manhattan and the superintendent of the bureau of incumbrances to enjoin them from interfering with his stand. A temporary injunction was granted, which, after a hearing, was continued during the pendency of the action. This order purported in terms not only to restrain the defendants, but also "all persons having knowledge of this injunction order." Thereafter one Rosenblum, the son-in-law of Levy, landlord of the building, brought proceedings in the Municipal Court to dispossess Levy from his store. In these proceedings Levy made default, and a warrant for his removal was issued. Acting under this warrant, Loewenthal, a city marshal, and Dickman, the attorney for the landlord, removed and destroyed the plaintiff's stand. Thereafter application was made to punish Levy, Dickman, and Loewenthal for contempt. The proof tended to show that all of them were notified of the existence of the injunction. The Special Term adjudged the parties guilty of a civil contempt in impairing and prejudicing the plaintiff's rights, and fined them the sum of $150. Levy appealed to the Appellate Division, where the order was affirmed. The court afterward allowed an appeal to this court, certifying the question, "Do the papers submitted by the respondent state sufficient facts upon which the order adjudging the appellant in contempt could properly be made?" ... The Special Term found that the appellant "did, by trick and scheme, violate said injunction order (and caused said stand to be removed." It is doubtful whether the proof was sufficient to justify this

notice.

full stop
first ruling (lower court)

finding. Levy was not present at the removal of the stand, nor does it appear that he gave any instructions to the persons who actually removed the stand. It does appear that he was anxious to have the plaintiff ousted, and had some time previous to this occurrence threatened he would get the stand removed. It also appears that other summary proceedings had been taken by Rosenblum against Levy and the plaintiff to remove them. Those proceedings were dismissed. These facts, and the relationship between Levy and Rosenblum, create a very strong suspicion that Levy was a prime mover in all the transactions; but it is doubtful whether, in the face of Levy's sworn denial, they were sufficient in these proceedings, which are quasi criminal, to establish his guilt. However this may be, we are of opinion that the removal of the stand, though illegal, was not a violation of the injunction. The parties might have been sued for their trespass civilly, and, it is possible, criminally; but, however great their fault, it was not a contempt of court. The court had jurisdiction of the subject-matter of the action and of the defendants to the action, and the injunction was in all respects valid and binding on the parties. But the question is, what persons did it restrain? . . . In terms the Code authorizes an injunction against the defendants only, not the whole world. There are some exceptions to this rule—as in the case of proceedings for the dissolution of corporations which are in the nature of proceedings in rem, where the statute expressly authorizes an injunction against all creditors. Therefore, so far as the order purported to restrain all other persons having knowledge of the injunction, this provision was inoperative to enlarge its effect.

It is true that persons not parties to the action may be bound by an injunction if they have knowledge of it, provided they are servants or agents of the defendants, or act in collusion or combination with them. Such was the case of Daly v. Amberg, 126 N.Y. 490, 27 N.E. 1038, where the agents and employees of the manager of a theater disobeyed an injunction granted against their employer to restrain the representation of a play at his theater. . . . Authorities illustrating the rule might be cited to an indefinite extent, but the underlying principle in all cases of this class, on which is founded the power of the court to punish for the violation of its mandate persons not parties to the action, is that the parties so punished were acting either as the agents or servants of the defendants, or in combination or collusion with them, or in assertion of their rights or claims. Persons, however, who are not connected in any way with the parties to the action, are not restrained by the order of the court. . . . In People ex rel. Morris v. Randall, 73 N.Y. 416, . . . it was held that a stranger to the restraining orders of the court was in no way affected by or bound to obey them. In the present case the injunction order determined that prima facie the plaintiff was authorized to maintain his stand as against the city of New York and its authorities. This was the only right passed upon on the application for the injunction, and the only right which could have been passed upon. The injunction order therefore properly restrained the city authorities from interfering with the plaintiff's stand. Had any of the city officials, or their employees or agents, or any third parties acting in aid of or in connivance with them, interfered with the stand, they would have committed a contempt of court. But it is not pretended that the city officials against whom the action was brought, or either of them, in any way, directly or indirectly, by act or solicitation, took part in the subsequent trespass on the plaintiff's property. The parties who removed the stand neither acted nor assumed to act under any right or authority of the city officials, but in execution of the process of another court, issued on a judgment not based on any claim of the city that the stand was a nuisance, but on a right asserted by a landlord to dispossess a defaulting tenant. It is true that this process offered no justification for the trespass on the plaintiff's property. That fact did not make them guilty of contempt, but liable as trespassers. A thief might have come along in the night and stolen the plaintiff's stand. He would have been guilty of larceny, but not of contempt of court.

The order of the Special Term and of the Appellate Division should be reversed, and the application denied, but, under the circumstances, without costs.

■ PARKER, C.J., and GRAY, O'BRIEN, HAIGHT, and MARTIN, JJ., concur. VANN, J., dissents.

Orders reversed.

United Pharmacal Corp. v. United States

United States Court of Appeals, First Circuit, 1962.
306 F.2d 515.

[The United States filed a complaint against Metabolic Products Corp. for a temporary and permanent injunction restraining them from introducing a drug into interstate commerce on the ground that the drug was misbranded. After a hearing, the court issued a preliminary injunction ordering that the defendant Metabolic and its "agents, employees, representatives and all other persons in active concert or participation with any of them, be and they are hereby preliminarily restrained and enjoined ... from violating ... [the statute] by causing the introduction or the delivery for introduction into interstate commerce of said drug...." Certified copies of this decree were served on United Pharmacal Corp., which had a contractual relationship with Metabolic for sale of the drug. United sued for a declaratory judgment that it was not bound by the preliminary injunction. While this suit was pending, United sent the drug in interstate commerce to a customer, who was an agent of the Food and Drug Administration. The United States moved for an order to show cause why United should not be held in criminal contempt for violating the preliminary injunction. From a finding of guilty of criminal contempt, United appeals.]

■ WOODBURY, C.J.... We turn now to the question whether United and its two principal officers ... are bound by the preliminary injunction issued against Metabolic.

That injunction is couched in the terms of Rule 65(d) Fed.R.Civ.P., 28 U.S.C.A., which so far as material provides that every order granting an injunction "... is binding only upon the parties to the action, their officers, agents, servants, employees, and attorneys, and upon those persons in active concert or participation with them who receive actual notice of the order by personal service or otherwise."

United is not a subsidiary of Metabolic.... Nor has the United States shown that United is a mere pawn or tool in the hands of Metabolic. So far as appears they are wholly separate and independent corporations each going its separate way linked together only by Metabolic's minority stock ownership of United and the distributorship agreement entered into between them....

Since it is conceded that United had received actual notice of the order granting the preliminary injunction against Metabolic, and there is no basis for finding that United or its officers ... were agents, servants or employees of Metabolic, the only question is whether United and its officers were "in active concert or participation" with Metabolic when United made its shipment to the government agent in St. Albans.

It may very well be, although we do not need to decide, that prior to the preliminary injunction Metabolic and United had been actively collaborating in pushing the drug on the market. But the question is not what Metabolic and United had been doing. Their past contractual relationship is not controlling. The question is whether United and its officers aided and abetted Metabolic in violating the preliminary injunction for, as the late Judge Learned Hand pointed out in Alemite Mfg. Corp. v. Staff, 42 F.2d 832 (C.A.2, 1930): "... the only occasion when a person not a party may be punished, is when he has helped to bring about, not merely what the decree has forbidden, because it may have gone too far, but what it has power to forbid, an act of a party. This means that the respondent must either abet the defendant [i.e., the person enjoined], or must be legally identified with him."[1] Wherefore, as Judge Hand went on to point out, if the person enjoined is not involved in the contempt, an employee, and by the same token one in active concert or participation, cannot be either, because the decree has not been violated. The reason for this is clear: "... for it is not the act described which the decree may forbid, but only that act when the defendant does it."

Since it is conceded that Metabolic itself did not violate the injunction, since United was not identified with Metabolic in the sense of being its agent, servant, subsidiary, tool, cat's paw or alter ego, and since it did not obtain the drug which it shipped to the government agent from Metabolic but from an outside source, it cannot be said to have acted in concert or participation with Metabolic in violating the injunction.

Judgment will be entered vacating the judgments of the District Court and remanding the case to that Court with directions to dismiss the government's petition for adjudication in criminal contempt.

United States v. Hall

United States Court of Appeals, Fifth Circuit, 1972.
472 F.2d 261.

■ WISDOM, J. This case presents the question whether a district court has power to punish for criminal contempt a person who, though neither a

---

1. [Prior to the above quote, Judge Hand had said: "We agree that a person who knowingly assists a defendant in violating an injunction subjects himself to civil as well as criminal proceedings for contempt. This is well settled law...."]

party nor bearing any legal relationship to a party, violates a court order designed to protect the court's judgment in a school desegregation case. We uphold the district court's conclusion that in the circumstances of this case it had this power, and affirm the defendant's conviction for contempt.

Holding

On June 23, 1971, the district court entered a "Memorandum Opinion and Final Judgment" in the case of Mims v. Duval County School Board. The court required the Duval County [Jacksonville], Florida school board to complete its desegregation of Duval County schools, in accordance with the Supreme Court's decision in Swann v. Charlotte–Mecklenburg Board of Education, 1971, 402 U.S. 1, 91 S.Ct. 1267, 28 L.Ed.2d 554, by pairing and clustering a number of schools which had theretofore been predominantly one-race schools. This order culminated litigation begun eleven years before. This Court affirmed the district court's order in Mims v. Duval County School Board, 5 Cir.1971, 447 F.2d 1330. The district court retained jurisdiction to enter such orders as might be necessary in the future to effectuate its judgment.

Among the schools marked for desegregation under the plan approved by the district court was Ribault Senior High School, a predominantly white school. The plan directed pairing of Ribault with William E. Raines Senior High School, a predominantly black school, so that the black enrollment would be 59 percent at Raines and 57 percent at Ribault. After the desegregation order was put into effect racial unrest and violence developed at Ribault, necessitating on one occasion the temporary closing of the school. On March 5, 1972, the superintendent of schools and the sheriff of Jacksonville filed a petition for injunctive relief in the *Mims* case with the district court. This petition alleged that certain black adult "outsiders" had caused or abetted the unrest and violence by their activities both on and off the Ribault campus. The petition identified the appellant Eric Hall, allegedly a member of a militant organization known as the "Black Front", as one of several such outsiders who, in combination with black students and parents, were attempting to prevent the normal operation of Ribault through student boycotts and other activities. As relief the petitioners requested an order "restraining all Ribault Senior High School students and any person acting independently or in concert with them from interfering with the orderly operation of the school and the Duval County School system, and for such other relief as the court may deem just and proper."

At an ex parte session on March 5, 1972, the district court entered an order providing in part:

1. All students of Ribault Senior High School, whether in good standing or under suspension, and other persons acting independently or in concert with them and having notice of this order are hereby enjoined and restrained from

(a) Obstructing or preventing the attendance in classes of students and faculty members;

(b) Harassing, threatening or intimidating any faculty, staff member or employee of Ribault Senior High School or the Duval County School Board;

(c) Harassing, threatening or intimidating any student en route to and from school;

(d) Destroying or attempting to destroy, defacing or attempting to deface any structure, buildings, materials or equipment of Ribault Senior High School or the Duval County School Board;

(e) Committing any other act to disrupt the orderly operation of Ribault Senior High School or any other school of the Duval County School System;

2. Until further order of this Court, no person shall enter any building of the Ribault Senior High School or go upon the school's grounds except the following:

(a) Students of Ribault Senior High School while attending classes or official school functions;

(b) The faculty, staff, and administration of Ribault Senior High School and other employees of the Duval County School Board having assigned duties at the school;

(c) Persons having business obligations which require their presence on the school's premises;

(d) Parents of Ribault Senior High School students or any other person who has the prior permission of the principal or his designee to be present on the school's premises;

(e) Law enforcement officials of the City of Jacksonville, the State of Florida or the United States Government.

The order went on to provide that "[a]nyone having notice of this order who violates any of the terms thereof shall be subject to arrest, prosecution and punishment by imprisonment or fine, or both, for criminal contempt under the laws of the United States of America...." The court ordered the sheriff to serve copies of the order on seven named persons, *including Eric Hall.* Hall was neither a party plaintiff nor a party defendant in the *Mims* litigation, and in issuing this order the court did not join Hall or any of the other persons named in the order as parties.

On March 9, 1972, four days after the court issued its order, Hall violated that portion of the order restricting access to Ribault High School by appearing on the Ribault campus. When questioned by a deputy United States marshal as to the reasons for his presence, Hall replied that he was on the grounds of Ribault for the purpose of violating the March 5, order. The marshal then arrested Hall and took him into custody. After a non-jury trial, the district court found Hall guilty of the charge of criminal contempt and sentenced him to sixty days' imprisonment.

Defenses

On this appeal Hall raises two related contentions. Both contentions depend on the fact that Hall was not a party to the *Mims* litigation and the fact that, in violating the court's order, he was apparently acting independently of the *Mims* parties① He first points to the common law rule that a nonparty who violates an injunction solely in pursuit of his own interests cannot be held in contempt. Not having been before the court as a party or as the surrogate of a party, he argues that in accordance with this common law rule he was not bound by the court's order②Second, he contends that

Rule 65(d) of the Federal Rules of Civil Procedure prevents the court's order from binding him, since Rule 65(d) limits the binding effect of injunctive orders to "parties to the action, their officers, agents, servants, employees, and attorneys, and ... those persons in active concert or participation with them who receive actual notice of the order by personal service or otherwise." We reject both contentions.

I.

For his first contention, that a court of equity has no power to punish for contempt a nonparty acting solely in pursuit of his own interests, the appellant relies heavily on the two leading cases of Alemite Manufacturing Corp. v. Staff, 2 Cir.1930, 42 F.2d 832, and Chase National Bank v. City of Norwalk, 1934, 291 U.S. 431, 54 S.Ct. 475, 78 L.Ed. 894. In *Alemite* the district court had issued an injunction restraining the defendant and his agents, employees, associates, and confederates from infringing the plaintiff's patent. Subsequently a third person, not a party to the original suit and acting entirely on his own initiative, began infringing the plaintiff's patent and was held in contempt by the district court. The Second Circuit reversed in an opinion by Judge Learned Hand, stating that "it is not the act described which the decree may forbid, but only that act when the defendant does it." In *Chase National Bank* the plaintiff brought suit against the City of Norwalk to obtain an injunction forbidding the removal of poles, wires, and other electrical equipment belonging to the plaintiff. The district court issued a decree enjoining the City, its officers, agents, and employees, "and all persons whomsoever to whom notice of this order shall come" from removing the equipment or otherwise interfering with the operation of the plaintiff's power plant. The Supreme Court held that the district court had violated "established principles of equity jurisdiction and procedure" insofar as its order applied to persons who were not parties, associates, or confederates of parties, but who merely had notice of the order.

This case is different. In *Alemite* and *Chase National Bank* the activities of third parties, however harmful they might have been to the plaintiffs' interests, would not have disturbed in any way the adjudication of rights and obligations as between the original plaintiffs and defendants. Infringement of the *Alemite* plaintiff's patent by a third party would not have upset the defendant's duty to refrain from infringing or rendered it more difficult for the defendant to perform that duty. Similarly, the defendant's duty in *Chase National Bank* to refrain from removing the plaintiff's equipment would remain undisturbed regardless of the activities of third parties, as would the plaintiff's right not to have its equipment removed by the defendant. The activities of Hall, however, threatened both the plaintiffs' right and the defendant's duty as adjudicated in the *Mims* litigation. In *Mims* the plaintiffs were found to have a constitutional right to attend an integrated school. The defendant school board had a corresponding constitutional obligation to provide them with integrated schools and a right to be free from interference with the performance of that duty. Disruption of the orderly operation of the school system, in the form of a racial dispute, would thus negate the plaintiffs' constitutional right and the defendant's constitutional duty. In short, the activities of persons contributing to racial disorder at Ribault imperiled the court's fundamental power to make a binding adjudication between the parties properly before it.

Courts of equity have inherent jurisdiction to preserve their ability to render judgment in a case such as this. This was the import of the holding in United States v. United Mine Workers of America.... This holding affirmed the power of a court of equity to issue an order to preserve the status quo in order to protect its ability to render judgment in a case over which it might have jurisdiction.

The integrity of a court's power to render a binding judgment in a case over which it has jurisdiction is at stake in the present case. In *Mine Workers* disruptive conduct prior to the court's decision could have destroyed the court's power to settle a controversy at least potentially within its jurisdiction. Here the conduct of Hall and others, if unrestrained, could have upset the court's ability to bind the parties in *Mims,* a case in which it unquestionably had jurisdiction. Moreover, the court retained jurisdiction in *Mims* to enter such further orders as might be necessary to effectuate its judgment. Thus disruptive conduct would not only jeopardize the effect of the court's judgment already entered but would also undercut its power to enter binding desegregation orders in the future.

The principle that courts have jurisdiction to punish for contempt in order to protect their ability to render judgment is also found in the use of in rem injunctions. Federal courts have issued injunctions binding on all persons, regardless of notice, who come into contact with property which is the subject of a judicial decree. A court entering a decree binding on a particular piece of property is necessarily faced with the danger that its judgment may be disrupted in the future by members of an undefinable class—those who may come into contact with the property. The in rem injunction protects the court's judgment. The district court here faced an analogous problem. The judgment in a school case, as in other civil rights actions, inures to the benefit of a large class of persons, regardless of whether the original action is cast in the form of a class action. At the same time court orders in school cases, affecting as they do large numbers of people, necessarily depend on the cooperation of the entire community for their implementation.

As this Court is well aware, school desegregation orders often strongly excite community passions. School orders are, like in rem orders, particularly vulnerable to disruption by an undefinable class of persons who are neither parties nor acting at the instigation of parties. In such cases, as in voting rights cases, courts must have the power to issue orders similar to that issued in this case, tailored to the exigencies of the situation and directed to protecting the court's judgment. The peculiar problems posed by school cases have required courts to exercise broad and flexible remedial powers. Similarly broad applications of the power to punish for contempt may be necessary, as here, if courts are to protect their ability to design appropriate remedies and make their remedial orders effective.

II.

The appellant also asserts that Rule 65(d) of the Federal Rules of Civil Procedure prevents the court's order from binding him. He points out that he was not a party to the original action, nor an officer, agent, servant, employee, or attorney of a party, and denies that he was acting in "active concert or participation" with any party to the original action.

In examining this contention we start with the proposition that Rule 65 was intended to embody "the common-law doctrine that a decree of injunction not only binds the parties defendant but also those identified with them in interest, in 'privity' with them, represented by them or subject to their control." Literally read, Rule 65(d) would forbid the issuance of in rem injunctions. But courts have continued to issue in rem injunctions notwithstanding Rule 65(d), since they possessed the power to do so at common law and since Rule 65(d) was intended to embody rather than to limit their common law powers.

Similarly, we conclude that Rule 65(d), as a codification rather than a limitation of courts' common-law powers, cannot be read to restrict the inherent power of a court to protect its ability to render a binding judgment. We hold that Hall's relationship to the *Mims* case fell within that contemplated by Rule 65(d). By deciding *Mims* and retaining jurisdiction the district court had, in effect, adjudicated the rights of the entire community with respect to the racial controversy surrounding the school system. Moreover, as we have noted, in the circumstances of this case third parties such as Hall were in a position to upset the court's adjudication. This was not a situation which could have been anticipated by the draftsmen of procedural rules. In meeting the situation as it did, the district court did not overstep its powers.

We do not hold that courts are free to issue permanent injunctions against all the world in school cases. Hall had notice of the court's order. Rather than challenge it by the orderly processes of law, he resorted to conscious, willful defiance.

It is true that this order was issued without a hearing, and that ordinarily injunctive relief cannot be granted without a hearing. But we need not hold that this order has the effect of a preliminary or permanent injunction. Rather, the portion of the court's order here complained of may be characterized as a temporary restraining order, which under Rule 65(b) may be issued ex parte. The prohibition directed to restricting access to the school grounds nowhere purported to be an injunction. Moreover, Hall's violation occurred within four days of the issuance of the order, well within the ten-day limitation period for temporary restraining orders. The present case is therefore distinguishable from the situation presented in Harrington v. Colquitt County Board of Education, 5 Cir.1971, 449 F.2d 161, a direct appeal from a permanent injunction, in which this Court struck language purporting to enjoin persons beyond the scope of Rule 65(d).

We hold, then, that the district court had the inherent power to protect its ability to render a binding judgment between the original parties to the *Mims* litigation by issuing an interim ex parte order against an undefinable class of persons. We further hold that willful violation of that order by one having notice of it constitutes criminal contempt. The judgment of the district court is affirmed.

———

3. THE DUTY TO OBEY: THE COLLATERAL BAR RULE

United States v. United Mine Workers of America

Supreme Court of the United States, 1947.
330 U.S. 258, 67 S.Ct. 677, 91 L.Ed. 884.

■ MR. CHIEF JUSTICE VINSON delivered the opinion of the Court.

In October, 1946, the United States was in possession of, and operating, the major portion of the country's bituminous coal mines.[1]

Terms and conditions of employment were controlled "for the period of Government possession" by an agreement entered into on May 29, 1946, between Secretary of Interior Krug, as Coal Mines Administrator, and John L. Lewis, as President of the United Mine Workers of America. The Krug–Lewis agreement embodied far reaching changes favorable to the miners; and, except as amended and supplemented therein, the agreement carried forward the terms and conditions of the National Bituminous Coal Wage Agreement of April 11, 1945.

On October 21, 1946, the defendant Lewis directed a letter to Secretary Krug and presented issues which led directly to the present controversy. According to the defendant Lewis, the Krug–Lewis agreement carried forward § 15 of the National Bituminous Coal Wage Agreement of April 11, 1945. Under that section either party to the contract was privileged to give ten days' notice in writing of a desire for a negotiating conference which the other party was required to attend; fifteen days after the beginning of the conference either party might give notice in writing of the termination of the agreement, effective five days after receipt of such notice. Asserting authority under this clause, the defendant Lewis in his letter of October 21 requested that a conference begin November 1 for the purpose of negotiating new arrangements concerning wages, hours, practices, and other pertinent matters appertaining to the bituminous coal industry.

Captain N.H. Collisson, then Coal Mines Administrator, answered for Secretary Krug. Any contractual basis for requiring negotiations for revision of the Krug–Lewis agreement was denied. In the opinion of the Government, § 15 of the 1945 agreement had not been preserved by the Krug–Lewis agreement; indeed, § 15 had been expressly nullified by the clause of the latter contract providing that the terms contained therein were to cover the period of Government possession. Although suggesting that any negotiations looking toward a new agreement be carried on with the mine owners, the Government expressed willingness to discuss matters affecting the operation of the mines under the terms of the Krug–Lewis agreement.

---

1. The United States had taken possession of the mines pursuant to Executive Order 9728 of May 21, 1946, in which the President, after determining that labor disturbances were interrupting the production of bituminous coal necessary for the operation of the national economy during the transition from war to peace, directed the Secretary of Interior to take possession of and operate the mines and to negotiate with representatives of the miners concerning the terms and conditions of employment.

. . . .

Conferences were scheduled and began in Washington on November 1, both the union and the Government adhering to their opposing views regarding the right of either party to terminate the contract. At the fifth meeting, held on November 11, the union for the first time offered specific proposals for changes in wages and other conditions of employment. On November 13 Secretary Krug requested the union to negotiate with the mine owners. This suggestion was rejected. On November 15 the union, by John L. Lewis, notified Secretary Krug that "Fifteen days having now elapsed since the beginning of said conference, the United Mine Workers of America, exercising its option hereby terminates said Krug–Lewis Agreement as of 12:00 o'clock P.M., Midnight, Wednesday, November 20, 1946."

Secretary Krug again notified the defendant Lewis that he had no power under the Krug–Lewis agreement or under the law to terminate the contract by unilateral declaration. The President of the United States announced his strong support of the Government's position and requested reconsideration by the union in order to avoid a national crisis. However, the defendant Lewis, as union president, circulated to the mine workers copies of the November 15 letter to Secretary Krug. This communication was for the "official information" of union members.

The United States on November 18 filed a complaint in the District Court for the District of Columbia against the United Mine Workers of America and John L. Lewis, individually and as president of the union. The suit was brought under the Declaratory Judgment Act and sought judgment to the effect that the defendants had no power unilaterally to terminate the Krug–Lewis agreement. And alleging that the November 15 notice was in reality a strike notice, the United States, pending the final determination of the cause, requested a temporary restraining order and preliminary injunctive relief.

The court, immediately and without notice to the defendants, issued a temporary order restraining the defendants from continuing in effect the notice of November 15, from encouraging the mine workers to interfere with the operation of the mines by strike or cessation of work, and from taking any action which would interfere with the court's jurisdiction and its determination of the case. The order by its terms was to expire at 3:00 p.m. on November 27 unless extended for good cause shown. A hearing on the preliminary injunction was set for 10:00 a.m. on the same date. The order and complaint were served on the defendants on November 18.

A gradual walkout by the miners commenced on November 18, and, by midnight of November 20, consistent with the miners' "no contract, no work" policy, a full-blown strike was in progress. Mines furnishing the major part of the nation's bituminous coal production were idle.

On November 21 the United States filed a petition for a rule to show cause why the defendants should not be punished as and for contempt, alleging a willful violation of the restraining order. The rule issued, setting November 25 as the return day and, if at that time the contempt was not sufficiently purged, setting November 27 as the day for trial on the contempt charge.

On the return day, defendants, by counsel, informed the court that no action had been taken concerning the November 15 notice, and denied the jurisdiction of the court to issue the restraining order and rule to show cause. Trial on the contempt charge was thereupon ordered to begin as scheduled on November 27. On November 26 the defendants filed a motion to discharge and vacate the rule to show cause. Their motion challenged the jurisdiction of the court, and raised the grave question of whether the Norris–LaGuardia Act prohibited the granting of the temporary restraining order at the instance of the United States.

After extending the temporary restraining order on November 27, and after full argument on November 27 and November 29, the court, on the latter date, overruled the motion and held that its power to issue the restraining order in this case was not affected by either the Norris–LaGuardia Act or the Clayton Act.

The defendants thereupon pleaded not guilty and waived an advisory jury. Trial on the contempt charge proceeded. The Government presented eight witnesses, the defendants none. At the conclusion of the trial on December 3, the court found that the defendants had permitted the November 15 notice to remain outstanding, had encouraged the miners to interfere by a strike with the operation of the mines and with the performance of governmental functions, and had interfered with the jurisdiction of the court. Both defendants were found guilty beyond reasonable doubt of both criminal and civil contempt dating from November 18. The court entered judgment on December 4, fining the defendant Lewis $10,000, and the defendant union $3,500,000. On the same day a preliminary injunction, effective until a final determination of the case, was issued in terms similar to those of the restraining order.

On December 5 the defendants filed notices of appeal from the judgments of contempt. The judgments were stayed pending the appeals. The United States on December 6 filed a petition for certiorari in both cases. Section 240(a) of the Judicial Code, authorizes a petition for certiorari by any party and the granting of certiorari prior to judgment in the Circuit Court of Appeals. Prompt settlement of this case being in the public interest, we granted certiorari on December 9, and subsequently, for similar reasons, granted petitions for certiorari filed by the defendants. The cases were consolidated for argument.

I.

Defendants' first and principal contention is that the restraining order and preliminary injunction were issued in violation of the Clayton and Norris–LaGuardia Acts. We have come to a contrary decision.

. . . .

II.

Although we have held that the Norris–LaGuardia Act did not render injunctive relief beyond the jurisdiction of the District Court, there are alternative grounds which support the power of the District Court to punish violations of its orders as criminal contempt.

. . . .

In the case before us, the District Court had the power to preserve existing conditions [by a temporary restraining order] while it was determining its own authority to grant injunctive relief. The defendants, in making their private determination of the law, acted at their peril. Their disobedience is punishable as criminal contempt.

Although a different result would follow were the question of jurisdiction frivolous and not substantial, such contention would be idle here. The applicability of the Norris–LaGuardia Act to the United States in a case such as this had not previously received judicial consideration, and both the language of the Act and its legislative history indicate the substantial nature of the problem with which the District Court was faced.

Proceeding further, we find impressive authority for the proposition that an order issued by a court with jurisdiction over the subject matter and person must be obeyed by the parties until it is reversed by orderly and proper proceedings. This is true without regard even for the constitutionality of the Act under which the order is issued. In Howat v. Kansas, 1922, 258 U.S. 181, 42 S.Ct. 277, 66 L.Ed. 550 this Court said:

> "An injunction duly issuing out of a court of general jurisdiction with equity powers, upon pleadings properly invoking its action, and served upon persons made parties therein and within the jurisdiction, must be obeyed by them, however erroneous the action of the court may be, even if the error be in the assumption of the validity of a seeming, but void law going to the merits of the case. It is for the court of first instance to determine the question of the validity of the law, and until its decision is reversed for error by orderly review, either by itself or by a higher court, its orders based on its decision are to be respected, and disobedience of them is contempt of its lawful authority, to be punished."

Violations of an order are punishable as criminal contempt even though the order is set aside on appeal or though the basic action has become moot.

We insist upon the same duty of obedience where, as here, the subject matter of the suit, as well as the parties, was properly before the court; where the elements of federal jurisdiction were clearly shown; and where the authority of the court of first instance to issue an order ancillary to the main suit depended upon a statute, the scope and applicability of which were subject to substantial doubt. The District Court on November 29 affirmatively decided that the Norris–LaGuardia Act was of no force in this case and that injunctive relief was therefore authorized. Orders outstanding or issued after that date were to be obeyed until they expired or were set aside by appropriate proceedings, appellate or otherwise. Convictions for criminal contempt intervening before that time may stand.

It does not follow, of course, that simply because a defendant may be punished for criminal contempt for disobedience of an order later set aside on appeal, that the plaintiff in the action may profit by way of a fine imposed in a simultaneous proceeding for civil contempt based upon a violation of the same order. The right to remedial relief falls with an injunction which events prove was erroneously issued, and a fortiori when the injunction or restraining order was beyond the jurisdiction of the court.... If the Norris–LaGuardia Act were applicable in this case, the conviction for civil contempt would be reversed in its entirety.

Assuming, then, that the Norris–LaGuardia Act applied to this case and prohibited injunctive relief at the request of the United States, we would set aside the preliminary injunction of December 4 and the judgment for civil contempt; but we would, subject to any infirmities in the contempt proceedings or in the fines imposed, affirm the judgments for criminal contempt as validly punishing violations of an order then outstanding and unreversed.

. . . .

V.

It is urged that, in any event, the amount of the fine of $10,000 imposed on the defendant Lewis and of the fine of $3,500,000 imposed on the defendant Union were arbitrary, excessive, and in no way related to the evidence adduced at the hearing.

Sentences for criminal contempt are punitive in their nature and are imposed for the purpose of vindicating the authority of the court.... The interests of orderly government demand that respect and compliance be given to orders issued by courts possessed of jurisdiction of persons and subject matter. One who defies the public authority and willfully refuses his obedience, does so at his peril. In imposing a fine for criminal contempt, the trial judge may properly take into consideration the extent of the willful and deliberate defiance of the court's order, the seriousness of the consequences of the contumacious behavior, the necessity of effectively terminating the defendant's defiance as required by the public interest, and the importance of deterring such acts in the future. Because of the nature of these standards, great reliance must be placed upon the discretion of the trial judge.

The trial court properly found the defendants guilty of criminal contempt. Such contempt had continued for 15 days from the issuance of the restraining order until the finding of guilty. Its willfulness had not been qualified by any concurrent attempt on defendants' part to challenge the order by motion to vacate or other appropriate procedures. Immediately following the finding of guilty, defendant Lewis stated openly in court that defendants would adhere to their policy of defiance. This policy, as the evidence showed, was the germ center of an economic paralysis which was rapidly extending itself from the bituminous coal mines into practically every other major industry of the United States. It was an attempt to repudiate and override the instrument of lawful government in the very situation in which governmental action was indispensable.

The trial court also properly found the defendants guilty of civil contempt. Judicial sanctions in civil contempt proceedings may, in a proper case, be employed for either or both of two purposes: to coerce the defendant into compliance with the court's order, and to compensate the complainant for losses sustained.... Where compensation is intended, a fine is imposed, payable to the complainant. Such fine must of course be based upon evidence of complainant's actual loss, and his right, as a civil litigant, to the compensatory fine is dependent upon the outcome of the basic controversy.

But where the purpose is to make the defendant comply, the court's discretion is otherwise exercised. It must then consider the character and magnitude of the harm threatened by continued contumacy, and the probable effectiveness of any suggested sanction in bringing about the result desired.

It is a corollary of the above principles that a court which has returned a conviction for contempt must, in fixing the amount of a fine to be imposed as a punishment or as a means of securing future compliance, consider the amount of defendant's financial resources and the consequent seriousness of the burden to that particular defendant.

In the light of these principles, we think the record clearly warrants a fine of $10,000 against defendant Lewis for criminal contempt. A majority of the Court, however, does not think that it warrants the unconditional imposition of a fine of $3,500,000 against the defendant union. A majority feels that, if the court below had assessed a fine of $700,000 against the defendant union, this, under the circumstances, would not be excessive as punishment for the criminal contempt theretofore committed; and feels that, in order to coerce the defendant union into a future compliance with the court's order, it would have been effective to make the other $2,800,000 of the fine conditional on the defendant's failure to purge itself within a reasonable time. . . .

The temporary restraining order and the preliminary injunction were properly issued, and the actions of the District Court in these respects are affirmed. The judgment against the defendant Lewis is affirmed. The judgment against the defendant union is modified in accordance with this opinion, and, as modified, that judgment is affirmed. . . .

■ Mr. Justice Jackson joins in this opinion except as to the Norris–LaGuardia Act which he thinks relieved the courts of jurisdiction to issue injunctions in this class of case.

■ Mr. Justice Frankfurter, concurring in the judgment.

. . . .

. . . A majority of my brethren find that neither the Norris–LaGuardia Act nor the War Labor Disputes Act limited the power of the district court to issue the orders under review. I have come to the contrary view. But to suggest that the right to determine so complicated and novel an issue could not be brought within the cognizance of the district court, and eventually of this Court, is to deny the place of the judiciary in our scheme of government. And if the district court had power to decide whether this case was properly before it, it could make appropriate orders so as to afford the necessary time for fair consideration and decision while existing conditions were preserved. To say that the authority of the court may be flouted during the time necessary to decide is to reject the requirements of the judicial process.

It does not mitigate such defiance of law to urge that hard-won liberties of collective action by workers were at stake. The most prized liberties themselves pre-suppose an independent judiciary through which these liberties may be, as they often have been, vindicated. When in a real controversy, such as is now here, an appeal is made to law, the issue must be left to the judgment of courts and not the personal judgment of one of the parties. This principle is a postulate of our democracy.

And so I join the opinion of the Court insofar as it sustains the judgment for criminal contempt upon the broad ground of vindicating the process of law....

■ Mr. Justice Black and Mr. Justice Douglas, concurring in part and dissenting in part.

. . . .

Since the Norris–LaGuardia Act is inapplicable, we agree that the District Court had power in these proceedings to enter orders necessary to protect the Government against an invasion of the rights it asserted, pending adjudication of the controversy its complaint presented to the court. It is therefore unnecessary for us to reach the question of whether the District Court also had power to enter these orders under the doctrine [endorsed in Part II of the Court's opinion].

. . . .

■ [The dissenting opinion of Murphy, J., is omitted.]

■ Mr. Justice Rutledge, dissenting.

. . . .

Since in my opinion the order was jurisdictionally invalid when issued, by virtue of the War Labor Disputes Act and its adoption of the Norris–LaGuardia Act's policy, it follows that the violation gave no sufficient cause for sustaining the conviction for contempt. Lewis and the United Mine Workers necessarily took the risk that the order would be found valid on review and, in that event, that punishment for contempt would apply. They did not take the risk that it would apply in any event, even if the order should be found void as beyond the jurisdiction of the Court to enter....

. . . .

... The power of the federal courts to issue stay orders to maintain the status quo pending appeal, like other matters affecting their jurisdiction except in the case of this Court's original jurisdiction, is subject to Congress' control. That control has been exercised, in my view, to exclude such jurisdiction in cases of this character. And, this being true, I do not think either we or any other court subject to that mandate has power to punish as for contempt the violation of such an order issued in contravention of Congress' command....

■ Mr. Justice Murphy joins in this opinion.

NOTE

Consider the relevance of 28 U.S.C. §§ 1291, 1292, the pertinent portions of which are set forth below, to the practical problems facing

Lewis and the United Mine Workers after the temporary restraining order was entered.

§ 1291.   FINAL DECISIONS OF DISTRICT COURTS

The courts of appeals (other than the United States Court of Appeals for the Federal Circuit) shall have jurisdiction of appeals from all final decisions of the district courts of the United States, the United States District Court for the District of the Canal Zone, the District Court of Guam, and the District Court of the Virgin Islands, except where a direct review may be had in the Supreme Court. The jurisdiction of the United States Court of Appeals for the Federal Circuit shall be limited to the jurisdiction described in sections 1292(c) and (d) and 1295 of this title.

§ 1292.   INTERLOCUTORY DECISIONS

(a) Except as provided in subsections (c) and (d) of this section, the courts of appeals shall have jurisdiction of appeals from:

(1) Interlocutory orders of the district courts of the United States, the United States District Court for the District of the Canal Zone, the District Court of Guam, and the District Court of the Virgin Islands, or of the judges thereof, granting, continuing, modifying, refusing or dissolving injunctions, or refusing to dissolve or modify injunctions, except where a direct review may be had in the Supreme Court;

(2) Interlocutory orders appointing receivers, or refusing orders to wind up receiverships or to take steps to accomplish the purposes thereof, such as directing sales or other disposals of property;

(3) Interlocutory decrees of such district courts or the judges thereof determining the rights and liabilities of the parties to admiralty cases in which appeals from final decrees are allowed.

(b) When a district judge, in making in a civil action an order not otherwise appealable under this section, shall be of the opinion that such order involves a controlling question of law as to which there is substantial ground for difference of opinion and that an immediate appeal from the order may materially advance the ultimate termination of the litigation, he shall so state in writing in such order. The Court of Appeals may thereupon, in its discretion, permit an appeal to be taken from such order, if application is made to it within ten days after the entry of the order: *Provided, however,* That application for an appeal hereunder shall not stay proceedings in the district court unless the district judge or the Court of Appeals or a judge thereof shall so order.

Walker v. City of Birmingham

Supreme Court of the United States, 1967.
388 U.S. 307, 87 S.Ct. 1824, 18 L.Ed.2d 1210.

■ MR. JUSTICE STEWART delivered the opinion of the Court.

On Wednesday, April 10, 1963, officials of Birmingham, Alabama, filed a bill of complaint in a state circuit court asking for injunctive relief against

139 individuals and two organizations. The bill and accompanying affidavits stated that during the preceding seven days:

> "[R]espondents [had] sponsored and/or participated in and/or conspired to commit and/or to encourage and/or to participate in certain movements, plans or projects commonly called 'sit-in' demonstrations, 'kneel-in' demonstrations, mass street parades, trespasses on private property after being warned to leave the premises by the owners of said property, congregating in mobs upon the public streets and other public places, unlawfully picketing private places of business in the City of Birmingham, Alabama; violation of numerous ordinances and statutes of the City of Birmingham and State of Alabama...."

It was alleged that this conduct was "calculated to provoke breaches of the peace," "threaten[ed] the safety, peace and tranquility of the City," and placed "an undue burden and strain upon the manpower of the Police Department."

The bill stated that these infractions of the law were expected to continue and would "lead to further imminent danger to the lives, safety, peace, tranquility and general welfare of the people of the City of Birmingham," and that the "remedy by law [was] inadequate." The circuit judge granted a temporary injunction as prayed in the bill, enjoining the petitioners from, among other things, participating in or encouraging mass street parades or mass processions without a permit as required by a Birmingham ordinance.

Five of the eight petitioners were served with copies of the writ early the next morning. Several hours later four of them held a press conference. There a statement was distributed, declaring their intention to disobey the injunction because it was "raw tyranny under the guise of maintaining law and order." At this press conference one of the petitioners stated: "That they had respect for the Federal Courts, or Federal Injunctions, but in the past the State Courts had favored local law enforcement, and if the police couldn't handle it, the mob would."

That night a meeting took place at which one of the petitioners announced that "[i]njunction or no injunction we are going to march tomorrow." The next afternoon, Good Friday, a large crowd gathered in the vicinity of Sixteenth Street and Sixth Avenue North in Birmingham. A group of about 50 or 60 proceeded to parade along the sidewalk while a crowd of 1,000 to 1,500 onlookers stood by, "clapping, and hollering, and [w]hooping." Some of the crowd followed the marchers and spilled out into the street. At least three of the petitioners participated in this march.

Meetings sponsored by some of the petitioners were held that night and the following night, where calls for volunteers to "walk" and go to jail were made. On Easter Sunday, April 14, a crowd of between 1,500 and 2,000 people congregated in the midafternoon in the vicinity of Seventh Avenue and Eleventh Street North in Birmingham. One of the petitioners was seen organizing members of the crowd in formation. A group of about 50, headed by three other petitioners, started down the sidewalk two abreast. At least one other petitioner was among the marchers. Some 300 or 400 people from among the onlookers followed in a crowd that occupied the entire width of the street and overflowed onto the sidewalks. Violence occurred. Members of the crowd threw rocks that injured a newspaperman and damaged a police motorcycle.

The next day the city officials who had requested the injunction applied to the state circuit court for an order to show cause why the petitioners should not be held in contempt for violating it. At the ensuing hearing the petitioners sought to attack the constitutionality of the injunction on the ground that it was vague and overbroad, and restrained free speech. They also sought to attack the Birmingham parade ordinance upon similar grounds, and upon the further ground that the ordinance had previously been administered in an arbitrary and discriminatory manner.

The circuit judge refused to consider any of these contentions, pointing out that there had been neither a motion to dissolve the injunction, nor an effort to comply with it by applying for a permit from the city commission before engaging in the Good Friday and Easter Sunday parades. Consequently, the court held that the only issues before it were whether it had jurisdiction to issue the temporary injunction, and whether thereafter the petitioners had knowingly violated it. Upon these issues the court found against the petitioners, and imposed upon each of them a sentence of five days in jail and a $50 fine, in accord with an Alabama statute.

The Supreme Court of Alabama affirmed. That court, too, declined to consider the petitioners' constitutional attacks upon the injunction and the underlying Birmingham parade ordinance:

> "It is to be remembered that petitioners are charged with violating a temporary injunction. We are not reviewing a denial of a motion to dissolve or discharge a temporary injunction. Petitioners did not file any motion to vacate the temporary injunction until after the Friday and Sunday parades. Instead, petitioners deliberately defied the order of the court and did engage in and incite others to engage in mass street parades without a permit."

> . . . .

> "We hold that the circuit court had the duty and authority, in the first instance, to determine the validity of the ordinance, and, until the decision of the circuit court is reversed for error by orderly review, either by the circuit court or a higher court, the orders of the circuit court based on its decision are to be respected and disobedience of them is contempt of its lawful authority, to be punished. Howat v. State of Kansas, 258 U.S. 181, 42 S.Ct. 277, 66 L.Ed. 550 (1922)."

Howat v. State of Kansas was decided by this Court almost 50 years ago. That was a case in which people had been punished by a Kansas trial court for refusing to obey an antistrike injunction issued under the state industrial relations act. They had claimed a right to disobey the court's order upon the ground that the state statute and the injunction based upon it were invalid under the Federal Constitution. The Supreme Court of Kansas had affirmed the judgment, holding that the trial court "had general power to issue injunctions in equity, and that even if its exercise of the power was erroneous, the injunction was not void, and the defendants were precluded from attacking it in this collateral proceeding * * * that, if the injunction was erroneous, jurisdiction was not thereby forfeited, that the error was subject to correction only by the ordinary method of appeal, and disobedience to the order constituted contempt."

This Court, in dismissing the writ of error, not only unanimously accepted but fully approved the validity of the rule of state law upon which the judgment of the Kansas court was grounded:

> "An injunction duly issuing out of a court of general jurisdiction with equity powers, upon pleadings properly invoking its action, and served upon persons made parties therein and within the jurisdiction, must be obeyed by them, however erroneous the action of the court may be, even if the error be in the assumption of the validity of a seeming, but void law going to the merits of the case. It is for the court of first instance to determine the question of the validity of the law, and until its decision is reversed for error by orderly review, either by itself or by a higher court, its orders based on its decision are to be respected, and disobedience of them is contempt of its lawful authority, to be punished."

The rule of state law accepted and approved in Howat v. State of Kansas is consistent with the rule of law followed by the federal courts.

In the present case, however, we are asked to hold that this rule of law, upon which the Alabama courts relied, was constitutionally impermissible. We are asked to say that the Constitution compelled Alabama to allow the petitioners to violate this injunction, to organize and engage in these mass street parades and demonstrations, without any previous effort on their part to have the injunction dissolved or modified, or any attempt to secure a parade permit in accordance with its terms. Whatever the limits of Howat v. State of Kansas, we cannot accept the petitioners' contentions in the circumstances of this case.

Without question the state court that issued the injunction had, as a court of equity, jurisdiction over the petitioners and over the subject matter of the controversy. And this is not a case where the injunction was transparently invalid or had only a frivolous pretense to validity. We have consistently recognized the strong interest of state and local governments in regulating the use of their streets and other public places....

The generality of the language contained in the Birmingham parade ordinance upon which the injunction was based would unquestionably raise substantial constitutional issues concerning some of its provisions. The petitioners, however, did not even attempt to apply to the Alabama courts for an authoritative construction of the ordinance. Had they done so, those courts might have given the licensing authority granted in the ordinance a narrow and precise scope, as did the New Hampshire courts in Cox v. State of New Hampshire, 312 U.S. 569, 61 S.Ct. 762, 85 L.Ed. 1049, and Poulos v. State of New Hampshire, 345 U.S. 395, 73 S.Ct. 760, 97 L.Ed. 1105. Here, just as in Cox and Poulos, it could not be assumed that this ordinance was void on its face.

The breadth and vagueness of the injunction itself would also unquestionably be subject to substantial constitutional question. But the way to raise that question was to apply to the Alabama courts to have the injunction modified or dissolved. The injunction in all events clearly prohibited mass parading without a permit, and the evidence shows that the petitioners fully understood that prohibition when they violated it.

The petitioners also claim that they were free to disobey the injunction because the parade ordinance on which it was based had been administered in the past in an arbitrary and discriminatory fashion. In support of this claim they sought to introduce evidence that, a few days before the injunction issued, requests for permits to picket had been made to a member of the city commission. One request had been rudely rebuffed, and this same official had later made clear that he was without power to grant the permit alone, since the issuance of such permits was the responsibility of the entire city commission. Assuming the truth of this proffered evidence, it does not follow that the parade ordinance was void on its face. The petitioners, moreover, did not apply for a permit either to the commission itself or to any commissioner after the injunction issued. Had they done so, and had the permit been refused, it is clear that their claim of arbitrary or discriminatory administration of the ordinance would have been considered by the state circuit court upon a motion to dissolve the injunction.

This case would arise in quite a different constitutional posture if the petitioners before disobeying the injunction, had challenged it in the Alabama courts, and had been met with delay or frustration of their constitutional claims. But there is no showing that such would have been the fate of a timely motion to modify or dissolve the injunction. There was an interim of two days between the issuance of the injunction and the Good Friday march. The petitioners give absolutely no explanation of why they did not make some application to the state court during that period. The injunction had issued *ex parte;* if the court had been presented with the petitioners' contentions, it might well have dissolved or at least modified its order in some respects. If it had not done so, Alabama procedure would have provided for an expedited process of appellate review. It cannot be presumed that the Alabama courts would have ignored the petitioners' constitutional claims. Indeed, these contentions were accepted in another case by an Alabama appellate court that struck down on direct review the conviction under this very ordinance of one of these same petitioners.

The rule of law upon which the Alabama courts relied in this case was one firmly established by previous precedents. We do not deal here, therefore, with a situation where a state court has followed a regular past practice of entertaining claims in a given procedural mode, and without notice has abandoned that practice to the detriment of a litigant who finds his claim foreclosed by a novel procedural bar. This is not a case where a procedural requirement has been sprung upon an unwary litigant when prior practice did not give him fair notice of its existence.

The Alabama Supreme Court has apparently never in any criminal contempt case entertained a claim of nonjurisdictional error....

These precedents clearly put the petitioners on notice that they could not bypass orderly judicial review of the injunction before disobeying it. Any claim that they were entrapped or misled is wholly unfounded, a conclusion confirmed by evidence in the record showing that when the petitioners deliberately violated the injunction they expected to go to jail.

The rule of law that Alabama followed in this case reflects a belief that in the fair administration of justice no man can be judge in his own case, however exalted his station, however righteous his motives, and irrespective of his race, color, politics, or religion. This Court cannot hold that the petitioners were constitutionally free to ignore all the procedures of the law and carry their battle to the streets. One may sympathize with the petitioners' impatient commitment to their cause. But respect for judicial process is a small price to pay for the civilizing hand of law, which alone can give abiding meaning to constitutional freedom.

Affirmed.

■ MR. CHIEF JUSTICE WARREN, whom MR. JUSTICE BRENNAN and MR. JUSTICE FORTAS join, dissenting.

. . . .

Petitioners were served with copies of the injunction at various times on Thursday and on Good Friday. Unable to believe that such a blatant and broadly drawn prior restraint on their First Amendment rights could be valid, they announced their intention to defy it and went ahead with the planned peaceful demonstrations on Easter weekend. On the following Monday, when they promptly filed a motion to dissolve the injunction, the court found them in contempt, holding that they had waived all their First Amendment rights by disobeying the court order.

These facts lend no support to the court's charges that petitioners were presuming to act as judges in their own case, or that they had a disregard for the judicial process. They did not flee the jurisdiction or refuse to appear in the Alabama courts. Having violated the injunction, they promptly submitted themselves to the courts to test the constitutionality of the injunction and the ordinance it parroted. They were in essentially the same position as persons who challenge the constitutionality of a statute by violating it, and then defend the ensuing criminal prosecution on constitutional grounds. It has never been thought that violation of a statute indicated such a disrespect for the legislature that the violator always must be punished even if the statute was unconstitutional. On the contrary, some cases have required that persons seeking to challenge the constitutionality of a statute first violate it to establish their standing to sue. Indeed, it shows no disrespect for law to violate a statute on the ground that it is unconstitutional and then to submit one's case to the courts with the willingness to accept the penalty if the statute is held to be valid.

. . . The only circumstance that the court can find to justify anything other than a *per curiam* reversal is that Commissioner Connor had the foresight to have the unconstitutional ordinance included in an *ex parte* injunction issued without notice or hearing or any showing that it was impossible to have notice or a hearing, forbidding the world at large (insofar as it knew of the order) to conduct demonstrations in Birmingham without the consent of the city officials. This injunction was such potent magic that it transformed the command of an unconstitutional statute into an impregnable barrier, challengeable only in what likely would have been protracted legal proceedings and entirely superior in the meantime even to the United States Constitution.

I do not believe that giving this Court's seal of approval to such a gross misuse of the judicial process is likely to lead to greater respect for the law any more than it is likely to lead to greater protection for First Amendment freedoms. The *ex parte* temporary injunction has a long and odious history in this country, and its susceptibility to misuse is all too apparent from the facts of the case. As a weapon against strikes, it proved so effective in the hands of judges friendly to employers that Congress was forced to take the drastic step of removing from federal district courts the jurisdiction to issue injunctions in labor disputes. The labor injunction fell into disrepute largely because it was abused in precisely the same way that the injunctive power was abused in this case. Judges who were not sympathetic to the union cause commonly issued, without notice or hearing, broad restraining orders addressed to large numbers of persons and forbidding them to engage in acts that were either legally permissible or, if illegal, that could better have been left to the regular course of criminal prosecution. The injunctions might later be dissolved, but in the meantime strikes would be crippled because the occasion on which concerted activity might have been effective had passed. Such injunctions so long discredited as weapons against concerted labor activities, have now been given new life by this Court as weapons against the exercise of First Amendment freedoms. Respect for the courts and for judicial process was not increased by the history of the labor injunction.

Nothing in our prior decisions, or in the doctrine that a party subject to a temporary injunction issued by a court of competent jurisdiction with power to decide a dispute properly before it must normally challenge the injunction in the courts rather than by violating it, requires that we affirm the convictions in this case. The majority opinion in this case rests essentially on a single precedent, and that a case the authority of which has clearly been undermined by subsequent decisions. Howat v. State of Kansas, was decided in the days when the labor injunction was in fashion. Kansas had adopted an Industrial Relations Act, the purpose of which in effect was to provide for compulsory arbitration of labor disputes by a neutral administrative tribunal, the "Court of Industrial Relations." Pursuant to its jurisdiction to investigate and perhaps improve labor conditions in the coal mining industry, the "Court" subpoenaed union leaders to appear and testify. In addition, the State obtained an injunction to prevent a strike while the matter was before the "Court." The union leaders disobeyed both the subpoena and the injunction, and sought to challenge the constitutionality of the Industrial Relations Act in the ensuing contempt proceeding. The Kansas Supreme Court held that the constitutionality of the Act could not be challenged in a contempt proceeding, and this Court upheld that determination.

Insofar as Howat v. State of Kansas might be interpreted to approve an absolute rule that any violation of a void court order is punishable as contempt, it has been greatly modified by later decisions. In In re Green, 369 U.S. 689, 82 S.Ct. 1114, 8 L.Ed.2d 198 (1962), we reversed a conviction for contempt of a state injunction forbidding labor picketing because the petitioner was not allowed to present evidence that the labor dispute was arguably subject to the jurisdiction of the National Labor Relations Board and hence not subject to state regulation. If an injunction can be challenged on the ground that it deals with a matter arguably subject to the jurisdiction of the National Labor Relations Board, then *a fortiori* it can be challenged on First Amendment grounds.

It is not necessary to question the continuing validity of the holding in Howat v. State of Kansas, however, to demonstrate that neither it nor the *Mine Workers* case supports the holding of the majority in this case. In *Howat* the subpoena and injunction were issued to enable the Kansas Court of Industrial Relations to determine an underlying labor dispute. In the *Mine Workers* case, the District Court issued a temporary anti-strike injunction to preserve existing conditions during the time it took to decide whether it had authority to grant the Government relief in a complex and difficult action of enormous importance to the national economy. In both cases the orders were of questionable legality, but in both cases they were reasonably necessary to enable the court or administrative tribunal to decide an underlying controversy of considerable importance before it at the time. This case involves an entirely different situation. The Alabama Circuit Court did not issue this temporary injunction to preserve existing conditions while it proceeded to decide some underlying dispute. There was no underlying dispute before it, and the court in practical effect merely added a judicial signature to a preexisting criminal ordinance. Just as the court had no need to issue the injunction to preserve its ability to decide some underlying dispute, the city had no need of an injunction to impose a criminal penalty for demonstrating on the streets without a permit. The ordinance already accomplished that. In point of fact, there is only one apparent reason why the city sought this injunction and why the court issued it: to make it possible to punish petitioners for contempt rather than for violating the ordinance, and thus to immunize the unconstitutional statute and its unconstitutional application from any attack. I regret that this strategy has been so successful.

It is not necessary in this case to decide precisely what limits should be set to the *Mine Workers* doctrine in cases involving violations of the First Amendment. Whatever the scope of that doctrine, it plainly was not intended to give a State the power to nullify the United States Constitution by the simple process of incorporating its unconstitutional criminal statutes into judicial decrees. I respectfully dissent.

■ MR. JUSTICE DOUGLAS, with whom the CHIEF JUSTICE, MR. JUSTICE BRENNAN, and MR. JUSTICE FORTAS concur, dissenting.

. . . .

The right to defy an unconstitutional statute is basic in our scheme. Even when an ordinance requires a permit to make a speech, to deliver a sermon, to picket, to parade, or to assemble, it need not be honored when it is invalid on its face.

By like reason, where a permit has been arbitrarily denied one need not pursue the long and expensive route to this Court to obtain a remedy. The reason is the same in both cases. For if a person must pursue his judicial remedy before he may speak, parade, or assemble, the occasion when protest is desired or needed will have become history and any later speech, parade, or assembly will be futile or pointless.

Howat v. State of Kansas states the general rule that court injunctions are to be obeyed until error is found by normal and orderly review procedures. But there is an exception where "the question of jurisdiction" is "frivolous and not substantial." Moreover, a state court injunction is not *per se* sacred where federal constitutional questions are involved. In re Green held that contempt could not be imposed without a hearing where the state decree bordered the federal domain in labor relations and only a hearing could determine whether there was federal pre-emption. In the present case the collision between this state court decree and the First Amendment is so obvious that no hearing is needed to determine the issue.

. . . .

A court does not have *jurisdiction* to do what a city or other agency of a State lacks *jurisdiction* to do. The command of the Fourteenth Amendment, through which the First Amendment is made applicable to the States, is that no "State" shall deprive any person of "liberty" without due process of law. The decree of a state court is "state" action in the constitutional sense, as much as the action of the state police, the state prosecutor, the state legislature, or the Governor himself. An ordinance—unconstitutional on its face or patently unconstitutional as applied—is not made sacred by an unconstitutional injunction that enforces it. It can and should be flouted in the manner of the ordinance itself. Courts as well as citizens are not free "to ignore all the procedures of the law," to use the Court's language. The "constitutional freedom" of which the Court speaks can be won only if judges honor the Constitution.

■ MR. JUSTICE BRENNAN, with whom the CHIEF JUSTICE, MR. JUSTICE DOUGLAS, and MR. JUSTICE FORTAS join, dissenting.

. . . .

Like the Court, I start with the premise that States are free to adopt rules of judicial administration designed to require respect for their courts' orders. But this does not mean that this valid state interest does not admit of collision with other and more vital interests. Surely the proposition requires no citation that a valid state interest must give way when it infringes on rights guaranteed by the Federal Constitution. The plain meaning of the Supremacy Clause requires no less.

In the present case we are confronted with a collision between Alabama's interest in requiring adherence to orders of its courts and the constitutional prohibition against abridgment of freedom of speech, more particularly "the right of the people peaceably to assemble," and the right "to petition the Government for a redress of grievances." . . .

The vitality of First Amendment protections has . . . been deemed to rest in large measure upon the ability of the individual to take his chances and express himself in the face of such restraints, armed with the ability to challenge those restraints if the State seeks to penalize that expression. The most striking examples of the right to speak first and challenge later, and of peculiar moment for the present case, are the cases concerning the ability of an individual to challenge a permit or licensing statute giving broad discretion to an individual or group, such as the Birmingham permit ordinance, despite the fact that he did not attempt to obtain a permit or license. . . .

Yet by some inscrutable legerdemain these constitutionally secured rights to challenge prior restraints invalid on their face are lost if the State takes the precaution to have some judge append his signature to an *ex parte* order which recites the words of the invalid statute. The State neatly insulates its legislation from challenge by mere incorporation of the identical stifling, overbroad, and vague restraints on exercise of the First Amendment freedoms into an even more vague and pervasive injunction obtained invisibly and upon a stage darkened lest it be open to scrutiny by those affected. The *ex parte* order of the judicial officer exercising broad equitable powers is glorified above the presumably carefully considered, even if hopelessly invalid, mandates of the legislative branch. I would expect this tribunal, charged as it is with the ultimate responsibility to safeguard our constitutional freedoms, to regard the *ex parte* injunctive tool to be far more dangerous than statutes to First Amendment freedoms. One would expect this Court particularly to remember the stern lesson history taught courts, in the context of the labor injunction, that the *ex parte* injunction represents the most devastating of restraints on constitutionally protected activities. . . .

The Court's religious deference to the state court's application of the *Mine Workers'* rule in the present case is in stark contrast to the Court's approach in In re Green. The state court issued an *ex parte* injunction against certain labor picketing. Green, counsel for the union, advised the union that the order was invalid and that it should continue to picket so that the order could be tested in a contempt hearing. The court held Green in contempt without allowing any challenge to the order. This Court stated that the issue was "whether the state court was trenching on the federal domain." It remanded for a hearing to determine whether the activity enjoined was "arguably" subject to Labor Board jurisdiction. In *Green,* therefore, we rejected blind effectuation of the State's interest in requiring compliance with its court's *ex parte* injunctions because of the "arguable" collision with federal labor policy. Yet in the present case the Court affirms the determination of a state court which was willing to assume that its *ex parte* order and the underlying statute were repugnant on their face to the First Amendment of the Federal Constitution. One must wonder what an odd inversion of values it is to afford greater respect to an "arguable" collision with federal labor policy than an assumedly patent interference with constitutional rights so high in the scale of constitutional values that this Court has described them as being "delicate and vulnerable, as well as supremely precious in our society."

. . . .

The suggestion that petitioners be muffled pending outcome of dissolution proceedings without any measurable time limits is particularly inappropriate in the setting of this case. Critical to the plain exercise of the right of protest was the timing of that exercise. . . .

The Court today lets loose a devastatingly destructive weapon for infringement of freedoms jealously safeguarded not so much for the benefit of any given group of any given persuasion as for the benefit of all of us. We cannot permit fears of "riots" and "civil disobedience" generated by slogans like "Black Power" to divert our attention from what is here at stake—not violence or the right of the State to control its streets and sidewalks, but the insulation from attack of *ex parte* orders and legislation upon which they are based even when patently impermissible prior restraints on the exercise of First Amendment rights, thus arming the state courts with the power to punish as a "contempt" what they otherwise could not punish at all. Constitutional restrictions against abridgments of First Amendment freedoms limit judicial equally with legislative and executive power. Convictions for contempt of court orders which invalidly abridge First Amendment freedoms must be condemned equally with convictions for violation of statutes which do the same thing. I respectfully dissent.

NOTES ON *WALKER* AND THE COLLATERAL BAR RULE

1. One of the petitioners in Walker v. City of Birmingham was Dr. Martin Luther King. A number of the participants in the Easter Sunday march were prosecuted for violation of the same Birmingham parade ordinance. Included among their number was the Rev. Fred L. Shuttlesworth, who had also been one of the petitioners in *Walker*. The Supreme Court reversed his conviction on the ground that the ordinance was unconstitutional. Shuttlesworth v. Birmingham, 394 U.S. 147, 89 S.Ct. 935, 22 L.Ed.2d 162 (1969). Writing for the Court, Justice Stewart remarked,

> This ordinance as it was written ... fell squarely within the ambit of the many decisions of this Court over the last 30 years, holding that a law subjecting the exercise of First Amendment freedoms to the prior restraint of a license, without narrow, objective, and definite standards to guide the licensing authority, is unconstitutional.... And our decisions have made clear that a person faced with such an unconstitutional licensing law may ignore it and engage with impunity in the exercise of the right of free expression for which the law purports to require a license.

2. *Mine Workers* and *Walker* reinforce the proposition that an order issued by a court with jurisdiction over the subject matter and the person must be obeyed until it is reversed, modified, or dissolved by orderly and proper proceedings. Failure to obey such an order may, as *Mine Workers* and *Walker* illustrate, result in contempt sanctions. An order issued by a court lacking either subject matter jurisdiction or personal jurisdiction is generally void, and contempt sanctions cannot be imposed for disobedience. The *Mine Workers* case, however, held that courts have jurisdiction to determine their own jurisdiction. In making this preliminary determination, courts have the requisite jurisdiction to issue some valid orders, like the preliminary injunction in *Mine Workers*, and violation of these orders is punishable by contempt.

3. Willy v. Coastal Corporation, 503 U.S. 131, 112 S.Ct. 1076, 117 L.Ed.2d 280 (1992) presented the question of whether a district court may impose Rule 11 sanctions when it is later determined that the court lacked subject matter jurisdiction. Plaintiff Willy commenced a wrongful discharge

action against his employer in state court and the employer removed the action to federal court. Willy challenged the jurisdiction of the district court, arguing that the claim did not arise under federal law. The district court concluded that it had subject matter jurisdiction, granted the employer's motion to dismiss, and imposed sanctions on plaintiff's attorney for filing papers that "created a blur of absolute confusion," (including a 1,200 page, unindexed, unnumbered pile of materials) and for relying on a nonexistent Federal Rule of Evidence. On appeal, the Fifth Circuit Court of Appeals reversed and remanded the case to the state court holding that the district court was without subject matter jurisdiction. The court, however, upheld the Rule 11 sanctions. The Supreme Court affirmed, stating that "the maintenance of orderly procedure, even in the wake of a jurisdiction ruling later found to be mistaken, justifies the conclusion that the sanction ordered here need not be upset." *Willy*, 112 S.Ct. at 1080.

---

4. CONTEMPT

Spry, Equitable Remedies

344 (2d ed. 1980).

A person who wilfully disobeys the order of a court of equity is, if he knows of its terms, to be regarded as in contempt of court, although whether he will be punished for, or compelled to purge, his contempt will be found to depend on the precise circumstances which are in question. It is perhaps not surprising that the means availed of to compel obedience to equitable orders include penalties of considerable rigour.... They are used primarily to compel obedience rather than to punish disobedience; for equity acts in personam, and historically the purpose of the processes of the Court of Chancery was to rectify and reform the conscience of the wrongdoer. The jurisdiction was, to use Professor Ashburner's phrase, "a cathartic jurisdiction".

Anonymous

Court of the King's Bench, 1631.
Dyer 188b, 73 Eng.Rep. 416n.

■ RICHARDSON, CHIEF JUSTICE of C.B. at the assizes at Salisbury in the summer of 1631 was assaulted by a prisoner condemned there for felony, who after his condemnation threw a brickbat at the said Judge, which narrowly missed; and for this an indictment was immediately drawn by Noy against the prisoner, and his right hand cut off and fixed to the gibbet, upon which he was himself immediately hanged in the presence of the Court.

International Union, United Mine Workers of America v. Bagwell

Supreme Court of the United States, 1994.
512 U.S. 821, 114 S.Ct. 2552, 129 L.Ed.2d 642

■ JUSTICE BLACKMUN delivered the opinion of the Court.

We are called upon once again to consider the distinction between civil and criminal contempt. Specifically, we address whether contempt fines levied against a union for violations of a labor injunction are coercive civil fines, or are criminal fines that constitutionally could be imposed only through a jury trial. We conclude that the fines are criminal and, accordingly, we reverse the judgment of the Supreme Court of Virginia.

I

Petitioners, the International Union, United Mine Workers of America, and United Mine Workers of America, District 28 (collectively, the union), engaged in a protracted labor dispute with the Clinchfield Coal Company and Sea "B" Mining Company (collectively, the companies) over alleged unfair labor practices. In April 1989, the companies filed suit in the Circuit Court of Russell County, Virginia, to enjoin the union from conducting unlawful strike-related activities. The trial court entered an injunction which, as later amended, prohibited the union and its members from, among other things, obstructing ingress and egress to company facilities, throwing objects at and physically threatening company employees, placing tire-damaging "jackrocks" on roads used by company vehicles, and picketing with more than a specified number of people at designated sites. The court additionally ordered the union to take all steps necessary to ensure compliance with the injunction, to place supervisors at picket sites, and to report all violations to the court. . . .

As a result of . . . contempt proceedings, the court levied over $64 million in fines against the union, approximately $12 million of which was ordered payable to the companies. Because the union objected to payment of any fines to the companies and in light of the law enforcement burdens posed by the strike, the court ordered that the remaining roughly $52 million in fines be paid to the Commonwealth of Virginia and Russell and Dickenson Counties, "the two counties most heavily affected by the unlawful activity."

While appeals from the contempt orders were pending, the union and the companies settled the underlying labor dispute, agreed to vacate the contempt fines, and jointly moved to dismiss the case. A special mediator representing the Secretary of Labor, and the governments of Russell and Dickenson Counties, supported the parties' motion to vacate the outstanding fines. The trial court granted the motion to dismiss, dissolved the injunction, and vacated the $12 million in fines payable to the companies. After reiterating its belief that the remaining $52 million owed to the counties and the Commonwealth were coercive, civil fines, the trial court refused to vacate these fines, concluding they were "payable in effect to the public." . . .

The Court of Appeals of Virginia reversed and ordered that the contempt fines be vacated pursuant to the settlement agreement. . . .

On consolidated appeals, the Supreme Court of Virginia reversed. The court held that whether coercive, civil contempt sanctions could be settled by private parties was a question of state law, and that Virginia public policy disfavored such a rule, "if the dignity of the law and public respect for the judiciary are to be maintained." 244 Va. 463, 478, 423 S.E.2d 349, 358 (1992). The court also rejected petitioners' contention that the outstanding fines were criminal and could not be imposed absent a criminal trial. Because the trial court's prospective fine schedule was intended to coerce compliance with the injunction and the union could avoid the fines through obedience, the court reasoned, the fines were civil and coercive and properly imposed in civil proceedings. . . .

II

A

"Criminal contempt is a crime in the ordinary sense," Bloom v. Illinois, 391 U.S. 194, 201, (1968), and "criminal penalties may not be imposed on someone who has not been afforded the protections that the Constitution requires of such criminal proceedings," Hicks v. Feiock, 485 U.S. 624, 632. For "serious" criminal contempts involving imprisonment of more than six months, these protections include the right to jury trial. In contrast, civil contempt sanctions, or those penalties designed to compel future compliance with a court order, are considered to be coercive and avoidable through obedience, and thus may be imposed in an ordinary civil proceeding upon notice and an opportunity to be heard. Neither a jury trial nor proof beyond a reasonable doubt is required.

Although the procedural contours of the two forms of contempt are well established, the distinguishing characteristics of civil versus criminal contempts are somewhat less clear. In the leading early case addressing this issue in the context of imprisonment, Gompers v. Bucks Stove & Range Co., 221 U.S. at 441, the Court emphasized that whether a contempt is civil or criminal turns on the "character and purpose" of the sanction involved. Thus, a contempt sanction is considered civil if it "is remedial, and for the benefit of the complainant. But if it is for criminal contempt the sentence is punitive, to vindicate the authority of the court." Ibid.

As Gompers recognized, however, the stated purposes of a contempt sanction alone cannot be determinative. "[W]hen a court imposes fines and punishments on a contemnor, it is not only vindicating its legal authority to enter the initial court order, but it also is seeking to give effect to the law's purpose of modifying the contemnor's behavior to conform to the terms required in the order." Hicks, 485 U.S. at 635. Most contempt sanctions, like most criminal punishments, to some extent punish a prior offense as well as coerce an offender's future obedience. The Hicks Court accordingly held that conclusions about the civil or criminal nature of a contempt sanction are properly drawn, not from "the subjective intent of a State's laws and its courts," ibid., but "from an examination of the character of the relief itself," id. at 636.

The paradigmatic coercive, civil contempt sanction, as set forth in Gompers, involves confining a contemnor indefinitely until he complies with an affirmative command such as an order "to pay alimony, or to surrender property ordered to be turned over to a receiver, or to make a conveyance." 221 U.S. at 442. Imprisonment for a fixed term similarly is coercive when the contemnor is given the option of earlier release if he complies. In these circumstances, the contemnor is able to purge the contempt and obtain his release by committing an affirmative act, and thus " 'carries the keys of his prison in his own pocket.' " Gompers, 221 U.S. at 442 (quoting In re Nevitt, 117 F. 448, 451 (C.A.8 1902)).

By contrast, a fixed sentence of imprisonment is punitive and criminal if it is imposed retrospectively for a "completed act of disobedience," Gompers, 221 U.S. at 443, such that the contemnor cannot avoid or abbreviate the confinement through later compliance. Thus, the Gompers Court concluded that a 12–month sentence imposed on Samuel Gompers for violating an anti-boycott injunction was criminal. When a contempt involves the prior conduct of an isolated, prohibited act, the resulting sanction has no coercive effect. "[T]he defendant is furnished no key, and he cannot shorten the term by promising not to repeat the offense." Id. at 442.

This dichotomy between coercive and punitive imprisonment has been extended to the fine context. A contempt fine accordingly is considered civil and remedial if it either "coerce[s] the defendant into compliance with the court's order, [or] . . . compensate[s] the complainant for losses sustained." United States v. Mine Workers, 330 U.S. 258, 303–304 (1947). Where a fine is not compensatory, it is civil only if the contemnor is afforded an opportunity to purge. Thus, a "flat, unconditional fine" totaling even as little as $50 announced after a finding of contempt is criminal if the contemnor has no subsequent opportunity to reduce or avoid the fine through compliance. Id. at 588.

A close analogy to coercive imprisonment is a per diem fine imposed for each day a contemnor fails to comply with an affirmative court order. Like civil imprisonment, such fines exert a constant coercive pressure, and once the jural command is obeyed, the future, indefinite, daily fines are purged. Less comfortable is the analogy between coercive imprisonment and sus-pended, determinate fines. In this Court's sole prior decision squarely addressing the judicial power to impose coercive civil contempt fines, Mine Workers, supra, it held that fixed fines also may be considered purgable and civil when imposed and suspended pending future compliance. Mine Workers involved a $3,500,000 fine imposed against the union for nation-wide post-World War II strike activities. Finding that the determinate fine was both criminal and excessive, the Court reduced the sanction to a flat criminal fine of $700,000. The Court then imposed and suspended the remaining $2,800,000 as a coercive civil fine, conditioned on the union's ability to purge the fine through full, timely compliance with the trial court's order. The Court concluded, in light of this purge clause, that the civil fine operated as "a coercive imposition upon the defendant union to compel obedience with the court's outstanding order." 330 U.S., at 307.

This Court has not revisited the issue of coercive civil contempt fines addressed in Mine Workers. Since that decision, the Court has erected substantial procedural protections in other areas of contempt law, such as criminal contempts, and summary contempts. Lower federal courts and state courts such as the trial court here nevertheless have relied on Mine Workers to authorize a relatively unlimited judicial power to impose noncompensatory civil contempt fines.

B

Underlying the somewhat elusive distinction between civil and criminal contempt fines, and the ultimate question posed in this case, is what procedural protections are due before any particular contempt penalty may be imposed. Because civil contempt sanctions are viewed as nonpunitive and avoidable, fewer procedural protections for such sanctions have been required. To the extent that such contempts take on a punitive character, however, and are not justified by other considerations central to the contempt power, criminal procedural protections may be in order.

The traditional justification for the relative breadth of the contempt power has been necessity: Courts independently must be vested with "power to impose silence, respect, and decorum, in their presence, and submission to their lawful mandates, and . . . to preserve themselves and their officers from the approach and insults of pollution." Anderson v. Dunn, 6 Wheat. 204, 227 (1821). Courts thus have embraced an inherent contempt authority, as a power "necessary to the exercise of all others," United States v. Hudson, 7 Cranch 32, 34 (1812).

But the contempt power also uniquely is " 'liable to abuse.' " Bloom, 391 U.S., at 202, quoting Ex parte Terry, 128 U.S. 289, 313 (1888). Unlike most areas of law, where a legislature defines both the sanctionable conduct and the penalty to be imposed, civil contempt proceedings leave the offended judge solely responsible for identifying, prosecuting, adjudicating, and sanctioning the contumacious conduct. Contumacy "often strikes at the most vulnerable and human qualities of a judge's temperament," Bloom, 391 U.S. at 202, and its fusion of legislative, executive, and judicial powers "summons forth . . . the prospect of 'the most tyrannical licentiousness,' " Young v. United States ex rel. Vuitton et Fils S.A., 481 U.S. 787, 822 (1987) (SCALIA, J., concurring in judgment), quoting Anderson, 6 Wheat. at 228. Accordingly, "in [criminal] contempt cases an even more compelling argument can be made [than in ordinary criminal cases] for providing a right to jury trial as a protection against the arbitrary exercise of official power." Bloom, 391 U.S. at 202.

Our jurisprudence in the contempt area has attempted to balance the competing concerns of necessity and potential arbitrariness by allowing a relatively unencumbered contempt power when its exercise is most essential, and requiring progressively greater procedural protections when other considerations come into play. The necessity justification for the contempt authority is at its pinnacle, of course, where contumacious conduct threatens a court's immediate ability to conduct its proceedings, such as where a witness refuses to testify, or a party disrupts the court. Thus, petty, direct contempts in the presence of the court traditionally have been subject to summary adjudication, "to maintain order in the courtroom and the integrity of the trial process in the face of an 'actual obstruction of justice.'" Codispoti v. Pennsylvania, 418 U.S. at 513. In light of the court's substantial interest in rapidly coercing compliance and restoring order, and because the contempt's occurrence before the court reduces the need for extensive factfinding and the likelihood of an erroneous deprivation, summary proceedings have been tolerated.

Summary adjudication becomes less justifiable once a court leaves the realm of immediately sanctioned, petty direct contempts. If a court delays punishing a direct contempt until the completion of trial, for example, due process requires that the contemnor's rights to notice and a hearing be respected. There "it is much more difficult to argue that action without notice or hearing of any kind is necessary to preserve order and enable [the court] to proceed with its business," id. at 498, particularly "in view of the heightened potential for abuse posed by the contempt power," id. at 500. Direct contempts also cannot be punished with serious criminal penalties absent the full protections of a criminal jury trial.

Still further procedural protections are afforded for contempts occurring out of court, where the considerations justifying expedited procedures do not pertain. Summary adjudication of indirect contempts is prohibited, and criminal contempt sanctions are entitled to full criminal process. Certain indirect contempts nevertheless are appropriate for imposition through civil proceedings. Contempts such as failure to comply with document discovery, for example, while occurring outside the court's presence, impede the court's ability to adjudicate the proceedings before it and thus touch upon the core justification for the contempt power. Courts traditionally have broad authority through means other than contempt—such as by striking pleadings, assessing costs, excluding evidence, and entering default judgment—to penalize a party's failure to comply with the rules of conduct governing the litigation process. Such judicial sanctions never have been considered criminal, and the imposition of civil, coercive fines to police the litigation process appears consistent with this authority. Similarly, indirect contempts involving discrete, readily ascertainable acts, such as turning over a key or payment of a judgment, properly may be adjudicated through civil proceedings since the need for extensive, impartial factfinding is less pressing.

For a discrete category of indirect contempts, however, civil procedural protections may be insufficient. Contempts involving out-of-court disobedience to complex injunctions often require elaborate and reliable factfinding. Such contempts do not obstruct the court's ability to adjudicate the proceedings before it, and the risk of erroneous deprivation from the lack of a neutral factfinder may be substantial. Under these circumstances, criminal procedural protections such as the rights to counsel and proof beyond a reasonable doubt are both necessary and appropriate to protect the due process rights of parties and prevent the arbitrary exercise of judicial power.

C

In the instant case, neither any party nor any court of the Commonwealth has suggested that the challenged fines are compensatory. At no point did the trial court attempt to calibrate the fines to damages caused by the union's contumacious activities or indicate that the fines were "to compensate the complainant for losses sustained." Mine Workers, 330 U.S. at 303–304. The nonparty governments, in turn, never requested any compensation or presented any evidence regarding their injuries, never moved to intervene in the suit, and never actively defended the fines imposed. The issue before us accordingly is limited to whether these fines, despite their noncompensatory character, are coercive civil or criminal sanctions.

The parties propose two independent tests for determining whether the fines are civil or criminal. Petitioners argue that because the injunction primarily prohibited certain conduct rather than mandated affirmative acts, the sanctions are criminal. Respondents in turn urge that because the trial court established a prospective fine schedule that the union could avoid through compliance, the fines are civil in character.

Neither theory satisfactorily identifies those contempt fines that are criminal and thus must be imposed through the criminal process. Petitioners correctly note that Gompers suggests a possible dichotomy "between refusing to do an act commanded,—remedied by imprisonment until the party performs the required act; and doing an act forbidden,—punished by imprisonment for a definite term." 221 U.S. at 443. The distinction between mandatory and prohibitory orders is easily applied in the classic contempt scenario, where contempt sanctions are used to enforce orders compelling or forbidding a single, discrete act. In such cases, orders commanding an affirmative act simply designate those actions that are capable of being coerced.

But the distinction between coercion of affirmative acts and punishment of prohibited conduct is difficult to apply when conduct that can recur is involved, or when an injunction contains both mandatory and prohibitory provisions. Moreover, in borderline cases injunctive provisions containing essentially the same command can be phrased either in mandatory or prohibitory terms. Under a literal application of petitioners' theory, an injunction ordering the union: "Do not strike," would appear to be prohibitory and criminal, while an injunction ordering the union: "Continue working," would be mandatory and civil. In enforcing the present injunction, the trial court imposed fines without regard to the mandatory or prohibitory nature of the clause violated. Accordingly, even though a parsing of the injunction's various provisions might support the classification of contempts such as rock throwing and placing tire-damaging "jack-rocks" on roads as criminal and the refusal to place supervisors at picket sites as civil, the parties have not asked us to review the order in that manner. In a case like this involving an injunction that prescribes a detailed code of conduct, it is more appropriate to identify the character of the entire decree.

Despite respondents' urging, we also are not persuaded that dispositive significance should be accorded to the fact that the trial court prospectively announced the sanctions it would impose. Had the trial court simply levied the fines after finding the union guilty of contempt, the resulting "determinate and unconditional" fines would be considered "solely and exclusively punitive." Id. at 632–633. Respondents nevertheless contend that the trial court's announcement of a prospective fine schedule allowed the union to "avoid paying the fine[s] simply by performing the . . . act required by the court's order," Hicks, 485 U.S. at 632, and thus transformed these fines into coercive, civil ones. Respondents maintain here, as the Virginia Supreme Court held below, that the trial court could have imposed a daily civil fine to coerce the union into compliance, and that a prospective fine schedule is indistinguishable from such a sanction.

Respondents' argument highlights the difficulties encountered in parsing coercive civil and criminal contempt fines. The fines imposed here concededly are difficult to distinguish either from determinate, punitive fines or from initially suspended, civil fines. Ultimately, however, the fact that the trial court announced the fines before the contumacy, rather than after the fact, does not in itself justify respondents' conclusion that the fines are civil or meaningfully distinguish these penalties from the ordinary criminal law. Due process traditionally requires that criminal laws provide prior notice both of the conduct to be prohibited and of the sanction to be imposed. The trial court here simply announced the penalty determinate fines of $20,000 or $100,000 per violation—that would be imposed for future contempts. The union's ability to avoid the contempt fines was indistinguishable from the ability of any ordinary citizen to avoid a criminal sanction by conforming his behavior to the law. The fines are not coercive day fines, or even suspended fines, but are more closely analogous to fixed, determinate, retrospective criminal fines which petitioners had no opportunity to purge once imposed. We therefore decline to conclude that the mere fact that the sanctions were announced in advance rendered them coercive and civil as a matter of constitutional law.

Other considerations convince us that the fines challenged here are criminal. The union's sanctionable conduct did not occur in the court's presence or otherwise implicate the court's ability to maintain order and adjudicate the proceedings before it. Nor did the union's contumacy involve simple, affirmative acts, such as the paradigmatic civil contempts examined in Gompers. Instead, the Virginia trial court levied contempt fines for widespread, ongoing, out-of-court violations of a complex injunction. In so doing, the court effectively policed petitioners' compliance with an entire code of conduct that the court itself had imposed. The union's contumacy lasted many months and spanned a substantial portion of the State. The fines assessed were serious, totaling over $52 million. Under such circumstances, disinterested factfinding and evenhanded adjudication were essential, and petitioners were entitled to a criminal jury trial.

In reaching this conclusion, we recognize that this Court generally has deferred to a legislature's determination whether a sanction is civil or criminal, and that "[w]hen a State's proceedings are involved, state law provides strong guidance about whether or not the State is exercising its authority 'in a nonpunitive, noncriminal manner.'" Hicks, 485 U.S. at 631. We do not deviate from either tradition today. Where a single judge, rather than a legislature, declares a particular sanction to be civil or criminal, such deference is less appropriate. Moreover, this Court has recognized that even for state proceedings, the label affixed to a contempt ultimately "will not be allowed to defeat the applicable protections of federal constitutional law." Hicks v. Feiock, 485 U.S. at 631. We conclude that the serious contempt fines imposed here were criminal and constitutionally could not be imposed absent a jury trial.

III

Our decision concededly imposes some procedural burdens on courts' ability to sanction widespread, indirect contempts of complex injunctions through noncompensatory fines. Our holding, however, leaves unaltered the longstanding authority of judges to adjudicate direct contempts summarily, and to enter broad compensatory awards for all contempts through civil proceedings. Because the right to trial by jury applies only to serious criminal sanctions, courts still may impose noncompensatory, petty fines for contempts such as the present ones without conducting a jury trial. We also do not disturb a court's ability to levy, albeit through the criminal contempt process, serious fines like those in this case.

Ultimately, whatever slight burden our holding may impose on the judicial contempt power cannot be controlling. The Court recognized more than a quarter century ago:

> "We cannot say that the need to further respect for judges and courts is entitled to more consideration than the interest of the individual not be subjected to serious criminal punishment without the benefit of all the procedural protections worked out carefully over the years and deemed fundamental to our system of justice. Genuine respect, which alone can lend true dignity to our judicial establishment, will be engendered, not by the fear of unlimited authority, but by the firm administration of the law through those institutionalized procedures which have been worked out over the centuries."

Bloom, 391 U.S. at 208.

Where, as here, "a serious contempt is at issue, considerations of efficiency must give way to the more fundamental interest of ensuring the even-handed exercise of judicial power." Id. at 209.

The judgment of the Supreme Court of Virginia is reversed.

It is so ordered.

■ Concurring opinion of JUSTICE SCALIA omitted; Concurring opinion of JUSTICE GINSBURG, with whom the CHIEF JUSTICE joins, omitted.

NOTES ON CIVIL AND CRIMINAL CONTEMPT

1. A criminal contempt proceeding is a criminal case separate from the underlying proceeding. A civil contempt proceeding, on the other hand, is a civil proceeding (but not a "case at common law") adjunct to the underlying case. For the quotation of contemnors carrying "the keys of their prison in their own pockets," see In re Nevitt, 117 Fed. 448 (8th Cir.1902).

The difference between civil and criminal contempt affects such matters as consequences of the plaintiff's voluntary dismissal of the equity suit, the application of the Statute of Limitations for crimes, the availability of the privilege against self-incrimination, the burden of proof, the procedure and scope of appellate review, and the power of the executive to pardon the person adjudged to be in contempt.

2. Although there was traditionally no right to jury trial in criminal contempt proceedings, the Supreme Court ruled in Bloom v. Illinois, 391 U.S. 194, 88 S.Ct. 1477, 20 L.Ed.2d 522 (1968), that the Sixth Amendment right to trial by jury applies in cases of criminal contempt. The Sixth Amendment guarantees a right to trial by jury in prosecutions for serious, as opposed to petty, crimes. The distinction between serious and petty crimes turns upon the penalty that the courts are legislatively authorized to impose on convicted offenders. In the event that no such maximum penalty exists, as is often the case with respect to contempt, the actual punishment imposed upon the contemnor is determinative. If the relevant punishment is a jail term in excess of six months, the crime is serious. If it is a sentence of six months or less, the crime is presumed petty. Blanton v. City of North Las Vegas, Nevada, 489 U.S. 538, 109 S.Ct. 1289, 103 L.Ed.2d 550 (1989), found that a possible fine of $1,000 did not make a drunk driving offense with a maximum six month prison term a serious crime. Muniz v. Hoffman, 422 U.S. 454, 95 S.Ct. 2178, 45 L.Ed.2d 319 (1975), held that there was no right to jury trial in a criminal contempt proceeding where a fine of $10,000 was imposed on a union with 13,000 dues-paying members. But the Court has not ruled out the possibility that a fine alone could bring the jury trial right into play in a case of criminal contempt.

3. Vuitton informed a federal district court that Klayminc and others were violating its injunction barring the infringement of Vuitton's trademark. The judge appointed Vuitton's lawyers to investigate and prosecute this contempt on behalf of the United States. They did so, and Klayminc and several associates were convicted of criminal contempt. On appeal, the Supreme Court reversed their convictions. Young v. United States ex rel. Vuitton et Fils S.A., 481 U.S. 787, 107 S.Ct. 2124, 95 L.Ed.2d 740 (1987). A majority of the Justices agreed "that courts possess inherent authority to initiate contempt proceedings for disobedience to their orders, authority which necessarily encompasses the ability to appoint a private attorney to prosecute the contempt." Nonetheless, the Court invoked its supervisory authority to hold that, because of the potential conflict of interest, a federal court may not appoint "counsel for a party that is the beneficiary of a court order ... as prosecutor in a [criminal] contempt action alleging a violation of that order."

4. Mayberry was proceeding *pro se* in a criminal case. In the course of the trial, he spoke most abusively to the judge. He also attempted to disrupt the proceedings when the judge charged the jury. The attempt was unsuccessful, and Mayberry was found guilty as charged. When he appeared for sentencing, the judge said that he was guilty of contempt and sentenced him to 11–22 years imprisonment for his contemptuous behavior. On appeal, the Supreme Court held that, given the sting of Mayberry's personal attacks upon the trial judge and the judge's decision to delay the contempt proceedings until the end of the trial, due process required that a different judge preside over the adjudication of Mayberry's contempt.

Mayberry v. Pennsylvania, 400 U.S. 455, 91 S.Ct. 499, 27 L.Ed.2d 532 (1971).

5. In Spallone v. United States, 493 U.S. 265, 110 S.Ct. 625, 107 L.Ed.2d 644 (1990), the Supreme Court held that a District Court order against four Yonkers city councilmembers for refusing to vote in favor of legislation implementing a consent decree earlier approved by the city, constituted an abuse of discretion. The consent decree was aimed at terminating residential racial segregation within the city of Yonkers. The City of Yonkers was a party to the action, but the individual councilmembers were not. The Court stated:

> We hold that the District Court, in view of the "extraordinary" nature of the imposition of sanctions against the individual councilmen, should have proceeded with such contempt sanctions first against the city alone in order to secure compliance with the remedial orders. Only if that approach failed to produce compliance within a reasonable time should the question of imposing contempt sanctions against petitioners even have been considered. "This limitation accords with the doctrine that a court must exercise '[t]he least possible power adequate to the end proposed.' "

In Re Yengo

Supreme Court of New Jersey, 1980.
84 N.J. 111, 417 A.2d 533.

■ POLLOCK, J. . . .

The trial judge concluded that the absence of the attorney constituted direct contempt in the presence of the court and disobedience of a court order prohibiting involvement in other proceedings. She found him guilty of contempt and imposed a $500 fine. The Appellate Division reversed and remanded, concluding that the offense was an indirect contempt requiring notice and hearing in accordance with R. 1:10–2 to . . . .

I

Respondent, John W. Yengo, represented Leo Leone, one of ten defendants in a multiple defendant gambling conspiracy trial. The nature of the case, the number of defendants and their counsel, together with the complexity of the evidence, presented difficult trial problems. The intricate proofs, which included wiretaps or monitored telephone conversations by court-authorized electronic surveillance, made attorney attendance throughout the trial a matter of highest priority. Both court and counsel recognized the special problems inherent in the management of the case. . . .

Anticipating scheduling difficulties among the numerous defense attorneys, the judge stressed the need for regular attendance. She instructed counsel that she would not tolerate tardiness or absence without her prior approval. On February 8, 1978, she pointedly advised counsel:

"Now you are considered on trial before me.... [Y]ou are to advise all other courts and all other judges that you are on trial before me. If you have any problem with any judge, you let me know.... So, don't get involved in any other case or trial...."

On February 14, the judge again emphasized the importance of punctuality:

"Now, I just want to advise you that it is my intention to move this case along as rapidly as I can. The case itself has enough problems involved with the law involved in it without us having practical problems on a day-to-day basis with regard to time and otherwise....

"However, I am putting you all on notice that I intend, once we get going with this case, to abide by the time restrictions on this case. All of you have got to be here at 9 o'clock because I am going to be out on the bench at 9 o'clock. I intend to impose sanctions on any attorney who is not here on time....

"So, all of you get yourselves here on time as we move throughout the case....

"As for your clients, most of them are here. I want to advise all of you that you are all to make appropriate arrangements to get yourselves here on time. I intend to proceed with the case and move along with the case in accordance with the time restrictions and if you are not here, I will consider you to have voluntarily absented yourself.

"So, what I am asking from you is your cooperation in telling you I am going to give you every consideration I can under the circumstances, but because of the nature of the case, the number of attorneys, the number of defendants, we have to be strict with regard to the time requirements. I intend to impose those and if they are violated, I will impose sanctions."

Yengo was not only aware of the instructions, but on February 22 he requested Judge Loftus to call another judge before whom he had a matter pending.

Testimony began on February 21, and Yengo appeared regularly until March 2. On that date, without previously informing the judge, he failed to appear at trial. Although Yengo failed to notify the court of his planned absence, he had discussed the matter with the prosecutor, several of the other defense attorneys and his client. In his place, Lawrence Burns ... appeared on behalf of Leone. Burns shared office space with Yengo, received cases from him, and described himself as Yengo's associate. Burns arrived late for the trial.

Leone advised the court that he consented to representation by Burns in Yengo's absence....

The trial judge acknowledged Burns' authorization to represent Leone, and heard testimony ... until lunchtime. Following the initial hour of testimony, Judge Loftus became concerned about the extent of Burns' knowledge of the case. During the lunchtime recess, the judge questioned Burns in her chambers about Yengo's absence....

In response to questions from the court, Burns informed the judge that Yengo had called Burns at 9 o'clock the preceding evening to advise that he was going out of the country. Burns stated further that he had reviewed the file with Yengo for 15 minutes at 11:00 p.m. on that evening and that previously he had spent two days reviewing the file and discussing it with Yengo.

The trial proceeded with Burns acting as counsel for Leone. Judge Loftus tried several times to locate Yengo through calls placed by her secretary to his answering service. Judge Loftus also called Yengo's home and spoke with his daughter, who told the judge that Yengo had gone to Bermuda on a four day vacation and would return on Sunday, March 5. However, the daughter was unable to inform the court where Yengo was staying in Bermuda.

The trial court concluded that she had no alternative but to let the trial continue. . . .

The judge . . . sent a telegram to his home ordering and directing him to appear before her at 9:00 a.m. on Monday, March 6, 1978, the next trial date.

On that date, Yengo appeared in court. The trial judge cleared the courtroom, except for court personnel and Yengo. He explained that he had been in Bermuda on business for a supermarket. He stated that he did not communicate with the court because he did not know if he would be going to Bermuda until late Wednesday, March 1. . . .

In the course of the colloquy with the court, the trial judge stated:

"I called you here this morning and gave you the opportunity to speak because I thought that maybe the information that had come to my attention by the various phone calls I had to make, that you had gone to Bermuda for the weekend, was wrong. I thought maybe there was even some kind of explanation for it . . . but that is not so. There is absolutely no emergent necessity for you to leave this Country and go to Bermuda. Your actions just bespeak nothing but irresponsible professional conduct toward your client and towards this court."

She then cited him for contempt in the presence of the court and stated he would be "dealt with further at another time with regard to the disposition of this particular citation."

On April 14, 1978, Yengo appeared before Judge Loftus. She affirmed the determination of contempt and imposed a fine of $500. In her certification on April 21, 1978, the trial court stated:

"The action of John Yengo, Esq., in going to Bermuda for two court days in the third week of a five-week, complex wiretap gambling conspiracy case with ten defendants and a seventeen-member jury without prior notice and approval of the Court and without leaving word as to where he could be reached, constituted a disruption in the Court proceedings, disobedience of the Court order prohibiting involvement in other proceedings, a lack of respect for the Court, a lack of professional responsibility, as well as conduct prejudicial to the administration of justice."

The certification concluded by stating that Yengo was adjudged guilty of contempt in the presence of the court on March 6, 1978. See R. 1:10–1.

II

The law of contempt is derived from statutes, rules of court, and judicial decisions. In general, contempt includes disobedience of a court order or misbehavior in the presence of the court by any person or misbehavior by an officer of the court in his official transactions....

. . . .

III

Where the conduct of an attorney disrupts the orderliness of a trial, the speed with which a court should respond depends on the offensiveness of the lawyer's conduct and the need to assure the continuity and fairness of the proceeding.

When the contempt is in the presence of the court, the judge may act summarily without notice or order to show cause. R. 1:10–1. On other occasions, the proceedings shall be on notice and on an order for arrest or an order to show cause. R. 1:10–2. In addition, the matter may not be heard by the judge allegedly offended, except with the consent of the person charged. R. 1:10–4.

The reasons for notice and hearing for a contempt occurring outside the presence of the court "are, first, that there is no need to deal so abruptly with an offense which does not constitute an obstruction within the courtroom itself, and second, that since the court does not know by its own senses all of the facts constituting the offense, there must be a trial to adduce them."

That rationale is consistent with a dual test established by the United States Supreme Court to determine the justification for the exercise of summary contempt powers: (1) the act or omission must occur in the presence of the court so that no further evidence need be adduced for the judge to certify to the observation of the contumacious behavior and (2) the act must impact adversely on the authority of the court.

Both this Court and the United States Supreme Court have demonstrated sensitivity to the potential for abuse in summary contempt proceedings. The United States Supreme Court has stated that summary contempt powers should be limited to the "least possible power adequate to the end proposed." That limitation has been followed in New Jersey as well as in federal and other state courts.

[handwritten margin note: ▷ important maxim.]

Since the power to punish directly inevitably diminishes the procedural due process accorded to the alleged contemnor, the power must be permitted only where necessary. If proof of the contempt depends on evidence from persons other than the judge, the better practice is to proceed on order to show cause even where the contempt is in the face of the court. That procedure comports more closely with concepts of procedural due process and eliminates unseemly confrontations between the court and the contemnor.

IV

The critical question is whether an unexcused absence of an attorney should be classified as a direct or indirect contempt for procedural purposes. The essence of a direct contempt, or contempt in the face of the court, is conduct that a judge can determine through his own senses is offensive and that tends to obstruct the administration of justice. Generally a disruptive act in the presence of the court, such as the use of offensive words or conduct, is a direct contempt.

However, an act may be a direct contempt although it is not committed in the presence of the court. Examples include: threatening letter from an attorney to the clerk in chancery; assault on one incorrectly thought to be a witness; letter from father of husband in divorce proceeding to wife and threats to her attorney; sending an abusive letter to the Ordinary [(an appellate judge)] denouncing and abusing the court below. More recent examples include: letter from recipient of parking ticket to clerk of municipal court containing obscenities and alleging "ugly" methods of collecting money; letter to judge from recipient of traffic ticket alleging he would not receive a fair trial.

A useful definition of indirect contempt is even more difficult to find. One writer suggests: "Probably the only all-embracing and accurate definition of indirect contempt is that it is composed of all contempts that are not direct." R. Goldfarb, The Contempt Power 70 (Colum.Univ.Press 1963). Stated otherwise, an indirect contempt "is an act committed not in the presence of the court, but at some distance therefrom." [C]f. Van Sweringen v. Van Sweringen, 22 N.J. 440, 126 A.2d 334 (1956)(by telling a corespondent in a divorce case that he could obtain a favorable decision for money, an attorney committed criminal contempt outside presence of the court which reflected on the integrity of judge, who should have disqualified himself).

By itself, the unexplained absence of an attorney from a courtroom is an enigma. It demands an explanation. Aside from the unlikely event of complete disappearance of an attorney, the absence will be followed, as here, by a subsequent appearance before the court. At that time, the court invariably will ask for an explanation from the attorney. Generally, the absence alone does not constitute contempt. An essential element of the offense is the inadequacy of the explanation. As Justice Traynor has written, "The absence of a valid excuse is an indispensable element of the contempt."

Although we have not determined when the absence of an attorney is a direct contempt, the Appellate Division has held that an unexplained absence or tardiness together with a refusal to explain or a wholly inadequate excuse will constitute a direct contempt. In re Clawans, 69 N.J.Super. 373, 174 A.2d 367 (App.Div.1961), certif. den. 36 N.J. 296, 177 A.2d 340 (1962), cert. den. 370 U.S. 905, 82 S.Ct. 1250, 8 L.Ed.2d 401 (1962), involved two separate contempts. The first consisted of insulting statements in open court about the trial judge, and the second, which occurred several months later, was a flat refusal to explain her absence. In State v. Dias, 76 N.J.Super. 337, 184 A.2d 535 (App.Div.1962), the defendant-attorney gave a "wholly inadequate excuse" for his tardiness in appearing at a peremptorily scheduled hearing. On appeal, he did not deny that the alleged contempt was one that occurred in the presence of the court.

Federal courts and other state courts have divided on the issue, but the majority view is that an attorney's unexcused absence is not contempt in the actual presence of the court. The rationale is that, although the absence or late arrival of an attorney can be perceived directly by the court, the conclusion that the absence is inexcusable requires reference to facts not immediately within the court's perception.

As with the state courts, the majority view among the federal courts is to treat the absence of an attorney as an indirect contempt.

We conclude that the mere unexplained absence of an attorney is a hybrid. In fashioning the appropriate judicial response, we adhere to our prior declaration that the summary contempt power should be exercised sparingly. However, we recognize also that strict compliance with the requirement of referring absent attorneys to another judge may not be in the interests of the judiciary, attorneys, or the public. Time would be wasted needlessly if, after observing the absence of an attorney, a judge could not ask, "Where were you?" The answer to that question frequently will obviate the need for further proceedings. Preclusion of the inquiry would prevent any dialogue between court and counsel on an issue that might be resolved without complicated proceedings. The characterization of the contempt as direct or indirect should be deferred until after the attorney has an opportunity to explain his absence.

V

If there is an adequate explanation, the matter should proceed no further. However, if the attorney refuses to explain, the judge may treat the offense as a direct contempt. Both the absence and the refusal are in the presence of the judge, who may determine the matter summarily. Similarly if the attorney offers an insulting, frivolous, or clearly inadequate explanation, both elements of the offense are in the presence of the judge, who may treat the matter as a direct contempt. Of equal importance the refusal to explain or an offensive explanation creates the need in the court to deal immediately with the matter. The need for immediate adjudication and punishment outweighs the procedural safeguards that would ensue from referring the matter to another judge. . . .

If there is some evidence of the adequacy of the explanation, the judge should characterize the matter as an indirect contempt and proceed by order to show cause returnable before another judge. R. 1:10–2,–4. The semblance of adequacy dilutes the offensiveness of the explanation and diminishes the need for dealing instantly with the offense. If the proffered explanation may require proof of facts occurring outside the presence of the court, the better practice is to proceed before another judge.

To the extent the inconvenience of the preferred practice unduly encourages some trial judges to hear the matter themselves, the power of the appellate court to make an independent review of the facts and law provides an adequate safeguard for the allegedly contumacious attorney.

The competing interests create a spectrum for selecting the appropriate procedure. The determination of the procedure depends on where the explanation falls on the spectrum. Where the explanation is clearly inadequate, the need to maintain the authority of the court should predominate. The offense should be treated as a direct contempt. Where there is a good faith excuse, although another judge may find it to be inadequate, the predominant consideration should be enhancement of procedural due process for the alleged contemnor. The offense should be treated as an indirect contempt. The explanation and the factual background color the characterization of the offense and affect the determination of the appropriate procedure as well as the ultimate outcome.

Whether the hearing proceeds before the same or another judge, there must be proof of criminal intent to establish contempt as a public offense. . . .

In this case, the explanation was frivolous. Respondent went to Bermuda in the middle of winter. Whether he went for a vacation, as his daughter stated, or for business, as he asserted, the explanation was clearly inadequate. His unexcused absence was particularly egregious when viewed against the background of a multiple defendant criminal gambling conspiracy case and the admonitions of the trial judge.

There is no evidence of intemperate conduct on the part of the trial judge. . . .

Accordingly the judgment of the Appellate Division is reversed, and the judgment of conviction by the trial court and the $500 fine are reinstated.

Pounders v. Watson

Supreme Court of the United States, 1997.
521 U.S. 982, 117 S.Ct. 2359, 138 L.Ed.2d 976.

■ PER CURIAM.

In this case the Court of Appeals for the Ninth Circuit granted respondent's habeas corpus petition and held invalid on due process grounds her conviction for summary contempt before a state court judge for conduct in open court. The Court of Appeals misinterpreted the constitutional requirements for imposition of a summary contempt order. We grant the petition for a writ of certiorari and reverse.

Respondent Penelope Watson is an attorney who represented William Mora in a multidefendant murder trial in the Superior Court of the State of California in and for the County of Los Angeles. The Honorable William Pounders presided over the case, and he is the petitioner here. On April 7, 1994, counsel for one of Mora's codefendants repeatedly raised in open court the issue of the punishment defendants might receive if they were convicted. Judge Pounders stated that possible punishment " 'is not a subject that's open to discussion. It should not be explored.' " App. to Pet. for Cert. 20. Though it is not clear whether this was said at a bench conference only or reiterated in open court, it seems respondent remained at the defense table during the bench conference. Her co-counsel, Joseph Gutierrez, was at the bench on behalf of their client Mora. In later proceedings, Judge Pounders noted that "Miss Watson is no more than six feet away from us when we're at the side bar conference. She's at the end of the center table closest to the bench and only a matter of feet away." Id., at 36.

On April 20, counsel for a different codefendant again raised the issue of punishment. Judge Pounders stated in open court: " '[T]he subject of sentencing of Mr. Fernandez is not part of the conversation. But more than that, it is prejudicial under [Cal. Evid.Code Ann. §]352 [(West 1966)]. It's not a subject the jury is entitled to discuss. This is not a death penalty case, so penalties are not something to discuss. . . .' " Id., at 21.

The next day, petitioner's co-counsel Gutierrez asked a series of questions in which he stated that defendants were "looking at life in prison." At a bench conference, while respondent remained at the defense table, Judge Pounders told Gutierrez:

" 'You had an ulterior motive in bringing out the amount of time [the witness] spent [in prison], and I think it's to show the contrast between what he got and what your clients may be facing, and you continue to say life. . . . I'm saying that's the last time I want to hear anything about a sentence. . . . You've covered it. Do not cover it again.' " Watson v. Block, 102 F.3d 433, 435 (C.A.9 1996).

After the side bar, Gutierrez apologized in open court:

" 'Judge, I would just like the record to reflect that I apologize to this court for asking the question as to or informing this witness through my question that he served six months in jail and three years probation. . . . I obviously defied the Court Order, and I misunderstood the Court and I apologize.' " Ibid.

In response, Judge Pounders said in open court: " 'It's simply that punishment is not an issue for this jury to decide, and the more that counsel want to harp on this issue of punishment, the more inappropriate it becomes.' " Ibid.

On June 21, while respondent was questioning Mora, the following examination and colloquy occurred:

By Ms. Watson: "[T]hroughout this trial sometimes you've had to get up at 4:00 in the morning and not go to sleep until 10:00 at night?

"Ms. Walker [for the People of California]: Objection, your honor, relevance.

"The Court: Sustained.

"By Ms. Watson: And during that four years [that you have been in prison], you were facing the death penalty until just the day before we started.

"Ms. Walker: Your honor, People are going to object.

"The Court: Sustained.

"Ms. Walker: Ask Miss Watson to be admonished and the Court—

"The Court: Sustained. We've already talked about this at side bar. Follow the Court's admonitions.

"By Ms. Watson: You're facing life without possibility of parole?" App. to Pet. for Cert. 30–31.

At that point, Judge Pounders called counsel to the bench. The judge asked respondent why he should not hold her in contempt for discussing punishment after he had "at least twice ordered counsel not to cover" the issue. Respondent replied, "I think it goes to [Mora's] state of mind as to why he would take this risk at this point in revealing that he was the person who called 911." When the judge asked why respondent did not raise the point at sidebar, particularly when her co-counsel Gutierrez had been admonished for raising the issue, Watson responded: "I wasn't at side bar with any of that involving Mr. Gutierrez...." The judge said, "You're in violation of a court order. You do not think that's relevant to anything?" Watson responded, "I didn't think it was." Id., at 31, 32.

Judge Pounders then found respondent in contempt for violating Cal.Civ.Proc.Code Ann. § 1209(a)(5) (West 1997), which provides that "[d]isobedience of any lawful judgment, order, or process of the court" is grounds for contempt. The next day, on June 22, the judge issued a written order of contempt finding that "the questions asked by contemnor of Defendant Mora in the presence of the jury had as its [sic] sole purpose improperly advising the jury of the potential penalty for the defendants in violation of the court order." Id., at 26. He found "contemnor was aware of the Order," since she was

> "at all times ... present (a) at or immediately adjacent to all side bar conferences and (b) present in open court on April 7, 1994, when the initial warning was given, and (c) on April 20, 1994, when the warning was repeated in open court, and (d) on April 21, 1994, when co-counsel Mr. Gutierrez apologized in open court for defying that same order." Ibid.

The court imposed a 2–day jail sentence to be served after trial.

On July 8, two days after the murder case was submitted to the jury, Judge Pounders gave respondent another opportunity to justify her actions. She again explained and argued through her counsel that she thought her questions were relevant and " 'not covered by the court's previous rulings or admonitions.' " 102 F.3d, at 436. Judge Pounders was not convinced. Respondent, he noted, did not ask for a side bar for clarification. He found:

> " 'I think she has permanently prejudiced this jury in favor of her client.... They know the penalty he's facing ... and they know that the person that was killed [a gang member] isn't worth that penalty, and so they are not going to find him guilty of the major charge.
>
> . . . .
>
> " 'And when the penalty is as extreme as this one is presented to the jury, I think that's a prejudice that cannot be overcome....
>
> . . . .
>
> " 'And I believe that the result is going to be that [the jury] will not find Mr. Mora guilty of the main offense, which is murder, that they may not find him guilty of much at all.' " Ibid.

Respondent's habeas petitions to the District Court of Appeals and the California Supreme Court were denied summarily. She filed this federal habeas corpus action in the United States District Court for the Central District of California. The District Court denied the petition on September 8, 1994, finding "[t]he record makes it quite clear that multiple statements made in open court gave Petitioner adequate warning to put a person of reasonable intelligence on notice as to what conduct Judge Pounders had prohibited, satisfying due process notice requirements." App. to Pet. for Cert. 15.

Respondent appealed to the United States Court of Appeals for the Ninth Circuit, arguing that her due process rights were violated because she did not have notice of the prohibited conduct and because the trial judge could not have known without a hearing whether her conduct was willful. The Court of Appeals did not dispute the state trial court's findings on these points. Instead, it held that "her conduct was not so disruptive as to justify use of summary contempt procedure," 102 F.3d, at 437.

Longstanding precedent confirms the power of courts to find summary contempt and impose punishment. See, e.g., Ex parte Terry, 128 U.S. 289, 9 S.Ct. 77, 32 L.Ed. 405 (1888). In Cooke v. United States, 267 U.S. 517, 45 S.Ct. 390, 69 L.Ed. 767 (1925), the Court said:

"To preserve order in the court room for the proper conduct of business, the court must act instantly to suppress disturbance or violence or physical obstruction or disrespect to the court when occurring in open court. There is no need of evidence or assistance of counsel before punishment, because the court has seen the offense. Such summary vindication of the court's dignity and authority is necessary. It has always been so in the courts of the common law and the punishment imposed is due process of law." Id., at 534, 45 S.Ct., at 394.

As we have recognized, however, the contempt power may be abused. We have held the summary contempt exception to the normal due process requirements, such as a hearing, counsel, and the opportunity to call witnesses, "includes only charges of misconduct, in open court, in the presence of the judge, which disturbs the court's business, where all of the essential elements of the misconduct are under the eye of the court, are actually observed by the court, and where immediate punishment is essential to prevent 'demoralization of the court's authority' before the public." In re Oliver, 333 U.S. 257, 275, 68 S.Ct. 499, 509, 92 L.Ed. 682 (1948) (quoting Cooke, supra, at 536, 45 S.Ct., at 395).

We have stressed the importance of confining summary contempt orders to misconduct occurring in court. Where misconduct occurs in open court, the affront to the court's dignity is more widely observed, justifying summary vindication. See In re Green, 369 U.S. 689, 692, 82 S.Ct. 1114, 1116–1117, 8 L.Ed.2d 198 (1962) (relying on due process cases); Harris v. United States, 382 U.S. 162, 164, 86 S.Ct. 352, 354, 15 L.Ed.2d 240 (1965) (defining boundary between summary and ordinary contempt under Fed. Rule Crim. Proc. 42).

. . .

In this case the state trial court made an express finding that respondent willfully refused to comply with the court's order. Again and again the trial court admonished counsel, both in open court and at bench conferences when respondent was sitting a few feet away, not to discuss punishment. After respondent asked her client whether he had been facing the death penalty, the court sustained an objection and said " 'We've already talked about this at side bar. Follow the Court's admonitions.' " App. to Pet. for Cert. 24. Undaunted, respondent's next question was, " 'You're facing life without possibility of parole?' " Id., at 25.

The Court of Appeals did not question the willfulness finding in its opinion. 102 F.3d, at 438 ("[W]e do not decide the issue whether Ms. Watson willfully disobeyed a court order"). Instead, the Court of Appeals held her conduct was not sufficiently disruptive because she herself "did not engage in a pattern of repeated violations that pervaded the courtroom and threatened the dignity of the court" and because the record did not indicate she would have repeated the references to punishment unless she were held in summary contempt. Ibid.

All that is before us is the ruling that respondent's conduct was not disruptive enough to justify contempt, and on this issue we are in disagreement with the Court of Appeals. Nothing in our cases supports a requirement that a contemnor "engage in a pattern of repeated violations that pervaded the courtroom" ibid. before she may be held in summary contempt. To the contrary, in Wilson, the summary contempt convictions were upheld after a single refusal to give immunized testimony, "not delivered disrespectfully." 421 U.S., at 314, 95 S.Ct., at 1805. We nevertheless held that the conduct there "disrupt[ed] and frustrat[ed] an ongoing proceeding." Id., at 316, 95 S.Ct., at 1806. And we have not required that a court determine a contemnor would have repeated the misconduct but for summary punishment. While we have approved, in the context of reviewing a federal contempt order, the equitable principle that only " 'the least possible power adequate to the end proposed' should be used in contempt cases," id., at 319, 95 S.Ct., at 1808 (quoting Anderson v. Dunn, 6 Wheat. 204, 231, 5 L.Ed. 242 (1821)), we found that principle satisfied in the circumstances in Wilson because, during an ongoing trial, the court is justified in acting swiftly "to prevent a breakdown of the proceedings." 421 U.S., at 319, 95 S.Ct., at 1808. Likewise, in Sacher v. United States, 343 U.S. 1, 5, 72 S.Ct. 451, 453, 96 L.Ed. 717 (1952), the Court upheld summary contempt convictions of counsel where the misconduct had the following characteristics: "It took place in the immediate presence of the trial judge; it consisted of breaches of decorum and disobedience in the presence of the jury of his orders and rulings upon the trial; the misconduct was professional in that it was that of lawyers" and conviction was based "upon a course of conduct long-continued in the face of warnings that it was regarded by the court as contemptuous." See also Groppi v. Leslie, 404 U.S. 496, 506, 92 S.Ct. 582, 588, 30 L.Ed.2d 632 (1972). Cf. Illinois v. Allen, 397 U.S. 337, 343, 90 S.Ct. 1057, 1061, 25 L.Ed.2d 353 (1970) ("We believe trial judges confronted with disruptive, contumacious, stubbornly defiant defendants must be given sufficient discretion to meet the circumstances of each case.")

Here the trial court expressly found that respondent's questions had "permanently prejudiced the jury in favor of her client" and that the prejudice "cannot be overcome." The Court of Appeals glossed over the state court finding, saying "we can understand Judge Pounders' concern that her two questions might prejudice jurors in favor of her client," 102 F.3d, at 438 (emphasis added). Seriously prejudicing the jury is comparable in terms of damage to the administration of justice to the refusals to testify in Wilson. The trial court's finding that respondent's comments had prejudiced the jury—together with its assessment of the flagrance of respondent's defiance—support the finding of the need for summary contempt to vindicate the court's authority.

While the Due Process Clause no doubt imposes limits on the authority to issue a summary contempt order, the states must have latitude in determining what conduct so infects orderly judicial proceedings that contempt is permitted. . . .

On the record before us, the Court of Appeals was in error. It was error for the Court of Appeals to rule, as a matter of law, that the contempt order went beyond those necessities pertaining to the ordered administration of justice. The ruling of the Court of Appeals, not reviewed en banc, introduced uncertainty into routine proceedings of the many state courts within the Court of Appeals' large geographical jurisdiction. The judgment is reversed.

It is so ordered.

■ JUSTICE STEVENS, with whom JUSTICE BREYER joins, dissenting.

As the Court correctly explains, the record supports the conclusion that respondent defied a court order when she asked two questions about her client's potential punishment. I assume therefore that she acted in contempt of court. The record also demonstrates, however, that no further misconduct or disruption of the trial occurred. The question the Court of Appeals addressed was whether these circumstances justified a summary contempt proceeding conducted by the judge before whom the contempt occurred. I do not agree with the Court that the answer to this question is so clear as to justify summary reversal. . . .

. . .

Given that the respondent in this case asked two inappropriate questions over the course of a three and a half month long trial and that the trial continued without incident for two weeks after her contemptuous conduct, a substantial question exists as to whether fair procedure required a hearing before another judge. Neither the Court nor the petitioner contends that this summary contempt power was exercised to prevent the "actual obstruction of justice," such that a hearing before an entirely disinterested judge would have been impractical. Because I believe that these questions are important and not clearly answered by our precedents—indeed, the Court does not cite a single case that is at all comparable to this one on its facts—it is unwise to answer it without full briefing and argument.

Accordingly, I respectfully dissent.

. . . .

NOTES ON CONTEMPT BY ATTORNEYS

1. Martina, an attorney, went before a trial judge to explain his failure to appear on behalf of his client. He stated that he had had "an agreement with [police prosecutor] Whitmarsh that my client could attend on her own, with my instructions on how to proceed." The court, troubled that Mr. Martina had entered an appearance on his client's behalf and failed to appear, did not accept this explanation. Mr. Martina then stated, "My reasons for not showing up were personal reasons. I am trying to make a living. This was a pro bono matter and I felt that my client was not unintelligent. She was fully informed. I simply entered an appearance to expedite it." The court, again, did not accept this explanation. Rather than hold him in indirect contempt (which might have been warranted), the court informed Mr. Martina that the matter would be referred to the Professional Conduct Committee. Upon hearing this Mr. Martina remarked, "Thank you, and I should advise the court I intend to bring you to the Judicial Conduct Committee. I think your actions before this Bench were quite frankly ignominious." The court responded by summarily punishing him for direct criminal contempt, imposing a fine of five hundred dollars and sentencing him to fifteen days in jail. The Supreme Court of New Hampshire upheld the trial court's use of the summary contempt procedure, but ultimately remanded the case for further proceedings (on the ground that the defendant was not notified of the precise conduct punished). State v. Martina, 135 N.H. 111, 600 A.2d 132 (1991).

2. Wendy, an attorney, was held in contempt when he refused to proceed with a scheduled criminal trial. Wendy had substituted for his law partner, who was busy in another court at the time, and represented a client at an arraignment and during some pretrial matters. When the case was called for trial, Wendy explained that he was a tax lawyer, had never tried a case in court, and had merely substituted for his partner during the earlier stages of the proceedings. On appeal, the court held that he could not be held in contempt for refusing to proceed with the trial of the criminal case. United States v. Wendy, 575 F.2d 1025 (2d Cir.1978).

3. A lawyer, whose application for a fee for representing an indigent defendant under the Criminal Justice Act had been returned to him for additional documentation, wrote the district judge a letter which stated in part:

> "In the first place, I am appalled by the amount of money which the federal court pays for indigent criminal defense work. The reason that so few attorneys in Bismarck accept this work is for that exact reason. We have, up to this point, still accepted the indigent appointments, because of a duty to our profession, and the fact that nobody else will do it.

> "Now, however, not only are we paid an amount of money which does not even cover our overhead, but we have to go through extreme gymnastics even to receive the puny amounts which the federal courts authorize for this work. We have sent you everything we have concern-

ing our representation, and I am not sending you anything else. You can take it or leave it.

"Further, I am extremely disgusted by the treatment of us by the Eighth Circuit in this case, and you are instructed to remove my name from the list of attorneys who will accept criminal indigent defense work. I have simply had it.

"Thank you for your time and attention."

The district judge forwarded the letter to the chief judge of the circuit, who is responsible under the Act for approving expenditures in excess of $1,000.00. The chief judge found the letter disrespectful and ultimately suspended the attorney from practice in the federal courts in the circuit when he refused to apologize for his remarks. In re Snyder, 472 U.S. 634, 105 S.Ct. 2874, 86 L.Ed.2d 504 (1985), held that the attorney's conduct did not warrant his suspension from practice.

4.   Ernest, an attorney, caused the circuit court clerk to issue a deposition subpoena on the presiding judge in a probate case. The testator's will had made cash bequests in excess of $300,000 while the net probate estate amounted to less than $98,000. The executor proposed to distribute the estate by fully satisfying the bequests contained in each succeeding paragraph of the will until the funds were exhausted. Under the distribution plan general bequests contained in the latter part of the will would go unsatisfied. Notice of the hearing on the final account had been provided only to those beneficiaries who were to receive funds under the executor's proposal. The executor of the estate and counsel appeared before the trial judge who approved the proposed distribution. Attorney Ernest, representing those beneficiaries whose bequests had not been funded by the plan, subsequently petitioned the court to reopen the estate, alleging, among other things, that the executor failed to abate the bequests by distributing the assets of the estate proportionately among the general legatees, as required by statute. Ernest filed a motion for substitution of judge, believing that the judge would be a material witness concerning the representations made by the executor at the hearing in which the judge approved the initial distribution plan. Concerned that permitting a litigant to call the presiding judge as a witness could lead to disqualification in almost every case, the judge denied the motion. Uninhibited by the judge's ruling on the substitution motion, Ernest subpoenaed the judge for a deposition. Upon learning of the subpoena, the judge requested Ernest to appear before him. The judge told Ernest that the issuance of the subpoena was contrary to the "spirit and intent" of the denial of the substitution motion, and the judge told the attorney he could withdraw the subpoena or be cited for contempt. The defendant elected not to withdraw the subpoena, and the judge issued a formal contempt citation. In a subsequent hearing before another judge, Ernest was found guilty of direct criminal contempt.

On appeal, the Supreme Court of Illinois, upheld the finding of direct criminal contempt, without ruling on the propriety of the trial judge's ruling on the substitution motion. The court stated, "In causing the issuance of the subpoena, defendant acted in apparent defiance of [the trial judge's] reason for denying the substitution motion. [The trial judge] believed that it would be improper for any of the parties to subpoena the presiding judge in the case. We must conclude that by doing so, defendant's conduct disparaged the court's authority and dignity." People v. Ernest, 141 Ill.2d 412, 422, 566 N.E.2d 231, 236, 152 Ill.Dec. 544 (1990).

5.   H. Beauty Chadwick, an attorney, was accused of hiding $2.5 million during his divorce proceeding, and had been in jail since 1995 on civil contempt charges. He asserted that he had lost the money in a bad investment. In Chadwick v. Janecka, No Civ. A. 00–1130, 2002 WL 12292 (E.D. Pa. Jan. 3, 2002), the U.S. district judge ruled that he should be released, holding that his incarceration had "crossed the line from coercive to punitive." A three judge panel of the Court of Appeals for the Third Cicuit reversed the order of the district judge. See Chadwick v. Janecka, 312 F.3d 597 (3d Cir. 2002), cert. denied, 538 U.S. 1000, 123 S.Ct. 1914, 155 L.Ed.2d 828 (2003).

See MCR 3.606

In Re Little

Supreme Court of the United States, 1972.
404 U.S. 553, 92 S.Ct. 659, 30 L.Ed.2d 708.

■ PER CURIAM. Petitioner was convicted of committing a direct contempt of a judge of the District Court Division of the Forsyth County, North Carolina, General Court of Justice. He was sentenced to 30 days in jail as summary punishment authorized by General Statutes of North Carolina §§ 5–1(1) and 5–6. He sought habeas corpus in the Superior Court Division of the General Court. That court denied relief after hearing oral argument but without receiving evidence. Both the North Carolina Court of Appeals and the North Carolina Supreme Court denied review by certiorari.

Neither the order of the District Court nor the judgment of the Superior Court details the events leading to the conviction. The petition recites these events, however, and the State's response does not challenge the accuracy of the recital. Petitioner's trial on a charge of carrying a concealed weapon was scheduled for March 8, 1971, in the District Court at Winston–Salem. Petitioner appeared and filed a written motion for continuance by reason of another trial engagement of his retained counsel in Charlotte. The trial judge denied the motion and proceeded with the trial. Without benefit of counsel petitioner attempted to defend himself. In summation following the close of the evidence petitioner made statements that the court was biased and had prejudged the case and that petitioner was a political prisoner. The trial judge adjudged petitioner in contempt for these statements. The court's order recites that "[t]he Court at this point informed the [petitioner] that he was in contempt as the Court felt that these remarks were very disrespectful and tended to subvert and prevent justice," and further recites that "[t]he Court concludes on the foregoing facts that the conduct of the [petitioner] and the words spoken by him in the presence of the Court were contemptuous, that they reflected on the integrity of the Court and tended to subvert and prevent justice."

The order also recites, "As the defendant was being removed from the courtroom by deputy sheriff [following the contempt adjudication], he spoke out and called the undersigned presiding judge a M____ F____." This language in a courtroom is, of course, reprehensible and cannot be tolerated. But this was not relied upon by either the District Court or the Superior Court for the conviction and sentence and the State defends the conviction in this Court without any reference to it. We therefore also lay it aside for the purpose of our decision.

The Superior Court had the District Court order before it but no other evidence. The Superior Court judgment tracks the statutory language in reciting that petitioner's statements "directly tended to interrupt its proceedings and to impair the respect due the District Court's authority," and, further, the District Court's conclusion that the statements " 'reflected on the integrity of the Court and tended to subvert and prevent justice' amounted to a finding by the District Court that the words were wilful and intentionally used and that the words used tended to interrupt the Court's proceedings and to impair the respect due its authority."*

We hold that in the context of this case petitioner's statements in summation did not constitute criminal contempt. The court's denial of the continuance forced petitioner to argue his own cause. He was therefore clearly entitled to as much latitude in conducting his defense as we have held is enjoyed by counsel vigorously espousing a client's cause. There is no indication, and the State does not argue, that petitioner's statements were uttered in a boisterous tone or in any wise actually disrupted the court proceeding. Therefore, "The vehemence of the language used is not alone the measure of the power to punish for contempt. The fires which it kindles must constitute an imminent, not merely a likely, threat to the administration of justice. The danger must not be remote or even probable; it must immediately imperil ... [T]he law of contempt is not made for the protection of judges who may be sensitive to the winds of public opinion. Judges are supposed to be men of fortitude, able to thrive in a hardy climate." "Trial courts ... must be on guard against confusing offenses to their sensibilities with obstruction to the administration of justice."

The reversal of this conviction is necessarily required under our holding in Holt v. Virginia, 381 U.S. 131, 85 S.Ct. 1375, 14 L.Ed.2d 290 (1965). There attorneys filed motions that the trial judge recuse himself and for a change of venue, alleging that the judge was biased. The motion for change of venue, alleged that the judge intimidated and harassed the attorneys' client. The court adjudged the attorneys in contempt for filing these motions. We reversed for reasons also applicable here:

> "It is not charged that petitioners here disobeyed any valid court order, talked loudly, acted boisterously, or attempted to prevent the judge or any other officer of the court from carrying on his court duties. Their convictions rest on nothing whatever except allegations made in motions for change of venue and disqualification of Judge Holladay because of alleged bias on his part."

The petition for certiorari is granted and the judgment is reversed.

It is so ordered.

---

* Section 5–1(1) makes punishable for contempt "[d]isorderly, contemptuous, or insolvent behavior committed during the sitting of any court of justice in immediate view and presence of the court, and directly tending to interrupt its proceedings, or to impair the respect due to its authority."

■ MR. CHIEF JUSTICE BURGER, with whom MR. JUSTICE REHNQUIST joins, concurring.

I agree with the Court's disposition of the case but something more needs to be said.

A contempt holding depends in a very special way on the setting, and such elusive factors as the tone of voice, the facial expressions, and the physical gestures of the contemnor; these cannot be dealt with except on full ventilation of the facts. Those present often have a totally different impression of the events from what would appear even in a faithful transcript of the record. Some measure of the flavor of what really occurred in this episode, and of the petitioner's attitude and demeanor, how his spoken words impressed those present, may be gleaned from the events and utterances described in the Court's *per curiam* opinion.

The North Carolina court is, of course, free to promptly summon this petitioner before it and, observing the strictures of Mayberry v. Pennsylvania, 400 U.S. 455, 91 S.Ct. 499, 27 L.Ed.2d 532 (1971), issue process requiring him to show cause why he should not be held in contempt for the conduct and utterances following the contempt adjudication.

NOTES ON CRIMINAL CONTEMPT

1. In answering a question on cross-examination at his trial, in the Municipal Court of Tulsa, Oklahoma, for violating a municipal ordinance, the defendant referred to an alleged assailant as "chicken shit." In consequence, he was prosecuted and convicted under an information that charged him with "direct contempt," in violation of another Tulsa ordinance, "by his insolent behavior during open court and in the presence of [the judge], to wit: by using the language 'chicken-shit'." The Supreme Court held that this incident could not constitutionally support a conviction for criminal contempt. Eaton v. City of Tulsa, 415 U.S. 697, 94 S.Ct. 1228, 39 L.Ed.2d 693 (1974).

2. Malone and Kennedy were spectators in a courtroom. Because they felt that courts do not always serve the cause of justice, they refused to rise, as requested by the bailiff, when the judge entered and left the courtroom. The judge held them in contempt of court and the appellate court affirmed. United States ex rel. Robson v. Malone, 412 F.2d 848 (7th Cir. 1969).

---

5.   WRITS OF ASSISTANCE

Hamilton v. Nakai

United States Court of Appeals, Ninth Circuit, 1971.
453 F.2d 152.

■ DUNIWAY, J. The action in which this proceeding was filed was authorized by P.L. 85–547, the Act of July 22, 1958, 72 Stat. 403. The purpose of the action, which was brought by the Hopi Indian Tribe against the Navajo

on final

Indian Tribe and the Attorney General on behalf of the United States, was to determine the rights and interests of the Hopi and Navajo Indian Tribes and individual Indians in a reservation in northeastern Arizona established by an Executive Order of December 16, 1882, and to quiet title to that reservation. A three-judge United States District Court held that, subject to the trust title of the United States, the Hopi Tribe had the exclusive interest in that part of the reservation lying within the boundaries of a land management district administratively defined in 1943, and that the Hopi and Navajo Tribes each had an undivided and equal interest in all the reservation lying outside the boundaries of the land management district. The Supreme Court affirmed this judgment.

On March 13, 1970, the Hopi Indian Tribe petitioned the District Court for an order of compliance or writ of assistance to enforce its rights as a co-tenant. More specifically, in paragraphs 3 and 4 of their prayer for relief, the Hopi requested an order:

"3. Directing the defendants to forthwith grant and permit the joint use and possession of the surface, including all resources, in and to all of the executive order reservation of December 16, 1882, lying outside of the boundaries of land management district 6, as defined on April 24, 1943 to the Hopi Indian Tribe and Navajo Indian Tribe, share and share alike, and to remove such Navajo livestock from said lands as is necessary to accomplish such joint use without further damage to said lands."

"4. Directing the Clerk of this court to issue a writ of assistance to compel performance of the judgment of [the] court entered herein on September 28, 1962, and to allow the plaintiff, the Hopi Tribe, to enter upon said joint use area, and with the Navajo Tribe to jointly and equally use and benefit from the grazing forage and all other surface resources of said area, for the benefit of the respective members of said tribes until further order of this court."

The District Court denied the Hopi's petition on August 3, 1970. The Hopi appeal and we reverse.

. . . .

The equitable jurisdiction of a federal court extends to supplemental or ancillary bills brought for the purpose of effectuating a decree of the same court. See Root v. Woolworth, 1893, 150 U.S. 401, 14 S.Ct. 136, 37 L.Ed. 1123. In *Root* the Court emphasized that "[t]he jurisdiction of courts of equity to interfere and effectuate their own decrees by injunctions or writs of assistance, in order to avoid the relitigation of questions once settled between the same parties, is well settled." Furthermore, in *Root* the appellant contended that no relief should be granted because the present bill sought possession, a matter that was not covered in the original decree. The Court held that this fact did not preclude the relief requested. . . .

Here, as in *Root,* the power of the court to issue the order requiring compliance or to enforce the judgment by a writ of assistance follows from the principle that a court's power to afford a remedy must be coextensive with its jurisdiction over the subject matter. The decision in *Healing* adjudged joint and equal title in the Hopi and Navajo Tribes to a portion of the 1882 reservation, and the right to joint possession follows that title even though, as in *Root,* the original decree did not make explicit provisions concerning possession.

These principles have found expression not only in judicial decisions, but also in a specific statutory enactment, the "All Writs" Act, 28 U.S.C. § 1651(a):

"The Supreme Courts and all courts established by Act of Congress may issue all writs necessary or appropriate in aid of their respective jurisdictions and agreeable to the usages and principles of law."

The present case meets all the requirements of § 1651(a). First, if the allegations of the Hopi's petition are true, "necessity" rests on the side of the Hopi. They allege that the Navajo have denied to the Hopi the joint use and benefit of the property in question, and that the United States, as trustee and guardian of the property, has neglected its duty to see that the original decree was effectively implemented.

A writ of assistance is also "appropriate" under § 1651(a). Of course, this statutory provision does not confer original jurisdiction, but rather, prescribes the scope of relief that may be granted when jurisdiction otherwise exists. But once jurisdiction has attached, powers under § 1651(a) should be broadly construed. In *Dixie,* a case that involved a three-judge panel, the court concluded, "The universal rule is that every court has the inherent power to enforce its judgment and decrees. The All Writs Statute appears as a Congressional reaffirmation of that power."

Finally, a writ of assistance in a suit to quiet title is also "agreeable to the usages and principles of law." In *Healing* the court did not direct that joint possession of the joint use area be delivered to the Hopi, but the court did quiet their title, as co-tenants, and determined that both tribes, for the common use and benefit of their respective members, have joint undivided and equal rights. In these circumstances a writ of assistance is "agreeable to the usages and principles of law." Montgomery v. Tutt, 1858, 11 Cal. 190. In *Montgomery* there was a decree of sale that did not require or provide for the delivery of possession of the premises to the purchaser. After the possessor refused to surrender possession, a writ of assistance was sought. The Supreme Court of California held that the writ should issue:

"The power of the court to issue the judicial writ, or to make the order, and enforce the same by a writ of assistance, rests upon the obvious principle that the power of the Court to afford a remedy must be co-extensive with its jurisdiction over the subject matter. Where the Court possesses jurisdiction to make a decree, it possesses the power to enforce its execution. It is true that in the present case the decree does not contain a direction that the possession of the premises be delivered to the purchaser. It is usual to insert a clause to that effect, but it is not essential.... [A]s the right to the possession ... follows title, it would be a useless and vexatious course to require the purchaser to obtain such possession by another suit. Such is not the course of procedure adopted by a Court of Equity."

Nor does it matter that the request for a writ of assistance or possession follows by a number of years the rendering of the decree quieting title. . . .

Neither P.L. 85–547 nor 28 U.S.C. § 2284, to which it refers, contains any restrictions on the power of the court to enforce its judgment. The Act authorizes suit "in the United States District Court for the District of Arizona." It is beyond the possibility of argument that a United States District Court has power to enforce its judgments. Absent some contrary provision in the jurisdictional statute, that power exists in this case.

. . . .

We are told that it would not be possible to grant the relief sought because many Navajo are permanently settled on the lands in question. In support of the argument we are then confronted with a parade of horribles. Are the Navajo to be ordered to share their hogans [structure or cabin of logs and mud] with the Hopi? Must they share such gardens as they have, or stock corrals, etc.? Obviously, where the tract of land is large and the population is sparse, these are straw men. A District Judge is not a creature without judgment or imagination. He can hear testimony from the parties and from representatives of the United States as to what the actual situation is, and can tailor the relief to be afforded to the facts that confront him, always bearing in mind that the objective is to achieve what the court has decreed, the exercise by the Hopi and the Navajo of their "joint, undivided and equal interests as to the surface and subsurface and all resources appertaining thereto [in the lands in question], subject to the trust title of the United States."

The order is reversed and the matter is remanded to the district court for further proceedings consistent with this opinion.

———

NOTE

For an explanation of how a writ of assistance works, see the excerpt from Langdell's Summary of Equity Pleading in Section A of Chapter 2, *supra* pp. 39–41.

———

6. WRITS OF SEQUESTRATION

North, Life of Lord Keeper Guilford

197 (1742).

But Sequestrations were not heard of till the Lord Coventry's Time [(1625–40)], when Sir John Read lay in the Fleet (with 10,000 *l.* in an Iron Cash–Chest in his Chamber) for Disobedience to a Decree, and would not submit and pay the Duty. This being represented to the Lord Keeper as a great Contempt and Affront put upon the Court, he authorised Men to go and break up his Iron Chest, and pay the Duty and Costs, and leave the rest to him, and discharged his Commitment: From thence came Sequestrations; which now are so established as to run of course after all other Process fails, and is but in Nature of a grand Distress, the best Process at Common Law after a Summons, such as a Subpoena is; what need all that Grievance and Delay of the intervening Process?

Shaw v. Wright

Chancery, 1795.
3 Ves. 22, 20 Eng.Rep. 872.

Bill against a trustee to have the trusts of a will carried into execution. A sequestration issued for want of answer, under which some leasehold houses were taken. The plaintiffs petitioned that the sequestrators be ordered to sell the houses and account for the proceeds. This relief was denied. Loughborough, L.C.: "The order would do you no good. I should not have much difficulty in selling, not only perishable commodities, but if the sequestrators were in possession of rents paid in kind, or the natural produce of a farm; but how shall I make a title? By whom? I cannot well order the sequestrators to sell without at the same time warranting the title: then I do not know how I can do that. It does not transfer the term to the sequestrators. It is only a process to compel an appearance, the performance of a duty. All profits I will direct them to apply. The difficulty is this: if the sequestrators sell, and the purchasers should be brought before this Court to complete their contracts, I could not compel them to pay the money. I cannot make a man take a title, which he is to support a bill for an injunction. You will not find any instance of an order to sell under a sequestration a subject, which passes by title and not by delivery."

———

NOTES

1.   For further discussion of the writ of sequestration, see the excerpt from Langdell's Summary of Equity Pleading in Section A of Chapter 2, *supra* pp. 39–41.

2.   Spry, Equitable Remedies 344–45 (1980):

However there are cases where imprisonment is not appropriate because, for example, the contemnor is outside the jurisdiction or is a corporation, and here it may be found desirable that a writ of sequestration shall issue instead. Accordingly although a corporation cannot be imprisoned it is possible to sequester its property, as well as to attach or commit its officers to the extent to which they have been parties to the disobedience to the order of the court. It must here be remembered that sequestration of the property of a contemnor is, just as much as his committal or attachment, part of the process of executing equitable decrees and that it has thus a double aspect. On the one hand, contumacy to the court is, should it be thought fit, required; and on the other hand, the contemnor is compelled to satisfy the original equitable decree or order which the applicant has obtained.

———

7. EXECUTION OF DECREES FOR MONEY

If contempt sanctions could not force a defendant to comply with an order commanding the payment of money, recourse could be had to sequestration. If that failed to satisfy the decree (or coerce the defendant into doing so), an equity court once had no further means of effectuating its decree.

However, beginning in 1785, American legislatures began to enact statutes authorizing the execution of money decrees in the same manner as legal judgments. Such laws now exist throughout the country. This change in attitude towards the enforcement of money decrees has been so complete that Fed.R.Civ.P. 69(a), for example, now states, "Process to enforce a judgment for the payment of money shall be a writ of execution, unless the court directs otherwise."

Reeves v. Crownshield

Court of Appeals of New York, 1937.
274 N.Y. 74, 8 N.E.2d 283.

■ FINCH, J. The uncollectibility of money judgments has ever been a subject of concern to bench and bar. A large part of the statute law of this State is designed to enable a judgment creditor to obtain satisfaction upon his money judgment. That a large percentage of these money judgments have remained uncollectible has been confirmed by statistical surveys. Many debtors who were in a position to pay have evaded their legal obligations by unlawful and technical means. Discontent with this situation resulted in agitation for reform in collection procedure. Finally, in 1935, upon the recommendation of the Judicial Council, a law was enacted creating a new mode of enforcing the payment of judgments.

Section 793 of the Civil Practice Act now provides that, in addition to the garnishee provisions of the old law, the court may make an order directing a judgment debtor to make payments in installments out of the income which he receives. Such orders must be made upon notice to the judgment debtor and after he has had an opportunity to show inability to pay, and with due regard to the reasonable requirements of the judgment debtor and his family, as well as of payments required to be made by him to other creditors. Section 801 of the Civil Practice Act provides that refusal to pay after such an order of the court is punishable as a contempt....[2]

This new procedure was invoked against the appellant, in an attempt to collect a judgment for approximately $400. The examination in supple-

---

2. [See Section 5101 N.Y. CPLR "Enforcement of money judgment or order." Article 52, Sections 5201–5252 of the N.Y. CPLR contains provision for the "enforcement of money judgments."]

mentary proceedings disclosed that he was employed by the Federal government as a steamship inspector at a salary of $230 per month, less a small pension deduction. He has no children, and the whereabouts of his wife are unknown. Aside from $48 a month paid as rent and his living expenses, he has no financial obligations. The court ordered the appellant to pay installments of $20 per month until the judgment was satisfied. Upon his failure to pay, he was held in contempt and fined the sum of $20, commitment being provided for in default of payment.

An appeal was taken directly to this court from the City Court of New York City on the ground that a constitutional question was involved.

. . . .

The judgment debtor challenges the constitutionality of section 793 and section 801 on the ground that in effect, they provide for imprisonment for debt. It is admitted that neither the State nor the Federal Constitutions contain provisions expressly prohibiting imprisonment for debt, and that the statutory provision forbidding imprisonment for debt found in section 21 of the New York Civil Rights Law excepts cases otherwise specially prescribed by law. It is asserted, however, that imprisonment for debt is barred by the due process clauses of the State and Federal Constitutions. No cases so holding are cited, but reliance is had upon vague dicta found in Bailey v. Alabama (219 U.S. 219, 244, 31 S.Ct. 145, 55 L.Ed. 191) and Henderson v. Mayor (92 U.S. 259, 268, 23 L.Ed. 543). Whatever doubt there may exist as to whether imprisonment for debt without regard to ability to pay may be treated as a deprivation of liberty without due process of law, there can be no doubt that imprisonment for failure to obey an order of a court to make payment out of income, which order is made with due regard to the needs of the debtor and his family, is not violative of the due process clause.

. . . .

"The amelioration of the condition of poor debtors has also proceeded through the enactment of insolvency laws. But in construing legislation having this end in view, courts cannot keep too constantly in mind the fundamental theory upon which it is based, namely, that none of the exemptions thereby afforded debtors should enable them to avoid the payment of debts when able to pay them." (3 Freeman on The Law of Executions [3d ed.], p. 2394 et seq.)

In the case at bar the judgment debtor has not complained that the order directing the payment of $20 per month is unjust, inequitable or harsh. His position is an arbitrary refusal to pay. It is based upon the ground that the courts are powerless to compel him to pay out of his income an amount fixed after deducting the sum necessary for his reasonable needs.

The Legislature has seen fit to provide a creditor with a direct remedy for the collection of his just debts. A refusal to recognize such an order by the judgment debtor entitles the creditor to move to have him punished for contempt. Without this right, there would be no power in the court to enforce its order. To compel the judgment debtor to obey the order of the court is not imprisonment for debt, but only imprisonment for disobedience of an order with which he is able to comply. His refusal is contumacious conduct, the same as a refusal to obey any other lawful order of the court.

. . . .

It follows that the orders appealed from should be affirmed, with costs.

NOTES

1. Garnishment is another ancillary remedy that can be used to collect a money judgment. Garnishment involves a proceeding against a third party (the "garnishee") who owes the debtor money (e.g., wages or funds in a bank account). Unless the garnishee proves that it owes the debtor nothing, it will be held liable to the creditor. Of course, the garnishee's obligation to the debtor (and the latter's to the creditor) is reduced by the amount paid by it to the judgment creditor.

2. At common law, the writ of attachment could also be used to help collect a money judgment. Thus, a judgment debtor could simply be imprisoned until the judgment was satisfied. The debtor's ability to pay was immaterial.

Most states have constitutional or statutory rules barring imprisonment for debt. These prohibitions apply when the underlying obligation is a contract claim, but they often do not apply to other obligations, including tort claims, alimony and child support claims, claims for taxes owed, and claims against fiduciaries. The federal courts are statutorily required to follow state practice in this respect.

3. In Bearden v. Georgia, 461 U.S. 660, 103 S.Ct. 2064, 76 L.Ed.2d 221 (1983), the Supreme Court held that the imprisonment of an indigent probationer for failing to pay a fine and restitution was unconstitutional if he had "made all reasonable efforts to pay," but was unable to do so "through no fault of his own."

----

8. ENFORCEMENT OF DECREES "IN REM"

Legislation Giving Equity Power to Transfer Property[3]

The difficulties arising from the circumstance that a decree requiring the defendant to transfer property was enforceable in classical equity only by pressure on the person of the defendant exerted by imprisonment for contempt or by sequestration of his property were quite serious in some cases. Even if the defendant was served with a subpoena or appeared in the suit, the decree might be nugatory for various reasons. The defendant might be insane, or an infant, or persistently contumacious, or he might leave the jurisdiction and take all his property with him if no *ne exeat* had been issued.[4] Moreover, where the defendant was a nonresident who was

----

3. Reprinted from SCOTT & SIMPSON, CASES AND OTHER MATERIALS ON CIVIL PROCEDURE, 338–40 (1951).

4. The writ *ne exeat regno* [do not leave the Kingdom] is an equitable remedy in the nature of bail at common law. It is directed to a sheriff, commanding the Sheriff to com-

not served with a subpoena within the state and did not appear, no decree in personam could be made against him at all. Suppose for example that a resident of Massachusetts owns land in New York and contracts to sell it. Under the view of classical equity that the contract could be specifically enforced only by compelling the Massachusetts vendor by personal pressure on him to give a deed to the land, the courts of New York could not enforce the contract except by getting and keeping personal jurisdiction, over the vendor although the subject-matter of the contract was New York land. To be sure, they could sequester the land to compel appearance, but they could not, it was thought, transfer legal title.

To meet these difficulties, statutes extending the power of equity to transfer property came to be enacted. The first of these were English statutes relating to particular situations, such as infant trustees or mortgagees, and lunatics. But before there had been more than piecemeal legislation in England, statutes of much broader effect were being enacted in the United States. The first of these was a Maryland statute of 1785 which provided that if a decree "for a conveyance, release or acquittance" was not obeyed, "such decree shall stand, be considered and taken, in all courts of law and equity, to have the same operation and effect as if the conveyance, release or acquittance, had been executed conformably to such decree." Similar statutes were soon enacted in other states. Then, in 1808, Kentucky initiated a somewhat different way of dealing with the problem, enacting a statute which provided that where a defendant did not comply with a decree for the conveyance of land the court might "appoint one or more commissioners to make a conveyance of said title to the plaintiff or plaintiffs by deed agreeably to the decree of said court," which deed, when recorded in the court, "shall effectually vest legal title in said plaintiff or plaintiffs." The same method was adopted in England in 1830 and has been followed in several of the United States. Most of the states now have one or the other type of statute, and some have both.

It will be noted that these two types of statutes, which may be described as the *vesting* and the *appointive* type respectively, reach the same result. They permit the execution *in rem* between the parties of a decree in equity for the transfer of property in cases which fall within the particular statute. Under a vesting statute, the decree executes itself *in rem;* under an appointive statute, it is executed *in rem.*

NOTE

Consider the approach of Fed. R. Civ. P. 70 to this problem:

Judgment for Specific Acts; Vesting Title

If a judgment directs a party to execute a conveyance of land or to deliver deeds or other documents or to perform any other specific act and the party fails to comply within the time specified, the court may

mit the party to prison until the party gives security not to leave the jurisdiction without the permission of the court. See De Rivafinoli v. Corsetti, *infra* p. 403.

direct the act to be done at the cost of the disobedient party by some other person appointed by the court and the act when so done has like effect as if done by the party. On application of the party entitled to performance, the clerk shall issue a writ of attachment or sequestration against the property of the disobedient party to compel obedience to the judgment. The court may also in proper cases adjudge the party in contempt. If real or personal property is within the district, the court in lieu of directing a conveyance thereof may enter a judgment divesting the title of any party and vesting it in others and such judgment has the effect of a conveyance executed in due form of law. When any order or judgment is for the delivery of possession, the party in whose favor it is entered is entitled to a writ of execution or assistance upon application to the clerk.

Garfein v. McInnis

Court of Appeals of New York, 1928.
248 N.Y. 261, 162 N.E. 73.

The following questions were certified:

"1. Has any jurisdiction been obtained by the Supreme Court of New York State in an action brought by the vendee in the Supreme Court, Westchester county, for the specific performance of a contract to convey real property situated in said county of Westchester, where the vendor is a resident of Connecticut, and has not been personally served within the State of New York, nor appeared in the action, but was personally served with a summons and verified complaint in the State of Connecticut?

"2. Under the circumstances as set forth in the above question, if the court decrees specific performance for the vendee, can the court direct the sheriff to convey the property, under section 979 of the Civil Practice Act?"

■ LEHMAN, J. . . . .

. . . The question presented by this appeal is whether a judgment in an action for specific performance is only a decree *in personam* against the party who has agreed to convey property, or whether the court in such an action may grant a judgment which will operate upon the property itself and result in a transfer of the title to a successful party though the defendant fail or refuse to obey a command of the judgment directed to him.

That a court of chancery acts only upon the person is a recognized maxim of equity jurisprudence. "A decree of chancery spoke in terms of personal command to the defendant, but its directions could only be carried into effect by his personal act. . . . The decree never stood as a title in the place of an actual conveyance by the defendant; nor was it ever carried into effect by any officer acting in the defendant's name." (Pomeroy on Equity Jurisprudence, section 428.) In jurisdictions where the decrees of a court of equity still retain the traditional form and effect of a mere command, a court of equity cannot obtain jurisdiction over a nonresident by service without the State.

It has been doubted whether the jurisdiction of courts of equity was ever subject to any inherent limitation that its decrees must operate solely *in personam,* though the early chancellors adopted the "method of acting, as they said, upon the conscience of defendants." In this country "the statutes of the several states have virtually abolished the ancient doctrine that the decrees in equity can only act upon the person of a party, and have generally provided that in all cases where the ends of justice require such an effect, and where it is possible, a decree shall either operate *ex proprio vigore* [by its own force] to create, transfer, or vest the intended right, title, estate, or interest, or else that the acts required to be done in order to accomplish the object of the decree shall be performed by an officer of the court acting for and in the name of the party against whom the adjudication is made." (Pomeroy's Equity Jurisprudence, sec. 135.) "A bill for the specific execution of a contract to convey real estate is not strictly a proceeding *in rem,* in ordinary cases; but where such a procedure is authorized by statute, on publication, without personal service of process, it is, substantially, of that character."

It has been held that the power of a court of equity to pronounce a judgment *in rem* is not dependent upon statute and may be exercised against a non-resident whenever the Legislature has authorized constructive service. In Silver Camp Mining Co. v. Dickert (31 Mont. 488, 78 P. 967) the court reached opposite conclusion. We need not now decide between such conflicting decisions. A court of equity, undoubtedly, may by constructive service, in accordance with statute, acquire jurisdiction over a non-resident in an action for specific performance whenever it has power, whether granted by statute or inherent, to make a decree which will result directly, or through conveyance by an officer, in the transfer of title or interest in land.

In this State the Legislature has provided in section 979 of the Civil Practice Act[5] that where a "judgment directs a party ... to convey real property, if the direction is disobeyed, the court, by order, besides punishing the disobedience as a contempt, may require the sheriff ... to convey the real property, in conformity with the direction of the court." A decree of the court is enforceable not merely by punishment of a disobedient party but may be carried into effect by action of the sheriff operating directly upon the property. It may be that the primary purpose of the Legislature was to grant additional force to a decree in a case where the court had acquired jurisdiction of the person of a disobedient party. Its effect extends beyond such a case. It has changed the nature of the action from an action *in personam,* to an action substantially *in rem.* Though the court cannot by constructive service obtain jurisdiction of the person of a non-resident defendant and cannot compel such a defendant to obey its decree, where the court has the power to make a decree which will affect the interests of a party in property within the State, whether that party obeys the decree or not, the action is not purely *in personam.* The court's decree acts upon the

5. [See Section 5102 N.Y. CPLR "Enforcement of judgment or order awarding possession of real property or a chattel" and Section 5107 "Conveyance by sheriff."]

property as well as the person of the non-resident defendant. In such case the objection that the court by constructive service obtains no jurisdiction over the person of a non-resident is without force. The Legislature has expressly provided that in an action for specific performance a court may enforce its decree by other means than direction to the defendant.

The order should be affirmed, with costs, and the questions certified answered "Yes."

NOTES

1.   The severe constraints imposed during the reign of Pennoyer v. Neff, 95 U.S. (5 Otto) 714, 24 L.Ed. 565 (1877), upon the states' power to exercise *in personam* jurisdiction have been greatly loosened by the "minimum contacts" rule of International Shoe Co. v. Washington, 326 U.S. 310, 66 S.Ct. 154, 90 L.Ed. 95 (1945), and its progeny. Nonetheless, not all of the states have chosen to adopt long arm statutes taking full advantage of this change.

2.   In a controversy concerning right to part of the corpus of a trust established in Delaware by the settlor who later became domiciled in Florida, the U.S. Supreme Court held that, since the Florida court had no personal jurisdiction over the trustee and no *in rem* jurisdiction over the trust, it was without jurisdiction to determine the validity of the trust. Hanson v. Denckla, 357 U.S. 235, 78 S.Ct. 1228, 2 L.Ed.2d 1283 (1958). Discussing the question of *in rem* jurisdiction over the trust, Warren, C.J., stated:

. . . Founded on physical power, the *in rem* jurisdiction of a state court is limited by the extent of its power and by the coordinate authority of sister States. The basis of the jurisdiction is the presence of the subject property within the territorial jurisdiction of the forum State. Tangible property poses no problem for the application of this rule, but the situs of intangibles is often a matter of controversy. . . .

The Florida court held that the presence of the subject property was not essential to its jurisdiction. Authority over the probate and construction of its domiciliary's will, under which the assets might pass, was thought sufficient to confer the requisite jurisdiction. But jurisdiction cannot be predicated upon the contingent role of this Florida will. Whatever the efficacy of a so-called *"in rem"* jurisdiction over assets admittedly passing under a local will, a State acquires no *in rem* jurisdiction to adjudicate the validity of *inter vivos* dispositions simply because its decision might augment an estate passing under a will probated in its courts. If such a basis of jurisdiction were sustained, probate courts would enjoy nationwide service of process to adjudicate interests in property with which neither the State nor the decedent could claim any affiliation. The settlor-decedent's Florida domicile is equally unavailing as a basis for jurisdiction over the trust assets. For the purpose of jurisdiction *in rem* the maxim that personalty has its situs at the domicile of its owner is a fiction of limited utility. The maxim is no less suspect when the domicile is that of a decedent. . . .

B. DECREES AS TO FOREIGN PROPERTY

1. CONVEYANCES OF FOREIGN LAND

Penn v. Lord Baltimore

Chancery, 1750.
1 Vesey Senior 444, 27 Eng.Rep. 1132.

[This case involved a dispute over the boundary line between Pennsylvania and Maryland. Plaintiffs claim that the parties entered into a settlement agreement of the boundary dispute and seek specific performance of the settlement provisions. Defendants entered a number of objections, including the claim that the court could not decree specific performance of an agreement regarding foreign lands, nor could it enforce its judgment if it decreed specific performance.]

LORD CHANCELLOR [LORD HARDWICKE]. I directed this cause to stand over for judgment, not so much from any doubt of what was the justice of the case, as by reason of the nature of it, the great consequence and importance, and the great labour and ability of the argument on both sides; it being for the determination of the right and boundaries of two great provincial governments and three counties; of a nature worthy the judicature of a Roman senate rather than of a single judge: and my consolation is, that if I should err in my judgment, there is a judicature equal in dignity to a Roman senate that will correct it [(i.e., the House of Lords)].

It is unnecessary to state the case on all the particular circumstances of evidence; which will fall in more naturally, and very intelligibly, under the particular points arising in the cause.

The relief prayed must be admitted to be the common and ordinary equity dispensed by this court; the specific performance of agreements being one of the great heads of this court, and the most useful one, and better than damages at law, so far as relates to the thing in specie; and more useful in a case of this nature than in most others; because no damages in an action of covenant could be at all adequate to what is intended by the parties, and to the utility to arise from this agreement, *viz.* the settling and fixing these boundaries in peace, to prevent the disorder and mischief, which in remote countries, distant from the seat of government, are most likely to happen, and most mischievous. Therefore the remedy prayed by a specific performance is more necessary here than in other cases: provided it is proper in all respect: and the relief sought must prevail, unless sufficient objections are shewn by defendant; who has made many and various for that purpose.

First, the point of jurisdiction ought in order to be considered: and though it comes late, I am not unwilling to consider it.... It is certain, that the original jurisdiction in cases of this kind relating to boundaries between provinces, the dominion, and proprietary government, is in the King and council.... This court therefore has no original jurisdiction on the direct question of the original right of the boundaries; and this bill does not stand in need of that. It is founded on articles executed in *England* under seal for mutual consideration; which gives jurisdiction to the King's courts both of law and equity, whatever be the subject matter.... The conscience of the party was bound by this agreement; and being within the jurisdiction of this court, which acts *in personam,* the court may properly decree it as an agreement, if a foundation for it....

. . . .

As to the court's not inforcing the execution of their judgment; if they could not at all, I agree, it would be in vain to make a decree; and that the court cannot inforce their own decree *in rem,* in the present case: but that is not an objection against making a decree in the cause; for the strict primary decree in this court as a court of equity is *in personam,* long before it was settled, whether this court could issue to put into possession in a suit of lands in England; which was first begun and settled in the time of James I. [(r. 1603–25)] but ever since done by injunction or writ of assistance to the sheriff: but the court cannot to this day as to lands in Ireland or the plantations. In Lord King's time [(Ch. 1725–33)] in the case of Richardson v. Hamilton, Attorney–General of Pennsylvania, which was a suit of land and a house in the town of Philadelphia, the court made a decree, though it could not be inforced *in rem.* In the case of Lord Anglesey of land lying in Ireland, I decreed for distinguishing and settling the parts of the estate, though impossible to inforce that decree *in rem,* but the party being in England, I could inforce it by process of contempt *in personam* and sequestration, which is the proper jurisdiction of this court....

I am of opinion therefore to decree a specific performance of this agreement.

NOTES

1. The order entered by Lord Hardwicke, which appears at 3 Ves.Sr. * 194, 28 Eng.Rep. 498 (1750), decreed

> that the said articles, and the several matters and things therein contained, should be performed and carried into execution by and between the said parties, and every of them; and to that end, that the Plaintiffs T.P. and R.P. the father, in their own right, and as standing in the place of J.P. deceased; and the Defendant, the Lord B. should respectively, before the end of three calendar months from that day, execute, under their hands and seals, two several proper instruments, appointing and authorizing proper persons, not more than seven on each side, with full powers to the said seven persons respectively, or any three or more of them, for the actual running, marking, and laying out the part of a circle, and the several lines in the said articles mentioned: and such commissioners were to give due notice to each other, and to fix and agree upon a time or times to begin and proceed in the running, marking, and laying out the same.
>
> ... that the same should be begun, at the furthest, some time in the month of November then next, and be proceeded in according to

the said article; and that the said lines should be marked out by visible stones, posts, trees, pillars, buildings, land marks, or other certain boundaries, which might remain and continue; and that such boundaries should be marked on one side with the arms of the Defendant the Lord B.; and on the other side, with the arms of the Plaintiffs the Penns; and that such lines should be completely so run, marked, and laid out, on or before the last day of April 1752; and when so done, that a true and exact plan and survey thereof, with the best, and most exact, and certain description that could be given of the same, should be made up, signed, and sealed by the commissioners on both sides, and by their principals, and be entered in all the public offices in the provinces of Maryland and Pennsylvania, and the three lower counties of Newcastle, Kent, and Sussex; and that a true copy of such respective instruments for appointing commissioners, when prepared, should be delivered by the solicitor of the one party, to the solicitor of the other party; and in case the parties should differ about such instruments, or either of them, the Master was to settle the same. . . . and that after the said limits and boundaries should be so set out and ascertained by the commissioners, the Plaintiffs . . . and the Defendant . . . should respectively release and convey to each other, and their heirs, their respective rights, titles, interests, powers, prerogatives, claims, demands, and pretensions, in or to the respective territories, districts, and lands severally allotted to them, according to the tenth article contained in the said articles of agreement.

2.   In 1763, the responsibility for completing the survey was put in the hands of Jeremiah Mason and Charles Dixon. Part of the boundary drawn by these two men is still known as the Mason–Dixon line.

3.   Arglasse filed a bill in England to be relieved against a grant of annuity or rent-charge upon his lands in Ireland. He claimed that this grant was obtained by fraud. The defendant's plea to the court's jurisdiction, that the matter was examinable only in the Irish Court of Chancery, was overruled. Arglasse v. Muschamp, 1 Vern. 75, 135, 23 Eng.Rep. 322, 369 (Ch. 1682). Nottingham, L.C., said:

This is surely only a jest put upon the jurisdiction of this court by the common lawyers; for when you go about to bind the lands, and grant a sequestration to execute a decree, then they readily tell you, that the authority of this court is only to regulate a man's conscience, and ought not to affect the estate, but that this court must *agere in personam* only; and when, as in this case, you prosecute the person for a fraud, they tell you, you must not intermeddle here, because the fraud, though committed here, concerns lands that lie in Ireland, which makes the jurisdiction local; and so would wholly elude the jurisdiction of this court. But certainly they forget the case of Archer and Preston, in which case, if in any, the jurisdiction was local, the matter there being not only for land that lay in Ireland, but of a title under the act of settlement there; yet the defendant coming into England, a bill was exhibited against him here, and a *ne exeat regno* [writ to restrain a person from leaving the kingdom] granted, and he put to answer a contract made for those lands; and when he departed into Ireland without answering, he was sent for over by a special order from the King, and made to answer the contempt, and to abide the justice of this court; for the King will maintain the authority of his courts, when they act according to law and reason. . . . [A]nd as to the objection, that this court was deficient in power in this case to compel a performance of its decree, because it could not sequester the lands in question, he looked upon that as an objection of no weight; and it did not appear to him, but the defendant might have other lands in England.

4. Watts, the holder of a prior equity in Ohio land, brought an equity action against Massie, a resident of Kentucky, in the federal court in Kentucky. Watts sought a decree ordering Massie to convey to him legal title to the Ohio land. Watts prevailed, and Massie appealed on the ground that the federal court in Kentucky lacked jurisdiction over the case. The Supreme Court rejected this argument and affirmed the decree. Massie v. Watts, 10 U.S. (6 Cranch) 148, 3 L.Ed. 181 (1810). Marshall, C.J., explained:

> where the defendant in the original action is liable to the plaintiff, either in consequence of contract, or as trustee, or as the holder of a legal title acquired by any species of *mala fides* practised on the plaintiff, the principles of equity give a court jurisdiction wherever the person may be found, and the circumstance, that a question of title may be involved in the inquiry, and may even constitute the essential point on which the case depends, does not seem sufficient to arrest that jurisdiction.

---

2. EXTRATERRITORIAL EFFECT OF DECREES FOR CONVEYANCE

Deschenes v. Tallman

Court of Appeals of New York, 1928.
248 N.Y. 33, 161 N.E. 321.

■ CARDOZO, C.J. The complaint is for the foreclosure of a purchase-money mortgage. The answer is a counterclaim for breach of a covenant of seizin [(i.e., an assurance that the seller had the estate conveyed)]. Whether seizin was lacking is the question to be answered.

Plaintiffs sold the land to the defendant Francis Tallman in April, 1925. A predecessor in title was Miller & Lockwell, Limited, a Canadian corporation. By a decree of the courts of the Province of Quebec, made in 1911, the corporation was adjudged insolvent, and its property, real and personal, was ordered to be sold by two liquidators duly appointed according to the laws of the Province. The liquidators conveyed the land to the plaintiffs, who thereafter sold to Tallman with covenant of seizin. The land is located in the city of New York. The defendants insist that the title does not pass under a deed by foreign liquidators.

A second and confirmatory deed, made in December, 1926, is also the subject of attack. After the sale to Tallman, the plaintiffs procured the execution of a quitclaim deed by the Canadian corporation. This deed, made by the corporation to the defendant Francis Tallman, contains a recital that it is given "in confirmation of a deed" made by the liquidators, "it being the opinion of the liquidators that this deed is necessary for the beneficial winding up of the party of the first part and they having requested the execution of the same." The statutes of Canada are to the effect that the corporate life survives the appointment of a liquidator until the winding up is finished, but that the powers of the directors cease "except in so far as the court or liquidator sanctions the continuance of the same." The defendants insist that the later deed, being made under compulsion, adds nothing to the first one, and leaves the title where it was.

The answer demands judgment for the cancellation of the purchase-money mortgage, the return of the cash payment, and reimbursement for the value of subsequent improvements.

We think the counterclaim must fail.

There is no need to determine what effect would be given to the liquidators' deed considered by itself. . . .

If the deed by the liquidators be assumed to be inoperative, there was none the less a conveyance of title upon delivery by the corporation of a confirmatory deed of grant. A judgment of a foreign court will not avail of its own force to transfer the title to land located in this State. It will not avail though a conveyance be executed by the sheriff or a master or other agent of the court in fulfillment of its mandate. "The court, not having jurisdiction of the *res,* cannot affect it by its decree, nor by a deed made by a master in accordance with the decree." But the rule is different where the conveyance is executed by the owner, though he act under compulsion. The conveyance, and not the judgment, is then the source of title. As to this the law has been undoubted since Penn v. Lord Baltimore. The distinction is between a judgment directed against the *res* itself, and one directed against the person of the owner, who acts upon the *res.* His deed transmits the title irrespective of the pressure exerted on his will.

. . . .

The order of the Appellate Division and that of the Special Term should be reversed, with costs in the Appellate Division and in this court, and judgment ordered in favor of the plaintiffs for the relief demanded in the complaint.

Burnley v. Stevenson

Supreme Court of Ohio, 1873.
24 Ohio St. 474.

[General Scott agreed to convey certain lands, originally part of the Virginia military district and now part of Ohio, to Evans in return for his services as a surveyor. After the services were performed, but before the lands were conveyed, Scott died. In a suit by Evans for specific performance of the contract with Scott, a Circuit Court in Kentucky, having jurisdiction of the heirs and legal representatives of Scott, ordered the lands to be conveyed to Evans. A commissioner appointed by the court executed and delivered to Evans a deed in fee simple for the lands. Plaintiffs, claiming through Scott's heirs and legal representatives, now sue in Ohio to recover possession of the lands.]

The defendant in his answer further sets forth, that he has succeeded to all the rights and title of said John Evans in and to said lands, and avers that he and those under whom he claims, are now lawfully in possession thereof, and have so been in possession, claiming under said decree and the deed from said master, ever since the dates thereof.

To this defense the plaintiffs below filed their reply, to which the defendant demurred. The demurrer was sustained, to which ruling the plaintiffs excepted.

Judgment was therefore rendered in favor of the defendant below, which was afterward, on error, affirmed by the District Court.

To reverse these judgments, this proceeding is now instituted.

Plaintiffs in error admit that their reply in the court below was insufficient, if the above matters and things contained in the answer, constituted a good defense to the action.

McIlvaine, J. The main proposition submitted in this case is, whether, under and by virtue of the decree of the Circuit Court of Kentucky and the master's deed made in pursuance thereof, or of either of them, such an estate or right was vested in John Evans as entitles the defendant, who has succeeded to all the rights of Evans, to the possession of the lands in controversy, as against the plaintiffs, whose claim of title is derived from the parties against whom the decree was rendered.

1. The jurisdiction of the Circuit Court to pronounce the decree, is the first inquiry involved in this proposition.

It appears from the record before us, that the Circuit Court of Kentucky which pronounced the decree, was a court of general equity jurisdiction; that some of the defendants in the cause were properly served with the process of the court, and that all others voluntarily appeared and submitted themselves to its jurisdiction, and that the subject-matter of the bill on which the decree was rendered, was the enforcement of a trust and the specific performance of a contract to convey lands situate in the State of Ohio.

That courts exercising chancery powers in one state have jurisdiction to enforce a trust, and to compel the specific performance of a contract in relation to lands situate in another state, after having obtained jurisdiction of the persons of those upon whom the obligation rests, is a doctrine fully settled by numerous decisions.

2. It does not follow, however, that a court having power to compel the parties before it to convey lands situated in another state, may make its own decree to operate as such conveyance. Indeed, it is well settled that the decree of such court can not operate to transfer title to lands situate in a foreign jurisdiction. And this, for the reason that a judgment or decree *in rem* can not operate beyond the limits of the jurisdiction or state wherein it is rendered. And if a decree in such case can not effect the transfer of the title to such lands, it is clear that a deed executed by a master, under the

direction of the court, can have no greater effect. The master's deed to Evans must therefore be regarded as a nullity.

The next inquiry then is as to the force and effect of the decree rendered by the Circuit Court directing the heirs of Gen. Scott to convey the land in Ohio to Evans. This decree was *in personam,* and bound the consciences of those against whom it was rendered. In it, the contract of their ancestor to make the conveyance was merged. The fact that the title which had descended to them was held by them in trust for Evans, was thus established by the decree of a court of competent jurisdiction. Such decree is record evidence of that fact, and also of the fact that it [had] become and was their duty to convey the legal title to him. The performance of that duty might have been enforced against them in that court by attachment as for contempt; and the fact that the conveyance was not made in pursuance of the order, does not affect the validity of the decree in so far as it determined the equitable rights of the parties in the land in controversy. In our judgment, the parties, and those holding under them with notice, are still bound thereby.

3.   Under our code of practice, equitable as well as legal defenses may be set up in an action for the recovery of land. The defendant in the court below set up this decree of the Circuit Court of Kentucky as a defense to the plaintiffs' action. That it did not constitute a good defense at law may be admitted, but we think, in equity, it was a sufficient defense.

The constitution of the United States declares that full faith and credit shall be given in each state to the records and judicial proceedings of every other state, and provides that Congress may prescribe the mode of proving such records and proceedings, and the effect thereof. By an act of May 26, 1790, Congress declared that the "records and judicial proceedings of the state courts," when properly authenticated, "shall have the same faith and credit given to them in every court within the United States, as they have, by law or usage, in the courts of the state from whence they are or shall be taken." When, therefore, a decree rendered by a court in a sister state, having jurisdiction of the parties and of the subject-matter, is offered as evidence, or pleaded as the foundation of a right, in any action in the courts of this state, it is entitled to the same force and effect which it had in the state where it was pronounced. That this decree had the effect in Kentucky of determining the equities of the parties to the land in this state, we have already shown; hence the courts of this state must accord to it the same effect. True, the courts of this state can not enforce the performance of that decree, by compelling the conveyance through its process of attachment; but when pleaded in our courts as a cause of action, or as a ground of defense, it must be regarded as conclusive of all the rights and equities which were adjudicated and settled therein, unless it be impeached for fraud.

Motion overruled.

NOTE

In addition to the full faith and credit clause of the Constitution, Article 4 § 1, Congress has statutorily required state and federal courts to give full faith and credit to each others' "judicial proceedings." 28 U.S.C. § 1738.

McElreath v. McElreath

Supreme Court of Texas, 1961.
162 Tex. 190, 345 S.W.2d 722.

■ NORVELL, J. This is a suit to enforce an Oklahoma equitable decree ordering James Dorsey McElreath to convey lands in Texas to Evelyn Ann McElreath. Both courts below refused the relief prayed for.

The decree sought to be enforced was entered in a divorce suit between the parties both of whom were residents of Oklahoma and Oklahoma was their matrimonial domicile [(i.e., where they lived together as husband and wife, in fact or in the eyes of the law)] .... It appears without dispute that the order is valid and enforceable in Oklahoma and has been affirmed by the court of last resort in that State. However, after the decree had been entered, but before the Oklahoma court could enforce its order, McElreath crossed the Red River and now asserts sanctuary in Texas.

Insofar as marital property is concerned, the laws of Oklahoma are different from those of Texas. However, upon the dissolution of a marriage, Oklahoma like Texas seeks to provide equitable distribution of properties and property rights between its residents. Quite obviously one authority must settle these rights if anything approaching fairness and equity is to be secured. Jurisdiction for such purpose rests with the courts of the matrimonial domicile which, in this case, is the State of Oklahoma. A competent court of that state having acted, and presumably having made a proper and equitable adjustment of the property rights of the divorcing parties, it is anomalous to say the least, to assert that the work of that court may be set at naught by the defendant's crossing the state line and coming to Texas. There is no doubt but that had he remained in Oklahoma, the decree could and would have been enforced by contempt proceedings. As a matter of justice, good order and common sense, the Oklahoma decree should be enforced in Texas, unless contrary to some well defined public policy of this State. There is something incongruous and out of keeping with the concept of orderly processes to tolerate a situation wherein solemn court decrees may be flouted by playing hop-skip with state boundaries. This case involves Oklahomans and it is not against the public policy of Texas for Oklahoma to maintain a different system of property ownership for its residents than that provided by Texas for Texans.

. . . .

... Under our laws, permanent alimony is not recognized, nor is a Texas court authorized to divest either spouse of his or her title to separate property, but the wife, in the main, must look to the community property for her share of the material gains incident to an ill-starred marriage. We expect other states to recognize our system of marital property ownership, so should we respect their schemes of property ownership and attendant plans for the adjustment of property rights upon the dissolution of a marriage. Texas public policy does not relate to and is not concerned with the settlement by Oklahoma courts of marital property problems which arise between Oklahoma citizens. . . .

The matter of enforcing the equitable decrees of one state which affect lands in another state has been the subject of much writing, largely occasioned by a few unsatisfactory court decisions. Only a small portion of this legal literature need be noticed. Most of the authorities discuss the problem of the extra-territorial effect of an equitable decree from the standpoint of the full faith and credit clause of the United States Constitution, Article 4, § 1. That doctrine need not be adverted to here. It is similar, but much broader in scope than the doctrine of comity. However, persuasive and helpful, the decisions relating to "Full Faith and Credit" may be, the doctrine itself need not be invoked when the state of the situs as a matter of comity recognizes the rights upon which the decree of a sister state is based and decides that the enforcement of such rights does not violate any principle of public policy of the situs state. . . .

. . . .

Our differences with the courts below rest primarily upon a divergence of opinions as to the proper construction of the Oklahoma court decree. The trial court and the Court of Civil Appeals treated the decree as being one which directly affected the title to Texas lands. We regard it as being an equitable order operating in personam which orders James Dorsey McElreath to execute a deed conveying land in Texas to Evelyn Ann McElreath. As so construed, the Oklahoma decree should be enforced as a matter of comity.

. . . .

The distinction between the decree which purports to directly affect title to lands in another state *ex proprio vigore* [by its own force] and one which acts upon the parties in personam is important. In essence, the validity of the decree in rem or *ex proprio vigore* depends upon rules applicable to jurisdiction of courts, while the enforceability of an equitable decree in personam depends upon the public policy of the forum state insofar as comity is concerned. . . . Our inquiry relates to public policy and not jurisdiction. The Texas courts, like the courts of Oklahoma, possess the power and authority to award equitable relief in the nature of an order for specific performance and to enforce the same by appropriate contempt action. The enforcement of the rights established by the Oklahoma decree do not involve the use of remedies and processes unknown to the law of Texas, nor the recognition of rights and estates in property unknown to Texas law.

The argument of respondents which was accepted by the Court of Civil Appeals stems from Bullock v. Bullock, 52 N.J.Eq. 561, 30 A. 676, and Fall v. Fall, 75 Neb. 104, 106 N.W. 412, 113 N.W. 175, which follows the Bullock case. In Fall v. Fall, the following statement of the New Jersey court is quoted with approval:

> "[T]he doctrine that jurisdiction respecting lands in a foreign state is not in rem, but one in personam, is bereft of all practical force, if the decree in personam is conclusive and must be enforced by the courts of the situs."

From this premise, it is asserted that a decree of a Washington court in a suit between Washington citizens which directs a party to that suit to execute a conveyance of Nebraska lands is contrary to the public policy of the State of Nebraska. . . .

. . . .

In Weesner v. Weesner, 168 Neb. 346, 95 N.W.2d 682 [1959] it was said that:

> "[I]t is universally held that a court of one state cannot directly affect or determine the title to land in another state. However, it is also now well established that a court of competent jurisdiction in one state with all necessary parties properly before it in an action for divorce, generally has the power and authority to render a decree ordering the execution and delivery of a deed to property in another state in lieu of alimony for the wife. Such an order is personam in character, and when final it is generally res judicata, bringing into operation the doctrine of collateral estoppel."

. . . .

It seems settled that the situs state is not required to give full faith and credit to the judgment of a sister state which purports to act in rem and would directly affect the title to land in the situs state. When, however, as in this case, it is contended that the enforcement of an in personam decree of a sister state would be contrary to the public policy of the situs state, the path to be followed is not so clear. In some cases of conflict of public policies, the state policy may be forced to give way. Fauntleroy v. Lum, 210 U.S. 230, 28 S.Ct. 641, 52 L.Ed. 1039. It is peculiarly the function of the Supreme Court of the United States to decide these delicate questions of policy conflict. Comity, in the absence of a controlling decision by the United States Supreme Court under the "Full Faith and Credit" clause, seems the preferable basis for a state court decision. In that way there is no danger of restricting the scope of state public policy by a prediction of what the United States Supreme Court may hold in any given situation. Our holding therefore is that as a matter of comity we will enforce the equitable decrees of a sister state affecting Texas land so long as such enforcement does not contravene an established public policy in this State. As a corollary to this holding and as applicable to this case, we hold that the enforcement of an equitable decree entered by a sister state in a divorce case between nonresidents of the State of Texas who possess no peculiar property rights growing out of Texas marital laws, does not violate the public policy of this State. Other factual situations are not before us and hence are not decided.

. . . .

The judgments of the courts below are reversed and the cause remanded to the trial court with directions to render judgment for the petitioner in accordance with this opinion and the stipulation of the parties. . . .

■ THE CHIEF JUSTICE and ASSOCIATE JUSTICES GRIFFIN, SMITH, and WALKER dissented.

■ GRIFFIN, J. (dissenting). This is the first case in the history of American jurisprudence in which a court of the situs state has recognized the judgment of a sister state adjudging title to land on the ground of comity, where, without question, that judgment violates the plain and unambiguous provisions of the statute of the situs state.

I cannot agree to the disposition of this case for the following reasons:

1. The majority, in holding that the Oklahoma judgment is a decree *in personam* rather than a decree *in rem,* is directly contrary to the plain wording of the judgment and to the construction placed on the judgment by the parties themselves.

2. The Oklahoma judgment which the majority opinion enforces is void and may be collaterally attacked under the decisions of the Oklahoma Supreme Court. Thus the argument that the effect of the decree can be changed by the defendant's crossing the state line is without force.

3. The majority opinion would have our trial courts pass title to realty of one spouse to the other spouse, which power is prohibited to our courts in Texas in divorce matters by legislative enactment; to wit, Art. 4638, R.C.S.1925. This necessarily has the effect of permitting the other 49 states to decree a division of Texas land, while Texas courts are expressly prohibited from doing so. Thus we have one rule of law for Texas citizens who own land in Texas and another, more favorable rule, for nonresidents who may own Texas land. This is the rankest kind of discrimination of our own citizens.

4. The judgment of the Oklahoma court is not entitled to recognition under the doctrine of comity because it violates the public policy of Texas as established by legislative enactment.

5. The Oklahoma judgment is not *res judicata* as to the interest petitioner has in the Texas real estate.

6. The majority decision will create interminable confusion and uncertainty as to land titles and particularly as to land titles in divorce suits, and, as a matter of policy, the decision of the majority should not prevail.

. . . .

. . . [There is a] distinction between this case and those in which the courts of a state of the situs of land will recognize and enforce a judgment of a sister state ordering specific performance of a contract to convey. In those cases the right to the conveyance is not grounded in or created by a judgment which purports to adjudicate title to real property over which the court has no jurisdiction; rather, the right to the conveyance is grounded in and created by a contract of the parties which the court having the parties properly before it has jurisdiction to interpret and order performed.

. . . .

Being a judgment in rem, the Oklahoma judgment is clearly not entitled to full faith and credit. "A divorce court does not have jurisdiction to enter a decree in rem which will directly affect the legal title to real estate situated in another state, even though it has jurisdiction in personam over the defendant, and if the person who is ordered to execute the deed does not do so the courts of the state in which the land is situated are not bound to give *full faith and credit* to a decree concerning the title or the right to it." (Emphasis added.) 17A Am.Jur. 172, § 991 and 17 Am.Jur. 733, § 669.

. . . .

The case of Weesner v. Weesner, 168 Neb. 346, 95 N.W.2d 682, not only does not support the majority view, but supports my view that the foreign decree should not be given effect, when to do so would be contrary to the statutes and therefore to the public policy of the state of the situs of the land. After discussing Fall v. Fall, 75 Neb. 104, 106 N.W. 412, 113 N.W. 175, which was affirmed by the U.S. Supreme Court as Fall v. Eastin, 215 U.S. 1, 30 S.Ct. 3, 54 L.Ed. 65, the court holds that a foreign judgment which adjudges title to land in another state will be given effect only ". . . if the related public policy of the situs state is in substantial accord with that of the other state."

. . . .

In conclusion, I believe we will have more certainty to land titles and less confusion if Texas continues her present policy of determining the title to Texas lands in accordance with its law and decrees, rather than permitting decrees of the 49 other states to affect titles to Texas lands.

I would affirm the judgments of both courts below.

On Motion for Rehearing.

◼ NORVELL, J. Respondent has filed an able motion for rehearing and a supplement thereto, wherein he strongly reurges two propositions, namely, that the decree here involved is actually an in rem decree, and alternatively, that if the decree be considered one in personam, nevertheless the equitable rights supporting the same cannot be enforced in Texas because of local policy considerations.

. . . In this case, the order of the Oklahoma court entered in accordance with the law which controls the marital rights of the parties was an order operating in personam and one which the Oklahoma court had jurisdiction to render . . . .

We pass next to the second contention which presents the paramount issue in this suit. Do public policy considerations prevent a Texas court from ordering respondent to do what the Oklahoma court has ordered him to do, namely, convey land in Texas to the petitioner?

. . . .

The question of the enforceability of equitable decrees arising out of divorce cases relating to lands in states other than the matrimonial domicile is one of growing importance. It demands some solution which is hardly met by the adoption of a strictly "hands off" or "do nothing" policy on the part of the courts of the states wherein the real property may be located . . . .

We do not regard the objection to the enforcement of the Oklahoma decree as being a valid one. Texas courts have asserted their authority to issue equitable in personam decrees relating to property outside the state. It seems that there should be no valid objection to the recognition of a like right in the Oklahoma court which had undisputed jurisdiction of the parties. . . .

Respondent's motion for rehearing overruled.

[Four judges again dissented.]

NOTES

1.   Under the Full Faith and Credit Clause, a final judgment in a civil action at law must be recognized by the courts of sister states. This does not require those courts to issue execution on the judgment. But the sister state must (1) consider the judgment as *res judicata,* and (2) allow the maintenance of an action on the judgment if it is for money. Thus, in Fauntleroy v. Lum, 210 U.S. 230, 28 S.Ct. 641, 52 L.Ed. 1039 (1908), which is cited in *McElreath,* a Mississippi court was compelled to grant recovery on a Missouri money judgment, although the original cause of action was an agreement made in Mississippi and unenforceable there because of a statute expressly making it illegal.

2.   Divorce actions may be brought wherever either party is domiciled. However, a property settlement can only be rendered by a court with personal jurisdiction over both parties.

3.   Various difficult problems of conflict of laws and domestic relations are raised by a suit in one state upon the alimony decree of another state or a foreign country. Much depends (1) on whether the suit is for accrued installments only, or also seeks to obtain an order in the second suit for the payment of future installments; and (2) on whether the original decree is capable of modification by the court which rendered it, either as to future installments or as to past installments still unpaid.

---

3.   FORECLOSURE AND PARTITION

Eaton v. McCall

Supreme Judicial Court of Maine, 1894.
86 Me. 346, 29 A. 1103.

■ WISHWELL, J. Bill in equity between parties resident in this state to foreclose a mortgage upon real estate situated in Nova Scotia.

The defendant failing to appear, the bill was taken pro confesso. Afterwards, on motion for a decree, the justice presiding at nisi prius, being doubtful as to the jurisdiction of this court, with the consent of counsel for the complainant, reported the case to the law court to determine whether the bill should be sustained, and what decree, if any, should be made.

. . . .

. . . [T]his court has the power to make a decree compelling a mortgagor, over whom it has jurisdiction, to make a conveyance of the mortgaged premises, after failure to pay the amount ascertained to be due, within the time fixed by a decree of the court, which time should not be less than the statutory period allowed for redemption in the place where the land is situated.

But as to when and under what circumstances this power should be exercised by the court, is, we think, another and quite different question. It must be remembered that no decree of the court would be operative except one against the mortgagor, or person having the right to redeem, commanding a conveyance. The court could not proceed in the usual and customary method by decreeing either a strict foreclosure or a foreclosure by a judicial sale. Neither the decree itself nor any conveyance under it, except by the person in whom the title is vested, can operate beyond the jurisdiction of the court. A court cannot send its process into another State nor can it deliver possession of land in another jurisdiction. It can only accomplish foreclosure of such a mortgage by its decree *in personam,* compelling a conveyance.

We do not think that a chancery court should exercise this power except under unusual or extraordinary circumstances. Wherever it is necessary in order to prevent loss or to protect the rights of a mortgagee it may be done, for instance in the case of a mortgage upon property situated both within and without the State, where, unless a sale of the entire property could be made at one time, great loss might ensue, or in other cases where an equally good reason existed. But ordinarily we think that the holder of a mortgage should be required to resort to the remedies or the courts of the jurisdiction in which the land is situated. This is in accordance with the principle, than which none is better established, that the disposition of real estate, whether by deed, descent, or by any other mode, must be governed by the law of the state where the same is situated.

In this case there are no reasons, either alleged or apparent, why the holder of this mortgage cannot foreclose the same according to the law of the place where the land is situated, without loss or great inconvenience.

We think, therefore, that the entry should be,

Bill dismissed without prejudice.

Wimer v. Wimer

Supreme Court of Appeals of Virginia, 1888.
82 Va. 890, 5 S.E. 536.

Appeal from decree of circuit court of Highland county ... The purpose of this suit was to have partition of the lands whereof George Wimer, of Philip, died seized in fee, among the several parties then owning it as tenants in common. These lands consisted of several adjoining tracts ... situated on Dry Run, partly in said county and partly in Pendleton county, in West Virginia. Defendants demurred to the bill and answered it, ... denying the jurisdiction of the said circuit court to make partition of land situated in West Virginia, & c. The court appointed commissioners to make the partition, if practicable, as prayed for, and accordingly they did make and report such partition as well of the lands lying in West Virginia as of those lying in Virginia. Defendants made exceptions to the report, .

which were overruled and the report confirmed. From the decree the said [defendants] obtained an appeal and *supersedeas* [(a stay)] from one of the judges of this court.

■ HINTON, J., delivered the opinion of the court. The question in this case is one of importance, but of little intrinsic difficulty. It is this: Has a court in Virginia, when the defendants have appeared and answered, jurisdiction to partition lands, the major part of which lies within another State?

Now, it is a fundamental maxim of international jurisprudence that every State or nation possesses an exclusive sovereignty and jurisdiction within its own territory, and the "direct consequence of this rule is," says a learned author, "that the laws of every State affect and bind directly all property, whether real or personal, within its territory." Story's Conflict of Laws, 5, 18. Another consequence of this maxim is, that no State can, by its laws, and no court, which is but a creature of the State, can, by its judgments or decrees, directly bind or affect property beyond the limits of that State; and hence it is axiomatic that no writ of sequestration, or execution, or any order, judgment or decree of a foreign court, can be directly enforced against real estate situate without the limits of the foreign State. . . .

". . . [I]t is undoubtedly well settled that in cases of fraud, trust or contract, courts of equity will, whenever jurisdiction over the parties has been acquired, administer full relief without regard to the nature or situation of the property in which the controversy had its origin, and even where the relief sought consists in a decree for the conveyance of property which lies beyond the control of the court, provided it can be reached by the exercise of its powers over the person, and the relief asked is of such a nature as the court is capable of administering." But even as to these cases it must be borne in mind that the decrees of the foreign court do not directly affect the land, but operate upon the person of the defendant, and compel him to execute the conveyance, and it is the conveyance which has the effect, and not the decree. If, however, the relief asked cannot be administered by a decree *in personam*, without going further and acting upon the land, the court will refuse to entertain the bill. . . .

Now, tested by these principles, it is perfectly manifest that a court of chancery in Virginia has no jurisdiction to decree a partition of lands in another State, and this, for the plain reason before given that the right to transfer, partition and change real estate, belongs exclusively to the State within whose territory it is situate. In order to make a partition the court must invade by its officers the soil of another State, and divide up and allot its lands to suit the views of a foreign jurisdiction. This cannot be done.

For these reasons the decree of the circuit court of Highland County must be reversed, and the bill will be dismissed.

NOTES

1. Tenants in common hold an undivided interest in the land; i.e., each has a right of possession with respect to the whole tract. The parties

in *Wimer* became tenants in common when George Wimer died without bequeathing the land to anyone in his will.

2. For an explanation of how partition is carried out, see the excerpt from Langdell's Summary of Equity Pleading in Section A of Chapter 2, *supra* p. 39.

———

C. Injunctions Against Foreign Suits

———

1. Grounds for Issuance

———

Lord Portarlington v. Soulby

Chancery, 1834.
3 Myl. & K. 104, 40 Eng.Rep. 40.

THE LORD CHANCELLOR [LORD BROUGHAM]. This was a motion to dissolve an injunction, granted to restrain the Defendants from suing in Ireland upon a bill of exchange for £1000,[6] accepted by the Plaintiff,[7] payable to a person of the name of Aldridge, by whom it was indorsed and passed away to Mr. Brook, a retail dealer in wines, and by him to the Defendants.

The ground of the injunction is, that the bill was given by Lord Portarlington for money lost at play. . . .

The case is reduced to this. An illegal consideration distinctly stated and not denied, with several circumstances leading to the belief, that the Defendants now know such to have been the origin of the bill; and several circumstances also shewing that it was taken by their late partner under suspicion, and yet without inquiry.

It is, then, impossible to doubt that the injunction was well granted, and the whole question would be free from difficulty but for one peculiarity in the case; the action is brought in Ireland, and the interposition of this Court is sought to stop proceedings there. That this is an unusual proceeding must be admitted, but I do not see any ground for questioning the competency of it.

Soon after the restoration [(1660)], and when this like every other branch of the Court's jurisdiction was, if not in its infancy, at least far from that maturity which it attained under the illustrious series of chancellors, the Nottinghams and Macclesfields, the parents of equity, the point re-

---

6. [A bill of exchange is an instrument in which A orders B to pay C a sum certain at a definite future time. A check is a demand bill of exchange.]

7. [The person who promises to pay a bill is called the acceptor. In the previous footnote, B is the acceptor.]

ceived a good deal of consideration in a case which came before Lord Clarendon, and which is reported shortly in Freeman's Reports, (2 Freem. 125) and somewhat more fully in Chancery Cases, under the name of Love v. Baker, 1 Ch.Cas. 67 [1665]. In Love v. Baker it appears that one only of several parties who had begun proceedings in the Court of Leghorn [(i.e., Livorno, Italy)] was resident within the jurisdiction here, and the Court allowed the *subpoena* to be served on him, and that this should be good service on the rest. So far there seems to have been very little scruple in extending the jurisdiction. Lord Clarendon refused the injunction to restrain those proceedings at Leghorn, after advising with the other judges, but the report adds, "[but examine this further], for all the bar was of another opinion;" and it is said that, when the argument against issuing it was used, that this Court had no authority to bind a foreign court, the answer was given that the injunction was not directed to the foreign court, but to the party within the jurisdiction here. A very sound answer, as it appears to me; for the same argument might apply to a Court within this country, which no order of this Court ever affects to bind, our orders being only pointed at the parties to restrain them from proceeding.

Accordingly this case of Love v. Baker has not been recognized or followed in later times. Two instances are mentioned in Mr. Hargrave's collection of the jurisdiction being recognized; and in the case of Wharton v. May, 5 Ves. 71, which underwent so much discussion, part of the decree was to restrain the Defendants from entering up any judgment, or carrying on any action, in what is called "the Court of Great Session in Scotland," meaning, of course, the Court of Session.

I have directed a search to be made for precedents in case the jurisdiction had been exercised in any instances which have not been reported; and one has been found directly in point. It is the case of Campbell v. Houlditch in 1820, where Lord Eldon ordered an injunction to restrain the Defendant from further proceeding in an action which he had commenced before the court of session in Scotland. From the note which his Lordship himself wrote upon the petition, requiring a further affidavit, and from his refusing the injunction to the extent prayed, it is clear that he paid particular attention to it. This precedent, therefore, is of very high authority.

In truth, nothing can be more unfounded than the doubts of the jurisdiction. That is grounded, like all other jurisdiction of the Court, not upon any pretension to the exercise of judicial and administrative rights abroad, but on the circumstance of the person of the party on whom this order is made being within the power of the Court. If the Court can command him to bring home goods from abroad, or to assign chattel interests, or to convey real property locally situate abroad;—if, for instance, as in Penn v. Lord Baltimore, it can decree the performance of an agreement touching the boundary of a province in North America; or, as in the case of Toller v. Carteret [2 Vern. 494 (1705)], can foreclose a mortgage on the isle of Sark, one of the channel islands; in precisely the like manner it can restrain the party being within the limits of its jurisdiction from doing anything abroad, whether the thing forbidden be a conveyance or other act *in pais* [(done without legal proceedings)], or the instituting or prosecution of an action in a foreign court.

. . . .

As to the argument that the Courts of Equity in Ireland can, if applied to, restrain the action, the same consideration would prevent an injunction from ever issuing to stay proceedings in this country; for it might be said that the Court of Exchequer has the power of restraining, and therefore there needs no interposition of the Court of Chancery.[8] It suffices to say that the court in which the action is brought is a court of common law, and has no jurisdiction as such to stop the proceeding upon the ground now set forth.

I am, therefore, of opinion that this injunction was well issued, and that it must be continued, and that this motion must be refused with costs.

Castanho v. Brown & Root (U.K.), Ltd.

House of Lords, 1980.
[1981] A.C. 557.

■ LORD SCARMAN.

This is an appeal by defendants from an order of the Court of Appeal, with the leave of that court, whereby, allowing the plaintiff's appeal from the judge, the court restored the plaintiff's notice of discontinuance of his action in England and discharged an injunction which the judge had granted restraining the plaintiff from proceeding with his claim in America. Put shortly, the judge required the plaintiff to proceed in England; the Court of Appeal allowed him to proceed in America.

. . . .

The defendants' reaction to his decision to sue in America was understandable and predictable, bearing in mind how much more they stood to lose if he proceeded there. They moved to set aside, or stay, the American proceedings, and did all they could to move along the English proceedings. On the 30th April they delivered a defence in the English action; and on the 1st May they issued two summonses, one for directions and the other for an injunction to restrain the plaintiff from prosecuting or continuing proceedings in the U.S.A.

. . . .

The judge in chambers had before him two applications, one (on the summons for directions) to strike out the notice of discontinuance and the other for the injunction. He made the two orders sought, delivering a judgment in open court. He held that the notice of discontinuance was in the circumstances an abuse of the process of the court and struck it out. Having so held, he had no difficulty in deciding—indeed, it was conceded— that he had jurisdiction to grant the injunction: and, in the exercise of his discretion, he granted it.

. . . .

8. [The Court of Exchequer had equity jurisdiction, which was abolished in 1842.]

The question in the appeal is, therefore, whether the plaintiff should be restrained by the English court from pursuing his claim for damages in the American courts. It is a question of great importance to the parties. In the American courts the plaintiff claims punitive as well as compensatory damages ($5m. compensation, and "at least" $10m. punitive or exemplary). In England he has no claim for punitive damages: and the scale of compensatory damages is much less. . . .

. . . .

In the Court of Appeal no majority *ratio decidendi* emerged. The Master of the Rolls, though he preferred a declaration to an injunction, agreed with the judge. Shaw L.J. based his judgment on lack of jurisdiction: as the English action had been ended, in his view, by the notice of discontinuance, the court had no jurisdiction to grant an injunction. Brandon L.J. assuming without deciding that there was jurisdiction, concluded (implicitly rather than expressly) that the judge had erred in the exercise of his discretion, and gave detailed reasons why in his view no injunction ought to have been granted.

In this welter of judicial differences it becomes necessary for your Lordships' House to trace a clear path based on accepted principle. . . .

Injunction, being an equitable remedy, operates *in personam*. It has been used to order parties amenable to the court's jurisdiction "to take, or to omit to take, any steps and proceedings in any other court of justice, whether in this country or in a foreign country". The English court, as the Vice–Chancellor went on to say, "does not pretend to any interference with the other court; it acts upon the defendant by punishment for his contempt in his disobedience to the order of the court." The jurisdiction, which has been frequently exercised since 1821, was reviewed by the Court of Appeal in Ellerman Lines Ltd. v. Read [1928] 2 K.B. 144. Scrutton L.J. in that case quoted with approval a passage from the judgment of Lord Brougham in Portarlington v. Soulby where the Lord Chancellor affirmed that "the injunction was not directed to the foreign court, but to the party within the jurisdiction here." I would not, however, leave *Ellerman's* case without a reference to the warning of Eve J. at p. 158: "No doubt, the jurisdiction is to be exercised with caution".

The considerable case law to which your Lordships have been referred does not, in terms, express any limitation upon the sort of cases in which it may be appropriate to exercise the jurisdiction. Counsel for the plaintiff however, submitted that it is to be found to have been exercised only in two classes of case: "(1) *'lis alibi pendens'* [a suit pending elsewhere], where the object is to prevent harassment . . .; and (2) where there is a right justiciable in England, which the court seeks to protect."

In support of his second class, counsel cited a passage from the speech of my noble and learned friend, Lord Diplock, in The Siskina, [1979] A.C. 210, 256:

> "A right to obtain an interlocutory injunction is not a cause of action. . . . It is dependent upon there being a pre-existing cause of action against the defendant arising out of an invasion, actual or threatened by him, of a legal or equitable right of the plaintiff for the

enforcement of which the defendant is amenable to the jurisdiction of the court.''

No doubt, in practice, most cases fall within one or other of these two classes. But the width and flexibility of equity are not to be undermined by categorisation. Caution in the exercise of the jurisdiction is certainly needed: but the way in which the judges have expressed themselves from 1821 onwards amply supports the view for which the defendants contend that the injunction can be granted against a party properly before the court, where it is appropriate to avoid injustice.

The plaintiff went home to Portugal after his accident (in fact, on the 1st November 1977), where he has ever since remained. He is neither a British subject nor resident in England. . . .

There remains the point that to grant an injunction in the circumstances of this case against the respondent would be useless, a mere [empty threat]. The answer was given succinctly by the Court of Appeal in In re Liddell's Settlement Trusts [1936] 1 Ch. 365: Romer L.J., at p. 374, observing that: ''It is not the habit of this court in considering whether or not it will make an order to contemplate the possibility that it will not be obeyed,'' and Slesser L.J. at p. 373: ''We are not to assume that the lady will necessarily disobey the court. . . .''

I turn to consider what criteria should govern the exercise of the court's discretion to impose a stay or grant an injunction. It is unnecessary now to examine the earlier case law. The principle is the same whether the remedy sought is a stay of English proceedings or a restraint upon foreign proceedings. The modern statement of the law is to be found in the majority speeches in The Atlantic Star [1974] A.C. 436. It had been thought that the criteria for staying (or restraining) proceedings were two-fold: (1) that to allow the proceedings to continue would be oppressive or vexatious, and (2) that to stay (or restrain) them would not cause injustice to the plaintiff. In The Atlantic Star this House . . . extended and re-formulated, the criteria, treating the epithets ''vexatious'' ''oppressive'' as illustrating but not confining the jurisdiction. My noble and learned friend Lord Wilberforce put it in this way. The ''critical equation,'' he said, was between ''any advantage to the plaintiff'' and ''any disadvantage to the defendant''. Though this is essentially a matter for the court's discretion, it is possible, he said, to ''make explicit'' some elements. He then went on, at pp. 468–469:

> ''The cases say that the advantage must not be 'fanciful'—that a 'substantial advantage' is enough. . . . A bona fide advantage to a plaintiff is a solid weight in the scale, often a decisive weight, but not always so. Then the disadvantage to the defendant: to be taken into account at all this must be serious, more than mere disadvantage of multiple suits; . . . I think too that there must be a relative element in assessing both advantage and disadvantage—*relative to the individual circumstances of the plaintiff and defendant.*''

In MacShannon v. Rockware Glass Ltd. [1978] A.C. 795, 812 my noble and learned friend Lord Diplock interpreted the majority speeches in The Atlantic Star as an invitation to drop the use of the words ''vexatious'' and "oppressive" (an invitation which I gladly accept) and formulated his distillation of principle in words which are now very familiar:

> "In order to justify a stay two conditions must be satisfied, one positive and the other negative: (a) the defendant must satisfy the court that there is another forum to whose jurisdiction he is amenable in which justice can be done between the parties at substantially less inconvenience or expense, and (b) the stay must not deprive the plaintiff of a legitimate personal or juridical advantage which would be available to him if he invoked the jurisdiction of the English court."

Transposed into the context of the present case, this formulation means that to justify the grant of an injunction the defendants must show: (*a*) that the English court is a forum to whose jurisdiction they are amenable in which justice can be done at substantially less inconvenience and expense, *and (b)* the injunction must not deprive the plaintiff of a legitimate personal or juridical advantage which would be available to him if he invoked the American jurisdiction.

The formula is not, however, to be construed as a statute. No time should be spent in speculating as to what is meant by "legitimate." It, like the whole of the context, is but a guide to solving in the particular circumstances of the case the "critical equation" between advantage to the plaintiff and disadvantage to the defendants.

... The judge directed himself correctly as to the applicable law, founding himself on the MacShannon formulation and dealing with (b) at length....

    ....

Having acknowledged that the prospect of higher damages in America can be a legitimate advantage for a plaintiff, he gives two reasons for considering the advantage to be of little weight in this case. First, he instances a situation in which two plaintiffs "suffering identical personal injuries" sue in England but one sues also in Texas because his defendant has an office and assets there. The judge considers it would be unjust to allow the second plaintiff to recover more in Texas than the first can recover in England. But this example, upon which he heavily relies for his conclusion, is an irrelevancy. The criterion, as was emphasised in The Atlantic Star, is the critical equation between the advantage to the plaintiff and the disadvantage to the defendant; but not, as the judge assumes, a comparison between different plaintiffs in their separate claims against different defendants. The judge, though he pays lip service to the principle that he must do justice *between* the parties, relies in this instance upon a comparison not between them but with others. He ignores "the relative element" of which my noble and learned friend spoke in The Atlantic Star.

Secondly, he treats as "the question of real importance" whether the plaintiff is likely to obtain a lower award in England than he would in the country where he lives, i.e. Portugal. There being no evidence that an English award would be treated as unjustly low in Portugal, he considers the prospect of a higher recovery in Texas to be "of little weight." I reject the reasoning and its relevance. The fact that the plaintiff can sue in Texas defendants who have an office and substantial assets in Texas and that under the law there he has the legitimate personal and juridical advantage of the prospect of a much greater recovery than if he were to sue in England cannot be discarded as of little weight merely because an English award would not be regarded as unjustly low in Portugal. The discretion is not to be exercised upon such a comparison, even if there were (which there was not) any evidence to guide the judge's speculation as to the Portuguese possibilities. The balance is between the English and the American proceedings; the relative elements of plaintiff's advantage and defendant's disadvantage in each have to be weighed. The balance is not to be confused by uncertain legal, social and economic elements arising outside the two sets of litigation.

It is, therefore, open to this House to review the exercise of the judge's discretion. My Lords, upon this aspect of the case I find the judgment of Brandon L.J. convincing. He found that to restrain the plaintiff from proceeding in Texas would deprive him of a legitimate personal or juridical advantage: I agree. If he had been advised early enough to sue the J.M.C. group in Texas first, they could not have compelled him to sue in England. The only additional expense incurred by the defendants as a result of the plaintiff suing first in England has been that of legal costs, which are recoverable by the defendants. Texas is as natural and proper a forum for suing a group of Texan-based companies as England—even though England, as the scene of the accident, is also a natural and proper forum. . . . For the reasons which the Lord Justice gives I agree with his conclusion "that the balance comes down clearly in the plaintiff's favour."

My conclusion is, therefore, that the Court of Appeal was right to discharge the injunction: . . . .

[LORD WILBERFORCE, LORD DIPLOCK, LORD KEITH OF KINKEL, and LORD BRIDGE OF HARWICH, each having had the benefit of reading in advance the speech to be delivered by LORD SCARMAN, agree with the order which he proposes for dismissing the appeal.]

Kaepa, Inc. v. Achilles Corporation

United States Court of Appeals, Fifth Circuit, 1996.
76 F.3d 624.

■ WIENER, CIRCUIT JUDGE:

The primary issue presented by this appeal is whether the district court erred by enjoining Defendant–Appellant Achilles Corporation from prosecuting an action that it filed in Japan as plaintiff, which essentially mirrored a lawsuit previously filed by Plaintiff–Appellee Kaepa, Inc. in state court and then being prosecuted in federal district court by Kaepa. Given the private nature of the dispute, the clear indications by both parties that claims arising from their contract should be adjudicated in this country, and the duplicative and vexatious nature of the Japanese action, we conclude that the district court did not abuse its discretion by barring the prosecution of the foreign litigation. Accordingly, we affirm the grant of the antisuit injunction.

I.

FACTS AND PROCEEDINGS

This case arises out of a contractual dispute between two sophisticated, private corporations: Kaepa, an American company which manufactures athletic shoes; and Achilles, a Japanese business enterprise with annual sales that approximate one billion dollars. In April 1993, the two companies entered into a distributorship agreement whereby Achilles obtained exclusive rights to market Kaepa's footwear in Japan. The distributorship agreement expressly provided that Texas law and the English language would govern its interpretation, that it would be enforceable in San Antonio, Texas, and that Achilles consented to the jurisdiction of the Texas courts.

Kaepa grew increasingly dissatisfied with Achilles's performance under the contract. Accordingly, in July of 1994, Kaepa filed suit in Texas state court, alleging (1) fraud and negligent misrepresentation by Achilles to induce Kaepa to enter into the distributorship agreement, and (2) breach of contract by Achilles. Thereafter, Achilles removed the action to federal district court, and the parties began a laborious discovery process which to date has resulted in the production of tens of thousands of documents. In February 1995, after appearing in the Texas action, removing the case to federal court, and engaging in comprehensive discovery, Achilles brought its own action in Japan, alleging mirror-image claims: (1) fraud by Kaepa to induce Achilles to enter into the distributorship agreement, and (2) breach of contract by Kaepa.

Back in Texas, Kaepa promptly filed a motion asking the district court to enjoin Achilles from prosecuting its suit in Japan (motion for an antisuit injunction). Achilles in turn moved to dismiss the federal court action on the ground of forum non conveniens. The district court denied Achilles's motion to dismiss and granted Kaepa's motion to enjoin, ordering Achilles to refrain from litigating the Japanese action and to file all of its counterclaims with the district court. Achilles timely appealed the grant of the antisuit injunction.

II.

ANALYSIS

A.   PROPRIETY OF THE ANTISUIT INJUNCTION

Achilles's primary argument is that the district court failed to give proper deference to principles of international comity when it granted Kaepa's motion for an antisuit injunction. We review the decision to grant injunctive relief for abuse of discretion. Under this deferential standard, findings of fact are upheld unless clearly erroneous, whereas legal conclusions " 'are subject to broad review and will be reversed if incorrect.' "

It is well settled among the circuit courts—including this one—which have reviewed the grant of an antisuit injunction that the federal courts have the power to enjoin persons subject to their jurisdiction from prosecuting foreign suits. The circuits differ, however, on the proper legal standard to employ when determining whether that injunctive power should be exercised. We have addressed the propriety of an antisuit injunction on two prior occasions, in *In re Unterweser Reederei Gmbh*[7] and *Bethell v. Peace*.[8] Emphasizing in both cases the need to prevent vexatious or oppressive litigation, we concluded that a district court does not abuse its discretion by issuing an antisuit injunction when it has determined "that allowing simultaneous prosecution of the same action in a foreign forum thousands of miles away would result in 'inequitable hardship' and 'tend to frustrate and delay the speedy and efficient determination of the cause.' " The Seventh and the Ninth Circuits have either adopted or "incline[d] toward" this approach, but other circuits have employed a standard that elevates principles of international comity to the virtual exclusion of essentially all other considerations.[12]

Achilles urges us to give greater deference to comity and apply the latter, more restrictive standard. We note preliminarily that, even though the standard espoused in *Unterweser* and *Bethell* focuses on the potentially vexatious nature of foreign litigation, it by no means excludes the consideration of principles of comity. We decline, however, to require a district court to genuflect before a vague and omnipotent notion of comity every time that it must decide whether to enjoin a foreign action.

In the instant case, for example, it simply cannot be said that the grant of the antisuit injunction actually threatens relations between the United States and Japan. First, no public international issue is implicated by the case: Achilles is a private party engaged in a contractual dispute with another private party. Second, the dispute has been long and firmly ensconced within the confines of the United States judicial system: Achilles consented to jurisdiction in Texas; stipulated that Texas law and the English language would govern any dispute; appeared in an action brought in Texas; removed that action to a federal court in Texas; engaged in extensive discovery pursuant to the directives of the federal court; and only then, with the federal action moving steadily toward trial, brought identical claims in Japan. Under these circumstances, we cannot conclude that the district court's grant of an antisuit injunction in any way trampled on notions of comity.

On the contrary, the facts detailed above strongly support the conclusion that the prosecution of the Japanese action would entail "an absurd duplication of effort" and would result in unwarranted inconvenience, expense, and vexation. Achilles's belated ploy of filing as putative plaintiff in Japan the very same claims against Kaepa that Kaepa had filed as plaintiff against Achilles smacks of cynicism, harassment, and delay. Accordingly, we hold that the district court did not abuse its discretion by granting Kaepa's motion for an antisuit injunction.

B. RULE 65 REQUIREMENTS

Achilles also argues that the district court erred by failing to meet several requirements of Federal Rule of Civil Procedure 65 before issuing

---

7. *Unterweser*, 428 F.2d 888.

8. *Bethell*, 441 F.2d 495.

12. *See, e.g., Gau Shan*, 956 F.2d at 1355; *China Trade*, 837 F.2d at 36; *Laker Airways*, 731 F.2d at 927, 937. The weakness in the foundation of the dissent's opinion is that it relies extensively on these cases while virtually disregarding our holdings in *Unterweser* and *Bethell*.

[handwritten marginalia: "Achilles argument", "rule"]

the antisuit injunction. Rule 65(a)(1) provides that "[n]o preliminary injunction shall be issued without notice to the adverse party." We have interpreted the notice requirement of Rule 65(a)(1) to mean that "where factual disputes are presented, the parties must be given a fair opportunity and a meaningful hearing to present their differing versions of those facts before a preliminary injunction may be granted." If no factual dispute is involved, however, no oral hearing is required; under such circumstances the parties need only be given "ample opportunity to present their respective views of the legal issues involved." In the instant case, the district court did not rely on any disputed facts in determining whether it could properly grant an antisuit injunction. Moreover, both parties presented comprehensive memoranda in support of their positions on the issue. Accordingly, the district court did not violate Rule 65(a)(1) by failing to conduct an oral hearing before granting the antisuit injunction.

[handwritten marginalia: "No bond discretion of court"]

Achilles also argues that the district court violated Rule 65(c) by not requiring Kaepa to post a bond. Rule 65(c) provides that "[n]o ... preliminary injunction shall issue except upon the giving of security by the applicant, in such sum as the court deems proper...." In holding that the amount of security required pursuant to Rule 65(c) "is a matter for the discretion of the trial court," we have ruled that the court "may elect to require no security at all." Thus, the district court did not violate Rule 65(c) by failing to compel Kaepa to post a bond.

III.

CONCLUSION

For the foregoing reasons, the district court's grant of Kaepa's motion to enjoin the litigation of Achilles's action in Japan is

AFFIRMED.

■ EMILIO M. GARZA, dissenting:

International comity represents a principle of paramount importance in our world of ever increasing economic interdependence. Admitting that "comity" may be a somewhat elusive concept does not mean that we can blithely ignore its cautionary dictate. Unless we proceed in each instance with respect for the independent jurisdiction of a sovereign nation's courts, we risk provoking retaliation in turn, with detrimental consequences that may reverberate far beyond the particular dispute and its private litigants. Amicable relations among sovereign nations and their judicial systems depend on our recognition, as federal courts, that we share the international arena with co-equal judicial bodies, and that we therefore act to deprive a foreign court of jurisdiction only in the most extreme circumstances. Because I feel that the majority's opinion does not grant the principle of international comity the weight it deserves, I must respectfully dissent.

I

A

I do not quarrel with the well established principle, relied on by the majority, that our courts have the power to control the conduct of persons subject to their jurisdiction, even to the extent of enjoining them from prosecuting in a foreign jurisdiction. I write to emphasize, however, that under concurrent jurisdiction, "parallel proceedings on the same in person-am claim should ordinarily be allowed to proceed simultaneously, at least until a judgment is reached in one which can be pled as res judicata in the other." Laker Airways Ltd. v. Sabena, Belgian World Airlines, 731 F.2d 909, 926–27 (D.C.Cir.1984). The filing of a second parallel action in another jurisdiction does not necessarily conflict with or prevent the first court from exercising its legitimate concurrent jurisdiction. Id. at 926. In the ordinary case, both forums should be free to proceed to a judgment, unhindered by the concurrent exercise of jurisdiction in another court. . . .

B

In holding that the district court in this case did not abuse its discretion by enjoining Achilles, a Japanese corporation, from proceeding with its lawsuit filed in the sovereign nation of Japan, the majority appears to rely primarily on the duplicative nature of the Japanese suit and the resulting "unwarranted inconvenience, expense, and vexation." The inconvenience, expense and vexation, however, are factors likely to be present whenever there is an exercise of concurrent jurisdiction by a foreign court. *Sea Containers Ltd. v. Stena AB*, 890 F.2d 1205, 1213–14 (D.C.Cir.1989). The majority's standard can be understood to hold, therefore, that "a duplication of the parties and issues, alone, is sufficient to justify a foreign antisuit injunction." *Gau Shan Co.*, 956 F.2d at 1353; *see also Laker Airways*, 731 F.2d at 928 (concluding that this rationale "is *prima facie* inconsistent with the rule permitting parallel proceedings in concurrent in personam actions"). Under this standard, concurrent jurisdiction involving a foreign tribunal will rarely, if ever, withstand the request for an antisuit injunction.

By focusing on the potential hardship to Kaepa of having to litigate in two forums, the majority applies an analysis that is more appropriately brought to bear in the context of a motion to dismiss for *forum non conveniens*. *See Laker Airways*, 731 F.2d at 928. Considerations that are appropriate in deciding whether to decline jurisdiction are not as persuasive when deciding whether to deprive another court of jurisdiction. "The policies of avoiding hardships to the parties and promoting the economies of consolidation litigation 'do not outweigh the important principles of comity that compel deference and mutual respect for concurrent foreign proceedings. Thus, the better rule is that duplication of parties and issues alone is not sufficient to justify issuance of an antisuit injunction.'" *Gau Shan Co.*, 956 F.2d at 1355 (quoting *Laker Airways*, 731 F.2d at 928); *see also China Trade & Dev. Corp. v. M.V. Choong Yong*, 837 F.2d 33, 36 (2nd Cir.1987); *Compagnie des Bauxites de Guinea v. Insurance Co. of N. Am.*, 651 F.2d 877, 887 (3d Cir.1981), *aff'd on other grounds sub nom. Insurance Corp. of Ireland, Ltd. v. Compagnie des Bauxites de Guinee*, 456 U.S. 694, 102 S.Ct. 2099, 72 L.Ed.2d 492 (1982). A dismissal on grounds of *forum non conveniens* by either court in this case would satisfy the majority's concern with avoiding hardship to the parties, without harming the interests of international comity. The district court is not in a position, however, to make the *forum non conveniens* determination on behalf of the Japanese court. In light of the important interests of international comity, the decision by a United States court to deprive a foreign court of jurisdiction must be supported by far weightier factors than would otherwise justify that court's decision to decline its own jurisdiction on *forum non conveniens* grounds.

C

Accordingly, I believe that the standard followed by the Second, Sixth, and D.C. Circuits more satisfactorily respects the principle of concurrent jurisdiction and safeguards the important interests of international comity. Under this stricter standard, a district court should look to only two factors in determining whether to issue an antisuit injunction: (1) whether the foreign action threatens the jurisdiction of the district court; and (2) whether the foreign action was an attempt to evade important public policies of the district court. *Gau Shan Co.*, 956 F.2d at 1355; *China Trade*, 837 F.2d at 36; *Laker Airways*, 731 F.2d at 927. Neither of these factors are present in this case.

II

Because neither factor supports the issuance of an antisuit injunction in this case, I believe the district court abused its discretion by enjoining Achilles from prosecuting an action filed in Japan. Accordingly, I respectfully dissent.

NOTES

1. For a thorough discussion of the applicability of the antitrust laws of the United States and the doctrine of comity in cases involving relations with other countries, see the Laker Airways Litigation, British Airways Board v. Laker Airways Ltd., House of Lords, 1984, [1985] A.C. 58. The Laker litigation in the United States included motion by Laker to restrain British Airways and British Caledonian Airways from proceeding with their action in the High Court of Justice in the United Kingdom. The motion was granted by the district court. On appeal, this ruling was affirmed. Laker Airways Ltd. v. Sabena, Belgian World Airlines, 731 F.2d 909 (D.C.Cir. 1984).

2. Equity will enjoin foreign proceedings by a resident that are in evasion of domestic legislation embodying a strong local policy. For example, a domestic creditor will be enjoined from suing outside the jurisdiction to reach property of a domestic debtor which would be protected by exemption statutes in a domestic suit. But a non-resident creditor, who is personally served, will not be enjoined from taking advantage of foreign exemption laws. Attempts by local creditors to make use of a more stringent procedure for collection in another state will not ordinarily be enjoined.

Vanneck v. Vanneck

Court of Appeals of New York, 1980.
49 N.Y.2d 602, 427 N.Y.S.2d 735, 404 N.E.2d 1278.

■ Cooke, C.J.

John and Isabelle Vanneck were married in New York in 1965 and lived together with their three children in this State until December, 1978.

On the 19th of that month, during the children's winter school recess, Isabelle Vanneck took the children to the family's home in North Stamford, Connecticut, and decided to remain. Alleging the irretrievable breakdown of the marriage, Isabelle, defendant here, commenced an action in Connecticut on December 30, 1978 ... seeking dissolution of the marriage, alimony and custody of the children. Two weeks later, on January 13, 1979, plaintiff commenced this New York action for divorce on the ground of cruelty or, in the alternative, for separation on the ground of abandonment. He too sought custody of the parties' three children.

Plaintiff moved in the New York court to enjoin defendant from prosecuting the divorce action in Connecticut, contending that defendant's move was undertaken to establish divorce jurisdiction in that State to enable her to exploit its equitable distribution laws. Plaintiff also sought temporary custody of the children, urging that daily transportation to New York schools was not in the children's best interest. In opposition, defendant asserted the *bona fides* of her residence in Connecticut, as well as that of the children, and in support of her custody of the children, that they had been enrolled in Connecticut schools for the spring 1979 term.

Traditionally, an injunction against prosecution of a foreign divorce would be granted when the rights of a resident spouse were threatened. The grant of such relief involves the exercise of discretion after consideration of such factors as the *bona fides* of the domicile established in the other State, the motivation for commencing an action there and the substantiality of contacts with that forum. When the parties to a divorce proceeding seek as ancillary relief a child custody determination, however, the [Uniform Child Custody Jurisdiction Act] is applicable. A separate inquiry, with proper weight accorded to the provisions of the act, is required for determining whether the custody phase of the litigation may proceed in the foreign court. To assure that the best interests of the child and salutary provisions of the act are not subordinated to the parents' interest in obtaining the best terms of the divorce, the court should determine whether to enjoin prosecution of the divorce only after the inquiry concerning the custody issues has been undertaken. Of course, the decision whether to exercise custody jurisdiction is a factor in determining the propriety of injunctive relief against the divorce phase, and the weight to be accorded this factor may vary depending on the circumstances of the particular case. The preliminary decision concerning New York's exercise of jurisdiction over the custody issues, however, must have as its foundation the proper application of the UCCJA.

The UCCJA represents a considered effort to give stability to child custody decrees, minimize jurisdictional competition between sister States, promote co-operation and communication between the courts of different States, all to the end of resolving custody disputes in the best interests of the child. The act offers a standard for determining in the first instance whether the necessary predicate for jurisdiction exists. Custody may be determined in the child's "home state," defined as "the state in which the child at the time of the commencement of the custody proceeding, has resided with his parents, a parent, or a person acting as parent, for at least six consecutive months", or in the State that had been the child's home State within six months before commencement of the proceeding where the child is absent from the State through removal by a person claiming custody and a parent lives in the State. A jurisdictional predicate also exists in New York when "it is in the best interest of the child that a court of this state assume jurisdiction because (i) the child and his parents, or the child and at least one contestant, have a significant connection with this state, and (ii) there is within the jurisdiction of the court substantial evidence concerning the child's present or future care, protection, training, and personal relationships."

The inquiry is not completed merely by a determination that a jurisdictional predicate exists in the forum State, for then the court must determine whether to exercise its jurisdiction. There, too, the act guides the determination, commanding the court to consider whether it is an inconvenient forum or whether the conduct of the parties militates against an exercise of jurisdiction. Notwithstanding that this State has jurisdiction, a court "shall not exercise its jurisdiction under this article if at the time of filing the petition a proceeding concerning the custody of the child was pending in a court of another state exercising jurisdiction substantially in conformity with this article". Once a court of this State learns of the pendency of another proceeding, the court "shall stay [its own] proceeding and communicate with the court in which the other proceeding is pending to the end that the issue may be litigated in the more appropriate forum and that information be exchanged in accordance with sections seventy-five-s through seventy-five-v of this article."

The express statutory command of section 75–g was all but ignored by Special Term. Given the pendency of the Connecticut action, the question with which the court should have been concerned was not whether New York had jurisdiction to determine the custody dispute, nor whether New York was the most appropriate forum. Rather, at that stage of the proceeding, the focus of inquiry should have been whether Connecticut was "exercising jurisdiction substantially in conformity" with article 5–A.

The instant case calls into play the jurisdictional predicate of section 75–d, which provides that a State may exercise jurisdiction when it serves the best interests of the child because there is a significant connection to the forum and there is available substantial evidence concerning the child's present or future welfare. Particularly relevant to the jurisdictional determination is whether the forum in which the litigation is to proceed has "optimum access to relevant evidence" (Prefatory Note of Commissioners on Uniform State Laws, 9 ULA [Master Ed.], § 3, p. 124). Maximum rather than minimum contacts with the State are required. The general language of this subdivision permits a flexible approach to various fact patterns. This imprecision, however, must not destroy the legislative design "to limit jurisdiction rather than to proliferate it".

. . . .

Thus, defendant's assertions here, at least as a threshold matter, support an exercise of jurisdiction by the Connecticut court (cf. Prefatory Note of Commissioners on Uniform State Laws, 9 ULA [Master Ed.], § 3,

p. 124 [suggesting that a parent's return to a State of former residence in which the children each year spent several months might provide the requisite connection to the State]), and required Special Term to open channels of communication with the Connecticut court before enjoining prosecution of the action there. The New York court's unilateral decision to exercise jurisdiction and prevent Connecticut's exercise of jurisdiction is contrary to the avowed purposes of the legislation adopted by both States. Rather than promote co-operation between courts, it fosters the very jurisdictional competition sought to be avoided.

The Appellate Division therefore properly determined that the injunction against prosecuting the action in Connecticut was inappropriate. The Appellate Division, in the exercise of discretion, could have enjoined only the divorce phase of the litigation, for, as noted above, that question is separate from the question whether jurisdiction exists to entertain a custody dispute. . . .

Accordingly, the order of the Appellate Division should be affirmed, with costs.

NOTES

1. *Concurrent Litigation*: The existence of concurrent litigation in another state furnishes a ground of equitable jurisdiction, but there are reasons for caution in its exercise. The rule of "first come, first served" ordinarily applies in such situations: i.e., a foreign court will not enjoin the prosecution of a previously filed litigation involving the same dispute.

2. *Child Custody*: Child custody decrees are modifiable upon a showing of changed circumstances. Moreover, child custody disputes could easily lie within the jurisdiction of several different states' courts. As a result, forum-shopping, kidnapping, and seemingly endless relitigation of custody disputes became all too common. In response to this problem, every state adopted some version of the UCCJA. The federal government enacted the Parental Kidnapping Prevention Act of 1980. See Thompson v. Thompson, infra p. 1056.

---

2. EFFECT OF INJUNCTIONS AGAINST SUIT

Dobson v. Pearce

Court of Appeals of New York, 1854.
12 N.Y. 156.

The action was commenced in the New-York superior court, on the 26th of September, 1850. The complaint was upon a judgment for $612.93, recovered in that court in April, 1846, in favor of one Olney against Pearce, the defendant in this suit, alleging an assignment thereof from Olney to Dobson, the plaintiff, just previous to the commencement of the action.

The defendant by his answer alleged that the judgment was entered in a suit commenced against him, in favor of Olney, by the service of a *capias* [(a writ formerly used to start actions at law)] upon him in February, 1846, when he was casually in New–York, he then and ever after being a resident of Connecticut; that Olney had no just or legal demand against him, when the *capias* was served, and that he was induced by fraudulent representations and assurances of Olney, made to him after the *capias* was served, and upon which he relied, to the effect that no further proceedings would be taken in the suit, not to appear therein; and that afterwards Olney fraudulently and without the knowledge of the defendant procured the judgment mentioned in the complaint to be entered in the suit upon a false and unfounded claim, and known so to be by Olney at the time; that in 1848 Olney commenced an action of debt on the judgment, against the defendant, in the superior court of the State of Connecticut. Thereupon the defendant commenced a suit in chancery against Olney, before the same court in Connecticut alleging that the judgment was procured to be entered by fraud on the part of Olney, and praying the court to perpetually enjoin him from further prosecuting it. Olney appeared in and defended the chancery suit by attorney; and on the 10th of September, 1850, a decree was made therein, declaring the judgment fraudulent and perpetually enjoining Olney from further prosecuting the action upon it; that in submission to this decree the action upon the judgment in the superior court of Connecticut was discontinued; and that the pretended assignment to the plaintiff was made after the decree and with full knowledge of it and of the fraud in procuring the judgment. The plaintiff replied, denying the allegations in the answer.

... The ... trial was had before Justice Duer and a jury, in 1853. On this trial the plaintiff proved the judgment described in the complaint, and the assignment thereof by Olney to the plaintiff, on the 11th of September, 1850, and rested.

The defendant offered in evidence a duly authenticated copy of the record of the proceedings in the suit in chancery in the superior court of Connecticut, mentioned in the answer. The counsel for the plaintiff objected to it as evidence; the objection was overruled and the same received and read in evidence, and plaintiff's counsel excepted....

The counsel for the defendant read in evidence a duly authenticated copy of the record of the proceedings in the action of debt on the judgment rendered in the New–York superior court, commenced by Olney in the superior court of Connecticut. To the admission of this record in evidence the counsel for the plaintiff duly objected; the objection was overruled and he excepted.... The justice before whom the cause was tried instructed the jury that the record of the proceedings, finding and decree of the superior court of Connecticut in the chancery suit, was conclusive evidence against the plaintiff to sustain the allegations in the defendant's answer, if the jury found that Olney appeared in that suit by an attorney who was authorized by him to do so; that if the jury did not so find, then this record did not affect the plaintiff. The counsel for the plaintiff excepted to such instructions. The jury rendered a verdict in favor of the defendant. The judgment rendered on this verdict was affirmed at a general term of the superior court. The plaintiff appealed to this court.

■ W.F. ALLEN, J. A judgment rendered by a court of competent jurisdiction cannot be impeached collaterally for error or irregularity, but is conclusive until set aside or reversed by the same court or some other court having appellate jurisdiction. The jurisdiction of the court in which a judgment has been recovered is, however, always open to inquiry; and if it has exceeded its jurisdiction, or has not acquired jurisdiction of the parties by the due service of process or by a voluntary appearance, the proceedings are *coram non judice* [(i.e., extra-judicial)] and the judgment void. The want of jurisdiction has always been held to be a valid defence to an action upon the judgment, and a good answer to it when set up for any purpose.

So, fraud and imposition invalidate a judgment as they do all acts; and it is not without semblance of authority that it has been suggested that at law the fraud may be alleged, whenever the party seeks to avail himself of the results of his own fraudulent conduct by setting up the judgment, the fruits of his fraud. But whether this be so or not, it is unquestionable that a court of chancery has power to grant relief against judgments when obtained by fraud. Any fact which clearly proves it to be against conscience to execute a judgment, and of which the injured party could not avail himself at law, but was prevented by fraud or accident, unmixed with any fault or negligence in himself or his agents, will justify an interference by a court of equity.

Under our present judiciary system, the functions of the courts of common law and of chancery are united in the same court, and the distinctions between actions at law and suits in equity, and the forms of all such actions and suits, are abolished, and the defendant may set forth by answer as many defences as he may have, whether they be such as have been heretofore denominated legal or equitable, or both. The Code also authorizes affirmative relief to be given to a defendant in an action by the judgment. The intent of the legislature is very clear, that all controversies respecting the subject matter of the litigation should be determined in one action, and the provisions are adapted to give effect to that intent. Whether, therefore, fraud or imposition in the recovery of a judgment could heretofore have been alleged against it collaterally at law or not, it may now be set up as an equitable defence to defeat a recovery upon it. Under the head of equitable defences are included all matters which would before have authorized an application to the court of chancery for relief against a legal liability, but which, at law, could not have been pleaded in bar. The facts alleged by way of defence in this action would have been good cause for relief against the judgment in a court of chancery, and under our present system are, therefore, proper matters of defence; and there was no necessity or propriety for a resort to a separate action to vacate the judgment. In Connecticut, although law and equity are administered by the same judges, still the distinction between these systems is preserved, and justice is administered under the head of common law and chancery jurisdiction by distinct and appropriate forms of procedure; and hence, as it was at least doubtful whether at law the fraud alleged would bar a recovery upon the judgment, a resort to the chancery powers of the court of that state was proper if not necessary.

The right of the plaintiff in the judgment was a personal right and followed his person; and, aside from the fact that he had resorted to the courts of Connecticut to enforce his claim under the judgment, the courts of that state, having obtained jurisdiction of his person by due service of process within the state, had full power to pronounce upon the rights of the parties in respect to the judgment and to decree concerning it. It necessarily follows that the decree of the superior court of Connecticut, sitting as a court of chancery, directly upon the question of fraud, is conclusive upon the parties to that litigation and all persons claiming under them with notice of the adjudication. The judgment of a court of competent jurisdiction upon a point litigated between the parties is conclusive in all subsequent controversies where the same point comes again in question between the same parties. In the State of Connecticut, it is quite clear the question of fraud would not be an open question between the parties, but would be considered entirely settled by the decree of the court of that state; and as full faith and credit are to be given by each state to the judicial proceedings of every other state, that is, the same credit, validity and effect as they would have in the state in which they were had, the parties are concluded in the courts of this state by the judgment of the court in Connecticut directly upon the question in issue. The decree of the court of chancery of the State of Connecticut as an operative decree, so far as it enjoined and restrained the parties, had and has no extraterritorial efficacy, as an injunction does not affect the courts of this state; but the judgment of the court upon the matters litigated is conclusive upon the parties everywhere and in every forum where the same matters are drawn in question. It is not the particular relief which was granted which affects the parties litigating in the courts of this state; but it is the adjudication and the determination of the facts by that court, the final decision that the judgment was procured by fraud, which is operative here and necessarily prevents the plaintiff from asserting any claim under it. The court acquired jurisdiction of the parties by the commencement of the action, and the service of process upon the defendant therein, and his appearance by an authorized attorney; and the withdrawal of the action of debt upon the judgment did not deprive it of jurisdiction thus acquired.

The judgment of the superior court must be affirmed, with costs.

James v. Grand Trunk Western Railroad Co.

Supreme Court of Illinois, 1958.
14 Ill.2d 356, 152 N.E.2d 858.

[A Michigan administratrix brought an action in Illinois under the Michigan wrongful death statute to recover against the defendant Illinois railroad corporation for death arising out of an accident occurring in the county of administratrix' residence in Michigan. The defendant railroad then sought and obtained an injunction against the administratrix in Michigan, enjoining her from proceeding with her action in Illinois. The administratrix now seeks to restrain the defendant railroad from enforcing its injunction. From an order denying her motion, plaintiff appeals.]

■ BRISTOW, J. . . . The issues are essentially whether the Illinois court, having prior jurisdiction of a wrongful death action instituted by a nonresident plaintiff, must recognize an out-of-State injunction restraining the plaintiff from proceeding with that action; and whether the Illinois court, to protect its jurisdiction of the wrongful death action, may issue a counter injunction restraining defendant from enforcing its injunction against plaintiff in the State of her residence. . . .

On this appeal plaintiff argues that she had an unquestionable right to file the action in the Illinois court; that where a court has obtained prior jurisdiction of an action, injunctive relief is proper to prevent defendant from transferring the action elsewhere through an action in another forum; and that neither the full-faith-and-credit clause nor comity require the Illinois court to respect the Michigan venue statute and the decision of the Michigan court in this case.

The defendant argues, however, that this court will not, by counterinjunction, aid a citizen of another State to violate an injunction against prosecuting an action in Illinois; that the counterinjunction cannot be justified to protect the prior injunction of the Illinois court, since the Michigan injunction was *in personam* only; and that such counterinjunction would compel a party to give up vested rights and would violate the full-faith-and-credit and due-process clauses of the Federal constitution. . . .

With reference to the Michigan injunction, while we quite agree with defendant's repeated assertion that a court of equity has power to restrain persons within its jurisdiction from instituting or proceeding with foreign actions, we note that the exercise of such power by equity courts has been deemed a matter of great delicacy, invoked with great restraint to avoid distressing conflicts and reciprocal interference with jurisdiction.

Illinois has consistently followed the course of refusing to restrain the prosecution of a prior instituted action pending in a sister State unless a clear equity is presented requiring the interposition of the court to prevent a manifest wrong and injustice; and neither a difference of remedy afforded by the domicile and the forum nor mere inconvenience and expense of defending will constitute grounds for such an injunction. . . .

Conversely, where other States have enjoined litigants from proceeding with a previously instituted Illinois action, this jurisdiction has followed the overwhelming judicial opinion that neither the full-faith-and-credit clause nor rules of comity require compulsory recognition of such injunctions so as to abate or preclude the disposition of the pending case. . . .

It would serve no purpose to discuss each of the aforementioned citations, which are in accord. Suffice to note, there is negligible authority for the recognition of foreign injunctions in the local court where the case is pending, as urged by defendant. . . .

In the instant case the Michigan injunction was apparently issued pursuant to the policy of the State embodied in a Michigan venue statute restricting venue in suits against railroads to the county in which plaintiff resides, if the railroad lines traverse that county.

While it is not the province of this court to adjudge the constitutionality of the Michigan venue statute, it may be noted that similar statutes confining transitory actions to the State of plaintiff's residence have been held unconstitutional. Atchison, Topeka & Santa Fe Railway Co. v. Sowers, 213 U.S. 55, 29 S.Ct. 397, 53 L.Ed. 695; Tennessee Coal, Iron, & Railroad Co. v. George, 233 U.S. 354, 34 S.Ct. 587, 58 L.Ed. 997. In the Tennessee Coal Company case the court stated at page 360 of 233 U.S., at page 589 of 34 S.Ct.: "But venue is no part of the right; and a state cannot create a transitory cause of action and at the same time destroy the right to sue on that transitory cause of action in any court having jurisdiction. That jurisdiction is to be determined by the law of the court's creation, and cannot be defeated by the extraterritorial operation of a statute of another state, even though it created the right of action."

In the light of this reasoning, we cannot escape the observation that if statutes prohibiting or circumscribing the export of causes of action may not be given extraterritorial effect, it is hard to see why an equity decree should be entitled to any greater recognition. A court should be subject to the same limitations.

Therefore, it is evident that legal consistency, as well as the weight of authority, do not require us to recognize the Michigan injunction, and we may retain jurisdiction and proceed with plaintiff's wrongful death action. Such a course, however, is not practicable in the instant case, unless plaintiff, who is subject to imprisonment and other coercive tactics if she fails to dismiss her Illinois action, is protected by enjoining defendant from enforcing the Michigan injunction by contempt proceedings. A plaintiff cannot be expected or required to risk imprisonment so that the court may retain jurisdiction of a cause.

This brings us to the ultimate issue in this case: whether the court which first acquires jurisdiction of the parties and of the merits of the cause can issue a counterinjunction restraining a party before it from enforcing an out-of-State injunction which requires the dismissal of the local cause and ousts the forum of jurisdiction.

There is no quarrel with the basic principle that a court has a duty, as well as power, to protect its jurisdiction over a controversy in order to decree complete and final justice between the parties and may issue an injunction for that purpose, restraining proceedings in other courts.

Defendant, however, claims that there is no reason to invoke this principle in the instant case since the Michigan injunction in no way interferes with the jurisdiction of this court, but merely affects the litigants. In support thereof defendant cites the equitable maxim, "equity acts *in personam,*" invoked since the days of Coke and Bacon to obviate open conflicts between law and equity courts, and the general principle that courts of equity have the power to prevent those amenable to their own process from instituting or carrying on suits in other States which will result in injury or fraud.

In applying these principles to the instant case, we cannot close our eyes to the fact that the intended effect of the Michigan injunction, though directed at the parties and not at this court, is to prevent the Illinois court from adjudicating a cause of action of which it had proper jurisdiction. For it is patent that if the litigants are coerced to dismiss the Illinois action, it is our rightfully acquired jurisdiction that is thereby destroyed. Therefore, the Michigan injunction was in everything but form an order restraining the Illinois court and determining the cases it may properly try....

Under our analysis of the authorities, if Illinois were not the appropriate forum to try this, or any other transitory action, the defense of *forum non conveniens* could be interposed, and, if meritorious, the Illinois court would dismiss the case. However, this court need not, and will not, countenance having its right to try cases, of which it has proper jurisdiction, determined by the courts of other States, through their injunctive process. We are not only free to disregard such out-of-State injunctions, and to adjudicate the merits of the pending action, but we can protect our jurisdiction from such usurpation by the issuance of a counterinjunction restraining the enforcement of the out-of-State injunction.

It was therefore error for the trial court to dismiss plaintiff's supplemental complaint and her motion for a counterinjunction, and its order, and the judgment of the Appellate Court affirming it, must be reversed and the cause remanded to the trial court to proceed in accordance with views expressed in this opinion.

Reversed and remanded, with directions.

■ SCHAEFER, JUSTICE (dissenting)....

... I agree with the majority that the Michigan injunction is not entitled to full faith and credit.

But the question in this case goes a step beyond the issue as to full faith and credit. What is here sought is a counter-injunction to restrain the railroad from enforcing the injunction entered by the Michigan court. The difficulties that attend the kind of injunction that the Michigan court entered were stated long ago by Chancellor Walworth: "If this court should sustain an injunction bill to restrain proceedings previously commenced in a sister state, the court of that state might retaliate upon the complainant, who was defendant in the suit there; and, by process of attachment, might compel him to relinquish the suit subsequently commenced here. By this course of proceeding, the courts of different states would indirectly be brought into collision with each other in regard to jurisdiction; and the rights of suitors might be lost sight of in a useless struggle for what might be considered the legitimate powers and rights of courts." What was there said with respect to an initial injunction applies with added force to a counterinjunction. Just as the first injunction sired the second, so the second might sire a third. The ultimate end is not foreseeable.

The place to stop this unseemly kind of judicial disorder is where it begins....

I think that the trial court and the Appellate Court were right, and so I would affirm.

————

D.   STATE COURT INJUNCTIONS AGAINST FEDERAL COURT PROCEEDINGS

Donovan v. City of Dallas

Supreme Court of the United States, 1964.
377 U.S. 408, 84 S.Ct. 1579, 12 L.Ed.2d 409.

■ MR. JUSTICE BLACK delivered the opinion of the Court.

The question presented here is whether a state court can validly enjoin a person from prosecuting an action *in personam* in a district or appellate court of the United States which has jurisdiction both of the parties and of the subject matter.

The City of Dallas, Texas, owns Love Field, a municipal airport. In 1961, 46 Dallas citizens who owned or had interests in property near the airport filed a class suit in a Texas court to restrain the city from building an additional runway and from issuing and selling municipal bonds for that purpose. The complaint alleged many damages that would occur to the plaintiffs if the runway should be built and charged that issuance of the bonds would be illegal for many reasons. The case was tried, summary judgment was given for the city, the Texas Court of Civil Appeals affirmed, the Supreme Court of Texas denied review, and we denied certiorari. Later 120 Dallas citizens, including 27 of the plaintiffs in the earlier action, filed another action in the United States District Court for the Northern District of Texas seeking similar relief. A number of new defendants were named in addition to the City of Dallas, all the defendants being charged with taking part in plans to construct the runway and to issue and sell bonds in violation of state and federal laws. The complaint sought an injunction against construction of the runway, issuance of bonds, payment on bonds already issued, and circulation of false information about the bond issue, as well as a declaration that all the bonds were illegal and void. None of the bonds would be approved, and therefore under Texas law none could be issued, so long as there was pending litigation challenging their validity. The city filed a motion to dismiss and an answer to the complaint in the federal court. But at the same time the city applied to the Texas Court of Civil Appeals for a writ of prohibition to bar all the plaintiffs in the case in the United States District Court from prosecuting their case there. The Texas Court of Civil Appeals denied relief, holding that it was without power to enjoin litigants from prosecuting an action in a federal court and that the defense of *res judicata* on which the city relied could be raised and adjudicated in the United States District Court. On petition for mandamus the Supreme Court of Texas took a different view, however, held it the duty of the Court of Civil Appeals to prohibit the litigants from further prosecuting the United States District Court case, and stated that a writ of mandamus would issue should the Court of Civil Appeals fail to perform this duty. The Court of Civil Appeals promptly issued a writ prohibiting all the plaintiffs in the United States District Court case from any further prosecution of that case and enjoined them "individually and as a class . . . from filing or instituting . . . any further litigation, law suits or actions in any court, the purpose of which is to contest the validity of the airport revenue bonds . . . or from in any manner interfering with . . . the proposed bonds. . . ." The United States District Court in an unreported opinion dismissed the case pending there. Counsel Donovan, who is one of the petitioners here, excepted to the dismissal and then filed an appeal from that dismissal in the United States Court of Appeals for the Fifth Circuit. The Texas Court of Civil Appeals thereupon cited Donovan and the other United States District Court claimants for contempt and convicted 87 of them on a finding that they had violated its "valid order." Donovan was sentenced to serve 20 days in jail, and the other 86 were fined $200 each, an aggregate of $17,200. These penalties were imposed upon each contemner for having either (1) joined as a party plaintiff in the United States District Court case; (2) failed to request and contested the dismissal of that case; (3) taken exceptions to the dismissal preparatory to appealing to the Court of Appeals; or (4) filed a separate action in the Federal District Court seeking to enjoin the Supreme Court of Texas from interfering with the original federal-court suit. After the fines had been paid and he had served his jail sentence, counsel Donovan appeared in the District Court n behalf of himself and all those who had been fined and moved to dismiss the appeal to the United States Court of Appeals. His motion stated that it was made under duress and that unless the motion was made "the Attorney for Defendant City of Dallas and the Chief Judge of the Court of Civil Appeals have threatened these Appellants and their Attorney with further prosecution for contempt resulting in additional fines and imprisonment." The United States District Court then dismissed the appeal.

We declined to grant certiorari to review the United States District Court's dismissal of the case before it or its dismissal of the appeal brought on by the state court's coercive contempt judgment, but we did grant certiorari to review the State Supreme Court's judgment directing the Civil Court of Appeals to enjoin petitioners from prosecuting their action in the federal courts and also granted certiorari to review the Civil Court of Appeals' judgment of conviction for contempt. We think the Texas Court of Civil Appeals was right in its first holding that it was without power to enjoin these litigants from prosecuting their federal-court action, and we therefore reverse the State Supreme Court's judgment upsetting that of the Court of Appeals. We vacate the later contempt judgment of the Court of Civil Appeals, which rested on the mistaken belief that the writ prohibiting litigation by the federal plaintiffs was "valid."

Early in the history of our country a general rule was established that state and federal courts would not interfere with or try to restrain each other's proceedings. That rule has continued substantially unchanged to this time. An exception has been made in cases where a court has custody of property, that is, proceedings *in rem* or *quasi in rem.* In such cases this Court has said that the state or federal court having custody of such property has exclusive jurisdiction to proceed. In Princess Lida v. Thompson, 305 U.S. 456, 59 S.Ct. 275, 83 L.Ed. 285 (1939), this Court said "where the judgment sought is strictly in personam, both the state court and the federal court, having concurrent jurisdiction, may proceed with the litigation at least until judgment is obtained in one of them which may be set up as res judicata in the other." It may be that a full hearing in an appropriate court would justify a finding that the state-court judgment in favor of Dallas in the first suit barred the issues raised in the second suit, a question as to which we express no opinion. But plaintiffs in the second suit chose to file that case in the federal court. They had a right to do this, a right which is theirs by reason of congressional enactments passed pursuant to congressional policy. And whether or not a plea of *res judicata* in the second suit would be good is a question for the federal court to decide. While Congress has seen fit to authorize courts of the United States to restrain state-court proceedings in some special circumstances, it has in no way relaxed the old and well-established judicially declared rule that state courts are completely without power to restrain federal-court proceedings in *in personam* actions like the one here. And it does not matter that the prohibition here was addressed to the parties rather than to the federal court itself. For the heart of the rule as declared by this Court is that:

> "... where the jurisdiction of a court, and the right of a plaintiff to prosecute his suit in it, have once attached, that right cannot be arrested or taken away by proceedings in another court.... The fact, therefore, that an injunction issues only to the parties before the court, and not to the court, is no evasion of the difficulties that are the necessary result of an attempt to exercise that power over a party who is a litigant in another and independent forum."

Petitioners being properly in the federal court had a right granted by Congress to have the court decide the issues they presented, and to appeal to the Court of Appeals from the District Court's dismissal. They have been punished both for prosecuting their federal-court case and for appealing it. They dismissed their appeal because of threats to punish them more if they did not do so. The legal effect of such a coerced dismissal on their appeal is not now before us, but the propriety of a state court's punishment of a federal-court litigant for pursuing his right to federal-court remedies is. That right was granted by Congress and cannot be taken away by the State. The Texas courts were without power to take away this federal right by contempt proceedings or otherwise.

It is argued here, however, that the Court of Civil Appeals' judgment of contempt should nevertheless be upheld on the premise that it was petitioners' duty to obey the restraining order whether that order was valid or invalid. The Court of Civil Appeals did not consider or pass upon this question, but acted on the assumption that petitioners were guilty of "willful disobedience of a *valid* order." Since we hold the order restraining petitioners from prosecuting their case in the federal courts was not valid, but was invalid, petitioners have been punished for disobeying an invalid order. Whether the Texas court would have punished petitioners for contempt had it known that the restraining order petitioners violated was invalid, we do not know. However, since that question was neither considered nor decided by the Texas court, we leave it for consideration by that court on remand. We express no opinion on that question at this time.

The judgment of the Texas Supreme Court is reversed, the judgment of the Texas Court of Civil Appeals is vacated, and the case is remanded to the

Court of Civil Appeals for further proceedings not inconsistent with this opinion.

It is so ordered.

Judgment of Texas Supreme Court reversed, judgment of Texas Court of Civil Appeals vacated, and case remanded with directions.

■ MR. JUSTICE HARLAN, whom MR. JUSTICE CLARK and MR. JUSTICE STEWART join, dissenting.

The question presented by this case is not the general one stated by the Court at the outset of its opinion, but a much narrower one: May a state court enjoin resident state-court suitors from prosecuting in the federal courts vexatious, duplicative litigation which has the effect of thwarting a state-court judgment already rendered against them? Given the Texas Supreme Court's finding, amply supported by the record and in no way challenged by this Court, that this controversy "has reached the point of vexatious and harassing litigation," I consider both the state injunction and the ensuing contempt adjudication to have been perfectly proper.

I.

The power of a court in equity to enjoin persons subject to its jurisdiction from conducting vexatious and harassing litigation in another forum has not been doubted until now. In Cole v. Cunningham, 133 U.S. 107, 10 S.Ct. 269, 33 L.Ed. 538, this Court affirmed "a decree of the supreme judicial court of Massachusetts, restraining citizens of that commonwealth from the prosecution of attachment suits in New York, brought by them for the purpose of evading the laws of their domicile...." The Court stated:

> "The jurisdiction of the English court of chancery to restrain persons within its territorial limits and under its jurisdiction from doing anything abroad whether the thing forbidden be a conveyance or other act, *in pais,* or the institution or the prosecution of an action in a foreign court, is well settled."

The Court quoted with approval the following passage from Mr. Justice Story's Equity Jurisprudence, Vol. II (10th ed. 1870), 89: "It is now held that whenever the parties are resident within a country the courts of that country have full authority to act upon them personally with respect to the subject of suits in a foreign country, as the ends of justice may require, and with that view to order them to take or to omit to take any steps and proceedings in any other court of justice, whether in the same country or in any foreign country."[2]

This Court, in 1941, expressly recognized the power of a state court to do precisely what the Texas court did here. In Baltimore & Ohio R. Co. v. Kepner, 314 U.S. 44, 62 S.Ct. 6, 86 L.Ed. 28, the Court, although denying the state court's power to issue an injunction in that case, said:

2. In the next sentence, Story stated that there was an exception to this doctrine, based "upon peculiar grounds of municipal and constitutional law"; state courts could not enjoin proceedings in federal courts and vice versa. Ibid. It is apparent from the cases cited to support this exception that Story had in mind the kind of situation presented in cases like those relied on by the present majority, which ... deal not with injunctions to prevent vexatious litigation but with injunctions issued in very different contexts.

"The real contention of petitioner is that despite the admitted venue respondent is acting in a vexatious and inequitable manner in maintaining the federal court suit in a distant jurisdiction when a convenient and suitable forum is at respondent's doorstep. Under such circumstances petitioner asserts power, abstractly speaking, in the Ohio court to prevent a resident under its jurisdiction from doing inequity. *Such power does exist.*" (emphasis supplied.)

Mr. Justice Frankfurter, dissenting because of disagreement with the particular basis for the Court's refusal to give effect to the general principle, ... observed that the opinion of the Court did "not deny the historic power of courts of equity to prevent a misuse of litigation by enjoining resort to vexatious and oppressive foreign suits," and that the decision did not "give new currency to the discredited notion that there is a general lack of power in the state courts to enjoin proceedings in federal courts."

In light of the foregoing, there was no impropriety in the issuance of the state court's injunction in the present case.

II.

None of the cases on which the Court relies deals with, or in any way negatives, the power of a state court to enjoin federal litigation in circumstances such as those involved here. None of them was concerned with vexatious litigation.

. . . .

In short, today's decision rests upon confusion between two distinct lines of authority in this Court, one involving vexatious litigation and the other not.

I would affirm.

NOTES

1. On remand, the Texas Court of Civil Appeals declined to hold the *Donovan* petitioners in contempt for having violated the invalid writ of prohibition. Instead, the court remitted the fines and costs that they had paid. City of Dallas v. Brown, 384 S.W.2d 724 (Tex.Civ.App.1964).

2. *Donovan* was essentially an attempt to enjoin further prosecution of a pending federal suit. In General Atomic Co. v. Felter, 434 U.S. 12, 98 S.Ct. 76, 54 L.Ed.2d 199 (1977)(per curiam), the Court held that *Donovan* bars injunctions aimed entirely at prospective litigation in the federal courts.

E. FEDERAL COURT INJUNCTIONS AGAINST STATE COURT PROCEEDINGS

Younger v. Harris

Supreme Court of the United States, 1971.
401 U.S. 37, 91 S.Ct. 746, 27 L.Ed.2d 669.

■ MR. JUSTICE BLACK delivered the opinion of the Court.

Appellee, John Harris, Jr., was indicted in a California state court, charged with violation of the California Penal Code §§ 11400 and 11401, known as the California Criminal Syndicalism Act, set out below.[1] He then filed a complaint in the Federal District Court, asking that court to enjoin the appellant, Younger, the District Attorney of Los Angeles County, from prosecuting him, and alleging that the prosecution and even the presence of the Act inhibited him in the exercise of his rights of free speech and press, rights guaranteed him by the First and Fourteenth Amendments. Appellees Jim Dan and Diane Hirsch intervened as plaintiffs in the suit, claiming that the prosecution of Harris would inhibit them as members of the Progressive Labor Party from peacefully advocating the program of their party, which was to replace capitalism with socialism and to abolish the profit system of production in this country. Appellee Farrell Broslawsky, an instructor in history at Los Angeles Valley College, also intervened claiming that the prosecution of Harris made him uncertain as to whether he could teach about the doctrines of Karl Marx or read from the Communist Manifesto as part of his classwork. All claimed that unless the United States court restrained the state prosecution of Harris each would suffer immediate and irreparable injury. A three-judge Federal District Court, convened pursuant to 28 U.S.C. § 2284, held that it had jurisdiction and power to restrain the District Attorney from prosecuting, held that the

---

1. "§ 11400. *Definition*

" 'Criminal syndicalism' as used in this article means any doctrine or precept advocating, teaching or aiding and abetting the commission of crime, sabotage (which word is hereby defined as meaning wilful and malicious physical damage or injury to physical property), or unlawful acts of force and violence or unlawful methods of terrorism as a means of accomplishing a change in industrial ownership or control, or effecting any political change."

"§ 11401. *Offense; punishment*

"Any person who:

"1. By spoken or written words or personal conduct advocates, teaches or aids and abets criminal syndicalism or the duty, necessity or propriety of committing crime, sabotage, violence or any unlawful method of terrorism as a means of accomplishing a

change in industrial ownership or control, or effecting any political change; or

"2. Wilfully and deliberately by spoken or written words justifies or attempts to justify criminal syndicalism or the commission or attempt to commit crime, sabotage, violence or unlawful methods of terrorism with intent to approve, advocate or further the doctrine of criminal syndicalism; or

"3. Prints, publishes, edits, issues or circulates or publicly displays any book, paper, pamphlet, document, poster or written or printed matter in any other form, containing or carrying written or printed advocacy, teaching, or aid and abetment of, or advising, criminal syndicalism; or

"4. Organizes or assists in organizing, or is or knowingly becomes a member of, any organization, society, group or assemblage of persons organized or assembled to advocate, teach or aid and abet criminal syndicalism; or

State's Criminal Syndicalism Act was void for vagueness and overbreadth in violation of the First and Fourteenth Amendments, and accordingly restrained the District Attorney from "further prosecution of the currently pending action against plaintiff Harris for alleged violation of the Act."

The case is before us on appeal by the State's District Attorney Younger, pursuant to 28 U.S.C. § 1253. In his notice of appeal and his jurisdictional statement appellant presented two questions: (1) whether the decision of this Court in Whitney v. California, 274 U.S. 357, 47 S.Ct. 641, 71 L.Ed. 1095, holding California's law constitutional in 1927 was binding on the District Court and (2) whether the State's law is constitutional on its face. In this Court the brief for the State of California, filed at our request, also argues that only Harris, who was indicted, has standing to challenge the State's law, and that issuance of the injunction was a violation of a longstanding judicial policy and of 28 U.S.C. § 2283, which provides:

> "A court of the United States may not grant an injunction to stay proceedings in a State court except as expressly authorized by Act of Congress, or where necessary in aid of its jurisdiction, or to protect or effectuate its judgments."

Without regard to the questions raised about Whitney v. California, supra, since overruled by Brandenburg v. Ohio, 395 U.S. 444, 89 S.Ct. 1827, 23 L.Ed.2d 430 (1969), or the constitutionality of the state law, we have concluded that the judgment of the District Court, enjoining appellant Younger from prosecuting under these California statutes, must be reversed as a violation of the national policy forbidding federal courts to stay or enjoin pending state court proceedings except under special circumstances. We express no view about the circumstances under which federal courts may act when there is no prosecution pending in state courts at the time the federal proceeding is begun.

I

Appellee Harris has been indicted, and was actually being prosecuted by California for a violation of its Criminal Syndicalism Act at the time this suit was filed. He thus has an acute, live controversy with the State and its prosecutor. But none of the other parties plaintiff in the District Court, Dan, Hirsch, or Broslawsky, has such a controversy. None has been indicted, arrested, or even threatened by the prosecutor.... Whatever right Harris, who is being prosecuted under the state syndicalism law may have, Dan, Hirsch, and Broslawsky cannot share it with him.... [They] do not claim ... even that a prosecution is remotely possible....

II

Since the beginning of this country's history Congress has, subject to few exceptions, manifested a desire to permit state courts to try state cases free from interference by federal courts. In 1793 an Act unconditionally provided: "[N]or shall a writ of injunction be granted to stay proceedings in any court of a state...." A comparison of the 1793 Act with 28 U.S.C.

"5. Wilfully by personal act or conduct, practices or commits any act advised, advocated, taught or aided and abetted by the doctrine or precept of criminal syndicalism, with intent to accomplish a change in indus-

trial ownership or control, or effecting any political change;

"Is guilty of a felony and punishable by imprisonment in the state prison not less than one nor more than 14 years."

§ 2283, its present-day successor, graphically illustrates how few and minor have been the exceptions granted from the flat, prohibitory language of the old Act. During all this lapse of years from 1793 to 1970 the statutory exceptions to the 1793 congressional enactment have been only three: (1) "except as expressly authorized by Act of Congress"; (2) "where necessary in aid of its jurisdiction"; and (3) "to protect or effectuate its judgments." [1a] In addition, a judicial exception to the longstanding policy evidenced by the statute has been made where a person about to be prosecuted in a state court can show that he will, if the proceeding in the state court is not enjoined, suffer irreparable damages. See Ex parte Young, 209 U.S. 123, 28 S.Ct. 441, 52 L.Ed. 714 (1908).

The precise reasons for this longstanding public policy against federal court interference with state court proceedings have never been specifically identified but the primary sources of the policy are plain. One is the basic doctrine of equity jurisprudence that courts of equity should not act, and particularly should not act to restrain a criminal prosecution, when the moving party has an adequate remedy at law and will not suffer irreparable injury if denied equitable relief. The doctrine may originally have grown out of circumstances peculiar to the English judicial system and not applicable in this country, but its fundamental purpose of restraining equity jurisdiction within narrow limits is equally important under our Constitution, in order to prevent erosion of the role of the jury and avoid a duplication of legal proceedings and legal sanctions where a single suit would be adequate to protect the rights asserted. This underlying reason for restraining courts of equity from interfering with criminal prosecutions is reinforced by an even more vital consideration, the notion of "comity," that is, a proper respect for state functions, a recognition of the fact that the entire country is made up of a Union of separate state governments, and a continuance of the belief that the National Government will fare best if the States and their institutions are left free to perform their separate functions in their separate ways. This, perhaps for lack of a better and clearer way to describe it, is referred to by many as "Our Federalism," and one familiar with the profound debates that ushered our Federal Constitution into existence is bound to respect those who remain loyal to the ideals and dreams of "Our Federalism." The concept does not mean blind deference to "States' Rights" any more than it means centralization of control over every important issue in our National Government and its courts. The Framers rejected both these courses. What the concept does represent is a system in which there is sensitivity to the legitimate interests of both State and National Governments, and in which the National Government, anxious though it may be to vindicate and protect federal rights and federal interests, always endeavors to do so in ways that will not unduly interfere with the legitimate activities of the States. It should never be forgotten that this slogan, "Our Federalism," born in the early struggling days of our Union of States, occupies a highly important place in our Nation's history and its future. This brief discussion should be enough to suggest some of the reasons why it has been perfectly natural for our cases to repeat time and time again that the normal thing to do when

1a. [All three had their origin in judicially-created exceptions to the statutory bar.]

federal courts are asked to enjoin pending proceedings in state courts is not to issue such injunctions. In Fenner v. Boykin, 271 U.S. 240, 46 S.Ct. 492, 70 L.Ed. 927 (1926), suit had been brought in the Federal District Court seeking to enjoin state prosecutions under a recently enacted state law that allegedly interfered with the free flow of interstate commerce. The Court, in a unanimous opinion made clear that such a suit, even with respect to state criminal proceedings not yet formally instituted, could be proper only under very special circumstances:

> "Ex parte Young, 209 U.S. 123, 28 S.Ct. 441, 52 L.Ed. 714, and following cases have established the doctrine that, when absolutely necessary for protection of constitutional rights, courts of the United States have power to enjoin state officers from instituting criminal actions. But this may not be done, except under extraordinary circumstances, where the danger of irreparable loss is both great and immediate. Ordinarily, there should be no interference with such officers; primarily, they are charged with the duty of prosecuting offenders against the laws of the state, and must decide when and how this is to be done. The accused should first set up and rely upon his defense in the state courts, even though this involves a challenge of the validity of some statute, unless it plainly appears that this course would not afford adequate protection."

These principles, made clear in the *Fenner* case, have been repeatedly followed and reaffirmed in other cases involving threatened prosecutions.

In all of these cases the Court stressed the importance of showing irreparable injury, the traditional prerequisite to obtaining an injunction.

In addition, however, the Court also made clear that in view of the fundamental policy against federal interference with state criminal prosecutions, even irreparable injury is insufficient unless it is "both great and immediate." Certain types of injury, in particular, the cost, anxiety, and inconvenience of having to defend against a single criminal prosecution, could not by themselves be considered "irreparable" in the special legal sense of that term. Instead, the threat to the plaintiff's federally protected rights must be one that cannot be eliminated by his defense against a single criminal prosecution. Thus, in the *Buck* case, we stressed:

> "Federal injunctions against state criminal statutes, either in their entirety or with respect to their separate and distinct prohibitions, are not to be granted as a matter of course, even if such statutes are unconstitutional. 'No citizen or member of the community is immune from prosecution, in good faith, for his alleged criminal acts. The imminence of such a prosecution even though alleged to be unauthorized and hence unlawful is not alone ground for relief in equity which exerts its extraordinary powers only to prevent irreparable injury to the plaintiff who seeks its aid.'"

And similarly, in *Douglas,* we made clear, after reaffirming this rule, that:

> "It does not appear from the record that petitioners have been threatened with any injury other than that incidental to every criminal proceeding brought lawfully and in good faith...."

This is where the law stood when the Court decided Dombrowski v. Pfister, 380 U.S. 479, 85 S.Ct. 1116, 14 L.Ed.2d 22 (1965), and held that an injunction against the enforcement of certain state criminal statutes could properly issue under the circumstances presented in that case. In *Dombrowski,* unlike many of the earlier cases denying injunctions, the complaint made substantial allegations that:

> "the threats to enforce the statutes against appellants are not made with any expectation of securing valid convictions, but rather are part of a plan to employ arrests, seizures, and threats of prosecution under color of the statutes to harass appellants and discourage them and their supporters from asserting and attempting to vindicate the constitutional rights of Negro citizens of Louisiana."

The appellants in *Dombrowski* had offered to prove that their offices had been raided and all their files and records seized pursuant to search and arrest warrants that were later summarily vacated by a state judge for lack of probable cause. They also offered to prove that despite the state court order quashing the warrants and suppressing the evidence seized, the prosecutor was continuing to threaten to initiate new prosecutions of appellants under the same statutes, was holding public hearings at which photostatic copies of the illegally seized documents were being used, and was threatening to use other copies of the illegally seized documents to obtain grand jury indictments against the appellants on charges of violating the same statutes. These circumstances, as viewed by the Court sufficiently establish the kind of irreparable injury, above and beyond that associated with the defense of a single prosecution brought in good faith, that had always been considered sufficient to justify federal intervention. Indeed, after quoting the Court's statement in *Douglas* concerning the very restricted circumstances under which an injunction could be justified, the Court in *Dombrowski* went on to say:

> "But the allegations in this complaint depict a situation in which defense of the State's criminal prosecution will not assure adequate vindication of constitutional rights. They suggest that a substantial loss of or impairment of freedoms of expression will occur if appellants must await the state court's disposition and ultimate review in this Court of any adverse determination. These allegations, if true, clearly show irreparable injury."

And the Court made clear that even under these circumstances the District Court issuing the injunction would have continuing power to lift it at any time and remit the plaintiffs to the state courts if circumstances warranted. Similarly, in Cameron v. Johnson, 390 U.S. 611, 88 S.Ct. 1335, 20 L.Ed.2d 182 (1968), a divided Court denied an injunction after finding that the record did not establish the necessary bad faith and harassment; the dissenting Justices themselves stressed the very limited role to be allowed for federal injunctions against state criminal prosecutions and differed with the Court only on the question whether the particular facts of that case were sufficient to show that the prosecution was brought in bad faith.

It is against the background of these principles that we must judge the propriety of an injunction under the circumstances of the present case.

Here a proceeding was already pending in the state court, affording Harris an opportunity to raise his constitutional claims. There is no suggestion that this single prosecution against Harris is brought in bad faith or is only one of a series of repeated prosecutions to which he will be subjected. In other words, the injury that Harris faces is solely "that incidental to every criminal proceeding brought lawfully and in good faith," and therefore under the settled doctrine we have already described he is not entitled to equitable relief "even if such statutes are unconstitutional."

The District Court, however, thought that the *Dombrowski* decision substantially broadened the availability of injunctions against state criminal prosecutions and that under that decision the federal courts may give equitable relief, without regard to any showing of bad faith or harassment, whenever a state statute is found "on its face" to be vague or overly broad, in violation of the First Amendment. We recognize that there are some statements in the *Dombrowski* opinion that would seem to support this argument. But, as we have already seen, such statements were unnecessary to the decision of that case, because the Court found that the plaintiffs had alleged a basis for equitable relief under the long-established standards. In addition, we do not regard the reasons adduced to support this position as sufficient to justify such a substantial departure from the established doctrines regarding the availability of injunctive relief. It is undoubtedly true, as the Court stated in *Dombrowski,* that "[a] criminal prosecution under a statute regulating expression usually involves imponderables and contingencies that themselves may inhibit the full exercise of First Amendment freedoms." But this sort of "chilling effect," as the Court called it, should not by itself justify federal intervention. In the first place, the chilling effect cannot be satisfactorily eliminated by federal injunctive relief. In *Dombrowski* itself the Court stated that the injunction to be issued there could be lifted if the State obtained an "acceptable limiting construction" from the state courts. The Court then made clear that once this was done, prosecutions could then be brought for conduct occurring before the narrowing construction was made, and proper convictions could stand so long as the defendants were not deprived of fair warning. The kind of relief granted in *Dombrowski* thus does not effectively eliminate uncertainty as to the coverage of the state statute and leaves most citizens with virtually the same doubts as before regarding the danger that their conduct might eventually be subjected to criminal sanctions. The chilling effect can, of course, be eliminated by an injunction that would prohibit any prosecution whatever for conduct occurring prior to a satisfactory rewriting of the statute. But the States would then be stripped of all power to prosecute even the socially dangerous and constitutionally unprotected conduct that had been covered by the statute, until a new statute could be passed by the state legislature and approved by the federal courts in potentially lengthy trial and appellate proceedings. Thus, in *Dombrowski* itself the Court carefully re-affirmed the principle that even in the direct prosecution in the State's own courts, a valid narrowing construction can be applied to conduct occurring prior to the date when the narrowing construction was made, in the absence of fair warning problems.

Moreover, the existence of a "chilling effect," even in the area of First Amendment rights, has never been considered a sufficient basis, in and of itself, for prohibiting state action. Where a statute does not directly abridge free speech, but—while regulating a subject within the State's power—tends to have the incidental effect of inhibiting First Amendment rights, it is well settled that the statute can be upheld if the effect on speech is minor in relation to the need for control of the conduct and the lack of alternative means for doing so. Just as the incidental "chilling effect" of such statutes does not automatically render them unconstitutional, so the chilling effect that admittedly can result from the very existence of certain laws on the statute books does not in itself justify prohibiting the State from carrying out the important and necessary task of enforcing these laws against socially harmful conduct that the State believes in good faith to be punishable under its laws and the Constitution.

Beyond all this is another, more basic consideration. Procedures for testing the constitutionality of a statute "on its face" in the manner apparently contemplated by *Dombrowski,* and for then enjoining all action to enforce the statute until the State can obtain court approval for a modified version, are fundamentally at odds with the function of the federal courts in our constitutional plan. The power and duty of the judiciary to declare laws unconstitutional is in the final analysis derived from its responsibility for resolving concrete disputes brought before the courts for decision; a statute apparently governing a dispute cannot be applied by judges, consistently with their obligations under the Supremacy Clause, when such an application of the statute would conflict with the Constitution. But this vital responsibility, broad as it is, does not amount to an unlimited power to survey the statute books and pass judgment on laws before the courts are called upon to enforce them. Ever since the Constitutional Convention rejected a proposal for having members of the Supreme Court render advice concerning pending legislation it has been clear that, even when suits of this kind involve a "case or controversy" sufficient to satisfy the requirements of Article III of the Constitution, the task of analyzing a proposed statute, pinpointing its deficiencies, and requiring correction of these deficiencies before the statute is put into effect, is rarely if ever an appropriate task for the judiciary. The combination of the relative remoteness of the controversy, the impact on the legislative process of the relief sought, and above all the speculative and amorphous nature of the required line-by-line analysis of detailed statutes, see, *e.g.,* Landry v. Daley, 280 F.Supp. 938 (N.D.Ill.1968), rev'd sub nom. Boyle v. Landry, 401 U.S. 77, 91 S.Ct. 758, 27 L.Ed.2d 696, ordinarily results in a kind of case that is wholly unsatisfactory for deciding constitutional questions, whichever way they might be decided. In light of this fundamental conception of the Framers as to the proper place of the federal courts in the governmental processes of passing and enforcing laws, it can seldom be appropriate for these courts to exercise any such power of prior approval or veto over the legislative process.

For these reasons, fundamental not only to our federal system but also to the basic functions of the Judicial Branch of the National Government under our Constitution, we hold that the *Dombrowski* decision should not be regarded as having upset the settled doctrines that have always confined very narrowly the availability of injunctive relief against state criminal prosecutions. We do not think that opinion stands for the proposition that a federal court can properly enjoin enforcement of a statute solely on the basis of a showing that the statute "on its face" abridges First Amendment rights. There may, of course, be extraordinary circumstances in which the necessary irreparable injury can be shown even in the absence of the usual prerequisites of bad faith and harassment. For example, as long ago as the *Buck* case, we indicated:

> "It is of course conceivable that a statute might be flagrantly and patently violative of express constitutional prohibitions in every clause, sentence and paragraph, and in whatever manner and against whomever an effort might be made to apply it."

Other unusual situations calling for federal intervention might also arise, but there is no point in our attempting now to specify what they might be. It is sufficient for purposes of the present case to hold, as we do, that the possible unconstitutionality of a statute "on its face" does not in itself justify an injunction against good-faith attempts to enforce it, and that appellee Harris has failed to make any showing of bad faith, harassment, or any other unusual circumstance that would call for equitable relief. Because our holding rests on the absence of the factors necessary under equitable principles to justify federal intervention, we have no occasion to consider whether 28 U.S.C. § 2283, which prohibits an injunction against state court proceedings "except as expressly authorized by Act of Congress" would in and of itself be controlling under the circumstances of this case.

The judgment of the District Court is reversed, and the case is remanded for further proceedings not inconsistent with this opinion.

Reversed.

■ MR. JUSTICE STEWART, with whom MR. JUSTICE HARLAN joins, concurring.

The questions the Court decides today are important ones. Perhaps as important, however, is a recognition of the areas into which today's holdings do not necessarily extend. In all of these cases, the Court deals only with the proper policy to be followed by a federal court when asked to intervene by injunction or declaratory judgment in a criminal prosecution which is contemporaneously pending in a state court.

In basing its decisions on policy grounds, the Court does not reach any questions concerning the independent force of the federal anti-injunction statute, 28 U.S.C. § 2283. Thus we do not decide whether the word "injunction" in § 2283 should be interpreted to include a declaratory judgment, or whether an injunction to stay proceedings in a state court is "expressly authorized" by § 1 of the Civil Rights Act of 1871, now 42 U.S.C. § 1983. And since all these cases involve state criminal prosecutions, we do not deal with the considerations that should govern a federal court when it is asked to intervene in state civil proceedings, where, for various reasons, the balance might be struck differently.[2] Finally, the Court today

---

2. Courts of equity have traditionally shown greater reluctance to intervene in criminal prosecutions than in civil cases. The offense to state interests is likely to be less in a civil proceeding. A State's decision to classify conduct as criminal provides some indication of the importance it has ascribed to prompt and unencumbered enforcement of

does not resolve the problems involved when a federal court is asked to give injunctive or declaratory relief from *future* state criminal prosecutions.

The Court confines itself to deciding the policy considerations that in our federal system must prevail when federal courts are asked to interfere with pending state prosecutions. Within this area, we hold that a federal court must not, save in exceptional and extremely limited circumstances, intervene by way of either injunction or declaration in an existing state criminal prosecution.[3] Such circumstances exist only when there is a threat of irreparable injury "both great and immediate." A threat of this nature might be shown if the state criminal statute in question were patently and flagrantly unconstitutional on its face, or if there has been bad faith and harassment—official lawlessness—in a statute's enforcement. In such circumstances the reasons of policy for deferring to state adjudication are outweighed by the injury flowing from the very bringing of the state proceedings, by the perversion of the very process that is supposed to provide vindication, and by the need for speedy and effective action to protect federal rights.

■ MR. JUSTICE BRENNAN with whom MR. JUSTICE WHITE and MR. JUSTICE MARSHALL join, concurring in the result.

I agree that the judgment of the District Court should be reversed. Appellee Harris had been indicted for violations of the California Criminal Syndicalism Act before he sued in federal court. He has not alleged that the prosecution was brought in bad faith to harass him. His constitutional contentions may be adequately adjudicated in the state criminal proceeding, and federal intervention at his instance was therefore improper.*

Appellees Hirsch and Dan have alleged that they "feel inhibited" by the statute and the prosecution of Harris from advocating the program of the Progressive Labor Party. Appellee Broslawsky has alleged that he "is uncertain" whether as an instructor in college history he can under the statute give instruction relating to the Communist Manifesto and similar

its law. By contrast, the State might not even be a party in a proceeding under a civil statute.

These considerations would not, to be sure, support any distinction between civil and criminal proceedings should the ban of 28 U.S.C. § 2283, which makes no such distinction, be held unaffected by 42 U.S.C. § 1983.

3. The negative pregnant in this sentence—that a federal court may, as a matter of policy, intervene when such "exceptional and extremely limited circumstances" are found—is subject to any further limitations that may be placed on such intervention by 28 U.S.C. § 2283.

* ... The court below also thought it significant that appellee Harris had raised his constitutional claim in the state courts in a motion to dismiss the indictment and in petitions in the state appellate courts for a writ of prohibition. It was questioned at oral argument whether constitutional issues could properly be raised by the procedures invoked by Harris, and it was suggested that the denial of Harris' motions did not necessarily involve rejection of his constitutional claims. However, even if the California courts had at that interlocutory stage rejected Harris' constitutional arguments, that rejection would not have provided a justification for intervening by the District Court. Harris could have sought direct review of that rejection of his constitutional claims or he could have renewed the claims in requests for instructions, and on direct review of any conviction in the state courts and in this Court. These were the proper modes for presentation and these the proper forums for consideration of the constitutional issues.

revolutionary works. None of these appellees has stated any ground for a reasonable expectation that he will actually be prosecuted under the statute for taking the actions contemplated. The court below expressly declined to rely on any finding "that * * * Dan, Hirsch or Broslawsky stand[s] in any danger of prosecution by the [State], because of the activities that they ascribed to themselves in the complaint * * *." It is true, as the court below pointed out, that "[w]ell-intentioned prosecutors and judicial safeguards do not neutralize the vice of a vague law," but still there must be a live controversy under Art. III. No threats of prosecution of these appellees are alleged. Although Dan and Hirsch have alleged that they desire to advocate doctrines of the Progressive Labor Party, they have not asserted that their advocacy will be of the same genre as that which brought on the prosecution of Harris. In short, there is no reason to think that California has any ripe controversy with them.

■ MR. JUSTICE DOUGLAS, dissenting.

The fact that we are in a period of history when enormous extrajudicial sanctions are imposed on those who assert their First Amendment rights in unpopular causes emphasizes the wisdom of Dombrowski v. Pfister, 380 U.S. 479, 85 S.Ct. 1116, 14 L.Ed.2d 22. There we recognized that in times of repression, when interests with powerful spokesmen generate symbolic programs against nonconformists, the federal judiciary, charged by Congress with special vigilance for protection of civil rights, has special responsibilities to prevent an erosion of the individual's constitutional rights.

Dombrowski represents an exception to the general rule that federal courts should not interfere with state criminal prosecutions. The exception does not arise merely because prosecutions are threatened to which the First Amendment will be the proffered defense. *Dombrowski* governs statutes which are a blunderbuss by themselves or when used *en masse*—those that have an "overbroad" sweep. "If the rule were otherwise, the contours of regulation would have to be hammered out case by case—and tested only by those hardy enough to risk criminal prosecution to determine the proper scope of regulation." It was in the context of overbroad state statutes that we spoke of the "chilling effect upon the exercise of First Amendment rights" caused by state prosecutions.

As respects overbroad statutes we said at least as early as 1940 that when dealing with First Amendment rights we would insist on statutes "narrowly drawn to prevent the supposed evil."

The special circumstances when federal intervention in a state criminal proceeding is permissible are not restricted to bad faith on the part of state officials or the threat of multiple prosecutions. They also exist where for any reason the state statute being enforced is unconstitutional on its face. As Mr. Justice Butler, writing for the Court, said in Terrace v. Thompson, 263 U.S. 197, 44 S.Ct. 15, 68 L.Ed. 255;

> "Equity jurisdiction will be exercised to enjoin the threatened enforcement of a state law which contravenes the federal Constitution wherever it is essential in order effectually to protect property rights and the rights of persons against injuries otherwise irremediable; and in such a case a person, who as an officer of the state is clothed with the duty of

enforcing its laws and who threatens and is about to commence proceedings, either civil or criminal, to enforce such a law against parties affected, may be enjoined from such action by a Federal court of equity."

Our *Dombrowski* decision was only another facet of the same problem.

In *Younger,* "criminal syndicalism" is defined so broadly as to jeopardize "teaching" that socialism is preferable to free enterprise.

Harris' "crime" was distributing leaflets advocating change in industrial ownership through political action. The statute under which he was indicted was the one involved in Whitney v. California, 274 U.S. 357, 47 S.Ct. 641, 71 L.Ed. 1095, a decision we overruled in Brandenburg v. Ohio, 395 U.S. 444, 89 S.Ct. 1827, 23 L.Ed.2d 430.

If the "advocacy" which Harris used was an attempt at persuasion through the use of bullets, bombs, and arson, we would have a different case. But Harris is charged only with distributing leaflets advocating political action toward his objective. He tried unsuccessfully to have the state court dismiss the indictment on constitutional grounds. He resorted to the state appellate court for writs of prohibition to prevent the trial, but to no avail. He went to the federal court as a matter of last resort in an effort to keep this unconstitutional trial from being saddled on him.

The "anti-injunction" statute, 28 U.S.C. § 2283, is not a bar to a federal injunction under these circumstances. That statute was adopted in 1793, and reflected the early view of the proper role of the federal courts within American federalism.

Whatever the balance of the pressures of localism and nationalism prior to the Civil War, they were fundamentally altered by the war. The Civil War Amendments made civil rights a national concern. Those Amendments, especially § 5 of the Fourteenth Amendment, cemented the change in American federalism brought on by the war. Congress immediately commenced to use its new powers to pass legislation. Just as the first Judiciary Act and the "anti-injunction" statute represented the early views of American federalism, the Reconstruction statutes, including the enlargement of federal jurisdiction,[4] represent a later view of American federalism.

One of the jurisdiction-enlarging statutes passed during Reconstruction was the Act of April 20, 1871. Beyond its jurisdictional provision that statute, now codified as 42 U.S.C. § 1983 provides:

"Every person who, under color of any statute, ordinance, regulation, custom, or usage, of any State or Territory, subjects, or causes to be subjected, any citizen of the United States or other person within the jurisdiction thereof *to the deprivation of any rights, privileges, or immunities secured by the Constitution* and laws, shall be liable to the party injured in an action at law, *suit in equity,* or other proper proceeding for redress." (Emphasis added.)[4a]

---

4. What is now 28 U.S.C. § 1343(3) was added in 1871, and the federal-question jurisdiction of 28 U.S.C. § 1331 was added in 1875.

4a. [When the claimed "deprivation" is a result of federal, rather than state, action, the Court has "implied" a cause of action

A state law enforcement officer is someone acting under "color of law" even though he may be misusing his authority. And prosecution under a patently unconstitutional statute is a "deprivation of . . . rights, privileges, or immunities secured by the Constitution." "Suit[s] in equity" obviously includes injunctions.

I hold to the view that § 1983 is included in the "expressly authorized" exception to § 2283. . . . There is no more good reason for allowing a general statute dealing with federalism passed at the end of the 18th century to control another statute also dealing with federalism, passed almost 80 years later, than to conclude that the early concepts of federalism were not changed by the Civil War.

. . . .

As the standards of certainty in statutes containing criminal sanctions are higher than those in statutes containing civil sanctions, so are the standards of certainty touching on freedom of expression higher than those in other areas. "There must be ascertainable standards of guilt. Men of common intelligence cannot be required to guess at the meaning of the enactment. The vagueness may be from uncertainty in regard to persons within the scope of the act . . . or in regard to the applicable tests to ascertain guilt."

Where freedom of expression is at stake these requirements must be more sedulously enforced.

In *Younger* there is a prosecution under an unconstitutional statute and relief is denied. . . . Allegations of a prosecution or harassment under facially unconstitutional statutes should be sufficient for the exercise of federal equity powers.

Dombrowski and 42 U.S.C. § 1983 indicate why in [a companion case] federal intervention against enforcement of the state laws is appropriate. The case of *Younger* is even stronger. There the state statute challenged is the prototype of the one we held unconstitutional in Brandenburg v. Ohio.

The eternal temptation, of course, has been to arrest the speaker rather than to correct the conditions about which he complains. I see no reason why these appellees should be made to walk the treacherous ground of these statutes. They, like other citizens, need the umbrella of the First Amendment as they study, analyze, discuss, and debate the troubles of these days. When criminal prosecutions can be leveled against them because they express unpopular views, the society of the dialogue is in danger.

NOTES

1. *Younger* did not decide whether 42 U.S.C. § 1983 suits come within 28 U.S.C. § 2283's "expressly authorized" exception. The Court decided this question in Mitchum v. Foster, 407 U.S. 225, 92 S.Ct. 2151, 32 L.Ed.2d 705 (1972), which held the exception applicable.

2. In Samuels v. Mackell, 401 U.S. 66, 91 S.Ct. 764, 27 L.Ed.2d 688 (1971), decided the same day as *Younger,* the Court held that federal courts

and a damage remedy from the Constitution
itself. See Chapter 17A.]

may not grant declaratory relief when *Younger* forbids them from granting injunctive relief. Although the Court has not decided the question, two Justices have expressed the opinion that the *Younger* principles apply equally to damage actions filed under § 1983. Deakins v. Monaghan, 484 U.S. 193, 205–210, 108 S.Ct. 523, 531–33, 98 L.Ed.2d 529, 542–45 (1988)(White, J., joined by O'Connor, J., concurring).

3. In the absence of a pending state prosecution, the *Younger* rule does not bar federal courts from granting either injunctive or declaratory relief. See Wooley v. Maynard, 430 U.S. 705, 97 S.Ct. 1428, 51 L.Ed.2d 752 (1977); Steffel v. Thompson, 415 U.S. 452, 94 S.Ct. 1209, 39 L.Ed.2d 505 (1974). However, abstention is required if a state prosecution is begun "before any proceedings of substance on the merits have taken place in the federal court." See Hicks v. Miranda, 422 U.S. 332, 95 S.Ct. 2281, 45 L.Ed.2d 223 (1975).

O'Shea v. Littleton

Supreme Court of the United States, 1974.
414 U.S. 488, 94 S.Ct. 669, 38 L.Ed.2d 674.

■ MR. JUSTICE WHITE delivered the opinion of the Court.

The respondents are 19 named individuals who commenced this civil rights action, individually and on behalf of a class of citizens of the city of Cairo, Illinois, against the State's Attorney for Alexander County, Illinois, his investigator, the Police Commissioner of Cairo, and the petitioners here, Michael O'Shea and Dorothy Spomer, Magistrate and Associate Judge of the Alexander County Circuit Court, respectively, alleging that they have intentionally engaged in, and are continuing to engage in, various patterns and practices of conduct in the administration of the criminal justice system in Alexander County that deprive respondents of rights secured by the First, Sixth, Eighth, Thirteenth, and Fourteenth Amendments, and by 42 U.S.C. §§ 1981, 1982, 1983, and 1985. The complaint, as amended, alleges that since the early 1960's, black citizens of Cairo, together with a small number of white persons on their behalf, have been actively, peaceably and lawfully seeking equality of opportunity and treatment in employment, housing, education, participation in governmental decisionmaking and in ordinary day-to-day relations with white citizens and officials of Cairo, and have, as an important part of their protest, participated in, and encouraged others to participate in, an economic boycott of city merchants who respondents consider have engaged in racial discrimination. Allegedly, there had resulted a great deal of tension and antagonism among the white citizens and officials of Cairo.

The individual respondents are 17 black and two white residents of Cairo. The class, or classes, which they purport to represent are alleged to include "all those who, on account of their race or creed and because of their exercise of First Amendment rights, have in the past and continue to be subjected to the unconstitutional and selectively discriminatory enforcement and administration of criminal justice in Alexander County," as well as financially poor persons "who, on account of their poverty, are unable to afford bail, or are unable to afford counsel and jury trials in city ordinance violation cases." The complaint charges the State's Attorney, his investigator, and the Police Commissioner with a pattern and practice of intentional racial discrimination in the performance of their duties, by which the state criminal laws and procedures are deliberately applied more harshly to black residents of Cairo and inadequately applied to white persons who victimize blacks, to deter respondents from engaging in their lawful attempt to achieve equality. Specific supporting examples of such conduct involving some of the individual respondents are detailed in the complaint as to the State's Attorney and his investigator.

With respect to the petitioners, the county magistrate and judge, a continuing pattern and practice of conduct, under color of law, is alleged to have denied and to continue to deny the constitutional rights of respondents and members of their class in three respects: (1) petitioners set bond in criminal cases according to an unofficial bond schedule without regard to the facts of a case or circumstances of an individual defendant in violation of the Eighth and Fourteenth Amendments; (2) "on information and belief" they set sentences higher and impose harsher conditions for respondents and members of their class than for white persons, and (3) they require respondents and members of their class when charged with violations of city ordinances which carry fines and possible jail penalties if the fine cannot be paid, to pay for a trial by jury in violation of the Sixth, Eighth, and Fourteenth Amendments. Each of these continuing practices is alleged to have been carried out intentionally to deprive respondents and their class of the protections of the county criminal justice system and to deter them from engaging in their boycott and similar activities. The complaint further alleges that there is no adequate remedy at law and requests that the practices be enjoined. No damages were sought against the petitioners in this case, nor were any specific instances involving the individually named respondents set forth in the claim against these judicial officers.

The District Court dismissed the case for want of jurisdiction to issue the injunctive relief prayed for and on the ground that petitioners were immune from suit with respect to acts done in the course of their judicial duties. The Court of Appeals reversed, holding that Pierson v. Ray, 386 U.S. 547, 554, 87 S.Ct. 1213, 1217, 18 L.Ed.2d 288 (1967), on which the District Court relied, did not forbid the issuance of injunctions against judicial officers if it is alleged and proved that they have knowingly engaged in conduct intended to discriminate against a cognizable class of persons on the basis of race. Absent sufficient remedy at law, the Court of Appeals ruled that in the event respondents proved their allegations, the District Court should proceed to fashion appropriate injunctive relief to prevent petitioners from depriving others of their constitutional rights in the course of carrying out their judicial duties in the future.[1] We granted certiorari.

1. While the Court of Appeals did not attempt to specify exactly what type of injunctive relief might be justified, it at least suggested that it might include a requirement of "periodic reports of various types of aggregate data on actions on bail and sentencing." The dissenting judge urged that a federal district court has no power to supervise and regulate by mandatory injunction the discretion which state court judges may exercise within the limits of the powers vested in them by law, and that any relief con-

I

We reverse the judgment of the Court of Appeals. The complaint failed to satisfy the threshold requirement imposed by Art. III of the Constitution that those who seek to invoke the power of federal courts must allege an actual case or controversy. Plaintiffs in the federal courts "must allege some threatened or actual injury resulting from the putatively illegal action before a federal court may assume jurisdiction." There must be a "personal stake in the outcome" such as to "assure that concrete adverseness which sharpens the presentation of issues upon which the court so largely depends for illumination of difficult constitutional questions." Nor is the principle different where statutory issues are raised. Abstract injury is not enough. It must be alleged that the plaintiff "has sustained or is immediately in danger of sustaining some direct injury" as the result of the challenged statute or official conduct. The injury or threat of injury must be both "real and immediate," not "conjectural" or "hypothetical." Moreover, if none of the named plaintiffs purporting to represent a class establishes the requisite of a case or controversy with the defendants, none may seek relief on behalf of himself or any other member of the class.

In the complaint that began this action, the sole allegations of injury are that petitioners "have engaged in, and continue to engage in, a pattern and practice of conduct ... all of which has deprived, and continues to deprive, plaintiffs and members of their class of their" constitutional rights and, again, that petitioners "have denied and continue to deny to plaintiffs and members of their class their constitutional rights" by illegal bond, sentencing, and jury fee practices. None of the named plaintiffs is identified as having himself suffered any injury in the manner specified. In sharp contrast to the claim for relief against the State's Attorney where specific instances of misconduct with respect to particular individuals are alleged, the claim against petitioners alleges injury in only the most general terms. At oral argument, respondents' counsel stated that some of the named plaintiffs-respondents, who could be identified by name if necessary, had actually been defendants in proceedings before petitioners and had suffered from the alleged unconstitutional practices. Past exposure to illegal conduct does not in itself show a present case or controversy regarding injunctive relief, however, if unaccompanied by any continuing, present adverse effects. Neither the complaint nor respondents' counsel suggested that any of the named plaintiffs at the time the complaint was filed was himself serving an allegedly illegal sentence or was on trial or awaiting trial before petitioners. Indeed, if any of the respondents were then serving an assertedly unlawful sentence, the complaint would inappropriately be seeking relief from or modification of current, existing custody. Furthermore, if any were then on trial or awaiting trial in state proceedings, the complaint would be seeking injunctive relief that a federal court should not provide.

templated by the majority holding which might be applicable to the pattern and practice alleged, if proven, would subject the petitioners to the continuing supervision of the District Court, the necessity of defending their motivations in each instance when the fixing of bail or sentence was challenged by a Negro defendant as inconsistent with the equitable relief granted, and the possibility of a contempt citation for failure to comply with the relief awarded.

We thus do not strain to read inappropriate meaning into the conclusionary allegations of this complaint.

Of course, past wrongs are evidence bearing on whether there is a real and immediate threat of repeated injury. But here the prospect of future injury rests on the likelihood that respondents will again be arrested for and charged with violations of the criminal law and will again be subjected to bond proceedings, trial, or sentencing before petitioners. Important to this assessment is the absence of allegations that any relevant criminal statute of the State of Illinois is unconstitutional on its face or as applied or that plaintiffs have been or will be improperly charged with violating criminal law. If the statutes that might possibly be enforced against respondents are valid laws, and if charges under these statutes are not improvidently made or pressed, the question becomes whether any perceived threat to respondents is sufficiently real and immediate to show an existing controversy simply because they anticipate violating lawful criminal statutes and being tried for their offenses, in which event they may appear before petitioners and, if they do, will be affected by the allegedly illegal conduct charged. Apparently, the proposition is that *if* respondents proceed to violate an unchallenged law and *if* they are charged, held to answer, and tried in any proceedings before petitioners, they will be subjected to the discriminatory practices that petitioners are alleged to have followed. But it seems to us that attempting to anticipate whether and when these respondents will be charged with crime and will be made to appear before either petitioner takes us into the area of speculation and conjecture. The nature of respondents' activities is not described in detail and no specific threats are alleged to have been made against them. Accepting that they are deeply involved in a program to eliminate racial discrimination in Cairo and that tensions are high, we are nonetheless unable to conclude that the case or controversy requirement is satisfied by general assertions or inferences that in the course of their activities respondents will be prosecuted for violating valid criminal laws. We assume that respondents will conduct their activities within the law and so avoid prosecution and conviction as well as exposure to the challenged course of conduct said to be followed by petitioners.

As in Golden v. Zwickler, supra, we doubt that there is "sufficient immediacy and reality" to respondents' allegations of future injury to warrant invocation of the jurisdiction of the District Court. There, "it was wholly conjectural that another occasion might arise when Zwickler might be prosecuted for distributing the handbills referred to in the complaint." Here we can only speculate whether respondents will be arrested, either again or for the first time, for violating a municipal ordinance or a state statute, particularly in the absence of any allegations that unconstitutional criminal statutes are being employed to deter constitutionally protected conduct. Even though *Zwickler* attacked a specific statute under which he had previously been prosecuted, the threat of a new prosecution was not sufficiently imminent to satisfy the jurisdictional requirements of the federal courts. Similarly, respondents here have not pointed to any imminent prosecutions contemplated against any of their number and they naturally do not suggest that any one of them expects to violate valid criminal laws. Yet their vulnerability to the alleged threatened injury from which relief is sought is necessarily contingent upon the bringing of prosecutions against one or more of them. Under these circumstances, where respondents do not claim any constitutional right to engage in conduct proscribed by therefore presumably permissible state laws, or that it is otherwise their intention to so conduct themselves, the threat of injury from the alleged course of conduct they attack is simply too remote to satisfy the "case or controversy" requirement and permit adjudication by a federal court. . . .

II

The foregoing considerations obviously shade into those determining whether the complaint states a sound basis for equitable relief; and even if we were inclined to consider the complaint as presenting an existing case or controversy, we would firmly disagree with the Court of Appeals that an adequate basis for equitable relief against petitioners had been stated. The Court has recently reaffirmed the "basic doctrine of equity jurisprudence that courts of equity should not act, and particularly should not act to restrain a criminal prosecution, when the moving party has an adequate remedy at law and will not suffer irreparable injury if denied equitable relief." Additionally, recognition of the need for a proper balance in the concurrent operation of federal and state courts counsels restraint against the issuance of injunctions against state officers engaged in the administration of the State's criminal laws in the absence of a showing of irreparable injury which is "both great and immediate." In holding that 42 U.S.C. § 1983 is an Act of Congress that falls within the "expressly authorized" exception to the absolute bar against federal injunctions directed at state court proceedings provided by 28 U.S.C. § 2283, the Court expressly observed that it did not intend to "question or qualify in any way the principles of equity, comity, and federalism that must restrain a federal court when asked to enjoin a state court proceeding." Those principles preclude equitable intervention in the circumstances present here.

Respondents do not seek to strike down a single state statute, either on its face or as applied; nor do they seek to enjoin any criminal prosecutions that might be brought under a challenged criminal law. In fact, respondents apparently contemplate that prosecutions will be brought under seemingly valid state laws. What they seek is an injunction aimed at controlling or preventing the occurrence of specific events that might take place in the course of future state criminal trials. The order the Court of Appeals thought should be available if respondents proved their allegations would be operative only where permissible state prosecutions are pending against one or more of the beneficiaries of the injunction. Apparently the order would contemplate interruption of state proceedings to adjudicate assertions of non-compliance by petitioners. This seems to us nothing less than an ongoing federal audit of state criminal proceedings which would indirectly accomplish the kind of interference that Younger v. Harris and related cases sought to prevent.

A federal court should not intervene to establish the basis for future intervention that would be so intrusive and unworkable. In concluding that injunctive relief would be available in this case because it would not interfere with prosecutions to be commenced under challenged statutes, the Court of Appeals misconceived the underlying basis for withholding federal equitable relief when the normal course of criminal proceedings in the state courts would otherwise be disrupted. The objection is to unwarranted anticipatory interference in the state criminal process by means of continuous or piecemeal interruptions of the state proceedings by litigation in the federal courts; the object is to sustain "the special delicacy of the adjustment to be preserved between federal equitable power and State administration of its own law."[5] ... An injunction of the type contemplated by respondents and the Court of Appeals would disrupt the normal course of proceedings in the state courts via resort to the federal suit for determination of the claim *ab initio,* just as would the request for injunctive relief from an ongoing state prosecution against the federal plaintiff which was found to be unwarranted in *Younger.* Moreover, it would require for its enforcement the continuous supervision by the federal court over the conduct of the petitioners in the course of future criminal trial proceedings involving any of the members of the respondents' broadly-defined class. The Court of Appeals disclaimed any intention of requiring the District Court to sit in constant day-to-day supervision of these judicial officers, but the "periodic reporting" system it thought might be warranted[7] would constitute a form of monitoring of the operation of state court functions that is antipathetic to established principles of comity. Moreover, because an injunction against acts which might occur in the course of future criminal proceedings would necessarily impose continuing obligations of compliance, the question arises of how compliance might be enforced if the beneficiaries of the injunction were to charge that it had been disobeyed. Presumably, any member of respondents' class who appeared as an accused before petitioners could allege and have adjudicated a claim that petitioners were in contempt of the federal court's injunction order, with review of adverse decisions in the Court of Appeals and, perhaps, in this Court. Apart from the inherent difficulties in defining the proper standards against which such claims might be measured, and the significant problems of proving noncompliance in individual cases, such a major continuing intrusion of the equitable power of the federal courts into the daily conduct of state criminal proceedings is in sharp conflict with the principles of equitable restraint which this Court has recognized in the decisions previously noted.

Respondents have failed, moreover, to establish the basic requisites of the issuance of equitable relief in these circumstances—the likelihood of substantial and immediate irreparable injury, and the inadequacy of remedies at law. We have already canvassed the necessarily conjectural nature of the threatened injury to which respondents are allegedly subjected. And if any of the respondents are ever prosecuted and face trial, or if they are illegally sentenced, there are available state and federal procedures which could provide relief from the wrongful conduct alleged. Open to a victim of the discriminatory practices asserted under state law are the right to a

---

5. ... [I]n suits brought under 42 U.S.C. § 1983 "we have withheld relief in equity even when recognizing that compara- ble facts would create a cause of action for damages."

7. See n. 1 supra.

substitution of judge or a change of venue, review on direct appeal or on postconviction collateral review, and the opportunity to demonstrate that the conduct of these judicial officers is so prejudicial to the administration of justice that available disciplinary proceedings, including the possibility of suspension or removal, are warranted. In appropriate circumstances, moreover, federal habeas relief would undoubtedly be available.

Nor is it true that unless the injunction sought is available federal law will exercise no deterrent effect in these circumstances. Judges who would willfully discriminate on the ground of race or otherwise would willfully deprive the citizen of his constitutional rights, as this complaint alleges, must take account of 18 U.S.C. § 242. That section provides:

> "Whoever, under color of any law, statute, ordinance, regulation, or custom, willfully subjects any inhabitant of any State ... to the deprivation of any rights, privileges, or immunities secured or protected by the Constitution or laws of the United States, or to different punishments, pains, or penalties, on account of such inhabitant being an alien, or by reason of his color, or race, than are prescribed for the punishment of citizens, shall be fined ... or imprisoned...."

Whatever may be the case with respect to civil liability generally, see Pierson v. Ray, 386 U.S. 547, 87 S.Ct. 1213, 18 L.Ed.2d 288 (1967),[7a] or civil liability for willful corruption, we have never held that the performance of the duties of judicial, legislative, or executive officers, requires or contemplates the immunization of otherwise criminal deprivations of constitutional rights. On the contrary, the judicially fashioned doctrine of official immunity does not reach "so far as to immunize criminal conduct proscribed by an Act of Congress...."

Considering the availability of other avenues of relief open to respondents for the serious conduct they assert, and the abrasive and unmanageable intercession which the injunctive relief they seek would represent, we conclude that, apart from the absence of an existing case or controversy presented by respondents for adjudication, the Court of Appeals erred in deciding that the District Court should entertain respondents' claim.

Reversed.

■ MR. JUSTICE BLACKMUN, concurring in part.

I join the judgment of the Court and Part I of the Court's opinion which holds that the complaint "failed to satisfy the threshold requirement imposed by Art. III of the Constitution that those who seek to invoke the power of federal courts must allege an actual case or controversy."

When we arrive at that conclusion, it follows, it seems to me, that we are precluded from considering any other issue presented for review. Thus, the Court's additional discussion of the question whether a case for equitable relief was stated amounts to an advisory opinion that we are powerless to render....

7a. [*Pierson* held that judges are absolutely immune from damage suits under Section 1983 for judicial acts performed by them within their jurisdiction. Also see Stump v. Sparkman, 435 U.S. 349, 98 S.Ct. 1099, 55 L.Ed.2d 331 (1978).]

■ MR. JUSTICE DOUGLAS, with whom MR. JUSTICE BRENNAN and MR. JUSTICE MARSHALL concur, dissenting.

The respondents in this case are black and indigent citizens of Cairo, Illinois. Suing in federal court, they alleged that since the early 1960's black citizens of Cairo have been actively seeking equal opportunity and treatment in employment, housing, education, and ordinary day-to-day relations with the white citizens and officials of Cairo. In this quest, blacks have engaged in a boycott of local merchants deemed to have engaged in racial discrimination.

Alleging that this quest for equality has generated substantial antagonism from white governmental officials, respondents brought a class action under 42 U.S.C. §§ 1981, 1982, 1983, and 1985, seeking to represent citizens of Cairo who have been subjected in the past, and continue to be subjected, to the allegedly discriminatory and unconstitutional administration of criminal justice in Alexander County, Illinois, which includes Cairo. Among their other claims, respondents alleged that petitioners Michael O'Shea and Dorothy Spomer, both now judges in Alexander County, engage in acts which deprive them and members of their class of their constitutional rights. These judges allegedly set bond in criminal cases without regard to the facts of individual cases and as punishment, and not merely to assure the appearance of defendants at trial; impose higher sentences and harsher conditions of sentencing on blacks than on white citizens; and require respondents and members of their class, when charged with violations of city ordinances which carry fines and possible jail penalties, to pay for a trial by jury if the fine cannot be paid.

I

An injunction was sought against this conduct. The District Court referred obliquely to want of jurisdiction, but, focusing on the fact that the complaint sought review of matters of judicial discretion, concluded that the action should be dismissed because judges and magistrates are immune from liability for acts done in performance of their duties. In reversing and remanding the case to the District Court, the Court of Appeals held that the action was not barred by the doctrine of judicial immunity. The Court of Appeals also held that the complaint contained sufficiently specific factual averments to satisfy Rule 8(a) of the Federal Rules of Civil Procedure.

This Court now decides for the first time in the course of this litigation that the complaint is deficient because it does not state a "case or controversy" within the meaning of Art. III.

The fact that no party has raised that issue in this closely contested case is no barrier of course to our consideration of it....

. . . .

It is also alleged that the police commissioner in Cairo "has denied and continues to deny to plaintiffs and members of their class their constitutional rights in the following ways:

"(a) Defendant has made or caused to be made or cooperated in the making of arrests and the filing of charges against plaintiffs and members of their class where such charges are not warranted and are merely for the purpose of harassment and to discourage and prevent plaintiffs and their class from exercising their constitutional rights.

"(b) Defendant has made or caused to be made or cooperated in the making of arrests and the filing of charges against plaintiffs and members of their class where there may be some colorable basis to the arrest or charge, but the crime defined in the charge is much harsher than is warranted by the facts and is far more severe than like charges would be against a white person."

These allegations support the likelihood that the named plaintiffs as well as members of their class will be arrested in the future and therefore will be brought before O'Shea and Spomer and be subjected to the alleged discriminatory practices in the administration of justice.

What we have alleged here is not only wrongs done to named plaintiffs but a recurring pattern of wrongs which establishes, if proved, that the legal regime under control of the whites in Cairo, Illinois, is used over and over again to keep the Blacks from exercising First Amendment rights, to discriminate against them, to keep from the Blacks the protection of the law in their lawful activities, to weight the scales of justice repeatedly on the side of white prejudices and against Black protests, fears, and suffering. This is a more pervasive scheme for suppression of Blacks and their civil rights than I have ever seen. It may not survive a trial. But if this case does not present a "case or controversy" involving the named plaintiffs, then that concept has been so watered down as to be no longer recognizable. This will please the white super-structure, but it does violence to the conception of even-handed justice envisioned by the Constitution.

Suits under 42 U.S.C. § 1983 are exceptions to the absolute bar against federal injunctions directed at state court proceedings provided in 28 U.S.C. § 2283. It will be much more appropriate to pass on the nature of any equitable relief to be granted after the case has been tried. It may be that when the case is ended, no injunction against any state proceeding will be asked for or will seem appropriate. Or the injunctive relief in final analysis may come down to very narrow and discrete orders prohibiting precise practices. The Court labels this an "ongoing federal audit of state criminal proceedings." That of course is a regime that we do not foster. But the federal Constitution is supreme and if the power of the white power-structure in Cairo, Illinois, is so great as to disregard it, extraordinary relief is demanded. I would cross the bridge of remedies only when the precise contours of the problem have been established after a trial.

To repeat, in the instant case, there are allegations that state lower-court judges are willfully discriminating in their sentencing determinations and are imposing excessive bail. The effects of such results may well persist quite aside from the disposition of the underlying substantive charges at trial or on appeal, and may well be functionally unreviewable. The Court of Appeals observed, that the individual defendant in a criminal case will find it difficult, if not impossible, to obtain review of a sentence within statutory limits unless it is manifestly harsh or unjustified, citing the Illinois rule that "imposition of sentence is a matter of judicial discretion, and in the absence of a manifest abuse of that discretion it will not be altered by a reviewing court."

Furthermore, the respondents do not primarily allege individual instances of excessively harsh treatment, on an absolute scale, of black and indigent defendants, but rather a pattern of discriminatory treatment, especially in favor of prosperous white defendants. Such allegations would amount to denials of equal protection even if blacks and poor whites were not subject to sentences which were so excessive that they constituted manifest abuses of discretion, as long as wealthy whites were at the same time receiving relatively lenient sentences from the same judges. A single instance of sentencing by itself might not strike the conscience of a reviewing court, but when coupled with a pattern of discriminatory treatment could well justify the equitable intervention of a federal court. A class suit where evidence could be developed showing a pattern of discriminatory bail and sentencing decisions by the petitioners would be the one appropriate vehicle in which these claims could be developed.

Whether respondents could come forward with such evidence, and whether the Federal District Court in the exercise of its equitable discretion could frame suitable relief are, of course, questions which can be answered only after a trial on the merits. The resolution of those issues would then be properly reviewable. But the principles of abstention and comity should not bar this suit *ab initio*.

II

Because I believe that the complaint is sufficient to state an actual "case or controversy," I reach the further question, on the merits, whether equitable relief may be warranted in the circumstances of this case. I agree, nonetheless, with by brother Blackmun that the Court's discussion in Part II of its opinion, whether a case for equitable relief was stated, is an advisory opinion since the Court has determined that there is no "case or controversy" in the Article III sense.

APPENDIX

There are seven statutes in addition to § 1983 which the Court has recognized constitute "express exceptions" to the policy of nonintervention in state proceedings enunciated by the anti-injunction statute: (1) The Bankruptcy Act specifically recognized by Congress as an exception to § 2283. (2) The Interpleader Act of 1926, allowing federal courts to restrain prosecution of state court suits involving property involved in federal interpleader actions. (3) The 1851 Act limiting the liability of shipowners by providing for the cessation of proceedings against them when they have made a deposit equal to the value of their ships with a federal court. (4) The Frazier–Lemke Farm Mortgage Act. (5) The Federal Habeas Corpus Act, permitting a stay of state court proceedings when a federal habeas action is pending. (6) Section 205(a) of the Emergency Price Control Act of 1942. (7) Legislation providing for the removal of litigation to federal courts and the simultaneous cessation of state court proceedings.

This Court has also recognized the power of a federal court to stay proceedings in a state court to prevent relitigation of an issue already decided in a federal proceeding. It has recognized the power of a federal court to enjoin state court proceedings to protect the jurisdiction which a federal court has already acquired over a *res*. And we have found it proper for a federal court to directly enjoin state proceedings when the injunction was sought by either the United States, or by a federal agency asserting superior federal interests.

NOTES

1.   Illinois law essentially allowed criminal defendants two peremptory challenges of judges. A showing of cause was required, however, to obtain a change of venue.

2.   Gibson v. Berryhill, 411 U.S. 564, 93 S.Ct. 1689, 36 L.Ed.2d 488 (1973), involved a controversy over whether Alabama optometrists could lawfully work for business corporations. Employees of Lee Optical Co. were charged with unprofessional conduct, and the Alabama Board of Optometry was asked to revoke their licenses. Thirteen optometrists employed by Lee Optical then filed a § 1983 suit in federal court, challenging the Board's ability to give them the fair and impartial hearing to which they felt entitled under the Due Process Clause. The trial court found the Board members biased, and so it granted the plaintiffs' request for an injunction against the pending license revocation proceedings.

On appeal, the Supreme Court rejected the Board's contention that *Younger* required the federal trial court to abstain and dismiss the injunction action. The Court explained that

[*Younger* abstention] naturally presupposes the opportunity to raise and have timely decided by a competent state tribunal the federal issues involved. Here the predicate for a Younger v. Harris dismissal was lacking, for the appellees alleged, and the District Court concluded, that the State Board of Optometry was incompetent by reason of bias to adjudicate the issues pending before it. If the District Court's conclusion was correct in this regard [and the Supreme Court held it was], it was also correct that it need not defer to the Board. Nor, in these circumstances, would a different result be required simply because judicial review, *de novo* or otherwise, would be forthcoming at the conclusion of the administrative proceedings.

Huffman v. Pursue, Ltd.

Supreme Court of the United States, 1975.
420 U.S. 592, 95 S.Ct. 1200, 43 L.Ed.2d 482.

■ MR. JUSTICE REHNQUIST delivered the opinion of the Court.

This case requires that we decide whether our decision in Younger v. Harris, 401 U.S. 37, 91 S.Ct. 746, 27 L.Ed.2d 669 (1971), bars a federal district court from intervening in a state civil proceeding such as this, when the proceeding is based on a state statute believed by the district court to be unconstitutional. A similar issue was raised in Gibson v. Berryhill, 411 U.S. 564, 93 S.Ct. 1689, 36 L.Ed.2d 488 (1973), but we were not required to decide it because there the enjoined state proceedings were before a biased administrative body which could not provide a necessary predicate for a *Younger* dismissal, that is, "the opportunity to raise and have timely decided by a competent state tribunal the federal issues involved." ... Today we do reach the issue, and conclude that in the circumstances presented here the principles of *Younger* are applicable even though the state proceeding is civil in nature.

I

Appellants are the sheriff and prosecuting attorney of Allen County, Ohio. This case arises from their efforts to close the Cinema I Theatre, in Lima, Ohio. Under the management of both its current tenant, appellee Pursue, Ltd., and appellee's predecessor, William Dakota, the Cinema I has specialized in the display of films which may fairly be characterized as pornographic, and which in numerous instances have been adjudged obscene after adversary hearings.

Appellants sought to invoke the Ohio public nuisance statute against appellee. Section 3767.01(C) provides that a place which exhibits obscene films is a nuisance, while § 3767.06 requires closure for up to a year of any place determined to be a nuisance. The statute also provides for preliminary injunctions pending final determination of status as a nuisance, for sale of all personal property used in conducting the nuisance, and for release from a closure order upon satisfaction of certain conditions (including a showing that the nuisance will not be re-established).

Appellants instituted a nuisance proceeding in the Court of Common Pleas of Allen County against appellee's predecessor, William Dakota. During the course of the somewhat involved legal proceedings which followed, the Court of Common Pleas reviewed 16 movies which had been shown at the theater. The court rendered a judgment that Dakota had engaged in a course of conduct of displaying obscene movies at the Cinema I, and that the theater was therefore to be closed ... "for any purpose for a period of one year unless sooner released by Order of [the] Court pursuant to defendant-owners fulfilling the requirements provided in Section 3767.04 of the Revised Code of Ohio." The judgment also provided for the seizure and sale of personal property used in the theater's operations.

Appellee, Pursue, Ltd., had succeeded to William Dakota's leasehold interest in the Cinema I prior to entry of the state-court judgment. Rather than appealing that judgment within the Ohio court system, it immediately filed suit in the United States District Court for the Northern District of Ohio. The complaint was based on 42 U.S.C. § 1983 and alleged that appellants' use of Ohio's nuisance statute constituted a deprivation of constitutional rights under the color of state law. It sought injunctive relief and a declaratory judgment that the statute was unconstitutional and unenforceable.[10] Since the complaint was directed against the constitutionality of a state statute, a three-judge court was convened. The District

---

10. Because the state-court judgment was primarily directed against a property interest to which Pursue had succeeded, the District Court concluded that Pursue had standing to challenge the nuisance statute.

Similarly, counsel for Pursue conceded at oral argument that Pursue could have appealed the judgment of the Court of Common Pleas within the Ohio court system.

Court concluded that while the statute was not vague, it did constitute an overly broad prior restraint on First Amendment rights insofar as it permanently or temporarily prevented the showing of films which had not been adjudged obscene in prior adversary hearings. Fashioning its remedy to match the perceived constitutional defect, the court permanently enjoined the execution of that portion of the state court's judgment that closed the Cinema I to films which had not been adjudged obscene. The judgment and opinion of the District Court give no indication that it considered whether it should have stayed its hand in deference to the principles of federalism which find expression in Younger v. Harris, 401 U.S. 37, 91 S.Ct. 746, 27 L.Ed.2d 669 (1971).

On this appeal, appellants raise the *Younger* problem, as well as a variety of constitutional and statutory issues. We need consider only the applicability of *Younger*.

II

. . . .

III

The seriousness of federal judicial interference with state civil functions has long been recognized by this Court. We have consistently required that when federal courts are confronted with requests for such relief, they should abide by standards of restraint that go well beyond those of private equity jurisprudence. For example, Massachusetts State Grange v. Benton, 272 U.S. 525, 47 S.Ct. 189, 71 L.Ed. 387 (1926), involved an effort to enjoin the operation of a state daylight savings act. Writing for the Court, Mr. Justice Holmes cited Fenner v. Boykin, and emphasized a rule that "should be very strictly observed," "that no injunction ought to issue against officers of a State clothed with authority to enforce the law in question, unless in a case reasonably free from doubt and when necessary to prevent great and irreparable injury."

Although Mr. Justice Holmes was confronted with a bill seeking an injunction against state executive officers, rather than against state judicial proceedings, we think that the relevant considerations of federalism are of no less weight in the latter setting. If anything, they counsel more heavily toward federal restraint, since interference with a state judicial proceeding prevents the state not only from effectuating its substantive policies, but also from continuing to perform the separate function of providing a forum competent to vindicate any constitutional objections interposed against those policies. Such interference also results in duplicative legal proceedings, and can readily be interpreted "as reflecting negatively upon the state courts' ability to enforce constitutional principles."

The component of *Younger* which rests upon the threat to our federal system is thus applicable to a civil proceeding such as this quite as much as it is to a criminal proceeding. *Younger* however, also rests upon the traditional reluctance of courts of equity, even within a unitary system, to interfere with a criminal prosecution. Strictly speaking, this element of *Younger* is not available to mandate federal restraint in civil cases. But whatever may be the weight attached to this factor in civil litigation involving private parties, we deal here with a state proceeding which in important respects is more akin to a criminal prosecution than are most civil cases. The State is a party to the Court of Common Pleas proceeding, and the proceeding is both in aid of and closely related to criminal statutes which prohibit the dissemination of obscene materials. Thus, an offense to the State's interest in the nuisance litigation is likely to be every bit as great as it would be were this a criminal proceeding. Similarly, while in this case the District Court's injunction has not directly disrupted Ohio's criminal justice system, it has disrupted that State's efforts to protect the very interests which underlie its criminal laws and to obtain compliance with precisely the standards which are embodied in its criminal laws.

IV

In spite of the critical similarities between a criminal prosecution and Ohio nuisance proceedings, appellee nonetheless urges that there is also a critical difference between the two which should cause us to limit *Younger* to criminal proceedings. This difference, says appellee, is that whereas a state-court criminal defendant may, after exhaustion of his state remedies, present his constitutional claims to the federal courts through habeas corpus, no analogous remedy is available to one, like appellee, whose constitutional rights may have been infringed in a state proceeding which cannot result in custodial detention or other criminal sanction.

A civil litigant may, of course, seek review in this Court of any federal claim properly asserted in and rejected by state courts. Moreover, where a final decision of a state court has sustained the validity of a state statute challenged on federal constitutional grounds, an appeal to this Court lies as a matter of right. Thus, appellee in this case was assured of eventual consideration of its claim by this Court. But quite apart from appellee's right to appeal had it remained in state court, we conclude that it should not be permitted the luxury of federal litigation of issues presented by ongoing state proceedings, a luxury which, as we have already explained, is quite costly in terms of the interests which *Younger* seeks to protect.

Appellee's argument, that because there may be no civil counterpart to federal habeas it should have contemporaneous access to a federal forum for its federal claim, apparently depends on the unarticulated major premise that every litigant who asserts a federal claim is entitled to have it decided on the merits by a federal, rather than a state, court. We need not consider the validity of this premise in order to reject the result which appellee seeks. Even assuming, *arguendo,* that litigants are entitled to a federal forum for the resolution of all federal issues, that entitlement is most appropriately asserted by a state litigant when he seeks to *relitigate* a federal issue adversely determined in *completed* state court proceedings.[18] We do not understand why the federal forum must be available prior to

---

18. We in no way intend to suggest that there is a right of access to a federal forum for the disposition of all federal issues, or that the normal rules of res judicata and judicial estoppel do not operate to bar relitigation in actions under 42 U.S.C. § 1983 of federal issues arising in state court proceedings. Our assumption is made solely as a means of disposing of appellee's contentions without confronting issues which have not been briefed or argued in this case.

completion of the state proceedings in which the federal issue arises, and the considerations canvassed in *Younger* militate against such a result.

The issue of whether federal courts should be able to interfere with ongoing state proceedings is quite distinct and separate from the issue of whether litigants are entitled to subsequent federal review of state-court dispositions of federal questions. *Younger* turned on considerations of comity and federalism peculiar to the fact that state proceedings were pending; it did *not* turn on the fact that in any event a criminal defendant could eventually have obtained federal habeas consideration of his federal claims. The propriety of federal-court interference with an Ohio nuisance proceeding must likewise be controlled by application of those same considerations of comity and federalism.

... For the purposes of the case before us, ... we need make no general pronouncements upon the applicability of *Younger* to all civil litigation. It suffices to say that for the reasons heretofore set out, we conclude that the District Court should have applied the tests laid down in *Younger* in determining whether to proceed to the merits of appellee's prayer for relief against this Ohio civil nuisance proceeding.

V

Appellee contends that even if *Younger* is applicable to civil proceedings of this sort, it nonetheless does not govern this case because at the time the District Court acted there was no longer a "pending state court proceeding" as that term is used in *Younger*. *Younger* and subsequent cases such as *Steffel* have used the term "pending proceeding" to distinguish state proceedings which have already commenced from those which are merely incipient or threatened. Here, of course, the state proceeding had begun long before appellee sought intervention by the District Court. But appellee's point, we take it, is not that the state proceeding had not begun, but that it had ended by the time its District Court complaint was filed.[19]

Appellee apparently relies on the facts that the Allen County Court of Common Pleas had already issued its judgment and permanent injunction when this action was filed, and that no appeal from that judgment has ever been taken to Ohio's appellate courts. As a matter of state procedure, the judgment presumably became final, in the sense of being nonappealable, at some point after the District Court filing, possibly prior to entry of the District Court's own judgment, but surely after the single judge stayed the state court's judgment. We need not, however, engage in such inquiry. For regardless of when the Court of Common Pleas' judgment became final, we believe that a necessary concomitant of *Younger* is that a party in appellee's posture must exhaust his state appellate remedies before seeking relief in the District Court, unless he can bring himself within one of the exceptions specified in *Younger*.

19. It would ordinarily be difficult to consider this problem, that of the duration of *Younger's* restrictions after entry of a state trial court judgment, without also considering the res judicata implications of such a judgment. However, appellants did not plead res judicata in the District Court, and it is therefore not available to them here.

Virtually all of the evils at which *Younger* is directed would inhere in federal intervention prior to completion of state appellate proceedings, just as surely as they would if such intervention occurred at or before trial. Intervention at the later stage is if anything more highly duplicative, since an entire trial has already taken place, and it is also a direct aspersion on the capabilities and good faith of state appellate courts. Nor, in these state-initiated nuisance proceedings, is federal intervention at the appellate stage any the less a disruption of the State's efforts to protect interests which it deems important. Indeed, it is likely to be even more disruptive and offensive because the State has already won a *nisi prius* determination that its valid policies are being violated in a fashion which justifies judicial abatement.

Federal post-trial intervention, in a fashion designed to annul the results of a state trial, also deprives the States of a function which quite legitimately is left to them, that of overseeing trial court dispositions of constitutional issues which arise in civil litigation over which they have jurisdiction. We think this consideration to be of some importance because it is typically a judicial system's appellate courts which are by their nature a litigant's most appropriate forum for the resolution of constitutional contentions. Especially is this true when, as here, the constitutional issue involves a statute which is capable of judicial narrowing. In short, we do not believe that a State's judicial system would be fairly accorded the opportunity to resolve federal issues arising in its courts if a federal district court were permitted to substitute itself for the State's appellate courts. We therefore hold that *Younger* standards must be met to justify federal intervention in a state judicial proceeding as to which a losing litigant has not exhausted his state appellate remedies.[21]

At the time appellee filed its action in the United States District Court, it had available the remedy of appeal to the Ohio appellate courts. Appellee nonetheless contends that exhaustion of state appellate remedies should not be required because an appeal would have been "futile." This claim is based on the decision of the Supreme Court of Ohio in State ex rel. Keating v. A Motion Picture Film Entitled "Vixen," 27 Ohio St.2d 278, 272 N.E.2d 137 (1971), which had been rendered at the time of the proceedings in the Court of Common Pleas. While *Keating* did uphold the use of a nuisance statute against a film which ran afoul of Ohio's statutory definition of obscenity, it had absolutely nothing to say with respect to appellee's principal contention here, that of whether the First and Fourteenth Amendments prohibit a blanket injunction against a showing of all films, including those which have not been adjudged obscene in adversary proceedings. We therefore have difficulty understanding appellee's belief that an appeal was doomed to failure.

---

21. By requiring exhaustion of state appellate remedies for the purposes of applying *Younger* we in no way undermine Monroe v. Pape, 365 U.S. 167, 81 S.Ct. 473, 5 L.Ed.2d 492 (1961). There we held that one seeking redress under 42 U.S.C. § 1983 for a deprivation of federal rights need not first initiate state proceedings based on related state causes of action. Monroe v. Pape had nothing to do with the problem presently before us, that of the deference to be accorded state proceedings which have already been initiated and which afford a competent tribunal for the resolution of federal issues.

. . .

More importantly, we are of the opinion that the considerations of comity and federalism which underlie *Younger* permit no truncation of the exhaustion requirement merely because the losing party in the state court of general jurisdiction believes that his chances of success on appeal are not auspicious. Appellee obviously believes itself possessed of a viable federal claim, else it would not so assiduously seek to litigate in the District Court. Yet, Art. VI of the United States Constitution declares that "the Judges in every State shall be bound" by the Federal Constitution, laws, and treaties. Appellee is in truth urging us to base a rule on the assumption that state judges will not be faithful to their constitutional responsibilities. This we refuse to do. The District Court should not have entertained this action, seeking pre-appeal interference with a state judicial proceeding, unless appellee established that early intervention was justified under one of the exceptions recognized in *Younger*.[22]

VI

Younger, and its civil counterpart which we apply today, do of course allow intervention in those cases where the District Court properly finds that the state proceeding is motivated by a desire to harass or is conducted in bad faith, or where the challenged statute is " 'flagrantly and patently violative of express constitutional prohibitions in every clause, sentence and paragraph, and in whatever manner and against whomever an effort might be made to apply it.' " As we have noted, the District Court in this case did not rule on the *Younger* issue, and thus apparently has not considered whether its intervention was justified by one of these narrow exceptions. Even if the District Court's opinion can be interpreted as a *sub silentio* determination that the case fits within the exception for statutes which are " 'flagrantly and patently violative of express constitutional prohibitions,' " such a characterization of the statute is not possible after the subsequent decision of the Supreme Court of Ohio in State ex rel. Ewing v. A Motion Picture Film Entitled "Without a Stitch," 37 Ohio St.2d 95, 307 N.E.2d 911 (1974). That case narrowly construed the Ohio nuisance statute, with a view to avoiding the constitutional difficulties which concerned the District Court.

We therefore think that this case is appropriate for remand so that the District Court may consider whether irreparable injury can be shown in light of *"Without a Stitch,"* and if so, whether that injury is of such a nature that the District Court may assume jurisdiction under an exception to the policy against federal judicial interference with state court proceedings of this kind. The judgment of the District Court is vacated and the cause is remanded for further proceedings consistent with this opinion.

It is so ordered.

■ MR. JUSTICE BRENNAN, with whom MR. JUSTICE DOUGLAS and MR. JUSTICE MARSHALL join, dissenting.

---

22. *While appellee had the option to appeal in state courts at the time it filed this action, we do not know for certain whether such remedy remained available at the time the District Court issued its permanent injunction, or whether it remains available now. In any event, appellee may not avoid the standards of Younger by simply failing to comply* with the procedures of perfecting its appeal within the Ohio judicial system.

I dissent. The treatment of the state *civil* proceeding as one "in aid of and closely related to criminal statutes" is obviously only the first step toward extending to state *civil* proceedings generally the holding of Younger v. Harris, 401 U.S. 37, 91 S.Ct. 746, 27 L.Ed.2d 669 (1971), that federal courts should not interfere with pending state *criminal* proceedings except under extraordinary circumstances. Similarly, today's holding that the plaintiff in an action under 42 U.S.C. § 1983 may not maintain it without first exhausting state appellate procedures for review of an adverse state trial court decision is but an obvious first step toward discard of heretofore settled law that such actions may be maintained without first exhausting state judicial remedies.

Younger v. Harris was basically an application, in the context of the relation of federal courts to pending state criminal prosecutions, of "the basic doctrine of equity jurisprudence that courts of equity ... particularly should not act to restrain a criminal prosecution." "The maxim that equity will not enjoin a criminal prosecution summarizes centuries of weighty experience in Anglo–American law." But Younger v. Harris was also a decision enforcing "the national policy forbidding federal courts to stay or enjoin pending state court [criminal] proceedings except under special circumstances." For in decisions long antedating Younger v. Harris, the Court had invested the basic maxim with particular significance as a restraint upon federal equitable interference with pending state prosecutions. Not a showing of irreparable injury alone but of irreparable injury "both great and immediate" is required to justify federal injunctive relief against a pending state prosecution. Injury merely "incidental to every criminal proceeding brought lawfully and in good faith" is not irreparable injury that justifies an injunction. The line of decisions culminating in Younger v. Harris reflects this Court's longstanding recognition that equitable interference by federal courts with pending state prosecutions is incompatible in our federal system with the paramount role of the States in the definition of crimes and the enforcement of criminal laws. Federal-court noninterference with state prosecution of crimes protects against "the most sensitive source of friction between States and Nation."

The tradition, however, has been quite the opposite as respects federal injunctive interference with pending state civil proceedings. Even though legislation as far back as 1793 has provided in "seemingly uncompromising language," that a federal court "may not grant an injunction to stay proceedings in a State court" with specified exceptions, the Court has consistently engrafted exceptions upon the prohibition. Many, if not most, of those exceptions have been engrafted under the euphemism "implied." ... Indeed, when Congress became concerned that the Court's 1941 decision in Toucey v. New York Life Ins. Co., 314 U.S. 118, 62 S.Ct. 139, 86 L.Ed. 100, forecast the possibility that the 1793 Act might be enforced according to its literal terms, Congress amended the Act in 1948 "to restore 'the basic law as generally understood and interpreted prior to the Toucey decision.'"

Thus today's extension of Younger v. Harris turns the clock back and portends once again the resuscitation of the literal command of the 1793 Anti–Injunction Act—that the state courts should be free from interference by federal injunction even in civil cases. This not only would overrule some 18 decades of this Court's jurisprudence but would heedlessly flout Congress' evident purpose in enacting the 1948 amendment to acquiesce in that jurisprudence.

The extension also threatens serious prejudice to the potential federal-court plaintiff not present when the pending state proceeding is a criminal prosecution. That prosecution does not come into existence until completion of steps designed to safeguard him against spurious prosecution—arrest, charge, information, or indictment. In contrast, the civil proceeding, as in this case, comes into existence merely upon the filing of a complaint, whether or not well founded. To deny by fiat of this Court the potential federal plaintiff a federal forum in that circumstance is obviously to arm his adversary (here the public authorities) with an easily wielded weapon to strip him of a forum and a remedy that federal statutes were enacted to assure him. The Court does not escape this consequence by characterizing the state civil proceeding involved here as "in aid of and closely related to criminal statutes." The nuisance action was brought into being by the mere filing of the complaint in state court, and the untoward consequences for the federal plaintiff were thereby set in train without regard to the connection, if any, of the proceeding to the State's criminal laws.

Even if the extension of Younger v. Harris to pending state civil proceedings can be appropriate in any case, and I do not think it can be, it is plainly improper in the case of an action by a federal plaintiff, as in this case, grounded upon 42 U.S.C. § 1983. That statute serves a particular congressional objective long recognized and enforced by the Court. Today's extension will defeat that objective. After the War Between the States, "nationalism dominated political thought and brought with it congressional investiture of the federal judiciary with enormously increased powers." Section 1983 was enacted at that time as § 1 of the Civil Rights Act of 1871. That Act, and the Judiciary Act of 1875, which granted the federal courts general federal-question jurisdiction, completely altered Congress' pre-Civil War policy of relying on state courts to vindicate rights arising under the Constitution and federal laws. These statutes constituted the lower federal courts " 'the *primary* and powerful reliances for vindicating every right given by the Constitution, the laws, and treaties of the United States.' " The fact, standing alone, that state courts also must protect federal rights can never justify a refusal of federal courts to exercise that jurisdiction. This is true notwithstanding the possibility of review by this Court of state decisions for, "even when available by appeal rather than only by discretionary writ of certiorari [that possibility] is an inadequate substitute for the initial District Court determination ... to which the litigant is entitled in the federal courts."

Consistently with this congressional objective of the 1871 and 1875 Acts we held in Monroe v. Pape, 365 U.S. 167, 81 S.Ct. 473, 5 L.Ed.2d 492 (1961), that a federal plaintiff suing under § 1983 need not exhaust state administrative or judicial remedies before filing his action under § 1983 in federal district court. "The federal remedy is supplementary to the state remedy, and the latter need not be first sought and refused before the federal one is invoked." The extension today of Younger v. Harris to require exhaustion in an action under § 1983 drastically undercuts Monroe v. Pape and its numerous progeny—the mere filing of a complaint against a potential § 1983 litigant forces him to exhaust state remedies.

Mitchum v. Foster, holding that actions under § 1983 are excepted from the operation of the federal anti-injunction statute, 28 U.S.C. § 2283, is also undercut by today's extension of *Younger*. *Mitchum* canvassed the history of § 1983 and concluded that it extended "federal power in an attempt to remedy the state courts' failure to secure federal rights." *Mitchum* prompted the comment that if Younger v. Harris were extended to civil cases, "much of the rigidity of section 2283 would be reintroduced, the significance of *Mitchum* for those seeking relief from state civil proceedings would largely be destroyed, and the recognition of section 1983 as an exception to the Anti–Injunction Statute would have been a Pyrrhic victory."[4] Today's decision fulfills that gloomy prophecy. I therefore dissent from the remand and would reach the merits.

■ MR. JUSTICE DOUGLAS, while joining in the opinion of MR. JUSTICE BRENNAN, wishes to make clear that he adheres to the view he expressed in Younger v. Harris, that federal abstention from interference with state criminal prosecutions is inconsistent with demands of our federalism where important and overriding civil rights (such as those involved in the First Amendment) are about to be sacrificed.

NOTES

1. As the Supreme Court subsequently held in Allen v. McCurry, 449 U.S. 90, 101 S.Ct. 411, 66 L.Ed.2d 308 (1980), "the normal rules of collateral estoppel" do apply when plaintiffs in § 1983 actions attempt to relitigate matters previously decided in state criminal proceedings.

2. Since *Huffman*, the Court has held *Younger* applicable to civil cases in a number of different contexts. In two decisions, the Court has applied it to civil enforcement proceedings. See Moore v. Sims, 442 U.S. 415, 99 S.Ct. 2371, 60 L.Ed.2d 994 (1979)(child custody proceedings); Trainor v. Hernandez, 431 U.S. 434, 97 S.Ct. 1911, 52 L.Ed.2d 486 (1977) (action to recover welfare payments wrongly received). In the same vein, Middlesex County Ethics Committee v. Garden State Bar Association, 457 U.S. 423, 102 S.Ct. 2515, 73 L.Ed.2d 116 (1982), required abstention in the face of a state attorney disciplinary proceeding. In another group of cases, abstention was required to preclude federal interference with "orders ... in furtherance of the state courts' ability to perform their judicial functions." Pennzoil Co. v. Texaco, Inc., 481 U.S. 1, 107 S.Ct. 1519, 95 L.Ed.2d 1 (1987) (judgment lien and supersedeas bond); Juidice v. Vail, 430 U.S. 327, 97 S.Ct. 1211, 51 L.Ed.2d 376 (1977) (civil contempt order). Finally, there is Ohio Civil Rights Commission v. Dayton Christian Schools, Inc., the next principal case.

3. *Younger* itself suggests that abstention is only required when the constitutional claim can be raised in the pending state court proceeding. Pronouncing *Younger* abstention "appropriate unless state law clearly bars

4. Note, The Supreme Court, 1971 Term. 86 Harv.L.Rev. 50, 217–218 (1972).

the interposition of the constitutional claims," Moore v. Sims approved its application where some of those claims could only be raised in the state court by counterclaim. Beyond this, *Middlesex County Ethics Committee* deemed it sufficient that a state forum becomes available while the question of abstention is being litigated in the federal appellate courts.

Ohio Civil Rights Commission v. Dayton Christian Schools, Inc.

Supreme Court of the United States, 1986.
477 U.S. 619, 106 S.Ct. 2718, 91 L.Ed.2d 512.

■ JUSTICE REHNQUIST delivered the opinion of the Court.

[Appellee Dayton Christian Schools, Inc. (Dayton), a private nonprofit corporation that provides elementary and secondary education, requires that its teachers subscribe to a particular set of religious beliefs, including belief in the internal resolution of disputes through the "biblical chain of command." As a contractual condition of employment, teachers must agree to present any grievance to their immediate supervisor and to acquiesce in the final authority of Dayton's board of directors, rather than to pursue a remedy in civil court. After a pregnant teacher was told that her employment contract would not be renewed because of Dayton's religious doctrine that mothers should stay home with their preschool age children, she contacted an attorney, who threatened Dayton with litigation under state and federal sex discrimination laws if it did not agree to rehire the teacher for the coming school year. Dayton then rescinded its nonrenewal decision, but terminated the teacher because of her violation of the internal dispute resolution doctrine. The teacher then filed a charge with appellant Ohio Civil Rights Commission, alleging that under Ohio statutes Dayton's original nonrenewal decision constituted unlawful sex discrimination and its termination decision unlawfully penalized her for asserting her rights. Ultimately, the Commission initiated administrative proceedings against Dayton, which answered the complaint by asserting that the First Amendment prevented the Commission from exercising jurisdiction over it since its actions had been taken pursuant to sincerely held religious beliefs. While the administrative proceedings were pending, Dayton and others (also appellees here) filed this action in Federal District Court, seeking an injunction against the state administrative proceedings on the ground that any investigation of Dayton's hiring process or any imposition of sanctions for its nonrenewal or termination decisions would violate the Religion Clauses of the First Amendment. Without addressing the commission's argument that the court should abstain from exercising its jurisdiction, the District Court refused to issue an injunction, holding, *inter alia*, that the Commission's proposed action would not violate the First and Fourteenth Amendments. The Court of Appeals reversed, holding that the Commission's exercise of jurisdiction would violate both the Free Exercise and the Establishment Clauses of the First Amendment.]

We conclude that the District Court should have abstained from adjudicating this case under Younger v. Harris and later cases. The Commission urged such abstention in the District Court, and on oral argument here. Dayton has filed a post argument brief urging that the Commission has waived any claim to abstention because it had stipulated in the District Court that that court had jurisdiction of the action. We think, however, that this argument misconceives the nature of *Younger* abstention. It does not arise from lack of jurisdiction in the District Court, but from strong policies counseling against the exercise of such jurisdiction where particular kinds of state proceedings have already been commenced. A State may of course voluntarily submit to federal jurisdiction even though it might have had a tenable claim for abstention. But in each of these cases the State expressly urged this Court or the District Court to proceed to an adjudication of the constitutional merits. We think there was no similar consent or waiver here, and we therefore address the issue of whether the District Court should have abstained from deciding the case.

In [*Younger*], we held that a federal court should not enjoin a pending state criminal proceeding except in the very unusual situation that an injunction is necessary to prevent great and immediate irreparable injury. We justified our decision both on equitable principles, and on the "more vital consideration" of the proper respect for the fundamental role of States in our federal system. Because of our concerns for comity and federalism, we thought that it was

> "perfectly natural for our cases to repeat time and time again that the *normal* thing to do when federal courts are asked to enjoin pending proceedings in state courts is not to issue such injunctions."

We have since recognized that our concern for comity and federalism is equally applicable to certain other pending state proceedings. We have applied the *Younger* principle to civil proceedings in which important state interests are involved. We have also applied it to state administrative proceedings in which important state interests are vindicated, so long as in the course of those proceedings the federal plaintiff would have a full and fair opportunity to litigate his constitutional claim. We stated in Gibson v. Berryhill, 411 U.S. 564, 93 S.Ct. 1689, 36 L.Ed.2d 488 (1973), that "administrative proceedings looking toward the revocation of a license to practice medicine may in proper circumstances command the respect due court proceedings." Similarly, we have held that federal courts should refrain from enjoining lawyer disciplinary proceedings initiated by state ethics committees if the proceedings are within the appellate jurisdiction of the appropriate State Supreme Court. Middlesex County Ethics Committee v. Garden State Bar Assn., 457 U.S. 423, 102 S.Ct. 2515, 73 L.Ed.2d 116 (1982). Because we found that the administrative proceedings in *Middlesex* were "judicial in nature" from the outset, it was not essential to the decision that they had progressed to state court review by the time we heard the federal injunction case.[2]

---

2. . . .

The application of the *Younger* principle to pending state administrative proceedings is fully consistent with Patsy v. Florida Board of Regents, 457 U.S. 496, 102 S.Ct. 2557, 73 L.Ed.2d 172 (1982), which holds that litigants need not exhaust their administrative reme- dies prior to bringing a § 1983 suit in federal court. Unlike *Patsy*, the administrative proceedings here are coercive rather than remedial, began before any substantial advancement in the federal action took place, and involve an important state interest.

We think the principles enunciated in these cases govern the present one. We have no doubt that the elimination of prohibited sex discrimination is a sufficiently important state interest to bring the present case within the ambit of the cited authorities. We also have no reason to doubt that Dayton will receive an adequate opportunity to raise its constitutional claims. Dayton contends that the mere exercise of jurisdiction over it by the state administrative body violates its First Amendment rights. But we have repeatedly rejected the argument that a constitutional attack on state procedures themselves "automatically vitiates the adequacy of those procedures for purposes of the *Younger–Huffman* line of cases." Even religious schools cannot claim to be wholly free from some state regulation. We therefore think that however Dayton's constitutional claim should be decided on the merits, the Commission violates no constitutional rights by merely investigating the circumstances of [the teacher's] discharge in this case, if only to ascertain whether the ascribed religious-based reason was in fact the reason for the discharge.

Dayton also contends that the administrative proceedings do not afford the opportunity to level constitutional challenges against the potential sanctions for the alleged sex discrimination. In its reply brief in this Court, the Commission cites several rulings to demonstrate that religious justifications for otherwise illegal conduct are considered by it. Dayton in turn relies on a decision of the Supreme Court of Ohio in which that court held that a local zoning commission could not consider constitutional claims. But even if Ohio law is such that the Commission may not consider the constitutionality of the statute under which it operates, it would seem an unusual doctrine, and one not supported by the cited case, to say that the Commission could not construe its own statutory mandate in the light of federal constitutional principles. In any event, it is sufficient under Middlesex that constitutional claims may be raised in state-court judicial review of the administrative proceeding. Section 4112.06 of Ohio Rev.Code Ann. (1980) provides that any "respondent claiming to be aggrieved by a final order of the commission . . . may obtain judicial review thereof." Dayton cites us to no Ohio authority indicating that this provision does not authorize judicial review of claims that agency action violates the United States Constitution.

The judgment of the Court of Appeals is therefore reversed and the case remanded for further proceedings consistent with this opinion.

It is so ordered.

■ JUSTICE STEVENS, with whom JUSTICE BRENNAN, JUSTICE MARSHALL, and JUSTICE BLACKMUN join, concurring in the judgment.

. . . .

Like the majority, I agree with the District Court that neither the investigation of certain charges nor the conduct of a hearing on those charges is prohibited by the First Amendment: "the Commission violates no constitutional rights by merely investigating the circumstances of Hoskinson's discharge in this case, if only to ascertain whether the ascribed religious-based reason was in fact the reason for the discharge."

I further agree with the District Court that any challenge to a possibly intrusive remedy is premature at this juncture. As the majority points out, the Commission recognizes religious justifications for conduct that might otherwise be illegal.... It bears emphasis that the Commission dismissed these complaints only *after* investigating charges of discrimination, finding probable cause that the statute had been violated, and holding a hearing on the complaint. It therefore follows that the Commission's finding of probable cause and decision to schedule a hearing in this case does not also mean that the Commission intends to impose *any* sanction, let alone a sanction in derogation of the First Amendment's Religion Clauses. In view of this fact, the District Court was entirely correct in concluding that appellees' constitutional challenge to the remedial provisions of the Ohio statute is not ripe for review. Accordingly, I concur in the judgment.[5]

New Orleans Public Service, Inc. v. Council of City of New Orleans

Supreme Court of the United States, 1989.
491 U.S. 350, 109 S.Ct. 2506, 105 L.Ed.2d 298.

■ JUSTICE SCALIA delivered the opinion of the Court.

In Nantahala Power & Light Co. v. Thornburg, 476 U.S. 953, 106 S.Ct. 2349, 90 L.Ed.2d 943 (1986), we held that for purposes of setting intrastate retail rates a State may not differ from the Federal Energy Regulatory Commission's allocations of wholesale power by imposing its own judgment of what would be just and reasonable. Last Term, in Mississippi Power & Light Co. v. Mississippi ex rel. Moore, 487 U.S. 354, 108 S.Ct. 2428, 101 L.Ed.2d 322 (1988), we held that FERC's allocation of the $3 billion-plus cost of the Grand Gulf 1 nuclear reactor among the operating companies that jointly agreed to finance its construction and operation pre-empted Mississippi's inquiry into the prudence of a utility retailer's decision to participate in the joint venture. Today we confront once again a legal issue arising from the question of who must pay for Grand Gulf 1. Here the state ratemaking authority deferred to FERC's implicit finding that New Orleans Public Service, Inc.'s decision to participate in the Grand Gulf venture was reasonable, but determined that the costs incurred thereby should not be completely reimbursed because, it asserted, the utility's management was negligent in failing later to diversify its supply portfolio by selling a portion of its Grand Gulf power. Whether the State's decision to provide less than full reimbursement for the FERC-allocated wholesale costs conflicts with

---

5. I do not agree with the majority that the doctrine of abstention associated with Younger v. Harris, 401 U.S. 37, 91 S.Ct. 746, 27 L.Ed.2d 669 (1971), required the District Court to dismiss appellees' complaint. That disposition would presumably deny the School a federal forum to adjudicate the constitutionality of a provisional administrative remedy, such as reinstatement pending resolution of the complainant's charges, even though the constitutional issues have become ripe for review by the Commission's entry of a coercive order and the Commission refuses to address the merits of the constitutional claims. *Younger* abstention has never been applied to subject a federal-court plaintiff to an allegedly unconstitutional state administrative order when the constitutional challenge to that order can be asserted, if at all, only in state-court judicial review of the administrative proceeding.

our holdings in *Nantahala* and *Mississippi Power & Light* is not at issue in this case. Rather, we address the threshold question whether the District Court, which the utility petitioned for declaratory and injunctive relief from the state ratemaking authority's order, properly abstained from exercising jurisdiction in deference to the state review process.

I

. . . Petitioner New Orleans Public Service, Inc. (NOPSI), a producer, wholesaler, and retailer of electricity that provides retail electrical service to the city of New Orleans, is one of four wholly-owned operating subsidiaries of Middle South Utilities, Inc. Middle South operates an integrated "power pool" in which each of the four operating companies transmits produced electricity to a central dispatch center and draws back from the dispatch center the power it needs to meet customer demand. In 1974, NOPSI and its fellow operating companies entered a contract with Middle South Energy, Inc. (MSE), another wholly-owned Middle South subsidiary, whereby the operating companies agreed to finance MSE's construction and operation of two 1250 megawatt nuclear reactors, Grand Gulf 1 and 2, in return for the right to the reactors' electrical output. The estimated cost of completing the two reactors was $1.2 billion.

During the late 1970s, consumer demand turned out to be far lower than expected, and regulatory delays, enhanced construction requirements, and high inflation led to spiraling costs. As a result, construction of Grand Gulf 2 was suspended, and the cost of completing Grand Gulf 1 alone eventually exceeded $3 billion. Not surprisingly, the cost of the electricity produced by the reactor greatly exceeded that of power generated by Middle South's conventional facilities.

Acting pursuant to its exclusive regulatory authority over interstate wholesale power transactions, FERC conducted extensive proceedings to determine "just and reasonable" rates for Grand Gulf 1 power and to prescribe a "just, reasonable, and nondiscriminatory" allocation of Grand Gulf's costs and output. In June 1985, the Commission issued a final order, in which it concluded that, because the planned nuclear reactors had been designed "to meet overall System needs and objectives," the Middle South subsidiaries should pay for the Grand Gulf project "roughly in proportion to each company's share of System demand." The Commission allocated 17 percent of Grand Gulf costs (approximately $13 million per month) to NOPSI, rejecting Middle South's proposal of 29.8 percent as well as the 9 percent figure favored by the respondent here, the New Orleans City Council.

"Although it did not expressly discuss the 'prudence' of constructing Grand Gulf and bringing it on line, FERC implicitly accepted the uncontroverted testimony of [Middle South] executives who explained why they believed the decisions to construct and to complete Grand Gulf 1 were sound, and approved the finding that 'continuing construction of Grand Gulf Unit No. 1 was prudent because Middle South's executives believed Grand Gulf would enable the Middle South system to diversify its base load fuel mix and, it was projected, at the same time, produce power for a total cost (capacity and energy) which would be less than existing alternatives on the system.'"

When NOPSI sought from the New Orleans City Council—the local ratemaking body with final authority over the utility's retail rates—a rate increase to cover the increase in wholesale rates resulting from FERC's allocation of Grand Gulf costs, the Council denied an immediate rate adjustment, explaining that a public hearing was necessary to explore " 'the legality and prudency [*sic*] of the [contracts relating to Grand Gulf 1, and] the prudency and reasonableness of the said expenses.' " ...

. . . .

By resolution of October 10, 1985 ... the Council initiated an investigation into the prudence of NOPSI's involvement in Grand Gulf 1. Resolution R–85–636 stated the Council's intention to examine all aspects of NOPSI's relationship with Grand Gulf, including NOPSI's " 'efforts to minimize its total cost exposure for the purchase,' " and Grand Gulf's " 'impact on its other power supply opportunities,' " " 'for the purpose of determining what portion, if any, of NOPSI's Grand Gulf 1 expense shall be assumed by [NOPSI's] shareholders.' " The resolution specifically provided, however, that in setting the appropriate retail rate, the Council would " 'not seek to invalidate any of the agreements surrounding Grand Gulf 1 or to order NOPSI to pay MSE a rate other than that approved by the FERC.' "

. . . .

The Council completed its prudence review on February 4, 1988, and immediately entered a final order disallowing $135 million of the Grand Gulf costs. The order was based on the Council's determinations that "NOPSI's ... oversight and review of its Grand Gulf obligation ... was uncritical and severely deficient" and that NOPSI acted imprudently in failing to reduce the risk of its Grand Gulf commitment, in the wake of the Three Mile Island nuclear incident in March 1979, "by selling all or part of its share off-system."

Upon receipt of the Council's decree, NOPSI turned once again to the District Court for the Eastern District of Louisiana, seeking declaratory and injunctive relief on the ground that, in light of this Court's recent decision in Nantahala Power & Light Co. v. Thornburg, 476 U.S. 953, 106 S.Ct. 2349, 90 L.Ed.2d 943 (1986), the Council's rate order was pre-empted by federal law. Although the District Court expressed considerable doubt as to the merits of the Council's position on the pre-emption question, it concluded that, notwithstanding *Nantahala,* it should still abstain from deciding the suit.

Anticipating that the District Court might again abstain, NOPSI had filed a petition for review of the Council's Order in the Civil District Court for the Parish of Orleans, Louisiana. As filed, NOPSI's petition raised only state-law claims and federal due process and takings claims, but NOPSI informed the state court by letter that it would amend to raise its federal pre-emption claim if the federal court once again dismissed its complaint. When that happened, it did so.

In the parallel federal proceedings, the Fifth Circuit affirmed the District Court's dismissal, agreeing ... that *Burford* and *Younger* abstention applied....

II

Before proceeding to the merits of the abstention issues, it bears emphasis that the Council does not dispute the District Court's *jurisdiction* to decide NOPSI's pre-emption claim. Our cases have long supported the proposition that federal courts lack the authority to abstain from the exercise of jurisdiction that has been conferred.... Underlying these assertions is the undisputed constitutional principle that Congress, and not the judiciary, defines the scope of federal jurisdiction within the constitutionally permissible bounds.

That principle does not eliminate, however, and the categorical assertions based upon it do not call into question, the federal courts' discretion in determining whether to grant certain types of relief—a discretion that was part of the common-law background against which the statutes conferring jurisdiction were enacted. Thus, there are some classes of cases in which the withholding of authorized equitable relief because of undue interference with state proceedings is "the normal thing to do." We have carefully defined, however, the areas in which such "abstention" is permissible, and it remains " 'the exception, not the rule.' " As recently as last Term we described the federal courts' obligation to adjudicate claims within their jurisdiction as " 'virtually unflagging.' "

With these principles in mind, we address the question whether the District Court, relying on Burford v. Sun Oil Co., 319 U.S. 315, 63 S.Ct. 1098, 87 L.Ed. 1424 (1943), and Younger v. Harris properly declined to exercise its jurisdiction in the present case. While we acknowledge that "[t]he various types of abstention are not rigid pigeonholes into which federal courts must try to fit cases," the policy considerations supporting *Burford* and *Younger* are sufficiently distinct to justify independent analyses.

A

In *Burford,* a Federal District Court sitting in equity was confronted with a Fourteenth Amendment challenge to the reasonableness of the Texas Railroad Commission's grant of an oil drilling permit. The constitutional challenge was of minimal federal importance, involving solely the question whether the Commission had properly applied Texas' complex oil and gas conservation regulations. Because of the intricacy and importance of the regulatory scheme, Texas had created a centralized system of judicial review of Commission orders, which "permit[ted] the state courts, like the Railroad Commission itself, to acquire a specialized knowledge" of the regulations and industry. We found the state courts' review of Commission decisions "expeditious and adequate," and, because the exercise of equitable jurisdiction by comparatively unsophisticated Federal District Courts alongside state court review had repeatedly led to "[d]elay, misunderstanding of local law, and needless federal conflict with the state policy," we concluded that "a sound respect for the independence of state action requir[ed] the federal equity court to stay its hand."

. . . .

From these cases, and others on which they relied, we have distilled the principle now commonly referred to as the *"Burford* doctrine." Where timely and adequate state court review is available, a federal court sitting in equity must decline to interfere with the proceedings or orders of state administrative agencies: (1) when there are "difficult questions of state law bearing on policy problems of substantial public import whose importance transcends the result in the case then at bar"; or (2) where the "exercise of federal review of the question in a case and in similar cases would be disruptive of state efforts to establish a coherent policy with respect to a matter of substantial public concern."

The present case does not involve a state law claim, nor even an assertion that the federal claims are "in any way entangled in a skein of state law that must be untangled before the federal case can proceed." The Fifth Circuit acknowledged as much in *NOPSI I,* but found "the absence of a state law claim . . . not fatal" because, it thought, "[t]he motivating force behind *Burford* abstention is . . . a reluctance to intrude into state proceedings where there exists a complex state regulatory system." Finding that this case involved a complex regulatory scheme of "paramount local concern and a matter which demands local administrative expertise," it held that the District Court appropriately applied *Burford.*

While *Burford* is concerned with protecting complex state administrative processes from undue federal interference, it does not require abstention whenever there exists such a process, or even in all cases where there is a "potential for conflict" with state regulatory law or policy. Here, NOPSI's primary claim is that the Council is prohibited by federal law from refusing to provide reimbursement for FERC-allocated wholesale costs. Unlike a claim that a state agency has misapplied its lawful authority or has failed to take into consideration or properly weigh relevant state-law factors, federal adjudication of this sort of pre-emption claim would not disrupt the State's attempt to ensure uniformity in the treatment of an "essentially local problem."

. . . [I]n the case at bar, no inquiry beyond the four corners of the Council's retail rate order is needed to determine whether it is facially pre-empted by FERC's allocative decree and relevant provisions of the Federal Power Act. Such an inquiry would not unduly intrude into the processes of state government or undermine the State's ability to maintain desired uniformity. It may, of course, result in an injunction against enforcement of the rate order, but "there is . . . no doctrine requiring abstention merely because resolution of a federal question may result in the overturning of a state policy."

It is true that in its initial complaint, NOPSI asserted, as an alternative to its facial pre-emption challenge, that the rate order's nominal emphasis on NOPSI's failure in 1979–1980 to diversify its power supply by selling off a portion of its Grand Gulf allocation was merely a cover for the determination that the original Grand Gulf investment was itself unwise.

Unlike the facial challenge, this claim cannot be resolved on the face of the rate order, because it hinges largely on the plausibility of the Council's finding that NOPSI should have, and could have, diversified its supply portfolio and thereby lowered its average wholesale costs. Analysis of this pretext claim requires an inquiry into industry practice, wholesale rates, and power availability during the relevant time period, an endeavor that demands some level of industry-specific expertise. But since, as the facts of this case amply demonstrate, wholesale electricity is not bought and sold within a predominantly local market, it does *not* demand significant familiarity with, and will not disrupt state resolution of, distinctively local regulatory facts or policies. The principles underlying *Burford* are therefore not implicated.

B

. . . .

The state-court proceeding at issue here is not a criminal prosecution, and one of the issues in the present case is whether the principle of *Younger* can properly be extended to this type of suit. NOPSI argues that that issue does not have to be reached, however, for several reasons. First, NOPSI argues that *Younger* does not require abstention in the face of a substantial claim that the challenged state action is completely pre-empted by federal law. Such a claim, NOPSI contends, calls into question the prerequisite of *Younger* abstention that the State have a legitimate, substantial interest in its pending proceedings. Thus, it contends, a district court presented with a pre-emption-based request for equitable relief should take a quick look at the merits; and if upon that look the claim appears substantial, the court should endeavor to resolve it.

We disagree. There is no greater federal interest in enforcing the supremacy of federal statutes than in enforcing the supremacy of explicit constitutional guaranties, and constitutional challenges to state action, no less than pre-emption-based challenges call into question the legitimacy of the State's interest in its proceedings reviewing or enforcing that action. Yet it is clear that the mere assertion of a substantial constitutional challenge to state action will not alone compel the exercise of federal jurisdiction. That is so because when we inquire into the substantiality of the State's interest in its proceedings we do not look narrowly to its interest in the *outcome* of the particular case—which could arguably be offset by a substantial federal interest in the opposite outcome. Rather, what we look to is the importance of the generic proceedings to the state. . . . Because pre-emption-based challenges merit a similar focus, the appropriate question here is not whether Louisiana has a substantial, legitimate interest in reducing NOPSI's retail rate below that necessary to recover its wholesale costs, but whether it has a substantial, legitimate interest in regulating intrastate retail rates. It clearly does. "[T]he regulation of utilities is one of the most important of the functions traditionally associated with the police power of the States."

NOPSI attempts to avoid this conclusion by stressing that it challenges not only the result of the Council's deliberations, but the very right of the Council to conduct those deliberations. (This argument assumes, of course, that enjoining the Louisiana state courts can be equated with enjoining the Council proceedings, a point we shall address in due course.) But that is simply not true, if the reference to "the Council's deliberations" is as generic as it should be. NOPSI does not deny that the State has an interest affirmatively protected by federal law in conducting proceedings to set intrastate retail electricity rates; rather, it contends that under the particular facts of the present case its FERC-allocated wholesale costs are not a proper subject for such proceedings. That is no different from the contention in *Younger* that the defendant's violation of the particular (allegedly unconstitutional) state statute was not a proper subject of prosecution. In other words, this argument of NOPSI ultimately reduces once again to insistence upon too narrow an analytical focus.

NOPSI's second argument to the effect that abstention is improper even assuming the state proceedings here are the sort to which *Younger* applies rests upon the principle that abstention is not appropriate if the federal plaintiff will "suffer irreparable injury" absent equitable relief. Irreparable injury may possibly be established, *Younger* suggested, by a showing that the challenged state statute is " 'flagrantly and patently violative of express constitutional prohibitions....' " ... NOPSI asserts that *Younger*'s posited exception for state statutes "flagrantly and patently violative of express constitutional prohibitions" ought to apply equally to state proceedings and orders flagrantly and patently violative of federal pre-emption (which is unlawful only because it violates the express constitutional prescription of the Supremacy Clause). Thus, NOPSI argues, even if a *substantial* claim of federal pre-emption is not sufficient to render abstention inappropriate, at least a *facially conclusive* claim is. Perhaps so. But we do not have to decide the matter here, since the proceeding and order at issue do not meet that description. The Council has not sought directly to regulate interstate wholesale rates; nor has it questioned the validity of the FERC-prescribed allocation of power within the Grand Gulf system, or the FERC-prescribed wholesale rates; nor has it reexamined the prudence of NOPSI's agreement to participate in Grand Gulf 1 in the first place. Rather, the Council maintains that it has examined the prudence of NOPSI's failure, after the risks of nuclear power became apparent, to diversify its supply portfolio, and that finding that failure negligent, it has taken the normal ratemaking step of making NOPSI's shareholders rather than the ratepayers bear the consequences. Nothing in this is directly or even indirectly foreclosed by the federal statute, the regulations implementing it, or the case law applying it. There may well be reason to doubt the Council's necessary factual finding that NOPSI would have saved money had it diversified. But we cannot conclusively say it is wrong without further factual inquiry—and what requires further factual inquiry can hardly be deemed "flagrantly" unlawful for purposes of a threshold abstention determination.

We conclude, therefore, that NOPSI's challenge must stand or fall upon the answer to the question whether the Louisiana court action is the type of proceeding to which *Younger* applies. Viewed in isolation, it plainly is not. Although our concern for comity and federalism has led us to expand the protection of *Younger* beyond state criminal prosecutions, to civil enforcement proceedings, and even to civil proceedings involving certain orders that are uniquely in furtherance of the state courts' ability to perform their judicial functions, it has never been suggested that *Younger* requires abstention in deference to a state judicial proceeding reviewing legislative or executive action. Such a broad abstention requirement would make a mockery of the rule that only exceptional circumstances justify a federal court's refusal to decide a case in deference to the States.

In asserting that *Younger* is applicable, however, respondents focus not upon the Louisiana court action in isolation, but upon that action as a mere continuation of the Council proceeding. Their contention is that "[t]he Council's own ratemaking and prudence inquiry, even though complete, constitutes an 'ongoing proceeding' because it is subject to state judicial review." The proper question, they contend, is whether the *Council proceeding* qualified for *Younger* treatment—because if it did, the proceeding is not complete until judicial review is concluded. Respondents argue by analogy to the treatment of court proceedings, for *Younger* purposes, as an uninterruptible whole. When, in a proceeding to which *Younger* applies, a state trial court has entered judgment, the losing party cannot, of course, pursue equitable remedies in federal district court while concurrently challenging the trial court's judgment on appeal. For *Younger* purposes, the State's trial-and-appeals process is treated as a unitary system, and for a federal court to disrupt its integrity by intervening in mid-process would demonstrate a lack of respect for the State as sovereign. For the same reason, a party may not procure federal intervention by terminating the state judicial process prematurely—forgoing the state appeal to attack the trial court's judgment in federal court. "[A] necessary concomitant of *Younger* is that a party [wishing to contest in federal court the judgment of a state judicial tribunal] must exhaust his state appellate remedies before seeking relief in the District Court." Respondents urge that these principles apply equally where the initial adjudicatory tribunal is an agency—*i.e.,* that the litigation, from agency through courts, is to be viewed as a unitary process that should not be disrupted, so that federal intervention is no more permitted at the conclusion of the administrative stage than during it.

We will assume, without deciding, that this is correct.[4] Respondents' case for abstention still requires, however, that the *Council proceeding* be the sort of proceeding entitled to *Younger* treatment. We think it is not. While we have expanded *Younger* beyond criminal proceedings, and even beyond proceedings in courts, we have never extended it to proceedings

---

4. In Ohio Civil Rights Comm'n v. Dayton Christian Schools, Inc., 477 U.S. 619, 106 S.Ct. 2718, 91 L.Ed.2d 512 (1986), we held that the *Younger* doctrine prevented an injunction against an *ongoing* sex-discrimination proceeding before the Ohio Civil Rights Commission. The only other decision of ours arguably applying *Younger* to an administrative proceeding, Middlesex County Ethics Comm. v. Garden State Bar Assn., 457 U.S. 423, 102 S.Ct. 2515, 73 L.Ed.2d 116 (1982), similarly involved a situation in which the proceeding was not yet at an end. The fact that *Dayton Christian Schools* relied, as an alternative argument, upon the fact that the federal challenge could be made upon appeal to the state courts suggests, perhaps, that an administrative proceeding to which *Younger* applies cannot be challenged in federal court even after the administrative action has become final. But we have never squarely faced the question.

that are not "judicial in nature." The Council's proceedings in the present case were not judicial in nature.

. . . .

. . . Since the state-court review is not an extension of the legislative process, NOPSI's pre-emption claim was ripe for federal review when the Council's order was entered.

As a challenge to completed legislative action, NOPSI's suit represents neither the interference with ongoing judicial proceedings against which *Younger* was directed, nor the interference with an ongoing legislative process against which our ripeness holding in Prentis v. Atlantic Coast Line Co., 211 U.S. 210, 29 S.Ct. 67, 53 L.Ed. 150 (1908), was directed. It is, insofar as our policies of federal comity are concerned, no different in substance from a facial challenge to an allegedly unconstitutional statute or zoning ordinance—which we would assuredly not require to be brought in state courts. It is true, of course, that the federal court's disposition of such a case may well affect, or for practical purposes pre-empt, a future—or, as in the present circumstances, even a pending—state-court action. But there is no doctrine that the availability or even the pendency of state judicial proceedings excludes the federal courts. Viewed, as it should be, as no more than a state-court challenge to completed legislative action, the Louisiana suit comes within none of the exceptions that *Younger* and later cases have established.

For the reasons stated, the judgment of the Court of Appeals is reversed and the case remanded for further proceedings consistent with this opinion.

So ordered.

■ JUSTICE BRENNAN, with whom JUSTICE MARSHALL joins, concurring.

I join the Court's opinion. I continue to adhere to my view, however, that the abstention doctrine of Younger v. Harris is in general inapplicable to civil proceedings.

■ CHIEF JUSTICE REHNQUIST, concurring in Parts I and II–B and concurring in the judgment.

I agree with the Court that our prior cases extending *Younger* beyond criminal prosecutions to civil proceedings have limited its application to proceedings which are "judicial in nature," and that, under our long-standing characterization of the distinction between "judicial" and "legislative" proceedings, the Council ratemaking proceedings at issue here were not judicial in nature. Under these circumstances, I agree that *Younger* abstention is inappropriate, despite the pendency of state-court review of the Council's rate-making order. Nothing in the Court's opinion curtails our prior application of *Younger* to certain administrative proceedings which *are* "judicial in nature"; nor does it alter our prior case law indicating that such proceedings should be regarded as "ongoing" for the purposes of *Younger* abstention until state appellate review is completed, see *Dayton Christian Schools*. With this understanding, I join the portion of the Court's opinion holding that *Younger* abstention is inappropriate here.

I agree with the Court's conclusion that *Burford* abstention is inappropriate on the facts of this case. But I would not foreclose the possibility of *Burford* abstention in a case like this had the State consolidated review of the orders of local ratemaking bodies in a specialized state court with power to hear a federal pre-emption claim. Accordingly, I concur only in the judgment as to *Burford* abstention.

■ JUSTICE BLACKMUN, concurring in the judgment.

I concur in the judgment in this case. I also agree with what I take to be the core of the majority's reasoning: in the posture of this case, a legislative proceeding ended when the Council entered its ratemaking order; after that point, adjudication in the District Court would not have interfered with any *ongoing* proceeding, be it judicial, quasi-legislative, or legislative. I find, however, that the majority's understanding of *Burford* abstention is much narrower than my own in respects not relevant to the disposition of this case, and that there is considerable tension between its discussion of the nature of the State's interests in the *Burford* context and its discussion of the State's interests in the *Younger* context. Furthermore, I am not entirely persuaded that this Court's decisions applying *Younger* abstention to administrative proceedings that are judicial in nature leave open the question whether abstention must continue through the judicial review process. In my view, the majority's observations on these questions are not necessary to the result or to the legal standard the majority has adopted.

NOTES

1. A third federal abstention doctrine was explained by the Supreme Court in the following terms:

> In Railroad Comm'n v. Pullman Co., 312 U.S. 496, 61 S.Ct. 643, 85 L.Ed. 971 (1941), this Court held that federal courts should abstain from decision when difficult and unsettled questions of state law must be resolved before a substantial federal constitutional question can be decided. By abstaining in such cases, federal courts will avoid both unnecessary adjudication of federal questions and "needless friction with state policies...." However, federal courts need not abstain on *Pullman* grounds when a state statute is not "fairly subject to an interpretation which will render unnecessary" adjudication of the federal constitutional question. *Pullman* abstention is limited to uncertain questions of state law because "[a]bstention from the exercise of federal jurisdiction is the exception, not the rule."

Hawaii Housing Authority v. Midkiff, 467 U.S. 229, 236, 104 S.Ct. 2321, 2327, 81 L.Ed.2d 186 (1984). Unlike abstention under *Younger* and *Burford, Pullman* abstention generally results in the stay, rather than the dismissal, of the federal action pending the outcome of state court proceedings.

2. Yet another doctrine, whose aim is the avoidance of duplicative proceedings, may also counsel the refusal of a federal court to decide a case when the same issues are pending in the state courts. This doctrine made

its first appearance in the Supreme Court in Colorado River Water Conservation District v. United States, 424 U.S. 800, 96 S.Ct. 1236, 47 L.Ed.2d 483 (1976), in which the Court made the following comments:

> . . . Generally, as between state and federal courts, the rule is that "the pendency of an action in the state court is no bar to proceedings concerning the same matter in the Federal court having jurisdiction. . . ." As between federal district courts, however, though no precise rule has evolved, the general principle is to avoid duplicative litigation. This difference in general approach between state-federal concurrent jurisdiction and wholly federal concurrent jurisdiction stems from the virtually unflagging obligation of the federal courts to exercise the jurisdiction given them. Given this obligation, and the absence of weightier considerations of constitutional adjudication and state-federal relations, the circumstances permitting the dismissal of a federal suit due to the presence of a concurrent state proceeding for reasons of wise judicial administration are considerably more limited than the circumstances appropriate for abstention. The former circumstances, though exceptional, do nevertheless exist.

> It has been held, for example, that the court first assuming jurisdiction over property may exercise that jurisdiction to the exclusion of other courts. . . . In assessing the appropriateness of dismissal in the event of an exercise of concurrent jurisdiction, a federal court may also consider such factors as the inconvenience of the federal forum, the desirability of avoiding piecemeal litigation, and the order in which jurisdiction was obtained by the concurrent forums. No one factor is necessarily determinative; a carefully considered judgment taking into account both the obligation to exercise jurisdiction and the combination of factors counselling against that exercise is required. Only the clearest of justifications will warrant dismissal.

In Moses H. Cone Memorial Hospital v. Mercury Construction Corp., 460 U.S. 1, 103 S.Ct. 927, 74 L.Ed.2d 765 (1983), the Court identified two other factors that are important to determining whether such "exceptional" circumstances exist: whether the case is governed by state or federal law and "the probable inadequacy of the state-court proceeding to protect [the federal plaintiff's] rights."

Rizzo v. Goode

Supreme Court of the United States, 1976.
423 U.S. 362, 96 S.Ct. 598, 46 L.Ed.2d 561.

■ MR. JUSTICE REHNQUIST delivered the opinion of the Court.

The District Court for the Eastern District of Pennsylvania, after parallel trials of separate actions filed in 1970, entered an order in 1973 requiring petitioners "to submit to [the District] Court for its approval a comprehensive program for improving the handling of citizen complaints alleging police misconduct" in accordance with a comprehensive opinion filed together with the order. The proposed program, negotiated between petitioners and respondents for the purpose of complying with the order, was incorporated six months later into a final judgment. Petitioner City Police Commissioner was thereby required, *inter alia,* to put into force a directive governing the manner by which citizens' complaints against police officers should henceforth be handled by the department. The Court of Appeals for the Third Circuit, upholding the District Court's finding that the existing procedures for handling citizen complaints were "inadequate," affirmed the District Court's choice of equitable relief: "The revisions were ... ordered because they appeared to have the potential for prevention of future police misconduct." We granted certiorari to consider petitioners' claims that the judgment of the District Court represents an unwarranted intrusion by the federal judiciary into the discretionary authority committed to them by state and local law to perform their official functions. We find ourselves substantially in agreement with these claims, and we therefore reverse the judgment of the Court of Appeals.

[handwritten margin notes: "Petitioner claims." and "— Holding."]

I

The central thrust of respondents' efforts in the two trials was set to lay a foundation for equitable intervention, in one degree or another, because of an assertedly pervasive pattern of illegal and unconstitutional mistreatment by police officers. This mistreatment was said to have been directed against minority citizens in particular and against all Philadelphia residents in general. The named individual and group respondents were certified to represent these two classes. The principal petitioners here—the Mayor, the City Managing Director, and the Police Commissioner—were charged with conduct ranging from express authorization or encouragement of this mistreatment to failure to act in a manner so as to assure that it would not recur in the future.

[handwritten margin note: "original complaint in lower court."]

Hearing some 250 witnesses during 21 days of hearings, the District Court was faced with a staggering amount of evidence; each of the 40–odd incidents might alone have been the *pièce de résistance* of a short, separate trial. The District Court carefully and conscientiously resolved often sharply conflicting testimony, and made detailed findings of fact, which both sides now accept, with respect to eight of the incidents presented by the *Goode* respondents and with respect to 28 of those presented by *COPPAR*.

The principal antagonists in the eight incidents recounted in *Goode* were Officers DeFazio and D'Amico, members of the city's "Highway Patrol" force. They were not named as parties to the action. The District Court found the conduct of these officers to be violative of the constitutional rights of the citizen complainants in three of the incidents, and further found that complaints to the police Board of Inquiry had resulted in one case in a relatively mild five-day suspension and in another case a conclusion that there was no basis for disciplinary action.

In only two of the 28 incidents recounted in *COPPAR* (which ranged in time from October 1969 to October 1970) did the District Court draw an explicit conclusion that the police conduct amounted to a deprivation of a federally secured right; it expressly found no police misconduct whatsoever in four of the incidents; and in one other the departmental policy complained of was subsequently changed. As to the remaining 21, the District Court did not proffer a comment on the degree of misconduct that had occurred: whether simply improvident, illegal under police regulations or state law, or actually violative of the individual's constitutional rights. Respondents' brief asserts that of this latter group, the facts as found in 14 of them "reveal [federal] violations." While we think that somewhat of an overstatement, we accept it, *arguendo,* and thus take it as established that, insofar as the *COPPAR* record reveals, there were 16 incidents occurring in the city of Philadelphia over a year's time in which numbers of police officers violated citizens' constitutional rights. Additionally, the District Court made reference to citizens' complaints to the police in seven of those 16; in four of which, involving conduct of constitutional dimension, the police department received complaints but ultimately took no action against the offending officers.

The District Court made a number of conclusions of law, not all of which are relevant to our analysis. It found that the evidence did not establish the existence of any policy on the part of the named petitioners to violate the legal and constitutional rights of the plaintiff classes, but it did find that evidence of departmental procedure indicated a tendency to discourage the filing of civilian complaints and to minimize the consequences of police misconduct. It found that as to the larger plaintiff class, the residents of Philadelphia, only a small percentage of policemen commit violations of their legal and constitutional rights, but that the frequency with which such violations occur is such that "they cannot be dismissed as rare, isolated instances." In the course of its opinion, the District Court commented:

> In the course of these proceedings, [much of the argument has been directed toward the proposition that courts should not attempt to supervise the functioning of the police department.] Although, contrary to the defendants' assertions [the Court's legal power to do just that is firmly established] . . . I am not persuaded that any such drastic remedy is called for, at least initially, in the present cases.

The District Court concluded by directing petitioners to draft, for the court's approval, "a comprehensive program for dealing adequately with civilian complaints," to be formulated along the following "guidelines" suggested by the court:

> (1) Appropriate revision of police manuals and rules of procedure spelling out in some detail, in simple language, the "dos and don'ts" of permissible conduct in dealing with civilians (for example, manifestations of racial bias, derogatory remarks, offensive language, etc.; unnecessary damage to property and other unreasonable conduct in executing search warrants; limitations on pursuit of persons charged only with summary offenses; recording and processing civilian complaints, etc.). (2) Revision of procedures for processing complaints against police, including (a) ready availability of forms for use by civilians in lodging complaints against police officers; (b) a screening procedure for eliminating frivolous complaints; (c) prompt and adequate investigation of complaints; (d) adjudication of nonfrivolous complaints by an impartial individual or body, insulated so far as practicable from chain of command pressures, with a fair opportunity afforded the complaint to present his complaint, and to the police

officer to present his defense; and (3) prompt notification to the concerned parties, informing them of the outcome.

While noting that the "guidelines" were consistent with "generally recognized minimum standards" and imposed "no substantial burdens" on the police department, the District Court emphasized that respondents had no constitutional *right* to improved police procedures for handling civilian complaints. But given that violations of constitutional rights of citizens occur in "unacceptably" high numbers, and are likely to continue to occur, the court-mandated revision was a "necessary first step" in attempting to prevent future abuses. On petitioners' appeal the Court of Appeals affirmed.

reasoning of lower court.

II

These actions were brought, and the affirmative equitable relief fashioned, under the Civil Rights Act of 1871, 42 U.S.C. § 1983. It provides that "[e]very person who, under color of [law] subjects, or causes to be subjected, any ... person within the jurisdiction [of the United States] to the deprivation of any rights ... secured by the Constitution and laws, shall be liable to the party injured in an action at law [or] suit in equity...." The plain words of the statute impose liability—whether in the form of payment of redressive damages or being placed under an injunction—only for conduct which "subjects, or causes to be subjected" the complainant to a deprivation of a right secured by the Constitution and laws.

fed law lower court action brought under

The findings of fact made by the District Court at the conclusion of these two parallel trials—in sharp contrast to that which respondents sought to prove with respect to petitioners—disclose a central paradox which permeates that court's legal conclusions. Individual police officers *not named as parties* to the action were found to have violated the constitutional rights of particular individuals, only a few of whom were parties plaintiff. As the facts developed, there was no affirmative link between the occurrence of the various incidents of police misconduct and the adoption of any plan or policy by petitioners—express or otherwise—showing their authorization or approval of such misconduct. Instead, the *sole* causal connection found by the District Court between petitioners and the individual respondents was that in the absence of a change in police disciplinary procedures, the incidents were likely to continue to occur, *not* with respect to them, but as to the members of the classes they represented. In sum, the genesis of this lawsuit—a heated dispute between individual citizens and certain policemen—has evolved into an attempt by the federal judiciary to resolve a "controversy" between the entire citizenry of Philadelphia and the petitioning elected and appointed officials over what steps might, in the Court of Appeals' words, "[appear] to have the potential for prevention of future police misconduct." The lower courts have, we think, overlooked several significant decisions of this Court in validating this type of litigation and the relief ultimately granted.

reason for lower court's remedy.

A

We first of all entertain serious doubts whether on the facts as found there was made out the requisite Art. III case or controversy between the

"question of case or controversy"

individually named respondents and petitioners.... [T]he individual respondents' claim to "real and immediate" injury rests not upon what the named petitioners might do to them in the future—such as set a bond on the basis of race—but upon what one of a small, unnamed minority of policemen might do to them in the future because of that unknown policeman's perception of departmental disciplinary procedures. This hypothesis is even more attenuated than those allegations of future injury found insufficient in *O'Shea* to warrant invocation of federal jurisdiction. Thus, insofar as the individual respondents were concerned, we think they lacked the requisite "personal stake in the outcome," i.e., the order overhauling police disciplinary procedures.

B

That conclusion alone might appear to end the matter, for *O'Shea* also noted that "if none of the named plaintiffs ... establishes the requisite of a case or controversy with the defendants, none may seek relief on behalf of himself or any other member of the class" which they purport to represent. But, unlike *O'Shea,* this case did not arise on the pleadings. The District Court, having certified the plaintiff classes, bridged the gap between the facts shown at trial and the classwide relief sought with an unprecedented theory of § 1983 liability. [It held that the classes' § 1983 actions for equitable relief against petitioners were made out on a showing of an "unacceptably high" number of those incidents of constitutional dimension—some 20 in all—occurring at large in a city of three million inhabitants, with 7,500 policemen.] *— lower court holding*

. . . .

Court court reasoning

Respondents stress that the District Court not only found an "unacceptably high" number of incidents but held, as did the Court of Appeals, that "when a *pattern* of frequent police violations of rights is shown, the law is clear that injunctive relief may be granted." However, there was no showing that the behavior of the Philadelphia police was different in kind or degree from that which exists elsewhere; indeed, the District Court found "that the problems disclosed by the record ... are fairly typical of [those] afflicting police departments in major urban areas.".....

Court court reasoning

The theory of liability underlying the District Court's opinion, and urged upon us by respondents, is that even without a showing of direct responsibility for the actions of a small percentage of the police force, petitioners' *failure* to act in the face of a statistical pattern is indistinguishable from the active conduct enjoined in [two prior cases]. Respondents posit a constitutional "duty" on the part of petitioners (and a corresponding "right" of the citizens of Philadelphia) to "eliminate" future police misconduct; a "default" of that affirmative duty being shown by the statistical pattern, the District Court is empowered to act in petitioners' stead and take whatever preventive measures are necessary, within its discretion, to secure the "right" at issue. Such reasoning, however, blurs accepted usages and meanings in the English language in a way which would be quite inconsistent with the words Congress chose in § 1983. We have never subscribed to these amorphous propositions, and we decline to do so now.

. . . .

... Here, the District Court found that none of the petitioners had
deprived the respondent classes of any rights secured under the Constitution. Under the well-established rule that federal "judicial powers may be
exercised only on the basis of a constitutional violation," this case presented no occasion for the District Court to grant equitable relief against
petitioners.

C

Going beyond considerations concerning the existence of a live controversy and threshold statutory liability, we must address an additional and
novel claim advanced by respondent classes. They assert that given the
citizenry's "right" to be protected from unconstitutional exercises of police
power, and the "need for protection from such abuses," respondents have a
right to mandatory equitable relief in some form when those in supervisory
positions do not institute steps to reduce the incidence of unconstitutional
police misconduct. The scope of federal equity power, it is proposed, should
be extended to the fashioning of prophylactic procedures for a state agency
designed to minimize this kind of misconduct on the part of a handful of its
employees. But on the facts of this case, not only is this novel claim quite at
odds with the settled rule that in federal equity cases "the nature of the
violation determines the scope of the remedy," important considerations of
federalism are additional factors weighing against it. Where, as here, the
exercise of authority by state officials is attacked, federal courts must be
constantly mindful of the "special delicacy of the adjustment to be preserved between federal equitable power and State administration of its own
law."

Section 1983 by its terms confers authority to grant equitable relief as
well as damages, but its words "allow a suit in equity only when that is the
proper proceeding for redress, and they refer to existing standards to
determine what is a proper proceeding." Even in an action between private
individuals, it has long been held that an injunction is "to be used
sparingly, and only in a clear and plain case." When a plaintiff seeks to
enjoin the activity of a government agency, even within a unitary court
system, his case must contend with "the well-established rule that the
Government has traditionally been granted the widest latitude in the
'dispatch of its own internal affairs.'" The District Court's injunctive order
here, significantly revising the internal procedures of the Philadelphia
police department, was indisputably a sharp limitation on the department's
"latitude in the 'dispatch of its own internal affairs.'"

When the frame of reference moves from a unitary court system,
governed by the principles just stated, to a system of federal courts
representing the Nation, subsisting side by side with 50 state judicial,
legislative, and executive branches, appropriate consideration must be
given to principles of federalism in determining the availability and scope of
equitable relief.

So strongly has Congress weighted this factor of federalism in the case
of a state criminal proceeding that it has enacted 28 U.S.C. § 2283 to
actually deny to the district courts the authority to issue injunctions

against such proceedings unless the proceedings come within narrowly specified exceptions. Even though an action brought under § 1983, as this was, is within those exceptions, the underlying notions of federalism which Congress has recognized in dealing with the relationships between federal and state courts still have weight. Where an injunction against a criminal proceeding is sought under § 1983, "the principles of equity, comity, and federalism" must nonetheless restrain a federal court. —Rule

But even where the prayer for injunctive relief does not seek to enjoin the state criminal proceedings themselves, we have held that the principles of equity nonetheless militate heavily against the grant of an injunction except in the most extraordinary circumstances. In O'Shea v. Littleton, we held that "a major continuing intrusion of the equitable power of the federal courts into the daily conduct of state criminal proceedings is in sharp conflict with the principles of equitable restraint which this Court has recognized in the decisions previously noted." And the same principles of federalism may prevent the injunction by a federal court of a state civil proceeding once begun.

Thus the principles of federalism which play such an important part in governing the relationship between federal courts and state governments, though initially expounded and perhaps entitled to their greatest weight in cases where it was sought to enjoin a criminal prosecution in progress, have not been limited either to that situation or indeed to a criminal proceeding itself. We think these principles likewise have applicability where injunctive relief is sought, not against the judicial branch of the state government, but against those in charge of an executive branch of an agency of state or local governments such as respondents here. Indeed, in the recent case of Mayor v. Educational Equality League, 415 U.S. 605, 94 S.Ct. 1323, 39 L.Ed.2d 630 (1974), in which private individuals sought injunctive relief against the Mayor of Philadelphia, we expressly noted the existence of such considerations, saying: "There are also delicate issues of federal-state relationships underlying this case."

Contrary to the District Court's flat pronouncement that a federal court's legal power to "supervise the functioning of the police department ... is firmly established," it is the foregoing cases and principles that must govern consideration of the type of injunctive relief granted here. When it injected itself by injunctive decree into the internal disciplinary affairs of this state agency, the District Court departed from these precepts.

For the foregoing reasons the judgment of the Court of Appeals which affirmed the decree of the District Court is

Reversed.

■ MR. JUSTICE STEVENS took no part in the consideration or decision of this case.

■ MR. JUSTICE BLACKMUN, with whom MR. JUSTICE BRENNAN and MR. JUSTICE MARSHALL join, dissenting.

To be sure, federal-court intervention in the daily operation of a large city's police department, as the Court intimates, is undesirable and to be avoided if at all possible. The Court appropriately observes, however, that what the Federal District Court did here was to engage in a careful and conscientious resolution of often sharply conflicting testimony and to make detailed findings of fact, now accepted by both sides, that attack the problem that is the subject of the respondents' complaint. The remedy was one evolved with the defendant officials' assent, reluctant though that assent may have been, and it was one that the police department concededly could live with. Indeed, the District Court, in its memorandum of December 18, 1973, stated that "the resolution of all the disputed items was more nearly in accord with the defendants' position than with the plaintiffs' position," and that the relief contemplated by the earlier orders of March 14, 1973, "did not go beyond what the defendants had always been willing to accept." No one, not even this Court's majority, disputes the apparent efficacy of the relief or the fact that it effectuated a betterment in the system and should serve to lessen the number of instances of deprival of constitutional rights of members of the respondent classes. What is worrisome to the Court is abstract principle, and, of course, the Court has a right to be concerned with abstract principle that, when extended to the limits of logic, may produce untoward results in other circumstances on a future day.

But the District Court here, with detailed, careful, and sympathetic findings, ascertained the existence of violations of citizens' *constitutional* rights, of a *pattern* of that type of activity, of its likely continuance and recurrence, and of an official indifference as to doing anything about it. . . .

The Court entertains "serious doubt" as to whether there is a case of controversy here, citing O'Shea v. Littleton, 414 U.S. 488, 94 S.Ct. 669, 38 L.Ed.2d 674 (1974). *O'Shea,* however, presented quite different facts. There, the plaintiff-respondents had alleged a fear of injury from actions that would be subsequent to some future, valid arrest. . . . Here, by contrast, plaintiff-respondents are persons injured by past unconstitutional conduct (an allegation not made in the *O'Shea* complaint) and fear injury at the hands of the police regardless of whether they have violated a valid law.

To the extent that Part II–A of the Court's opinion today indicates that some constitutional violations might be spread so extremely thin as to prevent any individual from showing the requisite case or controversy, I must agree. I do not agree, however, with the Court's substitution of its judgment for that of the District Court on what the evidence here shows. The Court states that what was shown was minimal, involving only a few incidents out of thousands of arrests in a city of several million population. Small as the ratio of incidents to arrests may be, the District Court nevertheless found a pattern of operation, even if no policy and one sufficiently significant that the violations "cannot be dismissed as rare, isolated instances." Nothing the Court has said demonstrates for me that there is no justification for that finding on this record. The Court's criticism about numbers would be just as forceful, or would miss the mark just as much, with 100 incidents or 500 or even 3,000, when compared with the overall number of arrests made in the city of Philadelphia. The pattern line will appear somewhere. The District Court drew it this side of the number of proved instances. One properly may wonder how many more instances actually existed but were unproved because of the pressure of time upon the trial court, or because of reluctant witnesses, or because of inherent fear to question constituted authority in any degree, or because of a despairing belief, unfounded though it may be, that nothing can be done about it anyway and that it is not worth the effort. That it was worth the effort is convincingly demonstrated by the result in the District Court, by the affirmance, on the issues before us, by a unanimous panel of the Third Circuit, and by the support given the result below by the Commonwealth of Pennsylvania, the Philadelphia Bar Association, the Greater Philadelphia Movement, and the other entities that have filed briefs as *amici curiae* here in support of the respondents.

The Court today appears to assert that a state official is not subject to the strictures of 42 U.S.C. § 1983 unless he directs the deprivation of constitutional rights. In so holding, it seems to me, the Court ignores both the language of § 1983 and the case law interpreting that language....

I do not find it necessary to reach the question under what circumstances failure to supervise will justify an award of money damages, or whether an injunction is authorized where the superior has no consciousness of the wrongs being perpetrated by his subordinates. It is clear that an official may be enjoined from consciously permitting his subordinates, in the course of their duties, to violate the constitutional rights of persons with whom they deal....

In the instant case, the District Court found that although there was no departmental policy of racial discrimination, "such violations do occur, with such frequency that they cannot be dismissed as rare, isolated instances; and that little or nothing is done by the city authorities to punish such infractions, or to prevent their recurrence," and that it "is the policy of the department to discourage the filing of such complaints, to avoid or minimize the consequences of proven police misconduct, and to resist disclosure of the final disposition of such complaints." Needless to say, petitioners were under a statutory duty to supervise their subordinates. I agree with the District Court that its findings are sufficient to bring petitioners within the ambit of § 1983.

Further, the applicability of § 1983 to controlling officers allows the district courts to avoid the necessity of injunctions issued against individual officers and the consequent continuing supervision by the federal courts of the day-to-day activities of the men on the street....

I would regard what was accomplished in this case as one of those rightly rare but nevertheless justified instances ... of federal-court "intervention" in a state or municipal executive area. The facts, the deprival of constitutional rights, and the pattern are all proved in sufficient degree. And the remedy is carefully delineated, worked out within the administrative structure rather than superimposed by edict upon it, and essentially, and concededly, "livable." In the City of Brotherly Love—or in any other American city—no less should be expected. It is a matter of regret that the Court sees fit to nullify what so meticulously and thoughtfully has been evolved to satisfy an existing need relating to constitutional rights that we cherish and hold dear.

NOTES

1. In Pennhurst State School & Hospital v. Halderman, 465 U.S. 89, 104 S.Ct. 900, 79 L.Ed.2d 67 (1984), the Supreme Court held that the Eleventh Amendment forbids the issuance of federal court injunctions designed to vindicate, and require state officials to comply with, state law.

2. Section 1983 actions may be brought in state courts. See Howlett v. Rose, 496 U.S. 356, 110 S.Ct. 2430, 110 L.Ed.2d 332 (1990).

Missouri v. Jenkins

Supreme Court of the United States, 1995.
515 U.S. 70, 115 S.Ct. 2038, 132 L.Ed.2d 63.

■ CHIEF JUSTICE REHNQUIST delivered the opinion of the Court.

As this school desegregation litigation enters its 18th year, we are called upon again to review the decisions of the lower courts. In this case, the State of Missouri has challenged the District Court's order of salary increases for virtually all instructional and noninstructional staff within the Kansas City, Missouri, School District (KCMSD) and the District Court's order requiring the State to continue to fund remedial "quality education" programs because student achievement levels were still "at or below national norms at many grade levels."

I

A general overview of this litigation is necessary for proper resolution of the issues upon which we granted certiorari. This case has been before the same United States District Judge since 1977. Missouri v. Jenkins, 491 U.S. 274, 276 (1989) (Jenkins I). In that year, the KCMSD, the school board, and the children of two school board members brought suit against the State and other defendants. Plaintiffs alleged that the State, the surrounding suburban school districts (SSD's), and various federal agencies had caused and perpetuated a system of racial segregation in the schools of the Kansas City metropolitan area. The District Court realigned the KCMSD as a nominal defendant and certified as a class, present and future KCMSD students. The KCMSD brought a cross-claim against the State for its failure to eliminate the vestiges of its prior dual school system.

After a trial that lasted 7 1/2 months, the District Court dismissed the case against the federal defendants and the SSD's, but determined that the State and the KCMSD were liable for an intradistrict violation, i.e., they had operated a segregated school system within the KCMSD. Jenkins v. Missouri, 593 F.Supp. 1485 (W.D.Mo.1984). The District Court determined that prior to 1954 "Missouri mandated segregated schools for black and white children." Id., at 1490. Furthermore, the KCMSD and the State had failed in their affirmative obligations to eliminate the vestiges of the State's dual school system within the KCMSD. Id., at 1504.

In June 1985, the District Court issued its first remedial order and established as its goal the "elimination of all vestiges of state imposed segregation." Jenkins v. Missouri, 639 F.Supp. 19, 23 (W.D.Mo.1985). The District Court determined that "[s]egregation ha[d] caused a system wide reduction in student achievement in the schools of the KCMSD." Id. at 24. The District Court made no particularized findings regarding the extent that student achievement had been reduced or what portion of that reduction was attributable to segregation. The District Court also identified 25 schools within the KCMSD that had enrollments of 90% or more black students.

The District Court, pursuant to plans submitted by the KCMSD and the State, ordered a wide range of quality education programs for all students attending the KCMSD. First, the District Court ordered that the KCMSD be restored to an AAA classification, the highest classification awarded by the State Board of Education. Second, it ordered that the number of students per class be reduced so that the student-to-teacher ratio was below the level required for AAA standing. The District Court justified its reduction in class size as "an essential part of any plan to remedy the vestiges of segregation in the KCMSD. Reducing class size will serve to remedy the vestiges of past segregation by increasing individual attention and instruction, as well as increasing the potential for desegregative educational experiences for KCMSD students by maintaining and attracting non-minority enrollment." 639 F. Supp. at 29.

The District Court also ordered programs to expand educational opportunities for all KCMSD students: full-day kindergarten; expanded summer school; before-and after-school tutoring; and an early childhood development program. Finally, the District Court implemented a state-funded "effective schools" program that consisted of substantial yearly cash grants to each of the schools within the KCMSD. Under the "effective schools" program, the State was required to fund programs at both the 25 racially identifiable schools as well as the 43 other schools within the KCMSD.

The KCMSD was awarded an AAA rating in the 1987–1988 school year, and there is no dispute that since that time it has " 'maintained and greatly exceeded AAA requirements.' " 19 F.3d 393, 401 (CA8 1994) (Beam, J., dissenting from denial of rehearing en banc). The total cost for these quality education programs has exceeded $220 million. Missouri Department of Elementary and Secondary Education, KCMSD Total Desegregation Program Expenditures (Sept. 30, 1994) (Desegregation Expenditures).

The District Court also set out to desegregate the KCMSD but believed that "[t]o accomplish desegregation within the boundary lines of a school district whose enrollment remains 68.3% black is a difficult task." 639 F.Supp. at 38. Because it had found no interdistrict violation, the District Court could not order mandatory interdistrict redistribution of students between the KCMSD and the surrounding SSD's. Ibid.; see also Milliken v. Bradley, 418 U.S. 717 (1974) (Milliken I). The District Court refused to order additional mandatory student reassignments because they would "increase the instability of the KCMSD and reduce the potential for desegregation." 639 F.Supp. at 38. Relying on favorable precedent from the Eighth Circuit, the District Court determined that "[a]chievement of AAA status, improvement of the quality of education being offered at the KCMSD schools, magnet schools, as well as other components of this desegregation plan can serve to maintain and hopefully attract non-minority student enrollment." Ibid.

In November 1986, the District Court approved a comprehensive magnet school and capital improvements plan and held the State and the KCMSD jointly and severally liable for its funding. Under the District Court's plan, every senior high school, every middle school, and one-half of the elementary schools were converted into magnet schools. The District Court adopted the magnet-school program to "provide a greater educational opportunity to all KCMSD students," id., at 131–132, and because it believed "that the proposed magnet plan [was] so attractive that it would draw non-minority students from the private schools who have abandoned or avoided the KCMSD, and draw in additional non-minority students from the suburbs." Id., at 132. The District Court felt that "[t]he long-term benefit of all KCMSD students of a greater educational opportunity in an integrated environment is worthy of such an investment." Id., at 133. Since its inception, the magnet-school program has operated at a cost, including magnet transportation, in excess of $448 million. See Desegregation Expenditures. In April 1993, the District Court considered, but ultimately rejected, the plaintiffs' and the KCMSD's proposal seeking approval of a long-range magnet renewal program that included a 10–year budget of well over $500 million, funded by the State and the KCMSD on a joint-and-several basis.

In June 1985, the District Court ordered substantial capital improvements to combat the deterioration of the KCMSD's facilities. In formulating its capital-improvements plan, the District Court dismissed as "irrelevant" the "State's argument that the present condition of the facilities [was] not traceable to unlawful segregation." 639 F.Supp. at 40. Instead, the District Court focused on its responsibility to "remed[y] the vestiges of segregation" and to "implemen[t] a desegregation plan which w[ould] maintain and attract non-minority enrollment." Id. at 41. The initial phase of the capital-improvements plan cost $37 million. Ibid. The District Court also required the KCMSD to present further capital-improvements proposals "in order to bring its facilities to a point comparable with the facilities in neighboring suburban school districts." Ibid. In November 1986, the District Court approved further capital improvements in order to remove the vestiges of racial segregation and "to ... attract non-minority students back to the KCMSD."

In September 1987, the District Court adopted, for the most part, KCMSD's long-range capital-improvements plan at a cost in excess of $187 million. The plan called for the renovation of approximately 55 schools, the closure of 18 facilities, and the construction of 17 new schools. The District Court rejected what it referred to as the " 'patch and repair' approach proposed by the State" because it "would not achieve suburban comparability or the visual attractiveness sought by the Court as it would result in floor coverings with unsightly sections of mismatched carpeting and tile, and individual walls possessing different shades of paint." Id. at 404. . . . [T]he total cost of capital improvements ordered has soared to over $540 million. . . .

As part of its desegregation plan, the District Court has ordered salary assistance to the KCMSD. . . . The total cost of this component of the desegregation remedy since 1987 is over $200 million.

The District Court's desegregation plan has been described as the most ambitious and expensive remedial program in the history of school desegregation. The annual cost per pupil at the KCMSD far exceeds that of the neighboring SSD's or of any school district in Missouri. Nevertheless, the KCMSD, which has pursued a "friendly adversary" relationship with the plaintiffs, has continued to propose ever more expensive programs. As a result, the desegregation costs have escalated and now are approaching an annual cost of $200 million. These massive expenditures have financed

> "high schools in which every classroom will have air conditioning, an alarm system, and 15 microcomputers; a 2,000–square-foot planetarium; green houses and vivariums; a 25–acre farm with an air-conditioned meeting room for 104 people; a Model United Nations wired for language translation; broadcast capable radio and television studios with an editing and animation lab; a temperature controlled art gallery; movie editing and screening rooms; a 3,500–square-foot dust-free diesel mechanics room; 1,875–square-foot elementary school animal rooms for use in a zoo project; swimming pools; and numerous other facilities."

Jenkins II, 495 U.S. at 77, (Kennedy, J., concurring in part and concurring in judgment).

Not surprisingly, the cost of this remedial plan has "far exceeded KCMSD's budget, or for that matter, its authority to tax." Id. at 60. The State, through the operation of joint-and-several liability, has borne the brunt of these costs. The District Court candidly has acknowledged that it has "allowed the District planners to dream" and "provided the mechanism for th[ose] dreams to be realized." In short, the District Court "has gone to great lengths to provide KCMSD with facilities and opportunities not available anywhere else in the country."

II

With this background, we turn to the present controversy. First, the State has challenged the District Court's requirement that it fund salary increases for KCMSD instructional and noninstructional staff. The State claimed that funding for salaries was beyond the scope of the District Court's remedial authority. Second, the State has challenged the District Court's order requiring it to continue to fund the remedial quality education programs for the 1992–1993 school year. (District Court's Order of June 17, 1992). The State contended that under Freeman v. Pitts, 503 U.S. 467 (1992), it had achieved partial unitary status with respect to the quality education programs already in place. As a result, the State argued that the District Court should have relieved it of responsibility for funding those programs.

The District Court rejected the State's arguments. . . .

III

. . .

Almost 25 years ago, in Swann v. Charlotte–Mecklenburg Bd. of Ed., 402 U.S. 1 (1971), we dealt with the authority of a district court to fashion remedies for a school district that had been segregated in law in violation of the Equal Protection Clause of the Fourteenth Amendment. Although recognizing the discretion that must necessarily adhere in a district court in fashioning a remedy, we also recognized the limits on such remedial power:

> "[E]limination of racial discrimination in public schools is a large task and one that should not be retarded by efforts to achieve broader purposes lying beyond the jurisdiction of the school authorities. One vehicle can carry only a limited amount of baggage. It would not serve the important objective of Brown [v. Board of Education, 347 U.S. 483 (1954),] to seek to use school desegregation cases for purposes beyond their scope, although desegregation of schools ultimately will have impact on other forms of discrimination."

Rule.

Id. at 22–23.

Three years later, in Milliken I, 418 U.S. 717 (1974), we held that a District Court had exceeded its authority in fashioning interdistrict relief where the surrounding school districts had not themselves been guilty of any constitutional violation. We said that a desegregation remedy "is necessarily designed, as all remedies are, to restore the victims of discriminatory conduct to the position they would have occupied in the absence of such conduct." Id. at 746. . .

rule.

Three years later, in Milliken v. Bradley, 433 U.S. 267 (1977) (Milliken II), we articulated a three-part framework derived from our prior cases to guide district courts in the exercise of their remedial authority.

> "In the first place, like other equitable remedies, the nature of the desegregation remedy is to be determined by the nature and scope of the constitutional violation. Swann v. Charlotte–Mecklenburg Board of Education, 402 U.S., at 16. The remedy must therefore be related to 'the condition alleged to offend the Constitution. . . .' Milliken I, 418 U.S. at 738. Second, the decree must indeed be remedial in nature, that is, it must be designed as nearly as possible 'to restore the victims of discriminatory conduct to the position they would have occupied in the absence of such conduct.' Id. at 746. Third, the federal courts in devising a remedy must take into account the interests of state and local authorities in managing their own affairs, consistent with the Constitution." Id., at 280–281.

① ② ③

We added that the "principle that the nature and scope of the remedy are to be determined by the violation means simply that federal-court decrees must directly address and relate to the constitutional violation itself." Id. at 281–282. In applying these principles, we have identified "student assignments, . . . 'faculty, staff, transportation, extracurricular activities and facilities'," as the most important indicia of a racially segregated school system.

+4

most important indicia of a racially segregated school system

Because "[f]ederal supervision of local school systems was intended as a temporary measure to remedy past discrimination," Dowell, supra, at 247, 111 S.Ct., at 637, we also have considered the showing that must be made by a school district operating under a desegregation order for complete or partial relief from that order. In Freeman, we stated that "[a]mong the factors which must inform the sound discretion of the court in ordering partial withdrawal are the following: [1] whether there has been <u>full and satisfactory compliance</u> with the decree in those aspects of the system where supervision is to be withdrawn; [2] whether <u>retention of judicial control is necessary</u> or practicable to achieve compliance with the decree in other facets of the school system; and [3] whether the school district has <u>demonstrated, to the public and to the parents and students of the once disfavored race,</u> its <u>good-faith commitment to the whole of the courts' decree and to those provisions of the law and the Constitution</u> that were the predicate for judicial intervention in the first instance."

503 U.S., at 491.

The ultimate inquiry is " 'whether the [constitutional violator] ha[s] complied in good faith with the desegregation decree since it was entered, and whether the vestiges of past discrimination ha[ve] been eliminated to the extent practicable.' " Id., at 492 (quoting Dowell, 498 U.S. at 249–250).

Proper analysis of the District Court's orders challenged here, then, must rest upon their serving as proper means to the end of restoring the victims of discriminatory conduct to the position they would have occupied in the absence of that conduct and their eventual restoration of "state and local authorities to the control of a school system that is operating in compliance with the Constitution." 503 U.S., at 489.

The State argues that the order approving salary increases is beyond the District Court's authority because it was crafted to serve an "interdistrict goal," in spite of the fact that the constitutional violation in this case is "intradistrict" in nature. "[T]he nature of the desegregation remedy is to be determined by the nature and scope of the constitutional violation." Milliken II, 433 U.S. at 280. The proper response to an intradistrict violation is an intradistrict remedy, that serves to eliminate the racial identity of the schools within the affected school district by eliminating, as far as practicable, the vestiges of de jure segregation in all facets of their operations.

Here, the District Court has found, and the Court of Appeals has affirmed, that this case involved no interdistrict constitutional violation that would support interdistrict relief. Thus, the proper response by the District Court should have been to eliminate to the extent practicable the vestiges of prior de jure segregation within the KCMSD: a systemwide reduction in student achievement and the existence of 25 racially identifiable schools with a population of over 90% black students.

The District Court and Court of Appeals, however, have felt that because the KCMSD's enrollment remained 68.3% black, a purely intradistrict remedy would be insufficient. But, as noted in Milliken I, 418 U.S. 717 (1974), we have rejected the suggestion "that schools which have a majority of Negro students are not 'desegregated' whatever the racial makeup of the school district's population and however neutrally the district lines have been drawn and administered." Id., 418 U.S. at 747, n. 22. see Milliken II, 433 U.S. at 280, n. 14,

Instead of seeking to remove the racial identity of the various schools within the KCMSD, the District Court has set out on a program to create a school district that was equal to or superior to the surrounding SSD's. Its remedy has focused on "desegregative attractiveness," coupled with "suburban comparability." Examination of the District Court's reliance on "desegregative attractiveness" and "suburban comparability" is instructive for our ultimate resolution of the salary-order issue.

The purpose of desegregative attractiveness has been not only to remedy the systemwide reduction in student achievement, but also to attract nonminority students not presently enrolled in the KCMSD. This remedy has included an elaborate program of capital improvements, course enrichment, and extracurricular enhancement not simply in the formerly identifiable black schools, but in schools throughout the district. The District Court's remedial orders have converted every senior high school, every middle school, and one-half of the elementary schools in the KCMSD into "magnet" schools. The District Court's remedial order has all but made the KCMSD itself into a magnet district.

We previously have approved of intradistrict desegregation remedies involving magnet schools. Magnet schools have the advantage of encouraging voluntary movement of students within a school district in a pattern that aids desegregation on a voluntary basis, without requiring extensive busing and redrawing of district boundary lines. As a component in an intradistrict remedy, magnet schools also are attractive because they promote desegregation while limiting the withdrawal of white student enrollment that may result from mandatory student reassignment.

The District Court's remedial plan in this case, however, is not designed solely to redistribute the students within the KCMSD in order to eliminate racially identifiable schools within the KCMSD. Instead, its purpose is to attract nonminority students from outside the KCMSD schools. But this interdistrict goal is beyond the scope of the intradistrict violation identified by the District Court. In effect, the District Court has devised a remedy to accomplish indirectly what it admittedly lacks the remedial authority to mandate directly: the interdistrict transfer of students. . . .

What we meant in Milliken I by an interdistrict violation was a violation that caused segregation between adjoining districts. Nothing in Milliken I suggests that the District Court in that case could have circumvented the limits on its remedial authority by requiring the State of Michigan, a constitutional violator, to implement a magnet program designed to achieve the same interdistrict transfer of students that we held was beyond its remedial authority. Here, the District Court has done just that: created a magnet district of the KCMSD in order to serve the interdistrict goal of attracting nonminority students from the surrounding SSD's and redistributing them within the KCMSD. The District Court's pursuit of "desegregative attractiveness" is beyond the scope of its broad remedial authority.

Respondents argue that the District Court's reliance upon desegregative attractiveness is justified in light of the District Court's statement that segregation has "led to white flight from the KCMSD to suburban districts." The lower courts' "findings" as to "white flight" are both inconsistent internally, and inconsistent with the typical supposition, bolstered here by the record evidence, that "white flight" may result from desegregation, not de jure segregation. . . .

In Freeman, we stated that "[t]he vestiges of segregation that are the concern of the law in a school case may be subtle and intangible but nonetheless they must be so real that they have a causal link to the de jure violation being remedied." 503 U.S. at 496. The record here does not support the District Court's reliance on "white flight" as a justification for a permissible expansion of its intradistrict remedial authority through its pursuit of desegregative attractiveness.

Justice Souter claims that our holding effectively overrules Hills v. Gautreaux, 425 U.S. 284 (1976). In Gautreaux, the Federal Department of Housing and Urban Development (HUD) was found to have participated, along with a local housing agency, in establishing and maintaining a racially segregated public housing program. After the Court of Appeals ordered " 'the adoption of a comprehensive metropolitan area plan,' " id. at 291, we granted certiorari to consider the "permissibility in light of [Milliken I] of 'inter-district relief for discrimination in public housing in the absence of a finding of an inter-district violation.' " Gautreaux at 292. Because the "relevant geographic area for purposes of the [plaintiffs'] housing options [was] the Chicago housing market, not the Chicago city limits," 425 U.S. at 299, we concluded that "a metropolitan area remedy . . . [was] not impermissible as a matter of law," id. at 306.

In Gautreaux, we did not obligate the District Court to "subjec[t] HUD to measures going beyond the geographical or political boundaries of its violation." Instead, we cautioned that our holding "should not be interpreted as requiring a metropolitan area order." Gautreaux, 425 U.S. at 306. . . .

Our decision today is fully consistent with Gautreaux. A district court seeking to remedy an intradistrict violation that has not "directly caused" significant interdistrict effects, Milliken I, 418 U.S. at 744–745, exceeds its remedial authority if it orders a remedy with an interdistrict purpose. This conclusion follows directly from Milliken II, decided one year after Gautreaux, where we reaffirmed the bedrock principle that "federal-court decrees exceed appropriate limits if they are aimed at eliminating a condition that does not violate the Constitution or does not flow from such a violation." 433 U.S. at 282. In Milliken II, we also emphasized that "federal courts in devising a remedy must take into account the interests of state and local authorities in managing their own affairs, consistent with the Constitution." Id. at 280–281. Gautreaux, however, involved the imposition of a remedy upon a federal agency. Thus, it did not raise the same federalism concerns that are implicated when a federal court issues a remedial order against a State.

The District Court's pursuit of "desegregative attractiveness" cannot be reconciled with our cases placing limitations on a district court's remedial authority. It is certainly theoretically possible that the greater the expenditure per pupil within the KCMSD, the more likely it is that some unknowable number of nonminority students not presently attending schools in the KCMSD will choose to enroll in those schools. Under this reasoning, however, every increased expenditure, whether it be for teachers, noninstructional employees, books, or buildings, will make the KCMSD in some way more attractive, and thereby perhaps induce nonminority students to enroll in its schools. But this rationale is not susceptible to any objective limitation. Cf. Milliken II at 280 (remedial decree "must be designed as nearly as possible 'to restore the victims of discriminatory conduct to the position they would have occupied in the absence of such conduct' "). This case provides numerous examples demonstrating the limitless authority of the District Court operating under this rationale.

Nor are there limits to the duration of the District Court's involvement. The expenditures per pupil in the KCMSD currently far exceed those in the neighboring SSD's. Sixteen years after this litigation began, the District Court recognized that the KCMSD has yet to offer a viable method of financing the "wonderful school system being built." Each additional program ordered by the District Court—and financed by the State—to increase the "desegregative attractiveness" of the school district makes the KCMSD more and more dependent on additional funding from the State; in turn, the greater the KCMSD's dependence on state funding, the greater its reliance on continued supervision by the District Court. But our cases recognize that local autonomy of school districts is a vital national tradition, and that a district court must strive to restore state and local authorities to the control of a school system operating in compliance with the Constitution.

The District Court's pursuit of the goal of "desegregative attractiveness" results in so many imponderables and is so far removed from the task of eliminating the racial identifiability of the schools within the KCMSD that we believe it is beyond the admittedly broad discretion of the District Court. In this posture, we conclude that the District Court's order of salary increases, which was "grounded in remedying the vestiges of segregation by improving the desegregative attractiveness of the KCMSD," is simply too far removed from an acceptable implementation of a permissible means to remedy previous legally mandated segregation.

Similar considerations lead us to conclude that the District Court's order requiring the State to continue to fund the quality education programs because student achievement levels were still "at or below national norms at many grade levels" cannot be sustained.

Our review in this respect is needlessly complicated because the District Court made no findings in its order approving continued funding of the quality education programs. Although the Court of Appeals later recognized that a determination of partial unitary status requires "careful factfinding and detailed articulation of findings," 11 F.3d, at 765, it declined to remand to the District Court. Instead it attempted to assemble an adequate record from the District Court's statements from the bench and subsequent orders. Id., at 761. In one such order relied upon by the Court of Appeals, the District Court stated that the KCMSD had not reached anywhere close to its "maximum potential because the District is still at or below national norms at many grade levels."

But this clearly is not the appropriate test to be applied in deciding whether a previously segregated district has achieved partially unitary status. The basic task of the District Court is to decide whether the reduction in achievement by minority students attributable to prior de jure segregation has been remedied to the extent practicable. Under our precedents, the State and the KCMSD are "entitled to a rather precise statement of [their] obligations under a desegregation decree." Freeman, 503 U.S. at 246. Although the District Court has determined that "[s]egregation has caused a system wide reduction in achievement in the schools of the KCMSD," 639 F.Supp. at 24, it never has identified the incremental effect that segregation has had on minority student achievement or the specific goals of the quality education programs.

In reconsidering this order, the District Court should apply our three-part test from Freeman v. Pitts, 503 U.S., at 491. The District Court should consider that the State's role with respect to the quality education programs has been limited to the funding, not the implementation, of those programs. As all the parties agree that improved achievement on test scores is not necessarily required for the State to achieve partial unitary status as to the quality education programs, the District Court should sharply limit, if not dispense with, its reliance on this factor. Just as demographic changes independent of de jure segregation will affect the racial composition of student assignments, so too will numerous external factors beyond the control of the KCMSD and the State affect minority student achievement. So long as these external factors are not the result of segregation, they do not figure in the remedial calculus. Insistence upon academic goals unrelated to the effects of legal segregation unwarrantably postpones the day when the KCMSD will be able to operate on its own.

The District Court also should consider that many goals of its quality education plan already have been attained: the KCMSD now is equipped with "facilities and opportunities not available anywhere else in the country." KCMSD schools received an AAA rating eight years ago, and the present remedial programs have been in place for seven years. It may be that in education, just as it may be in economics, a "rising tide lifts all boats," but the remedial quality education program should be tailored to remedy the injuries suffered by the victims of prior de jure segregation. See Milliken II, 433 U.S. at 287. Minority students in kindergarten through grade 7 in the KCMSD always have attended AAA-rated schools; minority students in the KCMSD that previously attended schools rated below AAA have since received remedial education programs for a period of up to seven years.

On remand, the District Court must bear in mind that its end purpose is not only "to remedy the violation" to the extent practicable, but also "to restore state and local authorities to the control of a school system that is operating in compliance with the Constitution." Freeman, 503 U.S. at 489.

The judgment of the Court of Appeals is reversed.

It is so ordered.

■ Justice O'Connor, concurring....

On the merits, the Court's resolution of the dispute comports with Hills v. Gautreaux, 425 U.S. 284 (1976). There, we held that there is no "per se rule that federal courts lack authority to order parties found to have violated the Constitution to undertake remedial efforts beyond the municipal boundaries of the city where the violation occurred," id. at 298.... More important for our purposes here, Gautreaux in no way contravenes the underlying principle that the scope of desegregation remedies, even those that are solely intradistrict, is "determined by the nature and extent of the constitutional violation." Milliken I, 418 U.S. at 744. Gautreaux simply does not give federal courts a blank check to impose unlimited remedies upon a constitutional violator.

As an initial matter, Gautreaux itself may not even have concerned a case of interdistrict relief, at least not in the sense that Milliken I and other school desegregation cases have understood it. Our opinion made clear that the authority of the Department of Housing and Urban Development (HUD) extends beyond the Chicago city limits. Thus, "[t]he relevant geographic area for purposes of the respondents' housing options is the Chicago housing market, not the Chicago city limits." 425 U.S. at 299....

Here, where the District Court found that KCMSD students attended schools separated by their race and that facilities have "literally rotted," Jenkins v. Missouri, 672 F.Supp. 400, 411 (W.D.Mo.1987), it of course should order restorations and remedies that would place previously segregated black KCMSD students at par with their white KCMSD counterparts. The District Court went further, however, and ordered certain improvements to KCMSD as a whole, including schools that were not previously segregated; these district-wide remedies may also be justified (the State does not argue the point here) in light of the finding that segregation caused "a system wide reduction in student achievement in the schools of the KCMSD," Jenkins v. Missouri, 639 F.Supp. 19, 24 (W.D.Mo.1985). Such remedies obviously may benefit some who did not suffer under—and, indeed, may have even profited from—past segregation. There is no categorical constitutional prohibition on nonvictims enjoying the collateral, incidental benefits of a remedial plan designed "to restore the victims of discriminatory conduct to the position they would have occupied in the absence of such conduct." Milliken I, 418 U.S. at 746. Thus, if restoring KCMSD to unitary status would attract whites into the school district, such a reversal of the white exodus would be of no legal consequence.

What the District Court did in this case, however, and how it transgressed the constitutional bounds of its remedial powers, was to make desegregative attractiveness the underlying goal of its remedy for the specific purpose of reversing the trend of white flight. However troubling that trend may be, remedying it is within the District Court's authority only if it is "directly caused by the constitutional violation." Id. at 745. The Court and the dissent attempt to reconcile the different statements by the lower courts as to whether white flight was caused by segregation or desegregation. One fact, however, is uncontroverted. When the District Court found that KCMSD was racially segregated, the constitutional violation from which all remedies flow in this case, it also found that there was neither an interdistrict violation nor significant interdistrict segregative effects. Whether the white exodus that has resulted in a school district that is 68% black was caused by the District Court's remedial orders or by natural, if unfortunate, demographic forces, we have it directly from the District Court that the segregative effects of KCMSD's constitutional violation did not transcend its geographical boundaries. In light of that finding, the District Court cannot order remedies seeking to rectify regional demographic trends that go beyond the nature and scope of the constitutional violation.

. . .

For these reasons, I join the opinion of the Court.

■ JUSTICE THOMAS, concurring.

It never ceases to amaze me that the courts are so willing to assume that anything that is predominantly black must be inferior. Instead of focusing on remedying the harm done to those black schoolchildren injured by segregation, the District Court here sought to convert the Kansas City, Missouri, School District (KCMSD) into a "magnet district" that would reverse the "white flight" caused by desegregation. In this respect, I join the Court's decision concerning the two remedial issues presented for review.

I

A

The mere fact that a school is black does not mean that it is the product of a constitutional violation. A "racial imbalance does not itself establish a violation of the Constitution." United States v. Fordice, 505 U.S. 717, 745 (1992) (Thomas, J., concurring). Instead, in order to find unconstitutional segregation, we require that plaintiffs "prove all of the essential elements of de jure segregation—that is, stated simply, a current condition of segregation resulting from intentional state action directed specifically to the [allegedly segregated] schools." Keyes v. School Dist. No. 1, Denver, 413 U.S. 189, 205–206 (1973) (emphasis added). "[T]he differentiating factor between de jure segregation and so-called de facto segregation . . . is purpose or intent to segregate." Id., at 208.

In the present case, the District Court inferred a continuing constitutional violation from two primary facts: the existence of de jure segregation in the KCMSD prior to 1954, and the existence of de facto segregation today. For the District Court, it followed that the KCMSD had not dismantled the dual system entirely. Id., at 1493. The District Court also concluded that because of the KCMSD's failure to "become integrated on a system-wide basis," the dual system still exerted "lingering effects" upon KCMSD black students, whose "general attitude of inferiority" produced "low achievement . . . which ultimately limits employment opportunities and causes poverty." 593 F.Supp. at 1492.

Without more, the District Court's findings could not have supported a finding of liability against the State. It should by now be clear that the existence of one-race schools is not by itself an indication that the State is practicing segregation. . . . The continuing "racial isolation" of schools after de jure segregation has ended may well reflect voluntary housing choices or other private decisions. . . .

According to the District Court, the schools whose student bodies were more than 90% black constituted "vestiges" of the prior de jure segregation, which the State and the KCMSD had an obligation to eliminate. Later, in the course of issuing its first "remedial" order, the District Court added that a "system wide reduction in student achievement in the schools of . . . KCMSD" was also a vestige of the prior de jure segregation. Jenkins v. Missouri, 639 F.Supp. 19, 24 (W.D.Mo.1985). In a subsequent order, the District Court indicated that post–1954 "white flight" was another vestige of the pre–1954 segregated system.

In order for a "vestige" to supply the ground for an exercise of remedial authority, it must be clearly traceable to the dual school system. . . . District courts must not confuse the consequences of de jure segregation with the results of larger social forces or of private decisions. . . .

B

Without a basis in any real finding of intentional government action, the District Court's imposition of liability upon the State of Missouri improperly rests upon a theory that racial imbalances are unconstitutional. That is, the court has "indulged the presumption, often irrebuttable in practice, that a presently observed [racial] imbalance has been proximately caused by intentional state action during the prior de jure era." United States v. Fordice, 505 U.S. at 745. In effect, the court found that racial imbalances constituted an ongoing constitutional violation that continued to inflict harm on black students. This position appears to rest upon the idea that any school that is black is inferior, and that blacks cannot succeed without the benefit of the company of whites. . . .

Given that desegregation has not produced the predicted leaps forward in black educational achievement, there is no reason to think that black students cannot learn as well when surrounded by members of their own race as when they are in an integrated environment. Indeed, it may very well be that what has been true for historically black colleges is true for black middle and high schools. Despite their origins in "the shameful history of state-enforced segregation," these institutions can be " 'both a source of pride to blacks who have attended them and a source of hope to black families who want the benefits of . . . learning for their children.' " Fordice, 505 U.S. at 748. Because of their "distinctive histories and traditions," ibid., black schools can function as the center and symbol of black communities, and provide examples of independent black leadership, success, and achievement.

Thus, even if the District Court had been on firmer ground in identifying a link between the KCMSD's pre–1954 de jure segregation and the present "racial isolation" of some of the district's schools, mere de facto segregation (unaccompanied by discriminatory inequalities in educational resources) does not constitute a continuing harm after the end of de jure segregation. "Racial isolation" itself is not a harm; only state-enforced segregation is. After all, if separation itself is a harm, and if integration therefore is the only way that blacks can receive a proper education, then there must be something inferior about blacks. Under this theory, segregation injures blacks because blacks, when left on their own, cannot achieve. To my way of thinking, that conclusion is the result of a jurisprudence based upon a theory of black inferiority. . . .

II

. . .

The District Court's unwarranted focus on the psychological harm to blacks and on racial imbalances has been only half of the tale. Not only did the court subscribe to a theory of injury that was predicated on black inferiority, it also married this concept of liability to our expansive approach to remedial powers. . . .

A

I assume for purposes of this case that the remedial authority of the federal courts is inherent in the "judicial Power," as there is no general equitable remedial power expressly granted by the Constitution or by statute. As with any inherent judicial power, however, we ought to be reluctant to approve its aggressive or extravagant use, and instead we should exercise it in a manner consistent with our history and traditions.

Motivated by our worthy desire to eradicate segregation, however, we have disregarded this principle and given the courts unprecedented authority to shape a remedy in equity. . . .

It is perhaps understandable that we permitted the lower courts to exercise such sweeping powers. . . . Our impatience with the pace of desegregation and with the lack of a good-faith effort on the part of school boards led us to approve such extraordinary remedial measures. But such powers should have been temporary and used only to overcome the widespread resistance to the dictates of the Constitution. The judicial overreaching we see before us today perhaps is the price we now pay for our approval of such extraordinary remedies in the past. . . .

B

Such extravagant uses of judicial power are at odds with the history and tradition of the equity power and the Framers' design. The available historical records suggest that the Framers did not intend federal equitable remedies to reach as broadly as we have permitted. . . .

C

Two clear restraints on the use of the equity power—federalism and the separation of powers—derive from the very form of our Government. Federal courts should pause before using their inherent equitable powers to intrude into the proper sphere of the States. . . . A structural reform decree eviscerates a State's discretionary authority over its own program and budgets and forces state officials to reallocate state resources and funds to the desegregation plan at the expense of other citizens, other government programs, and other institutions not represented in court. When district courts seize complete control over the schools, they strip state and local governments of one of their most important governmental responsibilities, and thus deny their existence as independent governmental entities.

. . .

The separation of powers imposes additional restraints on the judiciary's exercise of its remedial powers...

In this case, not only did the District Court exercise the legislative power to tax, it also engaged in budgeting, staffing, and educational decisions, in judgments about the location and esthetic quality of the schools, and in administrative oversight and monitoring. These functions involve a legislative or executive, rather than a judicial power....

D

The dissent's approval of the District Court's treatment of salary increases is typical of this Court's failure to place limits on the equitable remedial power....

Much of the District Court's overreaching in this case occurred because it employed this hit-or-miss method to shape, and reshape, its remedial decree. Using its authority of continuing jurisdiction, the court pursued its goal of decreasing "racial isolation" regardless of the cost or of the difficulties of engineering demographic changes. Wherever possible, district courts should focus their remedial discretion on devising and implementing a unified remedy in a single decree. This method would still provide the lower courts with substantial flexibility to tailor a remedy to fit a violation, and courts could employ their contempt power to ensure compliance....

Second, the District Court failed to target its equitable remedies in this case specifically to cure the harm suffered by the victims of segregation....

To ensure that district courts do not embark on such broad initiatives in the future, we should demand that remedial decrees be more precisely designed to benefit only those who have been victims of segregation....

■ JUSTICE SOUTER, with whom JUSTICE STEVENS, JUSTICE GINSBURG, and JUSTICE BREYER join, dissenting....

I

In 1984, 30 years after our decision in Brown v. Board of Education, 347 U.S. 483 (1954), the District Court found that the State of Missouri and the Kansas City, Missouri, School District (KCMSD) had failed to reform the segregated scheme of public school education in the KCMSD, previously mandated by the State, which had required black and white children to be taught separately according to race. Jenkins v. Missouri, 593 F.Supp. 1485, 1490–1494, 1503–1505 (W.D.Mo.1984). After Brown, neither the State nor the KCMSD moved to dismantle this system of separate education "root and branch," id. at 1505, despite their affirmative obligation to do that under the Constitution. "Instead, the [KCMSD] chose to operate some completely segregated schools and some integrated ones," Jenkins, 593 F.Supp. at 1492, using devices like optional attendance zones and liberal transfer policies to "allo[w] attendance patterns to continue on a segregated basis." Id. at 1494. Consequently, on the 20th anniversary of

Brown in 1974, 39 of the 77 schools in the KCMSD had student bodies that were more than 90 percent black, and 80 percent of all black schoolchildren in the KCMSD attended those schools. Ten years later, in the 1983–1984 school year, 24 schools remained racially isolated with more than 90 percent black enrollment. Because the State and the KCMSD intentionally created this segregated system of education, and subsequently failed to correct it, the District Court concluded that the State and the district had "defaulted in their obligation to uphold the Constitution." Id. at 1505.

Neither the State nor the KCMSD appealed this finding of liability, after which the District Court entered a series of remedial orders aimed at eliminating the vestiges of segregation. Since the District Court found that segregation had caused, among other things, "a system wide reduction in student achievement in the schools of the KCMSD," 639 F.Supp. 19, 24 (W.D.Mo.1985), it ordered the adoption, starting in 1985, of a series of remedial programs to raise educational performance. . . .

II

A

While the Court recognizes the three-part showing that the State must make under Freeman in order to get a finding of partial unitary status, it fails to acknowledge that the State did not even try to make a Freeman showing in the litigation leading up to the District Court's Order. . . . [T]he State failed even to allege its compliance with two of the three prongs of the Freeman test.

The State did not claim that implementation of the Milliken II component of the decree had remedied the reduction in student achievement in the KCMSD to the extent practicable; it simply argued that various Milliken II programs had been implemented. . . .

Nor did the State focus on its own good faith in complying with the District Court's decree; it emphasized instead the district's commitment to the decree and to the constitutional provisions on which the decree rested. . . .

Thus, it was the State's failure to meet or even to recognize its burden under Freeman that led the Court of Appeals to reject the suggestion that it make a finding of partial unitary status as to the district's Milliken II education programs. . . .

In the development of a proper unitary status record, test scores will undoubtedly play a role. It is true, as the Court recognizes, that all parties to this case agree that it would be error to require that the students in a school district attain the national average test score as a prerequisite to a finding of partial unitary status, if only because all sorts of causes independent of the vestiges of past school segregation might stand in the way of the goal. That said, test scores will clearly be relevant in determining whether the improvement programs have cured a deficiency in student achievement to the practicable extent. . . .

B

The other question properly before us has to do with the propriety of the District Court's recent salary orders. While the Court suggests otherwise, the District Court did not ground its orders of salary increases solely on the goal of attracting students back to the KCMSD. From the start, the District Court has consistently treated salary increases as an important element in remedying the systemwide reduction in student achievement resulting from segregation in the KCMSD. As noted above, the Court does not question this remedial goal, which we expressly approved in Milliken II. . . .

There is nothing exceptionable in the lower courts' findings about the relationship between salaries and the District Court's remedial objectives, and certainly nothing in the record suggests obvious error as to the amounts of the increases ordered. If it is tempting to question the place of salary increases for administrative and maintenance personnel in a desegregation order, the Court of Appeals addressed the temptation in specifically affirming the District Court's finding that such personnel are critical to the success of the desegregation effort, and did so in the circumstances of a district whose schools have been plagued by leaking roofs, defective lighting, and reeking lavatories. . . .

III

The two discrete questions that we actually accepted for review are, then, answerable on their own terms without any need to consider whether the District Court's use of the magnet school concept in its remedial plan is itself constitutionally vulnerable. . . .

The attractiveness of the Court's analysis disappears, . . ., as soon as we recognize two things. First, the District Court did not mean by an "intradistrict violation" what the Court apparently means by it today. The District Court meant that the violation within the KCMSD had not led to segregation outside of it, and that no other school districts had played a part in the violation. It did not mean that the violation had not produced effects of any sort beyond the district. . . .

A

[T]he District Court and the Court of Appeals concurred in finding that "the preponderance of black students in the [KCMSD] was due to the State and KCMSD's constitutional violations, which caused white flight. . . . [T]he existence of segregated schools led to white flight from the KCMSD to suburban districts and to private schools." Jenkins, 855 F.2d at 1302. . . .

Without the contradiction [between the finding of no interdistrict segrative effect and findings about white flight], the Court has nothing to justify its rejection of the District Court's finding that segregation caused white flight but its supposition that flight results from integration, not segregation. The supposition, and the distinction on which it rests, are untenable. At the more obvious level, there is in fact no break in the chain of causation linking the effects of desegregation with those of segregation. There would be no desegregation orders and no remedial plans without prior unconstitutional segregation as the occasion for issuing and adopting them, and an adverse reaction to a desegregation order is traceable in fact to the segregation that is subject to the remedy. When the Court quotes the

District Court's reference to abundant evidence that integration caused flight to the suburbs, then, it quotes nothing inconsistent with the District Court's other findings that segregation had caused the flight. The only difference between the statements lies in the point to which the District Court happened to trace the causal sequence. . . .

I respectfully dissent.

■ JUSTICE GINSBURG, dissenting.

■ I join JUSTICE SOUTER's illuminating dissent and emphasize a consideration key to this controversy.

The Court stresses that the present remedial programs have been in place for seven years. But compared to more than two centuries of firmly entrenched official discrimination, the experience with the desegregation remedies ordered by the District Court has been evanescent.

. . .

Today, the Court declares illegitimate the goal of attracting nonminority students to the Kansas City, Missouri, School District, and thus stops the District Court's efforts to integrate a school district that was, in the 1984/1985 school year, sorely in need and 68.3% black. Given the deep, inglorious history of segregation in Missouri, to curtail desegregation at this time and in this manner is an action at once too swift and too soon.

F. INJUNCTIONS AND DECREES AS TO FOREIGN ACTS

The Salton Sea Cases

United States Court of Appeals, Ninth Circuit, 1909.
172 Fed. 792.

[Plaintiff, a salt company, sued to enjoin defendant, a land development company, from diverting water from the Colorado River without suitable controls. The water flooded plaintiff's valuable salt deposits and damaged plaintiff's property. To divert the water, defendant had built a canal through Mexican territory and north into the Imperial Valley of California. Title to the canal and water works in Mexico was vested in a Mexican corporation, one of defendant's subsidiaries. The lower court perpetually enjoined defendant from diverting more water than was necessary for domestic and irrigation purposes, restrained defendant from diverting the water in such a way as to cause injury to the plaintiff, and awarded damages to the plaintiff. Defendant appealed.]

■ MORROW, J. . . .

It is objected that the court had no jurisdiction to compel the defendants to construct headgates in the republic of Mexico for the reason that the defendant would not have been permitted by the laws of Mexico to construct such headgates until the plans for such structures had been approved by the proper engineering authority of Mexico. The answer to this objection is the fact shown by the evidence that the only site for controlling headgates on the river below what is known as the Laguna dam, above Yuma, is at Hanlon's Heading, in California. This point was originally selected for that purpose and the title to the land for such headworks was acquired by the California Development Company. . . . The decree does not compel the defendant to construct headgates in Mexico. The flow of the river into the Salton Sink was finally placed under control in February, 1907, but this was done by placing permanent dams across the breaks in the river bank with a concrete heading in the canal about eight or nine miles below Yuma, and this appears to be the only permanent and effective control that can be placed upon the river below the international boundary line. There is no evidence that the consent of the republic of Mexico was necessary or ever obtained or asked for the building of these dams or the placing of the concrete heading.

It is further objected that the court had no jurisdiction to decree an injunction in effect abating a nuisance caused by the construction of intakes in the republic of Mexico, and it is claimed that there is a rule supporting this objection to the effect that a court of equity can never compel a defendant to do anything which is not capable of being physically done within the territorial jurisdiction of the court. This rule undoubtedly obtains where the property injured is itself outside the jurisdiction of the court. . . .

        . . . .

The injury charged in the present case was an injury to property within the jurisdiction of the court, and the party charged with the commission of the injury was also within the jurisdiction of the court. The cause of the injury was not serving a useful purpose for any one, and the relief asked for was that the party causing the injury might be enjoined from continuing to injure complainant's property within the jurisdiction of the court. Why may not a court restrain a party over whom it has jurisdiction from injuring property within its jurisdiction? How does it affect the question of jurisdiction or venue to say that the party on whom the court must act may find it necessary to do things outside the jurisdiction of the court in order to comply with the order of the court? May this not often happen, and would it not happen oftener, if it were determined that such an excuse was sufficient to defeat the jurisdiction of the court? In criminal law he who on one side of a boundary shoots a person on the other side is amenable where the blow is received. . . .

        . . . .

In civil actions the jurisdiction of the court depends upon the question whether the action is local or transitory. . . .

        . . . .

In England the rule has been stated to be that where the action is founded on two things done in several counties, and both are material or traversable, and the one without the other does not maintain the action, the plaintiff may bring his action in which county he will. . . .

. . . .

In Phelps v. McDonald, 99 U.S. 298, 25 L.Ed. 473, the court said:

> Where the necessary parties are before a court of equity, it is immaterial that the res of the controversy, whether it be real or personal property, is beyond the territorial jurisdiction of the tribunal. It has the power to compel the defendant to do all things necessary, according to the lex loci rei sitae, which he could do voluntarily, to give full effect to the decree against him. Without regard to the situation of the subject-matter, such courts consider the equities between the parties, and decree in personam.

In Miller & Lux v. Rickey, 127 F. 573, the action was brought in the Circuit Court for the District of Nevada to restrain the defendants from the wrongful diversion of the waters naturally flowing down the stream of both forks of the Walker river having their source in California, and flowing down into and through the state of Nevada, where the lands of the complainant were situated. The alleged diversion was in the state of California, and the injury caused by such diversion was in the state of Nevada. It was contended on behalf of the defendant that the Circuit Court in Nevada was without jurisdiction, first, because the suit was of a local nature, and could not be brought outside of the state of California; second, because the water right in controversy was in California; third, because the wrongs and injury alleged to have been committed by the defendant were committed wholly in the state of California; fourth, that complete relief could not be decreed by the Nevada court in favor of the complainant without reaching the property rights of the defendant which were situated wholly in California. Judge Hawley in an elaborate opinion considered the question of jurisdiction as presented by these objections, and reviewed the authorities upon the subject, meeting and answering the objection raised and urged by the defendants in this case that the court could not send its process to execute its decree into foreign territory. The court says on page 580:

> That this court has jurisdiction over the person of the defendant is unquestioned. It can reach him by injunction, and punish him for contempt if he violates it. This doctrine had its foundation in the equity courts of England at an early day. . . .

. . . .

The court accordingly maintained its jurisdiction of the action, and on appeal to this court the question was fully considered and the jurisdiction of the Circuit Court sustained. It may be further stated that in Massie v. Watts, 6 Cranch 148, Chief Justice Marshall cited the case of *Penn v. Lord Baltimore*, and made the same application of the doctrine of jurisdiction of courts of equity as was made by Judge Hawley in *Miller & Lux v. Rickey*. We are of the opinion, therefore, that the court had jurisdiction in the present case to protect property within its jurisdiction, and to restrain the defendant from diverting the waters of the Colorado river to the damage of such property, notwithstanding the defendant may find it necessary in complying with the decree of the court to perform acts beyond the jurisdiction of the court.

. . . .

The decree of the Circuit Court is affirmed.

NOTE

The following map may help readers visualize the facts of this case:

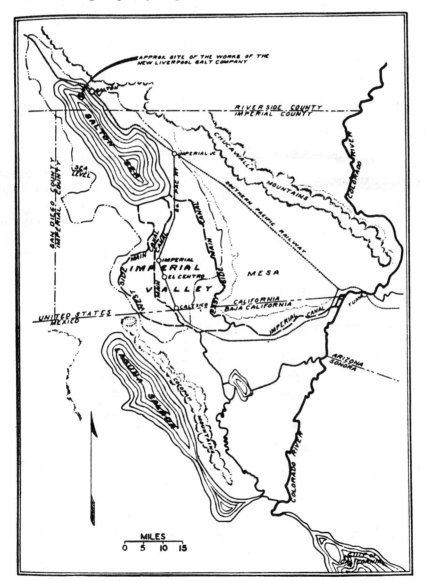

MAP OF COLORADO DELTA AND IMPERIAL VALLEY

Madden v. Rosseter

Supreme Court of New York, New York County, 1921.
114 Misc. 416, 187 N.Y.S. 462.

■ FORD, J. Plaintiff is a resident of New York and the defendant of California. Each owns a half interest in the thoroughbred stallion Friar Rock, which the plaintiff now values at $250,000. In fact the defendant paid the plaintiff $30,000 for a half interest in the horse more than two and half years ago.

Under the written agreement of sale dated June 29, 1918, the defendant was to have possession and use of Friar Rock in California during the seasons of 1919 and 1920, the plaintiff to have him for use in Kentucky during the seasons of 1921 and 1922; "thereafter on new arrangements mutually satisfactory."

The season of 1921 is now open or opening and plaintiff by the agreement is entitled in his turn to possess and use the stallion, but defendant flatly refuses to abide by his agreement, unless the plaintiff enters into a new agreement which is unsatisfactory to him.

The defendant has utterly no right to insist upon any conditions of any kind for returning the horse to plaintiff except those expressed in the agreement of sale and those require his shipment forthwith to the plaintiff's stock farm in Kentucky. Indeed he has already been kept by the defendant so far beyond the reasonable time of shipment as to substantially prejudice the plaintiff's rights. The horse should have been sent in August or September of 1920 in order to get the stallion acclimated and fit for the season of 1921, during which the plaintiff is entitled to his possession.

Personal service of the summons upon the defendant has been made in this state and he has duly appeared by his attorneys. Upon the verified complaint and affidavits the plaintiff now asks for a mandatory injunction requiring the defendant to ship Friar Rock to Kentucky as provided in the agreement and enjoining other disposition of him; also for a receiver of the stallion with power to proceed to California and to take appropriate steps there or elsewhere, including the invoking of the aid of the courts of that or any other state, or of the Federal courts, to gain possession of the animal and ship him to the plaintiff's stock farm in Kentucky.

Plaintiff's application for relief is quite novel but so is the situation in which he finds himself. Already his rights have been prejudiced and further irreparable damage is threatening him. There must be a remedy and I do not believe this court is powerless to give it to him. The relief prayed for seems to be the most practicable and appropriate which is available to him. The courts of sister states may be relied upon to aid in serving the ends of justice whenever our own process falls short of effectiveness.

The motion will be granted and the amount of the receiver's bond will be fixed upon settlement of the order.

Motion granted.

NOTE

Madden v. Rosseter was affirmed without opinion, 196 App.Div. 891, 187 N.Y.S. 943 (1921). The receiver carried out the order of the court "with tact and diplomacy," and was allowed a fee of $5,000 for his services. 117 Misc. 244, 245, 192 N.Y.S. 113, 114 (1921).

Equitable receiverships are discussed in Section F of Chapter 4, pp. 333–339.

CHAPTER 4

THE INJUNCTION

Of the various coercive equitable remedies, none is as useful and effective as the *injunction*, the in personam order by the court to a defendant, to do or to refrain from doing something. Injunctive relief is perhaps the most widely requested equitable relief. It has been decreed in the widest variety of cases and hundreds of examples can be found to demonstrate its expanding utility and flexibility. The importance of a knowledge of the injunction cannot be overstated. Professor Chafee, writing about equity, two years before his death, stated the following about the injunction:

> Injunctions are a kit of tools which can be employed effectively in all sorts of ways after one has been thoroughly accustomed to handling them. They are equally helpful against abuses of power by government officials and commissions. The operation and limitations of a particular tool, for instance the temporary mandatory injunction, are not adequately understood unless one has become familiar with the use of this tool in several different parts of the law. Again, the problem whether an injunction should be phrased in general terms or should tell the defendant just what he may do and mustn't do, is illuminated by cases on nuisances, unfair competition, family law, labor law, pollution of streams and atmosphere, and the enforcement of the Sherman Anti-trust Act.[1]

The cases seeking injunctive relief are some of the most interesting and fascinating cases to be found in the law reports. They prove the accuracy of Professor Chafee's statement as to the importance and usefulness of injunctions as a "kit of tools which can be employed effectively in all sorts of ways after one has been thoroughly accustomed to handling them."

Injunctive relief may be sought to preserve the status quo pending litigation, or to prevent a threatened injury. It may be denied if it is premature, oppressive, impractical, or impossible to enforce. It is an effective remedy enforceable by the court's power to punish for contempt.

For a thought-provoking article on the concept of "prophylactic" remedy, see Tracy A. Thomas, *The Prophylactic Remedy: Normative Principles and Definitional Parameters of Broad Injunctive Relief,* 52 BUFF. L. REV. 301 (2004). In this article, Professor Thomas states that *The Prophylactic Remedy* imposes specific measures directing defendant's legal conduct affiliated with the proven wrong to prevent future harm; and that, "[p]rophylaxis has become the remedy of choice for violations of intangible rights

---

1. CHAFEE, *FOREWORD TO RE*, SELECTED ESSAYS ON EQUITY iii (1955).

protecting constitutional, personal, and community values because of its effectiveness in preventing hard that is otherwise difficult to redress." *Id.* at 302.

———

A. INTERLOCUTORY INJUNCTIONS

Hughes v. Cristofane

United States District Court, District of Maryland, 1980.
486 F.Supp. 541.

[handwritten: P — owner of 3 Captains Restaurant. D — Mayor & councilmen]

■ MURRAY, J. The plaintiffs are the owners and major shareholders of the Three Captains House of Seafood Restaurant in Bladensburg, Maryland; the defendants are the mayor and town councilmen of Bladensburg. The plaintiffs, whose restaurant has until recently provided entertainment in the form of "topless" dancing, seek a temporary restraining order enjoining enforcement of a recently-enacted Bladensburg town ordinance which prohibits such entertainment in establishments that serve alcoholic beverages or food. After hearing oral argument on the matter from both sides, and having considered the applicable law, the court has concluded that the restraining order should issue as the plaintiffs have requested.

. . . .

[handwritten: TRO.]

In order to obtain relief by a temporary restraining order under Rule 65 of the Federal Rules, the plaintiffs must show:

(1) that unless the restraining order issues, they will suffer irreparable harm;

(2) that the hardship they will suffer absent the order outweighs any hardship the defendants would suffer if the order were to issue;

(3) that they are likely to succeed on the merits of their claims;

(4) that the issuance of the order will cause no substantial harm to the public; and

(5) that they have no adequate remedy at law.

The plaintiffs have satisfied each of the prerequisites.

If a restraining order did not issue, the owners of the Three Captains Restaurant would suffer irreparable harm both to their financial interests and to their interest in the free exercise of constitutional rights. According to the affidavit of plaintiff Bernard Hughes, filed with the court on February 20, 1980, the gross income of his restaurant was "generally" over $1000 and rarely less than $800 per day before he clothed his dancers on February 14th in order to comply with Ordinance 3–80. Since he has complied, the business has averaged $700 a day. Because Mr. Hughes requires at least $750 to $800 gross income per day to meet expenses, he has been operating at a loss since the topless dancing ceased. He anticipates that his business may fail if the dancers must continue to comply with the ordinance. Other courts have found that loss of revenue, when specifically described, constitutes irreparable harm, and this court believes Mr. Hughes has made an adequate showing under that standard.

More importantly, the plaintiffs have made an adequate showing that if enforcement of the ordinance is not enjoined, the law might operate to infringe the first and fourteenth amendment freedoms not only of the plaintiffs, but also of other proprietors and entertainers subject to the law's requirements. Such a showing satisfies not only the irreparable harm requirement, but also the likelihood-of-success requirement.

In the first place, the weight of authority in the federal courts is that nude dancing which cannot be characterized as obscene is a form of expression entitled to some protection under the first amendment. Although several state courts have held nude dancing not to be protected under the first amendment, those cases are arguably distinguishable on their facts, and do not necessarily support the proposition that topless dancing *per se* is never protected expression.[2]

. . . .

The plaintiffs have also made an adequate showing that Ordinance 3–80 may be unconstitutionally overbroad, and may violate principles of equal protection. . . .

. . . .

Given the plaintiffs' substantial showing of threatened irreparable harm, it is not difficult to conclude that the balance of hardships tips in the plaintiffs' favor. If the temporary restraining order should issue, the only resulting hardship to the defendants will be a return to the status quo before the ordinance took effect. Because the defendants have not shown that the status quo injured anything other than their moral sensibilities, the court feels that the importance of the plaintiffs' constitutional rights outweighs the defendants' interests. For the same reasons, the court finds that enjoining the enforcement of Ordinance 3–80 will not substantially harm the public interest.

The plaintiffs have also satisfied the court that they have no adequate remedy at law. If the status quo is not preserved, the passage of time required to litigate the plaintiffs' claims will work the irreparable injury the plaintiffs have described.

The plaintiffs have thus met all the prerequisites for obtaining a temporary restraining order. The court is mindful that the remedy is an extraordinary one, but is persuaded that the case presents the urgency and special circumstances that make extraordinary relief necessary.

---

2. [In Barnes v. Glen Theatre, Inc., 501 U.S. 560, 111 S.Ct. 2456, 115 L.Ed.2d 504 (1991), the Supreme Court ultimately held that the first amendment does not bar the prohibition of non-obscene nude dancing in this type of setting. In *Barnes*, two establishments that wished to provide totally nude dancing as entertainment sought to enjoin the enforcement of Indiana's public indecency law on first amendment grounds. In upholding the public indecency statute, Chief Justice Rehnquist stated that the statute was "narrowly tailored" and that Indiana's "requirement that the dancers wear at least pasties and a G-string is modest, and the bare minimum necessary to achieve the State's purpose."]

Accordingly, the Town of Bladensburg and its agents will be temporarily enjoined from enforcing Ordinance 3–80, and the court will issue a separate order to that effect. However, nothing in this opinion or in the order should be deemed to affect any state proceedings stemming from enforcement of the ordinance prior to today's date.

Order

For the reasons set forth in the Memorandum Opinion dated this 22nd day of February, 1980, it is this same date, by the United States District Court for the District of Maryland,

ORDERED:

(1) that the plaintiffs' request for a temporary restraining order be, and the same hereby is *Granted;*

(2) that effective immediately, defendants Mayor and Councilmen of the Town of Bladensburg and their agents be, and the same hereby are *Restrained* from enforcing Ordinance 3–80 of the Town of Bladensburg for a period of ten days from the date of this Order;

(3) that plaintiffs give security by filing forthwith with the Clerk of this Court a bond in the sum of $500.00 for the payment of such costs and damages as may be incurred or suffered by defendants if found to be wrongfully enjoined or restrained;

(4) that this matter be heard on plaintiffs' request for preliminary injunction at 4:30 p.m. on Monday, March 3, 1980.

———

NOTES

1. Fed.R.Civ.P. 65 provides, in part:

(a) Preliminary Injunction.

(1) *Notice.* No preliminary injunction shall be issued without notice to the adverse party....

(b) Temporary Restraining Order; Notice; Hearing; Duration. A temporary restraining order may be granted without written or oral notice to the adverse party or his attorney only if (1) it clearly appears from specific facts shown by affidavit or by the verified complaint that immediate and irreparable injury, loss, or damage will result to the applicant before the adverse party or his attorney can be heard in opposition, and (2) the applicant's attorney certifies to the court in writing the efforts, if any, which have been made to give the notice and the reasons supporting his claim that notice should not be required. Every temporary restraining order granted without notice shall be indorsed with the date and hour of issuance; shall be filed forthwith in the clerk's office and entered of record; shall define the injury and state why it is irreparable and why the order was granted without notice; and shall expire by its terms within such time after entry, not to exceed 10 days, as the court fixes, unless within the time so fixed the order, for good cause shown, is extended for a like period or unless the party against whom the order is directed consents that it may be extended for a longer period. The reasons for the extension shall be entered of record. In case a temporary restraining order is granted without notice, the motion for a preliminary injunction shall be set down for hearing at the earliest possible time and takes precedence of all matters except older matters of the same character; and when the motion comes on for hearing the party who obtained the temporary restraining order shall proceed with the application for a preliminary injunction and, if he does not do so, the court shall dissolve the temporary restraining order. On 2 days' notice to the party who obtained the temporary restraining order without notice or on such shorter notice to that party as the court may prescribe, the adverse party may appear and move its dissolution or modification and in that event the court shall proceed to hear and determine such motion as expeditiously as the ends for justice require.

(c) Security. No restraining order or preliminary injunction shall issue except upon the giving of security by the applicant, in such sum as the court deems proper, for the payment of such costs and damages as may be incurred or suffered by any party who is found to have been wrongfully enjoined or restrained. No such security shall be required of the United States or of an officer or agency thereof. . . .

2.   Temporary restraining orders, unlike preliminary injunctions, are generally not appealable. For the relevant federal statutes, see the note on page 88.

3.   See factors considered in request for preliminary equitable relief in United States v. Price, p. 297.

4.   On preliminary injunctive relief, see Thomas R. Lee, Preliminary Injunctions and the Status Quo, 58 Wash. & Lee L. Rev. 109 (2001).

Abbott Laboratories v. Mead Johnson & Company

United States Court of Appeals, Seventh Circuit, 1992.
971 F.2d 6.

[Manufacturer of oral electrolyte maintenance solution ("Abbott—Pedialyte") sought preliminary injunction against rival manufacturer ("Mead—Ricelyte") in suit under the Lanham Act for false advertising and trade dress infringement. The District Court denied the request for injunctive relief. The Court of Appeals reversed and remanded the case for further consideration of less drastic preliminary injunctive measures.]

■ Flaum, Circuit Judge.

Abbott Laboratories (Abbott) filed this interlocutory appeal, 28 U.S.C. § 1292(a)(1), after the district court denied its motion for a preliminary injunction against Mead Johnson & Company (Mead). Abbott seeks relief under § 43(a) of the Lanham Act (the Act), 15 U.S.C. § 1125(a), to halt Mead's alleged false advertising and trade dress infringement practices in the oral electrolyte maintenance solution (OES) market. We vacate the district court's denial of preliminary relief, and remand with directions to promptly commence a full trial on the merits.

I.

Oral electrolyte maintenance solutions are over-the-counter medical products used to prevent dehydration in infants suffering from acute diarrhea or vomiting. They are clear liquids, comprised almost exclusively of water, electrolytes and dissolved carbohydrates, and are ingested orally. While OES products do not actually cure diarrhea or nausea, they maintain the fluid balance of infants inflicted with these maladies by facilitating the body's absorption of fluids and electrolytes. The OES market is a small (approximately $45 million in annual sales) but important one[.] ...

Abbott and Mead are, for all practical purposes, the only two competitors in the United States OES market. Abbott's product is called "Pedialyte," while Mead's is called "Ricelyte". Competition in this market is of surprisingly recent vintage, as Pedialyte enjoyed a virtual monopoly until Mead introduced Ricelyte in 1990. The two products are virtually identical; only their carbohydrate components differ....

The OES market, unlike typical consumer product markets, is "professionally driven," meaning that Abbott and Mead do not promote their product directly to consumers, but rather to physicians and nurses, who in turn recommend them to consumers....

Since Pedialyte is the incumbent and Ricelyte the challenger, Mead launched a promotional campaign designed to convince physicians and nurses to recommend Ricelyte over Pedialyte....

Abbott did not take kindly to Mead's promotional and advertising campaign. It filed suit, alleging that the campaign, up to and including the "Ricelyte" name, was false and misleading in violation of § 43(a)(2) of the Act. Abbott also alleged that Ricelyte's bottle, label and overall packaging infringed upon Pedialyte's trade dress in violation of § 43(a)(1) of the Act. Abbott asked for a preliminary injunction, seeking a wide variety of relief, ranging in severity from a product recall to modifications in Mead's advertising and promotional materials. The district court approved an expedited discovery schedule submitted by the parties, held a ten-day evidentiary hearing, and heard one day of oral argument. Shortly thereafter it issued an order, accompanied by a lengthy and thorough memorandum opinion, denying Abbott's preliminary injunction motion in full.

....

II.

Despite our recent efforts to clarify the law of preliminary injunctions, confusion persists, as demonstrated by the contrasting spins both parties place upon the four-part preliminary injunction standard. To guide our analysis, as well as assist litigants in future cases, we briefly outline the following precepts, and note the parties' deviation therefrom in the margin.

As a threshold matter, a party seeking a preliminary injunction must demonstrate (1) some likelihood of succeeding on the merits, and (2) that it has "no adequate remedy at law" and will suffer "irreparable harm" if preliminary relief is denied. If the moving party cannot establish either of these prerequisites, a court's inquiry is over and the injunction must be denied. If, however, the moving party clears both thresholds, the court must then consider: (3) the irreparable harm the non-moving party will suffer if preliminary relief is granted, balancing that harm against the irreparable harm to the moving party if relief is denied; and (4) the public interest, meaning the consequences of granting or denying the injunction to non-parties.

The court, sitting as would a chancellor in equity, then "weighs" all four factors in deciding whether to grant the injunction, seeking at all times to "minimize the costs of being mistaken." American Hosp. Supply Corp. v. Hospital Prods. Ltd., 780 F.2d 589 (7th Cir.1986). We call this process the "sliding scale" approach: the more likely it is the plaintiff will succeed on the merits, the less the balance of irreparable harms need weigh towards its side; the less likely it is the plaintiff will succeed, the more the balance need weigh towards its side.[2] This weighing process, as noted, also takes into consideration the consequences to the public interest of granting or denying preliminary relief.[3] While we have at times framed the sliding

---

2.   Mead, pointing to an isolated dictum in Maxim's Ltd. v. Badonsky, 772 F.2d 388, 391 (7th Cir.1985), states that if the balance of irreparable harms (factor number 3 in the text) tips toward the defendant, the preliminary injunction must be denied regardless of the strength of plaintiff's case on the merits. This statement is erroneous. It is the balance of harms discounted by the parties' relative chances of succeeding on the merits (and taking account of the public interest), not the undiscounted balance of harms, that must weigh in plaintiff's favor for a preliminary injunction to issue. To buttress its position, Mead also relies upon a passage in Diginet, 958 F.2d at 1394, which reads: "Given the exceptionally one-sided balance of harms [in defendant's favor], it is plain that the injunction should not have been issued, regardless of the likely merits of the [plaintiff's] claim." When read in context, however, this passage does not support Mead's position. We characterized the balance of harms as "exceptionally one sided" because the plaintiff in Diginet failed to demonstrate that it would suffer any irreparable harm in the event preliminary relief were denied; in fact, we found that the plaintiff would benefit from a denial. Id. As such, the plaintiff could not clear the second preliminary injunction threshold (factor number 2 in the text), and hence was doomed to lose regardless of its chances of succeeding on the merits. To illustrate our point, consider the following. Plaintiff X seeks a preliminary injunction against defendant Y. Suppose that the (undiscounted) balance of irreparable harms tips slightly toward Y—in other words, that X will be irreparably harmed 9x if the court denies preliminary relief, while Y will be harmed 10x if the court grants it.

Suppose further that X has a 99 percent chance of succeeding on the merits, Y a one percent chance, and that the public interest is not implicated by the case. The proper course in this instance—recognizing, of course, that quantifying the factors to this degree of precision is likely impossible— would be to grant preliminary relief, for that is the course that would minimize the cost of error. Weighing the equities as a whole favors X, making preliminary relief appropriate, even though the undiscounted balance of harms favors Y.

3.   Both parties state that a plaintiff, to obtain a preliminary injunction, must show that the injunction would not harm the public interest. This, in effect, adds a third threshold to our preliminary injunction standard by making the public interest factor dispositive. Although the statement finds support from a dictum in Brunswick Corp. v. Jones, 784 F.2d 271, 274 n. 1 (7th Cir. 1986)(as a prerequisite, plaintiff must establish that "an injunction would not harm the public interest"), we question whether it accurately characterizes the law of the circuit. The public interest is one factor courts must consider in weighing the equities; it is not dispositive. Suppose, to take a simple example, that the balance of harms tips significantly in plaintiff's favor, that plaintiff has an overwhelming chance of succeeding on the merits, but that granting the injunction would ever so slightly impair the public interest (e.g., by removing one of ten products from a given product market). In this instance, preliminary relief would be proper even though it might harm the public interest.

scale approach in mathematical terms, it is more properly characterized as subjective and intuitive, one which permits district courts to "weigh the competing considerations and mold appropriate relief." Lawson Prods., Inc. v. Avnet, Inc., 782 F.2d 1429, 1436 (7th Cir.1986).

. . . .

III.

The district court, as noted, denied Abbott's request to enter a preliminary injunction under § 43(a)(2) of the Act to halt Ricelyte's allegedly false and misleading promotional campaign. The court found that Abbott had demonstrated a likelihood of succeeding on the merits, but determined that the remaining three preliminary injunction factors favored Mead. We find that the court misconstrued the legal principles underlying each of those three factors, and hence that it abused its discretion in completely denying preliminary relief.

A.

Section 43(a)(2) of the Act prohibits the use of false or misleading statements or representations of fact in commercial advertising, and establishes a private remedy for any violation thereof. The provision applies with equal force to (1) statements which are literally false and (2) statements which, while literally true or ambiguous, convey a false impression or are misleading in context, as demonstrated by actual consumer confusion. The district court determined that Abbott had established a likelihood of prevailing at trial on the merits. Mead, advancing an alternative ground for affirmance, contends otherwise. We consider separate aspects of Mead's promotional campaign in turn, keeping in mind throughout that to pass this threshold Abbott need only demonstrate some likelihood of prevailing on the merits, not that it will definitely prevail.

. . . .

[W]e agree with the district court's determination that Abbott has established a likelihood of succeeding on the merits of its § 43(a)(2) cause of action.

B.

The second preliminary injunction threshold requires Abbott to establish that it will be irreparably harmed if it does not receive preliminary relief, and that money damages and/or an injunction ordered at final judgment would not rectify that harm. The district court determined that Abbott did not clear this threshold. In so holding, the court acknowledged the well-established presumption that injuries arising from Lanham Act violations are irreparable, even absent a showing of business loss. This presumption, it appears, is based upon the judgment that it is virtually impossible to ascertain the precise economic consequences of intangible harms, such as damage to reputation and loss of goodwill, caused by such violations.

There can be no doubt that Mead's Ricelyte campaign, which attempts to convince consumers that Pedialyte is an inferior OES product, has dented Abbott's reputation. The district court nonetheless found the presumption of irreparable harm rebutted owing to the unusual structure of the OES market. It reasoned as follows: Pedialyte enjoyed a virtual monopoly prior to Ricelyte's entry into the market. Any injunction, entered after a full trial, would remove Ricelyte from the market, thereby restoring Pedialyte's monopoly and lost market share. Under these circumstances, one could easily measure the sales Abbott lost while waiting for final judgment. As far as the future is concerned, Abbott's reputational damage will have no tangible economic impact because Pedialyte will have regained its monopoly, leaving those who need OES products with no other choice. It appears, then, that we are faced with a rare situation—any harm to Abbott's reputation and goodwill wreaked by Mead's promotional campaign between now and final judgment will be fully compensable in money damages, and therefore cannot be considered irreparable. Put another way, the fact that injunctive relief in Abbott's favor at final judgment would boot Ricelyte from the market renders compensable any injuries Abbott will have suffered in the interim.

The district court's conclusion rests upon two assumptions. First, the court assumed that if final judgment forced Mead to withdraw Ricelyte, Abbott's losses would be limited to past lost sales in the OES market. In our view, this assumption overlooks the fact that Mead's promotional campaign will probably have lingering, incalculable economic consequences even if final relief on the merits drives Ricelyte from the market. Any monopoly Abbott regains is unlikely to last very long. (We of course do not mean to imply that Abbott deserves a monopoly, or that a monopoly would benefit the OES market, but only that Abbott's damages would be difficult to calculate in the event it could not sustain a monopoly.) It is almost certain that Mead will re-enter, or some other company will enter, the OES market shortly after Ricelyte departs; the market has a proven potential for growth, see Dist.Op. at 80, and the dominant player has proven potentially vulnerable. Pedialyte's loss of goodwill will have tangible economic consequences once competition reemerges, because doubts planted by the Ricelyte campaign will linger in the minds of consumers and physicians, who may avail themselves of an alternative to Pedialyte if given the choice. Moreover, any shifts in the OES market between now and final judgment will affect the closely related competition between Abbott and Mead in the immense infant formula market, which accounts for more than $1.5 billion in annual sales. Mead acknowledged as much in its 1991 Marketing Plan, which opined that "[t]he more market share Ricelyte takes from Pedialyte, the more opportunities Ricelyte creates to" shift infant formula sales from Abbott to Mead. Any suggestion that forcing Ricelyte from the market after a full trial would completely reverse this shift is simply implausible.

The loss of market share Abbott will likely suffer in both the OES market (once competition reemerges) and the infant formula market was not considered by the district court. As an original matter, one could have concluded that Abbott would suffer these harms were preliminary relief denied, and that the difficulty, indeed practical impossibility, of quantifying them would render monetary relief inadequate, and hence Abbott's injuries irreparable. It is more difficult, however, to determine whether the court's decision not to consider these harms constitutes an abuse of discretion.

We need not resolve that issue here, for the district court erred by assuming in the first instance that granting final injunctive relief to Abbott would necessarily mean the end of Ricelyte. Granted, some of the relief sought by Abbott—e.g., an order requiring Mead to recall Ricelyte, change its label, and immediately cease use of the "Ricelyte" name—would eliminate Ricelyte from the market at least temporarily, and perhaps permanently. But other relief—e.g., an order prohibiting Mead from purveying the false "rice claims" and directing it to issue corrective advertisements and brochures—would not have such drastic consequences. These less severe remedies would leave Ricelyte a viable, albeit somewhat discredited, competitor with at least part of its current market share.

The district court did not address the possibility of ordering these intermediate forms of relief after a full trial on the merits. This, we believe, constitutes an error of law. It is axiomatic that injunctions, preliminary as well as permanent, have their basis in equity. When faced with a motion for a preliminary injunction, a district court must remain flexible, and weigh the equities as to each element of preliminary relief sought by the plaintiff. The same applies to final relief if, as here, the potential parameters of a permanent injunction will influence the equities that govern the propriety of issuing a preliminary injunction. The importance of flexibility is enhanced where those equities depend in great measure upon which preliminary and permanent remedies are ordered. We therefore find that the district court abused its discretion by restricting its focus to those final remedies, to the exclusion of all others, that would eliminate Ricelyte from the market.

If on remand the district court should revisit the topic of preliminary relief, it should explicitly consider whether Abbott's injuries between now and final judgment would be irreparable if some intermediate form of relief were eventually ordered after a full trial. We take no formal stand on this issue, but offer the following observations. Any inquiry must start with the well-established, and in this case unchallenged, presumption that Lanham Act injuries are irreparable. While the district court found this presumption rebutted, we have concluded that an assumption underlying the court's rebuttal was erroneous as a matter of law. Absent any considerations we have not had occasion to address, we can see no reason why the presumption should not stand here. Less severe relief, as we just observed, would leave Ricelyte a viable competitor in the OES market, making it extremely difficult to measure Abbott's damages. Some consumers, particularly new parents, would choose Ricelyte for reasons unrelated to Mead's promotional campaign. Other consumers would inevitably choose Ricelyte on the basis of impressions formed during that campaign; this group includes, for example, consumers who accepted their physicians' initial recommendation to purchase Ricelyte but who were not subsequently informed that the recommendation rested upon false premises. In theory, one could differentiate between the two groups of consumers, and thus calculate the damages arising from Mead's campaign. In practice, however, it would "be very difficult to distinguish the effect of the [campaign] from the effect of other [factors causing consumers to purchase Ricelyte], and to project that effect into the distant future." This difficulty would appear to render monetary relief inadequate, and hence Abbott's injury irreparable.

Again, by offering these thoughts we do not intend to foreclose the possibility that Mead could rebut, in some other way, the presumption of irreparable harm. We certainly do not intend to suggest that the court must enter the forms of final relief, if any, that would render Abbott's interim injuries irreparable. Finding that, given certain assumptions regarding the potential scope of final relief, Abbott's injuries are irreparable only would mean that it has cleared the second preliminary injunction threshold; the wisdom of granting preliminary relief would then depend upon the discretionary weighing of all four preliminary injunction factors. Id. at 593. We conclude only that the district court's analysis of the second preliminary injunction threshold was erroneous as a matter of law.

C.

We next consider the public interest. The district court concluded that granting Abbott's request for a preliminary injunction would disserve the public interest. Ricelyte, the court reasoned, is a safe and effective product whose presence in the market has promoted the public welfare by focusing attention upon OES products and increasing their use. The court also believed that forcing Ricelyte from the market would restore Abbott's former virtual monopoly, dousing competitive incentives to invest in additional research and develop more effective OES products.

We agree with the district court that forcing Ricelyte from the market would harm the public interest. It is a rare case where purging a safe and effective product serves broad societal interests. This is particularly so when the purged product is one of only two in a given market; monopolies, as a general rule, carry substantial social costs, including higher prices, lower output, and a reduced incentive to engage in product innovation beneficial to consumers. The costs are even higher when, as here, important health concerns are involved.

But we decline to accept the court's implicit assumption that granting Abbott preliminary relief would necessarily mean the demise of Ricelyte, for the same reasons we just rejected that assumption with regard to final injunctive relief. As noted, some forms of intermediate relief, such as ordering Mead to purge the false aspects of its promotional campaign and issue corrective advertising, would leave Ricelyte a viable competitor. In fact, such relief would serve, rather than disserve, the public interest in truthful advertising, an interest that lies at the heart of the Lanham Act. The court therefore committed an error of law by not addressing less severe remedies that would have addressed the allegedly false and misleading aspects of Ricelyte's campaign without eliminating it from the market.

D.

The district court also determined that the balance of hardships tilted in Mead's favor—in other words, that the irreparable harm to Mead of granting preliminary relief would outweigh the irreparable harm to Abbott of denying such relief. It based this ruling upon a finding that the relief requested by Abbott, most notably an injunction prohibiting Mead's further use of the name Ricelyte, would drive Ricelyte from the market for some period of time, and hence might be "fatal" to the product's survival. This, the court stated, would work a "significant" irreparable harm to Mead, a harm which would far outweigh the "possible damage" to Abbott of denying preliminary relief. We believe that the court's analysis contains two legal errors which led it to understate the harm to Abbott of denying an injunction and to overstate the harm to Mead of granting an injunction.

The first error we have already discussed: the court abused its discretion in concluding that Abbott would not suffer any irreparable harm if preliminary relief were denied. The second we have discussed as well. The district court's assessment that Mead would be significantly harmed by a preliminary injunction purging Ricelyte from the market rests on the supposition that any injunction entered would do just that. This supposition is unfounded, for imposing a less severe remedy would most likely wound, but not kill, Ricelyte. Consequently, the sting of a preliminary injunction would depend upon its scope, and could have been less injurious to Mead than the court surmised. These two errors of law, we believe, distorted the district court's assessment of the balance of irreparable harms.

Having found that the district court (1) overstated the irreparable harm to Mead and the public interest of granting a preliminary injunction, and (2) possibly overlooked the irreparable harm to Abbott of denying an injunction, we cannot accept its conclusion that the equities weigh in Mead's favor as to Abbott's false advertising claim under § 43(a)(2).

IV.

The district court also denied Abbott's request under § 43(a)(1) of the Act to enter a preliminary injunction to halt Mead's alleged infringement of Pedialyte's trade dress. The court concluded that Pedialyte's trade dress is "functional," and therefore that Abbott had failed to establish that it was likely to prevail on the merits under § 43(a)(1), thus sinking its chances for preliminary relief at the outset. We disagree with the court's conclusion, . . .

. . . .

B.

We proceed to the second threshold inquiry: whether Abbott has an adequate remedy at law and whether it will suffer an irreparable harm if it does not obtain preliminary relief on its trade dress claim. Our prior discussion of the irreparable harm issue, although made in the context of Abbott's false advertising claim, applies with equal, if not greater, force here. We observe (again) only that enjoining Mead's alleged infringement of Pedialyte's trade dress after a full trial would not necessarily force Ricelyte from the market. For example, the court could permit Mead to continue using Ricelyte's current packaging, but order it to print new labels and/or develop a non-square bottle as soon as commercially feasible.

Our prior discussion of the public interest factor in § III.C, *supra*, also applies with equal force here, as does our discussion of the balance of hardships in § III.D, *supra*. For the foregoing reasons, we cannot accept the district court's conclusion that Abbott was not entitled to preliminary relief on its § 43(a)(1) trade dress infringement claim.

* * * * * *

In cases such as this, we traditionally have done one of two things: reverse and direct the district court to order the preliminary relief we deem appropriate, or vacate and remand for renewed consideration under the proper legal standards. We decline to do the former because the district court, owing to its superior familiarity with the underlying facts of this case, is in a far better position than we to weigh the equities and fashion a proper remedy. We also decline to do the latter in the interests of expediency and judicial economy; the parties indicated at argument that they are virtually ready for a full trial on the merits and need only limited time for additional discovery. We therefore vacate the district court's denial of Abbott's request for a preliminary injunction, and remand with directions to commence a full trial on the merits within 60 days. If, contrary to our assumptions, there is no prospect for a trial within that time, we remand with directions to fashion appropriate preliminary relief, if any, in accordance with this opinion.

One final note. As we have emphasized throughout, the district court's analysis suffered from its near exclusive focus upon the most drastic remedies requested by Abbott (e.g., product recall) to the exclusion of less severe remedies (e.g., corrective advertising). This focus, we learned at argument, resulted from the district court's decision to adopt, nearly verbatim, the proposed findings of fact and conclusions of law submitted by the parties; obviously, the court selected some of Abbott's proposals and some of Mead's. Each party, it appears, tried to hit a home run, Abbott by submitting conclusions of law granting it all the relief it sought, and Mead by submitting conclusions of law granting Abbott nothing. Neither offered alternative conclusions that steered a reasonable middle ground. So, when it came time for the court to assess the impact upon the parties and the public of granting or denying preliminary relief, the court considered only the impact of either granting the most severe relief or shutting Abbott out altogether.

Of course there is nothing wrong and everything right with zealous advocacy. But counsel, when drafting proposed conclusions of law for the district court, should bear in mind a crucial observation to which we alluded above: courts retain a great deal of flexibility when fashioning preliminary relief, and the equities weighed under the four-part preliminary injunction standard can shift as the nature of that relief varies. Nor do we cast aspersions upon the widespread practice in the busy district courts of adopting many or most of the parties' proposed findings of fact and conclusions of law, particularly if skillfully and wisely drafted. Nonetheless, district judges also should bear in mind our observations regarding the nature of preliminary relief, and, when presented with proposed findings and conclusions that hug the extremes, consider developing alternatives of their own.

Vacated and Remanded, with Directions.

———

NOTE

In LeSportsac, Inc. v. K Mart Corp., 754 F.2d 71 (2d Cir.1985), the court stated:

A party seeking a preliminary injunction in this circuit must establish both possible irreparable injury and either (1) a likelihood of success on the merits or (2) sufficiently serious questions going to the merits to make them a fair ground for litigation and a balance of hardships tipping decidedly in the movant's favor. . . .

————

Coyne–Delany Co. v. Capital Development Board

United States Court of Appeals, Seventh Circuit, 1983.
717 F.2d 385.

■ POSNER, J. The principal questions for decision are the extent of the district court's power to deny damages to a defendant injured by the issuance of a preliminary injunction that is later reversed on appeal, and the proper standard for exercising that power.

The genesis of this case is an otherwise unrelated civil rights suit brought by inmates of the Illinois state prison at Stateville complaining about living conditions. A decree was entered requiring the prison to replace all of the plumbing fixtures in one of the prison's cellhouses. The state's Capital Development Board let a contract for the first of two projected phases of the work to Naal Plumbing & Heating Co., which subcontracted with Coyne–Delany Company for the flush valves required in the project ... The valves were installed, and malfunctioned. After Coyne–Delany shipped redesigned valves which also malfunctioned, the prison authorities asked the Capital Development Board to designate another valve subcontractor in the bidding specifications for the second phase of the contract. The Board complied, designating Sloan [Company].

Bids were received, but on May 7, 1979, two days before they were to be opened, Coyne–Delany sued the Board under section 1 of the Civil Rights Act of 1871, 42 U.S.C. § 1983, and on May 8 it obtained a temporary restraining order against the Board's opening the bids. The state asked that Coyne–Delany be ordered to post a $50,000 bond, pointing out that the temporary restraining order was preventing it from proceeding with the entire project and that indefinite delay could be extremely costly. But Judge Perry ... required a bond of only $5,000, in the belief that the temporary restraining order would be in effect for only a week until Judge Bua could hear the motion for a preliminary injunction. However, at the preliminary-injunction hearing Judge Bua issued the injunction but refused to increase the bond.

    . . . .

The premise of Coyne–Delany's civil rights suit against the Capital Development Board was that under Illinois law as expounded by the Illinois Appellate Court in Polyvend, Inc. v. Puckorius, 61 Ill.App.3d 163, 18 Ill.Dec. 524, 377 N.E.2d 1160 (1978), Coyne–Delany, as an indirect bidder on the plumbing contract for the Stateville cellhouse, had a property right of which it was deprived without due process of law by the Board's requiring Naal to use Sloan valves merely because the prison authorities had determined—unreasonably in Coyne–Delany's opinion—that Coyne–Delany's valves were defective. When he issued the preliminary injunction Judge Bua said that Coyne–Delany was likely to prevail on the merits, especially given the Board's refusal to submit the dispute over the quality of Coyne–Delany's valves to an impartial expert for binding determination, as Coyne–Delany had proposed. This court reversed the grant of the preliminary injunction, however. Noting that *Polyvend* had been reversed by the Illinois Supreme Court, after Judge Bua had granted the preliminary injunction to Coyne–Delany, we held that under Illinois law a bidder, and *a fortiori* an indirect bidder, has no property right in being allowed to bid on a public contract and that Coyne–Delany therefore had no claim against the Board under the Fourteenth Amendment.

Our decision came down on February 22, 1980, and a few days later the Board at last opened the bids that had been submitted back in May 1979. Naal was the low bidder, with a bid of $214,000, but its bid had lapsed because of the passage of time, and the Board had to solicit new bids. The new bids were opened on May 9, 1980. Although Naal's new bid, $270,000, was higher than its old bid had been, Naal was again the low bidder and was awarded the contract.

The Board then joined Hanover Insurance Company, the surety on the injunction bond, as an additional defendant in Coyne–Delany's civil rights suit, pursuant to Rule 65.1 of the Federal Rules of Civil Procedure, and moved the district court to award the Board damages of $56,000 for the wrongfully issued preliminary injunction and statutory costs (filing fees and the like, see 28 U.S.C. § 1920) of $523 which the Board had incurred in the district court. Judge Bua refused to award either costs or damages. His opinion states, "the Court must weigh the equitable factors of the case, including whether the case was filed in good faith or is frivolous....[T]he parties have stipulated that the case was filed in good faith and without malice. Further, it is apparent that the case was not frivolous. The law as it existed at the time the case was filed clearly favored the plaintiffs. It would be unreasonable to require a party to anticipate a change in the law and would be unconscionable to label a suit filed in good faith as frivolous where there is such a subsequent change."

There is no dispute over the amount of costs claimed by the Board; and while Coyne–Delany has not conceded that the Board incurred damages of $56,000 as a result of the delay of the project and the district court made no finding with respect to those damages, they undoubtedly exceeded $5,000, the amount of the injunction bond....The specifications for the second round of bids were apparently the same as those for the first round. The Board must therefore have lost much more than $5,000 on the difference in the bids alone. And it may well have incurred other costs from the delay of the project by a year.

. . . .

The language of Rule 65(c), governing damages on an injunction bond, is ...: "No restraining order or preliminary injunction shall issue except upon the giving of security by the applicant, in such sum as the court deems proper, for the payment of such costs and damages as may be incurred or suffered by any party who is found to have been wrongfully enjoined or restrained." The court is not told in so many words to order the applicant to pay the wrongfully enjoined party's damages. But it is told to require a bond or equivalent security in order to ensure that the plaintiff will be able to pay all or at least some of the damages that the defendant incurs from the preliminary injunction if it turns out to have been wrongfully issued. The draftsmen must have intended that when such damages were incurred the plaintiff ... would normally be required to pay the damages, at least up to the limit of the bond.

Yet some courts treat the district court's discretion to award or deny damages under an injunction bond as completely open-ended unless the plaintiff acted in bad faith in seeking the preliminary injunction. The principal cases, Page Communications Engineers, Inc. v. Froehlke, 475 F.2d 994 (D.C.Cir.1973)(per curiam), and H & R Block, Inc. v. McCaslin, 541 F.2d 1098 (5th Cir.1976)(per curiam), rely on Russell v. Farley, 105 U.S. 433, 26 L.Ed. 1060 (1881), where the Supreme Court stated that "in the absence of an imperative statute to the contrary, the court should have the power to mitigate the terms imposed [in granting the injunction], or to relieve from them altogether, whenever in the course of the proceedings it appears that it would be inequitable or oppressive to continue them." Although the statement partakes of dictum because the injunction had not been dissolved completely, a more important point is the absence, at the time the case was decided, of any statute or rule of court dealing with security for federal court injunctions. The Court discussed state statutes and rules, precursors of Rule 65(c), requiring injunction bonds, and only then stated that because of the absence of a federal statute or rule the federal courts "must *still* be governed in the matter by the general principles and usages of equity." The implication is that a rule requiring an injunction bond would have changed the Court's result—would have been the "imperative statute" to which it referred.

Page and *H & R Block* do not consider this reading of Russell or cite Houghton v. Cortelyou, 208 U.S. 149, 28 S.Ct. 234, 52 L.Ed. 432 (1908), where the Court narrowed the discretion that *Russell* had given district courts to relieve from liability under an injunction bond. And they dismiss Rule 65(c)'s requirement of a bond or other security by pointing out that the district court can require a bond of nominal amount in appropriate cases, for example if the plaintiff is indigent. But it is one thing to say that the requirement of a bond can in effect be waived when there is a good reason for doing so ... and another to say that where a substantial bond is clearly required by the equities of the case the district court nevertheless has carte blanche to excuse the plaintiff from paying any damages on the bond.

Most cases hold, contrary to *Page* and *H & R Block,* that a prevailing defendant is entitled to damages on the injunction bond unless there is a good reason for not requiring the plaintiff to pay in the particular case. We agree with the majority approach. Not only is it implied by the text of Rule 65(c) but it makes the law more predictable and discourages the seeking of preliminary injunctions on flimsy (though not necessarily frivolous) grounds.

When rules prescribe a course of action as the norm but allow the district court to deviate from it, the court's discretion is more limited than it would be if the rules were nondirective.... The judge must have a good reason for departing from such a principle in a particular case. It is not a sufficient reason for denying costs or damages on an injunction bond that the suit had as in this case been brought in good faith. That would be sufficient only if the presumption were against rather than in favor of awarding costs and damages on the bond to the prevailing party.... The award of damages on the bond is not punitive but compensatory.

A good reason for not awarding such damages would be that the defendant had failed to mitigate damages. The district court made no reference to any such failure in this case and we can find no evidence that there was any; the Board's requesting and obtaining a 30–day extension of time for filing its appeal brief, the factor stressed by Coyne–Delany, did not create material or unreasonable delay. A good reason not for denying but for awarding damages in this case, unmentioned by the district court, was that the bond covered only a small fraction of the defendant's damages. The Board asked for and should have been granted a much larger bond; and when the heavy damages that the Board had predicted in asking for the larger bond materialized, it had a strong equitable claim to recover its damages up to the limit of the bond....

Although the district court's decision cannot stand, both because it applies an incorrect standard and because it fails to consider and evaluate the full range of factors (which might in an appropriate case include, but is not exhausted by, the plaintiff's good faith) that would be relevant under the proper standard, we are not prepared to hold that the Board is entitled as a matter of law to its costs and to its injunction damages up to the limit of the bond. The district court did allude to one factor, besides mere absence of bad faith, that supported its ruling—the change in the applicable law after the preliminary injunction was issued. The law on which the court had relied in issuing the injunction was contained in an intermediate state appellate court decision and of course such decisions are reversed with some frequency. We do not believe that a change in the law is always a good ground for denying costs and injunction damages to a prevailing party, but it is a legitimate consideration, perhaps especially where the prevailing party is a state agency that benefited from a change in the law of its state. In a sense, this is a case where one state agency (the Board) is seeking to benefit from the confusing signals sent out by another state agency (the court system)—though we do not mean to suggest that the Illinois Supreme Court was rushing fraternally to the aid of another state agency when it reversed *Polyvend*. In any event, a remand is necessary to allow Judge Bua to consider and weigh all the relevant factors identified in this opinion—bearing in mind the principle of preference that we have indicated should guide his equitable determination.

It remains to consider whether on remand the Board should be allowed to seek injunction damages above the limit of the bond. The surety cannot be required to pay more than the face amount of the bond, but it is a separate question whether the plaintiff can be. However, the Ninth Circuit has held in a scholarly opinion that the bond is the limit of the damages the defendant can obtain for a wrongful injunction, even from the plaintiff, provided the plaintiff was acting in good faith, which is not questioned here. Buddy Systems, Inc. v. Exer–Genie, Inc., 545 F.2d 1164, 1167–68 (9th Cir.1976). (Another exception might be where the plaintiff was seeking restitution rather than damages.) The Supreme Court has cited *Buddy Systems* in dictum for the proposition that "a party injured by the issuance of an injunction later determined to be erroneous has no action for damages in the absence of a bond." Although there was a bond in the present case, it states unequivocally: "The obligation of this bond is limited to $5,000.00." In asking for more, the Board is necessarily relying not on the bond but on some principle of equity that [the Court] says does not exist.

Rightly or wrongly, American common law, state and federal, does not attempt to make the winner of a lawsuit whole by making the loser reimburse the winner's full legal expenses, even when the winner is the defendant, who unlike a prevailing plaintiff does not have the consolation of a damage recovery. In noninjunctive suits, except those brought (or defended) in bad faith, the winner can recover only his statutory costs, invariably but a small fraction of his expenses of suit. It would be incongruous if a prevailing defendant could obtain the full, and potentially the staggering, consequential damages caused by a preliminary injunction. The preliminary injunction in this case halted work on a major construction project for a year; it could easily have been two or three years, and the expenses imposed on the defendant not $56,000 but $560,000. . . .

. . . .

A defendant's inability to obtain damages in excess of the bond unless the plaintiff was acting in bad faith can have unfortunate results, which are well illustrated by this case where the district court required too small a bond. But a defendant dissatisfied with the amount of bond set by the district court can, on appeal from the preliminary injunction, ask the court of appeals to increase the bond, which the defendant here did not do. . . .

Since Coyne–Delany is conceded to have brought this suit in good faith, the Board is not entitled to any damages above the $5,000 fixed in the bond. . . .

REVERSED AND REMANDED.

B.   MANDATORY INJUNCTIONS

Vane v. Lord Barnard

Court of Chancery, 1716.
2 Vern. 738, 23 Eng.Rep. 1082.

The defendant, on the marriage of the plaintiff, his eldest son, with the daughter of Morgan Randyll and 10,000*l.* portion, settled (*inter alia*) Raby

Castle on himself for life, without impeachment of waste,[5] remainder to his son for life, and to his first and other sons in tail male.

The defendant, the Lord Barnard, having taken some displeasure against his son, got two hundred workmen together, and of a sudden in a few days, stript the castle of the lead, iron, glass doors, and boards, & c., to the value of 3000*l.*

The court [LORD COWPER, L.C.], upon filing the bill (and plea and answer put in by Lord Barnard), granted an injunction to stay committing of waste, in pulling down the castle; and now, upon the hearing of the cause, decreed, not only the injunction to continue, but that the castle should be repaired, and put into the same condition it was in, in August, 1714, and for that purpose a commission was to issue to ascertain what ought to be repaired, and a master to see it done at the expense and charge of the defendant, the Lord Barnard; and decreed the plaintiff his costs.

NOTES

1.   As Sir George Jessel, M.R., observed in Smith v. Smith, L.R. 20 Eq. 500 (1875), "At one point it was supposed that the [Equity] Court would not issue mandatory injunctions at all." A reluctance to grant mandatory interlocutory injunctive relief has lingered long after judicial discomfort towards mandatory permanent injunctions abated.

2.In 1908, Professor Langdell was able to write,

When ... justice requires that a tort should be specifically repaired, it would seem to be much more feasible for a court of equity itself to undertake the repair of it at the expense of the tortfeasor, than to attempt to compel the latter to repair it....[Yet the only instance seems to be Vane v. Barnard.] The decree directed the master to see the castle repaired at the defendant's expense. Whether the decree was ever performed or not does not appear. It is said not to have been performed during the defendant's life.

LANGDELL, BRIEF SURVEY OF EQUITABLE JURISDICTION 36, 37 (2d ed. 1908).

3.   Fed.R.Civ.P. 70 authorizes the type of relief granted in Vane. See *supra* pp. 154–55.

Cooling v. Security Trust Co.

Court of Chancery of Delaware, 1946.
29 Del.Ch. 286, 49 A.2d 121.

■ SEITZ, V.C. This is the decision on defendant's motion to dissolve a mandatory preliminary injunction heretofore entered in this cause.

The bill of complaint was filed by Emily R. Cooling as guardian ad litem by appointment of this court for her two minor children who are beneficiaries under a certain trust, the terms of which are set forth in an

---

5. [This means that the tenant—i.e.,   in the law courts for waste committed during
Lord Barnard—could not be called to account   his tenure.]

opinion filed in this court in the case of Security Trust Company et al. v. Cooling et al., 28 Del.Ch. 303, 42 A.2d 784 [1945].

The defendant is the Security Trust Company, trustee under the last will of Severson B. Cooling, Sr., and as such is trustee of the estate of which the minors heretofore mentioned are beneficiaries.

It also appears that the defendant Security Trust Company is the guardian of the same minor children by appointment of the Orphans' Court of this state. It is also a coexecutor of the estate of Severson B. Cooling, Sr., and its activities in that behalf should be challenged by the defendant as trustee, according to the complainant.

The bill had attached thereto what were described as exceptions, which the complainant contended the defendant as trustee should file to its accounts as coexecutor. It also set forth that though requested defendant refused to file the exceptions mentioned. The bill then recited that the complainant as guardian ad litem for the minor children had no way of knowing whether or not the defendant trustee had received from the executors the written notice required under the Constitution and Laws of the State of Delaware of the filing of the executors' accounts so as to bar the trustee from filing exceptions to such accounts.

The complainant then alleged as follows: "Your Complainant alleges that an irreparable damage will be done to the estate of the said minors if said Exceptions are not filed, and filed immediately, unless an admission is made by the Executors that they have not complied with the Constitution and Statute of the State of Delaware, in respect to the sending of notice of the filing of the account; . . ."

The bill prayed for a mandatory preliminary injunction directing the defendant trustee to file in the Orphans' Court exceptions to the final account filed by it as a coexecutor of the estate of Severson B. Cooling, Sr., and also to file exceptions to all other accounts to which written notice has not been received of the filing.

. . . .

Moreover, and of extreme importance, I concluded that this court had the power under the circumstances to grant the mandatory preliminary injunction, and that the Delaware cases . . . do not hold that this court is powerless in all cases to grant a preliminary injunction, mandatory in character.

The application for the preliminary injunction had to be heard and disposed of on the same day due to the possible running of the statute of limitations against the filing of exceptions to the accounts of the executors. As a consequence, no opinion was filed.

The defendant trustee now moves to dissolve the mandatory preliminary injunction for the reason that this court "has no power, authority, or jurisdiction to direct the issuance of a Preliminary Injunction, mandatory in nature and such action was an abuse of discretion."

Defendant's solicitor argues that the above-cited cases clearly hold "that the Court of Chancery has no jurisdiction, power or authority to decree the issuance of a preliminary injunction, mandatory in nature". I cannot agree that such a generalization is justified from a reading of the cases. True it is that the courts in the cases mentioned concluded that the power did not exist under the attendant facts to grant the mandatory preliminary injunction requested. It seems to me, however, that "power" as used in the Delaware cases is no more than a conclusion that in the ordinary situation the issuance of a mandatory preliminary injunction would violate the sound legal discretion which the Chancellor is required to exercise. Language and quotations contained in certain of the Delaware cases relied upon by defendant's solicitor indicate quite clearly that the court recognized the possibility of the existence of an unusual case where a mandatory preliminary injunction would issue. . . . Such a situation was described in some of the cases as an "exception" to the general rule. However, without regard to nomenclature, I feel that as applied to the present facts, the question involved the case where the power exists and should be exercised whether such a situation be considered an exception to the usual rule, or—as I prefer it—merely a principle of law applicable to a particular set of facts.

To consider the problem as a question of power rather than one of discretion is to fail to take cognizance of the situation which warranted and necessitated the creation of equity jurisdiction, viz., the limited and rigid remedies at law. The power to grant a mandatory preliminary injunction is lacking in this court only if the court so concludes of its own initiative, because I know of no constitutional or statutory limitation in this respect. If the exercise of the power is susceptible of such abuse that it should not be available to a court of equity, then let the appropriate body remove such power. I prefer to believe that the power exists in a proper case, and that it becomes the duty of this court to determine whether, under the circumstances, it should be exercised. Such a conclusion to my mind is not inconsistent with the Delaware authorities, and is by no means unusual. As Mr. Pomeroy states in a footnote in his Treatise on Equity Jurisprudence, Vol. 4, 5th ed., § 1359a: "16. Preliminary mandatory injunctions have undoubtedly been granted more freely by the English courts than by the American. Indeed, it has been said in some American decisions that a mandatory *interlocutory* injunction would never be granted. This doctrine is not only opposed to the overwhelming weight of authority, but is contrary to the principle which regulates the administration of preventive relief, and is manifestly absurd."

     . . . .

However, it is equally important to emphasize that a mandatory preliminary injunction should only issue to preserve the status quo in the true sense of that term. In my opinion, the issuance of the injunction here served that purpose. This court recognizes that the power exists, but it also realizes that there are stringent prerequisites to the exercise of the power.

Only by the issuance of the mandatory preliminary injunction could it be assured that a possible trust asset would not be lost here. When such a showing is made, I feel that this court has the power and the duty to issue an appropriate injunction. I conclude, therefore, that this court had the power, authority, and jurisdiction to direct the issuance of the mandatory preliminary injunction under the facts shown.

. . . .

The motion to dissolve the mandatory preliminary injunction heretofore entered in this cause is denied.

An order accordingly will be advised.

NOTE

Moreno Mutual Irrigation Co. claimed that Trautwein was a common carrier of water, a status that Trautwein disclaimed. Moreno Mutual sought, and was awarded, an injunction pendente lite permitting it to transport water to plaintiff Moreno Water Co. through Trautwein's irrigation system. Trautwein v. Moreno Mutual Irrigation Company, 22 F.2d 374 (9th Cir.1927). The court wrote:

The right of the plaintiffs to the injunction granted is not entirely clear. It has been held in many cases that a mandatory injunction will not be issued on an interlocutory application. "But this view is against the weight of authority, which recognizes the power of a court of equity to award preliminary mandatory injunctions, and holds that it is proper to do so in extreme cases, where the right is very clear indeed, and where considerations of the relative inconvenience bear strongly in complainant's favor; and especially is this so where the acts complained of are willful and fraudulent and without any pretense of right. While it is generally true that the office of a preliminary injunction is to preserve the status quo until, upon final hearing the court may grant full relief, and that this can be accomplished by an injunction prohibitory in form, it sometimes happens that the status quo is a condition, not of rest, but of action, and the condition of rest is what will inflict the irreparable injury complained of, in which circumstances courts of equity may issue mandatory writs before the case is heard on its merits." Inasmuch as the defendants were not transporting or carrying water for the plaintiffs immediately prior to the demand in question, it is doubtful whether the status quo in this case was a condition of action; but, after all, the question rests very largely in the discretion of the court, and the principal consideration is the relative inconvenience to the parties that will result from granting or refusing the relief.

United States v. Price

United States Court of Appeals, Third Circuit, 1982.
688 F.2d 204.

■ RE, C.J.* In this action, brought under section 7003 of the Resource Conservation and Recovery Act (RCRA), 42 U.S.C. § 6973, and section 1431 of the Safe Drinking Water Act (SDWA), 42 U.S.C. § 300i, plaintiff United States, on behalf of the Administrator of the Environmental Protection Agency (EPA), appeals from the denial of its application for a preliminary injunction. The requested injunction would have required defendants to (1) fund a diagnostic study of the threat to Atlantic City's public water supply

---

* Sitting by designation pursuant to 28
U.S.C. § 293(a).

posed by toxic substances emanating from Price's Landfill, a former commercial landfill, and (2) provide an alternate water supply to homeowners whose private wells have been contaminated by substances leaching from the landfill.

The question presented on this appeal, whether the district court abused its discretion in denying plaintiff's request for preliminary relief, is answered in the negative. Therefore, we affirm and direct the district court to proceed as expeditiously as possible with a trial on the merits of this action. In view of certain findings and conclusions of the district court, we deem it necessary to comment on the availability of equitable relief in actions brought under these provisions.

. . . .

While we agree with the district court that in this case it was not required to grant the requested preliminary relief, its reasoning casts doubt upon the powers of federal courts to grant the requested preliminary equitable relief. In its conclusions of law, the district court expressed an unduly restrictive view of its remedial powers both under traditional equitable doctrines as well as under the endangerment provisions of RCRA and SDWA.

A court of equity has traditionally had the power to fashion any remedy deemed necessary and appropriate to do justice in the particular case. As stated in Hecht Co. v. Bowles, 321 U.S. 321, 329, 64 S.Ct. 587, 591, 88 L.Ed. 754 (1944):

> The essence of equity jurisdiction has been the power of the Chancellor to do equity and to mould each decree to the necessities of the particular case. Flexibility rather than rigidity has distinguished it. The qualities of mercy and practicality have made equity the instrument for nice adjustment and reconciliation between the public interest and private needs. . . .

Equity, in addition to achieving an individualization of justice, is also, in the words of Professor Zechariah Chafee, "a set of effective and flexible remedies admirably adapted to the needs of a complex society.". . . .

By enacting the endangerment provisions of RCRA and SDWA, Congress sought to invoke the broad and flexible equity powers of the federal courts in instances where hazardous wastes threatened human health. Indeed, these provisions have enhanced the courts' traditional equitable powers by authorizing the issuance of injunctions when there is but a risk of harm, a more lenient standard than the traditional requirement of threatened irreparable harm.

Whether authorized by statute or traditional equitable powers, a request for preliminary equitable relief requires a court of equity to weigh several factors in the effort to determine whether the request should be granted. Among the factors which guide the exercise of the courts' equitable discretion are: "(1) the probability of irreparable injury to the moving party in the absence of relief; (2) the possibility of harm to the non-moving party if relief is granted; (3) the likelihood of success on the merits; and (4) the public interest." The process of balancing these factors should not be abandoned merely because the preliminary relief requested is uncommon, non-traditional or novel.

In the case before us, the district court explained that, because plaintiff's request for funds to conduct a diagnostic study would have required monetary payments, it was an inappropriate form of preliminary equitable relief. In the eyes of the district court, it was an attempt to transform a claim for damages into an equitable action by asking for an injunction that orders the payment of money. This perception was based on the district court's reading of Jaffee v. United States, 592 F.2d 712 (3d Cir.1979). In *Jaffee,* the plaintiff alleged that, as a soldier in the United States Army, he and other soldiers had been ordered to stand in an open field where they were exposed to radiation without their knowledge or consent. Plaintiff further alleged that, as a result of this exposure, he had developed inoperable cancer. This court affirmed the district court's denial of plaintiff's request for a preliminary injunction requiring the government to pay medical expenses, stating that the relief requested was a traditional form of damages in tort, and not a proper subject for equitable relief. The court of appeals, however, reversed the district court's denial of plaintiff's request for a preliminary injunction requiring the government to warn members of plaintiff's class about possible medical risks. The court stated: "Although providing the warning will impose an expense on the Government, the creation of an expense does not necessarily remove a form of relief from the category of equitable remedies."

We do not agree that *Jaffee* leads to the conclusion that, in this case, plaintiff's request for an injunction was actually a claim for damages. Damages are awarded as a form of substitutional redress. They are intended to compensate a party for an injury suffered or other loss. A request for funds for a diagnostic study of the public health threat posed by the continuing contamination and its abatement is not, in any sense, a traditional form of damages. The funding of a diagnostic study in the present case, though it would require monetary payments, would be preventive rather than compensatory. The study is intended to be the first step in the remedial process of abating an existing but growing toxic hazard which, if left unchecked, will result in even graver future injury, i.e., the contamination of Atlantic City's water supply.

The appropriateness of issuing a mandatory preliminary injunction in a case in which the status quo "is a condition not of rest, but of action" was recognized in Toledo, A.A. & N.M. Ry. Co. v. Pennsylvania Co., 54 F. 730, 741 (C.C.N.D.Ohio 1893). There the court stated:

> The office of a preliminary injunction is to preserve the status quo until, upon final hearing, the court may grant full relief. Generally this can be accomplished by an injunction prohibitory in form, but it sometimes happens that the status quo is a condition not of rest, but of action, and the condition of rest is exactly what will inflict the irreparable injury upon complainant.... In such a case courts of equity issue mandatory writs before the case is heard on its merits.
>
> .... The facts of the present case show clearly that the status quo is a condition of action which, if allowed to continue or proceed unchecked and unrestrained, will inflict serious irreparable injury. Therefore, a mandatory

preliminary injunction designed to prevent that injury would have been appropriate if the other criteria relevant to issuing preliminary injunctions were satisfied. A preliminary injunction designed to prevent an irreparable injury is conceptually distinct from a claim for damages.

The fact that an injunction may require the payment or expenditure of money does not necessarily foreclose the possibility of equitable relief. In Crawford v. University of North Carolina, 440 F.Supp. 1047 (M.D.N.C. 1977), the district court issued a mandatory preliminary injunction ordering the university to procure and compensate an interpreter for the benefit of a deaf student. In granting the requested relief the court stated:

> Mandatory injunctions should be used sparingly. Moreover, an injunction should not work so as to give a party the full relief which he seeks on the merits, especially when the order would require the payment of money. Notwithstanding, it would appear that in a case where a party requests a mandatory preliminary injunction, the test is still one of balancing the competing interests.

In C.B.S., Inc. v. ASCAP, 320 F.Supp. 389, 392 (S.D.N.Y.1970), it was stated that:

> Although courts are rarely called upon to issue mandatory injunctions calling for the payment of moneys pendente lite, they have done so when the equities and the circumstances of the case demonstrated the appropriateness of the remedy.

Thus, even though funding a diagnostic study would require payments of money, it may still be an appropriate form of preliminary relief if the traditional balancing process tips decidedly in favor of plaintiff.

It is not unusual for a defendant in equity to expend money in order to obey or perform the act mandated by an injunction. Injunctions, which by their terms compel expenditures of money, may similarly be permissible forms of equitable relief. In all cases the question the court must decide is whether, considering all of the circumstances, it is appropriate to grant the specific relief requested.

An example is found in the case of Wheelock v. Noonan, 108 N.Y. 179, 15 N.E. 67 (1888). In *Wheelock,* plaintiff brought an action to compel defendant to remove from certain lots owned by plaintiff a quantity of rocks and boulders deposited there by defendant. In granting the requested relief the court explained:

> It is now said that the remedy was at law; that the owner could have removed the stone and then recovered of the defendant for the expense incurred. But to what locality could the owner remove them? He could not put them in the street; the defendant presumably had no vacant lands of his own on which to throw the burden; and it would follow that the owner would be obliged to hire some vacant lot or place of deposit, become responsible for the rent, and advance the cost of men and machinery to effect the removal. If any adjudication can be found throwing such burden upon the owner, compelling him to do in advance for the trespasser what the latter is bound to do, I should very much doubt its authority. On the contrary the law is the other way.

Judicial precedents indicate that the preliminary relief requested by plaintiff in this action was not inappropriate. Furthermore, it seems clear that it falls within the range of remedies contemplated and specifically authorized by Congress when it enacted the endangerment provisions of RCRA and SDWA.

. . . .

Although it was within the power of the district court to grant the requested preliminary relief, the procedural posture of this litigation militates against granting it on this appeal. It would bind only a few of more than 35 defendants, and to require these few to bear the entire cost of the requested relief might prove impractical and unfair.

The district court found that an imminent danger existed at the time of the hearing. Nevertheless, it may well be that the public interest counseled against the grant of the requested preliminary relief. Very large sums of money were required to pay for the diagnostic study, and there may have been some question about the original defendants' financial ability to fund it. In those circumstances, the most practical and effective solution may well have been to refuse the government's request for a preliminary injunction thereby necessitating the study be undertaken by EPA without delay. Prompt preventive action was the most important consideration. Reimbursement could thereafter be directed against those parties ultimately found to be liable.

. . . .

The judgment of the district court will be affirmed.

Friends for All Children, Inc. v. Lockheed Aircraft Corporation

United States Court of Appeals, District of Columbia Circuit, 1984.
746 F.2d 816.

■ STARR, J. This is a tort action on behalf of Vietnamese orphans for injuries suffered in a tragic aviation accident in South Vietnam in 1975. The suit is over eight years old, and this appeal is the fourth before this court. Seven years after the action was filed, the District Court granted partial summary judgment on a motion on behalf of the Vietnamese children adopted by non-U.S. parents, holding that Lockheed was liable for the cost of diagnostic examinations of the children. Finding that approximately forty adopted Vietnamese children living in France faced irreparable injury unless they promptly obtained diagnostic examinations, the court entered a mandatory injunction *pendente lite*. The injunction ordered Lockheed to create a $450,000 fund from which reasonable expenses of diagnostic examinations would be paid.

. . . .

Lockheed claims that even if partial summary judgment was appropriate, the entry of a preliminary mandatory injunction, ordering it to pay $450,000 into the Registry of the District Court, was improper. Lockheed argues that it is always impermissible for a court to provide interim equitable relief in a suit the ultimate objective of which is the recovery of money damages—the classic remedy at law. Lockheed invokes no less an authority than Learned Hand as the *fons et origo* of this doctrine. In Sims v. Stuart, 291 F. 707 (S.D.N.Y.1922), Judge Hand displayed no hesitation in rejecting the plaintiff's motion for a mandatory injunction ordering a collector of customs in advance of trial to return money that the plaintiff contended had illegally been seized. Judge Hand stated:

> The acts charged constitute, on the plaintiff's theory, a conversion, nothing more. Under the guise of a mandatory injunction I do not see how I can give final relief in advance of answer and trial in such a case. It is, of course, true that equity will at times affirmatively restore the status quo ante pending the suit. But never, so far as I know, will it take jurisdiction over a legal claim merely to hurry it along by granting final relief at the outset of a cause. . . . I cannot suppose that it would anywhere be seriously contended that upon a conversion of money the victim might file a bill in equity and get final relief by mandatory injunction.

Judge Hand's remarks have enjoyed wide and lasting currency. In Enercons Virginia, Inc. v. American Security Bank, N.A., 720 F.2d 28 (D.C.Cir.1983), this court recently had occasion to quote *Sims* in reversing a temporary restraining order enjoining a bank from refusing to honor a cashier's check payable to the plaintiff. The *Enercons* court emphasized that since the plaintiff's action was a "straightforward action on a negotiable instrument," the plaintiff possessed an adequate remedy at law and the injunction was impermissible.

We have no quarrel whatever with *Sims'* result. But, critically, the *Sims* line of cases differs from the instant case in one vital respect: in those cases liability had not yet been determined, whereas here the defendant has already been adjudicated as *liable* for the costs of reasonable diagnostic testing. Only the computation of the *amount* of damages remains for the trier of fact. In our view, the *Sims* rule should not rigidly be erected as an absolute bar to a limited intervention by equity designed to prevent irreparable harm in those circumstances where, as here, the defendant's liability has already been determined through stipulation or partial summary judgment prior to trial. The invocation of equity in such a case reflects a common-sense notion of fairness that undergirds equity jurisprudence: it is more just that a defendant already adjudged liable bear the risk that an interim computation of damages will be fixed too high by the court than to have the plaintiff bear the risk of receiving damages too late to be of any use.

To be sure, the language of *Sims* and other cases cited by Lockheed seems to announce flatly that courts should not entertain interim equitable relief when a remedy at law—money damages—is deemed adequate to provide final relief in the plaintiff's action. In short, equity is perceived in these cases as an interloper threatening to trample law's well-cultivated garden. We cannot agree, however, that equity should never, under any circumstances, be permitted to provide interim relief in an action at law. While our legal system quite properly views damages ultimately as an adequate compensation for a particular kind of loss, it simply does not follow that equity may never be properly called upon, in order to prevent irreparable injury, to accelerate recovery of a portion of damages likely to be awarded when liability has already been determined. Lockheed's counsel commendably admitted at oral argument that once summary judgment was granted, the only circumstance preventing the award of damages for diagnostic examinations was the need to conduct individual trials for the approximately forty French plaintiffs on the issue of the reasonable cost for such examinations. The inability of normal legal channels to provide plaintiffs the necessary relief to prevent their suffering irreparable harm provides under these circumstances the classic case warranting the chancellor's intervention.

Moreover, in the circumstances of this case, we believe that a slavish adherence to *Sims'* dictum would be inconsistent with the deep-rooted power of equity to do what is necessary and appropriate to achieve justice in the individual case. Other courts have refused to forbid rigidly the entry of preliminary injunctions that create monetary funds, the proceeds of which are to be used to prevent injury. For instance, in United States v. Price, 688 F.2d 204 (3d Cir.1982) [infra, p. 297], the District Court had refused to grant a preliminary injunction which would have ordered a company to provide funds for a diagnostic study of the environmental hazards to the Atlantic City water supply created by the company's landfill, because interim equitable relief that granted monetary damages was in its view inappropriate. The Third Circuit affirmed the District Court's denial of preliminary relief, but rejected its rationale. The court noted that funds for a diagnostic study were not a traditional form of compensatory damages but rather a "first step in [a] remedial process" designed to prevent serious irreparable injury. Similarly in the instant case, the funds for diagnostic examinations do not simply represent compensation for past injury, but are required to prevent future injury. To allow this injunction to stand therefore creates no new equitable principle.

. . . .

Finally, appropriate to the novelty of the case before us, we emphasize the narrowness of today's holding. We hold only that a preliminary injunction requiring the defendant to create a fund to pay for diagnostic exams is proper when the defendant has been held liable for the cost of such examinations and when the delay inherent in trying the case to compute the amount of the defendant's liability will result in irreparable injury. Moreover, under our holding, plaintiffs must show that they meet the traditional standards governing the award of equitable relief, and the District Court must seek to minimize the prospect that a plaintiff will receive any funds that a trier of fact will subsequently fail to award.

. . . .

Having concluded that the traditional factors favor the granting of equitable relief, we affirm the judgment of the District Court.

Affirmed.

C.   SPECIFICITY

Collins v. Wayne Iron Works

Supreme Court of Pennsylvania, 1910.
227 Pa. 326, 76 A. 24.

■ Opinion by MR. JUSTICE MOSCHZISKER.

The plaintiff below, appellee here, filed a bill against the defendant below, appellant here, alleging a nuisance from the noise created by the operation of defendant's works.

. . . .

... The learned court below found: "The noises of which complaint is made are not reasonably endurable or bearable, and render the dwelling of complainant during the operation of said iron works uncomfortable and unfit for use as the residence of a reasonable and ordinary person." The following decree was entered: "It is ordered, adjudged and decreed that you, Wayne Iron Works, your servants, agents and employees do abate the nuisance complained of in said bill, and you are hereby enjoined and restrained from the operation of your works by at any time making noises with air drills, power hammers, power chippers, riveting machines or other tools or apparatus so as to render the premises of the plaintiff described in the said bill unfit for use and enjoyment as a residence by a reasonable and normal person."

The defendant contends: first, that the decree does not specifically point out the things that it is required to do or to refrain from doing in order to abate the nuisance which the court found to exist; and, second, that the evidence in the case does not justify such a sweeping decree as the one entered.

The entry of an injunction is, in some respects, analogous to the publication of a penal statute; it is a notice that certain things must be done or not done, under a penalty to be fixed by the court. Such a decree should be as definite, clear and precise in its terms as possible, so that there may be no reason or excuse for misunderstanding or disobeying it; and when practicable it should plainly indicate to the defendant all of the acts which he is restrained from doing, without calling upon him for inferences or conclusions about which persons may well differ. In the present instance, the only definite thing that the defendant is ordered to do is "to abate the nuisance complained of in said bill." As the evidence does not show any improper or negligent operation of the machinery, and as the defendant's conclusion as to what constitutes "a reasonable and normal person" may well differ from that of the plaintiff, it would seem that the only safe way to comply with the decree would be to entirely stop the running of its machinery. Where the facts and equities call for it, a chancellor is required to give relief by injunction; but such injunction should never go beyond the requirements of the particular case; and under no circumstances should a decree be entered the apparent practical effect of which will be to close an industrial plant, if it is possible to frame another form of decree which will give such relief as the plaintiff is entitled to. . . .An important question is, Can the noise by any reasonable means be so moderated so as to accord with the degree of quietness the plaintiff has a right to enjoy; and if it can, by what means?

   . . . .

   . . . We find no manifest error in any of the findings of fact made by the court below; but in addition thereto, the testimony suggests and is sufficient to sustain the further finding that the disturbance of the standard of comfort normally prevailing in the neighborhood of the plaintiff's residence, and the consequent annoyance to the plaintiff, are caused by the defendant's permitting the use of tools and apparatus of a noisy character on its premises outside of its buildings; by their use inside of certain of its buildings with the windows and doors open; and at times by the use of such tools and apparatus until late in the evenings.

On this finding, a definite decree can be entered enjoining the defendant from operating tools, machines or apparatus of a noisy character between certain hours, and requiring it to carry on all such operations on the inside of buildings with windows securely closed and with doors shut. This decree will probably afford the relief required. At least such a measure of relief should be first tried before the entry of a decree that may mean the closing of the defendant's works, the ruin of a prosperous business, and the loss of employment to many men.

   . . . .

The twenty-second assignment of error, which goes to the form of the decree, is sustained, and the decree entered by the court below is modified; and it is now adjudged, ordered and decreed that the Wayne Iron Works, its servants, agents and employees are restrained from working its plant in such a manner as to create the nuisance complained of, and to that end they are enjoined from operating drills, power hammers, power chippers, riveting machines or other tools, machines or apparatus of a noisy character between the hours of 7 p.m. and 7 a.m.; and from operating such tools, machines and apparatus of a noisy character at any time unless on the inside of buildings with all windows securely closed with double sash, and with the doors shut. . . .

NOTES

1.   In Swift & Co. v. United States, 196 U.S. 375, 25 S.Ct. 276, 49 L.Ed. 518 (1905), Justice Holmes wrote,

> The general words of the injunction "or by any other method or device, the purpose and effect of which is to restrain commerce as aforesaid," should be stricken out. The defendants ought to be informed, as accurately as the case permits, what they are forbidden to do. Specific devices are mentioned in the bill, and they stand prohibited. The words quoted are a sweeping injunction to obey the law, and

are open to the objection which we stated at the beginning, that it was our duty to avoid.

2.   An *ex parte* injunction in a separation suit, restraining the defendant from "annoying, following," etc., his wife or children, was modified on application for dissolution and cross-application for attachment of the husband for contempt for annoying his wife by a letter, Laurie v. Laurie, 9 Paige Ch. 234 (1841). Walworth, C., stated:

> As the defendant is bound to obey the process of the court at his peril, the language of the injunction should in all cases be so clear and explicit that an unlearned man can understand its meaning, without the necessity of employing counsel to advise him what he has a right to do to save him from subjecting himself to punishment for a breach of injunction. And the language of the writ should at the same time be so restricted as not to deprive him of any rights which the case made by the bill does not require that he should be restrained from exercising.

3.   In many cases the decree is framed so as not to prohibit the defendant's business altogether, by the use in the injunction of such general words as "to the injury of the plaintiff." Usually the defendant is content with the form of the decree and does not request more specific words.

This kind of relief, like the remedial approach approved in *Collins,* is known as an experimental decree. Experimental decrees have been used in many other cases, with varying results. For example, in Georgia v. Tennessee Copper Co., 206 U.S. 230, 27 S.Ct. 618, 51 L.Ed. 1038 (1907), a suit by the State of Georgia to bar the discharge of noxious gas from two Tennessee smelting plants, the Supreme Court held, "If the State of Georgia adheres to its determination, there is no alternative to issuing an injunction, after allowing a reasonable time to the defendants to complete the structures that they now are building, and the efforts that they are making, to stop the fumes." One defendant's efforts cut its emissions in half, but, because Georgia continued to demand an injunction, the Court ordered that defendant to keep detailed records and appointed an expert to make recommendations. 237 U.S. 474, 35 S.Ct. 631, 59 L.Ed. 1054 (1915). After receiving the expert's report, the Court issued a final decree regulating the amount of gas that the defendant could permit to escape into the air. 240 U.S. 650, 36 S.Ct. 465, 60 L.Ed. 846 (1916). In the end, this litigation resulted in the reduction of emissions and the emergence of sulphuric acid as a profitable commercial by-product of copper smelting. The Court had much less success with the experimental decree entered in Brown v. Board of Education, 349 U.S. 294, 75 S.Ct. 753, 99 L.Ed. 1083 (1955), which ordered the end of segregation in the public schools "with all deliberate speed."

Schmidt v. Lessard

Supreme Court of the United States, 1974.
414 U.S. 473, 94 S.Ct. 713, 38 L.Ed.2d 661.

■ Per curiam.

In October and November 1971, appellee Alberta Lessard was subjected to a period of involuntary commitment under the Wisconsin State

Mental Health Act, Wis.Stat. § 51.001 et seq. While in confinement, she filed this suit in the United States District Court for the Eastern District of Wisconsin, on behalf of herself and all other persons 18 years of age or older who were being held involuntarily pursuant to the Wisconsin involuntary-commitment laws, alleging that the statutory scheme was violative of the Due Process Clause of the Fourteenth Amendment. Jurisdiction was predicated on 28 U.S.C. § 1343(3) and 42 U.S.C. § 1983. . . .

. . . [T]he District Court filed a comprehensive opinion, declaring the Wisconsin statutory scheme unconstitutional. The opinion concluded by stating that

"Alberta Lessard and other members of her class are entitled to declaratory and injunctive relief against further enforcement of the present Wisconsin scheme against them. . . .[Miss Lessard] is also entitled to an injunction against any further extensions of the invalid order which continues to make her subject to the jurisdiction of the hospital authorities."

Over nine months later, the District Court entered a judgment, which simply stated that

"It is Ordered and Adjudged that judgment be and hereby is entered in accordance with the Opinion heretofore entered."

. . . .

. . . [A]lthough sufficient to invoke our appellate jurisdiction, the District Court's order provides a wholly inadequate foundation upon which to premise plenary judicial review. Rule 65(d) of the Federal Rules of Civil Procedure provides, in relevant part:

"Every order granting an injunction and every restraining order shall set forth the reasons for its issuance; shall be specific in terms; shall describe in reasonable detail, and not by reference to the complaint or other document, the act or acts sought to be restrained."

The order here falls far short of satisfying the second and third clauses of Rule 65(d). Neither the brief judgment order nor the accompanying opinion is "specific" in outlining the "terms" of the injunctive relief granted; nor can it be said that the order describes "in reasonable detail . . . the act or acts sought to be restrained." Rather, the defendants are simply told not to enforce "the present Wisconsin scheme" against those in the appellees' class.

As we have emphasized in the past, the specificity provisions of Rule 65(d) are no mere technical requirements. The Rule was designed to prevent uncertainty and confusion on the part of those faced with injunctive orders, and to avoid the possible founding of a contempt citation on a decree too vague to be understood. Since an injunctive order prohibits conduct under threat of judicial punishment, basic fairness requires that those enjoined receive explicit notice of precisely what conduct is outlawed.

The requirement of specificity in injunction orders performs a second important function. Unless the trial court carefully frames its orders of injunctive relief, it is impossible for an appellate tribunal to know precisely what it is reviewing. We can hardly begin to assess the correctness of the judgment entered by the District Court here without knowing its precise bounds. In the absence of specific injunctive relief, informed and intelligent appellate review is greatly complicated, if not made impossible.

. . . .

Vacated and remanded.

■ MR. JUSTICE DOUGLAS dissents.

D.   MODIFICATION OR DISSOLUTION

Ladner v. Siegel

Supreme Court of Pennsylvania, 1930.
298 Pa. 487, 148 A. 699.

[Petition for modification of decree. The earlier injunction by the Court of Common Pleas read:]

And now, to wit, March 2, 1928, in consideration of the foregoing case, it is ordered, adjudged and decreed as follows:

1. That the defendants, Clarence R. Siegel and William M. Anderson be and are hereby enjoined as follows:

(a) From maintaining and operating garage building built in the center of the block of ground surrounded by Forty–Seventh, Forty–Eighth, Pine and Spruce Streets, Philadelphia, as a public garage.

Defendants to bear the cost.

On May 14, 1929, the same court, after reciting the 1928 decree, ordered that the same be amended to read as follows:

1. That the defendants, Clarence R. Siegel and William M. Anderson be and are hereby enjoined.

(a) From maintaining and operating garage buildings built in the center of the block of ground surrounded by Forty–Seventh, Forty–Eighth, Pine and Spruce Streets, Philadelphia, as a public garage.

(b) Nothing in this injunction, however, shall prevent the defendants, Clarence R. Siegel and William M. Anderson, from using the said garage building for the storage of automobiles by the tenants of Garden Court Apartments, situate at the northeast corner 47th and Pine Streets in the City of Philadelphia or by the tenants of the apartment houses now being erected at the northwest corner 47th and Pine Streets or by any other apartment house erected in the block bounded by Forty–Seventh, Forty–Eighth, Pine and Spruce Streets. Leave is hereby given to the plaintiffs and any of them to apply to this court at any time for specific orders in connection with the operation of the building as actual operation shall show to be necessary or proper to effectuate the conclusions and decisions of the Supreme Court and the law of the case as found and established by the Supreme Court.

Defendants appealed.[3]

■ KEPHART, J. This is the fourth appeal to this court in the present case, and it is high time the controversy is put to rest. . . .

. . . .

It is contended, first, that a court of equity has no power to modify a final decree after the term at which it was entered, except by a bill of review based on sufficient grounds. Without discussing the matter at length, we may say, in the first place, that in this State there are no term times in equity. Hence the common law rules as to term time do not apply. Our equity rules providing for a decree nisi [(a provisional decree that becomes final unless cause is shown)], exceptions, and final decree contemplate finality apart from term rules in all cases where the nature of the decree calls for finality. An appeal to a higher court may of itself suspend the force of such a decree, but, when action is taken by that tribunal affirming the decree, the suspension is lifted, and the decree is in full force; if the time for appeal is allowed to run, at the expiration thereof the decree becomes unchangeable as though it had been affirmed on appeal. . . . [A] rehearing must be requested before the time for an appeal expires. Under these proceedings our decrees possess all the attributes of finality. . . . Such are the general rules governing final decrees in equity.

There are many equitable proceedings that illustrate the general rule, such as specific performance, bills to reform instruments, and others. A final decree in such equitable proceeding is unchangeable except possibly through gross mistake to be corrected by a bill of review, and not then if any intervening right has appeared since entering the decree. In all such proceedings the decree calls for definite action and the law presumes such action to follow the order.

. . . .

An injunction is the form of equitable proceeding which protects civil rights from irreparable injury, either by commanding acts to be done, or preventing their commission, there being no adequate remedy at law. Granting an injunction rests in the sound discretion of the court, that discretion to be exercised under well-established principles and there are no statutory limitations on the power of the court in relation thereto. While the decree in such action is an adjudication of the facts and the law applicable thereto, it is none the less executory and continuing as to the purpose or object to be attained; in this it differs from other equitable actions. It operates until vacated, modified, or dissolved. An injunction contemplates either a series of continuous acts or a refraining from action. A preventive injunction constantly prevents one party from doing that which would cause irreparable damage to his neighbor's property rights.

3. [Owen J. Roberts, who was an Associate Justice of the Supreme Court from   1930–45, was one of the plaintiff's counsel.]

The final decree continues the life of such proceeding, not only for the purpose of execution, but for such other relief as a chancellor may in good conscience grant under the law....

The injunction in this case prevented an anticipated injury to a property right. The chancellor in granting it placed the protecting arm of the court about this right and prevented Siegel from using his property in such a way as would injure his neighbors. It was to remain as long as the court felt that protection necessary to complainant's rights, or until conditions demanded a modification of that protection or its entire removal. The power of the chancellor to modify in such cases cannot be controlled by term rules, otherwise equity would cease to be equity and become a hard and fast taskmaster.

. . . .

The modification of a decree in a preventive injunction is inherent in the court which granted it, and may be made, (a) if, in its discretion judicially exercised, it believes the ends of justice would be served by a modification, and (b) where the law, common or statutory, has changed, been modified or extended, and (c) where there is a change in the controlling facts on which the injunction rested.

. . . .

... An injunction decree does not create a right; it protects the right of the owner to the enjoyment of his property from injurious interference by the uses of other land. The right protected is an attribute of property existing through the application of common-law principles. A decree preventing its injury does not give to the complaining party a perpetual or vested right either in the remedy, the law governing the order or the effect of it. He is not entitled to the same measure of protection at all times and under all circumstances. A decree protecting a property right is given subject to the rules governing modification, suspension or dissolution of an injunction. The decree is an ambulatory one, and marches along with time affected by the nature of the proceeding.

. . . .

Having carefully considered all matters before us, the order of the court below modifying the injunction is affirmed; costs to be paid by appellants.

NOTES

1. At common law, a legal judgment was not subject to reconsideration after the end of the term of court during which it had been rendered. At that point, the judgment could be challenged in the law courts only if it could be appealed or was subject to collateral attack by way of one of the narrow extraordinary writs. (It may also have been possible to attack the judgment by petitioning the chancellor to bar its execution.)

Some American equity courts adopted an analogous set of rules to give their orders a comparable measure of finality. In these courts, an order could be attacked after the end of the term in which it was rendered only if an appeal was still timely or if it was subject to collateral attack by means of one of two narrow bills: the "bill of review" and the "bill in the nature of a bill of review." The former bill was available when the moving party could show "new matter" (i.e., newly discovered evidence existing at the time the decree was rendered) or "error apparent" in the decree (i.e., that the ruling represented an incorrect application of the law as it stood at the time the decree was rendered). The latter bill would lie when the movant could show that the decree had been obtained by fraud, mistake, or duress.

2. In Pennsylvania, as in the federal courts, formal trial court terms have been abolished, and non-ambulatory equity decrees generally become final when the time for appeal has expired. At the same time, the bill of review and the bill in the nature of a bill of review, as well as the analogous extraordinary legal writs, have largely been supplanted in civil procedure by what is called a motion for relief from judgment. This statutory remedy, which liberalizes the rules under which post-judgment relief may be obtained, is exemplified by Fed.R.Civ.P. 60, which provides as follows:

(a) Clerical Mistakes. Clerical mistakes in judgments, orders or other parts of the record and errors therein arising from oversight or omission may be corrected by the court at any time of its own initiative or on the motion of any party and after such notice, if any, as the court orders. During the pendency of an appeal, such mistakes may be so corrected before the appeal is docketed in the appellate court, and thereafter while the appeal is pending may be so corrected with leave of the appellate court.

(b) Mistakes; Inadvertence; Excusable Neglect; Newly Discovered Evidence; Fraud, etc. On motion and upon such terms as are just, the court may relieve a party or a party's legal representative from a final judgment, order, or proceeding for the following reasons: (1) mistake, inadvertence, surprise, or excusable neglect; (2) newly discovered evidence which by due diligence could not have been discovered in time to move for a new trial under Rule 59(b); (3) fraud (whether heretofore denominated intrinsic or extrinsic), misrepresentation, or other misconduct of an adverse party; (4) the judgment is void; (5) the judgment has been satisfied, released, or discharged, or a prior judgment upon which it is based has been reversed or otherwise vacated, or it is no longer equitable that the judgment should have prospective application; or (6) any other reason justifying relief from the operation of the judgment. The motion shall be made within a reasonable time, and for reasons (1), (2), and (3) not more than one year after the judgment, order, or proceeding was entered or taken. A motion under this subdivision (b) does not affect the finality of a judgment or suspend its operation. This rule does not limit the power of a court to entertain an independent action to relieve a party from a judgment, order, or proceeding, or to grant relief to a defendant not actually personally notified as provided in Title 28, U.S.C. § 1655, or to set aside a judgment for fraud upon the court. Writs of coram nobis, coram vobis, audita querela, and bills of review and bills in the nature of a bill of review, are abolished, and the procedure for obtaining any relief from a judgment shall be by motion as prescribed in these rules or by an independent action.[4]

Emergency Hospital of Easton v. Stevens

Court of Appeals of Maryland, 1924.
146 Md. 159, 126 A. 101.

[Dr. Stevens filed a bill of complaint against the hospital, charging it refused to permit him to perform surgical operations, contrary to its constitution and by-laws. He sought an injunction. The defendant's answer alleged that the constitution and by-laws on which he relied had been amended, so that he was not entitled to operate in the hospital without the permission of its directors and staff, which he had not obtained. A decree dismissing the bill was reversed, on the ground that the amendments on which the hospital relied were void because proper notice had not been given as required by Maryland law. The cause was remanded in order that a perpetual injunction might issue as prayed. On February 21, 1923, an injunction was issued as directed:

> That the Emergency Hospital of Easton, its officers, directors, agents, superintendent, nurses, servants, and employees, they and each of them, are hereby enjoined and perpetually restrained from interfering with or failing to aid and assist Dr. James A. Stevens, the plaintiff, in the surgical treatment of his patients in the said hospital, as fully as aid and assistance is given to any other physician or surgeon operating upon or engaged in the treatment of patients in said hospital, and from interfering with or discriminating against any patient of said James A. Stevens presenting himself or herself for the medical or surgical treatment of said James A. Stevens at the said hospital.

Three months later, on May 29, 1923, the hospital validly adopted the following by-law:

> *Physicians and Surgeons.* Any physician in good standing can practice medicine, exclusive of surgery, in this hospital; and any surgeon in good standing may operate in this hospital with the approval of the staff and the board of directors.

About September 26, 1923, Dr. Stevens filed a petition in the cause, praying that the hospital be attached and punished for violation of the injunction.

Upon that petition a *nisi* order was passed, and by way of cause the defendant on September 13, 1923, filed an answer, in which it averred that subsequent to the filing of the decree for a perpetual injunction it had validly and regularly amended its constitution and by-laws, and that, under

---

4.   [*Coram nobis* lay to correct factual errors not apparent on the face of the record and whose previous correction was not due to the moving party's negligence (e.g., the lack of jurisdiction over a defendant against whom an adverse default judgment had been entered). *Coram nobis* served the same function, except that the correction was done by an appellate court, rather than the trial court. *Audita querela* was available when a defense or discharge becoming available after the entry of judgment entitled the losing party to relief against the judgment or its execution.]

these as amended, the plaintiff had no right to operate in said hospital without the approval and consent of the hospital staff, which he had not obtained. The answer also admitted the refusal of the operation room and other surgical facilities, but alleged that Dr. Stevens and all other Easton doctors had received notice of the new by-law; that the hospital had not discriminated against him; that it had not denied him the right to treat any private patient medically; that he had not applied to its surgical staff for permission to operate; "and this defendant denies that it has disobeyed any order of this court, and denies that it is in contempt of the injunction of this Honorable Court or of any order or ruling thereof, but has acted solely in accordance with the amended constitution and by-laws and in strict accord with its legal rights."

The plaintiff demurred to this answer on October 11, 1923, when the defendant asked and was granted leave to move for dissolution of the injunction. On the same day, before any such motion was filed, the court sustained the demurrer to the answer and continued the injunction. It reserved the question of punishment for the contempt until the hearing of the motion to dissolve the injunction.

From this order the hospital appealed.]

OFFUTT, J. This appeal is the second chapter in an unfortunate controversy between Dr. James A. Stevens, a physician and surgeon in good standing practicing his profession in Talbot County, Maryland, and the Emergency Hospital of Easton, a corporation organized and maintained to afford the inhabitants of that part of the State necessary hospital facilities for surgical operations and the treatment of disease.

The . . . only other, question in the case is whether the facts set up in the defendant's answer presented a sufficient defense to the charge that it had deliberately and wilfully violated the court's order, and was thereby guilty of contempt of that court. It is admitted that the defendant wilfully and deliberately did the very thing which the court in its decree expressly enjoined and prohibited it from doing, and there can be no question but that such conduct was in flagrant and open contempt of the injunction of the court from which it issued, unless excused or explained by some act or event which justified such extraordinary conduct. But the only excuse offered by the appellant was that it, by its own act, had, after the appellee's right to the injunction had been established by this Court, so changed the conditions upon which that decision rested that the injunction no longer controlled its conduct. That is to say, by way of excuse it submitted the proposition that it was clothed with the power of determining for itself when it should obey and when it should not obey an explicit and peremptory order of a court of competent jurisdiction passed in a cause to which it was a party. In support of that proposition it contends that in no other way could it exercise rights which had accrued to it through changes in the conditions upon which the decree was based occurring after its passage which, if they did not nullify the authority of the injunction as a continuing command, at least made its continued operation inequitable and unjust. And as a corollary of that proposition it contends that, if its interpretation of the facts relied upon and the legal consequences flowing therefrom, as nullifying the continuing authority of the injunction, is correct, it should be exonerated from the charge of contempt and that only in the event that such interpretation is erroneous can it be deemed guilty of the contempt charged.

That contention assumes that the court granting the injunction had no power to rescind or modify its final decree after it had become enrolled, no matter what changes had occurred in the conditions or the relations of the parties after the decree. There is obviously no force in these contentions.

. . . .

It is true as a general principle that a final enrolled decree will not be opened to relitigate any question dealt with in it by the court passing such a decree, but that rule does not mean that, where events have occurred since the decree which would necessarily make the continuance of the injunction an absurdity, or unjust or oppressive, that the court which granted it could not in a proper proceeding change its decree to conform to the changed conditions. By way of illustration, if one were enjoined from obstructing a way appurtenant to land, and he afterwards acquired the land and its appurtenances, it cannot be supposed that the court which granted the injunction could not under such circumstances, open the decree and dissolve it. . . .

. . . .

From what has been said it is apparent that, in our opinion, the order appealed from must be affirmed. In reaching this conclusion we have treated the appeal as presenting a purely procedural question and have not attempted to discuss the substantial question which must ultimately control the litigation, i.e., whether the appellant has the power to regulate and control the management and operation of its own hospital because, as recognized by counsel, that question is not before us, and the record does not contain facts sufficient to enable us to consider it.

. . . .

Decree affirmed, with costs to appellee, "and the case remanded in order that further proceedings may be had therein, in conformity with the views expressed in this opinion, and especially that application may be made to the lower court to open the decree for a perpetual injunction passed therein and to rescind the same."

———

Board of Education of Oklahoma City Public Schools v. Dowell

Supreme Court of the United States, 1991.
498 U.S. 237, 111 S.Ct. 630, 112 L.Ed.2d 715.

■ Chief Justice Rehnquist delivered the opinion of the Court.

Petitioner Board of Education of Oklahoma City sought dissolution of a decree entered by the District Court imposing a school desegregation plan. The District Court granted relief over the objection of respondents Robert L. Dowell, et al., black students and their parents. The Court of Appeals for the Tenth Circuit reversed, holding that the Board would be entitled to such relief only upon " '[n]othing less than a clear showing of grievous wrong evoked by new and unforeseen conditions....' " We hold that the Court of Appeals' test is more stringent than is required either by our cases dealing with injunctions or by the Equal Protection Clause of the Fourteenth Amendment.

I

This school desegregation litigation began almost 30 years ago. In 1961, respondents, black students and their parents, sued petitioners, the Board of Education of Oklahoma City (Board), to end *de jure* segregation in the public schools. In 1963, the District Court found that Oklahoma City had intentionally segregated both schools and housing in the past, and that Oklahoma City was operating a "dual" school system—one that was intentionally segregated by race. In 1965, the District Court found that the School Board's attempt to desegregate by using neighborhood zoning failed to remedy past segregation because residential segregation resulted in one-race schools. Residential segregation had once been state imposed, and it lingered due to discrimination by some realtors and financial institutions. The District Court found that school segregation had caused some housing segregation. In 1972, finding that previous efforts had not been successful at eliminating state imposed segregation, the District Court ordered the Board to adopt the "Finger Plan," under which kindergarteners would be assigned to neighborhood schools unless their parents opted otherwise; children in grades 1–4 would attend formerly all white schools, and thus black children would be bused to those schools; children in grade five would attend formerly all black schools, and thus white children would be bused to those schools; students in the upper grades would be bused to various areas in order to maintain integrated schools; and in integrated neighborhoods there would be stand-alone schools for all grades.

In 1977, after complying with the desegregation decree for five years, the Board made a "Motion to Close Case." The District Court held in its "Order Terminating Case":

"The Court has concluded that [the Finger Plan] worked and that substantial compliance with the constitutional requirements has been achieved. The School Board, under the oversight of the Court, has operated the Plan properly, and the Court does not foresee that the termination of its jurisdiction will result in the dismantlement of the Plan or any affirmative action by the defendant to undermine the unitary system so slowly and painfully accomplished over the 16 years during which the cause has been pending before this court....

"... The School Board, as now constituted, has manifested the desire and intent to follow the law. The court believes that the present members and their successors on the Board will now and in the future continue to follow the constitutional desegregation requirements.

"Now sensitized to the constitutional implications of its conduct and with a new awareness of its responsibility to citizens of all races, the Board is entitled to pursue in good faith its legitimate policies without the continuing constitutional supervision of this Court....

. . . .

"... Jurisdiction in this case is terminated ipso facto subject only to final disposition of any case now pending on appeal."

This unpublished order was not appealed.

In 1984, the School Board faced demographic changes that led to greater burdens on young black children. As more and more neighborhoods became integrated, more stand-alone schools were established, and young black students had to be bused further from their inner-city homes to outlying white areas. In an effort to alleviate this burden and to increase parental involvement, the Board adopted the Student Reassignment Plan (SRP), which relied on neighborhood assignments for students in grades K–4 beginning in the 1985–1986 school year. Busing continued for students in grades 5–12. Any student could transfer from a school where he or she was in the majority to a school where he or she would be in the minority. Faculty and staff integration was retained, and an "equity officer" was appointed.

In 1985, respondents filed a "Motion to Reopen the Case," contending that the School District had not achieved "unitary" status and that the SRP was a return to segregation. Under the SRP, 11 of 64 elementary schools would be greater than 90% black, 22 would be greater than 90% white plus other minorities, and 31 would be racially mixed. The District Court refused to reopen the case, holding that its 1977 finding of unitariness was res judicata as to those who were then parties to the action, and that the district remained unitary. The District Court found that the School Board, administration, faculty, support staff, and student body were integrated, and transportation, extracurricular activities and facilities within the district were equal and nondiscriminatory. Because unitariness had been achieved, the District Court concluded that court-ordered desegregation must end.

The Court of Appeals for the Tenth Circuit reversed. It held that, while the 1977 order finding the district unitary was binding on the parties, nothing in that order indicated that the 1972 injunction itself was terminated. The court reasoned that the finding that the system was unitary merely ended the District Court's active supervision of the case, and because the school district was still subject to the desegregation decree, respondents could challenge the SRP. The case was remanded to determine whether the decree should be lifted or modified.

On remand, the District Court found that demographic changes made the Finger Plan unworkable, that the Board had done nothing for 25 years to promote residential segregation, and that the school district had bused students for more than a decade in good-faith compliance with the court's orders. The District Court found that present residential segregation was the result of private decisionmaking and economics, and that it was too attenuated to be a vestige of former school segregation. It also found that the district had maintained its unitary status, and that the neighborhood assignment plan was not designed with discriminatory intent. The court concluded that the previous injunctive decree should be vacated and the school district returned to local control.

The Court of Appeals again reversed, holding that " 'an injunction takes on a life of its own and becomes an edict quite independent of the law it is meant to effectuate.' " That court approached the case "not so much as one dealing with desegregation, but as one dealing with the proper application of the federal law on injunctive remedies." Relying on United States v. Swift & Co., 286 U.S. 106, 52 S.Ct. 460, 76 L.Ed. 999 (1932), it held that a desegregation decree remains in effect until a school district can show "grievous wrong evoked by new and unforeseen conditions" and "dramatic changes in conditions unforeseen at the time of the decree that ... impose extreme and unexpectedly oppressive hardships on the obligor." 890 F.2d, at 1490 (quoting T. Jost, From Swift to Stotts and Beyond: Modification of Injunctions in the Federal Courts, 64 Tex.L.Rev. 1101, 1110 (1986)). Given that a number of schools would return to being primarily one-race schools under the SRP, circumstances in Oklahoma City had not changed enough to justify modification of the decree. The Court of Appeals held that, despite the unitary finding, the Board had the " 'affirmative duty ... not to take any action that would impede the process of disestablishing the dual system and its effects.' "

We ... reverse the Court of Appeals.

II

We must first consider whether respondents may contest the District Court's 1987 order dissolving the injunction which had imposed the desegregation decree. Respondents did not appeal from the District Court's 1977 order finding that the school system had achieved unitary status, and petitioners contend that the 1977 order bars respondents from contesting the 1987 order. We disagree, for the 1977 order did not dissolve the desegregation decree, and the District Court's unitariness finding was too ambiguous to bar respondents from challenging later action by the Board.

The lower courts have been inconsistent in their use of the term "unitary." Some have used it to identify a school district that has completely remedied all vestiges of past discrimination. Under that interpretation of the word, a unitary school district is one that has met the mandate of Brown v. Board of Education, 349 U.S. 294, 75 S.Ct. 753, 99 L.Ed. 1083 (1955), and Green v. New Kent County School Board, 391 U.S. 430, 88 S.Ct. 1689, 20 L.Ed.2d 716 (1968). Other courts, however, have used "unitary" to describe any school district that has currently desegregated student assignments, whether or not that status is solely the result of a court-imposed desegregation plan. In other words, such a school district could be called unitary and nevertheless still contain vestiges of past discrimination....

We think it is a mistake to treat words such as "dual" and "unitary" as if they were actually found in the Constitution. The constitutional command of the Fourteenth Amendment is that "[n]o State shall ... deny to any person ... the equal protection of the laws." Courts have used the terms "dual" to denote a school system which has engaged in intentional segregation of students by race, and "unitary" to describe a school system which has been brought into compliance with the command of the Constitution. We are not sure how useful it is to define these terms more precisely, or to create subclasses within them. But there is no doubt that the differences in usage described above do exist. The District Court's 1977 order is unclear with respect to what it meant by unitary and the necessary result of that finding. We therefore decline to overturn the conclusion of the Court of Appeals that while the 1977 order of the District Court did bind the parties as to the unitary character of the district, it did not finally terminate the Oklahoma City school litigation. In Pasadena City Bd. of Education v. Spangler, 427 U.S. 424, 96 S.Ct. 2697, 49 L.Ed.2d 599 (1976), we held that a school board is entitled to a rather precise statement of its obligations under a desegregation decree. If such a decree is to be terminated or dissolved, respondents as well as the school board are entitled to a like statement from the court.

III

The Court of Appeals relied upon language from this Court's decision in United States v. Swift and Co., for the proposition that a desegregation decree could not be lifted or modified absent a showing of "grievous wrong evoked by new and unforeseen conditions." It also held that "compliance alone cannot become the basis for modifying or dissolving an injunction," relying on United States v. W.T. Grant Co., 345 U.S. 629, 73 S.Ct. 894, 97 L.Ed. 1303 (1953). We hold that its reliance was mistaken.

In *Swift*, several large meat-packing companies entered into a consent decree whereby they agreed to refrain forever from entering into the grocery business. The decree was by its terms effective in perpetuity. The defendant meat-packers and their allies had over a period of a decade attempted, often with success in the lower courts, to frustrate operation of the decree. It was in this context that the language relied upon by the Court of Appeals in this case was used.

United States v. United Shoe Machinery Corp., 391 U.S. 244, 88 S.Ct. 1496, 20 L.Ed.2d 562 (1968), explained that the language used in *Swift* must be read in the context of the continuing danger of unlawful restraints on trade which the Court had found still existed. "*Swift* teaches ... a decree may be changed upon an appropriate showing, and it holds that it may not be changed ... if the purposes of the litigation as incorporated in the decree ... have not been fully achieved." In the present case, a finding by the District Court that the Oklahoma City School District was being operated in compliance with the commands of the Equal Protection Clause of the Fourteenth Amendment, and that it was unlikely that the school board would return to its former ways, would be a finding that the purposes of the desegregation litigation had been fully achieved. No additional showing of "grievous wrong evoked by new and unforeseen conditions" is required of the school board.

In Milliken v. Bradley (*Milliken II*), 433 U.S. 267, 97 S.Ct. 2749, 53 L.Ed.2d 745 (1977), we said:

> "[F]ederal-court decrees must directly address and relate to the constitutional violation itself. Because of this inherent limitation upon federal judicial authority, federal-court decrees exceed appropriate limits if they are aimed at eliminating a condition that does not violate the Constitution or does not flow from such a violation. ..."

From the very first, federal supervision of local school systems was intended as a temporary measure to remedy past discrimination. . . .

Considerations based on the allocation of powers within our federal system, we think, support our view that quoted language from *Swift* does not provide the proper standard to apply to injunctions entered in school desegregation cases. Such decrees, unlike the one in *Swift,* are not intended to operate in perpetuity. Local control over the education of children allows citizens to participate in decisionmaking, and allows innovation so that school programs can fit local needs. The legal justification for displacement of local authority by an injunctive decree in a school desegregation case is a violation of the Constitution by the local authorities. Dissolving a desegregation decree after the local authorities have operated in compliance with it for a reasonable period of time properly recognizes that "necessary concern for the important values of local control of public school systems dictates that a federal court's regulatory control of such systems not extend beyond the time required to remedy the effects of past intentional discrimination."

The Court of Appeals, as noted, relied for its statement that "compliance alone cannot become the basis for modifying or dissolving an injunction" on our decision in *United States v. W.T. Grant Co.* That case, however, did not involve the dissolution of an injunction, but the question of whether an injunction should be issued in the first place. This Court observed that a promise to comply with the law on the part of a wrongdoer did not divest a district court of its power to enjoin the wrongful conduct in which the defendant had previously engaged.

A district court need not accept at face value the profession of a school board which has intentionally discriminated that it will cease to do so in the future. But in deciding whether to modify or dissolve a desegregation decree, a school board's compliance with previous court orders is obviously relevant. In this case the original finding of *de jure* segregation was entered in 1961, the injunctive decree from which the Board seeks relief was entered in 1972, and the Board complied with the decree in good faith until 1985. Not only do the personnel of school boards change over time, but the same passage of time enables the District Court to observe the good faith of the school board in complying with the decree. The test espoused by the Court of Appeals would condemn a school district, once governed by a board which intentionally discriminated, to judicial tutelage for the indefinite future. Neither the principles governing the entry and dissolution of injunctive decrees, nor the commands of the Equal Protection Clause of the Fourteenth Amendment, require any such Draconian result.

Petitioners urge that we reinstate the decision of the District Court terminating the injunction, but we think that the preferable course is to remand the case to that court so that it may decide, in accordance with this opinion, whether the Board made a sufficient showing of constitutional compliance as of 1985, when the SRP was adopted, to allow the injunction to be dissolved.[1] The District Court should address itself to whether the

---

1. The Court of Appeals viewed the Board's adoption of the SRP as a violation of its obligation under the injunction, and tech- nically it may well have been. But just as the Court of Appeals held that the respondent should not be penalized for failure to appeal

Board had complied in good faith with the desegregation decree since it was entered, and whether the vestiges of past discrimination had been eliminated to the extent practicable.[2]

In considering whether the vestiges of *de jure* segregation had been eliminated as far as practicable, the District Court should look not only at student assignments, but "to every facet of school operations—faculty, staff, transportation, extracurricular activities and facilities."

After the District Court decides whether the Board was entitled to have the decree terminated, it should proceed to decide respondent's challenge to the SRP. A school district which has been released from an injunction imposing a desegregation plan no longer requires court authorization for the promulgation of policies and rules regulating matters such as assignment of students and the like, but it of course remains subject to the mandate of the Equal Protection Clause of the Fourteenth Amendment. If the Board was entitled to have the decree terminated as of 1985, the District Court should then evaluate the Board's decision to implement the SRP under appropriate equal protection principles.

The judgment of the Court of Appeals is reversed, and the case is remanded to the District Court for further proceedings consistent with this opinion.

It is so ordered.

■ JUSTICE SOUTER took no part in the consideration or decision of this case.

■ JUSTICE MARSHALL, with whom JUSTICE BLACKMUN and JUSTICE STEVENS join, dissenting.

Oklahoma gained statehood in 1907. For the next 65 years, the Oklahoma City School Board maintained segregated schools—initially relying on laws requiring dual school systems; thereafter, by exploiting residential segregation that had been created by legally enforced restrictive covenants. In 1972—18 years after this Court first found segregated schools unconstitutional—a federal court finally interrupted this cycle, enjoining the Oklahoma City School Board to implement a specific plan for achieving actual desegregation of its schools.

The practical question now before us is whether, 13 years after that injunction was imposed, the same School Board should have been allowed to return many of its elementary schools to their former one-race status. The majority today suggests that 13 years of desegregation was enough. The Court remands the case for further evaluation of whether the purposes of the injunctive decree were achieved sufficient to justify the decree's

from an order that by hindsight was ambiguous, we do not think that the Board should be penalized for relying on the express language of that order. The District Court in its decision on remand should not treat the adoption of the SRP as a breach of good faith on the part of the Board.

2. As noted above, the District Court earlier found that present residential segregation in Oklahoma City was the result of private decisionmaking and economics, and that it was too attenuated to be a vestige of former school segregation. Respondents contend that the Court of Appeals held this finding was clearly erroneous, but we think its opinion is at least ambiguous on this point.... To dispel any doubt, we direct the District Court and the Court of Appeals to treat this question as *res nova* upon further consideration of the case.

dissolution. However, the inquiry it commends to the District Court fails to recognize explicitly the threatened reemergence of one-race schools as a relevant "vestige" of *de jure* segregation.

In my view, the standard for dissolution of a school desegregation decree must reflect the central aim of our school desegregation precedents. In Brown v. Board of Education, 347 U.S. 483, 74 S.Ct. 686, 98 L.Ed. 873 (1954)(*Brown I*), a unanimous Court declared that racially "[s]eparate educational facilities are inherently unequal." This holding rested on the Court's recognition that state-sponsored segregation conveys a message of "inferiority as to th[e] status [of Afro–American school children] in the community that may affect their hearts and minds in a way unlikely ever to be undone." Remedying this evil and preventing its recurrence were the motivations animating our requirement that formerly *de jure* segregated school districts take all feasible steps to *eliminate* racially identifiable schools.

I believe a desegregation decree cannot be lifted so long as conditions likely to inflict the stigmatic injury condemned in *Brown I* persist and there remain feasible methods of eliminating such conditions. Because the record here shows, and the Court of Appeals found, that feasible steps could be taken to avoid one-race schools, it is clear that the purposes of the decree have not yet been achieved and the Court of Appeals' reinstatement of the decree should be affirmed. I therefore dissent.[1]

I

In order to assess the full consequence of lifting the decree at issue in this case, it is necessary to explore more fully than does the majority the history of racial segregation in the Oklahoma City schools. This history reveals nearly unflagging resistance by the Board to judicial efforts to dismantle the City's dual education system.

When Oklahoma was admitted to the Union in 1907, its Constitution mandated separation of Afro–American children from all other races in the public school system. In addition to laws enforcing segregation in the schools, racially restrictive covenants, supported by state and local law, established a segregated residential pattern in Oklahoma City. Petitioner Board of Education of Oklahoma City (Board) exploited this residential segregation to enforce school segregation, locating "all-Negro" schools in the heart of the City's northeast quadrant, in which the majority of the City's Afro–American citizens resided.

Matters did not change in Oklahoma City after this Court's decision in *Brown I* and Brown v. Board of Education, 349 U.S. 294, 75 S.Ct. 753, 99 L.Ed. 1083 (1955)(*Brown II*). Although new school boundaries were established at that time, the Board also adopted a resolution allowing children to continue in the schools in which they were placed or to submit transfer requests that would be considered on a case-by-case basis. Because it

---

1. The issue of decree *modification* is not before us. However, I would not rule out the possibility of petitioner demonstrating that the purpose of the decree at issue could be realized by less burdensome means. Under such circumstances a modification affording petitioner more flexibility in redressing the lingering effects of past segregation would be warranted.

allowed thousands of white children each year to transfer to schools in which their race was the majority, this transfer policy undermined any potential desegregation.

Parents of Afro–American children relegated to schools in the northeast quadrant filed suit against the Board in 1961. Finding that the Board's special transfer policy was "designed to perpetuate and encourage segregation," the District Court struck down the policy as a violation of the Equal Protection Clause. Undeterred, the Board proceeded to adopt another special transfer policy which, as the District Court found in 1965, had virtually the same effect as the prior policy—"perpetuat[ion] [of] a segregated system."

The District Court also noted that, by failing to adopt an affirmative policy of desegregation, the Board had reversed the desegregation process in certain respects. For example, eight of the nine new schools planned or under construction in 1965 were located to serve all-white or virtually all-white school zones. Rather than promote integration through new school locations, the District Court found that the Board destroyed some integrated neighborhoods and schools by adopting inflexible neighborhood school attendance zones that encouraged whites to migrate to all-white areas. Because the Board's pupil assignments coincided with residential segregation initiated by law in Oklahoma City, the Board also preserved and augmented existing residential segregation.

Thus, by 1972, 11 years after the plaintiffs had filed suit and 18 years after our decision in *Brown I,* the School Board continued to resist integration and in some respects the Board had worsened the situation. Four years after this Court's admonition to formerly *de jure* segregated school districts to come forward with realistic plans for *immediate* relief, the Board still had offered no meaningful plan of its own. Instead, "[i]t rationalize[d] its intransigence on the constitutionally unsound basis that public opinion [was] opposed to any further desegregation." The District Court concluded: "This litigation has been frustratingly interminable, not because of insuperable difficulties of implementation of the commands of the Supreme Court ... and the Constitution ... but because of the unpardonable recalcitrance of the ... Board." Consequently, the District Court ordered the Board to implement the only available plan that exhibited the promise of achieving actual desegregation—the "Finger Plan" offered by the plaintiffs.

In 1975, after a mere three years of operating under the Finger Plan, the Board filed a "Motion to Close Case," arguing that it had " 'eliminated all vestiges of state imposed racial discrimination in its school system.' " In 1977, the District Court granted the Board's motion and issued an "Order Terminating Case." The court concluded that the Board had "operated the [Finger] Plan properly" and stated that it did not "foresee that the termination of ... jurisdiction will result in the dismantlement of the [Finger] Plan or any affirmative action by the defendant to undermine the unitary system." The order ended the District Court's active supervision of the school district but did not dissolve the injunctive decree. The plaintiffs' did not appeal this order.

The Board continued to operate under the Finger Plan until 1985, when it implemented the Student Reassignment Plan (SRP). The SRP superimposed attendance zones over some residentially segregated areas. As a result, considerable racial imbalance reemerged in 33 of 64 elementary schools in the Oklahoma City system with student bodies either greater than 90% Afro–American or greater than 90% non–Afro–American. More specifically, 11 of the schools ranged from 96.9% to 99.7% Afro–American, and approximately 44% of all Afro–American children in grades K–4 were assigned to these virtually all–Afro–American schools.

In response to the SRP, the plaintiffs moved to reopen the case. Ultimately, the District Court dissolved the desegregation decree, finding that the school district had been "unitary" since 1977 and that the racial imbalances under the SRP were the consequence of residential segregation arising from "personal preferences." The Court of Appeals reversed, finding that the Board had not met its burden to establish that "the condition the [decree] sought to alleviate, a constitutional violation, has been eradicated."

II

I agree with the majority that the proper standard for determining whether a school desegregation decree should be dissolved is whether the purposes of the desegregation litigation, as incorporated in the decree, have been fully achieved.[3] I strongly disagree with the majority, however, on what must be shown to demonstrate that a decree's purposes have been fully realized. In my view, a standard for dissolution of a desegregation decree must take into account the unique harm associated with a system of racially identifiable schools and must expressly demand the elimination of such schools.

A

Our pointed focus in *Brown I* upon the stigmatic injury caused by segregated schools explains our unflagging insistence that formerly *de jure* segregated school districts extinguish all vestiges of school segregation. The concept of stigma also gives us guidance as to what conditions must be eliminated before a decree can be deemed to have served its purpose.

In the decisions leading up to *Brown I,* the Court had attempted to curtail the ugly legacy of Plessy v. Ferguson, 163 U.S. 537, 16 S.Ct. 1138, 41 L.Ed. 256 (1896), by insisting on a searching inquiry into whether "separate" Afro–American schools were genuinely "equal" to white schools in terms of physical facilities, curricula, quality of the faculty and certain "intangible" considerations. In *Brown I,* the Court finally liberated the

3. I also strongly agree with the majority's conclusion that, prior to the dissolution of a school desegregation decree, plaintiffs are entitled to a precise statement from a district court. Because of the sheer importance of a desegregation decree's objectives, and because the dissolution of such a decree will mean that plaintiffs will have to mount a new constitutional challenge if they wish to contest the segregative effects of the school board's subsequent actions, the district court must give a detailed explanation of how the standards for dissolution have been met. Because the District Court's 1977 order terminating its "active jurisdiction" did not contain such a statement, that order does not bar review of its 1987 order expressly dissolving the decree.

Equal Protection Clause from the doctrinal tethers of *Plessy,* declaring that "in the field of public education the doctrine of 'separate but equal' has no place. Separate educational facilities are inherently unequal."

The Court based this conclusion on its recognition of the particular social harm that racially segregated schools inflict on Afro–American children. . . .

Just as it is central to the standard for evaluating the formation of a desegregation decree, so should the stigmatic injury associated with segregated schools be central to the standard for dissolving a decree. The Court has indicated that "the ultimate end to be brought about" by a desegregation remedy is "a unitary, nonracial system of public education." We have suggested that this aim is realized once school officials have "eliminate[d] from the public schools *all* vestiges of state-imposed segregation," whether they inhere in the school's "faculty, staff, transportation, extracurricular activities and facilities," or even in "the community and administration['s] attitudes toward [a] school." Although the Court has never explicitly defined what constitutes a "vestige" of state-enforced segregation, the function that this concept has performed in our jurisprudence suggests that it extends to any condition that is likely to convey the message of inferiority implicit in a policy of segregation. So long as such conditions persist, the purposes of the decree cannot be deemed to have been achieved.

B

The majority suggests a more vague and, I fear, milder standard. Ignoring the harm identified in *Brown I,* the majority asserts that the District Court should find that the purposes of the decree have been achieved so long as "the Oklahoma City School District [is now] being operated in compliance with the commands of the Equal Protection Clause" and "it [is] unlikely that the school board would return to its former ways." Insofar as the majority instructs the District Court, on remand, to "conside[r] whether the vestiges of *de jure* segregation ha[ve] been eliminated as far as practicable," the majority presumably views elimination of vestiges as part of "operat[ing] in compliance with the commands of the Equal Protection Clause." But as to the scope or meaning of "vestiges," the majority says very little.

By focusing heavily on present and future compliance with the Equal Protection Clause, the majority's standard ignores how the stigmatic harm identified in *Brown I* can persist even after the State ceases actively to enforce segregation. It was not enough in *Green,* for example, for the school district to withdraw its own enforcement of segregation, leaving it up to individual children and their families to "choose" which school to attend. For it was clear under the circumstances that these choices would be shaped by and perpetuate the state-created message of racial inferiority associated with the school district's historical involvement in segregation. In sum, our school-desegregation jurisprudence establishes that the *effects* of past discrimination remain chargeable to the school district regardless of its lack of continued enforcement of segregation, and the remedial decree is required until those effects have been finally eliminated.

III

Applying the standard I have outlined, I would affirm the Court of Appeals' decision ordering the District Court to restore the desegregation decree. For it is clear on this record that removal of the decree will result in a significant number of racially identifiable schools that could be eliminated.

. . . .

IV

Consistent with the mandate of *Brown I,* our cases have imposed on school districts an unconditional duty to eliminate *any* condition that perpetuates the message of racial inferiority inherent in the policy of state-sponsored segregation. The racial identifiability of a district's schools is such a condition. Whether this "vestige" of state-sponsored segregation will persist cannot simply be ignored at the point where a district court is contemplating the dissolution of a desegregation decree. In a district with a history of state-sponsored school segregation, racial separation, in my view, *remains* inherently unequal.

I dissent.

NOTES

1. In a school desegregation case subsequent to *Dowell,* the Supreme Court stated:

> A federal court in a school desegregation case has the discretion to order an incremental or partial withdrawal of its supervision and control. This discretion derives both from the constitutional authority which justified its intervention in the first instance and its ultimate objectives in formulating the decree. The authority of the court is invoked at the outset to remedy particular constitutional violations. In construing the remedial authority of the district courts, we have been guided by the principles that "judicial powers may be exercised only on the basis of a constitutional violation," and that "the nature of the violation determines the scope of the remedy." [Swann v. Charlotte–Mecklenburg Bd. of Education, 402 U.S. 1, 16, 91 S.Ct. 1267, 1282]. A remedy is justifiable only insofar as it advances the ultimate objective of alleviating the initial constitutional violation.

> ... In Dowell, we emphasized that federal judicial supervision of local school systems was intended as a "temporary measure." 498 U.S. at 247, 111 S.Ct. at 636. Although this temporary measure has lasted decades, the ultimate objective has not changed—to return school districts to the control of local authorities. Just as a court has the obligation at the outset of a desegregation decree to structure a plan so that all available resources of the court are directed to comprehensive supervision of its decree, so too must a court provide an orderly means for withdrawing from control when it is shown that the school district has attained the requisite degree of compliance. A transition phase in

which control is relinquished in a gradual way is an appropriate means to this end.

We hold that, in the course of supervising desegregation plans, federal courts have the authority to relinquish supervision and control of school districts in incremental stages, before full compliance has been achieved in every area of school operations. While retaining jurisdiction over the case, the court may determine that it will not order further remedies in areas where the school district is in compliance with the decree. That is to say, upon a finding that a school system subject to a court-supervised desegregation plan is in compliance in some but not all areas, the court in appropriate cases may return control to the school system in those areas where compliance has been achieved, limiting further judicial supervision to operations that are not yet in full compliance with the court decree. In particular, the district court may determine that it will not order further remedies in the area of student assignments where racial imbalance is not traceable, in a proximate way, to constitutional violations.

A court's discretion to order the incremental withdrawal of its supervision in a school desegregation case must be exercised in a manner consistent with the purposes and objectives of its equitable power. Among the factors which must inform the sound discretion of the court in ordering partial withdrawal are the following: whether there has been full and satisfactory compliance with the decree in those aspects of the system where supervision is to be withdrawn; whether retention of judicial control is necessary or practicable to achieve compliance with the decree in other facets of the school system; and whether the school district has demonstrated, to the public and to the parents and students of the once disfavored race, its good-faith commitment to the whole of the court's decree and to those provisions of the law and the Constitution that were the predicate for judicial intervention in the first instance.

In considering these factors, a court should give particular attention to the school system's record of compliance. A school system is better positioned to demonstrate its good-faith commitment to a constitutional course of action when its policies form a consistent pattern of lawful conduct directed to eliminating earlier violations. And, with the passage of time, the degree to which racial imbalances continue to represent vestiges of a constitutional violation may diminish, and the practicability and efficacy of various remedies can be evaluated with more precision.

Freeman v. Pitts, 503 U.S. 467, 489–491, 112 S.Ct. 1430, 1444–1446, 118 L.Ed.2d 108 (1992).

2. Courts have applied the standards articulated in *Dowell* when called upon to modify or dissolve consent decrees or injunctive orders designed to curb other constitutional violations. For example, in *King v. Greenblatt*, 53 F.Supp.2d 117, the Commonwealth of Massachusetts moved to vacate or terminate consent decrees put in place twenty five years earlier that governed operations at treatment facilities for civilly committed sexually dangerous persons. The standard of review applied by the district court to decide the motion was derived from the school desegregation cases:

I repeat the standard to be applied in this case. It is derived from the standard used by courts when deciding whether to end injunctive orders in school desegregation cases. See Board of Educ. v. Dowell, 498 U.S. 237, 111 S.Ct. 630, 112 L.Ed.2d 715 (1991), and more recently, Freeman v. Pitts, 503 U.S. 467, 112 S.Ct. 1430, 118 L.Ed.2d 108 (1992). The First Circuit has relied on this standard in cases involving consent decrees which pertain to conditions at correctional facilities, Inmates of Suffolk County v. Rufo, 12 F.3d 286 (1st Cir.1993), In Re Pearson, 990 F.2d 653 (1st Cir.1993); and to the treatment of mentally ill persons, Consumer Advisory Bd. v. Glover, 989 F.2d 65 (1st Cir. 1993).

Under *Dowell*, I must determine that the underlying constitutional wrong has been remedied and that the authorities have complied with the decrees in good faith for a reasonable period of time since they were entered. *Dowell*, 498 U.S. at 247, 249–50, 111 S.Ct. 630. In *Rufo*, the First Circuit said that the district court must be satisfied that there is little or no likelihood that the original constitutional violations will return when the decree is lifted. *Rufo*, 12 F.3d at 292, citing *Dowell*, 498 U.S. at 247, 111 S.Ct. 630. This Circuit also said that the district court may consider the defendants' past record of compliance; present attitudes towards the reforms mandated by the decrees; and the way in which demographic, economic, and political forces may be expected to influence local authorities and the institution once the shelter of the decrees has been lost. Id.

At first reading, the standards appear to require a straightforward application of the law to the factual record. But, as usual in the context of the unique and changing environment of the Treatment Center, the application is not so straightforward. If the issue is whether the consent decrees are necessary to correct the conditions that existed at the Treatment Center at the time the decrees were entered, and continue to be necessary to maintain the improved conditions so that the constitutional rights asserted in *King* and *Williams* are not violated, I conclude that the evidence clearly shows that the consent decrees have served the purpose of correcting those conditions and are no longer necessary to maintain those improvements.

On the other hand, if the issue is whether the consent decrees continue to be necessary because of concerns that once the shelter of the decrees has been lost, "the original constitutional violations will promptly be repeated," then the test becomes one of the sincerity, willingness and commitment of DOC to the Treatment Center's mission. The resolution of this issue requires an examination of DOC's past record, its attitude toward treatment and behavior management, and the influence of outside forces. With these issues in mind, I turn to the record.

King v. Greenblatt, 53 F.Supp.2d 117, 124–125 (D.Mass.1999). After review of the record, the Court granted the motion to *terminate*, rather than *vacate*, the consent decrees:

The Commonwealth has phrased its motion alternatively, to vacate or terminate the consent decrees. In *Rufo*, the defendants asked the district court to enter an order that vacated the consent decree. In that case, the district court decided to terminate, but not vacate, the decrees. As the district judge stated in that case, a consent decree is "an adjudication of an ongoing obligation based on a claim of 'violation of a Federal right' that was at least one part of the subject matter of the civil action in which the Consent Decree was entered. That adjudication may still have pragmatic consequences even after the prospective relief that had earlier been included in the Consent Decree has been terminated." *Rufo*, 952 F.Supp. at 883–84. The First Circuit upheld the trial court's decision to terminate, rather than vacate, the consent decrees, noting that the distinction between the terms has practical significance. "While terminating a consent decree strips it of future potency, the decree's past puissance is preserved and certain of its collateral effects may endure." *Rouse*, 129 F.3d at 662. I believe a record of the past should be preserved and, accordingly, I grant the motion to terminate the consent decrees. The *King* and *Williams* cases are to be closed by the Clerk.

53 F.Supp.2d 117, 139.

E.   Appeal

In Re O'Connell

District Court of Appeal of California, First District, 1925.
75 Cal.App. 292, 242 P. 741.

■ Knight, J. The petitioner, Daniel O'Connell, by virtue of a writ of injunction issued in a divorce proceeding to which he was a party, was ordered excluded, during the pendency of said action, from the dwelling-house theretofore occupied by him with his wife under the marital relation, and, for violating said injunction, was adjudged guilty of contempt of court and sentenced to pay a fine and to be imprisoned. He now seeks release on *habeas corpus*.

The circumstances leading up to the contempt proceedings are as follows: On June 2, 1923, petitioner, upon his cross-complaint, obtained an interlocutory judgment of divorce from Mrs. O'Connell, whereby the property in question was assigned to him as his sole and separate property. Later, by a decree in equity, rendered in a suit commenced by Mrs. O'Connell in June, 1925, said interlocutory judgment was annulled, upon the ground that said interlocutory judgment had been obtained through extrinsic fraud [(i.e., fraud with respect to matters collateral to the issues in the case)]. Thereupon Mrs. O'Connell, upon notice to petitioner, applied for and was granted, in the divorce proceeding, said writ of injunction, enjoining petitioner, during the pendency of said action, "from entering the dwelling-house now occupied by the said plaintiff and known and designated as No. 900 Balboa Street in the City and County of San Francisco, State of California, and from living in said dwelling-house during the pendency of said action and from annoying or harassing the said plaintiff in any way during the pendency of said action and from attempting to cause or causing or ordering or employing any person whatsoever to alter, repair or do any work whatsoever on said dwelling during the pendency of said action." Petitioner perfected an appeal from the order granting said injunction and filed a stay bond, but nevertheless was thereafter adjudged guilty of contempt for having continued in the occupation of the premises in violation of the injunction.

[The decree entered in the equity suit, until declared void or reversed on appeal, rendered the interlocutory judgment in the divorce proceedings nugatory for all purposes; and the operation of the equity decree was not stayed by the appeal therefrom, so as to revive that interlocutory judgment or any of the rights granted thereunder.]

The controlling question presented for determination in this particular proceeding, however, relates to said writ of injunction, and not to said decree in equity. The question is whether said writ of injunction is mandatory or prohibitory in its nature and effect. If it be mandatory, its operation was stayed by appeal, and it was beyond the power of the court to punish as a contempt failure to comply with its mandatory terms pending appeal; but if it be prohibitory its operation could not be stayed by appeal and the enforcement thereof was at all times within the jurisdiction of the court.

. . . .

In the instant case, upon the rendition of said decree in equity, the parties to said divorce proceeding, by operation of law as well as by the express declaration of said decree itself, were restored to the same position as if said interlocutory judgment had never been entered. . . . It follows that the effect of said decree was merely to again place said divorce action at issue, Mrs. O'Connell claiming, in her pleadings therein, absolute owner-ship in said property by virtue of a deed to her from petitioner, and petitioner alleging in his pleadings that said property constituted a home-stead and that Mrs. O'Connell's title was merely that of a trustee; and both parties were in actual possession of said property. In that state of the record the plain effect of said injunction *pendente lite,* in relation to the occupancy of said premises was to oust petitioner from the possession which he theretofore held and to compel him to turn over to the other party to the litigation, prior to final determination of their respective rights in said property, the sole and exclusive possession thereof. Manifestly, said injunction, in the respect noted, did not operate merely to preserve *in statu quo* the subject of the litigation, but went further to the extent of attempt-ing to change the *status* of the parties in relation to the possession of the property in dispute. Therefore . . . it must be held that in so far as said injunction sought to exclude petitioner from said premises, it was mandato-ry in its effect and consequently its operation was stayed by the appeal therefrom.

. . . .

The remaining features of said injunction, wherein petitioner was enjoined from harassing and annoying or otherwise interfering with the person of Mrs. O'Connell, and from making any alterations in said premises, are, we believe, purely prohibitive in their nature, and therefore self-executing and not stayed by appeal. Those features become immaterial here, however, owing to the fact that the act for which petitioner was adjudged guilty of contempt was his refusal to discontinue in the occupation of the premises no point being made on behalf of Mrs. O'Connell of any other contemptuous act.

Having reached the conclusion that the appeal from the order granting said injunction *pendente lite* stayed the operation of that injunction in so far as it attempted to compel petitioner to surrender the possession theretofore held by him, it becomes unnecessary to consider the other points raised by petitioner in this proceeding.

The writ is granted and the petitioner is discharged from custody.

■ TYLER, P.M., and CASHIN, J., concurred.

Super Tire Engineering Co. v. McCorkle

Supreme Court of the United States, 1974.
416 U.S. 115, 94 S.Ct. 1694, 40 L.Ed.2d 1.

■ MR. JUSTICE BLACKMUN delivered the opinion of the Court.

. . . .

The complaint alleged that many of the striking employees had received and would continue to receive public assistance through two New Jersey public welfare programs, pursuant to regulations issued and administered by the named defendants. The petitioners sought a declaration that these interpretive regulations, according benefits to striking workers, were null and void because they constituted an interference with the federal labor policy of free collective bargaining expressed in the Labor Management Relations Act, 1947, 29 U.S.C. § 141 et seq., and with other federal policy pronounced in provisions of the Social Security Act of 1935, viz., 42 U.S.C. §§ 602(a)(8)(C), 606(e)(1), and 607(b)(1)(B). The petitioners also sought injunctive relief against the New Jersey welfare administrators' making public funds available to labor union members engaged in the strike.

With their complaint, the petitioners filed a motion for a preliminary injunction. . . .

. . . Counsel for the union contended that "this entire matter . . . has been mooted" because "these employees voted to return to work and are scheduled to return to work tomorrow morning." The District Court, nonetheless, proceeded to the merits of the dispute and, on the basis of the holding in ITT Lamp Division v. Minter, 435 F.2d 989 (C.A.1 1970), cert. denied 402 U.S. 933, 91 S.Ct. 1526, 28 L.Ed.2d 868 (1971), ruled that the appropriate forum for the petitioners' claim was the Congress, and that the New Jersey practice of according aid to striking workers was not violative of the Supremacy Clause of the Constitution. The court denied the motion for preliminary injunction and dismissed the complaint. On appeal, the United States Court of Appeals for the Third Circuit, by a divided vote, did not reach the merits but remanded the case with instructions to vacate and dismiss for mootness. We granted certiorari to consider the mootness issue.

II

The respondent union invites us to conclude that this controversy between the petitioners and the State became moot when the particular economic strike terminated upon the execution of the new collective-bargaining agreement and the return of the strikers to work in late June. That conclusion, however, is appropriate with respect to only one aspect of the lawsuit, that is, the request for injunctive relief made in the context of official state action during the pendency of the strike.

The petitioners here have sought, from the very beginning, *declaratory* relief as well as an injunction. Clearly, the District Court had "the duty to decide the appropriateness and the merits of the declaratory request irrespective of its conclusion as to the propriety of the issuance of the injunction." Thus, even though the case for an injunction dissolved with the subsequent settlement of the strike and the strikers' return to work, the parties to the principal controversy, that is, the corporate petitioners and the New Jersey officials, may still retain sufficient interests and injury as to justify the award of declaratory relief. The question is "whether the facts alleged, under all the circumstances, show that there is a substantial controversy, between parties having adverse legal interests, of sufficient immediacy and reality to warrant the issuance of a declaratory judgment." And since this case involves governmental action, we must ponder the broader consideration whether the short-term nature of that action makes the issues presented here "capable of repetition, yet evading review," so that petitioners are adversely affected by government "without a chance of redress."

A.   We hold that the facts here provide full and complete satisfaction of the requirement of the Constitution's Art. III, § 2, and the Declaratory Judgment Act, that a case or controversy exist between the parties. Unlike the situations that prevailed in Oil Workers Unions v. Missouri, 361 U.S. 363, 80 S.Ct. 391, 4 L.Ed.2d 373 (1960), on which the Court of Appeals' majority chiefly relied, and in Harris v. Battle, 348 U.S. 803, 75 S.Ct. 34, 99 L.Ed. 634 (1954), the challenged governmental activity in the present case is not contingent, has not evaporated or disappeared, and, by its continuing and brooding presence, casts what may well be a substantial adverse effect on the interests of the petitioning parties.

. . . .

... As in *Harris* and *Oil Workers*, the strike here was settled before the litigation reached this Court. But, unlike those cases, the challenged governmental action has not ceased. The New Jersey governmental action does not rest on the distant contingencies of another strike and the discretionary act of an official. Rather, New Jersey has declared positively that able-bodied striking workers who are engaged, individually and collectively, in an economic dispute with their employer are eligible for economic benefits. This policy is fixed and definite. It is not contingent upon executive discretion. Employees know that if they go out on strike, public funds are available. The petitioners' claim is that this eligibility affects the collective-bargaining relationship, both in the context of a live labor dispute when a collective-bargaining agreement is in process of formulation, *and* in the ongoing collective relationship, so that the economic balance between labor and management, carefully formulated and preserved by Congress in the federal labor statutes, is altered by the State's beneficent policy toward strikers. It cannot be doubted that the availability of state welfare assistance for striking workers in New Jersey pervades every work stoppage, affects every existing collective-bargaining agreement, and is a factor lurking in the background of every incipient labor contract. The question, of course, is whether Congress, explicitly or implicitly, has ruled out such assistance in its calculus of laws regulating labor-management disputes. In this sense petitioners allege a colorable claim of injury from an extant and fixed policy directive of the State of New Jersey. That claim deserves a hearing.

. . . .

B. If we were to condition our review on the existence of an economic strike, this case most certainly would be of the type presenting an issue "capable of repetition, yet evading review." To require the presence of an active and live labor dispute would tax the litigant too much by arbitrarily slighting claims of adverse injury from concrete governmental action (or the immediate threat thereof). It is sufficient, therefore, that the litigant show the existence of an immediate and definite governmental action or policy that has adversely affected and continues to affect a present interest. Otherwise, a state policy affecting a collective-bargaining arrangement, except one involving a fine or other penalty, could be adjudicated only rarely, and the purposes of the Declaratory Judgment Act would be frustrated.

Certainly, the pregnant appellants in Roe v. Wade, supra, and in Doe v. Bolton, 410 U.S. 179, 93 S.Ct. 739, 35 L.Ed.2d 201 (1973), had long since outlasted their pregnancies by the time their cases reached this Court. Yet we had no difficulty in rejecting suggestions of mootness. Similar and consistent results were reached in . . . [several] cases concerning various challenges to state election laws. The important ingredient in these cases was governmental action directly affecting, and continuing to affect, the behavior of citizens in our society.

The issues here are no different. Economic strikes are of comparatively short duration. There are exceptions, of course. But the great majority of economic strikes do not last long enough for complete judicial review of the controversies they engender. A strike that lasts six weeks as this one did, may seem long, but its termination, like pregnancy at nine months and elections spaced at year-long or biennial intervals, should not preclude challenge to state policies that have had their impact and that continue in force, unabated and unreviewed. The judiciary must not close the door to the resolution of the important questions these concrete disputes present.

The judgment of the Court of Appeals is reversed and the case is remanded for further proceedings on the merits of the controversy.

It is so ordered.

■ MR. JUSTICE STEWART, with whom THE CHIEF JUSTICE, MR. JUSTICE POWELL, and MR. JUSTICE REHNQUIST join, dissenting.

The Court today reverses the Court of Appeals and holds that this case is not moot, despite the fact that the underlying labor dispute that gave rise to the petitioners' claims ended even before the parties made their initial appearance in the District Court. I think this holding ignores the limitations placed upon the federal judiciary by Art. III of the Constitution and disregards the clear teachings of prior cases. Accordingly, I dissent.

. . . .

In short, I think that this case is completely controlled by *Harris* and *Oil Workers.* The doctrine of mootness is already a difficult and complex one, and I think that the Court today muddies the waters further by straining unnecessarily to distinguish and limit some of the few clear precedents available to us.

For these reasons I would affirm the judgment of the Court of Appeals.

———

F. NONCOERCIVE ANCILLARY REMEDIES: MASTERS, RECEIVERS, AND ACCOUNTING

Hurst v. Papierz

Appellate Court of Illinois, First District, 1973.
16 Ill.App.3d 574, 306 N.E.2d 532.

■ MORAN, J. Counterdefendants appeal from the following decree entered by the Circuit Court of Cook County:

"DECREE

This cause coming on to be heard on all of the pleadings herein and the Court having considered the Appellate Court Opinion, Judgment and Mandate rendered in this cause, reversing the May 22, 1968, Decree of this Court, and the Court having considered the arguments of counsel and being fully advised in the premises, FINDS:

(A) That this Court has jurisdiction of the parties hereto and the subject matter hereof.

(B) That the Appellate Court found that the equities in this cause are with the counterclaimant, ROBERT RAUTH, and against the counterdefendants, STANLEY PAPIERZ, THERESA PAPIERZ and STANLEY PAPIERZ BUILDERS . . .

(C) That the counterdefendants, STANLEY PAPIERZ, THERESA PAPIERZ and STANLEY PAPIERZ BUILDERS, INC., were found by the Appellate Court to have wrongfully and fraudulently denied ROBERT RAUTH's 30% interest as a joint venturer in the Villa Venice apartment building complex; it was further found that since 1963 said defendants excluded ROBERT RAUTH from the operation and profits of said apartment building complex and that said counterdefendants possessed and operated said apartment buildings and refused to account to ROBERT RAUTH.

(D) That the Appellate Court found that the counterdefendants, STANLEY PAPIERZ and THERESA PAPIERZ, and the counterplaintiff ROBERT RAUTH, were joint venturers in the real estate development known as "Villa Venice West" and that ROBERT RAUTH owned a 30% interest therein.

. . . .

IT IS THEREFORE ORDERED, ADJUDGED AND DECREED:

. . . .

2. That ROBERT RAUTH is hereby decreed to be the owner of a 30% interest in the real estate development known as "Villa Venice West" as represented by his ownership of 30% of the outstanding common stock of S.P. Construction, Inc.

3. That defendants, STANLEY A. PAPIERZ, THERESA PAPIERZ, STANLEY PAPIERZ BUILDERS, INC., and any other person, firm or corporation asserting any interest in the following described property shall forthwith convey to S.P. Construction, Inc., a corporation, said premises located in the Village of La Grange, Illinois:

. . . .

4. From and after the entry of this Decree, all income, receipts, revenues and proceeds thereafter derived from the operation of "Villa Venice West", in whatsoever form, and all assets, including cash on hand, shall become the property of S.P. Construction, Inc.

5. Michael P. Giambrone is hereby appointed Receiver to manage "Villa Venice West" until further order of this Court. Said Receiver shall be paid for his services the usual and customary charges paid therefor in the metropolitan Chicago area from the gross collections made by him from "Villa Venice West." Said Receiver shall be responsible for the collection of all rentals and payment of all expenses. No extraordinary payments for capital improvements, or otherwise, shall be made by the Receiver without the consent of the parties hereto, and failing such consent, by order of Court. Said Receiver shall submit to the parties a monthly statement with respect to his operation and conduct of "Villa Venice West."

6. From and after the entry of this Decree, all parties hereto shall be and they are hereby enjoined and restrained, until further order of this Court, from paying or disbursing any proceeds derived from the operation of "Villa Venice West" to any person, firm, or corporation other than S.P. Construction, Inc., excepting the Receiver for the purposes hereinabove described in paragraph 5.

7. That from and after the entry of this Decree and until further order of this Court, S.P. Construction, Inc. is enjoined and restrained from paying any salaries, dividends, fees, allowances, or emoluments of

any kind or description to any of the parties hereto, their transferees or assigns.

8.   That S.P. Construction, Inc. is, from and after the date of this Decree, enjoined and restrained from expending or employing any of its income, assets, or funds in connection with the litigation herein involved, or any other subsequent related cause, whether by way of attorneys' fees, court costs, or otherwise.

. . . .

. . . .

Counterdefendants also contend that even though we determine that the trial court properly ordered an accounting, the method by which it is to be taken is contrary to Illinois law. After ordering an accounting, the trial court appointed an accounting firm to determine the net sums due and payable to Robert Rauth from the counterdefendants. We find no authority in law for a method of accounting which does not set forth a procedure by which evidentiary questions may be adjudicated. Whether the suit is referred to a master or is heard by the court itself, each party has a right to be heard in support of his rights. On the hearing they have a right to introduce evidence, cross-examine witnesses and take the various steps authorized by law to protect their rights.

Appellants suggest that the trial court should follow the rules of the Circuit Court of Cook County in taking the accounting, and refer the accounting to a master-in-chancery. Counterdefendants would then submit their accounts before the master and Rauth could then review the accounting and have complete access to the books and records. Rauth could then file objections to the accounting and counterdefendants could then respond to his objections which would establish the issues. An evidentiary hearing could then be held to adjudicate the disputed items and objections to the master's report could then be filed before the circuit court. They state that this is the only procedure deemed proper by the Illinois Supreme Court in complicated accounting suits.

Prior to the passage of the new Illinois Constitution, there was a long line of cases in Illinois which held that in the case of a complicated accounting, the taking of such should be referred to a master in chancery. However, Section 8 of Article VI of the Illinois Constitution now provides that "there shall be no masters in chancery or other fee officers in the judicial system".

In view of the foregoing, the trial court itself must conduct the accounting, try all the issues, administer full relief to the parties and grant a judgment for the balance found due. In so doing, it is suggested that the trial court should follow established accounting procedures, except that it should not refer the case to a master or other fee officer as prohibited by the Illinois Constitution. In addition, it is suggested that the parties use the broad discovery tools available to them in the Supreme Court Rules.

. . . .

Appointment of a receiver is considered generally to be a harsh remedy. Nevertheless, it resides in the arsenal of equitable remedies to be used when in the sound discretion of the chancellor it is needed to insure complete justice is done between the parties. In equity, the particular circumstances surrounding the case are the criteria by which to judge whether or not the appointment of a receiver was reasonable, i.e., not arbitrary, capricious and an abuse of discretion. Considering that counter-defendants were found to be joint venturers with Rauth and defrauded him and have contumaciously and consistently resisted this conclusion in various ways, including behavior which appears to be continuing bad faith and at the very least a badge of fraud, we hold the appointment of a receiver and the imposition of the complained of temporary injunctions were proper in this case. It is reasonable to fear that there is a danger in this case that the property which belongs to the joint venture may be placed beyond the jurisdiction of the court or in some way involved in transfers, conveyances or subjected to other claims, so as to render it more difficult for the court to give and enforce final relief to which counterclaimant may be found entitled at the conclusion of the accounting.

For the foregoing reasons the judgment of the trial court is affirmed except for that portion which provided for the appointment of the accounting firm to take the accounting.

. . . .

NOTES ON ACCOUNTING, MASTERS AND RECEIVERS

1. An accounting is an audit conducted to ascertain the amount of money that one party owes to another. It is a form of relief ancillary to a decree for the payment of money. These remedies were available to Rauth because equity imposed a duty on fiduciaries to account. Traditionally, equity was also willing to grant an accounting in at least some circumstances where the accounts between the parties were deemed too complex for a jury to understand.

2. Courts of equity (and courts exercising equitable powers) frequently appoint a master or receiver to facilitate their work. Masters have been appointed to assist chancellors in a number of ways.[14] They have been used, for example, to conduct hearings and investigations, make determinations of fact or law, recommend appropriate sanctions, verify accounts, determine the value of property, and compute damages. More recently, they have also been used to propose and oversee the implementation of plans to desegregate schools and reform prisons.

The use of masters in the federal courts is governed by FED.R.CIV.P. 53. That Rule provides as follows:

Rule 53. Masters

(a) **Appointment and Compensation.** The court in which any action is pending may appoint a special master therein. As used in these rules the word "master" includes a referee, an auditor, an examiner, and an assessor. The compensation to be allowed to a master

---

14. See Madden v. Rosseter, *supra* p. 274.

shall be fixed by the court, and shall be charged upon such of the parties or paid out of any fund or subject matter of the action, which is in the custody and control of the court as the court may direct; provided that this provision for compensation shall not apply when a United States magistrate is designated to serve as a master pursuant to Title 28, U.S.C. § 636(b)(2). The master shall not retain the master's report as security for the master's compensation; but when the party ordered to pay the compensation allowed by the court does not pay it after notice and within the time prescribed by the court, the master is entitled to a writ of execution against the delinquent party.

(b) Reference. A reference to a master shall be the exception and not the rule. In actions to be tried by a jury, a reference shall be made only when the issues are complicated; in actions to be tried without a jury, save in matters of account and of difficult computation of damages, a reference shall be made only upon a showing that some exceptional condition requires it. Upon the consent of the parties, a magistrate may be designated to serve as a special master without regard to the provisions of this subdivision.

(c) Powers. The order of reference to the master may specify or limit the master's powers and may direct the master to report only upon particular issues or to do or perform particular acts or to receive and report evidence only and may fix the time and place for beginning and closing the hearings and for the filing of the master's report. Subject to the specifications and limitations stated in the order, the master has and shall exercise the power to regulate all proceedings in every hearing before the master and to do all acts and take all measures necessary or proper for the efficient performance of the master's duties under the order. The master may require the production before the master of evidence upon all matters embraced in the reference, including the production of all books, papers, vouchers, documents, and writings applicable thereto. The master may rule upon the admissibility of evidence unless otherwise directed by the order of reference and has the authority to put witnesses on oath and may examine them and may call the parties to the action and examine them upon oath. When a party so requests, the master shall make a record of the evidence offered and excluded in the same manner and subject to the same limitations as provided in the Federal Rules of Evidence for a court sitting without a jury.

(d) Proceedings.

(1) *Meetings.* When a reference is made, the clerk shall forthwith furnish the master with a copy of the order of reference. Upon receipt thereof unless the order of reference otherwise provides, the master shall forthwith set a time and place for the first meeting of the parties or their attorneys to be held within 20 days after the date of the order of reference and shall notify the parties or their attorneys. It is the duty of the master to proceed with all reasonable diligence. Either party, on notice to the parties and master, may apply to the court for an order requiring the master to speed the proceedings and to make the report. If a party fails to appear at the time and place appointed, the master may proceed ex parte or, in the master's discretion, adjourn the proceedings to a future day, giving notice to the absent party of the adjournment.

(2) *Witnesses.* The parties may procure the attendance of witnesses before the master by the issuance and service of subpoenas as provided in Rule 45. If without adequate excuse a witness fails to appear or give evidence, the witness may be punished as for a contempt and be subjected to the consequences, penalties, and remedies provided in Rules 37 and 45.

(3) *Statement of Accounts.* When matters of accounting are in issue before the master, the master may prescribe the form in which the accounts shall be submitted and in any proper case may require or receive in evidence a statement by a certified public accountant who is called as a witness. Upon objection of a party to any of the items thus submitted or upon a showing that the form of statement is insufficient, the master may require a different form of statement to be furnished, or the accounts or specific items thereof to be proved by oral examination of the accounting parties or upon written interrogatories or in such other manner as the master directs.

(e) Report.

(1) *Contents and Filing.* The master shall prepare a report upon the matters submitted to the master by the order of reference and, if required to make findings of fact and conclusions of law, the master shall set them forth in the report. The master shall file the report with the clerk of the court and in an action to be tried without a jury, unless otherwise directed by the order of reference, shall file with it a transcript of the proceedings and of the evidence and the original exhibits. The clerk shall forthwith mail to all parties notice of the filing.

(2) *In Non–Jury Actions.* In an action to be tried without a jury the court shall accept the master's findings of fact unless clearly erroneous. Within 10 days after being served with notice of the filing of the report any party may serve written objections thereto upon the other parties. Application to the court for action upon the report and upon objections thereto shall be by motion and upon notice as prescribed in Rule 6(d). The court after hearing may adopt the report or may modify it or may reject it in whole or in part or may receive further evidence or may recommit it with instructions.

(3) *In Jury Actions.* In an action to be tried by a jury the master shall not be directed to report the evidence. The master's findings upon the issues submitted to the master are admissible as evidence of the matters found and may be read to the jury, subject to the ruling of the court upon any objections in point of law which may be made to the report.

(4) *Stipulation as to Findings.* The effect of a master's report is the same whether or not the parties have consented to the reference; but, when the parties stipulate that a master's findings of fact shall be

final, only questions of law arising upon the report shall thereafter be considered.

(5) *Draft Report.* Before filing the master's report a master may submit a draft thereof to counsel for all parties for the purpose of receiving their suggestions.

(f) [Application to Magistrate]. A magistrate is subject to this rule only when the order referring a matter to the magistrate expressly provides that the reference is made under this Rule.

3. Receivers are appointed to manage property. Because a receiver is an officer of the appointing court, the law considers the appointing court to be the true possessor of property within the receiver's custody. Consequently, any improper interference with or attempt to disturb the receiver's possession may be punishable as contempt.

Receivers are not only used to manage private property. In recent years, they have also been appointed to aid courts in implementing decrees reforming schools, prisons, and other institutions.

MCR 2.622 Receivers

CHAPTER 5

THE DECLARATORY JUDGMENT AND RELATED REMEDIES

A. QUIA TIMET RELIEF

Fletcher v. Bealey

High Court of Justice, Chancery Division, 1885.
28 Ch.D. 688.

[The plaintiff was a manufacturer of the finest classes of paper, from linen that had to be bleached to as pure a white as possible. For this purpose he used a large quantity of water, which was pumped from the River Irwell, filtered, and returned after use to the river. The defendants were alkali manufacturers about six miles higher up the same river. Their process of manufacture produced a very large quantity of a refuse called "vat waste." After a large heap of this, the product possibly of many years, has been stored, there flows from it a liquid of a greenish color, which contains very destructive chemical elements. The defendants for some years carted this refuse bodily into the river, but in 1881 were enjoined at the suit of the municipality, and hired from a railway a piece of land on the bank of the river one mile and a half above the plaintiff's works. The plaintiff says that if the defendants proceed to deposit this refuse on this land, depositing, as they do at the present moment, at the rate of 1000 tons a month, the result will be that, sooner or later, there will necessarily come from the heap a large quantity of this green liquid, which will find its way into the River Irwell, and finding its way into the river, will be carried down to his works, and when he pumps the water from the river he will take in with it this chemical matter which will be destructive to his paper. There is no dispute between the parties that in process of time a liquid of that character does come from these heaps. There is no dispute that if any reasonably large quantity of that liquid should find its way into the plaintiff's bleaching works, that is, if it should be pumped by him from the river into his reservoir, it would be very destructive to his manufacture. But the defendants say: "You need be under no apprehension. We have not the slightest intention of injuring you; we intend to conduct our works in such a way that no appreciable quantity of that liquid shall find its way into the Irwell, and consequently no appreciable quantity will find its way from our heap into your works." There was no allegation that the plaintiff had in fact received any injury from the defendants' operations.]

■ PEARSON, J. . . .

340

It is admitted that the action is brought, not to obtain damages for a past injury, but to prevent that which is feared as a future injury, or, to use the more technical expression, the action is a *quia timet* action.

That being so, the objection has been taken that, under the particular circumstances of this case, a *quia timet* action will not lie, and, as that seems to me to be really the only point in the case, I think that I had better consider, first, what are the rules which have been laid down with regard to *quia timet* actions, and then I will consider whether the evidence in this case brings it within those circumstances which have been held to justify such an action. I need not refer to many of the cases which have been cited, because there is really no dispute as to the law.

. . . .

. . . I do not think, therefore, that I shall be very far wrong if I lay it down that there are at least two necessary ingredients for a *quia timet* action. There must, if no actual damage is proved, be proof of imminent danger, and there must also be proof that the apprehended damage will, if it comes, be very substantial. I should almost say it must be proved that it will be irreparable, because, if the danger is not proved to be so imminent that no one can doubt that, if the remedy is delayed, the damage will be suffered, I think it must be shewn that, if the damage does occur at any time, it will come in such a way and under such circumstances that it will be impossible for the plaintiff to protect himself against it if relief is denied to him in a *quia timet* action.

Now the circumstances of the present case are these. In the first place, it is said that, do what the Defendants may, if they proceed to cover, as they propose to do, two acres and a half of the land with this refuse, at the rate of 1000 tons a month, necessarily, although not immediately, there will ooze from the heap a large quantity of this pernicious liquid. Moreover, it is said that, inasmuch as the Defendants have taken a lease of the land from the railway company only for the purpose of depositing this refuse on it, and they have the power of giving up the lease when they have made as much use of the land as they can for the purpose, at the end of ten years, at which time it is reasonably concluded they will have deposited on the land as much of the refuse as it will hold, they will give up the lease, and then the heap will be left without any person whose duty it is to take care of it, and the liquid will continue to ooze out of it for a period of forty or fifty years, or even longer, and the Plaintiff will be under a risk, an increasing risk, certainly a much greater risk than he incurs at the present moment, of having the water of the Irwell polluted, and of pumping into his works the water which is so polluted. The quantity of water which the Plaintiff takes from the Irwell is very large indeed, amounting, I think, sometimes to one-third of the water in the river; 1,000,000 gallons in the twenty-four hours.

Now, if that stood alone, would there be a sufficient ground for a *quia timet* action? I think not. There was some conflict in the evidence as to what amount of the liquid would be sufficient to pollute the water so as to injure the plaintiff. . . . But the answer of the defendants is this. They do not intend that any appreciable amount of this liquid should get into the Irwell, and, inasmuch as it is perfectly practicable, according to all that we know to prevent the liquid which comes from the heap from getting into the Irwell, I cannot think that at the present moment the evidence on this point is sufficient to justify the Court in interfering. In Attorney–General v. Corporation of Kingston, 13 W.R. 888, Wood, V.C., spoke of injurious results at the end of 100 years. If an injury does result in the present case it will result in a much shorter time, and, if the heap were left alone without any protection to the river to prevent the liquid from oozing into it, I have no doubt that at the end of ten years the water would be polluted sufficiently to do a great amount of injury to the Plaintiff. But Wood, V.C., pointed out that in 100 years' time chemical processes might be invented which would prevent the sewage from doing any injury to the River Thames, and I think that in ten years time it is highly probable that science (which is now at work on the subject) may have discovered some means for rendering this green liquid innocuous. But, even if no such discovery should be made in that time, I cannot help seeing that there are contrivances, such as tanks and pumps, and other things of that kind, by which the liquid may, as the Defendants say, be kept out of the river altogether. Therefore, upon that ground alone, I do not think that the action can be supported.

There is another observation to be made on this point of the case. In the first place I think the danger is not imminent, because it must be some years before any such quantity of the liquid will be found issuing from the heap as would pollute the Irwell to the detriment of the plaintiff. And, in the next place, if any such quantity of liquid did get into the river so as to injure the plaintiff, I think it would be discovered immediately, and it would be perfectly possible for him then to apply to the court for relief, and to obtain an immediate injunction restraining the defendants from allowing the liquid to get into the river. For both these reasons I think there is not sufficient in this part of the case to sustain a *quia timet* action.

. . . .

I think the plaintiff has been premature in bringing his action, and that, according to the rules which have been laid down (and I cannot go beyond precedent), I must refuse to grant an injunction, and I believe, according to the practice in these cases, I have no choice but to dismiss the action with costs. But I observe that in Attorney–General v. Corporation of Kingston Wood, V.C., guarded the dismissal of the information by a declaration of the right of the plaintiff to bring another action thereafter if there should be actual damage, or damage which he could prove to be imminent or likely to be irreparable. The Vice–Chancellor said: "The proper course would be to dismiss the information, such dismissal being prefaced by a declaration that the court was of opinion that the evidence did not establish the existence of any nuisance in respect of the works executed, or intended to be executed, by the defendants, or any case for the interference of the court in respect of nuisance to be apprehended, if such works were carried into effect. The order would be without prejudice to any future proceedings on the part of the Attorney–General in case the works should occasion a nuisance." Though I do not think it is necessary, yet, if the plaintiff's counsel desire it, I have no objection to inserting a similar declaration in the order which I am now making.

Cozens–Hardy said that he wished to have the declaration inserted.

Escrow Agents' Fidelity Corp. v. Abelman

Court of Appeal, Second District, Division 5, California., 1992.
4 Cal.App.4th 491, 5 Cal.Rptr.2d 698.

■ BOREN, ASSOCIATE JUSTICE.

Petitioners challenge an order of the respondent court sustaining, without leave to amend, the demurrer of real party Linda Abelman ("Abelman") to the first cause of action of petitioners' complaint. In that cause of action, petitioners sought relief based on the theory of quia timet, an equitable remedy which allows an aggrieved party to obtain pre-judgment relief to prevent an anticipated injury. Abelman persuaded the respondent court that quia timet was a remedy which no longer exists in the State of California, having been "taken over by, consumed in and now part of a whole statutory scheme of rights."

Although quia timet has by and large been abandoned in favor of other legal and equitable pre-judgment remedies, it is by no means obsolete. Although rarely utilized in general practice, it is widely and effectively used in fidelity and surety bond cases. The respondent court erred, therefore, in sustaining Abelman's demurrer to petitioners' quia timet cause of action.

FACTS AND PROCEDURAL HISTORY

Petitioner Escrow Agents' Fidelity Corporation (EAFC) is a nonprofit corporation established by the Legislature pursuant to the Escrow Law (Fin.Code Sect. 17000 et seq.) to act as the fidelity surety for the trust obligations of licensed escrow agents in California. The purpose of EAFC is to indemnify its member agents against loss of trust obligations as a result of embezzlement, theft, or mysterious disappearance. (See 30 Cal.Jur.3d, Escrows, §§ 57–66.) The surety coverage is underwritten by petitioner National Union Fire Insurance Company, which issued a "Blanket Crime Policy" for the benefit of EAFC and each of its member agents.

One such agent, Abelman, is alleged to have embezzled over $4 million from Citi Escrow ("Citi") and a related company, 1031 Exchange ("Exchange"). On June 11, 1990, both of those entities filed voluntary Chapter 11 petitions in bankruptcy court. On Citi's behalf, Citi's trustee in bankruptcy made a claim with petitioners in excess of four million dollars, a claim which petitioners are statutorily obligated to pay. (Fin.Code, §§ 17330, 17314.)

On November 21, 1990, petitioners filed the underlying superior court action against Abelman, to which Abelman demurred. On May 8, 1991, the respondent court sustained, without leave to amend, the demurrer to the first cause of action for equitable relief quia timet and imposition of a constructive trust. [footnote omitted]

On August 5, 1991, while this petition was pending, Abelman filed a voluntary Chapter 7 bankruptcy petition in the U.S. Bankruptcy Court in Hawaii. Oral argument in this case was continued several times so that petitioners could obtain a transfer of Abelman's bankruptcy case to California, then obtain relief from the automatic stay imposed by 11 U.S.C. § 362. On February 5, 1992, the United States Bankruptcy Court for the Central District of California entered its order granting petitioners' motion for relief from the automatic stay, for the limited purpose of allowing this court to rule on the petition for writ of mandate.

DISCUSSION

Quia timet (literal translation, "because he fears"), is an action for equitable relief against an anticipated injury. "Bills quia timet are in the nature of writs known at the common law as brevia anticipantia, or writs of prevention, to accomplish the ends of precautionary justice. They are ordinarily applied to prevent wrongs or anticipated mischief, and not merely to redress them when done. The party asks the aid of the court because he fears some future probable injury to his rights or interests, and not because an injury has already occurred which requires compensation or other relief." (Conners, California Surety & Fidelity Bond Practice (C.E.B. 1969), § 13.13, p. 176, citing Roman Catholic Archbishop of San Francisco v. Shipman (1886) 69 Cal. 586, 589, 11 P. 343.)

Traditionally, the equitable remedy of quia timet was used in California in real property cases (and, to a lesser extent in personal property cases), "to prevent a mischief, rather than redress it." (Martin v. Holm (1925) 197 Cal. 733, 746, 242 P. 718 [threatened violation of building restriction]; see also Newport v. Hatton (1924) 195 Cal. 132, 231 P. 987 ["writ of prevention" to protect remainderman's interest in real property]; German Savings and Loan Society v. Collins (1904) 145 Cal. 192, 78 P. 637 [quia timet action to determine claims and liabilities of parties to $2,500 drawn on forged checks]; Benson v. Shotwell (1890) 87 Cal. 49, 25 P. 249 [specific performance of a contract to purchase waterfront property in San Francisco]; McGrath v. Wallace (1890) 85 Cal. 622, 24 P. 793 [action to enjoin a foreclosure sale]; United Land Assn. v. Knight (1890) 85 Cal. 448, 24 P. 818 [suit over title to real property]; Roman Catholic Archbishop of San Francisco, supra [action to enjoin a foreclosure sale].)

Even at the time the above cases were decided, quia timet relief was used sparingly. (Roman Catholic Archbishop of San Francisco, supra, 69 Cal. at p. 586, 11 P. 343.) Today, it has for the most part been forsaken in favor of statutory remedies. For example, a party who wants to enjoin a foreclosure sale, prevent a nuisance, or otherwise assert a right to real property (the traditional uses for quia timet), would seek injunctive relief and make effective use of the lis pendens statutes (Code Civ.Proc., §§ 409 et seq.). An aggrieved creditor might avail himself of the attachment law (Code Civ.Proc., § 481.010 et seq.), provided he is fortunate enough to have a debtor with assets to attach. An individual with a claim to personal property has at his disposal the claim and delivery statutes (Code Civ.Proc., § 511.010 et seq.).

Had these statutory remedies completely replaced quia timet, however, it would have been news to the fidelity and surety bond industry, and to those judges of the Los Angeles Superior court who have granted relief in cases similar to this one.[2] " 'No principle in equity is more familiar, or more firmly established, than that a surety, after the debt for which he is liable has become due, without paying or being called on to pay it, may file a bill in equity in the nature of a bill quia timet to compel the principal to exonerate him from liability by its payment, provided no rights of the creditor are prejudiced thereby.' ... The doctrine is not premised on mere fear of loss or liability prior to an obligation's maturity. Rather, only after the obligation becomes payable, the surety, before he pays it, may maintain a suit in equity against the debtor in the nature of a bill quia timet to compel the latter to pay the debt or perform the obligation, provided the creditor could enforce payment or performance but neglects or refuses to do it." (Fireman's Fund Ins. Co. v. S.E.K. Construction Co. (10th Cir.1971) 436 F.2d 1345, 1349; emphasis in original; see also Northwestern Nat. Ins. v. Alberts (S.D.N.Y.1990) 741 F.Supp. 424, 429–430, and cases cited therein.)

Quia timet is in fact especially suited to surety cases. (See, e.g., examples cited in Conners, Fidelity & Surety Bond Practice, supra, pp. 177–178.) "A surety or guarantor is one who promises to answer for the debt, default, or miscarriage of another ..." (Civ.Code, § 2787.) A surety is obligated by law to pay the creditor of its defaulting principal immediately upon the principal's default or defalcation. (Civ.Code, § 2807). Although a surety may file an action at law to compel its principal to perform the obligation on a bond when due (Civ.Code, § 2846), the fact that it may eventually obtain a judgment against the principal is of little comfort to the surety if, in the interim, the principal has absconded with the very funds which could have been used to satisfy the bond. Quia timet allows the surety to prevent the principal from dissipating those funds if the surety knows it will be called upon to "pay the debt or perform the obligation" on the bond, suspects that the principal has some or all of the necessary funds to do so, and fears that the principal may abscond with those funds.

Abelman, without citing any specific authority to support her argument, persuaded the respondent court that quia timet was "a concept that pre-dates movable type, and has virtually no application in modern society." Petitioners have persuaded us otherwise.

DISPOSITION

Let a peremptory writ of mandate issue directing the respondent court to vacate that portion of its order of May 8, 1991, sustaining, without leave to amend, the demurrer of defendant Linda Abelman to the first cause of action of plaintiffs' complaint, and enter a new and different order overruling the demurrer.

■ TURNER, P.J., and GRIGNON, J., concur.

2. EAFC asked this court to take judicial notice of temporary restraining orders or injunctions which it obtained in several escrow cases. At petitioners' request, we published this opinion to provide current authority on the viability of quia timet relief. (Cal. Rules of Court, rule 976(b)(3).)

NOTES

1.   By a bill *quia timet,* a plaintiff invokes equity jurisdiction "because he fears," i.e., because the complainant apprehends or fears injury to his property rights or other interests by the wrongdoing or neglect of the defendant. In view of the generality of the words *quia timet*—"because he fears"—many equity actions might loosely be deemed to request *quia timet* relief. For example, in an action for specific performance of a contract, it might be said that plaintiff is suing because of fear that the defendant will not perform the contract. Also, in the sense that plaintiff sues because of fear of litigation, it may be deemed to include bills of peace and interpleader. Dean Ames even regarded bills to remove a cloud on title as *quia timet* relief, although the removal of a cloud on title invariably deals with a present injury to the marketability of the title, rather than a prospective injury.

In a narrower sense, the purposes of the bill were to guard against prospective injury, and to preserve the means to protect existing rights from future violation or infringement.

2.   Professor Bispham wrote that the principle upon which a court acts in the granting of *quia timet* relief "is that justice sometimes requires that a man shall not be compelled to have hanging over him, or his title, for an indefinite time, some claim or demand or liability, which, if enforced, would subject him to loss; but that he is entitled to have the questions relating to his rights settled at once forever, to have the claim against his rights immediately enforced, or to be presently made secure against any future liability." Bispham, Principles of Equity 853 (10th ed. 1924). Beyond this, he argued that this equitable relief "goes one step further than the relief by injunction." Id. Unlike an injunction, Bispham maintained, the bill *quia timet* secures rights against invasion without the requirement that the threatened invasion be imminent and certain. Courts, however, have been more demanding than suggested by Professor Bispham in the granting of *quia timet* relief.

3.   One may "fear" that a negotiable instrument may be negotiated to a holder in due course (and thereby cut off personal defenses that might otherwise be asserted by the maker). Since equity acts in personam, an injunction against the negotiation of a negotiable note does not destroy the negotiability of the note. Also, the doctrine of *lis pendens* would not apply to the negotiable instrument. Hence, the most effective remedy would be a *quia timet* action to cancel the note. Note the following provisions of the California Civil Code on the cancellation of instruments:

§ 3412. When cancellation may be ordered. A written instrument, in respect to which there is a reasonable apprehension that if left outstanding it may cause serious injury to a person against whom it is void or voidable, may, upon his application, be so adjudged, and ordered to be delivered up or canceled.

§ 3413. Instrument obviously void. An instrument, the invalidity of which is apparent upon its face, or upon the face of another instrument which is necessary to the use of the former in evidence, is not to be deemed capable of causing injury, within the provisions of the last section.

———

B.   BILLS OF PEACE

Yuba Consolidated Gold Fields v. Kilkeary

United States Court of Appeals, Ninth Circuit, 1953.
206 F.2d 884.

■ BYRNE, J. The appellant, as plaintiff below, filed a complaint in the nature of a "bill of peace" seeking to avoid a multiplicity of legal actions by determining in one equity suit the liability asserted in hundreds of claims for damages resulting from floods of the Yuba River in the winter of 1950. The complaint was dismissed for failure to state a claim upon which relief can be granted and this appeal followed.

The material allegations of the complaint may be summarized as follows: Plaintiff is a citizen of the State of Maine; defendants are all citizens of the State of California; the amount in controversy exceeds $3,000; since March 18, 1905, the plaintiff has been engaged in mining gold by the dredging process in Yuba County; during the month of November, 1950, a series of storms brought heavy precipitation to the section of the Sierra Nevada from the Feather River on the north to the Kern River on the south; the rainfall caused the Yuba River to carry a greater volume of water than had ever before passed down the stream during its recorded history; the flood waters overflowed the south natural banks of the river and broke the south training wall—a cobble embankment that the plaintiff had constructed about the year 1925 as a part of approved projects of flood and debris control; the river's overflow spread over an area of approximately 100 square miles in Yuba County which included large acreages of farm lands, about 2669 separate ownerships of real property, and more than seven residential and business communities; the flood caused an unascertainable amount of heavy damage; claimed items include damage to agricultural lands, orchards, crops, highways, farm produce, machinery, walls and foundations of buildings, furnishings and personal effects in dwellings, automobiles, business, residential and industrial property and lost profits due to interruption of business; a state of emergency was declared in Yuba County, lasting from November 20, 1950, to December 11, 1950, during which about 8,000 persons were forced from their homes for varying lengths of time and received flood and disaster relief from the American Red Cross and others in Marysville; during and after the flood the charge was publicly made that the plaintiff's dredging in the Yuba River had caused the flood and that the plaintiff was responsible for the damage; during November and December, 1950, meetings were held at which various defendants discussed ways and means of prosecuting their claims against the plaintiff, and agreements were circulated providing for payment by claimants of 1% of their respective claims into a fund to be expended for the prosecution of actions against the plaintiff; six actions involving more than one hundred claimants and $853,964.98[1] in claims have been filed against the plaintiff in the Superior Court of Yuba County, California, in which the claimants assert that the plaintiff's operations in the Yuba River were responsible for the flood and the resulting damages, which assertions are unfounded; plaintiff's operations had no causal connection with the flood, were at all times conducted with due care in accordance with good engineering practice and in conformity with the requirements of Federal permits duly issued by statutory authority, and were part of projects approved by statute for debris and flood control that have been in progress on the Yuba River for more than 50 years; the potential claims of the unnamed defendants may run into sums aggregating millions of dollars and if the claims should be asserted and established in amounts comparable with the damage prayers of the suits on file, the resulting liability would exceed the value of the plaintiff's assets and would be beyond its ability to pay.

It is further alleged that the plaintiff has no adequate remedy at law; unless relief in equity is granted plaintiff will be subjected to a multiplicity of actions by the defendants; such actions will involve identical questions of law and fact with respect to the alleged liability of plaintiff; such actions involve damage claims beyond plaintiff's ability to pay and the defendants, therefore, have a common interest in pending and proposed litigation to enforce such claim; and the trial of such actions, potentially numbering hundreds or thousands, cannot be practically or fairly conducted at law.

The prayer of the complaint asks that the court permanently enjoin the defendants from the prosecution, "except in this court and cause," of any suit against the plaintiff for the recovery of any damage alleged to have been caused by the flood; that the court hear and determine all claims of the defendants against the plaintiff and decree such claims to be without right; that declaratory relief be granted "with respect to plaintiff's rights under the statutes pursuant to which said federal permits were issued to plaintiff".

Jurisdiction of the Subject Matter and "Equity Jurisdiction."

This case is permeated with serious questions relating to jurisdiction which requires, at the threshold of our discussion, that we point out the distinction between the term "jurisdiction" in its strict sense, and as commonly used in equity jurisprudence. "Jurisdiction," in the strict meaning of the term, is the *power* to hear and determine the subject matter of the class of actions to which the particular case belongs. Reference to "equity jurisdiction" does not relate to the power of the court to hear and determine a controversy but relates to *whether it ought to assume* the jurisdiction and decide the cause. The distinction is of the utmost impor-

---

1. At the time of the oral argument before this court, the appellant filed a memorandum with respect to the then pending actions at law which disclosed 22 actions pending by 1022 plaintiffs with a total prayer of $2,834,595.08. Subsequently counsel informed the court, by letter, that about 100 of the pending claims have been concluded by compromise and approximately 25 new claims asserted and that there are still pending against appellant actions involving more than 900 claimants for alleged damages exceeding $2,000,000.

tance here, as this case involves problems of both "equity jurisdiction" and "jurisdiction" in its strict sense.

The trial court's jurisdiction of *this* case is not disputed by any of the parties. The motions to dismiss were on the ground of failure to state a claim upon which relief can be granted.

The suits in equity of which federal courts may exercise jurisdiction constitute that body of remedies, procedures, and practices which had been evolved in the English Court of Chancery prior to the adoption of the First Judiciary Act, except as modified by Congress. The granting of relief against multiplicity of legal actions in appropriate situations is part of that historic jurisdiction.

The general doctrine that equity will take cognizance of a matter to prevent a multiplicity of suits is asserted in innumerable decisions, but when one seeks an answer to the question of the extent of the doctrine he finds uncertainty and a direct conflict of decisions.

Much of the confusion and uncertainty surrounding the doctrine flows from the failure to recognize that its extent and limitations are not identical in every class of cases which furnishes an occasion for its exercise. The class of cases with which we are here concerned is that class wherein a number of persons have separate and individual claims and rights of action against the same party arising from a common cause of transaction and the law defendant seeks to have all of the claims settled in a single suit in equity.

Equity jurisdiction in this class of cases will not be recognized unless there is a common bond or interest held by the number of persons against the single person. The character and essential elements of this common bond or interest constitute the fundamental question upon which the recognition of the equity jurisdiction rests, and it is in the solution of this question that most of the conflict of opinion among the courts has arisen.

Is it necessary that the common bond or interest be a community of interest in the subject matter of the controversy to such an extent as to create *a privity between the individual members of the group,* as well as between each of them and the single adversary party? Or is it sufficient that the common bond or interests consists solely in the fact that the claims of the members of the group have arisen from the same source and all involve and depend upon similar questions of law and fact, so that while the same positive relation exists between the single party on the one side and *each* individual member of the group on the other, *no such legal relation exists between the individual members themselves?*

The leading case supporting the restricted view is Tribbette v. Illinois C.R. Co., 1892, 70 Miss. 182, 12 So. 32, which has been followed by a number of courts including the Fourth Circuit. This restricted view has never been approved by the Supreme Court and is against the great weight of authority.

The majority view is succinctly stated [in Pomeroy, Equity Jurisprudence, 5th ed. 1941, Vol. I, sec. 269]:

"... notwithstanding the positive denials by some American courts, the weight of authority is simply overwhelming that the jurisdiction may and should be exercised, either on behalf of a numerous body of separate claimants against a single party, or on behalf of a single party against such a numerous body, although there is no 'common title,' no 'community of right' or of 'interest in the subject-matter,' among these individuals, but where there is and because there is merely a community of interest among them in the questions of law and fact involved in the general controversy, or in the kind and form of relief demanded and obtained by or against each individual member of the numerous body."

The appellees rely upon Hale v. Allinson, 1903, 188 U.S. 56, 23 S.Ct. 244, 47 L.Ed. 380. The case does not support their position. It is true that that court denied a bill of peace, but the denial was on the ground that each of the defenses of the multiple parties depended upon different facts. There is no dispute that common questions of law and fact must exist before a court of equity will interfere. The question is whether in addition to common questions of law and fact there must exist a *common title or community right or interest in the subject matter among the defendants*. The Hale v. Allinson court said such a community interest was not necessary.... In Bitterman v. Louisville & Nashville R.R., 1907, 207 U.S. 205, 28 S.Ct. 91, 98, 52 L.Ed. 171, the Supreme Court sustained a bill of peace and cited Hale v. Allinson for the principle that equity jurisdiction would be recognized where "the relief sought against each defendant was the same, and the defenses which might be interposed were common to each defendant and involved like legal questions."

There is an important distinction between the recognition of equity jurisdiction as authorized and the actual exercise of such jurisdiction. If the bill alleges a situation authorizing a bill of peace, equity jurisdiction will be recognized and a motion to dismiss will be denied. However it does not necessarily follow that equity jurisdiction will be exercised. Whether it will be exercised rests in the sound discretion of the chancellor. The basis of all equitable rules is the principle of discretionary application. In the instant case the trial court thought that there must exist among the defendants a common title or community right or interest in the subject matter. Under this belief, the court granted a motion to dismiss for failure to state a claim upon which relief can be granted. The bill did state facts sufficient to authorize the intervention of equity and an allegation of such a community of interest was not required. On a motion to dismiss the facts properly pleaded in the bill must be taken as established; therefore the motion to dismiss should have been denied. A ruling on a motion to dismiss for failure to state a claim upon which relief can be granted is a ruling on a question of law and does not admit the exercise of discretion.

Exercise of Discretion.

Equity jurisdiction being recognized, the question whether it will be exercised rests in the sound discretion of the chancellor. It must be a legal discretion based on principles of law and not on the arbitrary will of the chancellor. The discretion of the chancellor is directed primarily to the question of whether there is a plain, adequate and complete remedy at law.

The relief Yuba is here seeking is in the form of an injunction enjoining the defendants from the prosecution, except in this proceeding, of any claim for damages alleged to have been caused by the flood. If the chancellor in his discretion, determines that there is no plain, adequate remedy at law and that this is a proper case for the exercise of equity jurisdiction to prevent a multiplicity of suits, he should grant the injunction and proceed to the disposal of all the litigation and claims in this single equity suit. If he determines that this is not a proper case for the exercise of equity jurisdiction he should withhold such exercise, deny the injunction and leave the parties to their legal remedies, thus ending this particular proceeding.

Some of the factors to be considered by the chancellor are referred to in Hale v. Allinson, where the Supreme Court said each case "must, as we think, be decided upon its own merits and upon a survey of the real and substantial convenience of all parties, the adequacy of the legal remedy, the situations of the different parties, the points to be contested and the result which would follow if jurisdiction should be assumed or denied; these various matters being factors to be taken into consideration upon the question of equitable jurisdiction on this ground, and whether within reasonable and fair grounds the suit is calculated to be in truth one which will practically prevent a multiplicity of litigation, and will be an actual convenience to all parties, and will not unreasonably overlook or obstruct the material interests of any. The single fact that a multiplicity of suits may be prevented by this assumption of jurisdiction is not in all cases enough to sustain it. It might be that the exercise of equitable jurisdiction on this ground, while preventing a formal multiplicity of suits, would nevertheless be attended with more and deeper inconvenience to the defendants than would be compensated for by the convenience of a single plaintiff; and where the case is not covered by any controlling precedent the inconvenience might constitute good ground for denying jurisdiction."

Although the jury trial policy should be considered where the issues are basically legal in their nature, it must be borne in mind "that to sustain a suit in equity in the federal courts it must appear there is no plain, adequate, and complete remedy at law, and, if the remedy at law is not adequate, the right to a jury trial does not exist." The possibility of consolidating the actions at law has a direct bearing on the question of the adequacy of the legal remedy, and the question of removal of all of the actions at law to the federal court, in turn, affects the matter of consolidation.

. . . .

There is considerable discussion in the briefs of the parties and in the memorandum opinion of the trial court with respect to whether the damages resulted from the negligence of Yuba or were incidental or consequential damages flowing from work performed for the government in accordance with its requirements, by a government contractor. This is a question of fact to be determined by the court in a trial on the merits regardless of whether the trial is at law or in equity. We do not reach that question in the present posture of the case.

The appellant suggests that this court is in as good a position as the trial court to determine whether equity jurisdiction should be exercised. We do not agree. Where equity jurisdiction to entertain a bill of peace is authorized, the question of whether it will be exercised rests in the sound discretion of the chancellor. Because of an imperfect perception of the principles involved, the trial court thought that equity jurisdiction could not be recognized, and dismissed the complaint for failure to state a claim upon which relief can be granted. It was a ruling on a question of law and resulted in a failure to exercise discretion.

The complaint, accepting the facts properly pleaded as established, does state a claim authorizing the exercise of the trial court's discretion. Whether equity jurisdiction should be assumed to prevent a multiplicity of suits, is a question for the trial court. The determination must rest on sound principles of law and the court may require such proof as shall be deemed necessary for the proper exercise of its discretion. We therefore must reverse and remand the case for further proceedings in the trial court not inconsistent with the views expressed here.

NOTES

1. Consider the bearing of the following Federal Rules of Civil Procedure on the need for a bill of peace in a case like *Yuba Consolidated Gold Fields:*

Rule 19. Joinder of Persons Needed for Just Adjudication

(a) Persons to be Joined if Feasible. A person who is subject to service of process and whose joinder will not deprive the court of jurisdiction over the subject matter of the action shall be joined as a party in the action if (1) in the person's absence complete relief cannot be accorded among those already parties, or (2) the person claims an interest relating to the subject of the action and is so situated that the disposition of the action in the person's absence may (i) as a practical matter impair or impede the person's ability to protect that interest or (ii) leave any of the persons already parties subject to a substantial risk of incurring double, multiple, or otherwise inconsistent obligations by reason of the claimed interest. If the person has not been so joined, the court shall order that the person be made a party. If the person should join as a plaintiff but refuses to do so, the person may be made a defendant, or, in a proper case, an involuntary plaintiff. If the joined party objects to venue and joinder of that party would render the venue of the action improper, that party shall be dismissed from the action.

(b) Determination by Court Whenever Joinder not Feasible. If a person as described in subdivision (a)(1)–(2) hereof cannot be made a party, the court shall determine whether in equity and good conscience the action should proceed among the parties before it, or should be dismissed, the absent person being thus regarded as indispensable. The factors to be considered by the court include: first, to what extent a judgment rendered in the person's absence might be prejudicial to the person or those already parties; second, the extent to which, by protective provisions in the judgment, by the shaping of relief, or other measures, the prejudice can be lessened or avoided; third, whether a judgment rendered in the person's absence will be adequate; fourth, whether the plaintiff will have an adequate remedy if the action is dismissed for nonjoinder.

. . . .

Rule 23. Class Actions

(a) **Prerequisites to a Class Action.** One or more members of a class may sue or be sued as representative parties on behalf of all only if (1) the class is so numerous that joinder of all members is impracticable, (2) there are questions of law or fact common to the class, (3) the claims or defenses of the representative parties are typical of the claims or defenses of the class, and (4) the representative parties will fairly and adequately protect the interests of the class.

(b) **Class Actions Maintainable.** An action may be maintained as a class action if the prerequisites of subdivision (a) are satisfied, and in addition:

(1) the prosecution of separate actions by or against individual members of the class would create a risk of

(A) inconsistent or varying adjudications with respect to individual members of the class which would establish incompatible standards of conduct for the party opposing the class, or

(B) adjudications with respect to individual members of the class which would as a practical matter be dispositive of the interests of the other members not parties to the adjudications or substantially impair or impede their ability to protect their interests; or

(2) the party opposing the class has acted or refused to act on grounds generally applicable to the class, thereby making appropriate final injunctive relief or corresponding declaratory relief with respect to the class as a whole; or

(3) the court finds that the questions of law or fact common to the members of the class predominate over any questions affecting only individual members, and that a class action is superior to other available methods for the fair and efficient adjudication of the controversy. The matters pertinent to the findings include: (A) the interest of members of the class in individually controlling the prosecution or defense of separate actions; (B) the extent and nature of any litigation concerning the controversy already commenced by or against members of the class; (C) the desirability or undesirability of concentrating the litigation of the claims in the particular forum; (D) the difficulties likely to be encountered in the management of a class action.

(c) **Determination by Order Whether Class Action to be Maintained; Notice; Judgment; Actions Conducted Partially as Class Actions.**

(1) As soon as practicable after the commencement of an action brought as a class action, the court shall determine by order whether it

is to be so maintained. An order under this subdivision may be conditional, and may be altered or amended before the decision on the merits.

(2) In any class action maintained under subdivision (b)(3), the court shall direct to the members of the class the best notice practicable under the circumstances, including individual notice to all members who can be identified through reasonable effort. The notice shall advise each member that (A) the court will exclude the member from the class if the member so requests by a specified date; (B) the judgment, whether favorable or not, will include all members who do not request exclusion; and (C) any member who does not request exclusion may, if the member desires, enter an appearance through counsel.

(3) The judgment in an action maintained as a class action under subdivision (b)(1) or (b)(2), whether or not favorable to the class, shall include and describe those whom the court finds to be members of the class. The judgment in an action maintained as a class action under subdivision (b)(3), whether or not favorable to the class, shall include and specify or describe those to whom the notice provided in subdivision (c)(2) was directed, and who have not requested exclusion, and whom the court finds to be members of the class.

(4) When appropriate (A) an action may be brought or maintained as a class action with respect to particular issues, or (B) a class may be divided into subclasses and each subclass treated as a class, and the provisions of this rule shall then be construed and applied accordingly.

(d) Orders in Conduct of Actions. In the conduct of actions to which this rule applies, the court may make appropriate orders: (1) determining the course of proceedings or prescribing measures to prevent undue repetition or complication in the presentation of evidence or argument; (2) requiring, for the protection of the members of the class or otherwise for the fair conduct of the action, that notice be given in such manner as the court may direct to some or all of the members of any step in the action, or of the proposed extent of the judgment, or of the opportunity of members to signify whether they consider the representation fair and adequate, to intervene and present claims or defenses, or otherwise to come into the action; (3) imposing conditions on the representative parties or on intervenors; (4) requiring that the pleadings be amended to eliminate therefrom allegations as to representation of absent persons, and that the action proceed accordingly; (5) dealing with similar procedural matters. The orders may be combined with an order under Rule 16, and may be altered or amended as may be desirable from time to time.

(e) Dismissal or Compromise. A class action shall not be dismissed or compromised without the approval of the court, and notice of the proposed dismissal or compromise shall be given to all members of the class in such manner as the court directs.

Rule 42. Consolidation; Separate Trials

(a) Consolidation. When actions involving a common question of law or fact are pending before the court, it may order a joint hearing or trial of any or all the matters in issue in the actions; it may order all the actions consolidated; and it may make such orders concerning proceedings therein as may tend to avoid unnecessary costs or delay.

(b) Separate Trials. The court, in furtherance of convenience or to avoid prejudice, or when separate trials will be conducive to expedition and economy, may order a separate trial of any claim, cross-claim, counterclaim, or third-party claim, or of any separate issue or of any number of claims, cross-claims, counterclaims, third-party claims, or issues, always preserving inviolate the right of trial by jury as declared by the Seventh Amendment to the Constitution or as given by a statute of the United States.

2.   There is a second kind of bill of peace, one to prevent the vexatious recurrence of litigation, which is essentially an injunction ordering the defendant to stop filing motions or suits without judicial consent. Cf. Wrenn v. Benson, 490 U.S. 89, 109 S.Ct. 1629, 104 L.Ed.2d 80 (1989)(per curiam)(directing Supreme Court Clerk "not to accept any further filings from petitioner in which he seeks leave to proceed in forma pauperis ... unless the affidavit submitted with the filing indicates that petitioner's financial condition has substantially changed"); In re McDonald, 489 U.S. 180, 109 S.Ct. 993, 103 L.Ed.2d 158 (1989)(per curiam)(directing Clerk to reject future in forma pauperis requests for extraordinary writs, including habeas corpus, from pro se litigant).

C.   BILLS TO QUIET OR REMOVE A CLOUD ON TITLE

Wathen v. Brown

Court of Special Appeals of Maryland, 1981.
48 Md.App. 655, 429 A.2d 292.

■ LOWE, J. Appellee is the record title holder to a parcel of land and right of way in St. Mary's County. Alleging that appellant claimed ownership by adverse possession, appellee filed a Bill of Complaint to Quiet Title in the Circuit Court for St. Mary's County. Appellant answered, admitting her claim of ownership by adverse possession but denying all else save record title in appellee which was neither admitted nor denied.

Appellant tells us that appellee "elected to vest her claim of ownership and right of disposition on proof that she had paper title. Her proof consisted of the introduction into evidence of her deed ... and of a plat" which set out the parcel and the right of way.

"At the close of Appellee's case, Appellant moved to dismiss upon the ground that Appellee had not alleged or proved the conditions for maintenance of a cause of action and a right of relief pursuant to Real

Property Article, Section 14–108. The court denied the motion. The appellant declined to go forward.

The lower court declared that Appellee ... was the owner of the land and had the right to dispose of the property in dispute...."

Appellant's appeal, like her case below, rests upon two questions which may be answered as one:

"I. Is possession, actual or constructive, required to be proven by the plaintiff to establish a cause of action and a right to relief pursuant to Real Property Article, Section 14–108?

II. Did the evidence in this case permit the lower court to conclude that a cause of action and a right to relief pursuant to Real Property Article, Section 14–108 had been established by Appellee?"

Section 14–108 is one of the "Miscellaneous Rules" set forth in Title 14 of the recent recodification of the Real Property Laws. It was originally enacted in 1955 as a statutory section for the equitable remedy of quieting title to real estate, by authorizing courts of equity to do substantially what they had been doing prior to its enactment.

"§ 14–108. Quieting title.

(a) *Conditions.* Any person in actual peaceable possession of property, or, if the property is vacant and unoccupied, in constructive and peaceable possession of it, either under color of title or claim by right by reason of his or his predecessor's adverse possession for the statutory period, when his title to the property is denied or disputed, or when any other person claims, of record or otherwise to own the property, or any part of it, or to hold any lien encumbrance on it, regardless of whether or not the hostile outstanding claim is being actively asserted, and if an action at law or proceeding in equity is not pending to enforce or test the validity of the title, lien, encumbrance, or other adverse claim, the person may maintain a suit in equity in the county where the property lies to quiet or remove any cloud from the title, or determine any adverse claim.

(b) *Proceeding.* The proceeding shall be deemed in rem or quasi in rem so long as the only relief sought is a decree that the plaintiff has absolute ownership and the right of disposition of the property, and an injunction against the assertion by the person named as the party defendant, of his claim by any action at law or otherwise. Any person who appears of record, or claims to have a hostile outstanding right, shall be made a defendant in the proceedings."

Appellant argues that this statute established a burden of proving actual or constructive possession and that mere evidence of record title (which she concedes in appellee) is insufficient to constitute constructive possession.

The object of a bill to quiet title is to protect the owner of legal title "from being disturbed in his possession and from being harassed by suits in regard to his title by persons setting up unjust and illegal pretensions...." The statutory requirement of "possession" is that which originally provided equity with jurisdiction; otherwise the complainant would have had to resort to law, having an adequate legal remedy there.

"In such cases, one being in possession, he cannot have a remedy at law and is obliged therefore to seek the aid of a Court of Equity. If, however, the possession is in another person, his remedy is by action of ejectment, and there is no ground for the interposition of a Court of Equity, and for the reason that he has an adequate remedy at law."

The alternative to "actual" possession (i.e., title plus vacancy) was early recognized in the case of Baumgardner v. Fowler, 82 Md. 631, 640, 34 A. 537 (1896), which noted that:

". . . Courts have held that where a plaintiff has the legal title to lands that are wild, uncultivated and unoccupied, he may invoke the aid of a Court of Equity to remove a cloud upon his title, although he has no other than constructive possession resulting from legal ownership."

In *Baumgardner* this conclusion was coupled with, and apparently predicated upon, the fact that there was no proof that the adverse claimants under a tax sale had taken possession of the lands in dispute under the tax sale deed. Consequently, the plaintiffs could *not* have sued in ejectment to recover the property and thus decide ownership.

Although these cases arose prior to the statute, the statute was seemingly based upon them, and when enacted, it did not dispense with the necessity of showing possession, actual or constructive. Presumably then, if actual possession is not alleged in the Bill of Complaint although title is claimed, the bill is demurrable unless it is alleged that the lands are vacant and unoccupied.

The bill of complaint in this case was clearly demurrable if a demurrer had been filed. In five succinct paragraphs it alleged: (1) that appellee had record title to "Lot Number 5" (a copy of the deed was appended thereto); (2) that appellee had a twenty-foot right of way (evidenced by an appended deed); (3) that appellant's husband had acknowledged the land and right of way in a survey (which was also appended); (4) that appellant claimed both land and right of way by adverse possession; and (5) that the survey was acknowledged on August 29, 1960 and that therefore adverse possession could not have ripened until August 29, 1980. The suit was filed on September 27, 1979, obviously with the intention of tolling the twenty-year adverse possession period. There being no assertion of facts indicative either of actual possession or that the land was vacant and unoccupied (which coupled with the record title would have satisfied constructive possession), had appellant demurred she would have been successful since the bill failed to state on its face a case within the jurisdiction of the court of equity. A bill to quiet title in equity would not have been appropriate because it did not appear that the complainant was in possession of the property in dispute.

Through oversight or cunning, appellant chose not to educate appellee during the crucial twentieth year and elected to answer rather than demur. By admitting that *she claimed* the land and right of way by adverse *possession* as contended by appellee, she underscored the questionable jurisdiction of the equity court, but did naught to raise the issue at that time. On July 14, 1980, just over a month before the crucial date noted in the complaint, a hearing was held. Appellee as noted, rested upon her record title, and appellant, apparently hesitant to chance supplying any defects in appellee's case moved for dismissal and rested upon her motion urging that appellee had failed to supply by proof what she had failed to assert by pleading. Had that proof of right to equity jurisdiction been supplied, even in the absence of a question of the sufficiency of a bill to confer jurisdiction, the court could have based its decree on the evidence without regard to the allegations of the bill. But the evidence was not supplied and the bill was not amended even then, and if a bill fails to state on its face a case within the jurisdiction of equity, that error is fatal at every stage of the case.

The judge sought to avoid this dilemma when faced with the *fait accompli* presented him by the motion to dismiss at the end of appellee's case, by asserting that a fact-finder might draw an inference (which he subsequently seems to have done) of possession from the evidence, which consisted only of the deed and a plat.

"So, the fact of Title Owner, I think an inference may be drawn from [sic. 'of?'] the fact of possession, and for that reason, the Motion to Dismiss will be denied."

No such inference, however, can be drawn from mere paper and the appellee's express contention, admitted by appellant, claimed that appellant was an adverse possessor, which claim necessitates "actual" possession by the possessor. The statutory requirement for constructive possession furthermore, is that the property be "vacant and unoccupied."[2] An inference of vacancy is not available from the proof of bare paper title any more than actual possession by appellee would be inferable in the face of her claim that appellant was claiming possession adversely.

Thus, it did not appear and was not alleged in the present case that appellee was in possession actually or constructively. The object of the suit was to try the question not of possession, but only of right to possession, and such a proceeding is not within the province and jurisdiction of a court of chancery. Paraphrasing the holding of Crook v. Brown, 11 Md. 158 (1857), the Court of Appeals has noted:

"There is no head of equity jurisprudence under which a party in possession of land can be brought into Court, and made to show his title, in order that that title may be defeated and the possession delivered to the complainants, for this would be substantially to give a chancery suit the effect of an action in ejectment."

Therefore absent actual or constructive possession, appellee could not bring appellant, who claimed possession adversely, into court to defeat appellant's claim to title.

In Barnes v. Webster, 220 Md. 473, 154 A.2d 918 (1959), cited to us by appellant, a similar deficiency was found to exist in the Bill of Complaint.

---

2. The statutory requirement is obviously a codification of the holding of *Baum-* *gardner.*

However, that case was never reached upon its merits. The trial court had sustained a demurrer without leave to amend for the wrong reason. When the Court of Appeals reviewed and discovered the error, it also found that the Bill was demurrable for failure to allege that complainants were in possession. In that case the Court of Appeals remanded the case without affirmance or reversal for further proceedings, saying that:

> "Since we think the demurrer was sustainable only on the ground that there was not a sufficient showing of equity jurisdiction, we shall remand this case for further proceedings, which may include the granting of leave to file an amended bill of complaint, the filing of all relevant documents, or, if necessary the transfer of the suit to the law side of the court under Maryland Rule 515."

In this case we believe that a like remedy will provide substantial justice to both parties. We will vacate the decree entered below and remand the case for further proceedings which may include the granting of leave to amend the bill of complaint, the introduction of evidence, if any, solely relating to the jurisdictional question of the equity court, or, if necessary, the transfer of the suit to the law side of the court under Md. Rule 515. By doing so, neither party will be improperly prejudiced by a denial of the right to assert fully a claim of ownership in the proper form. Any other remedy appropriately applied would do no more than honor form over substance because a court of conscience erred.

Decree of July 24, 1980 Vacated. Case Remanded Without Affirmance or Reversal for Further Proceedings. Costs to Be Paid by Appellee.

NOTES

1. The origins of the bill to quiet title, and the relationship of that bill to the bill of peace, were clearly stated by Justice Brown in Wehrman v. Conklin, 155 U.S. 314, 15 S.Ct. 129, 39 L.Ed. 167 (1894):

> The general principles of equity jurisprudence, as administered both in this country and in England, permit a bill to quiet title to be filed only by a party in possession against a defendant who has been ineffectually seeking to establish a legal title by repeated actions of ejectment, and as a prerequisite to such bill it was necessary that the title of the plaintiff should have been established by at least one successful trial at law. At common law a party might by successive fictitious demises bring as many actions of ejectment as he chose, and a bill to quiet title was only permitted for the purpose of preventing the party in possession being annoyed by repeated and vexatious actions. The jurisdiction was, in fact, only another exercise of the familiar power of a court of equity to prevent a multiplicity of suits by bills of peace. A statement of the underlying principles of such bills is found in the opinion of this court in Holland v. Challen, 110 U.S. 15, 3 S.Ct. 495, 28 L.Ed. 52 (1884), in which it is said: "To entitle the plaintiff to relief in such cases, the concurrence of three particulars was essential: He must have been in possession of the property; he must have been disturbed in its possession by repeated actions at law; and he must have established his right by successive judgments in his favor. Upon

these facts appearing, the court would interpose and grant a perpetual injunction to quiet the possession of the plaintiff against any further litigation from the same source. It was only in this way that adequate relief could be afforded against vexatious litigation and the irreparable mischief which it entailed."

2. The limitations of this bill were many. Perhaps most important, it gave no relief to anyone whose claim of title had not been challenged at law. Of course, the existence of a rival claim may nonetheless have affected the possessor's rights by impairing the property's marketability. And this possibility caused the equity courts to create the bill to remove a cloud on title, a kind of *quia timet* action. (Unfortunately, this remedy was also referred to on occasion as a bill to quiet title.)

However, the bill to remove a cloud had shortcomings of its own. For example, it was only available if the competing claim was based on a document that the court believed would deter an average person from buying the property. Moreover, it only determined the validity of any claims based on the document; it did not resolve the broader issue of title to the property.

3. Many jurisdictions have enacted statutes eliminating some of the limitations on the availability of these equitable remedies. These laws are commonly designed to settle all of the parties' conflicting claims to the property. Although they may allow "quiet title" actions to be brought even by non-possessory plaintiffs, these acts often leave the parties' access to jury trial undisturbed.

D. INTERPLEADER

State Farm Fire & Casualty Co. v. Tashire

Supreme Court of the United States, 1967.
386 U.S. 523, 87 S.Ct. 1199, 18 L.Ed.2d 270.

■ MR. JUSTICE FORTAS delivered the opinion of the Court.

Early one September morning in 1964, a Greyhound bus proceeding northward through Shasta County, California, collided with a southbound pickup truck. Two of the passengers aboard the bus were killed. Thirty-three others were injured, as were the bus driver, the driver of the truck and its lone passenger. One of the dead and 10 of the injured passengers were Canadians; the rest of the individuals involved were citizens of five American States. The ensuing litigation led to the present case, which raises important questions concerning administration of the interpleader remedy in the federal courts.

The litigation began when four of the injured passengers filed suit in California state courts, seeking damages in excess of $1,000,000. Named as defendants were Greyhound Lines, Inc., a California corporation; Theron

Nauta, the bus driver; Ellis Clark, who drove the truck; and Kenneth Glasgow, the passenger in the truck who was apparently its owner as well. Each of the individual defendants was a citizen and resident of Oregon. Before these cases could come to trial and before other suits were filed in California or elsewhere, petitioner State Farm Fire & Casualty Company, an Illinois corporation, brought this action in the nature of interpleader in the United States District Court for the District of Oregon.

In its complaint State Farm asserted that at the time of the Shasta County collision it had in force an insurance policy with respect to Ellis Clark, driver of the truck, providing for bodily injury liability up to $10,000 per person and $20,000 per occurrence and for legal representation of Clark in actions covered by the policy. It asserted that actions already filed in California and others which it anticipated would be filed far exceeded in aggregate damages sought the amount of its maximum liability under the policy. Accordingly, it paid into court the sum of $20,000 and asked the court (1) to require all claimants to establish their claims against Clark and his insurer in this single proceeding and in no other, and (2) to discharge State Farm from all further obligations under its policy—including its duty to defend Clark in lawsuits arising from the accident. Alternatively, State Farm expressed its conviction that the policy issued to Clark excluded from coverage accidents resulting from his operation of a truck which belonged to another and was being used in the business of another. The complaint, therefore, requested that the court decree that the insurer owed no duty to Clark and was not liable on the policy, and it asked the court to refund the $20,000 deposit.

Joined as defendants were Clark, Glasgow, Nauta, Greyhound Lines, and each of the prospective claimants. Jurisdiction was predicated upon 28 U.S.C. § 1335, the federal interpleader statute,[1] and upon general diversity of citizenship, there being diversity between two or more of the claimants to the fund and between State Farm and all of the named defendants.

---

1. 28 U.S.C. § 1335 provides: "The district courts shall have original jurisdiction of any civil action of interpleader or in the nature of interpleader filed by any person, firm, or corporation, association, or society having in his or its custody or possession money or property of the value of $500 or more, or having issued a [note, bond, certificate,] policy of insurance[, or other instrument] of value or amount of $500 or more[, or providing for the delivery or payment or the loan of money or property of such amount or value, or being under any obligation written or unwritten to the amount of $500 or more,] if

"(1) Two or more adverse claimants, of diverse citizenship as defined in section 1332 of this title, are claiming or may claim to be entitled to such money or property, or to any one or more of the benefits arising by virtue of any [note, bond, certificate,] policy [or other instrument, or arising by virtue of any such obligation]; and if (2) the plaintiff has [deposited such money or property or has] paid [the amount of or the loan or other value of such instrument or] the amount due under such obligation into the registry of the court, there to abide the judgment of the court or has given bond payable to the clerk of the court in such amount and with such surety as the court or judge may deem proper, conditioned upon the compliance by the plaintiff with the future order or judgment of the court with respect to the subject matter of the controversy.

"(b) Such an action may be entertained although the titles or claims of the conflicting claimants do not have a common origin, or are not identical, but are adverse to and independent of one another."

An order issued, requiring the defendants to show cause why they should not be restrained from filing or prosecuting "any proceeding in any state or United States Court affecting the property or obligation involved in this interpleader action, and specifically against the plaintiff and the defendant Ellis D. Clark." Personal service was effected on each of the American defendants, and registered mail was employed to reach the 11 Canadian claimants. Defendants Nauta, Greyhound, and several of the injured passengers responded, contending that the policy did cover this accident and advancing various arguments for the position that interpleader was either impermissible or inappropriate in the present circumstances. Greyhound, however, soon switched sides and moved that the court broaden any injunction to include Nauta and Greyhound among those who could not be sued except within the confines of the interpleader proceeding.

When a temporary injunction along the lines sought by State Farm was issued by the United States District Court for the District of Oregon, the present respondents moved to dismiss the action and, in the alternative, for a change of venue—to the Northern District of California, in which district the collision had occurred. After a hearing, the court declined to dissolve the temporary injunction, but continued the motion for a change of venue. The injunction was later broadened to include the protection sought by Greyhound, but modified to permit the filing—although not the prosecution—of suits. The injunction, therefore, provided that all suits against Clark, State Farm, Greyhound, and Nauta be prosecuted in the interpleader proceeding.

On interlocutory appeal, the Court of Appeals for the Ninth Circuit reversed. The court found it unnecessary to reach respondents' contentions relating to service of process and the scope of the injunction, for it concluded that interpleader was not available in the circumstances of this case. It held that in States like Oregon which do not permit "direct action" suits against insurance companies until judgments are obtained against the insured, the insurance companies may not invoke federal interpleader until the claims against the insured, the alleged tortfeasor, have been reduced to judgment. Until that is done, said the court, claimants with unliquidated tort claims are not "claimants" within the meaning of § 1335, nor are they "[p]ersons having claims against the plaintiff" within the meaning of Rule 22 of the Federal Rules of Civil Procedure.[3] In accord with that view, it

---

3. We need not pass upon the Court of Appeals' conclusions with respect to the interpretation of interpleader under Rule 22, which provides that "(1) Persons having claims against the plaintiff may be joined as defendants and required to interplead when their claims are such that the plaintiff is or may be exposed to double or multiple liability. [It is not ground for objection to the joinder that the claims of the several claimants or the titles on which their claims depend do not have a common origin or are not identical but are adverse to and independent of one another, or that the plaintiff avers that he is not liable in whole or in part to any

or all of the claimants. A defendant exposed to similar liability may obtain such interpleader by way of cross-claim or counterclaim. The provisions of this rule supplement and do not in any way limit the joinder of parties permitted in Rule 20.

"(2) The remedy herein provided is in addition to and in no way supersedes or limits the remedy provided by Title 28, U.S.C. §§ 1335, 1397, and 2361. Actions under those provisions shall be conducted in accordance with these rules."]

First, as we indicate today, this action was properly brought under § 1335. Second,

directed dissolution of the temporary injunction and dismissal of the action. Because the Court of Appeals' decision on this point conflicts with those of other federal courts, and concerns a matter of significance to the administration of federal interpleader, we granted certiorari. Although we reverse the decision of the Court of Appeals upon the jurisdictional question, we direct a substantial modification of the District Court's injunction for reasons which will appear.

I.

Before considering the issues presented by the petition for certiorari, we find it necessary to dispose of a question neither raised by the parties nor passed upon by the courts below. Since the matter concerns our jurisdiction, we raise it on our own motion. The interpleader statute, 28 U.S.C. § 1335, applies where there are "Two or more adverse claimants, of diverse citizenship. . . ." This provision has been uniformly construed to require only "minimal diversity," that is, diversity of citizenship between two or more claimants, without regard to the circumstance that other rival claimants may be co-citizens. The language of the statute, the legislative purpose broadly to remedy the problems posed by multiple claimants to a single fund, and the consistent judicial interpretation tacitly accepted by Congress, persuade us that the statute requires no more. There remains, however, the question whether such a statutory construction is consistent with Article III of our Constitution, which extends the federal judicial power to "Controversies . . . between citizens of different States . . . and between a State, or the Citizens thereof, and foreign States, Citizens or Subjects." In Strawbridge v. Curtiss, 3 Cranch 267, 2 L.Ed. 435 (1806), this Court held that the diversity of citizenship statute required "complete diversity": where co-citizens appeared on both sides of a dispute, jurisdiction was lost. But Chief Justice Marshall there purported to construe only "The words of the act of congress," not the Constitution itself. And in a variety of contexts this Court and the lower courts have concluded that Article III poses no obstacle to the legislative extension of federal jurisdiction, founded on diversity, so long as any two adverse parties are not co-citizens. Accordingly, we conclude that the present case is properly in the federal courts.

II.

We do not agree with the Court of Appeals that, in the absence of a state law or contractual provision for "direct action" suits against the insurance company, the company must wait until persons asserting claims against its insured have reduced those claims to judgment before seeking to invoke the benefits of federal interpleader. That may have been a tenable

---

State Farm did not purport to invoke Rule 22. Third, State Farm could not have invoked it in light of venue and service of process limitations. Whereas statutory interpleader may be brought in the district where any claimant resides (28 U.S.C. § 1397), Rule interpleader based upon diversity of citizenship may be brought only in the district where all plaintiffs or all defendants reside (28 U.S.C. § 1391(a)). And whereas statutory interpleader enables a plaintiff to employ nationwide service of process (28 U.S.C. § 2361), service of process under Rule 22 is confined to that provided in Rule 4.

. . . .

position under the 1926 and 1936 interpleader statutes. These statutes did not carry forward the language in the 1917 Act authorizing interpleader where adverse claimants "may claim" benefits as well as where they "are claiming" them. In 1948, however, in the revision of the Judicial Code, the "may claim" language was restored. Until the decision below, every court confronted by the question has concluded that the 1948 revision removed whatever requirement there might previously have been that the insurance company wait until at least two claimants reduced their claims to judgments. The commentators are in accord.

Considerations of judicial administration demonstrate the soundness of this view which, in any event, seems compelled by the language of the present statute, which is remedial and to be liberally construed. Were an insurance company required to await reduction of claims to judgment, the first claimant to obtain such a judgment or to negotiate a settlement might appropriate all or a disproportionate slice of the fund before his fellow claimants were able to establish their claims. The difficulties such a race to judgment pose for the insurer, and the unfairness which may result to some claimants, were among the principal evils the interpleader device was intended to remedy.

III.

The fact that State Farm had properly invoked the interpleader jurisdiction under § 1335 did not, however, entitle it to an order both enjoining prosecution of suits against it outside the confines of the interpleader proceeding and also extending such protection to its insured, the alleged tortfeasor. Still less was Greyhound Lines entitled to have that order expanded so as to protect itself and its driver, also alleged to be tortfeasors, from suits brought by its passengers in various state or federal courts. Here, the scope of the litigation, in terms of parties and claims, was vastly more extensive than the confines of the "fund," the deposited proceeds of the insurance policy. In these circumstances, the mere existence of such a fund cannot, by use of interpleader, be employed to accomplish purposes that exceed the needs of orderly contest with respect to the fund.

There are situations, of a type not present here, where the effect of interpleader is to confine the total litigation to a single forum and proceeding. One such case is where a stakeholder, faced with rival claims to the fund itself, acknowledges—or denies—his liability to one or the other of the claimants.[16] In this situation, the fund itself is the target of the claimants. It marks the outer limits of the controversy. It is, therefore, reasonable and sensible that interpleader, in discharge of its office to protect the fund, should also protect the stakeholder from vexatious and multiple litigation. In this context, the suits sought to be enjoined are squarely within the language of 28 U.S.C. § 2361, which provides in part:

In any civil action of interpleader or in the nature of interpleader under section 1335 of this title, a district court may issue its process for all claimants and enter its order restraining them from instituting or prosecuting *any proceeding* in any State or United States court *affecting the*

16. This was the classic situation envisioned by the sponsors of interpleader.

property, instrument or obligation involved in the interpleader action . . . .
(Emphasis added.)

But the present case is another matter. Here, an accident has happened. Thirty-five passengers or their representatives have claims which they wish to press against a variety of defendants: the bus company, its driver, the owner of the truck, and the truck driver. The circumstance that one of the prospective defendants happens to have an insurance policy is a fortuitous event which should not of itself shape the nature of the ensuing litigation. For example, a resident of California, injured in California aboard a bus owned by a California corporation should not be forced to sue that corporation anywhere but in California simply because another prospective defendant carried an insurance policy. And an insurance company whose maximum interest in the case cannot exceed $20,000 and who in fact asserts that it has no interest at all, should not be allowed to determine that dozens of tort plaintiffs must be compelled to press their claims—even those claims which are not against the insured and which in no event could be satisfied out of the meager insurance fund—in a single forum of the insurance company's choosing. There is nothing in the statutory scheme, and very little in the judicial and academic commentary upon that scheme, which requires that the tail be allowed to wag the dog in this fashion.

State Farm's interest in this case, which is the fulcrum of the interpleader procedure, is confined to its $20,000 fund. That interest receives full vindication when the court restrains claimants from seeking to enforce against the insurance company any judgment obtained against its insured, except in the interpleader proceeding itself. To the extent that the District Court sought to control claimants' lawsuits against the insured and other alleged tortfeasors, it exceeded the powers granted to it by the statutory scheme.

We recognize, of course, that our view of interpleader means that it cannot be used to solve all the vexing problems of multiparty litigation arising out of a mass tort. But interpleader was never intended to perform such a function, to be an all-purpose "bill of peace."[17] Had it been so intended, careful provision would necessarily have been made to insure that a party with little or no interest in the outcome of a complex controversy should not strip truly interested parties of substantial rights— such as the right to choose the forum in which to establish their claims, subject to generally applicable rules of jurisdiction, venue, service of process, removal, and change of venue. None of the legislative and academic sponsors of a modern federal interpleader device viewed their accomplish-

---

17. There is not a word in the legislative history suggesting such a purpose. And Professor Chafee, upon whose work the Congress heavily depended, has written that little thought was given to the scope of the "second stage" of interpleader, to just what would be adjudicated by the interpleader court. See Chafee, Broadening the Second Stage of Federal Interpleader, 56 Harv.L.Rev. 929, 944–945 (1943). We note that in Professor Chafee's own study of the bill of peace as a device for dealing with the problem of multiparty litigation, he fails even to mention interpleader. See Chafee, Some Problems of Equity 149–198 (1950). In his writing on interpleader, Chafee assumed that the interpleader court would allocate the fund "among all the claimants who get judgment within a reasonable time. . . ." Chafee, The Federal Interpleader Act of 1936: II, 45 Yale L.J. 1161, 1165 (1936). See also Chafee, 49 Yale L.J., at 420–421.

ment as a "bill of peace," capable of sweeping dozens of lawsuits out of the various state and federal courts in which they were brought and into a single interpleader proceeding. And only in two reported instances has a federal interpleader court sought to control the underlying litigation against alleged tortfeasors as opposed to the allocation of a fund among successful tort plaintiffs. Another district court, on the other hand, has recently held that it lacked statutory authority to enjoin suits against the alleged tortfeasor as opposed to proceedings against the fund itself.

In light of the evidence that federal interpleader was not intended to serve the function of a "bill of peace" in the context of multiparty litigation arising out of a mass tort, of the anomalous power which such a construction of the statute would give the stakeholder, and of the thrust of the statute and the purpose it was intended to serve, we hold that the interpleader statute did not authorize the injunction entered in the present case. Upon remand, the injunction is to be modified consistently with this opinion.

IV.

The judgment of the Court of Appeals is reversed, and the case is remanded to the United States District Court for proceedings consistent with this opinion.

It is so ordered.

Judgment of Court of Appeals reversed and case remanded to the District Court.

■ MR. JUSTICE DOUGLAS, dissenting.

While I agree with the Court's view as to "minimal diversity" and that the injunction, if granted, should run only against prosecution of suits against the insurer, I feel that the use which we today allow to be made of the federal interpleader statute is, with all deference, unwarranted. How these litigants are "claimants" to this fund in the statutory sense is indeed a mystery. If they are not "claimants" of the fund, neither are they in the category of those who "are claiming" or who "may claim" to be entitled to it.

This insurance company's policy provides that it will "pay on behalf of the insured all sums which the insured shall become legally obligated to pay." To date the insured has not become "legally obligated" to pay any sum to any litigant. Since nothing is owed under the policy, I fail to see how any litigant can be a "claimant" as against the insurance company. If that is doubtful the doubt is resolved by two other conditions:

(1) The policy states "[n]o action shall lie against the company ... until the amount of the insured's obligation to pay shall have been finally determined either by judgment against the insured after actual trial or by written agreement of the insured, the claimant and the company."

(2) Under California law where the accident happened and under Oregon law where the insurance contract was made, a direct action against the insurer is not allowable until after a litigant receives a final judgment against the insured.

Thus under this insurance policy as enforced in California and in Oregon a "claimant" against the insured can become a "claimant" against the insurer only after final judgment against the insured or after a consensual written agreement of the insurer, a litigant, and the insured. Neither of those two events has so far happened.

This construction of the word "claimant" against the fund is borne out, as the Court of Appeals noted, by Rule 22(1) of the Federal Rules of Civil Procedure. That Rule, also based on diversity of citizenship, differs only in the district where the suit may be brought and in the reach of service of process, as the Court points out. But it illuminates the nature of federal interpleader for it provides that only "[p]ersons having claims against the plaintiff [insurer] may be joined as defendants and required to interplead."

Can it be that we have two kinds of interpleader statutes as between which an insurance company can choose: one that permits "claimants" against the insurer ("persons having claims against the plaintiff") to be joined and the other that permits "claimants" against the insured to be joined for the benefit of the insurer even though they may never be "claimants" against the insurer? I cannot believe that Congress launched such an irrational scheme.

The Court rests heavily on the fact that the 1948 Act contains the phrase "may claim," while the 1926 and 1936 interpleader statutes contained the phrase "are claiming." From this change in language the Court infers that Congress intended to allow an insurance company to interplead even though a judgment has not been entered against the insured and there is no direct-action statute. This inference is drawn despite the fact that the Reviser's Note contains no reference to the change in wording or its purpose; the omission is dismissed as "inadvertent." But it strains credulity to suggest that mention would not have been made of such a drastic change, if in fact Congress intended to make it. And, despite the change in wording, under the 1948 Act there must be "adverse claimants ... [who] are claiming or may claim to be entitled to such money ..., or to any one or more of the benefits arising by virtue of any ... policy...." Absent a direct-action statute, the victims are not "claimants" against the insurer until their claims against the insured have been reduced to judgment. Understandably, the insurance company wants the best of two worlds. It does not want an action against it until judgment against its insured. But, at the same time, it wants the benefits of an interpleader statute. Congress could of course confer such a benefit. But it is not for this Court to grant dispensations from the effects of the statutory scheme which Congress has erected.

I would construe its words in the normal sense and affirm the Court of Appeals.

NOTES ON INTERPLEADER

1. Interpleader, from the Anglo–French entrepleder, in essence, is a proceeding in which the applicant, who has money or goods claimed by two

or more persons, requests that the claimants litigate the title between themselves.[1] The proceeding permits a person who is ready to perform a duty to determine to whom the duty is owed. The adverse claimants are thereby compelled to litigate the matter between themselves thus relieving the applicant from the various suits that might have been brought against the applicant.

In the widest sense, the applicant who brings interpleader relief in the nature of *quia timet,* i.e., the fear of being subjected to double litigation, and possibly made to pay twice for the one liability. The applicant is basically a defendant who takes the initiative to determine to whom the obligation is properly owed.

Interpleader is available if the applicant can establish that adverse claims that have a reasonable foundation are being asserted against the applicant. If there are two adverse claims, and one is obviously valid and the other obviously void, interpleader is unnecessary. The question is to be determined as of the moment that the proceedings are commenced. If, as of that moment, there are two or more adverse claims, and the applicant's liability is limited to only one of them, interpleader should b e available.

Liberal provisions for the joinder of parties, found in all modern codes, have greatly diminished the need for the equitable remedy of interpleader. Today, in the states, the right to interpleader is regulated by modern codes and rules of court.

2. Writing about interpleader, Professor Charles Alan Wright, in Federal Courts 493–94 (4th ed.1983), states, "The contemporary importance of interpleader is in large measure due to the efforts of Professor Zechariah Chafee, Jr., who, in a notable group of articles, paved the way for the series of reforms by which federal interpleader was modernized and made available in situations where no state court could provide an adequate remedy. There are two kinds of interpleader available in federal court. A statute, 28 U.S.C. § 1335, authorizes interpleader and makes very liberal provisions as to jurisdiction, venue, and service of process. Nonstatutory interpleader is available under Rule 22, but the jurisdictional and procedural requirements there are the same as in an ordinary civil action."

"Before enactment of the federal interpleader statute, there was no effective procedure whereby rival claimants of diverse citizenship and residence could be sued in any district in federal court, while territorial limitation on service of process barred state courts from giving relief. This situation is cured by the statute, and the rule supplements the statute."

---

1. *Interpleader* is not to be confused with *impleader*. Impleader or "third party practice," refers to the procedure whereby a person sought to be held liable on a claim, usually a defendant, in turn and in the same action, makes a claim against a third person for all or part of plaintiff's claim against him. See Rule 14 of the Federal Rules of Civil Procedure. It implies a primary claim against one person, and a subsidiary claim against a third party. *Interpleader* implies adverse claims against the same party.

E. THE DECLARATORY JUDGMENT

There are instances when a plaintiff resorts to equity for the purpose of obtaining a judicial declaration of rights, i.e., a declaratory decree or judgment. In order to obtain the relief, the dispute has to be a real or actual controversy, but the declaration of rights is the relief sought, whether or not the plaintiff requests or may obtain further relief.

Judgments or decrees may be said to be coercive or declaratory. A coercive judgment is enforceable by execution issued against the person or property of the defendant or by contempt proceedings. By a declaratory judgment the court declares the rights of the parties. It does not order the defendant to perform or do or undo anything. It is, therefore, distinguished from other relief, in that, as of course, no executory process follows. This, however, does not detract from the value and importance of the declaratory relief. The declaratory judgment constitutes a determination on the merits, and by virtue of the principle of res judicata precludes a relitigation of the same issue.

It is to be noted that many equity proceedings have, as an ultimate goal, a declaration of rights of the plaintiff. Examples are actions to rescind or reform a contract. Certain examples are furnished in the cases reproduced herein. In Huntworth v. Tanner, 87 Wash. 670, 152 P. 523 (1915), plaintiff sued to restrain a threatened arrest and prosecution for the alleged violation of a penal statute. The real relief sought was a declaration that plaintiff's activities did not constitute a violation of the penal law.

As in all equitable relief, declaratory relief does not lie as a matter of course. However, as stated by Mr. Justice Cardozo, in Evangelical Lutheran Church of the Ascension v. Sahlem, 254 N.Y. 161, 172 N.E. 455 (1930), an action for declaratory judgment to declare a restrictive covenant no longer in effect:

In the award of equitable remedies there is often an element of discretion, but never a discretion that is absolute or arbitrary. In equity as at law there are signposts for the traveler. "Discretion ... must be regulated upon grounds that will make it judicial."

Further, Mr. Justice Harlan noted in Abbott Laboratories v. Gardner, 387 U.S. 136, 155, 87 S.Ct. 1507, 1519, 18 L.Ed.2d 681 (1967), the declaratory judgment and injunctive remedies are equitable in nature, and other equitable defenses may be interposed.

Nashville, Chattanooga & St. Louis Ry. v. Wallace

Supreme Court of the United States, 1933.
288 U.S. 249, 53 S.Ct. 345, 77 L.Ed. 730.

■ MR. JUSTICE STONE delivered the opinion of the Court.

Appellant brought suit in the Chancery Court of Davidson county, Tenn., under the Uniform Declaratory Judgments Act of that state, to secure a judicial declaration that a state excise tax levied on the storage of gasoline, is, as applied to appellant, invalid under the commerce clause and the Fourteenth Amendment of the Federal Constitution. A decree for appellees was affirmed by the Supreme Court of the state, and the case comes here on appeal under section 237(a) of the Judicial Code.

After the jurisdictional statement required by Rule 12 was submitted, this Court, in ordering the cause set down for argument, invited the attention of counsel to the question "whether a case or controversy is presented, in view of the nature of the proceedings in the state courts." This preliminary question, which has been elaborately briefed and argued, must first be considered, for the judicial power with which this Court is invested by article 3, § 1, of the Constitution, extends by article 3, § 2, only to "cases" and "controversies"; if no "case" or "controversy" is presented for decision, we are without power to review the decree of the court below.

In determining whether this litigation presents a case within the appellate jurisdiction of this Court, we are concerned, not with form, but with substance. Hence, we look not to the label which the Legislature has attached to the procedure followed in the state courts, or to the description of the judgment which is brought here for review, in popular parlance, as "declaratory," but to the nature of the proceeding which the statute authorizes, and the effect of the judgment rendered upon the rights which the appellant asserts.

Section 1 of the Tennessee Declaratory Judgments Act confers jurisdiction on courts of record "to declare rights . . . whether or not further relief is or could be claimed" and provides that "no action or proceeding shall be open to objection on the ground that a declaratory judgment or decree is prayed for. The declaration may be either affirmative or negative in form and effect; and such declaration shall have the force and effect of a final judgment or decree." By section 2 it is provided that "any person . . . whose rights, status or other legal relations are affected by a statute . . . may have determined any question of construction or validity arising under the . . . statute . . . and obtain a declaration of rights . . . thereunder."

Under section 6, the court may refuse to render a declaratory judgment where, if rendered, it "would not terminate the uncertainty or controversy giving rise to the proceeding." Declaratory judgments may, in accordance with section 7, be reviewed as are other orders, judgments, or decrees, and under section 8 "further relief based on a declaratory judgment or decree may be granted whenever necessary or proper." Section 11 requires that, "when declaratory relief is sought, all persons shall be made parties who have or claim any interest which would be affected by the declaration, and no declaration shall prejudice the rights of persons not parties to the proceeding."

This statute has often been considered by the highest court of Tennessee, which has consistently held that its provisions may only be invoked when the complainant asserts rights which are challenged by the defendant, and presents for decision an actual controversy to which he is a party, capable of final adjudication by the judgment or decree to be rendered. It has also held that no judgment or decree will be rendered when all the parties who will be adversely affected by it are not before the court.

Proceeding in accordance with this statute, appellant filed its bill of complaint in the state chancery court, joining as defendants the appellees, the Attorney General and the state officials charged with the duty of collecting the gasoline privilege tax imposed by the Tennessee statute. The complaint alleged that appellant is engaged in purchasing gasoline outside the state, which it stores within the state pending its use within and without the state in the conduct of appellant's business as an interstate rail carrier; that appellees assert that the statute taxes the privilege of storing gasoline within the state and is applicable to appellant; that they have demanded payment of the tax in a specified amount and have determined to enforce their demand; and that, under the circumstances alleged, the statute as applied to appellant is invalid under the commerce clause and the Fourteenth Amendment. The relief prayed was that the Taxing Act be declared unconstitutional as applied to appellant. The chancery court sustained the appellees' demurrer to the sufficiency in law of the allegations relied on to establish the unconstitutionality of the tax. Its final decree dismissing the bill on the merits has been affirmed by the highest court of the state.

That the issues thus raised and judicially determined would constitute a case or controversy if raised and decided in a suit brought by the taxpayer to enjoin collection of the tax cannot be questioned. The proceeding terminating in the decree below ... was between adverse parties, seeking a determination of their legal rights upon the facts alleged in the bill and admitted by the demurrer.... [V]aluable legal rights asserted by the complainant and threatened with imminent invasion by appellees, will be directly affected to a specific and substantial degree by the decision of the question of law; and ... the question lends itself to judicial determination and is of the kind which this court traditionally decides. The relief sought is a definitive adjudication of the disputed constitutional right of the appellant, in the circumstances alleged, to be free from the tax; and that adjudication is not ... subject to revision by some other and more authoritative agency. Obviously the appellant, whose duty to pay the tax will be determined by the decision of this case, is not attempting to secure an abstract determination by the Court of the validity of a statute or a decision advising what the law would be on an uncertain or hypothetical state of facts.... Thus the narrow question presented for determination is whether the controversy before us, which would be justiciable in this Court if presented in a suit for injunction, is any the less so because through a modified procedure appellant has been permitted to present it in the state courts, without praying for an injunction or alleging that irreparable injury will result from the collection of the tax.

While the ordinary course of judicial procedure results in a judgment requiring an award of process or execution to carry it into effect, such relief is not an indispensable adjunct to the exercise of the judicial function. This court has often exerted its judicial power to adjudicate boundaries between states, although it gave no injunction or other relief beyond the determination of the legal rights which were the subject of controversy between the parties, and to review judgments of the Court of Claims, although no process issues against the government. As we said in Fidelity National Bank & Trust Co. v. Swope, 274 U.S. 123, 47 S.Ct. 511, 71 L.Ed. 959,

"Naturalization proceedings; suits to determine a matrimonial or other status; suits for instructions to a trustee or for the construction of a will; bills of interpleader, so far as the stakeholder is concerned; bills to quiet title where the plaintiff rests his claim on adverse possession—are familiar examples of judicial proceedings which result in an adjudication of the rights of litigants, although execution is not necessary to carry the judgment into effect, in the sense that no damages are required to be paid or acts to be performed by the parties."

The issues raised here are the same as those which under old forms of procedure could be raised only in a suit for an injunction or one to recover the tax after its payment. But the Constitution does not require that the case or controversy should be presented by traditional forms of procedure, invoking only traditional remedies. The judiciary clause of the Constitution defined and limited judicial power, not the particular method by which that power might be invoked. It did not crystallize into changeless form the procedure of 1789 as the only possible means for presenting a case or controversy otherwise cognizable by the federal courts. Whenever the judicial power is invoked to review a judgment of a state court, the ultimate constitutional purpose is the protection, by the exercise of the judicial function, of rights arising under the Constitution and laws of the United States. The states are left free to regulate their own judicial procedure. Hence changes merely in the form or method of procedure by which federal rights are brought to final adjudication in the state courts are not enough to preclude review of the adjudication by this Court, so long as the case retains the essentials of an adversary proceeding, involving a real, not a hypothetical, controversy, which is finally determined by the judgment below. As the prayer for relief by injunction is not a necessary prerequisite to the exercise of judicial power, allegations of threatened irreparable injury which are material only if an injunction is asked, may likewise be dispensed with if, in other respects, the controversy presented is, as in this case, real and substantial. . . . Accordingly, we must consider the constitutional questions raised by the appeal.

. . . .

Affirmed.

NOTES

1. The Federal Declaratory Judgment statutes, 28 U.S.C. §§ 2201, 2202 (as amended), read as follows:

§ 2201. CREATION OF REMEDY.

(a) In a case of actual controversy within its jurisdiction, except with respect to Federal taxes other than actions brought under section 7428 of the Internal Revenue Code of 1986, a proceeding under section 505 or 1146 of title 11, or in any civil action involving an antidumping or countervailing duty proceeding regarding a class or kind of Canadian merchandise, as determined by the administering authority, any court of the United States, upon the filing of an appropriate pleading, may declare the rights and other legal relations of any interested party seeking such declaration, whether or not further relief is or could be sought. Any such declaration shall have the force and effect of a final judgment or decree and shall be reviewable as such.

(b) For limitations on actions brought with respect to drug patents see section 505 or 512 of the Federal Food, Drug, and Cosmetic Act.

§ 2202.   FURTHER RELIEF.

Further necessary or proper relief based on a declaratory judgment or decree may be granted, after reasonable notice and hearing, against any adverse party whose rights have been determined by such judgment.

2.   FED.R.CIV.P. 57 provides as follows:

The procedure for obtaining a declaratory judgment pursuant to Title 28, U.S.C. § 2201, shall be in accordance with these rules, and the right to trial by jury may be demanded under the circumstances and in the manner provided in Rules 38 and 39. The existence of another adequate remedy does not preclude a judgment for declaratory relief in cases where it is appropriate. The court may order a speedy hearing of an action for a declaratory judgment and may advance it on the calendar.

CHAPTER 6

SPECIFIC PERFORMANCE OF CONTRACTS

At common law, an action for damages was the ordinary or usual remedy for breach of contract. The party who breached the contract, by failing to convey property, or otherwise perform, was liable in damages to compensate for the breach. When damages were deemed to be inadequate, equity could order that the contract be performed specifically according to its terms. Furthermore, equity did not recognize an option either to perform or pay damages. In essence, the question was whether the "remedy at law was inadequate."

The question that must be answered is whether, under the circumstances presented, damages are inadequate and the court should order specific performance of the contract. Since specific performance is an equitable remedy, the court, in the exercise of equitable discretion, will consider a variety of factors in determining whether to grant or deny the remedy of specific performance. In general terms, it is said that equity will grant specific performance of contracts to convey land, and, of contracts to sell chattels and goods, only when they are unique and damages are "inadequate." The materials in this chapter illustrate the various factors that are considered by the courts in granting or denying the remedy of specific performance in contract cases.

A. CONTRACTS FOR THE SALE OR LEASE OF PROPERTY

1. ADEQUACY OF LEGAL REMEDIES

Eastern Rolling Mill Co. v. Michlovitz

Court of Appeals of Maryland, 1929.
157 Md. 51, 145 A. 378.

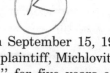

■ PARKE, J., delivered the opinion of the Court. [On September 15, 1927, defendant, Eastern Rolling Mill Co., agreed to supply plaintiff, Michlovitz & Co. with "crop end scrap" and "bundle steel scrap" for five years commencing October 1, 1927 until September 30, 1932. These contracts (one for each type of scrap) superseded previous agreements between the parties.] . . .

. . . .

By these contracts, the defendant agreed to sell its entire accumulation of the two kinds of scrap during the period of five years at prices to be fixed at the beginning of every quarter for the next succeeding three months in the following manner: The plaintiffs were to accept delivery of the scrap as it accumulated, and its price, when loaded by defendant on gondola cars at its plant, was, (a) with respect to the pressed bundled sheet steel scrap, three dollars a ton less than what was quoted in the "Iron Age," a trade publication, at the beginning of every quarter, as the Philadelphia market for bundled steel sheets; and, (b) with respect to the crop end scrap, three dollars a ton less than what was quoted in said journal, at the beginning of every quarter, as the Philadelphia market for No. 1 heavy melting steel. The contracts required the plaintiffs to pay $5,000 on account of both contracts at the time of their formation; and the defendant agreed to give credit to this amount on the scrap to be delivered, the plaintiffs promising to pay whatever was in excess of this sum in accordance with the terms then in force between the parties.

These contracts went into effect according to their stipulations; the plaintiffs paid to the defendant the required $5,000; the prices for bundled sheet steel scrap and for crop end scrap were fixed on September 29th, 1927, in accordance with the provisions of the contracts, for the ensuing last quarter, October, November and December, 1927; and the scrap for this quarter was regularly delivered by the defendant and paid for by the plaintiffs. No controversy of any kind arose until the death of John M. Jones, who had been the president and general manager of the defendant from its inception, and who, in these capacities, had made with the plaintiffs all the contracts for the sale of scrap to the plaintiffs. Jones died about November 1st, 1927, and in the following month, under the direction of A.J. Hazlett, the new president, an effort was made to induce the plaintiffs to agree to a rescission of the contracts. The defendant's objection to the contracts was their duration and the prices, but it was willing to enter into new contracts for not over a year, upon the other terms, including the prices, of the original contracts.... In performance of these contracts, the defendant and plaintiffs agreed in December, 1927, upon the prices for scrap for the ensuing first quarter of the year, and, similarly, agreed in March, 1928, upon the price basis for the second quarter, and, accordingly, the defendant delivered, and the plaintiffs received and paid for, all the scrap which accumulated during the first six months of 1928.

Since the June, 1928, deliveries, the defendant has refused to comply with its contracts, although the plaintiffs have demanded their performance, and the defendant does not question plaintiffs' willingness and ability to complete and discharge fully their obligations. Under these circumstances, and because of the alleged irreparable loss and injury to the plaintiffs resulting from the defendant's refusal to fulfill its continuing contracts, the plaintiffs brought a bill to enforce specifically the contracts. After answer, and the taking of proof by the parties in open court, the chancellor decreed the relief prayed for, and this appeal raises the question of the right of the plaintiffs to relief.

    . . . .

Rule →. [T]he court as a general rule will refuse to decree specific performance in respect of chattels because damages are a sufficient remedy. This
principle does not apply in all cases of chattels, so there are many
exceptions to this rule, because, principally, of the inadequacy of the
remedy at law in the particular case, or of the special nature and value of
the subject matter of the contract. Passing by other illustrations of the
exceptions to one more clearly in point, Pomeroy on Specific Performance
(3rd ed.) sec. 15, puts it thus: "Again, contracts for the delivery of goods
will be specifically enforced, when by their terms the deliveries are to be
made and the purchase price paid in installments running through a
considerable number of years. Such contracts 'differ from those that are
immediately to be executed.' Their profits depending upon future events,
cannot be estimated in present damages, which must, of necessity, be
almost wholly conjectural. To compel a party to accept damages under such
circumstances is to compel him to sell his possible profits at a price
depending upon a mere guess." This statement of the law is supported by
the Maryland decisions.

Rule   Under the cases the right to specific performance turns upon whether
the plaintiffs can be properly compensated at law. The plaintiffs are
entitled to compensatory damages, and if an action at law cannot afford
them adequate redress, equity will specifically enforce the contracts, which
would not impose upon the court any difficulties in enforcement, as the
subject matter of the contracts is the accumulated scrap at the plant of the
defendant. . . .

The scrap is not to be delivered according to specified tonnage, but as
it accumulates, which in the past has been at the rate of one and two and
occasionally three car loads of scrap a day, so the quantities vary from
quarter to quarter. If the plant should cease to operate or suffer an
interruption, there would be no scrap accumulating for delivery under the
contracts, and its deliveries would end or be lessened. Neither are the
prices for the scrap constant during the period of the contracts, but change
from quarter to quarter according to the quotations of two specified
materials on the Philadelphia market whose quarterly prices are accepted
as the standards upon which the contract prices are quarterly computed.
The contracts run to September 30th, 1932. By what method would a jury
determine the future quarterly tonnage, the quarterly contract price, and
quarterly market price, during these coming years? How could it possibly
arrive at any fair ascertainment of damages? Any estimate would be
speculative and conjectural, and not, therefore, compensatory. It follows
that the defendant's breach of its contracts is not susceptible of fair and
proper compensation by damages; and that to refuse to compel the defendant to do merely what it bound itself to do, and to remit the plaintiffs to
their action at law, is to permit the defendant to relieve itself of the
contracts, and to force the plaintiffs to sell their profits at a conjectural
price. To substitute damages by guess for due performance of contract
could only be because "there's no equity stirring."

. . . .

. . . [T]he property about which the parties to this appeal bargained is
not an undistinguished portion of a quantity of similar goods. From the

time the scrap is produced and pressed into bundles, it is identified, and nothing further remains to be done to put it in condition for delivery. This scrap, and none other, is the exclusive subject-matter of the contracts. A sale of a pound of it to a third party is a breach of the contracts; and not until every pound of this scrap—and none other—is delivered to the plaintiffs, is the contract fulfilled.

Under the special circumstances of this case, the scrap sold is "specific or ascertained goods" within the meaning of section 89 of the Sale of Goods Act [(§ 68 of the Uniform Sales Act)]; and the chancellor was empowered to pass the decree for specific performance. The logic of the facts leads to this conclusion, which was anticipated by eminent authority.

For the reasons given, the decree will be affirmed.

Decree affirmed, with costs.

NOTES

1.   Bromage sued Genning for specific performance of a covenant to lease land. In turn, Genning got a writ of prohibition (an order directing a lower court not to exceed its authority) from the Court of King's Bench. Bromage v. Genning, 1 Rolle 368, 81 Eng.Rep. 540 (K.B.1616). As Chief Justice Coke saw it, a decree ordering specific performance would "subvert the intent of the covenantor, for he intends to be at his election either to lose the damages or to make the lease. . . ."

2.   Wilson made a contract to sell Fortner a new Chevrolet car, but he later refused to go through with the deal. Because of wartime shortages, new cars were hard to get, so Fortner sought specific performance of his contract with Wilson. Fortner prevailed in the trial court. However, that decision was reversed on appeal on the ground that there was "nothing unique in any way about [the car] which would cause it to come under the exceptions to the rule that specific performance will not be granted as to personal property." Fortner v. Wilson, 202 Okl. 563, 216 P.2d 299 (1950).

3.   Welton claimed that General Securities Corporation agreed to sell him 60 shares of stock in St. Louis Aviation Corporation, but that GSC refused to give him the stock certificate when he tendered payment. Welton alleged further that SLAC stock was not listed on any stock exchange and that its market value was thus not readily ascertainable. He requested specific performance of the contract. The trial court overruled GSC's demurrer to Welton's bill, and its decision was affirmed on appeal. General Securities Corp. v. Welton, 223 Ala. 299, 135 So. 329 (1931).

4.   In 1952, the American Law Institute and the Commissioners on Uniform State Laws adopted the Uniform Commercial Code. U.C.C. § 2–716, which superseded § 68 of the Uniform Sales Act, provides as follows:

Buyer's Right to Specific Performance or Replevin.

(1) Specific performance may be decreed where the goods are unique or in other proper circumstances.

(2) The decree for specific performance may include such terms and conditions as to payment of the price, damages, or other relief as the court may deem just.

(3) The buyer has a right of replevin for goods identified to the contract if after reasonable effort he is unable to effect cover for such goods or the circumstances reasonably indicate that such effort will be unavailing or if the goods have been shipped under reservation and satisfaction of the security interest in them has been made or tendered.

The official comment accompanying this provision explains why the drafters modified section 68. The "[p]urposes" of the "[c]hanges" were

[t]o make it clear that:

1. The present section continues in general prior policy as to specific performance and injunction against breach. However, without intending to impair in any way the exercise of the court's sound discretion in the matter, this Article seeks to further a more liberal attitude than some courts have shown in connection with the specific performance of contracts of sale.

2. In view of this Article's emphasis on the commercial feasibility of replacement, a new concept of what are "unique" goods is introduced under this section. Specific performance is no longer limited to goods which are already specific or ascertained at the time of contracting. The test of uniqueness under this section must be made in terms of the total situation which characterizes the contract. Output and requirements contracts involving a particular or peculiarly available source or market present today the typical commercial specific performance situation, as contrasted with contracts for the sale of heirlooms or priceless works of art which were usually involved in the older cases. However, uniqueness is not the sole basis of the remedy under this section for the relief may also be granted "in other proper circumstances" and inability to cover is strong evidence of "other proper circumstances".

3. The legal remedy of replevin is given the buyer in cases in which cover is reasonably unavailable and goods have been identified to the contract. This is in addition to the buyer's right to recover identified goods on the seller's insolvency (Section 2–502).

4. This section is intended to give the buyer rights to the goods comparable to the seller's rights to the price.

5. If a negotiable document of title is outstanding, the buyer's right of replevin relates of course to the document not directly to the goods. . . .

5. In Heilman v. Union Canal Co., 37 Pa. 100 (1860), the court made these remarks:

The fact, if it be so, that this remedy may not be successful in realizing the fruits of a recovery at law, on account of the insolvency of the defendants, is not of itself a ground of equitable interference. The remedy is what is to be looked at. If it exist, and is ordinarily adequate, its possible want of success is not a consideration. It is not intended here to say that insolvency is never a consideration moving a chancellor. It frequently does, but not alone. The equitable remedy must exist independently. In balancing cases, it is a consideration that gives preponderance to the remedy. Hence, the alleged insolvency of the company, and the supposed inability to collect damages that may be recovered from it, is no reason for interfering by injunction.

6. Under the ordinary rules as to sales of personal property, title to a specific identified chattel ordinarily passes to the buyer immediately upon the conclusion of the contract. Thus, unjustified retention by the seller when the time for delivery has arrived is a tort as well as a breach of an implied term of the contract of sale. When given a choice, buyers prefer to proceed in equity on the theory of securing specific reparation for a tort rather than on a theory of specific performance.

Kitchen v. Herring

Supreme Court of North Carolina, 1851.
42 N.C. 190.

■ PEARSON, J. In December 1846, the defendant, Herring, executed a contract in writing in these words, "Rec'd. of John L. Kitchen payment in full for a certain tract of land lying on the South west side of Black River, adjoining the lands of William Haffland and Martial, for which I am to give him a good deed etc." The defendant Pridgen wrote the contract and is a subscribing witness. The plaintiff was put into possession in March 1847. Pridgen united with him; and the other defendant, Musgrove, under a contract with Pridgen, with a large number of hands, commenced cutting down the timber, which constitutes the chief value of the land. Pridgen was the surety of the plaintiff, to a note of $325, given payable at three months for the price of the land. In January, Herring executed a deed for the land to Pridgen, and under this title the plaintiff was turned out of possession.

The prayer of the Bill is for a specific performance, for an account of the profits and for an injunction. After the Bill was filed, an arrangement was made, by which Musgrove continued his operations in getting timber, and agreed to account with the successful party. . . .

. . . .

It was further insisted, that, as it appears by the plaintiff's own showing, that "the land is chiefly valuable on account of the timber," this case does not come within the principle, on which a specific performance is decreed.

The position is new, and the Counsel admitted, that there was no authority to sustain it, but he contended with earnestness, that it was so fully sustained by "the reason of the thing," as to justify a departure from a well settled rule of this Court under the maxim, *cessante ratione cessat lex* [the reason for the law ceasing, the law ceases].

The argument failed wholly to prove, that "the reason of the thing" called for an exception. The principle in regard to land was adopted, not because it was fertile or rich in minerals, or *valuable for timber,* but simply because it was *land*—a favorite and favored subject in England, and every country of Anglo Saxon origin. Our constitution gives to land preeminence over every other species of property; and our law, whether administered in Courts of law or of equity, gives to it the same preference. Land, whether rich or poor, cannot be taken to pay debts until the personal property is exhausted. Contracts concerning land must be in writing. Land must be sold at the Court House, must be conveyed by deeds duly registered, and other instances "too tedious to mention." The principle is, that land is *assumed* to have a peculiar value, so as to give an equity for a specific performance, without reference to its quality or quantity. The same is assumed as to slaves, while in regard to other property, less favored, a specific performance will not be decreed, unless there be peculiar circumstances; for, if with the money, an article of the same description can be bought in market—corn, cotton, etc., the remedy at law is adequate.

There must be a decree for the plaintiff with costs.

NOTE

1. The RESTATEMENT (SECOND) OF CONTRACTS § 360 comment e:

Contracts for the sale of land. Contracts for the sale of land have traditionally been accorded a special place in the law of specific performance. A specific tract of land has long been regarded as unique and impossible of duplication by the use of any amount of money. Furthermore, the value of land is to some extent speculative. Damages have therefore been regarded as inadequate to enforce a duty to transfer an interest in land,.... Under this traditional view, the fact that the buyer has made a contract for the resale of the land does not deprive him of the right to specific performance. If he cannot convey the land to his purchaser, he will be held for damages for breach of the resale contract, and it is argued that these damages cannot be accurately determined without litigation. Granting him specific performance enables him to perform his own duty and to avoid litigation and damages.

Similarly, the seller who has not yet conveyed is generally granted specific performance on breach by the buyer. Here it is argued that, because the value of land is to some extent speculative, it may be difficult for him to prove with reasonable certainty the difference between the contract price and the market price of the land....

Van Wagner Advertising Corp. v. S & M Enterprises

Court of Appeals of New York, 1986.
67 N.Y.2d 186, 501 N.Y.S.2d 628, 492 N.E.2d 756.

■ KAYE, J....

By agreement dated December 16, 1981, Barbara Michaels leased to plaintiff, Van Wagner Advertising, for an initial period of three years plus option periods totaling seven additional years space on the eastern exterior wall of a building on East 36th Street in Manhattan. Van Wagner was in the business of erecting and leasing billboards, and the parties anticipated that Van Wagner would erect a sign on the leased space, which faced an exit ramp of the Midtown Tunnel and was therefore visible to vehicles entering Manhattan from that tunnel.

In early 1982 Van Wagner erected an illuminated sign and leased it to Asch Advertising, Inc. for a three-year period commencing March 1, 1982. However, by agreement dated January 22, 1982, Michaels sold the building to defendant S & M Enterprises. Michaels informed Van Wagner of the sale in early August 1982, and on August 19, 1982 S & M sent Van Wagner a letter purporting to cancel the lease as of October 18 pursuant to section 1.05, which provided:

> "Notwithstanding anything contained in the foregoing provisions to the contrary, Lessor (or its successor) may terminate and cancel this lease on not less than 60 days prior written notice in the event and only in the event of:
>
>> "a) a bona fide sale of the building to a third party unrelated to Lessor."

Van Wagner abandoned the space under protest and in November 1982 commenced this action for declarations that the purported cancellation was ineffective and the lease still in existence, and for specific performance and damages.

[The trial court concluded that the "parties to the lease intended that only an owner making a bona fide sale could terminate the lease. They did not intend that once a sale had been made that any future purchaser could terminate the lease at will." The trial court, however, declined to order specific performance.]

. . . .

Given defendant's unexcused failure to perform its contract, we next turn to a consideration of remedy for the breach: Van Wagner seeks specific performance of the contract, S & M urges that money damages are adequate but that the amount of the award was improper.[2]

Whether or not to award specific performance is a decision that rests in the sound discretion of the trial court, and here that discretion was not abused. Considering first the nature of the transaction, specific performance has been imposed as the remedy for breach of contracts for the sale of real property, but the contract here is to lease rather than sell an interest in real property. While specific performance is available, in appropriate circumstances, for breach of a commercial or residential lease, specific performance of real property leases is not in this State awarded as a matter of course (see, Gardens Nursery School v. Columbia Univ., 94 Misc.2d 376, 378).[3]

---

2. We note that the parties' contentions regarding the remedy of specific performance in general, mirror a scholarly debate that has persisted throughout our judicial history, reflecting fundamentally divergent views about the quality of a bargained-for promise. While the usual remedy in Anglo–American law has been damages, rather than compensation "in kind", the current trend among commentators appears to favor the remedy of specific performance but the view is not unanimous.

3. But see, 5A Corbin, Contracts § 1143, at 131; at 7, n. 62; 11 Williston, Contracts § 1418A [3d ed.]; Pomeroy and Mann, Specific Performance of Contracts § 9,

Van Wagner argues that specific performance must be granted in light of the trial court's finding that the "demised space is unique as to location for the particular advertising purpose intended". The word "uniqueness" is not, however, a magic door to specific performance. A distinction must be drawn between physical difference and economic interchangeability. The trial court found that the leased property is physically unique, but so is every parcel of real property and so are many consumer goods. Putting aside contracts for the sale of real property, where specific performance has traditionally been the remedy for breach, uniqueness in the sense of physical difference does not itself dictate the propriety of equitable relief.

By the same token, at some level all property may be interchangeable with money. Economic theory is concerned with the degree to which consumers are willing to substitute the use of one good for another (see, Kronman, Specific Performance, 45 U.Chi.L.Rev. 351, 359), the underlying assumption being that "every good has substitutes, even if only very poor ones", and that "all goods are ultimately commensurable" (id.). Such a view, however, could strip all meaning from uniqueness, for if all goods are ultimately exchangeable for a price, then all goods may be valued. Even a rare manuscript has an economic substitute in that there is a price for which any purchaser would likely agree to give up a right to buy it, but a court would in all probability order specific performance of such a contract on the ground that the subject matter of the contract is unique.

The point at which breach of a contract will be redressable by specific performance thus must lie not in any inherent physical uniqueness of the property but instead in the uncertainty of valuing it: "What matters, in measuring money damages, is the volume, refinement, and reliability of the available information about substitutes for the subject matter of the breached contract. When the relevant information is thin and unreliable, there is a substantial risk that an award of money damages will either exceed or fall short of the promisee's actual loss. Of course this risk can always be reduced—but only at great cost when reliable information is difficult to obtain. Conversely, when there is a great deal of consumer behavior generating abundant and highly dependable information about substitutes, the risk of error in measuring the promisee's loss may be reduced at much smaller cost. In asserting that the subject matter of a particular contract is unique and has no established market value, a court is really saying that it cannot obtain, at reasonable cost, enough information about substitutes to permit it to calculate an award of money damages without imposing an unacceptably high risk of undercompensation on the injured promisee. Conceived in this way, the uniqueness test seems economically sound." (45 U.Chi.L.Rev. at 362.) This principle is reflected in the case law, and is essentially the position of the Restatement (Second) of Contracts, which lists "the difficulty of proving damages with reasonable certainty" as the first factor affecting adequacy of damages (Restatement [Second] of Contracts § 360[a]).

at 18–19 [3d ed. 1926]; Restatement [Second] of Contracts § 360 comment a, illustration 2; Restatement [Second] of Contracts § 360 comment e.

Thus, the fact that the subject of the contract may be "unique as to location for the particular advertising purpose intended" by the parties does not entitle a plaintiff to the remedy of specific performance.

Here, the trial court correctly concluded that the value of the "unique qualities" of the demised space could be fixed with reasonable certainty and without imposing an unacceptably high risk of undercompensating the injured tenant. Both parties complain: Van Wagner asserts that while lost revenues on the Asch contract may be adequate compensation, that contract expired February 28, 1985, its lease with S & M continues until 1992, and the value of the demised space cannot reasonably be fixed for the balance of the term. S & M urges that future rents and continuing damages are necessarily conjectural, both during and after the Asch contract, and that Van Wagner's damages must be limited to 60 days—the period during which Van Wagner could cancel Asch's contract without consequence in the event Van Wagner lost the demised space. S & M points out that Van Wagner's lease could remain in effect for the full 10–year term, or it could legitimately be extinguished immediately, either in conjunction with a bona fide sale of the property by S & M, or by a reletting of the building if the new tenant required use of the billboard space for its own purposes. Both parties' contentions were properly rejected.

First, it is hardly novel in the law for damages to be projected into the future. Particularly where the value of commercial billboard space can be readily determined by comparisons with similar uses—Van Wagner itself has more than 400 leases—the value of this property between 1985 and 1992 cannot be regarded as speculative. Second, S & M having successfully resisted specific performance on the ground that there is an adequate remedy at law, cannot at the same time be heard to contend that damages beyond 60 days must be denied because they are conjectural. If damages for breach of this lease are indeed conjectural, and cannot be calculated with reasonable certainty, then S & M should be compelled to perform its contractual obligation by restoring Van Wagner to the premises. Moreover, the contingencies to which S & M points do not, as a practical matter, render the calculation of damages speculative. While S & M could terminate the Van Wagner lease in the event of a sale of the building, this building has been sold only once in 40 years; S & M paid several million dollars, and purchased the building in connection with its plan for major development of the block. The theoretical termination right of a future tenant of the existing building also must be viewed in light of these circumstances. If any uncertainty is generated by the two contingencies, then the benefit of that doubt must go to Van Wagner and not the contract violator. Neither contingency allegedly affecting Van Wagner's continued contractual right to the space for the balance of the lease term is within its own control; on the contrary, both are in the interest of S & M. Thus, neither the need to project into the future nor the contingencies allegedly affecting the length of Van Wagner's term render inadequate the remedy of damages for S & M's breach of its lease with Van Wagner.

The trial court, additionally, correctly concluded that specific performance must be denied on the ground that such relief "would be inequitable in that its effect would be disproportionate in its harm to defendant and its assistance to plaintiff.'' It is well settled that the imposition of an equitable remedy must not itself work an inequity, and that specific performance would not be an undue hardship. This conclusion is "not within the absolute discretion of the Supreme Court." Here, however, there was no abuse of discretion; the finding that specific performance would disproportionately harm S & M and benefit Van Wagner has ... support in the proof regarding S & M's projected development of the property.

. . . .

Order modified, etc.

NOTE

1.   The RESTATEMENT (SECOND) OF CONTRACTS § 360 reads as follows:

FACTORS AFFECTING ADEQUACY OF DAMAGES.

In determining whether the remedy in damages would be adequate, the following circumstances are significant:

(a) the difficulty of proving damages with reasonable certainty,

(b) the difficulty of procuring a suitable substitute performance by means of money awarded as damages, and

(c) the likelihood that an award of damages could not be collected.

Rubinstein v. Rubinstein

Court of Appeals of New York, 1968.
23 N.Y.2d 293, 296 N.Y.S.2d 354, 244 N.E.2d 49.

■ KEATING, J. Henry and Leo Rubinstein are distant relatives. For some years they had successfully operated a number of joint enterprises. In July, 1965 they owned an equal number of shares in two corporations, one of which operated a grocery business on Third Avenue in New York City ("Premium") and the other a delicatessen business on First Avenue ("Kips Bay"). In addition, the cousins had equal interests in two other corporations. One held title to real property on which the Kips Bay delicatessen was conducted and the other to the adjoining parcel.

Prior to July, 1965 differences arose. The cousins decided on a parting of the ways. On July 20, 1965, with each party represented by his own counsel, an agreement was signed. Its basic outline was this. Each business was valued at $70,000. Henry was to choose immediately between the two businesses. Leo would get the other. The agreement also provided that whoever took the Kips Bay delicatessen would also take the realty located there. Although the agreement established a procedure by which the realty was to be valued, it appears that the realty played an insignificant part in the negotiations.

At the time the agreement was executed, Henry and Leo deposited $5,000 with their respective lawyers. The agreement stated this sum would "be held in escrow by each respective attorney, to be applied towards the payment that each of the parties may have to make to the other party upon the closing of the above transaction." Any surplus, after the necessary adjustments, was to be returned to Henry and Leo at the time of the closing. These two provisions, which appear in paragraph numbered "8", are then followed by this clause: "In the event that either of the parties hereto shall default or refuse to consummate this transaction, then the aforesaid $5,000.00 deposited by such defaulting party shall be forfeited as liquidated damages and such sum shall be paid by the escrowee thereof to the other party."

The day after the execution of the agreement Henry sent a letter to Leo's lawyer in which he elected to take the Kips Bay property. The agreement provided that the closing would take place within one week. Apparently, disputes arose as to how various details of the transaction should be worked out, and in October of 1965 the deal still had not been consummated. At this point, Henry instituted this suit in Supreme Court, New York County, for specific performance. An answer was interposed by the defendant in which he counterclaimed for specific performance, also alleging the lack of an adequate remedy at law.

Leo thereafter had a complete change of mind. He changed lawyers and in September, 1966 moved to strike the complaint from the equity calendar on the ground that the quoted provision of the agreement relegated Henry to an action at law for $5,000. Henry cross-moved for summary judgment for specific performance. Leo then moved for leave to serve a proposed amended answer to remove the counterclaim for equitable relief.

Special Term found that it "is clear that the defendant does not desire to go through with the contract", and ruled that plaintiff was entitled to summary judgment, but held that the clause quoted above constituted not only a liquidated damages provision but, as a matter of law, it constituted the sole relief to which plaintiff was entitled. The correctness of this holding is the principal legal issue presented by this appeal.

. . . .

We conclude that the pertinent clause does not preclude the relief of specific performance, that plaintiff does not have an adequate remedy at law and that the agreement is enforceable by a court of equity. Therefore, plaintiff's motion for summary judgment for specific performance should have been granted.

We may immediately dispose of a preliminary argument, namely, that plaintiff has an adequate remedy at law. On its face the principal aim of this agreement was to sever the parties' relationship and to enable each party to own completely, separately and without interference by the other one half the joint business. It is evident that this result cannot be achieved by a damage award, and respondent does not seriously argue that plaintiff has an adequate remedy at law.

We turn then to the main question presented by this appeal, whether the agreement by its terms or in light of surrounding circumstances precludes specific performance. Nothing in the language of the contract explicitly states that the liquidated damages provision was to be plaintiff's sole and exclusive remedy, but both Special Term and the Appellate Division majority found the liquidated damages provision itself precluded specific performance. This is made clear by the following language in the prevailing opinion: "Properly considered, clause Eight in the contract relating to the $5,000 was nothing more than an option, affording the plaintiff a choice not to go forward, if he was willing to forfeit $5,000."

In relying on the liquidated damages clause alone the majority was clearly in error. The law is now well settled that a liquidated damages provision will not in and of itself be construed as barring the remedy of specific performance. For there to be a complete bar to equitable relief there must be something more, such as explicit language in the contract that the liquidated damages provision was to be the sole remedy....

. . . .

It is interesting to note that nowhere in this contract can be found the word "option" although this is the term used by the Appellate Division majority to describe the instant contract. Absent, therefore, an unambiguous provision, the majority below was in error in finding that the language itself precluded specific performance and for a very sound reason. Generally, the law presumes that the primary purpose of a contract, not expressly stated to be an option, is performance of the act promised and not nonperformance. Penalty clauses and even liquidated damages clauses are generally inserted to help secure performance and to avoid litigation as to quantum of damages. In this way, it is hoped to induce performance by making delay or breaches unprofitable.

Moreover, the first reference to the $5,000 is that it was to be used in connection with the "closing". This clause signifies that the escrow deposit was not even intended to assure performance, which was presumed, but it was contemplated that it would be used in connection with the performance of the contract in question. Also to be considered is the fact that the closing—originally scheduled to take place within 48 hours—was set for a week later. This surely evinces an intent that the contract be specifically performed.

The agreement grew out of a deterioration in the personal relations of the two cousins. Its first goal was the severance of their partnership. Defendant's interpretation would only provide Henry with the "right" to continue as Leo's partner if Leo did not like the division. It would be preposterous for the parties to enter into an agreement providing that, at the risk of $5,000, the parties shall see if they can agree to a division. We may not presume persons act so irrationally. If the defendant desired the Kips Bay property as well as a severance, he could have demanded the right of first choice. Or some alternative method for dividing the business would have been devised. The fact that defendant was willing to give plaintiff the right to select the property indicates that his major desire was to terminate a relationship, which was no longer bearable, rather than to obtain a right to pay $5,000 for the privilege of being restored to the *status quo ante*.

Nor is there anything in the surrounding circumstances which discloses a design that the liquidated damages clause is intended to bar specific performance. On this point it is of significance that the same lawyer who represented the defendant at the time the agreement was made counterclaimed for specific performance. Defendant thus indicated that it was his understanding that the agreement could be specifically enforced.

The conclusion is clear. The agreement here does not bar plaintiff from seeking the remedy of specific performance. There being no question that defendant defaulted, plaintiff has his choice of remedies and he has elected specific performance.

A final point raised by the respondent is that equitable relief should not be granted since the agreement is allegedly ambiguous, vague, preliminary in nature and incomplete. This contention is distinctly without merit.

. . . .

If any serious difficulties as to the meaning of various terms of the agreement do ultimately arise, and at present defendant has shown none, oral testimony as to the meaning of the term in the agreement would appear proper. In any event, the propriety of equitable relief is one which should be resolved by the trial court since it is clear that the agreement does not, as a matter of law, bar equitable relief.

Accordingly, the order of the Appellate Division should be reversed and plaintiff's motion for summary judgment for specific performance should be granted, with costs in all courts.

BURKE, SCILEPPI, BREITEL, and JASEN, JJ., concur with KEATING, J.

FULD, C.J., and BERGAN, J., dissent and vote to affirm for the reasons stated in the concurring memorandum of EAGER, J., at the Appellate Division.

Order reversed, with costs in all courts, and matter remitted to Special Term for further proceedings in accordance with the opinion herein.[1]

––––––––

2.   RELIEF FOR AND AGAINST THIRD PERSONS
Liabilities of Purchaser's Assignee

Langel v. Betz

Court of Appeals of New York, 1928.
250 N.Y. 159, 164 N.E. 890.

■ POUND, J. Plaintiff, on August 1, 1925, made a contract with Irving W. Hurwitz and Samuel Hollander for the sale of certain real property. This contract the vendees assigned to Benedict, who in turn assigned it to Isidor Betz, the defendant herein. The assignment contains no delegation to the assignee of the performance of the assignor's duties. The date for performance of the contract was originally set for October 2, 1925. This was extended to October 15, 1925, at the request of the defendant, the last assignee of the vendees. The ground upon which the adjournment was asked for by defendant was that the title company had not completed its search and report on the title to the property. Upon the adjourned date the defendant refused to perform. The vendor plaintiff was ready, able, and

---

1. See also Truck Rent–A–Center, Inc. v. Puritan Farms 2nd, Inc., *infra* p. 831.

willing to do so, and was present at the place specified with a deed, ready to tender it to the defendant, who did not appear.

The plaintiff as vendor brought this action against the defendant assignee for specific performance of the contract. Upon the foregoing undisputed facts he has had judgment therefor.

The question is: "Can the vendor obtain specific performance of a contract for the sale of real estate against the assignee of the vendee, where the assignee merely requests and obtains an extension of time within which to close title?"

Here we have no novation, no express assumption of the obligations of the assignor in the assignment, and no demand for performance by the assignee.

The mere assignment of a bilateral executory contract may not be interpreted as a promise by the assignee to the assignor to assume the performance of the assignor's duties, so as to have the effect of creating a new liability on the part of the assignee to the other party to the contract assigned. The assignee of the vendee is under no personal engagement to the vendor where there is no privity between them. The assignee may, however, expressly or impliedly, bind himself to perform the assignor's duties. This he may do by contract with the assignor or with the other party to the contract. It has been held (Epstein v. Gluckin, 233 N.Y. 490, 135 N.E. 861) that, where the assignee of the vendee invokes the aid of a court of equity in an action for specific performance, he impliedly binds himself to perform on his part and subjects himself to the conditions of the judgment appropriate thereto. "He who seeks equity must do equity." The converse of the proposition, that the assignee of the vendee would be bound when the vendor began the action, did not follow from the decision in that case. On the contrary, the question was wholly one of remedy rather than right, and it was held that mutuality of remedy is important only so far as its presence is essential to the attainment of the ends of justice. This holding was necessary to sustain the decision. No change was made in the law of contracts nor in the rule for the interpretation of an assignment of a contract.

A judgment requiring the assignee of the vendee to perform at the suit of the vendor would operate as the imposition of a new liability on the assignee which would be an act of oppression and injustice, unless the assignee had, expressly or by implication, entered into a personal and binding contract with the assignor or with the vendor to assume the obligations of the assignor.

It has been urged that the probable intention of the assignee is ordinarily to assume duties as well as rights, and that the contract should be so interpreted in the absence of circumstances showing a contrary intention. The American Law Institute's Restatement of the Law of Contracts (section 164) proposes a change in the rule of interpretation of assigned contracts to give as full effect to the assumed probable intention of the parties as the law permits. The following statement is proposed:

"Section 164. Interpretation of Words Purporting to Assign a Bilateral Contract and Effect of Acceptance of the Assignment by the Assignee.

"(1) Where a party to a bilateral contract which is at the time wholly or partially executory on both sides, purports to assign the whole contract, his action is interpreted, in the absence of circumstances showing a contrary intention, as an assignment of the assignor's rights under the contract and a delegation of the performance of the assignor's duties.

"(2) Acceptance by the assignee of such an assignment is interpreted, in the absence of circumstances showing a contrary intention, as both as assent to become an assignee of the assignor's rights and as a promise to the assignor to assume the performance of the assignor's duties."

This promise to the assignor would then be available to the other party to the contract. Lawrence v. Fox, 20 N.Y. 268; 1 Williston on Contracts, s 412. The proposed change is a complete reversal of our present rule of interpretation as to the probable intention of the parties. It is, perhaps, more in harmony with modern ideas of contractual relations than is "the archaic view of a contract as creating a strictly personal obligation between the creditor and debtor" (Pollock on Contracts [9th Ed.] 232), which prohibited the assignee from suing at law in his own name and which denied a remedy to third party beneficiaries. "The fountains out of which these resolutions issue" have been broken up if not destroyed (Seaver v. Ransom, 224 N.Y. 233, 237, 120 N.E. 639, 2 A. L. R. 1187), but the law remains that no promise of the assignee to assume the assignor's duties is to be inferred from the acceptance of an assignment of a bilateral contract, in the absence of circumstances surrounding the assignment itself which indicate a contrary intention.

With this requirement of the interpretation of the intention of the parties controlling we must turn from the assignment to the dealings between the plaintiff and the defendant to discover whether the defendant entered into relations with the plaintiff whereby he assumed the duty of performance. The assignment did not bring the parties together, and the request for a postponement differs materially from the commencement of an action in a court of equity, whereby the plaintiff submits himself to the jurisdiction of the court or from a contractual assumption of the obligations of the assignor. If the substance of the transaction between the vendor and the assignee of the vendee could be regarded as a request on the part of the latter for a postponement of the closing day and a promise on his part to assume the obligations of the vendee if the request were granted, a contractual relation arising from an expression of mutual assent, based on the exchange of a promise for an act, might be spelled out of it; but the transaction is at least as consistent with a request for time for deliberation as to the course of conduct to be pursued as with an implied promise to assume the assignor's duties if the request were granted. The relation of promisor and promisee was not thereby expressly established, and such relation is not a necessary inference from the nature of the transaction. When we depart from the field of intention and enter the field of contract, we find no contractual liability; no assumption of duties based on a consideration.

Plaintiff contends that the request for an adjournment should be construed (time not being the essence of the contract) as an assertion of a right to such adjournment, and therefore as a binding act of enforcement, whereby defendant accepted the obligations of the assignee. Here again we have an equivocal act. There was no demand for an adjournment as a matter of right. The request may have been made without any intent to assert a right. It cannot be said that by that act alone the assignee assumed the duty of performance.

Furthermore, no controlling authority may be found which holds that a mere demand for performance by the vendee's assignee creates a right in the complaining vendor to enforce the contract against him. H. & H. Corporation v. Broad Holding Corporation, 204 App. Div. 569, 198 N.Y. S. 763. See 8 Cornell Law Quarterly, 374; 37 Harvard Law Review, 162. That question may be reserved until an answer is necessary.

The judgment of the Appellate Division and that of the Special Term should be reversed and the complaint dismissed, with costs in all courts.

■ Cardozo, C. J., and Crane, Andrews, Lehman, Kellogg, and O'Brien, JJ., concur.

NOTES

1.   Implied Assumption—Farnsworth,[2] Contracts § 11.11 at 832–33 (2d ed. 1990): "Even if a delegate does not promise in so many words to perform the duty of the delegating party, a court may infer such a promise from the delegate's conduct. Thus, if a party transfers the entire contract, assigning rights as well as delegating performance, an assumption of those duties by the transferee will be inferred from the acceptance of the transfer, unless the language or the situation indicates to the contrary. Both Restatements declare this to be the law, and the Uniform Commercial Code incorporates such a rule for contracts for the sale of goods. However, a notorious New York case, decided over a half a century ago, refused to apply the rule of the first Restatement to a transfer by a purchaser under a contract for the sale of land, and in deference to this case the Restatement Second declines to decide whether its rule covers such a case."

Section 328 of the Restatement Second of Contracts succeeds § 164 of the First Restatement, and states:

(1) Unless the language or the circumstances indicate the contrary, as in an assignment for security, an assignment of "the contract" or of "all my rights under the contract" or an assignment in similar general terms is an assignment of the assignor's rights and a delegation of his unperformed duties under the contract.

(2) Unless the language or the circumstances indicate the contrary, the acceptance by an assignee of such an assignment operates as a promise to the assignor to perform the assignor's unperformed duties, and the obligor of the assigned rights is an intended beneficiary of the promise.

2.   Professor Farnsworth was the Reporter for the Restatement (Second) of Contracts.

Caveat: The Institute expresses no opinion as to whether the rule stated in Subsection (2) applies to an assignment by a purchaser of his rights under a contract for the sale of land.

. . .

Comment c. Land contracts. By virtue of the right of either party to obtain specific performance of a contract for the sale of land, such contracts are treated for many purposes as creating a property interest in the purchaser and thus as partially executed. The vendor's interest resembles the interest of a mortgagee under a mortgage given as security for the purchase price. An assignment of the vendor's rights under the contract is similar to an assignment of a right to payment for goods or services: ordinarily no assumption of the vendor's duties by the assignee is implied merely from the acceptance of the assignment.

When the purchaser under a land contract assigns his rights, the assignment has commonly been treated like a sale of land "subject to" a mortgage. In this view acceptance of the assignment does not amount to an assumption of the assignor's duties unless the contract of assignment so provides either expressly or by implication. A provision in the land contract that it will bind the "assigns" of the parties does not change this result. See Comment b to § 323. The assignee may, however, bind himself by later action such as bringing a suit for specific performance [as was the case in Epstein v. Gluckin, 233 N.Y. 490, 135 N.E. 861 (1922)]. Decisions refusing to infer an assumption of duties by the assignee have been influenced by doctrinal difficulties in the recognition of rights of assignees and beneficiaries. Those difficulties have now been overcome, and it is doubtful whether adherence to such decisions carries out the probable intention of the parties in the usual case. But since the shift in doctrine has not yet produced any definite change in the body of decisions, the Institute expresses no opinion on the application of Subsection (2) to an assignment by a purchaser under a land contract.

Illustration:

4. A contracts to purchase land from B. The contract provides that it is to bind the assigns of the parties. A assigns "the contract" to C, and B assigns "the contract" to D. These facts themselves do not show a promise by D; the Institute expresses no opinion as to whether they show a promise by C.

The Reporter's note to the section states, "The application of Subsection (2) to land contracts is subjected to a new caveat because of the rejection of the rule stated in former § 164 in Langel v. Betz, 250 N.Y. 159, 164 N.E. 890 (1928)."

2. In Epstein v. Gluckin, 233 N.Y. 490, 135 N.E. 861 (1922), referred to in *Langel v. Betz*, the court held that, by bringing an action for specific performance, the assignee of the vendee was impliedly bound to perform the duties of the assignor. The court stated: "What equity exacts today as a condition of relief is the assurance that the decree, [of specific performance] if rendered, will operate without injustice or oppression either to plaintiff or to defendant."

3. The infant plaintiff in Weinberger v. Van Hessen, 260 N.Y. 294, 183 N.E. 429 (1932), was living in the custody of an uncle in Holland. Defendant and plaintiff's mother agreed that, if the latter brought the child to New York and let defendant raise him, defendant would "direct his education and control his religious and moral upbringing" and support him financially. Pursuant to this agreement, defendant took care of plaintiff for two years. When defendant stopped, plaintiff sought specific performance of the agreement. The Court of Appeals affirmed the lower courts' denial of defendant's motion to dismiss the complaint. In response to the suggestion that specific performance should be unavailable to plaintiff because "[t]here was no promise . . . under which defendant could have an enforceable right to direct the child's education and to control his religious and moral upbringing," the court made the following argument:

[Assuming that no such promise existed], the contract has been performed up to the present; and the child and his guardian have assumed the duty of performance by invoking the aid of equity. Their continued performance may be made a condition of the decree, if a decree be entered. . . . Suit may be maintained under the contract by plaintiff. It is sufficient that there is a close relationship between the promisee and the beneficiary. . . .

4. EQUITABLE CONVERSION—WARNER, J., Panushka v. Panushka, 221 Or. 145, 349 P.2d 450 (1960): "In equity a binding and enforceable contract for the sale and purchase of real estate is recognized for most purposes in this court, as well as in other jurisdictions, as if specifically executed and performed. This concept is derived from the maxim that equity considers as done that which was agreed to be done." See Maxims of Equity, pp. 33–35.

"An equitable conversion," therefore, takes place when a contract for the sale of real property becomes binding upon the parties. Thenceforth, the purchaser of the land is deemed the equitable owner thereof, and the seller is considered the owner of the purchase price. Upon the execution of the contract, the two contracting parties change positions. The purchaser's interest is "land," and the right and interest conferred by the contract upon the vendor is "personal property," i.e., ownership of the right to receive the purchase money. The naked legal title, which the vendor holds in trust as security for the payment of the purchase money, descends to his heirs to be held by them for the benefit of the purchaser, but the vendor has no *interest* in the *land* which is subject to descent. Upon the vendor's death, his interest in the purchase money passes to his personal representative as personalty, and is distributable among the deceased vendor's next of kin. In short, as a result of the equitable conversion, the vendor holds an encumbered legal title, charged with the equitable interest of the purchaser, which is subject to be defeated by the purchaser's performance of the contract but so long as the contract remains executory, no title to the land is conveyed in law to the purchaser. Subsequent holders of the legal title with notice are likewise treated as trustees for the purchaser, as are heirs and devisees. This trust cannot be terminated either by the vendor or by anyone, with notice of the trust, claiming under, by or through the vendor, except for a breach by the purchaser of the conditions of the contract. The purchaser is called, by some courts, the trustee of the purchase money for the vendor. Other courts, adhering in strict theory, do not say "trustee," but designate the purchaser a contracting party bound by an obligation to pay the vendor or his personal representative money for the land purchased. . . .

"In the absence of a showing that the parties have manifested an intention that the property should retain its present character, the general rule is that the conversion takes place when the contract is executed by the parties. . . ."

Rights and Liabilities of Vendor's Assignee and Transferee

Walker & Trenholm v. Kee

Supreme Court of South Carolina, 1881.
16 S.C. 76.

■ McGOWAN, A.J. [On December 18, 1876, Stevens & Cureton agreed to sell several tracts of land to Kee for $9,025. In payment Kee conveyed a house valued at $1,500 and gave four promissory notes maturing at successive dates in 1877–1879. The contract provided that if all the notes were paid the vendor would give a warranty deed; but if any note was not paid, then the contract should become void, and the parties of the first part should have the right to peaceable possession of the lands, with a forfeiture on Kee's part of all previous payments. By a series of indorsements the second and third notes were transferred for value before maturity to Walker & Trenholm and the fourth note to a bank. In February, 1878, Stevens & Cureton made an assignment for the benefit of creditors, in which they included the said lands "subject to a contract of sale to A.M. Kee." In January, 1879, Walker & Trenholm sued Kee on the notes transferred to them; the assignees were parties and denied the plaintiffs' title to the notes. The plaintiffs recovered judgment, which was affirmed.]

A.M. Kee being insolvent, Walker & Trenholm . . . and the bank . . . have united and instituted this action to compel specific performance of the land agreement, and, as incidental thereto, to sell the land in payment of their debts. [Kee makes no defense, but only desires to know to whom he can rightfully make payment if able. The co-defendants, the assignees for the benefit of creditors, claim the land, and deny the right of the plaintiffs in any manner to subject it to the payment of the judgment and notes which they hold against Kee.] Judge Hudson heard the case and decreed for the plaintiffs, and ordered the land sold.

It seems that Kee, the purchaser, upon failure to comply with the terms of sale, acknowledged his liability to pay rent, and gave an obligation to pay it, which, under some agreement, had been deposited with the clerk of the court, "to be turned over to the parties who may be entitled by the judgment of the court." In a supplemental order Judge Hudson directed the clerk to collect this obligation and hold the proceeds subject to the future order of the court. From these orders the defendants appeal to this court. . . .

     . . . .

... It is insisted that even if the transfer of the notes to the plaintiffs respectively were valid, and gave them the legal title thereto, that the transfer alone did not operate as an assignment of the land or any charge upon it, the legal title to which is still in the defendants as assignees of Stevens & Cureton, and, consequently, the plaintiffs are not entitled to have it sold towards payment of the notes.

It is true that Kee executed no mortgage to secure the purchase-money of the land. It is also true that, according to our decided cases, we have not, in this State, what is known technically as "the vendor's lien," as declared and enforced in the English Chancery—that is, a lien upon land sold to secure the purchase-money, whether the vendor has, or has not, executed titles to the vendee. But as to all executory contracts for the sale of land in which the title-deed is not executed, but the vendor gives a bond for titles, we have what is equivalent to the vendor's lien in the well-recognized equity doctrine of specific performance of contracts for the sale of land.... The contract in this case was executory, and the vendors, Stevens & Cureton, had the right to require specific performance, and the only question is whether the assignees of the notes have the same right.

Some confusion seems to have arisen from regarding the notes as nothing more than promissory notes, pure and simple. The fact is, they sprung out of the agreement for the sale of the land and are only a part of it. They were executed at the same time with the agreement, and have on their face the statement that they were given "in part payment for a tract of land," & c. They must be considered in connection with the agreement, and, thus considered, the papers constitute, both in form and substance, an executory contract for the sale of land. The transfer of these notes, accompanied with the agreement or with knowledge of its existence and contents, carried to those who acquired title to them all the rights which attached to them in the hands of Stevens & Cureton. The transfer was in fact, as it was intended to be, not merely an endorsement of the paper as promissory notes, but a sale and transfer of the land trade and all rights incident thereto. The plaintiffs, before they accepted the notes, were informed of the nature of the land trade and the connection of the notes therewith; indeed, the notes, upon their face, gave such information, and the plaintiffs have now the same rights which Stevens & Cureton had originally to ask specific performance.

Judge Story says: "It may also be stated that, in general, where the specific execution of a contract respecting lands will be decreed between the parties, it will be decreed between all persons claiming under them in privity of estate, or of representation, or of title, unless other controlling equities are interposed. If a person purchases lands with knowledge of a prior contract to convey them, he is, as we have seen, affected by all the equities which affected the lands in the hands of the vendor. The lien of the vendor for the purchase-money attaches to them, and such purchaser may be compelled either to pay the purchase-money, or to surrender up the land, or to have it sold for the benefit of the vendor.... On the other hand, if the vendee, under such a contract, conveys the same to a third person, the latter, upon paying the purchase-money, may compel the vendor, and any person claiming under him in privity, or as a purchaser with notice, to complete the contract and convey the title to him. The general principle upon which this doctrine proceeds is, that from the time of the contract for the sale of the land, the vendor as to the land becomes a trustee for the vendee, and the vendee as to the purchase-money a trustee for the vendor, who has a lien upon the land therefor. And every subsequent purchaser from either, with notice, becomes subject to the same equities as the party would from whom he purchased." Story Eq. §§ 788, 789.

We are not called upon to decide whether A.M. Kee, who entered upon the land under a contract to purchase, and paid part of the purchase-money, would be liable, in an action for specific performance, to account for rents and profits of the lands before judgment. It seems that under the provision in the agreement as to forfeiture, or for some other reason, the purchaser admitted his liability to pay rent after a certain time, and gave a rent obligation, which is now in the hands of the clerk, "to be turned over to the parties who may be entitled by the judgment of the court." Having determined that all the rights of Stevens & Cureton, [as to] the notes, were transferred to the respondents and that they have the right to ask specific performance of the agreement as to the land for their payment, it would seem to follow that the rents, an incident of the land, should go with it. In the view we take, Stevens & Cureton have been paid in full for the land, and they have no further interest in it or its products. In the beginning they got the "Kee lot," and, as we suppose, the first note when it fell due, and then they transferred, in payment of their debts, the remaining notes. True, their assignees have still the legal title to the land, but they hold it as trustees for the payment of the notes still due, and, surely, they cannot claim the rents by any higher right. The notes having been transferred only as collateral to secure debts to the plaintiffs, respectively, the rights of plaintiffs, as herein determined, must, of course, cease as soon as their debts are paid.

. . . .

The judgment of this court is that the judgment of the Circuit Court be affirmed and the appeal dismissed.

NOTES

1.   3 POMEROY, EQUITY JURISPRUDENCE § 1260 (5th ed. 1941):

. . . There is a plain distinction between the lien of the grantor after a conveyance, and the interest of the vendor before conveyance. The former is not a legal estate, but is a mere equitable charge on the land; it is not even, in strictness, an equitable lien until declared and established by judicial decree. In the latter, although possession may have been delivered to the vendee, and although under the doctrine of conversion the vendee may have acquired an equitable estate, yet the vendor retains the *legal title,* and the vendee cannot prejudice that legal title, or do anything by which it shall be divested, except by performing the very obligation on his part which the retention of such title was intended to secure,—namely, by paying the price according to the terms of the contract. To call this complete legal title a lien, is certainly a misnomer. In case of a conveyance, the grantor has a lien, but no title. In case of a contract for sale before conveyance the vendor has the legal title, and has no need of any lien; his title is a more efficient security, since the vendee cannot defeat it by any act or transfer even to or with a *bona fide* purchaser.

2. If a land contract fails of performance without the purchaser's default, e.g., because of defects of title, delay by the vendor, or non-compliance with the Statute of Frauds, the general rule is that the purchaser has an action against the vendor to recover any payments made on account of the purchase price. The purchaser also has an equitable lien on the land to the extent of his payments, which is enforceable in equity against the vendor's grantee unless for value without notice. This lien is implied by law without mention in the contract, like the grantor's lien of which it has been called the counterpart. However, the destruction of the grantor's lien in many states by statute or otherwise does not usually destroy the purchaser's lien.

---

3. DEVOLUTION ON DEATH—EQUITABLE CONVERSION
Rights Between Vendor and Purchaser

Taylor v. Kelly

Supreme Court of North Carolina, 1857.
56 N.C. 240.

Cause removed from the Court of Equity of Moore County.

The bill was filed against the defendants, for a specific performance of a contract to convey a tract of land. . . .

. . . .

■ PEARSON, J. The defendant Kelly opposes the plaintiff's right to a decree, on three grounds. . . . 3. He avers that, before the bill was filed, he had sold and conveyed the land, for a valuable consideration, to the other defendants, and so a specific performance by him is impracticable. Admitting this allegation, the plaintiff insists that, if she is not able to get the land from the other defendants, who are made parties by the amended bills, on the ground that they had notice of her equity, then, she is at liberty, under the general prayer for a relief, to fall back upon her secondary equity, and by ratifying the sale, charge the defendant Kelly with the price he received for the land, deducting the amount of the purchase-money, with its interest, that is still due on her contract.

It is held in Scarlett v. Hunter, 56 N.C. 84 (1856), and is, in fact, a familiar principle, that where there is a contract for the sale of land, the vendee is considered in Equity as the owner, and the vendor retains the title as a security for the purchase-money. So, the effect of the contract was, that the defendant held the land as trustee to secure the balance of the purchase-money, and then in trust for the plaintiff. This brings the case within another familiar principle: that where a trustee converts the fund, the *cestui que use* [(beneficiary)] has a right to follow the fund and take it in its changed shape; as, where a guardian invests the ward's money in the purchase of land, the ward may elect to have the land; so here, we can see no reason why the *cestui que use* may not, if she chooses, have the price which was realized by a sale of the land. What right has the trustee to say that he should be allowed to retain the profit made by his sale? It was a breach of trust. Can he take advantage of his own wrong, and ask a Court of Equity to drive the injured *cestui que use* to her action at law, for damages on the contract?

. . . .

There will be a decree for plaintiff, and a reference to ascertain the amount of the price received by Kelly, and the balance of the purchase-money with its interest still due by plaintiff, so as to fix the sum to which the plaintiff is entitled.

PER CURIAM.

Decree accordingly.

NOTES

1. Colby and his wife signed a pre-nuptial agreement providing that she would marry him and remain his wife until death do them part, and that she would inherit his residence if she survived him. Colby also executed a will devising the land to her. The marriage ceremony followed. Some of Colby's heirs subsequently convinced him to revoke the will and replace it with one leaving the land to his heirs. However, his wife did not learn of this event and the couple lived together at Colby's residence until his death. Finally, the wife sued the heirs for enforcement of the pre-nuptial contract. The trial court sustained a demurrer to the complaint. The appeals court reversed. Colby v. Colby, 30 N.Y.S. 677 (1894).

> There was a legal binding contract alleged in the complaint, made upon a good and sufficient consideration, which the plaintiff fully and faithfully performed upon her part; the deceased failed to perform on his part; he failed to vest her with the title to the property in question, and in consequence of such failure on the part of the deceased, the title to the house and lot descended to the defendants who are his heirs at law; the relief to which the plaintiff is entitled is a conveyance from these heirs of the title to the premises in fulfillment of the contract of their ancestor.

> While an agreement to make a certain disposition of property by a last will is one which, strictly speaking, is not capable of a specific execution, yet it has been held to be within the jurisdiction of a court of equity to do what is equivalent to a specific performance of such an agreement, by requiring those upon whom the legal title has descended to convey the property in accordance with its terms. And the court will not allow this *post mortem* remedy to be defeated by any devise inconsistent with the agreement.

2. The doctrine of equitable conversion was first enunciated in cases involving the devolution of rights and liabilities under land contracts upon

the death of one of the parties. Classical equity viewed a deceased vendor as leaving behind a money claim secured by a vendor's lien. A deceased buyer was seen as leaving land and a debt. Thus, if a vendor died intestate, legal title was taken from the heir to enable the administrator to recover the purchase price for the benefit of the next-of-kin; if a buyer died intestate, the heir received the land at the expense of the next-of-kin.

With the abolition of primogeniture and the enactment of modern statutes of descent and distribution, heirs and next-of-kin are commonly the same persons taking in the same shares, so that the application of the doctrine of equitable conversion frequently does not change devolution on intestacy. In this instance, legislation in no way directed at modification of the theory of conversion has had a large effect on the application of the theory and has rendered it of little practical importance in a substantial class of cases. But these statutes have had no such effect on testate devolution. Subject to some qualifications based on the actual or inferred intention of the testator, the same principles as to conversion are applicable between devisee and executor as between heir and administrator.

Several aspects of the law of equitable conversion as applied in devolution cases have attracted legislative attention. For example, a series of mid-nineteenth century English statutes, known as Locke King's Acts, abolished the right of exoneration (in the absence of explicit language to the contrary in a will). 40 & 41 Vict. c. 34 (1877); 17 & 18 Vict. c. 113 (1854), amended by 30 & 31 Vict. c. 69 (1867). The effect of these Acts is to leave the executor or administrator liable for the purchase money or mortgage debt due from the decedent, but to make that indebtedness ultimately payable out of the purchased or mortgaged land, if sufficient for the purpose, rather than out of the intestate or residuary personal estate. The heir or devisee thus takes subject to the vendor's lien or the mortgage, and the personal estate going to the next-of-kin or residuary legatees is unaffected unless the land is insufficient to pay the indebtedness due to the vendor or mortgagee, or unless, in the case of death testate, the testator expressly provides for exoneration.

Consider also this statute:

> An agreement made by a testator to convey any property does not revoke a prior testamentary disposition of such property; but such property passes under the will to the beneficiaries, subject to whatever rights were created by such agreement.

N.Y.—McKINNEY'S EST. POWERS & TRUSTS LAW § 3–4.2.

In Re Boyle's Estate

Supreme Court of Iowa, 1912.
154 Iowa 249, 134 N.W. 590.

In form, this is an action or claim for rent against the administrator of P.J. Boyle. The controversy, however, is between the plaintiff and the intervener who claims a part of the rent as the vendee of the leased premises, and as having acquired the same before the rent accrued. There was a judgment for the plaintiff, and the intervenor appeals.

■ EVANS, J. . . .

There is no controversy over the general rule that a conveyance of land carries with it to the grantee as an incident of the title and possession the right to receive unaccrued rent under an existing lease. The point in dispute here is whether the particular contract is such as to entitle the intervener to the advantage of this rule. There are many of our own cases where the rule has been applied, but they are all cases of complete conveyance by deed. . . . In the case before us the contract is wholly executory on the part of the plaintiff. It specifically provides for a conveyance in the future. It is silent upon the subject of possession.

    . . . .

. . . [T]he intervener has chosen to rest his claim solely upon the written contract and upon the proposition that the equitable ownership acquired by the contract necessarily carried the possession. In view of the fact already indicated that the contract in its terms was wholly executory as to the appellee and bound it to no performance even in part, until full performance was made by appellant, and in view of the further fact that the contract contained no terms of "present assurance," it devolved upon the intervener to plead and to prove either by way of reformation of the contract, or by way of oral agreement, if competent (a question we do not decide), that he was to have possession of the premises, and the date thereof. Unless he could prove that he was entitled to possession before the rent accrued, he was in no position to claim unaccrued rents. The case of Nun[n]gesser v. Hart, 122 Iowa 647, 98 N.W. 505, is quite in point, but by no means controlling of this case. In that case a contract similar to the one before us was entered into in the fall of the year and partial payment made thereon. It also provided that a deed and possession would be given on March 1st following. It was held that the purchaser did not become the "owner" of the land until March 1st. The fact that the contract contained no words of "present assurance," and that it expressly provided for a future conveyance, was deemed controlling on that question. In Toerring v. Lamp, 77 Iowa 488, 42 N.W. 378, the rule as to unaccrued rents is stated in these words: "Rents unaccrued pass with an unconditional conveyance." Putting this statement of the rule alongside of that in Hall v. Hall, 150 Iowa 277, 129 N.W. 960, they both impeach the sufficiency of the contract before us.

It is our conclusion, therefore, that the trial court properly sustained the demurrer, and its order is accordingly affirmed.

NOTE

Moses Bros. entered into an installment land sale contract with Johnson. The contract provided that Johnson would get title if he paid the accruing taxes and the unpaid purchase money (plus interest) as due. It also provided that, should Johnson default on any installment payment, Moses Bros. could cancel the contract and retake possession, keep some of the money paid by Johnson as rent (at a rate of $60 per year), and return the rest to Johnson.

Johnson took possession of the land when the contract was signed. Before his first payment was due, Moses Bros. sought an injunction barring him from cutting timber on the land, "except for repairs, fences, and other necessary purposes." A temporary restraining order was granted, but it was dissolved on Johnson's motion. This ruling was reversed on appeal. Moses v. Johnson, 88 Ala. 517, 7 So. 146 (1890).

When a vendor of real estate enters into an executory agreement to convey title on the payment of the purchase-money, he sustains, in substance, the same relation to the vendee, as a mortgagee does to a mortgagor. Each has a legal title, which, in the absence of stipulations for possession, will maintain an action of ejectment. Each can retain his legal title against the other party, until the purchase-money, or mortgage debt is paid unless he permits the other to remain in undisturbed possession for twenty years. And yet each is at last but a trustee of the legal title for the mortgagee or vendee, if the purchase-money, or mortgage debt, as the case may be, is paid, or seasonably tendered. The same mutual rights and remedies, legal and equitable, and the same limitation to the right of recovery, obtain in the one relation and in the other.

. . . .

In King v. Smith, 2 Har. 239, 24 Eng.Ch.Rep. 239 it was said to be an established rule, "that if the security of the mortgagee is insufficient, and the court is satisfied of that fact, the mortgagor will not be allowed to do that which would directly impair the security—cut timber upon the mortgaged premises. . . . The cases decide, that a mortgagee out of possession is not, of course, entitled to an injunction to restrain the mortgagor from cutting timber on the mortgaged property. If the security is sufficient, the court will not grant an injunction merely because the mortgagor cuts, or threatens to cut timber. There must be a special case made out before the court will interfere. The difficulty is in determining what is meant by a 'sufficient security.' Suppose the mortgage debt, with all the expenses, to be £1,000, and the property to be worth £1,000, that is, in one sense, a sufficient security; but no mortgagee, who is well advised, would lend his money, unless the mortgaged property was worth one-third more than the amount lent at the time of the mortgage." This was considered the rule, and the only safe rule, under English values. In that country, land values were, in a measure, stationary. In this, they are fluctuating. To be a "sufficient security," with us, there should be a much broader margin between the amount of the debt and the estimated value of the property mortgaged for its security, than is considered sufficient in that older country.

. . . .

The bill charges, and the answer admits, that the land, which is the subject of this suit, is in value not exceeding the sum of the purchase-money that remains unpaid. The bill also charges that the defendant is insolvent. To this charge the answer interposes a general denial, but accompanies it with a statement [to the effect] that defendant's other property will pay his other debts; but we can not interpret it as affirming that it will pay any certain sum above his other debts. This leaves the land in controversy as the sole security for its promised purchase-money. . . .

It may be, as contended, that the right to clear the land, sell the timber, and put the land in cultivation, were inducements—controlling inducements—to enter into the purchase. They were not expressed as terms of the contract, and defendant failed to stipulate for any such privilege. Considering the proximity of the land to a market for the firewood—an averment not denied, but admitted—we feel forced to presume, as charged in the bill, that the land is more valuable with the timber on it, than if cleared and put in cultivation. Hence, we hold, that the averment to the effect that the value of the land would be enhanced by clearing it, is affirmative matter, the burden of proving which is on the defendant. We may state here, that injunction is the only relief prayed, and is the only proper relief in a case like the present one.

However it may be made to appear by proof, the pleadings do not make a case for a dissolution of the injunction; and the decretal order dissolving the injunction must be reversed, and the injunction reinstated.

4. RISK OF LOSS, COMPENSATION AND ABATEMENT

Skelly Oil Co. v. Ashmore

Supreme Court of Missouri, 1963.
365 S.W.2d 582.

[Skelly Oil Co. contracted to buy land from the Ashmores. A building on the land, which Skelly intended to demolish, was destroyed by fire before the closing date. The day after the fire, Skelly notified the Ashmores that the fire would have no effect on the deal; Skelly, in turn, learned that the Ashmores had insurance on the building. The Ashmores received $10,000 on the insurance policy. Skelly sought specific performance of the contract with a $10,000 abatement in the price. The trial court gave it this relief and the Ashmores appealed.]

■ HYDE, J. . . .

The contract of sale here involved contained no provision as to who assumed the risk of loss occasioned by a destruction of the building, or for protecting the building by insurance or for allocating any insurance proceeds received therefor. When the parties met to close the sale on April 16, the purchaser's counsel informed vendors and their attorney he was relying on Standard Oil Co. v. Dye, 223 Mo.App. 926, 20 S.W.2d 946, for purchaser's claim to the $10,000 insurance proceeds on the building. Purchaser made no claim to the $4,000 paid vendors for the loss of the furniture and fixtures. It is stated in 3 American Law of Property, § 11.30, p. 90, that in the circumstances here presented at least five different views have been advanced for allocating the burden of fortuitous loss between vendor and purchaser of real estate. We summarize those mentioned: (1) The view first enunciated in Paine v. Meller (Ch. 1801, 6 Ves.Jr. 349, 31 Eng.Reprint 1088) is said to be the most widely accepted; holding that from the time of the contract of sale of real estate the burden of fortuitous loss was on the purchaser even though the vendor retained possession. (2) The loss is on the vendor until legal title is conveyed, although the purchaser is in possession, stated to be a strong minority. (3) The burden of loss should be on the vendor until the time agreed upon for conveying the legal title, and thereafter on the purchaser unless the vendor be in such default as to preclude specific performance, not recognized in the decisions. (4) The burden of the loss should be on the party in possession, whether vendor or purchaser, so considered by some courts. (5) The burden of loss should be on the vendor unless there is something in the contract or in the relation of the parties from which the court can infer a different intention, stating "this rather vague test" has not received any avowed judicial acceptance, although it is not inconsistent with jurisdictions holding the loss is on the vendor until conveyance or jurisdictions adopting the possession test. . . .

We do not agree that we should adopt the arbitrary rule of Paine v. Meller and Standard Oil Co. v. Dye, that there is equitable conversion from the time of making a contract for sale and purchase of land and that the risk of loss from destruction of buildings or other substantial part of the property is from that moment on the purchaser. Criticisms of this rule by eminent authorities have been set out in the dissenting opinion of Storckman, J., herein and will not be repeated here.

We take the view stated in an article on Equitable Conversion by Contract, 13 Columbia Law Review 369, 386, Dean Harlan F. Stone, later Chief Justice Stone, in which he points out that the only reason why a contract for the sale of land by the owner to another operates to effect conversion is that a court of equity will compel him specifically to perform his contract. He further states: "A preliminary to the determination of the question whether there is equitable ownership of land must therefore necessarily be the determination of the question whether there is a contract which can be and ought to be specifically performed *at the very time when the court is called upon to perform it*. This process of reasoning is, however, reversed in those jurisdictions where the "burden of loss" is cast upon the vendee. The question is whether there shall be a specific performance of the contract, thus casting the burden on the vendee, by compelling him to pay the full purchase price for the subject matter of the contract, a substantial part of which has been destroyed. The question is answered somewhat in this wise: equitable ownership of the vendee in the subject matter of the contract can exist only where the contract is one which equity will specifically perform. The vendee of land is equitably entitled to land, therefore the vendee may be compelled to perform, although the vendor is unable to give in return the performance stipulated for by his contract. The *non sequitur* involved in the proposition that performance may be had because of the equitable ownership of the land by the vendee, which in turn depends upon the right of performance, is evident. The doctrine of equitable conversion, so far as it is exemplified by the authorities hitherto considered, cannot lead to the result of casting the burden of loss on the vendee, since the *conversion depends upon the question whether the contract should in equity be performed*. In all other cases where the vendee is

plaintiff → seller

treated as the equitable owner of the land, it is only because the contract is one which equity first determines should be specifically performed.

"Whether a plaintiff, in breach of his contract by a default which goes to the essence, as in the case of the destruction of a substantial part of the subject matter of the contract, should be entitled to specific performance, is a question which is answered in the negative in every case except that of destruction of the subject matter of the contract. To give a plaintiff specific performance of the contract when he is unable to perform the contract on his own part, violates the fundamental rule of equity that … *equity will not compel a defendant to perform when it is unable to so frame its decree as to compel the plaintiff to give in return substantially what he has undertaken to give* or to do for the defendant.

"The rule of casting the 'burden of loss' on the vendee by specific performance if justifiable at all can only be explained and justified upon one of two theories: first, that since equity has for most purposes treated the vendee as the equitable owner, it should do so for all purposes, although *this ignores the fact that in all other cases the vendee is so treated only because the contract is either being performed or in equity ought to be performed;* or, second, which is substantially the same proposition in a different form, the specific performance which casts the burden on the vendee is an incident to and a consequence of an equitable conversion, whereas in all other equity relations growing out of the contract, the equitable conversion, if it exists, is an incident to and consequence of, a specific performance. Certainly nothing could be more illogical than this process of reasoning." (Emphasis ours.)

For these reasons, we do not agree with the rule that arbitrarily places the risk of loss on the vendee from the time the contract is made. Instead we believe the Massachusetts rule is the proper rule. It is thus stated in Libman v. Levenson, 236 Mass. 221, 128 N.E. 13, 22 A.L.R. 560: When "the conveyance is to be made of the whole estate, including both land and buildings, for an entire price, and the value of the buildings constitutes a large part of the total value of the estate, and the terms of the agreement show that they constituted an important part of the subject matter of the contract … the contract is to be construed as subject to the implied condition that it no longer shall be binding if, before the time for the conveyance to be made, the buildings are destroyed by fire. The loss by the fire falls upon the vendor, the owner; and if he has not protected himself by insurance, he can have no reimbursement of this loss; but the contract is no longer binding upon either party. If the purchaser has advanced any part of the price, he can recover it back. If the change in the value of the estate is not so great, or if it appears that the buildings did not constitute so material a part of the estate to be conveyed as to result in an annulling of the contract, specific performance may be decreed, *with compensation for any breach of agreement,* or relief may be given in damages." (Emphasis ours.) … The reason for the Massachusetts rule is that specific performance is based on what is equitable; and it is not equitable to make a vendee pay the vendor for something the vendor cannot give him.

However, the issue in this case is not whether the vendee can be compelled to take the property without the building but whether the vendee is entitled to enforce the contract of sale, with the insurance proceeds substituted for the destroyed building. We see no inequity to defendants in such enforcement since they will receive the full amount ($20,000.00) for which they contracted to sell the property. Their contract not only described the land but also specifically stated they sold it "together with the buildings, driveways and all construction thereon." While the words "Service Station Site" appeared in the caption of the option contract and that no doubt was the ultimate use plaintiff intended to make of the land, the final agreement made by the parties was that plaintiff would take it subject to a lease of the building which would have brought plaintiff about $6,150.00 in rent during the term of the lease. Moreover, defendants' own evidence showed the building was valued in the insurance adjustment at $16,716.00 from which $4,179.00 was deducted for depreciation, making the loss $12,537.00. Therefore, defendants are not in a very good position to say the building was of no value to plaintiff. Furthermore, plaintiff having contracted for the land with the building on it, the decision concerning use or removal of the building, or even for resale of the entire property, was for the plaintiff to make. Statements were in evidence about the use of the building and its value to plaintiff made by its employee who negotiated the purchase but he was not one of plaintiff's chief executive officers nor possessed of authority to bind its board of directors. The short of the matter is that defendants will get all they bargained for; but without the building or its value plaintiff will not.

We therefore affirm the judgment and decree of the trial court.

Eager, Leedy and Hollingsworth, JJ., concur.

Westhues, C.J., and Dalton, J., dissent and concur in separate dissenting opinion of Storckman, J.

Storckman, Judge (dissenting). . . .

The evidence is convincing that Skelly Oil Company was buying the lot as a site for a service station and that in so using it they not only wanted the Jones's lease terminated but intended to tear down and remove the building in question. . . .

. . . .

The claim of neither party is particularly compelling insofar as specific performance in this case is concerned. The destruction of the building by fire, its insurance, and the disposition of the insurance proceeds were matters not contemplated by the parties and not provided for in the purchase contract documents. Skelly's representative did not know that Mr. Ashmore carried insurance on the building until after the fire, and he then told Mr. Ashmore that despite the fire the deal would be closed on the agreed date. Skelly's present claims are an afterthought inconsistent with its conduct throughout the negotiations and prior to the closing date.

In short, as to both Skelly and the Ashmores, the destruction of the insured building was a fortuitous circumstance supplying the opportunity to rid the property of a vexatious lease, to dispose of the building, and at the same time resulting in a windfall of $10,000. And the problem, in fact the only seriously contested issue between the parties, is which of them is to have the advantage of this piece of good fortune. Skelly contracted to pay

$20,000 for the property. If it is awarded the $10,000 windfall, it will receive a $20,000 lot for $10,000. If the Ashmores retain the $10,000, they will in fact have realized $30,000 for a piece of property they have agreed to sell for $20,000.

In claiming the proceeds of the Ashmores' fire insurance policy, Skelly did not contend that the value of the real estate as a service station site had decreased. After learning of the fire and the existence of the insurance policy, Skelly's counsel did some research and, as he announced when the parties met in Joplin to close the deal, Skelly was relying on a case he had found, Standard Oil Company v. Dye, 223 Mo.App. 926, 20 S.W.2d 946. And in its basic facts the case, admittedly, is quite similar to this one although there were no attendant circumstances such as we have in the present case.... The doctrine [relied on in *Dye*], laboriously evolved from Paine v. Meller, (1801) 6 Ves.Jr. 349, 31 Eng.Reprint 1088, is "that a contract to sell real property vests the equitable ownership of the property in the purchaser, with the corollary that any loss by destruction of the property through casualty during the pendency of the contract must be borne by the purchaser." Annotation 27 A.L.R.2d 444, 446. The two-fold rationale of this doctrine is a maxim that "equity regards as done that which should have been done," from which it is said the "vendor becomes a mere trustee, holding the legal title for the benefit of the purchaser or as security for the price." 27 A.L.R.2d 444, 448, 449. All of the experts and scholars seem to agree that this doctrine and its rationale is misplaced if not unsound. To illustrate see only 4 Williston, Contracts, §§ 928–943B, pp. 2605–2639. As to the maxim, Williston said, "Only the hoary age and frequent repetition of the maxim prevents a general recognition of its absurdity." 4 Williston, Contracts, § 929, p. 2607. As to the corollary, Williston points out that while the purchaser may have an interest in the property, it is equally clear that the vendor likewise has an interest, and as for the vendor's being a trustee for the purchaser observes, "However often the words may be repeated, it cannot be true that the vendor is trustee for the purchaser." 4 Williston, Contracts, § 936, p. 2622.

Nevertheless, adapting this doctrine and following a majority opinion in another English case, Rayner v. Preston, (1881) L.R. 18 Ch.Div. 1 (CA), the rule as stated in the Dye case has evolved: "Where the purchaser as equitable owner will bear the loss occasioned by a destruction of the property pending completion of the sale, and the contract is silent as to insurance, the rule quite generally followed is that the proceeds of the vendor's insurance policies, even though the purchaser did not contribute to their maintenance, constitute a trust fund for the benefit of the purchaser to be credited on the purchase price of the destroyed property, the theory being that the vendor is a trustee of the property for the purchaser." Annotation 64 A.L.R.2d 1402, 1406. Many jurisdictions have modified or do not follow this doctrine, some take the view that the vendor's insurance policy is personal to him, and Parliament has enacted a statute which entirely changes the English rule. 4 Mo.L.R. 290, 296. The rule is not as general as the annotator indicated, and as with the rule upon which it is founded, all the experts agree that it is unsound, their only point of disagreement is as to what the rule should be....

Professor Williston was of the view that the risk of loss should follow possession (4 Williston, Contracts, §§ 940, 942), and that view has been written into the Uniform Vendor and Purchaser Risk Act. 9C U.L.A., p. 314 and 1960 Supp., p. 82. Eight states have adopted that act and four of those, California, New York, South Dakota, and Oregon, are listed among the fifteen jurisdictions said by the A.L.R. annotator (64 A.L.R. 1406) to follow the Dye case. . . .

Vance is of the opinion that a rule of "business usage" should be adopted, but he ruefully adds, "Here we have another instance in which business usage substitutes the insurance money for the insured property, despite the general rule that the two are not legally connected; and, as usual, the courts are sluggishly following business." Vance, Insurance, § 131, p. 781. Dean Pound assails Vance's contention that the insurance money is any part of the thing bargained for and he also vigorously attacks the theory that the vendor is a trustee for the vendee.

Professor Vanneman has pointed out that the basic problem in all these cases is, "should there be a decree for specific performance at all?" He is of the view that the important and controlling factor should be the intention of the parties. If the building was a material part of the transaction, the vendor intending to sell and the vendee intending to buy "land with a building upon it," the vendee should have the benefit of the insurance. . . . This view has the merit of avoiding resort to the legal fictions of equitable ownership and trusteeship.

A similar approach to this troublesome question was espoused by Dean Harlan F. Stone in his article entitled, "Equitable Conversion by Contract", 13 Columbia Law Review 369, 386, wherein he stated: "A preliminary to the determination of the question whether there is equitable ownership of land must therefore necessarily be the determination of the question whether there is a contract which can be and ought to be specifically performed at the very time when the court is called upon to perform it."

Automatic application of the doctrine that "equity regards that as done which ought to be done", in the circumstances of this case, begs the question of *what ought to be done*. Because the insurance proceeds may be a windfall to those legally entitled does not necessarily mean that justice will be accomplished by transferring them elsewhere. The substance of the purchase contract and the use to which the property is to be put must be considered. A resort to equity should involve a consideration of other equitable principles or maxims such as the equally important maxims that "equity follows the law" and "between equal equities the law will prevail".

A valid legal excuse is a sufficient reason for refusal of specific performance. . . . Destruction of a particular thing upon which the contract depends is generally regarded as a legal excuse for nonperformance. . . .

. . . .

If plaintiff's contention is that there has been a substantial failure or impairment of the consideration of the contract by reason of the destruction of the building, then I do not think that the Ashmores should be entitled to specific performance, and because of the theory of mutuality it would seem that Skelly would not be entitled to specific performance unless it was willing to perform its legal obligations under the purchase contract as drawn. We would not be justified in making a new contract for the parties to cover the building insurance, and a court of equity will not decree specific performance of a contract that is incomplete, indefinite or uncertain. Nor can the courts supply an important element that has been omitted from the contract.

. . . .

But Skelly did not after the fire or in this action elect to abandon the contract although the Ashmores gave it the opportunity to do so rather than to sell at the reduced price. It is quite evident that Skelly has received one windfall as the result of the fire in that the lease is terminated and the site can be cleared at less cost. It has not shown itself to be entitled to another, the one now legally vested in the Ashmores. Ideally the purchase contract should be set aside so that the parties could negotiate a new one based on the property in its present condition. But the plaintiff by its election to take title has foreclosed this possibility.

. . . [T]he majority opinion, employs conflicting rules or theories. It purports to adopt one but applies another. It professes to repudiate the equitable conversion theory and to adopt unequivocally the Massachusetts rule, stating: "Instead we believe the Massachusetts rule is the proper rule." This rule as shown by the opinion's quotation from Libman v. Levenson, 236 Mass. 221, 128 N.E. 13, 22 A.L.R. 560, is that the sales contract will no longer be binding if the buildings are destroyed by fire and "the value of the buildings constitutes a large part of the total value of the estate, and the terms of the agreement show that they constituted an important part of the subject matter of the contract". In the same quotation from the Libman case, the circumstances and terms under which specific performance is granted are stated as follows: "If the change in the value of the estate is not so great, or if it appears that the buildings did not constitute so material a part of the estate to be conveyed as to result in an annulling of the contract, specific performance may be decreed, *with compensation for any breach of agreement, or relief may be given in damages.*" Emphasis added.

Obviously the majority opinion did not find that the value of the building constituted "a large part of the total value of the estate" or "an important part of the subject matter of the contract", else it would have declared the sales contract no longer binding under the Massachusetts rule. What it had to find was that the value of the building was not so great or such a material part of the estate to be conveyed as to interfere with the decree of specific performance.

But at this point the majority opinion abandons any pretense of following the Massachusetts rule and switches back to the equitable conversion theory and awards the insurance proceeds as such to the vendee without a determination of compensation for breach or relief to be given in damages. The value of the building for insurance purposes or as a structure to house a retail store is not necessarily the proper measure of the compensation or damages to which the plaintiff is entitled. It might be considerably less than such a figure if Skelly intended to remove the building as soon as it had the legal right to do so. Obviously the Massachusetts rule is not tied in with insurance at all and that is as it should be. Logically the majority opinion should have remanded the case for a determination of the amount of actual damages suffered by Skelly or the compensation to which it is entitled if it still wants specific performance. This is undoubtedly what the Massachusetts rule contemplates. I would find no fault with such a procedure.

. . . .

On the present record the plaintiff has failed to show a superior equity in the insurance proceeds under the Massachusetts rule or otherwise, and on well-established equitable principles I would leave the legal title to that fund where it is. I would . . . award [Skelly] specific performance . . . on the condition that it pay to the defendants the agreed purchase price of $20,000 less the amount of compensation or damages, if any, that it could establish against the defendants (not the insurance funds) at a plenary hearing of that issue in the trial court.

Dixon v. Salvation Army

Court of Appeal, Fourth District, 1983.
142 Cal.App.3d 463, 191 Cal.Rptr. 111.

■ COLOGNE, ACTING PRESIDING JUSTICE. The Salvation Army appeals an order granting Albert D. Dixon's motion for summary judgment in Dixon's action for declaratory relief.

. . . Dixon and the Salvation Army entered a real estate purchase and sale agreement. The Salvation Army agreed to sell to Dixon two parcels, described herein as "8th & K property" and "8th & J property." Both parcels were improved with commercial structures. The 8th & K property included a two-story office building and warehouse building and the 8th and J property included a three-story brick warehouse.

The parties opened an escrow, and the escrow instructions were later amended to reduce the sales price from $1,100,000 to $900,000 because the parties discovered the 8th & J property had certain structural deficiencies.

Before the escrow closed and before either title or possession passed from the Salvation Army to Dixon, one of the two buildings on the 8th & K property was destroyed by fire. The Salvation Army received $240,000 as fire insurance proceeds, but it became apparent during the negotiations following the fire that the destroyed building was significantly underinsured. The Salvation Army could not, of course, deliver the property in the "same general condition minus normal wear and tear as when inspected prior to opening of escrow" as the contract provided and the parties could not agree to a new price of the property as is. This litigation resulted.

Dixon sought and obtained a court declaration that "as a result of the destruction by fire of the improvements on the . . . '8th & K property,' the total purchase price to be paid . . . should be abated to reflect the loss—if any—of the proportionate value of the improvements on the 8th and K property to the total value of all of the property sold" under the agreement. The effect of this order was to authorize Dixon to seek specific enforcement of the contract at an abated price. This price was to be determined by the parties' negotiation or future litigation. The Salvation Army had requested a declaration that the contract should be rescinded or, alternatively, the contract could be enforced without an abatement of the sales price.

The Uniform Vendor and Purchaser Risk Act (Uniform Act) was adopted in California and codified as Civil Code section 1662. This statute provides:

"Any contract hereafter made in this State for the purchase and sale of real property shall be interpreted as including an agreement that the parties shall have the following rights and duties, unless the contract expressly provides otherwise:

"(a) If, when neither the legal title nor the possession of the subject matter of the contract has been transferred, all or a material part thereof is destroyed without fault of the purchaser or is taken by eminent domain, the vendor cannot enforce the contract, and the purchaser is entitled to recover any portion of the price that he has paid;

"(b) If, when either the legal title or the possession of the subject matter of the contract has been transferred, all or any part thereof is destroyed without fault of the vendor or is taken by eminent domain, the purchaser is not thereby relieved from a duty to pay the price, nor is he entitled to recover any portion thereof that he has paid.

"This section shall be so interpreted and construed as to effectuate its general purpose to make uniform the law of those states which enact it.

. . . ."

Since neither title nor possession had passed to Dixon, the provisions of subdivision (a) apply and the Salvation Army had the risk of loss. This rule prohibits the Salvation Army from enforcing the contract and permits Dixon to rescind and recover any consideration. The statute is silent, however, on whether Dixon can specifically enforce the contract with or without an abatement in price.

Of the other jurisdictions which have enacted the Uniform Act, New York appears to be the only one which has previously resolved whether the vendee may obtain specific enforcement of the contract at an abated purchase price.

In Rizzo v. Landmark Realty Corp. (1950) 277 App.Div.1094, 101 N.Y.S.2d 151, the court held the Uniform Act precludes a vendor from specifically enforcing a real estate sales contract when a material part of the subject property has been destroyed, but it does not destroy any common law rights of the purchaser to specific performance with abatement. . . .

In Lucenti v. Cayuga Apartments, Inc. (1977) 59 App.Div.2d 438, 400 N.Y.S.2d 194, the court discussed the New York modified version of the Uniform Act. Section 5–1311 of New York's General Obligations Law is in essence the Uniform Act but with the added provision that "if an immaterial part thereof is destroyed without fault of the purchaser or is taken by eminent domain, neither the vendor nor the purchaser is thereby deprived of the right to enforce the contract, but there shall be, to the extent of the destruction or taking, an abatement of the purchase price."

Thus, the New York Legislature has expressly provided for the situation where the vendor has the risk of loss and an immaterial part of the property is destroyed. In *Lucenti,* the court considered a similar situation except found the destruction to the subject property was material. Finding "no logical basis for distinguishing between a loss to a 'material' and an 'immaterial' portion of the premises," the court allowed the vendee to specifically enforce the contract at an abated price. It is clear the court was also applying the common law rule of New York (which permitted the vendee to enforce a contract at an abated purchase price), thus providing no assistance in interpreting the California statute. In applying the common law rule, the New York court recognized, but chose not to follow, the recommendation of the New York Law Revision Commission report of 1936 (the same year New York enacted the Uniform Act), which suggested rescission of the contract was the best remedy when a material part of the subject property was destroyed.

The long established rule in California, stemming from cases occurring after the San Francisco fire of 1906, differs from the common law of New York. In Potts Drug Co. v. Benedict (1909) 156 Cal. 322, at page 334, 104 P. 432, the court stated in dictum:

> "Where there is a mere agreement to sell, and title therefore has not passed, the loss falls on the vendor for the same reason. In such a case the vendor is excused from the performance of his contract under *the rule we have discussed* by reason of the destruction of the thing, but he cannot retain money already paid on account of the proposed purchase, or recover moneys remaining unpaid." (Italics added.)[4]

Thus, we hold where a material part of the subject property is destroyed without the fault of either party and neither title nor possession has passed to the purchaser, the vendor's performance is excused and the purchaser is entitled to the return of any consideration paid.

We believe the more equitable approach and one more compatible with the Uniform Act is to place the parties in their original position, free to make a new bargain. A rule that denies a vendor the ability to specifically enforce the sales agreement where the material part of the consideration is lost or destroyed calls out for the converse also to be applied. It would be grossly unfair to require either party to accept consideration less than the whole of what was bargained for under these circumstances. If it is unfair to force the purchaser to receive materially damaged property, it is equally

---

4. The rule the court discussed was: "Where from the nature of the contract it is evident that the parties contracted on the basis of the continued existence of the person or thing to which it relates, the subsequent perishing of the person or thing will excuse the performance. Thus where the contract relates to the use or possession or any dealing with specific things in which the perform- ance necessarily depends on the existence of the particular thing, the condition is implied by the law that the impossibility arising from the perishing or destruction of the thing, without default in the party, shall excuse performance, because from the nature of the contract, it is apparent that the parties contracted on the basis of the continued existence of the subject of the contract."

unfair to compel the vendor to accept a price substantially below what he bargained for.[5] Although a court in equity has broad powers, it should not use its jurisdiction to remake the contract for the parties, particularly on the critical term of the purchase price. This task is better left to the further negotiations of the parties, with neither compelled to strike an agreement. Specific performance with abatement of the purchase price is not an appropriate remedy for the purchaser.

Judgment reversed.

■ STANIFORTH, J., concurs.

■ WORK, J., dissenting.

I respectfully dissent:

Because I find the trial court's disposition properly places the risk of loss, especially on the facts of this case, I would affirm.

The majority opinion omits several significant portions of the dealings between these parties. As a result, it overlooks the equities of this specific transaction and ignores commercial reality.

First, an unusually lengthy escrow period (one year) was given at Salvation Army's request to accommodate its moving out. Seller retained title and possession until close of escrow.

The escrow agreement stated buyer was to evaluate the properties and allocate the purchase price between the buildings and property.

The fire occurred eight months after opening of escrow.

The property consisted of two contiguous parcels of real property in a desirable downtown San Diego location, one (8th and J) improved by a single structure (three-story warehouse) and the other (8th and K) containing two buildings (a warehouse and a two-story office building). Only the two-story office building was destroyed in the fire, leaving two parcels of real property and two buildings.

The allocation was made and the value was generally assessed at $700,000 for the 8th and K property and structures, and $200,000 for the 8th and J parcel and building.[6]

. . . .

. . . Clearly, a seller bears the risk of loss under the *Potts* analysis until title or possession passes. Civil Code section 1662, adopted after *Potts,* does not change this rule. Consistent with *Potts,* subparagraph (b) imposes the risk of loss upon a buyer when either legal title or possession of the subject property is transferred before destruction. Also, under subparagraph (a) where neither legal title nor possession has passed when all "or a material

---

5. We do not suggest by this opinion that the vendee could not enforce the sales agreement where the land alone is the major or material element of the bargain and the buildings an immaterial part of the consideration, because the statute upon which we rely speaks of a loss of the material part of the subject matter of the contract.

6. Before the purchase price was reduced from $1,100,000 to $900,000, the allocation for 8th and J was $400,000. It was reduced after determining structural changes to bring the J Street warehouse up to seismic code would be $550,000 and it was probably more economical to tear the building down and rebuild.

part" of the premises are destroyed through no fault of the buyer, the seller cannot force performance of the contract and the buyer may recover any prepaid portion of the purchase price.

Potts does refer, in passing, to the elementary rule of the law of sales, i.e., where the loss falls upon the seller because title has not passed, the seller is excused from performing the contract. However, *Potts* only discusses the complete destruction of property, talking in terms of impossibility of performance from the perishing of the person or thing.

The majority assume the loss of one of the three buildings on the two parcels of scarce downtown San Diego real estate materially destroyed the essence of the bargain. This ignores the commercial reality readily visible through our chambers windows. However, it is necessary to engage in this fiction to set aside the ruling of the trial court for, where there is an immaterial destruction and the vendor may enforce the contract against the vendee, the vendee is entitled to abatement.[7] . . .

Although the majority opinion states, a rule denying seller the right to specifically enforce a sales agreement where a material (but not immaterial) part of the consideration is lost or destroyed calls out for the converse to be true, this statement lacks foundation. Nor is it relevant, in the context of our fact situation, whether the abatement requested is related to a material or immaterial part of the consideration. The reason a buyer is entitled to abatement for immaterial diminutions of the value of the consideration is because the seller, both statutorily and by common law, may enforce the contract over the buyer's objections. Certainly, if the seller could force the buyer to perform where there is a material part, but less than all, of the consideration destroyed, then an abatement for the reduction of the total value of the contract based upon the destruction of that material part would be equally required. Where the risk of loss remains with the seller, neither an immaterial *or* material loss should bar the buyer from purchasing the remainder at an abated price.

If the risk is foreseeable, a commercial practice by which a party might be expected to insure himself against a risk militates against shifting it to the other party.

Here, the risk of fire was foreseen by seller and specifically insured against. It is only the probability the coverage was inadequate which smarts. It is equitable to place this consciously self-assumed risk upon the seller who was allowed to remain in possession for one year at its own request to obtain benefits it desired.

The majority also make much ado of the fact the destroyed building was underinsured. Whether the building was fully insured, underinsured or completely uninsured is not relevant to the issues involved. It relates only to whether there is in fact an economic loss to seller.

Under the majority analysis, buyer is denied his right to specifically enforce even those land contracts where adequate insurance coverage would give seller its entire contract price, or even more.

---

7. In total context, the buyer claims the loss of one building does not materially destroy the essence of this bargain. The trial court found in his favor, and buyer's position is commercially realistic.

If we adhere to the concept that real property is unique and such sales may be specifically enforced, the destruction of one or all structures placed upon a piece of land should not prevent a buyer from electing to specifically enforce a sale even though the sale originally contemplated the land in its improved state. The policy reasons for denying a seller the right to force a materially different package upon an unwilling buyer are far different than those permitting an originally willing seller to refuse to specifically perform a contract to convey real property to the extent the property still exists when enforcement is requested. The majority does not quarrel with the harshness of the rule which forces a buyer in the *Potts* case to pay full value for a leasehold interest which has been totally destroyed before possession was even turned over to him on a rule the risk of loss passed when paper title was transferred. Why it is so solicitous of concern for hardships which are only imaginary and which the statute, and common law, properly impose upon sellers retaining both title and legal possession when the risk is realized, is beyond me. If the agreement was to sell two parcels of unimproved property for a total of $1,000,000, and one parcel was condemned by the State before title or possession passed, what unfairness is there in permitting the buyer to specifically enforce that portion of the contract regarding the other parcel and, if the parties cannot agree on the proper abatement of the price, to have it determined judicially? (See Skelly Oil Co. v. Ashmore (Mo.) 365 S.W.2d 582, 589.) I find no substantive difference here.

NOTES

1. Section 2–406(b) of the Uniform Land Transactions Act provides as follows:

> (b) ... In case of a casualty loss or taking by eminent domain while the risk is on the seller:
>
> (1) if the loss or taking results in a substantial failure of the real estate to conform to the contract, the buyer may cancel the contract and recover any portion of the price he has paid, or accept the real estate with his choice of (i) a reduction of the contract price equal to the decrease in fair market value caused by the loss or taking, or (ii) the benefit of the seller's insurance coverage or the eminent domain payment for the loss or taking, but without further right against the seller; or
>
> (2) if the real estate substantially conforms to the contract after the loss or taking, the buyer must accept the real estate, but is entitled to his choice of (i) a reduction of the contract price equal to the decrease in fair market value caused by the loss or taking or (ii) the benefit of the seller's insurance coverage or the eminent domain payment with respect to the loss or taking but without further right against the seller.

2. Rudd agreed to buy Lascelles' land for £3500. As Rudd knew, Lascelles had inherited the property from her husband and knew virtually nothing about her rights thereto. Hence, "[t]here was no representation as to the title the defendant could make to the property nor as to the nature

of her interest, nor any provision for compensation for defects." When he learned of restrictive covenants which significantly reduced the value of the land, Rudd sought specific performance of the contract at a price of £2500. The bill was dismissed. Rudd v. Lascelles, 1 Ch. 815 (1900).

In my opinion the jurisdiction to enforce specific performance with compensation on a vendor, where the contract is silent as to compensation, rests on the equitable estoppel referred to in Mortlock v. Buller, 10 Ves. 292, 315, namely, that a vendor representing and contracting to sell an estate as his own cannot afterwards be heard to say he has not the entirety. It probably first arose in cases of small deficiency in the quantity of the land sold, e.g., if a vendor contracted to sell 100 acres and only had 90 acres, he could not resist specific performance on the ground that the contract was to sell 100 acres. This cy-près execution was a purely equitable remedy.... In the present case there is obviously no direct representation of that kind, and though a mere offer to sell real property prima facie implies that the vendor has the unincumbered fee simple therein, still, if the purchaser, as in this case, knows that the vendor is ignorant as to the title, he cannot set up any such implication as a representation inducing the contract. The present case, therefore, does not come within the above category.

. . . .

Further, the compensation could not be fairly ascertained. If I am to make a new contract for the parties, I must see that it is at a fair price; but I do not ascertain this if I merely find out what would be the value of the property if it were subject to no restrictions, and how much less it is worth because of the restrictions. It would be necessary to find out further what the purchaser would have given and what the vendor would have taken for it under the altered conditions. Now, according to the plaintiff's own shewing, he has lost a resale at an advance of 1000*l.*, and, as he put the compensation at 1000*l.*, it looks as if he had contracted to give the right price for the property as it stands. How then can I assume that the purchaser would not still give 3500*l.?* I must not make any bargain that might be unjust to either party. The proposed new bargain would be extremely hard on the vendor. She sells on the basis of income, and she has contracted to sell property producing 125*l.* a year for 3500*l.*, and if the purchaser is right, she is to lose about one-third of the purchase-money. It would be a great hardship to enforce the contract against her with so large an abatement in respect of covenants which do not affect her enjoyment, and I cannot assume that she would have sold for such a reduced sum. . . .

3.   Radel contracted to buy land which the seller incorrectly told him brought in a particular rent. When Radel discovered the error, he sought specific performance of the contract at a lower price. However, he alleged neither that the seller knew that its claim regarding the rent was mistaken nor that he relied upon the false statement. Radel prevailed in the trial court, but, by a vote of 2–1, the appellate court ordered the complaint dismissed with leave to amend. Radel v. One Hundred Thirty–Four West

Twenty–Fifth Street Building Corp., 222 A.D. 617, 226 N.Y.S. 560 (1928). The majority stated:

> We do not believe that the doctrine of specific performance with abatement should be extended to cover defects other than deficiencies in title or in the area of the land to be conveyed. In Rutherford v. Acton–Adams (L.R. [1915] A.C. 866, 870) Viscount Haldane said that the purchaser "may elect to take all he can get, and to have a proportionate abatement from the purchase-money. But this right applies only to a deficiency in the subject-matter described in the contract. It does not apply to a claim to make good a representation about the subject-matter made not in the contract but collaterally to it. In the latter case the remedy is rescission, or a claim for damages for deceit where there has been fraud, or for breach of a collateral contract if there has been such a contract."

> In effect the plaintiff here, by way of diminution of price, seeks damages for false representations, which he could not get in an action at law, since he has failed to allege scienter and reliance. Without scienter he could at most secure rescission. He cannot accomplish in equity by indirection what he could not accomplish in an action at law. Nor does the circumstance that he has already conveyed his own land to the defendant change the legal situation. If he requires and is entitled to equitable relief in respect to this conveyance, his remedy would be either to demand a reconveyance to himself as on a rescission, or, if that were impossible, to declare a vendee's lien for the value of the property conveyed by him upon the property of the defendant.

The dissenter thought *Rutherford* inapposite and unwise.

> . . . Here the representation was not collateral to, but a part of the contract. Under present-day conditions when the value of property, particularly when bought for investment purposes, is based largely upon its income-producing power, equity should assume jurisdiction and decree specific performance with abatement in the circumstances here disclosed. Moreover, the action being by a vendee rather than a vendor, equity is more liberal in the exercise of its jurisdiction.

4.   Stringer agreed to sell Barnes a fee simple estate in land, but he had no such estate. As Barnes later learned, Stringer's wife had a remainder interest in the land, which she refused to release. Barnes sought specific performance of the contract and, in Barnes v. Wood, L.R. 8 Eq. 424 (Ch. 1869), the court ruled as follows:

> . . . The purchaser entered into his contract with the husband in total ignorance of the state of the title, and without any knowledge that the husband could only sell with the concurrence of his wife. The husband, therefore, is bound to convey all the interest that he has according to the principle of the authorities that have been cited, and the Court must endeavor to find out, in the best way it can, what compensation is to be made in respect of the interest which he is unable to convey. . . .

Billy Williams Builders & Developers, Inc. v. Hillerich

Court of Appeals of Kentucky, 1969.
446 S.W.2d 280.

■ HILL, J. Appellees (hereinafter Hillerich) sued appellant (hereinafter Williams) for specific performance of a contract to convey a house and a lot, for damages growing out of the defective construction of the house, and for damages due to delay in performance. Equity directed specific performance and transferred the case to the common law docket, where a jury later returned a verdict for appellees for $3318 in damages resulting from defective construction and for $910.38 in damages occasioned by delay in performance. Williams appeals.

Williams forcefully argues that: (1) Hillerich cannot have specific performance and damages; (2) Hillerich did not prove damages; (3) the verdict is excessive; (4) Hillerich judicially admitted a breach of contract, precluding recovery; (5) Hillerich first breached the contract by failure to make a down payment; and (6) the court erred in directing a verdict for Hillerich on Williams' counterclaim.

The main thrust of Williams' argument concerns the right of the buyer to have two remedies (1) specific performance of a contract to purchase real estate (a house and a lot) and (2) damages for defective construction and for delay in performance. Williams argues that by complying with the judgment for specific performance and by accepting the deed to the property, Hillerich elected to have one of two inconsistent remedies; and by so doing, he cannot back up to the "forks of the road" and take a road different from the one on which he "first embarked."

In a proper case there can be little doubt that one may be entitled to the specific performance of a contract to purchase real estate and damages for delay in performance. But damages for deficiency of quantity or quality present a more complex question, on which there is some conflict among the authorities. We look to the writings of text writers and then to the recorded opinions here and elsewhere for guidance.

First we note comments by text writers.

In Restatement of the Law, volume 2, Contracts, § 365, at page 659, it is said:

> "Specific Enforcement in Part, With Compensation for the Remainder.

> "The fact that a part of the promised performance cannot be rendered, or is otherwise such that its specific enforcement would violate some of the rules stated in §§ 360–380, does not prevent the specific enforcement of the remainder, if in all other respects the requisites for specific enforcement of that remainder exist. Compensation for the partial breach that still remains may be awarded in the same proceeding, either as damages, restitution, or an abatement in price.

> . . . .

> "A contracts to transfer land to B and also to make certain repairs and to complete an unfinished building on the land. In case of repudia-

tion by A, B may be given a decree for specific performance, with an abatement in the price or other compensation sufficient in amount to enable him to make the repairs and complete the building himself."

We find in Thompson on Real Property, volume 8A, chapter 57, § 4482, at page 487, the remedies available to both vendor and purchaser clearly defined in this fashion:

> "Whether the vendor or purchaser is the plaintiff there are three alternatives presented when the vendor is able to give only a performance nonconforming in quantity, *quality* or value: (1) to refuse the remedy of specific performance; (2) to enforce the contract without any regard to the partial failure; (3) to decree a conveyance and allow the vendee an abatement from price equal to the value of the deficiency in the performance. If the vendor cannot convey the agreed quantity of the estate the vendee may have specific performance with pro tanto abatement of purchase price." (Emphasis ours.)

As will be seen from annotations in some of the authorities above cited, the state courts are not of one accord in following the rule announced above. They seldom are.

Up to now, it has been extremely difficult to determine the position of this court on the specific questions here discussed. . . .

It is recognized that specific performance is an equitable remedy devised to apply in cases where common law actions for damages were found inadequate to afford a full remedy. The doctrine, first adopted in England, met with formidable opposition, but it has survived. In fact, its scope has been enlarged down through the years.

We need to keep in mind that in the contract in question vendor (appellant) agreed to sell lot 102 and to construct a house according to "submitted plans and specifications." Not only did appellant agree to convey the lot and residence to be built, but he undertook to build the house according to the "plans and specifications."

Appellees argue that their purpose in entering into the contract was to obtain this particular property in this particular neighborhood due to aged relatives nearby; that they are entitled to specific performance notwithstanding appellant's breach of the contract to construct the house according to plans and specifications. . . .

This court decided in Preece v. Wolford, 196 Ky. 710, 246 S.W. 27, that vendee may have "specific performance as to such title as the vendor can furnish, and may also have a just abatement from the purchase money for the deficiency of title or quantity or *quality* of the estate." (Our emphasis.) We can see no reason for a distinction between a deficiency in quantity (short acreage or lack of title) and deficiency of quality (defective construction).

We conclude that appellees' remedies were not inconsistent so as to require an election of remedies and that the chancellor did not err in granting specific performance and directing that damages be ascertained by the common law division of the court.

Appellant's second and third points, that appellees did not prove damages and that the amount of the verdict is excessive, will be treated as one. . . .

On this item we conclude the evidence supported the verdict and that the amount is not excessive. In addition appellees introduced evidence of two architects that it would cost $4200 to $6000 to remedy the claimed defects in construction.

Concerning damages occasioned from delay in performance, appellee Hillerich testified to itemized damages amounting to $2638.44. The jury found $910.38 for appellees on this item. We do not find this part of the verdict excessive.

We also treat appellant's fourth and fifth points as one. They state that appellees "judicially" admitted a breach of contract, precluding recovery (failure to make a down payment), and that to make the down payment was a condition precedent to the right of the specific performance (appellees completely ignore this argument in their brief).

The contract stipulates that the consideration was as follows:

> . . . [T]he sum of twenty-one thousand dollars ($21000.00) payable as follows, $6300 down, balance of $14700 thru first mortgage, payable $110 per month, principal, interest, taxes, & insurance included, 30 years.

The contract did not provide specifically when the down payment was to be made. We think it implied it was to be made on delivery of the deed due to the following circumstances: Appellant never at any time during their negotiations, nor at the time the contract was signed, demanded the down payment; appellant did not object to the entry of decree of specific performance but accepted the full contract price and executed deed. Of course, it may be said that appellant did so pursuant to the decree and that his act in so doing was in obedience to the decree and was therefore involuntary, which is perhaps true. Appellants did not object to the instructions or offer any instruction for the jury. It should be pointed out, in fairness to appellant's present counsel, that during all the proceedings in the trial court appellant had counsel other than the one representing him on this appeal.

Appellant's final argument is that the trial court erred in directing a verdict for appellees on appellant's counterclaim.

The trial court, both the equity and the common law divisions, we think, correctly determined the issues favorable to appellees. Obviously the court could not find for appellees and for appellant both on their antagonistic contentions. We find this argument without merit.

The judgment is affirmed.

All concur.

B. CONTRACTS TO BUILD OR REPAIR

Lane v. Newdigate

Chancery, 1804.
10 Ves.Jun. 192, 32 Eng.Rep. 818.

The plaintiff was assignee of a lease, granted by the defendant, for the purpose of erecting mills and other buildings; with covenants for the supply of water from canals and reservoirs on the defendant's estates, reserving to the defendant the right of working and using his then or future collieries coal mines together with their buildings and machinery, either with regard to the supply of water, or other uses of the collieries, or any locks for the passage of his boats or otherwise: the liberties and privileges granted being, as expressed in the lease, intended to be subordinate to the use and enjoyment of the collieries: the defendant to have due regard to the mills, & c. and doing as little mischief as the nature of the case would admit.

The bill prayed, that the defendant may be decreed so to use and manage the waters of the canals as not to injure the plaintiff in the occupation of his manufactory; and, in particular, that he may be restrained from using the locks, and thereby drawing off the waters which would otherwise run to and supply the manufactory; and that he may be decreed to restore the cut for carrying the waste waters from the Arbury Canal to Kenilworth Pool, and to restore Kenilworth Stopgate and the banks of the canal to their former height; and also to repair such stop-gates, bridges, canals, and towing-paths, as were made previously to granting the lease; and that he may be decreed to make compensation for the injury sustained by their having been suffered to go out of repair; and that he may be decreed to remove the locks, which have been made since the lease, and to make compensation for the injury sustained by the said locks having been made so near the manufactory; thereby injuring the machinery; and, that he may be decreed to pay the plaintiff the expense he has been put to by working the steam engine, to supply the want of water.

THE LORD CHANCELLOR [LORD ELDON], upon the motion for the injunction, expressed a difficulty, whether it is according to the practice of the court to decree or order repairs to be done.

Mr. Romilly, in support of the injunction, said the repairs to be done in this case are in effect nothing more than was done in Robinson v. Lord Byron, 1 Bro.C.C. 588, viz. raising the damheads, so that the water shall not escape; as it will otherwise.

THE LORD CHANCELLOR. So, as to restoring the stop-gate, the same difficulty occurs. The question is, whether the court can specifically order that to be restored. I think I can direct it in terms that will have that effect. The injunction, I shall order, will create the necessity of restoring the stop-gate; and attention will be had to the manner in which he is to use these locks; and he will find it difficult, I apprehend, to avoid completely repairing these works.

The order pronounced was, that the defendant, his agents, & c., be restrained until farther order, from farther impeding, obstructing, or hindering, the plaintiff from navigating the canal for the necessary purposes of the mill, or from using and enjoying the demised premises, and the mills and buildings erected thereon, or the liberties and privileges, granted by the indenture of lease, & c., contrary to the covenant, by continuing to keep the said canals, or the banks, gates, locks, or works of the same respectively, out of good repair, order, or condition; and also from farther troubling, molesting, and preventing, the plaintiff, contrary to the covenant, in the use and enjoyment of the said mills and buildings, or the liberty, privilege, and power of drawing for the use of the said mill from the canals, & c., a sufficient quantity of water for the use and working of the said mill, by diverting, draining, or drawing off water; or preventing the same by the use of any lock or locks, erected by the defendant, from remaining and continuing in the said canals, or by continuing the removal of the stop-gate, mentioned in the pleadings in the action brought by the plaintiff, to have been erected; and by means of which the water could and would have been kept and retained in the said pool for the use of the mill; but nothing in this order is to extend, to diminish, lessen, hinder, or prejudice the working, using, or enjoying, by the defendant of his present and future collieries, either with regard to the supply of water for his fire engine, or other uses of the collieries, or of any locks to be erected for the passage of his boats, or otherwise: the defendant having due regard to the said mills, and doing as little damage thereto, as the nature of the case will admit.

Jones v. Parker

Supreme Judicial Court of Massachusetts, 1895.
163 Mass. 564, 40 N.E. 1044.

■ HOLMES, J. The case of Jones v. Parker is a bill in equity brought by a lessee upon a lease purporting to begin on September 1, 1893, and to demise part of a basement in a building not yet erected. The lessor "covenants to deliver possession of the same to the lessee upon completion of said building, and thereafter, during the term of this lease, reasonably to heat and light the demised premises." It is alleged that the building has been completed, but that the defendants refuse to complete the premises with apparatus sufficient to heat and light the same, and to deliver the same to the plaintiff. It also is alleged that the occupancy of the premises for the purpose contemplated in the lease was impossible without the construction in the premises of proper apparatus for heating and lighting them before delivery to the plaintiff. The prayer is for specific performance of the covenant quoted, and for damages. The defendant demurs.

It does not need argument to show that the covenant is valid. Whether it should be enforced specifically admits of more doubt, the questions being whether it is certain enough for that purpose and whether a decree for specific performance would not call on the court to do more than it is in the habit of undertaking. We are of opinion that specific performance should be decreed. With regard to the want of certainty of the covenant, if the plaintiff were left to an action at law, a jury would have to determine whether what was done amounted to a reasonable heating and lighting. A judge sitting without a jury would find no difficulty in deciding the same question. We do not doubt that an expert would find it as easy to frame a scheme for doing the work. The other question is practical rather than a matter of precedent. It fairly is to be supposed, in the present case, that the difference between the plaintiff and the defendants is only with regard to the necessity of some more or less elaborate apparatus for light and heat, a difference which lies within a narrow compass and which can be adjusted by the court. There is no universal rule that courts of equity never will enforce a contract which requires some building to be done. They have enforced such contracts from the earliest days to the present time.

Demurrer overruled.

City Stores Co. v. Ammerman

United States District Court, District of Columbia, 1967.
266 F.Supp. 766.

Channel Homes v. Grossman 795 F.2d 297 testable?

[A group of developers wanted to build a shopping center. In exchange for City Stores' help in getting the property rezoned, the developers promised to "give [it] the opportunity to become one of . . . [the] center's major tenants with rental and terms at least equal to that of any other major department store in the center." City Stores provided the sought-after assistance and the land was rezoned. However, the developers did not offer to lease space in the shopping center to City Stores. It responded by bringing an action for specific performance.]

Gasch, J. . . . [In Part I of this opinion, the court held that the parties had made a valid contract.]

II

Whether the option contract secured by plaintiff in this case is sufficiently definite to be the subject of a decree for specific performance is *Issue* quite another question, which does not concern the validity or existence of the contract but only the nature of the remedy available to plaintiff.

It is not contested by the plaintiff that if it were to accept a lease tendered by defendants in accordance with the contract, there would be numerous complex details left to be worked out. The crucial elements of rate of rental and the amount of space can readily be determined from the Hecht and Woodward & Lothrop leases. But some details of design, construction and price of the building to be occupied by plaintiff at Tyson's Corner would have to be agreed to by the parties, subject to further negotiation and tempered only by the promise of equal terms with other tenants. The question is whether a court of equity will grant specific *Issue* performance of a contract which has left such substantial terms open for future negotiation.

The defendants have cited a number of cases in support of their argument that a court of equity will not grant specific performance of a contract in which some terms are left for further negotiations by the parties, or which would require a great deal of supervision by the court. I have examined those cases cited which were decided in this jurisdiction, because unless the precedents here establish a clear policy one way or the other, this court may exercise its discretion in fashioning an equitable decree. Moreover, this is an area of law in which not all jurisdictions are in agreement, and whichever way this court were to decide the case, there would be cases holding to the contrary in other parts of the country.

. . . .

Thus, defendants have cited no cases in this jurisdiction that would support the contention that an option contract involving further negotiations on details and construction of a building may not be specifically enforced.

On the other hand, the 1926 case of Morris v. Ballard, 56 App.D.C. 383, 16 F.2d 175, 49 A.L.R. 1461, held that an option to purchase property which contained a provision as to price "on terms to be agreed upon" was specifically enforceable by a court of equity. The court in that case held that "it became the duty of defendant, upon proper demand, either to accept the agreed purchase price in cash or to specify such terms as were acceptable to him. He had no right to refuse arbitrarily and unconditionally to accept payment solely for the purpose of defeating the option. Such a refusal would operate as a fraud upon the plaintiff." The court further held that the clause "on terms to be agreed upon"

> *"was in good conscience a stipulation that he would in fact agree with plaintiff upon reasonable terms of payment, and would not arbitrarily refuse to proceed with the sale. . . ."* [Emphasis added.]

The court also quoted Pomeroy, Specific Performance § 145 to the following effect:

> "when a contract has been partly performed by the plaintiff, and the defendant has received and enjoys the benefits thereof, and the plaintiff would be virtually remediless unless the contract were enforced, the court, from the plainest considerations of equity and common justice, does not regard with favor any objections raised by the defendant merely on the ground of the incompleteness or uncertainty of the agreement."

I therefore hold as a matter of law that the mere fact that a contract, definite in material respects, contains some terms which are subject to further negotiation between plaintiff and defendant will not bar a decree for specific performance, if in the court's discretion specific performance should be granted. . . .

The question whether a contract which also calls for construction of a building can or should be specifically enforced apparently never has been decided before in this jurisdiction.[3] The parties have cited no cases on this point.

---

3. Virginia has allowed specific performance of building contracts. See Grubb v. Sharkey, 90 Va. 831, 20 S.E. 784 (1894), where the Supreme Court of Appeals of Virginia said:

> "[A] court of equity has jurisdiction to enforce specific performance of a con-

At the outset, it should be noted that where specific performance of such contracts has been granted the essential criterion has not been the nature or subject of the contract, but rather the inadequacy or impracticability of legal remedies.... It is apparent from the nature of the contract involved in this case that even were it possible to arrive at a precise measure of damages for breach of a contract to lease a store in a shopping center for a long period of years—which it is not—money damages would in no way compensate the plaintiff for loss of the right to participate in the shopping center enterprise and for the almost incalculable future advantages that might accrue to it as a result of extending its operations into the suburbs. Therefore, I hold that the appropriate remedy in this case is specific performance.

Some jurisdictions in the United States have opposed granting specific performance of contracts for construction of buildings and other contracts requiring extensive supervision of the court, but the better view, and the one which increasingly is being followed in this country, is that such contracts should be specifically enforced unless the difficulties of supervision outweigh the importance of specific performance to the plaintiff. This is particularly true where the construction is to be done on land controlled by the defendant, because in that circumstance the plaintiff cannot employ another contractor to do the construction for him at defendant's expense. In the case at bar, the fact that more than mere construction of a building is involved reinforces the need for specific enforcement of the defendants' duty to perform their entire contractual obligation to the plaintiff.

. . . .

Joy v. City of St. Louis, 138 U.S. 1, 11 S.Ct. 243, 34 L.Ed. 843 (1891), is the leading Supreme Court case on specific performance of contracts where the relations between the parties were of a complex nature and might require continuous supervision by the court granting the decree. The Court said on this point:

> "In the present case, it is urged that the court will be called upon to determine from time to time what are reasonable regulations to be made by the Wabash Company for the running of trains upon its tracks by the Colorado Company. But this is no more than a court of equity is called upon to do whenever it takes charge of the running of a railroad by means of a receiver. Irrespectively of this, the decree is complete in itself, and disposes of the controversy; and it is not unusual for a court of equity to take supplemental proceedings to carry out its decree, and make it effective under altered circumstances."

. . . .

The defendants contend that the granting of specific performance in this case will confront the court with insuperable difficulties of supervision, but after reviewing the evidence, I am satisfied that the standards to be

tract by a defendant to do defined work upon his own property, in the performance of which the plaintiff has a material interest, and which is not capable of adequate compensation in damages; as, for example, an agreement on the part of a railway company to make an archway under its tracks, or to construct a siding at a particular point for the convenience of an adjoining landowner."

observed in construction of the plaintiff's store are set out in the Hecht and Woodward & Lothrop leases with sufficient particularity (Plaintiff's Ex. F) as to make design and approval of plaintiff's store a fairly simple matter, if the parties deal with each other in good faith and expeditiously, as I shall hereafter order.

For example, Article VIII, Sec. 8.1, Paragraph (G) of the Hecht lease (the Woodward & Lothrop lease contains a similar provision) says:

> "The quality of (i) the construction, (ii) the construction components, (iii) the decorative elements (including landscaping irrigation systems for the landscaping) and (iv) the furnishings; and the general architectural character and general design, the materials selection, the decor and the treatment values, approach and standards of the Enclosed Mall shall be comparable, at minimum, to the qualities, values, approaches and standards as of the date hereof of the enclosed mall at Topanga Plaza Shopping Center, Los Angeles, California. * * * "

The existing leases contain further detailed specifications which will be identical to those in the lease granted to plaintiff. The site for plaintiff's store has already been settled by the design of the center. Although the exact design of plaintiff's store will not be identical to the design of any other store, it must be remembered that all of the stores are to be part of the same center and subject to its overall design requirements. If the parties are not in good faith able to reach an agreement on certain details, the court will appoint a special master to help settle their differences, unless they prefer voluntarily to submit their disagreements to arbitration.

. . . .

During the course of this proceeding, the plaintiff has examined the leases executed between defendants and Hecht and Woodward & Lothrop and has indicated its willingness to accept a lease with terms equal to the Hecht lease. I therefore find that the plaintiff has exercised its option, and is entitled to specific performance of a lease on terms equal to those contained in the Hecht lease.

NOTES

1. In Kearns–Gorsuch Bottle Co. v. Hartford–Fairmont Co., 1 F.2d 318 (S.D.N.Y.1921) the court made these observations:

> The tendency of the times is to "take on" harder and longer jobs. . . . As a judge of first instance I would not nowadays hesitate to undertake any business enterprise for which, with the support of competent receivers, I thought a reasonably intelligent judge reasonably fit. Yet it might easily be that most appellate courts would still reverse that discretionary order. But the reversal could only logically or lawfully rest on an ascertained abuse of discretion; the error would be in degree, not kind.

2. Consider also Rule 70, Fed.R.Civ.P., which provides, in pertinent part:

> If a judgment directs a party to execute a conveyance of land or to deliver deeds or other documents or to perform any other specific act and the party fails to comply within the time specified, the court may

direct the act to be done at the cost of the disobedient party by some other person appointed by the court and the act when so done has like effect as if done by the party. . . .

————

C.   CONTRACTS FOR PERSONAL SERVICES

De Rivafinoli v. Corsetti

Court of Chancery of New York, 1833.
4 Paige 264.

[handwritten margin note: Personal service (k) — courts do not like to grant specific performance.]

This case came before the chancellor on an order for the complainant to show cause why a ne exeat a writ forbidding a person from entering the country or jurisdiction of the court granted against the defendant should not be discharged, or the amount for which the defendant was held to bail reduced. The bill, which was filed in September, 1833, stated that the defendant, in the March preceding, had agreed with the complainant, as manager of the Italian theatre in the City of New–York, to sing, gesticulate and recite, in the capacity of *primo basso,* in all the operas, serious, semi-serious and comic, farces, oratorios, concerts, cantatas and benefits, which should be ordered by the complainant, or his authorized agents, in any city of the United States, where the complainant should think proper; and that he should be present at the times which should be appointed for rehearsals, and contribute to the interest and good conduct of the enterprise, submitting himself to the regulations made by the complainant, and to the fines in such regulations established, for the term of eight months, commencing on the first of November, 1833. For which singing, gesticulating, reciting, etc. the complainant agreed to pay him $1192, in sixteen half monthly payments; each payment to be made in advance, at the commencement of the half month for which the same was to be paid; and to allow the defendant one benefit, he bearing half the expense thereof. And that the defendant also agreed not to make use of his talents in any other theatre, or public hall, without the permission of the complainant, or his agents. For the performance of which agreement each party bound himself to the other, under the penalty of a fine of one third of the salary of the defendant; which fine was to be paid by the party in default, without objection, or exception. The bill further alleged that the complainant had entered into a contract with the trustees of the Italian opera house, in New–York, under heavy penalties, to commence the performance of Italian operas, with a first rate company, on the first of November, 1833; and that he had engaged the defendant as one of such company, and had gone to Europe to procure others to make up a troupe, complete in all its departments. That the defendant was a skilful musician, and was well qualified to sing, perform and exhibit Italian operas, in the capacity in which he had been engaged by the complainant; who had made all his arrangements, and his selections of other performers, in this country and in Europe, on the faith of the defendant's performing his engagement. That the services of the defendant were necessary, in the capacity in which he was engaged, to make up the troupe, or company, and his place could not be supplied without great expense and delay. And also that the complainant would be exposed to great damage, loss and inconvenience, and be liable to fail in his contract to obtain a first rate company by the first of November, if the defendant did not perform his engagement. The bill further charged that the defendant, since the making of the agreement, and in violation thereof, had entered into a contract with another person to go to the Havana as an opera singer, and to be there on the same day on which, by his agreement with the complainant, his services were to commence at New–York; and that he was about to leave this state for Cuba, in fraud and violation of the rights of the complainant. The bill therefore prayed for a specific performance of the contract with the complainant; that the defendant might be decreed to sing, gesticulate and recite, in the capacity of *primo basso,* according to his said agreement; that he might be restrained from leaving the state; and for general relief. The bill also prayed for a ne exeat; which was granted by an injunction master. And the defendant being unable to find bail, was committed to prison. . . .

The CHANCELLOR [WALWORTH]. The material facts alleged in the complainant's bill are not denied; and for the purpose of this application, they must be taken to be true. There is an affidavit, annexed to the bill, that the defendant has declared his intention of going to the Havana; and the defendant has not denied such intention, although he swears he has not made any engagement to go there. Upon the merits of the case, I suppose it must be conceded that the complainant is entitled to a specific performance of this contract; as the law appears to have been long since settled that a bird that can sing and will not sing must be made to sing. (*Old adage.*) In this case it is charged in the bill, not only that the defendant can sing, but also that he has expressly agreed to sing, and to accompany that singing with such appropriate gestures as may be necessary and proper to give an interest to his performance. And from the facts disclosed, I think it is very evident also that he does not intend to gratify the citizens of New–York, who may resort to the Italian opera either by his singing, or by his gesticulations. Although the authority before cited shows the law to be in favor of the complainant, so far at least as to entitle him to a decree for the singing, I am not aware that any officer of this court has that perfect knowledge of the Italian language, or possesses that exquisite sensibility in the auricular nerve which is necessary to understand, and to enjoy with a proper zest, the peculiar beauties of the Italian opera, so fascinating to the fashionable world. There might be some difficulty, therefore, even if the defendant was compelled to sing under the direction and in the presence of a master in chancery, in ascertaining whether he performed his engagement according to its spirit and intent. It would also be very difficult for the master to determine what effect coercion might produce upon the defendant's singing, especially in the livelier airs; although the fear of imprisonment would unquestionably deepen his seriousness in the graver parts of the drama. But one thing at least is certain; his songs will be neither comic, or even semi-serious, while he remains confined in that dismal cage, the debtor's prison of New–York. I will therefore proceed to inquire whether the complainant had any legal right thus to change the character of his native warblings, by such a confinement, before the appointed season for the dramatic singing had arrived.

From the terms of the agreement, as stated in the bill it is evident that there can be no breach thereof until the 1st of November next, when the engagement of the defendant was to commence. Even when that time arrives, the complainant will not be entitled to the defendant's services until he shall have paid, or tendered to him, a half month's salary in advance. A specific performance cannot be decreed, upon the present bill, because at the time it was filed, the complainant had no right of action against the defendant, either at law or in equity. And I believe this court has never yet gone so far as to sustain a bill quia timet, because the complainant apprehended that the defendant might not be willing to perform an engagement for personal services; and where, from the peculiar nature of those services, they could not be performed until a future day. The writ of ne exeat is in the nature of equitable bail; and to entitle the complainant to such bail, there must be a present debt or duty, or some existing right to relief against the defendant or his property, either at law, or in equity. The writ in this case therefore was prematurely granted; and the rule to discharge it must be made absolute.

NOTES

1. On De Rivafinoli and Corsetti, see 3 G. Odell, Annals of the New York Stage (1927).

2. Title VII of the Civil Rights Act of 1964 bars employment discrimination on the basis of race, color, religion, sex, or national origin. The remedies that courts are authorized to use to redress violations of Title VII are set forth in 42 U.S.C. § 2000e–5(g):

> If the court finds that the respondent has intentionally engaged in or is intentionally engaging in an unlawful employment practice charged in the complaint, the court may enjoin the respondent from engaging in such unlawful employment practice, and order such affirmative action as may be appropriate, which may include, but is not limited to, reinstatement or hiring of employees, with or without back pay (payable by the employer, employment agency, or labor organization, as the case may be, responsible for the unlawful employment practice), or any other equitable relief as the court deems appropriate. . . .

————

D. NEGATIVE CONTRACTS

Lumley v. Wagner

Chancery, 1852.
1 DeG.M. & G. 604, 42 Eng.Rep. 687.

The bill in this suit was filed on the 22d April 1852, by Benjamin Lumley, the lessee of Her Majesty's Theatre, against Johanna Wagner,

Albert Wagner, her father, and Frederick Gye, the lessee of Covent Garden Theatre: it stated that in November 1851 Joseph Bacher, as the agent of the Defendants Albert Wagner and Johanna Wagner, came to and concluded at Berlin an agreement in writing in the French language, bearing date the 9th November 1851, and which agreement, being translated into English, was as follows:—

[Mlle. Wagner agreed to sing at Drury Lane for three months, beginning April 1, 1852. She also agreed "not to use her talents at any other theatre ... without the written authorization of Mr. Lumley."]

The bill then stated that J. and A. Wagner subsequently made another engagement with the Defendant F. Gye, by which it was agreed that the Defendant J. Wagner should, for a larger sum than that stipulated by the agreement with the Plaintiff, sing at the Royal Italian Opera, Covent Garden, and abandon the agreement with the Plaintiff. The bill then stated that the Defendant F. Gye had full knowledge of the previous agreement with the Plaintiff, and that the Plaintiff had received a protest from the Defendants J. and A. Wagner, repudiating the agreement on the allegation that the Plaintiff had failed to fulfil the pecuniary portion of the agreement.

The bill prayed that the defendants Johanna Wagner and Albert Wagner might be restrained from violating or committing any breach of the [quoted] article of the agreement; that the defendant Johanna Wagner might be restrained from singing and performing or singing at the Royal Italian Opera, Covent Garden, or at any other theatre or place without the sanction or permission in writing of the plaintiff during the existence of the agreement with the plaintiff; and that the defendant Albert Wagner might be restrained from permitting or sanctioning the defendant Johanna Wagner singing and performing or singing as aforesaid; that the defendant Frederick Gye might be restrained from accepting the professional services of the defendant Johanna Wagner as a singer and performer or singer at the said Royal Italian Opera, Covent Garden, or at any other theatre or place, and from permitting her to sing and perform or to sing at the Royal Italian Opera, Covent Garden, during the existence of the agreement with the plaintiff, without the permission or sanction of the plaintiff.

... The plaintiff having obtained an injunction from the Vice–Chancellor, Sir James Parker, on the 9th May, 1852, the defendants now moved by way of appeal before the Lord Chancellor, to discharge ... [this] order.

The LORD CHANCELLOR [LORD ST. LEONARDS]. The question which I have to decide in the present case arises out of a very simple contract the effect of which is that the defendant Johanna Wagner should sing at Her Majesty's Theatre for a certain number of nights, and that she should not sing elsewhere (for that is the true construction) during that period. As I understand the points taken by the defendants' counsel in support of this appeal, they in effect come to this, namely, that a court of equity ought not to grant an injunction except in cases connected with specific performance, or where the injunction being to compel a party to forbear from committing an act (and not to perform an act), that injunction will complete the whole of the agreement remaining unexecuted.

I have then to consider how the question stands on principle and on authority, and in so doing I shall observe upon some of the cases which have been referred to and commented upon by the defendants in support of their contention. The first was that of Martin v. Nutkin, 2 P.W. 266 [1725], in which the court issued an injunction restraining an act from being done where it clearly could not have granted any specific performance: but then it was said that that case fell within one of the exceptions which the defendants admit are proper cases for the interference of the court, because there the ringing of the bells, sought to be restrained, had been agreed to be suspended by the defendant in consideration of the erection by the plaintiffs of a cupola and clock, the agreement being in effect the price stipulated for the defendant's relinquishing bell-ringing at stated periods; the defendant having accepted the benefit, but rejected the corresponding obligation, Lord Macclesfield first granted the injunction which the Lords Commissioners, at the hearing of the cause, continued for the lives of the plaintiffs. That case, therefore, however it may be explained as one of the exceptional cases, is nevertheless a clear authority showing that this court has granted an injunction prohibiting the commission of an act in respect of which the court could never have interfered by way of specific performance.

. . . .

It was also contended that the plaintiff's remedy, if any, was at law; but it is no objection to the exercise of the jurisdiction by injunction, that the plaintiff may have a legal remedy. The case of Robinson v. Lord Byron, 1 Bro.C.C. 588 [1785], before Lord Thurlow, so very often commented upon by succeeding judges, is a clear illustration of that proposition, because in that case the defendant, Lord Byron, who had large pieces of water in his park which supplied the plaintiff's mills, was abusing his right by preventing a regular supply to the plaintiff's mill, and although the plaintiff had a remedy at law, yet this court felt no difficulty in restraining Lord Byron by injunction from preventing the regular flow of the water. Undoubtedly there are cases such as that cited for the defendants of Collins v. Plumb, 16 Ves. 454 [1810], before Lord Eldon, in which this court has declined to exercise the power (which in that instance it was assumed to have had) of preventing the commission of an act, because such power could not be properly and beneficially exercised. In that case the negative covenant, not to sell water to the prejudice of the plaintiffs, was not enforced by Lord Eldon, not because he had any doubt about the jurisdiction of the court (for upon that point he had no doubt), but because it was impossible to ascertain every time the water was supplied by the defendants, whether it was or not to the damage of the plaintiffs; but whether right or wrong, that learned judge, in refusing to exercise the jurisdiction on very sufficient grounds, meant in no respect to break in on the general rules deducible from the previous authorities.

At an early stage of the argument I adverted to the familiar cases of attorneys' clerks and surgeons' and apothecaries' apprentices, and the like, in which this court has constantly interfered, simply to prevent the violation of negative covenants; but it was said that in such cases the court only acted on the principle that the clerk or apprentice had received all the benefit and that the prohibition operated upon a concluded contract, and that therefore the injunction fell within one of the exceptional cases. I do not, however, apprehend that the jurisdiction of the court depends upon any such principle: it is obvious that in those cases the negative covenant does not come into operation until the servitude is ended, and therefore that the injunction cannot be required or applied for before that period.

The present is a mixed case, consisting not of two correlative acts to be done, one by the plaintiff and the other by the defendants, which state of facts may have and in some cases has introduced a very important difference—but of an act to be done by J. Wagner alone, to which is superadded a negative stipulation on her part to abstain from the commission of any act which will break in upon her affirmative covenant—the one being ancillary to, concurrent, and operating together with the other. The agreement to sing for the plaintiff during three months at his theatre, and during that time not to sing for anybody else, is not a correlative contract, it is in effect one contract; and though beyond all doubt this court could not interfere to enforce the specific performance of the whole of this contract, yet in all sound construction, and according to the true spirit of the agreement, the engagement to perform for three months at one theatre must necessarily exclude the right to perform at the same time at another theatre. It was clearly intended that J. Wagner was to exert her vocal abilities to the utmost to aid the theatre to which she agreed to attach herself. I am of opinion, that if she had attempted, even in the absence of any negative stipulation, to perform at another theatre, she would have broken the spirit and true meaning of the contract as much as she would now do with reference to the contract into which she has actually entered.

Wherever this court has not proper jurisdiction to enforce specific performance, it operates to bind men's consciences, as far as they can be bound, to a true and literal performance of their agreements; and it will not suffer them to depart from their contracts at their pleasure, leaving the party with whom they have contracted to the mere chance of any damages which a jury may give. The exercise of this jurisdiction has, I believe, had a wholesome tendency towards the maintenance of that good faith which exists in this country to a much greater degree perhaps than in any other; and although the jurisdiction is not to be extended, yet a judge would desert his duty who did not act up to what his predecessors have handed down as the rule for his guidance in the administration of such an equity.

It was objected that the operation of the injunction in the present case was mischievous, excluding the defendant J. Wagner from performing at any other theatre while this court had no power to compel her to perform at Her Majesty's Theatre. It is true, that I have not the means of compelling her to sing, but she has no cause of complaint, if I compel her to abstain from the commission of an act which she has bound herself not to do, and thus possibly cause her to fulfil her engagement. The jurisdiction which I now exercise is wholly within the power of the court, and being of opinion that it is a proper case for interfering, I shall leave nothing unsatisfied by the judgment I pronounce. The effect too of the injunction, in restraining J. Wagner from singing elsewhere may, in the event of an action being brought against her by the plaintiff, prevent any such amount of vindictive damages being given against her as a jury might probably be inclined to give if she had carried her talents and exercised them at the rival theatre: the injunction may also, as I have said, tend to the fulfillment of her engagement; though, in continuing the injunction, I disclaim doing indirectly what I cannot do directly.

Referring again to the authorities, I am well aware that they have not been uniform, and that there undoubtedly has been a difference of decision on the question now revived before me; but, after the best consideration which I have been enabled to give to the subject, the conclusion at which I have arrived is, I conceive, supported by the greatest weight of authority. The earliest case most directly bearing on the point is that of Morris v. Colman, 18 Ves. 437 [1812]. . . .

Thus far, I think, the authorities are very strong against the defendants' contention; but the case of Kemble v. Kean, 6 Sim. 333, [1829] [decided by Vice–Chancellor Shadwell], . . . is the first case which has in point of fact introduced all the difficulties on this part of the law. There Mr. Kean entered into an agreement precisely similar to the present: he agreed that he would perform for Mr. Kemble at Drury Lane, and that he would not perform anywhere else during the time that he had stipulated to perform for Mr. Kemble. Mr. Kean broke his engagement, a bill was filed, and the Vice–Chancellor Shadwell was of opinion that he could not grant an injunction to restrain Mr. Kean from performing elsewhere, which he was either about to do or actually doing, because the court could not enforce the performance of the affirmative covenant that he would perform at Drury Lane for Mr. Kemble. Being pressed by that passage which I have read from in the Lord Chancellor's judgment in Morris v. Colman [that the court may enforce personal service contracts by injunction], he put that paraphrase or commentary upon it which I have referred to; that is, he says: "Lord Eldon is speaking of a case where the parties are in partnership together." I have come to a different conclusion; and I am bound to say that, in my apprehension, the case of Kemble v. Kean was wrongly decided and cannot be maintained.

. . . .

From a careful examination of all these authorities I am of opinion that the principles and rules deducible from them are in direct contravention of those principles and rules which were so elaborately pressed upon me during the argument; and I wish it to be distinctly understood that I entertain no doubt whatever that the point of law has been properly decided in the court below. . . .

NOTES

1.   The parties in this case were distinguished figures in the world of music. See Z. Chafee, S. Simpson & J. Maloney, Cases on Equity 288–90 (3d ed. 1951). Gye was also well-known in the field of law, for he was involved in what became leading cases in equity, torts, contracts, and partnership. Besides the principal case, see Lumley v. Gye, 2 E. & B. 216, 118 Eng.Rep. 749 (1853); Bettini v. Gye, L.R. 1 Q.B.D. 183 (1876); S. Williston, Cases on

Contracts 571 (6th ed. 1954); Knox v. Gye, L.R. 5 H.L.C. 656 (1871–72); J. Ames, Cases on Partnership 163 (1894).

2.   In spite of the continuance of the injunction restraining her from singing for Gye, Mlle. Wagner did not perform her contract to sing for Lumley. After the decision in the principal case, Lumley sued Gye at law for damages for inducing Mlle. Wagner to break her contract with Lumley, alleging that Gye had "maliciously enticed and procured her" to leave Lumley's employment. A demurrer to Lumley's declaration was overruled in the leading case of Lumley v. Gye, 2 E. & B. 216, 118 Eng.Rep. 749 (1853). Thereafter, at the trial of the action Lumley was awarded nominal damages. See B. Lumley, Reminiscences of the Opera 328–33 (1864); Z. Chafee, *Equitable Servitudes on Chattels,* 41 Harv.L.Rev. 945, 975 and n. 89 (1928).

3.   The leading American case involved an attempt by Napoleon Lajoie, the Philadelphia Phillies' Hall of Fame second baseman, to repudiate his contract with the Phillies and play with their crosstown rivals, the Athletics. The trial court refused to enjoin him from breaching the exclusivity clause of his contract, but the state supreme court reversed. Philadelphia Ball Club v. Lajoie, 202 Pa. 210, 51 A. 973 (1902).

> The learned judge who filed the opinion in the court below, with great industry and painstaking care, collected and reviewed the English and American decisions bearing upon the question involved, and makes apparent the wide divergence of opinion which has prevailed. We think, however, that in refusing relief unless the defendant's services were shown to be of such a character as to render it impossible to replace him he has taken extreme ground. It seems to us that a more just and equitable rule is laid down in Pom. Spec. Perf. p. 31, where the principle is thus declared: "Where one person agrees to render personal services to another, which require and presuppose a special knowledge, skill, and ability in the employé, so that in case of a default the same service could not easily be obtained from others, although the affirmative specific performance of the contract is beyond the power of the court, its performance will be negatively enforced by enjoining its breach. . . . The damages for breach of such contract cannot be estimated with any certainty, and the employer cannot, by means of any damages, purchase the same service in the labor market." . . .

> The court below finds from the testimony that "the defendant is an expert baseball player in any position; that he has a great reputation as a second baseman; that his place would be hard to fill with as good a player; that his withdrawal from the team would weaken it, as would the withdrawal of any good player, and would probably make a difference in the size of the audiences attending the game." We think that, in thus stating it, he puts it very mildly, and that the evidence would warrant a stronger finding as to the ability of the defendant as an expert ball player. He has been for several years in the service of the plaintiff club, and has been re-engaged from season to season at a constantly increasing salary. He has become thoroughly familiar with the action and methods of the other players in the club, and his own

work is peculiarly meritorious as an integral part of the team work which is so essential. In addition to these features which render his services of peculiar and special value to the plaintiff, and not easily replaced, Lajoie is well known, and has great reputation among the patrons of the sport, for ability in the position which he filled, and was thus a most attractive drawing card for the public. He may not be the sun in the baseball firmament, but he is certainly a bright particular star. We feel, therefore, that the evidence in this case justifies the conclusion that the services of the defendant are of such a unique character, and display such a special knowledge, skill, and ability, as renders them of peculiar value to the plaintiff, and so difficult of substitution that their loss will produce "irreparable injury," in the legal significance of that term, to the plaintiff. The action of the defendant in violating his contract is a breach of good faith, for which there would be no adequate redress at law, and the case, therefore, properly calls for the aid of equity in negatively enforcing the performance of the contract by enjoining against its breach.

Despite this decision, Lajoie did not return to the Phillies.

4. Montague hired Flockton to act in his theater for a season. They later renewed their agreement for another season. Flockton received a few better offers during the second season and refused to complete the season with Montague, who hired Palmer to perform in Flockton's place in his next play. When Montague learned that Flockton was going to act in other theaters before the end of the season, he obtained an injunction barring Flockton from doing so. Montague v. Flockton, L.R. 16 Eq. 189 (1873). Although there was no explicit exclusivity provision in Flockton's contract with Montague, the judge thought it plain that "a man agreeing to act in one particular theatre during the season" is agreeing to "act there and not anywhere else." Given the retention of Palmer, an injunction would leave Flockton unemployed, but the court viewed this as a problem of his own making.

Ticor Title Insurance Co. v. Cohen

United States Court of Appeals, Second Circuit, 1999.
173 F.3d 63

[Title insurance companies brought action against former senior vice president in charge of several major sales accounts, asserting breach of noncompete covenant and seeking injunctive relief. The United States District Court for the Southern District of New York, permanently enjoined former vice president from working in title insurance business in New York and from appropriating title companies' corporate opportunities for six months. Former vice president appealed.]

■ CARDAMONE, CIRCUIT JUDGE:

Defendant Kenneth C. Cohen (defendant or appellant) appeals from a judgment entered July 1, 1998 in the United States District Court for the Southern District of New York (Martin, J.) that issued a permanent injunction against him and in favor of plaintiffs Ticor Title Insurance Co. and Chicago Title Insurance Co. (Ticor). This panel filed a summary order affirming the judgment of the district court on November 19, 1998, and stating that this opinion would follow.

A principal question to be resolved is whether appellant's services as an employee were so unique to his employer as to provide a basis for injunctive relief. In analyzing whether an employee's services are unique, the focus today is less on the uniqueness of the individual person of the employee, testing whether such person is extraordinary in the sense, for example, of Beethoven as a composer, Einstein as a physicist, or Michelangelo as an artist, where one can fairly say that nature made them and then broke the mold. Instead, now the inquiry is more focused on the employee's relationship to the employer's business to ascertain whether his or her services and value to that operation may be said to be unique, special or extraordinary; that inquiry, because individual circumstances differ so widely, must of necessity be on a case-by-case basis.

BACKGROUND

Facts Relating to Employment

A.   The Parties

Plaintiffs are affiliated companies that sell title insurance nationwide. Title insurance insures the buyer of real property, or a lender secured by real property, against defects in the legal title to the property, and guarantees that, in the event a defect in title surfaces, the insurer will reimburse the insured for losses associated with the defect, or will take steps necessary to correct it. This kind of insurance is almost always purchased when real estate is conveyed. Ticor has been, and remains today, the leading title insurance company in New York State. It focuses primarily on multi-million dollar transactions that are handled by real estate lawyers. On large transactions more than one title insurance company is often employed in order to spread the risk.

Defendant Cohen was employed by Ticor as a title insurance salesman. Title insurance salespeople contact real estate attorneys, handle title searches for them, and sell them policies; those salespeople from different title insurance companies compete to insure the same real estate transaction, seeking their business from the same group of widely-known attorneys. Due to the nature of the business, those attorneys commonly have relationships with more than one title insurance company.

Cohen began working for Ticor in 1981, shortly after graduating from college, as a sales account manager and within six years was a senior vice president in charge of several major accounts. Thus, he has been a title insurance salesman for Ticor for nearly all of his professional career. His clients have consisted almost exclusively of real estate attorneys in large New York law firms. As his supervisor testified, Cohen obtains his business due to his knowledge of the business, his professionalism, his ability to work through problems, and his ability to get things done.

B. Employment Contract

Ticor and Cohen, both represented by counsel, entered into an Employment Contract on October 1, 1995. There were extensive negotiations over its terms, including the covenant not to compete, which is at issue on this appeal. The contract's stated term is until December 31, 1999, although Cohen—but not Ticor—could terminate it without cause on 30 days' notice.

The non-compete provision, enforced by the district court, stated that during his employment with Ticor and "for a period ending on the earlier of ... June 30, 2000 or ... 180 days following [his] termination of employment," Cohen would not:

for himself, or on behalf of any other person, or in conjunction with any other person, firm, partnership, corporation or other entity, engage in the business of Title Insurance ... in the State of New York.

For the purposes of this provision, the Employment Contract provides that:

"Title Insurance" shall be defined ... as the sale, service or rental of any product, process or service [of Ticor] ... which had been developed, sold or offered for sale by [Ticor] in the State of New York during the 365 days preceding the date of [Cohen's] termination of employment ...

It also contains the following express representation regarding the material nature of the covenant not to compete:

[Ticor] is willing to enter into this Contract only on condition that [Cohen] accept certain post-employment restrictions with respect to subsequent reemployment set forth herein and [Cohen] is prepared to accept such condition.

Negotiation of the post-employment non-competition provision of the Employment Contract (¶ 9) culminated in a fax from Cohen's counsel to Ticor's counsel dated October 27, 1995 in which Cohen's counsel provided a proposed final version that included some additional modifications. Ticor accepted this proposed final version, and it was embodied, verbatim, in the final executed agreement. Thus, the non-compete provision defendant now asserts is unenforceable was drafted (in its final form) by his own lawyer.

Cohen enjoyed exclusive responsibility for key Ticor accounts throughout the entire term of his employment. A number of the accounts for which defendant had exclusive responsibility predated his 17–year employment, and no other Ticor sales representative was permitted to service them during the term of the Employment Contract.

In consideration for Cohen's agreeing to the recited post-employment restrictions, he was made one of the highest paid Ticor sales representatives, being guaranteed during the term of the Employment Contract annual compensation of $600,000, consisting of a base salary of $200,000 plus commissions. His total compensation in 1997 exceeded $1.1 million.

In addition to compensation, defendant received expense account reimbursements that by 1997 exceeded $150,000 per year, and which included fully paid memberships in exclusive clubs, as well as tickets to New York's professional sporting events and Broadway shows. His fringe benefits went far beyond those provided other Ticor sales representatives whose expense reimbursements are generally limited to $30,000 per year. Cohen also had his own six person staff at Ticor, all of whom reported directly to him. No other Ticor representative had such staff support.

C.   Breach of Contract

On April 20, 1998 TitleServ, a direct competitor of Ticor, offered to employ Cohen. As part of that offer, TitleServ agreed to indemnify Cohen by paying him a salary during the six-month period (i.e., the 180 days hiatus from employment) in the event that the covenant not to compete was enforced. Defendant sent plaintiff a letter on April 21, 1998 notifying it of his resignation effective May 21, 1998 and agreed to begin working for TitleServ on May 27, 1998.

Appellant commenced employment with his new employer on that date. His employment contract there guarantees him a minimum salary of $750,000 and a signing bonus of $2 million dollars, regardless of the outcome of this litigation. Cohen has received this signing bonus and has begun receiving salary payments, as scheduled. He admits to speaking with 20 Ticor customers about TitleServ before submitting his letter of resignation, and telling each of them that he was considering leaving Ticor and joining a competitor firm. Cohen maintains that this was an effort on his part to learn more information about TitleServ, including its ability to service the New York market and the opportunity he was being offered.

During the course of this due diligence, Cohen insists he never discussed transferring any business from Ticor to TitleServ, nor did he discuss any specific deals. However, this assertion is undermined by defendant's deposition testimony concerning conversations with Martin Polevoy of the Bachner Tally law firm, in which he admits he directly solicited Polevoy's business for TitleServ and, after initial resistance from Polevoy, eventually secured a promise that Polevoy would follow him by taking his firm's insurance business to TitleServ.

Prior Proceedings

Ticor commenced this action on June 5, 1998 and applied that day for a temporary restraining order and preliminary injunction. After receiving Cohen's opposition papers and hearing argument, the district court entered a temporary restraining order. The parties conducted expedited discovery and briefed the relevant issues over the ensuing ten days. On June 19, 1998 the district court heard further argument and extended the temporary restraining order for an additional ten days. It scheduled an evidentiary hearing, held on June 29, 1998, at the close of which the parties consented to consolidate the hearing with a trial on the merits of Ticor's cause of action seeking a permanent injunction.

On July 1, 1998 the district court issued its opinion and order permanently enjoining Cohen from working in the title insurance business and from appropriating Ticor's corporate opportunities with its current or prospective customers for a period of six months. Applying New York law, it found this case indistinguishable from Maltby v. Harlow Meyer Savage,

Inc., 166 Misc.2d 481, 486, 633 N.Y.S.2d 926 (Sup.1995), aff'd, 223 A.D.2d 516, 637 N.Y.S.2d 110 (1st Dep't 1996).

It also relied on two other independent grounds for enjoining Cohen. First, the trial court held an injunction was justified to protect Ticor's confidential information. Second, it ruled that Cohen had breached his fiduciary duties to Ticor because Cohen had expressly asked one client to follow him to TitleServ, and he had inquired of others if they would be willing to follow him. From the grant of a permanent injunction, Cohen appeals. We affirm.

DISCUSSION

There are five issues before us. Several require discussion, including those upon which the trial court relied in enjoining defendant. First, however, as a threshold matter, we discuss whether the injunction was properly issued; second, we analyze the district court's finding that defendant Cohen enjoyed a "special" or "unique" relationship with Ticor's clients; third, we consider a finding that defendant possessed "confidential information" of his employer's business and owed a fiduciary duty to plaintiff on that account. The fourth issue is whether under New York law, a contract not to compete violates public policy and is therefore unenforceable; and the last issue questions whether in construing the covenant—assuming its validity—it was appropriate to apply it to transactions originating in New York State concerning real property outside New York State.

I Injunctive Relief

A. Irreparable Harm

An award of an injunction is not something a plaintiff is entitled to as a matter of right, but rather it is an equitable remedy issued by a trial court, within the broad bounds of its discretion, after it weighs the potential benefits and harm to be incurred by the parties from the granting or denying of such relief. See Yakus v. United States, 321 U.S. 414, 440, 64 S.Ct. 660, 88 L.Ed. 834 (1944). An order involving injunctive relief will not be reversed unless it is contrary to some rule of equity or results from a discretion improvidently exercised. See Meccano, Ltd. v. John Wanamaker, N.Y., 253 U.S. 136, 141, 40 S.Ct. 463, 64 L.Ed. 822 (1920). In other words, such an order is subject to reversal only for an abuse of discretion or for a clear error of law. See Malarkey v. Texaco, Inc., 983 F.2d 1204, 1214 (2d Cir.1993); Plaza Health Labs., Inc. v. Perales, 878 F.2d 577, 581 (2d Cir.1989).

An injunction should be granted when the intervention of a court of equity is essential to protect a party's property rights against injuries that would otherwise be irremediable. See Cavanaugh v. Looney, 248 U.S. 453, 456, 39 S.Ct. 142, 63 L.Ed. 354 (1919). The basic requirements to obtain injunctive relief have always been a showing of irreparable injury and the inadequacy of legal remedies. See Weinberger v. Romero–Barcelo, 456 U.S. 305, 312, 102 S.Ct. 1798, 72 L.Ed.2d 91 (1982); New York State Nat'l Org. for Women v. Terry, 886 F.2d 1339, 1362 (2d Cir.1989) (to obtain permanent injunction the lack of an adequate remedy at law and irreparable harm must be shown). Appellant maintains that an injunction was improvidently granted in the instant case because there was no showing that Ticor would suffer irreparable harm in the absence of its issuance.

To the contrary, we think for several reasons irreparable harm was shown to be present in this case. Initially, it would be very difficult to calculate monetary damages that would successfully redress the loss of a relationship with a client that would produce an indeterminate amount of business in years to come. In fact, the employment contract sought to be enforced concedes that in the event of Cohen's breach of the post-employment competition provision, Ticor shall be entitled to injunctive relief, because it would cause irreparable injury. Such, we think, might arguably be viewed as an admission by Cohen that plaintiff will suffer irreparable harm were he to breach the contract's non-compete provision. Further, the district court thought as a matter of law, as stated in a footnote to its written decision, that New York cases in the covenant-not-to-compete context apparently assume an irreparable injury to plaintiff. We agree with the district court that irreparable injury exists in this case.

II Covenant Not to Compete

A. In General

We turn to the merits. To gain some insight into the subject of non-competition contracts, we look to an early common law case in England where much of the law in this area was set forth. That case is Mitchel v. Reynolds, 1 P. Wms. 181, 24 Eng. Rep. 347 (Q.B.1711), which has, through the ensuing 290 years, been frequently cited and followed. There, plaintiff alleged defendant had for good consideration assigned him his bakehouse in Liquorpond Street for five years, and defendant had agreed not to engage in trade as a baker in that neighborhood for that time, and if he did he had to pay plaintiff 50 pounds. When defendant began baking again, seeking the local trade, plaintiff sued. Defendant declared that because he was a baker by trade, the bond not to engage in that trade was void as a restraint on a person's ability to earn his livelihood. Queens Bench disagreed and held that this particular restraint of trade was not void, because a "man may, upon a valuable consideration, by his own consent, and for his own profit, give over his trade; and part with it to another in a particular place." Id. at 186, 24 Eng. Rep. at 349. The English court added that all contracts containing only a bare restraint of trade and no more must be void, but where circumstances are shown that make it a "reasonable and useful contract," the contract will be ruled good and enforced by the courts. Id. at 192, 24 Eng. Rep. at 351.

The issue of whether a restrictive covenant not to compete is enforceable by way of an injunction depends in the first place upon whether the covenant is reasonable in time and geographic area. See Reed, Roberts Assocs. v. Strauman, 40 N.Y.2d 303, 307, 386 N.Y.S.2d 677, 353 N.E.2d 590 (1976). In this equation, courts must weigh the need to protect the employer's legitimate business interests against the employee's concern regarding the possible loss of livelihood, a result strongly disfavored by public policy in New York. See id.

A scholarly commentator described the tension between these competing concerns, which we face in the case at hand, in this fashion: An employer will sometimes believe its clientele is a form of property that belongs to it and any new business a salesperson drums up is for its benefit because this is what the salesperson was hired and paid to do. The employee believes, to the contrary, that the duty to preserve customer relationships ceases when employment ends and the employee's freedom to use contacts he or she developed may not be impaired by restraints that inhibit competition and an employee's ability to earn a living. The always present potential problem is whether a customer will come to value the salesperson more than the employer's product. When the product is not that much different from those available from competitors, such a customer is ripe to abandon the employer and follow the employee should he go to work for a competitor. See Harlan M. Blake, Employee Agreements Not To Compete, 73 Harv. L.Rev. 625, 654 (1960).

That scenario fits the circumstances revealed by the present record. The way to deal with these conflicting interests is by contract, which is what the parties before us purported to do, only now appellant insists, just as was argued in Mitchel, that the non-compete provision is void as a contract in restraint of trade and therefore violates public policy.

The law points in a different direction. Over a hundred years ago New York's highest court observed, in conformance with Mitchel, that contracts in partial restraint of trade, if reasonable, are permitted. See Diamond Match Co. v. Roeber, 106 N.Y. 473, 482, 13 N.E. 419 (1887). Because of strong public policy militating against the sanctioning of a person's loss of the ability to earn a livelihood, New York law subjects a non-compete covenant by an employee to "an overriding limitation of reasonableness" which hinges on the facts of each case. Karpinski v. Ingrasci, 28 N.Y.2d 45, 49, 320 N.Y.S.2d 1, 268 N.E.2d 751 (1971). Assuming a covenant by an employee not to compete surmounts its first hurdle, that is, that it is reasonable in time and geographic scope, enforcement will be granted to the extent necessary (1) to prevent an employee's solicitation or disclosure of trade secrets, (2) to prevent an employee's release of confidential information regarding the employer's customers, or (3) in those cases where the employee's services to the employer are deemed special or unique. See Purchasing Assocs. v. Weitz, 13 N.Y.2d 267, 272–73, 246 N.Y.S.2d 600, 196 N.E.2d 245 (1963) (Fuld, J.). In the case at hand we are satisfied that the reasonableness test was met because the duration of the covenant was relatively short (six months) and the scope was not geographically overbroad. In any event, appellant does not argue that the covenant is unreasonable in time and scope. Rather, he argues that the services he provided to Ticor were not sufficiently unique to justify injunctive relief.

B. Unique Services

New York, following English law, recognizes the availability of injunctive relief where the non-compete covenant is found to be reasonable and the employee's services are unique. See Reed, Roberts, 40 N.Y.2d at 308, 386 N.Y.S.2d 677, 353 N.E.2d 590. Services that are not simply of value to the employer, but that may also truly be said to be special, unique or extraordinary may entitle an employer to injunctive relief. See American Broadcasting Companies v. Wolf, 52 N.Y.2d 394, 402, 438 N.Y.S.2d 482, 420

N.E.2d 363 (1981); Columbia Ribbon & Carbon Mfg. Co. v. A–1–A Corp., 42 N.Y.2d 496, 499, 398 N.Y.S.2d 1004, 369 N.E.2d 4 (1977); Purchasing Assocs., 13 N.Y.2d at 272–74, 246 N.Y.S.2d 600, 196 N.E.2d 245. An injunction may be used to bar such person from working elsewhere. If the unique services of such employee are available to a competitor, the employer obviously suffers irreparable harm. See American Broadcasting Companies, 52 N.Y.2d at 402–03, 438 N.Y.S.2d 482, 420 N.E.2d 363.

Unique services have been found in various categories of employment where the services are dependent on an employee's special talents; such categories include musicians, professional athletes, actors and the like. In those kinds of cases injunctive relief has been available to prevent the breach of an employment contract where the individual performer has such ability and reputation that his or her place may not easily be filled. See 42 Am.Jur.2d Injunctions § 110 (1969). We recognized this category of uniqueness in the case of the services of an acrobat who, in his performance, with one hand lifted his co-performer, a grown man, from a full length position on the floor, an act described as "the most marvelous thing that has ever been [done] before." Shubert Theatrical Co. v. Rath, 271 F. 827, 829–30 (2d Cir.1921). We later said that where services are unique the issuance of an injunction "is not an open question in this court," and commented that this "principle is equally well settled in the courts of New York." Associated Newspapers v. Phillips, 294 F. 845, 850 (2d Cir.1923) (citing Shubert Theatrical Co. and collecting New York cases) (employee writer of feature articles for the daily press provided unique services).

It has always been the rule, however, that to fall within this category of employees against whom equity will enforce a negative covenant, it is not necessary that the employee should be the only "star" of his employer, or that the business will grind to a halt if the employee leaves. See Comstock v. Lopokowa, 190 F. 599, 601 (C.C.S.D.N.Y.1911). Hence, as noted earlier, in determining uniqueness the inquiry now focuses more on the employee's relationship to the employer's business than on the individual person of the employee.

The "unique services" category has not often been the basis upon which a New York court has granted an injunction, and thus its full ambit there is unclear. See American Broad. Cos., 52 N.Y.2d at 403 n. 6, 438 N.Y.S.2d 482, 420 N.E.2d 363. However, in Maltby v. Harlow Meyer Savage, Inc., the Supreme Court in New York County found that several currency traders were unique employees because they had "unique relationships with the customers with whom they have been dealing," which were developed while they were employed and, partially at the employer's expense. Id. at 486, 633 N.Y.S.2d 926. The district court found the facts in Maltby so similar to those in the case at hand that it felt compelled in applying New York law to grant an injunction. Like Maltby, all of Cohen's clients came to him during his time at Ticor, and were developed, in part, at Ticor's expense. For example, about half of Cohen's clients he had attracted himself, but the other half were inherited from other departing Ticor salesmen. Cohen maintained these relationships, at least in part, by the use of the substantial entertainment expense account provided by

Ticor. For instance, in 1997 Cohen spent $170,000 entertaining clients, and in the first five months of 1998 he spent about $138,000.

The trial court found Cohen's relationships with clients were "special" and qualified as unique services. It deemed these relationships unique for several reasons. First, since the costs and terms of title insurance in New York are fixed by law, competition for business relies more heavily on personal relationships. Second, since potential clients—New York law firms with real estate practices—are limited and well known throughout the industry, maintaining current clients from this established group is crucial. Third, the trial court noted that, as in Maltby, Cohen had negotiated his employment contract and the non-compete clause with the assistance of counsel and not from an inferior bargaining position.

Maltby found a trader's absence from the market for six months did not make him unemployable or affect his ability to earn a living in the industry. Id. Here, the non-compete period is also six months, and quite plainly Cohen is not disabled from reviving his relationships with clients after the six months' absence, which would allow a new Ticor salesman sufficient opportunity to establish a fledgling relationship with Cohen's clients at Ticor.

Appellant maintains that Maltby can be distinguished, because in that case the employees were paid their base salary during the restricted period, while Cohen will receive nothing during his six-month hiatus. The significance of the salary paid in Maltby was that it helped alleviate the policy concern that non-compete provisions prevent a person from earning a livelihood. Here, by the same token, part of Cohen's $600,000 per year salary was in exchange for his promise not to compete for six months after termination, and since the employer had given Cohen sufficient funds to sustain him for six months, the public policy concern regarding impairment of earning a livelihood was assuaged. The district court's conclusion appears correct and its issuance of an injunction based on its finding of unique services clearly does not rise to the level of an abuse of discretion.

Cohen also insists that the trial court was wrong to apply Maltby, which dealt with trade brokers instead of insurance salesmen, because he suggests that New York law has specifically determined that "insurance salesmen" and the relationships they develop with clients can never be "unique." But many of the cases Cohen cites are simply ones where the court refused to find—on facts that differ from the current case—that the salesperson was unique, but those same cases did not make a blanket rule that no salesperson could ever be unique. Such, of course, is not the law.

We recognize that New York decisions reveal many situations where a particular employee was found not to be "special, unique or extraordinary." See Columbia Ribbon, 42 N.Y.2d at 500, 398 N.Y.S.2d 1004, 369 N.E.2d 4 (salesmen here provide standard services and are therefore not unique); Clark Paper & Mfg. Co. v. Stenacher, 236 N.Y. 312, 140 N.E. 708 (1923) (same); Kaumagraph Co. v. Stampagraph Co., 235 N.Y. 1, 138 N.E. 485 (1923) (printers of fabric designs not unique); Frederick Bros. Artists Corp. v. Yates, 271 A.D. 69, 62 N.Y.S.2d 714 (1st Dep't 1946), aff'd without opinion, 296 N.Y. 820, 72 N.E.2d 13 (1947) (theatrical booking agent); Corpin v. Wheatley, 227 A.D. 212, 237 N.Y.S. 205 (4th Dep't 1929) (beauty parlor employee); Magid v. Tannenbaum, 164 A.D. 142, 149 N.Y.S. 445 (1st Dep't 1914) (traveling representative for tailors); Small v. Kronstat, 175 Misc. 626, 24 N.Y.S.2d 535 (Sup.Ct.1940) (skilled watch artisan).

Yet, it still remains true that where the employee's services are "special, unique or extraordinary," then injunctive relief is available to enforce a covenant not to compete, if the covenant is reasonable, and even though competition does not involve disclosure of trade secrets or confidential lists. See Purchasing Assocs., 13 N.Y.2d at 273, 246 N.Y.S.2d 600, 196 N.E.2d 245. In a similar vein, we ruled in Bradford v. New York Times Co., 501 F.2d 51 (2d Cir.1974), that an employee can be unique. Bradford, an employee of the New York Times, left the publisher where he had been serving as general manager, vice-president and director, to go to work for a competitor, Scripps–Howard Newspapers, where he took the post of assistant general manager. As part of an incentive compensation plan with his former employer he had signed a non-compete contract and upon seeking the plan's benefits was told he had breached the non-compete clause and thus had been terminated from the plan. His suit against the New York Times was dismissed by the district court. We affirmed, holding that since Bradford was a unique employee the non-compete clause was enforceable. See id. at 58.

As stated in Service Sys. Corp. v. Harris, 41 A.D.2d 20, 23–24, 341 N.Y.S.2d 702 (4th Dep't 1973), "[a]n employer has sufficient interest in retaining present customers to support an employee covenant where the employee's relationship with the customers is such that there is a substantial risk that the employee may be able to divert all or part of the business." In the present case this risk is clearly evidenced by the fact that in 1997 another employee, Neil Clarke, left Ticor for TitleServ and took 75 percent of his clients with him. And, this is further demonstrated by appellant's successful solicitation of a law firm to follow him to TitleServ. Moreover, one appellate court in New York affirmed the grant of an injunction in favor of an employer in a restrictive employment covenant case where the employee was held to be a "star" salesman. Uniform Rental Div., Inc. v. Moreno, 83 A.D.2d 629, 441 N.Y.S.2d 538 (2d Dep't 1981). Thus, we do not think our holding contravenes established law in New York.

III Other Issues

The other issues we earlier noted are insubstantial and require only a brief discussion. These three issues are: (1) whether Cohen possessed confidential information regarding Ticor's business; (2) whether a non-compete contract is void under New York law; (3) whether the contract between the parties could be applied to transactions involving property located outside New York State.

Having decided that the district court correctly found that Cohen had a unique relationship with Ticor and its clients, it is unnecessary for us to decide whether Cohen possessed and misused confidential information of his employer's on whose account he owed a fiduciary duty not to divulge such knowledge. We recognize that the district court issued its injunction on the additional ground of defendant's divulging Ticor's trade secrets and confidential information. Cohen insists that knowledge of pending transactions was publicly available or was common knowledge in the industry, but the trial court made a finding that the information Ticor had developed and Cohen possessed went well beyond that which could be compiled from public sources.

Cohen's second argument, that it was error to uphold the covenant not to compete as a bargained for contract when such contracts are void as against public policy in New York, was disposed of in our analysis under Point II. As discussed earlier, these covenants are not per se void and may, if fairly and reasonably drawn, be enforced by injunction.

Finally, it was not error to rule that the covenant covered transactions that originated in New York dealing with real property outside New York State. The Employment Contract prohibits Cohen from working on sales originating in New York, and the contract does not specify that this prohibition is limited only to those transactions where the property is located in New York. The main limitation on covenants not to compete is that they will be enforced only to the extent necessary to protect the employer's legitimate interests. See Reed, Roberts, 40 N.Y.2d at 307, 386 N.Y.S.2d 677, 353 N.E.2d 590. Here, approximately one-half of Cohen's business on Ticor's behalf involved sale of title insurance to New York attorneys and other New York customers in connection with real property located outside of New York. As a consequence, to protect the legitimate business interests of the employer necessarily means construing the covenant not to compete as including sales originating in New York, but which cover out-of-state property.

CONCLUSION

For the reasons stated, therefore, the judgment entered in district court enjoining defendant under the non-competition contract is affirmed.

Rogers v. Runfola & Associates, Inc.

Supreme Court of Ohio, 1991.
57 Ohio St.3d 5, 565 N.E.2d 540.

[Court reporters filed declaratory judgment action challenging validity of covenants not to compete in employment contracts. Employer counterclaimed, seeking specific performance of covenants, injunctive relief, and damages. The trial court held in favor of employees. The Court of Appeals affirmed. The Supreme Court granted in part the relief sought by the employer.]

■ DOUGLAS, J.

The primary issue we are asked to decide is whether the covenants not to compete contained within appellees' employment contracts are reasonable in light of the guidelines pronounced by this court in Raimonde v. Van Vlerah (1975), 42 Ohio St.2d 21, 71 O.O.2d 12, 325 N.E.2d 544.

. . . .

II

Having found that appellees' employment contracts are valid, we now turn our discussion to the covenants not to compete contained therein.

In *Raimonde*, at paragraphs one and two of the syllabus, we stated:

"1. A covenant not to compete which imposes unreasonable restrictions upon an employee will be enforced to the extent necessary to protect an employer's legitimate interests. (Paragraphs two and three of the syllabus in Extine v. Williamson Midwest [(1964)] 176 Ohio St. 403 [200 N.E.2d 297] overruled.)

"2. A covenant restraining an employee from competing with his former employer upon termination of employment is reasonable if the restraint is no greater than is required for the protection of the employer, does not impose undue hardship on the employee, and is not injurious to the public." (Emphasis added.)

Further, in Raimonde, we acknowledged that courts are empowered to fashion a reasonable covenant between the parties and, in so doing, they should consider the following factors:

" * * * '[T]he absence or presence of limitations as to time and space, * * * whether the employee represents the sole contact with the customer; whether the employee is possessed with confidential information or trade secrets; whether the covenant seeks to eliminate competition which would be unfair to the employer or merely seeks to eliminate ordinary competition; whether the covenant seeks to stifle the inherent skill and experience of the employee; whether the benefit to the employer is disproportional to the detriment to the employee; whether the covenant operates as a bar to the employee's sole means of support; whether the employee's talent which the employer seeks to suppress was actually developed during the period of employment; and whether the forbidden employment is merely incidental to the main employment.' * * * " (Citations omitted.) *Raimonde,* 42 Ohio St.2d at 25, 71 O.O.2d at 14, 325 N.E.2d at 547.

Keeping the foregoing factors in mind, we conclude that the restraints and resultant hardships on appellees do exceed that which is reasonable to protect Runfola's legitimate business interests. Geographically, appellees are prohibited from engaging in court reporting or public stenography in Franklin County for two years. Appellees are also restricted, for a lifetime, from soliciting or diverting any of Runfola's clients. Court reporting is a unique profession. Appellees attended school to become court reporters and have worked as reporters for most of their adult lives. Rogers' and Marrone's testimony indicated that court reporting is the only profession in which they have become proficient. Imposing such space and time restrictions is unreasonable and will create an undue hardship on appellees.

Although we conclude that the covenants not to compete create an excessive hardship on appellees, our inquiry, nevertheless, cannot end here. We must also determine whether some restrictions prohibiting appellees from competing are necessary to protect Runfola's business interests. The record reflects that Runfola played a large role in appellees' development as successful court reporters. While employed by Runfola, Rogers and Marrone gained valuable experience in the business which included the use of computerized technology. Runfola invested time and money in equipment, facilities, support staff and training. Much of this training and support, undoubtedly, inured to the benefit of the appellees. Runfola also developed a clientele with which appellees had direct contact. Appellees' assignments were taken under the Runfola name. Indeed, Runfola has a legitimate commercial interest to protect.

Thus, balancing the restraints and projected hardships on appellees with Runfola's interests, and upon the authority of Raimonde, we modify the restrictions as to space and time as set forth infra.

Apparently, in 1988, soon after the trial court rendered its judgment, appellees started a court reporting business and, to date, are still in operation. Notwithstanding this, Runfola requests that we enjoin appellees from engaging in competitive activities with Runfola and that we remand the case to the trial court on the issue of damages. Runfola seeks to have appellees enjoined as of the date of our decision. Appellees, on the other hand, urge us to follow Moraine Industrial Supply, Inc. v. Sterling Rubber Products Co. (C.A.6, 1989), 891 F.2d 133, and Premix, Inc. v. Zappitelli (N.D.Ohio 1983), 561 F.Supp. 269, and find that an injunction would be extremely harsh or inappropriate because the restrictive period, by its own terms, has expired.

Upon balancing these competing interests, we find appellees' authority unpersuasive and conclude that the better view is to grant Runfola, in part, the relief sought. In *Raimonde*, this court held it was entirely proper for a trial court to enjoin an employee who breached a covenant not to compete " * * * for three years *from the date of the court's order * * * * [and] [t]o hold otherwise would emasculate the clear intent of * * * Civ.R. 54(C)." (Emphasis added.)

Therefore, we hold that appellees shall, sixty days from the date of this order, be prohibited for a period of one year from engaging in court reporting or public stenography as a business, as employees, or otherwise, within the city limits of Columbus, Ohio, and be prohibited for a period of one year from engaging in court reporting or the stenography business with any person, firm or other business entity with an office located within the city limits of Columbus, Ohio. Further, appellees shall, from the date of this order, be prohibited for a period of one year from soliciting or diverting any of Runfola's clients that have employed Runfola seeking advice, assistance or services. Finally, we remand this case to the trial court on the sole issue of damages. Upon remand, the trial court should determine what damages, if any, appellees have caused Runfola by disregarding the covenant not to compete, as modified, by this court.

Judgment affirmed in part, reversed in part and cause remanded.

[J. Herbert's separate opinion, concurring in part and dissenting in part has been omitted].

NOTES ON RESTRICTIVE COVENANTS IN EMPLOYMENT
   CONTRACTS

1. In Purchasing Associates, Inc. v. Weitz, 13 N.Y.2d 267, 246 N.Y.S.2d 600, 196 N.E.2d 245 (1963), the court made the following observations:

At one time, a covenant not to compete, basically an agreement in restraint of trade, was regarded with high disfavor by the courts and denounced as being "against the benefit of the commonwealth." It later became evident, however, that there were situations in which it was not only desirable but essential that such covenants not to compete be enforced.

Where, for instance, there is a sale of a business, involving as it does the transfer of its good will as a going concern, the courts will enforce an incidental covenant by the seller not to compete with the buyer after the sale. This rule is grounded, most reasonably, on the premise that a buyer of a business should be permitted to restrict his seller's freedom of trade so as to prevent the latter from recapturing and utilizing, by his competition, the good will of the very business which he transferred for value. This court has applied the "sale of a business" rationale where an owner, partner, or major stockholder of a commercial enterprise has sold his interest for an immediate consideration which was, in part, payment for the good will of the business, in terms of "continuity of place" and "continuity of name". The sole limitation on the enforceability of such a restrictive covenant is that the restraint imposed be "reasonable," that is, not more extensive, in terms of time and space, than is reasonably necessary to the buyer for the protection of his legitimate interest in the enjoyment of the asset bought.

Also enforceable is a covenant given by an employee that he will not compete with his employer when he quits his employ, and the general limitation of "reasonableness", to which we have just referred, applies equally to such a covenant. However, since in the case of such a covenant the element of good will, or its transfer, is not involved and since there are powerful considerations of public policy which militate against sanctioning the loss of a man's livelihood, the courts have generally displayed a much stricter attitude with respect to covenants of this type. Thus, a covenant by which an employee simply agrees, as a condition of his employment, not to compete with his employer after they have severed relations is not only subject to the overriding limitation of "reasonableness" but is enforced only to the extent necessary to prevent the employee's use or disclosure of his former employer's trade secrets, processes or formulae or his solicitation of, or disclosure of any information concerning, the other's customers. If, however, the employee's services are deemed "special, unique, or extraordinary", then, the covenant may be enforced by injunctive relief, if "reasonable," even though the employment did not involve the possession of trade secrets or confidential customer lists.

2. Consider Rule 5.6 of the Model Rules of Professional Conduct:

Rule 5.6 Restrictions on Right to Practice

A lawyer shall not participate in offering or making:

(a) A partnership or employment agreement that restricts the right of a lawyer to practice after termination of the relationship, except an agreement concerning benefits upon retirement; or

(b) An agreement in which a restriction on the lawyer's right to practice is part of the settlement of a controversy between private parties.

3.   Cullins worked for Smith, Bell & Co., an insurance company. His contract said that he would not work in a competing insurance business in the same county for three years after the end of his employment with Smith, Bell & Co. Over the next eleven years, he attained "a position of prominence" in the company. Finally, the company was sold. Cullins rejected the new owner's offer to stay with the firm in the capacity of vice president and director. He decided instead to form his own agency. Although the trial court found that Cullins "intend[ed] to use the knowledge, experience and customer contacts which he acquired during his service with Smith, Bell & Company, Inc., to further the business interests of his newly formed agency," it refused to enforce Cullins' covenant not to compete. Its decision was affirmed on appeal on the ground that the covenant was not assignable. Smith, Bell & Hauck, Inc. v. Cullins, 123 Vt. 96, 183 A.2d 528 (1962).

4.   In addition to noncompetition clauses that prohibit employees from competing against the employer during and for some time after their employment, there are "nonsolicitation" clauses that prohibit former employees from soliciting and attempting to attract business from their former employer's customers and prospects. The following case addresses the enforceability of such a clause.

BDO Seidman v. Hirshberg

Court of Appeals of New York, 1999.
93 N.Y.2d 382, 712 N.E.2d 1220, 690 N.Y.S.2d 854

Opinion of the Court

■ LEVINE, J.:

BDO Seidman (BDO), a general partnership of certified public accountants, appeals from the affirmance of an order of Supreme Court granting summary judgment dismissing its complaint against defendant, who was formerly employed as an accountant with the firm. The central issue before us is whether the "reimbursement clause" in an agreement between the parties, requiring defendant to compensate BDO for serving any client of the firm's Buffalo office within 18 months after the termination of his employment, is an invalid and unenforceable restrictive covenant. The courts below so held.

Facts and Procedural History

BDO is a national accounting firm having 40 offices throughout the United States, including four in New York State. Defendant began employment in BDO's Buffalo office in 1984, when the accounting firm he had been working for was merged into BDO, its partners becoming BDO partners. In 1989, defendant was promoted to the position of manager, apparently a step immediately below attaining partner status. As a condition of receiving the promotion, defendant was required to sign a "Manager's Agreement," the provisions of which are at issue. In Paragraph "SIXTH" defendant expressly acknowledged that a fiduciary relationship existed between him and the firm by reason of his having received various disclosures which would give him an advantage in attracting BDO clients. Based upon that stated premise, defendant agreed that if, within 18 months following the termination of his employment, he served any former client of BDO's Buffalo office, he would compensate BDO "for the loss and damages suffered" in an amount equal to one and one half times the fees BDO had charged that client over the last fiscal year of the client's patronage. Defendant was to pay such amount in five annual installments.

Defendant resigned from BDO in October 1993. This action was commenced in January 1995. During pretrial discovery, BDO submitted a list of 100 former clients of its Buffalo office, allegedly lost to defendant, who were billed a total of $138,000 in the year defendant left the firm's practice. Defendant denied serving some of the clients, averred that a substantial number of them were personal clients he had brought to the firm through his own outside contacts, and also claimed that with respect to some clients, he had not been the primary BDO representative servicing the account.

Following discovery, the parties exchanged motions for summary judgment. BDO's submissions on the motion did not contain any evidence that defendant actually solicited former clients, and did not rely in any way on claims that defendant used confidential information in acquiring BDO clients. Supreme Court granted summary judgment to defendant, concluding that the reimbursement clause was an overbroad and unenforceable anti-competitive agreement. The Appellate Division agreed, holding that the entire agreement was invalid (247 AD2d 923).

Discussion

Concededly, the Manager's Agreement defendant signed does not prevent him from competing for new clients, nor does it expressly bar him from serving BDO clients. Instead, it requires him to pay "for the loss and damages" sustained by BDO in losing any of its clients to defendant within 18 months after his departure, an amount equivalent to one and one half times the last annual billing for any such client who became the client of defendant. Nonetheless, it is not seriously disputed that the agreement, in its purpose and effect, is a form of ancillary employee anti-competitive agreement that will be carefully scrutinized by the courts (see, Columbia Ribbon & Carbon Mfg. Co. v. A–1–A Corp., 42 NY2d 496, 499). Reported cases adjudicating the validity of post-employment restrictive covenants go back almost 300 years (see, Blake, Employee Agreements Not To Compete, 73 Harv L Rev 625, 629, citing, inter alia, Mitchel v Reynolds, 24 Eng. Rep. 347 [Q.B. 1711]). In the 19th century, a standard of reasonableness for judging the validity of such agreements developed in case law here and in England, balancing the need of fair protection for the benefit of the employer against the opposing interests of the former employee and the public (Blake, op. cit., at 639–640).

The modern, prevailing common law standard of reasonableness for employee agreements not to compete applies a three-pronged test. A restraint is reasonable only if it: (1) is no greater than is required for the protection of the legitimate interest of the employer, (2) does not impose undue hardship on the employee, and (3) is not injurious to the public (see, e.g., Technical Aid Corp. v. Allen, 134 NH 1, 8, 591 A2d 262, 265–266; Blake, op. cit., at 648–649; Restatement [Second] of Contracts § 188). A violation of any prong renders the covenant invalid.

New York has adopted this prevailing standard of reasonableness in determining the validity of employee agreements not to compete. "In this context a restrictive covenant will only be subject to specific enforcement to the extent that it is reasonable in time and area, necessary to protect the employer's legitimate interests, not harmful to the general public and not unreasonably burdensome to the employee" (Reed, Roberts Assocs. v. Strauman, 40 NY2d 303, 307).

In general, we have strictly applied the rule to limit enforcement of broad restraints on competition. Thus, in Reed, Roberts Assocs. (supra), we limited the cognizable employer interests under the first prong of the common law rule to the protection against misappropriation of the employer's trade secrets or of confidential customer lists, or protection from competition by a former employee whose services are unique or extraordinary (40 NY2d, at 308).

With agreements not to compete between professionals, however, we have given greater weight to the interests of the employer in restricting competition within a confined geographical area. In Gelder Med. Group v. Webber (41 NY2d 680) and Karpinski v. Ingrasci (28 NY2d 45), we enforced total restraints on competition, in limited rural locales, permanently in Karpinski and for five years in Gelder. The rationale for the differential application of the common law rule of reasonableness expressed in our decisions was that professionals are deemed to provide "unique or extraordinary" services (see, Reed, Roberts Assocs. v Strauman, supra, 40 NY2d, at 308).

BDO urges that accountancy is entitled to the status of a learned profession and, as such, the Karpinski and Gelder Medical Group precedents militate in favor of the validity of the restrictive covenant here. We agree that accountancy has all the earmarks of a learned profession. CPAs are required to have extensive formal training and education (Education Law § 7404[1][2], [3]; 8 NYCRR 70.1); they must pass a written examination (Education Law § 7404[1][4]; 8 NYCRR 70.3); and they are subject to mandatory continuing education requirements (Education Law § 7409; 8 NYCRR 70.6). Their professional conduct is regulated by the Board of Regents under statutory disciplinary procedures (Education Law §§ 6509–6511). Moreover, there is a national code of professional conduct for certified public accountants which provides that "[m]embers should accept the obligation to act in a way that will serve the public interest, honor the public trust, and demonstrate commitment to professionalism" (American Institute of Certified Public Accountants Code of Professional Conduct § 53, art II). The foregoing factors closely correspond to the criteria for a learned profession listed in Matter of Freedman (34 NY2d 1, 7).[1] Nonethe-

---

1. Law firm partnership agreements represent an exception to the liberality with which we have previously treated restraints on competition in the learned professions (see, Cohen v. Lord, Day & Lord, 75 NY2d 95; Denburg v. Parker Chapin Flattau & Klimpl, 82 NY2d 375). Our decisions invalidating anti-competitive clauses in such agree-

less, Gelder Medical Group and Karpinski do not dictate the result here. As we noted in Karpinski, the application of the test of reasonableness of employee restrictive covenants focuses on the particular facts and circumstances giving context to the agreement (28 NY2d, at 49; see also, Reed, Roberts Assocs. v Strauman, supra, 40 NY2d, at 307). This Court's rationale for giving wider latitude to covenants between members of a learned profession because their services are unique or extraordinary (Reed, Roberts Assocs., supra) does not realistically apply to the actual context of the anti-competitive agreement here. In the instant case, BDO is a national accounting firm seeking to enforce the agreement within a market consisting of the entirety of a major metropolitan area. Moreover, defendant's unchallenged averments indicate that his status in the firm was not based upon the uniqueness or extraordinary nature of the accounting services he generally performed on behalf of the firm, but in major part on his ability to attract a corporate clientele. Nor was there any proof that defendant possessed any unique or extraordinary ability as an accountant that would give him a competitive advantage over BDO. Moreover, the contexts of the agreements not to compete in Karpinski and Gelder Medical Group were entirely different. In each case, the former associate would have been in direct competition with the promisee-practitioner for referrals from a narrow group of primary health providers in a rural, geographical market for their medical or dental practice specialty.

Thus, our learned profession precedents do not obviate the need for independent scrutiny of the anti-competitive provisions of the Manager's Agreement under the tripartite common law standard. Close analysis of Paragraph SIXTH of the agreement under the first prong of the common law rule, to identify the legitimate interest of BDO and determine whether the covenant is no more restrictive than is necessary to protect that interest, leads us to conclude that the covenant as written is overbroad in some respects. BDO claims that the legitimate interest it is entitled to protect is its entire client base, which it asserts a modern, large accounting firm expends considerable time and money building and maintaining. However, the only justification for imposing an employee agreement not to compete is to forestall unfair competition (see, Columbia Ribbon & Carbon Mfg. Co. v A–1–A Corp., 42 NY2d, supra, at 499). It seems self-evident that a former employee may be capable of fairly competing for an employer's clients by refraining from use of unfair means to compete. If the employee abstains from unfair means in competing for those clients, the employer's interest in preserving its client base against the competition of the former employer is no more legitimate and worthy of contractual protection than when it vies with unrelated competitors for those clients.

Legal scholars and courts have more circumspectly identified the employer's legitimate interest in employee anti-competitive agreements than that of preservation of the employer's entire client base where, as

---

ments were not based on application of the common law rule, but upon enforcement of the public policy reflected in DR 2–108(A) of the Code of Professional Responsibility (see, 22 NYCRR 1200.13). There is no counterpart to DR 2–108(A) in the rules regulating the ethical conduct of accountants. Hence, Cohen and Denburgdo not require invalidation of the restrictive covenant here (see, Faw, Casson & Co. v. Cranston, 375 A2d 463, 468 [Del Ch]; Mailman, Ross, Toyes & Shapiro v. Edelson, 183 NJ Super 434, 440; 444 A2d 75, 78).

here, there is no evidence that the employee obtained a competitive advantage by using confidential information. Professor Blake, in his seminal article in the Harvard Law Review, explains that the legitimate purpose of an employer in connection with employee restraints is "to prevent competitive use, for a time, of information or relationships which pertain peculiarly to the employer and which the employee acquired in the course of employment" (Blake, op. cit., at 647 [emphasis supplied]). Protection of customer relationships the employee acquired in the course of employment may indeed be a legitimate interest (id., at 653). "The risk to the employer reaches a maximum in situations in which the employee must work closely with the client or customer over a long period of time, especially when his services are a significant part of the total transaction" (id., at 661). Then, the employee has been enabled to share in the goodwill of a client or customer which the employer's overall efforts and expenditures created. The employer has a legitimate interest in preventing former employees from exploiting or appropriating the goodwill of a client or customer, which had been created and maintained at the employer's expense, to the employer's competitive detriment (see, Technical Aid Corp. v Allen, supra, 134 NH, at 9, 591 A2d, at 266; Peat Marwick Main & Co. v. Haass, 818 SW2d 381, 387 [Tex Sup Ct]).

It follows from the foregoing that BDO's legitimate interest here is protection against defendant's competitive use of client relationships which BDO enabled him to acquire through his performance of accounting services for the firm's clientele during the course of his employment (Blake, op. cit., at 647–661). Extending the anti-competitive covenant to BDO's clients with whom a relationship with defendant did not develop through assignments to perform direct, substantive accounting services would, therefore, violate the first prong of the common law rule: it would constitute a restraint "greater than is needed to protect" these legitimate interests (Restatement [Second] of Contracts § 188[1][a]).[2]

The foregoing overbreadth was the basis upon which a number of State courts have invalidated restrictive covenant agreements prohibiting employees from providing post-employment accounting services to any client of the employer without regard to whether the employee served the client during the course of employment (see, Peat Marwick Main & Co. v. Haass, 818 SW2d 381, supra; Singer v. Habif, Arogeti & Wynne, 250 Ga 376, 297 SE2d 473; Smith Batchelder & Rugg v. Foster, 119 NH 679, 406 A2d 1310; Philip G. Johnson & Co. v. Salmen, 211 Neb 123, 317 NW2d 900). Although other courts have enforced employee restrictive covenants extending to an accounting firm's entire client base, they have either failed adequately to identify the employer's legitimate interest (see, Dobbins, De Guire & Tucker, P.C. v. Rutherford, MacDonald & Olson, 218 Mont 392, 708 P2d 577; Follmer, Rudzewicz & Co. v. Kosco, 420 Mich 394, 362 NW2d 676), or having properly identified the interest, did not engage in analysis as to whether the restriction was greater than necessary to protect it (see, Perry

2. A different result might obtain had BDO submitted any proof that defendant had used confidential firm information to attract BDO clients with whom he had not had a relationship while employed there.

v. Moran, 109 Wash 2d 691, 748 P2d 224, modified on reh. 111 Wash 2d 885, 766 P2d 1096).

To the extent, then, that paragraph SIXTH of the Manager's Agreement requires defendant to compensate BDO for lost patronage of clients with whom he never acquired a relationship through the direct provision of substantive accounting services during his employment, the covenant is invalid and unenforceable. By a parity of reasoning, it would be unreasonable to extend the covenant to personal clients of defendant who came to the firm solely to avail themselves of his services and only as a result of his own independent recruitment efforts, which BDO neither subsidized nor otherwise financially supported as part of a program of client development. Because the goodwill of those clients was not acquired through the expenditure of BDO's resources, the firm has no legitimate interest in preventing defendant from competing for their patronage. Indeed, enforcement of the restrictive covenant as to defendant's personal clients would permit BDO to appropriate goodwill created and maintained through defendant's efforts, essentially turning on its head the principal justification to uphold any employee agreement not to compete based on protection of customer or client relationships.

Except for the overbreadth in the foregoing two respects, the restrictions in paragraph SIXTH do not violate the tripartite common law test for reasonableness. The restraint on serving BDO clients is limited to 18 months, and to clients of BDO's Buffalo office. The time constraint appears to represent a reasonably brief interlude to enable the firm to replace the client relationship and goodwill defendant was permitted to acquire with some of its clients. Defendant is free to compete immediately for new business in any market and, if the overbroad provisions of the covenant are struck, to retain his personal clients and those clients of BDO's that he had not served to any significant extent while employed at the firm. He has averred that BDO's list of lost accounts contains a number of clients in both categories. Thus, there is scant evidence suggesting that the covenant, if cured of overbreadth, would work an undue hardship on defendant.

Moreover, given the likely broad array of accounting services available in the greater Buffalo area, and the limited remaining class of BDO clientele affected by the covenant, it cannot be said that the restraint, as narrowed, would seriously impinge on the availability of accounting services in the Buffalo area from which the public may draw, or cause any significant dislocation in the market or create a monopoly in accounting services in that locale. These factors militate against a conclusion that a reformed paragraph SIXTH would violate the third prong of the common law test, injury to the public interest (see, Gelder Med. Group v Webber, supra, 41 NY2d, at 685; Blake, op. cit., at 686–687; Restatement [Second] of Contracts § 188, comment g).

Severance or Partial Enforcement

We conclude that the Appellate Division erred in holding that the entire covenant must be invalidated, and in declining partially to enforce the covenant to the extent necessary to protect BDO's legitimate interest. The Appellate Division rejected partial enforcement or severance of the invalid part of the covenant, because "the court would thereby be required to rewrite the entire contract" (247 AD2d, at 923). In Karpinski v Ingrasci (28 NY2d, supra, at 51–52), this Court expressly recognized and applied the judicial power to sever and grant partial enforcement for an overbroad employee restrictive covenant. The Court refused to give effect to the portion of the covenant which barred the practice of general dentistry, but enforced it respecting the practice of oral surgery, that being the employer's actual, specialized dental practice.

The issue of whether a court should cure the unreasonable aspect of an overbroad employee restrictive covenant through the means of partial enforcement or severance has been the subject of some debate among courts and commentators (see, Blake, op. cit., at 682–683). A legitimate consideration against the exercise of this power is the fear that employers will use their superior bargaining position to impose unreasonable anti-competitive restrictions, uninhibited by the risk that a court will void the entire agreement, leaving the employee free of any restraint (id.). The prevailing, modern view rejects a per se rule that invalidates entirely any overbroad employee agreement not to compete. Instead, when, as here, the unenforceable portion is not an essential part of the agreed exchange, a court should conduct a case specific analysis, focusing on the conduct of the employer in imposing the terms of the agreement (see, Restatement [Second] of Contracts § 184). Under this approach, if the employer demonstrates an absence of overreaching, coercive use of dominant bargaining power, or other anti-competitive misconduct, but has in good faith sought to protect a legitimate business interest, consistent with reasonable standards of fair dealing, partial enforcement may be justified (see, Blake, op. cit., at 633; Restatement [Second] of Contracts § 184[1], [2]). We essentially adopted this more flexible position in Karpinski (supra).

Here, the undisputed facts and circumstances militate in favor of partial enforcement. The covenant was not imposed as a condition of defendant's initial employment, or even his continued employment, but in connection with promotion to a position of responsibility and trust just one step below admittance to the partnership. There is no evidence of coercion or that the Manager's Agreement was part of some general plan to forestall competition. Moreover, no proof was submitted that BDO imposed the covenant in bad faith, knowing full well that it was overbroad. Indeed, as already discussed, the existence of our "learned profession" precedents, and decisions in other States upholding the full terms of this type of agreement, support the contrary conclusion. Therefore, partial enforcement of Paragraph SIXTH is warranted.

The Appellate Division's fear that partial enforcement will require rewriting the parties' agreement is unfounded. No additional substantive terms are required. The time and geographical limitations on the covenant remain intact. The only change is to narrow the class of BDO clients to which the covenant applies (cf., Karpinski v Ingrasci, supra [narrowing the scope of the prohibitive post-employment activity]). Moreover, to reject partial enforcement based solely on the extent of necessary revision of the contract resembles the now-discredited doctrine that invalidation of an entire restrictive covenant is required unless the invalid portion was so divisible that it could be mechanically severed, as with a "judicial blue pencil" (see, Blake, op. cit., at 681). The Restatement (Second) of Contracts rejected that rigid requirement of strict divisibility before a covenant could be partially enforced (see, Reporter's Note, Restatement [Second] of Contracts § 184, at 32). Thus, we conclude that severance is appropriate, rendering the restrictive covenant partially enforceable.

Damages

Since defendant does not dispute that at least some BDO clients to which the restrictive covenant validly applies were served by him during the contractual duration of the restraint, plaintiff is entitled to partial summary judgment on the issue of liability. Remittal is required in order to establish plaintiff's damages, including resolution of any contested issue as to which of BDO's former clients served by defendant the restrictive covenant validly covers.

As to those clients, the measure of plaintiff's damages will depend in the first instance on the validity of the clause in paragraph SIXTH of the Manager's Agreement requiring defendant to compensate BDO "for the loss and damages suffered" in an amount equal to one and one half times the fees charged each lost client over the last full year the client was served by the firm. This provision essentially represents a liquidated damages clause, as BDO conceded at nisi prius.

Liquidated damages provisions, under our precedents, are valid if the "damages flowing from a breach are difficult to ascertain [and under] a provision fixing damages in advance * * * the amount is a reasonable measure of the anticipated probable harm" (City of Rye v. Public Serv. Mut. Ins. Co., 34 NY2d 470, 473). On the other hand, if "the amount fixed is plainly or grossly disproportionate to the probable loss, the provision calls for a penalty and will not be enforced" (Truck Rent–A–Center, Inc. v. Puritan Farms 2nd, Inc., 41 NY2d 420, 425).

The damages here are sufficiently difficult to ascertain to satisfy the first requirement of a valid liquidated damages provision. Because of the inability to project with any degree of certainty how long a given client would have remained with BDO if defendant had not made himself available as an alternative source of accounting services, BDO's actual lost profits from defendant's breach would be impossible to determine with any precision.

BDO submits that the second requirement is also met, in that the agreed upon amount is not grossly disproportionate to the anticipated probable harm. In rationalizing this measure of damages, BDO relies upon the affidavit of the managing partner of its Buffalo office that "the amount of liquidated damages was tied to a commonly accepted way of valuing a client account of a professional services firm as an asset" (emphasis supplied). It is apparent that BDO's rationale for the liquidated damages formula likens the value of BDO's loss of a client account to what an arms-length purchaser would have paid for it as a firm asset on a sale of the practice. Various courts reviewing accountants' employee agreements not to compete have been persuaded of the reasonableness of a liquidated damages formula based on the prevalent use of client gross billings to value an accounting practice for purpose of acquisition (see, Holloway v. Faw, Casson & Co., 319 Md 324, 355, 572 A2d 510, 525; Foti v. Cook, 220 Va 800, 807, 263 SE2d 430, 434; Knight, Vale & Gregory v. McDaniel, 37 Wash App 366, 372, 680 P2d 448, 453).

In our view, however, the averment regarding the basis of the liquidated damages formula by no means conclusively demonstrates the absence of gross disproportionality. Indeed, the nonspecific averment in the affidavit, quoted above, which BDO relies upon, is the only record evidence supporting the reasonableness of the liquidated damages clause. We note that other courts have remitted on the issue of the validity of these types of liquidated damages provisions in accountant employee anti-competitive agreements when they found the record insufficiently developed to establish that the amount fixed in the agreement was not so excessive to actual damages as to constitute a penalty (see, Perry v Moran, supra, 111 Wash, at 887, 766 P2d, at 1097; Follmer Rudzewicz & Co. v Kosco, supra, 420 Mich, at 409, 362 NW2d, at 684). The sparse proof on this issue here persuades us that we, similarly, should remit for further development of the record on the liquidated damages formula.

Accordingly, the order of the Appellate Division, insofar as appealed from, should be modified, without costs, by denying defendant's motion for summary judgment, granting plaintiff's motion for partial summary judgment declaring the restrictive covenant enforceable as here provided, and remitting to Supreme Court for further proceedings in accordance with this Opinion and, as so modified, affirmed.

Order, insofar as appealed from, modified, without costs, by denying defendant's motion for summary judgment, granting plaintiff's motion for partial summary judgment declaring the restrictive covenant enforceable as provided in the opinion, and remitting to Supreme Court for further proceedings in accordance with the opinion herein and, as so modified, affirmed. Opinion by Judge Levine. Chief Judge Kaye and Judges Bellacosa, Smith, Ciparick, Wesley and Rosenblatt concur.

1.   Note that in *BDO Seidman*, the New York Court of Appeals partially enforced the covenant, rather than invalidate the covenant entirely. In Peat Marwick Main & Company v. Haass, 818 S.W.2d 381 (Texas 1991), the Supreme Court of Texas reviewed a similar type of nonsolicitation clause, and like the New York Court of Appeals, the Supreme Court of Texas found the covenant overbroad, but unlike the New York Court of Appeals, the Supreme Court of Texas refused partial enforcement and invalidated the entire covenant.

Consider the following Michigan statute:

445.774a. Agreements not to compete; application

Sec. 4a. (1) An employer may obtain from an employee an agreement or covenant which protects an employer's reasonable competitive business interests and expressly prohibits an employee from engaging in employment or a line of business after termination of employment if the agreement or covenant is reasonable as to its duration, geographical area, and the type of employment or line of business. *To the extent any such agreement or covenant is found to be unreasonable in any respect, a court may limit the agreement to render it reasonable in light of the circumstances in which it was made and specifically enforce the agreement as limited.*

(2) This section shall apply to covenants and agreements which are entered into after March 29, 1985.

MICH. COMP. LAWS ANN. § 445.774a (West 1999) (emphasis supplied).

Post v. Merrill Lynch, Pierce, Fenner & Smith, Inc.

Court of Appeals of New York, 1979.
48 N.Y.2d 84, 421 N.Y.S.2d 847, 397 N.E.2d 358.

■ WACHTLER, J. The narrow issue presented by this appeal . . . is the efficacy of a private pension plan provision permitting the employer to forfeit pension benefits earned by an employee who competes with the employer after being involuntarily discharged.

. . . .

Merrill Lynch employed Post and Maney as account executives at its Rochester offices beginning April 20, 1959, and May 15, 1961, respectively. Both men elected to be paid a salary and to participate in the firm's pension and profit-sharing plans rather than take a straight commission . . .

The employment of both plaintiffs by Merrill Lynch terminated August 30, 1974. On September 4, 1974, both began working for Bache & Company, admittedly a competitor of Merrill Lynch, in Rochester. Merrill Lynch learned about their new employment in September, 1974.

Fifteen months after their termination, and following repeated inquiries by the plaintiffs into the status of their pensions, the plaintiffs were informed by Merrill Lynch that all of their rights in the company-funded pension plan had been forfeited pursuant to a provision of the plan which permitted forfeiture in the event that an employee directly or indirectly competed with the firm.

Plaintiffs brought this action against Merrill Lynch for conversion and breach of contract, to recover amounts allegedly owed them on account of the pension plan and for punitive damages. They aver that they were discharged by Merrill Lynch without cause. Merrill Lynch does not, for the purpose of this motion, dispute plaintiffs' version, contending, rather, that for this purpose the reason for termination is irrelevant.

The Appellate Division granted Merrill Lynch's motion for summary judgment and dismissed the complaint, relying principally on the Appellate Division decision in Kristt v. Whelan, 4 A.D.2d 195, 164 N.Y.S.2d 239, affd., 5 N.Y.2d 807, 181 N.Y.S.2d 205, 155 N.E.2d 116 to sustain the validity of the forfeiture provision. As the Appellate Division in *Kristt* held: "It is no unreasonable restriction of the liberty of a man to earn his living if he may be relieved of the restriction by forfeiting a contract right or by adhering to the provisions of his contract. The provision for forfeiture here involved did not bar plaintiff from other employment. He had the choice of preserving his rights under the trust by refraining from competition with [his former employer] or risking forfeiture of such rights by exercising his right to compete with [him]."

Now, in determining the effect to be accorded a forfeiture-for-competition provision in an employees' pension, we are for the first time invited to distinguish between voluntary and involuntary termination of employment of the affected employee. Examination of our cases discloses no prior instance in which enforcement of such a forfeiture clause has been sought in circumstances where the employment has been terminated by the employer without cause. Rather, as in *Kristt*, they have involved claims by an employee who sought pension benefits from his former employer despite having voluntarily left the employer and joined forces with a competitor. In such situations effect has been given to the forfeiture-for-competition provision, and the employee's claim has been rejected.

... [W]e find no dispositive judicial precedent in our State where the employee has been terminated by the employer without cause.... [W]e also must take into account the declaration of a strong public policy against forfeiture of employee benefits manifested by the Employee Retirement Income Security Act of 1974 (ERISA)(U.S.Code, tit. 29, § 1001 et seq.). Indeed, had the relevant provisions of ERISA been in effect at the time of termination of these appellants' employment, its mandatory provisions might well have been dispositive in this case and have precluded the forfeiture countenanced by the court below.

Impelled as we are then by that powerfully articulated congressional policy, and confronted with no decisions which command a contrary result, we now conclude that our own policies—those in favor of permitting individuals to work where and for whom they please, and against forfeiture—preclude the enforcement of a forfeiture-for-competition clause where the termination of employment is involuntary and without cause.

In the case at bar we note that the particular provision in the pension plan was not drawn explicitly to cover employees whose employment had been involuntarily terminated; it indiscriminately mandates forfeiture by any "Participant who enters employment or engages directly or indirectly in any business deemed by the Committee to be competitive." Therefore we need not consider now what would have been our decision had the draftsman of this pension plan manifested an unmistakable intention to impose the heavy penalty of forfeiture for engaging in competition even after discharge of an employee without cause.

Acknowledging the tension between the freedom of individuals to contract, and the reluctance to see one barter away his freedom, the State enforces limited restraints on an employee's employment mobility where a mutuality of obligation is freely bargained for by the parties. An essential aspect of that relationship, however, is the employer's continued willingness to employ the party covenanting not to compete. Where the employer terminates the employment relationship without cause, however, his action necessarily destroys the mutuality of obligation on which the covenant rests as well as the employer's ability to impose a forfeiture. An employer should not be permitted to use offensively an anticompetition clause coupled with a forfeiture provision to economically cripple a former employee and simultaneously deny other potential employers his services.

Under the circumstances of the case at bar it would be unconscionable to tolerate a forfeiture, precipitated as it is by the unwarranted action of the employer. We find, therefore, that in the case of an involuntary discharge, the rule stated in *Kristt v. Whelan* ... does not apply. Further, we hold, that where an employee is involuntarily discharged by his employer without cause and thereafter enters into competition with his former employer, and where the employer, based on such competition, would forfeit the pension benefits earned by his former employee, such a forfeiture is unreasonable as a matter of law and cannot stand.

. . . .

Order, insofar as appealed from, reversed, with costs, defendants' motion for summary judgment denied and the complaint reinstated.

———

E. CONTRACTS FOR ARBITRATION

Arbitration and arbitration agreements have not always been honored by law. This formerly negative attitude has greatly changed in recent years as may be noted by statutes that favor arbitration as a method of dispute resolution.

It is now clearly established that a court will confirm and enforce by specific performance an arbitral award even in cases where there was doubt or discretion as to whether a court would have granted the specific relief granted by the additional award. Edward D. Re, *The Lawyer's Bookshelf*, N.Y.L.J., Nov. 28, 2003, at 2 (reviewing LAURENCE CRAIG, WILLIAM W. PARK & JAN PAULSON, INTERNATIONAL CHAMBER OF COMMERCE ARBITRATION (2000)).

Grayson–Robinson Stores, Inc. v. Iris Constr. Corp.
Court of Appeals of New York, 1960.
8 N.Y.2d 133, 202 N.Y.S.2d 303, 168 N.E.2d 377.

■ DESMOND, C.J. Again, as in Matter of Staklinski (Pyramid Elec. Co.), 6 N.Y.2d 159, 188 N.Y.S.2d 541, 160 N.E.2d 78, the courts are called upon to confirm an arbitration award which, conformably to the express powers given by the parties to the arbitrators, directed specific performance of a contract. Appellant, defaulting in performance and losing its case before the arbitrators, now argues to the courts, as did the losing party in Staklinski and in Matter of Ruppert (Egelhofer), 3 N.Y.2d 576, 170 N.Y.S.2d 785, 148 N.E.2d 129, that enforcement of this award would be contrary to public policy. Specific performance of a contract to construct a building, argues appellant, is never ordered by courts of equity because of the necessity of continuous judicial supervision and control of performance. Therefore, so the argument runs, the same courts will not confirm and enforce an arbitration award which decrees specific performance of the same kind of agreement. We disagree. There is no hard and fast rule against applying the remedy of specific performance to such contracts, especially when the parties have by agreement provided for just that remedy.

In 1955 appellant Iris, owner of vacant land in Levittown, Nassau County, entered into a written agreement with respondent Grayson (later assigned by Grayson to its subsidiary respondent Klein) whereby Iris undertook to erect on the Iris tract a building (part of a "shopping center") to be rented by Iris to Grayson for use as a retail department store for a term of 25 years after completion with certain optional provisions for renewals of the term. Possession was to be turned over to Grayson "on or before September 1, 1957, time being of the essence". The agreement called for arbitration of all disputes and incorporated the rules of the American Arbitration Association which in terms empower the arbitrator in his award to grant any just or equitable remedy or relief "including ... specific performance."

There were several amendments and extensions of the original contract, but none of these are relevant to our discussion. The plans and specifications for the building were completed or practically completed, a public ground-breaking ceremony was held and excavation commenced, then Iris notified Grayson–Klein that, because of difficulties in getting mortgage money, Iris could not go further unless Grayson–Klein agreed to increase the agreed rent. The tenant declined to pay more. The building has never been completed.

It was, apparently, always the intention of Iris to obtain by mortgage loan the money it needed for construction but there is nothing in the agreement relieving Iris of its obligation, in the event it should find such borrowing to be difficult or impossible. At the arbitration and in the courts Iris has argued "impossibility" but the arbitrators disposed of that issue by ordering Iris to "proceed forthwith with the improvements of the leased premises in accordance with the terms of the said lease, as amended." There was no proof before the arbitrators of any physical or actual impossibility as distinguished from difficulty of financing or additional expense of construction.

It would be quite remarkable if, after these parties had agreed that arbitrators might award specific performance and after the arbitrators had so ordered, the courts would, contrary to the command of article 84 of the Civil Practice Act [see McKinney's N.Y. CPLR art. 75], frustrate the whole arbitration process by refusing to confirm the award. The only ground suggested for such a refusal is that confirmation would involve the court in supervision of a complex and extended construction contract. We hold that this apprehension or speculation is no deterrent to confirmation by the courts.

There is of course, an old tradition or approach according to which courts have been reluctant to enforce "Contracts which require the performance of varied and continuous acts, or the exercise of special skill, taste, and judgment" because "the execution of the decree would require such constant superintendence as to make judicial control a matter of extreme difficulty." In some instances courts of equity in other States have for some such reasons refused to order specific performance of building contracts. Other courts of equity have gone the other way (see Jones v. Parker, 163 Mass. 564, 40 N.E. 1044, which also was a contract to build for a lessee). "There is no universal rule that courts of equity never will enforce a contract which requires some building to be done. They have enforced such contracts from the earliest days to the present time." On varying facts our New York decisions take one or the other position. Modern writers think that the "difficulty of enforcement" idea is exaggerated and that the trend is toward specific performance. Clearly there is no binding rule that deprives equity of jurisdiction to order specific performance of a building contract. At most there is discretion in the court to refuse such a decree. And here we do not even have an equity suit but a motion made as of right to confirm a completely valid arbitration award conforming in all respects to the express conferral of authority on the arbitrators and meeting all statutory requirements for confirmation.

Assuming that the equity court in an original suit would have discretion to refuse specific performance, and even making the very large assumption that the court would have similar discretionary power to refuse to confirm this award, it remains that such discretion, if any, was exercised the other way in this case, and unanimously affirmed by the Appellate Division. That exercise of discretion was justified on the facts. There is nothing extraordinary about this ordinary building contract. Appellant is simply being required to fulfill its promise. . . .

Arbitration is by consent and those who agree to arbitrate should be made to keep their solemn, written promises. Such is New York State's public policy, plainly written in article 84 of the Civil Practice Act. The courts should follow a "liberal policy of promoting arbitration both to accord with the original intention of the parties and to ease the current congestion of court calendars."

The judgment should be affirmed, with costs.

■ VAN VOORHIS, J. (dissenting). If "Arbitration is not merely a step in judicial enforcement of a claim nor auxiliary to a main proceeding, but the full relief sought," it would relieve the courts if the arbitrators enforced their own awards in specific performance instead of delegating that essential function to the courts after they have been discharged from further duty. Only recently was it settled that an arbitration award will be enforced by the courts which grants, under an appropriate arbitration clause, equitable relief by injunction. More recently it was held that our courts would enforce specific performance of an employment contract on an arbitration award (Matter of Staklinski [Pyramid Elec. Co.], 6 N.Y.2d 159, 188 N.Y.S.2d 541, 160 N.E.2d 78) even though a court of equity would not compel a man to work for another or to continue another in his employment. The decision in the present case lends the enforcement machinery of the courts to implement specific performance directed by arbitration that extends beyond any equitable relief which the courts have heretofore granted either on arbitrations or after trial.

. . . .

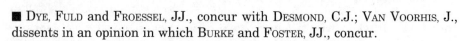

■ DYE, FULD and FROESSEL, JJ., concur with DESMOND, C.J.; VAN VOORHIS, J., dissents in an opinion in which BURKE and FOSTER, JJ., concur.

Judgment affirmed.

Sprinzen v. Nomberg

Court of Appeals of New York, 1979.
46 N.Y.2d 623, 415 N.Y.S.2d 974, 389 N.E.2d 456.

■ JASEN, J. This appeal requires us to determine whether an arbitrator's award which enforces the terms of a restrictive covenant of employment is unenforceable as being contrary to public policy.

Respondent Murray Nomberg was employed by the petitioner Local 1115 Joint Board in April, 1973 as a business agent in its health-care division. Nomberg's responsibilities included, among other tasks, the negotiation of collective bargaining agreements, the processing of members' grievances, and the general organization of employees at various facilities. Practically all of Nomberg's service occurred in New Jersey, although he did, on occasion, work in Connecticut and Pennsylvania.

Upon commencement of his employment with Local 1115 in April 1973, Nomberg signed an agreement which contained a restrictive covenant. The terms of such covenant provided for a perpetual prohibition against the divulgence of the identity and addresses of union members or the terms and conditions embodied in the union agreements or the revelation of any information obtained by Nomberg during the course of his employment. Further, Nomberg agreed that "[u]pon the termination of his employment . . . he shall not directly or indirectly, within the States of New York, Pennsylvania, New Jersey and Connecticut . . . enter into or engage in organizing workers, either as an individual or as a part of a labor organization, for a period of five (5) years after the date of termination of his employment hereunder." The agreement also contained a sweeping arbitration clause which prescribed that "[a]ll complaints, disputes whatsoever of whatever kind or nature . . . concerning any provision of this contract . . . or otherwise . . . shall be submitted for arbitration" pursuant to a clearly delineated process.

In February, 1976, Nomberg left Local 1115 and began employment as a business representative for Local 144 of the Hotel, Hospital, Nursing Home and Allied Services Union, a union also involved in organizing and representing employees in the healthcare field. With Local 144, Nomberg's geographical responsibilities included only Manhattan and Staten Island, areas with which he had no previous dealings.

Petitioner Local 1115 demanded arbitration to compel compliance with the terms of the restrictive covenant and to enjoin Nomberg from employment as a business representative for Local 144. The parties proceeded to arbitration, where Nomberg, after unsuccessfully contesting the partiality of the arbitrator named in the April, 1973 agreement, walked out of the hearing, refusing to participate further. After petitioner presented its case, the arbitrator ruled that Local 1115 was entitled to the relief sought and issued an award enjoining Nomberg from working for Local 144 until February 6, 1981, five years after his employment ceased with Local 1115, and further restrained Nomberg from engaging in any of the other practices and acts specifically prohibited by the restrictive covenant.

Petitioner moved to confirm the arbitrator's award, and Nomberg cross-moved to vacate the same, contending that his rights were prejudiced by the arbitrator's partiality and that the award itself was unjust. Special Term confirmed the award and denied Nomberg's cross motion in all respects. On appeal, the Appellate Division, with two Justices dissenting, reversed and vacated the award, holding that "the arbitration award under the circumstances of this case [is] in contravention of public policy." There should be a reversal and the judgment of Special Term confirming the award of the arbitrator reinstated.

Controversies involving questions of public policy can rarely, if ever, be resolved by the blind application of sedentary legal principles. The very nature of the concept of public policy itself militates against any attempt to define its ingredients in a manner which would allow one to become complacent in the thought that those precepts which society so steadfastly embraces today will continue to serve as the foundation upon which society will function tomorrow. Public policy, like society, is continually evolving and those entrusted with its implementation must respond to its ever-changing demands.

Over the years, courts have had not infrequent occasion to test restrictive covenants against the fabric of prevailing public policy. While it has been consistently asserted that the policy considerations against depriving the public of a person's industry and precluding an individual from pursuing his occupation, thereby preventing him from supporting himself and his family, must be weighed against the enforcement of such covenants, no hard-and-fast rules have yet been formulated and courts have been continuously engaged in the ongoing task of determining what restrictions are reasonable given the peculiar circumstances and context of each individual case. Thus, it can be said with apparent certainty that cases involving restrictive covenants cannot be decided in a vacuum free from external influences. Courts must respond to each case as it presents itself, and often times, as in the present case, must resolve seemingly divergent considerations of public policy.

The issue presented in this case comes to us in an increasingly recurrent posture—to wit: the review of a judgment confirming an arbitrator's award. An agreement to submit to arbitration disputes arising out of a contract, once condemned by the judiciary of this State as tending to oust the courts of their jurisdiction and, thus, declared void as contrary to settled policy, is now favorably recognized as an efficacious procedure whereby parties can select their own nonjudicial forum for the "private and practical" resolution of their disputes "with maximum dispatch and at minimum expense."

In furtherance of the laudable purposes served by permitting consenting parties to submit controversies to arbitration, the law has adopted a policy of noninterference, with few exceptions, in this mode of dispute resolution. Quite simply, it can be said that the arbitrator is not bound to abide by, absent a contrary provision in the arbitration agreement, those principles of substantive law or rules of procedure which govern the traditional litigation process. An arbitrator's paramount responsibility is to reach an equitable result, and the courts will not assume the role of overseers to mold the award to conform to their sense of justice. Thus, an arbitrator's award will not be vacated for errors of law and fact committed by the arbitrator and "[e]ven where the arbitrator states an intention to apply a law, and then misapplies it, the award will not be set aside."

Despite this policy of according an arbitrator seemingly unfettered discretion in matters submitted to him by the consent of the parties, it is the established law in this State that an award which is violative of public policy will not be permitted to stand. The courts, however, must exercise due restraint in this regard, for the preservation of the arbitration process and the policy of allowing parties to choose a nonjudicial forum, embedded in freedom to contract principles, must not be disturbed by courts, acting under the guise of public policy, wishing to decide the dispute on its merits, for arguably every controversy has at its core some issue requiring the application, or weighing, of policy considerations. Thus, there are now but a few matters of concern which have been recognized as so intertwined with overriding public policy considerations as to either place them beyond the bounds of the arbitration process itself or mandate the vacatur of awards which do violence to the principles upon which such matters rest.

Some examples would be instructive. It has been held that an arbitrator is without power to award punitive damages, a sanction reserved solely to the State and that an agreement to arbitrate, when sought to be enforced by a lender, cannot divest the courts of their responsibility to determine whether a purported sales agreement is in fact a usurious loan, and thus illegal. Matters involving the enforcement of our State's antitrust laws, recognized as representing "public policy of the first magnitude", cannot be left to commercial arbitration, and claims concerning the liquidation of insolvent insurance companies have been held to be beyond the reach of an arbitrator's discretion where a State statute bestows upon the Supreme Court exclusive jurisdiction over these proceedings.

In public school matters, it has been held that agreements which purportedly reflect a bargain by a board of education not to inspect teacher personnel files cannot be enforced through arbitration insofar as such right is supported by statute and public policy. Nor can a board of education surrender its authority to discharge a nontenured teacher at the end of his probationary period to the arbitration process pursuant to a collective bargaining agreement, and an award the terms of which would bestow upon a probationary teacher tenure, as distinguished from procedural guarantees, will be struck down as violative of public policy.

These illustrations of instances where courts will intervene in the arbitration process are, without apparent exception, cases in which public policy considerations, embodied in statute or decisional law, prohibit, in an absolute sense, particular matters being decided or certain relief being granted by an arbitrator. Stated another way, the courts must be able to examine an arbitration agreement or an award on its face, without engaging in extended factfinding or legal analysis, and conclude that public policy precludes its enforcement. This is so because, as has been previously noted, an arbitrator is free to apply his own sense of law and equity to the facts as he has found them to be in resolving a controversy.

Applying these principles to this case, we now hold that disputes involving restrictive covenants of employment can be, by mutual consent of the parties, submitted to arbitration, and an arbitrator's award which specifically enforces such covenants, even to the extent of enjoining an individual from engaging in like employment for a reasonable period of years in the future, will not be vacated on public policy grounds.

While it is true that considerations of public policy militate against the enforcement of restrictive covenants of future employment, these covenants are not per se unenforceable as being null and void. Each case turns upon its own distinct facts. If the restrictive covenant is found, under all the circumstances, to be "reasonable in time and area, necessary to protect the employer's legitimate interests, not harmful to the general public and not unreasonably burdensome to the employee", it will be subject to specific enforcement.

Here, the parties, by reason of a broad arbitration clause contained in their signed agreement, submitted the issue of the enforceability of the restrictive covenant to arbitration, clearly a proper forum for the resolution of their dispute in this private matter. By so doing, the parties placed upon the arbitrator, not the courts, the responsibility of passing upon the merits of their controversy with the expectation that a just, yet practical, result would be reached. While there may be some doubt whether we would have enforced the restrictive covenant now before us had this dispute been adjudicated in the courts, such consideration is irrelevant to the disposition of this case, for courts will not second-guess the factual findings or the legal conclusions of the arbitrator. The utility of the arbitration process itself is derived from its autonomy, and courts must honor the choice of the parties to have their controversy decided within this framework. Insofar as public policy considerations do not absolutely preclude the enforcement of restrictive covenants of future employment for a reasonable period of time or related business concerns, we conclude that the arbitrator had the power to pass upon the issue of both the reasonableness and the necessity of the restrictions imposed upon the employee. Having thus concluded, and acknowledging the wide latitude afforded arbitrators in formulating just relief, the award rendered should not now be disturbed.

In passing, we reject respondent's contention that the award must be vacated on the ground of the arbitrator's alleged bias. . . .

Accordingly, the order of the Appellate Division should be reversed, with costs, and the judgment of Supreme Court, New York County, confirming the arbitrator's award reinstated.

Order reversed, etc.

NOTES ON ENFORCEABILITY OF ARBITRATION AGREEMENTS

1. As *Sprinzen* suggests, arbitration agreements have not always been favored by the law. Consider the following passages from SIMPSON, *Specific Performance of Arbitration Contracts*, 83 U. PA. L. REV. 160 (1934):

> Arbitration as a method of settling disputes has a long and honorable history. Agreements to arbitrate existing controversies have been held valid at common law from an early date, as have arbitration clauses in contracts applying to disputes arising under such contracts. And once an award has been made pursuant to an arbitration agreement, equity will enforce it specifically if a contract between the parties in the same terms as the award would be specifically enforceable. . . .

2. Statutes have greatly changed any former negative attitude. Most states have adopted some variant of the Uniform Arbitration Act, which abolishes the "revocability" doctrine and declares arbitration agreements specifically enforceable. Under the Act, specific performance of an agreement to arbitrate existing or future controversies may be ordered directly (i.e., by ordering the breaching party to arbitrate) or indirectly (i.e., by staying litigation brought in violation of the agreement or appointing people with the power to act as arbitrators). Other states have adopted statutory reforms of a less comprehensive nature.

On the federal level, the Federal Arbitration Act, 9 U.S.C.A. §§ 1–14, which applies to contracts relating to "maritime transactions" and "transactions involving interstate commerce" other than contracts of employment, is similar to the Uniform Act. Agreements to arbitrate disputes arising out of labor-management contracts to which federal labor law applies are governed by, and specifically enforceable under, section 301 of the Labor Management Relations Act, 29 U.S.C.A. § 185. The Supreme Court has found a presumption of arbitrability under both the federal arbitration act, see Mitsubishi Motors Corp. v. Soler Chrysler–Plymouth, Inc., 473 U.S. 614, 626, 105 S.Ct. 3346, 87 L.Ed.2d 444 (1985), and the Labor Management Relations Act, see generally Steelworkers v. Enterprise Wheel & Car Corp., 363 U.S. 593, 80 S.Ct. 1358, 4 L.Ed.2d 1424 (1960).

In Wright v. Universal Maritime Service, 525 U.S. 70, 119 S.Ct. 391, 142 L.Ed.2d 361 (1998), the Supreme Court addressed whether a general arbitration clause in a collective bargaining agreement requires an employee to use an arbitration procedure for a federal statutory discrimination claim arising from an alleged violation of the Americans with Disabilities Act. The Court held that petitioner's statutory claim was not subject to a presumption of arbitrability and that any collective bargaining agreement to arbitrate such a claim must be "particularly clear." The Court held that a union-negotiated waiver of an employee's statutory right to a judicial forum for claims of employment discrimination must be "clear and unmistakable."

3. Arbitrating the Scope of Arbitration:

Generally, "any doubts concerning the scope of arbitrable issues should be resolved in favor of arbitration." Moses H. Cone Mem'l Hosp. v. Mercury Constr. Corp., 460 U.S. 1, 24–25, 103 S.Ct. 927 (1983); . . . . This presumption, however, does not apply to the issue of which claims are arbitrable. "[T]he general policy-based, federal presumption in favor of arbitration . . . is not applied as a rule of contract interpretation to resolve questions of the arbitrability of arbitrability issues themselves." Virginia Carolina Tools, Inc. v. International Tool Supply, Inc., 984 F.2d 113, 117 (4th Cir.1993). Thus, "Courts should not assume that the parties agreed to arbitrate arbitrability." First Options of Chicago, Inc. v. Kaplan, 514 U.S. 938, 944, 115 S.Ct. 1920, 131 L.Ed.2d 985 (1995).

The Supreme Court has explained the reasons for this reverse presumption. It has stated that the "willingness of parties to enter into agreements that provide for arbitration of specified disputes would be drastically reduced . . . if a labor arbitrator had the power to determine his own jurisdiction." AT & T Techs., 475 U.S. at 651 (internal quotation marks omitted). And, it has noted that a "party often might not focus upon that question or upon the significance of having arbitrators decide the scope of their own powers." First Options, 514 U.S. at 945.

Nevertheless, the parties can agree to let an arbitrator determine the scope of his own jurisdiction. Their agreement must, however, "clearly and unmistakably" provide that the arbitrator shall determine what disputes the parties agreed to arbitrate. AT & T Techs., 475 U.S. at 649; accord First Options, 514 U.S. at 944 ("Courts should not assume that the parties agreed to arbitrate arbitrability unless there is clear and unmistakable evidence that they did so." (internal quotation marks omitted)).

Defendants argue that the [collective bargaining agreements (CBAs)] here clearly and unmistakably committed arbitrability to arbitration. They note that the CBAs provided for the arbitration of "any grievance or dispute aris[ing] between the parties regarding the terms of this Agreement" and any "controversy, dispute or disagreement . . . concerning the interpretation of the provisions of this Agreement." Because the dispute over whether statutory discrimination claims are arbitrable requires an interpretation of the terms of the CBAs, defendants assert that the parties agreed to resolve this threshold dispute by arbitration. Thus, defendants claim that the parties agreed to arbitrate arbitrability.

. . . The "clear and unmistakable" test set forth by the Supreme Court requires more than simply saying that the arbitrator determines the meaning of any disputed contractual terms. The courts have repeatedly rejected the assertion that general arbitration clauses, like the ones at issue here, commit to arbitration disputes over an arbitrator's jurisdiction.

. . . [B]road arbitration clauses that generally commit all interpretive disputes "relating to" or "arising out of" the agreement do not satisfy the clear and unmistakable test.

. . .

The lesson from these cases is that if contracting parties wish to let an arbitrator determine the scope of his own jurisdiction, they must indicate that intent in a clear and specific manner. Expansive general arbitration clauses will not suffice to force the arbitration of arbitrability disputes.

. . .

We stress, however, that arbitration of arbitrability disputes—like other contractual matters—remains a question of the parties' intent. Those who wish to let an arbitrator decide which issues are arbitrable need only state that "all disputes concerning the arbitrability of particular disputes under this contract are hereby committed to arbitration," or words to that clear effect. Absent such clarity, we are compelled to find that disputes over the arbitrability of claims are for judicial resolution.

Carson v. Giant Food, Inc., 175 F.3d 325, 329–331 (4th Cir. 1999).

CHAPTER 7

EQUITABLE RELIEF AGAINST TORTIOUS INTERFERENCE WITH LAND AND CHATTELS

The Emergence of Equitable Relief Against Torts[1]

While there are some cases of equitable relief against torts in the early law, both in the common-law courts and in the Courts of Chancery, the development of this jurisdiction was on the whole less extensive until comparatively recent times than the development of jurisdiction over contracts. The first extensive development was with regard to injunctions against waste, where the Court of Chancery came to grant relief not only in cases of waste which were cognizable at law but also in cases of so-called equitable waste, where the defendant was not liable at law at all. Here there was a distinct contractual element.

The growth of equitable jurisdiction to prevent or require reparation for other torts, particularly trespass and nuisance, was much slower. The reasons for this appear to have been several. In the first place, it was thought that the plaintiff should be required to establish his right at law. Second, particularly in cases of trespass, the decision of an injunction suit was likely to require an investigation of the title to the premises involved which the Court of Chancery was loath to undertake. Third, the Court was much occupied with many other important matters—trusts, administration suits, specific performance, mortgages, and others—and may well have been reluctant further to clog its burdened docket.

In the time of Lord Eldon, this reluctance to deal with tort cases other than those involving waste (which had a certain contractual aspect) began to diminish to some extent. Even before that time injunctions to protect legal monopolies such as patents had begun to be granted. Injunctions against certain types of trespass became more frequent. Jurisdiction was exercised to prevent obstruction of easements, and an increasing degree of relief was allowed in cases of nuisance. There were still difficulties with respect to establishment of the legal right and trial of title, but the general lines of the jurisdiction in cases involving injuries to land were beginning to be established and precedents for relief in certain cases of injuries to business were being developed.

Later there was a large expansion of the jurisdiction exercised in patent and copyright cases, and the field of relief against interference with advantageous relations broadened greatly. In particular, equity has come to

---

1. Adapted from SCOTT & SIMPSON, CASES AND OTHER MATERIALS ON CIVIL PROCEDURE 218– 20 (1951).

give relief in cases of unfair competition and other tortious interferences with business expectations which has become one of the most important specialized fields of equity jurisdiction today. Moreover, there has been in the United States much resort to equity in labor disputes, mainly by employers, and the so-called "labor injunction" has had a rather unhappy history terminating for the present in substantial statutory curtailment of the jurisdiction of equity courts in labor cases.

Equitable relief against torts has been mostly given in connection with either such wrongs as trespass to land, conversion of chattels, and nuisance, or relatively novel types of torts such as interference with business and other advantageous relations. For obvious reasons there is little scope for the preventive relief of equity in cases of trespass to the person, negligence or deceit. Defamation raises special problems closely related to injuries to interests of personality, and equitable relief in this field has a rather different history from specific reparation and prevention of torts to property and business relations.

Establishing the Tort

In Leonard v. Hart, 42 N.J.Eq. 416, 7 A. 865 (1886) the plaintiff claimed to have acquired a right of way across the land of the defendant. Plaintiff claimed "user for over twenty years", but the defendant contered that the use was with the defendant's express permission as an act of neighborly accommodation. Judge Dixon enumerated nine "heads" or areas when equity may, by decree and injunction, protect legal rights in real estate, and concluded, "The case in hand does not come within any of these classes," and dismissed the bill.

In a discussion of this case, Professor Chafee wrote: "This question of *Leonard v. Hart* is very important, for it shows the danger in our system of law which has grown up from concrete cases rather than from abstract reasoning, of using precedents as principles *per se* and not as illustrations of a principle. Equity relieves against torts when the remedy at law is inadequate. It was inadequate in Dixon's nine classes, and may be equally so in a dozen new classes." CHAFEE, *Progress of the Law–Equitable Relief Against Torts*, 34 HARV. L. REV. 388, 391–92 (1921). Of course, one may add to Professor Chafee's observation that the very concept of "tort" is destined to become even more expansive in response to the demands of the modern social and moral order.

A. WASTE

Earl Bathurst v. Burden

Chancery, 1786.
2 Bro.C.C. 64, 29 Eng.Rep. 37.

Bill that the defendants, lessees of the plaintiff, may be decreed to keep the sills [of fish-ponds] in repair, and be restrained by injunction from obstructing them; and from erecting any further buildings, they having begun such as would interrupt the prospect from the plaintiff's house and would be disagreeable objects.

This was a general demurrer for want of equity.

. . . .

MASTER OF THE ROLLS [KENYON]. This Court will not interpose where the matter is merely in damages; but here a nobleman, having a seat [(i.e., a residence)], has granted privileges to the defendants, which they are using in such a way, as interferes with his pleasurable enjoyment of his property. The Duke of Beaufort obtained an injunction against persons who were building near him, to prevent their building so high as to obstruct the light of his windows, in the house now Gloucester House. So, in Lord Kilmorey v. Thackeray, Lord Kilmorey had granted lands on the river Dee, with covenant to keep the banks in repair, the Court of Exchequer were of opinion it was a proper subject for an injunction, as the verdict of a jury would be an imperfect remedy. So, in a case where a tenant was plowing up a bowling-green. In this case a damage is expected to be done to the fish-ponds, which in many cases are very valuable. I think I should not stop this cause in the first step; I should have been desirous, if compelled to it, to have made a precedent; but am glad to be able to find that of Lord Kilmorey v. Thackeray.

Demurrer overruled.[2]

Doherty v. Allman

House of Lords, 1878.
3 App.Cas. 709.

Appeal against an order of the Court of Appeal in Ireland, dissolving a perpetual injunction granted by the Vice–Chancellor of Ireland, made on the 4th of July, 1876, in a cause in which Mr. Doherty was the plaintiff, and the two respondents were defendants.

. . . .

THE LORD CHANCELLOR [CAIRNS]. The question in this case arises upon two leases which are now vested in the respondent. One of them is dated in the year 1798, and is for the long term of 999 years; the other was granted in 1824, and is for the term of 988 years; the first being at the rent of £10, and the second at a rent of £32 19s. The reversion to both these leases is vested in the present appellant.

. . . .

[The property consisted of buildings for the storing of corn. In fifty years the neighborhood changed, and the lessee intends to convert the buildings into dwellings.]

The appellant objects to this being done. The owner of the reversion subject to this long term of years objects to that which the holder of the lease proposes to do.

---

2. [See also Vane v. Lord Barnard and accompanying notes, *supra* p. 293].

There is no doubt that the Court of Chancery exercises a jurisdiction in restraining waste, and where waste is committed in requiring an account of the waste for the purpose of recompensing the person who has suffered; but I apprehend it is perfectly clear that the Court of Chancery, acting in that case in advance of the common law right, will, in the first place, consider whether there is, or is not, any substantial damage which would accrue, and which is sought to be prevented, and will make that inquiry. In the present case it appears to me to be extremely doubtful whether any jury could be found, who, after this work shall be executed in the way that is proposed, would say that any damage had been done by the work to the inheritance. And I doubt, farther, whether it must not be taken as clear from the evidence here that any jury, or any tribunal judging upon the question of fact, would not say that, if there be technically what in the eye of the common law is called waste, still it is that ameliorating waste which has been spoken of in several of the cases cited at the bar. That which is done, if it be technically waste—and here again I will assume in favor of the appellant that it is technically, according to the common law, waste—yet it seems to be that ameliorating waste which so far from doing injury to the inheritance, improves the inheritance. Now, there again, the course which the Court of Chancery ought undoubtedly to adopt would be to leave those who think they can obtain damages at common law to try what damages they can so obtain. Certainly, I think here again, the Court of Chancery would be doing very great injury to the one side for the purpose of securing to the other that slightest possible sum which would at common law be considered the full equivalent to which he was entitled. My lords, this was the view, in substance, taken by the Lord Chancellor of Ireland and the Lord Justice of the Court of Appeal, who in this respect differed from the Vice–Chancellor. I must say that I entirely concur with the decision at which they arrived, and therefore I would advise your lordships, and move your lordships, to dismiss this appeal with costs.

Order of the Court of Appeal in Ireland affirmed; and appeal dismissed with costs.

Travelers Insurance Co. v. 633 Third Associates

United States Court of Appeals, Second Circuit, 1994.
14 F.3d 114.

[In 1986 plaintiff loaned defendant $145 million secured by a nonrecourse mortgage on the defendant's sole property, a 41 story office building in New York City. In 1992 defendant failed to pay property taxes and failed to meet a payment on its loan, defaulting on its obligations. Traveler's filed for foreclosure of the property and brought an equitable action for waste to enjoin distribution of the defendant's cash assets. The district court refused to recognize the willful failure to pay property taxes as actionable waste. The Court of Appeals reversed and remanded the case.]

■ Oakes, Senior Circuit Judge:

. . .

A. Failure to Pay Property Taxes as Waste

The central issue in this appeal is whether failure to pay property taxes constitutes waste under New York law....

. . . .

The common law doctrine of waste emerged in response to problems of divided ownership that occurred when, say, an owner in fee simple granted a tenant an estate in years. The tenant had an incentive to maximize the stream of benefits that could be realized from the property during the period of his tenancy. The owner, on the other hand, preferred that the property be managed so as to maximize the stream of benefits that could be realized over the life of the property. An action for waste gave the owner a remedy against a tenant who undermined the long-term profit maximizing potential of the property in order to realize short-term gains. At first the doctrine of waste prohibited any change in the property. Over time, however, it came to prohibit only those changes that reduced the long-term value of the property. In this way, it has been suggested by one commentator, the doctrine of waste developed to force tenants to manage the property as if they were the owner of the property.

New York has codified a common law cause of action for waste: An action for waste lies against a tenant by the curtesy, in dower, for life, or for years, or the assignee of such a tenant, who, during his estate or term, commits waste upon the real property held by him, without a special and lawful written license so to do; or against such a tenant who lets or grants his estate and still retaining possession thereof commits waste without a like license. This cause of action provides for both legal and equitable relief.

New York Courts have recognized two general categories of waste. First, as this court observed in the previous appeal, New York courts recognize " 'a substantive cause of action for waste against one in control of real property who does no more than allow the property to deteriorate and decrease in value....' " Second, New York courts recognize a cause of action for waste by a mortgagee against a mortgagor who impairs the mortgage.

The difference between the two categories of an action for waste can best be illustrated by an example. Under New York law, an action for waste will lie against a tenant who fails to undertake certain repairs on the property. If a mortgagor were to undertake these repairs through, say, a contractor, the mortgagor could satisfy its duty and escape liability for waste for physical injury. If the mortgagor failed to pay the contractor, however, a mechanic's lien would attach against the property. The mortgagor would then be liable for waste for the impairment of a mortgage even though no injury were done to the property. If an action for waste for the impairment of the mortgage would not lie, it would be possible for mortgagors to escape liability for permissive waste by contracting for necessary repairs, defaulting on repair bills, and allowing a mechanic's lien to attach to the property.

It is uncertain whether New York law recognizes the willful failure to pay taxes as actionable waste. In the previous appeal, this court wrote that it "believe[d] an equitable action ... may be available to plaintiff in this case, although it has not yet been adequately pled." . . . [I]t is necessary to determine whether New York state law would recognize willful failure to pay property taxes as waste remediable by an action in equity.

While the New York cases on waste tend to deal with mortgage impairment resulting from physical injury to real property, at least one case clearly contemplates that, in certain circumstances, an action in waste will lie for financial injury to real property.

A line of New York cases has interpreted the scope of an action for waste broadly. In Van Pelt v. McGraw, 4 N.Y. 110, 111–12 (1850), the New York Court of Appeals said: It forms no objection to this action that the circumstances of the case are novel, and that no case precisely similar in all respects has previously arisen. The action is based upon very general principles, and is designed to afford relief in all cases where one man is injured by the wrongful act of another, where no other remedy is provided. This injury may result from some breach of positive law, or some violation of a right or duty growing out of the relations existing between the parties. . . . The defendant . . . in this case, came into possession of the land subject to the mortgage. The rights of the holder of the mortgage were therefore paramount to his rights, and any attempt on his part to impair the mortgage as a security, was a violation of the plaintiff's rights. Justice Kimball of the New York Supreme Court has written, Such an action [for waste], whether against a mortgagor, a stranger, or other person seems to have been of ancient origin and came into use by reason of the exigencies of the particular set of circumstances, the law not being without a remedy for a wrong. Syracuse Sav. Bank, 14 N.Y.S.2d at 358, 171 Misc. 993. The Appellate Division's Third Department has observed, '[I]t has been well remarked that courts of equity will exercise a liberal jurisdiction in respect to waste, and in its restraint.' Vandemark v. Schoonmaker, 9 Hun (N.Y.) 16, 19 (App.Div. 3d Dep't 1876).

Together with this line of New York cases interpreting the cause of action for waste broadly, the contemplation by the Appellate Division's First Department of an action for waste for failure to pay taxes suggests that an equitable action for waste would lie under New York law for the intentional failure to pay property taxes where there is an obligation to do so or the failure is intentional or fraudulent.

As we have previously noted, other courts have recognized the failure to pay property taxes as waste. See Pike v. Wassell, 94 U.S. 711, 715, 24 L.Ed. 307 (1876); Hausmann v. Hausmann, 231 Ill.App.3d 361, 172 Ill.Dec. 937, 596 N.E.2d 216 (App.Ct. 5th Dist.1992); Chapman v. Chapman, 526 So.2d 131, 135 (Fla.Ct.App.1988); First Nat'l Bank v. Clark & Lund Boat Co., 68 Wis.2d 738, 229 N.W.2d 221, 223 (Sup.Ct.1975); Farmers' Mut. Fire & Lightning Ins. Co. v. Crowley, 354 Mo. 649, 653, 190 S.W.2d 250, 253 (1945); Thayer v. Shorey, 287 Mass. 76, 191 N.E. 435 (Sup.Jud.Ct.1934); Straus v. Wilsonian Inv. Co., 171 Wash. 359, 17 P.2d 883 (Sup.Ct.1933); Mutual Benefit Life Ins. Co. v. Canby Inv. Co., 190 Minn. 144, 147, 251 N.W. 129, 131 (Sup.Ct.1933).

We hold that the intentional failure to pay property taxes where there is an obligation to do so or where the failure is fraudulent constitutes waste under the law of New York. We note, however, the narrow limits of this holding. Not every failure to comply with loan obligations will constitute waste actionable by the mortgagee. First, the failure must be intentional or fraudulent. Second, the failure must result in the impairment of the security of the mortgage. The mere failure to pay principal and interest, for example, will not constitute waste. Such failure does not impair the mortgage. Instead, such failure triggers default provisions and gives the mortgagee the right to foreclose on the mortgaged property. By contrast the intentional failure to pay property taxes does impair the mortgage. Under New York Real Property Tax law, a lien attaches against real property immediately upon the failure to pay assessed property taxes. Further, under the New York City Administrative Code, interest accrues on the unpaid real estate taxes at the rate of 18 percent per annum compounded daily. A mortgagee who attempts to foreclose on real property must pay the accrued taxes and interest in order to assume title to the property free of these liens.

. . . .

B. Possession and the Consequences of the Appointment of a Receiver

. . . .

1. Travelers' Claim for Waste

a. Waste After the Appointment of the Receiver

To the extent that Travelers' claims of waste relate to conduct that occurred after the appointment of the receiver, they were properly dismissed.

. . . .

Travelers does not cite, nor has this court found, any decision of the courts of New York suggesting that an action in waste will lie for waste committed by one with a contingent possessory interest. In addition, extension of the action to those who retain an "equity of redemption" would sever the doctrine of waste from its underlying rationale. If an action for waste exists to induce persons in possession or control of real property to manage it as if they were the owners, because the Partnership here is out of possession and control, it has no opportunity to exploit the property, regardless of its equity of redemption.

b. Waste Before the Appointment of the Receiver

It is undisputed that the Partnership was in possession of the Property before the Receiver's appointment and at the time of the original complaint. To the extent, therefore, that Travelers' claims of waste relate to conduct occurring before the appointment of the receiver, they were improperly dismissed.

. . . .

III. CONCLUSION

The order of the District Court dismissing Travelers' amended complaint is affirmed insofar as Travelers' claims of waste and for specific performance relate to conduct occurring after the appointment of the Receiver. Insofar as Travelers' claims of waste relate to conduct occurring before the appointment of the Receiver, the District Court's order dismissing Travelers' amended complaint is reversed. The District Court's order dismissing Travelers' claims under New York fraudulent conveyance law is reversed insofar as those claims relate to a portion of the distributions against which Travelers could have brought an equitable action for waste.

Remanded for proceedings consistent with this opinion.

■ Mishler, Senior District Judge, dissenting:

I record my disagreement with the holding by the majority that under New York law, the willful failure to pay property taxes and the failure to discharge the lien is a basis for a claim of waste by the mortgagee.

. . . .

I agree with the majority's observation that New York law is unclear as to whether the failure to pay property taxes constitutes waste. The New York Court of Appeals has not spoken on the issue.

. . . .

Wisconsin denies a right of action by a mortgagee for waste based on the failure to pay property taxes. Chetek State Bank v. Barberg, 170 Wis.2d 516, 489 N.W.2d 385 (1992). California would deny such a right. Krone v. Goff, 53 Cal.App.3d 191, 127 Cal.Rptr. 390 (1975); but see Osuna v. Albertson, 134 Cal.App.3d 71, 78, 184 Cal.Rptr. 338, 342 (1982)("Other authorities in California and elsewhere are in conflict, some holding that failure to pay taxes constitutes waste, and others holding that failure to pay taxes does not constitute waste.") New Jersey would also deny a claim of waste based on the failure to pay property taxes. Camden Trust Co. v. Handle, 132 N.J.Eq. 97, 26 A.2d 865 (1942).

States upholding an action by a mortgagee for waste for willful failure to pay property taxes, which become a prior lien, declare that the rental income during the period covered by the tax lien, after paying maintenance expenses, must be used to discharge the tax lien. Straus v. Wilsonian Inv. Co., 171 Wash. 359, 17 P.2d 883 (1933); Mutual Ben. Life Ins. Co. v. Canby Inv. Co., 190 Minn. 144, 251 N.W. 129 (1933).

. . . .

I believe the New York Court of Appeals would deny a right of action to Travelers based on the failure of the mortgagor to pay the property taxes due January 1, 1992. I find that if New York law permitted such an action, the claim would be dismissed on the ground that the rental income, after payment of maintenance expenses, was available for the discharge of the tax lien and therefore the mortgage security was not diminished.

NOTES ON "WRIT OF WASTE"

1. Most states have enacted statutes modeled, at least in part, on the Statute of Gloucester. That statute, which was repealed in 1879, read as follows:

It is provided that a man from henceforth shall have a Writ of Waste in the Chancery against him that holdeth by the law of England or otherwise for term of life or for term of years or a woman in dower. And he which shall be attainted of waste shall lose the thing that he hath wasted, and moreover shall recompense thrice so much as the waste shall be taxed at.

2.   For a discussion of the doctrine of equitable waste, see Vane v. Lord Barnard, which appears in Chapter 4B, *supra* p. 293.

B.   TRESPASS

Wheelock v. Noonan

Court of Appeals of New York, 1888.
108 N.Y. 179, 15 N.E. 67.

■ FINCH, J. The findings of the trial court establish that the defendant, who was a total stranger to the plaintiff, obtained from the latter a license to place upon his unoccupied lots in the upper part of the city of New York a few rocks for a short time, the indefiniteness of the period having been rendered definite by the defendant's assurance that he would remove them in the spring. Nothing was paid or asked for this permission, and it was not a contract in any just sense of the term but merely a license which by its terms expired in the next spring. During the winter, and in the absence and without the knowledge of plaintiff, the defendant covered six of the lots of plaintiff with "huge quantities of rock," some of them ten or fifteen feet long, and piled to the height of fourteen to eighteen feet. This conduct was a clear abuse of the license and in excess of its terms, and so much so that if permission had been sought upon a truthful statement of the intention it would undoubtedly have been refused. In the spring the plaintiff, discovering the abuse of his permission, complained bitterly of defendant's conduct and ordered him to remove the rocks to some other locality. The defendant promised to do so but did not, and in the face of repeated demands has neglected and omitted to remove the rocks from the land.

The court found as matter of law from these facts that the original permission given did not justify what was done either, as it respected the quantity of rock or the time allowed; that after the withdrawal of the permission in the spring, and the demand for the removal of the rock, the defendant was a trespasser, and the trespass was a continuing one which entitled plaintiff to equitable relief; and awarded judgment requiring defendant to remove the rocks before March 15, 1886, unless for good cause shown the time for such removal should be extended by the court.

. . . It is now said that the remedy was at law; that the owner could have removed the stone and then recovered of the defendant for the expense incurred. But to what locality could the owner remove them? He could not put them in the street; the defendant presumably had no vacant lands of his own on which to throw the burden; and it would follow that the owner would be obliged to hire some vacant lot or place of deposit, become responsible for the rent, and advance the cost of men and machinery to effect the removal. If any adjudication can be found throwing such burden upon the owner, compelling him to do in advance for the trespasser what the latter is bound to do, I should very much doubt its authority. On the contrary the law is the other way. And all the cases which give to the injured party successive actions for the continuance of the wrong are inconsistent with the idea that the injured party must once for all remove it. Such is neither an adequate remedy nor one which the plaintiff was bound to adopt.

But it is further said that he could sue at law for the trespass. That is undoubtedly true. The case of Uline v. New York Central and Hudson River Company, 101 N.Y. 98, 4 N.E. 536, demonstrates upon abundant authority that in such action only damages to its date could be recovered, and for the subsequent continuance of the trespass new actions following on in succession would have to be maintained. But in a case like the present would that be an adequate remedy? In each action the damages could not easily be anything more than the fair rental of the lot. It is difficult to see what other damages could be allowed, not because they would not exist, but because they would be quite uncertain in amount and possibly somewhat speculative in their character. The defendant, therefore, might pay those damages, and continue his occupation, and if there were no other adequate remedy, defiantly continue such occupation, and in spite of his wrong make of himself in effect a tenant who could not be dispossessed. The wrong in every such case is a continued unlawful occupation, and any remedy which does not or may not end it is not adequate to redress the injury or restore the injured party to his rights. On the other hand, such remedy in a case like the present might result to the wrong-doer in something nearly akin to persecution. He is liable to be sued every day, *die de diem,* for the renewed damages following from the continuance of the trespass; and while, ordinarily, there is no sympathy to be wasted on a trespasser, yet such multiplicity of suits should be avoided, and especially under circumstances like those before us. The rocks could not be immediately removed. The courts have observed that peculiarity of the case, and shaped their judgment to give time. It may take a long time, and during the whole of it the defendant would be liable to daily actions.

For reasons of this character it has very often been held that while ordinarily courts of equity will not wield their power merely to redress a trespass, yet they will interfere under peculiar circumstances, and have often done so where the trespass was a continuing one, and a multiplicity of suits at law was involved in the legal remedy. . . .

It is a general rule that a court of equity will act in such cases only after the plaintiff's right has been established at law, but that rule has its exceptions. Where the facts are in doubt, and the right not clear, such undoubtedly would be a just basis of decision, though the modern system of trying equity cases makes the rule less important. Where, as in an intrusion by railroad companies whose occupation threatens to be continuous, the injury partakes of that character, an action at law to establish the right has not been required. Indeed, I am inclined to deem it more a rule of discretion than of jurisdiction.

In Avery v. New York Central and Hudson River Railroad Company, 106 N.Y. 142, 12 N.E. 619, to which we have been referred since the argument, we were disposed to sustain a mandatory injunction requiring defendant to remove so much of a fence as obstructed plaintiff's right of way, although the obstruction was not a nuisance but an invasion of a private right. In that case, the equitable remedy was not challenged by either counsel or the court, and evidently stood upon the grounds here invoked; those of a continuing trespass the remedy for which at law would be inadequate, and involve repeated actions by the injured party for damages daily occurring.

These views of the case enable us to support the judgment rendered. It should be affirmed, with costs.

■ All concur, except RUGER, CH. J., not voting.

Judgment affirmed.

NOTES

1. Equity was reluctant to grant injunctive relief against trespass. At least in part, this reluctance stemmed from the Chancellors' belief that disputes about title ought to be resolved in the law courts. In America, that attitude was reinforced by the popularity of jury trials and the ignorance of equity on the part of many lawyers.

2. In Martin v. Reynolds Metals Co., 221 Or. 86, 342 P.2d 790 (1959), a landowner brought an action of trespass against an aluminum manufacturer. The court held that the manufacturing operation of an aluminum reduction plant which caused certain fluoride compounds in the form of gases and particulates, invisible to the naked eye, to become airborne and settle upon the owner's land, rendering it unfit for raising livestock during this period, constituted a direct trespass. The court therefore ruled that the action was not barred (with respect to the damages awarded for 1951–53) by the statute of limitations for nuisance.

Trespass and private nuisance are separate fields of tort liability relating to actionable interference with the possession of land. They may be distinguished by comparing the interest invaded; an actionable invasion of a possessor's interest in the exclusive possession of land is a trespass; an actionable invasion of a possessor's interest in the use and enjoyment of his land is a nuisance.

The same conduct on the part of a defendant may and often does result in the actionable invasion of both of these interests, in which case the choice between the two remedies is, in most cases, a matter of little consequence. Where the action is brought on the theory of nuisance alone the court ordinarily is not called upon to determine whether the conduct would also result in a trespassory invasion. In such cases the courts' treatment of the invasion solely in terms of the law of nuisance does not mean that the same conduct could not also be regarded as a trespass. Some of the cases relied upon by the defendant are of this type; cases in which the court holds that the interference with the plaintiff's possession through soot, dirt, smoke, cinders, ashes and similar substances constitutes a nuisance, but where the court does not discuss the applicability of the law of trespass to the same set of facts.

However, there are cases which have held that the defendant's interference with plaintiff's possession resulting from the settling upon his land of effluents emanating from defendant's operations is exclusively nontrespassory. Although in such cases the separate particles which collectively cause the invasion are minute, the deposit of each of the particles constitutes a physical intrusion and, but for the size of the particle, would clearly give rise to an action of trespass. The defendant asks us to take account of the difference in size of the physical agency through which the intrusion occurs and relegate entirely to the field of nuisance law certain invasions which do not meet the dimensional test, whatever that is. In pressing this argument upon us the defendant must admit that there are cases which have held that a trespass results from the movement or deposit of rather small objects over or upon the surface of the possessor's land.

. . . .

And liability on the theory of trespass has been recognized where the harm was produced by the vibration of the soil or by the concussion of the air which, of course, is nothing more than the movement of molecules one against the other. . . . The view recognizing a trespassory invasion where there is no "thing" which can be seen with the naked eye undoubtedly runs counter to the definition of trespass expressed in some quarters. It is quite possible that in an earlier day when science had not yet peered into the molecular and atomic world of small particles, the courts could not fit an invasion through unseen physical instrumentalities into the requirement that a trespass can result only from a *direct* invasion. But in this atomic age even the uneducated know the great and awful force contained in the atom and what it can do to a man's property if it is released. In fact, the now famous equation $E = mc^2$ has taught us that mass and energy are equivalents and that our concept of "things" must be reframed. If these observations on science in relation to the law of trespass should appear theoretical and unreal in the abstract, they become very practical and real to the possessor of land when the unseen force cracks the foundation of his house. The force is just as real if it is chemical in nature and must be awakened by the intervention of another agency before it does harm.

If, then, we must look to the character of the instrumentality which is making an intrusion upon another's land we prefer to emphasize the object's energy or force rather than its size. Viewed in this way we may define trespass as any intrusion which invades the possessor's protected interest in exclusive possession, whether that intrusion is by visible or invisible pieces of matter or by energy which can be measured only by the mathematical language of the physicist.

3. Consider the following excerpt from Brooks v. Wheeler, 243 N.Y. 28, 152 N.E. 454 (1926):

The controversy is over a right of way claimed by plaintiffs. . . . The complaint alleges that defendant has erected encroachments on the

right of way and asks that he be required to remove them. . . .
Defendant put in issue the existence of the right of way.

When the case came on for trial it was tried by jury as an action in
ejectment. . . .

. . . .

The rule is elementary that an incorporeal hereditament may not be
recovered in ejectment. Plaintiffs were not wrongfully disseized of an actual
possession of corporeal property. Defendant's motion to dismiss on the
ground that plaintiffs had not shown title to the land was sufficient to raise
the point. The proper remedy against one who bars another from possessing and exercising his incorporeal rights is in equity. City of Syracuse v.
Hogan, 234 N.Y. 457, 138 N.E. 406, does not modify this rule. It was there
held that where the title to land is in question defendant has a right to a
jury trial.

The complaint is sufficiently broad to sustain an action in equity.

Hirschberg v. Flusser

Court of Chancery of New Jersey, 1917.
87 N.J.Eq. 588, 101 A. 191.

■ LANE, V.C. This is a motion to strike out a bill. The bill alleges that
complainant is the owner of certain property; that defendant, who is the
owner of adjoining property, on or about May 3d, 1911, intending to build
an addition to his building, excavated to a depth of twenty-four feet, and in
so doing excavated a portion of complainant's property substantially twenty-six feet five inches by nine inches; that defendant then proceeded to
build on his own land and also on the land of complainant his foundation
and side wall up to the level of the ground, but that above the level of the
ground the defendant continued with his building on his own land; that
about the 3d day of July, 1911, complainant brought suit in the New Jersey
supreme court to recover possession of the land occupied by defendant's
foundation and side wall below the level of the ground, and on the 25th day
of September, 1913, procured a judgment against the defendant, and it was
therein found that the complainant was entitled to recover the possession
of the premises referred to in the bill of complaint; that the defendant did
not remove the foundation wall or side wall, and the complainant has been
unable by means of execution to get the sheriff of the county of Essex to
remove such encroachment because a large part of the wall which encroaches on the complainant's land is built with stones so large that they
not only encroach upon complainant's land but extend into and form part
of the wall of defendant's building on defendant's land, and it is impossible
to remove the part that encroaches without trespassing upon defendant's
land and injuring his building.

I assume that the bill may be considered as charging that the complainant actually issued execution and that the sheriff has failed or refused
to remove the encroachment. The motion to strike out is based upon: First,
that there is an adequate remedy at law. . . . It is insisted by the defendant
that the complainant by virtue of the judgment in ejectment has been

awarded the possession of the property in dispute and may remove whatever may be thereon; further, that he may compel the sheriff, if the nature of the defendant's property on the land in question is such that it may be removed, to remove it and put him in an actual physical possession of the soil as it was prior to defendant's interference with it, that the sheriff may, however, require indemnity, and if any part of the defendant's building is injured by the action of the sheriff acting under the writ the complainant will be responsible; and, finally, that if the nature of the property of the defendant upon the land of complainant is such that it may not be removed without injuring defendant's property, then the complainant is entitled only to constructive possession.

Where the injury is irreparable this court will enjoin continuous trespasses. In cases where the fundamental right of the complainant to equitable relief depends upon legal title in dispute the court of errors and appeals has said that it is the duty of the court to retain the bill and to send the complainant to law so that the legal title may be settled; the complainant in the meantime proceeding with the building at his peril. The logical result of Todd v. Staats, 60 N.J.Eq. 507, 46 A. 645, is that the legal right having been settled in favor of the complainant a mandatory injunction will go to compel the defendant to remove the offending structure if equitable considerations do not prevent and if the remedy obtained at law be not adequate. In Stanford v. Lyon, 37 N.J.Eq. 94, Vice–Chancellor Van Fleet held that the court would grant a mandatory injunction compelling defendants to remove portions of buildings erected by them which prevented complainant from exercising rights in a yard. The court of errors and appeals, in 42 N.J.Eq. 411 [7 A. 869], modified the decree so as to define the complainant's rights as they were defined in an action at law which he had previously brought against the defendants and in which his rights had been determined. The court of errors and appeals did not question the power of the court of equity to, after the right had been settled at law, protect the right by mandatory injunction if that were necessary. The first head of equitable jurisdiction stated in Leonard v. Hart, 42 N.J.Eq. 416, 7 A. 865, is that of cases where the legal right has been established in a suit at law and the bill in equity is filed to ascertain the extent of the right and enforce or protect it in a manner not attainable by legal procedure. And see the sixth and ninth head....

I am inclined to think that the jurisdiction is in the last analysis based upon the impossibility of securing at law any adequate relief for the damage done, either by ejectment or by numerous suits in trespass. In Baron v. Korn, 127 N.Y. 224 [27 N.E. 804], opinion by Parker, Judge, the New York court of appeals in an action to restrain the erection of a portion of a building on land of complainant said:

> "Assuming plaintiff's title to be established, the authority of the court in a suit in equity to interfere and prevent an appropriation of their lands to the use of another for building purposes cannot be longer questioned, not only for the purpose of avoiding multiplicity of actions, but also because they are without adequate remedy at law.... The sheriff might not regard it as his duty to deliver possession by taking down the wall, which would burden him with the risk of injury to other

portions of defendant's building, not included within the nine inches. (It is to be observed that the amount of land involved in that case was almost precisely what it is in this, at least so far as width is concerned.) But in equity the obligation to remove can be placed directly on the parties who caused the wall to be erected.''

The court did not consider the question as to whether it was necessary that the title should first be determined at law, holding that the question had not been properly raised. Upon the authority of the foregoing cases, I think that the bill may be maintained. The title and right of complainant has been settled at law. The law courts are not by reason of the nature of their processes able to give complete and adequate relief. Neither the sheriff nor the complainant should be compelled to take the risk, on removal of this structure, of injuring property of the defendant. To give the complainant constructive possession is no remedy at all; he has always had that. To remit him to actions for trespass will not afford adequate relief. He is entitled to the enjoyment of the land in the position it was before the defendant encroached upon it. It is only by the process of mandatory injunction that the obligation to remove, in the language of the New York court, can be placed directly on the party who caused the wall to be erected. . . .

. . . .

[Motion denied.]

Lucy Webb Hayes National Training School v. Geoghegan

United States District Court, District of Columbia, 1967.
281 F.Supp. 116.

■ HOLTZOFF, J. The plaintiff's prima facie case tends to show the following facts: that defendant Ellen S. Geoghegan has been a patient for a considerable length of time at Sibley Memorial Hospital, which is maintained and operated by the plaintiff corporation. The hospital is a private hospital. Evidence has been further introduced tending to show that the hospital came to the conclusion that the patient no longer needs hospital care but can be adequately provided for at a nursing home.

After a series of negotiations on June 2nd, 1967 the president of the hospital corporation made a formal demand on the defendant Thomas Geoghegan, the husband of the other defendant, that Ellen Geoghegan, his wife, be transferred from Sibley Memorial Hospital. This demand is worded as follows: "I again, request you to make arrangements for the transfer of your wife, Ellen Geoghegan, from Sibley Memorial Hospital." The mere fact that the polite word "request" is used does not detract from the tenor of the letter as a demand.

What, then, is the status of the defendant Ellen Geoghegan when her departure from the hospital has been demanded by the hospital? Manifestly she becomes a trespasser. This action is brought for an injunction to require her removal from the hospital as a trespasser. Obviously an action for damages would be an inadequate remedy.

A private hospital has a right to accept or decline any patient. It has a moral duty to reserve its accommodations for persons who actually need medical and hospital care and it would be a deviation from its purposes to act as a nursing home for aged persons who do not need constant medical care but who need nursing care. There are homes for the aged, there are nursing homes and similar institutions. Hospitals have a duty not to permit their facilities to be diverted to the uses for which hospitals are not intended.

The correspondence introduced in evidence shows that the male defendant takes the position that his wife should remain in the hospital for the remainder of her life. For the hospital to permit that would be to allow a diversion of its facilities to purposes for which they are not intended and would not be in the public interest. An action for damages, of course, would present no solution so far as the plaintiff is concerned because the husband is able and willing to pay whatever the hospital would charge.

It has been established for a great many years that equity will enjoin a continuing trespass or a series of repeated trespasses where an action for damages would not be an adequate remedy.... The Court of Appeals of New York State in Wheelock v. Noonan, 108 N.Y. 179, 15 N.E. 67, [p. 453 *supra*] stated, "It has very often been held that while, ordinarily, courts of equity will not wield their power merely to redress a trespass, yet they will interfere under peculiar circumstances, and have often done so where the trespass was a continuing one, and a multiplicity of suits at law was involved in the legal remedy."

This Court had occasion to consider this matter in Potomac Electric Power Co. v. Washington Chapter of the Congress of Racial Equality, 210 F.Supp. 418, 419, and stated, "it is well established that equity may enjoin continuing trespasses, repeated or irreparable injuries to property, or a course of illegitimate interference with business activities, if a remedy by an action for damages is not adequate. This is one of the traditional functions of equity."

It is argued by counsel for the defendants that the plaintiff has a remedy by way of an action of ejectment in this court. Such an action is a very cumbersome one and resort is had to it very rarely. It is also argued by counsel for the defendants that an action may be brought for forcible entry and detainer in the Court of General Sessions under the local statute, D.C. Code, Title 11, Section 735. These considerations do not detract from the power of equity to exercise its power to grant redress by way of injunction.

It is clear that in this case the damages in an action at law would obviously be inadequate, as has already been stated.

In light of these considerations the defendants' motion to dismiss is denied.

Peters v. Archambault

Supreme Judicial Court of Massachusetts, 1972.
361 Mass. 91, 278 N.E.2d 729.

■ CUTTER, J. The plaintiffs by this bill seek to compel the defendants (the Archambaults) to remove a portion of the Archambault house which encroaches on the plaintiffs' land in Marchfield. The plaintiffs and the Archambaults owned adjoining ocean-front lots. Both lots are registered (G.L. c. 185). Neither certificate of title shows the Archambault lot to have any rights in the plaintiffs' lot.

The Archambaults' predecessor in title obtained a building permit in 1946 and built a house partly on their own lot and partly on the plaintiffs' lot, of which the total area is about 4,900 square feet. Each lot had a frontage of only fifty feet on the adjacent way. The encroachment contains 465 square feet, and the building extends fifteen feet, three inches, onto the plaintiffs' lot, to a depth of thirty-one feet, four inches. The trial judge found that it will be expensive to remove the encroaching portion of the Archambaults' building. He ruled ... that there had been established no estoppel of, or laches on the part of, the plaintiffs in seeking to have the encroachment removed. It appears from the evidence that the Archambaults bought their lot from one vendor and the plaintiffs on June 14, 1966, bought their lot from another vendor. The judge found no evidence of any permission by the owners of the plaintiffs' lot for the encroachment. The encroachment was discovered on July 14, 1966, when the plaintiffs had a survey of their land made.

A final decree ordered the removal of the encroachment. The Archambaults appealed....

In Massachusetts a landowner is ordinarily entitled to mandatory equitable relief to compel removal of a structure significantly encroaching on his land, even though the encroachment was unintentional or negligent and the cost of removal is substantial in comparison to any injury suffered by the owner of the lot upon which the encroachment has taken place. In rare cases, referred to in our decisions as "exceptional", courts of equity have refused to grant a mandatory injunction and have left the plaintiff to his remedy of damages, "where the unlawful encroachment has been made innocently, and the cost of removal by the defendant would be greatly disproportionate to the injury to the plaintiff from its continuation, or where the substantial rights of the owner may be protected without recourse to an injunction, or where an injunction would be oppressive and inequitable.... But these are the exceptions. What is just and equitable in cases of this sort depends very much upon the particular facts and circumstances disclosed."

We here are considering the remedies to be applied with respect to registered land. Such land is protected to a greater extent than other land from unrecorded and unregistered liens, prescriptive rights, encumbrances, and other burdens. Adverse possession does not run against such land. To recognize the encumbrance created by the Archambaults' encroachment would tend to "defeat the purpose of the land registration act."

The present record discloses no circumstances which would justify denial of a mandatory injunction for removal of an encroachment taking away over nine per cent ($^{465}/_{4900}$) of the plaintiffs' lot. The exceptions ... to the general Massachusetts rule, hitherto recognized as sufficient to justify denial of mandatory relief, have related to much less significant invasions of a plaintiff's land, or have involved circumstances not here present. The invasion of the plaintiffs' lot is substantial and not de minimis. Photographs and maps in evidence, portraying the encroachment, show that the intrusion of the Archambaults' building on the plaintiffs' small lot greatly increases the congestion of that lot. The plaintiffs were entitled to receive whatever was shown by the land registration certificate as belonging to their grantor, unencumbered by any unregistered prescriptive easement or encroachment.

The Massachusetts rule in cases like this is well established. There is no occasion for resort to cases from other jurisdictions.

Decree affirmed with costs of appeal.

■ TAURO, C.J. (dissenting). The plaintiffs and defendants are owners of adjoining lots, with dwellings, both registered under G.L. c. 185. The defendants acquired title to their lot on June 18, 1954, and the plaintiffs acquired their title on June 14, 1966. The plaintiffs seek removal of a portion of the defendants' dwelling which encroaches on their land. This encroachment existed in full view from June, 1946, when the defendants' predecessor in title erected the dwelling, until July 14, 1966, when the plaintiffs had their property surveyed for the purpose of erecting a retaining wall. During this period, neither the plaintiffs' predecessor in title nor the plaintiffs raised any objection to the location of the defendants' dwelling. It is reasonable to infer that prior to taking title the plaintiffs viewed the property. Thus they had actual notice of the location of the defendants' dwelling and its relative position to their own dwelling.

The plaintiffs do not seek money damages but rather a decree for the removal of the encroachment on their land which, in effect, would result in the destruction of the defendants' dwelling. The Superior Court made, and the majority today affirm, such a decree. I cannot agree with the opinion of the majority that, in the proper exercise of the court's discretion, "[t]he present record discloses no circumstances which would justify denial of a mandatory injunction" compelling the removal of the encroaching structure. To the contrary, I believe that the record before us sets forth unusual circumstances which would justify this court in denying a mandatory injunction and leaving the plaintiffs to seek their remedy at law for damages. Moreover, the granting of injunctive relief in the circumstances of this case would be "oppressive and inequitable."

To conclude, as does the majority opinion, that this court must grant a mandatory injunction because the facts in the instant case do not precisely fit the factual pattern adjudged to be "exceptional" in prior Massachusetts cases is illogical and untenable. Courts, especially courts of equity, should not be restricted to so fossilized a concept of what the law is or should be. The cause of justice deserves a better fate. The overwhelming weight of authority in other jurisdictions recognizes and applies the doctrine I urge be adopted here. . . .

. . . .

In the totality of circumstances, I conclude that equity does not, in the exercise of our sound discretion, require us to grant injunctive relief. Removal imposes upon the defendants substantial cost and inconvenience which are entirely disproportionate to the injury to the plaintiffs. Where, as here, it appears that the plaintiffs were content with the status quo until fortuitous discovery of the encroachment, it would be oppressive and inequitable for this court to grant a mandatory injunction against the defendants who have acted in good faith, albeit their predecessor in title made a mistake which remained undiscovered for some twenty years. Hardship alone is of course not a ground for denial of injunctive relief, but this court should take relative hardship into account, if, as in the instant case, the owner of the encroaching structure is not guilty of an intentional trespass. The view I express is not only in accordance with our own case law but also in accordance with decisions in other jurisdictions. Here, it appears not only that the defendants have always acted in good faith but that the initial trespass was committed many years before they acquired title to their lot. . . .

. . . .

Upon reviewing the present record, I conclude that this is an exceptional case which does not require injunctive relief. . . .

If we were to refuse injunctive relief, common sense suggests that, in all probability, this dispute would be settled eventually without the need for the destruction of the defendants' dwelling. This could be accomplished through an agreement by the plaintiffs to voluntarily relocate their boundary line in return for payment by the defendants of an amount negotiated between them. The parties would then have their certificates of title reformed to reflect the agreement. In the alternative, the plaintiffs could bring an action at law and the court would make an impartial assessment of damages. The placing of the potent weapon of injunctive relief in the hands of the plaintiffs is hardly conducive to a fair and just settlement. In circumstances such as those in the instant case, the court in Christensen v. Tucker, 114 Cal.App.2d 554, 563, 250 P.2d 660, 665, said: "[T]he injunction should be denied, otherwise, the court would lend itself to what practically amounts to extortion." I would dismiss the bill and relegate the plaintiffs to their remedy at law.[3]

NOTE ON THE RESTATEMENT'S DEFINITION OF BALANCING OF EQUITIES

RESTATEMENT, SECOND, TORTS § 941(1979). *"Relative Hardship—"Balancing of Equities.'* The relative hardship likely to result to the defendant if an injunction is granted and to the plaintiff if it is denied, is one of the factors to be considered in determining the appropriateness of injunction against tort.

"**Comment a. Relative Hardship—'Balancing of equities.'** When a plaintiff proves that a tort has been committed or is threatened and shows that other remedies will not make him whole, an injunction is not to be issued as a matter of course. Elementary justice requires consideration of the hardship the defendant would be caused by an injunction as compared with the hardship the plaintiff would suffer if the injunction should be refused. Though the expression 'balance of convenience' is

3. [See also Miceli v. Riley, *supra* p. 20; Somerville v. Jacobs, *infra* p. 20; California "good faith improver statute," *infra* p. 20]

sometimes used to designate the weighing process here involved, it does not state the proper test. This term suggests a nice measurement of relative advantages and a denial of the injunction if the scales tip in the defendant's favor. The law does not grant an injunction merely because of the advantage that the plaintiff might reap from it, and it does not refuse an injunction merely because of the convenience that the refusal might afford the defendant. The problem is more complicated than that. It cannot be summed up in any phrase less elastic than 'relative hardship.' "

C. NUISANCE

State of Tennessee v. Feezell

Supreme Court of Tennessee, 1966.
218 Tenn. 17, 400 S.W.2d 716.

■ WHITE, J. The Honorable Glenn W. Woodlee, Chancellor ... heard this case which was brought in the name of the State of Tennessee, under T.C.A. § 23–301 et seq., on behalf of twenty-six citizens of Blount County, all similarly situated, to enjoin the establishment of a crematory by Defendant Feezell in a "rural or rural residential" area in said county.

. . . .

Petitioners aver in their bill that the proposed establishment and operation of the crematory is a public or private nuisance and said establishment and operation should be enjoined immediately....

A demurrer was filed to the petition stating essentially that it sought an injunction for an anticipated injury which constitutes no basis for injunctive relief. Excellent trial briefs were prepared by both parties, and in a memorandum opinion and decree, the chancellor sustained the demurrer and dismissed the petition on the ground that the suit was premature. Motion for a new trial having been overruled, appeal was perfected to this Court.

The question presented for determination by the Court is essentially this: Does a cause of action exist to enjoin, as a nuisance, a proposed cremation establishment in a rural or rural residential area under averments of the residents of the area that it will cause mental anguish, depressed feelings, physical discomfort and lower property values? We do not think so.

We believe that for an injunction suit to be sustained prior to the alleged nuisance coming into being, it must be sufficiently shown in the original bill or petition that the proposed establishment is a nuisance *per se;* that is within itself.

A nuisance at law or a nuisance per se is an act, occupation, or structure which is a nuisance at all times and under any circumstances, *regardless of location or surroundings.* Nuisances in fact or per accidens are those which become nuisances by reason of circumstances and surroundings and an act may be found to be a nuisance as a matter of fact where the natural tendency of the act is to create danger or inflict injury on person or property. 66 C.J.S. Nuisances § 3 (1950). (Emphasis supplied.)

Other definitions are: any act or omission or use of property or thing which is of itself hurtful to the health, tranquility, or morals, or which outrages the decency of the community; that which *cannot* be so *conducted* or *maintained* as to be *lawfully carried on* or *permitted* to *exist;* and, as related to private persons, an act or use of property of a continuing nature, offensive to and legally injurious to health and property, or both. 39 Am.Jur., Nuisances, § 11 (1942). (Emphasis supplied.)

It is perhaps misleading to define a nuisance per se as one which exists "at all times and under any circumstances, regardless of location or surroundings." Actually, a nuisance cannot exist without surrounding circumstances, because it is the surrounding circumstances that determine whether an injury is occasioned; and it is axiomatic that some injury must be occasioned or be at least imminent because of the alleged "nuisance."

There is, in at least one case in this State, an indication that the difference between a nuisance per se, and a nuisance per accidens is that in the former, injury in some form is certain to be inflicted, while in the latter, the injury is uncertain or contingent until it actually occurs. This case held that where injury from a nuisance is not real and immediate and certain to occur, but only uncertain or contingent, the nuisance will not be enjoined anticipatory to its going into operation. . . .

. . . .

We do not say that an anticipatory nuisance is not enjoinable under any circumstances. If the injury anticipated is imminent and certain to occur, there may, in fact, be a proper case for immediate abatement, provided, of course, the injury is recognized as otherwise actionable at law and equity. We do not say that mental disturbances or "psychic" injuries caused by a nuisance, public or private, are not such as may be actionable at law or equity. They can, in fact, be very real to the complainants. We do say, however, that allegations in the petition must be sufficient, in defining the circumstances and mode of operation surrounding the undertaking, to persuade the court, if they are proved, that injury is imminent and certain. We are convinced that proof of the alleged location of defendant's crematory and the alleged mode of operation and physical appearance of the same will be insufficient to foretell certain injury.

Our research has uncovered no case involving the attempted abatement of a human cremation establishment. Possibly the closest analogy would be the operation of a funeral parlor—at least as regards "psychic" injuries and lowered property values.

. . . .

As regards funeral parlors or undertaking establishments, the majority rule in this country, according to an annotation in 39 A.L.R.2d 1000 (1955), is . . . that if an undertaking establishment in a purely residential section causes from its normal operations, depressing feelings to families in the immediate neighborhood, and, as a constant reminder of death, appreciably impairs their happiness or weakens their powers of resistance and depreciates the values of their properties, such an establishment constitutes a nuisance.

. . . .

Our holding in the instant cases does not, perhaps, coincide precisely with some of the cases following the majority rule. . . . Nevertheless, we are limited in the instant case to an examination of those factors alleged in the petition, proof of which would not indicate certain injury, either emotional or physical, to petitioners. Residences in a rural area are sparsely situated and there is no allegation in the bill that any residence is in close proximity to the proposed crematory, but that it is to be located in "an entirely rural area."

There is, of course, a minority rule, the gist of which is that mental suffering or depressed feelings are not actionable injuries where funeral parlors are proposed for residential areas. . . .

. . .

Because we find the allegations in the petition insufficient, even if proved, to persuade us that a nuisance is sure to be created by the operation of a crematory in this particular location, we, therefore, affirm the ruling of the trial court as set forth in a splendid memorandum opinion.

Affirmed.

Campbell v. Seaman

Court of Appeals of New York, 1876.
63 N.Y. 568.

Appeal from a judgment in favor of the plaintiff entered upon the report of a referee. The action was brought to recover damages resulting from an alleged nuisance, and to restrain the continuance thereof. . . .

■ EARL, J. The plaintiffs owned about forty acres of land, situate in the village of Castleton, on the east bank of the Hudson river, and had owned it since about 1849. During the years 1857, 1858 and 1859 they built upon it an expensive dwelling-house, and during those years, and before and since, they improved the land by grading and terracing, building roads and walks through the same, and planting trees and shrubs, both ornamental and useful.

The defendant had for some years owned adjoining lands, which he had used as a brick-yard. The brick-yard is southerly of plaintiff's dwelling-house about 1,320 feet, and southerly of their woods about 567 feet. In burning bricks defendant had made use of anthracite coal. During the burning of a kiln sulphuric acid gas is generated, which is destructive to some kinds of trees and vines. The evidence shows, and the referee found, that gas coming from defendant's kilns had, during the years 1869 and 1870, killed the foliage of plaintiff's white and yellow pines and Norway spruce, and had, after repeated attacks, killed and destroyed from 100 to 150 valuable pine and spruce trees, and had injured their grape vines and plum trees, and he estimated plaintiff's damages from the gas during those years at $500.

This gas did not continually escape during the burning of a kiln, but only during the last two days, and was carried into and over plaintiff's land only when the wind was from the south.

It is a general rule that every person may exercise exclusive dominion over his own property, and subject it to such uses as will best subserve his private interests. Generally, no other person can say how he shall use or what he shall do with his property. But this general right of property has its exceptions and qualifications. *Sic utere tuo ut alienum non laedas* [to use your property as not to injure your neighbor's] is an old maxim which has a broad application. It does not mean that one must never use his own so as to do any injury to his neighbor or his property. Such a rule could not be enforced in civilized society. Persons living in organized communities must suffer some damage, annoyance and inconvenience from each other. For these they are compensated by all the advantages of civilized society. If one lives in the city he must expect to suffer the dirt, smoke, noisome odors, noise and confusion incident to city life. . . .

But every person is bound to make a reasonable use of his property so as to occasion no unnecessary damage or annoyance to his neighbor. If he make an unreasonable, unwarrantable or unlawful use of it, so as to produce material annoyance, inconvenience, discomfort or hurt to his neighbor, he will be guilty of a nuisance to his neighbor. And the law will hold him responsible for the consequent damage. As to what is a reasonable use of one's own property cannot be defined by any certain general rules, but must depend upon the circumstances of each case. A use of property in one locality and under some circumstances may be lawful and reasonable, which, under other circumstances, would be unlawful, unreasonable and a nuisance. To constitute a nuisance, the use must be such as to produce a tangible and appreciable injury to neighboring property, or such as to render its enjoyment specially uncomfortable or inconvenient.

Within the rules thus referred to, that defendant's brick burning was a nuisance to plaintiffs cannot be doubted. . . .

. . . .

But the claim is made that although the brick burning in this case is a nuisance, a court of equity will not and ought not to restrain it, and the plaintiffs should be left to their remedy at law to recover damages, and this claim must now be examined.

. . . .

The plaintiffs had built a costly mansion and had laid out their grounds and planted them with ornamental and useful trees and vines, for their comfort and enjoyment. How can one be compensated in damages for the destruction of his ornamental trees, and the flowers and vines which surrounded his home? How can a jury estimate their value in dollars and cents? The fact that trees and vines are for ornament or luxury entitles them no less to the protection of the law. Everyone has the right to surround himself with articles of luxury, and he will be no less protected than one who provides himself only with articles of necessity. The law will protect a flower or a vine as well as an oak. These damages are irreparable too, because the trees and vines cannot be replaced, and the law will not compel a person to take money rather than the objects of beauty and utility which he places around his dwelling to gratify his taste or to promote his comfort and his health.

Here the injunction also prevents a multiplicity of suits. The injury is a recurring one, and every time the poisonous breath from defendant's brick-kiln sweeps over plaintiffs' land they have a cause of action. Unless the nuisance be restrained the litigation would be interminable. The policy of the law favors, and the peace and good order of society are best promoted by the termination of such litigations by a single suit.

The fact that this nuisance is not continual, and that the injury is only occasional, furnishes no answer to the claim for an injunction. The nuisance has occurred often enough within two years to do the plaintiffs large damage. Every time a kiln is burned some injury may be expected, unless the wind should blow the poisonous gas away from plaintiffs' lands. Nuisances causing damage less frequently have been restrained.

It matters not that the brick-yard was used before plaintiffs bought their lands or built their houses. One cannot erect a nuisance upon his land adjoining vacant lands owned by another and thus measurably control the uses to which his neighbor's land may in the future be subjected. He may make a reasonable and lawful use of his land and thus cause his neighbor some inconvenience, and probably some damage which the law would regard as *damnum absque injuria* [loss or harm without injury in the legal sense]. But he cannot place upon his land anything which the law would pronounce a nuisance, and thus compel his neighbor to leave his land vacant, or to use it in such way only as the neighboring nuisance will allow.

It is claimed that the plaintiffs so far acquiesced in this nuisance as to bar them from any equitable relief. I do not perceive how any acquiescence short of twenty years can bar one from complaining of a nuisance, unless his conduct has been such as to estop him. There is no proof that plaintiffs, when they bought their lands, knew that any one intended to burn any bricks upon the land now owned by defendant. From about 1840 to 1853 no bricks were burned there. Then from 1853 to 1857 bricks were burned there, and then not again until 1867. From 1857 to 1867 the brick yard was plowed and used for agricultural purposes. Before suit brought, plaintiffs objected to the brick burning. No act or omission of theirs induced the defendant to incur large expenses or to take any action which could be the basis of an estoppel against them, and therefore there was no acquiescence or laches which should bar the plaintiffs, within any rule laid down in any reported case.

. . . .

The defendant claims a prescriptive right to burn bricks upon his land and to cause the poisonous vapors to flow over plaintiffs' lands. Assuming that defendant could acquire by lapse of time and continuous user the prescriptive right which he claims, there has not here been a continuous use and exercise of the right for twenty consecutive years. . . .

. . . .

We cannot apprehend that our decision in this case can improperly embarrass those engaged in the useful trade of brick making. Similar decisions in England, where population and human habitations are more dense, do not appear to have produced any embarrassment. In this country there can be no trouble to find places where brick can be made without damage to persons living in the vicinity. It certainly cannot be necessary to make them in the heart of a village or in the midst of a thickly settled community.

It follows from these views that the judgment should be confirmed.

All concur.

Judgment affirmed.

Tushbant v. Greenfield's, Inc.

Supreme Court of Michigan, 1944.
308 Mich. 626, 14 N.W.2d 520.

Suit by Fred Tushbant and another, doing business as Griswold Sporting Goods Company, a copartnership, against Greenfield's Incorporated, to enjoin defendant from operating its restaurant business in such manner as to cause its patrons to form a line-up in front of plaintiff's adjacent store. From a decree for plaintiffs, defendant appeals.

■ BOYLES, J. Plaintiffs have established to some extent the existence of a private nuisance which can be sufficiently abated by defendant to minimize the resulting harm to plaintiffs' business. Plaintiffs are entitled to some relief.

The record before us is convincing that defendant's manner of conducting its restaurant business is harmful to plaintiffs and results in their loss of business. It is possible to minimize the damage without imposing undue hardship on defendant. The decree entered in the circuit court should be modified. It is not necessary to require defendant to form a line-up of its customers on the outside edge of the sidewalk with not more than two persons standing abreast of each other, with an opening in crossing the sidewalk. The obstruction of view of plaintiffs' show windows for a short period of time is unimportant as compared with the inconvenience to the public use of the street that would be caused by trying to compel users of the street to pass through a double line-up of persons from curb to door. Unobstructed entrance to plaintiffs' store can readily be accomplished by defendant by means of an employee of defendant supervising the line-up of its customers. Plaintiffs may propose a decree for entry in this court in accordance herewith. No costs of appeal allowed either party.

■ REID, J. (dissenting). . . .

. . . .

The question involved herein is novel.

There are many occasions of waiting lines of patrons observed in many cities at ballparks, theaters, and several other places where lawful business is conducted. The situation in the instant case results in something of a damage to the neighbor's property for which the law affords no remedy as between the parties concerned. Instead the remedy is in the power of the police and it is their plain duty to reasonably control street conditions.

. . . .

The police have exclusive charge of the matter of conduct of persons on the streets. It is erroneous to order a private party to assume any control of persons on the streets whatsoever. . . .

In this case the record shows that the defendant addressed a communication to the police commissioner requesting police control of the situation. A sincere insistence on such police action is all that could be expected of defendant.

Danielson v. Local 275, Laborers Intern. Union of North America

United States Court of Appeals, Second Circuit, 1973.
479 F.2d 1033.

■ MULLIGAN, J. This is an appeal from an order of the United States District Court for the Southern District of New York which denied a petition of Sidney Danielson, Regional Director of the National Labor Relations Board (the Board) for a preliminary injunction pursuant to Section 10(*l*) of the National Labor Relations Act, 29 U.S.C. § 160(*l*) (the Act). . . .

The petition for the Section 10(*l*) injunction filed on January 29, 1973 was precipitated by a charge filed with the Board on January 10, 1973 by S.B. Apartments, Inc. (S.B.) alleging that Local 275, Laborers International Union of North America, AFL–CIO; Painters District Council No. 20 of Westchester and Putnam Counties, New York, Brotherhood of Painters, Decorators and Paperhangers of America, AFL–CIO; Local 55, Bricklayers, Masons and Plasterers; and Local 323, United Brotherhood of Carpenters and Joiners of America, AFL–CIO, had engaged in and are engaging in unfair labor practices within the meaning of Section 8(b)(7)(C) of the Act, 29 U.S.C. § 158(b)(7)(C). This Section, in essence, proscribes recognitional or organizational picketing for more than 30 days without filing with the Board a petition for an election under Section 9(c) of the Act, 29 U.S.C. § 159(c). No such petition has been filed. After investigation, the Regional Director concluded that there was reasonable cause to believe that the Unions were engaging in the unfair labor practices charged and that a complaint should issue. Accordingly, the Regional Director filed the petition in the District Court for injunctive relief pursuant to Section 10(*l*) of the Act, pending final disposition by the Board of the unfair labor practice charge. The Unions filed answers which denied the allegations of the petition. The Board has not finally adjudicated the charges.

S.B., the charging party, is the owner of real estate in Cold Spring, New York, where a 63 unit garden apartment complex is being constructed by James A. Klein, Inc. (Klein), a general contractor. Klein and S.B. (collectively referred to as the Employer) are commonly owned and controlled and constitute a single, integrated business enterprise. On October 31, 1972 the representatives of the Employer met in a pre-job conference with the Unions who stated that the job site had to be completely unionized and sought unsuccessfully to have the Employer sign a collective bargaining agreement. On November 1, 1972 the Unions began picketing the job site with between 2 and 200 pickets. The picketing by the Unions has been continuous except for a two week period in late March, 1973, and is still continuing. No petition for an election has been filed with the Board and no charge is before the Board under Section 8(a)(2) of the Act, 29 U.S.C. § 158(a)(2), alleging that the Employer has unlawfully recognized or assisted any labor organization. None of the Unions are now certified as bargaining representatives of any employees of the Employer. On this basis the Board contended that the picketing was not for informational purposes but had as its object forced recognition or bargaining by the Employer with the Unions and forced acceptance by the employees of the Unions as their bargaining agents. The Court below found that the Board has reasonable cause to believe that the Unions have engaged and are engaging in unfair labor practices in violation of Section 8(b)(7)(C) of the Act. Moreover the Court rejected the Unions' claims that the picketing was informational and educational stating:

> "the picture that emerges to this Court is clearly one of a series of coercive tactics designed to achieve organizational and recognitional objects. The petitioner's claim that the charging party has been subjected to a campaign of harassment is an accurate assessment of the events which followed the October 31st meeting when the employer refused to agree to the job being 100% union."

Despite these findings of reasonable cause, the lower Court refused to enjoin the union activity on the ground that in a 10(*l*) proceeding general equitable principles must be applied and since it found no "irreparable" damage, the Court concluded that it would not be "just and proper" to issue the extraordinary relief of a preliminary injunction. We reverse and remand for the entry of a preliminary injunction enjoining the unfair labor practices charged pending disposition of the charges before the Board.

... The sole issue posed by the parties is whether the issuance of a preliminary injunction under Section 10(*l*) depends upon the application of general equitable principles which the Court below interpreted to require a showing of irreparable harm to the Employer, or whether as the Board contends the irreparable harm concept applicable in private actions is not pertinent in a Section 10(*l*) case. The Board reasons that the purpose of 10(*l*) was not to prevent irreparable damage to the Employer but to protect the public interest in maintaining the free flow of commerce and to encourage collective bargaining.

The Supreme Court has not yet passed upon the criteria for granting a preliminary injunction under either Section 10(j) or 10(*l*). In McLeod v. Local 25, IBEW, [344 F.2d 634, 638 (2d Cir.1965)]this Court in discussing the question stated:

> "In § 10(*l*) proceedings the function of the federal district court consists of determining (1) whether the temporary injunctive relief would be 'just and proper' in terms of general equitable principles and (2) whether there is 'reasonable cause' for the Regional Director 'to believe such [unfair labor practice] charge is true and that a complaint should issue.' "

We see no reason here to depart from this statement of the law. Section 10(*l*) *in haec verba* provides that the District Court shall have jurisdiction to grant such injunctive relief "as it deems just and proper." The Section therefore does not mandate the preliminary injunction simply because the District Court concludes that the Board has reasonable ground to believe that an unfair labor practice has occurred. The Act gives the Court discretion by employing the "just and proper" language. In *Local 25,* supra, our Court simply held that in applying the "just and proper" norm the District Court should be guided by the application of general equitable principles. We see no impropriety in this since the District Court albeit authorized by the statute to grant injunctive relief, is exercising its equity powers.

We see no point in now deciding whether irreparable harm to the Employer must always be shown in a Section 10(*l*) case because in any event there was a clear showing of substantial and irreparable harm to the Employer which under any construction of the Act should have resulted in the issuance of the preliminary injunction sought by the Board.

We believe that the Court below was perhaps misled not by the language we have quoted from *Local 25* which stated that "general equitable principles" must be applied, but by the further statement in that case that Local 25's picketing "posed an imminent threat of irreparable injury, viz., halting the construction of the additional wing of the hospital." We cannot read this language as implying that anything less than a total work stoppage does not amount to irreparable injury. The Court below found that construction at the job site was not substantially halted; however, that the progress of the work was delayed and that extra expense was incurred and prospective rentals, lost, emerges clearly from the other findings of the Court and the record before us. . . .

While the Court below found that no irreparable injury to the Employer has been shown since December 1972, it is inescapable that the initial deliberate blockage of supplies and vandalism have a continued delaying effect upon the completion of the project, its availability to tenants and a postponement of rentals. The picketing concededly continues and there is reasonable cause to believe that it is unlawful. We do not agree therefore that it is just and proper to withhold equitable relief simply because the picketing has failed to shut down the operation but only delays performance which results in the incurring of expenses and prevention of profits.

The concept of irreparable injury in equity traces back to the early assumption of jurisdiction by the Courts of Chancery to enjoin waste, continuing trespass and nuisance. Irreparable injury is suffered where monetary damages are difficult to ascertain or are inadequate. (See cases collected in Z. [Chafee] & E. Re, Cases and Materials on Equity chap. 15 (5th ed. 1967)). A construction contract is characteristically one where a breach or interference with performance results in damages which are not readily or accurately determinable. In this case assuming that the Unions would be responsible for damages the amount of damage attributable specifically to union activity is clearly difficult to assess and measure.

As we have had occasion to point out recently a basic purpose of a preliminary injunction is to maintain the *status quo.* The failure to issue an injunction here maintains not the *status quo*, but protects what the Court below has found the Board had reasonable ground to believe, is a violation of the statute.

In applying general equitable principles, we fail to see how there is any possible weighing of hardships in favor of the Unions. . . .

Reversed and remanded for entry of a preliminary injunction enjoining the unfair labor practices pending disposition of the charges by the Board.

Boomer v. Atlantic Cement Co.

Court of Appeals of New York, 1970.
26 N.Y.2d 219, 309 N.Y.S.2d 312, 257 N.E.2d 870.

■ BERGAN, J. Defendant operates a large cement plant near Albany. These are actions for injunction and damages by neighboring land owners alleging injury to property from dirt, smoke and vibration emanating from the plant. A nuisance has been found after trial, temporary damages have been allowed; but an injunction has been denied.

The public concern with air pollution arising from many sources in industry and in transportation is currently accorded ever wider recognition accompanied by a growing sense of responsibility in State and Federal Governments to control it. Cement plants are obvious sources of air pollution in the neighborhoods where they operate.

But there is now before the court private litigation in which individual property owners have sought specific relief from a single plant operation. The threshold question raised by the division of view on this appeal is whether the court should resolve the litigation between the parties now before it as equitably as seems possible; or whether, seeking promotion of the general public welfare, it should channel private litigation into broad public objectives.

A court performs its essential function when it decides the rights of parties before it. Its decision of private controversies may sometimes greatly affect public issues. Large questions of law are often resolved by the manner in which private litigation is decided. But this is normally an incident to the court's main function to settle controversy. It is a rare exercise of judicial power to use a decision in private litigation as a purposeful mechanism to achieve direct public objectives greatly beyond the rights and interests before the court.

Effective control of air pollution is a problem presently far from solution even with the full public and financial powers of government. In large measure adequate technical procedures are yet to be developed and some that appear possible may be economically impracticable.

It seems apparent that the amelioration of air pollution will depend on technical research in great depth; on a carefully balanced consideration of the economic impact of close regulation; and of the actual effect on public health. It is likely to require massive public expenditure and to demand more than any local community can accomplish and to depend on regional and interstate controls.

A court should not try to do this on its own as a by-product of private litigation and it seems manifest that the judicial establishment is neither equipped in the limited nature of any judgment it can pronounce nor prepared to lay down and implement an effective policy for the elimination of air pollution. This is an area beyond the circumference of one private lawsuit. It is a direct responsibility for government and should not thus be undertaken as an incident to solving a dispute between property owners and a single cement plant—one of many—in the Hudson River valley.

The cement making operations of defendant have been found by the court at Special Term to have damaged the nearby properties of plaintiffs in these two actions. That court, as it has been noted, accordingly found defendant maintained a nuisance and this has been affirmed at the Appellate Division. The total damage to plaintiffs' properties is, however, relatively small in comparison with the value of defendant's operation and with the consequences of the injunction which plaintiffs seek.

The ground for the denial of injunction, notwithstanding the finding both that there is a nuisance and that plaintiffs have been damaged substantially, is the large disparity in economic consequences of the nuisance and of the injunction. This theory cannot, however, be sustained without overruling a doctrine which has been consistently reaffirmed in several leading cases in this court and which has never been disavowed here, namely that where a nuisance has been found and where there has been any substantial damage shown by the party complaining an injunction will be granted.

The rule in New York has been that such a nuisance will be enjoined although marked disparity be shown in economic consequence between the effect of the injunction and the effect of the nuisance.

The problem of disparity in economic consequence was sharply in focus in Whalen v. Union Bag & Paper Co. (208 N.Y. 1). A pulp mill entailing an investment of more than a million dollars polluted a stream in which plaintiff, who owned a farm, was "a lower riparian owner". The economic loss to plaintiff from this pollution was small. This court, reversing the Appellate Division, reinstated the injunction granted by the Special Term against the argument of the mill owner that in view of "the slight advantage to plaintiff and the great loss that will be inflicted on defendant" an injunction should not be granted. "Such a balancing of injuries cannot be justified by the circumstances of this case", Judge Werner noted. He continued: "Although the damage to the plaintiff may be slight as compared with the defendant's expense of abating the condition, that is not a good reason for refusing an injunction".

Thus the unconditional injunction granted at Special Term was reinstated. The rule laid down in that case, then, is that whenever the damage resulting from a nuisance is found not "unsubstantial", viz., $100 a year, injunction would follow. This states a rule that had been followed in this court with marked consistency.

There are cases where injunction has been denied. McCann v. Chasm Power Co. (211 N.Y. 301) is one of them. There, however, the damage shown by plaintiffs was not only unsubstantial, it was nonexistent. Plaintiffs owned a rocky bank of the stream in which defendant had raised the level of the water. This had no economic or other adverse consequence to plaintiffs, and thus injunctive relief was denied. Similar is the basis for denial of injunction in Forstmann v. Joray Holding Co. (244 N.Y. 22) where no benefit to plaintiffs could be seen from the injunction sought. Thus if, within Whalen v. Union Bag & Paper Co., which authoritatively states the rule in New York, the damage to plaintiffs in these present cases from defendant's cement plant is "not unsubstantial", an injunction should follow.

Although the court at Special Term and the Appellate Division held that injunction should be denied, it was found that plaintiffs had been damaged in various specific amounts up to the time of the trial and damages to the respective plaintiffs were awarded for those amounts. The effect of this was, injunction having been denied, plaintiffs could maintain successive actions at law for damages thereafter as further damage was incurred.

The court at Special Term also found the amount of permanent damage attributable to each plaintiff, for the guidance of the parties in the event both sides stipulated to the payment and acceptance of such permanent damage as a settlement of all the controversies among the parties. The total of permanent damages to all plaintiffs thus found was $185,000. This basis of adjustment has not resulted in any stipulation by the parties.

This result at Special Term and at the Appellate Division is a departure from a rule that has become settled; but to follow the rule literally in these cases would be to close down the plant at once. This court is fully agreed to avoid that immediately drastic remedy; the difference in view is how best to avoid it.

One alternative is to grant the injunction but postpone its effect to a specified future date to give opportunity for technical advances to permit defendant to eliminate the nuisance; another is to grant the injunction conditioned on the payment of permanent damages to plaintiffs which would compensate them for the total economic loss to their property present and future caused by defendant's operations. For reasons which will be developed the court chooses the latter alternative.

If the injunction were to be granted unless within a short period—e.g., 18 months—the nuisance be abated by improved methods, there would be no assurance that any significant technical improvement would occur.

The parties could settle this private litigation at any time if defendant paid enough money and the imminent threat of closing the plant would build up the pressure on defendant. If there were no improved techniques found, there would inevitably be applications to the court at Special Term for extensions of time to perform on showing of good faith efforts to find such techniques.

Moreover, techniques to eliminate dust and other annoying by-products of cement making are unlikely to be developed by any research the defendant can undertake within any short period, but will depend on the total resources of the cement industry nationwide and throughout the world. The problem is universal wherever cement is made.

For obvious reasons the rate of the research is beyond control of defendant. If at the end of 18 months the whole industry has not found a technical solution a court would be hard put to close down this one cement plant if due regard be given to equitable principles.

On the other hand, to grant the injunction unless defendant pays plaintiffs such permanent damages as may be fixed by the court seems to do justice between the contending parties. All of the attributions of economic loss to the properties on which plaintiffs' complaints are based will have been redressed.

The nuisance complained of by these plaintiffs may have other public or private consequences, but these particular parties are the only ones who have sought remedies and the judgment proposed will fully redress them. The limitation of relief granted is a limitation only within the four corners of these actions and does not foreclose public health or other public agencies from seeking proper relief in a proper court.

It seems reasonable to think that the risk of being required to pay permanent damages to injured property owners by cement plant owners would itself be a reasonable effective spur to research for improved techniques to minimize nuisance.

The power of the court to condition on equitable grounds the continuance of an injunction on the payment of permanent damages seems undoubted....

    . . . .

Thus it seems fair to both sides to grant permanent damages to plaintiffs which will terminate this private litigation. The theory of damage is the "servitude on land" of plaintiffs imposed by defendant's nuisance....

The judgment, by allowance of permanent damages imposing a servitude on land, which is the basis of the actions, would preclude future recovery by plaintiffs or their grantees.

This should be placed beyond debate by a provision of the judgment that the payment by defendant and the acceptance by plaintiffs of permanent damages found by the court shall be in compensation for a servitude on the land.

Although the Trial Term has found permanent damages as a possible basis of settlement of the litigation, on remission the court should be entirely free to re-examine this subject. It may again find the permanent damage already found; or make new findings.

The orders should be reversed, without costs, and the cases remitted to Supreme Court, Albany County to grant an injunction which shall be vacated upon payment by defendant of such amounts of permanent damage to the respective plaintiffs as shall for this purpose be determined by the court.

■ JASEN, J. (dissenting). I agree with the majority that a reversal is required here, but I do not subscribe to the newly enunciated doctrine of assessment of permanent damages, in lieu of an injunction, where substantial property rights have been impaired by the creation of a nuisance.

It has long been the rule in this State, as the majority acknowledges, that a nuisance which results in substantial continuing damage to neighbors must be enjoined. To now change the rule to permit the cement company to continue polluting the air indefinitely upon the payment of permanent damages is, in my opinion, compounding the magnitude of a very serious problem in our State and Nation today.

In recognition of this problem, the Legislature of this State has enacted the Air Pollution Control Act (Public Health Law, Consol.Laws, c. 45, §§ 1264 to 1299–m) declaring that it is the State policy to require the use of all available and reasonable methods to prevent and control air pollution.

The harmful nature and widespread occurrence of air pollution have been extensively documented. Congressional hearings have revealed that air pollution causes substantial property damage, as well as being a contributing factor to a rising incidence of lung cancer, emphysema, bronchitis and asthma.

The specific problem faced here is known as particulate contamination because of the fine dust particles emanating from defendant's cement plant. The particular type of nuisance is not new, having appeared in many cases for at least the past 60 years. It is interesting to note that cement production has recently been identified as a significant source of particulate contamination in the Hudson Valley. This type of pollution, wherein very small particles escape and stay in the atmosphere, has been denominated as the type of air pollution which produces the greatest hazard to human health. We have thus a nuisance which not only is damaging to the plaintiffs, but also is decidedly harmful to the general public.

I see grave dangers in overruling our long-established rule of granting an injunction where a nuisance results in substantial continuing damage. In permitting the injunction to become inoperative upon the payment of permanent damages, the majority is, in effect, licensing a continuing wrong. It is the same as saying to the cement company, you may continue to do harm to your neighbors so long as you pay a fee for it. Furthermore, once such permanent damages are assessed and paid, the incentive to alleviate the wrong would be eliminated, thereby continuing air pollution of an area without abatement.

It is true that some courts have sanctioned the remedy here proposed by the majority in a number of cases, but none of the authorities relied upon by the majority are analogous to the situation before us. In those cases, the courts, in denying an injunction and awarding money damages, grounded their decision on a showing that the use to which the property was intended to be put was primarily for the public benefit. Here, on the other hand, it is clearly established that the cement company is creating a continuing air pollution nuisance primarily for its own private interest with no public benefit.

This kind of inverse condemnation may not be invoked by a private person or corporation for private gain or advantage. Inverse condemnation should only be permitted when the public is primarily served in the taking or impairment of property. The promotion of the interests of the polluting cement company has, in my opinion, no public use or benefit.

Nor is it constitutionally permissible to impose servitude on land, without consent of the owner, by payment of permanent damages where the continuing impairment of the land is for a private use. . . .

In sum, then, by constitutional mandate as well as by judicial pronouncement, the permanent impairment of private property for private purposes is not authorized in the absence of clearly demonstrated public benefit and use.

I would enjoin the defendant cement company from continuing the discharge of dust particles upon its neighbors' properties unless, within 18 months, the cement company abated this nuisance.

It is not my intention to cause the removal of the cement plant from the Albany area, but to recognize the urgency of the problem stemming from this stationary source of air pollution, and to allow the company a specified period of time to develop a means to alleviate this nuisance.

I am aware that the trial court found that the most modern dust control devices available have been installed in defendant's plant, but, I submit, this does not mean that *better* and more effective dust control devices could not be developed within the time allowed to abate the pollution.

Moreover, I believe it is incumbent upon the defendant to develop such devices, since the cement company, at the time the plant commenced production (1962), was well aware of the plaintiffs' presence in the area, as well as the probable consequences of its contemplated operation. Yet, it still chose to build and operate the plant at this site.

In a day when there is a growing concern for clean air, highly developed industry should not expect acquiescence by the courts, but should, instead, plan its operations to eliminate contamination of our air and damage to its neighbors.

Accordingly, the orders of the Appellate Division, insofar as they denied the injunction, should be reversed, and the actions remitted to Supreme Court, Albany County to grant an injunction to take effect 18 months hence, unless the nuisance is abated by improved techniques prior to said date.

Sawyer v. Davis

Supreme Judicial Court of Massachusetts, 1884.
136 Mass. 239.

Bill of Review, alleging the following facts:

The plaintiffs, who were manufacturers in Plymouth, were restrained by a decree of this court, made on October 1, 1881, upon a bill in equity brought by the present defendants, from ringing a bell on their mill before the hour of six and one half o'clock in the morning; which decree was affirmed by the full court on September 7, 1882. On March 28, 1883, the legislature passed an act, which took effect upon its passage, as follows: "Manufacturers and others employing workmen are authorized, for the purpose of giving notice to such employees, to ring bells and use whistles and gongs of such size and weight, in such manner and at such hours as the board of aldermen of cities and the selectmen of towns may in writing designate." St.1883, c. 84. On April 18, 1883, the selectmen of Plymouth granted to the plaintiffs a written license to ring the bell on their mill in such manner, and at such hours beginning at five o'clock in the morning, as they were accustomed to do prior to the injunction of this court.

The prayer of the bill was that the injunction might be dissolved, or that the decree might be so modified as to enable the plaintiffs to act under their license without violating the decree of this court; and for other and further relief.

The defendants demurred to the bill, assigning, among other grounds of demurrer, that the St. of 1883, c. 84, was unconstitutional, so far as applicable to the defendants.

Hearing on bill and demurrer, before Colburn, J., who reserved the case for the consideration of the full court.

ALLEN, J. Nothing is better established than the power of the legislature to make what are called police regulations, declaring in what manner property shall be used and enjoyed, and business carried on, with a view to the good order and benefit of the community, even although they may to some extent interfere with the full enjoyment of private property, and although no compensation is given to a person so inconvenienced. In this conflict of rights, police regulations by the legislature find a proper office in determining how far and under what circumstances the individual must yield with a view to the general good. For example, if, in a neighborhood thickly occupied by dwelling-houses, any one, for his own entertainment or the gratification of a whim, were to cause bells to be rung and steam-whistles to be blown to the extent that is usual with the bells and steam-whistles of locomotive engines near railroad stations in large cities, there can be no doubt that it would be an infringement of the rights of the residents, for which they could find ample remedy and vindication in the courts. But if the legislature, with a view to the safety of life, provides that bells shall be rung and whistles sounded, under those circumstances, persons living nearby must necessarily submit to some annoyance from this source, which otherwise they would have a right to be relieved from.

It is ordinarily a proper subject for legislative discretion to determine by general rules the extent to which those who are engaged in customary and lawful and necessary occupations shall be required or allowed to give signals or warnings by bells or whistles, or otherwise, with a view either to the public safety, as in the case of railroads, or to the necessary or convenient operation and management of their own works; and ordinarily such determination is binding upon the courts, as well as upon citizens generally. And when the legislature directs or allows that to be done which would otherwise be a nuisance, it will be valid, upon the ground that the legislature is ordinarily the proper judge of what the public good requires, unless carried to such an extent that it can fairly be said to be an unwholesome and unreasonable law....

. . . .

... Courts are compelled to recognize the distinction between such serious disturbances as existed in the case referred to, and comparatively slight ones, which differ in degree only, and not in kind, from those suffered by others in the same vicinity. Slight infractions of the natural rights of the individual may be sanctioned by the legislature under the proper exercise of the police power, with a view to the general good. Grave ones will fall within the constitutional limitation that the legislature is only authorized to pass reasonable laws. The line of distinction cannot be so laid down as to furnish a rule for the settlement of all cases in advance. The difficulty of marking the boundaries of this legislative power, or of prescribing limits to its exercise, was declared in Commonwealth v. Alger, 7 Cush. 53, 85, and is universally recognized. Courts, however, must determine the rights of parties in particular cases as they arise; always recognizing that the ownership of property does not of itself imply the right to use or enjoy it in every possible manner, without regard to corresponding rights of others as to the use and enjoyment of their property; and also that the rules of the common law, which have from time to time been established, declaring or limiting such rights to use and enjoyment, may themselves be changed as occasion may require.

In the case before us, looking at it for the present without regard to the decree of this court in the former case between these parties, we find nothing in the facts set forth which show that the statute relied on as authorizing the plaintiffs to ring their bell (St.1883, c. 84) should be declared unconstitutional....

... But the argument is urged upon us with great force, that in the present case there had been a judicial determination that the ringing of the bell, at the hours now authorized by the terms of the statute and the designation of the selectmen, was a private nuisance to the defendants, not growing out of any public right, and that the statute ought not, as a matter of construction, to be held applicable to this case; or, if such is its necessary construction, that it is unconstitutional, as interfering with their vested rights.

... The legislature must be deemed to have determined that the benefit is greater than the injury and annoyance; and to have intended to enact that the public must submit to the disturbance, for the sake of the greater advantage that would result from this method of carrying on the business of manufacturing. It must be considered, therefore, in this case, that a legislative sanction has been given to the very act which this court found to create a private nuisance.

It is then argued that the legislature cannot legalize a nuisance, and cannot take away the rights of the defendants as they have been ascertained and declared by this court; and this is undoubtedly true, so far as such rights have become vested....

The injunction which was awarded by the court, upon the facts which appeared at the hearing, did not imply a vested right in the present defendants to have it continued permanently. Though a final determination of the case before the court, and though binding and imperative upon the present plaintiffs, and enforceable against them by all the powers vested in a court of equity, yet they were at liberty at any time, under new circumstances making it inequitable for it to be longer continued, to apply to the court for a review of the case and a dissolution of the injunction. In respect to such a state of facts, an injunction can never be said to be final, in the sense that it is absolute for all time. Even without any new legislation affecting the rights of the parties, with an increase of their own business and a general increase of manufacturing and other business in the vicinity, and of a general and pervading change in the character of the neighborhood, it might be very unreasonable to continue an injunction which it was in the first instance entirely reasonable and proper to grant. The ears of the court could not under such new circumstances be absolutely shut to an application for its modification, without any new statute declaring the policy of the Commonwealth in respect to any branch of business or employment. But a declaration by the legislature that, in its judgment, it is reasonable and necessary for certain branches of business to be carried on in particular ways, notwithstanding the incidental disturbance and annoyance to citizens, is certainly a change of circumstances which is entitled to the highest consideration of the court; and in the present case we cannot doubt that it is sufficient to entitle the plaintiffs to relief from the operation of the injunction.

The method of procedure to which the plaintiffs have resorted is the usual and proper one in such circumstances. And, for authorities tending to show that the plaintiffs are entitled to the relief which they seek, in consequence of a subsequent statute changing the rights of the parties, see [citations omitted].

Demurrer overruled.

Spur Industries, Inc. v. Del E. Webb Development Co.

Supreme Court of Arizona, 1972.
108 Ariz. 178, 494 P.2d 700.

[Action by real estate developer to enjoin cattle feeding operation.]

■ CAMERON, V.C.J. From a judgment permanently enjoining the defendant, Spur Industries, Inc., from operating a cattle feedlot near the plaintiff Del E. Webb Development Company's Sun City, Spur appeals. Webb cross-appeals. Although numerous issues are raised, we feel that it is necessary to answer only two questions. They are:

"1. Where the operation of a business, such as a cattle feedlot is lawful in the first instance, but becomes a nuisance by reason of a nearby residential area, may the feedlot operation be enjoined in an action brought by the developer of the residential area?

"2. Assuming that the nuisance may be enjoined, may the developer of a completely new town or urban area in a previously agricultural area be required to indemnify the operator of the feedlot who must move or cease operation because of the presence of the residential area created by the developer?"

[The cattle feeding operation was begun in 1956 by Spur's predecessors in interest. Del Webb began to plan the development of the area, to be known as Sun City, in 1959. The residential development expanded until, because of the odors from the Spur feed pens, the parcels became difficult if not impossible to sell.] . . .

By December 1967, Del Webb's property had extended south to Olive Avenue and Spur was within 500 feet of Olive Avenue to the north. Del Webb filed its original complaint alleging that in excess of 1,300 lots in the southwest portion were unfit for development for sale as residential lots because of the operation of the Spur feedlot.

Del Webb's suit complained that the Spur feeding operation was a public nuisance because of the flies and the odor which were drifting or being blown by the prevailing south to north wind over the southern portion of Sun City. At the time of the suit, Spur was feeding between 20,000 and 30,000 head of cattle, and the facts amply support the finding of the trial court that the feed pens had become a nuisance to the people who resided in the southern part of Del Webb's development. The testimony indicated that cattle in a commercial feedlot will produce 35 to 40 pounds of wet manure per day, per head, or over a million pounds of wet manure per day for 30,000 head of cattle, and that despite the admittedly good feedlot management and good housekeeping practices by Spur, the resulting odor and flies produced an annoying if not unhealthy situation as far as the senior citizens of southern Sun City were concerned. There is no doubt that some of the citizens of Sun City were unable to enjoy the outdoor living which Del Webb had advertised and that Del Webb was faced with sales resistance from prospective purchasers as well as strong and persistent complaints from the people who had purchased homes in that area.

Trial was commenced before the court with an advisory jury. The advisory jury was later discharged and the trial was continued before the court alone. Findings of fact and conclusions of law were requested and given. The case was vigorously contested, including special actions in this court on some of the matters. In one of the special actions before this court, Spur agreed to, and did, shut down its operation without prejudice to a determination of the matter on appeal. On appeal the many questions raised were extensively briefed.

It is noted, however, that neither the citizens of Sun City nor Youngtown are represented in this lawsuit and the suit is solely between Del E. Webb Development Company and Spur Industries, Inc.

May Spur Be Enjoined?

The difference between a private nuisance and a public nuisance is generally one of degree. A private nuisance is one affecting a single individual or a definite small number of persons in the enjoyment of private rights not common to the public, while a public nuisance is one affecting the rights enjoyed by citizens as a part of the public. To constitute a public nuisance, the nuisance must affect a considerable number of people or an entire community or neighborhood.

Where the injury is slight, the remedy for minor inconveniences lies in an action for damages rather than in one for an injunction. Moreover, some courts have held, in the "balancing of conveniences" cases, that damages may be the sole remedy.

Thus, it would appear from the admittedly incomplete record as developed in the trial court, that, at most, residents of Youngtown would be entitled to damages rather than injunctive relief.

We have no difficulty, however, in agreeing with the conclusion of the trial court that Spur's operation was an enjoinable public nuisance as far as the people in the southern portion of Del Webb's Sun City were concerned.

§ 36–601, subsec. A reads as follows:

"§ 36–601. Public nuisances dangerous to public health

"A. The following conditions are specifically declared public nuisances dangerous to the public health:

"1. Any condition or place in populous areas which constitutes a breeding place for flies, rodents, mosquitoes and other insects which are capable of carrying and transmitting disease-causing organisms to any person or persons."

By this statute, before an otherwise lawful (and necessary) business may be declared a public nuisance, there must be a "populous" area in which people are injured:

"... [I]t hardly admits a doubt that, in determining the question as to whether a lawful occupation is so conducted as to constitute a nuisance as a matter of fact, the locality and surroundings are of the first importance. A business which is not per se a public nuisance may become such by being carried on at a place where the health, comfort, or convenience of a populous neighborhood is affected.... What might amount to a serious nuisance in one locality by reason of the density of the population, or character of the neighborhood affected, may in another place and under different surroundings be deemed proper and unobjectionable...."

It is clear that as to the citizens of Sun City, the operation of Spur's feedlot was both a public and a private nuisance. They could have successfully maintained an action to abate the nuisance. Del Webb, having shown a special injury in the loss of sales, had a standing to bring suit to enjoin the nuisance. The judgment of the trial court permanently enjoining the operation of the feedlot is affirmed.

Must Del Webb Indemnify Spur?

A suit to enjoin a nuisance sounds in equity and the courts have long recognized a special responsibility to the public when acting as a court of equity:

§ 104.   Where public interest is involved.

"Courts of equity may, and frequently do, go much further both to give and withhold relief in furtherance of the public interest than they are accustomed to go when only private interests are involved. Accordingly, the granting or withholding of relief may properly be dependent upon considerations of public interest...." 27 Am.Jur.2d, Equity, page 626.

In addition to protecting the public interest, however, courts of equity are concerned with protecting the operator of a lawfully, albeit noxious, business from the result of a knowing and willful encroachment by others near his business.

In the so-called "coming to the nuisance" cases, the courts have held that the residential landowner may not have relief if he knowingly came into a neighborhood reserved for industrial or agricultural endeavors and has been damaged thereby:

> . . . .
>
> "People employed in a city who build their homes in suburban areas of the county beyond the limits of a city and zoning regulations do so for a reason. Some do so to avoid the high taxation rate imposed by cities, or to avoid special assessments for street, sewer and water projects. They usually build on improved or hard surface highways, which have been built either at state or county expense and thereby avoid special assessments for these improvements. It may be that they desire to get away from the congestion of traffic, smoke, noise, foul air and the many other annoyances of city life. But with all these advantages in going beyond the area which is zoned and restricted to protect them in their homes, they must be prepared to take the disadvantages."

And:

> ". . . a party cannot justly call upon the law to make that place suitable for his residence which was not so when he selected it. . . ."

Were Webb the only party injured, we would feel justified in holding that the doctrine of "coming to the nuisance" would have been a bar to the relief asked by Webb, and, on the other hand, had Spur located the feedlot near the outskirts of a city and had the city grown toward the feedlot, Spur would have to suffer the cost of abating the nuisance as to those people locating within the growth pattern of the expanding city:

> "The case affords, perhaps, an example where a business established at a place remote from population is gradually surrounded and becomes part of a populous center, so that a business which formerly was not an interference with the rights of others has become so by the encroachment of the population. . . ."

We agree, however, with the Massachusetts court that:

> "The law of nuisance affords no rigid rule to be applied in all instances. It is elastic. It undertakes to require only that which is fair and reasonable under all the circumstances. In a commonwealth like this, which depends for its material prosperity so largely on the continued growth and enlargement of manufacturing of diverse varieties, 'extreme rights' cannot be enforced. . . ."

There was no indication in the instant case at the time Spur and its predecessors located in western Maricopa County that a new city would spring up, full-blown, alongside the feeding operation and that the developer of that city would ask the court to order Spur to move because of the new city. Spur is required to move not because of any wrongdoing on the

part of Spur, but beca   egard of the courts for
the rights and interest

Del Webb, on the   relief prayed for (a
permanent injunction),   but because of the
damage to the people who   hase homes in Sun
City. It does not equitab   that Webb, being
entitled to the injunction, is   ur if Webb has in
fact been the cause of the   t does not seem
harsh to require a developer   the lesser land
values in a rural area as well   cts of land on
which to build and develop a   to indemnify
those who are forced to leave as

Having brought people to th   letriment of
Spur, Webb must indemnify Spu   the cost of
moving or shutting down. It sho   to Spur is
limited to a case wherein a develop   brought into
a previously agricultural or indust   lation which makes
necessary the granting of an injunct   a lawful business and for
which the business has no adequate re   .

It is therefore the decision of this court that the matter be remanded to
the trial court for a hearing upon the damages sustained by the defendant
Spur as a reasonable and direct result of the granting of the permanent
injunction. Since the result of the appeal may appear novel and both sides
have obtained a measure of relief, it is ordered that each side will bear its
own costs.

Affirmed in part, reversed in part, and remanded for further proceedings consistent with this opinion.

D. CONVERSION (EQUITABLE REPLEVIN)

Burr v. Bloomsburg

Court of Chancery of New Jersey, 1927.
101 N.J.Eq. 615, 138 A. 876.

■ BERRY, V.C. This bill seeks the recovery from the defendant of a diamond
ring which came into defendant's possession on the death of her husband,
and to which she claims title by virtue of her husband's will. The complainant claims the ring as her own property by virtue of a gift from her mother,
now deceased, and seeks the aid of this court on the ground that the ring
has a peculiar sentimental value by reason of its associations and because
damages at law would be an inadequate remedy. This suit is in the nature
of an equitable replevin. The evidence submitted at the final hearing
showed that the complainant's father, Robert Bloomsburg, died at Bordentown, N.J., in 1899; that many years before his death he purchased an
unset diamond for his wife, the mother of the complainant, and with the

intention of having it set in a ring for her; and that at the time of the purchase the complainant accompanied her father. On their return home the complainant's father took the unset stone from his pocketbook and handed it to his wife, telling her it was for her, and that she could have it set any way that she liked. Because she thought the stone was too large for her, however, she declined to have it set in a ring for herself, and after some months it was set in a ring for complainant's father, and he wore it until his death in 1899. While on his deathbed, and in the presence of the complainant, he handed the ring to his wife and said:

"This is the last gift, Jennie, I will ever give you. If you are hungry, you can sell it for food; if not, it goes to Mary, then to Pud, and then to the baby."

"Mary" was a daughter of Robert Bloomsburg, and "Pud" was the complainant; "Pud" being the father's pet name for her. The "baby" was the daughter of the complainant. These, together with a brother, George Bloomsburg, the husband of the defendant, comprised the family of Robert Bloomsburg. All of Robert Bloomsburg's family, with the exception of complainant, are now dead.

After the father's death, complainant's mother wore the ring until after the death of her daughter Mary, about three years later. She then gave the ring to complainant in George's presence. Complainant retained the ring until June 10, 1909, when, at his request, she loaned it to her brother and took from him a receipt in his own handwriting, in the following form:

"In case of my death I promise to return my father's ring to his family. [Signed] George A. Bloomsburg, June 10, 1909."

Some time later in a letter written by George Bloomsburg to complainant, he said:

"About the paper regarding the ring, won't you kindly send it to me, and I will make it all right with you in some other way. It would make things a great deal more pleasant for me if you will do this."

It seems that the defendant had started some family controversy about this ring and importuned her husband to get it from the complainant, which he finally did in an effort to appease the defendant. Complainant, however, refused to surrender the receipt.

When complainant's father died, he left a will of which he appointed his wife and his daughter Mary, executrices, and his son George, executor. The ring was inventoried as a part of the assets of the estate and appraised at $250. The estate was not formally settled through the courts, but apparently was adjusted out of court by agreement between complainant and her brother long after the death of their mother and the complainant's sister.

Some time before June 10, 1909, when the ring was delivered by complainant to her brother, the controversy then having arisen over its possession and ownership, he insisted that if she desired to retain the ring she would have to pay him $400, which she finally consented to do, and gave him her note for that amount. The note was finally paid on June 16,

1910, by complainant's check drawn to the order of George A. Bloomsburg for $416. It is significant that this payment was made over a year after the ring was delivered by complainant to her brother. If she did not own the ring at that time, I cannot understand why she would have paid the note, as it is reasonable to suppose that upon a surrender of her claim to the ring the note would have been canceled.

George Bloomsburg retained possession of the ring until his death in 1925. He left a will dated December 16, 1905, in which he devised all of his property to his wife, who is the defendant in this suit. A codicil to that will, dated October 9, 1914, contains the following paragraph:

"Whereas, since the making of my last will and testament to which this codicil is attached, I have executed a certain writing which might be considered a bequest of my diamond ring left me by my father, Robert Bloomsburg. I do hereby give and bequeath to my beloved wife, Mary A. Bloomsburg, the said diamond ring above referred to, absolutely for her benefit, behoof and use forever."

It is by virtue of this provision of the codicil that defendant claims title to the ring in question. The truth is, however, that the diamond ring had not been left to him by his father, and the statement in the codicil that it had been was a plain attempt to evade his obligation to return it to his sister.

Undoubtedly "this court has jurisdiction to enforce the restitution or delivery of a specific chattel which has a peculiar artificial value, and for which therefore adequate compensation cannot be obtained at law; and that, too, whether possession has been got by the wrongdoer through a trust or not." ... This jurisdiction has been exercised by the Court of Chancery since very early times.

The earliest leading case on the subject, and perhaps the one most frequently cited, is Pusey v. Pusey, 1 Vernon, 273 (1684). That case involved the possession of a horn anciently given to the Pusey family by the Danish King Canute and which time out of mind had gone along with the plaintiff's estate. The horn bore this inscription:

"Kyng Knowd geve Wyllyam Pewse This horne to hold, by they lond."

It was held the bill was maintainable for the recovery of the specific chattel. The next reported case pertinent to this inquiry, and to which my attention has been directed, is Duke of Somerset v. Cookson, 3 P. Wms. 389 (1735). It involved the possession of an old silver patera [sacrificial plate or saucer] bearing a Greek inscription and dedication to Hercules, which had been dug up on the plaintiff's estate. It had come into defendant's possession, and the Duke brought a bill in equity to compel its delivery in specie undefaced. Defendant demurred on the ground that the remedy was at law, but the demurrer was overruled. In Fells v. Read, 3 Vesey, 70 (1796), a suit was brought to recover a tobacco box of a remarkable kind which had belonged to a club, and the Lord Chancellor stated the reason of the equitable remedy as follows:

"The Pusey horn, the patera of the Duke of Somerset, were things of that sort of value, that a jury might not give two-pence beyond the weight. It was not to be cast to the estimation of people, who had not those feelings. In all cases, where the object of the suit is not liable to a compensation by damages, it would be strange, if the law of this country did not afford any remedy. It would be great injustice, if an individual cannot have his property without being liable to the estimate of people, who have not his feelings upon it."

In the later case of Nutbrown v. Thornton, 10 Vesey, 163, Lord Eldon, speaking of the Pusey Horn Case, said:

"It turned upon the pretium affections, independent of the circumstance as to tenure, which could not be estimated in damages."

. . . .

In Pomeroy's Specific Performance of Contracts, supra, the rule is expressed as follows:

"It is well settled that where chattels have some special peculiar value to their owner over and above any market value which could be placed upon them in accordance with strict legal rules, an interest which has happily been termed pretium affectionis, such as an heirloom; . . . contracts concerning them will be specifically enforced in equity, and a delivery of them will be decreed, although they might be recovered in the common-law actions of detinue or replevin. The reasons of this rule are the utter inadequacy of any mere pecuniary compensation, and the incompleteness of the relief afforded by the legal actions in which the defendant might easily evade an actual delivery of the chattel itself. . . . The equitable jurisdiction has not been confined to contracts; it is freely exercised to enforce the surrender and delivery of chattels in specie which have been tortiously obtained, or are wrongfully detained. . . . Equity, however, will not interfere to specifically enforce a contract concerning even such a special and unique chattel, or to compel its delivery, when its pecuniary value has already been fixed by the parties or can be readily ascertained, so that an adequate compensation in the form of debt or damages can be recovered in a legal action."

. . . .

It is also objected that this is a suit for specific performance of an agreement by defendant's husband to return the ring to his father's family, and that, therefore, the executrix of her husband's will (who is the defendant herself) should have been made a party as such executrix. But while the equitable principles here involved are usually treated under the head of "Specific Performance" in works on equity jurisprudence, the jurisdiction of this court is not confined to that head; "it is freely exercised to enforce the surrender of chattels *in specie* which have been *tortiously obtained or are wrongfully detained.*" (Italics mine.) Pomeroy, supra.

But here suit is not brought to enforce a written agreement. It is rather to enforce the right of the complainant to the return of the ring by reason of her ownership, amply proved, and the written instrument, the receipt signed by the defendant's husband, is merely evidential of that ownership and an admission against interest. The right parties are in court; namely, the owner of the chattel, as complainant, and the person, the defendant, who wrongfully detains the chattel from its rightful owner.

. . . .

It is also insisted that mere sentiment or personal desire for a particular object affords no basis for an equitable action such as this. That may be true as an abstract proposition; but when that sentiment or desire is based upon or born of facts and circumstances which endow the chattel with a special, aside from its intrinsic, value, to the extent of a pretium affectionis, it is not true. In such cases there is and can be no measure of damages in money. While this ring itself, as a piece of jewelry, may have a definite value in dollars and cents, how can the sentiment, the imaginary value put upon it by complainant's fancy, because of her affection for the one from whom she obtained it, be valued in terms of money any more than could a value be placed upon the "touch of a vanished hand" or "the sound of a voice that is still?" The real question here is whether or not this ring has a "pretium affectionis." If it has, whether because of sentiment, desire, or what not, provided it be real, "not . . . founded in weakness and folly", and not assumed for the occasion, then this court has jurisdiction, and relief should not be denied.

"Pretium affectionis" is defined in Wharton's Law Dictionary as:

"The imaginary value put upon a thing by the fancy of the owner in his affection for it."

In Bouvier's Law Dictionary, it is defined as:

"An imaginary value put upon a thing by the fancy of the owner in his affection for it, or *for the person from whom he obtained it.*" (Italics mine.)

There is here an abundance of proof to establish a "pretium affectionis" in this ring. The stone had been bought by complainant's father for her mother; it was later set in a ring which he wore during the balance of his lifetime, and which, on his deathbed, and in complainant's presence, he gave to her mother with the injunction not to part with it except that she be hungry and it was needed for bread, and that after her death it was to go first to the daughter Mary, then to complainant, and eventually to complainant's daughter.

That it does have a real and not a pretended sentimental value is evidenced by the fact that the complainant cherished it from then until now; that she refused to sell it even to her own brother; that rather than be deprived of it she acquiesced in her brother's demands for the payment of a considerable sum of money to him on the pretense that it was property of the father's estate, when, in fact, it was her very own; that after the loan of the ring to her brother, ostensibly to prevent domestic discord, she refused to surrender the receipt which he had given for it and finally instituted this suit to recover the ring itself rather than its money value.

These facts show conclusively to my mind that the ring has had the pretium affectionis impressed upon it. To the defendant, it is merely a piece of jewelry, necessary to the gratification of envy or avarice, but to the complainant it recalls the daydreams of youth and the childhood memories of maturer years. It is endowed with a sentimental fancy, which, even though imaginary, can no more be estimated in dollars and cents than can mother love or the guileless and trusting affection of the child. "There is no standard by which the price of affection can be adjusted, and no scale to graduate the feelings of the heart." To agree with defendant's argument would be to admit that sentiment should be commercialized; but when sentiment and the finer feelings of the heart are measured in terms of money, then will this world cease to be a fit habitation for man. "It would be a reproach to the country not to indulge" the complainant in her desire.

If necessary, it would not be difficult to spell out a trust here, the performance of which would be incumbent upon the defendant....

It is also contended by defendant that the value of this ring has already been fixed by the complainant herself; first, by assenting to the appraisement in the inventory, and second, by the payment of some $400 to her brother for it....

... In my judgment she has not. The value appearing in the inventory was not her valuation, but the valuation of strangers, the appraisers. It is claimed that she assented to it, and that this binds her; but, as already indicated, this estate was not formally settled through the courts, but was adjusted by the parties themselves out of court. I do not consider the complainant to have been bound by that appraisal. In fact, the appraisers had no right to include the ring in their inventory. It did not belong to the decedent, Robert Bloomsburg, as he had effectively disposed of it before his death.

As to the payment of some $400 to the brother, the surviving executor of her father's will, she did not fix this value. It was not a price set upon the article by her; it was a demand of the defendant's husband, reluctantly complied with by the complainant under duress. It was, in effect, the price of peace, and I do not consider that by paying this price the complainant has in any way set a value on the chattel in controversy which could bind her or prejudice her in this action. The fact is, she was under no obligation in law or otherwise to pay a dollar. The property was already hers. The payment was no more than a gratuity or a peace offering.

For the reasons above expressed I will advise a decree for the complainant.

NOTES ON REPLEVIN

1. *Burr v. Bloomsburg* is an example of a court granting specific relief in a case involving a unique chattel. Since damages are inadequate, the court proceeds in equity on the theory of securing specific reparation of a tort.

2. Replevin provides specific relief at law for the tortious taking or retention of personal property. A successful plaintiff may obtain a writ authorizing the sheriff to seize and turn over the property in question. Moreover, by posting a bond with the court, the plaintiff may obtain an order authorizing the sheriff to seize the property and deliver it to the plaintiff pending the resolution of the case. However, defendants are usually allowed to recover possession *pendente lite* by posting a counter bond.

CHAPTER 8

EQUITABLE DEFENSES

A. THE "CLEAN HANDS" DOCTRINE

Carmen v. Fox Film Corp.

United States Court of Appeals, Second Circuit, 1920.
269 Fed. 928.

[Jewel Carmen was a moving picture actress, residing in California. On July 31, 1917, while still a minor, she executed a contract with each of the two defendants, New York corporations engaged in manufacturing and producing photoplays. The William Fox Vaudeville Company agreed to employ her for six months, with an option in the company to extend the employment for successive periods of six months until October 17, 1919. The salary, if the options were exercised, began at $125 per week, and increased to $200 per week, with an additional consideration of $650 for each option. After October 17, 1919, the Fox Film Corporation agreed to employ her for one year at $175 per week; and in return for an additional consideration of $1300 was given options to continue the employment for another year. If the options were exercised, the salary was to be gradually increased to $250 per week.

While these two agreements had several years to run, the plaintiff received a telegram from Frank A. Keeney, the president of the Frank A. Keeney Pictures Corporation, asking whether she was open to an engagement. She replied that she was free to accept employment. Thereupon he sent her a contract, which she executed on March 28, 1918, a few months before she attained her majority. This provided for her exclusive appearance in motion pictures with the Keeney Corporation for two years commencing on or about July 15, 1918, with options to continue the employment for four years more. The weekly compensation was to begin at $450, and rise $50 each six months until July, 1923, when she would receive $1000 every week.

At the time this contract was made, Keeney had no knowledge that the plaintiff had contracts with the Fox companies extending beyond the beginning of his contract. He would not have made it if he had known the facts. On July 13, 1918, the plaintiff came of age, and two days later repudiated the Fox contracts because made during her infancy. The defendants insisted on her performance and threatened the Keeney Corporation with suit if it assisted her breach by allowing her to render it services. On September 19, 1918, the various photoplay companies made an agreement, whereby the Keeney Corporation was to refrain from using the plaintiff's services pending the determination of the rights of the respective parties, and the Fox Company was to indemnify the Keeney Corporation and Keeney from any damage they might suffer through any action the plaintiff might bring against them. After this, the Keeney Corporation refused to employ her.

The plaintiff sues the two Fox companies in equity, in the District Court for the Southern District of New York, to have the contracts which she made with them during her minority declared void, having been disaffirmed by her with reasonable diligence after she reached her majority; and she prays that an injunction be issued restraining the defendants from asserting that the contracts are valid and from interfering with her contract relations with any person, firm or corporation in employing the plaintiff and availing himself or itself of her services under any contract of employment entered into with her. Damages are also asked. From a decree by Manton, J., for the complainant, the defendants appeal.]

■ ROGERS, C.J. . . . [T]he conduct of the plaintiff has been such as entitles her to no relief in this court. According to her own allegations in her complaint, she was a minor when she entered into the contract with Keeney, and she misled him into making the contract by representing that she was free to make it, when in fact she was morally not free to make the contract, and there was doubt whether she was legally free to make it. If the contracts with defendants were valid, she was under a legal and moral obligation not to make the contract with the Keeney corporation. And if the contracts were voidable because of her infancy, then, while she was under no legal obligation to recognize them, she was under a moral obligation to abide by them, and good faith required her to continue to render the services she had agreed to give. In either case her action in repudiating her pledged word was misconduct of which no person of honor and conscience would have been guilty. That no action could be brought against her at law because of what she did does not alter the moral character of her act. And when she comes into a court of conscience and asks its affirmative aid to assist her in carrying into effect the inequitable arrangement into which she unfaithfully entered, the appeal falls on deaf ears. One who comes into equity must come with clean hands, and her hands are not clean. The testimony discloses that reliance cannot be placed upon her agreements which the law does not oblige her to keep, and that for a money gain to herself she unscrupulously disregarded her express contracts.

In Story's Equity Jurisprudence (14th Ed.) vol. 1, § 99, the rule is laid down as follows:

> "Equity imperatively demands of suitors in courts fair dealing and righteous conduct with reference to the matters concerning which they seek relief. He who has acted in bad faith, resorted to trickery and deception, or been guilty of fraud, injustice, or unfairness will appeal in vain to a court of conscience, even though in his wrongdoing he may have kept himself strictly 'within the law.' Misconduct which will bar relief in a court of equity need not necessarily be of such a nature as to be punishable as a crime or to constitute the basis of a legal action. Under this maxim, any willful act in regard to the matter in litigation, which would be condemned and pronounced wrongful by honest and fairminded men, will be sufficient to make the hands of the applicant

unclean. Both courts and text-writers have repeatedly spoken upon this subject in no uncertain language.''

. . . .

The maxim that one who comes into equity must come with clean hands expresses rather a principle of inaction than one of action. It means that equity will refuse its aid in any manner to one seeking its active interposition if he has been guilty either of unlawful or inequitable conduct respecting the subject-matter of the litigation.

An illustration of the maxim is found in the attitude of courts of equity in the matter of specific performance. A court of equity always refuses specific performance of a contract which has been obtained by the plaintiff by sharp and unscrupulous practices, by overreaching, by concealment of important facts, even though not actually fraudulent. The contract may be a legal one, against which no defense could be set up at law, and one which a court of equity would not cancel. But if it has been procured by unconscientious means a court of equity refuses specific performance.

The right which one seeks to enforce in a court of equity must be one which in and of itself appeals to the conscience of a chancellor. Mr. Justice Brewer, speaking for the court in Deweese v. Reinhard, 165 U.S. 386, 17 S.Ct. 340 [41 L.Ed. 757], said:

> "A court of equity acts only when and as conscience commands, and if the conduct of the plaintiff be offensive to the dictates of natural justice, then, whatever may be the rights he possesses and whatever use he may make of them in a court of law, he will be held remediless in a court of equity."

. . . .

In 1816 a case came before Vice Chancellor Plumer, Cory v. Gerteken, 2 Maddox 40, in which an infant who was nearly of age prevailed upon his trustees to transfer to him certain stock to which he was entitled on coming of age, and represented to them that they ran no risk in doing it. After coming of age he assigned his rights to an assignee, and suit was brought against the trustees on the ground that payment to an infant was bad. The bill was dismissed and the Vice Chancellor said:

> "The concealment of his infancy, under such circumstances, certainly was a fraud, and precludes him, or his assigns, who stand precisely in his situation, from calling for a repayment."

The fact that a contract has been dishonestly or dishonorably obtained is a bar to relief in equity.

Decree reversed.[1]

NOTES ON *CARMEN*

1.   Carmen subsequently sued Fox Film Corp. for damages in tort. In Carmen v. Fox Film Corp., 204 App.Div. 776, 198 N.Y.S. 766 (1923), the

---

1. [See reference to "clean hands doc-   *fra.*]
trine" in Firebaugh v. Hanback, p. 569 *in-*

court held that the dismissal of her bill in equity was no bar to her legal action, because the dismissal was not an adjudication on the merits of her cause of action for tort. The jury awarded her $43,500 and $17,182 more for interest.

2. One should not be misled by the successful outcome of Carmen's lawsuit. An empirical study has observed that "a defeat because of the defense in equity is in fact final, regardless of theoretical reservations" that there may be a recovery "at law". Frank & Endicott, *Defenses in Equity and "Legal Rights"*, 14 LA. L. REV. 380, 389 (1954). For additional evidence of the practical significance of equitable defenses, see Newman, *The Renaissance of Good Faith in Contracting in Anglo–American Law*, 54 CORN.L.REV. 553 (1969) and Yorio, *A Defense of Equitable Defenses*, 51 OHIO ST. L.J. 1201 (1990).

Claire v. Rue de Paris, Inc.

Supreme Court of Georgia, 1977.
239 Ga. 191, 236 S.E.2d 272.

■ BOWLES, J.... [P]laintiff in the court below filed identical petitions in Fulton Superior Court against the respective defendants, alleging in each that he is a shareholder in each of the defendant corporations, owning 33⅓ per cent of all outstanding shares. Each complaint says that the acts of those in control of each corporation are illegal and/or fraudulent and the corporations and the plaintiff will suffer irreparable injury unless a dissolution is ordered. He alleges that the corporation assets are being misapplied and/or wasted. Each complaint is brought under Georgia Code Ann. § 22–1317. He seeks to recover attorney fees and by way of relief, asks that an injunction issue enjoining the officers and directors of each corporation from disposing of the corporate assets, that each corporation be dissolved, that costs be taxed against the defendant and general relief....

. . . .

Georgia Code Section 22–1317(a)(1)(B). "Jurisdiction of court to liquidate assets and business of corporation.—(a) the superior courts shall have full power to liquidate the assets and business of a corporation: (1) In an action by a shareholder when it is established: ... (B) That the acts of the directors or those in control of the corporation are illegal or fraudulent;"

Code Section 22–1318 authorizes the court in such instances to issue injunctions, to appoint a receiver and to afford to the complaining party other equitable relief.

Plaintiff's complaint in each case seeks equitable relief. While plaintiff does not have to illustrate all of his evidence upon meeting a motion for summary judgment, the only evidence he has illustrated here is that the places of business sold alcoholic beverages on Sunday; they sold "watered down" drinks to the customers; and the principals of the corporation including plaintiff took money out of the business each week without proper accounting. He readily admits that he has personally taken money from the business. He also admits he took food and beverages from the business. He, therefore, comes into court with unclean hands and must be denied the relief he seeks. The defendants need not invoke the clean hands maxim as the court will apply it of its own accord.

The rule is firmly established that "... where stockholders in a corporation participate in the performance of an act, or acquiesce in and ratify the same, they are estopped to complain thereof in equity." This applies to derivative shareholder claims as well as direct actions against corporations.

Under the " 'clean hands' maxim, 'whenever a party, who, as actor, seeks to set the judicial machinery in motion and obtain some remedy, has violated conscience, or good faith, or other equitable principle, in his prior conduct, then the doors of the court will be shut against him in limine; the court will refuse to interfere on his behalf, to acknowledge his right, or to award him any remedy.' "

It would contravene the principles of equity and good conscience to allow a director and stockholder to complain about the acts of the other directors of the corporation in taking money from the business, when the moving party himself readily admits that he had acted in concert with the managing officers in doing the very same thing. Additionally, where a plaintiff readily admits that he has personally taken money and properties of the corporation for his personal use his hands are "unclean" within the meaning of the term, and they are not made clean by his removal from office and subsequently filing suit against the corporation asking dissolution.

. . . .

Judgment affirmed. . . .

All the Justices concur, except HALL, J., who dissents.

Seagirt Realty Corp. v. Chazanof

Court of Appeals of New York, 1963.
13 N.Y.2d 282, 246 N.Y.S.2d 613, 196 N.E.2d 254.

■ BURKE, J. This action, brought by plaintiff as the owner of real property, seeks, in effect, to remove a cloud on title. Defendant, the owner of record, conveyed the property to plaintiff in 1950. Plaintiff did not record this deed and it is now lost. The specific relief requested is a decree compelling the execution of a replacement deed. Although these simple affirmed findings of fact warrant the relief requested, the Appellate Division has reversed a judgment for plaintiff and dismissed the complaint on the theory of "unclean hands" because of a certain transaction concerning the property that occurred prior to that sued on here.

In 1934 Jacob Landau, the sole stockholder and concededly alter ego of plaintiff corporation, caused it to convey the subject property, together with other property, to his son, Alfred Landau, without consideration, and for the purpose of concealing it from his creditors. Alfred agreed to hold the property for his father's benefit. It also appears that Jacob Landau filed a petition in bankruptcy in 1945 in which he swore that he had no interest in real property. In 1950, Alfred, at his father's request, discharged his oral promise of 1934 by conveying the subject property to the defendant Chazanof, the son-in-law of Jacob Landau. This conveyance was also without consideration. The courts below have found that, simultaneously with the conveyance to him, defendant orally promised to convey to plaintiff, and did in fact execute and deliver a deed to plaintiff.

In view of the ground upon which the Appellate Division has reversed, it is important to note that any connection between defendant's promise to convey to plaintiff and the illegality of the conveyance to Alfred Landau in 1934 would be relevant only if plaintiff were suing on that promise. In such a case we would be called upon to apply the rule that the unclean hands doctrine bars only causes of action *founded in* illegality or immorality. This, in turn, would require an examination into the motive and circumstances surrounding the conveyance to defendant, to which his promise to convey to plaintiff was incident.

This case, however, presents no such issue. Plaintiff is not seeking to enforce a contractual duty of defendant against which illegality could be argued, or to enforce an "inequitable" interest in real property, in bar of which unclean hands could be raised (as where the "equity" lay in a promise given in consideration of a fraudulent conveyance). However vulnerable to attack may have been defendant's promise to convey to plaintiff, and we express no opinion on this, that promise has been fully performed. The property has been conveyed to plaintiff, who now holds title, both legal and equitable. Defendant has no interest whatever in the property. It is established by the unanimous assent of authority that a voluntary reconveyance to the fraudulent grantor, even from the immediate fraudulent grantee, is effective as between the parties and is entitled to the protection of the courts in its enjoyment. . . .

It is suggested, nevertheless, that moral considerations of fundamental importance require a different result in this case. The short answer, given at Trial Term (per Livoti, J.), is that equity is not an avenger at large. Conceding that the relief sought in this case is of equitable origin, the maxim must be applied only where the plaintiff has dealt unjustly in the very transaction of which he complains. It must also be remembered, as we are reminded by the late Professor Zechariah Chafee, that moral indignation against the plaintiff must operate, not in a vacuum, but in harmony with other important purposes and functions of the substantive law involved. As he criticized the application of the unclean hands doctrine in a situation similar to that here present, "This ethical attitude seems entirely out of place. What ought to count is the strong social policy in favor of making the land records furnish an accurate map of the ownership of all land in the community. Whatever A's old misdeeds, he *is* the lawful owner of this lot and the records ought to show this fact. The existing record falsely makes R owner. It may mislead scores of honest citizens—people who have strong reasons for wishing to buy the lot, such as creditors of A, creditors of R, or lawyers drawing deeds of adjoining lots who are anxious to insert an accurate description. What is the sense of perpetuating an erroneous land record in order to penalize A for past misdeeds by causing him inconvenience? Better regard his dirty hands as washed during the lapse of twenty years rather than mess up the recording system." (Chafee, Some Problems of Equity, 21–22 [1950].)

We find this reasoning persuasive. When equitable relief is sought, not to enforce an executory obligation arising out of an illegal transaction, but to protect a status of legal ownership, wrongs done by Jacob Landau to creditors in respect of the property at some time prior to the acquisition of the title now in issue may not now be raised by this defendant to defeat otherwise available relief.

The judgment of the Appellate Division should be reversed and that of the Supreme Court reinstated, without costs.

■ DESMOND, C.J. (dissenting). I vote to affirm the judgment below because it is an absolutely correct application of an ancient maxim honored and followed by this and other American and English courts in decisions innumerable. Variously articulated ("ex dolo malo non oritur actio"; "ex turpi causa non oritur actio"; "in aequali juri melior est conditio possidentis"; "pacta quae turpem causam continent non sunt observanda") the maxim means that no right of action can spring from an illegal contract and that courts do not sit to give protection to cheaters or to act "as paymaster[s] of the wages of crime." As Justice Johnson explained it for the Supreme Court in 1829, "no court of justice can in its nature be made the handmaid of iniquity" or "become auxiliary to the consummation of violations of law." . . .

Despite all these precedents, plaintiff is being awarded a decree which will crown with final success a fraudulent transaction begun by its sole stockholder Jacob Landau in 1934 when he conveyed this same land to his son Alfred Landau, without consideration and in fraud of his creditors. The fraudulent transaction was carried a step further in 1945 when Jacob Landau took bankruptcy proceedings but swore in the schedules that he had no real property. In 1950 son Alfred conveyed the property to son-in-law defendant Chazanof, again without consideration, and Chazanof simultaneously conveyed the land to Jacob Landau's corporation, plaintiff Seagirt Realty Corporation. The latter deed was never recorded but was lost and plaintiff now asks the court to require the son-in-law to deliver another deed. This a court of equity cannot do without ignoring a whole series of cases. . . .

. . . .

The judgment should be affirmed, with costs.

■ SCILEPPI, J. (dissenting). I cannot agree that the plaintiff is entitled to the relief sought herein. The majority is permitting this plaintiff corporation's president to invoke the aid of the court to bring to a successful conclusion that which he admits was a scheme to defraud his creditors.

. . . .

To say that the conveyance from the son to the defendant was a separate transaction and, therefore, does not come within the "clean hands" doctrine is to overlook the realities of these family conveyances, all of which were initiated at the direction and for the benefit of Landau.

Moreover, in my opinion, the separate transaction concept was rejected by this court in ... [an earlier] case....

. . . .

The judgment should be affirmed, with costs.

NOTES ON CLEAN HANDS

1.   Heller & Merz Co.'s bluing (a coloring agent used on fabrics) had long been known to the public under the names of "American Ball Blue" and "American Wash Blue." The Shavers and their associates adopted the same names for their bluing, and an injunction was granted. This ruling was affirmed on appeal. Shaver v. Heller & Merz Co., 108 Fed. 821 (8th Cir.1901). In response to the argument that the plaintiff had unclean hands because it had recently been manufacturing and selling other brands, "Germania" and "Bavarian" Ball Blue, in boxes simulating foreign products, Sanborn, J., said:

The principle that "he who comes into equity must do so with clean hands" ... does not repel all sinners from courts of equity, nor does it disqualify any complainant from obtaining relief there who has not dealt unjustly in the very transaction concerning which he complains. The iniquity which will repel him must have an immediate and necessary relation to the equity for which he sues. There is no evidence that the appellee has been guilty of any injustice, fraud, or wrong in acquiring the good will of its business in the American ball blue and the American wash blue, which is the subject of this suit, or in its relations with the appellants, and relief cannot be denied to it because it may have been wicked in other transactions which affect neither the appellants nor the equity here under consideration.

2.   American University, a fraudulent institution for instruction in chiropractic, falsely stated in its advertising that it had a professional staff of teachers with a consulting staff of practitioners, and gave the income of some of its graduates, of whom none actually existed. Wood, a discharged employee who had assisted in these frauds, was using American's lists of actual and prospective students to organize an equally fraudulent school of his own, and to conduct a campaign to destroy American's business. The trial judge granted American's request for injunctive relief. This decision was reversed by the appellate court, and its judgment was affirmed by the state supreme court. American University v. Wood, 294 Ill. 186, 128 N.E. 330 (1920).

... [A]s a general rule it is required that the wrongdoing or fraud of the complainant, to bar him from relief on the ground that he comes with unclean hands, must be connected with the subject of the litigation and have some relation to the rights of the parties arising out of the transaction. That rule is not applicable to the facts in this record. It is true the fraud and wrongdoing of complainant did not affect the private rights of defendants, and afforded no justification in morals for their seeking to profit by exposing them, but on the ground of the public interest and policy we do not think complainant's grievance is of a character to be redressed in a court of equity. The misrepresentations of complainant in the conduct of its business affected the public, and it would seem a strange thing if a court of conscience should be required to protect a suitor in the commission of a fraud upon the public.

A court of equity is a court of conscience and will exercise its extraordinary powers only to enforce the requirements of conscience. It is no part of its function to aid a litigant in the promotion of a fraud upon the public. . . .

3.   Consider the Supreme Court's decision in Morton Salt Co. v. G.S. Suppiger Co., 314 U.S. 488, 62 S.Ct. 402, 86 L.Ed. 363 (1942).

STONE, C.J. Respondent brought this suit in the district court for an injunction and an accounting for infringement of its Patent . . . on a machine for depositing salt tablets, a device said to be useful in the canning industry for adding predetermined amounts of salt in tablet form to the contents of the cans.

. . . [T]he trial court, without passing on the issues of validity and infringement, granted summary judgment dismissing the complaint. It took the ground that respondent was making use of the patent to restrain the sale of salt tablets in competition with its own sale of unpatented tablets, by requiring licensees to use with the patented machines only tablets sold by respondent. The Court of Appeals for the Seventh Circuit reversed, because it thought that respondent's use of the patent was not shown to violate § 3 of the Clayton Act, 15 U.S.C.A. § 14, as it did not appear that the use of its patent substantially lessened competition or tended to create a monopoly in salt tablets. . . .

. . . The question we must decide is not necessarily whether respondent has violated the Clayton Act, but whether a court of equity will lend its aid to protect the patent monopoly when respondent is using it as the effective means of restraining competition with its sale of an unpatented article.

. . . .

It is a principle of general application that courts, and especially courts of equity, may appropriately withhold their aid where the plaintiff is using the right asserted contrary to the public interest. Respondent argues that this doctrine is limited in its application to those cases where the patentee seeks to restrain contributory infringement by the sale to licensees of a competing unpatented article, while here respondent seeks to restrain petitioner from a direct infringement, the manufacture and sale of the salt tablet depositor. It is said that the equitable maxim that a party seeking the aid of a court of equity must come into court with clean hands applies only to the plaintiff's wrongful conduct in the particular act or transaction which raises the equity, enforcement of which is sought; that where, as here, the patentee seeks to restrain the manufacture or use of the patented device, his conduct in using the patent to restrict competition in the sale of salt tablets does not foreclose him from seeking relief limited to an injunction against the manufacture and sale of the infringing machine alone.

Undoubtedly "equity does not demand that its suitors shall have led blameless lives," but additional considerations must be taken into account where maintenance of the suit concerns the public interest as well as the private interests of suitors. Where the patent is used as a means of restraining competition with the patentee's sale of an unpatented product, the successful prosecution of an infringement suit even against one who is not a competitor in such sale is a powerful aid to the maintenance of the attempted monopoly of the unpatented article, and is thus a contributing factor in thwarting the public policy underlying the grant of the patent. Maintenance and enlargement of the attempted monopoly of the unpatented article are dependent to some extent upon persuading the public of the validity of the patent, which the infringement suit is intended to establish. Equity may rightly withhold its assistance from such a use of the patent by declining to entertain a suit for infringement, and should do so at least until it is made to appear that the improper practice has been abandoned and that the consequences of the misuse of the patent have been dissipated.

... It is the adverse effect upon the public interest of a successful infringement suit in conjunction with the patentee's course of conduct which disqualifies him to maintain the suit, regardless of whether the particular defendant has suffered from the misuse of the patent. Similarly equity will deny relief for infringement of a trademark where the plaintiff is misrepresenting to the public the nature of his product either by the trademark itself or by his label. The patentee, like these other holders of an exclusive privilege granted in the furtherance of a public policy, may not claim protection of his grant by the courts where it is being used to subvert that policy.

It is unnecessary to decide whether respondent has violated the Clayton Act, for we conclude that in any event the maintenance of the present suit to restrain petitioner's manufacture or sale of the alleged infringing machines is contrary to public policy and that the district court rightly dismissed the complaint for want of equity.

Reversed.

B.   LACHES AND THE STATUTE OF LIMITATIONS

Talmash v. Mugleston

Chancery, 1826.
4 L.J. Ch. O.S. 200.

The bill was filed for the specific performance of an agreement, dated in 1806, by which the defendants agreed to sell certain premises to the plaintiff: 100*l*. had been paid as a deposit. Great mutual delays had taken place; and the bill stated a correspondence between the solicitors of the parties, which continued at intervals throughout several years. The last letter was dated in 1815, and was written on the subject of the title, by the solicitor of the plaintiff to the solicitor for the defendants. The bill averred that the contract had not been rescinded or abandoned. [To this bill the defendants pleaded the text of the statute of limitations, the plea averring in addition only the fact that the said bill was filed on the 15th day of October, 1825.]

Mr. Koe appeared in support of the plea. The contract was made nearly twenty years ago; and the last transaction, mentioned in the bill, precedes the institution of the suit by much more than six years. If the plaintiff brought an action of damages for non-performance of the contract, the statute would be a bar to him: and, by analogy, it will be a defence to a suit in equity. It is not the practice of the court to decree a specific performance, if the party has lain by for more than six years.

Mr. Shadwell contra. The plea of the statute of limitations cannot by itself be a good plea: it must always be supported by averments bringing the case within the statute. In this plea there is nothing which meets the allegation in the bill, that the contract has never been abandoned or rescinded.

The only averment in it is that the bill was filed on a certain day.

◼ VICE-CHANCELLOR [SIR JOHN LEACH]. It was not necessary to plead on what day the bill was filed; that is apparent on the record. But what has the statute of limitations to do with the specific performance of a contract? The rule of this court, which refuses to enforce the specific performance of a contract after a certain interval, does not result from the statute of limitations. Suppose the rule to be adopted by analogy to the statute, that would not enable the defendant to plead the statute.

The statute of limitations never can be made available in any court, unless pleaded; for a party may abandon the protection which it throws round him. But this court, like every other, is bound to take notice of every public statute for the purposes of analogy, and of the statute of limitations among the rest. Where a court of equity proceeds by analogy to the statute, it is bound to know the statute, in order to apply the analogy. It is not necessary, therefore, to plead the statute; nor can the rule of the court, and the analogy on which it is founded, enable the party to protect himself by such a plea. If the case stated in the bill is of such a kind, that the Court, according to its known rules, will refuse to decree specific performance, the defendant ought to demur. It can serve no end for him to put in a plea, which only states an act of parliament, to which the Court, in applying its rules by analogy to that statute, would be bound to advert. It is impossible that the statute can be a bar to a species of suit to which it has no reference.

If the case appears sufficiently on the bill to lay a proper foundation for the application of the principle alluded to in the cases which have been cited, the defendant ought to have demurrer; and, in support of that demurrer, the argument would have been, that it appears by the plaintiff's own showing, that, if he were to proceed at law, he could not recover damages, and consequently the court, adopting by analogy the legal rule, will refuse to assist him.

If the circumstances did not appear on the bill so as to warrant the application of the rule, it would then be necessary to plead the facts, which were suppressed by the bill, and which were supposed to bring the case within the range of the equitable principle. . . .

NOTES ON LACHES

1.   The equitable doctrine of laches involves two elements: unreasonable delay by the plaintiff and prejudice to the defendant. Where these elements are present, the plaintiff's request for equitable relief ordinarily will be denied.

2.   Although the Court of Chancery did not directly apply the English statutes of limitations, the Court would apply the statutes "by analogy" and deny equitable relief to a plaintiff asserting legal rights in equity after the limitation period at law had run. Chancery termed this denial of equitable relief laches, even though the defendant did not have to show prejudice.

Most states have statutes of limitations covering suits in equity. Nevertheless, the doctrine of laches is still important, even in these jurisdictions, in that a delay for a time shorter than the statutory period, if unreasonable and prejudicial to the defendant, may bar equitable relief.

3.   A buyer (Grosbeck) was granted specific performance of a contract to sell land. An intermediate appellate court affirmed, but the judgment was reversed by the state's highest court. Groesbeck v. Morgan, 206 N.Y. 385, 99 N.E. 1046 (1912).

No doctrine of equity jurisprudence is better settled than the rule that specific performance is not a strict legal right and is never granted when the lapse of time renders such relief inequitable in its consequences, or as many judges have phrased it, "against equity and good conscience." The defense of laches, in a suit for specific performance, is to be considered wholly independent of the Statute of Limitations. Although the action is brought within the period prescribed by the statute, it may have been so delayed as to preclude the granting of equitable relief, and, if so, the complainant must be relegated to his action at law for damages. In determining whether such delay is fatal in the domain of equity, regard must always be had to the peculiar circumstances of each case ... a purchaser seeking specific performance must be "ready, desirous, prompt and eager." The vendee in the present contract manifested none of these attributes. He allowed nearly five years to elapse after he became aware that the defendant had acquired an unincumbered title before he instituted the present suit. No excuse is offered for the delay, while the effect of it now is to make the defendant convey to the plaintiff land which has increased in value by many thousands of dollars. . . . "He cannot be suffered to lie by and speculate on the rise of the estate."

Beresovski v. Warszawski

Court of Appeals of New York, 1971.
28 N.Y.2d 419, 322 N.Y.S.2d 673, 271 N.E.2d 520.

■ GIBSON, J. In this action, brought for specific performance of a stockholders' agreement, the complaint was dismissed, following a nonjury trial, on the ground that the action was barred by the 6–year Statute of Limitations applicable to an action upon a contractual obligation or liability....The Appellate Division, First Department, unanimously affirmed upon the opinion of the trial court; and appeal to this court was taken by our leave.

We find inapplicable the 6–year statute pleaded in bar and conclude that the 10–year Statute of Limitations provided by section 53 of the Civil Practice Act, and recognized as governing actions in equity, applies and will be effective in this case, if the cause of action, which had accrued prior to the effective date of the CPLR, was not barred at that time....

Plaintiff owns 25% of the stock of Joint Property Owners, Inc., and defendants, who are father and son, own the remaining shares. The agreement in suit is between them and provides, among other things, that all three stockholders shall be directors and that a fourth director shall be elected annually; that any action taken by the board shall require the vote of at least three directors; that any action taken by the stockholders shall require the affirmative vote of 85% of the issued shares; that the real property of the corporation shall not be mortgaged without the written consent of stockholders owning 100% of the issued shares, and that, "[i]n the event any of the provisions of this agreement shall be deemed illegal or against public policy, the validity or legality of any of the other provisions or any part thereof shall not be thereby affected. However, if any illegal provision can be cured by amending the certificate of incorporation, the parties agree to take such action immediately."

Recognizing, apparently, the invalidity of the contractual provisions for supermajority control unless they should be embodied in the certificate of incorporation, plaintiff, according to his testimony, made repeated demands for appropriate amendment of the certificate of incorporation, which defendants as consistently refused. There is evidence that the first demand to meet with a refusal, thereby accruing the cause of action, was made on June 5, 1957, and thus within 10 years of the commencement of the action on May 15, 1967. In the present state of the record, however, it could, in any event, be found, absent proof by defendants in rebuttal of the presumption of their absence, that the limiting statute of 10 years was tolled.

The 10–year statute is found in section 53 of the Civil Practice Act, providing that: "An action, the limitation of which is not specifically prescribed in this article, must be commenced within ten years after the cause of action accrues." This limitation was not carried over into the CPLR but remains in force in the cases specified in the transitional provisions of the new act.[2]

The trial court's application of the 6–year statute was grounded on the fact that the cause of action arose out of a contract, but this consideration is not the conclusive test. Thus, it was held in an early case that the remedy of specific performance of a contract for the sale of land "does not depend and is not based solely upon the contract, but upon other circumstances in connection with the contract" and, further, that "specific per-

---

2. [The present N.Y. CPLR Section 213 enumerates the causes of action that must be commenced within six years. Subdivision 1 of Section 213 provides: "An action for which no limitation is specifically prescribed by law."]

formance is granted or refused according to the circumstances of each case irrespective of the character or form of the contract or the foundation of the liability. The contract gives the right of action; that is, without it no right of action would exist, but other circumstances enter into the question, whether the party is entitled to this particular relief." Much later, in Hearn 45 St. Corp. v. Jano, 283 N.Y. 139, 27 N.E.2d 814, judgment creditors sued in equity to set aside transfers and follow the assets of the business, and a bona fide equity suit, susceptible of the 10–year statute, was made out despite the fact that it was possible for plaintiff to disregard the transfers and attach or levy execution upon the property conveyed. The court stated:

> "Plaintiff was not forced to take such action, but could instead adopt the action which it did. . . . Thus there is clearly no remedy at law comparable to that available in equity, and, therefore, the period of limitation which would bar an action at law does not reduce the period which ordinarily limits a suit in equity."

These specific performance cases seem to us completely analogous to this and the concept underlying them—the absence of an "adequate" or "comparable" remedy at law—determinative here.

Thus tested, plaintiff's cause of action is clearly dependent, for adequate enforcement, upon the equitable remedy of specific performance. According to his proof, plaintiff has suffered real detriment in that, among other things, a fourth director was elected in his absence and thereafter plaintiff was ousted from the board on the votes of but two directors. Were the agreement to be performed and the charter amended, the supermajority provisions would become effective, thus preventing actions of this nature in future and, indeed, enabling plaintiff to procure the rescission of the actions of which he complains. There appears no other suitable recourse; and, indeed, the deprivation of the minority control of a business corporation, as envisioned by the agreement, creates substantial but nonetheless intangible damage that cannot, in this instance at least, readily be measured monetarily. Defendants have not demonstrated the existence of any comparable legal remedy nor have they otherwise presented any effective argument to deny the consequent application of the 10–year statute.

. . . .

The order of the Appellate Division should be reversed and a new trial granted, with costs to abide the event.

Order reversed, etc.

Environmental Defense Fund, Inc. v. Alexander

United States Court of Appeals, Fifth Circuit, 1980.
614 F.2d 474.

■ RUBIN, J. This attempt to halt the construction of a federally financed waterway because the width of the waterway exceeds the size authorized by Congress was dismissed by the district court on the basis that it was barred by laches—delay in presenting the claim resulting in prejudice to the defendants. . . .

I.

The headwater of this litigation commenced to flow forty years ago when the Army Corps of Engineers presented Congress with a preliminary design for the proposed Tennessee–Tombigbee Waterway. The design was reviewed and modified in a report submitted to Congress in 1946. In that year Congress authorized construction of the waterway in accordance with the plans presented to it. . . .

Shortly after authorizing construction, Congress decided that the waterway was not economically feasible, and for some time it did not appropriate any funds for construction. However, studies continued. In June, 1966, in response to a request by Congress for restudy of the economic desirability of the project, the Corps of Engineers recommended that the proposed plan be modified to provide for a 300–foot channel (for convenience we refer to this as the 300–foot channel although this is its minimum width at its bottom). . . .

On May 18, 1967, the Association of American Railroads, on behalf of the L & N Railroad Company and other railroad companies in the waterway area, submitted a report to the Senate Appropriations Committee specifically suggesting the need for a reevaluation of the project authorization because of the increase in the project's width from 170 feet to 300 feet. Subsequently, the Appropriations Committees recommended appropriation of construction funds for the waterway with the increased bottom width. During the budget hearings for fiscal year 1971, representatives of appellants L & N Railroad and Committee for Leaving the Environment of America Natural (CLEAN) appeared before the House and Senate Appropriations Committees to oppose funding of the waterway.

Congress appropriated construction funds of $1 million for fiscal year 1971 and $6 million for fiscal year 1972. CLEAN and the Environmental Defense Fund (EDF) filed suit to enjoin the construction of the waterway in 1971. . . . Actual construction of the waterway began in 1972. Ultimately, the 1971 suit was dismissed by the court, and construction proceeded.

In November, 1976, this suit was filed, again seeking to enjoin construction. Plaintiffs alleged that the project under construction differed substantially from the project authorized by Congress and would have a greater impact on the environment and economic conditions of the surrounding areas, violating both statutory limitations and administrative regulations. . . . Over a year later, on January 30, 1978, an amended complaint was filed questioning, for the first time, the authority of the Corps to build a 300–foot channel.

When this suit was filed, the Corps had spent $36,000,000 out of a total estimated cost of $604,000,000 for channels and canals. By January 30, 1978, when the amended complaint was filed, it estimates it had completed 18% of the total project and spent over $265,000,000. After filing the lack of authority claims, the plaintiffs made no effort to obtain immediate injunctive relief and thus halt the further expenditure of funds or work on the project.

The Corps is now obligated on outstanding construction contracts in the amount of $864,302,200. If the project is restricted to a 170–foot channel, some of these funds may be recouped by sale of the unnecessary right of way and by renegotiation of contracts. Those who question authority to proceed urge that a substantial part of the $864 million could be saved if the project were restricted to 170 feet. In response to inquiry by this court concerning amounts spent for construction, the Corps estimates that by September 30, 1978, $408,651,600 had been spent for construction and $616,007,156 has been spent to the present. The opponents of the waterway state that the following sums have been spent on actual project construction:

As of September 30, 1976: $93,314,300.

As of September 30, 1977: $176,324,100.

As of September 30, 1978: $286,862,900....

The district judge did not decide whether the Secretary was authorized to increase the width of the channel because he concluded that the challenge was barred by laches. Deciding only that issue, he directed entry of a final judgment....

II.

... What is sought here is an injunction, an equitable form of relief. The doctrine of laches was developed by chancellors of equity to prevent the assertion of stale claims and to remedy an injustice that sometimes arose from the existence of the separate system of equity: when an equitable remedy was sought, the statute of limitations that ordinarily would apply to a legal right was inapplicable.

The doctrine was eventually adopted by common law courts and, following the merger of law and equity, became part of the general body of rules governing relief in the federal court system. Its interpretation in equity courts was not uniform; at times the courts required a showing of prejudice to the defendants, at other times the chancellor applied it if a plaintiff had unreasonably delayed the assertion of his claim whether or not the defendant had been prejudiced. One basic principle has, however, been consistently followed: equitable remedies are not available if granting the remedy would be inequitable to the defendant because of the plaintiff's long delay.

Today, three independent criteria must be met before laches can be invoked to bar litigation. "The defendant must show: (1) a delay in asserting a right or claim; (2) that the delay was not excusable; and (3) that there was undue prejudice to the party against whom the claim is asserted." Whether laches bars an action in a given case depends upon the circumstances of that case and is "a question primarily addressed to the discretion of the trial court."

As we have recently said, the applicability of the doctrine of laches to environmental litigation is no longer open to doubt. It is equally applicable to suits questioning public authority to act.

The record, which we have already summarized, amply supports the district judge's finding that on November 3, 1966, about a decade before the suit was filed, the Corps gave public notice of its recommendation to expand the width of the canal together with an invitation to the public to submit written comments. . . .

There is also ample evidence that the waterway opponents who appear in this suit were aware of this change: the 1967 opposition to a 300–foot channel by the Association of American Railroads, in part on L & N RR's behalf; the opposition to funding of the 300–foot channel project by CLEAN and EDF in Congress; and the suit to halt construction in 1971. The present waterway opponents did not challenge that decision until 1978, eleven years later. Even if we assume the challenge to have been effective when the complaint was filed in 1976, the delay was nine years. If we accept the contention that appellants remained blissfully ignorant of the increased dimensions throughout the congressional hearings on the waterway and despite the public attention the project received, they were aware of the width increase no later than 1971, when they sought to enjoin construction and stipulated to that width. This suit was not filed until five years thereafter, and the issue of authority to make the width increase was not injected until two years later.

Mere neglect to challenge action is not sufficient to establish laches in any case. When government action is involved, members of the public are entitled to assume that public officials will act in accordance with law. Therefore, apart from the question of prejudice, which we will discuss later, the government must show that those whom it seeks to bar by invoking laches were or should have been aware of the questionable nature of the governmental activity. The waterway opponents in this case had an adequate indication that the Secretary of the Army had unilaterally expanded the width of the canal beyond its statutorily authorized channel width. This was enough to alert them to the claim that the authorities were not acting legally.

. . . .

Because there is no evidence of any excuse for the lengthy delay, we next consider the final prerequisite to laches: prejudice. Measuring prejudice entails balancing equities. Under the rule as applied in Save Our Wetlands, Inc. (SOWL) v. United States Army Corps of Engineers, 549 F.2d 1021 (5th Cir.), cert. denied, 434 U.S. 836, 98 S.Ct. 126, 54 L.Ed.2d 98 (1977), we are required to consider the expenditures made by the defendants against the benefits claimed if their efforts were halted. Environmental concerns are not presented to us; therefore, unlike the situation in Ecology Center of Louisiana, Inc. v. Coleman, 515 F.2d 860 (5th Cir.1975), detriment to the environment cannot be a factor in our balance; the benefits we must weigh that could accrue by arresting work can be only those arising from the claimed vindication of congressional authority.

The amounts expended may be large in absolute terms but this does not tilt the scales if it represents a relatively small percentage of the total expenditures anticipated. See, e.g., Ecology Center of Louisiana, Inc. v. Coleman, 515 F.2d 860 (5th Cir.1975)($1 million had been spent out of a total estimated cost of $667 million). Here by the most conservative estimates, between $176 million and $286 million had been spent before the no-authority claim was asserted. This represented about 11% of the total project cost, far more than the ⅙ of 1% expended in *Coleman*. Vast amounts of soil had been excavated, locks had been built, and local authorities had constructed bridges. Reshaping the project would not only entail waste of much of those expenditures but also the outlay of additional funds to narrow the channel; moreover, there is substantial evidence that the narrower channel would be economically impractical and would never have been constructed.

. . . .

Laches is a clement doctrine. It assures that old grievances will some day be laid to rest, that litigation will be decided on the basis of evidence that remains reasonably accessible and that those against whom claims are presented will not be unduly prejudiced by delay in asserting them. Inevitably it means that some potentially meritorious demands will not be entertained. But there is justice too in an end to conflict and in the quiet of peace. The district court concluded that the day for battle on the authorization issue had come and gone and that the question should now be laid to rest unheard. Finding his factual premises supported by the record and his conclusions of law correct, we AFFIRM his judgment.

Addison v. State

Supreme Court of California, 1978.
21 Cal.3d 313, 146 Cal.Rptr. 224, 578 P.2d 941.

■ TOBRINER, A.C.J. . . .

Plaintiffs originally filed a tort action against defendants, the State of California and the County of Santa Clara, in federal court, alleging violations of both state and federal law. After defendants moved to dismiss the federal action for lack of jurisdiction and after the expiration of the six-month period provided in section 945.6 [of the Government Code] plaintiffs filed the present action in the Santa Clara County Superior Court. Upon defendants' motion, the federal suit was dismissed shortly thereafter, without prejudice to the prosecution of the superior court proceeding. The superior court then sustained defendants' subsequent demurrer to the Santa Clara County action because of the late filing of the complaint presently before us and notwithstanding the fact, which all parties acknowledge, that plaintiffs had filed the federal action in timely fashion. Plaintiffs appeal.

We will apply the well established doctrine of "equitable tolling." . . .

. . . .

The complaint herein alleges the following facts: Plaintiffs, whose business was the sale of automobiles at auction, were investigated by state and county officials for allegedly fraudulent practices in the conduct of these sales. On March 11, 1975, officers of the Department of Motor Vehicles and the deputy district attorney of Santa Clara County allegedly entered plaintiffs' place of business in San Jose and, pursuant to a search warrant, seized numerous records. . . . Defendants publicized this raid and made available to the news media the contents of the warrant and supporting affidavits. Plaintiffs assert that defendants' action was improper and constituted defamation, abuse of process, and conversion.

Plaintiffs filed timely damage claims with both the state and county pursuant to the provisions of the Tort Claims Act referred to above. These claims were rejected on May 22 and May 27, 1975, respectively. Each letter of rejection included the admonition required by the act (§ 913) that: "WARNING . . . you have only six (6) months from the date [of service of this notice] to file a *court action* on this claim." (Italics added.)

Three and one-half months later, on September 11, 1975, plaintiffs filed a complaint in the United States District Court, Northern District of California, alleging both a federal civil rights violation and, on the basis of the federal court's pendent jurisdiction, the state law causes of action for defamation, conversion, and abuse of process for which claims had been filed and rejected. On November 26, 1975, defendants moved to dismiss this action for lack of jurisdiction. On February 9, 1976, plaintiffs, anticipating an adverse ruling on the motion, filed their complaint in the present Santa Clara County action. The federal court granted the motion to dismiss on February 17, 1976, after determining that a federal civil rights action would not lie against public entities. Having dismissed the federal causes of action, the court decided not to retain the state causes of action and dismissed them, allegedly without prejudice to refiling in state court.

It is fundamental that the primary purpose of statutes of limitation is to prevent the assertion of stale claims by plaintiffs who have failed to file their action until evidence is no longer fresh and witnesses are no longer available. "[T]he right to be free of stale claims in time comes to prevail over the right to prosecute them." The statutes, accordingly, serve a distinct public purpose, preventing the assertion of demands which through the unexcused lapse of time, have been rendered difficult or impossible to defend. However, courts have adhered to a general policy which favors relieving plaintiff from the bar of a limitations statute when, possessing several legal remedies he, reasonably and in good faith, pursues one designed to lessen the extent of his injuries or damage.

In like fashion and more recently, in Elkins v. Derby (1974) 12 Cal.3d 410, 115 Cal.Rptr. 641, 525 P.2d 81, we unanimously held that the statute of limitations on a personal injury action is tolled while plaintiff asserts a workers' compensation remedy against defendant. In such a case, we noted, defendant can claim no substantial prejudice, having received timely notice of possible tort liability upon filing of the compensation claim, and having ample opportunity to gather defense evidence in the event a court action ultimately is filed. We also noted the long settled rule that whenever exhaustion of administrative remedies is a prerequisite to a civil action the running of the limitations period is suspended during the administrative proceedings and we stated that "regardless of whether the exhaustion of one remedy is a prerequisite to the pursuit of another, if the defendant is not prejudiced thereby, the running of the limitations period is tolled '[w]hen an injured person has several legal remedies and, reasonably and in good faith, pursues one.' "

Similarly, in Bollinger v. National Fire Ins. Co. (1944) 25 Cal.2d 399, 154 P.2d 399, plaintiff had filed in a timely manner a previous action against an insurer but the action had been improperly dismissed as premature under the terms of the insurance policy. Plaintiff promptly filed a new action, but by then the period of limitations had run. Nevertheless, we allowed the action, based upon the broad policy which is implicit in Code of Civil Procedure section 355, permitting the plaintiff to file a new action within one year if a judgment in his favor is reversed on appeal.

The rule announced in *Bollinger* is a general equitable one which operates independently of the literal wording of the Code of Civil Procedure. As we observed in that case: "[T]his court is not powerless to formulate rules of procedure where justice demands it. Indeed, it has shown itself ready to adapt rules of procedure to serve the ends of justice where technical forfeitures would unjustifiably prevent a trial on the merits."

As demonstrated by *Bollinger* and *Elkins,* application of the doctrine of equitable tolling requires timely notice, and lack of prejudice, to the defendant, and reasonable and good faith conduct on the part of the plaintiff. These elements seemingly are present here. As noted, the federal court, without prejudice, declined to assert jurisdiction over a timely filed state law cause of action and plaintiffs thereafter promptly asserted that cause in the proper state court. . . .

Furthermore, since the federal court action was timely filed, defendants were notified of the action and had the opportunity to begin gathering their evidence and preparing their defense. No prejudice to defendants is shown, for plaintiffs' state court action was filed within one week of the dismissal of the federal suit. To apply the doctrine of equitable tolling in this case, in our view, satisfies the policy underlying the statute of limitations without ignoring the competing policy of avoiding technical and unjust forfeitures.

. . . .

. . . As with other general equitable principles, application of the equitable tolling doctrine requires a balancing of the injustice to the plaintiff occasioned by the bar of his claim against the effect upon the important public interest or policy expressed by the Tort Claims Act limitations statute.

In our view, the balance in this case must be struck in plaintiffs' favor. If the tolling doctrine were not applied, plaintiffs would be denied a hearing on the merits of their claim. The doctrine's application, on the other hand, should not substantially undermine the policy of prompt resolution of claims. As we have noted, plaintiffs filed their state court action within nine months after their right to sue arose and by reason of the federal suit, defendants were fully notified within the six-month statutory period of plaintiffs' claims and their intent to litigate. Defendants were informed at all times of the nature of plaintiffs' claims. Any delay resulting from plaintiffs' original erroneous choice of forum was minimal. . . .

The judgment is reversed and the cause remanded to the superior court with directions to overrule the defendants' demurrer.

1.   On the subject of equitable tolling in federal tax cases, the Supreme Court has held that the federal statute of limitations for tax refunds

is not subject to equitable tolling. United States v. Brockamp, 519 U.S. 347, 117 S.Ct. 849 (1997).

———

C.   Estoppel

Barry v. Donnelly

United States Court of Appeals, Fourth Circuit, 1986.
781 F.2d 1040.

■ James Dickson Phillips, Circuit Judge:

In this declaratory judgment action, Honoria and William Donnelly appeal from a summary judgment declaring that they are barred by the Virginia statute of limitations from suing to recover from Ellen Barry, a close family friend and alleged bailee, a painting by Mrs. Donnelly's father, Gerald Murphy. Because we conclude that there are genuine issues of fact material to the Donnellys' claim that Ellen Barry should be precluded from asserting the statute of limitations under the doctrine of equitable estoppel, we vacate the district court's order and remand for further proceedings.

I

Gerald Murphy and his wife, Sara, lived in Paris during the 1920s and counted, among their friends, many of the principal artists and writers of that era, including Picasso, Hemingway, and Fitzgerald. Although his work was not at that time particularly well known, Murphy was himself a serious painter. Since his death in 1964, his paintings have become very valuable.

In 1964, Gerald Murphy brought his painting entitled "Cocktail" to the Washington, D.C., apartment of Ellen Barry, an old and dear friend of the Murphy family. According to Honoria Donnelly, Murphy contemplated that Barry would use and enjoy the painting for as long as she liked, but that she would ultimately return the artwork to his family. Barry maintains that the painting was a gift.

The painting has remained in Ellen Barry's possession and over the years she has loaned it to various museums, each time identifying the work as from the collection of Mrs. Phillip Barry. In October of 1978, Ellen Barry wrote to Honoria Donnelly requesting, for purposes of her "records and insurance," a written confirmation that the painting had been a gift from Gerald Murphy. In March of 1979, Mrs. Donnelly, who now resides in Virginia, responded with a letter indicating that she understood the arrangement to be merely a loan and suggesting that, in order to avoid future estate tax problems, the parties "put something in writing" to this effect.

Honoria Donnelly's letter referred to a conversation that the parties agree transpired sometime previously, probably during 1965, in which Barry indicated that she would eventually give or bequeath the painting to the Donnellys for their son, John. Accordingly, around this time, Mrs. Barry tagged the back of the painting with instructions to "Give to Honoria

Donnelly for John Donnelly." The parties disagree, however, as to whether this promise was later reaffirmed by Ellen Barry in discussions that ensued following the correspondence of 1978–79. Thus, Honoria Donnelly claims that notwithstanding Ellen Barry's 1978 assertion of ownership, Barry later confirmed that she would ultimately return the painting to the Donnellys. According to Mrs. Barry, on the other hand, there was no further discussion concerning the disposition of the painting after 1965.

On June 12, 1979, Ellen Barry wrote once more to Honoria Donnelly, again insisting that Gerald Murphy intended the painting as a gift and not as a loan for an indefinite term. According to Honoria Donnelly, it was not until 1983 that she learned that Ellen Barry no longer intended to give or bequeath the work to the Donnellys for their son, John.

On December 5, 1984, Ellen Barry, invoking diversity jurisdiction, sought a declaratory judgment pursuant to 28 U.S.C. s 2201, to resolve this controversy, in which she claims entitlement to the painting as a gift or, alternatively, assuming that the painting was merely loaned, by the running of Virginia's five-year statute of limitations on actions to recover property. Va.Code s 8.01–243(B)(1950). Solely for purposes of her motion for summary judgment, Ellen Barry conceded the Donnellys' characterization of the transaction as a bailment as well as their claim that Barry renewed her promise to return the painting even after her assertions of ownership in 1978–79.

The district court granted summary judgment in favor of Barry, holding that her letter of October 1978 was an act inconsistent with the asserted bailment and therefore triggered the applicable Virginia statute of limitations. The court characterized Barry's representations that she would return the painting as merely "a promise to do something in the future" rather than fraud sufficient to toll the statute of limitations. Apparently considering that under controlling state law only fraud could have that effect, the court therefore concluded that on the undisputed facts the statute barred any claim by the Donnellys so that Barry was entitled to judgment as a matter of law under Fed.R.Civ.P. 56(c). This appeal followed.

II

Assuming, as the district court found, that on the summary judgment record the undisputed evidence revealed no conduct amounting to fraud, this did not entitle Barry to judgment as a matter of law. Under Virginia law, one may be estopped to plead the bar of a statute of limitations by conduct short of fraud, under the general doctrine of equitable estoppel. Under that doctrine, estoppel occurs where "the aggrieved party reasonably relied on the words and conduct of the person to be estopped in allowing the limitations period to expire." City of Bedford v. James Leffel & Co., 558 F.2d 216, 218 (4th Cir.1977). As applied to the statute of limitations, the "central premise is that 'one cannot justly or equitably lull his adversary into a false sense of security, and thereby cause his adversary to subject his claim to the bar of the statute [of limitations], and then be permitted to plead the very delay caused by his course of conduct as a defense to the action when brought.' " Id. at 218, quoting Howard v. West Jersey & S.S.R.

Co., (1928), 102 N.J.Eq. 517, 141 A. 755, 757–58, aff'd mem. 104 N.J.Eq. 201, 144 A. 919 (1929).

While equitable estoppel in both its general applications as well as in its special application to statutes of limitations pleas frequently involves fraud or deceit and is "most clearly applicable" when it does, "deceit is not an essential element of estoppel" in either its general or special applications under Virginia law. City of Bedford, 558 F.2d at 218; T . . . v. T . . ., 216 Va. 867, 224 S.E.2d 148, 152 (1976) ("[t]o establish equitable estoppel, it is not necessary to show actual fraud, but only that the person to be estopped has misled another to his prejudice"); see also Lataif v. Commercial Industrial Construction, Inc., 223 Va. 59, 286 S.E.2d 159, 161 (1982)(citing City of Bedford on elements of equitable estoppel). The essential elements of equitable estoppel, in both its general applications and in its special application to statutes of limitation pleas under Virginia law are only those stated in T . . . v. T . . ., 224 S.E.2d at 152: "absent a showing of fraud and deception, . . . a representation, reliance, a change of position, and detriment" (citing United States v. Fidelity and Casualty Co. of New York, 402 F.2d 893, 898 (4th Cir.1968)).

III

Applying Virginia equitable estoppel doctrine, as stated in City of Bedford and T . . . v. T . . ., to the statute of limitations plea as here invoked by Barry, we conclude that genuine issues of material fact exist which made summary judgment inappropriate. Specifically, we hold that whether Barry reaffirmed her promise to return the painting after her assertion of ownership in 1978–79, and whether, if she did, the Donnellys reasonably relied upon that reaffirmation in failing to sue within the limitations period are issues requiring resolution by trial.

Accordingly, we vacate the summary judgment entered by the district court and remand for further proceedings consistent with this opinion.

So Ordered.

Office of Personnel Management v. Richmond

Supreme Court of the United States, 1990.
496 U.S. 414, 110 S.Ct. 2465, 110 L.Ed.2d 387.

■ JUSTICE KENNEDY delivered the opinion of the Court.

This case presents the question whether erroneous oral and written advice given by a Government employee to a benefit claimant may give rise to estoppel against the Government, and so entitle the claimant to a monetary payment not otherwise permitted by law. We hold that payments of money from the Federal Treasury are limited to those authorized by statute, and we reverse the contrary holding of the Court of Appeals.

I

Not wishing to exceed a statutory limit on earnings that would disqualify him from a disability annuity, respondent Charles Richmond sought advice from a federal employee and received erroneous information. As a result he earned more than permitted by the eligibility requirements of the relevant statute and lost six months of benefits. Respondent now claims that the erroneous and unauthorized advice should give rise to equitable estoppel against the Government, and that we should order payment of the benefits contrary to the statutory terms. Even on the assumption that much equity subsists in respondent's claim, we cannot agree with him or the Court of Appeals that we have authority to order the payment he seeks.

Respondent was a welder at the Navy Public Works Center in San Diego, California. He left this position in 1981 after petitioner, the Office of Personnel Management (OPM), approved his application for a disability retirement. OPM determined that respondent's impaired eyesight prevented him from performing his job and made him eligible for a disability annuity under 5 U.S.C. § 8337(a). Section 8337(a) provides this benefit for disabled federal employees who have completed five years of service. The statute directs, however, that the entitlement to disability payments will end if the retired employee is "restored to an earning capacity fairly comparable to the current rate of pay of the position occupied at the time of retirement." 5 U.S.C. § 8337(d).

The statutory rules for restoration of earning capacity are central to this case. Prior to 1982, an individual was deemed restored to earning capacity, and so rendered ineligible for a disability annuity, if

> "in *each of 2 succeeding calendar years* the income of the annuitant from wages or self-employment ... equals at least 80 percent of the current rate of pay of the position occupied immediately before retirement." 5 U.S.C. § 8337(d) (1976 ed.) (emphasis added).

The provision was amended in 1982 ... to change the measuring period for restoration of earning capacity from two years to one:

> "Earning capacity is deemed restored if *in any calendar year* the income of the annuitant from wages or self-employment or both equals at least 80 percent of the current rate of pay of the position occupied immediately before retirement." 5 U.S.C. § 8337(d)(emphasis added).

After taking disability retirement for his vision impairment, respondent undertook part-time employment as a school bus driver. From 1982 to 1985, respondent earned an average of $12,494 in this job, leaving him under the 80% limit for entitlement to continued annuity payments. In 1986, however, he had an opportunity to earn extra money by working overtime. Respondent asked an Employee Relations Specialist at the Navy Public Works Center's Civilian Personnel Department for information about how much he could earn without exceeding the 80% eligibility limit. Relying upon the terms of the repealed pre–1982 statute, under which respondent could retain the annuity unless his income exceeded the 80% limit in *two* consecutive years, the specialist gave respondent incorrect advice. The specialist also gave respondent a copy of Attachment 4 to Federal Personnel Manual Letter 831–64, published by petitioner OPM, which also stated the former 2–year eligibility rule. The OPM form was correct when written in 1981; but when given to respondent, the form was out of date and therefore inaccurate. Respondent returned to the Navy in

January 1987, and again was advised in error that eligibility would be determined under the old 2–year rule.

After receiving the erroneous information, respondent concluded that he could take on the extra work as a school bus driver in 1986 while still receiving full disability benefits for impaired vision so long as he kept his income for the previous and following years below the statutory level. He earned $19,936 during 1986, exceeding the statutory eligibility limit. OPM discontinued respondent's disability annuity on June 30, 1987. The annuity was restored on January 1, 1988, since respondent did not earn more than allowed by the statute in 1987. Respondent thus lost his disability payments for a 6–month period, for a total amount of $3,993.

Respondent appealed the denial of benefits to the Merit Systems Protection Board (MSPB). He argued that the erroneous advice given him by the Navy personnel should estop OPM and bar its finding him ineligible for benefits under the statute. The MSPB rejected this argument, noting that the officials who misinformed respondent were from the Navy, not OPM. The MSPB observed that, "[h]ad [respondent] directed his request for information to the OPM, presumably, he would have learned of the change in the law." The MSPB held that "OPM cannot be estopped from enforcing a statutorily imposed requirement for retirement eligibility." The MSPB denied respondent's petition for review, and respondent appealed to the Court of Appeals for the Federal Circuit.

A divided panel of the Court of Appeals reversed, accepting respondent's contention that the misinformation from Navy personnel estopped the Government, and that the estoppel required payment of disability benefits despite the statutory provision to the contrary. . . .

. . . .

II

From our earliest cases, we have recognized that equitable estoppel will not lie against the Government as against private litigants. . . .

. . . .

Despite the clarity of these earlier decisions, dicta in our more recent cases have suggested the possibility that there might be some situation in which estoppel against the Government could be appropriate. The genesis of this idea appears to be an observation found at the end of our opinion in Montana v. Kennedy, 366 U.S. 308, 81 S.Ct. 1336, 6 L.Ed.2d 313 (1961). In that case, the petitioner brought a declaratory judgment action seeking to establish his American citizenship. After discussing the petitioner's two statutory claims at length, we rejected the final argument that a consular official's erroneous advice to petitioner's mother that she could not return to the United States while pregnant prevented petitioner from having been born in the United States and thus deprived him of United States citizenship. Our discussion was limited to the observation that in light of the fact that no legal obstacle prevented petitioner's mother from returning to the United States, what may have been only the consular official's well-meant advice—"I am sorry, Mrs., you cannot [return to the United States] in that condition"—falls far short of misconduct such as might prevent the United

States from relying on petitioner's foreign birth. In this situation, we need not stop to inquire whether, as some lower courts have held, there may be circumstances in which the United States is estopped to deny citizenship because of the conduct of its officials.

The proposition about which we did not "stop to inquire" in *Kennedy* has since taken on something of a life of its own. Our own opinions have continued to mention the possibility, in the course of rejecting estoppel arguments, that some type of "affirmative misconduct" might give rise to estoppel against the Government.

The language in our decisions has spawned numerous claims for equitable estoppel in the lower courts. As Justice Marshall stated in dissent in [a prior case], "[t]he question of when the Government may be equitably estopped has divided the distinguished panel of the Court of Appeals in this case, has received inconsistent treatment from other Courts of Appeals, and has been the subject of considerable ferment." Since that observation was made, federal courts have continued to accept estoppel claims under a variety of rationales and analyses. In sum, courts of appeals have taken our statements as an invitation to search for an appropriate case in which to apply estoppel against the Government, yet we have reversed every finding of estoppel that we have reviewed. Indeed, no less than three of our most recent decisions in this area have been summary reversals of decisions upholding estoppel claims. Summary reversals of courts of appeals are unusual under any circumstances. The extraordinary number of such dispositions in this single area of the law provides a good indication that our approach to these cases has provided inadequate guidance for the federal courts and served only to invite and prolong needless litigation.

The Solicitor General proposes to remedy the present confusion in this area of the law with a sweeping rule. As it has in the past, the Government asks us to adopt "a flat rule that estoppel may not in any circumstances run against the Government." The Government bases its broad rule first upon the doctrine of sovereign immunity. Noting that the "United States, as sovereign, is immune from suit save as it consents to be sued," the Government asserts that the courts are without jurisdiction to entertain a suit to compel the Government to act contrary to a statute, no matter what the context or circumstances. The Government advances as a second basis for this rule the doctrine of separation of powers. The Government contends that to recognize estoppel based on the misrepresentations of Executive Branch officials would give those misrepresentations the force of law, and thereby invade the legislative province reserved to Congress. This rationale, too, supports the Government's contention that estoppel may never justify an order requiring executive action contrary to a relevant statute, no matter what statute or what facts are involved.

We have recognized before that the "arguments the Government advances for the rule are substantial." And we agree that this case should be decided under a clearer form of analysis than "we will know an estoppel when we see one." But it remains true that we need not embrace a rule that no estoppel will lie against the Government in any case in order to decide this case. We leave for another day whether an estoppel claim could ever succeed against the Government. A narrower ground of decision is sufficient to address the type of suit presented here, a claim for payment of money from the Public Treasury contrary to a statutory appropriation.

III

The Appropriations Clause of the Constitution, Art. I, § 9, cl. 7, provides that: "No Money shall be drawn from the Treasury, but in Consequence of Appropriations made by Law." For the particular type of claim at issue here, a claim for money from the Federal Treasury, the Clause provides an explicit rule of decision. Money may be paid out only through an appropriation made by law; in other words, the payment of money from the Treasury must be authorized by a statute. All parties here agree that the award respondent seeks would be in direct contravention of the federal statute upon which his ultimate claim to the funds must rest, 5 U.S.C. § 8337. The point is made clearer when the appropriation supporting the benefits sought by respondent is examined. In the same subchapter of the United States Code as the eligibility requirements, Congress established the Civil Service Retirement and Disability Fund. 5 U.S.C. § 8348. That section states in pertinent part: "The Fund . . . is appropriated for the payment of . . . benefits *as provided by* this subchapter . . ." (emphasis added). The benefits respondent claims were not "provided by" the relevant provision of the subchapter; rather, they were specifically denied. It follows that Congress has appropriated no money for the payment of the benefits respondent seeks, and the Constitution prohibits that any money "be drawn from the Treasury" to pay them.

. . . .

We have not had occasion in past cases presenting claims of estoppel against the Government to discuss the Appropriations Clause, for reasons that are apparent. Given the strict rule against estoppel applied as early as 1813 in Lee v. Munroe & Thornton, 7 Cranch 366, 3 L.Ed. 373 (1813), claims of estoppel could be dismissed on that ground without more. In our cases following Montana v. Kennedy, 366 U.S. 308, 81 S.Ct. 1336, 6 L.Ed.2d 313 (1961), reserving the possibility that estoppel might lie on some facts, we have held only that the particular facts presented were insufficient. As discussed above, we decline today to accept the Solicitor General's argument for an across-the-board no-estoppel rule. But this makes it all the more important to state the law and to settle the matter of estoppel as a basis for money claims against the Government.

Our decision is consistent with both the holdings and the rationale expressed in our estoppel precedents. Even our recent cases evince a most strict approach to estoppel claims involving public funds. The course of our jurisprudence shows why: Opinions have differed on whether this Court has ever accepted an estoppel claim in other contexts, but not a single case has upheld an estoppel claim against the Government for the payment of money. And our cases denying estoppel are animated by the same concerns that prompted the Framers to include the Appropriations Clause in the Constitution. As Justice Story described the Clause,

> "The object is apparent upon the slightest examination. It is to secure regularity, punctuality, and fidelity, in the disbursements of the public money. As all the taxes raised from the people, as well as revenues

arising from other sources, are to be applied to the discharge of the expenses, and debts, and other engagements of the government, it is highly proper, that congress should possess the power to decide how and when any money should be applied for these purposes. If it were otherwise, the executive would possess an unbounded power over the public purse of the nation; and might apply all its moneyed resources at his pleasure. The power to control and direct the appropriations, constitutes a most useful and salutary check upon profusion and extravagance, as well as upon corrupt influence and public peculation. . . ." 2 J. Story, Commentaries on the Constitution of the United States § 1348 (3d ed. 1858).

The obvious practical consideration cited by Justice Story for adherence to the requirement of the Clause is the necessity, existing now as much as at the time the Constitution was ratified, of preventing fraud and corruption. We have long ago accepted this ground as a reason that claims for estoppel cannot be entertained where public money is at stake, refusing to "introduce a rule against an abuse, of which, by improper collusions, it would be very difficult for the public to protect itself." But the Clause has a more fundamental and comprehensive purpose, of direct relevance to the case before us. It is to assure that public funds will be spent according to the letter of the difficult judgments reached by Congress as to the common good, and not according to the individual favor of Government agents or the individual pleas of litigants.

Extended to its logical conclusion, operation of estoppel against the Government in the context of payment of money from the Treasury could in fact render the Appropriations Clause a nullity. If agents of the Executive were able, by their unauthorized oral or written statements to citizens, to obligate the Treasury for the payment of funds, the control over public funds that the Clause reposes in Congress in effect could be transferred to the Executive. If, for example, the President or Executive Branch officials were displeased with a new restriction on benefits imposed by Congress to ease burdens on the fisc (such as the restriction imposed by the statutory change in this case) and sought to evade them, agency officials could advise citizens that the restrictions were inapplicable. Estoppel would give this advice the practical force of law, in violation of the Constitution.

It may be argued that a rule against estoppel could have the opposite result, that the Executive might frustrate congressional intent to appropriate benefits by instructing its agents to give claimants erroneous advice that would deprive them of the benefits. But Congress may always exercise its power to expand recoveries for those who rely on mistaken advice should it choose to do so. In numerous other contexts where Congress has been concerned at the possibility of significant detrimental reliance on the erroneous advice of Government agents, it has provided appropriate legislative relief.

One example is of particular relevance. In Schweiker v. Hansen, 450 U.S. 785, 101 S.Ct. 1468, 67 L.Ed.2d 685 (1981), we rejected an estoppel claim made by a Social Security claimant who failed to file a timely written application for benefits as required by the relevant statute. Congress then addressed such situations in the Budget Reconciliation Act of 1989, by providing that for claims to old age, survivors, and disability insurance, and for supplemental security income,

"In any case in which it is determined to the satisfaction of the Secretary that an individual failed as of any date to apply for monthly insurance benefits under this title by reason of misinformation provided to such individual by any officer or employee of the Social Security Administration relating to such individual's eligibility for benefits under this title, such individual shall be deemed to have applied for such benefits on the later of [the date on which the misinformation was given or the date upon which the applicant became eligible for benefits apart from the application requirement]."

The equities are the same whether executive officials' erroneous advice has the effect of frustrating congressional intent to withhold funds or to pay them. In the absence of estoppel for money claims, Congress has ready means to see that payments are made to those who rely on erroneous Government advice. Judicial adoption of estoppel based on agency misinformation would, on the other hand, vest authority in these agents that Congress would be powerless to constrain.

The provisions of the Federal Torts Claims Act also provide a strong indication of Congress' general approach to claims based on governmental misconduct, and suggest that it has considered and rejected the possibility of an additional exercise of its appropriation power to fund claims similar to those advanced here. The FTCA provides authorization in certain circumstances for suits by citizens against the Federal Government for torts committed by Government agents. Yet the FTCA by its terms excludes both negligent and intentional misrepresentation claims from its coverage. The claim brought by respondent is in practical effect one for misrepresentation, despite the application of the "estoppel" label. We would be most hesitant to create a judicial doctrine of estoppel that would nullify a congressional decision against authorization of the same class of claims.

Indeed, it would be most anomalous for a judicial order to require a Government official, such as the officers of petitioner OPM, to make an extrastatutory payment of federal funds. It is a federal crime, punishable by fine and imprisonment, for any Government officer or employee to knowingly spend money in excess of that appropriated by Congress. If an executive officer on his own initiative had decided that, in fairness, respondent should receive benefits despite the statutory bar, the official would risk prosecution. That respondent now seeks a court order to effect the same result serves to highlight the weakness and novelty of his claim.

The whole history and practice with respect to claims against the United States reveals the impossibility of an estoppel claim for money in violation of a statute. Congress' early practice was to adjudicate each individual money claim against the United States, on the ground that the Appropriations Clause forbade even a delegation of individual adjudicatory functions where payment of funds from the treasury was involved. As the business of the federal legislature has grown, Congress has placed the individual adjudication of claims based on the Constitution, statutes, or contracts, or on specific authorizations of suit against the Government, with the Judiciary. But Congress has always reserved to itself the power to address claims of the very type presented by respondent, those founded not on any statutory authority, but upon the claim that "the equities and circumstances of a case create a moral obligation on the part of the Government to extend relief to an individual." Subcommittee on Administrative Law and Governmental Relations of the House Committee on the Judiciary, Supplemental Rules of Procedure for Private Claims Bills, 101st Cong., 1st Sess., 2 (Comm.Print 1989).

In so-called "congressional reference" cases, Congress refers proposed private bills to the United States Claims Court for an initial determination of the merits of the claim, but retains final authority over the ultimate appropriation. Congress continues to employ private legislation to provide remedies in individual cases of hardship. Where sympathetic facts arise, cf. post (opinion of Stevens, J.), these examples show the means by which they can be addressed. In short, respondent asks us to create by judicial innovation an authority over funds that is assigned by the Constitution to Congress alone, and that Congress has not seen fit to delegate.

Congress has, of course, made a general appropriation of funds to pay judgments against the United States rendered under its various authorizations for suits against the Government, such as the Tucker Act and the FTCA. But respondent's claim for relief does not arise under any of these provisions. Rather, he sought and obtained an order of enrollment in the disability annuity plan in direct violation of that plan's requirements.

The general appropriation for payment of judgments, in any event, does not create an all-purpose fund for judicial disbursement. A law that identifies the source of funds is not to be confused with the conditions prescribed for their payment. Rather, funds may be paid out only on the basis of a judgment based on a substantive right to compensation based on the express terms of a specific statute. . . . Given this rule, as well as our many precedents establishing that authorizations for suits against the Government must be strictly construed in its favor, we cannot accept the suggestion that the terms of a statute should be ignored based on the facts of individual cases. Here the relevant statute by its terms excludes respondent's claim, and his remedy must lie with Congress.

Respondent would have us ignore these obstacles on the ground that estoppel against the Government would have beneficial effects. But we are unwilling to "tamper with these established principles because it might be thought that they should be responsive to a particular conception of enlightened governmental policy." And respondent's attempts to justify estoppel on grounds of public policy are suspect on their own terms. Even short of collusion by individual officers or improper Executive attempts to frustrate legislative policy, acceptance of estoppel claims for Government funds could have pernicious effects. It ignores reality to expect that the Government will be able to "secure perfect performance from its hundreds of thousands of employees scattered throughout the continent." To open the door to estoppel claims would only invite endless litigation over both real and imagined claims of misinformation by disgruntled citizens, imposing an unpredictable drain on the public fisc. Even if most claims were rejected in the end, the burden of defending such estoppel claims would itself be substantial.

Also questionable is the suggestion that if the Government is not bound by its agents' statements, then citizens will not trust them, and will instead seek private advice from lawyers, accountants, and others, creating wasteful expenses. Although mistakes occur, we may assume with confidence that Government agents attempt conscientious performance of their duties, and in most cases provide free and valuable information to those who seek advice about Government programs. A rule of estoppel might create not more reliable advice, but less advice. The natural consequence of a rule that made the Government liable for the statements of its agents would be a decision to cut back and impose strict controls upon Government provision of information in order to limit liability. Not only would valuable informational programs be lost to the public, but the greatest impact of this loss would fall on those of limited means, who can least afford the alternative of private advice. The inevitable fact of occasional individual hardship cannot undermine the interest of the citizenry as a whole in the ready availability of Government information. The rationale of the Appropriations Clause is that if individual hardships are to be remedied by payment of Government funds, it must be at the instance of Congress.

Respondent points to no authority in precedent or history for the type of claim he advances today. Whether there are any extreme circumstances that might support estoppel in a case not involving payment from the Treasury is a matter we need not address. As for monetary claims, it is enough to say that this Court has never upheld an assertion of estoppel against the Government by a claimant seeking public funds. In this context there can be no estoppel, for courts cannot estop the Constitution. The judgment of the Court of Appeals is

Reversed.

■ JUSTICE WHITE, with whom JUSTICE BLACKMUN joins, concurring.

I agree that the Government may not be estopped in cases such as this one and therefore join the opinion and judgment of the Court. I write separately to note two limitations to the Court's decision. First, the Court wisely does not decide that the Government may not be estopped under any circumstances. . . .

Second, although the Court states that "[a]ny exercise of a power granted by the Constitution to one of the other Branches of Government is limited by a valid reservation of congressional control over funds in the Treasury," the Court does not state that statutory restrictions on appropriations may never fall even if they violate a command of the Constitution such as the Just Compensation Clause, or if they encroach on the powers reserved to another Branch of the Federal Government. Although Knote v. United States, 95 U.S. 149, 154, 24 L.Ed. 442 (1877), held that the President's pardon power did not extend to the appropriation of moneys in the treasury without authorization by law for the benefit of pardoned criminals, it did not hold that Congress could impair the President's pardon power by denying him appropriations for pen and paper.

■ JUSTICE STEVENS, concurring in the judgment.

Although I join the Court's judgment, I cannot accept its reasoning. The Appropriations Clause of the Constitution has nothing to do with this case. Payments of pension benefits to retired and disabled federal servants are made "in Consequence of Appropriations made by Law" even if in particular cases they are the product of a mistaken interpretation of a statute or regulation. The Constitution contemplates appropriations that cover programs—not individual appropriations for individual payments. The Court's creative reliance on constitutional text is nothing but a red herring.

The dispute in this case is not about whether an appropriation has been made; it is instead about what rules govern administration of an appropriation that has been made. Once the issue is appropriately framed, it quickly becomes obvious that the Court's resolution of it is untenable. Three hypothetical changes in the facts of this case will illustrate the error in the Court's approach. Assume, first, that the forfeiture involved a permanent and total loss of pension benefits rather than a 6–month hiatus. Suppose also that respondent was a disabled serviceman, totally incapable of productive work, who was promised that his benefits would be unaffected if he enlisted in the reserve forces to show his continuing commitment to his country. Finally, assume that respondent was activated briefly for the sole purpose of enhancing his earnings, thereby depriving him of his pension permanently. Would the Court apply the harsh rule against estoppel that it announces today? I think not. Unless it found in the statute some unambiguous abrogation of estoppel principles, the Court would apply them to nullify the forfeiture. In doing so, the Court would construe the statute in a way consistent with congressional intent, and would ensure that the Executive administered the funds appropriated in a manner consistent with the terms of the appropriation.

This case, however, does not involve such extreme facts. Respondent's loss of benefits was serious but temporary, and, even if we assume that respondent was not adequately compensated for the stress of his increased workload, his additional earnings certainly mitigated the shortfall in benefits. I agree with Justice Marshall that there are strong equities favoring respondent's position, but I am persuaded that unless the 5–to–4 decision in [the case referred to by the Court as "the leading case in our modern line of estoppel decisions"] is repudiated by Congress or this Court, this kind of maladministration must be tolerated. . . .

■ JUSTICE MARSHALL, with whom JUSTICE BRENNAN joins, dissenting.

Respondent, a recipient of a federal disability annuity, was unsure whether he could accept limited overtime work without forfeiting his right to disability payments. He went to his former Government employer seeking an answer, asked the right questions, received an answer in the form of both oral advice and an official Government publication, and relied on that answer. Unfortunately, the publication the Government gave Richmond was years out of date, and the oral information was similarly erroneous. In this case, we must decide who should bear the burden of the Government's error.

The majority hints that it is unsympathetic to Richmond's claim that he was treated unfairly, but it does not rule on that basis. Rather, the majority resolves the issue by holding as a general rule that a litigant may not succeed on a claim for payment of money from the Treasury in the absence of a statutory appropriation. Although the Constitution generally forbids payments from the Treasury without a congressional appropriation, that proposition does not resolve this case. Most fundamentally, Richmond's collection of disability benefits would be fully consistent with the relevant appropriation. And even if the majority is correct that the statute cannot be construed to appropriate funds for claimants in Richmond's position, the Government may nonetheless be estopped, on the basis of its prelitigation conduct, from arguing that the Appropriations Clause bars his recovery. Both the statutory construction and the estoppel arguments turn on the equities, and the equities favor Richmond. I therefore dissent.

I

As the majority notes, the Appropriations Clause generally bars recovery from the Treasury unless the money sought " 'has been appropriated by an Act of Congress.' " The majority acknowledges that Congress *has* appropriated funds to pay disability annuities in 5 U.S.C. § 8348(a), but holds that the fund created is intended for the payment of benefits only "as provided by" law. Section 8337(d) provides that a disability annuity terminates when the annuitant's earning capacity is restored and that such capacity is "deemed restored" if in any calendar year the annuitant makes more than 80% of the current rate of pay of the position he left. The majority contends on the basis of this provision that paying benefits to an annuitant who has exceeded the 80% limit would violate the Appropriations Clause because such benefits are not "provided by" the statute.

The Court need not read the statute so inflexibly, however. When Congress passes a law to provide a benefit to a class of people, it intends and assumes that the executive will fairly implement that law. Where necessary to effectuate Congress' intent that its statutory schemes be fully implemented, this Court therefore often interprets the apparently plain words of a statute to allow a claimant to obtain relief where the statute on its face would bar recovery. . . .

. . . Where strict adherence to the literal language of the statute would produce results that Congress would not have desired, this Court has interpreted . . . statutes to authorize equitable exceptions though the plain language of the statute suggested a contrary result. . . .

Respect for Congress' purposes in creating the federal disability annuity system and principles of elementary fairness require that we read the statute in this case as not barring Richmond's claim. Perhaps "[t]he equities do not weigh in favor of modifying statutory requirements when the procedural default is caused by petitioners' 'failure to take the minimal steps necessary' to preserve their claims." But the equities surely *do* weigh in favor of reading the disability annuity statute to authorize payment of the claim of an annuitant rendered ineligible for benefits by his reliance on misinformation from the responsible federal authorities.

II

Even if the majority is correct that the statute does not itself require an exception where the executive has misled a claimant, Richmond should still prevail. Although the Government has an Appropriations Clause argument against any claim for money not authorized by a statutory appropriation, a court is not invariably required to entertain that argument. A number of circumstances may operate to estop the Government from invoking the Appropriations Clause in a particular case. For example, this Court's normal practice is to refuse to consider arguments not presented in the petition for certiorari. This Court customarily applies a similar rule to questions that were not raised in the Court of Appeals. These rules apply to *all* arguments, even those of constitutional dimension. Thus, had the Government failed to raise the argument on which it now prevails either in its petition for certiorari or in the Court of Appeals, we likely would have refused to consider it. Of course, we would have had the power to consider the claim. We would not, however, have been obligated to do so.

The grounds on which a court may refuse to entertain an argument are many, but most have an equitable dimension. The courts' general refusal to consider arguments not raised by the parties, for example, is founded in part on the need to ensure that each party has fair notice of the arguments to which he must respond. Thus, the Appropriations Clause's bar against litigants' collection of money from the Treasury where payment is not authorized by statute may not be enforced in a particular case if a court determines that the equities counsel against entertaining the Government's Appropriations Clause argument.

The question here is thus similar to ones that we have posed and answered in any number of recent cases: should the Government *in this case* be barred from invoking the statutory eligibility requirement (and through it, the Appropriations Clause) because Richmond's ineligibility for benefits was due entirely to the Government's own error? The majority refuses to answer this question. The Court of Appeals addressed it directly, concluding that the facts in this case were so "unusual and extreme" that the Government should be estopped from applying the statutory restrictions to bar Richmond's recovery. I agree with the Court of Appeals' ruling.

III

The majority argues that policy concerns justify its general refusal to apply estoppel against the Government in cases in which a claimant seeks unappropriated funds from the Treasury. Such a rule is necessary, says the majority, to protect against "fraud and corruption" by executive branch officials. If such officials are "displeased" with a statute, the argument goes, they may misinform the public as to the statute's meaning, thereby binding the Government to the officials' representations. The majority's concern with such dangers is undercut, however, by its observation that "Government agents attempt conscientious performance of their duties." The majority also contends that even if most claims of equitable estoppel are rejected in the end, "open[ing] the door" to such claims would impose "an unpredictable drain on the public fisc." The door has been open for almost 30 years, with an apparently unnoticeable drain on the public fisc. This reality is persuasive evidence that the majority's fears are overblown.

Significant policy concerns would of course be implicated by an indiscriminate use of estoppel against the Government. But estoppel is an equitable doctrine. As such, it can be tailored to the circumstances of particular cases, ensuring that fundamental injustices are avoided without seriously endangering the smooth operation of statutory schemes. In this case, the Federal Circuit undertook a thorough examination of the circumstances and concluded that denying Richmond his pension simply because he followed the Government's advice would be fundamentally unjust.

The majority does not reject the court's findings on the facts but rejects Richmond's claim on the theory that, except where the Constitution requires otherwise, equitable estoppel may not be applied against the Government where the claimant seeks unappropriated funds from the Treasury. This Court has never so much as mentioned the Appropriations Clause in the context of a discussion of equitable estoppel, nor has the majority's theory ever before been discussed, much less adopted, by any court. This lack of precedent for the majority's position is not surprising because the Appropriations Clause does not speak either to the proper interpretation of any statute or to the question whether the Government should be estopped from invoking the Clause in a particular case.

I dissent.

CHAPTER 9

EQUITABLE DEFENSES PECULIAR TO SPECIFIC PERFORMANCE; RESCISSION AND REFORMATION

NOTE

APPLICABILITY OF EQUITABLE PRINCIPLES LIMITATION IN THE INTERPRETATION AND ENFORCEMENT OF CONTRACTS

In a merged system of law and equity it is well to remember that equitable principles apply in all cases where parties to a contract request equitable remedies, such as injunctive relief or specific performance. The applicability of equitable principles may be referred to as an *equitable principles limitation* that applies in all cases where a party seeks to enforce specific provisions of a contract or obtain relief under a contract. This equitable principles limitation has not been limited to the availability of equitable remedies but has been given a broader applicability and may govern the relief that the court will grant under the contract. It reveals the intervention of the court in infusing equitable notions of justice, right conduct and fairness into all aspects of the contract.

A. FRAUD, MISREPRESENTATION, CONCEALMENT, AND NONDISCLOSURE

FRAUD

Fraud in Equity: A discussion of the meaning of fraud may commence with the following quotation from Reddaway v. Benham [1896] A.C. 199, 221 (per Lord Macnaghten):

> . . . Fraud is infinite in variety; sometimes it is audacious and unblushing; sometimes it pays a sort of homage to virtue, and then it is modest and retiring; it would be honesty itself if it could only afford it. But fraud is fraud all the same; and it is the fraud, not the manner of it, which calls for the imposition of the Court.

The difficulty of defining fraud, of course, stems from the supremacy of the individual facts of each case. It is for this reason that Pomeroy refused to define it and would merely say:

> Every fraud, in its most general and fundamental conception, consists in obtaining an undue advantage by means of some act or omission which is unconscientious or a violation of good faith in the

broad meaning given to the term by equity,—the *bona fides* of the Roman law.[1]

After stating that it was "utterly impossible to formulate any single statement which shall accurately define the equitable conception of fraud, and which shall contain all of the elements which enter into that conception, ..." Pomeroy, in § 873 entitled "Description–Essential Elements," not only "describes" fraud, but devotes 206 pages to "Actual Fraud" and 259 pages to "Constructive Fraud."

Fraud, or, rather, equitable relief against fraud, is an "ancient head of equity jurisdiction." Maitland refers to an "old rhyme": "These three give place in a court of conscience, Fraud, accident and breach of confidence." A similar couplet is ascribed to Sir Thomas More, the first lay person to be Chancellor.

As indicated by the cases, fraud and related wrongs may be raised in several different ways, such as:

(1) affirmatively at law as a ground for an action of deceit, and also as a ground of an informal rescission through an action of trover or conversion;

(2) defensively at law in an action for damages on a contract;

(3) affirmatively in equity as a ground for rescinding an executory or executed contract;

(4) defensively in equity in a suit for specific performance

(5) affirmatively at law or in equity to avoid or prevent the operation of the Statute of Frauds.

Kelly v. Central Pacific Railroad Co.

Supreme Court of California, 1888.
74 Cal. 557, 16 P. 386.

[The defendant railroad offered certain tracts of land for sale to settlers and actual occupants of the lands. Pursuant to this offer, the defendant agreed to convey certain lands to the plaintiff Kelly upon his false representation that he was the bona fide occupant. Upon learning of the deception, defendant's agent notified plaintiff that he couldn't have the lands and tendered back the first payment. Plaintiff refused to accept the money and sued for specific performance of the contract to convey the lands. The lower court ordered the lands to be conveyed to the person in actual possession, who had intervened, and plaintiff appeals.]

■ HAYNE, C. . . .

The point made on Kelly's appeal is, that the false representation was not productive of injury to the railroad company. . . .

. . . [W]e think there are two answers to the argument for the appellant.

---

1. POMEROY, EQUITY JURISPRUDENCE § 873, at 421 (5th ed. 1941).

1. Assuming the correctness of appellant's major proposition,—viz., that in order to defeat a suit for specific performance on the ground of fraud, the fraud must be productive of injury,—it is not necessary that the injury should result *to the vendor*. It is sufficient if it would result to third persons. It is upon this principle that the relief is refused, where the thing to be done would operate as a fraud upon the public. Thus a court will refuse to decree specific performance of an agreement to publish a book purporting to be written by one person, but in fact written by another. So, upon the same principle, the relief is refused where the agreement was in fraud of the rights of creditors, or in fraud of the rights of other parties. So it is refused where the act sought to be enforced would operate to the injury of interests in remainder; or to a wife's right in a homestead; or to subsequent purchasers from the same vendor. The court will not make itself an instrument to carry out the fraud, whether the person to be injured be a party to the contract or not. It will not assist the plaintiff to get the benefit of the intervenor's labor and improvements upon the tract in controversy.

2. But we do not think that in order to defeat a suit for the specific performance of a contract to convey land, upon the ground of fraud, the fraud must be productive of damage either to the vendor or to third persons. If the misrepresentation was intentional, and made for the purpose of deceiving the vendor, and the vendor relies upon it, and was deceived by it, and would not have entered into the contract but for the fact that he was so deceived, then we think a court of equity will not enforce the contract, whether it be accompanied by damage or not. So far as this kind of suit is concerned, such a misrepresentation is material although not accompanied by damage.

The counsel for the appellant cite in this connection the case of Morrison v. Lods, 39 Cal. 381, as affirming the contrary doctrine. The report of that case is somewhat obscure. It does not show what the representation was, nor whether it was intentionally false or a mere innocent misrepresentation. But if the court meant to decide that a court of equity will enforce a contract obtained solely through a false and fraudulent representation, then we think the decision is in violation of established principles. It is perfectly true, as stated in the opinion, that an action at law cannot be maintained for fraud unless accompanied by damage. It is also true, as stated in the opinion, that a court of equity will not set aside a contract obtained through fraud unless it be productive of injury. But it is not true that this applies to suits for specific performance. It is well settled that a court of equity may refuse specific performance of a contract which it would not set aside.

Although the court will refuse to destroy the contract, it will not further in any way the fraudulent design. In such cases, by an application of the maxim, that he who comes into equity must come with clean hands, the court is enabled to give greater effect to the principles of morality than can be done in ordinary cases. The leading textwriters are agreed in this view....

And it is evident that such must be the rule. To say otherwise is to place suits for specific performance on the same level with actions at law. . . .

In the present case the false and fraudulent representation of plaintiff was the inducing cause of the contract. This is apparent from the fact that so soon as the company discovered the fraud which had been practiced upon it, it repudiated the contract. And it is expressly found that "the land agent, but for such deception, would not have awarded said south half of northeast quarter to said Kelly, but would have awarded it to said Cole."

This state of facts well illustrates the wisdom of the doctrine which does not insist upon measuring everything by the standard of damage, but so far as can be done, allows parties to determine what is for their own interests, and to contract or refuse to contract accordingly. It is evident from the circulars contained in the record that it was the policy of the company to encourage the settlement of its vast tracts of unoccupied land. To carry out this policy it offered special inducements to settlers. It ought to be allowed to fulfill its promises to those who have relied upon its good faith. It is not for one who falsely pretends to be entitled to the benefit of those promises to say that it is all the same to the company because he pays the same price as the other would. The case is one where the vendor has special motives for selling to one person at a price which it would not accept from another.

. . . His [Kelly's] case against the company, therefore, fails. And this being so, he cannot inquire into the correctness of the decree directing the company to convey to the intervenor. For if he is not entitled to the specific thing, it is of no consequence to him what becomes of it, and he cannot concern himself with that question. . . .

We therefore advise that, upon the appeal of the plaintiff, the judgment be affirmed.

NOTES ON INNOCENT MISREPRESENTATION AND CONCEALMENT

1. INNOCENT MISREPRESENTATION MAY JUSTIFY DENIAL OF SPECIFIC PERFORMANCE: Wisherd v. Bollinger, 293 Ill. 357, 127 N.E. 657 (1920). Bollinger contracted to buy Wisherd's farm for $18,000, subject to a $10,000 mortgage. Wisherd and his real estate agent, Lawyer, made honest but false representations as to number of acres under cultivation, rent received, value per acre, and other facts. The actual value of the farm was little, if any, more than the amount of the mortgage. A degree granting Wisherd specific performance was reversed, and the bill dismissed. DUNCAN, J., said: "It is only on the principle that it is unjust and inequitable to permit a contract to remain unexecuted that a court of chancery assumes jurisdiction to enforce it. . . . Appellee [V] does not in this case come into a court of equity with clean hands and with a cause that appeals to equity for relief. We may assume that lawyer made only such representations as were made to him by appellee and without knowledge of their falsity. We may also assume that appellee himself did not know that he was misrepresenting this farm in the matters aforesaid. It is absolutely immaterial whether these material representations were made without knowledge of the real

truth or with an actual intent to deceive, because when representations are false and material they justify a court of chancery in refusing specific performance when the truth of the representations was relied upon by the other party to his injury, as in this case."

See also, FARNSWORTH, CONTRACTS § 4.11 at 252 (2d ed. 1990)("If the failure to diclose is unintentional, as when it is due to inadvertence or forgetfulness, it amounts to a nonfraudulent misrepresentation and will give a right to avoidance only if it is material.")

2. FARWELL, J., in BARNES v. CADOGAN DEVELOPMENTS, LTD., [1930] 1 Ch. 479, 488–89: "But if the vendor contracts to sell Blackacre, and states that it has certain advantages and the purchaser contracts to buy it, it is not a breach of contract on the vendor's part, if those advantages are absent." The vendor says: "Here is Blackacre. I will convey it to you." That carries out his contract. If the misdescription of Blackacre's advantages induced the purchaser to enter into the contract, he may have a remedy, but he cannot say: "I repudiate the contract and claim damages for breach." His only remedy is this. If the misrepresentation is innocent he may be in a position to ask the Court to refuse the vendor specific performance, as he was only buying on the footing that the representation was true. In such a case the Court will not enforce specific performance. But if the misrepresentation is innocent, the purchaser cannot recover damages. There has been no breach by the vendor. He can still sue on the contract. The only possible relief that the purchaser can get is the refusal by the Court to give the vendor specific performance. Of course if the misrepresentation is fraudulent, i.e., deliberately untrue, or reckless, other considerations arise. No man can be compelled to carry out a contract induced by fraud, and in such a case the purchaser is entitled to avoid the contract and to damages for fraudulent misrepresentation.

3. CONCEALMENT: Stewart v. Wyoming Cattle Ranche Co., 128 U.S. 383, 9 S.Ct. 101, 32 L.Ed. 439 (1888), was an action of deceit against a seller of a herd of cattle, who prevented the buyer's agent from prosecuting inquiries as to size of herd. Gray, J., made these observations:

In an action of deceit, it is true that silence as to a material fact is not necessarily, as matter of law, equivalent to a false representation. But mere silence is quite different from concealment; [to be silent is one thing, to conceal another;] a suppression of the truth may amount to a suggestion of falsehood; and if, with intent to deceive, either party to a contract of sale conceals or suppresses a material fact, which he is in good faith bound to disclose, this is evidence of and equivalent to a false representation, because the concealment or suppression is in effect a representation that what is disclosed is the whole truth. The gist of the action is fraudulently producing a false impression upon the mind of the other party; and if this result is accomplished, it is unimportant whether the means of accomplishing it are words or acts of the defendant, or his concealment or suppression of material facts not equally within the knowledge or reach of the plaintiff . . . each party must take care not to say or do anything tending to impose upon the other . . . .

Standard Steel Car Co. v. Stamm

Supreme Court of Pennsylvania, 1904.
207 Pa. 419, 56 A. 954.

[Anderson negotiated an option to buy Stamm's land in Butler, Pa. without disclosing his knowledge that a manufacturing plant would probably come to Butler. Anderson assigned the option to Standard Steel Car Company. Upon tender of payment, Stamm refused to convey the property. Anderson and Standard Steel Car Company sued for specific performance of the contract. The lower court refused specific performance on the ground that Anderson's concealment of the probability of a new manufacturing plant was a fraud upon Stamm. Anderson and Standard appeal.]

■ BROWN, J. . . .

In Anderson's negotiations with Stamm for the option it is not pretended that he made any misstatement or practiced any deception or imposition, or refused, at Stamm's request, to disclose any information which he possessed. As a matter of fact, he was in possession of no definite information. It was limited to the probability that a company, unknown and unnamed to him, might locate in Butler, and, among other lands, might need that of the defendant for its business purposes. As we gather from the testimony, he, with other citizens of the place, was anxious to have the manufacturing company come among them, and, most naturally, was willing to assist in the movement to induce it to do so. With not the slightest evidence of any intention to deceive Stamm or to practice a fraud upon him, he negotiated with him on a pure business basis. Each dealt with the other at arm's length, the prospective seller trying to obtain the best possible price paid for his land, and the option was given only after the prospective buyer had agreed to give all that was asked for it. There is nothing to show that the price agreed to be paid was not full and adequate at the time the option was given. And now, for no other conceivable reason than that the value of his land has greatly increased, the defendant would avoid performance of a contract in which there is involved nothing dishonest in law or in morals. Before the option was exercised the appellee heard that the manufacturing company might come to the town, but he made no objection on that account when Anderson notified him that he would exercise it. Such exercise turned it into a contract, enforceable by either party, whether the company came or not, and, if it had not come, Anderson would have had to pay the purchase money, though the same might have been much more than the property was worth and than anybody else would have paid for it. What Anderson is alleged to have concealed was nothing more than a rumor which might have been true or false. He concealed no fact the in existence that had actually affected the real market value of the property. But, even if he had, and the concealment under what took place between him and the prospective vendor had not amounted to actual deception, no fraud would have been practiced.

The complaint of the appellee is, that Anderson did not speak when it was his duty to speak. "A concealment to be material must be the concealment of something that the party concealing was under some legal or equitable obligation to disclose:" Kerr on Fraud (Am. ed.), 95. "Concealment which amounts to fraud in the sense of a court of equity, and for which it will grant relief, is the nondisclosure of those facts and circumstances which one party is under some legal or equitable obligation to communicate, and which the other party has a right, not merely in foro conscientiae, but juris et de jure, to know." In Neill v. Shamburg, 158 Pa. 263 [27 A. 992], the plaintiff sought to set aside her sale of an oil lease, alleging as one of her reasons concealment by the purchaser at the time of the purchase of the fact that oil was being produced upon a neighboring leasehold owned by him, and we held that the failure of the purchaser to make such disclosure was not a fraud upon her. If the information had been imparted to her, she might have refused to sell, or demanded more, but it was said by the present chief justice: "Unless there is some exceptional circumstance to put on him the duty of speaking, it is the right of every man to keep his business to himself." There was no exceptional circumstance here requiring Anderson to repeat to Stamm the rumor of the probability of the location of the manufacturing company in their town. On the contrary, common business prudence required him to remain silent, for, if he had spoken of the rumor, he might not have been able to negotiate at all.

... In Guaranty Safe Deposit and Trust Co. v. Liebold, [207 Pa.] 399 [56 A. 951], we said what we repeat as applicable to the facts here:

"In this commercial age options are daily procured by those in possession of information, from which they expect to profit simply because those from whom the options are sought are ignorant of it. When the prospective seller knows as much as the prospective buyer, options can rarely, if ever, be procured.... The prospective buyer seeks an option instead of at once entering into a contract for the purchase of land, because, no matter what information he may possess exclusively, he is unwilling to act upon it until it becomes a certainty. In the meantime, on the contingency of its becoming so, he makes his contingent bargain to purchase. This is fair in law and in morals."

The reason given for dismissing plaintiff's bill and refusing a decree for specific performance is untenable and cannot be sanctioned in this practical age. The decree of the court below is reversed, and it is now ordered, adjudged and decreed that the bill be reinstated and that, upon the tender of $8,000 of the purchase money by J.F. Anderson to the appellee, and the execution and delivery by him of the mortgage to secure the three annual payments of $2,000 each—balance of the purchase money—the appellee, J. George Stamm, execute and deliver to him, the said J.F. Anderson, a deed for the land described in the bill, the costs on this appeal and below to be paid by the appellee.

NOTE ON IMPLIED COVENANT OF GOOD FAITH AND FAIR DEALING

In addition to the applicability of equitable maxims and principles such as "equity abhors a forfeiture," "clean hands," estoppel and waiver, one must also consider the applicability of an *implied covenant of good faith and fair dealing*. In applying this doctrine of good faith and fair dealing, the courts consider and analyze the equities of the parties in the particular case. As a consequence, the courts have looked beyond the actual language of the contract to ascertain what in the specific case constitutes good faith and fair dealing. Indeed, it may be said that the courts uniformly hold that "[a]ll contracts contain an implied covenant of good faith and fair dealing." Hence, since good faith is now considered a doctrine or "covenant" implied in all contracts, it need not be considered strictly as an equitable defense. Indeed, it is statutorily imposed in all contracts covered by the Uniform Commercial Code.

Although not strictly an equitable defense, it is an essential requirement of fairness that is an equitable consideration in the interpretation of the rights and duties of the parties under the contract. Indeed, the *"implied doctrine of good faith and fair dealing"* is now so well established that basic and authoritative sources, under the heading of *good faith, fair dealing and cooperation*, state categorically that

> [e]very contract implies good faith and fair dealing between the parties to it. A duty of co-operation on the part of both parties is also implied in every contract. These principles lead to the implication of various negative covenants, such as that neither party will do anything which will have the effect of destroying or injuring the right of the other party to receive the fruits of the contract, that one party will not intentionally and purposely do anything to prevent the other party from carrying out the agreement on that party's part, and that an innocent party will be protected from overreaching adversaries.

Section 230, Vol. 22 NY JUR. 2d. 1996.

Many cases may be found that have applied the *equitable principles limitation* and *covenant of good faith and fair dealing* in litigation involving the interpretation and enforcement of contracts. See note on applicability of equitable principles. Hence, in interpreting the literal language of contracts, the courts have intervened to give effect to notions of justice and fairness in determining the rights and obligations of parties under a contract. Whether a more specific doctrine, such as "clean hands," waiver, estoppel or "equity abhors a forfeiture," also applies, it is clear that a test of reasonableness and fairness is applied by the courts in a way that may dilute the effect of the literal language of certain obligations as set forth in the contract.

In addition to the equitable principles and doctrines discussed must be added the power of courts, in the exercise of a wise and equitable discretion, to relieve parties of clauses that, if enforced literally, would produce an oppressive and unconscionable result. In view of the fusion or merger of law and equity, in order to reach a fair and equitable result in the decision of all cases, courts apply relevant principles whether formerly denominated "legal" or "equitable." Examples are cases such as Spalding v. Agri–Risk Services, See Note Infra p. 654, involving waiver and estoppel, J.N.A. Realty Corp. v. Cross Bay Chelsea Inc., infra p. 649, involving "equity abhors a forfeiture," Market Street Associates Ltd. v. Frey, p. 556 immediately below applying the "duty of good faith into every contract," and Rogers v. Runfola & Associates, Inc. infra p. 443, in which the court modified, as to "space and time," non-competition covenants in an employment contract because the provisions were "unreasonable" and created an "undue hardship." These cases are illustrative of the modern tendency of the courts in applying doctrines that lead to a fair and equitable result.

———

BREACH OF THE DUTY OF GOOD FAITH

Market Street Associates Ltd. v. Frey

United States Court of Appeals, Seventh Circuit, 1994.
21 F.3d 782.

[Lessee ("Market Street") of commercial property brought suit for specific performance of contract to force sale of the property. Under paragraph 34 of the lease, the lessee could request the lessor (the "Trust") to finance the costs and expenses of improvements upon the premises. If the lessor declined to finance the improvements, the lessee could give notice within 60 days of lessor's rejection that the lessee would purchase the property according to a contractual formula. The market value of the property at the time of the suit was approximately 3 million dollars. The contractual formula specified in paragraph 34 of the lease set the price of the property at roughly 1 million dollars. The District Court denied specific performance, and lessee appealed. The Court of Appeals held that lessee's violation of its duty of good faith in negotiating the financing of improvements (by failing to inform the lessor of its intentions under paragraph 34) precluded specific performance.]

■ HARLINGTON WOOD, JR., CIRCUIT JUDGE.

In 1988 Market Street and the Trust negotiated over the financing of improvements on, or possible sale of, the West Allis property. They did not reach an agreement, and Market Street filed this suit for specific performance of the contract to force sale of the property under the formula contained in paragraph 34. Whether Market Street acted in good faith when negotiating financing terms and, thus, whether they are entitled to specific performance were the issues faced by the district court on remand.

Following a bench trial the district court made key findings of fact concerning the events that occurred between Market Street and the Trust during the negotiation process. These findings are the basis upon which the district court determined that Market Street did not perform the contract in good faith and, thus, was not entitled to specific performance of the contract. The findings of fact focus on the contents and dates of a series of letters and phone calls between Orenstein and David Erb, an investment manager in the real estate department at General Electric Investment Corporation ("Investment Corp."). Investment Corp. serves as the investment advisor to the Trust's Trustees.

Before discussing financing options with the Trust, Market Street inquired into the possible purchase of the property. Market Street wanted to purchase the property because it determined that it would then be easier to finance and eventually sell the property. Orenstein first notified the

Trust by a June 8, 1988, letter to Erb stating that he wished to "open a discussion and perhaps a negotiation" regarding Market Street's possible purchase of the West Allis property. Erb does not remember receiving Orenstein's letter, but testified that his normal practice was to give a copy of such letters to an analyst to review the file so that a response could be prepared. When Erb did not respond to this letter, Orenstein contacted Erb. Erb told Orenstein that someone would get back to him, and then referred the matter to Gregory Fletcher, an investment analyst.

Fletcher called Orenstein on June 29 and told him that the Trust was willing to sell the West Allis property for $3 to $3.1 million. This price was significantly more than the calculated purchase price under paragraph 34 of the lease, though Orenstein testified that he does not remember whether he had calculated the price under paragraph 34 at the time of this correspondence. After receiving Fletcher's call, Orenstein felt the Trust had no interest in continuing negotiations with Market Street.

Market Street then turned its eye towards financing options. In a July 28, 1988 letter to Erb, Orenstein tried to determine whether the Trust was interested in providing financing for improvements to the property. The letter states: Market Street Associates is in the process of negotiating a lease with Phar–Mor, Inc. for an addition to be built at the [West Allis property].... The cost of the addition is ... $2,000,000. We propose to begin construction in September and are presently investigating financing opportunities.... We would like to discuss the financing with you and would appreciate it if you would call us as soon as possible. On behalf of the Trust, in an August 10, 1988 letter, Erb rejected this request for financing because it did not meet the Trust's current investment criteria. Before receiving the Trust's rejection letter, on August 16, 1988, Orenstein wrote a second letter to Erb regarding the proposed financing. He wrote:

By letter dated July 28, 1988, we advised you that Market Street Associates was negotiating a lease with Phar–Mor, Inc. for an addition to the captioned [West Allis] shopping center.... Although we requested that you call us as soon as possible, to date we have had no response. As in all real estate transactions, and especially in this one, timing is crucial. The purpose of this letter is to ask again that you advise us immediately if you are willing to provide the financing pursuant to the lease. If you are willing, we propose to enter into negotiation to amend the ground lease appropriately. If you are unwilling to provide the financing, please let us know that so that we can proceed accordingly. This letter did not refer to paragraph 34 or otherwise mention the buyout clause. This omission, Orenstein testified, is a result of an office practice never to refer to specific lease provisions for fear of referring to the wrong provision or neglecting to reference all relevant portions of the contract or lease.

On August 17, Orenstein received the Trust's August 10 form rejection letter, prompting Orenstein to respond by an August 22 letter in which he expressed disappointment with the Trust's rejection and stated that Market Street would attempt to obtain financing from another source. Orenstein did not mention paragraph 34 until September 27, 1988 when he sent Erb a letter, written by counsel, indicating that Market Street was exercising its option to purchase under that paragraph. Erb testified that it was not until he received this letter that the Trust became aware of paragraph 34.

On December 15, 1988, Erb and Orenstein met in Milwaukee and Erb offered to negotiate financing for the deal. Orenstein refused this offer stating that Market Street had already made previous commitments. When the date for closing arrived, the Trust refused to convey the property. In response, Market Street filed this suit for specific performance of the contract under paragraph 34 asking the court to command sale of the property.

II. Analysis

. . .

Wisconsin law, which governs this case, implies the duty of good faith into every contract. In our first opinion we discussed at length the meaning of the duty of good faith in contract law. Market Street, 941 F.2d at 593–96. Courts use good faith as a protection device to approximate terms not actually contained in the contract, but those that would have been included "expressly if at the time of making the contract [the parties] had had complete knowledge of the future and the costs of negotiating and adding provisions to the contract had been zero." Id. at 596. During the performance of a contract, this duty prohibits one party from taking "deliberate advantage of an oversight by your contract partner concerning his rights under the contract." Id. at 594. Here, the focus of the good faith inquiry should be on the correspondence and conversations that occurred between the parties during the summer and fall of 1988.[2] "The dispositive question in the present case is simply whether Market Street Associates tried to trick the pension trust and succeeded in doing so. If it did, this would be the type of opportunistic behavior in an ongoing contractual relationship that would violate the duty of good faith performance however the duty is formulated." Id. at 596. As we review the facts found by the district court we note that the plaintiffs do not contest any of the district court's findings, only the conclusion or ultimate finding of fact that Orenstein intended to trick the Trust.

Three letters from Orenstein to Erb constitute the extent of Market Street's sharing of information with the Trust, the contents of which are a sound basis upon which the district court determined that Market Street did not act in good faith.

Correspondence began on June 8 when Orenstein, in his letter to Erb, first offered to buy the West Allis property. After an exchange of letters and phone calls between Orenstein and other representatives of the Trust, the Trust offered to sell the property for $3 to $3.1 million dollars, an amount significantly above the paragraph 34 price. Once Orenstein realized that Market Street would not be able to purchase the West Allis property at an acceptable price, he turned to the option of financing. Orenstein's July 28 letter to Erb was the first request to discuss financing the $2 million in

2. ["Every contract implies good faith and fair dealing between the parties. A duty of cooperation on the part of both parties is also implied in every contract." 22 N.Y. Jur. 2d, Contracts, Section 230 (1996).]

proposed improvements to the property. The Trust was not interested in financing projects of less than $10 million and routinely rejected such requests. Accordingly, the Trust sent its form rejection letter on August 10.

But before receiving the August 10 letter, Orenstein sent a letter dated August 16 stating "[t]he purpose of this letter is to ask again that you advise us immediately if you are willing to provide the financing pursuant to the lease." While this is the first time Orenstein mentions the lease, he does not reference paragraph 34 or otherwise identify the buyout provision. One day later, on August 17, Orenstein received the August 10 rejection, and, as found by the district court, at that time knew the Trust was unaware of paragraph 34. Orenstein then sent another letter on August 22 which stated: Although your letter in connection with the captioned matter was dated August 10, 1988, we didn't receive it until August 17th. That was a day after our August 16th letter addressed to you. Apparently the two letters crossed. Anyway, we were sorry to hear that GE is not interested in the financing of our proposed addition in West Allis. We have opened negotiations with Great-West and First Interstate Bank who, as you know, were the principal lenders in our acquisition of the property from J.C. Penney. Orenstein wrote this August 22 letter before giving Erb a chance to respond to the August 16 letter, thereby seizing the opportunity to take advantage of the August 10 rejection letter. He informed the Trust that Market Street was obtaining financing from another source and in doing so, gave the Trust a reason to conclude that they need not take further action or respond to the August 16 letter. After receiving the August 22 letter, as far as the Trust knew, the matter was closed. It was not until September 27 that the trap was sprung and Market Street disclosed its intention to purchase the property pursuant to paragraph 34.

Based on this scenario, the district court found that once Orenstein received the form rejection letter, he knew that the Trust was not operating under paragraph 34, thus implying that Market Street had tried to trick the Trust in violation of the duty of good faith. We see no clear error in this finding of fact, and the district court's judgment is supported by substantial evidence. In fact, plaintiffs agree entirely with these factual findings. Instead plaintiffs complain that the district court did not make a determination about Orenstein's state of mind and intent, the specific purpose for which this Court remanded the case. The district court did, however, make this finding when it concluded that after receiving Erb's August 10 letter, "Orenstein knew that the Trust had not considered paragraph 34." Mem.Op. at 9. The district court further stated: While Orenstein initially assumed that the Trust would review the lease and make its determination as to whether it should provide financing to Market Street in light of paragraph 34, he subsequently recognized that the Trust was not operating under paragraph 34. While Orenstein knew this fact, he did not bring the matter to the Trust's attention, and continued to write ambiguous letters, until he wished to utilize the purchase option, thereby purchasing the property at a discounted cost. By so doing, this court concludes that Orenstein breached his duty to use good faith in his dealings with the Trust, and Market Street is not entitled to specific performance. Id. Implicit in these statements is the finding that Orenstein intended to trick the Trust by implementing a plan designed to acquire a valuable piece of real property at a price substantially below its market value. Even though this finding is taken from the "Conclusions of Law" section of the district court's opinion, it is still a finding of fact, and we will not remand the case simply to allow the district court to extract the factual determinations and place them in the fact section. As evidenced by the district court's numerous citations to our first opinion, it clearly knew its task on remand, followed our instructions, and made the appropriate findings. We will not remand this case again simply to allow the district court to use the explicit language sought by plaintiffs.

As plaintiffs' last argument, they contend that their conduct did not constitute a breach of good faith under the facts found by the district court, focusing our attention on the correspondence that occurred in August, 1988. Plaintiffs argue that even accepting the district court's finding that Orenstein knew the Trust was ignorant of paragraph 34 after receiving the August 10 rejection letter, that this mistake of fact was corrected by Orenstein's August 16 letter to Erb specifically referring to the lease. "Unless one concludes that Orenstein believed that Erb would not even read the letter of August 16, 1988, one cannot conclude that Orenstein believed that after August 19, 1988 [the Trust] was ignorant that financing was being sought pursuant to the Lease." Appellants' Brief at 22–23. This argument misses the mark. It is not the lease that should have been referenced but instead paragraph 34. Alternatively, Orenstein could simply have indicated Market Street's intention to buy the property at the discounted price if the Trust declined the request for financing. Orenstein recognized the importance and implications of paragraph 34 and knew or should have known that the Trust was unaware of the clause. By remaining silent about paragraph 34, the district court determined that he intended to trick the Trust, thus violating Market Street's duty of good faith in performing the contract. The district court could reasonably conclude that the language of Orenstein's letters and the failure to mention paragraph 34 specifically or describe its consequences was intentionally designed to keep the Trust blind and stupid, and that this constitutes a breach of the implied duty of good faith in performance of a contract. It is not the failure to specifically refer to a part of the lease that constitutes the breach, but instead the failure to mention what Market Street clearly preferred to do: purchase the West Allis property at the discounted price calculated under paragraph 34.

We find no clear error in the district court's finding that Orenstein intended to deceive the Trust through a series of vague and ambiguous letters, and took advantage of the Trust's unilateral, inadvertent mistake of fact, thereby violating its duty of good faith in performance of the contract. The record fully supports these findings. Specific performance is therefore not appropriate and the judgment for the defendants is

AFFIRMED.

Dalton v. Educational Testing Service, Appellant.

Court of Appeals of New York, 1995.

87 N.Y.2d 384, 663 N.E.2d 289, 639 N.Y.S.2d 977.

[Student brought suit for specific performance and money damages after testing service refused to release student's Scholastic Aptitude Test

(SAT) scores based on suspicion that imposter had taken second test. The lower court held that testing service breached its contract with student and ordered testing service to release SAT score. The Appellate Division affirmed. Testing service appealed. The Court of Appeals, Kaye, C.J., held that: (1) testing service breached implicit duty of good faith and fair dealing by failing to release score without considering material submitted by student which was relevant to issue of whether he took test, and (2) student was entitled to specific performance consisting of good faith consideration of material he submitted, but not release of his test score.]

■ KAYE, CHIEF JUDGE.

The primary question before us is whether defendant, Educational Testing Service (ETS), a standardized testing firm, complied with procedures specified in its contract with high school senior Brian Dalton in refusing to release Dalton's Scholastic Aptitude Test (SAT) score. Because the factual findings underlying the trial court's determination that ETS failed to act in good faith in following those procedures were affirmed by the Appellate Division, have support in the record and are consequently beyond the scope of our review, we conclude—as did the trial court and Appellate Division—that ETS breached its contract with Dalton. Though we agree, moreover, with the courts below that specific performance is the appropriate remedy, we nevertheless conclude that the promised performance was good-faith compliance with the stated procedures, not release of the questioned scores as ordered by those courts.

I

In May 1991, Brian Dalton took the SAT, which was administered by ETS, at Holy Cross High School in Queens where Dalton was a junior. Six months later, in November, he took the examination a second time, as a senior, this time at John Bowne High School in Queens, and his combined score increased 410 points.

Because Dalton's score increased by more than 350 points, his test results fell within the ETS category of "Large Score Differences" or "discrepant scores." In accordance with ETS policy, members of the ETS Test Security Office therefore reviewed his May and November answer sheets. Upon a finding of disparate handwriting, the answer sheets were submitted to a document examiner, who opined that they were completed by separate individuals. Dalton's case was then forwarded to the Board of Review, which preliminarily decided that substantial evidence supported cancelling Dalton's November score.

Upon registering for the November SAT, Dalton had signed a statement agreeing to the conditions in the New York State edition of the Registration Bulletin, which reserved to ETS "the right to cancel any test score ... if ETS believes that there is reason to question the score's validity." The Registration Bulletin further provided that, if "the validity of a test score is questioned because it may have been obtained unfairly, ETS [will] notif[y] the test taker of the reasons for questioning the score" and offer the test-taker the following five options: (1) the opportunity to provide additional information, (2) confirmation of the score by taking a free retest, (3) authorization for ETS to cancel the score and refund all fees,

(4) third-party review by any institution receiving the test score or (5) arbitration.

As specified in the Registration Bulletin, ETS apprised Dalton of its preliminary decision to cancel his November SAT score in a letter from Test Security Specialist Celeste M. Eppinger. Noting the handwriting disparity and the substantial difference between his May and November test results, Eppinger informed Dalton that "[t]he evidence suggests that someone else may have completed your answer sheet and that the questioned scores may be invalid." She advised him that he could supply "any additional information that will help explain" this or, alternatively, elect one of the other options.

Eppinger enclosed the Procedures for Questioned Scores pamphlet with her letter, which reiterated the test-taker's right to "submit additional relevant information" to the Board of Review supporting the validity of questioned scores. In cautioning test-takers to provide only information "relevant to the questions being raised," the Procedures for Questioned Scores explained, "[f]or example, character references or testimonial letters do not explain handwriting differences." As to the four additional options, the guide further explained, "ETS also offers other options . . . if additional information doesn't resolve the questions about the validity of the scores. The option to provide additional information to resolve these questions may be used in combination with one or more of the[se] options."

Dalton opted to present additional information to the Board of Review, including the following: verification that he was suffering from mononucleosis during the May examination; diagnostic test results from a preparatory course he took prior to the November examination (he had taken no similar course prior to the May SAT) that were consistent with his performance on that test; a statement from an ETS proctor who remembered Dalton's presence during the November examination; and statements from two students—one previously unacquainted with Dalton—that he had been in the classroom during that test. Dalton further provided ETS with a report from a document examiner obtained by his family who concluded that Dalton was the author of both sets of answer sheets.

ETS, after several Board of Review meetings, submitted the various handwriting exemplars to a second document examiner who, like its first, opined that the May and November tests were not completed by the same individual. As a result, ETS continued to question the validity of Dalton's November score.

At this point plaintiff Peter Dalton, father and natural guardian of Brian Dalton, filed a CPLR article 78 proceeding, later converted to an action at law, to prohibit ETS from cancelling Dalton's November SAT score and to compel immediate release of the score. Following a 12–day nonjury trial, the trial court found that ETS failed "to make even rudimentary efforts to evaluate or investigate the information" furnished by Dalton and thus concluded that ETS failed to act in good faith in determining the legitimacy of Dalton's score, thereby breaching its contract (155 Misc 2d 214, 225). The trial court premised this conclusion on its determination that the ETS Board of Review members failed to evaluate the information submitted because they believed Dalton's presence at the November SAT to be wholly irrelevant to the handwriting issue and that he could controvert the Board's preliminary finding that the score was invalid solely by taking a retest. As a remedy for the contractual breach, the trial court ordered ETS to release the November SAT score.

The Appellate Division affirmed. It too found that ETS ignored the documentation provided by Dalton and considered only the reports of its own document examiners. Like the trial court, the Appellate Division concluded that this failure to evaluate as well as to investigate Dalton's information constituted a breach of contract. In light of these factual determinations, we agree that ETS breached its contract with Dalton but differ as to the scope of the relief.

II

By accepting ETS' standardized form agreement when he registered for the November SAT, Dalton entered into a contract with ETS (see, AEB & Assocs. Design Group v. Tonka Corp., 853 F Supp 724, 732). Implicit in all contracts is a covenant of good faith and fair dealing in the course of contract performance (see, Van Valkenburgh, Nooger & Neville v. Hayden Publ. Co., 30 NY2d 34, 45, cert denied 409 US 875).

Encompassed within the implied obligation of each promisor to exercise good faith are " 'any promises which a reasonable person in the position of the promisee would be justified in understanding were included' " (Rowe v. Great Atl. & Pac. Tea Co., 46 NY2d 62, 69, quoting 5 Williston, Contracts § 1293, at 3682 [rev ed 1937]). This embraces a pledge that "neither party shall do anything which will have the effect of destroying or injuring the right of the other party to receive the fruits of the contract" (Kirke La Shelle Co. v. Armstrong Co., 263 NY 79, 87). Where the contract contemplates the exercise of discretion, this pledge includes a promise not to act arbitrarily or irrationally in exercising that discretion (see, Tedeschi v. Wagner Coll., 49 NY2d 652, 659)[*]. The duty of good faith and fair dealing, however, is not without limits, and no obligation can be implied that "would be inconsistent with other terms of the contractual relationship" (Murphy v. American Home Prods. Corp., 58 NY2d 293, 304).

The parties here agreed to the provisions in the Registration Bulletin, which expressly permit cancellation of a test score so long as ETS found "reason to question" its validity after offering the test-taker the five specified options. Nothing in the contract compelled ETS to prove that the test-taker cheated. Nor did the invitation to the test-taker to furnish ETS with relevant information reasonably and realistically translate into any requirement that ETS conduct a field investigation or gather evidence to verify or counter the test-taker's documentation. Indeed, such an obligation would be inconsistent with the contractual language placing the burden squarely on the test-taker to overcome the ETS finding of score invalidity. ETS, therefore, was under no duty, express or implied, to initiate an external investigation into a questioned score.

The contract, however, did require that ETS consider any relevant material that Dalton supplied to the Board of Review. The Registration

---

*   Reprinted at p. 1218.

Bulletin explicitly afforded Dalton the option to provide ETS with relevant information upon notification that ETS questioned the legitimacy of his test score. Having elected to offer this option, it was certainly reasonable to expect that ETS would, at the very least, consider any relevant material submitted in reaching its final decision.

Dalton triggered this implied-in-law obligation on the part of ETS by exercising his contractual option to provide ETS with information (compare, Matter of Yaeger v. Educational Testing Serv., 158 AD2d 602 [where test-taker declined to invoke any of the proffered options, ETS cancelled score in good faith and in accordance with terms of the contract]). Significantly, Dalton heeded the advice in the Procedures for Questioned Scores and tendered numerous documents that did more than simply deny allegations of wrongdoing or attest to his good character, such as medical evidence regarding his physical condition, statements by fellow test-takers, the statement of a classroom proctor and consistent diagnostic test results (compare, Swencki v Educational Testing Serv., No. C 81–0689 [WD KY] [test-taker sent letter to ETS explaining that he could not have cheated]; Matter of K. D. v. Educational Testing Serv., 87 Misc 2d 657 [test-taker submitted sworn statement that he did not cheat]).

Nevertheless, with the exception of the document examiner's report, ETS disputes the relevancy of this information. Specifically, ETS maintains that the sole issue before the Board of Review was the disparate handwriting and that evidence regarding Dalton's health (apart from a damaged arm) or presence during both examinations is irrelevant to resolving that issue.

To be sure, the Procedures for Questioned Scores warned Dalton "to provide only additional information that is relevant to the questions being raised." The Eppinger letter to Dalton, however, informed him that his November score was possibly invalid precisely because ETS believed "that someone else may have completed [his] answer sheet." Thus, ETS expressly framed the dispositive question as one of suspected impersonation. Because the statements from the classroom proctor and November test-takers corroborated Dalton's contention that he was present at and in fact took the November examination, they were relevant to this issue.

Likewise, inasmuch as the medical documentation concerning Dalton's health at the time of the May SAT provided an explanation for his poor performance on that examination, and the consistent diagnostic test results demonstrated his ability to achieve such a dramatic score increase, these items were also germane to the question whether it was Dalton or an imposter who completed the November examination. Indeed, in its manual, Policies and Procedures Concerning Scores of Questionable Validity—which details internal ETS procedure regarding questioned scores—ETS offers several examples of "relevant information" that a test-taker might provide, including "a doctor's report that the candidate was under the influence of medication at the time the low score was earned." Regarding "a case of possible impersonation" in particular, the manual suggests that "other test results might demonstrate that the questioned score is not inconsistent with other measures of the candidate's abilities." Thus, Dalton's material fell within ETS' own definition of relevancy, as expressed in its manual and letter to Dalton.

The critical question then is whether the Board of Review made any effort to consider this relevant information submitted by Dalton. That is a factual inquiry. Both the trial court and the Appellate Division concluded that the Board utterly failed to evaluate the material. Given these affirmed findings, "our scope of review is narrow. This Court is without power to review findings of fact if such findings are supported by evidence in the record" (Humphrey v. State of New York, 60 NY2d 742, 743).

Several Board of Review members—each member alone had the power to order release of Dalton's November score—testified that they believed information establishing Dalton's presence during the November examination to be irrelevant to their determination and, moreover, that only a successful retest would validate Dalton's score. Thus, there is support in the record for the factual determinations of the trial court and Appellate Division and they are binding on us. This is so notwithstanding inconsistent testimony by Board members that the Board did review Dalton's information but found it unpersuasive. In light of the affirmed findings, the Court of Appeals simply does not have authority to weigh conflicting evidence and make its own factual determinations, as the dissent would do.

Consequently, this case is factually distinct from those relied upon by ETS, where the testing service considered but then rejected information provided by the test-taker (see, e.g., Langston v. ACT, 890 F2d 380; Denburg v. Educational Testing Serv., No. C–1715–83 [NJ Super Ct]; cf., Johnson v. Educational Testing Serv., 754 F2d 20, 26, cert denied 472 US 1029 [noting that ETS provided test-taker with opportunity to be heard and to be represented by counsel]). When ETS fulfills its contractual obligation to consider relevant material provided by the test-taker and otherwise acts in good faith, the testing service—not the courts—must be the final arbiter of both the appropriate weight to accord that material and the validity of the test score. This Court will not interfere with that discretionary determination unless it is performed arbitrarily or irrationally.

Where, however, ETS refuses to exercise its discretion in the first instance by declining even to consider relevant material submitted by the test-taker, the legal question is whether this refusal breached an express or implied term of the contract, not whether it was arbitrary or irrational. Here, the courts below agreed that ETS did not consider the relevant information furnished by Dalton. By doing so, ETS failed to comply in good faith with its own test security procedures, thereby breaching its contract with Dalton.

. . .

In an analogous context, we have refused to compel a university to issue a degree to a student who had not fulfilled the academic requirements (see, Matter of Olsson v. Board of Higher Educ., 49 NY2d 408). This reluctance to interfere with the exercise of academic discretion is motivated by sound considerations of public policy. "When an educational institution issues a diploma to one of its students, it is, in effect, certifying to society that the student possesses all of the knowledge and skills that are required by his [or her] chosen discipline'' (id., at 413). Likewise, we have held that a college did not act arbitrarily in declining to ''round off'' a student's failing grade so that she could graduate (see, Matter of McIntosh v. Borough of Manhattan Community Coll., 78 AD2d 839, affd 55 NY2d 913).

The comparison between ETS and academic institutions is surely not exact, inasmuch as judicial restraint in matters of academic achievement is based, in part, on the inherently subjective nature of the evaluation to be made by professional educators (see, Tedeschi v. Wagner Coll., 49 NY2d 652, 658, supra). Still, similar policy concerns militate against directing ETS to release a questioned score. When a standardized testing service reports a score, it certifies to the world that the test-taker possesses the requisite knowledge and skills to achieve the particular score. Like academic credentials, if courts were to require testing services to release questioned scores, ''the value of these credentials from the point of view of society would be seriously undermined'' (Olsson, supra, at 413). Given the reliance that students, educational institutions, prospective employers and others place on the legitimacy of scores released by ETS, requiring challenged scores to be reported would be contrary to the public interest and exceed the scope of ETS' promised performance.

While courts as a matter of policy are reluctant to intrude upon academic discretion in educational matters, they stand ready as a matter of law and equity to enforce contract rights. Where a contract is breached, moreover, and the injured party is entitled to specific performance, the remedy must be a real one, not an exercise in futility.

Dalton is entitled to relief that comports with ETS' contractual promise—good-faith consideration of the material he submitted to ETS. We cannot agree with Dalton's assumption that ETS will merely rubber-stamp its prior determination without good-faith attention to his documentation and that reconsideration by ETS will be an empty exercise. Our conclusion that the contract affords Dalton a meaningful remedy rests also on the provision in the Procedures for Questioned Scores allowing Dalton to utilize one or more of the remaining four options in combination with renewed consideration by the Board of Review. Those options—including third-party review by any institution receiving the test score as well as arbitration—remain available should ETS determine that the information submitted fails to resolve its concerns about the validity of the November score.

Accordingly, the Appellate Division order should be modified in accordance with this opinion and, as so modified, affirmed, without costs.

■ LEVINE, JUDGE, dissenting.

I agree with the majority that the Educational Testing Service (ETS) had no duty, express or implied, to investigate the information submitted by Brian Dalton. However, I do not agree that we are bound by the factual determinations of the lower courts, which are based on an erroneous legal standard, or that the record contains any evidence that ETS arbitrarily failed to consider the materials submitted by Dalton. I, therefore, respectfully dissent.

. . .

■ JUDGES TITONE, BELLACOSA, SMITH and CIPARICK concur with CHIEF JUDGE KAYE; JUDGE LEVINE dissents and votes to reverse in a separate opinion in which JUDGE SIMONS concurs.

Order modified in accordance with the opinion herein and, as so modified, affirmed, without costs.

NOTE ON IMPLIED COVENANT OF GOOD FAITH AND "EMPLOYMENT AT WILL DOCTRINE"

1.   Wieder v. Skala, 80 N.Y.2d 628, 609 N.E.2d 105, 593 N.Y.S.2d 752 (1992). Plaintiff, a member of the Bar, sued his former employer, a law firm, claiming that he was wrongfully discharged as an associate because of his insistence that the firm comply with the governing disciplinary rules by reporting professional misconduct allegedly committed by another associate. The question presented was whether plaintiff stated a claim for relief either for breach of contract or for the tort of wrongful discharge in violation of the State's public policy. The lower courts dismissed both causes of action as legally insufficient on the strength of the State's employment-at-will doctrine.

Plaintiff asserted that he was wrongfully discharged as a result of his insistence that the misconduct of an associate be reported as required by DR 1–103 (A) of the Code of Professional Responsibility. In the fifth cause of action, plaintiff claimed that his discharge was in violation of public policy and constituted a tort for which he sought compensatory and punitive damages.

Concluding that plaintiff failed to state a cause of action because, as an at-will employee, the firm could terminate him without cause, the lower courts dismissed.

On appeal the question was "whether, notwithstanding our firmly established employment-at-will doctrine, plaintiff has stated a legal claim for breach of contract. . . ." The highest court of the State reversed, stating that "[I]t is the law that in 'every contract there is an implied undertaking on the part of each party that he will not intentionally and purposely do anything to prevent the other party from carrying out the agreement on his part'. . . . The idea is simply that when A and B agree that B will do something it is understood that A will not prevent B from doing it. The concept is rooted in notions of common sense and fairness (see, Farnsworth, The Law of Contracts Section 7.16, at 524 [1982]). 'What courts are doing [when an omitted term is implied'], Professor Corbin explains, 'whether calling the process "implication" of promises, or interpreting the requirements of "good faith," as the current fashion may be, is but a recognition that the parties occasionally have understanding or expectations that were so fundamental that they did not need to negotiate about those expectations'. . . . Just such fundamental understanding, though unexpressed, was inherent in the relationship, between plaintiff and defendant law firm. . . . Defendants hired plaintiff to practice law, and this objective was the only basis for the employment relationship. Intrinsic to this relationship, of course, was the unstated but essential compact that in conducting the firms' legal practice both the plaintiff and the firm would do so in compliance with the prevailing rules of conduct and ethical standards of the profession."

Hence, the court stated that "the case is distinguishable from [those cases] where giving effect to the implied obligation would have been 'inconsistent with' and 'destructive of' an elemental term in the [at will employment] agreement. We conclude, therefore, that plaintiff has stated a valid claim for breach of contract based on an implied-in-law obligation in his relationship with defendants." Wieder v. Skala, 80 N.Y.2d 628, 637, 638, 593 N.Y.S.2d 752, 609 N.E.2d 105 (1992).

2. Horn v. The New York Times, 100 N.Y.2d 85, 790 N.E.2d 753, 760 N.Y.S.2d 378 (2003). The recent case of Horn v. The New York Times is important because it considered the applicability of the exception of the "hiring at will doctrine" enunciated in Wieder v. Skala. Under the "at will" doctrine, an employee not hired for a specific term but "at will" may be discharged "without any cause." An exception to the ability to discharge the employee "at will," i.e., without cause, is found in Wieder v. Skala, a case that dealt with the discharge of a lawyer who was a member and employee of a law firm. The recent Horn case must be reconciled because the court did not apply the exception that was enunciated in the Wieder v. Skala case to the New York rule relating to the "employment at will doctrine."

In a nutshell, the question raised in Horn was whether the exception enunciated in Wieder, relating to the New York rule as to employment at will, should be "extended" or "expanded" and applied to a "physician" employed by a non-medical corporate entity. The Supreme Court of the State of New York (the trial court) held that the Wieder exception applied to a lawyer should also apply to a physician. The Appellate Division (two judges dissenting) affirmed, and subsequently certified the following question to the Court of Appeals (the highest court of the State).

"Was the order of the Appellate Division which affirmed the order of the Supreme Court properly made?"

In an opinion by Judge Read, the Court of Appeals reversed the order of the Appellate Division and answered the certified question in the negative. Judge Smith of the Court of Appeals dissented and voted to affirm. Chief Judge Kaye took no part.

In summary, the Wieder case established an exception to the "at will employment doctrine" on the basis of the ethical duties and professional responsibilities that were known to the parties, and were therefore implied conditions of the contract of employment with the lawyer's law firm.

In Wieder the Court of Appeals held that, a law firm that employed a lawyer, could not discharge a lawyer at will, i.e., a lawyer of the firm if the reason or purpose was to prevent the lawyer from adhering to or complying with a professional responsibility or duty set forth in the canons of legal or professional ethics. Hence, the Wieder Court held that, by virtue of the doctrine of good faith and fair dealing, the professional and ethical responsibilities and duties of the lawyer had to be complied with, and the law firm could not discharge a lawyer because the lawyer insisted on complying with the rules and canons of ethics of the legal profession.

It is essential to note the factual differences of the two cases. In the Horn case the plaintiff was not a lawyer working for a law firm but a medical doctor employed by the New York Times, a non-medical entity. The duties of Dr. Horn were to give an opinion or to determine whether an illness or injury sustained by an employee of the New York Times was "work related." The purpose of the opinion of Dr. Horn was to determine whether the employee would be entitled to receive Workers Compensation benefits. The Court of Appeals in Horn held that the doctor was not entitled to receive Workers Compensation benefits. The Court of Appeals in Horn held that the doctor was not entitled to the exception to the "at will doctrine" as set forth in the Wieder cases. The majority opinion in Horn indicated clearly that the court did not wish to expand or extend the exception set forth in Wieder to the "at will" employment doctrine that prevails in the State of New York.

Judge Smith, who believed that the application of the doctrine to the Horn case would not be an expansion, in the dissenting opinion set forth the reasons why, in his opinion, the Wieder exception should have been applied to Dr. Horn, who was a physician.

Is there not a vast difference between a lawyer being employed by a law firm, as in Wieder, and a medical doctor being employed by a non medical entity to perform a limited function of giving an opinion to help the employer make a corporate management decision?

The medical doctor in Horn served a specific and limited purpose i.e., to give an opinion or whether an illness or injury sustained by an employee of the New York Times was "work related" for the sole purpose of determining eligibility for Worker's Compensation benefits. Hence, the determination, although of a medical nature, was merely for the purpose of determining a corporate management decision and not for the medical or health benefit of a "patient," i.e., the employee who had sustained an injury. Hence, it was not a professional medical decision essential to the core values and mission of the medical profession.

Would you agree with the holding of the court in Horn because in that case the doctor was not employed as a physician for the benefit of the health and well being of the patient, but was employed in a capacity to assist the employer in the making of a corporate decision?

BREACH OF A FIDUCIARY DUTY

Firebaugh v. Hanback

Supreme Court of Virginia, 1994.
247 Va. 519, 443 S.E.2d 134.

[Real estate brokers brought action seeking specific performance of contract to purchase real estate owned by their principal. Brokers marketed property for principal as a sale in gross, not per acre. The principals believed the property to be roughly 126 acres in size. Several buyers expressed an interest in the property but declined to go to contract. The brokers finally extended an offer to purchase land themselves and went to contract with the principals. A subsequent survey revealed that the property was only 89.5 acres, and brokers sued for specific performance of the contract with an abatement of the purchase price. The trial court denied brokers request for specific performance because of their inequitable conduct. The Supreme Court held that agents, who breached fiduciary duty owed to principal, were not entitled to specific performance of contract.]

■ POFF, SENIOR JUSTICE.

We awarded this appeal to consider whether two real estate agents who had entered into a contract to purchase real estate owned by their principal were entitled to specific performance of that contract. We will uphold the chancellor's judgment denying the prayer of the purchasers' bill of complaint.

The chancellor based his decision on a finding that the agents breached the fiduciary duty they owed to their principal. We will summarize the evidence underlying that finding as it was adduced in hearings conducted by a commissioner in chancery.

Eugene D. Lunsford, a licensed real estate agent associated with Real Estate III, solicited a listing agreement for his firm from Edwin Murray Hanback and John C. Richards, Trustees for Ye Old Hunters Club (the club). In its original form dated April 2, 1990, the agreement listed for sale "126.669 acres located on the East side of Route 600 South of Deerfield". Lunsford mailed a copy of that form to Quinlan H. Hancock, one of the five members of the club. In a letter to Lunsford, Hancock returned what he identified as a "modified listing agreement which is necessary under the circumstances." The description of the property was modified by a handwritten note to read "126.669 acres plus or minus", and the date of the document was changed to May 15, 1990.

The evidence showed that, following an appraisal performed on site by Richard C. Firebaugh, the club had acquired the property in 1973. The deed, which reserved life estates to the grantors and the survivor, described the property as "120.80 acres, more or less, this being a sale in gross and not by the acre, and being ... a tract formerly containing 193.80 acres, more or less". Lunsford had obtained the information required to draft the listing agreement by examining that deed and the county tax records. Those records showed that the club had paid all annual assessments against property identified as containing 126.669 acres.

In September 1990, Lunsford enclosed in a letter to Hancock a written offer to purchase signed by Raymond R. Wittekind and Margaret B. Wittekind. As drafted the offer identified the property as "126 acres more or less" but provided: Seller to provide purchaser at closing with boundary survey not more than 10 years old. If not available Purchaser and Seller to equally share the cost of a new survey. Deviations in acreage in excess of 10 acres shall increase the purchase price by $500 per acre for overage and decrease the price by $500 per acre for underage. In a letter to Lunsford dated September 11, 1990, Hancock returned the document, executed as a contract by Hanback and Richards, but in a modified form. The language concerning a survey and its effect upon the purchase price was stricken and the deletions were initialed by the trustees of the club. In his letter, Hancock stated that he could "only represent that the acreage is the same as when we acquired it" and that the "executed contract" was "for the sale of the . . . farm in an 'as is' condition." Hancock explained at the hearing that "what I mean by that [language] is just exactly what was there" and that he had "communicated" that meaning to Lunsford "[m]any, many times."

The Wittekinds signed a counter offer at a higher price, and Lunsford submitted it to the club. Hancock testified that this offer "was rejected by the members because it had a provision that deviation in acreage from 126 acres of five acres or more . . . shall result in a price adjustment". Further, he stated that he "again, explained to Mr. Lunsford . . . the fact that we were selling the farm as such, without regard to acreage".

In a telephone conversation conducted with Hancock in November 1990, Lunsford relayed a third offer at a still higher price submitted by the Wittekinds. As appears from the exhibit introduced at the hearing, the document contained similar language concerning a survey and acreage deviation price changes as that included in the two prior Wittekind offers, and the club rejected that offer as well.

Lunsford testified that the cause of the failure to obtain a final contract with the Wittekinds was "not being able to get a release signed on [the life estate]" and that Hancock had "said he and the Hunt Club would pay half of [the cost of a survey]." Asked if he had discussed such a solution with Lunsford, Hancock replied, "Absolutely not."

In December 1990, Lunsford referred to trustees of the club an offer made by a third party. That offer described the property as "126 acres, Map #40–46" and contained no language concerning a survey or acreage deviation. The club rejected that offer but only because it contained a provision for deferred payment of a portion of the purchase price.

The listing agreement the club executed in May 1990 with Real Estate III expired on December 31, 1990. Lunsford prepared an extension agreement dated January 1, 1991. His description of the property failed to include the words "plus or minus" which Hancock had added to the original draft of the listing agreement. Lunsford acknowledged at the hearing that he had signed the names of the trustees of the club to the extension agreement without their permission.

Lunsford left Real Estate III and joined Richard C. Firebaugh in the firm of Dick Firebaugh Real Estate, Inc. Lunsford explained to Firebaugh the reasons he had been unsuccessful in his attempts to negotiate a sale of the club's farm. At Lunsford's invitation, the club executed a listing agreement with his new firm. After taking a view of the farm, Firebaugh and Lunsford became interested in acquiring the property themselves.

Lunsford testified that he and Firebaugh "discussed the writing of the contract" and that "he told me what to put on the contract." Lunsford's wife filled in the blank spaces on the printed form as he instructed. Lunsford testified that "Mr. Firebaugh looked at it, was not happy with it, changed some of the things on it'' and that ''[w]e redid it at least once, maybe twice.''

As submitted to the club, the contract, dated April 20, 1991, defined the term ''real property'' as ''the land, and all improvements thereon ... described as ... 126 acres, more or less''. The contract further provided that the ''[p]roperty is being purchased in 'as is' condition unless otherwise noted'', fixed the purchase price at $110,000, and waived the broker's commission.

The trustees executed the contract in that form. Hancock testified that his understanding was that the club was selling ''exactly what we got from [the prior owners], regardless of what it was'', and that he assumed that the closing attorney would insert a provision in the deed identifying the transaction as a sale in gross.

Lunsford and Firebaugh construed the language of the contract differently. Lunsford testified that ''had we been buying the property by the gross, I would have put [it] in [the contract]''. Reaffirming his earlier testimony, Hancock said that he intended the ''as is'' language to address the acreage as well as the condition of the premises and that the subject of the sale was to be ''something close to the acreage that's in the contract.'' Hancock added that the purchasers' interpretation of the language of the contract was not communicated to the trustees of the club before they signed the document.

After the trustees signed, the purchasers employed Robert E. Funk to conduct a survey. Funk reported that his preliminary calculations showed that the farm contained only 89.5 acres, and the purchasers did not close the sale on the date scheduled. The purchasers' attorney advised the club by letter that there was a ''deficiency in acreage of 36.5 acres'' and that Firebaugh and Lunsford were prepared to close at a later date at an ''abated purchase price of $90,967.80''.

The club refused a tender of a cashier's check for that amount, and the purchasers filed a bill of complaint asking the court to ''order the Defendants specifically to perform the contract and ... order an abatement in the purchase price of $19,032.20''. In responsive pleadings seeking, inter alia, rescission of the contract, the trustees of the club alleged that Firebaugh and Lunsford had breached a duty as their agents ''to advise [them] that they ... considered the offer to be a sale by the acre rather than in gross.''

A commissioner in chancery conducted a hearing on the questions framed by the parties and issued his report. The commissioner found that the contract contemplated a sale by the acre; that the acreage deficiency was approximately 30%; that the purchasers were entitled to specific performance with an abatement in the purchase price; that a survey should be completed in order to determine the amount of the abatement; and that neither party is liable to the other for costs.

In a letter opinion, the chancellor ruled: The exceptions ... are sustained to the extent that they object to the ruling that the plaintiffs performed all fiduciary duties owed to the defendants. Having breached their duties, the plaintiffs are not entitled to specific performance of the contract. Having breached the contract, they are not now entitled to enforce it according to the original terms and conditions....

. . .

Our review of the record shows that the purchasers intended the contract they drafted and revised to be a contract of sale by the acre rather than a sale in gross; that the purchasers were aware that the sellers, who had repeatedly rejected other contract offers containing explicit provisions for a survey and a sale by the acre, intended to execute nothing other than a contract of sale in gross; and that the purchasers failed to advise the sellers of their interpretation of the language they had chosen until the trustees of the club had executed what they thought was a contract of sale in gross.

Firebaugh and Lunsford were engaged by the owners in the listing agreement as their selling agents. "An agent is a fiduciary with respect to the matters within the scope of his agency." H–B Partnership v. Wimmer, 220 Va. 176, 179, 257 S.E.2d 770, 773 (1979). As a fiduciary, a broker owes his principal the duty to use utmost fidelity to him and must disclose to him all facts within the broker's knowledge which may be material to the transaction, or which might influence the principal in deciding upon a course of action.

As a general rule, it is true, as the purchasers say, that [w]hen the seller is unable to convey the entire estate in the land that he has contracted to sell, the buyer may compel the seller to convey whatever estate he may have and the buyer will be allowed an abatement of the purchase price to compensate him for the deficiency in title.

However, we have recognized exceptions to the general rule. Specific performance of a contract is not a matter of right, but rests in the discretion of the trial court to be granted or refused according to established principles and the facts of each case. Thus, we have denied specific performance of contracts executed under a mutual mistake of fact.

"[H]e who asks equity must do equity, and he who comes into equity must come with clean hands." Walker v. Henderson, 151 Va. 913, 927–28, 145 S.E. 311, 315 (1928) The court in Walker explained that "[f]ailure to communicate facts material under the circumstances, or conduct leading to misapprehension, may influence a court to refuse specific performance." Id. at 931, 145 S.E. at 316. Reaffirming this principle, we have recently held that a court of equity may be justified in applying the "clean hands" doctrine against a litigant who fails to communicate material facts, even when he owes no fiduciary duty to do so.

As we have said, Firebaugh and Lunsford had a fiduciary relationship with the club. We are of opinion that the record fully supports the chancellor's conclusion that the purchasers breached their fiduciary duties and, applying the "clean hands" doctrine, we hold that a correct application of the law supports the chancellor's decision that the purchasers "are not entitled to specific performance of the contract ... [or] to enforce it according to the original terms and conditions."

. . .

Affirmed.

––––––––

NOTES ON NONDISCLOSURE AND FIDUCIARY DUTIES

1. THE FIDUCIARY RELATION—CARDOZO, THE NATURE OF THE JUDICIAL PROCESS 109–10 (1922): "Some relations in life impose a duty to act in accordance with the customary morality and nothing more. In those the customary morality must be the standard for the judge. *Caveat emptor* is a maxim that will often have to be followed when the morality which it expresses is not that of sensitive souls. Other relations in life, as, e.g., those of trustee and beneficiary, or principal and surety, impose a duty to act in accordance with the highest standards which a man of the most delicate conscience and the nicest sense of honor might impose upon himself. In such cases, to enforce adherence to those standards becomes the duty of the judge."

CARDOZO, C.J. in Meinhard v. Salmon, 249 N.Y. 458, 164 N.E. 545 (1928): "Many forms of conduct permissible in a workaday world for those acting at arm's length, are forbidden to those bound by fiduciary ties. A trustee is held to something stricter than the morals of the marketplace. Not honesty alone, but the punctilio of an honor most sensitive, is then the standard of behavior."

2. The Securities and Exchange Commission sought a preliminary injunction requiring a registered investment adviser "to disclose to his clients, not all his security holdings, but only his dealings in recommended securities just before and after the issuance of his recommendations." The trial court denied this relief and the court of appeals affirmed its decision. Both courts felt that the defendant's conduct was not "fraud" or "deceit" within the meaning of the applicable statute. The Supreme Court reversed. Securities and Exchange Commission v. Capital Gains Research Bureau, Inc., 375 U.S. 180, 84 S.Ct. 275, 11 L.Ed.2d 237 (1963). Responding to the lower courts' assertion that a broader reading of the statute would be "in derogation of the common law of fraud," Goldberg, J., wrote:

> To the contrary, it finds support in the process by which the courts have adapted the common law of fraud to the commercial transactions of our society. It is true that at common law intent and injury have been deemed essential elements in a damage suit between parties to an arm's-length transaction. But this [is] ... not such an action....

The content of common-law fraud has not remained static as the courts below seem to have assumed. It has varied, for example, with the nature of the relief sought, the relationship between the parties, and the merchandise in issue. It is not necessary in a suit for equitable or prophylactic relief to establish all the elements required in a suit for monetary damages.

"Law had come to regard fraud ... as primarily a tort, and hedged about with stringent requirements, the chief of which was a strong moral, or rather immoral element, while equity regarded it, as it had all along regarded it, as a conveniently comprehensive word for the expression of a lapse from the high standard of conscientiousness that it exacted from any party occupying a certain contractual or fiduciary relation towards another party.''[4]

. . . .

Nor is it necessary in a suit against a fiduciary, which Congress recognized the investment adviser to be, to establish all the elements required in a suit against a party to an arm's-length transaction. Courts have imposed on a fiduciary an affirmative duty of "utmost good faith, and full and fair disclosure of all material facts,''[5] as well as an affirmative obligation "to employ reasonable care to avoid misleading''[6] his clients. There has also been a growing recognition by common-law courts that the doctrines of fraud and deceit which developed around transactions involving land and other tangible items of wealth are illsuited to the sale of such intangibles as advice and securities, and that, accordingly, the doctrines must be adapted to the merchandise in issue. . . .

3.   2 J. KENT, COMMENTARIES *490–91 and n. (d) (12th ed. 1873), (after saying that a sale would not be rescinded for the purchaser's nondisclosure of a mine, not known to the seller): "From this and other cases it would appear, that human laws are not so perfect as the dictates of conscience; and the sphere of morality is more enlarged than the limits of civil jurisdiction. There are many duties that belong to the class of imperfect obligations, which are binding on conscience, but which human laws do not, and cannot undertake directly to enforce. But when the aid of a court of equity is sought, to carry into execution such a contract, then the principles of ethics have a more extensive sway; and a purchase, made with such a reservation of superior knowledge, would be of too sharp a character to be aided and forwarded in its execution by the powers of the Court of Chancery. . . . It is a rule in equity, that all the material facts must be known to both parties, to render the agreement fair and just in all its parts; and it is against all the principles of equity, that one party, knowing a material ingredient in an agreement, should be permitted to suppress it, and still call for specific performance. . . .

"Cicero de Officiis, lib. 3 sec. 12–17, states the case of a corn-merchant of Alexandria arriving at Rhodes in a time of great scarcity, with a cargo of grain, and with knowledge that a number of other vessels, with similar cargoes, had already sailed from Alexandria for Rhodes, and which he had passed on the voyage. He then puts the question, whether the Alexandrian merchant was bound in conscience to inform the buyers of that fact, or to keep silence, and sell his wheat for an extravagant price; and he answers it by saying, that, in his opinion, good faith would require of a just and candid man, a frank disclosure of the fact.''[7]

4.   J.N. POMEROY, SPECIFIC PERFORMANCE 634n (3d ed. 1926), "It will be observed that in most cases where specific performance was refused because of non-disclosure by the vendee, such non-disclosure was coupled

---

4.   Hanbury, Modern Equity 643 (8th ed. 1962).

5.   Prosser, Law of Torts 534–35 (1955)(citing cases).

6.   1 Harper and James, The Law of Torts 541 (1956).

7.   [Kent goes on to say that Grotius, Pufendorf, Pothier, and others dissent from Cicero's opinion.]

with other facts of inequality between the parties, inadequacy of price so as to work hardship on the vendor, overreaching or 'sharp practice' so as to render the contract unfair and relief inequitable.''

B.   MISTAKE

1.   MISTAKE AS A GROUND FOR RESCISSION OR REFORMATION

Mistake of one or both parties in connection with the formation or attempted formation of a contract may have various effects:

(1) *Mistake may prevent there being any contract at law.* The classic case of this sort is Raffles v. Wichelhaus, 2 H. & C. 906 (1864), where the parties had contracted for a cargo by the ship "Peerless" from Bombay. There were two ships from Bombay of that name, and each party understood a different ship. The court held that no contract had been made.

(2) It has been suggested that *mistake may prevent there being any contract in equity.* Under this view, although there may be an unambiguous concurrence of expressed intents, yet if there is no "meeting of the minds" because the parties did not mean the same thing, there is said to be "no contract in equity" on the theory that equity looks at the substance and not at the outward acts. If this view be accepted, equity will of course deny specific performance in such a case, and, it would seem, might well grant rescission, although, in strict theory, cancellation would appear to be the more appropriate remedy. But it is now generally recognized that the requisites for a valid contract are the same at law and in equity in all ordinary cases, and the requirement of actual mental assent for a valid contract, even in equity, seems clearly out of accord with the modern theory of contracts.

(3) Mistake may result in erroneous integration of a contract actually made—i.e., the written embodiment of the contract may be a contract of a different sort, as where V agrees to sell and P to purchase Blackacre and the written contract calls for the sale and purchase of Whiteacre. Here the appropriate remedy is reformation. *See* Nash v. Kornblum, p. 576 *infra*.

(4) Even in the case of a contract which the parties intended to and did make and which is properly reduced to writing, there may be *mistake such as will be ground for rescission in equity.* Thus, if there is a mutual mistake as to some essential feature of the transaction (such as, e.g., it nature, object or personnel), either party may apply for a rescission of the contract.

(5) *Mistake knowingly induced is equivalent to fraud, and hence ground for rescission.*

(6) *Mistake may be such as to bar specific performance.* The cases in this section will not only show the circumstances under which

rescission or reformation may be granted, but also that "specific performance will be denied upon less proof than is required to set aside a contract."

RESCISSION

Costello v. Sykes

Supreme Court of Minnesota, 1919.
143 Minn. 109, 172 N.W. 907.

Action in the district court for Hennepin county to cancel a sale of bank stock and to recover $1,300. . . .

■ LEES, C. Appeal from order sustaining a demurrer to the complaint on the ground that it failed to state a cause of action. In substance the material allegations are as follows:

> The Calhoun State Bank was a Minnesota banking corporation, having, according to its books, a paid-in capital of $35,000, a surplus of $5,250 and undivided profits of $6,000. Respondents were stockholders. The par value of a share of stock was $100. If the bank's capital was unimpaired and it had the surplus and undivided profits shown by its books, a share of stock was worth at least $136. Respondents sold ten shares of stock to appellant for $1,360. At the time of the sale the parties to the transaction believed that the bank's capital had not been impaired; that its assets and liabilities were as set forth in its books; that it had the surplus and profits referred to; that its books were kept correctly, and that the book value of its stock was not less than $136 per share. In fact it had neither surplus nor undivided profits. Its employees had kept its books so as to conceal defalcations of which they were guilty, and its assets had been depleted until its stock was worth but $60 per share. Such employees are insolvent and there is no way of making good their defalcations. The parties to the sale were mutually mistaken as to the assets of the bank, the actual value and the book value of its stock, and the amount of its surplus and undivided profits. Upon discovering the truth, appellant tendered the stock to respondents and demanded repayment of the purchase price, and, his demand being refused, sues for a rescission of the contract of sale.

The sole question presented is whether the mistake alleged is of such a character as to give rise to a right to rescind.

The subject matter of the contract of sale was ten shares of the capital stock of the bank. There was no mistake as to its identity or existence. A mistake relating merely to the attributes, quality or value of the subject of a sale does not warrant a rescission. Neither does a mistake respecting something which was a matter of inducement to the making of the contract, where the means of information were open alike to both parties and each was equally innocent and there was no concealment of facts and no imposition.

A leading case is Kennedy v. Panama, etc., Mail Co., L.R. 2 Q.B. Cas. 580. Like the one at bar, it involved a contract for the sale of corporate stock. The corporation owned and operated a line of steamships. Both parties *bona fide* believed that it had obtained a valuable contract to carry government mails, but it turned out that the contract was made without authority. The government refused to ratify it, and so the value of the stock was much less than the parties supposed. It was contended, as it is here, that there was a difference in substance between shares in a company with and shares in a company without such a contract; that this was a difference which went to the very root of the matter involved, and that, therefore, the purchaser was entitled to rescind. The contention did not meet with the court's approval, and it was held that the case was one of innocent misapprehension, that a rescission could not be had, and that there was not such a complete difference in substance between what was supposed to be and what was taken as would constitute a failure of consideration. The purchaser got the very shares he intended to buy and they were far from being of no value.

Such are the facts in the case at bar, for appellant got the shares he intended to buy. His complaint is that they are worth but $60, instead of $136 each. The *Kennedy* case has been widely and approvingly cited by courts of last resort in this country....

. . . .

... The weight of authority is with the respondents so far as the general principle under consideration is here involved.

If the question were one of first impression, we should not be inclined to open up a new field for litigation by adopting the rule that a contract for the sale of corporate stock may be rescinded merely because both parties were mistaken about the nature or extent of the assets or liabilities of the corporation, if the means of information are open alike to both and there is no concealment of facts or imposition. Upon the sale of a note both parties may be mistaken as to the solvency of the maker or of an indorser or guarantor of payment, and may deal on the assumption that the paper is good, when in fact the unknown insolvency of the parties liable for its payment makes it worthless.

In the absence of fraud or inequitable conduct on the part of the seller of property of that kind, we had supposed the buyer could not have a rescission. He can always protect himself against possible loss by requiring the seller to guarantee or secure the payment of the paper. We think this should be the rule when stock in a corporation is the subject of a contract of sale, and conclude that the learned trial judge correctly disposed of the case and the order sustaining the demurrer is affirmed.

■ HALLAM, J. I dissent. In my opinion the following statement by Williston:

"If parties enter into a bargain on the assumption that certain things are true, it is inequitable to enforce the bargain, to allow it to stand, if the mistake relates to a matter so fundamental that it must be assumed that the parties would not have entered into the transaction had they known the truth." Williston on Sales, § 656.

And the following statement by Benjamin:

> "When there has been a common mistake as to some essential fact forming an inducement to the sale, that is, when the circumstances justify the inference that no contract would have been made if the whole truth had been known to the parties, the sale is voidable." Benjamin on Sales (7th Ed.) § 415

—are good law.

. . . .

This court has repeatedly re-affirmed and applied the same principles. I do not think we should depart from them. It cannot be said that no mistake as to either "attributes, quality, or value" gives grounds for rescission. . . . It seems to me there was a mutual mistake, not as to quality or value, but as to certain tangible facts so fundamental that it must be assumed that the parties would not have entered into the contract, had they known the truth.

Panco v. Rogers

Superior Court of New Jersey, Chancery Division, 1952.
19 N.J.Super. 12, 87 A.2d 770.

■ HANEMAN, J.S.C. The plaintiffs herein seek the rescission of a written agreement to sell real estate, upon the ground of mutual mistake. The defendant seeks specific performance of said agreement, by way of counterclaim. The alleged mistake lies in the consideration to be paid for the conveyance of the realty, plaintiffs alleging that it should have been $12,500 and defendant alleging it should have been $5,500, as expressed in said agreement.

I find the following facts in connection herewith:

> John Panco, a man of some 77 years of age, had been the owner of the realty here involved since 1913, the purchase of which was his only transaction involving real estate until that now under consideration. Being a carpenter by trade, he had, by his own efforts, constructed the home there situated. He had had very little formal schooling and was, at the time of the execution of the agreement, quite deaf.

In the fore part of the year 1951 the plaintiffs had decided to sell the premises here involved and to move to Florida. In furtherance of such a plan, with the aid of their daughter, Alice Panco, they prepared an advertisement which was inserted in the *Philadelphia Inquirer,* and placed a sign in the window of the house, advertising said property for sale. In response to these advertisements, several prospective purchasers arrived at the premises, but none accepted at the asking price of $12,500. The defendant, who lived in the neighborhood, came to the property on or about May 15, 1951. He was escorted through the property by the plaintiff Mary Panco, in the absence of her husband, John Panco. Mary Panco is apparently of foreign extraction and speaks with an accent. Upon inquiring the

price, defendant alleges that he was advised by Mary Panco that it was
$5,500. The plaintiff Mary Panco denies the price as so stated, but alleges
that the price asked was $12,500. The said defendant brought his intended
bride to examine the premises upon the following Thursday. Upon this
occasion there was no further discussion of price. On the succeeding
Tuesday, May 22, 1951, the defendant, as per arrangements made the
preceding night, took John Panco to his, defendant's, attorney, where the
agreement was prepared. The plaintiff, John Panco, took very little vocal
part in the discussion at the attorney's office.

. . . .

The defendant, after the agreement had been signed by him and John
Panco, drove the latter to his home, where the signature of Mary Panco
was obtained. That evening, when Alice Panco returned home from work,
the plaintiffs for the first time, upon her explanation, understood that the
agreement called for a consideration of $5,500. John Panco insisted that
the $5,500 related to a part payment on account of the purchase price of
$12,500. They immediately contacted a son-in-law of the plaintiffs who, in
turn, contacted the defendant. A conference ensued at plaintiff's residence.
Although plaintiffs contend that the defendant agreed to cancel the transaction, the defendant states that he did not definitely agree to do so. The
plaintiffs then offered to repay to the defendant not only his deposit, but
whatever expenses he had been put to, including attorney's fees. This offer
they still make.

The testimony satisfies me that the property here involved is worth
considerably in excess of $5,500, and is worth at least $10,000, and that the
plaintiffs had established their sale price at $12,500 and believed that they
were obtaining $12,500.

Mistake has been defined in Santamaria v. Shell Eastern Petroleum
Products, Inc., 116 N.J.Eq. 26, 172 A. 339, 341 (Ch. 1934), as follows:
"Mistake exists when a person, under some erroneous conviction of law or
fact, does, or omits to do, some act which but for the erroneous conviction
he would not have done or omitted. It may arise either from unconsciousness, ignorance, forgetfulness, imposition or misplaced confidence. Where it
arises from imposition or misplaced confidence, relief may be had on the
ground of fraud. Where it arises from unconsciousness, ignorance or
forgetfulness, no fraud exists and redress must be on the basis of mistake."

I am satisfied that there was a mutual mistake in the parol negotiations, i.e., the defendant conceived that he was purchasing the property for
$5,500 and the plaintiffs that they were selling at $12,500. It is understandable that such an error might have arisen when it is noted that Mary
Panco, the only person with whom the defendant discussed price before the
preparation of the agreement, speaks with an accent.

Insofar as the provisions of the final written agreement are concerned,
there was a unilateral mistake, i.e., the defendant knew that the agreement
provided for a sales price of $5,500 and the plaintiffs believed that the
agreement provided for $12,500.

Normally, rescission cannot be enforced on account of the mistake of
one party only, which the other party did not share and where such other

party was not guilty of fraud, undue influence, concealment or bad faith and would not derive any unconscionable advantage from the enforcement of the contract.

Rescission may be had on the ground of unilateral mistake under the above circumstances, provided the mistake is not attributable to the negligence of the party seeking such relief. The party seeking relief must be free of that want of care and diligence in the transaction which should be used by every person of reasonable prudence, and the absence of which would be a violation of a legal duty.

There can be no rescission unless the parties can be restored to their original positions.

To rescind one must act promptly. Failure to rescind promptly is plenary evidence of the party's election not to do so.

Considering all of the essential elements concerned, I find that although the plaintiffs are free of such negligence as would prevent them from relief, and acted promptly, and that the defendant can be restored to his original position, that there was no actual fraud, undue influence or concealment on the part of the defendant, and hence the plaintiffs may not have a rescission of the contract.

However, insofar as the affirmative relief demanded by the defendant is concerned, the specific performance of the contract, such an application is addressed to the sound discretion of a court of equity, which may grant or deny, as the circumstances of the case warrant. Upon an application for specific performance the court must be satisfied that the claim is fair, reasonable and just, and in judging of its fairness, the court will look not only at the terms of the contract itself, but at all of the surrounding circumstances, including the relations of the parties.

One seeking a specific performance may, upon a proper finding, be relegated to his remedy at law. A decree of specific performance will never be made unless substantial justice is done thereby, but the parties will be left to their remedies at law.

not anymore

Although inadequacy of price is not in and of itself a sufficient ground for refusing specific performance, it may be so gross as to shock the conscience of the court and amount to conclusive and decisive evidence of fraud in the transaction, even in the absence of affirmative proof of fraud or misrepresentation. Actual proof of fraud is, under those circumstances, not necessary.

. . . .

Where the enforcement of a contract for the sale of land would be harsh, oppressive or manifestly unjust to one of the parties thereto, its specific performance will not be decreed, but the parties will be left to their remedy at law. To succeed in a suit for specific performance, the court must be satisfied that the claim is fair, reasonable and equal in all its parts, and to so determine. The court will look not merely at the terms of the agreement but at the relation of the parties and the surrounding circumstances as well.

. . . .

The question is not what must the court do, but what should it do, in view of the circumstances, to further justice.

Therefore, taking into consideration all of the elements of this case, including the age, lack of education and deafness of John Panco, the foreign extraction of his wife, the original mistake as to the consideration, the manner in which the contract was prepared, and the attendant circumstances, the price, which I find inadequate, and as well the fact that a refusal to direct specific performance will result in no damage to defendant except the loss of a bargain, it is here held that a judgment of specific performance would be harsh, oppressive, unjust, inequitable and unfair to the plaintiffs; and defendant's counterclaim will as well be dismissed.

Volpe v. Schlobohm

Court of Civil Appeals of Texas, 1981.
614 S.W.2d 615.

■ CORNELIUS, C.J. Appellees, Charles H. and Joneen Lou Schlobohm, brought this suit against appellant, Robert M. Volpe, seeking rescission of a partnership agreement. The partnership was originally composed of the Schlobohms, Volpe and Edward R. Wright. Wright withdrew from the partnership before the suit was filed and was not a party. Volpe answered and counterclaimed seeking dissolution, accounting, damages and other relief.

In a trial to the court without the aid of a jury, judgment was rendered for the Schlobohms rescinding the partnership and vesting in them the title to all partnership assets. The judgment decreed that Volpe take nothing on his counterclaim but awarded him ... the ... value of his 30% interest in the partnership....

The Schlobohms have been engaged in the food distributing business in Dallas since 1966. Prior to February 1, 1978, they operated a proprietorship which consisted of various distributorships with companies in the prepared food business. Volpe became associated with the Schlobohms as a jobber on June 10 of 1972. On January 28, 1978, the Schlobohms, Volpe and Wright met to discuss the formation of a partnership. Mrs. Schlobohm made notes of the discussions which later formed the basis of a written partnership agreement. The agreement was accepted and agreed to by all parties on February 1, 1978, although it was never signed.

At the commencement of the partnership, Charles Schlobohm was a franchisee of Pepperidge Farms, Volpe was a franchisee of Stella D'Oro, and Wright was a franchisee of Pepperidge Farms. The Schlobohms testified that their Pepperidge Farms franchise was to be excluded from the partnership. Wright also testified that neither of the Pepperidge Farms franchises was to be contributed as a partnership asset. However, the revenues from these franchises were deposited in the partnership account and were divided among the partners according to their percentage interests in the firm. Mr. Volpe testified that he understood that the Pepperidge Farms franchises were to be contributed as partnership assets and that he also understood that he was contributing his Stella D'Oro franchise.

In June of 1978, some four months after the creation of the partnership, Wright withdrew taking his Pepperidge Farms franchise with him. His interest in the partnership was purchased by the Schlobohms with their own funds. Volpe testified that he was not given the opportunity to purchase his pro rata share of Wright's interest; the Schlobohms asserted that he was given the opportunity but declined to do so because they would not agree to his use of partnership funds to purchase his proportionate interest. Volpe did, however, insist that he was entitled to his proportionate share of Wright's profits and partnership assets; and ultimately this disagreement and the misunderstanding concerning the contribution of the Pepperidge Farms franchises as partnership assets resulted in a deterioration of the relationships between the Schlobohms and Volpe and gave rise to this suit.

Mr. Volpe contends that rescission was improper because it was not supported by ... the evidence.

The Schlobohms pleaded that the partnership should be rescinded because of "... a mutual mistake of material substance ..., namely, that the parties are unable and/or unwilling to work together to fulfill the purposes and intent of the intended partnership...." At the trial, however, the Schlobohms asserted that the mistake related to the question of whether the Pepperidge Farms franchises were partnership assets, and it was that mistake which formed the basis for the court's grant of rescission.

. . . .

A partnership agreement, like any other agreement or relationship, may be rescinded when proper grounds exist. Rescission may be authorized either because of a mutual mistake of the parties, or because of a unilateral mistake if the elements of remediable mistake are present.

Although the trial court here based its judgment on remediable mistake, characterizing the misunderstanding about the franchises as a unilateral mistake, the facts found by the trial court actually reveal a mutual mistake of a type which will warrant rescission.

Ordinarily a mutual mistake sufficient to justify rescission exists when both of the parties are laboring under the same misconception as to a common fact, as when the parties know what they have agreed to, but through their common mistake the expression of their contract fails to correctly state that agreement, or when the parties contract on the assumption of a matter material to the contract but not expressed in it, and their common assumption is incorrect. But the mutual mistakes need not be identical. If they relate to the same matter, equitable relief is available even though the mistakes of the parties as to that fact are not the same. Rescission may be granted when there is a mistake of this kind which results in the parties' never having reached a meeting of the minds and thus prevents, ab initio, the formulation of a valid contract. Examples of this type of mistake are found in cases in which the parties, when attempting to formulate their agreement, were laboring under different conceptions as to the subject matter of the agreement, or as to the identity, character or quantity of a matter or thing with reference to which they were attempting to contract.... [W]hen one party understands that he is contracting on one set of terms and the other understands that he is contracting on another set of terms, there is no contract unless the circumstances are such as preclude one of the parties from denying that he agreed to the terms set by the other. Of course, this type of mistake will justify relief only if the expression or writing evidencing the purported agreement is uncertain and ambiguous, for if there is no ambiguity with respect to the written or oral expression of the terms neither party will be heard to say that, by his subjective intent, he meant something different from what was actually expressed.

The written partnership agreement involved in this case makes no specific provision concerning whether or not the parties' franchises would be contributed to the firm as partnership assets, and the agreement as a whole is unclear as to whether the franchises were or were not to be included. On the basis of the testimony the trial judge concluded that the franchises were not to be contributed as partnership assets, but he also found that the parties were laboring under opposite understandings with reference to that issue—the Schlobohms thinking that they were not to become partnership assets and Volpe thinking that they were—and that there was no meeting of the minds of the parties on that material issue. Rescission is a proper remedy in such a situation, provided it is possible to restore the contracting parties to their original positions, and provided the rights of innocent third parties have not otherwise intervened.

The judgment is affirmed.

Krezinski v. Hay

Supreme Court of Wisconsin, 1977.
77 Wis.2d 569, 253 N.W.2d 522.

■ DAY, J. . . .

The plaintiff brought action against Ms. Izetta Hay and her insurer for damages resulting from Ms. Hay's negligent operation of her automobile on State Trunk Highway 31 in Racine county on September 28, 1963. According to the complaint, the plaintiff was driving north on the highway when the defendant negligently drove her car onto the highway from a driveway causing the two automobiles to collide. The plaintiff alleged that she sustained injuries, "among others, traumatic epilepsy, contusions to scalp—occipito parietal area, cervical sprain and right dorsal myositis; numerous other abrasions, contusions and lacerations; severe pain and suffering, shock and mental anguish."

The defendants' answer denied negligent conduct and set forth various affirmative defenses, among which was that on September 5, 1969, the plaintiff, while represented by counsel, executed a release of all claims against the defendants, "in any way growing out of, any and all known and unknown personal injuries, developed or undeveloped, including death and property damage resulting or to result from an accident that occurred on or about the 28th day of September, 1968." The agreement acknowledged receipt by plaintiff of $2,300 as consideration for the release.

The plaintiff filed a reply admitting execution of the release but alleging she and the defendants relied and acted upon a mutual mistake of fact. That mistake was their ignorance the plaintiff was suffering from a latent but present condition as a result of the accident which later manifested itself by grand mal epileptic seizures. This epileptic condition was not observed by plaintiff's physician prior to execution of the release.

The defendant moved for summary judgment. . . .

. . . .

Releases will be set aside on the ground of mistake only where the mistake is mutual and not unilateral. The mistake of fact must be past or present "for it is obvious that the coming into existence of any future fact must at the time of contracting have been understood to rest in conjecture, and the contingency thereof to have been assumed by both parties."

The seemingly all-inclusive language of the release before us is not dispositive of whether there was a mutual mistake of fact.

"(E)ven though a release expressly covers unknown injuries, it is not a bar to an action for such unknown injuries if it can be shown that such unknown injuries were not within the contemplation of the parties when the settlement was agreed upon; however, if the parties did in fact intentionally agree upon a settlement for unknown injuries, such release will be binding. Whether the parties intended the release to cover unknown injuries is usually a question of fact."

. . . .

The nature and extent of a party's reliance on a mutually accepted medical diagnosis is a question of fact. If the diagnosis failed to ascertain a then-existing but unknown condition caused by the incident which led to the suit, and the parties relied on the diagnosis as the basis for settlement, the release may be set aside.

. . . .

———

REFORMATION

———

Mutual of Omaha Insurance Co. v. Russell

United States Court of Appeals, Tenth Circuit, 1968.
402 F.2d 339.

■ BROWN, J. Does the speed of the modern jet age and the restless, irrepressible, increased tempo of all who are in its vortex impose on a flight insurer the obligation toward prospective policy buyers of explaining the distinctive differences of the several available coverages? Does the insurer's attractive sales booth, neon signs heralding the need for and availability of "flight insurance," and the other catchy advertising come-ons carry the inevitable message to scurrying people on the move the notion that the coverage is for the traveler's intended round trip rather than for a definitive period of time? And to avoid this misreading by people in a hurry of printed contracts plain enough that even those who run may read, must the insurer affirmatively take steps by extra-contract informational statements to overcome such misapprehension?

The District Judge, in effect, answered these broad inquiries in the affirmative. The failure to give such informational advice became, in his analysis, a constructive fraud upon which to base reformation of a flight insurance policy which, all now agree, did not by its terms cover the death of the Assured. In more austere terms the main issue presented for decision is whether the Assured is entitled to reformation of a general accident flight insurance policy purchased at Insurer's sales booth in the lobby of an airport. The District Court reformed the contract and awarded plaintiff $20,000. We hold that under the unusual fact situation of this case the insurance policy should not have been reformed and the decision of the District Court must be reversed.

To understand fully the Assured's theory a full recitation of the facts is helpful. Rev. and Mrs. Russell were residents of Kansas City, Kansas. On Thursday, January 24, 1963, upon receiving word that one of her brothers had died in Lubbock, Texas, Mrs. Russell decided to fly to Lubbock for the funeral. Reservations were made for a flight the next day, Friday, but the return flight was left open because the funeral date had not been set. On Friday Rev. and Mrs. Russell and their son went to the airport in Kansas City, Missouri, picked up their tickets at the Continental Airlines counter, and proceeded toward the awaiting plane.

As the three Russells passed one of Insurer's vending machines for dispensing flight insurance, Rev. Russell decided that Mrs. Russell should have insurance to cover her during the trip. This machine dispensed Insurer's policy T–20. In many ways the T–20 affords severely limited coverage in that it provides protection only for accidents while aboard an airplane or in established limousines going to or coming from the airport. On the other hand, the T–20's coverage expressly remains in effect for the duration of the round trip or for twelve months, whichever occurs first. Similarly, since events and covered occurrences were more restrictive, the face amount of insurance per premium dollar was larger than other policies. Had a T–20 been machine-issued the Assured's death would have been covered. But no one had the proper change to operate the machine, so the Russells stepped just south of the machine to one of Insurer's staffed insurance booths. The booth had signs overhead reading "Flight Insurance" and was attended by a Miss Fletcher.

Rev. Russell asked either for flight insurance or insurance to cover his wife on her round trip to Lubbock. Miss Fletcher then asked "How much?", meaning what amount of insurance coverage. Mrs. Russell asked for the least amount and $20,000 was the amount agreed upon. Without then explaining various policies available, Miss Fletcher took out an application form and began to fill it out. She then asked either how long would Mrs. Russell be gone or when would she be returning. Mrs. Russell turned to her husband and asked "Three days?". Rev. Russell said she should allow herself more than that—at least four days. Miss Fletcher completed the form and turned it around for Mrs. Russell's signature. Mrs. Russell signed and paid the $2.25 premium. Miss Fletcher stapled the policy together and handed it to Rev. Russell.

The policy purchased was not, however, the T–20; rather it was the T–18, a significantly different policy. The T–18 is a general accident policy that covers almost all risks—whether air related or not—during the life of the policy. The policy term is stated in terms of twenty-four hour periods on a daily basis up to thirty-one days. The premium is higher on the T–18 for the same dollar amount of insurance, and the T–18 is not sold in vending machines. As the Schedule signed by Mrs. Russell shows, the T–18 was issued for only four days, and expired at 11:00 a.m., Tuesday, January 29, 1963, about twelve hours prior to the Assured's death.

The District Court credited Rev. Russell's testimony that Miss Fletcher never mentioned any other available policies, did not explain the T–18, and did not warn plaintiff that the policy would expire at 11:00 a.m. on Tuesday, January 29, 1963. The Judge also found that the Assured intended to buy insurance that would cover Mrs. Russell's round trip, which both she and her husband thought would occur within four days.

After buying the insurance, Mrs. Russell boarded her plane and arrived safely in Lubbock, Texas. There the funeral was delayed because a son of the deceased had not arrived from England. The funeral was finally held on Tuesday, January 29, and Mrs. Russell was fatally injured when her airplane crashed that night at 10:45 p.m. while attempting to land at the Kansas City, Missouri, airport. The insurance policy had expired by its own terms about twelve hours earlier. The Insurer denied liability.

The Assured then pursued Insurer in this diversity of citizenship suit in Kansas on the theories that either (1) the insurance contract should be construed to cover the death of Mrs. Russell, or (2) the policy should be reformed to provide coverage for the return flight from Lubbock to Kansas City. The District Judge held that the contract was clear and unambiguous and as written did not cover the accident. But now of direct importance he held that as a matter of equity the policy should be reformed to cover the accident. Judgment for $20,000 was entered for the Assured. Insurer appealed contending that it is not liable since the policy had expired and the company was not guilty of any inequitable conduct that would give rise to the remedy of reformation. The Assured cross-appealed contending that the judgment should have been for $90,000, the amount of straight flight insurance (T–20) that $2.25 would have bought, but the Assured did not appeal the decision that the policy could not be construed to cover the accident. Thus the only substantive problem before us is whether the contract should, as a matter of equity, be reformed.

. . . .

Neither party disagrees about the general principles of equity applicable here. The rub comes in the proper application of those principles to the facts of this case. Reformation is an ancient remedy used to reframe written contracts to reflect accurately the real agreement between contracting parties when, either through mutual mistake or unilateral mistake coupled with actual or equitable fraud by the other party, the writing does not embody the contract as actually made.

But reformation is an extraordinary remedy, and courts exercise it with great caution. Even in situations where obvious mistakes have been made, courts will not rewrite the contract between the parties, but will only enforce the legal obligations of the parties according to their original agreement. Here, of course, the Assured does not contend that mutual mistake occurred and it is well that he does not do so for obviously the Insurer intended to sell the exact policy with the exact coverage that it did. Rather, the Assured's theory rests on another accepted reformation doctrine—mistake by one party coupled with constructive or equitable fraud by the other.

Thus the whole case boils down in reality to one question: Did Insurer have a duty to tell the Assured that several insurance policies were available and to explain fully the provisions and limitations of those policies? Without this supposed duty (and its breach) the District Judge would have had no basis for judge-reformation of the contract to conform to a regular straight flight insurance policy which Insurer was offering for sale. Rules of construction, either generally or with particular reference to the liberalizing impact of traveler haste in acquiring air-flight insurance, are of little help since on construction the Assured fails altogether. The problem is one of the proper scope of the doctrine of equitable fraud and the manner in which that doctrine relates to the duty of an insurer to warn the customer about what he is buying.

As in nearly all cases, an inquiry of this type involves consideration of the competing interests. On the one hand we have the right of the public to be free of fraud and oppression wrought by those in a superior bargaining position. But on the other hand we are confronted with the realities of doing business, the enforcement of contracts, and instability which flows from opening up written contracts to oral accretions.

The Assured urges, and the District Court declared, that an explanation was owing. By whom was it to be given? In what form was it to be offered? Orally or in writing? If orally, how would an insurer conscious of its duty of fair dealing toward a peripatetic public in a hurry assure that an adequate, reliable statement was made? The "explanation" would vary as work shifts changed and sales personnel rotated. They would be expansive or restrictive as the loquacious or taciturn quality of the employee predominated. If the insurer turned to a written statement, how or in what manner would it assure itself that the impatient prospect would pay any more heed to it than the terms of the policy contract? And what happens when, out of an abundance of good faith, an effort is made to explain (in nonlegalese) what a legal document prescribes? And as to either method or a mixture of both, what are the significant distinctions to be pointed out? Which ones to emphasize? To minimize? To omit? How many policies need to be explained? Just the two most common—T–20 and T–18? Or all eleven? In the meantime what is happening to time—that precious irreplaceable which accounts for the traveler's pressure at the airport facing either dispensing machine or an attractive sales person who may well try harder but without benefit of a legal education? The flight would either be missed or the "offer" of flight insurance withdrawn for want of adequate time for equity's mandated "explanation." Hardship, or what seems to be hardship, may sometimes occur if the law adheres to its long-held notions of the non-variability of written contracts. But a too-quick relaxation in the contrails of the jet age might well be worse, not better.

We think that imposing a duty to offer such explanations under circumstances of this kind—requiring as it does an effort by lay persons to interpret the legal meaning of the proposed contract as well as others available—would be fraught with great danger to the stability of contracts. We do not think Kansas would embrace such a view and for Kansas we decline to skywrite such an *Erie* judgment.

The printed contract controls. There it ends.

Reversed.

Nash v. Kornblum

Court of Appeals of New York, 1962.
12 N.Y.2d 42, 234 N.Y.S.2d 697, 186 N.E.2d 551.

■ FOSTER, J. The question before us is whether reformation should be granted where the written executed contract contains an essential term which does not represent the term as originally agreed upon in the oral negotiations. The remaining essential terms were not fixed until the execution of the formal contract.

The development of the negotiations and agreement are set forth as follows. Plaintiff, a fence building company, through its sales estimator, Mr. Harkness, and defendant, who conducted a Summer camp, entered into negotiations on March 17, 1958 concerning new fencing around three tennis courts. Harkness offered to prepare estimates, and by telephone told defendant that he had made an estimate "on 484 feet, of ten-foot high chain-link fence ... in one width" at $2,040. Because of the amount of money, defendant asked if there was anything else that could be done, to which Harkness replied for less money "we could figure that in hex netting, otherwise the specifications the same as in the chain-link". Although defendant testified Harkness personally came to the camp and viewed the area at this time, which Harkness denied, the realm of discussion was over the cost of fence material. Even with a possible idea of enclosing an additional handball court because of the savings in the use of hex netting, the 484–foot figure, defendant testified, "was a fair estimate of the whole area". In any event, defendant requested both estimates.

Harkness prepared the two estimates, one for chain-link, the other for hex netting, gave them to a stenographer, who typed them on two separate contract forms. Harkness looked them over quickly, and mailed them to defendant. Except as to the differences about to be noted, they are identical.

The first proposal dated March 21, 1958 specifies "Length *484* linear feet", "Height 10—", "Fabric 2—mesh #9 gauge galv. chain link", "Price TWO THOUSAND FORTY DOLLARS ($2,040.00)". This proposal was not accepted by defendant. The second proposed contract dated the same day specifies

"Length *968* linear feet", "Height 10", "Fabric 1½—mesh #16 ga. Hex Netting *in two widths of 5 each*". "Price ONE THOUSAND EIGHT HUNDRED TWENTY NINE DOLLARS ($1,829.00)" (emphasis supplied). Each proposal provides "If more or less fence is erected, an adjustment in price will be made." It should be noted that the second proposal did not state 968 linear feet of fence but simply 968 linear feet; to erect a 10–foot–high fence 484 feet long requires 968 linear feet of 5–foot–wide hex netting. During the first week in April, defendant signed and returned the second proposal, the hex netting offer, together with the requested $600 deposit.

When construction around the tennis courts was almost completed, defendant inquired about enclosing the handball court. Harkness quoted a price based on the tennis court price and, although a letter from plaintiff was sent on May 22, 1958 confirming the estimate and requesting a duplicate letter be signed and returned, the work went on without this additional approval.

At the completion of the fencing work, the job superintendent measured the area fenced. The perimeter of the tennis courts turned out to be 534 feet, and in addition there were 50 feet on each side of the handball court, a total of 634 feet. The total amount of hex netting used was thus 1,268 feet, since the fence was put up in 2 widths of 5 feet each. Plaintiff sent defendant a bill dated May 31, 1958, stating a balance due of $1,794.50. This sum was arrived at by adding $1,829 "as per Contract dated 4/2/58" plus "150—additional fence furnished and installed @ $3.77 per ft. as per estimate dated 5/22/58", a total of $2,394.50 less $600 deposit. On July 5, more than a month later, and without any protest meanwhile, defendant mailed plaintiff a check for only $597.92 together with a letter stating:

"Enclosed find $597.92 which pays up for 634 feet installed, and which was based on the original contract price. I find you made an error in your calculations. 968 linear feet priced at $1829.00 makes 634 feet equal to $1197.92. Six Hundred dollars has been paid, leaving a balance of $597.92.

"I would like to enclose another area which I estimate about 300 feet. Kindly get in touch with me to make arrangements as we then can use up the remaining 334 feet of our contract."

Thereafter, plaintiff instituted this action to reform the executed contract to read 484 linear feet.

There is no contention in the record that the two original proposals, identical in the most part except for the type of fence material, were not intended for exactly the same ground area. As noted previously, the problem here is that the *ground* linear feet involved in the original estimate (disregarding the actual measurement) was 484 feet. This would mean 484 feet of 10–foot–high chain-link fence; but 968 feet of 5–foot hex-netting fence since a double width was necessary to make the hex-netting fence 10 feet high. Plaintiff contends this contract, as signed, containing the reference to 968 linear feet, was merely a typographical or inadvertent error on the part of the plaintiff's secretary in exactly doubling the ground linear feet, perhaps to reflect the length of 5-foot width fencing, not coming to his attention until the fence was nearly finished, and did not represent the agreement previous to its reduction to writing. Defendant asserts that he signed the contract as written, he tendered payment on the basis of that contract and is even willing to "use up" the remaining ground linear feet of fencing.

The sole issue before us is whether reformation should have been granted. In Ross v. Food Specialties (6 N.Y.2d 336, 341, 189 N.Y.S.2d 857, 859, 860, 160 N.E.2d 618, 620, 621) this court stated: "We have consistently and repeatedly held that before a reformation can be granted the plaintiff '*must establish his right to such relief by clear, positive and convincing evidence*. Reformation may not be granted upon a probability nor even upon a mere preponderance of evidence, but only upon a certainty of error' nor may the plaintiff 'secure reformation merely upon a showing that he or his attorney made a mistake. In the absence of fraud, the mistake shown "must be one made by both parties to the agreement so that the intentions of neither are expressed in it"' . . . . Reformation is not designed for the purpose of remaking the contract agreed upon but, rather, solely for the purpose of stating correctly a mutual mistake shared by both parties to the contract; in other words, it provides an equitable remedy for use when it clearly and convincingly appears that the contract, as written does not embody the true agreement as mutually intended". However, in Hart v. Blabey (287 N.Y. 257, 262, 39 N.E.2d 230, 232), this court invoked the equitable doctrine of reformation on the following basis: "Where there is no mistake about the agreement, and the only mistake alleged is in the reduction of that agreement to writing, such mistake of the scrivener, or of either party, no matter how it occurred, may be corrected. In such a case equity will conform the written instrument to the parol agreement which it was intended to embody."

It clearly and convincingly appears from the record here that this is a case of a mistake on the part of the plaintiff's agent in typing the erroneous linear ground measurement, which plaintiff did not discover before submission to the defendant, and the latter, with knowledge of the mistake, trying to take advantage of the error. The writing itself did not represent the understanding of either party as to the area to be fenced which had been agreed upon previous to the writing, and thus did not embody the true agreement, as mutually intended, relating to the area.

This is not a case where the plaintiff unilaterally and mistakenly estimated the linear feet and defendant, without a duty to speak and absent fraud, agreed to the proposal. Should these circumstances have been present in the contract's reduction to writing, there would be no scrivener's mistake or mutual mistake of fact, the agreement would be the intended one by the parties, and equity would not "reform" the executed contract. This set of circumstances is not presented here by the record.

There is clear and convincing evidence that there was an agreement between the parties as to the area to be fenced before the formal written contract was executed, and *then* an error was made, albeit by plaintiff, in the reduction of the antecedent expression of the parties into the complete contract. The only question between the parties on the execution of the written contract was the type of fencing to be constructed and cost thereof, and admittedly these essential terms were not fixed until the formal contract was signed. These latter terms are not sought to be reformed.

The situation presented clearly calls for relief, and the only practicable method of achieving such a result is by the equitable remedy of reformation. The Trial Judge dismissed the complaint with the finding that the proof failed to show fraud on the part of the defendant. In our view of the case it was unnecessary for the plaintiff to establish fraud on the part of the defendant. Perhaps reformation could have been predicated upon a unilateral mistake on one side and deceptive conduct on the other side which tended to obscure the true agreement. However, the situation presented as a result of the scrivener's error was closely akin, if not precisely, to a mutual mistake of fact, and as such was sufficient to call for the application of the equitable doctrine of reformation. Therefore, the judgment should be reversed and the case remitted to Special Term for proceedings not inconsistent with this opinion.

NOTES ON RESCISSION AND REFORMATION

1. RESCISSION AND REFORMATION FOR FRAUD AND THE PAROL EVIDENCE RULE: Sabo brought an action for rescission of his contract with Delman on the ground of fraud. The trial court granted Delman's motion for judgment on the pleadings and dismissed the complaint. An appellate court affirmed this judgment, but its decision was reversed by the Court of Appeals. Sabo v. Delman, 3 N.Y.2d 155, 164 N.Y.S.2d 714, 143 N.E.2d 906 (1957). One argument rejected by the latter court was "that, since the alleged representations were not set forth in the written contracts, they could not be asserted or relied upon by the plaintiff." The Court of Appeals' discussion of the point follows:

The agreements being attached to the complaint, we are brought to a consideration of the impact of the recital in each of them that "No verbal understanding or conditions, not herein specified, shall be binding on either party."

The parol evidence rule forbids proof of extrinsic evidence to contradict or vary the terms of a written instrument and, accordingly, one who seeks, in a breach of contract action, to *enforce* an oral representation or promise relating to the subject matter of the contract cannot succeed. However, the parol evidence rule has no application in a suit brought to *rescind* a contract on the ground of fraud. In such a case, it is clear [that] evidence of the assertedly fraudulent oral misrepresentation may be introduced to avoid the agreement.

The provision to which we above referred—that no verbal undertakings or conditions not contained in the writing were to be binding on either party—sometimes termed a merger clause, merely furnishes another reason for applying the parol evidence rule, and, just as that rule is ineffectual to exclude evidence of fraudulent misrepresentations, so this provision may not be invoked to keep out such proof. Indeed, if it were otherwise, a defendant would have it in his power to perpetrate a fraud with immunity, depriving the victim of all redress, if he simply has the foresight to include a merger clause in the agreement. Such, of course, is not the law.

"I assume," Judge O'Brien long ago declared on behalf of a unanimous court in Bridger v. Goldsmith, 143 N.Y. 424, 38 N.E. 458, "that there is no authority that we are required to follow in support of the proposition that a party who has perpetrated a fraud upon his neighbor may nevertheless contract with him, in the very instrument by means of which it was perpetrated, for immunity against its consequences, close his mouth from complaining of it, and bind him never to seek redress. Public policy and morality are both ignored if such an agreement can be given effect in a court of justice. The maxim that fraud vitiates every transaction would no longer be the rule, but the exception. It could be applied then only in such case as the guilty party neglected to protect himself from his fraud by means of such a stipulation. Such a principle would in a short time break down every barrier which the law has erected against fraudulent dealing." In other words, "the law does not temporize with trickery or duplicity. A contract, the making of which was induced by deceitful methods or crafty device, is nothing more than a scrap of paper, and it makes no difference whether the fraud goes to the factum or whether it is preliminary to the execution of the agreement itself." And in the Ernst Iron Works case, 270 N.Y. 165, 200 N.E. 683, the court wrote, "A rogue cannot protect himself from liability for his fraud by inserting a printed clause in his contract. This principle disposes of the blanket clause providing that no representation shall be binding unless incorporated in the agreement."

In short, a contractual promise made with the undisclosed intention not to perform it constitutes fraud and, despite the so-called merger clause, the plaintiff is free to prove that he was induced by false and fraudulent misrepresentations. . . .

2.   Brandwein v. Provident Mutual Life Ins. Co., 3 N.Y.2d 491, 168 N.Y.S.2d 964, 146 N.E.2d 693 (1957) involved an action by a former general insurance agent to recover from insurance company certain collection fees allegedly due agent after termination of his agency under an agreement which by its written terms did not provide for any collection fees after termination. The Court of Appeals held that the allegation that, before the agent would sign the agreement, the insurance company orally promised that he would be entitled to collect fees after termination of the agreement, provided premiums on particular policies continued to be paid, was sufficient to state a cause of action for reformation of the contract.

Plaintiff would not have stated a cause of action had he limited himself to alleging that besides the payments set out in the formal written agreement he had a separate oral promise from defendant for the payment of other commissions. Attempted proof of such a "side agreement" would probably be inadmissible under the parol evidence rule. The oral agreement itself would be unenforceable under the Statute of Frauds since on its face and as pleaded it would be such an agreement as could not be performed within a year or before the end of a lifetime. But this complaint contains much more than that. It says that plaintiff's signature on the written agreement was procured from him by a fraudulent representation that defendant intended to write onto its records the collateral agreement. Plaintiff asserts that he does not know whether such record was ever made but that he was at one time assured by defendant that it had been made and later told that it had not. If it is not to be found on defendant's books, says plaintiff, its absence is due to a mutual mistake of the parties or to a mistake on plaintiff's part and a fraud by defendant. Those are the classic grounds for reformation of an instrument in equity.

As to the alleged defenses, it is settled that neither the Statute of Frauds nor the parol evidence prohibition forbids reformation of a written contract to include material orally agreed upon but, because of mutual mistake or unilateral mistake plus fraud, not inserted in the writing. The authorities so holding are numerous and consistent.... The latest application of that rule in this court is Sabo v. Delman (3 N.Y.2d 155, 164 N.Y.S.2d 714, 143 N.E.2d 906), the difference between the two cases being that Sabo sued for rescission while the present plaintiff prays for reformation.

----

2.   MISTAKE AS A DEFENSE TO SPECIFIC PERFORMANCE

Mansfield v. Sherman

Supreme Judicial Court of Maine, 1889.
81 Me. 365, 17 A. 300.

[Sherman, the respondent, living in New York, agreed to sell to Mansfield, the complainant, a certain lot in Bar Harbor, Maine, which, he believed, did not contain a valuable building site. By mistake, Sherman named a lot which had a building site. Mansfield knew that the price was very low for lots containing these sites. He now sues to compel Sherman to specifically perform the contract and to convey the lot with the building site at the low price agreed between the parties. Sherman refused to perform on the ground that he had made a mistake as to a material fact and not merely an error in judgment.]

■ EMERY, J. This is a bill in equity, in which the court is asked to decree the specific performance of a contract for the conveyance of two lots of land, as marked upon a plan.

Such an application is addressed to the sound discretion of the court. Not every party, who would be entitled as of right to damages for the breach of a contract, is entitled to a decree for its specific performance. Before granting such a decree, the court should be satisfied not only of the existence of a valid contract, free from fraud, and enforceable in law, but also of its fairness and its harmony with equity and good conscience. However strong, clear and emphatic the language of the contract, however plain the right at law if a specific performance would, for any reason, cause a result, harsh, inequitable or contrary to good conscience, the court should refuse such a decree and leave the parties to their remedies at law. In an equity proceeding, the complainant must do equity and can obtain only equity.

In this case the answer sets up the defense among others, that the respondent made his offer to sell the land, and named the price under a material mistake, as to the extent and boundaries of one of the lots,—that he did not understand that the lots included a certain valuable building site, which he never intended to sell at such a price—that by reason of such mistake, he named an inadequate price for the lot and that for the complainant to seek to compel him to convey at that price is inequitable, and is taking an unfair advantage of his mistake.

. . . .

Of course, if there was a valid contract, Mr. Sherman should answer in damages for all the loss his mistake and refusal to convey have occasioned Mr. Mansfield. The court when appealed to in an action at law can only consider whether there was a valid contract and a breach. The mere mistake of one party however great, will not excuse him from making full compensation. When however application is made to the court, not to determine and enforce legal rights, but "to do equity" between the parties, the court will be careful to do only equity, and will not aid one party to take advantage of the mistake of the other party. We think in this case, we should decline to decree a specific performance, and should leave the parties to their rights and remedies at law. It does not appear that pecuniary damages for the breach would not fully compensate Mr. Mansfield for all losses he has sustained in the matter.

. . . .

Bill dismissed.

NOTES ON MISTAKE AS DEFENSE TO SPECIFIC PERFORMANCE

1.   Suit was brought under the Federal Employers' Liability Act by an injured employee against the railroad for which he worked. The case was transferred to equity on motion of the railroad seeking specific performance of the employee's agreement to compromise. It was held that evidence sustained findings of trial court that the agreement sought to be enforced was founded upon mistake of employee as to the existence of a material fact, that is, his physical qualification to return to work immediately, and that some of the railroad's agents had knowledge of physician's report casting doubt on that qualification but did not disclose such information to the employee. Louisville and Nashville Railroad Co. v. Solchenberger, 270 Ala. 536, 120 So.2d 704 (1960). The court stated:

"... In an application to a court of equity, the defendant may rebut the *prima facie* case made by the contract alone, and show, by proof of extrinsic facts, that specific performance would not be strictly equitable. From our own decisions the following principles governing the discretion of the court in decreeing the enforcement of contracts may be regarded as settled: The agreement must be free from unfairness, hardship, or mistake going to its essence. A fraudulent representation or concealment, sufficient to avoid it at law, or for its rescission or cancellation in equity, is not essential to a denial of specific performance. If the contract is obtained by the suppression of material facts known to the party seeking performance, and unknown to the defendant; or if the defendant was led into making it by surprise without fault on his part, though not misled by positive representations of the other party; or if it is impressed with any inequitable feature, the court will refuse to enforce the contract."

The chancellor concluded that the agreement here sought to be enforced was founded on mistake of plaintiff as to the existence of a material fact, that is his physical qualification, that some of defendant's agents or employees had knowledge of the existence of the report of the August examination but did not disclose that information to plaintiff. We cannot escape the conclusion that knowledge of that report was a material fact unknown to plaintiff. We think it is clear that the record does not show any deliberate withholding of that information from plaintiff on the part of defendant or any of its agents, and certainly the record does not show any intentional misrepresentation or withholding of information by defendant's claim agent. None the less, we are also clear to the conclusion, that withholding of the August report coupled with plaintiff's belief based on the depositions of Dr. Batson and Dr. Baranco constitute sufficient reason for denying specific performance in this case.

2. In Earl of Durham v. Legard, 34 Beav. 611, 55 Eng.Rep. 771 (Ch.1865), plaintiff agreed to purchase from the defendant an estate described on the written contract as "Kidland Estate containing 21,750 acres." The estate actually contained 11,814 acres and the representation was the bona fide mistake of defendant's agent. Plaintiff sued for specific performance "on payment of the purchase money, less a proper compensation for the deficiency in quantity." The Master of the Rolls, Sir John Romilly, held that this was not a case for partial performance with compensation, but "simply a case of mistake." He added that the purchaser "may elect to perform the contract without compensation."

C. HARDSHIP OR UNFAIRNESS

Patel v. Ali

Chancery Division, 1984.
[1984] Ch. 283.

■ GOULDING, J. . . . .

The material facts are not in dispute and can be shortly stated. In the year 1979 the defendant was living in the property with her husband, Mr. Ali. They occupied it as their matrimonial home. Another couple, Mr. and Mrs. Nazir Ahmed, were also living in the house. Mr. Ahmed is the second defendant to the action. The property was freehold and was registered in the name of Mr. Ahmed and the defendant, who claim to be not only legally but beneficially entitled thereto. On 31 July 1979 the contract was entered into between both defendants as vendors and the plaintiffs, Mr. and Mrs. Patel, as purchasers. The price was £24,000, the contractual completion date 28 August 1979.

The performance of the contract has been subject—and this is a circumstance which, to my mind, is of the greatest importance in the case— to a quite extraordinary delay, for which neither side on this appeal has sought to blame the other. The causes of the delay have not been explored in detail in the evidence, but it appears that a great deal of it can be put down to two difficulties. In the first place, the trustee in bankruptcy of Mr. Ali has made claim to a beneficial interest in the property.... The second cause of delay, so it is said, was a succession of difficulties experienced by the plaintiffs in effecting service of proceedings on Mr. Ahmed, who has returned to Pakistan....

Meanwhile, the circumstances of the defendant had changed disastrously. At the date of the contract she had one child who was still a baby; and, so far as she knew, she was in good health. She was about 23 years old. She spoke and still speaks, in the words of her solicitor's affidavit, "virtually no English at all." In the summer of 1980 she was found to have a bone cancer in her right thigh. On 24 July 1980, that is three days after the order of Fox J. in the bankruptcy proceedings, her right leg was amputated at the hip joint. She was then in an advanced state of pregnancy and gave birth to her second child on 31 August 1980. In the spring of 1981 her husband went to prison and remained there until mid-summer 1982. After his release she became pregnant again and her third child was born in August 1983.

The defendant has been fitted with an artificial leg. She is able to walk about the house and dress herself, but not to do shopping, and she needs help with household duties and with the children. She is greatly dependent on friends and relations to enable her to keep her home going and to look after her children, especially on her sister who, I was told, lives only a few doors away, and on a friendly neighbour, Mrs. Dhillon.

It is in these circumstances that the defendant asks the court to refuse specific performance of the contract and to leave the plaintiffs to their remedy in damages....

That the hardship to the defendant of enforced removal from the property would be great is, on the evidence, beyond doubt....

The hardship which would be caused to the plaintiffs if specific performance were refused and adequate pecuniary compensation were available is not, so far as the evidence reveals, greater than what is necessarily involved in being disappointed of the purchase after so long a delay. Since the contractual date for completion in 1979 the plaintiffs have lived in accommodation rented from their local authority, Brent London Borough Council.

It is not in dispute that, like other equitable relief, the specific performance of contracts is a discretionary remedy; but, in the ordinary case of a sale of land or buildings, the court normally grants it as of course and withholds it only on proof of special facts. The textbooks and reported decisions have long recognised hardship as one ground on which, in a proper case, a purchaser or vendor may be refused specific performance and be left to his right to damages for breach of contract at law. The difficulty is to determine within what limits hardship to a defendant can properly be said to justify this exercise of judicial discretion. There is no doubt that, in the majority of cases, the hardship which moves the court to refuse specific performance is either a hardship existing at the date of the contract or a hardship due in some way to the plaintiff. In the present case, neither of those conditions being satisfied, the plaintiffs rely strongly on that principle or practice, which is stated in varying terms in all the well-known textbooks. It is sufficient for me to cite a passage from Fry on Specific Performance, 6th ed. (1921), p. 199:

> It is a well-established doctrine that the court will not enforce the specific performance of a contract, the result of which would be to impose great hardship on either of the parties to it; and this although the party seeking specific performance may be free from the least impropriety of conduct. The question of the hardship of a contract is generally to be judged of at the time at which it is entered into: if it be then fair and just and not productive of hardship, it will be immaterial that it may, by the force of subsequent circumstances or change of events, have become less beneficial to one party, except where these subsequent events have been in some way due to the party who seeks the performance of the contract. For whatever contingencies may attach to a contract, or be involved in the performance of either part, have been taken upon themselves by the parties to it. It has been determined that the reasonableness of a contract is to be judged of at the time it is entered into, and not by the light of subsequent events, and we have already seen that the same principle applies in considering the fairness of a contract.

However, the principle so stated cannot be erected into a fixed limitation of the court's equitable jurisdiction. It is recognised, both by Fry L.J. in his book and in the argument of Mr. Simpkiss for the plaintiffs in the present action, that the court has sometimes refused specific performance because of a change of circumstances supervening after the making of the contract and not in any way attributable to the plaintiff. One such case is City of London v. Nash (1747) 1 Ves.Sen. 11, 12, where Lord Hardwicke L.C. refused specific performance of a contract which required the demolition of houses and building of new ones, because he thought that the demolition would be a public loss and no benefit to the plaintiffs, who would be sufficiently compensated by damages at law. This seems a strong case, because the difficulties were due to breaches of contract by the defendant himself.... Another relevant case is Webb v. Direct London and Portsmouth Railway Co. (1852) 1 De.G.M. & G. 521, where the Court of Appeal refused specifically to enforce a purchase of land by the company after it had abandoned its proposed enterprise of constructing a railway from Epsom to Portsmouth. Similar in principle are the cases where the court has refused injunctions to compel specific performance of restrictive covenants by reason of a change in the character of the neighbourhood, even where the plaintiff and his predecessors in title have in no way contributed thereto. Thus, I am satisfied that the court's discretion is wide enough, in an otherwise proper case, to refuse specific performance on the ground of hardship subsequent to the contract and not caused by the plaintiff.

Another limitation suggested by Mr. Simpkiss was that, in the reported cases, as he said, hardship successfully relied on has always related to the subject matter of the contract and has not been just a personal hardship of the defendant. Certainly, mere pecuniary difficulties, whether of purchaser or of vendor, afford no excuse from performance of a contract. In a wider sense than that, I do not think the suggested universal proposition can be sustained. In *Webb's* case, 1 De G.M. & G. 521, the hardship in no way affected the title to the property or its physical condition. It was a hardship to the railway company to be compelled to pay for land it could never use, just as it is a hardship to the defendant here to be compelled to convey a house she cannot now well do without.

The important and true principle, in my view, is that only in extraordinary and persuasive circumstances can hardship supply an excuse for resisting performance of a contract for the sale of immovable property. A person of full capacity who sells or buys a house takes the risk of hardship to himself and his dependents, whether arising from existing facts or unexpectedly supervening in the interval before completion. This is where, to my mind, great importance attaches to the immense delay in the present case, not attributable to the defendant's conduct. Even after issue of the writ, she could not complete, if she had wanted to, without the concurrence of the absent Mr. Ahmed. Thus, in a sense, she can say she is being asked to do what she never bargained for, namely to complete the sale after more than four years, after all the unforeseeable changes that such a period entails. I think that in this way she can fairly assert that specific performance would inflict upon her "a hardship amounting to injustice" to use the phrase employed by James L.J., in a different but comparable context, in Tamplin v. James (1880) 15 Ch.D. 215, 221. Equitable relief may, in my view, be refused because of an unforeseen change of circumstances not amounting to legal frustration, ...

In the end, I am satisfied that it is within the court's discretion to accede to the defendant's prayer if satisfied that it is just to do so. And, on the whole, looking at the position of both sides after the long unpredictable delay for which neither seeks to make the other responsible, I am of opinion that it *is* just to leave the plaintiffs to their remedy in damages if that can indeed be effective.

. . . .

Order accordingly.

NOTES ON HARDSHIP OR UNFAIRNESS

1. UNCONSCIONABLE BARGAINS: Cornell v. T.V. Development Corp., 24 A.D.2d 471, 260 N.Y.S.2d 865 (1965), was an action brought against a former employer and others to recover damages for wrongful discharge and for other relief. In a memorandum opinion, the court stated:

. . . As plaintiff's action was in part cast in equity and was tried on the equity side of the court, equitable principles must dictate the determination of all the issues in the action.

Where an agreement which plaintiff submits as the basis for the relief he seeks is unreasonable or unconscionable, a court of equity will not grant specific performance or its equivalent, but may in its discretion "consider the particular facts of each case and deal with it on its merits" (5 Williston on Contracts [Rev. Ed.], § 1425, p. 3990).

By virtue of this doctrine, under the facts and circumstances at bar, the trial justice was free to conclude that plaintiff was equitably entitled to damages only up to the date he entered into business on his own, even though on this phase of the case plaintiff's cause of action for damages for wrongful discharge was one at law wherein normally plaintiff's measure of damages was *prima facie* the entire amount of compensation to accrue during the balance of the term of the employment contract. A court of equity, trying mixed questions of law and equity, "will mold its decrees to suit the needs of the particular case" without distinction as to whether it chooses legal or equitable principles as the basis for its determination.

2.   UNIFORM COMMERCIAL CODE § 2–302: Unconscionable Contract or Clause.

(1) If the court as a matter of law finds the contract or any clause of the contract to have been unconscionable at the time it was made the court may refuse to enforce the contract, or it may enforce the remainder of the contract without the unconscionable clause, or it may so limit the application of any unconscionable clause as to avoid any unconscionable result.

(2) When it is claimed or appears to the court that the contract or any clause thereof may be unconscionable the parties shall be afforded a reasonable opportunity to present evidence as to its commercial setting, purpose and effect to aid the court in making the determination.

Comment 1 to this section states that the "principle is one of the prevention of oppression and unfair surprise and not of disturbance of allocation of risks because of superior bargaining power."

3.   In Williams v. Walker–Thomas Furniture Co., 350 F.2d 445 (D.C.Cir.1965), a furniture company sued to recover on contracts under which the balance due on every item purchased continued until the balance due on all items, whenever purchased, was liquidated. (Installment sales legislation in many states prohibits contracts containing such provisions.) Relying on U.C.C. § 2–302, the court held that where the element of unconscionability is present at the time the contract is made, the contract should not be enforced. The case was remanded for further proceedings. A dissenting judge felt that the contract was not unconscionable within U.C.C. § 2–302 since "the appellant seems to have known precisely where she stood."

D. INADEQUACY OF CONSIDERATION

Jefferys v. Jefferys

Chancery, 1841.
138, 41 Eng.Rep. 443.

By articles of agreement, dated the 25th of July 1834, and made between John Jefferys of the one part, and Bowden and Thorn of the other part, John Jefferys, after reciting that he was desirous of making some certain and irrevocable provision for the support and maintenance of his daughters Martha, Charlotte, and Sarah Jefferys, covenanted with [(i.e., made a sealed promise to)] Bowden and Thorn, as trustees, forthwith to settle all his real estate to the same uses, ends, intents, and purposes as were expressed in his will, dated the 25th of May 1834; and, accordingly, he executed certain indentures [(i.e., deeds)] of lease and release[8] of the 16th and 17th of September 1834, whereby, in consideration of the natural love and affection which he had for his three daughters, and for divers other good causes and considerations, he conveyed certain freehold[9] hereditaments, subject to the incumbrances affecting the same, and covenanted to surrender certain copyhold[10] hereditaments, to Bowden and Thorn, upon trust, out of the rents and profits thereof to pay to him an annuity of 80*l.* for his life; and after his death to sell the freehold and copyhold hereditaments, and out of the monies arising therefrom to pay off certain incumbrances, and to stand possessed of the residue of such monies, upon certain trusts, for the benefit of his three daughters.

By the will of Sarah Jefferys, who died in April 1835, all her interest under the settlement became vested in her two sisters. John Jefferys never surrendered the copyholds, pursuant to the covenant. In September 1836, he died, having, by will, dated the 18th of August 1836, given part of the before-mentioned freehold and copyhold estates to his wife Isabella, who was, shortly after his death, admitted to part of the copyhold estates.

In July 1837 this bill was filed by Martha and Charlotte Jefferys against Isabella Jefferys and Bowden and Thorn, praying that the trusts of the indenture of the 17th September 1834 might be carried into execution; and that Isabella Jefferys might be decreed to surrender the copyholds, to which she had been admitted, to Bowden and Thorn, as trustees of that indenture.

By the will of Martha Jefferys, who died in April 1838, all her interest under the settlement became vested in her sister Charlotte Jefferys, the surviving Plaintiff; and Isabella Jefferys having, since the filing of the bill, married one Abraham Peacock, a bill of revivor and supplement was filed by the surviving Plaintiff.

. . . .

The Lord Chancellor [Lord Cottenham]. The title of the Plaintiffs to the freehold is complete; and they may have a decree for carrying the settlement into effect so far as the freeholds are concerned. With respect to the copyholds, I have no doubt that the Court will not execute a voluntary [(i.e., gratuitous)] contract; and my impression is, that the principle of the Court to withhold its assistance from a volunteer applies equally, whether he seeks to have the benefit of a contract, a covenant, or a settlement. As, however, the decision in [a prior case] is entitled to the highest consider-

8. [An indenture of lease and release was a conveyance used to avoid the Statute of Uses.]

9. [A freehold estate is an estate for life or in fee.]

10. [A copyhold was an estate held at the will of the lord, which was constrained by manorial custom.]

ation, I will not dispose of this case absolutely, without looking at a former case, in which I had occasion to refer to that decision. Unless I alter the opinion I have expressed, the bill must be dismissed with costs, so far as the copyholds are concerned.

On this day[11] his Lordship said he had looked at the case alluded to, and that he saw no reason for altering the opinion he had before expressed.

Seymour v. Delancey

Court of Chancery of New York, 1822.
6 Johnson's Chancery Reports 222.
Court for the Trial of Impeachments and the Correction of Errors of New York, 1824.
3 Cowen 445.

■ THE CHANCELLOR [KENT]. The question in this case is, whether it be fit and proper, under all the circumstances, to decree a specific performance of the contract of sale.

The main objection to the exercise of this power of the Court, in the present case, is the great inadequacy of price which the plaintiff was to allow for the two farms, of which he seeks title.

By the articles of agreement, Thomas Ellison, the ancestor of the defendants, was to convey, by the first of June, 1820, two farms, lying in the towns of Montgomery and Wallkill, in Orange county, and containing, in the whole, 763 acres of land, and the plaintiff was to give, in exchange, the one equal undivided third part of two lots of land, in the village of Newburgh. The agreement was executed on the 14th of January, 1820, and, by the terms of it, each party was at liberty to take possession of the estate to be conveyed to him, and to receive the profits to his own use; and it is in proof, that each party did enter into possession, on the execution of the agreement.

The witnesses differ greatly in their estimates of the value of these respective pieces of land. . . . It is impossible to be precise in ascertaining the difference in value between the lands of the two parties, but I am satisfied, that at the date of the agreement, the village lots were not worth half the value of the country farms; and we should make an ample advance of the one, and an ample diminution of the other, in value, if we were to fix the one third of the Newburgh lots at 6,000 dollars, and the farms at 12,000 dollars.

The question then recurs, is it the dictate of sound legal discretion, that this agreement should be specifically carried into execution by the authority of this Court? It is an application to sound discretion. . . . A Court of equity must be satisfied, that the claim for a deed is fair and just, and reasonable, and the contract equal in all its parts, and founded on an adequate consideration, before it will interpose with this extraordinary assistance. If there be any well founded objection on any of these grounds, the practice of the Court is to leave the party to his remedy at law for a compensation in damages.

11. [February 1, 1841. The prior judgment of Lord Cottenham had been given January 26, 1841, apparently at the conclusion of the arguments.]

. . . .

The doctrine involved in this inquiry has been repeatedly brought into discussion since the time of Lord Eldon . . .

. . . .

. . . [I]n these later cases, there is a doubt thrown over the question, whether inadequacy of price alone, though not so great as to be evidence of fraud, will be sufficient, in any case, and without any other ingredient, as infirmity of mind, surprise, & c., to withhold the decree for a specific performance. But, after so much recognition of the general doctrine, that equity will not enforce hard, or unreasonable, or unequal bargains, but rather leave them to a jury at law, to mitigate or apportion the damages, as the justice of the case shall appear; . . . I do not perceive the necessity or even the propriety of that doubt and distrust, if not disapprobation, which Lord Eldon and the Master of the Rolls, have been pleased to express. . . .

I conclude, then, that inadequacy of price may, of itself, and without fraud or other ingredient, be sufficient to stay the application of the power of this Court to *enforce* a specific performance of a private contract to sell land; though it may be true, as the Lord Ch. Baron [Eyre] said, in Griffith v. Spratley [1 Cox Eq. 383], that mere inadequacy of price, independent of other circumstances, is not sufficient to *set aside* the transaction. In the present case, the inadequacy is so great as to give the character of hardship, unreasonableness and inequality to the contract, and to render it discreet and proper, under the established principles of the Court, to refuse to decree a specific performance, and to leave the plaintiff to seek his compensation in damages at law.

The civil law went far beyond the English law on this subject, and a contract for the sale of land was rescinded by judicial authority, though made in good faith, if the price was below half the value. . . . This was the law in France before the revolution. Though by the Napoleon Code, the ratio is fixed at 7–12ths below the real value.

If it were to be granted that an inadequacy, great as that in the present case, was not sufficient to stay the powers of the Court, without the weight of some additional ingredient, we have that ingredient in this case.

Ellison, the ancestor of the defendants, was, in the last year or two of his life, rendered, for a considerable part of his time, unfit for business, by habitual intoxication. His mind must have felt the pernicious effects of that habit, and have lost its original strength, when he made the bargain in question. The proof is abundantly sufficient to render the fact of his competency to contract, with the requisite judgment, doubtful. One of the witnesses says, that for the greater part of the last two years of his life, he was incompetent. The answer sets up this defence, in terms sufficiently intelligible to admit the proof, and to prevent the objection of surprise. It states, that for some time previous to his death, he was occasionally incapable of attending to business. The contract was made in January, and he died in August, 1820; and this language is, perhaps, as direct and explicit as children could have been inclined to use, and it was, no doubt, well understood by the plaintiff, for the habitual intoxication of Ellison appears to have been a matter of public notoriety in the village of Newburgh. This fact adds greatly to the force of the considerations growing out of the inadequacy of the price, and is clearly sufficient, within the view of all the cases, to render it highly discreet and just to refuse the aid of the Court to a specific performance of so hard and so extravagant a bargain, gained from a habitual drunkard, in the last year of his life, and just before his infirmities had begun to incapacitate him entirely for business.

There is another circumstance in the case which ought to be taken into consideration, when the plaintiff comes here seeking a specific performance. He was not in a condition to give a good title to the village lots, either when he contracted, or when the deeds were to be exchanged, or at the time of the death of Ellison. The lots were under mortgage for 5000 dollars, which I consider as their full value, and that mortgage was not redeemed until after Ellison's death. The plaintiff was in default on the first of June, 1820. He ought to have shown himself able and ready to convey on that day. One of his witnesses, who is a physician, says, that Ellison, from June to within a week of his death, was competent in mind to do business. The plaintiff shows no sufficient excuse for his want of readiness and ability; and I cannot but persuade myself, after having examined most of the English cases, that the united force of the circumstances of this case would have overcome the scruples of the most cautious mind that has ever investigated and expressed any opinion on the subject, and that a bill with so much fact against the equity of the claim, has never been sustained.

. . . .

I am, consequently, of opinion, that the bill be dismissed, without costs.

. . . .

[The plaintiff appealed to the Court for the Trial of Impeachments and the Correction of Errors. This court consisted of the Lieutenant–Governor, the Chancellor, the Chief Justice and the two Associate Justices of the Supreme Court, and the 32 members of the state Senate. Kent had retired as Chancellor prior to the hearing of the appeal, and had been succeeded by Nathan Sanford, who, however, took no part in the hearing or decision of the appeal. Neither of the Associate Justices of the Supreme Court took part in the decision, one (Woolworth, J.) because he had not heard the argument, the other (Sutherland, J.) because of illness. By a vote of 14–10, the high court reversed Chancellor Kent's decision.]

■ SAVAGE, C.J . . . .

[T]he question [whether inadequacy of price alone is a ground for refusing specific performance] is one upon which very great men have differed, and have administered the equity of the Court upon diametrically opposite principles. The one class maintain, that the Court will not lend its aid to enforce the performance of contracts, unless they are fair, just and reasonable, and founded on adequate consideration. The other class maintain, that unless the inadequacy of price is such as shocks the conscience, and amounts in itself to decisive and conclusive evidence of fraud in the transaction, it is not of itself a sufficient ground for refusing a specific performance.

The most distinguished of those who support the latter doctrine is Lord Eldon. To him may be added Sir William Grant, Lord Keeper Wright, and probably some others . . . .

. . . .

Upon authority, therefore, as well as upon principle, I am clearly of opinion that a Court of Equity ought not to lend its aid in enforcing an executory contract unless it is fair, just, reasonable and equal in all its parts, and founded upon adequate consideration.

It is undoubtedly well settled that inadequacy of price, alone, is not a sufficient reason for setting aside a contract executed, unless its grossness amount to fraud; but there is a wide difference between enforcing an executory contract, and setting aside a contract deliberately executed; and the two subjects admit of very different views and considerations.

. . . .

. . . [O]n the question of decreeing specific performance of executory contracts, the Court of Chancery must exercise its discretion; not an arbitrary, but a sound judicial discretion. If the contract be free from objection, it is the duty of the Court to decree performance. But if there are circumstances of unfairness, though not amounting to fraud or oppression, or if the inadequacy of consideration be so great as to render the bargain hard and unconscionable; on either ground the Court may refuse its aid to enforce the contract, and leave the parties to contest their rights in a Court of law.

. . . .

I concur, therefore, with his honor the Chancellor, and am of opinion that his decree should be affirmed . . . .

■ Sudam, S. . . .

The first point made by the respondents, that this contract for exchange of lands was *hard, disproportionate and unequal in its terms,* is the main point in the cause, and has been so treated by the Chancellor in his opinion . . . .

. . . .

To determine whether, in fact, the agreement for exchange was hard, unequal, and disproportionate, and whether it was free from *fraud, surprise,* & c., it will be necessary to examine, with as much brevity as possible, the history of this transaction . . . .

. . . .

The next question which presents itself to the consideration of the Court is, whether the contract between the appellant and Ellison is so *hard, unreasonable, or unequal,* that this Court will not aid to enforce it.

In reviewing this part of the case, it will be the duty of the Court to investigate the evidence as to the value of the Newburgh lots, and the farms to be exchanged for them. Should they arrive at the conclusion that *mere inadequacy* in value, where there is *no fraud, misrepresentation, imposition, or concealment of facts, is of itself sufficient to avoid the contract,* it will save a great deal of the labor and investigation which might otherwise be required. I admit, however, that where the inadequacy of price in a contract is so flagrant and palpable as to convince a man at the first blush, that one of the contracting parties had been imposed on by some false pretense, such a contract ought not to be enforced by this, or any other Court of Equity. It is not to be denied, that it is the settled doctrine of the Court of Chancery, that it will not carry into effect, specifically, a contract where the inadequacy of price amounts to conclusive evidence of fraud. In this view of the case, therefore, as well as in reference to the objection of mere inadequacy, I shall briefly examine the evidence of value.

It may be proper to premise, that there is a distinction between a Court of Chancery, refusing to decree the specific performance of a contract, and setting it aside. It is also well settled, that a Court of Equity will not disturb an agreement that *has been executed,* although they would not have decreed a specific performance. In the first case, the court would leave the party to his remedy at law. In the second, they would refuse to interfere by directing the agreement to be cancelled, the party having consummated his own act. But if there should be fraud, circumvention, dec[e]it, or misrepresentation, a Court of Chancery would order the contract to be delivered up to be cancelled. This case, then, being free from fraud, concealment and misrepresentation, and from the charge of a hasty and unadvised contract, one important question appears to be, can a Court of Equity interfere, under such circumstances, to avoid the contract? For, in my opinion, not to carry this contract into effect is to avoid it wholly. It would be well to consider whether this is a case coming within the rule. For if it be true that the respondents must rest the decree of the Chancellor, principally, on the inadequacy in value of the property to be exchanged; and if it be true that, in order to avoid such a contract, the inadequacy of price must amount to conclusive evidence of fraud, I do not see in what manner the opinion of his Honor the Chancellor can be supported.

There is no question so well calculated to generate a variety of opinion, as that which regards the value of a village lot, or a farm in the country; and unless the disproportion should be gross and palpable, it would be very difficult to estimate how much more had been given by A. for a lot than the price at which B. would value it.

This, by the proofs, is the precise case before us. The average value of the appellant's interest in the lots at Newburgh, as sworn to by six witnesses, is $10,856; and this is corroborated by the fact, that the father of the appellant estimated the lot east of Water street, several years since, at $30,000. The average of the farms, as sworn to by witnesses, is $12,686, and the difference about $2186, according to the highest estimate made by the witnesses of the respondents. The lowest estimate of the Newburgh lots, by the respondents' witnesses, is between 5 and 6000 dollars. That a difference of opinion should exist among the witnesses, both as to the value of the lots in Newburgh and the farms of Ellison, is very natural. . . . There is no ground for saying that there was, in this case, either fraud, surprise, misrepresentation, or deceit. The bargain was conducted by him throughout with great deliberation, and he consummated it with his eyes open. Under such circumstances, we are called on to say, that mere inadequacy of price, and where there is much contradictory evidence, is of itself sufficient to prevent the Court of Chancery from decreeing the specific performance of the contract.

In the case of Coles v. Trecothick, (9 Ves. 246,) Lord Eldon observed, that inadequacy of price, unless it amounted to *conclusive evidence* of fraud, was not itself a sufficient ground for refusing a specific performance; and, although this was the case of an auction sale, the opinion was pronounced on the general question. In Mortlock v. Buller, (10 Ves. 292,) the Lord Chancellor declined giving an opinion on the doctrine of inadequacy. In Western v. Russell (3 Ves. & Bea. 187) the defence was *gross inadequacy of consideration*. The Master of the Rolls said that it was not necessary to determine the general question whether inadequacy of price might not be a ground for refusing performance, and he decided the case upon its special circumstances, and held that, as the vendor was not alleged to be under any incapacity or deficiency of judgment, and *set his own price and obtained it,* and never expressed any dissatisfaction, but accused the purchaser of delay, the agreement should be carried into execution. Chancellor Kent admits, that Lord Eldon and the Master of the Rolls had thrown doubt and distrust on this doctrine that inadequacy of price is of itself sufficient to prevent a specific execution.

. . . .

I cannot assent to the doctrine, that inadequacy of price may, of itself and without fraud or other ingredient, be sufficient to stay the application of the power of a Court of Chancery, to enforce a specific performance of a private contract to sell land.

. . . To say, when all is fair, and the parties deal on equal terms, that a Court of Equity will not interfere, does not appear to me to be supported by authority; and unless I am bound down by some rigid rule of law, I, for one cannot consent to its introduction into our equity code.

. . . .

Upon the whole, I am of opinion, that there is not in the present case such an inadequacy of price, as, of itself, amounts to conclusive evidence of fraud; that the contract between the appellant and Ellison, in his lifetime, was entered into with a full knowledge of all the circumstances by Ellison, and after much deliberation; and that it is fair in all its parts; and that the respondents ought to be compelled specifically to carry it into effect.

. . . .

The cause must therefore be remitted to the Court of Chancery that the Chancellor may direct a Master to inquire whether the appellant can give to the respondents a clear and unincumbered title to the Newburgh lots; and if he can, a decree for a specific performance, according to the contract, must be entered against the respondents. . . .

McKinnon v. Benedict

Supreme Court of Wisconsin, 1968.
38 Wis.2d 607, 157 N.W.2d 665.

This is an appeal from a judgment of the county court of Vilas county for damages for a trespass on the property owned by Roderick W. McKinnon and Dorothy D. McKinnon, and from an injunction which restrained the defendants, Roy A. Benedict, Jr., and Evelyn M. Benedict, from operating a trailer park and campsite on certain resort property located in Vilas county. The Benedicts have appealed from this judgment.

The Benedict property is approximately an 80–acre tract located on the shores of Mamie Lake, one of the chain of Cisco Lakes, on the Michigan–Wisconsin border. It is operated as a resort known as Bent's Camp. The Benedict property is completely surrounded by the McKinnon tract of approximately 1,170 acres. The McKinnons have lived on Mamie Lake since 1925, although at the present time they reside there only during the summer months and during the Christmas holidays. During the remainder of the year, the McKinnons reside in Arizona, where Roderick McKinnon is an investment counsellor. He is a member of the Wisconsin State Bar and at various times practiced law with the Milwaukee firms of Miller, Mack & Fairchild and Whyte, Hirschboeck, Minahan, Harding & Harland. During World War II, he was in intelligence work for the United States government. He served with the United States State Department and was, at one time, vice president of Cleaver–Brooks Company.

Until 1961, Bent's Camp was operated by a Mr. and Mrs. L.L. Dorsey. This property, although abutting Mamie Lake, is divided by county trunk B. The resort area is located near the lakeshore to the northeast of county trunk B and consists of 14 cabins and a main lodge. The area of Bent's Camp southwest of county trunk B is a small, undeveloped parcel of timberland. During 1960 the Dorseys were interested in selling the property. Their agent, one Handlos, located the Benedicts as prospective buyers. They, however, were in need of financial assistance to make the purchase, and they were referred to Roderick W. McKinnon, who agreed to loan the Benedicts the sum of $5,000 as a partial down payment. This loan was made on the basis of an understanding that the Benedicts would continue to operate Bent's Camp as an American plan family resort. On August 31, 1960, McKinnon wrote a letter to the Benedicts incorporating the terms on which the advance was made:

"Dear Roy:

"It is my understanding that in consideration of my advancing you $5000, for use as a downpayment on Bent's Camp we agree between one another as follows:

"(1) You and Mrs. Benedict will sign a non-interest bearing note for $5000, due January 1, 1961, and a first mortgage on your cottage in Gogebic County, Michigan. If you should sell this property or your property in Wheaton, Illinois prior to the time the note is paid, you will pay the note out of the proceeds.

"(2) As soon as convenient after your acquisition of Bent's Camp, we will sign a recordable agreement providing that for a period of 25 years no trees will be cut between my land and Bent's Camp, nor between Bent's Camp and County Highway 'B' nor will any improvements be constructed or placed closer to my property than the present buildings. This restriction will have no application to any of your land lying west of County Trunk 'B' nor to your separate 40–acre 'woodlot'. If you wish, we will supply trees to be planted in this area at no cost to you.

"(3) In the event you desire, we will from time to time designate certain trees or certain areas on our property where you may cut fire wood at no cost to you.

"(4) I will help you try to reach a satisfactory solution concerning the lease held by Mrs. J. Stuart Vair. I will also try to generate business for your camp and to otherwise assist you in getting the operation well organized.

"If the foregoing meets with your approval, will you and Mrs. Benedict please sign below and return one copy for my files."

The approval was signed by both of the Benedicts, and the letter was returned to McKinnon. Thereafter, the Benedicts executed a note in the sum of $5,000 and a mortgage on their cottage property in Michigan. The promised $5,000 was shortly thereafter transmitted and used as a down payment. The loan was paid in full in the spring of 1961. The Benedicts thus had the use of the $5,000 from early September, 1960, to April, 1961, a period of about seven months. The Benedicts purchased the property from the Dorseys on a land contract at a price of $60,000. That land contract provided that, while the Benedicts continued to be obligated to the Dorseys under the terms of the contract, they would replace all personal property so as to maintain it in substantially the same state as at the time of the agreement. They also agreed that no timber would be cut except for firewood without the written consent of the Dorseys and that the premises were to be operated substantially in the same manner as they had been operated by the Dorseys in the previous years.

At the time the land contract was executed, Bent's Camp consisted of 14 cottages, only five of which could be used for resort purposes. Between 1961 and 1964, the Benedicts invested $20,000 in cottages, installing bathrooms and kitchens so that all of the cabins were habitable. Roy Benedict testified that during the period between 1961 and 1964, the income from the operations of the American Plan resort substantially decreased and that it became increasingly difficult to make the land-contract payments.

One of the conditions of the letter of August 31, 1960, was that McKinnon would attempt to reach a satisfactory solution concerning the lease held by Mrs. J. Stuart Vair. The record shows that Mrs. Vair held a fifty-year lease on one of the cabins at an annual rental of $5 per year. The record reveals only one attempt, and that unsuccessful, on the part of McKinnon to "reach a satisfactory solution." The agreement also provided that McKinnon would try to generate business for the camp and otherwise assist in getting the operation well organized. The record indicates no attempt whatsoever on the part of McKinnon to get the operation "well organized." There was evidence that at least one small group had spent a few days at Bent's Camp at the suggestion of McKinnon, but it is apparent that the amount of business generated by him was almost nil.

Because of financial pressures, the Benedicts, in the fall of 1964, decided to add to a trailer park and facilities for a tent camp. A trailer park was laid out just to the northeast of county trunk B. In the fall of 1964, Roy Benedict bulldozed the hills in that area and installed sewer, water, and electric facilities for 18 trailers at a cost of approximately $8,000. In the spring of 1965 work was commenced on a campsite on a hill located to the south of the cottages and across the bay from the McKinnon property. The Benedicts have invested to date approximately $1,200 on this campsite, most of which was expended for grading.

In June of 1965, McKinnon wrote to Benedict stating:

"I have heard indirectly that you are making some fairly major changes in the operation of Bent's Camp.

"Although I do not know the exact nature of the changes, I am confident that you and Ev will bear in mind our agreement of August 31, 1960. . . . I enclose a photostatic copy."

When the McKinnons returned to Wisconsin in June of 1965, they became aware of the nature of the work done by Benedict and immediately commenced suit to enjoin defendants "from the acts done or being done and uses to be made or being made" of the property. The McKinnons relied not only on the agreement of August 31, 1960, but also alleged the violation of county zoning and trailer ordinances and alleged a trespass across a point of land, wholly surrounded by the Benedict property, which was owned by McKinnon.

After a trial before the court, the trial judge found for the plaintiffs in accordance with the demands of the complaint enjoining the defendants from further bulldozing or hill leveling and from conducting on the premises a trailer park or a mobile home camp. The renting of any portion of the land for trailers or campers was prohibited by the judgment, and the Benedicts were restrained from using the premises for any other purpose than as an American Plan summer resort until August 31, 1985. It is from this judgment the defendants appeal.

■ HEFFERNAN, J.

Are the restrictions contained in the letter agreement
of August 31, 1960, enforceable in equity . . .

. . . We are thus not confronted with the question of damages that may result from the breach of this contract and confine ourselves solely to the right of the plaintiffs to invoke the equitable remedy of specific performance, in this case the enjoining of the defendants from the breach of the contract. . . .

Restatement, 2 Contracts, sec. 367, page 665, "Effect of Unfairness, Hardship, Mistake and Inequitable Conduct," cites three bases for a court of equity refusing specific performance of a contract. They are:

"(a) the consideration for it is grossly inadequate or its terms are otherwise unfair, or

"(b) its enforcement will cause unreasonable or disproportionate hardship or loss to the defendant or to third persons, or "(c) it was induced by some sharp practice, misrepresentation, or mistake." [12]

. . . .

These, of course, are ancient principles of equity. . . .

. . . .

Coupled with the general equitable principle that contracts that are oppressive will not be enforced in equity is the principle of public policy that restrictions on the use of land "are not favored in the law", and that restrictions and prohibitions as to the use of real estate should be resolved, if a doubt exists, in favor of the free use of the property.

. . .

The facts in this case must be examined in light of these accepted principles of equity.

The bargain between the McKinnons and the Benedicts has proved to be a harsh one indeed. If the terms of the agreement of August 31, 1960, are to be enforced literally, the Benedicts have for a period of twenty-five years stripped themselves of the right to make an optimum and lawful use of their property. The agreement provides that no improvements can be constructed closer to the McKinnon property than those buildings and improvements that were in existence in 1960. . . .

There was clear testimony that Benedict found difficulty in meeting his land-contract obligations, and his efforts to construct a campsite and trailer camp were motivated by the desire to put the resort on a more stable financial basis. While it is understandable that McKinnon may object to the erection of a trailer park and a campsite on adjacent property, nevertheless, they are legal and proper uses, assuming that they conform with the ordinances and statutes and do not constitute a nuisance; and any contract that seeks to prohibit them on a neighbor's property must be supported by consideration that has some relationship to the detriment to be sustained by the property owner whose uses are thus curtailed.

The great hardship sought to be imposed upon the Benedicts is apparent. What was the consideration in exchange for this deprivation of use? The only monetary consideration was the granting of a $5,000 loan, interest free, for a period of seven months. The value of this money for that period of time, if taken at the same interest rate as the 5 percent used on the balance of the land contract, is approximately $145; and it should be noted that this was not an unsecured loan, since McKinnon took a mortgage on the cottage property of the Benedicts in Michigan. In addition,

---

12. [Comment b to § 367 reads as follows:

Mere pecuniary inadequacy of consideration will not generally make the terms of a contract seem too unfair for enforcement unless the degree of inadequacy is extreme. The court will consider all the other facts of the case before determining the existence of the necessary degree of unfairness. A slight inadequacy of consideration, accompanied by other facts . . . may prevent specific enforcement, even though no one of the existing facts, standing alone, would be sufficient. Such facts exist in varying combinations and in each case must be considered as a whole. The application of the rule . . . must depend upon the moral standards of enlightened judges.]

McKinnon stated that he would "help you try" to reach a solution of the problem posed by Mrs. Vair's occupancy of one of the cottages on a fifty-year lease at $5 per year. His one attempt, as stated above, was a failure; and McKinnon's promise to generate business resulted in an occupancy by only one group for less than a week. For this pittance and these feeble attempts to help with the operational problems of the camp, the Benedicts have sacrificed their right to make lawful and reasonable use of their property.

In oral argument it was pointed out that the value of the $5,000 loan could not be measured in terms of the interest value of the money, since, without this advance, Benedict would have been unable to purchase the camp at all. To our mind, this is evidence of the fact that Benedict was not able to deal at arm's length with McKinnon, for his need for these funds was obviously so great that he was willing to enter into a contract that results in gross inequities. Lord Chancellor Northington said "necessitous men are not, truly speaking, free men."

We find that the inadequacy of consideration is so gross as to be unconscionable and a bar to the plaintiffs' invocation of the extraordinary equitable powers of the court.

While there is no doubt that there are benefits from this agreement to McKinnon, they are more than outweighed by the oppressive terms that would be imposed upon the Benedicts. McKinnon testified that he and his wife spend only the summer months on their property. Undoubtedly, these are the months when it is most important that there be no disruption of the natural beauty or the quiet and pleasant enjoyment of the property, nevertheless, there was testimony that the trailer camp could not be seen from the McKinnon home, nor could the campsite be seen during the summer months of the year, when the leaves were on the trees. Thus, the detriment of which the McKinnons complain, that would be cognizable in an equity action, is minimal, while the damage done to the Benedicts is severe.

Considering all the factors—the inadequacy of the consideration, the small benefit that would be accorded the McKinnons, and the oppressive conditions imposed upon the Benedicts—we conclude that this contract failed to meet the test of reasonableness that is the *sine qua non* of the enforcement of rights in an action in equity.

5A Corbin, Contracts, sec. 1164, p. 219, points out that, although a contract is harsh, oppressive, and unconscionable, it may nevertheless be enforceable at law; but, in the discretion of the court, equitable remedies will not be enforced against one who suffers from such harshness and oppression.

A fair reading of the transcript indicates no sharp practice, dishonesty, or overreaching on the part of McKinnon. However, there was a wide disparity between the business experience of the parties. McKinnon was a man of stature in the legal field, an investment counsellor, a former officer of a major corporation, and had held posts of responsibility with the United States government, while, insofar as the record shows, Benedict was a retail jeweler and a man of limited financial ability. He no doubt overvalued the promises of McKinnon to assist in getting the operation "well organized" and to solve the lease problem and to "generate business." These factors, in view of Benedict's financial inability to enter into an arms-length transaction, may be explanatory of the reason for the agreement, but the agreement viewed even as of the time of its execution was unfair and based upon inadequate consideration. We, therefore, have no hesitancy in denying the plaintiffs the equitable remedy of injunction.

. . . .

Judgment affirmed in part, reversed in part, and the cause is remanded to the trial court for further proceedings not inconsistent with this opinion.

E.   THE STATUTE OF FRAUDS

An Act for Prevention of Frauds and Perjuries[13]

Statutes, 29 Charles II, Chapter 3 (1677).

For Prevention of many Fraudulent Practices which are commonly endeavoured to be upheld by Perjury, and Subornation of Perjury; Be it Enacted by the Kings most Excellent Majesty, by and with the Advice and Consent of the Lords Spiritual and Temporal, and the Commons in this present Parliament assembled, and by the Authority of the same, That from and after the Four and Twentieth day of *June,* which shall be in the year of our Lord, One thousand six hundred seventy and seven. . . .

[IV]   And be it further Enacted by the Authority aforesaid, That from and after the said Four and Twentieth day of *June,* no Action shall be brought [1] whereby to charge any Executor or Administrator upon any special promise to answer Damages out of his own Estate, [2] or whereby to charge the Defendant upon any special promise to answer for the debt, default or miscarriages of another person, [3] or to charge any person upon any Agreement made upon consideration of Marriage, [4] or upon any Contract or Sale of Lands, Tenements, or Hereditaments, or any Interest in or concerning them, [5] or upon any Agreement that is not to be performed within the space of One year from the making thereof, [6] unless the Agreement upon which such Action shall be brought, or some *Memorandum* or Note thereof shall be in Writing, and signed by the party to be charged therewith, or some other person thereunto by him lawfully authorized. . . .

[XVII]   And be it further Enacted by the Authority aforesaid, That from and after the said Four and Twentieth day of *June,* no Contract for the sale of any Goods, Wares or Merchandises, for the Price of Ten Pounds

---

13. [Only so much of the statute as is or may be applicable to contracts for the sale of goods or the conveyance of land is reprinted. The section and subsection numbers are inserted as they appear in later editions of the statute.]

Sterling, or upwards, shall be allowed to be good, except the Buyer shall accept part of the Goods so sold, and actually receive the same, or give something in earnest to bind the Bargain, or in part of payment, or that some Note or *Memorandum* in writing of the said Bargain, be made and Signed by the parties to be charged by such Contract, or their Agents thereunto lawfully Authorized....

---

1. SATISFACTION BY A MEMORANDUM IN WRITING

Mentz v. Newwitter

Court of Appeals of New York, 1890.
122 N.Y. 491, 25 N.E. 1044.

This action was brought to recover from the defendant the difference between the sum bid for certain real estate at an auction sale thereof and the sum for which said real estate was resold upon the refusal of the defendant to complete his purchase.

The referee found the following facts:

On April 28, 1886, the plaintiff was the owner of premises known as No. 311 East One Hundred and Fourth street, in the city of New York, and authorized and empowered Richard V. Harnett & Co., auctioneers, to sell the same at public auction at the Real Estate Exchange in said city, and on the date aforesaid said Harnett & Co. did offer said premises for sale, and they were struck off and sold to the defendant at his bid of $11,800. Said Harnett & Co. thereupon made and signed a memorandum of said sale. Defendant failed to pay ten per cent of the purchase-money, and to sign a memorandum of the purchase so made. Prior to May 26, 1886, a notice was served upon defendant that said premises would be resold on his account, on the date aforesaid, at the real estate auction rooms, and that the plaintiff would hold him for the deficiency arising between the price bid by said defendant and the price the same would bring at such resale. At such resale the premises were resold for $10,200.

And as a conclusion of law the referee found that the plaintiff was entitled to judgment for $1,600, with interest and auction fees.

The only evidence of a written contract between the parties for the sale of lands was a memorandum in the auctioneer's book of sales, as follows:

Wed. 28 April '86.

311 E 104	Terms Sale
11000	7000
250	at 5 per cent
250	2 m
11750	3000
11800	at 6 per cent
J.N. Newwitter	
4 Pine St	can be paid

This memorandum was signed by Harnett on the margin of the book at the close of the sale.

The book also contained a printed slip or advertisement of the sale, but such slip did not name or describe the owner or make mention of any such person.

■ BROWN, J. The exceptions to the referee's finding that the premises in question were sold by Harnett & Company, the auctioneers, to the defendant, and that said auctioneers thereupon made and signed a memorandum of sale present the question of the sufficiency of the memorandum recorded in the auctioneers' books.

It is upon that memorandum that the judgment is founded, and it is upon that that the respondent relies as a compliance with the Statute of Frauds. The Statute is as follows:

"Every contract ... for the sale of any lands ... shall be void, unless the contract, or some note or memorandum thereof, ... be in writing and be subscribed by the party by whom the sale is to be made.

"Every instrument required to be signed by any party under the last preceding section, may be subscribed by the agent of such party lawfully authorized."

The writing of the auctioneer's name upon the margin of the book may be regarded as sufficient subscription of the contract by the vendor in this instance, and for the purpose of disposing of this appeal, we may assume that the instrument created a valid and binding contract if it be such a note, or memorandum thereof, as the statute requires. And the precise question we are to determine is, whether a memorandum, which does not name or describe the vendor, fulfills the requirements of the law.

A note or memorandum in writing of the contract is necessary to give validity not only to agreements for the sale of land, but also to agreements not to be performed within a year, to answer for other's debts, and for the sales of goods and chattels and things in action, for the price of fifty dollars or more.

In considering, therefore, the question, what is a sufficient "note or memorandum," within the meaning of the statute, cases decided under any of these several provisions of the statute may be examined as authorities.

. . . .

The leading English case on the subject is Champion v. Plummer (1 Bos. & P. [N.R.] 252), where Champion, by his agent, wrote down in a memorandum book the terms of a verbal sale to him by the defendant and defendant signed the writing. The words were "Bought of W. Plummer," etc., etc., with no name of the person who bought. Sir James Mansfield, C.J., said: "How can that be said to be a contract or memorandum of a contract which does not state who are the contracting parties. By the note, it does not appear to whom the goods were sold. It would prove a sale to any other person as well as to the plaintiff."

. . . .

The American cases are to the same effect.

. . . .

In nearly all the cases in this state Champion v. Plummer was cited with approval. And the whole current of authority in this state is that the memorandum must contain substantially the whole agreement, and all its material terms and conditions, so that one reading it can understand from it what the agreement is.

No case holding a different rule is cited by the General Term and none by the counsel for the respondent, except Salmon Falls Manfg. Co. v. Goodard (14 How. 446).

There was a strong dissent in that case, and it was said in Grafton v. Cummings [99 U.S. 100, 25 L.Ed. 366] that it was to be doubted whether the opinion of the majority was sound law. It is clearly in conflict with the general current of authority and may well be disregarded in view of the later decision of the same court.

Tested by the rule established by the adjudged cases, the memorandum in this case was insufficient to answer the requirements of the statute.

It must be such that when it is produced in evidence it will inform the court or jury of the essential facts set forth in the pleading, and which go to make a valid contract.

Such essentials must appear without the aid of parol proof, either from the memorandum itself or from a reference therein to some other writing or thing, and such essentials to make a complete agreement must consist of the subject-matter of the sale, the terms and the names, or a description of the parties.

The memorandum in suit failed to state the name of the vendor or to give any description by which he or she could be identified, and this omission was fatal. In the potent language of the statute the contract was void.

The judgment should be reversed and a new trial granted, costs to abide the event.

All concur.

Judgment reversed.

NOTES

1. Lynch orally agreed to sell and Tobias to purchase a house and lot, and both signed the following memorandum: "Agreement between Mrs. Annie E. Lynch and Edward Tobias for sale of house No. 1142 E. 13th Street, Brooklyn, sale price $4250 subject to 1st of $3000 and lease to Sam J. Heines expiring May 1, 1920. Deposit $50.00." Tobias sued for specific performance, and, at the trial, offered evidence that Lynch was the owner of the property described in the memorandum. This evidence was held admissible to establish the meaning of the memorandum, and the judgment for the plaintiff was affirmed. Tobias v. Lynch, 192 App.Div. 54, 182 N.Y.S. 643 (1920), aff'd, 233 N.Y. 515, 135 N.E. 898 (1922).

2. Thurlow v. Perry, 107 Me. 127, 77 A. 641 (1910) was an action of assumpsit by a vendor for breach of contract to purchase his farm. After Perry made a verbal agreement to purchase the farm, correspondence passed between the parties, including a letter of October 27 in which Perry stated he told Thurlow he would buy the farm and he would do as he agreed. The letter did not describe the property more fully and did not indicate the purchase price or the terms of payment. In holding that this letter did not contain the necessary terms to take the agreement out of the Statute of Frauds, the court stated:

... The letter of October 27th, taken in connection with the other correspondence, is sufficiently definite in its designation of the property, which is the subject of the contract, and contains a clear statement of an intention to purchase in accordance with the terms which had been previously agreed upon, but it fails to set out these terms and particularly omits any reference to the purchase price. It therefore amounts to nothing more than an admission that a verbal agreement previously made for the purchase of the plaintiff's farm existed. To comply with the statute both in letter and in spirit, as must be done to maintain the action, it is necessary that all essential elements and terms of the contract be made to appear in writing signed by the party to be charged therewith or by some person thereunto lawfully authorized, in order that no part of the agreement needs to be proved by parol evidence.

Among such essential terms the amount of the purchase price is to be included where the contract contains a stipulation as to price.

3. As noted in 4 S. WILLISTON, CONTRACTS § 574 (3d ed. Jaeger 1961), if the agreement in fact did not include a fixed price, none need be mentioned in the memorandum; the law will imply an obligation to pay a reasonable price and the memorandum need be no more definite than was the contract itself.... The law will make the same implications in regard to the memorandum that it does in regard to the promise.

Laythoarp v. Bryant

Court of Common Pleas, 1836.
2 Bing.N.C. 735, 132 Eng.Rep. 283.

This was an action against the Defendant to recover damages for loss occasioned to the Plaintiff by the Defendant's refusing to pay for certain leasehold premises he had purchased at an auction, on the 3d of December 1833, for 441*l.*

The particulars and conditions of sale announced, that the lease and goodwill of the premises, situate in Stoke Newington, in which the coke, coal, and seed trades had been carried on, would be peremptorily sold by auction by Mr. Thomas Ross, at the Auction Mart, on the 3d of December, by order of Mr. W. Laythoarp, the proprietor, retiring from the trade.

The Defendant signed a memorandum of the purchase at the back of a paper containing the particulars and conditions of sale, but, being known to the auctioneer, was not required to pay any deposit. On the 12th of December the Plaintiff's solicitor sent Defendant an abstract of the Plaintiff's title, and by letter called on him to proceed with the purchase, when the Defendant, saying he had only bid at the Plaintiff's request, refused to complete the purchase, and returned the abstract. An assignment of the lease, prepared by the solicitor of the ground landlord, accompanied with a letter from the Plaintiff's solicitor, was then sent to the Defendant; this he also returned, still refusing to complete the contract, but making no objection to the title. The Plaintiff thereupon sold the premises again, for 194*l.* 5*s.*, and brought this action to recover the difference between that sum and 441*l.*, the price which the Defendant had agreed to pay.

A verdict having been found for the Plaintiff,

Atcherley Serjt., pursuant to leave reserved at the trial, moved to set aside the verdict, and enter a nonsuit instead, on the ground that the Plaintiff's name was not in the contract, which appeared to be made with Ross, the auctioneer: that it was not binding on the Plaintiff; that therefore, for want of mutuality, the contract was inoperative; and also as not being signed pursuant to the fourth section of the Statute of Frauds. . . .

. . . .

■ TINDAL, C.J. This case comes before the Court on two objections.

First, that when the contract is inspected it does not contain the name of one of the parties. . . .

The second objection is of great importance: that the contract has not been signed by the vendor. In order to determine the validity of the objection we must look to section 4, of the Statute of Frauds. . . . And the object of the statute was, that no action should lie unless where it could be proved at the trial that the agreement had been signed by the party to be charged. First, no action against any executor or administrator; that is, where an executor is defendant; then, "or to charge the defendant upon any special promise, & c.,"—there, the term is, expressly, defendant,— "unless the agreement upon which such action shall be brought, or some memorandum or note thereof, shall be in writing, and signed by the party—" By what party? By "the party to be charged therewith,"—the defendant in the action.

But then it is said, unless the plaintiff signs there is a want of mutuality. Whose fault is that? The defendant might have required the vendor's signature to the contract; but the object of the statute was to secure the defendant's. The preamble runs, "For prevention of many fraudulent practices, which are commonly endeavoured to be upheld by perjury and subornation of perjury." And the whole object of the legislature is answered when we put this construction on the statute. Here, when this party who has signed is the party to be charged, he cannot be subject to any fraud. And there has been a little confusion in the argument between the consideration of an agreement and mutuality of claims. It is true the consideration must appear on the face of the agreement. Wain v. Warlters [5 East 10 (1804)] was decided on the express ground that an agreement under the fourth section imports more than a bargain under the seventeenth. But I find no case, nor any reason for saying that the signature of both parties is that which makes the agreement. The agreement, in truth, is made before any signature.

Let us apply this to several of the cases pointed out in the fourth section. I agree that the same principle must be applied to all; but let us see whether in any it has been dreamed of that there must be a signature by both parties. In the first place, take the case of a letter from an executor. Who ever heard that in order to charge him there must also be a letter from the party addressed? If the executor's letter contain merely an offer, that offer indeed must be accepted before it can be binding; but if it contain a promise on adequate consideration, no further signature is wanting to its validity. Let us look at the next case,—an engagement to pay the debt of a third person. Is it not every day's practice to put in a guaranty signed by the surety? But I never heard it objected that unless you shew also the signature of the other party the guaranty is void. No such objection was made in Wain v. Warlters, although it would have afforded an easy answer to the Plaintiff's claim.

The word agreement, therefore, is satisfied, if the writing states the subject-matter of the contract; the consideration; and is signed by the party to be charged.

. . . .

[The concurring opinions of Park and Vaughan, JJ., are omitted.]

■ BOSANQUET, J. . . . In the fourth section, the language is, expressly, *the party to be charged*. It is said there must be an agreement, and, to be binding, it must be signed. No doubt that is so; and the question is, is this an agreement? It states the particulars of the property to be sold; it incorporates the name of the purchaser, the seller, the property and the price; it includes all the requisites of an agreement, and the Defendant testifies by his signature that such an agreement exists. The question is, can the vendor enforce it, if it be not signed by himself?

The statute requires that it shall be signed by the party to be charged; and it was not intended to impose on the vendor the burden of the proof of some other paper in the hands of the opposite party, and which the vendor may have no means of producing; for it often happens that each party delivers to the other the part signed by himself. A common case, is, where an agreement arises out of a correspondence; it often happens that a party is unable to give evidence of his own letter; and he is not [to] be defeated because he cannot produce a formal agreement signed by both the parties to the contract.

. . . .

Rule discharged.

NOTES ON STATUTE OF FRAUDS

1. The Statute of Frauds in several states requires that a contract for the sale or lease of an interest in land or some memorandum thereof be "subscribed by the lessor or grantor" or "by the party by whom the lease or sale is to be made." Under such statutes, the vendor cannot enforce the contract unless the Vendor has subscribed. And the same conclusion has been reached in a few states under statutes requiring signature by "the party to be charged," on the theory that the party to be charged is the vendor or owner of the land as such.

These statutes and decisions do not require that the contract or memorandum shall have been subscribed by the purchaser/defendant.

But it does not follow that the vendor may enforce an oral executory contract against the purchaser merely by writing and subscribing a memorandum of the bargain. . . . The note or memorandum, although subscribed by the lessor or grantor, becomes enforceable by him only when the lessee or grantee is shown in some manner to have accepted it as evidence of a valid and operative agreement between the parties.

300 West End Ave. Corp. v. Warner, 250 N.Y. 221, 165 N.E. 271 (1929).

2. Sweeting orally agreed to buy goods from Bailey. A carrier damaged them in shipping, and Sweeting refused to accept delivery. Bailey then brought an action for the price of the goods. The Court of Common Pleas held that the requirements of Section 14 of the English Statute of Frauds were satisfied by a letter sent by Sweeting to Bailey, which said, "the only parcel of goods selected for ready money was, the chimney-glasses, amounting to 38*l.* 10s. 6d., which goods I have never received, and have long since declined to have, for reasons made known to you at the time." Bailey v. Sweeting, 9 C.B.N.S. 834, 142 Eng.Rep. 332 (C.B.1861).

3. With respect to the oral modification of a contract within the Statute of Frauds, consider the following sections of the Restatement (Second) of Contracts:

§ 149. ORAL MODIFICATION

(1) For the purpose of determining whether the Statute of Frauds applies to a contract modifying but not rescinding a prior contract, the second contract is treated as containing the originally agreed terms as modified. The Statute may, however, apply independently of the original terms to a contract to modify a transfer of property.

(2) Where the second contract is unenforceable by virtue of the Statute of Frauds and there has been no material change of position in reliance on it, the prior contract is not modified.

§ 150. RELIANCE ON ORAL MODIFICATION

Where the parties to an enforceable contract subsequently agree that all or part of a duty need not be performed or of a condition need not occur, the Statute of Frauds does not prevent enforcement of the subsequent agreement if reinstatement of the original terms would be unjust in view of a material change of position in reliance on the subsequent agreement.

———

2. FRAUD AND ACCIDENT

Mullett v. Halfpenny

Chancery, 1699.
Precedents in Chancery 404.

. . . the Defendant on a Treaty of Marriage for his Daughter with the Plaintiff, signed a Writing, comprising the Terms of the Agreement; and afterwards designing to elude the Force thereof, and get loose from his Agreement, order'd his Daughter to put on a good Humour, and get the Plaintiff to deliver up that Writing, and then to marry him, which she accordingly did, and the Defendant stood at the Corner of a Street, to see them go by to be married, and afterwards forced the Plaintiff to bring his Bill in this Court to be relieved; and my Lord Chancellor [LORD COWPER] said, he remembered very well, that this Cause was heard before the Master of the Rolls [SIR JOHN TREVOR], and the Plaintiff had a Decree; but he said, this was on the Point of Fraud, which was proved in the Cause, and Halfpenny walked backwards and forwards in the Court, and bid the Master of the Rolls observe the Statute, which he humorously said, I do, I do.

Gilbert v. Gilbert

Superior Court of New Jersey, Chancery Division, 1960.
61 N.J.Super. 476, 161 A.2d 295.

■ WICK, J.S.C. This is a motion to dismiss the complaint for failure to state a claim upon which relief can be granted.

The facts, as presented by the complaint, are as follows: The plaintiff met John E. Gilbert in 1949 and, after some acquaintance with him, he sought to persuade her to marry him, but she refused to do so unless he would make a suitable property settlement on her prior to the marriage. He thus offered to provide her with a home of her own and a housekeeper and plaintiff accepted this offer with the proviso that the agreement be reduced to writing and signed by them. They fixed September 10, 1949 as the date of the marriage. On August 27, 1949, she having become insistent that she would not marry him unless a written agreement was executed, he, in order to further induce the marriage, executed a will (a copy of which is attached to the complaint) in which he left her certain real property, a Buick automobile and one-third of whatever cash he had in the bank. In reliance on the provisions of the will for her benefit and his representations that it would be his last will, she entered into the marriage on September 10, 1949. In October or November of 1949 he made a further will which, as she is advised and believes, left her his entire estate. On October 27, 1950 he executed a further will leaving his entire estate to his children, Margaret E. Gilbert and John E. Gilbert, Jr. This is the last will he left on his death on March 1, 1960. She has filed a caveat with the Surrogate of Burlington County against the probate of that will and the admissibility of that will to probate has not yet been adjudicated.

She seeks judgment that the execution of that will by him was a breach of their antenuptial agreement and a fraud; the probate of that will would constitute a breach of the antenuptial agreement and perpetrate a fraud on her; the will of August 27, 1949 was irrevocable without her consent except by a will more favorable to her and is valid and entitled to probate; she is the owner of the property that was to be left to her under either the will of August 27, 1949, or that of October or November, 1949; the probate of the will of October 27, 1950 would create a cloud on her title to the real and personal property which is hers under the earlier two wills. She would further have the probate of the October 27, 1950 will restrained.

. . . .

The will of October 27, 1950 makes John E. Gilbert, Jr., Margaret E. Gilbert, and Alexander Denbo executors. They have been made defendants as the prospective executors of that will and John and Margaret also as the perspective devisees and legatees under that will. John's wife, Elizabeth, is also made a party defendant evidently as the prospective holder of an inchoate right of dower in the real property passing to her husband under that will.

It might be noted that the first cause of action comprehends two related agreements. One is to provide the plaintiff with a home of her own and a housekeeper coupled with the promise that this agreement would be reduced to writing. The other is the promise or representation by John E. Gilbert, Sr. that he would not change the will of August 27, 1949. (It should be noted that we are not now concerned with the question of whether the second agreement constituted a vacation of the first.) The complaint demonstrates no consideration for either other than the marriage and neither is evidenced by any written memorandum. The defendants thus raise the defense of the statute of frauds as it relates to agreements made upon consideration of marriage. They make no reference to the statute as it relates to contracts concerning real estate, but such would also appear to be applicable to this agreement insofar as it concerns the transfer of real property. The plaintiff counters that the breach of the antenuptial agreements constitutes a fraud and the statute of frauds may not be raised to shield a fraud.

The breach of an antenuptial agreement is not such a fraud as will prevent the application of the statute of frauds. It has also been decided that mere breach of the further agreement to reduce the antenuptial agreement to writing is not such a fraud as will prevent the application of the statute. In Alexander v. Alexander, 96 N.J.Eq. 10, 124 A. 523 (Ch. 1924) it is stated by Leaming, V.C., as follows:

"Fraud, alone, will deny the intervention of the statute. Equity at all times will lend its aid to defeat a fraud, notwithstanding the statute of frauds. But the fraud against which equity will relieve in this class of cases, notwithstanding the statute, is not the mere moral wrong of repudiating a contract actually entered into, which, by reason of the statute, a party is not bound to perform for want of its being in writing. The fraud must be inherent in the transaction, such as a false representation that a contemplated written agreement has been executed pursuant to the parol agreement, or other similar artifices. The authorities do not appear to support the dictum of Mr. Justice Wells, in Glass v. Hulbert, 102 Mass. 24 ... to the effect that the assurance that a settlement would be executed, will remove the case from the bar of the statute. In the counterclaim here presented no written agreement or settlement was contemplated by the parties, and no fraud appears."

This statement is evidently based primarily on the noted citation to [2] Story Eq.Jur. [(13th ed.) § 768].

It might be said that the line of distinction developed by these authorities is that an assurance with a subsequent change of mind is a mere moral wrong while an assurance with a present intention never to follow through with it is a fraud which will prevent the application of the statute. This, certainly, is a correct statement of the two different situations. However, there is further involved, as is implicit in the principles quoted above, the problem of what is sufficient proof of the fraudulent intention. That is, may the court, upon mere proof that there was an assurance and a later breach of it raise the inference that this was not a mere change of mind, but a deliberate plan. It seems to me that the two authorities noted above require something more. A reference to the comments made by Leaming, V.C. in Alexander v. Alexander, supra, concerning Glass v. Hulbert, 102 Mass. 24, 3 Am.Rep. 418 (Sup.Jud.Ct.1869), further support this conclusion. The dictum in Glass v. Hulbert, referred to by Leaming, V.C., states as follows:

"... In such cases the marriage, although not regarded as a part performance of the agreement for a marriage settlement, is such an irretrievable change of situation, that, if procured by artifice, upon the faith that the settlement had been, or the assurance that it would be executed, the other party is held to make good the agreement, and not permitted to defeat it by pleading the statute."

It is to be noted that the court here speaks of an assurance that the settlement would be executed which is used as an artifice, with a present intention never to fulfill them. Nevertheless, Leaming, V.C. feels that this is not enough. The reason for this conclusion is clear. Both the statement that the agreement had been made and the statement that it would be made amount, in essence, to the same thing if the latter is made with an intention not to fulfill. It is the insincerity, the lie, that makes the fraud, but, as a practical matter, Leaming, V.C. feels that the finding of a lie cannot be based on a mere inference drawn from the existence of an assurance and its subsequent breach.

A similar conclusion is reached in Hackney v. Hackney [27 Tenn. 452], 8 Humph. 452 (Sup.Ct.1847), Chafee & Simpson, Cas.Eq.2d ed., p. 561 (1946)....

Chafee and Simpson take the position that Peek v. Peek, 77 Cal. 106, 19 P. 227 (Sup.Ct.1888) and Green v. Green, 34 Kan. 740, 10 P. 156 (Sup.Ct.1886) are *contra* to the decision just noted. In the latter, the husband was induced into the marriage upon the representation by the wife that she owned a 160–acre farm and that its proceeds should go to their support after they were married so long as they lived, and then to her children. They were married on August 31, 1882. However, on August 30, 1882, she had executed, without his knowledge, deeds conveying her farm to her children. After the marriage she controlled and rented the farm in her own name, but he received none of the proceeds. The deeds were delivered to the children on March 5, 1884. She deserted her husband, whether before or after delivery of the deeds does not appear. In the former the wife married the husband on the assurance that he would, on or before the marriage, make a conveyance to her of certain real property. On the day before the marriage he told her he was going to have the deeds drawn, but returned in a few minutes saying that it could not be done that day.

The next morning he again said he would have the deeds drawn but returned saying that they were too busy at the court house, but that he would have it done as soon as practicable. She accordingly married him that night. That very same morning, however, when he was making excuses, he had a deed executed conveying the property to his son by a former marriage.

These cases, although literally they may not come within statements and examples found in Hackney v. Hackney, supra, seem to be consistent with the fundamental premise of that case, and certainly, on their facts would appear consistent with the proposition laid down by Story and Leaming. In both, the fraud is evidenced by more than the mere assurance and subsequent breach, rather there is positive evidence of the fraudulent purpose.

. . . .

It is thus apparent that the complaint fails to allege or demonstrate a fraud that will prevent the application of the statute. Nothing appears more than a subsequent breach of the several interrelated promises. There is no allegation that the reduction of the agreement to writing was prevented by the contrivance or artifice of the husband similar to or in the nature of those indicated by the authorities above.

The plaintiff further argues that the execution of the will in pursuance of the antenuptial agreement followed by the marriage constitutes such part performance as to take the case out of the statute. A case in point, which plaintiff relies on, is Adams v. Swift, 169 App.Div. 802, 155 N.Y.S. 873 (1915). This, however, would not appear to be the law in New Jersey. In Alexander v. Alexander, 96 N.J.Eq. 10, 124 A. 523 (Ch.1924), Leaming, V.C., states as follows:

"The rule in equity that part performance may remove a parol contract from the operation of the statute of frauds does not extend to antenuptial parol agreements made in consideration of marriage. The act of marriage is not regarded as part performance in that class of cases; indeed, it has been stated by our court of errors and appeals that the equitable doctrine that part performance will remove the inhibition of the statute of frauds applies only to contracts relating to lands, and does not extend to contracts relating to other matters."

It might be said that this statement was too broad inasmuch as the court did not have before it a will executed in pursuance of the agreement and the case of McElroy v. Ludlum involved an employment contract.

However, the point seems to have been laid at rest in Russell v. Russell, 60 N.J.Eq. 282, 287, 47 A. 37, 39 (Ch.1900), affirmed 63 N.J.Eq. 282, 49 A. 1081 (E. & A. 1901). . . .

An order dismissing the complaint will be entered accordingly.

Finucane v. Kearney

Superior Court of Chancery of Mississippi, 1843.
Freeman, Chancery Reports 65.

This bill was filed to enforce the specific performance of a contract for the sale of a town lot, in the city of Jackson, which contract failed to be executed in writing in consequence of the death of the vendor.... Two of the defendants demurred to the bill, relying upon the statute of frauds.

THE CHANCELLOR [BUCKNER]....

. . . .

In the case now before me, it is distinctly alleged that the entire purchase money has been paid, and that possession of the lot was given under the contract, thus bringing it within the pale of the authorities referred to.

There is another allegation in the bill, which I think places it beyond the reach of the statute of frauds. It is alleged that Dickson *agreed* to sign the bond, but was prevented by his death. An acknowledged exception to the statute is where the agreement is intended to be reduced to writing according to the statute, but is prevented by the fraud of one of the parties. And so I apprehend the rule would be, where, as in this case, the contract was written out and one of the parties promised to sign it, but was prevented by inevitable accident. It is the peculiar province of courts of equity to relieve against accidents as well as fraud....

I think, then, that the grounds of demurrer are not well taken. Although a bill seeking the enforcement of a parol contract for land, without other circumstances, is a proper subject of demurrer, yet if the bill, besides the agreement, states matter in avoidance of the statute, such as part performance, a demurrer will not lie.

The demurrer must be overruled, with leave to answer.

————

3.   JUSTIFIABLE CHANGE OF POSITION

Steadman v. Steadman

House of Lords, 1974.
[1976] A.C. 536.

The appellant, Sylvia Emily Lila Steadman, brought proceedings in the Bromley County Court against her former husband, the respondent, Norman Leslie Steadman, for a declaration that the house, 9 Brookmead Close, Orpington, was jointly owned by the parties and for an order that it should be sold and the net proceeds of sale divided equally between the parties. On January 23, 1973, Mr. Registrar Miller found that there had been an act of part performance by the husband of an oral agreement made by the parties on March 2, 1972, by which the wife had agreed to transfer her interest in the house to the husband for £1,500. He therefore held that the wife had compromised the proceedings.

The wife appealed. On May 24, 1973, Judge Fife found that there had been no act of part performance on the part of the husband and, therefore, under section 40(1) of the Law of Property Act 1925, the agreement was unenforceable.

The husband appealed to the Court of Appeal and, on July 30, 1973, the court held that there had been an act of part performance on the part of the husband and, notwithstanding that the act was not referable to the term of the agreement for the disposition of the interest in land, it was sufficient part performance for the purposes of section 40(2) of the Act. The wife appealed.

. . . .

■ LORD REID. My Lords, the marriage of the appellant, the wife, and the respondent, the husband, was dissolved in 1970. They were then joint owners of a house which had been bought in 1963 for £3,600. Prior to the divorce the husband had been ordered to pay maintenance of £2 per week to the wife and £2.50 per week for their child. The husband remained in occupation of the house.

In 1970 the wife applied under section 17 of the Married Women's Property Act 1882, for, inter alia, an order for the sale of the house and division of the proceeds, but no further steps were taken until 1972. At that time the husband was in arrears in paying the wife's maintenance in a sum of £194. There were long negotiations between the parties' solicitors, and ultimately on March 2, 1972, the matter came before the magistrates' court. The husband's solicitor met the wife before the hearing. Unfortunately her solicitor was not present, but there is no suggestion that the husband's solicitor took advantage of his absence.

The parties then reached an oral agreement with regard to both the maintenance and the house. The court were to be asked to authorise discharge of the maintenance order against the husband and continuation of the order with regard to the child, to order the husband to pay £100 of the arrears of her maintenance and to order remission of the balance. In addition the court were to be informed of the agreement with regard to the house that the husband should pay £1,500 to the wife and the wife would transfer to the husband her interest in the house. The magistrates made orders in accordance with the agreement and the husband paid £100 to the wife.

The husband then borrowed £1,500 from a building society and paid that sum to his solicitor and the solicitor prepared a deed of transfer of the wife's interest in the house and sent it for her signature. But the wife refused to sign, thinking that £1,500 was less than she ought to have. She renewed her application under section 17 to have the house sold. The husband pleaded the parties' agreement as a binding compromise but the wife pleaded that the agreement was unenforceable.

She relied on section 40 of the Law of Property Act 1925, which provides:

"(1) No action may be brought upon any contract for the sale or other disposition of land or any interest in land, unless the agreement upon which such action is brought, or some memorandum or note thereof, is in writing, and signed by the party to be charged or by some other person thereunto by him lawfully authorised. (2) This section ... does not affect the law relating to part performance...."

The husband relied on subsection (2) and the registrar held that there had been part performance so that subsection (1) did not apply....

. . . .

The sole question for your Lordships' decision is whether the admitted facts amount to part performance within the meaning of section 40(2). In my view it is clear that the oral agreement of March 2, 1972, is indivisible and not severable. The whole must stand or fall. Indeed the contrary was not seriously argued. And it is clear that the payment of £100 to the wife as ordered by the magistrates' court was, taking the words in their ordinary sense, in part performance of the agreement. The husband also relies on the following other acts by him or his solicitor as being further part performance; (1) the intimation of the agreement to the magistrates and his abandonment of his attempts to have all arrears of maintenance remitted and (2) sending to the wife the transfer which she refused to sign and incurring the cost of its preparation. I am very doubtful about the first of these but I am inclined to think that the second could be regarded as part performance. It is the universal custom that a deed of transfer of an interest in land is prepared by the solicitor of the transferee so the wife or her solicitor as her agent must have known that the husband would incur the cost of preparation of the deed in carrying out the agreement.

But the wife's case is that we must not take "part performance" in its ordinary meaning because the phrase has acquired a highly technical meaning over the centuries.

This matter has a very long history. Section 40 replaced a part of section 4 of the Statute of Frauds 1677, and very soon after the passing of that Act authorities on this matter began to accumulate. It is now very difficult to find from them any clear evidence of general application. But it is not difficult to see at least one principle behind them. If one party to an agreement stands by and lets the other party incur expense or prejudice his position on the faith of the agreement being valid he will not then be allowed to turn round and assert that the agreement is unenforceable. Using fraud in its older and less precise sense, that would be fraudulent on his part and it has become proverbial that courts of equity will not permit the statute to be made an instrument of fraud.

It must be remembered that this legislation did not and does not make oral contracts relating to land void: it only makes then unenforceable. And the statutory provision must be pleaded; otherwise the court does not apply it. So it is in keeping with equitable principles that in proper circumstances a person will not be allowed "fraudulently" to take advantage of a defence of this kind. There is nothing about part performance in the Statute of Frauds. It is an invention of the Court of Chancery and in deciding any case not clearly covered by authority I think that the equitable nature of the remedy must be kept in mind.

A large number of the authorities are cases where a purchaser under an oral agreement has been permitted to take possession of or to do things on the land which he has agreed to buy. But sometimes rules appropriate to that situation have been sought to be applied to other cases of part performance where they are not appropriate. Indeed the courts have sometimes seemed disinclined to apply the principle at all to such other cases.

Normally the consideration for the purchase of land is a sum of money and there are statements that a sum of money can never be treated as part performance. Such statements would be reasonable if the person pleading the statute tendered repayment of any part of the price which he had received and was able thus to make restitution in integrum. That would remove any "fraud" or any equity on which the purchaser could properly rely. But to make a general rule that payment of money can never be part performance would seem to me to defeat the whole purpose of the doctrine and I do not think that we are compelled by authority to do that.

The argument for the wife, for which there is a good deal of authority, is that no act can be relied on as an act of part performance unless it relates to the land to be acquired and can only be explained by the existence of a contract relating to the land. But let me suppose a case of an oral contract where the consideration for the transfer of the land was not money but the transfer of some personal property or the performance of some obligation. The personal property is then transferred or the obligation is performed to the knowledge of the owner of the land in circumstances where there can be no *restitutio in integrum* [restoration or restitution to the previous condition]. On what rational principle could it be said that the doctrine of part performance is not to apply? And we were not referred to any case of that kind where the court had refused to apply it. The transfer of the personal property or the performance of the obligation would indicate the existence of a contract but it would not indicate that that contract related to that or any other land.

I think that there has been some confusion between this supposed rule and another perfectly good rule. You must not first look at the oral contract and then see whether the alleged acts of part performance are consistent with it. You must first look at the alleged acts of part performance to see whether they prove that there must have been a contract and it is only if they do so prove that you can bring in the oral contract.

. . . .

A thing is proved in civil litigation by showing that it is more probably true than not; and I see no reason why there should be any different standard of proof here. If there were, what would the standard be? The only other recognised standard of proof is beyond reasonable doubt, but why should that apply here?

I am aware that it has often been said that the acts relied on must necessarily or unequivocally indicate the existence of a contract. It may well be that we should consider whether any prudent reasonable man would have done those acts if there had not been a contract but many people are neither prudent nor reasonable and they might often spend money or prejudice their position not in reliance on a contract but in the optimistic expectation that a contract would follow. So if there were a rule that acts relied on as part performance must of their own nature unequivocally show that there was a contract, it would be only in the rarest case that all other possible explanations could be excluded.

In my view, unless the law is to be divorced from reason and principle, the rule must be that you take the whole circumstances, leaving aside evidence about the oral contract, to see whether it is proved that the acts relied on were done in reliance on a contract: that will be proved if it is shown to be more probable than not.

Authorities which seem to require more than that appear to be based on an idea, never clearly defined, to the effect that the law of part performance is a rule of evidence rather than an application of an equitable principle. I do not know on what ground any court could say that, although you cannot produce the evidence required by the Statute of Frauds, some other kind of evidence will do instead. But I can see that if part perform-ance is simply regarded as evidence, then it would be reasonable to hold not only that the acts of part performance must relate to the land but that they must indicate the nature of the oral contract with regard to the land. But that appears to me to be a fundamental departure from the true doctrine of part performance, and it is not supported by recent authorities such as Kingswood Estate Co. Ltd. v. Anderson [1963] 2 Q.B. 169.

. . . I would therefore dismiss the appeal.

■ Lord Morris of Borth-y-Gest . . . .

The problem that is raised in this case is whether there was any act which qualified to be regarded as an act of part performance of the contract. The view of the learned registrar was that being released from the maintenance order was not such an act nor was the arrangement regarding the arrears nor was the making of arrangements with the building society. The only act of part performance held by the learned registrar was the incurring by the husband of solicitor's costs of about £25 in connection with the contemplated transfer. That view did not find favour with any member of the Court of Appeal.

The learned judge in the county court considered that there was no act of part performance. On appeal to the Court of Appeal, the notice of appeal set out five acts which it was submitted were sufficient acts of part performance. In the result the act that appealed to the majority in the Court of Appeal was the payment of £100. They found it unnecessary to discuss certain other suggested acts.

It is difficult out of the richness of learning and authority to make selection, but the theme running through the speech of Lord Selborne L.C. in Maddison v. Alderson, 8 App.Cas. 467 is, I think, made clear. At p. 476 he drew the line between the simple case where a person is charged upon a contract only and the case in which "there are equities resulting from res gestae subsequent to and arising out of the contract." Lord Selborne said:

> "So long as the connection of those res gestae with the alleged contract does not depend upon the mere parol testimony, but is reasonably to be inferred from the res gestae themselves . . ."

then justice seemed to require some limitation upon the scope of the Statute of Frauds. He also added, at p. 478:

> "It is not enough that an act done should be a condition of, or good consideration for, a contract, unless it is, as between the parties, such a

part execution as to change their relative positions as to the subject matter of the contract."

Lord FitzGerald thus expressed himself, at p. 491:

"... the acts relied on as performance to take the case out of the statute must be unequivocally and in their own nature referable to some such agreement as that alleged, and I may add must necessarily relate to and affect the land the subject matter of that agreement."

The passage in Fry on Specific Performance, 6th ed. (1921), p. 278 reads:

"The true principle, however, of the operation of acts of part performance seems only to require that the acts in question be such as must be referred to some contract, and may be referred to the alleged one; that they prove the existence of some contract, and are consistent with the contract alleged."

That I take to be in full accord with the first of the four circumstances which Fry states must concur to withdraw a contract from the operation of the statute. The acts of part performance must be such that they point unmistakingly and can only point to the existence of some contract such as the oral contract alleged. But of course the acts of part performance need not show the precise terms of the oral contract. The terms of the oral contract must be proved by acceptable evidence but effect to them can only be given if and when acts of part performance establish that there must have been some such contract. Until then a door is, so to speak, closed against them.

. . . .

I would allow the appeal.

Viscount Dilhorne. . . .

. . . I am of the opinion that this appeal should be dismissed.

Lord Simon of Glaisdale. . . .

This is one of those difficult situations where two legal principles are in competition. The first legal principle is embodied in section 40(1) of the Law of Property Act 1925, which states:

"No action may be brought upon any contract for the sale or other disposition of land or any interest in land, unless the agreement upon which such action is brought, or some memorandum or note thereof, is in writing, and signed by the party to be charged or by some other person thereunto by him lawfully authorised."

This provision replaced that part of section 4 of the Statute of Frauds 1677 which related to interests in land. The preamble to the Statute of Frauds explained its object: "For prevention of many fraudulent practices, which are commonly endeavoured to be upheld by perjury and subornation of perjury; ..." The "mischief" for which the statute was providing a remedy was, therefore, that some transactions were being conducted orally in such a way that important interests were liable to be adversely affected by a mode of operation that invited forensic mendacity. The remedy was to require some greater formality in the record of such transaction than mere word of mouth if it was to be enforced. The continuing need for such a remedy for such a mischief was apparently recognised as subsisting when the law of landed property was recast in 1925.

The second, competing, legal principle was evoked when, almost from the moment of passing of the Statute of Frauds, it was appreciated that it was being used for a variant of unconscionable dealing, which the statute itself was designed to remedy. A party to an oral contract for the disposition of an interest in land could, despite performance of the reciprocal terms by the other party, by virtue of the statute disclaim liability for his own performance on the ground that the contract had not been in writing. Common Law was helpless. But Equity, with its purpose of vindicating good faith and with its remedies of injunction and specific performance, could deal with the situation. The Statute of Frauds did not make such contracts void but merely unenforceable; and, if the statute was to be relied on as a defence, it had to be specifically pleaded. Where, therefore, a party to a contract unenforceable under the Statute of Frauds stood by while the other party acted to his detriment in performance of his own contractual obligations, the first party would be precluded by the Court of Chancery from claiming exoneration, on the ground that the contract was unenforceable, from performance of his reciprocal obligations; and the court would, if required, decree specific performance of the contract. Equity would not, as it was put, allow the Statute of Frauds "to be used as an engine of fraud." This became known as the doctrine of part performance—the "part" performance being that of the party who had, to the knowledge of the other party, acted to his detriment in carrying out irremediably his own obligations (or some significant part of them) under the otherwise unenforceable contract. This competing principle has also received statutory recognition, as regards contracts affecting interests in land, in section 40(2) of the Law of Property Act 1925.

But what was in origin a rule of substantive law designed to vindicate conscientious dealing seems to have come in time sometimes to have been considered somewhat as a rule of evidence. It is easy to appreciate how this happened. Part performance could be viewed as a way of proving an agreement falling within section 4 notwithstanding the absence of writing. Seen as such, it was no doubt considered necessary to frame stringent requirements to prevent the doctrine from carting a sedan chair through the provisions of the statute. If part performance was to be evidence of a contract which could not otherwise and directly be proved, the acts of part performance should themselves intrinsically be capable of proving some such contract as that alleged. Oral evidence was not admissible to connect them with the alleged contract: otherwise, it was held, the statutory object would be defeated by allowing an interest in land to pass on mere oral testimony. As the Earl of Selborne L.C. put it in Maddison v. Alderson, 8 App.Cas. 467, 478, 479:

"The doctrine ... has been confined ... within limits intended to prevent a recurrence of the mischief which the statute was passed to suppress.... All the authorities show that the acts relied upon as part performance must be unequivocally, and in their own nature, referable to some such agreement as that alleged."

It may be questionable whether it was direct respect for the statute which led to such confinement of the doctrine, or whether it was not rather because part performance seems sometimes to have been regarded as an alternative way of proving an oral agreement; for Equity allowed a person to prove by parol evidence that land conveyed to another was so conveyed on trust for himself, notwithstanding section 7 of the Statute of Frauds: Rochefoucauld v. Boustead [1897] 1 Ch. 196, 206; Bannister v. Bannister [1948] 2 All E.R. 133, 136—the passages show that here, too, the guiding rule was that the court would not allow the statute to be used as a cloak for fraud. However that may be, the speech of the Earl of Selborne L.C. has always been regarded as authoritative, notwithstanding that what he said about part performance was, strictly, obiter.

But Lord Selborne went on to effect a complete reconciliation between the provisions of the statute and the doctrine of part performance in a passage (pp. 475–476) which is of crucial importance to the instant appeal . . .:

"In a suit founded on such part performance, the defendant is really 'charged' upon the equities resulting from the acts done in execution of the contract, and not (within the meaning of the statute) upon the contract itself. If such equities were excluded, injustice of a kind which the statute cannot be thought to have had in contemplation would follow . . . All the acts done must be referred to the actual contract, which is the measure and test of their legal and equitable character and consequences. . . . The matter has advanced beyond the stage of contract; and the equities which arise out of the stage which it has reached cannot be administered unless the contract is regarded. . . ."

. . . .

In the instant case the husband proved to the satisfaction of the registrar the following acts which were to his detriment: (i) procuring his solicitor to consent to an order by the justices which placed him under a continuing legal obligation; (ii) procuring his solicitor to forbear from seeking from the justices orders which might have been more advantageous to himself; (iii) paying £100 to the wife before March 30, 1972; (iv) procuring his solicitor to draft a conveyance for execution by the wife. Even if, contrary to my view, these matters could be considered in isolation from the statements inviting the justices to play their part in implementing them, they still, in my opinion, make it more probable than not that the husband acted as he did because he had contracted with the wife to do so; and they are consistent with the agreement which the husband alleges. This makes it inequitable for the wife to allege that the agreement was unenforceable because the formalities required by section 40(1) were not complied with. The registrar, therefore, rightly admitted oral and affidavit evidence to establish the agreement alleged by the husband, which he found proved.

I would therefore dismiss the appeal.

Lord Salmon. . . .

During the last 300 years there has been a mass of authority on this topic. Unfortunately many of the cases are irreconcilable with each other and it is by no means easy to discover the true answer to the question with which we are faced, namely, what are the essential elements of part performance in relation to contracts disposing of an interest in land. One rule, however, emerges clearly: a parol contract relating to land cannot be enforced unless the acts relied on as part performance, of themselves, establish a prima facie case that they were done in the performance of a contract. Then, but only then, may parol evidence of the contract be accepted. In order to discover the significance of the alleged acts of part performance, the circumstances in which they were performed must, I think, clearly be relevant. What is perhaps not so clear is whether the acts are sufficient to constitute part performance if they establish only that they were done in the performance of some contract which might but equally well might not be a contract disposing of an interest in land. There is certainly powerful authority for the view that this is not enough but that the acts relied on must of themselves show prima facie that they were done in performance of a contract disposing of such an interest.

It is perhaps not very difficult to see the reason for this view. Acts relied on as part performance which show that a parol contract of the kind referred to in the statute was probably made and that it has been partly performed by the party who seeks to enforce it, raises a substantially stronger equity in his favour than acts which are equally consistent with the existence and part performance of a contract having nothing to do with land. The object of the statute was to prevent a dishonest person from fraudulently inventing a parol contract under which someone was supposed to have disposed of an interest in land to him and then bringing perjured evidence in support of his claim under the spurious contract. An act which proves that probably a contract for the disposal of an interest in land had been concluded and that the person seeking to enforce it had done his part under it goes further to obviate the mischief at which the statute was aimed than an act which shows merely the existence of some contract which may equally well have nothing to do with land.

. . . .

My Lords, let us assume evidence of the following facts: A is anxious to sell an attractive house at a reasonable price of, say, £ 20,000. Full particulars of the house are sent to B by A's estate agents. The estate agents tell B, truthfully, that there are several people anxious to buy the house for the price asked but that owing to present economic conditions they have not yet been able to complete the necessary financial arrangements. They are expecting to do so at any moment. The estate agent, at B's request, makes an immediate appointment for B to inspect the house and meet A. B keeps the appointment. No written contract of sale comes into existence. B's cheque in favour of A for £ 20,000 is specially cleared by A the day after the appointment. A then refuses to convey the house to B and there is good reason to suppose that he is unable to repay the £ 20,000. Can anyone doubt that this evidence, unexplained, establishes a strong prima facie case that A orally agreed with B to sell him the house for £ 20,000 and that B performed his part of the contract by paying A the purchase price? If B sues A for specific performance of the parol agreement and applies for an interlocutory injunction to restrain A from parting with the house pending the trial of the action, it is surely inconceivable that our law can be so defective that it would allow A to shelter behind the statute. Yet A could succeed in doing so if the authorities which hold that payment can never substitute part performance for the purpose of taking a contract out of the statute were correctly decided. In my opinion, they were not.

Suppose another set of facts. B sues A for specific performance of a parol contract for the sale of A's house to him for £ X,000 and alleges that he has paid A the £ X,000. B gives evidence of the payment. A pleads the statute. A would have no case to answer because there would be no evidence of any circumstances surrounding the payment to connect it with the parol agreement. Suppose, however, that B, who is unrepresented, says to the judge at the trial: "Of course I agreed with A to sell him my house for £ X,000 and he has certainly paid me that sum which unfortunately, I cannot repay." A's admission would, in my view, be sufficient to connect the payment with the parol contract, establish part performance and deprive A of his defence under the statute. Once a party to a parol contract relating to land admits to any court the existence of the contract and that he has received a benefit under it which he is unable or unwilling to restore, the mischief aimed at by the statute disappears. It would be most unreasonable and unjust that, in such circumstances, he should be able to rely on the statute in order to break his word and evade performing his part under the contract. There is certainly no authority binding on this House which would enable him to do so.

In the present case, the payment of £ 100 by the husband to his wife who had divorced him—looked at without regard to its surrounding circumstances—would not be any evidence of any contract, let alone of a contract concerning land. . . .

If, in the present case, the payment of the £ 100 is looked at in the light of its surrounding circumstances, it is, in my opinion, quite plain that that sum was paid in part performance of a parol contract concerning land. The correspondence prior to March 2, 1972, shows that the only outstanding differences between the husband and the wife were then (a) the amount which he was to pay to her for transferring to him the interest which she claimed in the former matrimonial home and (b) what was to be done about the amount of arrears of maintenance to the wife which were then outstanding.

     . . . .

The wife's admission in open court plainly connected the payment of the £ 100 with the parol agreement relating to the disposition of an interest in land and showed that the payment was in part performance of that agreement. She has not repaid or ever offered to repay any part of the £ 100. This payment, in my opinion, bars the wife from relying on the statute and she is accordingly bound to perform her part of the agreement.

     . . . .

My Lords, for these reasons I would dismiss the appeal. Appeal dismissed.

NOTES

1. RESTATEMENT (SECOND) OF CONTRACTS:

§ 129. ACTION IN RELIANCE; SPECIFIC PERFORMANCE

A contract for the transfer of an interest in land may be specifically enforced notwithstanding failure to comply with the Statute of Frauds if it is established that the party seeking enforcement, in reasonable reliance on the contract and on the continuing assent of the party against whom enforcement is sought, has so changed his position that injustice can be avoided only by specific enforcement.

§ 139. ENFORCEMENT BY VIRTUE OF ACTION IN RELIANCE

(1) A promise which the promisor should reasonably expect to induce action or forbearance on the part of the promisee or a third person and which does induce the action or forbearance is enforceable notwithstanding the Statute of Frauds if injustice can be avoided only by enforcement of the promise. The remedy granted for breach is to be limited as justice requires.

(2) In determining whether injustice can be avoided only by enforcement of the promise, the following circumstances are significant:

(a) the availability and adequacy of other remedies, particularly cancellation and restitution;

(b) the definite and substantial character of the action or forbearance in relation to the remedy sought;

(c) the extent to which the action or forbearance corroborates evidence of the making and terms of the promise, or the making and terms are otherwise established by clear and convincing evidence;

(d) the reasonableness of the action or forbearance;

(e) the extent to which the action or forbearance was foreseeable by the promisor.

2. In Butcher v. Stapely, 1 Vern. 363, 23 Eng.Rep. 524 (Ch. 1685), Lord Chancellor Jeffreys pronounced the delivery of the property to the buyer sufficient to take the case out of the Statute of Frauds. On the other hand, Palumbo v. James, 266 Mass. 1, 164 N.E. 466 (1929), deemed the doctrine of part performance inapplicable where the buyer had both moved into the house on the property and planted what the court called a "substantial" garden on the premises. Indeed, some American courts have rejected the part performance rule entirely.

3. As an alternative ground of decision, the *Palumbo* court held that a seller may not avoid the Statute of Frauds by proving that the defendant/buyer had done acts that would entitle the latter to invoke the doctrine of part performance and specifically enforce the oral contract against the seller.

———

White v. Production Credit Association of Alma

Court of Appeals of Michigan, 1977.
76 Mich.App. 191, 256 N.W.2d 436.

■ BURNS, J. . . .

Plaintiff is a cattle farmer who has been buying, raising, and selling feeder cattle since 1960. The business requires periodic financing to cover basic operating expenses and the purchase of cattle. Defendant is a federally-chartered lending institution.

In the fall of 1970, James Orr, a representative of defendant, represented to plaintiff that defendant could and would provide exclusive financial assistance to plaintiff. Plaintiff accepted Orr's offer, submitted a financial statement and a loan application for $128,000. The loan was approved within two days.

Due to drought and other problems, 1970 was a poor year for plaintiff. He and Orr discussed the feasibility of irrigation and both agreed that it would be the answer to plaintiff's problem. According to plaintiff, defendant agreed to finance the irrigation project and provide financing for the balance of plaintiff's operation, including the purchase of cattle each year, for a period of 7 to 10 years, the time period anticipated to pay off the irrigation equipment loan. This irrigation loan was to be repaid in seven equal installments.

Plaintiff agreed to maintain a herd of approximately 500 cattle each year. As security for the financing, plaintiff agreed to deliver mortgages and security agreements to defendant covering all of the farm's real estate and fixtures, all crops, both present and future, all livestock on hand and to be acquired, and all machinery and equipment, including the irrigation system.

Defendant advanced the long-term loan for the irrigation project and plaintiff executed the security agreements.

Within five months, and seven months before the first payment was due, defendant reversed its position and wrote to plaintiff requesting he refinance the irrigation loan with another institution. Plaintiff was unable to acquire another source to refinance the irrigation project. Defendant then refused to loan plaintiff money to finance the purchase of cattle for the 1972 and the 1973 seasons. Plaintiff was unable to secure other financing because all of his security was pledged to defendant. Orr admitted at trial that the only reason defendant did not finance plaintiff's cattle operations for the years 1972 and 1973 was that plaintiff did not refinance the long-term irrigation project with another lending institution.

After numerous attempts, plaintiff finally obtained FHA refinancing in March, 1974, and the obligation to defendant was paid in full, including over $25,000 in interest. During the 2–year period, plaintiff was unable to purchase any cattle due to lack of financing. Testimony established that plaintiff lost $85,304 in 1972 and $34,445 in 1973.

These damages were essentially unchallenged and the jury returned a verdict for plaintiff of $100,000.

At the close of plaintiff's opening statement, defendant moved for a summary judgment on the basis that the alleged oral contract was within the statute of frauds because it could not have been completed within one year. M.C.L.A. § 566.132(1); M.S.A. § 26.922(1).[14]

---

14. [This provision declares that contracts which cannot be performed within one year are void unless evidenced by an adequate writing.]

Plaintiff's attorney argued that the statute did not apply because the defendant was estopped to assert the statute as the plaintiff had relied on the oral contract to his detriment.

The doctrine of equitable estoppel is set forth in 3 Williston, Contracts (3d ed.), § 533A, p. 796:

"Where one has acted to his detriment solely in reliance on an oral agreement, an estoppel may be raised to defeat the defense of the Statute of Frauds."

In Oxley v. Ralston Purina Co., 349 F.2d 328, 336 (C.A.6, 1965), a factually similar case, the Court quoted the aforementioned doctrine from Williston and then stated:

"We agree with the rule as above stated and believed that the Michigan Supreme Court would have applied the foregoing language had the problem in this case been before it."

The doctrine was again applied in [a lower court decision].

In the instant case the plaintiff relied upon the defendant's promise, installed an irrigation system and granted defendant a security interest in all of his collateral, to his detriment. It was proper for the trial judge to apply the doctrine.

. . . .

Affirmed. Costs to plaintiff.

---

4. REMEDIES AVAILABLE WHEN THE STATUTE HAS BEEN SUCCESSFULLY PLEADED

Burns v. McCormick

Court of Appeals of New York, 1922.
233 N.Y. 230, 135 N.E. 273.

■ CARDOZO, J. In June, 1918, one James A. Halsey, an old man and a widower, was living, without family or housekeeper, in his house in Hornell, New York. He told the plaintiffs, so it is said, that if they gave up their home and business in Andover, New York, and boarded and cared for him during his life, the house and lot, with its furniture and equipment, would be theirs upon his death. They did as he asked, selling out an interest in a little draying business in Andover, and boarding and tending him till he died, about five months after their coming. Neither deed nor will, nor memorandum subscribed by the promisor, exists to authenticate the promise. The plaintiffs asked specific performance. The defense is the statute of frauds.

We think the defense must be upheld. Not every act of part performance will move a court of equity though legal remedies are inadequate, to enforce an oral agreement affecting rights in land. There must be performance "unequivocally referable" to the agreement, performance which alone and without the aid of words of promise is unintelligible or at least extraordinary unless as an incident of ownership, assured, if not existing. "An act which admits of explanation without reference to the alleged oral contract or a contract of the same general nature and purpose is not, in general, admitted to constitute a part performance."

What is done must itself supply the key to what is promised. It is not enough that what is promised may give significance to what is done. The housekeeper who abandons other prospects of establishment in life and renders service without pay upon the oral promise of her employer to give her a life estate in land must find her remedy in an action to recover the value of the service. Her conduct, separated from the promise, is not significant of ownership, either present or prospective. On the other hand, the buyer who not only pays the price, but possesses and improves his acre, may have relief in equity without producing a conveyance. His conduct is itself the symptom of a promise that a conveyance will be made. Laxer tests may prevail in other jurisdictions. We have been consistent here.

Promise and performance fail when these standards are applied. The plaintiffs make no pretense that during the lifetime of Mr. Halsey they occupied the land as owners or under claim of present right. They did not even have possession. The possession was his; and those whom he invited to live with him were merely his servants or his guests. He might have shown them the door, and the law would not have helped them to return. Whatever rights they had were executory and future. The tokens of their title are not, then, to be discovered in acts of possession or dominion. The tokens must be found elsewhere if discoverable at all. The plaintiffs did, indeed, while occupants of the dwelling, pay the food bills for the owner as well as for themselves, and do the work of housekeepers. One who heard of such service might infer that it would be rewarded in some way. There could be no reasonable inference that it would be rewarded at some indefinite time thereafter by a conveyance of the land. The board might be given in return for lodging. The outlay might be merely an advance to be repaid in whole or part. "Time and care" might have been bestowed "from vague anticipation that the affection and gratitude so created would, in the long run, insure some indefinite reward." This was the more likely since there were no ties of kinship between one of the plaintiffs and the owner. Even if there was to be a reward, not merely as of favor, but as of right, no one could infer, from knowledge of the service, without more, what its nature or extent would be. Mr. Halsey paid the taxes. He paid also for the upkeep of the land and building. At least, there is no suggestion that the plaintiffs had undertaken to relieve him of those burdens. He was the owner while he lived. Nothing that he had accepted from the plaintiffs evinces an agreement that they were to be the owners when he died.

We hold, then, that the acts of part performance are not solely and unequivocally referable to a contract for the sale of land. Since that is so, they do not become sufficient because part of the plaintiffs' loss is without a remedy at law. At law the value of board and services will not be difficult of proof. The loss of the draying business in Andover does not permit us to disregard the statute, though it may go without requital. We do not ignore decisions to the contrary in other jurisdictions. They are not law for us. Inadequacy of legal remedies, without more, does not dispense with the requirement that acts, and not words, shall supply the framework of the promise. That requirement has its origin in something more than an arbitrary preference of one form over others. It is "intended to prevent a recurrence of the mischief" which the statute would suppress. The peril of perjury and error is latent in the spoken promise. Such, at least, is the warning of the statute, the estimate of policy that finds expression in its mandate. Equity, in assuming what is in substance a dispensing power, does not treat the statute as irrelevant, nor ignore the warning altogether. It declines to act on words, though the legal remedy is imperfect, unless the words are confirmed and illuminated by deeds. A power of dispensation, departing from the letter in supposed adherence to the spirit, involves an assumption of jurisdiction easily abused, and justified only within the limits imposed by history and precedent. The power is not exercised unless the policy of the law is saved.

In conclusion, we observe that this is not a case of fraud. No confidential relation has been abused. No inducement has been offered with the preconceived intention that it would later be ignored. The most that can be said against Mr. Halsey is that he made a promise which the law did not compel him to keep, and that afterwards, he failed to keep it. We cannot even say of his failure that it was willful. He had made a will before the promise. Negligence or mere inertia may have postponed the making of another. The plaintiffs left the preservation of their agreement, if they had one, to the fallible memory of witnesses. The law exacts a writing.

The judgment of the Appellate Division and that entered on the report of the referee should be reversed, and the complaint dismissed, with costs in all courts.

Judgments reversed, etc.

NOTES

1. When specific performance is barred by the Statute of Frauds, an action for restitution is usually allowed. This is permissible because the Statute is only a defense to actions to enforce oral contracts.

2. Smith and Hatch orally agreed that Hatch would sell Smith a farm. Payment was to take the form of Smith's wild land plus cash, the amount of which would depend on the price for which Hatch could sell the wild land. Smith conveyed his land to Hatch, who sold it. However, Hatch kept the proceeds and the farm.

Smith then filed an action for restitution. He prevailed in the trial court, and its judgment was affirmed on appeal. Smith v. Hatch, 46 N.H. 146 (1865). Hatch argued that, inasmuch as the doctrine of part performance allowed Smith to have the agreement specifically enforced, he could not elect any other remedy. But the court disagreed.

In Allen v. Webb, 24 N.H. 278, it is held that "where one party to a contract refuses to perform his part of the same, the other party may insist upon the contract being carried out, or he may avail himself of the refusal and rescind the contract." Without considering, therefore, whether the part performance by plaintiff was such as to take the case out of the statute, and enable him to enforce a specific performance on the part of defendant, we think that if such were the admitted fact, the plaintiff might elect his remedy, and either enforce the contract, or rescind it and recover back the value of the land he had conveyed. If the defendant had not sold this land, the count for money had and received could not have been maintained, though the count for land sold would then have been well enough. But the plaintiff may now, by adopting the act of selling on the part of defendant and ratifying the same, recover the money which defendant received for the land under the count for money had and received.

3. As noted in Comment, *The Confidential Relationship Theory of Constructive Trusts—An Exception to the Statute of Frauds*, 29 Fordham L.Rev. 561, 561 (1961):

Promises to convey or to hold property in trust, which would ordinarily be unenforceable under the statute [of Frauds], have often resulted in the imposition of a constructive trust when the abuse of a confidential relationship has been found. The "abuse of confidence" exception to the statute, which defies accurate definition, has provided courts of equity with an elastic means for intervention whenever such is considered just and proper.

Hewitt v. Parmenter

Supreme Court of Minnesota, 1930.
181 Minn. 454, 232 N.W. 919.

■ Stone, J. Action by lessee against lessor to recover damages for wrongful eviction. Defendant had a directed verdict, and plaintiff appeals from the order denying his motion for a new trial.

September 19, 1928, plaintiff was a tenant and in possession, under a written lease expiring March 1, 1929, of a farm owned by defendant. An oral agreement was then made by them for a lease of the same premises upon the same terms for another year, expiring March 1, 1930. The oral lease was not subject to sale. After it was made but before its term was to begin, defendant sold the farm to one Berry, undertaking to give possession upon the expiration of plaintiff's first and written lease expiring March 1, 1929. As that date approached, she unequivocally demanded that he surrender possession, thereby in effect repudiating the oral lease. Her demand not being complied with, she commenced, March 3, 1929, an action of unlawful detainer. Plaintiff, as defendant in that action, did not interpose a defense but elected to consider plaintiff's action a constructive eviction and voluntarily surrendered possession. After the making of the oral lease and before defendant's repudiation of it, plaintiff did a substantial quantity of plowing, stump-pulling and quack grass eradication which he now claims to have been such a part performance as to remove the agreement from the operation of the statute of frauds.

The doctrine of part performance, so called, is a creature of equity and resorted to only for the award of an equitable remedy. Part performance will not support an action at law for damages for breach of a contract within the statute of frauds. That is the general rule and was settled as the law of this state by Cram v. Thompson, 87 Minn. 172 [91 N.W. 483 (1902)]. The principle "is applicable only where the action is one in equity for specific performance." In that connection it is not to be overlooked that part performance of a contract within the statute of frauds may make a cause of action in quasi contract. Or, in the case of a vendor under such an agreement, his performance or willingness to perform may be a defense to such an action. But this is the ordinary action for breach of contract, and his part performance does not help plaintiff. With his possible remedy against defendant in quasi contract for the betterment of her land or against a third party upon an alleged assumption of the obligation, we are not now concerned.

Order affirmed.

————

F. PLAINTIFF'S DEFAULT

1. NONPERFORMANCE OF CONDITIONS PRECEDENT

Lord Ranelagh v. Melton

Chancery, 1864.
2 Dr. & Sm. 278, 62 Eng.Rep. 627.

This was a suit for specific performance.

By articles of agreement, bearing date the 22nd day of December, 1857, the Defendant, William Melton, agreed to lease certain plots of land in Richmond Road, Round Hill Park, Brighton, to Henry Banks and Joseph Vinall, for a term of ninety-nine years from June, 1856, subject to certain ground-rents;[15] and the articles of agreement contained the following clause:

"In case, at any time within the space of seven years from the 23rd day of June, 1856, the lessees shall be desirous of purchasing the fee simple and inheritance of all or any one of the said plots of ground, and of such their desire shall give three months' notice to the lessor, and shall, at the expiration of such notice, pay unto him the sum of 210*l.* in respect of each plot mentioned in such notice, and all rent payable to and including the current quarter, then the lessor shall and will convey the freehold and inheritance of the plot or plots mentioned in such notice unto and to the use of the lessees, or as they shall appoint."

15. [A "ground rent" is a "perpetual rent reserved to himself and his heirs, by the grantor of land in fee-simple, out of the land conveyed." Black's Law Dictionary 633 (5th ed. 1979).]

The articles of agreement provided that the terms lessor and lessee, as used therein, should apply to their assigns in the event of either party disposing of his interest in the premises.

. . . .

The interest of the lessees, Banks, and Vinall, subsequently became vested in the present Plaintiffs.

The Plaintiffs being desirous of exercising their right, under the clause in the articles of agreement, of purchasing from the Defendant the fee simple and inheritance in the said plots of land, on the 20th day of March, 1863, served on the Defendant notice, as provided by the articles of agreement, of their desire so to do. It was admitted that this notice was regular in all respects. After the service of this notice, some communications took place between the parties, in the course of which the Defendant expressed his wish to have the draft conveyances sent to him for perusal.

The period of three months from the date of the notice expired on the 20th of June, and the seven years from the date of the articles of agreement expired on the 24th of June, but nothing further took place till the 1st of July, when the Plaintiff's solicitor sent the Defendant draft conveyances for his perusal.

On the receipt of these draft conveyances the Defendant wrote the Plaintiff's solicitor that he did not consent to excuse the default to complete on or before the 20th or 24th day of June; and finally, on this ground, the Defendant refused to complete the sale to the Plaintiffs of the fee in the said plots of land. It appeared that the purchase-money had never been tendered.

Under these circumstances, the Plaintiffs filed their bill to enforce specific performance, by the Defendant, of the agreement to sell the fee simple to them.

The cause now came on upon motion for a decree.

THE VICE-CHANCELLOR [SIR R.T. KINDERSLEY]—I apprehend the rule of law applicable to cases like the present is perfectly clear. No doubt, if an owner of land and an intending purchaser enter into a contract constituting between them the relation of vendor and purchaser, and there is a stipulation in the contract that the purchase-money shall be paid and the contract completed on a certain day, this Court in ordinary cases has established the principle that time is not of the essence of the contract, and that the circumstance of the day fixed for the payment of the money and completion of the purchase being past does not entitle either party to refuse to complete. On the other hand, it is well settled that where there is a contract between the owner of land and another person, that if such person shall do a specified act, then he (the owner) will convey the land to him in fee; the relation of vendor and purchaser does not exist between the parties unless and until the act has been done as specified. The court regards it as the case of a condition on the performance of which the party performing it is entitled to a certain benefit; but in order to obtain such benefit he must perform the condition strictly. Therefore, if there be a day fixed for its performance, the lapse of that day without its being performed prevents him from claiming the benefit. Applying that rule to the present case: if the agreement fixes a day for the payment of the money, then it is clear that if that day is past without the payment, the right to compel a conveyance is lost.

The question then is, whether any time is fixed in this agreement for the payment of the money. The language is, that if the lessees shall at the expiration of three months after the notice (which notice was duly given) pay the money, *then* the lessor shall convey the freehold and inheritance; and the matter resolves itself into a question of construction,—What is the meaning of the words "at the expiration of three months"?

The Plaintiffs contend that these words mean, not *at* the time at which the three months expire, but at any time afterwards. If that be the true construction, the consequence would be, that not only a day or a week after, but a year or any number of years after the expiration of the three months, the plaintiffs would have a right to tender the money and demand a conveyance; and this is what the law will not permit. But besides that, if the lessees should think fit not to pay the money, could the owner file a bill to compel them to do so? I apprehend, clearly not; for there is nothing in the agreement to make it obligatory on the lessees to pay the money. It is impossible to put such a construction on the words. "At the expiration of three months" must mean, not at any time after such expiration, but on the day on which the three months expire.

This case is not open to the argument which might arise in ordinary cases between vendor and purchaser, that the investigation of the title would occupy some time, inasmuch as the agreement provides that the lessees shall accept the title; so that there was nothing to be done but the conveyance. Unfortunately for the Plaintiffs, they have allowed the time limited for the payment of the money to elapse, and therefore they are not entitled to a conveyance.

Bill dismissed, with costs.

---

2. BREACH

Gannett v. Albree

Supreme Judicial Court of Massachusetts, 1869.
103 Mass. 372.

Bill in equity for specific performance of an agreement to renew the lease of a dwelling-house numbered 28 on Pemberton Square in Boston.

At the hearing in this court, before Morton, J., it appeared that the defendant demised the premises to George W. Bassett for the term of three years from August 1, 1866, by an indenture in which the lessee covenanted not to lease nor underlet the premises, nor permit any other person or persons to occupy or improve the same without the written approbation of the lessor, and the lessor agreed that the lessee should have the right to renew the lease at his option for the term of two years; that on the indenture, before its delivery, was made the following indorsement under the hand and seal of the defendant: "In case the lessee shall cease to occupy the premises as a residence, he shall have the right to underlet the same for the remainder of the term, to any respectable person, to be used strictly as a private dwelling, and not for any public or objectionable purpose;" and that on September 12, 1866, Bassett, with the written consent of the defendant assigned the premises and all his interest therein to the plaintiff. It also appeared that the premises "from the time of the assignment till April 9, 1868, were used and occupied by the plaintiff, in connection with his school for young ladies, for sleeping-rooms, with the knowledge and consent of the defendant; that on or about April 9, 1869, the plaintiff leased the same to Lucy E. Small, for the unexpired term of the lease, for the purposes of a boarding-house, though not mentioned in the written lease, reserving to himself one room which had been occupied by his brother, a clergyman, as a sleeping-room; that Small occupied the house for a boarding-house, using a portion of the house for her own family, and the balance for boarders who lodged in the house; and that the plaintiff agreed that, when he obtained a renewal of the lease from the defendant, he would renew the lease for the same term to Small."

The judge ruled "that such use of the house was in violation of the provisions of the lease and the agreement, and, by reason thereof, declined to order a specific performance of the agreement" for renewal, and reported the case for the determination of the full court.

■ AMES, J. By the terms of the lease, the lessor had a right to insist that the house should be occupied as a residence, and used "strictly as a private dwelling," and not for any "public or objectionable purpose." When the lease was assigned to the plaintiff, he took it subject to all the covenants which it reserved or contained, to be kept and fulfilled on the part of the original lessee. The consent of the lessor that the plaintiff might occupy and use the house himself, in connection with his school for young ladies, cannot fairly be construed as a general or absolute waiver of the limitations as to the nature of the occupation. It is not the case of a condition which, when once dispensed with, is discharged for all purposes, and cannot be revived, but of a covenant which can be modified by consent. The lessor might be willing to consider such a use of the house as not an entire departure from its intended character of a private dwelling, and not an appropriation to a public or objectionable purpose. But, its conversion into a public boarding-house is an entirely different matter. In making the original lease, with its restrictions, the lessor may have supposed that such a use would subject the house to greater wear and tear, or to greater depreciation in value, or require more frequent repairs, or increase the rate of insurance. All these considerations may have had their influence upon her mind as to the rate of the rent and the length of the term. The use of the house as a boarding-house is in violation of the terms of the lease, and would subject it to very different conditions. For that reason, the plaintiff is not entitled to a decree for the specific performance of the contract for its renewal.

Bill dismissed, with costs.

———

3.   TIME PROVISIONS

Parkin v. Thorold

Chancery, 1852.
16 Beav. 59, 51 Eng.Rep. 698.

On the 25th of July, 1850, the Plaintiff agreed to sell to the Defendant a freehold estate. The abstract was to be delivered within ten days, and by the fifth condition of sale it was stipulated as follows: the purchaser shall pay a deposit, "and sign an agreement for completing the purchase and for payment of the residue of the purchase money on or before the 25th of October next," at the office of Mr. F., "*at which time and place the purchase is to be completed.*"

The seventh condition provided, "that in case the completion of the purchase, through the default of the purchaser, shall not take place on the 25th of October next, the purchaser shall pay interest, at five per cent., up to the time of actually completing the purchase."

The fifteenth condition provided, that if the purchaser "should neglect or fail to comply with the conditions and to complete his purchase by the time and in manner aforesaid," his deposit should be forfeited to the vendor, who should be at liberty to resell, & c.

The conditions were signed by both parties, and the deposit paid.

The abstract was delivered, but difficulties arose, in consequence of a settlement dated in 1804 having been mislaid. A correspondence took place respecting it, and on the 17th of October the vendor's solicitor stated: "I only require time to be able to find the settlement. I believe I have found out where it is."

On the 21st of October the purchaser's solicitor gave notice that unless the settlement were produced and the other requisitions satisfied on or before the 5th of November, he would treat the contract as at an end, and require a return of the deposit.

On the 7th of November the deposit was formally demanded. The vendor, on the 8th of January, 1851, offered to produce the deed, but the purchaser then stated, that he had long abandoned the contract, and on the 28th of February, 1851, he brought an action for the recovery of the deposit. On the following day (1st of March), the vendor instituted this suit for the specific performance of the contract.

On a motion to dissolve the common injunction to stay the proceedings at law, Lord Cranworth, holding that time was at law and in equity of the essence of the contract, and that it had not been waived, dissolved the injunction. The action went on, but was afterwards discontinued, and the cause now came on for hearing.

THE MASTER OF THE ROLLS [SIR JOHN ROMILLY]....

The case appears to me to be resolvable into the following questions: The first is, whether time was of the essence of this contract; if it was, the contract was not performed within the time. If it be determined that time was an essential part of the contract, then a second question will arise, whether this part of the contract was waived by the Defendant. If it be determined that time was not originally of the essence of the contract, the next question will be, whether the notice of the 21st of October, specifying the 5th of November as the time for the completion of the contract, made that time an essential part of the contract, or if not, whether the conduct of the Plaintiffs, by acquiescence in that notice, or by laches in not actively enforcing their rights, have deprived them of any right to relief in this Court.

Upon the first question, there is no great difficulty in stating the rule, although there may be considerable in applying it to the facts of individual cases. At law, time is always of the essence of the contract. When any time is fixed for the completion of it, the contract must be completed on the day specified, or an action will lie for the breach of it. This is not the doctrine of a Court of Equity; and although the dictum of Lord Thurlow, that time could not be made of the essence of the contract in equity, has long been exploded, yet time is held to be of the essence of the contract in equity, only in cases of direct stipulation, or of necessary implication. The cases of direct stipulation are, where the parties to the contract introduce a clause expressly stating that time is to be of the essence of the contract. The implication that time was of the essence of the contract is derived from the circumstances of the case, such as where the property sold is required for some immediate purpose, such as trade or manufacture; or where the property is of a determinable character, as an estate for life. It is needless to refer to the authorities, which are numerous, to support these propositions. Unless I am wholly mistaken, they establish that unless in the cases of direct stipulation, or of necessary implication, time is not considered in Courts of Equity to form such a portion of the contract, as either party can treat to be an essential part of it.

. . . .

... A contract is undoubtedly construed alike both in equity and at law; nay more, a Court of Law is the proper tribunal for determining the construction of it; and if a serious doubt should arise as to the effect of the words contained in a contract, a case would be directed to a Court of Law for its opinion as to the true construction to be put upon the words, which construction would be adopted in equity. But Courts of Equity make a distinction in all cases between that which is matter of substance and that which is matter of form; and if it find, that by insisting on the form, the substance will be defeated, it holds it to be inequitable to allow a person to insist on such form, and thereby defeat the substance. For instance, A. has contracted to sell an estate to B., and to complete the title by the 25th of October; but no stipulation is introduced that either party considers time of the essence of the contract. A. completes the title by the 26th; at law the contract is at an end, and B. may bring an action for the non-performance of the contract, and obtain damages for the breach; but equity holds, that unless B. can show that the delay of twenty-four hours really produced some injury to him, he is not to be permitted to bring this action, or to avoid the performance of the contract; not certainly on the ground that the 25th of October was not a part of the contract, but on the ground that it is unjust that B. should escape the performance of a contract, which has been substantially performed by A., by reason of some omission in a formal but immaterial portion of it.

The jurisdiction of equity in the execution of the specific performance of contracts accordingly is eminently discretionary; it will not enforce a contract where doing so would be productive of peculiar hardship on one party to it.... Neither will equity enforce a contract, where, though the Court considers the title good, yet considers it sufficiently doubtful that it might reasonably give rise to litigation hereafter between the purchasers and persons not bound by the decree of the Court in the suit for specific performance. It is, I apprehend, on a similar principle, that the Court has regarded the question of time in these matters, when it has not been specifically and precisely contracted for, as an essential clause in the contract. It then considers how far either party is injured by the delay, and will not permit one to insist upon that, which, although a formal part of the contract, would, in reality, defeat the object which both had in view, at the time when it was made. It is, I apprehend, on a similar principle, also, that the whole doctrine relating to equities of redemption, as administered by this Court, is founded. The contract between the mortgagor and mortgagee is precise; if the money and interest is not repaid on the day twelve-month on which the mortgage is made, the estate is to be the property of the mortgagee: the contract is positive and unambiguous, but a Court of Equity will not permit that contract to be enforced, and will restrain the parties from enforcing it at law. It treats the substance of the contract to be a security for the repayment of money advanced, and that portion of the contract which gives the estate to the mortgagee as mere form; and accordingly, in direct violation of the contract, it compels the mortgagee, so soon as he has been repaid his principal money and interest and the costs he has been put to, to restore the estate: and this, although the parties have acted on the contract, and the mortgagee has taken possession on the day when default arose, and has continued in possession for many years; in truth, as a general rule it may be said, any number of years not exceeding twenty, acknowledging no title in the mortgagor.

I am of opinion, therefore, that the later decisions of the Court have not altered the doctrine I have stated as to the cases where time is of the essence of the contract.

I turn therefore to this contract, for the purpose of examining it by the principles I have already laid down. In the first place, the time specified is not, by express words, made an essential part of it. This was, in truth, admitted at the bar and could not be denied; nay, more, the seventh condition of sale appears to me to be inconsistent with such a proposition, even if any such could have been maintained on the rest of the contract; and except that it is confined to the default of the purchaser, it is the condition which, in the precedents at ... [2 E. Sugden,] Vendors and Purchasers [1077 (11th ed. 1846)], is suggested as proper to be introduced, when it is intended by both parties that time shall not be of the essence of the contract.

Do then any such circumstances exist in this case, analogous to those to which I have already referred, as raising the presumption that time was an essential part of the contract? I find none. The property is not of a perishable nature, the interest in it sold is not of a determinable character, and possession is not required for any purpose of trade or manufacture. I have therefore, on the first question, come to the conclusion that time was not originally of the essence of this contract.

Having come to this conclusion on the first question, it may be superfluous to express my opinion on the next subordinate point, which would have arisen had I come to an opposite conclusion; but as it may have some bearing on the subsequent part of this case, I think it desirable to do so. I am of opinion then, that if time had been originally of the essence of this contract, the Defendant has waived that part of it. The time mentioned in the contract for the completion of the purchase is the 25th of October, 1850, but the Defendant, by his solicitor, on the 21st of October, 1850, extends that time till the 5th of November, 1850. If time was of the essence of the contract, the contract was at an end, if the title had not been made out on or before the 25th of October, 1850, but after that letter, the Defendant would, beyond all question, have been compellable in equity to complete the purchase, if the title had been completed by the 1st November, 1850, or any other day before the 5th November, 1850. It appears to me, therefore, that, after writing this letter, the Defendant abandoned his right to insist on the completion of the title on the 25th of October, 1850, which was the day specified in the contract.

[Romilly, M.R., then said that the purchaser's waiver would be effective even if made at the vendor's request, which was not the fact; and that the waiver was not conditioned on November 5 being made an essential part of the contract, nor was it so accepted by the vendor.]

. . . It is obvious, that one party to a contract cannot, at his will, vary one of the terms of it; the assent of both parties to the variation must be obtained, and this was not done. . . .

The next question I have to consider is, whether the notice contained in the letter of the 21st of October, 1850, specifying the 5th of November, 1850, as the time for the completion of the contract, made that time an essential part of the contract; or rather, whether it bound the Plaintiffs to complete within that period of time or to abandon the contract. It is, I consider, the undoubted law of this Court, that although time was not originally an essential part of the contract, still that either party may, by a proper notice, bind the other to complete within a reasonable time to be specified in such notice; and if the party receiving such notice do not complete within the time so specified, equity will not enforce a specific performance of the contract, but leave the parties to their remedies and their liabilities at law.

[Romilly, M.R., then decided that the notice did not obligate Plaintiffs to complete by November 5 because "fourteen days . . . was not a reasonable time within which to require Plaintiffs to produce the deed in question and complete the title."]

But although the notice was not sufficient, then the next question arises, the Plaintiffs may have acquiesced in it, or they may, by *laches,* have waived their right to seek for any relief from this Court. Heaphy v. Hill [2 S. & S. 29] and Watson v. Reid [1 Russ. & Myl. 236] establishes this proposition, which I apprehend to be the settled law of the Court, viz., that if one of two parties to a contract for the sale of land, give to the other notice that he will not perform the contract, and the person receiving the notice does not, within a reasonable time after the receipt of such notice, take steps to enforce the contract, equity will consider him to have acquiesced in the abandonment of the contract, and will leave the parties to it to their remedies at law; and the tendency of modern decisions has been to diminish the time allowed to either party for enforcing his right under the contract. It remains to apply these principles to the facts of the present case. Even though the time given by the notice of the 21st October, 1850, be not, in my opinion, sufficient, the Defendant is entitled to have it treated as an express notice of his abandonment of the contract on the 5th of November, 1850; then the question is, whether the Plaintiffs have acquiesced in this notice, or been guilty of such *laches,* as to prevent them from seeking the assistance of a Court of Equity.

. . . .

I am convinced that no Court, having regard to these decisions on this subject, will hold that under these circumstances the Plaintiffs can be said to have forfeited what rights they had in equity, by reason of any implied acquiescence in the notice of the 21st of October, 1850, or by reason of their having been too negligent and dilatory in the enforcement of their claim.

The short result of the opinion that I have come to is,

First.—That time was not originally of the essence of the contract.

Secondly.—That although express notice will make time of the essence of the contract, where a reasonable time is specified, that the notice of the 21st October did not specify a reasonable time for this purpose.

Thirdly.—That although acquiescence in the abandonment of a contract or *laches* in seeking the assistance of a Court of Equity will bar a party to a contract enforcing his rights, yet that there are not any facts in evidence before me to justify the Court in holding that the Plaintiffs acquiesced in such abandonment, or that he has been guilty of such *laches* as will prevent this Court from enforcing the specific performance of this contract.

. . . .

The decree pronounced by me will be the common decree for specific performance, with a reference to the Master as to title, unless that be accepted; and as the suit has been rendered necessary by the resistance of the Defendant to perform the contract, it follows, as a necessary consequence, from my decision, that the Defendant must pay the costs of the suit, so far as the same has been incurred by reason of his resisting his liability specifically to perform the contract.

J.N.A. Realty Corp. v. Cross Bay Chelsea, Inc.

Court of Appeals of New York, 1977.
42 N.Y.2d 392, 397 N.Y.S.2d 958, 366 N.E.2d 1313.

■ WACHTLER, J. J.N.A. Realty Corp., the owner of a building in Howard Beach, commenced this proceeding to recover possession of the premises claiming that the lease has expired. The lease grants the tenant, Cross Bay Chelsea, Inc., an option to renew and although the notice was sent, through negligence or inadvertence, it was not sent within the time prescribed in the lease. The landlord seeks to enforce the letter of the agreement. The tenant asks for equity to relieve it from a forfeiture.

The Civil Court, after trial, held that the tenant was entitled to equitable relief. The Appellate Term affirmed, without opinion, but the Appellate Division, after granting leave reversed and granted the petition. The tenant has appealed to this court.

Two primary questions are raised on the appeal. First, will the tenant suffer a forfeiture if the landlord is permitted to enforce the letter of the agreement. Secondly, if there will be a forfeiture, may a court of equity grant the tenant relief when the forfeiture would result from the tenant's own neglect or inadvertence.

At the trial it was shown that J.N.A. Realty Corp. (hereafter JNA) originally leased the premises to Victor Palermo and Sylvester Vascellero for a 10–year term commencing on January 1, 1964. Paragraph 58 of the lease, which was attached as part of 12–page rider, granted the tenants an option to renew for a 10–year term provided "that Tenant shall notify the landlord in writing by registered or certified mail six (6) months prior to the last day of the term of the lease that tenant desires such renewal." The tenants opened a restaurant on the premises. In February, 1964 they formed the Foro Romano Corp. (Foro) and assigned the lease to the corporation.

By December of 1967 the restaurant was operating at a loss and Foro decided to close it down and offer it for sale or lease. In March, 1968 Foro entered into a contract with Cross Bay Chelsea, Inc. (hereafter Chelsea), to sell the restaurant and assign the lease. As a condition of the sale Foro was required to obtain a modification of the option to renew so that Chelsea would have the right to renew the lease for an additional term of 24 years.

The closing took place in June of 1968. First JNA modified the option and consented to the assignment. The modification, which consists of a separate document to be attached to the lease, states: "the Tenant shall have a right to renew this lease for a further period of Twenty–Four (24) years, instead of Ten (10) years, from the expiration of the original term of said lease.... All other provisions of Paragraph #58 in said lease, ... shall remain in full force and effect, except as hereinabove modified." Foro then assigned the lease and sold its interest in the restaurant to Chelsea for $155,000. The bill of sale states that "the value of the fixtures and chattels included in this sale is the sum of $40,000 and that the remainder of the purchase price is the value of the leasehold and possession of the restaurant premises." At that point five and one-half years remained on the original term of the lease.

In the summer of 1968 Chelsea reopened the restaurant. JNA's president, Nicholas Arena, admitted on the stand that throughout the term of the tenancy he was "most assuredly" aware of the time limitation on the option. In fact there is some indication in the record that JNA had previously used this device in an attempt to evict another tenant. Nevertheless it was not until November 12, 1973 that JNA took any action to inform the tenant that the option had lapsed. Then it sent a letter noting that the date had passed and, the letter states, "not having heard from you as prescribed by paragraph #58 in our lease we must assume you will vacate the premises" at the expiration of the original term, January 1, 1974. By letter dated November 16, 1973 Chelsea, through its attorney, sent written notice of intention to renew the option which, of course, JNA refused to honor.

At the trial Chelsea's principals claimed that they were not aware of the time limitation because they had never received a copy of paragraph 58 of the rider. They had received a copy of the modification but they had assumed that it gave them an absolute right to retain the tenancy for 24 years after the expiration of the original term. However, at the trial and later at the Appellate Division, it was found that Chelsea had knowledge of, or at least was "chargeable with notice" of, the time limitation in the rider and thus was negligent in failing to renew within the time prescribed.

. . . .

It is a settled principle of law that a notice exercising an option is ineffective if it is not given within the time specified. "At law, of course, time is always of the essence of the contract" (De Funiak, Modern Equity, § 80, p. 223). Thus the tenant had no legal right to exercise the option when it did, but to say that is simply to pose the issue; it does not resolve it. Of course the tenant would not be asking for equitable relief if it could establish its rights at law.

The major obstacle to obtaining equitable relief in these cases is that default on an option usually does not result in a forfeiture. The reason is that the option itself does not create any interest in the property, and no rights accrue until the condition precedent has been met by giving notice within the time specified. Thus equity will not intervene because the loss of the option does not ordinarily result in the forfeiture of any vested rights. The general rule is customarily stated as follows: "There is a wide distinction between a condition precedent, where no title has vested and none is to vest until the condition is performed, and a condition subsequent, operating by way of a defeasance. In the former case equity can give no relief. The failure to perform is an inevitable bar. No right can ever vest. The result is very different where the condition is subsequent. There equity will interpose and relieve against the forfeiture." It has been suggested that even when the option has been paid for, nothing is forfeited when it expires, because the amount paid "is the exact agreed equivalent" of the power to exercise the right for the time allotted (see 1 Corbin, Contracts, § 35, p. 147).

But when a tenant in possession under an existing lease has neglected to exercise an option to renew, he might suffer a forfeiture if he has made valuable improvements on the property. This of course generally distinguishes the lease option, to renew or purchase, from the stock option or the option to buy goods. This was a distinction which some of the older cases failed to recognize. More recently it has been noted that "although the tenant has no legal interest in the renewal period until the required notice is given, yet an equitable interest is recognized and protected against forfeiture in some cases where the tenant has in good faith made improvements of a substantial character, intending to renew the lease, if the landlord is not harmed by the delay in the giving of the notice and the lessee would sustain substantial loss in case the lease were not renewed" (2 Pomeroy, Equity Jurisprudence [5th ed.], § 453b, p. 296).

The leading case on this point is Fountain Co. v. Stein, 97 Conn. 619, 118 A. 47, and the rule has been accepted by noted commentators. It has also been accepted and applied by this court. In Jones v. Gianferante, 305 N.Y. 135, 138, 111 N.E.2d 419, 420, citing the *Fountain* case we held that the tenant was entitled to "the benefit of the rule or practice in equity which relieves against such forfeitures of valuable lease terms when default in notice has not prejudiced the landlord, and has resulted from an honest mistake, or similar excusable fault." The rule was extended in Sy Jack Realty Co. v. Pergament Syosset Corp., 27 N.Y.2d 449, 453, 318 N.Y.S.2d 720, 722, 267 N.E.2d 462, 464, to preserve the tenant's interest in a "long-standing location for a retail business" because this is "an important part of the good will of that enterprise, [and thus] the tenant stands to lose a substantial and valuable asset."

In neither of those cases were we asked to consider whether the tenant would be entitled to equitable relief from the consequences of his own neglect or "mere forgetfulness" as the court had held in the *Fountain* case.... But the principle involved is well established in this State. A tenant or mortgagor should not be denied equitable relief from the consequences of his own neglect or inadvertence if a forfeiture would result. The rule applies even though the tenant or mortgagor, by his inadvertence, has neglected to perform an affirmative duty and thus breached a covenant in the agreement.

On occasion the court has cautioned that equitable relief would be denied where there has been a willful or gross neglect, but it has been reluctant to employ the sanction when a forfeiture would result....

. . . .

Here, as noted, the tenant has made a considerable investment in improvements on the premises—$40,000 at the time of purchase, and an additional $15,000 during the tenancy. In addition, if the location is lost, the restaurant would undoubtedly lose a considerable amount of its customer good will. The tenant was at fault, but not in a culpable sense. It was, as Cardozo says, "mere venial inattention." There would be a forfeiture and the gravity of the loss is certainly out of all proportion to the gravity of the fault. Thus, under the circumstances of this case, the tenant would be entitled to equitable relief if there is no prejudice to the landlord.

However, it is not clear from the record whether JNA would be prejudiced if the tenant is relieved of its default.... This ... must be resolved at a new trial.

. . . .

Accordingly, the order of the Appellate Division should be reversed and a new trial granted.

■ BREITEL, C.J. (dissenting)....

Had an honest mistake or similar "excusable fault", as opposed to what is undoubtedly mere carelessness, occasioned the tenant's tardiness, absent prejudice to the landlord, equitable relief would be available. At issue, instead, is the availability of equitable relief where the only excuse for the commercial tenant's dilatory failure to exercise its option to renew is sheer carelessness.

Enough has been said to uncover a common situation. Experienced and even hardened businessmen at cross-purposes over the renewal of a valuable lease term seek on the one hand to stand by the written agreement, and on the other, to loosen the applicable rules to receive *ad hoc* adjustment of equities and relief from economic detriment. The landlord wants a higher return. The tenant wants to keep the old bargain. Which of the profit-seeking parties in this particular case should prevail as a matter of morals is not within the province of the courts. The well-settled doctrine is that with respect to options, whether they be lease renewal options, options to purchase real or personal property, or stock options, time is of the essence. The exceptions, namely, estoppel, fraud, mistake, accident, or overreaching, are few. Commercial stability and certainty are paramount, and always the dangers of unsolvable issues of fact and speculative manipulation (as with stock options) are to be avoided.

The landlord should be awarded possession of the premises in accordance with the undisputed language and manifested intention of the written lease, its 12–page rider, and modification. It does not suffice that the tenant may suffer an economic detriment in losing the renewal period. Nor does it suffice that the delay in giving notice may have caused the landlord no "prejudice", other than loss of the opportunity to relet the property or renegotiate the terms of a lease on a fresh basis. Once an option to renew a lease has been conditioned upon the tenant's giving timely notice, the commercial lessee should not be heard to complain that through carelessness a valued asset has been lost, anymore than one would allow the landlord to complain of the economic detriment to him in agreeing to an improvident option to renew.

. . . .

NOTES ON HARDSHIP, WAIVER, AND ESTOPPEL

1. Reconsider Graf v. Hope Building Corp., supra page 16. In *Graf*, a mortgagor inadvertently paid the incorrect amount on an interest installment payment, triggering acceleration of the entire mortgage. The mortgagee refused the mortgagor's tender of the correct installment amount and instead foreclosed on the property. The court, with Chief Judge Cardozo dissenting, permitted foreclosure and refused to entertain any equitable defenses of the mortgagor. Judge Wachtler's majority opinion in *J.N.A. Realty* parallels the dissent in *Graf*, wherein Chief Judge Cardozo stated: "In this case, the hardship is so flagrant, the misadventure so undoubted, the oppression so apparent, as to justify holding that only through an acceptance of the [late] tender will equity be done." Graf v. Hope Building Corp., 254 N.Y. 1, 171 N.E. 884 (1930).

2.   Plaintiff, Jean Spalding, sued in the United States District Court to recover on a life insurance policy on a stallion after the stallion was destroyed for humane purposes. The Court entered summary judgment in favor of the insurer and agent, finding that, pursuant to a clause in the policy, the gelding of the stallion effected a forfeiture or cancellation of the policy. The insurance policy provided that: "In the event of an animal being operated upon for castration or spaying this insurance shall cease to cover such animal at midnight, local standard time, immediately prior to the day of the operation."

Defendants assert that since the stallion had been "operated upon," the insurance policy, by its terms, ceased to cover the insured animal. Plaintiff contends that defendants' failure to cancel the policy and return the premium payments, during a 4–month period, when defendants were made aware and knew of the facts which led to the humane destruction of the animal, raises issues of waiver or estoppel sufficient to defeat a motion for summary judgment.

The question presented was whether, under Missouri law, there was a material question of fact sufficient to defeat a motion for summary judgment as to whether the insurance company, by its silence or inaction, had waived its rights, or was estopped from asserting a condition of the insurance contract which provided for the cancellation of the coverage if the insured animal had been "operated upon," i.e., gelded. The Court of Appeals reversed and held that the record raised questions of material fact as to either waiver or estoppel, as alleged by plaintiff, and therefore reversed. Spalding v. Agri–Risk Services, 855 F.2d 586 (8th Cir. 1988).

---

4.   Forfeiture Provisions

Heckard v. Sayre

Supreme Court of Illinois, 1864.
34 Ill. 142.

This was a bill in chancery brought by the purchaser of a tract of land against the vendor to compel a specific performance. The Circuit Court [of Peoria county] granted the prayer of the bill, and the defendant sued out a writ of error. The facts appear in the opinion.

■ Mr. Justice Beckwith delivered the opinion of the Court. This is a suit in equity to enforce the specific performance of a contract for the sale of a tract of land in Fulton county.

On the 18th of September, 1857, the plaintiff in error bargained with the defendant in error, to sell him the land for the sum of $900. One hundred and five ⁸⁹⁄₁₀₀ dollars were then paid, and two notes were given for the residue; one for $494¹¹⁄₁₀₀ payable on or before October 25, 1857, and the other for $300, payable on or before September 1, 1858.

The contract between the parties provided, that the above notes should be paid at maturity; that the time stipulated for their payment should be regarded as of the essence of the contract; and that the nonpayment of either of the notes when they should become due, should be considered as an avoidance of the vendor's obligation, and as an absolute forfeiture of all payments previously made. The note maturing first was paid at maturity, and a tender of the amount due upon the other note was made on the 7th day of Sept., 1858, six days after it fell due.

The bill alleges a waiver by the vendor of the prompt performance of the agreement; and sets up as an excuse for the vendee's neglect to make the last payment at the time required that he was engaged in the discharge of his official duties as clerk of the circuit court of Fulton county.

There is no evidence of any waiver by the vendor of the stipulation in regard to time, and we think the excuse alleged is entirely insufficient. The term of the court at which the defendant in error was required to attend commenced on the 6th day of July, 1858, and he might have employed some one to transact his business with the plaintiff in error, if it was not convenient to attend to it in person. Such an excuse, if allowed, would exempt the clerks of many courts in this State from ever discharging their obligations.

From the allegations of the bill it appears that the complainant did not have the money to make the last payment at the time it became due; and stipulations like the one in the contract under consideration, would be of little value if they were to be enforced only in cases where parties making them had the money with which they might be discharged. No rule is more firmly settled than that parties may make time of the essence of a contract. In this case the parties have so made it, in plain and unambiguous language.

At law the defendant in error has no remedy for a breach of the agreement by reason of his own non-performance. He was not hindered or prevented in the discharge of his obligations by any fraud, accident or mistake; and under such circumstances equity must follow the law. A court of equity has no more right than a court of law to dispense with an express stipulation of parties in regard to time, in contracts of this nature, where no fraud, accident or mistake has intervened. To relieve from the effect of such stipulations, except on the grounds named, would practically deny the right of parties to make them. Such relief would result in great injustice to vendors. Usually the price of lands in this country is fixed with reference to prompt payment; and where they are an article of commerce, it is often of the last importance to a vendor to receive his money promptly. We have all known men of affluence reduced to penury by neglect in making such payments as they became due. A vendor may require the payments to be made promptly to enable him to meet his own engagements; and for that purpose a stipulation may be inserted in the contract that time shall be of its essence. If courts were to allow a vendee to neglect to make his payments at the stipulated times, where he is not hindered or prevented from so doing by fraud, accident or mistake, the consequences of his negligence would be visited upon his vendor. Justice does not require relief from the result of one's own negligence. Courts of equity in such cases refuse to interfere; and leave the parties to their remedies at law, if any they have, for the reason that there is no equity requiring such an interposition.

It was urged in argument that the plaintiff in error might compel the payment of the note of the defendant in error, but if he should do so, an equitable right to a conveyance of the land would then exist which, upon proper application, would be enforced. Equity would not allow the plaintiff in error to collect the residue of the purchase money and hold the land, but until he attempts its collection no such equity arises.

The decree of the court below is reversed, and the cause remanded.

Decree reversed.

NOTES

1. Edgerton v. Peckham, 11 Paige 352 (N.Y.Ch.1844), involved a contract to sell land for three annual payments of $1000 each, any default to end the contract and result in the forfeiture of prior payments. Edgerton tendered his last payment 17 days late. Specific performance was granted. Gridley, V.C., wrote:

Time may be of the essence of the contract when there is an express stipulation to that effect, and where the contract is executory at the time of the default; no part or no considerable part of the purchase money having been paid. And this is on a very plain principle, to wit: that the performance, by the vendee, is a condition precedent to the performance of the contract by the vendor. It is believed that most of the modern cases which have been supposed to establish the rule that a mere naked default will *ipso facto* work a forfeiture, not relievable in equity, will be found to fall within this class of cases.... None of them are cases of the purchase of premises accompanied with a long enjoyment, and the expenditure of moneys on them, and the payment of two-thirds of the purchase money....

. . . .

The proposition which is maintained by the defendant's counsel is a bold and startling one. If that proposition be the law of the court of equity, then a purchaser and holder of lands, under such a contract as this, may have paid, upon purchasing a farm, $1000 annually, for many years, may have expended thousands of dollars in improvements, may be in truth one of the wealthiest farmers and land-holders in the country, and may, from forgetfulness, or some other accidental cause, (which of course is not susceptible of other proof than his own assertion) omit to pay the last instalment of $1000, by the exact hour prescribed by the contract; and although he may be ready with the money, an hour after the default, and offer it to his inexorable creditor, yet he may be doomed to see the whole of his estate, the reward of years of toil and industry, swept from him in a moment by this unyielding rule of law; and may invoke in vain the benign powers of the court of chancery for his relief.... It seems to me, that this is too monstrous a proposition to be maintained in the nineteenth century. For while the application of this rule to the case of a contract which is not executed, by the payment of any part of the purchase money, is strictly just and proper, it is clear that to apply it to cases such as I have supposed, or to the very case at bar, would work the greatest injustice; and would require the court of chancery to be the organ of every Shylock, who chose to insist upon the rigorous exaction of his pound of flesh.

2.   A defaulting buyer was granted restitution of some of his previously made payment in Freedman v. Rector, 37 Cal.2d 16, 230 P.2d 629 (1951), where the court said:

Since defendant resold the property for $2,000 more than plaintiff had agreed to pay for it, it is clear that defendant suffered no damage as a result of plaintiff's breach. If defendant is allowed to retain the amount of the down payment in excess of its expenses in connection with the contract it will be enriched and plaintiff will suffer a penalty in excess of any damages he caused. Under our recent holdings in Barkis v. Scott, 34 Cal.2d 116, 208 P.2d 367, and Baffa v. Johnson, 35 Cal.2d 36, 216 P.2d 13, plaintiff could recover that excess under section 3275 of the Civil Code, if his breach was neither wilful, fraudulent, nor grossly negligent.

3.   Consider Henry Uihlein Realty Co. v. Downtown Development Corp., 9 Wis.2d 620, 101 N.W.2d 775 (1960). Downtown Development Corporation and Atomic Security Corporation appealed from a judgment granting Henry Uihlein Realty Company strict foreclosure of real estate sold under a land contract, subject to a period of redemption, and dismissing Atomic's counterclaim for restitution on a theory of unjust enrichment. In the course of affirming the judgment, the court stated:

The purchase price was $1,000,000. $100,000 was paid at execution, and the balance was to be paid as follows: $100,000 or more on or before May 27, 1956; $100,000 or more on or before May 27, 1957, and $700,000 or the balance on May 27, 1958. . . .

. . . . The premises are operated as a parking lot in possession of defendants.

. . . .

As an affirmative defense the defendant Atomic Security Corporation alleges the payment of $448,000 on principal, the expenditure of more than $100,000 in capital improvements to the property, that the fair market value of the property exceeds $1,250,000 and that to grant relief by way of strict foreclosure would result in unjust enrichment to the plaintiff.

The same facts are pleaded by defendant Atomic Security Corporation by way of counterclaim for judgment of restitution in the sum of $558,000.

Defendant Atomic Security Corporation prays for judgment allowing a period of at least 18 months for redemption and in the event the premises are not redeemed by defendant, and in the alternative, that judgment be entered in defendant's favor for $558,000.

. . . .

The trial court found that the fair market value of the parcel of land is between $875,000 and $900,000. Only time and the money market will determine whether the plaintiff and vendor will receive upon a sale the amount due on the contract.

The counterclaim and amended counterclaim state that the defendant Atomic Security Corporation had provided improvements in the land totaling $100,000. The original building was wrecked and the excavation was filled and surfaced so as to be used as a parking lot. This certainly did not constitute the type of improvement contemplated under the terms of the contract.

The trial court granted judgment of strict foreclosure and placed the reasonable time for the redemption at ten months from the 23d day of December, 1958, provided the defendants, or either or any of them, pay to the plaintiff on or before October 23, 1959, the amount due under the land contract and in default of such payment, the defendants, and each of them, and all persons claiming under them or any or more of them, subsequent to the date of the filing of the notice of lis pendens, shall be forever barred and foreclosed of all right, title, interest, claim or equity of redemption in and to the real estate remaining under the land contract.

This state has long recognized the right of a vendor to the remedy of strict foreclosure for the vendee's default of the terms of a land contract. This court stated in Oconto Co. v. Bacon, 1923, 181 Wis. 538, 195 N.W. 412:

> "... Parties should have some regard and respect for the terms of their own contracts and ought to make the terms thereof conform to their real understanding and not rely wholly or even largely upon a court of equity for protection from their own acts."

It is likewise an elementary principle of law in this state that in a land contract providing for the conveyance of land upon the future payment of the purchase price, the vendor withholds the legal title as security for the unpaid purchase price. The transaction is held to create between the vendor and the vendee a legal relationship similar to that of equitable mortgagee and mortgagor, giving to the mortgagee the right of foreclosure and the right of equity of redemption to the mortgagor.

The foreclosure of the land contract being a proceeding in equity does not seek a forfeiture, but affirms the contract and thereby recognizes that the vendee has an equitable interest in the real estate. It treats the contract as in full force and effect. The vendor offers to perform his covenants and asks that the vendee perform its, and only in case the vendee fails to perform within a time set by the court are the vendee's rights thereunder foreclosed. The period of redemption is a matter committed to the sound discretion of the trial court and the factor bearing upon the reasonable period of the equity of redemption is dependent largely on the amount paid by the vendee under the terms of the land contract.

Fifty States Management Corp. v. Pioneer Auto Parks, Inc.

Court of Appeals of New York, 1979.
46 N.Y.2d 573, 415 N.Y.S.2d 800, 389 N.E.2d 113.

■ COOKE, C.J. The question posed on this appeal is whether equity will intervene to prevent enforcement of a provision in a 20–year lease between commercial parties providing for the acceleration of the rent due for the entire lease term upon the tenant's default in the payment of a monthly rental installment. Reasoning that enforcement of the acceleration clause would exact an unconscionable forfeiture, the Appellate Division affirmed the dismissal of the landlord's complaint by Supreme Court, Erie County.

. . . .

Fifty States Management Corp. (referred to variously as "Fifty States" and "landlord") and Pioneer Auto Parks, Inc. (referred to variously as "Pioneer" and the "tenant"), entered into a 20–year lease of commercial property located in Buffalo in 1972. In return for possession, Pioneer covenanted to make rental payments the first of each month throughout the term of the lease. To secure these payments, Fifty States insisted that Pioneer supply a financially responsible guarantor. It also bargained for and received a clause in the lease giving it the option of accelerating future rent due for the balance of the lease term following default in the payment of a monthly installment from which the frequent provisions requiring the landlord to give formal notice of default and granting the tenant a grace period within which to cure its default were conspicuously absent. Defendant Lyon executed and delivered to Fifty States an instrument in which he unconditionally guaranteed the payment of rent fixed and the performance by Pioneer of all terms and conditions of the lease.

No claim has been made that the acceleration clause is boilerplate, unknowingly assented to by the tenant as a result of its being compelled to enter into a contract of adhesion. . . .

The first three rental payments were timely made. However, the check covering the August, 1973 rent was never received by the landlord. The envelope containing the check was incorrectly addressed and was returned to the tenant while its president was on vacation. During that period, however, Pioneer was on notice that the check had not been delivered. Fifty States informed Pioneer's president that there had been no receipt of the August rental payment and the guarantor inquired of him the reason tenant failed to make payment as required by its lease. On August 20, 1973, the parties met in Buffalo to discuss the problem. When there was no tender of payment by Pioneer, its president was served with a summons and complaint seeking acceleration of the rent payments in accordance with the terms of the lease. . . .

Pioneer resists enforcement of the acceleration clause on the ground that it constitutes a penal forfeiture, long disfavored by equity. It is true that equity will often intervene to prevent a substantial forfeiture occasioned by a trivial or technical breach. To permit literal enforcement of an instrument in such circumstances, it is reasoned, is to elevate the nonperformance of some collateral act into the cornerstone for the exaction of a penalty. Similarly, equity may relieve against the effect of a good faith mistake, promptly cured by the party in default with no prejudice to the creditor to prevent unconscionable overreaching. And, of course, equity abhors forfeitures and courts will examine the sum reserved under an instrument as liquidated damages to insure that it is not disproportionate to the damages actually arising from the breach or designed to coerce the performance of a party.

Thus, in rare cases, agreements providing for the acceleration of the entire debt upon the default of the obligor may be circumscribed or denied enforcement by utilization of equitable principles. In the vast majority of instances, however, these clauses have been enforced at law in accordance with their terms. Absent some element of fraud, exploitive overreaching or unconscionable conduct on the part of the landlord to exploit a technical breach, there is no warrant, either in law or equity, for a court to refuse enforcement of the agreement of the parties. Here, Pioneer points to no circumstances which would justify relieving it of the consequences of its bargain and subsequent default.

Generally, where a lease provides for acceleration as a result of a breach of any of its terms, however trivial or inconsequential, such a provision is likely to be considered an unconscionable penalty and will not be enforced by a court of equity. For example, a clause authorizing acceleration for failure to comply with a covenant collateral to the primary obligation of the tenant is generally held to constitute a forfeiture, for the damages reserved in the lease are disproportionate to any loss which could possibly accrue to the landlord. A covenant to pay rent at a specified time, however, is an essential part of the bargain as it represents the consideration to be received for permitting the tenant to remain in possession of the property of the landlord. Often the landlord relies on timely payment of rent to meet his own outstanding obligations, such as a mortgage on the demised premises. Thus, an acceleration clause, so common in other commercial transactions, is merely a device in the landlord-tenant relationship intended to secure the tenant's obligation to perform a material element of the bargain and its enforcement works no forfeiture. This, of course, presumes that the sum reserved for liquidated damages is no greater than the amount the tenant would have paid had it fully performed and that the tenant would be entitled to possession upon payment.

There can be no claim that the sum reserved under the acceleration clause here bears no relationship to the damages sustained by landlord as a result of the breach....

. . . .

In sum, the facts of this case do not justify equitable intervention....

Accordingly, the order of the Appellate Division should be reversed, with costs, and the case remitted to Supreme Court, Erie County for a determination of the amount due appellant under the lease in accordance with this opinion.

PART III

Restitution and Unjust Enrichment

CHAPTER 10

QUASI-CONTRACT

The Prevention of Unjust Enrichment

Many cases can be found where the basis of the recovery is the prevention of the defendant's unjust enrichment. The obligation is said to be *quasi–contractual*. The word is derived from the Roman Law which classified obligations as *ex contractu, quasi ex contractu, ex delicto* and *quasi ex delicto*. In Anglo–American law the prefix, quasi denotes a fiction designed to achieve a socially desirable goal, namely the imposition of a contractual liability even though there was no contract. In the law of contracts they are classified as "contracts implied in law." In a "contract implied in law" the obligation is imposed by law without regard to assent, or indeed, in spite of the lack of assent or even express dissent. Clearly, considerations of equity and good conscience underlie the imposition of this quasi contractual obligation or liability.

The basic purpose of the result reached in these cases is to prevent the defendant from being unjustly enriched. Hence, the restitutionary recovery is not, as in damages, the *harm* to the plaintiff, but rather the *benefit* received by the defendant.

In an attempt to stem the increasing role or expansion of equity, the law courts utilized the device of the common count in general assumpsit. The fictional promise on the part of the defendant, to pay or return money or goods obtained, was the procedural vehicle to prevent the unjust enrichment.

Quasi–contracts is a subject which originated in the law courts largely under the influence of Lord Mansfield, and is closely related to equitable principles. In a book review of Hansbury's Essays in Equity, in comparing the English and American law of quasi–contracts, Professor Chafee notes: "Everybody knows that the 'implied contract' is no contract at all.... The implied contract is only a fairy tale character who makes everything turn out right at the end of the story. Such a fiction was necessary in the days when forms of action were a rigid reality, and judges had to point to some labeled compartment in which to file a new kind of relief. Now that forms of action have vanished, it is only a mischievous survival." CHAFEE, BOOK REVIEW, 48 HARV. L. REV. 523, 526 (1935).

Lord Mansfield, in the landmark case of Moses v. Macpherlan, 1 W.Bl. 219 (K.B.1760), expressed the moral basis of the restitutionary remedy by stating: "In one word, the gist of this kind of action is that the defendant, upon the circumstances of the case, is obliged by the ties of natural justice and equity to refund the money.''

The American Law Institute will soon complete the *Restatement of the Law (Third), Restitution and Unjust Enrichment*. The Second Restatement of Restitution resulted in the Tentative Drafts before the project was terminated. The goal of the Restatement Third project ''is to replace the original Restatement of Restitution promulgated in 1936.'' Restatement Third restores the full title Restitution and Unjust Enrichment that appeared in the Tentative Drafts of the original Restatement, but was dropped when the original text was published, thus emphasizing that the subject matter encompasses an independent and coherent body of law, the law of unjust enrichment, and not simply the remedy of restitution. The new *Restatement Third* should be consulted on any of the cases or materials covered in Part III.*

A. GENERAL PRINCIPLES

Moses v. Macpherlan[1]

Court of King's Bench, 1760.
1 W.Bl. 219, 96 Eng.Rep. 120; 2 Burr. 1005, 97 Eng.Rep. 676.

Moses had four notes of one Chapman Jacob, dated 11th July, 1757, value 30s. each. Macpherlan, 7th November, 1758, prevailed upon Moses to indorse these notes to him, upon an express written agreement to indemnify Moses against all consequences of such indorsement, and that no suit should be brought against Moses the indorser, but only against Jacob the drawer. Notwithstanding which, Macpherlan brought four actions in the Court of Conscience[2] upon these very notes against Moses; and, upon trial of the first, the commissioners refused to go into any evidence of this agreement; whereupon the plaintiff recovered, and the defendant paid in the whole 6*l.* And now Moses, the defendant below, brought indebitatus assumpsit[3] against Macpherlan, the plaintiff below, for money had and received to his use, and obtained a verdict for 6*l.*, subject to the opinion of this Court.

---

* See Peter B.H. Birks, *A Letter to America: The New Restatement of Restitution*, 3 GLOBAL JURIST FRONTIERS 1 (2003); David F. Partlett & Russell L. Weaver, *Restitution: Restitution: Ancient Wisdom*, 36 LOY. L.A. L. REV. 975 (2003); Doug Rendleman, *When is Enrichment Unjust? Restitution Visits an Onyx Bathroom*, 36 LOY. L.A. L. REV. 991 (2003).

1. [Excerpt for the bracketed paragraphs in the opinion of Mansfield, C.J., Blackstone's report of the case is reprinted here.]

2. [Also called Court of Requests, the Court of Conscience was an inferior law court for the recovery of small debts. Its decisions were unappealable.]

3. [The English translation of this phrase, the name of a form of action, is ''owing a debt, he promised.'']

. . . .

On the argument, Mansfield, C.J., doubted if the action would lie, after a judgment in the Court of Conscience; but wished to extend this remedial action as far as might be: to which Dennison, J., agreed, and inclined strongly that the action would lie. Foster, J., was afraid of the consequences of overhauling the judgment of a Court of a competent jurisdiction. Wilmot, J., was clear that the action would not lie; because this action always arises from a contract of re-payment, implied by law; and it would be absurd, if the law were to raise an implication in one Court, contrary to its own express judgment in another Court. . . . But afterwards,

■ LORD MANSFIELD, C.J., delivered the opinion of the Court.—It has been objected to this action: 1st, that debt will not lie upon this ground of complaint; therefore indebitatus assumpsit will not lie. But there is no foundation for this argument. It is held, indeed, in *Slade's case,* 4 Rep. 93, that where debt will lie, assumpsit will also lie; but the negative doctrine, e converso, is not any where held; it is rather a general rule, that where debt will not lie, indebitatus assumpsit will. 2dly, that in this case no implied contract can arise, whereupon to ground an assumpsit. But surely, if a man is bonâ fide obliged to refund whatever money he has unlawfully received, an implied debt is thereby raised, quasi ex contractu. 3dly, that where money is recovered in a Court having a competent jurisdiction, it cannot be overhauled in another Court, but by writ of error or false judgment. But the verdict given in this cause is consistent with the determination of the Court of Conscience. The commissioners determined merely upon the indorsement, and refused to go into the collateral matter of the agreement; in which they did right; else, upon such a matter as a note of 30s., they might go into a large and extensive account; and might settle the balance of a series of merchantile transactions, much superior to their conusance. And yet, though the judgment was right, the iniquity of keeping the money so adjudged to be paid may appear in another Court. Suppose an insurer is condemned to pay money on the death of a person who afterwards appears to be alive; would not a new action lie for him, against the person who recovered upon the former judgment. The admission that an action will lie upon the express agreement, is conclusive upon this case. For the great benefit of this action (upon an implied contract) is, that the plaintiff need not set out the particular circumstances, on which, ex aequo et bono [in equity and good conscience], he demands a satisfaction; but may declare generally for money had and received to his use, and may give the special matter in evidence. And it is equally beneficial to defendant, who may give in evidence any equitable matter, in order to discharge himself. Therefore, if it stood merely upon principles, there is no reason why the plaintiff should be confined to his action on the special agreement, and be debarred his remedy on the assumpsit implied by law. But the point has been expressly determined in *Dutch* and *Warren* M. 7 Geo. 1, Common Pleas: wherein it was held, that it was at the election of the party, either to affirm an express contract, by bringing an action on the special agreement, or to disaffirm it, and rest on an implied one, by bringing indebitatus assumpsit. In this case, the plaintiff had paid to the defendant 262*l.* 10s. for five shares in copper mines, to be transferred on the 22d of February, which defendant failed to do. Plaintiff brought indebitatus assumpsit, for money had and received to his use: and the jury, who in these actions can go into all the equity of the transaction, gave him 175*l.* only, which he recovered; being the value which the shares had fallen to on the said 22d of February.

[And a case being made for the opinion of the Court of Common Pleas, the action was resolved to be well brought; and that the recovery was right, being not for the whole money paid, but for the damages, in not transferring the stock at the time; which was a loss to the plaintiff, and an advantage to the defendant, who was a receiver of the difference money to the plaintiff's use.

The Court said, that the extending those actions depends on the notion of fraud. If one man takes another's money to do a thing, and refuses to do it; it is a fraud: and it is at the election of the party injured, either to affirm the agreement, by bringing an action for the non-performance of it; or to disaffirm the agreement ab initio, by reason of the fraud, and bring an action for money had and received to his use.

The damages recovered in that case, shew the liberality with which this kind of action is considered: for though the defendant received from the plaintiff 262*l.* 10s. yet the difference money only, 175*l.* was retained by him against conscience: and therefore the plaintiff, ex aequo et bono, ought to recover no more . . .

If the five shares had been of much more value, yet the plaintiff could only have recovered the 262*l.* 10s. by this form of action.

The notion of fraud holds much more strongly in the present case, than in that: for here it is express. The indorsement, which enabled the defendant to recover, was got by fraud and falsehood, for one purpose, and abused to another.

This kind of equitable action, to recover back money, which ought not in justice to be kept, is very beneficial, and therefore much encouraged. It lies only for money which, ex aequo et bono, the defendant ought to refund: it does not lie for money paid by the plaintiff, which is claimed of him as payable in point of honor and honesty, although it could not have been recovered from him by any course of law; as in payment of a debt barred by the Statute of Limitations, or contracted during his infancy, or to the extent of principal and legal interest upon an usurious contract, or, for money fairly lost at play: because in all these cases, the defendant may retain it with a safe conscience, though by positive law he was barred from recovering. But it lies for money paid by mistake; or upon a consideration which happens to fail; or for money got through imposition, (express, or implied;) or extortion; or oppression; or an undue advantage taken of the plaintiff's situation, contrary to laws made for the protection of persons under those circumstances.

In one word, the gist of this kind of action is, that the defendant, upon the circumstances of the case, is obliged by the ties of natural justice and equity to refund the money.]

Therefore we are all of opinion, that the defendant ought in justice to refund this money thus malâ fide recovered; and though an action on the agreement would also have indemnified him for his costs in the Court below, yet he may waive this advantage and pursue the present remedy.

The postea must be delivered to the plaintiff.[4]

Kossian v. American National Insurance Co.

Court of Appeal of California, Fifth District, 1967.
254 Cal.App.2d 647, 62 Cal.Rptr. 225.

■ STONE, A.J. On February 19, 1964, fire destroyed a portion of the Bakersfield Inn, owned by one Reichert. At the time, the property was subject to a first deed of trust in which defendant was the beneficiary. Pursuant to the requirements of the deed of trust, defendant's interest in the property was protected by policies of fire insurance. On March 16, 1964, Reichert, as owner in possession, entered into a written contract with plaintiff whereby plaintiff agreed to clean up and remove the debris from the fire damaged portion of the Inn for the sum of $18,900. Defendant had no knowledge of the execution of the agreement between plaintiff and Reichert.

Plaintiff commenced work in the middle of March 1964, and completed it in early April. During the entire time work was in progress Reichert was in possession of the premises as owner, although defendant caused a notice of Reichert's default under the deed of trust to be filed four days after the contract for demolition was entered into between plaintiff and Reichert. The record does not reflect that plaintiff had actual knowledge of the notice of default until after the work was completed.

Some time after plaintiff had fully performed the contract, Reichert filed a petition in bankruptcy. The trustee in bankruptcy abandoned the premises comprising the Bakersfield Inn, together with any interest in the four fire insurance policies up to the amount of $424,000. Each policy contained a provision insuring against the cost of cleaning up and removing debris caused by fire damage.

Following abandonment of the policies by the trustee in bankruptcy, Reichert and his wife assigned their interest in them to defendant in accordance with the terms of the deed of trust. Defendant submitted proofs of loss, claiming a total of $160,000, including the sum of $18,000 as the estimated cost for removing and cleaning up debris. These claims were rejected by the carriers; negotiations followed; the compromise figure of $135,620 was agreed upon and this amount paid to defendant. We do not have an itemization of the adjusted claims of loss upon which the compromised loss settlement was made, so that the record is not clear as to what part of the $18,900 cost of debris removal defendant received. It is clear, however, that the insurance payment included at least a part of the cost of debris removal and demolition.

Defendant demonstrates, by a careful analysis of the facts, that there was no direct relationship between plaintiff and defendant in regard to

---

4. [The "postea", in common law practice, was the statement indorsed on the *nisi prius* record which gave an account of the proceedings at the trial. The court where the action started would then pronounce judg-ment given the facts that the report showed to have been found by the jury. The task of writing the postea was given to the prevailing party's lawyer.]

either the work performed on the property after the fire or in relation to the fire insurance policies. The contract for debris removal was between plaintiff and Reichert, and defendant did not induce plaintiff, directly or indirectly, to enter into that contract. Plaintiff had no lien against the property resulting from his work, and if he had such a lien it would have been wiped out by defendant's foreclosure of its first deed of trust.

Had the circumstances been simply that defendant, by foreclosure, took the property improved by plaintiff's debris removal, there would be a benefit conferred upon defendant by plaintiff, but no unjust enrichment. It is the additional fact that defendant made a claim to the insurance carriers for the value of work done by plaintiff that is the nub of the case.

Defendant argues that plaintiff was not a party to the insurance contracts, while defendant had a contract right to collect indemnity for losses resulting from the fire, including the debris removal cost. This contract right was embodied in the insurance policies. Defendant relies upon Russell v. Williams, 58 Cal.2d 487, 24 Cal.Rptr. 859, 374 P.2d 827, where it is said:

> "It is a principle of long standing that a policy of fire insurance does not insure the property covered thereby, but is a personal contract indemnifying the insured against loss resulting from the destruction of or damage to his interest in that property. This principle gives rise to the supplemental rule that, in the absence of a special contract, the proceeds of a fire insurance policy are not a substitute for the property the loss of which is the subject of indemnity."

Defendant says it made no agreement, express or implied, with plaintiff that it would pay for the debris removal or that any part of the insurance proceeds would be applied for that purpose. Therefore, concludes defendant, there being no privity of relationship between it and plaintiff, and no fraud or deceit alleged or proved, defendant has the right to the property benefited by plaintiff's work and labor expended in removing the debris and to the insurance payments as well.

Plaintiff makes no claim to the insurance "fund" upon the ground he relied thereon similar to the reliance of a mechanic or materialman that forms the basis of an equitable claim to a building fund. He relies upon the basic premise that defendant should not be allowed to have the fruits of plaintiff's labor and also the money value of that labor. This, of course, is a simplified pronouncement of the doctrine of unjust enrichment, a theory which can, in some instances, have validity without privity of relationship. The most prevalent, implied-in-fact contract recognized under the doctrine of unjust enrichment is predicated upon a relationship between the parties from which the court infers an intent. However, the doctrine also recognizes an obligation *imposed* by law regardless of the intent of the parties. In these instances there need be no relationship that gives substance to an implied intent basic to the "contract" concept, rather the obligation is imposed because good conscience dictates that under the circumstances the person benefited should make reimbursement.

Plaintiff's claim does not rest upon a quasi contract implied in fact, but upon an equitable obligation imposed by law. It is true that defendant's right to the insurance payment was a contract right embodied in the policies of insurance, as explicated in Russell v. Williams, supra, 58 Cal.2d 487, 24 Cal.Rptr. 859, 374 P.2d 827, nevertheless the indemnity payment was based in part upon a claim of loss that did not exist because plaintiff had already remedied the loss by his work for which he was not paid.

We are cited no California cases that are close aboard, and independent research reveals none. Lack of precedent applicable to the facts peculiar to this case is not surprising, however, as the authors of the Restatement recognize that the essential nature of equity cases concerned with problems of restitution makes definitive precedent unlikely. We are guided by the "Underlying Principles" delineated in the Restatement on Restitution:

> "The rules stated in the Restatement of this Subject depend for their validity upon certain basic assumptions in regard to what is required by justice in the various situations. In this Topic, these are stated in the form of principles. They cannot be stated as rules since either they are too indefinite to be of value in a specific case or, for historical or other reasons, they are not universally applied. They are distinguished from rules in that they are intended only as general guides for the conduct of the courts. . . ." (P. 11.)

The governing principle is expressed in the opening sentence of the Restatement on Restitution, as follows:

> "The Restatement of this Subject deals with situations in which one person is accountable to another on the ground that otherwise he would unjustly benefit or the other would unjustly suffer loss." (P. 1.)

The question, simply stated, is whether in a jurisdiction that recognizes the equitable doctrine of unjust enrichment one party should be indemnified twice for the same loss, once in labor and materials and again in money, to the detriment (forfeiture) of the party who furnished the labor and materials. We conclude that the doctrine of unjust enrichment is applicable to the facts of this case, and that plaintiff is entitled to reimbursement out of the insurance proceeds paid defendant for work done by plaintiff.

The facts concerning the amount of insurance recovered by defendant and the percentage of the total proof of loss attributable to plaintiff's work are not altogether clear, probably because this is a proceeding for summary judgment before trial of the action. In any event, it is clear that defendant, in addition to taking over the property which plaintiff cleared of debris, also received indemnity insurance payments covering at least part of the cost for clearing that property of debris. The amount can be made certain by a trial on the merits, and if it develops that defendant recovered only a part of the cost for debris removal, this fact does not preclude a partial recovery by plaintiff. We learn from the Restatement, page 611:

> "Where a person is entitled to restitution from another because the other, without tortious conduct, has received a benefit, the measure of recovery for the benefit thus received is the value of what was received. . . ."

Thus, to the extent defendant received insurance for debris removal performed by plaintiff, plaintiff should recover. If defendant received less than the value of plaintiff's work, as defendant seems to contend, then plaintiff should recover *pro tanto*.

The judgment is reversed.

Seegers v. Sprague

Supreme Court of Wisconsin, 1975.
70 Wis.2d 997, 236 N.W.2d 227.

■ HANLEY, J. The sole issue on this appeal is whether the contractor here may recover the value of goods and services rendered to a general contractor property owner.

The key paragraph in Seegers' complaint was:

"That on or about the 13th day of October, 1970 at the special instance and the request of the defendant, plaintiffs agreed to furnish certain materials and labor to wit: . . ."

With a further allegation that the agreed labor and materials necessary for septic systems were furnished, demand was made for their value.

The trial court adopted the allegations of the complaint as its findings of fact. Implicit in Sprague's argument on appeal, however, is the contention that the Seegers were always subcontractors of Keller and were without privity to Sprague, contrary to the conclusion accepted by the court.

Defendant Sprague places heavy reliance on Utschig v. McClone (1962), 16 Wis.2d 506, 114 N.W.2d 854, for the proposition that a subcontractor cannot obtain direct relief against a property owner without an express contract. *Utschig* acknowledged that the subcontractor may avail himself of a construction lien, but his primary remedy was to proceed against the main contractor who employed him. No attempt was made to prove an express contract between Sprague and the Seegers. The lien remedy has been terminated. Further, contractor Keller is "among the missing." This was brought out through the testimony of Sprague. Apparently some dispute over Keller's workmanship had arisen and he had commenced suit. Sprague counterclaimed, seemingly for the costs of defective work. The absence of Keller has suspended that action. Sprague claimed, however, to have paid Keller for the septic systems.

The latter testimony is argued as defeating the Seegers' claim which is denominated by Sprague as "unjust enrichment." *Utschig* had contained language that an owner is not liable on an implied contract simply because he received subcontractors services, but did not state that such theory would be unsuccessful under all circumstances. After losing at the demurrer stage, the plaintiff in *Utschig* argued that he had rendered extra services at the instance of the owner, but the lack of allegations on this privity contact in his complaint made this claim against demurrer unavailing.

In Superior Plumbing Co. v. Tefs (1965), 27 Wis.2d 434, 134 N.W.2d 430, an implied contract theory was also argued. The plaintiff corporation was a subcontractor and the defendant owner knew of this status and knew that he had received materials and services from it. Suit was commenced on the basis of unjust enrichment. Because the complaint as drafted admitted the possibility that the general contractor had been paid but had not in turn disbursed to the subcontractor, this court reversed an order overruling the demurrer. Underlying this approval of the demurrer was the belief that an owner was not unjustly enriched when he had paid the general contractor for all the work done.

Respondents claim to avoid this line of cases restricting unjust enrichment by denying that this theory was involved. They reiterate that the action is on quantum meruit. They also deny that the evidence establishes that they were subcontractors. Rather than argue that they were contractors with the owner, though, they concisely repeat the findings of the fact of the court which merely repeated the allegations of their complaint.

In an oral decision after the trial, the court stated:

"Well, there is conflicting testimony in the matter concerning Mr. Sprague's contact with one or both of the Seegers Brothers prior to commencement.... Eugene Seegers testified that he saw Mr. Sprague on the job and discussed with him the change in the size of the tanks.... It would lead the court to believe that Mr. Sprague was aware that some person other than Mr. Keller, the plumber, was installing the septic system.

" . . . .

" . . . [T]he court is satisfied that the plaintiffs have established the installation of the septic system . . . that Mr. Sprague was aware of the installation and is responsible for payment of the cost of the installation of the septic system."

Awareness of the subcontractor and his work does not establish unjust enrichment, but is an essential element of recovery. The above quoted language, read in connection with the findings, indicates that the court found some privity contact but did not find that [the] Seegers were "in the position of contractors with Donald Sprague" as the respondents would hope.

The trial court's conclusion is inevitable from the testimony adduced.... The testimony of Sprague refutes the conclusion that the Seegers were contractors with him....

Quantum meruit [as much as one deserves] was allowed despite the testimony of payment to Keller. The respondent apparently feels that this factor, which prevented an award under similar facts on a theory denominated as unjust enrichment, does not apply to his action. This contention is erroneous.

In reviewing the English law of implied in law contracts or quasi-contract, one treatise noted that the current basis for indebitatus assumpsit, quantum meruit and quantum valebat could be summarized by one theory:

"Quasi-contractual claims are, therefore, those which fall within the scope of the actions for money had and received or for money paid, or of *quantum meruit* or *quantum valebat* [as much as it is worth] claims, and which are founded upon the principle of unjust enrichment. There are, however, other claims of different origin which are also founded on that principle." Goff & Jones, Law of Restitution 4 (1966).

American cases also recognize this relationship:

> "A prominent characteristic of the concept of quantum meruit is as a device for the prevention of unjust enrichment of one party at the expense of another."

The full spectrum of quasi-contract law, specifically including quantum meruit has apparently been long recognized by one state as grounded in the doctrine of unjust enrichment.

This interrelationship in restitution theory has not gone unrecognized in Wisconsin. By implication in *Superior Plumbing,* and definitely in Gebhardt Bros., Inc. v. Brimmel (1966), 31 Wis.2d 581, 143 N.W.2d 479, this court recognized that subcontractors may have a basis for recovery in the quasi-contract action of unjust enrichment. In Don Ganser & Assoc., Inc. v. MHI, Inc., (1966), 31 Wis.2d 212, 142 N.W.2d 781, [t]he elements of such action were listed as:

> " . . . (1) a benefit conferred upon the defendant by the plaintiff, (2) appreciation by the defendant of the fact of such benefit, and (3) acceptance and retention by the defendant of the benefit, under circumstances such that it would be inequitable to retain the benefit without payment of the value thereof."

The operative facts in these cases were the same as presented here, of recovery for goods and services benefiting the property owner. Respondent's desire to call their action quantum meruit and to frame their complaint in terms of language from cases following that theory by name does not avoid the clear decisional law that regards unjust enrichment as an element necessary for recovery in these circumstances.

As in *Utschig,* there is also a lack of proof that an *independent* request or invitation for their services was made by Sprague. Quantum meruit as a measure of recovery for an implied in fact contract would demand as much. An owner is not liable on a contract implied by the facts simply because he has received goods or services or knows that services have been rendered. . . .

The respondents' right to recover here rested on the theory denominated in past construction cases as unjust enrichment. On the basis of *Superior Plumbing,* no unjust enrichment has occurred here. Payments by Sprague to Keller to cover his work and the work of his subcontractors has not left Sprague enriched. The absence of payment to Seegers is due to Keller's actions.

Although Sprague was also a general contractor as well as owner, this status does not add distinguishment that makes the *Superior Plumbing* rationale inapplicable. The claimant there was a subcontractor once removed from the defendant, as are the Seegers here.

Under the circumstances of this case we conclude that it is inequitable to compel the owner to pay the Seegers after payment had been made to

Keller. The owner had a right to rely upon his agreement with Keller. There was also no implied agreement to compensate the Seegers brothers.

Judgment reversed.

Recovery of Money Paid by Mistake and "Discharge for Value"

Banque Worms v. BankAmerica Int'l

Court of Appeals of New York, 1991.
77 N.Y.2d 362, 568 N.Y.S.2d 541, 570 N.E.2d 189.

[Security Pacific International Bank mistakenly wired $1,974,267.97 on behalf of a client bank into the account of Banque Worms, a French Bank. Security Pacific sought a return of the money on a theory of restitution, arguing that Banque Worms would have to demonstrate detrimental reliance to retain the funds mistakenly wired, (which it probably could not do because the mistake was discovered within hours). The United States Court of Appeals for the Second Circuit certified question to New York Court of Appeals inquiring whether New York would apply "discharge for value" rule to case involving mistaken wire transfer, rather than rule that money paid under mistake may be recovered, unless payment has caused change in position that it would be unjust. The Court of Appeals answered that New York applies the "discharge for value" rule in the interest of finality of business transactions, entitling Banque Worms to retain the funds mistakenly transferred without the necessity of demonstrating detrimental reliance.]

■ ALEXANDER, J.

. . . .

I

A

In the area of restitution, New York has long recognized the rule that "if A pays money to B upon the erroneous assumption of the former that he is indebted to the latter, an action may be maintained for its recovery. The reason for the rule is obvious. Since A was mistaken in the assumption that he was indebted to B, the latter is not entitled to retain the money acquired by the mistake of the former, even though the mistake is the result of negligence." (Ball v. Shepard, 202 N.Y. 247, 253, 95 N.E. 719.) This rule has been applied where the cause of action has been denominated as one for money had and received (Parsa v. State of New York, 64 N.Y.2d 143, 148, 485 N.Y.S.2d 27, 474 N.E.2d 235), for unjust enrichment or restitution (Paramount Film Distrib. Corp. v. State of New York, 30 N.Y.2d 415, 421, 334 N.Y.S.2d 388, 285 N.E.2d 695), or upon a theory of quasi contract (Miller v. Schloss, 218 N.Y. 400, 113 N.E. 337). Where, however, the receiving party has changed its position to its detriment in reliance upon the mistake so that requiring that it refund the money paid would be "unfair," recovery has been denied (Paramount Film Distrib. Corp. v. State of New York, supra, 30 N.Y.2d at 422, 334 N.Y.S.2d 388, 285 N.E.2d 695; Ball v. Shepard, supra, 202 N.Y. at 254, 95 N.E. 719).

This rule has evolved into the "mistake of fact" doctrine, in which detrimental reliance is a requisite factor, and which provides that "money paid under a mistake of fact may be recovered back, however negligent the party paying may have been in making the mistake, unless the payment has caused such a change in the position of the other party that it would be unjust to require him to refund." (National Bank v. National Mechanics' Banking Assn., 55 N.Y. 211, 213; see also, Hathaway v. County of Delaware, 185 N.Y. 368, 78 N.E. 153; Mayer v. City of N.Y., 63 N.Y. 455, 457 ["general rule that money paid under a mistake of material fact may be recovered back * * * is subject to the qualification that the payment cannot be recalled when the position of the party receiving it has been changed in consequence of the payment, and it would be inequitable to allow a recovery."].)

The Restatement of Restitution, on the other hand, has established the "discharge for value" rule which provides that "[a] creditor of another or one having a lien on another's property who has received from a third person any benefit in discharge of the debt or lien, is under no duty to make restitution therefor, although the discharge was given by mistake of the transferor as to his interests or duties, if the transferee made no misrepresentation and did not have notice of the transferor's mistake" (Restatement of Restitution § 14[1]).

The question as to which of these divergent rules New York will apply to electronic fund transfers divides the parties and prompts the certified question from the Second Circuit. Security Pacific argues that New York has rejected the "discharge for value" rule and has required that detrimental reliance under the "mistake of fact" rule be demonstrated in all cases other than where the mistake was induced by fraud. Banque Worms, on the other hand, invokes the "discharge for value" rule, arguing that because it is a creditor of Spedley and had no knowledge that the wire transfer was erroneous, it is entitled to keep the funds. It points out, as indicated by the official comment to section 14(1) of the Restatement of Restitution, that the "discharge for value" rule is simply a "specific application of the underlying principle of bona fide purchase" set forth in section 13 of the Restatement (Restatement of Restitution § 14, comment a).

Banque Worms cites to various decisions of New York courts in support of its contention that New York has adopted and applied the "discharge for value" rule (see, e.g., Ball v. Shepard, 202 N.Y. 247, 95 N.E. 719, supra; Consolidated Natl. Bank v. First Natl. Bank, 199 N.Y. 599, 92 N.E. 1081, affg. 129 App.Div. 538, 114 N.Y.S. 308; Oddie v. National City Bank, 45 N.Y. 735). Indeed, both parties rely to a significant degree upon Ball v. Shepard in support of their respective positions. Security Pacific relies upon the Court's observation in the first of two classes of cases discussed, that "the mistake of fact is usually one which arises inter partes, and in order to justify recovery in any such case it must appear that the defendant was not, in the first instance, entitled to receive the money; and that his circumstances have not been so changed through its receipt as to render it unjust to compel him to refund." (202 N.Y. at 256, 95 N.E. 719 [emphasis added].) Banque Worms, on the other hand, refers to the same discussion but relies upon the Court's description of the second class where "the mistake of the payor is usually superinduced by the fraud of a third person and the payee is not only ignorant of the fraud or mistake, but receives the money in good faith in the regular course of business and for valuable consideration." (Id. [emphasis added].)

Indeed one may find, as does Banque Worms, language in a myriad of cases that arguably lends support to the proposition that New York, long ago, embraced the "discharge for value" rule (see, e.g., Carlisle v. Norris, 215 N.Y. 400, 415, 109 N.E. 564 ["If defendants received the proceeds in good faith and without any notice of any wrong and credited them on an indebtedness due them, plaintiff is not entitled to recover them back."]; White v. Continental Natl. Bank, 64 N.Y. 316 [right of a party paying money to another to recover it from one who is not entitled to receive it, is well established]; Smith & McCrorken v. Chatham Phenix Natl. Bank & Trust Co., 239 App.Div. 318, 320, 267 N.Y.S. 153 ["where a bank honors and pays a check under a mistake of fact, it may sue for recovery of the money, at least, against one receiving payment thereon, who is not a bona fide holder for value."]; see also, New York Tit. & Mtge. Co. v. Title Guar. & Trust Co., 206 App.Div. 490, 201 N.Y.S. 529, affd. 237 N.Y. 626, 143 N.E. 769; State Farm Mut. Auto. Ins. Co. v. Stokos, 65 Misc.2d 316, 317 N.Y.S.2d 706; see generally, 44 NY Jur. Payment, s 107).

On the other hand, cases can also be cited where the language employed supports the contrary view—that New York not only eschews the "discharge for value" rule, as Security Pacific argues, but also embraces exclusively the detrimental reliance rule-mistake of fact doctrine (see, e.g., Hathaway v. County of Delaware, 185 N.Y. 368, 78 N.E. 153, supra; Mayer v. Mayor of City of N.Y., 63 N.Y. 455, supra; National Bank v. National Mechanics' Banking Assn., 55 N.Y. 211, supra; Citibank v. Warner, 113 Misc.2d 748, 449 N.Y.S.2d 822). These cases for the most part, however, present issues involving more traditional aspects of mistake and restitution, and do not satisfactorily address the unique problems presented by electronic funds transfer technology.

While courts have attempted in wire transfer cases to employ, by analogy, the rules of the more traditional areas of law, such as contract law, the law of negotiable instruments and the special relations between banks, these areas are governed by principles codified in articles 3 and 4 of the Uniform Commercial Code. Various commentators found these efforts ineffective and inadequate to deal with the problems presented (see, Official Comment to UCC 4A–102; Revisions of UCC Article 4A Postponed Due to Federal Preemption, ABA is Told, 51 Banking Rep. 282 [BNA] [Aug. 15, 1988]). As pointed out by the Official Comment to article 4A, "attempts to define rights and obligations in funds transfers by general principles or by analogy to rights and obligations in negotiable instruments law or the law of check collection have not been satisfactory" (Official Comment to UCC 4A–102, 2A ULA [Master ed.], 1990 Supp.Pamph.; see also, Revisions of UCC Article 4A Postponed Due to Federal Preemption, ABA is Told, 51 Banking Rep. 282 [BNA] [Aug. 15, 1988]). Consequently, it was concluded, as the Prefatory Note to the new article 4A of the UCC approved by the National Conference of Commissioners on Uniform State Law and the American Law Institute observes, that a new article was needed because "[t]here is no comprehensive body of law that defines the rights and obligations that arise from wire transfers." (2A ULA [Master ed.], at 143, 1990 Supp.Pamph.)

B

Electronic funds transfers have become the preferred method utilized by businesses and financial institutions to effect payments and transfers of a substantial volume of funds. These transfers, commonly referred to as wholesale wire transfers, differ from other payment methods in a number of significant respects, a fact which accounts in large measure for their popularity. Funds are moved faster and more efficiently than by traditional payment instruments, such as checks. The transfers are completed at a relatively low cost, which does not vary widely depending on the amount of the transfer, because the price charged reflects primarily the cost of the mechanical aspects of the funds transfer (Prefatory Note to UCC art. 4A). Most transfers are completed within one day and can cost as little as $10 to carry out a multimillion dollar transaction (see generally, Farley, Article 4A: Funds Transfers, NYS 7720–A, NYA 10431–A; Prefatory Note to UCC art. 4A). The popularity of wholesale wire transfers is evidenced by the fact that nearly $1 trillion in transactions occur each day, averaging $5 million per transfer and on peak days, this figure often approaches $2 trillion (see generally, Ring, Wholesale Funds Transfers: New Article 4A to the UCC, NYA 10431–A, NYS 7720–A).

Wholesale wire transfers are generally made over the two principal wire payment systems: the Federal Reserve Wire Transfer Network (Fedwire) and the CHIPS.[2] The CHIPS network handles 95% of the international transfers made in dollars, transferring an average of $750 billion per day (see generally, Note, Liability for Lost or Stolen Funds in Cases of Name and Number Discrepancies in Wire Transfers: Analysis of the Approaches Taken in the United States and Internationally, 22 Cornell Intl.L.J. 91 [1990]). These funds are transferred through participating banks located in New York because all of the banks belonging to the CHIPS network must maintain a regulated presence in New York. As a result, this State is considered the national and international center for wholesale wire transfers.

The low cost of electronic funds transfers is an important factor in the system's popularity and this is so even though banks executing wire transfers often risk significant liability as a result of losses occasioned by mistakes and errors, the most common of which involve the payment of funds to the wrong beneficiary or in an incorrect amount (see, American Law Institute Approves UCC Article Governing Wire Transfers, 52 Banking Rep. 1150 [BNA] [June 5, 1989]). Thus, a major policy issue facing the drafters of UCC article 4A was determining how the risk of loss might best

---

2. CHIPS is owned and operated by the New York Clearing House Association and the Federal Reserve Bank owns and operates Fedwire, the largest American wire transfer network.

be allocated, while preserving a unique price structure. In order to prevent or minimize losses, the industry had adopted and employed various security procedures designed to prevent losses such as the use of codes, identifying words or numbers, call-back procedures and limits on payment amounts or beneficiaries that may be paid.

As indicated above, it was the consensus among various commentators that existing rules of law did not adequately address the problems presented by these wholesale electronic funds transfers. Thus, the National Conference of Commissioners on Uniform State Laws (NCCUSL) and the American Law Institute (ALI) undertook to develop a body of unique principles of law that would address every aspect of the electronic funds transfer process and define the rights and liabilities of all parties involved in such transfers (Prefatory Note to UCC art. 4A, op. cit.). After extensive investigation and debate and through a number of drafts, in 1989, both the NCCUSL and the ALI approved a new article 4A of the Uniform Commercial Code (see generally, Ballen, Baxter, Davenport, Rougeau, and Veltri, Commercial Paper, Bank Deposits and Collections, and Other Payment Systems, 45 Bus.Law 2341 [Aug. 1990]). In 1990, the New York State Legislature adopted the new article 4A and incorporated it into the New York Uniform Commercial Code (N.Y. UCC art. 4–A). Although the new statute, which became effective January 1, 1991, may not be applied retroactively to resolve the issues presented by this litigation, the statute's legislative history and the history of article 4A of the Uniform Commercial Code from which it is derived and the policy considerations addressed by this legislation, can appropriately inform our decision and serve as persuasive authority in aid of the resolution of the issue presented in this case (see, Matter of Pell v. Coveney, 37 N.Y.2d 494, 373 N.Y.S.2d 860, 336 N.E.2d 421; Matter of Albano v. Kirby, 36 N.Y.2d 526, 369 N.Y.S.2d 655, 330 N.E.2d 615; MVAIC v. Eisenberg, 18 N.Y.2d 1, 271 N.Y.S.2d 641, 218 N.E.2d 524; see also, Shawmut Worcester County Bank v. First Am. Bank & Trust, 731 F.Supp. 57 [D Mass]).

II

Both the NCCUSL and ALI drafters of article 4A and the New York Legislature sought to achieve a number of important policy goals through enactment of this article. National uniformity in the treatment of electronic funds transfers is an important goal, as are speed, efficiency, certainty (i.e., to enable participants in fund transfers to have better understanding of their rights and liabilities), and finality. Establishing finality in electronic fund wire transactions was considered a singularly important policy goal (American Law Institute Approves UCC Article Governing Wire Transfers, 52 Banking Rep. 1150 [BNA] [June 5, 1989]). Payments made by electronic funds transfers in compliance with the provisions of article 4A are to be the equivalent of cash payments, irrevocable except to the extent provided for in article 4A (see, Assn of Bar of City of NY, Committee on Banking Law, Report on proposed New York UCC art. 4–A; see also, Delbrueck & Co. v. Manufacturers Hanover Trust Co., 609 F.2d 1047, 1049–1051 [2d Cir.] [once an electronic fund transfer is completed and the funds released, the transaction is final and irrevocable under the CHIPS system]).

This concern for finality in business transactions has long been a significant policy consideration in this State. In a different but pertinent context, we observed in Hatch v. Fourth Natl. Bank, 147 N.Y. 184, 192, 41 N.E. 403 that "to permit in every case of the payment of a debt an inquiry as to the source from which the debtor derived the money, and a recovery if shown to have been dishonestly acquired, would disorganize all business operations and entail an amount of risk and uncertainty which no enterprise could bear".

A consequence of this concern has been the adoption of a rule which precludes recovery from a third person, who as the result of the mistake of one or both of the parties to an original transaction receives payment by one of them in good faith in the ordinary course of business and for a valuable consideration (see, Ball v. Shepard, 202 N.Y. 247, 95 N.E. 719, supra). This rule is grounded in "considerations of public policy and convenience for the protection and encouragement of trade and commerce by guarding the security and certainty of business transactions, since to hold otherwise would obviously introduce confusion and danger into all commercial dealings" (44 N.Y.Jur., Payment, s 107; see also, Southwick v. First Natl. Bank, 84 N.Y. 420). We have previously held that from these considerations, "[t]he law wisely * * * adjudges that the possession of money vests the title in the holder as to third persons dealing with him and receiving it in due course of business and in good faith upon a valid consideration." (Stephens v. Board of Educ., 79 N.Y. 183, 187–188.)

The "discharge for value" rule is consistent with and furthers the policy goal of finality in business transactions and may appropriately be applied in respect to electronic funds transfers. When a beneficiary receives money to which it is entitled and has no knowledge that the money was erroneously wired, the beneficiary should not have to wonder whether it may retain the funds; rather, such a beneficiary should be able to consider the transfer of funds as a final and complete transaction, not subject to revocation.

We believe such an application accords with the legislative intent and furthers the policy considerations underlying article 4–A of the New York Uniform Commercial Code. Although no provision of article 4–A calls, in express terms, for the application of the "discharge for value" rule, the statutory scheme and the language of various pertinent sections, as amplified by the Official Comments to the UCC, support our conclusion that the "discharge for value" rule should be applied in the circumstances here presented.

Subject to certain exceptions not here relevant, N.Y. UCC 4–A–209(2) provides that a beneficiary's bank accepts a payment order when the bank pays the beneficiary by crediting the beneficiary's account and notifying the beneficiary of the right to withdraw the credit (see, UCC 4–A–209[2][a]; 4–A–405[1][i]). When a payment order has been accepted by the beneficiary's bank, cancellation or amendment of that payment order is not effective unless, for example, the order was issued because of a mistake of the sender resulting in a duplicate payment order or an order that directs payment to a beneficiary not entitled to receive the funds (see, UCC 4–A–211[3][b][i], [ii]). Where a duplicate payment order is erroneously executed or the payment order is issued to a beneficiary different from the beneficiary intended by the sender, the receiving bank in either case is entitled to recover the erroneously paid amount from the beneficiary "to the extent allowed by the law governing mistake and restitution" (see, UCC 4–A–303[1], [3]).

More specifically, UCC 4–A–303(3) instructs that "[i]f a receiving bank executes the payment order of the sender by issuing a payment order to a beneficiary different from the beneficiary of the sender's order and the funds transfer is completed on the basis of that error, the sender * * * [is] not obliged to pay the payment order[ ]. The issuer of the erroneous order is entitled to recover from the beneficiary * * * to the extent allowed by the law governing mistake and restitution." The Official Comment to UCC 4A–303 from which the identical New York statute is derived, explains that although section 4A–402(c) obligates the sender to pay the transfer order to the beneficiary's bank if that bank has accepted the payment order, section 4A–303 takes precedence and "states the liability of the sender and the rights of the receiving bank in various cases of erroneous execution" (see, Official Comment to UCC 4A–303, comment 1, 2A ULA [Master ed.], 1990 Supp.Pamph.).

Thus, as in the example discussed in comment 2, where the originator's bank mistakenly directs payment of $2,000,000 to the beneficiary's bank but payment of only $1,000,000 was directed by the originator, the originator's bank is obligated to pay the $2,000,000 if the beneficiary's bank has accepted the payment, although the originator need only pay its bank the $1,000,000 ordered. The originator's bank ordinarily would be entitled to recover the excess payment from the beneficiary. The comment points out, however, that "if Originator owed $2,000,000 to Beneficiary and Beneficiary received the extra $1,000,000 in good faith in discharge of the debt, Beneficiary may be allowed to keep it. In this case Originator's Bank has paid an obligation of Originator and under the law of restitution * * * Originator's Bank would be subrogated to Beneficiary's rights against Originator on the obligation paid by Originator's Bank" (see, Official Comment to UCC 4A–303, comment 2, 2A ULA [Master ed.], 1990 Supp. Pamph.).

A further example discussed in comment 3 of the Official Comment is of a duplicate payment order erroneously made, which transfers a second $1,000,000 payment to beneficiary's bank and beneficiary's bank accepts the payment. Although the originator's bank is only entitled to receive $1,000,000 from the originator, it must pay $2,000,000 to beneficiary's bank and would be relegated to a remedy the same as "that of a receiving bank that executes by issuing an order in an amount greater than the sender's order. It may recover the overpayment from Beneficiary to the extent allowed by the law governing mistake and restitution and in a proper case * * * may have subrogation rights if it is not entitled to recover from Beneficiary" (Official Comment to UCC 4A–303, comment 3, 2A ULA [Master ed.], 1990 Supp.Pamph.).

Although it seems clear from these provisions of article 4A and the Official Comments that the drafters of UCC article 4A contemplated that the "discharge for value" rule could appropriately be applied in respect to electronic fund transfers, Security Pacific argues that to do so would undermine the low cost structure of wholesale electronic fund transfers and impose extraordinary risks upon banks implementing these enormously large transactions. This argument is unpersuasive. Article 4A contemplates, in the first instance, that a mistake such as occurred here can be effectively held to a minimum through the utilization of "commercially reasonable" security procedures in effecting wire transfers. These security procedures are for the purpose of verifying the authenticity of the order or detecting error in the transmission or content of the payment order or other communication (see, e.g., N.Y. UCC 4–A–201).

For example, under N.Y. UCC 4–A–202(2), if a bank accepts a payment order that purports to be that of its customer after verifying its authenticity through an agreed upon security procedure, the customer is bound to pay the order even if the payment order was not authorized. The customer will be liable, however, only if the court finds that the security procedure was a "commercially reasonable" method of providing security against unauthorized payment orders (id.). If the bank accepts an unauthorized payment order without verifying it in compliance with a security procedure, the loss will fall on the bank.

Other mechanisms for preventing loss are also provided for in the statute. A bank may avoid a loss resulting from the insolvency of a sending bank by accepting the payment order on the condition that it first receives payment from the sending bank (see, N.Y. UCC 4–A–209[2][a][ii]; [c]; 4–A–403 [1][a], [b]; see also, American Law Institute Approves UCC Article Governing Wire Transfers, 52 Banking Rep 1150 [BNA] [June 5, 1989]; Prefatory Note to UCC art. 4A [a receiving bank can always avoid this risk by accepting a payment order after the bank has received payment]). Risk of loss can also be minimized by the institution keeping track of all transactions with a particular bank so that over-all debits and credits can be netted.

Application of the "discharge for value" rule to the circumstances presented here is particularly appropriate. The undisputed facts demonstrate that Security Pacific executed Spedley's initial order directing payment to Banque Worms notwithstanding having already received a cancellation of that order. The District Court also found that the second transfer to Natwest USA was executed despite the fact that Spedley's account did not have sufficient funds to cover this second transfer. Moreover, it appears that, as a creditor of Spedley, Banque Worms was a beneficiary entitled to the funds who made no "misrepresentation and did not have notice of the transferor's mistake."

Accordingly, we conclude, in answer to the certified question, that the "discharge for value" rule as set forth at section 14 of the Restatement of Restitution, should be applied in the circumstances in this case.

■ WACHTLER, C.J., and SIMONS, KAYE, TITONE, HANCOCK and BELLACOSA, JJ., concur.

Following certification of a question by the United States Court of Appeals for the Second Circuit and acceptance of the question by this Court pursuant to section 500.17 of the Rules of Practice of the New York State

Court of Appeals (22 NYCRR 500.17), and after hearing argument by counsel for the parties and consideration of the briefs and the record submitted, certified question answered as follows: New York would apply the "discharge for value" rule as set forth at section 14 of the Restatement of Restitution.

Owen v. Tate

Court of Appeal, 1974.
[1976] Q.B. 402.

■ SCARMAN, L.J. . . .

Mr. Unwin, who argued the case for the plaintiff [(Norman Owen)], the appellant in this court, makes this submission. He says that one who without being asked to do so guarantees payment of another's debt is entitled upon paying the debt to be indemnified, and he submits that this is a rule that brooks of no exceptions. He gives as the reason for the rule that, at the time when the obligation to pay arises, that is to say, when the guarantor is called upon by the creditor to pay the debt, he, the guarantor, is compelled by law to make the payment sought by the creditor. He relies on a dictum of Greene L.J. in In re A Debtor [1937] Ch. 156:

"A question may arise as to the application of the subsection" that is the subsection being considered in that case "... where a guarantee is given without any antecedent request on the part of the debtor. That case is merely one example of a number of cases where the law raises an obligation to indemnify irrespective of any actual antecedent contractual relationship between the parties."

Mr. Stephenson, who has argued the case for the defendants [(Elizabeth and Peter John Tate)], who are the respondents to this appeal, says that there is no such general rule as that for which Mr. Unwin contends. He takes his stand upon the general rule that a volunteer cannot claim repayment of that which he has purely voluntarily paid, or in respect of which he has purely voluntarily assumed the obligation to pay.

The case was tried in the Gateshead County Court by Judge Sharp and, on March 12, 1974, he gave judgment dismissing the plaintiff's claim for reimbursement. He based himself simply on the ground that, in his view of the facts and the law, the plaintiff was properly to be considered as a volunteer.

I can take the facts from the very succinct statement to be found in the county court judge's judgment. He said:

"On February 26, 1965, the defendants obtained a loan from Lloyds Bank, Sunderland. This loan was secured by a charge by way of legal mortgage upon the property of a Miss Lightfoot. The plaintiff was in no way concerned with this transaction, and received no money from the defendants. In 1969 Miss Lightfoot became concerned that her deeds were being held by the bank to secure the defendants' loan. She consulted the plaintiff, who offered to help her to get her deeds back. Miss Lightfoot was a former employee of the plaintiff. The plaintiff knew that Miss Lightfoot had cohabited with a Mr. Russell, who had

had a dispute with the defendants concerning money. Mr. Russell is now deceased. In order to oblige Miss Lightfoot, and in order to obtain her deeds and keep them in a safe place, the plaintiff deposited £350 with Lloyds Bank and signed a form of guarantee by which he guaranteed payment of all money, limited to £350, due, owing or incurred to Lloyds Bank by the defendants. He did not consult the defendants before doing this. He was not asked to do this by the defendants. His motive was only to help Miss Lightfoot. He did not speak to the defendants at all about the matter. On December 17, 1970, Lloyds Bank applied £350, held by them in support of the plaintiff's said guarantee, in repayment of the defendants' debt. On January 15, 1971, the plaintiff's solicitor demanded from the defendants reimbursement of this sum. The defendants refused and the battle was joined."

. . . .

I turn to consider the law. As I understand the law, there are two general rules, both of them well known. The first is conveniently set out in Chitty on Contracts, 23rd ed. (1968), vol. 1, para. 1736, on which Mr. Stephenson, for the defendants, naturally strongly relied. There it is said: "If the payment is regarded by the law as voluntary, it cannot be recovered." . . .

The second general rule which calls for consideration in this appeal was stated authoritatively by Lord Wright M.R. in Brook's Wharf and Bull Wharf Ltd. v. Goodman Brothers [1937] 1 K.B. 534. The rule applied in that case was formulated by Lord Tenterden C.J. in an earlier case [Pownal v. Ferrand (1827) 6 B. & C. 439] in language which received the express approval of Lord Wright M.R. I take Lord Tenterden's words from p. 545 of the reports in the *Brook's Wharf* case. Lord Tenterden C.J. said, at p. 443:

"... one man, who is compelled to pay money which another is bound by law to pay, is entitled to be reimbursed by the latter."

This appeal requires us to consider the interaction of the two rules in the particular circumstances of this case. . . . I would add that neither rule can be treated as one to which there can conceivably be no exception. The first rule, that a volunteer who makes a payment on behalf of another cannot obtain repayment, does appear to me to have been one to which over the centuries the common law recognised exceptions. The exceptions have been constructed by the judges through a readiness to imply from the circumstances of the case a request or an authority to make the payment. Good illustrations of that readiness are to be found in the books.

When one turns to the second general rule, namely, the rule that where a person is compelled by law to make a payment for which another is primarily liable he is entitled to be indemnified, notwithstanding the lack of any request or consent, one again finds that the law recognises exceptions. This rule has been subjected to very careful treatment in Goff and Jones, The Law of Restitution (1966), p. 207. The authors say, after stating the rule in general terms:

"To succeed in his claim, however, the plaintiff must satisfy certain conditions. He must show (1) that he has been compelled by law to make the payment; (2) that he did not officiously expose himself to the liability to make the payment; (3) that his payment discharged a *liability* of the defendant; and (4) that both he and the defendant were subject to a common demand by a third party, for which, as between the plaintiff and the defendant, the latter was primarily responsible."

In the present case we are very much concerned with the first two of those conditions: whether the plaintiff had been compelled by law to make the payment, and whether he did or did not officiously expose himself to the liability to make the payment.

The editors, at p. 214, discuss the exceptions to the general rule which fall under their second condition, namely, the officious assumption of a liability to make the payment. If they are right—as I think they are, and as I think the cases show that they are—then there are exceptions to the second general rule; that is to say, the law does recognise that there may be exceptions, even when a man is legally liable to pay the debt of another, to the general rule that he has a right to an indemnity.

. . . .

We are, therefore, in this appeal faced with two recognised and well-established general rules, each of which admits of exceptions. . . . The broad analysis of a guarantor situation suffices, and it is this: if, as in this case, there is no antecedent request, no consideration or consensual basis for the assumption of the obligation of a guarantor, he who assumes that obligation is a volunteer. That, of course, is not the end of the transaction. The time comes, or may come, and in this case did come, when the guarantor is called upon by the creditor to honour his guarantee. At that moment undoubtedly the guarantor, having entered into his guarantee, is under an obligation by law, or, in the words of the old cases, "is compelled by law" to make the payment.

. . . .

For myself, I think the reconciliation (if that is what is needed) of the two general rules is easily achieved. I doubt whether it is necessary to consider in any case, and certainly I do not think it necessary to consider in this case, at what moment the volunteer guarantor becomes compellable at law to make the payment on behalf of the principal debtor. A right of indemnity is a right of restitution. It can arise, as the cases reveal, notwithstanding the absence of any consensual basis. . . .

In . . . Exall v. Partridge, 8 Term Rep. 308 [1799] and England v. Marsden, L.R. 1 C.P. 529 [1866] the courts were faced with the owner of goods who had deposited them on the land of another, and that other had failed to pay either rates or rent, with the result that a distraint was levied, and the owner in order to release his goods paid their value to the distrainer. In Exall v. Partridge, Lord Kenyon C.J. was at pains to discover in the circumstances an implied request or authority from the mere fact that the goods were on the land with the consent of the occupier. In England v. Marsden no such consent was spelt out by implication by the court. But in Edmunds v. Wallingford, 14 Q.B.D. 811 Lindley L.J. said it should have been. We can, therefore, take that class of case as an illustration of where the law will grant a right of indemnity notwithstanding the absence really of any consensual basis. In the *Brook's Wharf* case a warehouseman who paid import duties for which his customer—the owner of the goods—was primarily liable, and did so because of an obligation imposed by statute and without any prior request from the owner of the goods, was also held to be entitled to an indemnity.

These cases, to my mind, amply support the proposition that a broad approach is needed to the question whether in circumstances such as these a right of indemnity arises, and that broad approach requires the court to look at all the circumstances of the case. It follows that the way in which the obligation came to be assumed is a relevant circumstance. If, for instance, the plaintiff has conferred a benefit upon the defendant behind his back in circumstances in which the beneficiary has no option but to accept the benefit, it is highly likely that the courts will say that there is no right of indemnity or reimbursement. But (to take the other extreme) if the plaintiff has made a payment in a situation not of his own choosing, but where the law imposes an obligation upon him to make the payment on behalf of the principal debtor, then clearly the right of indemnity does arise. Not every case will be so clear-cut: the fundamental question is whether in the circumstances it was reasonably necessary in the interests of the volunteer or the person for whom the payment was made, or both, that the payment should be made—whether in the circumstances it was "just and reasonable" that a right of reimbursement should arise.

I think now one can see the importance to this case of Greene L.J.'s dictum upon which Mr. Unwin so strongly relied. In this case it matters not when the obligation to make the payment arose. What is important to Mr. Unwin's case is that the dictum recognises that, even when an obligation is voluntarily assumed, the volunteer may be entitled at law to a right of indemnity.

. . . .

Looking, therefore, at the circumstances as a whole, and giving weight to both phases of the transaction, I come to the conclusion that the plaintiff has failed to make out a case that it would be just and reasonable in the circumstances to grant him a right to reimbursement. Initially he was a volunteer; he has, as I understand the findings of fact of the judge and as I read the documents in the case, established no facts, either initially when he assumed the obligation, or later when he was called upon to make the payment, such as to show that it was just and reasonable that he should have a right of indemnity. I think, therefore, that on the facts as found this appeal fails.

In my judgment, the true principle of the matter can be stated very shortly, without reference to volunteers or to the compulsions of the law, and I state it as follows. If without an antecedent request a person assumes an obligation or makes a payment for the benefit of another, the law will, as a general rule, refuse him a right of indemnity. But if he can show that in the particular circumstances of the case there was some necessity for the obligation to be assumed, then the law will grant him a right of reimbursement if in all the circumstances it is just and reasonable to do so. In the present case the evidence is that the plaintiff acted not only behind the backs of the defendants initially, but in the interests of another, and despite their protest. When the moment came for him to honour the obligation thus assumed, the defendants are not to be criticised, in my judgment, for having accepted the benefit of a transaction which they neither wanted nor sought.

I therefore think the county court judge was right in the conclusion that he reached, and I would dismiss the appeal.

■ STEPHENSON, L.J. . . . I would uphold the judge's judgment, and I agree that the appeal should be dismissed.

■ ORMROD, L.J. . . . I agree that the appeal should be dismissed.

Appeal dismissed with costs.

NOTES ON BENEFITS CONFERRED WITHOUT REQUEST

1.   Note the terminology employed in the Restatements of Restitution, as defined in this provision of the Restatement (Second) (Tent. Draft No. 1 1983):

> § 2   DENIAL OF RESTITUTION FOR BENEFIT OFFICIOUSLY CONFERRED
>
> A person who receives a benefit through conduct officious as to him does not owe restitution to the person so acting. A person acts officiously when he intervenes in the affairs of another without adequate justification, such as that which may be afforded by a request or a mistake.

2.   Savage's building material accidentally fell into a river. Savage being absent, Glenn recovered it at his own expense. When Savage refused to compensate Glenn for this good deed, Glenn sued for the value of his and his employees' services. Glenn prevailed in the trial court, but its judgment was reversed on appeal. Glenn v. Savage, 14 Or. 567, 13 P. 442 (1887). The state's highest court explained:

> . . . The facts enumerated . . . could not create a legal liability on the part of Savage. They may have been meritorious, and probably beneficial, to Savage, but this was not enough. To make him liable, he must either have requested the performance of the service, or, after he knew of the service, he must have promised to pay for it. The great and leading rule of law is to deem an act done for the benefit of another, without his request, as a voluntary act of courtesy, for which no action can be sustained. The world abounds with acts of this kind, done upon no request; but would more abound with ruinous litigation, and the overthrow of personal rights and civil freedom, if the law was otherwise. The law will never permit a friendly act, or such as was intended to be an act of kindness or benevolence, to be afterwards converted into a pecuniary demand. It would be doing violence to some of the kindest and best effusions of the heart to suffer them afterwards to be perverted by sordid avarice. Whatever differences may arise afterwards among men, let those meritorious and generous acts remain lasting monuments of the good offices, intended in the days of good neighborhood and friendship; and let no after-circumstances ever tarnish or obliterate them from the recollection of the parties. So, in Bartholo-

mew v. Jackson, 20 Johns. 29, it is said: "The plaintiff performed the service without the privity or request of the defendant, and there was, in fact, no promise express or implied. If a man humanely bestows his labor, and even risks his life, in voluntarily aiding to preserve his neighbor's house from destruction by fire, the law considers the service rendered as gratuitous, and it therefore forms no ground of action."

. . .

3.   Harrison was unconscious as a result of a street car accident. Doctors contacted by a spectator tried, unsuccessfully, to save his life. They then sued Cotnam, his administrator, for the value of their services. On appeal from a judgment for the plaintiffs, the court decided that restitution was proper. Cotnam v. Wisdom, 83 Ark. 601, 104 S.W. 164 (1907). The court noted that quasi-contract "sustains recovery for physicians and nurses who render services for" people who are "incapable of contracting."

Earhart v. William Low Co.

Supreme Court of California, 1979.
25 Cal.3d 503, 158 Cal.Rptr. 887, 600 P.2d 1344.

■ TOBRINER, J. In this case we must determine whether a party who expends funds and performs services at the request of another, under the reasonable belief that the requesting party will compensate him for such services, may recover in quantum meruit although the expenditures and services do not directly benefit property owned by the requesting party.

. . . .

Plaintiff Fayette L. Earhart is the president and owner of Earhart Construction Company. For approximately two months in early 1971, plaintiff and defendant William Low, on behalf of defendant William Low Company, engaged in negotiations for the construction of the Pana Rama Mobile Home Park. These negotiations culminated in a construction contract which was to become binding when defendant obtained the requisite financing to build the park and when plaintiff secured a labor and material or performance bond for the work. Neither condition was ever fulfilled.

The proposed park was to cover a number of acres, some of which defendant owned, and the balance of which were owned by Ervie Pillow. In May 1971 defendant and Pillow entered into an escrow agreement in which Pillow agreed to sell her tract to defendant on the condition that defendant obtain financing for the mobile home park. According to plaintiff, a "special use permit" allowing the construction of a mobile home park on Pillow's land was of particular interest to defendant. Plaintiff claimed that the permit would expire on May 27, 1971, without possibility of renewal, unless work on the property were "diligently under way" by that date.

Plaintiff maintained that on May 25, 1971, defendant telephoned him to inform him that he had secured the necessary financing for the park, and, waiving all conditions to the contract, urged plaintiff to move equipment onto the property and commence work immediately in order to "save" the special use permit. Plaintiff's crew began work at once and continued to work for one week, often in the presence of defendant. On

June 1, 1971, plaintiff submitted a progress bill to defendant and at that time learned that defendant had not secured the requisite financing. Defendant refused to pay plaintiff's bill, revealing that in the interim he had signed a construction contract for the park with another firm.

. . . .

At the conclusion of the trial, the court determined that plaintiff was entitled to recover from defendant on a theory of quantum meruit. . . .

In assessing the amount of the damages to which plaintiff was entitled under quantum meruit, however, the court limited plaintiff's recovery to the reasonable value of the work done on defendant's tract, declining to award damages for the reasonable value of services rendered in construction on the Pillow property. Acknowledging that plaintiff's services "were furnished both to the Pillow property and to the Low property," the trial court interpreted this court's decision in Rotea v. Izuel, (1939) 14 Cal.2d 605, 95 P.2d 927, as precluding plaintiff's recovery with respect to the work on the Pillow property. The court stated in this regard: "[I]t is an established proposition of law in California . . . that you can't get recovery for services furnished to a third person, even though the services were furnished at the request of the defendant. . . . So the plaintiff can't recover for services furnished Mrs. Pillow. . . . [E]ven though the plaintiff renders services or delivers a product, if it is of no value to the defendant, then the defendant doesn't pay for it. All he pays for is the value of what he got, notwithstanding how much it cost the plaintiff to produce it. That's the proper measure in this case."

. . . .

Since the action for money had and received—the predecessor to the action for reasonable value of services rendered—originated in an equitable bill for the recovery of money tortiously retained by the defendant, the medieval courts inevitably held the action to apply in cases in which the defendant had received an actual "benefit." Thus the courts used the action to force disgorgement from anyone who wrongfully came by money or property to which the plaintiff was entitled; the law implied an obligation to pay in order to restore sums, or "benefit," unfairly retained by the defendant.

While the unfair receipt of a tangible benefit to the defendant may have inspired the common law courts to order restitution, the court in Rotea need not have interpreted the ancient principle of unjust enrichment so literally. Even under contemporary authorities, the court could have recognized, consistent with the orthodox principle of unjust enrichment, that a defendant who receives the satisfaction of obtaining another person's compliance with the defendant's request to perform services incurs an obligation to pay for labor and materials expended in reliance on that request.

Section 1 of the Restatement of Restitution, which predates the decision in Rotea, provides that "[a] person who has been unjustly enriched at the expense of another is required to make restitution to the other." (Rest., Restitution (1937) § 1.) A person is enriched if he has "received a benefit." (Id., com. a., p. 12.) Furthermore, "[a] person confers a benefit upon another if he ... performs services *beneficial to or at the request of the other...."* (Emphasis added.) (Id., com. b., p. 12.) While the Restatement does not establish that performance of services at the request of another uniformly results in the unjust retention of "benefit," the Restatement recognizes, unlike the decision in *Rotea,* that performance of services at another's behest may itself constitute "benefit" such that an obligation to make restitution may arise.[5]

. . . .

Indeed, the issue whether we should broaden the basis of quasi-contractual recovery so as to prevent any unconscionable injury to the plaintiff, is not a novel one for our court. In his dissenting opinion in Coleman Engineering Co. v. North American Aviation, Inc. (1966) 65 Cal.2d 396, 55 Cal.Rptr. 1, 420 P.2d 713, Chief Justice Traynor cogently urged that we abandon the unconscionable requirement of "benefit" to the defendant and allow recovery in quantum meruit whenever a party acts to his detriment in reliance on another's representation that he will give compensation for the detriment suffered.

. . . .

Thus Chief Justice Traynor would have awarded plaintiff recovery notwithstanding defendant's lack of "benefit." As the Chief Justice concluded, "the one rendering performance and incurring expenses at the request of the other should receive reasonable compensation therefor without regard to benefit conferred upon the other. Such a rule places the loss where it belongs—on the party whose requests induced performance in justifiable reliance on the belief that the requested performance would be paid for."

The determination to protect "justifiable reliance" forms not only the inspiration for Chief Justice Traynor's application of a quasi-contractual remedy in *Coleman,* but also provides the basis for several parallel contractual doctrines as well. The first of these doctrines rests on the theory that "part performance" of an otherwise invalid contract may satisfy the purposes of the statute of frauds. Thus a court may award damages based on an unenforceable contract if unconscionable injury would result from denying enforcement after one party has been induced to make a serious change of position. Closely allied to the doctrine of part performance is the notion that reliance by one party on an oral contract may "estop" the other from setting up a defense based upon the statute of frauds.

Finally, section 90 of the Restatement of Contracts—the so-called "promissory estoppel" section—provides that reasonably expected reliance may under some circumstances make binding a promise for which nothing

5. We note that while restitution ordinarily connotes the return of something which one party has "received" from another, the term may also refer to a broader obligation to pay. Thus, "[i]t is enough that the plaintiff has rendered the very performance for which the defendant bargained.... Service or forbearance rendered at the defendant's request is regarded as having been received by him; and the fair price that it would have cost to obtain this service or forbearance from a person in the plaintiff's position can be recovered. Judgment will be given for the value of services so rendered, ... even though there never was any product created by the service that added to the wealth of the defendant." (Rest., Contracts (1932) § 348, com. a., pp. 591–592.)

has been given or promised in exchange.[9] In Raedeke v. Gibraltar Savings & Loan Assn. (1974) 10 Cal.3d 665, 111 Cal.Rptr. 693, 517 P.2d 1157 we explained that a court may invoke the doctrine of promissory estoppel embodied in section 90 to bind a promisor " 'when he should reasonably expect a substantial change of position, either by act or forbearance, in reliance on his promise, if injustice can be avoided only by its enforcement.' "

In view of the equitable considerations lying at the foundation of these several doctrines, and reflected in the opinion in *Coleman*, we conclude that compensation for a party's performance should be paid by the person whose request induced the performance. In light of this conclusion, the portion of the judgment denying plaintiff recovery with respect to the Pillow property must be reversed. . . .

. . . .

The judgment is reversed and the case is remanded to the trial court for further proceedings consistent with this opinion.

■ CLARK, J., concurring and dissenting. . . .

Neither principles of unjust enrichment nor of implied in fact contracts require imposing upon defendant an obligation to pay for improvement to the Pillow property in the circumstances before us.

Unjust enrichment presumes some benefit to the persons unjustly enriched sufficient to warrant implication of a promise to pay. Restatement, Restitution (1937) section 1, comment a, provides: "A person is unjustly enriched if the retention of the benefit would be unjust (see Comment c)."

Comment c provides: "Even where a person has received a benefit from another, he is liable to pay therefor only if the circumstances of its receipt or retention are such that, as between the two persons, it is unjust for him to retain it. The mere fact that a person benefits another is not of itself sufficient to require the other to make restitution therefor. Thus, one who improves his own land ordinarily benefits his neighbors to some extent, and one who makes a gift or voluntarily pays money which he knows he does not owe confers a benefit; in neither case is he entitled to restitution. . . ."

In Rotea v. Izuel, (1939) 14 Cal.2d 605, 95 P.2d 927, it was held that an obligation will not be implied in law "where the direct benefit is received by a third party and the only benefit received by the defendant is the incidental benefit which he may find in the satisfaction of obtaining compliance with his request." Absent promise of payment, a person who does no more than request an attorney to consult with a potential client does not incur an obligation to pay the attorney for the consultation.

The same rule should apply where the only benefit obtained by the defendant from the requested performance is substantially similar to the

---

9. Section 90 provides, "A promise which the promisor should reasonably expect to induce action or forbearance of a definite and substantial character on the part of the promisee and which does induce such action or forbearance is binding if injustice can be avoided only by enforcement of the promise." (Rest., Contracts (1932) p. 110.)

benefit received by the plaintiff from the same act. The hitchhiker should not be held to have promised to pay for his ride in the absence of a promise to pay. He and the person providing the ride receive the same benefit from the ride. A defendant who has solicited bids should not be held to have promised to pay the expenses incurred in preparing the bids unless he has expressly promised to do so. The bid provides substantially the same benefit to the one who solicits and the bidder—the opportunity to enter into a contract. Absent express agreement to pay, the potential customer does not obtain a cause of action for services rendered when he accepts the retailer's request to examine his merchandise, nor does the salesman who responds to the potential customer's requests for assistance. Again, the benefits are substantially the same—the opportunity to consummate a transaction.

When the defendant receives benefits in addition to those received by the plaintiff or which are substantially different, unjust enrichment may be remedied through imposition of a duty to pay. But so long as the only benefits received by the defendant from plaintiff's conduct are substantially equivalent to those obtained by the plaintiff, mere compliance with a request is not a sufficient benefit to warrant imposition of such duty absent a promise to pay. Absent agreement to pay, it would be mere speculation to conclude the benefit to the defendant rather than the substantially equivalent benefit to plaintiff was the motivating force for plaintiff's performance.

The improvements made to the defendant company's property inured to the benefit of defendant company, and the trial court properly determined those improvements warranted imposition of a duty to pay their reasonable value. However, the improvements made to the Pillow property did not inure to the use and enjoyment of defendant company but to the owner of that property and recovery was properly denied.

In one respect plaintiff's performance on the Pillow property did confer a benefit to the defendant company which in other circumstances might warrant recovery. Defendant received an advantage comparable to the extension of time to perform a contract or exercise an option. If the use permit had lapsed, the value of defendant company's right to purchase the Pillow property would have been impaired. It is doubtful whether defendant company would have continued its search for financing, and whether potential lenders would still be interested in the project. The fact that defendant company did not ultimately acquire the Pillow property does not mean it failed to receive contractual advantage from plaintiff's activity in preserving the use permit. To the contrary, some benefit was realized through increasing the time for defendant company to obtain financing for its project.

However, plaintiff secured a substantially similar benefit from his performance. Plaintiff had a contract to build the mobile home park for $892,557.86 contingent upon defendant obtaining financing. If the use permit lapsed, it would be unlikely that the transaction would go forward. By commencing work to maintain the permit, thereby increasing the time to obtain financing, plaintiff also increased the likelihood that his contract would be effective. Because the benefits to plaintiff are substantially similar to those to defendant company, there is no unjust enrichment, and no basis for finding an implied in fact promise to pay.

. . . .

I would affirm the judgment.

————

B.   MEASURE OF THE RESTITUTION INTEREST

Olwell v. Nye & Nissen Co.

Supreme Court of Washington, 1946.
26 Wash.2d 282, 173 P.2d 652.

■ MALLERY, J. On May 6, 1940, plaintiff, E.L. Olwell, sold and transferred to the defendant corporation his one-half interest in Puget Sound Egg Packers, a Washington corporation having its principal place of business in Tacoma. By the terms of the agreement, the plaintiff was to retain full ownership in an "Eggsact" egg-washing machine, formerly used by Puget Sound Egg Packers. The defendant promised to make it available for delivery to the plaintiff on or before June 15, 1940. It appears that the plaintiff arranged for and had the machine stored in a space adjacent to the premises occupied by the defendant but not covered by its lease. Due to the scarcity of labor immediately after the out-break of the war, defendant's treasurer, without the knowledge or consent of the plaintiff, ordered the egg washer taken out of storage. The machine was put into operation by defendant on May 31, 1941, and thereafter for a period of three years was used approximately one day a week in the regular course of the defendant's business. Plaintiff first discovered this use in January or February of 1945 when he happened to be at the plant on business and heard the machine operating. Thereupon plaintiff offered to sell the machine to defendant for $600 or half of its original cost in 1929. A counter offer of $50 was refused and approximately one month later this action was commenced to recover the reasonable value of defendant's use of the machine, and praying for $25 per month from the commencement of the unauthorized use until the time of trial. A second cause of action was alleged but was not pressed and hence is not here involved. The court entered judgment for plaintiff in the amount of $10 per week for the period of 156 weeks covered by the statute of limitations, or $1,560, and gave the plaintiff his costs.

Defendant has appealed to this court assigning error upon the judgment, upon the trial of the cause on the theory of unjust enrichment, upon the amount of damages, and upon the court's refusal to make a finding as to the value of the machine and in refusing to consider such value in measuring damages.

The theory of the respondent was that the tort of conversion could be "waived" and suit brought in quasi-contract, upon a contract implied in law, to recover, as restitution, the profits which inured to appellant as a result of its wrongful use of the machine. With this the trial court agreed and in its findings of facts found that the use of the machine "resulted in a benefit to the users, in that said use saves the users approximately $1.43 per hour of use as against the expense which would be incurred were eggs to be washed by hand; that said machine was used by Puget Sound Egg Packers and defendant, on an average of one day per week from May of 1941, until February of 1945 at an average saving of $10.00 per each day of use."

In substance, the argument presented by the assignments of error is that the principle of unjust enrichment, or quasi-contract, is not of universal application, but is imposed only in exceptional cases because of special facts and circumstances and in favor of particular persons; that respondent had an adequate remedy in an action at law for replevin or claim and delivery; that any damages awarded to the plaintiff should be based upon the use or rental value of the machine and should bear some reasonable relation to its market value. Appellant therefore contends that the amount of the judgment is excessive.

It is uniformly held that in cases where the defendant *tort feasor* has benefited by his wrong, the plaintiff may elect to "waive the tort" and bring an action in assumpsit for restitution. Such an action arises out of a duty imposed by law devolving upon the defendant to repay an unjust and unmerited enrichment.

It is clear that the saving in labor cost which appellant derived from its use of respondent's machine constituted a benefit.

According to the Restatement of Restitution, § 1(b),

"A person confers a benefit upon another if he gives to the other possession of or some other interest in money, land, chattels, or choses in action, performs services beneficial to or at the request of the other, satisfies a debt or a duty of the other, or in any way adds to the other's security or advantage. *He confers a benefit not only where he adds to the property of another, but also where he* saves the other from expense or loss. The word 'benefit', therefore denotes any form of advantage." (Italics ours)

It is also necessary to show that while appellant benefited from its use of the egg-washing machine, respondent thereby incurred a loss. It is argued by appellant that since the machine was put into storage by respondent, who had no present use for it, and for a period of almost three years did not know that appellant was operating it and since it was not injured by its operation and the appellant never adversely claimed any title to it, nor contested respondent's right of repossession upon the latter's discovery of the wrongful operation, that the respondent was not damaged because he is as well off as if the machine had not been used by appellant.

The very essence of the nature of property is the right to its exclusive use. Without it, no beneficial right remains. However plausible, the appellant cannot be heard to say that his wrongful invasion of the respondent's property right to exclusive use is not a loss compensable in law. To hold otherwise would be subversive of all property rights since his use was admittedly wrongful and without claim of right. The theory of unjust enrichment is applicable in such a case.

We agree with appellant that respondent could have elected a "common garden variety of action," as he calls it, for the recovery of damages. It is also true that except where provided for by statute, punitive damages are not allowed, the basic measure for the recovery of damages in this state being compensation. If, then, respondent had been *limited* to redress *in tort* for damages, as appellant contends, the court below would be in error in refusing to make a finding as to the value of the machine. In such case the award of damages must bear a reasonable relation to the value of the property.

But respondent here had an election. He chose rather to waive his right of action *in tort* and to sue *in assumpsit* on the implied contract. Having so elected, he is entitled to the measure of restoration which accompanies the remedy.

"Actions for restitution have for their primary purpose taking from the defendant and restoring to the plaintiff something to which the plaintiff is entitled, or if this is not done, causing the defendant to pay the plaintiff an amount which will restore the plaintiff to the position in which he was before the defendant received the benefit. If the value of what was received and what was lost were always equal, there would be no substantial problem as to the amount of recovery, since actions of restitution are not punitive. In fact, however, the plaintiff frequently has lost more than the defendant has gained, and sometimes the defendant has gained more than the plaintiff has lost.

"In such cases the measure of restitution is determined with reference to the tortiousness of the defendant's conduct or the negligence or other fault of one or both of the parties in creating the situation giving rise to the right to restitution. If the defendant was tortious in his acquisition of the benefit he is required to pay for what the other has lost although that is more than the recipient benefited. *If he was consciously tortious in acquiring the benefit, he is also deprived of any profit derived from his subsequent dealing with it.* If he was no more at fault than the claimant, he is not required to pay for losses in excess of benefit received by him and he is permitted to retain gains which result from his dealing with the property." (Italics ours) Restatement of Restitution, pp. 595, 596.

Respondent may recover the profit derived by the appellant from the use of the machine.

Respondent has prayed "on his first cause of action for the sum of $25.00 per month from the time defendant first commenced to use said machine subsequent to May 1940 (1941) until present time."

In computing judgment, the court below computed recovery on the basis of $10 per week. This makes the judgment excessive since it cannot exceed the amount prayed for.

. . . .

We therefore direct the trial court to reduce the judgment, based upon the prayer of the complaint, to $25 per month for thirty-six months, or $900.

The judgment as modified is affirmed. Appellant will recover its costs.

Bradkin v. Leverton

Court of Appeals of New York, 1970.
26 N.Y.2d 192, 309 N.Y.S.2d 192, 257 N.E.2d 643.

■ FULD, C.J. On this appeal from the dismissal of the complaint on motion before trial, we are called upon to say whether—accepting its allegations as true and reading them most liberally in favor of the pleader—it states a cause of action.

The complaint recites that the plaintiff, employed by H.L. Federman & Co., Inc., to find corporations which needed financing, procured for his employer the business of financing Mauchly Associates, Inc. By a letter dated October 25, 1966, Federman acknowledged not only that the plaintiff had earned $10,000 for having arranged $200,000 worth of financing in Mauchly but, in addition, that he was "to receive 10% of [any] net profit" which it (Federman) might realize "[s]hould there be a second financing, or any other financing ... concerning Mauchly in the year 1967". The complaint further recites that the defendant was an officer, director and nonvoting stockholder of Federman, that he became acquainted with Mauchly only through the plaintiff and that he knew or should have known that the plaintiff was to receive 10% of any profits derived from financing Mauchly. However, the complaint continues, solely through the "business relations between Mauchly and Federman created by the plaintiff", the defendant was enabled, without the plaintiff's knowledge, to "arrange private financing transactions" with Mauchly. The plaintiff, who learned of the defendant's actions later, charges that there was an implied promise by the defendant to pay the plaintiff 10% of his net profit—which amounted to more than $1,000,000—and that, although "due demand" was made by him, the defendant refused to compensate him "out of the profit from his Mauchly financing". In a second cause of action, the plaintiff, claiming that he is entitled to 10% of the profits realized by the defendant, seeks an accounting.

The defendant moved to dismiss the complaint, pursuant to CPLR 3211 (subd. [a])on the ground (1) that the causes of action were barred by the Statute of Frauds (par. 5) and (2) that the complaint failed to state a cause of action (par. 7). Although not admitting that the plaintiff introduced Mauchly to Federman or that he learned of Mauchly through the plaintiff in the first instance, the defendant does admit that some time in 1966, and again in January and June, 1967, he or his wife loaned Mauchly more than $200,000 and that he became a director of that corporation. He contends, however, that, even if there had been an agreement between him and the plaintiff, the Statute of Frauds (General Obligations Law, Consol.Laws, c. 24–A, § 5–701, subd. 10) renders it unenforceable since there was no writing; that the complaint fails to state a cause of action since he, as an officer of Federman, was not individually liable under the plaintiff's agreement with Federman.

The court at Special Term granted the defendant's motion and dismissed the complaint. It was its view that, since the plaintiff was, in effect, seeking a "finder's fee," the Statute of Frauds required a writing signed by the defendant and that the letter from Federman did not remove the statute's bar. The Appellate Division affirmed the resulting order of dismissal without opinion. Two justices dissented; concluding that the complaint stated a cause of action in tort, they interpreted it "as alleging both a breach of the contract induced by the defendant and an interference by defendant in the performance of the contract."

We agree with the Appellate Division dissenters that the complaint should be upheld but we read it, as does its draftsman, as stating a cause of action in quasi contract.

Quasi contracts are not contracts at all, although they give rise to obligations more akin to those stemming from contract than from tort. The contract is a mere fiction, a form imposed in order to adapt the case to a given remedy. Briefly stated, a quasi-contractual obligation is one imposed by law where there has been no agreement or expression of assent, by word or act, on the part of either party involved. The law creates it, regardless of the intention of the parties, to assure a just and equitable result....

Although there was no agreement between them, express or implied, the defendant received a benefit from the plaintiff's services under circumstances which, in justice, preclude him from denying an obligation to pay for them. As already noted, the plaintiff had, according to the complaint, introduced Mauchly to Federman and, under his written agreement with Federman, he was to receive from that party, in addition to an introduction fee of $10,000, "10% of [its] net profit" on a "second financing ... concerning Mauchly in the year 1967". It was solely from this relationship, which the plaintiff had created between Federman and Mauchly, that the defendant's dealings with Mauchly arose. By intruding into the transaction set up by the plaintiff, the defendant made use of his corporate position to promote his own private interests. More specifically, when the plaintiff procured Mauchly for Federman, he fully performed his part of the contract with Federman and thereupon became entitled, without more, to 10% of any profit which that corporation would have realized from any further financing of Mauchly. Since the defendant, an officer and director of Federman, intruded into the transaction and took unto himself the Mauchly financing, he obtained the benefit of the plaintiff's labors and must compensate him for such services.

This brings us to the defendant's contention—actually his threshold argument—that the absence of a writing between him and the plaintiff defeats the plaintiff's claim. It is true that quasi contract denotes a contract implied in law and that the Statute of Frauds' requirement of a writing to enforce an agreement for finders' or brokers' commissions expressly applies "to a contract implied in fact or in law" (General Obligations Law, § 5–701, subd. 10). It is on the basis of such reasoning that the defendant asserts the bar of the statute. Thus, in his brief, he urges that the plaintiff may not avoid its impact by casting his action in a guise other than one for a finder's fee through the "mere expediency" of labeling such a claim as one in "quantum meruit".

A contract to pay a finder's fee must, of course, be in writing and, obviously, this requirement may not be avoided by an action for compensation in *quantum meruit*. However, the contract required to be in writing is one between the finder and the principal or employer with whom he has assertedly contracted and from whom he seeks compensation. This is apparent from the evils at which the statute is aimed. " 'The nature of the transactions' ", we wrote in [a prior] case, quoting from the Law Revision Commission's Report recommending the enactment of subdivision 10 of section 31 of the Personal Property Law—the predecessor of subdivision 10 of section 5–701 of the General Obligations Law is such that, " 'in the absence of the requirement of a writing, unfounded and multiple claims for commissions [by business brokers and finders] are frequently asserted, and employers often seek to escape liability by denying the fact of employment. These controversies are commonly resolved by juries on conflicting testimony, with the consequent danger of erroneous verdicts' (1949 Report of N.Y.Law Rev.Comm. [N.Y.Legis.Doc., 1949, No. 65(G), p. 615])."

Quite manifestly, the purpose of the statute is to protect against fraudulent dealings *between the finder and his employer,* not between the finder and a third party, such as the defendant before us. Since there is no danger of "unfounded and multiple claims for commissions" where a third party is concerned, the Statute of Frauds provides no defense to him. When, therefore, a finder's contract meets all the requirements of the statute, a third party may not "take over" that contract and then evade his obligation to the finder by relying upon the statute. This is precisely what the present defendant is attempting to do. Federman had promised in writing to pay the plaintiff a finder's fee on any Mauchly financing and, when the defendant took over the corporation's financing arrangements, he assumed its obligation to the plaintiff for commissions. He is not privileged to assert the defense of the statute, which would not have been available to Federman.

In sum, given the facts alleged, it would be against good conscience for the defendant to retain the benefits of the contract which the plaintiff made with the defendant's corporation without compensating the plaintiff for the services he fully performed pursuant to that contract. Accordingly, if the plaintiff proves the allegations of his complaint, he will be entitled to recover from the defendant, as damages, the amount which the defendant's corporation had obligated itself to pay him if there was a "second financing . . . concerning Mauchly."[4]

The order appealed from should be reversed, with costs in all courts, and the case remitted to the Supreme Court, Kings County, for further proceedings in accordance with this opinion.

Farash v. Sykes Datatronics, Inc.

Court of Appeals of New York, 1983.
59 N.Y.2d 500, 465 N.Y.S.2d 917, 452 N.E.2d 1245.

■ COOKE, C.J. Plaintiff claims that he and defendant entered an agreement whereby defendant would lease a building owned by plaintiff, who was to

---

4. In view of the fact that there was no fiduciary relationship between the plaintiff and the defendant, the plaintiff has no right to the accounting sought by the second cause of action.

complete its renovation and make certain modifications on an expedited basis. Defendant, however, never signed any contract and never occupied the building. Plaintiff commenced this litigation, and defendant unsuccessfully moved to dismiss for failure to state a cause of action. On appeal, the Appellate Division reversed, with two Justices dissenting in part. For the reasons that follow, we now modify.

Plaintiff pleaded three causes of action in his complaint. The first was to enforce an oral lease for a term longer than one year. This is clearly barred by the Statute of Frauds (General Obligations Law, § 5–703, subd. 2). The third cause of action is premised on the theory that the parties contracted by exchanging promises that plaintiff would perform certain work in his building and defendant would enter into a lease for a term longer than one year. This is nothing more than a contract to enter into a lease; it is also subject to the Statute of Frauds. Hence, the third cause of action was properly dismissed.

Plaintiff's second cause of action, however, is not barred by the Statute of Frauds. It merely seeks to recover for the value of the work performed by plaintiff in reliance on statements by and at the request of defendant. This is not an attempt to enforce an oral lease or an oral agreement to enter a lease, but is in disaffirmance of the void contract and so may be maintained. That defendant did not benefit from plaintiff's efforts does not require dismissal; plaintiff may recover for those efforts that were to his detriment and that thereby placed him in a worse position. "The contract being void and incapable of enforcement in a court of law, the party ... rendering the services in pursuance thereof, may treat it as a nullity, and recover ... the value of the services."

The dissent's primary argument is that the second cause of action is equivalent to the third, and so is also barred by the Statute of Frauds. It is true that plaintiff attempts to take the contract outside the statute's scope and render it enforceable by arguing that the work done was unequivocally referable to the oral agreement. This should not operate to prevent recovery under a theory of quasi contract as a contract implied by law, which "is not a contract at all but an obligation imposed by law to do justice even though it is clear that no promise was ever made or intended" (Calamari and Perillo, Contracts [2d ed.], § 1–12, p. 19). Obviously, the party who seeks both to enforce the contract that is unenforceable by virtue of the Statute of Frauds and to recover under a contract implied in law will present contradictory characterizations. This, however, is proper in our courts where pleading alternative theories of relief is accepted. Moreover, the existence of any real promise is unnecessary; plaintiff's attempt to make his acts directly referable to the unenforceable contract simply is irrelevant.

The authorities all recognize that a promisee should be able to recover in the present situation. "[I]f the improvements made by the plaintiff are on land that is not owned by the defendant and in no respect add to his wealth, the plaintiff will not be given judgment for restitution of their value, even though he may have made such improvements in reliance upon the contract that the defendant has broken. For such expenditures as these in reliance on a contract, the plaintiff can get judgment only in the form of damages for consequential injury" (5 Corbin, Contracts, p. 578). Thus, plaintiff may recover for those expenditures he made in reliance on defendant's representations and that he otherwise would not have made. The Restatement provides that an injured party who has not conferred a benefit may not obtain restitution, but he or she may "have an action for damages, including one for recovery based on . . . reliance" (Restatement, Contracts 2d, § 370, Comment *a*). "[T]he injured party has a right to damages based on his reliance interest, including expenditures made in preparation for performance or in performance, less any loss that the party in breach can prove with reasonable certainty the injured party would have suffered had the contract been performed" (Restatement, Contracts 2d, § 349). The Restatement recognizes an action such as is involved here (see Restatement, Contracts 2d §§ 139, 349, Comment *b*).

The dissent relies on Bradkin v. Leverton, 26 N.Y.2d 192, 309 N.Y.S.2d 192, 257 N.E.2d 643 and Miller v. Schloss, 218 N.Y. 400, 113 N.E. 337 for the proposition that plaintiff can recover only if there is an actual benefit to the defendant. Those cases do not state that there can be no recovery for work performed in the absence of any real benefit to defendant. As stated by Professor Williston (12 Williston, Contracts [3d ed.] pp. 282–284, 286–287):

> "Again, even though the defendant's liability is imposed by law irrespective of the agreement of the parties, and may, therefore, be called quasi contractual, where the defendant is a wrongdoer the plaintiff may well be preferred, and if a complete restoration of the *status quo* or its equivalent is impossible the plaintiff should at least be replaced in as good a position as he originally was in, although the defendant is thereby compelled to pay more than the amount which the plaintiff's performance has benefited him.
>
> . . . .
>
> "That is, the law should impose on the wrongdoing defendant a duty to restore the plaintiff's former status, not merely to surrender any enrichment or benefit that he may unjustly hold or have received; although if the market value or, in the absence of a market value, the benefit to the defendant of what has been furnished exceeds the cost or value to the plaintiff, there is no reason why recovery of this excess should not be allowed.
>
> "These different possible situations, as has been said, have often been confused with one another, because the form of action in each of them was identical at common law—general assumpsit on a *quantum meruit or quantum valebat* count; and this tended to induce courts and others to inquire what is the rule of damages under such counts—a question not susceptible of a single answer."

A lesson in this area can be taken from Professors Calamari and Perillo: "The basic aim of restitution is to place the plaintiff in the same economic position as he enjoyed prior to contracting. Thus, unless specific restitution is obtained in Equity, the plaintiff's recovery is for the reasonable value of services rendered, goods delivered, or property conveyed less the reasonable value of any counter-performance received by him. The plaintiff recovers the reasonable value of his performance whether or not the defendant in any economic sense benefitted from the performance. The quasi-contractual concept of benefit continues to be recognized by the rule that the defendant must have received the plaintiff's performance; acts merely preparatory to performance will not justify an action for restitution. 'Receipt,' however, is a legal concept rather than a description of physical fact. If what the plaintiff has done is part of the agreed exchange, it is deemed to be 'received' by the defendant." (Calamari and Perillo, Contracts [2d ed.], § 15–4, p. 574).

We should not be distracted by the manner in which a theory of recovery is titled. On careful consideration, it becomes clear that the commentators do not disagree in result, but only in nomenclature. Whether denominated "acting in reliance" or "restitution," all concur that a promisee who partially performs (e.g., by doing work in a building or at an accelerated pace) at a promisor's request should be allowed to recover the fair and reasonable value of the performance rendered, regardless of the enforceability of the original agreement.

Accordingly, the order of the Appellate Division should be modified, with costs to appellant, by reinstating plaintiff's second cause of action and, as so modified, affirmed.

■ JASEN, J. (dissenting). Plaintiff's second cause of action alleges that "[p]laintiff, in reliance on statements made [by] the defendant and at its request, performed work, provided labor and material to the defendant" and that "[d]efendant has failed to compensate the plaintiff for monies and other expenses incurred by the plaintiff in preparing the property at 49 East Avenue to the defendants' needs", causing damage to the defendant in the amount of $400,000.

. . . .

The majority fails to specify the theory of recovery upon which it bases its conclusion that "plaintiff may recover for those efforts that were to his detriment and that thereby placed him in a worse position". Insofar as this conclusion is based upon quasi contract, it is incorrect for the well-established rule in this State is that in order for a plaintiff to recover under such a cause of action, he must demonstrate that the defendant was unjustly enriched by his efforts. The rule has been clearly set forth by this court and consistently followed: " '[a] *quasi* or constructive contract rests upon the equitable principle that a person shall not be allowed to enrich himself unjustly at the expense of another. In truth it is not a contract or promise at all. It is an obligation which the law creates, in the absence of any agreement, when and because the acts of the parties or others have placed in the possession of one person money, or its equivalent, under such circumstances that in equity and good conscience he ought not to retain it, and which *ex aequo et bono* belongs to another.' " Since as the majority correctly points out, defendant did not benefit from plaintiff's efforts, no recovery under quasi contract may be had.

The "lesson" provided by Professors Calamari and Perillo, cited by the majority, is inapposite to the case before us because section 15–4 of their text deals exclusively with actions based on breach while plaintiff does not allege in his second cause of action that defendant breached any agreement. Additionally, I note that insofar as this statement would allow recovery by the plaintiff under a theory of restitution, even though the defendant has not been benefited by any of plaintiff's efforts, such is not the law in New York. The majority itself concedes this point in stating, "an injured party who has not conferred a benefit may not obtain restitution." Moreover, assuming *arguendo* the accuracy of the legal principle stated by Calamari and Perillo, this principle does not accord relief to the plaintiff in the instant appeal. As the two professors correctly note, "the defendant must have received the plaintiff's performance; acts merely preparatory to performance will not justify an action for restitution." First, defendant received nothing from the plaintiff, as the majority accurately points out. Second, plaintiff's acts in renovating his building were "merely preparatory to performance" of the alleged oral contract whereby plaintiff and defendant agreed to enter into a two-year lease. Thus, even if section 15–4 were applicable, plaintiff would not be entitled to the relief which the majority is offering.

I also fail to see how sections 998 and 1011 of Corbin's treatise and sections 349 and 370 of the Restatement of Contracts, Second, support the majority's position. Corbin's discussion of reliance damages in sections 998 and 1011 (like Calamari and Perillo's) is concerned solely with a remedy available to a plaintiff injured by a defendant who has *breached a contract*. Since there was no such contract entered into by the parties here, and accordingly no breach thereof, those sections of Corbin's text do not even address the issue involved here.

Similarly, the Restatement lends no support to the majority's view. While it is true that section 370 would allow a party to maintain "an action for damages, including one for recovery based on . . . reliance", a reading of the entire section, *including its cite to section 349 as the sole authority for this proposition,* makes clear that such an action is based strictly on a theory of promissory estoppel, a theory which, as is discussed more fully below, has never been asserted by the parties and which this court has heretofore declined to adopt.[5]

The majority also mistakenly relies on a quote from section 349 of the Restatement of Contracts, Second—"[T]he injured party has a right to damages based on his reliance interest, including expenditures made in preparation for performance or in performance, less any loss that the party in *breach* can prove with reasonable certainty the injured party would have suffered had the *contract* been performed" (emphasis supplied). This passage, by its very terms, deals solely with remedies available where a party has breached an existing contract. Plaintiff, however, does not allege in his second cause of action the existence of any contract. Nor does he allege that defendant committed any breach. In the majority's view, plaintiff's second cause of action is not based upon breach of contract, but, rather, "is in disaffirmance of the void contract". Thus, section 349 of the Restatement

---

5. [Section 370 reads as follows:

Requirement That Benefit Be Conferred. A party is entitled to restitution under the rules stated in this Restatement only to the extent that he has conferred a benefit on the other party by way of part performance or reliance.]

does not address the situation presented on this appeal and, accordingly, provides no support for the majority's position.

It appears that the majority, in holding that plaintiff can recover the value of his efforts expended in reliance on defendant's alleged statements, is recognizing a cause of action sounding in promissory estoppel. This is implicit in its reference to the Restatement of Contracts, Second, section 139 and section 349, Comment *b,* as support for its conclusion that "[t]he Restatement recognizes an action such as is involved here". Section 139 is quite simply one of the estoppel sections of the Restatement. (See Restatement, Contracts 2d, § 139, Comment *a.*) . . .

While the doctrine of promissory estoppel has been recognized and applied in certain cases, to do so here, where the issue has not been pleaded or addressed in the parties' affidavits and has neither been argued nor briefed, is ill-advised. . . .

In the absence of either a contract requiring defendant to pay for plaintiff's renovation or some evidence that defendant was unjustly enriched, thus allowing plaintiff to recover under a cause of action sounding in quasi contract, defendant should not be held potentially liable to plaintiff for such renovation costs. Accordingly, I would affirm the order of the Appellate Division.

NOTES

1. Pursuant to a written contract, Oliver agreed to represent Campbell in a divorce action. A fee of $750 was to be paid after the trial. The trial took 29 days. After the judge announced his intended decision, but before argument on proposed findings of fact and conclusions of law, Campbell discharged Oliver and stated that he would proceed *pro se.* When Oliver replied that he would expect to be paid the reasonable value of his services if he was discharged before completing his obligations under the contract, Campbell said he would not pay "one cent more" than the $450 he had already paid. Oliver then brought an action for restitution seeking $9550, which he claimed to represent the reasonable value of his services less the $450 previously paid by Campbell. (The opposing lawyer in the divorce suit had been paid $9000.) The trial court found that the reasonable value of Oliver's services was $5000, but it held that his recovery was limited by the contract. The state supreme court agreed. Oliver v. Campbell, 43 Cal.2d 298, 273 P.2d 15 (1954). The Supreme Court of California stated that a nonbreaching party like Oliver " 'may treat the contract as rescinded and recover upon a quantum meruit so far as he has performed.' " However, it also recognized the rule, now embodied in Restatement (Second) of Contracts § 373(2), that the contract limits the recovery of a nonbreaching party who "has performed all of his duties under the contract [when] no performance by the other party remains due other than payment of a definite sum of money for that performance." Because it felt that Oliver "had performed practically all of the services he was employed to perform when he was discharged," the court held that his recovery must be limited to $300.

2.   The restitutionary rights of the breaching party have been touched upon in Chapter 10. Consider in this regard Restatement (Second) of Contracts § 374:

RESTITUTION IN FAVOR OF PARTY IN BREACH

(1) Subject to the rule stated in Subsection (2), if a party justifiably refused to perform on the ground that his remaining duties of performance have been discharged by the other party's breach, the party in breach is entitled to restitution for any benefit that he has conferred by way of part performance or reliance in excess of the loss that he has caused by his own breach.

(2) To the extent that, under the manifested assent of the parties, a party's performance is to be retained in the case of breach, that party is not entitled to restitution if the value of the performance as liquidated damages is reasonable in the light of the anticipated or actual loss caused by the breach and the difficulties of proof of loss.

Jersey City v. Hague

Supreme Court of New Jersey, 1955.
18 N.J. 584, 115 A.2d 8.

[The City of Jersey City seeks to recover money from former city officials, two former mayors and a deputy mayor, that they allegedly extorted from city employees. According to the complaint the defendants "did steal and did unlawfully, fraudulently, corruptly and with gross breach of trust, extort and appropriate to themselves property of the City, to wit, money," in the sum of $15,000,000. It charged that the "thefts and defrauds" were accomplished by extorting from the employees of the City 3% of the annual salary of each employee during each year from 1917 to 1949.]

■ VANDERBILT, C.J. Defendant Frank Hague moved, without supporting affidavit, to dismiss the complaint "for failure to state a claim upon which relief can be granted" and the trial court granted the motion. The plaintiff appealed to the Appellate Division of the Superior Court and we certified the case on our own motion while it was pending there.

I.   The Facts of the Complaint.

. . . .

The complaint then concludes:

"Wherefore, plaintiff demands judgment against the defendants, jointly and severally, in the amount of $15,000,000. plus interest; and for the impressment of a trust in the amount of $15,000,000. plus interest, upon the property and assets of the defendants for the use and benefit of the plaintiff as beneficiary, or in the name of plaintiff as trustee for the use and benefit of all employees (or their heirs and administrators) of the plaintiff from whom the defendants extorted payroll percentage amounts as alleged herein; and for the costs of this suit; and for such other relief as may be just, equitable and proper."

The complaint will be examined first with respect to the substantive law and then in its procedural aspects.

II.   The Substantive Law of the Complaint.

The complaint in effect alleges that the defendants by force of their official positions systematically extorted from the employees of the plaintiff municipality 3% of their official income from 1917 to 1949 as a condition of their employment and continued employment and retained these funds for their own use. The substantial question before us is whether they can be permitted in law to do this.

We do not have to look far for an answer. In Driscoll v. Burlington–Bristol Bridge Co., 8 N.J. 433, at page 474 et seq., 86 A.2d 201, at page 221 (1952), this court said without dissent:

"The members of the board of chosen freeholders and of the bridge commission are public officers holding positions of public trust. They stand in a fiduciary relationship to the people whom they have been elected or appointed to serve. As fiduciaries and trustees of the public weal they are under an inescapable obligation to serve the public with the highest fidelity. In discharging the duties of their office they are required to display such intelligence and skill as they are capable of, to be diligent and conscientious, to exercise their discretion not arbitrarily but reasonably, and above all to display good faith, honesty and integrity. They must be impervious to corrupting influences and they must transact their business frankly and openly in the light of public scrutiny so that the public may know and be able to judge them and their work fairly. When public officials do not so conduct themselves and discharge their duties, their actions are inimicable to and inconsistent with the public interest, and not only are they individually deserving of censure and reproach but the transactions which they have entered into are contrary to public policy, illegal and should be set aside to the fullest extent possible consistent with protecting the rights of innocent parties.

"These obligations are not mere theoretical concepts or idealistic abstractions of no practical force and effect; they are obligations imposed by the common law on public officers and assumed by them as a matter of law upon their entering public office. The enforcement of these obligations is essential to the soundness and efficiency of our government, which exists for the benefit of the people who are its sovereign. The citizen is not at the mercy of his servants holding positions of public trust nor is he helpless to secure relief from their machinations except through the medium of the ballot, the pressure of public opinion or criminal prosecution. He may secure relief in the civil courts either through an action brought in his own name, or through proceedings instituted on his behalf by the Governor. Under the former practice the great prerogative writs, especially *certiorari,* were generally available to the aggrieved citizen, but by art. VI, sec. V, par. 4 of the Constitution of 1947 the relief theretofore granted in such matters as a matter of judicial discretion became a matter of right...."

Manifestly the instant case falls within the pattern of the *Driscoll* case.

Restitution was likewise invoked in such cases as United States v. Carter, 217 U.S. 286, 30 S.Ct. 515, 54 L.Ed. 769 (1910), where the defendant, an army officer in charge of procurement, entered into an arrangement with two contractors by which he exercised his official discretion in such a way as to give them more contracts and more profits. The court traced his share in this enterprise into the hands of other defendants, who were not purchasers in good faith, and subjected the money to a constructive trust, saying:

"It would be a dangerous precedent to lay down as law that unless some affirmative fraud or loss can be shown, the agent may hold on to any secret benefit he may be able to make out of his agency. The larger interests of public justice will not tolerate, under any circumstances, that a public official shall retain any profit or advantage which he may realize through the acquirement of an interest in conflict with his fidelity as an agent. If he takes any gift, gratuity, or benefit in violation of his duty, or acquires any interest adverse to his principal, without a full disclosure, it is a betrayal of his trust and a breach of confidence, and he must account to his principal for all he has received.

"The doctrine is well established and has been applied in many relations of agency or trust. The disability results not from the subject-matter, but from the fiduciary character of the one against whom it is applied. It is founded on reason and the nature of the relation, and is of paramount importance. 'It is of no moment,' said Lord Thurlow, in The York Bldgs. Co. v. Mackenzie, 3 Paton, 378, 'what the particular name or description, whether of character or office, situation or position, is, on which the disability attaches.' "

. . . .

This view of the law is borne out by the American Law Institute *Restatement on Restitution:*

"Section 190, *General Rule:* Where a person in a fiduciary relation to another acquires property, and the acquisition or retention of the property is in violation of his duty as a fiduciary, he holds it upon a constructive trust for the other."

"Section 197, *Bonus or Commission Received by Fiduciary:* Where a fiduciary in violation of his duty to the beneficiary receives or retains a bonus or commission or other profit, he holds what he receives upon a constructive trust for the beneficiary."

"Comment: a) *Bribes and Commissions.* The rule stated in this section is applicable not only where the fiduciary receives something in the nature of a bribe given him by a third person in order to induce him to violate his duty as a fiduciary but also where something is given to him and received by him in good faith, if it was received for an act done by him in connection with the performance of his duties as fiduciary. . . ."

"c) *Where no Harm to Beneficiary.* The rule stated in this Section is applicable although the profit received by the fiduciary is not at the expense of the beneficiary. . . ."

As these decisions and the *Restatement* show, the development of the principle of restitution, both at law and in equity, as a remedy for breach by a public official of his fiduciary obligations has obviously been salutary. Restitution, by virtue of its adaptability to individual cases on equitable principles may, as we have seen, reach situations beyond the grasp of other civil or criminal remedies and do justice on equitable principles; see Driscoll v. Burlington–Bristol Bridge Co., 8 N.J. 433, at pages 497–504, 86 A.2d 201, where various alternatives were weighed with a view to working out justice so far as possible to all concerned, but always on the fundamental basis of preventing the unfaithful public official or public body profiting from his or its wrongdoing.

Applying these principles to the substance of the complaint we find that ... The first count sounds in restitution to permit the city to recover its property wrongfully taken by the defendant from it. Confusion results only from the language concerning the manner and means by which the taking of the property from the city was accomplished. On this count the city has the power to bring suit for the recovery of its property in the same manner as natural persons. The city itself is the real party in interest. The general description of the method used by the plaintiff satisfies R.R. 4:9–1, and to hold otherwise would do violence to the new practice.

To sustain the complaint all we need to find is that it sets forth at least one sufficient claim....

But the second count also alleges basically that it was unlawful for the employees of the city to pay consideration for obtaining or holding city employment, and that all such money extorted by the defendants "were subject to be forfeited [1] to the City for its own use and benefit, or [2] as trustee for the use and benefit of the employees." The second count involves at least the elements of a cause of action arising from the wrongful acts of the defendants, for the reasons set forth in Driscoll v. Burlington–Bristol Bridge Co., 8 N.J. 433, especially at pages 474–476, 86 A.2d 201, hereinbefore quoted. The general theory of recovery in the second count is that a constructive trust exists in favor of the city for the profit realized by its officials.

It was urged at the oral argument that the payments of city employees were voluntary political contributions, but the complaint contains no such allegations and therefore such facts are not before us.

. . . .

The acts alleged in the complaint, if true, were unlawful, improper, fraudulent and corrupt and it would be unconscionable for a court with equitable powers to add any dignity to such misconduct by refusing relief to a proper party. The City of Jersey City is the proper party, by the very nature of the allegations of the complaint, to seek to recover its own property wrongfully taken, to seek to recover property which in good conscience as between the parties to the suit belongs to the city or to right a wrong perpetrated upon its servants and inhabitants. Furthermore, it must be remembered that the court will not permit a trust to fail for the want of a trustee and that equity has the power to provide a trustee, if it should be necessary.

From the standpoint of substantive law the complaint states claims on which relief may be based.

. . . .

IV.   Conclusion.

The order appealed from is reversed and the cause remanded for further proceedings consistent herewith.

■ HEHER, J. (dissenting). The complaint is vague and uncertain in its allegations and fundamentally incongruous in the right of action pleaded and the relief sought.

. . . .

I would affirm the judgment, as grounded upon a complaint deficient in the statement of a cause of action.

Somerville v. Jacobs

Supreme Court of Appeals of West Virginia, 1969.
153 W.Va. 613, 170 S.E.2d 805.

■ HAYMOND, P. The plaintiffs, W.J. Somerville and Hazel M. Somerville, herein sometimes referred to as the plaintiffs, the owners of Lots 44, 45 and 46 in the Homeland Addition to the city of Parkersburg, in Wood County, believing that they were erecting a warehouse building on Lot 46 which they owned, mistakenly constructed the building on Lot 47 owned by the defendants, William L. Jacobs and Marjorie S. Jacobs, herein some-times referred to as the defendants. Construction of the building was completed in January 1967 and by deed dated January 14, 1967 the Somervilles conveyed Lots 44, 45 and 46 to the plaintiffs Fred C. Engle and Jimmy C. Pappas who subsequently leased the building to the Parkersburg Coca–Cola Bottling Company, a corporation. Soon after the building was completed but not until then, the defendants learned that the building was on their property and claimed ownership of the building and its fixtures on the theory of annexation. The plaintiffs then instituted this proceeding for equitable relief in the Circuit Court of Wood County and in their complaint prayed, among other things, for judgment in favor of the Somervilles for $20,500.00 as the value of the improvements made on Lot 47, or, in the alternative, that the defendants be ordered to convey their interest in Lot 47 to the Somervilles for a fair consideration. The Farmers Building and Loan Association, a corporation, the holder of a deed of trust lien upon the land of the defendants, was on motion permitted to intervene and be made a defendant in this proceeding.

. . . .

By final judgment rendered June 11, 1968, the circuit court required the defendants within 60 days to elect whether they would (1) retain the building and pay W.J. Somerville $17,500.00 or suffer judgment against themselves in his favor in that amount, or (2) convey title to Lot 47 of Homeland Addition to W.J. Somerville for the sum of $2,000.00 cash. From that judgment this Court granted an appeal and supersedeas upon applica-tion of the defendants on October 17, 1968.

. . . .

The controlling question for decision is whether a court of equity can award compensation to an improver for improvements which he has placed upon land not owned by him, which, because of mistake, he had reason to believe he owned, which improvements were not known to the owner until after their completion and were not induced or permitted by such owner, who is not guilty of any fraud or inequitable conduct, and require the owner to pay the fair value of such improvements or, in the alternative, to convey the land so improved to the improver upon his payment to the owner of the fair value of the land less the value of the improvements.

. . . .

Though the precise question here involved has not been considered and determined in any prior decision of this Court, the question has been considered by appellate courts in other jurisdictions and though the cases are conflicting the decisions in some jurisdictions, upon particular facts, recognize and sustain the jurisdiction of a court of equity to award compensation to the improver to prevent unjust enrichment to the owner and in the alternative to require the owner to convey the land to the improver upon his payment to the owner of the fair value of the land less the improvements.

In the early case of Bright v. Boyd, 4 Fed.Cas. p. 127, No. 1875, 1 Story 478 and 4 Fed.Cas. p. 134, No. 1876, 2 Story 605, a Federal trial court held in an opinion by Justice Story that an improving occupant could institute and maintain a suit in equity to secure compensation for his improvements on land of the owner and that as a doctrine of equity an innocent purchaser for valuable consideration, without notice of any infirmity in his title, who by his improvements added to the permanent value of the owner is entitled to compensation for the value of the improvements and to a lien upon the land which its owner must discharge before he can be restored to his original rights in the land.

. . . .

From the foregoing authorities it is manifest that equity has jurisdiction to, and will, grant relief to one who, through a reasonable mistake of fact and in good faith, places permanent improvements upon land of another, with reason to believe that the land so improved is that of the one who makes the improvements, and that the plaintiffs are entitled to the relief which they seek in this proceeding.

The undisputed facts, set forth in the agreed statement of counsel representing all parties, is that the plaintiff W.J. Somerville in placing the warehouse building upon Lot 47 entertained a reasonable belief based on the report of the surveyor that it was Lot 46, which he owned, and that the building was constructed by him because of a reasonable mistake of fact and in the good faith belief that he was constructing a building on his own property and he did not discover his mistake until after the building was completed. It is equally clear that the defendants who spent little if any time in the neighborhood were unaware of the construction of the building until after it was completed and were not at any time or in any way guilty of any fraud or inequitable conduct or of any act that would constitute an estoppel. In short, the narrow issue here is between two innocent parties and the solution of the question requires the application of principles of equity and fair dealing between them.

It is clear that the defendants claim the ownership of the building. Under the common law doctrine of annexation, the improvements passed to them as part of the land. This is conceded by the plaintiffs but they assert that the defendants can not keep and retain it without compensating them for the value of the improvements, and it is clear from the testimony of the defendant William L. Jacobs in his deposition that the defendants intend to keep and retain the improvements and refuse to compensate the plaintiffs for their value. The record does not disclose any express request by the plaintiffs for permission to remove the building from the premises if that could be done without its destruction, which is extremely doubtful as the building was constructed of solid concrete blocks on a concrete slab, and it is reasonably clear, from the claim of the defendants of their ownership of the building and their insistence that certain fixtures which have been removed from the building be replaced, that the defendants will not consent to the removal of the building even if that could be done.

In that situation if the defendants retain the building and refuse to pay any sum as compensation to the plaintiff W.J. Somerville they will be unjustly enriched in the amount of $17,500.00, the agreed value of the building, which is more than eight and one-half times the agreed $2,000.00 value of the lot of the defendants on which it is located, and by the retention of the building by the defendants the plaintiff W.J. Somerville will suffer a total loss of the amount of the value of the building. If, however, the defendants are unable or unwilling to pay for the building which they intend to keep but, in the alternative, would convey the lot upon which the building is constructed to the plaintiff W.J. Somerville upon payment of the sum of $2,000.00, the agreed value of the lot without the improvements, the plaintiffs would not lose the building and the defendants would suffer no financial loss because they would obtain payment for the agreed full value of the lot and the only hardship imposed upon the defendants, if this were required, would be to order them to do something which they are unwilling to do voluntarily. To compel the performance of such an act by litigants is not uncommon in litigation in which the rights of the parties are involved and are subject to determination by equitable principles. And the right to require the defendants to convey the lot to the plaintiff W.J. Somerville is recognized and sustained by numerous cases cited earlier in this opinion. Under the facts and circumstances of this case, if the defendants refuse and are not required to exercise their option either to pay W.J. Somerville the value of the improvements or to convey to him the lot on which they are located upon his payment of the agreed value, the defendants will be unduly and unjustly enriched at the expense of the plaintiff W.J. Somerville who will suffer the complete loss of the warehouse building which by bona fide mistake of fact he constructed upon the land of the defendants. Here, in that situation, to use the language of the Supreme Court of Michigan in Hardy v. Burroughs, 251 Mich. 578, 232 N.W. 200, "It is not equitable ... that defendants profit by plaintiffs' innocent mistake, that defendants take all and plaintiffs nothing."

To prevent such unjust enrichment of the defendants, and to do equity between the parties, this Court holds that an improver of land owned by another, who through a reasonable mistake of fact and in good faith erects a building entirely upon the land of the owner, with reasonable belief that such land was owned by the improver, is entitled to recover the value of the improvements from the landowner and to a lien upon such property which may be sold to enforce the payment of such lien, or, in the alternative, to purchase the land so improved upon payment to the landowner of the value of the land less the improvements and such landowner, even though free from any inequitable conduct in connection with the construction of the building upon his land, who, however, retains but refuses to pay for the improvements, must, within a reasonable time, either pay the improver the amount by which the value of his land has been improved or convey such land to the improver upon the payment by the improver to the landowner of the value of the land without the improvements.

It is pertinent to observe that, in cases involving the right to recover for improvements placed by mistake upon land owned by one other than the improver, the solution of the questions involved depends largely upon the circumstances and the equities involved in each particular case. Here, under the facts as stipulated by the parties, the equities which control the decision are clearly in favor of the plaintiffs.

. . . .

The judgment of the Circuit Court of Wood County is affirmed.

Affirmed.

■ CAPLAN, J., dissenting: . . . .

. . . .

In my opinion for the court to permit the plaintiff to force the defendants to sell their property contrary to their wishes is unthinkable and unpardonable. This is nothing less than condemnation of private property by private parties for private use. . . .

I am aware of the doctrine that equity frowns on unjust enrichment. However, contrary to the view expressed by the majority, I am of the opinion that the circumstances of this case do not warrant the application of such doctrine. It clearly is the accepted law that as between two parties in the circumstances of this case he who made the mistake must suffer the hardship rather than he who was without fault.

I would reverse the judgment of the Circuit Court of Wood County and remand the case to that court with directions that the trial court give the defendant, Jacobs, the party without fault, the election of purchasing the building, of selling the property, *or* of requiring the plaintiff to remove the building from defendant's property.

I am authorized to say that Judge Berry concurs in the views expressed in this dissenting opinion.

Shick v. Dearmore

Supreme Court of Arkansas, 1969.
246 Ark. 1209, 442 S.W.2d 198.

■ SMITH, J. In 1967 the appellee, Ben Dearmore, sold a vacant residential lot to Norbert Nelson, who was to pay for the lot in monthly installments over a period of two years. Nelson took possession of the lot by moving a trailer house to it and began the construction of a permanent dwelling house on the land. Nelson employed the appellant [(Shick)], a well driller, to drill a water well on the property. Shick successfully completed a well by drilling to a depth of 284 feet and installing 191 feet of pipe. Nelson ran out of money without having paid Dearmore for the lot or Shick for the water well. Nelson abandoned the project and apparently left the state, his whereabouts thereafter being unknown.

Later on it was learned that Nelson and Shick had made a mistake in locating the well, which was actually drilled at a point a few inches past Nelson's boundary line and upon an adjoining lot also owned by Dearmore. When Shick threatened to assert a well-driller's lien against the lot, Dearmore brought this suit in equity to enjoin Shick from either claiming a lien or destroying the well. By counter-claim Shick asserted that Nelson had acted as Dearmore's agent in employing Shick to drill the well. Shick asked that he be given judgment against Dearmore for the contract price of $992, that the judgment be declared a lien upon the land, that the lien be foreclosed, and that Shick have such other relief as he might be entitled to.

At the trial Shick, not having Nelson as a witness, was unable to prove the asserted agency. Dearmore testified that Nelson had not been authorized by Dearmore to contract for the well and that Dearmore knew nothing about the drilling until the well had been completed. At the end of the trial the chancellor apparently ruled in Dearmore's favor but went on to say that Shick might remove the pipe and restore the land as nearly as possible to its original condition. Upon objection, however, the court invited briefs on the question and later rendered a decree holding that the casing installed in the well was a permanent improvement that became part of the realty; so Shick had no right to remove it. This appeal is from that decree.

. . . .

We are convinced that in a court of equity Shick should be given the right to remove the casing and restore the land to its original condition, if that can be done without damaging the land. Any other holding would allow Dearmore to be unjustly enriched by obtaining a flowing water well to which he has no equitable claim.

The chancellor followed the strict common-law rule in holding that a permanent improvement placed upon another's land by mistake becomes a part of the realty and cannot be removed. Such a rule is obviously unjust when the improvement can be removed without damage to the freehold. Justice Joseph Story, while trying a case in Maine as circuit justice, first pointed out the inequities of the common-law rule and refused to follow it in a proceeding in equity. . . . [M]any cases . . . have adopted Justice Story's view. . . .

When the Restatement of Restitution was published in 1937 the American Law Institute took the position in § 42 that the harshness of the common-law rule had been mitigated in most states at least to the extent of allowing restitution as a defense or set-off to affirmative relief sought by the landowner. Since then the steady trend of the decisions has been to allow the removal of the improvements in an equitable proceeding whenever that course can be followed without substantial damage to the land. . . .

We are so strongly in favor of the equitable view that has been taken more and more widely in the past several decades that we have no hesitancy in adopting it in the case at hand. Thus the chancellor's immediate reaction at the close of the proof was right—that Shick should be allowed to remove his casing and restore the land to its original condition. It is not entirely clear, however, that such a course can be followed without damage to the land that might fairly be considered to be substantial when compared to the pecuniary loss that Shick would otherwise sustain. Pursuant to our discretionary power to remand a chancery case for further proof, we think it best to remand this cause to give the parties an opportunity to develop the proof upon the point mentioned, with leave to the chancellor to dispose of the matter by an award according to the principles of equity.

Reversed and remanded.

■ FOGLEMAN, J. (dissenting). I respectfully dissent. The majority opinion, based upon the chancellor's finding that this fixture is a permanent improvement, allows appellant to come upon the land and reclaim it. However equitable this result may seem in this case, it amounts to an overruling of a long standing rule of property, i.e., that permanent fixtures become part of the realty and belong to the owner thereof. We have held on several occasions, upon a finding that the fixture was a permanent improvement, that it cannot be removed from the land because it has become a part of the realty.

The cases cited by the majority, except one, all involve situations where equity has granted some sort of remunerative relief to a person who has mistakenly placed a permanent improvement on another's property. They are not support for the relief granted by the court here. Admittedly Citizens & Southern Nat. Bank v. Modern Homes Const. Co., 248 S.C. 130, 149 S.E.2d 326 (1966) allows the removal of improvements where it can be done without substantial damage to the land, but the short answer to this is that it is not the law in Arkansas. . . .

. . . .

■ HARRIS, C.J., joins in this dissent.

NOTES

1. *Jersey City, Somerville,* and *Shick* involve restitution in equity rather than law. The first two cases illustrate the fact that equity can, in cases within its jurisdiction, give a form of restitutionary relief that is analogous to quasi-contract.

2. Traditionally, equity alone addressed the question, raised by *Somerville* and *Shick,* of the rights of a good faith improver of land. This question has been resolved in a number of other ways by different courts. Consider, for example, the approaches taken in Peters v. Archambault (Chapter 7, *supra* p. 482) and Miceli v. Riley, which is discussed in the notes accompanying Graf v. Hope Building Corp. (in Chapter 1, *supra* p. 16).

In Comer v. Roberts, 252 Or. 189, 448 P.2d 543 (1968), the defendant mistakenly drilled a well on Roberts' adjacent property. Comer brought ejectment, and Roberts sought affirmative equitable relief. The trial court's decree ordering Comer to transfer to Roberts the one-eleventh of an acre on which the well stood in return for a payment of $500 was affirmed.

3. Section 42 of the Restatement of Restitution, which is referred to in *Schick,* reads as follows:

IMPROVEMENTS UPON LAND OR CHATTELS.

(1) Except to the extent that the rule is changed by statute, a person who, in the mistaken belief that he or a third person on whose account he acts is the owner, has caused improvements to be made upon the land of another, is not thereby entitled to restitution from the owner for the value of such improvements; but if his mistake was reasonable, the owner is entitled to obtain judgment in an equitable proceeding or in an action of trespass or other action for the mesne profits only on condition that he makes restitution to the extent that the land has been increased in value by such improvements, or for the value of the labor and materials employed in making such improvements, whichever is least.

Comment on Subsection (1):

c. Aside from statute, the harshness of the common law rule which allows no action for restitution has been mitigated in certain situations. Thus a court of equity requires one seeking its assistance against an improver of land to do equity by making compensation a condition to relief, and in actions at law brought to recover damages for the improver's occupation of the land he is entitled to have deducted from the claim against him the value of his improvements. . . .

Illustrations:

1. In a jurisdiction in which there is no statute with reference thereto, A, in possession of and mistakenly believing that he owns Blackacre, builds a house thereon. A is not thereby entitled to restitution from B, the owner.

2. Same facts as in Illustration 1, except that B brings an action of ejectment against A. A is not entitled to have the judgment of ejectment contain a proviso that B shall reimburse A, except in those jurisdictions in which the action of ejectment is equitable in nature.

3. Same facts as in Illustration 1, except that B gains possession of the land and brings a bill to remove the cloud on title created by A's occupancy. B is entitled to relief only upon paying A the reasonable value of the improvements.

4. Same facts as in Illustration 1, except that B brings an action for mesne profits because of A's occupancy. A is entitled to have the value of the improvements deducted from the sum otherwise found to be due.

Some statutes deal with the question of the "good faith improver." The West's Ann.Cal.Code Civ.Proc. § 871.3(b), for example, provides that:

In every case, the burden is on the good faith improver to establish that he is entitled to relief under this chapter, and the degree of negligence of the good faith improver should be taken into account by the court in determining whether the improver acted in good faith and in determining the relief, if any, that is consistent with substantial justice to the parties under the circumstances of the particular case.

Paramount Film Distributing Corp. v. State

Court of Appeals of New York, 1972.
30 N.Y.2d 415, 334 N.Y.S.2d 388, 285 N.E.2d 695.

■ Breitel, J. Claimant, a motion picture distributor, seeks recovery of $128,322.50 in motion picture license fees paid to the State from June 10, 1959 to June 10, 1965 when the applicable statutes were nullified (Education Law, Consol.Laws, c. 16, §§ 120–132; Matter of Trans–Lux Distr. Corp. v. Board of Regents, 16 N.Y.2d 710, 261 N.Y.S.2d 903, 209 N.E.2d 558, on remand from the United States Supreme Court, 380 U.S. 259, 85 S.Ct. 952, 13 L.Ed.2d 959). The fee for original films was $3.50 for each 1,000 feet of film while the fee for copies was $3 plus an additional dollar for each 1,000 feet. Although over a six-year period the fees aggregate an impressive sum, the fee per motion picture distributed in New York was only an inconsiderable expense compared to the cost of production, most often less than $10. Claimant had paid all but a trivial portion of the fees without protest and had not otherwise ever resisted the statutory procedure for licensing or the payment of fees.

On the prior appeal in the Trans–Lux case this court, in upholding the denial of a motion picture license, passed only on the propriety of denying a license for the particular motion picture in suit. The validity of the licensing statute, extant in some form since 1927, its procedure, and the fees charged were not in issue. Motion picture licensing generally had been held valid by the Supreme Court, and indeed in Freedman v. Maryland, 380 U.S. 51, 85 S.Ct. 734, 13 L.Ed.2d 649, the case upon which the *Trans–Lux* order was reversed, the Supreme Court went out of its way to observe that a requirement of prior submission of motion pictures to a licensing board need not be unconstitutional. The *Freedman* case nullified the Maryland statute only because its procedural "apparatus" violated due process in not providing for prompt judicial review. Since the New York procedure was similar to Maryland's, this court on remand declared the New York statute null.

A majority at the Appellate Division sustained claimant's right to recover all fees paid since 1959. While $128,322.50 plus interest is now involved, other cases pending bring the claims to just under $2,000,000.

As posed by the parties, the issue is whether the payments of the license fees were voluntary, or involuntary under duress entitling the payor to recover, albeit the payments were made without protest or other action to resist the payments or to recover them.

Two leading New York cases mark clearly when there is a right to recover unprotested taxes or fees.

In Mercury Mach. Importing Corp. v. City of New York, 3 N.Y.2d 418, 165 N.Y.S.2d 517, 144 N.E.2d 400 this court, over vigorous dissent it is true, held that corporate taxpayers who voluntarily paid an illegally levied tax without protest were not entitled to refunds although the statute under which the taxes were paid was subsequently held unconstitutional. The fulcrum of the determination was the relatively new section of the Civil Practice Act which provided that a mistake being one of law for that reason alone did not forbid recovery for mistake. The taxpayers had made a mistake of law, namely, as to the validity of the taxing statute, but it was held that the mistake did not render the payment involuntary. It was pointed out that in a sense no tax is paid willingly, free from the coercion of law. The precedents were collated and classified and it is unnecessary to repeat what was done there.

In Five Boro Elec. Contrs. Assn. v. City of New York, 12 N.Y.2d 146, 237 N.Y.S.2d 315, 187 N.E.2d 774 this court again in an opinion by Judge Van Voorhis, who had written for the court in the *Mercury* case, but this time with unanimous concurrence of the court, permitted the recovery of license fees paid under a city local law without protest by licensed electricians. The distinction was made that the payments then in question were involuntary and under duress, because the electricians would otherwise have been barred from engaging in their occupations. The court held that protest was not required "under the circumstances of this case ... in view of the compulsory nature of the payment of these exorbitant license fees." Most important, the fees themselves had been the subject of a previous successful attack and the exaction declared unconstitutional because the amounts bore no reasonable relation to the licensing and regulation of electricians under a nonrevenue statute. Again the same authorities cited in the *Mercury* case were reviewed and the distinctions there made repeated to explain the difference in result between the two cases.

The *Mercury* and *Five Boro* cases are not aberrational. They conform generally with distinctions made throughout the country between voluntary and involuntary payments of taxes or fees later declared void, and the necessity for protest in the case of voluntary payments.

Applying the distinctions to this case, the payments by claimant were voluntary, and in the absence of protest at the time, claimant is not entitled to recover the fees it paid just because in a collateral matter on grounds not applicable to it or ever raised by it, the statute has been declared null.

The test of voluntariness in cases involving taxes and fees is sometimes elusive and difficult of application. As noted earlier by Judge Van Voorhis, all taxes and fees in a sense are paid "involuntarily". The difference is often, if not always, one of degree and turns on many factors, including the right of taxing authorities to rely on objection if there be resistance to payment, the likelihood that authentic resistance will be asserted, the unavoidable drastic impact of the taxes or fees on the claimant, and the impact on the public fisc, if revenues raised long ago and expended are subject to reimbursement. Surely one would expect motion picture distributors, and especially a corporation as large as claimant with its staff of lawyers, to protest if the fees were thought illegal. Indeed, the failure to protest indicates that there was no authentic resistance to making the minimal payments for the extensive procedures in licensing motion pictures whose gross yield would be massive compared to the trivial fees imposed.

Moreover, the fees as such have never been held illegal or excessive but on the contrary sustained, and the regulatory services which the fees financed have long ago been rendered and the cost undoubtedly passed on to the patrons of the films. The *Trans–Lux* case and the *Freedman* case each involved a license requirement to exhibit a motion picture, and the requirements were overturned because of the invalid procedure under the statute. On the other hand, the fees sought to be recovered in this case were reasonable tariffs for motion picture licensing and the films were actually licensed. Notably, in the *Freedman* case the Supreme Court reiterated its prior holdings that motion pictures were properly subject to licensing and the payment of license fees. . . .

What has been said so far assumes, as the parties have assumed, that restitution is appropriate unless it can be shown that claimant paid its license fees voluntarily. But, if general principles of restitution were to be reached, even if one assumes involuntary or coerced payment, those general principles do not support restitution.

The essential inquiry in any action for unjust enrichment or restitution is whether it is against equity and good conscience to permit the defendant to retain what is sought to be recovered. Such a claim is undoubtedly equitable and depends upon broad considerations of equity and justice. Generally, courts will look to see if a benefit has been conferred on the defendant under mistake of fact or law, if the benefit still remains with the defendant, if there has been otherwise a change of position by the defendant, and whether the defendant's conduct was tortious or fraudulent.

It is difficult to say that the State has received any benefit, let alone unjust enrichment. The fees defrayed the cost of the licensing program, a program which, at least, was intended to further the interests of both the industry and the public. The statute was not a revenue measure, and, *inter alia,* it exacted a regulatory fee to support the program. The difference between regulatory fees and revenue imposts, the latter including unauthorized excessive regulatory fees paid involuntarily, also distinguishes this case from the *Five Boro* case.

Moreover, the funds have been disbursed long ago. Nor has the State acted tortiously or fraudulently in exacting the fees. The implications of this court's holding in *Trans–Lux* invalidating the statute for reasons distinct from the power to collect fees has already been noted. That the exactions were themselves proper and not tortious, fraudulent, or illegal, and that they have been consumed is significant. Generally, if a plaintiff's recovery will lead to an undue net loss to a defendant by reason of a changed position, as will often be the case when the funds have been disbursed, then the parties being equally innocent, recovery may be denied.

In summary, the payment of license fees without protest was voluntary for purposes of recovery of moneys paid as fees or taxes; hence, no recovery for the fees collected without protest or other resistance may be allowed. Since a small percentage of fees were paid under protest between March and June, 1965, the matter should be remanded so that such fees may be computed, and recovery allowed.

Accordingly, the order of the Appellate Division should be reversed, with one bill of costs, and the action remanded for further proceedings in accordance with this opinion.

■ BERGAN, J. (dissenting). . . .

[On remand in *Trans–Lux,* the court held] that the entire statute "is null and void", a decision embracing the fee provisions. This much must be said about the belief of the majority that the fees as such have never been held illegal.

. . . .

What seems decisive in the majority's summation of the grounds for decision here is that claimant's "payment of license fees without protest was voluntary for purposes of recovery of moneys paid as fees or taxes". On this aspect of the case, at least, *Five Boro* appears to be indistinguishable and it should be overruled or followed. The need for protest, and not the uses to which the fees were put, was decisive in *Five Boro*. The rule for licensed electricians and licensed motion picture exhibitors should be pretty much the same.

Thus the difference between regulatory fees and revenue imposts played no part in the announced reasons for decision in *Five Boro* and is not a ground to distinguish the present case. . . .

That the State used the proceeds of the license fees collected under the statute in the licensing operation itself does not for the purposes of this case distinguish it from one where the fee or tax is used for general State purposes. Here the program of inspection and licensing expressed in the statute was responsive to the State's belief in the value of censorship to protect public morals and elevate public taste, and so in furtherance of a general public policy. No benefit to the business of motion picture exhibitors was intended or demonstrated in the experience with censorship.

It is true, as the majority has observed, that an action for recovery for unjust enrichment or restitution should appeal to equity and good conscience and this principle ought to apply to an action such as the present one.

Here the good conscience in issue is that of the sovereign which collected the fees under the compulsion of a statute which the sovereign State itself, by its highest court, advisedly held to be "null and void". It seems the part of fair dealing to turn the money back.

The sum is large for the taxpayers as well as the State. As Judge Fuld noted in dissent in *Mercury*: "Modern and enlightened tax administration frowns upon the imposition of technical obstacles to the refunding of illegally collected taxes."

The order should be affirmed.

■ BURKE, SCILEPPI and JASEN, JJ., concur with BREITEL, J.

■ BERGAN, J., dissents and votes to affirm in a separate opinion in which FULD, C.J., and GIBSON, J., concur.

Order reversed, with costs, and case remitted to the Court of Claims for further proceedings in accordance with the opinion herein.

CHAPTER 11

THE CONSTRUCTIVE TRUST AND RELATED REMEDIES

A. THE CONSTRUCTIVE TRUST: A REMEDIAL DEVICE[1]

POUND, *PROGRESS OF THE LAW, 1918–1919—EQUITY*, 33 HARV. L. REV. 420–421 (1920). "An express trust is a substantive institution. Constructive trust, on the other hand, is purely a remedial institution. As the chancellor acted *in personam,* one of the most effective remedial expedients at his command was to treat a defendant as if he were a trustee and put pressure upon his person to compel him to act accordingly. Thus constructive trust could be used in a variety of situations, sometimes to provide a remedy better suited to the circumstances of the particular case, where the suit was founded on another theory, as in cases of reformation, of specific performance, of fraudulent conveyance, and of what the civilian would call exclusion of unworthy heirs, and sometimes to develop a new field of equitable interposition, as in what we have come to think the typical case of constructive trust, namely, specific restitution of a received benefit in order to prevent unjust enrichment. In the latter case, constructive trust appears as what might be called a remedial doctrine. . . ."

NOTE BY DEAN AMES ON "TRUSTS OF CHATTELS" [2]

"An express trust of a chattel is of course, enforceable in equity. Indeed, since the trustee has the legal title, and there is no common law contract, the jurisdiction of equity is exclusive.

"As to the constructive trusts a distinction must be made.

"If one acquires from the plaintiff by a tort the title to a chattel, or unconscionably retains a title, honestly acquired from the plaintiff, equity might, with propriety, compel him, as a constructive trustee, to reconvey the chattel, just as in early times decrees were made for the payment of money got by fraud, or though properly acquired, unjustly withheld, as in the case of failure of consideration. But at the present day the defrauded person must seek his relief at law, unless damages for the deceit would be

---

1. *See* Gegan, *Constructive Trusts: A New Basis for Tracing Equities*, 53 ST. JOHN'S L. REV. 593 (1979).

2. [This note was a footnote to the case of Wood v. Rowcliffe, 3 Hare 304 (Chancery 1844) set forth in 1 AMES, A SELECTION OF CASES IN EQUITY JURISDICTION (with notes and citations) 43–44 (1923). Prior editions appeared in 1902 and 1904. Professor Chafee, in later editions, placed the note in the text. 1 CHAFEE AND SIMPSON, CASES ON EQUITY 257 (1934). Many cases are cited.]

an inadequate remedy, either because of the peculiar nature of the chattel, or because of the insolvency of the defendant.

"If, on the other hand, a wrongdoer acquires the title to a chattel from a third person by the misuse of the plaintiffs property; if, for example, a fiduciary, a fraudulent purchaser, or a converter, by a breach of trust or a wrongful transfer of the fraudulently acquired or converted property, acquires in exchange the legal title to a chattel, equity will compel him to hold the newly acquired chattel in trust for the plaintiff. The cases in support of the doctrine that a fiduciary holds the product of the trust fund for the beneficiary are legion.... The authorities in favor of the rule that a fraudulent purchaser or a converter come within the same rule, though less numerous, are decisive...."—AMES.

———

RESTATEMENT, SECOND, RESTITUTION § 30 (Tent. Draft No. 2, 1984). *"Constructive Trust and Equitable Lien,*

"(1) A constructive trust or an equitable lien as described in this Chapter is a right to restitution from property, conferred as a means of preventing unjust enrichment. Such a trust or lien attaches only to the extent that the property is held by a person who owes restitution to the claimant.

"(2) If property is held subject to a constructive trust, the holder must account to the claimant as having beneficial ownership of the property. If property is held subject to an equitable lien, the holder must account for the property as security for his obligation to make restitution to the claimant. A constructive trust or an equitable lien may be appropriate means of effecting restitution in identical circumstances.

"(3) Property subject to a constructive trust or an equitable lien may be title to, or a limited or fractional interest in, one or more assets, either tangible or intangible."

RESTATEMENT, SECOND, RESTITUTION § 32 (Tent.Draft No. 2, 1984). *"Right to Restitution from Property: Relation of Property to Claim*

"A person claiming restitution from property under § 30 (Constructive Trust and Equitable Lien) will be granted such a remedy only if his claim relates to the property in one of the following ways:

"(a) the property was acquired from the claimant by wrongful conduct, or was transferred by the claimant's mistake,

"(b) the claimant was prevented from acquiring the property through wrongdoing or mistaken action,

"(c) loss was caused to the claimant by such an acquisition, or act of prevention, and the existence or value of the property

"(d) the existence or value of the property represents, at least in part, an infringement of an interest of the claimant, or "(e) the holder of the property contributed to its existence or value in knowing disregard of duty to the claimant, so that the remedy is required to prevent injustice (see 8 33)."

RESTATEMENT, SECOND, RESTITUTION § 33 (Tent. Draft No. 2, 1984). *"Restitution from Property Based on Particular Wrongs*

"(1) If a holder of property has prevented an exact showing of the relation between his interest and a claimant's right to restitution from him, and the requirements of §§ 30 and 32 would otherwise be satisfied, a constructive trust or an equitable lien will be imposed on that interest according to any reasonably certain standard by which the extent of the remedy can be determined.

"(2) If the holder of property has acquired it as a replacement for another asset of known value, and owes restitution to a claimant who could have enforced against the holder an agreement to preserve or replace that asset, a constructive trust or an equitable lien will be imposed on the holder's interest according to § 30 and clause (e) of § 32."

■ CARDOZO, J., IN BEATTY v. GUGGENHEIM EXPLORATION CO., 225 N.Y. 380, 122 N.E. 378 (1919): "We think the situation is one where an employer, not consenting to the investment, would have the privilege, if he so elected, to hold the plaintiff as trustee.

"The plaintiff [agent] was sent to the Yukon to investigate mining claims which were the subject of an option. He found certain other claims which were not included in the option, but which he believed to be essential to the successful operation of those that were included. In conjunction with Perry, he purchased rights in the new claims. The two were partners in the venture. Later his employer, appreciating the importance of the claims, determined to buy them for itself. We think it had the right to say to the agent that he must renounce the profits of the transaction and transfer the claims at cost. A different situation would be presented if the claims had no relation to those which the plaintiff was under a duty to investigate. But they had an intimate relation. One could not profitably be operated without the other. Let us suppose that the plaintiff, instead of buying the claims as a partner with Perry, had bought them alone. No one, we think, would say that he could have retained them against his employer, and held out for an extravagant price, as, of course, he could have done if the purchase was not affected by a trust. It is not an answer to say that he was not bound to risk his money as he did, or to go into the enterprise at all. *Rose v. Hayden*, 35 Kan. 106, 118, 10 Pac. 554. He might have kept out of it altogether, but if he went in he could not withhold from his employer the benefit of the bargain.

"We think, therefore, that aside from the special provisions of this contract, the agent became a trustee at the election of the principal. But the contract re–enforces that conclusion. A constructive trust is the formula through which the conscience of equity finds expression. When property has been acquired in such circumstances that the holder of the legal title may not in good conscience retain the beneficial interest, equity converts him into a trustee. *Moore v. Crawford*, 130 U.S. 122, 128, 9 Sup.Ct. 447, 32 L.Ed. 878; POMEROY, EQ. JUR. § 1053. We think it would be against good conscience for the plaintiff to retain these profits unless his employer has consented. The tie was close between the employer's business and the forbidden venture. The profits which the agent claims have come from the employer's coffers. If the agent must account as a trustee, the price which the employer pays is to that extent diminished. If the agent retains the profit, the price is to that extent increased. Of course it is true that if Perry had made the purchase alone, without the aid of plaintiff, the employer might be no better off. That is true whenever an agent goes into some competing venture. His associates might have succeeded in diverting equal profits without him. The disability is personal to him. Others may divert profits from the business of the principal. He may not. If he does, he must account for them.

"We conclude, therefore, that the plaintiff was chargeable as a trustee if the employer so elected. . . .

"A court of equity in decreeing a constructive trust is bound by no unyielding formula. The equity of the transaction must shape the measure of relief . . . "

Snepp v. United States

Supreme Court of the United States, 1980.
444 U.S. 507, 100 S.Ct. 763, 62 L.Ed.2d 704.

■ PER CURIAM. . . .

I

Based on his experiences as a CIA agent, Snepp published a book about certain CIA activities in South Vietnam. Snepp published the account without submitting it to the Agency for prepublication review. As an express condition of his employment with the CIA in 1968, however, Snepp had executed an agreement promising that he would "not . . . publish . . . any information or material relating to the Agency, its activities or intelligence activities generally, either during or after the term of [his] employment . . . without specific prior approval of the Agency." The promise was an integral part of Snepp's concurrent undertaking "not to disclose any classified information relating to the Agency without proper authorization." Thus, Snepp had pledged not to divulge *classified* information and not to publish *any* information without prepublication clearance. The Government brought this suit to enforce Snepp's agreement. It sought a declaration that Snepp had breached the contract, an injunction requiring Snepp to submit future writings for prepublication review, and an order imposing a constructive trust for the Government's benefit on all profits that Snepp might earn from publishing the book in violation of his fiduciary obligations to the Agency.[2]

---

2. At the time of suit, Snepp already had received about $60,000 in advance payments. His contract with his publisher provides for royalties and other potential profits.

The District Court found that Snepp had "willfully, deliberately and surreptitiously breached his position of trust with the CIA and the [1968] secrecy agreement" by publishing his book without submitting it for prepublication review. The court also found that Snepp deliberately misled CIA officials into believing that he would submit the book for prepublication clearance. Finally, the court determined as a fact that publication of the book had "caused the United States irreparable harm and loss." The District Court therefore enjoined future breaches of Snepp's agreement and imposed a constructive trust on Snepp's profits.

The Court of Appeals accepted the findings of the District Court and agreed that Snepp had breached a valid contract.[3] It specifically affirmed the findings that Snepp's failure to submit his manuscript for prepublication review had inflicted "irreparable harm" on intelligence activities vital to our national security. Thus, the court upheld the injunction against future violations of Snepp's prepublication obligation. The court, however, concluded that the record did not support imposition of a constructive trust. The conclusion rested on the court's perception that Snepp had a First Amendment right to publish unclassified information and the Government's concession—for the purposes of this litigation—that Snepp's book divulged no classified intelligence. In other words, the court thought that Snepp's fiduciary obligation extended only to preserving the confidentiality of classified material. It therefore limited recovery to nominal damages and to the possibility of punitive damages if the Government—in a jury trial— could prove tortious conduct.

Judge Hoffman, sitting by designation, dissented from the refusal to find a constructive trust. The 1968 agreement, he wrote, "was no ordinary contract; it gave life to a fiduciary relationship and invested in Snepp the trust of the CIA." Prepublication clearance was part of Snepp's undertaking to protect confidences associated with his trust. Punitive damages, Judge Hoffman argued, were both a speculative and inappropriate remedy for Snepp's breach. We agree with Judge Hoffman that Snepp breached a fiduciary obligation and that the proceeds of his breach are impressed with a constructive trust.

II

Snepp's employment with the CIA involved an extremely high degree of trust. In the opening sentence of the agreement that he signed, Snepp

---

3. The Court of Appeals and the District Court rejected each of Snepp's defenses to the enforcement of his contract. In his petition for certiorari, Snepp relies primarily on the claim that his agreement is unenforceable as a prior restraint on protected speech.

When Snepp accepted employment with the CIA, he voluntarily signed the agreement that expressly obligated him to submit any proposed publication for prior review.... Moreover, this Court's cases make clear that—even in the absence of an express agreement—the CIA could have acted to protect substantial government interests by imposing reasonable restrictions on employee activities that in other contexts might be protected by the First Amendment. The Government has a compelling interest in protecting both the secrecy of information important to our national security and the appearance of confidentiality so essential to the effective operation of our foreign intelligence service. The agreement that Snepp signed is a reasonable means for protecting this vital interest.

explicitly recognized that he was entering a trust relationship. The trust agreement specifically imposed the obligation not to publish *any* information relating to the Agency without submitting the information for clearance. Snepp stipulated at trial that—after undertaking this obligation—he had been "assigned to various positions of trust" and that he had been granted "frequent access to classified information, including information regarding intelligence sources and methods." Snepp published his book about CIA activities on the basis of this background and exposure. He deliberately and surreptitiously violated his obligation to submit all material for prepublication review. Thus, he exposed the classified information with which he had been entrusted to the risk of disclosure.

Whether Snepp violated his trust does not depend upon whether his book actually contained classified information. The Government does not deny—as a general principle—Snepp's right to publish unclassified information. Nor does it contend—at this stage of the litigation—that Snepp's book contains classified material. The Government simply claims that, in light of the special trust reposed in him and the agreement that he signed, Snepp should have given the CIA an opportunity to determine whether the material he proposed to publish would compromise classified information or sources. Neither of the Government's concessions undercuts its claim that Snepp's failure to submit to prepublication review was a breach of his trust.

Both the District Court and the Court of Appeals found that a former intelligence agent's publication of unreviewed material relating to intelligence activities can be detrimental to vital national interests even if the published information is unclassified. When a former agent relies on his own judgment about what information is detrimental, he may reveal information that the CIA—with its broader understanding of what may expose classified information and confidential sources—could have identified as harmful. In addition to receiving intelligence from domestically based or controlled sources, the CIA obtains information from the intelligence services of friendly nations and from agents operating in foreign countries. The continued availability of these foreign sources depends upon the CIA's ability to guarantee the security of information that might compromise them and even endanger the personal safety of foreign agents.

. . . In view of this and other evidence in the record, both the District Court and the Court of Appeals recognized that Snepp's breach of his explicit obligation to submit his material—classified or not—for prepublication clearance has irreparably harmed the United States Government.

III

The decision of the Court of Appeals denies the Government the most appropriate remedy for Snepp's acknowledged wrong. Indeed, as a practical matter, the decision may well leave the Government with no reliable deterrent against similar breaches of security. No one disputes that the actual damages attributable to a publication such as Snepp's generally are unquantifiable. Nominal damages are a hollow alternative, certain to deter no one. The punitive damages recoverable after a jury trial are speculative and unusual. Even if recovered, they may bear no relation to either the Government's irreparable loss or Snepp's unjust gain.

The Government could not pursue the only remedy that the Court of Appeals left it without losing the benefit of the bargain it seeks to enforce. Proof of the tortious conduct necessary to sustain an award of punitive damages might force the Government to disclose some of the very confidences that Snepp promised to protect. The trial of such a suit, before a jury if the defendant so elects, would subject the CIA and its officials to probing discovery into the Agency's highly confidential affairs.... When the Government cannot secure its remedy without unacceptable risks, it has no remedy at all.

A constructive trust, on the other hand, protects both the Government and the former agent from unwarranted risks. This remedy is the natural and customary consequence of a breach of trust. It deals fairly with both parties by conforming relief to the dimensions of the wrong. If the agent secures prepublication clearance, he can publish with no fear of liability. If the agent publishes unreviewed material in violation of his fiduciary and contractual obligation, the trust remedy simply requires him to disgorge the benefits of his faithlessness. Since the remedy is swift and sure, it is tailored to deter those who would place sensitive information at risk. And since the remedy reaches only funds attributable to the breach, it cannot saddle the former agent with exemplary damages out of all proportion to his gain. The decision of the Court of Appeals would deprive the Government of this equitable and effective means of protecting intelligence that may contribute to national security. We therefore reverse the judgment of the Court of Appeals in so far as it refused to impose a constructive trust on Snepp's profits, and we remand the case to the Court of Appeals for reinstatement of the full judgment of the District Court.

So ordered.

■ MR. JUSTICE STEVENS, with whom MR. JUSTICE BRENNAN and MR. JUSTICE MARSHALL join, dissenting....

I

The rule of law the Court announces today is not supported by statute, by the contract, or by the common law. Although Congress has enacted a number of criminal statutes punishing the unauthorized dissemination of certain types of classified information, it has not seen fit to authorize the constructive trust remedy the Court creates today. Nor does either of the contracts Snepp signed with the agency provide for any such remedy in the event of a breach. The Court's per curiam opinion seems to suggest that its result is supported by a blend of the law of trusts and the law of contracts. But neither of these branches of the common law supports the imposition of a constructive trust under the circumstances of this case.

Plainly this is not a typical trust situation in which a settlor has conveyed legal title to certain assets to a trustee for the use and benefit of designated beneficiaries. Rather, it is an employment relationship in which the employee possesses fiduciary obligations arising out of his duty of loyalty to his employer. One of those obligations, long recognized by the common law even in the absence of a written employment agreement, is the duty to protect confidential or "classified" information. If Snepp had breached that obligation, the common law would support the implication of a constructive trust upon the benefits derived from his misuse of confidential information.

But Snepp did not breach his duty to protect confidential information. Rather, he breached a contractual duty, imposed in aid of the basic duty to maintain confidentiality, to obtain prepublication clearance. In order to justify the imposition of a constructive trust, the majority attempts to equate this contractual duty with Snepp's duty not to disclose, labeling them both as "fiduciary." I find nothing in the common law to support such an approach.

Employment agreements often contain covenants designed to ensure in various ways that an employee fully complies with his duty not to disclose or misuse confidential information. One of the most common is a covenant not to compete. Contrary to the majority's approach in this case, the courts have not construed such covenants broadly simply because they support a basic fiduciary duty; nor have they granted sweeping remedies to enforce them. On the contrary, because such covenants are agreements in restraint of an individual's freedom of trade, they are enforceable only if they can survive scrutiny under the "rule of reason." That rule, originally laid down in the seminal case of Mitchel v. Reynolds, 1 P.Wms. 181, 24 Eng.Rep. 347 (1711), requires that the covenant be reasonably necessary to protect a legitimate interest of the employer (such as an interest in confidentiality), that the employer's interest not be outweighed by the public interest, and that the covenant not be of any longer duration or wider geographical scope than necessary to protect the employer's interest.

The Court has not persuaded me that a rule of reason analysis should not be applied to Snepp's covenant to submit to prepublication review. Like an ordinary employer, the CIA has a vital interest in protecting certain types of information; at the same time, the CIA employee has a countervailing interest in preserving a wide range of work opportunities (including work as an author) and in protecting his First Amendment rights. The public interest lies in a proper accommodation that will preserve the intelligence mission of the Agency while not abridging the free flow of unclassified information. When the Government seeks to enforce a harsh restriction on the employee's freedom, despite its admission that the interest the agreement was designed to protect—the confidentiality of classified information—has not been compromised, an equity court might well be persuaded that the case is not one in which the covenant should be enforced.

But even assuming that Snepp's covenant to submit to prepublication review should be enforced, the constructive trust imposed by the Court is not an appropriate remedy. If an employee has used his employer's confidential information for his own personal profit, a constructive trust over those profits is obviously an appropriate remedy because the profits are the direct result of the breach. But Snepp admittedly did not use confidential information in his book; nor were the profits from his book in any sense a product of his failure to submit the book for prepublication review. For, even if Snepp had submitted the book to the agency for prepublication review, the Government's censorship authority would surely have been limited to the excision of classified material. In this case, then, it would have been obliged to clear the book for publication in precisely the same form as it now stands. Thus, Snepp has not gained any profits as a result of his breach; the Government, rather than Snepp, will be unjustly enriched if he is required to disgorge profits attributable entirely to his own legitimate activity.

Despite the fact that Snepp has not caused the Government the type of harm that would ordinarily be remedied by the imposition of a constructive trust, the Court attempts to justify a constructive trust remedy on the ground that the Government has suffered *some* harm. The Court states that publication of "unreviewed material" by a former CIA agent "can be detrimental to vital national interests even if the published information is unclassified." . . .

In support of its position that Snepp's book had in fact had such an impact, the Government introduced testimony by the Director of the CIA, Admiral Stansfield Turner, stating that Snepp's book and others like it had jeopardized the CIA's relationship with foreign intelligence services by making them unsure of the Agency's ability to maintain confidentiality. Admiral Turner's truncated testimony does not explain, however, whether these unidentified "other" books actually contained classified information. If so, it is difficult to believe that the publication of a book like Snepp's, which does not reveal classified information, has significantly weakened the Agency's position. Nor does it explain whether the unidentified foreign agencies who have stopped cooperating with the CIA have done so because of a legitimate fear that secrets will be revealed or because they merely disagree with our Government's classification policies.

In any event, to the extent that the Government seeks to punish Snepp for the generalized harm he has caused by failing to submit to prepublication review and to deter others from following in his footsteps, punitive damages is, as the Court of Appeals held, clearly the preferable remedy "since a constructive trust depends on the concept of unjust enrichment rather than deterrence and punishment."

II

. . . .

. . . Despite the fact that the Government has specifically stated that the punitive damages remedy is "sufficient" to protect its interests, the Court forges ahead and summarily rejects that remedy on the grounds that (a) it is too speculative and thus would not provide the Government with a "reliable deterrent against similar breaches of security," and (b) it might require the Government to reveal confidential information in court, the Government might forego damages rather than make such disclosures, and the Government might thus be left with "no remedy at all." It seems to me that the Court is foreclosed from relying upon either ground by the Government's acquiescence in the punitive damages remedy. Moreover, the second rationale is entirely speculative and, in this case at least, almost certainly wrong. . . . [U]nder the Court of Appeals' opinion the Government would be entitled to punitive damages simply by proving that Snepp deceived it into believing that he was going to comply with his duty to submit the manuscript for prepublication review and that the Government relied on these misrepresentations to its detriment. I fail to see how such a showing would require the Government to reveal any confidential information or to expose itself to "probing discovery into the Agency's highly confidential affairs."

III

The uninhibited character of today's exercise in lawmaking is highlighted by the Court's disregard of two venerable principles that favor a more conservative approach to this case.

First, for centuries the English-speaking judiciary refused to grant equitable relief unless the plaintiff could show that his remedy at law was inadequate. Without waiting for an opportunity to appraise the adequacy of the punitive damages remedy in this case, the Court has jumped to the conclusion that equitable relief is necessary.

Second, and of greater importance, the Court seems unaware of the fact that its drastic new remedy has been fashioned to enforce a species of prior restraint on a citizen's right to criticize his government.[17] Inherent in this prior restraint is the risk that the reviewing agency will misuse its authority to delay the publication of a critical work or to persuade an author to modify the contents of his work beyond the demands of secrecy. The character of the covenant as a prior restraint on free speech surely imposes an especially heavy burden on the censor to justify the remedy it seeks. It would take more than the Court has written to persuade me that that burden has been met.

I respectfully dissent.

Sharp v. Kosmalski

Court of Appeals of New York, 1976.
40 N.Y.2d 119, 386 N.Y.S.2d 72, 351 N.E.2d 721.

■ GABRIELLI, J. Plaintiff commenced this action to impose a constructive trust upon property transferred to defendant on the ground that the retention of the property and the subsequent ejection of the plaintiff therefrom was in violation of a relationship of trust and confidence and constituted unjust enrichment. The Trial Judge dismissed plaintiff's complaint and his decision was affirmed without opinion by the Appellate Division.

Upon the death of his wife of 32 years, plaintiff, a 56–year–old dairy farmer whose education did not go beyond the eighth grade, developed a very close relationship with defendant, a school teacher and a woman 16 years his junior. Defendant assisted plaintiff in disposing of his wife's

---

17. ... In view of the national interest in maintaining an effective intelligence service, I am not prepared to say that the restraint is necessarily intolerable in this context. I am, however, prepared to say that, certiorari having been granted, the issue surely should not be resolved in the absence of full briefing and argument.

belongings, performed certain domestic tasks for him such as ironing his shirts and was a frequent companion of the plaintiff. Plaintiff came to depend upon defendant's companionship and, eventually, declared his love for her, proposing marriage to her. Notwithstanding her refusal of his proposal of marriage, defendant continued her association with plaintiff and permitted him to shower her with many gifts, fanning his hope that he could induce defendant to alter her decision concerning his marriage proposal. Defendant was given access to plaintiff's bank account, from which it is not denied that she withdrew substantial amounts of money. Eventually, plaintiff made a will naming defendant as his sole beneficiary and executed a deed naming her a joint owner of his farm. The record reveals that numerous alterations in the way of modernization were made to plaintiff's farmhouse in alleged furtherance of "domestic plans" made by plaintiff and defendant.

In September, 1971, while the renovations were still in progress, plaintiff transferred his remaining joint interest to defendant. At the time of the conveyance, a farm liability policy was issued to plaintiff naming defendant and her daughter as additional insureds. Furthermore, the insurance agent was requested by plaintiff, in the presence of defendant, to change the policy to read "J. Rodney Sharp, life tenant. Jean C. Kosmalski, owner." In February, 1973, the liaison between the parties was abruptly severed as defendant ordered plaintiff to move out of his home and vacate the farm. Defendant took possession of the home, the farm and all the equipment thereon, leaving plaintiff with assets of $300.

Generally, a constructive trust may be imposed "[w]hen property has been acquired in such circumstances that the holder of the legal title may not in good conscience retain the beneficial interest." In the development of the doctrine of constructive trust as a remedy available to courts of equity, the following four requirements were posited: (1) a confidential or fiduciary relation, (2) a promise, (3) a transfer in reliance thereon and (4) unjust enrichment.

Most frequently, it is the existence of a confidential relationship which triggers the equitable considerations leading to the imposition of a constructive trust. Although no marital or other family relationship is present in this case, such is not essential for the existence of a confidential relation. The record in this case clearly indicates that a relationship of trust and confidence did exist between the parties and, hence, the defendant must be charged with an obligation not to abuse the trust and confidence placed in her by the plaintiff. The disparity in education between the plaintiff and defendant highlights the degree of dependence of the plaintiff upon the trust and honor of the defendant.

Unquestionably, there is a transfer of property here, but the Trial Judge found that the transfer was made "without a promise or understanding of any kind." Even without an express promise, however, courts of equity have imposed a constructive trust upon property transferred in reliance upon a confidential relationship. In such a situation, a promise may be implied or inferred from the very transaction itself. As Judge Cardozo so eloquently observed: "Though a promise in words was lacking, the whole transaction, it might be found, was 'instinct with an obligation' imperfectly expressed. In deciding that a formal writing or express promise was not essential to the application of the doctrine of constructive trust, Judge Cardozo further observed in language that is most fitting in the instant case:

> "Here was a man transferring to his sister the only property he had in the world . . . He was doing this, as she admits, in reliance upon her honor. Even if we were to accept her statement that there was no distinct promise to hold for his benefit, the exaction of such a promise, in view of the relation, might well have seemed to be superfluous."

. . . Indeed, in the case before us, it is inconceivable that plaintiff would convey all of his interest in property which was not only his abode but the very means of his livelihood without at least tacit consent upon the party of the defendant that she would permit him to continue to live on and operate the farm. I would therefore reject the Trial Judge's conclusion, erroneously termed a finding of fact, that no agreement or limitation may, as a matter of law, be implied from the circumstances surrounding the transfer of plaintiff's farm.

The salutary purpose of the constructive trust remedy is to prevent unjust enrichment and it is to this requirement that I now turn. The Trial Judge in his findings of fact, concluded that the transfer did not constitute unjust enrichment. In this instance also, a legal conclusion was mistakenly labeled a finding of fact. . . . Having determined that the relationship between plaintiff and defendant in this case is of such a nature as to invoke consideration of the equitable remedy of constructive trust, it remains to be determined whether defendant's conduct following the transfer of plaintiff's farm was in violation of that relationship and, consequently, resulted in the unjust enrichment of the defendant. This must be determined from the circumstances of the transfer since there is no express promise concerning plaintiff's continued use of the land. Therefore, the case should be remitted to the Appellate Division for a review of the facts.

. . . This case seems to present the classic example of a situation where equity should intervene to scrutinize a transaction pregnant with opportunity for abuse and unfairness. It was for just this type of case that there evolved equitable principles and remedies to prevent injustices. Equity still lives. To suffer the hands of equity to be bound by misnamed "findings of fact" which are actually conclusions of law and legal inferences drawn from the facts is to ignore and render impotent the rich and vital impact of equity on the common law and, perforce, permit injustice. Universality of law requires equity.

Accordingly, the order of the Appellate Division should be reversed and the case remitted to that court for a review of the facts, or, if it be so advised, in its discretion, to order a new trial in the interests of justice.

■ CHIEF JUDGE BREITEL and JUDGES WACHTLER and Fuchsburg concur with JUDGE GABRIELLI; JUDGES JASEN, JONES and COOKE dissent and vote to affirm in the following memorandum: In view of the affirmed findings of fact that the appellant knowingly and voluntarily conveyed his property without agreement or condition of any kind, express or implied, and with full knowledge of their legal effect, it cannot be said that a constructive trust should be imposed as a matter of law. Although we are sympathetic to the appellant who has been doubly aggrieved by the loss of his wife and property, we are limited to consideration of questions of law and, therefore, in light of the factual findings, would affirm.

Order reversed and the case remitted to the Appellate Division, Fourth Department, for further proceedings in accordance with the opinion herein, with costs to abide the event.

Simonds v. Simonds

Sleedy grandmer

Court of Appeals of New York, 1978.
45 N.Y.2d 233, 408 N.Y.S.2d 359, 380 N.E.2d 189.

■ Breitel, C.J. Plaintiff Mary Simonds, decedent's first wife, seeks to impress a constructive trust on proceeds of insurance policies on decedent's life. The proceeds had been paid to the named beneficiaries, defendants Reva Simonds, decedent's second wife, and their daughter Gayle. Plaintiff, however, asserts as superior an equitable interest arising out of a provision in her separation agreement with decedent.

Special Term granted partial summary judgment to plaintiff and impressed a constructive trust to the extent of $7,000 plus interest against proceeds of a policy naming the second wife as beneficiary, and the Appellate Division affirmed.* Defendant Reva Simonds, the second wife, appeals.

The separation agreement required the husband to maintain in effect, with the wife as beneficiary to the extent of $7,000, existing life insurance policies or, if the policies were to be canceled or to lapse, insurance policies of equal value. The issue is whether that provision entitles the first wife to impress a constructive trust on proceeds of insurance policies subsequently issued, despite the husband's failure to name her as the beneficiary on any substitute policies once the original life insurance policies had lapsed.

There should be an affirmance. The separation agreement vested in the first wife an equitable right in the then existing policies. Decedent's substitution of policies could not deprive the first wife of her equitable interest, which was then transferred to the new policies. Since the proceeds of the substituted policies have been paid to decedent's second wife, whose interest in the policies is subordinate to plaintiff's, a constructive trust may be imposed.

On March 9, 1960, decedent Frederick Simonds and his wife of 14 years, plaintiff Mary Simonds, entered into a separation agreement which, on March 31, 1960, was incorporated into an Illinois divorce decree granted to plaintiff on grounds of desertion. The agreement provided, somewhat inartfully: "The husband agrees that he will keep all of the policies of Insurance now in full force and effect on his life. Said policies now being in the sum of $21,000.00 and the Husband further agrees that the Wife shall be the beneficiary of said policies in an amount not less than $7,000.00 and

---

* Special Term dismissed the cause of action against defendant Gayle Simonds. No   appeal of that dismissal was taken to the Appellate Division.

the Husband further agrees that he shall pay any and all premiums necessary to maintain such policies of Insurance and if for any reason any of them now existing the policies shall be cancelled or be caused to lapse. He shall procure additional insurance in an amount equal to the face value of the policies having been cancelled or caused to lapse." Thus, the husband was to maintain, somehow, at least $7,000 of life insurance for the benefit of his first wife as a named beneficiary.

On May 26, 1960, less than two months after the divorce, decedent husband married defendant Reva Simonds. Defendant Gayle Simonds was born to the couple shortly thereafter.

Sometime after the separation agreement was signed, the then existing insurance policies were apparently canceled or permitted to lapse. It does not appear from the record why, how, or when this happened, but the policies were not extant at the time of decedent husband's death on August 1, 1971. In the interim, however, decedent has acquired three other life insurance policies, totaling over $55,000, none of which named plaintiff as a beneficiary. At his death, decedent had one policy in the amount of $16,138.83 originally issued in 1962 by Metropolitan Life Insurance Company, a second policy for $34,000 issued in 1967 through decedent's employer by Travelers Insurance Company, and a third policy for $5,566 issued in 1962 by the Equitable Life Assurance Society of Iowa. The first two policies named Reva Simonds, defendant's second wife, as beneficiary, and the third policy named their daughter. Hence, at the time of decedent's death he had continuously violated the separation agreement by maintaining no life insurance naming the first wife as a beneficiary.

. . . .

There is no question that decedent breached his obligation to maintain life insurance with his first wife as beneficiary. Consequently, the first wife would of course be entitled to maintain an action for breach against the estate. The estate's insolvency, however, would make such an action fruitless. Thus, the controversy revolves around plaintiff's right, in equity, to recover $7,000 of the insurance proceeds.

Born out of the extreme rigidity of the early common law, equity in its origins drew heavily on Roman law, where equitable notions had long been accepted (see 1 Pomeroy, Equity Jurisprudence [5th ed.], §§ 2–29). "Its great underlying principles, which are the constant sources, the neverfailing roots, of its particular rules, are unquestionably principles of right, justice, and morality, so far as the same can become the elements of a positive human jurisprudence" (id., § 67, at p. 90). Law without principle is not law; law without justice is of limited value. Since adherence to principles of "law" does not invariably produce justice, equity is necessary. Equity arose to soften the impact of legal formalisms; to evolve formalisms narrowing the broad scope of equity is to defeat its essential purpose.

Whatever the legal rights between insurer and insured, the separation agreement vested in the first wife an equitable interest in the insurance policies then in force. An agreement for sufficient consideration, including a separation agreement, to maintain a claimant as a beneficiary of a life insurance policy vests in the claimant an equitable interest in the policies designated. This interest is superior to that of a named beneficiary who has given no consideration, notwithstanding policy provisions permitting the insured to change the designated beneficiary freely.

This is not to say that an insurance company may not rely on the insured's designation of a beneficiary. None of this opinion bears on the rights or responsibilities of the insurer in law or in equity.

Obviously, the policies now at issue are not the same policies in existence at the time of the separation agreement. But it has been held that mere substitution of policies, or even substitution of insurance companies, does not defeat the equitable interest of one who has given sufficient consideration for a promise to be maintained as beneficiary under an insurance policy. The persistence of the promisee's equitable interest is all the more evident where the agreement expressly provides for a change in policies, and in effect provides further that the promisee's right shall attach to the new policies.

For a certainty, the first wife's equitable interest would be easier to trace if the new policies were quid pro quo replacements for the original policies. The record does not reveal whether this was so. But inability to trace plaintiff's equitable rights precisely should not require that they not be recognized, much as in the instance of damages difficult to prove. The separation agreement provides nexus between plaintiff's rights and the later acquired policies. The later policies were expressly contemplated by the parties, and it was agreed that plaintiff would have an interest in them. No reason in equity appears for denying plaintiff that interest, so long as no one who has given value for the policies or otherwise suffered a detriment is involved. The second wife's innocence does not offset the wrong by the now deceased husband.

The conclusion is an application of the general rule that equity regards as done that which should have been done. Thus, if an insured, upon lapse or cancellation of insurance, followed by replacement with new insurance, has a contractual obligation to designate a particular person as beneficiary, equity will consider the obligee as a beneficiary.

In this case, then, the first wife's interest in the original policies extended as well to the later acquired policies. The husband, upon lapse or cancellation of the earlier policies, had by virtue of the separation agreement an obligation to name her as beneficiary on the later policies, an obligation enforceable in equity despite the husband's failure to comply with the terms of the separation agreement. Due to the husband's failure to do what he should have done, the first wife acquired not only a right at law to sue his estate for breach of contract, a right now worthless, but also an equitable right in the policies, a right which, upon the husband's death, attached to the proceeds.

And, since the first wife was entitled to $7,000 of the insurance proceeds at the time of the husband's death, she is no less entitled because the proceeds have already been converted by being paid, erroneously, to the named beneficiaries. Her remedy is imposition of a constructive trust.

In the words of Judge Cardozo, "[a] constructive trust is the formula through which the conscience of equity finds expression. When property has been acquired in such circumstances that the holder of the legal title may not in good conscience retain the beneficial interest, equity converts him into a trustee." Beatty v. Guggenheim Exploration Co., 225 N.Y. 380, 386, 122 N.E. 378, 380. Thus, a constructive trust is an equitable remedy. It is perhaps more different from an express trust than it is similar (5 Scott Trusts [3d ed.], § 461). As put so well by Scott and restated at the Appellate Division, "[the constructive trustee] is not compelled to convey the property because he is a constructive trustee; it is because he can be compelled to convey it that he is a constructive trustee" (id., § 462, at p. 3413).

More precise definitions of a constructive trust have been termed inadequate because of the failure to recognize the broad scope of constructive trust doctrine. As another leading scholar has said of constructive trusts, "[t]he Court does not restrict itself by describing all the specific forms of inequitable holding which will move it to grant relief, but rather reserves freedom to apply this remedy to whatever knavery human ingenuity can invent" (Bogert, Trusts and Trustees [2d ed. rev., 1978], § 471, at p. 29).

Four factors were posited in Sharp v. Kosmalski, 40 N.Y.2d 119, 386 N.Y.S.2d 72, 351 N.E.2d 721. Although the factors are useful in many cases constructive trust doctrine is not rigidly limited. For a single example, one who wrongfully prevents a testator from executing a new will eliminating him as beneficiary will be held as a constructive trustee even in the absence of a confidential or fiduciary relation, a promise by the "trustee", and a transfer in reliance by the testator (see, e.g., Latham v. Father Divine, 299 N.Y. 22, 26–27, 85 N.E.2d 168, 169–170). As then Judge Desmond said in response to the argument that a breach of a promise to the testator was necessary for imposition of a constructive trust (at p. 27, 85 N.E.2d at p. 170), "[a] constructive trust will be erected whenever necessary to satisfy the demands of justice ... [I]ts applicability is limited only by the inventiveness of men who find new ways to enrich themselves unjustly by grasping what should not belong to them."

It so happens, as an added argument, if it were necessary, that the four factors enumerated in Sharp v. Kosmalski are perceptible in this case: a promise, a transfer in reliance on the promise, the fiduciary relation between decedent and his first wife, and the "unjust enrichment" of the second wife. Because decedent and plaintiff were husband and wife, there is a duty of fairness in financial matters extending even past the contemplated separation of the spouses. Hence, a separation agreement based on one party's misrepresentation of financial condition is voidable. A similar rule applies in Illinois, where the instant separation agreement was made. Thus, at the time of the separation agreement decedent and plaintiff remained in a confidential or fiduciary relationship.

It is agreed that the purpose of the constructive trust is prevention of unjust enrichment.

Unjust enrichment, however, does not require the performance of any wrongful act by the one enriched. Innocent parties may frequently be unjustly enriched. What is required, generally, is that a party hold property "under such circumstances that in equity and good conscience he ought not to retain it." A bona fide purchaser of property upon which a constructive trust would otherwise be imposed takes free of the constructive trust, but a gratuitous donee, however innocent, does not.

The unjust enrichment in this case is manifest. At a time when decedent was certainly, anxious to remarry, he entered into a separation agreement with his wife of 14 years. As part of the agreement, he promised to maintain $7,000 in life insurance with the first wife as beneficiary. Later he broke his promise, and died with insurance policies naming only the second wife and daughter as beneficiaries. They have collected the proceeds, amounting to more than $55,000, while the first wife has collected nothing. Had the husband kept his promise, the beneficiaries would have collected $7,000 less in proceeds. To that extent, the beneficiaries have been unjustly enriched, and the proceeds should be subjected to a constructive trust.

Moreover, the second wife's complaint, if that it be, over the distinction drawn below between her daughter and herself is to no avail. The first wife's equitable interest attached to all the substituted insurance policies, whether they named the second wife or the daughter as beneficiary. At the time each substituted policy was issued, decedent had an obligation to make the first wife a beneficiary. None of the named beneficiaries can escape the superior equitable interest of the first wife by pointing to other policies. True, plaintiff might also be entitled to impose a constructive trust on the policy naming the daughter as beneficiary. But that provides no cause for prorating the constructive trust. The beneficiaries are jointly and severally liable, if the analogy applicable to express trusts be applied. Plaintiff's choice not to appeal the dismissal against the daughter should not bar her from collecting in full against the second wife, who may have a right of contribution against the daughter, a question not before the court and not passed on.

The issues in this case should not generate significant controversy. The action is in equity, and the equities are clear. True, some courts have decided the issues differently. Those cases, however, rely heavily on formalisms and too little on basic equitable principles, long established in Anglo–American law and in this State and especially relevant when family transactions are involved. "A court of equity in decreeing a constructive trust is bound by no unyielding formula. The equity of the transaction must shape the measure of relief."

Accordingly, the order of the Appellate Division should be affirmed, with costs.

———

B.   OTHER FORMS OF RESTITUTION FROM PROPERTY

The great contribution of equity can be readily seen by an examination of those cases where equity sought to prevent the unjust enrichment of a wrongdoer. It fashioned flexible and effective remedies which imposed obligations in order that justice and equity might prevail. In addition to the constructive trust, equity devised the *equitable lien* in favor of a plaintiff upon property held by a defendant. Equity could compel the sale of the property to satisfy plaintiff's equitable lien.

Another example is where the facts did not give rise to a legally enforceable assignment. Equity might deal with the transaction as though an assignment had taken place *in equity*. Assignments of expectancies, things not *in esse*, and property to be acquired in the future are some examples. Either to effectuate the intent of the parties, or to prevent an injustice, equity established an *equitable assignment*—even though the transaction was ineffectual as an assignment at law.

The factual complexity was no challenge to the ingenuity of equity. For example, what would result if defendant mingled money wrongfully acquired with his own? The identity of the wrongfully acquired money could no longer be determined. Equity would, nevertheless, hold that the plaintiff had an interest in the mingled fund, i.e., equity would give him an equitable claim upon the fund to the extent of his proportionate interest.

Regardless of deficiencies in logic or analysis, the utility of the constructive trust remedy in preventing unjust enrichment cannot be questioned. For example, by treating a thief as the constructive trustee of stolen funds, the owner may trace the trust–res and acquire property that the thief has purchased with the stolen funds. Even though the thief may have title to the property that he has purchased, and replevin would therefore not lie, the constructive trust is impressed to prevent unjust enrichment.

Furthermore, in a particular case, a plaintiff was not limited to any one of the equitable remedies. After the facts were unraveled several remedies could have been implemented to undo the wrong. Countless cases can be cited where equitable remedies were implemented to deprive a defendant of property or money to which he was not entitled in equity and good conscience. The case of Perry v. Perry that follows is a good example.

Perry v. Perry

Supreme Court of Missouri, 1972.
484 S.W.2d 257.

■ COTTEY, S.J. Alfred Perry, at the time of his divorce from Isabel in 1961, had three policies of insurance in force on his life, in each of which his mother, Mary was named as beneficiary. Two of these, in amounts of $5,000 and $2,000, were group policies written under a plan sponsored by Alfred's union, on which the premiums were paid by his employer; the third, commonly known as a G.I. policy in the amount of $10,000, had been issued in 1946 and all premiums on it from its inception were paid by Mary. Although each of the policies contained the usual provision authorizing the insured to change the beneficiary at will, at no time did Alfred ever exercise that privilege, in a formal manner on the books of the issuing companies.

As an incident of his divorce, by way of making provision for the parties' minor children, Alfred entered into a contract with Isabel whereby he agreed "to change the present beneficiary or beneficiaries on his life insurance and accident insurance policy or policies, making his minor children the beneficiaries on same, so that the minor children would receive the proceeds of said insurance policy or policies, and that he will make proper arrangements with the insurance company or companies in which his policy or policies are in force to pay said amounts in certain definite installments so as to enable said children to have their living expenses, as well as their educational needs, covered." On settled authority, that contract constituted an equitable assignment of the policies for the children's benefit and gave them a vested right to proceeds, subject to be defeated only by proof of a superior right.

Nothing further was done, however; the issuing companies were never directed to change the beneficiary of the policies, and, in consequence, on Alfred's death in 1965 they paid the proceeds to Mary. It stands admitted that Mary was informed of the contract at the time of Alfred's divorce, and that she nevertheless continued to pay the premiums on the G.I. policy. Ultimately she collected the money from all three policies, commingled it with her own funds, and rejected the children's demand for it. Isabel thereupon filed this suit on behalf of the children to impress a constructive trust on the policy proceeds for their benefit. The case followed a languid and desultory course through several hearings to eventual decision in the trial court, by which time Mary had spent the money in the payment of debts and living expenses, so she said, and there was no possibility of following the fund into the hands of any who had received it or of tracing it into any property into which it may have been converted.

That circumstance, Mary argued at the trial, entitled her to a decree in her favor in spite of her defalcation. This, because the fund was gone and no specific property could be identified as the product of its misappropriation; there was therefore nothing on which a trust could be impressed, and the equity jurisdiction of the court had consequently been exhausted in futility and frustration. The children's only recourse, so the argument concluded, was to start over again as common creditors of Mary and seek a general judgment against her in a court of law for the sum of the dissipated funds, because an action of that kind and a remedy of that sort is outside the cognizance and concern of a court of equity.

The trial court rejected that argument, and properly so. It is a settled maxim that equity, once having acquired jurisdiction of a cause, will not relinquish it without doing full and effective justice between the parties, even though, to right the wrong complained of, resort must be had to a remedy within the traditional province of law, as by a judgment for money by way of restitution.

A corollary rule, in cases of this kind, is that where a defaulting trustee has first commingled the trust funds with his own and then paid them out in satisfaction of his own debts, it will be presumed that the payment was made from his own contribution to the commingled fund, "and not out of the trust money," so that whatever is left is the money for which he is accountable in his fiduciary capacity. And if the depleted account is subsequently augmented by deposits of the trustee's personal funds, the resultant balance will be treated as trust funds on the theory that these deposits were "made by way of restitution of the trust funds previously withdrawn." Restatement of the Law, Trusts 2d, Ch. 7, § 202, p. 453. No proof of the fiduciary character of the balance remaining in the commingled account is necessary beyond that supplied by the presumption. "[T]he entire fund will be held to be a trust fund out of which the cestui que trust may be paid." Nor is it necessary, in order to fasten a constructive trust on the commingled account at any stage of its balance, to prove the trustee's fraud other than by the fact of his defalcation; "a breach of the confidential relationship is, in itself, a constructive fraud."

The trial chancellor entered a decree in favor of the children for the sum of the two group policies, with interest, which it was within his proper discretion to allow. But he impressed no trust on any balance standing to Mary's credit in the commingled account, possibly because counsel did not trouble themselves to go into that aspect of their case. As to the G.I. policy, however, the chancellor found in Mary's favor, on the declared ground that, as to it, "Mary Perry has a superior right." Both sides, after consolidated appeals to the wrong court, have at last got the matter to us for review.

We are unable to follow the reasoning that led to the award to Mary of the proceeds of the G.I. policy. The only difference between it and the others was that on it Mary paid the premiums, but that difference is illusory. There was neither pleading nor proof that she did so as the result of any contract between her and the insured that in anywise impaired his right to change the beneficiary at will. Absent such a contract, the payment of premiums by one who is merely hopeful of receiving the proceeds vests no right in him, "and the insured may change the beneficiary without the latter's consent." It follows that Alfred's assignment of the G.I. policy was just as valid in every way as his assignment of the group policies, and the law of the one is the law of the other.

It does not follow, however, that Mary should lose the money she has paid to keep the policy alive, even though she was under no obligation to make the payments and was, therefore, a volunteer to whom relief is ordinarily denied at law. The equitable doctrine is that one who pays the premiums on a policy to keep it in force, in the reasonable expectation of being the beneficiary of it, will, upon the disappointment of that expectation, be entitled to reimbursement for his outlay from the one who ultimately profits from it by receiving the policy proceeds. . . . It is said that this right of reimbursement does not exist, however, with respect to premiums paid after the payor's interest in the policy has been terminated by a change of beneficiaries. No doubt that limitation would be proper in a case where the supplanted beneficiary continued to pay the premiums after any reasonable hope he had of receiving the proceeds had been dispelled, for it would then be presumed that he intended the payments as a gift for the benefit of his successor, but that is not this case. Here the fact that Alfred made the change of beneficiaries in an unconventional manner and thereafter failed to confirm it by any "proper arrangements" of a formal nature as his contract required, viewed in the light of Isabel's apparent indifference to that neglect, was hardly calculated to dispel Mary's hope; and the fact that her payment of subsequent premiums was not made with the intent of keeping the policy alive for the children's benefit is demonstrated by her rejection of their demand for its proceeds. Misguided she may have been in paying those later premiums, but it is enough to deny her the fund without requiring her to forfeit the payments that made it available. Equity will not look a gift horse in the mouth in order to find a tooth to criticize.

The decree is reversed, and the cause remanded to the trial chancellor with directions:

1.   To enter a general judgment against Mary for the proceeds of all three policies, with interest, minus the sum of the premiums she has paid to keep the G.I. policy alive, also with interest, and to impress a constructive trust for the net debt on the balance, if any, standing to her credit in the commingled account.

2.   To ascertain by a further hearing the facts necessary to carry out the foregoing instruction.

NOTES ON EQUITABLE ASSIGNMENTS, EQUITABLE LIENS, AND SUBROGATION

1.   Equitable assignments are also used to provide restitutionary relief. When there is no legally enforceable assignment and an assignment is deemed necessary to prevent unjust enrichment, equity recognizes a duty to assign, which it can specifically enforce when (and to the extent that) justice requires.

2.   The equitable lien yet another remedial tool available to provide restitutionary relief. It was well described (and contrasted with the constructive trust) in Monaghan, *Constructive Trust and Equitable Lien: Status of the Conscious and the Innocent Wrongdoer in Equity*, 38 U. Det. L.J. 10, 12–13 (1960):

> [T]he theory of the constructive trust must not be confused with that of the equitable lien. The constructive trust proceeds upon the rationale that the specific res must be considered in equity as the property of the plaintiff and not of the title holder. The decree entered recognizes this and orders the defendant constructive trustee to deliver up the property. On the other hand, a lien is a right to have specific property subjected to the payment of the debt since the property is viewed as belonging to the defendant but subject to a security interest on behalf of the plaintiff. [Hence, equity could compel the sale of the property to satisfy the lien.] Now the property subject to the lien or trust may have a value in excess of or below the amount of the plaintiff's claim. Thus, the choice of remedy will often be determinative of the amount of recovery....

The nature of that choice is explored in greater detail in the following passage from Ames, *Following Misappropriated Property Into Its Product*, 19 Harv. L. Rev. 511 (1906):

> If a trustee wrongfully sells the trust-*res* or exchanges it for other property, the *cestui que trust* may charge him as a constructive trustee of the money or newly acquired property, or of any subsequent product of either; or, if he prefers, he may enforce an equitable lien to the amount of the misappropriation upon any property in the hands of the wrongdoer, which is the traceable product of the original trust-*res*. If,

at the time of relief given, the new property is worth less than the original trust-*res,* the *cestui que trust,* after exhausting his lien, will have a personal claim against the trustee for the difference. If the new property is worth as much as or more than the original trust-*res,* the enforcement of the constructive trust or of the equitable lien will be a full satisfaction of all claims founded on the breach of the express trust. When the value of the new property exceeds that of the original trust, the *cestui que trust,* by enforcing the constructive trust, makes a profit by the trustee's breach of the express trust, and this profit may be very large, as when the trust fund is invested in land or corporate shares which advance rapidly, or, to put the most conspicuous instance of great profit, when the trustee invests trust money in taking out a policy of life insurance which becomes payable soon afterwards by the death of the insured. The *cestui que trust* takes the whole of the insurance money, although ten times as much as the trust money misappropriated. This excess above full compensation is not given to the *cestui que trust* by reason of any merit on his part. It comes to him as a mere windfall. Public policy demands that the faithless trustee should not retain any advantage derived from his breach of trust. Hence the wholesome rule that whatever a trustee loses in the misuse of the trust fund he loses for himself, and whatever he wins, he wins for the beneficiary.

3.   Section 203 of the Restatement of Restitution covers the equitable remedies available against an innocent converter:

Where a person converts the property of another without notice of the facts which make him a converter and being still without such notice exchanges it for other property, the other is entitled to an equitable lien upon the property received in exchange to secure his claim for restitution, but is not entitled to enforce a constructive trust of the property.

4.   With respect to the problem of commingled funds, the Restatement of Restitution states:

§ 210   Effect of Acquisition of Other Property With Mingled Funds

(1) Where a person wrongfully mingles money of another with money of his own and with the mingled fund acquires property, the other is entitled to an equitable lien upon the property to secure his claim for reimbursement.

(2) If the wrongdoer knew that he was acting wrongfully, the other is entitled at his option to a share of the property in such proportion as his money bore to the whole amount of the fund.

§ 211   Effect of Withdrawals From Mingled Fund

(1) Where a person wrongfully mingles money of another with money of his own and subsequently makes withdrawals from the mingled fund, the other is entitled to an equitable lien upon the part which remains and the part which is withdrawn or upon their product, except as stated in Subsection (3).

(2) If the wrongdoer knew that he was acting wrongfully, the other is entitled at his option to a proportionate share both of the part which remains and of the part which is withdrawn or of their product, except as stated in Subsection (3).

(3) Where the wrongdoer has effectively separated the money of the other from his own money, the other is entitled to, and only to, his own money or its product.

5. Subrogation is an additional equitable remedy that provides restitutionary relief. It enables a "surety" (a party that is secondarily liable on a debt) who has paid the debt to be made whole. Subrogation allows the surety who has paid the debt to assume the creditor's rights against the principal debtor.

A simple illustration may be helpful: D (debtor) is indebted to C (creditor) in the sum of $1,000, and S (surety) is the surety for D on the debt. S pays C the $1,000 and the debt is discharged. S is entitled to be subrogated to C's rights against D. This implies that S is entitled to enforce such rights as C had against D before the debt was discharged by S's payment to C. If C held any securities of D, S is entitled to an assignment, and may proceed against them in the same manner as C might have proceeded.

The underlying theory of the remedy is similar to the constructive trust. After payment by S, C has no further claim on the securities. Since D has not paid the debt, he is not entitled to have the securities returned to him. It is S who having paid the debt is entitled to the securities, whether or not S knew that securities were being held by C. As in related cases, the remedy is not available to a volunteer or intermeddler, or, in the language of the Restatement, to someone who pays officiously. The remedy is available only to a surety or someone who paid another's debt under a necessity to save loss. The surety who is subrogated to the rights of the creditor is known as the subrogee.

The Restatement (Second) of Restitution states:

§ 31 SUBROGATION

(1) By subrogation, a person is vested with rights of another if, but for such relief, unjust enrichment would result from a payment or other transfer

(a) that discharged or was credited to an obligation of the other, or

(b) that discharged, in whole or in part, an encumbrance on the other's property.

(2) Except as otherwise required to prevent unjust enrichment, or as provided by statute, the rights a person acquires by subrogation are equivalent to the claim or encumbrance discharged by the application of his property, but are not greater in amount than his prior right to restitution.

PART IV

DAMAGES

739

CHAPTER 12

THE MEASURE OF DAMAGES: CONTRACT OR TORT

Rules for the Measure of Damages

When the remedy that plaintiff seeks is money only, what are the rules and principles that determine the amount?

In the words of Lord Hold in Ferrer v. Beale, 1 Lord Raym. 692 (1707), "[e]very one shall recover damages in proportion to the prejudice which he hath sustained."

Thus begins the inquiry as to the appropriate *measure* of damages. The law of damages pertains to those rules and principles which determine the measure and quantum of recovery allowed.

In contract cases it is stated broadly that a plaintiff may recover the *direct* pecuniary loss sustained; conversely, one cannot recover for an *indirect* loss.

Hadley v. Baxendale

Court of Exchequer, 1854.
9 Ex. 341, 156 Eng.Rep. 145.

At the trial before Crompton, J., at the last Gloucester Assizes, it appeared that the plaintiffs carried on an extensive business as millers at Gloucester; and that, on the 11th of May, their mill was stopped by a breakage of the crank shaft by which the mill was worked. The steam-engine was manufactured by Messrs. Joyce & Co., the engineers, at Greenwich, and it became necessary to send the shaft as a pattern for a new one to Greenwich. The fracture was discovered on the 12th, and on the 13th the plaintiffs sent one of their servants to the office of the defendants, who are the well-known carriers trading under the name of Pickford & Co., for the purpose of having the shaft carried to Greenwich. The plaintiffs' servant told the clerk that the mill was stopped, and that the shaft must be sent immediately; and in answer to the inquiry when the shaft would be taken, the answer was, that if it was sent up by twelve o'clock any day, it would be delivered at Greenwich on the following day. On the following day the shaft was taken by the defendants, before noon, for the purpose of being conveyed to Greenwich, and the sum of 2l. 4s. was paid for its carriage for the whole distance; at the same time the defendants' clerk was told that a special entry, if required, should be made to hasten its delivery. The delivery of the shaft at Greenwich was delayed by some neglect; and the consequence was, that the plaintiffs did not receive the new shaft for several days after they would otherwise have done, and the working of their mill was thereby delayed, and they thereby lost the profits they would otherwise have received.

On the part of the defendants, it was objected that these damages were too remote, and that the defendants were not liable with respect to them. The learned Judge left the case generally to the jury, who found a verdict with 25l. damages beyond the amount [previously] paid into Court [by defendants in satisfaction of this claim].

Whateley, in last Michaelmas Term, obtained a rule nisi for a new trial, on the ground of misdirection.

The judgment of the Court was now delivered by

■ ALDERSON, B. We think that there ought to be a new trial in this case; but, in so doing, we deem it to be expedient and necessary to state explicitly the rule which the Judge, at the next trial, ought, in our opinion, to direct the jury to be governed by when they estimate the damages.

It is, indeed, of the last importance that we should do this; for, if the jury are left without any definite rule to guide them, it will, in such cases as these, manifestly lead to the greatest injustice. The Courts have done this on several occasions; and, in Blake v. Midland Railway Company (18 Q.B. 93), the Court granted a new trial on this very ground, that the rule had not been definitely laid down to the jury by the learned Judge at Nisi Prius.

"There are certain established rules," this Court says, in Alder v. Keighley (15 M. & W. 117), "according to which the jury ought to find." And the Court, in that case, adds: "and here there is a clear rule, that the amount which would have been received if the contract had been kept, is the measure of damages if the contract is broken."

Now we think the proper rule in such a case as the present is this:— Where two parties have made a contract which one of them has broken, the damages which the other party ought to receive in respect of such breach of contract should be such as may fairly and reasonably be considered either arising naturally, i.e., according to the usual course of things, from such breach of contract itself, or such as may reasonably be supposed to have been in the contemplation of both parties, at the time they made the contract, as the probable result of the breach of it. Now, if the special circumstances under which the contract was actually made were communicated by the plaintiffs to the defendants, and thus known to both parties, the damages resulting from the breach of such a contract, which they would reasonably contemplate, would be the amount of injury which would ordinarily follow from a breach of contract under these special circumstances so known and communicated. But, on the other hand, if these special circumstances were wholly unknown to the party breaking the contract, he, at the most, could only be supposed to have had in his contemplation the amount of injury which would arise generally, and in the great multitude of cases not affected by any special circumstances, from such a breach of contract. For, had the special circumstances been known, the parties might have specially provided for the breach of contract by special terms as to the damages in that case; and of this advantage it would be very unjust to deprive them. Now the above principles are those by which we think the jury ought to be guided in estimating the damages arising out of any breach of contract. It is said, that other cases such as breaches of contract in the non-payment of money, or in the not making a good title to land, are to be treated as exceptions from this, and as governed by a conventional rule. But as, in such cases, both parties must be supposed to be cognisant of that well-known rule, these cases may, we think, be more properly classed under the rule above enunciated as to cases under known special circumstances, because there both parties may reasonably be presumed to contemplate the estimation of the amount of damages according to the conventional rule. Now, in the present case, if we are to apply the principles above laid down, we find that the only circumstances here communicated by the plaintiffs to the defendants at the time the contract was made, were, that the article to be carried was the broken shaft of a mill, and that the plaintiffs were the millers of that mill. But how do these circumstances shew reasonably that the profits of the mill must be stopped by an unreasonable delay in the delivery of the broken shaft by the carrier to the third person? Suppose the plaintiffs had another shaft in their possession put up or putting up at the time, and that they only wished to send back the broken shaft to the engineer who made it; it is clear that this would be quite consistent with the above circumstances, and yet the unreasonable delay in the delivery would have no effect upon the intermediate profits of the mill. Or, again, suppose that, at the time of the delivery to the carrier, the machinery of the mill had been in other respects defective, then, also, the same results would follow. Here it is true that the shaft was actually sent back to serve as a model for a new one, and that the want of a new one was the only cause of the stoppage of the mill, and that the loss of profits really arose from not sending down the new shaft in proper time, and that this arose from the delay in delivering the broken one to serve as a model. But it is obvious that, in the great multitude of cases of millers sending off broken shafts to third persons by a carrier under ordinary circumstances, such consequences would not, in all probability, have occurred; and these special circumstances were here never communicated by the plaintiffs to the defendants. It follows, therefore, that the loss of profits here cannot reasonably be considered such a consequence of the breach of contract as could have been fairly and reasonably contemplated by both the parties when they made this contract. For such loss would neither have flowed naturally from the breach of this contract in the great multitude of such cases occurring under ordinary circumstances, nor were the special circumstances, which, perhaps, would have made it a reasonable and natural consequence of such breach of contract, communicated to or known by the defendants. The Judge ought, therefore, to have told the jury, that, upon the facts then before them, they ought not to take the loss of profits into consideration at all in estimating the damages. There must therefore be a new trial in this case.

Rule absolute.

NOTES ON *HADLEY v. BAXENDALE*

1.   Under the rule enunciated in Hadley v. Baxendale, 9 Ex. 341 (1854), plaintiff can only recover for a loss which, in the ordinary course of events, would result from the defendant's act or omission, or for a loss

which was in the contemplation of the parties. There are limits to the compensation allowed. For example, it is stated that plaintiff cannot recover for a loss which reasonably could have been prevented.

2. In another action against the same carrier it was stated that "whether any particular class of expenses is reasonable or not [and therefor recoverable] depends upon the usage of trade, and other circumstances. It is not a question for the Judge, but for the jury, to decide what are reasonable expenses." Chief Baron Pollock in Balck v. Baxendale, 1 Exch. 410 (1847).

3. In Victoria Laundry (Windsor) Ltd. v. Newman Industries, Ltd., [1949] 2 K.B. 528, Asquith, L.J., made the following comments about the "two rules" of Hadley v. Baxendale:

> In cases of breach of contract the aggrieved party is only entitled to recover such part of the loss actually resulting as was at the time of the contract reasonably foreseeable as liable to result from the breach.
>
> What was at that time reasonably so foreseeable depends on the knowledge then possessed by the parties, or, at all events, by the party who later commits the breach.
>
> For this purpose, knowledge "possessed" is one of two kinds; one imputed, the other actual. Everyone, as a reasonable person, is taken to know the "ordinary course of things" and consequently what loss is liable to result from a breach of contract in that ordinary course. This is the subject matter of the "first rule" in Hadley v. Baxendale. But to this knowledge, which a contract-breaker is assumed to possess whether he actually possesses it or not, there may have to be added in a particular case knowledge which he actually possesses, of special circumstances outside the "ordinary course of things," of such a kind that a breach in those special circumstances would be liable to cause more loss. Such a case attracts the operation of the "second rule" so as to make additional loss also recoverable.
>
> In order to make the contract-breaker liable under either rule it is not necessary that he should actually have asked himself what loss is liable to result from a breach. As has often been pointed out, parties at the time of contracting contemplate not the breach of the contract, but its performance. It suffices that, if he had considered the question, he would as a reasonable man have concluded that the loss in question was liable to result.
>
> Nor, finally, to make a particular loss recoverable, need it be proved that upon a given state of knowledge the defendant could, as a reasonable man, foresee that a breach must necessarily result in that loss. It is enough if he could foresee it was likely so to result.

H. Parsons (Livestock) Ltd. v. Uttley Ingham & Co.

Court of Appeal, 1977.
[1978] Q.B. 791.

■ LORD DENNING, M.R. . . . .

The plaintiffs, H. Parsons (Livestock) Ltd., have a fine herd of nearly 700 pigs at their farm in Derbyshire. . . . They feed the pigs on special pignuts. They use about 10 tons a month of these pignuts. In order to store and handle the pignuts, the plaintiffs bought in 1968 a big hopper called a bulk feed storage hopper. They bought it from the makers, the defendants, Uttley Ingham & Co. Ltd., who are sheet-metal workers. The plaintiffs paid £270 for it. . . .

The first hopper was so successful that in 1971 the plaintiffs ordered a second one to be just the same as the first. It cost £275. The defendants accepted the order in a letter of April 23, 1971, in these terms:

> "We are very pleased to book your order for one bulk hopper exactly as supplied in 1968. . . . Hopper fitted with ventilated top and complete with filler and breather pipes . . . Ex works price £275. Carriage charges £15. We deliver in an upright position on your prepared concrete base and bolt down . . . tipping the hopper off the back of the vehicle."

On August 2, 1971, the defendants delivered the hopper to the site. It was exactly the same as the first, but when the delivery man erected it in position he forgot to adjust the ventilator. He left it closed. . . . No one noticed the mistake, because the ventilator was at the top of the hopper 28 feet above the ground. . . . The plaintiffs used the hopper. They put pignuts into it just as they did with the first hopper. On August 12, 1971, they filled it with 9½ tons of pignuts; on September 10, 8½ tons; on October 1, 8 tons.

At first all was well. But on September 28 a small number of the nuts appeared to be mouldy. The plaintiffs did not think this would harm the pigs. So they went on feeding them. Early in October more nuts turned mouldy. But still the plaintiffs were not unduly concerned. As a rule, mouldy nuts do not harm pigs. On Saturday, October 9, there was a bigger proportion of mouldy nuts; and some of the pigs were showing signs of illness. About six of the 21 sows suckling litters were very loose, and about seven or eight were not eating all their ration of nuts. Over the weekend the plaintiffs became really concerned. They did not know the cause. They telephoned the suppliers of the nuts. They telephoned the veterinary surgeon. The suppliers of nuts came. The veterinary surgeon came. They stopped feeding the pigs with nuts from the hopper. They got some bagged foods and fed them from the bags. They telephoned the defendants. On Friday, October 15, a representative of the defendants came. He climbed up to the top of the hopper. He found the ventilator closed. He opened it. When he came down, he said to the plaintiffs: "That appears to be your trouble."

It was indeed the trouble. After much evidence by experts, the judge found that the closed ventilator was the cause. But the effects remained so as to affect the herd greatly. A large number of the pigs suffered an attack of E. coli, which is very bad for pigs. It was triggered off by the eating of the mouldy nuts. The infection spread rapidly; 254 pigs died of a value of £10,000. They also lost sales and turnover resulting in big financial loss. The total claim is £20,000 or £30,000. The question is whether that damage is recoverable from the makers of the hopper, or whether it is too remote.

The judge's findings

The judge had before him the speeches in the House of Lords in C. Czarnikow Ltd. v. Koufos [1969] 1 A.C. 350 about remoteness of damage. That case draws a distinction between contract and tort. Remoteness in contract depends on what the parties "reasonably contemplated at the time of the contract," whereas in tort it depends on what could "reasonably be foreseen at the time of the wrongful act or omission." ...

. . . .

As I read the judge's findings of fact, he was of opinion that the makers of the hopper could reasonably contemplate the following consequences as the result of the breach: (i) that the ventilator would remain closed whilst the hopper was in use; (ii) that the pignuts stored in it would become mouldy for want of proper ventilation; (iii) that the pignuts would be fed to the pigs in a mouldy condition.

By making that last finding the judge has presented us with a nice problem of remoteness of damage. . . .

There is no problem here about causation. The closed ventilator was clearly the cause, or one of the causes, of the deaths of the pigs. . . . The only problem here is with remoteness of damage.

The law as to remoteness

Remoteness of damage is beyond doubt a question of law. In C. Czarnikow Ltd. v. Koufos [1969] A.C. 350 the House of Lords said that, in remoteness of damage, there is a difference between contract and tort. In the case of a *breach of contract*, the court has to consider whether the consequences were of such a kind that a reasonable man, at the time of making the contract, would *contemplate* them as being of a very substantial degree of probability. . . .

In the case of a *tort,* the court has to consider whether the consequences were of such a kind that a reasonable man, at the time of the tort committed, would *foresee* them as being of a much lower degree of probability. . . .

I find it difficult to apply those principles universally to all cases of contract or to all cases of tort: and to draw a distinction between what a man "contemplates" and what he "foresees." I soon begin to get out of my depth. . . . I go back with relief to the distinction drawn in legal theory by Professors Hart and Honoré in their book Causation in the Law (1959), at pp. 281–287. They distinguish between those cases in contract in which a man has suffered no damage to person or property, but only *economic loss,* such as, loss of profit or loss of opportunities for gain in some future transaction: and those in which he claims damages for an *injury actually done* to his person or *damage actually done* to his property (including his livestock) or for ensuing expense (damnum emergens) to which he has actually been put. In the law of *tort,* there is emerging a distinction between economic loss and physical damage. It underlies the words of Lord Wilberforce in Anns v. Merton London Borough Council [1978] A.C. 728, recently, where he classified the recoverable damage as "material, physical damage." ...

It seems to me that in the law of *contract,* too, a similar distinction is emerging. It is between loss of profit consequent on a breach of contract and physical damage consequent on it.

Loss of profit cases

I would suggest as a solution that in the former class of case—loss of profit cases—the defaulting party is only liable for the consequences if they are such as, at the time of the contract, he ought reasonably to have *contemplated* as a *serious* possibility or real danger. You must assume that, at the time of the contract, he had the very kind of breach in mind—such a breach as afterwards happened, as for instance, delay in transit—and then you must ask: ought he reasonably to have *contemplated* that there was a *serious* possibility that such a breach would involve the plaintiff in loss of profit? If yes, the contractor is liable for the loss unless he has taken care to exempt himself from it by a condition in the contract—as, of course, he is able to do if it was the sort of thing which he could reasonably contemplate. The law on this class of case is now covered by the three leading cases of Hadley v. Baxendale, 9 Exch. 341; Victoria Laundry (Windsor) Ltd. v. Newman Industries Ltd. [1949] 2 K.B. 528; and C. Czarnikow Ltd. v. Koufos [1969] 1 A.C. 350. These were all "loss of profit" cases: and the test of "reasonable contemplation" and "serious possibility" should, I suggest, be kept to that type of loss or, at any rate, to economic loss.

Physical damage cases

In the second class of case—the physical injury or expense case—the defaulting party is liable for any loss or expense which he ought reasonably to have *foreseen* at the time of the breach as a possible consequence, even if it was only a *slight* possibility. You must assume that he was aware of his breach, and then you must ask: ought he reasonably to have foreseen, at the time of the breach, that something of this kind might happen in consequence of it? This is the test which has been applied in cases of tort ever since *The Wagon Mound* cases. But there is a long line of cases which support a like test in cases of contract.

One class of case which is particularly apposite here concerns latent defects in goods: in modern words "product liability." In many of these cases the manufacturer is liable in contract to the immediate party for a breach of his duty to use reasonable care and is liable in tort to the ultimate consumer for the same want of reasonable care. The ultimate consumer can either sue the retailer in contract and pass the liability up the chain to the manufacturer, or he can sue the manufacturer in tort and thus by-pass the chain. The liability of the manufacturer ought to be the same in either case. In nearly all these cases the defects were outside the range of anything that was in fact contemplated, or could reasonably have been contemplated, by the manufacturer or by anyone down the chain to the retailers. Yet the manufacturer and others in the chain have been held liable for the damage done to the ultimate user. . . .

Another familiar class of case is where the occupier of premises is under the common duty of care, either in pursuance of a contract with a visitor or under the Occupiers' Liability Act 1957. If he fails in that duty and a visitor is injured, the test of remoteness must be the same no matter whether the injured person enters by virtue of a contract or as a visitor by permission without a contract. No matter whether in contract or tort, the damages must be the same. Likewise, when a contractor is doing work on premises for a tenant—and either the tenant or a visitor is injured—the test of remoteness is the same no matter whether the person injured is a tenant under the contract or a visitor without a contract.

. . . .

Conclusion

The present case falls within the class of case where the breach of contract causes physical damage. The test of remoteness in such cases is similar to that in tort. The contractor is liable for all such loss or expense as could reasonably have been foreseen, at the time of the breach, as a possible consequence of it. Applied to this case, it means that the makers of the hopper are liable for the death of the pigs. . . .

So I reach the same result as the judge, but by a different route. I would dismiss the appeal.

■ ORR, L.J. I agree with Lord Denning, M.R., and also with Scarman, L.J., whose judgment I have had the opportunity of reading, that this appeal should be dismissed, but with respect to Lord Denning, M.R., I would dismiss it for the reasons to be given by Scarman, L.J. . . .

. . . .

■ SCARMAN, L.J . . .

My conclusion in the present case is the same as that of Lord Denning, M.R. but I reach it by a different route. I would dismiss the appeal. I agree with him in thinking it absurd that the test for remoteness of damage should, in principle, differ according to the legal classification of the cause of action, though one must recognise that parties to a contract have the right to agree on a measure of damages which may be greater, or less, than the law would offer in the absence of agreement. I also agree with him in thinking that ... the law is not so absurd as to differentiate between contract and tort save in situations where the agreement, or the factual relationship, of the parties with each other requires it in the interests of justice. I differ from him only to this extent: the cases do not, in my judgment, support a distinction in law between loss of profit and physical damage. Neither do I think it necessary to develop the law judicially by drawing such a distinction. Of course (and this is a reason for refusing to draw the distinction in law) the type of consequence—loss of profit or market or physical injury—will always be an important matter of fact in determining whether in all the circumstances the loss or injury was of a type which the parties could reasonably be supposed to have in contemplation.

In C. Czarnikow Ltd. v. Koufos [1969] 1 A.C. 350 (a case of a contract of carriage of goods by sea) the House of Lords resolved some of the difficulties in this branch of the law. The law which the House in that case either settled or recognised as already settled may be stated as follows. (1) The general principle regulating damages for breach of contract is that "where a party sustains a loss by reason of a breach of contract, he is, so far as money can do it, to be placed in the same situation ... as if the contract had been performed." (2) The formulation of the remoteness test is not the same in tort and in contract because the relationship of the parties in a contract situation differs from that in tort. (3) The two rules formulated by Alderson B. in Hadley v. Baxendale, 9 Exch. 341 are but two aspects of one general principle—that to be recoverable in an action for damages for breach of contract the plaintiff's loss must be such as may reasonably be supposed would have been in the contemplation of the parties as a serious possibility had their attention been directed to the possibility of the breach which has, in fact, occurred.

Two problems are left unsolved by C. Czarnikow Ltd. v. Koufos: (1) the law's reconciliation of the remoteness principle in contract with that in tort where, as, for instance, in some product liability cases, there arises the danger of differing awards, the lesser award going to the party who has a contract, even though the contract is silent as to the measure of damages and all parties are, or must be deemed to be, burdened with the same knowledge, or enjoying the same state of ignorance; and (2) what is meant by "serious possibility" or its synonyms: is it a reference to the type of consequence which the parties might be supposed to contemplate as possible though unlikely or must the chance of it happening appear to be likely?

As to the first problem, I agree with Lord Denning M.R. in thinking that the law must be such that, in a factual situation where all have the same actual or imputed knowledge and the contract contains no term limiting the damages recoverable for breach, the amount of damages recoverable does not depend upon whether, as a matter of legal classification, the plaintiff's cause of action is breach of contract or tort.... It may be that the necessary reconciliation is to be found ... in holding that the difference between "reasonably foreseeable" (the test in tort) and "reasonably contemplated" (the test in contract) is semantic, not substantial....

The second problem—what is meant by a "serious possibility"—is, in my judgment, ultimately a question of fact. I shall return to it, therefore, after analysing the facts, since I believe it requires of the judge no more—and no less—than the application of common sense in the particular circumstances of the case.

Finally, there are two legal rules relevant to the present case which were not considered in C. Czarnikow Ltd. v. Koufos. The first relates to sale of goods. Section 53(2) of the Sale of Goods Act 1893 provides that "The measure of damages for breach of warranty is the estimated loss directly and naturally resulting, in the ordinary course of events, from the breach of warranty." This subsection, clearly a statutory formulation of the first rule in Hadley v. Baxendale, is not, however, intended to oust the second rule, where appropriate....

Secondly, the breach does not have to be foreseen, or contemplated. In a breach of warranty case the point may be put in this way: it does not matter if the defect is latent....

The court's task, therefore, is to decide what loss to the plaintiffs it is reasonable to suppose would have been in the contemplation of the parties as a serious possibility had they had in mind the breach when they made their contract.

. . . .

I would agree with McGregor on Damages, 13th ed. (1972), pp. 131–132 that

"... in contract as in tort, it should suffice that, if physical injury or damage is within the contemplation of the parties, recovery is not to be limited because the degree of physical injury or damage could not have been anticipated."

This is so, in my judgment, not because there is, or ought to be, a specific rule of law governing cases of physical injury but because it would be absurd to regulate damages in such cases upon the necessity of supposing the parties had a prophetic foresight as to the exact nature of the injury that does in fact arise. It is enough if upon the hypothesis predicated physical injury must have been a serious possibility. Though in loss of market or loss of profit cases the factual analysis will be very different from cases of physical injury, the same principles, in my judgment, apply. Given the situation of the parties at the time of contract, was the loss of profit, or market, a serious possibility, something that would have been in their minds had they contemplated breach?

It does not matter, in my judgment, if they thought that the chance of physical injury, loss of profit, loss of market, or other loss as the case may be, was slight, or that the odds were against it, provided they contemplated as a serious possibility the type of consequence, not necessarily the specific consequence, that ensued upon breach. Making the assumption as to breach that the judge did, no more than common sense was needed for them to appreciate that food affected by bad storage conditions might well cause illness in the pigs fed upon it.

As I read the judgment under appeal, this was how the judge ... reached this decision. In my judgment, he was right, upon the facts as found, to apply the first rule in Hadley v. Baxendale, 9 Exch. 341 or, if the case be one of breach of warranty, as I think it is, the rule in section 53(2) of the Sale of Goods Act 1893 without inquiring as to whether, upon a juridical analysis, the rule is based upon a presumed contemplation. At the end of a long and complex dispute the judge allowed common sense to prevail. I would dismiss the appeal.

Appeal dismissed with costs.

Leave to appeal on condition that no application to vary order as to costs.

———

NOTE

Foreseeability in Contract and Tort

Plaintiff Hampton, sued individually and on behalf of his infant son, Carl. He alleged that Federal Express, a common carrier, negligently failed to deliver blood samples of his son, a cancer patient in need of a bone marrow donor. He appealed from judgment of the district court which granted the partial summary judgment motion of the defendant carrier, Federal Express, limiting Hampton's recovery to $100 in damages.

Plaintiff's son, Carl, a 13–year old cancer patient at Children's Memorial Hospital in Omaha, Nebraska, was awaiting a bone marrow transplant. A transplant operation was scheduled at the University of Iowa Hospital in Iowa City. The shipper, the Children's Memorial Hospital, entered into a contract with the carrier, Federal Express, for the transport of blood samples, which limited "damages or loss" to $100.

In a paragraph entitled "Damage or Loss," the contract of carriage, set forth in the airbill, stated:

We are liable for no more than $100 per package in the event of physical loss or damage, unless you fill in a higher Declared Value to the left and document higher actual loss in the event of a claim. We charge 30 cents for each additional $100 of declared value up to the maximum shown in our Service Guide.

It was not disputed that the blood samples were never received; that Carl Hampton, the infant cancer patient, never obtained a bone marrow transplant, and that he died on May 19, 1988. On the facts presented, the U.S. District Court held that the nature and extent of damages suffered by plaintiff Hampton were not reasonably foreseeable by the carrier. Hence, it granted partial summary judgment for the carrier under the released value doctrine, limiting its liability to $100, the amount stated in the contract of carriage between it and the shipper.

In affirming, the U.S. Court of Appeals stated:

... even if it were to be assumed that Hampton may sue as a third party beneficiary of the contract between the shipper and the carrier, on the facts presented he still cannot recover in contract....

It is a fundamental principle of the law of damages that, in contract cases, a plaintiff can only recover for a loss which, in the ordinary course of events, would result from the defendant's breach or for a loss which was in the contemplation of the parties. In the words of the Restatement, "[d]amages are not recoverable for loss that the party in breach did not have reason to foresee as a probable result of the breach when the contract was made." Restatement (Second) of Contracts § 351(1) (1981). This rule of damages may be traced to Hadley v. Baxendale, [supra p. 740] ... Hampton, in this case, cannot dispute that Federal Express had no knowledge of Hampton or of the contents of the package that it accepted for delivery. Hence, even apart from the limitation of liability provision, since the damages suffered by Hampton were not reasonably foreseeable, they would not be recoverable in a breach of contract action.

. . .

... If Federal Express had known of the contents of the package, it might have charged a higher rate, exercised additional care, have obtained insurance, or might not have accepted the responsibility. Since Federal Express had no knowledge of the contents, and hence could not reasonably foresee the injury and damages that could be suffered, plaintiff Hampton cannot recover on its cause of action founded in tort.

Hampton v. Federal Express Corp., 917 F.2d 1119 (8th Cir. 1990).

———

Evra Corp. v. Swiss Bank Corp.

United States Court of Appeals, Seventh Circuit, 1982.
673 F.2d 951.

■ POSNER, J. The question—one of first impression—in this diversity case is the extent of a bank's liability for failure to make a transfer of funds when requested by wire to do so. The essential facts are undisputed. In 1972 Hyman–Michaels Company, a large Chicago dealer in scrap metal, entered into a two-year contract to supply steel scrap to a Brazilian corporation. Hyman–Michaels chartered a ship, the *Pandora,* to carry the scrap to Brazil. The charter was for one year, with an option to extend the charter for a second year; specified a fixed daily rate of pay for the hire of the ship during both the initial and the option period, payable semi-monthly "in advance"; and provided that if payment was not made on time the *Pandora's* owner could cancel the charter. Payment was to be made by deposit to the owner's account in the Banque de Paris et des Pays–Bas (Suisse) in Geneva, Switzerland.

The usual method by which Hyman–Michaels, in Chicago, got the payments to the Banque de Paris in Geneva was to request the Continental Illinois National Bank and Trust Company of Chicago, where it had an account, to make a wire transfer of funds. Continental would debit Hyman–Michaels' account by the amount of the payment and then send a telex to its London office for retransmission to its correspondent bank in Geneva—Swiss Bank Corporation—asking Swiss Bank to deposit this amount in the Banque de Paris account of the *Pandora's* owner. The transaction was completed by the crediting of Swiss Bank's account at Continental by the same amount.

When Hyman–Michaels chartered the *Pandora* in June 1972, market charter rates were very low, and it was these rates that were fixed in the charter for its entire term—two years if Hyman–Michaels exercised its option. Shortly after the agreement was signed, however, charter rates began to climb and by October 1972 they were much higher than they had been in June. The *Pandora's* owners were eager to get out of the charter if they could. At the end of October they thought they had found a way, for the payment that was due in the Banque de Paris on October 26 had not arrived by October 30, and on that day the *Pandora's* owner notified Hyman–Michaels that it was canceling the charter because of the breach of the payment term. Hyman–Michaels had mailed a check for the October 26 installment to the Banque de Paris rather than use the wire-transfer method of payment. It had done this in order to have the use of its money for the period that it would take the check to clear, about two weeks. But the check had not been mailed in Chicago until October 25 and of course did not reach Geneva on the twenty-sixth.

When Hyman–Michaels received notification that the charter was being canceled it immediately wired payment to the Banque de Paris, but the *Pandora's* owner refused to accept it and insisted that the charter was indeed canceled. The matter was referred to arbitration in accordance with the charter. On December 5, 1972, the arbitration panel ruled in favor of Hyman–Michaels. The panel noted that previous arbitration panels had "shown varying degrees of latitude to Charterers"; "In all cases, a pattern of obligation on Owners' part to protest, complain, or warn of intended withdrawal was expressed as an essential prerequisite to withdrawal, in spite of the clear wording of the operative clause. No such advance notice was given by Owners of M/V Pandora." One of the three members of the panel dissented; he thought the *Pandora's* owner was entitled to cancel.

Hyman–Michaels went back to making the charter payments by wire transfer. On the morning of April 25, 1973, it telephoned Continental Bank and requested it to transfer $27,000 to the Banque de Paris account of the *Pandora's* owner in payment for the charter hire period from April 27 to May 11, 1973. Since the charter provided for payment "in advance," this payment arguably was due by the close of business on April 26. The requested telex went out to Continental's London office on the afternoon of April 25, which was nighttime in England. Early the next morning a telex operator in Continental's London office dialed, as Continental's Chicago office had instructed him to do, Swiss Bank's general telex number, which rings in the bank's cable department. But that number was busy, and after trying unsuccessfully for an hour to engage it the Continental telex operator dialed another number, that of a machine in Swiss Bank's foreign exchange department which he had used in the past when the general number was engaged. We know this machine received the telexed message because it signaled the sending machine at both the beginning and end of the transmission that the telex was being received. Yet Swiss Bank failed to comply with the payment order, and no transfer of funds was made to the account of the *Pandora's* owner in the Banque de Paris.

No one knows exactly what went wrong. One possibility is that the receiving telex machine had simply run out of paper, in which event it would not print the message although it had received it. Another is that whoever took the message out of the machine after it was printed failed to deliver it to the banking department. Unlike the machine in the cable department that the Continental telex operator had originally tried to reach, the machines in the foreign exchange department were operated by junior foreign exchange dealers rather than by professional telex operators, although Swiss Bank knew that messages intended for other departments were sometimes diverted to the telex machines in the foreign exchange department.

At 8:30 a.m. the next day, April 27, Hyman–Michaels in Chicago received a telex from the *Pandora's* owner stating that the charter was canceled because payment for the April 27–May 11 charter period had not been made. Hyman–Michaels called over to Continental and told them to keep trying to effect payment through Swiss Bank even if the *Pandora's* owner rejected it. This instruction was confirmed in a letter to Continental dated April 28, in which Hyman–Michaels stated: "please instruct your London branch to advise their correspondents to persist in attempting to make this payment. This should be done even in the face of a rejection on the part of Banque de Paris to receive this payment. It is paramount that in order to strengthen our position in an arbitration that these funds continue to be readily available." Hyman–Michaels did not attempt to wire the money directly to the Banque de Paris as it had done on the occasion of its previous default. Days passed while the missing telex message was hunted unsuccessfully. Finally Swiss Bank suggested to Continental that it retransmit the telex message to the machine in the cable department and this was done on May 1. The next day Swiss Bank attempted to deposit the $27,000 in the account of the *Pandora's* owner at the Banque de Paris but the payment was refused.

Again the arbitrators were convened and rendered a decision. In it they ruled that Hyman–Michaels had been "blameless" up until the morning of April 27, when it first learned that the Banque de Paris had not received payment on April 26, but that "being faced with this situation," Hyman–Michaels had "failed to do everything in [its] power to remedy it. The action taken was immediate but did not prove to be adequate, in that [Continental] Bank and its correspondent required some ⅚ days to trace and effect the lost instruction to remit. [Hyman–Michaels] could have ordered an immediate duplicate payment—or even sent a Banker's check by hand or special messengers, so that the funds could have reached owner's Bank, not later than April 28th." By failing to do any of these things Hyman–Michaels had "created the opening" that the *Pandora's* owner was seeking in order to be able to cancel the charter. It had "acted imprudently." The arbitration panel concluded, reluctantly but unanimously, that this time the *Pandora's* owner was entitled to cancel the agreement. The arbitration decision was confirmed by a federal district court in New York.

Hyman–Michaels then brought this diversity action against Swiss Bank, seeking to recover its expenses in the second arbitration proceeding plus the profits that it lost because of the cancellation of the charter. The contract by which Hyman–Michaels had agreed to ship scrap steel to Brazil had been terminated by the buyer in March 1973 and Hyman–Michaels had promptly subchartered the *Pandora* at market rates, which by April 1973 were double the rates fixed in the charter. Its lost profits are based on the difference between the charter and subcharter rates.

. . . .

The case was tried to a district judge without a jury. In his decision, he ... ruled that ... Swiss Bank had been negligent and under Illinois law was liable to Hyman–Michaels for $2.1 million in damages. This figure was made up of about $16,000 in arbitration expenses and the rest in lost profits on the subcharter of the *Pandora*. ... The case comes to us on Swiss Bank's appeal from the judgment in favor of Hyman–Michaels ...

. . . .

When a bank fails to make a requested transfer of funds, this can cause two kinds of loss. First, the funds themselves or interest on them may be lost, and of course the fee paid for the transfer, having bought nothing, becomes a loss item. These are "direct" (sometimes called "general") damages. Hyman–Michaels is not seeking any direct damages in this case and apparently sustained none. It did not lose any part of the $27,000; although its account with Continental Bank was debited by this amount prematurely, it was not an interest-bearing account so Hyman–Michaels lost no interest; and Hyman–Michaels paid no fee either to Continental or to Swiss Bank for the aborted transfer. A second type of loss, which either the payor or the payee may suffer, is a dislocation in one's business triggered by the failure to pay. Swiss Bank's failure to transfer funds to the Banque de Paris when requested to do so by Continental Bank set off a chain reaction which resulted in an arbitration proceeding that was costly to Hyman–Michaels and in the cancellation of a highly profitable contract. It is those costs and lost profits—"consequential" or, as they are sometimes called, "special" damages—that Hyman–Michaels seeks in this lawsuit, and recovered below. It is conceded that if Hyman–Michaels was entitled to consequential damages, the district court measured them correctly. The only issue is whether it was entitled to consequential damages.

. . . .

The rule of *Hadley v. Baxendale*—that consequential damages will not be awarded unless the defendant was put on notice of the special circumstances giving rise to them—has been applied in many Illinois cases, and *Hadley* cited approvingly. See, e.g., Siegel v. Western Union Tel. Co., 312 Ill.App. 86, 92–93, 37 N.E.2d 868, 871 (1941). In *Siegel,* the plaintiff had delivered $200 to Western Union with instructions to transmit it to a friend of the plaintiff's. The money was to be bet (legally) on a horse, but this was not disclosed in the instructions. Western Union misdirected the money order and it did not reach the friend until several hours after the race had taken place. The horse that the plaintiff had intended to bet on won and would have paid $1650 on the plaintiff's $200 bet if the bet had been placed. He sued Western Union for his $1450 lost profit, but the court held that under the rule of *Hadley v. Baxendale* Western Union was not liable, because it "had no notice or knowledge of the purpose for which the money was being transmitted."

The present case is similar, though Swiss Bank knew more than Western Union knew in *Siegel;* it knew or should have known, from Continental Bank's previous telexes, that Hyman–Michaels was paying the Pandora Shipping Company for the hire of a motor vessel named *Pandora.* But it did not know when payment was due, what the terms of the charter were, or that they had turned out to be extremely favorable to Hyman–Michaels. And it did not know that Hyman–Michaels knew the *Pandora's* owner would try to cancel the charter, and probably would succeed, if Hyman–Michaels was ever again late in making payment, or that despite this peril Hyman–Michaels would not try to pay until the last possible moment and in the event of a delay in transmission would not do everything in its power to minimize the consequences of the delay. Electronic funds transfers are not so unusual as to automatically place a bank on notice of extraordinary consequences if such a transfer goes awry. Swiss Bank did not have enough information to infer that if it lost a $27,000 payment order it would face a liability in excess of $2 million.

It is true that in both *Hadley* and *Siegel* there was a contract between the parties and here there was none. We cannot be certain that the Illinois courts would apply the principles of those cases outside of the contract area. As so often in diversity cases, there is an irreducible amount of speculation involved in attempting to predict the reaction of a state's courts to a new issue. The best we can do is to assume that the Illinois courts would look to the policies underlying cases such as *Hadley* and *Siegel* and, to the extent they found them pertinent, would apply those cases here. We must therefore ask what difference it should make whether the parties are or are not bound to each other by a contract. On the one hand, it seems odd that the absence of a contract would enlarge rather than limit the extent of liability. After all, under Swiss law the absence of a contract would be devastating to Hyman–Michaels' claim. Privity is not a wholly artificial concept. It is one thing to imply a duty to one with whom one has a contract and another to imply it to the entire world.

On the other hand, contract liability is strict. A breach of contract does not connote wrongdoing; it may have been caused by circumstances beyond the promisor's control—a strike, a fire, the failure of a supplier to deliver an essential input. And while such contract doctrines as impossibility, impracticability, and frustration relieve promisors from liability for some failures to perform that are beyond their control, many other such failures are actionable although they could not have been prevented by the exercise of due care. The district judge found that Swiss Bank had been negligent in losing Continental Bank's telex message and it can be argued that Swiss Bank should therefore be liable for a broader set of consequences than if it had only broken a contract. But *Siegel* implicitly rejects this distinction. Western Union had not merely broken its contract to deliver the plaintiff's money order; it had "negligently misdirected" the money order. "The company's negligence is conceded." Yet it was not liable for the consequences.

Siegel, we conclude, is authority for holding that Swiss Bank is not liable for the consequences of negligently failing to transfer Hyman–Michaels' funds to Banque de Paris; reason for such a holding is found in the animating principle of *Hadley v. Baxendale,* which is that the costs of the untoward consequence of a course of dealings should be borne by that party who was able to avert the consequence at least cost and failed to do so. In *Hadley* the untoward consequence was the shutting down of the mill. The carrier could have avoided it by delivering the engine shaft on time. But the mill owners, as the court noted, could have avoided it simply by having a spare shaft. Prudence required that they have a spare shaft anyway, since a replacement could not be obtained at once even if there was no undue delay in carting the broken shaft to and the replacement shaft from the manufacturer. The court refused to imply a duty on the part of the carrier to guarantee the mill owners against the consequences of their own lack of prudence, though of course if the parties had stipulated for such a guarantee the court would have enforced it. The notice requirement of *Hadley v. Baxendale* is designed to assure that such an improbable guarantee really is intended.

This case is much the same, though it arises in a tort rather than a contract setting. Hyman–Michaels showed a lack of prudence throughout. It was imprudent for it to mail in Chicago a letter that unless received the next day in Geneva would put Hyman–Michaels in breach of a contract that was very profitable to it and that the other party to the contract had every interest in canceling. It was imprudent thereafter for Hyman–Michaels, having narrowly avoided cancellation and having (in the words of its appeal brief in this court) been "put . . . on notice that the payment provision of the Charter would be strictly enforced thereafter," to wait till arguably the last day before payment was due to instruct its bank to transfer the necessary funds overseas. And it was imprudent in the last degree for Hyman–Michaels, when it received notice of cancellation on the last possible day payment was due, to fail to pull out all the stops to get payment to the Banque de Paris on that day, and instead to dither while Continental and Swiss Bank wasted five days looking for the lost telex message. Judging from the obvious reluctance with which the arbitration panel finally decided to allow the *Pandora*'s owner to cancel the charter, it might have made all the difference if Hyman–Michaels had gotten payment to the Banque de Paris by April 27 or even by Monday, April 30, rather than allowed things to slide until May 2.

This is not to condone the sloppy handling of incoming telex messages in Swiss Bank's foreign department. But Hyman–Michaels is a sophisticated business enterprise. It knew or should have known that even the Swiss are not infallible; that messages sometimes get lost or delayed in transit among three banks, two of them located 5000 miles apart, even when all the banks are using reasonable care; and that therefore it should take its own precautions against the consequences—best known to itself—of a mishap that might not be due to anyone's negligence.

We are not the first to remark the affinity between the rule of *Hadley v. Baxendale* and the doctrine, which is one of tort as well as contract law and is a settled part of the common law of Illinois, of avoidable consequences. If you are hurt in an automobile accident and unreasonably fail to seek medical treatment, the injurer, even if negligent, will not be held liable for the aggravation of the injury due to your own unreasonable behavior after the accident. If in addition you failed to fasten your seat belt, you may be barred from collecting the tort damages that would have been prevented if you had done so. Hyman–Michaels' behavior in steering close to the wind prior to April 27 was like not fastening one's seat belt; its failure on April 27 to wire a duplicate payment immediately after disaster struck was like refusing to seek medical attention after a serious accident. The seat-belt cases show that the doctrine of avoidable consequences applies whether the tort victim acts imprudently before or after the tort is committed. Hyman–Michaels did both.

The rule of *Hadley v. Baxendale* links up with tort concepts in another way. The rule is sometimes stated in the form that only foreseeable damages are recoverable in a breach of contract action. So expressed, it corresponds to the tort principle that limits liability to the foreseeable consequence of the defendant's carelessness. The amount of care that a person ought to take is a function of the probability and magnitude of the harm that may occur if he does not take care. See, e.g., United States v. Carroll Towing Co., 159 F.2d 169 (2d Cir.1947). If he does not know what that probability and magnitude are, he cannot determine how much care to take. That would be Swiss Bank's dilemma if it were liable for consequential damages from failing to carry out payment orders in timely fashion. To estimate the extent of its probable liability in order to know how many and how elaborate fail-safe features to install in its telex rooms or how much insurance to buy against the inevitable failures, Swiss Bank would have to collect reams of information about firms that are not even its regular customers. It had no banking relationship with Hyman–Michaels. It did not know or have reason to know how at once precious and fragile Hyman–Michaels' contract with the *Pandora*'s owner was. These were circumstances too remote from Swiss Bank's practical range of knowledge to have affected its decisions as to who should man the telex machines in the foreign department or whether it should have more intelligent machines or should install more machines in the cable department, any more than the falling of a platform scale because a conductor jostled a passenger who was carrying fireworks was a prospect that could have influenced the amount of care taken by the Long Island Railroad. See *Palsgraf v. Long Island R.R.,* 248 N.Y. 339, 162 N.E. 99 (1928).

In short, Swiss Bank was not required in the absence of a contractual undertaking to take precautions or insure against a harm that it could not measure but that was known with precision to Hyman–Michaels, which could by the exercise of common prudence have averted it completely. As Chief Judge Cardozo (the author of *Palsgraf*)remarked in discussing the application of *Hadley v. Baxendale* to the liability of telegraph companies for errors in transmission, "The sender can protect himself by insurance in one form or another if the risk of nondelivery or error appears to be too great. . . . The company, if it takes out insurance for itself, can do no more than guess at the loss to be avoided."

. . . .

The legal principles that we have said are applicable to this case were not applied below. Although the district judge's opinion is not entirely clear, he apparently thought the rule of *Hadley v. Baxendale* inapplicable and the imprudence of Hyman–Michaels irrelevant. He did state that the damages to Hyman–Michaels were foreseeable because "a major international bank" should know that a failure to act promptly on a telexed request to transfer funds could cause substantial damage; but *Siegel* . . . make clear that that kind of general foreseeability, which is present in virtually every case, does not justify an award of consequential damages.

We could remand for new findings based on the proper legal standard, but it is unnecessary to do so. The undisputed facts, recited in this opinion, show as a matter of law that Hyman–Michaels is not entitled to recover consequential damages from Swiss Bank.

. . . .

. . . The judgment in favor of Hyman–Michaels against Swiss Bank is reversed with directions to enter judgment for Swiss Bank. . . . The costs of the appeals shall be borne by Hyman–Michaels (EVRA Corporation).

So ORDERED.

East River Steamship Corp. v. Transamerica Delaval, Inc.

Supreme Court of the United States, 1986.
476 U.S. 858, 106 S.Ct. 2295, 90 L.Ed.2d 865.

■ JUSTICE BLACKMUN delivered the opinion of the Court.

In this admiralty case, we must decide whether a cause of action in tort is stated when a defective product purchased in a commercial transaction malfunctions, injuring only the product itself and causing purely economic loss. . . .

[A shipbuilder contracted with Transamerica Delaval, Inc., to design, manufacture, and supervise the installation of turbines that would be the main propulsion units for four oil-transporting supertankers constructed by the shipbuilder. After each ship was completed, it was chartered to one of the petitioners. When the ships were put into service, the turbines on all four ships malfunctioned due to design and manufacturing defects. Only the products themselves were damaged. The charterers sued Delaval on a products liability theory. The trial court entered summary judgment for Delaval, and the court of appeals affirmed.]

. . . .

IV

Products liability grew out of a public policy judgment that people need more protection from dangerous products than is afforded by the law of warranty. It is clear, however, that if this development were allowed to progress too far, contract law would drown in a sea of tort. We must determine whether a commercial product injuring itself is the kind of harm against which public policy requires manufacturers to protect, independent of any contractual obligation.

A

The paradigmatic products-liability action is one where a product "reasonably certain to place life and limb in peril," distributed without reinspection, causes bodily injury. The manufacturer is liable whether or not it is negligent because "public policy demands that responsibility be fixed wherever it will most effectively reduce the hazards to life and health inherent in defective products that reach the market."

For similar reasons of safety, the manufacturer's duty of care was broadened to include protection against property damage. Such damage is considered so akin to personal injury that the two are treated alike.

In the traditional "property damage" cases, the defective product damages other property. In this case, there was no damage to "other" property. Rather, the first, second, and third counts allege that each supertanker's defectively designed turbine components damaged only the turbine itself. Since each turbine was supplied by Delaval as an integrated package, each is properly regarded as a single unit. "Since all but the very simplest of machines have component parts, [a contrary] holding would require a finding of 'property damage' in virtually every case where a product damages itself. Such a holding would eliminate the distinction between warranty and strict products liability." The fifth count also alleges injury to the product itself. Before the high-pressure and low-pressure turbines could become an operational propulsion system, they were connected to piping and valves under the supervision of Delaval personnel. Delaval's supervisory obligations were part of its manufacturing agreement. The fifth count thus can best be read to allege that Delaval's negligent manufacture of the propulsion system—by allowing the installation in reverse of the astern guardian valve—damaged the propulsion system. Obviously, damage to a product itself has certain attributes of a products-liability claim. But the injury suffered—the failure of the product to function properly—is the essence of a warranty action, through which a contracting party can seek to recoup the benefit of its bargain.

B

The intriguing question whether injury to a product itself may be brought in tort has spawned a variety of answers. At one end of the spectrum, the case that created the majority land-based approach, Seely v. White Motor Co., 63 Cal.2d 9, 45 Cal.Rptr. 17, 403 P.2d 145 (1965)(defective truck), held that preserving a proper role for the law of warranty precludes imposing tort liability if a defective product causes purely monetary harm.

At the other end of the spectrum is the minority land-based approach, whose progenitor, Santor v. A and M Karagheusian, Inc., 44 N.J. 52, 207 A.2d 305 (1965)(marred carpeting), held that a manufacturer's duty to make nondefective products encompassed injury to the product itself, whether or not the defect created an unreasonable risk of harm. The courts adopting this approach, including the majority of the Courts of Appeals sitting in admiralty that have considered the issue, find that the safety and insurance rationales behind strict liability apply equally where the losses are purely economic. These courts reject the *Seely* approach because they find it arbitrary that economic losses are recoverable if a plaintiff suffers bodily injury or property damage, but not if a product injures itself. They also find no inherent difference between economic loss and personal injury or property damage, because all are proximately caused by the defendant's conduct. Further, they believe recovery for economic loss would not lead to unlimited liability because they think a manufacturer can predict and insure against product failure.

Between the two poles fall a number of cases that would permit a products-liability action under certain circumstances when a product injures only itself. These cases attempt to differentiate between "the disappointed users ... and the endangered ones," and permit only the latter to sue in tort. The determination has been said to turn on the nature of the defect, the type of risk, and the manner in which the injury arose. The Alaska Supreme Court allows a tort action if the defective product creates a situation potentially dangerous to persons or other property, and loss occurs as a proximate result of that danger and under dangerous circumstances.

We find the intermediate and minority land-based positions unsatisfactory. The intermediate positions, which essentially turn on the degree of risk, are too indeterminate to enable manufacturers easily to structure their business behavior. Nor do we find persuasive a distinction that rests on the manner in which the product is injured. We realize that the damage may be qualitative, occurring through gradual deterioration or internal breakage. Or it may be calamitous. But either way, since by definition no person or other property is damaged, the resulting loss is purely economic. Even when the harm to the product itself occurs through an abrupt, accident-like event, the resulting loss due to repair costs, decreased value, and lost profits is essentially the failure of the purchaser to receive the benefit of its bargain—traditionally the core concern of contract law.

We also decline to adopt the minority land-based view espoused by *Santor* and *Emerson*. Such cases raise legitimate questions about the theories behind restricting products liability, but we believe that the countervailing arguments are more powerful. The minority view fails to account for the need to keep products liability and contract law in separate spheres and to maintain a realistic limitation on damages.

C

Exercising traditional discretion in admiralty, we adopt an approach similar to *Seely* and hold that a manufacturer in a commercial relationship has no duty under either a negligence or strict products-liability theory to prevent a product from injuring itself.

"The distinction that the law has drawn between tort recovery for physical injuries and warranty recovery for economic loss is not arbitrary and does not rest on the 'luck' of one plaintiff in having an accident causing physical injury. The distinction rests, rather, on an understanding of the nature of the responsibility a manufacturer must undertake in distributing his products." When a product injures only itself the reasons for imposing a tort duty are weak and those for leaving the party to its contractual remedies are strong.

The tort concern with safety is reduced when an injury is only to the product itself. When a person is injured, the "cost of an injury and the loss of time or health may be an overwhelming misfortune," and one the person is not prepared to meet. In contrast, when a product injures itself, the commercial user stands to lose the value of the product, risks the displeasure of its customers who find that the product does not meet their needs, or, as in this case, experiences increased costs in performing a service. Losses like these can be insured. Society need not presume that a customer needs special protection. The increased cost to the public that would result from holding a manufacturer liable in tort for injury to the product itself is not justified.

Damage to a product itself is most naturally understood as a warranty claim. Such damage means simply that the product has not met the customer's expectations, or, in other words, that the customer has received "insufficient product value." The maintenance of product value and quality is precisely the purpose of express and implied warranties. Therefore, a claim of a nonworking product can be brought as a breach-of-warranty action. Or, if the customer prefers, it can reject the product or revoke its acceptance and sue for breach of contract.

Contract law, and the law of warranty in particular, is well suited to commercial controversies of the sort involved in this case because the parties may set the terms of their own agreements. The manufacturer can restrict its liability, within limits, by disclaiming warranties or limiting remedies. In exchange, the purchaser pays less for the product. Since a commercial situation generally does not involve large disparities in bargaining power, we see no reason to intrude into the parties' allocation of the risk.

While giving recognition to the manufacturer's bargain, warranty law sufficiently protects the purchaser by allowing it to obtain the benefit of its bargain. The expectation damages available in warranty for purely economic loss give a plaintiff the full benefit of its bargain by compensating for forgone business opportunities. Recovery on a warranty theory would give the charterers their repair costs and lost profits, and would place them in the position they would have been in had the turbines functioned properly. Thus, both the nature of the injury and the resulting damages indicate it is more natural to think of injury to a product itself in terms of warranty.

A warranty action also has a built-in limitation on liability, whereas a tort action could subject the manufacturer to damages of an indefinite amount. The limitation in a contract action comes from the agreement of the parties and the requirement that consequential damages, such as lost profits, be a foreseeable result of the breach. In a warranty action where the loss is purely economic, the limitation derives from the requirements of foreseeability and of privity, which is still generally enforced for such claims in a commercial setting.

In products-liability law, where there is a duty to the public generally, foreseeability is an inadequate brake. Permitting recovery for all foreseeable claims for purely economic loss could make a manufacturer liable for vast sums. It would be difficult for a manufacturer to take into account the expectations of persons downstream who may encounter its product. In this case, for example, if the charterers—already one step removed from the transaction—were permitted to recover their economic losses, then the companies that subchartered the ships might claim their economic losses from the delays, and the charterers' customers also might claim their economic losses, and so on.

And to the extent that courts try to limit purely economic damages in tort, they do so by relying on a far murkier line, one that negates the charterers' contention that permitting such recovery under a products-liability theory enables admiralty courts to avoid difficult line drawing.

D

. . . .

[W]e affirm the entry of judgment for Delaval.

CHAPTER 13

DAMAGES FOR BREACH OF CONTRACT

A. FORESEEABILITY

Pipkin v. Thomas Hill, Inc.

Supreme Court of North Carolina 1979.
298 N.C. 278, 258 S.E.2d 778.

Plaintiffs, as individuals and general partners doing business under the name of P.W.D. & W., brought this action for damages against defendant, a West Virginia corporation engaged in the mortgage banking business, to recover damages for its breach of an alleged contract to make plaintiffs a long-term loan to repay a construction loan from Central Carolina Bank (CCB)....

. . .

■ SHARP, C.J.

... A borrower's claim for damages resulting from a lender's breach of a contract to lend money is primarily circumscribed by the rule of Hadley v. Baxendale, 156 Eng.Rep. 145, 151 (Ex.1854). This rule limits generally the recovery of damages in actions for breach of contract. To recover, a disappointed borrower must not only prove his damages with reasonable certainty, he must also show that they resulted naturally according to the usual course of things from the breach or that, at the time the contract was made, such damages were in the contemplation of the parties as a probable result of the breach. Additionally, the borrower must demonstrate that, upon the lender's breach, he minimized his damages by securing the money elsewhere if available. When alternative funds are unavailable, however, the borrower may recover the damages actually incurred because of the breach, subject to the general rules of foreseeability and certainty of proof. See 5 Corbin, Contracts s 1078 (1964); 11 Williston on Contracts, § 1411 (3d Ed. Jaeger 1968); Annot., 36 A.L.R. 1408 (1925); 22 Am.Jur.2d Damages ss 68, 69 (1965); Coles v. Lumber Co., 150 N.C. 183, 63 S.E. 736 (1909); Anderson v. Hilton and Dodge Lumber Co., 121 Ga. 688, 49 S.E. 725, 727 (1905); Bond Street Knitters, Inc. v. Peninsula National Bank, 266 App.Div. 503, 42 N.Y.S.2d 744 (1943); Davis v. Small Business Investment Co. of Houston, 535 S.W.2d 740, 742–43 (Tex.Civ.App.Texarkana 1976).

The rule governing damages for breach of a contract to lend money is nowhere stated more succinctly than in Restatement of Contracts s 343 (1932):

Damages for breach of a contract to lend money are measured by the cost of obtaining the use of money during the agreed period of credit, less interest at the rate provided in the contract, plus compensation for other unavoidable harm that the defendant had reason to foresee when the contract was made.

Comment:

a. This Section is an application of the general rules of damages to a special class of contracts. The damages awarded are affected by the fact that money is nearly always obtainable in the market. If the loan was to be repayable on demand, or if the contract rate of interest is as much as the current market rate and the money is available to the borrower in the market, his recoverable damages are nominal only. He is expected to avoid other harm by borrowing elsewhere if he can, the reasonable expenses being chargeable to the defendant. Sometimes inability to borrow elsewhere or the delay caused by the lender's action results in loss of a specific advantageous bargain, an unfinished building, or an equity of redemption in mortgaged land; damages are recoverable for losses if the lender had reason to foresee them.

Clearly, the plaintiffs in this case have been injured by defendant's breach of contract. Without defendant's commitment to provide long-term financing they would not have begun construction of the motel project. When it was completed and the construction loan from CCB became due they were unable to obtain alternative long-term financing because none was available at any rate of interest. Plaintiffs were able to forestall foreclosure only by refinancing the construction loan with a demand note at a fluctuating rate of interest which varied from 2 to 3% Above CCB's prime rate and was always in excess of the contract rate....

. . .

... Thus, the question remaining is whether, in order to avoid foreclosure, a disappointed borrower to whom a defaulting lender had committed long-term financing to pay off a temporary construction loan, is entitled to obtain temporary refinancing at a higher rate of interest and to recover the cost of this refinancing as special damages.

On the ground that such refinancing was an unforeseeable consequence of the breach defendant argues that the trial court properly denied plaintiffs any recovery of the interest they paid on the demand note which refinanced the temporary construction loan. In our view, this contention by a defaulting lender, fully aware of the purpose for which plaintiffs had secured its commitment, is entirely unrealistic. In 11 Williston on Contracts § 1411 (3d Ed. Jaeger 1968) it is stated:

It will frequently happen that the borrower is unable to get money elsewhere, and, if the defendant had notice of the purpose for which the money was desired, he will be liable for damages caused by the plaintiff's inability to carry out his purpose, if the performance of the promise would have enabled him to do so.

The case of St. Paul at Chase Corp. v. Manufacturers Life Ins. Co., 262 Md. 192, 278 A.2d 12, Cert. denied, 404 U.S. 857, 92 S.Ct. 104, 30 L.Ed.2d 98 (1971), grew out of the defendant's breach of a commitment to provide the plaintiff with permanent financing "to take out" a construction loan on a high rise apartment building. When the defendant canceled its commitment and the plaintiff was unable to obtain a substitute loan, the bank carrying the construction loan foreclosed the property and obtained a deficiency judgment against the plaintiff, which then sued the defendant for damages. In affirming the trial court's award of compensatory damages which would enable the plaintiff to pay the deficiency judgment and other "consequential damages," the Court of Appeals of Maryland also adopted both the judge's rationale and his succinct statement of it. After noting that in loan transactions such as the one in suit "the parties, of course, anticipate that everything will proceed according to Hoyle that there will be no breach by either party," Judge Proctor added:

> On the other hand, the would be permanent mortgage lender *must contemplate* that if, at the last minute, it cancels its commitment such action would be disastrous to the borrower; that in such event obtaining a new permanent mortgage loan would be well-nigh impossible, for the reason that whatever brought about the cancellation would in all likelihood prevent another lender from entering the fray; that one doesn't find someone willing and able to lend $4,800,000 at a moment's notice; that, under such circumstances, foreclosure under the construction mortgage would not only be a probability, it would be almost inevitable. (Emphasis added.) 262 Md. at 243, 278 A.2d at 36.

Whether the loan commitment be for $4,800,000 or $1,162,500, we harbor no doubt that a committed permanent lender on a substantial building project certainly must foresee that a breach of his commitment a relatively short time before the date he has contracted to provide the money to pay off the interim construction loan will result in substantial harm to the borrower. . . .

———

B. EXPECTATION INTEREST

1. CONTRACTS FOR THE SALE OR LEASE OF PROPERTY

Wilson v. Hays

Court of Civil Appeals of Texas, 1976.
544 S.W.2d 833.

■ JAMES, JUSTICE. This is a suit by the buyer against the seller for breach of an oral contract to sell and deliver used bricks. Trial was had to a jury, which rendered a verdict favorable to the Plaintiff buyer, pursuant to which verdict the trial court entered judgment. We affirm in part and reverse and render in part.

Plaintiff–Appellee W.D. Hays was in the business of buying and selling used building materials. Defendant–Appellant Bobby Wilson doing business as Wilson Salvage Co. was in the business of wrecking or demolishing buildings. In March 1972, Defendant Wilson was in the process of wrecking some buildings in Midland, Texas. Plaintiff Hays became interested in buying the used, uncleaned brick from Defendant Wilson's demolition work. Whereupon, Hays and Wilson entered into an oral agreement whereby Wilson agreed to sell and deliver 600,000 used uncleaned bricks to Hays at a price of one cent per brick, and Hays agreed to buy said bricks at said price. Hays paid Wilson $6,000.00 in advance. Wilson delivered the uncleaned brick to a designated area where Hays had people hired to clean and stack the bricks. Wilson delivered a lesser number of bricks than 600,000, thereby precipitating this suit.

Plaintiff–Appellee Hays brought this suit for the return of the proportionate part of the purchase price paid for the bricks he did not get, plus damages. In answer to special issues the jury found:

(1) That Bobby Wilson orally agreed with Hays that he, Bobby Wilson, would sell and deliver to Hays at least 600,000 bricks at a price of one cent per brick;

. . . .

(6) That Bobby Wilson did not deliver 600,000 uncleaned bricks to Hays (but)

(6A) delivered only 400,000 bricks to Hays;

(7) The market value of used bricks in Midland, Texas in April 1972, was five cents per brick;

(8) Hays suffered lost profits in the amount of $6250.00 by virtue of the failure of Bobby Wilson to deliver to Hays at least 600,000 bricks;

(9) That Hays saved $2605.00 in expenses in consequence of the failure of Bobby Wilson to deliver to him (Hays) at least 600,000 bricks.

Pursuant to the jury verdict, the trial court entered judgment in favor of Plaintiff Hays against Defendant Bobby Wilson in the amount of $13,645.00, plus accrued interest at 6% per annum from and after May 15, 1972, up to Jan. 27, 1976, same being the date of the trial court's judgment, plus interest at 9% per annum from and after the date of said judgment. From this judgment, Defendant Wilson appeals.

. . . .

By Appellant's remaining three points, he challenges the $13,645.00 judgment upon the ground, among other things, that there is no evidence to support the jury's findings in answer to Special Issues No. 8 (lost profits) and No. 9 (expenses). We sustain these points of error insofar as they assert no evidence to support the jury's findings concerning lost profits less expenses, and in all other respects we overrule such points.

Plaintiff–Appellee Hays's remedies and measures of damages as a buyer of goods in the case at bar are governed by Sections 2.711, 2.712, 2.713, and 2.715 of the Texas Business and Commerce Code. We herewith quote the portions of said sections that bear upon the case at bar:

"Sec. 2.711. Buyer's Remedies in General; . . . .

(a) Where the seller fails to make delivery or repudiates ... the buyer may cancel and whether or not he has done so may in addition to recovering so much of the price as has been paid

(1) 'cover' and have damages under the next section as to all the goods affected whether or not they have been identified to the contract; or

(2) recover damages for non-delivery as provided in this chapter (Section 2.713)."

. . . .

"Section 2.712. 'Cover'; Buyer's Procurement of Substitute Goods

(a) After a breach within the preceding section the buyer may 'cover' by making in good faith and without unreasonable delay any reasonable purchase of or contract to purchase goods in substitution for those due from the seller.

(b) The buyer may recover from the seller as damages the difference between the cost of cover and the contract price together with any incidental or consequential damages as hereinafter defined (Section 2.715), but less expenses saved in consequence of the seller's breach.

(c) Failure of the buyer to effect cover within this section does not bar him from any other remedy."

"Section 2.713. Buyer's Damages for Non–Delivery or Repudiation

(a) ... the measure of damages for non-delivery or repudiation by the seller is the difference between the market price at the time when the buyer learned of the breach and the contract price together with any incidental and consequential damages provided in this chapter (Sec. 2.715), but less expenses saved in consequence of the seller's breach."

"Section 2.715. Buyer's Incidental and Consequential Damages

(a) Incidental damages ... (not applicable).

(b) Consequential damages resulting from the seller's breach include

(1) any loss resulting from general or particular requirements and needs of which the seller at the time of contracting had reason to know and which could not reasonably be prevented by cover or otherwise; . . . . "

Let us analyze the verdict and judgment in the light of the foregoing statutory provisions. In the first place, it is established that Plaintiff Hays paid $6000.00 for 600,000 used bricks at the rate of one cent per brick, whereas he received only 400,000 bricks. Therefore he paid $2000 for 200,000 bricks that he never got, and he is thereby entitled to recover $2000.00 under Section 2.711 for "recovering so much of the price as has been paid."

Next, under Section 2.713, he is entitled to damages for "non-delivery or repudiation," and here his measure of damages is the difference between the market price and the contract price. The contract price of the 200,000 bricks not delivered is established at $2000.00. The market price at the appropriate time and place of the undelivered bricks was five cents per brick or $10,000.00. This jury finding of market value (five cents per brick) although challenged by Appellant for legal and factual insufficiency, is amply supported by the evidence and is well within the range of probative testimony. Therefore under Section 2.713 and appropriate jury findings, Plaintiff is entitled to $8000.00 damages (or $10,000.00 market price less $2000.00 contract price) for non-delivery.

Now we come to the problem of "consequential damages ... less expenses saved in consequence of the seller's breach" as mentioned in Sec. 2.713 and which damages are provided for in Sec. 2.715. As stated, the jury found Hays sustained lost profits of $6250.00 (Special Issue No. 8) and saved $2605.00 expenses (No. 9), thereby suffering a lost profits net of $3645.00, which last-named amount was included in the $13,645.00 judgment total. This $3645.00 lost profits amount has no support in the evidence. Under Sec. 2.715, "consequential damages" includes "any loss ... which could not reasonably be prevented by cover or otherwise." There is no evidence in the record whatever that Plaintiff Hays at any time made any effort to cover or in any other manner attempt to prevent or mitigate a loss resulting from the Defendant Wilson's non-delivery of the 200,000 bricks in question. In the absence of such a showing these consequential damages are unauthorized under Section 2.715. The burden of proving the extent of loss incurred by way of consequential damage is on the buyer. This being so, we are of the opinion that there is no evidence to support these jury findings concerning consequential damages, and that the trial court's judgment insofar as it awarded Plaintiff Hays $3645.00 lost profits is improper and this amount should be deleted from said judgment.

As stated before, the judgment is proper and should be affirmed for the amount of $10,000.00, same being composed of $2000.00 paid by Plaintiff for which he received no bricks plus $8000.00 damages for non-delivery.

We therefore affirm in part and reverse and render in part the trial court's judgment as follows: Plaintiff–Appellee Hays is hereby awarded judgment against Defendant–Appellant Wilson in the amount of $10,000.00, plus interest at six percent per annum from and after May 15, 1972 up until January 27, 1976, the date of entry of the trial court's judgment, together with interest from the date of the trial court's judgment upon the amount then due at the rate of nine percent per annum until paid.

Costs of the trial court and of this appeal are taxed one-half each to Appellant and Appellee.

AFFIRMED IN PART AND REVERSED AND RENDERED IN PART.

Neri v. Retail Marine Corp.

Court of Appeals of New York, 1972.
30 N.Y.2d 393, 334 N.Y.S.2d 165, 285 N.E.2d 311.

■ GIBSON, JUDGE. The appeal concerns the right of a retail dealer to recover loss of profits and incidental damages upon the buyer's repudiation of a contract governed by the Uniform Commercial Code. This is, indeed, the correct measure of damage in an appropriate case and to this extent the code (§ 2–708, subsection [2]) effected a substantial change from prior law, whereby damages were ordinarily limited to "the difference between the contract price and the market or current price".[1] Upon the record before us, the courts below erred in declining to give effect to the new statute and so the order appealed from must be reversed.

The plaintiffs contracted to purchase from defendant a new boat of a specified model for the price of $12,587.40, against which they made a deposit of $40. They shortly increased the deposit to $4,250 in consideration of the defendant dealer's agreement to arrange with the manufacturer for immediate delivery on the basis of "a firm sale", instead of the delivery within approximately four to six weeks originally specified. Some six days after the date of the contract plaintiffs' lawyer sent to defendant a letter rescinding the sales contract for the reason that plaintiff Neri was about to undergo hospitalization and surgery, in consequence of which, according to the letter, it would be "impossible for Mr. Neri to make any payments". The boat had already been ordered from the manufacturer and was delivered to defendant at or before the time the attorney's letter was received. Defendant declined to refund plaintiffs' deposit and this action to recover it was commenced. Defendant counterclaimed, alleging plaintiffs' breach of the contract and defendant's resultant damage in the amount of $4,250, for which sum defendant demanded judgment. Upon motion, defendant had summary judgment on the issue of liability tendered by its counterclaim; and Special Term directed an assessment of damages, upon which it would be determined whether plaintiffs were entitled to the return of any portion of their down payment.

Upon the trial so directed, it was shown that the boat ordered and received by defendant in accordance with plaintiffs' contract of purchase was sold some four months later to another buyer for the same price as that negotiated with plaintiffs. From this proof the plaintiffs argue that defendant's loss on its contract was recouped, while defendant argues that but for plaintiffs' default, it would have sold two boats and have earned two profits instead of one. Defendant proved, without contradiction, that its profit on the sale under the contract in suit would have been $2,579 and that during the period the boat remained unsold incidental expenses aggregating $674 for storage, upkeep, finance charges and insurance were incurred. . . .

The trial court found "untenable" defendant's claim for loss of profit, inasmuch as the boat was later sold for the same price that plaintiffs had contracted to pay; found, too, that defendant had failed to prove any incidental damages; further found "that the terms of section 2–718, subsection 2(b), of the Uniform Commercial Code are applicable and same make adequate and fair provision to place the sellers in as good a position as performance would have done" and, in accordance with paragraph (b) of subsection (2) thus relied upon, awarded defendant $500 upon its counterclaim and directed that plaintiffs recover the balance of their deposit,

---

1. Personal Property Law, Consol.Laws, c. 41, § 145, repealed by Uniform Commercial Code, § 10–102 (L.1962, ch. 553, eff. Sept. 27, 1964).

amounting to $3,750. The ensuing judgment was affirmed, without opinion, at the Appellate Division, and defendant's appeal to this court was taken by our leave.

The issue is governed in the first instance by section 2–718 of the Uniform Commercial Code which provides, among other things, that the buyer, despite his breach, may have restitution of the amount by which his payment exceeds: (a) reasonable liquidated damages stipulated by the contract or (b) absent such stipulation, 20% of the value of the buyer's total performance or $500, whichever is smaller (§ 2–718, subsection [2], pars. [a], [b]). As above noted, the trial court awarded defendant an offset in the amount of $500 under paragraph (b) and directed restitution to plaintiffs of the balance. Section 2–718, however, establishes, in paragraph (a) of subsection (3), an alternative right of offset in favor of the seller, as follows: "(3) The buyer's right to restitution under subsection (2) is subject to offset to the extent that the seller establishes (a) a right to recover damages under the provisions of this Article other than subsection (1)".

Among "the provisions of this Article other than subsection (1)" are those to be found in section 2–708, which the courts below did not apply. Subsection (1) of that section provides that "the measure of damages for non-acceptance or repudiation by the buyer is the difference between the market price at the time and place for tender and the unpaid contract price together with any incidental damages provided in this Article (Section 2–710), but less expenses saved in consequence of the buyer's breach." However, this provision is made expressly subject to subsection (2), providing: "(2) If the measure of damages provided in subsection (1) is inadequate to put the seller in as good a position as performance would have done then the measure of damages is the profit (including reasonable overhead) which the seller would have made from full performance by the buyer, together with any incidental damages provided in this Article (Section 2–710), due allowance for costs reasonably incurred and due credit for payments or proceeds of resale."

The provision of the code upon which the decision at Trial Term rested (§ 2–718, subsection [2], par. [b]) does not differ greatly from the corresponding provisions of the prior statute, except as the new act includes the alternative remedy of a lump sum award of $500. Neither does the present reference (in § 2–718, subsection [3], par. [a]) to the recovery of damages pursuant to other provisions of the article differ from a like reference in the prior statute to an alternative measure of damages under section 145 of that act; but section 145 made no provision for recovery of lost profits as does section 2–708 (subsection [2]) of the code. The new statute is thus innovative and significant and its analysis is necessary to the determination of the issues here presented.

Prior to the code, the New York cases "applied the 'profit' test, contract price less cost of manufacture, only in cases where the seller [was] a manufacturer or an agent for a manufacturer" (1955 Report of N.Y.Law Rev.Comm., vol. 1, p. 693). Its extension to retail sales was "designed to eliminate the unfair and economically wasteful results arising under the older law when fixed price articles were involved. This section permits the recovery of lost profits in all appropriate cases, which would include all standard priced goods." (Official Comment 2, McKinney's Cons.Laws of N.Y., Book 62½, Part 1, p. 605, under Uniform Commercial Code, § 2–708.) Additionally, and "[i]n all cases the seller may recover incidental damages" (*id.*, Comment 3). The buyer's right to restitution was established at Special Term upon the motion for summary judgment, as was the seller's right to proper offsets, in each case pursuant to section 2–718; and, as the parties concede, the only question before us, following the assessment of damages at Special Term, is that as to the proper measure of damage to be applied. The conclusion is clear from the record—indeed with mathematical certainty—that "the measure of damages provided in subsection (1) is inadequate to put the seller in as good a position as performance would have done" (Uniform Commercial Code, § 2–708, subsection [2]) and hence—again under subsection (2)—that the seller is entitled to its "profit (including reasonable overhead) ... together with any incidental damages ..., due allowance for costs reasonably incurred and due credit for payments or proceeds of resale."

It is evident, first, that this retail seller is entitled to its profit and, second, that the last sentence of subsection (2), as hereinbefore quoted, referring to "due credit for payments or proceeds of resale" is inapplicable to this retail sales contract.[2] Closely parallel to the factual situation now before us is that hypothesized by Dean Hawkland as illustrative of the operation of the rules: "Thus, if a private party agrees to sell his automobile to a buyer for $2,000, a breach by the buyer would cause the seller no loss (except incidental damages, i.e., expense of a new sale) if the seller was able to sell the automobile to another buyer for $2000. But the situation is different with dealers having an unlimited supply of standard-priced goods. Thus, if an automobile dealer agrees to sell a car to a buyer at the standard price of $2000, a breach by the buyer injures the dealer, even though he is able to sell the automobile to another for $2000. If the dealer has an inexhaustible supply of cars, the resale to replace the breaching buyer costs the dealer a sale, because, had the breaching buyer performed, the dealer would have made two sales instead of one. The buyer's breach, in such a case, depletes the dealer's sales to the extent of one, and the measure of damages should be the dealer's profit on one sale. Section 2–708 recognizes this, and it rejects the rule developed under the Uniform Sales Act by many courts that the profit cannot be recovered in this case." (Hawkland, Sales and Bulk Sales [1958 ed.], pp. 153–154.)

The record which in this case establishes defendant's entitlement to damages in the amount of its prospective profit, at the same time confirms defendant's cognate right to "any incidental damages provided in this Article (Section 2–710)"[3] (Uniform Commercial Code, § 2–708, subsection

---

2. The concluding clause, "due credit for payments or proceeds of resale", is intended to refer to "the privilege of the seller to realize junk value when it is manifestly useless to complete the operation of manufacture" (Supp. No. 1 to the 1952 Official Draft of Text and Comments of the Uniform Commercial Code, as Amended by the Action of the American Law Institute of the National

Conference of Commissioners on Uniform Laws [1954], p. 14)....

3. "Incidental damages to an aggrieved seller include any commercially reasonable charges, expenses or commissions incurred in stopping delivery, in the transportation, care and custody of goods after the buyer's breach, in connection with return or resale of

[2]). From the language employed it is too clear to require discussion that the seller's right to recover loss of profits is not exclusive and that he may recoup his "incidental" expenses as well. Although the trial court's denial of incidental damages in the uncontroverted amount of $674 was made in the context of its erroneous conclusion that paragraph (b) of subsection (2) of section 2–718 was applicable and was "adequate . . . to place the sellers in as good a position as performance would have done", the denial seems not to have rested entirely on the court's mistaken application of the law, as there was an explicit finding "that defendant completely failed to show that it suffered any incidental damages." We find no basis for the court's conclusion with respect to a deficiency of proof inasmuch as the proper items of the $674 expenses (being for storage, upkeep, finance charges and insurance for the period between the date performance was due and the time of the resale) were proven without objection and were in no way controverted, impeached or otherwise challenged, at the trial or on appeal. Thus the court's finding of a failure of proof cannot be supported upon the record and, therefore, and contrary to plaintiffs' contention, the affirmance at the Appellate Division was ineffective to save it.

. . . .

It follows that plaintiffs are entitled to restitution of the sum of $4,250 paid by them on account of the contract price less an offset to defendant in the amount of $3,253 on account of its lost profit of $2,579 and its incidental damages of $674.

The order of the Appellate Division should be modified, with costs in all courts, in accordance with this opinion, and, as so modified, affirmed.

Ordered accordingly.

Bumann v. Maurer

Supreme Court of North Dakota, 1972.
203 N.W.2d 434.

■ MAXWELL, J. This is our second look at this case. It was previously here on certified questions of law. This Court declined to rule on the questions then submitted for the reason "the certified answers would not be dispositive of the case." It was remanded for trial.

The facts were ably presented in Justice Paulson's opinion on that appeal, and need no reiteration at length here. In essence the suit was instituted by the plaintiffs (respondents) for two purposes. One was to require the defendants (appellants) to specifically perform an agreement to convey real estate. The other was to recover damages imputable to tardiness in transferring possession of the land.

After issue was joined, and when trial was first imminent, the defendants relented and did convey the property to the plaintiffs. That left open

the goods or otherwise resulting from the breach" (Uniform Commercial Code, § 2– 710).

only the issue of damages alleged to have sprouted from laggardly performance.

Trial of that question was had in Kidder County District Court on February 1, 1972. A jury verdict for the plaintiffs was brought in for the sum of $8,292.33. Judgment in that amount was thereafter entered.

Defendants' dual motion for judgment notwithstanding the verdict, or for a new trial followed; it was denied in toto. A host of defendants' grievances have now been brought here for review. Not all of the specifications of error will require our attention, however, due to the course we intend the case to take.

The leading issue on this appeal we esteem to be propriety of a portion of the trial court's jury charge. The defendants, (whom we shall for simplicity hereinafter call "sellers") press upon us with skill and zeal the criticism that one of the trial court's instructions obliged the jurors to use an inappropriate guide for measuring damages. With this view we are disposed to agree. The challenged instruction was, we find, inappropriate under the facts.

At the trial, the plaintiffs (hereinafter "buyers") advocated, and the court gave instructions on damages based upon Sec. 32–03–09 NDCC. That section reads:

> "For the breach of an obligation arising from contract, the measure of damages, except when otherwise expressly provided by the laws of this state, is the amount which will compensate the party aggrieved for all the detriment proximately caused thereby or which in the ordinary course of things would be likely to result therefrom. No damages can be recovered for a breach of contract if they are not clearly ascertainable in both their nature and origin."

The sellers resisted use of this statute as the legal basis for damages. Noting that this section, by its own terms, applied only when no other specific law controlled, sellers insisted there was a specifically applicable statute. They claimed Sec. 32–03–13 was singularly designed for this type of case. It states:

> "The detriment caused by the breach of an agreement to convey an estate in real property is the difference between the price agreed to be paid and the value of the estate agreed to be conveyed at the time of the breach and the expenses properly incurred in examining the title, and in preparing to enter upon the land, and the amount paid on the purchase price, if any, with interest thereon from the time of the breach."

While we do, as already mentioned, adopt sellers' position that the trial court erred by giving an instruction founded on Sec. 32–03–09, we do not find the alternative suggestion to be appropriate either. On the contrary, we believe the trial court properly resisted sellers' solicitations to give instructions based on Sec. 32–03–13. Use of that statute is warranted only when specific performance is impossible or impracticable. The appellate court in California, recently construed the very statute of that state from which ours was copied; it said: "A simple reading of the statute discloses that by its explicit terms it is adaptable only to a failure to convey, and not to a delay in conveying."

The sellers here rely on the case Missouri Slope Auction v. Wachter, 107 N.W.2d 349, decided by this court in 1961. We there approved as a measure of damages "the difference between the price to be paid under the contract and the value of the land at the time of the breach." However, in that case, conveyance could not be accomplished under any circumstances. The sellers had agreed to sell property to which they had no title. Here there was no such an impediment. The contract did not fail—it merely suffered long delay.

The damages in this case arose because, in defiance of their contractual obligation to convey and deliver, the sellers wrongfully occupied and used the real estate. There is a specific statute governing damages in such circumstances. Sec. 32–03–21 is titled "Damages for wrongful occupation of realty" and the pertinent part reads as follows:

> "The detriment caused by the wrongful occupation of real proper-
> ty . . . is deemed to be the value of the use of the property for the time
> of such occupation . . . and the costs, if any, of recovering the posses-
> sion." . . .

Sec. 32–03–21 speaks of "the value of the use" as the proper gauge of recovery for the period of wrongful occupation. This value may be found by either of two routes. The aggrieved party may require the party at fault to make an accounting and deliver over the fruits of the illegitimate posses-sion. Or he may, at his election, recover the fair rental value of the property.

It was also error for the court to instruct that "the measure of damages is the amount which will compensate for all detriment proximate-ly caused by the act or omission *whether it could have been anticipated or not.*" (Emphasis added.) This instruction is for a tort case. The emphasized portion is a verbatim quote from Sec. 32–03–20 entitled "Measure of Damages for Tort." That section reads:

> "For the breach of an obligation not arising from contract, the
> measure of damages, except when otherwise expressly provided by law,
> is the amount which will compensate for all the detriment proximately
> caused thereby, whether it could have been anticipated or not."

Such an instruction has no place in a contract case where the limit of liability is narrower than in a tort case. Unlike a tortfeasor, a contracting party is not liable for unforeseeable injury consequent to his breach.

The authorities seem generally to concur in the view that delay in performance of an agreement to convey can be the root of special as well as general damages. Implicit in an agreement to convey is the rudimentary doctrine that performance, unless otherwise specified, must be accom-plished in a reasonable time. Unwarranted and unreasonable tardiness of performance may very well result in special damages to the buyer.

Care, however, must be taken that double compensation is not given for the same element of injury, first as general damages, and again as an item of special damages.

"... there can be but one recovery for each element of damages, whether claimed as general or special damages."

. . . .

Evidence of several other items of special damage was admitted by the court. This evidence included (1) the expense of locating a new farm, (2) the cost of moving to it, (3) additional expense for school transportation, and (4) extra school tuition paid. It was not error to submit these matters to the jury—provided, of course, they were accompanied by proper instructions.

Recoverable special damages must meet the orthodox text laid down in the celebrated English case Hadley v. Baxendale, 156 Eng.Rep. 145 (1854). They must be "such as may reasonably be supposed to have been in the contemplation of the parties at the time they made the contract, as the probable result of the breach of it." The burden is upon the party claiming special damages to show that the injury was reasonably within the contemplation of the parties.

The question of foreseeability of the special damage is generally for the jury. . . .

. . . .

The Order denying motion for judgment notwithstanding the verdict is affirmed; the judgment is reversed and a new trial is ordered.

F. Enterprises, Inc. v. Kentucky Fried Chicken Corp.

Supreme Court of Ohio, 1976.
47 Ohio St.2d 154, 351 N.E.2d 121.

■ STEPHENSON, J . . . .

On January 20, 1968, appellees entered into an option with the H. Corporation for the purchase of a parcel of real estate fronting 170 feet on Morse Road in Franklin County for the sum of $85,000. Shortly thereafter, negotiations began between appellees and appellant, resulting in a contract between the parties for a 20–year lease at a monthly rental of $1,100 for 85 feet of the frontage on Morse Road, which was about 50 percent of the whole of the tract under option by appellees. It was agreed that as a part of the lease, appellees would construct a building on the leased premises not to exceed a cost of $40,000, appellees having the option to require appellant to erect the building with appellant being reimbursed by appellees in a sum not to exceed $40,000.

On August 12, 1968, appellant notified appellees by letter that it would not enter into the lease. On November 18, 1968, appellees exercised their option for the whole tract. The fair rental value of the 85–foot tract, if improved with a building, was $9,025 per year; without improvement, the fair rental value was $3,825 per year. The judgment of $28,508.89 was determined by the trial court in accordance with the opinion of the Court of Appeals.*

---

* The method of calculation by the trial court was as follows:

In their brief in the Court of Appeals, appellees state an arithmetical error was

Appellant urges this method of calculation is erroneous in that, upon appellant's breach of the contract, appellees were required to minimize their damage, and, since appellees were not *required* to exercise their option, even though, in fact, they did so, that appellant's liability for damages should be further reduced by a deduction for interest income for 20 years on one-half of the purchase price of the whole tract. Appellant then asserts that since over the twenty-year period such interest income, which is $51,000, when added to the interest income on the sum unexpended for the building, $48,000, would exceed the difference between the fair market rental and the proposed lease rental for the term of lease, appellees suffered no damage and should recover nothing, except, perhaps, nominal damages. In short, appellant's argument is that appellees either suffered no damage or were, in fact, benefited by appellant's breach of the contract. Such conclusion is untenable and unsupportable under the record. We conclude that not only is appellant not entitled to the further reduction asserted, but also, that the courts below erred in allowing the deduction for the interest upon the $40,000 cost of the proposed building.

We agree with the Court of Appeals that the general rule of damages to be applied when there is an anticipatory breach by a proposed lessee of a contract to make a lease, which is a contract that vests no estate in the prospective lessee, is the difference between the fair market rental of the property proposed to be leased and the agreed rental to be paid in the proposed lease, such sum discounted to present value, together with any special damages arising from the breach. Such rule is one of almost universal application, is consistent with general contract law, and represents the weight of authority. The general rule of necessity is formulated upon the basis of, and takes into consideration, any expenditures for improvements the lessor is required to make under the contract, inasmuch as the agreed payments in the proposed lease reflect such improvements. Such rule, therefore, gives to the defaulting prospective lessee the benefit of any expenditures, such as erection of a building, the prospective of such expenditures in rental obtainable for the improved property on the open market.

Where the courts below erred in their computation of the damage award was, after giving appellant the benefit of the investment by appellees of the $40,000 to help produce the rental income of $9,025, to again give appellant credit for the interest income upon the $40,000. Such $40,000, if invested in the building, could not be at the same time retained by appellees and also constitute a source of interest income to them.

made in such calculation and that the correct figure should have been $28,842.58. Appellees waived any claim of error in such respect and such is not an issue in this appeal.

Contract rental per year	$ 13,200
Market rental value per year	(9,025)
Difference	4,175
Interest income on unexpended $40,000 for building, per year	(2,400)

Difference	1,775
Term of lease in years	× 20
Result	$ 35,500
Discounted value of $35,500 to current value	$20,809.41
Interest at six percent	7,699.48
Damage Award	$28,508.89

When a contract is repudiated at a time when the injured party has not yet performed, ordinarily a savings to the injured party occurs by reason of not having to perform his promise. Such savings is deducted from the compensation under the contract the injured party would have received from the breaching party had the contract been fully performed, since the injured party is only entitled to a damage award which places him in as good a position as he would have been had the contract been fully performed. It is upon this principle that appellant relies; although, in its brief, appellant's argument is framed in the context of the doctrine of avoidable consequences. As will be seen hereafter non-exercise of the purchase of the land by the appellees, under the facts of this case, would not have effected a saving to appellees but actually increased their damages from the breach of the contract by appellant.

The doctrine of avoidable consequences is a rule also arising from the cardinal principle that the damage award should put the injured party in as good a position had the contract not been breached at the least cost to the defaulting party. It is applied, in substance, to prevent an inclusion in the damage award of such damages that could have been avoided by reasonable affirmative action by the injured party without substantial risk to such party.

Whatever should be the rule with respect to the breach of a lease by a lessee, a question not before us, as to the breach by a prospective lessee of a contract to make a lease, we agree with the rule, representing the weight of authority, that recovery of damages by the prospective lessor is limited to only those damages arising from the breach which could not, by reasonable effort on his part without undue risk or expense, have been averted or reduced.

It is to be noted that the general rule of damages gives recognition to a prospective lessor's obligation to minimize damages by renting on the open market to others. Thus, as stated in Branning Mfg. Co. v. Norfolk–Southern R. Co. (1924), 138 Va. 43, 121 S.E. 74, "[I]n effect, the measure of damages stated minimizes the damages of the plaintiff in such case, which is a duty which rests upon the plaintiff in all such cases." To the extent that the prospective lessor has made a "good" or "bad" bargain, it will be reflected in a difference between the agreed rental and market rental. Conceivably, the market rental could exceed the agreed rental so that no pecuniary loss is suffered by the prospective lessor by the prospective lessee's breach.

In order to comply with the contract to make a lease, the prospective lessor at the time of execution of the lease, must own or otherwise have an interest in the premises to let to the prospective lessee. In the ordinary case where the prospective lessor owns the premises at the time of contract, the value thereof, whatever the actual cost, is reflected both in the agreed rental and the fair market rental. What should be the rule, however, if, as here, the parcel is not owned by the prospective lessor but is only the subject of an option? If the prospective lessee does not breach the contract but demands compliance, the prospective lessor is legally required, irrespective of the market value, to exercise his option for whatever sum was agreed to in order to perform his obligation under the contract for the lease.

Conceivably, by the expenditure of the option price, coupled with his obligations under the proposed contract of lease, the result would not be a pecuniary gain but, rather, a loss by the prospective lessor. In such a situation the prospective lessor suffers no damage and might monetarily gain by the breach of the contract by the prospective lessee. Since the general rule of damages would not reflect such fact in such a situation, a deduction from the sum arrived at by application of the general rule of damages above set forth would be proper. However, under the facts of this case it is manifest that the non-exercise of the option would have been to appellees' monetary detriment and not benefit.

Appellees assert, and we agree, three alternatives were available to them upon the breach of the contract. First, they could decline exercise of the option and take no further action under the contract. In this event, they would have expended no funds and, as a result, had available to them the $42,500 (unexpended for land) and $40,000 (unexpended for building) to invest for a return of interest for the term of the proposed lease. Secondly, they could expend the $42,500 in buying the land and invest the $40,000 and receive interest for the term of the lease. Under this alternative they would derive the return from the fair market rental of the unimproved parcel ($3,825 per year) in addition to the interest return upon the $40,000 for the 20–year period. Thirdly, they could have exercised the option for $42,500 as to the parcel here considered, erected the building and rented the improved tract upon the open market for $9,025, effecting an eleven percent return upon the investment.

Simple mathematical calculation of the above alternatives discloses that the non-exercise of the option, would have resulted in the greatest damage to appellees. Additionally, the non-exercise of the option would have required appellees to forego any profit that could be realized by a sale of the other half of the parcel not the subject of the proposed lease. The exercise of the option was thus a prerequisite to appellees' minimization of their damage. It follows, therefore, that since the exercise of the option did not increase but, rather, decreased appellees' pecuniary loss, no deduction from the difference between the agreed rental and fair market rental was warranted.

It follows that appellant is not entitled to the further reduction sought in the award of damages entered by the trial court.

. . . .

The judgment of the Court of Appeals is therefore affirmed.

Austin Hill Country Realty, Inc. v. Palisades Plaza, Inc.

Supreme Court of Texas 1997.
948 S.W.2d 293.

■ SPECTOR, JUSTICE, delivered the opinion for a unanimous Court.

The issue in this case is whether a landlord has a duty to make reasonable efforts to mitigate damages when a tenant defaults on a lease.

The court of appeals held that no such duty exists at common law. We hold today that a landlord has a duty to make reasonable efforts to mitigate damages. Accordingly, we reverse the judgment of the court of appeals and remand for a new trial.

I.

Palisades Plaza, Inc., owned and operated an office complex consisting of four office buildings in Austin. Barbara Hill, Annette Smith, and David Jones sold real estate in Austin as a Re/Max real estate brokerage franchise operating through Austin Hill Country Realty, Inc. On September 15, 1992, the Palisades and Hill Country executed a five-year commercial office lease for a suite in the Palisades' office complex. An addendum executed in connection with the lease set the monthly base rent at $3,128 for the first year, $3,519 for the second and third years, and $3,910 for the fourth and fifth years. The parties also signed an improvements agreement that called for the Palisades to convert the shell office space into working offices for Hill Country. The lease was to begin on the "commencement date," which was defined in the lease and the improvements agreement as either (1) the date that Hill Country occupied the suite, or (2) the date that the Palisades substantially completed the improvements or would have done so but for "tenant delay." All parties anticipated that the lease would begin on November 15, 1992.

By the middle of October 1992, the Palisades had nearly completed the improvements. Construction came to a halt on October 21, 1992, when the Palisades received conflicting instructions about the completion of the suite from Hill on one hand and Smith and Jones on the other. By two letters, the Palisades informed Hill Country, Hill, Smith, and Jones that it had received conflicting directives and would not continue with the construction until Hill, Smith, and Jones collectively designated a single representative empowered to make decisions for the trio. Hill, Smith, and Jones did not reply to these letters.

In a letter dated November 19, 1992, the Palisades informed Hill Country, Hill, Smith, and Jones that their failure to designate a representative was an anticipatory breach of contract. The parties tried unsuccessfully to resolve their differences in a meeting. The Palisades then sued Hill Country, Hill, Smith, and Jones (collectively, "Hill Country") for anticipatory breach of the lease.

At trial, Hill Country attempted to prove that the Palisades failed to mitigate the damages resulting from Hill Country's alleged breach. In particular, Hill Country introduced evidence that the Palisades rejected an offer from Smith and Jones to lease the premises without Hill, as well as an offer from Hill and another person to lease the premises without Smith and Jones. Hill Country also tried to prove that, while the Palisades advertised for tenants continuously in a local newspaper, it did not advertise in the commercial-property publication "The Flick Report" as it had in the past. Hill Country requested an instruction asking the jury to reduce the Palisades' damage award by "any amount that you find the [Palisades] could have avoided by the exercise of reasonable care." The trial judge rejected this instruction, stating, "Last time I checked the law, it was that a landlord doesn't have any obligation to try to fill the space." The jury returned a verdict for the Palisades for $29,716 in damages and $16,500 in attorney's fees. The court of appeals affirmed that judgment. 938 S.W.2d 469.

II.

In its only point of error, Hill Country asks this Court to recognize a landlord's duty to make reasonable efforts to mitigate damages when a tenant breaches a lease. This Court's most recent, and most thorough, discussion of mitigation appeared in Brown v. RepublicBank First National Midland, 766 S.W.2d 203 (Tex.1988). The issues in Brown were whether a termination right in one contract was impliedly included in a sublease agreement between the same parties and, if not, whether the landlord had a duty to mitigate damages upon the tenant's breach. Id. at 204. We held that the termination right was incorporated into the sublease. Id. The tenant thus had properly terminated the sublease agreement, and we did not reach the mitigation issue. Id.

Five justices of this Court, however, expressed that they would hold that a landlord has a duty to mitigate damages after a tenant defaults. Id. at 204 (Kilgarlin, J., concurring, joined by Spears, Gonzalez, and Mauzy, JJ.); id. at 207–08 (Phillips, C.J., dissenting). The concurrence emphasized the contractual nature of modern leases, noting that a covenant to pay rent is like any other contractual promise to pay. Id. at 206 (citing Schneiker v. Gordon, 732 P.2d 603, 610 (Colo.1987)). The concurring justices and the dissenting Chief Justice concluded that public policy requires a landlord, like all other aggrieved parties to a contract, to mitigate damages. Id. at 206 (Kilgarlin, J., concurring); id. at 207–08 (Phillips, C.J., dissenting).

Today we face the issue that Brown did not reach: whether a landlord has a duty to make reasonable efforts to mitigate damages upon the tenant's breach. Because there is no statute addressing this issue, we look to the common law. John F. Hicks, The Contractual Nature of Real Property Leases, 24 Baylor L.Rev. 443, 446–53 (1972).

The traditional common law rule regarding mitigation dictates that landlords have no duty to mitigate damages. See Dawn R. Barker, Note, Commercial Landlords' Duty upon Tenants' Abandonment—To Mitigate?, 20 J. Corp. L. 627, 629 (1995). This rule stems from the historical concept that the tenant is owner of the property during the lease term; as long as the tenant has a right to possess the land, the tenant is liable for rent. See Reid v. Mutual of Omaha Ins. Co., 776 P.2d 896, 902, 905 (Utah 1989). Under this rule, a landlord is not obligated to undertake any action following a tenant's abandonment of the premises but may recover rents periodically for the remainder of the term. See Gruman v. Investors Diversified Servs., 247 Minn. 502, 78 N.W.2d 377, 379–80 (1956).

In Texas, the traditional common law rule was first adopted in Racke v. Anheuser–Busch Brewing Ass'n, 17 Tex.Civ.App. 167, 42 S.W. 774, 775 (Galveston 1897, no writ). In Racke, a landlord sued to determine the extent of the tenant's liability for holding over past the lease term.

Concluding that the holdover rendered the tenant liable under a new tenancy for one year, the Court of Civil Appeals held that the landlord could not "be subjected to damages for failing to let the premises to another, to prevent rents accruing the [tenant]." Id.

Texas courts have consistently followed this no-mitigation rule in cases involving a landlord's suit for past due rent. . . .

Some Texas courts have, however, required a landlord to mitigate damages when the landlord seeks a remedy that is contractual in nature, such as anticipatory breach of contract, rather than a real property cause of action. See Employment Advisors, Inc. v. Sparks, 364 S.W.2d 478, 480 (Tex.Civ.App.—Waco), writ ref'd n.r.e. per curiam, 368 S.W.2d 199, 200 (Tex.1963); see also Evons v. Winkler, 388 S.W.2d 265, 269 (Tex.Civ.App.—Corpus Christi 1965, writ ref'd n.r.e.). In Sparks, the landlord sued the tenant for anticipatory repudiation of the lease. The court of appeals observed that, because the landlord pursued a contractual remedy, the landlord's damage recovery was "subject, of course, to the usual rules concerning mitigation." 364 S.W.2d at 480. In refusing writ per curiam, this Court expressed no opinion on the appellate court's holding. 368 S.W.2d at 200.

Other Texas courts have required a landlord to mitigate damages when the landlord reenters or resumes control of the premises. See John Church Co. v. Martinez, 204 S.W. 486, 489 (Tex.Civ.App.—Dallas 1918, writ ref'd); Robinson Seed & Plant Co. v. Hexter & Kramer, 167 S.W. 749, 751 (Tex.Civ.App.—Dallas 1914, writ ref'd). Thus, a landlord currently may be subject to a mitigation requirement depending upon the landlord's actions following breach and the type of lawsuit the landlord pursues.

III.

In discerning the policy implications of a rule requiring landlords to mitigate damages, we are informed by the rules of other jurisdictions. Forty-two states and the District of Columbia have recognized that a landlord has a duty to mitigate damages in at least some situations: when there is a breach of a residential lease, a commercial lease, or both.[1]

---

1. Lennon v. United States Theatre Corp., 920 F.2d 996, 1000 (D.C.Cir.1990) (holding that both residential and commercial landlords have duty to mitigate); Alaska Stat. § 34.03.230(c) (Michie 1990) (residential); Ariz.Rev.Stat.Ann. § 33–1370 (West 1974) (residential); Tempe Corporate Office Bldg. v. Arizona Funding Servs., 167 Ariz. 394, 807 P.2d 1130, 1135 (App.1991) (commercial); Baston v. Davis, 229 Ark. 666, 318 S.W.2d 837, 841 (1958) (commercial); Cal.Civ.Code § 1951.2(a)(2), (c)(2) (West 1985) (residential); Sanders Constr. Co. v. San Joaquin First Fed. Sav. & Loan Ass'n, 136 Cal.App.3d 387, 186 Cal.Rptr. 218, 226 (1982) (commercial); Schneiker v. Gordon, 732 P.2d 603, 611 (Colo.1987) (commercial); Danpar Assocs. v. Somersville Mills Sales Room, Inc., 182 Conn. 444, 438 A.2d 708, 710 (1980) (commercial); Del.Code Ann. tit. 25, § 5507 (1996) (residential), Del.Code Ann. tit. 25, §§ 5101, 5507(d) (1996) (commercial); Fla.Stat.Ann. § 83.595 (West 1995) (residential); In re PAVCO Enters., Inc., 172 B.R. 114, 117 (Bankr.M.D.Fla. 1994) (commercial); Haw.Rev.Stat. § 521–70(d) (Supp.1975) (residential); Marco Kona Warehouse v. Sharmilo, Inc., 7 Haw.App. 383, 768 P.2d 247, 251, cert. denied, 70 Haw. 665, 796 P.2d 501 (1989) (commercial); Olsen v. Country Club Sports, Inc., 110 Idaho 789, 718 P.2d 1227, 1232–33 (App.1985) (commercial); 735 Ill.Comp.Stat. 5/9–213.1 (West 1992) (residential and commercial); Nylen v. Park Doral Apartments, 535 N.E.2d 178, 183 (Ind.Ct.App.1989) (residential); Sandor Dev. Co. v. Reitmeyer, 498 N.E.2d 1020, 1023 (Ind.

Only six states have explicitly held that a landlord has no duty to mitigate in any situation.[2] In South Dakota, the law is unclear.[3]

Ct.App.1986) (commercial); Hirsch v. Merchants Nat'l Bank & Trust Co. of Ind., 166 Ind.App. 497, 336 N.E.2d 833, 836 (1975) (commercial); Iowa Code § 562A.29(3) (1996) (residential); Harmsen v. Dr. MacDonald's, Inc., 403 N.W.2d 48, 51 (Iowa Ct.App.1987) (commercial); Kan.Stat.Ann. §§ 58–2532 to–2567 (1976)(residential); Gordon v. Consolidated Sun Ray, Inc., 195 Kan. 341, 404 P.2d 949, 953–54 (1965) (commercial); Ky.Rev. Stat.Ann. § 383.670(3) (Michie 1994) (residential); Gray v. Kanavel, 508 So.2d 970, 973 (La.Ct.App.1987) (residential); La.Civ.Code Ann. art. 2002 (West 1990) (commercial); Me. Rev.Stat.Ann. tit. 14, § 6010–A (West 1995) (residential and commercial); Md.Code Ann., Real Prop. § 8–207 (1995) (residential); Atkinson v. Rosenthal, 33 Mass.App.Ct. 219, 598 N.E.2d 666, 669 (1992) (commercial); Jefferson Dev. Co. v. Heritage Cleaners, 109 Mich.App. 606, 311 N.W.2d 426, 428 (1981) (commercial); MRI Northwest Rentals Invs. v. Schnucks–Twenty–Five. Inc., 807 S.W.2d 531, 534 (Mo.Ct.App.1991) (limited duty in commercial leases); Mont.Code Ann. § 70–24–426 (1995); Properties Inv. Group of Mid-America v. JBA, Inc., 242 Neb. 439, 495 N.W.2d 624, 628–29 (1993) (commercial); Nev.Rev.Stat. § 118.175 (1991) (residential); Deasy v. Dernham Co. (In re Blondheim Modular Mfg., Inc.), 65 B.R. 856, 861 (Bankr. D.N.H.1986) (residential and commercial); Sommer v. Kridel, 74 N.J. 446, 378 A.2d 767, 768 (1977) (residential); McGuire v. City of Jersey City, 125 N.J. 310, 593 A.2d 309, 314 (1991) (commercial); N.M.Stat.Ann. § 47–8–6 (Michie 1978) (residential); Isbey v. Crews, 55 N.C.App. 47, 284 S.E.2d 534, 537 (1981) (residential); Weinstein v. Griffin, 241 N.C. 161, 84 S.E.2d 549, 552 (1954) (commercial); N.D.Cent.Code § 47–16–13.4 to .5 (1993) (residential); MAR–SON, Inc. v. Terwaho Enters., 259 N.W.2d 289, 291–92 (N.D.1977) (commercial); Stern v. Taft, 49 Ohio App.2d 405, 361 N.E.2d 279, 281 (1976) (residential); Master Lease of Ohio, Inc. v. Andrews, 20 Ohio App.3d 217, 485 N.E.2d 820, 823 (1984) (commercial); Okla.Stat.Ann. tit. 41, § 129 (West 1986) (residential); Carpenter v. Riddle, 527 P.2d 592, 594 (Okla.1974) (limited duty in commercial leases); Or.Rev.Stat. § 90.410 (1995) (residential); United States Nat'l Bank of Oregon v. Homeland, Inc., 291 Or. 374, 631 P.2d 761, 765 (1981) (commercial); In re New York City Shoes, Inc., 86 B.R. 420, 424 (Bankr.E.D.Pa.1988) (commercial); R.I. Gen. Laws § 34–18–40 (1994) (residential); Lovell v. Kevin J. Thornton Enters., Inc. (In re Branchaud), 186 B.R. 337, 340 (Bankr.D.R.I.1995) (commercial); S.C.Code Ann. § 27–40–730 (Law Co-op.1993) (residential); United States Rubber Co. v. White Tire Co., 231 S.C. 84, 97 S.E.2d 403, 409 (1956) (commercial); Tenn.Code Ann. § 66–28–515 (1995) (residential); Jaffe v. Bolton, 817 S.W.2d 19, 26–27 (Tenn. Ct. App.1991) (commercial); Reid v. Mutual of Omaha Ins. Co., 776 P.2d 896, 906 (Utah 1989) (residential and commercial); O'Brien v. Black, 162 Vt. 448, 648 A.2d 1374, 1376 (1994) (commercial); Va.Code Ann. tit. 55 § 248.35 (Michie 1995) (residential); Wash.Rev.Code § 59.18.310 (1990) (residential); Hargis v. Mel–Mad Corp., 46 Wash.App. 146, 730 P.2d 76, 79 (1986) (commercial); Wis. Stat. § 704.29 (1993–94) (residential); First Wis. Trust Co. v. L. Wiemann Co., 93 Wis.2d 258, 286 N.W.2d 360, 366 (1980) (commercial); System Terminal Corp. v. Cornelison, 364 P.2d 91, 95 (Wyo.1961) (commercial). See generally 52 C.J.S. Landlord and Tenant § 498 (1968); 21 Am.Jur. 3d Damages—Mitigation by Landlord §§ 1–9 (1968 & Supp. 1994); 5 A. Corbin, Corbin on Contracts § 1039A (Supp.1993).

2. Ryals v. Laney, 338 So.2d 413, 415 (Ala.Civ.App.1976) (holding that there is no duty to mitigate in residential leases); Crestline Ctr. v. Hinton, 567 So.2d 393, 396 (Ala. Civ.App.1990) (commercial); Love v. McDevitt, 114 Ga.App. 734, 152 S.E.2d 705, 706 (1966) (residential); Lamb v. Decatur Fed. Sav. & Loan Ass'n, 201 Ga.App. 583, 411 S.E.2d 527, 530 (1991) (commercial); Markoe v. Naiditch & Sons, 303 Minn. 6, 226 N.W.2d 289, 291 (1975) (residential and commercial); Alsup v. Banks, 68 Miss. 664, 9 So. 895, 895 (1891) (residential); Duda v. Thompson, 169 Misc.2d 649, 647 N.Y.S.2d 401, 403–04 (N.Y.Sup.Ct.1996) (residential); Holy Properties, Ltd. v. Kenneth Cole Prods., Inc., 87 N.Y.2d 130, 637 N.Y.S.2d 964, 661 N.E.2d 694, 696 (1995) (commercial); Arbenz v. Exley, Watkins & Co., 52 W.Va. 476, 44 S.E. 149, 151 (1903) (commercial). Mississippi has reported no cases regarding a commercial landlord's duty to mitigate, and West Virginia has reported no cases regarding a residential landlord's duty to mitigate.

3. South Dakota has apparently reported no cases on this issue.

Those jurisdictions recognizing a duty to mitigate have emphasized the change in the nature of landlord-tenant law since its inception in medieval times. At English common law, the tenant had only contractual rights against the landlord and therefore could not assert common-law real property causes of action to protect the leasehold. Over time, the courts recognized a tenant's right to bring real property causes of action, and tenants were considered to possess an estate in land. 2 R. POWELL, THE LAW OF REAL PROPERTY § 221[1], at 16–18 (1969). The landlord had to give the tenant possession of the land, and the tenant was required to pay rent in return. As covenants in leases have become more complex and the structures on the land have become more important to the parties than the land itself, courts have begun to recognize that a lease possesses elements of both a contract and a conveyance. See, e.g., Schneiker v. Gordon, 732 P.2d 603, 607–09 (Colo.1987); Reid v. Mutual of Omaha Ins. Co., 776 P.2d 896, 902, 904 (Utah 1989). Under contract principles, the lease is not a complete conveyance to the tenant for a specified term such that the landlord's duties are fulfilled upon deliverance of the property to the tenant. Rather, a promise to pay in a lease is essentially the same as a promise to pay in any other contract, and a breach of that promise does not necessarily end the landlord's ongoing duties. Schneiker, 732 P.2d at 610; Wright v. Baumann, 239 Or. 410, 398 P.2d 119, 121 (1965). Because of the contractual elements of the modern lease agreement, these courts have imposed upon the landlord the contractual duty to mitigate damages upon the tenant's breach.

Public policy offers further justification for the duty to mitigate. First, requiring mitigation in the landlord-tenant context discourages economic waste and encourages productive use of the property. As the Colorado Supreme Court has written:

Under traditional property law principles a landlord could allow the property to remain unoccupied while still holding the abandoning tenant liable for rent. This encourages both economic and physical waste. In no other context of which we are aware is an injured party permitted to sit idly by and suffer avoidable economic loss and thereafter to visit the full adverse economic consequences upon the party whose breach initiated the chain of events causing the loss.

Schneiker, 732 P.2d at 610. A mitigation requirement thus returns the property to productive use rather than allowing it to remain idle. Public policy requires that the law "discourage even persons against whom wrongs have been committed from passively suffering economic loss which could be averted by reasonable efforts." Wright, 398 P.2d at 121 (quoting C. McCOR-MICK, HANDBOOK ON THE LAW OF DAMAGES, § 33 (1935)).

Second, a mitigation rule helps prevent destruction of or damage to the leased property. If the landlord is encouraged to let the property remain unoccupied, "the possibility of physical damage to the property through accident or vandalism is increased." Schneiker, 732 P.2d at 610.

Third, the mitigation rule is consistent with the trend disfavoring contract penalties. Reid, 776 P.2d at 905–06. Courts have held that a liquidated damages clause in a contract must represent a reasonable estimate of anticipated damages upon breach. See, e.g., Warner v. Rasmussen, 704 P.2d 559, 561, 563 (Utah 1985). "Similarly, allowing a landlord to leave property idle when it could be profitably leased and forc[ing] an absent tenant to pay rent for that idled property permits the landlord to recover more damages than it may reasonably require to be compensated for the tenant's breach. This is analogous to imposing a disfavored penalty upon the tenant." Reid, 776 P.2d at 905–06.

Finally, the traditional justifications for the common law rule have proven unsound in practice. Proponents of the no-mitigation rule suggest that the landlord-tenant relationship is personal in nature, and that the landlord therefore should not be forced to lease to an unwanted tenant. See Wohl v. Yelen, 22 Ill.App.2d 455, 161 N.E.2d 339, 343 (1959). Modern lease arrangements, however, are rarely personal in nature and are usually business arrangements between strangers. Edwin Smith, Jr., Comment, Extending the Contractual Duty to Mitigate Damages to Landlords when a Tenant Abandons the Lease, 42 Baylor L.Rev. 553, 559 (1990). Further, the landlord's duty to make reasonable efforts to mitigate does not require that the landlord accept replacement tenants who are financial risks or whose business was precluded by the original lease. Note, Landlord and Tenant—Mitigation of Damages, 45 Wash.L.Rev. 218, 225 (1970).

The overwhelming trend among jurisdictions in the United States has thus been toward requiring a landlord to mitigate damages when a tenant abandons the property in breach of the lease agreement. Those courts adopting a mitigation requirement have emphasized the contractual elements of a lease agreement, the public policy favoring productive use of property, and the practicalities of the modern landlord-tenant arrangement as supporting such a duty.

IV.

We are persuaded by the reasoning of those courts that recognize that landlords must mitigate damages upon a tenant's abandonment and failure to pay rent. This Court has recognized the dual nature of a lease as both a conveyance and a contract. See Davidow v. Inwood North Prof'l Group—Phase I, 747 S.W.2d 373, 375–76 (Tex.1988); Kamarath v. Bennett, 568 S.W.2d 658, 660–61 (Tex.1978). Under a contract view, a landlord should be treated no differently than any other aggrieved party to a contract. Further, the public policy of the state of Texas calls for productive use of property as opposed to avoidable economic waste. Brown, 766 S.W.2d at 204 (Kilgarlin, J., concurring). As Professor McCormick wrote over seventy years ago, the law which permits the landlord to stand idly by the vacant, abandoned premises and treat them as the property of the tenant and recover full rent, [should] yield to the more realistic notions of social advantage which in other fields of the law have forbidden a recovery for damages which the plaintiff by reasonable efforts could have avoided.

Charles McCormick, The Rights of the Landlord Upon Abandonment of the Premises by the Tenant, 23 Mich.L.Rev. 211, 221–22 (1925). Finally, we have recognized that contract penalties are disfavored in Texas. Stewart v. Basey, 150 Tex. 666, 245 S.W.2d 484, 486 (1952) (landlord should not receive more or less than actual damages upon tenant's breach). A landlord should not be allowed to collect rent from an abandoning tenant when the landlord can, by reasonable efforts, relet the premises and avoid incurring some damages. We therefore recognize that a landlord has a duty to make reasonable efforts to mitigate damages when the tenant breaches the lease and abandons the property, unless the commercial landlord and tenant contract otherwise.

V.

To ensure the uniform application of this duty by the courts of this state, and to guide future landlords and tenants in conforming their conduct to the law, we now consider several practical considerations that will undoubtedly arise. We first consider the level of conduct by a landlord that will satisfy the duty to mitigate. The landlord's mitigation duty has been variously stated in other jurisdictions. See, e.g., Reid, 776 P.2d at 906 ("objective commercial reasonableness"); Schneiker, 732 P.2d at 611 ("reasonable efforts"); Cal. Civ.Code § 1951.2(c)(2) ("reasonably and in a good-faith effort"). Likewise, the courts of this state have developed differing language regarding a party's duty to mitigate in other contexts. See City of San Antonio v. Guidry, 801 S.W.2d 142, 151 (Tex.App.—San Antonio 1990, no writ) (collecting cases). We hold that the landlord's duty to mitigate requires the landlord to use objectively reasonable efforts to fill the premises when the tenant vacates in breach of the lease.

We stress that this is not an absolute duty. The landlord is not required to simply fill the premises with any willing tenant; the replacement tenant must be suitable under the circumstances. Nor does the landlord's failure to mitigate give rise to a cause of action by the tenant. Rather, the landlord's failure to use reasonable efforts to mitigate damages bars the landlord's recovery against the breaching tenant only to the extent that damages reasonably could have been avoided. Similarly, the amount of damages that the landlord actually avoided by releasing the premises will reduce the landlord's recovery.

Further, we believe that the tenant properly bears the burden of proof to demonstrate that the landlord has mitigated or failed to mitigate damages and the amount by which the landlord reduced or could have reduced its damages. The traditional rule in other contexts is that the breaching party must show that the nonbreaching party could have reduced its damages. See, e.g., Sorbus, Inc. v. UHW Corp., 855 S.W.2d 771, 775 (Tex.App.—El Paso 1993, writ denied) (mitigation of damages following tortious interference with contract); Texas Dep't of Human Servs. v. Green, 855 S.W.2d 136, 151 (Tex.App.—Austin 1993, writ denied) (mitigation of damages following wrongful discharge); see generally E. ALLEN FARNSWORTH, CONTRACTS § 12.12 (2d ed. 1990). In the landlord-tenant context, although there is some split of authority, many other jurisdictions have placed the burden of proving mitigation or failure to mitigate upon the breaching tenant. See Barker, 20 J. Corp. L. at 639 n. 86.

When the tenant contends that the landlord has actually mitigated damages, the breaching tenant need not plead the landlord's actual mitigation as an affirmative defense. Rather, the tenant's evidence of the landlord's mitigation tends to rebut the measure of damages under the landlord's claim of breach and may be admitted under a general denial. See

Greater Fort Worth & Tarrant County Community Action Agency v. Mims, 627 S.W.2d 149, 151 (Tex.1982). The tenant's contention that the landlord failed to mitigate damages, in contrast, is similar to an avoidance defense; evidence of failure to mitigate is admissible only if the tenant pleads the failure to mitigate as an affirmative defense. W.L. Moody & Co. v. Rowland, 100 Tex. 363, 99 S.W. 1112, 1114–16 (1907); see also Professional Servs., Inc. v. Amaitis, 592 S.W.2d 396, 397 (Tex.Civ.App.—Dallas 1979, writ ref'd n.r.e.).

The final issue to resolve regarding the duty to mitigate is to which types of actions by the landlord the duty will apply. Traditionally, Texas courts have regarded the landlord as having four causes of action against a tenant for breach of the lease and abandonment. See Speedee Mart v. Stovall, 664 S.W.2d 174, 177 (Tex.App.—Amarillo 1983, no writ); Jerry D. Johnson, Landlord Remedies in Texas: Confusion Reigns Where Certainty Should Prevail, 33 S. Tex.L.Rev. 417, 419–20 (1992). First, the landlord can maintain the lease, suing for rent as it becomes due. Second, the landlord can treat the breach as an anticipatory repudiation, repossess, and sue for the present value of future rentals reduced by the reasonable cash market value of the property for the remainder of the lease term. Third, the landlord can treat the breach as anticipatory, repossess, release the property, and sue the tenant for the difference between the contractual rent and the amount received from the new tenant. Fourth, the landlord can declare the lease forfeited (if the lease so provides) and relieve the tenant of liability for future rent. Speedee Mart, 664 S.W.2d at 177.

The landlord must have a duty to mitigate when suing for anticipatory repudiation. Because the cause of action is contractual in nature, the contractual duty to mitigate should apply. The landlord's option to maintain the lease and sue for rent as it becomes due, however, is more troubling. To require the landlord to mitigate in that instance would force the landlord to reenter the premises and thereby risk terminating the lease or accepting the tenant's surrender. See Johnson, 33 S. Tex.L.Rev. at 437; Hicks, 24 Baylor L.Rev. at 517. We thus hold that, when exercising the option to maintain the lease in effect and sue for rent as it becomes due following the tenant's breach and abandonment, the landlord has a duty to mitigate only if (1) the landlord actually reenters, or (2) the lease allows the landlord to reenter the premises without accepting surrender, forfeiting the lease, or being construed as evicting the tenant. See Robinson Seed & Plant Co. v. Hexter & Kramer, 167 S.W. 749, 751 (Tex.Civ.App.—Dallas 1914, writ ref'd); 21 A.L.R.3d at 556–63. A suit for anticipatory repudiation, an actual reentry, or a contractual right of reentry subject to the above conditions will therefore give rise to the landlord's duty to mitigate damages upon the tenant's breach and abandonment.

VI.

In their first amended answer, Hill Country and Barbara Hill specifically contended that the Palisades failed to mitigate its damages. Because the court of appeals upheld the trial court's refusal to submit their mitigation instruction, we reverse the judgment of the court of appeals and remand for a new trial.

---

2. Contracts for Personal Services

Parker v. Twentieth Century–Fox Film Corp.

Supreme Court of California, 1970.
3 Cal.3d 176, 89 Cal.Rptr. 737, 474 P.2d 689.

■ Burke, J. . . .

Plaintiff is well known as an actress [by the name of Shirley MacLaine], and in the contract between plaintiff and defendant is sometimes referred to as the "Artist." Under the contract, dated August 6, 1965, plaintiff was to play the female lead in defendant's contemplated production of a motion picture entitled "Bloomer Girl." The contract provided that defendant would pay plaintiff a minimum "guaranteed compensation" of $53,571.42 per week for 14 weeks commencing May 23, 1966, for a total of $750,000. Prior to May 1966 defendant decided not to produce the picture and by a letter dated April 4, 1966, it notified plaintiff of that decision and that it would not "comply with our obligations to you under" the written contract.

By the same letter and with the professed purpose "to avoid any damage to you," defendant instead offered to employ plaintiff as the leading actress in another film tentatively entitled "Big Country, Big Man" (hereinafter, "Big Country"). The compensation offered was identical, as were 31 of the 34 numbered provisions or articles of the original contract. Unlike "Bloomer Girl," however, which was to have been a musical production, "Big Country" was a dramatic "western type" movie. "Bloomer Girl" was to have been filmed in California; "Big Country" was to be produced in Australia. Also certain terms in the proffered contract varied from those of the original. Plaintiff was given one week within which to accept; she did not and the offer lapsed. Plaintiff then commenced this action seeking recovery of the agreed compensation.

. . . .

Plaintiff moved for summary judgment . . ., the motion was granted, and summary judgment for $750,000 plus interest was entered in plaintiff's favor. This appeal by defendant followed.

The general rule is that the measure of recovery by a wrongfully discharged employee is the amount of salary agreed upon for the period of service, less the amount which the employer affirmatively proves the employee has earned or with reasonable effort might have earned from other employment. However, before projected earnings from other employment opportunities not sought or accepted by the discharged employee can be applied in mitigation, the employer must show that the other employment was comparable, or substantially similar, to that of which the employee has been deprived; the employee's rejection of or failure to seek other available employment of a different or inferior kind may not be resorted to in order to mitigate damages.

In the present case defendant has raised no issue of *reasonableness of efforts* by plaintiff to obtain other employment; the sole issue is whether plaintiff's refusal of defendant's substitute offer of "Big Country" may be used in mitigation. Nor, if the "Big Country" offer was of employment different or inferior when compared with the original "Bloomer Girl" employment, is there an issue as to whether or not plaintiff acted reasonably in refusing the substitute offer. Despite defendant's arguments to the contrary, no case cited or which our research has discovered holds or suggests that reasonableness is an element of a wrongfully discharged employee's option to reject, or fail to seek, different or inferior employment lest the possible earnings therefrom be charged against him in mitigation of damages.[5]

. . . .

Applying the foregoing rules to the record in the present case, with all intendments in favor of the party opposing the summary judgment motion—here, defendant—it is clear that the trial court correctly ruled that plaintiff's failure to accept defendant's tendered substitute employment could not be applied in mitigation of damages because the offer of the "Big Country" lead was of employment both different and inferior, and that no factual dispute was presented on that issue. The mere circumstance that "Bloomer Girl" was to be a musical review calling upon plaintiff's talents as a dancer as well as an actress, and was to be produced in the City of Los Angeles, whereas "Big Country" was a straight dramatic role in a "Western Type" story taking place in an opal mine in Australia, demonstrates the difference in kind between the two employments; the female lead as a dramatic actress in a western style motion picture can by no stretch of imagination be considered the equivalent of or substantially similar to the lead in a song-and-dance production.

Additionally, the substitute "Big Country" offer proposed to eliminate or impair the director and screenplay approvals accorded to plaintiff under the original "Bloomer Girl" contract . . . , and thus constituted an offer of inferior employment. No expertise or judicial notice is required in order to hold that the deprivation or infringement of an employee's rights held under an original employment contract converts the available "other employment" relied upon by the employer to mitigate damages, into inferior employment which the employee need not seek or accept.

. . . .

In view of the determination that defendant failed to present any facts showing the existence of a factual issue with respect to its sole defense—plaintiff's rejection of its substitute employment offer in mitigation of damages—we need not consider plaintiff's further contention that for

---

5. Instead, in each case the reasonableness referred to was that of the *efforts* of the employee to obtain other employment that was not different or inferior; his right to reject the latter was declared as an unqualified rule of law. . . .

various reasons, ... plaintiff was excused from attempting to mitigate damages.[5a]

The judgment is affirmed.

■ SULLIVAN, A.C.J. (dissenting). The basic question in this case is whether or not plaintiff acted reasonably in rejecting defendant's offer of alternate employment. The answer depends upon whether that offer (starring in "Big Country, Big Man") was an offer of work that was substantially similar to her former employment (starring in "Bloomer Girl") or of work that was of a different or inferior kind. To my mind this is a factual issue which the trial court should not have determined on a motion for summary judgment. The majority have not only repeated this error but have compounded it by applying the rules governing mitigation of damages in the employer-employee context in a misleading fashion. Accordingly, I respectfully dissent.

The familiar rule requiring a plaintiff in a tort or contract action to mitigate damages embodies notions of fairness and socially responsible behavior which are fundamental to our jurisprudence. Most broadly stated, it precludes the recovery of damages which, through the exercise of due diligence, could have been avoided. Thus, in essence, it is a rule requiring reasonable conduct in commercial affairs.

This general principle governs the obligations of an employee after his employer has wrongfully repudiated or terminated the employment contract. Rather than permitting the employee simply to remain idle during the balance of the contract period, the law requires him to make a reasonable effort to secure other employment. He is not obliged, however, to seek or accept any and all types of work which may be available. Only work which is in the same field and which is of the same quality need be accepted.

. . . .

... The inquiry in cases such as this should not be whether differences between the two jobs exist (there will always be differences) but whether the differences which are present are substantial enough to constitute differences in the *kind* of employment or, alternatively, whether they render the substitute work employment of an *inferior kind*.

It seems to me that *this* inquiry involves, in the instant case at least, factual determinations which are improper on a motion for summary judgment. Resolving whether or not one job is substantially similar to another or whether, on the other hand, it is of a different or inferior kind, will often (as here) require a critical appraisal of the similarities and differences between them in light of the importance of these differences to the employee. This necessitates a weighing of the evidence, and it is precisely this undertaking which is forbidden on summary judgment.

. . . .

[5a] In a wrongful discharge action, whether in contract or tort, the mitigation of damage rule requires that the discharged employee exercised reasonable diligence in seeking and obtaining comparable employment. See vol. 2 Mark A. Rothstein, Employment Law 8. 21, p. 321 (2d.ed. 19).

Indiana State Symphony Society, Inc. v. Ziedonis

Court of Appeals of Indiana, 1976.
171 Ind.App. 292, 359 N.E.2d 253.

■ WHITE, J. Plaintiff-appellee (Ziedonis), formerly employed by defendant-appellant (Symphony) as a violinist in the Indianapolis Symphony Orchestra, recovered a verdict and judgment of $6,335.00 as damages for his discharge in alleged violation of his written employment contract. Symphony's appeal charges error . . . in the amount of damages.

. . . .

Symphony contends that the verdict is too large by at least $3,430, which is the amount Ziedonis testified in his own case-in-chief he was paid for playing with two out-of-town orchestras during the period for which the verdict awards him the full amount of his Symphony salary. Ziedonis counters with argument to the effect that Symphony has failed to sustain its burden of proving mitigation in that it has failed to prove that the $3,430 is profit and that, inasmuch as his Symphony employment was only part-time, Symphony has failed to prove that he could not have earned this income had he not been discharged.

As to the last point, Symphony says that it is obvious that Ziedonis could not have played for those orchestras had he also been employed by Symphony. Since neither orchestra appears to have played in or near Indianapolis that proposition is irrefutable.

A majority of this court is of the opinion, for the reasons stated in Presiding Judge Buchanan's concurring opinion, that the entire $3,430 should have been deducted in mitigation of Ziedonis' damages. Therefore a remittitur will be ordered.

It is the writer's opinion, however, that the burden of *proving* mitigation, if any, rested on Symphony, and that it failed to prove that his earning this $3,430 actually reduced his loss. It was Ziedonis' duty to use reasonable efforts to avoid loss by securing employment elsewhere and, although it was not his burden to do so, he did prove that he had discharged that duty. The fact that in so doing he also proved that he earned a gross sum for out-of-town work in which he incurred expenses does not shift to him the burden of proving whether or not his earnings exceeded his expenses. . . .

. . . .

Reversed and Remanded with directions.

■ BUCHANAN, P.J., concurs with opinion, in which HOFFMAN, J., (participating by designation) joins.

■ BUCHANAN, P.J. (concurring). I concur in the result reached by the majority, but solely on the basis that once it was proved that Ziedonis had incurred mitigating damages, the burden was on him (not the Defendant) to prove that he also had expenses which otherwise would not have been incurred.

It has long been the rule in Indiana that one wrongfully discharged must attempt to seek alternate employment in order to mitigate damages.

... it is the duty of a person, when unlawfully discharged, to make reasonable effort to obtain work elsewhere, and that in no event could he recover more than what his actual loss might have been had he made such reasonable effort to obtain employment.

When a discharged employee obtains alternate employment there is no question that the proper measure of his damages is the amount of compensation agreed upon for the remainder of the contract period involved, less the amount which he earns from other employment. Thus, the jury should have reduced Ziedonis's award by Three Thousand Four Hundred and Thirty ($3,430.00) Dollars, the amount he earned in alternate employment.

The majority rightfully place the burden on the Defendant Symphony of showing that other employment was available to plaintiff or that the plaintiff did not use diligence in seeking other employment. This is the rule in Indiana.

In this case it was unnecessary for the Symphony to carry this burden because Ziedonis testified that he had earned Three Thousand Four Hundred and Thirty ($3,430.00) Dollars in other employment during the remainder of the contract period. However, I am aware of no Indiana cases which would require the Symphony to show that this employment was profitable to Ziedonis, i.e. because Ziedonis had certain expenses of an unspecified amount during the time he earned the Three Thousand Four Hundred and Thirty ($3,430.00) Dollars the Symphony has failed to show that such employment was profitable.

The defendant is in no position to know plaintiff's expenses and should not reasonably be saddled with the burden of proving them. As expenses are peculiarly within the cognizance of plaintiff, *he* should prove them.

Presumably, something more than love of music led Ziedonis to seek employment with out-of-town symphony orchestras. He certainly had income from this employment. If he had expenses which reduced his income, he should have proved them.

———

3. Construction Contracts

———

Appalachian Power Co. v. John Stewart Walker, Inc.

Supreme Court of Virginia, 1974.
214 Va. 524, 201 S.E.2d 758.

■ Poff, J. On a bill of complaint filed by John Stewart Walker, Inc., (Walker) against Appalachian Power Company (Appalachian) seeking *inter alia* damages of $10,000.00 for breach of an alleged contract to install, free of charge, underground electrical service, the trial court by order dated October 13, 1972 entered final judgment on the jury's verdict awarding Walker damages in the sum of $6,000.00....

. . . .

Walker's evidence tended to show that the lack of underground electrical facilities reduced the sale value of the 20 lots by $8,000.00. Appalachian's evidence tended to show that the cost of installation was $3,546.00. The trial court granted Walker's instruction based on the "value" formula, refused Appalachian's instruction based on the "cost" formula, and overruled Appalachian's motion to set aside the jury verdict based on the "value" formula.

A successful plaintiff is entitled to recover those damages which are "the natural and direct result of the breach of the contract". And "[t]he object of the law in awarding damages is to make amends or reparations by putting the party injured in the same position, as far as money can do it, as he would have been if the contract had been performed."

Whether the "value" formula or the "cost" formula is applicable "will depend upon the facts and [the] circumstances of the particular case." We have recognized application of the "value" formula in an appropriate case. The test is the nature of the motivation which induced the promisee to make the contract. If his primary interest was the value of the result performance would have produced, then the "value" formula is applicable; if performance itself, then the "cost" formula.

The uncontradicted evidence was that Walker was developing Locksview Subdivision to sell lots; that his reason for wanting underground electrical service was to enhance the marketability and market price of the lots; and that the lack of such service impaired both by a measurable degree. The first jury found that such impairment was the natural and direct result of Appalachian's breach of a contractual duty. We find no error in the formula applied by the trial court's instructions.

Accordingly, the decree is

Affirmed.

[CARRICO, J., joined by HARRISON and COCHRAN, JJ., dissented on other grounds.]

Eastlake Construction Company v. Hess

Supreme Court of Washington, 1984.
102 Wash.2d 30, 686 P.2d 465.

■ PEARSON, J. . . . .

Plaintiff Eastlake Construction Company (Eastlake) brought this action in King County Superior Court to recover $13,719 allegedly owing on a construction contract. Eastlake had entered the contract with defendants Leroy and Jean Hess to erect a 5–unit condominium building in Issaquah. Defendants counterclaimed, alleging damages for breach of the contract. . . . The trial court awarded defendants damages for breach of contract, less the amount owing to Eastlake under the contract. . . .

. . . .

. . . It was not disputed at trial that Eastlake had not been paid $13,719 of the contract price of $118,600. The principal factual dispute centered around the nature and extent of Eastlake's breaches of the contract and the measure of damages for those breaches. The trial court heard considerable testimony that Eastlake had delayed completion of the project, had failed to complete the work contracted for, and had performed work and used materials not in accordance with the contract specifications. The trial court found that Eastlake had breached the construction contract in a number of respects. These findings, and the damages allowed by the trial court, may be summarized as follows.

A.   Breaches for which the trial court allowed damages.

1.   Eastlake wrongfully abandoned the project in February 1978, and defendants were allowed the reasonable cost of completing construction to make the condominiums habitable, $7,979.90.

2.   Defendants were allowed the reasonable rental value of the condominiums from the time construction should have been completed until the actual completion date, $4,262.50.

3.   Defendants were allowed damages for the reasonable cost of work specified in the plans, but not completed by Eastlake: insulating waste pipes, $807.44; installing recirculating fans, $1,031.10.

4.   Defendants were allowed damages for the reasonable cost of repairing and replacing work performed by Eastlake which did not conform to the specifications: repairing the roof, $4,414.01; replacing balcony guardrails, $1,580.76; repairing and replacing washer and dryer closets, $751.84; replacing nonvented kitchen hood fans, $926.53; and replacing interior doors, $787.22.

5.   Defendants were also allowed $75 for installation of cable television and $200 for light fixture underrun.

6.   Defendants were also allowed damages for the installation of kitchen cabinets not in accordance with contract specifications.

The court declined to award the cost of replacement of these cabinets because this would constitute unreasonable economic waste. Instead, the measure of damages was the difference between the value of the specified cabinets ($8,725.50) and the cost of the cabinets actually installed ($3,700): $5,0252.50 [sic.].

B.   Breaches for which the trial court allowed no damages.

The trial court found that Eastlake had breached the construction contract in a number of other respects, but that these breaches "did not result in substantial damage to the building nor result in a substantial loss of value to the building". Defendants were not allowed damages for these breaches.

The trial court found that Eastlake departed from the specifications as follows:

1.   Installation of 1-inch foam insulation under the concrete floors, rather than 1½ inches.

2.   Installation of plastic rather than cast iron waste lines.

3.   Installation of electrical service panels in the bedrooms rather than the hallways.

4. Installation of the wrong grade of felt under the siding.

5. Use of insufficient caulking materials and exterior stain.

6. Installation of galvanized roof jacks rather than lead roof jacks.

7. Installation of acoustic ceiling materials rather than orange peel texture.

8. Installation of one piece of insulation in a party wall instead of two pieces.

9. Installation of blown-in rock wool rather than fiberglass batts for ceiling insulation.

. . . .

The trial court found a total of $27,841.70 in damages to defendants, against which was offset the $13,719 owing on the construction contract, for an award on the counterclaim of $14,122.70.

. . . .

. . . The Court of Appeals upheld the trial court's measuring damages by the cost of remedying defects.

On the cross appeal, the Court of Appeals increased the damages awarded by the trial court. First, it concluded that the issue of economic waste was a question of law, and that the trial court had erred in concluding that replacing the kitchen cabinets would constitute economic waste. Accordingly, the Court of Appeals allowed the cost of removing the existing cabinets ($4,060) plus the cost of the cabinets specified ($8,725.50), thus increasing the trial court's award by $7,760. Second, the Court of Appeals allowed damages for the cost of replacing some of the materials which did not conform to specifications: textured ceiling, $3,754.16; party walls, $1,488.27; ceiling insulation, $3,013.99; and exterior stain, $1,677.43. The court concluded that correction of these defects would not constitute unreasonable economic waste and that therefore the trial court erred in not awarding damages. . . . Both parties appeal from this decision.

We turn now to consider the . . . issue before us—the appropriate measure of damages. In its petition for review, Eastlake raises two objections to the Court of Appeals' resolution of the damages issues. First, Eastlake contends that the Court of Appeals improperly applied the "cost of remedying defects" measure of damages to a contract which had not been substantially performed. Second, Eastlake contends that the Court of Appeals improperly concluded as a matter of law that replacement of nonconforming materials did not constitute unreasonable economic waste. Both of these matters require consideration of the general principles applying to the measure of damages in construction contract cases.

. . . .

. . . [D]amages should put the injured party in the position which he would have enjoyed without the breach. In many cases this will be achieved by awarding the costs of repairing defective construction so as to conform to the contract. Some defects, however, cannot be remedied without great expense and substantial damage to the rest of the structure. . . . In such cases, the cost of remedying the defect would far exceed the value to the injured party of the improvement. An award of the cost of repairs in such cases would therefore constitute a substantial windfall to the injured party. The cost of repairs should not be awarded if that cost is clearly disproportionate to the value to the injured party of those repairs.

This idea was recognized by Professor McCormick in his treatise on damages:

> In whatever way the issue arises, the generally approved standards for measuring the owner's loss from defects in the work are two: First, in cases where the defect is one that can be repaired or cured *without undue expense,* so as to make the building conform to the agreed plan, then the owner recovers such amount as he has reasonably expended, or will reasonably have to spend, to remedy the defect. Second, if, on the other hand, the defect in material or construction is one that cannot be remedied without an *expenditure for reconstruction disproportionate to the end to be attained,* or without endangering unduly other parts of the building, then the damages will be measured not by the cost of remedying the defect, but by the difference between the value of the building as it is and what it would have been worth if it had been built in conformity with the contract.

(Italics ours.) C. McCormick, *Damages* § 168, 648–49 (1935).

The crux of the determination of which measure of damages to apply is therefore the proportionality of the cost to the corresponding benefits. This is a factual question which must be resolved, as Professor Corbin points out, according to "prevailing practices and opinions (the mores) of men, involving their emotions as well as reason and logic". A. Corbin, *Contracts* § 1089, at 492 (1964).

The authors of the Restatement have recently recognized in Restatement (Second) of Contracts (1981) that the concept of unreasonable economic waste is unhelpful in determining damages, and have turned instead to consider the proportionality of the cost of repairs to the value conferred. The second Restatement provides a convenient and effective means of clarifying and regularizing the rules governing this issue.

The general rule of damages is stated in Restatement (Second) of Contracts § 347, at 112:

Subject to the limitations stated in §§ 350–53, the injured party has a right to damages based on his expectation interest as measured by

> (a) the loss in the value to him of the other party's performance caused by its failure or deficiency, plus

> (b) any other loss, including incidental or consequential loss, caused by the breach, less

> (c) any cost or other loss that he has avoided by not having to perform.

Comment *a* to this rule explains the rationale for damages under the second Restatement.

> *a.   Expectation interest.* Contract damages are ordinarily based on the injured party's expectation interest and are intended to give him

the benefit of his bargain by awarding him a sum of money that will, to the extent possible, put him in as good a position as he would have been in had the contract been performed.

Further comments to section 347 recognize that in some cases it may be difficult to determine with sufficient certainty the damage to the injured party's expectation interest. Comment *b* states, in part:

Where the injured party's expected advantage consists largely or exclusively of the realization of profit, it may be possible to express this loss in value in terms of money with some assurance. In other situations, however, this is not possible and compensation for lost value may be precluded by the limitation of certainty. In order to facilitate the estimation of loss with sufficient certainty to award damages, the injured party is sometimes given a choice between alternative bases of calculating his loss in value. The most important of these are stated in § 348.

The alternatives set out in Restatement (Second) of Contracts § 348 include measures of damages specifically applicable to construction contracts.

(1) If a breach delays the use of property and the loss in value to the injured party is not proved with reasonable certainty, he may recover damages based on the rental value of the property or on interest on the value of the property.

(2) If a breach results in defective or unfinished construction and the loss in value to the injured party is not proved with sufficient certainty, he may recover damages based on

(a) the diminution in the market price of the property caused by the breach, or

(b) the reasonable cost of completing performance or of remedying the defects if that cost is not clearly disproportionate to the probable loss in value to him.

The comments to section 348 include a helpful discussion of the considerations applicable to a determination of damages for a breach of the construction contract. Comment *c* is especially relevant to this case and is here set out in full:

c. Incomplete or defective performance. If the contract is one for construction, including repair or similar performance affecting the condition of property, and the work is not finished, the injured party will usually find it easier to prove what it would cost to have the work completed by another contractor than to prove the difference between the values to him of the finished and the unfinished performance. Since the cost to complete is usually less than the loss in value to him, he is limited by the rule on avoidability to damages based on cost to complete. If he has actually had the work completed, damages will be based on his expenditures if he comes within the rule stated in § 350(2).

Sometimes, especially if the performance is defective as distinguished from incomplete, it may not be possible to prove the loss in value to the injured party with reasonable certainty. In that case he can usually recover damages based on the cost to remedy the defects.

Even if this gives him a recovery somewhat in excess of the loss in value to him, it is better that he receive a small windfall than that he be undercompensated by being limited to the resulting diminution in the market price of his property.

Sometimes, however, such a large part of the cost to remedy the defects consists of the cost to undo what has been improperly done that the cost to remedy the defects will be clearly disproportionate to the probable loss in value to the injured party. Damages based on the cost to remedy the defects would then give the injured party a recovery greatly in excess of the loss in value to him and result in a substantial windfall. Such an award will not be made. It is sometimes said that the award would involve "economic waste," but this is a misleading expression since an injured party will not, even if awarded an excessive amount of damages, usually pay to have the defects remedied if to do so will cost him more than the resulting increase in value to him. If an award based on the cost to remedy the defects would clearly be excessive and the injured party does not prove the actual loss in value to him, damages will be based instead on the difference between the market price that the property would have had without the defects and the market price of the property with the defects. This diminution in market price is the least possible loss in value to the injured party, since he could always sell the property on the market even if it had no special value to him.

The Restatement formulation of the rule represents a sensible and workable approach to measuring damages in construction contract cases. It achieves a fair measure of damages while avoiding the potentially confusing concepts of substantial completion and unreasonable economic waste. We therefore adopt Restatement (Second) of Contracts § 348 as the appropriate rule for determining damages in cases such as the present one.

This conclusion requires us to remand the issue of damages to the trial court for reconsideration in light of Section 348. The trial court should award defendants the cost of replacing defective items, unless the cost of replacement is "clearly disproportionate" to the value of the benefit conferred by replacement. Section 348(2)(a) and (b).

Of course, we do not disturb the trial court's award of damages for the loss of rental value, the costs of completing the project, and the costs of remedying various defects. These items of damages are clearly recoverable under Section 348. The trial court, therefore, need only apply the "clearly disproportionate" test to the kitchen cabinets and to the 9 breaches for which the trial court allowed no damages . . .

. . . .

The case is remanded for reconsideration of the issue of damages in light of Restatement (Second) of Contracts § 348 (1981). . . .

Bellizzi v. Huntley Estates, Inc.

Court of Appeals of New York, 1957.
3 N.Y.2d 112, 164 N.Y.S.2d 395, 143 N.E.2d 802.

■ DYE, J. The defendant-respondent, a real estate developer, on or about August 19, 1950, contracted to sell to the plaintiff-appellant a lot designated as No. 235 in its development and to build a house thereon in accordance with its demonstration model known as "The 1951 Kent" which, among other features, had an attached garage with an access driveway substantially at street level. When the construction work was commenced, the defendant encountered rock close to the surface and, instead of excavating same, as might have been done without too much trouble at the time, it placed the house thereon, with the result that from the entrance of the garage to the street, a distance of 43 feet, there was a difference in elevation of 9 feet and 8 inches. This amounted to a 22½% grade, which is so steep that the driveway cannot be used safely and conveniently. As a matter of fact, the evidence shows that a grade of 12% is considered the permissive maximum. While the plans are silent as to the grade of the driveways, the defendant does not now claim that the grade of the existing driveway is reasonable or that plaintiff has no cause for complaint. It defends against plaintiff's claim for damages on the sole ground that the trial court erred when it excluded evidence offered by it as to the value of the property and should not have refused to charge that the measure of damages "is the difference between the value of the building as constructed and its value had it been constructed conformably to the contract or the cost of repairs, whichever is the lesser." Instead, the trial court charged in substance that the measure of damage is "the fair and reasonable cost to remedy the defect in this controversy or to get a reasonably usable driveway".

The Appellate Division adopted the defendant's contention largely in reliance on Jacob & Youngs v. Kent (230 N.Y. 239, 244, 129 N.E. 889, 891). In that case, we had applied the "difference in value" rule simply because the proof failed to show any substantial damage or loss in value, since the wrought iron galvanized pipe, as furnished, was substantially the same in quality, weight, market price, serviceability and appearance as pipe of "Reading" manufacture called for in the contract specifications and that the cost of replacing same with the "Reading" pipe as specified "would be great, but the difference in value ... would be either nominal or nothing"; in other words, replacement of the pipe, under the circumstances in that case, would have constituted economic waste.

However, this litigation poses an entirely different kind of breach, the consequence of which is to burden plaintiff with an unusable, unsafe and unsightly driveway. While it is unfortunate that the defendant elected to build the garage at an unsuitable elevation in order to avoid the cost of excavating unforeseen rock and that to correct the defect will now cost much more than initially, nonetheless, that loss should not fall on the innocent owner whose protests made at the time were put off by the president of the defendant corporation with assurances not to worry, that when finished the grade would not exceed 10% and that the plaintiff would be happy when he got into his home.

The "difference in value" rule in defective performance of construction contracts seems to be applied only when it would be unfair to apply the general rule. In a case such as the present when the variance is so substantial as to render the finished building partially unusable and unsafe, the measure of damage is "the market price of completing or correcting the performance'' (5 Williston on Contracts [Rev. ed.], § 1363, p. 3825.) It is only "If the defect is not thus remediable, damages are based on the difference between the value of the defective structure and that of the structure if properly completed." (5 Williston on Contracts, supra, pp. 3825–3826.) This rule we have long applied.

Here, there is uncontradicted evidence that the dangerous and unsatisfactory driveway can be corrected. When that is done, the plaintiff will have received no more than he was entitled to under his contract and the defendant will have given no more than it obligated itself to furnish.

The order appealed from should be reversed, and the judgment of the County Court reinstated, with costs in this court and in the Appellate Division.

Ordered accordingly.

C. CERTAINTY

United Virginia Bank v. Dick Herriman Ford, Inc.

Supreme Court of Virginia, 1974.
215 Va. 373, 210 S.E.2d 158.

■ COCHRAN, J. On September 7, 1972, United Virginia Bank of Fairfax (Bank) filed its motion for judgment against Dick Herriman Ford, Inc. (Dealer), alleging damages resulting from breach of a contract to record a first lien in favor of the Bank on the application for title to an automobile purchased from the Dealer by Scott Burdette, to whom the Bank made a loan for a portion of the purchase price.

The case was tried before the court, sitting without a jury. At the conclusion of the Bank's evidence the Dealer moved to strike the evidence on the ground that a prima facie case had not been made out. The trial court granted the motion and on October 12, 1973, entered a final order awarding summary judgment for the Dealer. In the final order, however, the court held that there was a contract between the Bank and the Dealer, that the Dealer had breached the contract and had thereby damaged the Bank and was liable therefor, but that the Bank had "failed to establish the value of the automobile at the time that its right to repossession accrued," so that the court could not assess the measure of damages.

. . . .

The trial court's action in entering summary judgment for the Dealer would have been permissible . . . had it followed a finding that there was no liability on the part of the Dealer. But the court erred in taking such action after finding that the Dealer was liable to the Bank and that the Bank had been damaged by the Dealer's breach of contract.

The Bank was not required to prove the value of the vehicle at the time of Burdette's default. The Bank is entitled to be put in the same position as it would have been in if the contract had been performed. If the Dealer had fulfilled its contractual obligations the Bank would have been protected by a first lien on the title certificate issued in the name of the borrower covering the amount of his indebtedness to the Bank. Damages within the reasonable contemplation of the parties at the time the contract was made would comprise the amount of the indebtedness to be secured, diminished by payments actually received.

The general rule is that damages are to be determined at the time of breach of a contract. Evidence of fluctuations in value after the breach is irrelevant.

To require the Bank to prove the value of the automobile as of the date its right of repossession accrued would be to reward the Dealer, at the Bank's expense, for the Dealer's breach of contract. We hold, therefore, that the general rule should apply in this case and that damages should be determined as of the date of breach of the contract between the Bank and the Dealer.

A litigant is not required to prove his damages with precision, particularly where the violator of the contract has made it impossible for him to do so, provided the evidence permits an intelligent and reasonable estimate of the damages. Here, the amount of the obligation to be protected by the first lien that was never perfected was $4,525.92. This is rebuttable evidence that the value of the vehicle at the time the contract was breached was not less than that amount. The title application, however, signed by the Dealer, disposes of the question of value, for it shows that the purchase price paid for the vehicle was $4,560.00. We hold that $4,525.92 was the measure of damages caused by the Dealer's breach of contract, less credits for payments received by the Bank after the contract was breached, reducing the damages to $3,771.98.

As value has been established by the evidence, we reverse the final order of October 12, 1973, and enter final judgment for the Bank in the amount of $3,771.98.

Reversed and final judgment [entered].

Beverly Hills Concepts, Inc. v. Schatz And Schatz, Ribicoff and Kotkin

Supreme Court of Connecticut, 1998.
247 Conn. 48, 717 A.2d 724.

[Failed business brought action against its former law firm and individual attorneys for, inter alia, alleged legal malpractice. The Superior Court rendered judgment for plaintiff and awarded approximately $15.9 million in lost profits calculated over a period of 12 years. On appeal, the Connecticut Supreme Court reversed and remanded, holding that lost profits for reasonable period of time may serve as appropriate measure of damages for destruction of nascent business, but that plaintiff had failed to prove lost profits damages with reasonable certainty.]

■ Before Norcott, Katz, Palmer, Peters and Edward Y. O'Connell, JJ.

■ Katz, Associate Justice.

The principal issue in this appeal is the proper method for calculating damages for the destruction of a nascent business. We conclude that: (1) unestablished enterprises must be permitted to recover damages for legal malpractice and that a flexible approach in determining those damages generally is appropriate; (2) lost profits for a reasonable period of time may serve as an appropriate measure of damages under certain circumstances; and (3) the plaintiff bears the burden of proving lost profits to a reasonable certainty. As applied to the facts of this case, however, we conclude that the plaintiff has not sustained its burden of proof regarding damages.

This appeal arises from a malpractice action brought by Beverly Hills Concepts, Inc. (plaintiff) against the named defendant, the law firm, Schatz and Schatz, Ribicoff and Kotkin (Schatz & Schatz), and the individual defendants, attorneys Stanford Goldman, Ira Dansky and Jane Seidl.... On January 27, 1997, following a trial to the court, Hon. Robert J. Hale, judge trial referee, rendered judgment for the plaintiff.... The trial court awarded the plaintiff damages in the amount of $15,931,289.

The trier of fact reasonably could have found the following facts. Charles Remington, Wayne Steidle, and Jeannie Leitao, incorporated the plaintiff as a Massachusetts corporation in April, 1987. They sold fitness equipment with a distinctive color scheme and logo, as well as a plan for operating a fitness club for women. The plaintiff's system included everything an owner would need to run a club, including equipment, training, sales and marketing support, and advertising and promotional materials. The plaintiff incorporated in Connecticut on August 17, 1987, and opened a corporate headquarters in Rocky Hill. From its Rocky Hill headquarters, the plaintiff licensed purchasers to use its concept, and sold distributorships to investors who gained the exclusive right to sell the plaintiff's products and to sublicense its name within a regional territory.

In October, 1987, prompted by a legal problem regarding the plaintiff's trademark in California, Leitao contacted the law firm of Schatz & Schatz. On October 28, 1987, the plaintiff met with Goldman, a partner at Schatz & Schatz, and Seidl, an associate in the firm. Leitao advised them that she recently had filed a trademark application for the name "Beverly Hills Concepts" in Washington, D.C. Goldman assumed incorrectly that this meant that the plaintiff had a "federally registered trademark," which would have alleviated the need to register as a "business opportunity" pursuant to the Connecticut Business Opportunity Investment Act (act). General Statutes (Rev. to 1987) § 36–503 et seq.[5] He told Leitao that Schatz & Schatz possessed expertise in the field of franchising, and that the firm was well qualified to handle the plaintiff's legal affairs. Goldman also

---

5. General Statutes (Rev. to 1987) § 36–508 provides in relevant part: "Registration and application by seller of business opportunity. Financial statement. Registration fee. Exemptions. (a) Unless exempted by subsection (e) of this section, any person who advertises, sells, contracts, offers for sale or promotes any business opportunity in this state or from this state must register with the commissioner and file, in a form prescribed by said commissioner, an application...."

said that he would be involved personally in the firm's representation of the plaintiff.

In fact, beginning in late 1987, Goldman turned the plaintiff's file over to Seidl, a junior associate, and Ira Dansky, a "contract" lawyer not yet admitted to the Connecticut bar. Neither Seidl nor Dansky possessed expertise in the law of franchising and business opportunities. Schatz & Schatz billing records revealed that Goldman spent only about two hours on the plaintiff's matter between December, 1987, and June, 1988.

Before turning the plaintiff's file over to Seidl, Goldman visited the plaintiff's headquarters in Rocky Hill and examined its distributorship and licensing agreements and promotional materials. Despite the plaintiff's request for guidelines regarding the sale of its equipment and "system" pending its franchise registration, Schatz & Schatz failed to advise the plaintiff that it was violating the act by selling fitness club packages without first registering with the state banking commissioner. Rather, after analyzing the plaintiff's documents, Goldman told Remington that the question of whether the plaintiff was offering business opportunities within the meaning of the act was a "gray area" of the law.

Recognizing that the plaintiff would need financial statements in order to file its franchise documents, Schatz & Schatz referred the plaintiff to the accounting firm of Coopers and Lybrand (Coopers). Schatz & Schatz advised Coopers, however, only of the financial statements required under federal law. It failed to inform Coopers of the requirements of the act.

In the winter of 1987–88, Seidl began drafting the plaintiff's franchise documents. On February 8, 1988, another Schatz & Schatz associate, who had been assigned the task of researching the franchise registration requirements of fourteen states, including Connecticut, informed Seidl that the plaintiff was not exempt from the registration requirements of the act. That same day, Schatz & Schatz contacted the plaintiff's Washington, D.C., trademark attorney, who confirmed that the plaintiff's trademark application was pending, and that no federal registration had been issued. Under these circumstances, Schatz & Schatz lawyers should have realized that the plaintiff was not exempt from the filing requirements of the act. Yet no one from the defendant law firm apprised the plaintiff of that fact.[6]

In June, 1988, Dansky terminated Schatz & Schatz's representation of the plaintiff, stating that he was concerned that the plaintiff's franchise offering documents overstated its financial position. Shortly afterwards, the plaintiff retained Martin Clayman, an attorney with the firm of Clayman, Markowitz and Tapper, to complete the plaintiff's franchise registration. Within a few weeks, Clayman and his partner, Holly Abery–Wetstone, had prepared an application for the plaintiff to register as a business opportunity in Connecticut. The plaintiff decided not to file the registration documents, however, until its trademark had been approved, an event that its

---

6. In fact, also in February, 1988, Dansky advised the plaintiff to merge its Massachusetts and Connecticut corporations, retaining the Connecticut entity. Because Massachusetts has no business opportunity laws and filing requirements, that merger foreclosed a route by which the plaintiff could have curtailed its violation of the act.

Washington, D.C., attorney had estimated would occur within a few months.

On September 15, 1988, an official acting for the banking commissioner notified the plaintiff that its marketing of franchises violated the act. The plaintiff contacted Clayman and Abery–Wetstone, who began preparing a postsale registration for the plaintiff's previous sales. The plaintiff complied immediately with advice from Abery–Wetstone that it should stop advertising and selling franchises. The plaintiff filed a postsale registration application on December 7, 1988, in an effort to comply with the act. Nevertheless, on June 28, 1989, the banking commissioner issued a cease and desist order and a notice of intent to fine the plaintiff up to $10,000 for each sale made in violation of the act. The commissioner further issued a stop order invalidating the plaintiff's postsale registration. On June 26, 1991, following hearings in September and November of 1989 and May of 1990, the commissioner issued a final cease and desist order, stating that the plaintiff had violated the act repeatedly by selling unregistered business opportunities in Connecticut. This malpractice action followed.

For purposes of this appeal, the defendants do not challenge the trial court's determination that they breached the applicable professional standard of care. Rather, they raise claims regarding the issues of causation and damages. . . .

. . .

III

The defendants' third claim on appeal challenges the trial court's award of damages. The defendants argue that the trial court improperly: (1) concluded that the plaintiff's expert witness was qualified to render an opinion as to the value of the plaintiff; (2) awarded damages based on lost profits rather than the going concern value of the business at the date of destruction; (3) awarded the plaintiff approximately $15.9 million in lost profits calculated over a period of twelve years; and (4) included prejudgment interest in the damages award. We conclude that: (1) the plaintiff's expert was qualified; (2) unestablished enterprises must be permitted to recover damages for legal malpractice and that a flexible approach in determining those damages generally is appropriate; (3) lost profits for a reasonable period of time may serve as an appropriate measure of damages under certain circumstances; and (4) the plaintiff bears the burden of proving lost profits to a reasonable certainty. As applied to the facts of this case, however, we conclude that the plaintiff has not sustained its burden of proof regarding damages.

We begin with a brief overview of additional facts that are relevant to the correct determination of damages in this case. The plaintiff had been operating for approximately one year at the time it retained the defendants. It therefore had a business track record by which to measure the likely success of its planned franchising operation. As the defendants correctly point out, despite its initial sales of exercise equipment, the plaintiff was in poor financial condition. The plaintiff owed approximately $80,000 in unpaid federal and state payroll taxes and had never paid unemployment taxes, a decision that its own expert witness, Thomas Ferreira, a certified public accountant, characterized as not a good business practice. Significantly, the plaintiff had not filed federal or state income tax returns for 1987, 1988 or 1989. The plaintiff's financial statement, prepared by Coopers, revealed that it was insolvent as of November 30, 1987, and its situation had deteriorated even further by January, 1988. It is particularly telling that the plaintiff had attempted to obtain financing from a number of banks as well as from the Small Business Administration and that it had been rejected by all of these institutions. According to Charles Remington, one of the plaintiff's officers, this financing was necessary to the proposed franchising operation. Additionally, the model franchise opened by the plaintiff in East Hartford quickly failed. Finally, despite several months of trying, the plaintiff never sold a single franchise. Moreover, its own damages expert, Ferreira, characterized the plaintiff as a poor credit risk. These facts serve to indicate that the plaintiff was not financially stable and that its prospects for earning profits in the future were, at best, questionable.

A

We first address the defendants' claim that Ferreira was not qualified to render an expert opinion regarding the value of the plaintiff. We conclude that the trial court did not abuse its discretion in determining that Ferreira was sufficiently qualified.

. . .

B

We next address the question of whether lost profits are an appropriate measure of damages for the destruction of a nascent enterprise. The defendants argue that the appropriate measure of damages for the destruction of a business is its going concern value at the time of its destruction rather than lost profits. The plaintiff argues that the present value of a stream of expected future profits is an appropriate way to value a business and that it is therefore an appropriate measure of damages. We conclude that it is proper to award damages for the destruction of an unestablished enterprise and that lost profits may constitute an appropriate measure of damages for the destruction of such an enterprise.

We begin with a brief history of the evolution of the law on the determination of damages with respect to a business that has been destroyed by the conduct of a third party. A principle component of damages in such a situation is the present value of the profits lost as a result of the defendant's wrongdoing. See Westport Taxi Service, Inc. v. Westport Transit District, supra, 235 Conn. at 32–33, 664 A.2d 719 (noting that plaintiff entitled to recover probable value of business at time of its destruction and that going concern value of business may be calculated based on lost profits). Although the guiding principle of tort law is to compensate parties for harm to their protected interests; W. Prosser & W. Keeton, Torts (5th Ed.1984) § 1, pp. 5–6; recovery for lost profits has not always been available. The "new business rule" in particular forbade the recovery of lost profits for an unestablished enterprise. See, e.g., Evergreen Amusement Corp. v. Milstead, 206 Md. 610, 618, 112 A.2d 901 (1955) (holding lost profits not generally recoverable but creating exception for established businesses). "Originally the speculative and contingent nature of profits was regarded as a complete bar to their recovery in any case. Gradually, however, came recognition that difficulties of proof and the speculative nature of profits were not uniform for all situations; and the rigid prohibition has given way to a more flexible requirement of 'reasonable certainty.'" 4 F. Harper, F. James & O. Gray, Torts (2d Ed.1986) § 25.3, pp. 502–503. "A common thread running through opinions expressing the liberal standard of proof in lost profit damages cases is that there is really no alternative: [A][d]efendant will get away with its wrongdoing if the court requires [the] plaintiff to prove damages to the dollar.... The wrongdoer has created the problem; its conduct has interfered with [the] plaintiff and caused damages. The wrongdoer cannot now complain that the damages cannot be measured exactly." 1 R. Dunn, supra, § 5.2, p. 314. The former rule forbidding lost profit damages for new enterprises has thus given way to the general view that such damages ought to be recoverable where the likelihood of future profits can be established with reasonable certainty.

The approach taken by the Restatement (Second) of Torts, as it relates to the destruction of a new enterprise, is also instructive in that it places the burden on the plaintiff who is attempting to prove damages for harm to a new enterprise to come forward with specific evidence regarding future profits.[9] The Restatement states that "[w]hen the tortfeasor has prevented the beginning of a new business or the prosecution of a single transaction, all factors relevant to the likelihood of the success or lack of success of the business or transaction that are reasonably provable are to be considered, including general business conditions and the degree of success of similar enterprises. Because of a justifiable doubt as to the success of new and untried enterprises, more specific evidence of their probable profits is required than when the claim is for harm to an established business." 4 Restatement (Second), Torts § 912, comment (d), p. 483 (1979).[10] The Restatement does not place a higher burden on plaintiffs attempting to prove lost profits relative to a new business but, instead, points out that new enterprises must provide specific evidence in order to meet the same burden that applies to established businesses.[11]

9. The Restatement (Second), Torts § 912 (1979) provides with respect to the quantum of proof needed to prove damages generally:

"Certainty

"One to whom another has tortiously caused harm is entitled to compensatory damages for the harm if, but only if, he establishes by proof the extent of the harm and the amount of money representing adequate compensation with as much certainty as the nature of the tort and the circumstances permit."

10. The Restatement provides that the plaintiff must "[establish] by proof the extent of the harm and the amount of money representing adequate compensation with as much

certainty as the nature of the tort and the circumstances permit." 4 Restatement (Second), supra, § 912.

11. The following illustration set forth in the Restatement exemplifies the standard by which a plaintiff must prove lost profits. "A pays B $10,000 for a license to sell in specified territory a new drink, produced and extensively advertised by B. Before a shipment has been made, C tortiously causes B to refuse to make delivery. A is not entitled to substantial damages from C on proof that the gross profit would have been 20 per cent, that other drinks have had a ready sale in the same locality, that in other localities large quantities of the same drink have been sold, and that in the past A has been successful in

The Supreme Court of Alabama has stated that "the weight of modern authority does not predicate recovery of lost profits upon the artificial categorization of a business as 'unestablished,' 'existing,' or 'new,' particularly where the defendant itself has wrongfully prevented the business from coming into existence and generating a track record of profits. Instead, the courts focus on whether the plaintiff has adduced evidence that provides a basis from which the [fact finder] could, with 'reasonable certainty' calculate the amount of lost profits." Super Valu Stores, Inc. v. Peterson, 506 So.2d 317, 330 (Ala.1987) (upholding $5 million verdict for breach of contract to open grocery store where plaintiff projected profits of $20 million over fifteen years and defendant conceded that statistical evaluation of future profit, which it had itself generated, was reliable).

In accordance with these principles, we have approved the recovery of lost profits where the defendant has destroyed the plaintiff's opportunity to earn profits in the future. See, e.g., Westport Taxi Service, Inc. v. Westport Transit District, supra, 235 Conn. at 32–33, 664 A.2d 719; Torosyan v. Boehringer Ingelheim Pharmaceuticals, Inc., 234 Conn. 1, 33, 662 A.2d 89 (1995); West Haven Sound Development Corp. v. West Haven, supra, 201 Conn. at 319, 514 A.2d 734. Furthermore, we note that, "[i]n economic theory . . . the current market value of a company is the discounted present value of the estimated flow of future earnings." Note, "Private Treble Damage Antitrust Suits: Measure of Damages For Destruction of All or Part of a Business," 80 Harv. L.Rev. 1566, 1580 (1967). Thus, determining a business' future lost profits is one generally accepted way of calculating its market value at the time of its destruction.

For example, in Westport Taxi Service, Inc., an antitrust case, we stated that "[w]here the plaintiff's business is totally or partially destroyed by [the] defendant's violation . . . damages may be measured by lost goodwill or the going concern value of [the] plaintiff's business." (Internal quotation marks omitted.) Westport Taxi Service, Inc. v. Westport Transit District, supra, 235 Conn. at 32–33, 664 A.2d 719. We further explained that "[a] plaintiff injured by an antitrust violation may recover both lost past profits and the probable value of the business [at the time of its destruction]." Id., at 33, 664 A.2d 719. The trial court in that case calculated the going concern value of the business at the time of its destruction by capitalizing the plaintiff's projected profits over a certain period of time at a given rate of return. Id., at 33–34, 664 A.2d 719.

Similarly, in West Haven Sound Development Corp. v. West Haven, supra, 201 Conn. at 319, 514 A.2d 734, a case involving breach of contract, the trial court allowed a certified public accountant to testify to the value that the plaintiff's restaurant would have attained had the defendant performed its contract obligations. The accountant valued the plaintiff's business by calculating the net present value of its future earnings, using a rate of capitalization appropriate to the restaurant industry. Id., at 317, 514 A.2d 734. In other words, he "determined the value of the plaintiff's business by estimating future profits, and then by capitalizing those expected profits to their net present value at an appropriate interest rate."

other enterprises." 4 Restatement (Second), supra, § 912, illustration (12), p. 485.

Id., at 319, 514 A.2d 734. We concluded that his "opinion as to the going concern value of the plaintiff's restaurant business before the breach was based on reasonable estimates of lost profits." Id., at 321, 514 A.2d 734.

For the foregoing reasons, we conclude that lost profits may provide an appropriate measure of damages for the destruction of an unestablished enterprise, and further, that a flexible approach is best suited to ensuring that new businesses are compensated fully if they suffer damages as a result of a breach of contract, professional malpractice, or similar injuries.

C

We next consider whether the trial court improperly awarded the plaintiff approximately $15.9 million in lost profits calculated over a period of twelve years. In challenging the award, the defendants contest the assumptions upon which Ferreira based his projections and the court's acceptance of his choice of a twelve year time span. We conclude that the trial court abused its discretion because the plaintiff did not prove the lost profit damages to a reasonable certainty.

We recognize that "[t]he trial court has broad discretion in determining damages. Buckman v. People Express, Inc., 205 Conn. 166, 175, 530 A.2d 596 (1987); Amwax Corp. v. Chadwick, 28 Conn.App. 739, 745, 612 A.2d 127 (1992). The determination of damages involves a question of fact that will not be overturned unless it is clearly erroneous. Beckman v. Jalich Homes, Inc., 190 Conn. 299, 309–10, 460 A.2d 488 (1983); Gerber & Hurley, Inc. v. CCC Corp., 36 Conn.App. 539, 545, 651 A.2d 1302 (1995)." Westport Taxi Service, Inc. v. Westport Transit District, supra, 235 Conn. at 27–28, 664 A.2d 719; see also Johnson v. Flammia, 169 Conn. 491, 499, 363 A.2d 1048 (1975). "[W]hether the decision of the trial court is clearly erroneous ... involves a two part function: where the legal conclusions of the court are challenged, we must determine whether they are legally and logically correct and whether they find support in the facts set out in the memorandum of decision; where the factual basis of the court's decision is challenged we must determine whether the facts set out in the memorandum of decision are supported by the evidence or whether, in light of the evidence and the pleadings in the whole record, those facts are clearly erroneous.... In a case tried before a court, the trial judge is the sole arbiter of the credibility of the witnesses and the weight to be given specific testimony.... On appeal, we will give the evidence the most favorable reasonable construction in support of the verdict to which it is entitled.... A factual finding may be rejected by this court only if it is clearly erroneous.... A finding is clearly erroneous when although there is evidence to support it, the reviewing court on the entire evidence is left with the definite and firm conviction that a mistake has been committed." (Citation omitted; internal quotation marks omitted.) Barbara Weisman v. Kaspar, 233 Conn. 531, 541, 661 A.2d 530 (1995).

We are, therefore, constrained to accord substantial deference to the fact finder on the issue of damages. In deciding whether damages properly have been awarded, however, we are guided by the well established principle that such damages must be proved with reasonable certainty. Gargano v. Heyman, 203 Conn. 616, 621, 525 A.2d 1343 (1987). "Although we recognize that damages for lost profits may be difficult to prove with exactitude; see Conaway v. Prestia, [191 Conn. 484, 494, 464 A.2d 847 (1983)]; Burr v. Lichtenheim, 190 Conn. 351, 360, 460 A.2d 1290 (1983); Humphrys v. Beach, 149 Conn. 14, 21, 175 A.2d 363 (1961); such damages are recoverable only to the extent that the evidence affords a sufficient basis for estimating their amount with reasonable certainty. Conaway v. Prestia, supra [at 494, 464 A.2d 847]; Simone Corporation v. Connecticut Light & Power Co., 187 Conn. 487, 494–95, 446 A.2d 1071 (1982); Humphrys v. Beach, supra [at 21, 175 A.2d 363]." (Emphasis added.) Gargano v. Heyman, supra, at 621, 525 A.2d 1343. Consequently, we have permitted lost profits to be calculated by extrapolating from past profits. See, e.g., Westport Taxi Service, Inc. v. Westport Transit District, supra, 235 Conn. at 32–33, 664 A.2d 719 (proper to base lost profits award on profits from preceding year); Humphrys v. Beach, supra, at 21, 175 A.2d 363 ("[i]n the absence of evidence to the contrary, the court was entitled to draw the inference that the plaintiff's business would continue to be as profitable as it had been in the year and a half before the fire"). We have stated, however, that the plaintiff cannot recover for "the mere possibility" of making a profit. See Goldman v. Feinberg, 130 Conn. 671, 674–75, 37 A.2d 355 (1944) (in context of tortious interference claim, plaintiff must show more than that he was "about to" enter into contract and must, instead, show that he "would have" done so). "A damage theory may be based on assumptions so long as the assumptions are reasonable in light of the record evidence." (Internal quotation marks omitted.) Westport Taxi Service, Inc. v. Westport Transit District, supra, at 28, 664 A.2d 719.

In order to recover lost profits, therefore, the plaintiff must present sufficiently accurate and complete evidence for the trier of fact to be able to estimate those profits with reasonable certainty. The trial court in this case, although cognizant of this standard, nevertheless assessed damages based upon assumptions that were not supported by the record. The trial court's determination that the plaintiff would have earned approximately $15.9 million in profits over the course of twelve years had it not been for the defendants' conduct, therefore, constituted an abuse of discretion.

We will first address the defendants' claims regarding the assumptions upon which the plaintiff's expert, Ferreira, based his projections. Ferreira assumed that a substantial number of the people who had purchased toning tables would also have purchased franchises. He also assumed that the plaintiff would sell twenty franchises per year for the first five years and would progressively increase sales until it was selling forty franchises per year by year twelve. The defendants have claimed that these assumptions were speculative and therefore could not have formed a reasonable basis from which to estimate damages with any degree of certainty. We agree with the defendants and therefore conclude that the trial court abused its discretion in determining that the plaintiff had established lost profits to a reasonable certainty.

The weakness underlying the assumptions challenged by the defendants is that the plaintiff's sales of toning tables, which had been declining, could be extrapolated to predict future success in selling franchises. The testimony indicates that there is no reasonable basis to compare the two products other than the possibility that they might be marketed to the same customer base. The toning table transactions cost from $45,000 to $50,000 per location, whereas each franchise cost $116,500 to $172,500. That figure included a $20,000 franchise fee and $90,000 in equipment, or approximately twice the initial expenditure required for toning table packages. Additionally, a franchise involves a much greater commitment in terms of expenditures, opportunity costs and effort than does the purchase of equipment. Purchasers of toning tables were not required to make any further expenditures. Franchisees, on the other hand, would have been required to pay the plaintiff a monthly service fee of 5 percent of gross revenue, but not less than $349 per month and would have had to contribute 3 percent of monthly gross revenues, but not less than $200, to an advertising fund. It is also significant that the plaintiff, by its own estimate, needed $300,000 in new capital to launch its proposed franchising business and, in its investment proposal, stated that it was seeking to raise between $250,000 and $500,000 for that purpose. Ferreira's projections, however, were based on the assumption that the plaintiff needed only $100,000 to enter the franchise business.

Ferreira's assumption that the plaintiff would, in fact, have sold franchises is also directly contradicted by the record. The model franchise opened by the plaintiff failed shortly after it began operation. Additionally, the plaintiff attempted for months to sell franchises but was unable to sell even one. Ferreira's reliance on the performance of World Gym Licensing Limited (World Gym) as a model for predicting the plaintiff's future success was also unreasonable. Ferreira himself conceded that World Gym and the plaintiff were not similar. Additionally, he appears to have based his information about World Gym on a magazine article. Although he assumed that the plaintiff would grow at a slower rate than World Gym, Ferreira did not explain how he arrived at the projected rate of sale for the plaintiff's franchises other than to state that he had discounted the rates reported by World Gym. Therefore, even reducing the plaintiff's sales of sixty-five toning tables in a one and one-half year period to a projection that twenty franchises per year would be sold is contradicted by the available evidence of the plaintiff's failed attempts to sell the actual franchises. Moreover, no evidence was presented to support the contention that even the sales of toning tables would continue at their prior rate.

This court and courts of other jurisdictions have looked to a number of factors in evaluating whether the plaintiff has proved lost profits to a reasonable certainty. A plaintiff's prior experience in the same business has been held to be probative; see, e.g., Kay Petroleum Corp. v. Piergrossi, 137 Conn. 620, 624–25, 79 A.2d 829 (1951) (profits earned by plaintiff in year prior to breach may be extrapolated to time remaining on contract breached by defendant); Tull v. Gundersons, Inc., 709 P.2d 940, 945 (Colo.1985) (trial court improperly excluded evidence of plaintiff's "past profit experience on other projects"); White v. Southwestern Bell Telephone Co., 651 S.W.2d 260, 263 (Tex.1983) (profits earned by plaintiff's florist shop prior to defendant's breach of contract relevant to determination of lost profits caused by defendant's failure to list plaintiff's business properly in telephone directory); as has a plaintiff's experience in the same enterprise subsequent to the interference. See, e.g., El Fredo Pizza, Inc. v. Roto–Flex

Oven Co., 199 Neb. 697, 698, 261 N.W.2d 358 (1978) (increased profits earned after faulty pizza oven replaced indicative of profits lost as result of defendant's breach of warranty of merchantability); Guady v. Seaman, 188 Pa.Super. 475, 477–78, 149 A.2d 523 (1959) (plaintiff's success at different location admissible to show lost profits from defendant's breach of lease); Ferrell v. Elrod, 63 Tenn.App. 129, 146–47, 469 S.W.2d 678 (1971) (same); Cook Associates v. Warnick, 664 P.2d 1161 (Utah 1983) (plaintiff's experience at unaffected plant relevant to lost profits projected for affected plant). In jurisdictions that have been faced with assessing damages for the destruction of a new business, the experience of the plaintiff and that of third parties in a similar business have been admitted to prove lost profits. See, e.g., Lucky Auto Supply v. Turner, 244 Cal.App.2d 872, 884, 53 Cal.Rptr. 628 (1966) (evidence regarding 48 percent increase in business at other locations admissible to prove loss of profits at affected location where plaintiff testified that other locations were comparable to affected location); Chung v. Kaonohi Center Co., 62 Haw. 594, 611, 618 P.2d 283 (1980) (proper to base future profit calculation on experience of third party conducting virtually identical business at same location); Vickers v. Wichita State University, 213 Kan. 614, 618, 518 P.2d 512 (1974) (approving reliance on experience of others in same line of business); Ellwest Stereo Theatres, Inc. v. Davilla, 436 So.2d 1285, 1288–89 (La.App.1983) (evidence of profitability of other locations in chain of stores owned by plaintiff held admissible to show lost profits where plaintiff testified that variables among locations were similar and that expected profit at unestablished location was expected to be greater than for existing locations); Smith Development Corp. v. Bilow Enterprises, Inc., 112 R.I. 203, 214, 308 A.2d 477 (1973) (evidence of profitability of nearby McDonald's franchises held admissible to show lost profits from tortious interference with establishment of new McDonald's location); cf. Kenford Co. v. County of Erie, 108 App.Div.2d 132, 134, 489 N.Y.S.2d 939 (1985), rev'd on other grounds, 73 N.Y.2d 312, 537 N.E.2d 176, 540 N.Y.S.2d 1 (1989) (evidence of profitability and expenses of nearby established domed stadiums inadmissible to prove lost profits for stadium never built where plaintiff failed to establish existing stadiums were comparable and where too many variables existed). In addition, the average experience of participants in the same line of business as the injured party has been approved as a method of proving lost profits. See, e.g., Vermont Food Industries, Inc. v. Ralston Purina Co., 514 F.2d 456, 457 (2d Cir.1975) (average egg production when proper chicken feed used compared with egg production when defendant's deficient feed used). Similarly, prelitigation projections, particularly when prepared by the defendant, have also been approved. See, e.g., Super Valu Stores, Inc. v. Peterson, supra, 506 So.2d at 330. The underlying requirement for each of these types of evidence is a substantial similarity between the facts forming the basis of the profit projections and the business opportunity that was destroyed.

A review of several cases relied upon by the plaintiff in which jury verdicts based upon lost profits were upheld serves to illustrate the relatively poor evidence of future profitability offered by the plaintiff in the present case. In Super Valu Stores, Inc. v. Peterson, supra, 506 So.2d 317, the Supreme Court of Alabama upheld a $5 million jury verdict for breach of a contract to construct and lease a grocery store to the plaintiff. In that case, the plaintiff had introduced evidence that the store would have generated profits of $20 million over the proposed fifteen year lease term. Id., at 326. The statistical studies introduced by the plaintiff to support that contention had been prepared by the defendant and were acknowledged by the defendant to be accurate. Id., at 330–31. In the present case, by contrast, the defendant did not prepare the data relied upon by the plaintiff nor did it concede that the figures were reliable.

In Chung v. Kaonohi Center Co., supra, 62 Haw. at 611, 618 P.2d 283, the Supreme Court of Hawaii upheld a jury verdict of $175,000 for the loss of anticipated profits relating to the breach of a contract to enter into a ten year lease for a restaurant. In that case, the projected profits were based on the actual earnings and expenses of the restaurant experienced by the person who eventually contracted with the defendants for the same enterprise. Id., at 610–11, 618 P.2d 283. It is not reasonable to compare projections based on the actual experience of a business that is identical in nature and in location to the one that the plaintiff in Chung had intended to form with the hypothetical projections based on an untried enterprise offered by the plaintiff in the present case.

In Fera v. Village Plaza, Inc., 396 Mich. 639, 647, 242 N.W.2d 372 (1976), the Michigan Supreme Court upheld a $200,000 award for lost profits where the plaintiff had claimed that breach of a ten year lease to operate a liquor store would result in $270,000 in lost profits. In that case, the plaintiffs presented several days of testimony from a number of experts in the liquor sales business and from liquor distribution firms to support their claim. In the present case, by contrast, the plaintiff's expert had no experience in the fitness industry and had based his projections on informal interviews and articles in the lay press about the industry.

We note that lack of prior profitability does not necessarily prohibit a trial court from awarding future lost profits, although it serves as a strong indicator that future profits are uncertain. The plaintiff must carry the burden of proving that prior losses will be turned around to provide future gains. In the present case, the plaintiff has failed to come forward with evidence showing, to a reasonable degree of certainty, that it would become profitable.

Finally, we disagree with the trial court's decision to award lost profits over a twelve year period. We agree with the plaintiff that there is nothing inherently improper about allowing damages for lost profits over a twelve year period. What is improper, however, is to award damages over such a long time span when there is no evidence that the plaintiff would have survived for twelve years, let alone that it would have remained profitable for that length of time. In order to remove the assessment of damages from the realm of speculation, it is necessary to tie the award of damages to objective verifiable facts that bear a logical relationship to projected future profitability.

Where the lost business opportunity is grounded in a contract or a lease, it is sometimes appropriate to award damages for a period commensurate with the term of that contract or lease. We have stated that, where the claimed damages are not the result of a breach of contract or lease of express duration, damages for future losses are permitted "as long as they are limited to a reasonable time and are supported by the evidence." (Emphasis added.) Torosyan v. Boehringer Ingelheim Pharmaceuticals, Inc., supra, 234 Conn. at 33–34, 662 A.2d 89 (analogizing future earnings to lost profits). In Torosyan, this court approved an award of lost wages for wrongful termination of an implied employment contract. Damages for lost wages were awarded from the date of discharge, in May, 1985, to the end of 1992, which was approximately one year beyond the end of trial. Id., at 32, 662 A.2d 89. In Westport Taxi Service, Inc. v. Westport Transit District, supra, 235 Conn. at 33–36, 664 A.2d 719, this court approved the trial court's damage award consisting of one year of lost profits and the value of the business based on its actual earnings in the year before it ceased operating. Cf. Olympia Equipment Leasing Co. v. Western Union Tele-graph, 797 F.2d 370, 383 (7th Cir.1986), cert. denied, 480 U.S. 934, 107 S.Ct. 1574, 94 L.Ed.2d 765 (1987) (lost profit award for ten year period not appropriate where plaintiff failed to demonstrate that it would have survived and remained profitable for that length of time).

A survey of cases permitting the recovery of lost profits over long periods of time reveals that, in these cases, the recovery period frequently is based on contracts or lease terms of fixed duration. See, e.g., Super Valu Stores, Inc. v. Peterson, supra, 506 So.2d 317 (breach of contract to lease and operate grocery store for fifteen years); Chung v. Kaonohi Center Co., supra, 62 Haw. 594, 618 P.2d 283 (breach of contract to enter into ten year lease for fast food restaurant); Fera v. Village Plaza, Inc., supra, 396 Mich. 639, 242 N.W.2d 372 (breach of ten year lease for liquor store). In the present case, by contrast, the choice of a twelve year time span appears quite arbitrary. The example case study prepared by the American Institute of Certified Public Accountants that was introduced by the plaintiff, and noted by the trial court in its memorandum of decision, was based on a proposed twelve year contractual agreement, and was therefore not comparable to the present case. The time span applied in the present case was not tied to any objective facts that reasonably could be construed as supporting the plaintiff's claim that the sale of fitness center franchises would have become profitable and would have remained so for twelve years. We conclude, therefore, that the trial court abused its discretion in failing to limit the recovery of lost profits to a reasonable time period.

We recognize that our decision that the plaintiff failed to prove damages means that the defendants, whose malpractice caused the plaintiff's harm, escape virtually unscathed. "Injury is the illegal invasion of a legal right; damage is the loss, hurt, or harm which results from the injury; and damages are the recompense or compensation awarded for the damage suffered. 22 Am.Jur.2d [Damages] § 1 [1988]. Ballentine's Law Dictionary (3d Ed.1969) p. 303." (Internal quotation marks omitted.) DiNapoli v. Cooke, 43 Conn.App. 419, 427–28, 682 A.2d 603, cert. denied, 239 Conn. 951, 686 A.2d 124 (1996). In this case, the defendants argued that Ferreira's testimony failed to remove the question of damages from the realm of speculation and, consequently, the plaintiff failed to satisfy its burden of proof on the issue of damages. This is a case in which we reverse the judgment not for lack of "mathematical exactitude"; Falco v. James Peter Associates, Inc., 165 Conn. 442, 445, 335 A.2d 301 (1973); but because the plaintiff failed to provide sufficient evidence.[14] This outcome is a direct result of the plaintiff's choice of evidence.

. . .

The judgment with respect to the appeal is reversed and the case is remanded with direction to render judgment for the defendants; the judgment is affirmed with respect to the cross appeal.

■ In this opinion NORCOTT, PALMER and EDWARD Y. O'CONNELL, JJ., concurred.

[PETERS, ASSOCIATE JUSTICE, filed a dissenting opinion, which has been omitted].

Fairfax County Redevelopment and Housing Authority v. Worcester Brothers Company, Inc.

Supreme Court of Virginia 1999.
257 Va. 382, 514 S.E.2d 147.

■ KOONTZ, JUSTICE.

In this appeal, we consider whether the trial court's award of unabsorbed home office expenses to the contractor on a public construction project following an unreasonable delay by the contracting government agency was based upon sufficient proof of the existence and amount of those damages.

BACKGROUND

Under well established principles, we recount only those facts relevant to our resolution of the appeal. On September 14, 1995, the Fairfax County Redevelopment and Housing Authority (the Authority) entered into a contract with Worcester Brothers Company, Inc. (Worcester Brothers), a general construction contractor, for site renovations and improvements of Washington Plaza in Lake Anne Village (the project) in Reston.

The Authority had originally solicited bids for the project based on a projected start date in July 1995, with completion of the work in 150 calendar days from the notice to proceed. Thus, the proposed date of substantial completion at the time bids were solicited was mid-December 1995. Worcester Brothers based its bid on these conditions. However, because the Authority did not award the contract to Worcester Brothers until September 14, 1995, the substantial completion date for the project was moved back to mid-February 1996.

---

14. Generally, proof of a legal injury entitles a plaintiff to, at least, token or nominal damages even if no specific actual damages are proven. "Nominal damages mean no damages. They exist only in name and not in amount." (Internal quotation marks omitted.) Sessa v. Gigliotti, 165 Conn. 620, 622, 345 A.2d 45 (1973). To recover more than nominal damages, it was incumbent upon the plaintiff to prove the extent of those damages for the actions of the defendants. This the plaintiff failed to do, and, accordingly, it is entitled only to nominal damages. Because, however, the plaintiff does not seek nominal damages, we do not remand the case for such an award.

It is not disputed that at the time Worcester Brothers commenced work on the project, the Authority had not yet obtained the necessary clearances from an adjoining property owner to allow work to proceed on a portion of the project site. The Authority did not obtain the clearances until March 6, 1996.

After the work was completed, Worcester Brothers filed notice of potential change #15 (NPC 15) with the Authority's architect seeking additional payment for field office expenses incurred on the job site due to the Authority's delay in obtaining the clearances. Worcester Brothers also claimed it had unabsorbed home office expenses attributable to the delay. In NPC 15, Worcester Brothers calculated its additional field office expenses based upon its daily field office overhead rate multiplied by the 98 days of delay it attributed to the Authority.[1] To calculate its unabsorbed home office expenses, Worcester Brothers used the so-called "[Appeal of] Eichleay [Corp., 1960 WL 538 (1960)] formula,"[2] to determine a daily home office overhead rate and multiplied that rate by the same 98 days of delay. The architect, acting on behalf of the Authority, denied the claims made in NPC 15.

On November 4, 1996, Worcester Brothers filed a motion for judgment against the Authority seeking damages for breach of contract based upon the failure to pay NPC 15. The Authority filed an answer denying the allegations of the motion for judgment and raising as an affirmative defense the claim that "[h]ome office damages based on the Eichleay formula are prohibited by Virginia law."

At trial, Worcester Brothers contended that during the delay it incurred both additional field office expenses as a result of having to maintain its personnel at the job site and unabsorbed home office expenses. It presented evidence of its actual field office expenses related to the delay in the amount of $46,359.11. Worcester Brothers' accounting system did not allocate its home office expenses to particular contracts. However, Joseph P. Noonan, Worcester Brothers' president, testified that the unabsorbed home office expenses attributable to the delay amounted to $34,495.89. According to Noonan, that figure was calculated from statements prepared by Worcester Brothers' accountants reflecting the total general and administrative expenses of the company during the relevant contract period and the application of the Eichleay formula to those expenses.

The Authority asserted numerous objections to Worcester Brothers' evidence of damages. Pertinent to the issue presented on appeal, the Authority contended that Worcester Brothers had proven no actual damages as a result of the delay. It contended that the Eichleay formula calculation did not constitute proof of actual damages to a reasonable degree of certainty, but, rather, is merely a method for determining the

---

1. This figure was later revised to represent the actual costs Worcester Brothers incurred in maintaining its workforce on the project site during the delay period.

2. The Eichleay formula is "the prevailing method" used for calculating a contrac-

tor's home office expenses attributable to a government-caused delay on a federal contract. Capital Electric Company v. United States, 729 F.2d 743, 744 (Fed.Cir.1984).

amount of unabsorbed home office expenses attributable to a particular contract once the existence of such damages has been proven by other evidence. The Authority contended that Worcester Brothers had not shown that its workforce was actually idle as a result of the delay in obtaining the clearances and, thus, that none of its home office expenses was incurred as a result of the delay. Moreover, the Authority contended that the Eichleay formula was "totally and wholly irrelevant" to "a contract governed by state law."

At the conclusion of the evidence, the trial court addressed the Authority's contentions and reasoned that in order to succeed on a breach of contract damage claim for unabsorbed home office expenses resulting from a delay, the contractor was first required to show that it had incurred such damages by establishing that the government had caused the delay; that the contractor's workforce was placed on standby as a result; and that the contractor was not free to engage in work on other projects during the delay. The trial court then found that the Authority's delay was "manifest on this record" and was "egregious" and "frankly inexcusable." The trial court further found that Worcester Brothers' workforce had been on "standby" because the Authority "never could advise the contractor that the area would not be available until a particular date. Instead it was a rolling deadline." Finally, the trial court found that the "rolling deadline" also inhibited Worcester Brothers from seeking other contracts, and thereby minimizing the damage caused by the delay, since it could not be assured of the availability of its workforce for another project.

Having found that Worcester Brothers had satisfied its initial "burden of proving [home office] damages with reasonable certainty," the trial court turned to the question whether the Eichleay formula could be used to calculate the amount of those damages. Recognizing that other courts had found the Eichleay formula to be "a fair way of approximating" such damages, the trial court noted that after auditing Worcester Brothers' books, the Authority did not contend that any of the specific expenses were inappropriately claimed and that the Authority's witnesses failed "to present any reasoned analysis of why Eichleay is inappropriate." Accordingly, the trial court entered judgment for Worcester Brothers for both the field office expenses ($46,359.11) and the unabsorbed home office expenses as calculated by the Eichleay formula ($34,495.89). The trial court granted the Authority's motion to reconsider, and, after receiving briefs from the parties, sustained its original ruling. We awarded the Authority this appeal.

DISCUSSION

The Authority does not challenge the trial court's determination that the Authority was liable for damages caused by the delay. Nor does the Authority challenge that portion of the judgment attributable to field office expenses. Accordingly, our discussion is necessarily limited to a determination of whether, as specified by the Authority's assignment of error, "[t]he trial court erred in finding that a contractor had proved its home office damages with reasonable certainty." (Emphasis added.) We agree with the trial court's reasoning that the resolution of this issue requires that we first consider whether Worcester Brothers established that it suffered damages in the form of unabsorbed home office expenses attributable to the Authority's delay, and, if so, whether there was adequate proof of the amount of those damages.

Home office expenses, commonly called overhead, include those costs that a contractor must expend for the benefit of its business as a whole. These expenses include, for example, the salaries of office staff, accounting expenses, dues and subscriptions, equipment costs, and utility services. Unabsorbed home office expenses comprise "those overhead costs needlessly consumed by a partially or totally idle contractor. A contractor continues to incur overhead costs during periods of reduced activity or delay on a particular contract. When this occurs, the 'reduced activity' contract no longer 'absorbs' its share of overhead costs." Michael W. Kauffman and Craig A. Holman, The Eichleay Formula: A Resilient Means for Recovering Unabsorbed Overhead, 24 Pub. Contr. L.J. 319, 321 (1995)(footnotes omitted).

When a breach by one party imposes a delay on the ability of the other party to perform its obligations under a contract, "the damages are to be measured by the direct cost of all labor and material . . . plus fair and reasonable overhead expenses properly chargeable . . . during the reasonable time required" to complete performance. E.I. duPont deNemours & Co. v. Universal Moulded Prod., 191 Va. 525, 581, 62 S.E.2d 233, 259 (1950)(emphasis added). In such cases, while the plaintiff must prove its damages with reasonable certainty, " '[a]n absolute certainty as to the amount of the damages is not essential when the existence of a loss has been established. The quantum may be fixed when the facts and circumstances are such as to permit . . . an intelligent and probable estimate thereof.' " Pebble Building Co. v. G.J. Hopkins, Inc., 223 Va. 188, 191, 288 S.E.2d 437, 438 (1982) (citation omitted).

We recognize that not every instance of a delay caused by the other party to a contract will result in a contractor incurring either direct or overhead damages. However, where the evidence shows that a contractor has incurred direct damages as a result of the delay such as additional cost of labor and material, the question whether the contractor also suffered unabsorbed overhead damages necessarily must be determined from the facts and circumstances of the individual case. It is not necessary for the contractor to show that its overhead was increased as a result of the delay, but only that it could not otherwise reasonably recoup its pro rata home office expenses incurred while its workforce was idled by the delay.

Here, the evidence showed that Worcester Brothers incurred actual direct damages as a result of having to maintain its personnel on the job site far beyond the anticipated date of substantial completion. The record supports the trial court's finding that the Authority was responsible for a delay that caused Worcester Brothers' workforce to be "on standby" and this further prohibited Worcester Brothers from recouping its unabsorbed home office expenses by seeking other contracts during the delay period. Accordingly, we agree with the trial court's ruling that Worcester Brothers met its burden of proof with respect to the existence of unabsorbed home office expenses attributable to the Authority's delay.

The Authority contends, however, that even if Worcester Brothers proved that it incurred unabsorbed home office expenses as a result of the Authority's delay, the trial court erred in accepting the Eichleay formula as the method for determining the amount of these expenses. The Authority asserts that the contract provides that disputes between the parties will be governed by Virginia law and, since no legislative act, administrative rule, or case law in Virginia has "adopt[ed] the use of the Eichleay formula in claims against public bodies in Virginia," the use of the formula "was not within the parties' contemplation at the time the contract was executed."

The Authority is correct in noting that use of the Eichleay formula has not been previously approved in this Commonwealth by legislative or administrative act, nor has its use been addressed in a published appellate court decision relating to a public contract. However, we are not persuaded by the Authority's contention that a lack of prior authoritative application of the Eichleay formula to a Virginia public contract prevents its application in this instance. The Eichleay formula is not a legal standard that must be formally approved or adopted; rather, it is merely a mathematical method of prorating a contractor's total overhead expenses for a particular contract.[5] As such, the question before the trial court was not whether, in the absence of an express term, the parties contemplated using the Eichleay formula, or any other method of calculating unabsorbed overhead damages, but whether the resulting quantum was "an intelligent and probable estimate" of the actual damages. Pebble, 223 Va. at 191, 288 S.E.2d at 438.

As an abstract proposition, the Eichleay formula has been criticized as an inadequate substitute for direct evidence of the actual amount of damages and "no less speculative" than other unsupported opinion evidence simply "because it was cast in a mathematical milieu." Berley Indus., Inc. v. City of New York, 45 N.Y.2d 683, 412 N.Y.S.2d 589, 385 N.E.2d 281, 283 (1978). In Berley, the New York Court of Appeals rejected the use of the Eichleay formula as an "administrative convenience," where there was no supporting evidence that any of the home office expenses were attributable to the delay. Id.

Distinguishing Berley, the Florida District Court of Appeals held that use of the Eichleay formula for calculating unabsorbed home office expenses attributable to a delay is proper so long as there is competent evidence of actual damage having been sustained by the party seeking relief. Broward County v. Russell, Inc., 589 So.2d 983, 984 (Fla.Dist.Ct.App. 1991). Similarly, other jurisdictions have held that where there is sufficient proof that the plaintiff has suffered damages as a result of the delay, the

---

5. To make that proration, the total amount billed on the particular contract by the contractor (B subc) is divided by the contractor's total billings during the contract period (B subt) and this quotient is then multiplied by the contractor's home office expenses attributable to the contract period (H subt) to determine the amount of home office expenses allocable to the contract. Next, the amount of home office expenses allocable to the contract is divided by the total number of days of the contractor's performance under the contract (D subt) to determine a daily contract home office expense rate. Finally, the daily contract home office expense rate is multiplied by the number of days of delay (D subd) to determine the amount of damages (A). See Capital Electric, 729 F.2d at 747.

Eichleay formula affords a reasonable basis for estimating the amount of those damages with respect to unabsorbed home office expenses. See, e.g., Conti Corp. v. Ohio Dept. of Admin. Serv's, 90 Ohio App.3d 462, 629 N.E.2d 1073, 1077 (1993); Golf Landscaping, Inc. v. Century Const. Co., 39 Wash.App. 895, 696 P.2d 590, 593 (1984).

We are of opinion that the rationale of the latter cases is in accord with the general principles of law applicable to proving damages for delay as outlined in the duPont and Pebble, cases. Accordingly, where, as here, there is evidence that a contractor has suffered actual damages as a result of an unreasonable owner-caused delay, the Eichleay formula is an acceptable method, though not the only possible method, of calculating the portion of home office expenses attributable to delay. Cf. Southern New England Contracting Co. v. State, 165 Conn. 644, 345 A.2d 550, 559–60 (1974); PDM Plumbing & Heating, Inc. v. Findlen, 13 Mass.App.Ct. 950, 431 N.E.2d 594, 595 (1982).

In recognizing the adequacy of the evidence in this case to support the use of the Eichleay formula to determine unabsorbed overhead damages for the delay in this contract, we do not adopt it as the standard for determining such damages generally. Rather, as with any fact-specific question, the individual circumstances of a given case will determine whether "an intelligent and probable estimate" of such damages has been proven. Pebble, 223 Va. at 191, 288 S.E.2d at 438.

CONCLUSION

For the reasons stated above, we will affirm the judgment of the trial court.

Affirmed.

D. RELIANCE INTEREST

Sullivan v. O'Connor

Supreme Judicial Court of Massachusetts, 1973.
363 Mass. 579, 296 N.E.2d 183.

■ KAPLAN, J. The plaintiff patient secured a jury verdict of $13,500 against the defendant surgeon for breach of contract in respect to an operation upon the plaintiff's nose....

... [T]he plaintiff[, an entertainer,] alleged that she, as patient, entered into a contract with the defendant, a surgeon, wherein the defendant promised to perform plastic surgery on her nose and thereby to enhance her beauty and improve her appearance; that he performed the surgery but failed to achieve the promised result; rather the result of the surgery was to disfigure and deform her nose, to cause her pain in body and mind, and to subject her to other damage and expense....

. . . .

The judge instructed the jury, first, that the plaintiff was entitled to recover her out-of-pocket expenses incident to the operations. Second, she could recover the damages flowing directly, naturally, proximately, and foreseeably from the defendant's breach of promise. These would comprehend damages for any disfigurement of the plaintiff's nose—that is, any change of appearance for the worse—including the effects of the consciousness of such disfigurement on the plaintiff's mind, and in this connection the jury should consider the nature of the plaintiff's profession. Also consequent upon the defendant's breach, and compensable, were the pain and suffering involved in the third operation, but not in the first two. As there was no proof that any loss of earnings by the plaintiff resulted from the breach, that element should not enter into the calculation of damages.

By his exceptions the defendant contends that the judge erred in allowing the jury to take into account anything but the plaintiff's out-of-pocket expenses (presumably at the stipulated amount). . . .

. . . .

It has been suggested on occasion that agreements between patients and physicians by which the physician undertakes to effect a cure or to bring about a given result should be declared unenforceable on grounds of public policy. But there are many decisions recognizing and enforcing such contracts, and the law of Massachusetts has treated them as valid, although we have had no decision meeting head on the contention that they should be denied legal sanction. These causes of action are, however, considered a little suspect, and thus we find courts straining sometimes to read the pleadings as sounding only in tort for negligence, and not in contract for breach of promise, despite sedulous efforts by the pleaders to pursue the latter theory.

. . . .

If an action on the basis of contract is allowed, we have next the question of the measure of damages to be applied where liability is found. Some cases have taken the simple view that the promise by the physician is to be treated like an ordinary commercial promise, and accordingly that the successful plaintiff is entitled to a standard measure of recovery for breach of contract—"compensatory" ("expectancy") damages, an amount intended to put the plaintiff in the position he would be in if the contract had been performed, or, presumably, at the plaintiff's election, "restitution" damages, an amount corresponding to any benefit conferred by the plaintiff upon the defendant in the performance of the contract disrupted by the defendant's breach. Thus in Hawkins v. McGee, 84 N.H. 114, 146 A. 641, the defendant doctor was taken to have promised the plaintiff to convert his damaged hand by means of an operation into a good or perfect hand, but the doctor so operated as to damage the hand still further. The court, following the usual expectancy formula, would have asked the jury to estimate and award to the plaintiff the difference between the value of a good or perfect hand, as promised, and the value of the hand after the operation. (The same formula would apply, although the dollar result would be less, if the operation had neither worsened nor improved the condition of the hand.) If the plaintiff had not yet paid the doctor his fee, that amount would be deducted from the recovery. There could be no recovery for the pain and suffering of the operation, since that detriment would have been incurred even if the operation had been successful; one can say that this detriment was not "caused" by the breach. But where the plaintiff by reason of the operation was put to more pain than he would have had to endure, had the doctor performed as promised, he should be compensated for that difference as a proper part of his expectancy recovery.... The New Hampshire court further refined the *Hawkins* analysis in McQuaid v. Michou, 85 N.H. 299, 157 A. 881, all in the direction of treating the patient-physician cases on the ordinary footing of expectancy.

Other cases, including a number in New York, without distinctly repudiating the *Hawkins* type of analysis, have indicated that a different and generally more lenient measure of damages is to be applied in patient-physician actions based on breach of alleged special agreements to effect a cure, attain a stated result, or employ a given medical method. This measure is expressed in somewhat variant ways, but the substance is that the plaintiff is to recover any expenditures made by him and for other detriment (usually not specifically described in the opinions) following proximately and foreseeably upon the defendant's failure to carry out his promise. This, be it noted, is not a "restitution" measure, for it is not limited to restoration of the benefit conferred on the defendant (the fee paid) but includes other expenditures, for example, amounts paid for medicine and nurses; so also it would seem according to its logic to take in damages for any worsening of the plaintiff's condition due to the breach. Nor is it an "expectancy" measure, for it does not appear to contemplate recovery of the whole difference in value between the condition as promised and the condition actually resulting from the treatment. Rather the tendency of the formulation is to put the plaintiff back in the position he occupied just before the parties entered upon the agreement, to compensate him for the detriments he suffered in reliance upon the agreement. This kind of intermediate pattern of recovery for breach of contract is discussed in the suggestive article by Fuller and Perdue, The Reliance Interest in Contract Damages, 46 Yale L.J. 52, 373, where the authors show that, although not attaining the currency of the standard measures, a "reliance" measure has for special reasons been applied by the courts in a variety of settings, including noncommercial settings. See 46 Yale L.J. at 396–401.[4]

For breach of the patient-physician agreements under consideration, a recovery limited to restitution seems plainly too meager, if the agreements are to be enforced at all. On the other hand, an expectancy recovery may well be excessive.... Where ... the doctor has been absolved of negligence by the trier, an expectancy measure may be thought harsh. We should recall here that the fee paid by the patient to the doctor for the alleged promise would usually be quite disproportionate to the putative expectation recovery. To attempt, moreover, to put a value on the condition that would

---

4. Some of the exceptional situations mentioned where reliance may be preferred to expectancy are those in which the latter measure would be hard to apply or would impose too great a burden; performance was interfered with by external circumstances; the contract was indefinite.

or might have resulted had the treatment succeeded as promised, may sometimes put an exceptional strain on the imagination of the factfinder. . . .

There is much to be said, then, for applying a reliance measure to the present facts, and we have only to add that our cases are not unreceptive to the use of that formula in special situations. We have, however, had no previous occasion to apply it to patient-physician cases.[5]

The question of recovery on a reliance basis for pain and suffering or mental distress requires further attention. We find expressions in the decisions that pain and suffering (or the like) are simply not compensable in actions for breach of contract. The defendant seemingly espouses this proposition in the present case. True, if the buyer under a contract for the purchase of a lot of merchandise, in suing for the seller's breach, should claim damages for mental anguish caused by his disappointment in the transaction, he would not succeed; he would be told, perhaps, that the asserted psychological injury was not fairly foreseeable by the defendant as a probable consequence of the breach of such a business contract. But there is no general rule barring such items of damage in actions for breach of contract. It is all a question of the subject matter and background of the contract, and when the contract calls for an operation on the person of the plaintiff, psychological as well as physical injury may be expected to figure somewhere in the recovery, depending on the particular circumstances. . . . Again, it is said in a few of the New York cases, concerned with the classification of actions for statute of limitations purposes, that the absence of allegations demanding recovery for pain and suffering is characteristic of a contract claim by a patient against a physician, that such allegations rather belong in a claim for malpractice. These remarks seem unduly sweeping. Suffering or distress resulting from the breach going beyond that which was envisaged by the treatment as agreed, should be compensable on the same ground as the worsening of the patient's condition because of the

---

5. In Mt. Pleasant Stable Co. v. Steinberg, 238 Mass. 567, 131 N.E. 295, the plaintiff company agreed to supply teams of horses at agreed rates as required from day to day by the defendant for his business. To prepare itself to fulfill the contract and in reliance on it, the plaintiff bought two "Cliest" horses at a certain price. When the defendant repudiated the contract, the plaintiff sold the horses at a loss and in its action for breach claimed the loss as an element of damages. The court properly held that the plaintiff was not entitled to this item as it was also claiming (and recovering) its lost profits (expectancy) on the contract as a whole. (The loss on sale of the horses is analogous to the pain and suffering for which the patient would be disallowed a recovery in Hawkins v. McGee, 84 N.H. 114, 146 A. 641, because he was claiming and recovering expectancy damages.) The court in the Mt. Pleasant case referred, however, to Pond v.

Harris, 113 Mass. 114, as a contrasting situation where the expectancy could not be fairly determined. There the defendant had wrongfully revoked an agreement to arbitrate a dispute with the plaintiff (this was before such agreements were made specifically enforceable). In an action for the breach, the plaintiff was held entitled to recover for his preparations for the arbitration which had been rendered useless and a waste, including the plaintiff's time and trouble and his expenditures for counsel and witnesses. The context apparently was commercial but reliance elements were held compensable when there was no fair way of estimating an expectancy. A noncommercial example is Smith v. Sherman, 4 Cush. 408, 413–414, suggesting that a conventional recovery for breach of promise of marriage included a recompense for various efforts and expenditures by the plaintiff preparatory to the promised wedding.

breach. Indeed it can be argued that the very suffering or distress "contracted for"—that which would have been incurred if the treatment achieved the promised result—should also be compensable on the theory underlying the New York cases. For that suffering is "wasted" if the treatment fails. Otherwise stated, compensation for this waste is arguably required in order to complete the restoration of the status quo ante.[6]

In the light of the foregoing discussion, all the defendant's exceptions fail: the plaintiff was not confined to the recovery of her out-of-pocket expenditures; she was entitled to recover also for the worsening of her condition, and for the pain and suffering and mental distress involved in the third operation. These items were compensable on either an expectancy or a reliance view. We might have been required to elect between the two views if the pain and suffering connected with the first two operations contemplated by the agreement, or the whole difference in value between the present and the promised conditions, were being claimed as elements of damage. But the plaintiff waives her possible claim to the former element, and to so much of the latter as represents the difference in value between the promised condition and the condition before the operations.

. . . .

Defendant's exceptions overruled.

E.   NOMINAL DAMAGES

Freund v. Washington Square Press, Inc.

Court of Appeals of New York, 1974.
34 N.Y.2d 379, 357 N.Y.S.2d 857, 314 N.E.2d 419.

RABIN, J. In this action for breach of a publishing contract, we must decide what damages are recoverable for defendant's failure to publish plaintiff's manuscript. In 1965, plaintiff, an author and a college teacher, and defendant, Washington Square Press, Inc., entered into a written agreement which, in relevant part, provided as follows. Plaintiff ("author") granted defendant ("publisher") exclusive rights to publish and sell in book form plaintiff's work on modern drama. Upon plaintiff's delivery of the manuscript, defendant agreed to complete payment of a nonreturnable $2,000 "advance". Thereafter, if defendant deemed the manuscript not "suitable for publication", it had the right to terminate the agreement by

---

6. Recovery on a reliance basis for breach of the physician's promise tends to equate with the usual recovery for malpractice, since the latter also looks in general to restoration of the condition before the injury. But this is not paradoxical, especially when it is noted that the origins of contract lie in tort. A few cases have considered possible recovery for breach by a physician of a promise to sterilize a patient, resulting in birth of a child to the patient and spouse. If such an action is held maintainable, the reliance and expectancy measures would, we think, tend to equate, because the promised condition was preservation of the family status quo.

written notice within 60 days of delivery. Unless so terminated, defendant agreed to publish the work in hardbound edition within 18 months and afterwards in paperbound edition. The contract further provided that defendant would pay royalties to plaintiff, based upon specified percentages of sales. (For example, plaintiff was to receive 10% of the retail price of the first 10,000 copies sold in the continental United States.) If defendant failed to publish within 18 months, the contract provided that "this agreement shall terminate and the rights herein granted to the Publisher shall revert to the Author. In such event all payments theretofore made to the Author shall belong to the Author without prejudice to any other remedies which the Author may have." ...

Plaintiff performed by delivering his manuscript to defendant and was paid his $2,000 advance. Defendant thereafter merged with another publisher and ceased publishing in hardbound. Although defendant did not execute its 60–day right to terminate, it has refused to publish the manuscript in any form.

[The trial court found that the cost of hardcover publication to the plaintiff was the natural and probable consequence of the breach and, based upon expert testimony, awarded $10,000.00 to cover this cost.]

The Appellate Division, affirmed, finding that the cost of publication was the proper measure of damages. In support of its conclusion, the majority analogized to the construction contract situation where the cost of completion may be the proper measure of damages for a builder's failure to complete a house or for use of wrong materials. The dissent concluded that the cost of publication is not an appropriate measure of damages and consequently, that plaintiff may recover nominal damages only. We agree with the dissent. In so concluding, we look to the basic purpose of damage recovery and the nature and effect of the parties' contract.

It is axiomatic that, except where punitive damages are allowable, the law awards damages for breach of contract to compensate for injury caused by the breach—injury which was foreseeable, i.e., reasonably within the contemplation of the parties, at the time the contract was entered into. Money damages are substitutional relief designed in theory "to put the injured party in as good a position as he would have been put by full performance of the contract, at the least cost to the defendant and without charging him with harms that he had no sufficient reason to foresee when he made the contract." (5 Corbin, Contracts, § 1002, pp. 31–32.) In other words, so far as possible, the law attempts to secure to the injured party the benefit of his bargain, subject to the limitations that the injury—whether it be losses suffered or gains prevented—was foreseeable, and that the amount of damages claimed to be measurable with a reasonable degree of certainty and of course, adequately proven. But it is equally fundamental that the injured party should not recover more from the breach than he would have gained had the contract been fully performed.

Measurement of damages in this case according to the cost of publication to the plaintiff would confer greater advantage than performance of the contract would have entailed to plaintiff and would place him in a far better position than he would have occupied had the defendant fully performed. Such measurement bears no relation to compensation for plaintiff's actual loss or anticipated profit. Far beyond compensating plaintiff for the interests he had in the defendant's performance of the contract— whether restitution, reliance or expectation an award of the cost of publication would enrich plaintiff at defendant's expense.

Pursuant to the contract, plaintiff delivered his manuscript to the defendant. In doing so, he conferred a value on the defendant which, upon defendant's breach, was required to be restored to him. Special Term, in addition to ordering a trial on the issue of damages, ordered defendant to return the manuscript to plaintiff and plaintiff's restitution interest in the contract was thereby protected.

At the trial on the issue of damages, plaintiff alleged no reliance losses suffered in performing the contract or in making necessary preparations to perform. Had such losses, if foreseeable and ascertainable, been incurred, plaintiff would have been entitled to compensation for them.

As for plaintiff's expectation interest in the contract, it was basically two-fold—the "advance" and the royalties. (To be sure, plaintiff may have expected to enjoy whatever notoriety, prestige or other benefits that might have attended publication, but even if these expectations were compensable, plaintiff did not attempt at trial to place a monetary value on them.) There is no dispute that plaintiff's expectancy in the "advance" was fulfilled—he has received his $2,000. His expectancy interest in the royalties—the profit he stood to gain from sale of the published book—while theoretically compensable, was speculative. Although this work is not plaintiff's first, at trial he provided no stable foundation for a reasonable estimate of royalties he would have earned had defendant not breached its promise to publish. In these circumstances, his claim for royalties fails for uncertainty.

Since the damages which would have compensated plaintiff for anticipated royalties were not proved with the required certainty, we agree with the dissent in the Appellate Division that nominal damages alone are recoverable. Though these are damages in name only and not at all compensatory, they are nevertheless awarded as a formal vindication of plaintiff's legal right to compensation which has not been given a sufficiently certain monetary valuation.

In our view, the analogy by the majority in the Appellate Division to the construction contract situation was inapposite. In the typical construction contract, the owner agrees to pay money or other consideration to a builder and expects, under the contract, to receive a completed building in return. The value of the promised performance to the owner is the properly constructed building. In this case, unlike the typical construction contract, the value to plaintiff of the promised performance—publication—was a percentage of sales of the books published and not the books themselves. Had the plaintiff contracted for the printing, binding and delivery of a number of hardbound copies of his manuscript, to be sold or disposed of as he wished, then perhaps the construction analogy, and measurement of damages by the cost of replacement or completion, would have some application.

Here, however, the specific value to plaintiff of the promised publication was the royalties he stood to receive from defendant's sales of the published book. Essentially, publication represented what it would have cost the defendant to confer that value upon the plaintiff, and, by its breach, defendant saved that cost. The error by the courts below was in measuring damages not by the value to plaintiff of the promised performance but by the cost of that performance to defendant. Damages are not measured, however, by what the defaulting party saved by the breach, but by the natural and probable consequences of the breach *to the plaintiff*. In this case, the consequence to plaintiff of defendant's failure to publish is that he is prevented from realizing the gains promised by the contract—the royalties. But, as we have stated, the amount of royalties plaintiff would have realized was not ascertained with adequate certainty and, as a consequence, plaintiff may recover nominal damages only.

Accordingly, the order of the Appellate Division should be modified to the extent of reducing the damage award of $10,000 for the cost of publication to six cents, but with costs and disbursements to the plaintiff.

Order modified, with costs and disbursements to plaintiff-respondent, in accordance with opinion herein and, as so modified, affirmed.

———

F. EMOTIONAL DISTRESS

Awarding Damages

B & M Homes, Inc. v. Hogan

Supreme Court of Alabama, 1979.
376 So.2d 667.

■ EMBRY, J. . . .

. . . The Hogans entered into a written agreement to buy both a lot and a house to be constructed on that lot. . . . The agreed purchase price was $37,500. . . .

During the construction of the house, Mrs. Hogan discovered a hairline crack in the concrete slab that extended from the front porch through the den and informed Morrow of this. He informed her that such cracks were common and told her not to worry about it. B & M Homes completed construction of the house and the Hogans received a warranty of completion of construction signed by Morrow on behalf of B & M Homes. The Hogans then moved into the house. After they moved in they reported several defects in the house to Morrow and repairmen were sent to fix those defects. After a couple of months the crack in the slab widened and extended through the house causing severe damage.

Again, Morrow was notified. He sent a man to repair some of the damage caused by the crack in the slab; however, nothing was done to repair the slab itself. There is expert testimony to the effect the slab probably could not be permanently repaired. There is also testimony the defective slab seriously decreased the value of the house; the Hogan's expert witness testified the defective slab made the house worthless....

I

Appellants contend the trial court erred by failing to grant their motion to strike mental anguish as an element of damages from the Hogans' complaint. We find mental anguish a proper element of damages in this case.

... [T]he Hogans' case was submitted to the jury on two theories stated in separate counts: one for breach of an implied covenant, to their written purchase contract, to build their home in a workmanlike manner using first class materials; and one for breach of express warranty. In both counts, appellees alleged damages for mental anguish as follows:

"... the plaintiffs have suffered mental anguish and are still suffering mental anguish with regard to the condition of such home in that they fear for their safety in the house not being structurally sound;...."

At the close of the trial, B & M Homes filed a motion to strike the above allegation from both causes of action. The motion was denied. It can be assumed the jury awarded damages for mental anguish since the verdict was for $75,000 and the highest appraisal of the value of the house had it been built without defects was $42,500.

Evidence was introduced, over appellants' objection, that the Hogans were worried and concerned for their safety due to these facts: (1) the house was structurally defective and they believed its defective condition might cause the gas and water lines to burst; and (2) they were forced to live in the defective house because they could not afford to move.

In Alabama the general rule is that mental anguish is not a recoverable element of damages arising from breach of contract. Stead v. Blue Cross–Blue Shield of Alabama, 346 So.2d 1140 (Ala.1977). This court, however, has traditionally recognized exceptions to this rule in certain cases. F. Becker Asphaltum Roofing Co. v. Murphy, 224 Ala. 655, 141 So. 630 (1932). The exceptions are stated in the following excerpt from F. Becker Asphaltum Roofing Co. v. Murphy ...

"The general rule is that damages cannot be recovered for mental anguish in an action of assumpsit. The ground on which the right to recover such damages is denied, is that they are too remote, were not within the contemplation of the parties, and that the breach of the contract is not such as will naturally cause mental anguish. 'Yet where the contractual duty or obligation is so coupled with matters of mental concern or solicitude, or with the feelings of the party to whom the duty is owed, that a breach of that duty will necessarily or reasonably result in mental anguish or suffering, it is just that damages therefor be taken into consideration and awarded.'

"Another exception is where the breach of the contract is tortious, or attended with personal injury, damages for mental anguish may be awarded.

"The facts of this case, if the plaintiff's evidence was believed, brings the case within these two exceptions.

"The contract related to placing a roof on the plaintiff's residence, her 'castle,' the habitation which she had provided to protect her against the elements, and to shelter her belongings that she thought essential to her comfort and well-being, the very things against which she made the contract to protect herself and her property, and as a result of the breach of the obligation which defendants assumed, the roof leaked to such extent that she was disturbed in her comfort, her household belongings were soaked with water, her house was made damp, she was made sick, as the jury were authorized to find. And the defendants, though repeatedly notified, took no steps to meet their obligation, were not only guilty of a breach of the contract, but were negligent in respect to the performance of the duty which it imposed on them. Charge 12 was therefore refused without error.

"She was also entitled to recover for inconvenience and annoyance, resulting proximately from such breach."

This case clearly falls within the first exception delineated in *F. Becker Asphaltum*. It was reasonably foreseeable by appellants that faulty construction of appellees' house would cause them severe mental anguish. The largest single investment the average American family will make is the purchase of a home. The purchase of a home by an individual or family places the purchaser in debt for a period ranging from twenty (20) to thirty (30) years. While one might expect to take the risk of acquiring a defective home if that person bought an older home, he or she certainly would not expect severe defects to exist in a home they contracted to have newly built. Consequently, any reasonable builder could easily foresee that an individual would undergo extreme mental anguish if their newly constructed house contained defects as severe as those shown to exist in this case. In any event, this court long ago set down the principle that the person who contracts to do work concerning a person's residence subjects himself to possible liability for mental anguish if that work is improperly performed and causes severe defects in that residence or home. The court clearly indicated this when it referred to the plaintiff's residence in *F. Becker Asphaltum* as "... her 'castle,' the habitation which she had provided to protect her against the elements...." While such language might be dramatic, it is a clear indication that contracts dealing with residences are in a special category and are exceptions to the general damages rule applied in contract cases which prohibits recovery for mental anguish.

In the recent case of Hill v. Sereneck, 355 So.2d 1129 (Ala.Civ.App. 1978), the Court of Civil Appeals dealt with the issue of damages for mental anguish where a builder had breached an agreement to build a residence in a workmanlike manner. The major defects in the house in *Hill* were almost exactly the same as the major defects in the house in this case. The appellate court in *Hill* found that cases of this type fall within the first exception set out in *F. Becker Asphaltum* and that evidence of mental anguish caused by such defects was relevant and admissible. The *Hill* court stated:

> "... Such evidence was relevant to the first exception to the general proposition that damages cannot be recovered for mental anguish in a civil action for breach of contract. In instances where it is demonstrated that the breach of the contractual duty actually caused the complaining party mental anguish or suffering and that the breach was such that it would necessarily result in emotional or mental detriment to the plaintiff, damages for annoyance and inconvenience may be awarded."

We concur with the Court of Civil Appeals in the accuracy of the above statement. Appellants contend, that before recovery for mental anguish or suffering can be allowed, the mental anguish has to be corroborated by physical symptoms, i.e., becoming physically sick or ill. We reject this contention. The cases have not required mental anguish to be corroborated by the presence of physical symptoms. This is demonstrated by the fact that the cases have allowed recovery for annoyance and inconvenience. Appellees were only required to present evidence of their mental anguish, which they did; the question of damages for mental anguish then became a question of fact for the jury to decide.

. . . .

NOTE ON RECOVERY FOR EMOTIONAL DISTRESS

1. In Hancock v. Northcutt, 808 P.2d 251 (Alaska 1991), the Supreme Court of Alaska stated:

> The view that contracts pertaining to one's dwelling are not among those contracts which, if breached, are particularly likely to result in serious emotional disturbance is reflected in numerous cases. E.g., Mack v. Hugh W. Comstock Associates, Inc., 225 Cal.App.2d 583, 37 Cal.Rptr. 466, 469 (1964); Maere v. Churchill, 116 Ill.App.3d 939, 72 Ill.Dec. 441, 452 N.E.2d 694 (1983); Groh v. Broadland Builders, Inc., 120 Mich.App. 214, 327 N.W.2d 443 (1982); Caradonna v. Thorious, 17 Mich.App. 41, 169 N.W.2d 179 (1969); Jankowski v. Mazzotta, 7 Mich.App. 483, 152 N.W.2d 49 (1967); Young v. Abalene Pest Control Services, Inc., 122 N.H. 287, 444 A.2d 514 (1982); Emerman v. Baldwin, 186 Pa.Super. 561, 142 A.2d 440 (1958). There is contrary authority as well, B & M Homes, Inc. v. Hogan, 376 So.2d 667 (Ala.1979); Jack v. Henry, 128 So.2d 62 (La.App.1961).
>
> In our view, breach of a house construction contract is not especially likely to result in serious emotional disturbance. Such contracts are not so highly personal and laden with emotion as contracts where emotional damages have typically been allowed to stand on their own. Examples of the latter include contracts to marry, to conduct a funeral, to sell a sealed casket, to conduct a cesarean birth, to surgically rebuild a nose, to provide promised maternity medical coverage, to provide medical services, and to keep a daughter informed of her mother's health. Further, the typical damages for breach of house construction

contracts can appropriately be calculated in terms of monetary loss. By contrast, the damages in contracts of a more personal nature in which emotional disturbance damages are allowed are usually intangible. Thus, there would ordinarily be only a nominal recovery unless emotional disturbance damages were allowed.

808 P.2d at 258–59.

Valentine v. General American Credit, Inc.

Supreme Court of Michigan, 1984.
420 Mich. 256, 362 N.W.2d 628.

■ LEVIN, J. Sharon Valentine seeks to recover mental distress damages arising out of the alleged breach of an employment contract. Valentine claims that, under the contract, she was entitled to job security and the peace of mind that is associated with job security. Because an employment contract providing for job security has a personal element, and breach of such a contract can be expected to result in mental distress, Valentine argues that she should be able to recover mental distress damages....

> . . . .

Valentine may not recover mental distress damages for breach of the employment contract, although such damages may have been foreseeable and she might not be "made whole" absent an award of mental distress damages.

Valentine relies on the rule of Hadley v. Baxendale, 9 Exch. 341, 156 Eng.Rep. 145 (1854), which provides that damages recoverable for a breach of contract are those that "may fairly and reasonably be considered either arising naturally, i.e., according to the usual course of things, from such breach of contract itself, or such as may reasonably be supposed to have been in the contemplation of both parties at the time they made the contract, as the probable result of the breach of it."

Although courts frequently begin analysis with a reference to the rule stated in Hadley v. Baxendale, that rule has not been applied scrupulously. As stated by Professor Dobbs in his treatise on remedies, a "difficulty in the Hadley type case is that the test of foreseeability [i.e., whether damages 'arise naturally'] has little or no meaning. The idea is so readily subject to expansion or contraction that it becomes in fact merely a technical way in which the judges can state their conclusion."[7]

Under the rule of Hadley v. Baxendale, literally applied, damages for mental distress would be recoverable for virtually every breach of contract. Professor Dobbs said:

> "When a defendant breaches a contract, this may and often does cause pecuniary loss to the other party, at least temporarily. It is a common experience of mankind that pecuniary loss almost invariably causes some form and degree of mental distress."[8]

---

7. Dobbs, Remedies, § 12.3, p. 814.   **8.** Dobbs, Remedies, § 12.4, p. 819.

In Stewart v. Rudner, 349 Mich. 459, 84 N.W.2d 816 (1957), this Court said that "all breaches of contract do more or less" cause "vexation and annoyance".....

Yet the general rule, with few exceptions, is to "uniformly den[y]" recovery for mental distress damages although they are "foreseeable within the rule of Hadley v. Baxendale."[10] The rule barring recovery of mental distress damages—a gloss on the generality of the rule stated in Hadley v. Baxendale—is fully applicable to an action for breach of an employment contract.

The denial of mental distress damages, although the result is to leave the plaintiff with less than a full recovery, has analogy in the law. The law does not generally compensate for all losses suffered.... In contract actions, the market price is the general standard.

In determining what damages are recoverable, the courts of this state have qualified the general rule, pursuant to which mental distress damages for breach of contract are not recoverable, with a narrow exception. Rather than look to the foreseeability of loss to determine the applicability of the exception, the courts have considered whether the contract "has elements of personality"[19] and whether the "damage suffered upon the breach of the agreement is capable of adequate compensation by reference to the terms of the contract."

The narrow scope of those verbal formulas appears on consideration of the limited situations in which this Court has allowed the recovery of mental distress damages for breach of contract. In Vanderpool v. Richardson, 52 Mich. 336, 17 N.W. 936 (1883), recovery was allowed for breach of a promise to marry. In Stewart v. Rudner, 349 Mich. 459, 84 N.W.2d 816 (1957), a doctor who failed to fulfill his promise to deliver a child by caesarean section was required to pay mental distress damages. In Miholevich v. Mid–West Mutual Auto Ins. Co., 261 Mich. 495, 246 N.W. 202 (1933), the plaintiff, who was jailed for failure to pay a liability judgment, recovered mental distress damages from an insurer who had failed to pay the judgment.

Loss of a job is not comparable to the loss of a marriage or a child and generally results in estimable monetary damages. In *Miholevich*, the breach resulted in a deprivation of personal liberty.

An employment contract will indeed often have a personal element. Employment is an important aspect of most persons' lives, and the breach of an employment contract may result in emotional distress. The primary purpose in forming such contracts, however, is economic and not to secure the protection of personal interests. The psychic satisfaction of the employment is secondary.

Mental distress damages for breach of contract have not been awarded where there is a market standard by which damages can be adequately

---

10. Grismore, Contracts (rev. ed.), § 203, p. 320.

19. In *Stewart*, [Stewart v. Rudner] the Court also said that mental distress damages are recoverable in cases "where a contract is *made* to secure relief from a particular inconvenience or annoyance, or to confer a particular enjoyment." (Emphasis supplied.)

determined. Valentine's monetary loss can be estimated with reasonable certainty according to the terms of the contract and the market for, or the market value of, her service. Mental distress damages are not awarded an employee found to have been wrongfully discharged in violation of a collective bargaining agreement.

We conclude, because an employment contract is not entered into primarily to secure the protection of personal interests and pecuniary damages can be estimated with reasonable certainty, that a person discharged in breach of an employment contract may not recover mental distress damages.

. . . .

Affirmed.

_____

G. LIQUIDATED DAMAGES[1]

Truck Rent–A–Center, Inc. v. Puritan Farms 2nd, Inc.

Court of Appeals of New York, 1977.
41 N.Y.2d 420, 393 N.Y.S.2d 365, 361 N.E.2d 1015.

■ JASEN, J. The principal issue on this appeal is whether a provision in a truck lease agreement which requires the payment of a specified amount of money to the lessor in the event of the lessee's breach is an enforceable liquidated damages clause, or, instead, provides for an unenforceable penalty.

Defendant Puritan Farms 2nd, Inc. (Puritan), was in the business of furnishing milk and milk products to customers through home delivery. In January, 1969, Puritan leased a fleet of 25 new milk delivery trucks from plaintiff Truck Rent–A–Center for a term of seven years commencing January 15, 1970. Under the provisions of a truck lease and service agreement entered into by the parties, the plaintiff was to supply the trucks and make all necessary repairs. Puritan was to pay an agreed upon weekly rental fee. It was understood that the lessor would finance the purchase of the trucks through a bank, paying the prime rate of interest on the date of the loan plus 2%. The rental charges on the trucks were to be adjusted in the event of a fluctuation in the interest rate above or below specified levels. The lessee was granted the right to purchase the trucks, at any time after 12 months following commencement of the lease, by paying to the lessor the amount then due and owing on the bank loan, plus an additional $100 per truck purchased.

Article 16 of the lease agreement provided that if the agreement should terminate prior to expiration of the term of the lease as a result of the lessee's breach, the lessor would be entitled to damages, "liquidated for all purposes", in the amount of all rentals that would have come due from the

_____

1. See also Rubinstein v. Rubinstein, p. 384 *supra*.

date of termination to the date of normal expiration of the term less the "re-rental value" of the vehicles, which was set at 50% of the rentals that would have become due. In effect, the lessee would be obligated to pay the lessor, as a consequence of breach, one half of all rentals that would have become due had the agreement run its full course. The agreement recited that, in arriving at the settled amount of damage, "the parties hereto have considered, among other factors, Lessor's substantial initial investment in purchasing or reconditioning for Lessee's service the demised motor vehicles, the uncertainty of Lessor's ability to re-enter the said vehicles, the costs to Lessor during any period the vehicles may remain idle until re-rented, or if sold, the uncertainty of the sales price and its possible attendant loss. The parties have also considered, among other factors, in so liquidating the said damages, Lessor's saving in expenditures for gasoline, oil and other service items."

The bulk of the written agreement was derived from a printed form lease which the parties modified by both filling in blank spaces and typing in alterations. The agreement also contained several typewritten indorsements which also made changes in the provisions of the printed lease. The provision for lessee's purchase of the vehicles for the bank loan balance and $100 per vehicle was contained in one such indorsement. The liquidated damages clause was contained in the body of the printed form.

Puritan tendered plaintiff a security deposit, consisting of four weeks' rent and the lease went into effect. After nearly three years, the lessee sought to terminate the lease agreement. On December 7, 1973, Puritan wrote to the lessor complaining that the lessor had not repaired and maintained the trucks as provided in the lease agreement. Puritan stated that it had "repeatedly notified" plaintiff of these defaults, but plaintiff had not cured them. Puritan, therefore, exercised its right to terminate the agreement "without any penalty and *without purchasing the trucks*". (Emphasis added.) On the date set for termination, December 14, 1973, plaintiff's attorneys replied to Puritan by letter to advise it that plaintiff believed it had fully performed its obligations under the lease and, in the event Puritan adhered to the announced breach, would commence proceedings to obtain the liquidated damages provided for in article 16 of the agreement. Nevertheless, Puritan had its drivers return the trucks to plaintiff's premises, where the bulk of them have remained ever since. At the time of termination, plaintiff owed $45,134.17 on the outstanding bank loan.

Plaintiff followed through on its promise to commence an action for the payment of the liquidated damages. Defendant counterclaimed for the return of its security deposit. At the nonjury trial, plaintiff contended that it had fully performed its obligations to maintain and repair the trucks. Moreover, it was submitted, Puritan sought to cancel the lease because corporations allied with Puritan had acquired the assets, including delivery trucks, of other dairies and Puritan believed it cheaper to utilize this "shadow fleet". The home milk delivery business was on the decline and plaintiff's president testified that efforts to either re-rent or sell the truck fleet to other dairies had not been successful. Even with modifications in the trucks, such as the removal of the milk racks and a change in the floor of the trucks, it was not possible to lease the trucks to other industries, although a few trucks were subsequently sold. The proceeds of the sales were applied to the reduction of the bank balance. The other trucks remained at plaintiff's premises, partially protected by a fence plaintiff erected to discourage vandals. The defendant countered with proof that plaintiff had not repaired the trucks promptly and satisfactorily.

At the close of the trial, the court found, based on the evidence it found to be credible, that plaintiff had substantially performed its obligations under the lease and that defendant was not justified in terminating the agreement. Further, the court held that the provision for liquidated damages was reasonable and represented a fair estimate of actual damages which would be difficult to ascertain precisely. "The parties, at the time the agreement was entered into, considered many factors affecting damages, namely: the uncertainty of the plaintiff's ability to re-rent the said vehicles; the plaintiff's investment in purchasing and reconditioning the vehicles to suit the defendant's particular purpose; the number of man hours not utilized in the non-service of the vehicles in the event of a breach; the uncertainty of reselling the vehicles in question; the uncertainty of the plaintiff's savings or expenditures for gasoline, oil or other service items, and the amount of fluctuating interest on the bank loan." The court calculated that plaintiff would have been entitled to $177,355.20 in rent for the period remaining in the lease and, in accordance with the liquidated damages provision, awarded plaintiff half that amount, $88,677.60. The resulting judgment was affirmed by the Appellate Division, with two Justices dissenting.

The primary issue before us is whether the "liquidated damages" provision is enforceable. Liquidated damages constitute the compensation which, the parties have agreed, should be paid in order to satisfy any loss or injury flowing from a breach of their contract. In effect, a liquidated damage provision is an estimate, made by the parties at the time they enter into their agreement, of the extent of the injury that would be sustained as a result of breach of the agreement. Parties to a contract have the right to agree to such clauses, provided that the clause is neither unconscionable nor contrary to public policy. Provisions for liquidated damage have value in those situations where it would be difficult, if not actually impossible, to calculate the amount of actual damage. In such cases, the contracting parties may agree between themselves as to the amount of damages to be paid upon breach rather than leaving that amount to the calculation of a court or jury.

On the other hand, liquidated damage provisions will not be enforced if it is against public policy to do so and public policy is firmly set against the imposition of penalties or forfeitures for which there is no statutory authority. It is plain that a provision which requires, in the event of contractual breach, the payment of a sum of money grossly disproportionate to the amount of actual damages provides for penalty and is unenforceable. A liquidated damage provision has its basis in the principle of just compensation for loss. A clause which provides for an amount plainly disproportionate to real damage is not intended to provide fair compensation but to secure performance by the compulsion of the very disproportion.

A promisor would be compelled, out of fear of economic devastation, to continue performance and his promisee, in the event of default, would reap a windfall well above actual harm sustained. As was stated eloquently long ago, to permit parties, in their unbridled discretion, to utilize penalties as damages, "would lead to the most terrible oppression in pecuniary dealings."

The rule is now well established. A contractual provision fixing damages in the event of breach will be sustained if the amount liquidated bears a reasonable proportion to the probable loss and the amount of actual loss is incapable or difficult of precise estimation. If, however, the amount fixed is plainly or grossly disproportionate to the probable loss, the provision calls for a penalty and will not be enforced. In interpreting a provision fixing damages, it is not material whether the parties themselves have chosen to call the provision one for "liquidated damages", as in this case, or have styled it as a penalty. Such an approach would put too much faith in form and too little in substance. Similarly, the agreement should be interpreted as of the date of its making and not as of the date of its breach.

— Rule

In applying these principles to the case before us, we conclude that the amount stipulated by the parties as damages bears a reasonable relation to the amount of probable actual harm and is not a penalty. . . .

Looking forward from the date of the lease, the parties could reasonably conclude, as they did, that there might not be an actual market for the sale or re-rental of these specialized vehicles in the event of the lessee's breach. To be sure, plaintiff's lost profit could readily be measured by the amount of the weekly rental fee. However, it was permissible for the parties, in advance, to agree that the re-rental or sale value of the vehicles would be 50% of the weekly rental. Since there was uncertainty as to whether the trucks could be re-rented or sold, the parties could reasonably set, as they did, the value of such mitigation at 50% of the amount the lessee was obligated to pay for rental of the trucks. This would take into consideration the fact that, after being used by the lessee, the vehicles would no longer be "shiny, new trucks", but would be used, possibly battered, trucks, whose value would have declined appreciably. The parties also considered the fact that, although plaintiff, in the event of Puritan's breach, might be spared repair and maintenance costs necessitated by Puritan's use of the trucks, plaintiff would have to assume the cost of storing and maintaining trucks idled by Puritan's refusal to use them. Further, it was by no means certain, at the time of the contract, that lessee would peacefully return the trucks to the lessor after lessee had breached the contract.

With particular reference to the dissent at the Appellate Division, it is true that the lessee might have exercised an option to purchase the trucks. However, lessee would not be purchasing 25 "shiny, new trucks" for a mere $2,500. Rather, lessee, after the passage of one year from the commencement of the term, could have purchased trucks that had been used for at least one year for the amount outstanding on the bank loan, in addition to the $2,500. Of course, the purchase price would be greater if the option were exercised early in the term rather than towards the end of the term since plaintiff would be making payments to the bank all the while.

More fundamental, the existence of the option clause has absolutely no bearing on the validity of the discrete, liquidated damages provision. The lessee could have elected to purchase the trucks but elected not to do so. In fact, the lessee's letter of termination made a point of the fact that the lessee did not want to purchase the trucks. The reality is that the lessee sought, by its wrongful termination of the lease, to evade all obligations to the plaintiff, whether for rent or for the agreed upon purchase price. Its effort to do so failed. That lessee could have made a better bargain for itself by purchasing the trucks for $48,134.17[3] pursuant to the option, instead of paying $92,341.79 in damages for wrongful breach of the lease is not availing to it now. Although the lessee might now wish, with the benefit of hindsight, that it had purchased the trucks rather than default on its lease obligations, the simple fact is that it did not do so.

We attach no significance to the fact that the liquidated damages clause appears on the preprinted form portion of the agreement. The agreement was fully negotiated and the provisions of the form, in many other respects, were amended. There is no indication of any disparity of bargaining power or of unconscionability. The provision for liquidated damages related reasonably to potential harm that was difficult to estimate and did not constitute a disguised penalty. We also find no merit in the claim of trial error advanced by Puritan.

Accordingly, the order of the Appellate Division should be affirmed, with costs.

NOTES ON LIQUIDATED DAMAGES

1. Consider Restatement (Second) of Contracts § 356(1) and U.C.C. § 2–718(1), dealing with liquidated damages:

§ 356. LIQUIDATED DAMAGES AND PENALTIES.

(1) Damages for breach by either party may be liquidated in the agreement but only at an amount that is reasonable in the light of the anticipated or actual loss caused by the breach and the difficulties of proof of loss. A term fixing unreasonably large liquidated damages is unenforceable on grounds of public policy as a penalty.

§ 2–718. LIQUIDATION . . . OF DAMAGES . . .

(1) Damages for breach by either party may be liquidated in the agreement but only at an amount which is reasonable in the light of the anticipated or actual harm caused by the breach, the difficulties of proof of loss, and the inconvenience or nonfeasibility of otherwise obtaining an adequate remedy. A term fixing unreasonably large liquidated damages is void as a penalty.

2. Mandle agreed to sell his house to Owens for $30,000. The contract for the sale provided in part:

---

3. This sum represents the $45,634.17 $2,500 ($100 for each of the 25 trucks). still owed by plaintiff on the bank loan, plus

We hereby deposit with you earnest money in the sum of Three Hundred ($300.00) Dollars, to be applied as part of the purchase price for said real estate at the time of delivery of deed.

This proposition shall be treated as made to the owner of said property, and shall remain open for acceptance for the period of ten (10) days from this date and if accepted, the above amount is to apply as part of purchase price, and if refused same is to be refunded. If offer is accepted and we fail to complete the purchase of the real estate herein mentioned as provided herein, the amount of Three Hundred ($300.00) dollars will be forfeited to you.

Subsequent to agreeing to purchase Mandle's house, Owens decided not to proceed with the sale. Mandle resold the property and then sued Owens for the resulting $3,000 loss. Owens argued that this claim was barred by the contractual language quoted above, which Owens called a liquidated damages clause. However, the court held that this was an invalid penalty provision, as there was "nothing to show that the stipulated sum has any relation to anticipated loss." Mandle v. Owens, 164 Ind.App. 607, 330 N.E.2d 362 (1975).

3. The Board of Trustees of State Institutions of Higher Learning adopted Rules and Regulations to govern loans to medical students designed to encourage needed medical practice in Mississippi communities of 10,000 and under. Dr. Elbert Homer Wood, Jr. applied for and was granted a loan at a time when the Rules and Regulations provided (1) for residency training only in the specialties of Family Practice, Internal Medicine and Pediatrics; (2) that the Board's Rules and Regulations were a part of every loan contract; and (3) that any breach of contract matured the loan and, upon demand, made liquidated damages of $5,000 for each unfulfilled year of the required five years of practice then due and payable.

Disregarding the Board's express refusal of his request to waive the residency training restrictions for him, Dr. Wood chose to pursue a residency in Obstetrics and Gynecology. The Board then brought suit to recover both the outstanding balance on the loan with interest and liquidated damages of $5000 for each of five years. Dr. Wood defended by arguing that the $5000 liquidated damages provision was a penalty. The Board prevailed. Board of Trustees of State Institutions of Higher Learning v. Wood, 779 F.2d 1106 (5th Cir.1986). As the court put it, " '[w]here it is inherently difficult to approximate the actual damages that a breach will cause,' Mississippi courts 'tend to be particularly indulgent of contractual provisions that prescribe a crude but convenient liquidation of the parties' rights.' "

CHAPTER 14

DAMAGES FOR TORTIOUS CONDUCT

———

Damages awards in tort cases, like tort law itself, serve two principal functions. On the one hand, they make wrongdoers pay for the harm they do, which may be seen as intrinsically just. At the same time, by imposing upon tortfeasors the cost of their wrongful acts, they promote the deterrent value of tort law.

Either way, the law requires that the effects of tortious conduct be measured in dollars and cents. The difficult task of valuation is complex enough when a definite injury is inflicted upon property. The problems multiply greatly when the tortfeasor has brought about an actual or potential physical injury, emotional trauma, or death. Chapter 14 examines the law's response to these problems.

———

A. INJURY TO PROPERTY

Portland General Electric Company, an Oregon Corporation v. Taber

Court of Appeals of Oregon 1997.
146 Or.App. 735, 934 P.2d 538.

■ Before DEITS, P.J., and DE MUNIZ and HASELTON, JJ.

■ HASELTON, JUDGE.

The sole issue presented is whether the proper measure of damages when a motorist negligently destroys a wooden power pole is: (a) the undepreciated cost of the lost pole or (b) the full replacement cost of a new pole. The trial court determined that, as a matter of law, PGE's recovery was limited to the lost pole's undepreciated value. We affirm.

The material facts are undisputed. PGE owns and operates an electrical distribution system, which includes approximately 235,000 wooden power poles. The age of the poles varies, with roughly 40 percent being in service for more than 40 years; the oldest is 84 years old. Among the factors that affect the life of any individual pole may be rot and decay, insect infestation, lightning strikes, other accidental destruction, and systemic relocation or restructuring. Improved treatment processes have extended the useful life of properly treated wooden poles. PGE does not replace poles on a fixed schedule, but, instead, inspects and treats poles on a seven-year cycle and replaces them on an "as necessary" basis.

PGE depreciates its poles, as a capital asset, for tax and accounting purposes. Poles are depreciated as a group, rather than individually, based on the projected useful life of all wooden transmission poles in the system. The projected useful life, for tax and accounting purposes, is 37 years.

There is no market for used power poles, and such poles have no salvage or retirement value. Historically, until 1993, whenever one of its wooden transmission poles was negligently damaged or destroyed, PGE calculated its damages for the loss of the pole as the original cost of the pole less any depreciation previously taken (the "undepreciated cost" method). Thus, if a 17–year-old pole was damaged or destroyed, PGE would invoice damages for 20/37 of the pole's total original cost.[1] On July 1, 1993, PGE altered its methodology and began invoicing allegedly liable third parties for the full replacement cost of a new power pole, rather than the undepreciated cost of the damaged pole. Under the new "full replacement cost" method, if the third party actually pays the full cost of the new pole, PGE does not depreciate the new pole for tax and accounting purposes. If the third party pays for part of the new pole, PGE depreciates the balance of the cost.

On June 20, 1994, defendant Taber's pickup truck struck and damaged a wooden power pole owned by PGE, which had been installed in 1934 and was still fully functional. PGE brought this action, seeking to recover damages of $2,213 for removing and replacing the damaged pole and $407.85 for the cost of the new pole itself. Defendant agreed to pay PGE $2,213 for costs, exclusive of the actual cost of the new pole, but disputed PGE's claim for the full replacement cost of a new pole. In particular, defendant asserted that the "undepreciated value" measure of damages should control and that, under that method, PGE was not entitled to any damages, because the pole's actual age (60 years) exceeded the 37–year average useful life that PGE assumed for depreciation purposes.

On September 12, 1993, a car driven by intervenor Farmers' insured, Johnson, struck and damaged a PGE power pole that had been installed in 1976. As with Taber, PGE sought to recover the full cost of a new pole ($908.22),[2] rather than the pole's undepreciated value ($467.73). Farmers moved to intervene, ORCP 33, in the Taber litigation because the issue presented there, as to the correct measure of damages, was identical to that raised by PGE's claim against Johnson. Farmers sought a declaration that the "undepreciated cost" method was the correct measure of damages. Neither PGE nor Taber objected, and the trial court allowed Farmers' intervention.

PGE then moved for summary judgment, and Taber and Farmers cross-moved, on the dispositive replacement cost issue. The trial court granted Taber's and Farmers' cross-motions for summary judgment. PGE appeals.

---

1. In addition, PGE would seek damages for the costs of removing and replacing the damaged pole, excluding the pole's cost.

2. The record does not explain the difference between the replacement costs of the poles in the Taber and Johnson cases.

The question is one of first impression in Oregon. That question seems simple. Nevertheless, it has engendered a substantial division of opinion in other jurisdictions.[3] That disagreement suggests, quite correctly, that although the question is straight-forward, the answer is not.

Despite that complexity, the overarching principles that guide our inquiry are clear. In assessing compensatory damages for tortious injury to property, the measure of damages is to be determined " 'not only by what might be right for an injured person to receive in order to afford just compensation, but also by what is just to compel the other party to pay [.]' " Mock v. Terry, 251 Or. 511, 513, 446 P.2d 514 (1968) (quoting Hansen v. Oregon–Wash. R. & N. Co., 97 Or. 190, 201, 188 P. 963, 191 P. 655 (1920)). Generally, where property has been damaged, the measure of damages is the difference in value before and after the injury. Cutsforth v. Kinzua Corp., 267 Or. 423, 439, 517 P.2d 640 (1973). Similarly, where property is destroyed, the measure of damages is generally the market value of the property. Prettyman v. Railway etc. Co., 13 Or. 341, 343, 10 P. 634 (1886). Where, however, the property that is damaged or destroyed had no market value, "other means of valuation must necessarily be resorted to in order to appraise the property[.]" Id. at 344, 10 P. 634. See also Erickson Hardwood Co. v. North Pacific Lumber, 70 Or.App. 557, 568, 690 P.2d 1071 (1984), rev. den. 298 Or. 705, 695 P.2d 1371 (1985).

Here, it is undisputed that there was no market and, hence, no market value for used wooden power poles. Accordingly, our task is to identify the appropriate "other means of valuation," Prettyman, 13 Or. at 344, 10 P. 634, that justly compensates plaintiff while not unfairly assessing defendant.

The parties espouse starkly contrasting methodologies, with PGE invoking the "full replacement cost" rule adopted in 14 states, and Taber and Farmers urging a variation of the "depreciated value" approach adopted in five states. Each contends that the other's approach yields unconscionable windfalls, but that its own achieves, or at least approximates, just compen-

---

3. Pacific Gas & Elec. Co. v. Alexander, 90 Cal.App.3d 253, 153 Cal.Rptr. 319 (1979); Hartford Electric Light Company v. Beard, 3 Conn.Cir.Ct. 323, 213 A.2d 536 (1965); Horton v. Georgia Power Co., 149 Ga.App. 328, 254 S.E.2d 479 (1979); Kansas Power & Light Co. v. Thatcher, 14 Kan.App.2d 613, 797 P.2d 162 (1990); Louisiana Power & Light Co. v. Smith, 343 So.2d 367 (La.Ct.App.1977); Mississippi Power & Light Company v. Tillman, 291 So.2d 736 (Miss.1974); Board of Public Utilities v. Fenton, 669 S.W.2d 612 (Mo.Ct. App.1984); N.J. Power & Light Co. v. Mabee, 41 N.J. 439, 197 A.2d 194 (1964); Carolina Power & Light Company v. Paul, 261 N.C. 710, 136 S.E.2d 103 (1964); Polk v. Oklahoma Gas & Electric Co., 410 P.2d 547 (Okla. 1966); Duke Power Co. v. Thornton, 303 S.C. 454, 401 S.E.2d 195 (Ct.App.1991); Middle Tenn. Elec. Membership Corp. v. Barrett, 56 Tenn.App. 660, 410 S.W.2d 914 (1966); Puget Sound Power & Light Co. v. Strong, 117 Wash.2d 400, 816 P.2d 716 (1991); Appalachian Power Company v. Morrison, 152 W.Va. 638, 165 S.E.2d 809 (1969) (all adopting "full cost of replacement" rule).

See Central Illinois Light Company v. Stenzel, 44 Ill.App.2d 388, 195 N.E.2d 207 (1963); Public Serv. Co. of New Mexico v. Jasso, 96 N.M. 800, 635 P.2d 1003 (Ct.App. 1981); New York State Electric & Gas Corp. v. J.C.A. Truck Leasing, Inc., 19 N.Y.2d 926, 281 N.Y.S.2d 335, 228 N.E.2d 393 (1967); Ohio Power Co. v. Zemelka, 19 Ohio App.2d 213, 251 N.E.2d 2 (1969); Younger v. Appalachian Power Company, 214 Va. 662, 202 S.E.2d 866 (1974) (all adopting "depreciated value" approach).

sation. As described below, there is—notwithstanding their Manichean oversimplification—some merit in both positions.

The original, and most frequently quoted, "full cost of replacement" case is N.J. Power & Light Co. v. Mabee, 41 N.J. 439, 197 A.2d 194 (1964). The premise of that holding, which is reiterated in virtually every "majority rule" decision, is that, because it is impossible to predict the life of any particular power pole, only the full cost replacement ensures that the power company will be fully compensated for its loss:

> "If the life of every pole were 36 years and if it were clear that each pole would be replaced at the end of that period defendants could well urge that a new pole clearly conferred a benefit beyond the amount of the damage done. The difficulty is that there is no discernible life expectancy of an individual pole and that although the period of 36 years is used for accounting purposes, the pole that was destroyed might well have served for a much longer period and the new pole may last for but a few years. Moreover, because of changes in circumstances or in technology, it cannot be known whether the pole would ever have been replaced. In short, at least upon the record before us, we cannot say with reasonable assurance that the installation of a new pole did more than remedy the wrong done. An injured party should not be required to lay out money, as defendants' approach would require, upon a questionable assumption that one day its worth will be recaptured." Id. 197 A.2d at 195–96.[4]

See also Puget Sound Power & Light Co. v. Strong, 117 Wash.2d 400, 403, 816 P.2d 716, 717 (1991) (rejecting argument that full cost of replacement would confer windfall on utility: "We would agree with that reasoning if the actual life expectancy of a specific pole could be determined. It cannot.").

Conversely, the minority "undepreciated cost" rule turns on the premise that requiring a party to replace a used power pole with a new pole confers an unfair windfall on the utility and that relating damages to the pole's undepreciated cost, representing the loss of the balance of the average projected useful life, effects fair compensation. Younger v. Appalachian Power Company, 214 Va. 662, 202 S.E.2d 866, 868 (1974), exemplifies that view:

> "The record shows that Appalachian periodically inspects its transmission system and replaces poles deteriorated in normal usage. From this experience, Appalachian can determine the average useful life of poles in the system. Since in the normal course of doing business Appalachian must bear the expense of replacement costs at some reasonable ascertainable future time, recovery from a tortfeasor of full replacement costs at an earlier time would overcompensate the injury sustained. Thus, if a pole deteriorated in normal usage was to be replaced and an automobile damaged it an hour before the replacement

---

4. See Horton, 254 S.E.2d at 481; Kansas Power, 797 P.2d at 167–68; Mississippi Power, 291 So.2d at 738; Carolina Power, 136 S.E.2d at 103; Washington Water Power Co. v. Miller, 52 Wash.App. 565, 570–71, 762 P.2d 16, 19–20 (1988); Appalachian Power, 165 S.E.2d at 812 (all quoting N.J. Power with approval).

crew arrived with the new pole, Appalachian would gain a windfall if the tortfeasor is required to pay the full replacement costs Appalachian was about to expend. On the other hand, if an automobile damaged a pole an hour after it had been replaced in the normal course of replacement, Appalachian would be less than whole if the tortfeasor is permitted to pay less than full replacement costs. In each case, the actual injury sustained by Appalachian is related to the useful life of the pole. In the former case, Appalachian would have enjoyed the full anticipated use of its property and incurred no unanticipated expense. In the latter case, Appalachian would have been deprived of the full anticipated use of its property and would have incurred an expense which, but for the tort, would have been deferred for the useful life of the pole."

See also Puget Sound Power and Light Co. v. Strong, 59 Wash.App. 430, 434–35, 798 P.2d 1162, 1164 (1990), rev'd 117 Wash.2d 400, 816 P.2d 716 (1991) (rejecting "total cost replacement" in favor of "undepreciated value" measure where defendant destroyed 14–year-old pole: "Puget would gain an estimated additional fourteen years of service life if it were permitted to recover the cost of a new pole. Such compensation exceeds the loss incurred by Puget and, thus, would result in a windfall to Puget.").

In related fashion, in Ohio Power Co. v. Zemelka, 19 Ohio App.2d 213, 251 N.E.2d 2, 4–5 (1969), the court held that, just as the utility relied on "sound accounting principles," in projecting poles' useful life for accounting and taxation purposes and in assessing other costs associated with the removal and replacement of damaged poles, the same actuarial assumptions should bind the utility in determining the value of a lost pole:

We feel that justice is a two-way street. Just as plaintiff is entitled to be compensated for such items as cost of pole storage and administration and engineering expenses, because the application of sound accounting principles establishes that these indirect expenses are properly part of the damages suffered by a utility company when one of its utility poles is damaged, so defendants are entitled to use sound accounting principles to establish the life expectancy of a utility pole so that the depreciation of such a utility pole can be readily determined by the application of sound accounting principles.

It is true that a utility pole has a variable life expectancy, just as any other item of personal property, such as an automobile, furniture, etc., but sound accounting principles can establish a life expectancy of such items. * * * All variables can be attacked on the basis of uncertainty; however, for business and legal reasons, we need to establish uniform definite standards for variable expenses on the basis of sound accounting principles. We feel that there is no difference in the application of sound accounting principles to determine the accrued depreciation of a damaged utility pole with a variable life expectancy than to determine the indirect costs of repairing the damaged pole by the application of sound accounting principles to the variable costs of such expenses.

As the dispute is framed by the parties, we are, thus, faced with an "either/or" choice between two contending formulations. That choice is, frankly, less than satisfying for at least three reasons.

First, it is beyond dispute that either measure of damages will, at least in some circumstances, produce seemingly unjust results. For example, if the "full replacement cost" method were applied here, PGE would, in effect, be allowed to trade a 60–year-old pole, which has survived 23 years past its projected useful life, for a brand new pole. Conversely, if the "undepreciated cost" method were applied to the same 60–year-old pole, Taber would pay nothing for PGE's loss of a pole that was fully functioning and useful until Taber's pickup damaged it—and that might still be in use but for Taber's negligence.[5] Second, many, if not all, of the decisions that adopt either rule speak in terms of the speculative nature of projecting the life expectancy of any particular pole. It is true that "there is no discernible life expectancy to any individual pole[.]" N.J. Power, 197 A.2d at 195. However, with all respect to those courts, and to the present litigants who invoke their reasoning, their apparent preoccupation with that truism seems inapt. This dispute is special, perhaps unique, in that it concerns the appropriate valuation of (1) peculiar property (power poles), (2) that is owned by a very limited class of persons (utilities), and (3) whose valuation is the subject of frequent disputes and litigation. To be blunt: This dispute is not about the fairness or "speculativeness" of valuing the loss of a single 60–year-old power pole in Clackamas County; it is, instead, about the proper method of compensating PGE for the loss of any of the 235,000 poles in its transmission system. Our task, then, is to identify the measure of damages that most closely effects just compensation systemically, in power pole loss cases in the aggregate.[6]

Third, our performance of that task is skewed by the fact that the parties present us with only two options and the evidentiary record was tailored to those two options only. There are, at least in the abstract, alternative methodologies that might mitigate the cross-cutting "windfall" concerns and better effectuate just compensation.[7] However, because of the manner in which the record was developed on summary judgment, there is no basis on this record for determining the practicability of such ap-

---

5. The "windfall" consideration appears to be, at least in part, a factor of the pole's age. For example, if the damaged pole is only a year old, any "windfall" from employing a "full replacement cost" measure is seemingly less pronounced. Similarly, employing the "undepreciated cost" measure, which would require the tortfeasor to pay 36/37 of the pole's cost, would not seem to yield any appreciable windfall to the tortfeasor.

6. PGE advises us that at least eight cases involving claims for damage to its power poles are being held in abeyance in various courts pending the disposition of this appeal.

7. For example, during oral argument, we explored with counsel a method by which the life expectancy of power poles would be projected, actuarially, in a fashion similar to human life mortality tables. Thus, even if the average useful life of a wooden power pole in PGE's system were assumed to be 37 years, a 60–year-old pole might (hypothetically) have a projected remaining life of 12 years, and damages could be based on that period. Similarly, two-year-old power poles might, as a class, have an average projected life of 30 years, and damages to any particular two-year-old pole would be based on that 28 years of "lost life." In response to our inquiries, counsel explained that the record contained no evidence as to whether the actuarial data necessary to implement such an approach existed or could be practicably developed. Cf. Kansas Power, 797 P.2d at 164 ("The average age of a male tells us no more about how long John Doe will actually live than the average age of a utility pole tells us how long an individual pole will remain in service.").

proaches. We cannot prescribe them in an evidentiary void.[8]

Faced with the "either/or" choice, we opt for the "undepreciated cost" approach. That measure, although imperfect, comes closer to promoting just compensation in power pole damage cases as a whole than does the "full replacement cost" method.

Our holding rests on reasoning similar to Ohio Power's observation that "justice is a two-way street." 251 N.E.2d at 4. The only evidence in this record as to the average useful life of PGE's wooden power poles in the aggregate is that, for tax and accounting purposes, PGE depreciates the poles on the basis of a 37–year useful life. We fully appreciate that different considerations may underlie projections of useful life for tax and accounting purposes, as opposed to property loss valuation purposes. Nevertheless, PGE has not explained why it should reap the benefit of a 37–year useful life for tax depreciation purposes but, concurrently, claim that the 37–year figure is not an accurate benchmark of average projected life in crafting a measure of damages that applies to all power poles. Nor does PGE explain why the "undepreciated cost" approach, which it has applied historically, became somehow unjust or incompletely remedial as of July 1, 1993.

Conversely, adoption and application of the "full cost replacement" measure in every power pole loss case would systematically overcompensate PGE. In every case, PGE would be receiving a new pole for a used and depreciated pole. Regardless of whether that might yield an appreciable windfall in any given case, the inescapable consequence would be that PGE would be unjustly overcompensated in the aggregate.

The trial court did not err in adopting and applying the "undepreciated cost" measure of damages.

Affirmed.

Averett v. Shircliff

Supreme Court of Virginia, 1977.
218 Va. 202, 237 S.E.2d 92.

■ I'Anson, C.J. Plaintiff, James V. Shircliff, instituted this action against the defendant, Henry T. Averett, to recover damages to his automobile, certain personal property in the trunk of the car, and the loss of use of his vehicle as a result of defendant's negligence in the operation of an automobile which collided with plaintiff's vehicle. The defendant admitted liability, and the case was tried by a jury on the issue of damages only. The jury returned a verdict for the plaintiff and awarded $4,000 as damages to the car and $160 for damages to the personal property in the car.

Plaintiff moved the court to set aside the jury's verdict and award him judgment as a matter of law in the amount of $8,059 on the ground that under the Restatement of the Law of Torts, § 928,[1] he "had a right to

---

8. Other parties in other cases would, of course, be free to present arguments and supporting evidence for a measure of damage that differs from those that the parties espouse here.

1. Section 928 of the Restatement of the Law of Torts reads as follows:

elect" as his measure of damages the difference in the value of the automobile before and after the accident. Alternately, plaintiff moved that he be awarded a new trial on the grounds that the court had erred in instructing the jury and in refusing to admit certain evidence.

The trial judge, in a written opinion, held that the Restatement rule as set forth in refused Instruction 1, which would have told the jury that plaintiff's measure of damages was the difference in the value of the car before and after the accident, was the proper measure of plaintiff's damages; and that he had erred in granting Instruction 1a which told the jury that the proper measure of plaintiff's damages was the difference between the fair market value of the damaged vehicle immediately before the accident and the fair market value of the vehicle immediately after the accident, with the exception that if the vehicle could be restored to its former condition by repairs and the cost of repairs would be less than the diminution in value because of the injury, then the measure of damages was the cost of repairs plus any applicable depreciation. Thereupon, the court set aside the jury's verdict and entered final judgment for the plaintiff in the amount of $8,059, awarding $7,899 as damages to the automobile and $160 as damages for the loss of the personal property in the vehicle.

Defendant contends that Instruction 1a set forth the general rule for determining the proper measure of damages to plaintiff's automobile; and that the trial court erred in adopting plaintiff's interpretation of the Restatement rule as the proper measure of damages, and in setting aside the verdict of the jury and entering final judgment for the plaintiff rather than awarding a new trial because the evidence was conflicting.

. . . .

The question presented is what is the proper measure of damages in the present case. The precise issue has not heretofore been decided by us.

In Norview Cars v. Crews, 208 Va. 148, 156 S.E.2d 603 (1967), we quoted the general rule[2] with its exception and the Restatement rule. However, we found it unnecessary to adopt either the general rule and the contended for "special circumstances" exception thereto or the Restate-

---

"Where a person is entitled to a judgment for harm to chattels not amounting to a total destruction in value, the damages include compensation for

"(a) the difference between the value of the chattel before the harm and the value after the harm or, at the plaintiff's election, the reasonable cost of repair or restoration where feasible, with due allowance for any difference between the original value and the value after repairs, and

"(b) the loss of use."

2. The general rule was quoted from Riddle v. Baltimore & O.R. Co., 137 W.Va. 733, 73 S.E.2d 793 (1952), as follows:

"In the valuation of personal property, which has been damaged but not destroyed, the measure of damages is the difference between the market value of the property immediately before and immediately after the property was damaged, plus necessary and reasonable expenses incurred by the owner in connection with the injury. . . . An exception to this rule is that where tangible personal property can be restored by repairs and the repairs would be less than the diminution in value because of the injury, the amount recoverable is the reasonable cost of restoring the property to its former condition. . . ."

ment rule, "if there be, indeed, any real difference between the two rules," because of the stipulation plaintiff had entered into in the trial court.

In an annotation entitled "Damages—Injury to Pleasure Vehicles," at 169 A.L.R. 1100 (1947), numerous cases are collected, and the general rule with its exception is stated and applied to variant circumstances. The author of the annotation, in summarizing the principles on the issue, states:

"Where the automobile is totally destroyed the measure of damages is the market value of the automobile as at the time of destruction. . . .

"Where the automobile is damaged but not completely destroyed the measure of damages is basically the difference between market value at the time of the injury and market value after the injury, which, where the injury is susceptible of repairs, is ordinarily measured by the cost of reasonable repairs necessary to restore the automobile to its original condition . . . together with . . ."

the diminution in value of the injured property after repairs are made. Id. 1100–01.

Most jurisdictions confronted with situations such as exist in the present case have held that where an automobile has been damaged but not totally destroyed and it is reasonably susceptible of repairs, the measure of damages is the cost of repairs and any diminution of the automobile's market value which results from the car having been injured after the repairs; that is, the cost of repairs plus any amount of depreciation in value of the vehicle as repaired.

Instruction 1a granted by the trial court is in accord with the above principles. It reads, in pertinent part, as follows:

"The Court instructs the jury that in the valuation of personal property, which has been damaged but not destroyed, the measure of damages is the difference between the market value of the property immediately before and immediately after the property was damaged.

"The Court further instructs the jury that an exception to this rule is that where personal property can be restored by repairs and the repairs would be less than the diminution in value because of the injury, the amount recoverable is the reasonable cost of restoring the property to its former condition.

"Thus, if you believe from the preponderance of the evidence that the car involved could not be restored to its former condition by repairs, the measure of damages is the difference between the market value of the car immediately before and immediately after the accident.

"And if you believe from a preponderance of the evidence that the car involved could be restored to its former condition by repairs, the measure of damage is the reasonable cost of repairs, with reasonable allowance for depreciation."

There is little difference between the rule set out in Instruction 1a and the Restatement rule. Both rules are merely evidentiary methods for determining that amount which will reasonably compensate the owner for his actual pecuniary loss sustained as a result of a negligent or wrongful act. The reasonable cost of repairs is one of the evidentiary factors in determining the market value of an automobile after it has been damaged.

The only significant difference in the two rules is that under the Restatement rule a plaintiff has the option of recovering either the difference in the value of the vehicle immediately before and immediately after the accident or the reasonable cost of repairs plus any depreciation in value after repairs. But we think that the jury, not the plaintiff, should make that determination based on the evidence presented.

. . . .

For the reasons stated, we reverse the judgment, reinstate the verdict of the jury, and enter judgment thereon for the plaintiff in the amount of $4,160.

Judgment reversed, verdict of the jury reinstated, and judgment is here entered thereon.

Kaplan v. City of Winston–Salem

Supreme Court of North Carolina, 1974.
286 N.C. 80, 209 S.E.2d 743.

■ HIGGINS, J. The Court of Appeals ordered a new trial on all issues on the assigned ground that the trial court's instructions permitted the jury to consider the retail value of the damaged merchandise in fixing the amount of damages the plaintiffs were entitled to recover. While the court in the charge recited to the jury the respective contentions and claims of the parties respecting the amount of damages resulting from the defendant's acts of negligence and thereafter discussed the various claims of damages, the court gave the jury this mandate:

"... [Y]ou will award to the plaintiffs, if you award anything on this issue, the amount which you find represents the difference in the reasonable market value of the merchandise before and after it was damaged. The reasonable market value of any article being the amount which, the owner wanting to sell but not having to, would accept for it and the amount which a buyer who wanted the article but didn't have to have it would pay for it in a free, fair trade in which there is no compulsion on either side. In this case, that amount may be anywhere from one cent to forty-nine thousand nine hundred and seven dollars and seven cents.

"Now, in a case of this type involving the stock of merchandise, you may, in arriving at the fair market value of the items, take into consideration the replacement cost of the items which would be the wholesale price of the goods. You may consider but are not bound by the retail prices of the damaged items because that price would include profits which may or may not be realized and therefore would be a speculative value. In considering the cost of the merchandise to the plaintiff, you may also consider reasonable delivery charges and unpacking expenses involved in the goods or merchandise reaching the stage at which they were at the time that this damage was done to it. In other words, you will try by your verdict to put the plaintiffs in the same position they were in prior to the damage to their merchandise insofar as money can do so. If you reach this issue and decide the plaintiffs are entitled to recover anything as a result of the actionable negligence of the defendant, you will award them the amount you find will fully compensate them for their loss according to the rules I have given you with regard to damages in this kind of a case and you will base your verdict on the evidence in the case."

According to the decided cases in North Carolina, "The measure of damages for injury to personal property is the difference between the market value immediately before the injury and the market value immediately after the injury...." Where the injury is less than total destruction, the measure of damages is the difference between the market value of the article immediately before and immediately after the injury.

... [W]e are of the opinion that the trial court stated to the jury the correct rule to govern their determination of the amount of damages....

The decision of the Court of Appeals is reversed. The cause will be remanded to the Superior Court of Forsyth County with the direction that the original judgment entered therein be restored as the final judgment of the court.

Reversed.

■ SHARP, J. (dissenting): ...

Ordinarily the measure of damages for injury to personal property is the retail value of the property immediately before the damage and immediately thereafter. "But, that rule does not apply where the property involved is part of a stock in trade of a business concern." The authorities agree that the value of a stock of goods held for retail sale is the wholesale or replacement cost, "without the profit of resale which enters into the retail value." 1 Sedgwick on Damages, § 248a (9th ed. 1912).

The rule, which seems to have been almost universally adopted, is well stated in 4 Sutherland, Law of Damages, § 1098 (1916) as follows:

"The retail price of property held for sale is not the standard by which its value is to be determined. Where a quantity of merchandise is sued for, the retail price would be unjust, for the merchant in fixing that price takes into consideration not only the first cost of the goods, but store rent, clerk hire, insurance, and probable amount of bad debts, and adds to all these a percentage of profit. This must be understood of a considerable quantity, not of a single article. The owner must be entitled to recover at such rate as he would have to pay in the nearest market where a like quantity could be bought to replace the property taken; added to this, no doubt, should be the expense necessarily incurred in getting the property so purchased to the place where the trespass was committed. This would make the damages depend upon the value of the property taken at the place where the wrong was done. The rule is thus expressed in some cases, with the addition that the estimate is to be made as of the time the right of action accrued, and compensation for the time required to obtain other property to replace that destroyed."

A case which parallels this one is Millison v. Ades of Lexington, Inc., 262 Md. 319, 277 A.2d 579 (MDCA 1971), in which the plaintiff sued to recover for damage to a stock of merchandise ruined by water. As here, the trial judge, over objection, admitted in evidence a compilation of the value of the merchandise based on the retail selling price (price tag) of each item. He then charged the jury that the measure of damages was "the fair market value of the goods" on the date they were damaged and the cost of labor occasioned by the loss, less any salvaged value recovered upon a sale of the damaged goods.

In awarding a new trial upon the issue of damages only, the Maryland Court said, "It is obvious in this case that in the admission of evidence and in his instruction to the jury the trial judge equated 'fair market value of the goods on the date they were destroyed or lost' with the retail selling price as of that date. This was an erroneous conclusion."

. . . .

"Ades is entitled to recover the reasonable cost of replacing the goods on the shelf. This reasonable cost would include the wholesale cost at the time of the loss, plus any reasonable transportation charges that might be involved and the reasonable value of the labor involved in placing the goods on the shelf ... [and] the reasonable value of the labor involved in tabulating the loss and removing the damaged merchandise. . . . On the retrial of damages Ades must spell out with some particularity the net salvage value of the goods after the loss which will be properly deductible from the value otherwise determined. It must also spell out its efforts to mitigate damages. We do not state these criteria as an exclusive measure of damages, but as guidelines to assist the parties and the trial court at the new trial on the issue of damages." Accord, Chicago Title & Trust Co. v. W.T. Grant Co., 2 Ill.App.3d 483, 275 N.E.2d 670 (1971). (Proper measures of damages for harm to merchandise due to roof leakage was wholesale price, and not retail price, less salvage value.)

. . . .

For the reasons stated herein I vote to modify and affirm the decision of the Court of Appeals by remanding this case to the Superior Court for retrial upon the issue of damages alone.

■ BRANCH, J., joins in the dissenting opinion.

Matter of Rothko's Estate

Court of Appeals of New York, 1977.
43 N.Y.2d 305, 401 N.Y.S.2d 449, 372 N.E.2d 291.

■ COOKE, J. Mark Rothko, an abstract expressionist painter whose works through the years gained for him an international reputation of greatness, died testate on February 25, 1970. The principal asset of his estate consisted of 798 paintings of tremendous value, and the dispute underlying this appeal involves the conduct of his three executors in their disposition of these works of art. In sum, that conduct as portrayed in the record and sketched in the opinions was manifestly wrongful and indeed shocking.

Rothko's will was admitted to probate on April 27, 1970 and letters testamentary were issued to Bernard J. Reis, Theodoros Stamos and Morton Levine. Hastily and within a period of only about three weeks and by virtue of two contracts each dated May 21, 1970, the executors dealt with all 798 paintings.

By a contract of sale, the estate executors agreed to sell to Marlborough A.G., a Liechtenstein corporation (hereinafter MAG), 100 Rothko paintings as listed for $1,800,000, $200,000 to be paid on execution of the agreement and the balance of $1,600,000 in 12 equal interest-free installments over a 12–year period. Under the second agreement, the executors consigned to Marlborough Gallery, Inc., a domestic corporation (hereinafter MNY), "approximately 700 paintings listed on a Schedule to be prepared", the consignee to be responsible for costs covering items such as insurance, storage, restoration and promotion. By its provisos, MNY could sell up to 35 paintings a year from each of two groups, pre–1947 and post–1947, for 12 years at the best price obtainable but not less than the appraised estate value, and it would receive a 50% commission on each painting sold, except for a commission of 40% on those sold to or through other dealers.

Petitioner Kate Rothko, decedent's daughter and a person entitled to share in his estate by virtue of an election under EPTL 5–3.3, instituted this proceeding to remove the executors, to enjoin MNY and MAG from disposing of the paintings, to rescind the aforesaid agreements between the executors and said corporations, for a return of the paintings still in possession of those corporations, and for damages. . . .

. . . .

The measure of damages was the issue that divided the Appellate Division. The contention of Reis, Stamos, MNY and MAG, that the award of appreciation damages was legally erroneous and impermissible, is based on a principle that an executor authorized to sell is not liable for an increase in value if the breach consists only in selling for a figure less than that for which the executor should have sold. For example, Scott states:

> "The beneficiaries are not entitled to the value of the property at the time of the decree if it was not the duty of the trustee to retain the property in the trust and the breach of trust consisted *merely* in selling the property for too low a price" (3 Scott, Trusts [3d ed.], § 208.3, p. 1687 [emphasis added]).

> "If the trustee is guilty of a breach of trust in selling trust property for an inadequate price, he is liable for the difference between the amount he should have received and the amount which he did receive. He is not liable, however, for any subsequent rise in value of the property sold". (Id., § 208.6, pp. 1689–1690.)

A recitation of similar import appears in Comment *d* under Restatement, Trusts 2d (§ 205): "*d*. Sale for less than value. If the trustee is authorized to sell trust property, but in breach of trust he sells it for less than he should receive, he is liable for the value of the property at the time of the sale less the amount which he received. If the breach of trust consists *only* in selling it for too little, he is not chargeable with the amount of any subsequent increase in value of the property under the rule stated in

Clause (c), as he would be if he were not authorized to sell the property. See § 208." (Emphasis added.) However, employment of "merely" and "only" as limiting words suggests that where the breach consists of some misfeasance, other than solely for selling "for too low a price" or "for too little", appreciation damages may be appropriate. Under Scott and the Restatement, the trustee may be held liable for appreciation damages if it was his or her duty to retain the property, the theory being that the beneficiaries are entitled to be placed in the same position they would have been in had the breach not consisted of a sale of property that should have been retained. The same rule should apply where the breach of trust consists of a serious conflict of interest—which is more than merely selling for too little.

The reason for allowing appreciation damages, where there is a duty to retain, and only date of sale damages, where there is authorization to sell, is policy oriented. If a trustee authorized to sell were subjected to a greater measure of damages he might be reluctant to sell (in which event he might run a risk if depreciation ensued). On the other hand, if there is a duty to retain and the trustee sells there is no policy reason to protect the trustee; he has not simply acted imprudently, he has violated an integral condition of the trust.

"If a trustee in breach of trust transfers trust property to a person who takes with notice of the breach of trust, and the transferee has disposed of the property . . . [i]t seems proper to charge him with the value at the time of the decree, since if it had not been for the breach of trust the property would still have been a part of the trust estate" (4 Scott, Trusts [3d ed.], § 291.2.) This rule of law which applies to the transferees MNY and MAG also supports the imposition of appreciation damages against Reis and Stamos, since if the Marlborough corporations are liable for such damages either as purchaser or consignees with notice, from one in breach of trust, it is only logical to hold that said executors, as sellers and consignors, are liable also *pro tanto*.

Contrary to assertions of appellants and the dissenters at the Appellate Division, Menzel v. List, 24 N.Y.2d 91, 298 N.Y.S.2d 979, 246 N.E.2d 742, is authority for the allowance of appreciation damages. There, the damages involved a breach of warranty of title to a painting which at one time had been stolen from plaintiff and her husband and ultimately sold to defendant. Here, the executors, though authorized to sell, did not merely err in the amount they accepted but sold to one with whom Reis and Stamos had a self-interest. To make the injured party whole, in both instances the quantum of damages should be the same. In other words, since the paintings cannot be returned, the estate is therefore entitled to their value at the time of the decree, i.e., appreciation damages. These are not punitive damages in a true sense, rather they are damages intended to make the estate whole. Of course, as to Reis, Stamos, MNY and MAG, these damages might be considered by some to be exemplary in a sense, in that they serve as a warning to others, but their true character is ascertained when viewed in the light of overriding policy considerations and in the realization that the sale and consignment were not merely sales below value but inherently wrongful transfers which should allow the owner to be made whole.

. . . .

Accordingly, the order of the Appellate Division should be affirmed, with costs to the prevailing parties against appellants, and the question certified answered in the affirmative.

NOTE

1. Section 927 of the Restatement (Second) of Torts:

CONVERSION OR DETENTION OF A THING OR OF A LEGALLY PROTECTED INTEREST IN IT.

(1) When one is entitled to a judgment for the conversion of a chattel or the destruction or impairment of any legally protected interest in land or other thing, he may recover either

(a) the value of the subject matter or of his interest in it at the time and place of the conversion, destruction or impairment; or

(b) in the case of commodities of fluctuating value customarily traded on an exchange to which traders customarily resort, the highest replacement value of the commodity within a reasonable period during which he might have replaced it.

(2) His damages also include:

(a) the additional value of a chattel due to additions or improvements made by a converter not in good faith;

(b) the amount of any further pecuniary loss of which the deprivation has been a legal cause;

(c) interest from the time at which the value is fixed; and

(d) compensation for the loss of use not otherwise compensated.

Varjabedian v. City of Madera

Supreme Court of California, 1977.
20 Cal.3d 285, 142 Cal.Rptr. 429, 572 P.2d 43.

■ MOSK, J. Defendant City of Madera appeals from a judgment awarding plaintiffs approximately $73,000 for damages caused by the city's operation of a sewage treatment plant near plaintiffs' property. Recovery was on a nuisance theory. Plaintiffs cross-appeal from a judgment on the pleadings for defendant on plaintiffs' cause of action in inverse condemnation.

. . . .

Plaintiffs Michael and Judith Ann Varjabedian acquired a vineyard of approximately 80 acres in Madera County, and in 1971 moved onto the property with their three children. In 1972 defendant city began operation of a new waste water treatment plant on land located some 600 feet from plaintiffs' residence. The plant emits odors which are blown onto plaintiffs' property by the prevailing winds.

The Varjabedians noticed septic smells on their property as soon as sewage was delivered to the new plant in June 1972. There followed a lengthy period during which they repeatedly complained of the odors to city officials and were told that corrective efforts were being made and assured that the plant would eventually be odor-free. On advice of counsel, Michael Varjabedian began to keep a log of the occurrence and intensity of the smells, and of his attempts to persuade the city to remedy the situation. Finally, in July 1973 the instant lawsuit was filed against the city by all five family members.

In their complaint, plaintiffs set forth four theories of recovery; negligence in the design, construction and operation of the plant; maintenance of a nuisance; maintenance of a dangerous and defective condition; and inverse condemnation. When the case came to trial in June 1974, plaintiffs voluntarily dismissed the causes of action for negligence and maintenance of a defective condition. The remaining two counts were the object of defendant's motion for judgment on the pleadings. The trial judge granted the motion as to the inverse condemnation theory, stating his belief that recovery on that cause required "physical damage to the property."

As to the nuisance cause of action the motion was denied, and the case went to trial on that theory. Plaintiffs sought recovery for permanent diminution in the value of their property caused by the nuisance, as well as compensation for personal discomfort. They further sought special damages for the anticipated loss of a Cal–Vet loan which financed the purchase of the bulk of the vineyard. In support of this claim, plaintiffs contended they would be compelled to move off the property and would therefore forfeit their loan under Military and Veterans Code section 987.2. Damages were requested to cover the cost of refinancing the land purchase at a higher rate.

The jury returned a verdict for plaintiffs awarding damages as follows: $32,000 to the Varjabedians for the loss in value of their real property; $30,000 special damages for loss of the Cal–Vet loan; and $11,000 other damages distributed among the five named plaintiffs.

I

Defendant relies upon alleged error in the instructions to the jury regarding the measure of property damage for which the city could be liable in nuisance. The challenged instruction read: "In determining the compensation, if any, to be awarded Plaintiffs for damage to their property proximately caused by a permanent nuisance, in addition to other damage as to which I have instructed you or will instruct you, they are entitled to recover the difference, if any, in the present fair market value of the property as the same would have been without the construction of the sewage treatment plant by the City of Madera, and the present fair market value after said plant was constructed and put into operation."

. . . .

Defendant argues, however, that the instruction allowed the jury to consider effects of the sewage plant on the market value of the Varjabedians' property caused by aspects of the plant other than its production of odors. It is true that under the instruction, which simply calls for a comparison of the market value of the Varjabedians' land before and after the construction of the plant, the jury could have considered decreases in market value provoked by such considerations as the unappealing aesthetic qualities of the sewer plant or anxiety caused by mere knowledge of its proximity. Undoubtedly, not all of such factors fall within the definition of nuisance; in those respects, therefore, the instruction failed to satisfy the requirements of the law of nuisance. . . .

We decline to speculate, however, on which of the potentially depressive effects of sewer plant construction on property values—other than odors—constitute nuisances, or if nuisances, which are expressly authorized, because of our belief that any error in the instruction in this case was not prejudicial to defendant. There was no evidence of negative impact on plaintiffs' property value, to which the jury was exposed, which did not relate directly to the odors. The only testimony regarding the nonolfactory impact of the sewer plant was that of defendant's expert, one Freeman, who estimated that in the absence of constant foul odors there was no depreciation of the farmland. The testimony of plaintiff's expert, one Salaberry, that the sewage plant had caused a depreciation of $56,000 was based solely on the existence of the smells. Indeed, the court kept Salaberry's written report from the jury because it contained language which might have misled the jury into estimating damages before and after the construction of the plant rather than before and after the emission of odors. And although the challenged instruction gave some sanction to the jury's consideration of precisely the same erroneous comparison, this tendency was minimized by other instructions which tied damages to those proximately caused by a permanent nuisance. In the light of the evidence and the totality of the court's instructions, the potential for prejudice contained in the erroneous instruction on damages was minimal. We do not believe the error was "likely to mislead the jury and thus to become a factor in its verdict."

. . . .

III

Defendant next asserts that plaintiffs' recovery for the anticipated loss of their Cal–Vet loan was speculative and therefore improper (Civ.Code, § 3283). The trial court treated the certainty of the future loss of the loan as a question of fact for the jury, and instructed as follows: "If, under the evidence you should find that there is a permanent nuisance, and if you further find that it is reasonably certain that plaintiffs Michael C. and Judith Ann Varjabedian will by reason thereof move from their property, then you may consider any damages that it is reasonably certain they will suffer from the loss of their Cal Vet loan." The submission of the issue to the jury as a question of fact was proper, and the instruction requirement of "reasonable certainty" satisfied Civil Code section 3283.

. . . .

The total amount of damages awarded for loss of the loan was adequately supported by testimony of plaintiff's expert, a banker, that this was the present value of the additional obligations the Varjabedians would incur if forced to refinance their farm. We do not find the amount excessive.

For the above reasons, we affirm in its entirety that portion of the judgment which awards plaintiffs damages in nuisance.

IV

We turn now to plaintiffs' appeal from the judgment on the pleadings entered against their claim in inverse condemnation. Despite plaintiffs' successful nuisance recovery, we cannot say on the basis of the record before us that the challenged ruling, if erroneous, was necessarily harmless. We therefore reach the issue whether the court erred in denying plaintiffs' claim in inverse condemnation.

Article I, section 19 (formerly art. I, § 14) of the California Constitution requires that "just compensation" be paid when "private property" is "taken or damaged for public use." In this case, the trial judge gave as his reason for denying compensation under this provision plaintiffs' failure to allege "physical damage to the property" or a "trespass." Defendant urges no other grounds in support of the judgment, and we consider none.

In assessing whether plaintiffs' allegations may serve as a basis for inverse liability, we note that physical damage to property is not invariably a prerequisite to compensation. Rather, the determination of the scope of the just compensation clause rests on its construction " 'as a matter of interpretation and policy.' " The contending policies which guide that construction have often been described as follows: " 'on the one hand the policy underlying the eminent domain provision in the Constitution is to distribute throughout the community the loss inflicted upon the individual by the making of the public improvements. . . . On the other hand, fears have been expressed that compensation allowed too liberally will seriously impede, if not stop, beneficial public improvements because of the greatly increased cost.' "

Several factors present militate in favor of a distribution throughout the relevant community of the type of loss involved here. Plaintiffs' claim stems from the recurring violation of their property by a gaseous effluent. As such, the injury is not far removed from those core cases of direct physical invasion which indisputably require compensation. Thus, damage from invasions of water or other liquid effluents often provides the basis for inverse liability. Moreover, plaintiffs' complaint which includes, inter alia, the claim that their land was made "untenantable for residential purposes" is clearly sufficient to depict a permanent and "substantial impairment" in their use of the land.

At the same time, fears that "compensation . . . will seriously impede, if not stop" the beneficial construction of sewage treatment plants might be realized if courts were to award compensation for every objectionable odor, however insubstantial or widely dispersed, produced by such facilities. But the problem of reconciling this consideration with the competing policy of loss-distribution is not presented in its most difficult form by the appeal of the present judgment, since it appears from the Varjabedians' allegations that their property may have been peculiarly burdened by the odors so as to bring the case within the doctrine of Richards v. Washington Terminal Co. (1914) 233 U.S. 546, 34 S.Ct. 654, 58 L.Ed. 1088. In *Richards* the plaintiff complained of "inconvenience . . . in the occupation of his property" caused by "gases and smoke" emanating from a nearby railroad. The United States Supreme Court ruled that under the "taking" clause of the Fifth Amendment to the federal Constitution, the plaintiff could not recover for "those consequential damages that are necessarily incident to proximity to the railroad...." Yet the landowner was entitled to compensation for "gases and smoke emitted from locomotive engines while in [a] tunnel, and forced out of it by means of [a] fanning system through a portal located so near to plaintiff's property that these gases and smoke materially contribute to injure the furniture and to render the house less habitable than otherwise...." Construing federal statutes immunizing the railroad from nuisance liability "in light of the Fifth Amendment" the court concluded "they do not authorize the imposition of so direct and peculiar and substantial a burden upon plaintiff's property without compensation to him."

Of course, *Richards* may be distinguished from this case with respect to the nature of the public facility involved, or on the ground that there is no device here which directs the noxious gases onto plaintiffs' property. However, such factual differences do not render the underlying principle of *Richards* inapplicable to the problem at hand, particularly when it is considered together with the California Constitution, which protects a somewhat broader range of property values from government destruction than does the analogous federal provision. If a plaintiff can establish that his property has suffered a "direct and peculiar and substantial" burden as a result of recurring odors produced by a sewage facility—that he has, as in *Richards,* been in effect "singled out" to suffer the detrimental environmental effects of the enterprise—then the policy favoring distribution of the resulting loss of market value is strong and the likelihood that compensation will impede necessary public construction is relatively slight. In these circumstances, the necessity of breathing noxious sewage fumes may be a burden unfairly and unconstitutionally imposed on the individual landowner.

Here plaintiffs allege their farm was directly in the path of the odors as they were blown from defendant's facility by the prevailing winds. Plaintiffs should have been given the opportunity—through amendment of their pleadings if necessary—to demonstrate that the burden on their farm was sufficiently direct, substantial, and peculiar to come within the principle of *Richards,* as applied above. On that showing the Varjabedians can base a claim in inverse condemnation. It follows that the trial court's judgment on that count must be reversed.

The judgment is amended by adding thereto a paragraph dismissing the fourth cause of action of the complaint (inverse condemnation) and awarding judgment thereon to defendant. The portion of the judgment thus added is reversed. The remainder of the judgment is affirmed. Plaintiffs shall recover their costs on appeal.

NOTE

1.   The Restatement (Second) of Torts on tortious injury of land:

§ 929.   Harm to Land from Past Invasions

(1) If one is entitled to a judgment for harm to land resulting from a past invasion and not amounting to a total destruction of value, the damages include compensation for

(a) the difference between the value of the land before the harm and the value after the harm, or at his election in an appropriate case, the cost of restoration that has been or may be reasonably incurred,

(b) the loss of use of the land, and

(c) discomfort and annoyance to him as an occupant.

(2) If a thing attached to the land but severable from it is damaged, he may at his election recover the loss in value to the thing instead of the damage to the land as a whole.

§ 930.   DAMAGES FOR FUTURE INVASIONS

(1) If one causes continuing or recurrent tortious invasions on the land of another by the maintenance of a structure or acts or operations not on the land of the other and it appears that the invasions will continue indefinitely, the other may at his election recover damages for the future invasions in the same action as that for the past invasions.

(2) If the future invasions would not be enjoined because the defendant's enterprise is affected with a public interest, the court in its discretion may rule that the plaintiff must recover for both past and future invasions in the single action.

(3) The damages for past and prospective invasions of land include compensation for

(a) the harm caused by invasions prior to the time when the injurious situation became complete and comparatively enduring, and

(b) either the decrease in the value of the land caused by the prospect of the continuance of the invasion measured at the time when the injurious situation became complete and comparatively enduring, or the reasonable cost to the plaintiff of avoiding future invasions.

J'Aire Corp. v. Gregory

Supreme Court of California, 1979.
24 Cal.3d 799, 157 Cal.Rptr. 407, 598 P.2d 60.

■ BIRD, C.J. Appellant, a lessee, sued respondent, a general contractor, for damages resulting from the delay in completion of a construction project at the premises where appellant operated a restaurant. Respondent demurred successfully and the complaint was dismissed. This court must decide whether a contractor who undertakes construction work pursuant to a contract with the owner of premises may be held liable in tort for business losses suffered by a lessee when the contractor negligently fails to complete the project with due diligence.

I

The facts as pleaded are as follows. Appellant, J'Aire Corporation, operates a restaurant at the Sonoma County Airport in premises leased from the County of Sonoma. Under the terms of the lease the county was to provide heat and air conditioning. In 1975 the county entered into a contract with respondent for improvements to the restaurant premises, including renovation of the heating and air conditioning systems and installation of insulation.

As the contract did not specify any date for completion of the work, appellant alleged the work was to have been completed within a reasonable time as defined by custom and usage. Despite requests that respondent complete the construction promptly, the work was not completed within a reasonable time. Because the restaurant could not operate during part of the construction and was without heat and air conditioning for a longer period, appellant suffered loss of business and resulting loss of profits.

Appellant alleged two causes of action in its third amended complaint. The first cause of action was based upon the theory that it was a third party beneficiary of the contract between the county and respondent. The second cause of action sounded in tort and was based upon negligence in completing the work within a reasonable time. Damages of $50,000 were claimed.

Respondent demurred on the ground that the complaint did not state facts sufficient to constitute a cause of action. The trial court sustained the demurrer without leave to amend and the complaint was dismissed. On appeal only the sustaining of the demurrer to the second cause of action is challenged.

II

. . . .

Liability for negligent conduct may only be imposed where there is a duty of care owed by the defendant to the plaintiff or to a class of which the plaintiff is a member. A duty of care may arise through statute or by contract. Alternatively, a duty may be premised upon the general character of the activity in which the defendant engaged, the relationship between the parties or even the interdependent nature of human society. Whether a duty is owed is simply a shorthand way of phrasing what is " 'the essential question—whether the plaintiff's interests are entitled to legal protection against the defendant's conduct.' "

This court has held that a plaintiff's interest in prospective economic advantage may be protected against injury occasioned by negligent as well as intentional conduct. For example, economic losses such as lost earnings or profits are recoverable as part of general damages in a suit for personal injury based on negligence. Where negligent conduct causes injury to real or personal property, the plaintiff may recover damages for profits lost during the time necessary to repair or replace the property.

Even when only injury to prospective economic advantage is claimed, recovery is not foreclosed. Where a special relationship exists between the parties, a plaintiff may recover for loss of expected economic advantage through the negligent performance of a contract although the parties were not in contractual privity. Biakanja v. Irving (1958) 49 Cal.2d 647, 320 P.2d 16; Lucas v. Hamm (1961) 56 Cal.2d 583, 15 Cal.Rptr. 821, 364 P.2d 685 and Heyer v. Flaig (1969) 70 Cal.2d 223, 74 Cal.Rptr. 225, 449 P.2d 161 held that intended beneficiaries of wills could sue to recover legacies lost through the negligent preparation of the will.

In each of the above cases, the court determined that defendants owed plaintiffs a duty of care by applying criteria set forth in Biakanja v. Irving. Those criteria are (1) the extent to which the transaction was intended to affect the plaintiff, (2) the foreseeability of harm to the plaintiff, (3) the degree of certainty that the plaintiff suffered injury, (4) the closeness of the connection between the defendant's conduct and the injury suffered, (5) the moral blame attached to the defendant's conduct and (6) the policy of preventing future harm.[1]

Applying these criteria to the facts as pleaded, it is evident that a duty was owed by respondent to appellant in the present case. (1) The contract entered into between respondent and the county was for the renovation of the premises in which appellant maintained its business. The contract could not have been performed without impinging on that business. Thus respondent's performance was intended to, and did, directly affect appellant. (2) Accordingly, it was clearly foreseeable that any significant delay in completing the construction would adversely affect appellant's business beyond the normal disruption associated with such construction. Appellant alleges this fact was repeatedly drawn to respondent's attention. (3) Further, appellant's complaint leaves no doubt that appellant suffered harm since it was unable to operate its business for one month and suffered additional loss of business while the premises were without heat and air conditioning. (4) Appellant has also alleged that delays occasioned by the respondent's conduct were closely connected to, indeed directly caused its injury. (5) In addition, respondent's lack of diligence in the present case was particularly blameworthy since it continued after the probability of damage was drawn directly to respondent's attention. (6) Finally, public policy supports finding a duty of care in the present case. The willful failure or refusal of a contractor to prosecute a construction project with diligence, where another is injured as a result, has been made grounds for disciplining a licensed contractor. Although this section does not provide a basis for imposing liability where the delay in completing construction is due merely to negligence, it does indicate the seriousness with which the Legislature views unnecessary delays in the completion of construction.

In light of these factors, this court finds that respondent had a duty to complete construction in a manner that would have avoided unnecessary injury to appellant's business, even though the construction contract was with the owner of a building rather than with appellant, the tenant. It is settled that a contractor owes a duty to avoid injury to the person or property of third parties. As appellant points out, injury to a tenant's

---

1. Countervailing public policies may preclude recovery for injury to prospective economic advantage in some cases, such as the strong public policy favoring organized activity by workers. Accordingly, interference with the prospective economic advantage of an employer or business has traditionally not been considered tortious when it results from union activity, including picketing, striking, primary and secondary boycotts or similar activity, that is otherwise lawful and reasonably related to labor conditions. The present case does not alter this principle.

business can often result in greater hardship than damage to a tenant's person or property. Where the risk of harm is foreseeable, as it was in the present case, an injury to the plaintiff's economic interests should not go uncompensated merely because it was unaccompanied by any injury to his person or property.

To hold under these facts that a cause of action has been stated for negligent interference with prospective economic advantage is consistent with the recent trend in tort cases. This court has repeatedly eschewed overly rigid common law formulations of duty in favor of allowing compensation for foreseeable injuries caused by a defendant's want or ordinary care. Rather than traditional notions of duty, this court has focused on foreseeability as the key component necessary to establish liability: "While the question whether one owes a duty to another must be decided on a case-by-case basis, every case is governed by the rule of general application that all persons are required to use ordinary care to prevent others from being injured as a result of their conduct. . . . [F]oreseeability of the risk is a primary consideration in establishing the element of duty." Similarly, respondent is liable if his lack of ordinary care caused foreseeable injury to the economic interests of appellant.

In addition, this holding is consistent with the Legislature's declaration of the basic principle of tort liability, embodied in Civil Code section 1714, that every person is responsible for injuries caused by his or her lack of ordinary care. That section does not distinguish among injuries to one's person, one's property or one's financial interests. Damages for loss of profits or earnings are recoverable where they result from an injury to one's person or property caused by another's negligence. Recovery for injury to one's economic interests, where it is the foreseeable result of another's want of ordinary care, should not be foreclosed simply because it is the only injury that occurs.

. . . .

III

Accordingly, this court holds that a contractor owes a duty of care to the tenant of a building undergoing construction work to prosecute that work in a manner which does not cause undue injury to the tenant's business, where such injury is reasonably foreseeable. The demurrer to appellant's second cause of action should not have been sustained. The judgment of dismissal is reversed.

People Express Airlines, Inc. v. Consolidated Rail Corporation

Supreme Court of New Jersey, 1985.
100 N.J. 246, 495 A.2d 107.

■ HANDLER, J. This appeal presents a question that has not previously been directly considered: whether a defendant's negligent conduct that interferes with a plaintiff's business resulting in purely economic losses, unaccompanied by property damage or personal injury, is compensable in tort. The appeal poses this issue in the context of the defendants' alleged negligence that caused a dangerous chemical to escape from a railway tank car, resulting in the evacuation from the surrounding area of persons whose safety and health were threatened. The plaintiff, a commercial airline, was forced to evacuate its premises and suffered an interruption of its business operations with resultant economic losses.

. . . .

II.

The single characteristic that distinguishes parties in negligence suits whose claims for economic losses have been regularly denied by American and English courts from those who have recovered economic losses is, with respect to the successful claimants, the fortuitous occurrence of physical harm or property damage, however slight. It is well-accepted that a defendant who negligently injures a plaintiff or his property may be liable for all proximately caused harm, including economic losses. Nevertheless, a virtually *per se* rule barring recovery for economic loss unless the negligent conduct also caused physical harm has evolved throughout this century, based, in part, on Robins Dry Dock & Repair Co. v. Flint, 275 U.S. 303, 48 S.Ct. 134, 72 L.Ed. 290 (1927) and Cattle v. Stockton Waterworks Co., 10 Q.B. 453 (1875). This has occurred although neither case created a rule absolutely disallowing recovery in such circumstances.

The reasons that have been advanced to explain the divergent results for litigants seeking economic losses are varied. Some courts have viewed the general rule against recovery as necessary to limit damages to reasonably foreseeable consequences of negligent conduct. This concern in a given case is often manifested as an issue of causation and has led to the requirement of physical harm as an element of proximate cause. In this context, the physical harm requirement functions as part of the definition of the causal relationship between the defendant's negligent act and the plaintiff's economic damages; it acts as a convenient clamp on otherwise boundless liability. The physical harm rule also reflects certain deep-seated concerns that underlie courts' denial of recovery for purely economic losses occasioned by a defendant's negligence. These concerns include the fear of fraudulent claims, mass litigation, and limitless liability, or liability out of proportion to the defendant's fault.

The assertion of unbounded liability is not unique to cases involving negligently caused economic loss without physical harm. Even in negligence suits in which plaintiffs have sustained physical harm, the courts have recognized that a tortfeasor is not necessarily liable for *all* consequences of his conduct. While a lone act can cause a finite amount of physical harm, that harm may be great and very remote in its final consequences. A single overturned lantern may burn Chicago. Some limitation is required; that limitation is the rule that a tortfeasor is liable only for that harm that he proximately caused. Proximate or legal cause has traditionally functioned to limit liability for negligent conduct. Duty has also been narrowly defined to limit liability. Compare the majority and dissenting opinions in Palsgraf v. Long Island R.R., 248 N.Y. 339, 162 N.E. 99 (1928). Thus, we proceed from the premise that principles of duty and proximate cause are instrumental in limiting the amount of litigation and extent of liability in cases in which no physical harm occurs just as they are in cases involving physical injury.

Countervailing considerations of fairness and public policy have led courts to discard the requirement of physical harm as an element in defining proximate cause to overcome the problem of fraudulent or indefinite claims.... The asserted inability to define damages in cases arising under the cause of action for negligent infliction of emotional distress absent impact or near-impact has not hindered adjudication of those claims. Nor is there any indication that unfair awards have resulted.

The troublesome concern reflected in cases denying recovery for negligently-caused economic loss is the alleged potential for infinite liability, or liability out of all proportion to the defendant's fault. This objection is also not confined to negligently-caused economic injury. The same objection has been asserted and, ultimately, rejected by this Court and others in allowing recovery for other forms of negligent torts and in the creation of the doctrine of strict liability for defective products and ultrahazardous activities. The answer to the allegation of unchecked liability is not the judicial obstruction of a fairly grounded claim for redress. Rather, it must be a more sedulous application of traditional concepts of duty and proximate causation to the facts of each case.

It is understandable that courts, fearing that if even one deserving plaintiff suffering purely economic loss were allowed to recover, all such plaintiffs could recover, have anchored their rulings to the physical harm requirement. While the rationale is understandable, it supports only a limitation on, not a denial of, liability. The physical harm requirement capriciously showers compensation along the path of physical destruction, regardless of the status or circumstances of individual claimants. Purely economic losses are borne by innocent victims, who may not be able to absorb their losses. In the end, the challenge is to fashion a rule that limits liability but permits adjudication of meritorious claims. The asserted inability to fix chrystalline formulae for recovery on the differing facts of future cases simply does not justify the wholesale rejection of recovery in all cases.

Further, judicial reluctance to allow recovery for purely economic losses is discordant with contemporary tort doctrine. The torts process, like the law itself, is a human institution designed to accomplish certain social objectives. One objective is to ensure that innocent victims have avenues of legal redress, absent a contrary, overriding public policy. This reflects the overarching purpose of tort law: that wronged persons should be compensated for their injuries and that those responsible for the wrong should bear the cost of their tortious conduct.

Other policies underlie this fundamental purpose. Imposing liability on defendants for their negligent conduct discourages others from similar tortious behavior, fosters safer products to aid our daily tasks, vindicates reasonable conduct that has regard for the safety of others, and, ultimately, shifts the risk of loss and associated costs of dangerous activities to those who should be and are best able to bear them. Although these policies may be unevenly reflected or imperfectly articulated in any particular case, we strive to ensure that the application of negligence doctrine advances the fundamental purpose of tort law and does not unnecessarily or arbitrarily foreclose redress based on formalisms or technicalisms. Whatever the original common law justifications for the physical harm rule, contemporary tort and negligence doctrine allow—indeed, impel—a more thorough consideration and searching analysis of underlying policies to determine whether a particular defendant may be liable for a plaintiff's economic losses despite the absence of any attendant physical harm.

III.

We may appropriately consider two relevant avenues of analysis in defining a cause of action for negligently-caused economic loss. The first examines the evolution of various exceptions to the rule of nonrecovery for purely economic losses, and suggests that the exceptions have cast considerable doubt on the validity of the current rule and, indeed, have laid the foundation for a rule that would allow recovery. The second explores the elements of a suitable rule and adopts the traditional approach of foreseeability as it relates to duty and proximate cause molded to circumstances involving a claim only for negligently-caused economic injury.

A.

Judicial discomfiture with the rule of nonrecovery for purely economic loss throughout the last several decades has led to numerous exceptions in the general rule. Although the rationalizations for these exceptions differ among courts and cases, two common threads run throughout the exceptions. The first is that the element of foreseeability emerges as a more appropriate analytical standard to determine the question of liability than a *per se* prohibitory rule. The second is that the extent to which the defendant knew or should have known the particular consequences of his negligence, including the economic loss of a particularly foreseeable plaintiff, is dispositive of the issues of duty and fault.

One group of exceptions is based on the "special relationship" between the tortfeasor and the individual or business deprived of economic expectations. Many of these cases are recognized as involving the tort of negligent misrepresentation, resulting in liability for specially foreseeable economic losses. Importantly, the cases do not involve a breach of contract claim between parties in privity; rather, they involve tort claims by innocent third parties who suffered purely economic losses at the hands of negligent defendants with whom no direct relationship existed. Courts have justified their finding of liability in these negligence cases based on notions of a special relationship between the negligent tortfeasors and the foreseeable plaintiffs who relied on the quality of defendants' work or services, to their detriment. The special relationship, in reality, is an expression of the courts' satisfaction that a duty of care existed because the plaintiffs were particularly foreseeable and the injury was proximately caused by the defendant's negligence.

The special relationship exception has been extended to auditors, see H. Rosenblum, Inc. v. Adler, 93 N.J. 324, 461 A.2d 138 (1983); surveyors, termite inspectors, engineers, attorneys, see Lucas v. Hamm, 56 Cal.2d 583, 15 Cal.Rptr. 821, 364 P.2d 685 (1961), cert. den., 368 U.S. 987, 82 S.Ct.

603, 7 L.Ed.2d 525 (1962); notaries public, weighers, and telegraph companies.

. . . .

Courts have found it fair and just in all of these exceptional cases to impose liability on defendants who, by virtue of their special activities, professional training or other unique preparation for their work, had particular knowledge or reason to know that others, such as the intended beneficiaries of wills (e.g., Lucas v. Hamm) or the purchasers of stock who were expected to rely on the company's financial statement in the prospectus (e.g., H. Rosenblum, Inc. v. Adler), would be economically harmed by negligent conduct. In this group of cases, even though the particular plaintiff was not always foreseeable, the particular class of plaintiffs was foreseeable as was the particular type of injury.

A very solid exception allowing recovery for economic losses has also been created in cases akin to private actions for public nuisance. Where a plaintiff's business is based in part upon the exercise of a public right, the plaintiff has been able to recover purely economic losses caused by a defendant's negligence. The theory running throughout these cases, in which the plaintiffs depend on the exercise of the public or riparian right to clean water as a natural resource, is that the pecuniary losses suffered by those who make direct use of the resource are particularly foreseeable because they are so closely linked, through the resource, to the defendants' behavior.

Particular knowledge of the economic consequences has sufficed to establish duty and proximate cause in contexts other than those already considered. In Henry Clay v. Jersey City, 74 N.J.Super. 490, 181 A.2d 545 (Ch.Div.1962), aff'd, 84 N.J.Super. 9, 200 A.2d 787 (App.Div.1964), for example, a lessee-manufacturer had to vacate the building in which its business was located because of the defendant city's negligent failure to maintain its sewer line while the line was repaired. While there was some property damage, the court treated the tenant's and owner's claims separately; the tenant's claims were purely economic, stemming from the loss of use of its property right, as in the instant case. Further, the city had had notice of the leak since 1957 and should have known about it even earlier. Duty, breach and proximate cause were found to exist; the plaintiff-tenant recovered lost profits and expenses incurred during the shut-down.

These exceptions expose the hopeless artificiality of the *per se* rule against recovery for purely economic losses. When the plaintiffs are reasonably foreseeable, the injury is directly and proximately caused by defendant's negligence, and liability can be limited fairly, courts have endeavored to create exceptions to allow recovery. The scope and number of exceptions, while independently justified on various grounds, have nonetheless created lasting doubt as to the wisdom of the *per se* rule of nonrecovery for purely economic losses. Indeed, it has been fashionable for commentators to state that the rule has been giving way for nearly fifty years, although the cases have not always kept pace with the hypothesis.

One thematic motif that may be extrapolated from these decisions to differentiate between those cases in which recovery for economic losses was allowed and denied is that of foreseeability as it relates to both the duty owed and proximate cause. The traditional test of negligence is what a reasonably prudent person would foresee and do in the circumstances; duty is clearly defined by knowledge of the risk of harm or the reasonable apprehension of that risk. In the above-cited cases, the defendants knew or reasonably should have foreseen both that particular plaintiffs or an identifiable class of plaintiffs were at risk and that ascertainable economic damages would ensue from the conduct. Thus, knowledge or special reason to know of the consequences of the tortious conduct in terms of the persons likely to be victimized and the nature of the damages likely to be suffered will suffice to impose a duty upon the tortfeasor not to interfere with economic well-being of third parties.

The further theme that may be extracted from these decisions rests on the specificity and strictness that are infused into the definitional standard of foreseeability. The foreseeability standard that may be synthesized from these cases is one that posits liability in terms of where, along a spectrum ranging from the general to the particular, foreseeability is ultimately found. A broad view of these cases reasonably permits the conclusion that the extent of liability and degree of foreseeability stand in direct proportion to one another. The more particular is the foreseeability that economic loss will be suffered by the plaintiff as a result of defendant's negligence, the more just is it that liability be imposed and recovery allowed.

We hold therefore that a defendant owes a duty of care to take reasonable measures to avoid the risk of causing economic damages, aside from physical injury, to particular plaintiffs or plaintiffs comprising an identifiable class with respect to whom defendant knows or has reason to know are likely to suffer such damages from its conduct. A defendant failing to adhere to this duty of care may be found liable for such economic damages proximately caused by its breach of duty.

. . . .

B. INJURY TO THE PERSON

Cunningham v. Harrison

Court of Appeal, 1973.
[1973] Q.B. 942.

■ LORD DENNING, M.R. On December 18, 1970, Mr. Cunningham, the plaintiff, was severely injured in a road accident. He was in a car going along a major road across Epsom Downs. Another car came out of a side road and there was a collision.

. . . .

The accident was a disaster. There was a complete tetraplegia. That means that he was paralyzed in all four limbs and in his body. This is permanent. He will spend the rest of his life either in bed or in a wheelchair. He is entirely dependent on others for dressing, bath, evacuation of bowels, and partly feeding. He can move his arms a little, but his hands are useless. He can bring his arms round so as to lift a cup, but he has no feel in them so as to grip it or to know if it is hot or cold. Up till the trial all the expenses of his treatment in hospital were paid for by the state. So, I expect, also were the lifting apparatus at home, the wheelchair, and so forth.

One of the most disturbing features is the working of his inside. He has no sensation there. [Lord Denning then noted that he was unable to eliminate waste without manual assistance.] Yet with all this, his head is absolutely unimpaired. His mind, his eyes, his ears, and his tongue are as active as ever.

After he went back to his home in August 1971 his wife looked after him with entire devotion. She did everything for him from early morning till late at night. She helped him in all the distressing things that I have mentioned. The district nurse came in most days for 20 minutes or so. Some days before the trial the wife gave a proof to her solicitors in which she told it all:

"He is 13½ stone [Official British unit equal to 14 lb], and I am 8½. I do my best but I do not have the strength. I should have a nurse or another woman to live in, but we do not have either the money or the accommodation."

She described a typical day from 7:15 a.m. till midnight with every moment filled in doing things for him. She finished:

"Normally my sleep is broken during the night by his waking for spasms or other causes and needing drinks": and she added this last sentence in her own hand: "I am now in a very low state of health and don't weigh 8 stone."

It was indeed too much for her. On November 24, 1972, three days before the case was to be heard, she died from an overdose of barbiturates. She had perhaps foreseen it. In her proof she said: "If I were ill or not available, it would be necessary to employ at least two women full time and best for him to have trained nurses."

Now, how is he to be looked after? His personality makes it difficult. The judge heard his evidence and described him:

"He quite likes talking . . . when he was the chairman of the social club the club was run as he wanted it to be run. . . . He is a self-opinionated person, he calls himself autocratic. . . ."

With such a personality, it is quite clear as the judge said:

"He is not a man who should be in a home if it can be avoided . . . the Heatherly Cheshire Home . . . is the last place that this man should go to. One has but to see him to realise that he would not prosper there, and I do not think that he would be of great therapeutic assistance to those with whom he would be intimately closeted in such a place . . . This plaintiff would obviously be at his worst in a room with someone else. Therefore, I take the view that, in so far as it is possible, it will benefit him to live in some dwelling of his own where, attended by his housekeeper and the persons who do the nursing, he will be best able to overcome his disability for such period of life as remains to him."

Now, what is the period of life which remains to him? On that matter the doctors were divided in opinion. There are so many contingencies. He may get a urinary infection and die from that. His kidneys may deteriorate and he may have to seek help from a kidney machine. He may have some illness which normal people could throw off but he could not. The judge on the evidence gave him a life expectancy of about 12 years, possibly a shade longer. That means he may be expected to live to the age of 61 or 62.

. . . .

4. *Nursing expenses and accommodation*

The plaintiff's case was that his present council house was quite unsuitable for his accommodation; that it was not at all appropriate for him to be placed in a home for the disabled; and that, therefore, he should be provided with a bungalow specially built for the purpose: and nursing attention for all his needs. He called an architect who gave figures showing that the cost of such a bungalow would be something in the order of £28,000. He also claimed that he would need a housekeeper living in at £15 a week, two nurses at £42 a week each, and food for the three of them at £15 a week, making £114 a week, or nearly £6,000 a year. The consulting surgeon who supported this claim was asked by Mr. Laughton–Scott:

"Are we not really here setting up a high quality private nursing home? (A) I suppose one could admit that, but the alternative in my view is not really possible in the case of this man ... We are aiming, I believe, at a situation which will give this man the best possible chance of a future...."

. . . .

... [I]s it right to charge the defendants with the cost of running a fully equipped bungalow and nursing staff specially for him? He seems to be a very autocratic and talkative man who would not fit well with others in a home for the disabled. For his own sake, it would be better for him to be on his own. But should it all be charged on the defendant? It is often said that a wrongdoer must take his victim as he finds him. But I do not think that should be carried to the length here claimed. There should be moderation in all things, even in a claim for personal injuries. Let him have all such reasonable expenses as are appropriate to a normal person so placed, but let them not be increased by his exceptional personality. There is another point for consideration. Will it be practicable to obtain a housekeeper and nurses to staff such a home? We all know how difficult it is to get them. So difficult that it may be that the family will have to take advantage of the assistance now rendered by the state free of charge to disabled persons. The local authorities are under a statutory duty under the Chronically Sick and Disabled Persons Act 1970. They are to provide for many of the needs of a disabled person, such as the provision of suitable accommodation, nursing and general assistance, meals, television, holidays, and so forth. In the present case the manager of the Social Services

Department of the London Borough of Sutton area said that they were building ground floor flats in the borough which were specially designed for handicapped persons with a large living room, two bedrooms, doorways and access for the needs of a wheelchair. He said they would hope to offer accommodation suitable to Mr. Cunningham's needs in about two years. If and in so far as Mr. Cunningham accepted the assistance afforded by the state, it would cost him nothing, or, at any rate, much less. It would be like the medical and nursing services already provided by the National Health Services. It does not form an item in the damages for personal injuries.

In the light of this state assistance—to say nothing of the voluntary organisations—I think a claim for nursing expenses and accommodation should be kept to reasonable limits. If excessive claims are permitted, there might arise a very anomalous situation. A very large sum might be awarded in damages on the basis that the plaintiff would incur the expenses: and then he would find it better afterwards to accept the aid of the statutory and voluntary organisations at much less cost. To avoid this anomaly, the award for future expenses should be kept at a moderate figure.

In view of all this, I would rule out the cost of a bungalow, £28,000. That would give the freehold available as capital for him and his successors—when he is only expected to live for 12 years. That cannot be right. No doubt, as an alternative, it could be possible to award the yearly cost of any extra accommodation that he needed. That would be permissible. . . . But no figures were put forward on that basis. So I would rule that out, too.

Next, the cost of a housekeeper and nursing services. The plaintiff put it at £115 a week. The defendant offered £50 a week. The judge assessed it at £70 a week. In my opinion, the offer of £50 is generous. It should cover not only the nursing services but also the extra accommodation. I would assess the figure at £2,600 a year.

. . . .

[The concurring opinion of ORR, L.J., is omitted.]

■ LAWTON, L.J. . . .

The law imposed upon the trial judge the duty of assessing the compensation to be paid by, in the eyes of the law, the first defendant, but in reality by an insurance company. . . . The judge had to award a sum "which, so far as money can compensate, will give the injured party reparation for the wrongful act" and which would be reasonable and assessed with moderation and, as far as possible, comparable with awards for similar injuries.

When a judge in a case such as this tries to perform the task which the law sets him he moves at once into a world of unreal speculation. How long will the plaintiff live? The estimates of three eminent doctors of great experience varied between 5 and 20 years—and they may all be wrong. The judge found that the plaintiff will require the constant attendance of two persons, with relief from a third in order to cover rest days, holidays and occasional sickness. . . . Where are such persons to be found? What is to happen to the plaintiff when help is not available?

Is the plaintiff likely to get the benefit of the £18,000 which the judge awarded him for his loss of the so-called amenities of life? He will, no doubt, appreciate for the rest of his life a supply of books and gramophone records and the installation of a good television set and long playing record and tape players. He must be kept warm and fed and if possible from time to time given a change of surroundings and be accommodated near his children and his friends. But in the world of reality what more can be done for him? Who in fact will benefit from the award of damages under this head and for the loss of future earnings?

What will happen to the sum of £33,250 which the judge awarded to cover future expenses for the cost of looking after him for the rest of his life? In my judgment it is most unlikely that the whole of this sum, or even a substantial part of it, will be spent on domestic and nursing help. This will not be from any wish on the part of the plaintiff or his children to avoid this expenditure: but from the fact that the help will often not be available. There was evidence from two of the doctors that people can be found to look after tetraplegics and the court was informed that since the trial arrangements have been made for a married couple to look after the plaintiff as soon as a new house which has been bought has been adapted for his needs. Judges, however, cannot shut their eyes to the world outside the courts and it would be wrong for them to do so. I have no doubt at all that for long periods the plaintiff will be without full domestic and nursing help. This probability is not diminished by the fact that, as the judge found, the plaintiff has a personality which may not be congenial to many. During such times his children, friends and neighbours will, no doubt, do what they can, but he will inevitably have to spend longish periods in National Health Service hospitals and in homes run by charitable organisations to which he will be expected to make some contribution but in nothing like the amount for domestic and nursing help which the judge had in mind when deciding on the figure of £33,250.

This case graphically illustrates the difficulties which arise in the assessment of damages in cases of grave personal injury engendering acute, and probably insoluble, human and social problems. The judge who takes on the task, as Lord Morris of Borth-y-Gest said in H. West & Son Ltd. v. Shephard [1964] A.C. 326, 346, has to fix a sum which is "to a considerable extent conventional." Conventions, however, change; and if judges do not adjust their awards to changing conditions and rising standards of living, their assessments of damages will have even less contact with reality than they have had in the recent past or at the present time. Twenty-five years ago Parliament in section 2(4) of the Law Reform (Personal Injuries) Act 1948 provided that in an action for personal injuries there shall be disregarded, in determining the reasonableness of any expenses or part of them the possibility of avoiding them by taking advantage of facilities under the National Health Service. That service when it started is not the same as it is today and the public's attitude towards it is different. Had the plaintiff sustained his injuries in his own home by falling off a ladder whilst doing some decorating, the same medical, human and social problems would have arisen and would have been dealt with within the National Health Service and under the Chronically Sick and Disabled Persons Act 1970, in a way entirely different from what is now contemplated, probably not wholly to the plaintiff's satisfaction but substantially so; he personally would have been spared the worry of contemplating what was going to happen if one or more of his attendants gave notice of leaving him. It is the first defendant's momentary carelessness that makes all the difference and at a total cost, so the judge found, of £70,566 plus interest and two lots of legal costs, a burden which in the end all those who use motor vehicles (and that is a very large proportion of the population) will have to bear.

In the future there may be changes in the law following the findings and recommendations of the recently appointed Royal Commission on Civil Liability and Compensation for Personal Injury. In the meantime this court must continue to discover and apply what are the conventional awards for this class of case. Brabin J., with his extensive experience of personal injury litigation both at the bar and as a judge, is likely to be a reliable guide.

. . . .

As to the sum of £33,250 for domestic and nursing help (which counsel told us is the highest award known for this kind of damage) I find myself impelled to the view that it is unrealistic. I accept that it is a reasonable sum to award the plaintiff on the basis that if he did employ domestic and nursing help for the rest of his life this is the sort of sum which would be necessary to pay for it. For the reasons I have already given he will probably never be able to get the necessary help and will have to fall back on the National Health Service and the welfare services of the area in which he is living. Should the probability that he will have to rely upon the National Health Service be taken into account having regard to section 2(4) of the Law Reform (Personal Injuries) Act 1948? In my judgment the answer is that it should. The plaintiff is entitled to compensation for the expense to which he will be put in obtaining domestic and nursing help; and the defendant cannot say that he could avoid that expense by falling back on the National Health Service. The statute forbids that defence. What she can, however, submit is that he will probably not incur such expenses because he will be unable to obtain the domestic and nursing help which he requires. . . .

. . . .

I started this judgment by calling attention to the lack of reality about the speculation which the present law requires judges to make when assessing damages for grave injuries. I will end by referring to another unreal factor which seems to be making an appearance, namely, that judges should make financial prophesies about the probable rate of inflation in the period for which the award makes provision and should keep in mind factors affecting investment policy. I doubt whether many judges are competent to do anything of the kind; I know that I am not. If expert evidence is called the costs can be very great and the benefits of such evidence very meagre . . .

I would allow the appeal to the extent suggested by Lord Denning M.R.

Appeal allowed and cross-appeal dismissed with costs. Leave to appeal refused.

Hagerty v. L & L Marine Services, Inc.

United States Court of Appeals, Fifth Circuit, 1986.
788 F.2d 315.

■ REAVLEY, J. William L. Hagerty was accidently soaked with toxic chemicals while doing duty as a Jones Act seaman. He sues for his damages which include pain and suffering, mental anguish due to the fear of developing cancer, and the medical expense of regular checkups to monitor against that disease. The district court granted summary judgment for the defendants on the ground that no cause of action had accrued. We reverse and remand.

The traditional tort rules may be restated. A tortious cause of action accrues when the victim suffers harm caused by the defendant's wrong. The injury or harm may occur simultaneously with the tortious conduct in the case of a traumatic event or the injury may be latent and not manifested and discovered until some later date. When the fact of the injury does occur, if discovered by the victim, the cause of action accrues. The victim is then entitled to sue for his damages, past and present, as well as his probable future damages, and limitation also begins to run on the time within which suit may be instituted. The victim is entitled to only one cause of action and, if his injuries subsequently worsen, he has no further opportunity for recompense.

The present appeal raises, primarily, the question of whether a cause of action has accrued. We hold that Hagerty suffered physical injuries and was entitled to pursue this action. The element of fear of cancer and attendant medical costs will be urged upon remand, and we therefore address that issue. Finally, we volunteer our dissatisfaction with the single cause of action rule in face of the recurring problem of injured people facing the possibility of cancer. Those victims should be entitled to recover for present injuries and, also, for the cancer when and if it later develops; they should neither be entitled nor compelled to recover for cancer damages until those damages can be realistically assessed.

1. ACCRUAL OF CAUSE OF ACTION

. . . .

The cause of action has accrued if Hagerty's injury was discernible on the occasion when he was drenched with the toxic chemical. Albertson v. T.J. Stevenson & Co., Inc., 749 F.2d 223 (5th Cir.1984). Dizziness, leg cramps, and a persistent stinging sensation in feet and fingers suggest some harm or injury. The prospects of cancer are of some significance only because that affected Hagerty's appraisal of the significance of what had occurred. Whether a person has suffered harm and whether it is nominal or significant may depend upon that person's own feelings and response. One person might ignore headaches and temporary lassitude, while another—possibly because of a lower pain threshold or because of a greater awareness of the potential consequences—might be so disturbed as to suffer injury and be charged by law with the accrual of a cause of action. In *Albertson* we held that limitations barred the Jones Act and general maritime law claims because the plaintiff's headaches and nausea and a subsequent loss of consciousness gave the plaintiff knowledge of the critical facts that he had suffered more than a minor injury. While the early effects of Hagerty's exposure may not have been as severe as those of Albertson, we hold that they suffice to present an issue of physical injury and to render summary judgment improper.

2. THE ELEMENTS OF DAMAGES

Upon trial the plaintiff is entitled to recover damages for all of his past, present and probable future harm attributable to the defendant's tortious conduct. Those damages include pain and suffering and mental anguish. The present fear or anxiety due to the possibility of contracting cancer constitutes a present fact of mental anguish and may be included in recoverable damages. The increase in the risk of his contracting cancer may not be included, however.

a. *Cancerphobia*

Defendants contend that a plaintiff's cancerphobia should not be considered a present injury unless accompanied by "physical manifestations." Only a physical injury requirement, they argue, will ensure against the proliferation of "unworthy claims." It would also deny worthy claims, perhaps that of Hagerty. We believe the courts have better devices with which to choose between the worthy and the unworthy.

Cancerphobia is merely a specific type of mental anguish or emotional distress. Courts have long allowed plaintiffs to recover for psychic and emotional harm in Federal Employers' Liability Act or Jones Act/maritime cases. Indeed, these statutes are intended to provide broad coverage for all work-related "injuries," whether characterized as mental or physical. Furthermore, while neither the parties' nor our own research has uncovered any claims for cancerphobia under the Jones Act or FELA, courts have often recognized such claims in other contexts. E.g., Jackson v. Johns–Manville Sales Corp., 781 F.2d 394 (5th Cir.1986)(en banc).

The physical injury requirement, like its counterpart, the physical impact requirement, was developed to provide courts with an objective means of ensuring that the alleged mental injury is not feigned. We believe that notion to be unrealistic. It is doubtful that the trier of fact is any less able to decide the fact or extent of mental suffering in the event of physical injury or impact. With or without physical injury or impact, a plaintiff is entitled to recover damages for serious mental distress arising from fear of developing cancer where his fear is reasonable and causally related to the defendant's negligence. The circumstances surrounding the fear-inducing occurrence may themselves supply sufficient indicia of genuineness. It is for the jury to decide questions such as the existence, severity and reasonableness of the fear.

Here, Hagerty has testified that he studied the characteristics of the chemicals he dealt with and thus knew before his exposure that dripolene was a carcinogen. In addition, he felt physical effects after the first dousing; having previously watched benzene absorb into his finger, these effects triggered anxiety because he realized that his entire body had absorbed the chemical. He further testified that he saw a doctor after the exposure and advised his co-worker to do the same. His doctor advised him to undergo periodic medical testing for cancer. In addition to doing so, he subsequently left his job as a tankerman out of concern for future accidents. From this evidence, we conclude that Hagerty has presented sufficient indicia of genuineness so as to make summary judgment of his cancerphobia claim improper.

b. *Medical Expenses*

In addition to any damages for mental distress, Hagerty correctly asserts that he is entitled to recover for the continuing expense of his periodic medical checkups. A plaintiff ordinarily may recover reasonable medical expenses, past and future, which he incurs as a result of a demonstrated injury. Moreover, under the "avoidable consequences rule," he is required to submit to treatment that is medically advisable; failure to do so may bar future recovery for a condition he could thereby have alleviated or avoided. Hagerty testified that he undergoes the checkups at the advice of his physician to ensure early detection and treatment of a possible cancerous condition. We agree that the reasonable cost of those checkups may be included in a damage award to the extent that, in the past, they were medically advisable and, in the future, will probably remain so.

c. *Increased Risk*

Hagerty also urges that he be allowed to recover damages for his increased risk of contracting cancer in the future. In his brief, he does not specify exactly what he believes that "increased risk" to be; we assume, however, that it is not greater than fifty percent.

Recent commentators have argued for recognition of a claim for "increased risk," whether greater or less than fifty percent. To be consistent with our position in section 3 below and with other courts who have recently addressed this question, we conclude that a plaintiff can recover only where he can show that the toxic exposure more probably than not will lead to cancer. Because he does not allege that he has cancer or will probably develop it in the future, Hagerty does not state a claim for this possible effect of his dousing.

3.   THE SINGLE CAUSE OF ACTION RULE

In Albertson v. T.J. Stevenson & Co., 749 F.2d 223 (5th Cir.1984), this court decided that the single cause of action rule barred the plaintiff's suit for complications to his initial injury from trichloroethylene exposure. That result is consistent with the vast majority of latent diseases cases under state tort law, particularly those involving asbestos exposure. The victim of exposure to toxic substances which cause present harm and which may at some future time cause cancer or other serious disease is further victimized by the single cause of action rule. If Hagerty, for example, cannot prove a future probability of his contracting cancer when his trial is conducted but thereafter does contract the disease because of the 1982 exposure at Guyanilla, he will have no remedy for his damages suffered from cancer. He could not, however, have postponed this suit to protect himself from the catastrophic damages because, having suffered some injury, he was forced to sue or suffer the same fate as Albertson.

Even when there is evidence that the increased risk of cancer exceeds fifty percent, the rule does not work well. A plaintiff, if suffering any injury, is forced to seek cancer damages although the extent of those damages is yet highly speculative. They may be nothing at all because what was probable may not occur. The extent of the disease may be limited or the suffering and expenses may be enormous.

The rule has its disadvantages for all parties. Consider the case of *Jackson*. The prognosis of Jackson's future cancer was not predicated on the detection of any personal physiology, not from results of a cytogenetic test or a showing of immunodysfunction in Jackson himself. It was based entirely on the experience of all persons who have developed asbestosis from heavy exposure to asbestos dust; over fifty percent of those people have in the past died from bronchogenic carcinoma. Should all plaintiffs who make that showing recover for cancer damages, and if they match the experience upon which the testimony is based, over forty percent of them will not contract cancer even though they will have been awarded the damages. The onset of cancer, its extent and the amount of damages are too speculative to be decided in this manner.

At least in the toxic chemical or asbestos cases, the disease of cancer should be treated as a separate cause of action for all purposes. There should be no cause of action or beginning of the running of limitations until the diagnosis of the disease. Nor should damages for that disease be recoverable unless and until that time. A prior but distinct disease, though the tortfeasor may have paid reparations, should not affect the cause of action and damages for the subsequent disease.

A few courts have been willing to construe the "single injury" rule so as not to preclude a later suit for latent disease. . . .

When the proper case is presented, this panel hopes that the en banc court will consider this problem, if Congress has not acted upon it by that time.

The district court's judgment is REVERSED and the cause is RE-MANDED to that court.

McDougald v. Garber

Court of Appeals of New York, 1989.
73 N.Y.2d 246, 538 N.Y.S.2d 937, 536 N.E.2d 372.

■ WACHTLER, CHIEF JUDGE. This appeal raises fundamental questions about the nature and role of nonpecuniary damages in personal injury litigation. By nonpecuniary damages, we mean those damages awarded to compensate an injured person for the physical and emotional consequences of the injury, such as pain and suffering and the loss of the ability to engage in certain activities. Pecuniary damages, on the other hand, compensate the victim for the economic consequences of the injury, such as medical expenses, lost earnings and the cost of custodial care.

The specific questions raised here deal with assessment of nonpecuniary damages and are (1) whether some degree of cognitive awareness is a prerequisite to recovery for loss of enjoyment of life and (2) whether a jury should be instructed to consider and award damages for loss of enjoyment of life separately from damages for pain and suffering. We answer the first question in the affirmative and the second question in the negative.

I.

On September 7, 1978, plaintiff Emma McDougald, then 31 years old, underwent a Caesarean section and tubal ligation at New York Infirmary. Defendant Garber performed the surgery; defendants Armengol and Kulkarni provided anesthesia. During the surgery, Mrs. McDougald suffered oxygen deprivation which resulted in severe brain damage and left her in a permanent comatose condition. This action was brought by Mrs. McDougald and her husband, suing derivatively, alleging that the injuries were caused by the defendants' acts of malpractice.

A jury found all defendants liable and awarded Emma McDougald a total of $9,650,102 in damages, including $1,000,000 for conscious pain and suffering and a separate award of $3,500,000 for loss of the pleasures and pursuits of life. The balance of the damages awarded to her were for pecuniary damages—lost earnings and the cost of custodial and nursing care. Her husband was awarded $1,500,000 on his derivative claim for the loss of his wife's services. On defendants' posttrial motions, the Trial Judge reduced the total award to Emma McDougald to $4,796,728 by striking the entire award for future nursing care ($2,353,374) and by reducing the separate awards for conscious pain and suffering and loss of the pleasures and pursuits of life to a single award of $2,000,000. Her husband's award was left intact. On cross appeals, the Appellate Division affirmed and later granted defendants leave to appeal to this court.

II.

We note at the outset that the defendants' liability for Emma McDougald's injuries is unchallenged here....

Also unchallenged are the awards in the amount of $770,978 for loss of earnings and $2,025,750 for future custodial care—that is, the pecuniary damage awards that survived defendants' posttrial motions.

What remains in dispute, primarily, is the award to Emma McDougald for nonpecuniary damages. At trial, defendants sought to show that Mrs. McDougald's injuries were so severe that she was incapable of either experiencing pain or appreciating her condition. Plaintiffs, on the other hand, introduced proof that Mrs. McDougald responded to certain stimuli to a sufficient extent to indicate that she was aware of her circumstances. Thus, the extent of Mrs. McDougald's cognitive abilities, if any, was sharply disputed.

The parties and the trial court agreed that Mrs. McDougald could not recover for pain and suffering unless she were conscious of the pain. Defendants maintained that such consciousness was also required to support an award for loss of enjoyment of life. The court, however, accepted plaintiffs' view that loss of enjoyment of life was compensable without regard to whether the plaintiff was aware of the loss. Accordingly, because the level of Mrs. McDougald's cognitive abilities was in dispute, the court instructed the jury to consider loss of enjoyment of life as an element of nonpecuniary damages separate from pain and suffering. . . .

We conclude that the court erred, both in instructing the jury that Mrs. McDougald's awareness was irrelevant to their consideration of damages for loss of enjoyment of life and in directing the jury to consider that aspect of damages separately from pain and suffering.

III.

We begin with the familiar proposition that an award of damages to a person injured by the negligence of another is to compensate the victim, not to punish the wrongdoer. The goal is to restore the injured party, to the extent possible, to the position that would have been occupied had the wrong not occurred. To be sure, placing the burden of compensation on the negligent party also serves as a deterrent, but purely punitive damages—that is, those which have no compensatory purpose—are prohibited unless the harmful conduct is intentional, malicious, outrageous, or otherwise aggravated beyond mere negligence.

Damages for nonpecuniary losses are, of course, among those that can be awarded as compensation to the victim. This aspect of damages, however, stands on less certain ground than does an award for pecuniary damages. An economic loss can be compensated in kind by an economic gain; but recovery for noneconomic losses such as pain and suffering and loss of enjoyment of life rests on "the legal fiction that money damages can compensate for a victim's injury." We accept this fiction, knowing that although money will neither ease the pain nor restore the victim's abilities, this device is as close as the law can come in its effort to right the wrong. We have no hope of evaluating what has been lost, but a monetary award may provide a measure of solace for the condition created.

Our willingness to indulge this fiction comes to an end, however, when it ceases to serve the compensatory goals of tort recovery. When that limit is met, further indulgence can only result in assessing damages that are punitive. The question posed by this case, then, is whether an award of damages for loss of enjoyment of life to a person whose injuries preclude any awareness of the loss serves a compensatory purpose. We conclude that it does not.

Simply put, an award of money damages in such circumstances has no meaning or utility to the injured person. An award for the loss of enjoyment of life "cannot provide [such a victim] with any consolation or ease any burden resting on him ... He cannot spend it upon necessities or pleasures. He cannot experience the pleasure of giving it away."

We recognize that, as the trial court noted, requiring some cognitive awareness as a prerequisite to recovery for loss of enjoyment of life will result in some cases "in the paradoxical situation that the greater the degree of brain injury inflicted by a negligent defendant, the smaller the award the plaintiff can recover in general damages." The force of this argument, however—the temptation to achieve a balance between injury and damages—has nothing to do with meaningful compensation for the victim. Instead, the temptation is rooted in a desire to punish the defendant in proportion to the harm inflicted. However relevant such retributive symmetry may be in the criminal law, it has no place in the law of civil damages, at least in the absence of culpability beyond mere negligence.

Accordingly, we conclude that cognitive awareness is a prerequisite to recovery for loss of enjoyment of life. We do not go so far, however, as to require the fact finder to sort out varying degrees of cognition and determine at what level a particular deprivation can be fully appreciated. With respect to pain and suffering, the trial court charged simply that there must be "some level of awareness" in order for plaintiff to recover. We think that this is an appropriate standard for all aspects of nonpecuniary loss. No doubt the standard ignores analytically relevant levels of cognition, but we resist the desire for analytical purity in favor of simplicity. A more complex instruction might give the appearance of greater precision but, given the limits of our understanding of the human mind, it would in reality lead only to greater speculation.

We turn next to the question whether loss of enjoyment of life should be considered a category of damages separate from pain and suffering.

IV.

There is no dispute here that the fact finder may, in assessing nonpecuniary damages, consider the effect of the injuries on the plaintiff's capacity to lead a normal life. Traditionally, in this State and elsewhere, this aspect of suffering has not been treated as a separate category of damages; instead, the plaintiff's inability to enjoy life to its fullest has been considered one type of suffering to be factored into a general award for nonpecuniary damages, commonly known as pain and suffering.

Recently, however, there has been an attempt to segregate the suffering associated with physical pain from the mental anguish that stems from the inability to engage in certain activities, and to have juries provide a separate award for each.

Some courts have resisted the effort, primarily on the ground that duplicative and therefore excessive awards would result. Other courts have allowed separate awards, noting that the types of suffering involved are analytically distinguishable. Still other courts have questioned the propriety of the practice but held that, in the particular case, separate awards did not constitute reversible error.

In this State, the only appellate [courts] to address the question ... were persuaded that the distinctions between the two types of mental anguish justified separate awards and that the potential for duplicative awards could be mitigated by carefully drafted jury instructions. In addition, the courts opined that separate awards would facilitate appellate review concerning the excessiveness of the total damage award.

We do not dispute that distinctions can be found or created between the concepts of pain and suffering and loss of enjoyment of life. If the term "suffering" is limited to the emotional response to the sensation of pain, then the emotional response caused by the limitation of life's activities may be considered qualitatively different. But suffering need not be so limited—it can easily encompass the frustration and anguish caused by the inability to participate in activities that once brought pleasure. Traditionally, by treating loss of enjoyment of life as a permissible factor in assessing pain and suffering, courts have given the term this broad meaning.

If we are to depart from this traditional approach and approve a separate award for loss of enjoyment of life, it must be on the basis that such an approach will yield a more accurate evaluation of the compensation due to the plaintiff. We have no doubt that, in general, the total award for nonpecuniary damages would increase if we adopted the rule. That separate awards are advocated by plaintiffs and resisted by defendants is sufficient evidence that larger awards are at stake here. But a larger award does not by itself indicate that the goal of compensation has been better served.

The advocates of separate awards contend that because pain and suffering and loss of enjoyment of life can be distinguished, they must be treated separately if the plaintiff is to be compensated fully for each distinct injury suffered. We disagree. Such an analytical approach may have its place when the subject is pecuniary damages, which can be calculated with some precision. But the estimation of nonpecuniary damages is not amenable to such analytical precision and may, in fact, suffer from its application. Translating human suffering into dollars and cents involves no mathematical formula; it rests, as we have said, on a legal fiction. The figure that emerges is unavoidably distorted by the translation. Application of this murky process to the component parts of nonpecuniary injuries (however analytically distinguishable they may be) cannot make it more accurate. If anything, the distortion will be amplified by repetition.

Thus, we are not persuaded that any salutary purpose would be served by having the jury make separate awards for pain and suffering and loss of enjoyment of life. We are confident, furthermore, that the trial advocate's art is a sufficient guarantee that none of the plaintiff's losses will be ignored by the jury.

The errors in the instructions given to the jury require a new trial on the issue of nonpecuniary damages to be awarded to plaintiff Emma McDougald. . . .

Accordingly, the order of the Appellate Division, insofar as appealed from, should be modified, with costs to defendants, by granting a new trial on the issue of nonpecuniary damages of plaintiff Emma McDougald, and as so modified, affirmed.

■ TITONE, JUDGE (dissenting). The majority's holding represents a compromise position that neither comports with the fundamental principles of tort compensation nor furnishes a satisfactory, logically consistent framework for compensating nonpecuniary loss. Because I conclude that loss of enjoyment of life is an objective damage item, conceptually distinct from conscious pain and suffering, I can find no fault with the trial court's instruction authorizing separate awards and permitting an award for "loss of enjoyment of life" even in the absence of any awareness of that loss on the part of the injured plaintiff. Accordingly, I dissent.

. . . .

Unquestionably, recovery of a damage item such as "pain and suffering" requires a showing of some degree of cognitive capacity. Such a requirement exists for the simple reason that pain and suffering are wholly subjective concepts and cannot exist separate and apart from the human consciousness that experiences them. In contrast, the destruction of an individual's capacity to enjoy life as a result of a crippling injury is an objective fact that does not differ in principle from the permanent loss of an eye or limb. As in the case of a lost limb, an essential characteristic of a healthy human life has been wrongfully taken, and, consequently, the injured party is entitled to a monetary award as a substitute, if, as the majority asserts, the goal of tort compensation is "to restore the injured party, to the extent possible, to the position that would have been occupied had the wrong not occurred."

Significantly, this equation does not suggest a need to establish the injured's awareness of the loss. The victim's ability to comprehend the degree to which his or her life has been impaired is irrelevant, since, unlike "conscious pain and suffering," the impairment exists independent of the victim's ability to apprehend it. Indeed, the majority reaches the conclusion that a degree of awareness must be shown only after injecting a new element into the equation. Under the majority's formulation, the victim must be aware of the loss because, in addition to being compensatory, the award must have "meaning or utility to the injured person." This additional requirement, however, has no real foundation in law or logic. "Meaning" and "utility" are subjective value judgments that have no place in the law of tort recovery, where the primary goal is to find ways of quantifying, to the extent possible, the worth of various forms of human tragedy.

Moreover, the compensatory nature of a monetary award for loss of enjoyment of life is not altered or rendered punitive by the fact that the unaware injured plaintiff cannot experience the pleasure of having it. The fundamental distinction between punitive and compensatory damages is that the former exceed the amount necessary to replace what the plaintiff lost. As the Court of Appeals for the Second Circuit has observed, "[t]he fact that the compensation [for loss of enjoyment of life] may inure as a practical matter to third parties in a given case does not transform the nature of the damages."

Ironically, the majority's expressed goal of limiting recovery for nonpecuniary loss to compensation that the injured plaintiff has the capacity to appreciate is directly undercut by the majority's ultimate holding, adopted in the interest of "simplicity," that recovery for loss of enjoyment of life may be had as long as the injured plaintiff has " 'some level of awareness' ", however slight. Manifestly, there are many different forms and levels of awareness, particularly in cases involving brain injury. Further, the type and degree of cognitive functioning necessary to experience "pain and suffering" is certainly of a lower order than that needed to apprehend the loss of the ability to enjoy life in all of its subtleties. Accordingly, the existence of "some level of awareness" on the part of the injured plaintiff says nothing about that plaintiff's ability to derive some comfort from the award or even to appreciate its significance. Hence, that standard does not assure that loss of enjoyment of life damages will be awarded only when they serve "a compensatory purpose," as that term is defined by the majority.

. . . .

Having concluded that the injured plaintiff's awareness should not be a necessary precondition to recovery for loss of enjoyment of life, I also have no difficulty going on to conclude that loss of enjoyment of life is a distinct damage item which is recoverable separate and apart from the award for conscious pain and suffering. The majority has rejected separate recovery, in part because it apparently perceives some overlap between the two damage categories and in part because it believes that the goal of enhancing the precision of jury awards for nonpecuniary loss would not be advanced. However, the overlap the majority perceives exists only if one assumes, as the majority evidently has, that the "loss of enjoyment" category of damages is designed to compensate only for "*the emotional response* caused by the limitation of life's activities" and "*the frustration and anguish caused by* the inability to participate in activities that once brought pleasure" (emphasis added), both of which are highly *subjective* concepts.

In fact, while "pain and suffering compensates the victim for the physical and mental discomfort caused by the injury; . . . loss of enjoyment of life compensates the victim for the limitations on the person's life created by the injury", a distinctly *objective* loss. In other words, while the victim's "emotional response" and "frustration and anguish" are elements of the award for pain and suffering, the "limitation of life's activities" and the "inability to participate in activities" that the majority identifies are recoverable under the "loss of enjoyment of life" rubric. Thus, there is no real overlap, and no real basis for concern about potentially duplicative awards where, as here, there is a properly instructed jury.

Finally, given the clear distinction between the two categories of nonpecuniary damages, I cannot help but assume that permitting separate awards for conscious pain and suffering and loss of enjoyment of life would contribute to accuracy and precision in thought in the jury's deliberations on the issue of damages. . . .

. . . .

■ Simons, Kaye, Hancock and Bellacosa, JJ., concur with Wachtler, C.J.

■ Itone, J., dissents and votes to affirm in a separate opinion in which Alexander, J., concurs.

NOTE

On the question of whether damage elements for loss of enjoyment of one's life are separate and distinct from damage elements of pain and suffering, the Ohio Supreme Court has held:

> Courts throughout the United States have differed on whether damages may be awarded for loss of enjoyment of life in addition to, and separate from, an award for other elements of damages such as

pain and suffering, or an award for general damages. A number of state courts of last resort have recognized the loss of enjoyment of life as a proper element of damages for personal injuries which may be separate and distinct from pain and suffering and other categories of damages. Exemplary of these are: McAlister v. Carl (1964), 233 Md. 446, 197 A.2d 140; Mariner v. Marsden (Wyo.1980), 610 P.2d 6; and Swiler v. Baker's Super Market, Inc. (1979), 203 Neb. 183, 277 N.W.2d 697.

There are also a considerable number of cases from other states that, while disallowing or discouraging the claim of loss of enjoyment of life as a separate element of damages with its own separate jury instruction and separate award, have held that such claim could be properly considered by the jury in arriving at the amount for general damages. See, e.g., Leiker v. Gafford, 245 Kan. 325, 778 P.2d 823 (1989); McDougald v. Garber, 73 N.Y.2d 246, 538 N.Y.S.2d 937, 536 N.E.2d 372 (1989); Leonard v. Parrish, 420 N.W.2d 629 (Minn.App.1988); Nussbaum v. Gibstein, 73 N.Y.2d 912, 539 N.Y.S.2d 289, 536 N.E.2d 618 (1989); Huff v. Tracy, supra, 57 Cal. App.3d 939, 129 Cal.Rptr. 551. These courts have, in the main, determined that such a claim could not be a separate award, in that the plaintiff's loss of enjoyment of life is encompassed within one of the established elements of damages such as pain and suffering or permanency of injuries. Accordingly, the court in Leiker v. Gafford, supra, stated: "One of the strongest arguments that has been advanced as a reason for not recognizing loss of enjoyment of life as a separate category of damages is that it duplicates or overlaps other categories of damages, such as permanent disability or pain and suffering." Id., 245 Kan. at 339, 778 P.2d at 834. See, generally, Hermes, Loss of Enjoyment of Life—Duplication of Damages Versus Full Compensation (1987), 63 N.D.L.Rev. 561; Annotation, Loss of Enjoyment of Life as a Distinct Element or Factor in Awarding Damages for Bodily Injury (1984), 34 A.L.R. 4th 293; Comment, Loss of Enjoyment of Life as a Separate Element of Damages (1981), 12 Pac.L.J. 965.

How each jurisdiction has treated the issue of whether loss of enjoyment of life is an element of damage separate from other allowable damages such as pain and suffering, or permanent disability, has been dependent upon the elements of damages recognized in that particular state by statute, court rule, or case law. In like manner, in order to answer the query presented here, we have looked to our Ohio laws and to Ohio Jury Instructions (1992) ("OJI").

. . .

The damage with which we deal here is the claimed impairment of one's physical capacity to enjoy the amenities of life. This concept entails providing compensation for the deprivation of one's ability to engage in those activities, and perform those functions, which were part of, and provided pleasure to, one's life prior to the injury. This type of claimed damage is distinguishable from those types of damages that are based upon recognized categories of bodily pain and mental suffering. The claim of damages for deprivation or impairment of life's usual activities has, in other jurisdictions, been applied to a wide variety of pleasurable activities shown to have been curtailed by the injuries received by the plaintiff. Such damages include loss of ability to play golf, dance, bowl, play musical instruments, engage in specific outdoor sports, along with other activities. These types of experiences are all positive sensations of pleasure, the loss of which could provide a basis for an award of damages to the plaintiff in varying degrees depending upon his involvement, as shown by the evidence. Such proof differs from the elements of mental suffering occasioned by the plaintiff's injury such as nervousness, grief, shock, anxiety, and so forth. Although the loss of the ability to engage in a usual pleasant activity of life is an emotional experience, it is a loss of a positive experience rather than the infliction of a negative experience.

In a review and weighing of all factors involved in this discussion, we find it reasonable to treat the claimed inability to perform usual functions (both basic and hedonic) as a separate and distinct element of damage. As noted previously, such an element of damages has already been reflected in OJI Section 23.01(2). It would seem to follow that if Ohio has seen fit to provide for such a statement of law within its standard jury instructions, then the determination of such damage may be made by the jury separate from the other elements of allowable damage that it considers.

. . .

As noted previously, the many jurisdictions which have not permitted "loss of enjoyment of life" as a separate element of damages made their determination on the basis that this would lead to a duplication of damages, in that the jury would have included that loss within the element of pain and suffering or the permanency of the disability. We recognize the validity of such fears, and with the aim of avoiding the feared duplication, shall herewith set forth new provisions to Section 23.01 of OJI. Our intent is that the trial court shall henceforth instruct the jury that if it awards damages for loss of ability to perform usual activities (which will also encompass the permanency of the disability suffered), the jury must not award additional damages for that same loss when considering any other element of damages, such as physical and mental pain and suffering, as such additional award would be duplicative.

In the appropriate case, where there have been allegations of and evidence adduced on the plaintiff's inability to perform usual activities, occasioned by the injuries received, the trial court shall give these additional instructions to the jury:

> "If you find from the greater weight of the evidence that, as a proximate cause of the injuries sustained, the plaintiff has suffered a permanent disability which is evidenced by way of the inability to perform the usual activities of life such as the basic mechanical body movements of walking, climbing stairs, feeding oneself, driving a car, etc., or by way of the inability to perform the plaintiff's usual specific activities which had given pleasure to this particular plaintiff, you may consider, and make a separate award for, such damages.

> "Any amounts that you have determined will be awarded to the plaintiff for any element of damages shall not be considered again or added to any other element of damages. You shall be cautious in your consideration of the damages not to overlap or duplicate the amounts

of your award which would result in double damages. For example, any amount of damages awarded to the plaintiff for pain and suffering must not be awarded again as an element of damages for the plaintiff's inability to perform usual activities. In like manner, any amount of damages awarded to the plaintiff for the inability to perform usual activities must not be considered again as an element of damages awarded for the plaintiff's pain and suffering, or any other element of damages."

Fantozzi v. Sandusky Cement Prods. Co., 64 Ohio St.3d 601, 612–618, 597 N.E.2d 474, 483–487 (1992).

O'Shea v. Riverway Towing Co.

United States Court of Appeals, Seventh Circuit, 1982.
677 F.2d 1194.

■ POSNER, J. This is a tort case under the federal admiralty jurisdiction. We are called upon to decide questions of contributory negligence and damage assessment, in particular the question—one of first impression in this circuit—whether, and if so how, to account for inflation in computing lost future wages.

On the day of the accident, Margaret O'Shea was coming off duty as a cook on a towboat plying the Mississippi River. A harbor boat operated by the defendant, Riverway Towing Company, carried Mrs. O'Shea to shore and while getting off the boat she fell and sustained the injury complained of. The district judge found Riverway negligent and Mrs. O'Shea free from contributory negligence, and assessed damages in excess of $150,000. Riverway appeals only from the finding that there was no contributory negligence and from the part of the damage award that was intended to compensate Mrs. O'Shea for her lost future wages.

. . . .

The more substantial issues in this appeal relate to the computation of lost wages. Mrs. O'Shea's job as a cook paid her $40 a day, and since the custom was to work 30 days consecutively and then have the next 30 days off, this comes to $7200 a year although, as we shall see, she never had earned that much in a single year. She testified that when the accident occurred she had been about to get another cook's job on a Mississippi towboat that would have paid her $60 a day ($10,800 a year). She also testified that she had been intending to work as a boat's cook until she was 70—longer if she was able. An economist who testified on Mrs. O'Shea's behalf used the foregoing testimony as the basis for estimating the wages that she lost because of the accident. He first subtracted federal income tax from yearly wage estimates based on alternative assumptions about her wage rate (that it would be either $40 or $60 a day); assumed that this wage would have grown by between six and eight percent a year; assumed that she would have worked either to age 65 or to age 70; and then discounted the resulting lost-wage estimates to present value, using a discount rate of 8.5 percent a year. These calculations, being based on alternative assumptions concerning starting wage rate, annual wage increases, and length of employment, yielded a range of values rather than a single value. The bottom of the range was $50,000. This is the present value, computed at an 8.5 percent discount rate, of Mrs. O'Shea's lost future wages on the assumption that her starting wage was $40 a day and that it would have grown by six percent a year until she retired at the age of 65. The top of the range was $114,000, which is the present value (again discounted at 8.5 percent) of her lost future wages assuming she would have worked till she was 70 at a wage that would have started at $60 a day and increased by eight percent a year. The judge awarded a figure— $86,033—near the mid-point of this range. He did not explain in his written opinion how he had arrived at this figure, but in a preceding oral opinion he stated that he was "not certain that she would work until age 70 at this type of work," although "she certainly was entitled to" do so and "could have earned something"; and that he had not "felt bound by [the economist's] figure of eight per cent increase in wages" and had "not found the wages based on necessarily a 60 dollar a day job." If this can be taken to mean that he thought Mrs. O'Shea would probably have worked till she was 70, starting at $40 a day but moving up from there at six rather than eight percent a year, the economist's estimate of the present value of her lost future wages would be $75,000.

There is no doubt that the accident disabled Mrs. O'Shea from working as a cook on a boat. The break in her leg was very serious: it reduced the stability of the leg and caused her to fall frequently. It is impossible to see how she could have continued working as a cook, a job performed mostly while standing up, and especially on a boat, with its unsteady motion. But Riverway argues that Mrs. O'Shea (who has not worked at all since the accident, which occurred two years before the trial) could have gotten some sort of job and that the wages in that job should be deducted from the admittedly higher wages that she could have earned as a cook on a boat.

The question is not whether Mrs. O'Shea is totally disabled in the sense, relevant to social security disability cases but not tort cases, that there is no job in the American economy for which she is medically fit. It is whether she can by reasonable diligence find gainful employment, given the physical condition in which the accident left her. Here is a middle-aged woman, very overweight, badly scarred on one arm and one leg, unsteady on her feet, in constant and serious pain from the accident, with no education beyond high school and no work skills other than cooking, a job that happens to require standing for long periods which she is incapable of doing. It seems unlikely that someone in this condition could find gainful work at the minimum wage. True, the probability is not zero; and a better procedure, therefore, might have been to subtract from Mrs. O'Shea's lost future wages as a boat's cook the wages in some other job, discounted (i.e., multiplied) by the probability—very low—that she would in fact be able to get another job. But the district judge cannot be criticized for having failed to use a procedure not suggested by either party. The question put to him was the dichotomous one, would she or would she not get another job if she made reasonable efforts to do so? This required him to decide whether there was a more than 50 percent probability that she would. We cannot say that the negative answer he gave to that question was clearly erroneous.

Riverway argues next that it was wrong for the judge to award damages on the basis of a wage not validated, as it were, by at least a year's employment at that wage. Mrs. O'Shea had never worked full time, had never in fact earned more than $3600 in a full year, and in the year preceding the accident had earned only $900. But previous wages do not put a cap on an award of lost future wages. If a man who had never worked in his life graduated from law school, began working at a law firm at an annual salary of $35,000, and was killed the second day on the job, his lack of a past wage history would be irrelevant to computing his lost future wages. The present case is similar if less dramatic. Mrs. O'Shea did not work at all until 1974, when her husband died. She then lived on her inheritance and worked at a variety of part-time jobs till January 1979, when she started working as a cook on the towboat. According to her testimony, which the trial judge believed, she was then working full time. It is immaterial that this was her first full-time job and that the accident occurred before she had held it for a full year. Her job history was typical of women who return to the labor force after their children are grown or, as in Mrs. O'Shea's case, after their husband dies, and these women are, like any tort victims, entitled to damages based on what they would have earned in the future rather than on what they may or may not have earned in the past.

If we are correct so far, Mrs. O'Shea was entitled to have her lost wages determined on the assumption that she would have earned at least $7200 in the first year after the accident and that the accident caused her to lose that entire amount by disabling her from any gainful employment. And since Riverway neither challenges the district judge's (apparent) finding that Mrs. O'Shea would have worked till she was 70 nor contends that the lost wages for each year until then should be discounted by the probability that she would in fact have been alive and working as a boat's cook throughout the damage period, we may also assume that her wages would have been at least $7200 a year for the 12 years between the date of the accident and her seventieth birthday. But Riverway does argue that we cannot assume she might have earned $10,800 a year rather than $7200, despite her testimony that at the time of the accident she was about to take another job as a boat's cook where she would have been paid at the rate of $60 rather than $40 a day. The point is not terribly important since the trial judge gave little weight to this testimony, but we shall discuss it briefly. Mrs. O'Shea was asked on direct examination what "pay you would have worked" for in the new job. Riverway's counsel objected on the ground of hearsay, the judge overruled his objection, and she answered $60 a day. The objection was not well taken. Riverway argues that only her prospective employer knew what her wage was, and hence when she said it was $60 she was testifying to what he had told her. But an employee's wage is as much in the personal knowledge of the employee as of the employer. If Mrs. O'Shea's prospective employer had testified that he would have paid her $60, Riverway's counsel could have made the converse hearsay objection that the employer was really testifying to what Mrs. O'Shea had told him she was willing to work for. Riverway's counsel could on cross-examination have probed the basis for Mrs. O'Shea's belief that she was going t get $60 a day in a new job, but he did not do so and cannot complain now that the judge may have given her testimony some (though little) weight.

We come at last to the most important issue in the case, which is the proper treatment of inflation in calculating lost future wages. Mrs. O'Shea's economist based the six to eight percent range which he used to estimate future increases in the wages of a boat's cook on the general pattern of wage increases in service occupations over the past 25 years. During the second half of this period the rate of inflation has been substantial and has accounted for much of the increase in nominal wages in this period; and to use that increase to project future wage increases is therefore to assume that inflation will continue, and continue to push up wages. Riverway argues that it is improper as a matter of law to take inflation into account in projecting lost future wages. Yet Riverway itself wants to take inflation into account—one-sidedly, to reduce the amount of the damages computed. For Riverway does not object to the economist's choice of an 8.5 percent discount rate for reducing Mrs. O'Shea's lost future wages to present value, although the rate includes an allowance—a very large allowance—for inflation.

To explain, the object of discounting lost future wages to present value is to give the plaintiff an amount of money which, invested safely, will grow to a sum equal to those wages. So if we thought that but for the accident Mrs. O'Shea would have earned $7200 in 1990, and we were computing in 1980 (when this case was tried) her damages based on those lost earnings, we would need to determine the sum of money that, invested safely for a period of 10 years, would grow to $7200. Suppose that in 1980 the rate of interest on ultra-safe (i.e., federal government) bonds or notes maturing in 10 years was 12 percent. Then we would consult a table of present values to see what sum of money invested at 12 percent for 10 years would at the end of that time have grown to $7200. The answer is $2318. But a moment's reflection will show that to give Mrs. O'Shea $2318 to compensate her for lost wages in 1990 would grossly undercompensate her. People demand 12 percent to lend money risklessly for 10 years because they expect their principal to have much less purchasing power when they get it back at the end of the time. In other words, when long-term interest rates are high, they are high in order to compensate lenders for the fact that they will be repaid in cheaper dollars. In periods when no inflation is anticipated, the risk-free interest rate is between one and three percent. Additional percentage points above that level reflect inflation anticipated over the life of the loan. But if there is inflation it will affect wages as well as prices. Therefore to give Mrs. O'Shea $2318 today because that is the present value of $7200 10 years hence, computed at a discount rate—12 percent—that consists mainly of an allowance for anticipated inflation, is in fact to give her less than she would have been earning then if she was earning $7200 on the date of the accident, even if the only wage increases she would have received would have been those necessary to keep pace with inflation.

There are (at least) two ways to deal with inflation in computing the present value of lost future wages. One is to take it out of both the wages and the discount rate—to say to Mrs. O'Shea, "we are going to calculate your probable wage in 1990 on the assumption, unrealistic as it is, that there will be zero inflation between now and then; and, to be consistent, we are going to discount the amount thus calculated by the interest rate that would be charged under the same assumption of zero inflation." Thus, if we thought Mrs. O'Shea's real (i.e., inflation-free) wage rate would not rise in the future, we would fix her lost earnings in 1990 as $7200 and, to be consistent, we would discount that to present (1980) value using an estimate of the real interest rate. At two percent, this procedure would yield a present value of $5906. Of course, she would not invest this money at a mere two percent. She would invest it at the much higher prevailing interest rate. But that would not give her a windfall; it would just enable her to replace her lost 1990 earnings with an amount equal to what she would in fact have earned in that year if inflation continues, as most people expect it to do. (If people did not expect continued inflation, long-term interest rates would be much lower; those rates impound investors' inflationary expectations.)

An alternative approach, which yields the same result, is to use a (higher) discount rate based on the current risk-free 10–year interest rate, but apply that rate to an estimate of lost future wages that includes expected inflation. Contrary to Riverway's argument, this projection would not require gazing into a crystal ball. The expected rate of inflation can, as just suggested, be read off from the current long-term interest rate. If that rate is 12 percent, and if as suggested earlier the real or inflation-free interest rate is only one to three percent, this implies that the market is anticipating 9–11 percent inflation over the next 10 years, for a long-term interest rate is simply the sum of the real interest rate and the anticipated rate of inflation during the term.

Either approach to dealing with inflation is acceptable (they are, in fact, equivalent) and we by no means rule out others; but it is illogical and indefensible to build inflation into the discount rate yet ignore it in calculating the lost future wages that are to be discounted. That results in systematic undercompensation, just as building inflation into the estimate of future lost earnings and then discounting using the real rate of interest would systematically overcompensate.... We align ourselves instead with those circuits (a majority), notably the Second, that require that inflation be treated consistently in choosing a discount rate and in estimating the future lost wages to be discounted to present value using that rate....

Applying our analysis to the present case, we cannot pronounce the approach taken by the plaintiff's economist unreasonable. He chose a discount rate—8.5 percent—well above the real rate of interest, and therefore containing an allowance for inflation. Consistency required him to inflate Mrs. O'Shea's starting wage as a boat's cook in calculating her lost future wages, and he did so at a rate of six to eight percent a year. If this rate had been intended as a forecast of purely inflationary wage changes, his approach would be open to question, especially at the upper end of his range. For if the estimated rate of inflation were eight percent, the use of a discount rate of 8.5 percent would imply that the real rate of interest was only .5 percent, which is lower than most economists believe it to be for any substantial period of time. But wages do not rise just because of inflation.

Mrs. O'Shea could expect her real wages as a boat's cook to rise as she became more experienced and as average real wage rates throughout the economy rose, as they usually do over a decade or more. It would not be outlandish to assume that even if there were no inflation, Mrs. O'Shea's wages would have risen by three percent a year. If we subtract that from the economist's six to eight percent range, the inflation allowance built into his estimated future wage increases is only three to five percent; and when we subtract these figures from 8.5 percent we see that his implicit estimate of the real rate of interest was very high (3.5–5.5 percent). This means he was conservative, because the higher the discount rate used the lower the damages calculated.

If conservative in one sense, the economist was most liberal in another. He made no allowance for the fact that Mrs. O'Shea, whose health history quite apart from the accident is not outstanding, might very well not have survived—let alone survived and been working as a boat's cook or in an equivalent job—until the age of 70. The damage award is a sum certain, but the lost future wages to which that award is equated by means of the discount rate are mere probabilities. If the probability of her being employed as a boat's cook full time in 1990 was only 75 percent, for example, then her estimated wages in that year should have been multiplied by .75 to determine the value of the expectation that she lost as a result of the accident; and so, with each of the other future years. The economist did not do this, and by failing to do this he overstated the loss due to the accident.

But Riverway does not make an issue of this aspect of the economist's analysis. Nor of another: the economist selected the 8.5 percent figure for the discount rate because that was the current interest rate on Triple A 10-year state and municipal bonds, but it would not make sense in Mrs. O'Shea's federal income tax bracket to invest in tax-free bonds. If he wanted to use nominal rather than real interest rates and wage increases (as we said was proper), the economist should have used a higher discount rate and a higher expected rate of inflation. But as these adjustments would have been largely or entirely offsetting, the failure to make them was not a critical error.

Although we are not entirely satisfied with the economic analysis on which the judge, in the absence of any other evidence of the present value of Mrs. O'Shea's lost future wages, must have relied heavily, we recognize that the exactness which economic analysis rigorously pursued appears to offer is, at least in the litigation setting, somewhat delusive. Therefore, we will not reverse an award of damages for lost wages because of questionable assumptions unless it yields an unreasonable result—especially when, as in the present case, the defendant does not offer any economic evidence himself and does not object to the questionable steps in the plaintiff's economic analysis. We cannot say the result here was unreasonable. If the economist's method of estimating damages was too generous to Mrs. O'Shea in one important respect it was, as we have seen, niggardly in another. Another error against Mrs. O'Shea should be noted: the economist should not have deducted her entire income tax liability in estimating her future lost wages. While it is true that the damage award is not taxable, the interest she earns on it will be (a point the economist may have ignored because of his erroneous assumption that she would invest the award in tax-exempt bonds), so that his method involved an element of double taxation.

If we assume that Mrs. O'Shea could have expected a three percent annual increase in her real wages from a base of $7200, that the real risk-free rate of interest (and therefore the appropriate discount rate if we are considering only real wage increases) is two percent, and that she would have worked till she was 70, the present value of her lost future wages would be $91,310. This figure ignores the fact that she did not have a 100 percent probability of actually working till age 70 as a boat's cook, and fails to make the appropriate (though probably, in her bracket, very small) net income tax adjustment; but it also ignores the possibility, small but not totally negligible, that the proper base is really $10,800 rather than $7200.

So we cannot say that the figure arrived at by the judge, $86,033, was unreasonably high. But we are distressed that he made no attempt to explain how he had arrived at that figure, since it was not one contained in the economist's testimony though it must in some way have been derived from that testimony. Unlike many other damage items in a personal injury case, notably pain and suffering, the calculation of damages for lost earnings can and should be an analytical rather than an intuitive undertaking. Therefore, compliance with Rule 52(a) of the Federal Rules of Civil Procedure requires that in a bench trial the district judge set out the steps by which he arrived at his award for lost future earnings, in order to assist the appellate court in reviewing the award. The district judge failed to do that here. We do not consider this reversible error, because our own analysis convinces us that the award of damages for lost future wages was reasonable. But for the future we ask the district judges in this circuit to indicate the steps by which they arrive at damage awards for lost future earnings.

Judgment affirmed.

NOTE

McCarrell was injured when his automobile collided with a piece of pipe which Rieth–Riley Construction Company negligently allowed to enter the highway. McCarrell brought an action against Rieth–Riley Construction Company and the trial judge charged the jury as follows:

If you find for the plaintiff on the question of liability, you then must determine the amount of money which will fairly compensate plaintiff for those elements of damage which were proved by the evidence to have resulted from the negligence of defendant. You may consider:

. . . .

(f) The value of lost time, earnings or salary, and loss or impairment of earning capacity. . . .

A judgment was entered for McCarrell on the verdict of the jury. On appeal, Rieth–Riley contended that this instruction was erroneous in that it authorized a recovery for McCarrell for lost time when the evidence conclusively showed that McCarrell was unemployed. The appellate court rejected this argument, holding that even an unemployed person's time is worth money. See Rieth–Riley Constr. Co. v. McCarrell, 163 Ind.App. 613, 325 N.E.2d 844 (1975).

Jones & Laughlin Steel Corp. v. Pfeifer

Supreme Court of the United States, 1983.
462 U.S. 523, 103 S.Ct. 2541, 76 L.Ed.2d 768.

■ STEVENS, J. Respondent was injured in the course of his employment as a loading helper on a coal barge. As his employer, petitioner was required to compensate him for his injury under § 4 of the Longshoremen's and Harbor Workers' Compensation Act (the Act). 44 Stat. 1426, 33 U.S.C. § 904. As the owner *pro hac vice* of the barge, petitioner may also be liable for negligence under § 5 of the Act. 86 Stat. 1263, 33 U.S.C. § 905. We granted certiorari to decide ... whether the Court of Appeals correctly upheld the trial court's computation of respondent's damages.

. . . .

The District Court arrived at its final award by taking 12½ years of earnings at respondent's wage at the time of injury ($325,312.50), subtracting his projected hypothetical earnings at the minimum wage ($66,352) and the compensation payments he had received under § 4 ($33,079.14), and adding $50,000 for pain and suffering. The court did not increase the award to take inflation into account, and it did not discount the award to reflect the present value of the future stream of income. The Court instead decided to follow a decision of the Supreme Court of Pennsylvania, which had held "as a matter of law that future inflation shall be presumed equal to future interest rates with these factors offsetting." Kaczkowski v. Bolubasz, 491 Pa. 561, 583, 421 A.2d 1027, 1038–1039 (1980). . . .

. . . .

The Damages Issue

The District Court found that respondent was permanently disabled as a result of petitioner's negligence. He therefore was entitled to an award of damages to compensate him for his probable pecuniary loss over the duration of his career, reduced to its present value. It is useful at the outset to review the way in which damages should be measured in a hypothetical inflation-free economy. We shall then consider how price inflation alters the analysis. Finally, we shall decide whether the District Court committed reversible error in this case.

I

In calculating damages, it is assumed that if the injured party had not been disabled, he would have continued to work, and to receive wages at periodic intervals until retirement, disability, or death. An award for impaired earning capacity is intended to compensate the worker for the diminution in that stream of income.[4] The award could in theory take the

---

4. It should be noted that in a personal injury action such as this one, damages for   weekly or biweekly installments, virtually all calculations of lost earnings, including the

form of periodic payments, but in this country it has traditionally taken the form of a lump sum, paid at the conclusion of the litigation. The appropriate lump sum cannot be computed without first examining the stream of income it purports to replace.

The lost stream's length cannot be known with certainty; the worker could have been disabled or even killed in a different, non-work-related accident at any time. The probability that he would still be working at a given date is constantly diminishing. Given the complexity of trying to make an exact calculation, litigants frequently follow the relatively simple course of assuming that the worker would have continued to work up until a specific date certain. In this case, for example, both parties agreed that the petitioner would have continued to work until age 65 (12½ more years) if he had not been injured.

Each annual installment[11] in the lost stream comprises several elements. The most significant is, of course, the actual wage. In addition, the worker may have enjoyed certain fringe benefits, which should be included in an ideal evaluation of the worker's loss but are frequently excluded for simplicity's sake.[12] On the other hand, the injured worker's lost wages would have been diminished by state and federal income taxes. Since the damages award is tax-free, the relevant stream is ideally of *after-tax* wages and benefits. Moreover, workers often incur unreimbursed costs, such as transportation to work and uniforms, that the injured worker will not incur. These costs should also be deducted in estimating the lost stream.

In this case the parties appear to have agreed to simplify the litigation, and to presume that in each installment all the elements in the stream would offset each other, except for gross wages. However, in attempting to estimate even such a stylized stream of annual installments of gross wages, a trier of fact faces a complex task. The most obvious and most appropriate place to begin is with the worker's annual wage at the time of injury. Yet the "estimate of loss from lessened earnings capacity in the future need not be based solely upon the wages which the plaintiff was earning at the time of his injury." C. McCormick, Damages § 86 (1935). Even in an inflation-free economy—that is to say one in which the prices of consumer goods remain stable—a worker's wages tend to "inflate." This "real" wage inflation reflects a number of factors, some linked to the specific individual and some linked to broader societal forces.[13]

---

impaired earning capacity are awarded to compensate the injured person for his loss. In a wrongful death action, a similar but not identical item of damages is awarded for the manner in which diminished earning capacity harms either the worker's survivors or his estate. Since the problem of incorporating inflation into the award is the same in both types of action, we shall make occasional reference to wrongful death actions in this opinion.

11. Obviously, another distorting simplification is being made here. Although workers generally receive their wages in one made in this case, pretend that the stream would have flowed in large spurts, taking the form of annual installments.

12. These might include insurance coverage, pension and retirement plans, profit sharing, and in-kind services.

13. As will become apparent, in speaking of "societal" forces we are primarily concerned with those macroeconomic forces that influence wages in the worker's particular industry. The term will be used to encompass all forces that tend to inflate a worker's wage

With the passage of time, an individual worker often becomes more valuable to his employer. His personal work experiences increase his hourly contributions to firm profits. To reflect that heightened value, he will often receive "seniority" or "experience" raises, "merit" raises, or even promotions.[14] Although it may be difficult to prove when, and whether, a particular injured worker might have received such wage increases, see Feldman v. Allegheny Airlines, 524 F.2d 384, 392–393 (C.A.2 1975)(Friendly, J., concurring *dubitante*), they may be reliably demonstrated for some workers.

Furthermore, the wages of workers as a class may increase over time. Through more efficient interaction among labor, capital, and technology, industrial productivity may increase, and workers' wages may enjoy a share of that growth. Such productivity increases—reflected in real increases in the gross national product per worker-hour—have been a permanent feature of the national economy since the conclusion of World War II. Moreover, through collective bargaining, workers may be able to negotiate increases in their "share" of revenues, at the cost of reducing shareholders' rate of return on their investments. Either of these forces could affect the lost stream of income in an inflation-free economy. In this case, the plaintiff's proffered evidence on predictable wage growth may have reflected the influence of either or both of these two factors.

To summarize, the first stage in calculating an appropriate award for lost earnings involves an estimate of what the lost stream of income would have been. The stream may be approximated as a series of after-tax payments, one in each year of the worker's expected remaining career. In estimating what those payments would have been in an inflation-free economy, the trier of fact may begin with the worker's annual wage at the time of injury. If sufficient proof is offered, the trier of fact may increase that figure to reflect the appropriate influence of individualized factors (such as foreseeable promotions) and societal factors (such as foreseeable productivity growth within the worker's industry).[19]

Of course, even in an inflation-free economy the award of damages to replace the lost stream of income cannot be computed simply by totaling up the sum of the periodic payments. For the damages award is paid in a lump sum at the conclusion of the litigation, and when it—or even a part of it—is invested, it will earn additional money. It has been settled since our decision in Chesapeake & Ohio R. Co. v. Kelly, 241 U.S. 485, 36 S.Ct. 630, 60 L.Ed. 1117 (1916) that "in all cases where it is reasonable to suppose that interest may safely be earned upon the amount that is awarded, the ascertained future benefits ought to be discounted in the making up of the award."[20]

without regard to the worker's individual characteristics.

14. It is also possible that a worker could be expected to change occupations completely.

19. If foreseeable real wage growth is shown, it may produce a steadily increasing series of payments, with the first payment showing the least increase from the wage at the time of injury and the last payment showing the most.

20. Although this rule could be seen as a way of ensuring that the lump-sum award accurately represents the pecuniary injury as of the time of trial, it was explained by reference to the duty to mitigate damages.

The discount rate should be based on the rate of interest that would be earned on "the best and safest investments." Once it is assumed that the injured worker would definitely have worked for a specific term of years, he is entitled to a risk-free stream of future income to replace his lost wages; therefore, the discount rate should not reflect the market's premium for investors who are willing to accept some risk of default. Moreover, since under *Liepelt,* the lost stream of income should be estimated in after-tax terms, the discount rate should also represent the after-tax rate of return to the injured worker.[21]

Thus, although the notion of a damage award representing the present value of a lost stream of earnings in an inflation-free economy rests on some fairly sophisticated economic concepts, the two elements that determine its calculation can be stated fairly easily. They are: (1) the amount that the employee would have earned during each year that he could have been expected to work after the injury; and (2) the appropriate discount rate, reflecting the safest available investment. The trier of fact should apply the discount rate to each of the estimated installments in the lost stream of income, and then add up the discounted installments to determine the total award.[22]

II

Unfortunately for triers of fact, ours is not an inflation-free economy. Inflation has been a permanent fixture in our economy for many decades, and there can be no doubt that it ideally should affect both stages of the calculation described in the previous section. The difficult problem is how it can do so in the practical context of civil litigation under § 5(b) of the Act.

The first stage of the calculation required an estimate of the shape of the lost stream of future income. For many workers, including respondent, a contractual "cost-of-living adjustment" automatically increases wages each year by the percentage change during the previous year in the consumer price index calculated by the Bureau of Labor Statistics. Such a contract provides a basis for taking into account an additional societal factor—price inflation—in estimating the worker's lost future earnings.

---

21. The arithmetic necessary for discounting can be simplified through the use of a so-called "present value table," such as those found in R. Wixon, Accountants' Handbook, at 29.58–29.59 (1956 ed.), or S. Speiser, Recovery for Wrongful Death 2d § 8:4, at 713–718 (1975). These tables are based on the proposition that if i is the discount rate, then "the present value of $1 due in n periods must be $1/(1 + i)^n$." Wixon, *supra,* at 29.57. In this context, the relevant "periods" are years; accordingly, if "*i*" is a market interest rate, it should be the effective *annual* yield.

22. At one time it was thought appropriate to distinguish between compensating a plaintiff "for the loss of time from his work which has actually occurred up to the time of trial" and compensating him "for the time which he will lose in the future." C. McCormick, Damages § 86 (1935). This suggested that estimated future earning capacity should be discounted to the date of trial, and a separate calculation should be performed for the estimated loss of earnings between injury and trial. It is both easier and more precise to discount the entire lost stream of earnings back to the date of injury—the moment from which earning capacity was impaired. The plaintiff may then be awarded interest on that discounted sum for the period between injury and judgment, in order to ensure that the award when invested will still be able to replicate the lost stream.

The second stage of the calculation requires the selection of an appropriate discount rate. Price inflation—or more precisely, anticipated price inflation—certainly affects market rates of return. If a lender knows that his loan is to be repaid a year later with dollars that are less valuable than those he has advanced, he will charge an interest rate that is high enough both to compensate him for the temporary use of the loan proceeds and also to make up for their shrinkage in value.[23]

At one time many courts incorporated inflation into only one stage of the calculation of the award for lost earnings. In estimating the lost stream of future earnings, they accepted evidence of both individual and societal factors that would tend to lead to wage increases even in an inflation-free economy, but required the plaintiff to prove that those factors were not influenced by predictions of future price inflation. No increase was allowed for price inflation, on the theory that such predictions were unreliably speculative. In discounting the estimated lost stream of future income to present value, however, they applied the market interest rate.

The effect of these holdings was to deny the plaintiff the benefit of the impact of inflation on his future earnings, while giving the defendant the benefit of inflation's impact on the interest rate that is used to discount those earnings to present value. Although the plaintiff in such a situation could invest the proceeds of the litigation at an "inflated" rate of interest, the stream of income that he received provided him with only enough dollars to maintain his existing *nominal* income; it did not provide him with a stream comparable to what his lost wages would have been in an inflationary economy.[24] This inequity was assumed to have been minimal because of the relatively low rates of inflation.

23. The effect of price inflation on the discount rate may be less speculative than its effect on the lost stream of future income. The latter effect always requires a prediction of the future, for the existence of a contractual cost-of-living adjustment gives no guidance about how big that adjustment will be in some future year. However, whether the discount rate also turns on predictions of the future depends on how it is assumed that the worker will invest his award.

On the one hand, it might be assumed that at the time of the award the worker will invest in a mixture of safe short-term, medium-term, and long-term bonds, with one scheduled to mature each year of his expected worklife. In that event, by purchasing bonds immediately after judgment, the worker can be ensured whatever future stream of nominal income is predicted. Since all relevant effects of inflation on the market interest rate will have occurred at that time, future changes in the rate of price inflation will have no effect on the stream of income he receives.... On the other hand, it might be assumed that the worker will invest exclusively in safe short-term notes, reinvesting

them at the new market rate whenever they mature. Future market rates would be quite important to such a worker. Predictions of what they will be would therefore also be relevant to the choice of an appropriate discount rate, in much the same way that they are always relevant to the first stage of the calculation.... We perceive no intrinsic reason to prefer one assumption over the other, but most "offset" analyses seem to adopt the latter. See n. 26, infra.

24. As Judge Posner has explained it:

"But if there is inflation it will affect wages as well as prices. Therefore to give Mrs. O'Shea $2318 today because that is the present value of $7200 10 years hence, computed at a discount rate—12 percent—that consists mainly of an allowance for anticipated inflation, is in fact to give her less than she would have been earning then if she was earning $7200 on the date of the accident, even if the only wage increases she would have received would have been those necessary to keep pace with inflation." O'Shea v. Riverway Towing Co., 677 F.2d 1194, 1199 (C.A.7 1982).

In recent years, of course, inflation rates have not remained low. There is now a consensus among courts that the prior inequity can no longer be tolerated. There is no consensus at all, however, regarding what form an appropriate response should take.

Our sister common law nations generally continue to adhere to the position that inflation is too speculative to be considered in estimating the lost stream of future earnings; they have sought to counteract the danger of systematically undercompensating plaintiffs by applying a discount rate that is below the current market rate. Nevertheless, they have each chosen different rates, applying slightly different economic theories. In England, Lord Diplock has suggested that it would be appropriate to allow for future inflation "in a rough and ready way" by discounting at a rate of 4¾%. He accepted that rate as roughly equivalent to the rates available "[i]n times of stable currency." The Supreme Court of Canada has recommended discounting at a rate of seven percent, a rate equal to market rates on long-term investments minus a government expert's prediction of the long-term rate of price inflation. And in Australia, the High Court has adopted a 2% rate, on the theory that it represents a good approximation of the long-term "real interest rate."

In this country, some courts have taken the same "real interest rate" approach as Australia. They have endorsed the economic theory suggesting that market interest rates include two components—an estimate of anticipated inflation, and a desired "real" rate of return on investment—and that the latter component is essentially constant over time.[25] They have concluded that the inflationary increase in the estimated lost stream of future earnings will therefore be perfectly "offset" by all but the "real" component of the market interest rate.[26]

25. In his dissenting opinion in Pennant Hills Restaurant Pty. Ltd. v. Barrell Insurances Pty. Ltd., 55 A.L.J.R. 258, 266–267 (1981), Justice Stephen explained the real interest rate approach to discounting future earnings, in part, as follows:

"It rests upon the assumption that interest rates have two principal components: the market's own estimation of likely rates of inflation during the term of a particular fixed interest investment, and a 'real interest' component, being the rate of return which, in the absence of all inflation, a lender will demand and a borrower will be prepared to pay for the use of borrowed funds. It also relies upon the alleged economic fact that this 'real interest' rate, of about two per cent, will always be much the same and that fluctuations in nominal rates of interest are due to the other main component of interest rates, the inflationary expectation."

26. What is meant by the "real interest rate" depends on how one expects the plain-

tiff to invest the award, see n. 23, supra. If one assumes that the injured worker will immediately invest in bonds having a variety of maturity dates, in order to ensure a particular stream of future payments, then the relevant "real interest rate" must be the difference between (1) an average of short-term, medium-term, and long-term market interest rates in a given year and (2) the average rate of price inflation in *subsequent* years (i.e., during the terms of the investments)....

It appears more common for "real interest rate" approaches to rest on the assumption that the worker will invest in low-risk short-term securities and will reinvest frequently. Under that assumption, the relevant real interest rate is the difference between the short-term market interest rate in a given year and the average rate of price inflation during that same year. Several studies appear to have been done to measure this difference.

However one interprets the "real interest rate," there is a slight distortion intro-

Still other courts have preferred to continue relying on market interest rates. To avoid undercompensation, they have shown at least tentative willingness to permit evidence of what future price inflation will be in estimating the lost stream of future income.

Within the past year, two Federal Courts of Appeals have decided to allow litigants a choice of methods....

Finally, some courts have applied a number of techniques that have loosely been termed "total offset" methods. What these methods have in common is that they presume that the ideal discount rate—the after-tax market interest rate on a safe investment—is (to a legally tolerable degree of precision) completely offset by certain elements in the ideal computation of the estimated lost stream of future income. They all assume that the effects of future price inflation on wages are part of what offsets the market interest rate. The methods differ, however, in their assumptions regarding which if any other elements in the first stage of the damages calculation contribute to the offset.

Beaulieu v. Elliott, 434 P.2d 665 (Alaska 1967), is regarded as the seminal "total offset" case. The Supreme Court of Alaska ruled that in calculating an appropriate award for an injured worker's lost wages, no discount was to be applied. It held that the market interest rate was fully offset by two factors: price inflation and real wage inflation. Significantly, the Court did not need to distinguish between the two types of sources of real wage inflation—individual and societal—in order to resolve the case before it. It simply observed:

"It is a matter of common experience that as one progresses in his chosen occupation or profession he is likely to increase his earnings as the years go by. In nearly any occupation a wage earner can reasonably expect to receive wage increases from time to time. This factor is generally not taken into account when loss of future wages is determined, because there is no definite way of determining at the time of trial what wage increases the plaintiff may expect to receive in the years to come. However, this factor may be taken into account to some extent when considered to be an offsetting factor to the result reached when future earnings are not reduced to present value."

Thus, the market interest rate was deemed to be offset by price inflation and all other sources of future wage increases.

In State v. Guinn, 555 P.2d 530 (Alaska 1976), the Beaulieu approach was refined slightly. In that case, the plaintiff had offered evidence of "small, automatic increases in the wage rate keyed to the employee's length of service with the company," and the trial court had included those increases in the estimated lost stream of future income but had not discounted. It held that this type of "certain and predictable" individual raise was not the type of wage increase that offsets the failure to discount to present value. Thus, the market interest rate was deemed to be offset by price inflation, societal sources of wage inflation, and individual sources of wage inflation that are not "certain and predictable."

duced by netting out the two effects and discounting by the difference.

Kaczkowski v. Bolubasz, 491 Pa. 561, 421 A.2d 1027 (1980), took still a third approach. The Pennsylvania Supreme Court followed the approach of the District Court in *Feldman,* supra, and the Court of Appeals for the Fifth Circuit in Higginbotham v. Mobil Oil Corp., 545 F.2d 422 (C.A.5 1977), in concluding that the plaintiff could introduce all manner of evidence bearing on likely sources—both individual and societal—of future wage growth, except for predictions of price inflation. However, it rejected those courts' conclusion that the resulting estimated lost stream of future income should be discounted by a "real interest rate." Rather, it deemed the market interest rate to be offset by future price inflation.

The litigants and the amici in this case urge us to select one of the many rules that have been proposed and establish it for all time as the exclusive method in all federal trials for calculating an award for lost earnings in an inflationary economy. We are not persuaded, however, that such an approach is warranted. For our review of the foregoing cases leads us to draw three conclusions. First, by its very nature the calculation of an award for lost earnings must be a rough approximation. Because the lost stream can never be predicted with complete confidence, any lump sum represents only a "rough and ready" effort to put the plaintiff in the position he would have been in had he not been injured. Second, sustained price inflation can make the award substantially less precise. Inflation's current magnitude and unpredictability create a substantial risk that the damage award will prove to have little relation to the lost wages it purports to replace. Third, the question of lost earnings can arise in many different contexts. In some sectors of the economy, it is far easier to assemble evidence of an individual's most likely career path than in others.

These conclusions all counsel hesitation. Having surveyed the multitude of options available, we will do no more than is necessary to resolve the case before us. We limit our attention to suits under § 5(b) of the Act, noting that Congress has provided generally for an award of damages but has not given specific guidance regarding how they are to be calculated. Within that narrow context, we shall define the general boundaries within which a particular award will be considered legally acceptable.

III

. . . .

In calculating an award for a longshoreman's lost earnings caused by the negligence of a vessel, the discount rate should be chosen on the basis of the factors that are used to estimate the lost stream of future earnings. If the trier of fact relies on a specific forecast of the future rate of price inflation, and if the estimated lost stream of future earnings is calculated to include price inflation along with individual factors and other societal factors, then the proper discount rate would be the after-tax market interest rate. But since specific forecasts of future price inflation remain too unreliable to be useful in many cases, it will normally be a costly and ultimately unproductive waste of longshoremen's resources to make such forecasts the centerpiece of litigation under § 5(b). As Judge Newman has warned: "The average accident trial should not be converted into a graduate seminar on economic forecasting." For that reason, both plaintiffs and trial courts should be discouraged from pursuing that approach.

On the other hand, if forecasts of future price inflation are not used, it is necessary to choose an appropriate below-market discount rate. As long as inflation continues, one must ask how much should be "offset" against the market rate. Once again, that amount should be chosen on the basis of the same factors that are used to estimate the lost stream of future earnings. If full account is taken of the individual and societal factors (excepting price inflation) that can be expected to have resulted in wage increases, then all that should be set off against the market interest rate is an estimate of future price inflation. This would result in one of the "real interest rate" approaches described above. Although we find the economic evidence distinctly inconclusive regarding an essential premise of those approaches,[30] we do not believe a trial court adopting such an approach in a suit under § 5(b) should be reversed if it adopts a rate between 1 and 3% and explains its choice.

There may be a sound economic argument for even further setoffs. In 1976, Professor Carlson of the Purdue University Economics Department wrote an article in the American Bar Association Journal contending that in the long run the societal factors excepting price inflation—largely productivity gains—match (or even slightly exceed) the "real interest rate." Carlson, Economic Analysis v Courtroom Controversy, 62 ABAJ 628 (1976). He thus recommended that the estimated lost stream of future wages be calculated without considering either price inflation or societal productivity gains. All that would be considered would be individual seniority and promotion gains. If this were done, he concluded that the entire market interest rate, including both inflation and the real interest rate, would be more than adequately offset.

Although such an approach has the virtue of simplicity and may even be economically precise, we cannot at this time agree with the Court of Appeals for the Third Circuit that its use is mandatory in the federal courts. Naturally, Congress could require it if it chose to do so. And nothing prevents parties interested in keeping litigation costs under control from stipulating to its use before trial. But we are not prepared to impose it on unwilling litigants, for we have not been given sufficient data to judge how closely the national patterns of wage growth are likely to reflect the patterns within any given industry. The legislative branch of the Federal Government is far better equipped than we are to perform a comprehensive economic analysis and to fashion the proper general rule.

As a result, the judgment below must be set aside. In performing its damages calculation, the trial court applied the theory of *Kaczkowski* as a mandatory federal rule of decision, even though the petitioner had insisted that if compensation was to be awarded, it "must be reduced to its present worth." Moreover, this approach seems to have colored the trial court's evaluation of the relevant evidence. At one point, the court noted that respondent had offered a computation of his estimated wages from the date of the accident until his presumed date of retirement, including projected cost-of-living adjustments. It stated, "We do not disagree with these projec-

---

30. The key premise is that the real interest rate is stable over time. See n 25, supra. It is obviously not perfectly stable, but whether it is even relatively stable is hotly disputed among economists....

tions, but feel they are inappropriate in view of the holding in *Kacz-kowski*." Later in its opinion, however, the court declared, "We do not believe that there was sufficient evidence to establish a basis for estimating increased future productivity for the plaintiff, and therefore we will not inject such a factor in this award."

On remand, the decision on whether to reopen the record should be left to the sound discretion of the trial court. It bears mention that the present record already gives reason to believe a fair award may be more confidently expected in this case than in many. The employment practices in the longshoring industry appear relatively stable and predictable. The parties seem to have had no difficulty in arriving at the period of respondent's future work expectancy, or in predicting the character of the work that he would have been performing during that entire period if he had not been injured. Moreover, the record discloses that respondent's wages were determined by a collective-bargaining agreement that explicitly provided for "cost of living" increases, and that recent company history also included a "general" increase and a "job class increment increase." Although the trial court deemed the latter increases irrelevant during its first review because it felt legally compelled to assume they would offset any real interest rate, further study of them on remand will allow the court to determine whether that assumption should be made in this case.

IV

We do not suggest that the trial judge should embark on a search for "delusive exactness." It is perfectly obvious that the most detailed inquiry can at best produce an approximate result. And one cannot ignore the fact that in many instances the award for impaired earning capacity may be overshadowed by a highly impressionistic award for pain and suffering. But we are satisfied that whatever rate the District Court may choose to discount the estimated stream of future earnings, it must make a deliberate choice, rather than assuming that it is bound by a rule of state law.

The judgment of the Court of Appeals is vacated and the case is remanded for further proceedings consistent with this opinion.

It is so ordered.

NOTE

The Supreme Court clarified in Monessen Southwestern Railway Company v. Morgan, 486 U.S. 330, 108 S.Ct. 1837, 100 L.Ed.2d 349 (1988), that the trier of fact determines the appropriate present value discount rate to be applied to a damage award, and that it was error for the trial judge to instruct the jury that a zero discount rate was to be applied as a matter of law to the measure of future damages.

Helfend v. Southern California Rapid Transit District

Supreme Court of California, 1970.
2 Cal.3d 1, 84 Cal.Rptr. 173, 465 P.2d 61.

■ TOBRINER, A.C.J. Defendants appeal from a judgment of the Los Angeles Superior Court entered on a verdict in favor of plaintiff, Julius J. Helfend, for $16,400 in general and special damages for injuries sustained in a bus-auto collision that occurred on July 19, 1965, in the City of Los Angeles.

We have concluded that the judgment for plaintiff in this tort action against the defendant governmental entity should be affirmed. The trial court properly followed the collateral source rule in excluding evidence that a portion of plaintiff's medical bills had been paid through a medical insurance plan that requires the refund of benefits from tort recoveries.

1. *The facts.*

. . . .

Plaintiff filed a tort action against the Southern California Rapid Transit District, a public entity, and Mitchell, an employee of the transit district. At trial plaintiff claimed slightly more than $2,700 in special damages, including $921 in doctor's bills, a $336.99 hospital bill, and about $45 for medicines. Defendant requested permission to show that about 80 percent of the plaintiff's hospital bill had been paid by plaintiff's Blue Cross insurance carrier and that some of his other medical expenses may have been paid by other insurance. The superior court thoroughly considered the then very recent case of City of Salinas v. Souza & McCue Construction Company (1967) 66 Cal.2d 217, 57 Cal.Rptr. 337, 424 P.2d 921, distinguished the *Souza* case on the ground that *Souza* involved a contract setting, and concluded that the judgment should not be reduced to the extent of the amount of insurance payments which plaintiff received. The court ruled that defendants should not be permitted to show that plaintiff had received medical coverage from any collateral source.

. . . .

We must decide whether the collateral source rule applies to tort actions involving public entities and public employees in which the plaintiff has received benefits from his medical insurance coverage.

2. *The collateral source rule.*

The Supreme Court of California has long adhered to the doctrine that if an injured party receives some compensation for his injuries from a source wholly independent of the tortfeasor, such payment should not be deducted from the damages which the plaintiff would otherwise collect from the tortfeasor. As recently as August 1968 we unanimously reaffirmed our adherence to this doctrine, which is known as the "collateral source rule."

Although the collateral source rule remains generally accepted in the United States, nevertheless many other jurisdictions have restricted[5] or

---

5. The New York Court of Appeals has, for example, quite reasonably held that an injured physician may not recover from a tortfeasor for the value of medical and nursing care rendered gratuitously as a matter of professional courtesy. The doctor owed at least a moral obligation to render gratuitous services in return, if ever required; but he had neither paid premiums for the services under some form of insurance coverage nor manifested any indication that he would endeavor to repay those who had given him assistance. Thus this situation differs from that in which friends and relatives render assistance to the injured plaintiff with the expectation of repayment out of any tort re-

repealed it. In this country most commentators have criticized the rule and called for its early demise. In *Souza* we took note of the academic criticism of the rule, characterized the rule as "punitive," and held it inapplicable to the governmental entity involved in that case.

We must, however, review the particular facts of *Souza* in order to determine whether it applies to the present case. The City of Salinas brought suit against Souza & McCue Construction Company, a public works contractor, and its pipe supplier for breach of a contract to construct a sewer pipe line. Souza cross-complained against the city, alleging fraudulent misrepresentation and breach of implied warranty of site conditions; and against the pipe supplier, alleging a guarantee of performance of the piping and a promise to indemnify Souza for any losses. The trial court found that the city materially misrepresented soil conditions by failing to inform Souza of unstable conditions known to the city, that with the city's knowledge Souza relied upon the misrepresentations in bidding, and that Souza should recover damages proximately caused by the city's fraudulent breach.

We held that the trial court improperly determined damages against the city by refusing to allow the city to show that the supplier had recompensed Souza for some of the damages caused by the city's breach. In this contract setting in which the supplier did not constitute a wholly independent collateral source,[7] we held that the collateral source rule cannot be applied against public entities because the collateral source rule appears punitive in nature and punitive damages cannot be imposed on public entities.

Although *Souza's* reasoning as to punitive damages might appear to apply to private tortfeasors as well as public entities and to torts as well as contract actions, we did not there consider the collateral source rule in contexts different from the specific contractual setting and particular relationship of the parties involved. We distinguish the present case from *Souza* on the ground that in *Souza* the plaintiff received payments from his subcontractor which, in the contractual setting of that case, did not constitute a truly independent source. Obviously, such a "source" differs entirely from the instant one, which derives from plaintiff's payment of insurance premiums. Here plaintiff received benefits from his medical insurance coverage only because he had long paid premiums to obtain

covery; in that case, the rule has been applied. On the other hand, New York has joined most states in holding that a tortfeasor may not mitigate damages by showing that an injured plaintiff would receive a disability pension. In these cases the plaintiff had actually or constructively paid for the pension by having received lower wages or by having contributed directly to the pension plan.

7. In Laurenzi v. Vranizan (1945) 25 Cal.2d 806, 155 P.2d 633, this court held that "payments by one tort-feasor on account of a harm for which he and another are each liable, diminish the amount of the claim against the other whether or not it was so agreed at the time of payment and whether the payment was made before or after judgment. Since the plaintiff can have but one satisfaction, evidence of such payments is admissible for the purpose of reducing *pro tanto* the amount of the damages he may be entitled to recover." Hence, the rule applies only to payments that come from a source entirely independent of the tortfeasor and does not apply to payments by joint tortfeasors or to benefits the plaintiff receives from a tortfeasor's insurance coverage.

them. Such an origin does constitute a completely independent source. Hence, although we reaffirm the holding in *Souza,* we do not believe that its reasoning either compels the abolition of the collateral source rule in all cases or requires an unwarranted exemption from the rule of public entities and their employees involved in tort actions. . . .

The collateral source rule as applied here embodies the venerable concept that a person who has invested years of insurance premiums to assure his medical care should receive the benefits of his thrift. The tortfeasor should not garner the benefits of his victim's providence.

The collateral source rule expresses a policy judgment in favor of encouraging citizens to purchase and maintain insurance for personal injuries and for other eventualities. Courts consider insurance a form of investment, the benefits of which become payable without respect to any other possible source of funds. If we were to permit a tortfeasor to mitigate damages with payments from plaintiff's insurance, plaintiff would be in a position inferior to that of having bought no insurance, because his payment of premiums would have earned no benefit. Defendant should not be able to avoid payment of full compensation for the injury inflicted merely because the victim has had the foresight to provide himself with insurance.

Some commentators object that the above approach to the collateral source rule provides plaintiff with a "double recovery," rewards him for the injury, and defeats the principle that damages should compensate the victim but not punish the tortfeasor. We agree with Professor Fleming's observation, however, that "double recovery is justified only in the face of some exceptional, supervening reason, as in the case of accident or life insurance, where it is felt unjust that the tortfeasor should take advantage of the thrift and prescience of the victim in having paid the premiums." (Fleming, Introduction to the Law of Torts (1967) p. 131.) As we point out infra, recovery in a wrongful death action is not defeated by the payment of the benefit on a life insurance policy.

Furthermore, insurance policies increasingly provide for either subrogation or refund of benefits upon a tort recovery, and such refund is indeed called for in the present case. Hence, the plaintiff receives no double recovery; the collateral source rule simply serves as a means of by-passing the antiquated doctrine of non-assignment of tortious actions and permits a proper transfer of risk from the plaintiff's insurer to the tortfeasor by way of the victim's tort recovery. The double shift from the tortfeasor to the victim and then from the victim to his insurance carrier can normally occur with little cost in that the insurance carrier is often intimately involved in the initial litigation and quite automatically receives its part of the tort settlement or verdict.

Even in cases in which the contract or the law precludes subrogation or refund of benefits,[17] or in situations in which the collateral source waives

---

17. "Certain insurance benefits are regarded as the proceeds of an investment rather than as an indemnity for damages. Thus it has been held that the proceeds of a life insurance contract made for a fixed sum rather than for the damages caused by the death of the insured are proceeds of an investment and can be received independently of the claim for damages against the person who caused the death of the insured. The

such subrogation or refund, the rule performs entirely necessary functions in the computation of damages. For example, the cost of medical care often provides both attorneys and juries in tort cases with an important measure for assessing the plaintiff's general damages. To permit the defendant to tell the jury that the plaintiff has been recompensed by a collateral source for his medical costs might irretrievably upset the complex, delicate, and somewhat indefinable calculations which result in the normal jury verdict.

We also note that generally the jury is not informed that plaintiff's attorney will receive a large portion of the plaintiff's recovery in contingent fees or that personal injury damages are not taxable to the plaintiff and are normally deductible by the defendant. Hence, the plaintiff rarely actually receives full compensation for his injuries as computed by the jury. The collateral source rule partially serves to compensate for the attorney's share and does not actually render "double recovery" for the plaintiff. Indeed, many jurisdictions that have abolished or limited the collateral source rule have also established a means for assessing the plaintiff's costs for counsel directly against the defendant rather than imposing the contingent fee system. In sum, the plaintiff's recovery for his medical expenses from both the tortfeasor and his medical insurance program will not usually give him "double recovery," but partially provides a somewhat closer approximation to full compensation for his injuries.

If we consider the collateral source rule as applied here in the context of the entire American approach to the law of torts and damages, we find that the rule presently performs a number of legitimate and even indispensible functions. Without a thorough revolution in the American approach to torts and the consequent damages, the rule at least with respect to medical insurance benefits has become so integrated within our present system that its precipitous judicial nullification would work hardship. In this case the collateral source rule lies between two systems for the compensation of accident victims: the traditional tort recovery based on fault and the increasingly prevalent coverage based on non-fault insurance. Neither system possesses such universality of coverage or completeness of compensation that we can easily dispense with the collateral source rule's approach to meshing the two systems. The reforms which many academicians propose cannot easily be achieved through piecemeal common law development; the proposed changes, if desirable, would be more effectively accomplished through legislative reform. In any case, we cannot believe that the judicial repeal of the collateral source rule, as applied in the present case, would be the place to begin the needed changes.

same rule has been held applicable to accident insurance contracts. As to both kinds of insurance it has been stated: 'Such a policy is an investment contract giving the owner or beneficiary an absolute right, independent of the right against any third person responsible for the injury covered by the policy.' ... An insurer who fully compensates the insured, however, is subrogated to the rights of the insured against [or may receive a refund of benefits from] one who insured his property if the insurance was for the protection of the property of the insured, and was therefore an indemnity contract. In such cases subrogation [or refund of benefits] is the means by which double recovery by the owner is prevented and the ultimate burden shifted to the wrongdoer where it belongs...."

. . . .

Although in the special circumstances of *Souza* we characterized the collateral source rule as "punitive" in nature, we have pointed out the several legitimate and fully justified compensatory functions of the rule. In fact, if the collateral source rule were actually punitive, it could apply only in cases of oppression, fraud, or malice and would be inapplicable to most tort, and almost all negligence, cases regardless of whether a governmental entity were involved. We therefore reaffirm our adherence to the collateral source rule in tort cases in which the plaintiff has been compensated by an independent collateral source—such as insurance, pension, continued wages, or disability payments—for which he had actually or constructively paid or in cases in which the collateral source would be recompensed from the tort recovery through subrogation, refund of benefits, or some other arrangement. Hence, we conclude that in a case in which a tort victim has received partial compensation from medical insurance coverage entirely independent of the tortfeasor the trial court properly followed the collateral source rule and foreclosed defendant from mitigating damages by means of the collateral payments.

3.   *The collateral source rule, public entities, and public employees.*

Having concluded that the collateral source rule is not simply punitive in nature, we hold, for the reasons set out infra, that the rule as delineated here applies to governmental entities as well as to all other tortfeasors. We must therefore disapprove of any indications to the contrary in City of Salinas v. Souza & McCue Constr. Co.

Defendants would have this court create a special form of sovereign immunity as a novel exception to the collateral source rule for tortfeasors who are public entities or public employees. We see no justification for such special treatment. In the present case the nullification of the collateral source rule would simply frustrate the transfer of the medical costs from the medical insurance carrier, Blue Cross, to the public entity. The public entity or its insurance carrier is in at least as advantageous a position to spread the risk of loss as is the plaintiff's medical insurance carrier. To deprive Blue Cross of repayment for its expenditures on plaintiff's behalf merely because he was injured by a public entity rather than a private individual would constitute an unwarranted and arbitrary discrimination.

Furthermore, if we were to follow without careful analysis the *Souza* characterization of the collateral source rule as punitive in nature, we would immediately face a dilemma as to the proper treatment of the public employee's liability. In order to encourage public employees to perform their duties without the threat of untoward personal liability, we held in Johnson v. State of California (1968) 69 Cal.2d 782, 73 Cal.Rptr. 240, 447 P.2d 352, that a public entity must . . . indemnify and defend its employees against civil liability, except in cases of conduct outside the scope of employment or acts performed with actual fraud, corruption, or malice.

If we were to conclude that the collateral source rule cannot apply to public entities, we would be forced to reach one of three equally implausible results: (1) Since the public entity is immune from the rule and enjoys a deduction in damages, but the driver possesses no such immunity, the driver must bear the cost of the extra damages equivalent to the collateral source increment, despite our rule in *Johnson.* (2) Since the public entity is immune from the rule and enjoys a deduction in damages, the driver would initially bear the cost of the extra damages equivalent to the collateral source increment, but under *Johnson* he would be indemnified by the public entity for all the plaintiff's tort recovery. Hence, by suing both the public entity and the public employee the plaintiff can bypass the purported *Souza* rule through the *Johnson* decision. (3) Finally, since the public entity is immune from the rule and enjoys a deduction in damages, the only way to avoid untoward personal liability for the driver under *Johnson* would be for this court to extend the collateral source rule immunity from the public entity to the public employee.

The first alternative would patently conflict with this court's approach to the civil liability of public employees in *Johnson....*

The second alternative would mechanically follow the rules established in *Johnson* and *Souza,* but would totally undermine the effect of *Souza* by indirectly imposing the rule upon the public entity by means of the indemnification process....

The third approach would extend the collateral source rule immunity from the public entity to its employees and increase the unjustified discrimination against tort victims who happen to be injured by public entities rather than private individuals....

In view of the several legitimate and important functions of the collateral source rule in our present approach to the law of torts and damages, we find no appropriate justification for labelling the rule "punitive" or for not applying it to public entities and public employees ...

4. *The trial court properly refused to permit the defendant to inquire whether plaintiff had been compensated by a collateral source in the absence of some allegation that such information bears a proper relationship to the issues in the case.*

. . . .

The judgment is affirmed.

Norfolk and Western Railway v. Liepelt

Supreme Court of the United States, 1980.
444 U.S. 490, 100 S.Ct. 755, 62 L.Ed.2d 689.

■ MR. JUSTICE STEVENS delivered the opinion of the Court.

In cases arising under the Federal Employers' Liability Act,[1] most trial judges refuse to allow the jury to receive evidence or instruction concerning the impact of federal income taxes on the amount of damages to be awarded. Because the prevailing practice developed at a time when federal taxes were relatively insignificant, and because some courts are now following a different practice, we decided to answer the two questions presented by the certiorari petition in this wrongful death action: (1) whether it was error to exclude evidence of the income taxes payable on the

---

1. 35 Stat 65, as amended, 45 USC
§§ 51 et seq.

decedent's past and estimated future earnings; and (2) whether it was error for the trial judge to refuse to instruct the jury that the award of damages would not be subject to income taxation.

In 1973 a fireman employed by petitioner suffered fatal injuries in a collision caused by petitioner's negligence. Respondent, as administratrix of the fireman's estate, brought suit under the FELA to recover the damages that his survivors suffered as a result of his death. In 1976, after a full trial in the Circuit Court of Cook County, the jury awarded respondent $775,000. On appeal, the Appellate Court of Illinois held that it was "not error to refuse to instruct a jury as to the nontaxability of an award" and also that it was "not error to exclude evidence of the effect of income taxes on future earnings of the decedent." The Illinois Supreme Court denied leave to appeal.

The evidence supporting the damage award included biographical data about the decedent and his family and the expert testimony of an economist. The decedent, a 37–year–old man, was living with his second wife and two young children and was contributing to the support of two older children by his first marriage. His gross earnings in the 11 months prior to his death on November 22, 1973 amounted to $11,988. Assuming continued employment, those earnings would have amounted to $16,828.26 in 1977.

The expert estimated that the decedent's earnings would have increased at a rate of approximately five percent per year, which would have amounted to $51,600 in the year 2000, the year of his expected retirement. The gross amount of those earnings, plus the value of the services he would have performed for his family, less the amounts the decedent would have spent upon himself, produced a total which, when discounted to present value at the time of trial, amounted to $302,000.

Petitioner objected to the use of gross earnings, without any deduction for income taxes, in respondent's expert's testimony and offered to prove through the testimony of its own expert, an actuary, that decedent's federal income taxes during the years 1973 through 2000 would have amounted to about $57,000. Taking that figure into account, and making different assumptions about the rate of future increases in salary and the calculation of the present value of future earnings, petitioner's expert computed the net pecuniary loss at $138,327. As already noted, the jury returned a verdict of $775,000.

Petitioner argues that the jury must have assumed that its award was subject to federal income taxation; otherwise, it is argued, the verdict would not have exceeded respondent's expert's opinion by such a large amount. For that reason, petitioner contends that it was prejudiced by the trial judge's refusal to instruct the jury that "your award will not be subject to any income taxes, and you should not consider such taxes in fixing the amount of your award."

Whether it was error to refuse that instruction, as well as the question whether evidence concerning the federal taxes on the decedent's earnings was properly excluded, is a matter governed by federal law. . . .

I

In a wrongful death action under the FELA, the measure of recovery is "the damages ... [that] flow from the deprivation of the pecuniary benefits which the beneficiaries might have reasonably received...." The amount of money that a wage earner is able to contribute to the support of his family is unquestionably affected by the amount of the tax he must pay to the Federal Government. It is his after-tax income, rather than his gross income before taxes, that provides the only realistic measure of his ability to support his family. It follows inexorably that the wage earner's income tax is a relevant factor in calculating the monetary loss suffered by his dependents when he dies.

Although federal courts have consistently received evidence of the amount of the decedent's personal expenditures and have required that the estimate of future earnings be reduced by "taking account of the earning power of the money that is presently to be awarded," they have generally not considered the payment of income taxes as tantamount to a personal expenditure and have regarded the future prediction of tax consequences as too speculative and complex for a jury's deliberations.

Admittedly there are many variables that may affect the amount of a wage earner's future income tax liability. The law may change, his family may increase or decrease in size, his spouse's earnings may affect his tax bracket, and extra income or unforeseen deductions may become available. But future employment itself, future health, future personal expenditures, future interest rates, and future inflation are also matters of estimate and prediction. Any one of these issues might provide the basis for protracted expert testimony and debate. But the practical wisdom of the trial bar and the trial bench has developed effective methods of presenting the essential elements of an expert calculation in a form that is understandable by juries that are increasingly familiar with the complexities of modern life. We therefore reject the notion that the introduction of evidence describing a decedent's estimated after-tax earnings is too speculative or complex for a jury.

Respondent argues that if this door is opened, other equally relevant evidence must also be received. For example, she points out that in discounting the estimate of future earnings to its present value, the tax on the income to be earned by the damage award is now omitted. Logically, it would certainly seem correct that this amount, like future wages, should be estimated on an after-tax basis. But the fact that such an after-tax estimate, if offered in proper form, would also be admissible does not persuade us that it is wrong to use after-tax figures instead of gross earnings in projecting what the decedent's financial contributions to his survivors would have been had this tragic accident not occurred.

Respondent also argues that evidence concerning costs of litigation, including her attorneys' fees, is equally pertinent to a determination of what amount will actually compensate the survivors for their monetary loss. In a sense this is, of course, true. But the argument that attorneys' fees must be added to a plaintiff's recovery if the award is truly to make him whole is contrary to the generally applicable "American Rule." ... In any event, it surely is not proper for the Judiciary to ignore the demonstrably relevant factor of income tax in measuring damages in order to offset what may be perceived as an undesirable or unfair rule regarding attorney's fees.

II

Section 104(a)(2) of the Internal Revenue Code provides that the amount of any damages received on account of personal injuries is not taxable income. The section is construed to apply to wrongful death awards; they are not taxable income to the recipient.

Although the law is perfectly clear, it is entirely possible that the members of the jury may assume that a plaintiff's recovery in a case of this kind will be subject to federal taxation, and that the award should be increased substantially in order to be sure that the injured party is fully compensated. The Missouri Supreme Court expressed the opinion that "it is reasonable to assume that many jurors will believe [that its verdict will] be subject to such taxes." And Judge Aldisert, writing for the Third Circuit, agreed:

"We take judicial notice of the 'tax consciousness' of the American public. Yet, we also recognize, as did the court in Dempsey v. Thompson, 363 Mo. 339, 251 S.W.2d 42 (1952), that few members of the general public are aware of the special statutory exception for personal injury awards contained in the Internal Revenue Code.

" '[T]here is always danger that today's tax-conscious juries may assume (mistakenly of course) that the judgment will be taxable and therefore make their verdict big enough so that plaintiff would get what they think he deserves after the imaginary tax is taken out of it.'

"H. Harper & James, The Law of Torts § 25.12, at 1327–1328 (1956)."

A number of other commentators have also identified that risk.

In this case the respondents' expert witness computed the amount of pecuniary loss at $302,000, plus the value of the care and training that decedent would have provided to his young children; the jury awarded damages of $775,000. It is surely not fanciful to suppose that the jury erroneously believed that a large portion of the award would be payable to the Federal Government in taxes and that therefore it improperly inflated the recovery. Whether or not this speculation is accurate, we agree with petitioner that, as Judge Ely wrote for the Ninth Circuit,

"[t]o put the matter simply, giving the instruction can do no harm, and it can certainly help by preventing the jury from inflating the award and thus overcompensating the plaintiff on the basis of an erroneous assumption that the judgment will be taxable."

We hold that it was error to refuse the requested instruction in this case. That instruction was brief and could easily be understood. It would not complicate the trial by making additional qualifying or supplemental instructions necessary. It would not be prejudicial to either party, but would merely eliminate an area of doubt or speculation that might have an improper impact on the computation of the amount of damages.

The judgment is reversed and the case is remanded to the Appellate Court of Illinois for further proceedings consistent with this opinion.

It is so ordered.

■ MR. JUSTICE BLACKMUN, with whom MR. JUSTICE MARSHALL joins, dissenting.

. . . .

. . . In my view, by mandating adjustment of the award by way of reduction for federal income taxes that would have been paid by the decedent on his earnings, the Court appropriates for the tortfeasor a benefit intended to be conferred on the victim or his survivors. And in requiring that the jury be instructed that a wrongful-death award is not subject to federal income tax, the Court opens the door for a variety of admonitions to the jury not to "misbehave," and unnecessarily interjects what is now to be federal law into the administration of a trial in a state court.

. . . .

I

The employer-petitioner argues, and the Court holds, that federal income taxes that would have been paid by the deceased victim must be subtracted in computing the amount of the wrongful-death award. Were one able to ignore and set aside the uncertainties, estimates, assumptions and complexities involved in computing and effectuating that subtraction, this might not be an unreasonable legislative proposition in a compensatory tort system. Neither petitioner nor the Court, however, recognizes that the premise of such an argument is the nontaxability, under the Internal Revenue Code, of the wrongful-death award itself.

By not taxing the award, Congress has bestowed a benefit. Although the parties disagree over the origin of the tax-free status of the wrongful-death award, it is surely clear that the lost earnings could be taxed as income. . . .

While Congress has not articulated its reasons for not taxing a wrongful-death award, it is highly unlikely that it intended to confer this benefit on the tortfeasor. Two more probable purposes for the exclusion are apparent. First, taxing the award could involve the same uncertainties and complexities noted by respondent and the majority of the courts of this country as a reason for not taking income taxes into account in computing the award. Congress may have decided that it is simply not worthwhile to enact a complex and administratively burdensome system in order to approximate the tax treatment of the income if, in fact, it had been earned over a period of time by the decedent. Second, Congress may have intended to confer a humanitarian benefit on the victim or victims of the tort. . . .

Whichever of these concerns it was that motivated Congress, transfer of the tax benefit to the FELA tortfeasor-defendant is inconsistent with that purpose. If Congress felt that it was not worth the effort to estimate the decedent's prospective tax liability on behalf of the public fisc, it is unlikely that it would want to require this effort on behalf of the tortfeasor. And Congress would not confer a humanitarian benefit on tort victims or their survivors in the Internal Revenue Code, only to take it away from victims or their survivors covered by the FELA. I conclude, therefore, that any income tax effect on lost earnings should not be considered in the computation of a damages award under the FELA.

II

. . . .

The required instruction is purely cautionary in nature. It does not affect the determination of liability or the measure of damages. It does nothing more than call a basically irrelevant factor to the jury's attention, and then directs the jury to forget that matter. Even if federal law governed such an admonition to the jury not to misbehave, the instruction required by the Court seems to me to be both unwise and unjustified, and almost an affront to the practical wisdom of the jury.

It also is "entirely possible" that the jury "may" increase its damages award in the belief that the defendant is insured, or that the plaintiff will be obligated for substantial attorney's fees, or that the award is subject to state (as well as federal) income tax, or on the basis of any number of other extraneous factors. Charging the jury about every conceivable matter as to which it should not misbehave or miscalculate would be burdensome and could be confusing. Yet the Court's decision today opens the door to that possibility. There certainly is no evidence in this record to indicate that the jury is any more likely to act upon an erroneous assumption about an award's being subject to federal income tax than about any other collateral matter. Although the Court suggests that the difference in the expert's estimation of the pecuniary loss and the total amount of the award represents inflation of the award for federal income taxes, this is pure surmise. The jury was instructed that it could compensate for factors on which experts could not place a precise dollar value, and it is "entirely possible" that these, instead, were the basis of the award.

. . . .

NOTES ON TAX EXEMPTIONS

1. The Allens' son committed suicide while he was a patient in a psychiatric hospital. The parents sued the hospital, claiming that its negligence led to his death. Their $270,000 judgment was then affirmed on appeal. Psychiatric Institute of Washington v. Allen, 509 A.2d 619 (D.C.App.1986). The appeals court gave this response to the Institute's argument that the trial court's failure to give a tax exemption instruction was reversible error:

Because the *Liepelt* case arose under the FELA, the Supreme Court's opinion is not controlling in this case, an action brought under the District of Columbia wrongful death and survival statutes. This court has never been called upon to decide whether such an instruction should be given in any case. A majority of the state courts that have addressed the issue have held that the instruction need not be given, particularly when the court instructs the jury to confine itself to the evidence and not to award any damages that are speculative or remote. In fact, several courts have held that the instruction is not only unnecessary but improper.

Nevertheless, we find the Court's opinion in *Liepelt* persuasive, and accordingly we hold that in any case in which trial begins on or after the date of this opinion, the trial court should, upon request, instruct the jury that any damage award will not be subject to income taxation. Such an instruction, as the Supreme Court said, will "eliminate an area of doubt or speculation that might have an improper impact on the computation of the amount of damages." In the case at bar, however, . . . the court's refusal to give the instruction requested by the Institute was not prejudicial and does not warrant reversal.

2. In Otis Elevator Co. v. Reid, 101 Nev. 515, 706 P.2d 1378 (1985), the court made the following observations with respect to the propriety of tax exemption instructions under state law:

Jurisdictions which have considered the propriety of these instructions are divided into three groups. The majority prohibit tax instructions under any circumstances. The minority view, exemplified by the United States Supreme Court decision in Norfolk & Western R. Co. v. Liepelt, 444 U.S. 490, 100 S.Ct. 755, 62 L.Ed.2d 689 (1980), requires trial courts to give the instruction upon request of counsel. In a few jurisdictions, the instruction may be given at the discretion of trial court.

In determining whether a tax exemption instruction is appropriate under the latter rule, other jurisdictions have focused on whether the jury has been exposed to the issue of taxes during trial, either by the evidence or by comments by counsel. We conclude that tax exemption instructions are appropriate only as curative devices designed to eliminate any prejudice resulting from the jury's exposure to tax-related issues at trial.

NOTES ON REMITTITUR AND ADDITUR

1. Remittitur is a procedural device for limiting excessive damage awards. Additur is the analogous means of increasing awards which are held to be unacceptably low. Neither is applicable only to tort suits.

When a court decides that a damage award is not sustainable, these remedies allow the plaintiff (or defendant) to avoid a new trial by accepting a reduction (or increase) in the verdict. The result is the replacement of a jury determination of damages with a verdict acceptable to the court. For this reason, the Supreme Court has ruled that the seventh amendment bars the use of additur in the federal courts. Dimick v. Schiedt, 293 U.S. 474, 55 S.Ct. 296, 79 L.Ed. 603 (1935). Federal remittitur is permissible but plaintiff will have the option of a new jury trial on damages because the seventh amendment precludes the court from simply entering judgment for the lower amount. Hetzel v. Prince William County, 523 U.S. 208, 118 S.Ct. 1210 (1998)

2. California's Medical Injury Compensation Reform Act of 1975 (MICRA) limited "the amount of damages for noneconomic losses" to $250,000 and modified the collateral source rule to allow the use of evidence that the plaintiff received collateral source benefits (and the

amount plaintiff had paid to secure them). By a 4–3 vote, the California Supreme Court held these provisions to be rationally related to the state's legitimate interest in preserving affordable access to treatment by insured doctors, and therefore immune from challenge under the Due Process and Equal Protection Clauses of the United States Constitution. Fein v. Permanente Medical Group, 38 Cal.3d 137, 211 Cal.Rptr. 368, 695 P.2d 665 (1985).

Applying a "middle-tier" scrutiny test under its state's equal protection clause, the New Hampshire Supreme Court struck down two similar provisions in Carson v. Maurer, 120 N.H. 925, 424 A.2d 825 (1980). In Smith v. Department of Insurance, 507 So.2d 1080 (Fla.1987), the Florida Supreme Court held a state law limiting damages for noneconomic losses in tort actions generally to $450,000 to be unconstitutional by virtue of the state's constitutional guarantee that "[t]he courts shall be open to every person for redress of any injury."

C.   NOMINAL DAMAGES

Carey v. Piphus

Supreme Court of the United States, 1978.
435 U.S. 247, 98 S.Ct. 1042, 55 L.Ed.2d 252.

■ MR. JUSTICE POWELL delivered the opinion of the Court.

In this case, brought under 42 U.S.C. § 1983, we consider the elements and prerequisites for recovery of damages by students who were suspended from public elementary and secondary schools without procedural due process. The Court of Appeals for the Seventh Circuit held that the students are entitled to recover substantial nonpunitive damages even if their suspensions were justified, and even if they do not prove that any other actual injury was caused by the denial of procedural due process. We disagree, and hold that in the absence of proof of actual injury, the students are entitled to recover only nominal damages.

I

Respondent Jarius Piphus was a freshman at Chicago Vocational High School during the 1973–1974 school year. On January 23, 1974, during school hours, the school principal saw Piphus and another student standing outdoors on school property passing back and forth what the principal described as an irregularly shaped cigarette. The principal approached the students unnoticed and smelled what he believed was the strong odor of burning marihuana. He also saw Piphus try to pass a packet of cigarette papers to the other student. When the students became aware of the principal's presence, they threw the cigarette into a nearby hedge.

The principal took the students to the school's disciplinary office and directed the assistant principal to impose the "usual" 20–day suspension for violation of the school rule against the use of drugs. The students protested that they had not been smoking marihuana, but to no avail. Piphus was allowed to remain at school, although not in class, for the remainder of the school day while the assistant principal tried, without success, to reach his mother.

A suspension notice was sent to Piphus' mother, and a few days later two meetings were arranged among Piphus, his mother, his sister, school officials, and representatives from a legal aid clinic. The purpose of the meetings was not to determine whether Piphus had been smoking marihuana, but rather to explain the reasons for the suspension. Following an unfruitful exchange of views, Piphus and his mother, as guardian *ad litem*, filed suit against petitioners in Federal District Court under 42 U.S.C. § 1983 and its jurisdictional counterpart, 28 U.S.C. § 1343, charging that Piphus had been suspended without due process of law in violation of the Fourteenth Amendment. The complaint sought declaratory and injunctive relief, together with actual and punitive damages in the amount of $3,000. Piphus was readmitted to school under a temporary restraining order after eight days of his suspension.

Respondent Silas Brisco was in the sixth grade at Clara Barton Elementary School in Chicago during the 1973–1974 school year. On September 11, 1973, Brisco came to school wearing one small earring. The previous school year the school principal had issued a rule against the wearing of earrings by male students because he believed that this practice denoted membership in certain street gangs and increased the likelihood that gang members would terrorize other students. Brisco was reminded of this rule, but he refused to remove the earring, asserting that it was a symbol of black pride, not of gang membership.

The assistant principal talked to Brisco's mother, advising her that her son would be suspended for 20 days if he did not remove the earring. Brisco's mother supported her son's position, and a 20–day suspension was imposed. Brisco and his mother, as guardian *ad litem*, filed suit in Federal District Court under 42 U.S.C. § 1983 and 28 U.S.C. § 1343, charging that Brisco had been suspended without due process of law in violation of the Fourteenth Amendment. The complaint sought declaratory and injunctive relief, together with actual and punitive damages in the amount of $5,000. Brisco was readmitted to school during the pendency of proceedings for a preliminary injunction after 17 days of his suspension.

Piphus' and Brisco's cases were consolidated for trial and submitted on stipulated records. The District Court held that both students had been suspended without procedural due process. It also held that petitioners were not entitled to qualified immunity from damages ... because they "should have known that a lengthy suspension without any adjudicative hearing of any type" would violate procedural due process. Despite these holdings, the District Court declined to award damages because:

> Plaintiffs put no evidence in the record to qualify their damages, and the record is completely devoid of any evidence which could even form the basis of a speculative inference measuring the extent of their injuries. Plaintiffs' claims for damages therefore fail for complete lack of proof.

The court also stated that the students were entitled to declaratory relief and to deletion of the suspensions from their school records, but for reasons that are not apparent the court failed to enter an order to that effect. Instead, it simply dismissed the complaints. No finding was made as to whether respondents would have been suspended if they had received procedural due process.

On respondents' appeal, the Court of Appeals reversed and remanded. It first held that the District Court erred in not granting declaratory and injunctive relief. It also held that the District Court should have considered evidence submitted by respondents after judgment that tended to prove the pecuniary value of each day of school that they missed while suspended. The court said, however, that respondents would not be entitled to recover damages representing the value of missed school time if petitioners showed on remand "that there was just cause for the suspension[s] and that therefore [respondents] would have been suspended even if a proper hearing had been held."

Finally, the Court of Appeals held that even if the District Court found on remand that respondents' suspensions were justified, they would be entitled to recover substantial "nonpunitive" damages simply because they had been denied procedural due process.... We granted certiorari to consider whether, in an action under § 1983 for the deprivation of procedural due process, a plaintiff must prove that he actually was injured by the deprivation before he may recover substantial "nonpunitive" damages.

II

Title 42 U.S.C. § 1983, derived from § 1 of the Civil Rights Act of 1871, provides:

> Every person who, under color of any statute, ordinance, regulation, custom, or usage, of any State or Territory, subjects, or causes to be subjected, any citizen of the United States or other person within the jurisdiction thereof to the deprivation of any rights, privileges, or immunities secured by the Constitution and laws, shall be liable to the party injured in an action at law, suit in equity, or other proper proceeding for redress.

The legislative history of § 1983, elsewhere detailed, demonstrates that it was intended to "[create] a species of tort liability" in favor of persons who are deprived of "rights, privileges, or immunities secured" to them by the Constitution.

Petitioners contend that the elements and prerequisites for recovery of damages under this "species of tort liability" should parallel those for recovery of damages under the common law of torts. In particular, they urge that the purpose of an award of damages under § 1983 should be to compensate persons for injuries that are caused by the deprivation of constitutional rights; and, further, that plaintiffs should be required to prove not only that their rights were violated, but also that injury was caused by the violation, in order to recover substantial damages. Unless respondents prove that they actually were injured by the deprivation of procedural due process, petitioners argue, they are entitled at most to nominal damages.

Respondents seem to make two different arguments in support of the holding below. First, they contend that substantial damages should be awarded under § 1983 for the deprivation of a constitutional right *whether or not* any injury was caused by the deprivation. This, they say, is appropriate both because constitutional rights are valuable in and of themselves, and because of the need to deter violations of constitutional rights. Respondents believe that this view reflects accurately that of the Congress that enacted § 1983. Second, respondents argue that even if the purpose of a § 1983 damages award is, as petitioners contend, primarily to compensate persons for injuries that are caused by the deprivation of constitutional rights, every deprivation of procedural due process may be *presumed* to cause some injury. This presumption, they say, should relieve them from the necessity of proving that injury actually was caused.

A

Insofar as petitioners contend that the basic purpose of a § 1983 damages award should be to compensate persons for injuries caused by the deprivation of constitutional rights, they have the better of the argument. Rights, constitutional and otherwise, do not exist in a vacuum. Their purpose is to protect persons from injuries to particular interests, and their contours are shaped by the interests they protect.

Our legal system's concept of damages reflects this view of legal rights. "The cardinal principle of damages in Anglo–American law is that of *compensation* for the injury caused to plaintiff by defendant's breach of duty." 2 F. Harper & F. James, Law of Torts § 25.1, p. 1299 (1956) (emphasis in original). The Court implicitly has recognized the applicability of this principle to actions under § 1983 by stating that damages are available under that section for actions "found ... to have been violative of ... constitutional rights *and to have caused compensable injury....*" The lower federal courts appear generally to agree that damages awards under § 1983 should be determined by the compensation principle.

The Members of the Congress that enacted § 1983 did not address directly the question of damages, but the principle that damages are designed to compensate persons for injuries caused by the deprivation of rights hardly could have been foreign to the many lawyers in Congress in 1871.... To the extent that Congress intended that awards under § 1983 should deter the deprivation of constitutional rights, there is no evidence that it meant to establish a deterrent more formidable than that inherent in the award of compensatory damages.[11]

---

11. This is not to say that exemplary or punitive damages might not be awarded in a proper case under § 1983 with the specific purpose of deterring or punishing violations of constitutional rights. [citations omitted] Although we imply no approval or disapproval of any of these cases, we note that there is no basis for such an award in this case. The District Court specifically found that petitioners did not act with malicious intention to deprive respondents of their rights or to do them other injury, and the Court of Appeals approved only the award of "non-punitive" damages.

We also note that the potential liability of § 1983 defendants for attorney's fees, see

B

It is less difficult to conclude that damages awards under § 1983 should be governed by the principle of compensation than it is to apply this principle to concrete cases. But over the centuries the common law of torts has developed a set of rules to implement the principle that a person should be compensated fairly for injuries caused by the violation of his legal rights. These rules, defining the elements of damages and the prerequisites for their recovery, provide the appropriate starting point for the inquiry under § 1983 as well.

It is not clear, however, that common-law tort rules of damages will provide a complete solution to the damages issue in every § 1983 case. In some cases, the interests protected by a particular branch of the common law of torts may parallel closely the interests protected by a particular constitutional right. In such cases, it may be appropriate to apply the tort rules of damages directly to the § 1983 action. In other cases, the interests protected by a particular constitutional right may not also be protected by an analogous branch of the common law torts. In those cases, the task will be the more difficult one of adapting common-law rules of damages to provide fair compensation for injuries caused by the deprivation of a constitutional right.

Although this task of adaptation will be one of some delicacy—as this case demonstrates—it must be undertaken. The purpose of § 1983 would be defeated if injuries caused by the deprivation of constitutional rights went uncompensated simply because the common law does not recognize an analogous cause of action. In order to further the purpose of § 1983, the rules governing compensation for injuries caused by the deprivation of constitutional rights should be tailored to the interests protected by the particular right in question—just as the common-law rules of damages themselves were defined by the interests protected in the various branches of tort law. We agree with Mr. Justice Harlan that "the experience of judges in dealing with private [tort] claims supports the conclusion that courts of law are capable of making the types of judgment concerning causation and magnitude of injury necessary to accord meaningful compensation for invasion of [constitutional] rights." Bivens v. Six Unknown Fed. Narcotics Agents, supra, 403 U.S., at 409, 91 S.Ct., at 2011 (Harlan, J., concurring in judgment). With these principles in mind, we now turn to the problem of compensation in the case at hand.

C

The Due Process Clause of the Fourteenth Amendment provides:

"[N]or shall any State deprive any person of life, liberty, or property, without due process of law...."

This Clause "raises no impenetrable barrier to the taking of a person's possessions," or liberty, or life. Procedural due process rules are meant to

Civil Rights Attorney's Fees Awards Act of 1976, Pub.L. 94–559, 90 Stat. 2641, amending 42 U.S.C. § 1988, provides additional— and by no means inconsequential—assurance that agents of the State will not deliberately ignore due process rights. See also 18 U.S.C. § 242, the criminal counterpart of § 1983.

protect persons not from the deprivation, but from the mistaken or unjustified deprivation of life, liberty, or property . . .

In this case, the Court of Appeals held that if petitioners can prove on remand that "[respondents] would have been suspended even if a proper hearing had been held," then respondents will not be entitled to recover damages to compensate them for injuries caused by the suspensions. The court thought that in such a case, the failure to accord procedural due process could not properly be viewed as the cause of the suspensions. The court suggested that in such circumstances, an award of damages for injuries caused by the suspensions would constitute a windfall, rather than compensation, to respondents. We do not understand the parties to disagree with this conclusion. Nor do we.

The parties do disagree as to the further holding of the Court of Appeals that respondents are entitled to recover substantial—although unspecified—damages to compensate them for "the injury which is 'inherent in the nature of the wrong,' " even if their suspensions were justified and even if they fail to prove that the denial of procedural due process actually caused them some real, if intangible, injury. Respondents, elaborating on this theme, submit that the holding is correct because injury fairly may be "presumed" to flow from every denial of procedural due process. Their argument is that in addition to protecting against unjustified deprivations, the Due Process Clause also guarantees the "feeling of just treatment" by the government. They contend that the deprivation of protected interests without procedural due process, even where the premise for the deprivation is not erroneous, inevitably arouses strong feelings of mental and emotional distress in the individual who is denied this "feeling of just treatment." They analogize their case to that of defamation *per se,* in which "the plaintiff is relieved from the necessity of producing any proof whatsoever that he has been injured" in order to recover substantial compensatory damages.

Petitioners do not deny that a purpose of procedural due process is to convey to the individual a feeling that the government has dealt with him fairly, as well as to minimize the risk of mistaken deprivations of protected interests. They go so far as to concede that, in a proper case, persons in respondents' position might well recover damages for mental and emotional distress caused by the denial of procedural due process. Petitioners' argument is the more limited one that such injury cannot be presumed to occur, and that plaintiffs at least should be put to their proof on the issue, as plaintiffs are in most tort actions.

We agree with petitioners in this respect. As we have observed in another context, the doctrine of presumed damages in the common law of defamation *per se* "is an oddity of tort law, for it allows recovery of purportedly compensatory damages without evidence of actual loss." The doctrine has been defended on the grounds that those forms of defamation that are actionable *per se* are virtually certain to cause serious injury to reputation, and that this kind of injury is extremely difficult to prove. Moreover, statements that are defamatory *per se* by their very nature are likely to cause mental and emotional distress, as well as injury to reputation, so there arguably is little reason to require proof of this kind of injury either.[18] But these considerations do not support respondents' contention that damages should be presumed to flow from every deprivation of procedural due process.

First, it is not reasonable to assume that every departure from procedural due process, no matter what the circumstances or how minor, inherently is as likely to cause distress as the publication of defamation *per se* is to cause injury to reputation and distress. Where the deprivation of a protected interest is substantively justified but procedures are deficient in some respect, there may well be those who suffer no distress over the procedural irregularities. Indeed, in contrast to the immediately distressing effect of defamation *per se,* a person may not even know that procedures *were* deficient until he enlists the aid of counsel to challenge a perceived substantive deprivation.

Moreover, where a deprivation is justified but procedures are deficient, whatever distress a person feels may be attributable to the justified deprivation rather than to deficiencies in procedure. But as the Court of Appeals held, the injury caused by a justified deprivation, including distress, is not properly compensable under § 1983. This ambiguity in causation, which is absent in the case of defamation *per se,* provides additional need for requiring the plaintiff to convince the trier of fact that he actually suffered distress because of the denial of procedural due process itself.

Finally, we foresee no particular difficulty in producing evidence that mental and emotional distress actually was caused by the denial of procedural due process itself. Distress is a personal injury familiar to the law, customarily proved by showing the nature and circumstances of the wrong and its effect on the plaintiff. In sum, then, although mental and emotional distress caused by the denial of procedural due process itself is compensable under § 1983, we hold that neither the likelihood of such injury nor the difficulty of proving it is so great as to justify awarding compensatory damages without proof that such injury actually was caused.

. . . .

III

Even if respondents' suspensions were justified, and even if they did not suffer any other actual injury, the fact remains that they were deprived of their right to procedural due process. . . .

Common-law courts traditionally have vindicated deprivations of certain "absolute" rights that are not shown to have caused actual injury through the award of a nominal sum of money. By making the deprivation of such rights actionable for nominal damages without proof of actual injury, the law recognizes the importance to organized society that those rights be scrupulously observed; but at the same time, it remains true to the principle that substantial damages should be awarded only to compen-

---

18. The essence of libel *per se* is the publication in writing of false statements that tend to injure a person's reputation. The essence of slander *per se* is the publication by spoken words of false statements imputing to a person a criminal offense; a loathsome disease; matter affecting adversely a person's fitness for trade, business, or profession; or serious sexual misconduct.

sate actual injury or, in the case of exemplary or punitive damages, to deter or punish malicious deprivations of rights.

Because the right to procedural due process is "absolute" in the sense that it does not depend upon the merits of a claimant's substantive assertions, and because of the importance to organized society that procedural due process be observed, we believe that the denial of procedural due process should be actionable for nominal damages without proof of actual injury. We therefore hold that if, upon remand, the District Court determines that respondents' suspensions were justified, respondents nevertheless will be entitled to recover nominal damages not to exceed one dollar from petitioners.

The judgment of the Court of Appeals is reversed, and the case is remanded for further proceedings consistent with this opinion.

It is so ordered.

■ MR. JUSTICE MARSHALL concurs in the result.

■ MR. JUSTICE BLACKMUN took no part in the consideration or decision of this case.

Memphis Community School District v. Stachura

Supreme Court of the United States, 1986.
477 U.S. 299, 106 S.Ct. 2537, 91 L.Ed.2d 249.

■ JUSTICE POWELL delivered the opinion of the Court.

This case requires us to decide whether 42 U.S.C. § 1983 authorizes an award of compensatory damages based on the factfinder's assessment of the value or importance of a substantive constitutional right.

I

Respondent Edward Stachura is a tenured teacher in the Memphis, Michigan, public schools. When the events that led to this case occurred, respondent taught seventh-grade life science, using a textbook that had been approved by the School Board. The textbook included a chapter on human reproduction. During the 1978–1979 school year, respondent spent six weeks on this chapter. As part of their instruction, students were shown pictures of respondent's wife during her pregnancy. Respondent also showed the students two films concerning human growth and sexuality. These films were provided by the County Health Department, and the Principal of respondent's school had approved their use. Both films had been shown in past school years without incident.

After the showing of the pictures and the films, a number of parents complained to school officials about respondent's teaching methods. These complaints, which appear to have been based largely on inaccurate rumors about the allegedly sexually explicit nature of the pictures and films, were discussed at an open School Board meeting held on April 23, 1979. Following the advice of the School Superintendent, respondent did not attend the meeting, during which a number of parents expressed the view that respondent should not be allowed to teach in the Memphis school system. The day after the meeting, respondent was suspended with pay. The School Board later confirmed the suspension, and notified respondent that an "administration evaluation" of his teaching methods was underway. No such evaluation was ever made. Respondent was reinstated the next fall, after filing this lawsuit.

Respondent sued the School District, the Board of Education, various Board members and school administrators, and two parents who had participated in the April 23 School Board meeting. The complaint alleged that respondent's suspension deprived him of both liberty and property without due process of law and violated his First Amendment right to academic freedom. Respondent sought compensatory and punitive damages under 42 U.S.C. § 1983 for these constitutional violations.

At the close of trial on these claims, the District Court instructed the jury as to the law governing the asserted bases for liability. Turning to damages, the court instructed the jury that on finding liability it should award a sufficient amount to compensate respondent for the injury caused by petitioners' unlawful actions:

"You should consider in this regard any lost earnings; loss of earning capacity; out-of-pocket expenses; and any mental anguish or emotional distress that you find the Plaintiff to have suffered as a result of conduct by the Defendants depriving him of his civil rights."

In addition to this instruction on the standard elements of compensatory damages, the court explained that punitive damages could be awarded, and described the standards governing punitive awards. Finally, at respondent's request and over petitioners' objection, the court charged that damages also could be awarded based on the value or importance of the constitutional rights that were violated:

"If you find that the Plaintiff has been deprived of a Constitutional right, you may award damages to compensate him for the deprivation. Damages for this type of injury are more difficult to measure than damages for a physical injury or injury to one's property. There are no medical bills or other expenses by which you can judge how much compensation is appropriate. In one sense, no monetary value we place upon Constitutional rights can measure their importance in our society or compensate a citizen adequately for their deprivation. However, just because these rights are not capable of precise evaluation does not mean that an appropriate monetary amount should not be awarded.

"The precise value you place upon any Constitutional right which you find was denied to Plaintiff is within your discretion. You may wish to consider the importance of the right in our system of government, the role which this right has played in the history of our republic, [and] the significance of the right in the context of the activities which the Plaintiff was engaged in at the time of the violation of the right."

The jury found petitioners liable, and awarded a total of $275,000 in compensatory damages and $46,000 in punitive damages. The District Court entered judgment notwithstanding the verdict as to one of the defendants, reducing the total award to $266,750 in compensatory damages and $36,000 in punitive damages.

. . . .

We granted certiorari limited to the question whether the Court of Appeals erred in affirming the damages award in the light of the District Court's instructions that authorized not only compensatory and punitive damages, but also damages for the deprivation of "any constitutional right." We reverse, and remand for a new trial limited to the issue of compensatory damages.

. . . .

II

A

We have repeatedly noted that 42 U.S.C. § 1983 creates " 'a species of tort liability' in favor of persons who are deprived of 'rights, privileges, or immunities secured' to them by the Constitution." Accordingly, when § 1983 plaintiffs seek damages for violations of constitutional rights, the level of damages is ordinarily determined according to principles derived from the common law of torts.

Punitive damages aside, damages in tort cases are designed to provide "*compensation* for the injury caused to plaintiff by defendant's breach of duty." 2 F. Harper, F. James, & O. Gray, Law of Torts § 25.1, p. 490 (2d ed. 1986)(emphasis in original). To that end, compensatory damages may include not only out-of-pocket loss and other monetary harms, but also such injuries as "impairment of reputation ..., personal humiliation, and mental anguish and suffering." Deterrence is also an important purpose of this system, but it operates through the mechanism of damages that are *compensatory*—damages grounded in determinations of plaintiffs' actual losses. Congress adopted this common-law system of recovery when it established liability for "constitutional torts." Consequently, "the basic purpose" of § 1983 damages is "to *compensate persons for injuries* that are caused by the deprivation of constitutional rights." . . . .

The instructions at issue here cannot be squared with Carey v. Piphus, 435 U.S. 247, 98 S.Ct. 1042, 55 L.Ed.2d 252 (1978), or with the principles of tort damages on which *Carey* and § 1983 are grounded. The jurors in this case were told that, in determining how much was necessary to "compensate [respondent] for the deprivation" of his constitutional rights, they should place a money value on the "rights" themselves by considering such factors as the particular right's "importance ... in our system of government," its role in American history, and its "significance ... in the context of the activities" in which respondent was engaged. These factors focus, not on compensation for provable injury, but on the jury's subjective perception of the importance of constitutional rights as an abstract matter. *Carey* establishes that such an approach is impermissible. The constitutional right transgressed in *Carey*—the right to due process of law—is central to our system of ordered liberty. We nevertheless held that *no* compensatory damages could be awarded for violation of that right absent proof of actual injury. *Carey* thus makes clear that the abstract value of a constitutional right may not form the basis for § 1983 damages.[11]

11. We did approve an award of nominal damages for the deprivation of due process in *Carey*. Our discussion of that issue makes clear that nominal damages, and not

Respondent nevertheless argues that *Carey* does not control here, because in this case a *substantive* constitutional right—respondent's First Amendment right to academic freedom—was infringed. The argument misperceives our analysis in *Carey.* That case does not establish a two-tiered system of constitutional rights, with substantive rights afforded greater protection than "mere" procedural safeguards. We did acknowledge in *Carey* that "the elements and prerequisites for recovery of damages" might vary depending on the interests protected by the constitutional right at issue. But we emphasized that, whatever the constitutional basis for § 1983 liability, such damages must always be designed "to *compensate injuries* caused by the [constitutional] deprivation."[13] See also Hobson v. Wilson, 237 U.S.App.D.C. 219, 277–279, 737 F.2d 1, 59–61 (1984), cert. denied, 470 U.S. 1084, 105 S.Ct. 1843, 85 L.Ed.2d 142 (1985). That conclusion simply leaves no room for noncompensatory damages measured by the jury's perception of the abstract "importance" of a constitutional right.

Nor do we find such damages necessary to vindicate the constitutional rights that § 1983 protects. See n. 11, supra. Section 1983 presupposes that damages that compensate for actual harm ordinarily suffice to deter constitutional violations. Moreover, damages based on the "value" of constitutional rights are an unwieldy tool for ensuring compliance with the Constitution. History and tradition do not afford any sound guidance concerning the precise value that juries should place on constitutional protections. Accordingly, were such damages available, juries would be free to award arbitrary amounts without any evidentiary basis, or to use their unbounded discretion to punish unpopular defendants. Such damages would be too uncertain to be of any great value to plaintiffs, and would inject caprice into determinations of damages in § 1983 cases. We therefore hold that damages based on the abstract "value" or "importance" of constitutional rights are not a permissible element of compensatory damages in such cases.

B

Respondent further argues that the challenged instructions authorized a form of "presumed" damages—a remedy that is both compensatory in nature and traditionally part of the range of tort law remedies. Alternative-

---

damages based on some undefinable "value" of infringed rights, are the appropriate means of "vindicating" rights whose deprivation has not caused actual, provable injury....

13. *Carey* recognized that "the task ... of adapting common-law rules of damages to provide fair compensation for injuries caused by the deprivation of a constitutional right" is one "of some delicacy." We also noted that "the elements and prerequisites for recovery of damages appropriate to compensate injuries caused by the deprivation of one constitutional right are not necessarily appropriate

to compensate injuries caused by the deprivation of another." See also Hobson v. Wilson, 237 U.S.App.D.C., at 279–281, 737 F.2d, at 61–63. This "delicate" task need not be undertaken here. None of the parties challenges the portion of the jury instructions that permitted recovery for actual harm to respondent, and the instructions that *are* challenged simply do not authorize compensation for injury. We therefore hold only that damages based on the "value" or "importance" of constitutional rights are not authorized by § 1983, because they are not truly compensatory.

ly, respondent argues that the erroneous instructions were at worst harmless error.

Neither argument has merit. Presumed damages are a *substitute* for ordinary compensatory damages, not a *supplement* for an award that fully compensates the alleged injury. When a plaintiff seeks compensation for an injury that is likely to have occurred but difficult to establish, some form of presumed damages may possibly be appropriate. In those circumstances, presumed damages may roughly approximate the harm that the plaintiff suffered and thereby compensate for harms that may be impossible to measure. As we earlier explained, the instructions at issue in this case did not serve this purpose, but instead called on the jury to measure damages based on a subjective evaluation of the importance of particular constitutional values. Since such damages are wholly divorced from any compensatory purpose, they cannot be justified as presumed damages.[14] Moreover, no rough substitute for compensatory damages was required in this case, since the jury was fully authorized to compensate respondent for both monetary and nonmonetary harms caused by petitioners' conduct.

Nor can we find that the erroneous instructions were harmless. . . . For these reasons, the case must be remanded for a new trial on compensatory damages.

IV

The judgment of the Court of Appeals is reversed, and the case is remanded for further proceedings consistent with this opinion.

It is so ordered.

■ JUSTICE BRENNAN and JUSTICE STEVENS join the opinion of the Court and also join JUSTICE MARSHALL'S opinion concurring in the judgment.

■ JUSTICE MARSHALL, with whom JUSTICE BRENNAN, JUSTICE BLACKMUN, and JUSTICE STEVENS join, concurring in the judgment.

14. For the same reason, Nixon v. Herndon, 273 U.S. 536, 47 S.Ct. 446, 71 L.Ed. 759 (1927), and similar cases do not support the challenged instructions. In *Nixon,* the Court held that a plaintiff who was illegally prevented from voting in a state primary election suffered compensable injury. This holding did not rest on the "value" of the right to vote as an abstract matter; rather, the Court recognized that the plaintiff had suffered a particular injury—his inability to vote in a particular election—that might be compensated through substantial money damages.

Nixon followed a long line of cases, going back to Lord Holt's decision in Ashby v. White, 2 Ld.Raym. 938, 92 Eng.Rep. 126 (1703), authorizing substantial money damages as compensation for persons deprived of their right to vote in particular elections.

Although these decisions sometimes speak of damages for the value of the right to vote, their analysis shows that they involve nothing more than an award of presumed damages for a nonmonetary harm that cannot easily be quantified . . .

The "value of the right" in the context of these decisions is the money value of the particular loss that the plaintiff suffered—a loss of which "each member of the jury has personal knowledge." It is *not* the value of the right to vote as a general, abstract matter, based on its role in our history or system of government. Thus, whatever the wisdom of these decisions in the context of the changing scope of compensatory damages over the course of this century, they do not support awards of noncompensatory damages such as those authorized in this case.

I agree with the Court that this case must be remanded for a new trial on damages. Certain portions of the Court's opinion, however, can be read to suggest that damages in § 1983 cases are necessarily limited to "out-of-pocket loss," "other monetary harms," and "such injuries as 'impairment of reputation ..., personal humiliation, and mental anguish and suffering.'" I do not understand the Court so to hold, and I write separately to emphasize that the violation of a constitutional right, in proper cases, may itself constitute a compensable injury.

The appropriate starting point of any analysis in this area is this Court's opinion in Carey v. Piphus, 435 U.S. 247, 98 S.Ct. 1042, 55 L.Ed.2d 252 (1978) ...

. . . .

Following *Carey,* the Courts of Appeals have recognized that invasions of constitutional rights sometimes cause injuries that cannot be redressed by a wooden application of common-law damages rules. In Hobson v. Wilson, 237 U.S.App.D.C. 219, 275–281, 737 F.2d 1, 57–63 (1984), cert. denied, 470 U.S. 1084, 105 S.Ct. 1843, 85 L.Ed.2d 142 (1985), which the Court cites, plaintiffs claimed that defendant Federal Bureau of Investigation agents had invaded their First Amendment rights to assemble for peaceable political protest, to associate with others to engage in political expression, and to speak on public issues free of unreasonable government interference. The District Court found that the defendants had succeeded in diverting plaintiffs from, and impeding them in, their protest activities. The Court of Appeals for the District of Columbia Circuit held that that injury to a First Amendment-protected interest could itself constitute compensable injury wholly apart from any "emotional distress, humiliation and personal indignity, emotional pain, embarrassment, fear, anxiety and anguish" suffered by plaintiffs. The court warned, however, that that injury could be compensated with substantial damages only to the extent that it was "reasonably quantifiable"; damages should not be based on "the so-called inherent value of the rights violated."

I believe that the *Hobson* court correctly stated the law. When a plaintiff is deprived, for example, of the opportunity to engage in a demonstration to express his political views, "[i]t is facile to suggest that no damage is done." Loss of such an opportunity constitutes loss of First Amendment rights "'in their most pristine and classic form.'" There is no reason why such an injury should not be compensable in damages. At the same time, however, the award must be proportional to the actual loss sustained.

The instructions given the jury in this case were improper because they did not require the jury to focus on the loss actually sustained by respondent. Rather, they invited the jury to base its award on speculation about "the importance of the right in our system of government" and "the role which this right has played in the history of our republic," guided only by the admonition that "[i]n one sense, no monetary value we place on Constitutional rights can measure their importance in our society or compensate a citizen adequately for their deprivation." These instructions invited the jury to speculate on matters wholly detached from the real injury occasioned respondent by the deprivation of the right. Further, the instructions might have led the jury to grant respondent damages based on the "abstract value" of the right to procedural due process—a course directly barred by our decision in *Carey.*

The Court therefore properly remands for a new trial on damages. I do not understand the Court, however, to hold that deprivations of constitutional rights can never themselves constitute compensable injuries. Such a rule would be inconsistent with the logic of *Carey,* and would defeat the purpose of § 1983 by denying compensation for genuine injuries caused by the deprivation of constitutional rights.

D. LOSS OF CONSORTIUM

Spouse's Loss of Consortium

Whittlesey v. Miller

Supreme Court of Texas, 1978.
572 S.W.2d 665.

■ McGEE, J. The question presented by this appeal is whether one spouse has an independent action for loss of consortium as a result of physical injuries caused to the other spouse by the negligence of a third party. The vehicle Stewart Miller was driving was involved in a collision with a vehicle driven by David Whittlesey in June 1974. In March 1976, Miller and Whittlesey entered into a settlement agreement whereby Miller released Whittlesey from liability in connection with the accident for consideration of $9,650. In June 1976, Ann Miller, Stewart's wife, sued Whittlesey for damages, alleging that Whittlesey's negligence had caused personal injury to her husband, thereby depriving her of her husband's consortium. Whittlesey was granted a summary judgment on the basis that a Texas wife could not recover for loss of consortium for the alleged negligent injury to her husband. The court of civil appeals reversed and remanded. We affirm the judgment of the court of civil appeals.

The marital relationship is the primary familial interest recognized by the courts. The remedy for the negligent or intentional impairment of this relationship is a tort action for loss of consortium.[1] Consortium has been the subject of many different definitions by the courts, but it can generally be defined to include the mutual right of the husband and wife to that affection, solace, comfort, companionship, society, assistance, and sexual relations necessary to a successful marriage. This definition primarily consists of the emotional or intangible elements of the marital relationship. In Texas, it does not include the "services" rendered by a spouse to the

1. The phrase "loss of consortium" is more accurately described as an element of damage rather than a cause of action. But courts have so frequently used the phrase to denote those actions in which loss of consortium is the major element of damage that "loss of consortium" has come to be referred to as a cause of action.

marriage.[2] These elements have been referred to as a conceptualistic unity, and the action accrues upon the substantial impairment of them.

The loss of consortium can arise from either the intentional or negligent conduct of a third party toward the marital relationship. The intentional impairment of consortium can result in actions for either alienation of affections or criminal conversation. Both actions have been recognized by prior Texas decisions.

The husband's right to recover for the negligent impairment of consortium has existed at common law, although there are no decisions by this court expressly holding this. It has only been within the past 25 years, however, that the wife's cause of action in the United States has been recognized. The general acceptance of this action is reflected in the Restatement (Second) of Torts § 693 (1977), which now states:

"(1) One who by reason of his tortious conduct is liable to one spouse for illness or other bodily harm is subject to liability to the other spouse for the resulting loss of the society and services of the first spouse, including impairment of capacity for sexual intercourse...."

Comment a to the above characterizes the spouse who suffered the bodily harm as a result of the tortious conduct as the "impaired spouse"; the spouse who brings the independent consortium action is characterized as the "deprived spouse." We find these designations to be pertinent and will use them in the balance of this opinion to assist in simplifying the discussion.

The present action for negligent impairment of consortium contemplates a single tortious act which injures both spouses by virtue of their relationship to each other. While the impaired spouse sustains direct physical injuries, the deprived spouse sustains damage to emotional interests stemming from their relationship. In the respective causes of action, the impaired spouse would have the exclusive right to recover for the normal damages associated with such an injury—bodily injuries, medical expenses, pain and suffering, loss of earnings, et cetera. The deprived spouse would have the right to bring an action for the loss of consortium and seek recovery on the basis of harm to the intangible or sentimental elements. Finally, while the deprived spouse's suit for loss of consortium is considered to be derivative of the impaired spouse's negligence action to the extent that the tortfeasor's liability to the impaired spouse must be established, the consortium action is, nevertheless, independent and apart from that of the impaired spouse's negligence action.

It has been argued that the deprived spouse's loss of consortium is an injury that is too indirect to be compensated because the elements involved are too intangible or conjectural to be measured in pecuniary terms by a jury. We do not agree, for to do so would mean that a jury would also be

2. The term "services" is generally taken to include the performance by a spouse of household and domestic duties. In Texas, it is a concept that is entirely separate and distinct from that of consortium. In our community property system the husband and wife are equal; as such, a spouse's services counterbalance the other spouse's duty to support the community with earnings. Furthermore, the services of the spouse performing such are thus recoverable as a damage to the community.

incompetent to award damages for pain and suffering. The character of harm to the intangible or sentimental elements is not illusory. The loss of companionship, emotional support, love, felicity, and sexual relations are real, direct, and personal losses. It is recognized that these terms concern subjective states which present some difficulty in translating the loss into a dollar amount. The loss, however, is a real one requiring compensation, and "the issue generally must be resolved by the 'impartial conscience and judgment of jurors who may be expected to act reasonably, intelligently and in harmony with the evidence.' "

. . . .

. . . Providing either spouse with a cause of action for loss of consortium would allow us to keep pace with modern society by recognizing that the emotional interests of the marriage relationship are as worthy of protection from negligent invasion as are other legally protected interests.

Therefore, we hold that either spouse has a cause of action for loss of consortium that might arise as a result of an injury caused to the other spouse by a third party tortfeasor's negligence. This holding not only aligns Texas with the majority of jurisdictions recognizing the action for either spouse,[6] but it also corrects a paradox in the law of this state in that heretofore the marital relationship has been protected from only intentional invasions. . . .

. . . .

Accordingly, we affirm the judgment of the court of civil appeals.

———

Child's Loss of Parental Consortium

Reagan v. Vaughn

Supreme Court of Texas, 1990.
804 S.W.2d 463.

■ J. Gonzalez.

In this case, we are presented with the issue of whether a child has a right to recover damages for loss of consortium and mental anguish when a parent is injured but not killed by the tortious conduct of a third party. The court of appeals, stating that it did not have the authority to recognize such a cause of action,[1] modified the judgment of the trial court by deleting the award of damages for loss of parental consortium. The judgment was affirmed in all other respects. 784 S.W.2d 88. We reverse that portion of the

6.   Either by statute or judicial decision, the cause of action for either spouse for the loss of consortium has been recognized in the great majority of states. This has long been favored by legal commentators.

1.   "The phrase 'loss of consortium' is more accurately described as an element of damage rather than a cause of action. But courts have so frequently used the phrase to denote those actions in which loss of consortium is the major element of damage that 'loss of consortium' has come to be referred to as a cause of action." Whittlesey v. Miller, 572 S.W.2d 665, 666 (Tex.1978).

court of appeals' judgment deleting the damages awarded to Julia Reagan for lost parental consortium and otherwise affirm.

I. FACTS

David Reagan was involved in a fight with another patron in the parking lot of K–Jacs Saloon in Pasadena, Texas. During the course of the fight, the manager of the bar, Vaughn, struck Reagan on the head with a baseball bat. Reagan suffered a severe brain injury and now functions at the level of a six-or seven-year-old child. Reagan and his minor daughter, Julia, sued Vaughn as well as the owners of K–Jacs, Keith Nichols and Ernest Rosenovac. The jury found that Vaughn, Nichols, and Rosenovac were each 20% negligent and that Reagan was 40% negligent. The jury awarded damages in the amount of $2,432,000 to Reagan and $405,000 to Julia. ($200,000 for loss of "parental care, nurture and guidance:" $25,000 for mental anguish in the past and $180,000 for mental anguish in the future). The trial court rendered judgment in conformity with the verdict.

This court has never addressed the issue of whether a child may recover damages for the loss of parental companionship, love, and society when a parent is injured....

... In the present case, Reagan was not killed; thus our analysis does not include interpretation of the wrongful death statute. Rather, we must decide whether, given our previous recognition of the significance of injuries to the familial relationship, this court should recognize a common law cause of action for loss of consortium damages that result from injury to a parent.[4]

---

4. The following courts have recognized a cause of action for loss of parental consortium: Hibpshman v. Prudhoe Bay Supply, Inc., 734 P.2d 991 (Alaska 1987); Villareal v. State, 160 Ariz. 474, 774 P.2d 213 (1989); Weitl v. Moes, 311 N.W.2d 259 (Iowa 1981), modified by Audubon–Exira Ready Mix, Inc. v. Illinois Cent. Gulf R.R. Co., 335 N.W.2d 148 (Iowa 1983); Ferriter v. Daniel O'Connell's Sons, Inc., 381 Mass. 507, 413 N.E.2d 690 (1980); Berger v. Weber, 411 Mich. 1, 303 N.W.2d 424 (1981); Hay v. Medical Center Hosp., 145 Vt. 533, 496 A.2d 939 (1985); Ueland v. Reynolds Metals Co., 103 Wash.2d 131, 691 P.2d 190 (1984); Theama v. City of Kenosha, 117 Wis.2d 508, 344 N.W.2d 513 (1984); Nulle v. Gillette–Campbell County Joint Powers Fire Bd., 797 P.2d 1171 (Wyo. 1990). It is argued that because a majority of the states do not recognize this cause of action, we should follow suit. "[T]hat is no sufficient reason why an action should not be sustained." Hill v. Kimball, 76 Tex. 210, 13 S.W. 59, 59 (1890). This observation remains valid today. Commentators generally favor recognition of a cause of action for loss of parental consortium. See W. Prosser, The Law of Torts s 123, at 896 (4th ed. 1971); W. Keeton, D. Dobbs, R. Keeton & D. Owen, Prosser and Keeton on the Law of Torts § 125, at 936 (5th ed. 1984); Harper, James & Gray, The Law of Torts § 8.8 (May 1988 Supp.); Pound, Individual Interests in the Domestic Relations, 14 Mich.L.Rev. 177 (1916); see also Love, Tortious Interference with the Parent–Child Relationship; Loss of an Injured Persons' Society and Companionship, 51 Ind.L.J. 590 (1976); Petrilli, A Child's Right to Collect for Parental Consortium Where Parent is Seriously Injured, 26 J.Fam.L. 318 (1987–88); Comment, The Child's Right to Parental Consortium, 14 J. Marshall L.Rev. 341 (1981); Comment, The Child's Claim for Loss of Consortium Damages; A Logical and Sympathetic Appeal, 13 San Diego L.Rev. 231 (1975); Comment, The Child's Cause of Action for Loss of Consortium, 5 San Fern. V.L.Rev. 449 (1977); Comment, Actions for Loss of Consortium in Washington: The Children are Still Crying, 56 Wash.L.Rev. 487 (1981); Note, The Child's Right to Sue for Loss of a Parent's Love, Care, and Companionship Caused by Tortious Injury to the Parent, 56 B.U.L.Rev. 723 (1976); Note, Loss of Parental Consortium, 8 J.Juv.L. 457, 462–63 (1984); Note, Ipcock v. Gilmore: North

III.   SHOULD THE PARENT–CHILD RELATIONSHIP BE PROTECT-ED?

"The common law is not frozen or stagnant, but evolving, and it is the duty of this court to recognize the evolution." El Chico Corp. v. Poole, 732 S.W.2d 306, 309–10 (Tex.1987). "The law is not static; and the courts, whenever reason and equity demand, have been the primary instruments for changing the common law through a continual re-evaluation of common law concepts in light of current conditions." *Whittlesey*, 572 S.W.2d at 668. We fashion our analysis after that in Whittlesey and inquire whether the parent-child relationship in our modern society is "as worthy of protection from negligent invasion as are other legally protected interests." Id.

. . . .

In Sanchez, we recognized that the death of a child inflicts upon his parents a loss of love, advice, comfort, companionship and society. *Sanchez*, 651 S.W.2d at 251. Likewise, in Cavnar we held that a child suffers equivalent losses from the death of a parent. *Cavnar*, 696 S.W.2d at 551. And in *Whittlesey*, we acknowledged that nonfatal injury to a spouse can result in a real, direct, and personal loss to the other spouse. 572 S.W.2d at 667. We would be hard pressed to say that a serious, permanent and disabling injury to a parent does not potentially visit upon the child an equally serious deprivation. In the present case, Julia Reagan has been deprived of essentially any opportunity for further parent-child exchange with her father. A child faced with Julia's circumstances can no longer experience the joy of shared experiences with her parent, and she is denied the care, guidance, love, and protection ordinarily provided by her parent. There is no principled reason to accord the parent-child relationship second class status:

While all family members enjoy a mutual interest in consortium, the parent-child relationship is undeniably unique and the wellspring from which other family relationships derive. It is the parent-child relationship which most deserves protection and which, in fact, has received judicial protection in the past. (citations omitted). The loss of a parent's love, care, companionship, and guidance can severely impact a child's development and have a major influence on a child's welfare and personality throughout life. The obvious and unquestionable significance of the parent-child relationship compels our recognition of a cause of action for loss of parental consortium.

Respondents have suggested that recognition of this cause of action will somehow have the snowball effect of leading to recognition of actions in favor of siblings, grandparents, close friends, and so on. We have little difficulty limiting recovery to the parent-child relationship. We recognize, as did the Wisconsin Supreme Court, that the two relationships likely to be

Carolina's Refusal to Extend Recovery to the Infant Secondary Tort Victim, 66 N.C.L.Rev. 1337 (1988); Note, Torts—Loss of Consortium—Right of a Child to a Cause of Action for Loss of Society and Companionship When the Parent is Tortiously Injured, 28 Wayne L.Rev. 1877 (1982). The Restatement (Sec-ond) of Torts declares that the action should not be recognized. Restatement (Second) of Torts § 707A (1977). But cf. Norwest v. Presbyterian Intercommunity Hosp., 652 P.2d 318, 319–20 (Or.1982)(explaining that this section of the Restatement had less than whole-hearted support from the drafters).

most severely affected by a negligent injury to a person are the husband and wife relationship and that of the parent and child: The distinction between the interests of children and those of other relatives is rational and easily applied. Most children are dependent on their parents for emotional sustenance. This is rarely the case with more remote relatives. Thus, by limiting the plaintiffs in the consortium action to the victim's children, the courts would ensure that the losses compensated would be both real and severe. Consistent with our prior recognition that adult children may recover for the wrongful death of a parent, we decline to limit the right of recovery under this cause of action to minor children. "Although minors are the group most likely to suffer real harm due to a disruption of the parent-child relationship, we leave this to the jury to consider in fixing damages." Ueland, 691 P.2d at 195; see also Audubon–Exira Ready Mix, Inc. v. Illinois Cent. Gulf R. Co., 335 N.W.2d 148, 152 (Iowa 1983)("even adult and married children have the right to expect the benefit of good parental advice and guidance") (citing Schmitt v. Jenkins Truck Lines, Inc., 170 N.W.2d 632, 665 (Iowa 1969)).

IV. SHOULD RECOVERY INCLUDE DAMAGES FOR MENTAL ANGUISH?

Respondents assert that the jury's award of mental anguish damages to Julia violates Freeman v. City of Pasadena, in which we held that a stepfather who was not located at or near the scene of an accident involving injury to his stepsons could not recover for negligent infliction of mental anguish. 744 S.W.2d 923 (Tex.1988).

A claim for negligent infliction of mental anguish is separate and distinct from a child's claim for loss of parental consortium and loss of consortium does not include an element of mental anguish. A cause of action for loss of consortium is derivative of the parent's claim for personal injuries. In order to recover, the child must prove that the defendant is liable for the personal injuries suffered by her parent, and any defense that tends to constrict or exclude the defendant's liability to the injured parent will have the same effect on the child's consortium action.

On the other hand, a claim for negligent infliction of mental anguish that is not based upon the wrongful death statute requires that the plaintiff prove that he or she was, among other things, located at or near the scene of the accident, and that the mental anguish resulted from a direct emotional impact upon the plaintiff from the sensory and contemporaneous observance of the incident, as contrasted with learning of the accident from others after the occurrence. Julia has not met either of these requirements and therefore may not recover for mental anguish.

V. CONCLUSION

We hold that children may recover for loss of consortium when a third party causes serious, permanent, and disabling injuries to their parent. In order to successfully maintain a claim for loss of parental consortium resulting from injury to the parent-child relationship, the plaintiff must show that the defendant physically injured the child's parent in a manner that would subject the defendant to liability. The child may recover for such non-pecuniary damages as loss of the parent's love, affection, protection, emotional support, services, companionship, care, and society. Factors that the jury may consider in determining the amount of damages include, but are not limited to, the severity of the injury to the parent and its actual effect upon the parent-child relationship, the child's age, the nature of the child's relationship with the parent, the child's emotional and physical characteristics, and whether other consortium giving relationships are available to the child.

Julia Reagan adduced legally sufficient evidence to sustain her claim for lost parental consortium. We therefore reverse that portion of the court of appeals judgment deleting $200,000 damages awarded to Julia for loss of parental consortium and render judgment for Julia in this amount. In all other respects, the judgment of the court of appeals is affirmed.

OPINION ON MOTION FOR REHEARING

■ J. GONZALEZ.

. . . .

We also note that the cause of action for loss of parental consortium, like the cause of action for loss of spousal consortium is a derivative cause of action. As such, the defenses which bar all or part of the injured parent's recovery have the same effect on the child's recovery. Any percentage of negligence attributable against the parent under Texas' comparative negligence statute will reduce the amount of the child's recovery. In this case, however, the defendants' have waived their claim for this relief by failing to raise this point in their motion for rehearing.

Finally, when the facts are disputed, there must be a threshold finding by the finder of fact that the injury to the parent was a serious, permanent, and disabling injury before the finder of fact determines the consortium damage issue.

■ J. HECHT, concurring and dissenting.

Today the Court creates a new personal injury cause of action, holding for the first time that a person is entitled to money damages for a diminution in parental love, advice, comfort, companionship and society occasioned by tortious injury to the parent. The Court extends this newly allowed recovery to adult as well as minor children, although the only child in this case is a minor. It equivocates on the rather important matter of how seriously a parent must be injured before the child can recover, suggesting at several points in its opinion that recovery may be sought for any injury to a parent, and at other points, including the opinion on rehearing, that the injury must be "serious, permanent, and disabling". On rehearing, the Court considers for the first time the retroactive effect of its decision and partially restricts that effect. The Court never acknowledges the problems its decision poses for the judicial system. Henceforth every person whose parent is, or within any applicable limitations period has been, personally injured—either intentionally, or in a motor vehicle accident, or by a fall, or from using an unreasonably dangerous product, or while receiving medical or health care, or as a result of any other tortious misconduct—has a separate damage claim against the person causing the injuries. In the future, simple personal injury claims cannot be absolutely resolved without the concurrence of the injured person's children. Today's decision is breathtaking in its scope.

For so extreme a change in the common law the Court ought to have some compelling justification, yet I do not find it in the Court's opinion. Rather, the Court poses the rhetorical question—"Should the parent-child relationship be protected?"—and quickly provides the unsurprising affirmative answer. The question is irrelevant and the answer immaterial. Every personal relationship, not just the parent-child relationship, ought to be, in the Court's words, "worthy of protection"; at least the Court does not name the relationships which it thinks are un worthy of protection. Yet the Court holds that damages may not be recovered for every loss of consortium, such as between siblings. An affirmative answer to the Court's question simply does not decide this case. I suspect the Court phrases its inquiry to make its decision as appealing as it can. But rhetoric does not substitute well for reason.

I concur with the Court that damages should not be awarded for a child's mental anguish caused by injury to a parent in these circumstances. I disagree only with the Court's allowance of damages for loss of consortium, which is not justified either by the record in this case or what little analysis there is in the Court's opinion. Good reasons, totally ignored by the Court, strongly support the opposite conclusion. Because I think it is most unwise to allow recovery for loss of parental consortium whenever the parent is injured but not killed, I dissent.

I

If ever there were a case that cried out for recovery for loss of parental consortium, this is not it. The circumstances of David Reagan's injury and any consequent loss to his daughter, Julia, vivify the inappropriateness of awarding a person money because his or her parent has been hurt. Brushing facts aside, the Court simply idealizes that "[a] child faced with Julia's circumstances can no longer experience the joy of shared experiences with the parent and is denied the care, guidance, love, and protection ordinarily provided by a parent." Supra at 466. The Court is conspicuously vague about what Julia's circumstances are exactly, and about whether the evidence shows that she would have had the sort of relationship with her father, but for his injury, that other children "ordinarily" have. The concurring opinion picks up the Court's refrain, adding that children in Julia's circumstances—not Julia herself, but children like Julia—face "sorrow and grief ... on a daily basis." Supra at 489. There is absolutely no evidence in the record before us that Julia faces, or has ever faced, sorrow and grief on account of her father's injury. There is some evidence to the contrary.

These panegyrics, while moving as they are no doubt intended to be, have little to do with the reality of this case. The Court's preference for generalities calls for a recapitulation of the facts here in some detail.

A

When his wife of some four years filed for divorce, David Reagan left her and their four-year-old daughter, Julia, in Indiana and moved to

Houston. Unemployed, the 22–year-old Reagan became a "regular" at K–Jacs Saloon, a beer joint in a "rough" part of town. K–Jacs was owned by Keith Jack Nichols and Ernest Rosenovac, and managed by Lester Gene "Lucky" Vaughn. Vaughn's duties included protecting the barmaids and waitresses from harassment and breaking up fights among the patrons, routine occurrences at K–Jacs and other bars in its neighborhood. Reagan spent two or three nights a week at K–Jacs during the three months he stayed with his sister. Vaughn testified that he had seen Reagan in the bar on several prior occasions and that Reagan seemed like a nice kid.

On Friday, the thirteenth of June, Reagan arrived at K–Jacs early, about 3:30 or 4:00 p.m. One of the waitresses, Elizabeth "Tina" Lamb, testified that Reagan said he was very upset because he was about to return to Indiana to finish up his divorce. He began drinking immediately, Lamb stated, and continued to drink heavily throughout the evening, roaming around in the bar, increasingly intoxicated and increasingly violent. Reagan stayed until K–Jacs closed at 2:00 a.m. Nearly three hours later his blood alcohol level was .226 gm/dl, more than twice the level for legal intoxication.

Richard Lepper testified that he noticed while talking with Reagan during the evening that Reagan was unstable. Concerned that Reagan was in no condition to be driving, Lepper said he offered to take Reagan to get something to eat and then home. Lepper stated that as he and Reagan were walking out across the parking lot, Reagan stopped to talk to two girls in a car. When they drove off, Lepper said, Reagan got into an argument with three cowboys who were standing nearby. Lepper, who had been stabbed on the K–Jacs parking lot on a separate occasion, testified that he begged Reagan to leave, but the argument turned into a scuffle, and when he tried to pull Reagan away from the others, Reagan turned, enraged, and began to fight like a wild man.

About that time Ronnie Di Simone and his wife, Donna, were also leaving K–Jacs. They had been to a movie earlier in the evening and had stopped by on the way home. Di Simone testified that as he walked out of the bar he saw Reagan, whom he had seen at K–Jacs on prior occasions, grabbing through the open window of a car at a man inside and shouting, "I'm going to whip your ass." Di Simone said that he walked over to Reagan and tried to persuade him to leave, but Reagan whirled around and said, "If I can't whip him, I'm going to whip you." Di Simone said that Reagan hit him, and the two began to fight. After a few minutes, Di Simone stated, Vaughn came out of the bar and separated them, telling them that he had called the police and that they had better go home. Vaughn testified that he was cleaning up in the bar after it closed when he was told that there was fighting outside. He stated that he told one of the bartenders to call the police, went outside and stopped the fight, and then returned inside. Several spectators verified that Vaughn warned everyone to leave and told them that the police were on their way.

Reagan, however, was wild-eyed and uncontrollable, according to Di Simone, and came at him again. Vaughn testified that when he heard that Reagan and Di Simone were still fighting, he again instructed an employee to call the police and went outside to break them up. This time, Vaughn stated, he grabbed Reagan, threw him on the ground, and sat on him until Reagan promised he would go home if Vaughn would let him up. Di Simone stated that he tried to walk away while Vaughn pinned Reagan on the ground, but that as soon as Reagan got up he came at Di Simone again. Di Simone testified that Reagan shouted that "he was in a fighting mood and he was going to whip some son-of-a-bitch".

Vaughn testified that having failed in his efforts to separate Reagan and Di Simone, he went inside K–Jacs, instructed one of the waitresses again to call the police, retrieved a baseball bat he kept under the bar, and went back outside. By this time Reagan and Di Simone had been fighting off and on for nearly half an hour. Several witnesses testified that as Vaughn tried again to break up the pair, Di Simone hit Reagan so that he fell, striking his head against a concrete curb on the parking lot. Reagan got up and lunged, screaming, at Vaughn who was using the baseball bat to push Di Simone away. Lamb and another K–Jacs waitress, Diane Jackson, who were watching the fight, testified that Vaughn was only trying to settle the two down. But Reagan, Lamb stated, would not stop cursing and fighting. Another onlooker, Ronnie McFadden, testified that Reagan was fighting as if he were not afraid of anything.

As to some of the details of the events of the evening the recollections of the witnesses vary. But every witness present testified that when Reagan came up behind Vaughn, someone yelled that there was a knife. Waitresses Lamb and Jackson heard it, although they did not see anyone with a knife. McFadden heard someone shout, "Look out, Lucky, he's got a knife!" Don Morgan, a K–Jacs patron who was still inside the bar, heard the same thing. Neither McFadden nor Morgan actually saw a knife. However, Vaughn, Di Simone and Di Simone's wife all testified that they not only heard the shout but saw a knife in Reagan's hand. Henry Willis, a passerby who drove into the parking lot to see what was happening, also heard the same outcry and saw Reagan with a knife.

As soon as someone yelled that there was a knife, Di Simone kicked at Reagan, and as he did, Vaughn turned and swung the bat, hitting Reagan in the side of the head. Reagan fell to the ground motionless. Vaughn and several others immediately loaded Reagan into a vehicle to take him to the hospital. When the police arrived at 2:44 a.m., the parking lot was clear. The knife, if there was one, was never found.

As a result of his injury, Reagan suffered serious, permanent, debilitating brain damage. Although he is able to care for himself in many respects, he cannot function as an adult. A physician testified at trial that Reagan behaves much like a six-year-old child and will never significantly improve.

B

The only evidence of the nature of the relationship between Reagan and his daughter, Julia, is the testimony of Reagan's two sisters, Geneva Dale Showalter and Donita Cooper. Neither Julia, who was eleven years old at the time of trial, nor her mother, Tressa, appeared at trial or offered testimony. Reagan appeared but did not testify.

. . . .

II

The Court's decision today is well outside the mainstream of the common law which for centuries has restricted recovery of damages for tortious injury to personal relationships to very limited circumstances. Not until the past decade has any American jurisdiction extended that recovery to include loss of consortium for bodily injury to a parent. Only a very small minority of jurisdictions, at most three and perhaps only one, appear to have wandered so far as the Court does today.

. . . .

C

Section 707A of the Restatement (Second) of Torts states: "One who by reason of his tortious conduct is liable to a parent for illness or other bodily harm is not liable to a minor child for resulting loss of parental support and care." RESTATEMENT (SECOND) OF TORTS § 707A (1977). This provision and section 693 were both tentatively adopted by the American Law Institute in 1969. The Court alludes to the fact that section 707A was recommended "with some reluctance on the part of several of the drafting group, and under compulsion of the case law." AMERICAN LAW INSTITUTE, RESTATEMENT (SECOND) OF TORTS TENT. DRAFT NO. 14, at 28 (1969). Supra at 474 n. 4. What the Court omits is that section 707A was reported by Professor William Prosser and adopted without opposition at a general session of the American Law Institute.

The first state to depart from the rule of section 707A was Massachusetts, in 1980. Ferriter v. Daniel O'Connell's Sons, Inc., 381 Mass. 507, 413 N.E.2d 690 (1980). Since then, eight other states have followed suit. Berger v. Weber, 411 Mich. 1, 303 N.W.2d 424 (1981); Weitl v. Moes, 311 N.W.2d 259 (Iowa 1981), modified and overruled in part, Audubon–Exira Ready Mix, Inc. v. Illinois Cent. Gulf R.R., 335 N.W.2d 148 (Iowa 1983); Theama v. City of Kenosha, 117 Wis.2d 508, 344 N.W.2d 513 (1984); Ueland v. Reynolds Metals Co., 103 Wash.2d 131, 691 P.2d 190 (1984); Hay v. Medical Center Hosp. of Vt., 145 Vt. 533, 496 A.2d 939 (1985); Hibpshman v. Prudhoe Bay Supply, Inc., 734 P.2d 991 (Alaska 1987); Villareal v. State Dep't of Transp., 160 Ariz. 474, 774 P.2d 213 (1989); Nulle v. Gillette–Campbell County Joint Powers Fire Bd., 797 P.2d 1171 (Wyo.1990). Of these nine states, three have expressly limited recovery to cases in which the parent sustained very serious injuries. Weitl, 311 N.W.2d at 270 (recovery only when "significant disruption or diminution" of the relationship is shown); Hay, 496 A.2d at 946 (recovery only "when the parent has been rendered permanently comatose"); Villareal, 160 Ariz. at 480, 774 P.2d at 219 ("We limit our holding to allow loss of consortium claims only when the parent suffers serious, permanent, disabling injury rendering the parent unable to provide love, care, companionship, and guidance to the child. The parent's mental or physical impairment must be so overwhelming and severe that the parent-child relationship is destroyed or nearly destroyed."). Only one state has refused this limitation on recovery. Berger, 303 N.W.2d at 427. All but three states have limited recovery to minor, or at least dependent, children. See id.; Audubon–Exira, 335 N.W.2d at 152: Ueland, 691 P.2d at 195.

The Court acknowledges that it does not follow the rule adopted in a majority of states. What the Court does not say is that the rule it adopts has been expressly rejected by courts in twenty-seven states, decisions in twenty-one of which were in the past decade, and in the District of Columbia. Gray v. Suggs, 292 Ark. 19, 728 S.W.2d 148 (1987); Lewis v. Rowland, 287 Ark. 474, 701 S.W.2d 122 (1985); Borer v. American Airlines, 19 Cal.3d 441, 138 Cal.Rptr. 302, 563 P.2d 858 (1977), cited in Nix v. Preformed Line Products Co., 170 Cal.App.3d 975, 216 Cal.Rptr. 581 (1985), and Ledger v. Tippitt, 164 Cal.App.3d 625, 210 Cal.Rptr. 814 (1985); Lee v. Colorado Dep't of Health, 718 P.2d 221 (Colo.1986); Hinde v. Butler, 35 Conn.Sup. 292, 408 A.2d 668 (1979)(wrongful death action; loss of consortium is an element of a marital relationship and cannot be extended to children); Pleasant v. Washington Sand & Gravel Co., 262 F.2d 471 (D.C.Cir.1958); Zorzos v. Rosen, 467 So.2d 305 (Fla.1985), citing Clark v. Suncoast Hosp., Inc., 338 So.2d 1117 (Fla. 2d DCA 1976); W.J. Bremer Co. v. Graham, 169 Ga.App. 115, 312 S.E.2d 806 (1983); Halberg v. Young, 41 Haw. 634, 59 A.L.R.2d 445 (1957); Green v. A.B. Hagglund & Soner, 634 F.Supp. 790 (D.Idaho 1986)(applying Idaho law); Huter v. Ekman, 137 Ill.App.3d 733, 92 Ill.Dec. 369, 484 N.E.2d 1224 (1985), cited in Dralle v. Ruder, 124 Ill.2d 61, 124 Ill.Dec. 389, 529 N.E.2d 209 (1988); Dearborn Fabricating & Eng'g Corp. v. Wickham, 551 N.E.2d 1135 (Ind.1990); Schmeck v. City of Shawnee, 231 Kan. 588, 647 P.2d 1263 (1982)(parent's suit for injury to child), citing Hoffman v. Dautel, 189 Kan. 165, 368 P.2d 57 (1962); Kelly v. United States Fidelity & Guar. Co., 353 So.2d 349 (La.App.1977), appeal dism'd as moot, 357 So.2d 1144 (La.1978); Hickman v. Parish of E. Baton Rouge, 314 So.2d 486 (La.App.), writ denied 318 So.2d 59 (La.1975); Durepo v. Fishman, 533 A.2d 264 (Me.1987); Gaver v. Harrant, 316 Md. 17, 557 A.2d 210 (1989); Salin v. Kloempken, 322 N.W.2d 736 (Minn.1982); Barbera v. Brod–Dugan Co., 770 S.W.2d 318 (Mo.Ct.App. 1989); Hoesing v. Sears Roebuck & Co., 484 F.Supp. 478 (Dist.Neb. 1980)(applying Nebraska law); General Elec. Co. v. Bush, 88 Nev. 360, 498 P.2d 366 (1972); Russell v. Salem Transp. Co., 61 N.J. 502, 295 A.2d 862 (1972); DeAngelis v. Lutheran Medical Center, 84 A.D.2d 17, 445 N.Y.S.2d 188 (1981), aff'd, 58 N.Y.2d 1053, 462 N.Y.S.2d 626, 449 N.E.2d 406 (1983); Vaughn v. Clarkson, 324 N.C. 108, 376 S.E.2d 236 (1989)(per curiam); Morgel v. Winger, 290 N.W.2d 266 (N.D.1980); Sanders v. Mt. Sinai Hosp., 21 Ohio App.3d 249, 487 N.E.2d 588 (1985); Norwest v. Presbyterian Intercommunity Hosp., 293 Or. 543, 652 P.2d 318 (1982); Steiner v. Bell Tel. Co., 358 Pa.Super. 505, 517 A.2d 1348 (1986), aff'd without opinion, 518 Pa. 57, 540 A.2d 266 (1988); Turner v. Atlantic Coast Line R., 159 F.Supp. 590 (N.D.Ga.1958)(applying South Carolina law); Still v. Baptist Hosp., 755 S.W.2d 807 (Tenn. Ct. App.1988). By extending recovery to minors the Court adopts a rule rejected in thirty-three jurisdictions and adopted in only three. By failing to unambiguously limit recovery to cases involving very serious parental injuries, the Court aligns itself with exactly one other state in the country, Michigan.

III

With a few sentences in a footnote, the Court dismisses the fact that its decision today is the view of only a very small minority of American jurisdictions, adding lamely that it need not follow a rule just because the great majority of other states do. Of course, the validity of the Court's decision cannot be judged merely by counting the other jurisdictions that would seem to agree or disagree. The Court's position today is misguided, not simply because its adherents are few, although they certainly are, but for the very good reasons its adherents are few. The Court ignores these reasons and relies instead on analysis that is feeble and flawed.

A

The Court attempts to base its decision upon the fact that the common law is changing, that the parent-child relationship is worthy of protection, and that loss of consortium damages are allowed in other settings. Each of these facts is true; but, as will be shown, none supports the conclusion the Court reaches. Without support in law or logic, the Court's decision is not a natural development in the law but an anomaly.

1

The Court attempts to premise its analysis upon the proposition that the common law is ever developing and subject to reexamination in light of changing conditions. Supra at 465–466. This proposition, though true, proves nothing. The common law's fluvial course is altered by the naturally changing contours of the society through which it flows. It can also be diverted artificially. It does not follow logically from the fact that the course of the law can change that it should change in any particular case. And it cannot be determined from the mere fact that the common law does change, as it has today, whether its course was altered legitimately because of changing conditions, or simply by contrivance. That determination depends upon an analysis of current conditions which is noticeably lacking in the Court's opinion.

Certainly, there has not been much change in the law itself. As noted above, few states have deviated from the rule so as to cast much doubt upon its continued validity. The Court nevertheless argues that "[c]ommentators generally favor recognition of a cause of action for loss of parental consortium." Supra at 465 n. 4. In support of this perception of a changing trend in the law the Court cites articles by seven law students written over a period of twice as many years, articles of similar vintage by two lawyers and two professors, an article written by Roscoe Pound in 1916, and three recognized treatises. I would not ordinarily expect the highest court of a state to rely quite so heavily on the views of a few law students, lawyers and professors in law review articles in deciding to reject the considered views of the courts of other states. In citing the bulk of these materials the Court appears to be groping for whatever support it can find. Dean Pound's incisive article sheds some light on the issues in this case; but it certainly does not endorse the result the Court reaches today. To the contrary, I would say that Dean Pound expressed seventy-five years ago some of the same reservations about allowing recovery for loss of parental consortium which still persuade a majority of courts.[13] The treatis-

---

13. The Court may have in mind the following observations by Dean Pound:

As against the world at large a child has an interest in the relation [with a

es the Court cites certainly do not criticize the minority rule it follows, but they do stop short of actually "favor[ing] recognition of a cause of action for loss of parental consortium." Perhaps the weakness of this commentary accounts for the Court's failure to point to a single sentence that is very helpful. In any event, weighed against these academic views must be the contrary opinions of the majority of state judiciaries that have passed on the issue.

There also does not appear to have been much if any change in the nature of family relationships in what the Court calls "our modern society" to warrant recognizing recovery for loss of parental consortium for the first time. The significance of the parent-child relationship is, as the Court states, "obvious and unquestionable". Supra at 466. But this fact is hardly a recent discovery. Surely we cannot claim to have attained a more enlightened appreciation of the parental relationship in an age when divorce and child abuse are at least as commonplace as ever, and the Court does not say that we can.

In short, if "current conditions" compel today's decision, it is hard to see what they are. I agree that the Court is empowered to reexamine common law rules. But to make a legitimate change in common law rules the Court needs more than power; it needs a sound basis for doing so. I am not sure the Court recognizes this distinction.

2

According to the Court, the inquiry in this case should be "whether the parent-child relationship in our modern society is 'as worthy of protection from negligent invasion as are other legally protected interests.'" Supra at 466. The Court purports to derive this "worthy of protection" test from *Whittlesey*. The test is not supported by *Whittlesey*, nor can it be determinative of whether to allow damages for loss of consortium.

The holding in *Whittlesey* was not based upon its conclusion that the marital relationship was worthy of protection. *Whittlesey* gave two principal

parent] because of the support he may expect by virtue thereof while infancy or, after majority, circumstances precluding self-support render it improper or impossible for him to be left to himself. Also he has an interest in the society and affection of the parent, at least while he remains in the household. But the law has done little to secure these interests. At common law there are no legal rights which protect them.

Pound, Individual Interests in the Domestic Relations, 14 MICH.L.REV. 177, 185 (1916). Dean Pound did not conclude from these observations, however, that loss of consortium should be awarded when a family member was injured by a third party. Rather, he stated:

The reason for not securing the interest of wife or child in these cases seems to be that our modes of trial are such and our mode of assessment of damages by the verdict of a jury is necessarily so crude that if husband and wife were each allowed to sue, instead of each recovering an exact reparation, each would be pretty sure to recover what would repair the injury to both. Moreover the injury to wife or child is very hard to measure in money....

... Perhaps a no less cogent reason may be found in consciousness on the part of the courts that very little is actually achieved by the husband's actions, already in the law, which should be applied by analogy to make the law logically complete.
Id. at 194–95.

reasons for its holding: that it was following a majority of jurisdictions, and that it was correcting a paradox in Texas law that allowed compensation for direct, intentional injury to the marital relationship but not indirect, negligent injury. If the Court today followed *Whittlesey*, it would not reach the conclusion it does. If the Court followed the rule in a majority of jurisdictions, as *Whittlesey* did, it would deny recovery for loss of parental consortium in this case. And if the Court allowed the same recovery for indirect injury to the parental relationship as is allowed for direct injury, there would be none in these circumstances. Texas law, like the common law generally, has never allowed recovery for direct injury to the parental relationship. In fact, as noted above, Texas has, like most other American jurisdictions, abolished the right to recover for direct injury to the marital relationship on which *Whittlesey* relied.

The Court derives its "worthy of protection" test from the following sentence in *Whittlesey*: Providing either spouse with a cause of action for loss of consortium would allow us to keep pace with modern society by recognizing that the emotional interests of the marriage relationship are as worthy of protection from negligent invasion as are other legally protected interests. 572 S.W.2d at 668. The emphasis in this sentence seems to be more on keeping pace with modern society than on whether an interest is worthy of protection. To find in the phrase, "worthy of protection", the test which determined, albeit implicitly, the result in *Whittlesey* and which must therefore be the basis of analysis in this case requires a very expansive reading of this one sentence. More plausibly, the observation is merely another recognition of the majority rule that allowed recovery in that case.

The right to recover damages for loss of consortium resulting from injury to a personal relationship cannot depend upon whether the relationship is "worthy of protection". The test proves everything and nothing. The marital relationship found to be worthy of protection in *Whittlesey* is no longer protected from direct injury, yet the statutory abolition of actions for criminal conversation and alienation of affections has not prompted reconsideration of the holding in *Whittlesey*. The marital relationship has not become less worthy of protection in the past fifteen years, simply because it is entitled to less protection. The relationships between siblings, grandparents and grandchildren, other family members, and even friends are surely close, important relationships, sometimes as meaningful as those between spouses and between parents and children, and equally worthy of protection. The Court does not hold that these other relationships are not worthy of protection but nevertheless states that it has "little difficulty" denying recovery for injuries involving them. Supra at 466. It is quite obvious that the Court has "little difficulty" with this and the other conclusions it reaches, but it is not so obvious why.

The Court also says that it would be "hard pressed" to conclude that injury to a parent did not result in "an equally serious deprivation" as the death of that parent, or the death of a child, or the death or injury of a spouse. Supra at 466. Again, the argument proves too much or nothing at all. Almost any loss of a close friend or family member is a "serious deprivation".[15] If every such serious deprivation should be recompensed with money damages, then a person should be entitled to damages for loss of consortium whenever someone close is injured. The Court, however, would not allow recovery for every "serious deprivation", only for some.

To characterize certain close, personal relationships as "worthy of protection" and the loss of such relationships a "serious deprivation" is unavoidably demeaning to others. The very idea contemplates that some personal losses are not "serious", and that some relationships are unworthy of protection, or in the Court's ill-chosen words, have "second class status". Supra at 466. If it is reassuring to parents and children to know that this Court considers their relationships to be first class, it must be equally insulting to other family members to have their relationships judicially relegated to lesser status. To decide what relationships are "first" and "second class", and "worthy of protection" or "unworthy", and what personal losses are "serious" and "not serious", is grossly presumptuous. The Court ought not to place itself in the position of making such determinations, and it certainly should not generalize and divide relationships by category without considering their particular aspects in specific circumstances. If recovery for loss of consortium really depended upon whether the injured relationship was "worthy of protection"—and it certainly should not—that determination ought to be left to the finder of fact to be made from the evidence adduced in each case. Not even the Court is willing to go so far, preferring categorization over individual determination.

Whether to allow recovery for loss of consortium must not depend upon the worth of the relationship injured or the seriousness of the loss. The emotional, spiritual attributes of all kinds of personal relationships are immeasurable. The Court's "worthy of protection" standard is alluring rhetoric but very flawed and unfortunately offensive reasoning. Allowing damages for loss of consortium must instead depend on the ability of our legal system to determine appropriate monetary compensation for such intangible, emotional injuries, an ability Dean Pound characterized as "necessarily . . . crude". Pound, supra, at 194.

. . . .

4

. . . .

If David Reagan had simply decided to abandon Julia, she would have suffered as serious a deprivation of his care and affection as she has in this case, but she would not have a cause of action against him, no matter how reprehensible his actions. Although parents in this state are obliged to support their children financially, they have no legal duty to provide them affection. A daughter cannot sue her father for failing to love her.

---

15. "No man is an island, entire of itself; every man is a piece of the continent, a part of the main; if a clod be washed away by the sea, Europe is the less, as well as if a promontory were, as well as if a manor of thy friends or of thine own were; any man's death diminishes me, because I am involved in mankind; and therefore never send to know for whom the bell tolls; it tolls for thee." J. DONNE, DEVOTIONS UPON ENERGENT OCCASIONS, NO. 17.

If Julia had lost the care and love of her father not because he was negligently hit in the head in a fight at a beer joint but because one of the barmaids at the beer joint intentionally enticed him to abandon his family for her, Julia would have suffered the same loss of her father's consortium that she has suffered in this case, but she would not be entitled to recover damages either from her father or his Lorelei. The law has never afforded a child recovery for direct, intentional injury to the parental relationship. "If a claim is not allowed for an intentional tort, it would be strange indeed that it should be allowed for a negligent tort." Pleasant v. Washington Sand & Gravel Co., 262 F.2d 471, 473 (D.C.Cir.1958). Yet that is the result of the Court's decision.

Julia cannot recover for the loss of her father's consortium caused by her parents' decision to divorce and her mother's decision to remarry. She cannot sue her stepfather for damages for ordering Reagan not to telephone Julia. The injury to Julia's relationship with her father caused by her parents' divorce, her father's move to Texas, and her mother's remarriage is no less real than the injury caused by Lucky Vaughn; only the latter, however, is compensable under the Court's rule.

If the Court's purpose is to protect children from the wrongful deprivation of their parents' affection, then it has not accomplished much by today's ruling. If only it would extend its rule to cover other injuries to the parent-child relationship which are equally as serious as those it would recompense and very much more frequent, it might achieve real protection of children. As it is, the Court's ruling helps very few children. It surely goes without saying that awarding money to a child who cannot spend it until majority does nothing to help relieve the loss of relationship with the parent at all; rather, as one court has observed, it simply assures "that upon reaching adulthood, when plaintiffs will be in less need of [parental] guidance, they will be unusually wealthy men and women." Borer v. American Airlines, 19 Cal.3d 441, 138 Cal.Rptr. 302, 563 P.2d 858, 862 (1977). On the whole, the Court's ruling does little more than increase the stakes in high-dollar personal injury litigation.

B

The rule the Court adopts is unmanageable. It extends the right to recover monetary damages for an intangible loss which cannot be measured. It does nothing to prevent overlapping recovery when there are multiple claimants as a result of a single occurrence. It is not limited to claims by minor children, and is not clearly limited to instances involving serious injury to the parent. And it is likely that the recovery the Court allows will result in additional friction in relationships already marred by physical injury. The Court appears to be oblivious to these problems, for it chooses not to mention them or to refute this dissent.

1

The law recognizes that some intangible, non-economic injuries may be compensated with an award of money damages. Such injuries include physical pain, mental anguish, impairment and disfigurement resulting from personal injuries. No appraiser can testify to the value of such losses.

Yet juries must do what no one else can: they must set a specific dollar figure on these intangible injuries.

Like other intangible injuries, the loss of a family member's "love, affection, protection, emotional support, services, companionship, care, and society", supra at 467, cannot be measured in dollars and cents. Assessing damages for loss of consortium, however, is even harder than for other intangible losses. As Dean Pound observed, "in so far as these interests are in effect interests of personality, they are so peculiarly related to the mental and spiritual life of the individual as to involve in the highest degree the difficulties incident to all legal reparation of injuries to the person." Pound, supra, at 196.

The Court takes no notice of the immense difficulties inherent in the task. The Court holds that jurors awarding damages for loss of parental consortium may take into account "the severity of the injury to the parent and its actual effect upon the parent-child relationship, the child's age, the nature of the child's relationship with the parent, the child's emotional and physical characteristics, and whether other consortium giving relationships are available to the child." Supra at 467. I doubt whether jurors will find these factors to be of much help. Regarding the child's age, for example, I cannot tell whether the Court thinks injury is greater when the child has become close to the parent but is less in need of parental guidance, or when the child is an infant and does not know the parent but is very much in need of some parental care. Considering the child's personality, I do not know if the Court thinks that injury involving a well-adjusted, stable child is worth more or less than injury involving an emotionally insecure child. Regarding the availability of "other consortium giving relationships", I cannot tell whether the Court actually thinks that a child in a larger family suffers less from parental injury than an only child. I simply do not see how the Court can imagine that anyone, even a juror, can use these factors to arrive at a monetary value for loss of parental consortium. The factors are as imponderable as the loss itself, and applying them is mostly guesswork.

Consigning to a jury the task of assessing damages for loss of parental consortium does not make it any less difficult, or the result any more defensible. Consider the present case. No direct evidence of the dollar amount of Julia's damages was introduced in this case, no doubt because such evidence is not available and because, as any experienced litigator will appreciate, it is virtually impossible to speak of a loss like Julia's delicately and respectfully in terms of money. The bare mention of the relative value of a personal, intangible loss risks offending jurors. The only suggestion to the jury about what they should find from the facts before them came from counsel in closing arguments. Reagan's counsel's entire argument on the subject was the following: For Julie Reagan I think you ought to be $2,500 a year. You're talking about support in the past, support in the future. That's what I would do a year and just multiply it. Loss of parental care. What is that worth? I suggest $250,000. I suggest $250,000 on mental anguish in the past and mental anguish in the future. A lot of money? But I think she has suffered. This is in my career, without a doubt, one of the worst injuries I have ever seen, both as to consequences and injuries it caused. The guardian ad litem appointed for Julia never mentioned a dollar amount to the jury but argued briefly that Reagan would not be able to do the kinds of things for Julia that another father might do for his daughter. Defendants' counsel argued only: Now there's a little girl I know who will suffer more than anybody, but that's unfortunate. As you've heard, and I can't answer questions of these folks on the stand, the mother remarried and I know she's got a stepfather and I understand a stepfather is not the same as a father. She's the person that will suffer but, unfortunately, it's not because of anything that Lester Vaughn, Ernest Rosenovac or Keith Nichols did. It was because of what David Reagan did. Based upon this argument and the evidence summarized above, the jury awarded Julia $405,000 for lost parental care and past and future mental anguish.

There is nothing in the evidence in this case to indicate that Julia should get $405,000 for her loss. The jury appears simply to have accepted some of the figures suggested by Reagan's counsel in argument. The jury might just as well have assessed damages at $1,000 or $1,000,000; I doubt seriously whether either award would have been set aside as either inadequate or excessive. In future cases, some children will "hit the jackpot" while others will be awarded little or nothing, depending mostly on factors like which attorney is more persuasive, which party is more sympathetic, and the geographical location of the trial—none of which have anything whatever to do with any loss that may have been suffered. In no case will any real loss be restored. I can see very little justification for a rule which allows such lottery-like awards and serves as much or more to benefit lawyers than the children the rule professes to protect.

The difficulty in assessing compensation for intangible injuries is unavoidably present in most personal injury actions. Now, if the injured person is a parent, that difficulty is multiplied by the necessity of considering the more remote injuries to the children's relationships with the injured parent. The Court offers no justification for this result.

2

Further complicating assessment of damages for a child's loss of parental consortium is the difficulty in preventing such recovery from overlapping or conflicting with damages awarded to the injured parent or to any sibling. Apart from any claim by the child, the injured parent may ask the fact finder to consider as an element of any damages assessed the impairment in performing parental responsibilities that the parent claims to have suffered. If damages are assessed for this element of recovery, the injury to the parent-child relationship has been compensated at least in part. Under the rule the Court adopts today, each of the injured parent's children may also sue for damages to the parent-child relationship. To prevent multiple recovery for the same injury, the damages awarded the parent and each child should not overlap each other. Also, the damage awards should not be conflicting: that is, a child should not be awarded damages for loss of consortium when the injured parent has not recovered damages for any loss of ability to love and care for the child; and recovery by similarly situated children should not be greatly disparate.

. . . .

IV

A

The far-reaching effects of the Court's legislation today seem to have escaped its notice. Before today, the only persons who could claim damages resulting from the tortious infliction of nonfatal bodily injury were the injured person and his or her spouse. Now the children of the injured person may assert their own claims. The potential liability for a single incident of bodily injury has thus been multiplied. The liability for injury to a person with children may be greater than for a person who is childless, resulting in an unpredictable range of exposure. Someone who injures a single person may get off relatively lightly compared with someone else who inflicts no greater injury on a married person with children.

. . . .

B

The Court insists that it is only reexamining common law rules in light of current conditions. I was not aware that there was a public clamor for more personal injury lawsuits. Many of the damage claims allowed by the Court in today's decision will be paid ultimately by the public in the form of increased costs of goods and services, and increased insurance premiums. The continued viability of this wealth redistribution system is everyday more in doubt. The personal injury compensation business employs thousands, many of whom are attorneys who are rewarded quite handsomely, partially at the expense of its customers who must bear the terrible overhead of expenses, fees and costs, and partially at the expense of the public. The extent to which the unlimited growth of this business benefits society remains to be measured.

The Court does not even pause to acknowledge these current conditions in light of which it is to reexamine the established common law rule. It does not take evidence on the benefits and costs of the rule it adopts, as it might if it were a legislature. It does not seek expert prognosis on the probable effects of the rule. The Court does not need this kind of information regarding the effect of changes in the law to inform its decisions. The Court knows best. It simply announces that it is time to change the rule.

The Court's decision reflects an ever-expanding universe of tort liability. It is difficult to find in its opinion any principled parameters on the kinds of relational injuries or claimants which might be held to be compensable. For example, I suspect that the Court's opinion will soon be used to argue that having allowed recovery for loss of spousal and parental consortium, we should also allow recovery for loss of filial consortium. Two of the states which have recognized recovery of parental consortium have refused to extend recovery to filial consortium. Norman v. Massachusetts Bay Transp. Auth., 403 Mass. 303, 529 N.E.2d 139 (1988); Sizemore v. Smock, 430 Mich. 283, 422 N.W.2d 666 (1988). As the Massachusetts highest court recognized, courts should proceed with an awareness that "as a matter of sound public policy, the law cannot and should not attempt to right all wrongs. . . . '[T]ort liability cannot be extended without limit.'" Norman, 529 N.E.2d at 140.

* * * * * *

The decision in this case is founded almost entirely on nothing sturdier than the personal preferences of a majority of the members of the Court as to what the law should be. It is this Court's prerogative to develop the common law, but its stewardship of that jurisprudence does not authorize it to act as a judicial oligarchy imposing its individual whims of what is fair on the public. The rule the Court adopts is unwise; but the manner in which the Court adopts that rule is imperious.

Accordingly, I dissent.

■ [J. Doggett's concurring and dissenting opinion omitted.]

E. Wrongful Death

Liff v. Schildkrout

Court of Appeals of New York, 1980.
49 N.Y.2d 622, 427 N.Y.S.2d 746, 404 N.E.2d 1288.

■ Jasen, J. The issues on these appeals are whether a surviving spouse, in his or her individual capacity, may maintain a common-law cause of action for loss of consortium due to death and whether loss of consortium may be asserted as an element of damages within a wrongful death action.

. . . .

The first issue for our resolution is whether a surviving spouse, in his or her individual capacity, may maintain a common-law cause of action in this State for loss of consortium due to death which is independent and distinct from a statutory action for wrongful death. While we recognize the attractive nature of plaintiffs' arguments, we decline the invitation to change the law of this State and adhere to our pronouncement in Ratka v. St. Francis Hosp., 44 N.Y.2d 604, 407 N.Y.S.2d 458, 378 N.E.2d 1027, that all causes of action arising from the death of an individual must be maintained in accordance with statutory authority.

Although the origin of the common-law notion that "[i]n a civil court, the death of a human being could not be complained of as an injury" has been the subject of much speculation and the cited theoretical underpinnings of the rule itself have drawn serious questions as to their continued vitality, there is simply no room left for debate that the common law of this State, despite numerous opportunities and forceful requests to change, does not recognize suits to recover damages for the wrongful death of an individual. This is not to say that a decedent's distributees are without a remedy, for a cause of action for wrongful death has been expressly authorized by statute in this State since 1847 and is now embodied in EPTL 5–4.1. (See N.Y.Const., art. I, § 16 [right of action to recover for injuries resulting in death may not be abrogated].) Thus, the cause of action for wrongful death has been dubbed "a child of statute".

Perhaps the most forthright justification for the refusal by the courts of this State to establish a common-law cause of action for wrongful death is the very existence of the statutory right. This is the clear import of our holding in the *Ratka* case. The courts have deferred to the wisdom of the Legislature in striking the sensitive balance as to the causes of action which should be permitted to be maintained due to the wrongful death of another and also the measure of damages recoverable. In short, legislative enactments have pre-empted this area; the rights accorded by statute being in derogation of the common law, the right to sue for injury sustained due to the death of another must be founded in statutory authority.

Nor can it be said that a spouse's cause of action for loss of consortium exists in the common law independent of the injured spouse's right to maintain an action for injuries sustained. In this regard, we adopt the reasoning set forth in Osborn v. Kelley, 61 A.D.2d 367, 402 N.Y.S.2d 463, "that insofar as plaintiff is attempting to recover for loss of consortium for the period prior to decedent's death, a cause of action is stated. Such a cause of action, however, is a derivative one. The wrongful death statute created a new cause of action based not upon damage to the estate of the deceased because of death, but rather for the pecuniary injury to the surviving spouse and next of kin of the decedent. Since a decedent has no cause of action to recover damages for his death, plaintiff has no derivative cause of action to recover for loss of consortium due to decedent's death."

In sum, we decline the invitation to recognize a common-law cause of action on behalf of the surviving spouse for permanent loss of consortium due to the wrongful death of his or her marital partner. Any cause of action or, indeed, remedy predicated upon the loss of one's spouse must be founded in statutory authority.

Having so concluded, it becomes necessary to determine the issue whether loss of consortium can be claimed as an element of damages within a wrongful death action. Resolution of this issue centers upon an examination of the statutory language embodied in EPTL 5–4.3.

That section—which delineates the measure of damages in wrongful death actions—provides in pertinent part: "The damages awarded to the plaintiff may be such sum as the jury or, where issues of fact are tried without a jury, the court or referee deems to be fair and just compensation for the pecuniary injuries resulting from the decedent's death to the persons for whose benefit the action is brought. In every such action, in addition to any other lawful element of recoverable damages, the reasonable expenses of medical aid, nursing and attention incident to the injury causing death and the reasonable funeral expenses of the decedent paid by the distributees, or for the payment of which any distributee is responsible, shall also be proper elements of damage."

The qualifying phrase "pecuniary injuries" has been retained since the enactment of the first wrongful death statute in this State and has been consistently construed by the courts as excluding recovery for grief, and loss of society, affection and conjugal fellowship—all elements of the generic phrase "loss of consortium". While it is true that one factor often cited by courts in refusing recovery for loss of consortium—that loss of consortium is incapable of measurement in monetary terms—has been repudiated by this court, there still exists a fundamental reason why we should not change the present rule of law.

The Legislature, by including the pecuniary injury limitation in its statutory scheme, clearly intended that damages for loss of consortium should not be recoverable in wrongful death actions. The courts, under such circumstances, are not free to consider the relative merits of the arguments in favor of, or in opposition to, this limitation for the Legislature has "struck the balance for us." As shown, the courts of this State have consistently honored this legislative policy of limitation on damages and, given the failure of the Legislature to amend the statute, we conclude that the Legislature has approved this finding and implementation of legislative intent.

In short, we now reaffirm the principle that a claim for loss of consortium will not be recognized within a wrongful death action in this State. If a change should be made, it is for the Legislature, and not the courts, to make.

. . . .

NOTE ON *LIFF*

Compare with *Liff* the following passages from Krouse v. Graham, 19 Cal.3d 59, 137 Cal.Rptr. 863, 562 P.2d 1022 (1977):

The statutory cause of action for wrongful death, created in California in 1862, provided that "pecuniary or exemplary" damages were to be awarded by the jury in the amount found "just" under all the circumstances. Ten years after its enactment, the statute was amended to remove the words "pecuniary or exemplary," retaining the language that "damages may be given as under all the circumstances of the case, may be just, . . ." Nonetheless, in subsequent decisional law a theory developed that damages for wrongful death were recoverable only for the "pecuniary" losses suffered by the decedent's heirs.

California case law, however, has not restricted wrongful death recovery only to those elements with an ascertainable economic value, such as loss of household services or earning capacity. On the contrary, as early as 1911, we held that damages could be recovered for the loss of a decedent's "society, comfort and protection," though only the "pecuniary value" of these losses was held to be a proper element of recovery. Other cases have held admissible such evidence as the closeness of the family unit, the warmth of feeling between family members, and the character of the deceased as "kind and attentive" or "kind and loving". Not only was wrongful death compensation awarded historically to heirs who had been financially dependent upon their deceased relatives, but adult children received substantial awards for the wrongful death of retired, elderly parents and parents received compensatory damages for the death of young children. These cases suggest a realization that if damages truly were limited to "pecuniary" loss, recovery frequently would be barred by the heirs' inability to prove such loss. The services of children, elderly parents, or nonworking spouses often do not result in measurable net income to the family unit, yet unquestionably the death of such a person represents a substantial "injury" to the family for which just compensation should be paid.

. . . .

We think it significant that the United States Supreme Court (announcing the rule under maritime law) permits recovery in a wrongful death action for the loss of such elements as comfort, love or affection without any accompanying requirement that such loss be deemed to be pecuniary in nature. (Sea–Land Services, Inc. v. Gaudet (1974) 414 U.S. 573, 94 S.Ct. 806, 39 L.Ed.2d 9.) In *Sea–Land* the high court, in construing the federal Death on the High Seas Act, carefully assessed the issue presently before us. It concluded that the weight of state court authority favored recognition of the right of recovery for loss of the decedent's society, even in those jurisdictions which by statutory language or judicial interpretation restrict the remedy to pecuniary loss. Recognizing this national trend and "the humanitarian policy of the maritime law to show 'special solicitude' for those who are injured within its jurisdiction", the *Sea–Land* court held that recovery for wrongful death in an admiralty case could properly be had for the demonstrable and, in a monetary sense more easily measurable, services of the decedent to spouse and child. It is greatly persuasive with us that in doing so the Supreme Court interpreted the term "society" as including "a broad range of mutual benefits each family member receives from the others' continued existence, including love, affection, care, attention, companionship, comfort, and protection."

Yowell v. Piper Aircraft Corporation

Supreme Court of Texas, 1986.
703 S.W.2d 630.

■ SPEARS, J. This is a wrongful death and survival case. On February 22, 1977, Howard Reed Yowell, James Luther Ward, Jr., Jimmy Kenneth Fulkerson, and Fabe Ingram, Jr. were killed in a crash of a Piper PA–31–310 aircraft near Springdale, Arkansas. The airplane sustained a mid-air breakup at about 10,000 feet and crashed to the ground. There were no survivors.

. . . .

LOSS OF INHERITANCE

This court has not specifically addressed loss of inheritance damages in prior wrongful death cases. In San Antonio A.P. Ry. Co. v. Long, 87 Tex. 148, 27 S.W. 113 (1894), this court hinted that "under our statute the loss of prospective increase of inheritance may be an element of damages." In International–Great Northern R. Co. v. Acker, 128 S.W.2d 506 (Tex.Civ. App.—Eastland 1939, writ dism'd judgmt. cor.), the court stated that "[i]t is also the recognized law in this state that in such cases a child, whether adult or minor, may recover for wrongful death of a parent, and that in estimating the damages the loss of prospective accumulations of the deceased parent may be taken into consideration in estimating the amount of recovery."

Clearly, heirs or devisees may suffer pecuniary loss to the extent the decedent would have accumulated property and passed it on to the heirs at his later, natural death. In Texas, the plaintiffs do not receive a double recovery when they receive loss of inheritance damages because the decedent's estate has no cause of action for lost future earnings.

The Texas wrongful death statute gives a specified group of survivors a cause of action for losses they sustain as a result of their decedent's wrongful death. Some states' statutes give the decedent's estate, rather than certain classes of survivors, a cause of action for loss of future accumulated property occasioned by wrongful death. Loss of inheritance under the Texas statute is very similar to "loss of the estate." Under a loss of inheritance claim, however, the claimant must prove not only the probability that the deceased would have accumulated money or assets, but also the probability that the decedent would have left this accumulation by will or inheritance to the statutory beneficiaries.

Substantial federal and state authority allows a beneficiary to recover for loss of inheritance caused by a decedent's wrongful death. Such damages are recoverable under the Federal Employer's Liability Act, as well as the Death on High Seas Act.

Many states allow loss of inheritance damages.

The relatively few courts which have denied this type of recovery have done so not by excluding the loss from pecuniary damages but by holding the amount of the loss too speculative. Though probably nothing is more certain than the uncertainty of human life, presuming that thrifty persons will accumulate an estate and leave it to their heirs at death is no more speculative than finding any of the other recognized elements of pecuniary loss in a wrongful death action, such as lost support, guidance, and training. "Statutes giving damages for injuries resulting in death necessarily deal with probabilities," and necessarily indeterminate damages are properly left to the sound sense of the jury.

Recovery for loss of inheritance is proper. Had the injured person survived, his recovery would include lost future earnings which presumably would increase the personal estate and, at death, pass to heirs or beneficiaries. Preventing the heir's recovery would protect the wrongdoer from the consequences of the wrong.

We define loss of inheritance damages in Texas as the present value that the deceased, in reasonable probability, would have added to the estate and left at natural death to the statutory wrongful death beneficiaries but for the wrongful act causing the premature death. True, not every wrongful death beneficiary sustains loss of inheritance damages. If the decedent would have earned no more than he and his family would have used for support, or if the decedent would have outlived the wrongful death beneficiary, loss of inheritance damages would properly be denied. This is for the jury to decide.

. . . .

Mitchell v. Buchheit

Supreme Court of Missouri, 1977.
559 S.W.2d 528.

■ MORGAN, C.J. . . . . [T]he Court of Appeals . . . transferred the case to this court "for the purpose of [our] reexamining the existing law," relative to whether or not the surviving parents of a minor child, in an action for wrongful death, may recover for pecuniary benefits which they reasonably could have expected after majority of the deceased child.

Decedent was 19 years and 10 months of age, unmarried, and living with his parents when killed in an accident involving two motor vehicles. The parents instituted a wrongful death action; and, judgment was entered on a jury verdict in their favor for $12,500. . . .

. . . .

Plaintiffs' Appeal

. . . [P]laintiffs' contend that the award of $12,500 was inadequate, and that such an unacceptable result was caused by the trial court erroneously refusing to admit evidence or permit argument that circumstances were such that plaintiffs reasonably could have expected pecuniary benefits from their son after he reached majority. . . .

The Court of Appeals agreed with plaintiffs and would have remanded the cause for a new trial as to damages; but, being bound by the latest pronouncements of the substantive law by this court, ordered transfer. We agree that a reassessment of the issue is proper and necessary.

In this state, the Wrongful Death Act was enacted originally in 1855. It has been revised several times since, including 1879, 1905, 1955, 1967 and 1973 Amendments. Throughout, and to this date, the interpretation placed upon the statute by the courts of this state was delineated best in Oliver v. Morgan, 73 S.W.2d 993 (Mo.1934), wherein this court stated that:

"It is . . . clearly the law that the basis of the recovery [for the death of a minor child] is the value of the child's services to the parents during the child's minority, and that from this must be deducted the expenses of the support and maintenance of the child during that period. . . . So long as the statute permits a recovery in such a case of only the *pecuniary* loss to the plaintiffs, the plaintiffs must prove and the jury find an actual pecuniary loss in order to recover."

. . . .

The case of Parsons v. Missouri Pacific Ry. Co., 94 Mo. 286, 6 S.W. 464 (1888), relied on in the *Oliver* case, provided the predicate upon which the rule has continued to rest. . . .

. . . .

The statute was amended as seen in Laws 1905, page 135, (§ 5425, RSMo 1909) and survived as § 537.080(3). It provides, in part, that:

". . . if there be no husband, wife, minor child or minor children, natural born or adopted as hereinbefore indicated, or if the deceased be an unmarried minor and there be no father or mother, then in such case suit may be instituted and recovery had by the administrator or executor of the deceased and the amount recovered shall be distributed according to the laws of descent . . ."

Recovery, therefore, was no longer limited to the parents in a wrongful death case involving a minor. An administrator or executor could recover as a trustee. Logically, no framework remained for the idea a deceased had to be legally obligated to furnish support to the beneficiary. It was sufficient if there existed "a reasonable probability of pecuniary benefit to one from the continuing life of another ..."

Later cases, oddly enough, did not undertake to reassess the limitations created in the *Parsons* case, although doubts as to the validity thereof did appear. For instance, in McCrary v. Ogden, 267 S.W.2d 670 (Mo.1954), this court stated: "Whether our past interpretations of the section, to the effect that recovery is limited to pecuniary loss and in the case of an infant, to the value of services during minority only, are basically correct, may be debatable—but we have consistently so construed the section.". .

. . . .

We have concluded that the holding in the *Parsons* case is not tenable under the present statutory provisions, nor can it stand on its own logic. Parents, seeking to recover for the death of a minor child, should not be prohibited from trying to establish a reasonable probability of pecuniary benefit from the continued life of said child beyond the age of minority. . . .

. . . .

The judgment heretofore entered is affirmed except as to damages and the cause is remanded to the trial court for a new trial on that issue only.

Sanchez v. Schindler

Supreme Court of Texas, 1983.
651 S.W.2d 249.

■ SPEARS, J. Eugene and Angelica Sanchez brought this wrongful death action against Charles Schindler and his parents for the death of their minor son, Johnny Sanchez, arising from a collision between Johnny's motorcycle and Schindler's pick-up truck. The jury found for plaintiffs on the liability issues. On the damages issues, however, they found that Mr. and Mrs. Sanchez sustained no pecuniary loss, but awarded $102,500.00 in damages for the mental anguish suffered by Mrs. Sanchez. The trial court disregarded the jury's answers to the special issues on mental anguish. The court of appeals affirmed the trial court's denial of recovery for mental anguish. . . .

. . . .

The seminal question presented is whether damages for mental anguish are recoverable under the Texas Wrongful Death Act for the death of a child. More specifically, we must determine whether Texas should continue to follow the pecuniary loss rule as the proper measure of damages for the death of a child.

In the past a surviving parent's damages in an action for the death of a child under the Texas Wrongful Death Act have been limited to the pecuniary value of the child's services and financial contributions, minus the cost of his care, support and education. The Texas statute does not expressly limit recovery to pecuniary loss. Tex.Rev.Civ.Stat.Ann. article 4671 creates a cause of action for "actual damages on account of the injuries causing the death...." Article 4677 provides that "[t]he jury may give such damages as they may think proportionate to the injury resulting from such death." Like most states, Texas patterned its wrongful death statutes after Lord Campbell's Act. The Fatal Accident Act, 9 & 10 Vict., ch. 93 § 1 (1846). The English court ruled that Lord Campbell's Act limited recovery to pecuniary loss. In March v. Walker, 48 Tex. 372, 375 (1877), this court held that since the language of the Texas Wrongful Death Act was based on Lord Campbell's Act, the measure of damages under the Texas statute would also be restricted to pecuniary loss.

Sanchez argues the pecuniary loss rule is based on an antiquated concept of the child as an economic asset, and should be rejected. We agree. It is time for this court to revise its interpretation of the Texas Wrongful Death statutes in light of present social realities and expand recovery beyond the antiquated and inequitable pecuniary loss rule. If the rule is literally followed, the average child would have a negative worth. Strict adherence to the pecuniary loss rule could lead to the negligent tortfeasor being rewarded for having saved the parents the cost and expense of rearing a child. The real loss sustained by a parent is not the loss of any financial benefit to be gained from the child, but is the loss of love, advice, comfort, companionship and society. We, therefore, reject the pecuniary loss limitation and allow a plaintiff to recover damages for loss of companionship and society and damages for mental anguish for the death of his or her child. In this case, Mrs. Sanchez pleaded for the recovery of damages for mental anguish, and the jury awarded her $102,500 pursuant to the special issues on mental anguish. She has preserved her argument on appeal to this court.

. . . .

This court has recognized previously that injuries to the familial relationship are significant injuries and are worthy of compensation. In Whittlesey v. Miller, 572 S.W.2d 665 (Tex.1978), we held that either spouse has a cause of action for loss of consortium suffered as a result of an injury to the other spouse by a tortfeasor's negligence. We held that loss of affection, solace, comfort, companionship, society, assistance, and sexual relations were real, direct, and personal losses and said that these losses were not too intangible or conjectural to be measured in pecuniary terms. A parent's claim for damages for the loss of companionship of a child is closely analogous to the loss of consortium cause of action created in *Whittlesey.* In Selders v. Armentrout, 190 Neb. 275, 207 N.W.2d 686 (Neb.1973), the Nebraska Supreme Court noted this analogy with loss of consortium and said, "There is no logical reason for treating an injury to the family relationship resulting from the wrongful death of a child more restrictively."

Either by statute or judicial decision, thirty-five states allow recovery for loss of companionship and society in a wrongful death action brought by the parents. Presently, fourteen jurisdictions allow recovery for damages for loss of companionship and society under statutes containing language which traditionally had been interpreted as limiting recovery to pecuniary loss. Twenty one states recognize recovery for loss of society and companionship by statute. Nine of these statutes were amended to include these elements after their existing statutes were judicially interpreted to include society and companionship.

Commentators are virtually unanimous in their criticism of the pecuniary loss limitation and advocate recovery for nonpecuniary losses.

The jurisdictions that do not limit recovery to pecuniary loss realize that damages for loss of companionship and society of a child are not too uncertain to be measured in pecuniary terms in an attempt to redress the actual loss which a parent suffers. These elements of damage are not too speculative to be given a monetary value. Recovery is allowed in other tort areas for injuries which are equally intangible; e.g., pain and suffering. The fear of excessive verdicts is not a sufficient justification for denying recovery for loss of companionship. The judicial system has adequate safeguards to prevent recovery of damages based on sympathy or prejudice rather than fair and just compensation for the plaintiff's injuries.

A parent's recovery under the wrongful death statute includes the mental anguish suffered as a result of the child's wrongful death. The destruction of the parent-child relationship results in mental anguish, and it would be unrealistic to separate injury to the familial relationship from emotional injury. Injuries resulting from mental anguish may actually be less nebulous than pain and suffering, or injuries resulting from loss of companionship and consortium. A plaintiff should be permitted to prove the damages resulting from a tortfeasor's negligent infliction of emotional trauma. This includes recovery for mental anguish.

In this case Mrs. Sanchez proved she is suffering from traumatic depressive neurosis. She presented testimony that she is despondent and disoriented, has been forced to seek medical attention for her neurosis and has frequent neck and shoulder pains and headaches. Mrs. Sanchez has proved that she suffered mental anguish, and therefore, is entitled to recover the $102,500 awarded to her by the jury for her mental anguish.

Presently, the courts of several states allow recovery for mental anguish under statutes similar to Texas' statute. See, e.g., City of Tucson v. Wondergem, 105 Ariz. 429, 466 P.2d 383, 386 (Ariz.1970).[7] In City of Tucson v. Wondergem, the Arizona Supreme Court allowed a plaintiff to recover for mental anguish in a wrongful death action under a statute which provided "the jury shall give such damages as it deems fair and just with reference to the injury resulting from the death...." The Arizona court found the denial of recovery for mental anguish deprived the survivor of material damages "resulting from the death." The court noted that the Arizona Wrongful Death Act had already been interpreted to allow recovery for loss of companionship and comfort and said that these losses result in mental anguish.

. . . .

We, therefore, reverse the judgment of the court of appeals, and render judgment that Mrs. Angelica Sanchez recover $102,500 for the mental anguish she suffered as a result of her son's death in addition to the other damages awarded by the jury which have not been appealed.

---

7. Additionally, eight states allow recovery for mental anguish by statute.

[The dissenting opinion of POPE, C.J., is omitted.]

Farley v. Sartin Trucking Co.

Supreme Court of Appeals of West Virginia, 1995.
195 W.Va. 671, 466 S.E.2d 522.

■ CLECKLEY, JUSTICE:

The plaintiff below and appellant herein, Kenneth Farley, as the Administrator of the Estate of Baby Farley, his unborn child, appeals from the September 8, 1994, order of the Circuit Court of Wayne County. This order granted a motion for summary judgment by the defendants below and appellees herein, Billy R. Sartin and Lee Sartin Trucking Company, Inc., and dismissed the plaintiff's case with prejudice. The issue presented to this Court on appeal is whether the plaintiff can maintain a cause of action under West Virginia's wrongful death statute, W.Va.Code, 55–7–5 (1931), for the death of Baby Farley, who was eighteen to twenty-two weeks of gestation and, at best, of questionable viability in light of the evidence presented to the circuit court. Upon review, we conclude the plaintiff may maintain his cause of action regardless of viability and, therefore, we reverse the order of the circuit court.

I.

FACTS AND PROCEDURAL HISTORY

On November 6, 1991, the plaintiff's pregnant wife, Cynthia Farley, was killed in an automobile accident she had with the defendant, Billy R. Sartin, who was driving a tractor trailer owned by the defendant, Lee Sartin Trucking Company, Inc. The deposition of Mrs. Farley's treating obstetrician, Dr. Gary Gilbert, which was the only medical testimony in the record, adduced the following. Mrs. Farley was probably eighteen weeks and a few days pregnant when calculated from the date of the first day of her last menses, although she could have been as far along as twenty-two weeks pregnant.[2] Baby Farley was neither large enough nor developed enough to survive outside the womb.[3] "The earliest surviving infant that

---

2. Dr. Gilbert indicated that the gestational age of Baby Farley was an estimate because more accurate testing is not performed on a normal pregnant woman until her twentieth week of pregnancy and Mrs. Farley had not reached that point when calculated from her last menses.

3. At this gestational age of development, an unborn child often is referred to as a fetus. Biologically, a fetus is defined as "the unborn offspring in the post embryonic period after major structures have been outlined (in man from seven or eight weeks after fertilization until birth)." Black's Law Dictionary 621 (6th ed. 1990). Between the second and eighth week of development after fertilization is referred to as the "embryo" stage.

The first week after fertilization is called the "ovum" stage. See Taber's Cyclopedic Medical Dictionary E–19 (13th ed. 1977). Although we recognize the biological distinction among the ovum, embryo, and fetus stages, this distinction largely is irrelevant to this opinion because we are concerned with the concept of viability and the time frame from conception to viability and viability to birth.

Throughout the cases and literature reviewed and cited by this Court, the terms "fetus" and "unborn child" frequently are used interchangeably. (The common definition of "child" includes "an unborn ... person[.]" Webster's New Collegiate Dictionary, first definition, in part, 191 (1979)). By our use of the phrase "unborn child" in the con-

[the doctor knew] of was right at 500 grams, which would have been about 22 weeks." Dr. Gilbert concluded that if Mrs. Farley had not been killed in the accident, he had "no reason to believe that she would not have a normal pregnancy."

The plaintiff filed a wrongful death action as the Administrator of the Estate of Baby Farley. In response, the defendants filed a motion for summary judgment pursuant to Rule 56 of the West Virginia Rules of Civil Procedure on the basis that Baby Farley was not viable at the time of death; therefore, the defendants argued Baby Farley was not a "person" under the wrongful death statute, W.Va.Code, 55–7–5. After reviewing the parties' respective motions and supporting memoranda, the circuit court granted summary judgment in favor of the defendants.

The issue presented to this Court is narrow and one of first impression. Although the plaintiff first argues that this case presents a genuine issue of fact as to whether Baby Farley was a viable child at the time of the accident, we find the more critical issue is whether viability is the appropriate criterion to determine whether an unborn child is a "person" within the context of W.Va.Code, 55–7–5. Our discussion and holding are limited to this issue only, and what we say in this opinion should not be considered as indicative of our views on other unrelated issues, especially those on abortion. For reasons that will follow, we find that viability is not the appropriate criterion to determine whether an unborn child is a "person" within the context of W.Va.Code, 55–7–5.

. . .

IV.

A CAUSE OF ACTION FOR THE TORTIOUS DEATH OF A NONVIABLE UNBORN CHILD

First, we agree with those jurisdictions that hold a tortious injury suffered by a nonviable child en ventre sa mere who subsequently is born alive is compensable and no less meritorious than an injury inflicted upon a viable child who subsequently is born alive. [footnote omitted] To declare otherwise not only would lead to unjust and inequitable results but also would be contrary to the underlying philosophies of our tort law. In this

text of this opinion, we are sensitive to those who may have philosophical, religious, or other reasons why they prefer the term "fetus" over the phrase "unborn child" or vice versa. In this respect, our reference is not designed to pass judgment upon these reasons nor do we intend to invoke an emotional response on the part of the reader. For purposes of this opinion, we frame the issue in the context of the phrase "unborn child" to encompass all stages of development after conception where the medical definition of "fetus" limits the developmental time frame.

We also explicitly limit this holding to unborn children who are en ventre sa mere and decline to address the issues that may arise with advances in medical technology now enabling conception outside the womb. In addition, we decline to address the area of preconception torts that may result in the death of an unborn child.

In Black's Law Dictionary at 534, the phrase "en ventre sa mere" is defined as: "In its mother's womb. A term descriptive of an unborn child. For some purposes the law regards an infant en ventre as in being. It may take a legacy; have a guardian; an estate may be limited to its use, etc." (Citations omitted).

respect, viability at the time of the injury is "a mere theoretical abstraction" if a child born alive suffers from a pre-viability tort as opposed to a post-viability tort.

Turning to a cause of action for wrongful death, we confront the issue of whether "viability" is the proper line upon which we should permit a cause of action. With the exception of Georgia, which allows recovery after an unborn child is quick in the womb, and Missouri, which found legislative direction to hold a nonviable child is a "person" under its wrongful death statute, we are not aware of any other cases that permit recovery for injury prior to viability unless there is a live birth. As previously stated, however, a lack of precedent—standing alone—is an insufficient reason to deny a cause of action. Rather, we must examine the reasons for the dearth of precedent and determine whether those reasons give due cause for refusing to extend the law. After reviewing a number of nonviable unborn child decisions in jurisdictions that permit a cause of action for a viable unborn child, we can find no legitimate or persuasive reason to infuse the distinction into West Virginia's statute. We do not believe that proper application of stare decisis prevents us from rejecting an unjustified and unpersuasive majority position. Nor does abandoning the majority position in any way cause harm to any West Virginia interest. "Primary behavior is not affected: no rule of conduct is retroactively changed [.]" Allied–Bruce Terminix Cos., Inc. v. Dobson, ___ U.S. ___, ___, 115 S.Ct. 834, 845, 130 L.Ed.2d 753, 771 (1995). (Scalia, J., dissenting). The law merely is made applicable and beneficial to a broader class of litigants.

In jurisdictions where the viability standard is controlling, the tortfeasor remains unaccountable for the full extent of the injuries inflicted by his or her wrongful conduct. In our judgment, justice is denied when a tortfeasor is permitted to walk away with impunity because of the happenstance that the unborn child had not yet reached viability at the time of death. The societal and parental loss is egregious regardless of the state of fetal development. Our concern reflects the fundamental value determination of our society that life—old, young, and prospective—should not be wrongfully taken away. In the absence of legislative direction, the overriding importance of the interest that we have identified merits judicial recognition and protection by imposing the most liberal means of recovery that our law permits.

As explained by Justice Maddox in his dissent in Gentry v. Gilmore, 613 So.2d 1241, 1246 (Ala.1993), in construing Alabama's wrongful death statute, the phrase "minor child" should be interpreted to include a nonviable unborn child. To give it such a construction, Justice Maddox said, would

"(1) promote the purpose of the wrongful death statute, which is to prevent the wrongful termination of life, even potential life; (2) facilitate the legislature's intent to protect nonviable fetal life, as expressed in other statutes concerning abortion and fetal deaths; and (3) be logically consistent with prior decisions of this Court that have, in my opinion, rejected what I believe are artificial distinctions based on viability and live birth as conditions for recovery." 613 So.2d at 1245.

In addition, Justice Maddox stated that "in distinguishing between viability and nonviability of the fetus as a condition for the application of Alabama's Wrongful Death Act, [one] necessarily resurrect[s] the same distinctions that led to the adoption of wrongful death statutes in the first place." 613 So.2d at 1246. Justice Maddox further reasoned:

"To deny a cause of action rewards tortfeasors who inflict fatal injuries upon nonviable fetuses, by allowing them to escape liability based upon what I think is an artificial distinction that focuses more on the status of the life that has been wrongfully terminated than upon the wrongful conduct that caused the death. Such a holding produces an anomalous result." 613 So.2d at 1246.

These common-sense principles as set forth by Justice Maddox apply equally as well to the death of a nonviable unborn child as they do to a nonviable unborn child who suffers a tortious injury and survives birth and a viable unborn child who suffers a tortious injury and dies en ventre sa mere. Wrongful death statutes, after all, are designed to provide economic compensation to the surviving family. When a family loses a potential member because of tortious conduct, it suffers an injury of the same order[25] as that which occurs when it loses an existing member. The statute allows recovery for the loss of a life that would have provided love and sustenance but for the intervening tort.

As this Court previously has held, W.Va.Code, 55–7–5, is remedial in nature and should be liberally construed. Baldwin, 155 W.Va. at 437, 184 S.E.2d at 431. In light of our previous interpretation of W.Va.Code, 55–7–5, and the goals and purposes of wrongful death statutes generally, we, therefore, hold that the term "person," as used in this statute and the equivalent language in its counterpart, W.Va.Code, 55–7–6 (1992), encompasses a nonviable unborn child and, thus, permits a cause of action for the tortious death of such child.

We recognize that the closer one gets to the moment of conception, the more substantial becomes the potential for fraudulent claims and for increased difficulties in resolving some issues of causation and damages. However, those risks are no more of a justification to erect a bar to legitimate claims in this context than they were when we dismissed them as a reason for rejecting claims relating to viable unborn children in Baldwin. Moreover, our holding in this case eliminates the need for trial courts to decide what often could be an extremely difficult factual question, i.e., whether the fetus was "viable." For reasons stated above and in Baldwin, we also reject the argument that the legal question presented here should be left to the Legislature. Although we invite legislative direction on this matter, it is clear from the statute that the Legislature has not confronted the issue we must decide here, and, therefore, it is the duty of this Court to reach that decision which is most consistent with the purposes of the wrongful death law and which best comports with our sense of justice. We believe our holding meets that duty.

---

25. Concededly, the degree of bonding and love toward an unborn child may not be as great as that which would extend toward the deceased in the more typical wrongful death case. That fact, however, goes to the question of damages and not to actionability.

Several observations about today's decision are in order. Our definition of "person" within the confines of the wrongful death statute neither affects nor interferes with the constitutional protection afforded a woman who chooses to have an abortion, as was set forth originally in Roe v. Wade, 410 U.S. 113, 93 S.Ct. 705, 35 L.Ed.2d 147 (1973). The abortion question simply is not relevant to wrongful death. As Symonds, supra at 113 n. 68, stated, the United States Supreme Court in Roe v. Wade "limited its statement that an unborn child is not a person to the specific terms of the fourteenth amendment." (Citation omitted). Symonds then explained:

"[T]he decision to allow abortion does not depend on the same policies and justifications as does the decision to allow a cause of action for the wrongful death of a fetus. While the fetus may not be a 'person' for the purposes of the fourteenth amendment, it may be a 'person' for the purposes of a state's wrongful death statute. Furthermore, while a woman's right to privacy is the policy involved in the abortion decision, the policy that a tortfeasor should not escape liability is involved in the wrongful death decision. One decision does not solve the controversy of the other."

See also Lingle, supra at 490 ("recognizing a fetus as a 'person' for purposes of the Arkansas wrongful death statute does not run afoul of the decision in Roe v. Wade, nor should it be in conflict with the intent of the statute"); Meadows, supra at 112 n. 123 (given the different policies governing abortion and wrongful death decisions " 'it may be necessary to accept some inconsistency and conclude that prenatal life will be protected against intentional or negligent interference, absent some compelling countervailing interest' "), quoting David Kader, The Law of Tortious Prenatal Death Since Roe v. Wade, 45 Mo.L.Rev. 639, 660 (1980). (Emphasis in original). See generally Summerfield, 144 Ariz. at 477–78, 698 P.2d at 722–23 (the Supreme Court of Arizona stated that the definition of "person" for purposes of the Fourteenth Amendment to the United States Constitution does not control the way the term may be interpreted in another context, i.e., a wrongful death statute).[28] To be clear, a wrongful death action will not lie against a woman who chooses to exercise her constitutional right to have an abortion.[29] By definition, if a woman has a constitutional right to decide whether to carry an unborn child to term or abort it, then the act of aborting is not tortious. In such cases, the reasons for invoking the wrongful death statute do not apply; there is no tortious conduct to deter.

Although we have answered the question presented to this Court given the current language in our wrongful death statute, we strongly encourage

---

28. For the foregoing reasons, we disagree with those jurisdictions that appear to limit the use of the term "person" in wrongful death statutes to the United States Supreme Court's interpretation of "person" in the Fourteenth Amendment context. See Justus, 19 Cal.3d at 577–78, 139 Cal.Rptr. at 106, 565 P.2d at 131.

29. Similarly, we do not find that our determinations in a criminal context control our conclusions in a wrongful death context. See State ex. rel. Atkinson v. Wilson, 175 W.Va. 352, 355, 332 S.E.2d 807, 810 (1984) (recognizing "a distinction between a court's power to evolve common law principles in areas in which it has traditionally functioned, i.e., the tort law, and in those areas in which the legislature has primary or plenary power, i.e., the creation and definition of crimes and penalties." In Syllabus Point 2, we stated: "Neither our murder statute, W.Va.Code, 61-2-1, nor its attendant common law principles authorize prosecution of an individual for the killing of a viable unborn child").

the Legislature to define the word "person" to deal with future problems that may arise—especially with regard to medical technology that now enables conception outside the mother's womb and pre-conception torts.[30] As stated in note 3, supra, this opinion is limited to an unborn child who is en ventre sa mere.

V.

SUMMARY

In conclusion, we find that a nonviable unborn child who is tortiously injured but, nevertheless, is born alive may maintain a cause of action. In addition, if death ensues as a result of a tortiously inflicted injury to a nonviable unborn child, the personal representative of the deceased may maintain an action pursuant to our wrongful death statute. Our decision is a limited one and is in no way intended to be contrary to the constitutional right of a woman to have an abortion. We, therefore, reverse the judgment of the Circuit Court of Wayne County and remand this case for further proceedings.

Reversed and Remanded.

■ MILLER, RETIRED JUSTICE, sitting by temporary assignment.

■ ALBRIGHT, J., did not participate.

NOTE ON RECOVERY FOR INJURY OR DEATH OF A FETUS

Amadio v. Levin, 509 Pa. 199, 501 A.2d 1085 (1985), held that a cause of action lies for the injury or death of a fetus. The court reasoned as follows:

We have, since our decision in Sinkler v. Kneale, 401 Pa. 267, 164 A.2d 93 (1960), recognized that a child en ventre sa mere is a separate individual from the moment of conception, and have permitted that child to sue for injuries received during gestation when the child is born alive. Implicit in our holding in *Sinkler* is the acknowledgement that a child en ventre sa mere is an individual with the right to be free of prenatal injury. If a child en ventre sa mere is an individual at the time of its injury, then, *a fortiori,* the child is also an individual when those injuries cause its death, and it makes no difference in liability under the wrongful death and survival statutes whether the child dies of the injuries just prior to or just after birth.

. . . .

As we have observed in the past, our wrongful death and survival statutes create a derivative cause of action, but those statutes are remedial in nature and purpose, and as such should be liberally construed to accomplish the objective of the act, which is to provide a cause of action

---

30. The Legislature should take such action after careful and reflective consideration of the complexities of the issue before it. Any legislation adopted must provide in clear and plain language the intent of the Legislature. For current examples of state legislation, see Ill.Ann.Stat. ch. 740, Civ.Liab. Act 180, para. 2.2 (Smith–Hurd 1995); S.D. Codified Laws Ann. § 21–5–1 (1984); Tenn. Code Ann. § 20–5–106(c) (1991).

against one whose tortious conduct caused the death of another. By limiting the right to bring an action to those children born alive, we were giving the statute a narrow reading and thereby perpetuating the much criticized rule of the common law which made it "more profitable for the defendant to kill the plaintiff than to scratch him."

. . . .

Our prior concern that such actions create difficulties in establishing proof, upon closer examination, must also give way. Difficulty in obtaining proof of the wrong should never bar the right to bring an action, once it is determined that a cause of action does, indeed, exist. Our caution in extending the right of suit on behalf of the estates of stillborn children may have partly had to do with our unfamiliarity with the problems that this type of litigation would spawn, but any such difficulties in proving damages cannot be deemed greater or different in character from difficulties attending the determination of damages in the case of an injured child who survived delivery for a few minutes, hours or days. These actions have been part of our law for some time, and we are confident that the experience gained from handling such matters has matured our bench to the point when we can now extend the application of these cases to cases where the child is born dead due to death causing injury while en ventre sa mere.

This Court's former view that the real objective of these lawsuits was to compensate the parents of their deceased children twice for the parents' emotional distress is not only incorrect, but if accepted, merely perpetuates the notion that a child is inseparable from its mother while en ventre sa mere. That view lumped medical and funeral costs incurred due to the injury to the child as elements of damages recoverable by the mother. Once the child is recognized as a separate individual, however, medical and funeral costs incurred as well as any economic losses are recoverable by the child's estate, not the mother.

F. WRONGFUL CONCEPTION, WRONGFUL BIRTH, AND WRONGFUL LIFE

Hartke v. McKelway

United States Court of Appeals, District of Columbia Circuit, 1983.
707 F.2d 1544.

■ McGOWAN, J. . . . .

After a jury verdict for plaintiff on all claims, the District Court disallowed the award of childrearing expenses because it found the evidence clear that plaintiff had sought to be sterilized for therapeutic, not economic, reasons, and because she prized the child she bore. . . . We affirm.

. . . .

III

The District of Columbia courts have not offered the same kind of guidance as to the other major issue raised by this appeal: whether Hartke may recover some portion of the costs of raising to majority the child born after the failed sterilization. Moreover, as the District Court noted, the case law from other jurisdictions is almost evenly divided, some courts allowing some recovery under various formulas, others allowing no recovery whatsoever.

In large part, the differences appear to revolve around whether the child can be considered a kind of damage to the parents.[8] A number of courts have ruled that as a matter of law no healthy child can ever be considered an injury to its parents, because, as one court put it, "it is a matter of universally-shared emotion and sentiment that the intangible but all-important, incalculable but invaluable 'benefits' of parenthood far outweigh any of the mere monetary burdens involved." Other courts have found that there are some cases in which the addition of a child constitutes an injury to the family. One court provided the following explanation:

To say that for reasons of public policy contraceptive failure can result in no damage as a matter of law ignores the fact that tens of millions of persons use contraceptives daily to avoid the very result which the defendant would have us say is always a benefit, never a detriment. Those tens of millions of persons, by their conduct, express the sense of the community.

[S]ee also Terrell v. Garcia, 496 S.W.2d 124, 131 (Tex.Civ.App.1973) (Cadena, J., dissenting)("The birth of [an 'unwanted'] child may be a catastrophe not only for the parents and the child itself, but also for previously born siblings."), cert. denied, 415 U.S. 927, 94 S.Ct. 1434, 39 L.Ed.2d 484 (1974).

Though we need not finally decide the question given our ultimate result, we suspect that allowing the plaintiff to prove that raising a child constitutes damage is the course of greater justice, and the one the District of Columbia courts may well adopt. Usually, of course, it is true that the birth of a healthy child confers so substantial a benefit on its parents as to outweigh the physical, emotional, and financial burdens of bearing and raising it; "else, presumably, people would not choose to multiply so freely." But when a couple has chosen not to have children, or not to have any more children, the suggestion arises that for them, at least, the birth of

---

8. Cases that do not fit into the categorization outlined in text include those that recognize that the parents may suffer damage from the birth of a child, but find that those damages are too speculative for calculation. While the calculation of damages in a case like this may be difficult, we see no significant distinction between the task here and the analogous task of fixing damages for wrongful death, for pain and suffering, or for extended loss of consortium. Another argument that does not relate to whether the

birth of a child can be damage to the parents is that the children involved might be adversely affected when they found out that their birth was attributable to a doctor's negligence rather than to their parents' desires, or that their parents once claimed they were not worth the cost of raising them. We are not convinced that the effect on the child will be significantly detrimental in every case, or even in most cases; at least in the absence of that, we think the parents, not the courts, are the ones who must weigh the risk.

a child would not be a net benefit. That is their choice and the courts are required to respect it.

. . . .

Nevertheless, courts have recognized that there is an unusual difficulty in wrongful conception cases in setting the amount of compensation, because the extent, if any, to which the birth of a child is an injury to particular parents is not obvious but will vary depending on their circumstances and aspirations. The parents may in fact have ended up with a child that they adore and that they privately consider to be, on balance, an overwhelming benefit to their lives.[9] This is because the parents may have sought to avoid conception for any of a number of reasons. They may have done so for socio-economic reasons, seeking to avoid disruption of their careers or lifestyle, or to conserve family resources; for eugenic reasons, seeking to avoid the birth of a handicapped child; or for therapeutic reasons, seeking to avoid the dangers to the mother's health of pregnancy and childbirth.

When a couple chooses sterilization solely for therapeutic or eugenic reasons, it seems especially likely that the birth of a healthy child, although unplanned, may be, as it is for most parents, a great benefit to them. In such cases, a court will tend to feel that it is unjust to impose on the

9. It has been said that courts should not allow defendants in wrongful conception cases to thrust upon the plaintiff an unwanted benefit, and that therefore a plaintiff's recovery should not be reduced by any benefits conferred by the defendant's tort. For example, one commentator has written:

> Certainly, the birth of the child may confer certain intangible emotional benefits upon the parent, but these are benefits the parent did not ask for and quite possibly cannot afford. The defendant can be analogized to an officious intermeddler, and when he argues that the damages assessed against him should be offset by the unsolicited benefits of parenthood, the resemblance is quite striking indeed.

Kashi, The Case of the Unwanted Blessing: Wrongful Life, 31 U.Miami L.Rev. 1409, 1416 (1977).

Nevertheless, the courts that allow any recovery of childrearing damages have, with apparently only two exceptions, always required that the detriments of childrearing be offset against the benefits.

It may be, as one court has said, that allowing the benefits of childrearing to reduce the damages recoverable "is nothing more nor less than the application of an offset to reduce the magnitude of verdicts and lessen the monetary shock to the medical tortfeasor and his insurer." If this is so, it is nonetheless true that this desire to reduce the verdict is widely shared, and reflects deeply felt values. The desire may perhaps be based on a sense that, "even in this day of sophisticated contraception and family planning," couples are commonly faced with unanticipated pregnancies. Thus, the sense of wrong that may arise in cases where the defendant usurps the plaintiffs' right to use their property as they please, is tempered by the knowledge that the ability to be free of unwanted pregnancy has never been all that secure. The benefits that the parents of an unplanned child derive from parenthood are nonetheless real. The feeling in wrongful conception cases may be that, especially in view of the parents' concerted efforts to avoid pregnancy, they should recover something in addition to medical expenses and pain and suffering for the disruption of their planning and of their lifestyles. But to refuse to recognize the benefits of childrearing would be contrary to all the humanistic impulses that the law should seek to reinforce and would give plaintiffs a windfall with which to deal with a problem that many couples face without compensation. Whatever the reason, the virtual unanimity of opinion on this question convinces us that the District of Columbia courts would share the sense of justice evinced by the cases, and would adopt some form of the benefits rule.

defendant doctor the often huge costs of raising the child, and will fear that a jury that did so was motivated by passion or anti-doctor prejudice. Thus, in considering the question of whether childrearing expenses may be recoverable, many courts and commentators have placed great emphasis on the couple's reasons for undergoing sterilization. For example, the court in the earliest wrongful conception case, Christensen v. Thornby, 192 Minn. 123, 255 N.W. 620 (1934), made the point most clearly:

> The purpose of the operation was to save the wife from the hazards to her life which were incident to childbirth. It was not the alleged purpose to save the expense incident to pregnancy and delivery. The wife has survived. Instead of losing his wife, the plaintiff has been blessed with the fatherhood of another child. The expenses alleged are incident to the bearing of a child, and their avoidance is remote from the avowed purpose of the operation.

Other cases are to the same effect.

We tend to agree that a factfinder should place great weight on a couple's reason for undergoing sterilization in deciding whether the subsequent birth of a child, on balance, constitutes damage to the parents. Their reason for departing from the usual view that child-rearing is a positive experience is in effect a calculation of the way in which they anticipate the costs of childbirth to outweigh the benefits. That calculation, untainted by bitterness and greed, or by a sense of duty to a child the parents have brought into the world, is usually the best available evidence of the extent to which the birth of the child has in fact been an injury to them. Thus, for example, where a couple sought sterilization solely for therapeutic or eugenic reasons, there is a presumption raised that the uneventful birth of a healthy child constitutes damage to the parents only to the extent that they experienced abnormal fear of harm to the mother or of the birth of a handicapped child. Courts and juries may assume that the parents treasure the child and that the usual expenses of raising it will be outweighed by the benefits derived.

The presumption raised by the evidence of the parents' reason for seeking sterilization is, however, rebuttable. If it can be shown that the parents' situation has somehow significantly changed since the sterilization—by reliance on presumed infertility in making an income-reducing career change, for example, or by a sudden increase in wealth—it may be that the original calculation of anticipated injury has changed for better or worse.[11] Generally, however, the plaintiff's recovery will most accurately

---

11. We note that some courts appear to treat the reason for undergoing sterilization not as the best evidence of whether the birth of a child constitutes damage to the parents, but as conclusive evidence of that fact. The theory is that plaintiffs should recover only for those harms that they sought to avoid. We think such an approach conflicts with the standard tort damages rule that a defendant takes his plaintiff as he finds him, and pays for all damages proximately caused. Regardless of the reason for which the parents sought sterilization, there may be persuasive evidence that the birth of a child was, at the time of birth, damage to them; the parents may have guessed wrong in their initial calculation or they may have changed their minds. In the absence of intervening cause, the defendant must pay for that damage.

Since the approach outlined in the text is merely a guideline to be used in evaluating the evidence in the usual case, and not a conclusive test, it avoids placing undue weight on what the patient told the doctor. For any of a number of reasons, the patient

reflect the amount of injury incurred if it is limited to paying for those risks that the plaintiff specifically sought to avoid and that came to pass.[12]

. . . .

... It seems clear, then, that once the extraordinary dangers of childbirth for her were passed, Hartke shared the general view that having a child would, on balance, be a positive experience.[15]

In these circumstances, we agree that the jury could not rationally have found that the birth of this child was an injury to this plaintiff. Awarding childrearing expenses would only give Hartke a windfall.[16]

may not have given the doctor all the reasons involved or even the right ones. Also, we would not want to encourage doctors to take extra care with persons who provide "expensive" reasons, or to refuse to treat them altogether.

12. This approach will be primarily useful in cases in which the evidence of the reason for undergoing sterilization is unambiguous and overwhelming, as it is in this case. Where there is a mixture of motivations, and the socio-economic reasons are at least a but-for reason for undergoing the operation, the trier of fact will have to look to more direct, but perhaps less reliable, evidence of whether the birth of a child constitutes damage to the parents.

15. In view of the result we reach, we do not need to decide the related question of whether Hartke's failure to have an abortion or place the child for adoption would preclude her from recovering childrearing expenses. Conceivably, a holding based on Hartke's failure to mitigate damages by having an abortion might reduce the damages for medical expenses and pain and suffering that McKelway must pay under our present approach, see infra note 16. McKelway has not pressed this claim here, however, and has in any case provided no evidence as to what Hartke's medical expenses and suffering would have been had she aborted the fetus.

16. Conceivably, the benefits of childraising could be so weighty as to outweigh even the pain and anguish associated with the pregnancy and childbirth. Certainly, this is true in the usual case, since parents are apparently not deterred from having children by the usual prenatal pain and discomfort. Courts that have applied the rule of offsetting benefits against detriments in wrongful conception cases have done so in a variety of ways, however. Some have allowed the benefits of childrearing to be offset against all damages, so that it might happen that a plaintiff would not even recover for medical expenses or pain and suffering. Others limit the offset to reducing childrearing expenses, so that medical expenses and the pain and suffering of pregnancy would be separately recoverable. The Restatement (Second) of Torts offers the narrowest offset rule, requiring that the benefits conferred by a tortfeasor be considered in mitigation of damages only when the benefits are to the same "interest" of the plaintiff that was harmed. Restatement (Second) of Torts § 920 (1979). As applied in the comments, this would require that the pecuniary expenses of childraising be offset only by the monetary benefits that the child brings in, and not by the psychological or emotional rewards derived. Id. comment b (damages to husband for loss of consortium are not diminished by savings derived from no longer having to support wife). The overwhelming majority of courts that have invoked the benefits rule in wrongful conception cases have rejected the strict terms of the Restatement approach.

Few of these sources provide a clear rationale for the lines they draw. Perhaps the most logical approach, in light of the presumptions discussed in this opinion, would be to allow the benefits of childrearing to be offset against the normal pain and expenses of pregnancy and childbirth, but not against any extraordinary expenses and pain associated with the conditions that moved the parents to seek sterilization. This suggestion may, however, attempt to put too fine a point on an admittedly uncertain calculation. Once again, see supra note 9, it may be that the courts' motivations are most accurately stated in terms of rough justice or public policy, like the explanation once given of the concept that damages are limited to those proximately caused by a tort:

> What we ... mean by the word "proximate" is that, because of convenience, of public policy, of a rough sense of

IV

The judgment of the District Court is affirmed.

It is so ordered.

Reed v. Campagnolo

Court of Appeals of Maryland, 1993.
332 Md. 226, 630 A.2d 1145.

Argued before MURPHY, C.J., and ELDRIDGE, RODOWSKY, McAULIFFE, CHASANOW, KARWACKI and ROBERT M. BELL, JJ.

■ RODOWSKY, JUDGE.

This case of alleged medical malpractice comes to us from the United States District Court for the District of Maryland, pursuant to the Maryland Uniform Certification of Questions of Law Act (the Act), Md.Code (1974, 1989 Repl.Vol.), §§ 12–601 through 12–609 of the Courts and Judicial Proceedings Article (CJ). The certified questions are:

"i. Whether the State of Maryland recognizes a tort cause of action for wrongful birth when the doctor does not inform the patient about an available diagnostic test which might reveal the possibility of neural tube defects of the fetus, when these defects are genetically caused, when further diagnostic testing would be required to determine the nature and extent of any fetal defects, and when the plaintiff asserts she would have aborted the child had she been made aware of the fetus's deformities.

"ii. Whether the continuation of a pregnancy is a decision requiring the informed consent of the patient which can give rise to a Maryland tort cause of action for lack of informed consent when the allegedly negligent course of treatment is the defendant physician's failure to inform a pregnant patient about the availability, risks and benefits of diagnostic testing which might reveal birth defects, and failure to inform the patient about the benefits and risks associated with aborting a severely deformed fetus."

Reed v. Campagnolo, 810 F.Supp. 167, 172–73 (D.Md.1993).

. . .

Plaintiffs, Tina Smedley Reed and Frederick E. Reed, seek damages against defendants, Mary Campagnolo, M.D. and Bruce Grund, M.D. Defendants rendered prenatal care to Mrs. Reed and her unborn child at a

justice, the law arbitrarily declines to trace a series of events beyond a certain point. This is not logic. It is practical politics.

The District Court in this case allowed the benefits of childrearing to be offset against the expenses thereof, but not against the expenses and pain associated with the pregnancy itself. We think this was a fair place to draw the line. The latter expenses and pain are more clearly separable from the benefits of raising a child than are the expenses of raising it. More important, if the benefits of childrearing were offset against all damages, it might happen that the defendant would pay no damages whatsoever, which would not provide any disincentive to negligence. Therefore, we agree that Hartke may recover damages for her medical expenses and pain and suffering during pregnancy and childbirth without regard to the benefits of childraising.

Caroline County Health Department maternity clinic beginning in January 1986, the third month of Mrs. Reed's pregnancy.

The essence of the Reeds' allegations are

"that defendants failed in the course of pre-natal care to 'inform plaintiffs of the existence or need for routine [<⌈>-fetoprotein] ("AFP") testing of maternal serum to detect serious birth defects such as spina bifida and imperforate anus.' Had they been informed about AFP testing they would have requested it. Had such testing been done, it would have revealed elevated protein levels, indicative of an abnormal fetus, which would have led plaintiffs to request amniocentesis. Amniocentesis, claim plaintiffs, would have revealed the extent of the fetus's defects and plaintiffs ultimately would have chosen to terminate the pregnancy."

Reed, 810 F.Supp. at 169 (references to complaint omitted).

"The parties agree Mrs. Reed was never informed about AFP testing, a procedure which reveals abnormal levels of proteins produced by the fetus. Abnormal protein levels may indicate genetically caused neural tube defects, including spina bifida. This test must be performed between weeks 16 and 18 of the pregnancy to obtain reliable results."

Id. (footnotes omitted).

"The [Reeds'] child, Ashley Nicole, suffers from a variety of genetically caused abnormalities, including meningomyelocele (spina bifida), hydrocephaly, imperforate anus, and ambiguous genitalia. The infant also has only one kidney, a fistula connecting her bladder and intestines, and increased head circumference, which required the insertion of a cerebral-abdominal shunt after birth."

Id. at 168 (references to complaint omitted).

In August 1989 the plaintiffs and Ashley Nicole made claim through the Health Claims Arbitration Office under the Maryland Health Care Malpractice Claims Act, CJ §§ 3–2A–01 through 3–2A–09. Thereafter, the parties waived arbitration, see CJ § 3–2A–06(A), and in February 1991 the plaintiffs filed their complaint with the United States District Court.

Initially that complaint contained three counts, described by the federal court as follows:

"Count I (Wrongful Birth) alleges negligent failure to inform the parent plaintiffs about the existence, benefits, and risks of AFP testing, amniocentesis, and abortion of a severely deformed fetus, and negligent failure to recognize and evaluate the signs and symptoms of an abnormal pregnancy.

"Count II (Lack of Informed Consent) alleges failure to inform the parent plaintiffs about the various risks of birth defects, testing procedures for birth defects, and the option of aborting a severely deformed fetus.

"Count III (Third Party Beneficiary Maintenance After Age of Majority) alleges a duty owed to all plaintiffs, including the baby, to inform about risk of birth defects, tests available to detect defects, and the option of abortion of a severely deformed fetus."

Reed, 810 F.Supp. at 169.

The plaintiffs subsequently abandoned Count III, which the federal court had read as undertaking to allege "a cause of action for wrongful life." Id. at 169.

I

The first certified question asks whether the claim alleged in Count I of the complaint states a cause of action under Maryland law. The allegations undertake to state what has been called a "wrongful birth" claim. W.P. Keeton, Prosser & Keeton on the Law of Torts § 55, at 370 (5th ed. 1984), succinctly states the background and context of this theory of liability.

"The last couple of decades have witnessed the rapid development of tort claims concerning a variety of issues that arise when the tortfeasor's act or omission results in the birth of an unwanted child. The defendants in these cases are typically doctors charged with negligence in failing directly to prevent the conception or birth of the child, as by negligently performing a sterilization or abortion procedure, or in failing to diagnose or inform the parents that the child might be born deformed—because of a disease contracted by the mother or a genetic condition in one of the parents—in time to permit the termination of the pregnancy. These actions are now generally referred to as 'wrongful birth' claims, when brought by the parents for their own damages, and 'wrongful life' claims, when brought by or on behalf of the child for the harm of being born deformed."

(Footnote omitted).

The issue presented by the first certified question is whether the claim is simply a traditional negligence claim, as the Reeds contend, or whether the claim fails to withstand traditional tort analysis, as the defendants contend. If the latter, then the defendants submit that this Court should not recognize it as a new tort, but rather should defer to the General Assembly.

. . .

We now consider legal injury. The clear majority of courts that has considered the type of medical malpractice case alleged by the Reeds has concluded that there is legally cognizable injury, proximately caused by a breach of duty. See Robak v. United States, 658 F.2d 471 (7th Cir.1981) (applying Alabama law); Phillips v. United States, 508 F.Supp. 544 (D.S.C. 1981) (applying South Carolina law); Lininger v. Eisenbaum, 764 P.2d 1202 (Colo.1988); Garrison v. Medical Center of Delaware, Inc., 581 A.2d 288 (Del.1989); Haymon v. Wilkerson, 535 A.2d 880 (D.C.1987); Kush v. Lloyd, 616 So.2d 415 (Fla.1992); Moores v. Lucas, 405 So.2d 1022 (Fla.Dist.Ct. App.1981); Blake v. Cruz, 108 Idaho 253, 698 P.2d 315 (1984); Siemieniec v. Lutheran Gen. Hosp., 117 Ill.2d 230, 111 Ill.Dec. 302, 512 N.E.2d 691 (1987); Arche v. United States, 247 Kan. 276, 798 P.2d 477 (1990); Viccaro v. Milunsky, 406 Mass. 777, 551 N.E.2d 8 (1990); Proffitt v. Bartolo, 162 Mich.App. 35, 412 N.W.2d 232 (1987); Smith v. Cote, 128 N.H. 231, 513 A.2d 341 (1986); Berman v. Allan, 80 N.J. 421, 404 A.2d 8 (1979); Becker v. Schwartz, 46 N.Y.2d 401, 413 N.Y.S.2d 895, 386 N.E.2d 807 (1978); Jacobs v. Theimer, 519 S.W.2d 846 (Tex.1975); Naccash v. Burger, 223 Va. 406,

290 S.E.2d 825 (1982); Harbeson v. Parke–Davis, Inc., 98 Wash.2d 460, 656 P.2d 483 (1983); James G. v. Caserta, 175 W.Va. 406, 332 S.E.2d 872 (1985); Dumer v. St. Michael's Hosp., 69 Wis.2d 766, 233 N.W.2d 372 (1975). Contra Atlanta Obstetrics & Gynecology Group v. Abelson, 260 Ga. 711, 398 S.E.2d 557 (1990); Wilson v. Kuenzi, 751 S.W.2d 741 (Mo.1988); Azzolino v. Dingfelder, 315 N.C. 103, 337 S.E.2d 528 (1985).[5]

Although the majority of courts addressing the issue has recognized the form of medical malpractice asserted by the Reeds, those courts are not in agreement on the measure of damages. The certified questions do not ask this Court to define the measure of damages. For the purpose of answering the first certified question, it is sufficient to state that there is at least some economic harm to the parents in these cases—a harm that can be quantified under the general rules relating to tort damages. See Phillips v. United States, 508 F.Supp. at 551 ("While it would be premature to demarcate the ultimate limits of 'wrongful birth' damages at this stage in the litigation, '[b]ecause at least some damages are cognizable at law, the motion for judgment on the pleadings may not be granted for lack of damages.' " (Citation omitted)).

The principal contentions of the defendant physicians turn on how one conceptualizes the tort alleged by the Reeds. Highly relevant to that consideration are the observations by the Supreme Judicial Court of Massachusetts concerning the terminology, "wrongful life," "wrongful birth," and "wrongful conception."

"These labels are not instructive. Any 'wrongfulness' lies not in the life, the birth, the conception, or the pregnancy, but in the negligence of the physician. The harm, if any, is not the birth itself but the effect of the defendant's negligence on the [parents] resulting from the denial to the parents of their right, as the case may be, to decide whether to bear a child or whether to bear a child with a genetic or other defect."

Viccaro v. Milunsky, 551 N.E.2d at 10 n. 3.

The defendants' basic argument is that the Reeds have not suffered any legally cognizable injury. The argument adopts the analysis of the majority of the Supreme Court of North Carolina in its four-three decision in Azzolino v. Dingfelder, 337 S.E.2d 528. That court said:

Courts which purport to analyze wrongful birth claims in terms of 'traditional' tort analysis are able to proceed to this point [i.e., injury] but no further before their 'traditional' analysis leaves all tradition behind or begins to break down. In order to allow recovery such courts must then take a step into entirely untraditional analysis by holding that the existence of a human life can constitute an injury cognizable at law. Far from being 'traditional' tort analysis, such a step requires a

---

5. A number of states prohibit by statute an action based on a claim that, but for the act or omission of another, a person would not have been permitted to be born alive, but would have been aborted. See Idaho Code § 5–334 (1990) (legislating the opposite result from that reached in Blake v. Cruz, 108 Idaho 253, 698 P.2d 315 (1984)); Minn. Stat. § 145.424, Subd. 2 (1984) (constitutionality upheld in Hickman v. Group Health Plan, Inc., 396 N.W.2d 10 (Minn.1986)); Mo. Rev.Stat. § 188.130, Subd. 2 (1986); Pa.Cons. Stat.Ann., tit. 42, § 8305(a) (Supp.1993); Utah Code Ann. § 78–11–24 (1992).

view of human life previously unknown to the law of this jurisdiction. We are unwilling to take any such step because we are unwilling to say that life, even life with severe defects, may ever amount to a legal injury.

337 S.E.2d at 533–34. See also Atlanta Obstetrics & Gynecology Group v. Abelson, 398 S.E.2d at 560–63 (applying Azzolino analysis); J. Bopp et al., The "Rights" and "Wrongs" of Wrongful Birth and Wrongful Life: A Jurisprudential Analysis of Birth Related Torts, 27 Duq.L.Rev. 461 (1989).

The Azzolino analysis does not recognize even the economic impact on the parents and, in that respect, is contrary to Maryland law. In Jones v. Malinowski we replied to an argument similar to that advanced by the defendant physicians here when we said:

> "We reject the proposition that as a matter of law and public policy no legally cognizable claim for child rearing damages can ever arise in such cases where the unplanned child is born normal and healthy.... That the public policy of Maryland may foster the development and preservation of the family relationship does not, in our view, compel the adoption of a per se rule denying recovery by parents of child rearing costs from the physician whose negligence has caused their expenditure. In other words, it is not to disparage the value of human life and the societal need for harmonious family units to protect the parents' choice not to have children by recognizing child rearing costs as a compensable element of damages in negligent sterilization cases. We, therefore, decline to follow the majority rule of those jurisdictions which have held that in all cases, without regard to the circumstances, the benefits to the parents from the birth of a healthy child always outweigh child rearing costs and thus result in no injury or damage to the parents. Instead, we align ourselves with those jurisdictions which permit the trier of fact to consider awarding damages to parents for child rearing costs to the age of the child's majority, offset by the benefits derived by the parents from the child's aid, society and comfort."

299 Md. at 269–70, 473 A.2d at 435.

Thus, those courts that recognize the cause of action alleged by the Reeds permit, at a minimum, damages measured by the extraordinary cost, at least through minority, of supporting the child with severe birth defects as compared to supporting a child who is not so afflicted.... These courts are not in agreement as to the period of time over which the extraordinary expenses are projected. In Berman v. Allan, the New Jersey Supreme Court rejected damages based on extraordinary support expenses, but allowed damages for the parents' emotional distress. 404 A.2d at 14–15. Other courts allow both economic and emotional damages ..... We cite these authorities not for the purpose of defining or refining a measure of damages in these cases, but simply to demonstrate that there is legally cognizable injury to the parents in these cases.

The defendant physicians also suggest that they cannot be liable because they have not caused the impairments suffered by Ashley Nicole. This argument espouses the view advanced by the dissenting judge of the

New York Court of Appeals in Becker v. Schwartz, 413 N.Y.S.2d at 904, 386 N.E.2d at 816:

> The heart of the problem in these cases is that the physician cannot be said to have caused the defect. The disorder is genetic and not the result of any injury negligently inflicted by the doctor. In addition it is incurable and was incurable from the moment of conception. Thus the doctor's alleged negligent failure to detect it during prenatal examination cannot be considered a cause of the condition by analogy to those cases in which the doctor has failed to make a timely diagnosis of a curable disease. The child's handicap is an inexorable result of conception and birth.

That analysis was also adopted in the plurality opinion announcing the judgment of the Supreme Court of Missouri in Wilson v. Kuenzi, 751 S.W.2d at 744–46.

We do not agree, because this argument takes too narrow a view of proximate or legal cause. Under Restatement (Second) of Torts § 431 (1965), an actor's negligent conduct is a legal cause if it is "a substantial factor" and if no rule of law relieves the actor from liability because of the manner in which the negligence resulted in harm. Even though the physical forces producing Ashley Nicole's birth defects were already in operation at the time of the alleged negligence of the physicians, under the chain of causation alleged by the Reeds the physicians could have prevented the harm to the parents. Those allegations, if proved, would present sufficient evidence from which the trier of fact could find that the alleged negligence of the physicians was a substantial factor in the legal harm to the parents. See Restatement (Second) of Torts § 302, comment c.

In argument before this Court, counsel for the defendants also presented an "over utilization" argument. The submission is that, faced with the possibility of liability in these cases, physicians will order tests for which there is no medical justification, and that this form of defensive medicine will become so widespread that it would create the appearance of the standard of care. Obviously, whether the defendants should have offered or recommended certain tests to Mrs. Reed is a matter for proof at trial. Further, although we acknowledge a general public interest in medical cost containment, that public interest, as currently manifested in cost containment legislation, is not a prohibition against legally recognized medical malpractice actions.

For the foregoing reasons, the answer to the first certified question is that Maryland does recognize the tort cause of action therein described.

. . .

CERTIFIED QUESTIONS ANSWERED AS ABOVE SET FORTH. COSTS TO BE EVENLY DIVIDED BETWEEN THE PLAINTIFFS AND THE DEFENDANTS.

CHAPTER 15

PUNITIVE DAMAGES

A. TORTS

Smith v. Wade

Supreme Court of the United States, 1983.
461 U.S. 30, 103 S.Ct. 1625, 75 L.Ed.2d 632.

■ JUSTICE BRENNAN delivered the opinion of the Court.

We granted certiorari in this case to decide whether the District Court for the Western District of Missouri applied the correct legal standard in instructing the jury that it might award punitive damages under 42 U.S.C. § 1983.[1] The Court of Appeals for the Eighth Circuit sustained the award of punitive damages. We affirm.

I

The petitioner, William H. Smith, is a guard at Algoa Reformatory, a unit of the Missouri Division of Corrections for youthful first offenders. The respondent, Daniel R. Wade, was assigned to Algoa as an inmate in 1976. In the summer of 1976 Wade voluntarily checked into Algoa's protective custody unit. Because of disciplinary violations during his stay in protective custody, Wade was given a short term in punitive segregation and then transferred to administrative segregation. On the evening of Wade's first day in administrative segregation, he was placed in a cell with another inmate. Later, when Smith came on duty in Wade's dormitory, he placed a third inmate in Wade's cell. According to Wade's testimony, his cellmates harassed, beat, and sexually assaulted him.

Wade brought suit under 42 U.S.C. § 1983 against Smith and four other guards and correctional officials, alleging that his Eighth Amendment rights had been violated. At trial his evidence showed that he had placed himself in protective custody because of prior incidents of violence against him by other inmates. The third prisoner whom Smith added to the cell had been placed in administrative segregation for fighting. Smith had made no effort to find out whether another cell was available; in fact there was another cell in the same dormitory with only one occupant. Further, only a

---

1. Section 1983 reads in relevant part:

Every person who, under color of any statute, ordinance, regulation, custom, or usage, of any State or Territory or the District of Columbia, subjects, or causes to be subjected, any citizen of the United States or other person within the juris-

diction thereof to the deprivation of any rights, privileges, or immunities secured by the Constitution and laws, shall be liable to the party injured in an action at law, suit in equity, or other proper proceeding for redress.

few weeks earlier, another inmate had been beaten to death in the same dormitory during the same shift, while Smith had been on duty. Wade asserted that Smith and the other defendants knew or should have known that an assault against him was likely under the circumstances.

. . . .

The district judge also charged the jury that it could award punitive damages on a proper showing:

> "In addition to actual damages, the law permits the jury, under certain circumstances, to award the injured person punitive and exemplary damages, in order to punish the wrongdoer for some extraordinary misconduct, and to serve as an example or warning to others not to engage in such conduct.

> "If you find the issues in favor of the plaintiff, and if the conduct of one or more of the defendants is shown to be *a reckless or callous disregard of, or indifference to, the rights or safety of others,* then you may assess punitive or exemplary damages in addition to any award of actual damages.

> "... The amount of punitive or exemplary damages assessed against any defendant may be such sum as you believe will serve to punish that defendant and to deter him and others from like conduct."

The jury returned verdicts for two of the three remaining defendants. It found Smith liable, however, and awarded $25,000 in compensatory damages and $5,000 in punitive damages. The District Court entered judgment on the verdict, and the Court of Appeals affirmed.

In this Court, Smith attacks only the award of punitive damages. . . .

II

Section 1983 is derived from § 1 of the Civil Rights Act of 1871. It was intended to create "a species of tort liability" in favor of persons deprived of federally secured rights. We noted in Carey v. Piphus, 435 U.S. 247, 98 S.Ct. 1042, 55 L.Ed.2d 252 (1978), that there was little in the section's legislative history concerning the damages recoverable for this tort liability. In the absence of more specific guidance, we looked first to the common law of torts (both modern and as of 1871), with such modification or adaptation as might be necessary to carry out the purpose and policy of the statute. We have done the same in other contexts arising under § 1983, especially the recurring problem of common-law immunities.

Smith correctly concedes that "punitive damages are available in a 'proper' § 1983 action...." Although there was debate about the theoretical correctness of the punitive damages doctrine in the latter part of the last century, the doctrine was accepted as settled law by nearly all state and federal courts, including this Court. It was likewise generally established that individual public officers were liable for punitive damages for their misconduct on the same basis as other individual defendants. Further, although the precise issue of the availability of punitive damages under § 1983 has never come squarely before us, we have had occasion more than once to make clear our view that they are available; indeed, we have rested decisions on related questions on the premise of such availability.

Smith argues, nonetheless, that this was not a "proper" case in which to award punitive damages. More particularly, he attacks the instruction that punitive damages could be awarded on a finding of reckless or callous disregard of or indifference to Wade's rights or safety. Instead, he contends that the proper test is one of actual malicious intent—"ill will, spite, or intent to injure." He offers two arguments for this position: first, that actual intent is the proper standard for punitive damages in all cases under § 1983; and second, that even if intent is not always required, it should be required here because the threshold for punitive damages should always be higher than that for liability in the first instance. We address these in turn.

III

Smith does not argue that the common law, either in 1871 or now, required or requires a showing of actual malicious intent for recovery of punitive damages.

Perhaps not surprisingly, there was significant variation (both terminological and substantive) among American jurisdictions in the latter nineteenth century on the precise standard to be applied in awarding punitive damages—variation that was exacerbated by the ambiguity and slipperiness of such common terms as "malice" and "gross negligence." Most of the confusion, however, seems to have been over the degree of negligence, recklessness, carelessness, or culpable indifference that should be required—not over whether actual intent was essential. On the contrary, the rule in a large majority of jurisdictions was that punitive damages (also called exemplary damages, vindictive damages, or smart money) could be awarded without a showing of actual ill will, spite, or intent to injure.

This Court so stated on several occasions, before and shortly after 1871....

     . . . .

The large majority of state and lower federal courts were in agreement that punitive damage awards did not require a showing of actual malicious intent; they permitted punitive awards on variously stated standards of negligence, recklessness, or other culpable conduct short of actual malicious intent.

The same rule applies today. The Restatement (Second) of Torts (1977), for example, states: "Punitive damages may be awarded for conduct that is outrageous, because of the defendant's evil motive *or his reckless indifference to the rights of others.*" Id., § 908(2)(emphasis added). Most cases under state common law, although varying in their precise terminology, have adopted more or less the same rule, recognizing that punitive damages in tort cases may be awarded not only for actual intent to injure or evil motive, but also for recklessness, serious indifference to or disregard for the rights of others, or even gross negligence.

The remaining question is whether the policies and purposes of § 1983 itself require a departure from the rules of tort common law. As a general matter, we discern no reason why a person whose federally guaranteed rights have been violated should be granted a more restrictive remedy than a person asserting an ordinary tort cause of action. Smith offers us no persuasive reason to the contrary.

Smith's argument, which he offers in several forms, is that an actual intent standard is preferable to a recklessness standard because it is less vague. He points out that punitive damages, by their very nature, are not awarded to compensate the injured party. He concedes, of course, that deterrence of future egregious conduct is a primary purpose of both § 1983 and of punitive damages. But deterrence, he contends, cannot be achieved unless the standard of conduct sought to be deterred is stated with sufficient clarity to enable potential defendants to conform to the law and to avoid the proposed sanction. Recklessness or callous indifference, he argues, is too uncertain a standard to achieve deterrence rationally and fairly. A prison guard, for example, can be expected to know whether he is acting with actual ill will or intent to injure, but not whether he is being reckless or callously indifferent.

Smith's argument, if valid, would apply to ordinary tort cases as easily as to § 1983 suits; hence, it hardly presents an argument for adopting a different rule under § 1983. In any event, the argument is unpersuasive. While, *arguendo,* an intent standard may be easier to understand and apply to particular situations than a recklessness standard, we are not persuaded that a recklessness standard is too vague to be fair or useful. In ... Milwaukee & St. Paul R. Co. v. Arms, 91 U.S. 489, 23 L.Ed. 374 (1875), we adopted a recklessness standard rather than a gross negligence standard precisely because recklessness would better serve the need for adequate clarity and fair application. Almost a century later, in the First Amendment context, we held that punitive damages cannot be assessed for defamation in the absence of proof of "knowledge of falsity or reckless disregard for the truth." Our concern in Gertz v. Robert Welch, Inc., 418 U.S. 323, 94 S.Ct. 2997, 41 L.Ed.2d 789 (1974), was that the threat of punitive damages, if not limited to especially egregious cases, might "inhibit the vigorous exercise of First Amendment freedoms"—a concern at least as pressing as any urged by Smith in this case. Yet we did not find it necessary to impose an actual intent standard there. Just as Smith has not shown why § 1983 should give higher protection from punitive damages than ordinary tort law, he has not explained why it gives higher protection than we have demanded under the First Amendment.

More fundamentally, Smith's argument for certainty in the interest of deterrence overlooks the distinction between a standard for punitive damages and a standard of liability in the first instance. Smith seems to assume that prison guards and other state officials look mainly to the standard for punitive damages in shaping their conduct. We question the premise; we assume, and hope, that most officials are guided primarily by the underlying standards of federal substantive law—both out of devotion to duty, and in the interest of avoiding liability for compensatory damages. At any rate, the conscientious officer who desires clear guidance on how to do his job and avoid lawsuits can and should look to the standard for actionability in the first instance. The need for exceptional clarity in the standard for punitive damages arises only if one assumes that there are substantial numbers of officers who will not be deterred by compensatory damages; only such officers will seek to guide their conduct by the punitive damages standard. The presence of such officers constitutes a powerful argument *against* raising the threshold for punitive damages.

In this case, the jury was instructed to apply a high standard of constitutional right ("physical abuse of such base, inhumane and barbaric proportions as to shock the sensibilities"). It was also instructed, under the principle of qualified immunity, that Smith could not be held liable at all unless he was guilty of "a callous indifference or a thoughtless disregard for the consequences of [his] act or failure to act," or of "a flagrant or remarkably bad failure to protect" Wade. These instructions are not challenged in this Court, nor were they challenged on grounds of vagueness in the lower courts. Smith's contention that this recklessness standard is too vague to provide clear guidance and reasonable deterrence might more properly be reserved for a challenge seeking different standards of liability in the first instance. As for punitive damages, however, in the absence of any persuasive argument to the contrary based on the policies of § 1983, we are content to adopt the policy judgment of the common law—that reckless or callous disregard for the plaintiff's rights, as well as intentional violations of federal law, should be sufficient to trigger a jury's consideration of the appropriateness of punitive damages.

. . . .

V

We hold that a jury may be permitted to assess punitive damages in an action under § 1983 when the defendant's conduct is shown to be motivated by evil motive or intent, or when it involves reckless or callous indifference to the federally protected rights of others. We further hold that this threshold applies even when the underlying standard of liability for compensatory damages is one of recklessness. Because the jury instructions in this case are in accord with this rule, the judgment of the Court of Appeals is

Affirmed.

■ JUSTICE REHNQUIST, with whom THE CHIEF JUSTICE and JUSTICE POWELL join, dissenting.

. . . .

I

. . . [T]he doctrine of punitive damages permits the award of "damages" beyond even the most generous and expansive conception of actual injury to the plaintiff. This anomaly is rationalized principally on three grounds. First, punitive damages "are assessed for the avowed purpose of visiting *a punishment* upon the defendant." C. McCormick, Law of Damages 275 (1935)(emphasis added). Second, the doctrine is rationalized on the ground that it deters persons from violating the rights of others. Third, punitive damages are justified as a "bounty" that encourages private lawsuits seeking to assert legal rights.

Despite these attempted justifications, the doctrine of punitive damages has been vigorously criticized throughout the Nation's history. Countless cases remark that such damages have never been "a favorite in the law." The year after § 1983 was enacted, the New Hampshire Supreme Court declared, "The idea of [punitive damages] is wrong. It is a monstrous heresy. It is an unsightly and unhealthy excrescence, deforming the symmetry of the body of the law." Such remarks reflect a number of deeply held reservations regarding punitive damages, which can only be briefly summarized here.

Punitive damages are generally seen as a windfall to plaintiffs, who are entitled to receive full compensation for their injuries—but no more. Even assuming that a punitive "fine" should be imposed after a civil trial, the penalty should go to the state, not to the plaintiff—who by hypothesis is fully compensated. Moreover, although punitive damages are "quasi-criminal," their imposition is unaccompanied by the types of safeguards present in criminal proceedings. This absence of safeguards is exacerbated by the fact that punitive damages are frequently based upon the caprice and prejudice of jurors. We observed in Electrical Workers v. Foust, 442 U.S. 42, 99 S.Ct. 2121, 60 L.Ed.2d 698 (1979), that "punitive damages may be employed to punish unpopular defendants," and noted elsewhere that "juries assess punitive damages in wholly unpredictable amounts bearing no necessary relation to the harm caused." Finally, the alleged deterrence achieved by punitive damage awards is likely outweighed by the costs—such as the encouragement of unnecessary litigation and the chilling of desirable conduct—flowing from the rule, at least when the standards on which the awards are based are ill-defined.

Because of these considerations, a significant number of American jurisdictions refuse to condone punitive damage awards. Other jurisdictions limit the amount of punitive damages that may be awarded, for example, to the plaintiff's attorney's fees or otherwise.

Nonetheless, a number of states do permit juries to award punitive damages in certain circumstances. Historically, however, there has been little uniformity among the standards applied in these states for determining on what basis a jury might award punitive damages.

One fundamental distinction is essential to an understanding of the differences among the various standards for punitive damages. Many jurisdictions have required some sort of wrongful motive, actual intention to inflict harm or intentional doing of an act known to be unlawful—"express malice," "actual malice," "bad faith," "wilful wrong" or "ill will." Other states, however, have permitted punitive damage awards merely upon a showing of very careless or negligent conduct by the defendant—"gross negligence," "recklessness," or "extreme carelessness." In sharp contrast to the first set of terms noted above, which connote a requirement of actual ill will towards the plaintiff, these latter phrases import only a degree of negligence. This distinction between acts that are intentionally harmful and those that are very negligent, or unreasonable, involves a basic difference of kind, not just a variation of degree. The former typically demands inquiry into the actor's subjective motive and purpose, while the latter ordinarily requires only an objective determination of the relative risks and advantages accruing to society from particular behavior.

. . . .

II

At bottom, this case requires the Court to decide whether a particular remedy is available under § 1983 . . . The decisions of state courts decided well after 1871 . . . are largely irrelevant to what Members of the 42nd Congress intended by way of a standard for punitive damages.

. . . .

III

. . . .

In short, a careful examination of the decisions available to the members of the 42d Congress reveals a portrait different in important respects from that painted by the Court. While a few jurisdictions may have adopted a more lenient, if less precise, standard of recklessness, the majority's claim that the prevailing standard in 1871 was one of recklessness simply cannot be sustained. The decisions of this Court, which were likely well-known to federal legislators, supported an *animus* requirement. . . .

IV

Even apart from this historical background, I am persuaded . . . that the 42nd Congress intended a "wrongful intent" requirement. . . .

. . . .

An intent requirement, unlike a recklessness standard, is logically consistent with the underlying justification for *punitive* damages. It is a fundamental principal of American law that penal consequences generally ought to be imposed only where there has been some sort of wrongful *animus* creating the type of culpability warranting this treatment. . . . Given that punitive damages are meant to punish, it is difficult to believe that Congress would have departed from the "instinctive," "universal and persistent" linkage in our law between punishment and wrongful intent.

V

Finally, even if the evidence of congressional intent were less clear-cut, I would be persuaded to resolve any ambiguity in favor of an actual malice standard. It scarcely needs repeating that punitive damages are not a "favorite in the law," owing to the numerous persuasive criticisms that have been leveled against the doctrine. The majority reasons that these arguments apply to all awards of punitive damages, not just to those under § 1983; while this is of course correct, it does little to reduce the strength of the arguments, and, if they are persuasive, we should not blindly follow the mistakes other courts have made.

Much of what has been said above regarding the failings of a punitive damages remedy is equally appropriate here. It is anomalous, and counter to deep-rooted legal principles and common-sense notions, to punish persons who meant no harm, and to award a windfall, in the form of punitive damages, to someone who already has been fully compensated. These peculiarities ought to be carefully limited—not expanded to every case where a jury may think a defendant was too careless, particularly where a vaguely-defined, elastic standard like "reckless indifference" gives free reign to the biases and prejudices of juries. In short, there are persuasive reasons not to create a new punitive damages remedy unless it is clear that Congress so intended.

This argument is particularly powerful in a case like this, where the uncertainty resulting from largely random awards of punitive damages will have serious effects upon the performance by state and local officers of their official duties. One of the principal themes of our immunity decisions is that the threat of liability must not deter an official's "willingness to execute his office with the decisiveness and the judgment required by the public good." To avoid stifling the types of initiative and decisiveness necessary for the "government to govern," we have held that officials will be liable for compensatory damages only for certain types of conduct. Precisely the same reasoning applies to liability for punitive damages. Because punitive damages generally are not subject to any relation to actual harm suffered, and because the recklessness standard is so imprecise, the remedy poses an even greater threat to the ability of officials to take decisive, efficient action. After the Court's decision, governmental officials will be subjected to the possibility of damage awards unlimited by any harm they may have caused or the fact they acted with unquestioned good faith: when swift action is demanded, their thoughts likely will be on personal financial consequences that may result from their conduct—but whose limits they cannot predict—and not upon their official duties. It would have been difficult for the Court to have fashioned a more effective Damoclean sword than the open-ended, standardless and unpredictable liability it creates today.

Moreover, notwithstanding the Court's inability to discern them, there are important distinctions between a right to damages under § 1983 and a similar right under state tort law. A leading rationale seized upon by proponents of punitive damages to justify the doctrine is that "the award is . . . a covert response to the legal system's overt refusal to provide financing for litigation." D. Dobbs, Remedies 221 (1973). Yet, 42 U.S.C. § 1988 provides not just a "covert response" to plaintiffs' litigation expenses but an explicit provision for an award to the prevailing party in a § 1983 action of "a reasonable attorney's fee as part of the costs." By permitting punitive damages *as well as* attorney's fees, § 1983 plaintiffs, unlike state tort law plaintiffs, get not just one windfall but two—one for them, and one for their lawyer. This difference between the incentives that are present in state tort actions, and those in § 1983 actions, makes the Court's reliance upon the standard for punitive damages in the former entirely inapposite: in fashioning a new financial lure to litigate under § 1983 the Court does not act in a vacuum, but, by adding to existing incentives, creates an imbalance of inducements to litigate that may have serious consequences.

The staggering effect of § 1983 claims upon the workload of the federal courts has been decried time and again. The torrent of frivolous claims under that section threatens to incapacitate the judicial system's resolution of claims where true injustice is involved; those claims which truly warrant redress are in a very real danger of being lost in a sea of meritless suits. Yet, apparently oblivious to this, the Court today reads into the silent, inhospitable terms of § 1983 a remedy that is designed to serve as a "bounty" to encourage private litigation. Dobbs, supra, at 221. In a time when the courts are flooded with suits that do not raise colorable claims, in large part because of the existing incentives for litigation under § 1983, it is regrettable that the Court should take upon itself, in apparent disregard for the likely intent of the 42d Congress, the legislative task of encouraging yet more litigation. There is a limit to what the federal judicial system can bear.

Finally, by unquestioningly transferring the standard of punitive damages in *state* tort actions to *federal* § 1983 actions, the Court utterly fails to recognize the fundamental difference that exists between an award of punitive damages by a federal court, acting under § 1983, and a similar award by a state court acting under prevailing local laws. While state courts may choose to adopt such measures as they deem appropriate to punish officers of the jurisdiction in which they sit, the standards they choose to adopt can scarcely be taken as evidence of what it is appropriate for a federal court to do. When federal courts enforce punitive damage awards against local officials they intrude into sensitive areas of sovereignty of coordinate branches of our nation, thus implicating the most basic values of our system of federalism. Moreover, by yet further distorting the incentives that exist for litigating claims against local officials in federal court, as opposed to state courts, the Court's decision makes it even more difficult for state courts to attempt to conform the conduct of state officials to the Constitution.

I dissent.

■ JUSTICE O'CONNOR, dissenting.

Although I agree with the result reached in Justice Rehnquist's dissent, I write separately because I cannot agree with the approach taken by either the Court or Justice Rehnquist. Both opinions engage in exhaustive, but ultimately unilluminating, exegesis of the common law of the availability of punitive damages in 1871. Although both the Court and Justice Rehnquist display admirable skills in legal research and analysis of great numbers of musty cases, the results do not significantly further the goal of the inquiry: to establish the intent of the 42d Congress. In interpreting § 1983, we have often looked to the common law as it existed in 1871, in the belief that, when Congress was silent on a point, it intended to adopt the principles of the common law with which it was familiar. This approach makes sense when there was a generally prevailing rule of common law, for then it is reasonable to assume that Congressmen were familiar with that rule and imagined that it would cover the cause of action that they were creating. But when a significant split in authority existed, it strains credulity to argue that Congress simply assumed that one view rather than the other would govern. Particularly in a case like this one, in which those interpreting the common law of 1871 must resort to dictionaries in an attempt to translate the language of the late 19th century into terms that judges of the late 20th century can understand, and in an area in which the courts of the earlier period frequently used inexact and contradictory language, we cannot safely infer anything about congressional intent from the divided contemporaneous judicial opinions. The battle of the string citations can have no winner.

Once it is established that the common law of 1871 provides us with no real guidance on this question, we should turn to the policies underlying § 1983 to determine which rule best accords with those policies. In Newport v. Fact Concerts, Inc., 453 U.S. 247, 101 S.Ct. 2748, 69 L.Ed.2d 616 (1981), we identified the purposes of § 1983 as preeminently to compensate victims of constitutional violations and to deter further violations. The conceded availability of compensatory damages, particularly when coupled with the availability of attorney's fees under § 1988, completely fulfills the goal of compensation, leaving only deterrence to be served by awards of punitive damages. We must then confront the close question whether a standard permitting an award of unlimited punitive damages on the basis of recklessness will chill public officials in the performance of their duties more than it will deter violations of the Constitution, and whether the availability of punitive damages for reckless violations of the Constitution in addition to attorney's fees will create an incentive to bring an ever-increasing flood of § 1983 claims, threatening the ability of the federal courts to handle those that are meritorious. Although I cannot concur in Justice Rehnquist's wholesale condemnation of awards of punitive damages in any context or with the suggestion that punitive damages should not be available even for intentional or malicious violations of constitutional rights, I do agree with the discussion in Part V of his opinion of the special problems of permitting awards of punitive damages for the recklessness of public officials. Since awards of compensatory damages and attorney's fees already provide significant deterrence, I am persuaded that the policies counseling against awarding punitive damages for the recklessness of public officials outweigh the desirability of any incremental deterrent effect that such awards may have. Consequently, I dissent.

NOTES

1. In Ngo v. Reno Hilton Resort Corp., 140 F.3d 1299, as modified, 156 F.3d 988 (9th Cir. 1998), the Ninth Circuit held that section 1981a requires plaintiffs seeking punitive damages to make a showing beyond the threshold level of intent required for compensatory liability. The court noted:

In adopting this standard, we join five other circuits that also require evidence of conduct more egregious than intentional discrimination to support an award of punitive damages in Title VII cases.

The five other circuits are the First, Fourth, Sixth, Eighth and District of Columbia.

2. In State Farm Mutual Automobile Insurance Company, petitioner v. Inez Preece Campbell et al., 538 U.S. 408, 123 S.Ct. 1513, 155 L.Ed.2d 585 (2003), the insureds sued the automobile liability insurer for the insurer's bad faith failure to settle within the insurance policy limits, fraud

and intentional infliction of emotional distress. The state court entered judgment on the jury verdict in favor of the insureds, but remitted the jury's punitive and compensatory damages awards. On appeal by the parties, the Utah Supreme Court sought to apply the three guideposts enunciated in the Gore case, reinstated the $2.6 million award for compensatory damages and $145 million in punitive damages that the trial court had reduced to $1 million and $25 million respectively. Justice Kennedy, writing for the majority of the U.S. Supreme Court held that it was error to reinstate the jury's $145 million in punitive damages award, and that the award of $145 million in punitive damages on the $1 million compensatory judgment violated due process. Citing BMW v. Gore, 517 U.S. 559, 116 S.Ct. 1589, 134 L.Ed.2d 809 (1996), Justice Kennedy stated that "the wealth of a defendant cannot justify an otherwise unconstitutional punitive damages award." Justices Scalia, Thomas and Ginsburg dissented.

3. In Barnes et al. v. Jeffrey Gorman, 536 U.S. 181, 122 S.Ct. 2097, 153 L.Ed.2d 230 (2002), a wheelchair disabled person, under arrest, who was injured while being transported in a police van that was not equipped with wheelchair restraints, sued police officials and the police officer driving the van, under the Americans with Disabilities Act of 1990 and the Rehabilitation Act of 1973. The jury granted a verdict for both compensatory and punitive damages. The Supreme Court affirmed the vacating of the jury award of punitive damages, holding that they are unavailable in private suits, both under the Americans with Disabilities Act and the Rehabilitation Act.

Taylor v. Superior Court

Supreme Court of California, 1979.
24 Cal.3d 890, 157 Cal.Rptr. 693, 598 P.2d 854.

■ RICHARDSON, J. We consider whether punitive damages are recoverable in a personal injury action brought against an intoxicated driver....

. . . .

Section 3294 of the Civil Code authorizes the recovery of punitive damages in noncontract cases "where the defendant has been guilty of oppression, fraud, or malice, express or implied...." As we recently explained, "This has long been interpreted to mean that malice in fact, as opposed to malice implied by law, is required. The malice in fact, referred to ... as animus malus, may be proved under section 3294 either expressly (by direct evidence probative on the existence of hatred or ill will) or by implication (by indirect evidence from which the jury may draw inferences)."

Other authorities have amplified the foregoing principle. Thus it has been held that the "malice" required by section 3294 "implies an act conceived in a spirit of mischief or with criminal indifference towards the obligations owed to others." In Dean Prosser's words: "Where the defendant's wrongdoing has been intentional and deliberate, and has the character of outrage frequently associated with crime, all but a few courts have permitted the jury to award in the tort action 'punitive' or 'exemplary' damages ... [¶] Something more than the mere commission of a tort is always required for punitive damages. There must be circumstances of aggravation or outrage, such as spite or 'malice,' or a fraudulent or evil motive on the part of the defendant, *or such a conscious and deliberate disregard of the interests of others that his conduct may be called wilful or wanton.*" (W. Prosser, Law of Torts (4th ed. 1971) § 2, at pp. 9–10, italics added.)

Defendant's successful demurrer to the complaint herein was based upon plaintiff's failure to allege any actual intent of defendant to harm plaintiff or others. Is this an essential element of a claim for punitive damages? As indicated by Dean Prosser, courts have not limited the availability of punitive damages to cases in which such an intent has been shown. As we ourselves have recently observed, in order to justify the imposition of punitive damages the defendant " '... must act with the intent to vex, injure, or annoy, *or with a conscious disregard of the plaintiff's rights.*' " (Accord, G.D. Searle & Co. v. Superior Court (1975) 49 Cal.App.3d 22, 122 Cal.Rptr. 218.)

The *Searle* court, speaking through Justice Friedman, after reviewing many of the earlier decisions, concluded that "The phrase *conscious disregard* is sometimes used to describe the highly culpable state of mind which justifies an exemplary award.... [¶] We suggest *conscious disregard of safety* as an appropriate description of the *animus malus* which may justify an exemplary damage award when nondeliberate injury is alleged." The *Searle* court likewise rejected suggestions in earlier cases that mere *reckless* disregard or misconduct would be sufficient to sustain an award of punitive damages, because "The central spirit of the exemplary damage statute, the demand for evil motive, is violated by an award founded upon recklessness alone."

We concur with the *Searle* observation that a conscious disregard of the safety of others may constitute malice within the meaning of section 3294 of the Civil Code. In order to justify an award of punitive damages on this basis, the plaintiff must establish that the defendant was aware of the probable dangerous consequences of his conduct, and that he wilfully and deliberately failed to avoid those consequences.

Relying on Gombos v. Ashe (1958) 158 Cal.App.2d 517, 322 P.2d 933, defendant asserts that historically the act of driving while intoxicated has never been considered "malice" under section 3294. In *Gombos,* plaintiff has alleged that defendant drove his car in a " 'highly reckless manner with absolute disregard and callous indifference to the rights and safety' " of others, in that he became "knowingly and wilfully intoxicated" despite his knowledge that his intoxication "rendered him physically unfit" to drive safely. Despite these allegations, the court held that "... it is quite apparent that such facts fall short of alleging malice in fact, express or implied. One who becomes intoxicated, knowing that he intends to drive his automobile on the highway, is of course negligent, and perhaps grossly negligent. It is a reckless and wrongful and illegal thing to do. But it is not a malicious act."

Plaintiff seeks to distinguish *Gombos* by stressing the additional allegations in the present complaint which include defendant's history of alcoholism, his prior arrests and convictions for drunk driving, his prior accident attributable to his intoxication, and his acceptance of employment involving the transportation of alcoholic beverages. Certainly, the foregoing allegations may reasonably be said to confirm defendant's awareness of his inability to operate a motor vehicle safely while intoxicated. Yet the essence of the *Gombos* and present complaints remains the same: Defendant became intoxicated and thereafter drove a car while in that condition, despite his knowledge of the safety hazard he created thereby. This is the essential gravamen of the complaint, and while a history of prior arrests, convictions and mishaps may heighten the probability and foreseeability of an accident, we do not deem these aggravating factors essential prerequisites to the assessment of punitive damages in drunk driving cases.

We note that when *Gombos* was decided it was unclear whether, as a general principle, an award of punitive damages could be based upon a finding of defendant's conscious disregard of the safety of others. In the evolution of this area of tort law during the ensuing 20 years it has now become generally accepted that such a finding is sufficient. Examining the pleadings before us, we have no difficulty concluding that they contain sufficient allegations upon which it may reasonably be concluded that defendant consciously disregarded the safety of others. There is a very commonly understood risk which attends every motor vehicle driver who is intoxicated. One who wilfully consumes alcoholic beverages to the point of intoxication, knowing that he thereafter must operate a motor vehicle, thereby combining sharply impaired physical and mental faculties with a vehicle capable of great force and speed, reasonably may be held to exhibit a conscious disregard of the safety of others. The effect may be lethal whether or not the driver had a prior history of drunk driving incidents.

The allowance of punitive damages in such cases may well be appropriate because of another reason, namely, to deter similar future conduct, the "incalculable cost" of which is well documented. Section 3294 expressly provides that punitive damages may be recovered "for the sake of example." The applicable principle was well expressed in a recent Oregon case upholding an award of punitive damages against a drunken driver, "the fact of common knowledge that the drinking driver is the cause of so many of the more serious automobile accidents is strong evidence in itself to support the need for *all possible means of deterring* persons from driving automobiles after drinking, including exposure to awards of punitive damages in the event of accidents." (Harrell v. Ames (1973) 265 Or. 183, 190, 508 P.2d 211, 214–215, italics added.) According to a recent annotation, the *Harrell* case represents the view of a substantial majority of those courts of other states which have considered the matter. We think it also represents the better reasoned view.

. . . .

Let a peremptory writ of mandate issue directing the trial court to overrule defendant Stille's demurrer.

■ TOBRINER, MOSK AND MANUEL, JJ., concur.

[The concurring and dissenting opinion of BIRD, C.J., joined by NEWMAN, J., is omitted.]

■ CLARK, J., dissenting. I share the majority's dismay at the carnage on our highways. And if today's decision would significantly reduce the number of accidents involving drunk drivers, the majority might be justified in changing the law relating to punitive damage. However, today's decision clearly will not reduce the number of drunk drivers on our highways. We should therefore adhere to the traditional rule—enunciated in Strauss v. Buckley (1937) 20 Cal.App.2d 7, 65 P.2d 1352, and reiterated by Justice Peters in his careful and scholarly opinion in Gombos v. Ashe (1958) 158 Cal.App.2d 517, 322 P.2d 933—that driving while intoxicated does not establish the malice essential to an award of punitive damages.

Justice Peters commenced his analysis by pointing out: "Punitive damages are allowed in certain cases [for the sake of example] as a punishment of the defendant. They are not a favorite of the law and the granting of them should be done with the greatest caution. They are only allowed in the clearest of cases."

Considerations Governing Allowance of Punitive Awards

The reasons for hesitancy in awarding punitive damages are obvious. First, the plaintiff is fully compensated for injury by compensatory damages. An additional award or fine from the defendant may constitute unjust enrichment. Unlike fines paid into the public treasury for public use, we may assume fines paid to private persons will not be similarly used.

Second, civil law is concerned with vindicating rights and compensating persons for harm suffered when those rights are invaded. Criminal law is concerned with punishing wrongdoers. In our tripartite system of government, the Legislature prescribes punishment for criminal conduct. Ordinarily, the Legislature specifies the range of criminal punishment, and it is for trial judges or administrative specialists to determine the appropriate punishment within that range.

Punitive damage is awarded in the context of a civil trial. While the Legislature has provided punitive damage may be awarded in certain civil cases, it has not created standards to guide the jury in determining when such awards are justified. Consequently, punitive damage may be awarded at whim. Upon deciding to grant punitive damage, little if any guidance is given the jury as to the appropriate size of the award. Moreover, when the defendant's conduct also constitutes a crime for which he has been or will be punished, the punitive award constitutes double punishment—potentially in excess of the maximum punishment specified in the Penal Code and a dubious exception to the prohibition against multiple punishment.

Third, punitive damage trials interfere with policies governing trial procedures. Punishment ordinarily serves as a deterrent to future conduct. As Justice Peters pointed out, if the plaintiff can place punitive damages in issue, it means "that the plaintiffs can offer evidence of the financial status of the defendant. This would convert personal injury cases where intoxication or wilful misconduct are involved from the trial of a negligence case into a field day in which the financial standing of the defendant would become a major issue."

In addition, the trier of fact assessing deterrence should be advised whether the compensatory award will come out of the defendant's pocket—thereby reducing his assets—or whether it will be paid by a liability insurer. But "Section 1155 of the Evidence Code provides that evidence of insurance is inadmissible to prove negligence or wrongdoing. The obvious purpose of the provision is to prevent the prejudicial use of evidence of liability insurance in an action against an insured." It is apparent that to permit punitive damages in accident cases will distract the trier of fact from its liability function, interfering with sound policies governing trial procedures.

Fourth, although situations do exist where punitive awards have a substantial deterrent effect, others exist in which deterrence is marginal at best. Because restitution only requires a wrongdoer give up his unjustified gains, compensatory damage will not always constitute deterrence. If the conduct while clearly wrongful is not criminal, a punitive award may be necessary to deter. Otherwise persons contemplating the wrongful conduct may feel they are in a no-lose situation, only gaining by the wrongful conduct.

On the other hand, deterrent effect of a punitive award may be minimal or marginal where the conduct already constitutes a crime and the criminal statute is regularly and effectively enforced. Deterrence by punitive award is also marginal where wrongful conduct is as likely to result in injury to the wrongdoer as to others.

In addition, if application of punitive award depends upon a fortuitous rather than an intended consequence of wrongful conduct, potential wrongdoers will not be deterred. They will simply assume the unintended consequence will not occur. This consideration has particular relevance to the instant case because the majority seek to deter drunk driving by enhancing penalty only when an accident occurs. Drunk drivers not involved in accidents—comprising the vast majority—are not subject to the penalty....

Fifth, the prevalence of liability insurance in our society requires that any evaluation of punitive damage in accident cases, especially in the context of deterrence, must consider the insurance factor.

Under the traditional view, an award of punitive damage nullifies all insurance coverage. An insurer is not liable for loss intentionally caused by the insured, and any contract providing for liability is void as being against public policy. When an insured commits an intentional injury, he cannot require his insurer to indemnify him for either punitive or compensatory damage paid under a judgment. Because punitive damage is recoverable only for malicious or other intentional injury, a punitive award traditionally exonerated the insurance company from coverage.

. . . .

The practical significance of the majority's opinion is not that juries may assess punitive damage in accident cases involving drunk driving, but rather the undesirable result the liability insurers will now avoid all coverage in such cases. While a few victims injured by wealthy drunk drivers will receive both compensatory and punitive damages, the many unfortunately injured by drivers without assets will be unable to recover even compensatory damages from insurers.

Because wary plaintiffs are unlikely to jeopardize carrier coverage for compensatory damage, they will not seek punitive damage unless the defendant is either wealthy or uninsured. For this reason, the deterrent effect as to insured drivers who are not wealthy is further diluted.

Sixth, creation of the new punitive award appears contrary to the solicitude for injured wrongdoers reflected by the recent adoption of comparative fault. A plaintiff guilty of wilful misconduct may not recover any damages against a negligent defendant. Because malice imports wilfulness, intoxicated drivers will be barred from any recovery against negligent defendants.

The foregoing six considerations suggest we adhere rigidly to Justice Peters' fundamental principle that punitive damage should be awarded with "the greatest caution" in accident cases.

. . . .

Nardelli v. Stamberg

Court of Appeals of New York, 1978.
44 N.Y.2d 500, 406 N.Y.S.2d 443, 377 N.E.2d 975.

■ GABRIELLI, J. Plaintiff commenced this action seeking to recover damages for malicious prosecution. He was successful at trial, and was awarded both compensatory and punitive damages. On defendants' appeal, the Appellate Division, *inter alia,* reversed the judgment on the law insofar as it awarded punitive damages, and dismissed that part of plaintiff's complaint requesting such damages. The Appellate Division did, however, affirm the findings of fact with respect to defendants' liability for malicious prosecution. In view of its determination as to the facts, the Appellate Division's conclusion of law with respect to punitive damages may not stand.

A necessary element of the cause of action for malicious prosecution is "actual malice" or "malice in fact". The "actual malice" element of a malicious prosecution action does not require a plaintiff to prove that the defendant was motivated by spite or hatred, although it will of course be satisfied by such proof. Rather, it means that the defendant must have commenced the prior criminal proceeding due to a wrong or improper motive, something other than a desire to see the ends of justice served.

It has long been recognized in New York that punitive damages may be awarded in an action for malicious prosecution if the defendant was motivated by actual malice or acted in reckless disregard of the plaintiff's rights. While the latter phrase might at first seem to imply that something more than the "actual malice" essential to malicious prosecution is needed to support an award of exemplary damages, in fact this is so only in certain cases involving the imposition of vicarious liability. In a case such as this, in which liability is to be imposed upon the wrongdoer himself, a finding of liability for malicious prosecution precludes a determination as a matter of law that punitive damages are improper, for the actual malice necessary to support an action for malicious prosecution also serves to justify an award of exemplary damages. "[I]n torts which, like malicious prosecution, require a particular anti-social state of mind, the improper motive of the tortfeasor is both a necessary element in the cause of action and a reason for awarding punitive damages" (Restatement, Torts, Comment c, § 908). Thus, the Appellate Division incorrectly held as a matter of law that plaintiff had no claim for exemplary damages.

This is not to say, of course, that exemplary damages must be awarded in every such action, for the trier of facts is not required to make such an award simply because it may do so. Whether to award punitive damages in a particular case, as well as the amount of such damages, if any, are primarily questions which reside in the sound discretion of the original trier of the facts, in this case the jury, and such an award is not lightly to be disturbed. . . .

Here, . . . the Appellate Division erroneously concluded as a matter of law that plaintiff was not entitled to punitive damages. . . .

Accordingly, the order of the Appellate Division, insofar as it reversed so much of the judgment of Supreme Court as awarded exemplary damages, and dismissed the claim seeking such damages, should be reversed, and the case remitted to the Appellate Division for review of the award therefor in the exercise of discretion, with costs to abide the event.

Nappe v. Anschelewitz, Barr, Ansell & Bonello

Supreme Court of New Jersey, 1984.
97 N.J. 37, 477 A.2d 1224.

■ SCHREIBER, J. The primary issue raised by this case is whether a cause of action for legal fraud exists in the absence of compensatory damages. A related issue is whether punitive damages may be awarded in the absence of a compensatory damage award in an action for legal fraud. These issues arose when the jury awarded plaintiff $2 as nominal damages against the defendant Richard Bonello for fraud in each of two transactions and $50,000 in punitive damages for both frauds, without an allocation of the punitive award to either matter. These claims arose from two separate transactions—one involving plaintiff's loan to furnish a model apartment for a highrise condominium project, and the other, plaintiff's purchase of an interest in an office building.

. . . .

As early as 1791, this Court recognized that damages may appropriately be awarded "for *example's* sake, to prevent such offences in future ... [and] as would mark [the jury's] disapprobation. . . ." Subsequent cases reaffirmed our commitment that punitive or exemplary damages can be awarded to punish aggravated misconduct by the defendant and to deter him and others from repeating it. As Chief Justice Grummere observed many years ago in Dreimuller v. Rogow, 93 N.J.L. 1, 107 A. 144 (Sup.Ct. 1919):

The purpose of the award being to punish the wrongdoer, no reason is perceived for holding that the power to inflict punishment is dependent to any extent upon the form of the action by which the injured party seeks redress for the wrong done him by the malicious or wanton trespass committed against his property.

To warrant a punitive award, the defendant's conduct must have been wantonly reckless or malicious. There must be an intentional wrongdoing in the sense of an "evil-minded act" or an act accompanied by a wanton and wilful disregard of the rights of another. In Berg v. Reaction Motors Div., 37 N.J. at 414, 181 A.2d 487 (1962), this Court said:

Professor McCormick suggests that in order to satisfy the requirement of willfulness or wantonness there must be a "positive element of conscious wrongdoing." See *McCormick,* supra, at p. 280. Our cases indicate that the requirement may be satisfied upon a showing that there has been a deliberate act or omission with knowledge of a high degree of probability of harm and reckless indifference to consequences.

The key to the right to punitive damages is the wrongfulness of the intentional act. "The right to award exemplary damages primarily rests upon the single ground—wrongful motive...." ...

Because of the fortuitous circumstance that an injured plaintiff failed to prove compensatory damages, the defendant should not be freed of responsibility for aggravated misconduct. People should not be able with impunity to trench wilfully upon a right. Moreover, it is especially fitting to allow punitive damage for actions such as legal fraud, since intent rather than mere negligence is the requisite state of mind.

The punitive award is not required to have a fixed proportional relationship to the amount of compensatory damages. Instead, to further the punishment and deterrent goals in assessing punitive damages, the trier of fact should take into consideration all of the circumstances surrounding the particular occurrence including the nature of the wrongdoing, the extent of harm inflicted, the intent of the party committing the act, the wealth of the perpetrator, as well as any mitigating circumstances which may operate to reduce the amount of the damages.

Our [lower] courts have held that punitive damages could be awarded for egregious conduct in the absence of compensatory damages.

It should be noted that the punishment aspect is for the private wrong to the individual, rather than the wrong to the public. It is settled that if the wrong constitutes a criminal act, the punitive damage award may effectively supplement the criminal law in punishing the defendant.

The principle that punitive damages may be awarded in the absence of compensatory damages in actions for intentional torts furthers desirable policy goals. "[T]he nominal-damage cases are peculiarly appropriate for exemplary damages. If no compensable harm is done even though the defendant's conduct is very wrongful, the normal admonitory function of tort law is not brought into play unless exemplary damages are assessed." Note, "Exemplary Damages in the Law of Torts," 70 Harv.L.Rev. 517, 529 (1957).

We therefore hold that punitive damages may be assessed in an action for an intentional tort involving egregious conduct whether or not compensatory damages are awarded, at least where some injury, loss, or detriment to the plaintiff has occurred.

. . . .

[The concurring opinion of O'HERN, J., is omitted.]

NOTE

Oliver brought a strict products liability suit against GAF Corporation for injuries caused by exposure to asbestos made by it. The jury awarded Oliver no compensatory damages, but it awarded him $500,000 in punitive damages. The trial court denied GAF's motion for judgment notwithstanding the verdict. However, this judgment was reversed on appeal. Oliver v. Raymark Industries, Inc., 799 F.2d 95 (3d Cir.1986). The appellate court explained:

> We believe that the district court erred in its prediction of New Jersey law. New Jersey's adoption of strict products liability eliminated the element of *fault* (breach of duty) from a cause of action against the manufacturer of a defective product; it did not eliminate the element of *damages*. Thus, there is no valid cause of action in strict products liability absent compensatory damages. Employing the analysis of *Nappe,* a strict products liability action should, therefore, be treated as a negligence action (where compensatory damages are also required to establish a valid cause of action) rather than as an intentional tort action (where compensatory damages are not required). We believe that the proper prediction of New Jersey law is that in a strict products liability action—as in a negligence action—punitive damages cannot be awarded without compensatory damages.

> This rule is consistent with the position of the Restatement (Second) of Torts § 908, comment c (1979)(in awarding punitive damages "[i]t is essential ... that facts be established that, apart from punitive damages, are sufficient to maintain a cause of action."); see also comment b ("Although a defendant has inflicted no harm, punitive damages may be awarded because of, and measured by, his wrongful purpose or intent.... In all these cases, however, a cause of action for the particular tort must exist, at least for nominal damages."). It is also the position adopted by leading commentators. Moreover, the only other jurisdiction to directly address the availability of punitive damages under similar circumstances [i.e., Kansas] reaches a conclusion contrary to that of the district court.

Jackson v. Johns–Manville Sales Corporation

United States Court of Appeals, Fifth Circuit, 1986.
781 F.2d 394.

■ RANDALL, J. This Mississippi diversity case involves plaintiff Jackson's efforts to recover compensatory and punitive damages from Johns–Manville Sales Corporation, Raybestos–Manhattan, Inc., and H.K. Porter Company, all manufacturers of asbestos products. Jackson was injured as a result of his exposure to asbestos products during the course of his employment as a shipyard worker. The district court, after a lengthy trial, entered judgment in favor of Jackson against all defendants except H.K. Porter Company in the amount of $391,500 in compensatory damages and $625,000 in combined punitive damages. . . .

. . . .

The defendants argued before the instructions were given that the punitive damages issue should not go to the jury as a matter of law, and, after failing in that, they contended that the punitive damages award should be vacated. The defendants offered the identical legal theory in support of their objections to the jury instruction on both occasions: The uniqueness of the factual context in a mass tort case makes punitive damages inappropriate as a matter of law. . . .

. . . .

The focus of the defendants' argument is that the policies justifying punitive damages in Mississippi are not implicated in the mass tort case. They conclude that punitive damages should therefore be unavailable as a matter of law. The defendants note correctly that under Mississippi law, plaintiffs have no "right" to recover punitive damages. Rather, punitive damages are granted only in "extreme" cases, and they "should be allowed only with caution and within narrow limits". The law authorizes punitive damage awards somewhat reluctantly, because they alter the settled principle that a remedy in tort should simply make the plaintiff whole. However, greater societal concerns justify punitive damages in the exceptional case, because in extreme circumstances wrongdoers deserve punishment both as an expression of society's disfavor of their actions "and as an example so that others may be deterred from the commission of similar offenses." Further, punitive damages reward individuals who serve as "private attorneys general" in bringing wrongdoers to account.

Given these specific functions which punitive damages serve, the defendants and the United States insist that the Mississippi Supreme Court would not allow them here. As JM sums up Mississippi law:

> Mississippi courts . . . neither regard punitive damages as a right to which plaintiffs are entitled nor demonstrate such a callous disregard for the results of punitive damages which result in the financial destruction of a defendant. Rather, the Mississippi courts have recognized a duty for both trial and appellate courts to scrutinize carefully all punitive damages cases to be sure that societal interests are served and that punitive damages are not awarded except in the most extreme cases where the plaintiff is not motivated by vindictiveness, reprisal, or greed.

The defendants' counsel asserted to the trial judge that punitive damages should not be awarded since multiple punitive damage awards might preclude future plaintiffs from recovering even compensatory damages. They pointed out to the trial judge that punitive damages serve to punish defendants, and contended that, as a result of the voluminous asbestos litigation, they have already been punished enough. They stated to the trial judge that punitive damages serve to motivate "private attorneys general" to bring suit, but argued that persons injured by asbestos have motivation enough to sue. Finally, they acknowledged to the trial judge that punitive damages deter wrongful conduct, but they insisted that the asbestos litigation is deterrence enough.

The defendants' analysis neglects to pay any attention to the heavy burden the plaintiff must meet— . . . the burden Jackson *did* meet—before the punitive damage issue may properly be submitted to the jury and punitive damages may be awarded. That heavy burden is designed to take into account the interests of both society and defendants by ensuring that punitive damages are awarded in only the unusual case where the defendant must be made an example because of its especially egregious behavior.

. . . .

Yet the defendants do not directly contend that the jury instructions inadequately or incorrectly summarized the existing legal rules, which is the usual issue in a Rule 51 objection to jury instructions. They argue instead that "facts" not a part of this record mandate a drastic change in the law of remedies. They urge us to determine that when a defendant injures tens of thousands and manifests reckless disregard for the victims' lives and welfare, punitive damages should be unavailable as a matter of law.

. . . .

There appears to be no Mississippi case law directly on the issue of the availability of punitive damages in the mass tort context. Absent the controlling authority of the Mississippi Supreme Court or the guiding authority of lower Mississippi courts, we must look to the jurisprudence of other states in formulating substantive law, as a Mississippi court would.

The simple fact of the matter is that no appellate court has accepted the defendants' theory in a reported decision. In Oregon, for example, the Supreme Court recently ruled in a "mass tort" case that the "financial interests of the malicious and wanton wrongdoer must be considered in the context of societal concern for the injured and the future protection of society." An Illinois court recently explained that it did "not believe that defendants should be relieved of liability for punitive damages merely because, through outrageous misconduct, they may have managed to seriously injure a large number of persons." Pennsylvania, New Jersey, Florida, Tennessee, and Texas each permits plaintiffs to recover punitive damages in mass tort cases.

Moreover, several commentators writing on the issue of punitive damages in mass tort cases have concluded that punitive damages should be generally available in mass tort cases. The central thesis of much of the scholarly writing in this area is that the problems assertedly caused by awarding punitive damages in the mass tort context are typically more apparent than real. Further, in response to the speculation that punitive damage awards may prevent compensatory damage awards in the future due to financial pressures on the defendants, these authors conclude that if serious societal difficulties do *in fact* arise, they can be addressed by less drastic means than a complete bar to the availability of punitive damages as a matter of law.

The rule of law requested by the defendants would require a modification of Mississippi's approach to fashioning its substantive law, as well as a modification of the law itself. For this court to make such a modification in the absence of explicit guidance from the Mississippi courts would be to abdicate our proper role as a diversity court. As the Sixth Circuit concluded in a recent diversity case applying Tennessee law, the "serious public policy concerns" raised by asbestos case defendants seeking to avoid punitive damages were not "a proper basis upon which this Court can rest a diversity decision.... The relief sought by JM may be more properly granted by the state or federal legislature than by this Court."

. . . .

The defendants and the United States contend nevertheless that regardless of existing Mississippi law, punitive damages should not be awarded in this context, where there have been thousands of persons injured by asbestos and where thousands of plaintiffs have sued, since the potential ramifications of multiple damage awards on the defendants' financial viability may be severe, with the consequence that future plaintiffs may be unable to recover even compensatory damages. JM's position is that in "the asbestos litigation, punitive damages ... carry the very real prospect of financial destruction for the defendant [and] threaten the possible recovery of thousands of other injured parties." Similarly, the United States acknowledges that the "defendants' conduct would clearly warrant the lower court's punitive damage sanction if the full scope of the asbestos litigation were ignored, [but] the justifiable outrage at defendants' conduct should not permit a damage award that in fact runs counter to the public interest."

There is a fundamental inconsistency within this argument, an inconsistency which many other courts have pointed out and have ultimately found to be dispositive. Punitive damages exist in part to punish defendants whose conduct merits punishment. As the defendants repeatedly point out, punitive damages are awarded only in extreme cases. Yet the defendants and the United States argue that in the *most* extreme cases, when a defendant commits an especially pernicious act which injures a myriad of innocent persons, cases which one might imagine to be especially suitable for the imposition of punitive damages, the law should shield the defendant from punitive damages by the sheer magnitude of its wrong.

Mississippi law already provides that the defendants could have introduced to the jury evidence of their asserted dire financial straits, and of the possibility that punitive damage awards might prevent other plaintiffs from recovering even compensatory damages. They could have attempted to convince the finder of fact that they did not need to be deterred, or that the effect of punitive damage awards would cripple their companies. They could have produced evidence of their contingent liability and then requested that the trial judge specifically instruct the jury that this evidence be taken into account in assessing the amount of punitive damages, if any. If the defendants had done so, the finder of fact could have assessed the merits of their contentions. Thereafter, the trial judge could have reviewed the propriety of the award, in light of the evidence supporting the defendants' contentions, on either a motion for judgment notwithstanding the verdict or a motion to remit the punitive damages. However, the defendants did not elect to follow the path which was available to them under existing law to bring their concerns about insolvency and the lack of need for deterrence to the attention first of the finder of fact and then to the judge.

There is no basis for us to disturb the trial court's decision that punitive damages are available as a matter of law in mass tort contexts. We conclude that the Mississippi Supreme Court would not deny punitive damages in cases of strict liability or cases of mass tort as a matter of law.

. . . .

... Accordingly, the judgment of the district court is affirmed.

[The dissenting opinion of CLARK, C.J., joined by GEE, GARZA, POLITZ, and JOLLY, JJ., is omitted.]

Mattyasovszky v. West Towns Bus Co.

Supreme Court of Illinois, 1975.
61 Ill.2d 31, 330 N.E.2d 509.

■ SCHAEFFER J. Matyas Mattyasovszky, Jr., a 12–year–old boy, left a bus operated by the defendant, West Towns Bus Company, by the rear door at the wrong stop. When he attempted to reenter, his foot was apparently momentarily caught in the door, and he fell under the wheels and was killed as the bus moved forward. In this action, brought by his father as administrator of his estate, a jury found the defendant guilty of willful and wanton conduct and awarded the plaintiff $75,000 pecuniary damages and $50,000 punitive damages. The appellate court affirmed the award of pecuniary damages, but reversed the judgment which awarded punitive damages....

... Only two questions are presented: (1) are punitive damages recoverable under the "Survival Act", and (2) is there a common law action for wrongful death which includes the element of punitive damages.

The Survival Act, upon which the plaintiff relies primarily for a reversal of the judgment of the appellate court, reads as follows:

"In addition to the actions which survive by the common law, the following also survive: actions of replevin, actions to recover damages for an injury to the person (except slander and libel), actions to recover damages for an injury to real or personal property or for the detention or conversion of personal property...."

This statute has never been thought to authorize the award of punitive damages....

... [T]he plaintiff [also] relies upon the decisions of the courts of other States construing the language of their survival statutes. From them he argues that punitive damages should be allowed in the present case. We do not find those decisions persuasive. The actions which survive under our statute are "actions to recover damages for an injury to the person," and as we have pointed out, the very decisions that have recently expanded the right to recover under it have emphasized the compensatory nature of the recovery it authorizes.

In addition to his argument based upon the construction of the statute, the plaintiff urges that this court should now recognize a common law action for the death of a person which can include exemplary damages....

. . . .

... Historically, the practice of awarding punitive damages seems to have "originated in the English courts in the eighteenth century as a means of justifying awards of damages in excess of the plaintiff's tangible harm." But it is unnecessary to pursue the possible historical origins in connection with this case, for it is generally recognized today that punitive damages are awarded primarily to punish the offender and to discourage other offenses.

The underlying strength of these objectives of punishment and deterrence varies substantially from case to case. Where, for example, the defendant has benefited by his misconduct, a judgment which only compensates the plaintiff for what he has lost would permit the defendant to keep his wrongful gain. Apart from such cases, the situations in which punitive damages become an issue cover a broad spectrum that ranges from the intentional tort which is also a crime to what we characterize today as "willful and wanton" conduct, a characterization that shades imperceptibly into simple negligence.

The objectives of an award of punitive damages are the same as those which motivate the criminal law—punishment and deterrence. Yet in a criminal case the conduct which gives rise to the imposition of punishment must be clearly defined. That is not so when the question is whether the conduct of the defendant can be characterized as either negligence or as willful and wanton conduct. The fine that is imposed upon the defendant in a criminal case goes to the State. But in a civil case the exaction taken from the defendant, under the label of exemplary damages, becomes a windfall for the plaintiff. The maximum and minimum amounts of the fine imposed by way of punishment and deterrence in a criminal case are fixed by statute. In the civil case, however, the jury is left at large to take from the defendant and deliver to the plaintiff such amount as it sees fit....

Moreover, the punitive and admonitory justifications for the imposition of punitive damages are sharply diminished in those cases in which liability is imposed vicariously.... Serious questions inevitably arise in a case like the present, in which the driver of the bus, whose conduct was primarily responsible for the injury, is no longer a party defendant because he was dismissed by the plaintiff before the case went to the jury.

. . . .

Judgment affirmed.

[An Addendum to the opinion of SCHAEFER, J., and the dissenting opinion of GOLDENHERSH, J., are omitted.]

B. CONTRACTS

Miller Brewing Co. v. Best Beers of Bloomington, Inc.

Supreme Court of Indiana, 1993.
608 N.E.2d 975.

■ KRAHULIK, JUSTICE.

This case involves the interpretation of Ind.Code Ann. § 7.1–5–5–9 (West 1982) ("Termination Statute") pertaining to the termination of an agreement between a brewer and a wholesaler.... Several issues are raised in the petitions, which we restate as follows:

. . .

(3) Whether punitive damages are appropriate in this breach of contract action; . . .

3. Punitive Damages

Miller next attacks Best Beer's entitlement to punitive damages. We reverse the grant of a new trial on punitive damages because Best Beers failed to meet its burden of proof for punitive damages in this breach of contract case.

Opinions of this Court have consistently stated the general rule that punitive damages are not allowed in a breach of contract action. Such statements suggest that there are exceptions to this rule, but upon close examination of the opinions of this Court, we find that no exceptions have ever been applied. Today we hold that, in fact, no exception exists.

The notion that in some instances punitive damages are available for a breach of contract appears to have begun in Vernon Fire & Casualty v. Sharp, 264 Ind. 599, 349 N.E.2d 173. In that case, plaintiff sued his insurer for breach of an insurance contract, and the jury awarded compensatory damages for the breach. Plaintiff also alleged tortious conduct on part of the insurer for refusing to pay policy proceeds admittedly due, and was awarded punitive damages. In addressing whether punitive damages were available when a breach of contract was proven, this Court noted the general rule that such damages are not recoverable because a plaintiff is "not entitled to mulct the promisor in punitive damages" for a breach of contract. 264 Ind. at 608, 349 N.E.2d at 180. The Court reasoned that such damages were not legally appropriate because (1) "the well-defined parameters of compensatory and consequential damages which may be assessed against a promisor who decides for whatever reason not to live up to his bargain lend a needed measure of stability and predictability to the free enterprise system," and (2) the promisee will be compensated for all damages proximately resulting from the promisor's breach. 264 Ind. at 607, 349 N.E.2d at 180. The Court acknowledged, however, the widely-recognized principle that where the conduct of the breaching party independently establishes the elements of a common law tort, and where the proven tort is of the kind for which punitive damages are allowed, then punitive damages may be awarded. Id. In such a case, however, the punitive damages are awarded for the tort, and not for the breach of contract. The majority then found that the Vernon Fire plaintiff had established the elements of the common law tort of fraud and affirmed the award of punitive damages. 264 Ind. at 617, 349 N.E.2d at 184.

In spite of its conclusion that the plaintiff had established the elements of fraud as an independent tort, the majority proceeded to opine that the requirement of an independent tort was not very compelling "when it appears from the evidence as a whole that a serious wrong, tortious in nature, has been committed, but the wrong does not conveniently fit the confines of a pre-determined tort" and where "the public interest will be served by the deterrent effect punitive damages will have upon future conduct of the wrongdoer and parties similarly situated." 264 Ind. at 608, 349 N.E.2d at 180 (emphasis omitted). Such language has been cited in subsequent Indiana cases addressing the availability of punitive damages in a breach of contract action.

In reaching this conclusion, the court relied upon Sedgwick on Damages, which was cited in an early Indiana case, Taber v. Hutson (1854), 5 Ind. 322. We do not find this authority persuasive. As Justice Prentice wrote in his dissent to Vernon Fire:

Coming now to the majority statement that an independent tort is not a prerequisite to an award of punitive damages, the statement is not supported by case law. The majority has stated that a careful review of the case law leads to that conclusion, but it has cited no cases. Instead it cites Corbin on Contracts and Sedgwick on Damages. The quotation from 5 Corbin, § 1077 does refer to punitive damages in " * * * cases that contain elements that enable the court to regard them as falling within the field of tort or closely analogous thereto" indicating that only tort elements, as opposed to a tort or tortious conduct would be required. I believe this is an unfortunate and erroneous inference. The section quoted from is not a treatise upon the law of punitive damages in contract actions. Rather, it is a pronouncement that such damages are not recoverable for breach of contract, with the caveat that there are certain exceptions. A detailed enumeration of the exceptions and their interplay between certain actions that are a mixture of tort and contract was not required in the context of this portion of the treatise, and I believe the quoted statement was casual and unguarded. At any rate, none of the cases cited in the footnote support the inference. On the contrary, it appears that in each case cited and in which punitive damages were allowed, there had been a tort committed and not merely unsavory conduct.

The quote from Sedgwick was taken from Taber v. Hutson (1854), 5 Ind. 322, 325, as disclosed by the majority opinion. That case, however, was not a contract case but was one for assault and battery and false imprisonment. The quotation from Sedgwick was quite appropriate in that case. The formulation from Sedgwick obviously was related to tort cases. The word "mingle" accented in the majority opinion refers not to the mingling of the elements of fraud, malice, etc. in contract controversies but in tort controversies. The author, it appears was explaining that punitive damages are not allowable in all tort cases but only in those also embodying the especially reprehensible elements.

* * *

That evidence of tortious conduct, an independent tort, and not merely of "tort-like" conduct is a prerequisite to an award of punitive damages in contract actions is borne out by an abundance of cases, and we have been cited to none to the contrary.

264 Ind. at 632–35, 349 N.E.2d at 194–95.

A rule that requires establishment of an independent tort furthers the public interest in recognizing the existence of bona fide business disputes and separating them from breaches of contract achieved in a tortious manner. As we stated in Travelers, breaches of contract "will almost invariably be regarded by the complaining party as oppressive if not outright fraudulent." 442 N.E.2d at 363. "The public interest cannot be served by any policy that deters resort to the courts for the determination of bona fide business disputes," Travelers, 442 N.E.2d at 363, or prohibits one party to a contract from exercising his common law rights to breach a contract and pay a rightful amount of compensatory damages. Unlike torts, where the duty is owed to all and a broad measure of damages is available, contract obligations are owed only to the parties to the contract and damages are limited to those reasonably within the expectations of the parties when the contract is made. Vernon Fire, 264 Ind. at 607, 349 N.E.2d at 179, citing Prosser, Law of Torts, 613 (4th ed. 1971). Third, as the Court of Appeals noted in Indiana & Michigan Elec. Co. v. Terre Haute Indus. (1987), Ind.App., 507 N.E.2d 588, 617, "[i]t is not our prerogative to reopen the floodgates of punitive damages in contract cases, which were largely closed by the supreme court in Vernon, Travelers, and Orkin, and let all disputes and quarrels over broken contracts and disappointed business ventures become the subject of acrimonious litigation over punitive damages." Finally, as stated earlier, the dicta in Vernon Fire has never, in fact, been applied by this Court.

We note the Court of Appeals reached the opposite result in a case dealing with the same statute. Joseph Schlitz Brewing Co. v. Central Beverage Co., 172 Ind.App. 81, 359 N.E.2d 566. In Schlitz, the brewer sought to have the distributor adopt certain internal controls which it had no legal right to do. The court noted that although the brewer's conduct did not fall within the well-defined parameters of any common law tort, the conduct was tortious in nature because its conduct was "an exhibition of bad faith toward the rights of its wholesalers." 172 Ind.App. at 103–4, 359 N.E.2d at 580. We do not find that Schlitz compels us to affirm the award of punitive damages here. Although it may have been correctly decided at the time, such is no longer the law.

We hold that in order to recover punitive damages in a lawsuit founded upon a breach of contract, the plaintiff must plead and prove the existence of an independent tort of the kind for which Indiana law recognizes that punitive damages may be awarded.

Having stated the proper legal standard for punitive damages in contract cases, we now address the parties' contentions as to whether the evidence presented in this case was sufficient. Best Beers claims the following evidence supports the imposition of punitive damages:

 1) Miller employees made false statements (to their superiors) about Best Beers' sales efforts.

 2) Miller employees made false statements (to their superiors) about the conduct of Best Beers' employees.

 3) Miller made accusations in its termination letter which weren't supported by its own employees' reports.

4) Miller tolerated overage beer in the market after terminating Best Beers ostensibly because Best Beers had permitted overage beer to remain in the market.

5) A Miller employee said she would not rate Best Beers' performance as satisfactory no matter how well they did.

6) Miller solicited unfavorable comments about Best Beers in writing from selected retailers.

Best Beers does not seriously contend that there was sufficient evidence of an independent tort upon which punitive damages could have been awarded, but merely asserts that the above evidence is clear and convincing evidence of a "serious wrong tortious in nature." As discussed above, such evidence is insufficient to support an award of punitive damages in a breach of contract case. At best, such evidence establishes that Miller wrongfully terminated the contract, for which Best Beers was awarded compensatory damages. Under elementary contract principles, those compensatory damages fully compensate Best Beers to the extent allowed by law for all losses suffered by it as a result of the breach of contract. We discern nothing, based on the evidence presented at trial, compelling the conclusion that Best Beers is entitled to punitive damages.

. . .

Conclusion

Accordingly, we grant transfer, vacate the opinion of the Court of Appeals, affirm the award of compensatory damages, and vacate the award of punitive damages.

■ SHEPARD, C.J., and DEBRULER, J., concur.

■ GIVAN, J., dissents, without opinion.

■ DICKSON, J., dissents, with separate opinion, in which GIVAN, J., concurs.

■ DICKSON, JUSTICE, dissenting.

In Vernon Fire & Casualty Ins. Co. v. Sharp (1976), 264 Ind. 599, 349 N.E.2d 173, this Court recognized two exceptions to the general rule that punitive damages are not recoverable in a contract action. The first arises when conduct of the breaching party not only constitutes breach of contract but also independently establishes the elements of a common law tort. Id. at 608, 349 N.E.2d at 180. The second occurs when the evidence reveals that a serious wrong, tortious in nature, has been committed, although the wrong "does not conveniently fit the confines of a pre-determined tort." Id.

Judicial response to the Vernon exceptions has been both positive and widespread. Not only have Indiana courts consistently endorsed the opinion, but other jurisdictions have also cited Vernon while recognizing recovery of punitive damages within the context of a contractual relationship.[2]

---

2. McCullough v. Golden Rule Ins. Co. (1990), Wyo., 789 P.2d 855; Romero v. Mervyn's (1989), 109 N.M. 249, 784 P.2d 992; McCutchen v. Liberty Mut. Ins. Co. (N.D.Ind. 1988), 699 F.Supp. 701; Roberts v. Western– Southern Life Ins. Co. (N.D.Ill.1983), 568 F.Supp. 536; Canada Dry Corp. v. Nehi Beverage Co. (7th Cir.1983), 723 F.2d 512; Central Armature Works, Inc. v. American Motorists Ins. Co. (D.D.C.1980), 520 F.Supp.

The majority opines that the second Vernon exception has never been applied by this Court, noting that in several cases where we have permitted punitive damages in a contract action, we have found evidence of an independent tort. Bud Wolf Chevrolet, Inc. v. Robertson (1988), Ind., 519 N.E.2d 135; Art Hill Ford, Inc. v. Callender (1981), Ind., 423 N.E.2d 601; Hibschman Pontiac, Inc. v. Batchelor (1977), 266 Ind. 310, 362 N.E.2d 845. Examination of these cases, however, reveals that in each, prior to finding that punitive damages were justified, we specifically made reference to fraud, malice, gross negligence, or oppression which "mingle" in the controversy—the language we emphasized in Hibschman when explaining the second Vernon exception. Id. at 314, 362 N.E.2d at 847. Additionally, while we did not specifically identify the second exception as the basis of our affirmance of punitive damages in these cases, neither did we expressly articulate the finding of an independent tort. These opinions do not express greater reliance upon the first rather than the second Vernon exception. I respectfully disagree with the majority's conclusion that the second exception has never been utilized by this Court.

Furthermore, the second Vernon exception has long been employed by the Court of Appeals to award punitive damages in the context of a contract breach. In Liberty Mut. Ins. Co. v. Parkinson (1985), Ind.App., 487 N.E.2d 162, punitive damages were upheld when an insurance company demonstrated bad faith in settling a claim under uninsured motorist coverage. Relying on the second exception, the court observed: "we have found no reason to adopt bad faith as an independent tort in this state and we see no need to adopt such an action now." Id. at 165. Similarly affirming punitive damages against an insurer in the absence of an independent tort, the court instructed that "a complaint which requests punitive damages in an action for breach of contract need not contain all of the elements which must be specifically alleged for actionable fraud." State Farm Mut. Auto. Ins. Co. v. Shuman (1977), 175 Ind.App. 186, 196, 370 N.E.2d 941, 950. Likewise, when punitive damages were awarded where the seller of a defective mobile home fraudulently refused to refund the buyer's deposit, punitive damages were justified even though "as is often the case, the findings do not specifically set out all five elements of the tort of fraud...." Jones v. Abriani (1976), 169 Ind.App. 556, 580, 350 N.E.2d 635, 650.

The Court of Appeals, in a case somewhat similar to that before us, determined that conduct by a brewing company, while failing to meet the common law elements of tort, nevertheless was sufficiently tort-like to sustain an award of punitive damages. Jos. Schlitz Brewing Co. v. Central Beverage Co. (1977), 172 Ind.App. 81, 359 N.E.2d 566. The brewer's breach of a distribution contract, allegedly precipitated by the distributor's refusal to adopt internal management controls required by the brewer, was found to be tortiously oppressive conduct. Id. at 103, 359 N.E.2d at 580. The court observed that punitive damages properly served the public interest inasmuch as the brewer's conduct contravened principles of free market economy which could ultimately manifest itself in higher prices for consumers. Id. at 104, 359 N.E.2d at 581.

283; General Motors v. Piskor (1977), 281 Md. 627, 381 A.2d 16.

This Court is unanimous in its recognition of the continued viability of the first Vernon exception based upon the establishment of an independent tort. Today, however, the majority abruptly seeks to modify Vernon and its progeny by relegating to dicta the exception permitting punitive damages where a contract breach attended by egregiously culpable conduct falls short of an independently actionable tort. However attractive it may be to limit an award of punitive damages to such bright-line situations, reprehensible behavior often defies strict tort categorization and should not go undeterred merely because it fails to completely conform to the precise contours of pre-existing tort classifications.

The majority speculates that recovery of punitive damages under the second Vernon exception would "reopen" the floodgates of punitive damages in contract cases. I disagree. The gates have already been open for the 17 years since Vernon, and neither catastrophe nor havoc has resulted. Twin restraints of case law and statutory enactment are clearly in place. Punitive damages are appropriate only upon clear and convincing evidence showing that the defendant "acted with malice, fraud, gross negligence or oppressiveness" and that such conduct "was not the result of a mistake of fact or law, honest error o[f] judgment, overzealousness, mere negligence, or human failing." Bud Wolf, 519 N.E.2d at 137. Moreover, Ind.Code § 34–4–34–2 likewise emphasizes that facts supporting punitive damages must be established by "clear and convincing evidence." It is not surprising that, notwithstanding Vernon, there has been no flood of punitive damages judgments in Indiana courts.

Vernon's flexible and responsive application of the law to category-resistant dimensions of human behavior represents an enlightened approach to the infinite variations that elude rigid doctrinal formulations. Experience has shown this approach to be wise, effective, balanced, and just. It should not now be discarded.

■ GIVAN, J., concurs.

C.   EXCESSIVE AWARDS, AWARDS AGAINST PRINCIPALS FOR ACTS OF AGENTS AND INSURANCE

BMW, Inc. v. Gore

Supreme Court of the United States, 1996.
517 U.S. 559, 116 S.Ct. 1589, 134 L.Ed.2d 809.

■ JUSTICE STEVENS delivered the opinion of the Court.

The Due Process Clause of the Fourteenth Amendment prohibits a State from imposing a " 'grossly excessive' " punishment on a tortfeasor. TXO Production Corp. v. Alliance Resources Corp., 509 U.S. 443, 454, 113 S.Ct. 2711, 2718, 125 L.Ed.2d 366 (1993) (and cases cited). The wrongdoing involved in this case was the decision by a national distributor of automobiles not to advise its dealers, and hence their customers, of predelivery damage to new cars when the cost of repair amounted to less than 3 percent of the car's suggested retail price. The question presented is whether a $2 million punitive damages award to the purchaser of one of these cars exceeds the constitutional limit.

I

In January 1990, Dr. Ira Gore, Jr. (respondent), purchased a black BMW sports sedan for $40,750.88 from an authorized BMW dealer in Birmingham, Alabama. After driving the car for approximately nine months, and without noticing any flaws in its appearance, Dr. Gore took the car to "Slick Finish," an independent detailer, to make it look " 'snazzier than it normally would appear.' " 646 So.2d 619, 621 (Ala.1994). Mr. Slick, the proprietor, detected evidence that the car had been repainted.[3] Convinced that he had been cheated, Dr. Gore brought suit against petitioner BMW of North America (BMW), the American distributor of BMW automobiles. . . . The complaint prayed for $500,000 in compensatory and punitive damages, and costs.

At trial, BMW acknowledged that it had adopted a nationwide policy in 1983 concerning cars that were damaged in the course of manufacture or transportation. If the cost of repairing the damage exceeded 3 percent of the car's suggested retail price, the car was placed in company service for a period of time and then sold as used. If the repair cost did not exceed 3 percent of the suggested retail price, however, the car was sold as new without advising the dealer that any repairs had been made. Because the $601.37 cost of repainting Dr. Gore's car was only about 1.5 percent of its suggested retail price, BMW did not disclose the damage or repair to the Birmingham dealer.

Dr. Gore asserted that his repainted car was worth less than a car that had not been refinished. To prove his actual damages of $4,000, he relied on the testimony of a former BMW dealer, who estimated that the value of a repainted BMW was approximately 10 percent less than the value of a new car that had not been damaged and repaired. To support his claim for punitive damages, Dr. Gore introduced evidence that since 1983 BMW had sold 983 refinished cars as new, including 14 in Alabama, without disclosing that the cars had been repainted before sale at a cost of more than $300 per vehicle. Using the actual damage estimate of $4,000 per vehicle, Dr. Gore argued that a punitive award of $4 million would provide an appropriate penalty for selling approximately 1,000 cars for more than they were worth.

In defense of its disclosure policy, BMW argued that it was under no obligation to disclose repairs of minor damage to new cars and that Dr. Gore's car was as good as a car with the original factory finish. It disputed Dr. Gore's assertion that the value of the car was impaired by the repainting and argued that this good-faith belief made a punitive award

---

3. The top, hood, trunk, and quarter panels of Dr. Gore's car were repainted at BMW's vehicle preparation center in Brunswick, Georgia. The parties presumed that the damage was caused by exposure to acid rain during transit between the manufacturing plant in Germany and the preparation center.

inappropriate. BMW also maintained that transactions in jurisdictions other than Alabama had no relevance to Dr. Gore's claim.

The jury returned a verdict finding BMW liable for compensatory damages of $4,000. In addition, the jury assessed $4 million in punitive damages, based on a determination that the nondisclosure policy constituted "gross, oppressive or malicious" fraud. See Ala.Code §§ 6–11–20, 6–11–21 (1993).

BMW filed a post-trial motion to set aside the punitive damages award. The company introduced evidence to establish that its nondisclosure policy was consistent with the laws of roughly 25 States defining the disclosure obligations of automobile manufacturers, distributors, and dealers. The most stringent of these statutes required disclosure of repairs costing more than 3 percent of the suggested retail price; none mandated disclosure of less costly repairs. Relying on these statutes, BMW contended that its conduct was lawful in these States and therefore could not provide the basis for an award of punitive damages.

BMW also drew the court's attention to the fact that its nondisclosure policy had never been adjudged unlawful before this action was filed. Just months before Dr. Gore's case went to trial, the jury in a similar lawsuit filed by another Alabama BMW purchaser found that BMW's failure to disclose paint repair constituted fraud. Yates v. BMW of North America, Inc., 642 So.2d 937 (Ala.Civ.App.1993).[8] Before the judgment in this case, BMW changed its policy by taking steps to avoid the sale of any refinished vehicles in Alabama and two other States. When the $4 million verdict was returned in this case, BMW promptly instituted a nationwide policy of full disclosure of all repairs, no matter how minor.

In response to BMW's arguments, Dr. Gore asserted that the policy change demonstrated the efficacy of the punitive damages award. He noted that while no jury had held the policy unlawful, BMW had received a number of customer complaints relating to undisclosed repairs and had settled some lawsuits. Finally, he maintained that the disclosure statutes of other States were irrelevant because BMW had failed to offer any evidence that the disclosure statutes supplanted, rather than supplemented, existing causes of action for common-law fraud.

The trial judge denied BMW's post-trial motion, holding, inter alia, that the award was not excessive. On appeal, the Alabama Supreme Court also rejected BMW's claim that the award exceeded the constitutionally permissible amount. 646 So.2d 619 (1994). The court's excessiveness inquiry applied the factors articulated in Green Oil Co. v. Hornsby, 539 So.2d 218, 223–224 (Ala.1989), and approved in Pacific Mut. Life Ins. Co. v. Haslip, 499 U.S. 1, 21–22, 111 S.Ct. 1032, 1045–1046, 113 L.Ed.2d 1 (1991). 646 So.2d, at 624–625. Based on its analysis, the court concluded that BMW's conduct was "reprehensible"; the nondisclosure was profitable for

---

8. While awarding a comparable amount of compensatory damages, the Yates jury awarded no punitive damages at all. In Yates, the plaintiff also relied on the 1983 nondisclosure policy, but instead of offering evidence of 983 repairs costing more than $300 each, he introduced a bulk exhibit containing 5,856 repair bills to show that petitioner had sold over 5,800 new BMW vehicles without disclosing that they had been repaired.

the company; the judgment "would not have a substantial impact upon [BMW's] financial position"; the litigation had been expensive; no criminal sanctions had been imposed on BMW for the same conduct; the award of no punitive damages in Yates reflected "the inherent uncertainty of the trial process"; and the punitive award bore a "reasonable relationship" to "the harm that was likely to occur from [BMW's] conduct as well as . . . the harm that actually occurred." 646 So.2d, at 625–627.

The Alabama Supreme Court did, however, rule in BMW's favor on one critical point: The court found that the jury improperly computed the amount of punitive damages by multiplying Dr. Gore's compensatory damages by the number of similar sales in other jurisdictions. Id., at 627. Having found the verdict tainted, the court held that "a constitutionally reasonable punitive damages award in this case is $2,000,000," id., at 629, and therefore ordered a remittitur in that amount. [FN10] The court's discussion of the amount of its remitted award expressly disclaimed any reliance on "acts that occurred in other jurisdictions"; instead, the court explained that it had used a "comparative analysis" that considered Alabama cases, "along with cases from other jurisdictions, involving the sale of an automobile where the seller misrepresented the condition of the vehicle and the jury awarded punitive damages to the purchaser." Id., at 628.

Because we believed that a review of this case would help to illuminate "the character of the standard that will identify unconstitutionally excessive awards" of punitive damages, see Honda Motor Co. v. Oberg, 512 U.S. 415, 420, 114 S.Ct. 2331, 2335, 129 L.Ed.2d 336 (1994), we granted certiorari, 513 U.S. 1125, 115 S.Ct. 932, 130 L.Ed.2d 879 (1995).

II

Punitive damages may properly be imposed to further a State's legitimate interests in punishing unlawful conduct and deterring its repetition. In our federal system, States necessarily have considerable flexibility in determining the level of punitive damages that they will allow in different classes of cases and in any particular case. Most States that authorize exemplary damages afford the jury similar latitude, requiring only that the damages awarded be reasonably necessary to vindicate the State's legitimate interests in punishment and deterrence. Only when an award can fairly be categorized as "grossly excessive" in relation to these interests does it enter the zone of arbitrariness that violates the Due Process Clause of the Fourteenth Amendment. Cf. TXO Production Corp. v. Alliance Resources Corp., 509 U.S., at 456, 113 S.Ct., at 2719 (1993). For that reason, the federal excessiveness inquiry appropriately begins with an identification of the state interests that a punitive award is designed to serve. We therefore focus our attention first on the scope of Alabama's legitimate interests in punishing BMW and deterring it from future misconduct.

No one doubts that a State may protect its citizens by prohibiting deceptive trade practices and by requiring automobile distributors to disclose presale repairs that affect the value of a new car. But the States need not, and in fact do not, provide such protection in a uniform manner. Some States rely on the judicial process to formulate and enforce an appropriate disclosure requirement by applying principles of contract and tort law. Other States have enacted various forms of legislation that define the disclosure obligations of automobile manufacturers, distributors, and dealers. The result is a patchwork of rules representing the diverse policy judgments of lawmakers in 50 States.

That diversity demonstrates that reasonable people may disagree about the value of a full disclosure requirement. Some legislatures may conclude that affirmative disclosure requirements are unnecessary because the self-interest of those involved in the automobile trade in developing and maintaining the goodwill of their customers will motivate them to make voluntary disclosures or to refrain from selling cars that do not comply with self-imposed standards. Those legislatures that do adopt affirmative disclosure obligations may take into account the cost of government regulation, choosing to draw a line exempting minor repairs from such a requirement. In formulating a disclosure standard, States may also consider other goals, such as providing a "safe harbor" for automobile manufacturers, distributors, and dealers against lawsuits over minor repairs.

We may assume, arguendo, that it would be wise for every State to adopt Dr. Gore's preferred rule, requiring full disclosure of every presale repair to a car, no matter how trivial and regardless of its actual impact on the value of the car. But while we do not doubt that Congress has ample authority to enact such a policy for the entire Nation, it is clear that no single State could do so, or even impose its own policy choice on neighboring States. Similarly, one State's power to impose burdens on the interstate market for automobiles is not only subordinate to the federal power over interstate commerce, but is also constrained by the need to respect the interests of other States.

We think it follows from these principles of state sovereignty and comity that a State may not impose economic sanctions on violators of its laws with the intent of changing the tortfeasors' lawful conduct in other States. Before this Court Dr. Gore argued that the large punitive damages award was necessary to induce BMW to change the nationwide policy that it adopted in 1983. But by attempting to alter BMW's nationwide policy, Alabama would be infringing on the policy choices of other States. To avoid such encroachment, the economic penalties that a State such as Alabama inflicts on those who transgress its laws, whether the penalties take the form of legislatively authorized fines or judicially imposed punitive damages, must be supported by the State's interest in protecting its own consumers and its own economy. Alabama may insist that BMW adhere to a particular disclosure policy in that State. Alabama does not have the power, however, to punish BMW for conduct that was lawful where it occurred and that had no impact on Alabama or its residents. Nor may Alabama impose sanctions on BMW in order to deter conduct that is lawful in other jurisdictions.

In this case, we accept the Alabama Supreme Court's interpretation of the jury verdict as reflecting a computation of the amount of punitive damages "based in large part on conduct that happened in other jurisdictions." 646 So.2d, at 627. As the Alabama Supreme Court noted, neither the jury nor the trial court was presented with evidence that any of BMW's out-of-state conduct was unlawful. "The only testimony touching the issue showed that approximately 60% of the vehicles that were refinished were sold in states where failure to disclose the repair was not an unfair trade practice." Id., at 627, n. 6. The Alabama Supreme Court therefore properly eschewed reliance on BMW's out-of-state conduct, id., at 628, and based its remitted award solely on conduct that occurred within Alabama.[21] The award must be analyzed in the light of the same conduct, with consideration given only to the interests of Alabama consumers, rather than those of the entire Nation. When the scope of the interest in punishment and deterrence that an Alabama court may appropriately consider is properly limited, it is apparent—for reasons that we shall now address—that this award is grossly excessive.

III

Elementary notions of fairness enshrined in our constitutional jurisprudence dictate that a person receive fair notice not only of the conduct that will subject him to punishment, but also of the severity of the penalty that a State may impose. Three guideposts, each of which indicates that BMW did not receive adequate notice of the magnitude of the sanction that Alabama might impose for adhering to the nondisclosure policy adopted in 1983, lead us to the conclusion that the $2 million award against BMW is grossly excessive: the degree of reprehensibility of the nondisclosure; the disparity between the harm or potential harm suffered by Dr. Gore and his punitive damages award; and the difference between this remedy and the civil penalties authorized or imposed in comparable cases. We discuss these considerations in turn.

Degree of Reprehensibility

Perhaps the most important indicium of the reasonableness of a punitive damages award is the degree of reprehensibility of the defendant's conduct. As the Court stated nearly 150 years ago, exemplary damages imposed on a defendant should reflect "the enormity of his offense." Day v. Woodworth, 13 How. 363, 371, 14 L.Ed. 181 (1852). This principle reflects the accepted view that some wrongs are more blameworthy than others. Thus, we have said that "nonviolent crimes are less serious than crimes marked by violence or the threat of violence." Solem v. Helm, 463 U.S. 277, 292–293, 103 S.Ct. 3001, 3011, 77 L.Ed.2d 637 (1983). Similarly, "trickery and deceit," TXO, 509 U.S., at 462, 113 S.Ct., at 2722, are more reprehensible than negligence. In TXO, both the West Virginia Supreme Court and the Justices of this Court placed special emphasis on the principle that punitive damages may not be "grossly out of proportion to the severity of the offense." Id., at 453, 482, 113 S.Ct., at 2718, 2733. Indeed, for Justice

21. Of course, the fact that the Alabama Supreme Court correctly concluded that it was error for the jury to use the number of sales in other States as a multiplier in computing the amount of its punitive sanction does not mean that evidence describing out-of-state transactions is irrelevant in a case of this kind. To the contrary, as we stated in TXO Production Corp. v. Alliance Resources Corp., 509 U.S. 443, 462, n. 28, 113 S.Ct. 2711, 2722, n. 28, 125 L.Ed.2d 366 (1993), such evidence may be relevant to the determination of the degree of reprehensibility of the defendant's conduct.

KENNEDY, the defendant's intentional malice was the decisive element in a "close and difficult" case. Id., at 468, 113 S.Ct., at 2725.

In this case, none of the aggravating factors associated with particularly reprehensible conduct is present. The harm BMW inflicted on Dr. Gore was purely economic in nature. The presale refinishing of the car had no effect on its performance or safety features, or even its appearance for at least nine months after his purchase. BMW's conduct evinced no indifference to or reckless disregard for the health and safety of others. To be sure, infliction of economic injury, especially when done intentionally through affirmative acts of misconduct, id., at 453, 113 S.Ct., at 2717–2718, or when the target is financially vulnerable, can warrant a substantial penalty. But this observation does not convert all acts that cause economic harm into torts that are sufficiently reprehensible to justify a significant sanction in addition to compensatory damages.

Dr. Gore contends that BMW's conduct was particularly reprehensible because nondisclosure of the repairs to his car formed part of a nationwide pattern of tortious conduct. Certainly, evidence that a defendant has repeatedly engaged in prohibited conduct while knowing or suspecting that it was unlawful would provide relevant support for an argument that strong medicine is required to cure the defendant's disrespect for the law. Our holdings that a recidivist may be punished more severely than a first offender recognize that repeated misconduct is more reprehensible than an individual instance of malfeasance.

In support of his thesis, Dr. Gore advances two arguments. First, he asserts that the state disclosure statutes supplement, rather than supplant, existing remedies for breach of contract and common-law fraud. Thus, according to Dr. Gore, the statutes may not properly be viewed as immunizing from liability the nondisclosure of repairs costing less than the applicable statutory threshold. Second, Dr. Gore maintains that BMW should have anticipated that its failure to disclose similar repair work could expose it to liability for fraud.

We recognize, of course, that only state courts may authoritatively construe state statutes. As far as we are aware, at the time this action was commenced no state court had explicitly addressed whether its State's disclosure statute provides a safe harbor for nondisclosure of presumptively minor repairs or should be construed instead as supplementing common-law duties. A review of the text of the statutes, however, persuades us that in the absence of a state-court determination to the contrary, a corporate executive could reasonably interpret the disclosure requirements as establishing safe harbors. In California, for example, the disclosure statute defines "material" damage to a motor vehicle as damage requiring repairs costing in excess of 3 percent of the suggested retail price or $500, whichever is greater. Cal. Veh.Code Ann. § 9990 (West Supp.1996). The Illinois statute states that in cases in which disclosure is not required, "nondisclosure does not constitute a misrepresentation or omission of fact." Ill. Comp. Stat., ch. 815, § 710/5 (1994). Perhaps the statutes may also be interpreted in another way. We simply emphasize that the record contains no evidence that BMW's decision to follow a disclosure policy that coincided with the strictest extant state statute was sufficiently reprehensible to justify a $2 million award of punitive damages.

Dr. Gore's second argument for treating BMW as a recidivist is that the company should have anticipated that its actions would be considered fraudulent in some, if not all, jurisdictions. This contention overlooks the fact that actionable fraud requires a material misrepresentation or omission. This qualifier invites line-drawing of just the sort engaged in by States with disclosure statutes and by BMW. We do not think it can be disputed that there may exist minor imperfections in the finish of a new car that can be repaired (or indeed, left unrepaired) without materially affecting the car's value. There is no evidence that BMW acted in bad faith when it sought to establish the appropriate line between presumptively minor damage and damage requiring disclosure to purchasers. For this purpose, BMW could reasonably rely on state disclosure statutes for guidance. In this regard, it is also significant that there is no evidence that BMW persisted in a course of conduct after it had been adjudged unlawful on even one occasion, let alone repeated occasions.

Finally, the record in this case discloses no deliberate false statements, acts of affirmative misconduct, or concealment of evidence of improper motive, such as were present in Haslip and TXO. Haslip, 499 U.S., at 5, 111 S.Ct., at 1036; TXO, 509 U.S., at 453, 113 S.Ct., at 2717–2718. We accept, of course, the jury's finding that BMW suppressed a material fact which Alabama law obligated it to communicate to prospective purchasers of repainted cars in that State. But the omission of a material fact may be less reprehensible than a deliberate false statement, particularly when there is a good-faith basis for believing that no duty to disclose exists.

That conduct is sufficiently reprehensible to give rise to tort liability, and even a modest award of exemplary damages does not establish the high degree of culpability that warrants a substantial punitive damages award. Because this case exhibits none of the circumstances ordinarily associated with egregiously improper conduct, we are persuaded that BMW's conduct was not sufficiently reprehensible to warrant imposition of a $2 million exemplary damages award.

Ratio

The second and perhaps most commonly cited indicium of an unreasonable or excessive punitive damages award is its ratio to the actual harm inflicted on the plaintiff. The principle that exemplary damages must bear a "reasonable relationship" to compensatory damages has a long pedigree. Scholars have identified a number of early English statutes authorizing the award of multiple damages for particular wrongs. Some 65 different enactments during the period between 1275 and 1753 provided for double, treble, or quadruple damages. Our decisions in both Haslip and TXO endorsed the proposition that a comparison between the compensatory award and the punitive award is significant.

In Haslip we concluded that even though a punitive damages award of "more than 4 times the amount of compensatory damages" might be "close to the line," it did not "cross the line into the area of constitutional impropriety." 499 U.S., at 23–24, 111 S.Ct., at 1046. TXO, following dicta in Haslip, refined this analysis by confirming that the proper inquiry is " 'whether there is a reasonable relationship between the punitive damages award and the harm likely to result from the defendant's conduct as well as the harm that actually has occurred.' " TXO, 509 U.S., at 460, 113 S.Ct., at 2721 (emphasis in original), quoting Haslip, 499 U.S., at 21, 111 S.Ct., at 1045. Thus, in upholding the $10 million award in TXO, we relied on the difference between that figure and the harm to the victim that would have ensued if the tortious plan had succeeded. That difference suggested that the relevant ratio was not more than 10 to 1.

The $2 million in punitive damages awarded to Dr. Gore by the Alabama Supreme Court is 500 times the amount of his actual harm as determined by the jury. Moreover, there is no suggestion that Dr. Gore or any other BMW purchaser was threatened with any additional potential harm by BMW's nondisclosure policy. The disparity in this case is thus dramatically greater than those considered in Haslip and TXO.

Of course, we have consistently rejected the notion that the constitutional line is marked by a simple mathematical formula, even one that compares actual and potential damages to the punitive award. Indeed, low awards of compensatory damages may properly support a higher ratio than high compensatory awards, if, for example, a particularly egregious act has resulted in only a small amount of economic damages. A higher ratio may also be justified in cases in which the injury is hard to detect or the monetary value of noneconomic harm might have been difficult to determine. It is appropriate, therefore, to reiterate our rejection of a categorical approach. Once again, "we return to what we said ... in Haslip: 'We need not, and indeed we cannot, draw a mathematical bright line between the constitutionally acceptable and the constitutionally unacceptable that would fit every case. We can say, however, that [a] general concer[n] of reasonableness ... properly enter[s] into the constitutional calculus.' " Id., at 458, 113 S.Ct., at 2720 (quoting Haslip, 499 U.S., at 18, 111 S.Ct., at 1043). In most cases, the ratio will be within a constitutionally acceptable range, and remittitur will not be justified on this basis. When the ratio is a breathtaking 500 to 1, however, the award must surely "raise a suspicious judicial eyebrow." TXO, 509 U.S., at 481, 113 S.Ct., at 2732 (O'CONNOR, J., dissenting).

Sanctions for Comparable Misconduct

Comparing the punitive damages award and the civil or criminal penalties that could be imposed for comparable misconduct provides a third indicium of excessiveness. As Justice O'CONNOR has correctly observed, a reviewing court engaged in determining whether an award of punitive damages is excessive should "accord 'substantial deference' to legislative judgments concerning appropriate sanctions for the conduct at issue." Browning–Ferris Industries of Vt., Inc. v. Kelco Disposal, Inc., 492 U.S., at 301, 109 S.Ct., at 2934 (opinion concurring in part and dissenting in part). In Haslip, 499 U.S., at 23, 111 S.Ct., at 1046, the Court noted that although the exemplary award was "much in excess of the fine that could be imposed," imprisonment was also authorized in the criminal context. In this case the $2 million economic sanction imposed on BMW is substantially greater than the statutory fines available in Alabama and elsewhere for similar malfeasance.

The maximum civil penalty authorized by the Alabama Legislature for a violation of its Deceptive Trade Practices Act is $2,000; other States authorize more severe sanctions, with the maxima ranging from $5,000 to $10,000. Significantly, some statutes draw a distinction between first offenders and recidivists; thus, in New York the penalty is $50 for a first offense and $250 for subsequent offenses. None of these statutes would provide an out-of-state distributor with fair notice that the first violation— or, indeed the first 14 violations—of its provisions might subject an offender to a multimillion dollar penalty. Moreover, at the time BMW's policy was first challenged, there does not appear to have been any judicial decision in Alabama or elsewhere indicating that application of that policy might give rise to such severe punishment.

The sanction imposed in this case cannot be justified on the ground that it was necessary to deter future misconduct without considering whether less drastic remedies could be expected to achieve that goal. The fact that a multimillion dollar penalty prompted a change in policy sheds no light on the question whether a lesser deterrent would have adequately protected the interests of Alabama consumers. In the absence of a history of noncompliance with known statutory requirements, there is no basis for assuming that a more modest sanction would not have been sufficient to motivate full compliance with the disclosure requirement imposed by the Alabama Supreme Court in this case.

IV

We assume, as the juries in this case and in the Yates case found, that the undisclosed damage to the new BMW's affected their actual value. Notwithstanding the evidence adduced by BMW in an effort to prove that the repainted cars conformed to the same quality standards as its other cars, we also assume that it knew, or should have known, that as time passed the repainted cars would lose their attractive appearance more rapidly than other BMW's. Moreover, we of course accept the Alabama courts' view that the state interest in protecting its citizens from deceptive trade practices justifies a sanction in addition to the recovery of compensatory damages. We cannot, however, accept the conclusion of the Alabama Supreme Court that BMW's conduct was sufficiently egregious to justify a punitive sanction that is tantamount to a severe criminal penalty.

The fact that BMW is a large corporation rather than an impecunious individual does not diminish its entitlement to fair notice of the demands that the several States impose on the conduct of its business. Indeed, its status as an active participant in the national economy implicates the federal interest in preventing individual States from imposing undue burdens on interstate commerce. While each State has ample power to protect its own consumers, none may use the punitive damages deterrent as a means of imposing its regulatory policies on the entire Nation.

As in Haslip, we are not prepared to draw a bright line marking the limits of a constitutionally acceptable punitive damages award. Unlike that case, however, we are fully convinced that the grossly excessive award imposed in this case transcends the constitutional limit. Whether the appropriate remedy requires a new trial or merely an independent determination by the Alabama Supreme Court of the award necessary to vindicate the economic interests of Alabama consumers is a matter that should be addressed by the state court in the first instance.

It is so ordered.

■ JUSTICE BREYER, with whom JUSTICE O'CONNOR and JUSTICE SOUTER join, concurring.

The Alabama state courts have assessed the defendant $2 million in "punitive damages" for having knowingly failed to tell a BMW automobile buyer that, at a cost of $600, it had repainted portions of his new $40,000 car, thereby lowering its potential resale value by about 10%. The Court's opinion, which I join, explains why we have concluded that this award, in this case, was "grossly excessive" in relation to legitimate punitive damages objectives, and hence an arbitrary deprivation of life, liberty, or property in violation of the Due Process Clause. Members of this Court have generally thought, however, that if "fair procedures were followed, a judgment that is a product of that process is entitled to a strong presumption of validity." TXO, 509 U.S. at 457, 113 S.Ct., at 2720. And the Court also has found that punitive damages procedures very similar to those followed here were not, by themselves, fundamentally unfair. Thus, I believe it important to explain why this presumption of validity is overcome in this instance.

The reason flows from the Court's emphasis in Haslip upon the constitutional importance of legal standards that provide "reasonable constraints" within which "discretion is exercised," that assure "meaningful and adequate review by the trial court whenever a jury has fixed the punitive damages," and permit "appellate review [that] makes certain that the punitive damages are reasonable in their amount and rational in light of their purpose to punish what has occurred and to deter its repetition." Id., at 20–21, 111 S.Ct., at 1045.

This constitutional concern, itself harkening back to the Magna Carta, arises out of the basic unfairness of depriving citizens of life, liberty, or property, through the application, not of law and legal processes, but of arbitrary coercion. Requiring the application of law, rather than a decision-maker's caprice, does more than simply provide citizens notice of what actions may subject them to punishment; it also helps to assure the uniform general treatment of similarly situated persons that is the essence of law itself.

Legal standards need not be precise in order to satisfy this constitutional concern. But they must offer some kind of constraint upon a jury or court's discretion, and thus protection against purely arbitrary behavior. The standards the Alabama courts applied here are vague and open ended to the point where they risk arbitrary results. In my view, although the vagueness of those standards does not, by itself, violate due process, it does invite the kind of scrutiny the Court has given the particular verdict before us. This is because the standards, as the Alabama Supreme Court authoritatively interpreted them here, provided no significant constraints or protection against arbitrary results.

First, the Alabama statute that permits punitive damages does not itself contain a standard that readily distinguishes between conduct warranting very small, and conduct warranting very large, punitive damages awards. That statute permits punitive damages in cases of "oppression, fraud, wantonness, or malice." Ala.Code § 6–11–20(a) (1993). But the statute goes on to define those terms broadly, to encompass far more than the egregious conduct that those terms, at first reading, might seem to imply. An intentional misrepresentation, made through a statement or silence, can easily amount to "fraud" sufficient to warrant punitive damages. The statute thereby authorizes punitive damages for the most serious kinds of misrepresentations, say, tricking the elderly out of their life savings, for much less serious conduct, such as the failure to disclose repainting a car, at issue here, and for a vast range of conduct in between.

Second, the Alabama courts, in this case, have applied the "factors" intended to constrain punitive damages awards in a way that belies that purpose. Green Oil Co. v. Hornsby, 539 So.2d 218 (Ala.1989), sets forth seven factors that appellate courts use to determine whether or not a jury award was "grossly excessive" and which, in principle, might make up for the lack of significant constraint in the statute. But, as the Alabama courts have authoritatively interpreted them, and as their application in this case illustrates, they impose little actual constraint.

(a) Green Oil requires that a punitive damages award "bear a reasonable relationship to the harm that is likely to occur from the defendant's conduct as well as to the harm that actually has occurred." Id., at 223. But this standard does little to guide a determination of what counts as a "reasonable" relationship, as this case illustrates. The record evidence of past, present, or likely future harm consists of (a) $4,000 of harm to Dr. Gore's BMW; (b) 13 other similar Alabama instances; and (c) references to about 1,000 similar instances in other States. The Alabama Supreme Court, disregarding BMW's failure to make relevant objection to the out-of-state instances at trial (as was the court's right), held that the last mentioned, out-of-state instances did not count as relevant harm. It went on to find "a reasonable relationship" between the harm and the $2 million punitive damages award without "consider[ing] those acts that occurred in other jurisdictions." 646 So.2d 619, 628 (1994) (emphasis added). For reasons explored by the majority in greater depth, the relationship between this award and the underlying conduct seems well beyond the bounds of the "reasonable." To find a "reasonable relationship" between purely economic harm totaling $56,000, without significant evidence of future repetition, and a punitive award of $2 million is to empty the "reasonable relationship" test of meaningful content. As thus construed, it does not set forth a legal standard that could have significantly constrained the discretion of Alabama factfinders.

(b) Green Oil's second factor is the "degree of reprehensibility" of the defendant's conduct. Green Oil, supra, at 223. Like the "reasonable relationship" test, this factor provides little guidance on how to relate culpability to the size of an award. The Alabama court, in considering this factor, found "reprehensible" that BMW followed a conscious policy of not disclosing repairs to new cars when the cost of repairs amounted to less than 3% of the car's value. Of course, any conscious policy of not disclosing a repair—where one knows the nondisclosure might cost the customer resale value—is "reprehensible" to some degree. But, for the reasons discussed by the majority, ante, at 1599–1601, I do not see how the Alabama courts could find conduct that (they assumed) caused $56,000 of relevant economic harm especially or unusually reprehensible enough to warrant $2 million in punitive damages, or a significant portion of that award. To find to the contrary, as the Alabama courts did, is not simply unreasonable; it is to make "reprehensibility" a concept without constraining force, i.e., to deprive the concept of its constraining power to protect against serious and capricious deprivations.

(c) Green Oil's third factor requires "punitive damages" to "remove the profit" of the illegal activity and "be in excess of the profit, so that the defendant recognizes a loss." Green Oil, 539 So.2d, at 223. This factor has the ability to limit awards to a fixed, rational amount. But as applied, that concept's potential was not realized, for the court did not limit the award to anywhere near the $56,000 in profits evidenced in the record. Given the record's description of the conduct and its prevalence, this factor could not justify much of the $2 million award.

(d) Green Oil's fourth factor is the "financial position" of the defendant. Ibid. Since a fixed dollar award will punish a poor person more than a wealthy one, one can understand the relevance of this factor to the State's interest in retribution (though not necessarily to its interest in deterrence, given the more distant relation between a defendant's wealth and its responses to economic incentives). This factor, however, is not necessarily intended to act as a significant constraint on punitive awards. Rather, it provides an open-ended basis for inflating awards when the defendant is wealthy, as this case may illustrate. That does not make its use unlawful or inappropriate; it simply means that this factor cannot make up for the failure of other factors, such as "reprehensibility," to constrain significantly an award that purports to punish a defendant's conduct.

(e) Green Oil's fifth factor is the "costs of litigation" and the State's desire "to encourage plaintiffs to bring wrongdoers to trial." 539 So.2d, at 223. This standard provides meaningful constraint to the extent that the enhancement it authorized is linked to a fixed, ascertainable amount approximating actual costs, even when defined generously to reflect the contingent nature of plaintiffs' victories. But as this case shows, the factor cannot operate as a constraint when an award much in excess of costs is approved for other reasons. An additional aspect of the standard—the need to "encourage plaintiffs to bring wrongdoers to trial"—is a factor that does not constrain, but enhances, discretionary power—especially when unsupported by evidence of a special need to encourage litigation (which the Alabama courts here did not mention).

(f) Green Oil's sixth factor is whether or not "criminal sanctions have been imposed on the defendant for his conduct." This factor did not apply here.

(g) Green Oil's seventh factor requires that "other civil actions" filed "against the same defendant, based on the same conduct," be considered in mitigation. Id., at 224. That factor did not apply here.

Thus, the first, second, and third Green Oil factors, in principle, might sometimes act as constraints on arbitrary behavior. But as the Alabama courts interpreted those standards in this case, even taking those three factors together, they could not have significantly constrained the court system's ability to impose "grossly excessive" awards.

Third, the state courts neither referred to, nor made any effort to find, nor enunciated any other standard that either directly, or indirectly as background, might have supplied the constraining legal force that the statute and Green Oil standards (as interpreted here) lack. Dr. Gore did argue to the jury an economic theory based on the need to offset the totality of the harm that the defendant's conduct caused. Some theory of that general kind might have provided a significant constraint on arbitrary awards (at least where confined to the relevant harm-causing conduct). Some economists, for example, have argued for a standard that would deter illegal activity causing solely economic harm through the use of punitive damages awards that, as a whole, would take from a wrongdoer the total cost of the harm caused. My understanding of the intuitive essence of some of those theories, which I put in crude form (leaving out various qualifications), is that they could permit juries to calculate punitive damages by making a rough estimate of global harm, dividing that estimate by a similarly rough estimate of the number of successful lawsuits that would likely be brought, and adding generous attorney's fees and other costs. Smaller damages would not sufficiently discourage firms from engaging in the harmful conduct, while larger damages would "over-deter" by leading potential defendants to spend more to prevent the activity that causes the economic harm, say, through employee training, than the cost of the harm itself. Larger damages might also "double count" by including in the punitive damages award some of the compensatory, or punitive, damages that subsequent plaintiffs would also recover.

The record before us, however, contains nothing suggesting that the Alabama Supreme Court, when determining the allowable award, applied any "economic" theory that might explain the $2 million recovery. And courts properly tend to judge the rationality of judicial actions in terms of the reasons that were given, and the facts that were before the court, not those that might have been given on the basis of some conceivable set of facts (unlike the rationality of economic statutes enacted by legislatures subject to the public's control through the ballot box). Therefore, reference to a constraining "economic" theory, which might have counseled more deferential review by this Court, is lacking in this case.

Fourth, I cannot find any community understanding or historic practice that this award might exemplify and which, therefore, would provide background standards constraining arbitrary behavior and excessive awards. A punitive damages award of $2 million for intentional misrepresentation causing $56,000 of harm is extraordinary by historical standards, and, as far as I am aware, finds no analogue until relatively recent times....

The upshot is that the rules that purport to channel discretion in this kind of case, here did not do so in fact. That means that the award in this case was both (a) the product of a system of standards that did not significantly constrain a court's, and hence a jury's, discretion in making that award; and (b) grossly excessive in light of the State's legitimate punitive damages objectives.

■ JUSTICE SCALIA, with whom JUSTICE THOMAS joins, dissenting.

Today we see the latest manifestation of this Court's recent and increasingly insistent "concern about punitive damages that 'run wild.' " Pacific Mut. Life Ins. Co. v. Haslip, 499 U.S. 1, 18, 111 S.Ct. 1032, 1043, 113 L.Ed.2d 1 (1991). Since the Constitution does not make that concern any of our business, the Court's activities in this area are an unjustified incursion into the province of state governments.

In earlier cases that were the prelude to this decision, I set forth my view that a state trial procedure that commits the decision whether to impose punitive damages, and the amount, to the discretion of the jury, subject to some judicial review for "reasonableness," furnishes a defendant with all the process that is "due." See TXO Production Corp. v. Alliance Resources Corp., 509 U.S. 443, 470, 113 S.Ct. 2711, 2726, 125 L.Ed.2d 366 (1993) (SCALIA, J., concurring in judgment); Haslip, supra, at 25–28, 111 S.Ct., at 1046–1049 (SCALIA, J., concurring in judgment); cf. Honda Motor Co. v. Oberg, 512 U.S. 415, 435–436, 114 S.Ct. 2331, 2342, 129 L.Ed.2d 336 (1994) (SCALIA, J., concurring). I do not regard the Fourteenth Amendment's Due Process Clause as a secret repository of substantive guarantees against "unfairness"—neither the unfairness of an excessive civil compensatory award, nor the unfairness of an "unreasonable" punitive award. What the Fourteenth Amendment's procedural guarantee assures is an opportunity to contest the reasonableness of a damages judgment in state court; but there is no federal guarantee a damages award actually be reasonable.

This view, which adheres to the text of the Due Process Clause, has not prevailed in our punitive damages cases. When, however, a constitutional doctrine adopted by the Court is not only mistaken but also insusceptible of principled application, I do not feel bound to give it stare decisis effect—indeed, I do not feel justified in doing so. Our punitive damages jurisprudence compels such a response. The Constitution provides no warrant for federalizing yet another aspect of our Nation's legal culture (no matter how much in need of correction it may be), and the application of the Court's new rule of constitutional law is constrained by no principle other than the Justices' subjective assessment of the "reasonableness" of the award in relation to the conduct for which it was assessed.

Because today's judgment represents the first instance of this Court's invalidation of a state-court punitive assessment as simply unreasonably large, I think it a proper occasion to discuss these points at some length.

I

The most significant aspects of today's decision—the identification of a "substantive due process" right against a "grossly excessive" award, and the concomitant assumption of ultimate authority to decide anew a matter of "reasonableness" resolved in lower court proceedings—are of course not new. Haslip and TXO revived the notion, moribund since its appearance in the first years of this century, that the measure of civil punishment poses a question of constitutional dimension to be answered by this Court. Neither of those cases, however, nor any of the precedents upon which they relied, actually took the step of declaring a punitive award unconstitutional simply because it was "too big."

At the time of adoption of the Fourteenth Amendment, it was well understood that punitive damages represent the assessment by the jury, as the voice of the community, of the measure of punishment the defendant deserved. Today's decision, though dressed up as a legal opinion, is really no more than a disagreement with the community's sense of indignation or outrage expressed in the punitive award of the Alabama jury, as reduced by the State Supreme Court. It reflects not merely, as the concurrence candidly acknowledges, "a judgment about a matter of degree," but a judgment about the appropriate degree of indignation or outrage, which is hardly an analytical determination.

There is no precedential warrant for giving our judgment priority over the judgment of state courts and juries on this matter. The only support for the Court's position is to be found in a handful of errant federal cases, bunched within a few years of one other, which invented the notion that an unfairly severe civil sanction amounts to a violation of constitutional liberties. These were the decisions upon which the TXO plurality relied in pronouncing that the Due Process Clause "imposes substantive limits 'beyond which penalties may not go,'" 509 U.S., at 454, 113 S.Ct., at 2718 (quoting Seaboard Air Line R. Co. v. Seegers, 207 U.S. 73, 78, 28 S.Ct. 28, 30, 52 L.Ed. 108 (1907)). Although they are our precedents, they are themselves too shallowly rooted to justify the Court's recent undertaking. The only case relied upon in which the Court actually invalidated a civil sanction does not even support constitutional review for excessiveness, since it really concerned the validity, as a matter of procedural due process, of state legislation that imposed a significant penalty on a common carrier which lacked the means of determining the legality of its actions before the penalty was imposed. The amount of the penalty was not a subject of independent scrutiny. As for the remaining cases, while the opinions do consider arguments that statutory penalties can, by reason of their excessiveness, violate due process, not a single one of these judgments invalidates a damages award.

More importantly, this latter group of cases—which again are the sole precedential foundation put forward for the rule of constitutional law espoused by today's Court—simply fabricated the "substantive due process" right at issue. Seaboard assigned no precedent to its bald assertion that the Constitution imposes "limits beyond which penalties may not go," 207 U.S., at 78, 28 S.Ct., at 30. Waters–Pierce cited only Coffey v. County of Harlan, 204 U.S. 659, 27 S.Ct. 305, 51 L.Ed. 666 (1907), a case which inquired into the constitutionality of state procedure, id., at 662–663, 27 S.Ct., at 305–306. Standard Oil simply cited Waters–Pierce, and St. Louis, I.M. & S. R. Co. offered in addition to these cases only Collins v. Johnston,

237 U.S. 502, 35 S.Ct. 649, 59 L.Ed. 1071 (1915), which said nothing to support the notion of a "substantive due process" right against excessive civil penalties, but to the contrary asserted that the prescribing and imposing of criminal punishment were "functions peculiarly belonging to the several States," id., at 509–510, 35 S.Ct., at 652–653. Thus, the only authority for the Court's position is simply not authoritative. These cases fall far short of what is needed to supplant this country's longstanding practice regarding exemplary awards.

II

One might understand the Court's eagerness to enter this field, rather than leave it with the state legislatures, if it had something useful to say. In fact, however, its opinion provides virtually no guidance to legislatures, and to state and federal courts, as to what a "constitutionally proper" level of punitive damages might be.

We are instructed at the outset of Part II of the Court's opinion—the beginning of its substantive analysis—that "the federal excessiveness inquiry ... begins with an identification of the state interests that a punitive award is designed to serve." On first reading this, one is faced with the prospect that federal punitive damages law (the new field created by today's decision) will be beset by the sort of "interest analysis" that has laid waste the formerly comprehensible field of conflict of laws. The thought that each assessment of punitive damages, as to each offense, must be examined to determine the precise "state interests" pursued, is most unsettling. Moreover, if those "interests" are the most fundamental determinant of an award, one would think that due process would require the assessing jury to be instructed about them.

It appears, however (and I certainly hope), that all this is a false alarm. As Part II of the Court's opinion unfolds, it turns out to be directed, not to the question "How much punishment is too much?" but rather to the question "Which acts can be punished?" "Alabama does not have the power," the Court says, "to punish BMW for conduct that was lawful where it occurred and that had no impact on Alabama or its residents." That may be true, though only in the narrow sense that a person cannot be held liable to be punished on the basis of a lawful act. But if a person has been held subject to punishment because he committed an unlawful act, the degree of his punishment assuredly can be increased on the basis of any other conduct of his that displays his wickedness, unlawful or not. Criminal sentences can be computed, we have said, on the basis of "information concerning every aspect of a defendant's life," Williams v. New York, 337 U.S. 241, 250–252, 69 S.Ct. 1079, 1085, 93 L.Ed. 1337 (1949). The Court at one point seems to acknowledge this, observing that, although a sentencing court "[cannot] properly punish lawful conduct," it may in assessing the penalty "consider ... lawful conduct that bears on the defendant's character." That concession is quite incompatible, however, with the later assertion that, since "neither the jury nor the trial court was presented with evidence that any of BMW's out-of-state conduct was unlawful," the Alabama Supreme Court "therefore properly eschewed reliance on BMW's out-of-state conduct, ... and based its remitted award solely on conduct that occurred within Alabama." Why could the Supreme Court of Alabama not consider lawful (but disreputable) conduct, both inside and outside Alabama, for the purpose of assessing just how bad an actor BMW was?

The Court follows up its statement that "Alabama does not have the power . . . to punish BMW for conduct that was lawful where it occurred" with the statement: "Nor may Alabama impose sanctions on BMW in order to deter conduct that is lawful in other jurisdictions." The Court provides us no citation of authority to support this proposition—other than the barely analogous cases cited earlier in the opinion—and I know of none.

These significant issues pronounced upon by the Court are not remotely presented for resolution in the present case. There is no basis for believing that Alabama has sought to control conduct elsewhere. The statutes at issue merely permit civil juries to treat conduct such as petitioner's as fraud, and authorize an award of appropriate punitive damages in the event the fraud is found to be "gross, oppressive, or malicious," Ala.Code § 6–11–20(b)(1) (1993). To be sure, respondent did invite the jury to consider out-of-state conduct in its calculation of damages, but any increase in the jury's initial award based on that consideration is not a component of the remitted judgment before us. As the Court several times recognizes, in computing the amount of the remitted award the Alabama Supreme Court—whether it was constitutionally required to or not—"expressly disclaimed any reliance on acts that occurred in other jurisdictions." Thus, the only question presented by this case is whether that award, limited to petitioner's Alabama conduct and viewed in light of the factors identified as properly informing the inquiry, is excessive. The Court's sweeping (and largely unsupported) statements regarding the relationship of punitive awards to lawful or unlawful out-of-state conduct are the purest dicta.

III

In Part III of its opinion, the Court identifies "[t]hree guideposts" that lead it to the conclusion that the award in this case is excessive: degree of reprehensibility, ratio between punitive award and plaintiff's actual harm, and legislative sanctions provided for comparable misconduct. The legal significance of these "guideposts" is nowhere explored, but their necessary effect is to establish federal standards governing the hitherto exclusively state law of damages. Apparently (though it is by no means clear) all three federal "guideposts" can be overridden if "necessary to deter future misconduct,"—a loophole that will encourage state reviewing courts to uphold awards as necessary for the "adequat[e] protect[ion]" of state consumers. By effectively requiring state reviewing courts to concoct rationalizations—whether within the "guideposts" or through the loophole—to justify the intuitive punitive reactions of state juries, the Court accords neither category of institution the respect it deserves.

Of course it will not be easy for the States to comply with this new federal law of damages, no matter how willing they are to do so. In truth, the "guideposts" mark a road to nowhere; they provide no real guidance at all. As to "degree of reprehensibility" of the defendant's conduct, we learn that " 'nonviolent crimes are less serious than crimes marked by violence or the threat of violence,' " (quoting Solem v. Helm, 463 U.S. 277, 292–293, 103 S.Ct. 3001, 3011, 77 L.Ed.2d 637 (1983)), and that " 'trickery and deceit' " are "more reprehensible than negligence." As to the ratio of punitive to compensatory damages, we are told that a " 'general concer[n] of reasonableness . . . enter[s] into the constitutional calculus,' " (quoting TXO, 509 U.S., at 458, 113 S.Ct., at 2720)—though even "a breathtaking 500 to 1" will not necessarily do anything more than " 'raise a suspicious judicial eyebrow,' " (quoting TXO, supra, at 481, 113 S.Ct., at 2732 (O'CONNOR, J., dissenting), an opinion which, when confronted with that "breathtaking" ratio, approved it). And as to legislative sanctions provided for comparable misconduct, they should be accorded " 'substantial deference,' " (quoting Browning–Ferris Industries of Vt., Inc. v. Kelco Disposal, Inc., 492 U.S. 257, 301, 109 S.Ct. 2909, 2934, 106 L.Ed.2d 219 (1989) (O'CONNOR, J., concurring in part and dissenting in part)). One expects the Court to conclude: "To thine own self be true."

These crisscrossing platitudes yield no real answers in no real cases. And it must be noted that the Court nowhere says that these three "guideposts" are the only guideposts; indeed, it makes very clear that they are not—explaining away the earlier opinions that do not really follow these "guideposts" on the basis of additional factors, thereby "reiterat[ing] our rejection of a categorical approach." Ante, at 1602. In other words, even these utter platitudes, if they should ever happen to produce an answer, may be overridden by other unnamed considerations. The Court has constructed a framework that does not genuinely constrain, that does not inform state legislatures and lower courts—that does nothing at all except confer an artificial air of doctrinal analysis upon its essentially ad hoc determination that this particular award of punitive damages was not "fair."

The Court distinguishes today's result from Haslip and TXO partly on the ground that "the record in this case discloses no deliberate false statements, acts of affirmative misconduct, or concealment of evidence of improper motive, such as were present in Haslip and TXO." Ante, at 1601. This seemingly rejects the findings necessarily made by the jury—that petitioner had committed a fraud that was "gross, oppressive, or malicious," Ala.Code § 6–11–20(b)(1) (1993). Perhaps that rejection is intentional; the Court does not say.

The relationship between judicial application of the new "guideposts" and jury findings poses a real problem for the Court, since as a matter of logic there is no more justification for ignoring the jury's determination as to how reprehensible petitioner's conduct was (i.e., how much it deserves to be punished), than there is for ignoring its determination that it was reprehensible at all (i.e., that the wrong was willful and punitive damages are therefore recoverable). That the issue has been framed in terms of a constitutional right against unreasonably excessive awards should not obscure the fact that the logical and necessary consequence of the Court's approach is the recognition of a constitutional right against unreasonably imposed awards as well. The elevation of "fairness" in punishment to a principle of "substantive due process" means that every punitive award unreasonably imposed is unconstitutional; such an award is by definition excessive, since it attaches a penalty to conduct undeserving of punishment. Indeed, if the Court is correct, it must be that every claim that a state jury's award of compensatory damages is "unreasonable" (because not supported by the evidence) amounts to an assertion of constitutional injury. And the same would be true for determinations of liability. By today's logic, every dispute as to evidentiary sufficiency in a state civil suit poses a question of constitutional moment, subject to review in this Court. That is a stupefying proposition.

For the foregoing reasons, I respectfully dissent.

■ JUSTICE GINSBURG with whom THE CHIEF JUSTICE joins, dissenting.

The Court, I am convinced, unnecessarily and unwisely ventures into territory traditionally within the States' domain, and does so in the face of reform measures recently adopted or currently under consideration in legislative arenas. The Alabama Supreme Court, in this case, endeavored to follow this Court's prior instructions; and, more recently, Alabama's highest court has installed further controls on awards of punitive damages. I would therefore leave the state court's judgment undisturbed, and resist unnecessary intrusion into an area dominantly of state concern.

I

The respect due the Alabama Supreme Court requires that we strip from this case a false issue: No impermissible "extraterritoriality" infects the judgment before us; the excessiveness of the award is the sole issue genuinely presented. The Court ultimately so recognizes, but further clarification is in order.

Dr. Gore's experience was not unprecedented among customers who bought BMW vehicles sold as flawless and brand-new. In addition to his own encounter, Gore showed, through paint repair orders introduced at trial, that on 983 other occasions since 1983, BMW had shipped new vehicles to dealers without disclosing paint repairs costing at least $300; at least 14 of the repainted vehicles, the evidence also showed, were sold as new and undamaged to consumers in Alabama. 646 So.2d 619, 623 (Ala. 1994). Sales nationwide, Alabama's Supreme Court said, were admissible "as to the issue of a 'pattern and practice' of such acts." Id., at 627. There was "no error," the court reiterated, "in the admission of the evidence that showed how pervasive the nondisclosure policy was and the intent behind BMW NA's adoption of it." Id., at 628. That determination comports with this Court's expositions.

Alabama's highest court next declared that the

"jury could not use the number of similar acts that a defendant has committed in other jurisdictions as a multiplier when determining the dollar amount of a punitive damages award. Such evidence may not be considered in setting the size of the civil penalty, because neither the jury nor the trial court had evidence before it showing in which states the conduct was wrongful." 646 So.2d, at 627 (emphasis in original) (footnote omitted).

Because the Alabama Supreme Court provided this clear statement of the State's law, the multiplier problem encountered in Gore's case is not likely to occur again. Now, as a matter of Alabama law, it is plainly impermissible to assess punitive damages by multiplication based on out-of-state events not shown to be unlawful.

No Alabama authority, it bears emphasis—no statute, judicial decision, or trial judge instruction—ever countenanced the jury's multiplication of the $4,000 diminution in value estimated for each refinished car by the number of such cars (approximately 1,000) shown to have been sold nationwide. The sole prompt to the jury to use nationwide sales as a multiplier came from Gore's lawyer during summation. Notably, counsel for BMW failed to object to Gore's multiplication suggestion, even though BMW's counsel interrupted to make unrelated objections four other times during Gore's closing statement. Nor did BMW's counsel request a charge instructing the jury not to consider out-of-state sales in calculating the punitive damages award.

Following the verdict, BMW's counsel challenged the admission of the paint repair orders, but not, alternately, the jury's apparent use of the orders in a multiplication exercise. Curiously, during postverdict argument, BMW's counsel urged that if the repair orders were indeed admissible, then Gore would have a "full right" to suggest a multiplier-based disgorgement.

In brief, Gore's case is idiosyncratic. The jury's improper multiplication, tardily featured by petitioner, is unlikely to recur in Alabama and does not call for error correction by this Court.

Because the jury apparently (and erroneously) had used acts in other States as a multiplier to arrive at a $4 million sum for punitive damages, the Alabama Supreme Court itself determined " 'the maximum amount that a properly functioning jury could have awarded.' " 646 So.2d, at 630 (Houston, J., concurring specially) (quoting Big B, Inc. v. Cottingham, 634 So.2d 999, 1006 (Ala.1993)). The per curiam opinion emphasized that in arriving at $2 million as "the amount of punitive damages to be awarded in this case, [the court did] not consider those acts that occurred in other jurisdictions." 646 So.2d, at 628 (emphasis in original). As this Court recognizes, the Alabama high court "properly eschewed reliance on BMW's out-of-state conduct and based its remitted award solely on conduct that occurred within Alabama." In sum, the Alabama Supreme Court left standing the jury's decision that the facts warranted an award of punitive damages—a determination not contested in this Court—and the state court concluded that, considering only acts in Alabama, $2 million was "a constitutionally reasonable punitive damages award." 646 So.2d, at 629.

II

A

Alabama's Supreme Court reports that it "thoroughly and painstakingly" reviewed the jury's award, according to principles set out in its own pathmarking decisions and in this Court's opinions in TXO and Pacific Mut. Life Ins. Co. v. Haslip, 499 U.S. 1, 21, 111 S.Ct. 1032, 1045, 113 L.Ed.2d 1 (1991). 646 So.2d, at 621. The Alabama court said it gave weight to several factors, including BMW's deliberate ("reprehensible") presentation of refinished cars as new and undamaged, without disclosing that the value of those cars had been reduced by an estimated 10%, the financial position of the defendant, and the costs of litigation. These standards, we previously held, "impos[e] a sufficiently definite and meaningful constraint on the discretion of Alabama factfinders in awarding punitive damages." Haslip, 499 U.S., at 22, 111 S.Ct., at 1045. Alabama's highest court could have displayed its labor pains more visibly, but its judgment is nonetheless entitled to a presumption of legitimacy.

We accept, of course, that Alabama's Supreme Court applied the State's own law correctly. Under that law, the State's objectives—"punishment and deterrence"—guide punitive damages awards. Nor should we be quick to find a constitutional infirmity when the highest state court endeavored a corrective for one counsel's slip and the other's oversight—counsel for plaintiff's excess in summation, unobjected to by counsel for defendant, see supra, at 1615—and when the state court did so intending to follow the process approved in our Haslip and TXO decisions.

B

The Court finds Alabama's $2 million award not simply excessive, but grossly so, and therefore unconstitutional. The decision leads us further into territory traditionally within the States' domain, and commits the Court, now and again, to correct "misapplication of a properly stated rule of law." But cf. this Court's Rule 10 ("A petition for a writ of certiorari is rarely granted when the asserted error consists of erroneous factual findings or the misapplication of a properly stated rule of law."). The Court is not well equipped for this mission. Tellingly, the Court repeats that it brings to the task no "mathematical formula," no "categorical approach," no "bright line." It has only a vague concept of substantive due process, a "raised eyebrow" test, as its ultimate guide.

In contrast to habeas corpus review under 28 U.S.C. § 2254, the Court will work at this business alone. It will not be aided by the federal district courts and courts of appeals. It will be the only federal court policing the area. The Court's readiness to superintend state-court punitive damages awards is all the more puzzling in view of the Court's longstanding reluctance to countenance review, even by courts of appeals, of the size of verdicts returned by juries in federal district court proceedings....

For the reasons stated, I dissent from this Court's disturbance of the judgment the Alabama Supreme Court has made.

Cooper Industries, Inc. v. Leatherman Tool Group, Inc.

Supreme Court of the United States, 2001.
532 U.S. 424, 121 S.Ct. 1678, 149 L.Ed.2d 674.

■ JUSTICE STEVENS delivered the opinion of the court.

A jury found petitioner guilty of unfair competition and awarded respondent $50,000 in compensatory damages and $4.5 million in punitive damages. The District Court held that the punitive damages award did not violate the Federal Constitution. The Court of Appeals concluded that "the district court did not abuse its discretion in declining to reduce the amount of punitive damages." App. to Pet. for Cert. 4a. The issue in this case is whether the Court of Appeals applied the wrong standard of review in considering the constitutionality of the punitive damages award.

[I]n *Ornelas*, we held that trial judges' determinations of reasonable suspicion and probable cause should be reviewed *de novo* on appeal. The reasons we gave in support of that holding are equally applicable in this case. First, as we observed in *Ornelas*, the precise meaning of concepts like "reasonable suspicion" and "probable cause" cannot be articulated with precision; they are "fluid concepts that take their substantive content from the particular contexts in which the standards are being assessed." *Id.*, at 696, 116 S.Ct. 1657. That is, of course, also a characteristic of the concept of "gross excessiveness." Second, "the legal rules for probable cause and reasonable suspicion acquire content only through application. Independent review is therefore necessary if appellate courts are to maintain control of, and to clarify, the legal principles." Id., at 697, 116 S.Ct. 1657. Again, this is also true of the general criteria set forth in Gore; they will acquire more meaningful content through case-by-case application at the appellate level. "Finally, *de novo* review tends to unify precedent" and " 'stabilize the law.' " 517 U.S., at 697–698, 116 S.Ct. 1657. JUSTICE BREYER made a similar point in his concurring opinion in *Gore*:

> "Requiring the application of law, rather than a decisionmaker's caprice, does more than simply provide citizens notice of what actions may subject them to punishment; it also helps to assure the uniform general treatment of similarly situated persons that is the essence of law itself." 517 U.S., at 587, [116 S.Ct. 1589].

Our decisions in analogous cases, together with the reasoning that produced those decisions, thus convince us that courts of appeals should apply a *de novo* standard of review when passing on district courts' determinations of the constitutionality of punitive damages awards.

III

"Unlike the measure of actual damages suffered, which presents a question of historical or predictive fact ... the level of punitive damages is not really a 'fact' 'tried' by the jury." ... Because the jury's award of punitive damages does not constitute a finding of "fact," appellate review of the district court's determination that an award is consistent with due process does not implicate the Seventh Amendment concerns raised by respondent and its *amicus*. See Brief for Respondent 18–24; Brief for Association of Trial Lawyers of America as *Amicus Curiae* 17–20. Our decisions in *Gasperini* and *Hetzel v. Prince William County*, 523 U.S. 208, 118 S.Ct. 1210, 140 L.Ed.2d 336 (1998) (*per curiam*), both of which concerned compensatory damages, are not to the contrary.

It might be argued that the deterrent function of punitive damages suggests that the amount of such damages awarded is indeed a "fact" found by the jury and that, as a result, the Seventh Amendment is implicated in appellate review of that award. Some scholars, for example, assert that punitive damages should be used to compensate for the under-deterrence of unlawful behavior that will result from a defendant's evasion of liability. See Polinsky & Shavell, Punitive Damages: An Economic

Analysis, 111 Harv. L.Rev. 869, 890–891 (1998) (in order to obtain optimal deterrence, "punitive damages should equal the harm multiplied by . . . the ratio of the injurer's chance of escaping liability to his chance of being found liable"); see also *Ciraolo v. New York*, 216 F.3d 236, 244–245 (C.A.2 2000) (Calabresi, J., concurring). "The efficient deterrence theory thus regards punitive damages as merely an augmentation of compensatory damages designed to achieve economic efficiency." Galanter & Luban, Poetic Justice: Punitive Damages and Legal Pluralism, 42 Am. U.L. Rev. 1393, 1449 (1993).

However attractive such an approach to punitive damages might be as an abstract policy matter, it is clear that juries do not normally engage in such a finely tuned exercise of deterrence calibration when awarding punitive damages. See Sunstein, Schkade, & Kahneman, Do People Want Optimal Deterrence?, 29 J. Legal Studies 237, 240 (2000). After all, deterrence is not the only purpose served by punitive damages.[12] See *supra*, at 1683. And there is no dispute that, in this case, deterrence was but one of four concerns the jury was instructed to consider when setting the amount of punitive damages. Moreover, it is not at all obvious that even the *deterrent function* of punitive damages can be served *only* by economically "optimal deterrence." "[C]itizens and legislators may rightly insist that they are willing to tolerate some loss in economic efficiency in order to deter what they consider morally offensive conduct, albeit cost-beneficial morally offensive conduct; efficiency is just one consideration among many." Galanter & Luban, 42 Am. U.L. Rev., at 1450.[13] damages it determined was necessary to obtain economically optimal deterrence or if it defined punitive damages as a multiple of compensatory damages (e.g., treble damages).

Differences in the institutional competence of trial judges and appellate judges are consistent with our conclusion. In *Gore*, we instructed courts evaluating a punitive damages award's consistency with due process to consider three criteria: (1) the degree or reprehensibility of the defendant's misconduct, (2) the disparity between the harm (or potential harm) suffered by the plaintiff and the punitive damages award, and (3) the difference between the punitive damages awarded by the jury and the civil penalties authorized or imposed in comparable cases. 517 U.S., at 574–575, 116 S.Ct. 1589. Only with respect to the first *Gore* inquiry do the district

---

12. The jury was instructed to consider the following factors: (1) "The character of the defendant's conduct that is the subject of Leatherman's unfair competition claims"; (2) "The defendant's motive"; (3) "The sum of money that would be required to discourage the defendant and others from engaging in such conduct in the future"; and (4) "The defendant's income and assets." App. 14. Although the jury's application of these instructions may have depended on specific findings of fact, nothing in our decision today suggests that the Seventh Amendment would permit a court, in reviewing a punitive damages award, to disregard such jury findings. See,

e.g., Gore, 517 U.S., at 579–580, 116 S.Ct. 1589.

13. We express no opinion on the question whether *Gasperini* would govern—and *de novo* review would be inappropriate—if a State were to adopt a scheme that tied the award of punitive damages more tightly to the jury's finding of compensatory damages. This might be the case, for example, if the State's scheme constrained a jury to award only the exact amount of punitive damages it determined was necessary to obtain economically optimal deterrence or if it defined punitive damages as a multiple of compensatory damages (e.g., treble damages).

courts have a somewhat superior vantage over courts of appeals, and even then the advantage exists primarily with respect to issues turning on witness credibility and demeanor. Trial courts and appellate courts seem equally capable of analyzing the second factor. And the third *Gore* criterion, which calls for a broad legal comparison, seems more suited to the expertise of appellate courts. Considerations of institutional competence therefore fail to tip the balance in favor of deferential appellate review.

IV

It is possible that the standard of review applied by the Court of Appeals will affect the result of the *Gore* analysis in only a relatively small number of cases. ... Nonetheless, it does seem likely that in this case a thorough, independent review of the District Court's rejection of petitioner's due process objections to the punitive damages award might well have led the Court of Appeals to reach a different result. Indeed, our own consideration of each of the three *Gore* factors reveals a series of questionable conclusions by the District Court that may not survive *de novo* review.

When the jury assessed the reprehensibility of Cooper's misconduct, it was guided by instructions that characterized the deliberate copying of the PST as wrongful. The jury's selection of a penalty to deter wrongful conduct may, therefore, have been influenced by an intent to deter Cooper from engaging in such copying in the future. Similarly, the District Court's belief that Cooper acted unlawfully in deliberately copying the PST design might have influenced its consideration of the first *Gore* factor. See App. to Pet. for Cert. 23a. But, as the Court of Appeals correctly held, such copying of the functional features of an unpatented product is lawful. ... The Court of Appeals recognized that the District Court's award of attorney's fees could not be supported if based on the premise that the copying was unlawful, but it did not consider whether that improper predicate might also have undermined the basis for the jury's large punitive damages award.

In evaluating the second *Gore* factor, the ratio between the size of the award of punitive damages and the harm caused by Cooper's tortious conduct, the District Court might have been influenced by respondent's submission that it was not the actual injury—which the jury assessed at $50,000—that was relevant, but rather "the potential harm Leatherman would have suffered had Cooper succeeded in its wrongful conduct." ... Respondent calculated that "potential harm" by referring to the fact that Cooper had anticipated "gross profits of approximately $3 million during the first five years of sales." ... Even if that estimate were correct, however, it would be unrealistic to assume that all of Cooper's sales of the ToolZall would have been attributable to its misconduct in using a photograph of a modified PST in its initial advertising materials. As the Court of Appeals pointed out, the picture of the PST did not misrepresent the features of the original ToolZall and could not have deceived potential customers in any significant way. Its use was wrongful because it enabled Cooper to expedite the promotion of its tool, but that wrongdoing surely could not be treated as the principal cause of Cooper's entire sales volume for a 5–year period.

With respect to the third *Gore* factor, respondent argues that Cooper would have been subject to a comparable sanction under Oregon's Unlawful Trade Practices Act. Brief for Respondent 49. In a suit brought by a State under that Act, a civil penalty of up to $25,000 per violation may be assessed. Ore. Rev. Stat. § 646.642(3) (1997). In respondent's view, *each* of the thousands of pieces of promotional material containing a picture of the PST that Cooper distributed warranted the maximum fine. Brief for Respondent 49. Petitioner, on the other hand, argues that its preparation of a single "mock-up" for use in a single distribution would have been viewed as a single violation under the state statute. Reply Brief for Petitioner 2–3. The Court of Appeals expressed no opinion on this dispute. It did, however, observe that the unfairness in Cooper's use of the picture apparently had nothing to do with misleading customers but was related to its inability to obtain a "mock-up" quickly and cheaply. App. to Pet. for Cert. 3a. This observation is more consistent with the single-violation theory than with the notion that the statutory violation would have been sanctioned with a multimillion dollar fine.

We have made these comments on issues raised by application of the three *Gore* guidelines to the facts of this case, not to prejudge the answer to the constitutional question, but rather to illustrate why we are persuaded that the Court of Appeals' answer to that question may depend upon the standard of review. The *de novo* standard should govern its decision. Because the Court of Appeals applied a less demanding standard in this case, we vacate the judgment and remand the case for further proceedings consistent with this opinion.

It is so ordered.

State Farm Mutual Automobile Insurance Company v. Campbell

Supreme Court of the United States, 2003.
538 U.S. 408, 123 S.Ct. 1513, 155 L.Ed.2d 585.

■ JUSTICE KENNEDY delivered the opinion of the Court.

We address once again the measure of punishment, by means of punitive damages, a State may impose upon a defendant in a civil case. The question is whether, in the circumstances we shall recount, an award of $145 million in punitive damages, where full compensatory damages are $1 million, is excessive and in violation of the Due Process Clause of the Fourteenth Amendment to the Constitution of the United States.

I

In 1981, Curtis Campbell (Campbell) was driving with his wife, Inez Preece Campbell, in Cache County, Utah. He decided to pass six vans traveling ahead of them on a two-lane highway. Todd Ospital was driving a small car approaching from the opposite direction. To avoid a head-on collision with Campbell, who by then was driving on the wrong side of the highway and toward oncoming traffic, Ospital swerved onto the shoulder, lost control of his automobile, and collided with a vehicle driven by Robert

G. Slusher. Ospital was killed, and Slusher was rendered permanently disabled. The Campbells escaped unscathed.

In the ensuing wrongful death and tort action, Campbell insisted he was not at fault. Early investigations did support differing conclusions as to who caused the accident, but "a consensus was reached early on by the investigators and witnesses that Mr. Campbell's unsafe pass had indeed caused the crash." 65 P.3d 1134, 1141 (Utah 2001). Campbell's insurance company, petitioner State Farm Mutual Automobile Insurance Company (State Farm), nonetheless decided to contest liability and declined offers by Slusher and Ospital's estate (Ospital) to settle the claims for the policy limit of $50,000 ($25,000 per claimant). State Farm also ignored the advice of one of its own investigators and took the case to trial, assuring the Campbells that "their assets were safe, that they had no liability for the accident, that [State Farm] would represent their interests, and that they did not need to procure separate counsel." *Id.*, at 1142. To the contrary, a jury determined that Campbell was 100 percent at fault, and a judgment was returned for $185,849, far more than the amount offered in settlement.

At first State Farm refused to cover the $135,849 in excess liability. Its counsel made this clear to the Campbells: " 'You may want to put for sale signs on your property to get things moving.' " *Ibid.* Nor was State Farm willing to post a supersedeas bond to allow Campbell to appeal the judgment against him. Campbell obtained his own counsel to appeal the verdict. During the pendency of the appeal, in late 1984, Slusher, Ospital, and the Campbells reached an agreement whereby Slusher and Ospital agreed not to seek satisfaction of their claims against the Campbells. In exchange the Campbells agreed to pursue a bad faith action against State Farm and to be represented by Slusher's and Ospital's attorneys. The Campbells also agreed that Slusher and Ospital would have a right to play a part in all major decisions concerning the bad-faith action. No settlement could be concluded without Slusher's and Ospital's approval, and Slusher and Ospital would receive 90 percent of any verdict against State Farm.

In 1989, the Utah Supreme Court denied Campbell's appeal in the wrongful-death and tort actions. SLUSHER v. OSPITAL, 777 P.2d 437 (Utah 1989). State Farm then paid the entire judgment, including the amounts in excess of the policy limits. The Campbells nonetheless filed a complaint against State Farm alleging bad faith, fraud, and intentional infliction of emotional distress. The trial court initially granted State Farm's motion for summary judgment because State Farm had paid the excess verdict, but that ruling was reversed on appeal. 840 P.2d 130 (Utah App.1992). On remand State Farm moved *in limine* to exclude evidence of alleged conduct that occurred in unrelated cases outside of Utah, but the trial court denied the motion. At State Farm's request the trial court bifurcated the trial into two phases conducted before different juries. In the first phase the jury determined that State Farm's decision not to settle was unreasonable because there was a substantial likelihood of an excess verdict. . . .

The Utah Supreme Court sought to apply the three guideposts we identified in *Gore, supra*, at 574–575, 116 S.Ct. 1589, and it reinstated the $145 million punitive damages award. Relying in large part on the extensive evidence concerning the PP & R policy, the court concluded State

Farm's conduct was reprehensible. The court also relied upon State Farm's "massive wealth" and on testimony indicating that "State Farm's actions, because of their clandestine nature, will be punished at most in one out of every 50,000 cases as a matter of statistical probability," 65 P.3d, at 1153, and concluded that the ratio between punitive and compensatory damages was not unwarranted. Finally, the court noted that the punitive damages award was not excessive when compared to various civil and criminal penalties State Farm could have faced, including $10,000 for each act of fraud, the suspension of its license to conduct business in Utah, the disgorgement of profits, and imprisonment. Id., at 1154–1155. We granted certiorari. 535 U.S. 1111, 122 S.Ct. 2326, 153 L.Ed.2d 158 (2002).

II

We recognized in *Cooper Industries, Inc. v. Leatherman Tool Group, Inc.*, 532 U.S. 424, 121 S.Ct. 1678, 149 L.Ed.2d 674 (2001), that in our judicial system compensatory and punitive damages, although usually awarded at the same time by the same decisionmaker, serve different purposes. *Id.*, at 432, 121 S.Ct. 1678. Compensatory damages "are intended to redress the concrete loss that the plaintiff has suffered by reason of the defendant's wrongful conduct." *Ibid.* (citing Restatement (Second) of Torts § 903, pp. 453–454 (1979)). By contrast, punitive damages serve a broader function; they are aimed at deterrence and retribution. *Cooper Industries, supra*, at 432, 121 S.Ct. 1678; see also *Gore, supra*, at 568, 116 S.Ct. 1589 ("Punitive damages may properly be imposed to further a State's legitimate interests in punishing unlawful conduct and deterring its repetition"); *Pacific Mut. Life Ins. Co. v. Haslip*, 499 U.S. 1, 19, 111 S.Ct. 1032, 113 L.Ed.2d 1 (1991) ("[P]unitive damages are imposed for purposes of retribution and deterrence"). . . .

Although these awards serve the same purposes as criminal penalties, defendants subjected to punitive damages in civil cases have not been accorded the protections applicable in a criminal proceeding. This increases our concerns over the imprecise manner in which punitive damages systems are administered. We have admonished that "[p]unitive damages pose an acute danger of arbitrary deprivation of property. Jury instructions typically leave the jury with wide discretion in choosing amounts, and the presentation of evidence of a defendant's net worth creates the potential that juries will use their verdicts to express biases against big businesses, particularly those without strong local presences." *Honda Motor, supra*, at 432, 114 S.Ct. 2331; see also Haslip, supra, at 59, 111 S.Ct. 1032 (O'CONNOR, J., dissenting) ("[T]he Due Process Clause does not permit a State to classify arbitrariness as a virtue. Indeed, the point of due process—of the law in general—is to allow citizens to order their behavior. A State can have no legitimate interest in deliberately making the law so arbitrary that citizens will be unable to avoid punishment based solely upon bias or whim"). Our concerns are heightened when the decisionmaker is presented, as we shall discuss, with evidence that has little bearing as to the amount of punitive damages that should be awarded. Vague instructions, or those that merely inform the jury to avoid "passion or prejudice," App. to Pet. for Cert. 108a–109a, do little to aid the decisionmaker in its task of assigning appropriate weight to evidence that is relevant and evidence that is tangential or only inflammatory.

In light of these concerns, in *Gore, supra,* we instructed courts reviewing punitive damages to consider three guideposts: (1) the degree of reprehensibility of the defendant's misconduct; (2) the disparity between the actual or potential harm suffered by the plaintiff and the punitive damages award; and (3) the difference between the punitive damages awarded by the jury and the civil penalties authorized or imposed in comparable cases. *Id.,* at 575, 116 S.Ct. 1589. We reiterated the importance of these three guideposts in *Cooper Industries* and mandated appellate courts to conduct *de novo* review of a trial court's application of them to the jury's award. 532 U.S. 424, 121 S.Ct. 1678. Exacting appellate review ensures that an award of punitive damages is based upon an " 'application of law, rather than a decisionmaker's caprice.' " *Id.,* at 436, 121 S.Ct. 1678 (quoting *Gore, supra,* at 587, 116 S.Ct. 1589 (BREYER, J., concurring)).

III

Under the principles outlined in *BMW of North America, Inc. v. Gore,* this case is neither close nor difficult. It was error to reinstate the jury's $145 million punitive damages award. We address each guidepost of *Gore* in some detail.

A

"[T]he most important indicium of the reasonableness of a punitive damages award is the degree of reprehensibility of the defendant's conduct." *Gore,* 517 U.S., at 575, 116 S.Ct. 1589. We have instructed courts to determine the reprehensibility of a defendant by considering whether: the harm caused was physical as opposed to economic; the tortious conduct evinced an indifference to or a reckless disregard of the health or safety of others; the target of the conduct had financial vulnerability; the conduct involved repeated actions or was an isolated incident; and the harm was the result of intentional malice, trickery, or deceit, or mere accident. *Id.,* at 576–577, 116 S.Ct. 1589. The existence of any one of these factors weighing in favor of a plaintiff may not be sufficient to sustain a punitive damages award; and the absence of all of them renders any award suspect. It should be presumed a plaintiff has been made whole for his injuries by compensatory damages, so punitive damages should only be awarded if the defendant's culpability, after having paid compensatory damages, is so reprehensible as to warrant the imposition of further sanctions to achieve punishment or deterrence. *Id.,* at 575, 116 S.Ct. 1589.

Applying these factors in the instant case, we must acknowledge that State Farm's handling of the claims against the Campbells merits no praise. The trial court found that State Farm's employees altered the company's records to make Campbell appear less culpable. State Farm disregarded the overwhelming likelihood of liability and the near-certain probability that, by taking the case to trial, a judgment in excess of the policy limits would be awarded. State Farm amplified the harm by at first assuring the Campbells their assets would be safe from any verdict and by later telling them, postjudgment, to put a for-sale sign on their house.

While we do not suggest there was error in awarding punitive damages based upon State Farm's conduct toward the Campbells, a more modest punishment for this reprehensible conduct could have satisfied the State's legitimate objectives, and the Utah courts should have gone no further.

This case, instead, was used as a platform to expose, and punish, the perceived deficiencies of State Farm's operations throughout the country. The Utah Supreme Court's opinion makes explicit that State Farm was being condemned for its nationwide policies rather than for the conduct directed toward the Campbells. 65 P.3d, at 1143 ("[T]he Campbells introduced evidence that State Farm's decision to take the case to trial was a result of a national scheme to meet corporate fiscal goals by capping payouts on claims company wide"). This was, as well, an explicit rationale of the trial court's decision in approving the award, though reduced from $145 million to $25 million. App. to Pet. for Cert. 120a ("[T]he Campbells demonstrated, through the testimony of State Farm employees who had worked outside of Utah, and through expert testimony, that this pattern of claims adjustment under the PP & R program was not a local anomaly, but was a consistent, nationwide feature of State Farm's business operations, orchestrated from the highest levels of corporate management").

The Campbells contend that State Farm has only itself to blame for the reliance upon dissimilar and out-of-state conduct evidence. The record does not support this contention. From their opening statements onward the Campbells framed this case as a chance to rebuke State Farm for its nationwide activities. App. 208 ("You're going to hear evidence that even the insurance commission in Utah and around the country are unwilling or inept at protecting people against abuses"); *id.*, at 242 ("[T]his is a very important case.... [I]t transcends the Campbell file. It involves a nationwide practice. And you, here, are going to be evaluating and assessing, and hopefully requiring State Farm to stand accountable for what it's doing across the country, which is the purpose of punitive damages"). This was a position maintained throughout the litigation. In opposing State Farm's motion to exclude such evidence under *Gore*, the Campbells' counsel convinced the trial court that there was no limitation on the scope of evidence that could be considered under our precedents. App. to Pet. for Cert. 172a ("As I read the case [*Gore*], I was struck with the fact that a clear message in the case ... seems to be that courts in punitive damages cases should receive more evidence, not less. And that the court seems to be inviting an even broader area of evidence than the current rulings of the court would indicate"); *id.*, at 189a (trial court ruling).

A State cannot punish a defendant for conduct that may have been lawful where it occurred. *Gore, supra*, at 572, 116 S.Ct. 1589; *Bigelow v. Virginia*, 421 U.S. 809, 824, 95 S.Ct. 2222, 44 L.Ed.2d 600 (1975) ("A State does not acquire power or supervision over the internal affairs of another State merely because the welfare and health of its own citizens may be affected when they travel to that State"); *New York Life Ins. Co. v. Head*, 234 U.S. 149, 161, 34 S.Ct. 879, 58 L.Ed. 1259 (1914) ("[I]t would be impossible to permit the statutes of Missouri to operate beyond the jurisdiction of that State ... without throwing down the constitutional barriers by which all the States are restricted within the orbits of their lawful authority and upon the preservation of which the Government under the Constitution depends. This is so obviously the necessary result of the Constitution that it has rarely been called in question and hence authorities directly dealing with it do not abound"); *Huntington v. Attrill*, 146 U.S. 657, 669, 13 S.Ct. 224, 36 L.Ed. 1123 (1892) ("Laws have no force of themselves beyond the jurisdiction of the State which enacts them, and can have extraterritorial effect only by the comity of other States"). Nor, as a general rule, does a State have a legitimate concern in imposing punitive damages to punish a defendant for unlawful acts committed outside of the State's jurisdiction. Any proper adjudication of conduct that occurred outside Utah to other persons would require their inclusion, and, to those parties, the Utah courts, in the usual case, would need to apply the laws of their relevant jurisdiction. *Phillips Petroleum Co. v. Shutts*, 472 U.S. 797, 821–822, 105 S.Ct. 2965, 86 L.Ed.2d 628 (1985).

Here, the Campbells do not dispute that much of the out-of-state conduct was lawful where it occurred. They argue, however, that such evidence was not the primary basis for the punitive damages award and was relevant to the extent it demonstrated, in a general sense, State Farm's motive against its insured. Brief for Respondents 46–47 ("[E]ven if the practices described by State Farm were not malum in se or malum prohibitum, they became relevant to punitive damages to the extent they were used as tools to implement State Farm's wrongful PP & R policy"). This argument misses the mark. Lawful out-of-state conduct may be probative when it demonstrates the deliberateness and culpability of the defendant's action in the State where it is tortious, but that conduct must have a nexus to the specific harm suffered by the plaintiff. A jury must be instructed, furthermore, that it may not use evidence of out-of-state conduct to punish a defendant for action that was lawful in the jurisdiction where it occurred. *Gore*, 517 U.S., at 572–573, 116 S.Ct. 1589 (noting that a State "does not have the power ... to punish [a defendant] for conduct that was lawful where it occurred and that had no impact on [the State] or its residents"). A basic principle of federalism is that each State may make its own reasoned judgment about what conduct is permitted or proscribed within its borders, and each State alone can determine what measure of punishment, if any, to impose on a defendant who acts within its jurisdiction. *Id.*, at 569, 116 S.Ct. 1589 ("[T]he States need not, and in fact do not, provide such protection in a uniform manner").

For a more fundamental reason, however, the Utah courts erred in relying upon this and other evidence: The courts awarded punitive damages to punish and deter conduct that bore no relation to the Campbells' harm. A defendant's dissimilar acts, independent from the acts upon which liability was premised, may not serve as the basis for punitive damages. A defendant should be punished for the conduct that harmed the plaintiff, not for being an unsavory individual or business. Due process does not permit courts, in the calculation of punitive damages, to adjudicate the merits of other parties' hypothetical claims against a defendant under the guise of the reprehensibility analysis, but we have no doubt the Utah Supreme Court did that here. 65 P.3d, at 1149 ("Even if the harm to the Campbells can be appropriately characterized as minimal, the trial court's assessment of the situation is on target: 'The harm is minor to the individual but massive in the aggregate' ''). Punishment on these bases creates the possibility of multiple punitive damages awards for the same conduct; for in the usual case nonparties are not bound by the judgment some other plaintiff obtains. Gore, supra, at 593, 116 S.Ct. 1589 (BREYER, J., concurring) ("Larger damages might also 'double count' by including in the punitive damages award some of the compensatory, or punitive, damages that subsequent plaintiffs would also recover").

The same reasons lead us to conclude the Utah Supreme Court's decision cannot be justified on the grounds that State Farm was a recidivist. Although "[o]ur holdings that a recidivist may be punished more severely than a first offender recognize that repeated misconduct is more reprehensible than an individual instance of malfeasance," Gore, supra, at 577, 116 S.Ct. 1589, in the context of civil actions courts must ensure the conduct in question replicates the prior transgressions. TXO, 509 U.S., at 462, n. 28, 113 S.Ct. 2711 (noting that courts should look to " 'the existence and frequency of similar past conduct' " (quoting Haslip, 499 U.S., at 21–22, 111 S.Ct. 1032)). . . .

B

Turning to the second *Gore* guidepost, we have been reluctant to identify concrete constitutional limits on the ratio between harm, or potential harm, to the plaintiff and the punitive damages award. 517 U.S., at 582, 116 S.Ct. 1589 ("[W]e have consistently rejected the notion that the constitutional line is marked by a simple mathematical formula, even one that compares actual *and potential* damages to the punitive award"); *TXO, supra,* at 458, 113 S.Ct. 2711. We decline again to impose a bright-line ratio which a punitive damages award cannot exceed. Our jurisprudence and the principles it has now established demonstrate, however, that, in practice, few awards exceeding a single-digit ratio between punitive and compensatory damages, to a significant degree, will satisfy due process. In *Haslip,* in upholding a punitive damages award, we concluded that an award of more than four times the amount of compensatory damages might be close to the line of constitutional impropriety. 499 U.S., at 23–24, 111 S.Ct. 1032. We cited that 4-to-1 ratio again in *Gore.* 517 U.S., at 581, 116 S.Ct. 1589. The Court further referenced a long legislative history, dating back over 700 years and going forward to today, providing for sanctions of double, treble, or quadruple damages to deter and punish. *Id.,* at 581, and n. 33, 116 S.Ct. 1589. While these ratios are not binding, they are instructive. They demonstrate what should be obvious: Single-digit multipliers are more likely to comport with due process, while still achieving the State's goals of deterrence and retribution, than awards with ratios in range of 500 to 1, *id.,* at 582, 116 S.Ct. 1589, or, in this case, of 145 to 1.

Nonetheless, because there are no rigid benchmarks that a punitive damages award may not surpass, ratios greater than those we have previously upheld may comport with due process where "a particularly egregious act has resulted in only a small amount of economic damages." *Ibid.*; see also *ibid.* (positing that a higher ratio *might* be necessary where "the injury is hard to detect or the monetary value of noneconomic harm might have been difficult to determine"). The converse is also true, however. When compensatory damages are substantial, then a lesser ratio, perhaps only equal to compensatory damages, can reach the outermost limit of the due process guarantee. The precise award in any case, of course, must be based upon the facts and circumstances of the defendant's conduct and the harm to the plaintiff.

In sum, courts must ensure that the measure of punishment is both reasonable and proportionate to the amount of harm to the plaintiff and to the general damages recovered. In the context of this case, we have no doubt that there is a presumption against an award that has a 145–to–1 ratio. The compensatory award in this case was substantial; the Campbells were awarded $1 million for a year and a half of emotional distress. This was complete compensation. . . .

The Utah Supreme Court sought to justify the massive award by pointing to State Farm's purported failure to report a prior $100 million punitive damages award in Texas to its corporate headquarters; the fact that State Farm's policies have affected numerous Utah consumers; the fact that State Farm will only be punished in one out of every 50,000 cases as a matter of statistical probability; and State Farm's enormous wealth. . . . Since the Supreme Court of Utah discussed the Texas award when applying the ratio guidepost, we discuss it here. The Texas award, however, should have been analyzed in the context of the reprehensibility guidepost only. The failure of the company to report the Texas award is out-of-state conduct that, if the conduct were similar, might have had some bearing on the degree of reprehensibility, subject to the limitations we have described. Here, it was dissimilar, and of such marginal relevance that it should have been accorded little or no weight. The award was rendered in a first-party lawsuit; no judgment was entered in the case; and it was later settled for a fraction of the verdict. With respect to the Utah Supreme Court's second justification, the Campbells' inability to direct us to testimony demonstrating harm to the people of Utah (other than those directly involved in this case) indicates that the adverse effect on the State's general population was in fact minor.

The remaining premises for the Utah Supreme Court's decision bear no relation to the award's reasonableness or proportionality to the harm. They are, rather, arguments that seek to defend a departure from well-established constraints on punitive damages. While States enjoy considerable discretion in deducing when punitive damages are warranted, each award must comport with the principles set forth in *Gore*. . . .

C

The third guidepost in *Gore* is the disparity between the punitive damages award and the "civil penalties authorized or imposed in comparable cases." *Id.*, at 575, 116 S.Ct. 1589. We note that, in the past, we have also looked to criminal penalties that could be imposed. *Id.*, at 583, 116 S.Ct. 1589; *Haslip*, 499 U.S., at 23, 111 S.Ct. 1032. The existence of a criminal penalty does have bearing on the seriousness with which a State views the wrongful action. When used to determine the dollar amount of the award, however, the criminal penalty has less utility. Great care must be taken to avoid use of the civil process to assess criminal penalties that can be imposed only after the heightened protections of a criminal trial have been observed, including, of course, its higher standards of proof. Punitive damages are not a substitute for the criminal process, and the remote possibility of a criminal sanction does not automatically sustain a punitive damages award. . . .

An application of the Gore guideposts to the facts of this case, especially in light of the substantial compensatory damages awarded (a portion of which contained a punitive element), likely would justify a punitive damages award at or near the amount of compensatory damages. The punitive award of $145 million, therefore, was neither reasonable nor proportionate to the wrong committed, and it was an irrational and arbitrary deprivation of the property of the defendant. The proper calculation of punitive damages under the principles we have discussed should be resolved, in the first instance, by the Utah courts. . . .

The judgment of the Utah Supreme Court is reversed, and the case is remanded for further proceedings not inconsistent with this opinion.

It is so ordered.

■ JUSTICE SCALIA, dissenting.

I adhere to the view expressed in my dissenting opinion in *BMW of North America, Inc. v. Gore*, 517 U.S. 559, 598–99, 116 S.Ct. 1589, 134 L.Ed.2d 809 (1996), that the Due Process Clause provides no substantive protections against "excessive" or " 'unreasonable' " awards of punitive damages. I am also of the view that the punitive damages jurisprudence which has sprung forth from *BMW v. Gore* is insusceptible of principled application; accordingly, I do not feel justified in giving the case *stare decisis* effect. See *id.*, at 599, 116 S.Ct. 1589. I would affirm the judgment of the Utah Supreme Court.

■ JUSTICE THOMAS, dissenting.

I would affirm the judgment below because "I continue to believe that the Constitution does not constrain the size of punitive damages awards." *Cooper Industries, Inc. v. Leatherman Tool Group, Inc.*, 532 U.S. 424, 443, 121 S.Ct. 1678, 149 L.Ed.2d 674 (2001) (THOMAS, J., concurring) (citing *BMW of North America, Inc. v. Gore*, 517 U.S. 559, 599, 116 S.Ct. 1589, 134 L.Ed.2d 809 (1996) (SCALIA, J., joined by THOMAS, J., dissenting)). Accordingly, I respectfully dissent.

■ JUSTICE GINSBURG, dissenting.

Not long ago, this Court was hesitant to impose a federal check on state-court judgments awarding punitive damages. . . .

In *Gore*, I stated why I resisted the Court's foray into punitive damages "territory traditionally within the States' domain." 517 U.S., at 612, 116 S.Ct. 1589 (dissenting opinion). I adhere to those views, and note again that, unlike federal habeas corpus review of state-court convictions under 28 U.S.C. § 2254, the Court "work[s] at this business [of checking state courts] alone," unaided by the participation of federal district courts and courts of appeals. 517 U.S., at 613, 116 S.Ct. 1589. It was once recognized that "the laws of the particular State must suffice [to superintend punitive damages awards] until judges or legislators authorized to do so initiate system-wide change." *Haslip*, 499 U.S., at 42, 111 S.Ct. 1032 (KENNEDY, J., concurring in judgment). I would adhere to that traditional view.

I

The large size of the award upheld by the Utah Supreme Court in this case indicates why damages-capping legislation may be altogether fitting and proper. Neither the amount of the award nor the trial record, however, justifies this Court's substitution of its judgment for that of Utah's competent decisionmakers. In this regard, I count it significant that, on the key criterion "reprehensibility," there is a good deal more to the story than the Court's abbreviated account tells. . . .

I remain of the view that this Court has no warrant to reform state law governing awards of punitive damages. *Gore*, 517 U.S., at 607, 116 S.Ct. 1589 (GINSBURG, J., dissenting). Even if I were prepared to accept the flexible guides prescribed in *Gore*, I would not join the Court's swift conversion of those guides into instructions that begin to resemble marching orders. For the reasons stated, I would leave the judgment of the Utah Supreme Court undisturbed. . . .

NOTES

1.   State legislatures have also acted to limit punitive damage awards. Consider the following statutes:

N.H.Rev.Stat.Ann. § 507:16. PUNITIVE DAMAGES OUTLAWED.

No punitive damages shall be awarded in any action, unless otherwise provided by statute.

Va.Code Ann. § 8.01–38.1. LIMITATION ON RECOVERY OF PUNITIVE DAMAGES.

In any action accruing on or after July 1, 1988, including an action for medical malpractice under Chapter 21.1, the total amount awarded for punitive damages against all defendants found to be liable shall be determined by the trier of fact. In no event shall the total amount awarded for punitive damages exceed $350,000. The jury shall not be advised of the limitation prescribed by this section. However, if a jury returns a verdict for punitive damages in excess of the maximum amount specified in this section, the judge shall reduce the award and enter judgment for such damages in the maximum amount provided by this section.

Fla.Stat.Ann. § 768.73. PUNITIVE DAMAGES; LIMITATION.

(1)(a) Except as provided in paragraphs (b) and (c), an award of punitive damages may not exceed the greater of:

1.   Three times the amount of compensatory damages awarded to each claimant entitled thereto, consistent with the remaining provisions of this section; or

2.   The sum of $500,000.

(b) Where the fact finder determines that the wrongful conduct proven under this section was motivated solely by unreasonable financial gain and determines that the unreasonably dangerous nature of the conduct, together with the high likelihood of injury resulting from the conduct, was actually known by the managing agent, director, officer, or other person responsible for making policy decisions on behalf of the defendant, it may award an amount of punitive damages not to exceed the greater of:

1. Four times the amount of compensatory damages awarded to each claimant entitled thereto, consistent with the remaining provisions of this section; or

2. The sum of $2 million.

(c) Where the fact finder determines that at the time of injury the defendant had a specific intent to harm the claimant and determines that the defendant's conduct did in fact harm the claimant, there shall be no cap on punitive damages.

(d) This subsection is not intended to prohibit an appropriate court from exercising its jurisdiction under § 768.74 in determining the reasonableness of an award of punitive damages that is less than three times the amount of compensatory damages.

(2)(a) Except as provided in paragraph (b), punitive damages may not be awarded against a defendant in a civil action if that defendant establishes, before trial, that punitive damages have previously been awarded against that defendant in any state or federal court in any action alleging harm from the same act or single course of conduct for which the claimant seeks compensatory damages. For purposes of a civil action, the term "the same act or single course of conduct" includes acts resulting in the same manufacturing defects, acts resulting in the same defects in design, or failure to warn of the same hazards, with respect to similar units of a product.

(b) In subsequent civil actions involving the same act or single course of conduct for which punitive damages have already been awarded, if the court determines by clear and convincing evidence that the amount of prior punitive damages awarded was insufficient to punish that defendant's behavior, the court may permit a jury to consider awarding subsequent punitive damages, the court shall make specific findings of fact in the record to support its conclusion. In addition, the court may consider whether the defendant's act or course of conduct has ceased. Any subsequent punitive damage awards must be reduced by the amount of any earlier punitive damage awards rendered in state or federal court.

(3) The claimant attorney's fees, if payable from the judgment, are, to the extent that the fees are based on the punitive damages, calculated based on the final judgment for punitive damages. The subsection does not limit the payment of attorney's fees based upon an award of damages other than punitive damages.

(4) The jury may neither be instructed nor informed as to the provisions of this section.

(5) The provisions of this section shall be applied to all causes of action arising after the effective date of this act.

2. In Browning–Ferris Industries of Vermont, Inc. v. Kelco Disposal, Inc., 492 U.S. 257, 109 S.Ct. 2909, 106 L.Ed.2d 219 (1989), the Court held that the Excessive Fines Clause of the Eighth Amendment does not apply to awards of punitive damages in cases between private parties.

Norfolk and Western Railway Co. v. Hartford Accident and Indemnity Co.

United States District Court, Northern District of Indiana, 1976.
420 F.Supp. 92.

■ ESCHBACH, C.J. This cause is now before the court upon ... cross-motions for summary judgment as to both plaintiff's claim and defendant's counter-claim. As such, for reasons given below, plaintiff's motion will be granted and defendant's motion will be denied.

Plaintiff is a railroad corporation.... Defendant is an insurance company....

On or about January 1, 1971, defendant (hereinafter referred to as the insurer) issued a policy of multiple liability insurance to plaintiff.... The scope of insurance included "all sums which the insured shall become legally obligated to pay as damages because of ... bodily injury or ... property damage to which this insurance applies, caused by an occurrence and arising out of the ownership, maintenance or use ... of any automobile...." Persons insured under this contract included not only plaintiff itself but also "employee[s] of the named insured." ...

During the life of the policy, a truck owned by plaintiff and being operated by one of plaintiff's employees was involved in a collision with an automobile operated by Norbert Herman.... Suit was thereafter filed ... by Mr. and Mrs. Herman against the insured (Norfolk & Western) and its employee.... [T]he jury returned verdicts in favor of the Hermans totaling $67,000 in compensatory damages and $200,000 in punitive damages. Judgment was against both the insured and its employee. The insurer paid in full the compensatory damage award but refused to pay any part of the punitive damages. Ultimately, the insurer and the insured agreed to each pay one-half of the punitive damages, with a reservation of rights to determine coverage in court. The $200,000 amount was subsequently negotiated down to $187,500, with the insurer and the insured each paying $93,750. Plaintiff, the insured, now seeks payment of the $93,750 it paid; the insurer counterclaims for the $93,750 it paid....

. . . .

II

The principal question, and the only question seriously in dispute, is whether under the law of Indiana it contravenes public policy for an insured to avoid liability for a punitive damage award by means of insurance....

. . . .

Since the strong underlying purpose of the punitive damage award is to deter, the availability of insurance may totally undo the public policy of the state. Thus, "a person should not be permitted to insure against harms he may intentionally and unlawfully cause others, and thereby acquire a license to engage in such activity." So, also, on a guardian's bond, the surety is not obligated to pay a punitive damage award, although compensatory damages must be paid.

These cases reflect the concern that a punitive damage award may be shifted by insurance or surety, such that the deterrent effect of the award will be lost. To the extent, then, that the law imposes punitive damages upon an insured in order to shape or deter the insured's conduct, the insured may not avoid the penalty by means of insurance.

The rule against shifting the impact of a punitive damage award has an exception, however. An employer may be held liable for a punitive damage award against his agent when the agent acted within the scope of his employment. The exception was developed in terms of a corporation's freedom from criminal prosecution rather than in terms of any social policy favoring limited shifting of punitive damage awards.... In Jeffersonville R.R. Co. v. Rogers, 38 Ind. 116 (1871), ... the rule was stated to be that "It is also well established that vindictive or exemplary damages may be given against corporations for the tortious and wrongful acts of their agents." As authority for this proposition, the court cited the first *Jeffersonville Railroad* case, 28 Ind. 1 (1867). In that case, however, the Indiana Supreme Court had held that it was possible for a corporation itself to act willfully and maliciously, as where "[t]he instructions governing subordinate employees and agents [are] devised in such utter disregard of the rights of others that obedience to them will result in palpable oppression and gross wrong to individuals." There was no mention of vicarious liability for punitive damages.

The exception to the rule against shifting of punitive damages in the case of a corporate employer was explained thereafter as resting on the ground that since a corporation could not be held criminally liable, the assessment of punitive damages against it would not offend Indiana's prohibition against double punishment. The rule is still applied: "a corporation may remain liable for punitive damages since it cannot be prosecuted for the criminal acts of its agents."

Of course, it does not necessarily follow that because a corporation is not subject to criminal prosecution it is therefore liable vicariously for punitive damages awarded on account of an agent's torts. The first *Jeffersonville Railroad* case properly recognized that a corporation may itself act willfully and maliciously, and, as to such conduct, punitive damages may be had in a proper case. Nonetheless, the exception exists, and upon this exception the plaintiff herein was held liable for punitive damages because of the acts of its agent.

Where the corporation is strictly liable without fault, as where liability arises solely by operation of *respondeat superior,* the policy against shifting of punitive damages has already been put aside, and it would make no sense to revive that policy as between the innocent corporation and its insurer....

There is, accordingly, a distinction to be made in Indiana law between liability for punitive damages directly imposed and such liability when vicariously imposed. The former situation arises in cases similar to the first *Jeffersonville Railroad* case, 28 Ind. 1 (1867), in which the corporation itself is found to have acted maliciously or oppressively. The latter situation arises when the corporation, without itself being guilty of willful misconduct, is held to respond in damages for the intentional tort of its agent. In the former case, it would contravene public policy to allow the corporation to shift to an insurer the deterrent award imposed on account of the corporation's own wrongful acts; in the latter case, it would not be inconsistent with public policy to allow the corporation to shift to an insurer the punitive damage award when that award is placed upon the corporation solely as a matter of vicarious liability. The distinction is not a novel one; it has been fully considered and adopted by the courts of Florida. . . .

III

The only factual issue, then, is whether the insured (Norfolk & Western) was held liable in the state court trial on the basis of vicarious responsibility alone or whether its liability rested in whole or in part on its own misconduct. In this case it is quite clear that the insured was only vicariously liable.

. . . .

Accordingly, under Indiana law it is not contrary to public policy for Norfolk & Western to shift the punitive damage award to its liability insurer, ...

. . . .

NOTE

Consider the following provision of the Restatement (Second) of Torts:

§ 909. PUNITIVE DAMAGES AGAINST A PRINCIPAL.

Punitive damages can properly be awarded against a master or other principal because of an act by an agent if, but only if,

"(a) the principal or a managerial agent authorized the doing and the manner of the act, or

"(b) the agent was unfit and the principal or a managerial agent was reckless in employing or retaining him, or

"(c) the agent was employed in a managerial capacity and was acting in the scope of employment, or

"(d) the principal or a managerial agent of the principal ratified or approved the act."

CHAPTER 16

DAMAGES IN ADDITION TO OR IN LIEU OF EQUITABLE RELIEF

Johnson v. Agnew

House of Lords, 1979.
[1979] 1 All.E.R. 883.

By a contract dated 1st November 1973 the vendors agreed to sell a house and some grazing land to the purchaser. The properties were mortgaged under separate mortgages. The purchase price exceeded the amount required to pay off the mortgages and also a bank loan obtained by the vendors for the purchase of another property. The contract fixed the completion date as 6th December. The purchaser paid part of the deposit and accepted the vendors' title, but did not complete on that date. On 21st December the vendors served on the purchaser a notice making time of the essence of the contract and fixing 21st January 1974 as the final date by which completion was to take place. The purchaser failed to complete, and on 8th March the vendors commenced an action against her, claiming specific performance and damages in addition to, or in lieu of, specific performance, and alternatively, a declaration that the vendors were no longer bound to perform the contract, and further relief. . . .

LORD WILBERFORCE. . . .

. . . On 20th May the vendors issued a summons for specific performance, and the order sought was made in the usual form on 27th June 1974. It was not however drawn up and entered until 26th November 1974.

Meanwhile action was taken by the vendors' mortgagees. The building society obtained an order for possession of the grange on 22nd August 1974, they sold it on 20th June 1975 and completion took place on 18th July 1975. The finance company obtained an order for possession of the grazing land on 7th March 1975, they sold it on 3rd April 1975 and completion took place on 11th July 1975. Thus by 3rd April 1975 specific performance of the contract for sale had become impossible. The vendors took no action on the order for specific performance until 5th November 1976 when they issued a notice of motion seeking . . . an order that the purchaser should pay the balance of the purchase price and an enquiry as to damages. . . .

On 25th February 1977 Megarry V–C dismissed the motion. He rejected the . . . claim on the ground that, as specific performance was no longer possible, it would be unjust to order payment of the full purchase price. . . .

The vendors appealed to the Court of Appeal who again rejected [this request]. . . . However they held that the vendors could recover damages under the Chancery Amendment Act 1858 (Lord Cairns's Act), which enables the court to award damages in addition to or in substitution for specific performance. They accordingly made an order discharging the order for specific performance and an order for an enquiry as to damages. They fixed the date on which damages should be assessed as 26th November 1974, being the date of entry of the order for specific performance. The purchaser is now appealing against this order.

In this situation it is possible to state at least some uncontroversial propositions of law. First, in a contract for the sale of land, after time has been made, or has become, of the essence of the contract, if the purchaser fails to complete, the vendor can *either* treat the purchaser as having repudiated the contract, accept the repudiation, and proceed to claim damages for breach of the contract, both parties being discharged from further performance of the contract; *or* he may seek from the court an order for specific performance with damages for any loss arising from delay in performance. (Similar remedies are of course available to purchasers against vendors.) This is simply the ordinary law of contract applied to contracts capable of specific performance. Secondly, the vendor may proceed by action for the above remedies (viz specific performance or damages) in the alternative. At the trial he will however have to elect which remedy to pursue. Thirdly, if the vendor treats the purchaser as having repudiated the contract and accepts the repudiation, he cannot thereafter seek specific performance. This follows from the fact that, the purchaser having repudiated the contract and his repudiation having been accepted, both parties are discharged from further performance.

. . . .

Fourthly, if an order for specific performance is sought and is made, the contract remains in effect and is not merged in the judgment for specific performance. This is clear law, best illustrated by the judgment of Greene MR in Austins of East Ham Ltd. v. Macey should be [[1941] Ch. 338], in a passage which deals both with this point and with that next following. It repays quotation in full:

> "The contract is still there. Until it is got rid of, it remains as a blot on the title, and the position of the vendor, where the purchaser has made default, is that he is entitled, not to annul the contract by aid of the court, but to obtain the normal remedy of a party to a contract which the other party has repudiated. He cannot, in the circumstances, treat it as repudiated except by order of the court and the effect of obtaining such an order is that the contract, which until then existed, is brought to an end. The real position, in my judgment, is that, so far from proceeding to the enforcement of an order for specific performance, the vendor, in such circumstances is choosing a remedy which is alternative to the remedy of proceeding under the order for specific performance. He could attempt to enforce that order and could levy an execution which might prove completely fruitless. Instead of doing that, he elects to ask the court to put an end to the contract, and that is an alternative to an order for enforcing specific performance."

Fifthly, if the order for specific performance is not complied with by the purchaser, the vendor may *either* apply to the court for enforcement of the order, *or* may apply to the court to dissolve the order and ask the court to put an end to the contract. This proposition is as stated in Austins of East Ham Ltd. v. Macey ... and is in my opinion undoubted law, both on principle and authority. It follows, indeed, automatically from the facts that the contract remains in force after the order for specific performance and that the purchaser has committed a breach of it of a repudiatory character which he has not remedied....

These propositions being, as I think they are, uncontrovertible, there only remains the question whether, if the vendor takes the latter course, i.e., of applying to the court to put an end to the contract, he is entitled to recover damages for breach of the contract. On principle one may ask "Why ever not?" If, as is clear, the vendor is entitled (after and notwithstanding that an order for specific performance has been made) if the purchaser still does not complete the contract, to ask the court to permit him to accept the purchaser's repudiation and to declare the contract to be terminated, why, if the court accedes to this, should there not follow the ordinary consequences, undoubted under the general law of contract, that on such acceptance and termination the vendor may recover damages for breach of contract?

. . . .

This is however the first time that this House has had to consider the right of an innocent party to a contract for the sale of land to damages on the contract being put an end to by accepted repudiation, and I think that we have the duty to take a fresh look.... I quote first from a judgment of Dixon J. which with typical clarity sets out the principle, this, be it observed, in a case concerned with a contract for the sale of land:

> "When a party to a simple contract, upon a breach by the other contracting party of a condition of the contract, elects to treat the contract as no longer binding upon him, the contract is not rescinded as from the beginning. Both parties are discharged from the further performance of the contract, but rights are not divested or discharged which have already been unconditionally acquired. Rights and obligations which arise from the partial execution of the contract and causes of action which have accrued from its breach alike continue unaffected. When a contract is rescinded because of matters which affect its formation, as in the case of fraud, the parties are to be rehabilitated and restored, so far as may be, to the position they occupied before the contract was made. But when a contract, which is not void or voidable at law, or liable to be set aside in equity, is dissolved at the election of one party because the other has not observed an essential condition or has committed a breach going to its root, the contract is determined so far as it is executory only and the party in default is liable for damages for its breach."

Closer to the present case, in Holland v. Wiltshire, 90 C.L.R. 409 (1954), the High Court of Australia was directly concerned with a question of damages for breach of contract for the sale of land. The purchaser having failed to complete, the vendor claimed damages. Dixon C.J. said:

"The proper conclusion is that the vendor proceeded not under the contractual provision but on the footing that the purchasers had discharged him from the obligations of the contract. It follows that he is entitled to sue for unliquidated damages...."

....

Then, in McKenna v. Richey, [1950] V.L.R. 360, a case very similar to the present, it was decided by O'Bryan J. in the Supreme Court of Victoria that, after an order for specific performance had been made, which in the event could not be carried into effect, even though this was by reason of delay on the part of the plaintiff, the plaintiff could still come to the court and ask for damages on the basis of an accepted repudiation. The following passage is illuminating:

"The apparent inconsistency of a plaintiff suing for specific performance and for common law damages in the alternative arises from the fact that, in order to avoid circuity of action, there is vested in one Court jurisdiction to grant either form of relief. The plaintiff, in effect, is saying: 'I don't accept your repudiation of the contract but am willing to perform my part of the contract and insist upon your performing your part—but if I cannot successfully insist on your performing your part, I will accept the repudiation and ask for damages.' Until the defendant's repudiation is accepted the contract remains on foot, with all the possible consequences of that fact. But if, from first to last, the defendant continues unwilling to perform her part of the contract, then, if for any reason the contract cannot be specifically enforced, the plaintiff may, in my opinion, turn round and say: 'Very well, I cannot have specific performance; I will now ask for my alternative remedy of damages at common law.' This, in my opinion, is equally applicable both before and after decree whether the reason for the refusal or the failure of the decree of specific performance is due to inability of the defendant to give any title to the property sold, or to the conduct of the plaintiff which makes it inequitable for the contract to be specifically enforced."

Later the judge said of the case:

"It is an appropriate case for a Court of Equity to say: 'As a matter of discretion, this contract should not now be enforced specifically, but, in lieu of the decree for specific performance, the Court will award the plaintiff such damages as have been suffered by her in consequence of the defendant's breach. That is the best justice that can be done in this case.'"

...

My Lords, I am happy to follow the latter case....

....

There is one final point, on this part of the case, on which I should make a brief observation. Once the matter has been placed in the hands of a court of equity, or one exercising equity jurisdiction, the subsequent control of the matter will be exercised according to equitable principles. The court would not make an order dissolving the decree of specific performance and terminating the contract (with recovery of damages) if to do so would be unjust, in the circumstances then existing, to the other party, in this case to the purchaser.... This is why there was, in the Court of Appeal, rightly, a relevant and substantial argument, repeated in this House, that the non-completion of the contract was due to the default of the vendors; if this had been made good, the court could properly have refused them the relief sought. But the Court of Appeal came to the conclusion that this non-completion, and the ultimate impossibility of completion, was the fault of the purchaser. I agree with their conclusion and their reasons on this point and shall not repeat or add to them.

It is now necessary to deal with questions relating to the measure of damages. The Court of Appeal, while denying the vendors' right to damages at common law, granted damages under Lord Cairns's Act. Since on the view which I take, damages can be recovered at common law, two relevant questions now arise: (1) whether Lord Cairns's Act provides a different measure of damages from the common law? If so, the respondents would be in a position to claim the more favorable basis to them; and (2) if the measure of damages is the same, on what basis they should be calculated?

Since the decision of this House, by a majority, in Leeds Industrial Co-operative Society Ltd. v. Slack, [1924] A.C. 851 (H.L.), it is clear that the jurisdiction to award damages in accordance with § 2 of Lord Cairns's Act (accepted by the House as surviving the repeal of the Act) may arise in some cases in which damages could not be recovered at common law; examples of this would be damages in lieu of a quia timet injunction and damages for breach of a restrictive covenant to which the defendant was not a party. To this extent the Act created a power to award damages which did not exist before at common law. But apart from these, and similar cases where damages could not be claimed at all at common law, there is sound authority for the proposition that the Act does not provide for the assessment of damages on any new basis. The wording of § 2 that damages "may be assessed in such manner as the court shall direct" does not so suggest, but clearly refers only to procedure.

   . . . .

The general principle for the assessment of damages is compensatory, i.e., that the innocent party is to be placed, so far as money can do so, in the same position as if the contract had been performed. Where the contract is one of sale, this principle normally leads to assessment of damages as at the date of the breach, a principle recognized and embodied in § 51 of the Sale of Goods Act 1893. But this is not an absolute rule; if to follow it would give rise to injustice, the court has power to fix such other date as may be appropriate in the circumstances.

In cases where a breach of a contract for sale has occurred, and the innocent party reasonably continues to try to have the contract completed, it would to me appear more logical and just rather than tie him to the date of the original breach, to assess damages as at the date when (otherwise than by his default) the contract is lost....

In the present case if it is accepted, as I would accept, that the vendors acted reasonably in pursuing the remedy of specific performance, the date on which that remedy became aborted (not by the vendors' fault) should logically be fixed as the date on which damages should be assessed. Choice of this date would be in accordance both with common law principle, as indicated in the authorities I have mentioned, and with the wording of the Act "in substitution for ... specific performance". The date which emerges from this is 3rd April 1975, the first date on which mortgagees contracted to sell a portion of the property. I would vary the order of the Court of Appeal by substituting this date for that fixed by them, viz 26th November 1974.... Subject to [this] modification I would dismiss the appeal.

[LORD SALMON, LORD FRASER of Tullybelton, LORD KEITH of Kinkel, and LORD SCARMAN, each having had the opportunity to read in advance the speech of LORD WILBERFORCE, and finding themselves in agreement, would dismiss the appeal subject to the variation proposed by him in the order of the Court of Appeal:]

Appeal dismissed subject to variation of order of the Court of Appeal....

NOTES

1. Lord Cairns' Act is discussed in Chapter 2, *supra* pp. 43–44.

2. With respect to the matter of election of remedies, consider the following section of the Restatement (Second) of Contracts:

§ 378. Election Among Remedies.

If a party has more than one remedy ... his manifestation of a choice of one of them by bringing suit or otherwise is not a bar to another remedy unless the remedies are inconsistent and the other party materially changes his position in reliance on the manifestation.

Abbott v. 76 Land and Water Co.

Supreme Court of California, 1911.
161 Cal. 42, 118 P. 425.

[Action for damages by L.E. Abbott, as assignee of the cause of action from its original owner, O.L. Abbott (hereinafter called Abbott). The complaint alleged in part that on October 1, 1887, the defendant held the legal title to 320 acres of land with appurtenant water rights under a duty to convey to Abbott on receipt of $4,800, but refused to convey until March 4, 1892. It was further alleged that on October 1, 1887, the value of the premises was $16,000; that it rose to $24,000, for which Abbott would have sold the premises if legal title had not been withheld; and that the land then depreciated in value until at the time of the conveyance it was worth only $9,600, wherefore Abbott was damaged in the sum of $14,400.

The answer denied the allegations of damage by reason of the retention of legal title, and alleged as a special defense that, long before this action, Abbott began and prosecuted to final judgment on the merits an action against the defendant wherein all matters relating to the alleged depreciation could and should have been litigated.

The trial court found that Abbott took possession under a written lease from the defendant for one year from October 1, 1885, with the privilege of purchasing the demised premises for $4,800 at any time before October 1, 1886. On or about the latter date Abbott accepted a renewal lease for one year, which contained no such purchase clause. In September, 1887, Abbott claimed the right to purchase the land and tendered the specified price. The defendant in good faith denied the alleged right, and refused Abbott's demand for a deed. In 1889, Abbott began suit for specific performance, and in February, 1890, he obtained a decree directing the execution of a deed upon payment of $4,800 before October 1, 1890. This decree was affirmed. Since Abbott had not tendered the price after judgment and before October 1, 1890, the defendant claimed that Abbott's right under the decree had lapsed and still refused to execute the deed. Thereupon the defendant was adjudged guilty of contempt by order of the superior court, which was affirmed on certiorari. On March 4, 1892, the defendant complied with the decree by executing its deed. The alleged depreciation in value in the land occurred subsequent to the commencement of the action, and subsequent to the rendition of judgment by the superior court in the specific performance action. At the time of the defendant's original breach of contract no damages were sustained by Abbott, and he then elected the remedy of specific performance, and not to bring an action at law to recover damages for such breach. The trial court further found that the delay between such breach and the deed was caused by the specific performance suit and the necessary delay of the courts in adjudicating the rights of the parties. The trial court found that no damage was sustained; and that, if any was sustained, it was caused by the delay of litigation and was remote and speculative damage not otherwise recoverable at law.

Judgment was entered for the defendant, and a new trial was refused. The plaintiff appealed.]

■ ANGELLOTTI, J. . . .

So far as the land was concerned, it cannot be disputed that the findings above referred to are fully sustained by the evidence. In view of the facts thus shown, we know of no rule of law that authorizes a recovery in this action of the damage alleged in regard thereto. Certainly no authority has been cited by plaintiff that would sustain such a recovery. The sole cause of the damages alleged was defendant's breach of its contract to sell the land to plaintiff's assignor. The breach occurred in the year 1887, and was, as said by counsel for defendant, "a total breach and repudiation of the contract." The defendant claimed in good faith and with apparently much ground for its claim, that the contract relied on by plaintiff's assignor did not entitle him to purchase the land. Be this as it may, the contract, so far as it related to the matter of the sale of the land, was single and entire. The total abandonment or breach thereof by defendant gave plaintiff's assignor but a single cause of action, and this single cause of action could not be so split as to afford warrant for two or more actions. It is true that the vendee had an election of remedies. He might have brought an action to recover such damages as were caused him by the breach, or he might, as he did, bring his action for specific enforcement of the contract, and in such action obtain not only the specific enforcement of his contract, but also such damages as he was lawfully entitled to, for it is thoroughly settled that a court of equity taking jurisdiction for the purpose of specifically enforcing a contract takes full jurisdiction of all the rights of the parties, whether legal or equitable, and may award such legal damages as the vendee may have suffered by reason of the delay in performances. But, under elementary principles, he was bound to obtain all his relief on account of the breach in one action, and could not recover part in one and part in another. If he had brought his action at law for damages, thereby treating the contract as at an end, a judgment therein awarding him damages would have been conclusive on him as to the amount of damages sustained by reason of the breach, and a bar to any action for further damage on account thereof. Resorting as he did to an action in equity to compel specific performance of the contract, instead of an action at law for damages, the decree in his favor of the court having the power to give him all relief that he was entitled to on account of the breach is likewise conclusive and a bar to any subsequent action for relief based on the same contract. This is the necessary result of the application of the well settled principle that an entire claim arising either upon a contract or from a wrong cannot be divided and made the subject to several suits. In such a case it is no warrant for a second action that the party may not be able to actually prove in the first action all the items of the demand, or that all the damage may not then have been actually suffered. He is bound to prove in the first action not only such damage as has been actually suffered, but also such prospective damage by reason of the breach as he may be legally entitled to, for the judgment he recovers in such action will be a conclusive adjudication as to the total damage on account of the breach.

Appellant's claim for a contrary rule in this case must necessarily be that defendant's breach was what is known in the law as a continuous breach, continuing from the first repudiation of the contract to the day of the execution of the deed and giving rise to new causes of action as long as it continues. Of course, in such a case a judgment for damages accruing prior to the commencement of the action is not a bar to an action for damages accruing subsequently, for the claim for such damages is a new cause of action. This is recognized by section 1047 of the Code of Civil Procedure, but the rule there stated has no application to actions for additional damages on account of some particular breach involved in a former action.

But a continuous breach necessarily implies a continuous duty, such as the duty imposed by a stipulation to keep certain premises in repair during a specified term. There can be no such thing in the case of the absolute repudiation by the vendor of a contract for the sale of real estate. In the latter case there is a single breach, complete at the time of such repudiation, and a single and entire cause of action at once accrues. And it is especially true in such a case that a decree of specific performance of the contract of sale is a bar to any further relief based on the claim of the breach, for, as we have said, an action for specific performance necessarily involves not only the question of such performance, but also all claims for compensation and damage on account of the delay in performance.

. . . .

In accord with the views we have stated it has been held that the continued withholding of stocks or bonds after the bringing of action to enforce their delivery, pending the litigation and up to the time of the enforcement of the decree, is not a new wrong redressible by a new action, but is simply a continuation of the original wrong for which the only redress given by the law must be had in the original action, and that, consequently, a second action would not lie for the damage due to depreciation in the value of the stocks or bonds occurring between the time of the commencement of the first action and the determination of such action on appeal. . . .

That a decree of specific performance of a contract for the conveyance of real estate is a bar to any subsequent action by the vendee for damages on account of the breach of such contract is held in Head v. Meloney, 111 Pa. 99, 2 A. 195, and Thompson v. Myrick, 24 Minn. 4. In the Pennsylvania case it is said, among other things, that, as is plain, the suit for the specific performance was "an action upon the contract in its entirety," and it was substantially held that the decree in such a case must be taken as a complete and final adjudication of the rights of the parties growing out of said contract.

From what we have said it is manifest, we think, as was found by the trial court, that, so far as the land is concerned, all the rights and remedies of plaintiff's assignors here sought to be enforced were merged in and exhausted by the specific performance action.

. . . .

The judgment and order denying a new trial are affirmed.

Livingston v. Krown Chemical Manufacturing, Inc.

Supreme Court of Michigan, 1975.
394 Mich. 144, 229 N.W.2d 793.

■ LEVIN, J. Marsano, Inc. was engaged in the manufacture and sale of a product known as "Beauty Mate Comb." Leonard Marsano and his wife, Lillian Marsano, owned about 52½% of the capital stock and plaintiffs Jack K. Livingston, et al., owned about 47½%.

The stockholders, majority and minority, decided to sell their shares and placed an advertisement in the Wall Street Journal. Defendant Krown Chemical Manufacturing, Inc. negotiated with stockholders and a contract was signed on December 22, 1967.

For their shares, the Marsanos received $31,000 and 2,000 shares of Krown capital stock. The Krown shares were placed in escrow subject to certain conditions. Krown agreed to pay the plaintiff minority stockholders, 120 days after January 3, 1968, $46,000 for their shares which were escrowed.

Krown failed to pay the $46,000 and the minority stockholders commenced this action against Krown and the Marsanos.

The trial court, finding that there were misrepresentations by the sellers, denied the minority stockholders specific performance but, nevertheless, awarded them $46,000 as damages.... The Court of Appeals affirmed.

We affirm, but remand for further proceedings.

I.

Krown, relying on Farrell v. Hannan Real Estate Exchange, 251 Mich. 669, 232 N.W. 209 (1930), contends that damages cannot be awarded when specific performance has been denied because of the plaintiff's fraudulent conduct. In *Farrell,* this court adopted the trial court's opinion refusing to award money damages on denial of specific performance: "obviously, if the plaintiff has not made out such a case here as entitles him to consideration in a court of equity, money damages may not be properly awarded to him. Such damages are awarded only in lieu of equitable relief, in the strict sense of the term."

Krown would distinguish the two cases relied on by the Court of Appeals, Herpolsheimer v. A.B. Herpolsheimer Realty Co., 344 Mich. 657, 75 N.W.2d 333 (1956), and Michigan Sugar Co. v. Falkenhagen, 243 Mich. 698, 220 N.W. 760 (1928), where this Court said that money damages can be awarded in lieu of equitable relief. *Herpolsheimer* was not an action for specific performance; the plaintiff sought equitable superintendence of a claimed constructive trust, an accounting and ancillary relief. The plaintiff in *Michigan Sugar,* in contrast with the minority stockholders in this case, was not denied equitable relief because of inequitable or fraudulent conduct on its part.

Professor Corbin wrote, "[i]ndependently of codes of procedure and other statutes, it became generally established in the United States that a bill for specific performance would be retained for the assessment of damages, in lieu of the remedy asked, if the bill stated a case that was proper for equity jurisdiction and the only reason for refusal of the decree asked was because performance had become impossible or for some reason inequitable...." However, "[i]f the plaintiff's case is not one that is normally the subject of equity jurisdiction, one in which his own conduct has made an equitable remedy unavailable ... the plaintiff's bill will seldom be retained for assessment of his damages unless the case falls within the provisions of statutes like those referred to below." 5A Corbin on Contracts, § 1161, pp. 197, 199–200.

Michigan Sugar appears to be a case where specific performance "had become impossible or for some reason inequitable." Defendant had oversold and delivered the commodity, creating rights in a third party.

Corbin cites *Farrell* as a case in which plaintiff's conduct made an equitable remedy unavailable.

But Corbin further explained that as a result of modern codes of procedure in most jurisdictions:

> "a single system of courts has been established with both common law and equity jurisdiction. It is generally provided also that the court may grant other forms of relief than that expressly sought by the plaintiff. Under such statutes, the court may assess damages in lieu of specific performance if the facts established in the suit show the plaintiff to be

entitled to damages, *whether a former court of equity would have retained a bill for such a purpose or not.* The assessment of damages may rest upon the plaintiff's right thereto by virtue of common law rules or statute, as well as upon earlier doctrines of equity. Such statutes should be given the most liberal of application in order to avoid unnecessary litigation. It is true, however, that some courts with the combined jurisdiction have failed fully to understand their true function in this respect." 5A Corbin on Contracts, § 1161, pp. 201–203.

The Michigan constitutions of 1850 and 1908 provided, "The legislature shall, as far as practicable, abolish distinctions between law and equity proceedings." The 1963 Constitution provides, "The supreme court shall by general rules establish, modify, amend, and simplify the practice and procedure in all courts of this state. The distinctions between law and equity proceedings shall, as far as practicable, be abolished." The Judicature Act of 1915 and the Revised Judicature Act of 1961, adopted before the effective date of the 1963 Constitution, authorized the Supreme Court by general rules to abolish, as far as practicable, distinctions between law and equity.

Despite the 1850 and 1908 constitutional directives to the Legislature, the objective was not achieved. The Judicature Act of 1915 provided that "legal and equitable causes of action shall not be joined."

The long-sought reform was achieved in the General Court Rules of 1963. GCR 1963, 12 provides "There shall be 1 form of action to be known as a 'Civil Action.'" The accompanying committee comment states, "It is the intention of this rule to abolish all distinctions insofar as practicable between law and equity.... To carry out this philosophy, reference should be made to Rule 203 in which it is made clear that claims of legal and equitable nature may be joined under the circumstances as therein limited."

GCR 1963, 203.1 provides, "A complaint shall state as a claim every claim either legal or equitable" which the pleader has against any party arising out of the transaction or occurrence that is the subject-matter of the action and does not require the presence of third parties of whom the court cannot acquire jurisdiction. GCR 1963, 111.2, 111.9(2) provide that a pleader may state as many separate claims or defenses as he has "whether based upon legal or equitable grounds or upon both."

The minority stockholders, thus, could properly join claims seeking legal and equitable relief. However, they did not. Their complaint against Krown asserted that "compensation in damages would be inadequate and incalculable." The relief sought "as to Count One" was specific performance and such other and further relief "as shall be agreeable to equity and good conscience."

However, the Revised Judicature Act permits amendment after judgment has been entered "in affirmance of the judgment." The deficiencies in plaintiffs' pleadings do not preclude an award of damages as an alternative to specific relief.

No reason appears for concluding that Krown's trial defense against the assessment of damages was prejudiced by plaintiffs' failure to amend before judgment.

We are remanding for further proceedings for other reasons. On remand amendment may be allowed and Krown may be afforded an opportunity to introduce any additional evidence opposing the plaintiffs' damage claim.

. . . .

Affirmed and remanded. Costs to appellees.

NOTES

1. The existence of the equitable "clean-up" doctrine, and its significance with respect to questions of merger and bar, is noted in Chapter 2, *supra* pp. 38–42.

2. In connection with the passages from Corbin on Contracts set forth in *Livingston,* consider Margraf v. Muir, 57 N.Y. 155 (1874), and Gulbenkian v. Gulbenkian, 147 F.2d 173 (2d Cir.1945). In *Margraf,* the plaintiff's request for specific performance of a land sale contract was denied because he knowingly took advantage of the defendant's ignorance to obtain an unconscionably low purchase price. After noting that New York equity courts traditionally would have relegated plaintiff to an action at law to recover his damages under these circumstances, the court ruled that the merger of law and equity obviated the need for a second suit and allowed his recovery of damages in this action. In *Gulbenkian,* the court approved the exercise of "clean-up" jurisdiction to award damages for breach of a contract (to reorganize a business) that it found too indefinite to enforce specifically.

3. Rosario Mining & Milling Co. contracted to sell a mine to Clark and his associates, with a stipulation for liquidated damages upon failure to purchase. Rosario later sued for specific performance and general relief. The equity court denied specific performance because of the liquidated damages provision and awarded Rosario the amount of liquidated damages. This judgment was reversed on appeal on the ground that, the specific performance claim being frivolous, "clean-up" jurisdiction could not be invoked. Clark v. Rosario Mining & Milling Co., 176 Fed. 180 (9th Cir. 1910).

4. U.C.C. § 2–716(2) states that a decree giving a buyer specific performance "may include such terms and conditions as to payment of the price, damages or other relief as the court may deem just."

Lewis v. North Kingstown
Supreme Court of Rhode Island, 1887.
16 R.I. 15, 11 A. 173.

■ DURFEE, C.J. The bill sets out that the complainants are owners in possession of a lot of land situate on Washington Street in the village of Wickford, in the town of North Kingstown, in highway district No. 37 of said town, on which lot there is a building belonging to them; that the defendant, John H. Weeden, the surveyor of highways of said district, acting under order of the town council of said town, the members whereof are likewise made defendants, has entered on said lot, and is engaged in razing said building and taking away the foundations and grading said lot; thereby throwing the estate open to the public and obliterating its boundaries, to the irreparable injury of the complainants. The bill prays that the defendants may be enjoined from carrying out their purposes, and from further interfering in any way with the estate, and for general relief. The bill was filed February 28, 1885. The defendants by their answer filed May 27, 1885, admit that they are or were doing as charged, but deny that the lot is part and parcel of the estate of the complainants, and allege that it is and ever has been, from a time when the memory of man runneth not to the contrary, part and parcel of a public highway, and that the building had stood thereon by sufferance of the town. The defendants, also, by supplemental answer filed September 28, 1886, allege that their purposes have been fully carried out by removing the building and foundations and grading the lot, and set up that the complainants ought not to maintain their bill because their remedy is complete at law. To both answers the complainants have filed general replications.

In this state of the pleadings the defendants move that the bill be dismissed because the complainants have an adequate remedy at law, and in support of their motion contend: *first,* that the bill does not state a case for equitable relief; and *second,* if it does, that the case stated has ceased to exist by reason of the removal of the building and foundations and the grading of the lot.

We do not think the motion should be granted because of the statements of the supplemental answer, since those statements are controverted by the replication. Moreover, if they were admitted we do not think they would make a case for dismissal. It ought not to be in the power of a defendant in an injunction bill to oust the court of its jurisdiction by committing, *pendente lite,* the very acts to prevent which the suit was begun, and such, we think, is the law. "It is well settled," says the Supreme Judicial Court of Massachusetts, "with little or no conflict of authority, that when a defendant in a bill in equity disenables himself, pending the suit, to comply with an order for specific relief, the court will proceed to afford relief by way of compelling compensation to be made, and for this purpose will retain the bill and determine the amount of such compensation, although its nature and measure are precisely the same as the party would otherwise recover as damages in an action at law." See Milkman v. Ordway, 106 Mass. 232 (1870), a case which contains a very full citation and discussion of authorities, and goes even beyond the passage quoted. It may be that an amendment of the bill, setting forth the acts committed by the defendants *pendente lite,* will be necessary, notwithstanding the supplemental answer, if the complainants desire not only an injunction from further interference but also an award of damages, but if so the complainants should have an opportunity to make it.

Motion dismissed.

NOTE

Milkman v. Ordway, 106 Mass. 232 (1870), allowed an award of "clean-up" damages by invoking a broader rule than the one quoted in *Lewis:* viz., "provided the plaintiff brought his bill . . . in good faith," the exercise of "clean-up" jurisdiction is appropriate "when the [defendant's] disability was caused before suit, but after the date of the agreement relied on."

Cox v. City of New York

Court of Appeals of New York, 1934.
265 N.Y. 411, 193 N.E. 251.

■ LOUGHRAN, J. This is an action for a mandatory injunction against the disturbance of easements of the plaintiffs in a public highway, with damages to the time of trial. The cause of action has been established only against the defendant railroad company, and the controversy between that defendant and the plaintiffs is, in substance, now reduced to the question whether the trial court, after denying an injunction, was warranted in directing that, in exchange for their property rights, the plaintiffs have judgment for a sum of money only.

The act complained of is the removal by the defendant railroad company of two bridges which carried the highway over its tracks. That defendant in good faith supposed that it owned the easements in question under a conveyance from the defendant city of New York. The cost of restoration of the bridges would largely exceed the value of the rights invaded. Over their exception, the easements of the plaintiffs have been extinguished by the judgment for damages against the defendant railroad company. To the form of the judgment, the defendant railroad company expressly assented.

The result is challenged as transcending the equity jurisdiction of the court. The plaintiffs urge that, without their consent, they may not be made to accept relief which they did not and could not ask. They contend that they had no adequate opportunity to litigate an issue introduced by the court. A wrong has been sanctioned, so it is argued, because the wrongdoer is able and ready to pay money for the injury inflicted.

On the contrary, as we think, the discretion committed to the court was soundly exercised in the exceptional circumstances.

Originally the Court of Chancery, although it might exact an account of the profits of a wrong, could not award damages. The Supreme Court is vested with both legal and equitable powers, but this fusion of administration did not abolish "the essential and permanent difference between legal and equitable relief. For the distinction between a judgment that the plaintiff recover land, chattels or money, and a judgment that the defendant do or refrain from doing a certain thing, is as vital and far-reaching as ever." (Ames, Lectures on Legal History and Legal Essays, 311.)

The practice here adopted has no exact precedent in this court. "We have been referred to no case in this State where an equity court has assumed the authority to render judgment for prospective damages against a wrongdoer, and, we think, in the nature of the jurisdiction of such courts, a suit brought for such a purpose alone is not authorized. To say, therefore, that an action in which the plaintiff has no legal right to demand permanent damages, and the court owes no legal duty to award them, affords the owner an adequate remedy for such damages, is to pervert the plain character of the action. While equity courts have frequently suspended the remedy, as they did in this case, by injunction upon conditions, as for a specified time, or until the wrongdoer has been afforded an opportunity to condemn the property invaded, or has satisfied the owner's damages, they have never, to our knowledge, rendered judgment for such damages or authorized the collection thereof by the owner." (Galway v. Metropolitan Elevated Ry. Co., 128 N.Y. 132, 149, 28 N.E. 479.) When that language was written, the Supreme Court lacked competency to determine the compensation to be made for private property taken for public use. The power now exists except when such compensation is to be made by the State. It is not disputed that the easements of the plaintiffs could have been acquired by the defendant railroad company through condemnation. The rule of injunction and alternative damages established by the elevated railroad cases (Galway v. Metropolitan Elevated Ry. Co.) was declared in part upon the authority of English decisions which applied Lord Cairns' Act (21 & 22 Vict. ch. 27), authorizing an award of damages in substitution for an injunction.... Lord Cairns' Act has been repealed, but the jurisdiction to give damages in lieu of an injunction continues in England. So in this State, an action like the present is, in practical effect, a substitute for condemnation proceedings.

An injunction with its alternative damages would have been as unacceptable to the plaintiffs as the present judgment. They took the position that they would be content with nothing less than the unconditional injunction demanded by them. Certainly they have not been aggrieved by the acceleration of receipt of their damages. The Special Term was of opinion that proof had been supplied of all factors upon which full compensation for the easements of the plaintiffs was to be fixed. It is true that the plaintiffs asserted the contrary. There was, however, no request by them for the chance to present additional evidence. It was perhaps going too far to direct that the mere entry of judgment should put an end to their rights, but the judgment is not questioned in that particular.

The judicial discretion of the Special Term was, we repeat, validly exercised in the state of the record.

The Appellate Division modified the judgment upon new findings by reducing the damages awarded. We think that the new findings follow the weight of the evidence. The property to which the easements of the plaintiffs were appurtenant is situated in the county of Bronx, city of New York. The land is a mile distant from principal traffic arteries. It is vacant and unimproved, and has never been used for any purpose. Destruction of the easements in question leaves the property accessible over other thoroughfares. Upon a new trial of the issue of the amount of damages, the plaintiffs could add nothing to this record but further real estate expert testimony. That such proof would produce a substantially different result is quite unlikely.

The judgment dismissing the complaint against the defendant City of New York and the award to the plaintiff of $1,150 damages against the defendant railroad company should be affirmed, without costs. The appeal of the New York Central Railroad Company has been marked withdrawn in accordance with the concession of that defendant.

■ POUND, C.J., and CRANE, O'BRIEN, and HUBBS, JJ., concur; LEHMAN and CROUCH, JJ., dissent.

Judgment accordingly.

I. H. P. Corp. v. 210 Central Park South Corp.

Court of Appeals of New York, 1963.
12 N.Y.2d 329, 239 N.Y.S.2d 547, 189 N.E.2d 812.

■ BURKE, J. The principal law question on these cross appeals is whether the Supreme Court committed reversible error in awarding exemplary damages as incidental to injunctive relief.

Plaintiff's complaint alleged a "plain and concise statement of the material facts" and "[a] demand of the judgment to which [it] suppos[ed] [itself] entitled." The facts alleged were that plaintiff was the lessee in possession of the street level floor in the building of one of the defendants; that all of the defendants caused the premises to be broken into at night on two occasions during which certain damage was done to the leasehold; that each time barriers were placed on the means of access to bar plaintiff from the premises, all with the purpose of harassing plaintiff into surrendering its valuable lease; that similar acts will occur in the future unless restrained by the court. The relief requested was an injunction and treble damages. The note of issue repeated the request for injunction, and "$5,000 plus exemplary damages besides injunction".

Defendants challenge the propriety of the award, not as a matter of the law of damages but rather on the procedural ground that "the function of a court of equity goes no further than to award compensatory damages as incidental to injunctive relief: it may not assess exemplary damages." Defendants' position, aside from the right to a jury trial, which we think is waived here, is based on an erroneous concept of the court system of this State. We have one court of general jurisdiction which administers *all* of New York law, be that law of legal or equitable origin. Therefore, defendants are mistaken when they suggest that a Justice of the Supreme Court of the State of New York cannot apply a particular principle of New York law to a case before him for decision where that principle is properly applicable to the facts as determined. The court in Dunkel v. McDonald (272 App.Div. 267, 70 N.Y.S.2d 653, affd. on other issues, 298 N.Y. 586, 81 N.E.2d 323), which the Appellate Division overruled in reaching its conclusion in this case, mistook the issue in stating that "The court has no power in an action in equity to award exemplary or punitive damages.... The function of a court of equity goes no further than to award as incidental to other relief, or in lieu thereof, compensatory damages; it may not assess exemplary damages." This, as we have said, presupposes a court intrinsically limited to granting remedies solely equitable in historical origin. There is no such court in this State.

No amount of authority in other States should persuade us that Judge Cardozo was wrong when he said in Susquehanna S.S. Co. v. Andersen & Co. (239 N.Y. 285, 146 N.E. 381): "The whole body of principles, whether of law or of equity, bearing on the case, becomes the reservoir to be drawn upon by the court in enlightening its judgment". Maitland expressed the same view when he predicted that "The day will come when lawyers will cease to inquire whether a given rule be a rule of equity or a rule of common law; suffice it that it is a well-established rule administered by the High Court of Justice." (Maitland, Equity [1909], p. 20.) Needless to say, we have accepted Maitland's and Judge Cardozo's understanding of the consequences of the merger.

Of course, we are obliged to preserve inviolate "Trial by jury in all cases in which it has heretofore been guaranteed by constitutional provision" (N.Y.Const., art. I, § 2). It is to this sole remaining jurisdictional distinction between law and equity that we now turn.

Assuming that defendants had a constitutional right to a jury trial of the issues of fact supporting the award of exemplary damages (an assumption which is not free from uncertainty), it is clear that the failure to move to separately state and number the causes of action or to demand a jury trial constituted a waiver of any such right.

This waiver is unaffected by the amendment, granted at the close of plaintiff's case, conforming the pleadings to the proof by adding allegations of malice and adding to the prayer for relief the words "or the actual damages suffered by plaintiff plus adequate exemplary damages." As the Trial Judge observed, these amendments added little to the meaning of the existing allegations which stated the facts and the purpose for which they were designed. Since the complaint originally requested "treble ... damage", the additional request for "adequate exemplary damages" added nothing that was not there before. Accordingly, the only limitation on the court's power to award whatever relief the law calls for—the right to a jury trial on legal issues—is not present here.

The propriety of exemplary damages as a matter of substantive law is not contested by defendants if the finding of malice was proper. Defendants' only contention in this regard is that there was no malice. This affirmed finding of fact is amply supported by the record. The trespasses in the nighttime, the barring of the doors, all done while workmen were redecorating the premises during the daytime, render the denials of malice incredible.

The cross appeal contests the reduction of the amount of damages, both compensatory and exemplary. The Appellate Division's reduction in amount of exemplary damages to twice the amount of actual damages so as to match the statutory (Real Property Law, Consol.Laws, c. 50, § 535) amount is well within the discretion of that court.

The judgment should, therefore, be affirmed, without costs.

NOTES

1.   Hedworth v. Chapman, 135 Ind.App. 129, 192 N.E.2d 649 (1963) began as an action for ejectment. A cross-complaint was filed seeking reformation of a real estate contract and damages, including exemplary damages. In holding that, upon establishment of fraud entitling cross-complainants to reformation, an award of punitive damages was discretionary, the court said that "a court of equity may grant exemplary damages in a proper case and in doing so it is merely affording complete relief after it once has acquired jurisdiction."

2.   In Superior Construction Co. v. Elmo, 204 Md. 1, 104 A.2d 581 (1954), the court reversed an award of punitive damages which was made in conjunction with a decree enjoining a continuing trespass. According to the appellate court, the Elmos had waived any claim to punitive damages by bringing their case in equity. Moreover, the court continued, it would be inappropriate for equity courts to award "clean-up" damages without statutory authorization because "equity will permit only what is just and right with no element of vengeance."

PART V

REMEDIES IN CONTEXT

CHAPTER 17

REMEDIES AND PUBLIC LAW

A. IMPLIED CAUSES OF ACTION

1. VIOLATION OF A STATUTE

Thompson v. Thompson

Supreme Court of the United States, 1988.
484 U.S. 174, 108 S.Ct. 513, 98 L.Ed.2d 512.

■ JUSTICE MARSHALL delivered the opinion of the Court.

We granted certiorari in this case to determine whether the Parental Kidnaping Prevention Act of 1980, 28 U.S.C. § 1738A, furnishes an implied cause of action in federal court to determine which of two conflicting state custody decisions is valid.

I

The Parental Kidnaping Prevention Act (PKPA or Act) imposes a duty on the States to enforce a child custody determination entered by a court of a sister State if the determination is consistent with the provisions of the Act. In order for a state court's custody decree to be consistent with the provisions of the Act, the State must have jurisdiction under its own local law and one of five conditions set out in § 1738A(c)(2) must be met. Briefly put, these conditions authorize the state court to enter a custody decree if the child's home is or recently has been in the State, if the child has no home State and it would be in the child's best interest for the State to assume jurisdiction, or if the child is present in the State and has been abandoned or abused. Once a State exercises jurisdiction consistently with the provisions of the Act, no other State may exercise concurrent jurisdiction over the custody dispute, even if it would have been empowered to take jurisdiction in the first instance,[2] and all States must accord full faith and credit to the first State's ensuing custody decree.

. . . This case arises out of a jurisdictional stalemate that came to pass notwithstanding the strictures of the Act. In July 1978, respondent Susan Clay (then Susan Thompson) filed a petition in Los Angeles Superior Court asking the court to dissolve her marriage to petitioner David Thompson and seeking custody of the couple's infant son, Matthew. The court initially awarded the parents joint custody of Matthew, but that arrangement became infeasible when respondent decided to move from California to Louisiana to take a job. The court then entered an order providing that

---

2. The sole exception to this constraint occurs where the first State either has lost jurisdiction or has declined to exercise continuing jurisdiction.

respondent would have sole custody of Matthew once she left for Louisiana. This state of affairs was to remain in effect until the court investigator submitted a report on custody, after which the court intended to make a more studied custody determination.

Respondent and Matthew moved to Louisiana in December of 1980. Three months later, respondent filed a petition in Louisiana state court for enforcement of the California custody decree, judgment of custody, and modification of petitioner's visitation privileges. By order dated April 7, 1981, the Louisiana court granted the petition and awarded sole custody of Matthew to respondent. Two months later, however, the California court, having received and reviewed its investigator's report, entered an order awarding sole custody of Matthew to petitioner. Thus arose the current impasse.

In August 1983, petitioner brought this action in the District Court for the Central District of California. Petitioner requested an order declaring the Louisiana decree invalid and the California decree valid, and enjoining the enforcement of the Louisiana decree. Petitioner did not attempt to enforce the California decree in a Louisiana state court before he filed suit in federal court. The District Court granted respondent's motion to dismiss the complaint for lack of subject matter and personal jurisdiction. The Court of Appeals for the Ninth Circuit affirmed.... Canvassing the background, language, and legislative history of the PKPA, the Court of Appeals held that the Act does not create a private right of action in federal court to determine the validity of two conflicting custody decrees. We ... affirm.

II

In determining whether to infer a private cause of action from a federal statute, our focal point is Congress' intent in enacting the statute. As guides to discerning that intent, we have relied on the four factors set out in Cort v. Ash, see 422 U.S. 66, 95 S.Ct. 2080, 45 L.Ed.2d 26 (1975), along with other tools of statutory construction. Our focus on congressional intent does not mean that we require evidence that Members of Congress, in enacting the statute, actually had in mind the creation of a private cause of action. The implied cause of action doctrine would be a virtual dead letter were it limited to correcting drafting errors when Congress simply forgot to codify its evident intention to provide a cause of action. Rather, as an *implied* cause of action doctrine suggests, "the legislative history of a statute that does not expressly create or deny a private remedy will typically be equally silent or ambiguous on the question." We therefore have recognized that Congress' "intent may appear implicitly in the language or structure of the statute, or in the circumstances of its enactment." The intent of Congress remains the ultimate issue, however, and "unless this congressional intent can be inferred from the language of the statute, the statutory structure, or some other source, the essential predicate for implication of a private remedy simply does not exist." In this case, the essential predicate for implication of a private remedy plainly does not exist. None of the factors that have guided our inquiry in this difficult area points in favor of inferring a private cause of action. Indeed, the context, language, and legislative history of the PKPA all point sharply away from the remedy petitioner urges us to infer.

We examine initially the context of the PKPA with an eye toward determining Congress' perception of the law that it was shaping or reshaping. At the time Congress passed the PKPA, custody orders held a peculiar status under the full faith and credit doctrine, which requires each State to give effect to the judicial proceedings of other States, see U.S. Const., Art. IV, § 1; 28 U.S.C. § 1738. The anomaly traces to the fact that custody orders characteristically are subject to modification as required by the best interests of the child. As a consequence, some courts doubted whether custody orders were sufficiently "final" to trigger full faith and credit requirements, and this Court had declined expressly to settle the question. Even if custody orders were subject to full faith and credit requirements, the Full Faith and Credit Clause obliges States only to accord the same force to judgments as would be accorded by the courts of the State in which the judgment was entered. Because courts entering custody orders generally retain the power to modify them, courts in other States were no less entitled to change the terms of custody according to their own views of the child's best interest. For these reasons, a parent who lost a custody battle in one State had an incentive to kidnap the child and move to another State to relitigate the issue. This circumstance contributed to widespread jurisdictional deadlocks like this one, and more importantly, to a national epidemic of parental kidnaping. At the time the PKPA was enacted, sponsors of the Act estimated that between 25,000 and 100,000 children were kidnaped by parents who had been unable to obtain custody in a legal forum.

A number of States joined in an effort to avoid these jurisdictional conflicts by adopting the Uniform Child Custody Jurisdiction Act (UCCJA), 9 U.L.A. §§ 1–28 (1979). The UCCJA prescribed uniform standards for deciding which State could make a custody determination and obligated enacting States to enforce the determination made by the State with proper jurisdiction. The project foundered, however, because a number of States refused to enact the UCCJA while others enacted it with modifications. In the absence of uniform national standards for allocating and enforcing custody determinations, noncustodial parents still had reason to snatch their children and petition the courts of any of a number of haven States for sole custody.

The context of the PKPA therefore suggests that the principal problem Congress was seeking to remedy was the inapplicability of full faith and credit requirements to custody determinations. Statements made when the Act was introduced in Congress forcefully confirm that suggestion. The sponsors and supporters of the Act continually indicated that the purpose of the PKPA was to provide for nationwide enforcement of custody orders made in accordance with the terms of the UCCJA. . . .

The significance of Congress' full faith and credit approach to the problem of child snatching is that the Full Faith and Credit Clause, in either its constitutional or statutory incarnations, does not give rise to an implied federal cause of action. Rather, the clause "only prescribes a rule by which courts, Federal and state, are to be guided when a question arises in the progress of a pending suit as to the faith and credit to be given by the court to the public acts, records, and judicial proceedings of a State other than that in which the court is sitting." Because Congress' chief aim in enacting the PKPA was to extend the requirements of the Full Faith and Credit Clause to custody determinations, the Act is most naturally construed to furnish a rule of decision for courts to use in adjudicating custody disputes and not to create an entirely new cause of action. It thus is not compatible with the purpose and context of the legislative scheme to infer a private cause of action.

The language and placement of the statute reinforce this conclusion. The PKPA, is an addendum to the full faith and credit statute. This fact alone is strong proof that the Act is intended to have the same operative effect as the full faith and credit statute. Similarly instructive is the heading to the PKPA: "Full faith and credit given to child custody determinations." As for the language of the Act, it is addressed entirely to States and state courts. Unlike statutes that explicitly confer a right on a specified class of persons, the PKPA is a mandate directed to state courts to respect the custody decrees of sister States....

Finally, the legislative history of the PKPA provides unusually clear indication that Congress did not intend the federal courts to play the enforcement role that petitioner urges. Two passages are particularly revealing. The first of these is a colloquy between Congressmen Conyers and Fish.... This exchange suggests that Congress considered and rejected an approach to the problem that would have resulted in a "[f]ederal court litigating between two State court decrees."

The second noteworthy entry in the legislative history is a letter from then Assistant Attorney General Patricia Wald to the Chairman of the House Judiciary Committee, which was referred to extensively during the debate on the PKPA.... The letter endorsed the full faith and credit approach that eventually was codified in the PKPA. More importantly, it "strongly oppose[d] ... the creation of a federal forum for resolving custody disputes." ... That the views of the Justice Department and Congressman Conyers prevailed, and that Congress explicitly opted for a full faith and credit approach over reliance on enforcement by the federal courts, provide strong evidence against inferring a federal cause of action.

Petitioner discounts these portions of the legislative history. He argues that the cause of action that he asks us to infer arises only in cases of an actual conflict between two state custody decrees, and thus is substantially narrower than the cause of action proposed by Congressman Fish and rejected by Congress. The Fish bill would have extended federal-diversity jurisdiction to permit federal courts to enforce custody orders in the first instance, before a second State had created a conflict by refusing to do so. This cause of action admittedly is farther reaching than that which we reject today. But the considerations that prompted Congress to reject the Fish bill also militate against the more circumscribed role for the federal courts that petitioner proposes. Instructing the federal courts to play Solomon where two state courts have issued conflicting custody orders would entangle them in traditional state-law questions that they have little expertise to resolve.[4] This is a cost that Congress made clear it did not want the PKPA to carry.[5]

In sum, the context, language, and history of the PKPA together make out a conclusive case against inferring a cause of action in federal court to determine which of two conflicting state custody decrees is valid. Against this impressive evidence, petitioner relies primarily on the argument that failure to infer a cause of action would render the PKPA nugatory. We note, as a preliminary response, that ultimate review remains available in this Court for truly intractable jurisdictional deadlocks. In addition, the unspoken presumption in petitioner's argument is that the States are either unable or unwilling to enforce the provisions of the Act. This is a presumption we are not prepared, and more importantly, Congress was not prepared, to indulge. State courts faithfully administer the Full Faith and Credit Clause every day; now that Congress has extended full faith and credit requirements to child custody orders, we can think of no reason why the courts' administration of federal law in custody disputes will be any less vigilant. Should state courts prove as obstinate as petitioner predicts, Congress may choose to revisit the issue. But any more radical approach to the problem will have to await further legislative action; we "will not engraft a remedy on a statute, no matter how salutary, that Congress did not intend to provide." The judgment of the Court of Appeals is affirmed.

It is so ordered.

■ JUSTICE O'CONNOR, concurring in part and concurring in the judgment.

For the reasons expressed by Justice Scalia in Part I of his opinion in this case, I join all but the first full paragraph of Part II of the Court's opinion and judgment.

■ JUSTICE SCALIA, concurring in the judgment.

I write separately because in my view the Court is not being faithful to current doctrine in its dictum denying the necessity of an actual congressional intent to create a private right of action, and in referring to Cort v.

---

4. Petitioner argues that determining which of two conflicting custody decrees should be given effect under the PKPA would not require the federal courts to resolve the merits of custody disputes and thus would not offend the longstanding tradition of reserving domestic-relations matters to the States. Petitioner contends that the cause of action he champions would require federal courts only to analyze which of two States is given exclusive jurisdiction under a federal statute, a task for which the federal courts are well-qualified. We cannot agree with petitioner that making a jurisdictional determination under the PKPA would not involve the federal courts in substantive domestic-relations determinations. Under the Act, jurisdiction can turn on the child's "best interest" or on proof that the child has been abandoned or abused. In fact, it would seem that the jurisdictional disputes that are suffi-

ciently complicated as to have provoked conflicting state-court holdings are the most likely to require resolution of these traditional domestic-relations inquiries.

5. Moreover, petitioner's argument serves to underscore the extraordinary nature of the cause of action he urges us to infer. Petitioner essentially asks that federal district courts exercise appellate review of state-court judgments. This is an unusual cause of action for Congress to grant, either expressly or by implication. Petitioner's proposal is all the more remarkable in the present case, in which he seeks to have a California District Court enjoin enforcement of a Louisiana state-court judgment before the intermediate and supreme courts of Louisiana even have had an opportunity to review that judgment.

Ash, 422 U.S. 66, 95 S.Ct. 2080, 45 L.Ed.2d 26 (1975), as though its analysis had not been effectively overruled by our later opinions. I take the opportunity to suggest, at the same time, why in my view the law revision that the Court's dicta would undertake moves in precisely the wrong direction.

I

I agree that the Parental Kidnapping Prevention Act, 28 U.S.C. § 1738A (1982), does not create a private right of action in federal court to determine which of two conflicting child custody decrees is valid. I disagree, however, with the portion of the Court's analysis that flows from the following statement:

Our focus on congressional intent does not mean that we require evidence that members of Congress, in enacting the statute, actually had in mind the creation of a private cause of action.

I am at a loss to imagine what congressional intent to create a private right of action might mean, if it does not mean that Congress had in mind the creation of a private right of action. Our precedents, moreover, give no indication of a secret meaning, but to the contrary seem to use "intent" to mean "intent." ... We have said, to be sure, that the existence of intent may be inferred from various indicia; but that is worlds apart from today's delphic pronouncement that intent is required but need not really exist.

I also find misleading the Court's statement that, in determining the existence of a private right of action, "we have relied on the four factors set out in Cort v. Ash, ... along with other tools of statutory construction." That is not an accurate description of what we have done. It could not be plainer that we effectively overruled the Cort v. Ash analysis in Touche Ross & Co. v. Redington, 442 U.S. 560, 99 S.Ct. 2479, 61 L.Ed.2d 82 (1979) and Transamerica Mortgage Advisors, Inc. v. Lewis, 444 U.S. 11, 100 S.Ct. 242, 62 L.Ed.2d 146 (1979), converting one of its four factors (congressional intent) into *the determinative factor,* with the other three merely indicative of its presence or absence.

Finally, the Court's opinion conveys a misleading impression of current law when it proceeds to examine the "context" of the legislation for indication of intent to create a private right of action, after having found no such indication in either text or legislative history. In my view that examination is entirely superfluous, since context alone cannot suffice. We have held context to be relevant to our determination in only two cases—both of which involved statutory language that, in the judicial interpretation of related legislation prior to the subject statute's enactment, or of the same legislation prior to its reenactment, had been held to create private rights of action. Since this is not a case where such textual support exists, or even where there is any support in legislative history, the "context" of the enactment is immaterial.

Contrary to what the language of today's opinion suggests, this Court has long since abandoned its hospitable attitude towards implied rights of action. In the 23 years since Justice Clark's opinion for the court in J.I. Case Co. v. Borak, 377 U.S. 426, 84 S.Ct. 1555, 12 L.Ed.2d 423 (1964), we have *twice* narrowed the test for implying a private right, first in Cort v. Ash itself, and then again in Touche Ross & Co. v. Redington and Transamerica Mortgage Advisors, Inc. v. Lewis. The recent history of our holdings is one of repeated rejection of claims of an implied right. This has been true in nine of eleven recent private right of action cases heard by this Court, including the instant case. The Court's opinion exaggerates the difficulty of establishing an implied right when it surmises that "[t]he implied cause of action doctrine would be a virtual dead letter were it limited to correcting drafting errors when Congress simply forgot to codify its evident intention to provide a cause of action." That statement rests upon the erroneous premise that one never implies anything except when he forgets to say it expressly. It is true, however, that the congressional intent test for implying private rights of action as it has evolved since the repudiation of Cort v. Ash is much more stringent than the Court's dicta in the present case suggest.

II

I have found the Court's dicta in the present case particularly provocative of response because it is my view that, if the current state of the law were to be changed, it should be moved in precisely the opposite direction— away from our current congressional intent test to the categorical position that federal private rights of action will not be implied.

As Justice Powell observed in his dissent in *Cannon;*

Under Art. III, Congress alone has the responsibility for determining the jurisdiction of the lower federal courts. As the Legislative Branch, Congress also should determine when private parties are to be given causes of action under legislation it adopts. As countless statutes demonstrate, including Titles of the Civil Rights Act of 1964, Congress recognizes that the creation of private actions is a legislative function and frequently exercises it. When Congress chooses not to provide a private civil remedy, federal courts should not assume the legislative role of creating such a remedy and thereby enlarge their jurisdiction.

It is, to be sure, not beyond imagination that in a particular case Congress may intend to create a private right of action, but choose to do so by implication. One must wonder, however, whether the good produced by a judicial rule that accommodates this remote possibility is outweighed by its adverse effects. An enactment by implication cannot realistically be regarded as the product of the difficult lawmaking process our Constitution has prescribed. Committee reports, floor speeches, and even colloquies between congressmen are frail substitute for bicameral vote upon the text of a law and its presentment to the President. It is at best dangerous to assume that all the necessary participants in the law-enactment process are acting upon the same unexpressed assumptions. And likewise dangerous to assume that, even with the utmost self-discipline, judges can prevent the implications they see from mirroring the policies they favor.

I suppose all this could be said, to a greater or lesser degree, of *all* implications that courts derive from statutory language, which are assuredly numerous as the stars. But as the likelihood that Congress would leave the matter to implication decreases, so does the justification for bearing the risk of distorting the constitutional process. A legislative act so significant, and so separable from the remainder of the statute, as the creation of a private right of action seems to me so implausibly left to implication that the risk should not be endured.

If we were to announce a flat rule that private rights of action will not be implied in statutes hereafter enacted, the risk that that course would occasionally frustrate genuine legislative intent would decrease from its current level of minimal to virtually zero. It would then be true that the opportunity for frustration of intent "would be a virtual dead letter[,] ... limited to ... drafting errors when Congress simply forgot to codify its ... intention to provide a cause of action." I believe, moreover, that Congress would welcome the certainty that such a rule would produce. Surely conscientious legislators cannot relish the current situation, in which the existence or nonexistence of a private right of action depends upon which of the opposing legislative forces may have guessed right as to the implications the statute will be found to contain.

If a change is to be made, we should get out of the business of implied private rights of action altogether.

NOTES

1.   Borak claimed that the management of J.I. Case Co., in which he owned stock, violated Section 14(a) of the Securities Exchange Act of 1934 by using deceptive proxy statements to get shareholder approval of a merger. Although the Act makes such conduct unlawful and gives federal courts exclusive jurisdiction over suits brought to enforce the Act, it does not say that stockholders may sue for damages or the rescission of mergers resulting from violations of Section 14(a). Nonetheless, the Supreme Court unanimously decided that Borak could do so. J.I. Case Co. v. Borak, 377 U.S. 426, 84 S.Ct. 1555, 12 L.Ed.2d 423 (1964). The Court deduced that investor protection was one of the primary aims of Section 14(a). Because the Securities and Exchange Commission cannot check the accuracy of every proxy statement, the Court deemed "[p]rivate enforcement of the proxy rules ... a necessary supplement to Commission action" if this goal is to be achieved. "We, therefore, believe," the Court concluded, "that under the circumstances here it is the duty of the courts to be alert to provide such remedies as are necessary to make effective the congressional purpose."

2.   A federal law makes it a crime for a corporation to make "a contribution or expenditure in connection with any election at which Presidential and Vice Presidential electors ... are to be voted for." Claiming that the chairman of the board of a company in which he owned stock had violated this law, Ash brought a suit in federal court seeking damages under the statute. The Supreme Court unanimously ruled that Ash had not stated a cause of action. Cort v. Ash, 422 U.S. 66, 95 S.Ct. 2080, 45 L.Ed.2d 26 (1975). According to the Court, which spoke through Justice Brennan, Ash did not satisfy any of the relevant criteria for implying a cause of action:

In determining whether a private remedy is implicit in a statute not expressly providing one, several factors are relevant. First, is the plaintiff "one of the class for whose *especial* benefit the statute was enacted"—that is, does the statute create a federal right in favor of the plaintiff? Second, is there any indication of legislative intent, explicit or implicit, either to create such a remedy or to deny one? Third, is it consistent with the underlying purposes of the legislative scheme to imply such a remedy for the plaintiff? And finally, is the cause of action one traditionally relegated to state law, in an area basically the concern of the States, so that it would be inappropriate to infer a cause of action based solely on federal law?

3. Section 17(a) of the Securities Exchange Act of 1934 requires securities brokers and dealers to keep records and file reports as directed by the Securities and Exchange Commission. Touche Ross & Co. v. Redington, 442 U.S. 560, 99 S.Ct. 2479, 61 L.Ed.2d 82 (1979), presented the question whether the customers of a brokerage firm have an implied cause of action for damages under this statute against an accountant which improperly audited the firm's reports. A divided Court rejected their claim. Justice Rehnquist, writing for the majority, emphasized that "our task is limited solely to determining whether Congress intended to create the private right of action asserted by" the plaintiffs. While he acknowledged that *Cort* had identified four factors as "relevant" to the analysis of an "implied right of action" question, Justice Rehnquist denied that "each of these factors is entitled to equal weight." "Here," he continued,

the statute by its terms grants no private rights to any identifiable class and proscribes no conduct as unlawful. And ... the legislative history of the 1934 Act simply does not speak to the issue of private remedies under § 17(a). At least in such a case as this, the inquiry ends there.

Karahalios v. National Federation of Federal Employees, Local 1263

Supreme Court of the United States, 1989.
489 U.S. 527, 109 S.Ct. 1282, 103 L.Ed.2d 539.

■ JUSTICE WHITE delivered the opinion of the Court.

The question before the Court is whether Title VII of the Civil Service Reform Act of 1978 (CSRA or Act) confers on federal employees a private cause of action against a breach by a union representing federal employees of its statutory duty of fair representation. Because we decide that Congress vested exclusive enforcement authority over this duty in the Federal Labor Relations Authority (FLRA), and its General Counsel, we agree with the Court of Appeals that no private cause of action exists. Hence we affirm.

Petitioner, Efthimios Karahalios, is a Greek language instructor for respondent, the Defense Language Institute/Foreign Language Center, Presidio of Monterey, California (the Institute). Karahalios was not a union member but was within a bargaining unit of professional employees for which respondent, the National Federation of Federal Employees, Local 1263 (Union), was the exclusive bargaining agent. In 1976, the Institute reopened its "course developer" position, for which opening Karahalios applied. Previously, the position had been occupied by one Simon Kuntelos, who had been demoted to instructor in 1971, when the Institute first abolished the course developer position. Because Kuntelos declined to seek the reopened job through the competitive application process, Karahalios won the position after scoring 81 on the required examination.

Kuntelos filed a grievance, asserting that the Institute's job award to Karahalios infringed the collective-bargaining agreement, and that Kuntelos should have been assigned the position without a competitive application process. The Union agreed to arbitrate on behalf of Kuntelos (a Union board member), and successfully argued that the position be declared vacant for refilling. Because promotion selection procedures had altered, Kuntelos was permitted considerably more time on the examination. He scored 83, and in May 1978, the Institute reassigned the course developer opening to Kuntelos and demoted Karahalios to instructorship status.

The Institute denied Karahalios' direct protest against the substitution; likewise, the Union refused to prosecute his grievances because of a perceived conflict of interest with its previous Kuntelos advocacy. Karahalios filed unfair labor practice charges with the FLRA challenging both adverse decisions: He alleged first, that the Institute violated its collective-bargaining agreement; and second, that the Union breached its duty of fair representation. The General Counsel of FLRA upheld Karahalios' second charge, and ordered that a complaint be issued against the Union. The Union and FLRA's Regional Director, however, entered into a settlement whereby the Union posted notice guaranteeing representation to all employees seeking a single position. The General Counsel rejected Karahalios' contention on appeal that the settlement provided him no relief.

Karahalios then filed a damages suit in the District Court, restating his charges against the Institute and the Union. The District Court ... dismissed on jurisdictional grounds Karahalios' claim against the Institute, but declared judicially cognizable his unfair labor practice charge against the Union. Specifically, the District Court held that 28 U.S.C. § 1331 supports jurisdiction because CSRA's grant of exclusive union representation impliedly supplies to federal employees a private right of action to safeguard their right to fair representation. After trial, the District Court ruled that the Union's actions—notably its decisions to arbitrate for Kuntelos without consulting, or even notifying, Karahalios, and, subsequently, to refuse to represent Karahalios—breached its duty of fair representation owed to him. The court confined damages to attorney's fees, however, explaining that both applicants were too similarly matched to allow judicial distinction.

The Court of Appeals reversed, stating that CSRA's statutory scheme, which creates both an express duty of fair representation and a remedy in the FLRA for infringement of this duty, precludes implication of a parallel right to sue in federal courts. We granted Karahalios' petition for certiorari.

Prior to 1978, labor relations in the federal sector were governed by a 1962 Executive Order administered by a Federal Labor Relations Counsel whose decisions were not subject to judicial review. Since 1978, Title VII of the CSRA has been the controlling authority. Of particular relevance here, CSRA's § 7114(a)(1) provides that a labor organization that has been accorded the exclusive right of representing employees in a designated unit "is responsible for representing the interests of all employees in the unit it represents without discrimination and without regard to labor organization membership." This provision is "virtually identical" to that found in the Executive Order and is the source of the collective-bargaining agent's duty of fair representation. This duty also parallels the fair representation obligation of a union in the private sector that has been found implicit in the National Labor Relations Act (NLRA) and the Railway Labor Act (RLA).

Title VII also makes it clear that a breach of the duty of fair representation is an unfair labor practice. . . . Under § 7118, unfair labor practice complaints are adjudicated by the FLRA, which is authorized to order remedial action appropriate to carry out the purposes of Title VII, including an award of backpay against either the agency or the labor organization that has committed the unfair practice.

There is no express suggestion in Title VII that Congress intended to furnish a parallel remedy in a federal district court to enforce the duty of fair representation. The Title provides recourse to the courts in only three instances: with specified exceptions, persons aggrieved by a final FLRA order may seek review in the appropriate court of appeals, § 7123(a); the FLRA may seek judicial enforcement of its orders, § 7123(b); and temporary injunctive relief is available to the FLRA to assist it in the discharge of its duties. § 7123(d).

Petitioner nevertheless insists that a cause of action to enforce the Union's fair representation duty should be implied. Such a claim poses an issue of statutory construction: The "ultimate issue is whether Congress intended to create a private cause of action." Unless such "congressional intent can be inferred from the language of the statute, the statutory structure, or some other source, the essential predicate for implication of a private remedy simply does not exist." It is also an "elemental canon" of statutory construction that where a statute expressly provides a remedy, courts must be especially reluctant to provide additional remedies. In such cases, "[i]n the absence of strong indicia of contrary congressional intent, we are compelled to conclude that Congress provided precisely the remedies it considered appropriate."

These guideposts indicate that the Court of Appeals was quite correct in concluding that neither the language nor the structure of the Act shows any congressional intent to provide a private cause of action to enforce federal employees unions' duty of fair representation. That duty is expressly recognized in the Act, and an administrative remedy for its breach is expressly provided for before the FLRA, a body created by Congress to enforce the duties imposed on agencies and unions by Title VII, including the duty of fair representation. Nothing in the legislative history of Title VII has been called to our attention indicating that Congress contemplated direct judicial enforcement of the union's duty. Indeed, the General Counsel of the FLRA was to have exclusive and final authority to issue unfair labor practice complaints, and only those matters mentioned in § 7123 were to be judicially reviewable. All complaints of unfair labor practices were to be filed with the FLRA. Furthermore, Title VII contemplates the arbitration of unsettled grievances, but a House proposal that the duty to arbitrate could be enforced in federal court in the first instance was ultimately rejected. There exists no equivalent to § 301 of the Labor Management Relations Act, which permits judicial enforcement of private collective-bargaining contracts.

Petitioner, however, relies on another source to find the necessary congressional intent to provide him with a cause of action. Petitioner urges that Title VII was modeled after the NLRA and that the authority of the FLRA was meant to be similar to that of the National Labor Relations Board (NLRB). Because this Court found implicit in the NLRA a private cause of action against unions to enforce their fair representation duty even after the NLRB had construed the NLRA to make a breach of the duty an unfair labor practice, petitioner argues that Congress must have intended to preserve this judicial role under Title VII. Much of the argument rests on our decision in Vaca v. Sipes, 386 U.S. 171, 87 S.Ct. 903, 17 L.Ed.2d 842 (1967). There are, however, several difficulties with this argument.

In the first place, Title VII is not a carbon copy of the NLRA, nor is the authority of the FLRA the same as that of the NLRB. The NLRA, like the RLA, did not expressly make a breach of the duty of fair representation an unfair labor practice and did not expressly provide for the enforcement of such a duty by the NLRB. That duty was implied by the Court because members of bargaining units were forced to accept unions as their exclusive bargaining agents. Because employees had no administrative remedy for a breach of the duty, we recognized a judicial cause of action on behalf of the employee. This occurred both under the RLA, and also under the LMRA. Very dissimilar, Title VII of the CSRA not only expressly recognizes the fair representation duty but also provides for its administrative enforcement.

To be sure, prior to *Vaca,* the NLRB had construed §§ 7 and 8(b) of the NLRA to impose a duty of fair representation on union bargaining agents and to make its breach an unfair labor practice. See Miranda Fuel Co., 140 N.L.R.B. 181 (1962), enf. denied, NLRB v. Miranda Fuel Co., 326 F.2d 172 (C.A.2 1963). The issue in *Vaca,* some years later, was whether, in light of *Miranda Fuel Co.,* the courts still had jurisdiction to enforce the unions' duty. As we understood our inquiry, it was whether Congress, in enacting § 8(b) in 1947 had intended to oust the courts of their role enforcing the duty of fair representation implied under the NLRA. We held that the "tardy assumption" of jurisdiction by the NLRB was insufficient reason to abandon our prior cases, such as *Syres.*

In the case before us, there can be no mistaking Congress' intent to create a duty previously without statutory basis, and no mistaking the authority of the Board to enforce that duty. Also, because the courts played no role in enforcing a unions' fair representation duty under Executive Order No. 11491 § 10e and subsequent amended orders, under the pre-CSRA regulatory regime, there was not in this context any pre-existing judicial role that at least arguably Congress intended to preserve.

Moreover, in *Vaca* and the earlier cases, it was stressed that by providing for exclusive bargaining agents, the pertinent statutes deprived bargaining unit employees of their individual rights to bargain for wages, hours and working conditions. Hence it was critical that unions be required to represent all in good faith. Again, Title VII operates in a different context. As the United States as *amicus* explains, federal employment does not rest on contract in the private sector sense; nor is it clear that the deprivation a federal employee suffers from the election of a bargaining agent—if there is such a deprivation—is comparable to the private sector predicament. Moreover, the collective-bargaining mechanisms created by Title VII do not deprive employees of recourse to any of the remedies otherwise provided by statute or regulation.

We also note that *Vaca* rested in part on the fact that private collective-bargaining contracts were enforceable in the federal courts under LMRA § 301. Because unfair representation claims most often involve a claim of breach by the employer and since employers are suable under § 301, the implied fair representation cause of action allows claims against an employer and a union to be adjudicated in one action. Section 301 has no equivalent under Title VII; there is no provision in that Title for suing an agency in federal court.

We therefore discern no basis for finding congressional intent to provide petitioner with a cause of action against the union. Congress undoubtedly was aware from our cases such as Cort v. Ash, 422 U.S. 66, 95 S.Ct. 2080, 45 L.Ed.2d 26 (1975), that the Court had departed from its prior standard for resolving a claim urging that an implied statutory cause of action should be recognized, and that such issues were being resolved by a straightforward inquiry into whether Congress intended to provide a private cause of action. Had Congress intended the courts to enforce a federal employees union's duty of fair representation, we would expect to find some evidence of that intent in the statute or its legislative history. We find none. Just as in United States v. Fausto, 484 U.S. 439, 108 S.Ct. 668, 98 L.Ed.2d 830 (1988), we held that CSRA's "integrated scheme of administrative and judicial review" foreclosed an implied right to Court of Claims review, we follow a similar course here. To be sure, courts play a role in CSRA § 7116(b)(8) fair representation cases, but only sitting in review of the FLRA. To hold that the district courts must entertain such cases in the first instance would seriously undermine what we deem to be the congressional scheme, namely to leave the enforcement of union and agency duties under the Act to the General Counsel and the FLRA and to confine the courts to the role given them under the Act.

Accordingly the judgment of the Court of Appeals is

Affirmed.

Lieberman v. University of Chicago

United States Court of Appeals, Seventh Circuit, 1981.
660 F.2d 1185.

■ CAMPBELL, J. Plaintiff, Judy Lieberman, filed this lawsuit against the University of Chicago, its medical school (The Pritzker School of Medicine), the Dean of Students of the Division of Biological Sciences, and the Medical School Admissions Committee, claiming that she was denied admission to the medical school as a result of sexual discrimination in violation of Title IX of the Education Amendments of 1972, 20 U.S.C. § 1681(a). In her complaint, plaintiff sought . . . compensatory and punitive damages. Defendants' answer admits that the University of Chicago and its medical school receive federal financial assistance, but denies the allegations of discrimination.

. . . .

The defendants moved for and obtained summary judgment. The district court concluded that . . ., as a matter of law, Title IX does not provide a damage remedy. The plaintiff appeals. . . .

The issue of whether Title IX provides a damages remedy is conceded by the parties to be a question of first impression. The District Court based its decision on Cannon v. University of Chicago, 441 U.S. 677, 99 S.Ct. 1946, 60 L.Ed.2d 560 (1979), (hereafter *Cannon* I) and both sides argue that case as compelling support for their positions. In *Cannon* I, the court held that Title IX contains an implied private right of action for an individual injured by a violation of 20 U.S.C. § 1681(a), and found injunctive relief appropriate. The question whether the plaintiff was entitled to damages was not addressed.[3] The Supreme Court has stated that:

> the question whether a litigant has a "cause of action" is analytically distinct and prior to the question of what relief, if any, a litigant may be entitled to receive.[4]

Therefore, while *Cannon* I is certainly an important source of guidance for the issue before this court, we do not perceive it as dispositive of the question presented.

. . . .

Both Title IX and its legislative history are silent as to the existence of a damage remedy for sexual discrimination. However, appellant argues that it is a small step from the implied private cause of action created in *Cannon* I to an implied remedy in damages. But the decision in *Cannon* I did not significantly alter the conditions upon which the recipients accepted federal funds. The injunctive relief authorized in *Cannon* I merely permits the courts to require the institutions to comply with one of the unambiguous terms of the agreement. While the Court did expand the class of plaintiffs

---

3. The only mention of damages in *Cannon* I is a tangential reference in footnote 10, see footnote 7, infra.

4. While the Supreme Court has made it clear that the issue of an implied remedy is distinct from the issue of an implied cause of action, guidance beyond that point is conflicting. It is agreed that the analysis required is one of statutory construction, however, there is authority that where a statute expressly provides a particular remedy it is improper to imply the existence of other remedies, while

on the other hand the Court has stated that "the existence of a statutory right implies the existence of all necessary and appropriate remedies." We believe that the result in the case *sub judice* is mandated by the analysis formulated in Pennhurst State School and Hospital v. Halderman, 451 U.S. 1, 101 S.Ct. 1531, 67 L.Ed.2d 694 (1981). Therefore, we do not deem it necessary to attempt a resolution of the apparent inconsistency.

who could enforce the "contract," the remedy created did not impose any additional burdens on the recipients of the funds.[7]

. . . .

Appellant argues that the implication of a damages remedy would create an extremely effective means of enforcing § 1681. However, as noted previously, we do not perceive that remedy as entirely consistent with the legislative purpose. Furthermore, in light of the implied private cause of action for injunctive relief authorized by *Cannon* I, coupled with the provision for an award of attorneys' fees contained in 42 U.S.C. § 1988, aggrieved individuals have at least one effective means of enforcement. 20 U.S.C. § 1682 also provides means for federal administrative enforcement. Therefore, based upon the considerations discussed above, we consider it unwise to imply an additional remedy. If a damages remedy is to be created, it should be fashioned by Congress and not by the Courts, thus providing the institutions with ample notice and an opportunity to reconsider their acceptance of federal aid.

. . . .

For the above-stated reasons, the judgment of the District Court is affirmed.

[The dissenting opinion of SWYGERT, J., is omitted.]

---

2. VIOLATION OF THE CONSTITUTION

Bivens v. Six Unknown Named Agents of Federal Bureau of Narcotics

Supreme Court of the United States, 1971.
403 U.S. 388, 91 S.Ct. 1999, 29 L.Ed.2d 619.

■ MR. JUSTICE BRENNAN delivered the opinion of the Court.

The Fourth Amendment provides that:

"The right of the people to be secure in their persons, houses, papers, and effects, against unreasonable searches and seizures, shall not be violated. . . ."

In Bell v. Hood, 327 U.S. 678, 66 S.Ct. 773, 90 L.Ed. 939 (1946), we reserved the question whether violation of that command by a federal agent

---

7. The Court in *Cannon* I did refer to damages in a footnote quoting Texas & Pacific R. Co. v. Rigsby, 241 U.S. 33, 40, 36 S.Ct. 482, 484, 60 L.Ed. 874 (1916):

"A disregard of the command of the statute is a wrongful act, and where it results in damage to one of the class for whose especial benefit the statute was enacted, the right to recover the damages from the party in default is implied, ac-

cording to a doctrine of the common law . . ."

However, the legislation involved in that case, The Federal Safety Appliance Acts, was enacted pursuant to the Commerce Clause and subject to different considerations regarding the implication of a damages remedy. Therefore, we do not consider our decision herein to be inconsistent with that holding.

acting under color of his authority gives rise to a cause of action for damages consequent upon his unconstitutional conduct. Today we hold that it does.

This case has its origin in an arrest and search carried out on the morning of November 26, 1965. Petitioner's complaint alleged that on that day respondents, agents of the Federal Bureau of Narcotics acting under claim of federal authority, entered his apartment and arrested him for alleged narcotics violations. The agents manacled petitioner in front of his wife and children, and threatened to arrest the entire family. They searched the apartment from stem to stern. Thereafter, petitioner was taken to the federal courthouse in Brooklyn, where he was interrogated, booked, and subjected to a visual strip search.

On July 7, 1967, petitioner brought suit in Federal District Court. In addition to the allegations above, his complaint asserted that the arrest and search were effected without a warrant, and that unreasonable force was employed in making the arrest; fairly read, it alleges as well that the arrest was made without probable cause. Petitioner claimed to have suffered great humiliation, embarrassment, and mental suffering as a result of the agents' unlawful conduct, and sought $15,000 damages from each of them. The District Court, on respondents' motion, dismissed the complaint on the ground, *inter alia,* that it failed to state a cause of action.[2] The Court of Appeals, one judge concurring specially, affirmed on that basis. We ... reverse.

I

Respondents do not argue that petitioner should be entirely without remedy for an unconstitutional invasion of his rights by federal agents. In respondents' view, however, the rights that petitioner asserts—primarily rights of privacy—are creations of state and not of federal law. Accordingly, they argue, petitioner may obtain money damages to redress invasion of these rights only by an action in tort, under state law, in the state courts. In this scheme the Fourth Amendment would serve merely to limit the extent to which the agents could defend the state law tort suit by asserting that their actions were a valid exercise of federal power: if the agents were shown to have violated the Fourth Amendment, such a defense would be lost to them and they would stand before the state law merely as private individuals. Candidly admitting that it is the policy of the Department of Justice to remove all such suits from the state to the federal courts for decision,[4] respondents nevertheless urge that we uphold dismissal of peti-

---

2. The agents were not named in petitioner's complaint, and the District Court ordered that the complaint be served upon "those federal agents who it is indicated by the records of the United States Attorney participated in the November 25, 1965, arrest of the [petitioner]." Five agents were ultimately served.

4. ... In light of this, it is difficult to understand our Brother Blackmun's complaint that our holding today "opens the door

for another avalanche of new federal cases." In estimating the magnitude of any such "avalanche," it is worth noting that a survey of comparable actions against state officers under 42 U.S.C. § 1983 found only 53 reported cases in 17 years (1951–1967) that survived a motion to dismiss. Increasing this figure by 900% to allow for increases in rate and unreported cases, every federal district judge could expect to try one such case every 13 years.

tioner's complaint in federal court, and remit him to filing an action in the state courts in order that the case may properly be removed to the federal court for decision on the basis of state law.

We think that respondents' thesis rests upon an unduly restrictive view of the Fourth Amendment's protection against unreasonable searches and seizures by federal agents, a view that has consistently been rejected by this Court. Respondents seek to treat the relationship between a citizen and a federal agent unconstitutionally exercising his authority as no different from the relationship between two private citizens. In so doing, they ignore the fact that power, once granted, does not disappear like a magic gift when it is wrongfully used. An agent acting—albeit unconstitutionally—in the name of the United States possesses a far greater capacity for harm than an individual trespasser exercising no authority other than his own. Accordingly, as our cases make clear, the Fourth Amendment operates as a limitation upon the exercise of federal power regardless of whether the State in whose jurisdiction that power is exercised would prohibit or penalize the identical act if engaged in by a private citizen. It guarantees to citizens of the United States the absolute right to be free from unreasonable searches and seizures carried out by virtue of federal authority. And "where federally protected rights have been invaded, it has been the rule from the beginning that courts will be alert to adjust their remedies so as to grant the necessary relief."

. . . .

Third. That damages may be obtained for injuries consequent upon a violation of the Fourth Amendment by federal officials should hardly seem a surprising proposition. Historically, damages have been regarded as the ordinary remedy for an invasion of personal interests in liberty. Of course, the Fourth Amendment does not in so many words provide for its enforcement by an award of money damages for the consequences of its violation. But "it is ... well settled that where legal rights have been invaded, and a federal statute provides for a general right to sue for such invasion, federal courts may use any available remedy to make good the wrong done." The present case involves no special factors counselling hesitation in the absence of affirmative action by Congress. We are not dealing with a question of "federal fiscal policy," as in United States v. Standard Oil Co., 332 U.S. 301, 67 S.Ct. 1604, 91 L.Ed. 2067 (1947). In that case we refused to infer from the Government-soldier relationship that the United States could recover damages from one who negligently injured a soldier and thereby caused the Government to pay his medical expenses and lose his services during the course of his hospitalization. Noting that Congress was normally quite solicitous where the federal purse was involved, we pointed out that "the United States [was] the party plaintiff to the suit. And the United States has power at any time to create the liability." Nor are we asked in this case to impose liability upon a congressional employee for actions contrary to no constitutional prohibition, but merely said to be in excess of the authority delegated to him by the Congress. Finally, we cannot accept respondents' formulation of the question as whether the availability of money damages is necessary to enforce the Fourth Amendment. For we have here no explicit congressional declaration that persons injured by a federal officer's violation of the Fourth Amendment may not recover money damages from the agents, but must instead be remitted to another remedy, equally effective in the view of Congress. The question is merely whether petitioner, if he can demonstrate an injury consequent upon the violation by federal agents of his Fourth Amendment rights, is entitled to redress his injury through a particular remedial mechanism normally available in the federal courts. "The very essence of civil liberty certainly consists in the right of every individual to claim the protection of the laws, whenever he receives an injury." Having concluded that petitioner's complaint states a cause of action under the Fourth Amendment, we hold that petitioner is entitled to recover money damages for any injuries he has suffered as a result of the agents' violation of the Amendment.

II

In addition to holding that petitioner's complaint had failed to state facts making out a cause of action, the District Court ruled that in any event respondents were immune from liability by virtue of their official position. This question was not passed upon by the Court of Appeals, and accordingly we do not consider it here. The judgment of the Court of Appeals is reversed and the case is remanded for further proceedings consistent with this opinion.

So ordered.

Judgment reversed and case remanded.

■ MR. JUSTICE HARLAN, concurring in the judgment.

My initial view of this case was that the Court of Appeals was correct in dismissing the complaint, but for reasons stated in this opinion I am now persuaded to the contrary. Accordingly, I join in the judgment of reversal.

. . . .

. . . Chief Judge Lumbard's opinion [for the Court of Appeals] reasoned, in essence, that: (1) the framers of the Fourth Amendment did not appear to contemplate a "wholly new federal cause of action founded directly on the Fourth Amendment," and (2) while the federal courts had power under a general grant of jurisdiction to imply a federal remedy for the enforcement of a constitutional right, they should do so only when the absence of alternative remedies renders the constitutional command a "mere 'form of words.'" The Government takes essentially the same position here. And two members of the Court add the contention that we lack the constitutional power to accord Bivens a remedy for damages in the absence of congressional action creating "a federal cause of action for damages for an unreasonable search in violation of the Fourth Amendment."

For the reasons set forth below, I am of the opinion that federal courts do have the power to award damages for violation of "constitutionally protected interests" and I agree with the Court that a traditional judicial remedy such as damages is appropriate to the vindication of the personal interests protected by the Fourth Amendment.

I

I turn first to the contention that the constitutional power of federal courts to accord Bivens damages for his claim depends on the passage of a statute creating a "federal cause of action." Although the point is not entirely free of ambiguity, I do not understand either the Government or my dissenting Brothers to maintain that Bivens' contention that he is entitled to be free from the type of official conduct prohibited by the Fourth Amendment depends on a decision by the State in which he resides to accord him a remedy. Such a position would be incompatible with the presumed availability of federal equitable relief, if a proper showing can be made in terms of the ordinary principles governing equitable remedies. However broad a federal court's discretion concerning equitable remedies, it is absolutely clear ... that in a nondiversity suit a federal court's power to grant even equitable relief depends on the presence of a substantive right derived from federal law.

Thus the interest which Bivens claims—to be free from official conduct in contravention of the Fourth Amendment—is a federally protected interest. Therefore, the question of judicial *power* to grant Bivens damages is not a problem of the "source" of the "right"; instead, the question is whether the power to authorize damages as a judicial remedy for the vindication of a federal constitutional right is placed by the Constitution itself exclusively in Congress' hands.

II

The contention that the federal courts are powerless to accord a litigant damages for a claimed invasion of his federal constitutional rights until Congress explicitly authorizes the remedy cannot rest on the notion that the decision to grant compensatory relief involves a resolution of policy considerations not susceptible of judicial discernment. Thus, in suits for damages based on violations of federal statutes lacking any express authorization of a damage remedy, this Court has authorized such relief where, in its view, damages are necessary to effectuate the congressional policy underpinning the substantive provisions of the statute.[4]

If it is not the nature of the remedy which is thought to render a judgment as to the appropriateness of damages inherently "legislative," then it must be the nature of the legal interest offered as an occasion for invoking otherwise appropriate judicial relief. But I do not think that the

---

4. The *Borak* case is an especially clear example of the exercise of federal judicial power to accord damages as an appropriate remedy in the absence of any express statutory authorization of a federal cause of action. There we "implied"—from what can only be characterized as an "exclusively procedural provision" affording access to a federal forum—a private cause of action for damages for violation of § 14(a) of the Securities Exchange Act of 1934. We did so in an area where federal regulation has been singularly comprehensive and elaborate administrative enforcement machinery had been provided. The exercise of judicial power involved in *Borak* simply cannot be justified in terms of statutory construction; nor did the *Borak* Court purport to do so. The notion of "implying" a remedy, therefore, as applied to cases like *Borak,* can only refer to a process whereby the federal judiciary exercises a choice among *traditionally available* judicial remedies according to reasons related to the substantive social policy embodied in an act of positive law.

fact that the interest is protected by the Constitution rather than statute or common law justifies the assertion that federal courts are powerless to grant damages in the absence of explicit congressional action authorizing the remedy. Initially, I note that it would be at least anomalous to conclude that the federal judiciary—while competent to choose among the range of traditional judicial remedies to implement statutory and common-law policies, and even to generate substantive rules governing primary behavior in furtherance of broadly formulated policies articulated by statute or Constitution—is powerless to accord a damages remedy to vindicate social policies which, by virtue of their inclusion in the Constitution, are aimed predominantly at restraining the Government as an instrument of the popular will.

More importantly, the presumed availability of federal equitable relief against threatened invasions of constitutional interests appears entirely to negate the contention that the status of an interest as constitutionally protected divests federal courts of the power to grant damages absent express congressional authorization. . . .

If explicit congressional authorization is an absolute prerequisite to the power of a federal court to accord compensatory relief regardless of the necessity or appropriateness of damages as a remedy simply because of the status of a legal interest as constitutionally protected, then it seems to me that explicit congressional authorization is similarly prerequisite to the exercise of equitable remedial discretion in favor of constitutionally protected interests. Conversely, if a general grant of [federal question] jurisdiction to the federal courts by Congress is thought adequate to empower a federal court to grant equitable relief for all areas of subject-matter jurisdiction enumerated therein, then it seems to me that the same statute is sufficient to empower a federal court to grant a traditional remedy at law. Of course, the special historical traditions governing the federal equity system, might still bear on the comparative appropriateness of granting equitable relief as opposed to money damages. That possibility, however, relates, not to whether the federal courts have the power to afford one type of remedy as opposed to the other, but rather to the criteria which should govern the exercise of our power. To that question, I now pass.

III

The major thrust of the Government's position is that, where Congress has not expressly authorized a particular remedy, a federal court should exercise its power to accord a traditional form of judicial relief at the behest of a litigant, who claims a constitutionally protected interest has been invaded, only where the remedy is "essential," or "indispensable for vindicating constitutional rights." While this "essentiality" test is most clearly articulated with respect to damage remedies, apparently the Government believes the same test explains the exercise of equitable remedial powers. It is argued that historically the Court has rarely exercised the power to accord such relief in the absence of an express congressional authorization and that "[i]f Congress had thought that federal officers should be subject to a law different than state law, it would have had no difficulty in saying so, as it did with respect to state officers. . . ." [S]ee 42 U.S.C. § 1983. Although conceding that the standard of determining whether a damage remedy should be utilized to effectuate statutory policies is one of "necessity" or "appropriateness," the Government contends that questions concerning congressional discretion to modify judicial remedies relating to constitutionally protected interests warrant a more stringent constraint on the exercise of judicial power with respect to this class of legally protected interests.

These arguments for a more stringent test to govern the grant of damages in constitutional cases[7] seem to be adequately answered by the point that the judiciary has a particular responsibility to assure the vindication of constitutional interests such as those embraced by the Fourth Amendment. To be sure, "it must be remembered that legislatures are ultimate guardians of the liberties and welfare of the people in quite as great a degree as the courts." But it must also be recognized that the Bill of Rights is particularly intended to vindicate the interests of the individual in the face of the popular will as expressed in legislative majorities; at the very least, it strikes me as no more appropriate to await express congressional authorization of traditional judicial relief with regard to these legal interests than with respect to interests protected by federal statutes.

The question then, is, as I see it, whether compensatory relief is "necessary" or "appropriate" to the vindication of the interest asserted. In resolving that question, it seems to me that the range of policy considerations we may take into account is at least as broad as the range of a legislature would consider with respect to an express statutory authorization of a traditional remedy. In this regard I agree with the Court that the appropriateness of according Bivens compensatory relief does not turn simply on the deterrent effect liability will have on federal official conduct. Damages as a traditional form of compensation for invasion of a legally protected interest may be entirely appropriate even if no substantial deterrent effects on future official lawlessness might be thought to result. Bivens, after all, has invoked judicial processes claiming entitlement to compensation for injuries resulting from allegedly lawless official behavior, if those injuries are properly compensable in money damages. I do not think a court of law—vested with the power to accord a remedy—should deny him his relief simply because he cannot show that future lawless conduct will thereby be deterred.

And I think it is clear that Bivens advances a claim of the sort that, if proved, would be properly compensable in damages. The personal interests protected by the Fourth Amendment are those we attempt to capture by the notion of "privacy"; while the Court today properly points out that the type of harm which officials can inflict when they invade protected zones of an individual's life are different from the types of harm private citizens inflict on one another, the experience of judges in dealing with private trespass and false imprisonment claims supports the conclusion that courts of law are capable of making the types of judgment concerning causation

7. I express no view on the Government's suggestion that congressional authority to simply discard the remedy the Court today authorizes might be in doubt; nor do I understand the Court's opinion today to express any view on that particular question.

and magnitude of injury necessary to accord meaningful compensation for invasion of Fourth Amendment rights.[9]

On the other hand, the limitations on state remedies for violation of common-law rights by private citizens argue in favor of a federal damages remedy. The injuries inflicted by officials acting under color of law, while no less compensable in damages than those inflicted by private parties, are substantially different in kind, as the Court's opinion today discusses in detail. It seems to me entirely proper that these injuries be compensable according to uniform rules of federal law, especially in light of the very large element of federal law which must in any event control the scope of official defenses to liability. Certainly, there is very little to be gained from the standpoint of federalism by preserving different rules of liability for federal officers dependent on the State where the injury occurs.

Putting aside the desirability of leaving the problem of federal official liability to the vagaries of common-law actions, it is apparent that some form of damages is the only possible remedy for someone in Bivens' alleged position. It will be a rare case indeed in which an individual in Bivens' position will be able to obviate the harm by securing injunctive relief from any court. However desirable a direct remedy against the Government might be as a substitute for individual official liability, the sovereign still remains immune to suit. Finally, assuming Bivens' innocence of the crime charged, the "exclusionary rule" is simply irrelevant. For people in Bivens' shoes, it is damages or nothing.

The only substantial policy consideration advanced against recognition of a federal cause of action for violation of Fourth Amendment rights by federal officials is the incremental expenditure of judicial resources that will be necessitated by this class of litigation. There is, however, something ultimately self-defeating about this argument. For if, as the Government contends, damages will rarely be realized by plaintiffs in these cases because of jury hostility, the limited resources of the official concerned, etc., then I am not ready to assume that there will be a significant increase in the expenditure of judicial resources on these claims. Few responsible lawyers and plaintiffs are likely to choose the course of litigation if the statistical chances of success are truly *de minimis*. And I simply cannot agree with my Brother Black that the possibility of "frivolous" claims—if defined simply as claims with no legal merit—warrants closing the courthouse doors to people in Bivens' situation. There are other ways, short of that, of coping with frivolous lawsuits.

On the other hand, if—as I believe is the case with respect, at least, to the most flagrant abuses of official power—damages to some degree will be available when the option of litigation is chosen, then the question appears to be how Fourth Amendment interests rank on a scale of social values compared with, for example, the interests of stockholders defrauded by misleading proxies. Judicial resources, I am well aware, are increasingly scarce these days. Nonetheless, when we automatically close the courthouse

---

9. The same, of course, may not be true with respect to other types of constitutionally protected interests, and therefore the appropriateness of money damages may well vary with the nature of the personal interest asserted.

door solely on this basis, we implicitly express a value judgment on the comparative importance of classes of legally protected interests. And current limitations upon the effective functioning of the courts arising from budgetary inadequacies should not be permitted to stand in the way of the recognition of otherwise sound constitutional principles.

Of course, for a variety of reasons, the remedy may not often be sought. And the countervailing interests in efficient law enforcement of course argue for a protective zone with respect to many types of Fourth Amendment violations. But, while I express no view on the immunity defense offered in the instant case, I deem it proper to venture the thought that at the very least such a remedy would be available for the most flagrant and patently unjustified sorts of police conduct. Although litigants may not often choose to seek relief, it is important, in a civilized society, that the judicial branch of the Nation's government stand ready to afford a remedy in these circumstances. It goes without saying that I intimate no view on the merits of petitioner's underlying claim.

For these reasons, I concur in the judgment of the Court.

■ MR. CHIEF JUSTICE BURGER, dissenting.

I dissent from today's holding which judicially creates a damage remedy not provided for by the Constitution and not enacted by Congress. We would more surely preserve the important values of the doctrine of separation of powers—and perhaps get a better result—by recommending a solution to the Congress as the branch of government in which the Constitution has vested the legislative power. Legislation is the business of the Congress, and it has the facilities and competence for that task—as we do not.

. . . .

Today's holding seeks to fill one of the gaps of the suppression doctrine—at the price of impinging on the legislative and policy functions that the Constitution vests in Congress. Nevertheless, the holding serves the useful purpose of exposing the fundamental weaknesses of the suppression doctrine. Suppressing unchallenged truth has set guilty criminals free but demonstrably has neither deterred deliberate violations of the Fourth Amendment nor decreased those errors in judgment that will inevitably occur given the pressures inherent in police work having to do with serious crimes.

. . . .

The problems of both error and deliberate misconduct by law enforcement officials call for a workable remedy. Private damage actions against individual police officers concededly have not adequately met this requirement, and it would be fallacious to assume today's work of the Court in creating a remedy will really accomplish its stated objective. There is some validity to the claims that juries will not return verdicts against individual officers except in those unusual cases where the violation has been flagrant or where the error has been complete, as in the arrest of the wrong person or the search of the wrong house. . . . Jurors may well refuse to penalize a police officer at the behest of a person they believe to be a ''criminal'' and probably will not punish an officer for honest errors of judgment. In any event an actual recovery depends on finding non-exempt assets of the police officer from which a judgment can be satisfied.

I conclude, therefore, that an entirely different remedy is necessary but it is one that in my view is as much beyond judicial power as the step the Court takes today. Congress should develop an administrative or quasi-judicial remedy against the government itself to afford compensation and restitution for persons whose Fourth Amendment rights have been violated. The venerable doctrine of *respondeat superior* in our tort law provides an entirely appropriate conceptual basis for this remedy. . . .

A simple structure would suffice. For example, Congress could enact a statute along the following lines:

(a) a waiver of sovereign immunity as to the illegal acts of law enforcement officials committed in the performance of assigned duties;

(b) the creation of a cause of action for damages sustained by any person aggrieved by conduct of governmental agents in violation of the Fourth Amendment or statutes regulating official conduct;

(c) the creation of a tribunal, quasi-judicial in nature or perhaps patterned after the United States Court of Claims to adjudicate all claims under the statute;

(d) a provision that this statutory remedy is in lieu of the exclusion of evidence secured for use in criminal cases in violation of the Fourth Amendment; and

(e) a provision directing that no evidence, otherwise admissible, shall be excluded from any criminal proceeding because of violation of the Fourth Amendment.

. . . .

■ Mr. Justice Black, dissenting.

. . . If it wanted to do so, Congress could, of course, create a remedy against federal officials who violate the Fourth Amendment in the performance of their duties. But the point of this case and the fatal weakness in the Court's judgment is that neither Congress nor the State of New York has enacted legislation creating such a right of action. For us to do so is, in my judgment, an exercise of power that the Constitution does not give us.

Even if we had the legislative power to create a remedy, there are many reasons why we should decline to create a cause of action where none has existed since the formation of our Government. The courts of the United States as well as those of the States are choked with lawsuits. The number of cases on the docket of this Court have reached an unprecedented volume in recent years. A majority of these cases are brought by citizens with substantial complaints—persons who are physically or economically injured by torts or frauds or governmental infringement of their rights; persons who have been unjustly deprived of their liberty or their property; and persons who have not yet received the equal opportunity in education, employment, and pursuit of happiness that was the dream of our forefathers. Unfortunately, there have also been a growing number of frivolous lawsuits, particularly actions for damages against law enforcement officers whose conduct has been judicially sanctioned by state trial and appellate courts and in many instances even by this Court. My fellow Justices on this Court and our brethren throughout the federal judiciary know only too well the time-consuming task of conscientiously pouring over hundreds of thousands of pages of factual allegations of misconduct by police, judicial, and corrections officials. Of course, there are instances of legitimate grievances, but legislators might well desire to devote judicial resources to other problems of a more serious nature.

We sit at the top of a judicial system accused by some of nearing the point of collapse. Many criminal defendants do not receive speedy trials and neither society nor the accused are assured of justice when inordinate delays occur. Citizens must wait years to litigate their private civil suits. Substantial changes in correctional and parole systems demand the attention of the lawmakers and the judiciary. If I were a legislator I might well find these and other needs so pressing as to make me believe that the resources of lawyers and judges should be devoted to them rather than to civil damage actions against officers who generally strive to perform within constitutional bounds. There is also a real danger that such suits might deter officials from the *proper* and honest performance of their duties.

All of these considerations make imperative careful study and weighing of the arguments both for and against the creation of such a remedy under the Fourth Amendment. I would have great difficulty for myself in resolving the competing policies, goals, and priorities in the use of resources, if I thought it were my job to resolve those questions. But that is not my task. The task of evaluating the pros and cons of creating judicial remedies for particular wrongs is a matter for Congress and the legislatures of the States. Congress has not provided that any federal court can entertain a suit against a federal officer for violations of Fourth Amendment rights occurring in the performance of his duties. A strong inference can be drawn from creation of such actions against state officials that Congress does not desire to permit such suits against federal officials. Should the time come when Congress desires such lawsuits, it has before it a model of valid legislation, 42 U.S.C. § 1983, to create a damage remedy against federal officers. Cases could be cited to support the legal proposition which I assert, but it seems to me to be a matter of common understanding that the business of the judiciary is to interpret the laws and not to make them.

I dissent.

■ MR. JUSTICE BLACKMUN, dissenting.

I, too, dissent. I do so largely for the reasons expressed in Chief Judge Lumbard's thoughtful and scholarly opinion for the Court of Appeals. But I also feel that the judicial legislation, which the Court by its opinion today concededly is effectuating, opens the door for another avalanche of new federal cases.... This will tend to stultify proper law enforcement and to make the day's labor for the honest and conscientious officer even more onerous and more critical. Why the Court moves in this direction at this time of our history, I do not know. The Fourth Amendment was adopted in 1791, and in all the intervening years neither the Congress nor the Court has seen fit to take this step. I had thought that for the truly aggrieved person other quite adequate remedies have always been available. If not, it is the Congress and not this Court that should act.

NOTES

1. Alleging that Representative Otto E. Passman fired her from her job as his deputy administrative assistant because of her gender, Davis sued him for damages on the theory that his action had violated her right to equal protection under the Due Process Clause of the Fifth Amendment. The Supreme Court ruled that Davis' complaint stated a cause of action under the Fifth Amendment and that (questions of immunity aside) damages would be an appropriate remedy for a proven violation of her rights. Davis v. Passman, 442 U.S. 228, 99 S.Ct. 2264, 60 L.Ed.2d 846 (1979).

In reaching the former conclusion, the Court held the analysis of Cort v. Ash inapplicable in this context. Justice Brennan, once again writing for the majority, explained that "the question of who may enforce a *statutory* right is fundamentally different from the question of who may enforce a [constitutional] right" because the Framers intended the courts to be "the primary means through which [constitutional] rights may be enforced." Accordingly, he deemed these to be the governing principles where constitutional rights are violated:

At least in the absence of "a textually demonstrable constitutional commitment of [an] issue to a coordinate political department," we presume that justiciable constitutional rights are to be enforced through the courts. And, unless such rights are to become merely precatory, the class of those litigants who allege that their own constitutional rights have been violated, and who at the same time have no effective means other than the judiciary to enforce these rights, must be able to invoke the existing jurisdiction of the courts for the protection of their justiciable constitutional rights.

Bivens had suggested that, absent an "explicit congressional declaration that persons injured by a federal officer's violation of [constitutional rights] . . . must . . . be remitted to another remedy, equally effective in the view of Congress," a damage remedy against the wrongdoer would ordinarily be available unless "special factors counsel hesitation." Particularly in light of the fact that Passman's failure to obtain reelection meant that Davis could receive no other remedy, the Court felt damages should be available (questions of immunity aside) if Davis were to establish Passman's liability. While Congress excluded its own staff members from the scope of Title VII of the Civil Rights Act of 1964 (which bars sex-based employment discrimination), Justice Brennan stated that this did not prove Congress intended "to foreclose alternative remedies available to those not covered by the statute."

2. In Carlson v. Green, 446 U.S. 14, 100 S.Ct. 1468, 64 L.Ed.2d 15 (1980), the Court held that a cause of action for damages could be maintained against federal prison officials under the Cruel and Unusual Punishments Clause of the Eighth Amendment. Again speaking through Justice Brennan, the majority conceded that Green's claim was actionable under the Federal Tort Claims Act. However, there was no "explicit" congressional substitution of the FTCA for *Bivens* suits brought by victims of cruel and unusual punishment. In fact, the majority felt "that Congress views FTCA and *Bivens* as parallel, complementary causes of action." On

the one hand, the applicable provision of the FTCA, unlike some other parts of that Act, did not say that it was an exclusive remedy. On the other hand, the Court thought that the FTCA provided a less effective remedy than *Bivens:* because damages under the FTCA are paid by the federal government, they would lack the potential deterrent value of a *Bivens* remedy; neither punitive damages and jury trials were available under the FTCA; and a FTCA suit only lies if liability would exist under the law of "the State in which the alleged misconduct occurred."

3. For a discussion of the power of the judicial branch to create "remedies" and the "authority of Congress to enact remedies for the violation of constitutional rights" under Section 5 of the Fourteenth Amendment, see Tracy A. Thomas, *Congress' Section 5 Power and Remedial Rights*, 34 U.C. DAVIS L.REV. 673 (2001).

Schweiker v. Chilicky

Supreme Court of the United States, 1988.
487 U.S. 412, 108 S.Ct. 2460, 101 L.Ed.2d 370.

■ JUSTICE O'CONNOR delivered the opinion of the Court.

This case requires us to decide whether the improper denial of Social Security disability benefits, allegedly resulting from violations of due process by government officials who administered the Federal Social Security program, may give rise to a cause of action for money damages against those officials. We conclude that such a remedy, not having been included in the elaborate remedial scheme devised by Congress, is unavailable.

I

A

Under Title II of the Social Security Act (Act), the Federal Government provides disability benefits to individuals who have contributed to the Social Security program and who, because of a medically determinable physical or mental impairment, are unable to engage in substantial gainful work.... Title II, which is administered in conjunction with state welfare agencies, provides benefits only while an individual's statutory disability persists. In 1980, Congress noted that existing administrative procedures provided for reexamination of eligibility "only under a limited number of circumstances." Congress responded by enacting legislation requiring that most disability determinations be reviewed at least once every three years. Although the statute did not require this program for "continuing disability review" (CDR) to become effective before January 1, 1982, the Secretary of Health and Human Services initiated CDR in March 1981.

The administration of the CDR program was at first modeled on the previous procedures for reexamination of eligibility. Under these procedures, an individual whose case is selected for review bears the burden of demonstrating the continuing existence of a statutory disability. The appropriate state agency performs the initial review, and persons who are found to have become ineligible are generally provided with administrative review similar to the review provided to new claimants. Under the original CDR procedures, benefits were usually terminated after a state agency found a claimant ineligible, and were not available during administrative appeals.

Finding that benefits were too often being improperly terminated by state agencies, only to be reinstated by a federal administrative law judge (ALJ), Congress enacted temporary emergency legislation in 1983. This law provided for the continuation of benefits, pending review by an ALJ, after a state agency determined that an individual was no longer disabled. In the Social Security Disability Benefits Reform Act of 1984 (1984 Reform Act), Congress extended this provision until January 1, 1988, and provided for a number of other significant changes in the administration of CDR. In its final form, this legislation was enacted without a single opposing vote in either Chamber.

The problems to which Congress responded so emphatically were widespread. One of the cosponsors of the 1984 Reform Act, who had conducted hearings on the administration of CDR, summarized evidence from the General Accounting Office as follows:

"[T]he message perceived by the State agencies, swamped with cases, was to deny, deny, deny, and, I might add, to process cases faster and faster and faster. In the name of efficiency, we have scanned our computer terminals, rounded up the disabled workers in the country, pushed the discharge button, and let them go into a free [f]all toward economic chaos." (Sen. Cohen).

. . . The Social Security Administration itself apparently reported that about 200,000 persons were wrongfully terminated, and then reinstated, between March 1981 and April 1984. In the first year of CDR, half of those who were terminated appealed the decision, and "an amazing two-thirds of those who appealed were being reinstated." (Sen. Levin).

Congress was also made aware of the terrible effects on individual lives that CDR had produced. . . . Termination could also lead to the cut-off of Medicare benefits, so that some people were left without adequate medical care. There is little doubt that CDR led to many hardships and injuries that could never be adequately compensated.

B

Respondents are three individuals whose disability benefits under Title II were terminated pursuant to the CDR program in 1981 and 1982. Respondents Spencer Harris and Dora Adelerte appealed these determinations through the administrative process, were restored to disabled status, and were awarded full retroactive benefits. Respondent James Chilicky did not pursue these administrative remedies. Instead, he filed a new application for benefits about a year and a half after his benefits were stopped. His application was granted, and he was awarded one year's retroactive benefits; his application for the restoration of the other six months' benefits is apparently still pending. Because the terminations in these three cases occurred before the 1983 emergency legislation was enacted, respondents experienced delays of many months in receiving disability benefits to which they were entitled. All the respondents had been wholly dependent on their disability benefits, and all allege that they were unable to maintain themselves or their families in even a minimally adequate fashion after they were declared ineligible. Respondent James Chilicky was in the hospital recovering from open-heart surgery when he was informed that his heart condition was no longer disabling.

In addition to pursuing administrative remedies, respondents ... filed this lawsuit in the United States District Court for the District of Arizona. They alleged that petitioners—one Arizona and two federal officials who had policymaking roles in the administration of the CDR program—had violated respondents' due process rights. The thrust of the complaint, which named petitioners in their official and individual capacities, was that petitioners had adopted illegal policies that led to the wrongful termination of benefits by state agencies. Among the allegations were claims that petitioners improperly accelerated the starting date of the CDR program; illegally refused to acquiesce in decisions of the United States Court of Appeals for the Ninth Circuit; failed to apply uniform written standards in implementing the CDR program; failed to give effect to dispositive evidence in particular cases; and used an impermissible quota system under which state agencies were required to terminate predetermined numbers of recipients. Respondents sought injunctive and declaratory relief, and money damages for "emotional distress and for loss of food, shelter and other necessities proximately caused by [petitioners'] denial of benefits without due process."

The District Court dismissed the case on the ground that petitioners were protected by a qualified immunity. . . .

Respondents appealed, pressing only their claims for money damages against petitioners in their individual capacities. . . . The Court of Appeals ... affirm[ed] the District Court to the extent that it dismissed the claims involving acceleration of the CDR program and nonacquiescence in Ninth Circuit decisions. As to respondents' other claims, however, the Court of Appeals concluded that "[i]t cannot be determined as a matter of law that [respondents] could prove no state of facts ... that resulted in violations of their due process rights and consequent damages."[2] The case was accordingly remanded for further proceedings, including a trial if necessary.

The petition for certiorari presented one question: "Whether a *Bivens* remedy should be implied for alleged due process violations in the denial of social security disability benefits." We ... reverse.

II

A

The Constitution provides that federal courts may be given original jurisdiction over "all Cases, in Law and Equity, arising under this Constitu-

---

2. The Court of Appeals described the remaining allegations as follows:

"1. Knowing use of unpublished criteria and rules and standards contrary to the Social Security Act.

"2. Intentional disregard of dispositive favorable evidence.

"3. Purposeful selection of biased physicians and staff to review claims.

"4. Imposition of quotas.

"5. Failure to review impartially adverse decisions.

"6. Arbitrary reversal of favorable decisions.

"7. Denial of benefits based on the type of disabling impairment.

"8. Unreasonable delays in receiving hearings after termination of benefits."

tion, the Laws of the United States, and Treaties made, or which shall be made, under their Authority." Since 1875, Congress has provided the federal trial courts with general jurisdiction over such cases. The statute currently provides that the "district courts shall have original jurisdiction of all civil actions arising under the Constitution, laws, or treaties of the United States." 28 U.S.C. § 1331.

In 1971, this Court held that the victim of a Fourth Amendment violation by federal officers acting under color of their authority may bring suit for money damages against the officers in federal court. . . .

So-called "*Bivens* actions" for money damages against federal officers have subsequently been permitted under § 1331 for violations of the Due Process Clause of the Fifth Amendment and the Cruel and Unusual Punishment Clause of the Eighth Amendment. In each of these cases, as in *Bivens* itself, the Court found that there were no "special factors counselling hesitation in the absence of affirmative action by Congress," no explicit statutory prohibition against the relief sought, and no exclusive statutory alternative remedy.

Our more recent decisions have responded cautiously to suggestions that *Bivens* remedies be extended into new contexts. The absence of statutory relief for a constitutional violation, for example, does not by any means necessarily imply that courts should award money damages against the officers responsible for the violation. Thus, in Chappell v. Wallace, 462 U.S. 296, 103 S.Ct. 2362, 76 L.Ed.2d 586 (1983), we refused—unanimously—to create a *Bivens* action for enlisted military personnel who alleged that they had been injured by the unconstitutional actions of their superior officers and who had no remedy against the Government itself:

"The special nature of military life—the need for unhesitating and decisive action by military officers and equally disciplined responses by enlisted personnel—would be undermined by a judicially created remedy exposing officers to personal liability at the hands of those they are charged to command. . . .

"Also, Congress, the constitutionally authorized source of authority over the military system of justice, has not provided a damages remedy for claims by military personnel that constitutional rights have been violated by superior officers. *Any action to provide a judicial response by way of such a remedy would be plainly inconsistent with Congress' authority in this field.*

"Taken together, the unique disciplinary structure of the Military Establishment and Congress' activity in the field constitute 'special factors' which dictate that it would be inappropriate to provide enlisted military personnel a *Bivens*-type remedy against their superior officers." (emphasis added).

See also United States v. Stanley, 483 U.S. 669, 107 S.Ct. 3054, 97 L.Ed.2d 550 (1987)(disallowing *Bivens* actions by military personnel "whenever the injury arises out of activity 'incident to service' ").

Similarly, we refused—again unanimously—to create a *Bivens* remedy for a First Amendment violation "aris[ing] out of an employment relationship that is governed by comprehensive procedural and substantive provisions giving meaningful remedies against the United States." Bush v. Lucas, 462 U.S. 367, 103 S.Ct. 2404, 76 L.Ed.2d 648 (1983). In that case, a federal employee was demoted, allegedly in violation of the First Amendment, for making public statements critical of the agency for which he worked. He was reinstated through the administrative process, with retroactive seniority and full backpay, but he was not permitted to recover for any loss due to emotional distress or mental anguish, or for attorney's fees. Concluding that the administrative system created by Congress "provides meaningful remedies for employees who may have been unfairly disciplined for making critical comments about their agencies," the Court refused to create a *Bivens* action even though it assumed a First Amendment violation and acknowledged that "existing remedies do not provide complete relief for the plaintiff." The Court stressed that the case involved policy questions in an area that had received careful attention from Congress. Noting that the Legislature is far more competent than the Judiciary to carry out the necessary "balancing [of] governmental efficiency and the rights of employees," we refused to "decide whether or not it would be good policy to permit a federal employee to recover damages from a supervisor who has improperly disciplined him for exercising his First Amendment rights."

In sum, the concept of "special factors counselling hesitation in the absence of affirmative action by Congress" has proved to include an appropriate judicial deference to indications that congressional inaction has not been inadvertent. When the design of a government program suggests that Congress has provided what it considers adequate remedial mechanisms for constitutional violations that may occur in the course of its administration, we have not created additional *Bivens* remedies.

B

The administrative structure and procedures of the Social Security system, which affects virtually every American, "are of a size and extent difficult to comprehend." Millions of claims are filed every year under the Act's disability benefits programs alone, and these claims are handled under "an unusually protective [multi]-step process for the review and adjudication of disputed claims."

... The Act, however, makes no provision for remedies in money damages against officials responsible for unconstitutional conduct that leads to the wrongful denial of benefits. As respondents concede, claimants whose benefits have been fully restored through the administrative process would lack standing to invoke the Constitution under the statute's administrative review provision.

The case before us cannot reasonably be distinguished from Bush v. Lucas. Here, exactly as in *Bush,* Congress has failed to provide for "complete relief": respondents have not been given a remedy in damages for emotional distress or for other hardships suffered because of delays in their receipt of Social Security benefits. The creation of a *Bivens* remedy would obviously offer the prospect of relief for injuries that must now go unredressed. Congress, however, has not failed to provide meaningful safeguards or remedies for the rights of persons situated as respondents were. Indeed, the system for protecting their rights is, if anything, considerably more elaborate than the civil service system considered in *Bush*. The prospect of personal liability for official acts, moreover, would undoubtedly lead to new difficulties and expense in recruiting administrators for the programs Congress has established. Congressional competence at "balancing governmental efficiency and the rights of [individuals]" is no more questionable in the social welfare context than it is in the civil service context....

We agree that suffering months of delay in receiving the income on which one has depended for the very necessities of life cannot be fully remedies by the "belated restoration of back benefits." The trauma to respondents, and thousands of others like them, must surely have gone beyond what anyone of normal sensibilities would wish to see imposed on innocent disabled citizens. Nor would we care to "trivialize" the nature of the wrongs alleged in this case. Congress, however, has addressed the problems created by state agencies' wrongful termination of disability benefits. Whether or not we believe that its response was the best response, Congress is the body charged with making the inevitable compromises required in the design of a massive and complex welfare benefits program. Congress has discharged that responsibility to the extent that it affects the case before us, and we see no legal basis that would allow us to revise its decision.

Because the relief sought by respondents is unavailable as a matter of law, the case must be dismissed. The judgment of the Court of Appeals to the contrary is therefore

Reversed.

[The concurring opinion of Stevens, J., is omitted.]

■ JUSTICE BRENNAN, with whom JUSTICE MARSHALL and JUSTICE BLACKMUN join, dissenting.

Respondents ... allege, and petitioners do not dispute, that as a result of these deprivations [of disability benefits] which lasted from 7 to 19 months, they suffered immediate financial hardship, were unable to purchase food, shelter, and other necessities, and were unable to maintain themselves in even a minimally adequate fashion.

. . . .

I agree that in appropriate circumstances we should defer to a congressional decision to substitute alternative relief for a judicially created remedy. Neither the design of Title II's administrative review process, however, nor the debate surrounding its reform contain any suggestion that Congress meant to preclude recognition of a *Bivens* action for persons whose constitutional rights are violated by those charged with administering the program, or that Congress viewed this process as an adequate substitute remedy for such violations. Indeed, Congress never mentioned, let alone debated, the desirability of providing a statutory remedy for such constitutional wrongs. Because I believe legislators of "normal sensibilities" would not wish to leave such traumatic injuries unrecompensed, I find it inconceivable that Congress meant by mere silence to bar all redress for such injuries.

. . . .

II

A

In *Bivens* itself, we noted that, although courts have the authority to provide redress for constitutional violations in the form of an action for money damages, the exercise of that authority may be inappropriate where Congress has created another remedy that it regards as equally effective, or where "special factors counse[l] hesitation [even] in the absence of affirmative action by Congress." . . . The cases setting forth the "special factors" analysis upon which the Court relies, however, reveal, by way of comparison, both the inadequacy of Title II's "remedial mechanism" and the wholly inadvertent nature of Congress' failure to provide any statutory remedy for constitutional injuries inflicted during the course of previous review proceedings.

In Chappell v. Wallace, 462 U.S. 296, 103 S.Ct. 2362, 76 L.Ed.2d 586 (1983), where we declined to permit an action for damages by enlisted military personnel seeking redress from their superior officers for constitutional injuries, we noted that Congress, in the exercise of its "plenary constitutional authority over the military, has enacted statutes regulating military life, and has established a comprehensive internal system of justice to regulate military life. . . . The resulting system provides for the review and remedy of complaints and grievances such as [the equal protection claim] presented by respondents." That system not only permits aggrieved military personnel to raise constitutional challenges in administrative proceedings, it authorizes recovery of significant consequential damages, notably retroactive promotions. Similarly, in Bush v. Lucas, 462 U.S. 367, 103 S.Ct. 2404, 76 L.Ed.2d 648 (1983), we concluded that, in light of the "elaborate, comprehensive scheme" governing federal employment relations, recognition of any supplemental judicial remedy for constitutional wrongs was inappropriate. Under that scheme . . . "[c]onstitutional challenges . . . are fully cognizable" and prevailing employees are entitled not only to full backpay, but to retroactive promotions, seniority, pay raises, and accumulated leave. Indeed, Congress expressly "intended [to] put the employee 'in the same position he would have been in had the unjustified or erroneous personnel action not taken place.' "

It is true that neither the military justice system nor the federal employment relations scheme affords aggrieved parties full compensation for constitutional injuries; nevertheless, the relief provided in both is far more complete than that available under Title II's review process. Although federal employees may not recover damages for any emotional or dignitary harms they might suffer as a result of a constitutional injury, they, like their military counterparts, are entitled to redress for most economic consequential damages, including, most significantly, consequential damage to their Government careers. Here, by stark contrast, Title II recipients cannot even raise constitutional challenges to agency action in any of the four tiers of administrative review, and if they ultimately prevail on their eligibility claims in those administrative proceedings they can recover no consequential damages whatsoever. The only relief afforded persons unconstitutionally deprived of their disability benefits is retroactive payment of the very benefits they should have received all along. Such an award, of course, fails miserably to compensate disabled persons illegally stripped of the income upon which, in many cases, their very subsistence depends....

The mere fact, that Congress was aware of the prior injustices and failed to provide a form of redress for them, standing alone, is simply not a "special factor counselling hesitation" in the judicial recognition of a remedy. Inaction, we have repeatedly stated, is a notoriously poor indication of congressional intent, all the more so where Congress is legislating in the face of a massive breakdown calling for prompt and sweeping corrective measures.... I therefore think it altogether untenable to conclude, on the basis of mere legislative silence and inaction, that Congress intended an administrative scheme that does not even take cognizance of constitutional claims to displace a damages action for constitutional deprivations that might arise in the administration of the disability insurance program.

B

Our decisions in *Chappell* and *Bush* reveal yet another flaw in the "special factors" analysis the Court employs today. In both those cases, we declined to legislate in areas in which Congress enjoys a special expertise that the judiciary clearly lacks.

Ignoring the unique characteristics of the military and civil service contexts that made judicial recognition of a *Bivens* action inappropriate in those cases, the Court today observes that "[c]ongressional competence at 'balancing governmental efficiency and the rights of [individuals]' is no more questionable in the social welfare context than it is in the civil service context." This observation, however, avails the Court nothing, for in *Bush* we declined to create a *Bivens* action for aggrieved federal employees not because Congress is simply competent to legislate in the area of federal employment relations, but because Congress is far more capable of addressing the special problems that arise in those relations than are courts.... [The decision in *Bush* flowed] from our recognition that we lacked the special expertise Congress had developed in such matters, as well as the ability to evaluate the impact such a right of action would have on the civil service.

The Court's suggestion, therefore, that congressional authority over a given subject is itself a "special factor" that "counsel[s] hesitation [even] in the absence of affirmative action by Congress," is clearly mistaken. In *Davis,* we recognized a cause of action under the Fifth Amendment's Due Process Clause for a congressional employee who alleged that she had been discriminated against on the basis of her sex, even though Congress is competent to pass legislation governing the employment relations of its own Members, see 42 U.S.C. § 2000e–16(a)(excluding congressional employees from the coverage of § 717 of Title VII). Likewise, in *Carlson* we created a *Bivens* action for redress of injuries flowing from the allegedly unconstitutional conduct of federal prison officials, notwithstanding the fact that Congress had expressly (and competently) provided a statutory remedy in the Federal Tort Claims Act for injuries inflicted by such officials. In neither case was it necessary to inquire into Congress' competence over the subject matter. Rather, we permitted the claims because they arose in areas in which congressional competence is no greater than that of the courts, and in which, therefore, courts need not fear to tread even in the absence of congressional action.

The same is true here. Congress, of course, created the disability insurance program and obviously may legislate with respect to it. But unlike the military setting, where Congress' authority is plenary and entitled to considerable judicial deference, or the federal employment context, where Congress enjoys special expertise, social welfare is hardly an area in which the courts are largely incompetent to act. The disability insurance program is concededly large, but it does not involve necessarily unique relationships like those between enlisted military personnel and their superior officers, or Government workers and their federal employers. Rather, like the federal law enforcement and penal systems that gave rise to the constitutional claims in *Bivens* and *Carlson,* the constitutional issues that surface in the social welfare system turn on the relationship of the Government and those it governs—the relationship that lies at the heart of constitutional adjudication. Moreover, courts do not lack familiarity or expertise in determining what the dictates of the Due Process Clause are. In short, the social welfare context does not give rise to the types of concerns that make it an area where courts should refrain from creating a damages action even in the absence of congressional action.

. . . .

Finally, petitioners argue that the sheer size of the disability insurance program is a special factor militating against recognition of a *Bivens* action for respondents' claims. . . .

Petitioners' dire predictions are overblown in several respects. To begin with, Congress' provision for interim payments in both the 1983 emergency legislation and the 1984 Reform Act dramatically reduced the number of recipients who suffered consequential damages as a result of initial unconstitutional benefits termination. Similarly, the various other corrective measures incorporated in the 1984 legislation, which petitioners champion here as a complete remedy for past wrongs, should forestall future constitutional deprivations. Moreover, in order to prevail in any *Bivens* action, recipients such as respondents must both prove a deliberate abuse of governmental power rather than mere negligence and overcome the defense of qualified immunity. Indeed, these very requirements are designed to protect Government officials from liability for their "legitimate" actions; the prospect of liability for deliberate violations of known constitutional rights, therefore, will not dissuade well-intentioned civil servants either from accepting such employment or from carrying out the legitimate duties that employment imposes.

Petitioner's argument, however, is more fundamentally flawed. Both the federal law enforcement system involved in *Bivens* and the federal prison system involved in *Carlson* are vast undertakings, and the possibility that individuals who come in contact with these government entities will consider themselves aggrieved by the misuse of official power is at least as great as that presented by the social welfare program involved here. Yet in neither case did we even hint that such factors might legitimately counsel against recognition of a remedy for those actually injured by the abuse of such authority. Indeed, in *Bivens* itself we rejected the suggestion.... That the authority wielded by officials in this case may be used to harm an especially large number of innocent citizens, therefore, militates in *favor* of a cause of action, not against one, and petitioners' argument to the contrary perverts the entire purpose underlying our recognition of *Bivens* actions. In the modern welfare society in which we live, where many individuals such as respondents depend on government benefits for their sustenance, the Due Process Clause stands as an essential guarantee against arbitrary governmental action. The scope of any given welfare program is relevant to determining what process is due those dependent upon it, but it can never free the administrators of that program from all constitutional restraints, and should likewise not excuse those administrators from liability when they act in clear contravention of the Due Process Clause's commands.

IV

... Because I am convinced that Congress did not intend to preclude judicial recognition of a cause of action for such injuries, and because I believe there are no special factors militating against the creation of such a remedy here, I dissent.

NOTE

In Patsy v. Board of Regents, 457 U.S. 496, 102 S.Ct. 2557, 73 L.Ed.2d 172 (1982), the Court ruled that exhaustion of state administrative remedies is not a prerequisite to suit under 42 U.S.C. § 1983.

United States v. Stanley

Supreme Court of the United States, 1987.
483 U.S. 669, 107 S.Ct. 3054, 97 L.Ed.2d 550.

■ JUSTICE SCALIA delivered the opinion of the Court.

In February 1958, James B. Stanley, a master sergeant in the Army stationed at Fort Knox, Kentucky, volunteered to participate in a program ostensibly designed to test the effectiveness of protective clothing and equipment as defenses against chemical warfare. He was released from his then-current duties and went to the Army's Chemical Warfare Laboratories at the Aberdeen Proving Grounds in Maryland. Four times that month, Stanley was secretly administered doses of lysergic acid diethylamide (LSD), pursuant to an Army plan to study the effects of the drug on human subjects. According to his Second Amended Complaint (the allegations of which we accept for purposes of this decision), as a result of the LSD exposure, Stanley has suffered from hallucinations and periods of incoherence and memory loss, was impaired in his military performance, and would on occasion "awake from sleep at night and, without reason, violently beat his wife and children, later being unable to recall the entire incident." He was discharged from the Army in 1969. One year later, his marriage dissolved because of the personality changes wrought by the LSD.

On December 10, 1975, the Army sent Stanley a letter soliciting his cooperation in a study of the long-term effects of LSD on "volunteers who participated" in the 1958 tests. This was the Government's first notification to Stanley that he had been given LSD during his time in Maryland. After an administrative claim for compensation was denied by the Army, Stanley ... [sued nine named individuals, the University of Maryland Board of Regents, and others[2] for violating his constitutional rights.]

. . . .

... [The trial court denied defendants' motions to dismiss Stanley's *Bivens* claims and] certified its order for interlocutory appeal under § 1292(b), which the petitioners sought and the Court of Appeals for the Eleventh Circuit granted.

The Court of Appeals affirmed. . . .

. . . .

... In our view, the [Court of Appeals] took an unduly narrow view of the circumstances in which courts should decline to permit nonstatutory damages actions for injuries arising out of military service.

In *Bivens,* we held that a search and seizure that violates the Fourth Amendment can give rise to an action for damages against the offending federal officials even in the absence of a statute authorizing such relief. We suggested in dictum that inferring such an action directly from the Constitution might not be appropriate when there are "special factors counselling hesitation in the absence of affirmative action by Congress," or where there is an "explicit congressional declaration that persons injured by a federal officer's violation of the Fourth Amendment may not recover money damages from the agents, but must instead be remitted to another remedy, equally effective in the view of Congress." In Chappell v. Wallace, 462 U.S. 296, 103 S.Ct. 2362, 76 L.Ed.2d 586 (1983)(and in Bush v. Lucas, 462 U.S. 367, 103 S.Ct. 2404, 76 L.Ed.2d 648 (1983), decided the same day), that dictum became holding. *Chappell* reversed a determination that no "special factors" barred a constitutional damages remedy on behalf of minority servicemen who alleged that because of their race their superior officers "failed to assign them desirable duties, threatened them, gave them low performance evaluations, and imposed penalties of unusual severity." We found "factors counselling hesitation" in "[t]he need for special regulations in relation to military discipline, and the consequent need and justification for a special and exclusive system of military justice. . . ." We observed that the Constitution explicitly conferred upon Congress the power, *inter alia,* "To make Rules for the Government and Regulation of the land and naval

---

2. The named defendants are Joseph R. Bertino, M.D.; Board of Regents of the University of Maryland; H.D. Collier; Albert Dreisbach; Bernard G. Elfert; Sidney Gottlieb, M.D.; Richard Helms; Gerald Klee, M.D.; Van Sim, M.D.; Walter Weintraub, M.D.; and unknown individual federal and state agents and officers. Klee and Weintraub, who are not parties to this appeal, were employees of the University of Maryland in 1958; the rest of the individual defendants, the petitioners in this action, are alleged to have been federal employees or agents involved at some point in the drug testing program or follow-up. Stanley claims that these names first became available to him from the record in Sweet v. United States, 687 F.2d 246 (C.A.8 1982), a case raising near-identical claims.

Forces," thus showing that "the Constitution contemplated that the Legislative Branch have plenary control over rights, duties, and responsibilities in the framework of the Military Establishment...." Congress, we noted, had exercised that authority to "establis[h] a comprehensive internal system of justice to regulate military life, taking into account the special patterns that define the military structure." We concluded that "[t]aken together, the unique disciplinary structure of the Military Establishment and Congress' activity in the field constitute 'special factors' which dictate that it would be inappropriate to provide enlisted military personnel a *Bivens*-type remedy against their superior officers."

Stanley seeks to distance himself from this holding in several ways. First, he argues that the defendants in this case were not Stanley's superior military officers, and indeed may well have been civilian personnel, and that the chain-of-command concerns at the heart of *Chappell* ... are thus not implicated. Second, Stanley argues that there is no evidence that this injury was "incident to service," because we do not know the precise character of the drug testing program, the titles and roles of the various individual defendants, or Stanley's duty status when he was at the Maryland testing grounds. If that argument is sound, then even if *Feres* principles apply fully to *Bivens* actions,[2a] further proceedings are necessary to determine whether they apply to this case.

The second argument, however, is not available to Stanley here. The issue of service incidence, as that term is used in *Feres,* was decided adversely to him by the Court of Appeals in 1981, and there is no warrant for reexamining that ruling here. As for his first argument, Stanley and the lower courts may well be correct that *Chappell* implicated military chain-of-command concerns more directly than do the facts alleged here; in the posture of this case, one must assume that at least some of the defendants were not Stanley's superior officers, and that he was not acting under orders from superior officers when he was administered LSD. It is therefore true that *Chappell* is not strictly controlling, in the sense that no holding can be broader than the facts before the court. It is even true that some of the language of *Chappell,* explicitly focusing on the officer-subordinate relationship that existed in the case at hand, would not be applicable here. To give controlling weight to those facts, however, is to ignore our plain statement in *Chappell* that "[t]he 'special factors' that bear on the propriety of respondents' *Bivens* action also formed the basis of this Court's decision in *Feres v. United States,*" and that "[a]lthough this case concerns the limitations on the type of nonstatutory damages remedy recognized in *Bivens,* rather than Congress' intent in enacting the Federal Tort Claims Act, the Court's analysis in *Feres* guides our analysis in this case." Since *Feres* did not consider the officer-subordinate relationship crucial, but established instead an "incident to service" test, it is plain that our reasoning in *Chappell* does not support the distinction Stanley would rely on.

2a. [Feres v. United States, 340 U.S. 135, 71 S.Ct. 153, 95 L.Ed. 152 (1950), held that "the Government is not liable under the Federal Tort Claims Act for injuries to servicemen where the injuries arise out of or are in the course of activity incident to service."]

As we implicitly recognized in *Chappell,* there are varying levels of generality at which one may apply "special factors" analysis. Most narrowly, one might require reason to believe that in the particular case the disciplinary structure of the military would be affected—thus not even excluding *all* officer-subordinate suits, but allowing, for example, suits for officer conduct so egregious that no responsible officer would feel exposed to suit in the performance of his duties. Somewhat more broadly, one might disallow *Bivens* actions whenever an officer-subordinate relationship underlay the suit. More broadly still, one might disallow them in the officer-subordinate situation and also beyond that situation when it affirmatively appears that military discipline would be affected. (This seems to be the position urged by Stanley.) Fourth, as we think appropriate, one might disallow *Bivens* actions whenever the injury arises out of activity "incident to service." And finally, one might conceivably disallow them by servicemen entirely. Where one locates the rule along this spectrum depends upon how prophylactic one thinks the prohibition should be (i.e., how much occasional, unintended impairment of military discipline one is willing to tolerate), which in turn depends upon how harmful and inappropriate judicial intrusion upon military discipline is thought to be. This is essentially a policy judgment, and there is no scientific or analytic demonstration of the right answer. Today, no more than when we wrote *Chappell,* do we see any reason why our judgment in the *Bivens* context should be any less protective of military concerns than it has been with respect to FTCA suits, where we adopted an "incident to service" rule. In fact, if anything we might have felt more free to compromise military concerns in the latter context, since we were confronted with an explicit congressional authorization for judicial involvement that was, on its face, unqualified; whereas here we are confronted with an explicit constitutional authorization for *Congress* "[t]o make Rules for the Government and Regulation of the land and naval Forces," and rely upon inference for our own authority to allow money damages.[5] This is not to say, as Justice Brennan's dissent characterizes it, that all matters within congressional power are exempt from *Bivens.* What is distinctive here is the specificity of that technically superfluous grant of power,[6] and the insistence (evident from the number of Clauses devoted to the subject) with which the Constitution confers authority over the Army, Navy, and militia upon the political branches. All this counsels hesitation in our creation of damages remedies in this field.

The other major factor determining at which point, along the spectrum of generality, one should apply *Chappell*'s "special factors" analysis consists of the degree of disruption which each of them will in fact produce. This is an analytic rather than a policy judgment—but once again we see

---

5. This distinction also explains why the author of this opinion, who dissented in United States v. Johnson, 481 U.S. 681, 107 S.Ct. 2063, 95 L.Ed.2d 648 (1987), because he saw no justification for adopting a military affairs exception to the FTCA believes that consideration of such an exception to *Bivens* liability is appropriate. And if exception is to be made, there is, as *Chappell* recognized, no reason for it to be narrower under *Bivens* than under the FTCA.

6. Had the power to make rules for the military not been spelled out, it would in any event have been provided by the Necessary and Proper Clause—as is, for example, the power to make rules for the government and regulation of the postal service.

no reason why it should differ in the *Bivens* and the *Feres* contexts. Stanley underestimates the degree of disruption that would be caused by the rule he proposes. A test for liability that depends on the extent to which particular suits would call into question military discipline and decision-making would itself require judicial inquiry into, and hence intrusion upon, military matters. Whether a case implicates those concerns would often be problematic, raising the prospect of compelled depositions and trial testimony by military officers concerning the details of their military commands. Even putting aside the risk of erroneous judicial conclusions (which would becloud military decision-making), the mere process of arriving at correct conclusions would disrupt the military regime. The "incident to service" test, by contrast, provides a line that is relatively clear and that can be discerned with less extensive inquiry into military matters.

Contrary to the view of the Court of Appeals, it is irrelevant to a "special factors" analysis whether the laws currently on the books afford Stanley, or any other particular serviceman, an "adequate" federal remedy for his injuries. The "special facto[r]" that "counsel[s] hesitation" is not the fact that Congress has chosen to afford some manner of relief in the particular case, but the fact that congressionally uninvited intrusion into military affairs by the judiciary is inappropriate. Similarly irrelevant is the statement in *Chappell,* erroneously relied upon by Stanley and the lower courts, that we have "never held, nor do we now hold, that military personnel are barred from all redress in civilian courts for constitutional wrongs suffered in the course of military service." As the citations immediately following that statement suggest, it referred to redress designed to halt or prevent the constitutional violation rather than the award of money damages. Such suits, like the case of *Wilkes v. Dinsman,* 7 How.89, 12 L.Ed. 618 (1849), distinguished in *Chappell,* sought traditional forms of relief, and "did not ask the Court to imply a new kind of cause of action."

We therefore reaffirm the reasoning of *Chappell* that the "special factors counselling hesitation"—"the unique disciplinary structure of the Military Establishment and Congress' activity in the field,"—extend beyond the situation in which an officer-subordinate relationship exists, and require abstention in the inferring of *Bivens* actions as extensive as the exception to the FTCA established by *Feres* and United States v. Johnson. We hold that no *Bivens* remedy is available for injuries that "arise out of or are in the course of activity incident to service."

Part II of Justice Brennan's dissent argues in essence that because the refusal to entertain a *Bivens* action has the same effect as a grant of unqualified immunity, we should find "special factors" sufficient to preclude a *Bivens* action only when our immunity decisions would absolutely foreclose a money judgment against the defendant officials. The short answer to this argument is that *Chappell* made no reference to immunity principles, and *Bivens* itself explicitly distinguished the question of immunity from the question of whether the Constitution directly provides the basis for a damages action against individual officers. The analytic answer is that the availability of a damages action under the Constitution for particular *injuries* (those incurred in the course of military service) is a question logically distinct from immunity to such an action on the part of particular *defendants*. When liability is asserted under a statute, for example, no one would suggest that whether a cause of action exists should be determined by consulting the scope of common-law immunity enjoyed by actors in the area to which the statute pertains. Rather, one applies that immunity (unless the statute says otherwise) *to* whatever actions and remedies the terms of the statute are found to provide. Similarly, the *Bivens* inquiry in this case—whether a damages action for injury in the course of military service can be founded directly upon the Constitution—is analytically distinct from the question of official immunity from *Bivens* liability.

We do not understand the dissent to dispute this. Rather, the dissent argues that the answer to the former inquiry should be such that it produces a result coextensive with the answer to the latter. That is of course quite possible to achieve, since one can adjust the definition of a cause of action to produce precisely the same results as a given definition of immunity.... But what the dissent fails to produce is any *reason* for creating such an equivalency in the present case (and, presumably, in all *Bivens* actions). In the sole case it relies upon for its novel analysis, Davis v. Passman, 442 U.S. 228, 99 S.Ct. 2264, 60 L.Ed.2d 846 (1979), there was a reason. There the Constitution itself contained an applicable immunity provision—the Speech or Debate Clause, Art. I, § 6, cl. 1—which rendered Members of Congress immune from suit for their legislative activity. The Court held that the "special factors counselling hesitation" in the inference of *Bivens* actions in that area "are coextensive with the protections afforded by the Speech or Debate Clause." That is to say, the Framers addressed the special concerns in that field through an immunity provision—and had they believed further protection was necessary they would have expanded that immunity provision. It would therefore have distorted their plan to achieve the same effect as more expansive immunity by the device of denying a cause of action for injuries caused by Members of Congress where the constitutionally prescribed immunity does not apply.

Thus, Davis v. Passman would be relevant here if the Constitution contained a grant of immunity to military personnel similar to the Speech or Debate Clause. It does not, of course, and so we are compelled in the military field, as in others, to make our own assessment of whether, given the "special factors counselling hesitation," *Bivens* actions will lie. There is no more reason why court-created rules of immunity (as opposed to immunity specifically prescribed in the Constitution) should be held *a priori* to describe the limit of those concerns here than in any other field. Thus, the rule the dissent proposes is not an application but a repudiation of the "special factors" limitation upon the inference of *Bivens* actions. That limitation is quite hollow if it does nothing but duplicate pre-existing immunity from suit.

For the foregoing reasons, we ... reverse [the Court of Appeals'] judgment refusing to dismiss the *Bivens* claims against the petitioners....

    . . . .

■ JUSTICE O'CONNOR, concurring in part and dissenting in part.

... I agree with the Court that under Chappell v. Wallace, 462 U.S. 296, 103 S.Ct. 2362, 76 L.Ed.2d 586 (1983), there is generally no *Bivens* remedy available for injuries that arise out of the course of activity incident to military service. In Chappell v. Wallace, this Court unanimously held that enlisted military personnel may not maintain a suit to recover damages from a superior officer for alleged constitutional violations. The "special factors" that we found relevant to the propriety of a *Bivens* action by enlisted personnel against their military superiors "also formed the basis" of this Court's decision in Feres v. United States, 340 U.S. 135, 71 S.Ct. 153, 95 L.Ed. 152 (1950), that the Federal Tort Claims Act does not extend to injuries arising out of military service. In my view, therefore, *Chappell* and *Feres* must be read together; both cases unmistakably stand for the proposition that the special circumstances of the military mandate that civilian courts avoid entertaining a suit involving harm caused as a result of military service. Thus, no amount of negligence, recklessness or perhaps even deliberate indifference on the part of the military would justify the entertainment of a *Bivens* action involving actions incident to military service.

Nonetheless, the *Chappell* exception to the availability of a *Bivens* action applies only to "injuries that 'arise out of or are in the course of activity incident to service.'" In my view, conduct of the type alleged in this case is so far beyond the bounds of human decency that as a matter of law it simply cannot be considered a part of the military mission. The bar created by *Chappell*—a judicial exception to an implied remedy for the violation of constitutional rights—surely cannot insulate defendants from liability for deliberate and calculated exposure of otherwise healthy military personnel to medical experimentation without their consent, outside of any combat, combat training, or military exigency, and for no other reason than to gather information on the effect of lysergic acid diethylamide on human beings.

No judicially crafted rule should insulate from liability the involuntary and unknowing human experimentation alleged to have occurred in this case. Indeed, as Justice Brennan observes, the United States military played an instrumental role in the criminal prosecution of Nazi officials who experimented with human subjects during the Second World War, and the standards that the Nuremberg Military Tribunals developed to judge the behavior of the defendants stated that the "voluntary consent of the human subject is absolutely essential ... to satisfy moral, ethical and legal concepts." United States v. Brandt (The Medical Case), 2 Trials of War Criminals Before the Nuremberg Military Tribunals Under Control Council Law No. 10, p. 181 (1949). If this principle is violated the very least that society can do is to see that the victims are compensated, as best they can be, by the perpetrators. I am prepared to say that our Constitution's promise of due process of law guarantees this much. Accordingly, I would permit James Stanley's *Bivens* action to go forward, and I therefore dissent.

■ JUSTICE BRENNAN with whom JUSTICE MARSHALL joins, and with whom JUSTICE STEVENS joins as to Part III, dissenting.

In experiments designed to test the effects of lysergic acid diethylamide (LSD), the Government of the United States treated thousands of its citizens as though they were laboratory animals, dosing them with this dangerous drug without their consent. One of the victims, James B. Stanley, seeks compensation from the Government officials who injured him. The Court holds that the Constitution provides him with no remedy, solely because his injuries were inflicted while he performed his duties in the Nation's Armed Forces. If our Constitution required this result, the Court's decision, though legally necessary, would expose a tragic flaw in that document. But in reality, the Court disregards the commands of our Constitution, and bows instead to the purported requirements of a different master, "Military Discipline," declining to provide Stanley with a remedy because it finds "special factors counselling hesitation." This is abdication, not hesitation. I dissent.

I

Before addressing the legal questions presented, it is important to place the Government's conduct in historical context. The medical trials at Nuremberg in 1947 deeply impressed upon the world that experimentation with unknowing human subjects is morally and legally unacceptable. The United States Military Tribunal established the Nuremberg Code as a standard against which to judge German scientists who experimented with human subjects. Its first principle was:

> "1. *The voluntary consent of the human subject is absolutely essential.*

>   . . . .

> The duty and responsibility for ascertaining the quality of the consent rests upon *each individual* who initiates, directs or engages in the experiment. *It is a personal duty and responsibility which may not be delegated to another with impunity.*" United States v. Brandt (The Medical Case), 2 Trials of War Criminals Before the Nuremberg Military Tribunals Under Control Council Law No. 10, pp. 181–182 (1949)(emphasis added).

The United States military developed the Code, which applies to all citizens—soldiers as well as civilians.

In the 1950's, in defiance of this principle, military intelligence agencies and the Central Intelligence Agency (CIA) began surreptitiously testing chemical and biological materials, including LSD. These programs, which were "designed to determine the potential effects of chemical or biological agents when used operationally against individuals unaware that they had received a drug," included drug testing on "unwitting, nonvolunteer" Americans. S.Rep. No. 94–755, Book I, p. 385 (1976) (S.Rep.). James B. Stanley, a master sergeant in the Army, alleges that he was one of 1,000 soldiers covertly administered LSD by Army intelligence between 1955 and 1958.[4]

---

4. The intelligence community believed that it was necessary "to conceal these activities from the American public in general," because public knowledge of the "unethical and illicit activities would have serious repercussions in political and diplomatic circles and would be detrimental to the accomplishment of its mission." Id., at 394 (quoting CIA

The Army recognized the moral and legal implications of its conduct. In a 1959 Staff Study, the United States Army Intelligence Corps (USAINTC) discussed its covert administration of LSD to soldiers:

"It was always a tenet of Army Intelligence that the basic American principle of dignity and welfare of the individual will not be violated.... In intelligence, the stakes involved and the interests of national security may permit a more tolerant interpretation of moral-ethical values, but not legal limits, through necessity.... Any claim against the US Government for alleged injury due to EA 1729 [LSD] must be legally shown to have been due to the material. Proper security and appropriate operational techniques can protect the fact of employment of EA 1729."

That is, legal liability could be avoided by covering up the LSD experiments.

When the experiments were uncovered, the Senate agreed with the Army's conclusion that its experiments were of questionable legality, and issued a strong condemnation:

"[I]n the Army's tests, as with those of the CIA, individual rights were ... subordinated to national security considerations; informed consent and follow-up examinations of subjects were neglected in efforts to maintain the secrecy of the tests. Finally, the command and control problems which were apparent in the CIA's programs are paralleled by a lack of clear authorization and supervision in the Army's programs."

Having invoked national security to conceal its actions, the Government now argues that the preservation of military discipline requires that Government officials remain free to violate the constitutional rights of soldiers without fear of money damages. What this case and others like it demonstrate, however, is that government officials (military or civilian) must not be left with such freedom. See, e.g., Jaffee v. United States, 663 F.2d 1226 (C.A.3 1981)(en banc)(exposure of soldiers to nuclear radiation during atomic weapons testing); Schnurman v. United States, 490 F.Supp. 429 (E.D.Va.1980)(exposure of unknowing soldier to mustard gas); Thornwell v. United States, 471 F.Supp. 344 (D.D.C.1979)(soldiers used to test the effects of LSD without their knowledge); cf. Barrett v. United States, 660 F.Supp. 1291 (S.D.N.Y.1987)(death of mental hospital patient used as the unconsenting subject of an Army experiment to test mescaline derivative).[6]

Inspector General's Survey of the Technical Services Division, p. 217 (1957)).

6. ....

Between 1945 and 1963, an estimated 250,000 military personnel were exposed to large doses of radiation while engaged in maneuvers designed to determine the effectiveness of combat troops in nuclear battlefield conditions. Soldiers were typically positioned one to three miles from nuclear detonation. They were issued no protective clothing (although Atomic Energy Commission personnel were) and were not warned as to the possible dangers of radiation. They were instructed to cover their eyes at detonation; "soldiers with their eyes shut could see the bones in their forearms at the moment of the explosion." Schwartz, Making Intramilitary Tort Law More Civil: A Proposed Reform of the *Feres* Doctrine, 95 Yale L.J. 992, 994, n. 16 (1986)(discussing first-hand accounts in T.

II

Serious violations of the constitutional rights of soldiers, must be exposed and punished. Of course, experimentation with unconsenting soldiers, like any constitutional violation, may be enjoined *if* and when discovered. An injunction, however, comes too late for those already injured; for these victims, "it is damages or nothing." The solution for Stanley and other soldiers, as for any citizen, lies in a *Bivens* action—an action for damages brought directly under the Constitution for the violation of constitutional rights by federal officials. But the Court today holds that no *Bivens* remedy is available for service-connected injuries, because "special factors counse[l] hesitation." The practical result of this decision is absolute immunity from liability for money damages for all federal officials who intentionally violate the constitutional rights of those serving in the military.

First, I will demonstrate that the Court has reached this result only by ignoring governing precedent. The Court confers absolute immunity from money damages on federal officials (military and civilian alike) without consideration of longstanding case law establishing the general rule that such officials *are* liable for damages caused by their intentional violations of well-established constitutional rights. If applied here, that rule would require a different result. Then I will show that the Court denies Stanley's *Bivens* action solely on the basis of an unwarranted extension of the narrow exception to this rule created in Chappell v. Wallace, 462 U.S. 296, 103 S.Ct. 2362, 76 L.Ed.2d 586 (1983). The Court's reading of *Chappell* tears it from its analytical moorings, ignores the considerations decisive in our immunity cases, and leads to an unjust and illogical result.

A

. . . .

As the Court notes, I do not dispute that the question whether a *Bivens* action exists is "analytically distinct from the question of official immunity from *Bivens* liability." I contend only that the "special factors" analysis of *Bivens* and the functional analysis of immunity are based on identical judicial concerns which, when correctly applied, should not and do not (as either a logical or practical matter) produce different outcomes. . . . And *Davis* cannot be characterized, as the Court asserts, as a *unique* case in which the "special factors" of *Bivens* were coextensive with the immunity granted.[10]

Saffer & O. Kelly, Countdown Zero 43, 75, 152 (1982)). The exposed service members have been disproportionately likely to be afflicted with inoperable cancer and leukemia, as well as a number of nonmalignant disorders.

10. The Court does not provide an example of a situation in which the *Bivens* inquiry and the immunity inquiry might reach contrary conclusions. Of course, I cannot produce "any *reason* for creating" an equivalency between the two analyses as to this particular case. Neither I nor the Court has any idea what functions were performed by the petitioner officials, so I cannot argue that the considerations militating in favor of qualified immunity here also militate in favor of permitting a cause of action.

When performing the *Bivens* analysis here, therefore, the Court should examine our cases discussing immunity for federal officials.[11]

B

The Court historically has conferred absolute immunity on officials who intentionally violate the constitutional rights of citizens only in extraordinary circumstances. Qualified immunity (that is, immunity for acts that an official did not know, or could not have known, violated clearly established constitutional law) "represents the norm."

. . . .

Even when, as here, national security is invoked, federal officials bear the burden of demonstrating that the usual rule of qualified immunity should be abrogated. . . .

This analysis of official immunity in the national security context applies equally to officials giving orders to the military. . . .

Whoever the officials in this case are (and we do not know), and whatever their functions, it is likely that under the Court's usual analysis, they, like most government officials, are not entitled to absolute immunity. The record does not reveal what offices the individual respondents held, let alone what functions they normally performed, or what functions they were performing at the time they (somehow) participated in the decision to administer LSD to Stanley (and 1,000 other soldiers). The Court has no idea whether those officials can carry "the burden of showing that public policy requires [absolute immunity]" for effective performance of those functions. Yet the Court grants them absolute immunity, so long as they intentionally inflict only service-connected injuries, doing violence to the principle that "extension of absolute immunity from damages liability to all federal executive officials would seriously erode the protection provided by basic constitutional guarantees." The case should be remanded and respondents required to demonstrate that absolute immunity was necessary to the effective performance of their functions.

C

It is well-accepted that when determining whether and what kind of immunity is required for government officials, the Court's decision is informed by the common law. My conclusion that qualified, rather than absolute, immunity is the norm for government officials, even in cases involving military matters, is buttressed by common law. . . .

---

11. The Court's use of the doctrine of Feres v. United States, 340 U.S. 135, 71 S.Ct. 153, 95 L.Ed. 152 (1950), in its analysis of soldiers' *Bivens* actions reveals the connection between the "special factors" inquiry and the absolute immunity inquiry. In *Feres,* the Court decided that, in the Federal Tort Claims Act (FTCA), Congress had not waived sovereign immunity from damages for claims arising out of negligent acts of federal officials causing service-connected injury. When, as here, the Court decides whether a *Bivens* action exists, it necessarily decides whether the policies underlying *Feres* alter the usual rule of qualified immunity for federal officials. In both cases the question is how policies underpinning *Feres* affect immunity from money damages.

III

A

In *Chappell* the Court created a narrow exception to the usual rule of qualified immunity for federal officials. Repeatedly referring to the " 'peculiar and special relationship of the soldier to his superiors,' " and to the need for "immediate compliance with military procedures and orders," the Court held that "enlisted military personnel may not maintain a suit to recover damages from a superior officer for alleged constitutional violations." Although the Court concedes this central focus of *Chappell,* it gives short shrift to the obvious and important distinction between *Chappell* and the present case, namely that the defendants are not alleged to be Stanley's superior officers. Instead the Court seizes upon the statement in *Chappell* that our analysis in that case was guided by the concerns underlying the *Feres* doctrine, and dramatically expands the carefully limited holding in *Chappell,* extending its reasoning beyond logic and its meaning beyond recognition.

. . . .

. . . [The Court's] argument has a number of flaws. First, in *Chappell* we said with good reason that our analysis would be "guided," not governed, by concerns underlying *Feres.* The *Bivens* context differs significantly from the FTCA context; *Bivens* involves not negligent acts, but intentional constitutional violations that must be deterred and punished. Because *Chappell* involved the relationship at the heart of the *Feres* doctrine—the relationship between soldier and superior—the Court found *Feres* considerations relevant, and provided direct military superiors with absolute immunity from damages actions filed by their subordinates. Here, however, the defendants are federal officials who perform *unknown* functions and bear an *unknown* relationship to Stanley. . . .

Second, two of the three *Feres* rationales that decided *Johnson,* are entirely inapplicable here.[23] Thus, the Court relies solely upon the third *Feres* rationale—a solicitude for military discipline. The *Feres'* concern for military discipline itself has three components. The first, the concern for the instinctive obedience of soldiers to orders, is of central importance in the *Feres* doctrine.[24] That rationale profoundly and exclusively concerned the Court in *Chappell* which involved the relationship between a superior

23. First, in *Feres* the Court feared that allowing FTCA recovery, which varies from State to State, would impinge upon the military's need for uniformity. In contrast, *Bivens* actions are governed by uniform federal law. Second, the "swift," "efficient," and "generous statutory disability and death benefits" of the Veterans Benefits Act constitute "an independent reason why the *Feres* doctrine bars suit for service-related injuries." But the VBA fails to address the violation of constitutional rights unaccompanied by personal injury that is not defined as disabling. . . .

24. In *Johnson,* when the Court extended the application of *Feres* to preclude suits for service-connected injuries against civilian officials, the Court did not refer to, or rely upon, *Feres'* concern with obedience to orders. Of course, this aspect of military discipline would not be implicated in *Johnson,* or in any cases involving tortious conduct by a civilian official. But in *Johnson,* two of the three major rationales underlying *Feres*—the concern for uniformity and the congressional provision of thoroughgoing compensation—were relevant. Neither of these rationales applies here.

officer and those in his or her command.[25] This concern for instinctive obedience is not at all implicated where a soldier sues civilian officials.

As for the other components of the concern for military discipline, their application is entirely different in the *Bivens* context. The Court fears that military affairs might be disrupted by factual inquiries necessitated by *Bivens* actions. The judiciary is already involved, however, in cases that implicate military judgments and decisions, as when a soldier sues for nonservice-connected injury, when a soldier sues civilian contractors with the Government for service-connected injury, and when a civilian is injured and sues a civilian contractor with the military or a military tortfeasor. Although the desire to *limit* the number of such cases might justify the decision not to allow soldiers' FTCA suits arising from *negligent* conduct by civilian government employees, it is insufficient to preclude suits against civilians for *intentional* violations of constitutional rights. Unless the command relationship (or some other consideration requiring absolute immunity) is involved, these violations should receive moral condemnation and legal redress without limitation to that accorded negligent acts.

Finally, the Court fears that the vigor of military decisionmaking will be sapped if damages can be awarded for an incorrect (albeit intentionally incorrect) choice. Of course, this case involves civilian decisionmakers, but because the injury was service-connected, we must assume that these civilian judgments are somehow intertwined with conduct of the military mission. The significant difference between the *Feres* (FTCA) and *Bivens* (constitutional claim) contexts, however, is that, in the latter, the vigorous-decisionmaking concern has already been taken into account in our determination that qualified immunity is the general rule for federal officials, who *should* be required "on occasion ... to pause to consider whether a proposed course of action can be squared with the Constitution." The special requirements of command that concerned us in *Chappell* are not implicated in this case, and neither the Government nor the Court offer any plausible reason to extend absolute immunity to these civilian officials for their intentional constitutional violations.

. . . .

B

The second "special factor" in *Chappell*—congressional activity "provid[ing] for the review and remedy of complaints and grievances such as those presented by" the injured soldier—is not present here. The Veterans Benefits Act is irrelevant where, as here, the injuries alleged stem (in large part) from pain and suffering in forms not covered by the Act. The UCMJ assists only when the soldier is on active duty and the tortfeasor is another military member. Here, in contrast to the situation in *Chappell,* no intramilitary system "provides for the ... remedy" of Stanley's complaint.

Nonetheless, the Court finds Congress' activity (and inactivity) of particular significance here, because we are confronted with a constitutional authorization for Congress to " 'make Rules for the Government and

---

25. Stanley points out that he was administered LSD without his knowledge so that he could not have disobeyed any order given him....

Regulation of the land and naval Forces.' " First, the existence of a constitutional provision authorizing Congress to make intramilitary rules does not answer the question whether *civilian* federal officials are immune from damages in actions arising from service-connected injury. Second, *any time* Congress acts, it does so pursuant to either an express or implied grant of power in the Constitution. If a *Bivens* action were precluded any time Congress possessed a constitutional grant of authority to act in a given area, there would be no *Bivens*. In fact, many administrative agencies exist and function entirely at the pleasure of Congress, yet the Court has not hesitated to infer *Bivens* actions against these agencies' officials. This is so no matter how explicitly or frequently the Constitution authorizes Congress to act in a given area. Even when considering matters most clearly within Congress' constitutional authority, we have found that a *Bivens* action will lie. See Davis v. Passman, 442 U.S. 228, 99 S.Ct. 2264, 60 L.Ed.2d 846 (1979).

. . . .

Correctional Services Corporation, Petitioner, v. Malesko

Supreme Court of the United States, 2001.
534 U.S. 61, 122 S.Ct. 515, 151 L.Ed.2d 456.

REHNQUIST, C. J., delivered the opinion of the Court, in which O'CON-NOR, SCALIA, KENNEDY, and THOMAS, JJ., joined. SCALIA, J., filed a concurring opinion, in which THOMAS, J., joined, post, p. 523. STEVENS, J., filed a dissenting opinion, in which SOUTER, GINSBURG, and BREYER, JJ., joined, post, p. 524.

■ CHIEF JUSTICE REHNQUIST delivered the opinion of the Court.

We decide here whether the implied damages action first recognized in *Bivens v. Six Unknown Fed. Narcotics Agents*, 403 U.S. 388, 91 S.Ct. 1999, 29 L.Ed.2d 619 (1971), should be extended to allow recovery against a private corporation operating a halfway house under contract with the Bureau of Prisons. We decline to so extend *Bivens*.

Petitioner Correctional Services Corporation (CSC), under contract with the federal Bureau of Prisons (BOP), operates Community Corrections Centers and other facilities that house federal prisoners and detainees. Since the late 1980's, CSC has operated Le Marquis Community Correctional Center (Le Marquis), a halfway house located in New York City. Respondent John E. Malesko is a former federal inmate who, having been convicted of federal securities fraud in December 1992, was sentenced to a term of 18 months' imprisonment under the supervision of the BOP. During his imprisonment, respondent was diagnosed with a heart condition and treated with prescription medication. Respondent's condition limited his ability to engage in physical activity, such as climbing stairs.

In February 1993, the BOP transferred respondent to Le Marquis where he was to serve the remainder of his sentence. Respondent was assigned to living quarters on the fifth floor. On or about March 1, 1994, CSC instituted a policy at Le Marquis requiring inmates residing below the sixth floor to use the staircase rather than the elevator to travel from the first-floor lobby to their rooms. There is no dispute that respondent was exempted from this policy on account of his heart condition. Respondent alleges that on March 28, 1994, however, Jorge Urena, an employee of CSC, forbade him to use the elevator to reach his fifth-floor bedroom. Respondent protested that he was specially permitted elevator access, but Urena was adamant. Respondent then climbed the stairs, suffered a heart attack, and fell, injuring his left ear.

Three years after this incident occurred, respondent filed a *pro se* action against CSC and unnamed CSC employees in the United States District Court for the Southern District of New York. Two years later, now acting with counsel, respondent filed an amended complaint which named Urena as 1 of the 10 John Doe defendants. The amended complaint alleged that CSC, Urena, and unnamed defendants were "negligent in failing to obtain requisite medication for [respondent's] condition and were further negligent by refusing [respondent] the use of the elevator." App. 12. It further alleged that respondent injured his left ear and aggravated a pre-existing condition "[a]s a result of the negligence of the Defendants." *Ibid.* Respondent demanded judgment in the sum of $1 million in compensatory damages, $3 million in anticipated future damages, and punitive damages "for such sum as the Court and/or [j]ury may determine." *Id.,* at 13.

The District Court treated the amended complaint as raising claims under *Bivens v. Six Unknown Fed. Narcotics Agents, supra,* and dismissed respondent's cause of action in its entirety. App. to Pet. for Cert. 20a. Relying on our decision in *FDIC v. Meyer,* 510 U.S. 471, 114 S.Ct. 996, 127 L.Ed.2d 308 (1994), the District Court reasoned that "a *Bivens* action may only be maintained against an individual," and thus was not available against CSC, a corporate entity. App. to Pet. for Cert. 20a. With respect to Urena and the unnamed individual defendants, the complaint was dismissed on statute of limitations grounds.

The Court of Appeals for the Second Circuit affirmed in part, reversed in part, and remanded. 229 F.3d 374 (C.A.2 2000). That court affirmed dismissal of respondent's claims against individual defendants as barred by the statute of limitations. Respondent has not challenged that ruling, and the parties agree that the question whether a *Bivens* action might lie against a private individual is not presented here. With respect to CSC, the Court of Appeals remarked that Meyer expressly declined " 'to expand the category of defendants against whom Bivens-type actions may be brought to include not only federal agents, but federal agencies as well.' " 229 F.3d, at 378 (quoting *Meyer, supra,* at 484, 114 S.Ct. 996 (emphasis deleted)). But the court reasoned that private entities like CSC should be held liable under *Bivens* to "accomplish the ... important *Bivens* goal of providing a remedy for constitutional violations." 229 F.3d, at 380.

We granted certiorari ... and now reverse.[2]

2. The Courts of Appeals have divided on whether *FDIC v. Meyer,* 510 U.S. 471, 114 S.Ct. 996, 127 L.Ed.2d 308 (1994), forecloses the extension of Bivens to private entities. Compare *Hammons v. Norfolk Southern Corp.,* 156 F.3d 701, 705 (C.A.6 1998) ("Nothing in Meyer prohibits a Bivens claim against a private corporation that engages in

From this discussion, it is clear that the claim urged by respondent is fundamentally different from anything recognized in *Bivens* or subsequent cases. In 30 years of *Bivens* jurisprudence we have extended its holding only twice, to provide an otherwise nonexistent cause of action against *individual officers* alleged to have acted unconstitutionally, or to provide a cause of action for a plaintiff who lacked *any alternative remedy* for harms caused by an individual officer's unconstitutional conduct. Where such circumstances are not present, we have consistently rejected invitations to extend *Bivens*, often for reasons that foreclose its extension here.[4]

The purpose of *Bivens* is to deter individual federal officers from committing constitutional violations. *Meyer* made clear that the threat of litigation and liability will adequately deter federal officers for *Bivens* purposes no matter that they may enjoy qualified immunity, 510 U.S., at 474, 485, 114 S.Ct. 996, are indemnified by the employing agency or entity, *id.*, at 486, 114 S.Ct. 996, or are acting pursuant to an entity's policy, *id.*, at 473–474, 114 S.Ct. 996. *Meyer* also made clear that the threat of suit against an individual's employer was not the kind of deterrence contemplated by *Bivens*. See 510 U.S., at 485, 114 S.Ct. 996 ("If we were to imply a damages action directly against federal agencies ... there would be no reason for aggrieved parties to bring damages actions against individual officers. [T]he deterrent effects of the Bivens remedy would be lost"). This case is, in every meaningful sense, the same. For if a corporate defendant is available for suit, claimants will focus their collection efforts on it, and not the individual directly responsible for the alleged injury. See, *e.g., TXO Production Corp. v. Alliance Resources Corp.*, 509 U.S. 443, 464, 113 S.Ct. 2711, 125 L.Ed.2d 366 (1993) (plurality opinion) (recognizing that corporations fare much worse before juries than do individuals); *id.*, at 490–492, 113 S.Ct. 2711 (O'CONNOR, J., dissenting) (same) (citing authorities). On the logic of *Meyer*, inferring a constitutional tort remedy against a private entity like CSC is therefore foreclosed.

Harlow v. Fitzgerald

Supreme Court of the United States, 1982.
457 U.S. 800, 102 S.Ct. 2727, 73 L.Ed.2d 396.

■ JUSTICE POWELL delivered the opinion of the Court.

The issue in this case is the scope of the immunity available to the senior aides and advisers of the President of the United States in a suit for damages based upon their official acts.

federal action"), with *Kauffman v. Anglo–American School of Sofia*, 28 F.3d 1223, 1227 (C.A.D.C.1994) ("[Under] Meyer's conclusion that public federal agencies are not subject to Bivens liability, it follows that equivalent private entities should not be liable either"). We hold today that it does.

4. JUSTICE STEVENS' claim that this case does not implicate an "extension" of Bivens,

post, at 524, 527 (dissenting opinion), might come as some surprise to the Court of Appeals which twice characterized its own holding as "extending Bivens liability to reach private corporations." 229 F.3d 374, 381 (C.A.2 2000). See also ibid. ("Bivens liability should extend to private corporations").

I

In this suit for civil damages petitioners Bryce Harlow and Alexander Butterfield are alleged to have participated in a conspiracy to violate the constitutional and statutory rights of the respondent A. Ernest Fitzgerald. Respondent avers that petitioners entered the conspiracy in their capacities as senior White House aides to former President Richard M. Nixon. As the alleged conspiracy is the same as that involved in Nixon v. Fitzgerald, 457 U.S. 731, 102 S.Ct. 2690, 73 L.Ed.2d 349 (1982), the facts need not be repeated in detail.

[Fitzgerald was a management analyst for the Department of the Air Force. His 1968 testimony before a congressional subcommittee about cost-overruns and technical problems with the C–5A transport plane angered and embarrassed his superiors, including Air Force Secretary Harold Brown, whose staff prepared a memorandum outlining three ways of removing Fitzgerald from his post. One of them was a reduction in force.

Fourteen months later, Fitzgerald's job was eliminated as part of a departmental reduction in force. Although this reorganization was announced and implemented by the new Nixon administration, the congressional subcommittee was concerned that Fitzgerald had really been fired in retaliation for his earlier testimony. Hearings were held, and Fitzgerald's fate became even more of a cause célèbre.

When the White House proved unwilling to give him another job, Fitzgerald filed a complaint with the Civil Service Commission. After hearing extensive testimony, the Commission's Chief Examiner decided that Fitzgerald had been dismissed for "purely personal" reasons, in violation of civil service regulations. However, the Examiner also ruled that Fitzgerald had failed to prove that he was fired in retaliation for his congressional testimony.

After receiving the Commission's decision, Fitzgerald filed this *Bivens* suit against President Nixon and several members of his administration.]

Respondent claims that Harlow joined the conspiracy in his role as the Presidential aide principally responsible for congressional relations. At the conclusion of discovery the supporting evidence remained inferential. As evidence of Harlow's conspiratorial activity respondent relies heavily on a series of conversations in which Harlow discussed Fitzgerald's dismissal with Air Force Secretary Robert Seamans. The other evidence most supportive of Fitzgerald's claims consists of a recorded conversation in which the President later voiced a tentative recollection that Harlow was "all for canning" Fitzgerald.

Disputing Fitzgerald's contentions, Harlow argues that exhaustive discovery has adduced no direct evidence of his involvement in any wrongful activity. He avers that Secretary Seamans advised him that considerations of efficiency required Fitzgerald's removal by a reduction in force, despite anticipated adverse congressional reaction. Harlow asserts he had no reason to believe that a conspiracy existed. He contends that he took all his actions in good faith.

Petitioner Butterfield also is alleged to have entered the conspiracy not later than May 1969. Employed as Deputy Assistant to the President and

Deputy Chief of Staff to H.R. Haldeman, Butterfield circulated a White House memorandum in that month in which he claimed to have learned that Fitzgerald planned to "blow the whistle" on some "shoddy purchasing practices" by exposing these practices to public view. Fitzgerald characterizes this memorandum as evidence that Butterfield had commenced efforts to secure Fitzgerald's retaliatory dismissal. As evidence that Butterfield participated in the conspiracy to conceal his unlawful discharge and prevent his reemployment, Fitzgerald cites communications between Butterfield and Haldeman in December 1969 and January 1970. After the President had promised at a press conference to inquire into Fitzgerald's dismissal, Haldeman solicited Butterfield's recommendations. In a subsequent memorandum emphasizing the importance of "loyalty," Butterfield counseled against offering Fitzgerald another job in the administration at that time.

For his part, Butterfield denies that he was involved in any decision concerning Fitzgerald's employment status until Haldeman sought his advice in December 1969—more than a month after Fitzgerald's termination had been scheduled and announced publicly by the Air Force. Butterfield states that he never communicated his views about Fitzgerald to any official of the Defense Department. He argues generally that nearly eight years of discovery have failed to turn up any evidence that he caused injury to Fitzgerald.

Together with their codefendant Richard Nixon, petitioners Harlow and Butterfield moved for summary judgment on February 12, 1980. In denying the motion the District Court upheld the legal sufficiency of Fitzgerald's *Bivens* claim under the First Amendment and his "inferred" statutory causes of action under 5 U.S.C. § 7211 (1976 ed., Supp. IV) and 18 U.S.C. § 1505.[10] The court found that genuine issues of disputed fact remained for resolution at trial. It also ruled that petitioners were not entitled to absolute immunity.

Independently of former President Nixon, petitioners invoked the collateral order doctrine and appealed the denial of their immunity defense to the Court of Appeals for the District of Columbia Circuit. The Court of Appeals dismissed the appeal without opinion. . . .

II

As we reiterated today in Nixon v. Fitzgerald, 457 U.S. 731, 102 S.Ct. 2690, 73 L.Ed.2d 349, our decisions consistently have held that government officials are entitled to some form of immunity from suits for damages. As

---

10. The first of these statutes, 5 U.S.C. § 7211 (1976 ed., Supp.IV), provides generally that "[t]he right of employees ... to ... furnish information to either House of Congress, or to a committee or Member thereof, may not be interfered with or denied." The second, 18 U.S.C. § 1505, is a criminal statute making it a crime to obstruct congressional testimony. Neither expressly creates a private right to sue for damages. Petitioners argue that the District Court erred in finding that a private cause of action could be inferred under either statute, and that "special factors" present in the context of the federal employer-employee relationship preclude the recognition of respondent's *Bivens* action under the First Amendment. The legal sufficiency of respondent's asserted causes of action is not, however, a question that we view as properly presented for our decision in the present posture of this case. See n. 36, infra.

recognized at common law, public officers require this protection to shield them from undue interference with their duties and from potentially disabling threats of liability.

Our decisions have recognized immunity defenses of two kinds. For officials whose special functions or constitutional status requires complete protection from suit, we have recognized the defense of "absolute immunity." The absolute immunity of legislators, in their legislative functions, and of judges, in their judicial functions, now is well settled. Our decisions also have extended absolute immunity to certain officials of the Executive Branch. These include prosecutors and similar officials, executive officers engaged in adjudicative functions, and the President of the United States.

For executive officials in general, however, our cases make plain that qualified immunity represents the norm. In Scheuer v. Rhodes, 416 U.S. 232, 94 S.Ct. 1683, 40 L.Ed.2d 90 (1974), we acknowledged that high officials require greater protection than those with less complex discretionary responsibilities. Nonetheless, we held that a governor and his aides could receive the requisite protection from qualified or good-faith immunity. In Butz v. Economou, 438 U.S. 478, 98 S.Ct. 2894, 57 L.Ed.2d 895 (1978), we extended the approach of *Scheuer* to high federal officials of the Executive Branch. Discussing in detail the considerations that also had underlain our decision in *Scheuer,* we explained that the recognition of a qualified immunity defense for high executives reflected an attempt to balance competing values: not only the importance of a damages remedy to protect the rights of citizens, but also "the need to protect officials who are required to exercise their discretion and the related public interest in encouraging the vigorous exercise of official authority." Without discounting the adverse consequences of denying high officials an absolute immunity from private lawsuits alleging constitutional violations—consequences found sufficient in Spalding v. Vilas, 161 U.S. 483, 16 S.Ct. 631, 40 L.Ed. 780 (1896), and Barr v. Matteo, 360 U.S. 564, 79 S.Ct. 1335, 3 L.Ed.2d 1434 (1959), to warrant extension to such officials of absolute immunity from suits at common law—we emphasized our expectation that insubstantial suits need not proceed to trial. . . .

Butz continued to acknowledge that the special functions of some officials might require absolute immunity. But the Court held that "federal officials who seek absolute exemption from personal liability for unconstitutional conduct must bear the burden of showing that public policy requires an exemption of that scope." This we reaffirmed today in Nixon v. Fitzgerald.

III

A

Petitioners argue that they are entitled to a blanket protection of absolute immunity as an incident of their offices as Presidential aides. In deciding this claim we do not write on an empty page. In Butz v. Economou, the Secretary of Agriculture—a Cabinet official directly accountable to the President—asserted a defense of absolute official immunity from suit for civil damages. We rejected his claim. In so doing we did not question the power or the importance of the Secretary's office. Nor did we doubt the importance to the President of loyal and efficient subordinates in executing his duties of office. Yet we found these factors, alone, to be insufficient to justify absolute immunity. "[T]he greater power of [high] officials," we reasoned, "affords a greater potential for a regime of lawless conduct." Damages actions against high officials were therefore "an important means of vindicating constitutional guarantees." Moreover, we concluded that it would be "untenable to draw a distinction for purposes of immunity law between suits brought against state officials under [42 U.S.C.A.] § 1983 and suits brought directly under the Constitution against federal officials."

Having decided in *Butz* that Members of the Cabinet ordinarily enjoy only qualified immunity from suit, we conclude today that it would be equally untenable to hold absolute immunity an incident of the office of every Presidential subordinate based in the White House. Members of the Cabinet are direct subordinates of the President, frequently with greater responsibilities, both to the President and to the Nation, than White House staff. The considerations that supported our decision in *Butz* apply with equal force to this case. It is no disparagement of the offices held by petitioners to hold that Presidential aides, like Members of the Cabinet, generally are entitled only to a qualified immunity.

B

In disputing the controlling authority of *Butz,* petitioners rely on the principles developed in Gravel v. United States, 408 U.S. 606, 92 S.Ct. 2614, 33 L.Ed.2d 583 (1972). In *Gravel* we endorsed the view that "it is literally impossible ... for Members of Congress to perform their legislative tasks without the help of aides and assistants" and that "the day-to-day work of such aides is so critical to the Members' performance that they must be treated as the latter's alter egos...." Having done so, we held the Speech and Debate Clause derivatively applicable to the "legislative acts" of a Senator's aide that would have been privileged if performed by the Senator himself.

Petitioners contend that the rationale of *Gravel* mandates a similar "derivative" immunity for the chief aides of the President of the United States. Emphasizing that the President must delegate a large measure of authority to execute the duties of his office, they argue that recognition of derivative absolute immunity is made essential by all the considerations that support absolute immunity for the President himself.

Petitioners' argument is not without force. Ultimately, however, it sweeps too far. If the President's aides are derivatively immune because they are essential to the functioning of the Presidency, so should the Members of the Cabinet—Presidential subordinates some of whose essential roles are acknowledged by the Constitution itself—be absolutely immune. Yet we implicitly rejected such derivative immunity in *Butz*.[14]

---

14. *The Chief Justice argues that senior Presidential aides work "more intimately with the President on a daily basis than does a Cabinet officer," and that Butz therefore is* not controlling. In recent years, however, such men as Henry Kissinger and James Schlesinger have served in both Presidential advisory and Cabinet positions. Kissinger held both posts simultaneously. In our view it is impossible to generalize about the role of "offices" in an individual President's administration without reference to the functions

Moreover, in general our cases have followed a "functional" approach to immunity law. We have recognized that the judicial, prosecutorial, and legislative functions require absolute immunity. But this protection has extended no further than its justification would warrant. In *Gravel,* for example, we emphasized that Senators and their aides were absolutely immune only when performing "acts legislative in nature," and not when taking other acts even "in their official capacity." Our cases involving judges and prosecutors have followed a similar line. The undifferentiated extension of absolute "derivative" immunity to the President's aides therefore could not be reconciled with the "functional" approach that has characterized the immunity decisions of this Court, indeed including *Gravel* itself.[17]

C

Petitioners also assert an entitlement to immunity based on the "special functions" of White House aides. This form of argument accords with the analytical approach of our cases. For aides entrusted with discretionary authority in such sensitive areas as national security or foreign policy, absolute immunity might well be justified to protect the unhesitating performance of functions vital to the national interest. But a "special functions" rationale does not warrant a blanket recognition of absolute immunity for all Presidential aides in the performance of all their duties. This conclusion too follows from our decision in *Butz,* which establishes that an executive official's claim to absolute immunity must be justified by reference to the public interest in the special functions of his office, not the mere fact of high station.[19]

Butz also identifies the location of the burden of proof. The burden of justifying absolute immunity rests on the official asserting the claim. We have not of course had occasion to identify how a Presidential aide might carry this burden. But the general requisites are familiar in our cases. In order to establish entitlement to absolute immunity a Presidential aide first must show that the responsibilities of his office embraced a function so sensitive as to require a total shield from liability. He then must demonstrate that he was discharging the protected function when performing the act for which liability is asserted.

---

that particular officeholders are assigned by the President. *Butz v. Economou* cannot be distinguished on this basis.

17. Our decision today in *Nixon v. Fitzgerald* in no way abrogates this general rule. As we explained in that opinion, the recognition of absolute immunity for all of a President's acts in office derives in principal part from factors unique to his constitutional responsibilities and station. Suits against other officials—including Presidential aides—generally do not invoke separation-of-powers considerations to the same extent as suits against the President himself.

19. Gravel v. United States points to a similar conclusion. We fairly may assume that some aides are assigned to act as Presidential "alter egos" in the exercise of functions for which absolute immunity is "essential for the conduct of the public business." By analogy to *Gravel,* a derivative claim to Presidential immunity would be strongest in such "central" Presidential domains as foreign policy and national security, in which the President could not discharge his singularly vital mandate without delegating functions nearly as sensitive as his own.

Applying these standards to the claims advanced by petitioners Harlow and Butterfield, we cannot conclude on the record before us that either has shown that "public policy requires [for any of the functions of his office] an exemption of [absolute] scope." Nor, assuming that petitioners did have functions for which absolute immunity would be warranted, could we now conclude that the acts charged in this lawsuit—if taken at all—would lie within the protected area. We do not, however, foreclose the possibility that petitioners, on remand, could satisfy the standards properly applicable to their claims.

IV

Even if they cannot establish that their official functions require absolute immunity, petitioners assert that public policy at least mandates an application of the qualified immunity standard that would permit the defeat of insubstantial claims without resort to trial. We agree.

A

The resolution of immunity questions inherently requires a balance between the evils inevitable in any available alternative. In situations of abuse of office, an action for damages may offer the only realistic avenue for vindication of constitutional guarantees. It is this recognition that has required the denial of absolute immunity to most public officers. At the same time, however, it cannot be disputed seriously that claims frequently run against the innocent as well as the guilty—at a cost not only to the defendant officials, but to society as a whole. These social costs include the expenses of litigation, the diversion of official energy from pressing public issues, and the deterrence of able citizens from acceptance of public office. Finally, there is the danger that fear of being sued will "dampen the ardor of all but the most resolute, or the most irresponsible [public officials], in the unflinching discharge of their duties."

In identifying qualified immunity as the best attainable accommodation of competing values, in *Butz,* as in *Scheuer,* we relied on the assumption that this standard would permit "[i]nsubstantial lawsuits [to] be quickly terminated." Yet petitioners advance persuasive arguments that the dismissal of insubstantial lawsuits without trial—a factor presupposed in the balance of competing interests struck by our prior cases—requires an adjustment of the "good faith" standard established by our decisions.

B

Qualified or "good faith" immunity is an affirmative defense that must be pleaded by a defendant official. Gomez v. Toledo, 446 U.S. 635, 100 S.Ct. 1920, 64 L.Ed.2d 572 (1980).[24] Decisions of this Court have established that the "good faith" defense has both an "objective" and a "subjective" aspect. The objective element involves a presumptive knowledge of and respect for "basic, unquestioned constitutional rights." The subjective component re-

---

24. Although *Gomez* presented the question in the context of an action under 42 U.S.C. § 1983, the Court's analysis indicates that "immunity" must also be pleaded as a defense in actions under the Constitution and laws of the United States. *Gomez* did not decide which party bore the burden of proof on the issue of good faith.

fers to "permissible intentions." Characteristically the Court has defined these elements by identifying the circumstances in which qualified immunity would *not* be available. Referring both to the objective and subjective elements, we have held that qualified immunity would be defeated if an official *"knew or reasonably should have known* that the action he took within his sphere of official responsibility would violate the constitutional rights of the [plaintiff], *or* if he took the action *with the malicious intention* to cause a deprivation of constitutional rights or other injury. . . ."

The subjective element of the good-faith defense frequently has proved incompatible with our admonition in *Butz* that insubstantial claims should not proceed to trial. Rule 56 of the Federal Rules of Civil Procedure provides that disputed questions of fact ordinarily may not be decided on motions for summary judgment. And an official's subjective good faith has been considered to be a question of fact that some courts have regarded as inherently requiring resolution by a jury.[27]

In the context of *Butz'* attempted balancing of competing values, it now is clear that substantial costs attend the litigation of the subjective good faith of government officials. Not only are there the general costs of subjecting officials to the risks of trial—distraction of officials from their governmental duties, inhibition of discretionary action, and deterrence of able people from public service. There are special costs to "subjective" inquiries of this kind. Immunity generally is available only to officials performing discretionary functions. In contrast with the thought processes accompanying "ministerial" tasks, the judgments surrounding discretionary action almost inevitably are influenced by the decisionmaker's experiences, values, and emotions. These variables explain in part why questions of subjective intent so rarely can be decided by summary judgment. Yet they also frame a background in which there often is no clear end to the relevant evidence. Judicial inquiry into subjective motivation therefore may entail broad-ranging discovery and the deposing of numerous persons, including an official's professional colleagues.[28] Inquiries of this kind can be peculiarly disruptive of effective government.[29]

---

27. E.g., Landrum v. Moats, 576 F.2d 1320, 1329 (C.A.8 1978); Duchesne v. Sugarman, 566 F.2d 817, 832–833 (C.A.2 1977); cf. Hutchinson v. Proxmire, 443 U.S., at 120 n. 9, 99 S.Ct., at 2680, n. 9 (questioning whether the existence of "actual malice," as an issue of fact, may properly be decided on summary judgment in a suit alleging libel of a public figure).

28. In suits against a President's closest aides, discovery of this kind frequently could implicate separation-of-powers concerns. As the Court recognized in United States v. Nixon, 418 U.S. 683, 94 S.Ct. 3090, 41 L.Ed.2d 1039 (1974):

"A President and those who assist him must be free to explore alternatives in the process of shaping policies and making decisions and to do so in a way

many would be unwilling to express except privately. These are the considerations justifying a presumptive privilege for Presidential communications. The privilege is fundamental to the operation of Government and inextricably rooted in the separation of powers under the Constitution."

29. As Judge Gesell observed in his concurring opinion in Halperin v. Kissinger, 196 U.S.App.D.C. 285, 307, 606 F.2d 1192, 1214 (1979), aff'd in pertinent part by an equally divided Court, 452 U.S. 713, 101 S.Ct. 3132, 69 L.Ed.2d 367 (1981):

"We should not close our eyes to the fact that with increasing frequency in this jurisdiction and throughout the country plaintiffs are filing suits seeking damage awards against high government

Consistently with the balance at which we aimed in *Butz,* we conclude today that bare allegations of malice should not suffice to subject government officials either to the costs of trial or to the burdens of broad-reaching discovery. We therefore hold that government officials performing discretionary functions generally are shielded from liability for civil damages insofar as their conduct does not violate clearly established statutory or constitutional rights of which a reasonable person would have known.[30]

Reliance on the objective reasonableness of an official's conduct, as measured by reference to clearly established law, should avoid excessive disruption of government and permit the resolution of many insubstantial claims on summary judgment. On summary judgment, the judge appropriately may determine, not only the currently applicable law, but whether that law was clearly established at the time an action occurred.[32] If the law at that time was not clearly established, an official could not reasonably be expected to anticipate subsequent legal developments, nor could he fairly be said to "know" that the law forbade conduct not previously identified as unlawful. Until this threshold immunity question is resolved, discovery should not be allowed. If the law was clearly established, the immunity defense ordinarily should fail, since a reasonably competent public official should know the law governing his conduct. Nevertheless, if the official pleading the defense claims extraordinary circumstances and can prove that he neither knew nor should have known of the relevant legal standard, the defense should be sustained. But again, the defense would turn primarily on objective factors.

By defining the limits of qualified immunity essentially in objective terms, we provide no license to lawless conduct. The public interest in deterrence of unlawful conduct and in compensation of victims remains protected by a test that focuses on the objective legal reasonableness of an official's acts. Where an official could be expected to know that certain conduct would violate statutory or constitutional rights, he should be made to hesitate; and a person who suffers injury caused by such conduct may have a cause of action. But where an official's duties legitimately require action in which clearly established rights are not implicated, the public

officials in their personal capacities based on alleged constitutional torts. Each such suit almost invariably results in these officials and their colleagues being subjected to extensive discovery into traditionally protected areas, such as their deliberations preparatory to the formulation of government policy and their intimate thought processes and communications at the presidential and cabinet levels. Such discover [*sic*]is wide-ranging, time-consuming, and not without considerable cost to the officials involved. [. . .] The effect of this development upon the willingness of individuals to serve their country is obvious."

30.   This case involves no issue concerning the elements of the immunity available to state officials sued for constitutional violations under 42 U.S.C. § 1983. We have found previously, however, that it would be "untenable to draw a distinction for purposes of immunity law between suits brought against state officials under § 1983 and suits brought directly under the Constitution against federal officials."

. . . .

32.   As in Procunier v. Navarette, 434 U.S. 555, 98 S.Ct. 855, 55 L.Ed.2d 24 (1978), we need not define here the circumstances under which "the state of the law" should be "evaluated by reference to the opinions of this Court, of the Courts of Appeals, or of the local District Court."

interest may be better served by action taken "with independence and without fear of consequences."[34]

C

In this case petitioners have asked us to hold that the respondent's pretrial showings were insufficient to survive their motion for summary judgment. We think it appropriate, however, to remand the case to the District Court for its reconsideration of this issue in light of this opinion.[36] The trial court is more familiar with the record so far developed and also is better situated to make any such further findings as may be necessary.

V

The judgment of the Court of Appeals is vacated, and the case is remanded for further action consistent with this opinion.

So ordered.

■ JUSTICE BRENNAN, with whom JUSTICE MARSHALL, and JUSTICE BLACKMUN join, concurring.

I agree with the substantive standard announced by the Court today, imposing liability when a public-official defendant "knew or should have known" of the constitutionally violative effect of his actions. This standard would not allow the official who *actually knows* that he was violating the law to escape liability for his actions, even if he could not "reasonably have been expected" to know what he actually did know. Thus the clever and unusually well-informed violator of constitutional rights will not evade just punishment for his crimes. I also agree that this standard applies "across the board," to all "government officials performing discretionary functions." I write separately only to note that given this standard, it seems inescapable to me that some measure of discovery may sometimes be required to determine exactly what a public-official defendant did "know" at the time of his actions. Of course, as the Court has already noted, summary judgment will be readily available to public-official defendants whenever the state of the law was so ambiguous at the time of the alleged violation that it could not have been "known" then, and thus liability could not ensue. In my view, summary judgment will also be readily available whenever the plaintiff cannot prove, as a threshold matter, that a violation of his constitutional rights actually occurred. I see no reason why discovery

---

34. We emphasize that our decision applies only to suits for civil *damages* arising from actions within the scope of an official's duties and in "objective" good faith. We express no view as to the conditions in which injunctive or declaratory relief might be available.

36. Petitioners also have urged us, prior to the remand, to rule on the legal sufficiency of respondent's "implied" causes of action under 5 U.S.C. § 7211 (1976 ed., Supp. IV) and 18 U.S.C. § 1505 and his *Bivens* claim under the First Amendment. We do not view petitioners' argument on the statutory question as insubstantial. Nor is the *Bivens*

question. Cf. Bush v. Lucas, 647 F.2d 573 (C.A.5 1981)(holding that the "unique relationship between the Federal Government and its civil service employees is a special consideration which counsels hesitation in inferring a *Bivens* remedy"). As in Nixon v. Fitzgerald, however, we took jurisdiction of the case only to resolve the immunity question under the collateral order doctrine. We therefore think it appropriate to leave these questions for fuller consideration by the District Court and, if necessary, by the Court of Appeals.

of defendants' "knowledge" should not be deferred by the trial judge pending decision of any motion of defendants for summary judgment on grounds such as these.

■ JUSTICE BRENNAN, JUSTICE WHITE, JUSTICE MARSHALL and JUSTICE BLACKMUN, concurring.

We join the Court's opinion but, having dissented in Nixon v. Fitzgerald, we disassociate ourselves from any implication in the Court's opinion in the present case that Nixon v. Fitzgerald was correctly decided.

■ JUSTICE REHNQUIST concurring.

At such time as a majority of the Court is willing to re-examine our holding in Butz v. Economou, I shall join in that undertaking with alacrity. But until that time comes, I agree that the Court's opinion in this case properly disposes of the issues presented, and I therefore join it.

■ CHIEF JUSTICE BURGER, dissenting.

The Court today decides in Nixon v. Fitzgerald what has been taken for granted for 190 years, that it is implicit in the Constitution that a President of the United States has absolute immunity from civil suits arising out of official acts as Chief Executive. I agree fully that absolute immunity for official acts of the President is, like executive privilege, "fundamental to the operation of Government and inextricably rooted in the separation of powers under the Constitution."

In this case the Court decides that senior aides of the President do not have derivative immunity from the President. I am at a loss, however, to reconcile this conclusion with our holding in Gravel v. United States. The Court reads Butz v. Economou as resolving that question; I do not. *Butz* is clearly distinguishable.

. . . .

We very properly recognized in *Gravel* that the central purpose of a Member's absolute immunity would be "diminished and frustrated" if the legislative aides were not also protected by the same broad immunity . . . [W]ithout absolute immunity for these "elbow aides," who are indeed "alter egos," a Member could not effectively discharge all of the assigned constitutional functions of a modern legislator.

The Court has made this reality a matter of our constitutional jurisprudence. How can we conceivably hold that a President of the United States, who represents a vastly larger constituency than does any Member of Congress, should not have "alter egos" with comparable immunity? To perform the constitutional duties assigned to the Executive would be "literally impossible, in view of the complexities of the modern [Executive] process, . . . without the help of aides and assistants."[4] These words reflect

---

4. In the early years of the Republic, Members of Congress and Presidents performed their duties without staffs of aides and assistants. Washington and Jefferson spent much of their time on their plantations. Congress did not even appropriate funds for a Presidential clerk until 1857. Lincoln opened his own mail, Cleveland answered the phone at the White House, and Wilson regularly typed his own speeches. Whatever may have been the situation beginning under Washington, Adams, and Jefferson, we know today that the Presidency functions with a staff that exercises a wide

the precise analysis of *Gravel,* and this analysis applies with at least as much force to a President. The primary layer of senior aides of a President—like a Senator's "alter egos"—are literally at a President's elbow, with offices a few feet or at most a few hundred feet from his own desk. The President, like a Member of Congress, may see those personal aides many times in one day. They are indeed the President's "arms" and "fingers" to aid in performing his constitutional duty to see "that the laws [are] faithfully executed." Like a Member of Congress, but on a vastly greater scale, the President cannot personally implement a fraction of his own policies and day-to-day decisions.

For some inexplicable reason the Court declines to recognize the realities in the workings of the Office of a President, despite the Court's cogent recognition in *Gravel* concerning the realities of the workings of 20th-century Members of Congress. Absent equal protection for a President's aides, how will Presidents be free from the risks of "intimidation . . . by [Congress] and accountability before a possibly hostile judiciary?" Under today's holding in this case the functioning of the Presidency will inevitably be "diminished and frustrated."

Precisely the same public policy considerations on which the Court now relies in Nixon v. Fitzgerald, and that we relied on only recently in *Gravel,* are fully applicable to senior Presidential aides. The Court's opinion in Nixon v. Fitzgerald correctly points out that if a President were subject to suit, awareness of personal vulnerability to suit "frequently could distract a President from his public duties, to the detriment of not only the President and his office but also the Nation that the Presidency was designed to serve." This same negative incentive will permeate the inner workings of the Office of the President if the Chief Executive's "alter egos" are not protected derivatively from the immunity of the President. In addition, exposure to civil liability for official acts will result in constant judicial questioning, through judicial proceedings and pretrial discovery, into the inner workings of the Presidential Office beyond that necessary to maintain the traditional checks and balances of our constitutional structure.[6]

I challenge the Court and the dissenters in *Nixon v. Fitzgerald* who join in the instant holding to say that the effectiveness of Presidential aides will not "inevitably be diminished and frustrated," if they must weigh every act and decision in relation to the risks of future lawsuits. The *Gravel* Court took note of the burdens on congressional aides: the stress of long hours, heavy responsibilities, constant exposure to harassment of the political arena. Is the Court suggesting the stresses are less for Presidential aides? By construing the Constitution to give only qualified immunity to

spectrum of authority and discretion and directly assists the President in carrying out constitutional duties.

6. The same remedies for checks on Presidential abuse also will check abuses by the comparatively small group of senior aides who act as "alter egos" of the President. The aides serve at the pleasure of the President and thus may be removed by the President. Congressional and public scrutiny maintain a constant and pervasive check on abuses, and such aides may be prosecuted criminally. However, a criminal prosecution cannot be commenced absent careful consideration by a grand jury at the request of a prosecutor; the same check is not present with respect to the commencement of civil suits in which advocates are subject to no realistic accountability.

senior Presidential aides we give those key "alter egos" only lawsuits, winable lawsuits perhaps, but lawsuits nonetheless, with stress and effort that will disperse and drain their energies and their purses.[7]

. . . When we see the myriad irresponsible and frivolous cases regularly filed in American courts, the magnitude of the potential risks attending acceptance of public office emerges. Those potential risks inevitably will be a factor in discouraging able men and women from entering public service.

We—judges collectively—have held that the common law provides us with absolute immunity for ourselves with respect to judicial acts, however erroneous or ill-advised. Are the lowest ranking of 27,000 or more judges, thousands of prosecutors, and thousands of congressional aides—an aggregate of not less than 75,000 in all—entitled to greater protection than two senior aides of a President?

Butz v. Economou does not dictate that senior Presidential aides be given only qualified immunity. *Butz* held only that a Cabinet officer exercising discretion was not entitled to absolute immunity; we need not abandon that holding. A senior Presidential aide works more intimately with the President on a daily basis than does a Cabinet officer, directly implementing Presidential decisions literally from hour to hour.

. . . Cabinet officers . . . are department heads rather than "alter egos." It would be in no sense inconsistent to hold that a President's personal aides have greater immunity than Cabinet officers.

The Court's analysis in *Gravel* demonstrates that the question of derivative immunity does not and should not depend on a person's rank or position in the hierarchy, but on the *function* performed by the person and the relationship of that person to the superior. Cabinet officers clearly outrank United States Attorneys, yet qualified immunity is accorded the former and absolute immunity the latter; rank is important only to the extent that the rank determines the function to be performed. The function of senior Presidential aides, as the "alter egos" of the President, is an integral, inseparable part of the function of the President.[8] . . .

By ignoring *Gravel* and engaging in a wooden application of *Butz,* the Court significantly undermines the functioning of the Office of the President. Under the Court's opinion in *Nixon* today it is clear that Presidential immunity derives from the Constitution as much as congressional immunity comes from that source. Can there rationally be one rule for congressional aides and another for Presidential aides simply because the initial absolute immunity of each derives from different aspects of the Constitution? I find it inexplicable why the Court makes no effort to demonstrate

---

7. The Executive Branch may as a matter of grace supply some legal assistance. The Department of Justice has a longstanding policy of representing federal officers in civil suits involving conduct performed within the scope of their employment. In addition, the Department provides for retention of private legal counsel when necessary. The Congress frequently pays the expenses of defending its Members even as to acts wholly outside the legislative function.

8. This Court had no trouble reconciling *Gravel* with Kilbourn v. Thompson, 103 U.S. 168, 26 L.Ed. 377 (1881). In *Kilbourn* the Sergeant-at-Arms of the House of Representatives was held not to share the absolute immunity enjoyed by the Members of Congress who ordered that officer to act.

why the Chief Executive of the Nation should not be assured that senior staff aides will have the same protection as the aides of Members of the House and Senate.

NOTES

1.   In Clinton v. Jones, 520 U.S. 681, 117 S.Ct. 1636, 137 L.Ed.2d 945 (1997), the Supreme Court unanimously held that the President is not immune from suit while in office for unofficial conduct. The Court's assumption, however, that such private litigation would not interfere with the performance of Presidential duties proved to be incorrect.

2.   Scherer was fired from his job with the Florida Highway Patrol. Claiming that he had been dismissed without procedural due process, Scherer sued state officials for damages under Section 1983. The trial court concluded that, while Scherer's constitutional rights had been violated, the unconstitutionality of these procedures was not clearly established when he was fired. Nonetheless, the judge rejected the official's defense of qualified immunity and awarded Scherer damages. The judge decided that the officer's conduct was unreasonable, hence unprotected by immunity, because the procedures followed in this case clearly violated Highway Patrol regulations. The Court of Appeals affirmed.

The Supreme Court reversed. Davis v. Scherer, 468 U.S. 183, 104 S.Ct. 3012, 82 L.Ed.2d 139 (1984). A five Justice majority, speaking through Justice Powell, agreed with the lower courts that the defendants did not violate any of Scherer's clearly established constitutional rights. However, the majority rejected the notion that qualified immunity against constitutional tort claims is lost "merely because [an official's] conduct violates some statutory or administrative provision." Justice Powell argued that a contrary rule would subject state officers to excessive liability and force federal courts to resolve endless disputes about questions of state law. Indeed, he suggested that, given the number of laws on the books, it is not "always fair, or sound policy, to demand official compliance with statute and regulation on pain of money damages."

3.   Anderson, an FBI agent, took part in a warrantless search of the Creightons' home because he believed (wrongly, it turned out) that a suspected criminal was there. The Fourth Amendment forbids the warrantless search of a home in the absence of probable cause and exigent circumstances, and the Creightons filed a *Bivens* suit against Anderson. The trial judge awarded him summary judgment on the ground that the search was lawful, but the Court of Appeals, perceiving factual disputes about the existence of probable cause and exigent circumstances, disagreed. Because the right that the Creightons claimed Anderson violated was clearly established, the Court of Appeals also refused to uphold the judgment below on the ground that Anderson had a good defense of qualified immunity. A divided Supreme Court reversed. Anderson v. Creighton, 483 U.S. 635, 107 S.Ct. 3034, 97 L.Ed.2d 523 (1987). If the appeals court's view on the immunity issue was correct, Justice Scalia explained,

> [p]laintiffs would be able to convert [*Harlow*'s] rule of qualified immunity ... into a rule of virtually unqualified liability simply by

alleging violation of extremely abstract rights.... [T]he right the official is alleged to have violated must have been "clearly established" in a more particularized, and hence more relevant, sense: The contours of the right must be sufficiently clear that a reasonable official would understand that what he is doing violates that right.

4.   For a discussion of judicial immunity and the Judicial Councils Reform and Judicial Conduct and Disability Act of 1980, see Edward D. Re, *Judicial Independence and Accountability: The Judicial Councils Reform and Judicial Conduct and Disability Act of 1980*, 8 N. KY. L. REV. 221 (1981); Edward D. Re, *Article III Federal Judges*, 14 ST. JOHN'S J.LEGAL COMMENT. 79 (1999).

———

B.   INJUNCTIONS AGAINST CRIME

Gouriet v. Union of Post Office Workers

House of Lords, 1977.
[1978] A.C. 435.

LORD WILBERFORCE. My Lords, these appeals relate to certain orders made by the Court of Appeal in January 1977. The Attorney–General, Mr. J.P. Gouriet, and the two Post Office unions are each appealing against portions of these orders.... [B]riefly, the issues which have emerged for decision by this House are:

1.   Whether, in spite of the refusal of the Attorney–General to consent to the use of his name in relator proceedings, Mr. Gouriet, as a private citizen, was entitled to come to the court and ask for an injunction against the Post Office unions from soliciting interference with the mail to or with communications with the Republic of South Africa, and/or for a declaration that it would be unlawful for the unions to take such action.

2.   Whether Mr. Gouriet's claim against the Post Office unions to such injunctions or declarations is maintainable or ought to be struck out.

. . . .

[The speeches of Viscount Dilhorne and Lords Edmund–Davies and Frazier of Tullybelton are omitted. Like Lord Wilberforce, they voted with Lord Diplock.]

LORD DIPLOCK. My Lords, at the heart of the issues in these appeals lies the difference between private law and public law....

As the facts that have been narrated by my noble and learned friend Lord Wilberforce disclose, on Friday, January 14, 1977 the Union of Post Office Workers ("U.P.W.") was threatening to instruct its members to refuse to handle during the ensuing week any postal packets in course of transmission between England and the Republic of South Africa. That such conduct by the postal workers would constitute a criminal offence punishable upon indictment by imprisonment or a fine is, as Lord Wilberforce's citation of the relevant section of the Post Office Act 1953 shows, plain beyond argument. It is no less plain that if the U.P.W. were to carry out its proposal to instruct its members to "black" South African mail, the union would itself commit a criminal offence punishable by indictment. So the situation on that Friday was that a powerful trade union was threatening to defy the criminal law and to endeavour to procure its members to do likewise in such a way as would result in inconvenience and, it may be, in some cases serious financial loss, to those members of the public who during the coming week might want to make use of the postal services between England and South Africa for the purpose of their business or personal affairs.

It is understandable that, in the face of such a threat and the nationwide publicity that it had been accorded, the question should be put rhetorically, as it was by Lord Denning M.R. in his interlocutory judgment of January 17: "Are the courts to stand idly by?"

Courts of justice do not act of their own motion. In our legal system it is their function to stand idly by until their aid is invoked by someone recognized by law as entitled to claim the remedy in justice that he seeks. Courts of justice cannot compel anyone to invoke their aid who does not choose to do so; nor can they demand of him an explanation for his abstention. That is why it is now conceded that the Attorney–General cannot be called upon to disclose his reasons for refusing on January 14 to authorise the bringing of proceedings in his name against the U.P.W. when so requested by Mr. Gouriet.

So, Mr. Gouriet if he wanted to achieve his purpose of preventing the U.P.W. from carrying out its threatened defiance of the criminal law had to proceed alone. The remedy originally sought by him was an injunction against the U.P.W. to restrain their threatened conduct. . . .

Mr. Gouriet does not base his claim . . . upon the ground that any private legal right either of his own or of any other individual would be infringed if the Post Office were to suspend for a week transmission of postal packets between England and South Africa. . . . The conduct would be criminal; it would cause great public inconvenience and harm, but it would not be in breach of any duty in contract or quasi-contract owed by the Post Office to the sender or addressee of any postal packet; nor would it give rise to any cause of action in tort. For the harm it caused there would be no remedy available in private law.

The ordinary way of enforcing criminal law is by punishing the offender after he has acted in breach of it. Commission of the crime precedes the invocation of the aid of a court of criminal jurisdiction by a prosecutor. The functions of the court whose aid is then invoked are restricted to (1) determining (by verdict of a jury in indictable cases) whether the accused is guilty of the offence that he is charged with having committed and, (2) if he is found guilty, decreeing what punishment may be inflicted on him by the executive authority. In English public law every citizen still has the right, as he once had a duty (though of imperfect obligation), to invoke the aid of courts of criminal jurisdiction for the enforcement of the criminal law by this procedure. . . .

Mr. Gouriet could have initiated a private prosecution against the U.P.W.; but he would have had to wait until an offence under section 68 of the Post Office Act 1953 had been committed; and it is doubtful whether that could be proved until the officials of the union had acted on the resolution by actually sending out to its members instructions to "black" all South African mail.

So much for the ordinary way of enforcing the criminal law. There are, however, two procedures by which the aid of a court of justice may be anticipatively invoked before any crime, even inchoate, has actually been committed. Both these procedures are exceptional and in some respects anomalous....

The second exceptional procedure is that which has given rise to these appeals: the application to a court of civil jurisdiction for an injunction to restrain a potential offender from doing something in the future which although if done it would give the applicant no right to redress in private law, would nevertheless be a criminal offence.

My Lords, there is ample authority already cited by Lord Wilberforce that this procedure is undoubtedly available if applied for by the Attorney–General either ex officio or ex relatione.... It is in my view appropriate to be used only in the most exceptional of cases. It is not accurate to describe it as preventive justice. It is a deterrent and punitive procedure; but this is characteristic too of the enforcement of criminal law through the ordinary courts of criminal jurisdiction. The very creation by Parliament of a statutory offence constitutes a warning to potential offenders that if they are found guilty by a court of criminal jurisdiction of the conduct that is proscribed, they will be liable to suffer punishment up to a maximum authorised by the statute. When a court of civil jurisdiction grants an injunction restraining a potential offender from committing what is a crime but not a wrong for which there is redress in private law, this in effect is warning him that he will be in double jeopardy, for if he is found guilty by the civil court of committing the crime he will be liable to suffer punishment of whatever severity that court may think appropriate, whether or not it exceeds the maximum penalty authorised by the statute and notwithstanding that he will also be liable to be punished again for the same crime if found guilty of it by a court of criminal jurisdiction....

... The matters I have referred to are juristic considerations proper to be taken into account, no doubt with others of a less juristic character, in determining whether the public interest was likely to be best served by resorting to this exceptional and anomalous procedure for the enforcement of the criminal law.

The second reason why they are important is that they are relevant to the distinction between an injunction in restraint of crime simpliciter and an injunction to restrain conduct which, although amounting to a crime, would also infringe some right belonging to the plaintiff who is applying for the injunction, which is enforceable by him in private law. The supercession of private revenge for wrongs by remedies obtainable from courts of justice and enforceable by the executive authority of the state lies at the common origin both of the criminal law and of the civil private law of tort. So from the outset there have been many crimes which at common law were private wrongs to the person who suffered particular damage from them as well as public wrongs; and the policy of the law has been not to deprive the victim of a private wrong of his redress in civil private law against the wrongdoer merely because the wrongdoer is subject also to punitive sanctions under the criminal law for the same conduct....

In modern statutes whose object is to protect the health or welfare of a section of the public by prohibiting conduct of a particular kind, it is not infrequently the case that the prohibited conduct is made both a criminal offence and a civil wrong for which a remedy in private law is available to any individual member of that section of the public who has suffered damage as a result of it. So it creates a private right to be protected from loss or damage caused by the prohibited conduct.

For the protection of the private right created by such a statute a court of civil jurisdiction has jurisdiction to grant to the person entitled to the private right, *but to none other,* an injunction to restrain a threatened breach of it by the defendant. Upon the application for the injunction the issues are neither technically nor actually the same as they would be upon a subsequent prosecution for the criminal offence once the threat had been translated into action. They would still not be technically the same upon an application to the civil court to commit the defendant for contempt of court for breach of the injunction; though proof of commission of an offence would be a necessary step in the proof of the contempt where the only civil wrong involved was conduct prohibited by the penal provisions of the statute. This is a consideration that it would be proper for the court to bear in mind in exercising its discretion whether or not to grant an injunction in this type of case; but however sparingly it should be exercised, where the court is satisfied that grave and irreparable harm would otherwise be done to the plaintiff's private rights for which damages could not provide adequate compensation, it has undoubted jurisdiction to grant one.

The words italicised in the last paragraph are important words for they draw attention to the fact that the jurisdiction of a civil court to grant remedies in private law is confined to the grant of remedies to litigants whose rights in private law have been infringed or are threatened with infringement. To extend that jurisdiction to the grant of remedies for unlawful conduct which does not infringe any rights of the plaintiff in private law, is to move out of the field of private into that of public law with which analogies may be deceptive and where different principles apply.

. . . .

In my view the High Court has no jurisdiction to make any of the declarations now sought in the amended statement of claim. It should be struck out.

. . . .

Appeals of H.M. Attorney–General and of the Post Office unions allowed.

Appeal of the plaintiff dismissed.

People Ex Rel. Bennett v. Laman

Court of Appeals of New York, 1938.
277 N.Y. 368, 14 N.E.2d 439.

[This action is brought for an injunction to restrain the defendant permanently from practicing medicine in this State, in violation of article 48 of the Education Law. In their complaint the plaintiffs allege that the defendant is neither qualified nor licensed to practice medicine in this State; that he fraudulently represents himself as a qualified practitioner of medicine, in violation of the provisions of sections 1250 and 1263 of that law, and deceives large numbers of people thereby; that the defendant held and holds himself out in the city of Binghamton as able to diagnose and treat human disease, and that he undertook to do so, and did practice medicine within the meaning of such law, and continues to do so, and that such practice by the defendant endangers the public health, and is a public nuisance.

The complaint also alleges that in the year 1932, and again in the year 1935, the defendant was charged with crime, and was prosecuted in a criminal action by the People of the State, for unlawfully practicing medicine in the city of Binghamton, in violation of the sections above mentioned; that in those criminal actions the defendant was tried in the City Court of Binghamton, and was acquitted by the verdict of a jury in each instance.

Plaintiffs have alleged that "the constituted authorities ... are powerless to deal with defendant" on account of his unlawful practice of medicine; that a multiplicity of criminal prosecutions of the defendant will be necessary; that the penalties prescribed by law are insufficient punishment for defendant and do not afford protection to the health of the public against the defendant; and accordingly the plaintiffs have no adequate remedy at law, and seek to restrain the defendant from practicing medicine, or chiropractic, or maintaining an office therefor, or using the title chiropractor.

The complaint was dismissed by the trial court, whose judgment was affirmed by an intermediate appellate court.]

CRANE, C.J. . . .

. . . The question before us on this appeal is whether a court of equity of this State has jurisdiction to enjoin the unlawful activities of defendant, or whether jurisdiction over his acts exists only in the proper criminal courts.

That a court of equity will not undertake the enforcement of the criminal law, and will not enjoin the commission of a crime is a principle of equity jurisprudence that is settled beyond any question. There can equally be no doubt that the criminal nature of an act will not deprive equity of the jurisdiction that would otherwise attach. Whether or not the act sought to be enjoined is a crime, is immaterial. Equity does not seek to enjoin it simply because it is a crime; it seeks to protect some proper interest. If the interest sought to be protected is one of which equity will take cognizance, it will not refuse to take jurisdiction on the ground that the act which invades that interest is punishable by the penal statutes of the State.

Equity does not pretend to punish the perpetrator for the act; it attempts to protect the right of the party (here the People) seeking relief, and to prevent the performance of the act or acts, which here may injure many.

. . . .

Although invasion of property rights or pecuniary interests is emphasized in some of the earlier cases as a basis for equitable interference, there appeared later a recognition that public health, morals, safety and welfare of the community equally required protection from irreparable injury.

. . . .

In our own State, Chief Judge Ruger wrote: "The fact that the teas, the sale of which this action was brought to restrain, were adulterated, and that their possession for the purpose of sale to the general public was a nuisance subjecting the offenders to an indictment, and in case of sale, to actions for penalties for selling adulterated goods, cannot be successfully controverted; and yet this fact alone is insufficient to support the action. The plaintiffs have thereby established but one of the elements necessary to entitle them to the relief demanded. Courts will not in all cases interfere by way of injunction to restrain the continuance of an illegal trade, the abatement of a nuisance, or the prosecution of a dangerous employment. Its power, however, to do so in case of the exercise of any trade or business which is either illegal or dangerous to human life, detrimental to health, or the occasion of great public inconvenience, is not only conferred by the provisions of the statute, but *belongs to the general powers possessed by courts of equity to prevent irreparable mischief and obviate damages for which no adequate remedy exists at law.*"

. . . .

Section 1251 of the Education Law provides that: "No person shall practice medicine . . . unless licensed by the department and registered as required by this article." . . . The prohibition against the unlawful practice of medicine is made without relation to the imposition of a penalty. Equity is not concerned with the criminal feature of defendant's acts. Another section of the statute absolutely prohibits such unlawful practice. These provisions are designed to protect the people from the ministrations of incompetent, incapable, ignorant persons, and to avoid the consequent harm to their health and physical well-being. The interest of the state, the imminence of the danger and the irreparable character of the injury are here fully apparent. A court of equity is not powerless to lend its assistance.

We have pointed out that the fact that a criminal penalty is imposed for the performance of such acts will not deprive equity of its jurisdiction. In equity the court will consider the criminality of the act only to determine whether, under the particular circumstances, equitable intervention is necessary to give adequate protection to the interest invaded and whether justice will be best served by relegating the parties to the criminal court. It is not every violation of a statute, even of the statute under consideration, that calls for equitable interference. But where, as here, it is made to appear as a fact that real danger is threatened to the public health by the conduct of the defendant, that irreparable damage to the health of individuals is likely to result, and that criminal prosecution, even if successful, will not give adequate protection to those in danger, a proper case for injunction has been made out.

There are allegations in the complaint which charge that criminal prosecutions against defendant and others have been unsuccessful due to the reluctance of local juries to convict those defendants. That is not a factor calling for equitable intervention. It is no part of the office of equity to take over the duties of other public officers. Nor will equity sit in judgment on the criminal courts. As heretofore pointed out, equity interferes, in a proper case, not to punish the individual for his past acts, but to afford more complete protection to the complaining party by enjoining unlawful acts in the future.

In some of the other States, an injunction has been permitted in similar cases. Other States have refused to grant such an injunction....

. . . .

In the case at bar the People would not be entitled to an injunction upon a mere showing that the statute had been violated or that acts prohibited by the statute had been performed, in the absence of special statutory authority. However, they go much further than that. They allege facts showing that the acts of defendant imperil the health of the people of the community, and will continue to cause irreparable injury to the health of the people and perhaps to their lives. The relators invoke only the ordinary powers of a court of equity. The power of the court to restrain acts which are dangerous to human life, detrimental to the public health and the occasion of great public inconvenience and damage is one that is possessed by all courts of equity. Enough has been shown here, which if proven upon the trial, will warrant the issuance of an injunction.

The judgments should be reversed, and the motion denied, without costs.

■ O'BRIEN, HUBBS, LOUGHRAN and FINCH, JJ., concur; LEHMAN and RIPPEY, JJ., dissent.

Judgments reversed, etc.

State v. Red Owl Stores, Inc.

Supreme Court of Minnesota, 1958.
253 Minn. 236, 92 N.W.2d 103.

■ MURPHY, J. . . .

The complaints of the State of Minnesota seek to restrain the defendant corporations and certain of their officers from the alleged violation of certain provisions of M.S.A. c. 151 relating to the subject of pharmacy. The complaint against the Red Owl Stores, Inc., alleges that it operates a large number of retail food markets; that it is not registered or licensed with the Minnesota Board of Pharmacy to engage in selling at wholesale or at retail drugs and medicines; that it has been unlawfully selling and distributing various "drugs, medicines, chemicals and poisons" in the State of Minnesota, among them being Alka–Seltzer, Anacin, Bromo Seltzer, Bufferin, Pepto–Bismol, Pinex, Murene, Castoria, Ex–Lax, Feen-a-Mint, Sal Hepatica, and Vick's Va–Tru–Nol; . . . The complaint further alleges that the conduct of the defendants endangers the public health of the people of Minnesota and renders ineffectual the laws of the state for the protection of public health and asks that the defendant be permanently enjoined and restrained from selling at wholesale or retail drugs, medicines, etc., in violation of the section of the statute quoted, including the drugs named herein.

. . . .

The trial court held that . . . violation of the Pharmacy Act was a misdemeanor and that it was the duty of the city attorney of Minneapolis . . . to prosecute the alleged violations referred to in the complaint. The court further held that the remedy provided by criminal prosecution . . . is exclusive; that the legislature has not authorized injunctive relief to enforce the provisions of the Pharmacy Act; that no attempt has been made by the state to enforce the act by criminal prosecution; and that there is no evidence to prove that a multiplicity of actions would result from enforcement by criminal prosecution. The court concluded that a single prosecution would reach exactly the same number of persons and stores as might be enjoined in this proceeding. The court also found that the defendants are entitled to a trial by jury as to the alleged violations of the provisions of the Pharmacy Act and that these proceedings which seek injunctive relief circumvent the requirements of law and deny to the defendants a trial by which they are entitled to have proof of guilt established beyond a reasonable doubt.

. . . .

In support of their contention that the provisions for prosecution of the misdemeanor . . . represent the exclusive remedy reserved to the state for enforcement, the defendants cite numerous statutory provisions to the effect that, where the legislature has intended that equity should lend its aid in support of criminal law, express provision to that effect has been included in the statute. They point out that courts are reluctant to enforce criminal laws by injunction for the reason that "criminal equity" deprives the defendant of a jury trial and substitutes for the definite penalties fixed by the legislature whatever punishment for contempt a particular court may see fit to exact. . . .

. . . .

From an examination of the authorities it may be said that, where the acts complained of are violations of the criminal law, the courts of equity will not on that ground interfere by injunction to prevent their commission, since they will not exercise their preventive power for the purpose of enforcing criminal laws by restraining criminal acts. However, courts of equity will interfere by injunction to restrain acts amounting to a public nuisance if they affect public rights or privileges or endanger public health, regardless of whether such acts are denounced as crimes.

. . . .

It is also apparent that the exercise of the court's equity jurisdiction to grant injunctive relief must depend upon the facts in each particular case. The contending parties in the case before us view the issues from entirely different aspects. To the defendants this action is in essence a criminal prosecution instituted under the guise of an action in equity. The state on the other hand contends that this is a civil action to enforce a public health measure and that the criminal aspect is incidental.

It seems to us that the case before us involves something more than the prosecution of a misdemeanor. It involves the question of whether, under circumstances where the state is without an adequate remedy at law to enforce a measure adopted in the interest of public health, equity jurisdiction is suspended, merely because the measure in question makes no provision for an injunction. On the basis of the record before us, there are two parts to this question: (1) Does the misdemeanor provision of the act fail to provide the state with an adequate remedy at law? (2) Do the acts of the defendants constitute a danger to the public health?

. . . .

On the basis of this evidence the trial court was of the view that one prosecution in the city of Minneapolis would accomplish the same result as an injunction. We do not think the record warrants any such conclusion. Aside from the admitted policy of defendant Red Owl to contest enforcement wherever it is instituted, the defendant Groves–Kelco, in oral argument before this court, gives us to understand that rather than have a decision which would resolve the questions of law raised by the pleadings they insist upon a jury trial requiring proof beyond a reasonable doubt as to each particular violation. While courts jealously protect the constitutional rights of those charged with criminal offenses, respect for due process does not require that the courts in every instance should ignore other considerations merely because the act complained of may constitute a misdemeanor. The nuisance aspect of the act sought to be enjoined may be considered, as well as its social consequences. Here we are dealing not with an individual charged with an isolated offense but with an alleged widespread violation of a misdemeanor statute which penalizes breach of a law enacted to protect the public health. It should be recognized that for the state to undertake to prosecute each violation in face of resistance over a great area of the state would in effect set at nought the effective and uniform enforcement of the act.

While it is true that the legislature has not provided for injunctive relief, that fact should not place the pharmaceutical board in a position where, in the face of organized resistance, it must rely on one prosecution at a time to accomplish enforcement. We think that under the circumstances it was the duty of the attorney general as an agent of the state to institute injunctive proceedings to accomplish that purpose.

. . . .

. . . The statute here was not passed for the purpose of punishing crime; it was primarily enacted for the protection of the public health and welfare, and the criminal sanction included in the act was intended as a deterrent for the purpose of admonishing those engaged in the sale of drugs that they must comply with the terms of the statute and regulations. Under the circumstances the pharmaceutical board could make little progress toward enforcing the act if it was limited to prosecutions to recover the small penalties provided. Upon the record we are satisfied that the state's evidence is sufficient to establish, without evidence to the contrary, that the remedy at law is inadequate.

. . . .

The real issues in this case, which affect substantial business interests of the defendants as opposed to an important concern of the state in the area of public health, were never reached. We think the method adopted by the attorney general in resolving those opposing interests was appropriate.

. . . .

Reversed and new trial granted.

■ DELL, C.J. (dissenting). . . .

Two requirements must be satisfied in order to justify the issuance of an injunction: (1) The injury threatened must be real, substantial, and irreparable and (2) the remedy at law must be inadequate. It appears to me that on neither ground has the state made out its case.

There has been no showing of any injury, past, present, or future; real, substantial, or irreparable. The majority opinion admits that the state failed to present a single instance in which the use of any item enumerated in the complaint, purchased in a grocery store or supermarket, injured the safety, health, comfort, or welfare of anyone. . . .

. . . .

An injunction will not issue to enjoin purely criminal acts. It is only where criminal prosecutions have been wholly ineffective, and where repeated convictions have failed to deter violators, that equity will interpose its jurisdiction. Upon this principle the injunction proceedings herein were premature. There has never been a criminal prosecution. Nor is there any showing at all that defendants would persist in violating the statute if they were convicted and the state's assertion to that effect is mere speculation. Moreover, defendants' decision to continue marketing these items does not indicate any disregard of the law. . . .

The cases cited in the majority opinion are inapplicable. They fall into two categories which are clearly distinguishable from the instant case: (1) Instances where the statutes specifically provided for injunctive relief in lieu of a criminal prosecution and (2) cases upholding injunctions because no specific statutory prohibition was applicable other than the public nuisance provisions. . . . In the instant case, however, there are *both* a declared criminal violation *and* a declared method of enforcement which should be exhausted before attempting to proceed by injunction.

. . . .

NOTE

At the second trial, the lower court found that the preparations sold by the defendants were proprietary medicines and exempted from the provisions of the Pharmacy Act. It therefore denied injunctive relief. Plaintiff requested a new trial and appealed the denial of his request. The Minnesota Supreme Court held that the preparations were drugs within the Pharmacy Act, but that the sale of these drugs in defendants' unlicensed outlets did not constitute a nuisance or danger to the public health and would not be enjoined. State v. Red Owl Stores, Inc., 262 Minn. 31, 115 N.W.2d 643 (1962).

CHAPTER 18

REMEDIES FOR INVASIONS OF PERSONAL INTERESTS

A. DEFAMATION

Dun & Bradstreet, Inc. v. Greenmoss Builders, Inc.

Supreme Court of the United States, 1985.
472 U.S. 749, 105 S.Ct. 2939, 86 L.Ed.2d 593.

■ JUSTICE POWELL announced the judgment of the Court and delivered an opinion, in which JUSTICE REHNQUIST and JUSTICE O'CONNOR joined.

In Gertz v. Robert Welch, Inc., 418 U.S. 323, 94 S.Ct. 2997, 41 L.Ed.2d 789 (1974), we held that the First Amendment restricted the damages that a private individual could obtain from a publisher for a libel that involved a matter of public concern. More specifically, we held that in these circumstances the First Amendment prohibited awards of presumed and punitive damages for false and defamatory statements unless the plaintiff shows "actual malice," that is, knowledge of falsity or reckless disregard for the truth. The question presented in this case is whether this rule of *Gertz* applies when the false and defamatory statements do not involve matters of public concern.

I

Petitioner Dun & Bradstreet, a credit reporting agency, provides subscribers with financial and related information about businesses. All the information is confidential; under the terms of the subscription agreement the subscribers may not reveal it to anyone else. On July 26, 1976, petitioner sent a report to five subscribers indicating that respondent, a construction contractor, had filed a voluntary petition for bankruptcy. This report was false and grossly misrepresented respondent's assets and liabilities. That same day, while discussing the possibility of future financing with its bank, respondent's president was told that the bank had received the defamatory report. He immediately called petitioner's regional office, explained the error, and asked for a correction. In addition, he requested the names of the firms that had received the false report in order to assure them that the company was solvent. Petitioner promised to look into the matter but refused to divulge the names of those who had received the report.

After determining that its report was indeed false, petitioner issued a corrective notice on or about August 3, 1976, to the five subscribers who had received the initial report. The notice stated that one of respondent's former employees, not respondent itself, had filed for bankruptcy and that respondent "continued in business as usual." Respondent told petitioner that it was dissatisfied with the notice, and it again asked for a list of subscribers who had seen the initial report. Again petitioner refused to divulge their names.

Respondent then brought this defamation action in Vermont state court. It alleged that the false report had injured its reputation and sought both compensatory and punitive damages. The trial established that the error in petitioner's report had been caused when one of its employees, a 17–year-old high school student paid to review Vermont bankruptcy pleadings, had inadvertently attributed to respondent a bankruptcy petition filed by one of respondent's former employees. Although petitioner's representative testified that it was routine practice to check the accuracy of such reports with the businesses themselves, it did not try to verify the information about respondent before reporting it.

After trial, the jury returned a verdict in favor of respondent and awarded $50,000 in compensatory or presumed damages and $300,000 in punitive damages. Petitioner moved for a new trial.... The trial court indicated some doubt as to whether *Gertz* applied to "non-media cases," but granted a new trial "[b]ecause of ... dissatisfaction with its charge and ... conviction that the interests of justice require[d]" it.

The Vermont Supreme Court reversed.... It held that the balance between a private plaintiff's right to recover presumed and punitive damages without a showing of special fault and the First Amendment rights of "nonmedia" speakers "must be struck in favor of the private plaintiff defamed by a nonmedia defendant." Accordingly, the court held "that as a matter of federal constitutional law, the media protections outlined in *Gertz* are inapplicable to nonmedia defamation actions [like this one]."

Recognizing disagreement among the lower courts about when the protections of *Gertz* apply, we granted certiorari. We now affirm, although for reasons different from those relied upon by the Vermont Supreme Court.

. . . .

III

In New York Times Co. v. Sullivan, 376 U.S. 254, 84 S.Ct. 710, 11 L.Ed.2d 686 (1964), the Court for the first time held that the First Amendment limits the reach of state defamation laws. That case concerned a public official's recovery of damages for the publication of an advertisement criticizing police conduct in a civil rights demonstration. As the Court noted, the advertisement concerned "one of the major public issues of our time." Noting that "freedom of expression *upon public questions* is secured by the First Amendment," id., at 269, 84 S.Ct., at 720 (emphasis added), and that "debate *on public issues* should be uninhibited, robust, and wide-open," id., at 270, 84 S.Ct., at 721 (emphasis added), the Court held that a public official cannot recover damages for defamatory falsehood unless he proves that the false statement was made with " 'actual malice'—that is, with knowledge that it was false or with reckless disregard of whether it was false or not." In later cases, all involving public issues, the Court extended this same constitutional protection to libels of public figures, and in one case suggested in a plurality opinion that this constitutional rule should extend to libels of any individual so long as the defamatory statements involved a "matter of public or general interest," Rosenbloom v. Metromedia, Inc., 403 U.S. 29, 44, 91 S.Ct. 1811, 1820, 29 L.Ed.2d 296 (1971)(opinion of Brennan, J.).

In Gertz v. Robert Welch, Inc., 418 U.S. 323, 94 S.Ct. 2997, 41 L.Ed.2d 789 (1974), we held that the protections of *New York Times* did not extend as far as *Rosenbloom* suggested. *Gertz* concerned a libelous article appearing in a magazine called American Opinion, the monthly outlet of the John Birch Society. The article in question discussed whether the prosecution of a policeman in Chicago was part of a Communist campaign to discredit local law enforcement agencies. The plaintiff, Gertz, neither a public official nor a public figure, was a lawyer tangentially involved in the prosecution. The magazine alleged that he was the chief architect of the "frame-up" of the police officer and linked him to Communist activity. Like every other case in which this Court has found constitutional limits to state defamation laws, *Gertz* involved expression on a matter of undoubted public concern.

In *Gertz,* we held that the fact that expression concerned a public issue did not by itself entitle the libel defendant to the constitutional protections of *New York Times.* These protections, we found, were not "justified solely by reference to the interest of the press and broadcast media in immunity from liability." Rather, they represented "an accommodation between [First Amendment] concern[s] and the limited state interest present in the context of libel actions brought by public persons." In libel actions brought by private persons we found the competing interests different. Largely because private persons have not voluntarily exposed themselves to increased risk of injury from defamatory statements and because they generally lack effective opportunities for rebutting such statements, we found that the State possessed a "strong and legitimate ... interest in compensating private individuals for injury to reputation." Balancing this stronger state interest against the same First Amendment interest at stake in *New York Times,* we held that a State could not allow recovery of presumed and punitive damages absent a showing of "actual malice." Nothing in our opinion, however, indicated that this same balance would be struck regardless of the type of speech involved.

IV

We have never considered whether the *Gertz* balance obtains when the defamatory statements involve no issue of public concern. To make this determination, we must employ the approach approved in *Gertz* and balance the State's interest in compensating private individuals for injury to their reputation against the First Amendment interest in protecting this type of expression. This state interest is identical to the one weighed in *Gertz*. . . .

The First Amendment interest, on the other hand, is less important than the one weighed in *Gertz.* We have long recognized that not all speech is of equal First Amendment importance.[5] It is speech on " 'matters of public concern' " that is "at the heart of the First Amendment's protection." As we stated in Connick v. Myers, 461 U.S. 138, 145, 103 S.Ct. 1684, 1689, 75 L.Ed.2d 708 (1983), this "special concern [for speech on public issues] is no mystery":

> "The First Amendment 'was fashioned to assure unfettered interchange of ideas for the bringing about of political and social changes desired by the people.' '[S]peech concerning public affairs is more than self-expression; it is the essence of self-government.' Accordingly, the Court has frequently reaffirmed that speech on public issues occupies the ' "highest rung of the hierarchy of First Amendment values," ' and is entitled to special protection."

In contrast, speech on matters of purely private concern is of less First Amendment concern. As a number of state courts, including the court below, have recognized, the role of the Constitution in regulating state libel law is far more limited when the concerns that activated *New York Times* and *Gertz* are absent. . . .

While such speech is not totally unprotected by the First Amendment, its protections are less stringent. In *Gertz,* we found that the state interest in awarding presumed and punitive damages was not "substantial" in view of their effect on speech at the core of First Amendment concern. This interest, however, *is* "substantial" relative to the incidental effect these remedies may have on speech of significantly less constitutional interest. The rationale of the common-law rules has been the experience and judgment of history that "proof of actual damage will be impossible in a great many cases where, from the character of the defamatory words and the circumstances of publication, it is all but certain that serious harm has resulted in fact." W. Prosser, Law of Torts § 112, p. 765 (4th ed. 1971). As a result, courts for centuries have allowed juries to presume that some damage occurred from many defamatory utterances and publications. This rule furthers the state interest in providing remedies for defamation by ensuring that those remedies are effective. In light of the reduced constitutional value of speech involving no matters of public concern, we hold that

---

5. This Court on many occasions has recognized that certain kinds of speech are less central to the interests of the First Amendment than others. Obscene speech and "fighting words" long have been accorded no protection. In the area of protected speech, the most prominent example of reduced protection for certain kinds of speech concerns commercial speech. Such speech, we have noted, occupies a "subordinate position in the scale of First Amendment values." It also is more easily verifiable and less likely to be deterred by proper regulation. Accordingly, it may be regulated in ways that might be impermissible in the realm of noncommercial expression.

Other areas of the law provide further examples. In Ohralik v. Ohio State Bar Assn., 436 U.S. 447, 98 S.Ct. 1912, 56 L.Ed.2d 444 (1978), we noted that there are "[n]umerous examples ... of communications that are regulated without offending the First Amendment, such as the exchange of information about securities, corporate proxy statements, the exchange of price and production information among competitors, and employers' threats of retaliation for the labor activities of employees." Yet similar regulation of political speech is subject to the most rigorous scrutiny. Likewise, while the power of the State to license lawyers, psychiatrists, and public school teachers—all of whom speak for a living—is unquestioned, this Court has held that a law requiring licensing of union organizers is unconstitutional under the First Amendment.

the state interest adequately supports awards of presumed and punitive damages—even absent a showing of "actual malice."[7]

V

The only remaining issue is whether petitioner's credit report involved a matter of public concern. In a related context, we have held that "[w]hether ... speech addresses a matter of public concern must be determined by [the expression's] content, form, and context ... as revealed by the whole record." These factors indicate that petitioner's credit report concerns no public issue. It was speech solely in the individual interest of the speaker and its specific business audience. This particular interest warrants no special protection when—as in this case—the speech is wholly false and clearly damaging to the victim's business reputation. Moreover, since the credit report was made available to only five subscribers, who, under the terms of the subscription agreement, could not disseminate it further, it cannot be said that the report involves any "strong interest in the free flow of commercial information." There is simply no credible argument that this type of credit reporting requires special protection to ensure that "debate on public issues [will] be uninhibited, robust, and wide-open."

In addition, the speech here, like advertising, is hardy and unlikely to be deterred by incidental state regulation. It is solely motivated by the desire for profit, which, we have noted, is a force less likely to be deterred than others. Arguably, the reporting here was also more objectively verifiable than speech deserving of greater protection. In any case, the market provides a powerful incentive to a credit reporting agency to be accurate, since false credit reporting is of no use to creditors. Thus, any incremental "chilling" effect of libel suits would be of decreased significance.[3]

VI

We conclude that permitting recovery of presumed and punitive damages in defamation cases absent a showing of "actual malice" does not violate the First Amendment when the defamatory statements do not involve matters of public concern. Accordingly, we affirm the judgment of the Vermont Supreme Court.

It is so ordered.

---

7. ....

The dissent's "balance," moreover, would lead to the protection of all libels—no matter how attenuated their constitutional interest. If the dissent were the law, a woman of impeccable character who was branded a "whore" by a jealous neighbor would have no effective recourse unless she could prove "actual malice" by clear and convincing evidence. This is not malice in the ordinary sense, but in the more demanding sense of *New York Times.* The dissent would, in effect, constitutionalize the entire common law of libel.

3. The Court of Appeals for the Fifth Circuit has noted that, while most States provide a qualified privilege against libel suits for commercial credit reporting agencies, in those States that do not there is a thriving credit reporting business and commercial credit transactions are not inhibited. The court cited an empirical study comparing credit transactions in Boise, Idaho, where there is no privilege, with those in Spokane, Washington, where there is one.

■ CHIEF JUSTICE BURGER, concurring in the judgment.

. . . .

The single question before the Court today is whether *Gertz* applies to this case. The plurality opinion holds that *Gertz* does not apply because, unlike the challenged expression in *Gertz*, the alleged defamatory expression in this case does not relate to a matter of public concern. I agree that *Gertz* is limited to circumstances in which the alleged defamatory expression concerns a matter of general public importance, and that the expression in question here relates to a matter of essentially private concern. I therefore agree with the plurality opinion to the extent that it holds that *Gertz* is inapplicable in this case for the two reasons indicated. No more is needed to dispose of the present case.

I continue to believe, however, that *Gertz* was ill-conceived, and therefore agree with Justice White that *Gertz* should be overruled. I also agree generally with Justice White's observations concerning New York Times Co. v. Sullivan. *New York Times,* however, equates "reckless disregard of the truth" with malice; this should permit a jury instruction that malice may be found if the defendant is shown to have published defamatory material which, in the exercise of reasonable care, would have been revealed as untrue. But since the Court has not applied the literal language of *New York Times* in this way, I agree with Justice White that it should be reexamined. The great rights guaranteed by the First Amendment carry with them certain responsibilities as well.

Consideration of these issues inevitably recalls an aphorism of journalism that "too much checking on the facts has ruined many a good news story."

■ JUSTICE WHITE, concurring in the judgment.

Until New York Times Co. v. Sullivan, 376 U.S. 254, 84 S.Ct. 710, 11 L.Ed.2d 686 (1964), the law of defamation was almost exclusively the business of state courts and legislatures. Under the then prevailing state libel law, the defamed individual had only to prove a false written publication that subjected him to hatred, contempt, or ridicule. Truth was a defense; but given a defamatory false circulation, general injury to reputation was presumed; special damages, such as pecuniary loss and emotional distress, could be recovered; and punitive damages were available if common-law malice were shown. General damages for injury to reputation were presumed and awarded because the judgment of history was that "in many cases the effect of defamatory statements is so subtle and indirect that it is impossible directly to trace the effects thereof in loss to the person defamed." Restatement of Torts § 621, Comment *a,* p. 314 (1938). The defendant was permitted to show that there was no reputational injury; but at the very least, the prevailing rule was that at least nominal damages were to be awarded for any defamatory publication actionable *per se.* This rule performed "a vindicatory function by enabling the plaintiff publicly to brand the defamatory publication as false. The salutary social value of this rule is preventive in character since it often permits a defamed person to expose the groundless character of a defamatory rumor before harm to the reputation has resulted therefrom." Id. § 569, Comment *b,* p. 166.

Similar rules applied to slanderous statements that were actionable *per se*.[1]

. . . .

I joined the judgment and opinion in *New York Times*. I also joined later decisions extending the *New York Times* standard to other situations. But I came to have increasing doubts about the soundness of the Court's approach and about some of the assumptions underlying it. I could not join the plurality opinion in *Rosenbloom,* and I dissented in *Gertz,* asserting that the common-law remedies should be retained for private plaintiffs. I remain convinced that *Gertz* was erroneously decided. I have also become convinced that the Court struck an improvident balance in the *New York Times* case between the public's interest in being fully informed about public officials and public affairs and the competing interest of those who have been defamed in vindicating their reputation.

In a country like ours, where the people purport to be able to govern themselves through their elected representatives, adequate information about their government is of transcendent importance. That flow of intelligence deserves full First Amendment protection. Criticism and assessment of the performance of public officials and of government in general are not subject to penalties imposed by law. But these First Amendment values are not at all served by circulating false statements of fact about public officials. On the contrary, erroneous information frustrates these values. They are even more disserved when the statements falsely impugn the honesty of those men and women and hence lessen the confidence in government. As the Court said in *Gertz:* "[T]here is no constitutional value in false statements of fact. Neither the intentional lie nor the careless error materially advances society's interest in 'uninhibited, robust, and wide-open' debate on public issues." Yet in *New York Times* cases, the public official's complaint will be dismissed unless he alleges and makes out a jury case of a knowing or reckless falsehood. Absent such proof, there will be no jury verdict or judgment of any kind in his favor, even if the challenged publication is admittedly false. The lie will stand, and the public continue to be misinformed about public matters. This will recurringly happen because the putative plaintiff's burden is so exceedingly difficult to satisfy and can be discharged only by expensive litigation. Even if the plaintiff sues, he frequently loses on summary judgment or never gets to the jury because of insufficient proof of malice. If he wins before the jury, verdicts are often overturned by appellate courts for failure to prove malice. Furthermore, when the plaintiff loses, the jury will likely return a general verdict and there will be no judgment that the publication was false, even though it was without foundation in reality.[2] The public is left to conclude

---

1. *At the common law, slander, unlike libel, was actionable per se* only when it dealt with a narrow range of statements: those imputing a criminal offense, a venereal or loathsome and communicable disease, improper conduct of a lawful business, or unchastity of a woman. To be actionable, all other slanderous statements required additional proof of special damages other than an injury to reputation or emotional distress. The special damages most often took the form of material or pecuniary loss.

2. If the plaintiff succeeds in proving a jury case of malice, it may be that the jury will be asked to bring in separate verdicts on falsity and malice. In that event, there could be a verdict in favor of the plaintiff on falsity,

that the challenged statement was true after all. Their only chance of being accurately informed is measured by the public official's ability himself to counter the lie, unaided by the courts. That is a decidedly weak reed to depend on for the vindication of First Amendment interests—"it is the rare case where the denial overtakes the original charge. Denials, retractions, and corrections are not 'hot' news, and rarely receive the prominence of the original story."

Also, by leaving the lie uncorrected, the *New York Times* rule plainly leaves the public official without a remedy for the damage to his reputation. Yet the Court has observed that the individual's right to the protection of his own good name is a basic consideration of our constitutional system, reflecting " 'our basic concept of the essential dignity and worth of every human being—a concept at the root of any decent system of ordered liberty.' " The upshot is that the public official must suffer the injury, often cannot get a judgment identifying the lie for what it is, and has very little, if any, chance of countering that lie in the public press.

. . . .

In *New York Times,* instead of escalating the plaintiff's burden of proof to an almost impossible level, we could have achieved our stated goal by limiting the recoverable damages to a level that would not unduly threaten the press. Punitive damages might have been scrutinized as Justice Harlan suggested in *Rosenbloom,* or perhaps even entirely forbidden. Presumed damages to reputation might have been prohibited, or limited, as in *Gertz.* Had that course been taken and the common-law standard of liability been retained, the defamed public official, upon proving falsity, could at least have had a judgment to that effect. His reputation would then be vindicated; and to the extent possible, the misinformation circulated would have been countered. He might have also recovered a modest amount, enough perhaps to pay his litigation expenses. At the very least, the public official should not have been required to satisfy the actual malice standard where he sought no damages but only to clear his name. In this way, both First Amendment and reputational interests would have been far better served. . . . It could be suggested that even without the threat of large presumed and punitive damages awards, press defendants' communication will be unduly chilled by having to pay for the actual damages caused to those they defame. But other commercial enterprises in this country not in

but against him on malice. There would be no judgment in his favor, but the verdict on falsity would be a public one and would tend to set the record right and clear the plaintiff's name.

It might be suggested that courts, as organs of the government, cannot be trusted to discern what the truth is. But the logical consequence of that view is that the First Amendment forbids all libel and slander suits, for in each such suit, there will be no recovery unless the court finds the publication at issue to be factually false. Of course, no forum is perfect, but that is not a justification for leaving whole classes of defamed

individuals without redress or a realistic opportunity to clear their names. We entrust to juries and the courts the responsibility of decisions affecting the life and liberty of persons. It is perverse indeed to say that these bodies are incompetent to inquire into the truth of a statement of fact in a defamation case. I can therefore discern nothing in the Constitution which forbids a plaintiff to obtain a judicial decree that a statement is false—a decree he can then use in the community to clear his name and to prevent further damage from a defamation already published.

the business of disseminating information must pay for the damage they cause as a cost of doing business, and it is difficult to argue that the United States did not have a free and vigorous press before the rule in *New York Times* was announced. In any event, the *New York Times* standard was formulated to protect the press from the chilling danger of numerous large damages awards. Nothing in the central rationale behind *New York Times* demands an absolute immunity from suits to establish the falsity of a defamatory misstatement about a public figure where the plaintiff cannot make out a jury case of actual malice.

. . . .

It is interesting that Justice Powell declines to follow the *Gertz* approach in this case. I had thought that the decision in *Gertz* was intended to reach cases that involve any false statements of fact injurious to reputation, whether the statement is made privately or publicly and whether or not it implicates a matter of public importance. Justice Powell, however, distinguishes *Gertz* as a case that involved a matter of public concern, an element absent here. Wisely, in my view, Justice Powell does not rest his application of a different rule here on a distinction drawn between media and nonmedia defendants. On that issue, I agree with Justice Brennan that the First Amendment gives no more protection to the press in defamation suits than it does to others exercising their freedom of speech. None of our cases affords such a distinction; to the contrary, the Court has rejected it at every turn. It should be rejected again, particularly in this context, since it makes no sense to give the most protection to those publishers who reach the most readers and therefore pollute the channels of communication with the most misinformation and do the most damage to private reputation. If *Gertz* is to be distinguished from this case, on the ground that it applies only where the allegedly false publication deals with a matter of general or public importance, then where the false publication does not deal with such a matter, the common-law rules would apply whether the defendant is a member of the media or other public disseminator or a nonmedia individual publishing privately. Although Justice Powell speaks only of the inapplicability of the *Gertz* rule with respect to presumed and punitive damages, it must be that the *Gertz* requirement of some kind of fault on the part of the defendant is also inapplicable in cases such as this.

As I have said, I dissented in *Gertz,* and I doubt that the decision in that case has made any measurable contribution to First Amendment or reputational values since its announcement. Nor am I sure that it has saved the press a great deal of money. Like the *New York Times* decision, the burden that plaintiffs must meet invites long and complicated discovery involving detailed investigation of the workings of the press, how a news story is developed, and the state of mind of the reporter and publisher. That kind of litigation is very expensive. I suspect that the press would be no worse off financially if the common-law rules were to apply and if the judiciary was careful to insist that damages awards be kept within bounds. A legislative solution to the damages problem would also be appropriate. Moreover, since libel plaintiffs are very likely more interested in clearing their names than in damages, I doubt that limiting recoveries would deter or be unfair to them. In any event, I cannot assume that the press, as successful and powerful as it is, will be intimidated into withholding news that by decent journalistic standards it believes to be true.

The question before us is whether *Gertz* is to be applied in this case. For either of two reasons, I believe that it should not. First, I am unreconciled to the *Gertz* holding and believe that it should be overruled. Second, as Justice Powell indicates, the defamatory publication in this case does not deal with a matter of public importance. Consequently, I concur in the Court's judgment.

■ JUSTICE BRENNAN, with whom JUSTICE MARSHALL, JUSTICE BLACKMUN, and JUSTICE STEVENS join, dissenting.

... [We] would reverse the judgment of the Vermont Supreme Court. We believe that, although protection of the type of expression at issue is admittedly not the "central meaning of the First Amendment," *Gertz* makes clear that the First Amendment nonetheless requires restraints on presumed and punitive damages awards for this expression....

I

. . . .

Our cases since New York Times Co. v. Sullivan have proceeded from the general premise that all libel law implicates First Amendment values to the extent it deters true speech that would otherwise be protected by the First Amendment.... "When we deal with the complex of strands in the web of freedoms which make up free speech, the operation and effect of the method by which speech is sought to be restrained must be subjected to close analysis and critical judgment in the light of the particular circumstances to which it is applied." This general proscription against unnecessarily broad content-based regulation permeates First Amendment jurisprudence.

... The ready availability and unconstrained application of presumed and punitive damages in libel actions is too blunt a regulatory instrument to satisfy this First Amendment principle, even when the alleged libel does not implicate directly the type of speech at issue in New York Times Co. v. Sullivan....

. . . .

Thus, when an alleged libel involves criticism of a public official or a public figure, the need to nurture robust debate of public issues and the requirement that all state regulation of speech be narrowly tailored coalesce to require actual malice as a prerequisite to any recovery. When the alleged libel involves speech that falls outside these especially important categories, we have held that the Constitution permits States significant leeway to compensate for actual damage to reputation.[6] The requirement of

---

6. Such speech might at times involve issues of public or general interest within the meaning of *Rosenbloom* and thus implicate important First Amendment interests. To justify this cost, the Court in *Gertz* held that the State had an enhanced interest in protecting private reputation and cited the independent First Amendment difficulties inherent in case-by-case judicial determination of whether speech concerns a matter of public

narrowly tailored regulatory measures, however, always mandates at least a showing of fault and proscribes the award of presumed and punitive damages on less than a showing of actual malice....

II

The question presented here is narrow. Neither the parties nor the courts below have suggested that respondent Greenmoss Builders should be required to show actual malice to obtain a judgment and actual compensatory damages. Nor do the parties question the requirement of *Gertz* that respondent must show fault to obtain a judgment and actual damages. The only question presented is whether a jury award of presumed and punitive damages based on less than a showing of actual malice is constitutionally permissible. *Gertz* provides a forthright negative answer. To preserve the jury verdict in this case, therefore, the opinions of Justice Powell and Justice White have cut away the protective mantle of *Gertz*.

A

Relying on the analysis of the Vermont Supreme Court, respondent urged that this pruning be accomplished by restricting the applicability of *Gertz* to cases in which the defendant is a "media" entity. Such a distinction is irreconcilable with the fundamental First Amendment principle that "[t]he inherent worth of ... speech in terms of its capacity for informing the public does not depend upon the identity of its source, whether corporation, association, union, or individual." First Amendment difficulties lurk in the definitional questions such an approach would generate. And the distinction would likely be born an anachronism. Perhaps most importantly, the argument that *Gertz* should be limited to the media misapprehends our cases. We protect the press to ensure the vitality of First Amendment guarantees. This solicitude implies no endorsement of the principle that speakers other than the press deserve lesser First Amendment protection....

The free speech guarantee gives each citizen an equal right to self-expression and to participation in self-government. This guarantee also protects the rights of listeners to "the widest possible dissemination of information from diverse and antagonistic sources." Accordingly, at least six Members of this Court (the four who join this opinion and Justice White and The Chief Justice) agree today that, in the context of defamation law, the rights of the institutional media are no greater and no less than those enjoyed by other individuals or organizations engaged in the same activities.

B

....

interest. The decision in *Gertz* is also susceptible of an alternative justification. Speech allegedly defaming a private person will generally be far less likely to implicate matters of public importance than will speech allegedly defaming public officials or public figures. In light of the problems inherent in case-by-case judicial determination of what is in the public interest, the Court's result could be explained as a decision that the cost of case-by-case evaluation could be avoided without significant chilling of speech involving matters of public importance.

... Even accepting the notion that a distinction can and should be drawn between matters of public concern and matters of purely private concern, however, the analyses presented by both Justice Powell and Justice White fail on their own terms. Both, by virtue of what they hold in this case, propose an impoverished definition of "matters of public concern" that is irreconcilable with First Amendment principles. The credit reporting at issue here surely involves a subject matter of sufficient public concern to require the comprehensive protections of *Gertz*. Were this speech appropriately characterized as a matter of only private concern, moreover, the elimination of the *Gertz* restrictions on presumed and punitive damages would still violate basic First Amendment requirements.

(1)

. . . .

The credit reporting of Dun & Bradstreet falls within any reasonable definition of "public concern" consistent with our precedents.... [A]n announcement of the bankruptcy of a local company is information of potentially great concern to residents of the community where the company is located; ... such a bankruptcy "in a single factory may have economic repercussions upon a whole region." And knowledge about solvency and the effect and prevalence of bankruptcy certainly would inform citizen opinions about questions of economic regulation. It is difficult to suggest that a bankruptcy is not a subject matter of public concern when federal law requires invocation of judicial mechanisms to effectuate it and makes the fact of the bankruptcy a matter of public record.

. . . .

(2)

Even if the subject matter of credit reporting were properly considered—in the terms of Justice White and Justice Powell—as purely a matter of private discourse, ... the expression at issue in this case should receive protection from the chilling potential of unrestrained presumed and punitive damages awards in defamation actions.

Our economic system is predicated on the assumption that human welfare will be improved through informed decisionmaking. In this respect, ensuring broad distribution of accurate financial information comports with the fundamental First Amendment premise that "the widest possible dissemination of information from diverse and antagonistic sources is essential to the welfare of the public." The economic information Dun & Bradstreet disseminates in its credit reports makes an undoubted contribution to this private discourse essential to our well-being....

The credit reports of Dun & Bradstreet bear few of the earmarks of commercial speech that might be entitled to somewhat less rigorous protection. In *every* case in which we have permitted more extensive state regulation on the basis of a commercial speech rationale the speech being regulated was pure advertising—an offer to buy or sell goods and services or encouraging such buying and selling. Credit reports are not commercial advertisements for a good or service or a proposal to buy or sell such a product. We have been extremely chary about extending the "commercial speech" doctrine beyond this narrowly circumscribed category of advertising because often vitally important speech will be uttered to advance economic interests and because the profit motive making such speech hardy dissipates rapidly when the speech is not advertising.

. . . .

Even if Justice Powell's characterization of the credit reporting at issue here were accepted in its entirety, his opinion would have done no more than demonstrate that this speech is the equivalent of commercial speech. The opinion, after all, relies on analogy to advertising. Credit reporting is said to be hardy, motivated by desire for profit, and relatively verifiable. But this does not justify the elimination of restrictions on presumed and punitive damages. State efforts to regulate commercial speech in the form of advertising must abide by the requirement that the regulatory means chosen be narrowly tailored so as to avoid any unnecessary chilling of protected expression.

. . . .

(3)

Even if not at "the essence of self-government," the expression at issue in this case is important to both our public discourse and our private welfare. That its motivation might be the economic interest of the speaker or listeners does not diminish its First Amendment value. Whether or not such speech is sufficiently central to First Amendment values to require actual malice as a standard of liability, this speech certainly falls within the range of speech that *Gertz* sought to protect from the chill of unrestrained presumed and punitive damage awards.[7]

Of course, the commercial context of Dun & Bradstreet's reports is relevant to the constitutional analysis insofar as it implicates the strong state interest "in protecting consumers and regulating commercial transactions." The special harms caused by inaccurate credit reports, the lack of public sophistication about or access to such reports, and the fact that such reports by and large contain statements that are fairly readily susceptible of verification, all may justify appropriate regulation designed to prevent the social losses caused by false credit reports. And in the libel context, the States' regulatory interest in protecting reputation is served by rules permitting recovery for actual compensatory damages upon a showing of fault. Any further interest in deterring potential defamation through case-by-case judicial imposition of presumed and punitive damages awards on less than a showing of actual malice simply exacts too high a toll on First Amendment values. Accordingly, Greenmoss Builders should be permitted to recover for any actual damage it can show resulted from Dun & Bradstreet's negligently false credit report, but should be required to show actual malice to receive presumed or punitive damages. Because the jury

---

7. . . . .

... Dun & Bradstreet doubtless provides thousands of credit reports to thousands of subscribers who receive the information pursuant to the same strictures imposed on the recipients in this case. As a systemic matter, therefore, today's decision diminishes the free flow of information because Dun & Bradstreet will generally be made more reticent in providing information to all its subscribers.

was not instructed in accordance with these principles, we would reverse and remand for further proceedings not inconsistent with this opinion.

Mazzocone v. Willing

Superior Court of Pennsylvania, 1976.
246 Pa.Super. 98, 369 A.2d 829.

■ CERCONE, J.: This is an appeal from the following final decree of the court below sitting in equity:

> AND NOW, to wit, this 10th day of November, 1975, following a full and final hearing on the merits, it is hereby Ordered and Decreed that the Defendant herein, Helen R. Willing, be and is permanently enjoined from further demonstrating against and/or picketing Mazzocone and Quinn, Attorneys–at–Law, and from uttering or publishing defamatory, slanderous or libelous matter with respect to said attorneys.

As modified the decree is affirmed.

The record reveals that plaintiff's request for equitable relief was precipitated by the following undisputed facts: For several hours on Monday, September 29, and Wednesday, October 1, 1975, defendant demonstrated in front of the entrance to Number Two Penn Center Plaza—an office building located in Centre City, Philadelphia in which plaintiffs maintained their law offices. Defendant's demonstration consisted of her pushing a shopping cart while ringing a cow-bell and blowing on a whistle. While so engaged defendant wore a sign in the form of a sandwich board which read:

LAW–FIRM
OF
QUINN–MAZZOCONE
STOLE–MONEY FROM ME AND
SOLD ME OUT TO THE
INSURANCE COMPANY

When the plaintiffs' attempts to amicably terminate defendant's demonstrations failed, they instituted this action in equity to enjoin defendant's conduct.

The evidence before the Chancellor established, among other things, that plaintiffs, a two-member law firm, were retained by defendant in 1968 to prosecute her claim for workmen's compensation benefits. Although plaintiffs secured a favorable decision for defendant, it was ironically this event which spawned her animosity towards them. Specifically, defendant developed the belief that plaintiffs wrongfully diverted to themselves $25.00 of the settlement proceeds. This conviction apparently arose out of some confusion regarding the payment of $150.00 which, according to plaintiff's distribution schedule, was made to the defendant's treating psychiatrist, Dr. DeSilverio. Defendant maintains that plaintiffs only paid Dr. DeSilverio the sum of $125.00. In reply to this contention, plaintiffs introduced into evidence their records relating to Dr. DeSilverio, including cancelled checks. Furthermore, any possible doubt as to the truth or falsity of defendant's allegations was dispelled by Dr. DeSilverio himself, who testified that plaintiffs had indeed paid him $150.00 for his services. Defendant made no attempt to contradict or refute this evidence, but simply repeated her belief that plaintiffs had defrauded her out of $25.00, and no proof to the contrary would erase this conviction.

As the lower court well stated:

"Thus, the evidence adduced clearly establishes that defendant is a woman firmly in the thrall of the belief that plaintiffs defrauded her, an *idee fixe* which, either by reason of eccentricity or an even more serious mental instability, refuses to be dislodged by the most convincing proof to the contrary. It is equally clear that unless stayed by this Court, defendant will resume her bizarre parade before plaintiffs' office building, displaying her defamatory accusation which will not only offer plaintiffs continuous embarrassment and humiliation but do serious injury to their professional reputation as well."

Defendant's challenge to the lower court's injunction is predicated on the traditional view that equity does not have the power to enjoin the publication of defamatory matter. These cases indicate the reasons why equity has traditionally declined to enjoin defamation: (1) equity will afford protection only to property rights; (2) an injunction would deprive the defendant of his right to a jury trial on the issue of the truth of the publication; (3) the plaintiff has an adequate remedy at law; and (4) an injunction would be unconstitutional as a prior restraint on freedom of expression. However, the logic and soundness of these reasons have been severely criticized by numerous commentators. Our own analysis compels us to conclude that blind application of the majority view to the instant case would be antithetical to equity's historic function of maintaining flexibility and accomplishing total justice whenever possible.

First of all, the concept that equity will protect only property rights as opposed to personal rights has been expressly repudiated by our Supreme Court. In any event, the right to practice law is a property right.

The second objection often advanced for refusing to enjoin defamation is that the defendant would be denied the right to have a jury pass upon the truth or falsity of the publication.... In short, the jury trial objection vanishes where there are no controverted issues of fact to submit to the jury.... To refuse injunctive relief under the circumstances of this case on the grounds that defendant would be denied a jury trial is to elevate form over substance.

The third argument often invoked for denying injunctive relief in defamation cases is that the plaintiff has an adequate remedy at law. This reason is premised on the theory that an award of damages will sufficiently recompense the plaintiff for any harm occasioned by the defamatory publication. We, however, have difficulty accepting the idea that the payment of a sum of money is either an adequate or proper remedy in this case. In the first instance, it is obvious that a good professional and/or personal reputation is a unique and precious possession. Damage to this inestimable possession is, however, difficult to prove and measure accurately; in fact, in most cases, more difficult than measuring property damages.

More importantly, we cannot disregard the fact that in the present case an action for damages would be a pointless gesture since the defendant is indigent.... An additional consideration militating in favor of equitable jurisdiction is the avoidance of a multiplicity of suits. In view of the defendant's unshakeable conviction that plaintiffs have defrauded her, it is not unreasonable to assume that unless restrained she will persist in conducting her defamatory demonstrations secure in the knowledge that any monetary judgment would be unenforceable. To permit this would place plaintiffs in the oppressive position of resorting to ineffective actions at law whenever the defendant is inclined to denigrate them. Clearly this cannot be an "adequate remedy at law."

The final reason frequently advanced for equity's reluctance to enjoin defamation is that an injunction against the publication would be unconstitutional as a prior restraint on free expression. This is by far the most cogent of all the reasons offered in support of the traditional view. However, ... a pragmatic and modern rather than a theoretical and historical approach should be made in deciding the justiciability of an injunction against defamatory publications.

Of course, the Supreme Court has never declared that all injunctions of speech do not pass constitutional muster. This circumspection necessarily derives from the realization that the peculiar facts of a particular case may admit of no other alternative but injunction. We submit that this is such a case. Here we have a situation where an indigent person persists in defaming the plaintiffs despite the fact that her allegations have been irrefutably demonstrated to be untrue. Indeed, the evidence of their untruth is so overwhelming that one can only infer that the defendant's intent is purely malicious. Furthermore, her indigence allows her to proceed without fear of having to pay for her defamations; there is no economic incentive here for self-censorship. Similarly, her indigence deprives the plaintiffs of any fund upon which they might draw to repair, in some measure, the damage already done to their business and reputations. Hence, the suggestion is that the constitution requires the plaintiffs to endure a continuing and utterly false attack upon their reputations without affording any relief whatsoever, monetarily or otherwise. We cannot agree that the constitution permits any such inverse condemnation of these valuable personal rights....

Furthermore, there is an inconsistency with the majority view in that it approves injunctions in trade libel cases and frowns on injunctions against defamatory publications concerning the reputation of an individual. Purchasers have been enjoined from adorning their cars with drawings of lemons and similar decorations or against advertising the identification of a vendor. Carter v. Knapp Motor Co., 243 Ala. 600, 11 So.2d 383 (1943); Menard v. Houle, 298 Mass. 546, 11 N.E.2d 436 (1937); Saxon Motor Sales, Inc. v. Torino, 166 Misc. 863, 2 N.Y.S.2d 885 (1938). Demonstrative tenants have been restrained from picketing their landlord. Springfield Bayside Corporation v. Hochman, 44 Misc.2d 882, 255 N.Y.S.2d 140 (1964). The owner of a hospital has been protected against the disparagement of that facility. Wolf v. Gold, 9 A.D.2d 257, 193 N.Y.S.2d 36 (1959). The business interests of a real estate developer have been protected. West Willow Realty Corp. v. Taylor, 23 Misc.2d 867, 198 N.Y.S.2d 196 (1960).

There is definitely a curious inversion of logic in the view that gives property rights primacy over personal rights involving reputation. . . . There is as much threat in the potential destruction of a person's good name through malicious falsehoods as there is in coercive and threatening measures taken against one's property rights.

We are fully aware that equity cannot enjoin every utterance or publication, whether it be in a trade libel or a defamation case. Each case must stand on its own facts. . . . The pivotal question and its solution depend on the presence or absence of an overriding public interest in the utterance or publication. . . .

In the case at bar, we perceive no public interest so substantial or significant as to permit defendant's continuing false accusations concerning plaintiff's professional conduct. On the other hand, the injury to plaintiff's reputation can be extensive and irreparable if the defendant is permitted to continue her activities. Under these circumstances, the court below properly granted the injunction.

While we have concluded that the injunction was properly issued, we must agree with defendant's contention that the decree is constitutionally offensive insofar as it curtails any form of expression. . . . It is too broad since it imposes sanctions beyond the scope of her activities which have been adjudged defamatory and false in this case. The decree must be modified to read as follows:

"Helen R. Willing, be and is permanently enjoined from further demonstrating against and/or picketing Mazzocone and Quinn, Attorneys–at–Law, by uttering or publishing statements to the effect that Mazzocone and Quinn, Attorneys–at–Law stole money from her and sold her out to the insurance company."

Accordingly, the decree entered by the court below as modified is hereby affirmed.

■ Jacobs, J., dissenting: . . . .

      . . . .

The action taken below was clearly erroneous. Injunctive relief for defamation is simply not within "equity's traditional powers of interdiction". It is the general rule in Pennsylvania and in an overwhelming majority of other jurisdictions that, absent independent grounds for equitable jurisdiction, equity lacks the power to issue an injunction restraining the publication of defamatory matter. This long-standing rule may be summarized by reference to the following statement of law, which is particularly appropriate to the instant case: "Equity does not have jurisdiction to act for the sole purpose of restraining the publication or utterance of a libel or slander, regardless of whether the defamation is personal or relates to a property right. Nor will a publication be enjoined merely because it is false, misleading, or amounts to nothing more than an expression of opinion. . . ."

There are a few exceptions to the rule prohibiting an injunction against libel or slander. For example, an injunction may be granted where the false statements are part of a conspiracy to injure, or where there is intimidation or coercion. "... After a plaintiff has, by a judgment at law, established the fact that certain published statements are libelous, he may, on a proper showing, have an injunction to restrain any further publication of the same or similar statements...." 42 Am.Jur.2d Injunctions § 135 (1969).

The preceding general rule has been specifically followed in Pennsylvania, ... and my research has disclosed no decision suggesting subsequent adoption of a contrary rule. Moreover, it is the rule of and has been consistently followed in the federal courts. Furthermore, the general rule above stated has been universally applied to deny injunctions in cases in other states in which the parties and/or activities involved were substantially similar to those present in the case at bar. See Gariepy v. Springer, 318 Ill.App. 523, 48 N.E.2d 572 (1943)(defendant circulating letters to plaintiff attorney's clients, defaming him); Greenberg v. DeSalvo, 254 La.1019, 229 So.2d 83, cert. denied, 397 U.S. 1075, 90 S.Ct. 1521, 25 L.Ed.2d 809 (1970)(defendant calling attorney "crook", "crooked attorney", etc.); Schmoldt v. Oakley, 390 P.2d 882 (Okl.1964)(displaying sign on street near plaintiff's business disparaging auto sold to defendants by plaintiff); Stansbury v. Beckstrom, 491 S.W.2d 947 (Tex.Civ.App. 1973)(defendant parading, standing, sitting or lying in front of physician's office displaying libelous and false signs); Kwass v. Kersey, 139 W.Va. 497, 81 S.E.2d 237 (1954)(defendant widely circulating letters charging that plaintiff attorney was a "shyster" who had betrayed the interests of his client)....

... It is patently apparent that the injunction issued in the case at bar is violative not only of the general rule that equity will not enjoin a defamation, but also of each of the ... reasons for the rule. The court below, in deciding that appellant's statements were not true, precluded a jury determination of that issue. Furthermore, an adequate remedy at law is available in this case, in the form of an action for damages. Additionally, the injunction decreed unquestionably imposes a prior restraint on appellant's constitutional right to freedom of speech.

I am particularly troubled by the majority's treatment of the question of an adequate remedy at law in this case. The majority first notes that damages are particularly difficult to prove in a defamation case. The majority opinion then observes that the defendant was indigent and concludes that the combination of these factors makes the remedy at law inadequate. While I can agree that proof of damages in a defamation case is a difficult task I am unprepared to state that because proof of damages is difficult an action for defamation at law is inadequate. If this proposition were followed to its logical conclusion, all defamation cases could initially qualify for equitable relief. This is not the law, however, as is noted supra. Moreover, appellees made no attempt to establish their actual damages at the hearings below and did not show that they could not be adequately compensated by damages at law....

The majority also states that "we cannot disregard the fact that in the present case an action for damages would be a pointless gesture since the defendant is indigent." I simply cannot accept the proposition that the presence of an impecunious defendant in the case renders an otherwise adequate remedy at law inadequate. To so hold would be to create a ground for equity jurisdiction based on the defendant's wealth or lack of it....

The rule that equity will not enjoin defamation is not without limited exception. Equitable jurisdiction to interdict libelous publication has been assumed under some circumstances, such as where the libel or slander is accompanied by coercion, breach of trust or violence, where there is a conspiracy to maliciously injure a plaintiff's business or property, where a labor dispute is involved, where a right to privacy is invaded, or where the activity becomes a traditional nuisance. Evidence of the above factors is, however, undeveloped in the instant case and I dissent vigorously from the majority's creation of a new exception based on the defendant's indigency.

Nor am I convinced that appellant's activities were properly enjoined because her publication was accomplished in conjunction with picketing. Initially, it must be noted that predominant purpose and effect of the instant decree was to *enjoin defamation,* not *to halt unlawful picketing.* While *unlawful* picketing may be restrained, perfectly *lawful* picketing, unaccompanied by violence or violation of clearly defined law or public policy of the state is a constitutionally protected activity which could not justify the lower court's decree. There is no evidence in the present case that appellant's activities were accompanied by violence, coercion or other unlawful behavior. Moreover, it may not be said that her demonstration violated clearly defined law or public policy. The decree below enjoining appellant from defaming appellees may, therefore, not be upheld on the theory that the picketing accompanying the publication was enjoinable.

I would vacate the decree of the court below.

■ HOFFMAN and SPAETH, JJ., join in this dissenting opinion.

NOTE

The Superior Court's decision was reversed by a 4–3 vote of the Pennsylvania Supreme Court. Willing v. Mazzocone, 482 Pa. 377, 393 A.2d 1155 (1978). The majority felt both that damages were an adequate remedy for Willing's tort regardless of her indigence and that the injunction was an unconstitutional prior restraint. The lead opinion based the latter conclusion on Pennsylvania's state constitution, noting:

History supports the view that the framers of our state constitution intended to prohibit prior restraint on Pennsylvanians' right to speak.

"After the demise in 1694 of the last of the infamous English Licensing Acts, freedom of the press, at least freedom from administrative censorship, began in England, and later in the Colonies, to assume the status of a 'common law or natural right.' Blackstone so recognized (circa 1767) when he wrote, 'The liberty of the press is indeed essential to the nature of a free state; but this consists in laying no previous restraints upon publications, and not in freedom from censure for criminal matter when published. Every freeman had an undoubted right to lay what sentiments he pleases before the public; to forbid this is to destroy the freedom of the press; but if he publishes what is improper, mischievous, or illegal, he must take the consequence of his own temerity. To subject the press to the restrictive power of a licenser, as was formerly done, both before and since the revolution, is to subject all freedom of sentiment to the prejudices of one man, and make him the arbitrary and infallible judge of all controverted points in learning, religion, and government.'

. . . .

What Blackstone thus recognized as the law of England concerning freedom of the press came to be, 133 years later, an established constitutional right in Pennsylvania as to both speech and press; Article IX, Section 7, of the Constitution of 1790 so ordained; and, as already pointed out, the provision still endures as Article I, Section 7, of our present Constitution."

Organization for a Better Austin v. Keefe

Supreme Court of the United States, 1971.
402 U.S. 415, 91 S.Ct. 1575, 29 L.Ed.2d 1.

■ MR. CHIEF JUSTICE BURGER delivered the opinion of the Court.

We granted the writ in this case to consider the claim that an order of the Circuit Court of Cook County, Illinois, enjoining petitioners from distributing leaflets anywhere in the town of Westchester, Illinois, violates petitioners' rights under the Federal Constitution.

Petitioner Organization for a Better Austin (OBA) is a racially integrated community organization in the Austin neighborhood of Chicago. Respondent is a real estate broker whose office and business activities are in the Austin neighborhood. He resides in Westchester, Illinois, a suburb of Chicago, some seven miles from the Austin area.

OBA is an organization whose stated purpose is to "stabilize" the racial ratio in the Austin area. For a number of years the boundary of the Negro segregated area of Chicago has moved progressively west to Austin. OBA, in its efforts to "stabilize" the area—so it describes its program—has opposed and protested various real estate tactics and activities generally known as "blockbusting" or "panic peddling."

It was the contention of OBA that respondent had been one of those who engaged in such tactics, specifically that he aroused the fears of the local white residents that Negroes were coming into the area and then, exploiting the reactions and emotions so aroused, was able to secure listings and sell homes to Negroes. OBA alleged that since 1961 respondent had from time to time actively promoted sales in this manner by means of flyers, phone calls, and personal visits to residents of the area in which his office is located, without regard to whether the persons solicited had expressed any desire to sell their homes. As the "boundary" marking the furthest westward advance of Negroes moved into the Austin area, respondent is alleged to have moved his office along with it.

Community meetings were arranged with respondent to try to persuade him to change his real estate practices. Several other real estate agents were prevailed on to sign an agreement whereby they would not solicit property, by phone, flyer or visit, in the Austin community. Respondent who has consistently denied that he is engaging in "panic peddling" or "blockbusting" refused to sign, contending that it was his right under Illinois law to solicit real estate business as he saw fit.

Thereafter, during September and October of 1967, members of petitioner organization distributed leaflets in Westchester describing respondent's activities. There was no evidence of picketing in Westchester. The challenged publications, now enjoined, were critical of respondent's real estate practices in the Austin neighborhood; one of the leaflets set out the business card respondent used to solicit listings, quoted him as saying "I only sell to Negroes," cited a Chicago Daily News article describing his real estate activities and accused him of being a "panic peddler." Another leaflet, of the same general order, stated that "When he signs the agreement, we stop coming to Westchester." Two of the leaflets requested recipients to call respondent at his home phone number and urge him to sign the "no solicitation" agreement. On several days leaflets were given to persons in a Westchester shopping center. On two other occasions leaflets were passed out to some parishioners on their way to or from respondent's church in Westchester. Leaflets were also left at the doors of his neighbors. The trial court found that petitioners' "distribution of leaflets was on all occasions conducted in a peaceful and orderly manner, did not cause any disruption of pedestrian or vehicular traffic, and did not precipitate any fights, disturbances or other breaches of the peace." One of the officers of OBA testified at trial that he hoped that respondent would be induced to sign the no-solicitation agreement by letting "his neighbors know what he was doing to us."

Respondent sought an injunction in the Circuit Court of Cook County, Illinois, on December 20, 1967. After an adversary hearing the trial court entered a temporary injunction enjoining petitioners "from passing out pamphlets, leaflets or literature of any kind, and from picketing, anywhere in the City of Westchester, Illinois."

On appeal to the Appellate Court of Illinois, First District, that court affirmed. It sustained the finding of fact that petitioners' activities in Westchester had invaded respondent's right of privacy, had caused irreparable harm, and were without adequate remedy at law. The Appellate Court appears to have viewed the alleged activities as coercive and intimidating, rather than informative and therefore as not entitled to First Amendment protection. The Appellate Court rested its holding on its belief that the public policy of the State of Illinois strongly favored protection of the privacy of home and family from encroachment of the nature of petitioners' activities.

It is elementary, of course, that in a case of this kind the courts do not concern themselves with the truth or validity of the publication. Under Near v. Minnesota, 283 U.S. 697, 51 S.Ct. 625, 75 L.Ed. 1357 (1931), the injunction, so far as it imposes prior restraint on speech and publication, constitutes an impermissible restraint on First Amendment rights. Here, as in that case, the injunction operates not to redress alleged private wrongs, but to suppress, on the basis of previous publications, distribution of literature "of any kind" in a city of 18,000.

This Court has often recognized that the activity of peaceful pamphleteering is a form of communication protected by the First Amendment. In sustaining the injunction, however, the Appellate Court was apparently of the view that petitioners' purpose in distributing their literature was not to inform the public, but to "force" respondent to sign a no-solicitation agreement. The claim that the expressions were intended to exercise a coercive impact on respondent does not remove them from the reach of the First Amendment. Petitioners plainly intended to influence respondent's conduct by their activities; this is not fundamentally different from the function of a newspaper. Petitioners were engaged openly and vigorously in making the public aware of respondent's real estate practices. Those practices were offensive to them, as the views and practices of petitioners are no doubt offensive to others. But so long as the means are peaceful, the communication need not meet standards of acceptability.

Any prior restraint on expression comes to this Court with a "heavy presumption" against its constitutional validity. Respondent thus carries a heavy burden of showing justification for the imposition of such a restraint. He has not met that burden. No prior decisions support the claim that the interest of an individual in being free from public criticism of his business practices in pamphlets or leaflets warrants use of the injunctive power of a court. Designating the conduct as an invasion of privacy, the apparent basis for the injunction here, is not sufficient to support an injunction against peaceful distribution of informational literature of the nature revealed by this record. Rowan v. United States Post Office Dept., 397 U.S. 728, 90 S.Ct. 1484, 25 L.Ed.2d 736 (1970), relied on by respondent, is not in point; the right of privacy involved in that case is now shown here. Among other important distinctions, respondent is not attempting to stop the flow of information into his own household, but to the public. Accordingly, the injunction issued by the Illinois Court must be vacated.

Reversed.

[The opinion of HARLAN, J., who dissented on jurisdictional grounds, is omitted.]

NOTES

1. In New York Times Co. v. United States, 403 U.S. 713, 91 S.Ct. 2140, 29 L.Ed.2d 822 (1971), the Court invoked the prior restraint doctrine to strike down two injunctions barring the publication of a classified study of the Vietnam War the release of which would allegedly imperil national security. The Court did not determine whether the *Times* or the Washington Post (which was also enjoined) could be prosecuted for publishing these materials. However, the Justices indicated that a criminal prosecution for this conduct might well be held constitutional.

2. Pittsburgh Press Co. v. Pittsburgh Commission on Human Relations, 413 U.S. 376, 93 S.Ct. 2553, 37 L.Ed.2d 669 (1973), approved an injunction barring the Press from printing help-wanted ads in sex-designated columns. The Court rejected a claim that the order was improper under the prior restraint doctrine. Its rationale follows:

> ... The special vice of a prior restraint is that communication will be suppressed, either directly or by inducing excessive caution in the speaker, before an adequate determination that it is unprotected by the First Amendment.

> The present order does not endanger arguably protected speech. Because the order is based on a continuing course of repetitive conduct, this is not a case in which the Court is asked to speculate as to the effect of publication. Moreover, the order is clear and sweeps no more broadly than necessary. And because no interim relief was granted, the order will not have gone into effect before our final determination that the actions of Pittsburgh Press were unprotected.

3. Consider these remarks made by White, J., for the Court in Zauderer v. Office of Disciplinary Counsel of the Supreme Court of Ohio, 471 U.S. 626, 105 S.Ct. 2265, 85 L.Ed.2d 652 (1985):

> There is no longer any room to doubt that what has come to be known as "commercial speech" is entitled to the protection of the First Amendment, albeit to protection somewhat less extensive than that afforded "noncommercial speech." More subject to doubt, perhaps, are the precise bounds of the category of expression that may be termed commercial speech, but it is clear enough that the speech at issue in this case—advertising pure and simple—falls within those bounds. Our commercial speech doctrine rests heavily on "the 'common-sense' distinction between speech proposing a commercial transaction ... and other varieties of speech," and appellant's advertisements undeniably propose a commercial transaction. Whatever else the category of commercial speech may encompass, it must include appellant's advertisements.

> Our general approach to restrictions on commercial speech is also by now well-settled. The States and the Federal Government are free to prevent the dissemination of commercial speech that is false, deceptive, or misleading, or that proposes an illegal transaction. Commercial speech that is not false or deceptive and does not concern unlawful activities, however, may be restricted only in the service of a substantial governmental interest, and only through means that directly advance that interest. Our application of these principles to the commercial speech of attorneys has led us to conclude that blanket bans on price advertising by attorneys and rules preventing attorneys from using nondeceptive terminology to describe their fields of practice are impermissible, but that rules prohibiting in-person solicitation of clients by attorneys are, at least under some circumstances, permissible.

B.   PRIVACY AND PUBLICITY

Birnbaum v. United States

United States District Court, Eastern District of New York, 1977.
436 F.Supp. 967.

■ WEINSTEIN, J. In each of these three cases consolidated for trial the plaintiff complains that first-class mail was intercepted by the Central Intelligence Agency (CIA), opened without warrant and copied. Birnbaum and MacMillen each sent a letter abroad; Avery received one here. All the letters were resealed after copying and promptly returned to the mails. Plaintiffs ... seek to recover damages under the Federal Tort Claims Act.

. . . .

I.   FACTUAL BACKGROUND

From approximately 1953 until 1973, in violation of federal statutes and the Fourth Amendment of the United States Constitution, the Central Intelligence Agency conducted an extensive program of opening first-class mail passing in and out of the country through Hawaii, San Francisco, New Orleans, and New York.

Most of the correspondence opened, photographed and circulated within the CIA and the Federal Bureau of Investigation (FBI) was intercepted by the New York project, known within the CIA by either of the two code names HTLINGUAL or SRPOINTER. Various criteria were employed in selecting letters for inspection. Sometimes the name of either the intended recipient or sender appeared on a "watch list" of "suspect" persons and institutions compiled by CIA and FBI agents. In other instances envelopes were opened because of the country of origin or destination; any letter to or from the Soviet Union, for example, was subject to inspection. In still other situations mail was examined at random. When HTLINGUAL was at its peak, New York agents investigated some 13,000 letters a year; over the life of the project, at least 215,000 pieces of mail were copied.

Ultimately, the CIA collected and placed in computers a list of some 1.5 million names gleaned from its various mail-opening projects. Among those whose mail was read and photographed were author John Steinbeck and Senator Frank Church. Schwarz, Intelligence Activities and the Rights of Americans, 32 The Record of the Association of the Bar of the City of New York 43, 48 (1977). These operations were only part of a general pattern of post-World War II lawlessness and abuse of power exemplifying "contempt for the law and the Constitution" by government. Schwarz at 46. Breaking this pernicious pattern and preventing its recurrence is the task of Congress and the President. The limited question before this court is whether and how reparations can be made to individuals who were personally affected by this partial breakdown in official respect for individual liberties.

Plaintiff Norman Birnbaum is a professor of sociology at Amherst College in Massachusetts. In 1970, he wrote letters to two academic colleagues—one in Canada, and the other in Rumania—about an upcoming meeting of specialists in the sociology of religion. He sent copies of those letters to a third colleague at Moscow State University. HTLINGUAL agents copied the contents of this third letter while it was in transit through the foreign mail depot at Kennedy International Airport, and later distributed four copies to various units of the CIA. According to testimony by a member of the staff of the Inspector General of the CIA, this was done solely because intelligence agencies had an "interest" in correspondence to and from Moscow University.

Plaintiff Mary Rule MacMillen wrote a personal letter in 1973 to a Soviet dissident she had met on a trip to Russia. Her letter was intercepted at Kennedy, opened and photographed, and a copy filed by the agency. But, apparently because project HTLINGUAL was terminated two weeks later, no other reproductions were disseminated.

In the final case, that of B. Leonard Avery, a letter was written to him by his son, who was then an exchange student studying at Moscow State University. Ironically, Avery, concerned that his own letters to his son might be tampered with by Soviet authorities, attempted to avoid that possibility by sending them to the American Embassy in Vienna, where they were passed on to Moscow via diplomatic pouch. His son's replies, however, arrived by regular mail, and one of them, personal in nature, was opened here in 1968. Three copies of that letter were made, and one of these was sent to the FBI, which was described by a government witness as having "an interest in U.S. exchange students in Russia."

None of the plaintiffs were aware that their mail had been interfered with until the government responded to general requests made under the Freedom of Information Act. They were then notified that CIA files contained copies of the letters at issue.

These facts are not in dispute. The government concedes that the plaintiffs' mail was opened, read and copied. It does not contend that the actions were lawful. No judicial warrants were obtained, and no evidence was submitted to suggest the existence of probable cause for a warrantless search. Both the First and Fourth Amendments of the Constitution as well as applicable statutes and regulations support the conclusion that the opening and reading of these letters under these circumstances was illegal.

In addition, HTLINGUAL and other mail-opening projects probably violated several criminal statutes. . . .

The criminal liability—or lack of it—of government agents for the acts complained of is not an issue in this case. Plaintiffs seek a civil remedy: damages for injury suffered as a result of the operation of HTLINGUAL. They seek relief, not against the particular agents who opened their mail or who directed the program, but against the government, relying on the provisions of the Federal Tort Claims Act.

. . . .

Section 1346(b) of the Federal Tort Claims Act, 28 U.S.C. § 1346(b) provides that the United States may be sued for money damages caused by the wrongful act of any employee of the Government "under circumstances where the United States, if a private person, would be liable to the claimant in accordance with the law of the place where the act ... occurred." ...

Since the opening of mail complained of in these cases occurred at the international mail facility at John F. Kennedy International Airport in New York, the "law of the place where the act or omission occurred" is that of New York. Under the Supreme Court's interpretation of this language, a trial court hearing a federal tort action must look to the whole law of the state where the tort occurred, including that state's law of conflicts. Ordinarily, therefore, the court would first need to decide whether a New York court would apply its own law since the letters were neither mailed from or to a New York address. This issue need not be decided because the parties have stipulated that the substantive tort law of New York is applicable.

1.   Common Law Right To Privacy.

Most states recognize invasions of privacy as actionable torts.

In this context, the general rubric "right of privacy" encompasses four concepts. As described by the Restatement (Second) of Torts, they are:

(a) Intrusion upon the seclusion of another ... , or

(b) Appropriation of the other's name or likeness, ... or

(c) Publicity given to the other's private life [of a sort which is offensive and not of legitimate public concern], ... or

(d) Publicity which places the other in a false light before the public ...

....

3 Restatement (Second) of Torts, § 625A (1977).

Intrusion upon the seclusion of these plaintiffs is the branch of privacy involved in these cases. Comments to the Restatement make it plain that the tort is committed whenever an intrusive act is committed, even if the tortfeasor never reveals either the fact of the invasion or any information about the plaintiff to third persons.

The form of invasion of privacy covered by this Section *does not depend upon any publicity given to the person whose interest is invaded,* or to his affairs. It *consists solely of an intentional interference* with his interest in solitude or seclusion, either as to his person or as to his private affairs or concerns, of a kind that would be highly offensive to a reasonable man.

3 Restatement (Second) of Torts, § 652B, Comment a at 378 (1977)(emphasis added). This common law right extends beyond the plaintiff's immediate physical environment and is infringed by examinations of bank accounts or of personal records under false pretenses, or by opening of mail.

The invasion may be by physical intrusion into a place in which the plaintiff has secluded himself, as where the defendant forces his way into the plaintiff's room in a hotel, or insists over the plaintiff's objection in entering his home. It may also be by the use of the defendant's senses, with or without mechanical aids, to oversee or overhear the plaintiff's private affairs, as by looking into his upstairs windows with binoculars, or tapping his telephone wires. It may be by some other form of investigation or examination into his private concerns, *as by opening his private and personal mail,* searching his safe or his wallet, examining his private bank account, or compelling him by a forged court order to permit an inspection of his personal documents.

3 Restatement (Second) of Torts, § 652B, Comment b at 378–79 (1977) (emphasis added). The comment emphasizes that "The intrusion itself makes the defendant subject to liability, even though there is no publication or other use of any kind of the ... information...." Id. at 379. It is apparent, therefore, that, in the majority of states, case law would provide a right to recovery on the facts of these cases.

The law of New York is less clear. This state was the first to consider a case sounding in common law privacy following the publication of a leading article on the subject by Samuel Warren and Louis Brandeis, Warren & Brandeis, The Right To Privacy, 4 Harv.L.Rev. 193 (1890), and its lower courts quickly recognized the doctrine. The New York Court of Appeals at the turn of the century was, however, not yet prepared to accept the doctrine. In Roberson v. Rochester Folding Box Company, 171 N.Y. 538, 64 N.E. 442 (1902)—a case of commercial appropriation where defendant used the photograph of a woman in its advertisements without her permission—the Court by a four to three decision rejected the right to privacy as a distinct and independent tort. It stated that "The so-called right of privacy has not as yet found an abiding place in our jurisprudence". The court was careful to note, however, that it was speaking of the developments up to that point—"the doctrine cannot *now* be incorporated" and not predicting future development. *Roberson's* refusal to recognize commercial appropriations of names, faces and the like as torts was legislatively overruled by sections 50 and 51 of New York's Civil Rights Law, but the general right to privacy has not yet been recognized explicitly by the New York Court of Appeals. Were the question to be placed once more squarely before the Court of Appeals, strong evidence suggests that the court would follow the American "tide ... in favor of recognition." W.L. Prosser, The Law of Torts § 117 at 804 (4th ed. 1971).

. . . .

The evidence is overwhelming that New York would recognize the common law right of privacy sufficiently to compensate for the kind of intrusion by the government into private mails represented by the instant case.

. . . .

IV. MEASURE OF DAMAGES

A. Elements Generally

Recovery under the Federal Tort Claims Act is limited to compensatory damages. "The United States shall not be liable for ... punitive damages." 28 U.S.C. § 2674.

Neither may the award take into account injuries inflicted upon the structure of American democracy. Any theory which would allow private litigants to seek relief on behalf of the entire injured segment of the public as private attorneys general has no application in this case for two reasons. First, the effect would be punitive, and hence would contravene the limitation in section 2674. Second, it would make little sense to ask the citizenry as a whole to pay damages to these plaintiffs out of the public purse for injuries which the American population itself has suffered en masse. The remedy for the wrong against the nation, therefore, must be supplied by other branches of government.

The plaintiffs in these cases suffered none of the tangible indicia of harm for which a dollar value may easily be assigned. They experienced no financial losses. Their jobs, their reputations and prestige in their communities did not suffer. They were not subjected to intrusive or humiliating investigations by the government. Their homes were not broken into. They were not assaulted or detained. They lost no time from work and incurred no medical expenses. Plaintiff MacMillen did testify that she broke out in hives and suffered some respiratory difficulties shortly after she learned of the CIA action, but even she did not claim damages for physical injury or medical bills.

The lack of objective harm is, however, no bar to recovery. The law generally recognizes that where a person suffers an invasion of the right to privacy, awards are appropriate for general damages covering the injury of invasion itself, as well as for the resulting mental distress. The Restatement (Second) of Torts, § 652H, summarizes the rule in privacy cases:

One who has established a cause of action for unreasonable invasion of his privacy is entitled to recover damages for

(a) the harm to his interest in privacy resulting from the invasion;

(b) his mental distress proved to have been suffered if it is of a kind which normally results from such an invasion; and

(c) special damage of which the invasion is a legal cause.

3 Restatement (Second), Section 652H at 401 (1977).

. . . .

The court credits the testimony of the plaintiffs in these cases that they suffered actual mental pain, outrage and shock when they learned that government agents had interfered with their privacy by opening and reading their mail. They are entitled, therefore, to recovery for that injury under any of the three tort theories supporting liability.

The parties are entitled to recover for the invasion of their rights, without respect to the consequences. The Restatement (Second) of Torts suggests that a deprivation of common law privacy is an independent injury for which damages are appropriate. The comment to the damages section of the Restatement notes:

A cause of action for invasion of privacy, in any of its four forms, entitles the plaintiff to recover damages for the harm to the particular element of his privacy which is invaded. Thus one who suffers an intrusion upon his solitude or seclusion . . . may recover damages for the deprivation of his seclusion. One to whose private life publicity is given . . . may recover for the harm resulting to his reputation from such publicity. One who is publicly placed in a false light . . . may recover damages for the harm to his reputation from the position in which he is so placed. One whose name, likeness or identity is appropriated to the use of another ... may recover for the loss of the exclusive use of the value so appropriated.

3 Restatement (Second) of Torts, § 652H, Comment at 401–02 (1977). . . .

Valuation of intangibles is difficult, but not impossible. In ordinary tort suits, judges and juries commonly draw upon the evidence and their shared experience to assess the dollar worth of such imponderables as future pain and suffering. Over time, a range of awards appropriate for certain kinds of losses is established, enabling courts to decide whether a given recovery is reasonable. In this case, however, no precedents are available. For this reason the court decided to seek the assistance of an advisory jury.

B. Advisory Jury Recommendations

While trial by jury is specifically prohibited in Federal Tort Claims Act cases, use of an advisory jury is permitted. The verdict of such an advisory panel is only part of the data taken into consideration in arriving at the court's independent conclusion.

It was, nevertheless, instructive that this panel of average citizens— representing a broad range of economic, educational, social and political experience—uniformly found that the damages suffered by the plaintiffs in this case were substantial. Although the jurors were instructed that they could recommend nominal damages of one dollar if they found that the wrong done resulted only in slight harm, none chose this alternative. Three suggested that plaintiffs be awarded $10,000 each for their mental distress and for the encroachment upon their personal liberty; one suggested $2500; and the other eight jurors all agreed that $5000 was the compensation needed to make these plaintiffs whole.

In addition, the verdict of the advisory panel served to affirm the opinion of the court that the emotional distress these plaintiffs suffered was the sort that would be experienced by reasonable people under the almost unprecedented circumstances of these cases. Since normal principles of tort recovery in privacy do not permit compensation for unusual sensitivity, the consensus of the jurors on this point was particularly useful. The Restatement (Second) of Torts provides that:

The plaintiff [who has established a cause of action for invasion of his privacy] may also recover damages for emotional distress ... if it is of a kind that *normally* results from such an invasion and ... is normal and reasonable in its extent.

3 Restatement (Second) of Torts, § 652H, Comment b at 402 (1977)(emphasis added). It should also be noted that the jury did not find any difference in the degree of damage sustained by any of the three plaintiffs.

C. Court Findings

The court's findings on the damages issue agree substantially with those of the jury. The injuries suffered were substantial. It is entirely reasonable and normal for any citizen whose privacy has been invaded by the government, as it was in these cases, to experience comparable emotional distress. All three plaintiffs should be treated similarly in the absence of substantial proof that any one suffered perceptibly more than the others. Although plaintiff MacMillen's letter was more personal than those of the other plaintiffs, there was insufficient evidence that she suffered enough incremental embarrassment to justify a higher award.

The jurors' damage recommendations were somewhat high. Awards of the magnitude suggested by the advisory verdict have been found only where plaintiffs have suffered objective, observable injuries as a result of interferences with their civil liberties.

In the instant case it is possible to ameliorate the harm by the government's writing a letter of apology, a possibility raised by the jury. Assurance by the government that it regrets the injury to plaintiffs will serve to soothe their wounded faith in our democratic institutions, give assurances of non-recurrence in the future, and restore some confidence in our government. In analogous defamation cases, New York law recognizes that an apology will mitigate damages, or at least that a failure to apologize will enhance them. It is appropriate to apply these precedents to the special facts of this case.

In arriving at an appropriate figure some guidance is found in the amount declared by Congress as proper compensation in a similar context. Under the Omnibus Crime Control and Safe Streets Act of 1968, Congress created a right to civil recovery for individuals whose telephone or oral conversations were intercepted without legal sanction by wiretaps or eavesdropping. The basic damage figure was set at $100 a day, or $1000, whichever is larger; special damages, punitive damages and attorney's fees are also recoverable. Since the interests sought to be vindicated in these CIA cases and by the Omnibus Crime Control Act provisions are similar, comparability in the size of the non-punitive awards seems reasonable, even though it is the state rather than the federal law of damages that is being applied.

These considerations, as well as the documentary and testimonial evidence, lead to a conclusion that plaintiffs should recover for the violations they suffered, and for the mental distress which followed, in the sum of $1000 each, provided the government furnishes a suitable letter of regret and assurance of non-recurrence. Of the $1000, twenty-five per cent is to be paid to the counsel for these plaintiffs as attorney's fees. While this legal fee clearly does not compensate the plaintiffs' talented lawyers for the time devoted to these cases, it is the maximum permitted by statute. In addition to the $1000 in compensatory damages, plaintiffs are also entitled to recover costs.

V. CONCLUSION

The American people have already paid a considerable price for the CIA's illegal mail search activities. In addition to the large out-of-pocket expenditures in operating the program, there has been a perceptible widespread loss of confidence in the integrity of the mails and in the right of individuals to be free from surreptitious intrusions into their privacy by government officials. Adding to the taxpayers' burdens by awarding damages in these cases may seem like a regrettable additional disbursement for this ill-starred program. But the law requires that plaintiffs be compensated for their special loss. Moreover, knowledge by government officials that individuals have effective legal remedies to enforce their rights may deter future illegality. The existence of a court system capable of protecting the right to privacy by granting money damages and other relief against the government and its agents makes our Constitution and laws consequential to our citizens rather than pretentious, empty promises.

The court finds that the United States government, through its agents, committed torts against plaintiffs, causing compensable injury. Each plaintiff shall have judgment for $1000 plus costs.

So ordered.

NOTES

1. The court of appeals affirmed the district court's conclusion that the plaintiffs established the Government's liability for the CIA's violation of their right of privacy. It ruled further that the letter of apology was not an authorized remedy under the FTCA. Finally, it upheld the damage award of $1000 per plaintiff. While the plaintiffs should have known that the Soviet government might have read their mail and would not have suffered any distress had they not used the FOIA to discover that their mail had been read, the court held the tort to be a legal cause of the anguish that the trier of fact legitimately found the plaintiffs to have actually, and reasonably, suffered. Birnbaum v. United States, 588 F.2d 319 (2d Cir.1978).

2. Silver had a letter critical of government regulatory policies printed in a trade journal under the name of one of his company's employees, Jonap. Jonap neither wrote the letter, consented to its issuance in his name, nor agreed with the views expressed therein. A jury found that Silver and the company tortiously appropriated Jonap's name and placed him in a false light. It awarded Jonap $24,000 for the former tort and $32,000 for the latter. On appeal, however, these awards were deemed redundant and Jonap's recovery was limited to $32,000. Jonap v. Silver, 1 Conn.App. 550, 474 A.2d 800 (1984).

Zacchini v. Scripps–Howard Broadcasting Co.

Supreme Court of the United States, 1977.
433 U.S. 562, 97 S.Ct. 2849, 53 L.Ed.2d 965.

■ MR. JUSTICE WHITE delivered the opinion of the Court.

Petitioner, Hugo Zacchini, is an entertainer. He performs a "human cannonball" act in which he is shot from a cannon into a net some 200 feet away. Each performance occupies some 15 seconds. In August and September 1972, petitioner was engaged to perform his act on a regular basis at the Geauga County Fair in Burton, Ohio. He performed in a fenced area, surrounded by grandstands, at the fairgrounds. Members of the public attending the fair were not charged a separate admission fee to observe his act.

On August 30, a freelance reporter for Scripps–Howard Broadcasting Company, the operator of a television broadcasting station and respondent in this case, attended the fair. He carried a small movie camera. Petitioner noticed the reporter and asked him not to film the performance. The reporter did not do so on that day; but on the instructions of the producer of respondent's daily newscast, he returned the following day and videotaped the entire act. This film clip, approximately 15 seconds in length, was shown on the 11 o'clock news program that night, together with favorable commentary.

Petitioner then brought this action for damages, alleging that he is "engaged in the entertainment business," that the act he performs is one "invented by his father and ... performed only by his family for the last fifty years," that respondent "showed and commercialized the film of his act without his consent," and that such conduct was an "unlawful appropriation of plaintiff's professional property." Respondent answered and moved for summary judgment, which was granted by the trial court.

[The Ohio Court of Appeals reversed, but its decision in turn was reversed by the Ohio Supreme Court.] ...

We granted certiorari to consider an issue unresolved by this Court: whether the First and Fourteenth Amendments immunized respondent from damages for its alleged infringement of petitioner's state law "right of publicity." Insofar as the Ohio Supreme Court held that the First and Fourteenth Amendments of the United States Constitution required judgment for respondent, we reverse the judgment of that court.

. . . .

The Ohio Supreme Court held that respondent is constitutionally privileged to include in its newscasts matters of public interest that would otherwise be protected by the right of publicity, absent an intent to injure or to appropriate for some nonprivileged purpose. If under this standard respondent had merely reported that petitioner was performing at the fair and described or commented on his act, with or without showing his picture on television, we would have a very different case. But petitioner is not contending that his appearance at the fair and his performance could not be reported by the press as newsworthy items. His complaint is that respondent filmed his entire act and displayed that film on television for the public to see and enjoy. This, he claimed, was an appropriation of his professional property. The Ohio Supreme Court agreed that petitioner had "a right of publicity" that gave him "personal control over the commercial display and exploitation of his personality and the exercise of his talents." This right of "exclusive control over the publicity given to his performance" was said to be such a "valuable part of the benefit which may be attained by his talents and efforts" that it was entitled to legal protection. It was also observed, or at least expressly assumed, that petitioner had not abandoned his rights by performing under the circumstances present at the Geauga County Fair Grounds.

The Ohio Supreme Court nevertheless held that the challenged invasion was privileged, saying that the press "must be accorded broad latitude in its choice of how much it presents of each story or incident, and of the emphasis to be given to such presentation. No fixed standard which would bar the press from reporting or depicting either an entire occurrence or an entire discrete part of a public performance can be formulated which would not unduly restrict the 'breathing room' in reporting which freedom of the press requires." Under this view, respondent was thus constitutionally free to film and display petitioner's entire act.

The Ohio Supreme Court relied heavily on Time, Inc. v. Hill, 385 U.S. 374, 87 S.Ct. 534, 17 L.Ed.2d 456 (1967), but that case does not mandate a media privilege to televise a performer's entire act without his consent. Involved in Time, Inc. v. Hill was a claim under the New York "Right of Privacy" statute that Life Magazine, in the course of reviewing a new play, had connected the play with a long-past incident involving petitioner and his family and had falsely described their experience and conduct at that time. The complaint sought damages for humiliation and suffering flowing from these nondefamatory falsehoods that allegedly invaded Hill's privacy. The Court held, however, that the opening of a new play linked to an actual incident was a matter of public interest and that Hill could not recover without showing that the Life report was knowingly false or was published with reckless disregard for the truth—the same rigorous standard that had been applied in New York Times v. Sullivan.

Time, Inc. v. Hill, which was hotly contested and decided by a divided court, involved an entirely different tort than the "right of publicity" recognized by the Ohio Supreme Court. As the opinion reveals in Time, Inc. v. Hill, the Court was steeped in the literature of privacy law and was aware of the developing distinctions and nuances in this branch of the law. The Court, for example, cited Prosser, Handbook of the Law of Torts (3d ed. 1964), and the same author's well-known article, Privacy, 48 Calif.L.Rev. 383 (1960), both of which divided privacy into four distinct branches. The Court was aware that it was adjudicating a "false light" privacy case involving a matter of public interest, not a case involving "intrusion," "appropriation" of a name or likeness for the purposes of trade, or "private details" about a non-newsworthy person or event. It is also abundantly clear that Time, Inc. v. Hill did not involve a performer, a person with a name having commercial value, or any claim to a "right of publicity." This discrete kind of "appropriation" case was plainly identified in the literature cited by the Court and had been adjudicated in the reported cases.

The differences between these two torts are important. First, the State's interests in providing a cause of action in each instance are different. "The interest protected" in permitting recovery for placing the plaintiff in a false light "is clearly that of reputation, with the same overtones of mental distress as in defamation." Prosser, supra, 48 Calif.L.Rev., at 400. By contrast, the State's interest in permitting a "right of publicity" is in protecting the proprietary interest of the individual in his act in part to encourage such entertainment. As we later note, the State's interest is closely analogous to the goals of patent and copyright law, focusing on the right of the individual to reap the reward of his endeavors and having little to do with protecting feelings or reputation. Second, the two torts differ in the degree to which they intrude on dissemination of information to the public. In "false light" cases the only way to protect the interests involved is to attempt to minimize publication of the damaging matter, while in "right of publicity" cases the only question is who gets to do the publishing. An entertainer such as petitioner usually has no objection to the wide-spread publication of his act as long as he gets the commercial benefit of such publication. Indeed, in the present case petitioner did not seek to enjoin the broadcast of his act; he simply sought compensation for the broadcast in the form of damages.

Nor does it appear that our later cases, such as Rosenbloom v. Metromedia, Inc., 403 U.S. 29, 91 S.Ct. 1811, 29 L.Ed.2d 296 (1971); Gertz v. Robert Welch, Inc., 418 U.S. 323, 94 S.Ct. 2997, 41 L.Ed.2d 789 (1974); and Time, Inc. v. Firestone, 424 U.S. 448, 96 S.Ct. 958, 47 L.Ed.2d 154 (1976), require or furnish substantial support for the Ohio court's privilege ruling. These cases, like *New York Times,* emphasize the protection extended to the press by the First Amendment in defamation cases, particularly when suit is brought by a public official or a public figure. None of them involve an alleged appropriation by the press of a right of publicity existing under state law.

Moreover, *Time, Inc. v. Hill, New York Times, Metromedia, Gertz* and *Firestone* all involved the reporting of events; in none of them was there an attempt to broadcast or publish an entire act for which the performer ordinarily gets paid. It is evident, and there is no claim here to the contrary, that petitioner's state-law right of publicity would not serve to prevent respondent from reporting the newsworthy facts about petitioner's act. Wherever the line in particular situations is to be drawn between media reports that are protected and those that are not, we are quite sure that the First and Fourteenth Amendments do not immunize the media when they broadcast a performer's entire act without his consent. The Constitution no more prevents a State from requiring respondent to compensate petitioner for broadcasting his act on television than it would privilege respondent to film and broadcast a copyrighted dramatic work without liability to the copyright owner, or to film and broadcast a prize fight, or a baseball game where the promoters or the participants had other plans for publicizing the event. There are ample reasons for reaching this conclusion.

The broadcast of a film of petitioner's entire act poses a substantial threat to the economic value of that performance. As the Ohio court recognized, this act is the product of petitioner's own talents and energy, the end result of much time, effort and expense. Much of its economic value lies in the "right of exclusive control over the publicity given to his performance"; if the public can see the act for free on television, they will be less willing to pay to see it at the fair. The effect of a public broadcast of the performance is similar to preventing petitioner from charging an admission fee. "The rationale for [protecting the right of publicity] is the straight-forward one of preventing unjust enrichment by the theft of good will.[12] No social purpose is served by having the defendant get for free some

---

12. It is possible, of course, that respondent's news broadcast increased the value of petitioner's performance by stimulating the public's interest in seeing the act live. In

aspect of the plaintiff that would have market value and for which he would normally pay." Kalven, Privacy in Tort Law—Were Warren and Brandeis Wrong?, 31 Law and Contemporary Problems 326, 331 (1966). Moreover, the broadcast of petitioner's entire performance, unlike the unauthorized use of another's name for purposes of trade or the incidental use of a name or picture by the press, goes to the heart of petitioner's ability to earn a living as an entertainer. Thus in this case, Ohio has recognized what may be the strongest case for a "right of publicity"— involving not the appropriation of an entertainer's reputation to enhance the attractiveness of a commercial product, but the appropriation of the very activity by which the entertainer acquired his reputation in the first place.

Of course, Ohio's decision to protect petitioner's right of publicity here rests on more than a desire to compensate the performer for the time and effort invested in his act; the protection provides an economic incentive for him to make the investment required to produce a performance of interest to the public. This same consideration underlies the patent and copyright laws long enforced by this Court. As the Court stated in Mazer v. Stein, 347 U.S. 201, 74 S.Ct. 460, 98 L.Ed. 630 (1954):

"The economic philosophy behind the clause empowering Congress to grant patents and copyrights is the conviction that encouragement of individual effort by personal gain is the best way to advance public welfare through the talents of authors and inventors in 'Science and useful Arts.' Sacrificial days devoted to such creative activities deserve rewards commensurate with the services rendered."

These laws perhaps regard the "reward to the owner [as] a secondary consideration," but they were "intended definitely to grant valuable, enforceable rights" in order to afford greater encouragement to the production of works of benefit to the public. The Constitution does not prevent Ohio from making a similar choice here in deciding to protect the entertainer's incentive in order to encourage the production of this type of work.

There is no doubt that entertainment, as well as news, enjoys First Amendment protection. It is also true that entertainment itself can be important news. But it is important to note that neither the public nor respondent will be deprived of the benefit of petitioner's performance as long as his commercial stake in his act is appropriately recognized. Petitioner does not seek to enjoin the broadcast of his performance; he simply wants to be paid for it. Nor do we think that a state-law damages remedy against respondent would represent a species of liability without fault contrary to the letter or spirit of *Gertz*. Respondent knew exactly that petitioner objected to televising his act, but nevertheless displayed the entire film.

We conclude that although the State of Ohio may as a matter of its own law privilege the press in the circumstances of this case, the First and Fourteenth Amendments do not require it to do so.

these circumstances, petitioner would not be able to prove damages and thus would not recover. But petitioner has alleged that the broadcast injured him to the extent of $25,000, and we think the State should be allowed to authorize compensation of this injury if proved.

Reversed.

■ MR. JUSTICE POWELL, with whom MR. JUSTICE BRENNAN and MR. JUSTICE MARSHALL join, dissenting.

Disclaiming any attempt to do more than decide the narrow case before us, the Court reverses the decision of the Supreme Court of Ohio based on repeated incantation of a single formula: "a performer's entire act." The holding today is summed up in one sentence:

"Wherever the line in particular situations is to be drawn between media reports that are protected and those that are not, we are quite sure that the First and Fourteenth Amendments do not immunize the media when they broadcast a performer's entire act without his consent."

I doubt that this formula provides a standard clear enough even for resolution of this case. In any event, I am not persuaded that the Court's opinion is appropriately sensitive to the First Amendment values at stake, and I therefore dissent.

Although the Court would draw no distinction, I do not view respondent's action as comparable to unauthorized commercial broadcasts of sporting events, theatrical performances, and the like where the broadcaster keeps the profits. There is no suggestion here that respondent made any such use of the film. Instead, it simply reported on what petitioner concedes to be a newsworthy event, in a way hardly surprising for a television station—by means of film coverage. The report was part of an ordinary daily news program, consuming a total of 15 seconds. It is a routine example of the press' fulfilling the informing function so vital to our system.

The Court's holding that the station's ordinary news report may give rise to substantial liability[2] has disturbing implications, for the decision could lead to a degree of media self-censorship. Hereafter, whenever a television news editor is unsure whether certain film footage received from a camera crew might be held to portray an "entire act," he may decline coverage—even of clearly newsworthy events—or confine the broadcast to watered-down verbal reporting, perhaps with an occasional still picture. The public is then the loser. This is hardly the kind of news reportage that the First Amendment is meant to foster.

In my view the First Amendment commands a different analytical starting point from the one selected by the Court. Rather than begin with a quantitative analysis of the performer's behavior—is this or is this not his entire act?—we should direct initial attention to the actions of the news media: what use did the station make of the film footage? When a film is

---

2. At some points the Court seems to acknowledge that the reason for recognizing a cause of action asserting a "right of publicity" is to prevent unjust enrichment. But the remainder of the opinion inconsistently accepts a measure of damages based not on the defendant's enhanced profits but on harm to the plaintiff regardless of any gain to the defendant. Indeed, in this case there is no suggestion that respondent television station gained financially by showing petitioner's flight (although it no doubt received its normal advertising revenue for the news program—revenue it would have received no matter which news items appeared). Nevertheless, in the unlikely event that petitioner can prove that his income was somehow reduced as a result of the broadcast, respondent will apparently have to compensate him for the difference.

used, as here, for a routine portion of a regular news program, I would hold that the First Amendment protects the station from a "right of publicity" or "appropriation" suit, absent a strong showing by the plaintiff that the news broadcast was a subterfuge or cover for private or commercial exploitation.

I emphasize that this is a "reappropriation" suit, rather than one of the other varieties of "right of privacy" tort suits identified by Dean Prosser in his classic article. In those other causes of action the competing interests are considerably different. The plaintiff generally seeks to avoid any sort of public exposure, and the existence of constitutional privilege is therefore less likely to turn on whether the publication occurred in a news broadcast or in some other fashion. In a suit like the one before us, however, the plaintiff does not complain about the fact of exposure to the public, but rather about its timing or manner. He welcomes some publicity, but seeks to retain control over means and manner as a way to maximize for himself the monetary benefits that flow from such publication. But having made the matter public—having chosen, in essence, to make it newsworthy—he cannot, consistent with the First Amendment, complain of routine news reportage.

Since the film clip here was undeniably treated as news and since there is no claim that the use was subterfuge, respondent's actions were constitutionally privileged. I would affirm.

[The dissenting opinion of STEVENS, J., is omitted.]

Chappell v. Stewart

Court of Appeals of Maryland, 1896.
82 Md. 323, 33 A. 542.

■ BRYAN, J. Thomas C. Chappell filed a bill in equity against David Stewart. Without entering minutely into the details of the bill of complaint, it may be stated that he charged that the defendant had employed detectives to follow him and watch him wherever he should go; and that this conduct caused him great inconvenience and annoyance, interfered with his social intercourse and his business; and caused grave suspicions to be entertained about him, so as greatly to damage his financial credit. It is also alleged that the defendant intended to continue the same course of conduct towards the complainant. The bill prayed for an injunction to restrain and prohibit the defendant from the aforesaid conduct; and for a decree for damages; and for general relief. He also filed a special motion for a preliminary injunction. The defendant filed a demurrer and answer combined together. It was maintained that the bill of complaint did not entitle the complainant to any relief in equity, because it did not set forth any legal or equitable right which the defendant was injuring; because it did not set forth any danger of irreparable damage, and for other reasons. And the answer denied the charges of the bill. The court refused to grant the preliminary injunction. The defendant, by leave of the court, amended his pleading by changing its form so as to make it simply an answer and nothing more. Afterwards the court passed an order sustaining the demurrer and dismissing the bill with costs.

The court acted inadvertently in passing an order on the demurrer, when, in consequence of an amendment of the defendant's pleading, there was no longer a demurrer in the case. We shall see whether this oversight inflicted any injury on the plaintiff. As the answer denied the allegations of the bill, and the motion for a preliminary injunction was heard on bill and answer, it was of necessity that the motion should be denied. And as the bill, assuming that all its allegations were true, did not contain any matter cognizable in equity, it ought then and there to have been dismissed. Courts of equity exercise a very extensive jurisdiction in cases involving property rights. The occasion does not require us to state its precise limits. It is usually said in general terms that it does not exist where a plain, adequate, and complete remedy can be obtained at law. In this case it is alleged that rights affecting the complainant's person have been violated, and that there is a purpose to persist in violating them. The ordinary processes of the law are fully competent to redress all injuries of this character. They have always been considered beyond the scope of the powers of a court of equity. In Gee v. Pritchard, 2 Swanst. 402, Lord Eldon said: "The question will be whether the bill has stated facts of which the court can take notice, as a case of civil property, which it is bound to protect." In Bispham's Equity (5th ed.), 584, note 2, it is said: "But it is the rights of property, or rather rights in property, that equity interferes to protect; a party is not entitled to a writ of injunction for a matter affecting his person." In Kerr on Injunctions, pages 1 and 2, it is said: "A court of equity is conversant only with questions of property and the maintenance of civil rights. Injury to property, whether actual or prospective, is the foundation on which its jurisdiction rests. A court of equity has no jurisdiction in matters merely criminal or merely immoral, which do not affect any right to property. If a charge be of a criminal nature, or an offense against the public peace, and does not touch the enjoyment of property, jurisdiction cannot be entertained. The court has no jurisdiction to restrain or prevent crime, or to enforce the performance of a moral duty, except so far as the same is concerned with rights to property; nor can it interfere on the ground of any criminal offense committed, or for the purpose of getting a better remedy in the case of a criminal offense, or for putting a stop to acts, which, if permitted, would lead to a breach of the public peace." We, of course, do not intend to express an opinion on the merits of any action at law which the complainant may see fit to bring.

Decree affirmed with costs.

Galella v. Onassis

United States Court of Appeals, Second Circuit, 1973.
487 F.2d 986.

■ SMITH, J. Donald Galella, a free-lance photographer, appeals from a summary judgment dismissing his complaint against three Secret Service agents for false arrest, malicious prosecution and interference with trade, the dismissal after trial of his identical complaint against Jacqueline Onassis and the grant of injunctive relief to defendant Onassis on her counterclaim and to the intervenor, the United States, on its intervening complaint and a third judgment retaxing transcript costs to plaintiff. In addition to numerous alleged procedural errors, Galella raises the First Amendment as an absolute shield against liability to any sanctions. The judgments dismissing the complaints are affirmed; the grant of injunctive relief is affirmed as herein modified. Taxation of costs against the plaintiff is affirmed in part, reversed in part.

Galella is a free-lance photographer specializing in the making and sale of photographs of well-known persons. Defendant Onassis is the widow of the late President John F. Kennedy, mother of the two Kennedy children, John and Caroline, and is the wife of Aristotle Onassis, widely known shipping figure and reputed multimillionaire. John Walsh, James Kalafatis and John Connelly are U.S. Secret Service agents assigned to the duty of protecting the Kennedy children under 18 U.S.C. § 3056, which provides for protection of the children of deceased presidents up to the age of 16.

Galella fancies himself as a "paparazzo" (literally a kind of annoying insect, perhaps roughly equivalent to the English "gadfly.") Paparazzi make themselves as visible to the public and obnoxious to their photographic subject as possible to aid in the advertisement and wide sale of their works.

Some examples of Galella's conduct brought out at trial are illustrative. Galella took pictures of John Kennedy riding his bicycle in Central Park across the way from his home. He jumped out into the boy's path, causing the agents concern for John's safety. The agents' reaction and interrogation of Galella led to Galella's arrest and his action against the agents; Galella on other occasions interrupted Caroline at tennis, and invaded the children's private schools. At one time he came uncomfortably close in a power boat to Mrs. Onassis swimming. He often jumped and postured around while taking pictures of her party, notably at a theater opening but also on numerous other occasions. He followed a practice of bribing apartment house, restaurant and nightclub doormen as well as romancing a family servant to keep him advised of the movements of the family.

After detention and arrest following complaint by the Secret Service agents protecting Mrs. Onassis' son and his acquittal in the state court, Galella filed suit in state court against the agents and Mrs. Onassis. Galella claimed that under orders from Mrs. Onassis, the three agents had falsely arrested and maliciously prosecuted him, and that this incident in addition to several others described in the complaint constituted an unlawful interference with his trade.

Mrs. Onassis answered denying any role in the arrest or any part in the claimed interference with his attempts to photograph her, and counterclaimed for damages and injunctive relief, charging that Galella had invaded her privacy, assaulted and battered her, intentionally inflicted emotional distress and engaged in a campaign of harassment.

The action was removed under 28 U.S.C. § 1442(a) to the United States District Court....

Certain incidents of photographic coverage by Galella, subsequent to an agreement among the parties for Galella not to so engage, resulted in the issuance of a temporary restraining order to prevent further harassment of Mrs. Onassis and the children. Galella was enjoined from "harassing, alarming, startling, tormenting, touching the person of the defendant ... or her children ... and from blocking their movements in the public places and thoroughfares, invading their immediate zone of privacy by means of physical movements, gestures or with photographic equipment and from performing any act reasonably calculated to place the lives and safety of the defendant ... and her children in jeopardy." Within two months, Galella was charged with violation of the temporary restraining order; a new order was signed which required that the photographer keep 100 yards from the Onassis apartment and 50 yards from the person of the defendant and her children. Surveillance was also prohibited.

. . . .

After a six-week trial the court dismissed Galella's claim and granted relief to both the defendant and the intervenor. Galella was enjoined from (1) keeping the defendant and her children under surveillance or following any of them; (2) approaching within 100 yards of the home of defendant or her children, or within 100 yards of either child's school or within 75 yards of either child or 50 yards of defendant; (3) using the name, portrait or picture of defendant or her children for advertising; (4) attempting to communicate with defendant or her children except through her attorney.

We conclude that grant of summary judgment and dismissal of Galella's claim against the Secret Service agents was proper....

... Unquestionably the agents were acting within the scope of their authority.

. . . .

Discrediting all of Galella's testimony the court found the photographer guilty of harassment, intentional infliction of emotional distress, assault and battery, commercial exploitation of defendant's personality, and invasion of privacy. Fully crediting defendant's testimony, the court found no liability on Galella's claim. Evidence offered by the defense showed that Galella had on occasion intentionally physically touched Mrs. Onassis and her daughter, caused fear of physical contact in his frenzied attempts to get their pictures, followed defendant and her children too closely in an automobile, endangered the safety of the children while they were swimming, water skiing and horseback riding. Galella cannot successfully challenge the court's finding of tortious conduct.

Finding that Galella had "insinuated himself into the very fabric of Mrs. Onassis' life ..." the court framed its relief in part on the need to prevent further invasion of the defendant's privacy. Whether or not this accords with present New York law, there is no doubt that it is sustainable under New York's proscription of harassment.

Of course legitimate countervailing social needs may warrant some intrusion despite an individual's reasonable expectation of privacy and freedom from harassment. However the interference allowed may be no greater than that necessary to protect the overriding public interest. Mrs. Onassis was properly found to be a public figure and thus subject to news coverage. Nonetheless, Galella's action went far beyond the reasonable bounds of news gathering. When weighed against the *de minimis* public importance of the daily activities of the defendant, Galella's constant surveillance, his obtrusive and intruding presence, was unwarranted and unreasonable. If there were any doubt in our minds, Galella's inexcusable conduct toward defendant's minor children would resolve it.

Galella does not seriously dispute the court's finding of tortious conduct. Rather, he sets up the First Amendment as a wall of immunity protecting newsmen from any liability for their conduct while gathering news. There is no such scope to the First Amendment right. Crimes and torts committed in news gathering are not protected. There is no threat to a free press in requiring its agents to act within the law.

. . . .

Injunctive relief is appropriate. Galella has stated his intention to continue his coverage of defendant so long as she is newsworthy, and his continued harassment even while the temporary restraining orders were in effect indicate that no voluntary change in his technique can be expected. New York courts have found similar conduct sufficient to support a claim for injunctive relief.

The injunction, however, is broader than is required to protect the defendant. Relief must be tailored to protect Mrs. Onassis from the "paparazzo" attack which distinguishes Galella's behavior from that of other photographers; it should not unnecessarily infringe on reasonable efforts to "cover" defendant. Therefore, we modify the court's order to prohibit only (1) any approach within twenty-five (25) feet of defendant or any touching of the person of the defendant Jacqueline Onassis; (2) any blocking of her movement in public places and thoroughfares; (3) any act foreseeably or reasonably calculated to place the life and safety of defendant in jeopardy; and (4) any conduct which would reasonably be foreseen to harass, alarm or frighten the defendant.

Any further restriction on Galella's taking and selling pictures of defendant for news coverage is, however, improper and unwarranted by the evidence.

Likewise we affirm the grant of injunctive relief to the government modified to prohibit any action interfering with Secret Service agents' protective duties. Galella thus may be enjoined from (a) entering the children's schools or play areas; (b) engaging in action calculated or reasonably foreseen to place the children's safety or well being in jeopardy, or which would threaten or create physical injury; (c) taking any action which could reasonably be foreseen to harass, alarm, or frighten the children; and (d) from approaching within thirty (30) feet of the children.

. . . .

As modified, the relief granted fully allows Galella the opportunity to photograph and report on Mrs. Onassis' public activities. Any prior restraint on news gathering is miniscule and fully supported by the findings.

Affirmed in part, reversed in part and remanded for modification of the judgment in accordance with this opinion. Costs on appeal to be taxed in favor of appellees.

■ TIMBERS, J. (concurring in part and dissenting in part). With one exception, I concur in the judgment of the Court and in the able majority opinion of Judge Smith.

With the utmost deference to and respect for my colleagues, however, I am constrained to dissent from the judgment of the Court and the majority opinion to the extent that they modify the injunctive relief found necessary by the district court to protect Jacqueline Onassis and her children, Caroline B. and John F. Kennedy, Jr., from the continued predatory conduct of the self-proclaimed paparazzo Galella.

. . . .

. . . I feel very strongly that such findings should not be set aside or drastically modified by our Court unless they are clearly erroneous; and I do not understand the majority to suggest that they are.

. . . .

With deference, I believe the majority's modification of the injunction in the respects indicated above to be unwarranted and unworkable. . . . I most respectfully dissent.

NOTE

1. Subsequently, Galella was held in contempt of court for violating the injunction entered by the district court on remand. Galella v. Onassis, 533 F.Supp. 1076 (S.D.N.Y.1982). Galella avoided a fine and a prison sentence, however, by promising the district judge that he would in the future avoid taking any pictures of Jacqueline Onassis and her family.

2. On May 30, 2000, the *New York Times* reported that the French Parliament had adopted a law restricting news photography designed "to protect the dignity of people snapped in an incriminating or humiliating pose." See France Adopts Limits on Photographers, N.Y. Times, May 31, 2000, at A4.

———

C. THE FAMILY

Baumann v. Baumann

Court of Appeals of New York, 1929.
250 N.Y. 382, 165 N.E. 819.

■ HUBBS, J. The plaintiff has secured a declaratory judgment, which adjudges that she is the lawful wife of the defendant Charles Ludwig Baumann; that the defendants are not and never have been husband and wife; that an alleged divorce procured by the defendant Charles Ludwig Baumann from the plaintiff in Yucatan, Mexico, is null and void; and that an alleged marriage between the defendants on June 28, 1926, is null and void. The findings and evidence justify the judgment to that extent.

... We think the conclusion reached by the Appellate Division was justified by the facts in this case. The judgment entered, however, goes far beyond establishing the plaintiff's matrimonial status. It enjoins the defendants from representing or holding out that they are husband and wife, and from representing or holding out that the defendant Charles Ludwig Baumann was divorced from the plaintiff. It also restrains the defendant Ray Starr Einstein from assuming or using the name "Baumann." It also restrains the defendants from going through any marriage ceremony, or "attempting or purporting to have performed any further marriage ceremony between them" during the life of the plaintiff. In granting such injunctive relief, on the facts in this case, we think the court exceeded its jurisdiction.

. . . .

The declaratory judgment herein has established the matrimonial status of the plaintiff. Injunctive relief is not necessary to establish that status. It is elementary that a court of equity will not award the extraordinary relief of injunction, except in cases where some legal wrong has been done or is threatened, and where there exists in the moving party some substantial legal right to be protected. Whether there exists or is threatened a legal wrong to be restrained and a legal right to be protected is in the absence of disputed questions of fact, a question of law.

Does the fact that the defendants are living as man and wife, and holding themselves out as husband and wife, under the name of "Baumann," constitute a legal wrong, which infringes a substantial legal right of the plaintiff, under the facts in this case? If so, the court had jurisdiction in its discretion to grant the injunction. The acts of the defendants cannot affect the matrimonial status of the plaintiff. That is established by the provisions of the declaratory judgment, which also adjudges the Yucatan divorce and the attempted marriage of the defendants null and void. If the plaintiff has any property rights, that decree also protects those rights by legally establishing her status.

It cannot be questioned that the conduct of the defendants is reprehensible. That it is illegal has been determined by the judgment herein. That it is socially and morally wrong may be conceded, and doubtless it is annoying and humiliating to the plaintiff. Those considerations alone do not, however, justify the granting of an injunction. Equity cannot by injunction restrain conduct which merely injures a person's feelings and causes mental anguish.

The law does not remedy all social evils or moral wrongs. In [another] case, the court said: "Although injuries to feelings are recognized as a ground for increasing damages, the law has never given a right of action for an injury to feelings merely. . . ."

The most serious contention of the plaintiff is in relation to that part of the judgment which restrains the defendant Ray Starr Einstein from using the name "Baumann." Upon marriage a woman takes her husband's name. The plaintiff has a legal right to use the name "Baumann," but not necessarily an exclusive right to the use of that name. There is no pretense that said defendant is impersonating the plaintiff. She does not pretend to be Berenice L. Baumann, the plaintiff. There is no claim that the plaintiff will be injured because of a mistake in identity....

In the last analysis the only injury alleged is an injury to plaintiff's feelings. For such an injury an injunction will not be granted....

. . . .

The plaintiff is living apart from her husband under a separation agreement which secures to her $21,000 a year. She is conducting an independent business under the name of Berenice L. Baumann. She has secured a judgment which defines her matrimonial status, and protects her property rights, if any. The complaint does not allege that any of plaintiff's property rights are affected or endangered by the conduct of the defendants. Neither does it allege that the defendant Ray Starr Einstein has alienated the affections of plaintiff's husband, or that plaintiff has been excluded by any act or conduct of said defendant from the marital society of her husband. Under such circumstances the acts enjoined do not constitute legal wrongs, which invade substantial legal rights of the plaintiff that can be recognized in law and protected by injunction. It is not the province of courts of equity to administer paternal relief in domestic affairs. As a matter of fact, such decrees cannot be enforced....

. . . .

Attempts to govern the morals of people by injunctions can only result in making ridiculous the courts which grant such decrees.

We do not find it necessary to discuss the question of the jurisdiction of equity to grant injunctive relief in cases where there are no property rights involved. It is sufficient for the decision in this case that there exists no legal wrong which gives rise to a correlative legal right.

The judgment of the Appellate Division and that of the Special Term should be modified, by striking therefrom the restraining clauses thereof, and, as modified, affirmed, without costs.

■ CRANE, J. (dissenting in part). We must not recoil from an equity judgment because the law which it enforces is also good morals....

. . . .

■ O'BRIEN, J. (dissenting in part)....

Something unsound appears to lie in a rule which would deny to a court of equity the power to enjoin the masquerade of another's name and title and the infringement of the mingled personal and property rights which include that name and constitute the matrimonial status. This part of the judgment which grants an injunction can be reversed only because this court is prepared to concede a complete absence of power to protect that status in a manner substantially similar to the method adopted by the courts below. A mere declaration of rights will prove inadequate; I think that equity has jurisdiction to enforce some protective measure. An individual possesses an exclusive property right in a name....

. . . .

Among the most enlightened of modern equity cases is Greenberg v. Greenberg, 218 App.Div. 104 [218 N.Y.S. 87], where an injunction restrained a husband from prosecuting an action to obtain a judgment of divorce. The relief granted in that case was based upon the fact that "there are many conceivable uses to which such a judgment of divorce could be put, causing plaintiff expense, litigation, worry, annoyance, and misrepresentation." It was to protect the present plaintiff from the same factors of legal wrong that the Special Term and a unanimous Appellate Division issued the injunction which is now so vigorously and successfully assailed. To hold that the Supreme Court is without power to exercise its discretion on such facts as this record reveals seems to me to run counter to the expanding trend of equity.

Mark v. Kahn

Supreme Judicial Court of Massachusetts, 1956.
333 Mass. 517, 131 N.E.2d 758.

■ SPALDING, J. The plaintiff brings this bill in equity to enjoin the defendant Anna R. Kahn, his former wife who has remarried, from registering their minor children at school under the surname Kahn, which is her present name, or from representing that their name is Kahn. Although her husband is also a defendant we shall, for convenience, refer to Anna R. Kahn sometimes hereinafter as the defendant. The evidence is reported and the judge made findings of material facts.

[Defendant had obtained a decree nisi of divorce from plaintiff under which defendant was awarded custody of the two children and support. Defendant later married a man who had three children of a previous marriage. These children and plaintiff's daughter attend the same school. The lower court found that defendants were motivated by hostility toward plaintiff and enjoined them from registering plaintiff's children under the surname of Kahn. Defendants appealed.]

Whether a parent having custody of a minor child pursuant to a decree of divorce may change the surname of such child or cause him to be called by a different name in the face of opposition of the former spouse, is a question that has never been decided by this court. Such a question was presented in Lord v. Cummings, 303 Mass. 457, 22 N.E.2d 26, in a petition in equity brought in the Probate Court but the court refused to decide it because it was not a matter within the equity jurisdiction granted to the Probate Courts. The question whether the subject matter of the petition was within the general principles of equity jurisprudence was left open. In the present proceeding we are squarely faced with this question. To be sure, the point was not raised in the court below and it has not been raised here. But consent or waiver by the parties cannot confer jurisdiction over a cause where none exists. Hence it is our duty to notice the point of our own motion.

The question presented not only is one of first impression in this Commonwealth but from a careful search of the authorities does not appear to have been passed on elsewhere. There are several decisions dealing with the right of one spouse to change the surname of a minor child in the face of opposition of the other spouse, but these cases have arisen either under a statute expressly empowering the court to grant such relief or as incidental to divorce proceedings.... In some of these cases the petition to change the name of the minor child was granted and in others it was denied. But none is authority for the proposition that one spouse may invoke the aid of a court of equity to prevent the other from registering the child in school under a surname different from that of the complaining spouse or from representing that the child's name is different.

We are of opinion that the relief sought by the plaintiff here is one that a court of equity ought to grant in appropriate instances. The old notion that equity will protect only property rights, which stems from a dictum of Lord Eldon in Gee v. Pritchard, 2 Swanst. 402, was repudiated by this court recently in Kenyon v. Chicopee, 320 Mass. 528, 70 N.E.2d 241. There it was said, "We believe the true rule to be that equity will protect personal rights by injunction upon the same conditions upon which it will protect property rights by injunction. In general, these conditions are, that unless relief is granted a substantial right of the plaintiff will be impaired to a material degree; that the remedy at law is inadequate; and that injunctive relief can be applied with practical success and without imposing an impossible burden on the court or bringing its processes into disrepute." Tested by these principles the present case, we think, is one where the aid of a court of equity may properly be invoked.

Previously this court has said that at common law a person could change his name at will, without resort to legal proceedings, by merely adopting another name, provided that this was done for an honest purpose. The statute regulating the changing of name does not restrict a person's choice of name but aids him in securing an official record which definitely and specifically establishes his change of name.

In the present case no court action seeking to change the children's surname has been brought; rather their mother has attempted by her own act to have the children of her first marriage adopt the surname of their stepfather. It does not follow that because one may adopt any name he may choose, so long as such change is not made for fraudulent purposes, a parent may select for a child a name different from that by which such child is known. It does not appear here that the plaintiff's children have ever consented to being called Kahn. However, in view of their ages their consent would not necessarily be decisive. Until they reach an age when they are capable of making an intelligent choice in the matter of their name they ought not to have another name foisted upon them which they may later reject. Prior to that time one in the plaintiff's position ought to have the right to be heard to prevent a change or use of a name different from that of their birth. The bond between a father and his children in circumstances like the present is tenuous at best and if their name is changed that bond may be weakened if not destroyed. We recognize that here the defendant may not have effected an actual change of the children's name but by registering them at school under the name of Kahn she has gone far in that direction. We perceive no insuperable difficulties in enforcing decrees granting injunctive relief in cases of this sort.

In the cases cited above dealing with change of names of children either under statutes or as incidental to divorce proceedings the following factors have been deemed to be relevant. When a father supports a child, and manifests a continuing interest in his welfare, and without unreasonable delay objects to an attempted change of name, the court must decide the issue by determining what is for the child's best interest. A change of name may not be in the child's best interest if the effect of such change is to contribute to the further estrangement of the child from a father who exhibits a desire to preserve the parental relationship. Undoubtedly there are instances when an informal change to the surname of a stepfather would be in the best interests of the child. A father who completely abandons a child, or is indifferent to a child's welfare or has by his serious misconduct caused the child embarrassment, can by his actions lose the right to successfully protest the child's change of name. There may be other factors, but these are the ones likely to be decisive in most cases.

With these principles in mind we turn to the decision of the judge below. He found that "The use by the Mark children, at the insistence of the defendants, of the surname Kahn ... [was] motivated by a spirit of hostility on the part of the defendants toward ... [the father]." It is doubtful whether this finding is supported by the evidence. But be that as it may, there are lacking here sufficient findings to support the decree below. On the crucial and controlling issue whether the use of the name Kahn was for the best welfare of the children the findings tell us little. Conceivably the trial judge had that consideration in mind but his decision appears to have been based on the defendants' motive rather than what was best for the children. "Where the facts on which the rights of the parties depend have not been ascertained at the trial it is within the power of the court, in its discretion and of its own motion, to recommit the cause for retrial."

Accordingly the decree must be reversed and the case is to be further heard in conformity with this opinion.

In Re Marriage of Schiffman

Supreme Court of California, 1980.
28 Cal.3d 640, 169 Cal.Rptr. 918, 620 P.2d 579.

■ NEWMAN, J. Appellant challenges the portion of an interlocutory decree that changes her child's surname from appellant's birth name (formerly called "maiden name") to the surname of the father and enjoins each parent from any further change without court permission.

. . . .

Ms. Herdman and Mr. Schiffman were married on January 15, 1977, and separated six months later. She then was four months pregnant. On August 4, 1977 she petitioned for dissolution and noted that there was an unborn child. The child was born on November 2, and Ms. Herdman registered the name on the birth certificate as Aita Marie Herdman. The dissolution was called for trial on February 21, 1978, and essentially was uncontested. The trial ... court granted dissolution and awarded custody of Aita Marie to Ms. Herdman.

The court raised the question of the surname and, for its statement of the law, summarized two court of appeal decisions, In re Worms (1967) 252

Cal.App.2d 130, 60 Cal.Rptr. 88 and Montandon v. Montandon (1966) 242 Cal.App.2d 886, 52 Cal.Rptr. 43. They state the traditional rule that the father has a "primary right" or "protectible interest" in having the minor child bear his surname even after the mother is awarded custody. Under that rule a change is permitted not to save the child from "inconvenience and embarrassment" but only when there is "substantial" reason to do so, as "where the father's misconduct has been such as to justify a forfeiture of his rights or where his name is positively deleterious to the child...."

Relying on *Worms* and *Montandon* the trial court ruled that "the child's name is *as the law prescribes* the surname of the father." (Italics added.) It also ruled that Ms. Herdman "will have no authority" to change her daughter's surname without a court order giving her permission to do so, and it put teeth in the ruling by prescribing that "each party is enjoined from changing the child's surname from Schiffman." Ms. Herdman has appealed.

Should *Worms, Montandon, Trower,* and *Larson* be overturned? ...

Surnames have been used at least since the Norman Conquest. In early days they were derived from individual reputations, characteristics, occupations, or places of birth and residence and were not passed from generation to generation. The custom of patrilineal succession seems to have been a response to England's medieval social and legal system, which came to vest all rights of ownership and management of marital property in the husband. "[T]he inheritance of property was often contingent upon an heir's retention of the surname associated with that property." (Note, The Controversy Over Children's Surnames: Familial Autonomy, Equal Protection and the Child's Best Interests, 1979 Utah L.Rev. 303, 305 (Utah Note).) The trend toward paternal surnames was accelerated by Henry VIII, who required recordation of legitimate births in the name of the father. Thence the naming of children after the fathers became the custom in England.

At common law a married woman had little legal identity apart from her husband's. The fiction that husband and wife were one "worked out in reality to mean that ... the one [was] the husband...." After marriage, custom dictated that the wife give up her surname and assume the husband's. She could no longer contract or litigate in her own name; nor could she manage property or earn money. Allowing the husband to determine the surname of their offspring was part of that system, wherein he was sole legal representative of the marriage, its property, and its children.

Today those bases for patrimonial control of surnames have virtually disappeared. In the mid–19th century, Married Women's Property Acts returned to wives a separate legal identity. Progress toward marital and parental equality has accelerated in recent years. Most important for our purposes are many steps the California Legislature has taken to abolish outmoded distinctions in the rights of spouses and parents....

The Family Law Act enacted in 1969, effected changes including the adoption of "no-fault" divorce. In 1972 the Legislature deleted the preference accorded mothers in custody disputes involving young children

(§ 4600, as added by Stats. 1969, ch. 1608, p. 3330, § 8) and required that custody be awarded to "either parent according to the best interests of the child." In 1979 the Legislature strengthened section 4600, declaring that it is public policy to encourage divorced parents "to share the rights and responsibilities of child rearing. . . ." The Legislature decreed that, in awarding custody, the trial court "shall not prefer a parent as custodian because of that parent's sex."

The 1973 statutes eliminated virtually all sex-specific differences in property rights of spouses. The Legislature repealed the declaration that "The husband is the head of the family"; it provided that "either spouse" rather than "the husband" has the management and control of both the community personal property and the community real property; and throughout the Family Law Act it gave the wife the same property rights as the husband by use of the sex-neutral designation of "spouse".

In 1975 the Legislature adopted the California Uniform Parentage Act. One of its aims is to eliminate legal distinctions between legitimate and illegitimate children. . . . The major premise is that ". . . regardless of the marital status of the parents, all children and all parents have equal rights with respect to each other."

Recently the Court of Appeal ruled that the Uniform Parentage Act abrogates common law rules governing parental disputes over children's surnames. (Donald J. v. Evna M. (1978) 81 Cal.App.3d 929, 147 Cal.Rptr. 15.) . . .

      . . . .

[In *Donald J.,*] the court reasoned, "[w]ith the adoption of the California Uniform Parentage Act no longer can it be said that a parent has a primary right or protectible interest in having his or her child bear and maintain that parent's surname merely because of the parent's sex and marital status with respect to that child's other parent at the time the child is born. The controlling consideration in determining whether a change in a child's surname should be ordered against the objection of one of the parents, is the welfare of the child." Plaintiff therefore had the right to a determination of surname, *based on the legal standard of the child's best interest.*

We think that is the correct rule. While neither the Uniform Parentage Act nor other legislation expressly overrules the common law, is there not a compelling implication to that effect? The Legislature clearly has articulated the policy that irrational, sex-based differences in marital and parental rights should end and that parental disputes about children should be resolved in accordance with each child's best interest.

      . . . .

That test should neither consume inordinate judicial time nor engender confusion in the keeping of birth records. Here we are not presented with the question of what name originally should be entered on a birth certificate. Nothing we say is intended to change the established practice in that regard or disturb the prevalent custom of giving a child born in wedlock the paternal surname. Nor do we create any new right to involve the courts in surname disputes. Rather, we consider only the test to be applied when such a dispute does arise between natural parents.

Adoption of a "best interest" test is but an evolutionary change in the state's rules for resolving parental disputes over children's surnames. Even *Trower*, decided before the recent legislation that helps effect equality of spouses and parents, conceded that a father's interest in having his child bear his name "... is not absolute. The best interests of the child are paramount."

"When the reason for a rule ceases, so should the rule itself." (Civ. Code, § 3510.) "The true doctrine is, that the common law by its own principles adapts itself to varying conditions, and modifies its own rules so as to serve the ends of justice under the different circumstances...."

We conclude that the rule giving the father, as against the mother, a primary right to have his child bear his surname should be abolished. Henceforth, as in parental custody disputes, the sole consideration when parents contest a surname should be the child's best interest. Expressions to the contrary in *Trower, Worms, Montandon,* and *Larson* are disapproved.

Under the test thus revised the length of time that the child has used a surname is to be considered. If, as here, the time is negligible because the child is very young, other facts may be controlling. For instance, the effect of a name change on preservation of the father-child relationship, the strength of the mother-child relationship, and the identification of the child as part of a family unit are all pertinent. The symbolic role that a surname other than the natural father's may play in easing relations with a new family should be balanced against the importance of maintaining the biological father-child relationship....

In recognizing a father's right to have his child bear his surname, courts largely have ignored the impact a name may have on the mother-child relationship. Perhaps that is because mothers, usually given custodial preference in the past, generally had more regular contact and could maintain a psychological relationship without the need for the tie a surname provides. However, "the maternal surname might play a significant role in supporting the mother-child relationship, for example, in the cases where the father is the custodial parent or *where the custodial mother goes by her birth-given surname.*" ([Utah Note, p. 330]; italics added.) Ms. Herdman uses her birth name; and Aita Marie's future friends, neighbors, teachers, acquaintances, and family indeed may associate her with the name Herdman rather than Schiffman. The trial court apparently failed to weigh those considerations and relied exclusively on the anachronistic, father's "primary right" theory to decide the issue.

Accordingly, the portion of the interlocutory decree that changes the child's surname is reversed. The cause is remanded to the trial court for a finding whether the name change requested by the father is in the best interests of the child.

■ Mosk, J., concurring. I concur in the order but would qualify the rationale.

. . . .

. . . I would recognize a presumption that the parent with custody—whether custody was assumed without conflict, by agreement or by court order—has acted in the child's best interest in selecting the name. The selection may be the original name, or a name change for a child of tender years. The presumption, however, would be rebuttable. Just as the noncustodial parent can seek a corrective court order if the child's health, education or control are deleteriously affected by the abuse of custodial care, so the selection of name can be contested on the ground that it is not in the child's best interest. The burden, however, would be on the noncustodial parent to establish the intrusion on the child's best interest.

. . . .

[The concurring opinion of BIRD, C.J., is omitted.]

CLARK, J., dissenting. . . .

Whatever the ancient origins of the common law rule, it must be obvious to all that the rule reflects past and present custom and practice in California—legitimate children are given the paternal surname. Apart from adoptions—where the express purpose is to sever biological ties—we are unaware of any significant number of California parents refusing to use the paternal surname, and this case reflects no evidence that the traditional practice is even questioned.

Custom and practice have always been fundamental to our civil law because they necessarily define and assure reasonable expectations of the parties. When it appears a certain result will uniformly occur in the absence of dispute, the courts in a democracy should defer to popular determination unless Constitution or statute requires a different result. No constitutional or statutory law even suggests questioning the custom and practice at issue.

Neither the majority nor concurring opinion has shown that the common law rule favoring the paternal surname has resulted in any evil, and it is presumptuous—maybe even elitist—for this court to now reject long-settled California practice and custom.

I would affirm the trial court's judgment.

■ RICHARDSON, J., concurs.

Blazek v. Rose

Circuit Court of Illinois, Cook County, 1922.

As Reported in Pound, Cases on Equitable Relief Against Defamation and Injuries to Personality 138 (2d ed. Chafee 1930).

This suit begun in February, 1922, in the Circuit Court of Cook County, Illinois, has not been reported. The bill in equity filed by Frank Blazek, through his mother as next friend, against Ike Rose makes in substance the following allegations.

The plaintiff, aged eleven years, is the son of Rosa Blazek. His mother is an abnormal being, her body being joined or grown together with the body of her sister, Josefa Blazek. This physical anomaly renders the sisters available for public exhibitions. In 1920 the sisters made a written agreement in Germany with the defendant, placing themselves under his management for three years beginning January 1, 1921, for the purpose of being publicly exhibited in the United States. They came to this country with the plaintiff in February, 1921, and have frequently appeared for exhibition at various theaters, county fairs and other public places in the United States and Canada. The plaintiff is not a party to this agreement or mentioned in it, and it confers no right upon the defendant to exhibit him or to advertise his appearance. On the contrary, it was expressly understood between the plaintiff's mother and the defendant at the time of the execution of this contract that the plaintiff would not be required to take any part in public exhibitions, and that neither his name nor photograph would be used in advertisements or any reference made to him.

Immediately upon the plaintiff's arrival in this country, the defendant informed the plaintiff and his mother that he would be required to appear at the various exhibitions in company with his mother and be pointed out to the public as her son. The defendant began at once the publication of advertisements in newspapers and upon bulletins and billboards in Chicago and other cities containing photographs of the plaintiff and references to him in phrases such as "one son and two mothers." The protests of the plaintiff and his mother against his appearance in exhibitions and advertisements were ineffectual. The defendant has compelled the plaintiff to appear for exhibition with his mother by threats that he would cancel the contract and leave the Blazeks without means of support and by threatening them with deportation from the United States and with criminal prosecution. The plaintiff's mother, as the defendant knows, has no other means of support than the compensation derived from exhibitions. In states and cities where the employment of children is prohibited by law, the defendant seeks to evade the law by having the plaintiff occupy a conspicuous place in the audience instead of appearing upon the stage, but nevertheless points out the plaintiff to the audience as the son of Rosa Blazek, thereby violating the spirit if not the letter of the law and compelling the plaintiff to participate in such violation.

During the year after the plaintiff's arrival in the United States, he was forced to appear at more than 1000 exhibitions conducted by the defendant in the United States and Canada. . . .

The plaintiff and his mother have now been advised by counsel that his appearance at exhibitions cannot be legally demanded by the defendant, and he has refused to appear since February, 1922, but the defendant, despite protests, continues to publish the plaintiff's photographs and refer to him in various advertisements. The plaintiff has reason to fear that the defendant will persist in such conduct unless restrained by injunction. The right to the publication of the plaintiff's photograph in itself and in connection with advertisements of his public appearance as aforesaid is a valuable property right. The use of the photographs constitutes a violation of his right of property and of privacy. The publication of the photographs and references to the plaintiff, if continued, will bring him into unpleasant and embarrassing notoriety, and have caused, and if continued, will cause him to be made the subject of jesting, sneering, lewd, licentious, lascivious, and indecent remarks by many of the persons to whose attention the advertisements may be brought. The plaintiff has suffered and will suffer irreparable injury for which he will have no adequate remedy at law. The defendant, although claiming to be a resident of New York City, spends nearly all his time traveling, so that it would be difficult, if not wholly impossible, to obtain service upon him.

The plaintiff prays an answer; that all funds received by the defendant through such exhibitions may be declared to be trust funds of which the defendant is the joint trustee for himself and the plaintiff, and that the trust may be dissolved; that an accounting may be taken and the defendant be decreed to pay to the plaintiff what shall appear to be due from him, and such damages as the plaintiff has suffered by reason of the unauthorized use of his photographs and name in advertisements and the deprivation of schooling; that the defendant, his attorneys, agents, and employees, may be restrained until further order of the court from publishing the plaintiff's photograph or name, or any reference whatever to him, in any of said advertisements relating to the exhibition of the Blazek sisters, from interfering with the plaintiff, and from directing public attention to him in any manner whatsoever; and that upon a hearing the injunction may be made permanent; and for general relief and a writ of summons.

A temporary injunction was granted, and no appeal perfected.

In Re Sampson

Court of Appeals of New York, 1972.
29 N.Y.2d 900, 328 N.Y.S.2d 686, 278 N.E.2d 918.

■ PER CURIAM. In affirming the qualified court direction to operate on the then 15–year–old child over the mother's religious objections two observations only need be added to the exhaustive opinion at the Family Court. The holding by this court in Matter of Seiferth, 309 N.Y. 80, 127 N.E.2d 820, did not limit to drastic or mortal circumstances the statutory power of the Family Court or like court in neglect proceedings to order necessary surgery. In the *Seiferth* case the court was obliged to choose between the findings of the Children's Court and that of the Appellate Division on how best to exercise a court's discretionary powers in the circumstances. There was no disagreement over power, and that case, like this, involved a serious physiological impairment which did not threaten the physical life or health of the subject or raise the risk of contagion to the public. Indeed, the opinions in that case impliedly or expressly recognized the court's power to direct surgery even in the absence of risk to the physical health or life of the subject or to the public. Nor does the religious objection to blood transfusion present a bar at least where the transfusion is necessary to the success of required surgery. What doubt there may have been was laid to rest by the case of Jehovah's Witnesses in State of Wash. v. King County Hosp., 390 U.S. 598, 88 S.Ct. 1260, 20 L.Ed.2d 158, affg. 278 F.Supp. 488, rehearing den. 391 U.S. 961, 88 S.Ct. 1844, 20 L.Ed.2d 874.

The order of the Appellate Division, 37 A.D.2d 668, 323 N.Y.S.2d 253, should be affirmed, without costs.

Cruzan v. Director, Missouri Department of Health

Supreme Court of the United States, 1990.
497 U.S. 261, 110 S.Ct. 2841, 111 L.Ed.2d 224.

■ CHIEF JUSTICE REHNQUIST delivered the opinion of the Court.

Petitioner Nancy Beth Cruzan was rendered incompetent as a result of severe injuries sustained during an automobile accident. Co-petitioners Lester and Joyce Cruzan, Nancy's parents and co-guardians, sought a court order directing the withdrawal of their daughter's artificial feeding and hydration equipment after it became apparent that she had virtually no chance of recovering her cognitive faculties. The Supreme Court of Missouri held that because there was no clear and convincing evidence of Nancy's desire to have life-sustaining treatment withdrawn under such circumstances, her parents lacked authority to effectuate such a request. We granted certiorari, and now affirm.

On the night of January 11, 1983, Nancy Cruzan lost control of her car as she traveled down Elm Road in Jasper County, Missouri. The vehicle overturned, and Cruzan was discovered lying face down in a ditch without detectable respiratory or cardiac function. Paramedics were able to restore her breathing and heartbeat at the accident site, and she was transported to a hospital in an unconscious state. An attending neurosurgeon diagnosed her as having sustained probable cerebral contusions compounded by significant anoxia (lack of oxygen). The Missouri trial court in this case found that permanent brain damage generally results after 6 minutes in an anoxic state; it was estimated that Cruzan was deprived of oxygen from 12 to 14 minutes. She remained in a coma for approximately three weeks and then progressed to an unconscious state in which she was able to orally ingest some nutrition. In order to ease feeding and further the recovery, surgeons implanted a gastrostomy feeding and hydration tube in Cruzan with the consent of her then husband. Subsequent rehabilitative efforts proved unavailing. She now lies in a Missouri state hospital in what is commonly referred to as a persistent vegetative state: generally, a condition in which a person exhibits motor reflexes but evinces no indications of significant cognitive function. The State of Missouri is bearing the cost of her care.

After it had become apparent that Nancy Cruzan had virtually no chance of regaining her mental faculties her parents asked hospital employees to terminate the artificial nutrition and hydration procedures. All agree that such a removal would cause her death. The employees refused to honor the request without court approval. The parents then sought and received authorization from the state trial court for termination. . . .

The Supreme Court of Missouri reversed by a divided vote. The court recognized a right to refuse treatment embodied in the common-law doctrine of informed consent, but expressed skepticism about the application of that doctrine in the circumstances of this case. The court also declined to read a broad right of privacy into the State Constitution which would "support the right of a person to refuse medical treatment in every circumstance," and expressed doubt as to whether such a right existed under the United States Constitution. It then decided that the Missouri

Living Will statute embodied a state policy strongly favoring the preservation of life. The court found that Cruzan's statements to her roommate regarding her desire to live or die under certain conditions were "unreliable for the purpose of determining her intent," "and thus insufficient to support the co-guardians claim to exercise substituted judgment on Nancy's behalf." It rejected the argument that Cruzan's parents were entitled to order the termination of her medical treatment, concluding that "no person can assume that choice for an incompetent in the absence of the formalities required under Missouri's Living Will statutes or the clear and convincing, inherently reliable evidence absent here." ...

We granted certiorari to consider the question of whether Cruzan has a right under the United States Constitution which would require the hospital to withdraw life-sustaining treatment from her under these circumstances.

At common law, even the touching of one person by another without consent and without legal justification was a battery....This notion of bodily integrity has been embodied in the requirement that informed consent is generally required for medical treatment. The informed consent doctrine has become firmly entrenched in American tort law....

The logical corollary of the doctrine of informed consent is that the patient generally possesses the right not to consent, that is, to refuse treatment. Until about 15 years ago and the seminal decision in In re Quinlan, 70 N.J. 10, 355 A.2d 647, cert. denied sub nom., Garger v. New Jersey, 429 U.S. 922, 97 S.Ct. 319, 50 L.Ed.2d 289 (1976), the number of right-to-refuse-treatment decisions were relatively few. Most of the earlier cases involved patients who refused medical treatment forbidden by their religious beliefs, thus implicating First Amendment rights as well as common law rights of self-determination. More recently, however, with the advance of medical technology capable of sustaining life well past the point where natural forces would have brought certain death in earlier times, cases involving the right to refuse life-sustaining treatment have burgeoned.

In the *Quinlan* case, young Karen Quinlan suffered severe brain damage as the result of anoxia, and entered a persistent vegetative state. Karen's father sought judicial approval to disconnect his daughter's respirator. The New Jersey Supreme Court granted the relief, holding that Karen had a right of privacy grounded in the Federal Constitution to terminate treatment. Recognizing that this right was not absolute, however, the court balanced it against asserted state interests. Noting that the State's interest "weakens and the individual's right to privacy grows as the degree of bodily invasion increases and the prognosis dims," the court concluded that the state interests had to give way in that case. The court also concluded that the "only practical way" to prevent the loss of Karen's privacy right due to her incompetence was to allow her guardian and family to decide "whether she would exercise it in these circumstances."

After *Quinlan*, however, most courts have based a right to refuse treatment either solely on the common law right to informed consent or on both the common law right and a constitutional privacy right. In Superintendent of Belchertown State School v. Saikewicz, 373 Mass. 728, 370

N.E.2d 417 (1977), the Supreme Judicial Court of Massachusetts relied on both the right of privacy and the right of informed consent to permit the withholding of chemotherapy from a profoundly-retarded 67–year–old man suffering from leukemia. Reasoning that an incompetent person retains the same rights as a competent individual "because the value of human dignity extends to both," the court adopted a "substituted judgment" standard whereby courts were to determine what an incompetent individual's decision would have been under the circumstances. Distilling certain state interests from prior case law—the preservation of life, the protection of the interests of innocent third parties, the prevention of suicide, and the maintenance of the ethical integrity of the medical profession—the court recognized the first interest as paramount and noted it was greatest when an affliction was curable, "as opposed to the State interest where, as here, the issue is not whether, but when, for how long, and at what cost to the individual [a] life may be briefly extended."

In In re Storar, 52 N.Y.2d 363, 438 N.Y.S.2d 266, 420 N.E.2d 64, cert. denied, 454 U.S. 858, 102 S.Ct. 309, 70 L.Ed.2d 153 (1981), the New York Court of Appeals declined to base a right to refuse treatment on a constitutional privacy right. Instead, it found such a right "adequately supported" by the informed consent doctrine. In *In re Eichner* (decided with *In re Storar*) an 83–year–old man who had suffered brain damage from anoxia entered a vegetative state and was thus incompetent to consent to the removal of his respirator. The court, however, found it unnecessary to reach the question of whether his rights could be exercised by others since it found the evidence clear and convincing from statements made by the patient when competent that he "did not want to be maintained in a vegetative coma by use of a respirator." In the companion *Storar* case, a 52–year–old man suffering from bladder cancer had been profoundly retarded during most of his life. Implicitly rejecting the approach taken in *Saikewicz,* the court reasoned that due to such life-long incompetency, "it is unrealistic to attempt to determine whether he would want to continue potentially life prolonging treatment if he were competent." As the evidence showed that the patient's required blood transfusions did not involve excessive pain and without them his mental and physical abilities would deteriorate, the court concluded that it should not "allow an incompetent patient to bleed to death because someone, even someone as close as a parent or sibling, feels that this is best for one with an incurable disease."

Many of the alter cases build on the principles established in *Quinlan, Saikewicz* and *Storar/Eichner.* For instance, in In re Conroy, 98 N.J. 321, 486 A.2d 1209 (1985), the same court that decided *Quinlan* considered whether a nasogastric feeding tube could be removed from an 84–year–old incompetent nursing-home resident suffering irreversible mental and physical ailments. While recognizing that a federal right of privacy might apply in the case, the court, contrary to its approach in *Quinlan,* decided to base its decision on the common-law right to self-determination and informed consent. . . .

Reasoning that the right of self-determination should not be lost merely because an individual is unable to sense a violation of it, the court held that incompetent individuals retain a right to refuse treatment. It also held that such a right could be exercised by a surrogate decisionmaker using a "subjective" standard when there was clear evidence that the incompetent person would have exercised it. Where such evidence was lacking, the court held that an individual's right could still be invoked in certain circumstances under objective "best interest" standards. Thus, if some trustworthy evidence existed that the individual would have wanted to terminate treatment, but not enough to clearly establish a person's wishes for purposes of the subjective standard, and the burden of a prolonged life from the experience of pain and suffering markedly outweighed its satisfactions, treatment could be terminated under a "limited-objective" standard. Where no trustworthy evidence existed, and a person's suffering would make the administration of life-sustaining treatment inhumane, a "pure-objective" standard could be used to terminate treatment. If none of these conditions obtained, the court held it was best to err in favor of preserving life.

The court also rejected certain categorical distinctions that had been drawn in prior refusal-of-treatment cases as lacking substance for decision purposes: the distinction between actively hastening death by terminating treatment and passively allowing a person to die of a disease; between treating individuals as an initial matter versus withdrawing treatment afterwards; between ordinary versus extraordinary treatment; and between treatment by artificial feeding versus other forms of life-sustaining medical procedures....[4]

In contrast to *Conroy,* the Court of Appeals of New York recently refused to accept less than the clearly expressed wishes of a patient before permitting the exercise of her right to refuse treatment by a surrogate decisionmaker. In re Westchester County Medical Center on behalf of O'Connor, 72 N.Y.2d 517, 534 N.Y.S.2d 886, 531 N.E.2d 607 (1988) (*O'Connor*). There, the court, over the objection of the patient's family members, granted an order to insert a feeding tube into a 77–year–old woman rendered incompetent as a result of several strokes. While continuing to recognize a common-law right to refuse treatment, the court rejected the substituted judgment approach for asserting it "because it is inconsistent with our fundamental commitment to the notion that no person or court should substitute its judgment as to what would be an acceptable quality of life for another." ...

Other courts have found state statutory law relevant to the resolution of these issues. In Conservatorship of Drabick, 200 Cal.App.3d 185, 245 Cal.Rptr. 840, cert. denied, 488 U.S. 958, 109 S.Ct. 399, 102 L.Ed.2d 387 (1988), the California Court of Appeal authorized the removal of a nasogastric feeding tube from a 44–year–old man who was in a persistent vegeta-

---

4. In a later trilogy of cases, the New Jersey Supreme Court stressed that the analytic framework adopted in *Conroy* was limited to elderly, incompetent patients with shortened life expectancies, and established alternative approaches to deal with a different set of situations. See ... In re Jobes, 108 N.J. 394, 529 A.2d 434 (1987)(31–year–old woman in persistent vegetative state entitled to removal of jejunostomy feeding tube—even though hearsay testimony regarding patient's intent insufficient to meet clear and convincing standard of proof, under *Quinlan,* family or close friends entitled to make a substituted judgment for patient).

tive state as a result of an auto accident. Noting that the right to refuse treatment was grounded in both the common law and a constitutional right of privacy, the court held that a state probate statute authorized the patient's conservator to order the withdrawal of life-sustaining treatment when such a decision was made in good faith based on medical advice and the conservatee's best interests. While acknowledging that "to claim that [a patient's] 'right to choose' survives incompetence is a legal fiction at best," the court reasoned that the respect society accords to persons as individuals is not lost upon incompetence and is best preserved by allowing others "to make a decision that reflects [a patient's] interests more closely than would a purely technological decision to do whatever is possible."

In In re Estate of Longeway, 133 Ill.2d 33, 139 Ill.Dec. 780, 549 N.E.2d 292 (1989), the Supreme Court of Illinois considered whether a 76–year–old woman rendered incompetent from a series of strokes had a right to the discontinuance of artificial nutrition and hydration. Noting that the boundaries of a federal right of privacy were uncertain, the court found a right to refuse treatment in the doctrine of informed consent. The court further held that the State Probate Act impliedly authorized a guardian to exercise a ward's right to refuse artificial sustenance in the event that the ward was terminally ill and irreversibly comatose. Declining to adopt a best interests standard for deciding when it would be appropriate to exercise a ward's right because it "lets another make a determination of a patient's quality of life," the court opted instead for a substituted judgment standard. Finding the "expressed intent" standard utilized in *O'Connor* too rigid, the court noted that other clear and convincing evidence of the patient's intent could be considered. The court also adopted the "consensus opinion [that] treats artificial nutrition and hydration as medical treatment." Cf. McConnell v. Beverly Enterprises—Connecticut, Inc., 209 Conn. 692, 705, 553 A.2d 596, 603 (1989)(right to withdraw artificial nutrition and hydration found in the Connecticut Removal of Life Support Systems Act, which "provid[es] functional guidelines for the exercise of the common law and constitutional rights of self-determination"; attending physician authorized to remove treatment after finding that patient is in a terminal condition, obtaining consent of family, and considering expressed wishes of patient).[6]

As these cases demonstrate, the common-law doctrine of informed consent is viewed as generally encompassing the right of a competent individual to refuse medical treatment. Beyond that, these decisions demonstrate both similarity and diversity in their approach to decision of what all agree is a perplexing question with unusually strong moral and ethical overtones. State courts have available to them for decision a number of sources—state constitutions, statutes, and common law—which are not available to us. In this Court, the question is simply and starkly whether the United States Constitution prohibits Missouri from choosing the rule of decision which it did. This is the first case in which we have been squarely presented with the issue of whether the United States Constitution grants

---

6. [Every court that has] ... specifically considered and discussed the issue of withholding or withdrawing artificial nutrition and hydration from incompetent individuals....permitted or would permit the termination of such measures based on rights grounded in the common law, or in the State or Federal Constitution.

what is in common parlance referred to as a "right to die." We follow the judicious counsel of our decision in Twin City Bank v. Nebeker, 167 U.S. 196, 17 S.Ct. 766, 42 L.Ed. 134 (1897), where we said that in deciding "a question of such magnitude and importance ... it is the [better] part of wisdom not to attempt, by any general statement, to cover every possible phase of the subject."

The Fourteenth Amendment provides that no State shall "deprive any person of life, liberty, or property, without due process of law." The principle that a competent person has a constitutionally protected liberty interest in refusing unwanted medical treatment may be inferred from our prior decisions. In Jacobson v. Massachusetts, 197 U.S. 11, 25 S.Ct. 358, 49 L.Ed. 643 (1905), for instance, the Court balanced an individual's liberty interest in declining an unwanted smallpox vaccine against the State's interest in preventing disease. Decisions prior to the incorporation of the Fourth Amendment into the Fourteenth Amendment analyzed searches and seizures involving the body under the Due Process Clause and were thought to implicate substantial liberty interests.

Just this Term, in the course of holding that a State's procedures for administering antipsychotic medication to prisoners were sufficient to satisfy due process concerns, we recognized that prisoners possess "a significant liberty interest in avoiding the unwanted administration of antipsychotic drugs under the Due Process Clause of the Fourteenth Amendment." Still other cases support the recognition of a general liberty interest in refusing medical treatment.

But determining that a person has a "liberty interest" under the Due Process Clause does not end the inquiry;[7] "whether respondent's constitutional rights have been violated must be determined by balancing his liberty interests against the relevant state interests."

Petitioners insist that under the general holdings of our cases, the forced administration of life-sustaining medical treatment, and even of artificially-delivered food and water essential to life, would implicate a competent person's liberty interest. Although we think the logic of the cases discussed above would embrace such a liberty interest, the dramatic consequences involved in refusal of such treatment would inform the inquiry as to whether the deprivation of that interest is constitutionally permissible. But for purposes of this case, we assume that the United States Constitution would grant a competent person a constitutionally protected right to refuse lifesaving hydration and nutrition.

Petitioners go on to assert that an incompetent person should possess the same right in this respect as is possessed by a competent person. . . .

The difficulty with petitioners' claim is that in a sense it begs the question: an incompetent person is not able to make an informed and voluntary choice to exercise a hypothetical right to refuse treatment or any other right. Such a "right" must be exercised for her, if at all, by some sort

7. Although many state courts have held that a right to refuse treatment is encompassed by a generalized constitutional right of privacy, we have never so held. We believe this issue is more properly analyzed in terms of a Fourteenth Amendment liberty interest.

of surrogate. Here, Missouri has in effect recognized that under certain circumstances a surrogate may act for the patient in electing to have hydration and nutrition withdrawn in such a way as to cause death, but it has established a procedural safeguard to assure that the action of the surrogate conforms as best it may to the wishes expressed by the patient while competent. Missouri requires that evidence of the incompetent's wishes as to the withdrawal of treatment be proved by clear and convincing evidence. The question, then, is whether the United States Constitution forbids the establishment of this procedural requirement by the State. We hold that it does not.

Whether or not Missouri's clear and convincing evidence requirement comports with the United States Constitution depends in part on what interests the State may properly seek to protect in this situation. Missouri relies on its interest in the protection and preservation of human life, and there can be no gainsaying this interest. As a general matter, the States— indeed, all civilized nations—demonstrate their commitment to life by treating homicide as serious crime. Moreover, the majority of States in this country have laws imposing criminal penalties on one who assists another to commit suicide. We do not think a State is required to remain neutral in the face of an informed and voluntary decision by a physically-able adult to starve to death.

But in the context presented here, a State has more particular interests at stake. The choice between life and death is a deeply personal decision of obvious and overwhelming finality. We believe Missouri may legitimately seek to safeguard the personal element of this choice through the imposition of heightened evidentiary requirements. It cannot be disputed that the Due Process Clause protects an interest in life as well as an interest in refusing life-sustaining medical treatment. Not all incompetent patients will have loved ones available to serve as surrogate decisionmakers. And even where family members are present, "[t]here will, of course, be some unfortunate situations in which family members will not act to protect a patient." A State is entitled to guard against potential abuses in such situations. Similarly, a State is entitled to consider that a judicial proceeding to make a determination regarding an incompetent's wishes may very well not be an adversarial one, with the added guarantee of accurate factfinding that the adversary process brings with it.[9] Finally, we think a State may properly decline to make judgments about the "quality" of life that a particular individual may enjoy, and simply assert an unqualified interest in the preservation of human life to be weighed against the constitutionally protected interests of the individual.

In our view, Missouri has permissibly sought to advance these interests through the adoption of a "clear and convincing" standard of proof to govern such proceedings. "The function of a standard of proof, as that

---

9. Since Cruzan was a patient at a state hospital when this litigation commenced, the State has been involved as an adversary from the beginning. However, it can be expected that many of these types of disputes will arise in private institutions, where a guardian *ad* *litem* or similar party will have been appointed as the sole representative of the incompetent individual in the litigation. In such cases, a guardian may act in entire good faith, and yet not maintain a position truly adversarial to that of the family....

concept is embodied in the Due Process Clause and in the realm of factfinding, is to 'instruct the factfinder concerning the degree of confidence our society thinks he should have in the correctness of factual conclusions for a particular type of adjudication.' " "This Court has mandated an intermediate standard of proof—'clear and convincing evidence'—when the individual interests at stake in a state proceeding are both 'particularly important' and 'more substantial than mere loss of money.' " Thus, such a standard has been required in deportation proceedings, in denaturalization proceedings, in civil commitment proceedings, and in proceedings for the termination of parental rights.[10] Further, this level of proof, "or an even higher one, has traditionally been imposed in cases involving allegations of civil fraud, and in a variety of other kinds of civil cases involving such issues as ... lost wills, oral contracts to make bequests, and the like."

We think it self-evident that the interests at stake in the instant proceedings are more substantial, both on an individual and societal level, than those involved in a run-of-the-mine civil dispute. But not only does the standard of proof reflect the importance of a particular adjudication, it also serves as "a societal judgment about how the risk of error should be distributed between the litigants." The more stringent the burden of proof a party must bear, the more that party bears the risk of an erroneous decision. We believe that Missouri may permissibly place an increased risk of an erroneous decision on those seeking to terminate an incompetent individual's life-sustaining treatment. An erroneous decision not to terminate results in a maintenance of the status quo; the possibility of subsequent developments such as advancements in medical science, the discovery of new evidence regarding the patient's intent, changes in the law, or simply the unexpected death of the patient despite the administration of life-sustaining treatment, at least create the potential that a wrong decision will eventually be corrected or its impact mitigated. An erroneous decision to withdraw life-sustaining treatment, however, is not susceptible of correction....

It is also worth noting that most, if not all, States simply forbid oral testimony entirely in determining the wishes of parties in transactions which, while important, simply do not have the consequences that a decision to terminate a person's life does. At common law and by statute in most States, the parole evidence rule prevents the variations of the terms of a written contract by oral testimony. The statute of frauds makes unenforceable oral contracts to leave property by will, and statutes regulating the making of wills universally require that those instruments be in writing. There is no doubt that statutes requiring wills to be in writing, and statutes of frauds which require that a contract to make a will be in writing, on occasion frustrate the effectuation of the intent of a particular decedent, just as Missouri's requirement of proof in this case may have

---

10. We recognize that these cases involved instances where the government sought to take action against an individual. Here, by contrast, the government seeks to protect the interests of an individual, as well as its own institutional interests, in life. We do not see any reason why important individual interests should be afforded less protection simply because the government finds itself in the position of defending them....

frustrated the effectuation of the not-fully-expressed desires of Nancy Cruzan. But the Constitution does not require general rules to work faultlessly; no general rule can.

In sum, we conclude that a State may apply a clear and convincing evidence standard in proceedings where a guardian seeks to discontinue nutrition and hydration of a person diagnosed to be in a persistent vegetative state. We note that many courts which have adopted some sort of substituted judgment procedure in situations like this, whether they limit consideration of evidence to the prior expressed wishes of the incompetent individual, or whether they allow more general proof of what the individual's decision would have been, require a clear and convincing standard of proof for such evidence.

The Supreme Court of Missouri held that in this case the testimony adduced at trial did not amount to clear and convincing proof of the patient's desire to have hydration and nutrition withdrawn. In so doing, it reversed a decision of the Missouri trial court which had found that the evidence "suggest[ed]" Nancy Cruzan would not have desired to continue such measures, but which had not adopted the standard of "clear and convincing evidence" enunciated by the Supreme Court. The testimony adduced at trial consisted primarily of Nancy Cruzan's statements made to a housemate about a year before her accident that she would not want to live should she face life as a "vegetable," and other observations to the same effect. The observations did not deal in terms with withdrawal of medical treatment or of hydration and nutrition. We cannot say that the Supreme Court of Missouri committed constitutional error in reaching the conclusion that it did.

Petitioners alternatively contend that Missouri must accept the "substituted judgment" of close family members even in the absence of substantial proof that their views reflect the views of the patient....

No doubt is engendered by anything in this record but that Nancy Cruzan's mother and father are loving and caring parents. If the State were required by the United States Constitution to repose a right of "substituted judgment" with anyone, the Cruzans would surely qualify. But we do not think the Due Process Clause requires the State to repose judgment on these matters with anyone but the patient herself. Close family members may have a strong feeling—a feeling not at all ignoble or unworthy, but not entirely disinterested, either—that they do not wish to witness the continuation of the life of a loved one which they regard as hopeless, meaningless, and even degrading. But there is no automatic assurance that the view of close family members will necessarily be the same as the patient's would have been had she been confronted with the prospect of her situation while competent. All of the reasons previously discussed for allowing Missouri to require clear and convincing evidence of the patient's wishes lead us to conclude that the State may choose to defer only to those wishes, rather than confide the decision to close family members.[12]

---

12. We are not faced in this case with the question of whether a State might be required to defer to the decision of a surro- gate if competent and probative evidence established that the patient herself had expressed a desire that the decision to termi-

The judgment of the Supreme Court of Missouri is

Affirmed.

■ JUSTICE O'CONNOR, concurring.

I agree that a protected liberty interest in refusing unwanted medical treatment may be inferred from our prior decisions and that the refusal of artificially delivered food and water is encompassed within that liberty interest. I write separately to clarify why I believe this to be so.

As the Court notes, the liberty interest in refusing medical treatment flows from decisions involving the State's invasions into the body. . . . The State's imposition of medical treatment on an unwilling competent adult necessarily involves some form of restraint and intrusion. A seriously ill or dying patient whose wishes are not honored may feel a captive of the machinery required for life-sustaining measures or other medical interventions. Such forced treatment may burden that individual's liberty interests as much as any state coercion.

The State's artificial provision of nutrition and hydration implicates identical concerns. Artificial feeding cannot readily be distinguished from other forms of medical treatment. Whether or not the techniques used to pass food and water into the patient's alimentary tract are termed "medical treatment," it is clear they all involve some degree of intrusion and restraint. Feeding a patient by means of a nasogastric tube requires a physician to pass a long flexible tube through the patient's nose, throat and esophagus and into the stomach. Because of the discomfort such a tube causes, "[m]any patients need to be restrained forcibly and their hands put into large mittens to prevent them from removing the tube." Major, The Medical Procedures for Providing Food and Water: Indications and Effects, in By No Extraordinary Means: The Choice to Forgo Life–Sustaining Food and Water 25 (J. Lynn ed. 1986). A gastrostomy tube (as was used to provide food and water to Nancy Cruzan) or jejunostomy tube must be surgically implanted into the stomach or small intestine. Requiring a competent adult to endure such procedures against her will burdens the patient's liberty, dignity, and freedom to determine the course of her own treatment. Accordingly, the liberty guaranteed by the Due Process Clause must protect, if it protects anything, an individual's deeply personal decision to reject medical treatment, including the artificial delivery of food and water.

I also write separately to emphasize that the Court does not today decide the issue whether a State must also give effect to the decisions of a surrogate decisionmaker. In my view, such a duty may well be constitutionally required to protect the patient's liberty interest in refusing medical treatment. Few individuals provide explicit oral or written instructions regarding their intent to refuse medical treatment should they become incompetent. States which decline to consider any evidence other than such instructions may frequently fail to honor a patient's intent. Such failures might be avoided if the State considered an equally probative source of

nate life-sustaining treatment be made for   . . . .
her by that individual.

evidence: the patient's appointment of a proxy to make health care decisions on her behalf. Delegating the authority to make medical decisions to a family member or friend is becoming a common method of planning for the future. Several States have recognized the practical wisdom of such a procedure by enacting durable power of attorney statutes that specifically authorize an individual to appoint a surrogate to make medical treatment decisions. Some state courts have suggested that an agent appointed pursuant to a general durable power of attorney statute would also be empowered to make health care decisions on behalf of the patient. Other States allow an individual to designate a proxy to carry out the intent of a living will. These procedures for surrogate decisionmaking, which appear to be rapidly gaining in acceptance, may be a valuable additional safeguard of the patient's interest in directing his medical care. Moreover, as patients are likely to select a family member as a surrogate, giving effect to a proxy's decisions may also protect the "freedom of personal choice in matters of . . . family life."

. . . .

■ JUSTICE SCALIA, concurring.

The various opinions in this case portray quite clearly the difficult, indeed agonizing, questions that are presented by the constantly increasing power of science to keep the human body alive for longer than any reasonable person would want to inhabit it. The States have begun to grapple with these problems through legislation. I am concerned, from the tenor of today's opinions, that we are poised to confuse that enterprise as successfully as we have confused the enterprise of legislating concerning abortion—requiring it to be conducted against a background of federal constitutional imperatives that are unknown because they are being newly crafted from Term to Term. That would be a great misfortune.

While I agree with the Court's analysis today, and therefore join in its opinion, I would have preferred that we announce, clearly and promptly, that the federal courts have no business in this field; that American law has always accorded the State the power to prevent, by force if necessary, suicide—including suicide by refusing to take appropriate measures necessary to preserve one's life; that the point at which life becomes "worthless," and the point at which the means necessary to preserve it become "extraordinary" or "inappropriate," are neither set forth in the Constitution nor known to the nine Justices of this Court any better than they are known to nine people picked at random from the Kansas City telephone directory; and hence, that even when it *is* demonstrated by clear and convincing evidence that a patient no longer wishes certain measures to be taken to preserve her life, it is up to the citizens of Missouri to decide, through their elected representatives, whether that wish will be honored. It is quite impossible (because the Constitution says nothing about the matter) that those citizens will decide upon a line less lawful than the one we would choose; and it is unlikely (because we know no more about "life-and-death" than they do) that they will decide upon a line less reasonable.

The text of the Due Process Clause does not protect individuals against deprivations of liberty *simpliciter*. It protects them against deprivations of liberty "without due process of law." To determine that such a deprivation would not occur if Nancy Cruzan were forced to take nourishment against her will, it is unnecessary to reopen the historically recurrent debate over whether "due process" includes substantive restrictions. It is at least true that no "substantive due process" claim can be maintained unless the claimant demonstrates that the State has deprived him of a right historically and traditionally protected against State interference. That cannot possibly be established here.

. . . .

What I have said above is not meant to suggest that I would think it desirable, if we were sure that Nancy Cruzan wanted to die, to keep her alive by the means at issue here. I assert only that the Constitution has nothing to say about the subject. To raise up a constitutional right here we would have to create out of nothing (for it exists neither in text nor tradition) some constitutional principle whereby, although the State may insist that an individual come in out of the cold and eat food, it may not insist that he take medicine; and although it may pump his stomach empty of poison he has ingested, it may not fill his stomach with food he has failed to ingest. Are there, then, no reasonable and humane limits that ought not to be exceeded in requiring an individual to preserve his own life? There obviously are, but they are not set forth in the Due Process Clause. What assures us that those limits will not be exceeded is the same constitutional guarantee that is the source of most of our protection—what protects us, for example, from being assessed a tax of 100% of our income above the subsistence level, from being forbidden to drive cars, or from being required to send our children to school for 10 hours a day, none of which horribles is categorically prohibited by the Constitution. Our salvation is the Equal Protection Clause, which requires the democratic majority to accept for themselves and their loved ones what they impose on you and me. This Court need not, and has no authority to, inject itself into every field of human activity where irrationality and oppression may theoretically occur, and if it tries to do so it will destroy itself.

■ JUSTICE BRENNAN, with whom JUSTICE MARSHALL and JUSTICE BLACKMUN join, dissenting.

. . . .

. . . Because I believe that Nancy Cruzan has a fundamental right to be free of unwanted artificial nutrition and hydration, which right is not outweighed by any interests of the State, and because I find that the improperly biased procedural obstacles imposed by the Missouri Supreme Court impermissibly burden that right, I respectfully dissent. Nancy Cruzan is entitled to choose to die with dignity.

I

A

"[T]he timing of death—once a matter of fate—is now a matter of human choice." Office of Technology Assessment Task Force, Life Sustaining Technologies and the Elderly 41 (1988). Of the approximately two million people who die each year, 80% die in hospitals and long-term care institutions, and perhaps 70% of those after a decision to forgo life-sustaining treatment has been made. Nearly every death involves a decision whether to undertake some medical procedure that could prolong the process of dying. Such decisions are difficult and personal. They must be made on the basis of individual values, informed by medical realities, yet within a framework governed by law. The role of the courts is confined to defining that framework, delineating the ways in which government may and may not participate in such decisions.

The question before this Court is a relatively narrow one: whether the Due Process Clause allows Missouri to require a now-incompetent patient in an irreversible persistent vegetative state to remain on life-support absent rigorously clear and convincing evidence that avoiding the treatment represents the patient's prior, express choice. If a fundamental right is at issue, Missouri's rule of decision must be scrutinized under the standards this Court has always applied in such circumstances. As we said in Zablocki v. Redhail, 434 U.S. 374, 98 S.Ct. 673, 54 L.Ed.2d 618 (1978), if a requirement imposed by a State "significantly interferes with the exercise of a fundamental right, it cannot be upheld unless it is supported by sufficiently important state interests and is closely tailored to effectuate only those interests." The Constitution imposes on this Court the obligation to "examine carefully ... the extent to which [the legitimate government interests advanced] are served by the challenged regulation." An evidentiary rule, just as a substantive prohibition, must meet these standards if it significantly burdens a fundamental liberty interest. Fundamental rights "are protected not only against heavy-handed frontal attack, but also from being stifled by more subtle governmental interference."

B

The starting point for our legal analysis must be whether a competent person has a constitutional right to avoid unwanted medical care....

But if a competent person has a liberty interest to be free of unwanted medical treatment, as both the majority and Justice O'Connor concede, it must be fundamental. "We are dealing here with [a decision] which involves one of the basic civil rights of man." Whatever other liberties protected by the Due Process Clause are fundamental, "those liberties that are 'deeply rooted in this Nation's history and tradition'" are among them. "Such a tradition commands respect in part because the Constitution carries the gloss of history."

The right to be free from medical attention without consent, to determine what shall be done with one's own body, is deeply rooted in this Nation's traditions, as the majority acknowledges. This right has long been "firmly entrenched in American tort law" and is securely grounded in the earliest common law.... Thus, freedom from unwanted medical attention is unquestionably among those principles "so rooted in the traditions and conscience of our people as to be ranked as fundamental."

That there may be serious consequences involved in refusal of the medical treatment at issue here does not vitiate the right under our common law tradition of medical self-determination. It is "a well-established rule of general law ... that it is the patient, not the physician, who ultimately decides if treatment—any treatment—is to be given at all....

The rule has never been qualified in its application by either the nature or purpose of the treatment, or the gravity of the consequences of acceding to or foregoing it."

No material distinction can be drawn between the treatment to which Nancy Cruzan continues to be subject—artificial nutrition and hydration—and any other medical treatment....

. . . .

Nor does the fact that Nancy Cruzan is now incompetent deprive her of her fundamental rights. As the majority recognizes, the question is not whether an incompetent has constitutional rights, but how such rights may be exercised....

II

A

The right to be free from unwanted medical attention is a right to evaluate the potential benefit of treatment and its possible consequences according to one's own values and to make a personal decision whether to subject oneself to the intrusion. For a patient like Nancy Cruzan, the sole benefit of medical treatment is being kept metabolically alive. Neither artificial nutrition nor any other form of medical treatment available today can cure or in any way ameliorate her condition. Irreversibly vegetative patients are devoid of thought, emotion and sensation; they are permanently and completely unconscious. As the President's Commission concluded in approving the withdrawal of life support equipment from irreversibly vegetative patients:

"[T]reatment ordinarily aims to benefit a patient through preserving life, relieving pain and suffering, protecting against disability, and returning maximally effective functioning. If a prognosis of permanent unconsciousness is correct, however, continued treatment cannot confer such benefits. Pain and suffering are absent, as are joy, satisfaction, and pleasure. Disability is total and no return to an even minimal level of social or human functioning is possible." President's Commission 181–182.

There are also affirmative reasons why someone like Nancy might choose to forgo artificial nutrition and hydration under these circumstances. Dying is personal. And it is profound. For many, the thought of an ignoble end, steeped in decay, is abhorrent. A quiet, proud death, bodily integrity intact, is a matter of extreme consequence. "In certain, thankfully rare, circumstances the burden of maintaining the corporeal existence degrades the very humanity it was meant to serve." ...

Such conditions are, for many, humiliating to contemplate, as is visiting a prolonged and anguished vigil on one's parents, spouse, and children. A long, drawn-out death can have a debilitating effect on family members. For some, the idea of being remembered in their persistent vegetative states rather than as they were before their illness or accident may be very disturbing.[11]

11. What general information exists about what most people would choose or   would prefer to have chosen for them under these circumstances also indicates the impor-

B

Although the right to be free of unwanted medical intervention, like other constitutionally protected interests, may not be absolute, no State interest could outweigh the rights of an individual in Nancy Cruzan's position. Whatever a State's possible interests in mandating life-support treatment under other circumstances, there is no good to be obtained here by Missouri's insistence that Nancy Cruzan remain on life-support systems if it is indeed her wish not to do so. Missouri does not claim, nor could it, that society as a whole will be benefited by Nancy's receiving medical treatment. No third party's situation will be improved and no harm to others will be averted.[13]

The only state interest asserted here is a general interest in the preservation of life. But the State has no legitimate general interest in someone's life, completely abstracted from the interest of the person living that life, that could outweigh the person's choice to avoid medical treatment. "[T]he regulation of constitutionally protected decisions ... must be predicated on legitimate state concerns *other than* disagreement with the choice the individual has made.... Otherwise, the interest in liberty protected by the Due Process Clause would be a nullity." Thus, the State's general interest in life must accede to Nancy Cruzan's particularized and intense interest in self-determination in her choice of medical treatment. There is simply nothing legitimately within the State's purview to be gained by superseding her decision.

tance of ensuring a means for now-incompetent patients to exercise their right to avoid unwanted medical treatment. A 1988 poll conducted by the American Medical Association found that 80% of those surveyed favored withdrawal of life support systems from hopelessly ill or irreversibly comatose patients if they or their families requested it. Another 1988 poll conducted by the Colorado University Graduate School of Public Affairs showed that 85% of those questioned would not want to have their own lives maintained with artificial nutrition and hydration if they became permanently unconscious.

Such attitudes have been translated into considerable political action. Since 1976, 40 States and the District of Columbia have enacted natural death acts, expressly providing for self-determination under some or all of these situations. Thirteen States and the District of Columbia have enacted statutes authorizing the appointment of proxies for making health care decisions.

13. Were such interests at stake, however, I would find that the Due Process Clause places limits on what invasive medical procedures could be forced on an unwilling comatose patient in pursuit of the interests of a third party. If Missouri were correct that its interests outweigh Nancy's interest in avoiding medical procedures as long as she is free of pain and physical discomfort, it is not apparent why a State could not choose to remove one of her kidneys without consent on the ground that society would be better off if the recipient of that kidney were saved from renal poisoning. Nancy cannot feel surgical pain. Nor would removal of one kidney be expected to shorten her life expectancy. Patches of her skin could also be removed to provide grafts for burn victims, and scrapings of bone marrow to provide grafts for someone with leukemia. Perhaps the State could lawfully remove more vital organs for transplanting into others who would then be cured of their ailments, provided the State placed Nancy on some other life-support equipment to replace the lost function. Indeed, why could the State not perform medical experiments on her body, experiments that might save countless lives, and would cause her no greater burden than she already bears by being fed through the gastrostomy tube? This would be too brave a new world for me and, I submit, for our Constitution.

Moreover, there may be considerable danger that Missouri's rule of decision would impair rather than serve any interest the State does have in sustaining life. Current medical practice recommends use of heroic measures if there is a scintilla of a chance that the patient will recover, on the assumption that the measures will be discontinued should the patient improve. When the President's Commission in 1982 approved the withdrawal of life support equipment from irreversibly vegetative patients, it explained that "[a]n even more troubling wrong occurs when a treatment that might save life or improve health is not started because the health care personnel are afraid that they will find it very difficult to stop the treatment if, as is fairly likely, it proves to be of little benefit and greatly burdens the patient." President's Commission 75. A New Jersey court recognized that families as well as doctors might be discouraged by an inability to stop life-support measures from "even attempting certain types of care [which] could thereby force them into hasty and premature decisions to allow a patient to die."

III

This is not to say that the State has no legitimate interests to assert here. As the majority recognizes, Missouri has a *parens patriae* interest in providing Nancy Cruzan, now incompetent, with as accurate as possible a determination of how she would exercise her rights under these circumstances. Second, if and when it is determined that Nancy Cruzan would want to continue treatment, the State may legitimately assert an interest in providing that treatment. But *until* Nancy's wishes have been determined, the only state interest that may be asserted is an interest in safeguarding the accuracy of that determination.

Accuracy, therefore, must be our touchstone. Missouri may constitutionally impose only those procedural requirements that serve to enhance the accuracy of a determination of Nancy Cruzan's wishes or are at least consistent with an accurate determination. The Missouri "safeguard" that the Court upholds today does not meet that standard. The determination needed in this context is whether the incompetent person would choose to live in a persistent vegetative state on life-support or to avoid this medical treatment. Missouri's rule of decision imposes a markedly asymmetrical evidentiary burden. Only evidence of specific statements of treatment choice made by the patient when competent is admissible to support a finding that the patient, now in a persistent vegetative state, would wish to avoid further medical treatment. Moreover, this evidence must be clear and convincing. No proof is required to support a finding that the incompetent person would wish to continue treatment.

A

The majority offers several justifications for Missouri's heightened evidentiary standard.... Missouri's evidentiary standard, however, cannot rest on the State's own interest in a particular substantive result. To be sure, courts have long erected clear and convincing evidence standards to place the greater risk of erroneous decisions on those bringing disfavored claims. In such cases, however, the choice to discourage certain claims was a legitimate, constitutional policy choice. In contrast, Missouri has no such power to disfavor a choice by Nancy Cruzan to avoid medical treatment, because Missouri has no legitimate interest in providing Nancy with treatment until it is established that this represents her choice. Just as a State may not override Nancy's choice directly, it may not do so indirectly through the imposition of a procedural rule. . . .

. . . .

B

Even more than its heightened evidentiary standard, the Missouri court's categorical exclusion of relevant evidence dispenses with any semblance of accurate factfinding. The court adverted to no evidence supporting its decision, but held that no clear and convincing, inherently reliable evidence had been presented to show that Nancy would want to avoid further treatment. In doing so, the court failed to consider statements Nancy had made to family members and a close friend. The court also failed to consider testimony from Nancy's mother and sister that they were certain that Nancy would want to discontinue the artificial nutrition and hydration, even after the court found that Nancy's family was loving and without malignant motive. The court also failed to consider the conclusions of the guardian ad litem, appointed by the trial court, that there was clear and convincing evidence that Nancy would want to discontinue medical treatment and that this was in her best interests. The court did not specifically define what kind of evidence it would consider clear and convincing, but its general discussion suggests that only a living will or equivalently formal directive from the patient when competent would meet this standard.

Too few people execute living wills or equivalently formal directives for such an evidentiary rule to ensure adequately that the wishes of incompetent persons will be honored. While it might be a wise social policy to encourage people to furnish such instructions, no general conclusion about a patient's choice can be drawn from the absence of formalities. The probability of becoming irreversibly vegetative is so low that many people may not feel an urgency to marshal formal evidence of their preferences. Some may not wish to dwell on their own physical deterioration and mortality. Even someone with a resolute determination to avoid life-support under circumstances such as Nancy's would still need to know that such things as living wills exist and how to execute one. Often legal help would be necessary, especially given the majority's apparent willingness to permit States to insist that a person's wishes are not truly known unless the particular medical treatment is specified.

. . . When a person tells family or close friends that she does not want her life sustained artificially, she is "express[ing] her wishes in the only terms familiar to her, and . . . as clearly as a lay person should be asked to express them. To require more is unrealistic, and for all practical purposes, it precludes the rights of patients to forego life-sustaining treatment." When Missouri enacted a living will statute, it specifically provided that the absence of a living will does not warrant a presumption that a patient wishes continued medical treatment. Thus, apparently not even Missouri's own legislature believes that a person who does not execute a living will fails to do so because he wishes continuous medical treatment under all circumstances.

The testimony of close friends and family members, on the other hand, may often be the best evidence available of what the patient's choice would be. It is they with whom the patient most likely will have discussed such questions and they who know the patient best. "Family members have a unique knowledge of the patient which is vital to any decision on his or her behalf." Newman, Treatment Refusals for the Critically and Terminally Ill: Proposed Rules for the Family, the Physician, and the State, 3 N.Y.L.S. Human Rights Annual 35, 46 (1985). The Missouri court's decision to ignore this whole category of testimony is also at odds with the practices of other States.

The Missouri court's disdain for Nancy's statements in serious conversations not long before her accident, for the opinions of Nancy's family and friends as to her values, beliefs and certain choice, and even for the opinion of an outside objective factfinder appointed by the State evinces a disdain for Nancy Cruzan's own right to choose. The rules by which an incompetent person's wishes are determined must represent every effort to determine those wishes. The rule that the Missouri court adopted and that this Court upholds, however, skews the result away from a determination that as accurately as possible reflects the individual's own preferences and beliefs. . . .

. . . .

Finally, I cannot agree with the majority that where it is not possible to determine what choice an incompetent patient would make, a State's role as *parens patriae* permits the State automatically to make that choice itself. Under fair rules of evidence, it is improbable that a court could not determine what the patient's choice would be. Under the rule of decision adopted by Missouri and upheld today by this Court, such occasions might be numerous. But in neither case does it follow that it is constitutionally acceptable for the State invariably to assume the role of deciding for the patient. A State's legitimate interest in safeguarding a patient's choice cannot be furthered by simply appropriating it.

The majority justifies its position by arguing that, while close family members may have a strong feeling about the question, "there is no automatic assurance that the view of close family members will necessarily be the same as the patient's would have been had she been confronted with the prospect of her situation while competent." I cannot quarrel with this observation. But it leads only to another question: Is there any reason to suppose that a State is *more* likely to make the choice that the patient would have made than someone who knew the patient intimately? To ask this is to answer it. . . .

A State's inability to discern an incompetent patient's choice still need not mean that a State is rendered powerless to protect that choice. But I would find that the Due Process Clause prohibits a State from doing more than that. A State may ensure that the person who makes the decision on the patient's behalf is the one whom the patient himself would have selected to make that choice for him. And a State may exclude from consideration anyone having improper motives. But a State generally must either repose the choice with the person whom the patient himself would most likely have chosen as proxy or leave the decision to the patient's family.

IV

As many as 10,000 patients are being maintained in persistent vegetative states in the United States, and the number is expected to increase significantly in the near future.... Today, various forms of artificial feeding have been developed that are able to keep people metabolically alive for years, even decades. In addition, in this century, chronic or degenerative ailments have replaced communicable diseases as the primary causes of death. The 80% of Americans who die in hospitals are "likely to meet their end ... 'in a sedated or comatose state; betubed nasally, abdominally and intravenously; and far more like manipulated objects than like moral subjects.'"[24] A fifth of all adults surviving to age 80 will suffer a progressive dementing disorder prior to death.

"[L]aw, equity and justice must not themselves quail and be helpless in the face of modern technological marvels presenting questions hitherto unthought of." The new medical technology can reclaim those who would have been irretrievably lost a few decades ago and restore them to active lives. For Nancy Cruzan, it failed, and for others with wasting incurable disease it may be doomed to failure. In these unfortunate situations, the bodies and preferences and memories of the victims do not escheat to the State; nor does our Constitution permit the State or any other government to commandeer them. No singularity of feeling exists upon which such a government might confidently rely as *parens patriae*. The President's Commission, after years of research, concluded:

"In few areas of health care are people's evaluations of their experiences so varied and uniquely personal as in their assessments of the nature and value of the processes associated with dying. For some, every moment of life is of inestimable value; for others, life without some desired level of mental or physical ability is worthless or burdensome. A moderate degree of suffering may be an important means of personal growth and religious experience to one person, but only frightening or despicable to another." President's Commission 276.

Yet Missouri and this Court have displaced Nancy's own assessment of the processes associated with dying. They have discarded evidence of her will, ignored her values, and deprived her of the right to a decision as closely approximating her own choice as humanly possible. They have done so disingenuously in her name, and openly in Missouri's own. That Missouri and this Court may truly be motivated only by concern for incompetent patients makes no matter. As one of our most prominent jurists warned us decades ago: "Experience should teach us to be most on our guard to protect liberty when the government's purposes are beneficent.... The greatest dangers to liberty lurk in insidious encroachment by

24. Fadiman, The Liberation of Lolly and Gronky, Life Magazine, Dec. 1986, p. 72 (quoting medical ethicist Joseph Fletcher).

men of zeal, well meaning but without understanding." Olmstead v. United States, 277 U.S. 438, 479, 48 S.Ct. 564, 572–573, 72 L.Ed. 944 (1928)(Brandeis, J., dissenting).

I respectfully dissent.

■ JUSTICE STEVENS, dissenting.

Our Constitution is born of the proposition that all legitimate governments must secure the equal right of every person to "Life, Liberty, and the pursuit of Happiness." In the ordinary case we quite naturally assume that these three ends are compatible, mutually enhancing, and perhaps even coincident.

The Court would make an exception here. It permits the State's abstract, undifferentiated interest in the preservation of life to overwhelm the best interests of Nancy Beth Cruzan, interests which would, according to an undisputed finding, be served by allowing her guardians to exercise her constitutional right to discontinue medical treatment. Ironically, the Court reaches this conclusion despite endorsing three significant propositions which should save it from any such dilemma. First, a competent individual's decision to refuse life-sustaining medical procedures is an aspect of liberty protected by the Due Process Clause of the Fourteenth Amendment. Second, upon a proper evidentiary showing, a qualified guardian may make that decision on behalf of an incompetent ward. Third, in answering the important question presented by this tragic case, it is wise "not to attempt by any general statement, to cover every possible phase of the subject." Together, these considerations suggest that Nancy Cruzan's liberty to be free from medical treatment must be understood in light of the facts and circumstances particular to her.

I would so hold: in my view, the Constitution requires the State to care for Nancy Cruzan's life in a way that gives appropriate respect to her own best interests.

. . . .

III

It is perhaps predictable that courts might undervalue the liberty at stake here. Because death is so profoundly personal, public reflection upon it is unusual. As this sad case shows, however, such reflection must become more common if we are to deal responsibly with the modern circumstances of death. Medical advances have altered the physiological conditions of death in ways that may be alarming: highly invasive treatment may perpetuate human existence through a merger of body and machine that some might reasonably regard as an insult to life rather than as its continuation. But those same advances, and the reorganization of medical care accompanying the new science and technology, have also transformed the political and social conditions of death: people are less likely to die at home, and more likely to die in relatively public places, such as hospitals or nursing homes.

Ultimate questions that might once have been dealt with in intimacy by a family and its physician have now become the concern of institutions. When the institution is a state hospital, as it is in this case, the government itself becomes involved.[13] Dying nonetheless remains a part of "the life which characteristically has its place in the home." The "integrity of that life is something so fundamental that it has been found to draw to its protection the principles of more than one explicitly granted Constitutional right," and our decisions have demarcated a "private realm of family life which the state cannot enter." The physical boundaries of the home, of course, remain crucial guarantors of the life within it. Nevertheless, this Court has long recognized that the liberty to make the decisions and choices constitutive of private life is so fundamental to our "concept of ordered liberty" that those choices must occasionally be afforded more direct protection.

Respect for these choices has guided our recognition of rights pertaining to bodily integrity. The constitutional decisions identifying those rights, like the common-law tradition upon which they built, are mindful that the "makers of our Constitution ... recognized the significance of man's spiritual nature." It may truly be said that "our notions of liberty are inextricably entwined with our idea of physical freedom and self determination." Thus we have construed the Due Process Clause to preclude physically invasive recoveries of evidence not only because such procedures are "brutal" but also because they are "offensive to human dignity." We have interpreted the Constitution to interpose barriers to a State's efforts to sterilize some criminals not only because the proposed punishment would do "irreparable injury" to bodily integrity, but because "[m]arriage and procreation" concern "the basic civil rights of man." The sanctity, and individual privacy, of the human body is obviously fundamental to liberty. "Every violation of a person's bodily integrity is an invasion of his or her liberty." Yet, just as the constitutional protection for the "physical curtilage of the home ... is surely ... a result of solicitude to protect the privacies of the life within," so too the constitutional protection for the human body is surely inseparable from concern for the mind and spirit that dwell therein.

It is against this background of decisional law, and the constitutional tradition which it illuminates, that the right to be free from unwanted life-sustaining medical treatment must be understood. That right presupposes no abandonment of the desire for life. Nor is it reducible to a protection against batteries undertaken in the name of treatment, or to a guarantee against the infliction of bodily discomfort. Choices about death touch the core of liberty. Our duty, and the concomitant freedom, to come to terms with the conditions of our own mortality are undoubtedly "so rooted in the traditions and conscience of our people as to be ranked as fundamental," and indeed are essential incidents of the unalienable rights to life and liberty endowed us by our Creator.

---

13. ... The Court apparently believes that the absence of the State from the litigation would have created a problem, because agreement among the family and the independent guardian ad litem as to Nancy Cruzan's best interests might have prevented her treatment from becoming the focus of a "truly adversarial" proceeding. It may reasonably be debated whether some judicial process should be required before life-sustaining treatment is discontinued; this issue has divided the state courts. I tend, however, to agree with Judge Blackmar [of the Missouri Supreme Court] that the intervention of the State in these proceedings as an *adversary* is not so much a cure as it is part of the disease.

The more precise constitutional significance of death is difficult to describe; not much may be said with confidence about death unless it is said from faith, and that alone is reason enough to protect the freedom to conform choices about death to individual conscience. We may also, however, justly assume that death is not life's simple opposite, or its necessary terminus,[15] but rather its completion. Our ethical tradition has long regarded an appreciation of mortality as essential to understanding life's significance. It may, in fact, be impossible to live for anything without being prepared to die for something. Certainly there was no disdain for life in Nathan Hale's most famous declaration or in Patrick Henry's; their words instead bespeak a passion for life that forever preserves their own lives in the memories of their countrymen. From such "honored dead we take increased devotion to that cause for which they gave the last full measure of devotion."[17]

These considerations cast into stark relief the injustice, and unconstitutionality, of Missouri's treatment of Nancy Beth Cruzan. Nancy Cruzan's death, when it comes, cannot be an historic act of heroism; it will inevitably be the consequence of her tragic accident. But Nancy Cruzan's interest in life, no less than that of any other person, includes an interest in how she will be thought of after her death by those whose opinions mattered to her. There can be no doubt that her life made her dear to her family, and to others. How she dies will affect how that life is remembered. The trial court's order authorizing Nancy's parents to cease their daughter's treatment would have permitted the family that cares for Nancy to bring to a close her tragedy and her death. Missouri's objection to that order subordinates Nancy's body, her family, and the lasting significance of her life to the State's own interests. The decision we review thereby interferes with constitutional interests of the highest order.

To be constitutionally permissible, Missouri's intrusion upon these fundamental liberties must, at a minimum, bear a reasonable relationship to a legitimate state end. Missouri asserts that its policy is related to a state interest in the protection of life. In my view, however, it is an effort to define life, rather than to protect it, that is the heart of Missouri's policy. Missouri insists, without regard to Nancy Cruzan's own interests, upon equating her life with the biological persistence of her bodily functions....

... Nancy Cruzan is obviously *"alive"* in a physiological sense. But for patients like Nancy Cruzan, who have no consciousness and no chance of recovery, there is a serious question as to whether the mere persistence of their bodies is *"life"* as that word is commonly understood, or as it is used in both the Constitution and the Declaration of Independence. The State's unflagging determination to perpetuate Nancy Cruzan's physical existence is comprehensible only as an effort to define life's meaning, not as an attempt to preserve its sanctity.

15. Many philosophies and religions have, for example, long venerated the idea that there is a "life after death," and that the human soul endures even after the human body has perished. Surely Missouri would not wish to define its interest in life in a way antithetical to this tradition.

17. A. Lincoln, Gettysburg Address, 1 Documents of American History (H. Commager ed.)(9th ed. 1973).

This much should be clear from the oddity of Missouri's definition alone. Life, particularly human life, is not commonly thought of as a merely physiological condition or function. Its sanctity is often thought to derive from the impossibility of any such reduction. When people speak of life, they often mean to describe the experiences that comprise a person's history, as when it is said that somebody "led a good life." They may also mean to refer to the practical manifestation of the human spirit, a meaning captured by the familiar observation that somebody "added life" to an assembly. If there is a shared thread among the various opinions on this subject, it may be that life is an activity which is at once the matrix for and an integration of a person's interests. In any event, absent some theological abstraction, the idea of life is not conceived separately from the idea of a living person. Yet, it is by precisely such a separation that Missouri asserts an interest in Nancy Cruzan's life in opposition to Nancy Cruzan's own interests. The resulting definition is uncommon indeed.

The laws punishing homicide, upon which the Court relies, do not support a contrary inference. Obviously, such laws protect both the life *and* interests of those who would otherwise be victims. Even laws against suicide pre-suppose that those inclined to take their own lives have *some* interest in living, and, indeed, that the depressed people whose lives are preserved may later be thankful for the State's intervention. Likewise, decisions that address the "quality of life" of incompetent, but conscious, patients rest upon the recognition that these patients have *some* interest in continuing their lives, even if that interest pales in some eyes when measured against interests in dignity or comfort. Not so here. Contrary to the Court's suggestion, Missouri's protection of life in a form abstracted from the living is not commonplace; it is aberrant.

Nor does Missouri's treatment of Nancy Cruzan find precedent in the various state law cases surveyed by the majority.... Considered against the background of other cases involving patients in persistent vegetative states, instead of against the broader—and inapt—category of cases involving chronically ill incompetent patients, Missouri's decision is anomalous.

In short, there is no reasonable ground for believing that Nancy Beth Cruzan has any *personal* interest in the perpetuation of what the State has decided is her life. As I have already suggested, it would be possible to hypothesize such an interest on the basis of theological or philosophical conjecture. But even to posit such a basis for the State's action is to condemn it. It is not within the province of secular government to circumscribe the liberties of the people by regulations designed wholly for the purpose of establishing a sectarian definition of life.

My disagreement with the Court is thus unrelated to its endorsement of the clear and convincing standard of proof for cases of this kind. Indeed, I agree that the controlling facts must be established with unmistakable clarity. The critical question, however, is not how to prove the controlling facts but rather what proven facts should be controlling. In my view, the constitutional answer is clear: the best interests of the individual, especially when buttressed by the interests of all related third parties, must prevail over any general state policy that simply ignores those interests.[22] Indeed, the only apparent *secular* basis for the State's interest in life is the policy's persuasive impact upon people other than Nancy and her family. Yet, "[a]lthough the State may properly perform a teaching function," and although that teaching may foster respect for the sanctity of life, the State may not pursue its project by infringing constitutionally protected interests for "*symbolic* effect." ...

Only because Missouri has arrogated to itself the power to define life, and only because the Court permits this usurpation, are Nancy Cruzan's life and liberty put into disquieting conflict. If Nancy Cruzan's life were defined by reference to her own interests, so that her life expired when her biological existence ceased serving *any* of her own interests, then her constitutionally protected interest in freedom from unwanted treatment would not come into conflict with her constitutionally protected interest in life. Conversely, if there were *any* evidence that Nancy Cruzan herself defined life to encompass every form of biological persistence by a human being, so that the continuation of treatment would serve Nancy's own liberty, then once again there would be no conflict between life and liberty. The opposition of life and liberty in this case are thus not the result of Nancy Cruzan's tragic accident, but are instead the artificial consequence of Missouri's effort, and this Court's willingness, to abstract Nancy Cruzan's life from Nancy Cruzan's person.

IV

Both this Court's majority and the state court's majority express great deference to the policy choice made by the state legislature. That deference is, in my view, based upon a severe error in the Court's constitutional logic. The Court believes that the liberty interest claimed here on behalf of Nancy Cruzan is peculiarly problematic because "an incompetent person is not able to make an informed and voluntary choice to exercise a hypothetical right to refuse treatment or any other right." The impossibility of such an exercise affords the State, according to the Court, some discretion to interpose "a procedural requirement" that effectively compels the continuation of Nancy Cruzan's treatment.

There is, however, nothing "hypothetical" about Nancy Cruzan's constitutionally protected interest in freedom from unwanted treatment, and the difficulties involved in ascertaining what her interests are do not in any way justify the State's decision to oppose her interests with its own. As this case comes to us, the crucial question—and the question addressed by the Court—is not what Nancy Cruzan's interests are, but whether the State must give effect to them....

V

In this case, as is no doubt true in many others, the predicament confronted by the healthy members of the Cruzan family merely adds

---

22. Although my reasoning entails the conclusion that the best interests of the incompetent patient must be respected even when the patient is conscious, rather than in a vegetative state, considerations pertaining to the "quality of life," in addition to consid- erations about the definition of life, might then be relevant. The State's interest in protecting the life, and thereby the interests, of the incompetent patient would accordingly be more forceful, and the constitutional questions would be correspondingly complicated.

emphasis to the best interests finding made by the trial judge. Each of us has an interest in the kind of memories that will survive after death. To that end, individual decisions are often motivated by their impact on others. A member of the kind of family identified in the trial court's findings in this case would likely have not only a normal interest in minimizing the burden that her own illness imposes on others, but also an interest in having their memories of her filled predominantly with thoughts about her past vitality rather than her current condition. The meaning and completion of her life should be controlled by persons who have her best interests at heart—not by a state legislature concerned only with the "preservation of human life."

The Cruzan family's continuing concern provides a concrete reminder that Nancy Cruzan's interests did not disappear with her vitality or her consciousness. However commendable may be the State's interest in human life, it cannot pursue that interest by appropriating Nancy Cruzan's life as a symbol for its own purposes. Lives do not exist in abstraction from persons, and to pretend otherwise is not to honor but to desecrate the State's responsibility for protecting life. A State that seeks to demonstrate its commitment to life may do so by aiding those who are actively struggling for life and health. In this endeavor, unfortunately, no State can lack for opportunities: there can be no need to make an example of tragic cases like that of Nancy Cruzan.

I respectfully dissent.

NOTE

On remand, the State dropped out of the case and a probate judge found that there was clear and convincing evidence that Ms. Cruzan would want her treatment to be terminated. Accordingly, this was done, and she died six months after the Supreme Court decision reprinted above.

D. PROTECTION OF EDUCATION RIGHTS

----

1. ADMISSION

Lesser v. Board of Education of City of New York

Supreme Court, Appellate Division, Second Department, 1963.
18 A.D.2d 388, 239 N.Y.S.2d 776.

■ PER CURIAM. The petitioner (the mother and guardian ad litem of Melvin Lesser, an infant) instituted this proceeding under article 78 of the Civil

Practice Act, to compel the Board of Education of the City of New York, the Board of Higher Education of the City of New York, the president of Brooklyn College, and the principal of Lafayette High School, to review the scholastic records of her son Melvin, to make corrections in his scholastic records and to admit him to Brooklyn College. The petitioner's prayer for relief has been granted; and the Boards of Education and the school officials appeal.

Melvin was graduated from Lafayette High School in 1962. During his attendance there, he was a member of the "Scholarship Program" which consisted of a series of classes open to students of superior performance and in which a more enriched treatment of the subjects was offered, enabling the participating students to achieve the maximum of their capacity. His high school scholastic average was 84.3%. The petitioner complains that, despite her son's credible accomplishments, he has been denied admission to Brooklyn College, a municipal college under the jurisdiction of the Board of Higher Education.

Brooklyn College has adopted standards governing the admission of students: (1) the completion of 16 units of high school subjects in prescribed courses; and (2) the attainment of an average which is set for each term in order to accommodate the number of applicants as determined by budgetary allotments and college facilities. Like other institutions for higher education, Brooklyn College has received many more applications than may be accepted within the limits of its conveniences. Petitioner's son qualified under the first requirement, but his average of 84.3% was below the average of 85% set by the authorities for admission.[2] Nor did he achieve the average required under an alternative method of admission used by the authorities—a method which was based on the mark achieved by the student on the College Board Aptitude Test merged with the student's high school average.

The petitioner does not challenge the accuracy of the averages attributed to her son. She asserts instead that the admission officer should have given greater weight to the marks which her son had obtained in the subjects encompassed within the "Scholarship Program". Such an evaluation, she claims, would result in an average above the minimum 85%. Further, she attacks the fairness and validity of an admission policy which operates solely by means of a mechanically-applied average. The court below sustained her contentions; it directed the appellants to redetermine Melvin's marks so as to bring them up to the 85% average, and then to admit him to the College.

In our opinion, the court was without power to make such directions. Courts may not interfere with the administrative discretion exercised by agencies which are vested with the administration and control of educational institutions, unless the circumstances disclosed by the record leave no scope for the use of that discretion in the manner under scrutiny. Section 6202 of the Education Law provides in part that (subd. 1): "The control of

2. Some grasp of the keenness of the competition among the applicants may be obtained by noting that 170 students had averages above Melvin's average but below 85%. All such applicants were denied admission.

the educational work of such institutions [including Brooklyn College] shall rest solely in the board of higher education," and that it shall (subd. 5) "prescribe conditions of student admission, attendance and discharge." If the Board of Higher Education performs its discretion fairly and not arbitrarily, the court may not substitute its judgment for that of the Board.

More particularly, a court should refrain from interjecting its views within those delicate areas of school administration which relate to the eligibility of applicants and the determination of marketing standards, unless a clear abuse of statutory authority or a practice of discrimination or gross error has been shown. . . .

Petitioner's son was entitled to fair and equal treatment with other applicants in accordance with standards reasonably established. The record before us denotes no arbitrary, unfair, or unreasonable conduct by the appellants in denying him admission.

Whether, in computing the high school average, the marks given in special courses such as the "Scholarship Program" should be accorded more weight than the marks given in standard courses, was clearly a matter resting exclusively in the discretion of the school and college authorities. Equally, the determination as to what factors should enter into the standards set for college admission was within the exclusive province of the college authorities. The judicial task ends when it is found that the applicant has received from the college authorities uniform treatment under reasonable regulations fairly administered. In effect, by the order of the court below petitioner's son has been granted a preference over other applicants who may be equally worthy.[3] This the court may not do.

. . . .

Orders reversed on the law and the facts, without costs; motion for rehearing granted; and petition dismissed, without costs. Findings of fact contained or implicit in the decision of the Special Term which may be inconsistent herewith are reversed, and new findings are made as indicated herein.

2. DISMISSAL AND SUSPENSION

Goss v. Lopez

Supreme Court of the United States, 1975.
419 U.S. 565, 95 S.Ct. 729, 42 L.Ed.2d 725.

■ MR. JUSTICE WHITE delivered the opinion of the Court.

This appeal by various administrators of the Columbus, Ohio, Public School System ("CPSS") challenges the judgment of a three-judge federal court, declaring that appellees—various high school students in the CPSS— were denied due process of law contrary to the command of the Fourteenth Amendment in that they were temporarily suspended from their high

---

3. The record discloses that in Lafayette High School alone, another student besides Melvin in the "Scholarship Program" was not admitted to Brooklyn College because his scholastic average did not measure up to the admission standards.

schools without a hearing either prior to suspension or within a reasonable time thereafter, and enjoining the administrators to remove all references to such suspensions from the students' records.

I

Ohio law, Rev.Code § 3313.64, provides for free education to all children between the age of six and 21. Section 3313.66 of the Code empowers the principal of an Ohio public school to suspend a pupil for misconduct for up to 10 days or to expel him. In either case, he must notify the student's parents within 24 hours and state the reasons for his action. A pupil who is expelled, or his parents, may appeal the decision to the Board of Education and in connection therewith shall be permitted to be heard at the board meeting. The board may reinstate the pupil following the hearing. No similar procedure is provided in § 3313.66 or any other provision of state law for a suspended student. . . .

The nine named appellees, each of whom alleged that he or she had been suspended from public high school in Columbus for up to 10 days without a hearing pursuant to § 3313.66, filed an action against the Columbus Board of Education and various administrators of the CPSS under 42 U.S.C. § 1983. The complaint sought a declaration that § 3313.66 was unconstitutional in that it permitted public school administrators to deprive plaintiffs of their rights to an education without a hearing of any kind, in violation of the procedural due process component of the Fourteenth Amendment. It also sought to enjoin the public school officials from issuing future suspensions pursuant to § 3313.66 and to require them to remove references to the past suspensions from the records of the students in question.

The proof below established that the suspensions in question arose out of a period of widespread student unrest in the CPSS during February and March of 1971. . . .

. . . .

II

. . . .

Although Ohio may not be constitutionally obligated to establish and maintain a public school system, it has nevertheless done so and has required its children to attend. Those young people do not "shed their constitutional rights" at the schoolhouse door. . . . Among other things, the State is constrained to recognize a student's legitimate entitlement to a public education as a property interest which is protected by the Due Process Clause and which may not be taken away for misconduct without adherence to the minimum procedures required by that clause.

The Due Process Clause also forbids arbitrary deprivations of liberty. "Where a person's good name, reputation, honor, or integrity is at stake because of what the government is doing to him," the minimal requirements of the clause must be satisfied. School authorities here suspended appellees from school for periods of up to 10 days based on charges of misconduct. If sustained and recorded, those charges could seriously damage the students' standing with their fellow pupils and their teachers as well as interfere with later opportunities for higher education and employment. It is apparent that the claimed right of the State to determine unilaterally and without process whether that misconduct has occurred immediately collides with the requirements of the Constitution.

... A 10–day suspension from school is not *de minimis* in our view and may not be imposed in complete disregard of the Due Process Clause.

A short suspension is of course a far milder deprivation than expulsion. But, "education is perhaps the most important function of state and local governments," and the total exclusion from the educational process for more than a trivial period, and certainly if the suspension is for 10 days, is a serious event in the life of the suspended child. Neither the property interest in educational benefits temporarily denied nor the liberty interest in reputation, which is also implicated, is so insubstantial that suspensions may constitutionally be imposed by any procedure the school chooses, no matter how arbitrary.

III

. . . .

... "The fundamental requisite of due process of law is the opportunity to be heard," a right that "has little reality or worth unless one is informed that the matter is pending and can choose for himself whether to ... contest." At the very minimum, therefore, students facing suspension and the consequent interference with a protected property interest must be given *some* kind of notice and afforded *some* kind of hearing. . . .

It also appears from our cases that the timing and content of the notice and the nature of the hearing will depend on appropriate accommodation of the competing interests involved. . . .

. . . .

We do not believe that school authorities must be totally free from notice and hearing requirements if their schools are to operate with acceptable efficiency. Students facing temporary suspension have interests qualifying for protection of the Due Process Clause, and due process requires, in connection with a suspension of 10 days or less, that the student be given oral or written notice of the charges against him and, if he denies them, an explanation of the evidence the authorities have and an opportunity to present his side of the story. The clause requires at least these rudimentary precautions against unfair or mistaken findings of misconduct and arbitrary exclusion from school.

There need be no delay between the time "notice" is given and the time of the hearing. In the great majority of cases the disciplinarian may informally discuss the alleged misconduct with the student minutes after it has occurred. We hold only that, in being given an opportunity to explain his version of the facts at this discussion, the student first be told what he is accused of doing and what the basis of the accusation is. . . . Since the hearing may occur almost immediately following the misconduct, it follows that as a general rule notice and hearing should precede removal of the student from school. We agree with the District Court, however, that there are recurring situations in which prior notice and hearing cannot be insisted upon. Students whose presence poses a continuing danger to persons or property or an ongoing threat of disrupting the academic process may be immediately removed from school. In such cases, the necessary notice and rudimentary hearing should follow as soon as practicable, as the District Court indicated.

We stop short of construing the Due Process Clause to require, countrywide, that hearings in connection with short suspensions must afford the student the opportunity to secure counsel, to confront and cross-examine witnesses supporting the charge or to call his own witnesses to verify his version of the incident. Brief disciplinary suspensions are almost countless. To impose in each such case even truncated trial type procedures might well overwhelm administrative facilities in many places and, by diverting resources, cost more than it would save in educational effectiveness. Moreover, further formalizing the suspension process and escalating its formality and adversary nature may not only make it too costly as a regular disciplinary tool but also destroy its effectiveness as part of the teaching process.

On the other hand, requiring effective notice and informal hearing permitting the student to give his version of the events will provide a meaningful hedge against erroneous action. At least the disciplinarian will be alerted to the existence of disputes about facts and arguments about cause and effect. He may then determine himself to summon the accuser, permit cross-examination and allow the student to present his own witnesses. In more difficult cases, he may permit counsel. In any event, his discretion will be more informed and we think the risk of error substantially reduced.

Requiring that there be at least an informal give-and-take between student and disciplinarian, preferably prior to the suspension, will add little to the factfinding function where the disciplinarian has himself witnessed the conduct forming the basis for the charge. But things are not always as they seem to be, and the student will at least have the opportunity to characterize his conduct and put it in what he deems the proper context.

We should also make it clear that we have addressed ourselves solely to the short suspension, not exceeding 10 days. Longer suspensions or expulsions for the remainder of the school term, or permanently, may require more formal procedures. Nor do we put aside the possibility that in unusual situations, although involving only a short suspension, something more than the rudimentary procedures will be required.

IV

The District Court found each of the suspensions involved here to have occurred without a hearing, either before or after the suspension, and that each suspension was therefore invalid and the statute unconstitutional insofar as it permits such suspensions without notice or hearing. Accordingly, the judgment is

Affirmed.

■ MR. JUSTICE POWELL, with whom the CHIEF JUSTICE, MR. JUSTICE BLACKMUN, and MR. JUSTICE REHNQUIST join, dissenting.

The Court today invalidates an Ohio statute that permits student suspensions from school without a hearing "for not more than ten days." The decision unnecessarily opens avenues for judicial intervention in the operation of our public schools that may affect adversely the quality of education. The Court holds for the first time that the federal courts, rather than educational officials and state legislatures, have the authority to determine the rules applicable to routine classroom discipline of children and teenagers in the public schools. It justifies this unprecedented intrusion into the process of elementary and secondary education by identifying a new constitutional right: the right of a student not to be suspended for as much as a single day without notice and a due process hearing either before or promptly following the suspension.

The Court's decision rests on the premise that, under Ohio law, education is a property interest protected by the Fourteenth Amendment's Due Process Clause and therefore that any suspension requires notice and a hearing. In my view, a student's interest in education is not infringed by a suspension within the limited period prescribed by Ohio law. Moreover, to the extent that there may be some arguable infringement, it is too speculative, transitory and insubstantial to justify imposition of a *constitutional* rule. . . .

Not so long ago, state deprivations of the most significant forms of state largesse were not thought to require due process protection on the ground that the deprivation resulted only in the loss of a state provided "benefit." In recent years the Court, wisely in my view, has rejected the "wooden distinction between 'rights' and 'privileges,'" and looked instead to the significance of the state created or enforced right and to the substantiality of the alleged deprivation. Today's opinion appears to abandon this reasonable approach by holding in effect that government infringement of any interest to which a person is entitled, no matter what the interest or how inconsequential the infringement, requires *constitutional* protection. As it is difficult to think of any less consequential infringement than suspension of a junior high school student for a single day, it is equally difficult to perceive any principled limit to the new reach of procedural due process.

Board of Curators of the University of Missouri v. Horowitz

Supreme Court of the United States, 1978.
435 U.S. 78, 98 S.Ct. 948, 55 L.Ed.2d 124.

■ MR. JUSTICE REHNQUIST delivered the opinion of the Court.

Respondent, a student at the University of Missouri–Kansas City Medical School, was dismissed by petitioner officials of the school during her final year of study for failure to meet academic standards. Respondent sued petitioners under 42 U.S.C. § 1983 . . . alleging . . . that petitioners had not accorded her procedural due process prior to her dismissal. The

District Court, after conducting a full trial, concluded that respondent had been afforded all of the rights guaranteed her by the Fourteenth Amendment to the United States Constitution and dismissed her complaint. The Court of Appeals for the Eighth Circuit reversed.... We granted certiorari to consider what procedures must be accorded to a student at a state educational institution whose dismissal may constitute a deprivation of "liberty" or "property" within the meaning of the Fourteenth Amendment. We reverse the judgment of the Court of Appeals.

I

... During the final years of a student's education at the School, the student is required to pursue in "rotational units" academic and clinical studies pertaining to various medical disciplines such as Obstetrics–Gynecology, Pediatrics, and Surgery. Each student's academic performance at the School is evaluated on a periodic basis by the Council on Evaluation, a body composed of both faculty and students, which can recommend various actions including probation and dismissal. The recommendations of the Council are reviewed by the Coordinating Committee, a body composed solely of faculty members, and must ultimately be approved by the Dean. Students are not typically allowed to appear before either the Council or the Coordinating Committee on the occasion of their review of the student's academic performance.

In the spring of respondent's first year of study, several faculty members expressed dissatisfaction with her clinical performance during a pediatrics rotation. The faculty members noted that respondent's "performance was below that of her peers in all clinical patient-oriented settings," that she was erratic in her attendance at clinical sessions, and that she lacked a critical concern for personal hygiene. Upon the recommendation of the Council on Evaluation, respondent was advanced to her second and final year on a probationary basis.

Faculty dissatisfaction with the respondent's clinical performance continued during the following year.... In the middle of the year, the Council again reviewed respondent's academic progress and concluded that respondent should not be considered for graduation in June of that year; furthermore, the Council recommended that, absent "radical improvement," respondent be dropped from the School.

Respondent was permitted to take a set of oral and practical examinations as an "appeal" of the decision not to permit her to graduate.... Upon receipt of [the evaluations of these examinations], the Council on Evaluation reaffirmed its prior position.

The Council met again in mid-May to consider whether respondent should be allowed to remain in school beyond June of that year. Noting that the report on respondent's recent surgery rotation rated her performance as "low-satisfactory," the Council unanimously recommended that "barring receipt of any reports that Miss Horowitz has improved radically, [she] not be allowed to re-enroll in the ... School of Medicine." The Council delayed making its recommendation official until receiving reports on other rotations; when a report on respondent's emergency rotation also turned out to be negative, the Council unanimously reaffirmed its recommendation that respondent be dropped from the School. The Coordinating Committee and the Dean approved the recommendation and notified respondent, who appealed the decision in writing to the University's Provost for Health Sciences. The Provost sustained the School's actions after reviewing the record compiled during the earlier proceedings.

II

. . . .

B

. . . These procedures were sufficient under the Due Process Clause of the Fourteenth Amendment. We agree with the District Court that respondent

> "was afforded full procedural due process by the [school]. In fact, the Court is of the opinion, and so finds, that the school went beyond [constitutionally required] procedural due process by affording [respondent] the opportunity to be examined by seven independent physicians in order to be absolutely certain that their grading of the [respondent] in her medical skills was correct."

. . . [W]e have frequently emphasized that "[t]he very nature of due process negates any concept of inflexible procedures universally applicable to every imaginable situation." The need for flexibility is well illustrated by the significant difference between the failure of a student to meet academic standards and the violation by a student of valid rules of conduct. This difference calls for far less stringent procedural requirements in the case of an academic dismissal.

Since the issue first arose 50 years ago, state and lower federal courts have recognized that there are distinct differences between decisions to suspend or dismiss a student for disciplinary purposes and similar actions taken for academic reasons which may call for hearings in connection with the former but not the latter. . . . These prior decisions of state and federal courts, over a period of 60 years, unanimously holding that formal hearings before decisionmaking bodies need not be held in the case of academic dismissals, cannot be rejected lightly.

Reason, furthermore, clearly supports the perception of these decisions. A school is an academic institution, not a courtroom or administrative hearing room. In *Goss*, [Goss-Lopez *supra* p. 190] this Court felt that suspensions of students for disciplinary reasons have a sufficient resemblance to traditional judicial and administrative factfinding to call for a "hearing" before the relevant school authority. While recognizing that school authorities must be afforded the necessary tools to maintain discipline, the Court concluded:

> "[I]t would be a strange disciplinary system in an educational institution if no communication was sought by the disciplinarian with the student in an effort to inform him of his dereliction and to let him tell his side of the story in order to make sure that an injustice is not done.

. . . .

"[R]equiring effective notice and informal hearing permitting the student to give his version of the events will provide a meaningful hedge against erroneous action. At least the disciplinarian will be alerted to the existence of disputes about facts and arguments about cause and effect."

Even in the context of a school disciplinary proceeding, however, the Court stopped short of requiring a *formal* hearing since "further formalizing the suspension process and escalating its formality and adversary nature may not only make it too costly as a regular disciplinary tool but also destroy its effectiveness as a part of the teaching process."

Academic evaluations of a student, in contrast to disciplinary determinations, bear little resemblance to the judicial and administrative factfinding proceedings to which we have traditionally attached a full hearing requirement. In *Goss,* the school's decision to suspend the students rested on factual conclusions that the individual students had participated in demonstrations that had disrupted classes, attacked a police officer, or caused physical damage to school property. The requirement of a hearing, where the student could present his side of the factual issue, could under such circumstances "provide a meaningful hedge against erroneous action." The decision to dismiss respondent, by comparison, rested on the academic judgment of school officials that she did not have the necessary clinical ability to perform adequately as a medical doctor and was making insufficient progress toward that goal. Such a judgment is by its nature more subjective and evaluative than the typical factual questions presented in the average disciplinary decision. Like the decision of an individual professor as to the proper grade for a student in his course, the determination whether to dismiss a student for academic reasons requires an expert evaluation of cumulative information and is not readily adapted to the procedural tools of judicial or administrative decisionmaking.

Under such circumstances, we decline to ignore the historic judgment of educators and thereby formalize the academic dismissal process by requiring a hearing. The educational process is not by nature adversarial; instead it centers around a continuing relationship between faculty and students, "one in which the teacher must occupy many roles—educator, adviser, friend, and, at times, parent-substitute." This is especially true as one advances through the varying regimes of the educational system, and the instruction becomes both more individualized and more specialized. In *Goss,* this Court concluded that the value of some form of hearing in a disciplinary context outweighs any resulting harm to the academic environment. Influencing this conclusion was clearly the belief that disciplinary proceedings, in which the teacher must decide whether to punish a student for disruptive or insubordinate behavior, may automatically bring an adversarial flavor to the normal student-teacher relationship. The same conclusion does not follow in the academic context. We decline to further enlarge the judicial presence in the academic community and thereby risk deterioration of many beneficial aspects of the faculty-student relationship....

. . . .

The judgment of the Court of Appeals is therefore reversed.

[The concurring opinion of POWELL, J., and the opinion of BLACKMUN, J., joined by BRENNAN, J., concurring in part and dissenting in part, are omitted.]

■ MR. JUSTICE WHITE concurring in part and concurring in the judgment.

I join Parts I, II–A, and III of the Court's opinion and concur in the judgment.

I agree with my Brother Blackmun that it is unnecessary to decide whether respondent had a constitutionally protected property or liberty interest or precisely what minimum procedures were required to divest her of that interest if it is assumed she had one. Whatever that minimum is, the procedures accorded her satisfied or exceeded that minimum.

The Court nevertheless assumes the existence of a protected interest, proceeds to classify respondent's expulsion as an "academic dismissal," and concludes that no hearing of any kind or any opportunity to respond is required in connection with such an action. Because I disagree with this conclusion, I feel constrained to say so and to concur only in the judgment.

As I see it, assuming a protected interest, respondent was at the minimum entitled to be informed of the reasons for her dismissal and to an opportunity personally to state her side of the story. Of course, she had all this, and more. I also suspect that expelled graduate or college students normally have the opportunity to talk with their expellers and that this sort of minimum requirement will impose no burden that is not already being shouldered and discharged by responsible institutions.

■ MR. JUSTICE MARSHALL, concurring in part and dissenting in part.

I agree with the Court that, "[a]ssuming the existence of a liberty or property interest, respondent has been awarded at least as much due process as the Fourteenth Amendment requires." I cannot join the Court's opinion, however, because it contains dictum suggesting that respondent was entitled to even less procedural protection than she received. I also differ from the Court in its assumption that characterization of the reasons for a dismissal as "academic" or "disciplinary" is relevant to resolution of the question of what procedures are required by the Due Process Clause. Finally, I disagree with the Court's decision not to remand to the Court of Appeals for consideration of respondent's substantive due process claim.

. . . .

NOTE

In Regents of the University of Michigan v. Ewing, 474 U.S. 214, 106 S.Ct. 507, 88 L.Ed.2d 523 (1985), the Court rejected a student's charge that the university's refusal to allow him to retake an examination, and its consequent dismissal of the student, violated his substantive rights under the Due Process Clause. Writing for the Court, Stevens, J., noted:

> Considerations of profound importance counsel restrained judicial review of the substance of academic decisions. As Justice White has explained:

"Although the Court regularly proceeds on the assumption that the Due Process Clause has more than a procedural dimension, we must always bear in mind that the substantive content of the Clause is suggested neither by its language nor by preconstitutional history; that content is nothing more than the accumulated product of judicial interpretation of the Fifth and Fourteenth Amendments. This is ... only to underline Mr. Justice Black's constant reminder to his colleagues that the Court has no license to invalidate legislation which it thinks merely arbitrary or unreasonable."

Added to our concern for lack of standards is a reluctance to trench on the prerogatives of state and local educational institutions and our responsibility to safeguard their academic freedom, "a special concern of the First Amendment." If a "federal court is not the appropriate forum in which to review the multitude of personnel decisions that are made daily by public agencies," far less is it suited to evaluate the substance of the multitude of academic decisions that are made daily by faculty members of public educational institutions—decisions that require "an expert evaluation of cumulative information and [are] not readily adapted to the procedural tools of judicial or administrative decisionmaking."

Tedeschi v. Wagner College

Court of Appeals of New York, 1980.
49 N.Y.2d 652, 427 N.Y.S.2d 760, 404 N.E.2d 1302.

■ MEYER, J....

Plaintiff Nancy Jean Tedeschi was admitted to Wagner College, a private institution, in September, 1976. She was a part-time student taking courses in mathematics, Latin and psychology. Her performance during the fall semester presented both academic and social problems, however. Dr. Thompson, her Latin professor, testified that she did not participate in class, did not know the required material and only once of the several times called upon was able to answer correctly even a simple question about Latin grammar. Her conduct during class was also disruptive in that three or four times during each period she would pick up her handbag and leave the room, returning after two to five minutes.

On the evening of December 20, 1976 Ms. Tedeschi sat for her Latin examination, but at the end of it dramatically tore up her blue book and did not hand it in. In response to her question, Dr. Thompson advised her that without an examination score her grade for the course would be an F. Beginning at 4 a.m. the next morning and continuing until late in the evening of December 22, Dr. Thompson was subjected to a barrage of telephone calls in which Ms. Tedeschi repeatedly threatened to commit suicide, or to "fix" Dr. Thompson, and at one point appeared in a distraught condition at the front door of his home. Only when the police were summoned and advised plaintiff of the possible criminal consequences did the calls cease.

On January 10, 1977 through his secretary, Dr. Wendel, the academic dean, contacted plaintiff and her mother by telephone to arrange a meeting with them for the purpose of discussing plaintiff's academic situation, in view of her incomplete grades in two courses. Plaintiff, however, refused to meet stating that there was no problem. There followed, nevertheless, another series of harassing calls by plaintiff to Dr. Thompson. Later that evening in a telephone conversation between Dr. Thompson and Nancy's mother, Mrs. Tedeschi refused to discuss the matter with college officials and insisted that any problem should be presented to her in a formal letter from the college. The next day plaintiff was orally advised by Dr. Wendel that she was suspended by the college because of her bad character and the repeated disruption of her Latin class. Thereafter she met with the academic dean, the dean of students and an assistant to the president, who testified that during the interviews plaintiff's conduct was irrational and discussion fruitless. By letter dated January 13, 1977 plaintiff was advised by the dean of students, Dr. Guttu, that after consultation with Dr. Wendel and other members of the faculty and the administration, she was "withdrawn from classes for the 1977 spring semester" but could, if she wished, reapply in the fall. Shortly thereafter, plaintiff's tuition for the spring semester was refunded. Plaintiff's mother testified that she called the school several times to arrange a hearing, but without success.

Plaintiff then began this action alleging that she had not been granted a hearing or afforded an opportunity to defend herself and that she had been arbitrarily frustrated in completing her education. She asked for an order reinstating her and for damages. The trial court found that there was no constitutional violation since Wagner College was not State involved, that it could not review the decision to suspend plaintiff on the basis of her academic record, that the disciplinary aspects of her suspension were not arbitrary, that the college was obligated only to act in good faith, that the informal procedure followed was believed to be in plaintiff's best interests and that she had failed to prove any damage. On appeal from the judgment for defendant entered on that decision, the Appellate Division affirmed by a divided court. The majority took note of the college guideline quoted below but held that plaintiff had rebuffed several attempts by the college to arrange a conference; the dissenters reasoned that the relationship between a college and its students is contractual and that the college was bound to follow its own rules relating to suspension. Though we do not arrive at our conclusion by exactly the same reasoning, we agree with the dissenters below that the college has not conformed to the procedure its guidelines prescribed and that plaintiff is entitled to have it do so. We, therefore, reverse.

The guideline referred to is part of a publication distributed by the office of the dean of students entitled 1976–1977 Guidelines of Wagner College. The portion pertinent to this appeal reads:

"Whenever it shall appear that any student is not making satisfactory progress in his studies, and that his scholastic standing does not meet the requirements specified by the Committee on Academic Standards he shall be discharged from the College. If for any other cause a student is deemed to be an unfit member of the College, the Dean of Students may notify parents or guardians in order that they may have an opportunity to withdraw the student.

"A student may be suspended or expelled from the College by the Dean of Students or the Dean of Academic Affairs. If he is suspended or expelled for any cause other than failure in his academic work, and has not had recourse to a hearing before an established College Court, he shall have the right to be heard by the Student–Faculty Hearing Board which shall present its findings to the president of the college for final determination."

. . .

. . . .

. . . Whether by analogy to the law of associations, on the basis of a supposed contract between university and student, or simply as a matter of essential fairness in the somewhat one-sided relationship between the institution and the individual, we hold that when a university has adopted a rule or guideline establishing the procedure to be followed in relation to suspension or expulsion that procedure must be substantially observed.

We are brought then to a consideration of the guideline in question in relation to the suspension of Nancy Tedeschi. Had her suspension been solely for unsatisfactory progress in her studies, the guideline would have imposed no further obligation on the college and the only judicially review-able question would have been whether it had acted in good faith. . . .

The guideline permits either the dean of students or the dean of academic affairs to expel or suspend a student. The withdrawal letter forwarded on January 13, 1977 by the dean of students was, therefore, in conformance with its provisions. But the guideline does not stop there. It requires a further hearing by the Student–Faculty Hearing Board and review of that board's findings by the president of the college in any case in which suspension is for a cause other than academic failure and the student has not had a hearing before an established college court.

. . . .

Under the guideline plaintiff was properly suspended but was entitled to review of her suspension by the hearing board and the president. So much of the complaint as sought money damages and the right to a due process hearing based on claimed "state action" was properly dismissed, but she was entitled to judgment directing review by that body and that official as the guidelines require.

. . . .

Order reversed, with costs, and the case remitted to Supreme Court, Richmond County, with directions to enter judgment in accordance with the opinion herein.

———

3.   GRADUATION

Olsson v. Board of Higher Education

Court of Appeals of New York, 1980.
49 N.Y.2d 408, 426 N.Y.S.2d 248, 402 N.E.2d 1150.

■ GABRIELLI, J. This case presents the novel questions of whether and under what circumstances a court may intervene in the decision of an educational institution to withhold a diploma from one of its students on academic grounds. . . .

The petitioner in this case, Eugene Olsson, was a candidate for a Master's degree at the John Jay College of Criminal Justice, a branch of the City University of New York. Having completed the bulk of his studies with an "honors" average, Olsson elected to take a final "comprehensive" examination. . . .

Toward the end of the semester, one of the professors . . . undertook to describe to his class the criteria that would be used in the grading of the upcoming examination. Professor Kim apparently intended to inform his students that, in addition to attaining an over-all average score of 2.8 points on the examination, they would be required to score three out of a possible five points on each of four of the five examination questions answered. In the course of relating this information, however, Professor Kim misspoke, stating: "You must have at least three out of five *questions*" (emphasis supplied). This uncorrected misstatement, according to Olsson, left him and several of his classmates with the impression that they could achieve a passing grade on the examination by scoring at least three points on only three of the five questions. As a consequence, Olsson was unpleasantly surprised when he learned that, although his overall average score exceeded 2.8, he had nevertheless failed the examination because he had received passing scores on only three rather than four of the five questions he had answered.

Believing that the outcome was unfair, Olsson petitioned the academic appeals committee of the college for a reconsideration of his grade. He thought himself aggrieved because he had budgeted his time during the examination in such a way as to maximize his chances of achieving a passing score on three of the five questions. Had he known that he would be required to perform acceptably on four questions, Olsson asserted, he would have allocated his efforts more evenly and might therefore have passed the examination. The academic appeals committee, however, declined to change Olsson's test score to a "pass", concluding that it would be improper to do so in view of the fact that he had failed the examination under the uniformly applied criteria. Nevertheless, in the interest of fairness, the committee offered to expunge the results of Olsson's examination and permit Olsson to retake it without prejudice to his right to sit for the test a second time should he fail again.

Finding this offer to be unacceptable, Olsson commenced the instant article 78 proceeding in an effort to compel the college to award him a diploma on the strength of his existing examination score. Since he had relied on Professor Kim's classroom statements in allocating his time during the examination and had "passed" the test under the criteria delineated in those statements Olsson contended that the college should be estopped from applying the higher standard, which had resulted in his failing grade. Both the trial court and the Appellate Division accepted this argument and ordered the college to award Olsson a diploma in his chosen field *nunc pro tunc*. Both courts stressed that there existed no written regulations governing grading criteria at the time that Olsson took the examination, and both courts concluded that the college rather than the individual student should bear the ultimate responsibility for Professor Kim's unfortunate "slip-of-the-tongue". We disagree.

In reversing the determinations below, we are mindful that this case involves more than a simple balancing of equities among various competing commercial interests. While it is true that in the ordinary case, a principal must answer for the misstatements of his agent when the latter is clothed with a mantle of apparent authority, such hornbook rules cannot be applied mechanically where the "principal" is an educational institution and the result would be to override a determination concerning a student's academic qualifications. Because such determinations rest in most cases upon the subjective professional judgment of trained educators, the courts have quite properly exercised the utmost restraint in applying traditional legal rules to disputes within the academic community.

This judicial reluctance to intervene in controversies involving academic standards is founded upon sound considerations of public policy. When an educational institution issues a diploma to one of its students, it is, in effect, certifying to society that the student possesses all of the knowledge and skills that are required by his chosen discipline. In order for society to be able to have complete confidence in the credentials dispensed by academic institutions, however, it is essential that the decisions surrounding the issuance of these credentials be left to the sound judgment of the professional educators who monitor the progress of their students on a regular basis. Indeed, the value of these credentials from the point of view of society would be seriously undermined if the courts were to abandon their longstanding practice of restraint in this area and instead began to utilize traditional equitable estoppel principles as a basis for requiring institutions to confer diplomas upon those who have been deemed to be unqualified.

This is not, of course, to suggest that the decisions of educators are completely immune from judicial scrutiny. Consistent with the policy of ensuring that academic credentials truly reflect the knowledge and skills of the bearer, the courts have indicated that they will intervene if an institution exercises its discretion in an arbitrary or irrational fashion. In addition, it has been suggested that there exists an "implied contract" between the institution and its students such that "if [the student] complies with the terms prescribed by the [institution], he will obtain the degree which he sought." The essence of the implied contract is that an academic institution must act in good faith in its dealings with its students.

In this case, John Jay College amply fulfilled its obligation to act in good faith when it offered Eugene Olsson the opportunity to retake his comprehensive examination....

. . . .

In summary, it must be stressed that the judicial awarding of an academic diploma is an extreme remedy which should be reserved for the most egregious of circumstances. In light of the serious policy considerations which militate against judicial intervention in academic disputes, the courts should shun the "diploma by estoppel" doctrine whenever there is some question as to whether the student seeking relief has actually demonstrated his competence in accordance with the standards devised by the appropriate school authorities. Additionally, the courts should be particularly cautious in applying the doctrine in cases such as this, where a less drastic remedy, such as retesting, may be employed without seriously disrupting the student's academic or professional career.

For the foregoing reasons, the order of the Appellate Division should be reversed, without costs, and the petition should be dismissed.

E. PROTECTION OF SOCIAL AND PROFESSIONAL INTERESTS

Rigby v. Connol

High Court of Justice, Chancery Division, 1880.
14 Ch.D. 482.

This was an action by the plaintiff, who had been expelled from a trades union of which he was a member, against the committee and trustees of the union, claiming to be entitled to share in the benefits of the union, and that the defendants might be restrained from excluding him therefrom.

■ JESSEL, M.R. . . .

The first question that I will consider is, what is the jurisdiction of a court of equity as regards interfering at the instance of a member of a society to prevent his being improperly expelled therefrom? I have no doubt whatever that the foundation of the jurisdiction is the right of property vested in the member of the society, and of which he is unjustly deprived by such unlawful expulsion. There is no such jurisdiction that I am aware of reposed in this country at least, in any of the Queen's courts to decide upon the rights of persons to associate together when the association possesses no property. Persons, and many persons, do associate together without any property in common at all. A dozen people may agree to meet and play whist at each other's houses for a certain period, and if eleven of them refuse to associate with the twelfth any longer, I am not aware that there is any jurisdiction in any Court of Justice in this country to interfere. Or a dozen or a hundred scientific men may agree with each other in the same way to meet alternately at each other's houses, or at any place where there is a possibility of their meeting each other; but if the association has no property, and takes no subscriptions from its members, I cannot imagine that any Court of Justice could interfere with such an association if some of the members declined to associate with some of the others. That is to say, the courts, as such, have never dreamt of enforcing agreements strictly personal in their nature, whether they are agreements of hiring and service, being the common relation of master and servant, or whether they are agreements for the purpose of pleasure, or for the purpose of scientific pursuits, or for the purpose of charity or philanthropy—in such cases no Court of Justice can interfere so long as there is no property the right to which is taken away from the person complaining.

If that is the foundation of the jurisdiction, the plaintiff, if he can succeed at all, must succeed on the ground that some right of property to which he is entitled has been taken away from him. That this is the foundation of the interference of the courts as regards clubs I think is quite clear. If we look at the Lord Chancellor's judgment in the case of In re St. James's Club, 2 D.M. & G. 383, 387, he says this: "What, then, were the interests and liabilities of a member? He had an interest in the general assets as long as he remained a member, and, if the club was broken up while he was a member, he might file a bill to have its assets administered in this court, and he would be entitled to share in the furniture and effects of the club." So that he puts it that the member has an interest in the assets.

   . . . .

The present plaintiff certainly does not state in his statement of claim that there is any property at all here, and I think that that is a fatal objection to the statement of claim altogether, and I might, if I thought fit, dismiss the action simply on that ground. He states nothing but that there is an association which he calls a "trades union,"—the "Journeymen Hatters' Fair Trade Union"—as governed by rules. He says that he has been a member, and that he has been unfairly and improperly expelled, but he does not allege that there is any property of any kind or description belonging to the union or that he is entitled to any share of it. That is, however, a very technical ground, and I intend to base my judgment also on the larger ground that if he had stated fully the position and rules of this trades' union to which he belonged, the result would have been the same. . . .

   . . . .

The action will therefore be dismissed with costs.

Falcone v. Middlesex County Medical Society

Supreme Court of New Jersey, 1961.
34 N.J. 582, 170 A.2d 791.

■ JACOBS, J. The Law Division directed that the plaintiff Dr. Falcone be admitted to full membership in the Middlesex County Medical Society. . . . The County Medical Society appealed . . . and, while the appeal was pending . . . , we certified it on our own motion.

The Law Division's factual findings are amply supported by the record and need only be dealt with here briefly. . . .

In 1953 Dr. Falcone was admitted as an associate member of the Middlesex County Medical Society. The by-laws of the Society provide that a physician may not be an associate member for more than two years. In 1956 the Society declined to admit Dr. Falcone as an active member, assigning as its reason that he had been "licensed to practice as a Doctor of Osteopathy and, not as a Doctor of Medicine." This reason was unsound since Dr. Falcone's license unrestrictedly authorized him to practice medicine and surgery although it did refer to him as the holder of the degree of D.O. Nothing in the Society's written by-laws purports to preclude membership by a licensed physician who holds an M.D. from an A.M.A. approved medical school (as does Dr. Falcone) but the record does indicate that the Society's committee on medical ethics applies an unwritten membership requirement of four years of study at a medical college approved by the A.M.A. This requirement, if effective, would preclude membership by Dr. Falcone since the A.M.A. has not approved the Philadelphia School and Dr. Falcone's actual attendance at the A.M.A. approved school at Milan was not of the prescribed duration; and it would preclude his membership despite the uncontroverted evidence that he is a duly licensed and duly registered New Jersey physician who meets all of the qualifications prescribed in the written by-laws; that he has consistently practiced surgery and obstetrics and has never practiced osteopathy; that he is regarded by medical colleagues who are members of the Society, as a qualified physician and surgeon; and that he has not engaged in any conduct which would raise any question as to his professional ethics and competency.

The Society's declaration of his ineligibility and its refusal to admit him to membership have had seriously adverse economic and professional effects on Dr. Falcone. He was a member of the medical staffs of the Middlesex General Hospital and St. Peter's General Hospital in New Brunswick but was dropped because they, like other hospitals in the area, require that their staff physicians be members of the County Medical Society. It seems entirely evident that Dr. Falcone cannot successfully continue his practice of surgery and obstetrics or properly serve his surgical and obstetric patients without the use of local hospital facilities; he testified that in order to earn a livelihood it is necessary "to belong to the local society" for "otherwise, you cannot use the hospitals." The virtual monopoly which the Society possesses in fact over the use of local hospital facilities results from the well known inter-relationship between the County Society, the State Medical Society, the American Medical Association and the Joint Commission on Accreditation of Hospitals. Over thirty years ago Professor Chafee, in his discussion of nonprofit associations, pointed to the distinction between the customary social and fraternal organizations on the one hand and trade unions and professional societies on the other hand; he noted that whereas exclusion or expulsion from a social or fraternal organization may result in little more than hurt feelings, exclusion or expulsion from a trade union or a professional society may result, as here, in deprivation of the invaluable opportunity "to earn a livelihood." Chafee, The Internal Affairs of Associations Not for Profit, 43 Harv.L.Rev. 993, 1022 (1930). In a more recent discussion addressed specially to medical societies, the editors of the Yale Law Journal, after pointing out that exclusion or expulsion from a local medical society results, as a practical matter, in the deprivation of hospital facilities, descriptively noted that "nonmembership amounts to a partial revocation of licensure to practice medicine." Comment, The American Medical Association: Power, Purpose, and Politics in Organized Medicine, 63 Yale L.J. 938, 953 (1954).

After the County Society refused to admit him to full membership, Dr. Falcone appealed to the State Medical Society which gave him a hearing but refused to permit representation by legal counsel. The State Society declined to interfere with the County Society's action and on further appeal the American Medical Association took the position that it lacked jurisdiction. Dr. Falcone then instituted his proceeding in the Law Division seeking an order directing the County Society to admit him to membership. The only party named as a defendant was the County Society but no other parties were indispensable and we need not now consider whether others would have been proper parties since the issue was not raised in the Law Division and no move was made there towards joinder of the State Society, the hospitals, or others as parties. The County Society's position in the Law Division, repeated in this court, is that it is a voluntary organization which is at liberty to prescribe its own rules and that Dr. Falcone has "no judicially enforceable right of admission to membership." In the Law Division, Judge Vogel determined that, in the light of its virtual monopolistic control of the practice of medicine in the area, the County Society must be dealt with as involuntary in nature and subject to judicial scrutiny; he expressly found that the County Society's requirement of four years' study in a medical college approved by the A.M.A., as applied to Dr. Falcone, "contravenes the public policy of the State" and entered judgment directing that it admit him to full membership.

. . . .

Courts have been understandably reluctant to interfere with the internal affairs of membership associations and their reluctance has ordinarily promoted the health of society. Nevertheless, in particular situations, where the considerations of policy and justice were sufficiently compelling, judicial scrutiny and relief were not found wanting; for the most part these situations involved improper expulsions from pre-existing membership which called forth judicial directions for reinstatement or other suitable relief. In granting relief courts have, on various occasions, discussed specific legal theories resting on protection of the member's property interests, his contractual rights, and his advantageous relationships with the association; on other occasions they have, without discussion of specific legal theories, set aside the expulsion as being unreasonable, contrary to natural justice or violative of public policy. In Bernstein v. Alameda–Contra Costa Medical Ass'n, 139 Cal.App.2d 241, 293 P.2d 862 (1956), the court noted that any medical association's by-law which is found by the court to be against public policy is unenforceable and furnishes no legal support for an expulsion. It cited many supporting authorities including Spayd v. Ringing Rock Lodge No. 665, 270 Pa. 67, 113 A. 70, where the Pennsylvania Supreme Court sustained a lower court order restoring the plaintiff to membership in a labor union from which he had been expelled because he had petitioned the legislature for the repeal of a law which his union favored.

. . . .

The persistent movement of the common law towards satisfying the needs of the times is soundly marked by gradualness. Its step by step process affords the light of continual experience to guide its future course. When courts originally declined to scrutinize admission practices of membership associations they were dealing with social clubs, religious organizations and fraternal associations. Here the policies against judicial intervention were strong and there were no significant countervailing policies. When the courts were later called upon to deal with trade and professional associations exercising virtually monopolistic control, different factors were involved. The intimate personal relationships which pervaded the social, religious and fraternal organizations were hardly in evidence and the individual's opportunity of earning a livelihood and serving society in his chosen trade or profession appeared as the controlling policy consideration. Here there have been persuasive indications, ... that in a case presenting sufficiently compelling factual and policy considerations, judicial relief will be available to compel admission to membership. . . .

It must be borne in mind that the County Medical Society is not a private voluntary membership association with which the public has little or no concern. It is an association with which the public is highly concerned and which engages in activities vitally affecting the health and welfare of the people. . . .

. . . When the County Society engages in action which is designed to advance medical science or elevate professional standards, it should and will be sympathetically supported. When, however, as here, its action has no relation to the advancement of medical science or the elevation of professional standards but runs strongly counter to the public policy of our State and the true interests of justice, it should and will be stricken down. The judgment entered in the Law Division is in all respects:

Affirmed.

Blatt v. University of Southern California

Court of Appeal, Second District, Division 3, 1970.
5 Cal.App.3d 935, 85 Cal.Rptr. 601.

■ SCHWEITZER, A.J. Appeal from a judgment dismissing an action following an order sustaining a general demurrer without leave to amend to the second amended complaint. The complaint is for injunctive and declaratory relief and seeks to compel the admission of plaintiff to membership in the Order of the Coif, a national honorary legal society.

The Pleadings

Plaintiff was a June 1967 graduate of the School of Law, University of Southern California, and is a member of the California bar. Defendants are the University of Southern California, the national society known as the Order of the Coif, the local chapter of the society, and members of the committee of the local chapter having the authority and responsibility to elect members from graduating students.

The complaint alleges that the Order of the Coif (hereinafter referred to as the Order) gives recognition to high scholastic grade levels attained by law students; that members are elected from law students in the top 10 per cent in scholarship in those accredited law schools having a chapter; that defendant University of Southern California has a chapter; that "[e]lection to the Order of the Coif elevates the esteem, standing and position of the law student elected in the eyes of the school faculty, fellow students, judges, the legal profession and the public at large; and greatly enhances his employment possibilities and economic position after graduation and admittance to the Bar"; that plaintiff was a night law student at University of Southern California from September 1961 until graduation in June 1967; that the individual defendants were members of the selection committee of the local chapter of the Order and were authorized to establish the policy and rules for election of members within the limits of its constitution; that after plaintiff became a student the individual defendants represented to him that if he were in the top 10 per cent of his graduating class, he "would be eligible for election to membership in the Order;" that plaintiff relied on these representations in order to attain membership in the Order, ranked fourth scholastically in his graduating class of 135 students, and was thereby in the top 10 per cent of his class in scholarship.

. . . .

Plaintiff alleges that in June 1967 the committee elected seven or eight members to the Order who ranked below him in scholastic achievement; that plaintiff was not elected because "membership was restricted to students who, being eligible for the school's Law Review, accepted the invitation to work on the Law Review and completed their assignments successfully"; that said reason "was unreasonable, arbitrary and contrary to the representations" mentioned above, and was not applicable to plaintiff because it was a policy adopted after said representations were made to plaintiff. . . .

The complaint concludes by alleging that plaintiff is qualified and entitled to membership in the Order, that defendants breached their promises and representations, and that he was denied membership therein by arbitrary and discriminatory action based upon erroneous and invalid reasons. The complaint seeks a declaration of the rights and duties of the parties, a determination that plaintiff is entitled to election to membership in the Order, and an order directing defendants to admit plaintiff to membership.

Contentions

. . . We hold that each contention is without merit and that defendants' demurrer to the second amended complaint was properly sustained without leave to amend.

Judicial Review of Membership Exclusion

Plaintiff argues that organizations whose membership offers the member educational, professional or financial advantage cannot arbitrarily and discriminatorily deny admission to one who has met and complied with all the stated and represented requirements of membership. He admits that the courts in the past have refused to interfere with professional and honorary societies to compel one's admission but calls our attention to recent cases where courts have interfered to compel admission to membership in voluntary associations that have some effect upon the applicant's professional or economic success, or where the association has a professional or economic interest. He attributes this change in judicial attitude primarily to the recognition by the courts of the increasing effect that private and voluntary organizations have on the individual's ability and access to the economic marketplace and his opportunities to earn a living or practice his trade or profession.

. . . .

Plaintiff . . . contends that his allegation that nonelection will adversely affect his professional and economic interests is sufficient to bring him within the purview of the cited cases, that this is a question of fact, not of law, and therefore he should be permitted to offer evidence in support of this allegation. In effect he argues that the courts may compel admission to membership in voluntary organizations in *any* situation where membership may enhance or affect one's professional or economic interests. Such is not the law. The cited cases do not support this contention; they are expressly limited in application to situations affecting the right to work in a chosen occupation or specialized field thereof. We have been unable to find any authority that supports plaintiff's contention.

To adopt plaintiff's contention would subject to judicial review the membership selection activity and policies of *every* voluntary organization because it is difficult to conceive of any organization that does not in some respect involve or affect professional or economic interests of its members. It would also subject to judicial review procedures used in selecting persons for advanced and honorary degrees, and for selection of members for such honorary societies as Phi Beta Kappa, each of which presumably have some resultant professional or economic benefit. We know of no compelling factual or policy consideration for holding that judicial relief should be made available to compel admission to membership in *every* voluntary organization, especially in honorary organizations where outstanding scholars or leaders of a profession are best qualified to evaluate the record of those being considered for membership.

Membership in the Order does not give a member the right to practice the profession of law. It does not signify qualification for any specialized field of practice. It has no direct bearing on the number or type of clients that the attorney-member might have or on the income he will make in his professional practice. It does not affect his basic right to earn a living. We hold that in the absence of allegations of sufficient facts of arbitrary or discriminatory action, membership in the Order is an honor best determined by those in the academic field without judicial interference. Plaintiff's allegations of arbitrary or discriminatory action on the part of the election committee are insufficient to state a cause of action. No justiciable issue has been presented.

[The court then ruled that Blatt had not stated a cause of action for breach of contract or promissory estoppel, as no breach or reliance had been pleaded.]

Judgment affirmed.

Board of Directors of Rotary International v. Rotary Club of Duarte

Supreme Court of the United States, 1987.
481 U.S. 537, 107 S.Ct. 1940, 95 L.Ed.2d 474.

■ JUSTICE POWELL delivered the opinion of the Court.

We must decide whether a California statute that requires California Rotary Clubs to admit women members violates the First Amendment.

I

A

Rotary International (International) is a nonprofit corporation founded in 1905, with headquarters in Evanston, Illinois. It is "an organization of business and professional men united worldwide who provide humanitarian service, encourage high ethical standards in all vocations, and help build goodwill and peace in the world." Rotary Manual of Procedure 7 (1981) (hereinafter Manual), App. 35. Individual members belong to a local Rotary Club rather than to International. In turn, each local Rotary Club is a member of International. In August 1982, shortly before the trial in this case, International comprised 19,788 Rotary Clubs in 157 countries, with a total membership of about 907,750.

Individuals are admitted to membership in a Rotary Club according to a "classification system." The purpose of this system is to ensure "that each Rotary Club includes a representative of every worthy and recognized business, professional, or institutional activity in the community." 2 Rotary Basic Library, Club Service 67–69. Each active member must work in a leadership capacity in his business or profession. The general rule is that "one active member is admitted for each classification, but he, in turn, may propose an additional active member, who must be in the same business or professional classification." Id., p. 7. Thus, each classification may be represented by two active members. In addition, "senior active" and "past service" members may represent the same classifications as active members. There is no limit to the number of clergymen, journalists, or diplomats who may be admitted to membership.

Subject to these requirements, each local Rotary Club is free to adopt its own rules and procedures for admitting new members. International has promulgated Recommended Club By-laws providing that candidates for membership will be considered by both a "classifications committee" and a "membership committee." The classifications committee determines whether the candidate's business or profession is described accurately and fits an "open" classification. The membership committee evaluates the candidate's "character, business and social standing, and general eligibility." If any member objects to the candidate's admission, the final decision is made by the club's board of directors.

Membership in Rotary Clubs is open only to men. Herbert A. Pigman, the General Secretary of Rotary International, testified that the exclusion of women results in an "aspect of fellowship ... that is enjoyed by the present male membership," and also allows Rotary to operate effectively in foreign countries with varied cultures and social mores. Although women are not admitted to membership, they are permitted to attend meetings, give speeches, and receive awards. Women relatives of Rotary members may form their own associations, and are authorized to wear the Rotary lapel pin. Young women between 14 and 28 years of age may join Interact or Rotaract; organizations sponsored by Rotary International.

B

In 1977 the Rotary Club of Duarte, California admitted Donna Bogart, Mary Lou Elliott, and Rosemary Freitag to active membership. International notified the Duarte Club that admitting women members is contrary to the Rotary constitution. After an internal hearing, International's board of directors revoked the charter of the Duarte Club and terminated its membership in Rotary International. The Duarte Club's appeal to the International Convention was unsuccessful.

The Duarte Club and two of its women members filed a complaint in the California Superior Court for the County of Los Angeles. The complaint alleged, *inter alia,* that appellants' actions violated the Unruh Civil Rights Act.[2] Appellees sought to enjoin International from enforcing its restrictions against admitting women members, revoking the Duarte Club's charter, or compelling delivery of the charter to any representative of International. Appellees also sought a declaration that the appellants' actions had violated the Unruh Act. After a bench trial, the court concluded that neither Rotary International nor the Duarte Club is a "business establishment" within the meaning of the Unruh Act. The court recognized that "some individual Rotarians derive sufficient business advantage from Rotary to warrant deduction of Rotarian expenses in income tax calculations, or to warrant payment of those expenses by their employers...." But it found that "such business benefits are incidental to the principal purposes of the association ... to promote fellowship ... and ... 'service' activities." The court also found that Rotary clubs do not provide their members with goods, services, or facilities. On the basis of these findings and conclusions, the court entered judgment for International.

The California Court of Appeal reversed. It held that both Rotary International and the Duarte Rotary Club are business establishments subject to the provisions of the Unruh Act. For purposes of the Act, a " 'business' embraces everything about which one can be employed," and an "establishment" includes "not only a fixed location, ... but also a permanent 'commercial force or organization' or a 'permanent settled position (as in life or business).' " The Court of Appeal identified several "businesslike attributes" of Rotary International, including its complex structure, large staff and budget, and extensive publishing activities. The

---

2. The Unruh Civil Rights Act provides, in part: "All persons within the jurisdiction of this state are free and equal, and no matter what their sex, race, color, religion, ancestry, or national origin are entitled to the full and equal accommodations, advantages, facilities, privileges, or services in all business establishments of every kind whatsoever." Cal.Civ.Code Ann. § 51 (West 1982).

court held that the trial court had erred in finding that the business advantages afforded by membership in a local Rotary Club are merely incidental. It stated that testimony by members of the Duarte Club "leaves no doubt that business concerns are a motivating factor in joining local clubs," and that "business benefits [are] enjoyed and capitalized upon by Rotarians and their businesses or employers." The Court of Appeal rejected the trial court's finding that the Duarte Club does not provide goods, services, or facilities to its members. In particular, the court noted that members receive copies of the Rotary magazine and numerous other Rotary publications, are entitled to wear and display the Rotary emblem, and may attend conferences that teach managerial and professional techniques.

The court also held that membership in Rotary International or the Duarte Club does not give rise to a "continuous, personal, and social" relationship that "take[s] place more or less outside public view." The court further concluded that admitting women to the Duarte Club would not seriously interfere with the objectives of Rotary International. Finally, the court rejected appellants' argument that its policy of excluding women is protected by the First Amendment principles set out in Roberts v. United States Jaycees, 468 U.S. 609, 104 S.Ct. 3244, 82 L.Ed.2d 462 (1984). It observed that "[n]othing we have said prevents, or can prevent, International from adopting or attempting to enforce membership rules or restrictions outside of this state." The court ordered appellants to reinstate the Duarte Club as a member of Rotary International, and permanently enjoined them from enforcing or attempting to enforce the gender requirement against the Duarte Club.

The California Supreme Court denied appellants' petition for review. We ... affirm the judgment of the Court of Appeal.

II

In Roberts v. United States Jaycees, we upheld against First Amendment challenge a Minnesota statute that required the Jaycees to admit women as full voting members. *Roberts* provides the framework for analyzing appellants' constitutional claims. As we observed in *Roberts,* our cases have afforded constitutional protection to freedom of association in two distinct senses. First, the Court has held that the Constitution protects against unjustified government interference with an individual's choice to enter into and maintain certain intimate or private relationships. Second, the Court has upheld the freedom of individuals to associate for the purpose of engaging in protected speech or religious activities. In many cases, government interference with one form of protected association will also burden the other form of association. In *Roberts* we determined the nature and degree of constitutional protection by considering separately the effect of the challenged state action on individuals' freedom of private association and their freedom of expressive association. We follow the same course in this case.[4]

---

4. International, an association of thousands of local Rotary Clubs, can claim no constitutionally protected right of private association. Moreover, its expressive activities are quite limited. Because the Court of Appeal held that the Duarte Rotary Club also is a business establishment subject to the provisions of the Unruh Act, we proceed to consid-

A

The Court has recognized that the freedom to enter into and carry on certain intimate or private relationships is a fundamental element of liberty protected by the Bill of Rights. Such relationships may take various forms, including the most intimate. We have not attempted to mark the precise boundaries of this type of constitutional protection. The intimate relationships to which we have accorded constitutional protection include marriage, the begetting and bearing of children, child rearing and education, and cohabitation with relatives. Of course, we have not held that constitutional protection is restricted to relationships among family members. We have emphasized that the First Amendment protects those relationships, including family relationships, that presuppose "deep attachments and commitments to the necessarily few other individuals with whom one shares not only a special community of thoughts, experiences, and beliefs but also distinctively personal aspects of one's life." But in *Roberts* we observed that "[d]etermining the limits of state authority over an individual's freedom to enter into a particular association . . . unavoidably entails a careful assessment of where that relationship's objective characteristics locate it on a spectrum from the most intimate to the most attenuated of personal attachments." In determining whether a particular association is sufficiently personal or private to warrant constitutional protection, we consider factors such as size, purpose, selectivity, and whether others are excluded from critical aspects of the relationship.

The evidence in this case indicates that the relationship among Rotary Club members is not the kind of intimate or private relation that warrants constitutional protection. The size of local Rotary Clubs ranges from fewer than 20 to more than 900. There is no upper limit on the membership of any local Rotary Club. About ten percent of the membership of a typical club moves away or drops out during a typical year. The clubs therefore are instructed to "keep a flow of prospects coming" to make up for the attrition and gradually to enlarge the membership. The purpose of Rotary "is to produce an inclusive, not exclusive, membership, making possible the recognition of all useful local occupations, and enabling the club to be a true cross section of the business and professional life of the community." 1 Rotary Basic Library, Focus on Rotary 60–61. The membership undertakes a variety of service projects designed to aid the community, to raise the standards of the members' businesses and professions, and to improve international relations. Such an inclusive "fellowship for service based on diversity of interest," ibid., however beneficial to the members and to those they serve, does not suggest the kind of private or personal relationship to which we have accorded protection under the First Amendment. To be sure, membership in Rotary Clubs is not open to the general public. But each club is instructed to include in its membership "all fully qualified prospective members located within its territory," to avoid "arbitrary limits on the number of members in the club," and to "establish and maintain a membership growth pattern."

er whether application of the Unruh Act vio-   Clubs.
lates the rights of members of local Rotary

Many of the Rotary Clubs' central activities are carried on in the presence of strangers. Rotary Clubs are required to admit any member of any other Rotary Club to their meetings. Members are encouraged to invite business associates and competitors to meetings. At some Rotary Clubs, the visitors number "in the tens and twenties each week." Joint meetings with the members of other organizations, and other joint activities, are permitted. The clubs are encouraged to seek coverage of their meetings and activities in local newspapers. In sum, Rotary Clubs, rather than carrying on their activities in an atmosphere of privacy, seek to keep their "windows and doors open to the whole world," [Ibid.]. We therefore conclude that application of the Unruh Act to local Rotary Clubs does not interfere unduly with the members' freedom of private association.

B

The Court also has recognized that the right to engage in activities protected by the First Amendment implies "a corresponding right to associate with others in pursuit of a wide variety of political, social, economic, educational, religious, and cultural ends." For this reason, "[i]mpediments to the exercise of one's right to choose one's associates can violate the right of association protected by the First Amendment...." In this case, however, the evidence fails to demonstrate that admitting women to Rotary Clubs will affect in any significant way the existing members' ability to carry out their various purposes.

As a matter of policy, Rotary Clubs do not take positions on "public questions," including political or international issues. To be sure, Rotary Clubs engage in a variety of commendable service activities that are protected by the First Amendment. But the Unruh Act does not require the clubs to abandon or alter any of these activities. It does not require them to abandon their basic goals of humanitarian service, high ethical standards in all vocations, goodwill, and peace. Nor does it require them to abandon their classification system or admit members who do not reflect a cross-section of the community. Indeed, by opening membership to leading business and professional women in the community, Rotary Clubs are likely to obtain a more representative cross-section of community leaders with a broadened capacity for service.

Even if the Unruh Act does work some slight infringement on Rotary members' right of expressive association, that infringement is justified because it serves the State's compelling interest in eliminating discrimination against women. On its face the Unruh Act, like the Minnesota public accommodations law we considered in *Roberts,* makes no distinctions on the basis of the organization's viewpoint. Moreover, public accommodations laws "plainly serv[e] compelling state interests of the highest order." In *Roberts* we recognized that the State's compelling interest in assuring equal access to women extends to the acquisition of leadership skills and business contacts as well as tangible goods and services. The Unruh Act plainly serves this interest. We therefore hold that application of the Unruh Act to California Rotary Clubs does not violate the right of expressive association afforded by the First Amendment.[6]

6. Appellants assert that admission of women will impair Rotary's effectiveness as an international organization. This argument is undercut by the fact that the legal effect of

. . . .

The judgment of the Court of Appeal of California is affirmed.

It is so ordered.

■ JUSTICE SCALIA CONCURS IN THE JUDGMENT.

■ JUSTICE BLACKMUN and JUSTICE O'CONNOR took no part in the decision or consideration of this case.

Cleveland Board of Education v. Loudermill

Supreme Court of the United States, 1985.
470 U.S. 532, 105 S.Ct. 1487, 84 L.Ed.2d 494.

■ JUSTICE WHITE delivered the opinion of the Court.

In these cases we consider what pretermination process must be accorded a public employee who can be discharged only for cause.

I

In 1979 the Cleveland Board of Education ... hired respondent James Loudermill as a security guard. On his job application, Loudermill stated that he had never been convicted of a felony. Eleven months later, as part of a routine examination of his employment records, the Board discovered that in fact Loudermill had been convicted of grand larceny in 1968. By letter dated November 3, 1980, the Board's Business Manager informed Loudermill that he had been dismissed because of his dishonesty in filling out the employment application. Loudermill was not afforded an opportunity to respond to the charge of dishonesty or to challenge his dismissal. On November 13, the Board adopted a resolution officially approving the discharge.

. . . .

II

Respondents' federal constitutional claim depends on their having had a property right in continued employment. If they did, the State could not deprive them of this property without due process.

Property interests are not created by the Constitution, "they are created and their dimensions are defined by existing rules or understandings that stem from an independent source such as state law. . . ." The Ohio statute plainly creates such an interest. Respondents were "classified civil service employees," Ohio Rev.Code Ann. § 124.11 (1984), entitled to retain their positions "during good behavior and efficient service," who could not be dismissed "except . . . for . . . misfeasance, malfeasance, or nonfeasance in office," § 124.34. The statute plainly supports the conclusion, reached by both lower courts, that respondents possessed property rights in continued employment. . . .

the judgment of the California Court of Appeal is limited to the State of California. Appellants' argument also is undermined by

the fact that women already attend the Rotary Clubs' meetings and participate in many of its activities.

. . . .

III

An essential principle of due process is that a deprivation of life, liberty, or property "be preceded by notice and opportunity for hearing appropriate to the nature of the case." We have described "the root requirement" of the Due Process Clause as being "that an individual be given an opportunity for a hearing *before* he is deprived of any significant property interest." This principle requires "some kind of a hearing" prior to the discharge of an employee who has a constitutionally protected property interest in his employment. As we pointed out last Term, this rule has been settled for some time now. Even decisions finding no constitutional violation in termination procedures have relied on the existence of some pretermination opportunity to respond. . . .

The need for some form of pretermination hearing, recognized in these cases, is evident from a balancing of the competing interests at stake. These are the private interests in retaining employment, the governmental interest in the expeditious removal of unsatisfactory employees and the avoidance of administrative burdens, and the risk of an erroneous termination.

First, the significance of the private interest in retaining employment cannot be gainsaid. We have frequently recognized the severity of depriving a person of the means of livelihood. While a fired worker may find employment elsewhere, doing so will take some time and is likely to be burdened by the questionable circumstances under which he left his previous job.

Second, some opportunity for the employee to present his side of the case is recurringly of obvious value in reaching an accurate decision. Dismissals for cause will often involve factual disputes. Even where the facts are clear, the appropriateness or necessity of the discharge may not be; in such cases, the only meaningful opportunity to invoke the discretion of the decisionmaker is likely to be before the termination takes effect.

. . . .

The governmental interest in immediate termination does not outweigh these interests. As we shall explain, affording the employee an opportunity to respond prior to termination would impose neither a significant administrative burden nor intolerable delays. Furthermore, the employer shares the employee's interest in avoiding disruption and erroneous decisions; and until the matter is settled, the employer would continue to receive the benefit of the employee's labors. It is preferable to keep a qualified employee on than to train a new one. A governmental employer also has an interest in keeping citizens usefully employed rather than taking the possibly erroneous and counter-productive step of forcing its employees onto the welfare rolls. Finally, in those situations where the employer perceives a significant hazard in keeping the employee on the job, it can avoid the problem by suspending with pay.

IV

The foregoing considerations indicate that the pretermination "hearing," though necessary, need not be elaborate. We have pointed out that "[t]he formality and procedural requisites for the hearing can vary, depending upon the importance of the interests involved and the nature of the subsequent proceedings." In general, "something less" than a full evidentiary hearing is sufficient prior to adverse administrative action. Under state law, respondents were later entitled to a full administrative hearing and judicial review. The only question is what steps were required before the termination took effect.

. . . .

The essential requirements of due process, and all that respondents seek or the Court of Appeals required, are notice and an opportunity to respond. The opportunity to present reasons, either in person or in writing, why proposed action should not be taken is a fundamental due process requirement. The tenured public employee is entitled to oral or written notice of the charges against him, an explanation of the employer's evidence, and an opportunity to present his side of the story. To require more than this prior to termination would intrude to an unwarranted extent on the government's interest in quickly removing an unsatisfactory employee.

. . . .

VI

We conclude that all the process that is due is provided by a pretermination opportunity to respond, coupled with post-termination administrative procedures as provided by the Ohio statute. . . .

So ordered.

■ JUSTICE MARSHALL, concurring in part and concurring in the judgment.

. . . .

I write separately . . . to reaffirm my belief that public employees who may be discharged only for cause are entitled, under the Due Process Clause of the Fourteenth Amendment, to more than respondents sought in this case. I continue to believe that *before the decision is made to terminate an employee's wages,* the employee is entitled to an opportunity to test the strength of the evidence "by confronting and cross-examining adverse witnesses and by presenting witnesses on [their] own behalf, whenever there are substantial disputes in testimonial evidence." Because the Court suggests that even in this situation due process requires no more than notice and an opportunity to be heard before wages are cut off, I am not able to join the Court's opinion in its entirety.

. . . .

[The opinion of BRENNAN, J., concurring in part and dissenting in part, and the dissenting opinion of REHNQUIST, J., are omitted.]

Redgrave v. Boston Symphony Orchestra, Inc.

United States Court of Appeals, First Circuit, 1988.
855 F.2d 888.

OPINION EN BANC

■ COFFIN, J. . . . .

I. PROCEDURAL HISTORY

In March 1982, the Boston Symphony Orchestra (BSO) engaged Vanessa Redgrave to narrate Stravinsky's "Oedipus Rex" in a series of concerts in Boston and New York. Following announcement of the engagement, the BSO received calls from its subscribers and from community members protesting the engagement because of Redgrave's political support for the Palestine Liberation Organization and because of her views regarding the state of Israel. On or about April 1, 1982, the BSO cancelled its contract with Redgrave and its performances of "Oedipus Rex."

Redgrave sued the BSO for breach of contract and for violation of the [Massachusetts Civil Rights Act, or] MCRA. The BSO argued at trial that the contract rightfully was cancelled because the cancellation was the result of "a cause or causes beyond the reasonable control" of the BSO. In response to the civil rights claim, BSO agents testified that they had not cancelled the performances in order to punish Redgrave for her past speech or repress her future speech, but because it was felt that potential disruptions, given the community reaction, would implicate the physical safety of the audience and players and would detract from the artistic qualities of the production.

Following a sixteen-day trial, the jury found that the BSO wrongfully had breached its contract with Redgrave. On that basis, the district court awarded Redgrave her stipulated performance fee of $27,500. The jury also found that the BSO's cancellation had damaged Redgrave's career by causing loss of future professional opportunities, and awarded Redgrave $100,000 in consequential damages. The district court found that the question whether there was sufficient evidence to support a finding of $100,000 in consequential damages was a "close and debatable" one, but concluded that there was sufficient evidence to support the award. Nevertheless, the district court overturned the grant of consequential damages, finding that a First Amendment right of freedom of speech was implicated by the theory of consequential damages advanced by Redgrave and that Redgrave had not met the strict standards required by the First Amendment for recovery of damages.

Redgrave's MCRA claim was premised on the allegation that the BSO had interfered, "by threats, intimidation, or coercion," with Redgrave's exercise of free speech rights. The district court utilized the jury in an advisory capacity on this claim. In response to special interrogatories, the jury found that the BSO did not cancel the contract because of the disagreements of BSO agents with Redgrave's political views. The district court stated that this finding eliminated an "essential factual premise" of Redgrave's primary claim based on the MCRA.

But Redgrave also argued that, even if BSO agents had not themselves disagreed with Redgrave's political views and did not cancel the contract because they wished to punish her for past speech or to repress her future speech, the BSO did cancel the contract in response to pressure from third parties who disagreed with and wished to repress Redgrave's speech. Redgrave contended that such acquiescence to third parties on the part of the BSO made it liable under the MCRA. The district court concluded that acquiescence unaccompanied by express personal disagreement with Redgrave's views could not amount to the "threats, intimidation, or coercion" needed to establish a claim under the MCRA. The district court, therefore, rejected Redgrave's acquiescence theory and entered judgment for the BSO on Redgrave's MCRA claim.

Redgrave appealed from the district court's entry of judgment notwithstanding the verdict on the consequential damages claim and from the judgment against her on the MCRA claim. The BSO cross-appealed, arguing that even if the First Amendment should be found inapplicable to the consequential damages claim, the evidence of those damages was insufficient to support the verdict.

II. THE CONSEQUENTIAL DAMAGES CLAIM

A. *Consequential Damages for Loss of Professional Opportunities*

In response to special interrogatories, the jury found that the BSO's cancellation of the "Oedipus Rex" concerts caused consequential harm to Redgrave's professional career and that this harm was a foreseeable consequence within the contemplation of the parties at the time they entered the contract. A threshold question is whether Massachusetts contract law allows the award of such consequential damages for harm to a claimant's professional career.

Redgrave's consequential damages claim is based on the proposition that a significant number of movie and theater offers that she would ordinarily have received in the years 1982 and following were in fact not offered to her as a result of the BSO's cancellation in April 1982. The BSO characterizes this claim as one for damage to Redgrave's reputation, and argues that ... recent Massachusetts state court decisions ... establish that Massachusetts law does not permit plaintiffs in breach of contract actions to recover consequential damages for harm to reputation.

. . . .

The claim advanced by Redgrave is significantly different, however, from a general claim of damage to reputation. Redgrave is not claiming that her general reputation as a professional actress has been tarnished by the BSO's cancellation. Rather, she claims that a number of specific movie and theater performances that would have been offered to her in the usual course of events were not offered to her as a result of the BSO's cancellation. This is the type of specific claim that, with appropriate evidence, can meet the *Hadley v. Baxendale* rule. . . .

. . . .

Although we find that Redgrave did not present sufficient evidence to establish that the BSO's cancellation caused consequential harm to her professional career in the amount of $100,000, we hold that, as a matter of Massachusetts contract law, a plaintiff may receive consequential damages if the plaintiff proves with sufficient evidence that a breach of contract proximately caused the loss of identifiable professional opportunities. This type of claim is sufficiently different from a nonspecific allegation of damage to reputation that it appropriately falls outside the general rule that reputation damages are not an acceptable form of contract damage.

B. *First Amendment Restrictions*

The district court found that, although consequential damages for loss of professional opportunities could be a legitimate contract claim, it was required to overturn the jury's verdict of $100,000 because Redgrave had not met the strict standards required by the First Amendment for the recovery of such damages. According to the district court, the only theory that Redgrave could advance for establishing consequential damages necessarily implicated First Amendment concerns. As the court explained, "the only possible mechanism of harm to Redgrave's professional career, revealed by the evidence, is the alleged influence of some statement made by the BSO on later decisions of others—a statement of fact or opinion implied in BSO's cancellation, or express or implied in BSO's press release." In other words, "an inescapable element of the claimed causal connection between BSO's cancellation and consequential harm to Redgrave's professional career" was for "a factfinder reasonably [to] infer that others, upon receiving the news of BSO's cancellation, interpreted the cancellation as conveying a message about Redgrave."

Having concluded that Redgrave's theory of consequential damages necessarily rested on the premise that the BSO had conveyed a message about her to others, the district court felt it was required to apply heightened First Amendment scrutiny to any claim for damages stemming from such communicative activity. It made the threshold decision that state action would exist because it, as a court, would enter a judgment for such damages. The court then applied the standard governing damages in defamation cases. Accordingly, it required that Redgrave show that "BSO has impliedly communicated to others some material issue of fact (and not merely opinion) about Redgrave that it knew to be false, or that BSO acted with reckless disregard for the truth or falsity of a material statement of fact it impliedly communicated." The court concluded that, in any message the BSO could be said to have sent, no statement of fact to which the jury could apply a "reckless falsity" test could be disentangled from the BSO's statements of opinion. Further, any statements of opinion by the BSO would be protected absolutely under the First Amendment.[1] Thus, the court found that Redgrave had not overcome the significant obstacles created by the First Amendment to recovery of consequential damages.

The district court is correct in stating that an act can be a protected form of First Amendment activity.

The BSO's cancellation of its contract with Redgrave was not, however, an act intended to be a form of symbolic speech or a "statement" by the BSO. As BSO agents testified, the press release announcing the BSO's cancellation went through a number of drafts in order to remove any statement or implication that Redgrave was too controversial or dangerous to hire. In fact, the press release did not even refer to Redgrave by name. Indeed, in response to special verdict question 11A, the jury found that the BSO's cancellation and press release did not "impliedly state to others that

---

1. [The Supreme Court has since ruled that there is no separate, absolute, constitutional privilege for statements of opinion. Milkovich v. Lorain Journal Co., 497 U.S. 1, 110 S.Ct. 2695, 111 L.Ed.2d 1 (1990).]

BSO's managerial agents held the opinion that Vanessa Redgrave was so controversial because of her publicly expressed political views that the risks associated with the series of performances in Boston and New York, in which she was to appear as narrator, were too great to be acceptable to a prudently managed symphony orchestra." Thus, the evidence does not support an inference that the BSO intended its cancellation to act as a symbolic message to others.

An act not intended to be communicative does not acquire the stature of First–Amendment-protected expression merely because someone, upon learning of the act, might derive some message from it. Nor is such an act entitled to special protection merely because others speak about it. Accordingly, we believe the district court erred in reasoning that the causal link between the BSO's contract cancellation and Redgrave's harm necessarily involved protected expression by the BSO.

Redgrave's counsel presented two distinct avenues of causation through which the jury could find that the BSO's cancellation caused Redgrave consequential harm and the jury was instructed on both grounds. Besides contending that the BSO's cancellation and press release impliedly stated to others that Redgrave was too controversial to be acceptable to a prudently managed symphony orchestra, Redgrave also contended that "since BSO was a prestigious cultural organization, the very fact that it decided to cancel rather than proceed with performances in which Vanessa Redgrave was to appear would tend to influence others not to offer her future professional opportunities." The jury was instructed to "determine whether the evidence supports either, both, or neither of these contentions" in deciding whether the BSO's cancellation caused Redgrave consequential harm.

The jury rejected the "implied message" theory yet still found that the BSO's contract cancellation caused Redgrave to lose future professional opportunities. Apparently, the jury felt that the BSO's cancellation had caused harm to Redgrave's career, despite its conclusion that the BSO had not intentionally sent any implied message regarding Redgrave. Theodore Mann, a director, testified that he chose not to offer Redgrave a job in a theater performance because

[t]he Boston Symphony Orchestra had cancelled, terminated Ms. Redgrave's contract. This had a—this is the premier or one of the premier arts organizations in America who, like ourselves, seeks support from foundations, corporations, individuals; have subscribers; sell individual tickets. I was afraid ... and those in my organization were afraid that this termination would have a negative effect on us if we hired her.

Thus, the jury could appropriately have found that even though the BSO did not intend its contract cancellation to be a purposeful symbolic communication, other performing companies may have derived, or feared that their supporters might derive, some message from the cancellation, causing them concern about hiring Redgrave. Under this theory, the jury could have found that the act of cancellation, unprotected by the First Amendment, was the proximate cause of Redgrave's harm.

The district court correctly stated that "plaintiffs must prove that in some way information about BSO's action was communicated to others." However, as amici correctly point out, the trial court erred in confusing communication *about* the BSO's contract cancellation with the notion of an implied communication of a particular message *by* the BSO regarding Redgrave. Absent unusual circumstances suggesting primary interest in communicating an idea transcending the immediate act, a contract cancellation would not trigger the concerns ordinarily protected by the First Amendment. Indeed, under the district court's ruling, the cancellation of almost any contract with a notable figure could effectively be transformed into a statement protected by the First Amendment, thereby unnecessarily diluting the protections intended by contract law. Thus, although Redgrave must meet the ordinary strict contract requirements for finding consequential damages, no additional requirements need be imposed in this case because of the strictures of the First Amendment.

. . . .

III. THE MASSACHUSETTS CIVIL RIGHTS CLAIM AND THE DEFENSE OF ACQUIESCENCE TO THIRD-PARTY PRESSURE

The factor that converts this case from a garden variety, if not simple, contract action into an exotic plant without very apposite precedents is the MCRA (and its judicial gloss as added by the Massachusetts Supreme Judicial Court). As we shall see, the MCRA extends the 42 U.S.C. § 1983 concept of a civil rights claim against government officials to a claim against private individuals, so that it is no defense to the MCRA to show that the defendant's action was not "state action." Further, as with a typical civil rights claim against a government official, it is no defense to the MCRA to show that a defendant acted in response to third-party pressure. Finally, the sweeping liability resulting from the absence of these defenses may be limited by a constitutional right of free speech.

A. The Nature of the Claim

The MCRA creates a private cause of action for injunctive and other equitable relief, including damages, against "any person or persons, whether or not acting under color of law, [who] interfere by threats, intimidation or coercion, or attempt to interfere by threats, intimidation or coercion, with the exercise or enjoyment by any other person or persons of rights secured by the constitution or laws of the United States, or of rights secured by the constitution or laws of the commonwealth." A right is "secured" against private parties under the MCRA even though the constitutional provision from which it emanates applies only to government action. In this fashion the MCRA dispenses with the state action requirement of ordinary civil rights claims, by permitting a plaintiff to sue a private party for action that would be, absent the MCRA, forbidden only to state actors.

Redgrave alleged that the BSO interfered with her "secured" rights of free speech and free association under the First Amendment and the Massachusetts Constitution. Redgrave asserted that her secured rights were violated whether the BSO cancelled the contract because its own agents disagreed with her political views and intended to punish her for past speech or repress her future speech, or whether the BSO cancelled the contract because it acquiesced to pressure from third parties who disagreed with her views and intended to punish her or chill her expression.

B. *The Findings Below*

The jury, in answer to a special interrogatory, found that the BSO did not cancel the contract because its own agents disagreed with Redgrave's political views. Although the district court found that the BSO cancelled because of outside pressure, the court held that Redgrave's MCRA claim failed, because acquiescence to third party pressure, absent any discriminatory intent, did not constitute "threats, intimidation, or coercion" under the MCRA.

The court did not go further and make a finding as to the precise reason why the BSO cancelled, but it did find credible the testimony of BSO officials that the BSO cancelled because of concerns over the physical safety of the performers and audience and over disruptions that might jeopardize the artistic qualities of the performance. The court cited the testimony of, among others, Seiji Ozawa, the BSO's Music Director, who explained that his conception of "Oedipus Rex" required an "atmosphere of hearing" in which both performers and audience could concentrate, rather than an atmosphere influenced by shouting, booing, and the presence of uniformed police. Earlier in the case, the district court had noted that "the extent to which a broad interpretation of the MCRA could interfere with the BSO's First Amendment rights to make artistic judgments may depend upon whether the factfinder decides that the cancellation of the concerts was at least in part for artistic reasons." In ultimately ruling for the BSO on Redgrave's MCRA claim, however, the district court did not reach this constitutional issue.

C. *Our Certified Questions and the Answers*

Because we felt that Redgrave's MCRA claim turned on a significant question of Massachusetts law on which we found no controlling precedent, we certified two questions of law to the Supreme Judicial Court of the Commonwealth pursuant to Supreme Judicial Court Rule 1:03. The questions were as follows:

1. Under the Massachusetts Civil Rights Act, Mass.Gen.Laws ch. 12, § 11H and § 11I, may a defendant be held liable for interfering with the rights of another person, by "threats, intimidation, or coercion", if the defendant had no personal desire to interfere with the rights of that person but acquiesced to pressure from third parties who did wish to interfere with such rights?

2. If a defendant can be held liable under the Massachusetts Civil Rights Act for acquiescence to third party pressure, is it a defense for the defendant to show that its actions were independently motivated by additional concerns, such as the threat of extensive economic loss, physical safety, or particular concerns affecting the defendant's course of business?

The Supreme Judicial Court answered "Yes" to the first question. It held:

Making an exemption for civil rights deprivations resulting from third-party pressure "would reward and encourage" the very conduct which the substantive statutes prohibit. Whether the issue is phrased in terms of the existence of a specific intent requirement under the Massachusetts Civil Rights Act or a third-party pressure exemption from the statute, recognizing such an exemption would tend to eviscerate the statute and defeat the legislative policies behind the statute. Persons seeking to interfere with the civil rights of others in violation of the statute may not know or believe that the interference may lead to civil or criminal liability. Thus, to be effective, the provisions of §§ 11H and 11I must apply to any threatening, intimidating, or coercive behavior regardless of whether the defendant specifically intended to interfere with a right to which the plaintiff is entitled. Accordingly, we answer "yes" to the first question.

The second question was answered "No." The court held:

As an abstract proposition, fear of business disruption, fear for economic loss, or fear for physical safety are not justifications under §§ 11H and 11I. The legislative intent would be negated if such defenses were permitted. In an analogous context, the Supreme Court has rejected the notion that private biases and injuries that may be inflicted as a result of such biases are permissible justifications for deprivations of constitutional rights. Fear that the prejudice of third-party actors may lead to a breach of the peace has also been rejected as a justification for deprivations of civil rights. We recognize that explicit and imminent danger of physical harm might well in some circumstances justify interference with an individual's civil rights, but the certified question raises no such premise. Our answer to the second certified question is, "No."

These answers effectively disposed of the district court's view that acquiescence to third party pressure was a defense to an MCRA action. At first blush, this might suggest, as our dissenting colleagues insist, that we must now confront the BSO's additional argument for affirmance—that the First Amendment protects it from MCRA liability. The response of the SJC, however, significantly expanded upon and went beyond the answers to our specific questions. The nature and deliberateness of these additional remarks convince us that, as a matter of Massachusetts law, the BSO may not in these circumstances be held liable under the MCRA.

IV.   THE MASSACHUSETTS CIVIL RIGHTS ACT CLAIM: THE TEACHINGS OF THE SUPREME JUDICIAL COURT

The response of the Supreme Judicial Court to our questions was divided among three groups of Justices: the Chief Justice, writing for himself and Justices Liacos and Nolan; Justice Wilkins, joined by Justice Abrams, concurring; and Justice O'Connor, joined by Justice Lynch, dissenting. All three groups thought it necessary to identify an issue we had not raised expressly in our two certified questions. All three groups indicated, in tones ranging from strong suggestion to outright certainty, a view that the BSO should not be held liable under the MCRA for exercising its free speech right not to perform.

Although all of the Justices' reflections on this issue technically may fall under the heading of dicta, they are so deliberate, so unanimously expressed, and involve such a basic proposition, that we feel constrained to listen carefully. The certification process is the only opportunity for direct dialogue between a federal and a state court. We think it pointless to turn a deaf ear to all but the direct responses to formal questions where, as here, other important issues clearly are implicated. To do so would be to elevate form over substance, to ignore a helpful opportunity to interpret state law correctly, and to demean the principles of comity and federalism. "In the absence of a definitive ruling by the highest state court, a federal court may consider 'analogous decisions, considered dicta, scholarly works, and any other reliable data tending convincingly to show how the highest court in the state would decide the issue at hand,' taking into account the broad policies and trends so evinced."

As two commentators recently have noted:

[T]he ability of the answering court to reshape or add to the issues is necessary to further the goals of certification. The answering court may be best situated to frame the question for precedential value and to control the development of its laws. If state courts take offense at a poorly framed question, they may miss a genuine opportunity to settle state law on a particular point.

Corr & Robbins, Interjurisdictional Certification and Choice of Law, 41 Vand.L.Rev. 411, 426 (1988).

In order to understand the reaction of the Supreme Judicial Court, it is helpful to describe the difficulty of the free expression issues involved, and the uncommon relation of the MCRA to those issues.

A.   *A Conflict of Rights*

The MCRA is an unusual statute, a civil rights law that abolishes the state action requirement for constitutional claims of deprivation of rights. This is not difficult to understand in the context of racial discrimination, the prohibition of which was the statute's primary object. There, it makes sense to treat private individuals similarly to the state, just as Title VII is designed as a "private" analogue to the non-discrimination provisions of the Constitution. But where the issue is the plaintiff's "right" to free speech, the analogy is strained. Such a right traditionally has content only in relation to state action—the state must be neutral as to all expression, and must not unreasonably restrain speech or expression. The right *is* to be free of state regulation, so that all private speech is formally on equal footing as a legal matter. In the traditional context, this means that various private actors can, without state interference, battle it out in the market-place of ideas.

In the present case, this application of the statute is made doubly unusual because, unlike in the typical discrimination case, there are free speech interests on the defendant's side of the balance as well. The plaintiff's statutory "free speech" right against the defendant is to be measured against the defendant's constitutional right against the state. If it were to enforce the statute, the state would be entering the marketplace of ideas in order to restrict speech that may have the effect of "coercing" other speech.

We have grave concerns about the implications of such a conflict. If constitutional protections are effectively to protect private expression, they must do so, to some extent, even when the expression (or lack thereof) of one private person threatens to interfere with the expression of another. To permit a newspaper, for example, wide freedom to pick and choose what to print, freedom to turn down some who would write letters or columns with which a particular newspaper (or its readers) disagrees, is to permit the newspaper to deprive certain speakers of an audience (perhaps deliberately, perhaps for "speech-content-related" reasons) or to intimidate the expression of other voices outside the newspaper. But, for the government to guarantee even some of those speakers a "newspaper" platform (or guarantee that they will not be coerced by what the newspaper decides to write or not to write) itself risks interfering with the newspaper's editorial freedom. The freedom of mediating institutions, newspapers, universities, political associations, and artistic organizations and individuals themselves to pick and choose among ideas, to winnow, to criticize, to investigate, to elaborate, to protest, to support, to boycott, and even to reject is essential if "free speech" is to prove meaningful. The courts, noting that free speech guarantees protect citizens against *governmental* restraints upon expression, have hesitated to permit governments to referee disputes between speakers lest such mediation, even when it flies the banner of "protecting speech," interfere with the very type of interest it seeks to protect.[17]

We digress briefly to note that we disagree fundamentally with our dissenting colleagues' analysis of the constitutional questions implicated in this case. The BSO does *not* demand, as our dissenting colleagues claim, the constitutional right to perform without audience interruption, or an absolute right against any infringement of its artistic expression. Of course there are no such rights. The BSO merely alleges a constitutional right not to be penalized[18] for failing to perform an artistic work where *the BSO* believes that its expression will be compromised or ineffective. That the reason for its desire to cancel may be the potential for audience disruption does not mean that the decision should be immune from constitutional solicitude.[19] The BSO asserts, simply, a right to be free from compelled expression.

17. Of course, a defendant's freedom of expression interests can also be implicated in a traditional race or sex discrimination case under the MCRA. We do not think it at all obvious, as do our dissenting brethren, that liability should attach if a performing group replaces a black performer with a white performer (or vice versa) in order to further its expressive interests....

Finally, we note that, even if an artistic organization could not *discriminate* in favor of a white (or black, or male) performer, presumably it would have a much more compelling interest in cancelling the performance rather than acceding to the casting requirements imposed by the state, even if the reason for cancellation is fear of community reaction. Of course, we here simply point out some of the difficulties that arise when two important protected interests conflict—where there is a clash of rights. We express no view as to how, in particular cases, that clash might be resolved.

18. For constitutional purposes, it makes no difference whether the state seeks to compel expression directly by "forcing" the artist to perform, or by imposing civil liability for refusing to perform; either form of coercion is burdensome to rights of free expression.

19. There are numerous ways in which adverse performance conditions may disturb that synergistic interplay of performers and

It is clear that artistic expression in the performing arts enjoys substantial constitutional protection. Protection for free expression in the arts should be particularly strong when asserted against a state effort to *compel* expression, for then the law's typical reluctance to force private citizens to act augments its constitutionally based concern for the integrity of the artist. A distinguished line of cases has underscored a private party's right to refuse compelled expression. "[T]he First Amendment guarantees 'freedom of speech,' a term necessarily comprising the decision of both what to say and what *not* to say." We have been unable to find any case, involving the arts or otherwise, in which a state has been allowed to compel expression. The outcome urged by our dissenting colleagues would, to our knowledge, be completely unprecedented.

Redgrave conceded at oral argument, and presumably the dissent would not disagree, that persons picketing a Redgrave performance would have a free expression defense to MCRA liability. This principle logically would extend as well to persons boycotting Redgrave performances. These are activities that are *intended* to coerce the exercise of others' speech by means of public approbation and economic pressure. Indeed, that is their animating purpose. Yet they are protected, for the simple reason that we have always tolerated and encouraged private expression, rather than state compulsion, as the antidote to private speech with which we disagree. We see no reason why *less* protection should be provided where the artist refuses to perform; indeed, silence traditionally has been more sacrosanct than affirmative expression. The BSO argues that it desired simply to protect its own artistic expression, and it chose cancellation as the means of doing so. That this may have had a residual effect of coercing Redgrave's exercise of her speech should not mean that the cancellation is any less protected than expression intended to coerce such exercise.

We raise these points not to resolve the constitutional questions, but to point out how difficult those questions are to resolve, to indicate that expression-related interests appear on all sides, and to suggest that the dissent's resolution, while motivated by values we share, too easily reduces a very complex clash of rights to a simple equation that neglects the serious weight of the BSO's interests.[21]

We have no reason to think that the Massachusetts Legislature enacted the MCRA in an attempt to have its courts, at the insistence of private plaintiffs, oversee the editorial judgments of newspapers, the speech-related activities of private universities, or the aesthetic judgments of artists. To be more specific, our examination of these difficulties helps us understand why at least four, and perhaps as many as seven, members of the Supreme

---

audience that is so important to the content of the performance. . . .

21. The implications of the dissent's position underscore its problems. For instance, under the dissent's theory of the MCRA, a private university would be liable for denying tenure to a professor whose views it found politically reprehensible, or to a scholar who might cause turmoil on campus. A newspaper could not, without running afoul of the statute, cancel an opinion writer's column in response to outrage in the community, even if it meant that the newspaper's reputation was impugned or that great numbers of people stopped reading the paper. While we may commend those institutions and artists that resist such public pressure, no court has, to our knowledge, ever held legally accountable those private groups or artists that do succumb to public taste.

Judicial Court wrote opinions indicating that the statute does not impose liability upon the BSO in the circumstances of this case.

. . . .

There are at least four votes on the SJC denying liability on state law grounds. The concurring justices would establish a state constitutional defense, and the dissenters would interpret the statute, in light of constitutional concerns, to prohibit liability in the first instance. These two grounds are separate and not inconsistent. Because a majority of the SJC would foreclose liability on state law grounds, it is unnecessary and improper for us to reach the federal constitutional issues.

We are, moreover, confident that the *entire* SJC would, if explicitly asked to decide the issue, concur with the finding of no liability on both state law grounds. . . .

. . . .

Accordingly, we hold, in light of our understanding of state law, that the district court correctly entered judgment for the BSO on Redgrave's MCRA claim.

The judgment on the MCRA claim is AFFIRMED and the judgment on the contract claim is VACATED and REMANDED for entry of judgment for consequential damages to the extent approved herein. No costs.

■ Bownes, Circuit Judge, with whom Circuit Judge Selya joins, concurring in part and dissenting in part.

Although I concur wholeheartedly in part II of the majority opinion concerning Redgrave's consequential contract damages claim, I cannot agree with the majority's treatment of Redgrave's claim under the Massachusetts Civil Rights Act (MCRA). Accordingly, I write separately.

. . . .

Unlike the majority, I do not believe that state law provides a basis for ducking the important and difficult federal constitutional issues raised by this case. . . .

. . . .

. . . . It is true that four members of the SJC would not have held the BSO liable under the MCRA. The two dissenters found that the MCRA did not extend liability absent specific intent to interfere with secured rights, and the two concurring justices found a state constitutional defense. Therefore, had this exact case arisen in the Massachusetts state courts and proceeded in its present form to the SJC, the BSO would not have been subjected to liability, by virtue of the somewhat unusual combined effect of two *minority* positions. But that possibility is simply irrelevant to the issues here, because this case did not arise in the state courts, it arose in the federal courts. As a federal court sitting in a diversity case, our task is to apply the substantive law of Massachusetts on any given state law question, not to predict what quirky result might obtain in the state courts because a particular case contains multiple state law issues, each of which attracts a minority as well as a majority position.

The central state law issues in this case are the two questions of statutory interpretation we certified to the SJC. On those questions, we have received clear answers from a majority of five justices. That two justices disagreed with the majority's analysis should have no bearing on our handling of this case, for their view, however interesting it may be, failed to carry the day in the SJC. Certainly we have no business combining the two dissenting votes with the votes of the two concurring justices, who based their position on entirely different grounds and indeed explicitly rejected the dissent's analysis. In its eagerness to "defer" to the SJC, the majority of this court has confused the procedure of certifying questions of state law to a state court with the procedure of certifying entire cases to state courts. Federal courts do not certify cases to state courts. They certify questions of law and then apply the answers to those questions to reach a result which represents the combined effect of majority, not minority, positions.

. . . .

[Moreover,] . . . I do not agree with the majority's selective reading of the SJC's opinions. I find no basis in those opinions for rejecting Redgrave's claims on state law grounds. . . .

. . . .

The next issue, therefore, is whether the BSO has, as it asserts, a first amendment "artistic integrity" defense to its violation of the MCRA. Although the words "artistic integrity" evoke a positive response and sound as if they ought to come within the protective mantle of the first amendment, I have found no case explicitly recognizing a first amendment right of "artistic integrity." The term is hard to define. It can mean an actor's desire to perform a role as she wishes, the right of an artist to write, paint, or compose free of any outside restraints, or a myriad of other activities involving artistic creation and expression. In the context of this case, however, and as articulated by the BSO, it means the right of the BSO to refuse to perform *Oedipus Rex* under less than optimal audience conditions. I recognize that the BSO has a first amendment right to control its artistic expression but, like every other first amendment right, this one is not an absolute.

The MCRA provides a cause of action against "any person or persons, whether or not acting under color of law, [who] interfere by threats, intimidation of coercion" with the free speech rights of another. Redgrave argues that the BSO's refusal to perform with her as narrator was motivated, as it clearly was, by the public outcry over her open endorsement of the Palestine Liberation Organization (PLO). She claims that she was deprived of employment because of her political views and that this deprivation amounted to coercion. The SJC agreed, rejecting the BSO's proffered statutory defenses to MCRA liability.

This case thus presents a clash between Redgrave's right under the MCRA not to be punished for her public espousal of unpopular political views, and the BSO's asserted first amendment right to control its artistic expression. It requires the application of a standard approach to first amendment issues: the balancing of two competing rights. In a number of recent cases, the Supreme Court has considered similar challenges to state antidiscrimination laws that, like the MCRA, incidentally infringe the right to free speech. Under the Court's now well-established test, such laws survive so long as they are necessary to serve a compelling state interest that is unrelated to the suppression of ideas. E.g., Board of Directors of Rotary Int'l v. Rotary Club, 481 U.S. 537, 107 S.Ct. 1940, 95 L.Ed.2d 474 (1987); Roberts v. United States Jaycees, 468 U.S. 609, 628, 104 S.Ct. 3244, 82 L.Ed.2d 462 (1984).

In order to apply that test to this case, I begin by examining the MCRA and Massachusetts' interest in passing it. The effect of the MCRA in this case is to further the Commonwealth's interest in preventing the abridgement of speech. There can be no denying that this interest is substantial. Political speech, like the pro–PLO speech for which Redgrave has been made to suffer, is a particularly valuable and protected commodity. Neither the federal government nor the states may regulate such speech on the basis of its content absent a clear and present danger. And, unless accompanied by a present intent to overthrow the government and an actual likelihood of concrete harm, even subversive political speech is protected and may not be made the basis for discrimination by the government. The Commonwealth has reinforced the centrality of these first amendment values by passing a statute that broadens the reach of free speech rights. By eliminating the state action requirement of 42 U.S.C. § 1983, the MCRA proscribes the abridgement of speech rights by private actors, such as the BSO, as well as by state actors, such as the Commonwealth itself.

The Supreme Court has noted that the states and the federal government have a compelling interest in eliminating invidious discrimination by private persons on the basis of race and sex. Consequently, it routinely has upheld statutes aimed at eradicating such discrimination, even though they have the incidental effect of abridging the first amendment rights of the discriminators. I believe that a similar analysis should be applied to the MCRA, which, among other things, prohibits discrimination on the basis of speech or politics.

Branding it "an unusual statute," however, the majority attempts to distinguish the MCRA from "traditional" statutes such as Title VII, which forbid racial and gender discrimination. The majority declares that it "makes sense to treat private individuals similarly to the state" in order to combat racial discrimination. On the other hand, it does not "make sense" to the majority to accord similar treatment to individuals who discriminate on the basis of political speech. The majority asserts that, unlike the right to be free from racial discrimination, the right to free speech "traditionally has content only in relation to state action. . . . The right is to be free of state regulation."

I am at a loss to understand the majority's position except as the "common sense" of federal judges so wedded to "traditional" thinking that they simply refuse to accept the basis for Massachusetts' innovative antidiscrimination law. Certainly it is not true that the right to be free from racial discrimination is by definition less dependent on state action than the right to be free from restraints on speech. Even today, a primary legal guarantee against racial discrimination in this country is the equal protection clause of the fourteenth amendment which, of course, applies only to state action. Moreover, prior to the civil rights revolution of the 1960s, many Americans, including federal judges, thought that it did not "make sense," even through legislation, to extend that antidiscrimination mandate to private persons. See, e.g., Civil Rights Cases, 109 U.S. 3, 3 S.Ct. 18, 27 L.Ed. 835 (1883)(holding that public accommodations such as railroads and hotels were immune from federal legislation aimed at racial discrimination because they did not involve state action).

It is also important to note that the first amendment's free speech guarantee textually applies to action by the federal government alone. It is the fourteenth amendment's due process guarantee which extends to individuals a federal right to free speech enforceable against the states. Therefore, insofar as action by *states* is concerned, the same amendment—the fourteenth amendment—provides individuals with both their right to free speech and their right to be free from invidious racial discrimination. How, then, can the majority argue that the free speech right is inherently *more* dependent on state action than the antidiscrimination right?

Virtually all antidiscrimination rights, whether they pertain to discrimination on the basis of race, sex or political belief, find their "traditional" basis in constitutional guarantees which are limited to state action. However, just as Congress through Title VII extended rights against racial discrimination to encompass actions by private persons, so has Massachusetts through the MCRA extended protection to persons like Redgrave whose free speech rights are abridged by private persons. Certainly, laws against racial discrimination have a somewhat more established track record than the Redgrave's use of the MCRA, but I find particularly repugnant the majority's assertion that because Redgrave's claim is innovative, it does not "make sense."

Turning to the constitutional rights aspect of the balancing equation, the BSO argues, in its defense, that its own interest in interpreting and presenting *Oedipus Rex* as it wishes precludes liability to Redgrave under the MCRA. It asserts that the cancellation of her contract, in response to threats of audience disruption arising out of a disagreement with her prior political expression, was a legitimate means of maintaining artistic control over the production and did not give rise to liability under the MCRA.

It is necessary to state what the BSO has *not* alleged. The BSO has never claimed that it cancelled the contract with Redgrave as a symbolic act meant to communicate its disapproval of the PLO. Indeed this court unanimously has rejected the idea that the BSO's firing of Redgrave intended to be any kind of symbolic speech or "statement." Had the BSO intended to communicate such expression, we would be confronted by a more difficult case, with a conflict between two compelling speech interests: that of Redgrave to be free, under the MCRA, of economic retaliation by an employer for her views on matters of significant public import, and that of the BSO to be free, under the first amendment, of state encroachment on its right to express itself on those same matters.

. . . .

The only possible conclusion to be drawn from this record and from the findings of the district court is that the BSO cancelled its contract with Redgrave in acquiescence to pressure from persons who disagreed with her political views and who, therefore, sought to retaliate against her. The BSO's asserted first amendment right, then, was not an independent artistic judgment to cancel the performance of *Oedipus Rex* but an instance of caving in to third-party pressure. The BSO, by doing so, effectively has blacklisted Redgrave.

The Supreme Court previously has held that fear of community reaction is no defense to an action for discrimination on the basis of race. The BSO argues that in this case the acquiescence to third-party pressure was justified by the necessity of protecting the artistic integrity of its own performance. The BSO's musical director, Seiji Ozawa, testified to his belief that, if police were in the audience, the performers could not concentrate, and that, if somebody shouted or booed, the performance might not be able to continue. The artistic administrator, Bernell, referred to the possibility of police lining the halls as a threat to "artistic integrity." The BSO president, Darling, remembered a conversation in which Ozawa commented that the presence of security forces would change the artistic format of the performance.

By invoking a broad-based defense in the name of "artistic integrity," the BSO is, in essence, asserting a right to unlimited discretion in the presentation of its work. "Artistic integrity," as the BSO defines it, means the absolute and unrestricted power to determine everything about the performance—from the choice of the production to the hiring of performers, to the quality of the audience ambience. The effect of allowing such a defense would be that the BSO itself would determine when the MCRA would and would not apply simply by deciding what is "artistic" and what is not. Under the rubric of "artistic integrity," the BSO could insulate itself from any but the most superficial legal scrutiny.

The very breadth of this proposed defense renders it suspect. Although I recognize that the BSO does have a first amendment right to control its artistic expression, I do not believe that this right is so broad and so absolute as to outweigh Massachusetts' interest in protecting Redgrave's rights. Neither the majority of this court nor the BSO seriously has suggested that Massachusetts does not have a compelling state interest in enacting legislation to protect the free speech rights of citizens in the Commonwealth. Nor has anyone argued that the MCRA does not represent the least restrictive means of achieving that purpose. Rather, the BSO asserts an absolute right against *any* infringement of its artistic expression. Under established Supreme Court precedent, it is clear that this argument must be rejected.

In Board of Directors of Rotary Int'l v. Rotary Club, 481 U.S. 537, 107 S.Ct. 1940, 95 L.Ed.2d 474 (1987), Rotary International asserted that an absolute right of free association and expression under the first amendment immunized it from a California statute prohibiting discrimination on the basis of sex. The Court rejected Rotary International's claim, noting that even if the California act did "work some slight infringement on Rotary members' right of expressive association, that infringement is justified because it serves the State's compelling interest in eliminating discrimination against women." This holding was recently reaffirmed in New York State Club Ass'n v. City of New York, 487 U.S. 1, 108 S.Ct. 2225, 101 L.Ed.2d 1 (1988), where the Supreme Court rejected a facial challenge to a New York City ordinance prohibiting discrimination in certain private clubs. I believe these cases conclusively establish that the BSO's claim to absolute first amendment immunity from state antidiscrimination laws is contrary to governing constitutional precedent.[9]

If the Commonwealth were attempting to dictate how *Oedipus Rex* should be presented, an entirely different case would be presented. Such an extreme and probably unjustifiable exercise of state power would almost certainly be a violation of the first amendment. Here, however, the Massachusetts statute does not take control of the production away from the BSO. It merely holds the BSO to its own previously and voluntarily adopted contractual obligations. The BSO is still free to interpret and perform *Oedipus Rex* as it chooses. The only constraint imposed upon the BSO by operation of the MCRA is that the BSO cannot *cancel* the performance in reaction to anticipated audience disruption.

History and experience teach that the risk of catcalls, boos, disruptions, and even being the target of vegetable projectiles is inherent in any public performance by artists who seek to entertain and/or educate the public. Indeed, it could be argued that the audience has a first amendment right to object vociferously to an artistic performance. The record in this case contains a strong dissent from Peter Sellars, the stage director hired by the BSO for the production, to Ozawa's opinion that the presence of police or expressions of displeasure by the audience would affect adversely the BSO's performance. Sellars testified that there is a "rich history of disruption" in the history of musical concerts and that, rather than shocking, "it is an important part of the concert to have a strong audience reaction." He pointed out that at the first performance of Stravinsky's *Rites of Spring,* "there were riots [and] the audience was stampeding." But Sellars went even further. He stated that "music has a responsibility to incite and is very exciting in this way." He believed that, far from disrupting the performance, the presence of police officers in Symphony Hall could be incorporated into the drama of *Oedipus Rex.* Sellars declared that the political tensions surrounding Redgrave's performance could result in a "living recreation" or even a "living creation" of the moral essence of the drama of *Oedipus Rex.*

9. The majority has turned the BSO's absolutist first amendment claim on its head, instead suggesting that in order to apply the MCRA to the BSO, this court would have to adopt the absolutist position that there could *never* be a first amendment defense to the BSO. The majority thus marches out a "parade of horribles," asserting that under my interpretation of the MCRA, the statute would be used to control the editorial practices of newspapers. This far-fetched hypothetical, however, demonstrates that the majority has missed the point. First amendment claims are not made of absolutes, they involve the balancing of competing interests. Each case must be judged on its own specific facts, and I am more than willing to concede that certain applications of the MCRA, including the majority's newspaper hypothetical, would be plainly impermissible under the first amendment.

To recognize an absolute first amendment defense of "artistic integrity," as the BSO urges, would flout the very values that the first amendment and the MCRA protect. It would mean that a performing artist, or group of artists, could deny another artist her statutorily protected right to perform because of fear that the audience might interrupt the performance. This is the opposite of "artistic integrity"; it allows the audience to dictate who shall perform and what shall be played. "Artistic integrity" under this view would be a license for the heckler's veto in the arena of artistic expression.

But perhaps the strongest illustration of the weakness of the BSO's asserted absolute first amendment defense lies in examining the potentially nightmarish consequences of recognizing it. If the first amendment extends absolute protection to the BSO when it fired Redgrave in response to public outcry over her political views, why would it not also protect the BSO in caving in to public views about her sex, her race, or her religion? If, in another case, the BSO refused to hire a Black performer because it felt that protests by bigots would be so intense as to compromise the BSO's "artistic integrity," then the Black performer should have a cause of action under the MCRA against the BSO for infringing her rights under the equal protection clause and any analogous state constitutional provisions banning race discrimination. But the "artistic integrity" defense would impose a fatal barrier to the application of the MCRA. And there is no reason to assume that the same defense would not also extend to other institutions, such as newspapers and universities, that engage generally in first amendment activity. In order to qualify for protection, these institutions would only need to characterize their discriminatory acts as based on artistic or intellectual choices and thus effectively foreclose legislative or judicial scrutiny.

Ironically, the BSO conceded at oral argument that the first amendment would not protect it from liability for race or sex discrimination. But its attempt to portray laws against race or sex discrimination as having deeper historical roots than laws against discrimination on the basis of political views is not only doctrinally unsound, but historically incorrect. The first amendment, and not the equal protection clause, is the longstanding tradition. The passage of the equal protection clause, and its concomitant application to Blacks came over one hundred years after the passage of the Bill of Rights. And the application of the equal protection clause to women is too recent to characterize as anything short of an innovation.

In conclusion, it is important to point out that the elimination of the state action requirement by the MCRA puts the BSO in the place of the state. Of course, the BSO retains its first amendment rights against the Commonwealth. But now, by operation of the MCRA, it also has obligations like those of the Commonwealth itself not to abridge the free speech rights of others. In cancelling its contract with Redgrave, the BSO repudiated that obligation and thwarted the Commonwealth's compelling interest in preventing the abridgement of speech.

I respectfully dissent.

PART VI

COMPLETING THE REMEDY

CHAPTER 19

ATTORNEYS' FEES, COSTS, PREJUDGMENT INTEREST, & FOREIGN CURRENCY JUDGMENTS

———

The merits of the case have been determined. The parties' basic rights to relief have been fixed. A number of problems nonetheless remain, of which this Chapter addresses three. First, there is the matter of attorneys' fees: who should pay for the litigation? Then comes the question of prejudgment interest: to what extent should the plaintiff be reimbursed for the defendant's failure to provide compensation prior to the entry of judgment? Finally, there is the intriguing puzzle of foreign currency judgments: when wrongs occur abroad, in what currency (at what rate of exchange) should awards be fixed?

———

A. ATTORNEYS' FEES

———

Alyeska Pipeline Service Co. v. Wilderness Society

Supreme Court of the United States, 1975.
421 U.S. 240, 95 S.Ct. 1612, 44 L.Ed.2d 141.

■ MR. JUSTICE WHITE delivered the opinion of the Court.

This litigation was initiated by respondents Wilderness Society, Environmental Defense Fund, Inc., and Friends of the Earth in an attempt to prevent the issuance of permits by the Secretary of the Interior which were required for the construction of the trans-Alaska oil pipeline. The Court of Appeals awarded attorneys' fees to respondents against petitioner Alyeska Pipeline Service Co. based upon the court's equitable powers and the theory that respondents were entitled to fees because they were performing the services of a "private attorney general." Certiorari was granted to determine whether this award of attorneys' fees was appropriate. We reverse.

I

A major oil field was discovered in the North Slope of Alaska in 1968. In June 1969, the oil companies constituting the consortium owning

Alyeska submitted an application to the Department of the Interior for rights-of-way for a pipeline that would transport oil from the North Slope across land in Alaska owned by the United States, a major part of the transport system which would carry the oil to its ultimate markets in the lower 48 States. A special interdepartmental task force studied the proposal and reported to the President. An amended application was submitted in December 1969, which requested a 54–foot right-of-way, along with applications for "special land use permits" asking for additional space alongside the right-of-way and for the construction of a road along one segment of the pipeline.

Respondents brought this suit in March 1970, and sought declaratory and injunctive relief against the Secretary of the Interior on the grounds that he intended to issue the right-of-way and special land-use permits in violation of § 28 of the Mineral Leasing Act of 1920 and without compliance with the National Environmental Policy Act of 1969 (NEPA). On the basis of both the Mineral Leasing Act and the NEPA, the District Court granted a preliminary injunction against issuance of the right-of-way and permits.

Subsequently the State of Alaska and petitioner Alyeska were allowed to intervene. On March 20, 1972, the Interior Department released a six-volume Environmental Impact Statement and a three-volume Economic and Security Analysis. After a period of time set aside for public comment, the Secretary announced that the requested permits would be granted to Alyeska. Both the Mineral Leasing Act and the NEPA issues were at that point fully briefed and argued before the District Court. That court then decided to dissolve the preliminary injunction, to deny the permanent injunction, and to dismiss the complaint.

Upon appeal, the Court of Appeals for the District of Columbia Circuit reversed, basing its decision solely on the Mineral Leasing Act. Finding that the NEPA issues were very complex and important, that deciding them was not necessary at that time since pipeline construction would be enjoined as a result of the violation of the Mineral Leasing Act, that they involved issues of fact still in dispute, and that it was desirable to expedite its decision as much as possible, the Court of Appeals declined to decide the merits of respondents' NEPA contentions which had been rejected by the District Court.

Congress then enacted legislation which amended the Mineral Leasing Act to allow the granting of the permits sought by Alyeska and declared that no further action under the NEPA was necessary before construction of the pipeline could proceed.

With the merits of the litigation effectively terminated by this legislation, the Court of Appeals turned to the questions involved in respondents' request for an award of attorneys' fees. Since there was no applicable statutory authorization for such an award, the court proceeded to consider whether the requested fee award fell within any of the exceptions to the general "American rule" that the prevailing party may not recover attorneys' fees as costs or otherwise. The exception for an award against a party who had acted in bad faith was inapposite, since the position taken by the federal and state parties and Alyeska "was manifestly reasonable and assumed in good faith...." Application of the "common benefit" exception which spreads the cost of litigation to those persons benefiting from it would "stretch it totally outside its basic rationale...." The Court of Appeals nevertheless held that respondents had acted to vindicate "important statutory rights of all citizens ...;" had ensured that the governmental system functioned properly; and were entitled to attorneys' fees lest the great cost of litigation of this kind, particularly against well-financed defendants such as Alyeska, deter private parties desiring to see the laws protecting the environment properly enforced. Title 28 U.S.C. § 2412 was thought to bar taxing any attorneys' fees against the United States, and it was also deemed inappropriate to burden the State of Alaska with any part of the award.[16] But Alyeska, the Court of Appeals held, could fairly be required to pay one-half of the full award to which respondents were entitled for having performed the functions of a private attorney general....

II

In the United States, the prevailing litigant is ordinarily not entitled to collect a reasonable attorneys' fee from the loser. We are asked to fashion a far-reaching exception to this "American Rule"; but having considered its origin and development, we are convinced that it would be inappropriate for the Judiciary, without legislative guidance, to reallocate the burdens of litigation in the manner and to the extent urged by respondents and approved by the Court of Appeals.

At common law, costs were not allowed; but for centuries in England there has been statutory authorization to award costs, including attorneys' fees. Although the matter is in the discretion of the court, counsel fees are regularly allowed to the prevailing party.

During the first years of the federal-court system, Congress provided through legislation that the federal courts were to follow the practice with respect to awarding attorneys' fees of the courts of the States in which the federal courts were located, with the exception of district courts under admiralty and maritime jurisdiction which were to follow a specific fee schedule. Those statutes, by 1800, had either expired or been repealed.

In 1796, this Court appears to have ruled that the Judiciary itself would not create a general rule, independent of any statute, allowing awards of attorneys' fees in federal courts.... This Court has consistently adhered to that early holding.

The practice ... until 1853 continued as before, that is, with the federal courts referring to the state rules governing awards of counsel fees.... By legislation in 1842, Congress did give this Court authority to prescribe the items and amounts of costs which could be taxed in federal courts but the Court took no action under this statutory mandate.

16. "In the circumstances of this case it would be inappropriate to tax fees against appellee State of Alaska. The State voluntarily participated in this suit, in effect to present to the court a different version of the public interest implications of the trans-Alaska pipeline. Taxing attorneys' fees against Alaska would in our view undermine rather than further the goal of ensuring adequate spokesmen for public interests."

In 1853, Congress undertook to standardize the costs allowable in federal litigation. In support of the proposed legislation, it was asserted that there was great diversity in practice among the courts and that losing litigants were being unfairly saddled with exorbitant fees for the victor's attorney. The result was a far-reaching Act specifying in detail the nature and amount of the taxable items of cost in the federal courts. One of its purposes was to limit allowances for attorneys' fees that were to be charged to the losing parties. Although the Act disclaimed any intention to limit the amount of fees that an attorney and his client might agree upon between themselves, counsel fees collectible from the losing party were expressly limited to the amounts stated in the Act:

> "That in lieu of the compensation now allowed by the law to attorneys, solicitors, and proctors in the United States courts, to United States district attorneys, clerks of the district and circuit courts, marshals, witnesses, jurors, commissioners, and printers, in the several States, the following and no other compensation shall be taxed and allowed. But this act shall not be construed to prohibit attorneys, solicitors, and proctors from charging to and receiving from their clients, other than the Government, such reasonable compensation for their services, in addition to the taxable costs, as may be in accordance with general usage in their respective States, or may be agreed upon between the parties." Act of Feb. 26, 1853, 10 Stat. 161.

The Act then proceeds to list specific sums for the services of attorneys, solicitors, and proctors.

The intention of the Act to control the attorneys' fees recoverable by the prevailing party from the loser was repeatedly enforced by this Court....

Although, as will be seen, Congress has made specific provision for attorneys' fees under certain federal statutes, it has not changed the general statutory rule that allowances for counsel fees are limited to the sums specified by the costs statute. The 1853 Act was ... included in the Revised Code of 1948 as 28 U.S.C. §§ 1920 and 1923(a). Under § 1920, a court may tax as costs the various items specified, including the "docket fees" under § 1923(a). That section provides that "[a]ttorney's and proctor's docket fees in courts of the United States may be taxed as costs as follows...." Against this background, this Court understandably declared in 1967 that with the exception of the small amounts allowed by § 1923, the rule "has long been that attorney's fees are not ordinarily recoverable...." ...

To be sure, the fee statutes have been construed to allow, in limited circumstances, a reasonable attorneys' fee to the prevailing party in excess of the small sums permitted by § 1923. In Trustees v. Greenough, 105 U.S. 527, 26 L.Ed. 1157 (1882), the 1853 Act was read as not interfering with the historic power of equity to permit the trustee of a fund or property, or a party preserving or recovering a fund for the benefit of others in addition to himself, to recover his costs, including his attorneys' fees, from the fund or property itself or directly from the other parties enjoying the benefit. That rule has been consistently followed. Also, a court may assess attorneys' fees for the "willful disobedience of a court order ... as part of the fine to be levied on the defendant," or when the losing party has "acted in bad faith, vexatiously, wantonly, or for oppressive reasons...." These exceptions are unquestionably assertions of inherent power in the courts to allow attorneys' fees in particular situations, unless forbidden by Congress, but none of the exceptions is involved here.[31] The Court of Appeals expressly disclaimed reliance on any of them.

Congress has not repudiated the judicially fashioned exceptions to the general rule against allowing substantial attorneys' fees; but neither has it retracted, repealed, or modified the limitations on taxable fees contained in the 1853 statute and its successors. Nor has it extended any roving authority to the Judiciary to allow counsel fees as costs or otherwise whenever the courts might deem them warranted. What Congress has done, however, while fully recognizing and accepting the general rule, is to make specific and explicit provisions for the allowance of attorneys' fees under selected statutes granting or protecting various federal rights. These statutory allowances are now available in a variety of circumstances, but they also differ considerably among themselves. Under the antitrust laws, for instance, allowance of attorney's fees to a plaintiff awarded treble damages is mandatory. In patent litigation, in contrast, "[t]he court, in *exceptional* cases, *may* award reasonable attorney fees to the prevailing party." 35 U.S.C. § 285 (emphasis added). Under Title II of the Civil Rights Act of 1964, the prevailing party is entitled to attorneys' fees, at the discretion of the court, but we have held that Congress intended that the award should be made to the successful plaintiff absent exceptional circumstances. Under this scheme of things, it is apparent that the circumstances under which attorneys' fees are to be awarded and the range of discretion of the courts in making those awards are matters for Congress to determine.

It is true that under some, if not most, of the statutes providing for the allowance of reasonable fees, Congress has opted to rely heavily on private enforcement to implement public policy and to allow counsel fees so as to encourage private litigation. Fee shifting in connection with treble-damages awards under the antitrust laws is a prime example; and we have noted

---

31. A very different situation is presented when a federal court sits in a diversity case. "[I]n an ordinary diversity case where the state law does not run counter to a valid federal statute or rule of court, and usually it will not, state law denying the right to attorney's fees or giving a right thereto, which reflects a substantial policy of the state should be followed." 6 J. Moore, Federal Practice ¶ 54.77[2], pp. 1712–1713 (2d ed. 1974)(footnotes omitted). Prior to the decision in Erie R. Co. v. Tompkins, 304 U.S. 64, 58 S.Ct. 817, 82 L.Ed. 1188 (1938), this Court held that a state statute requiring an award of attorneys' fees should be applied in a case removed from the state courts to the federal courts: "[I]t is clear that it is the policy of the state to allow plaintiffs to recover an attorney's fee in certain cases, and it has made that policy effective by making the allowance of the fee mandatory on its courts in those cases. It would be at least anomalous if this policy could be thwarted and the right so plainly given destroyed by removal of the cause to the federal courts." The limitations on the awards of attorneys' fees by federal courts deriving from the 1853 Act were found not to bar the award. We see nothing after *Erie* requiring a departure from this result. The same would clearly hold for a judicially created rule, although the question of the proper rule to govern in awarding attorneys' fees in federal diversity cases in the absence of state statutory authorization loses much of its practical significance in light of the fact that most States follow the restrictive American Rule.

that Title II of the Civil Rights Act of 1964 was intended "not simply to penalize litigants who deliberately advance arguments they know to be untenable but, more broadly, to encourage individuals injured by racial discrimination to seek judicial relief under Title II." But congressional utilization of the private-attorney-general concept can in no sense be construed as a grant of authority to the Judiciary to jettison the traditional rule against nonstatutory allowances to the prevailing party and to award attorneys' fees whenever the courts deem the public policy furthered by a particular statute important enough to warrant the award.

Congress itself presumably has the power and judgment to pick and choose among its statutes and to allow attorneys' fees under some, but not others. But it would be difficult, indeed, for the courts, without legislative guidance, to consider some statutes important and others unimportant and to allow attorneys' fees only in connection with the former.... Moreover, should courts, if they were to embark on the course urged by respondents, opt for awards to the prevailing party, whether plaintiff or defendant, or only to the prevailing plaintiff? Should awards be discretionary or mandatory? Would there be a presumption operating for or against them in the ordinary case?[39]

---

39. Mr. Justice Marshall, after concluding that the federal courts have equitable power which can be used to create and implement a private-attorney-general rule, attempts to solve the problems of manageability which such a rule would necessarily raise. To do so, however, he emasculates the theory. Instead of a straightforward award of attorneys' fees to the winning plaintiff who undertakes to enforce statutes embodying important public policies, as the Court of Appeals proposed, Mr. Justice Marshall would tax attorneys' fees in favor of the private attorney general only when the award could be said to impose the burden on those who benefit from the enforcement of the law. The theory that he would adopt is not the private-attorney-general rule, but rather an expanded version of the common-fund approach to the awarding of attorneys' fees. When Congress has provided for allowance of attorneys' fees for the private attorney general, it has imposed no such common-fund conditions upon the award. The dissenting opinion not only errs in finding authority in the courts to award attorneys' fees, without legislative guidance, to those plaintiffs the courts are willing to recognize as private attorneys general, but also disserves that basis for fee shifting by imposing a limiting condition characteristic of other justifications.

That condition ill suits litigation in which the purported benefits accrue to the general public. In this Court's common-fund and common-benefit decisions, the classes of beneficiaries were small in number and easily identifiable. The benefits could be traced with some accuracy, and there was reason for confidence that the costs could indeed be shifted with some exactitude to those benefiting. In this case, however, sophisticated economic analysis would be required to gauge the extent to which the general public, the supposed beneficiary, as distinguished from selected elements of it, would bear the costs. The Court of Appeals, very familiar with the litigation and the parties after dealing with the merits of the suit, concluded that "imposing attorneys' fees on Alyeska will not operate to spread the costs of litigation proportionately among these beneficiaries...." ...

. . . .

We add that in the three-part test suggested by Mr. Justice Marshall for administering a judicially created private-attorney-general rule, the only criterion which purports to enable a court to determine which statutes should be enforced by application of the rule is the first: "the important right being protected is one actually or necessarily shared by the general public or some class thereof...." Absent some judicially manageable standard for gauging "importance," that criterion would apply to all substantive congressional legislation providing for rights and duties generally applicable, that is, to virtually all congressional output. That result would solve the problem of courts selectively applying the rule in accordance with their own

As exemplified by this case itself, it is also evident that the rational application of the private-attorney-general rule would immediately collide with the express provision of 28 U.S.C. § 2412. Except as otherwise provided by statute, that section permits costs to be taxed against the United States, "but not including the fees and expenses of attorneys," in any civil action brought by or against the United States or any agency or official of the United States acting in an official capacity. . . .

We need labor the matter no further. It appears to us that the rule suggested here and adopted by the Court of Appeals would make major inroads on a policy matter that Congress has reserved for itself. Since the approach taken by Congress to this issue has been to carve out specific exceptions to a general rule that federal courts cannot award attorneys' fees beyond the limits of 28 U.S.C. § 1923, those courts are not free to fashion drastic new rules with respect to the allowance of attorneys' fees to the prevailing party in federal litigation or to pick and choose among plaintiffs and the statutes under which they sue and to award fees in some cases but not in others, depending upon the courts' assessment of the importance of the public policies involved in particular cases. Nor should the federal courts purport to adopt on their own initiative a rule awarding attorneys' fees based on the private-attorney-general approach when such judicial rule will operate only against private parties and not against the Government.

We do not purport to assess the merits or demerits of the "American Rule" with respect to the allowance of attorneys' fees. It has been criticized in recent years, and courts have been urged to find exceptions to it. It is also apparent from our national experience that the encouragement of private action to implement public policy has been viewed as desirable in a variety of circumstances. But the rule followed in our courts with respect to attorneys' fees has survived. It is deeply rooted in our history and in congressional policy; and it is not for us to invade the legislature's province by redistributing litigation costs in the manner suggested by respondents and followed by the Court of Appeals.

The decision below must therefore be reversed.

So ordered.

Reversed.

[DOUGLAS and POWELL, JJ., took no part in the consideration or decision of this case. The dissenting opinion of BRENNAN, J., is omitted.]

particular substantive-law preferences and priorities, but its breadth requires more justification than Mr. Justice Marshall provides by citing this Court's common-fund and common-benefit cases.

Mr. Justice Marshall's application of his suggested rule to this case, however, demonstrates the problems raised by courts generally assaying the public benefits which particular litigation has produced. The conclusion of the dissenting opinion is that "[t]here is hardly room for doubt" that respondents' litigation has protected an "important right . . . actually or necessarily shared by the general public or some class thereof. . . ." Whether that conclusion is correct or not, it would appear at the very least that, as in any instance of conflicting public-policy views, there is room for doubt on each side. The opinions below are evidence of that fact. It is that unavoidable doubt which calls for specific authority from Congress before courts apply a private-attorney-general rule in awarding attorneys' fees.

MR. JUSTICE MARSHALL, dissenting.

In reversing the award of attorneys' fees to the respondent environmentalist groups, the Court today disavows the well-established power of federal equity courts to award attorneys' fees when the interests of justice so require. . . .

. . . Because the Court concludes that granting attorneys' fees to private attorneys general is beyond the equitable power of the federal courts, it does not reach the question whether an award would be proper against Alyeska in this case under the private-attorney-general rationale.

On my view of the case, both questions must be answered. I see no basis in precedent or policy for holding that the courts cannot award attorneys' fees where the interests of justice require recovery, simply because the claim does not fit comfortably within one of the previously sanctioned judicial exceptions to the American Rule. The Court has not in the past regarded the award of attorneys' fees as a matter reserved for the Legislature, and it has certainly not read the docketing-fees statute as a general bar to judicial fee shifting. The Court's concern with the difficulty of applying meaningful standards in awarding attorneys' fees to successful "public benefit" litigants is a legitimate one, but in my view it overstates the novelty of the "private attorney general" theory. The guidelines developed in closely analogous statutory and nonstatutory attorneys' fee cases could readily be applied in cases such as the one at bar. I therefore disagree with the Court's flat rejection of the private-attorney-general rationale for fee shifting. Moreover, in my view the equities in this case support an award of attorneys' fees against Alyeska. Accordingly, I must respectfully dissent.

. . . .

The statutory analysis aside, the Court points to the difficulties in formulating a "private attorney general" exception that will not swallow the American Rule. I do not find the problem as vexing as the majority does. In fact, the guidelines to the proper application of the private-attorney-general rationale have been suggested in several of our recent cases, both under statutory attorneys' fee provisions and under the common-benefit exception.

. . . .

. . . The reasonable cost of the plaintiff's representation should be placed upon the defendant if (1) the important right being protected is one actually or necessarily shared by the general public or some class thereof; (2) the plaintiff's pecuniary interest in the outcome, if any, would not normally justify incurring the cost of counsel; and (3) shifting that cost to the defendant would effectively place it on a class that benefits from the litigation.

There is hardly room for doubt that the first of these criteria is met in the present case. Significant public benefits are derived from citizen litigation to vindicate expressions of congressional or constitutional policy. As a result of this litigation, respondents forced Congress to revise the Mineral Leasing Act of 1920 rather than permit its continued evasion. The 1973 amendments impose more stringent safety and liability standards, and they require Alyeska to pay fair market value for the right-of-way and to bear the costs of applying for the permit and monitoring the right-of-way.

Although the NEPA issues were not actually decided, the lawsuit served as a catalyst to ensure a thorough analysis of the pipeline's environmental impact. Requiring the Interior Department to comply with the NEPA and draft an impact statement satisfied the public's statutory right to have information about the environmental consequences of the project, and also forced delay in the construction until safeguards could be included as conditions to the new right-of-way grants.

Petitioner contends that these "beneficial results ... might have occurred" without this litigation. But the record demonstrates that Alyeska was unwilling to observe and the Government unwilling to enforce congressional ... policy....

The second criterion is equally well satisfied in this case. Respondents' willingness to undertake this litigation was largely altruistic. While they did, of course, stand to benefit from the additional protections they sought for the area potentially affected by the pipeline, the direct benefit to these citizen organizations is truly dwarfed by the demands of litigation of this proportion. Extensive factual discovery, expert scientific analysis, and legal research on a broad range of environmental, technological, and land-use issues were required. The disparity between respondents' direct stake in the outcome and the resources required to pursue the case is exceeded only by the disparity between their resources and those of their opponents—the Federal Government and a consortium of giant oil companies.

Respondents' claim also fulfills the third criterion, for Alyeska is the proper party to bear and spread the cost of this litigation undertaken in the interest of the general public. The Department of the Interior, of course, bears legal responsibility for adopting a position later determined to be unlawful. And, since the class of beneficiaries from the outcome of this litigation is probably coextensive with the class of United States citizens, the Government should in fairness bear the costs of respondents' representation. But, the Court of Appeals concluded that it could not impose attorneys' fees on the United States, because in its view the statute providing for assessment of costs against the Government, 28 U.S.C. § 2412, permits the award of ordinary court costs, "but [does] not includ[e] the fees and expenses of attorneys." Since the respondents did not cross-petition on that point, we have no occasion to rule on the correctness of the court's construction of that statute.

Before the Department and the courts, Alyeska advocated adoption of the position taken by Interior, playing a major role in all aspects of the case. This litigation conferred direct and concrete economic benefits on Alyeska and its principals in affording protection of the physical integrity of the pipeline. If a court could be reasonably confident that the ultimate incidence of costs imposed upon an applicant for a public permit would indeed be on the general public, it would be equitable to shift those costs to the applicant. In this connection, Alyeska, as a consortium of oil companies that do business in 49 States and account for some 20% of the national oil market, would indeed be able to redistribute the additional cost to the general public. In my view the ability to pass the cost forward to the consuming public warrants an award here. The decision to bypass Congress and avoid analysis of the environmental consequences of the pipeline was made in the first instance by Alyeska's principals and not the Secretary of the Interior. The award does not punish the consortium for these actions but recognizes that it is an effective substitute for the public beneficiaries who successfully challenged these actions. Since the Court of Appeals held Alyeska accountable for a fair share of the fees to ease the burden on the public-minded citizen litigators, I would affirm the judgment below.

Fogerty v. Fantasy, Inc.

Supreme Court of the United States, 1994.
510 U.S. 517, 114 S.Ct. 1023, 127 L.Ed.2d 455.

■ CHIEF JUSTICE REHNQUIST delivered the opinion of the Court.

The Copyright Act of 1976, 17 U.S.C. § 505, provides in relevant part that in any copyright infringement action "the court may ... award a reasonable attorney's fee to the prevailing party as part of the costs."[1] The question presented in this case is what standards should inform a court's decision to award attorney's fees to a prevailing defendant in a copyright infringement action—a question that has produced conflicting views in the Courts of Appeals.

Petitioner John Fogerty is a successful musician, who, in the late 1960's, was the lead singer and songwriter of a popular music group known as "Creedence Clearwater Revival." In 1970, he wrote a song entitled "Run Through the Jungle" and sold the exclusive publishing rights to predecessors–in–interest of respondent Fantasy, Inc., who later obtained the copyright by assignment. The music group disbanded in 1972 and Fogerty subsequently published under another recording label. In 1985, he published and registered a copyright to a song entitled "The Old Man Down the Road," which was released on an album distributed by Warner Brothers Records, Inc. Respondent Fantasy, Inc., sued Fogerty, Warner Brothers, and affiliated companies, in District Court, alleging that "The Old Man Down the Road" was merely "Run Through the Jungle" with new words. The copyright infringement claim went to trial and a jury returned a verdict in favor of Fogerty.

After his successful defense of the action, Fogerty moved for reasonable attorney's fees pursuant to 17 U.S.C. § 505. The District Court denied the motion, finding that Fantasy's infringement suit was not brought frivolously or in bad faith as required by circuit precedent for an award of attorney's fees to a successful defendant. The Court of Appeals affirmed, 984 F.2d 1524 (C.A.9 1993), and declined to abandon the existing Ninth Circuit standard for awarding attorney's fees which treats successful plaintiffs and successful defendants differently. Under that standard, commonly termed the "dual" standard, prevailing plaintiffs are generally awarded attorney's

---

1. The section provides in full: "In any civil action under this title, the court in its discretion may allow the recovery of full costs by or against any party other than the United States or an officer thereof. Except as otherwise provided by this title, the court may also award a reasonable attorney's fee to the prevailing party as part of the costs." 17 U.S.C. § 505.

fees as a matter of course, while prevailing defendants must show that the original suit was frivolous or brought in bad faith. In contrast, some courts of appeals follow the so-called "evenhanded" approach in which no distinction is made between prevailing plaintiffs and prevailing defendants. The Court of Appeals for the Third Circuit, for example, has ruled that "we do not require bad faith, nor do we mandate an allowance of fees as a concomitant of prevailing in every case, but we do favor an evenhanded approach." Lieb v. Topstone Industries, Inc., 788 F.2d 151, 156 (C.A.3 1986).

We granted certiorari, to address an important area of federal law and to resolve the conflict between the Ninth Circuit's "dual" standard for awarding attorney's fees under § 505, and the so-called "evenhanded" approach exemplified by the Third Circuit. We reverse.

. . . .

The statutory language—"the court may also award a reasonable attorney's fee to the prevailing party as part of the costs"—gives no hint that successful plaintiffs are to be treated differently than successful defendants. But respondent contends that our decision in Christiansburg Garment Co. v. EEOC, 434 U.S. 412, 98 S.Ct. 694, 54 L.Ed.2d 648 (1978), in which we construed virtually identical language, supports a differentiation in treatment between plaintiffs and defendants.

Christiansburg construed the language of Title VII of the Civil Rights Act of 1964, which in relevant part provided that the court "in its discretion, may allow the prevailing party . . . a reasonable attorney's fee as part of the costs. . . ." 42 U.S.C. § 2000e–5(k). We had earlier held, interpreting the cognate provision of Title II of that Act, 42 U.S.C. § 2000a–3(b), that a prevailing plaintiff "should ordinarily recover an attorney's fee unless some special circumstances would render such an award unjust." Newman v. Piggie Park Enterprises, Inc., 390 U.S. 400, 402, 88 S.Ct. 964, 966, 19 L.Ed.2d 1263 (1968). This decision was based on what we found to be the important policy objectives of the Civil Rights statutes, and the intent of Congress to achieve such objectives through the use of plaintiffs as " 'private attorney[s] general.' " Ibid. In Christiansburg, supra, we determined that the same policy considerations were not at work in the case of a prevailing civil rights defendant. We noted that a Title VII plaintiff, like a Title II plaintiff in Piggie Park, is "the chosen instrument of Congress to vindicate 'a policy that Congress considered of the highest priority.' " 434 U.S., at 418, 98 S.Ct., at 698. We also relied on the admittedly sparse legislative history to indicate that different standards were to be applied to successful plaintiffs than to successful defendants.

Respondent points to our language in Flight Attendants v. Zipes, 491 U.S. 754, 758, n. 2, 109 S.Ct. 2732, 2735, n. 2, 105 L.Ed.2d 639 (1989), that "fee–shifting statutes' similar language is a 'strong indication' that they are to be interpreted alike." But here we think this normal indication is overborne by the factors relied upon in our Christiansburg opinion which are absent in the case of the Copyright Act. The legislative history of § 505 provides no support for treating prevailing plaintiffs and defendants differently with respect to the recovery of attorney's fees. The attorney's fees provision § 505 of the 1976 Act was carried forward verbatim from the

1909 Act with very little discussion. The relevant House Report provides simply:

"Under section 505 the awarding of costs and attorney's fees are left to the court's discretion, and the section also makes clear that neither costs nor attorney's fees can be awarded to or against 'the United States or an officer thereof.'" H.R.Rep. No. 94–1476, p. 163 (1976).

The goals and objectives of the two Acts are likewise not completely similar. Oftentimes, in the civil rights context, impecunious "private attorney general" plaintiffs can ill afford to litigate their claims against defendants with more resources. Congress sought to redress this balance in part, and to provide incentives for the bringing of meritorious lawsuits, by treating successful plaintiffs more favorably than successful defendants in terms of the award of attorney's fees. The primary objective of the Copyright Act is to encourage the production of original literary, artistic, and musical expression for the good of the public. See, infra, at 1029–1030. In the copyright context, it has been noted that "[e]ntities which sue for copyright infringement as plaintiffs can run the gamut from corporate behemoths to starving artists; the same is true of prospective copyright infringement defendants." Cohen, supra, at 622–623.

We thus conclude that respondent's argument based on our fee–shifting decisions under the Civil Rights Act must fail.

Respondent next argues that the policies and objectives of s 505 and of the Copyright Act in general are best served by the "dual approach" to the award of attorney's fees. The most common reason advanced in support of the dual approach is that, by awarding attorney's fees to prevailing plaintiffs as a matter of course, it encourages litigation of meritorious claims of copyright infringement.... Indeed, respondent relies heavily on this argument. We think the argument is flawed because it expresses a one–sided view of the purposes of the Copyright Act. While it is true that one of the goals of the Copyright Act is to discourage infringement, it is by no means the only goal of that Act. In the first place, it is by no means always the case that the plaintiff in an infringement action is the only holder of a copyright; often times, defendants hold copyrights too, as exemplified in the case at hand.

More importantly, the policies served by the Copyright Act are more complex, more measured, than simply maximizing the number of meritorious suits for copyright infringement....

Because copyright law ultimately serves the purpose of enriching the general public through access to creative works, it is peculiarly important that the boundaries of copyright law be demarcated as clearly as possible. To that end, defendants who seek to advance a variety of meritorious copyright defenses should be encouraged to litigate them to the same extent that plaintiffs are encouraged to litigate meritorious claims of infringement. In the case before us, the successful defense of "The Old Man Down the Road" increased public exposure to a musical work that could, as a result, lead to further creative pieces. Thus a successful defense of a copyright infringement action may further the policies of the Copyright Act every bit as much as a successful prosecution of an infringement claim by the holder of a copyright.

. . . .

In summary, neither of the two studies presented to Congress, nor the cases referred to by the studies, support respondent's view that there was a settled construction in favor of the "dual standard" under § 116 of the 1909 Copyright Act.

We thus reject each of respondent's three arguments in support of the dual standard. We now turn to petitioner's argument that § 505 was intended to adopt the "British Rule." Petitioner argues that, consistent with the neutral language of § 505, both prevailing plaintiffs and defendants should be awarded attorney's fees as a matter of course, absent exceptional circumstances. For two reasons we reject this argument for the British Rule.

First, just as the plain language of § 505 supports petitioner's claim for disapproving the dual standard, it cuts against him in arguing for the British Rule. The statute says that "the court may also award a reasonable attorney's fee to the prevailing party as part of the costs." The word "may" clearly connotes discretion. The automatic awarding of attorney's fees to the prevailing party would pretermit the exercise of that discretion.

Second, we are mindful that Congress legislates against the strong background of the American Rule. Unlike Britain where counsel fees are regularly awarded to the prevailing party, it is the general rule in this country that unless Congress provides otherwise, parties are to bear their own attorney's fees. While § 505 is one situation in which Congress has modified the American Rule to allow an award of attorney's fees in the court's discretion, we find it impossible to believe that Congress, without more, intended to adopt the British Rule. Such a bold departure from traditional practice would have surely drawn more explicit statutory language and legislative comment. Not surprisingly, no court has held that s 505 (or its predecessor statute) adopted the British Rule.

Thus we reject both the "dual standard" adopted by several of the Courts of Appeals, and petitioner's claim that § 505 enacted the British Rule for automatic recovery of attorney's fees by the prevailing party. Prevailing plaintiffs and prevailing defendants are to be treated alike, but attorney's fees are to be awarded to prevailing parties only as a matter of the court's discretion. "There is no precise rule or formula for making these determinations," but instead equitable discretion should be exercised "in light of the considerations we have identified." Hensley v. Eckerhart, 461 U.S. 424, 436–437, 103 S.Ct. 1933, 1941–1942, 76 L.Ed.2d 40 (1983). Because the Court of Appeals erroneously held petitioner, the prevailing defendant, to a more stringent standard than that applicable to a prevailing plaintiff, its judgment is reversed and the case is remanded for further proceedings consistent with this opinion.

It is so ordered.

[J. Thomas' concurring opinion omitted].

Chambers v. NASCO, Inc.

Supreme Court of the United States, 1991.
501 U.S. 32, 111 S.Ct. 2123, 115 L.Ed.2d 27.

■ JUSTICE WHITE delivered the opinion of the Court.

This case requires us to explore the scope of the inherent power of a federal court to sanction a litigant for bad-faith conduct. Specifically, we are asked to determine whether the District Court, sitting in diversity, properly invoked its inherent power in assessing as a sanction for a party's bad-faith conduct attorney's fees and related expenses paid by the party's opponent to its attorneys. We hold that the District Court acted within its discretion, and we therefore affirm the judgment of the Court of Appeals.

I

This case began as a simple action for specific performance of a contract, but it did not remain so. Petitioner G. Russell Chambers was the sole shareholder and director of Calcasieu Television and Radio, Inc.: (CTR), which operated television station KPLC–TV in Lake Charles, Louisiana. On August 9, 1983, Chambers, acting both in his individual capacity and on behalf of CTR, entered into a purchase agreement to sell the station's facilities and broadcast license to respondent NASCO, Inc., for a purchase price of $18 million. The agreement was not recorded in the parishes in which the two properties housing the station's facilities were located. Consummation of the agreement was subject to the approval of the Federal Communications Commission (FCC); both parties were obligated to file the necessary documents with the FCC no later than September 23, 1983. By late August, however, Chambers had changed his mind and tried to talk NASCO out of consummating the sale. NASCO refused. On September 23, Chambers, through counsel, informed NASCO that he would not file the necessary papers with the FCC.

NASCO decided to take legal action. On Friday, October 14, 1983, NASCO's counsel informed counsel for Chambers and CTR that NASCO would file suit the following Monday in the United States District Court for the Western District of Louisiana, seeking specific performance of the agreement, as well as a temporary restraining order (TRO) to prevent the alienation or encumbrance of the properties at issue. NASCO provided this notice in accordance with Federal Rule of Civil Procedure 65 and Rule 11 of the District Court's Local Rules (now Rule 10), both of which are designed to give a defendant in a TRO application notice of the hearing and an opportunity to be heard.

The reaction of Chambers and his attorney, A.J. Gray III, was later described by the District Court as having "emasculated and frustrated the purposes of these rules and the powers of [the District] Court by utilizing this notice to prevent NASCO's access to the remedy of specific performance." On Sunday, October 16, 1983, the pair acted to place the properties at issue beyond the reach of the District Court by means of the Louisiana Public Records Doctrine. Because the purchase agreement had never been recorded, they determined that if the properties were sold to a third party, and if the deeds were recorded before the issuance of a TRO, the District Court would lack jurisdiction over the properties.

To this end, Chambers and Gray created a trust, with Chambers' sister as trustee and Chambers' three adult children as beneficiaries. The pair then directed the president of CTR, who later became Chambers' wife, to execute warranty deeds conveying the two tracts at issue to the trust for a recited consideration of $1.4 million. Early Monday morning, the deeds were recorded. The trustee, as purchaser, had not signed the deeds; none of the consideration had been paid; and CTR remained in possession of the properties. Later that morning, NASCO's counsel appeared in the District Court to file the complaint and seek the TRO. With NASCO's counsel present, the District Judge telephoned Gray. Despite the judge's queries concerning the possibility that CTR was negotiating to sell the properties to a third person, Gray made no mention of the recordation of the deeds earlier that morning. That afternoon, Chambers met with his sister and had her sign the trust documents and a $1.4 million note to CTR. The next morning, Gray informed the District Court by letter of the recordation of the deeds the day before and admitted that he had intentionally withheld the information from the court.

Within the next few days, Chambers' attorneys prepared a leaseback agreement from the trustee to CTR, so that CTR could remain in possession of the properties and continue to operate the station. The following week, the District Court granted a preliminary injunction against Chambers and CTR and entered a second TRO to prevent the trustee from alienating or encumbering the properties. At that hearing, the District Judge warned that Gray's and Chambers' conduct had been unethical.

Despite this early warning, Chambers, often acting through his attorneys, continued to abuse the judicial process. In November 1983, in defiance of the preliminary injunction, he refused to allow NASCO to inspect CTR's corporate records. The ensuing civil contempt proceedings resulted in the assessment of a $25,000 fine against Chambers personally. Two subsequent appeals from the contempt order were dismissed for lack of a final judgment.

Undeterred, Chambers proceeded with "a series of meritless motions and pleadings and delaying actions." These actions triggered further warnings from the court. At one point, acting *sua sponte*, the District Judge called a status conference to find out why bankers were being deposed. When informed by Chambers' counsel that the purpose was to learn whether NASCO could afford to pay for the station, the court canceled the depositions consistent with its authority under Federal Rule of Civil Procedure 26(g).

At the status conference nine days before the April 1985 trial date,[5] the District Judge again warned counsel that further misconduct would not be tolerated. Finally, on the eve of trial, Chambers and CTR stipulated that

---

5. The trial date itself reflected delaying tactics. Trial had been set for February 1985, but in January, Gray, on behalf of Chambers, filed a motion to recuse the judge. The motion was denied, as was the subsequent writ of mandamus filed in the Court of Appeals.

the purchase agreement was enforceable and that Chambers had breached the agreement on September 23, 1983, by failing to file the necessary papers with the FCC. At trial, the only defense presented by Chambers was the Public Records Doctrine.

In the interlude between the trial and the entry of judgment during which the District Court prepared its opinion, Chambers sought to render the purchase agreement meaningless by seeking permission from the FCC to build a new transmission tower for the station and to relocate the transmission facilities to that site, which was not covered by the agreement. Only after NASCO sought contempt sanctions did Chambers withdraw the application.

The District Court entered judgment on the merits in NASCO's favor, finding that the transfer of the properties to the trust was a simulated sale and that the deeds purporting to convey the property were "null, void, and of no effect." Chambers' motions, filed in the District Court, the Court of Appeals, and this Court, to stay the judgment pending appeal were denied. Undeterred, Chambers convinced CTR officials to file formal oppositions to NASCO's pending application for FCC approval of the transfer of the station's license, in contravention of both the District Court's injunctive orders and its judgment on the merits. NASCO then sought contempt sanctions for a third time, and the oppositions were withdrawn.

When Chambers refused to prepare to close the sale, NASCO again sought the court's help. A hearing was set for July 16, 1986, to determine whether certain equipment was to be included in the sale. At the beginning of the hearing, the court informed Chambers' new attorney, Edwin A. McCabe, that further sanctionable conduct would not be tolerated. When the hearing was recessed for several days, Chambers, without notice to the court or NASCO, removed from service at the station all of the equipment at issue, forcing the District Court to order that the equipment be returned to service.

Immediately following oral argument on Chambers' appeal from the District Court's judgment on the merits, the Court of Appeals, ruling from the bench, found the appeal frivolous. The court imposed appellate sanctions in the form of attorney's fees and double costs, pursuant to Federal Rule of Appellate Procedure 38, and remanded the case to the District Court with orders to fix the amount of appellate sanctions and to determine whether further sanctions should be imposed for the manner in which the litigation had been conducted.

On remand, NASCO moved for sanctions, invoking the District Court's inherent power, Fed.Rule Civ.Proc. 11, and 28 U.S.C. § 1927. After full briefing and a hearing, the District Court determined that sanctions were appropriate "for the manner in which this proceeding was conducted in the district court from October 14, 1983, the time that plaintiff gave notice of its intention to file suit to this date." At the end of an extensive opinion recounting what it deemed to have been sanctionable conduct during this period, the court imposed sanctions against Chambers in the form of attorney's fees and expenses totaling $996,644.65, which represented the entire amount of NASCO's litigation costs paid to its attorneys.[5] In so doing, the court rejected Chambers' argument that he had merely followed the advice of counsel, labeling him "the strategist" behind a scheme devised "first, to deprive this Court of jurisdiction and, second, to devise a plan of obstruction, delay, harassment, and expense sufficient to reduce NASCO to a condition of exhausted compliance."

In imposing the sanctions, the District Court first considered Federal Rule of Civil Procedure 11. It noted that the alleged sanctionable conduct was that Chambers and the other defendants had "(1) attempted to deprive this Court of jurisdiction by acts of fraud, nearly all of which were performed outside the confines of this Court, (2) filed false and frivolous pleadings, and (3) attempted, by other tactics of delay, oppression, harassment and massive expense to reduce plaintiff to exhausted compliance." The court recognized that the conduct in the first and third categories could not be reached by Rule 11, which governs only papers filed with a court. As for the second category, the court explained that the falsity of the pleadings at issue did not become apparent until after the trial on the merits, so that it would have been impossible to assess sanctions at the time the papers were filed. Consequently, the District Court deemed Rule 11 "insufficient" for its purposes. The court likewise declined to impose sanctions under § 1927,[6] both because the statute applies only to attorneys, and therefore would not reach Chambers, and because the statute was not broad enough to reach "acts which degrade the judicial system," including "attempts to deprive the Court of jurisdiction, fraud, misleading and lying to the Court." The court therefore relied on its inherent power in imposing sanctions, stressing that "[t]he wielding of that inherent power is particularly appropriate when the offending parties have practiced a fraud upon the court."

The Court of Appeals affirmed. . . .

II

Chambers maintains that 28 U.S.C. § 1927 and the various sanctioning provisions in the Federal Rules of Civil Procedure[8] reflect a legislative

---

5. In calculating the award, the District Court deducted the amounts previously awarded as compensatory damages for contempt, as well as the amount awarded as appellate sanctions.

The court also sanctioned other individuals, who are not parties to the action in this Court. Chambers' sister, the trustee, was sanctioned by a reprimand; attorney Gray was disbarred and prohibited from seeking readmission for three years; attorney Richard A. Curry, who represented the trustee, was suspended from practice before the court for six months; and attorney McCabe was suspended for five years. Although these sanctions did not affect the bank accounts of these individuals, they were nevertheless substantial sanctions and were as proportionate to the conduct at issue as was the monetary sanction imposed on Chambers. Indeed, in the case of the disbarment of attorney Gray, the court recognized that the penalty was among the harshest possible sanctions and one which derived from its authority to supervise those admitted to practice before it.

6. That statute provides:

"Any attorney . . . who so multiples the proceedings in any case unreasonably and vexatiously may be required by the court to satisfy personally the excess costs, expenses, and attorneys' fees reasonably incurred because of such conduct." 28 U.S.C. § 1927.

8. A number of the rules provide for the imposition of attorney's fees as a sanction. See Fed.Rule Civ.Proc. 11 (certification

intent to displace the inherent power. At least, he argues that they obviate or foreclose resort to the inherent power in this case. We agree with the Court of Appeals that neither proposition is persuasive.

A

It has long been understood that "[c]ertain implied powers must necessarily result to our Courts of justice from the nature of their institution," powers "which cannot be dispensed with in a Court, because they are necessary to the exercise of all others." For this reason, "Courts of justice are universally acknowledged to be vested, by their very creation, with power to impose silence, respect, and decorum, in their presence, and submission to their lawful mandates." These powers are "governed not by rule or statute but by the control necessarily vested in courts to manage their own affairs so as to achieve the orderly and expeditious disposition of cases."

. . . .

Because of their very potency, inherent powers must be exercised with restraint and discretion. A primary aspect of that discretion is the ability to fashion an appropriate sanction for conduct which abuses the judicial process. . . . [O]utright dismissal of a lawsuit, which we [have] upheld . . . , is a particularly severe sanction, yet is within the court's discretion. Consequently, the "less severe sanction" of an assessment of attorney's fees is undoubtedly within a court's inherent power as well.

Indeed, "[t]here are ample grounds for recognizing . . . that in narrowly defined circumstances federal courts have inherent power to assess attorney's fees against counsel," even though the so-called "American Rule" prohibits fee-shifting in most cases. See Alyeska Pipeline Service Co. v. Wilderness Society, 421 U.S. 240, 95 S.Ct. 1612, 44 L.Ed.2d 141 (1975). As we explained in *Alyeska,* these exceptions fall into three categories. The first, known as the "common fund exception," derives not from a court's power to control litigants, but from its historic equity jurisdiction, and allows a court to award attorney's fees to a party whose litigation efforts directly benefit others. Second, a court may assess attorney's fees as a sanction for the " 'willful disobedience of a court order.' " Thus, a court's discretion to determine "[t]he degree of punishment for contempt" permits the court to impose as part of the fine attorney's fees representing the entire cost of the litigation.

Third, and most relevant here, a court may assess attorney's fees when a party has " 'acted in bad faith, vexatiously, wantonly, or for oppressive

requirement for papers), 16(f)(pretrial conferences), 26(g)(certification requirement for discovery requests), 30(g)(oral depositions), 37 (sanctions for failure to cooperate with discovery), 56(g)(affidavits accompanying summary judgment motions). In some instances, the assessment of fees is one of a range of possible sanctions, see, e.g., Fed.Rule Civ.Proc. 11, while in others, the court must award fees, see, e.g., Fed.Rule Civ.Proc. 16(f).

In each case, the fees that may be assessed are limited to those incurred as a result of the rule violation. In the case of Rule 11, however, a violation could conceivably warrant an imposition of fees covering the entire litigation, if, for example, a complaint or answer was filed in violation of the rule. The court generally may act *sua sponte* in imposing sanctions under the rules.

reasons.' " In this regard, if a court finds "that fraud has been practiced upon it, or that the very temple of justice has been defiled," it may assess attorney's fees against the responsible party, as it may when a party "shows bad faith by delaying or disrupting the litigation or by hampering enforcement of a court order." The imposition of sanctions in this instance transcends a court's equitable power concerning relations between the parties and reaches a court's inherent power to police itself, thus serving the dual purpose of "vindicat[ing] judicial authority without resort to the more drastic sanctions available for contempt of court and mak[ing] the prevailing party whole for expenses caused by his opponent's obstinacy."

B

We discern no basis for holding that the sanctioning scheme of the statute and the rules displaces the inherent power to impose sanctions for the bad-faith conduct described above. These other mechanisms, taken alone or together, are not substitutes for the inherent power, for that power is both broader and narrower than other means of imposing sanctions. First, whereas each of the other mechanisms reaches only certain individuals or conduct, the inherent power extends to a full range of litigation abuses. At the very least the inherent power must continue to exist to fill in the interstices. Even the dissent so concedes. Second, while the narrow exceptions to the American Rule effectively limit a court's inherent power to impose attorney's fees as a sanction to cases in which a litigant has engaged in bad-faith conduct or willful disobedience of a court's orders, many of the other mechanisms permit a court to impose attorney's fees as a sanction for conduct which merely fails to meet a reasonableness standard. . . .

It is true that the exercise of the inherent power of lower federal courts can be limited by statute and rule, for "[t]hese courts were created by act of Congress." Nevertheless, "we do not lightly assume that Congress has intended to depart from established principles" such as the scope of a court's inherent power. In *Alyeska* we determined that "Congress ha[d] not repudiated the judicially fashioned exceptions" to the American Rule, which were founded in the inherent power of the courts. Nothing since then has changed that assessment. . . .

The Court's prior cases have indicated that the inherent power of a court can be invoked even if procedural rules exist which sanction the same conduct. . . .

. . . .

There is, therefore, nothing in the other sanctioning mechanisms or prior cases interpreting them that warrants a conclusion that a federal court may not, as a matter of law, resort to its inherent power to impose attorney's fees as a sanction for bad-faith conduct. This is plainly the case where the conduct at issue is not covered by one of the other sanctioning provisions. But neither is a federal court forbidden to sanction bad-faith conduct by means of the inherent power simply because that conduct could also be sanctioned under the statute or the rules. A court must, of course, exercise caution in invoking its inherent power, and it must comply with the mandates of due process, both in determining that the requisite bad faith exists and in assessing fees. Furthermore, when there is bad-faith conduct in the course of litigation that could be adequately sanctioned under the rules, the court ordinarily should rely on the rules rather than the inherent power. But if in the informed discretion of the court, neither the statute nor the rules are up to the task, the court may safely rely on its inherent power.

Like the Court of Appeals, we find no abuse of discretion in resorting to the inherent power in the circumstances of this case. It is true that the District Court could have employed Rule 11 to sanction Chambers for filing "false and frivolous pleadings," and that some of the other conduct might have been reached through other rules. Much of the bad-faith conduct by Chambers, however, was beyond the reach of the rules, his entire course of conduct throughout the lawsuit evidenced bad faith and an attempt to perpetrate a fraud on the court, and the conduct sanctionable under the rules was intertwined within conduct that only the inherent power could address. In circumstances such as these in which all of a litigant's conduct is deemed sanctionable, requiring a court first to apply rules and statutes containing sanctioning provisions to discrete occurrences before invoking inherent power to address remaining instances of sanctionable conduct would serve only to foster extensive and needless satellite litigation, which is contrary to the aim of the rules themselves.

We likewise do not find that the District Court's reliance on the inherent power thwarted the purposes of the other sanctioning mechanisms. Although the dissent makes much of the fact that Rule 11 and Rule 26(g) "are cast in mandatory terms," the mandate of these provisions extends only to *whether* a court must impose sanctions, not to *which* sanction it must impose. Indeed, the language of both rules requires only that a court impose "an appropriate sanction." Thus, this case is distinguishable from Bank of Nova Scotia v. United States, 487 U.S. 250, 108 S.Ct. 2369, 101 L.Ed.2d 228 (1988), in which this Court held that a district court could not rely on its supervisory power as a means of circumventing the clear mandate of a procedural rule.

III

Chambers asserts that even if federal courts can use their inherent power to assess attorney's fees as a sanction in some cases, they are not free to do so when they sit in diversity, unless the applicable state law recognizes the "bad-faith" exception to the general rule against fee shifting. He relies on footnote 31 in *Alyeska*, in which we stated with regard to the exceptions to the American Rule that "[a] very different situation is presented when a federal court sits in a diversity case. '[I]n an ordinary diversity case where the state law does not run counter to a valid federal statute or rule of court, and usually it will not, state law denying the right to attorney's fees or giving a right thereto, which reflects a substantial policy of the state, should be followed.' 6 J. Moore, Federal Practice ¶ 54.77[2], pp. 1712–1713 (2d ed. 1974) (footnotes omitted)."

We agree with NASCO that Chambers has misinterpreted footnote 31. The limitation on a court's inherent power described there applies only to fee-shifting rules that embody a substantive policy, such as a statute which permits a prevailing party in certain classes of litigation to recover fees. . . .

Only when there is a conflict between state and federal substantive law are the concerns of Erie R. Co. v. Tompkins, 304 U.S. 64, 58 S.Ct. 817, 82 L.Ed. 1188 (1938), at issue. As we explained in Hanna v. Plumer, 380 U.S. 460, 85 S.Ct. 1136, 14 L.Ed.2d 8 (1965), the "outcome determinative" test of *Erie* and Guaranty Trust Co. v. York, 326 U.S. 99, 65 S.Ct. 1464, 89 L.Ed. 2079 (1945), "cannot be read without reference to the twin aims of the *Erie* rule: discouragement of forum-shopping and avoidance of inequitable administration of the laws." Despite Chambers' protestations to the contrary, neither of these twin aims is implicated by the assessment of attorney's fees as a sanction for bad-faith conduct before the court which involved disobedience of the court's orders and the attempt to defraud the court itself. . . . As the Court of Appeals expressed it, "*Erie* guarantees a litigant that if he takes his state law cause of action to federal court, and abides by the rules of that court, the result in his case will be the same as if he had brought it in state court. It does not allow him to waste the court's time and resources with cantankerous conduct, even in the unlikely event a state court would allow him to do so."

. . . .

Chambers argues that because the primary purpose of the sanction is punitive, assessing attorney's fees violates the State's prohibition on punitive damages. Under Louisiana law, there can be no punitive damages for breach of contract, even when a party has acted in bad faith in breaching the agreement. Indeed, "as a general rule attorney's fees are not allowed a successful litigant in Louisiana except where authorized by statute or by contract." It is clear, though, that this general rule focuses on the award of attorney's fees because of a party's success on the underlying claim. . . . This substantive state policy is not implicated here, where sanctions were imposed for conduct during the litigation.

Here the District Court did not attempt to sanction petitioner for breach of contract,[16] but rather imposed sanctions for the fraud he perpetrated on the court and the bad faith he displayed toward both his adversary and the court throughout the course of the litigation. We agree with the Court of Appeals that "[w]e do not see how the district court's inherent power to tax fees for that conduct can be made subservient to any state policy without transgressing the boundaries set out in *Erie, Guaranty Trust Co.,* and *Hanna*," for "[f]ee-shifting here is not a matter of substantive remedy, but of vindicating judicial authority."

IV

We review a court's imposition of sanctions under its inherent power for abuse of discretion. Based on the circumstances of this case, we find that the District Court acted within its discretion in assessing as a sanction

---

16. We therefore express no opinion as to whether the District Court would have had the inherent power to sanction Chambers for conduct relating to the underlying breach of contract, or whether such sanctions might implicate the concerns of *Erie*.

for Chambers' bad-faith conduct the entire amount of NASCO's attorney's fees.

. . . .

Second, Chambers claims that the fact that the entire amount of fees was awarded means that the District Court failed to tailor the sanction to the particular wrong. As NASCO points out, however, the District Court concluded that full attorney's fees were warranted due to the frequency and severity of Chambers' abuses of the judicial system and the resulting need to ensure that such abuses were not repeated.[20] Indeed, the court found Chambers' actions were "part of [a] sordid scheme of deliberate misuse of the judicial process" designed "to defeat NASCO's claim by harassment, repeated and endless delay, mountainous expense and waste of financial resources." It was within the court's discretion to vindicate itself and compensate NASCO by requiring Chambers to pay for all attorney's fees.

. . . .

. . . Chambers challenges the District Court's imposition of sanctions for conduct before other tribunals, including the FCC, the Court of Appeals, and this Court, asserting that a court may sanction only conduct occurring in its presence. Our cases are to the contrary, however. As long as a party receives an appropriate hearing, as did Chambers, the party may be sanctioned for abuses of process occurring beyond the courtroom, such as disobeying the court's orders. Here, for example, Chambers' attempt to gain the FCC's permission to build a new transmission tower was in direct contravention of the District Court's orders to maintain the status quo pending the outcome of the litigation, and was therefore within the scope of the District Court's sanctioning power.

. . . .

For the foregoing reasons, the judgment of the Court of Appeals for the Fifth Circuit is

Affirmed.

■ JUSTICE SCALIA, dissenting.

I agree with the Court that Article III courts, as an independent and coequal Branch of Government, derive from the Constitution itself, once they have been created and their jurisdiction established, the authority to do what courts have traditionally done in order to accomplish their assigned tasks. Some elements of that inherent authority are so essential to "[t]he judicial Power" that they are indefeasible, among which is a court's ability to enter orders protecting the integrity of its proceedings. . . .

I think some explanation might be useful regarding the "bad faith" limitation that the Court alludes to today. Since necessity does not depend upon a litigant's state of mind, the inherent sanctioning power must extend

---

20. In particular, Chambers challenges the assessment of attorney's fees in connection with NASCO's claim for delay damages and with the closing of the sale. As NASCO points out, however, Chambers' bad-faith conduct in the course of the litigation caused the delay for which damages were sought and greatly complicated the closing of the sale, through the cloud on the title caused by the fraudulent transfer.

to situations involving less than bad faith. For example, a court has the power to dismiss when counsel fails to appear for trial, even if this is a consequence of negligence rather than bad faith.... However, a "bad-faith" limitation upon the particular sanction of attorney's fees derives from our jurisprudence regarding the so-called American Rule, which provides that the prevailing party must bear his own attorney's fees, and cannot have them assessed against the loser. That rule, "deeply rooted in our history and in congressional policy," prevents a court (without statutory authorization) from engaging in what might be termed *substantive* fee-shifting, that is, fee-shifting as part of the merits award. It does not in principle bar fee-shifting as a sanction for procedural abuse. We have held, however—in my view as a means of preventing erosion or evasion of the American Rule—that even fee-shifting as a sanction can only be imposed for litigation conduct characterized by bad faith. But that in no way means that *all* sanctions imposed under the courts' inherent authority require a finding of bad faith. They do not.

Just as Congress may to some degree specify the manner in which the inherent or constitutionally assigned powers of the President will be exercised, so long as the effectiveness of those powers is not impaired, so also Congress may prescribe the means by which the courts may protect the integrity of their proceedings. A court must use the prescribed means unless for some reason they are inadequate. In the present case they undoubtedly were. Justice Kennedy concedes that some of the impairments of the District Court's proceedings in the present case were not sanctionable under the Federal Rules. I have no doubt of a court's authority to go beyond the Rules in such circumstances. And I agree with the Court that an overall sanction resting at least in substantial portion upon the court's inherent power need not be broken down into its component parts, with the actions sustainable under the Rules separately computed. I do not read the Rules at issue here to require that, and it is unreasonable to import such needless complication by implication.

I disagree, however, with the Court's statement that a court's inherent power reaches conduct "beyond the court's confines" that does not " 'interfer[e] with the conduct of trial.' " I emphatically agree with Justice Kennedy, therefore, that the District Court here had no power to impose any sanctions for petitioner's flagrant, bad-faith breach of contract; and I agree with him that it appears to have done so. For that reason, I dissent.

■ JUSTICE KENNEDY, with whom THE CHIEF JUSTICE and JUSTICE SOUTER join, dissenting.

Today's decision effects a vast expansion of the power of federal courts, unauthorized by rule or statute. I have no doubt petitioner engaged in sanctionable conduct that warrants severe corrective measures. But our outrage at his conduct should not obscure the boundaries of settled legal categories.

With all respect, I submit the Court commits two fundamental errors. First, it permits the exercise of inherent sanctioning powers without prior recourse to controlling rules and statutes, thereby abrogating to federal courts Congress' power to regulate fees and costs. Second, the Court upholds the wholesale shift of respondent's attorney's fees to petitioner, even though the District Court opinion reveals that petitioner was sanctioned at least in part for his so-called bad-faith breach of contract. The extension of inherent authority to sanction a party's prelitigation conduct subverts the American Rule and turns the *Erie* doctrine upside down by punishing petitioner's primary conduct contrary to Louisiana law. Because I believe the proper exercise of inherent powers requires exhaustion of express sanctioning provisions and much greater caution in their application to redress prelitigation conduct, I dissent.

. . . .

. . . The American Rule recognizes that the legislature, not the judiciary, possesses constitutional responsibility for defining sanctions and fees; the bad-faith exception to the Rule allows courts to assess fees not provided for by Congress "in narrowly defined circumstances." By allowing courts to ignore express Rules and statutes on point, however, the Court treats inherent powers as the norm and textual bases of authority as the exception. And although the Court recognizes that Congress in theory may channel inherent powers through passage of sanctioning rules, it create[s] a powerful presumption against congressional control of judicial sanctions.

The Court has the presumption backwards. Inherent powers are the exception, not the rule, and their assertion requires special justification in each case. Like all applications of inherent power, the authority to sanction bad-faith litigation practices can be exercised only when necessary to preserve the authority of the court.

The necessity limitation, which the Court brushes aside almost without mention, prescribes the rule for the correct application of inherent powers. Although this case does not require articulation of a comprehensive definition of the term "necessary," at the very least a court need not exercise inherent power if Congress has provided a mechanism to achieve the same end. Consistent with our unaltered admonition that inherent powers must be exercised "with great caution," the necessity predicate limits the exercise of inherent powers to those exceptional instances in which congressionally authorized powers fail to protect the processes of the Court. Inherent powers can be exercised only when necessary, and there is no necessity if a rule or statute provides a basis for sanctions. It follows that a district court should rely on text-based authority derived from Congress rather than inherent power in every case where the text-based authority applies.

. . . .

. . . [T]he Court ignores the commands of the Federal Rules of Civil Procedure, which support the conclusion that a court should rely on rules, and not inherent powers, whenever possible. Like the Federal Rules of Criminal Procedure, the Federal Rules of Civil Procedure are "as binding as any statute duly enacted by Congress, and federal courts have no more discretion to disregard the Rule[s'] mandate than they do to disregard constitutional or statutory provisions." Two of the most prominent sanctioning provisions, Rules 11 and 26(g), mandate the imposition of sanctions when litigants violate the Rules' certification standards.

The Rules themselves thus reject the contention that they may be discarded in a court's discretion. Disregard of applicable rules also circumvents the rulemaking procedures in 28 U.S.C. § 2071 *et seq.,* which Congress designed to assure that procedural innovations like those announced today "shall be introduced only after mature consideration of informed opinion from all relevant quarters, with all the opportunities for comprehensive and integrated treatment which such consideration affords."

. . . .

Upon a finding of bad faith, courts may now ignore any and all textual limitations on sanctioning power. By inviting district courts to rely on inherent authority as a substitute for attention to the careful distinctions contained in the rules and statutes, today's decision will render these sources of authority superfluous in many instances. A number of pernicious practical effects will follow.

The Federal Rules establish explicit standards for, and explicit checks against, the exercise of judicial authority. . . . These definite standards give litigants notice of proscribed conduct and make possible meaningful review for misuse of discretion—review which focuses on the misapplication of legal standards.

By contrast, courts apply inherent powers without specific definitional or procedural limits. True, if a district court wishes to shift attorney's fees as a sanction, it must make a finding of bad faith to circumvent the American Rule. But today's decision demonstrates how little guidance or limitation the undefined bad faith predicate provides. The Court states without elaboration that courts must "comply with the mandates of due process . . . in determining that the requisite bad faith exists," but the Court's bad-faith standard, at least without adequate definition, thwarts the first requirement of due process, namely, that "[a]ll are entitled to be informed as to what the State commands or forbids." This standardless exercise of judicial power may appear innocuous in this litigation between commercial actors. But the same unchecked power also can be applied to chill the advocacy of litigants attempting to vindicate all other important federal rights.

In addition, the scope of sanctionable conduct under the bad-faith rule appears unlimited. As the Court boasts, "whereas each of the other mechanisms [in Rules and statutes] reaches only certain individuals or conduct, the inherent power extends to a full range of litigation abuses." By allowing exclusive resort to inherent authority whenever "conduct sanctionable under the rules was intertwined within conduct that only the inherent power could address," the Court encourages all courts in the federal system to find bad-faith misconduct in order to eliminate the need to rely on specific textual provisions. This will ensure the uncertain development of the meaning and scope of these express sanctioning provisions by encouraging their disuse, and will defeat, at least in the area of sanctions, Congress' central goal in enacting the Federal Rules—" 'uniformity in the federal courts.' " Finally, as Part IV of the Court's opinion demonstrates, the lack of any legal requirement other than the talismanic recitation of the phrase "bad faith" will foreclose meaningful review of sanctions based on inherent authority.

Despite these deficiencies, the Court insists that concern about collateral litigation requires courts to place exclusive reliance on inherent authority in cases, like this one, which involve conduct, sanctionable under both express provisions and inherent authority.... We are bound, however, by the Rules themselves, not their "aim," and the Rules require that they be applied, in accordance with their terms, to much of the conduct in this case. We should not let policy concerns about the litigation effects of following the Rules distort their clear commands.

Nothing in the foregoing discussion suggests that the fee-shifting and sanctioning provisions in the Federal Rules and Title 28 eliminate the inherent power to impose sanctions for certain conduct. Limitations on a power do not constitute its abrogation. Cases can arise in which a federal court must act to preserve its authority in a manner not provided for by the Federal Rules or Title 28. But as the number and scope of rules and statutes governing litigation misconduct increase, the necessity to resort to inherent authority—a predicate to its proper application—lessens. Indeed, it is difficult to imagine a case in which a court can, as the District Court did here, rely on inherent authority as the exclusive basis for sanctions.

. . . .

The District Court's own findings concerning abuse of its processes demonstrate that the sanctionable conduct in this case implicated a number of rules and statutes upon which it should have relied....

. . . .

NOTES

1. The California Supreme Court approved an award of attorneys' fees on a "private attorney general" theory in Serrano v. Priest, 20 Cal.3d 25, 141 Cal.Rptr. 315, 569 P.2d 1303 (1977). However, in Bauguess v. Paine, 22 Cal.3d 626, 150 Cal.Rptr. 461, 586 P.2d 942 (1978), the court reversed a $700 fee award entered against opposing counsel as a sanction for alleged misconduct at trial. The award was defended as a proper exercise of the trial judge's inherent supervisory power, which allows "appropriate action to secure compliance with [court] orders, to punish contempt, and to control [court] proceedings," but court found that it "exceeded the limits of the trial court's inherent power." Bird, C.J., writing for the court, remarked:

> It would be both unnecessary and unwise to permit trial courts to use fee awards as sanctions apart from those situations authorized by statute. If an attorney's conduct is disruptive of court processes or disrespectful of the court itself, there is ample power to punish the misconduct as contempt. Moreover, unlike the [inherent supervisory] power advocated by respondent, a court's inherent power to punish contempt has been tempered by legislative enactment to provide procedural safeguards. Among these safeguards is the opportunity, in cases where the contempt occurs out of the immediate view and presence of the court, to disqualify the judge.... Additionally, the Legislature has limited the penalty for civil contempt to five days in jail and a $500

fine. Absent such safeguards, serious due process problems would result were trial courts to use their inherent powers, in lieu of the contempt power, to punish misconduct by awarding attorney's fees to an opposing party or counsel.

The use of courts' inherent power to punish misconduct by awarding attorney's fees may imperil the independence of the bar and thereby undermine the adversary system....

2.   Boeing announced that, for a limited time only, convertible debentures could be redeemed for cash or converted into common stock worth three times as much. The conversion option was to expire with the deadline. After that date passed, Van Gemert and others brought a class action lawsuit against Boeing in federal court. They proved that Boeing had not given debenture holders adequate notice of the redemption, that each class member (i.e., the nonconverting debenture holders) was entitled to "difference money damages", and the total amount of Boeing's liability to the class. On appeal, Boeing argued that the class attorneys' fees (some $2 million in fees were sought) "could not be awarded from the unclaimed portion of the judgment fund...." The Supreme Court decided otherwise. Boeing Co. v. Van Gemert, 444 U.S. 472, 100 S.Ct. 745, 62 L.Ed.2d 676 (1980). The Court's rationale, set forth by Powell, J., is as follows:

Since the decisions in Trustees v. Greenough, 105 U.S. 527, 26 L.Ed. 1157 (1882), and Central Railroad & Banking Co. v. Pettus, 113 U.S. 116, 5 S.Ct. 387, 28 L.Ed. 915 (1885), this Court has recognized consistently that a litigant or a lawyer who recovers a common fund for the benefit of persons other than himself or his client is entitled to a reasonable attorney's fee from the fund as a whole. The common-fund doctrine reflects the traditional practice in courts of equity and it ... rests on the perception that persons who obtain the benefit of a lawsuit without contributing to its cost are unjustly enriched at the successful litigant's expense. Jurisdiction over the fund involved in the litigation allows a court to prevent this inequity by assessing attorney's fees against the entire fund, thus spreading fees proportionately among those benefited by the suit.

In Alyeska Pipeline Co. v. Wilderness Society, we noted the features that distinguished our common-fund cases from cases where the shifting of fees was inappropriate. First, the classes of persons benefited by the lawsuits "were small in number and easily identifiable." Second, "[t]he benefits could be traced with some accuracy...." Finally, "there was reason for confidence that the costs [of litigation] could indeed be shifted with some exactitude to those benefiting." Those characteristics are not present where litigants simply vindicate a general social grievance. On the other hand, the criteria are satisfied when each member of a certified class has an undisputed and mathematically ascertainable claim to part of a lump sum judgment recovered on his behalf. Once the class representatives have established the defendant's liability and the total amount of damages, members of the class can obtain their share of the recovery simply by proving their individual claims against the judgment fund. This benefit devolves with certainty upon the identifiable persons whom the court has certified as members of the class. Although the full value of the benefit to each absentee member cannot be determined until he presents his claim, a fee awarded against the entire judgment fund will shift the costs of litigation to each absentee in the exact proportion that the value of his claim bears to the total recovery.

In this case, the named respondents have recovered a determinate fund for the benefit of every member of the class whom they represent. Boeing did not appeal the judgment awarding the class a sum certain. Nor does Boeing contend that any class member was uninjured by the company's failure adequately to inform him of his conversion rights. Thus, the damage to each class member is simply the difference between the redemption price of his debentures and the value of the common stock into which they could have been converted. To claim their logically ascertainable shares of the judgment fund, absentee class members need prove only their membership in the injured class. Their right to share the harvest of the lawsuit upon proof of their identity, whether or not they exercise it, is a benefit in the fund created by the efforts of the class representatives and their counsel. Unless absentees contribute to the payment of attorney's fees incurred on their behalves, they will pay nothing for the creation of the fund and their representatives may bear additional costs. The judgment entered by the District Court and affirmed by the Court of Appeals rectifies this inequity by requiring every member of the class to share attorney's fees to the same extent that he can share the recovery. Since the benefits of the class recovery have been "traced with some accuracy" and the costs of recovery have been "shifted with some exactitude to those benefiting," we conclude that the attorney's fee award in this case is a proper application of the common-fund doctrine.

. . . .

The common-fund doctrine, as applied in this case, is entirely consistent with the American rule against taxing the losing party with the victor's attorney's fees. The District Court's judgment assesses attorney's fees against a fund awarded to the prevailing class. Since there was no appeal from the judgment that quantified Boeing's liability, Boeing presently has no interest in any part of the fund. The members of the class, whether or not they assert their rights, are at least the equitable owners of their respective shares in the recovery. Any right that Boeing may establish to the return of money eventually unclaimed is contingent on the failure of absentee class members to exercise their present rights of possession. Although Boeing itself cannot be obliged to pay fees awarded to the class lawyers, its latent claim against unclaimed money in the judgment fund may not defeat each class member's equitable obligation to share the expenses of litigation.

Brandt v. Superior Court

Supreme Court of California, 1985.
37 Cal.3d 813, 210 Cal.Rptr. 211, 693 P.2d 796.

■ KAUS, J. When an insurer tortiously withholds benefits, are attorney's fees, reasonably incurred to compel payment of the policy benefits, recoverable as an element of the damages resulting from such tortious conduct? We hold that they are and accordingly issue a writ of mandate directing the trial court to reinstate the portion of the complaint seeking attorney's fees as damages.

According to the complaint real party in interest Standard Insurance Company (Standard) issued a group disability income insurance policy to Vicom Associates, petitioner's employer, under which petitioner was insured. Petitioner sustained a loss covered by the policy when he became totally disabled. He made a timely demand on Standard for benefits, which it unreasonably refused to pay. Petitioner therefore filed an action against Standard for (1) breach of contract, (2) breach of the covenant of good faith and fair dealing, and (3) for violation of the statutory prohibitions against unfair claims practices.

In his causes of action for breach of the duty of good faith and fair dealing and for the statutory violations, petitioner listed attorney's fees incurred in connection with the contract cause of action as part of the resulting damage. Standard successfully moved to strike the portions of the complaint seeking attorney's fees. Petitioner then filed the present mandate proceeding.

. . . .

> "It is well settled that if an insurer, in discharging its contractual responsibilities, 'fails to deal *fairly and in good faith* with its insured by refusing, without proper cause, to compensate its insured for a loss covered by the policy, such conduct may give rise to a cause of action in tort for breach of an implied covenant of good faith and fair dealing.' When such a breach occurs, the insurer is 'liable for any damages which are the proximate result of that breach.' "

When an insurer's tortious conduct reasonably compels the insured to retain an attorney to obtain the benefits due under a policy, it follows that the insurer should be liable in a tort action for that expense. The attorney's fees are an economic loss—damages—proximately caused by the tort. These fees must be distinguished from recovery of attorney's fees *qua* attorney's fees, such as those attributable to the bringing of the bad faith action itself. What we consider here is attorney's fees that are recoverable as damages resulting from a tort in the same way that medical fees would be part of the damages in a personal injury action.

> "When a pedestrian is struck by a car, he goes to a physician for treatment of his injuries, and the motorist, if liable in tort, must pay the pedestrian's medical fees. Similarly, in the present case, an insurance company's refusal to pay benefits has required the insured to seek the services of an attorney to obtain those benefits, and the insurer, because its conduct was tortious, should pay the insured's legal fees."

Code of Civil Procedure section 1021 does not preclude an award of attorney's fees under these circumstances. "Section 1021 leaves to the agreement of the parties 'the measure and mode of compensation of attorneys.' However, here, as in the third party tort situation, 'we are not dealing with "the measure and mode of compensation of attorneys" but with damages wrongfully caused by defendant's improper actions.' " In such cases there is no recovery of attorney's fees *qua* attorney's fees. This is also true in actions for false arrest and malicious prosecution, where damages may include attorney's fees incurred to obtain release from confinement or dismissal of the unjustified charges or to defend the prior suit.

The fact that—here as well as in Austero v. Washington National Ins. Co. (1982) 132 Cal.App.3d 408, 182 Cal.Rptr. 919—the fees claimed as damages are incurred in the very lawsuit in which their recovery is sought, does not in itself violate section 1021's general requirement that parties bear their own costs of legal representation, though it may make the identification of allowable fees more sophisticated. If the insured were to recover benefits under the policy in a separate action before suing on the tort, the distinction between fees incurred in the policy action, recoverable as damages, and those incurred in the tort action, nonrecoverable, would be unmistakable. As pointed out in Prentice v. North Amer. Title Guar. Corp. (1963) 59 Cal.2d 618, 30 Cal.Rptr. 821, 381 P.2d 645, "[i]n the usual case, the attorney's fees will have been incurred in connection with a prior action; but there is no reason why recovery of such fees should be denied simply because the two causes . . . are tried in the same court at the same time. [¶] There was no disadvantage to defendant in the fact that the causes, although separate, were concurrently tried."

The dual nature of the present action distinguishes this case from Lowell v. Maryland Casualty Co. (1966) 65 Cal.2d 298, 54 Cal.Rptr. 116, 419 P.2d 180, Patterson v. Insurance Co. of North America (1970) 6 Cal.App.3d 310, 85 Cal.Rptr. 665, and Carroll v. Hanover Insurance Co. (1968) 266 Cal.App.2d 47, 71 Cal.Rptr. 868. "*Lowell, Patterson,* and *Carroll* were not bad faith cases. The plaintiffs' entire actions there were comparable only to the first part of the present action, i.e., for benefits due under insurance policies. In none of those cases was any allegation of bad faith made, which is the gravamen of the second part of the present action. Thus [the] plaintiffs in *Lowell, Patterson,* and *Carroll* sought attorney's fees in an action for prosecution of that very action, or . . . attorney's fees qua attorney's fees. Plaintiff[ ]here, however, seek[s] recovery of attorney's fees as damages, like any other damages, proximately caused by defendant's breach of its duty to deal in good faith."

The *Austero* majority's reliance on *Lowell, Patterson,* and *Carroll* blurred the distinction between bad faith conduct and nontortious but erroneous withholding of benefits. "[A]n erroneous interpretation of an insurance contract by an insurer does not necessarily make the insurer liable in tort for violating the covenant of good faith and fair dealing; to be liable in tort, the insurer's conduct must also have been *unreasonable*. When no bad faith has been alleged and proved, *Lowell, Patterson,* and *Carroll* preclude the award of attorney's fees incurred in obtaining benefits that the insurer erroneously, but in good faith, withheld from the insured. However, when the insurer's conduct is unreasonable, a plaintiff is allowed to recover for all detriment proximately resulting from the insurer's bad faith, which detriment Mustachio v. Ohio Farmers Ins. Co. (1975) 44 Cal.App.3d 358, 118 Cal.Rptr. 581, has correctly held includes those attorney's fees that were incurred to obtain the policy benefits and that would not have been incurred but for the insurer's tortious conduct.'' The fees recoverable, however, may not exceed the amount attributable to the attorney's efforts to obtain the rejected payment due on the insurance contract. Fees attributable to obtaining any portion of the plaintiff's award which exceeds the amount due under the policy are not recoverable.

. . . .

The alternative writ is discharged. Let a peremptory writ of mandate issue, commanding the trial court to vacate its order striking portions of petitioner's complaint.

[The concurring opinion of MOSK, J., and the dissenting opinion of LUCAS, J., are omitted.]

Equitable Lumber Corp. v. IPA Land Development Corp.

Court of Appeals of New York, 1976.
38 N.Y.2d 516, 381 N.Y.S.2d 459, 344 N.E.2d 391.

■ GABRIELLI, J. In this case, one of first impression in this court,[1] the issue presented is the enforceability of a provision in a commercial sales contract which (1) stipulates that the seller may recover the reasonable value of attorney's fees incurred as a result of the buyer's breach and (2) attempts to liquidate such sum at 30% of the amount recovered by the plaintiff in the event that the buyer's failure to make payments due under the contract requires the services of an attorney for collection.

Plaintiff, a lumber company, entered into a contract with defendant, a builder and developer, in which plaintiff agreed to supply defendant with lumber and building materials required for construction projects on various plots of land in Suffolk County. The agreement, executed by defendant's president ... described the material to be provided and specified the purchase price. On the reverse side of the contract in a section entitled "TERMS AND CONDITIONS", the following provision was also specified:

> "If the Buyer breaches this contract and the enforcement thereof, or any provision thereof, or the collection of any monies due thereunder is turned over to an attorney, the Buyer herein agrees to pay, in addition to all of Seller's expenses, a reasonable counsel fee; and in the event the matter turned over is the collection of monies, such reasonable counsel fee is hereby agreed to be *thirty (30%) per cent*. The guarantor shall also be liable for such counsel fee and expenses." (Emphasis in original.)

Defendant took delivery of quantities of lumber and materials which it used in its construction projects. Thereafter, defendant refused to pay for this merchandise, terminated its operations and abandoned its office. Plaintiff instituted suit in the Supreme Court, Kings County, for the recovery of the purchase price of the materials and the attorney's fees

---

1. Indeed, research has revealed that the precise question raised here has not been considered by any other jurisdiction.

stipulated in the contract. . . . Special Term found that defendant was liable to plaintiff in the amount of $3,936.42, the unpaid purchase price of the goods sold and delivered; and the court held that plaintiff was entitled to recover the reasonable value of attorney's fees as provided in the contract, but declined to enforce the provision designating 30% of the amount recovered as a reasonable fee. Rather, the court conducted a hearing on the nature and extent of the services performed by plaintiff's attorney and determined that a maximum of 10 hours was required to handle the matter properly. The court then set the reasonable value of attorney's fees at $450 (approximately 11% of the amount recovered). The Appellate Division modified the award, raising the amount of attorney's fees recoverable by the plaintiff to $750 and, as so modified, affirmed the judgment of Special Term. Plaintiff now appeals to this court claiming that both courts below erred in disregarding the provision liquidating attorney's fees at 30%.

Because the contract in this case is one for the sale of goods, all its provisions are controlled by the rules governing remedies for breach of contract set forth in article 2 of the Uniform Commercial Code. Generally, attorney's fees are not recoverable as damages in an action for breach of contract under the Uniform Commercial Code or otherwise, unless expressly agreed to by the parties. The parties here have expressly agreed that the seller may recover reasonable attorney's fees from the buyer upon the latter's breach. Such variations on the code's damages scheme are permitted by subdivision (1) of section 2–719 which provides, in pertinent part, that:

> "Subject to the provisions [of subsections (2) and (3) and] of the preceding section on liquidation limitation of damages,

> "(a) the agreement may provide for remedies in addition to or in substitution for those provided in this Article and may limit or alter the measure of damages recoverable under this Article".

It has been recognized that this provision confers upon the parties a "broad latitude within which to fashion their own remedies for breach of contract". Despite the degree of latitude permitted under subdivision (1) of section 2–719 of the code, article 2 contains express limitations on the ability of the parties to alter its damages rules. Two primary restrictions may be found in sections 2–302 (pertaining to unconscionability) and 2–718 (governing liquidated damages clauses) of the Uniform Commercial Code.

Subdivision (1) of section 2–718 of the Uniform Commercial Code provides:

> "(1) Damages for breach by either party may be liquidated in the agreement but only at an amount which is reasonable in the light of the anticipated or actual harm caused by the breach, the difficulties of proof of loss, and the inconvenience or nonfeasibility of otherwise obtaining an adequate remedy. A term fixing unreasonably large liquidated damages is void as a penalty."

The test adopted by the Uniform Commercial Code is similar to that proposed by authorities prior to the code's enactment.

The first sentence of subdivision (1) of section 2–718 focuses on the situation of the parties both at the time of contracting and at the time of breach. Thus, a liquidated damages provision will be valid if reasonable with respect to either (1) the harm which the parties anticipate will result from the breach at the time of contracting or (2) the actual damages suffered by the nondefaulting party at the time of breach. Interestingly, subdivision (1) of section 2–718, does, in some measure, signal a departure from prior law which considered only the anticipated harm at the time of contracting since that section expressly contemplates that a court may examine the "actual harm" sustained in adjudicating the validity of a liquidated damages provision. Thus, decisions which have restricted their analysis of the validity of liquidated damages clauses solely to the anticipated harm at the time of contracting have, to this extent, been abrogated by the Uniform Commercial Code in cases involving transactions in goods.

Having satisfied the test set forth in the first part of subdivision (1) of section 2–718, a liquidated damages provision may nonetheless be invalidated under the last sentence of the section if it is so unreasonably large that it serves as a penalty rather than a good faith attempt to pre-estimate damages. Plaintiff may not manipulate the actual amount of damages by entering into any exorbitant fee arrangement with its attorney and, thus, it may be necessary to look beyond the actual fee arrangement between plaintiff and counsel to determine whether that arrangement was reasonable and proportionate to the normal fee chargeable by attorneys in the context of this case.

Our courts have, in the past, refused to enforce a liquidated damages provision which fixed damages grossly disproportionate to the harm actually sustained, or likely to be sustained, by the nonbreaching party. In Wirth & Hamid Fair Booking, 265 N.Y. p. 214, 192 N.E. p. 297, this court noted that "[l]iquidated damages constitute the compensation which the parties have agreed must be paid in satisfaction of the loss or injury which will follow from a breach of contract. They must bear reasonable proportion to the actual loss.... Otherwise an agreement to pay a fixed sum, upon a breach of contract, is an agreement to pay a penalty, though the parties have chosen to call it 'liquidated damages,' and is unenforceable."

Certain lower courts have had occasion to deal specifically with contractual clauses providing for the recovery of attorney's fees in a liquidated amount. Stipulations for the recovery of attorney's fees are commonly found in promissory notes, instruments which are not governed by article 2 of the Uniform Commercial Code. Courts dealing with such provisions have generally examined the reasonableness of the fee in deciding whether they should be enforced. These cases, of course, were not governed by the standards set forth in subdivision (1) of section 2–718 of the Uniform Commercial Code.

An alternative ground for invalidating a contractual alteration of the Uniform Commercial Code's damages provisions is section 2–302 of the code which articulates the principle of unconscionability. This section provides in pertinent part:

"If the court as a matter of law finds the contract or any clause of the contract to have been unconscionable at the time it was made the court may refuse to enforce the contract, or it may enforce the remainder of the contract without the unconscionable clause, or it may so limit the application of any unconscionable clause as to avoid any unconscionable result."

The principle underlying section 2–302 is "the prevention of oppression and unfair surprise ... and not of disturbance of allocation of risks" (Official Comment, McKinney's Cons.Laws of N.Y., Book 62½, part I, Uniform Commercial Code, § 2–302, p. 193). It should be emphasized that in contrast to subdivision (1) of section 2–718 of the code discussed above, section 2–302 is limited to and focuses only upon the time of contracting as the vantage point for the determination of unconscionability.

In the proper case a provision that one party to a contract pay the other party's attorney's fees in the event of breach may be unconscionable. Here, however, the parties are commercial entities dealing at arm's length with relative equality of bargaining power. There is no evidence that the contract is one of adhesion in that its terms were unfair or nonnegotiable, nor has it been shown that defendant would have been unable to obtain building supplies from another supplier without subjecting itself to possible liability for attorney's fees. Defendant cannot claim that it was ignorant of the challenged clause in the contract, especially in light of the fact that the contract was signed by defendant's president, a member of the New York Bar who fled to Spain following defendant's default. Defendant IPA, therefore cannot assume the posture of a commercially illiterate consumer beguiled into a grossly unfair bargain by a deceptive vendor or finance company. We are not confronted with the classic case of unconscionability.... Thus, we conclude that, under the circumstances of this case, the provision for payment of attorney's fees does not fail on the ground of unconscionability, although in a case involving disparity of bargaining power or oppressive practices this principle may be the basis for invalidating such a contractual term.

Subdivision (1) of section 2–718 of the Uniform Commercial Code, however, is directly applicable in this case. At the time of contracting the attorney's fees were arguably incapable of estimation. The amount required for attorney's fees would vary with the nature of the defaulting party's breach. For instance, a greater amount would be charged in the event that litigation was necessitated as opposed to settlement; and additional charges might be required for possible appellate procedures.

Special Term ruled that the 30% figure was disproportionate to the amount of time and effort which, according to its estimate, was required by the plaintiff's claim. This approach did not, however, result in the proper measure of damages sustained by the plaintiff. Analysis of the harm suffered by the injured party is the focal point of subdivision (1) of section 2–718 of the Uniform Commercial Code. Under both the "actual" and "anticipated" harm tests, the time expended by the attorney in obtaining collection is not necessarily the correct measure of damages, since an attorney would be expected to bill his client on a contingent fee basis. The liquidated damages provision would prove to be a reasonable pre-estimate of anticipated harm if it is related to the normal contingent fee charged by attorneys in the collection context.

On the other hand, if plaintiff actually entered into a contingent fee arrangement with its attorney for 30%, then the actual harm suffered by plaintiff would be consistent with the liquidated damages provision. However, even if the "actual harm" test is satisfied, it is then necessary, pursuant to the second sentence of subdivision (1) of section 2–718, to determine whether the liquidated damages provision is so unreasonably large as to be void as a penalty. If plaintiff entered into an exorbitant fee arrangement with counsel, knowing that defendant would suffer the consequences, then the liquidated damages provision would be void as a "term fixing unreasonably large liquidated damages". The commercial practice of attorneys in the area of debtor-creditor relations is relevant if plaintiff did, in fact, agree to pay its attorney 30% of the amount recovered on its claim against the defendant. While plaintiff may enter into any fee arrangement it wishes with counsel, it should not be permitted to manipulate the actual damage incurred by burdening the defendant with an exorbitant fee arrangement.

This case, therefore, should be remitted for the resolution of these factual issues: (1) was a 30% fee reasonable in light of the damages to be anticipated by one in the plaintiff's position, that is, was the fee reasonably related to the normal fee an attorney would charge for the collection of plaintiff's claim; or, alternatively, (2) was the fee commensurate with the actual arrangement agreed upon by this plaintiff and its attorney? Even if the 30% fee did correspond to the actual arrangement between plaintiff and its attorney, the court on remand should determine whether the amount stipulated was unreasonably large or grossly disproportionate to the damages which the plaintiff was likely to suffer from breach in the event it did not rely on respondent's agreement to pay its attorney's fees. If the amount is found to be unreasonably large, then the provision is void as a penalty.

. . . .

Order reversed, without costs, and case remitted to Supreme Court, Kings County, for further proceedings in accordance with the opinion herein.

NOTE

West's Ann.Cal.Civ.Code § 1717 provides:

ACTION ON CONTRACT; AWARD OF ATTORNEY'S FEES AND COSTS; PREVAILING PARTY; DEPOSIT OF AMOUNTS IN INSURED, INTEREST-BEARING ACCOUNT; DAMAGES NOT BASED ON CONTRACT

(a) In any action on a contract, where the contract specifically provides that attorney's fees and costs, which are incurred to enforce that contract, shall be awarded either to one of the parties or to the prevailing party, then the party who is determined to be the party prevailing on the contract, whether he or she is the party specified in the contract or not, shall be entitled to reasonable attorney's fees in addition to other costs.

Where a contract provides for attorney's fees, as set forth above, that provision shall be construed as applying to the entire contract, unless each party was represented by counsel in the negotiation and execution of the contract, and the fact of that representation is specified in the contract.

Reasonable attorney's fees shall be fixed by the court, and shall be an element of the costs of suit.

Attorney's fees provided for by this section shall not be subject to waiver by the parties to any contract which is entered into after the effective date of this section. Any provision in any such contract which provides for a waiver of attorney's fees is void.

(b)(1) The court, upon notice and motion by a party, shall determine who is the party prevailing on the contract for purposes of this section, whether or not the suit proceeds to final judgment. Except as provided in paragraph (2), the party prevailing on the contract shall be the party who recovered a greater relief in the action on the contract. The court may also determine that there is no party prevailing on the contract for purposes of this section.

(2) Where an action has been voluntarily dismissed or dismissed pursuant to a settlement of the case, there shall be no prevailing party for purposes of this section.

Where the defendant alleges in his or her answer that he or she tendered to the plaintiff the full amount to which he or she was entitled, and thereupon deposits in court for the plaintiff, the amount so tendered, and the allegation is found to be true, then the defendant is deemed to be a party prevailing on the contract within the meaning of this section.

Where a deposit has been made pursuant to this section, the court shall, on the application of any party to the action, order the deposit to be invested in an insured, interest-bearing account. Interest on the amount shall be allocated to the parties in the same proportion as the original funds are allocated.

(c) In an action which seeks relief in addition to that based on a contract, if the party prevailing on the contract has damages awarded against it on causes of action not on the contract, the amounts awarded to the party prevailing on the contract under this section shall be deducted from any damages awarded in favor of the party who did not prevail on the contract. If the amount awarded under this section exceeds the amount of damages awarded the party not prevailing on the contract, the net amount shall be awarded the party prevailing on the contract and judgment may be entered in favor of the party prevailing on the contract for that net amount.

Rosenberg v. Levin

Supreme Court of Florida, 1982.
409 So.2d 1016.

■ OVERTON, J. This is a petition to review a decision of the Third District Court of Appeal, reported as Levin v. Rosenberg, 372 So.2d 956 (Fla. 3d DCA 1979). The issue to be decided concerns the proper basis for compensating an attorney discharged without cause by his client after he has performed substantial legal services under a valid contract of employment.

We find conflict with our decision in Goodkind v. Wolkowsky, 132 Fla. 63, 180 So. 538 (1938).

We hold that a lawyer discharged without cause is entitled to the reasonable value of his services on the basis of quantum meruit, but recovery is limited to the maximum fee set in the contract entered into for those services. We have concluded that without this limitation, the client would be penalized for the discharge and the lawyer would receive more than he bargained for in his initial contract. In the instant case, we reject the contention of the respondent lawyer that he is entitled to $55,000 as the reasonable value of his services when his contract fee was $10,000. We affirm the decision of the district court and recede from our prior decision in *Goodkind*.

The facts of this case reflect the following. Levin hired Rosenberg and Pomerantz to perform legal services pursuant to a letter agreement which provided for a $10,000 fixed fee, plus a contingent fee equal to fifty percent of all amounts recovered in excess of $600,000. Levin later discharged Rosenberg and Pomerantz without cause before the legal controversy was resolved and subsequently settled the matter for a net recovery of $500,000. Rosenberg and Pomerantz sued for fees based on a "quantum meruit" evaluation of their services. After lengthy testimony, the trial judge concluded that quantum meruit was indeed the appropriate basis for compensation and awarded Rosenberg and Pomerantz $55,000. The district court also agreed that quantum meruit was the appropriate basis for recovery but lowered the amount awarded to $10,000, stating that recovery could in no event exceed the amount which the attorneys would have received under their contract if not prematurely discharged.

The issue submitted to us for resolution is whether the terms of an attorney employment contract limit the attorney's quantum meruit recovery to the fee set out in the contract. This issue requires, however, that we answer the broader underlying question of whether in Florida quantum meruit is an appropriate basis for compensation of attorneys discharged by their clients without cause where there is a specific employment contract. The Florida cases which have previously addressed this issue have resulted in confusion and conflicting views.

In Goodkind v. Wolkowsky, this Court held that an attorney who was employed for a specific purpose and for a definite fee, but who was discharged without cause after substantial performance, was entitled to recover the fee agreed upon as damages for breach of contract. The attorney in *Goodkind* was employed to represent several clients in a tax case for a fixed fee of $4,000 and was discharged without cause prior to his completion of the matter. He sought damages for breach of contract. The trial court sustained clients' demurrer to the complaint "on the ground that plaintiff's right to recover must be restricted to a reasonable compensation for the value of the services performed prior to the discharge." The attorney appealed and this Court, after an extensive survey of the authorities, reversed the attorney's quantum meruit recovery and found instead that he was entitled to recover under the contract. The *Goodkind* court, while following the traditional contract rule, did recognize the right of the client to discharge his attorney at any time with or without cause. The

Third District Court of Appeal later applied this contract rule to a contingent fee contract situation in Osius v. Hastings, 97 So.2d 623 (Fla. 3d DCA 1957), rev'd on other grounds, 104 So.2d 21 (Fla.1958).

In Milton Kelner, P.A. v. 610 Lincoln Road, Inc., 328 So.2d 193 (Fla.1976), we approved the enforcement of a specific attorney-client contract, but left open the issue of whether quantum meruit was the proper rule in a contingency fee case. The attorney in *Kelner* represented a client on an insurance claim under a contingency fee contract calling for "40% of all sums recovered." The insurer agreed to pay the face amount of the policy before trial, but the client rejected the settlement offer and discharged the attorney without cause. In effect, the maximum recovery from the insurance company had been obtained at the time of the discharge. The attorney then sought recovery under the contract in the trial court and was successful, with the jury resolving the dispute relating to fee calculation in favor of the attorney. On appeal, the district court reversed and limited the attorney's recovery to quantum meruit rather than the percentage of the insurance proceeds recovery provided by the contingency contract. The district court emphasized that recovery under the original contract might have a chilling effect on a client's exercise of the right to discharge. The district court then certified to this Court the question it had decided, whether quantum meruit should be the exclusive remedy in contingent fee cases. We chose to decide the *Kelner* case on its unique facts and held:

> Under the peculiar circumstances of this case, where the proceeds of the insurance policy were fully recovered and the real issue of how the contingency fee was to be computed was settled by a jury, we will not disturb the verdict and restrict the computation of the attorney's fee to quantum meruit. We do agree with the District Court that Goodkind v. Wolkowsky applies to a fixed fee contract and does not establish the precedent for contingent fee contracts.

We continued by stating:

> Quantum meruit may well be the proper standard when the discharge under a contingent fee contract occurs *prior* to the obtaining of the full settlement contracted for under the attorney-client agreement, with the cause of action accruing only upon the happening of the contingency to the benefit of the former client. That issue, however, is not factually before us and we do not make that determination in this cause.

The First District Court of Appeal, in Sohn v. Brockington, 371 So.2d 1089 (Fla. 1st DCA 1979), cert. denied, 383 So.2d 1202 (Fla.1980), subsequently determined that, based on the above-quoted language in *Kelner,* quantum meruit was the appropriate remedy when discharge occurred before the happening of the contingency. In *Sohn,* the attorney was employed under a forty percent contingent fee contract and was discharged without cause before filing the complaint. The client subsequently retained new counsel who secured a settlement of $75,000. The district court affirmed the trial court which had limited the attorney to a quantum meruit recovery and awarded him $950 as the reasonable value of his services. In so holding, the district court concluded that "the [modern] rule ... is the more logical and should be adopted in this state." That court also held that the attorney's cause of action accrued immediately upon discharge in accordance with the view expressed in Martin v. Camp, 219 N.Y. 170, 177, 114 N.E. 46, 49 (1916).

The existing case law in this state reflects that this Court is on record as favoring the traditional contract means of recovery. We have, however, inferred in dicta in *Kelner* that quantum meruit may be the proper basis for recovery in a contingent fee contract situation. The First District Court of Appeal in *Sohn* expressly held that quantum meruit is proper in a contingency contract. In the instant case, the Third District Court of Appeal held that quantum meruit is proper where the contingency does not control and limited such quantum meruit recovery to the maximum amount of the contract fee.

There are two conflicting interests involved in the determination of the issue presented in this type of attorney-client dispute. The first is the need of the client to have confidence in the integrity and ability of his attorney and, therefore, the need for the client to have the ability to discharge his attorney when he loses that necessary confidence in the attorney. The second is the attorney's right to adequate compensation for work performed. To address these conflicting interests, we must consider three distinct rules.

Contract Rule

The traditional contract rule adopted by a number of jurisdictions holds that an attorney discharged without cause may recover damages for breach of contract under traditional contract principles. The measure of damages is usually the full contract price, although some courts deduct a fair allowance for services and expenses not expended by the discharged attorney in performing the balance of the contract. Some jurisdictions following the contract rule also permit an alternative recovery based on quantum meruit so that an attorney can elect between recovery based on the contract or the reasonable value of the performed services.

Support for the traditional contract theory is based on: (1) the full contract price is arguably the most rational measure of damages since it reflects the value that the parties placed on the services; (2) charging the full fee prevents the client from profiting from his own breach of contract; and (3) the contract rule is said to avoid the difficult problem of setting a value on an attorney's partially completed legal work.

Quantum Meruit Rule

To avoid restricting a client's freedom to discharge his attorney, a number of jurisdictions in recent years have held that an attorney discharged without cause can recover only the reasonable value services rendered prior to discharge. This rule was first announced in Martin v. Camp, 219 N.Y. 170, 114 N.E. 46 (1916), where the New York Court of Appeals held that a discharged attorney could not sue his client for damages for breach of contract unless the attorney had completed performance of the contract. The New York court established quantum meruit recovery for the attorney on the theory that the client does not breach the contract by discharging the attorney. Rather, the court reasoned, there is an implied condition in every attorney-client contract that the client may discharge the attorney at any time with or without cause. With this right as part of the contract, traditional contract principles are applied to allow quantum meruit recovery on the basis of services performed to date. Under the New York rule, the attorney's cause of action accrues immediately upon his discharge by the client, under the reasoning that it is unfair to make the attorney's right to compensation dependent on the performance of a successor over whom he has no control.

The California Supreme Court, in Fracasse v. Brent, 6 Cal.3d 784, 494 P.2d 9, 100 Cal.Rptr. 385 (1972), also adopted a quantum meruit rule. That court carefully analyzed those factors which distinguish the attorney-client relationship from other employment situations and concluded that a discharged attorney should be limited to a quantum meruit recovery in order to strike a proper balance between the client's right to discharge his attorney without undue restriction and the attorney's right to fair compensation for work performed. The *Fracasse* court sought both to provide clients greater freedom in substituting counsel and to promote confidence in the legal profession while protecting society's interest in the attorney-client relationship.

Contrary to the New York rule, however, the California court also held that an attorney's cause of action for quantum meruit does not accrue until the happening of the contingency, that is, the client's recovery. If no recovery is forthcoming, the attorney is denied compensation. The California court offered two reasons in support of its position. First, the result obtained and the amount involved, two important factors in determining the reasonableness of a fee, cannot be ascertained until the occurrence of the contingency. Second, the client may be of limited means and it would be unduly burdensome to force him to pay a fee if there was no recovery. The court stated that: "[S]ince the attorney agreed initially to take his chances on recovering any fee whatever, we believe that the fact that the success of the litigation is no longer under his control is insufficient to justify imposing a new and more onerous burden on the client."

Quantum Meruit Rule Limited by the Contract Price

The third rule is an extension of the second that limits quantum meruit recovery to the maximum fee set in the contract. This limitation is believed necessary to provide client freedom to substitute attorneys without economic penalty. Without such a limitation, a client's right to discharge an attorney may be illusory and the client may in effect be penalized for exercising a right.

The Tennessee Court of Appeals, in Chambliss, Bahner & Crawford v. Luther, 531 S.W.2d 108 (Tenn. Ct. App.1975), expressed the need for limitation on quantum meruit recovery, stating: "It would seem to us that the better rule is that because a client has the unqualified right to discharge his attorney, fees in such cases should be limited to the value of the services rendered or the contract price, whichever is less." In rejecting the argument that quantum meruit should be the basis for the recovery even though it exceeds the contract fee, that court said:

> To adopt the rule advanced by Plaintiff would, in our view, encourage attorneys less keenly aware of their professional responsibilities than Attorney Chambliss, . . . to induce clients to lose confidence in them in cases where the reasonable value of their services has exceeded the original fee and thereby, upon being discharged, reap a greater benefit than that for which they had bargained.

Other authorities also support this position.

Conclusion

We have carefully considered all the matters presented, both on the original argument on the merits and on rehearing. It is our opinion that it is in the best interest of clients and the legal profession as a whole that we adopt the modified quantum meruit rule which limits recovery to the maximum amount of the contract fee in all premature discharge cases involving both fixed and contingency employment contracts. The attorney-client relationship is one of special trust and confidence. The client must rely entirely on the good faith efforts of the attorney in representing his interests. This reliance requires that the client have complete confidence in the integrity and ability of the attorney and that absolute fairness and candor characterize all dealings between them. These considerations dictate that clients be given greater freedom to change legal representatives than might be tolerated in other employment relationships. We approve the philosophy that there is an overriding need to allow clients freedom to substitute attorneys without economic penalty as a means of accomplishing the broad objective of fostering public confidence in the legal profession. Failure to limit quantum meruit recovery defeats the policy against penalizing the client for exercising his right to discharge. However, attorneys should not be penalized either and should have the opportunity to recover for services performed.

Accordingly, we hold that an attorney employed under a valid contract who is discharged without cause before the contingency has occurred or before the client's matters have concluded can recover only the reasonable value of his services rendered prior to discharge, limited by the maximum contract fee. We reject both the traditional contract rule and the quantum meruit rule that allow recovery in excess of the maximum contract price because both have a chilling effect on the client's power to discharge an attorney. Under the contract rule in a contingent fee situation, both the discharged attorney and the second attorney may receive a substantial percentage of the client's final recovery. Under the unlimited quantum meruit rule, it is possible, as the instant case illustrates, for the attorney to receive a fee greater than he bargained for under the terms of his contract. Both these results are unacceptable to us.

We further follow the California view that in contingency fee cases, the cause of action for quantum meruit arises only upon the successful occurrence of the contingency. If the client fails in his recovery, the discharged attorney will similarly fail and recover nothing. We recognize that deferring the commencement of a cause of action until the occurrence of the contingency is a view not uniformly accepted. Deferral, however, supports our goal to preserve the client's freedom to discharge, and any resulting harm to the attorney is minimal because the attorney would not have benefited earlier until the contingency's occurrence. There should, of course, be a presumption of regularity and competence in the performance of the services by a successor attorney.

In computing the reasonable value of the discharged attorney's services, the trial court can consider the totality of the circumstances surrounding the professional relationship between the attorney and client. Factors such as time, the recovery sought, the skill demanded, the results obtained, and the attorney-client contract itself will necessarily be relevant considerations.

We conclude that this approach creates the best balance between the desirable right of the client to discharge his attorney and the right of an attorney to reasonable compensation for his services. With this decision, we necessarily recede from our prior decision in Goodkind v. Wolkowsky. This decision has no effect on our *Kelner* decision concerning completed contracts, whether contingent, fixed fee, or mixed. We find the district court of appeal was correct in limiting the quantum meruit award to the contract price, and its decision is approved.

It is so ordered.

Buckhannon Board and Care Home, Inc. v. West Virginia Department of Health and Human Resources

Supreme Court of the United States, 2001.
532 U.S. 598, 121 S.Ct. 1835, 149 L.E.2d 855.

■ CHIEF JUSTICE REHNQUIST delivered the opinion of the Court.

Numerous federal statutes allow courts to award attorney's fees and costs to the "prevailing party." The question presented here is whether this term includes a party that has failed to secure a judgment on the merits or a court-ordered consent decree, but has nonetheless achieved the desired result because the lawsuit brought about a voluntary change in the defendant's conduct. We hold that it does not.

Buckhannon Board and Care Home, Inc., which operates care homes that provide assisted living to their residents, failed an inspection by the West Virginia Office of the State Fire Marshal because some of the residents were incapable of "self-preservation" as defined under state law. See W. Va.Code §§ 16–5H–1, 16–5H–2 (1998) (requiring that all residents of residential board and care homes be capable of "self-preservation," or capable of moving themselves "from situations involving imminent danger, such as fire"); W. Va.Code of State Rules, tit. 87, ser. 1, § 14.07(1) (1995) (same). On October 28, 1997, after receiving cease and desist orders requiring the closure of its residential care facilities within 30 days, Buckhannon Board and Care Home, Inc., on behalf of itself and other similarly situated homes and residents (hereinafter petitioners), brought suit in the United States District Court for the Northern District of West Virginia against the State of West Virginia, two of its agencies, and 18 individuals (hereinafter respondents), seeking declaratory and injunctive relief that the "self-preservation" requirement violated the Fair Housing

Amendments Act of 1988 (FHAA), 102 Stat. 1619, 42 U.S.C. § 3601 et seq., and the Americans with Disabilities Act of 1990 (ADA), 104 Stat. 327, 42 U.S.C. § 12101 et seq.

Respondents agreed to stay enforcement of the cease-and-desist orders pending resolution of the case and the parties began discovery. In 1998, the West Virginia Legislature enacted two bills eliminating the "self-preservation" requirement, see S. 627, I 1998 W. Va. Acts 983–986 (amending regulations); H.R. 4200, II 1998 W. Va. Acts 1198–1199 (amending statute), and respondents moved to dismiss the case as moot. The District Court granted the motion, finding that the 1998 legislation had eliminated the allegedly offensive provisions and that there was no indication that the West Virginia Legislature would repeal the amendments.

Petitioners requested attorney's fees as the "prevailing party" under the FHAA, 42 U.S.C. § 3613(c)(2) ("[T]he court, in its discretion, may allow the prevailing party ... a reasonable attorney's fee and costs"), and ADA, 42 U.S.C. § 12205 ("[T]he court ..., in its discretion, may allow the prevailing party ... a reasonable attorney's fee, including litigation expenses, and costs"). Petitioners argued that they were entitled to attorney's fees under the "catalyst theory," which posits that a plaintiff is a "prevailing party" if it achieves the desired result because the lawsuit brought about a voluntary change in the defendant's conduct. Although most Courts of Appeals recognize the "catalyst theory," the Court of Appeals for the Fourth Circuit rejected it in S–1 and S–2 v. State Bd. of Ed. of N. C., 21 F.3d 49, 51 (C.A.4 1994) (en banc) ("A person may not be a 'prevailing party' ... except by virtue of having obtained an enforceable judgment, consent decree, or settlement giving some of the legal relief sought"). The District Court accordingly denied the motion and, for the same reason, the Court of Appeals affirmed in an unpublished, per curiam opinion. Judgt. order reported at 203 F.3d 819 (C.A.4 2000).

To resolve the disagreement amongst the Courts of Appeals, we granted certiorari, 530 U.S. 1304, 121 S.Ct. 28, 147 L.Ed.2d 1050 (2000), and now affirm.

In the United States, parties are ordinarily required to bear their own attorney's fees—the prevailing party is not entitled to collect from the loser. See *Alyeska Pipeline Service Co. v. Wilderness Society*, 421 U.S. 240, 247, 95 S.Ct. 1612, 44 L.Ed.2d 141 (1975). Under this "American Rule," we follow "a general practice of not awarding fees to a prevailing party absent explicit statutory authority." *Key Tronic Corp. v. United States*, 511 U.S. 809, 819, 114 S.Ct. 1960, 128 L.Ed.2d 797 (1994). Congress, however, has authorized the award of attorney's fees to the "prevailing party" in numerous statutes in addition to those at issue here, such as the Civil Rights Act of 1964, 78 Stat. 259, 42 U.S.C. § 2000e–5(k), the Voting Rights Act Amendments of 1975, 89 Stat. 402, 42 U.S.C. § 1973*l* (e), and the Civil Rights Attorney's Fees Awards Act of 1976, 90 Stat. 2641, 42 U.S.C. § 1988. See generally *Marek v. Chesny*, 473 U.S. 1, 43–51, 105 S.Ct. 3012, 87 L.Ed.2d 1 (1985) (Appendix to opinion of Brennan, J., dissenting).

In designating those parties eligible for an award of litigation costs, Congress employed the term "prevailing party," a legal term of art. Black's Law Dictionary 1145 (7th ed.1999) defines "prevailing party" as "[a] party in whose favor a judgment is rendered, regardless of the amount of damages awarded <in certain cases, the court will award attorney's fees to the prevailing party>.—Also termed *successful party*." This view that a "prevailing party" is one who has been awarded some relief by the court can be distilled from our prior cases.

In *Hanrahan v. Hampton*, 446 U.S. 754, 758, 100 S.Ct. 1987, 64 L.Ed.2d 670 (1980) (*per curiam*), we reviewed the legislative history of § 1988 and found that "Congress intended to permit the interim award of counsel fees only when a party has prevailed on the merits of at least some of his claims." Our "[r]espect for ordinary language requires that a plaintiff receive at least some relief on the merits of his claim before he can be said to prevail." *Hewitt v. Helms*, 482 U.S. 755, 760, 107 S.Ct. 2672, 96 L.Ed.2d 654 (1987). We have held that even an award of nominal damages suffices under this test. See *Farrar v. Hobby*, 506 U.S. 103, 113 S.Ct. 566, 121 L.Ed.2d 494 (1992).

In addition to judgments on the merits, we have held that settlement agreements enforced through a consent decree may serve as the basis for an award of attorney's fees. See *Maher v. Gagne*, 448 U.S. 122, 100 S.Ct. 2570, 65 L.Ed.2d 653 (1980). Although a consent decree does not always include an admission of liability by the defendant, see, *e.g., id.*, at 126, n. 8, 100 S.Ct. 2570, it nonetheless is a court-ordered "chang[e][in] the legal relationship between [the plaintiff] and the defendant." *Texas State Teachers Assn. v. Garland Independent School Dist.*, 489 U.S. 782, 792, 109 S.Ct. 1486, 103 L.Ed.2d 866 (1989) (citing *Hewitt, supra*, at 760–761, 107 S.Ct. 2672, and *Rhodes v. Stewart*, 488 U.S. 1, 3–4, 109 S.Ct. 202, 102 L.Ed.2d 1 (1988) (*per curiam*)). These decisions, taken together, establish that enforceable judgments on the merits and court-ordered consent decrees create the "material alteration of the legal relationship of the parties" necessary to permit an award of attorney's fees. 489 U.S., at 792–793, 109 S.Ct. 1486; see also *Hanrahan, supra*, at 757, 100 S.Ct. 1987 ("[I]t seems clearly to have been the intent of Congress to permit . . . an interlocutory award only to a party who has established his entitlement to some relief on the merits of his claims, either in the *trial court or on appeal*" (emphasis added)).

We think, however, the "catalyst theory" falls on the other side of the line from these examples. It allows an award where there is no judicially sanctioned change in the legal relationship of the parties. Even under a limited form of the "catalyst theory," a plaintiff could recover attorney's fees if it established that the "complaint had sufficient merit to withstand a motion to dismiss for lack of jurisdiction or failure to state a claim on which relief may be granted." Brief for United States as *Amicus Curiae* 27. This is not the type of legal merit that our prior decisions, based upon plain language and congressional intent, have found necessary. Indeed, we held in *Hewitt* that an interlocutory ruling that reverses a dismissal for failure to state a claim "is not the stuff of which legal victories are made." 482 U.S., at 760, 107 S.Ct. 2672. See also *Hanrahan, supra*, at 754, 100 S.Ct. 1987 (reversal of a directed verdict for defendant does not make plaintiff a "prevailing party"). A defendant's voluntary change in conduct, although perhaps accomplishing what the plaintiff sought to achieve by the lawsuit, lacks the necessary judicial *imprimatur* on the change. Our precedents thus counsel against holding that the term "prevailing party" authorizes an award of attorney's fees *without* a corresponding alteration in the legal relationship of the parties.

The dissenters chide us for upsetting "long-prevailing Circuit precedent." Post, at 1850 (opinion of GINSBURG, J.) (emphasis added). But, as JUSTICE SCALIA points out in his concurrence, several Courts of Appeals have relied upon dicta in our prior cases in approving the "catalyst theory." See *post*, at 1849; see also *supra*, at 1839, n. 5. Now that the issue is squarely presented, it behooves us to reconcile the plain language of the statutes with our prior *holdings*. We have only awarded attorney's fees where the plaintiff has received a judgment on the merits, see, *e.g., Farrar, supra*, at 112, 113 S.Ct. 566, or obtained a court-ordered consent decree, *Maher, supra*, at 129–130, 100 S.Ct. 2570—we have not awarded attorney's fees where the plaintiff has secured the reversal of a directed verdict, see *Hanrahan*, 446 U.S., at 759, 100 S.Ct. 1987, or acquired a judicial pronouncement that the defendant has violated the Constitution unaccompanied by "*judicial* relief," *Hewitt, supra*, at 760, 107 S.Ct. 2672 (emphasis added). Never have we awarded attorney's fees for a nonjudicial "alteration of actual circumstances." *Post*, at 1856 (dissenting opinion). While urging an expansion of our precedents on this front, the dissenters would simultaneously abrogate the "merit" requirement of our prior cases and award attorney's fees where the plaintiff's claim "was at least colorable" and "not . . . groundless." *Post*, at 1852 (internal quotation marks and citation omitted). We cannot agree that the term "prevailing party" authorizes federal courts to award attorney's fees to a plaintiff who, by simply filing a nonfrivolous but nonetheless potentially meritless lawsuit (it will never be determined), has reached the "sought-after destination" without obtaining any judicial relief. *Post*, at 1856 (internal quotation marks and citation omitted).

Petitioners nonetheless argue that the legislative history of the Civil Rights Attorney's Fees Awards Act supports a broad reading of "prevailing party" which includes the "catalyst theory." We doubt that legislative history could overcome what we think is the rather clear meaning of "prevailing party"—the term actually used in the statute. Since we resorted to such history in *Garland*, 489 U.S., at 790, 109 S.Ct. 1486, *Maher*, 448 U.S., at 129, 100 S.Ct. 2570, and *Hanrahan, supra*, at 756–757, 100 S.Ct. 1987, however, we do likewise here. . . .

Given the clear meaning of "prevailing party" in the fee-shifting statutes, we need not determine which way these various policy arguments cut. In *Alyeska*, 421 U.S., at 260, 95 S.Ct. 1612, we said that Congress had not "extended any roving authority to the Judiciary to allow counsel fees as costs or otherwise whenever the courts might deem them warranted." To disregard the clear legislative language and the holdings of our prior cases on the basis of such policy arguments would be a similar assumption of a "roving authority." For the reasons stated above, we hold that the "catalyst theory" is not a permissible basis for the award of attorney's fees under the FHAA, 42 U.S.C. § 3613(c)(2), and ADA, 42 U.S.C. § 12205.

The judgment of the Court of Appeals is

Affirmed.

■ JUSTICE SCALIA, with whom JUSTICE THOMAS joins, concurring.

I join the opinion of the Court in its entirety, and write to respond at greater length to the contentions of the dissent.

I

"Prevailing party" is not some newfangled legal term invented for use in late–20th-century fee-shifting statutes. "[B]y the long established practice and universally recognized rule of the common law, in actions at law, the prevailing party is entitled to recover a judgment for costs...." *Mansfield, C. & L.M.R. Co. v. Swan*, 111 U.S. 379, 387, 4 S.Ct. 510, 28 L.Ed. 462 (1884).

> "Costs have usually been allowed to the prevailing party, as incident to the judgment, since the statute 6 Edw. I, c. 1, § 2, and the same rule was acknowledged in the courts of the States, at the time the judicial system of the United States was organized....

> "Weighed in the light of these several provisions in the Judiciary Act [of 1789], the conclusion appears to be clear that Congress intended to allow costs to the prevailing party, as incident to the judgment...." The Baltimore, 8 Wall. 377, 388, 390 [19 L.Ed. 463] (1869).

The term has been found within the United States Statutes at Large since at least the Bankruptcy Act of 1867, which provided that "[t]he party prevailing in the suit shall be entitled to costs against the adverse party." Act of Mar. 2, 1867, ch. 176, § 24, 14 Stat. 528. See also Act of Mar. 3, 1887, ch. 359, § 15, 24 Stat. 508 ("If the Government of the United States shall put in issue the right of the plaintiff to recover the court may, in its discretion, allow costs to the prevailing party from the time of joining such issue"). A computer search shows that the term "prevailing party" appears at least 70 times in the current United States Code; it is no stranger to the law.

■ JUSTICE GINSBURG, with whom JUSTICE STEVENS, JUSTICE SOUTER, and JUSTICE BREYER join, dissenting.

The Court today holds that a plaintiff whose suit prompts the precise relief she seeks does not "prevail," and hence cannot obtain an award of attorney's fees, unless she also secures a court entry memorializing her victory. The entry need not be a judgment on the merits. Nor need there be any finding of wrongdoing. A court-approved settlement will do.

The Court's insistence that there be a document filed in court—a litigated judgment or court-endorsed settlement—upsets long-prevailing Circuit precedent applicable to scores of federal fee-shifting statutes. The decision allows a defendant to escape a statutory obligation to pay a plaintiff's counsel fees, even though the suit's merit led the defendant to abandon the fray, to switch rather than fight on, to accord plaintiff sooner rather than later the principal redress sought in the complaint. Concomitantly, the Court's constricted definition of "prevailing party," and consequent rejection of the "catalyst theory," impede access to court for the less well heeled, and shrink the incentive Congress created for the enforcement of federal law by private attorneys general.

In my view, the "catalyst rule," as applied by the clear majority of Federal Circuits, is a key component of the fee-shifting statutes Congress adopted to advance enforcement of civil rights. Nothing in history, precedent, or plain English warrants the anemic construction of the term "prevailing party" the Court today imposes. . . .

Texas State Teachers Association v. Garland Independent School District

Supreme Court of the United States, 1989.
489 U.S. 782, 109 S.Ct. 1486, 103 L.Ed.2d 866.

■ Justice O'Connor delivered the opinion of the Court.

We must decide today the proper standard for determining whether a party has "prevailed" in an action brought under certain civil rights statutes such that the party is eligible for an award of attorney's fees under 42 U.S.C. § 1988. . . .

I

On March 31, 1981, petitioners, the Texas State Teacher's Association, its local affiliate the Garland Education Association, and several individual members and employees of both organizations brought suit under 42 U.S.C. § 1983 against respondent Garland Independent School District and various school district officials. Petitioners' complaint alleged that the school district's policy of prohibiting communications by or with teachers during the school day concerning employee organizations violated petitioners' First and Fourteenth Amendment rights. . . .

On cross motions for summary judgment, the District Court rejected petitioners' claims in almost all respects. . . .

On appeal, the Court of Appeals for the Fifth Circuit affirmed in part, reversed in part and remanded. The Court of Appeals agreed with the District Court that petitioners' claim that the First Amendment required the school district to allow union representatives access to school facilities during school hours was foreclosed by our decision in [an earlier case]. . . . The Court of Appeals, however, disagreed with the District Court's analysis of petitioners' claims relating to teacher-to-teacher discussion of employee organizations during the school day. It found that the prohibition of teacher speech promoting union activity during school hours was unconstitutional. It also found that there was a distinct possibility that the school district would discipline teachers who engaged in *any* discussion of employee organizations during the school day, and that such a policy had a chilling effect on teachers' First Amendment rights. Finally, the Court of Appeals held that the prohibition on teacher use of internal mail and billboard facilities to discuss employee organizations was unconstitutional. . . . As to these claims, the Court of Appeals granted petitioners' motion for summary judgment. Respondents filed an appeal in this Court, and we summarily affirmed the judgment of the Court of Appeals.

Petitioners then filed the instant application for an award of attorney's fees pursuant to 42 U.S.C. § 1988. The District Court found that under

Fifth Circuit precedent petitioners here were not "prevailing parties" within the meaning of § 1988 and thus were ineligible for any fee award. The court recognized that petitioners had achieved "partial success," but indicated that "[i]n this circuit the test for prevailing party status is whether the plaintiff prevailed on *the central issue* by acquiring the primary relief sought." Looking to "the background of the lawsuit" and the claims presented in petitioners' complaint, the District Court concluded that the central issue in this litigation was the constitutionality of the school district's policy of limiting employee organizations' access to teachers and school facilities during school hours. Because petitioners did not prevail on this issue, they had not carried the "central issue" in the lawsuit nor achieved "the primary relief sought" and were therefore precluded from recovering attorney's fees.

A divided panel of the Court of Appeals for the Fifth Circuit affirmed the District Court's judgment denying petitioners prevailing party status under § 1988. The majority ... found that while petitioners "did succeed on significant secondary issues," the "main thrust" of their lawsuit was nonetheless the desire to gain access to school campuses during school hours for outside representatives of employee organizations. Thus, under the "central issue" test, the District Court had correctly concluded that petitioners were not prevailing parties eligible for a fee award under § 1988.... We now reverse the judgment of the Court of Appeals.

II

As amended, 42 U.S.C. § 1988, provides in pertinent part:

> "In any action or proceeding to enforce a provision of sections 1981, 1982, 1983, 1985, and 1986 of this title, title IX of Public Law 92–318, or title VI of the Civil Rights Act of 1964, the court, in its discretion may allow the prevailing party, other than the United States, a reasonable attorney's fee as part of the costs."

In Hensley v. Eckerhart, 461 U.S. 424, 103 S.Ct. 1933, 76 L.Ed.2d 40 (1983), we dealt with the application of the attorney's fee provision of § 1988 to a situation much like the one before us today....

In *Hensley* this Court sought to clarify "the proper standard for setting a fee award where the plaintiff has achieved only limited success." At the outset we noted that no fee award is permissible until the plaintiff has crossed the "statutory threshold" of prevailing party status. In this regard, the Court indicated that "[a] typical formulation is that 'plaintiffs may be considered "prevailing parties" for attorney's fees purposes if they succeed on any significant issue in litigation which achieves some of the benefit the parties sought in bringing the suit.' " Id., at 433, 103 S.Ct., at 1939, quoting Nadeau v. Helgemoe, 581 F.2d 275, 278–279 (C.A.1 1978). The Court then went on to establish certain principles to guide the discretion of the lower courts in setting fee awards in cases where plaintiffs have not achieved complete success. Where the plaintiff's claims are based on different facts and legal theories, and the plaintiff has prevailed on only some of those claims, we indicated that "[t]he congressional intent to limit [fee] awards to prevailing parties requires that these unrelated claims be treated as if they had been raised in separate lawsuits, and therefore no fee may be awarded for services on the unsuccessful claim." In the more typical situation, where the plaintiff's claims arise out of a common core of facts, and involve related legal theories, the inquiry is more complex. In such a case, we indicated that "the most critical factor is the degree of success obtained." We noted that in complex civil rights litigation, "the plaintiff often may succeed in identifying some unlawful practices or conditions," but that "the range of possible success is vast," and the achievement of prevailing party status alone "may say little about whether the expenditure of counsel's time was reasonable in relation to the success achieved." We indicated that the district courts should exercise their equitable discretion in such cases to arrive at a reasonable fee award, either by attempting to identify specific hours that should be eliminated or by simply reducing the award to account for the limited success of the plaintiff.

We think it clear that the "central issue" test applied by the lower courts here is directly contrary to the thrust of our decision in *Hensley*. Although respondents are correct in pointing out that *Hensley* did not adopt one particular standard for determining prevailing party status, *Hensley* does indicate that the *degree of* the plaintiff's success in relation to the other goals of the lawsuit is a factor critical to the determination of the size of a reasonable fee, not to eligibility for a fee award at all.

Our decision in *Hensley* is consistent with congressional intent in this regard. Congress clearly contemplated that interim fee awards would be available "where a party has prevailed on an important matter in the course of litigation, even when he ultimately does not prevail on all issues." S.Rep. No. 94–1011, p. 5 (1976); see also H.R.Rep. No. 94–1558, p. 8 (1976), U.S.Code Cong. & Admin.News 1976, pp. 5908, 5912. In discussing the availability of fees *pendente lite* under § 1988, we have indicated that such awards are proper where a party "has established his entitlement to some relief on the merits of his claims, either in the trial court or on appeal." The incongruence of the "central issue" test in light of the clear congressional intent that interim fee awards be available to partially prevailing civil rights plaintiffs is readily apparent. In this case, our summary affirmance of the Court of Appeal's judgment for respondents on the union access issues and for petitioners on the teacher-to-teacher communication issues effectively ended the litigation. Because the Court of Appeals found that petitioners had not succeeded on what it viewed as the central issue in the suit, no fees were awarded. Yet, if petitioners' victory on the teacher-to-teacher communication issue had been only an interim one, with other issues remanded for further proceedings in the district court, petitioners would have been entitled to some fee award for their successful claims under § 1988. Congress cannot have meant "prevailing party" status to depend entirely on the timing of a request for fees: A prevailing party must be one who has succeeded on any significant claim affording it some of the relief sought, either *pendente lite* or at the conclusion of the litigation.

Nor does the central issue test have much to recommend it from the viewpoint of judicial administration of § 1988 and other fee shifting provisions. By focusing on the subjective importance of an issue to the litigants, it asks a question which is almost impossible to answer. Is the "primary relief sought" in a disparate treatment action under Title VII reinstatement, backpay, or injunctive relief? This question, the answer to which appears to depend largely on the mental state of the parties, is wholly irrelevant to the purposes behind the fee shifting provisions, and promises to mire district courts entertaining fee applications in an inquiry which one commentator has described as "excruciating." See M. Schwartz & J. Kirklin, Section 1983 Litigation: Claims, Defenses, and Fees § 15.11, p. 348 (1986). Creating such an unstable threshold to fee eligibility is sure to provoke prolonged litigation, thus deterring settlement of fee disputes and ensuring that the fee application will spawn a second litigation of significant dimension. In sum, the search for the "central" and "tangential" issues in the lawsuit, or for the "primary" as opposed to the "secondary" relief sought, much like the search for the Golden Fleece, distracts the district court from the primary purposes behind § 1988 and is essentially unhelpful in defining the term "prevailing party."

We think the language of Nadeau v. Helgemoe, quoted in our opinion in *Hensley,* adequately captures the inquiry which should be made in determining whether a civil rights plaintiff is a prevailing party within the meaning of § 1988. If the plaintiff has succeeded on "any significant issue in litigation which achieve[d] some of the benefit the parties sought in bringing suit" the plaintiff has crossed the threshold to a fee award of some kind. The floor in this regard is provided by our decision in Hewitt v. Helms, 482 U.S. 755, 107 S.Ct. 2672, 96 L.Ed.2d 654 (1987). As we noted there, "[r]espect for ordinary language requires that a plaintiff receive at least some relief on the merits of his claim before he can be said to prevail." Thus, at a minimum, to be considered a prevailing party within the meaning of § 1988 the plaintiff must be able to point to a resolution of the dispute which changes the legal relationship between itself and the defendant. Beyond this absolute limitation, a technical victory may be so insignificant, and may be so near the situations addressed in *Hewitt* and Rhodes v. Stewart, 488 U.S. 1, 109 S.Ct. 202, 102 L.Ed.2d 1 (1988), as to be insufficient to support prevailing party status. For example, in the context of this litigation, the District Court found that the requirement that non-school hour meetings be conducted only with prior approval from the local school principal was unconstitutionally vague. The District Court characterized this issue as "of minor significance" and noted that there was "no evidence that the plaintiffs were ever refused permission to use school premises during non-school hours." If this had been petitioners' only success in the litigation, we think it clear that this alone would not have rendered them "prevailing parties" within the meaning of § 1988. Where the plaintiff's success on a legal claim can be characterized as purely technical or *de minimis,* a district court would be justified in concluding that even the "generous formulation" we adopt today has not been satisfied. The touchstone of the prevailing party inquiry must be the material alteration of the legal relationship of the parties in a manner which Congress sought to promote in the fee statute. Where such a change has occurred, the degree of the plaintiff's overall success goes to the reasonableness of the award under *Hensley,* not to the availability of a fee award *vel non.*

III

Application of the principles enunciated above to the case at hand is not difficult. Petitioners here obtained a judgment vindicating the First Amendment rights of public employees in the workplace. Their success has materially altered the school district's policy limiting the rights of teachers to communicate with each other concerning employee organizations and union activities. Petitioners have thus served the "private attorney general" role which Congress meant to promote in enacting the Civil Rights Attorney's Fees Awards Act of 1976. They prevailed on a significant issue in the litigation and have obtained some of the relief they sought and are thus "prevailing parties" within the meaning of § 1988. We therefore reverse the judgment of the Court of Appeals and remand this case for a determination of a reasonable attorney's fee consistent with the principles established by our decision in *Hensley v. Eckerhart.*

It is so ordered.

NOTES ON ATTORNEY'S FEES

1.   In Kay v. Ehrler, 499 U.S. 432, 111 S.Ct. 1435, 113 L.Ed.2d 486 (1991), the question was whether an attorney who represented himself in a successful civil rights action should be awarded a "reasonable attorney's fee as part of the costs" under 42 U.S.C. 1988. In affirming the United States Court of Appeals denial of petitioner's request for attorney's fees, the Supreme Court stated: "A rule that authorizes awards of counsel fees to pro se litigants—even if limited to those who are members of the bar— would create a disincentive to employ counsel whenever such a plaintiff considered himself competent to litigate on his own behalf. The statutory policy of furthering the successful prosecution of meritorious claims is better served by a rule that creates an incentive to retain counsel in every such case."

2.   Hewitt v. Helms, discussed in *Texas State Teachers Ass'n.,* involved a claim that a prisoner's conviction in a disciplinary proceeding violated the Due Process Clause. Although a federal appeals court decided that Helms' substantive due process rights had been violated, the offending officials were held immune from damages, and Helms never moved for declaratory or injunctive relief. While his suit may have catalyzed a change in the rules governing disciplinary proceedings at the prison, Helms had been released before that development occurred. Based on its conclusion that Helms' suit had gotten him no relief, the Court held that he was not a "prevailing party", and therefore not eligible to recover attorneys' fees, under Section 1988.

3.   The prisoner-plaintiffs in Rhodes v. Stewart, which is also cited in *Texas State Teachers Association,* obtained a declaratory judgment that prison officials had violated their first amendment rights by refusing to let them subscribe to a magazine. They also won an award of attorneys' fees under Section 1988. However, it turned out that one of the plaintiffs had died and the other been released from custody before the declaratory judgment was entered. Because the judgment gave neither plaintiff any

relief, the Court held that neither was a "prevailing party" within the meaning of Section 1988.

4. A prevailing defendant is entitled to attorneys' fees under Section 1988 only where the action "was frivolous, unreasonable, or without foundation, even though not brought in subjective bad faith." The Court's reason for so interpreting this statute was first articulated in Christiansburg Garment Co. v. Equal Employment Opportunity Commission, 434 U.S. 412, 98 S.Ct. 694, 54 L.Ed.2d 648 (1978), which involved the construction of a similar law:

> That § 706(k) [of Title VII of the Civil Rights Act of 1964] allows fee awards only to *prevailing* private plaintiffs should assure that this statutory provision will not in itself operate as an incentive to the bringing of claims that have little chance of success. To take the further step of assessing attorney's fees against plaintiffs simply because they do not finally prevail would substantially add to the risks inherent in most litigation and would undercut the efforts of Congress to promote the vigorous enforcement of the provisions of Title VII. Hence, a plaintiff should not be assessed his opponent's attorney's fees unless a court finds that his claim was frivolous, unreasonable, or groundless, or that the plaintiff continued to litigate after it clearly became so. . . .

Pennsylvania v. Delaware Valley Citizens' Council for Clean Air

Supreme Court of the United States, 1986.
478 U.S. 546, 106 S.Ct. 3088, 92 L.Ed.2d 439.

■ JUSTICE WHITE delivered the opinion of the Court.

The questions presented in this case are first, whether the Clean Air Act authorizes attorney's fees awards for time spent by counsel participating in regulatory proceedings; second, whether a court may enhance an award to reflect superior quality of representation rendered by plaintiff's counsel; and third, whether enhancement of the fee is proper because of plaintiff's risk of not prevailing on the merits.

I

In 1977, the Delaware Valley Citizens' Council for Clean Air (Delaware Valley) and the United States each filed suit to compel the Commonwealth of Pennsylvania to implement a vehicle emission inspection and maintenance program (I/M program) as required by the Clean Air Act. Pursuant to a consent decree approved in 1978, the Commonwealth agreed to establish an I/M program for 10 counties in the Philadelphia and Pittsburgh areas by August 1, 1980. The decree called for the Pennsylvania Department of Transportation (PennDOT) to seek legislation instituting a franchise I/M system under which the Commonwealth would contract with garage owners for the establishment of inspection stations. If the legislature failed to approve such a system, then the decree required PennDOT to promulgate regulations allowing Pennsylvania to certify a number of private garage facilities to perform the inspections. In addition, the decree provided for Pennsylvania to pay Delaware Valley $30,000 for attorney's fees and costs incurred prior to the entry of the consent decree.

Entry of the consent decree marked only the beginning of this story, for implementation of the I/M program did not proceed smoothly. For simplicity's sake, we will summarize the relevant factual developments into nine phases, with each phase relating to a different aspect of the litigation. Not only is this the method used by the parties and followed by both lower courts, but it is a system for analyzing requests for attorney's fees and costs that appears to be useful in protracted litigation.

Phase I. After entry of the consent decree, the Pennsylvania Legislature refused to enact a franchise system. Under the decree, PennDOT then had until July 1, 1979 to publish the necessary regulations. When PennDOT failed to comply, Delaware Valley moved to have the Commonwealth held in contempt; PennDOT published the proposed regulations, however, before the scheduled hearing on the motion. The court thus refrained from finding the Commonwealth in contempt, but ordered the parties to establish a revised schedule for implementation of the I/M program approved by the consent decree.

Phase II. After PennDOT published the proposed I/M program regulations, Delaware Valley continued to monitor the Commonwealth's performance under the consent decree, and submitted comments on the regulations which were published in the Pennsylvania Bulletin.

Phase III. In late 1979, the Commonwealth requested a modification of the decree delaying implementation of the I/M program until May 1981. With Delaware Valley's approval, the District Court approved the extension in March 1980.

Phase IV. By February 1981, the Commonwealth still had not published final regulations covering the type of equipment which private garages needed to have in order to become certified inspection stations. The Commonwealth thus asked Delaware Valley to consent to a further postponement of the implementation date to January 1, 1983. The Commonwealth argued that the United States Environmental Protection Agency had recommended a type of emission analyzer different from the one required under the consent decree, but at that time no manufacturer had produced even a prototype of such machinery.

After extensive negotiations over this extension request, the parties failed to reach an agreement. The Commonwealth then filed a motion asking the District Court to grant the second extension and delay the starting date of the I/M program until January 1, 1983. In response, Delaware Valley sought to have the court declare the Commonwealth to be in violation of the consent decree, and requested numerous modifications to the consent decree. On May 20, 1981, the court issued an order finding the Commonwealth in violation of the decree, denying the motion for a further extension, and denying the modifications submitted by Delaware Valley. On June 16, the court denied the Commonwealth's motion for reconsideration, but approved May 1, 1982, as the new deadline for implementation of the

I/M program. The Commonwealth appealed both the May 20 and June 16 orders, both of which were affirmed by the Court of Appeals.

Phase V. Following the District Court's order of June 16, the Pennsylvania General Assembly enacted a statute, H.B. 456, over the Governor's veto, which prohibited the expenditure of state funds by the Executive Branch for the implementation of the I/M program. PennDOT and the remainder of the Executive Branch promptly ceased all activities related to implementing the I/M program, except for publication of the final regulations establishing specifications for the emissions analysis equipment to be used by garage owners wishing to participate as inspection locations.

The Commonwealth moved to stay implementation of the consent decree in light of H.B. 456. Delaware Valley opposed that motion, and sought to have the court declare the Commonwealth in contempt and apply sanctions. The court denied the Commonwealth's motion for a stay and held the Commonwealth in civil contempt. As a sanction, the court ordered the United States Secretary of Transportation to refrain from approving any projects, or awarding any grants, for highways in the two areas covered by the consent decree, except for projects required for purposes of safety, mass transit, or air quality improvement. Once again, the Commonwealth appealed, and once again, the Court of Appeals upheld the District Court's orders.

Phase VI. After the filing of the consent decree, the city of Pittsburgh and several groups of Pennsylvania legislators attempted to intervene in the litigation. Delaware Valley successfully opposed all of these attempts.

Phase VII. As noted above, a portion of the District Court's contempt order prevented the United States Secretary of Transportation from authorizing the expenditure of any federal funds for federal highway projects in Pennsylvania that did not fall into certain categories. In late 1982, the United States approved seven projects for funding, certifying that they would either improve safety or improve air quality. These certifications were submitted to both Delaware Valley and the District Court. The court found that five of the projects did not qualify as exemptions under the terms of its prior order, and only approved two proposals for federal funding.

Phase VIII. On May 3, 1983, the Pennsylvania General Assembly finally passed legislation authorizing the Commonwealth to proceed with implementation of the I/M program, and the Governor signed the bill into law the next day. Subsequently, Delaware Valley and the Commonwealth negotiated a new compliance schedule, under which the I/M program would begin by June 1, 1984. The District Court approved of this new schedule, and vacated its earlier contempt sanctions.

Phase IX. This phase includes work done by Delaware Valley in hearings before the Environmental Protection Agency, during which, *inter alia,* the Commonwealth unsuccessfully sought that agency's approval of an I/M program covering a smaller geographic area.[1]

---

1. This phase also includes work done by Delaware Valley in related state-court litigation ... brought by a group of state legislators to challenge the Executive Branch's au-

Delaware Valley then sought attorney's fees and costs for the work performed after issuance of the consent decree in 1978. The District Court awarded Delaware Valley $209,813 in attorney's fees and an additional $6,675.03 in costs. To calculate the legal fee award, the District Court first determined:

> "[T]he number of hours reasonably necessary to perform the legal services for which compensation is sought. The reasonable number of hours is then multiplied by a reasonable hourly rate for the attorney providing the services, the latter being based on the court's determination of the attorney's reputation, status and type of activity for which the attorney is seeking compensation. The sum of the two figures is the 'lodestar' which can then be adjusted upward or downward based on the contingency of success, and the quality of an attorney's work. In all instances plaintiffs have the burden of establishing entitlement to the award claimed and any adjustment to the 'lodestar.'"

The court used three separate hourly rates in making its award. Work which the court found to be "most difficult" was compensated at an hourly rate of $100. For work that could have been done "by an attorney working at the associate level," the hourly rate was set at $65. And for work "which required little or no legal ability," the court allowed an hourly rate of $25.

For the most part, the hours for which Delaware Valley sought compensation were those spent on the postdecree litigation itself.[2] In Phases II and IX, however, Pennsylvania objected that Delaware Valley was seeking compensation for work done in only tangentially related state and federal administrative proceedings. The District Court rejected this argument, and found that because the proposed regulations would have affected Delaware Valley's rights under the consent decree, it had a unique interest in the proceedings that made its work sufficiently related to the litigation to be compensable.

After determining the "lodestar" amounts for all phases of the litigation, the court next considered Delaware Valley's request for "multipliers" to adjust these figures for "the contingent nature of the case, the quality of the work performed and the results obtained." Given that the case involved new legal theories with little precedent, and that Delaware Valley was

---

thority to implement an I/M program. On appeal, Delaware Valley submitted an *amicus* brief supporting the Commonwealth. The Pennsylvania Supreme Court determined that state officials had no authority to enter into the federal consent decree in 1978, held the decree to be a "nullity," and remanded the case to the Commonwealth Court, which later enjoined PennDOT from following the terms of the decree. The Commonwealth then moved to vacate the consent decree pursuant to Federal Rule of Civil Procedure 60(b). The District Court denied the motion, and the Court of Appeals affirmed.

2. In determining the lodestar amounts, the District Court eliminated more than one-third of all of the hours submitted by Delaware Valley. Some of these hours were eliminated because they were not documented in sufficient detail. Additional hours were excluded because the court disallowed all time spent by attorneys in preparing for or in attending hearings in which another attorney for Delaware Valley was the principal advocate. The court also denied a certain number of hours for activities in related proceedings that it found were not necessary to protect Delaware Valley's rights under the consent decree. Finally, a significant number of hours were eliminated based on the court's conclusion that the time spent on the particular activity was "excessive," or that a less amount of time was "reasonable."

forced to go up against both the Federal Government and the Common-wealth of Pennsylvania to obtain the consent decree initially and then to protect it from being overturned, the court found "[t]he contingent nature of [Delaware Valley's] success [to have] been apparent throughout this litigation." The court also found that Delaware Valley's work during Phase V was "superior," and that an "[a]n increase based on the quality of work which culminated in an outstanding result is fully justified."

Accordingly, the District Court applied a multiplier of two to the awards in Phases IV, V, and VII to reflect the low likelihood of success Delaware Valley faced in those stages of the litigation. In addition, the court added a separate multiplier of two to Phase V to adjust the lodestar for the high quality of representation provided in that phase. The court's final calculation of the fee award for each of the nine phases was as follows:[3]

	Lodestar	Multiplier	Total
Phase I	$ 4,478.50	—	$ 4,478.50
Phase II	1,722.50	—	1,722.50
Phase III	1,745.00	—	1,745.00
Phase IV	36,711.50	2	73,423.00
Phase V	27,372.50	4	109,490.00
Phase VI	1,820.00	—	1,820.00
Phase VII	5,370.50	2	10,741.00
Phase VIII	1,560.00	—	1,560.00
Phase IX	1,453.00	—	1,453.00

The Court of Appeals for the Third Circuit affirmed....

....

... We ... affirm in part and reverse in part.

II

Section 304(d) of the Clean Air Act, 42 U.S.C. § 7604(d), provides, in pertinent part, as follows:

"The court, in issuing any final order in any action brought pursuant to subsection (a) of this section, may award costs of litigation (including reasonable attorney and expert witness fees) to any party, whenever the court determines such award is appropriate."

The Commonwealth argues that the plain language of the statute clearly limits the award of fees to "costs of litigation" for "action[s] brought" under the Act, and that the lower courts erred in awarding attorney's fees for Delaware Valley's activities in Phases II and IX, both of which involved the submission of comments on draft regulations to administrative agencies. The United States echoes these assertions, and contends that the "actions" contemplated by § 304(d) are judicial actions, not administrative proceedings. We reject these limiting constructions on the scope of § 304(d).

---

3. The District Court also awarded Delaware Valley an additional $3,380 in legal fees for the work done preparing the fee petition itself.

Although it is true that the proceedings involved in Phases II and IX were not "judicial" in the sense that they did not occur in a courtroom or involve "traditional" legal work such as examination of witnesses or selection of jurors for trial, the work done by counsel in these two phases was as necessary to the attainment of adequate relief for their client as was all of their earlier work in the courtroom which secured Delaware Valley's initial success in obtaining the consent decree. This case did not involve a single tortious act by the Commonwealth that resulted in a discrete injury to Delaware Valley, nor was the harm alleged the kind that could be remedied by a mere award of damages or the entry of declaratory relief. Instead, Delaware Valley filed suit to force the Commonwealth to comply with its obligations under the Clean Air Act to develop and implement an emissions inspection and maintenance program covering 10 counties surrounding two major metropolitan areas. To this end, the consent decree provided detailed instructions as to how the program was to be developed and the specific dates by which these tasks were to be accomplished.

Protection of the full scope of relief afforded by the consent decree was thus crucial to safeguard the interests asserted by Delaware Valley; and enforcement of the decree, whether in the courtroom before a judge, or in front of a regulatory agency with power to modify the substance of the program ordered by the court, involved the type of work which is properly compensable as a cost of litigation under § 304. In a case of this kind, measures necessary to enforce the remedy ordered by the District Court cannot be divorced from the matters upon which Delaware Valley prevailed in securing the consent decree.

Several courts have held that, in the context of the Civil Rights Attorney's Fees Awards Act of 1976, 42 U.S.C. § 1988, post-judgment monitoring of a consent decree is a compensable activity for which counsel is entitled to a reasonable fee. Although § 1988 authorizes fees in "any action or proceeding" brought to enforce the Civil Rights Acts, and § 304(d) applies only to "any action" brought under the Clean Air Act, this distinction is not a sufficient indication that Congress intended § 304(d) to apply only to judicial, and not administrative, proceedings.

. . . .

Given the common purpose of both § 304(d) and § 1988 to promote citizen enforcement of important federal policies, we find no reason not to interpret both provisions governing attorney's fees in the same manner. We hold, therefore, that the fact that the work done by counsel in Phases II and IX did not occur in the context of traditional judicial litigation does not preclude an award of reasonable attorney's fees under § 304(d) for the work done during these portions of the present action.

This conclusion is consistent with our opinion in Webb v. Board of Ed. of Dyer County, 471 U.S. 234, 105 S.Ct. 1923, 85 L.Ed.2d 233 (1985). There, we noted that for the time spent pursuing optional administrative proceedings properly to be included in the calculation of a reasonable attorney's fee, the work must be "useful and of a type ordinarily necessary" to secure the final result obtained from the litigation. Application of this standard is left to the discretion of the district court.

Here, the District Court found that, as for Phase II, Delaware Valley had a unique interest in the proposed regulation "based on a desire to ensure compliance with the consent decree and to protect [its] rights thereunder. The usefulness of [Delaware Valley's] comments was manifested in the revisions that were made to the original regulations." Similarly, the court found that counsel's work during Phase IX helped to protect the relief awarded under the consent decree, as any modification of the I/M program by the Environmental Protection Agency would have adversely affected Delaware Valley's rights under the decree. We agree that participation in these administrative proceedings was crucial to the vindication of Delaware Valley's rights under the consent decree and find that compensation for these activities was entirely proper and well within the "zone of discretion" afforded the District Court. We thus affirm the award of fees for work done in Phases II and IX.

III

A

It is well established that, under the "American Rule," "the prevailing litigant is ordinarily not entitled to collect a reasonable attorneys' fee from the loser." There are exceptions to this principle, the major one being congressional authorization for the courts to require one party to award attorney's fees to the other. There are over 100 separate statutes providing for the award of attorney's fees; and although these provisions cover a wide variety of contexts and causes of action, the benchmark for the awards under nearly all of these statutes is that the attorney's fee must be "reasonable."

Courts have struggled to formulate the proper measure for determining the "reasonableness" of a particular fee award. One method, first employed by the Fifth Circuit in Johnson v. Georgia Highway Express, Inc., 488 F.2d 714 (1974), involved consideration of 12 factors.[7] *Johnson* was widely followed by other courts, and was cited with approval by both the House and the Senate when § 1988 was enacted into law.

This approach required trial courts to consider the elements that go into determining the propriety of legal fees and was intended to provide appellate courts with more substantial and objective records on which to review trial court determinations. This mode of analysis, however, was not without its shortcomings. Its major fault was that it gave very little actual guidance to district courts. Setting attorney's fees by reference to a series of sometimes subjective factors placed unlimited discretion in trial judges and produced disparate results.

---

7. The 12 factors are: (1) the time and labor required; (2) the novelty and difficulty of the question; (3) the skill requisite to perform the legal service properly; (4) the preclusion of other employment by the attorney due to acceptance of the case; (5) the customary fee; (6) whether the fee is fixed or contingent; (7) time limitations imposed by the client or the circumstances; (8) the amount involved and the results obtained; (9) the experience, reputation, and ability of the attorney; (10) the "undesirability" of the case; (11) the nature and length of the professional relationship with the client; and (12) awards in similar cases. These factors were taken from the American Bar Association Code of Professional Responsibility, Disciplinary Rule 2–106 (1980).

For this reason, the Third Circuit developed another method of calculating "reasonable" attorney's fees. This method, known as the "lodestar"
approach, involved two steps. First, the court was to calculate the "lodestar," determined by multiplying the hours spent on a case by a reasonable
hourly rate of compensation for each attorney involved. Second, using the
lodestar figure as a starting point, the court could then make adjustments
to this figure, in light of "(1) the contingent nature of the case, reflecting
the likelihood that hours were invested and expenses incurred without
assurance of compensation; and (2) the quality of the work performed as
evidenced by the work observed, the complexity of the issues and the
recovery obtained." This formulation emphasized the amount of time
expended by the attorneys, and provided a more analytical framework for
lower courts to follow than the unguided "factors" approach provided by
Johnson. On the other hand, allowing the courts to adjust the lodestar
amount based on considerations of the "riskiness" of the lawsuit and the
quality of the attorney's work could still produce inconsistent and arbitrary
fee awards.

We first addressed the question of the proper manner in which to
determine a "reasonable" attorney's fee in Hensley v. Eckerhart, 461 U.S.
424, 103 S.Ct. 1933, 76 L.Ed.2d 40 (1983). We there adopted a hybrid
approach that shared elements of both *Johnson* and the lodestar method of
calculation. "The most useful starting point for determining the amount of
a reasonable fee is the number of hours reasonably expended on the
litigation multiplied by a reasonable hourly rate. This calculation provides
an objective basis on which to make an initial estimate of the value of a
lawyer's services." To this extent, the method endorsed in *Hensley* follows
the Third Circuit's description of the first step of the lodestar approach.
Moreover, we went on to state: "The product of reasonable hours times a
reasonable rate does not end the inquiry. There remain other considerations that may lead the district court to adjust the fee upward or
downward...." We then took a more expansive view of what those "other
considerations" might be, however, noting that "[t]he district court also
may consider [the] factors identified in Johnson v. Georgia Highway
Express, Inc., 488 F.2d 714, 717–719 (C.A.5 1974), though it should note
that many of these factors usually are subsumed within the initial calculation of hours reasonably expended at a reasonable hourly rate."

We further refined our views in Blum v. Stenson, 465 U.S. 886, 104
S.Ct. 1541, 79 L.Ed.2d 891 (1984). *Blum* restated that the proper first step
in determining a reasonable attorney's fee is to multiply "the number of
hours reasonably expended on the litigation times a reasonable hourly
rate." We emphasized, however, that the figure resulting from this calculation is more than a mere "rough guess" or initial approximation of the
final award to be made. Instead, we found that "[w]hen ... the applicant
for a fee has carried his burden of showing that the claimed rate and
number of hours are reasonable, the resulting product *is presumed* to be
the reasonable fee" to which counsel is entitled.

Blum also limited the factors which a district court may consider in
determining whether to make adjustments to the lodestar amount. Expanding on our earlier finding in *Hensley* that many of the *Johnson* factors "are

subsumed within the initial calculation" of the lodestar, we specifically held in *Blum* that the "novelty [and] complexity of the issues," "the special skill and experience of counsel," the "quality of representation," and the "results obtained" from the litigation are presumably fully reflected in the lodestar amount, and thus cannot serve as independent bases for increasing the basic fee award. Although upward adjustments of the lodestar figure are still permissible, such modifications are proper only in certain "rare" and "exceptional" cases, supported by both "specific evidence" on the record and detailed findings by the lower courts.

A strong presumption that the lodestar figure—the product of reasonable hours times a reasonable rate—represents a "reasonable" fee is wholly consistent with the rationale behind the usual fee-shifting statute, including the one in the present case. These statutes were not designed as a form of economic relief to improve the financial lot of attorneys, nor were they intended to replicate exactly the fee an attorney could earn through a private fee arrangement with his client. Instead, the aim of such statutes was to enable private parties to obtain legal help in seeking redress for injuries resulting from the actual or threatened violation of specific federal laws. Hence, if plaintiffs, such as Delaware Valley, find it possible to engage a lawyer based on the statutory assurance that he will be paid a "reasonable fee," the purpose behind the fee-shifting statute has been satisfied.

Moreover, when an attorney first accepts a case and agrees to represent the client, he obligates himself to perform to the best of his ability and to produce the best possible results commensurate with his skill and his client's interests. Calculating the fee award in a manner that accounts for these factors, either in determining the reasonable number of hours expended on the litigation or in setting the reasonable hourly rate, thus adequately compensates the attorney, and leaves very little room for enhancing the award based on his post-engagement performance. In short, the lodestar figure includes most, if not all, of the relevant factors constituting a "reasonable" attorney's fee, and it is unnecessary to enhance the fee for superior performance in order to serve the statutory purpose of enabling plaintiffs to secure legal assistance.

B

With this teaching from our prior cases in mind, we sustain the Commonwealth's contention that the lower courts erred in increasing the fee award to Delaware Valley in Phase V based on the "superior quality" of counsel's performance. . . .

. . . Because considerations concerning the quality of a prevailing party's counsel's representation normally are reflected in the reasonable hourly rate, the overall quality of performance ordinarily should not be used to adjust the lodestar, thus removing any danger of "double counting."

Furthermore, we are unpersuaded that the lodestar amount determined for Phase V in this case did not fully reflect the quality and competence of the legal services rendered by Delaware Valley's lawyers. For this portion of the litigation, counsel sought compensation for approximately 620 hours of work. Of these, the District Court allowed compensation for

324 hours. The District Court's elimination of a large number of hours on the grounds that they were unnecessary, unreasonable, or unproductive is not supportive of the court's later conclusion that the remaining hours represented work of "superior quality."

We also note that of the 324 hours compensated, 26 hours were compensated at $25 per hour, 88 hours were billed at an hourly rate of $65, and the remaining 210 hours were paid at $100 per hour.... Given that nearly one-third of all of the hours reasonably spent on this phase were not compensated at the hourly rate for work which the court found to be "most difficult," it is hard to see what made the quality of representation for those hours so "superior" that it was not reflected in the hourly rate used to determine the lodestar amount. This conclusion is reinforced by the fact that the Third Circuit expressly found that the $100 hourly rate for the attorney compensated for the 210 hours was "plainly appropriate" given that he was an "inexperienced attorne[y]" without "any prior significant litigation experience."

In sum, viewing the evidence submitted by Delaware Valley to support its petition for attorney's fees, there is no indication as to why the lodestar did not provide a reasonable fee award reflecting the quality of representation provided during Phase V of the litigation. Clearly, Delaware Valley was able to obtain counsel without any promise of reward for extraordinary performance. Furthermore, Delaware Valley presented no specific evidence as to what made the results it obtained during this phase so "outstanding," nor did it provide any indication that the lodestar figure for this portion of the case was far below awards made in similar cases where the court found equally superior quality of performance. Finally, neither the District Court nor the Court of Appeals made detailed findings as to why the lodestar amount was unreasonable, and in particular, as to why the quality of representation was not reflected in the product of the reasonable number of hours times the reasonable hourly rate. In the absence of such evidence and such findings, we find no reason to increase the fee award in Phase V for the quality of representation.

IV

There remains the question of upward adjustment, by way of multipliers or enhancement of the lodestar, based on the likelihood of success, or to put it another way, the risk of loss. This is the question that we left open in *Blum* and on which the Courts of Appeals are not entirely in accord. We are of the view that our resolution of the issue would be benefited by reargument and hence we do not decide it now. Accordingly, an order will issue restoring the case to the argument docket insofar as it raises the question whether attorney's fees chargeable to a losing defendant under the Clean Air Act and the comparable statutes may be enhanced based on the risk of loss, and if so, to what extent.

The judgment below is therefore affirmed insofar as it upheld the award of attorney's fees for the work done in Phases II and IX and, except for the multiplier for risk, is otherwise reversed.

It is so ordered.

■ JUSTICE BLACKMUN, with whom JUSTICE MARSHALL joins, and with whom JUSTICE BRENNAN joins ..., concurring in part and dissenting in part.

. . . .

I join only Parts I and II of the Court's opinion. In Part III, the Court purports to follow Blum v. Stenson, 465 U.S. 886, 104 S.Ct. 1541, 79 L.Ed.2d 891 (1984), in which we held that an adjustment for quality was available "in the rare case where the fee applicant offers specific evidence to show that the quality of service rendered was superior to that one reasonably should expect in light of the hourly rates charged and that the success was 'exceptional.'" The Court today, however, improperly heightens the showing required to the point where it may be virtually impossible for a plaintiff to meet.

Although the District Court's decision was issued before *Blum,* its quality adjustment in Phase V was in full accord with the standards subsequently laid down in *Blum.* The proper standard of review of an attorney's fee award is abuse of discretion. I do not think the District Court abused its discretion in multiplying by two the lodestar for Phase V in order to adjust for quality. If the majority applied the proper, deferential standard of review on the quality issue rather than substituting its judgment for that of the District Court, it may have reached the same result as I do.

Pennsylvania v. Delaware Valley Citizens' Council for Clean Air

Supreme Court of the United States, 1987.
483 U.S. 711, 107 S.Ct. 3078, 97 L.Ed.2d 585.

■ JUSTICE WHITE announced the judgment of the Court and delivered an opinion, Parts I, II, and III–A of which represent the views of the Court, and Parts III–B, IV, and V of which are joined by THE CHIEF JUSTICE, JUSTICE POWELL, and JUSTICE SCALIA.

. . . .

... The issue before us is whether, when a plaintiff prevails, its attorney should or may be awarded separate compensation for assuming the risk of not being paid. That risk is measured by the risk of losing rather than winning and depends on how unsettled the applicable law is with respect to the issues posed by the case and by how likely it is that the facts could be decided against the complainant. Looked at in this way, there are various factors that have little or no bearing on the question before us.

First is the matter of delay. When plaintiffs' entitlement to attorney's fees depends on success, their lawyers are not paid until a favorable decision finally eventuates, which may be years later, as in this case. Meanwhile, their expenses of doing business continue and must be met. In setting fees for prevailing counsel, the courts have regularly recognized the delay factor, either by basing the award on current rates or by adjusting the fee based on historical rates to reflect its present value. Although delay and the risk of nonpayment are often mentioned in the same breath, adjusting for the former is a distinct issue that is not involved in this case.

We do not suggest, however, that adjustments for delay are inconsistent with the typical fee-shifting statute.

Second, that a case involves an issue of public importance, that the plaintiff's position is unpopular in the community, or that defendant is difficult or obstreperous does not enter into assessing the risk of loss or determining whether that risk should be compensated. Neither does the chance that the court will find unnecessary and not compensate some of the time and effort spent on prosecuting the case.

Third, when the plaintiff has agreed to pay its attorney, win or lose, the attorney has not assumed the risk of nonpayment and there is no occasion to adjust the lodestar fee because the case was a risky one....

III

. . . .

B

... Neither the Clean Air Act nor § 1988 expressly provides for using the risk of loss as an independent basis for increasing an otherwise reasonable fee, and it is doubtful that the legislative history supports the use of this factor. In concluding that risk-enhancement is authorized, Justice Brennan[, concurring] in *Blum,* relied on the fact that one of the items to be relied on in setting a fee and enumerated in Johnson v. Georgia Highway Express, Inc., 488 F.2d 714 (C.A.5 1974), is whether the fee is fixed or contingent, and that Congress endorsed consideration of this factor. But a careful reading of *Johnson* shows that the contingency factor was meant to focus judicial scrutiny solely on the existence of any contract for attorney's fees which may have been executed between the party and his attorney. "The fee quoted to the client or the percentage of the recovery agreed to is helpful in demonstrating that attorney's fee expectations when he accepted the case." At most, therefore, *Johnson* suggests that the nature of the fee contract between the client and his attorney should be taken into account when determining the reasonableness of a fee award, but there is nothing in *Johnson* to show that this factor was meant to reflect the contingent nature of prevailing in the lawsuit as a whole.

... Given the divergence in both analysis and result between [the other] three cases [cited approvingly by Congress], the legislative history is, at best, inconclusive in determining whether Congress endorsed the concept of increasing the lodestar amount to reflect the risk of not prevailing on the merits.

We must nevertheless come to decision and have concluded that the judgment must be reversed.

IV

We are impressed with the view of the Court of Appeals for the District of Columbia Circuit that enhancing fees for risk of loss forces losing defendants to compensate plaintiff's lawyers for not prevailing against defendants in other cases. This result is not consistent with Congress' decision to adopt the rule that only prevailing parties are entitled to fees. If risk multipliers or enhancement are viewed as no more than compensating attorneys for their willingness to take the risk of loss and of nonpayment, we are nevertheless not at all sure that Congress intended that fees be denied when a plaintiff loses, but authorized payment for assuming the risk of an uncompensated loss. Such enhancement also penalizes the defendants who have the strongest case; and in theory, at least, would authorize the highest fees in cases least likely to be won and hence encourage the bringing of more risky cases, especially by lawyers whose time is not fully occupied with other work. Because it is difficult ever to be completely sure that a case will be won, enhancing fees for the assumption of the risk of nonpayment would justify some degree of enhancement in almost every case.

Weighing all of these considerations, we are unconvinced that Congress intended the risk of losing a lawsuit to be an independent basis for increasing the amount of any otherwise reasonable fee for the time and effort expended in prevailing. As the Senate Report observed: "In computing the fee, counsel for prevailing parties should be paid, as is traditional with attorneys compensated by a fee-paying client, 'for all time reasonably expended on a matter.' " S.Rep. 6, U.S.Code Cong. & Admin.News 1976, p. 5913.

The contrary argument is that without the promise of multipliers or enhancement for risk-taking, attorneys will not take cases for clients who cannot pay, and the fee-shifting statutes will therefore not serve their purpose. We agree that a fundamental aim of such statutes is to make it possible for those who cannot pay a lawyer for his time and effort to obtain competent counsel, this by providing lawyers with reasonable fees to be paid by the losing defendants. But it does not follow that fee enhancement for risk is necessary or allowable. Surely that is not the case where plaintiffs can afford to pay and have agreed to pay, win or lose. The same is true where any plaintiff, impecunious or otherwise, has a damages case that competent lawyers would take in the absence of fee-shifting statutes. Nor is it true in those cases where plaintiffs secure help from organizations whose very purpose is to provide legal help through salaried counsel to those who themselves cannot afford to pay a lawyer. It is also unlikely to be true in any market where there are competent lawyers whose time is not fully occupied by other matters.

The issue thus involves damages cases that lawyers would not take, not because they are too risky (the fee-shifting statutes should not encourage such suits to be brought), but because the damages likely to be recovered are not sufficient to provide adequate compensation to counsel, as well as those frequent cases in which the goal is to secure injunctive relief to the exclusion of any claim for damages. In both situations, the fee-shifting statutes guarantee reasonable payment for the time and effort expended if the case is won. Respondent's position is that without the prospect of being awarded fees exceeding such reasonable payment, plaintiffs with such cases will be unable to secure the help that the statutes aimed to provide.

We are not persuaded that this will be the case. Indeed, it may well be that using a contingency enhancement is superfluous and unnecessary under the lodestar approach to setting a fee. The reasons a particular lawsuit are considered to be "risky" for an attorney are because of the novelty and difficulty of the issues presented, and because of the potential for protracted litigation. Moreover, when an attorney ultimately prevails in such a lawsuit, this success will be primarily attributable to his legal skills and experience, and to the hours of hard work he devoted to the case. These factors, however, are considered by the court in determining the reasonable number of hours expended and the reasonable hourly rate for the lodestar, and any further increase in this sum based on the risk of not prevailing would result not in a "reasonable" attorney's fee, but in a windfall for an attorney who prevailed in a difficult case.

It may be that without the promise of risk enhancement some lawyers will decline to take cases; but we doubt that the bar in general will so often be unable to respond that the goal of the fee-shifting statutes will not be achieved. In any event, risk enhancement involves difficulties in administration and possible inequities to those who must pay attorney's fees; and in the absence of further legislative guidance, we conclude that multipliers or other enhancement of a reasonable lodestar fee to compensate for assuming the risk of loss is impermissible under the usual fee-shifting statutes.

Even if § 304(d) and other typical fee-shifting statutes are construed to permit supplementing the lodestar in appropriate cases by paying counsel for assuming the risk of nonpayment, for the reasons set out below, it was error to do so in this case.

V

Section 304(d), like § 1988, does not indicate that adjustment for risk should be the rule rather than the exception; neither does it require such an adjustment in any case. At most, it leaves the matter of risk-enhancement to the informed discretion of the courts. There are, however, severe difficulties and possible inequities involved in making upward adjustments for assuming the risk of nonpayment, and we deem it appropriate, in order to guide the exercise of the trial courts' discretion in awarding fees, to adopt here the approach followed in *Blum* in dealing with other multipliers. As in that case, payment for the time and effort involved—the lodestar—is presumed to be the reasonable fee authorized by the statute, and enhancement for the risk of nonpayment should be reserved for exceptional cases where the need and justification for such enhancement are readily apparent and are supported by evidence in the record and specific findings by the courts. For several reasons, the circumstances of this case do not justify the risk multiplier employed by the District Court.

... This case ... concerns only the reasonable fee for work done after the consent decree was entered, and fees have already been awarded for work done before that time. The risk of nonpayment should be determined at the beginning of the litigation. Whatever counsel thought the risk of losing was at the outset, it is doubtful that counsel anticipated a similar risk in enforcing a decree if plaintiff was successful in having one entered. In any event, the District Court did not specifically identify any new and novel issues, and we fail to discern any, that emerged in the long process of enforcing the court decree in accordance with its terms. And whether the

Commonwealth of Pennsylvania was a substantial opponent or whether it tried to circumvent the decree has little or nothing to do with whether there was a real risk of not persuading the District Court to enforce its own decree. The matter may have been difficult, wearing and time consuming, but that kind of effort has been recognized in the lodestar award.

Second, if it be assumed that this is one of the exceptional cases in which enhancement for assuming the risk of nonpayment is justified, we conclude that doubling the lodestar for certain phases of the work was excessive. We have alluded to the uncertainties involved in determining the risk of not prevailing and the burdensome nature of fee litigation. We deem it desirable and an appropriate application of the statute to hold that if the trial court specifically finds that there was a real risk of not prevailing issue in the case, an upward adjustment of the lodestar may be made, but, as a general rule, in an amount no more than ⅓ of the lodestar. Any additional adjustment would require the most exacting justification. This limitation will at once protect against windfalls for attorneys and act as some deterrence against bringing suits in which the attorney believes there is less than a 50–50 chance of prevailing. Riskier suits may be brought, and if won, a reasonable lodestar may be awarded, but risk enhancement will be limited to ⅓ of the lodestar, if awarded at all. Here, even assuming an adjustment for risk was justified, the multiplier employed was excessive.

Third: Whatever the risk of winning or losing in a specific case might be, a fee award should be informed by the statutory purpose of making it possible for poor clients with good claims to secure competent help. Before adjusting for risk assumption, there should be evidence in the record, and the trial court should so find, that without risk-enhancement plaintiff would have faced substantial difficulties in finding counsel in the local or other relevant market. Here, there were no such findings.

Accordingly, the judgment of the Court of Appeals is

Reversed.

■ JUSTICE O'CONNOR, concurring in part and concurring in the judgment.

For the reasons explained by the dissent I conclude that Congress did not intend to foreclose consideration of contingency in setting a reasonable fee under fee-shifting provisions such as that of the Clean Air Act, 42 U.S.C. § 7604(d), and the Civil Rights Attorney's Fees Awards Act, 42 U.S.C. § 1988. I also agree that compensation for contingency must be based on the difference in market treatment of contingent fee cases *as a class*, rather than on an assessment of the "riskiness" of any particular case. But in my view the plurality is also correct in holding that the "novelty and difficulty of the issues presented, and ... the potential for protracted litigation," are factors adequately reflected in the lodestar, and that the District Court erred in employing a risk multiplier in the circumstances of this case.

The private market commonly compensates for contingency through arrangements in which the attorney receives a percentage of the damages awarded to the plaintiff. In most fee-shifting cases, however, the private market model of contingency compensation will provide very little guidance. Thus it is unsurprising that when courts have enhanced fee awards to compensate for risk, "[p]inpointing the degree of risk [has been] one of the most subjective and difficult components of the fee computation process, and one which [has been] apt to lead to imprecision in the final award." 2 M. Derfner & A. Wolf, Court Awarded Attorney Fees, ¶ 16.04[c][i], p. 16–88 (1986). Although the dissent suggests a method of calculating compensation for contingency that is theoretically more satisfying than the practice of speculating on the riskiness of each case, the dissent does not explain how the theory should be put into practice. For example, how should a court translate the extra economic risk endured by smaller firms, or by firms that take unpopular cases, into a percentage enhancement?

Moreover, although the dissent offers no defense of this method of compensating for risk, it leaves the door open for "extra enhancement" for "exceptional cases" that pose great " 'legal' risk." The "extra enhancement" presumably would be calculated based on the likelihood at the time the litigation was commenced that the particular legal claims raised by the prevailing party would have been rejected by the court. This type of enhancement clearly is subject to the many difficulties described by the plurality. The dissent suggests that the plurality's objections "lose much of their force" because the cases in which "extra enhancement" is granted will be rare. But, an arbitrary or unjust result is no less so for its rarity. Furthermore, the difficulties created by this type of enhancement will arise not only when the enhancement is granted, but also whenever it is sought.

To be "reasonable," the method for calculating a fee award must be not merely justifiable in theory but also objective and nonarbitrary in practice. Moreover, if the concept of treating contingency cases as a class is to be more than symbolic, a court's determination of how the market in a community compensates for contingency should not vary significantly from one case to the next. I agree with the plurality that without guidance as to the trial court's exercise of discretion, adjustment for risk could result in "severe difficulties and possible inequities." In my view, certain constraints on a court's discretion in setting attorney's fees are appropriate.

First, District Courts and Courts of Appeals should treat a determination of how a particular market compensates for contingency as controlling future cases involving the same market. Haphazard and widely divergent compensation for risk can be avoided only if contingency cases are treated as a class; and contingency cases can be treated as a class only if courts strive for consistency from one fee determination to the next. Determinations involving different markets should also comport with each other. Thus, if a fee applicant attempts to prove that the relevant market provides greater compensation for contingency than the markets involved in previous cases, the applicant should be able to point to differences in the markets that would justify the different rates of compensation.

Second, at all times the fee applicant bears the burden of proving the degree to which the relevant market compensates for contingency. I would also hold that a court may not enhance a fee award any more than necessary to bring the fee within the range that would attract competent counsel. I agree with the plurality that no enhancement for risk is appropriate unless the applicant can establish that without an adjustment for risk the prevailing party "would have faced substantial difficulties in finding counsel in the local or other relevant market."

Finally, a court should not award any enhancement based on "legal" risks or risks peculiar to the case. The lodestar ... is flexible enough to account for great variation in the nature of the work performed in, and the challenges presented by, different cases.... Thus it is presumed that when counsel demonstrates considerable ability in overcoming unusual difficulties that have arisen in a case, counsel will be compensated for those accomplishments by means of an appropriate hourly rate multiplied by the hours expended.

Based on the above guidelines, the enhancement for risk awarded by the District Court in this case must be reversed. The enhancement is not supported by any findings of fact concerning the degree to which contingency is compensated in the relevant market. Neither the findings nor the evidence indicate that the large enhancements in this case were necessary to attract competent counsel in the relevant community. Moreover, it is clear that the District Court based the enhancement on "legal" risks and risks unique to the case. The considerations used by the District Court to justify the enhancement—the "new and novel issues" raised by the case, and the stubbornness of the defendants—should already be reflected in the number of hours expended and the hourly rate, and cannot be used again to increase the fee award.

Accordingly, I concur in parts I, II, and III–A of the plurality and concur in the judgment reversing the judgment of the Court of Appeals.

■ JUSTICE BLACKMUN, with whom JUSTICE BRENNAN, JUSTICE MARSHALL, and JUSTICE STEVENS join, dissenting.

... By not allowing an upward adjustment for a case taken on a contingent basis, the plurality undermines the basic purpose of statutory attorney fees—ensuring that "private citizens ... have a meaningful opportunity to vindicate the important Congressional policies which these laws contain." S.Rep. No. 94–1011, p. 2 (1976).

I

A

In the private market, lawyers charge a premium when their entire fee is contingent on winning....

The premium added for contingency compensates for the *risk* of nonpayment if the suit does not succeed and for the *delay* in payment until the end of the litigation—factors not faced by a lawyer paid promptly as litigation progresses. All else being equal, attorneys naturally will prefer cases where they will be paid regardless of the outcome, rather than cases where they will be paid only if they win. Cases of the latter type are inherently riskier and an attorney properly may expect greater compensation for their successful prosecution.

. . . .

B

In directing courts to award a "reasonable" attorney's fee to a litigant who vindicates various statutory rights, e.g., 42 U.S.C. § 7604(d)(Clean Air Act), Congress made clear that the winning lawyer should be paid at a rate that is basically competitive with what the lawyer is able to earn in other cases. Congress' purpose—extensively described in the legislative history of the Civil Rights Attorney's Fees Awards Act, 42 U.S.C. § 1988, but fully applicable to statutes that protect the environment—was to encourage the enforcement of federal law through lawsuits filed by private persons. Congress found that the market itself would not provide an adequate supply of interested lawyers because many potential plaintiffs lacked sufficient funds to hire such lawyers. Thus, fee awards were considered to be "an essential remedy" in order to encourage enforcement of the law. And unless the fee reimbursement was "full and complete," the statutory rights would be meaningless because they would remain largely unenforced.

. . . .

Congress found that a broad variety of factors go into the computation of a "reasonable" attorney's fee. One such consideration is the contingency that the attorney will be paid only if he wins the case. Three of the four major cases cited as examples of "the appropriate standards . . . correctly applied," S.Rep. No. 94–1011, at 6, . . . mentioned this risk as a factor for a court to weigh. . . .

As courts have gained more experience with fee calculations, many have begun to utilize as a "lodestar" the reasonable hours worked multiplied by a reasonable hourly rate. The lodestar, however, was designed to simplify, not to circumvent, application of the *Johnson* factors where appropriate. Thus, a statutory fee cannot be computed solely by reference to rates charged by corporate firms, which obtain many payments from their clients through monthly billings. Rather, in order to arrive at a "reasonable" attorney's fee, a court must incorporate a premium for the risk of nonrecovery, for the delay in payment, and for any economic risks aggravated by the contingency of payment, at a level similar to the premium incorporated in market rates. The risk premium can be reflected in the hourly rate that goes into the lodestar calculation, or, if the hourly rate does not include consideration of risk, in an enhancement of the lodestar. Under either approach, adding a premium simply brings the fee up to the "reasonable" level contemplated by Congress.

An adjustment for contingency is necessary if statutory fees are to be competitive with the private market and if competent lawyers are to be attracted in their private practice to prosecute statutory violations. This is simply the law of supply and demand. . . .

. . . .

C

If it were the law of the land, the plurality's decision, in Part IV of its opinion, to foreclose any compensation for the risk of nonrecovery would reduce statutory fees below the market rate and inevitably would obstruct the vindication of federal rights. Because fewer lawyers would be attracted to the work, some persons who now are able to bring valid claims would be unable to find a lawyer. They likely would be persons of modest means who could not afford to augment their lawyer's fee to what the market would charge—precisely the persons Congress sought to assist. Even plaintiffs who somehow could manage to attract lawyers at below the market rate usually would get what they pay for: lawyers who are less than fully employed or who are less capable.... As Congress recognized, effective enforcement of complex cases requires the services of experienced attorneys. Such lawyers are less likely to be underemployed. They therefore will tend to demand rates approaching what can be obtained in the private sector.

The plurality offers assurances that enforcement would not end completely because public interest groups would still take these cases.... But it is unrealistic to think that 600 public-interest lawyers in 90 public-interest law centers around the country would be able to pick up the slack from the rest of the bar, with its approximately 400,000 lawyers....

Significantly, the plurality's opinion would validate payment of public-interest lawyers at substantially less than what would be competitive with the private market. In *Blum,* however, this Court made clear that nonprofit legal-aid organizations should receive no less in fee awards than the hourly rate set by the private market for an attorney's services. The plurality today attempts to accomplish indirectly what the Court refused to do directly in *Blum.*

The plurality further defends its approach by asserting that plaintiffs bringing large damages claims could continue to attract private lawyers. But those plaintiffs might be able to hire counsel in any event through private contingency arrangements. Congress provided for fee-shifting precisely because it concluded that too many plaintiffs would be unable to obtain representation in this manner. The plurality's solution would slight actions that seek injunctive relief or relatively small damages awards, on which the vindication of many federal rights depends.

II

In view of Congress' desire that statutory fees be competitive with the private market, the plurality needs a compelling reason in order to reject the market approach for determining what constitutes a reasonable fee. Although the plurality suggests some reasons, its objections are all based on a fundamental mischaracterization of the enhancement for contingency in awarding attorney's fees....

The underlying flaw in all of these objections is that the appropriate enhancement for risk does not depend, in the first instance, on the *degree* of risk presented by a particular case. Enhancement for risk is not designed to equalize the prospective returns among contingent cases with different degrees of merit. Rather, it is designed simply to place contingent employment *as a whole* on roughly the same economic footing as noncontingent practice, in order that such cases receive the equal representation intended by Congress.

Once it is recognized that it is the fact of contingency, not the likelihood of success in any particular case, that mandates an increase in an attorney's fee, the frightening difficulties envisioned by the plurality disappear.... Rather, a court's job simply will be to determine whether a case was taken on a contingent basis, whether the attorney was able to mitigate the risk of nonpayment in any way, and whether other economic risks were aggravated by the contingency of payment....

. . . .

In most cases in which an enhancement for contingency is sought, therefore, a court will not need to inquire into the relative likelihood of success of the particular case before it. It is possible, however, that in a few, unusual cases the likelihood of success may appropriately be taken into account. Sometimes, the "legal" risks facing a case may be so apparent and significant that they will constitute an economic disincentive independent of that created by the basic contingency in payment. When the result achieved in such a case is significant and of broad public interest, an additional enhancement is justified in order to attract attorneys to take such cases, which otherwise might suffer from lack of representation. Extra enhancement for such cases, however, should be awarded in exceptional cases only. In most cases where the "legal" risks are high, and the case therefore novel and difficult, attorneys may be expected to spend a greater number of hours preparing and litigating the case. Courts should consider this seriously in determining the number of "reasonable" hours to be incorporated in the lodestar and should be careful not to reduce unduly the number of hours in a novel and difficult case. If a court finds, however, that an attorney has taken a significant legal risk in a case of important public interest, and that this risk has not been compensated adequately by the court in the number of hours represented in the lodestar, the court may then grant an enhancement above that awarded for the basic contingency risk. In such a case, the court must make detailed findings regarding the particular legal risks that were apparent at the outset of the litigation and the importance of the result obtained—findings that would justify the additional enhancement.

Almost all of the plurality's objections to enhancements for contingency become irrelevant once such enhancement is seen, as a general matter, to be completely independent from the likelihood of success in particular cases. Under the approach outlined above, there is no reason for a court to assess the success of a case retroactively, no cause for a conflict of interest to arise between attorney and client, and no possibility of a grant of huge multipliers simply because the odds against a case were significant. The only remaining objection is that awarding higher fees to lawyers who accept contingent cases gives such lawyers the economic stability with which to bring other, possibly unsuccessful, lawsuits. In the plurality's view, this contravenes Congress' intent to award attorney's fees only to prevailing parties. But this objection must ultimately fail. The fact is that an attorney still recovers fees only when that attorney's client prevails in a lawsuit.... That the attorney may use the fees obtained in the successful contingency lawsuit to bring other lawsuits—some of which will not be successful—does not contravene in any way Congress' mandate that fees be awarded solely to prevailing parties.... As in the private market, what a successful attorney does with earned fees is the attorney's own business.

. . . .

III

. . . .

I conclude that we should vacate the award and remand the case to the District Court for further findings. First, as I have explained, the District Court should determine whether respondent's attorneys took this case on a contingent basis, whether they were able to mitigate the risks of nonpayment in any way, and whether other economic risks were aggravated by the contingency of payment. The court then should arrive at an enhancement for risk that parallels, as closely as possible, the premium for contingency that exists in prevailing market rates. The court should thereby arrive at an enhancement that appropriately compensates the attorneys for the risks assumed.

Second, the court might also determine whether this case deserves an extra enhancement because of the significant legal risks apparent at the outset of the litigation and because of the importance of the case. I would note, however, that respondent's attorneys began this litigation in order to enforce a consent decree—a situation that does not usually entail difficult legal risks. If the District Court were to believe that the case nonetheless did involve significant legal risks at the outset of the litigation, it would make specific findings to that effect and would not simply state that the "case involved new and novel issues."

. . . .

I respectfully dissent.

NOTES ON FEES FOR LAW CLERKS, PARALEGALS AND EXPERTS

1. In Missouri v. Jenkins, 491 U.S. 274, 109 S.Ct. 2463, 105 L.Ed.2d 229 (1989), the Court ruled that the "reasonable attorney's fee" recoverable under Section 1988 includes separately billed paralegal and law clerk time.

... Clearly, a "reasonable attorney's fee" cannot have been meant to compensate only work performed personally by members of the bar. Rather, the term must refer to a reasonable fee for the work product of an attorney. Thus, the fee must take into account the work not only of attorneys, but also of secretaries, messengers, librarians, janitors, and others whose labor contributes to the work product for which an attorney bills her client; and it must also take account of other expenses and profit. The parties have suggested no reason why the work of [law clerks and] paralegals should not be similarly compensated, nor can we think of any. We thus take as our starting point the self-evident proposition that the "reasonable attorney's fee" provided for by statute should compensate the work of [law clerks and] paralegals, as well as that of attorneys....

2.   In West Virginia University Hospitals, Inc. v. Casey, 499 U.S. 83, 111 S.Ct. 1138, 113 L.Ed.2d 68 (1991), the Court ruled that fees paid to experts who aid in the preparation of, or testify in, civil rights suits are not recoverable under Section 1988. The six-Justice majority distinguished *Jenkins* in this manner:

> ... It was not remotely plain in *Jenkins* that the phrase "attorney's fee" did not include charges for law-clerk and paralegal services. Such services, like the services of "secretaries, messengers, librarians, janitors, and others whose labor contributes to the work product," had traditionally been included in calculation of the lawyers' hourly rates. Only recently had there arisen "the 'increasingly widespread custom of separately billing for [such] services.'" By contrast, there has never been, to our knowledge, a practice of including the cost of expert services within attorneys' hourly rates. There was also no record in *Jenkins*—as there is a lengthy record here—of statutory usage that recognizes a distinction between the charges at issue and attorney's fees.... In other words, *Jenkins* involved a respect in which the term "attorney's fees" (giving the losing argument the benefit of the doubt) was genuinely ambiguous; and we resolved that ambiguity not by invoking some policy that supersedes the text of the statute, but by concluding that charges of this sort had traditionally been included in attorney's fees, and that separate billing should make no difference. The term's application to expert fees is not ambiguous; and if it were the means of analysis employed in *Jenkins* would lead to the conclusion that since such fees have not traditionally been included within the attorney's hourly rate they are not attorney's fees.

City of Riverside v. Rivera

Supreme Court of the United States, 1986.
477 U.S. 561, 106 S.Ct. 2686, 91 L.Ed.2d 466.

■ JUSTICE BRENNAN announced the judgment of the Court and delivered an opinion in which JUSTICE MARSHALL, JUSTICE BLACKMUN, and JUSTICE STEVENS join.

The issue presented in this case is whether an award of attorney's fees under 42 U.S.C. § 1988 is *per se* "unreasonable" within the meaning of the statute if it exceeds the amount of damages recovered by the plaintiff in the underlying civil rights action.

I

Respondents, eight Chicano individuals, attended a party on the evening of August 1, 1975, at the Riverside, California, home of respondents Santos and Jennie Rivera. A large number of unidentified police officers, acting without a warrant, broke up the party using tear gas and, as found by the District Court, "unnecessary physical force." Many of the guests, including four of the respondents, were arrested. The District Court later found that "[t]he party was not creating a disturbance in the community at the time of the break-in." Criminal charges against the arrestees were ultimately dismissed for lack of probable cause.

On June 4, 1976, respondents sued the city of Riverside, its chief of police, and 30 individual police officers under 42 U.S.C. §§ 1981, 1983, 1985(3), and 1986 for allegedly violating their First, Fourth, and Fourteenth Amendment rights. The complaint, which also alleged numerous state-law claims, sought damages, and declaratory and injunctive relief.... The jury returned a total of 37 individual verdicts in favor of the respondents and against the city and five individual officers, finding 11 violations of § 1983, four instances of false arrest and imprisonment, and 22 instances of negligence. Respondents were awarded $33,350 in compensatory and punitive damages: $13,300 for their federal claims, and $20,050 for their state-law claims.

Respondents also sought attorney's fees and costs under § 1988. They requested compensation for 1,946.75 hours expended by their two attorneys at a rate of $125 per hour, and for 84.5 hours expended by law clerks at a rate of $25.00 per hour, a total of $245,456.25. The District Court found both the hours and rates reasonable, and awarded respondents $245,456.25 in attorney's fees....

Petitioners appealed only the attorney's fees award, which the Court of Appeals for the Ninth Circuit affirmed....

. . . .

Petitioners ... sought a writ of certiorari from this Court, alleging that the District Court's fee award was not "reasonable" within the meaning of § 1988, because it was disproportionate to the amount of damages recovered by respondents. We ... affirm the Court of Appeals.

. . . .

III

Petitioners, joined by the Solicitor General as *amicus curiae,* maintain that *Hensley*'s lodestar approach is inappropriate in civil rights cases where a plaintiff recovers only monetary damages. In these cases, so the argument goes, use of the lodestar may result in fees that exceed the amount of damages recovered and that are therefore unreasonable. Likening such cases to private tort actions, petitioners and the Solicitor General submit that attorney's fees in such cases should be proportionate to the amount of damages a plaintiff recovers. Specifically, they suggest that fee awards in damages cases should be modeled upon the contingent fee arrangements commonly used in personal injury litigation. In this case, assuming a 33% contingency rate, this would entitle respondents to recover approximately $11,000 in attorney's fees.

The amount of damages a plaintiff recovers is certainly relevant to the amount of attorney's fees to be awarded under § 1988. It is, however, only one of many factors that a court should consider in calculating an award of attorney's fees. We reject the proposition that fee awards under § 1988 should necessarily be proportionate to the amount of damages a civil rights plaintiff actually recovers.

A

As an initial matter, we reject the notion that a civil rights action for damages constitutes nothing more than a private tort suit benefiting only the individual plaintiffs whose rights were violated. Unlike most private tort litigants, a civil rights plaintiff seeks to vindicate important civil and constitutional rights that cannot be valued solely in monetary terms. And, Congress has determined that "the public as a whole has an interest in the vindication of the rights conferred by the statutes enumerated in § 1988, over and above the value of a civil rights remedy to a particular plaintiff...." ...

. . . .

Because damages awards do not reflect fully the public benefit advanced by civil rights litigation, Congress did not intend for fees in civil rights cases, unlike most private law cases, to depend on obtaining substantial monetary relief. Rather, Congress made clear that it "intended that the amount of fees awarded under [§ 1988] be governed by the same standards which prevail in other types of equally complex Federal litigation, such as antitrust cases and *not be reduced because the rights involved may be nonpecuniary in nature.*" Senate Report, at 6 (emphasis added). "[C]ounsel for prevailing parties should be paid, as is traditional with attorneys compensated by a fee-paying client, *'for all time reasonably expended on a matter.'*" Ibid. The Senate report specifically approves of the fee awards made in cases such as Stanford Daily v. Zurcher, 64 F.R.D. 680 (N.D.Cal. 1974), and Swann v. Charlotte–Mecklenburg Board of Education, 66 F.R.D. 483 (W.D.N.C.1975). In each of these cases, counsel received substantial attorney's fees despite the fact the plaintiffs sought no monetary damages. Thus, Congress recognized that reasonable attorney's fees under § 1988 are not conditioned upon and need not be proportionate to an award of money damages. The lower courts have generally eschewed such a requirement.

B

A rule that limits attorney's fees in civil rights cases to a proportion of the damages awarded would seriously undermine Congress' purpose in enacting § 1988. Congress enacted § 1988 specifically because it found that the private market for legal services failed to provide many victims of civil rights violations with effective access to the judicial process. These victims ordinarily cannot afford to purchase legal services at the rates set by the private market. Moreover, the contingent fee arrangements that make legal services available to many victims of personal injuries would often not encourage lawyers to accept civil rights cases, which frequently involve substantial expenditures of time and effort but produce only small monetary recoveries. As the House Report states:

> "[W]hile damages are theoretically available under the statutes covered by [§ 1988], it should be observed that, in some cases, immunity doctrines and special defenses, available only to public officials, preclude *or severely limit the damage remedy.* Consequently, awarding counsel fees to prevailing plaintiffs in such litigation is particularly important and necessary if Federal civil and constitutional rights are to be adequately protected." House Report, at 9. (emphasis added).

Congress enacted § 1988 specifically to enable plaintiffs to enforce the civil rights laws even where the amount of damages at stake would not otherwise make it feasible for them to do so. . . .

A rule of proportionality would make it difficult, if not impossible, for individuals with meritorious civil rights claims but relatively small potential damages to obtain redress from the courts. This is totally inconsistent with the Congress' purpose in enacting § 1988. Congress recognized that private-sector fee arrangements were inadequate to ensure sufficiently vigorous enforcement of civil rights. In order to ensure that lawyers would be willing to represent persons with legitimate civil rights grievances, Congress determined that it would be necessary to compensate lawyers for all time reasonably expended on a case.

This case illustrates why the enforcement of civil rights laws cannot be entrusted to private-sector fee arrangements. The District Court observed that "[g]iven the nature of this lawsuit and the type of defense presented, many attorneys in the community would have been reluctant to institute and to continue to prosecute this action." The court concluded, moreover, that "[c]ounsel for plaintiffs achieved excellent results for their clients, and their accomplishment in this case was outstanding. The amount of time expended by counsel in conducting this litigation was reasonable and reflected sound legal judgment under the circumstances." Nevertheless, petitioners suggest that respondents' counsel should be compensated for only a small fraction of the actual time spent litigating the case. In light of the difficult nature of the issues presented by this lawsuit and the low pecuniary value of the many of the rights respondents sought to vindicate, it is highly unlikely that the prospect of a fee equal to a fraction of the damages respondents might recover would have been sufficient to attract competent counsel. Moreover, since counsel might not have found it economically feasible to expend the amount of time respondents' counsel found necessary to litigate the case properly, it is even less likely that counsel would have achieved the excellent results that respondents' counsel obtained here. Thus, had respondents had to rely on private-sector fee arrangements, they might well have been unable to obtain redress for their grievances. It is precisely for this reason that Congress enacted § 1988.

IV

We agree with petitioners that Congress intended that statutory fee awards be "adequate to attract competent counsel, but ... not produce windfalls to attorneys." Senate Report, at 6. However, we find no evidence that Congress intended that, in order to avoid "windfalls to attorneys," attorney's fees be proportionate to the amount of damages a civil rights plaintiff might recover. Rather, there already exists a wide range of safeguards designed to protect civil rights defendants against the possibility of excessive fee awards. Both the House and Senate Reports identify standards for courts to follow in awarding and calculating attorney's fees; these standards are designed to insure that attorneys are compensated only for time *reasonably expended* on a case. The district court has the discretion to deny fees to prevailing plaintiffs under special circumstances, and to award attorney's fees against plaintiffs who litigate frivolous or vexatious claims. . . . We believe that these safeguards adequately protect against the possibility that § 1988 might produce a "windfall" to civil rights attorneys.

In the absence of any indication that Congress intended to adopt a strict rule that attorney's fees under § 1988 be proportionate to damages recovered, we decline to adopt such a rule ourselves. The judgment of the Court of Appeals is hereby

Affirmed.

■ JUSTICE POWELL, concurring in the judgment.

I join only the Court's judgment. . . . For me affirmance—quite simply—is required by the District Court's detailed findings of fact, which were approved by the Court of Appeals. On its face, the fee award seems unreasonable. But I find no basis for this Court to reject the findings made and approved by the courts below.

. . . .

Petitioners argue for a rule of proportionality between the fee awarded and the damages recovered in a civil rights case. Neither the decisions of this Court nor the legislative history of § 1988 support such a "rule." The facts and circumstances of litigation are infinitely variable. Under *Hensley,* of course, "the most critical factor [in the final determination of fee awards] is the degree of success obtained." Where recovery of private damages is the purpose of a civil rights litigation, a district court, in fixing fees, is obligated to give primary consideration to the amount of damages awarded as compared to the amount sought. In some civil rights cases, however, the court may consider the vindication of constitutional rights in addition to the amount of damages recovered. In this case, for example, the District Court made an explicit finding that the "public interest" had been served by the jury's verdict that the warrantless entry was lawless and unconstitutional. Although the finding of a Fourth Amendment violation hardly can be considered a new constitutional ruling, in the special circumstances of this case, the vindication of the asserted Fourth Amendment right may well have served a public interest, supporting the amount of the fees awarded.[3] As the District Court put it, there were allegations that the police misconduct was "motivated by a general hostility to the Chicano community in the area. . . ." The record also contained evidence of racial slurs by some of the police.

Finally, petitioners also contend that in determining a proper fee under § 1988 in a suit for damages the court should consider the prevailing contingent-fee rate charged by counsel in personal injury cases. The use of contingent-fee arrangements in many types of tort cases was customary long before Congress enacted § 1988. It is clear from the legislative history that § 1988 was enacted because existing fee arrangements were thought not to provide an adequate incentive to lawyers particularly to represent plaintiffs in unpopular civil rights cases. I therefore find petitioners' asserted analogy to personal injury claims unpersuasive in this context.

---

3. It probably will be the rare case in which an award of *private damages* can be said to benefit the public interest to an extent that would justify the disproportionality between damages and fees reflected in this case.

. . . .

[The dissenting opinion of BURGER, C.J., is omitted.]

■ JUSTICE REHNQUIST, with whom THE CHIEF JUSTICE, JUSTICE WHITE, and JUSTICE O'CONNOR, join, dissenting.

In Hensley v. Eckerhart, 461 U.S. 424, 103 S.Ct. 1933, 76 L.Ed.2d 40 (1983), our leading case dealing with attorney's fees awarded pursuant to 42 U.S.C. § 1988, we said that "[t]he most useful starting point for determining the amount of a reasonable fee is the number of hours reasonably expended on the litigation multiplied by a reasonable hourly rate." As if we had foreseen the case now before us, we went on to emphasize that "[t]he district court . . . should exclude from this initial fee calculation hours that were not 'reasonably expended'" on the litigation. Today . . . the plurality . . . acknowledges that "Hensley requires a fee applicant to exercise 'billing judgment' not because he should necessarily be compensated for less than the actual number of hours spent litigating a case, but because the hours he does seek compensation for must be reasonable." I see no escape from the conclusion that the District Court's finding that respondents' attorneys "reasonably" spent 1,946.75 hours to recover a money judgment of $33,350 is clearly erroneous, and that therefore the District Court's award of $245,456.25 in attorney's fees to respondents should be reversed. The Court's affirmance of the fee award emasculates the principles laid down in *Hensley,* and turns § 1988 into a relief act for lawyers.

. . . .

. . . The very "reasonableness" of the hours expended on a case by a plaintiff's attorney necessarily will depend, to a large extent, on the amount that may reasonably be expected to be recovered if the plaintiff prevails.

. . . .

In the context of § 1988, there would obviously be some exceptions to the general rules of "billing judgment" which I have been discussing, but none of these exceptions are applicable here. If the litigation is unnecessarily prolonged by the bad-faith conduct of the defendants, or if the litigation produces significant, identifiable benefits for persons other than the plaintiffs, then the purpose of Congress in authorizing attorney's fees under § 1988 should allow a larger award of attorney's fees than would be "reasonable" where the only relief is the recovery of monetary damages by individual plaintiffs. Nor do we deal here with a case such as Carey v. Piphus, 435 U.S. 247, 98 S.Ct. 1042, 55 L.Ed.2d 252 (1978), in which the deprivation of a constitutional right necessarily results in only nominal pecuniary damages. Here, respondents successfully claimed both compensatory and punitive damages for false arrest and imprisonment, negligence, and violations of their constitutional rights under the Fourth and Fourteenth Amendments, and the jury assessed damages as juries do in such cases. In short, this case shares none of the special aspects of certain civil rights litigation which the plurality suggests, in Part III of its opinion, would justify an award of attorney's fees totally divorced from the amount of damages awarded by the jury.

... Nearly 2,000 attorney-hours spent on a case in which the total recovery was only $33,000, in which only $13,300 of that amount was recovered for the federal claims, and in which the District Court expressed the view that, in such cases, juries typically were reluctant to award substantial damages against police officers, is simply not a "reasonable" expenditure of time....

. . . .

NOTES

1.   Blanchard was awarded $10,000 for a beating unconstitutionally inflicted upon him by a police officer. The trial court granted him $7,500 in attorney's fees, but the court of appeals reduced that award to $4,000, the amount to which the lawyer was entitled under a contingency fee agreement with Blanchard. The appellate court's decision was based upon its view that a contingency fee agreement sets a ceiling on the fee recoverable under Section 1988.

The Supreme Court reversed. Blanchard v. Bergeron, 489 U.S. 87, 109 S.Ct. 939, 103 L.Ed.2d 67 (1989). The statute, White, J., wrote for the Court, "contemplates reasonable compensation . . . for the time and effort expended by the attorney for the prevailing plaintiff, no more and no less." Even if Blanchard's fee contract had induced his lawyer to handle the case without any expectation of further recovery under Section 1988, that law ensures access of civil rights plaintiffs to competent legal assistance by requiring every losing defendant to pay every "prevailing" plaintiff a fee that a judge deems reasonable. Hence, even lawyers who are willing to handle civil rights cases on a *pro bono* basis are entitled to attorneys' fees under Section 1988. Finally, Justice White noted, a contrary result might lead to "an undesirable emphasis . . . on the importance of the recovery of damages" in these cases.

2.   Venegas charged police officers with violating his civil rights by falsely arresting him and lying at his trial. He hired Mitchell to represent him in his civil suit. Their contract set Mitchell's fee at 40% of the gross amount of any recovery. The contract also stated that Venegas would not waive any statutory right to recover attorneys' fees, that Mitchell could both "apply for and collect" such fees and intervene in the litigation in order to protect his interest a fee award, and that any statutory recovery would reduce the amount owed under the contingent fee agreement on a dollar-for-dollar basis.

After Venegas won a judgment of $2,800,000, the trial court assessed Mitchell's statutory fee at $75,000. After deciding not to handle the case on appeal (where Venegas once again prevailed), Mitchell withdrew and asked the trial court to place a lien on the judgment for the remaining amount due him under the contract. The court rejected Venegas' claim that the statutory award set a cap on Mitchell's recovery, holding that the contract set a reasonable fee that Mitchell could collect from Venegas. However, because it held that Mitchell could not intervene in this suit, the court did not decide whether an equitable lien should be imposed on Venegas' judgment. The appellate court upheld the former, and rejected the latter, ruling. It remanded the case for a decision on Mitchell's right to a lien.

The Supreme Court affirmed. Venegas v. Mitchell, 495 U.S. 82, 110 S.Ct. 1679, 109 L.Ed.2d 74 (1990). White, J., writing for the Court, decided that "§ 1988 controls what the losing defendant must pay, not what the prevailing plaintiff must pay his lawyer." He found support for this ruling in earlier cases holding that the plaintiff can waive the statutory right to recover attorneys' fees and the very right to sue under Section 1983.

3. A class of emotionally and mentally handicapped children sued Idaho officials for violating their civil rights by inadequately educating and treating them. Plaintiffs sought injunctive relief, costs, and attorneys' fees. The district court appointed Johnson, a lawyer from the Idaho Legal Aid Society, to represent them.

The parties quickly resolved the childrens' educational claims in an agreement which stipulated that each side would bear its "own attorney's fees and costs thus far incurred." The defendants later offered to settle the other claims. Their proposal provided almost all the injunctive relief sought by the class, which was "more than the district court in earlier hearings had indicated it was willing to grant." However, the proposal required the plaintiffs to waive any claim to attorneys' fees or costs. Johnson considered himself ethically obligated to accept the offer, but he did so subject to the court's approval (pursuant to Fed.R.Civ.P. 23(e)) of the waiver of attorneys' fees.

The district court approved the settlement, including the fee waiver clause. The court of appeals struck down that clause. The case then went to the Supreme Court, which reversed. Evans v. Jeff D., 475 U.S. 717, 106 S.Ct. 1531, 89 L.Ed.2d 747 (1986).

The three dissenting Justices, who spoke through Brennan, J., feared that the validation of attorneys' fee waivers would make it harder for civil rights plaintiffs to hire lawyers, frustrating the purpose of Section 1988. However, Stevens, J., writing for the majority, dismissed this prophecy as unrealistic. On the contrary, he suggested that the waivability of attorneys' fees might increase the negotiating leverage of civil rights plaintiffs and facilitate the vindication of their civil rights. He therefore thought it inappropriate to read a flat ban against waivers into Section 1988. Beyond this, he found no evidence that the defendants had demanded the waiver of fees as a matter of policy or to deter lawyers from handling civil rights cases against the State. Relying instead on the district court's implied finding that the waiver was "exchanged for injunctive relief of equivalent value," the Court held that the district court's approval of the settlement in this case was not an abuse of its discretion under Rule 23(e).

Marek v. Chesny

Supreme Court of the United States, 1985.
473 U.S. 1, 105 S.Ct. 3012, 87 L.Ed.2d 1.

■ CHIEF JUSTICE BURGER delivered the opinion of the Court.

We granted certiorari to decide whether attorney's fees incurred by a plaintiff subsequent to an offer of settlement under Federal Rule of Civil

Procedure 68 must be paid by the defendant under 42 U.S.C. § 1988, when the plaintiff recovers a judgment less than the offer.

I

Petitioners, three police officers, in answering a call on a domestic disturbance, shot and killed respondent's adult son. Respondent, in his own behalf and as administrator of his son's estate, filed suit against the officers in the United States District Court under 42 U.S.C. § 1983 and state tort law.

Prior to trial, petitioners made a timely offer of settlement "for a sum, including costs now accrued and attorney's fees, of ONE HUNDRED THOUSAND ($100,000) DOLLARS." Respondent did not accept the offer. The case went to trial and respondent was awarded $5,000 on the state-law "wrongful death" claim, $52,000 for the § 1983 violation, and $3,000 in punitive damages.

Respondent filed a request for $171,692.47 in costs, including attorney's fees. This amount included costs incurred after the settlement offer. Petitioners opposed the claim for post-offer costs, relying on Federal Rule of Civil Procedure 68, which shifts to the plaintiff all "costs" incurred subsequent to an offer of judgment not exceeded by the ultimate recovery at trial. Petitioners argued that attorney's fees are part of the "costs" covered by Rule 68. The District Court agreed with petitioners and declined to award respondent "costs, including attorney's fees, incurred after the offer of judgment." The parties subsequently agreed that $32,000 fairly represented the allowable costs, including attorney's fees, accrued prior to petitioner's offer of settlement. Respondent appealed the denial of post-offer costs.

The Court of Appeals reversed. The court rejected what it termed the "rather mechanical linking up of Rule 68 and section 1988." It stated that the District Court's reading of Rule 68 and § 1988, while "in a sense logical," would put civil rights plaintiffs and counsel in a "predicament" that "cuts against the grain of section 1988." Plaintiffs' attorneys, the court reasoned, would be forced to "think very hard" before rejecting even an inadequate offer, and would be deterred from bringing good faith actions because of the prospect of losing the right to attorney's fees if a settlement offer more favorable than the ultimate recovery were rejected. The court concluded that "[t]he legislators who enacted section 1988 would not have wanted its effectiveness blunted because of a little known rule of court."

We . . . reverse.

II

Rule 68 provides that if a timely pretrial offer of settlement is not accepted and "the judgment finally obtained by the offeree is not more favorable than the offer, the offeree must pay *the costs incurred after the making of the offer.*" (emphasis added). The plain purpose of Rule 68 is to encourage settlement and avoid litigation. The Rule prompts both parties to a suit to evaluate the risks and costs of litigation, and to balance them against the likelihood of success upon trial on the merits. This case requires us to decide ... whether the term "costs" as used in Rule 68 includes attorney's fees awardable under 42 U.S.C. § 1988.

A

. . . .

B

... By the time the Federal Rules of Civil Procedure were adopted in 1938, federal statutes had authorized and defined awards of costs to prevailing parties for more than 85 years. Unlike in England, such "costs" generally had not included attorney's fees; under the "American Rule," each party had been required to bear its own attorney's fees. The "American Rule" as applied in federal courts, however, had become subject to certain exceptions by the late 1930's. Some of these exceptions had evolved as a product of the "inherent power in the courts to allow attorney's fees in particular situations." But most of the exceptions were found in federal statutes that directed courts to award attorney's fees as part of costs in particular cases.

. . . .

The authors of Federal Rule of Civil Procedure 68 were fully aware of these exceptions to the American Rule. The Advisory Committee's Note to Rule 54(d) contains an extensive list of the federal statutes which allowed for costs in particular cases; of the 25 "statutes as to costs" set forth in the final paragraph of the Note, no fewer than 11 allowed for attorney's fees as part of costs. Against this background of varying definitions of "costs," the drafters of Rule 68 did not define the term; nor is there any explanation whatever as to its intended meaning in the history of the Rule.

In this setting, given the importance of "costs" to the Rule, it is very unlikely that this omission was mere oversight; on the contrary, the most reasonable inference is that the term "costs" in Rule 68 was intended to refer to all costs properly awardable under the relevant substantive statute or other authority. In other words, all costs properly awardable in an action are to be considered within the scope of Rule 68 "costs." Thus, absent Congressional expressions to the contrary, where the underlying statute defines "costs" to include attorney's fees, we are satisfied such fees are to be included as costs for purposes of Rule 68.

Here, respondents sued under 42 U.S.C. § 1983. Pursuant to the Civil Rights Attorney's Fees Awards Act of 1976, 42 U.S.C. § 1988, a prevailing party in a § 1983 action may be awarded attorney's fees "as part of the costs." Since Congress expressly included attorney's fees as "costs" available to a plaintiff in a § 1983 suit, such fees are subject to the cost-shifting provision of Rule 68. This "plain meaning" interpretation of the interplay between Rule 68 and § 1988 is the only construction that gives meaning to each word in both Rule 68 and § 1988.

Unlike the Court of Appeals, we do not believe that this "plain meaning" construction of the statute and the Rule will frustrate Congress' objective in § 1988 of ensuring that civil rights plaintiffs obtain "effective access to the judicial process." Merely subjecting civil rights plaintiffs to the settlement provision of Rule 68 does not curtail their access to the courts, or significantly deter them from bringing suit. Application of Rule 68 will serve as a disincentive for the plaintiff's attorney to continue litigation after the defendant makes a settlement offer. There is no evidence, however, that Congress, in considering § 1988, had any thought that civil rights claims were to be on any different footing from other civil claims insofar as settlement is concerned. Indeed, Congress made clear its concern that civil rights plaintiffs not be penalized for "helping to lessen docket congestion" by settling their cases out of court. See H.R.Rep. No. 94–1588, p. 7 (1976).

Moreover, Rule 68's policy of encouraging settlements is neutral, favoring neither plaintiffs nor defendants; it expresses a clear policy of favoring settlement of all lawsuits. Civil rights plaintiffs—along with other plaintiffs—who reject an offer more favorable than what is thereafter recovered at trial will not recover attorney's fees for services performed after the offer is rejected. But, since the Rule is neutral, many civil rights plaintiffs will benefit from the offers of settlement encouraged by Rule 68. Some plaintiffs will receive compensation in settlement where, on trial, they might not have recovered, or would have recovered less than what was offered. And, even for those who would prevail at trial, settlement will provide them with compensation at an earlier date without the burdens, stress, and time of litigation. In short, settlements rather than litigation will serve the interests of plaintiffs as well as defendants.

To be sure, application of Rule 68 will require plaintiffs to "think very hard" about whether continued litigation is worthwhile; that is precisely what Rule 68 contemplates. This effect of Rule 68, however, is in no sense inconsistent with the congressional policies underlying § 1983 and § 1988. Section 1988 authorizes courts to award only "reasonable" attorney's fees to prevailing parties. In Hensley v. Eckerhart, 461 U.S. 424, 103 S.Ct. 1933, 76 L.Ed.2d 40 (1983), we held that "the most critical factor" in determining a reasonable fee "is the degree of success obtained." We specifically noted that prevailing at trial "may say little about whether the expenditure of counsel's time was reasonable in relation to the success achieved." In a case where a rejected settlement offer exceeds the ultimate recovery, the plaintiff—although technically the prevailing party—has not received any monetary benefits from the post-offer services of his attorney. This case presents a good example: the $139,692 in post-offer legal services resulted in a recovery $8,000 less than petitioner's settlement offer. Given Congress' focus on the success achieved, we are not persuaded that shifting the post-offer costs to respondent in these circumstances would in any sense thwart its intent under § 1988.

Rather than "cutting against the grain" of § 1988, as the Court of Appeals held, we are convinced that applying Rule 68 in the context of a § 1983 action is consistent with the policies and objectives of § 1988. Section 1988 encourages plaintiffs to bring meritorious civil rights suits; Rule 68 simply encourages settlements. There is nothing incompatible in these two objectives.

III

Congress, of course, was well aware of Rule 68 when it enacted § 1988, and included attorney's fees as part of recoverable costs. The plain language of Rule 68 and § 1988 subjects such fees to the costshifting provision of Rule 68. Nothing revealed in our review of the policies underlying § 1988 constitutes "the necessary clear expression of congressional intent" required "to exempt ... [the] statute from the operation of" Rule 68. We hold that petitioners are not liable for costs of $139,692 incurred by respondent after petitioners' offer of judgment.

The judgment of the Court of Appeals is

Reversed.

[The concurring opinions of Powell and Rehnquist, JJ., are omitted.]

■ Justice Brennan, with whom Justice Marshall and Justice Blackmun join, dissenting.

The question presented by this case is whether the term "costs" as it is used in Rule 68 of the Federal Rules of Civil Procedure and elsewhere throughout the Rules refers simply to those taxable costs defined in 28 U.S.C. § 1920 and traditionally understood as "costs"—courts fees, printing expenses, and the like—or instead includes attorney's fees when an underlying fees-award statute happens to refer to fees "as part of" the awardable costs. Relying on what it recurrently emphasizes is the "plain language" of one such statute, 42 U.S.C. § 1988, the Court today holds that a prevailing civil-rights litigant entitled to fees under that statute is per se barred by Rule 68 from recovering any fees for work performed after rejecting a settlement offer where he ultimately recovers less than the proffered amount in settlement.

I dissent. The Court's reasoning is wholly inconsistent with the history and structure of the Federal Rules, and its application to the over 100 attorney's fees statutes enacted by Congress will produce absurd variations in Rule 68's operation based on nothing more than picayune differences in statutory phraseology. Neither Congress nor the drafters of the Rules could possibly have intended such inexplicable variations in settlement incentives. Moreover, the Court's interpretation will "seriously undermine the purposes behind the attorney's fees provisions" of the civil-rights laws,— provisions imposed by Congress pursuant to § 5 of the Fourteenth Amendment.[1] Today's decision therefore violates the most basic limitations on our rulemaking authority as set forth in the Rules Enabling Act, and as summarized in Alyeska Pipeline Co. v. Wilderness Society. Finally, both Congress and the Judicial Conference of the United States have been engaged for years in considering possible amendments to Rule 68 that would bring attorney's fees within the operation of the Rule. That process strongly suggests that Rule 68 has not previously been viewed as governing fee awards, and it illustrates the wisdom of deferring to other avenues of

1. [Justice Brennan pointed out that the Court's ruling would preclude recovery of post-offer attorney's fees under Section 1988 even if a plaintiff's rejection of the settlement offer was reasonable. Thus, he argued, the ruling would deter the litigation of civil rights cases whose prosecution Section 1988 was meant to encourage.]

amending Rule 68 rather than ourselves engaging in "standardless judicial lawmaking."

. . . .

NOTES

1. In Stefan v. Laurenitis, 889 F.2d 363 (1st Cir.1989), the plaintiffs moved pursuant to 42 U.S.C.A. § 1988 for reasonable attorney fees in a section 1983 case that had been settled. Plaintiffs originally sought compensatory and punitive damages of $1.9 million. The parties settled the case for $16,000, and sought reasonable attorney fees under FED. R. CIV. P. 68 as part of their costs. The issue before the court was whether the plaintiffs were prevailing parties within the meaning of 42 U.S.C.A. § 1988, entitling them to the award of reasonable attorney fees. The court held that the plaintiffs were, in fact, prevailing parties, in that the $16,000 settlement had changed the legal relationship of the parties in favor of the plaintiffs by conferring "some of the relief they originally sought in bringing the civil rights action."

2. See Buckhannon Bd. and Care Home, Inc. v. West Virginia Dept. of Health and Human Resources, 532 U.S. 598, 121 S.Ct. 1835 *infra* p. 1297.

Cooter & Gell v. Hartmarx Corp.

Supreme Court of the United States, 1990.
496 U.S. 384, 110 S.Ct. 2447, 110 L.Ed.2d 359.

■ JUSTICE O'CONNOR delivered the opinion of the Court.

This case presents three issues related to the application of Rule 11 of the Federal Rules of Civil Procedure: whether a district court may impose Rule 11 sanctions on a plaintiff who has voluntarily dismissed his complaint pursuant to Rule 41(a)(1)(i) of the Federal Rules of Civil Procedure; what constitutes the appropriate standard of appellate review of a district court's imposition of Rule 11 sanctions; and whether Rule 11 authorizes awards of attorney's fees incurred on appeal of a Rule 11 sanction.*

I

In 1983, Danik, Inc., owned and operated a number of discount men's clothing stores in the Washington, D.C., area. In June 1983, Intercontinental Apparel, a subsidiary of respondent Hartmarx Corp., brought a breach-of-contract action against Danik in the United States District Court for the District of Columbia. Danik, represented by the law firm of Cooter & Gell (petitioner), responded to the suit by filing a counterclaim against Intercontinental, alleging violations of the Robinson–Patman Act. In March 1984, the District Court granted summary judgment for Intercontinental in its suit against Danik, and, in February 1985, a jury returned a verdict for

---

* Because petitioners did not raise the argument that Rule 11 sanctions could only be imposed against the two attorneys who signed the complaint, either in the courts below or in their petition for certiorari here, we decline to consider it.

Intercontinental on Danik's counterclaim. Both judgments were affirmed on appeal.

While this litigation was proceeding, petitioner prepared two additional antitrust complaints against Hartmarx and its two subsidiaries, respondents Hart, Schaffner & Marx and Hickey–Freeman Co. One of the complaints, the one giving rise to the Rule 11 sanction at issue in this case, alleged a nationwide conspiracy to fix prices and to eliminate competition through an exclusive retail agent policy and uniform pricing scheme, as well as other unfair competition practices such as resale price maintenance and territorial restrictions.

Petitioner filed the two complaints in November 1983. Respondents moved to dismiss the antitrust complaint at issue, alleging, among other things, that Danik's allegations had no basis in fact. Respondents also moved for sanctions under Rule 11. In opposition to the Rule 11 motion, petitioner filed three affidavits setting forth the prefiling research that supported the allegations in the complaint. In essence, petitioner's research consisted of telephone calls to salespersons in a number of men's clothing stores in New York City, Philadelphia, Baltimore, and Washington, D.C. Petitioner inferred from this research that only one store in each major metropolitan area nationwide sold Hart, Schaffner & Marx suits.

In April 1984, petitioner filed a notice of voluntary dismissal of the complaint, pursuant to Rule 41(a)(1)(i). The dismissal became effective in July 1984.... In June 1984, before the dismissal became effective, the District Court heard oral argument on the Rule 11 motion. The District Court took the Rule 11 motion under advisement.

In December 1987, ... the District Court ordered respondents to submit a statement of costs and attorney's fees. Respondents filed a statement requesting $61,917.99 in attorney's fees. Two months later, the District Court granted respondent's motion for Rule 11 sanctions, holding that petitioner's prefiling inquiry was grossly inadequate. Specifically, the District Court found that the allegations in the complaint regarding exclusive retail agency arrangements for Hickey–Freeman clothing were completely baseless because petitioner researched only the availability of Hart, Schaffner & Marx menswear. In addition, the District Court found that petitioner's limited survey of only four Eastern cities did not support the allegation that respondents had exclusive retailer agreements in every major city in the United States. Accordingly, the District Court determined that petitioner violated Rule 11 and imposed a sanction of $21,452.52 against petitioner and $10,701.26 against Danik.

The Court of Appeals for the District of Columbia Circuit affirmed the imposition of Rule 11 sanctions....

. . . .

... [In addition,] the Court of Appeals held that an appellant who successfully defends a Rule 11 award was entitled to recover its attorney's fees on appeal and remanded the case to the district court to determine the amount of reasonable attorney's fees and to enter an appropriate award.

II

The Rules Enabling Act authorizes the Court to "prescribe general rules of practice and procedure and rules of evidence for cases in the United States district courts (including proceedings before Magistrates thereof) and courts of appeals." The Court has no authority to enact rules that "abridge, enlarge or modify any substantive right." Pursuant to this authority, the Court promulgated the Federal Rules of Civil Procedure to "govern the procedure in the United States district courts in all suits of a civil nature." Fed.Rule Civ.Proc. 1. We therefore interpret Rule 11 according to its plain meaning, in light of the scope of the congressional authorization.

Rule 11 provides, in full:

"Every pleading, motion, and other paper of a party represented by an attorney shall be signed by at least one attorney of record in the attorney's individual name, whose address shall be stated. A party who is not represented by an attorney shall sign the party's pleading, motion, or other paper and state the party's address. Except when otherwise specifically provided by rule or statute, pleadings need not be verified or accompanied by affidavit. The rule in equity that the averments of an answer under oath must be overcome by the testimony of two witnesses or of one witness sustained by corroborating circumstances is abolished. The signature of an attorney or party constitutes a certificate by the signer that the signer has read the pleading, motion, or other paper; that to the best of the signer's knowledge, information, and belief formed after reasonable inquiry it is well grounded in fact and is warranted by existing law or a good faith argument for the extension, modification, or reversal of existing law, and that it is not interposed for any improper purpose, such as to harass or to cause unnecessary delay or needless increase in the cost of litigation. If a pleading, motion, or other paper is not signed, it shall be stricken unless it is signed promptly after the omission is called to the attention of the pleader or movant. If a pleading, motion, or other paper is signed in violation of this rule, the court, upon motion or upon its own initiative, shall impose upon the person who signed it, a represented party, or both, an appropriate sanction, which may include an order to pay to the other party or parties the amount of the reasonable expenses incurred because of the filing of the pleading, motion, or other paper, including a reasonable attorney's fee."

An interpretation of the current Rule 11 must be guided, in part, by an understanding of the deficiencies in the original version of Rule 11 that led to its revision. The 1938 version of Rule 11 required an attorney to certify by signing the pleading "that to the best of his knowledge, information, and belief there is good ground to support [the pleading]; and that it is not interposed for delay ... or is signed with intent to defeat the purpose of this rule." An attorney who willfully violated the rule could be "subjected to appropriate disciplinary action." Moreover, the pleading could "be stricken as sham and false and the action [could] proceed as though the pleading had not been served." In operation, the rule did not have the deterrent effect expected by its drafters. The Advisory Committee identified two problems with the old Rule. First, the Rule engendered confusion regarding when a pleading should be struck, what standard of conduct would make an attorney liable to sanctions, and what sanctions were available. Second, courts were reluctant to impose disciplinary measures on attorneys, and attorneys were slow to invoke the rule.

To ameliorate these problems, and in response to concerns that abusive litigation practices abounded in the federal courts, the rule was amended in 1983. It is now clear that the central purpose of Rule 11 is to deter baseless filings in District Court and thus, consistent with the Rule Enabling Act's grant of authority, streamline the administration and procedure of the federal courts. Rule 11 imposes a duty on attorneys to certify that they have conducted a reasonable inquiry and have determined that any papers filed with the court are well-grounded in fact, legally tenable, and "not interposed for any improper purpose." An attorney who signs the paper without such a substantiated belief "shall" be penalized by "an appropriate sanction." Such a sanction may, but need not, include payment of the other parties' expenses. Although the rule must be read in light of concerns that it will spawn satellite litigation and chill vigorous advocacy, any interpretation must give effect to the rule's central goal of deterrence.

III

We first address the question whether petitioner's dismissal of its antitrust complaint pursuant to Rule 41(a)(1)(i) deprived the District Court of the jurisdiction to award attorney's fees. Rule 41(a)(1) states:

"(1) *By Plaintiff; by Stipulation.* Subject to the provisions of Rule 23(e), of Rule 66, and of any statute of the United States, an action may be dismissed by the plaintiff without order of court (i) by filing a notice of dismissal at any time before service by the adverse party of an answer or of a motion for summary judgment, whichever first occurs, or (ii) by filing a stipulation of dismissal signed by all parties who have appeared in the action. Unless otherwise stated in the notice of dismissal or stipulation, the dismissal is without prejudice, except that a notice of dismissal operates as an adjudication upon the merits when filed by a plaintiff who has once dismissed in any court of the United States or of any state an action based on or including the same claim."

... Once the defendant has filed a summary judgment motion or answer, the plaintiff may dismiss the action only by stipulation, or by order of the court, "upon such terms and conditions as the court deems proper." Rule 41(a)(2)....

Petitioner contends that filing a notice of voluntary dismissal pursuant to this rule automatically deprives a court of jurisdiction over the action, rendering the court powerless to impose sanctions thereafter....

The view more consistent with Rule 11's language and purposes, and the one supported by the weight of Circuit authority, is that district courts may enforce Rule 11 even after the plaintiff has filed a notice of dismissal under Rule 41(a)(1). The district court's jurisdiction, invoked by the filing of the underlying complaint, supports consideration of both the merits of the action and the motion for Rule 11 sanctions arising from that filing. As the "violation of Rule 11 is complete when the paper is filed," a voluntary dismissal does not expunge the Rule 11 violation. In order to comply with Rule 11's requirement that a court "shall" impose sanctions "[i]f a pleading, motion, or other paper is signed in violation of this rule," a court must have the authority to consider whether there has been a violation of the signing requirement regardless of the dismissal of the underlying action. In our view, nothing in the language of Rule 41(a)(1)(i), Rule 11, or other statute or Federal Rule terminates a district court's authority to impose sanctions after such a dismissal.

It is well established that a federal court may consider collateral issues after an action is no longer pending. For example, district courts may award costs after an action is dismissed for want of jurisdiction. This Court has indicated that motions for costs or attorney's fees are "independent proceeding[s] supplemental to the original proceeding and not a request for a modification of the original decree." Thus, even "years after the entry of a judgment on the merits" a federal court could consider an award of counsel fees. A criminal contempt charge is likewise " 'a separate and independent proceeding at law' " that is not part of the original action. A court may make an adjudication of contempt and impose a contempt sanction even after the action in which the contempt arose has been terminated. Like the imposition of costs, attorney's fees, and contempt sanctions, the imposition of a Rule 11 sanction is not a judgment on the merits of an action. Rather, it requires the determination of a collateral issue: whether the attorney has abused the judicial process, and, if so, what sanction would be appropriate. Such a determination may be made after the principal suit has been terminated.

Because a Rule 11 sanction does not signify a District Court's assessment of the legal merits of the complaint, the imposition of such a sanction after a voluntary dismissal does not deprive the plaintiff of his right under Rule 41(a) to dismiss an action without prejudice. "Dismissal without prejudice" is a dismissal that does not "operat[e] as an adjudication upon the merits," Rule 41(a)(1), and thus does not have a res judicata effect. Even if a district court indicated that a complaint was not legally tenable or factually well founded for Rule 11 purposes, the resulting Rule 11 sanction would nevertheless not preclude the refiling of a complaint. Indeed, even if the Rule 11 sanction imposed by the court were a prohibition against refiling the complaint (assuming that would be an "appropriate sanction" for Rule 11 purposes), the preclusion of refiling would be neither a consequence of the dismissal (which was without prejudice) nor a "term or condition" placed upon the dismissal (which was unconditional), see Rule 41(a)(2).

The foregoing interpretation is consistent with the policy and purpose of Rule 41(a)(1), which was designed to limit a plaintiff's ability to dismiss an action. Prior to the promulgation of the Federal Rules, liberal state and federal procedural rules often allowed dismissals or nonsuits as a matter of right up until the entry of the verdict or judgment. Rule 41(a)(1) was designed to curb abuses of these nonsuit rules. Where state statutes and common law gave plaintiffs expansive control over their suit, Rule 41(a)(1) preserved a narrow slice: it allowed a plaintiff to dismiss an action without the permission of the adverse party or the court only during the brief period before the defendant had made a significant commitment of time and money. Rule 41(a)(1) was not designed to give a plaintiff any benefit other than the right to take one such dismissal without prejudice.

Both Rule 41(a)(1) and Rule 11 are aimed at curbing abuses of the judicial system, and thus their policies, like their language, are completely compatible. Rule 41(a)(1) limits a litigant's power to dismiss actions, but allows one dismissal without prejudice. Rule 41(a)(1) does not codify any policy that the plaintiff's right to one free dismissal also secures the right to file baseless papers. The filing of complaints, papers, or other motions without taking the necessary care in their preparation is a separate abuse of the judicial system, subject to separate sanction. As noted above, a voluntary dismissal does not eliminate the Rule 11 violation. Baseless filing puts the machinery of justice in motion, burdening courts and individuals alike with needless expense and delay. Even if the careless litigant quickly dismisses the action, the harm triggering Rule 11's concerns has already occurred. Therefore, a litigant who violates Rule 11 merits sanctions even after a dismissal. Moreover, the imposition of such sanctions on abusive litigants is useful to deter such misconduct. If a litigant could purge his violation of Rule 11 merely by taking a dismissal, he would lose all incentive to "stop, think and investigate more carefully before serving and filing papers." Amendments to Rules, 97 F.R.D. 165, 192 (1983)(Letter from Judge Walter Mansfield, Chairman, Advisory Committee on Civil Rules)(March 9, 1982).

. . . .

IV

Petitioner further contends that the Court of Appeals did not apply a sufficiently rigorous standard in reviewing the District Court's imposition of Rule 11 sanctions. Determining whether an attorney has violated Rule 11 involves a consideration of three types of issues. The court must consider factual questions regarding the nature of the attorney's prefiling inquiry and the factual basis of the pleading or other paper. Legal issues are raised in considering whether a pleading is "warranted by existing law or a good faith argument" for changing the law and whether the attorney's conduct violated Rule 11. Finally, the district court must exercise its discretion to tailor an "appropriate sanction."

The Court of Appeals in this case did not specify the applicable standard of review. There is, however, precedent in the District of Columbia Circuit for applying an abuse of discretion standard to the determination whether a filing had an insufficient factual basis or was interposed for an improper purpose, but reviewing *de novo* the question whether a pleading or motion is legally sufficient. Petitioner contends that the Court of Appeals for the Ninth Circuit has adopted the appropriate approach. That Circuit reviews findings of historical fact under the clearly erroneous standard, the determination that counsel violated Rule 11 under a *de novo* standard, and the choice of sanction under an abuse-of-discretion standard. The majority of Circuits follow neither approach; rather, they apply a deferential standard to all issues raised by a Rule 11 violation.

Although the Courts of Appeal use different verbal formulas to characterize their standards of review, the scope of actual disagreement is narrow. No dispute exists that the appellate courts should review the district court's selection of a sanction under a deferential standard. In directing the district court to impose an "appropriate" sanction, Rule 11 itself indicates that the district court is empowered to exercise its discretion.

The Circuits also agree that, in the absence of any language to the contrary in Rule 11, courts should adhere to their usual practice of reviewing the district court's finding of facts under a deferential standard. See Fed.Rule Civ.Proc. 52(a)("Findings of fact ... shall not be set aside unless clearly erroneous, and due regard shall be given to the opportunity of the trial court to judge of the credibility of the witnesses"). In practice, the "clearly erroneous" standard requires the appellate court to uphold any district court determination that falls within a broad range of permissible conclusions. When an appellate court reviews a district court's factual findings, the abuse of discretion and clearly erroneous standards are indistinguishable: A court of appeals would be justified in concluding that a district court had abused its discretion in making a factual finding only if the finding were clearly erroneous.

The scope of disagreement over the appropriate standard of review can thus be confined to a narrow issue: whether the court of appeals must defer to the district court's legal conclusions in Rule 11 proceedings. A number of factors have led the majority of Circuits, as well as a number of commentators to conclude that appellate courts should review all aspects of a district court's imposition of Rule 11 sanctions under a deferential standard.

The Court has long noted the difficulty of distinguishing between legal and factual issues. Making such distinctions is particularly difficult in the Rule 11 context. Rather than mandating an inquiry into purely legal questions, such as whether the attorney's legal argument was correct, the rule requires a court to consider issues rooted in factual determinations. For example, to determine whether an attorney's prefiling inquiry was reasonable, a court must consider all the circumstances of a case. An inquiry that is unreasonable when an attorney has months to prepare a complaint may be reasonable when he has only a few days before the statute of limitations runs. In considering whether a complaint was supported by fact and law "to the best of the signer's knowledge, information, and belief," a court must make some assessment of the signer's credibility. Issues involving credibility are normally considered factual matters. The considerations involved in the Rule 11 context are similar to those involved in determining negligence, which is generally reviewed deferentially. Familiar with the issues and litigants, the district court is better situated than the court of appeals to marshall the pertinent facts and apply the fact-dependent legal standard mandated by Rule 11. Of course, this standard would not preclude the appellate court's correction of a district court's legal errors, e.g., determining that Rule 11 sanctions could be imposed upon the signing attorney's law firm, or relying on a materially incorrect view of the relevant law in determining that a pleading was not "warranted by existing law or a good faith argument" for changing the law. An appellate court would be justified in concluding that, in making such errors, the district ·

court abused its discretion. "[I]f a district court's findings rest on an erroneous view of the law, they may be set aside on that basis."

. . . .

. . . [An additional institutional factor supporting a deferential standard of review is the fact that] an appellate court reviewing legal issues in the Rule 11 context would be required to determine whether, at the time the attorney filed the pleading or other paper, his legal argument would have appeared plausible. Such determinations "will either fail to produce the normal law-clarifying benefits that come from an appellate decision on a question of law, or else will strangely distort the appellate process" by establishing circuit law in "a most peculiar, second-handed fashion."

[Moreover,] only deferential review [gives] the district court the necessary flexibility to resolve questions involving " 'multifarious, fleeting, special, narrow facts that utterly resist generalization.' " . . . The issues involved in determining whether an attorney has violated . . . involve "fact-intensive, close calls." C. Shaffer & P. Sandler, Sanctions: Rule 11 and Other Powers 15 (2d ed. 1988). . . .

Rule 11's policy goals also support adopting an abuse-of-discretion standard. The district court is best acquainted with the local bar's litigation practices and thus best situated to determine when a sanction is warranted to serve Rule 11's goal of specific and general deterrence. Deference to the determination of courts on the front lines of litigation will enhance these courts' ability to control the litigants before them. Such deference will streamline the litigation process by freeing appellate courts from the duty of reweighing evidence and reconsidering facts already weighed and considered by the district court; it will also discourage litigants from pursuing marginal appeals, thus reducing the amount of satellite litigation.

Although district courts' identification of what conduct violates Rule 11 may vary, some variation in the application of a standard based on reasonableness is inevitable. "Fact-bound resolutions cannot be made uniform through appellate review, de novo or otherwise." An appellate court's review of whether a legal position was reasonable or plausible enough under the circumstances is unlikely to establish clear guidelines for lower courts; nor will it clarify the underlying principles of law.

In light of our consideration of the purposes and policies of Rule 11 and in accordance with our analysis of analogous . . . provisions, we reject petitioner's contention that the Court of Appeals should have applied a three-tiered standard of review. Rather, an appellate court should apply an abuse-of-discretion standard in reviewing all aspects of a district court's Rule 11 determination. A district court would necessarily abuse its discretion if it based its ruling on an erroneous view of the law or on a clearly erroneous assessment of the evidence. Here, the Court of Appeals determined that the District Court "applied the correct legal standard and offered substantial justification for its finding of a Rule 11 violation." Its affirmance of the District Court's liability determination is consistent with the deferential standard we adopt today.

V

. . . .

On its face, Rule 11 does not apply to appellate proceedings. Its provision allowing the court to include "an order to pay to the other party or parties the amount of the reasonable expense, incurred because of the filing of the pleading, motion, or other paper, including a reasonable attorney's fee" must be interpreted in light of Federal Rule of Civil Procedure 1, which indicates that the rules only "govern the procedure in the United States district courts." Neither the language of Rule 11 nor the Advisory Committee Note suggests that the Rule could require payment for any activities outside the context of district court proceedings.

Respondents interpret the last sentence of Rule 11 as extending the scope of the sanction to cover any expenses, including fees on appeal, incurred "because of the filing." In this case, respondents argue, they would have incurred none of their appellate expenses had petitioner's lawsuit not been filed. This line of reasoning would lead to the conclusion that expenses incurred "because of" a baseless filing extend indefinitely. Such an interpretation of the rule is overbroad. We believe Rule 11 is more sensibly understood as permitting an award only of those expenses directly caused by the filing, logically, those at the trial level. A plaintiff's filing requires the defendant to take the necessary steps to defend against the suit in district court; if the filing was baseless, attorneys' fees incurred in that defense were triggered by the Rule 11 violation. If the district court imposes Rule 11 sanctions on the plaintiff, and the plaintiff appeals, the expenses incurred in defending the award on appeal are directly caused by the district court's sanction and the appeal of that sanction, not by the plaintiff's initial filing in district court.

The Federal Rules of Appellate Procedure place a natural limit on Rule 11's scope. On appeal, the litigants' conduct is governed by Federal Rule of Appellate Procedure 38, which provides: "If a court of appeals shall determine that an appeal is frivolous, it may award just damages and single or double costs to the appellee." If the appeal of a Rule 11 sanction is itself frivolous, Rule 38 gives appellate courts ample authority to award expenses. Indeed, because the district court has broad discretion to impose Rule 11 sanctions, appeals of such sanctions may frequently be frivolous. If the appeal is not frivolous under this standard, Rule 38 does not require the appellee to pay the appellant's attorney's fees. Respondent's interpretation of Rule 11 would give a district court the authority to award attorney's fees to the appellee even when the appeal would not be sanctioned under the appellate rules. To avoid this somewhat anomalous result, Rules 11 and 38 are better read together as allowing expenses incurred on appeal to be shifted onto appellants only when those expenses are caused by a frivolous appeal, and not merely because a Rule 11 sanction upheld on appeal can ultimately be traced to a baseless filing in district court.

Limiting Rule 11's scope in this manner accords with the policy of not discouraging meritorious appeals. If appellants were routinely compelled to shoulder the appellees' attorney's fees, valid challenges to district court decisions would be discouraged. The knowledge that, after an unsuccessful appeal of a Rule 11 sanction, the district court that originally imposed the sanction would also decide whether the appellant should pay his opponent's attorney's fee would be likely to chill all but the bravest litigants from taking an appeal. Moreover, including appellate attorney's fees in a Rule 11 sanction might have the undesirable effect of encouraging additional satellite litigation. For example, if a district court included appellate attorney's fees in the Rule 11 sanction on remand, the losing party might again appeal the amount of the award.

It is possible that disallowing an award of appellate attorney's fees under Rule 11 would discourage litigants from defending the award on appeal when appellate expenses are likely to exceed the amount of the sanction. There is some doubt whether this proposition is empirically correct. The courts of appeals have ample authority to protect the beneficiaries of Rule 11 sanctions by awarding damages and single or double costs under Rule 38—which they may do, as we have noted, when the appellant had no reasonable prospect of meeting the difficult standard of abuse of discretion. Beyond that protection, however, the risk of expending the value of one's award in the course of defending it is a natural concomitant of the American Rule, *i.e.*, that "the prevailing litigant is ordinarily not entitled to collect a reasonable attorneys' fee from the loser." Whenever damages awards at the trial level are small, a successful plaintiff will have less incentive to defend the award on appeal. As Rule 11 is not a fee-shifting statute, the policies for allowing district courts to require the losing party to pay appellate, as well as district court attorneys' fees, are not applicable. . . .

We affirm the Court of Appeals' conclusion that a voluntary dismissal does not deprive a district court of jurisdiction over a Rule 11 motion and hold that an appellate court should review the district court's decision in a Rule 11 proceeding for an abuse of discretion. As Rule 11 does not authorize a district court to award attorneys' fees incurred on appeal, we reverse that portion of the Court of Appeals' judgment remanding the case to the district court for a determination of reasonable appellate expenses. For the foregoing reasons, the judgment of the court below is affirmed in part and reversed in part.

It is so ordered.

■ JUSTICE STEVENS, concurring in part and dissenting in part.

Rule 11 and Rule 41(a)(1) are both designed to facilitate the just, speedy and inexpensive determination of cases in federal court. Properly understood, the two Rules should work in conjunction to prevent the prosecution of needless or baseless lawsuits. . . . The Court today, however, refuses to read the two Rules together in light of their limited, but valuable, purposes. By focusing on the filing of baseless complaints, without any attention to whether those complaints will result in the waste of judicial resources, the Court vastly expands the contours of Rule 11, eviscerates Rule 41(a)(1), and creates a federal common law of malicious prosecution inconsistent with the limited mandate of the Rules Enabling Act.

. . . .

The Court holds ... that a voluntary dismissal does not eliminate the predicate for a Rule 11 violation because a frivolous complaint that is withdrawn burdens "courts and individuals alike with needless expense and delay." That assumption is manifestly incorrect with respect to courts. The filing of a frivolous complaint which is voluntarily withdrawn imposes a burden on the court only if the notation of an additional civil proceeding on the court's docket sheet can be said to constitute a burden. By definition, a voluntary dismissal under Rule 41(a)(1) means that the court has not had to consider the factual allegations of the complaint or ruled on a motion to dismiss its legal claims.

The Court's observation that individuals are burdened, even if correct, is irrelevant. Rule 11 is designed to deter parties from abusing judicial resources, not from filing complaints. Whatever additional costs in reputation or legal expenses the defendant might incur, on top of those that are the product of being in a dispute, are likely to be either minimal or non-compensable. More fundamentally, the fact that the filing of a complaint imposes costs on a defendant should be of no concern to the rulemakers if the complaint does not impose any costs on the judiciary: the Rules Enabling Act does not give us authority to create a generalized federal common law of malicious prosecution divorced from concerns with the efficient and just processing of cases in federal court. The only result of the Court's interpretation will be to increase the frequency of Rule 11 motions and decrease that of voluntary dismissals.

I agree that dismissal of an action pursuant to Rule 41(a)(1) does not deprive the district court of jurisdiction to resolve collateral issues.[22] ... But when a plaintiff has voluntarily dismissed a complaint pursuant to Rule 41(a)(1), a collateral proceeding to examine whether the complaint is well grounded will stretch out the matter long beyond the time in which either the plaintiff or the defendant would otherwise want to litigate the merits of the claim. An interpretation that can only have the unfortunate consequences of encouraging the filing of sanction motions and discouraging voluntary dismissals cannot be a sensible interpretation of Rules that are designed "to secure the just, speedy, and inexpensive determination of every action." Fed.Rule Civil Proc. 1.

Despite the changes that have taken place at the bar since I left the active practice 20 years ago, I still believe that most lawyers are wise enough to know that their most precious asset is their professional reputation. Filing unmeritorious pleadings inevitably tarnishes that asset. Those who do not understand this simple truth can be dealt with in appropriate disciplinary proceedings, state law actions for malicious prosecution or abuse of process, or, in extreme cases, contempt proceedings. It is an unnecessary waste of judicial resources and an unwarranted perversion of the Federal Rules to hold such lawyers liable for Rule 11 sanctions in actions in federal court.

I respectfully dissent.

22. I also join Parts IV and V of the Court's opinion.

NOTES

1. Calloway brought a copyright suit against Marvel. Among other things, he claimed that papers giving Marvel the right to use his work were forged. At trial, the judge found this claim baseless. The court therefore directed a verdict for Marvel on the forgery issue. The jury's verdict rejected Calloway's other claims.

LeFlore, Calloway's lawyer, signed the complaint. After he entered a partnership with Pavelic, LeFlore signed court papers, some of which relied on the forgery claim, in the name of the firm "by" himself. After trial, the judge imposed a $100,000 Rule 11 sanction on the lawyers—$50,000 on Calloway and $50,000 on the firm—for failing sufficiently to investigate the forgery claim.

The court of appeals affirmed the imposition of liability on the partnership, but the Supreme Court reversed. Pavelic & LeFlore v. Marvel Entertainment Group, 493 U.S. 120, 110 S.Ct. 456, 107 L.Ed.2d 438 (1989). In an opinion by Scalia, J., the Court deemed the plain meaning of Rule 11 inconsistent with the notion that the partnership could be seen as the "person who signed" the offending court papers. Beyond this, it regarded the theory that the Rule's deterrence value would be greater were sanctions reserved for the individual "signer" as plausible enough to justify interpreting the Rule to mean "what it most naturally seems to say."

Marshall, J., dissented. Pointing out that the term "signer" is not used in the final sentence of Rule 11 (which authorizes the imposition of sanctions), he argued that "person who signed" should be read to include juridical persons. This would have the benefit, he asserted, of allowing judges to maximize the deterrent value of the Rule by sanctioning the signing attorney, his or her firm, or both, as appropriate.

2. Business Guides (BG) brought a suit requesting, among other things, a temporary restraining order to prevent Chromatic from pirating listings from its business directories. The application for the TRO was signed on behalf of BG by its president. BG also submitted sealed affidavits of its employees identifying the ten listings it claimed to have been stolen. After the judge's law clerk asked BG's lawyers for further details about the listings, BG filed a supplemental affidavit in which its research director stated that only six listings had been pilfered. The law clerk's independent inquiries revealed that the affidavits had identified at most a single stolen listing. In fact, it finally turned out that there were none.

No TRO was issued. Instead, hearings were held which led to the imposition of sanctions on BG for violation of Rule 11. While the judge concluded that BG had not acted in bad faith, he found that it had violated Rule 11 by filing the TRO application and the supplemental affidavit without first making reasonable inquiry into the facts. By way of sanction, the judge dismissed BG's case with prejudice and awarded Chromatic all of its legal expenses and out-of-pocket costs.

The Supreme Court granted certiorari to review the ruling that BG had violated Rule 11, which it affirmed by a 5–4 vote. Business Guides, Inc. v. Chromatic Communications Enterprises, Inc., 498 U.S. 533, 111 S.Ct. 922, 112 L.Ed.2d 1140 (1991). O'Connor, J., who spoke for the majority, considered the plain meaning of Rule 11 to be that "a party who signs a pleading or other paper without first conducting a reasonable inquiry shall be sanctioned." She judged this reading of the Rule to be eminently sensible, as it places on the parties, who may be in the best position to find the facts, the same responsibility as their lawyers to rid the courts of baseless claims. Rejecting the argument that the imposition of sanctions in this case was either a form of fee-shifting or a tort remedy in the nature of a federal law of malicious prosecution, she described the Rule as a "reasonably necessary" means of "maintain[ing] the integrity of the system of federal practice and procedure," and thus authorized by the Rules Enabling Act. Finally, although she found it unnecessary to rule on the question, given BG's failure to preserve it on appeal, Justice O'Connor asserted that there was no inconsistency between the imposition of vicarious liability on BG in this case and the decision in *Pavelic & LeFlore:*

> In *Pavelic & LeFlore,* we relied in part on Rule 11's unambiguous statement that papers must be signed by an attorney "in the attorney's individual name." A corporate entity, of course, cannot itself sign anything; it can act only through its agents. It would be anomalous to determine that an individual who is represented by counsel falls within the scope of Rule 11, but that a corporate client does not because it cannot itself sign a document.

Kennedy, J., dissented in an opinion which was joined by Marshall, Stevens, and (in most respects) Scalia, JJ. Drawing an analogy to the mode of analysis employed in *Pavelic & LeFlore,* the dissenters thought it proper to "correlate '[t]he signature of an attorney or party' that constitutes a Rule 11 certification with the signatures of attorneys and *unrepresented parties* provided for earlier in the Rule." Because Rule 11 does not require represented parties to sign or certify anything, and because they denied that affidavits required by other Rules are "papers" within the meaning of Rule 11's certification requirement (the Court did not suggest that they are "papers" within the meaning of Rule 11's signature requirement), these Justices asserted that the majority's contrary interpretation of Rule 11 would do nothing to further the deterrent policies behind it. Moreover, they maintained that the majority's equation of the signature of BG's officials with BG's signature was both inconsistent with the holding in *Pavelic & LeFlore* and wrong.

The dissenters found that BG's attorneys did not violate the Rule since they did not fail to make a reasonable inquiry regarding any paper signed by them. However, if the lawyers had violated the Rule, the dissenters felt that it would be improper to sanction the client (as seems to be allowed under the last sentence of the Rule) unless the client acted in bad faith, which was not the case here.

Three of the dissenters went further. These Justices hinted that the majority's recognition of a client's duty of reasonable inquiry was an improper and unwise intrusion on Congress' authority to set fee-shifting rules and an equally dubious displacement of state laws governing malicious prosecution and abuse of process. In any event, they argued that these concerns favored their view of the scope of Rule 11, which avoided any possible conflict with the Rules Enabling Act.

———

B.   PREJUDGMENT INTEREST

———

General Motors Corp. v. Devex Corp.

Supreme Court of the United States, 1983.
461 U.S. 648, 103 S.Ct. 2058, 76 L.Ed.2d 211.

■ JUSTICE MARSHALL delivered the opinion of the Court.

This case concerns the proper standard governing the award of prejudgment interest in a patent infringement suit under 35 U.S.C. § 284.

I

[Devex won its patent infringement suit against GMC. The final judgment included an award of over $8.8 million in royalties and some $11 million in prejudgment interest. The court of appeals affirmed.]

II

Prior to 1946 the provision of the patent laws concerning a plaintiff's recovery in an infringement action contained no reference to interest. The award of interest in patent cases was governed by the common law standard enunciated in several decisions of this Court. Under the *Duplate* standard, prejudgment interest was generally awarded from the date on which damages were liquidated, and could be awarded from the date of infringement in the absence of liquidation only in "exceptional circumstances," such as bad faith on the part of the infringer.[5]

In 1946 Congress adopted amendments to the provision of the patent laws governing recovery in infringement actions. One of the amended provisions, which has since been recodified as 35 U.S.C. § 284, states in relevant part:

"Upon finding for the claimant the court shall award the claimant damages adequate to compensate for the infringement, but in no event less than a reasonable royalty for the use made of the invention by the infringer, together with interest and costs as fixed by the court."

———

5. Under the common law rule a plaintiff's damages were often treated as liquidated if they were relatively certain and ascertainable by reference to established market values. Thus a plaintiff whose damages were determined by reference to an established royalty that the plaintiff charged for the use of the patent was entitled to prejudgment interest. In contrast, where a plaintiff's damages, as here, were based on a reasonable royalty determined by the court, they were unliquidated and not entitled to prejudgment interest absent exceptional circumstances.

The Courts of Appeals have reached differing conclusions as to whether § 284 incorporates the *Duplate* standard and more generally as to the standard governing the award of prejudgment interest under § 284.

We have little doubt that § 284 does not incorporate the *Duplate* standard. Under that standard, which evolved as a matter of federal common law, prejudgment interest could not be awarded where damages were unliquidated absent bad faith or other exceptional circumstances. By contrast, § 284 gives a court general authority to fix interest and costs. On the face of § 284, a court's authority to award interest is not restricted to exceptional circumstances, and there is no warrant for imposing such a limitation. When Congress wished to limit an element of recovery in a patent infringement action, it said so explicitly. With respect to attorney's fees, Congress expressly provided that a court could award such fees to a prevailing party only "in exceptional cases." 35 U.S.C. § 285. The power to award of interest was not similarly restricted.

. . . .

Having decided that § 284 does not incorporate the *Duplate* rule, we turn to a consideration of the proper standard for awarding prejudgment interest under that provision. Although the language of § 284 supplies little guidance as to the appropriate standard, for the reasons elaborated below we are convinced that the underlying purpose of the provision strongly suggests that prejudgment interest should ordinarily be awarded where necessary to afford the plaintiff full compensation for the infringement.

Both the background and language of § 284 provide evidence of this fundamental purpose. Under the pre–1946 statute, the owner of a patent could recover both his own damages and the infringer's profits. A patent owner's ability to recover the infringer's profits reflected the notion that he should be able to force the infringer to disgorge the fruits of the infringement even if it caused him no injury. In 1946 Congress excluded consideration of the infringer's gain by eliminating the recovery of his profits, the determination of which had often required protracted litigation. At the same time, Congress sought to ensure that the patent owner would in fact receive full compensation for "any damages" he suffered as a result of the infringement. Accordingly, Congress expressly provided in § 284 that the court "shall award the claimant damages *adequate to compensate* for the infringement."

The standard governing the award of prejudgment interest under § 284 should be consistent with Congress' overriding purpose of affording patent owners complete compensation. In light of that purpose, we conclude that prejudgment interest should ordinarily be awarded. In the typical case an award of prejudgment interest is necessary to ensure that the patent owner is placed in as good a position as he would have been in had the infringer entered into a reasonable royalty agreement.[10] An award

---

10. The traditional view, which treated prejudgment interest as a penalty awarded on the basis of the defendant's conduct, has long been criticized on the ground that pre-judgment interest represents "delay damages" and should be awarded as a component of full compensation. A rule denying prejudgment interest not only undercompensates the

of interest from the time that the royalty payments would have been received merely serves to make the patent owner whole, since his damages consist not only of the value of the royalty payments but also of the foregone use of the money between the time of infringement and the date of the judgment.

. . . .

III

Because we hold that prejudgment interest should ordinarily be awarded absent some justification for withholding such an award, a decision to award prejudgment interest will only be set aside if it constitutes an abuse of discretion. The District Court held that GMC infringed Devex's patent over the course of a number of years and awarded Devex a reasonable royalty as compensation. While GMC contends that Devex was guilty of causing unnecessary delay, the District Court rejected this contention when it concluded that "Devex has done no worse than fully litigate its claims achieving a large judgment in its favor" and awarded Devex costs on the basis of this conclusion. On these facts, we agree with the Court of Appeals that the award of prejudgment interest was proper.

Accordingly, the judgment of the Court of Appeals for the Third Circuit is

Affirmed.

[The concurring opinion of STEVENS, J., is omitted.]

Cavnar v. Quality Control Parking, Inc.

Supreme Court of Texas, 1985.
696 S.W.2d 549.

■ GONZALEZ, J. This is a wrongful death and survival action. The primary [issue is] . . . (2) whether prejudgment interest is recoverable in personal injury cases. The court of appeals[, like the trial court,] . . . denied prejudgment interest. We reverse that part of the judgment . . . and remand it to the trial court with instructions.

. . . .

The term "interest" encompasses two distinct forms of compensation: interest as interest (*eo nomine*) and interest as damages. Interest as interest is compensation allowed by law or fixed by the parties for the use or detention of money. Interest as damages is compensation allowed by law as additional damages for lost use of the money due as damages during the lapse of time between the accrual of the claim and the date of judgment.

In Phillips Petroleum Co. v. Stahl Petroleum Co., 569 S.W.2d 480, 485 (Tex.1978), this court recognized two separate bases for the award of prejudgment interest: (1) an enabling statute and (2) general principles of

patent owner but may also grant a windfall to the infringer and create an incentive to prolong litigation. There is no reason why an infringer should stand in a better position than a party who agrees to pay a royalty and then fails to pay because of financial difficulties.

equity.[1] Since no statute controls the award of prejudgment interest in personal injury cases, the Cavnars must rely upon equitable considerations in order to prevail on their prejudgment interest claim.

The primary objective of awarding damages in civil actions has always been to compensate the injured plaintiff, rather than to punish the defendant. A law that denies recovery of prejudgment interest frustrates this goal. If a judgment provides plaintiffs only the amount of damages sustained at the time of the incident, plaintiffs are not fully compensated. They have been denied the opportunity to invest and earn interest on the amount of damages between the time of the occurrence and the time of judgment.

Perhaps the lower courts would have relied upon the equitable ground of recovery set forth in *Stahl* had they not believed that the award of prejudgment interest was foreclosed based on *dicta* in Watkins v. Junker, 90 Tex. 584, 40 S.W. 11 (Tex.1897), and its progeny. *Watkins* involved a suit on a contract to recover money allegedly due for services and rental of boats. The court permitted the recovery of prejudgment interest but stated that "[i]nterest ... cannot be allowed upon damages arising from assault and battery, libel and slander, seduction, false imprisonment nor for personal injuries and the like."

The *Watkins* court justified its refusal to allow prejudgment interest in this class of cases because the measure of damages was not fixed at any particular time and because the jury was given considerable latitude in determining the amount of recovery in such cases. This limitation is echoed in Tex.Rev.Civ.Stat.Ann. art. 5069–1.03 (Vernon Supp.1985), which, by its terms, applies only to ascertainable sums. Later cases also rely on the *Watkins dicta* in denying recovery of prejudgment interest. However, the court in *Watkins* recognized that an award of prejudgment interest is necessary in order to fully compensate an injured plaintiff.

> It is objected in this case that interest is a creature of the statute, and cannot be allowed upon unliquidated damages. It is true that interest, strictly speaking, exists only by statutory law, but it is likewise true that courts have recognized the fact that compensation for detention of that which is due on account of injury inflicted is an element of damages necessary to the complete indemnity of the injured party....

The *Watkins* court based its decision on the assumption that interest under that name was not recoverable unless provided for by statute. Courts in subsequent cases therefore attempted to circumvent this limitation by allowing recovery of prejudgment interest under the guise of damages. However, the distinction between interest as damages and interest as interest was abolished in *Stahl* where the court stated:

> Our holding that Stahl is entitled to legal interest on that portion of his money which was held in suspense and used by Phillips is a mere extension of the equitable principles announced in *Watkins* and *Heid-*

---

1. The court in *Stahl* relied upon the "elemental equitable principle" that a defendant "ought not to be able to use someone else's money as it pleases ... thereby enjoying a very considerable benefit, and then pay nothing for the use of the money."

enheimer. The only difference is that we treat interest for the use of money under these circumstances as an equitable exception to the "interest *eo nomine* "rule. In such cases, *it is permissible but no longer necessary to continue the round-about method of allowing indemnity under the name of damages measured by the legal rate of interest.*

(Emphasis added). Thus, prejudgment interest is recoverable regardless of whether it is characterized as damages or as interest.

The rule set forth in *Stahl* actually was not a significant departure from the line of cases following *Watkins.* In an effort to fully compensate injured plaintiffs, the courts of this state have eroded the *Watkins* limitation on prejudgment interest until the distinction between claims in which the damages are or are not fixed and ascertainable has become forced and artificial. Plaintiffs have been permitted to recover prejudgment interest on both liquidated and unliquidated claims in both contract and tort disputes. As these cases demonstrate, the fact that the amount of damages is uncertain, disputed and therefore unliquidated has not barred recovery of prejudgment interest in any except personal injury cases. The distinctions drawn between these cases and personal injury cases are illogical because the measure of recovery for damages in a personal injury action is no more uncertain and unliquidated than that in many other tort and contractual disputes where prejudgment interest has been allowed.

The rationale underlying the distinction between liquidated and unliquidated damages as a basis for awarding or denying prejudgment interest has even been criticized by the Supreme Court of the United States.[2] The time has come to revise the prejudgment interest rule to make injured parties whole and restore equity and symmetry to this area of the law. We therefore hold that, as a matter of law, a prevailing plaintiff may recover prejudgment interest compounded daily (based on a 365–day year) on damages *that have accrued by the time of judgment.* To the extent that other cases conflict with this holding, they are overruled. Prejudgment interest shall accrue at the prevailing rate that exists on the date judgment is rendered according to the provisions of Tex.Rev.Civ.Stat.Ann. art. 5069–1.05 § 2 (Vernon Supp.1985). In addition to achieving full compensation, awarding prejudgment interest in personal injury cases at a rate close to the market rate will also serve to expedite both settlements and trials. It will remove the current incentives for defendants to delay as long as possible without creating incentives for plaintiffs to delay. These considerations were recognized by the 5th Circuit in Domangue v. Eastern Air Lines, Inc., where the court held:

2. It has been recognized that a distinction, in this respect simply as between cases of liquidated and unliquidated damages, is not a sound one. Whether the case is of the one class or the other, the injured party has suffered a loss which may be regarded as not fully compensated if he is confined to the amount found to be recoverable as of the time of breach and nothing is added for the delay in obtaining the award of damages. Because of this fact, the rule with respect to unliquidated claims has been in evolution ..., and in the absence of legislation the courts have dealt with the question of allowing interest according to their conception of the demands of justice and practicality. "The disinclination to allow interest on claim of uncertain amount seems based on practice rather than theoretical grounds." Williston on Contracts, vol. III, § 1413.

A potential award of pre-judgment interest advances the objective of encouraging speedy compensation to victims, and ensures that the aim of obtaining a high recovery for victims and their survivors is not defeated by a defendant's simple strategy of delaying payment or judgment until the award is diminished in actual value. We agree with the Supreme Court of New Jersey's reasoning in Busik v. Levine that the allowance of prejudgment interest on an unliquidated tort claim will induce prompt defense consideration of settlement possibilities. It is also likely to discourage delay if the case is taken to court.

722 F.2d 256, 264 (5th Cir.1984).

Accrual of Prejudgment Interest

We recognize that damages are typically incurred intermittently throughout the prejudgment period. This fact complicates the award of prejudgment interest because a plaintiff is not entitled to recover prejudgment interest on damages until those damages have actually been sustained. Until that time, the plaintiff has not lost the use of the money he ultimately receives from the defendant.

Yet a system which would force litigants to determine precisely when each element of a plaintiff's damage award was incurred would impose an onerous burden on both the trial bench and bar. We therefore adopt a method of calculation that, in our opinion, fairly compensates the plaintiff and avoids the difficulty of accruing prejudgment interest.

A few jurisdictions allow recovery of prejudgment interest as of the date the cause of action accrues. This approach, however, does not preserve the integrity of the principle that prejudgment interest is not meant to punish defendant's misbehavior, but to achieve full compensation for plaintiffs. Rather, it overcompensates the plaintiff by awarding interest on losses not yet incurred. While any accrual method is admittedly arbitrary, the method we adopt more closely approaches the goals underlying prejudgment interest compensation than would accrual as of the date the cause of action arises.

(1) Damages Suffered by a Plaintiff (Wrongful Death and Non–Death Personal Injury Actions)

In wrongful death and non-death personal injury cases, interest shall begin to accrue on both pecuniary and non-pecuniary damages from a date six months after the occurrence of the incident giving rise to the cause of action.

(2) Damages Suffered by a Decedent Prior to Death (Survival Actions)

In survival actions such as this one, the decedent typically sustains both out-of-pocket and non-pecuniary losses. However, the accrual problem is not critical in these cases because all of the decedent's damages must necessarily have accrued by the time of death or shortly thereafter. We therefore allow interest to accrue on the decedent's total damage award as of the date of death. In most cases, this method of calculation will yield the largest interest award. If, however, the decedent lingers for more than six months after the date of the occurrence that gave rise to the cause of action, interest shall begin to accrue from a date six months after the cause of action accrues. In other words, the decedent's estate is entitled to prejudgment interest either from the date of death or six months after the injury-causing incident occurred, whichever yields the larger interest award.

Punitive—Future Damages

Plaintiffs also contend that they are entitled to prejudgment interest for punitive damages and future damages. We disagree. Commentators are virtually unanimous in advocating that prejudgment interest not be awarded on future damages and punitive damages.

Punitive damages are intended to punish the defendant and to set an example to others. They are assessed over and above the amount of damages necessary to indemnify the plaintiff. The plaintiff can thus be made whole even if prejudgment interest is not awarded on punitive damages. The plaintiff is likewise unharmed by the defendant's retention of future damages prior to trial since these damages are, by their very nature, unaccrued. We therefore limit recovery of prejudgment interest to accrued damages.

. . . .

Our holding in this case applies to all future cases as well as those still in the judicial process involving wrongful death, survival and personal injury actions.

■ CAMPBELL, J., concurs with opinion.

I concur with the court that prejudgment interest should be allowed. However, I disagree with the part of the court's holding that allows prejudgment interest to be compounded daily. There should be one rule for determining prejudgment interest and post-judgment interest. I would hold that prejudgment interest, as allowed in this cause, be computed the same as post-judgment interest as provided in Article 5069–1.05.

NOTES

1. The Texas legislature responded to *Cavnar* by adopting Vernon's Ann.Tex.Civ.St. art. 5069–1.05(6), since repealed, which provided:

> (a) Judgments in wrongful death, personal injury, and property damage cases must include prejudgment interest. Except as provided by Subsections (b), (c), and (d) of this section, prejudgment interest accrues on the amount of the judgment during the period beginning on the 180th day after the date the defendant receives written notice of a claim or on the day the suit is filed, whichever occurs first, and ending on the day preceding the date judgment is rendered. [see Tex. Fin. § 304.104]

> (b) If judgment for a claimant is less than the amount of a settlement offer by the defendant, prejudgment interest does not accrue on the amount of the judgment for the period during which the offer may be accepted. [see Tex. Fin. § 305.105(a)]

(c) If judgment for a claimant is more than the amount of the settlement offer of the defendant, prejudgment interest does not include prejudgment interest on the amount of the settlement offer for the period during which the offer may be accepted. [see Tex. Fin. § 305.105(b)]

(d) In addition to the exceptions provided under Subsections (b) and (c) of this section, the court in its discretion may order that prejudgment interest does or does not accrue during periods of delay in the trial, taking into consideration:

(1) periods of delay caused by a defendant; and

(2) periods of delay caused by a claimant.

(e) In order for a settlement offer to toll the running of prejudgment interest in accordance with the provisions of this section, the offer must be communicated to a party or his attorney or representative in writing. [see Tex. Fin. § 304.106]

(f) If a settlement offer is made for other than present cash payment at the time of settlement, prejudgment interest on the amount of the settlement offer is computed on the basis of cost or fair market value of the settlement offer at the time it is made. [see Tex. Fin. § 304.107]

(g) The rate of prejudgment interest shall be the same as the rate of postjudgment interest at the time of judgment and shall be computed as simple interest. [see Tex. Fin. § 304.103]

2. Consider the following comments, made by Thornberry, J., in Crown Central Petroleum Corporation v. National Union Fire Insurance Company of Pittsburgh, Pennsylvania, 768 F.2d 632 (5th Cir.1985):

It is clear that in *Cavnar* the Supreme Court of Texas took the bold step of allowing prejudgment interest in personal injury cases. It is not so clear, however, whether the rule announced in *Cavnar* applies to all cases, or merely to that class of cases originally excepted from prejudgment interest awards in Watkins v. Junker, 90 Tex. 584, 40 S.W. 11 (Tex.1897). Nevertheless, after careful consideration we have concluded that although the holding in *Cavnar* is ostensibly limited to wrongful death, survival, and personal injury actions, logic dictates that the decision be read to create a new prejudgment interest rule for all cases. It would be incongruous indeed to assume that while attempting to "restore equity and symmetry to this area of the law" the court intended to create two entirely different branches of prejudgment interest jurisprudence, each involving different standards for determining whether and at what rate an award should be made. Moreover, the *Cavnar* court so thoroughly disapproved of the reasonable ascertainability standard employed in prior prejudgment interest cases that we cannot imagine that any rule other than that of *Cavnar* survives.

Prior to *Cavnar* the crucial issue in this appeal would have been whether the insurance policy between Crown and National Union fixed a measure by which the sum payable to Crown could be ascertained with reasonable certainty on the date of the injury. In its effort to discredit the *Watkins* rationale for exempting personal injury cases from prejudgment interest awards, however, the Supreme Court of Texas held that

> the distinction between claims in which the damages are or are not fixed and ascertainable has become forced and artificial. Plaintiffs have been permitted to recover prejudgment interest on both liquidated and unliquidated claims in both contract and tort disputes. As these cases demonstrate, the fact that the amount of damages is uncertain, disputed and therefore unliquidated has not barred recovery of prejudgment interest in any except personal injury cases. . . .

Despite National Union's protestations to the contrary, we could not in good conscience apply a standard that the Supreme Court of Texas has termed "forced and artificial." We must conclude that in contract as well as personal injury cases whether the plaintiff is entitled to prejudgment interest no longer depends on whether there is a fixed measure by which the sum payable is ascertainable to a reasonable certainty.

This conclusion is consistent with the *Cavnar* court's statement that the primary objective in awarding prejudgment interest is to fully compensate the plaintiff. A rule that discriminates between cases on the basis of whether a measure of damages is fixed does nothing to further this objective. If our aim is to compensate the plaintiff for the time value of the damages caused by the defendant, then it should be irrelevant whether the defendant could have ascertained prior to judgment the sum owed to the plaintiff. As the Supreme Court has stated, "[w]hether the case is of one class or the other, the injured party has suffered a loss which may be regarded as not fully compensated if he is confined to the amount found to be recoverable as of the time of the breach and nothing is added for the delay in obtaining the award of damages."

Bullis v. Security Pacific National Bank

Supreme Court of California, 1978.
21 Cal.3d 801, 148 Cal.Rptr. 22, 582 P.2d 109.

■ BIRD, C.J. [Heirs of an estate brought suit against a bank for damages allegedly occasioned when the bank failed to require the signatures of both of the estate's coexecutors for withdrawals from an estate account. The trial court found that the appellant bank breached its common law duty to act with reasonable care when it permitted the withdrawals with only one signature. This finding was affirmed.]

. . . .

Next, this court must decide whether the trial court abused its discretion when it awarded prejudgment interest. Relying on Civil Code section 3288, the trial court awarded respondents prejudgment interest on each unauthorized withdrawal from the date of the withdrawal. Appellant concedes respondents are entitled to prejudgment interest from the effective date of the filing of the complaint until the entry of judgment. However, appellant challenges any award of prejudgment interest calculated from the date of withdrawal rather than from the date the complaint was filed.

Under Civil Code section 3288, the trier of fact may award prejudgment interest "[i]n an action for the breach of an obligation not arising from contract, *and* in every case of oppression, fraud, or malice...." (Emphasis added.)[16] It is clear from this language that a party does not have to prove both a breach of a noncontractual obligation *and* oppression, fraud or malice. Even if plaintiff's damages are not liquidated, prejudgment interest may be awarded.

Respondents recovered damages because appellant breached its common law duty. Since this action was within the purview of section 3288, the decision to award prejudgment interest may not be overturned unless the trial court abused its discretion. A trial court's exercise of discretion will be upheld if it is based on a "reasoned judgment" and complies with the "legal principles and policies appropriate to the particular matter at issue."

Prejudgment interest is awarded to compensate a party for the loss of the use of his or her property. In the present case, the estate was deprived of the use of a quarter of a million dollars for several years due to appellant's negligence. The date on which the estate suffered the loss represented by each unauthorized withdrawal was readily ascertainable and stipulated to by the parties. Under these circumstances, the trial court's award of prejudgment interest to compensate respondents for the negligent loss of funds from the estate's checking account did not constitute an abuse of discretion.

. . . .

The judgment is affirmed.

Tripp v. Swoap

Supreme Court of California, 1976.
17 Cal.3d 671, 131 Cal.Rptr. 789, 552 P.2d 749.

■ SULLIVAN, J. This is an appeal from a judgment awarding plaintiff Kathy Tripp retroactive payment of welfare benefits with ... prejudgment interest.

. . . .

The same public policy which favors the award of retroactive [welfare] benefits would appear to favor the award of prejudgment interest on such benefits. Indeed, we have recognized in the context of an interest award on retroactive salary payments that "[i]f plaintiff had not been wrongfully suspended, he would have obtained the benefit of the moneys paid as of those dates; he has thus lost the natural growth and productivity of the withheld salary in the form of interest." (Mass v. Board of Education, supra, 61 Cal.2d at p. 625, 39 Cal.Rptr. at p. 748, 394 P.2d at p. 588.) The policy rationale behind awarding prejudgment interest articulated in *Mass*

---

16. While section 3288 only grants such authority to the "jury," the trial court, when acting as the trier of fact, may award prejudgment interest under this section.

takes on particular significance in the context of wrongfully withheld welfare benefits. In some instances, it may take long periods of time for an applicant to vindicate his entitlement to aid and in the interval the delay inevitably exacts its toll from that portion of our society least able to bear the deprivation.

The dual concept of debt and public policy ... supplies a strong rationale for the award of prejudgment interest in the case at bench. In the recent case of Luna v. Carleson (1975), 45 Cal.App.3d 670, 119 Cal.Rptr. 711, however, the court held as a matter of first impression that prejudgment interest was not available to the recipient of wrongfully withheld welfare benefits. In a brief opinion the court set forth essentially four grounds for its reversal of the trial court's award of interest in a proceeding brought under section 10962.[2] We are not persuaded that any of the grounds on which the court relied provide authority for the position which the court adopted.

First, the court appears to have misapplied the general rule that interest cannot be recovered against a state or municipality. While it is true that governmental entities traditionally have been immune from liability for interest, Civil Code section 3287 as amended in 1959 provides a clear statutory exception to the general rule, and this exception has been consistently recognized by this court as imposing liability for interest on such entities.

Second, the court was of the view that in the face of the provision in section 10962 for attorney's fees and costs, the Legislature's failure to include interest was not an inadvertence. The court was unable to find any legislative authorization for the payment of interest in a section 10962 proceeding. However, as we have pointed out above, the fact that the Legislature did not specify interest is not probative on the issue whether it is recoverable under the view that the purpose of section 10962 is to ensure access to judicial review and not to define the extent of recovery. Moreover, by failing to find any legislative authorization for the payment of interest in a section 10962 proceeding, the court completely ignored the general availability of interest under Civil Code section 3287, subdivision (a). As we have explained, we are satisfied that section 3287, subdivision (a), reaches actions brought to recover sums of money owing as a statutory obligation. In Mass v. Board of Education, the statute under which we awarded back salary did not provide for the recovery of interest. Rather than imply a legislative bar of interest from that fact, we awarded interest pursuant to the general authority of section 3287, subdivision (a).

Third, the *Luna* court observed that of the many cases decided by our appellate courts involving welfare payments, none of them discussed the matter of interest. As the court acknowledged, however, the fact that interest has not been discussed in similar decisions is not the most convincing authority for denying it.

---

2. [This section "permits an applicant or recipient of welfare benefits to seek judicial review of an adverse determination by the Director" of the State Department of Social Welfare.]

Finally, the court noted that the federal government funds a large share of the welfare payments made by the state and that there is no federal statute authorizing reimbursement to the state for interest payments. As amici have pointed out, however, whether federal reimbursement is available is irrelevant to the determination of the issue whether interest is recoverable against the state. The claims of a recipient such as plaintiff are based upon an entitlement to benefits as a matter of state law. The procedure for judicial review of a denial of benefits is a creature of state law under section 10962 and the entitlement to interest is a matter of state policy as articulated in Civil Code section 3287, subdivision (a).

We believe that sound statutory construction of section 10962 reveals no intent on the part of the Legislature to deny prejudgment interest to the recipient of wrongfully withheld welfare benefits. On the other hand, there is clear authority for awarding such interest pursuant to Civil Code section 3287, subdivision (a). We are further of the view that the award of such interest would be in conformity with the statutory mandate requiring the law relating to public assistance programs to be liberally construed.

Accordingly, we hold that where a recipient of welfare benefits is adjudged entitled to retroactive payment of benefits pursuant to the statutory obligation of the state, such recipient is entitled to an award of prejudgment interest at the legal rate from the time each payment becomes due. To the extent that Luna v. Carleson is inconsistent with the views expressed herein, it is disapproved.

The cause is remanded to the trial court with directions to modify its judgment by directing defendant to pay retroactive aid to plaintiff effective August 1, 1972, instead of July 25, 1972. As modified, the judgment is affirmed. . . . Plaintiff shall recover costs on appeal.

■ CLARK, J. (dissenting). The majority err in allowing a welfare recipient interest on unpaid aid, contravening both legislative intent and welfare's purpose.

The Legislature has provided the recipient judicial review, mentioning filing fees, attorney's fees and court costs. (Welf. & Inst.Code, § 10962.) But the same code makes no mention of interest.

The purpose of welfare is to provide subsistence to the needy. But it has not been shown that the addition of interest will alleviate Mrs. Tripp's needs.

The welfare fund is a limited resource, derived from the labor of others. By now adding interest to the aid of one, we reduce the aid available to another. Today's decision is inequitable to all.

■ McCOMB, J., concurs.

———

C.   FOREIGN CURRENCY JUDGMENTS

———

Owners of M.V. Eleftherotria v. Owners of M.V. Despina R

House of Lords, 1978.
[1979] A.C. 685.

■ LORD WILBERFORCE. My Lords, in Miliangos v. George Frank (Textiles) Ltd. [1976] A.C. 443, this House decided that a plaintiff suing for a debt payable in Swiss francs under a contract governed by Swiss law could claim and recover judgment in this country in Swiss francs. Whether the same, or a similar, rule could be applied to cases where (i) a plaintiff sues for damages in tort, or (ii) a plaintiff sues for damages for breach of contract, were questions expressly left open for later decision.... Now these questions are directly raised in the present appeals in each of which your Lordships have the advantage of judgments of the Court of Appeal and of judgments of high quality at first instance. These enable the House, as it could not have done in *Miliangos,* to consider some of the problems which may exist in the varied cases of torts and breaches of contract.

OWNERS OF M.V. ELEFTHEROTRIA *v.* OWNERS OF M.V. DESPINA R

These are two Greek vessels which collided in April 1974 off Shanghai. On July 7, 1976, a settlement was arrived at under which it was agreed that the appellants [(the owners of the *Despina R*)] should pay to the respondents 85 per cent. of the loss and damage caused to the respondents by the collision. This is therefore a tort case based upon negligence.

. . . .

My Lords, I do not think that there can now be any doubt that, given the ability of an English court (and of arbitrators sitting in this country) to give judgment or to make an award in a foreign currency, to give a judgment in the currency in which the loss was sustained produces a juster result than one which fixes the plaintiff with a sum in sterling taken at the date of the breach or of the loss. I need not expand upon this because the point has been clearly made both in Miliangos v. George Frank (Textiles) Ltd. [1976] A.C. 443, and in cases which have followed it, as well as in commentators who, prior to *Miliangos,* advocated abandonment of the breach-date-sterling rule. To fix such a plaintiff with sterling commits him to the risk of changes in the value of a currency with which he has no connection: to award him a sum in the currency of the expenditure or loss, or that in which he bears the expenditure or loss, gives him exactly what he has lost and commits him only to the risk of changes in the value of that currency, or those currencies, which are either his currency or those which he has chosen to use.

. . . .

My Lords, in my opinion, this question can be solved by applying the normal principles, which govern the assessment of damages in cases of tort (I shall deal with contract cases in the second appeal). These are the principles of restitutio in integrum [(restoration to the prior condition)] and that of the reasonable foreseeability of the damage sustained. It appears to me that a plaintiff, who normally conducts his business through a particular currency, and who, when other currencies are immediately involved, uses his own currency to obtain those currencies, can reasonably say that the loss he sustains is to be measured not by the immediate currencies in which the loss first emerges but by the amount of his own currency, which in the normal course of operation, he uses to obtain those currencies. This is the currency in which his loss is felt, and is the currency which it is reasonably foreseeable he will have to spend.

There are some objections to this, but I think they can be answered. First, it is said that to use the method of finding the loss in the plaintiff's currency would involve the court or arbitrators in complicated inquiries. I am not convinced of this. The plaintiff has to prove his loss: if he wishes to present his claim in his own currency, the burden is on him to show to the satisfaction of the tribunal that his operations are conducted in that currency and that in fact it was his currency that was used, in a normal manner, to meet the expenditure for which he claims or that his loss can only be appropriately measured in that currency (this would apply in the case of a total loss of a vessel which cannot be dealt with by the "expenditure" method). The same answer can be given to the objection that some companies, particularly large multi-national companies, maintain accounts and operate in several currencies. Here again it is for the plaintiff to satisfy the court or arbitrators that the use of the particular currency was in the course of normal operations of that company and was reasonably foreseeable. Then it is said that this method produces inequality between plaintiffs. Two claimants who suffer a similar loss may come out with different sums according to the currency in which they trade. But if the losses of both plaintiffs are suffered at the same time, the amounts awarded to each of them should be equivalent even if awarded in different currencies: if at different times, this might justify difference in treatment. If it happened that the currencies of the two plaintiffs relatively changed in value before the date of judgment, that would be a risk which each plaintiff would have to accept. Each would still receive, for himself, compensation for *his* loss.

Finally it is said (and this argument would apply equally if the expenditure currency were taken) that uncertainty will take the place of certainty under the present rule. Undoubtedly the present (sterling-breach-date) rule produces certainty—but it is often simpler to produce an unjust rule than a just one. The question is whether, in order to produce a just, or juster, rule, too high a price has to be paid in terms of certainty.

I do not think so. I do not see any reason why legal advisers, or insurers, should not be able, from their knowledge of the circumstances, to assess the extent of probable liability. The most difficult step is to assess the quantum of each head of damage. Once this is done, it should not be difficult, on the basis of information which the plaintiff must provide, to agree or disagree with his claim for the relevant currency. I wish to make it clear that I would not approve of a hard and fast rule that in all cases where a plaintiff suffers a loss or damage in a foreign currency the right currency to take for the purpose of his claim is "the plaintiff's currency." I should refer to the definition I have used of this expression and emphasise that it does not suggest the use of a personal currency attached, like nationality, to a plaintiff, but a currency which he is able to show is that in which he normally conducts trading operations. Use of this currency for assessment of damage may and probably will be appropriate in cases of international commerce. But even in that field, and still more outside it, cases may arise in which a plaintiff will not be able to show that in the normal course of events he would use, and be expected to use, the currency, or one of several currencies, in which he normally conducts his operations (the burden being on him to show this) and consequently the conclusion will be that the loss is felt in the currency in which it immediately arose. To say that this produces a measure of uncertainty may be true, but this is an uncertainty which arises in the nature of things from the variety of human experience. To resolve it is part of the normal process of adjudication. To attempt to confine this within a rigid formula would be likely to produce injustices which the courts and arbitrators would have to put themselves to much trouble to avoid.

. . . .

In my opinion the Court of Appeal reached a right conclusion on this case and I would dismiss the appeal.

SERVICES EUROPE ATLANTIQUE SUD (SEAS) OF PARIS *v.* STOCK-HOLMS REDERIAKTIEBOLAG SVEA OF STOCKHOLM

This case arises out of a charter party under which the appellants chartered the *Folias* to the respondents [(SEAS)] for a round voyage from the Mediterranean to the East Coast, South America. The hire was expressed to be payable in U.S. dollars, but there was a provision that in any general average adjustment disbursements in foreign currencies were to be exchanged in a European convertible currency or in sterling or in dollars (U.S.). The appellants are Swedish shipowners, the respondents are a French company which operates shipping services. The proper law of the contract was English law.

. . . .

My Lords, the effect of the decision of this House in Miliangos v. George Frank (Textiles) Ltd. [1976] A.C. 443 is that, in contractual as in other cases a judgment (in which for convenience I include an award) can be given in a currency other than sterling. Whether it should be, and, in a case where there is more than one eligible currency, in which currency, must depend on general principles of the law of contract and on rules of conflict of laws. The former require application, as nearly as possible, of the principle of restitutio in integrum, regard being had to what was in the reasonable contemplation of the parties. The latter involve ascertainment of the proper law of the contract, and application of that law. If the proper law is English, the first step must be to see whether, expressly or by implication, the contract provides an answer to the currency question. This may lead to selection of the "currency of the contract." If from the terms of the contract it appears that the parties have accepted a currency as the currency of account and payment in respect of all transactions arising under the contract, then it would be proper to give a judgment for damages in that currency—this is, I think, the case which Lord Denning M.R. had in mind when he said in Jugoslavenska Oceanska Plovidba v. Castle Investment Co. Inc. [1974] Q.B. 292:

"[arbitrators] should make their award in that currency because it is the proper currency of the contract. By that I mean that it is the currency with which the payments under the contract have the closest and most real connection."

But there may be cases in which, although obligations under the contract are to be met in a specified currency, or currencies, the right conclusion may be that there is no intention shown that damages for breach of the contract should be given in that currency or currencies. I do not think that Lord Denning M.R. was intending to exclude such cases. Indeed in the present case he said, in words which I would adopt "the plaintiff should be compensated for the expense or loss in the currency which most truly expresses his loss." In the present case the fact that U.S. dollars have been named as the currency in which payments in respect of hire and other contractual payments are to be made, provides no necessary or indeed plausible reason why damages for breach of the contract should be paid in that currency. The terms of other contracts may lead to a similar conclusion.

If then the contract fails to provide a decisive interpretation, the damage should be calculated in the currency in which the loss was felt by the plaintiff or "which most truly expresses his loss." This is not limited to that in which it first and immediately arose. In ascertaining which this currency is, the court must ask what is the currency, payment in which will as nearly as possible compensate the plaintiff in accordance with the principle of restitution, and whether the parties must be taken reasonably to have had this in contemplation. It would be impossible to devise a simple rule, other than the general principles I have mentioned, to cover cases on the sale of goods, on contracts of employment, on international carriage by sea or air: in any of these types of contract the terms of the individual agreement will be important.

My Lords, it is obvious that this analysis, involving as it does a reversion to the ordinary law governing damages for breach of contract, necessitates a departure from older cases decided upon the "breach-date-sterling" rule. . . .

    . . . .

The present case is concerned with a charter party for carriage by sea, the parties to which are Swedish and French. It was in the contemplation of the parties that delivery of the goods carried might be made in any of a number of countries with a currency different from that of either of the parties. Loss might be suffered, through non-delivery or incomplete delivery, or [(as happened in this case)] delivery of damaged or unsuitable goods, in any of those countries, and if any such loss were to fall upon the charterer, he in turn might have a claim against the shipowners. Although the proper law of the contract was accepted to be English by virtue of a London arbitration clause, neither of the parties to the contract, nor the contract itself, nor the claim which arose against the charterers, nor that by his charterers against the owners, had any connection with sterling, so that prima facie this would be a case for giving judgment in a foreign currency. This is not disputed in the present appeal, and the only question is which is the appropriate currency in which to measure the loss.

. . . .

In my opinion a decision in what currency the loss was borne or felt can be expressed as equivalent to finding which currency sum appropriately or justly reflects the recoverable loss. This is essentially a matter for arbitrators to determine. A rule that arbitrators may make their award in the currency best suited to achieve an appropriate and just result should be a flexible rule in which account must be taken of the circumstances in which the loss arose, in which the loss was converted into a money sum, and in which it was felt by the plaintiff. In some cases the "immediate loss" currency may be appropriate, in others the currency in which it was borne by the plaintiff. There will be still others in which the appropriate currency is the currency of the contract. Awards of arbitrators based upon their appreciation of the circumstances in which the foreign currency came to be provided should not be set aside for, as such, they involve no error of law.

The arbitrators' decision in the present case was both within the permissible area of decision, and further was in my opinion right.

I agree with the Court of Appeal that the award ought not to have been set aside and with the judgments in that court. I would dismiss the appeal.

[The statements of Lords Diplock, Salmon, and Keith of Kinkel, agreeing with the speech of Lord Wilberforce, are omitted. So, too, is the speech of Lord Russell of Killowen, who concurred in the result.]

Appeals dismissed.

Competex, S.A. v. Labow

United States Court of Appeals, Second Circuit, 1986.
783 F.2d 333.

■ NEWMAN, J. This appeal presents issues concerning currency conversion in the context of enforcing a foreign judgment. Specifically, the question is whether a judgment debtor may satisfy an American judgment that was based on an English judgment by paying the amount of the English judgment in pounds. Defendant-appellant Ronald LaBow appeals from an order . . . denying his motion under Fed.R.Civ.P. 60(b) for relief from the American judgment, previously entered by the late Judge Henry F. Werker in favor of plaintiff-appellee Competex, S.A. For reasons that follow, we affirm.

Background

LaBow, a New Yorker, lost a substantial sum of money through speculation in copper on the London Metal Exchange. His broker, Competex, a Swiss corporation, satisfied these debts. Competex sued LaBow for breach of contract in the English High Court of Justice, Queen's Bench Division, and obtained a default judgment for £187,929.82, which included principal, interest, and costs.

Competex then brought this diversity action to enforce the English judgment. Following a bench trial, Judge Werker held that the English judgment was entitled to recognition and enforcement. Because determination of the date on which to convert a foreign currency debt into dollars is a substantive question, Judge Werker was compelled to apply New York law. New York uses the breach-day conversion rule.

In applying the breach-day rule, Judge Werker reasoned that Competex's American claim was based on the English judgment rather than on the underlying contract. Competex's American claim had therefore accrued upon the date of entry of the English judgment, and Judge Werker applied the conversion rate prevailing on that date: £1 = $2.20. He entered judgment for $583,201.78, which included interest and a fee award pursuant to Fed.R.Civ.P. 56(g).[1] . . .

The pound depreciated substantially relative to the dollar between the dates of the English and American judgments. On the date of the American judgment, the conversion rate was: £1 = $1.50. The pound continued to depreciate. As a result, LaBow moved, pursuant to Fed.R.Civ.P. 60(b), for a clarification of the American judgment and a declaration that he could satisfy the American judgment by paying the underlying English judgment in pounds. While this motion was pending, LaBow borrowed the necessary funds and paid the English judgment, with interest, in pounds. Judge Sprizzo denied LaBow's Rule 60(b) motion and held that the American judgment could be satisfied only by paying the dollar amount specified in that judgment. He credited LaBow's payment against the American judgment at the conversion rate prevailing on the date of payment: £1 = $1.20. This calculation left a balance owing on the American judgment of approximately $236,000.[2] LaBow appeals the denial of his Rule 60(b) motion.

Discussion

Because of the procedural posture of this case, we are faced with a narrow issue: whether Judge Sprizzo's denial of LaBow's Rule 60(b) motion was proper. Rule 60(b) is not a substitute for appeal. LaBow may not relitigate the bases for the enforcing judgment entered by Judge Werker. Specifically, LaBow may not challenge Judge Werker's application of the breach-day conversion rule. However, review of the Rule 60(b) denial requires some exploration of the currency conversion problem because determination of a state's rule for deeming enforcing judgments satisfied turns on the rationale for the state's currency conversion rule.

For illustrative purposes, the following example will be helpful.[3] Defendant defaults on a contractual obligation to pay plaintiff £1. Plaintiff brings suit in an English court and receives judgment for that amount, at which time the prevailing conversion rate is: £1 = $1. For simplicity and to keep the discussion focused on the pertinent points, we assume that the value of the dollar remains constant (i.e., constant against gold and all currencies except the pound) but that fluctuation in the value of the pound causes a

1. The fee award has been paid, with interest, in dollars and forms no part of the instant controversy.

2. The parties disagree on the exact amount of the balance with LaBow ($236,-234.67), interestingly, claiming a higher amount than Competex ($236,089.68). Should this ultimately become an issue, we leave it for the District Court to resolve in the first instance.

3. Although we assume a judgment-on-a-judgment case, our analysis applies, *mutatis mutandis*, to a breach of contract case, on which the breach-day and judgment-day rules are based.

change in the exchange rate for the dollar. Initially, we consider what would happen if the pound depreciates relative to the dollar, so that £1 = $.60. Plaintiff then brings an action on the English judgment in an American state court. We will further assume that defendant has sufficient property in both jurisdictions to satisfy any judgments against it.

If the English judgment is entitled to enforcement, a state court applying New York's breach-day rule would enter judgment for $1, in accordance with the conversion rate prevailing on the date the English judgment debt became due. The asserted purpose of this rule is to assure that plaintiff will be made whole by protecting him against fluctuation in relative currency values. Thus, had defendant paid plaintiff £1 on the date of the English judgment and had plaintiff converted this amount into dollars on that date, plaintiff would be in possession of $1 on the date of the American judgment. On the surface, the breach-day rule appears to do no more than regard as done that which ought to have been done.

However, the breach-day rule does more than make plaintiff whole. It generously allows him to reap the benefit of appreciation in the value of the pound without risking loss as a result of the pound's depreciation. In our example, plaintiff was insulated from any loss as a result of the pound's depreciation. His right to receive $1 was completely unaffected by the pound's depreciation. However, had the pound appreciated relative to the dollar, so that £1 = $1.30, plaintiff would simply have executed on the English judgment. He would receive £1, the equivalent of $1.30. Since the original obligation was worth only $1, plaintiff would make $.30 as a result of the pound's appreciation.[4]

Of course, this game of creditor's choice is possible only if the judgment debtor has property in both jurisdictions sufficient to satisfy either judgment. The proposed *Restatement of Foreign Relations Law* suggests a more extreme rule of creditor's preference that can enable the creditor to benefit from currency fluctuations even if the debtor does not have property in both jurisdictions. See Restatement of Foreign Relations Law of the United States § 823 comment c (Tent. Draft No. 6, 1985). According to the Restatement, if the foreign currency has depreciated since the foreign obligation accrued, an American court should follow the breach-day rule and apply the conversion rate prevailing at the time of accrual. In our example, if the value of £1 goes from $1 to $.60, the American court enters judgment for $1, and plaintiff loses nothing as a result of the pound's depreciation. However, if the foreign currency appreciates, an American court, according to the Restatement, should follow the judgment-day rule and apply the conversion rate prevailing on the date of the American judgment. In our example, if the value of £1 goes from $1 to $1.30, the American court enters judgment for $1.30, and plaintiff makes $.30. Thus, under the Restatement's approach, the judgment debtor need not have

---

4. If the judgment debtor has property only in the United States, then the breach-day rule is one of neutrality rather than creditor's choice. If £1 = $1 on the date of the English judgment, the judgment creditor will receive an American judgment for $1 whether the pound appreciates or depreciates. Because the judgment creditor cannot execute in England to collect an appreciated pound (in which event he would have made $.30), he is not able to benefit from that appreciation.

property in England for the judgment creditor to be allowed to engage in currency speculation without risk.

It might be argued that the judgment debtor can avoid these unfavorable consequences by immediately satisfying the first judgment. Indeed, it could be argued that these consequences are fitting punishment for failure to pay debts justly due. However, these arguments assume that the original judgment is valid and enforceable. It might be that the original judgment is arguably not entitled to foreign recognition.[7] There is no justification for forcing defendant to choose between waiving all defenses to the enforcement action by satisfying the original judgment and assuming the risk of currency fluctuation.[8] Moreover, post-judgment interest, which compensates the judgment creditor for the time value of money, is ordinarily the only "punishment" for delay in paying judgment debts.

The gamesmanship of the breach-day rule can be avoided by selecting a conversion rule of general application that is neutral between the parties with respect to currency fluctuation. There are three methods by which neutrality can be achieved, depending on whether the original or the enforcing judgment is viewed as primary. If the original judgment is viewed as primary, which seems theoretically superior, neutrality can be achieved, first, by entering the enforcing judgment in the currency of the original jurisdiction (foreign-currency-judgment rule) or, second, by entering the enforcing judgment for an amount of dollars to be determined by converting the original judgment into dollars as of the date of payment (payment-day rule). If the enforcing judgment is viewed as primary, the third method for achieving neutrality is by converting the original judgment into dollars as of the date of the enforcing judgment (judgment-day rule).

Entry of judgment in a foreign currency is allowed in England, France, and Germany. Despite the obvious appeal of this approach, which preserves the original judgment inviolate and places on both parties the risk of fluctuation in the value of the currency of the original judgment, it has received little support in the United States for a procedural reason. Most American courts have assumed that American judgments must be entered in dollars. This assumption has rested on either common law notions of sovereignty or, at least in part, on the now repealed section 20 of the

---

7. The grounds on which foreign judgments may be refused recognition vary among jurisdictions. Although the majority rule is to the contrary, some jurisdictions continue to follow Hilton v. Guyot, 159 U.S. 113, 16 S.Ct. 139, 40 L.Ed. 95 (1895), in refusing to accord preclusive effect to judgments of foreign states that deny such effect to American judgments. Under the Uniform Foreign Money–Judgments Recognition Act of 1962, 13 U.L.A. 271 (1975), in force in nine states, recognition may be refused because: the tribunals of the rendering jurisdiction do not employ procedures comporting with due process, the rendering Court lacked jurisdiction over the person or subject matter, the judgment was obtained by fraud, the foreign court was a seriously inconvenient forum, the judgment conflicts with another judgment, or the judgment violates the public policy of the forum. Restatement (Second) of Conflict of Laws § 98 (1971) would allow recognition only of foreign judgments rendered in "contested proceeding[s]."

8. This point would seem even stronger in the breach-of-contract context than in the judgment-on-a-judgment context. There is no reason to require a defendant to pay a plaintiff merely because the plaintiff has a colorable contract claim.

Coinage Act of 1792. This assumption probably deserves reexamination in light of the repeal of section 20.[9]

The payment-day rule is economically equivalent to the foreign-currency-judgment rule. Indeed, the House of Lords recognized that, although entry of an enforcing judgment in a foreign currency may be the purest method of preserving the original judgment, there comes a time when that type of enforcing judgment, if paid in local currency, must be converted into that currency, at which point the foreign-currency-judgment rule becomes the payment-day rule. That point is reached no later than the time of execution, when a decision must be made as to how many units of the local currency satisfy the judgment entered in a foreign currency.[10] In France, the court has the option of adopting either the payment-day or judgment-day rule. However, in the United States, there has been some concern that a judgment must be entered in dollars for a sum certain. Cf. Forms 31 and 32, Appendix of Forms to Fed.R.Civ.P. Although the Federal Rules contain no explicit obstacle to the entry of a judgment for an amount of dollars to be determined in the future (by reference to ascertainable figures), the payment-day rule has found little favor in this country.

American courts wishing to avoid the procedural objections to the foreign-currency-judgment or payment-day rules while choosing a neutral conversion rule may apply the judgment-day rule. The neutrality of the judgment-day rule may be illustrated by a return to our example. If plaintiff holds an English judgment for £1 and the value of £1 depreciates from $1 to $.60 as of the date of the American judgment, the American court enters judgment for $.60, and plaintiff loses $.40. But that is merely the consequence of holding an obligation in pounds. Had plaintiff executed on his English judgment, he would have lost the equivalent of $.40 as a result of the pound's depreciation. Conversely, if the value of £1 appreciates from $1 to $1.30, the American court enters judgment for $1.30, and plaintiff makes $.30, the equivalent of what he would have made had he executed on the English judgment. Thus, the judgment-day rule allows the plaintiff to speculate in pounds for as long as he wishes, but he now engages in true speculation. His gains and losses are registered with equal force in England and in the United States, and any incentive for forum shopping disappears. After entry of the American judgment, the judgment

---

9. Section 20, now repealed, was formerly codified at 31 U.S.C. § 371, and stated:

> The money of account of the United States shall be expressed in dollars or units, dimes or tenths, cents or hundredths, ... and all accounts in the public offices and all proceedings in the courts shall be kept and had in conformity to this regulation.

Even before its repeal, doubt was expressed as to whether section 20 prohibited entry of judgments in foreign currencies. When the Coinage Act was reenacted without the units of account passage, the House Judiciary Committee noted that the statute expressed no view on the validity of judgments specifying payment in foreign currencies. It has therefore been suggested that such judgments are permissible.

10. In approving use of the payment-day rule for enforcing judgments entered in England, the House of Lords selected as the "payment day" the day on which a court authorizes execution upon the English judgment. This practice removes any question of how many pounds must be turned over to the judgment creditor after the execution sale. The court, in authorizing execution, converts the enforcing judgment into the currency of the forum for a sum certain.

creditor is insulated from fluctuation in the value of the pound but takes the risk of fluctuation in the value of the dollar. But that is merely the consequence of holding a judgment in dollars.

If we were free to choose a conversion rule, we would select either the judgment-day or the payment-day rule. However, as noted, we are not free to do so because the conversion question is one of New York law and because we are reviewing only the denial of LaBow's Rule 60(b) motion. Our task is to predict what satisfaction of judgment rule New York would apply.

Bearing in mind the consequences previously discussed of the various possible conversion rules, we believe that New York's choice of the breach-day conversion rule clearly implies that New York would require satisfaction of a New York enforcing judgment by payment of the dollar amount specified in that judgment and would not consider an enforcing judgment satisfied by payment of the amount of the underlying judgment in foreign currency. The breach-day rule protects the judgment creditor against fluctuation in currency values to the point of allowing him to speculate without risk. It would be anomalous to suggest that New York would allow its creditor's preference rule to be undercut by giving the judgment debtor the opportunity to satisfy his New York judgment by paying the underlying judgment in depreciated pounds. Therefore, Judge Sprizzo was correct in holding that Competex's American judgment could be satisfied only in dollars. As a corollary, any pounds paid must be credited in dollars at the rate prevailing on the date the pounds were paid.[15]

. . . .

The order of the District Court is affirmed.

---

15. A jurisdiction following the judgment-day rule would also require its enforcing judgments to be paid in local currency. . . .

INDEX

†